The Complete Crossword Puzzle Dictionary

SECOND EDITION

REDWOOD
EDITIONS

A GENUINE MERRIAM-WEBSTER

The name *Webster* alone is no guarantee of excellence. It is used by a number of publishers and may serve mainly to mislead an unwary buyer.

Merriam-Webster™ is the name you should look for when you consider the purchase of dictionaries or other fine reference books. It carries the reputation of a company that has been publishing since 1831 and is your assurance of quality and authority.

Published by
Redwood Editions
an imprint of
Hinkler Book Distributors Pty. Ltd.
17-23 Redwood Drive
Dingley, Victoria, Australia

Printed and bound in Australia

Preface

Merriam-Webster's Crossword Puzzle Dictionary, Second Edition, has been edited to meet the specific needs of crossword puzzle solvers. The extensive resources and editorial care that have placed Merriam-Webster® general dictionaries among the most respected and sought-after reference books in this country have been utilized in preparing this specialized dictionary.

Based on actual crossword puzzle clues, entries have been selected from Webster's Third New International Dictionary and its venerable predecessor, Webster's New International Dictionary, Second Edition, as well as from Merriam-Webster's Collegiate Thesaurus, Webster's New Geographical Dictionary, Merriam-Webster's Biographical Dictionary, Merriam-Webster's Collegiate Dictionary, and Encyclopædia Britannica, making this book one of the most comprehensive of its kind. Because of the wide range of information contained in this book, it can also be used as a source of much general reference material.

Merriam-Webster's Crossword Puzzle Dictionary, Second Edition, is based on the earlier Webster's Official Crossword Puzzle Dictionary and, as such, relies on work done by the writers and editors of that book, especially by its project editor, James G. Lowe. The text for this new edition was prepared by Michael G. Belanger. Production coordination was provided by Jennifer S. Goss. Proofreading was done by Rebecca R. Bryer, Jennifer N. Cislo, Michael G. Guzzi, Peter D. Haraty, Joan I. Narmontas, Donna L. Rickerby, Francine A. Roberts, Adrienne M. Scholz, and Amy West.

Introduction

Main Entries

The organization of Merriam-Webster's Crossword Puzzle Dictionary, Second Edition, is structured in accordance with the way in which crossword puzzles are constructed and solved. The main entries and their subcategories correspond to the numbered clues given in the puzzle, and the answer words that follow the main entries are possibilities for filling in the blanks provided.

Main entries appear in boldface type and are entered in alphabetical order letter by letter. Those beginning with *Mc-* are alphabetized as if spelled *Mac-*; thus **McTeague author** appears before **mad.** We have endeavored to make the range of entries as comprehensive as possible in a book of this size so as to enable the user to meet the challenges of even the most difficult puzzles.

These entries include names of persons (as biblical, famous, legendary, literary, and mythological), places (as countries, islands, mountains, rivers, states, and seas), and miscellaneous things (as chemical elements, coins, drinks, games, and wines). Also included are titles of famous books, operas, and works of art. The bulk of the main entries, however, consists of words that have synonyms or closely related words.

Entries may be a single word, a group of words, or a blank with a word or group of words (as **Damocles'** _____ or _____ **d'Azur**). Parts of speech are not indicated since they are not usually provided in puzzle clues.

Subcategories

When the main entry is a large category (as at **animal, composer,** and **river**), the list of answer words is broken down into alphabetically arranged subcategories for easy access. Each subcategory is introduced by an appropriate boldface italic word or words. If you want to find, for example, the name of a French composer, first look for the entry **composer** and then under it the subcategory *French.*

Subcategories may indicate various kinds of relationships to the main entry, for example, personal (father, mother, etc.), political (capital, kingdom, etc.), literary (author, character, etc.), or artistic (painter, sculptor, etc.). They may indicate a nationality, a language or dialect, or a particular example or type. Also included as subcategories are prefixes, suffixes, combining forms, and chemical symbols related to the main entry.

Answer Words

When more than one answer is possible to a clue represented by a main entry, the answer words are grouped together according to the number of letters they contain. The specific number appears in boldface before each numerical grouping, and within each grouping answer words are alphabetized. Even when only a single answer word is given, the boldface number of its letters precedes it. Answer words usually range from two to thirteen letters since longer answers are rarely asked for. However, some answers (as titles and nicknames) may consist of more than one word and may exceed thirteen letters. Some answers are not actual words; these include abbreviations, prefixes, suffixes, combining forms, and chemical symbols, which are commonly called for in crossword puzzles.

In a single list of answer words you may find grouped together words that seem unrelated to one another. This results when the answer words are of various parts of speech or are synonymous with only one meaning of a main entry that has more than one meaning. Thus, answer words, although related to the main entry, may not be synonymous with each other.

Guide Words

In order to facilitate finding a particular entry, the first main entry on each left-hand page is printed at the top of that page in large boldface type. Likewise, the last main entry on each right-hand page is printed at the top of that page. These two guide words indicate the alphabetical range of main entries on the two pages.

Cross-References

Occasionally a reduced boldface cross-reference to another main entry is given instead of answer words. For example, at **anywise** you are directed to see **anyhow** for answer words because these two main entries are synonymous, and at **Arthur** you are referred to **King Arthur** for the answer words. These cross-references save space and allow a greater number of main entries than would otherwise be possible.

A

Aaron *brother:* 5 Moses *father:* 5 Amram *sister:* 6 Miriam *son:* 5 Abiku, Nadab 7 Eleazer, Ithamar

aback 5 short 6 sudden 7 unaware 8 suddenly, unawares 10 unawaredly 12 unexpectedly

abacus *Chinese:* 7 swanpan 8 shwanpan

abaft 3 aft 4 back 5 after 6 astern, back of, behind

abalienate 4 cede, deed 5 alien 6 assign, convey, remise 8 make over, sign over, transfer

abalone 5 ormer

abandon 3 fun 4 cede, drop, ease, junk, play, quit 5 chuck, leave, scrap, sport, waive, yield 6 desert, disuse, give up, laxity, maroon, reject, resign, turn up 7 cast off, discard, forsake, freedom, laxness, liberty, license, unguard 8 hand over, renounce, wildness 9 looseness, repudiate, surrender, throw over 10 exuberance, relinquish, unruliness, wantonness 11 naturalness, spontaneity, unrestraint 12 heedlessness, incontinence, unconstraint 13 impulsiveness

abandoned 4 lewd, lorn 6 wanton 7 corrupt, debased, riotous; uncouth 8 depraved, derelict, deserted, desolate, forsaken, solitary 9 debauched, dissolute, lecherous, perverted, reprobate 10 degenerate, lascivious, licentious, profligate 12 incorrigible, unprincipled

abase 4 fawn, sink 5 cower, lower, toady 6 bemean, cringe, debase, demean, demote, grovel, humble, reduce 7 degrade, truckle 8 cast down, diminish 9 downgrade, humiliate

abash 4 faze 5 abase 6 demean, humble, rattle 7 confuse 8 confound 9 discomfit, embarrass, humiliate 10 disconcert

abashment 6 unease 9 confusion 10 uneasiness 12 discomfiture, discomposure 13 disconcertion, embarrassment

abate 3 ebb 4 fall, lull, wane 5 annul, close, let up, quash, taper 6 lessen, negate, recede, reduce, relent, weaken 7 abolish, die away, die down, dwindle, ease off, nullify, slacken, subside, vitiate 8 abrogate, decrease, diminish, moderate, taper off 9 drain away, eradicate 10 annihilate, invalidate 11 exterminate

abatement 6 rebate 8 discount 9 deduction, reduction 11 subtraction

abbot *female:* 6 abbess

abbreviate 3 cut 7 abridge, curtail, cut back, shorten

abbreviation 7 acronym 10 abridgment, shortening

abdicate 5 demit, leave 6 reject, resign 7 abandon 8 renounce, withdraw 9 surrender, throw away 10 relinquish

abdomen 3 gut, pot 5 belly, tummy 6 middle, paunch, venter 7 midriff, stomach 8 potbelly 9 bay window 10 midsection 11 breadbasket *combining form:* 6 ventri, ventro *depression:* 5 navel

abduct 5 seize 6 kidnap, snatch 10 spirit away

abecedarian 4 tyro 7 amateur, dabbier 9 smatterer 10 dilettante

Abel *brother:* 4 Cain, Seth *father:* 4 Adam *mother:* 3 Eve *slayer:* 4 Cain

Abelard *son:* 9 Astrolabe *wife:* 7 Heloise

abele 6 poplar

aberrant 3 odd 6 errant, erring 7 deviant, devious, strange, unusual 8 abnormal, atypical, peculiar 9 anomalous, deviative, different, disparate, divergent, eccentric, untypical 11 exceptional, heteroclite

aberration 4 slip 6 lunacy, oddity, rarity 7 madness, mistake, turning 8 insanity 9 curiosity, departure, deviation, diversion, unbalance 10 alienation, deflection, divergence, insaneness 11 abnormality, derangement, distraction, psychopathy

abet 3 aid, egg 4 goad, help, prod, spur, urge 6 assist, exhort, foment, incite, stir up 8 advocate 9 encourage, instigate 11 countenance

abettor 9 accessory 10 accomplice 11 confederate, conspirator 13 coconspirator

abeyance 5 break, pause 7 latency, respite 8 dormancy, interval 10 quiescence, quiescency, suspension 11 cold storage 12 intermission, interruption

abeyant 6 latent 7 dormant, lurking 8 deferred 9 postponed, quiescent, repressed 10 suppressed 11 intermitted

abhor 4 hate 5 scorn 6 detest, loathe 7 contemn, despise, disdain 8 execrate 9 abominate

abhorrence 4 hate 6 dismay, hatred, horror 8 aversion, distaste, loathing 9 repulsion, revulsion 10 repellency, repugnance 11 abomination, detestation

abhorrent 6 horrid, odious 7 hatable, hateful 8 hateable 9 invidious, obnoxious, repellent, repugnant, revulsive 10 abominable, detestable 11 uncongenial 12 antipathetic 13 unsympathetic

Abi *father:* 9 Zechariah *husband:* 4 Ahaz *mother:* 8 Hezekiah

abide 4 bear, last, live, stay, take, wait 5 brook, cling, dwell, exist, stand, stick, tarry 6 accede, accept, adhere, cleave, endure, linger, remain, reside, suffer 7 consent, hang out, perdure, persist, receive, stomach, subsist, swallow 8 continue, tolerate 11 stick around

abiding 4 firm, sure 6 steady 7 durable, lasting 8 enduring 9 steadfast 10 perdurable, persistent 11 unfaltering, unqualified 12 never-failing, wholehearted 13 unquestioning

Abiel *grandson:* 4 Saul 5 Abner *son:* 3 Ner 4 Kish

abigail 4 maid

Abigail's husband 5 David, Nabal

ability 5 knack, might, skill 6 talent 7 address, aptness, command, faculty, know-how, mastery, prowess 8 adequacy, aptitude, capacity, deftness, facility 9 dexterity, expertise, expertism, handiness, ingenuity 10 adroitness, capability, cleverness, competence, efficiency, expertness, mastership 11 proficiency 13 qualification, qualifiedness

Abital's husband 5 David

abject 9 underfoot 11 downtrodden

abjure 4 cede 5 unsay 6 desert, disown, recall, recant 7 abandon, disavow, forsake, retract 8 forswear, palinode, renounce, take back, withdraw 9 repudiate, surrender 10 relinquish

ablaze 5 afire, aglow, fiery 6 aflame, alight 7 burning, flaming, flaring, ignited 8 aflicker 11 conflagrant

able 4 good, keen 5 alert, sharp, smart 6 au fait, brainy, clever, expert, proper, wicked 7 capable, go-ahead, skilled 8 skillful 9 brilliant, competent, effective, effectual, efficient, qualified 10 proficient 11 intelligent 12 enterprising

abnegation 6 denial 10 self-denial 12 renouncement, renunciation

Abner *cousin:* 4 Saul *father:* 3 Ner *slayer:* 4 Joab

abnormal 3 odd 5 undue, weird 6 off-key 7 deviant, offtype, unusual 8 aberrant, atypical 9 anomalous, deviative, divergent, irregular, paratypic, unnatural, unregular, untypical 11 heteroclite, uncustomary

13 heteromorphic, preternatural *combining form:* 3 mal 4 anom, poly 5 anomo, pseud 6 pseudo *prefix:* 3 dys, par 4 para

abnormality 5 lusus

abode 4 home 5 house 8 domicile, dwelling 9 residence, residency 10 commorancy, habitation

abolish 4 undo 5 abate, annul, quash 6 cancel, negate, repeal, revoke, vacate 7 blot out, nullify, rescind, vitiate, wipe out 8 abrogate, disallow, disannul 9 eradicate, extirpate 10 annihilate, circumduct, extinguish, invalidate 11 exterminate

abolitionist 4 Mott (Lucretia), Weld (Theodore) 5 Lundy (Benjamin), Smith (Gerrit), Stowe (Harriet Beecher) 6 Birney (James), Lowell (James Russell), Parker (Theodore), Tappan (Arthur) 8 Douglass (Frederick), Garrison (William Lloyd), Phillips (Wendell), Whittier (John Greenlaef)

abominable 6 cursed, horrid, odious 7 hateful 8 accursed, hateable 9 abhorrent, loathsome, offensive, repugnant, revolting 10 detestable

abominable snowman 4 yeti

abominate 4 damn, hate 5 abhor, curse 6 detest, loathe 8 execrate 9 objurgate

abomination 4 hate, pest 5 bogey, scorn, trial 6 hatred, horror, plague 7 bugaboo, bugbear, disdain, dislike, incubus 8 anathema, aversion, contempt, disfavor, distaste, loathing 9 annoyance, bête noire, disrelish, repulsion, revulsion 10 abhorrence, black beast, repugnance, repugnancy 11 detestation

aboriginal 6 native, savage 7 endemic 8 barbaric, primeval 9 barbarian, barbarous, primitive 10 indigenous, primordial 13 autochthonous

aborigine 3 abo 6 native

abortive 4 vain 6 futile, unripe 7 useless 8 bootless, immature, unformed 9 fruitless 10 unavailing 11 ineffective, ineffectual, unavailable 12 unproductive

abound 4 flow, teem 5 crawl, swarm

abound in *suffix:* 5 ulent

abounding 4 full, rife 5 alive 6 jammed, packed 7 replete, stuffed, teeming 8 swarming, thronged 11 overflowing

abounding in *suffix:* 3 ose, ous 4 ious

about 2 on, re 4 as to, back, in re, most, much, near, nigh, over, upon, with 5 again, anent, circa, round 6 all but, almost, anyhow, around, nearby, nearly 7 anywise, apropos, through 8 at random, backward, casually, randomly, to and fro 9 aimlessly, as regards, haphazard, in reverse 10 carelessly, concerning, near-at-hand, respecting, throughout 11 any which way, haphazardly, practically 12 circuitously 13 approximately, helter-skelter

about-face 4 turn 7 reverse 8 reversal
9 reversion, volte-face 11 reversement
above 3 o'er 4 over, past 5 aloft, supra
6 beyond 8 overhead *combining form:*
6 supero *prefix:* 3 sur 4 over 5 hyper,
super, supra
above all 7 chiefly
aboveboard 4 open 7 artless 8 straight
9 ingenuous 10 forthright, scrupulous
12 plain dealing
abracadabra 4 cant 5 argot 6 jargon
7 mummery 9 gibberish 10 hocus-pocus,
mumbo jumbo 13 mystification
abrade 3 bug, irk, rub 4 burn, fret, gall,
rasp, wear 5 annoy, chafe, erode, grate,
graze 6 bother, flurry, ruffle, scrape 7 corrade, corrode, eat away, perturb, provoke
8 exercise 9 excoriate
Abraham *birthplace:* 2 Ur *brother:*
5 Haran, Nahor *concubine:* 5 Hagar
father: 5 Terah *grandfather:* 5 Nahor
grandson: 4 Esau *nephew:* 3 Lot *son:*
5 Isaac, Medan, Shuah 6 Midian, Zimran
7 Ishmael *well:* 9 Beer-Sheba *wife:*
5 Sarah 7 Keturah
Abraham's bosom 4 Zion 5 bliss
6 Canaan, heaven 7 elysium, nirvana
8 empyrean, paradise 10 Civitas Dei
12 New Jerusalem
abrasive 5 emery
abreast 2 up 6 au fait, versed 7 versant
8 familiar, informed, up-to-date 9 au courant 10 acquainted, conversant 12 contemporary
abridge 3 cut 5 limit, slash 6 lessen, minify, narrow, reduce 7 curtail, cut back,
shorten 8 condense, diminish, minimize,
restrict, retrench 10 abbreviate
abridgment 3 sum 5 brief 6 apercu,
digest, précis, sketch 7 capsule, epitome,
outline, summary 8 abstract, boildown, breviary, breviate, syllabus, synopsis 9 summation, summing-up 10 compendium, conspectus 12 condensation
abroad 6 afield 7 oversea 8 overseas
abrogate 4 ruin, undo, void 5 abate,
annul, quash, wreck 6 cancel, negate,
vacate 7 abolish, blot out, nullify, vitiate
8 dissolve 9 discharge 10 annihilate, extinguish, invalidate, obliterate
abrupt 4 curt 5 bluff, blunt, brief, brisk,
crisp, gruff, hasty, quick, ready, sharp,
sheer, short, steep 6 casual, crusty,
snippy, speedy, sudden 7 arduous,
brusque, hurried, rushing 8 headlong, informal 9 impetuous 11 precipitant, precipitate,
precipitous, short-spoken, subitaneous
13 unceremonious
abruptly 5 short 6 sudden 7 asudden
8 suddenly 9 forthwith
abruptness 10 brusquerie

Absalom *commander:* 5 Amasa *father:*
5 David *mother:* 7 Maachah *sister:*
5 Tamar *slayer:* 4 Joab
abscess 4 boil, sore 5 botch, ulcer
6 lesion, pimple, trauma 7 pustule 8 furuncle 9 carbuncle
abscond 2 go 3 fly 4 flee, quit 5 break,
leave, scape 6 decamp, escape 8 withdraw
absence 4 lack, need, void, want
6 dearth, defect, vacuum 7 default,
drought, failure 9 privation 10 deficiency
13 insufficiency
absent 4 away, gone, lost 7 bemused, faraway, lacking, missing, omitted, wanting
8 distrait, heedless 9 forgetful
10 abstracted
absentminded 4 lost 7 bemused, faraway 8 distrait, heedless, unseeing
10 abstracted, unnoticing 11 inattentive,
inconscient, preoccupied, unobserving
12 unperceiving
absent without leave 4 AWOL
absolute 4 hard, pure, real, true 5 ideal,
sheer, utter 6 actual, simple 7 eternal, factual, genuine, perfect, unmixed 8 complete,
despotic, flawless, infinite, outright, positive,
ultimate, unflawed 9 arbitrary, autarchic,
boundless, downright, fleckless, imperious,
masterful, out-and-out, sovereign, tyrannous, unalloyed, undiluted, unlimited
10 autocratic, autonomous, consummate,
impeccable, monocratic, tyrannical 11 categorical, dictatorial, domineering, independent, note-perfect, unmitigated, unqualified
12 indefectible, totalitarian, transcendent
13 authoritarian
absolutely 6 easily 9 doubtless 10 definitely, positively 11 doubtlessly 13 unequivocally
absolution 6 pardon 7 amnesty 11 con-
donation
absolutism 9 Caesarism 12 dictatorship
absolve 4 free 5 clear, spare 6 acquit,
excuse, exempt, let off, shrive 7 release,
relieve 8 dispense 9 discharge, exculpate,
exonerate, vindicate 10 disculpate
absorb 5 imbue 6 embody, engage,
imbibe, infuse, ingest, sponge 7 consume,
engross, immerse, inhaust, involve 8 permeate 9 preoccupy 10 assimilate, impregnate, monopolize 11 incorporate
absorbed 4 deep, rapt 6 intent
7 engaged, wrapped 8 immersed, involved
9 engrossed, wrapped up 11 preoccupied
absorbent cotton 7 pledget
absorbing 9 consuming 10 engrossing
12 monopolizing
abstain 4 curb, deny, keep 5 forgo, spurn
6 eschew, refuse, reject 7 decline, forbear,

refrain **8** abnegate, hold back, teetotal, withhold **9** constrain

abstemious **5** sober **7** ascetic, austere, sparing **9** abstinent, continent, temperate **11** self-denying

abstentious see **abstemious**

abstinence **8** sobriety **10** continence, temperance **12** renunciation

abstinent see **abstemious**

abstract **4** lift **5** annex, brief, filch, ideal, pinch, steal, swipe, unfix **6** detach, divide, pilfer **7** epitome, neutral, purloin, utopian **8** academic, boildown, breviary, breviate, detached, notional, separate, synopsis, uncouple **9** colorless, disengage, visionary **10** abridgment, conceptual, conspectus, disconnect, dissociate, impersonal, inconcrete **11** appropriate, impractical, speculative, theoretical, unpassioned **12** condensation, disassociate, hypothetical, transcendent **13** disinterested *being:* **3** ens

abstracted **4** lost, rapt **6** absent, intent **7** bemused, faraway **8** distrait, heedless **9** engrossed, oblivious, unmindful, unminding **11** inattentive, inconscient, preoccupied **12** absentminded

abstruse **4** deep **5** heavy, ideal **6** knotty, occult, orphic, secret **7** complex **8** esoteric, hermetic, profound **9** intricate, recondite **10** acroamatic **11** complicated **12** hypothetical

absurd **5** balmy, comic, crazy, droll, funny, loony, potty, silly, wacky **6** insane **7** asinine, fatuous, foolish **8** farcical **10** irrational **11** harebrained **12** preposterous, unreasonable

absurdity **5** folly **7** inanity **8** insanity, nonsense **9** craziness, dottiness, silliness **11** foolishness, witlessness **13** senselessness

abundance **4** ease **6** enough, galore, plenty **7** lashins **8** adequacy, lashings, thriving **10** lavishness, prosperity **11** prodigality, sufficiency *Scottish:* **5** routh, rowth

abundant **4** lush, rife **5** ample, thick **6** common, lavish, plenty **7** copious, crammed, crowded, liberal, profuse, replete **8** generous, prolific **9** bounteous, bountiful, luxuriant, plenteous, plentiful

abuse **3** mar, mud **4** harm, hurt **5** decry, spoil, wrong **6** damage, debase, impair, injure, mess up, misuse, rating, revile **7** calumny, corrupt, cursing, exploit, obloquy, oppress, outrage, pervert, profane, railing **8** belittle, berating, derogate, discount, illtreat, maltreat, minimize, misapply, mistreat, reviling, swearing **9** contumely, desecrate, disparage, dispraise, invective, manhandle, misemploy, mishandle, persecute, profanity **10** defamation, depreciate,

impose upon, malignment, scurrility **12** billingsgate, vilification, vituperation

abusive **5** dirty **6** odious **7** scurril **8** scurrile **9** aspersing, insulting, invective, maligning, offending, offensive, outraging, truculent, vilifying **10** affronting, scurrilous, vituperous **11** opprobrious **12** contumelious, vituperative, vituperatory

abut **4** join, line **5** flank, march, touch, verge **6** adjoin, border **8** neighbor **11** communicate

abutting **4** next **7** joining **8** adjacent, touching **9** adjoining, bordering, impinging **10** approximal, connecting, contiguous, juxtaposed **12** conterminous

abysm **4** gulf **5** chasm

abysmal **4** deep **8** infinite, profound **9** plumbless, soundless **10** bottomless, fathomless **11** illimitable, plummetless **12** unfathomable

abyss **3** pit **4** gulf, hell **5** chasm, depth, hades, Sheol **6** Tophet **7** Gehenna, inferno **8** deepness **9** perdition **10** profundity, underworld **11** netherworld **12** profoundness

academic **5** booky **6** closet **7** bookish, utopian **8** gownsman, pedantic **10** scholastic **11** book-learned, impractical, quodlibetic, speculative, theoretical

academic year *part* **4** term **7** quarter **8** semester **9** trimester

Academy Award Winner
picture:
1927-28: **5** Wings *1928-29:* **14** Broadway Melody *1929-30:* **25** All Quiet on the Western Front *1930-31:* **8** Cimarron *1931-32:* **10** Grand Hotel *1932-33:* **9** Calvalcade *1934:* **18** It Happened One Night *1935:* **17** Mutiny on the Bounty *1936:* **16** The Great Ziegfeld *1937:* **15** Life of Emile Zola *1938:* **20** You Can't Take It With You *1939:* **15** Gone With the Wind *1940:* **7** Rebecca *1941:* **19** How Green Was My Valley *1942:* **10** Mrs. Miniver *1943:* **10** Casablanca *1944:* **10** Going My Way *1945:* **14** The Lost Weekend *1946:* **22** The Best Years of Our Lives *1947:* **19** Gentleman's Agreement *1948:* **6** Hamlet *1949:* **14** All the King's Men *1950:* **11** All About Eve *1951:* **17** An American in Paris *1952:* **22** The Greatest Show on Earth *1953:* **18** From Here to Eternity *1954:* **15** On the Waterfront *1955:* **5** Marty *1956:* **26** Around the World in Eighty Days *1957:* **23** The Bridge on the River Kwai *1958:* **4** Gigi *1959:* **6** Ben-Hur *1960:* **12** The Apartment *1961:* **13** West Side Story *1962:* **16** Lawrence of Arabia *1963:* **8** Tom Jones *1964:* **10** My Fair Lady *1965:* **15** The Sound of Music *1966:*

17 A Man for All Seasons *1967:* 19 In the Heat of the Night *1968:* 6 Oliver *1969:* 14 Midnight Cowboy *1970:* 6 Patton *1971:* 19 The French Connection *1972:* 12 The Godfather *1973:* 8 The Sting *1974:* 12 The Godfather (Part Two) *1975:* 25 One Flew Over the Cuckoo's Nest *1976:* 5 Rocky *1977:* 9 Annie Hall *1978:* 13 The Deer Hunter *1979:* 14 Kramer vs. Kramer *1980:* 14 Ordinary People *1981:* 14 Chariots of Fire *1982:* 6 Gandhi *1983:* 17 Terms of Endearment *1984:* 7 Amadeus *1985:* 11 Out of Africa *1986:* 7 Platoon *1987:* 14 The Last Emperor *1988:* 7 Rain Man *1989:* 16 Driving Miss Daisy *1990:* 16 Dances With Wolves *1991:* 20 The Silence of the Lambs *1992:* 10 Unforgiven *1993:* 14 Schindler's List *1994:* 11 Forrest Gump *1995:* 10 Braveheart

actor:
1927-28: 8 Jannings (Emil) *1928-29:* 6 Baxter (Warner) *1929-30:* 6 Arliss (George) *1930-31:* 9 Barrymore (Lionel) *1931-32:* 5 Beery (Wallace), March (Fredric) *1932-33:* 8 Laughton (Charles) *1934:* 5 Gable (Clark) *1935:* 8 McLaglen (Victor) *1936:* 4 Muni (Paul) *1937:* 5 Tracy (Spencer) *1938:* 5 Tracy (Spencer) *1939:* 5 Donat (Robert) *1940:* 7 Stewart (James) *1941:* 6 Cooper (Gary) *1942:* 6 Cagney (James) *1943:* 5 Lukas (Paul) *1944:* 6 Crosby (Bing) *1945:* 7 Milland (Ray) *1946:* 5 March (Fredric) *1947:* 6 Colman (Ronald) *1948:* 7 Olivier (Laurence) *1949:* 8 Crawford (Broderick) *1950:* 6 Ferrer (Jose) *1951:* 6 Bogart (Humphrey) *1952:* 6 Cooper (Gary) *1953:* 6 Holden (William) *1954:* 6 Brando (Marlon) *1955:* 8 Borgnine (Ernest) *1956:* 7 Brynner (Yul) *1957:* 8 Guinness (Alec) *1958:* 5 Niven (David) *1959:* 6 Heston (Charlton) *1960:* 9 Lancaster (Burt) *1961:* 6 Schell (Maximilian) *1962:* 4 Peck (Gregory) *1963:* 7 Poitier (Sidney) *1964:* 8 Harrison (Rex) *1965:* 6 Marvin (Lee) *1966:* 8 Scofield (Paul) *1967:* 7 Steiger (Rod) *1968:* 9 Robertson (Cliff) *1969:* 5 Wayne (John) *1970:* 5 Scott (George C.) *1971:* 7 Hackman (Gene) *1972:* 6 Brando (Marlon) *1973:* 6 Lemmon (Jack) *1974:* 6 Carney (Art) *1975:* 9 Nicholson (Jack) *1976:* 5 Finch (Peter) *1977:* 8 Dreyfuss (Richard) *1978:* 6 Voight (Jon) *1979:* 7 Hoffman (Dustin) *1980:* 6 DeNiro (Robert) *1981:* 5 Fonda (Henry) *1982:* 8 Kingsley (Ben) *1983:* 6 Duvall (Robert) *1984:* 7 Abraham (F. Murray) *1985:* 4 Hurt (William) *1986:* 6 Newman (Paul) *1987:* 7 Douglas (Michael) *1988:* 7 Hoffman (Dustin) *1989:*

8 Day-Lewis (Daniel) *1990:* 5 Irons (Jeremy) *1991:* 7 Hopkins (Anthony) *1992:* 6 Pacino (Al) *1993:* 5 Hanks (Tom) *1994:* 5 Hanks (Tom) *1995:* 4 Cage (Nicholas)

actress:
1927-28: 6 Gaynor (Janet) *1928-29:* 8 Pickford (Mary) *1929-30:* 7 Shearer (Norma) *1930-31:* 8 Dressler (Marie) *1931-32:* 5 Hayes (Helen) *1932-33:* 7 Hepburn (Katharine) *1934:* 7 Colbert (Claudette) *1935:* 5 Davis (Bette) *1936:* 6 Rainer (Luise) *1937:* 6 Rainer (Luise) *1938:* 5 Davis (Bette) *1939:* 5 Leigh (Vivien) *1940:* 6 Rogers (Ginger) *1941:* 8 Fontaine (Joan) *1942:* 6 Garson (Greer) *1943:* 5 Jones (Jennifer) *1944:* 7 Bergman (Ingrid) *1945:* 8 Crawford (Joan) *1946:* 11 de Havilland (Olivia) *1947:* 5 Young (Loretta) *1948:* 5 Wyman (Jane) *1949:* 11 de Havilland (Olivia) *1950:* 8 Holliday (Judy) *1951:* 5 Leigh (Vivien) *1952:* 5 Booth (Shirley) *1953:* 7 Hepburn (Audrey) *1954:* 5 Kelly (Grace) *1955:* 7 Magnani (Anna) *1956:* 7 Bergman (Ingrid) *1957:* 8 Woodward (Joanne) *1958:* 7 Hayward (Susan) *1959:* 8 Signoret (Simone) *1960:* 6 Taylor (Elizabeth) *1961:* 5 Loren (Sophia) *1962:* 8 Bancroft (Anne) *1963:* 4 Neal (Patricia) *1964:* 7 Andrews (Julie) *1965:* 8 Christie (Julie) *1966:* 6 Taylor (Elizabeth) *1967:* 7 Hepburn (Katharine) *1968:* 7 Hepburn (Katharine) 9 Streisand (Barbara) *1969:* 5 Smith (Maggie) *1970:* 7 Jackson (Glenda) *1971:* 5 Fonda (Jane) *1972:* 8 Minnelli (Liza) *1973:* 7 Jackson (Glenda) *1974:* 7 Burstyn (Ellen) *1975:* 8 Fletcher (Louise) *1976:* 7 Dunaway (Faye) *1977:* 6 Keaton (Diane) *1978:* 5 Fonda (Jane) *1979:* 5 Field (Sally) *1980:* 6 Spacek (Sissy) *1981:* 7 Hepburn (Katharine) *1982:* 6 Streep (Meryl) *1983:* 8 MacLaine (Shirley) *1984:* 5 Field (Sally) *1985:* 4 Page (Geraldine) *1986:* 6 Matlin (Marlee) *1987:* 4 Cher *1988:* 6 Foster (Jodie) *1989:* 5 Tandy (Jessica) *1990:* 5 Bates (Kathy) *1991:* 6 Foster (Jodie) *1992:* 8 Thompson (Emma) *1993:* 6 Hunter (Holly) *1994:* 6 Lange (Jessica) *1995:* 8 Sarandon (Susan)

accede 3 let, yes 5 agree, allow 6 assent, concur, permit 7 consent 9 acquiesce, cooperate, subscribe

accelerate 5 hurry, impel, speed 6 hasten, step up 7 quicken, swiften

acceleration 7 speedup

accent 4 beat, tone 5 meter, pulse, throb 6 rhythm, stress 7 cadence 8 emphasis 9 pulsation 10 inflection, intonation *Irish:*

6 brogue *Scottish:* 4 burr *Southern:*
5 drawl

accent mark 5 acute, grave

accentuation see accent

accept 3 bow, buy, see 4 bear, take
5 adopt, agree, catch, favor, go for, grasp,
yield 6 admire, endure, esteem, follow,
pocket, take in 7 agree to, approve,
believe, compass, receive, respect, swallow
8 assent to, bear with, hold with, tolerate,
tough out 9 agree with, apprehend, approbate 10 capitulate, comprehend, understand 11 countenance, subscribe to

acceptable 4 good 6 decent 7 average
8 adequate, all right, bearable, ordinary
9 endurable, tolerable 10 sufficient
11 commonplace, supportable 12 satisfactory 13 unexceptional, unimpeachable

acceptably 4 well 5 amply, right 8 properly, suitably 9 fittingly 10 adequately,
becomingly 13 appropriately

acceptant 8 suasible, swayable 9 receptive 10 responsive 11 persuadable, persuasible 13 influenceable

acceptation 5 sense 6 import 7 meaning, message, purport 10 intendment
12 significance, significancy 13 signification, understanding

accepted 5 sound, usual 6 proper
7 chronic, correct, routine 8 habitual, orthodox, received 9 customary 10 accustomed,
recognized, sanctioned 11 established
12 conventional

access 3 fit, way 4 adit, door, gust, pang,
turn 5 burst, entry, onset, route, sally, spell,
throe 6 attack, entreé, stitch, taking, twinge
7 flare-up, ingress, passage, seizure
8 entrance, eruption, outburst 9 admission,
explosion 10 admittance

accessible 4 open 6 public, usable
9 operative 10 employable 11 practicable
12 approachable, unrestricted

accession 4 rise 5 raise 8 addition,
increase 9 accretion, increment 12 augmentation

accessory 7 abettor, adjunct, fitting
8 addition, adjuvant, appendix 9 accretion,
ancillary, appendage, auxiliary, increment,
secondary, tributary 10 accomplice, coincident, collateral, concurrent, incidental, subsidiary 11 appurtenant, concomitant, confederate, conspirator, subordinate,
subservient 12 adventitious, appurtenance,
contributory 13 accompaniment, coconspirator

accident 3 hap 4 fate, luck 5 fluke
6 chance, hazard, kismet, mishap 7 destiny, fortune 8 calamity, casualty, fortuity
9 mischance 10 misfortune 12 misadventure

accidental 3 odd 5 fluky 6 casual,
chance, random 7 unmeant 9 chromatic,
dependent, unplanned, unwitting 10 coincident, contingent, fortuitous, undesigned,
unintended, unpurposed 11 conditional,
inadvertent 13 unintentional

accidentally 5 haply

acclaim 4 hail 5 cheer, éclat, exalt, glory,
honor, roose 6 homage, kudize, praise
7 applaud, commend, glorify, magnify, ovation, root for 8 applause, plaudits 9 recommend, reverence 10 compliment

acclamation 8 applause, plaudits

acclimate 6 harden, season 7 toughen
9 climatize

acclimatize see acclimate

accolade 4 bays 5 award, badge, honor,
kudos 7 laurels 10 decoration 11 distinction

accommodate 3 fit 4 hold, suit, tune,
vary 5 adapt, alter, defer, favor, house,
humor, lodge, put up, yield 6 adjust, attune,
bestow, billet, change, encase, harbor, modify, oblige, square, submit, tailor 7 cater to,
conform, contain, enclose, indulge, quarter
8 domicile 9 entertain, harmonize, integrate, reconcile 10 coordinate, proportion
11 convenience, domiciliate 12 reconciliate

accommodations 4 keep, room 7 housing, lodging, shelter 8 lodgment 12 room
and board

accompaniment 4 mate 6 fellow 7 comrade, consort, partner 8 addition 9 accessory, associate, attendant, colleague, companion, corollary 10 assistance, complement, enrichment, equivalent, supplement
11 concomitant, enhancement 12 augmentation

accompany 4 join, lead 5 bring, guide,
pilot, steer 6 attend, convoy, escort 7 combine, conduct, consort, esquire 8 chaperon
9 associate 11 consort with

accompanying 8 incident 9 ancillary,
attendant, attending, satellite 10 coincident,
collateral 11 concomitant

accomplice 5 aider 6 flunky, helper,
stooge 7 abettor 9 accessory, assistant
11 confederate, conspirator 13 coconspirator

accomplish 3 win 4 gain 5 reach, score
6 attain, fulfil, rack up 7 achieve, fulfill, realize, succeed

accomplished 4 ripe 5 adept 6 expert
8 finished, masterly 9 all-around, many-
sided, perfected, versatile, virtuosic 10 consummate, proficient

accomplishment 3 act, art 4 deed
5 craft, doing, skill, thing 6 action, finish
8 fruition 9 adeptness, expertise 10 attainment, expertness 11 achievement, acquirement, acquisition, proficiency

accord 4 deal, fuse, give, jibe, tune
5 agree, award, blend, chime, fit in, grant,
merge, tally, union 6 chorus, concur, confer, square 7 concede, concert, conform,
empathy, harmony 8 affinity, coalesce,
coincide, dovetail, sympathy 9 agreement,
harmonize, vouchsafe 10 attraction, consonance, correspond, solidarity 11 concordance 13 understanding

accordant 9 congruous 10 harmonious

accordingly 2 so 4 ergo, then, thus
5 hence 9 therefore, thereupon 12 consequently

accost 3 dog 4 dare, face, hail 5 annoy,
front, greet, hound, worry 6 bother, call to,
halloo, pester, salute 7 address, affront,
apply to, bespeak, outface, outrage
8 approach, confront 9 challenge 10 buttonhole 11 memorialize

accouchement 7 lying in 8 childbed
11 confinement

account 3 tab, use 4 bill, deem, note,
rate, view 5 avail, favor, score, story, value,
worth 6 assess, esteem, reason, reckon,
regard, report, repute 7 dignity, explain,
expound, fitness, history, invoice, justify,
recital, respect, service, utility, version
8 appraise, consider, estimate, evaluate
9 advantage, chronicle, elucidate, narrative,
rationale, reckoning, relevance, statement,
valuation 10 admiration, estimation, reputation, usefulness 11 consequence, distinction, explain away, explanation, rationalize
13 applicability, consideration, justification

accountable 6 liable 8 amenable
10 answerable 11 responsible

account book 6 ledger

accounting *branch of:* 11 bookkeeping

accouter 3 arm, rig 4 deck, gear 5 adorn,
dress, equip, fix up, ready 6 attire, fit out,
outfit 7 appoint, furnish, prepare, turn out
8 decorate 9 embellish

accouterment 4 gear 6 outfit, tackle
7 bravery, regalia 8 matériel, tackling
9 apparatus, equipment, machinery, trappings 11 furnishings, habiliments
12 appointments 13 paraphernalia

accredit 2 OK 3 lay 4 okay 5 refer
6 assign, attest, charge, enable, impute
7 approve, ascribe, certify, commend,
empower, endorse, license 8 sanction,
vouch for 9 attribute, authorize, recommend 10 commission

accretion 4 rise 5 raise 7 adjunct 8 addition, increase 9 accession, appendage,
increment 10 attachment 11 enlargement
12 augmentation

accumulate 4 heap, hive, mass, pile
5 amass, hoard, lay by, lay in, lay up,
stock, uplay 6 garner, gather, roll up

7 backlog, collect, lay down, store up
8 assemble, treasure 9 stockpile

accumulation 4 bank, heap, mass, pile
5 hoard, stock, store, trove 7 buildup,
cumulus, reserve 9 amassment 10 collection 11 aggregation 13 agglomeration

accumulative 5 chain 8 additive, additory
9 summative 11 aggregative 12 augmenta-
tive

accuracy 9 exactness, precision 10 definition, exactitude 11 correctness, preciseness 12 definiteness

accurate 4 nice 5 exact, right 6 proper
7 certain, correct, precise 8 reliable, rigorous 9 authentic 10 dependable

accursed 6 odious 7 hateful 8 damnable
9 abhorrent, execrable, offensive, repugnant, revolting 10 abominable, detestable

accusation 6 charge 8 delation 10 allegation, indictment *false:* 7 calumny

accuse 3 tax 5 blame 6 charge, delate,
indict 7 arraign, censure, impeach
8 denounce 9 criminate, criticize, inculpate,
reprobate 11 incriminate

accustom 3 use 4 wont 5 adapt, inure
6 adjust, harden, season 9 habituate
11 acclimatize, familiarize

accustomed 5 usual 7 chronic, routine
8 accepted, everyday, habitual, standard
9 confirmed 10 habituated, regulation
11 commonplace 12 conventional

ace 3 bit, jot 4 atom, hair, iota, mite
5 crumb, minim, speck 7 whisker 8 molecule, particle 11 hairbreadth

ace and face card 7 natural 9 blackjack

acedia 5 sloth

acerb 3 dry 4 acid, sour, tart 7 acetose,
caustic 9 acidulous, corrosive, sarcastic
12 archilochian

acerbate 7 envenom 8 embitter

acerbic see acerb

acerbity 7 acidity, sarcasm 8 acrimony,
asperity, dourness, mordancy, sourness,
tartness 9 harshness, roughness, surliness
10 bitterness, causticity 11 crabbedness,
saturninity

Achates' companion 6 Aeneas

ache 3 yen 4 hurt, long, lust, pain, pang,
pine, pity, rack, sigh 5 crave, throe, yearn
6 hanker, hunger, injury, misery, stitch, suffer, thirst, twinge 7 feel for 8 yearning
10 sorrow over 11 commiserate 13 compassionate *Scottish:* 5 stoun 6 stound

acheronian 5 black, bleak, drear 6 dismal, gloomy 7 joyless 8 desolate, funereal
9 cheerless

achieve 2 do 3 get, win 4 gain 5 reach,
score 6 attain, finish, obtain, rack up,
secure 7 acquire, execute, perform, realize
8 complete, conclude 9 actualize
10 accomplish

achievement 4 deed, feat 6 finish
7 exploit 10 attainment 11 acquirement,
acquisition, tour de force
Achilles *adviser:* 6 Nestor *companion:*
9 Patroclus *father:* 6 Peleus *horse:* 7 Xan-
thus *lover:* 7 Briseis *mother:* 6 Thetis
slayer: 5 Paris *victim:* 6 Hector *vulnerable part:* 4 heel
Achilles' heel 8 soft spot
aching 4 sore 7 algetic, hurtful, hurting,
painful 10 afflictive
Achsah *father:* 5 Caleb *husband:* 7 Othniel
achy 4 sore
acicular 5 acute, peaky, piked, sharp
6 peaked 7 pointed
acid 3 dry 4 sour, tart 5 acerb 7 acerbic,
acetose *bleaching:* 6 oxalic *combining
form:* 3 oxy 4 acet 5 aceto *fatty:* 6 capric
7 caproic, stearic 8 caprylic *found in
apples:* 5 malic *found in cranberries:*
7 benzoic *found in grapes:* 8 tartaric
found in lemons: 6 citric *found in rhubarb:* 6 oxalic *found in sour milk:* 6 lactic
indicator: 6 litmus *kind:* 5 amino, boric,
iodic, malic, oleic 6 acetic, bromic, formic,
nitric, oxalic, tannic 7 chloric, nitrous, silicic
8 carbolic, carbonic, chlorous, muriatic, sul-
furic 9 aqua regia 12 hydrochloric *neutralizer:* 4 base 6 alkali *tanning:* 6 tannic
8 catechin *vinegar:* 6 acetic
acid radical *combining form:* 3 oyl
acidulous 3 dry 4 sour, tart 5 acerb,
sharp 6 biting 7 acerbic, acetose, cutting,
piquant, pungent
Acis *lover:* 7 Galatea *slayer:* 10 Polyphemus
acknowledge 3 own 4 avow, deem, tell,
view 5 admit, agree, allow, grant, let on,
own up 6 accept, fess up, reveal 7 concede, confess, declare, divulge
8 announce, consider, disclose, proclaim
9 recognize
acknowledgment 6 credit 11 recognition
acme 4 apex, peak 6 apogee, climax, summit, tiptop, vertex, zenith 8 capstone,
meridian, pinnacle 11 culmination
acorn *combining form:* 5 balan 6 balano
sprouter: 3 oak
acoustic 5 aural 6 audile 8 auditory
acquaint 4 clew, clue, post, tell, warn
6 advise, fill in, inform, notify, orient, wise
up 7 apprise, present 8 accustom 9 habituate, introduce
acquaintance 4 mate 5 amigo, crony
6 friend 7 comrade 8 familiar, intimacy, intimate 9 associate, companion, confidant
10 experience 11 familiarity
acquainted 6 au fait, versed 7 abreast,
versant 8 familiar, informed 9 au courant
10 conversant

acquiesce 3 bow, yes 5 agree 6 accede,
assent, concur 7 consent 9 reconcile, subscribe
acquiescence 9 deference 10 compliance, conformity 11 resignation 12 complaisance
acquiescent 7 passive 8 resigned, yielding 10 submissive 11 unresistant, unresisting 12 nonresistant, nonresisting
acquire 3 add, get, win 4 earn, form, gain,
land, make, reap 5 amass, annex, reach
6 garner, obtain, pick up, secure 7 bring in,
collect, develop, procure 8 cumulate
9 knock down 10 accumulate
acquirement 6 finish 7 advance 8 addition 9 accretion, erudition 10 attainment
11 achievement, acquisition, advancement
acquisition see acquirement
acquisitive 5 itchy 6 grabby, greedy
8 covetous, desirous, grasping 10 prehensile
acquit 3 act 4 bear, free 5 carry, clear
6 behave, deport 7 absolve, comport, conduct, release 8 liberate 9 discharge, exculpate, exonerate, vindicate 10 disculpate
acres 4 land 5 manor 6 estate 7 demesne
acrid 4 sour 5 harsh, sharp 6 biting, bitter
7 austere, caustic, cutting 9 amaroidal
10 astringent
acrimonious 3 mad 5 angry, cross, irate,
testy, wroth 6 cranky, ireful, wrathy, wrothy
8 wrathful, wrothful 9 indignant, irascible,
splenetic 11 belligerent, contentious, quarrelsome
acrimony 5 spite 6 animus, malice, rancor 7 ill will 8 acerbity, asperity, mordancy
9 animosity, antipathy, malignity 10 bitterness 11 malevolence
Acrisius *daughter:* 5 Danae *slayer:*
7 Perseus
across 4 over 6 beyond 7 athwart
12 transversely *prefix:* 2 di 3 dia 4 over
5 trans
act 2 do 3 run 4 bear, deed, fake, feat,
play, sham, work 5 bluff, doing, feign, put
on, serve 6 acquit, affect, assume, behave,
demean, deport 7 comport, conduct,
exploit, operate, perform, portray, pretend
8 function, simulate 9 discourse, officiate,
personate 10 masquerade 11 counterfeit,
impersonate *suffix:* 2 cy, th 3 ade, ate,
ice, ion, ism
acting 6 pro tem 7 interim 9 ad interim,
temporary 10 pro tempore
actinium *symbol:* 2 Ac
action 4 case, deed, fray, suit, work
5 cause, doing 6 affray, battle, combat
7 lawsuit, process, service 8 behavior, conflict, function 9 discharge, execution, operation, procedure 10 engagement, proceeding 11 performance *combining form:*

3 cin, kin **4** cino, kine, kino **5** cinet, kinet
6 cineto, kineto, praxia, praxis *suffix:* **2** al,
cy **3** ade, ing, sis **4** ance, ence, esis, ment,
osis **5** ation **7** isation, ization *unwise:*
8 impolicy

action painting **7** tachism

activate **4** stir, wake **5** rally, rouse, waken
6 arouse, awaken **8** energize, vitalize

activation *combining form:* **7** kinesis

active **4** busy, live, spry, yare **5** agile,
alert, alive, brisk, zippy **6** brisky, lively, nimble **7** driving, dynamic, running, working
8 animated, spirited, vigorous **9** assiduous,
energetic, operative, sprightly, vivacious
11 functioning, industrious **12** enterprising

activity **8** exercise, exertion **10** exercising

actor **4** mime **5** mimic, party **6** mummer,
player, sharer **7** trouper **8** histrion, par-
taker, thespian **9** performer **11** participant
12 impersonator, participator *name:* **3** Cox
(Wally), Dix (Richard), Fox (James, Michael
J.), Lee (Bruce), Lom (Herbert), Mix (Tom),
Ray (Aldo) **4** Alda (Alan, Robert), Bean
(Orson), Blue (Ben), Bond (Ward), Caan
(James), Cage (Nicholas), Cobb (Lee J.),
Coco (James), Culp (Robert), Dean
(James), Depp (Johnny), Dern (Bruce), Duff
(Howard), Egan (Richard), Falk (Peter),
Ford (Glenn, Harrison), Foxx (Redd), Geer
(Will), Gere (Richard), Grey (Joel), Hale
(Alan), Hill (Arthur), Hope (Bob), Hurt (John
William), Ives (Burl), Jory (Victor), Kaye
(Danny), Kean (Edmund), Keel (Howard),
Ladd (Alan), Lahr (Bert), Lord (Jack), Lowe
(Chad, Rob), Lunt (Alfred), Marx (Chico,
Groucho, Harpo), Muni (Paul), Ngor (Haing
S.), Noth (Christopher), Peck (Gregory),
Penn (Sean), Pitt (Brad), Raft (George),
Roth (Tim), Ryan (Robert), Shaw (Robert),
Todd (Richard), Tone (Franchot), Torn
(Rip), Tune (Tommy), Wahl (Ken), Webb
(Clifton, Jack), Wynn (Ed, Keenan), York
(Michael) **5** Adler (Luther), Allen (Tim,
Woody), Arkin (Adam, Alan), Asner (Ed),
Autry (Gene), Ayres (Lew), Bacon (Kevin),
Barry (Gene), Bates (Alan), Beery (Noah,
Wallace), Berle (Milton), Boone (Richard),
Brady (Scott), Brand (Neville), Burns
(George), Caine (Michael), Candy (John),
Chase (Chevy), Clark (Dane), Clift (Mont-
gomery), Conte (Richard), Cooke (Alistair),
Corey (Wendell), Cosby (Bill), Dafoe (Wil-
lem), Davis (Clifton, Ossie, Sammy Jr.),
Delon (Alain), Donat (Robert), Evans (Mau-
rice), Ewell (Tom), Finch (Peter), Firth
(Colin, Peter), Flynn (Errol), Fonda (Henry,
Peter), Franz (Dennis), Gabin (Jean),
Gable (Clark), Gould (Elliot), Grant (Cary,
Hugh), Gwenn (Edmund), Hanks (Tom),
Hardy (Oliver), Hauer (Rutger), Hawke
(Ethan), Hayes (Gabby), Irons (Jeremy),
Jaffe (Sam), Jones (Dean, James Earl,
Tommy Lee), Kazan (Elia), Keach (Stacy),
Keith (Brian, David), Kelly (Gene), Kiley
(Richard), Kline (Kevin), Kotto (Yaphet),
Lamas (Fernando, Lorenzo), Lanza (Mario),
Lewis (Jerry, Richard), Lloyd (Harold), Lorre
(Peter), Lukas (Paul), Lynde (Paul), March
(Fredric), McCoy (Tim), Mills (John), Mineo
(Sal), Moore (Dudley, Roger, Victor), Neill
(Sam), Nimoy (Leonard), Niven (David),
Nolan (Lloyd), Nolte (Nick), Oakie (Jack),
Oland (Warner), Olmos (Edward James),
O'Neal (Patrick, Ryan), Payne (John), Perry
(Luke, Matthew), Pesci (Joe), Power
(Tyrone), Price (Vincent), Pryce (Jonathan),
Quaid (Dennis, Randy), Quale (Anthony),
Quinn (Aidan Anthony), Rains (Claude),
Reeve (Christopher), Scott (Campbell,
George C., Randolph), Segal (George),
Sheen (Charlie, Martin), Smits (Jimmy),
Stack (Robert), Stamp (Terence), Tracy
(Spencer), Tufts (Sonny), Wayne (John),
Wilde (Cornel), Wills (Chill), Woods
(James), Young (Gig, Robert) **6** Abbott
(Bud), Albert (Eddie), Ameche (Don),
Arness (James), Backus (Jim), Balsam
(Martin), Barker (Lex), Baxter (Warner),
Beatty (Ned, Warren), Begley (Ed), Blades
(Ruben), Bogart (Humphrey), Bolger (Ray),
Bosley (Tom), Brando (Marlon), Brooks
(Albert, Mel), Burton (Richard), Caesar
(Sid), Cagney (James), Callan (Michael),
Cantor (Eddie), Cariou (Len), Carney (Art),
Carrey (Jim), Carvey (Dana), Chaney (Lon),
Coburn (Charles, James), Colman (Ron-
ald), Conrad (Robert, William), Conway
(Tim, Tom), Coogan (Jackie), Cooper
(Gary), Cotten (Joseph), Crabbe (Buster),
Crenna (Richard), Cronyn (Hume), Crosby
(Bing), Cruise (Tom), Culkin (Macaulay),
Curtis (Tony), Dailey (Dan), Dalton (Timo-
thy), Danson (Ted), Danton (Ray), Darren
(James), De Niro (Robert), De Vito
(Danny), Dillon (Matt), Downey (Robert),
Dullea (Keir), Duryea (Dan), Duvall (Rob-
ert), Ferrer (Jose, Mel), Fields (W.C.), Fin-
ney (Albert), Garcia (Andy), Garner
(James), Gibson (Hoot, Mel), Glover
(Danny), Gorcey (Leo), Gordan (Gale),
Graves (Peter), Greene (Lorne, Richard),
Grodin (Charles), Hamlin (Harry), Harris
(Ed, Richard), Harvey (Laurence), Hayden
(Sterling), Heflin (Van), Heston (Charlton),
Hingle (Pat), Holden (Bill), Hopper (Dennis,
William), Howard (Trevor), Hudson (Rock),
Hunter (Jeffrey, Tab), Huston (John, Wal-
ter), Hutton (Jim, Timothy), Jacobi (Lou),
Jagger (Dean), Keaton (Buster, Michael),
Keitel (Harvey), Kilmer (Val), Knotts (Don),
Kruger (Otto), Landau (Martin), Landon
(Michael), Laurel (Stan), Lemmon (Jack),

Liotta (Ray), Lugosi (Bela), MacRae (Gordon), Malden (Karl), Martin (Dean, Steve), Marvin (Lee), Massey (Raymond), Mature (Victor), McCrea (Joel), Meeker (Ralph), Menjou (Adolphe), Modine (Matthew), Morgan (Harry), Morley (Robert), Morris (Wayne), Morrow (Vic), Mostel (Josh, Zero), Murphy (Audie, Eddie), Murray (Bill, Don), Neeson (Liam), Nelson (Ozzie), Newley (Anthony), Newman (Paul), O'Brian (Hugh), O'Brien (Edmund, Pat), Oldman (Gary), O'Toole (Peter), Pacino (Al), Parker (Fess, Jameson), Poston (Tom), Powell (Dick), Reeves (Keanu, Steve), Reiner (Carl, Rob), Reiser (Paul), Rennie (Michael), Ritter (John, Tex), Rogers (Roy, Wayne, Will), Romero (Cesar), Rooney (Mickey), Rourke (Mickey), Schell (Maximilian), Seagal (Steven), Sharif (Omar), Slezak (Walter), Snipes (Wesley), Spacey (Kevin), Spader (James), Swayze (Patrick), Talbot (Lyle), Taylor (Robert, Rod), Thomas (Danny, Richard), Toomey (Regis), Tucker (Forrest), Turpin (Ben), Vaughn (Robert), Voight (Jon), Wagner (Jack, Robert), Walker (Robert), Warden (Jack), Wayans (Damon, Keenen Ivory), Weaver (Dennis, Fritz), Welles (Orson), Werner (Oskar), Wilder (Gene), Willis (Bruce) 7 Abraham (F. Murray), Andrews (Dana), Assante (Armand), Astaire (Fred), Aykroyd (Dan), Baldwin (Alec, Daniel, Stephen, William), Bellamy (Ralph), Bogarde (Dirk), Branagh (Kenneth), Bridges (Beau, Jeff, Lloyd), Bronson (Charles), Brosnan (Pierce), Brynner (Yul), Bushman (Francis X.), Buttons (Red), Calhern (Louis), Calhoun (Rory), Cameron (Rod), Carlson (Richard), Carroll (Leo G.), Chaplin (Charlie), Clooney (George), Connery (Sean), Connors (Chuck, Mike), Conried (Hans), Costner (Kevin), Crystal (Billy), Daniels (Jeff, William), da Silva (Howard), DeLuise (Dom), Dennehy (Brian), Donahue (Troy), Donlevy (Brian), Douglas (Kirk, Melvyn, Michael, Paul), Dreyfuss (Richard), Edwards (Vince), Feldman (Marty), Fiennes (Ralph), Freeman (Morgan), Garrick (David), Gazzara (Ben), Gielgud (John), Gleason (Jackie), Goodman (John), Gossett (Louis), Grammer (Kelsey), Granger (Farley, Stewart), Guiness (Alec), Hackman (Gene), Henreid (Paul), Hoffman (Dustin), Homeier (Skip), Homolka (Oscar), Hopkins (Anthony), Hoskins (Bob), Ireland (John), Janssen (David), Johnson (Ben, Don, Van), Jourdan (Louis), Jurgens (Curt), Karloff (Boris), Kennedy (Arthur, George), Klugman (Jack), Lawford (Peter), Leonard (Robert Sean, Sheldon), Lithgow (John), Macchio (Ralph), MacLane (Barton), Maharis (George), Mathers

(Jerry), Matthau (Walter), McCarey (Leo), McGavin (Darren), McQueen (Steve), Merrill (Gary), Milland (Ray), Mitchum (Robert), Montand (Yves), Navarro (Ramon), Newhart (Bob), O'Connor (Carroll, Donald), Olivier (Laurence), Palance (Jack), Paulsen (Pat), Peppard (George), Perkins (Anthony), Persoff (Nehemiah), Pickens (Slim), Pidgeon (Walter), Pinchot (Bronson), Poitier (Sidney), Preston (Robert), Randall (Tony), Redford (Robert), Rickman (Alan), Robards (Jason), Robbins (Tim), Robeson (Paul), Roberts (Pernell, Tony), Salvini (Tommaso), Sanders (George), Savalas (Telly), Scourby (Alexander), Selleck (Tom), Sellers (Peter), Shatner (William), Shepard (Sam), Silvers (Phil), Sinatra (Frank), Skelton (Red), Skinner (Otis), Steiger (Rod), Stewart (James, Patrick), Tamblyn (Russ), Ustinov (Peter), Vallone (Raf), Van Dyke (Dick, Jerry), Wallach (Eli), Widmark (Richard), Wilding (Michael), Winters (Jonathan), Woolley (Monty) 8 Banderas (Antonio), Basehart (Richard), Berenger (Tom), Bickford (Charles), Blackmer (Sidney), Borgnine (Ernest), Buchanan (Edgar), Buchholz (Horst), Carrillo (Leo), Chandler (Jeff), Costello (Lou), Crawford (Broderick, Michael), Cummings (Robert), Day-Lewis (Daniel), DiCaprio (Leonardo), Duchovny (David), Eastwood (Clint), Forsythe (John), Gardiner (Reginald), Garfield (John), Goldblum (Jeff), Harrison (Gregory, Noel, Rex), Hemmings (David), Holbrook (Hal), Holloway (Stanley), Jannings (Emil), Kilbride (Percy), Kingsley (Ben), Langella (Frank), Laughton (Charles), Lockhart (Gene), Marshall (E.G., Herbert), McDowall (Roddy), McDowell (Malcolm), McLaglen (Victor), Meredith (Burgess), Mitchell (Thomas), O'Connell (Arthur), O'Donnell (Chris), O'Herlihy (Dan), Rathbone (Basil), Redgrave (Michael), Reynolds (Burt), Ritchard (Cyril), Robinson (Edward G.), Sarrazin (Michael), Scofield (Paul), Stallone (Sylvester), Sullivan (Barry), Travolta (John), Turturro (John), Van Damme (Jean-Claude), Von Sydow (Max), Whitmore (James), Williams (Robin) 9 Amsterdam (Morey), Barrymore (John, Lionel), Brandauer (Klaus Maria), Broderick (Matthew), Carnovsky (Morris), Carradine (David, John, Keith, Robert), Courtenay (Tom), Depardieu (Gerard), Fairbanks (Douglas), Fishburne (Larry), Franciosa (Anthony), Hardwicke (Cedric), Harrelson (Woody), Hyde-White (Wilfrid), Lancaster (Burt), MacMurray (Fred), Malkovich (John), Montalban (Ricardo), Nicholson (Jack), Pleasance (Donald), Robertson (Cliff, Dale), Tarantino (Quentin), Zimbalist (Efrem) 10 Fitzgerald (Barry), Hasselhoff (David), Montgomery (Robert), Richardson (Ralph), Sutherland (Donald, Kiefer), Washington (Denzel) **11** Chamberlain (Richard), Greenstreet (Sydney), Larroquette (John), Mastroianni (Marcello) **13** Kristofferson (Kris) **14** Schwarzenegger (Arnold)

actor's *quest:* **4** part, role *signal:* **3** cue
actress 3 Bow (Clara), Cox (Courtney), Day (Doris), Dee (Sandra), Dru (Joanne), Gam (Rita), Loy (Myrna), May (Elaine), Rae (Charlotte) **4** Bara (Theda), Barr (Roseanne), Cass (Peggy), Cher, Coca (Imogene), Dahl (Arlene), Daly (Tyne), Dern (Laura), Duke (Patty), Eden (Barbara), Foch (Nina), Garr (Teri), Gish (Lillian), Hawn (Goldie), Holm (Celeste), Hunt (Helen, Linda, Marsha), Hyer (Martha), Kahn (Madeline), Kerr (Deborah), Lake (Veronica), Lisi (Virna), Main (Marjorie), Mayo (Virginia), Neal (Patricia), Olin (Lena), Raye (Martha), Rigg (Diana), Ross (Diana, Katharine), Rush (Barbara), Ryan (Meg, Peggy), Shue (Elisabeth), Weld (Tuesday), West (Mae), Wood (Natalie, Peggy), Wray (Fay), York (Susannah) **5** Adams (Maude), Aimee (Anouk), Allen (Joan, Karen, Nancy), Alley (Kirstie), Arden (Eve), Astor (Mary), Bates (Kathy), Berry (Halle), Bloom (Clair), Blyth (Ann), Booth (Shirley), Britt (May), Bruce (Virginia), Buzzi (Ruth), Caron (Leslie), Close (Glenn), Crain (Jeanne), Davis (Bette, Geena, Judy), Dunne (Irene), Eggar (Samantha), Field (Sally), Fonda (Bridget, Jane), Gabor (Eva, Zsa Zsa), Garbo (Greta), Gless (Sharon), Grant (Lee), Hagen (Uta), Hasso (Signe), Hayes (Helen), Henie (Sonja), Howes (Sally Ann), Jones (Jennifer, Shirley), Kelly (Patsy), Kurtz (Swoosie), Lahti (Christine), Lange (Hope, Jessica), Leigh (Janet, Jennifer Jason, Vivien), Lenya (Lotte), Lewis (Juliette), Loren (Sophia), Mason (Pamela), Meara (Anne), Miles (Sarah, Vera), Moore (Demi, Mary Tyler, Terry), North (Sheree), Novak (Kim), O'Hara (Maureen), Olson (Nancy), O'Neal (Tatum), Perez (Rosie), Picon (Molly), Pitts (Zasu), Roman (Ruth), Ruehl (Mercedes), Ryder (Winona), Saint (Eva Marie), Scott (Lizbeth, Martha), Smith (Alexis, Maggie), Storm (Gale), Tandy (Jessica), Tyson (Cicely), Welch (Raquel), Wiest (Dianne), Wyatt (Jane), Young (Sean Loretta) **6** Adjani (Isabelle), Angeli (Pier), Ashley (Elizabeth), Bacall (Lauren), Bardot (Brigitte), Barkin (Ellen), Barrie (Wendy), Baxter (Anne), Bening (Annette), Bergen (Candice, Polly), Bisset (Jacqueline), Blaine (Vivian), Bujold (Genevieve), Butler (Brett), Cannon (Dyan), Carter (Dixie, Lynda, Nell), Curtin (Jane), Curtis (Jamie Lee), Davies

(Marion), Delaney (Dana), Del Rio (Dolores), Dennis (Sandy), Diller (Phyllis), Duncan (Sandy), Durbin (Deanna), Fabray (Nanette), Farrow (Mia), Fisher (Carrie), Foster (Jodie), Garner (Peggy Ann), Garson (Greer), Gaynor (Mitzi), Gordon (Ruth), Grable (Betty), Grimes (Tammy), Hannah (Daryl), Harlow (Jean), Harper (Tess, Valerie), Harris (Julie, Rosemary), Hunter (Holly, Kim), Hussey (Ruth), Huston (Anjelica), Hutton (Betty), Keaton (Diane), Keeler (Ruby), Kidman (Nicole), Lamarr (Hedy), Lamour (Dorothy), Lasser (Louise), Laurie (Piper), Louise (Tina), Lupino (Ida), MacRae (Sheila), Malone (Dorothy), Martin (Mary), Matlin (Marlee), McGraw (Ali), Merkel (Una), Midler (Bette), Monroe (Marilyn), Moreau (Jeanne), Moreno (Rita), Oberon (Merle), O'Brien (Margaret), Palmer (Lili), Paquin (Anna), Parker (Eleanor, Mary-Louise, Sarah Jessica, Suzy), Powers (Stephanie), Prowse (Juliet), Rashad (Phylicia), Remick (Lee), Ritter (Thelma), Rogers (Ginger), Sidney (Sylvia), Spacek (Sissy), Streep (Meryl), Taylor (Elizabeth), Temple (Shirley), Thomas (Marlo), Tiffin (Pamela), Tomlin (Lily), Turner (Kathleen, Lana), Walker (Nancy), Weaver (Sigourney), Wilson (Marie), Winger (Debra), Wright (Teresa), Wynter (Dana) **7** Allyson (June), Andress (Ursula), Andrews (Julie), Bergman (Ingrid), Buckley (Betty), Bullock (Sandra), Burnett (Carol), Burstyn (Ellen), Collins (Joan, Pauline), Darnell (Linda), DeCarlo (Yvonne), Deneuve (Catherine), Dukakis (Olympia), Dunaway (Faye), Dunnock (Mildred), Fawcett (Farrah), Fleming (Rhonda), Fricker (Brenda), Gardner (Ava), Garland (Judy), Goddard (Paulette), Grayson (Kathryn), Hayward (Susan), Heckart (Eileen), Hepburn (Audrey, Katharine), Hershey (Barbara), Jackson (Ann, Glenda, Kate), Langtry (Lillie), Learned (Michael), Lombard (Carole), Madonna, Magnani (Anna), Mangano (Silvana), McGuire (Dorothy), McKenna (Siobhan), McQueen (Butterfly), Meadows (Audrey, Jayne), Mimieux (Yvette), Miranda (Carmen), Mulgrew (Kate), Natwick (Mildred), Perlman (Rhea), Perrine (Valerie), Podesta (Rosanna), Roberts (Julia), Russell (Jane, Rosalind, Theresa), Scacchi (Greta), Shearer (Norma), Simmons (Jean), Sorvino (Mira), Stevens (Connie, Stella), Swanson (Gloria), Thaxter (Phyllis), Tierney (Gene), Ullmann (Liv), Winfrey (Oprah), Winters (Shelley), Withers (Jane) **8** Anderson (Judith, Loni, Melissa Sue), Arquette (Patricia, Rosanna), Ashcroft (Peggy), Bancroft (Anne), Bankhead (Tallulah), Basinger (Kim), Blondell (Joan), Byington (Spring), Caldwell (Zoe), Channing (Carol, Stockard), Charisse (Cyd), Christie (Julie), Crawford (Joan), Dewhurst (Colleen), Dietrich (Marlene), Dressler (Marie), Fletcher (Louise), Fontaine (Joan), Fontanne (Lynn), Goldberg (Whoopi), Griffith (Melanie), Hayworth (Rita), Lansbury (Angela), Lawrence (Gertrude), Leachman (Cloris), Leighton (Margaret), Lindfors (Viveca), Lockhart (June), Lovelace (Linda), MacLaine (Shirley), Mercouri (Melina), Minnelli (Liza), Neuwirth (Bebe), O'Donnell (Rosie), Pfeiffer (Michelle), Pickford (Mary), Prentiss (Paula), Redgrave (Lynn, Vanessa), Roseanne, Rowlands (Gena), Sarandon (Susan), Shepherd (Cybill), Signoret (Simone), Stanwyck (Barbara), Sullavan (Margaret), Talmadge (Norma), Thompson (Emma, Sada), Williams (Esther), Woodward (Joanne) 9 Alexander (Jane), Barrymore (Drew, Ethel), Bernhardt (Sarah), Christian (Linda), Clayburgh (Jill), DeGeneres (Ellen), Dickinson (Angie), Kellerman (Sally), Mansfield (Jayne), McDonnell (Mary), Moorehead (Agnes), O'Sullivan (Maureen), Pleshette (Suzanne), Plowright (Joan), Schneider (Romy), Singleton (Penny), Stapleton (Jean, Maureen), Strasberg (Susan), Streisand (Barbra), Struthers (Sally), Thorndike (Sybil), Vera-Ellen 10 Lanchester (Elsa), Montgomery (Elizabeth), Richardson (Miranda, Natasha), Rutherford (Margaret), Tushingham (Rita) 11 Ann-Margaret, de Havilland (Olivia), McCambridge (Mercedes), Riefenstahl (Leni), Steenburgen (Mary) 12 Bonham-Carter (Helena), Lollabrigida (Gina), Mastrantonio (Mary Elizabeth)

actual 4 hard, real, true 6 extant 7 genuine 8 absolute, bona fide, concrete, existent, material, physical, positive, tangible, unfabled 9 authentic, objective, veridical 10 legitimate, phenomenal, undeniable 12 indisputable

actuality 4 fact 5 being 7 reality 9 existence, substance 10 embodiment 11 incarnation, materiality

actually 4 very 5 truly 6 really 7 de facto 9 genuinely, veritably

actuate 4 move, stir 5 drive, impel, rouse 6 arouse, propel, set off 7 provoke, trigger 8 mobilize, vitalize 9 circulate, galvanize

act up 9 misbehave

acumen 3 wit 8 astucity, keenness 9 acuteness, sharpness 10 astuteness, shrewdness 11 discernment, penetration, percipience 12 perspicacity

acute 4 dire, high, keen 5 peaky, piked, sharp 6 argute, peaked, piping, shrill, treble, urgent 7 crucial, cutting, exigent, pointed 8 acicular, critical, incisive, piercing, shooting, stabbing 9 aciculate, acumi-

nate, acuminous, cuspidate, desperate, knifelike, observant, sensitive, trenchant 10 perceptive 11 climacteric, penetrating, penetrative, quick-witted, sharp-witted *combining form:* 3 oxy

adage 3 saw 4 word 6 byword, saying, truism 7 proverb 8 aphorism, apothegm

Adah *husband:* 4 Esau 6 Lamech *son:* 5 Jabal, Jubal 7 Eliphaz

Adam *grandson:* 4 Enos 5 Enoch *rib:* 3 Eve *son:* 4 Abel, Cain, Seth *teacher:* 6 Raisel *wife:* 3 Eve 6 Lilith

Adam____ 4 Bede 5 Smith

adamant 5 rigid 8 immobile, obdurate 9 immovable, unbending, unswaying 10 inexorable, inflexible, relentless, unbendable, unyielding 12 unsubmitting

adapt 3 fit 4 suit 5 refit 6 adjust, square, tailor 7 conform 9 acclimate, reconcile 11 acclimatize, accommodate

adaptable 6 mobile, pliant, supple 7 ductile, plastic, pliable 8 moldable 9 all-around, malleable, many-sided, versatile

Ad astra per____ 6 aspera

add 3 sum, tot 4 cast, foot, tote 5 affix, annex, tally, total 6 append, attach, figure, reckon, tack on, take on 7 augment, compute, enlarge, subjoin, summate 8 compound, increase, totalize 9 calculate

added 3 new 4 else, more 5 fresh, other 7 another, farther, further 10 additional

addendum 5 rider 7 allonge 8 addition 10 supplement

ad design 4 logo

addict 3 fan 4 bias, buff 5 hound, lover 6 adjust, junkie, votary, zealot 7 devotee, fanatic, habitué, hophead 9 habituate 10 aficionado, enthusiast, predispose

addition 4 plus, rise 5 extra, raise, rider 7 accrual, adjunct 8 addendum, appanage, increase 9 accession, accessory, accretion, extension, increment 10 accruement, supplement 12 appurtenance, augmentation *number:* 6 addend 7 summand

additional 3 new 4 else, more 5 extra, fresh, other 7 another, farther, further 9 accessory 12 supplemental 13 supplementary

additionally 3 too, yea, yet 4 also, more, then 5 again 6 as well, withal 7 addedly, besides, further 8 likewise, moreover 11 furthermore

additive 5 chain 8 extender 9 summative 10 cumulative 12 accumulative

addle 5 mix up 6 ball up, fuddle 7 confuse, fluster, nonplus, perplex 8 befuddle, bewilder, confound, distract, throw off 9 dumbfound

address 3 aim, air, set, sue, woo 4 hail, mien, port, send, ship, tact, talk 5 apply, court, greet, level, point, poise, remit, route, skill, speak **6** accost, attend, call to, devote, direct, pursue, relate, salute, speech **7** bearing, bespeak, consign, forward, incline, know-how, lecture, prowess, tutoyer **8** appeal to, approach, converse, deftness, demeanor, dispatch, petition, presence, talk with, transmit **9** dexterity, diplomacy, expertise **10** adroitness, allocution, buckle down, competence, deportment, efficiency **11** comportment, memorialize, proficiency, savoir faire, superscribe, tactfulness **12** apostrophize

adduce 3 lay **4** cite **5** offer **6** allege, submit, tender **7** advance, present, proffer, propose, suggest **8** document **9** exemplify **10** illustrate

add up to 4 mean **5** spell **6** denote, import, intend **7** connote, express, signify

A Death in the Family author 4 Agee (James)

adept 4 deft, whiz **5** crack **6** adroit, expert, master, wizard **7** skilled **8** masterly, skillful, virtuoso **9** dexterous, masterful **10** proficient **11** crackerjack **12** professional

adequacy 5 might **6** enough **7** ability **8** capacity **10** capability, competence, sufficient **13** qualification

adequate 5 common, decent, enough **8** all right **9** competent, sufficing **10** acceptable, sufficient **11** comfortable **12** satisfactory **13** unexceptional, unimpeachable

adequately 4 well **5** amply, right **6** enough **8** properly, suitably **9** fittingly **10** becomingly **13** appropriately

adhere 5 cling, stick **6** adsorb, cleave, cohere

adherence 4 bond **5** cling **7** loyalty **8** adhesion, clinging, cohesion, fidelity, stickage, sticking **9** constancy **10** attachment, concretion **11** cementation **12** faithfulness **13** agglutination

adherent 6 cohort **7** sectary **8** disciple, follower, henchman, partisan, sectator, stalwart **9** satellite, supporter *suffix:* **3** ite

adhering 8 osculant

adhesion see **adherence**

adhesive 5 gluey, gooey, gummy, tacky **6** clingy, cloggy, sticky **7** stickum **8** mucilage

adieu 2 by **5** congé **6** bye-bye, so long **7** cheerio, good-bye, parting **8** farewell, toodle-oo **11** leave taking

ad interim 6 acting, pro tem, supply **9** temporary **10** pro tempore

adipose 3 fat **5** fatty

adiposity 7 fatness, obesity **10** corpulence, fleshiness

adit 3 way **4** door **5** entry **6** access, entrée **7** ingress **8** entrance **9** admission **10** admittance

adjacent 5 handy **6** nearby **7** close-by **8** abutting, touching **9** adjoining, bordering **10** approximal, contiguous, convenient, juxtaposed, near-at-hand **11** close-at-hand, neighboring **12** conterminous

adjoin 4 abut, line, meet **5** march, touch, verge **6** border, butt on **8** neighbor **11** communicate

adjoining see **abutting**

adjourn 4 rise, stay **5** close, defer, delay **6** hold up, put off, recess, shelve **7** break up, disband, hold off, suspend **8** dissolve, hold over, postpone, prorogue **9** prorogate, terminate

adjudge 6 umpire **7** referee **9** arbitrate **10** adjudicate

adjudicate see **adjudge**

adjunct 5 affix **8** addition, appanage, appendix **9** accessory, accretion, appendage **10** attachment **12** appurtenance

adjust 3 fit, fix, rig **4** suit, tune **5** adapt, order, right **6** accord, attune, orient, square, tailor, tune up **7** arrange, conform, correct, rectify **8** modulate, regulate **9** habituate, harmonize, reconcile **11** accommodate

adjuvant 9 accessory, ancillary, auxiliary **10** collateral, subsidiary **11** appurtenant, subservient **12** contributory

ad-lib 9 improvise **11** extemporize, improvisate

Admetus *father:* **6** Pheres *wife:* **8** Alcestis

administer 3 run **4** deal, give **5** issue **6** direct, govern, manage, render, strike **7** conduct, deal out, deliver, dole out, execute, give out, inflict, mete out **8** carry out, dispense, share out **9** apportion, supervise **10** distribute, portion out

administrate 6 govern, render **7** execute **8** carry out

administration *system of:* **11** bureaucracy

administrator 4 exec **7** manager, officer **8** official **9** executive

admirable 6 august, worthy **8** laudable **9** deserving, estimable, meritable, praisable **11** commendable, meritorious, thankworthy **12** praiseworthy

admiral *American:* **4** Byrd, Sims **5** Dewey, Stark **6** Halsey, Nimitz **7** Zumwalt **8** Farragut, Rickover, Spruance *Confederate:* **6** Semmes *Dutch:* **5** Tromp *English:* **6** Nelson, Rodney, Vernon **7** Hawkins **8** Beaufort, Jellicoe, Villiers **11** Mountbatten *French:* **10** Villeneuve *German:* **4** Spee **6** Donitz, Raeder **7** Tirpitz *Japanese:* **4** Togo **5** Yonai **8** Yamamoto *Spanish:* **8** Menendez

admiration 5 amaze, favor **6** esteem, regard, wonder **7** account, respect

9 amazement, marveling 10 estimation, wonderment 12 appreciation

admire 5 adore, prize, value 6 esteem, regard, relish, revere 7 adulate, cherish, lionize, respect, worship 8 consider, treasure, venerate 9 delight in, reverence 10 appreciate

admirer 3 fan 6 votary 7 amateur, devotee, fancier

admission 3 way 4 adit, door 5 entry 6 access, entrée 7 ingress 8 entrance 10 admittance

admit 3 own 4 avow, take 5 agree, allow, enter, grant, let on, lodge, own up 6 fess up, harbor, permit, suffer, take in 7 concede, confess, receive, shelter 9 entertain, introduce, recognize 11 acknowledge

admittance see admission

admix 5 merge 6 mingle 8 comingle, immingle 9 commingle 11 intermingle

admixture 4 dash 5 alloy, shade, smack, spice, taint, tinge 7 amalgam 8 compound 9 composite 10 adulterant, denaturant 12 amalgamation

admonish 4 warn 5 chide 6 lesson, monish, rebuke 7 caution, reprove, tick off 8 call down, reproach 9 reprimand

admonishing 7 warning 8 monitory 10 cautionary, cautioning, monitorial

admonition 3 rap, wig 6 caveat, rebuke 7 caution, chiding, reproof, warning 9 reprimand 11 forewarning

ado 4 fuss, stir 5 tizzy, whirl 6 bustle, flurry, furore, pother, uproar 7 turmoil 9 confusion

adolescence 5 youth 6 spring 7 puberty 9 greenness, youthhood 10 juvenility, pubescence, springtide, springtime 12 youthfulness

adolescent 4 teen 6 teener 8 preadult, teenager

Adonijah *brother:* 5 Amnon 7 Absalom, Chileab *father:* 5 David *mother:* 7 Haggith *slayer:* 7 Benaiah

Adonis *lover:* 5 Venus 9 Aphrodite *mother:* 5 Myrrh 6 Myrrha *slayer:* 4 boar

adopt 4 take 6 affect, assume, take on, take up 7 embrace, espouse

adoption 8 espousal 9 embracing 11 embracement

adorable 4 lush 7 darling, lovable 8 heavenly, lovesome, luscious 9 ambrosial, delicious 10 delectable, delightful 11 scrumptious

adoration 4 love 7 passion, worship 8 devotion, idolatry 9 affection 11 idolization

adore 4 love 6 admire, dote on, esteem, revere 7 idolize, worship 8 dote upon, enshrine, venerate 9 affection, delight in, reverence

adorn 4 deck, trim 5 prank, primp, prink 6 bedeck, doll up, enrich, pretty, richen 7 bedizen, dress up, enhance, furbish, garnish, smarten 8 beautify, decorate, ornament, prettify, spruce up, titivate 9 embellish

adornment 5 decor 6 finery 7 garnish 8 ornament 9 caparison 10 decoration 11 centerpiece 13 embellishment

ad rem 7 apropos, germane 8 apposite, material, pointful, relevant 9 pertinent 10 applicable 11 applicative, applicatory

adroit 3 sly 4 deft 5 canny, handy, smart 6 astute, clever, nimble, shrewd 7 cunning 8 dextrous, skillful 9 dexterous, ingenious, workmanly 11 intelligent, quick-witted, workmanlike 13 perspicacious

adroitness 3 art 5 craft, skill 7 address, cunning, know-how, prowess, sleight 8 deftness 9 dexterity, expertise, readiness

adulation 7 acclaim, blarney 8 applause, flattery, soft soap 12 blandishment

adult 4 aged, ripe 5 grown 6 mature 7 grown-up, matured, ripened 9 full-blown, full-grown 11 full-fledged

adulterant 5 alloy 9 admixture 10 denaturant

adulterate 4 thin 5 taint 6 debase, defile, dilute, doctor, dope up, weight 7 pollute 8 denature, impurify 10 tamper with

adumbrate 3 dim, fog 4 bode, call, hint, mist, murk 5 augur, cloud, draft 6 darken, shadow, sketch 7 becloud, bespeak, betoken, obscure, outline, portend, predict, presage, suggest 8 block out, chalk out, forebode, forecast, foretell, indicate, prophesy, rough out, skeleton 9 obfuscate, prefigure 10 foreshadow, vaticinate 11 prefigurate, skeletonize 12 characterize

adumbration 4 hint, sign 5 shade, umbra 6 shadow 7 umbrage 8 penumbra 10 intimation, suggestion

advance 3 aid 4 cite, help, lend, loan, move 5 get on, march, raise, serve 6 adduce, allege, assist, course, foster, mature, prefer, uplift 7 develop, elevate, forward, further, headway, ongoing, present, proceed, promote, upgrade 8 anabasis, approach, encroach, get along, heighten, increase, overture, progress 9 encourage, evolution 11 development, furtherance, improvement, progression 12 breakthrough

advanced 7 forward, liberal, radical 8 tolerant 10 precocious 11 broad-minded, progressive

advancement 5 march 7 headway 8 progress 9 promotion 10 preference

advantage 3 use 4 boon, edge, good, lead, odds, sake 5 asset, avail, bulge, serve 6 better, profit 7 account, benefit, fitness, godsend, mastery, service, welfare

8 blessing, handicap, interest, leverage
9 allowance, head start, relevance, upper hand, well-being 10 ascendancy, domination, leadership, prosperity, usefulness 11 benediction, superiority 12 running start

advantageous 4 good 6 paying, toward, useful 7 benefic, gainful, helpful 8 favoring, remedial, salutary 9 conducive, desirable, expedient, favorable, lucrative 10 beneficial, profitable, propitious, well-paying, worthwhile 11 moneymaking 12 remunerative

advent 6 coming 7 arrival, hearing 8 approach

adventitious 6 casual 10 accidental, contingent, fortuitous, incidental 12 supervenient

adventure 4 feat, gest, risk 5 quest, wager 6 chance 7 emprise, exploit 8 escapade 10 enterprise

adventuresome see adventurous

adventurous 4 bold, rash 5 brash 6 daring 7 doughty 8 intrepid, reckless 9 audacious, daredevil, foolhardy, impetuous, imprudent 11 temerarious

adversary 3 con 4 anti 5 match 7 opposer 8 opponent 9 oppugnant 10 antagonist

adverse 4 anti 7 counter, harmful, hurtful, opposed 8 contrary, negative, opposing 9 injurious, oppugnant 11 deleterious, detrimental, obstructive, unfavorable 12 antagonistic, antipathetic 13 counteractive

adversity 4 dole 6 misery, mishap 7 tragedy 8 distress 9 mischance, suffering 10 misfortune 11 contretemps

advert 4 note 5 refer 6 allude, notice, remark 7 bring up, observe 8 point out

advertent 6 arrect 7 heedful 9 attentive, intentive, observant, regardful

advertise 4 plug, puff, push 5 boost 6 blazon, report 7 build up, declare, promote, publish 8 announce, ballyhoo, proclaim 9 broadcast, publicize 10 annunciate, bruit about, promulgate

advertisement 2 ad 4 bill, plug, sign 5 blurb, flyer, promo 6 notice, poster 7 affiche 9 billboard, broadcast, promotion, publicity 10 commercial, propaganda 11 declaration, publication 12 announcement, proclamation, promulgation 13 pronouncement

advertising 7 buildup, puffery 9 publicity

advice 4 news, word 7 caution, counsel, tidings, warning 8 guidance, teaching 10 admonition 11 information, instruction 12 intelligence

advisable 4 wise 6 seemly 7 politic, prudent 8 sensible, suitable, tactical 9 expedient

advise 4 clew, clue, post, tell, warn 6 confab, confer, fill in, huddle, inform, notify, parley, powwow, wise up 7 apprise, caution, consult, counsel 8 acquaint, forewarn 9 recommend 11 confabulate

advised 7 studied 8 designed, intended, prepense, studious 10 considered, deliberate, thought-out 11 intentional 12 premeditated

advocacy 7 defense

advocate 4 back 5 favor 6 preach, uphold 7 promote, support 8 backstop, champion, exponent, side with 9 encourage, expounder, proponent, supporter 11 countenance *combining form:* 4 crat *suffix:* 5 arian

Aeacus *father:* 4 Zeus *mother:* 6 Aegina *son:* 6 Peleus 7 Telamon

Aedon *brother:* 7 Amphion *sister-in-law:* 5 Niobe *son (victim):* 6 Itylus

Aeetes *daughter:* 5 Medea *father:* 6 Helios

Aegaeon see Briareus

Aegeon's wife 7 Aemilia

Aegeus'son 7 Theseus

aegis 4 ward 5 armor, guard 6 shield 7 backing, defense 8 armament, auspices, security 9 patronage, safeguard 10 protection 11 sponsorship

Aegisthus *father:* 8 Thyestes *lover:* 12 Clytemnestra *mother:* 7 Pelopia *slayer:* 7 Orestes *victim:* 6 Atreus 9 Agamemnon

Aegyptus *brother:* 6 Danaus *father:* 5 Belus *mother:* 8 Anchinoe *son:* 7 Lynceus

Aeneas *companion:* 7 Achates *father:* 8 Anchises *mother:* 5 Venus 9 Aphrodite *son:* 5 Iulus 8 Ascanius *wife:* 6 Creusa 7 Lavinia

Aeneid *author:* 6 Vergil, Virgil *first words:* 16 arma virumque cano *hero:* 5 Aneas

Aeolus *brother:* 5 Dorus 6 Xuthus *daughter:* 6 Canace 7 Alcyone 8 Halcyone *father:* 6 Hellen 8 Poseidon *mother:* 9 Melanippe *son:* 7 Athamas 9 Salmoneus

aeon 3 age 7 dog's age 8 blue moon, coon's age, eternity

aerate 3 air 6 aerify 9 oxygenate, ventilate

aerial 4 airy 5 lofty 6 towery, vapory 7 soaring, spiring, topless 8 ethereal, towering, vaporous 9 pneumatic 10 impalpable 11 atmospheric

aerie, aery, eyrie 4 nest 5 brood 9 penthouse

aeronaut 4 Fogg 5 pilot 7 aviator 8 Zeppelin 10 balloonist

Aerope *husband:* 6 Atreus *lover:* 8 Thyestes *son:* 8 Menelaus 9 Agamemnon

aery 6 aerial 8 ethereal 9 visionary

Aesculapius *daughter:* 6 Hygeia 7 Panacea *father:* 6 Apollo *mother:* 7 Coronis *slayer:* 4 Zeus 7 Jupiter *son:* 7 Machaon 9 Podalirus *teacher:* 6 Chiron *wife:* 6 Epione

Aeson *brother:* 6 Pelias *son:* 5 Jason

aesthete 10 dilettante 11 cognoscente, connoisseur

Aether's father 6 Erebus

affable 6 genial, gentle, polite 7 amiable, cordial 8 gracious, sociable 9 congenial, courteous

affair 4 love 5 amour, thing 6 matter 7 concern, liaison, palaver, romance 8 business, intrigue 10 proceeding

affect 3 act, get 4 fake, move, sham, sway 5 bluff, carry, feign, haunt, put on, touch 6 assume, resort, strike 7 actuate, impress, inspire, pretend 8 frequent, simulate 9 influence 11 counterfeit

affectation 4 airs, lugs, pose 9 mannerism, prettyism

affected 5 put-on 6 chichi, la-di-da, tootoo 7 assumed, feigned, genteel, mincing, stilted 8 involved, mannered, overnice, précieux, precious, spurious 9 concerned, conscious 10 artificial, implicated, interested 11 alembicated, overrefined, pretentious 13 self-conscious

affected with/by *combining form:* 6 pathic *suffix:* 2 ic 4 ical

affecting 6 moving 8 poignant, touching 9 troubling 10 disturbing, impressive 11 distressful, distressing

affection 4 bias, love, mark 5 savor, trait 6 doting, malady, virtue, warmth 7 ailment, concern, disease, emotion, feature, feeling, leaning, passion, quality, worship 8 devotion, disorder, fondness, interest, penchant, property, sickness, sympathy, syndrome 9 attention, attribute, character, complaint, condition, infirmity, sentiment 10 attachment, propensity, tenderness 12 predilection

affectionate 4 dear, fond, warm 6 doting, loving, tender 7 devoted 8 lovesome 11 sympathetic

affective 6 moving 7 emotive 9 emotional

affectivity 7 emotion, feeling, passion 9 sentiment

affianced 7 engaged 8 intended, plighted, promised 9 betrothed 10 contracted

affiche 4 bill 6 poster 7 placard 8 handbill

affidavit certificate 5 jurat

affiliated 4 akin 6 agnate, allied 7 cognate, connate, kindred, related 8 incident 10 connatural 11 consanguine

affiliation 5 tie-up 6 hookup 7 cahoots 8 alliance 10 connection 11 association, combination, conjunction, partnership 12 conjointment

affinity 6 simile 7 analogy 8 likeness, sympathy 9 alikeness, semblance 10 attraction, comparison, similarity, similitude 11 resemblance *combining form:* 5 phily, trope 6 philia 7 tropism

affirm 3 say, yes 4 aver, avow 5 state, vouch 6 assert, attest, avouch, depose 7 certify, declare, profess, protest, witness 9 guarantee

affirmative 2 ay 3 aye, yes 8 positive

affix 3 add 5 annex, rivet 6 append, attach, fasten 7 subjoin

afflict 3 try, vex 4 rack 5 annoy, harry, press, smite, worry, wound, wring 6 bother, harass, harrow, martyr, pester, plague, strike 7 agonize, crucify, torment, torture 9 martyrize 10 excruciate

afflicted 6 dolent, rueful, woeful 7 doleful, ruthful 8 dolorous, stricken, wretched 9 miserable, sorrowful

affliction 3 rue, woe 4 care, dole 5 cross, grief, trial 6 mishap, ordeal, regret, sorrow 7 anguish, illness 8 disorder, sickness, unhealth 9 heartache, infirmity, mischance 10 heartbreak 11 tribulation *suffix:* 4 itis

afflictive 4 dire, sore 6 aching, bitter, woeful 7 algetic, galling, hurtful, hurting, painful 8 grievous 10 calamitous, deplorable, lamentable 11 distasteful, distressing, regrettable, unfortunate, unpalatable 13 heartbreaking

affluent 4 rich 7 moneyed, opulent, wealthy

affray 3 row 5 brawl, clash, fight, melee 6 fracas 7 ruction, scuffle 8 skirmish 9 scrimmage 10 donnybrook

affright 3 awe 5 alarm, scare, spook 7 startle, terrify 9 terrorize

affront 4 face, meet, slap 6 insult, offend, slight 7 despite, offense, outrage 8 dishonor 9 aspersion, contumely, criticize, encounter, indignity 10 defamation

aficionado 3 fan 4 buff 5 hound, lover 6 addict, votary 7 devotee, habitué

afield 4 away 5 amiss, badly, wrong 6 astray

afire see aflame

aflame 5 afire, aglow, fiery 6 ablaze, alight 7 blazing, burning, flaming, flaring, ignited 8 aflicker 11 conflagrant

afraid 3 shy 4 wary 5 chary, jumpy, loath, scary, timid 6 aghast, averse, scared, trepid 7 afeared, anxious, ascared, fearful, uneager 8 cautious, hesitant, skittish, timorous 9 reluctant, terrified, unwilling 10 frightened 11 disinclined 12 apprehensive

afresh 3 new 4 anew, over 5 again, newly 6 de novo, lately, of late 8 once more, recently

Africa *country:* 4 Chad, Mali, Togo
5 Benin, Congo, Egypt, Gabon, Ghana,
Kenya, Libya, Niger, Sudan, Zaire
6 Angola, Gambia, Guinea, Malawi,
Rwanda, Uganda, Zambia 7 Algeria,
Burundi, Comoros, Lesotho, Liberia,
Morocco, Namibia, Nigeria, Senegal,
Somalia, Tunisia 8 Botswana, Cameroon,
Djibouti, Ethiopia, Tanzania, Zimbabwe
9 Cape Verde, Mauritius, Swaziland
10 Ivory Coast, Madagascar, Mauritania,
Mozambique, Seychelles 11 Burkina Faso,
Sierra Leone, South Africa 12 Guinea Bis-
sau 13 Comoro Islands *ethnic group:*
3 Ibo 4 Akan, Arab, Boer, Copt, Fula, Issa,
Moor, Zulu 5 Bantu, Fulah, Galla, Hausa,
Kongo, Mande, Negro, Pygmy, Swazi,
Wolof 6 Beduin, Berber, Fulani, Hamite,
Herero, Kaffir, Kikuyu, Nubian, Somali, Tua-
reg, Ubangi, Yoruba 7 Ashanti, Bedouin,
Bushman, Malinke, Swahili 8 Egyptian,
Mandingo 9 Hottentot *language:* 3 Ibo
4 Urdu 5 Bantu, Galla, Hausa 6 Arabic,
Berber, Somali, Yoruba 7 Amharic, Bam-
bara, Swahili 8 Malagasy 9 Afrikaans
aft 6 astern
after 3 for 4 back, hind, next, past, rear
5 below, later, since 6 behind, beyond, hinder, retral 7 by and by, ensuing 8 hindmost, latterly 9 following, posterior 10 subsequent 12 postliminary, subsequently
after all 3 yet 5 still 6 though 7 howbeit,
however 11 nonetheless 12 nevertheless
aftereffect 5 issue 6 result, upshot 7 outcome 8 causatum 11 consequence, eventuality
afterlife 6 beyond 8 eternity 9 hereafter
aftermath see **aftereffect**
afterward 4 next, to-be 5 later 6 behind,
future, offing 7 by-and-by 8 latterly 9 hereafter 12 subsequently
afterword 8 epilogue
Agag *kingdom:* 6 Amalek *slayer:* 6 Samuel
again 4 also, anew, back, over 5 about
6 afresh, around, de novo 7 besides, further 8 once more 12 additionally *combining form:* 2 an 3 ana 4 pali *prefix:* 2 re
again and again 3 oft 4 much 5 often
8 ofttimes 10 frequently, oftentimes,
repeatedly
against 4 agin 6 contra, facing, toward,
versus 7 apropos, despite, vis-à-vis
8 fronting, touching 9 in spite of 10 concerning, respecting *prefix:* 2 ob 3 ant
4 anti 6 contra 7 counter
Agamemnon *avenger:* 7 Orestes
brother: 8 Menelaus *daughter:* 7 Electra
9 Iphigenia *father:* 6 Atreus *slayer:*
9 Aegisthus *son:* 7 Orestes *wife:* 12 Clytemnestra

agape 6 aghast 7 shocked 8 dismayed
10 confounded 11 dumbfounded, overwhelmed 13 thunderstruck
agate 3 mib, taw 6 marble 7 shooter
Agave *father:* 6 Cadmus *husband:*
6 Echion *mother:* 8 Harmonia *sister:*
3 Ino 6 Semele 7 Autonoe *son:* 8 Pentheus
age 3 eon, era 4 aeon, grow, ripe, time
5 epoch, ripen 6 grow up, mature, mellow,
period 7 develop 8 blue moon, caducity,
eternity, maturate
aged 3 old 4 ripe 5 hoary, olden 6 mellow,
senior 7 ancient, antique, elderly, matured,
ripened 8 Noachian, timeworn 9 senescent, venerable 11 patriarchal 12 antediluvian
ageless 7 eternal 8 dateless, timeless
10 intemporal
agency 4 mean 5 cause, organ 6 medium
7 channel, vehicle 8 ministry 10 instrument
agenda 6 docket 7 program 8 calendar,
schedule 9 timetable *entry:* 4 item
Agenor *brother:* 5 Belus *daughter:*
6 Europa *father:* 7 Antenor, Neptune
8 Poseidon *mother:* 5 Libya *son:* 6 Cadmus
agent 3 fed, spy 4 doer, mean, tool
5 actor, organ, proxy, spook 6 deputy, factor, medium 7 channel, proctor, steward,
vehicle 8 assignee, attorney, executor, insti-
tor, minister, ministry 9 activator, go-
between, middleman 10 instrument, procurator *combining form:* 4 stat *suffix:* 3 ant
age-old 7 ancient, antique 8 timeworn
9 venerable 12 antediluvian
agglomerate 4 heap, mass, pile 9 aggregate 11 aggregation
agglomeration 5 hoard, trove 9 aggregate, amassment 10 collection, cumulation
11 aggregation
aggrandize 5 boost, exalt, honor 6 beef
up, expand, extend 7 augment, build up,
dignify, enlarge, ennoble, glorify, magnify,
sublime 8 heighten, increase, multiply
11 distinguish
aggravate 4 gall 5 annoy, grate, mount,
peeve, pique, rouse, upset 6 burn up,
deepen, nettle, worsen 7 bedevil, disturb,
enhance, magnify, perturb, provoke
8 heighten, irritate 9 intensify 10 exasperate
aggravation 6 bother, pother 9 annoyance
aggregate 3 all, sum 4 body, bulk, floc
5 add up, gross, total; whole 6 amount,
budget, number 7 quantum 8 entirety,
quantity, totality 11 agglomerate 12 conglomerate 13 agglomeration *suffix:* 3 ery
aggregation 4 ruck 5 crowd, group,
hoard, trove 6 muster 7 company

8 assembly **9** amassment, congeries, gathering **10** assemblage, collection, cumulation **11** agglomerate **12** accumulation

aggression 4 raid **5** fight, onset **6** attack **7** assault, offense **8** invasion **9** incursion, offensive, onslaught, pugnacity **10** assailment **12** belligerence **13** combativeness

aggressive 5 pushy **6** fierce **7** scrappy, vicious **8** militant **9** assertive, combative, imperious **11** belligerent, contentious, domineering, hard-hitting

aggressiveness 11 bellicosity **12** belligerence, belligerency

aggrieve 4 hurt, pain **5** annoy, harry, worry, wrong **6** harass, injure, plague **7** afflict, oppress, torment **8** distress **9** constrain, persecute

aghast 4 agog, awed **5** agape **6** afraid, amazed, scared **7** anxious, fearful, shocked **8** appalled, dismayed, startled **9** horrified, terrified **10** astonished, confounded, frightened **11** awestricken, dumbfounded, overwhelmed **12** horror-struck **13** flabbergasted, thunderstruck

agile 4 deft, spry, yare **5** brisk, catty, lithe, zippy **6** active, adroit, limber, lively, nimble, supple, volant **7** lissome **8** dextrous **9** dexterous, sprightly

agitate 4 rile, rock **5** argue, drive, impel, peeve, shake, upset **6** bother, debate, flurry, joggle, ruffle **7** discuss, dispute, disturb, fluster, perturb, provoke, tempest, unhinge **8** convulse, irritate **9** thrash out **10** discompose, exasperate

agitation 4 flap, stew **6** bustle, dither, lather, pother, tumult **7** tempest, turmoil **9** commotion, confusion **10** turbulence

agitator 7 inciter **8** fomenter **10** instigator

Aglaia see **Graces**

Aglauros, Agraulos *father:* **7** Cecrops *sister:* **5** Herse **9** Pandrosos

aglow 5 afire **6** ablaze, aflame, alight, lucent **7** radiant, shining **8** aflicker, gleaming, luminous

agnate 4 akin, like **5** alike **6** allied **7** cognate, connate, kindred, related, similar **9** analogous **10** affiliated **11** consanguine **13** corresponding

agnostic 7 infidel, skeptic **11** disbeliever

"Agnus___" 3 Dei

ago 2 by **4** gone, past, syne, yore **5** since

agog 4 avid **5** eager **6** ardent, roused **7** excited, popeyed **9** impatient

agonize 4 fret, gall, rack **5** chafe **6** harrow, squirm, suffer, writhe **7** afflict, torment, torture, trouble **8** distress **10** excruciate

agonizing 7 intense, racking, tearing **9** harrowing, torturing, torturous **10** tormenting **12** excruciating

agony 4 pain **5** dolor **6** misery **7** passion **8** distress **9** suffering

agrarian 5 rural **6** rustic **8** agrestal, pastoral **10** campestral **12** agricultural

Agraulos see **Aglauros**

agree 3 yes **4** jibe, suit **5** admit, check, equal, fit in, match, tally **6** accede, accord, assent, concur, square **7** comport, concede, concert, concord, conform, consent **8** check out, coincide, dovetail **9** acquiesce, harmonize, recognize, subscribe **10** correspond **11** acknowledge

agreeable 4 nice **7** affable, welcome **8** amenable, pleasant, pleasing **9** congenial, congruous, consonant, favorable **10** compatible, consistent, gratifying **11** pleasurable, pleasureful, sympathetic

agreed 2 OK **3** aye, yea, yep, yes **4** okay **8** all right, okeydoke

agreement 4 bond, deal, pact **6** accord, treaty, unison **7** bargain, compact, concord, entente, harmony **8** contract, covenant **9** concordat **10** consonance **11** concordance

agree with 3 fit **4** suit **5** befit **6** become **10** go together

agricultural 8 agrarian *combining form:* **4** agro

agriculture 7 farming, tillage **8** agronomy **9** husbandry

Agrippina's son 4 Nero

aground 7 beached **8** stranded

Ahab *daughter:* **8** Athaliah *father:* **4** Omri *wife:* **7** Jezebel

Ahasuerus *kingdom:* **6** Persia *wife:* **6** Esther, Vashti

Ahaz *kingdom:* **5** Judah *son:* **8** Hezekiah *wife:* **3** Abi

Ahaziah *father:* **4** Ahab **5** Joram **7** Jehoram *kingdom:* **5** Judah **6** Israel *mother:* **7** Jezebel **8** Athaliah *sister:* **9** Jehosheba **11** Jehosobeath

ahead 4 alee, ante, fore **5** forth **6** before, onward **7** forward, onwards **8** forwards, previous **9** in advance **10** beforehand **11** precedently **12** antecedently

Ahinoam *father:* **7** Ahimaaz *husband:* **4** Saul **5** David *son:* **5** Amnon

aid 4 abet, hand, help, lift **6** assist, helper, relief, succor **7** ancilla, backing, comfort, help out, succour, support **8** benefact, succorer **9** assistant, attendant, coadjutor **10** assistance, benefactor, coadjutant, lieutenant, ministrant, mitigation **11** alleviation, assuagement

Aida *composer:* **5** Verdi *father:* **8** Amonasro *lover:* **7** Radames *rival:* **7** Amneris

aide 6 deputy, second **7** orderly **9** assistant, coadjutor **10** coadjutant, lieutenant

ail 4 cark **5** upset, worry **7** afflict, trouble **8** distress

ailing 3 ill, low **4** mean, weak **6** donsie, droopy, offish, poorly, sickly, unwell **8** off-color 9 enfeebled 10 indisposed 11 debilitated

ailment 3 ill 6 malady, unrest 7 disease, ferment, turmoil 8 disorder, disquiet, sickness, syndrome 9 affection, complaint, condition, infirmity 10 inquietude 11 disquietude, restiveness 12 restlessness

aim 3 try 4 cast, goal, head, mark, mean, plan, want, wish 5 angle, essay, focus, level, point, slant, train 6 aspire, design, desire, direct, intend, strive, target, zero in 7 address, attempt, propose, purpose 8 ambition, endeavor 9 objective 11 contemplate

aimless 6 random 9 desultory, haphazard, hit-or-miss, irregular, unplanned 10 designless 11 purposeless

air 3 sky 4 aura, feel, mien, mood, port, song, tune, vent 5 state, style 6 aerate, aerify, manner, melody, reveal, strain 7 bearing, declare, divulge, express, feeling, melisma, publish, quality 8 demeanor, presence, proclaim 9 broadcast, character, semblance, ventilate 10 atmosphere, deportment 11 comportment *combining form:* 3 aer, atm 4 aeri, aero, atmo 5 pneum 6 pneumo 7 pneumat 8 pneumato

aircraft 5 blimp, drone, plane 6 glider 7 airship, balloon, chopper 8 aerodyne, aerostat, airplane, jetliner, zeppelin 9 dirigible 10 helicopter *carrier:* 7 flattop 8 birdfarm *designer:* 6 Fokker, Martin 7 Junkers, Tupolev 8 Northrop, Sikorsky, Yakovlev 13 Messerschmitt

airless 5 close, stivy 6 stuffy, sultry 8 stifling 10 breathless 11 suffocating

airman 5 flier, pilot 6 fly-boy 7 aviator

air movement 5 draft 7 updraft 9 downdraft

air navigation system 5 loran, navar, radar

airplane 3 jet, SST 4 STOL, VTOL 5 avion, VSTOL 6 bomber 7 fighter 8 autogiro, autogyro 9 transport *A-bomb-dropper:* 8 Enola Gay *battle:* 8 dogfight *body:* 8 fuselage *commercial:* 5 liner *engine:* 3 jet 6 fanjet 7 propjet 8 turbofan, turbojet 9 turboprop *engine casing:* 7 nacelle *engineless:* 6 glider *instrument:* 5 radar, radio 7 compass 9 altimeter, gyroscope 10 tachometer 11 transponder *maneuver:* 4 buzz, dive, loop, roll 8 nosedive 9 chandelle 10 barrel roll *movement:* 3 yaw 4 bank, spin 5 pitch 8 tailspin *part:* 3 fin 4 flap, nose, prop, tail, wing 5 cabin, wheel 6 engine, rudder 7 aileron 8 airscrew, elevator 9 empennage, propeller 10 stabilator, stabilizer *pilotless:* 5 drone *shelter:* 6 hangar *target:* 6 drogue *vapor:* 8 contrail

airport 5 drome, field 7 helipad 8 airdrome, airfield, heliport 9 aerodrome *building:* 8 terminal *flag:* 8 windsock *name:*
Amsterdam: 8 Schiphol *Atlanta:* 10 Hartsfield *Boston:* 5 Logan *Chicago:* 5 O'Hare *Copenhagen:* 7 Kastrup *Dublin:* 7 Shannon *London:* 7 Gatwick 8 Heathrow *New York:* 3 JFK 7 Kennedy 9 La Guardia *Paris:* 4 Orly 8 DeGaulle 9 Le Bourget *Rome:* 7 Da Vinci *Washington:* 6 Dulles
part: 5 apron, tower 6 runway 7 taxiway

airs 4 lugs, pose, show 6 vanity 9 loftiness, mannerism, prettyism, vainglory 11 affectation, ostentation

airship 8 zeppelin 9 dirigible

airtight 8 hermetic, ironclad

airwaves nuisance 6 static

airy 4 rare, thin 5 blowy, gusty, light, lofty, windy 6 aerial, bouncy, breezy, dainty, towery, vapory 7 buoyant, gaseous, soaring, spiring, tenuous 8 animated, delicate, ethereal, rarefied, spirited, supernal, towering, vaporous, volatile 9 expansive, frivolous, pneumatic, resilient, windswept 10 diaphanous 11 atmospheric, skyscraping 12 effervescent, high-spirited

Ajax's father 6 Oileus 7 Telamon

akin 4 like 5 alike 6 agnate, allied 7 cognate, connate, kindred, related, similar, uniform 8 parallel 9 analogous, consonant 10 affiliated, comparable, connatural 11 consanguine 13 corresponding

Alabama *capital:* 10 Montgomery *college, university:* 5 Miles 6 Auburn, Mobile 8 Tuskegee 9 Talladega 10 Huntingdon *largest city:* 10 Birmingham *nickname:* 11 Cotton State 12 Heart of Dixie *state flower:* 8 camellia

alacrity 8 celerity, dispatch 9 briskness, eagerness, quickness, readiness 10 enthusiasm, expedition, promptness 11 promptitude

alamo 6 poplar 10 cottonwood

a la mode 4 chic, tony 6 modish, tonish, trendy 7 dashing, stylish 9 exclusive 11 fashionable

alarm 3 SOS 4 fear 5 alert, dread, larum, panic, scare, siren, spook, upset 6 dismay, fright, horror, terror, tocsin 7 startle, terrify, warning 8 affright, frighten 9 terrorize 11 forewarning, trepidation 13 consternation

alarmable 4 edgy 8 agitable, skittery, skittish, volatile 9 excitable, startlish 11 combustible

Alaska *capital:* 6 Juneau *largest city:* 9 Anchorage *state flower:* 11 forget-me-not

Albania *capital:* 6 Tirana, Tirane *monetary unit:* 3 lek

albatross 5 goony 6 gooney, goonie

albeit 5 while 6 much as, though 7 whereas 8 although

Alberta *capital:* 8 Edmonton *largest city:* 7 Calgary *university:* 7 Calgary 10 Lethbridge

Albion 7 England

album 3 ana 6 record 7 garland, omnibus 8 register 9 anthology 10 miscellany 11 florilegium

Alcestis *father:* 6 Pelias *husband:* 7 Admetus *rescuer:* 8 Heracles, Hercules

alchemist 10 Paracelsus

Alcina *sister:* 7 Morgana 10 Logistilla *victim:* 6 Rogero 8 Astolpho, Ruggiero

Alcinous *daughter:* 8 Nausicaa *wife:* 5 Arete

Alcmaeon *father:* 10 Amphiaraus *mother:* 8 Eriphyle *wife:* 10 Callirrhoe

Alcmene *husband:* 10 Amphitryon *son:* 8 Heracles, Hercules

alcohol 4 grog 5 booze, drink, hooch, juice 6 liquor, tipple 7 spirits 9 aqua vitae, firewater *name:* 4 amyl 5 butyl, cetyl, ethyl 6 glycol, methyl, sterol 7 butanol, ethanol, mannite, menthol 8 glycerin, glycerol, inositol, mannitol, methanol 9 isopropyl 11 cholesterol *used in perfumes:* 5 nerol 7 borneol, linalol 8 farnesol, geraniol, linalool

alcoholic 4 hard 8 bibulous 9 spiritous 10 spirituous 11 dipsomaniac 12 intoxicating

alcoholic drink see under **beverage**

alcoholized 5 drunk

alcove 4 nook 5 niche 6 gazebo, pagoda, recess 9 belvedere *Japanese:* 8 tokonoma

Alcyone *father:* 5 Atlas 6 Aeolus *husband:* 4 Ceyx *mother:* 7 Pleione *sisters:* 8 Pleiades

ale 3 nog 4 nogg

Alea 6 Athena

alehouse 3 pub 4 café 6 bistro 7 cabaret 8 beer hall 9 bierstube, brasserie, honkytonk, nightclub 10 beer garden 11 rathskellar

Alemanus *father:* 7 Histion *grandfather:* 6 Japhet

alert 3 SOS 4 keen, warn 5 alarm, quick, ready, sharp, smart 6 brainy, bright, clever, frisky, lively, tocsin 7 heedful, knowing, mindful, wakeful 8 animated, open-eyed, spirited, vigilant, watchful 9 attentive, brilliant, mercurial, sprightly, vivacious, wideawake 11 intelligent, quick-witted, readywitted *Scottish:* 4 gleg 8 wakerife

Alexander *birthplace:* 5 Pella *conquest:* 4 Tyre 5 Egypt, Issus 6 Arbela, Greece, Persia 7 Parthia 8 Granicus *father:*

6 Philip *general:* 9 Antipater *horse:* 10 Bucephalus *kingdom:* 9 Macedonia *mother:* 8 Olympias *teacher:* 9 Aristotle *wife:* 6 Roxana

alfalfa 6 lucern 7 lucerne

Alfonso's queen 3 Ena

alfresco 7 open-air, outdoor, outside 9 out-of-door 10 hypaethral

alga 6 desmid, diatom 7 seaweed *bluegreen:* 6 nostoc *brown:* 4 kelp 5 fucus 8 rockweed *combining form:* 7 phyceae *green:* 8 conferva 9 chlorella *red:* 4 nori 7 amanori

algebra term 4 root 6 factor 8 binomial, equation, monomial, variable 9 quadratic 10 polynomial

Algeria *capital:* 7 Algiers *ethnic group:* 4 Arab 6 Berber *monetary unit:* 5 dinar *port:* 4 Oran

algetic 4 sore 6 aching 7 hurtful, hurting, painful 10 afflictive

Ali *son:* 5 Hasan 6 Husayn *wife:* 6 Fatima

alias 3 AKA 6 anonym 7 pen name 9 pseudonym 10 nom de plume 11 nom de guerre

alibi 4 plea 6 excuse 7 pretext

alien 6 exotic 7 foreign, inconnu, strange 8 estrange, outcomer, outsider, stranger, transfer 9 auslander, extrinsic, foreigner, outlander 10 extraneous, outlandish

alienate 4 part, wean 6 assign, convey, remise 8 disunify, disunite, estrange, sign over, transfer 9 disaffect 10 relinquish

alienation 6 lunacy 7 madness 8 insanity 9 unbalance 10 aberration, insaneness 11 derangement, distraction, psychopathy 12 disaffection, estrangement

alight 4 land 5 afire, aglow, fiery, perch, roost 6 ablaze, aflame, bright, settle 7 blazing, burning, deplane, detrain, flaming, flaring, glowing, ignited, set down, sit down 8 aflicker, dismount 9 effulgent, refulgent, touch down 11 conflagrant

align 4 line, true 5 range 6 adjust, line up 8 regulate 9 allineate

alike 4 akin, same 7 similar, uniform 8 parallel 9 analogous, consonant 10 comparable 13 corresponding *combining form:* 2 is 3 hom, iso 4 homo

alikeness 6 simile 7 analogy 8 affinity 9 semblance 10 comparison, similarity, similitude 11 resemblance

aliment 3 pap 4 food 7 pabulum 9 nutriment 10 sustenance 11 nourishment

alimentary 9 nutritive 11 nutritional

alimentary canal 7 enteron

alimentation 4 keep 5 bread 6 living 7 support 10 livelihood, sustenance 11 maintenance, subsistence

alimony see alimentation

alive 4 rife 5 awake, aware, fresh, quick, vital 6 active, extant, living, zoetic 7 animate, dynamic, knowing, replete, running, teeming, working 8 animated, existent, existing, sensible, sentient, swarming, thronged 9 abounding, au courant, cognizant, conscious, operative, wide-awake 11 functioning, overflowing

alkali metal 6 cesium, sodium 7 lithium 8 francium, rubidium 9 potassium

alkaline substance 3 lye, reh 4 lime, soda, usar 5 borax 6 potash 7 ammonia, antacid 8 pearl ash, saltwort 11 caustic soda

alkali's opposite 4 acid

alkalize 6 basify

alkaloid 4 base *hallucinogenic:* 7 harmine 9 harmaline *medicinal:* 5 ergot 6 heroin 7 cocaine, codeine, emetine, eserine, harmine, quinine 8 atropine, caffeine, ecgonine, lobeline, morphine 9 ephedrine, harmaline, quinidine, reserpine 11 scopolamine *narcotic:* 6 heroin 7 cocaine, codeine 8 morphine *poisonous:* 6 conine 7 tropine 8 atropine, nicotine, solanine, thebaine 9 aconitine 11 scopolamine

all 3 sum 4 each 5 every, gross, quite, total, whole 6 apiece, entire, in toto, purely, wholly 7 exactly, totally, utterly 8 complete, entirety, everyone, outright, totality 9 aggregate, everybody 10 altogether, everything *combining form:* 3 omn, pam, pan 4 omni, pano, pant 5 panta, panto

all-around 7 general, overall 8 complete, sweeping, synoptic 9 adaptable, many-sided, panoramic, versatile 10 consummate 11 wide-ranging 13 comprehensive

allay 4 balm, calm, ease, lull 5 quiet, still 6 settle, soothe, subdue 7 assuage, compose, lighten, mollify, quieten, relieve 8 mitigate 9 alleviate 11 tranquilize

all but 4 most, much, nigh 5 about 6 almost, nearly 8 as good as, as much as, well-nigh 11 essentially, practically 13 approximately

allegation 8 pleading 9 assertion

allege 3 lay 4 cite 5 offer, state 6 adduce, assert 7 advance, declare, present, profess

alleged 7 dubious, would-be 8 doubtful, so-called, specious, supposed 9 pretended, professed, purported, soi-disant 10 ostensible, self-styled

allegiance 5 ardor, piety 6 fealty, homage 7 loyalty 8 devotion, fidelity 12 faithfulness

allegiant 4 true 5 liege, loyal 6 ardent 7 staunch 8 constant, faithful, resolute 9 steadfast

allegory 4 myth 5 fable 7 parable 8 apologue 9 symbolism 10 figuration 12 typification

allergy 5 atopy 8 aversion, dyspathy 9 antipathy, rejection, repulsion

alleviate 4 cure, ease 5 allay 6 remedy 7 assuage, lighten, mollify, relieve 8 mitigate

alleviation 4 ease 6 relief 8 easement 10 mitigation

all-fired 5 utter 6 blamed, dashed, deuced 7 blasted, blessed, doggone, goldarn 8 infernal

alliance 5 tie-up, union 6 hookup, league 7 cahoots 9 anschluss, coalition 10 connection, federation 11 affiliation, association, combination, confederacy, conjunction, partnership, unification 12 conjointment 13 confederation

allied 4 akin 6 agnate, linked, united 7 cognate, connate, kindred, related 8 incident 10 affiliated, connatural 11 consanguine

all in 5 spent 6 bleary, effete, used up 7 drained, far-gone, worn-out 8 depleted 9 exhausted, washed-out

all in all 5 quite 6 in toto, purely, wholly 7 en masse, totally, utterly 9 generally 10 altogether, by and large, on the whole

allineate 4 line 5 align, range 6 line up

aliness 8 entirety, totality

allocate 4 give 5 allot, allow 6 assign 7 earmark, mete out 9 admeasure, apportion, designate

allocution 4 talk 6 speech 7 address, lecture

allot 4 give 5 grant 6 accord, assign 7 deal out, dole out, mete out 8 allocate, dispense 9 admeasure, apportion 10 distribute

allotment 3 cut 4 bite, meed, part 5 quota, share, slice 6 ration 7 measure, partage, portion, quantum 9 allowance

all-out 5 total 9 full-blown, full-scale, unlimited 12 totalitarian

all over 10 everyplace, everywhere, far and near, far and wide, high and low, throughout

allow 3 let, lot, own 4 give 5 admit, allot, brook, grant, leave, let on, stand 6 assign, endure, fess up, permit, suffer 7 concede, confess, mete out 8 allocate, tolerate 9 admeasure, apportion 11 acknowledge

allowance 3 aid, cut, lot 4 bite, edge, help, meed, odds, part, tret 5 grant, leave, quota, share, slice 6 corody, permit, ration 7 consent, corrody, measure, partage, portion, quantum, subsidy, vantage 8 handicap, pittance, sanction 9 advantage, allotment, head start 10 assistance, concession, permission, sufferance 13 accommodation, apportionment, authorization

alloy 5 blend 6 fusion 7 amalgam, mixture 8 compound 9 admixture, composite 10 adulterant, denaturant 11 interfusion 12 amalgamation, intermixture *brass-like:* 6 latten, lattin *copper-sulfur:* 6 niello *copper-tin:* 6 bronze *copper-zinc:* 5 brass 6 tambac, tombac, tombak 8 arsedine *gold-like:* 6 oreide, ormolu, oroide *gold-silver:* 8 electrum *iron-carbon:* 5 steel *iron-nickel:* 5 invar 7 elinvar *mercury:* 7 amalgam *pewter-like:* 5 bidri *tin-lead:* 5 calin, terne 6 pewter, solder *tin-zinc:* 6 oreide, oroide *used in jewelry:* 6 oreide, oroide, tombac

all-powerful 8 almighty 10 omnipotent

all right 2 OK 3 aye, yea, yep, yes 4 good, jake, okay 6 agreed, decent 8 adequate, okeydoke 9 tolerable 10 acceptable 12 satisfactory

all round 7 overall 10 everyplace, everywhere, far and near, far and wide, high and low, throughout

all there 4 sane 5 lucid, right 6 normal 12 compos mentis

All the Way Home author 4 Agee (James)

allude 4 hint 5 imply, refer 6 advert 7 bring up, suggest 8 intimate

allure 4 bait, draw, take, tole, toll, wile 5 charm, decoy, tempt 6 appeal, entice, entrap, lead on, seduce 7 attract, bewitch, enchant, glamour 8 charisma, inveigle, witchery 9 captivate, fascinate, magnetism, magnetize 10 witchcraft 11 fascination

allurement 4 bait, call, draw, pull, trap 5 decoy, snare 6 appeal, come-on 9 seduction 10 attraction, enticement, seducement, temptation 12 drawing power, inveiglement

alluring 5 siren 8 charming 9 appealing, beguiling, glamorous, seductive 10 appetizing, attractive, bewitching, enchanting 11 captivating, fascinating

ally 4 join 5 unite 6 friend, helper 7 comrade, partner 8 federate 9 affiliate, associate, bedfellow, colleague, supporter 10 accomplice 11 confederate 12 collaborator

almighty 3 God 7 Creator 10 omnipotent 11 all-powerful

almost 4 nigh 5 about 6 all but, nearly 8 as good as, as much as, well-nigh 9 nearabout, virtually 11 essentially, practically 13 approximately *Scottish:* 6 feckly

alms 7 charity 8 donation, offering 11 benefaction, beneficence 12 contribution

Aloeus *father:* 7 Neptune 8 Poseidon *mother:* 6 Canace *son:* 4 Otus 9 Ephialtes *wife:* 9 Iphimedia

aloft 4 high, over 5 above 6 upward 7 skyward 8 overhead *combining form:* 4 hyps 5 hypsi, hypso

Aloha State 6 Hawaii

alone 4 only, sole, solo 5 apart, solus 6 lonely, singly, solely, unique 7 isolate, removed 8 detached, entirely, isolated, lonesome, peerless, singular, solitary 9 matchless, unequaled, unmatched, unrivaled 10 unexampled, unexcelled 11 exclusively, unsurpassed 12 unparalleled, unrepeatable 13 unaccompanied

aloneness 8 solitude 9 isolation

along 3 too, yet 4 also 5 forth 6 as well, onward 7 besides, forward 8 likewise, moreover 11 furthermore 12 additionally

alongside 2 by 6 beside, next to 7 fornent *prefix:* 3 par 4 para

along with *combining form:* 3 sym, syn

aloof 4 cold, cool 5 proud 6 casual, chilly, frigid, offish, remote 7 distant, haughty 8 arrogant, detached, reserved, reticent, solitary 9 unbending, uncurious, withdrawn 10 disdainful, restrained, unsociable 11 constrained, indifferent, standoffish, unconcerned 12 uninterested

alp 4 peak 5 mount 8 mountain

alpaca's habitat 4 Peru 5 Andes 7 Bolivia

alpha 4 dawn 5 start 6 outset 7 dawning, genesis, opening 8 outstart 9 beginning 12 commencement

alphabet 4 ABC's 7 grammar, letters 8 elements 9 rudiments 10 principles 12 fundamentals *Arabic:* 2 ba, fa, ha, ra, ta, ya, za 3 ayn, dad, dal, gaf, jim, kaf, kha, lam, mim, nun, sad, sin, tha, waw, zay 4 alif, dhal, shin 5 ghayn *Greek:* 2 mu, nu, pi, xi 3 chi, eta, phi, psi, rho, tau 4 beta, iota, zeta 5 alpha, delta, gamma, kappa, omega, sigma, theta 6 lambda 7 epsilon, omicron, upsilon *Hebrew:* 2 he, pe 3 mem, nun, sin, taf, tav, taw, tet, vav, waw, yod, yud 4 alef, ayin, beth, caph, heth, kaph, koph, qoph, resh, shin, teth 5 aleph, cheth, gimel, lamed, sadhe, tsade, zayin 6 daleth, samekh *Old Irish:* 4 ogam 5 ogham *runic:* 7 futhark, futhorc, futhork

Alphenor's mother 5 Niobe

Alpheus *beloved:* 8 Arethusa *father:* 7 Oceanus *form:* 5 river *mother:* 6 Tethys

Alpine *animal:* 4 ibex 7 chamois *climber:* 10 alpestrian *dance:* 5 gavot 7 gavotte *dress:* 6 dirndl *goat:* 4 ibex *herdsman:* 4 senn *house:* 6 chalet *lake:* 4 Como, Iseo 5 Garda 6 Geneva 7 Lucerne 8 Maggiore 9 Constance, Neuchatel *pass:* 3 col 5 Cenis 7 Brenner, Simplon 9 St. Bernard *peak:* 5 Blanc, Eiger 7 Bernina 8 Jungfrau 10 Matterhorn *plant:* 9 edelweiss *prim-*

rose: 8 auricula *resort:* 5 Davos 7 Bolzano, Zermatt 8 Chamonix, Grenoble 9 Innsbruck 10 Interlaken 11 Saint Moritz *river:* 5 Rhine, Rhone *snowfield:* 4 firn, neve *staff:* 10 alpenstock *state:* 5 Tirol, Tyrol 7 Bavaria *tunnel:* 5 Blanc, Cenis 7 Arlberg, Simplon 10 St. Gotthard *wind:* 4 bise, bora 5 foehn

already 4 even, once 6 before 7 earlier 8 formerly 9 erstwhile 10 heretofore, previously

also 3 too, yet 4 more 5 again, along, still 6 as well, withal 7 besides, further 8 likewise, moreover 9 similarly 10 in addition 11 furthermore 12 additionally

also-ran 5 loser

altar *boy:* 6 server 7 acolyte *cloth:* 4 pall 5 palla 7 frontal *constellation:* 3 Ara *hanging:* 6 dorsal, dossal, dossel *platform:* 8 predella *screen:* 7 reredos *shelf:* 6 gradin 7 gradine, retable *site:* 4 apse, bema *table:* 5 mensa *vessel:* 5 cruet, paten 7 chalice 8 ciborium 10 monstrance

alter 4 geld, turn, vary 5 adapt 6 adjust, change, jigger, modify, mutate, neuter, temper 8 moderate, modulate 9 refashion

alteration 4 turn 5 shift 6 change 8 mutation 9 variation 10 adaptation, adjustment, changeover, conversion, transition 12 modification 13 metamorphosis

altercate 4 spat, tiff 5 argue, scrap 6 bicker 7 brabble, dispute, quarrel, wrangle 8 squabble 9 caterwaul

altercation 3 row 4 tiff 6 combat, fracas 7 contest, dispute, quarrel, wrangle 8 argument, squabble 9 bickering 10 falling-out 11 controversy, embroilment

alternate 3 sub 5 proxy 6 fill-in, rotate 7 stand-in 8 periodic 9 change off, fluctuate, oscillate, recurrent, recurring, replacing, surrogate 10 equivalent, isochronal, periodical, substitute 11 isochronous, locum tenens, pinch hitter, replacement 12 intermittent

alternately 6 in lieu, rather 7 instead

alternative 5 proxy 6 choice, option 8 druthers, election 9 selection, surrogate 10 preference, substitute 11 contingency, possibility

Althaea *father:* 8 Thestius *husband:* 6 Oeneus *son:* 8 Meleager *victim:* 8 Meleager

although 4 when 5 while 6 albeit, much as 7 howbeit, whereas

altitude 6 height 9 elevation

altitudinous 4 high, tall

altogether 4 well 5 quite 6 in toto, wholly 7 en masse, exactly, totally, utterly 8 all in all, entirely 9 generally, perfectly 10 by and large, completely, on the whole, thoroughly

altruistic 6 humane 7 liberal 8 generous 9 unselfish 10 benevolent, bighearted, charitable, open-handed 11 magnanimous, noble-minded 12 eleemosynary, humanitarian 13 philanthropic

alum 4 grad 6 emetic 7 styptic 8 graduate 10 astringent

aluminum *symbol:* 2 Al

always 4 ever 7 forever 8 evermore 9 eternally 10 constantly, invariably 11 forevermore, in perpetuum, perpetually 12 continuously

amalgam see **amalgamation**

amalgamate 3 mix 4 fuse, meld 5 admix, merge, unify, unite 6 mingle 8 compound, intermix 9 interfuse 11 consolidate, intermingle

amalgamation 5 alloy, blend 6 fusion, merger 7 compost, mixture 8 compound 9 admixture, composite 10 commixture 13 consolidation

Amalthea *form:* 4 goat *horn:* 10 cornucopia *nursling:* 4 Zeus

Amasa *father:* 6 Hadlai, Jether *mother:* 7 Abigail

amass 4 bulk, hive 5 hoard, lay up, uplay 6 garner, gather, roll up 7 store up 8 cumulate 9 stockpile 10 accumulate

amassment 5 hoard, trove 9 colluvies 10 collection, cumulation 11 aggregation 12 accumulation 13 agglomeration

Amata's husband 7 Latinus

amateur 4 tyro 6 novice, tinker, votary 7 admirer, dabbler, devotee 8 beginner, neophyte, putterer 9 greenhorn, smatterer 10 apprentice, enthusiast, uninitiate 11 abecedarian

amateurish 3 raw 5 crude, green 6 clumsy, flawed 7 jackleg 8 dabbling 9 deficient, unskilled, untutored 10 dilettante, unfinished 12 dilettantist

amative 6 erotic 7 amorous 11 aphrodisiac

amaze 6 wonder 7 astound 8 astonish, surprise 9 dumbfound, marveling 10 admiration, wonderment 11 flabbergast 12 confoundment

amazement 6 wonder 8 surprise 9 marveling 10 admiration, wonderment 12 confoundment

amazing 7 strange 8 wondrous 9 marvelous, wonderful 10 astounding, miraculous, prodigious, stupendous, surprising 11 astonishing

amazon 5 harpy, scold, shrew, vixen 6 ogress, virago 8 fishwife 9 termagant, Xanthippe

ambassador 5 agent, envoy 6 legate 8 diplomat, emissary 9 messenger *papal:* 6 nuncio

ambience 6 medium, milieu 7 climate 10 atmosphere 11 environment, mise-en-scène 12 surroundings

ambiguity 7 evasion 9 equivoque, obscurity, vagueness 11 amphibology, uncertainty 12 equivocality, equivocation 13 double meaning

ambiguous 5 fishy, vague 6 opaque, unsure 7 dubious, obscure, suspect, unclear 8 doubtful 9 equivocal, tenebrous, uncertain, unsettled 10 inexplicit 11 problematic 12 questionable

ambit 5 limit, orbit, range, reach, scope, sweep 6 extent, radius 7 circuit, compass, purview 9 extension, perimeter, periphery 13 circumference

ambition 3 aim 4 goal, hope, mark, wish 5 dream, drive 6 desire, spirit, target 7 avidity, purpose 9 eagerness, intention, objective 10 aspiration, enterprise, get-up-and-go, initiative

ambitious 4 avid, bold, keen 5 eager 8 aspiring 9 energetic, grandiose, visionary 10 aggressive 11 hard-working 12 enterprising

ambivalent see equivocal

amble 4 mope 5 dally, drift, mosey 6 bummel, dawdle, linger, stroll 7 saunter

ambrosial 4 lush 5 balmy, spicy, sweet, yummy 6 aromal, savory 7 darling 8 adorable, aromatic, fragrant, heavenly, luscious, perfumed, redolent 9 delicious 10 delectable, delightful 11 scrumptious

ambulant 6 roving 7 nomadic, vagrant, walking 8 vagabond 9 itinerant 11 peripatetic

ambulate 4 hoof, pace, step, walk 5 tread, troop 6 foot it 7 traipse

ambulatory see ambulant

ambuscade 6 ambush 10 ambushment

ambush 4 trap 5 snare 6 assail, attack, entrap, lay for, waylay 7 assault, ensnare, scupper 8 surprise 9 ambuscade

ameliorate 4 help, mend 5 amend 6 better, perk up 7 improve, relieve 8 mitigate 10 convalesce, recuperate

amenable 4 tame 6 docile, liable, pliant 7 plastic, pliable, subdued, willing 8 biddable, obedient 9 adaptable, malleable, receptive, tractable 10 answerable, responsive 11 accountable, responsible

amend 4 help 5 right 6 better, repair 7 correct, improve, rectify 9 meliorate 10 ameliorate

amends 7 redress 8 reprisal 9 indemnity, quittance 10 recompense, reparation 11 restitution 12 compensation

amenities 5 mores 6 manner 8 decorums 9 etiquette 10 civilities 11 proprieties

amenity 5 charm, frill, luxus 6 luxury 7 comfort 8 civility, courtesy, facility 9 attention, gallantry, geniality, pleasance 10 affability, amiability, betterment, cordiality, enrichment, politeness 11 convenience, enhancement, improvement, sociability 12 agreeability, extravagance, graciousness, gratefulness, pleasantness 13 agreeableness, courteousness, enjoyableness

ament 4 fool, zany 5 idiot, moron 6 catkin, cretin 7 half-wit, natural 8 imbecile 9 simpleton

amerce 4 fine 5 mulct 6 punish 8 penalize

amercement 4 fine 5 mulct 7 forfeit, penalty

American *with Japanese-born parents:* 5 nisei

American League *Baltimore:* 7 Orioles *Boston:* 6 Red Sox *California:* 6 Angels *Chicago:* 8 White Sox *Cleveland:* 7 Indians *Detroit:* 6 Tigers *Kansas City:* 6 Royals *Milwaukee:* 7 Brewers *Minnesota:* 5 Twins *New York:* 7 Yankees *Oakland:* 9 Athletics *Seattle:* 8 Mariners *Texas:* 7 Rangers *Toronto:* 8 Blue Jays

America, the Beautiful *music:* 4 Ward (Samuel Augustus) *words:* 5 Bates (Katherine Lee)

americium *symbol:* 2 Am

Amfortas *father:* 7 Titurel *opera:* 8 Parsifal

amiability 7 amenity 9 geniality, pleasance 10 cordiality 12 gratefulness, pleasantness 13 agreeableness, enjoyableness

amiable 4 kind, mild, warm 6 benign, genial, gentle, kindly 7 affable, cordial, lenient 8 gracious, mannerly, obliging 9 courteous 10 responsive 11 complaisant, good-humored, good-natured, warmhearted 12 good-tempered

amicable 7 pacific 8 empathic, friendly, peaceful 9 congenial, peaceable 10 harmonious, like-minded, neighborly 11 sympathetic 13 understanding

amical 8 friendly 9 congenial 10 harmonious

amid 5 among, midst 6 during 10 throughout

amigo 4 mate 6 friend 8 familiar, intimate 9 confidant 12 acquaintance

amino acid 4 dopa 6 leucin, lysine, serine, toluid, valine 7 cystein, cystine, glycine, leucine, proline, toluide 8 cysteine, dopamine, histidin, thyroxin, toluidin, tyrosine

Amis novel 8 Lucky Jim

amiss 3 bad 4 awry, poor 5 badly, wrong 6 afield, astray, faulty, flawed, guilty, rotten, sinful, unholy 7 wrongly 8 blamable, blame-

ful, culpable, faultily 9 defective, imperfect
10 censurable 11 blameworthy, incorrectly,
unfavorably 12 inaccurately 13 demeritorious, reprehensible
amity 6 comity 7 concord, harmony
8 goodwill 10 friendship, kindliness
11 benevolence 12 friendliness
Ammonite god 6 Molech
Amneris's rival 4 Aida
amnesty 6 pardon 10 absolution
Amnon *father:* 5 David *half sister:*
5 Tamar *mother:* 7 Ahinoam
Amon *father:* 8 Manasseh *son:* 6 Josiah
Amonasro's daughter 4 Aida
among 3 mid 4 amid 5 midst 7 between
prefix: 5 inter
amorist 5 lover, Romeo 7 Don Juan, gallant 8 Casanova, lothario, paramour
amorous 6 erotic 7 amative, amatory, lustful 8 enamored 10 infatuated 11 aphrodisiac
amorousness 4 love 5 amour 7 passion
amorphous 8 formless, inchoate,
unformed, unshaped 9 shapeless
amount 4 body, bulk, core, dose 5 add
up, equal, price, reach, run to, sense, total,
touch 6 budget, burden, dosage, embody,
matter, number, thrust, upshot 7 include,
purport, quantum, run into, subsume
8 approach, comprise, quantity 9 aggregate, substance 12 correspond to *owed:*
4 debt *Scottish:* 4 haet 7 bittock *small:*
3 bit, jot 4 atom, drop, iota, mite, whit
5 minim, spark, speck, trace 7 modicum,
smidgen 8 molecule, particle 9 scintilla
amour 4 love 5 lover 6 affair 7 liaison,
passion, romance 8 intimacy, intrigue
10 love affair 12 entanglement, relationship
amour propre 5 pride 6 vanity 7 conceit
8 self-love, vainness 9 vainglory 10 narcissism, self-esteem, self-regard 11 self-conceit, self-respect 13 conceitedness
amphetamines 5 speed 6 dexies,
hearts, uppers 7 bennies, Dexoxyn
8 greenies, pep pills, Preludin 9 Dexedrine
10 Benzedrine, Methedrine
amphibian *burrowing:* 9 caecilian
extinct: 7 eryopid *family:* 7 Hylidae, Ranidae 9 Bufonidae, Proteidae, Sirenidae
genus: 4 Bufo, Hyla, Rana 5 Acris, Siren
7 Aneides, Eurycea 8 Ascaphus, Ensatina,
Manculus, Necturus, Triturus 9 Ambys-
toma, Plethodon *legless:* 9 caecilian *order:*
5 Anura 7 Caudata 9 Salientia *tailed:*
3 eft, olm 4 newt 7 caudate, proteus, ure-
dele 10 salamander *tailless:* 4 frog, hyla,
toad 8 bullfrog, tree toad 10 batrachian,
salientian *wormlike:* 9 caecilian *young:*
7 tadpole 8 polliwog

Amphion *brother:* 6 Zethus *conquest:*
6 Thebes *father:* 4 Zeus *mother:*
7 Antiope *sister:* 5 Aedon *wife:* 5 Niobe
Amphitrite *father:* 6 Nereus *husband:*
7 Neptune 8 Poseidon *mother:* 5 Doris
son: 6 Triton
Amphitryon's wife 7 Alcmene
ample 5 great, large, roomy 6 lavish,
plenty 7 copious, liberal, profuse 8 abundant, generous, handsome, prodigal, spacious 9 bounteous, bountiful, capacious,
plenteous, plentiful 10 commodious
amplify 5 swell 6 dilate, expand
7 develop, distend, enlarge, inflate
8 increase 9 elaborate
amplitude 4 size 5 scope, space
6 spread 7 bigness, breadth, expanse,
stretch 8 distance, fullness, wideness
9 expansion, greatness, largeness, magnitude, roominess 11 sizableness 12 size-
ableness, spaciousness 13 capaciousness
Amram *father:* 4 Bani 6 Dishon, Kohath
wife: 8 Jochebed
amulet 4 juju, luck, zemi 5 charm 6 fetish,
grigri, mascot 7 periapt 8 greegree, gris-
gris, talisman 10 lucky piece, phylactery,
rabbit-foot
Amulius' brother 7 Numitor
amuse 4 wile 5 charm 6 divert 7 animate,
beguile, delight, enchant, enliven 8 distract,
recreate 9 entertain, fascinate
amusement 9 diversion 10 recreation
11 dissipation, distraction 13 entertainment
amusement park 7 funfair
amusement show 8 carnival
amusing 5 droll, funny 7 comical, risible
8 humorous 9 laughable, ludicrous
Amycus *father:* 7 Neptune 8 Poseidon
friend: 8 Heracles, Hercules *mother:*
5 Melia
Amymone *father:* 6 Danaus *son:* 8 Nauplius
ana 5 varia 9 anecdotes 10 collection, miscellany 11 memorabilia
anabasis 5 march 7 advance, headway,
ongoing 8 progress 11 advancement, proficiency
anadem 5 crown 6 wreath 7 chaplet,
coronal, coronet, garland
anagogic 6 mystic, occult 8 mystical,
telestic 10 symbolical 11 allegorical
analects 4 posy 5 album 7 garland, omnibus 9 anthology 10 miscellany 11 florilegium
analgesic 7 anodyne 10 anesthetic, pain-
killer
analogous 4 akin, like 5 alike 7 kindred,
similar, uniform 8 parallel 9 consonant
10 comparable

analogue 5 match 7 cognate 8 congener, parallel 9 correlate 11 counterpart, countertype 13 correspondent

analogy 6 simile 8 affinity, likeness, metaphor 9 alikeness, semblance 10 comparison, similarity, similitude 11 resemblance

analysis 4 scan, view 5 audit 6 review, survey 7 breakup, checkup 8 exegesis, scrutiny 9 breakdown 10 dissection, inspection, resolution 11 examination 13 perlustration

analytic 4 keen 5 acute, sharp 6 subtle 7 logical 8 piercing 11 penetrating 13 ratiocinative

analyze 7 dissect, examine, inspect, resolve 8 classify 9 anatomize, break down, decompose 10 decompound, scrutinize 11 investigate

analyze grammatically 5 parse

Ananias 4 liar 6 fibber 7 fibster 8 perjurer 9 falsifier 11 storyteller 12 prevaricator *coconspirator:* 8 Sapphira *father:* 9 Nedebaeus *wife:* 8 Sapphira

anarch see anarchist

anarchism 4 riot 7 misrule 8 disorder 9 distemper

anarchist 5 rebel 8 frondeur, mutineer, revolter 9 insurgent 10 malcontent

anarchy 4 riot 5 chaos 7 misrule 8 disorder 9 distemper, mobocracy 10 ochlocracy 11 lawlessness

anathema 5 curse 6 pariah 7 bugbear, censure, malison, outcast, reproof 9 bête noire 10 black beast 11 abomination, commination, detestation, imprecation, malediction 12 condemnation, denunciation

anathematize 4 damn 5 curse 8 execrate 9 objurgate

anatomical depression 5 fossa, fovea

anatomical tube 3 vas 4 duct 5 canal

anatomist 5 Wolff (Kaspar) 6 Harvey (William) 8 Vesalius (Andreas)

anatomize 7 analyze, dissect, resolve 9 break down, decompose 10 decompound

Anaxarete's lover 5 Iphis

Anaxo *brother:* 10 Amphitryon *daughter:* 7 Alcmene *father:* 7 Alcaeus *husband:* 9 Electryon

ancestor 8 forebear, foregoer 9 ascendant, precursor, prototype 10 antecedent, antecessor, forefather, forerunner, progenitor 11 predecessor 12 primogenitor

ancestral sequence 8 pedigree 9 bloodline, genealogy

ancestry 4 race 5 blood, breed, stock 6 family, origin, source 7 descent, kindred, lineage 8 pedigree 10 derivation, extraction

Anchises' son 6 Aeneas

anchor 3 fix 4 moor 5 catch 6 fasten, secure 7 grapnel, killick, killock *line:* 7 catfall *part:* 4 ring 5 crown, fluke, shank

anchorage 4 port 5 chuck, haven, roads 6 harbor, riding 7 mooring 9 harborage, roadstead

anchorite 5 loner 6 hermit 7 recluse

anchors ____ 6 aweigh

ancient 3 old 4 aged 5 elder, hoary, olden 6 age-old, doting, primal, senior 7 antique, elderly, oldster 8 Noachian, old-timer, primeval, timeworn 9 doddering, venerable 10 primordial 12 antediluvian *combining form:* 4 pale 5 palae, paleo 6 archae, archeo, palaeo 7 archaeo

ancient capital 4 Susa 5 Balkh, Calah, Isker, Kalhu, Ninus, Sibir 6 Bactra, Nimrud 7 Nineveh, Shushan 10 Persepolis

ancient city *Asia Minor:* 4 Nice, Teos 5 Tyana 6 Edessa, Nicaea 7 Antioch 13 Halicarnassus *Babylonia:* 4 Sura 5 Accad, Agade, Akkad, Eridu, Larsa 7 Ellasar *Bengal:* 4 Gaur 9 Lakhnauti *Canaan:* 5 Gezer *Cyprus:* 7 Salamis *Egypt:* 2 On 5 Tanis 6 Thebes 7 Memphis 10 Heliopolis *Etruria:* 4 Veli *Euphrates River:* 7 Babylon *Greece:* 5 Crisa 6 Athens, Sparta 7 Calydon 10 Lacedaemon *Ionia:* 4 Myus, Teos 5 Chios, Samos 6 Priene 7 Ephesus, Lebedos, Miletus, Phocaea 8 Colophon, Erythrae 10 Clazomenae *Italy:* 5 Locri 7 Pompeii 11 Herculaneum *Latium:* 5 Gabii 9 Alba Longa *Mayan:* 4 Coba 5 Tikal *Nile River:* 5 Meroe *North Africa:* 5 Utica 8 Carthage *Palestine:* 4 Gaza 5 Ekron, Endor, Sodom 6 Beroea, Bethel, Gilead, Hebron 7 Jericho, Samaria 8 Ashkelon 9 Capernaum, Jerusalem *Peloponnesus:* 5 Tegea 6 Sparta 7 Corinth *Sumeria:* 2 Ur 4 Kish, Uruk 5 Erech, Larsa 6 Lagash *Turkey:* 5 Assos, Assus 9 Byzantium *Yucatan:* 5 Uxmal

ancient country *Adriatic coast:* 7 Illyria *Africa:* 10 Mauretania *Arabian Peninsula:* 5 Sheba *Asia:* 4 Aram 5 Media, Minni, Syria 7 Armenia, Ash Sham, Bactria *Asia Minor:* 5 Lydia, Mysia 6 Aeolis, Pontus 7 Cilicia, Phrygia 8 Bithynia *Balkan:* 7 Macedon 9 Macedonia *Black Sea:* 7 Colchis *Dead Sea:* 4 Edom *Euphrates River:* 9 Babylonia *Europe:* 4 Gaul 5 Dacia 6 Gallia *gold-rich:* 5 Ophir *Italy:* 6 Latium 7 Etruria *Nile valley:* 4 Cush *Peloponnesus:* 4 Elis 7 Arcadia *Syria:* 9 Phoenicia

ancient empire 6 Median 7 Hittite, Persian 8 Assyrian, Athenian, Chaldean, Egyptian, Seleucid 9 Ptolemaic 10 Babylonian

ancient kingdom *Anglo-Saxon:* 6 Wessex *Asia:* 4 Ghor, Ghur *Celtic:* 7 Cumbria

China: 3 Shu *Euphrates valley:* 4 Hira 7 Al-Hirah *Greece:* 8 Pergamon, Pergamum *North Of Assyria:* 3 Van 6 Ararat, Urartu *Palestine:* 5 Judah 6 Israel *Persian Gulf:* 4 Elam *Portugal:* 7 Algarve *Spain:* 4 Leon 6 Aragon 7 Castile, Galicia, Granada, Navarre *Syria:* 4 Moab *Welsh:* 5 Powys *West Sahara:* 4 Gana 5 Ghana

ancient monument 6 sphinx 7 obelisk, pyramid

ancient royal forest 4 Dean 8 Sherwood

ancient town *Africa:* 4 Zama *Armenia:* 4 Dwin, Tvin *Asia Minor:* 4 Soli 5 Derbe, Issus, Soloi *Attica:* 6 Icaria *Black Sea:* 5 Olbia 9 Apollonia *Greece:* 4 Abae, Opus 8 Marathon *Italy:* 4 Elea, Luna 5 Cumae, Velia *Latium:* 5 Ardea, Cures *Macedonia:* 5 Pydna, Stobi 9 Apollonia *Peloponnesus:* 5 Asine *Persia:* 6 Hormuz 8 Harmozia *Sicily:* 5 Hybla *Spain:* 5 Munda *Tatar:* 5 Isker, Sibir *Wendish:* 5 Julin

ancilla 3 aid 4 help 6 helper 7 striker 9 assistant, attendant

ancillary 8 adjuvant, incident 9 accessory, attendant, attending, auxiliary, satellite 10 coincident, collateral, subsidiary 11 appurtenant, concomitant, subservient 12 accompanying, contributory

Anderson, Maxwell *play:* 7 High Tor 8 Key Largo 9 Winterset 11 Valley Forge 14 What Price Glory

Anderson, Sherwood *book* 9 Poor White 10 Kit Brandon 12 Dark Laughter 13 Winesburg, Ohio

Andes native 4 Inca

andiron 7 firedog

androgynous 8 bisexual 13 hermaphrodite

android 5 robot 9 automaton

Andromache *husband:* 6 Hector 7 Helenus, Pyrrhus 11 Neoptolemus *son:* 8 Astyanax, Molossus

Andromeda *father:* 7 Cepheus *husband:* 7 Perseus *mother:* 10 Cassiopeia *rescuer:* 7 Perseus

___ and warp 4 woof

anecdote 4 tale, yarn 5 story 7 episode, recital 8 relation 9 narration, narrative

anemic 4 pale 6 pallid, watery 8 waterish 9 bloodless

anent 2 re 4 as to, in re 5 about, as for 7 apropos 8 touching 9 as regards 10 concerning 13 with respect to

anesthetic 4 dull, hard 5 rocky 7 anodyne 9 analgesic, bloodless, insensate 10 impassible, insensible, pain-killer 11 insensitive *combining form:* 5 caine *medical:* 5 ether 6 spinal 7 eucaine 8 morphine, procaine 9 halothane, novo-caine 10 benzocaine, chloroform, tetracaine 11 scopolamine

anesthetized 4 dead, numb 6 asleep, numbed 8 benumbed, deadened 9 senseless, unfeeling 10 insensible 11 insensitive

anew 4 over 5 again 6 afresh, de novo, lately, of late 8 once more, recently *combining form:* 2 an 3 ana 4 pali *prefix:* 2 re

angel 6 backer, cherub, patron, surety 7 sponsor 8 backer-up 9 celestial, guarantor *biblical:* 5 Uriel 7 Gabriel, Michael, Raphael *fallen:* 7 Lucifer *hierarchy:* 6 powers 7 thrones, virtues 8 cherubim, seraphim 9 dominions *Mormon:* 6 Moroni *of death:* 6 Azrael

Angel Clare's bride 4 Tess

angelic 4 holy 5 godly 7 saintly 8 cherubic

Angelica *father:* 9 Galaphron *husband:* 6 Medoro *lover:* 7 Orlando

anger 3 ire, irk, vex 4 bile, boil, burn, fume, fury, huff, rage, rant, rave, rile 5 annoy, pique, storm, wrath 6 blow up, choler, dander, enrage, madden, nettle, offend, seethe 7 affront, bristle, dudgeon, flare up, incense, outrage, provoke, steam up, umbrage 8 boil over, irritate 9 aggravate, annoyance, infuriate 10 exasperate 11 indignation, infuriation 12 exasperation

angered easily 4 rily 5 riley 9 irascible

angle 3 aim, bow 4 axil, bend, bias, fish, hand, hint, skew, turn 5 facet, phase, slant 6 aspect, crotch 7 flexure, outlook, turning 8 flection 9 direction, viewpoint 10 standpoint *combining form:* 3 gon 4 goni 5 gonio 6 anguli, angulo

Anglo-Saxon *army:* 4 fyrd *assembly:* 4 moot 5 gemot 6 gemote *coin:* 3 ora 5 sceat 6 mancus *council:* 9 heptarchy *county:* 5 shire *court:* 4 moot 5 gemot 6 gemote *crown tax:* 4 geld *epic:* 7 Beowulf *free servant:* 5 thane, thegn *god:* 3 Ing *goddess of fate:* 4 Wyrd *historian:* 4 Bede *king:* 3 Ine, Ini 4 Edwy 5 Edgar, Edred 6 Alfred, Edmund, Edward, Egbert 8 Ethelred *kingdom:* 4 Kent 5 Essex 6 Mercia, Sussex, Wessex 10 East Anglia 11 Northumbria *king's council:* 5 witan *letter:* 3 edh, eth, wen, wyn 4 wynn 5 thorn *nobleman:* 4 earl *poet:* 4 scop *prince:* 8 atheling *sheriff:* 5 reeve 6 gerefa *slave:* 4 esne *tenant:* 6 geneat *village:* 3 ham *warrior:* 5 thane, thegn

angry 3 mad 4 rily, sore, waxy 5 irate, riley, upset, vexed, wroth 6 heated, ireful, put out, shirty, wrathy, wrothy 7 enraged, furious, uptight 8 choleric, incensed, maddened, worked up, wrathful, wrothful 9 indignant, perturbed, wrought up

10 aggravated, infuriated 11 acrimonious, exasperated

anguish 3 rue, woe 4 ache, care, dole, pain, pang 5 grief, throe, worry 6 regret, sorrow, throes 7 anxiety, torment, torture 9 heartache 10 affliction, heartbreak

angular 4 bony, lank, lean 5 crude, gaunt, lanky, rough, spare 6 skinny 7 scraggy, scrawny 8 rawboned, unworked 9 rough-hewn, undressed 10 unfinished, unpolished 11 unfashioned

anima 4 soul 6 pneuma, psyche, spirit 9 élan vital 10 vital force

animadversion 4 slam, slur 7 censure, obloquy 9 aspersion, criticism, stricture 10 accusation, imputation, reflection 11 insinuation 12 reprehension

animadvert 5 state, utter 6 remark 7 comment, declare, observe 10 commentate

animal 5 beast, brute, feral 6 brutal, carnal, ferine 7 beastly, bestial, brutish, critter, fleshly, sensual, swinish, wilding 8 creature, wildling *antlered:* 3 elk 4 axis, deer 5 moose 7 caribou 8 reindeer *aquatic:* 3 eel 4 fish, frog, seal 5 otter, whale 6 dugong, sea cow, walrus 7 dolphin, manatee, octopus 8 bryozoan, porpoise 9 alligator, crocodile *arboreal:* 2 ai 4 bird, unau 5 chimp, coati, koala, lemur, sloth 6 gibbon, monkey 7 opossum, tarsier 8 kinkajou, marmoset, squirrel 9 orangutan *burrowing:* 4 mole 5 brock, ratel 6 badger, gopher, marmot, rabbit 7 echidna 9 armadillo, groundhog, woodchuck *castrated:* 2 ox 5 capon, spado, steer 6 barrow, wether 7 gelding *combining form:* 2 zo 3 zoa (plural), zoo 4 zoon 6 theria (plural) 7 therium *draft:* 2 ox 3 yak 4 mule, oxen (plural) 5 horse 6 donkey 8 elephant *exhibit:* 3 zoo *extinct:* 3 moa 4 dodo, urus 6 quagga 7 mammoth 8 dinosaur, eohippus, mastodon 9 solitaire, trilobite *female:* 3 cow, dam, doe, ewe, hen, pen, roe, sow 4 mare, puss 5 bitch, goose, jenny, nanny, vixen 6 jennet 7 lioness *four-footed:* 9 quadruped *four-limbed:* 8 tetrapod *free-swimming:* 6 nekton *hibernating:* 4 bear, frog, toad 5 skunk, snake 7 polecat 8 chipmunk 9 groundhog, woodchuck *horned:* 2 ox 3 ram, yak 4 bull, goat, ibex, kudu 5 addax, ariel, badak, bison, eland, rhino 6 cattle, koodoo 7 buffalo, gazelle, giraffe, unicorn 8 antelope *humped:* 2 ox 3 elk, yak 4 zebu 5 bison, camel, moose *imaginary:* 5 snark *insect-eating:* 4 mole, newt 5 gecko, shrew 6 numbat 7 echidna 8 aardvark, anteater, hedgehog, pangolin, tamandua 10 salamander *lover:* 8 zoophile *male:* 3 cob, ram, tom 4 boar, buck, bull, cock,

stag, stud 5 billy, steer 6 gander 7 gobbler, rooster 8 bachelor, stallion *many-celled:* 8 metazoan *many-footed:* 9 centipede, millipede *marsupial:* 4 tait 5 koala 6 cuscus, numbat, wombat 7 dasyure, opossum, wallaby 8 kangaroo 9 bandicoot, phalanger *meat-eating:* 9 carnivore *mythical:* 4 yale 5 hodag, Hydra, kylin 6 bunyip, dragon, kraken, sphinx 7 centaur, griffin, mermaid, Pegasus, unicorn 8 basilisk, Cerberus, Minotaur *one-celled:* 9 protozoan *Peruvian:* 5 llama 6 alpaca, vicuna *plant-eating:* 9 herbivore *skin disease:* 5 mange *snouted:* 5 coati, tapir 8 mongoose; (see also animal, insect-eating) *spotted:* 4 axis, paca 6 calico, jaguar, ocelot 7 cheetah, leopard, piebald 8 skewbald 9 dalmatian *striped:* 4 kudo 5 tiger, zebra 6 koodoo, quagga *suffix:* 4 acea (plural) 5 acean *trail:* 3 pug 4 foil, slot 5 spoor *tusked:* 6 walrus 7 warthog 8 elephant *two-footed:* 5 biped *web-footed:* 4 duck, frog, toad 5 goose, otter 6 beaver 8 duckbill, platypus *young:* 3 cub, kid, kit, pup 4 calf, colt, fawn, foal, joey, lamb 5 bunny, chick, kitty, poult, shoat, stirk, whelp 6 cygnet, farrow, heifer, kitten, piglet 7 bullock, gosling, lambkin 8 suckling, yeanling, yearling 9 fledgling

animal behavior *study of:* 8 ethology

animal fat 4 suet 6 tallow

animalism 7 lechery 9 carnality 10 sensualism, sensuality, unchastity 11 fleshliness, lustfulness 13 lecherousness

animalize 4 warp 6 debase 7 corrupt, deprave, pervert, vitiate 9 brutalize 10 bestialize, demoralize

animal life 5 fauna

animals *suffix:* 3 ata, ida, ini 4 idae, idea

animate 4 fire 5 cheer, drive, exalt, impel, liven, nerve, steel 6 inform, vivify 7 actuate, chirk up, enliven, hearten, inspire, quicken, refresh 8 activate, embolden, inspirit, motivate, vitalize 9 encourage, enhearten 10 invigorate, vivificate

animated 3 gay 4 cant, keen 5 alert, alive, canty, vital 6 lively, living, zoetic 7 zestful 8 spirited 9 exuberant, sprightly, vitalized, vivacious 12 high-spirited

animation 3 vim 4 brio, dash, élan, life, zing 5 oomph, verve 6 esprit, spirit

animosity 6 enmity, rancor 9 antipathy, hostility 10 antagonism

animus 4 plan, soul 6 design, enmity, intent, pneuma, psyche, rancor, spirit 7 meaning, purpose 9 antipathy, élan vital, hostility, intention 10 antagonism, intendment, vital force

Anius *daughter:* 4 Oeno 5 Elais 6 Spermo *father:* 6 Apollo *mother:* 5 Rhoeo

Anjou 4 pear
ankle 6 tarsus *combining form:* 4 tars
5 tarso
annals 7 history 9 chronicle
Anna's sister 4 Dido
annex 3 add, arm, cop, ell, nim, win
4 gain, hook, join, land, take, wing 5 affix,
seize, steal, unite 6 append, attach, fasten,
obtain, pick up, secure, take on 7 acquire,
preempt, procure, purloin, subjoin
8 accroach, addition, arrogate, superadd
9 extension, sequester 10 commandeer,
confiscate 11 appropriate, expropriate
Annie Oakley 4 pass
annihilate 4 raze, ruin, undo 5 abate,
annul, crush, quash, quell, wrack, wreck
6 murder, negate, quench, squash, uproot
7 abolish, blot out, destroy, expunge, nullify, put down, root out, vitiate, wipe out
8 abrogate, decimate, demolish, massacre,
suppress 9 eradicate, extirpate, slaughter
10 extinguish, invalidate, obliterate
11 exterminate
annihilative 7 ruinous 8 wrackful, wreckful 10 shattering 11 destructive
anniversary *hundredth:* 9 centenary
10 centennial *tenth:* 9 decennial *thousandth:* 10 millennial 11 millenniary
annotate 5 gloss 7 comment, explain
9 elucidate 10 commentate
announce 5 augur, sound 6 attest, blazon, herald 7 bespeak, betoken, declare,
forerun, presage, present, publish, testify,
witness 8 foreshow, foretell, indicate, proclaim 9 advertise, broadcast, harbinger
10 bruit about, promulgate 11 preindicate
announcement 9 broadcast 11 declaration, publication 12 proclamation, promulgation 13 advertisement
annoy 3 bug, irk, vex 4 bait, fret, gall,
gnaw, miff 5 chafe, chivy, harry, peeve,
tease, upset, worry 6 abrade, badger,
bother, harass, heckle, hector, pester,
plague, ruffle 7 agitate, bedevil, disturb,
hagride, perturb, provoke 8 distress, exercise, irritate 9 beleaguer *Scottish:* 4 fash
annoyance 3 ire 4 pest 5 anger, trial
6 bother, irking, pester, plague, pother, vexing 7 teasing 8 distress, irritant, nuisance,
vexation 9 besetment, bothering, pestering,
provoking 10 affliction, botherment, harassment 11 aggravation, botheration, indignation, provocation 12 exasperation
annoying 5 pesky
annual 5 plant 6 flower, yearly 7 almanac
8 yearbook
annul 4 undo, void 5 abate, erase, quash
6 cancel, delete, efface, negate, revoke,
vacate 7 abolish, blot out, expunge, nullify,
redress, rescind, vitiate, wipe out 8 abrogate, dissolve 9 cancel out, discharge, frus-

trate 10 annihilate, counteract, extinguish,
invalidate, neutralize, obliterate 11 countermand
annunciate 5 sound, state 7 declare, publish 8 proclaim 9 advertise, broadcast
10 bruit about, promulgate
anodyne 6 opiate 8 narcotic, nepenthe,
sedative 9 analgesic, calmative, soporific
10 anesthetic, depressant, pain-killer
12 tranquilizer
anointing 7 unction
anomalous 6 off-key 7 deviant, foreign,
strange 8 aberrant, abnormal, atypical,
peculiar 9 deviative, divergent, irregular,
unnatural, untypical 11 heteroclite 13 preternatural
anon 4 soon, then, when 5 again 7 by and
by, shortly 8 directly 9 presently
anonym 5 alias 11 nom de guerre
anonymous 7 unknown, unnamed
8 nameless 9 incognito 10 innominate
11 unspecified 12 undesignated, unidenti-
fied, unrecognized
another 3 new 4 else, more 5 added,
fresh 7 farther, further 10 additional
anschluss 5 union 6 league 8 alliance
9 coalition 10 federation 11 confederacy
13 confederation
anserine 5 silly 6 stupid 9 gooselike
answer 4 fill, meet 5 rebut, reply 6 come
in, refute, rejoin, result, retort, return 7 fulfill, respond, satisfy 8 antiphon, rebuttal,
response, solution 9 rejoinder 10 refutation
11 recriminate 13 countercharge
answerable 5 bound 6 liable 7 obliged
8 amenable 9 compelled, duty-bound, obligated 11 accountable, constrained, responsible
ant 5 emmet 9 carpenter *combining form:*
6 myrmec 7 myrmeco *male:* 4 aner *relating to:* 6 formic *worker:* 6 ergate
Antaean 4 huge 5 giant 6 heroic 7 titanic
8 colossal, gigantic 9 cyclopean, Herculean
10 gargantuan
Antaeus *father:* 7 Neptune 8 Poseidon
mother: 2 Ge 4 Gaea *slayer:* 8 Heracles,
Hercules
antagonism 3 con 6 animus, enmity, rancor 7 discord 8 friction, opposure 9 animosity, antipathy, hostility 10 antithesis,
opposition, oppugnancy, resistance 11 contrariety 12 disagreement
antagonist 3 con 4 anti 5 match
7 opposer 8 opponent 9 adversary, oppugnant
antagonistic 4 anti 6 averse, bitter
7 adverse, hostile, opposed 8 clashing,
contrary, inimical, opposing 9 oppugnant,
rancorous, vitriolic 10 antonymous, discordant 11 conflicting, contrariant, inconso-

nant 12 antipathetic, incompatible *combining form:* 7 enantio

ante 3 bet, pot 5 stake, wager

anteater see *animal, insect-eating*

antecede 7 forerun, precede, predate 8 foredate

antecedence 8 priority 12 previousness

antecedent 4 fore 5 cause, prior 6 former, reason 8 ancestor, anterior, forebear, foregoer, occasion, previous 9 condition, foregoing, precedent, preceding, precursor, prototype 10 forerunner 11 determinant, predecessor

antedate see *antecede*

antediluvian 3 old 4 aged, fogy 5 hoary 6 age-old, fogram, fossil, square 7 ancient, antique 8 mossback, Noachian, timeworn 10 fuddy-duddy 12 old-fashioned 13 stick-in-the-mud

antelope 3 gnu, kob 4 guib, koba, kudu, oryx, poku, puku, suni, tora 5 addax, beira, beisa, bongo, eland, goral, nagor, nyala, oribi, saiga, serow, tiang 6 dik-dik, duiker, grimme, impala, lechwe, leiwel, nilgai 7 blesbok, bubalis, chamois, defassa, dibatag, gazelle, gemsbok, gerenuk, grysbok, rooibok, sassaby 8 agacella, bontebok, bushbuck, reedbuck, sing-sing, steinbok 9 duikerbok, kleeneboc, sitatunga, springbok, waterbuck 10 hartebeest 12 klipspringer *extinct:* 7 blaubok 9 blaauwbok *family:* 7 Bovidae *female:* 3 doe *four-horned:* 6 chouka 7 chikara 10 chousingha *male:* 4 buck *mythical:* 4 yale *young:* 3 kid (see also *gazelle*)

antenna 4 yagi 6 aerial, dipole 8 monopole

Antenor *father:* 8 Aesyetes *son:* 6 Agenor *wife:* 6 Theano

anterior 4 past 5 prior 6 former 8 previous 9 foregoing, precedent, preceding 10 antecedent

Anteros *brother:* 4 Eros *father:* 4 Ares, Mars *mother:* 5 Venus 9 Aphrodite *opposite:* 4 Eros

anthology 3 ana 4 posy 5 album 7 garland, omnibus 8 analects, delectus, treasury 10 collection, miscellany 11 compilation, florilegium

anthropoid 3 ape 6 monkey 7 gorilla, manlike, primate 8 hominoid, humanoid 10 chimpanzee

anthropologist 4 Boas (Franz), Mead (Margaret) 5 Black (Davidson), Keith (Arthur), Sapir (Edward), Tylor (Edward Burnett) 6 Dubois (Eugène), Frazer (James George), Hooton (Earnest Albert), Leakey (Louis), Linton (Ralph), Morgan (Lewis Henry) 7 Kroeber (Alfred Louis), Wissler (Clark) 8 Benedict (Ruth), Washburn 10 Malinowski (Bronisław Kasper) 11 Wei-

denreich (Franz), Westermarck (Edward Alexander)

anti 3 con 7 adverse, opposed, opposer 8 opponent, opposing 9 adversary, oppugnant 10 antagonist 12 antagonistic, antipathetic

antiaircraft fire 4 flak

antibiotic 7 colicin 8 viomycin 9 polymyxin 10 bacitracin, novobiocin, penicillin 11 bacteriocin, tyrothricin 12 streptomycin, tetracycline

antic 4 dido, lark 5 caper, comic, prank, trick 6 frisky, frolic, lively, pranky, shines 7 bizarre, comical, foolish, playful, roguish 8 farcical, gamesome, prankful, prankish, spirited 9 fantastic, grotesque, laughable, ludicrous, sprightly 10 frolicsome, rollicking, shenanigan, tomfoolery 11 mischievous, monkeyshine

anticipate 3 see 5 await 6 divine, expect 7 foresee, preknow, presage, prevent, previse 8 forecast, forefeel, foreknow, foretell, outguess 9 apprehend, forestall, foretaste, prevision, visualize

anticipation 10 expectancy 11 expectation

anticipatory 7 atiptoe 9 expectant, expecting

Anticlea *father:* 9 Autolycus *husband:* 7 Laertes *son:* 7 Ulysses 8 Odysseus

antidote 4 cure 6 remedy 7 negator 9 nullifier 10 corrective 11 counterstep, neutralizer 12 counteragent 13 counteractant, counteractive

Antigone *brother:* 9 Polynices *father:* 7 Oedipus *mother:* 7 Jocasta *sister:* 6 Ismene *uncle:* 5 Creon

Antilochus *father:* 6 Nestor *friend:* 8 Achilles *slayer:* 6 Memnon

antimony 7 stibium *combining form:* 4 stib 5 stibi, stibo 6 stibio *symbol:* 2 Sb

Antiope *father:* 6 Asopus *husband:* 5 Lycus 7 Theseus *queen of:* 7 Amazons *son:* 6 Zethus 7 Amphion 10 Hippolytus

antipasto 4 whet 7 zakuska 9 appetizer 11 hors d'oeuvre

antipathetic 7 adverse, opposed 8 aversive, clashing, contrary, opposing, opposite, ungenial 9 abhorrent, antipodal, loathsome, obnoxious, oppugnant, repellent, repugnant, repulsive 10 antonymous, discordant, disgusting 11 conflicting, contrariant, distasteful, uncongenial 12 antagonistic 13 contradictory, unsympathetic

antipathy 6 animus, enmity, rancor 7 allergy, dislike 8 aversion, distaste, dyspathy 9 animosity, hostility 10 abhorrence, antagonism, repellency

antiphon 5 reply 6 answer, retort, return 7 respond 8 response 9 rejoinder

antipodal 5 polar 7 counter, reverse
8 contrary, converse, opposite 9 diametric
11 diametrical 12 antithetical 13 contradictory

antipode 6 contra 7 counter, reverse
8 contrary, converse, opposite 10 antithesis 11 counterpole 13 contradictory

antiquate 7 outdate, outmode 8 obsolete
9 obsolesce 12 superannuate

antiquated 5 dated, fusty, moldy, passé
7 antique, archaic 8 obsolete, old-timey,
outmoded 10 oldfangled 12 old-fashioned

antique 3 old 4 aged 5 dated, hoary,
passé 6 age-old 7 ancient, archaic 8 Noachian, old-timey, outdated, outmoded, timeworn 9 ancestral, out-of-date, venerable
10 antiquated, oldfangled 12 antediluvian,
old-fashioned

antiquity *combining form:* 6 archae,
archeo 7 archaeo

antiseptic 6 iodine 7 alcohol 8 peroxide
9 boric acid, carvacrol, germicide, merbro-
min 10 gramicidin 12 carbolic acid, disin-
fectant *pioneer:* 6 Lister (Joseph)

antisocial 7 ascetic, austere 8 eremitic,
reserved, solitary 9 reclusive, withdrawn
11 introverted, standoffish 12 misanthropic

antithesis 3 con 6 contra 7 counter,
reverse 8 antipode, antipole, contrary, converse, opposite, opposure 10 antagonism,
opposition 11 contrariety, counterpole
13 contradictory

antithetical 5 polar 7 counter, reverse
8 contrary, converse, opposite 9 antipodal,
diametric 10 antipodean 11 diametrical
13 contradictory

antitoxin 4 sera (plural) 5 serum

antlike 9 myrmecoid

Antony, Mark *defeat:* 6 Actium *friend:*
6 Caesar *lover:* 9 Cleopatra *wife:* 7 Octavia

Anubis' father 6 Osiris

anus *combining form:* 3 ano 5 proct
6 procta, procti, procto

anvil *combining form:* 5 incud 6 incudo

anxiety 4 care 5 doubt, dread, panic,
worry 6 unease 7 concern 8 disquiet, distress, mistrust, suspense 9 suffering
10 solicitude, uneasiness 11 concernment,
disquietude, uncertainty

anxious 4 agog, avid, keen 5 eager,
scary, upset 6 afraid, aghast, ardent,
scared, uneasy 7 alarmed, fearful, jittery,
worried 8 agitated, appetent, troubled
9 impatient, perturbed, terrified 10 breathless, disquieted, frightened 12 apprehensive

any 4 some

anyhow 6 random 8 at random, randomly
9 haphazard 11 any which way, haphazardly 13 helter-skelter

anytime 4 ever 5 at all

anyway 4 ever, once 5 at all

anywise see anyhow

A1 4 tops 5 prime 6 Grade A 8 five-star,
superior 9 excellent, first rate, front-rank,
number one, top-drawer 10 blue-ribbon,
first-class

apace 4 fast 7 flat-out, hastily, quickly,
rapidly, swiftly 8 speedily 9 posthaste
12 lickety-split 13 expeditiously

Apache chief 7 Cochise 8 Geronimo

apart 5 alone, aside 6 singly 7 asunder,
isolate, removed, sky-high 8 detached, isolated, one by one 9 severally 10 sepa-
rately 12 individually 13 independently,
unaccompanied *combining form:* 4 dich
5 chori, dicho *prefix:* 3 dis

apart from 3 bar, but 4 save 6 except,
saving 7 barring, besides 9 outside of
11 exclusive of

apartheid 10 separation, separatism
11 segregation 12 separateness

apartment 4 flat, room 5 rooms, suite
6 rental, walk-up 7 chamber, flatlet 8 lodgings, tenement

apathetic 3 dry 4 dull, limp 5 inert, stoic
6 stolid, torpid 7 callous, languid, unmoved
8 sluggish 9 impassive, untouched
10 anesthetic, insensible, phlegmatic, spiritless 11 indifferent, insensitive 12 matter-of-
fact

apathy 6 acedia, phlegm, torpor 8 cold-
ness, lethargy, obduracy, stoicism 9 disregard, inertness, lassitude, passivity, stolidity, torpidity, unconcern 10 detachment,
dispassion 11 callousness, disinterest,
impassivity, insouciance 12 heedlessness,
indifference, listlessness 13 insensibility,
insensitivity, unmindfulness

ape 4 copy, mime, mock 5 magot, mimic
6 baboon, gibbon, monkey, parody, pongid,
simian 7 copycat, gorilla, imitate, take off
8 travesty 9 burlesque, orangutan 10 caricature, chimpanzee, orangoutan *combining form:* 6 pithec 7 pitheco 8 pithecus

aperçu 6 digest, précis, sketch, survey
7 pandect, sylloge 8 syllabus 10 compendium

aperitif 4 whet 5 drink 8 cocktail 9 appetizer

aperitive 5 sapid, tasty 6 savory 8 saporous, tasteful 9 palatable, toothsome
10 appetizing, flavorsome 13 mouth-watering

aperture 3 gap 4 gash, hole, slit, vent
5 break, chasm, cleft, slash 6 breach, outlet 7 opening, orifice, pinhole 8 puncture
10 interstice 11 perforation 13 discontinuity

apery 7 mimicry

apex 3 cap, tip, top 4 acme, cusp, noon,
peak, roof 5 crest, crown, limit, point

6 apogee, climax, comble, culmen, summit, vertex, zenith **8** capsheaf, capstone, meridian, noontide, pinnacle, ultimate **9** crescendo, fastigium, sublimity **11** culmination, ne plus ultra **12** quintessence *combining form:* **3** ace **4** apic **5** apici, apico

Aphareus' son 4 Idas **7** Lynceus

aphorism 4 rule **5** axiom, gnome, maxim, moral **6** dictum, truism **7** brocard **8** apothegm

aphrodisia 4 itch, lust **6** desire **7** passion **9** eroticism, prurience, pruriency **11** lustfulness **13** concupiscence, lickerishness

aphrodisiac 6 erotic **7** amative, amatory, amorous

Aphrodite 5 Venus *consort:* **4** Ares **6** Vulcan **10** Hephaestus *father:* **4** Zeus **7** Jupiter *goddess of:* **4** love *mother:* **5** Dione *son:* **4** Eros **5** Cupid **6** Aeneas **7** Priapus

apiarist 6 beeman **9** beekeeper, beemaster

apical 3 top **7** highest, topmost **8** loftiest **9** uppermost

apiculture 10 beekeeping

apiece 3 all **4** each **5** aside **6** singly **8** one by one, per caput **9** per capita **12** individually, respectively

apish 7 slavish **9** emulative, imitative

aplomb 4 ease **5** poise **8** coolness, easiness **9** assurance, composure, sangfroid, self-trust **10** confidence, equanimity **11** nonchalance, savoir faire **13** self-assurance

apocalypse 6 oracle, vision **8** prophecy **10** revelation

apocalyptic 4 dire **5** vatic **6** mantic **7** baleful, baneful, direful, fateful, fatidic, ominous, unlucky **8** Delphian, oracular **9** ill-boding, prophetic, sibylline, vaticinal **11** prophetical, threatening **12** inauspicious

apocopate 5 elide

apocryphal 5 false, wrong **6** untrue **7** dubious **8** doubtful, spurious **9** incorrect, ungenuine **11** unauthentic

apogee 4 acme, apex, peak **6** climax, summit, zenith **8** capstone, meridian, pinnacle **11** culmination

Apollo 6 Helios **7** Phoebus *beloved:* **6** Cyrene, Daphne **8** Calliope *birthplace:* **5** Delos *father:* **4** Zeus **7** Jupiter *mother:* **4** Leto **6** Latona *oracle:* **6** Delphi *sister:* **5** Diana **7** Artemis *son:* **3** Ion **7** Orpheus *temple:* **6** Delphi

Apollyon 5 devil, fiend, Satan **6** diablo **7** Lucifer, Old Nick, serpent **9** Beelzebub **10** Old Scratch **13** Old Gooseberry

apologetic 5 sorry **7** defense **8** contrite, penitent **9** regretful, repentant **10** remorseful **11** attritional, penitential **12** compunctious **13** justification

apologia 7 defense **11** elucidation, explanation **13** clarification, justification

apologue 4 myth **5** fable **7** parable **8** allegory

apology 6 excuse **7** defense, redress, regrets, support **8** espousal, mea culpa **9** admission **10** advocating, advocation, concession, confession **11** championing **13** justification

aporetic 6 show-me **9** quizzical, skeptical **11** incredulous, questioning, unbelieving **12** disbelieving

apostasy 7 perfidy **9** defection, desertion, falseness, recreancy

apostate 8 defector, recreant, renegade, runagate, turncoat **9** turnabout **13** tergiversator

apostatize 4 turn **6** defect, desert **8** renounce **9** repudiate **10** tergiverse **12** tergiversate

a posteriori 9 inducible, inductive

apostle 4 John, Jude, Paul **5** James, Judas, Peter, Silas, Simon **6** Andrew, Philip, Thomas **7** Matthew **8** Barnabas, disciple, follower, Matthias, preacher **9** missioner **10** colporteur, evangelist, missionary **11** Bartholomew **12** propagandist *of Germany:* **8** Boniface *of Ireland:* **7** Patrick *of the English:* **9** Augustine *of the French:* **5** Denis *of the Gauls:* **8** Irenaeus *of the Gentiles:* **4** Paul *of the Goths:* **7** Ulfilas *to the Indians:* **9** John Eliot

apothecary 7 chemist **8** druggist **10** pharmacist

apothegm 4 rule **5** axiom, gnome, maxim, moral **6** dictum, truism **7** brocard **8** aphorism

apotheosis 6 height **7** epitome **8** last word, ultimate **9** elevation **10** exaltation **11** deification, ennoblement, idolization, lionization **12** enshrinement, quintessence **13** dignification, glorification

appall 3 awe **4** faze **5** daunt, shake **6** dismay **7** horrify, overawe **11** consternate

appalling 5 awful **7** fearful **8** daunting, dreadful, horrible, horrific, shocking, terrible, terrific **9** dismaying, frightful **10** formidable, horrifying

appanage 5 right **9** privilege **10** birthright, perquisite **11** prerogative

apparatus 4 gear, tool **6** outfit, tackle **7** utensil **8** materiel, tackling **9** equipment, implement, machinery **10** instrument **11** habiliments **13** accouterments, paraphernalia *combining form:* **4** stat

apparel 4 clad, duds, garb, togs **5** array, dress **6** attire, clothe **7** clothes, garment, raiment **8** clothing, enclothe **10** attirement **11** habiliments

apparent 5 clear, plain **6** patent **7** evident, obvious, seeming **8** distinct, illusive,

illusory, manifest, palpable, semblant
9 prominent 10 Barmecidal, noticeable,
observable, ostensible 11 discernible, perceivable, unambiguous, unequivocal

apparently *combining form:* 5 quasi

apparition 5 bogey, ghost, shade, spook,
umbra 6 shadow, spirit, wraith 7 eidolon,
phantom, specter 8 illusion, phantasm, revenant, spectrum 13 hallucination

appeal 3 beg 4 call, lure, plea, pray, pull,
suit 5 brace, charm, crave, plead 6 allure,
excite, invoke, orison, prayer, sue for
7 attract, beseech, entreat, glamour,
implore 8 charisma, entreaty, interest,
intrigue, petition 9 fascinate, importune,
magnetism, seduction 10 allurement,
attraction, supplicate 11 application, fascination, imploration 12 drawing power, solicitation, supplication

appealing 5 siren 8 alluring, charming
9 seductive 10 attracting, attractive,
bewitching, enchanting 11 captivating, fascinating

appear 4 look, loom, rise, seem, show
5 arise, issue, sound 6 arrive, emerge
7 emanate 11 materialize

appearance 3 air 4 face, look, mien,
pose, show 5 front, guise 6 aspect,
facade, facies, manner 7 bearing, seeming,
showing 8 demeanor 9 semblance 10 simulacrum 11 countenance *combining form:*
5 phane, phany

appease 4 calm 6 pacify, soothe
7 assuage, content, gratify, mollify, placate,
relieve, satisfy, sweeten 10 conciliate, propitiate

appellation 4 name 5 nomen, style, title
7 moniker 8 cognomen 11 designation
12 denomination

append 3 add 5 annex 6 take on 7 subjoin 8 superadd

appendage 3 arm, fin, leg, tab, tag
4 barb, flap, horn, limb, seta, tail, wing
5 extra 6 cercus 7 adjunct, antenna, elytron, stipule 8 pedipalp, pendicle, tentacle
9 accessory, auxiliary 10 collateral, incidental, supplement 12 appurtenance, nonessential

appendix 5 rider 7 adjunct, codicil
8 addendum 9 accessory 10 supplement
12 appurtenance

apperception 5 grasp 11 recognition
12 apprehension, assimilation 13 comprehension, understanding

appertain 5 apply 6 bear on, belong,
relate 8 bear upon

appetence 5 taste 7 stomach

appetent 4 agog, avid, keen 5 eager
6 ardent 7 anxious, athirst, craving, lusting,
thirsty 8 desirous, yearning 9 impatient
10 breathless

appetite 4 bent, bias, itch, lust, urge
5 taste 6 desire, hunger, liking 7 craving,
leaning, passion, stomach 8 cupidity, fondness, gluttony, penchant, soft spot, voracity, weakness 10 proclivity, propensity
11 inclination *combining form:* 6 orexia
insatiable: 7 bulimia

appetizer 4 whet 6 canapé, savory, tidbit
7 zakuska 8 delicacy 9 antipasto 11 hors
d'oeuvre

appetizing 5 sapid, tasty 6 savory
8 saporous 9 aperitive, palatable, relishing,
toothsome 10 flavorsome 13 mouth-watering

applaud 4 clap, hail, laud, root 5 bravo,
cheer, extol 6 kudize, praise, rise to
7 acclaim, commend 9 recommend
10 compliment

applause 4 hand 6 bravos, cheers
7 acclaim, ovation, rooting 8 cheering, clap-
ping, plaudits 11 acclamation

apple 4 crab, pome 6 pippin, russet
7 Baldwin, costard, Duchess, Stayman,
Wealthy, Winesap 8 Cortland, greening,
Jonathan, McIntosh, pearmain 9 Delicious
10 Rome Beauty 11 Granny Smith, Graven-
stein, Northern Spy, Transparent *combining form:* 4 pomi *dessert:* 5 crisp *genus:*
5 Malus *juice:* 5 cider *relating to:* 5 malic

applejack 5 cider 6 brandy

apple knocker 4 hick, jake 5 yokel
6 rustic 7 bucolic, bumpkin, hayseed, hoosier, redneck 10 provincial

apple-polish 4 fawn 5 cower, toady
6 cringe, grovel, kowtow 7 honey up,
truckle 8 bootlick 9 brownnose

apple-polisher 5 toady 8 bootlick, claw-
back, groveler, lickspit 9 brownnose, sycophant 10 bootlicker, brownnoser, footlicker
11 lickspittle

applesauce 5 fudge, hooey 6 bunkum
7 baloney, rubbish, twaddle 8 malarkey,
nonsense 9 poppycock 12 blatherskite

appliance 3 use 4 play 6 usance 9 operation 10 employment 11 application
kitchen: 4 oven 5 mixer, range, stove
7 blender, toaster 9 can opener 10 dishwasher 12 refrigerator

applicability 3 use 5 avail 7 account, fitness, utility 9 advantage, relevance
10 usefulness

applicable 3 apt, fit 4 just, meet 5 ad rem
6 seemly 7 apropos, correct, fitting, germane 8 apposite, material, pointful, relevant, suitable 9 befitting, pertinent 10 felicitous 11 applicative, applicatory,
appropriate

applicant 6 seeker 7 hopeful 8 aspirant
9 candidate

application 3 use 4 heed, plea, suit
5 study 6 appeal, debate, orison, prayer,

usance **8** entreaty, exercise, exertion, petition **9** appliance, attention, operation **10** employment, exercising **11** imploration, imprecation **12** deliberation, supplication **13** concentration, consideration

applicatory 5 ad rem **7** apropos, germane **8** apposite, material, pointful, relevant **9** pertinent

applied *combining form:* **6** techno

apply 3 dab, use **4** bend, give, turn, urge **5** press **6** accost, appeal, bear on, bestow, devote, direct, employ, handle, relate, resort, take on **7** address, beseech, entreat, implore, pertain, utilize **8** approach, bear upon, exercise, petition, set about **9** appertain, importune, undertake **10** buckle down

appoint 3 arm, rig, tap **4** gear, name **5** equip **6** assign, finger, fit out, outfit **7** dress up, furbish, furnish, turn out **8** accouter, accredit, delegate, nominate **9** authorize, designate, embellish **10** commission

appointment 3 job **4** date, post, spot **5** berth, place, tryst **6** billet, office **8** position **9** situation **10** connection, engagement, rendezvous **11** assignation

apportion 3 lot **4** give **5** allot, allow, divvy, quota, serve, share, split **6** assign, bestow, divide, parcel, ration **7** deal out, dish out, dole out, measure, mete out, prorate **8** allocate, dispense, separate, share out **9** admeasure, partition **10** administer, distribute

apportionment 4 meed, part **5** quota, share **6** ration **7** measure, quantum **9** allotment, allowance

apposite 5 ad rem **6** timely **7** apropos, germane **8** material, pointful, relevant **9** pertinent **10** applicable **11** applicative, applicatory

appositeness 5 order **9** propriety **10** expediency **11** suitability

appraisal 5 stock **8** estimate, judgment **9** valuation **10** assessment, estimation, evaluation

appraise 4 rate **5** assay, audit, judge, set at, value **6** assess, survey **7** adjudge, examine, inspect, valuate **8** estimate, evaluate **10** scrutinize

appreciable 5 clear, plain **7** evident, obvious **8** apparent, concrete, manifest, material, palpable, sensible, tangible **10** detectable, observable **11** discernible, perceptible, substantial

appreciate 4 know, like, love **5** enjoy, grasp, prize, savor, value **6** admire, esteem, fathom, regard, relish **7** apprize, cherish, cognize, respect **8** treasure **9** apprehend, delight in **10** comprehend, understand

appreciation 7 tribute **9** gratitude **11** recognition, testimonial **12** gratefulness

apprehend 3 dig, nab, see **4** bust, fear, know, take, twig **5** catch, grasp, pinch, run in, seize, sense **6** absorb, accept, arrest, detain, digest, divine, fathom, pick up, take in, wise up **7** catch on, cognize, compass, foresee, make out, preknow, previse, realize **8** conceive **9** penetrate, recognize, visualize **10** anticipate, appreciate, understand

apprehensible 5 lucid **8** knowable, luminous **10** fathomable

apprehension 4 care, fear, idea **5** alarm, angst, dread, pinch, worry **6** arrest, notion, pickup, unease **7** anxiety, capture, concern, thought **8** disquiet **9** agitation, detention, misgiving **10** conception, foreboding, perception, solicitude, uneasiness **11** disquietude, premonition

apprehensive 5 alive, awake, aware **6** afraid **7** anxious, fearful, knowing **8** sensible, sentient **9** cognizant, conscious

apprentice 4 colt, tyro **6** novice, rookie **7** learner, trainee **8** beginner, freshman, neophyte, newcomer **9** novitiate **10** tenderfoot

apprenticed 5 bound **8** articled **10** indentured

apprise 4 clue, post, tell, warn **6** advise, fill in, inform, notify, reveal, wise up **8** acquaint, announce **11** communicate

apprize 5 value **6** esteem **7** cherish **8** treasure **10** appreciate

approach 4 near, nigh **5** reach, rival, touch, verge **6** accost, advise, amount, border, trench **7** address, advance, apply to, attempt, bespeak, consult **8** endeavor, overture **11** approximate

approaching 6 coming **7** nearing **8** oncoming, upcoming **11** forthcoming

approbate 5 favor **6** accept **7** approve **11** countenance

approbation 2 OK **4** okay **5** favor **6** esteem **8** approval, blessing, goodwill, sanction **10** admiration **11** benediction

approbatory 9 favorable

appropinquity 9 immediacy, proximity **10** contiguity

appropriate 3 apt, cop, due, fit **4** grab, just, lift, meet, take, true **5** annex, claim, exact, filch, grasp, pinch, right, seize, steal, swipe, usurp **6** assume, pilfer, proper, snatch, snitch, timely, useful, worthy **7** condign, desired, fitting, germane, merited, preempt, purloin **8** accroach, apposite, arrogate, deserved, eligible, entitled, relevant, rightful, suitable **9** befitting, opportune, pertinent, requisite, sequester **10** acceptable, admissible, applicable, commandeer, confiscate, convenient, felicitous, seasonable

appropriately 4 well 5 amply, right
8 properly, suitably 9 fittingly 10 acceptably, adequately, becomingly

appropriateness 3 use 5 order
7 account, aptness, fitness, service, utility
8 meetness 9 advantage, propriety, relevance, rightness 10 expediency, usefulness

appropriation 5 grant 7 stipend, subsidy
9 allotment, allowance 10 subvention

approval 2 OK 4 okay 5 favor
8 applause, blessing, sanction, suffrage
10 acceptance, compliment 11 approbation, benediction, endorsement 12 commendation

approve 2 OK 4 okay 5 clear, favor, go
for 6 accept, back up, praise, ratify, uphold
7 applaud, certify, commend, condone,
confirm, endorse, initial, stand by, support,
sustain 8 accredit, hold with, sanction
9 approbate 10 compliment 11 countenance

approximal 8 abutting, adjacent, touching
9 adjoining, bordering 10 contiguous, juxtaposed 12 conterminous

approximate 4 near, nigh, rude 5 judge,
place, rough 6 reckon 8 approach, estimate, relative 11 comparative

approximately 4 most, nigh 5 about
6 all but, almost, nearly 8 well-nigh 9 nearabout 11 practically

appurtenance 7 adjunct 8 appendix
9 accessory, appendage, equipment, furniture 11 furnishings

appurtenant 8 adjuvant 9 accessory,
ancillary, auxiliary 10 collateral, subsidiary
11 subservient 12 contributory

a priori 8 dogmatic, reasoned 9 deducible,
deductive, derivable

apriorism 5 posit 6 thesis 7 premise
9 postulate 10 assumption 11 postulation,
presumption, supposition

apron 5 stage 8 pinafore

apropos 2 re 4 as to, in re, meet 5 about,
ad rem, anent, as for 6 proper 7 germane
8 apposite, material, pointful, relevant,
touching 9 as regards, pertinent, regarding
10 applicable, as respects, concerning,
respecting 11 applicative, applicatory, in
respect to 13 with respect to

Apsu *daughter:* 6 Lahamu *son:* 5 Lahmu
wife: 6 Tiamat

apt 3 fit 4 just, meet 5 alert, given, prone,
quick, ready 6 bright, liable, likely, prompt,
proper 7 apropos, fitting 8 apposite, disposed, inclined, relevant, suitable 9 befitting, pertinent 10 felicitous 11 appropriate

aptitude 4 bent, gift 5 flair, knack
6 genius, talent 7 ability, fitness 8 capacity,
tendency 10 propensity 11 disposition

aptness 4 bent, gift 5 flair, knack, order
6 genius, talent 7 faculty, fitness 8 meetness 9 propriety, rightness 10 expediency
11 suitability

aquake 5 shaky 7 aquiver, shaking
9 quivering, shivering, trembling, tremorous,
tremulant, tremulous

aqua vitae 4 grog 5 booze, drink, hooch
6 liquor, tipple 7 alcohol, spirits 9 firewater

aqueduct 5 canal 6 course 7 channel,
conduit 11 watercourse

Aquila star 6 Altair

aquiver see aquake

Arab chief 4 emir 5 sheik 6 sheikh, sultan

Arab country 4 Iraq, Oman 5 Egypt,
Libya, Qatar, Sudan, Syria, Yemen 6 Jor-
dan, Kuwait 7 Algeria, Bahrain, Lebanon,
Morocco, Tunisia 11 Saudi Arabia

arable 7 fertile 8 fruitful, tillable 10 cultivable, productive

Arachne *father:* 5 Idmon *form:* 6 spider
mother: 6 Cyrene *rival:* 6 Athena
7 Minerva

arachnid 4 mite, tick 6 acarus, spider
8 scorpion 9 phalangid, tarantula 10 har-
vestman

Aran *brother:* 2 Uz *father:* 6 Dishan

arbiter 5 judge 6 umpire 7 referee 9 moderator

arbitrary 4 rash 7 erratic, wayward
8 absolute, arrogant, despotic, freakish,
heedless, oracular, whimsied 9 autarchic,
impetuous, tyrannous, vagarious, whimsical
10 autocratic, capricious, monocratic, tyrannical 11 dictatorial, magisterial, precipitate
12 unreasonable 13 authoritarian

arbitrate 5 judge 6 umpire 7 adjudge,
mediate, referee 9 intervene 10 adjudicate
12 intermediate

arbitrator 5 judge 6 umpire 7 referee
8 mediator 9 moderator

arbor 5 bower 6 casino, gazebo 7 pergola
9 belvedere 11 summerhouse

arc 3 bow, lob 4 arch, bend 5 curve, round
7 rainbow 9 curvation, curvature

arcadia 4 Eden, Zion 6 heaven, utopia
8 paradise 9 Cockaigne, fairyland, Shangri-
la 10 lubberland, wonderland 12 promised
land

arcane 6 mystic, secret 8 numinous
10 cabalistic, mysterious, unknowable
11 inscrutable 12 impenetrable 13 unaccountable

Arcas *father:* 4 Zeus 7 Jupiter *mother:*
8 Callisto

arch 3 bow, coy 4 bend, hump, pert
5 chief, cocky, curve, first, fresh, roach,
round, saucy, vault 6 bantam, camber,
cheeky, cocket, impish 7 leading, playful,
premier, roguish 8 champion, flippant, fore-

most, malapert **9** curvation, curvature, principal **10** coquettish **11** mischievous *inner curve:* **8** intrados *kind:* **4** flat, ogee **5** ogive, round, Tudor **6** lancet **7** rampart, trefoil **9** horseshoe, primitive, segmental **10** shouldered **11** equilateral *outer curve:* **8** extrados *part:* **8** keystone, springer, voussoir *pointed:* **4** ogee **5** ogive

archaeological site *Africa:* **8** Zimbabwe *Crete:* **7** Knossos *Egypt:* **6** Naqada **9** Al-Bahnasa **11** Oxyrhynchus *England:* **10** Stonehenge *Greece:* **7** Mycenae, Olympia *Iraq:* **2** Ur **4** Isin, Nuzi **5** Issin **7** Babylon, Nineveh *Israel:* **7** Jericho *Italy:* **7** Pompeii *Turkey:* **4** Troy **9** Hissarlik

archaeologist 5 Evans (Arthur) **6** Carter (Howard) **7** Thomsen (Christian), Woolley (Leonard), Worsaae (Jens) **8** Breasted (James), Goodyear (William), Piranesi (Giambattista) **10** Schliemann (Heinrich) **11** Winckelmann (Johann)

archaic 3 old **5** dated, passé **6** bygone **7** antique **8** outdated **9** out-of-date, primitive, unevolved **10** antiquated **11** undeveloped **12** old-fashioned *combining form:* **4** pale **5** palae, paleo **6** palaeo

arched 4 bent **5** bowed, round **6** curved **7** arrondi, rounded **8** arciform **11** curvilinear *combining form:* **3** tox **4** toxi, toxo

archer 4 Tell (William) **5** Cupid **6** bowman **9** Robin Hood **11** Sagittarius, toxophilite

archery 9 toxophily *combining form:* **3** tox **4** toxi, toxo

archetypal 5 ideal, model **7** classic, typical **9** classical, exemplary **12** paradigmatic, prototypical

archetype 5 ideal, model **6** mirror **7** example, pattern **8** exemplar, original, paradigm, standard **9** beau ideal, prototype **10** protoplast

archfiend 5 demon, devil, Satan **8** succubus

Archimedes' cry 6 eureka

archipelago *Asian:* **5** Malay *Canada:* **6** Arctic *Japan:* **4** Goto **9** Gotoretto *Norway:* **11** Spitsbergen *off Scotland:* **7** Orcades, Orkneys **13** Orkney Islands *off South America:* **14** Tierra del Fuego

architect 4 sire **5** maker **6** author, father **7** creator, founder **8** designer, inventor **9** generator, patriarch **10** originator *American:* **3** Pei (leoh Ming) **5** McKim (Charles), Stone (Edward Durell), Weese (Harry), White (Stanford) **6** Breuer (Marcel), Rogers (Isaiah), Soleri (Paole), Upjohn (Richard), Walter (Thomas), Warren (William), Wright (Frank Lloyd) **7** Johnson (Philip), Latrobe (Benjamin), Renwick (James), Sturgis (John Hubbard) **8** Bulfinch (Charles), Saarinen (Eero, Eliel), Sullivan (Louis), Thornton

(William), Yamasaki (Minoru) **10** Richardson (Henry Hobson) *Brazilian:* **8** Niemeyer (Oscar) *English:* **4** Shaw (Richard), Wood (John), Wren (Christopher) **5** Jones (Inigo), Scott (George Gilbert), Wyatt (James) **6** Street (George Edmund), Voysey (Charles) **8** Vanbrugh (John) *Finnish:* **5** Aalto (Alvar) *French:* **6** Perret (Auguste) **11** Le Corbusier *German:* **8** Schinkel (Karl) *German-American:* **7** Gropius (Walter) *Italian:* **6** Romano (Giulio) **7** da Vinci (Leonardo), Orcagna, Peruzzi (Baldassare), Raphael, Vignola (Giacomo da) **8** Palladio (Andrea), Sangallo (Giuliano da), Terragni (Giuseppe) **9** Sansovino (Jacopo) **12** Michelangelo *Japanese:* **5** Tange (Kenzo) *Roman:* **9** Vitruvius

architecture 6 design, makeup **9** formation **11** composition **12** constitution, construction *ornament:* **4** boss, fret **5** gutta **6** finial, pampre, patera, volute **7** cabling, console, crocket, diglyph **8** encarpus, triglyph, vignette **9** arabesque, guilloche, modillion *style:* **5** Doric, Greek, Ionic, Tudor **6** Gothic, Norman, Rococo **7** Baroque **8** Colonial, Georgian **9** Byzantine, Victorian **10** Corinthian, Romanesque **11** Renaissance **13** Mediterranean

archive 6 record **7** library **8** document, monument **9** athenaeum

arch-shaped 8 arciform

arctic 3 icy **4** cold, cool **5** chill, gelid, nippy **6** chilly, frosty, hiemal **7** glacial, numbing **8** freezing, hibernal **11** hyperborean *animal:* **3** auk, fox **4** bear, hare, seal, vole **5** sable, whale **6** ermine, marten **7** caribou, lemming **8** reindeer *base:* **4** Etah (Greenland) *bird:* **3** auk **9** ptarmigan *cetacean:* **7** narwhal *current:* **8** Labrador *dog:* **5** husky **7** Samoyed **8** malamute, malemute *explorer:* **4** Byrd (Richard), Cook (Frederick) **5** Bylot (Robert), Davis (John), Peary (Robert) **6** Baffin (William), Bering (Vitus), Henson (Matthew), Hudson (Henry), Nansen (Fridtjof), Nobile (Umberto) **7** Barents (Willem), Bennet (Floyd), Wilkins (George), Wrangel (Ferdinand) **8** Amundsen (Roald) **9** Ellsworth (Lincoln), Mackenzie (Alexander), MacMillan (Donald) **10** Stefansson (Vilhjalmus) *forest:* **5** taiga *jacket:* **5** parka **6** anorak *people:* **4** Lapp **5** Aleut, Yakut **6** Eskimo, Koryak, Tungus, Zyrian **7** Chukchi, Samoyed **9** Kamchadal *sea:* **4** Kara **6** Laptev **7** Barents, Chukchi **8** Beaufort **9** Greenland *transport:* **7** dogsled *treeless plains:* **6** tundra

ardent 3 hot **4** agog, avid, keen, true **5** eager, fiery, loyal **6** fervid, heated, intent, red-hot, strong, torrid **7** anxious, athirst, blazing, burning, earnest, fervent, flaming, intense, staunch **8** appetent, constant, desirous, faithful, powerful, resolute, sizzling, vehement, white-hot **9** allegiant, impatient, impetuous, impulsive, scorching, steadfast **10** breathless, hot-blooded, passionate **11** impassioned **12** enthusiastic

ardor 4 fire, zeal, zest, zing **5** gusto, piety, verve **6** fealty, fervor, spirit, warmth **7** avidity, loyalty, passion **8** devotion, fidelity **9** calenture, eagerness **10** allegiance, enthusiasm **12** faithfulness

arduous 4 hard **5** rough, sheer, steep, tight **6** abrupt, trying, uphill **7** labored, operose, tricksy **8** sideling, toilsome **9** difficult, laborious, strenuous **11** precipitate, precipitous

area 4 belt, zone **5** field, place, range, realm, scene, space, tract **6** domain, locale, region, sector, sphere **7** expanse **8** district, locality, province, vicinage, vicinity **9** bailiwick, territory **12** neighborhood *combining form:* **3** gea **4** gaea *dark, shaded:* **5** umbra *unit:* **4** acre **7** hectare

arena 5 scene **7** stadium, theater **8** coliseum **10** hippodrome **12** amphi theater

Ares 4 Mars *consort:* **5** Venus **9** Aphrodite *father:* **4** Zeus **7** Jupiter *mother:* **4** Enyo, Hera, Juno *sister:* **4** Eris *son:* **5** Remus **7** Romulus

arête 5 crest, merit **6** virtue **7** quality **10** excellence, excellency, perfection

Arethusa's pursuer 7 Alpheus

argent 6 silver **7** silvern, silvery

Argentina *capital:* **11** Buenos Aires *monetary unit:* **4** peso

Arges 7 Cyclops *brother:* **7** Brontes **8** Steropes *father:* **6** Uranus *mother:* **4** Gaea

argon *symbol:* **2** Ar

Argonauts' leader 5 Jason

argot 4 cant **5** lingo, slang **6** jargon, patois, patter **7** dialect **10** vernacular

arguable 4 moot **7** dubious **8** doubtful **9** debatable, uncertain **10** disputable **11** problematic **12** questionable

argue 4 moot **5** claim, clash **6** assert, attest, bicker, debate, differ, hassle, object **7** agitate, bespeak, canvass, contend, discept, discuss, dispute, dissent, justify, protest, quarrel, quibble, stickle, testify, witness, wrangle **8** announce, conflict, disagree, indicate, maintain, polemize, squabble **9** thrash out **10** polemicize **11** expostulate, remonstrate

argument 3 row **4** fuss **5** theme, topic **6** debate, dustup, hassle, motive, reason, rumpus **7** dispute, polemic, sorites, subject, wrangle **8** rebuttal **10** contention, dissension, squabbling **11** controversy, disputation, embroilment **12** disagreement

argumentation 6 debate **7** dispute, mooting, oratory **8** forensic, rhetoric **9** dialectic **11** controversy, disputation

argumentative 9 litigious, polemical **11** contentious **12** disputatious **13** controversial

Argus *father:* **4** Zeus **7** Jupiter *mother:* **5** Niobe *slayer:* **6** Hermes **7** Mercury

argute 4 high **5** cagey, heady, savvy, sharp **6** piping, shrewd, shrill, treble **8** piercing **9** sagacious **13** perspicacious

aria 3 lay **4** hymn, lied, song **5** ditty **7** descant

Ariadne *father:* **5** Minos *husband:* **7** Theseus *mother:* **8** Pasiphae

arid 3 dry **4** drab, dull, sere **5** dusty, tepid **6** barren, boring, dreary **7** bone-dry, insipid, sterile, tedious, thirsty **8** bromidic, droughty, wearful **9** dryasdust, infertile, unwatered, waterless, wearisome **10** unfruitful **12** moistureless **13** uninteresting

Ariel's master 8 Prospero

Aries 3 ram

aright 4 well **5** fitly **6** justly, nicely **8** decently, properly **9** correctly, fittingly **10** decorously

arise 4 lift, soar **5** begin, get up, issue, mount, start **6** ascend, aspire, spring, uprear **7** emanate, proceed **8** commence **9** originate

Aristaeus *father:* **6** Apollo *mother:* **6** Cyrene *son:* **7** Actaeon *wife:* **7** Autonoe

aristarch 5 momus **6** carper, critic, Zoilus **7** caviler, knocker **10** criticizer **11** faultfinder

Aristocles 5 Plato

aristocracy 5 elite **6** bon ton, gentry, jet set **7** who's who **8** nobility, noblesse, smart set **9** beau monde, blue blood, gentility, haut monde **10** patricians, patriciate, upper class, upper crust **13** carriage trade

aristocrat 9 blue blood, gentleman, patrician *ancient Greek:* **8** eupatrid *Russian:* **5** boyar **6** boyard

Aristophanes play 6 Plutus **8** The Birds, The Frogs **9** The Clouds

arithmetic 4 math **8** figuring **9** ciphering, reckoning **11** calculation, computation, mathematics

Arizona *capital:* **7** Phoenix *college:* **11** Grand Canyon *motto:* **11** God Enriches *nickname:* **16** Grand Canyon State *state bird:* **10** cactus wren *state flower:* **13** saguaro cactus

Arkansas *capital:* **10** Little Rock *motto:* **13** The People Rule *state bird:* **11** mockingbird *state flower:* **12** apple blossom

ark landfall 6 Ararat

arm 3 bay, ell, gun, rig **4** cove, gear, gulf, wing **5** annex, bayou, equip, firth, force, inlet, power **6** fit out, harbor, muscle, outfit, slough, weapon **7** appoint, furnish, turn out **8** accouter, strength **9** extension *bone:* **4** ulna **6** radius **7** humerus *combining form:* **6** brachi **7** brachio *muscle:* **6** biceps **7** triceps

armada 4 navy **5** fleet

armadillo *genus:* **7** Dasypus *giant:* **4** tatu **5** tatou *nine-banded:* **4** peba, peva *relative:* **5** sloth **8** anteater *seven-banded:* **6** mulita *six-banded:* **5** poyou **6** peludo *small:* **5** pichi **10** pichiciago **11** quirquincho *three-banded:* **4** apar **5** apara *twelve-banded:* **7** tatouay

armament 4 ward **5** aegis, armor, guard **6** shield **7** defense **8** security **9** safeguard **10** protection

armamentarium 4 fund **5** stock, store **6** supply **9** inventory

armchair 8 fauteuil

armed *combining form:* **5** hoplo

armed attendant 9 bodyguard

armed forces 4 army, navy **6** troops **8** air force, military **10** servicemen

armistice 5 truce **9** cease-fire

armor 4 mail, ward **5** aegis, cover, guard **6** shield **7** buckler, defense, shelter **8** armament, security **9** safeguard **10** protection *arm:* **8** brassart *body:* **7** cuirass *armpit:* **8** pallette *buttocks:* **5** culet *coat:* **7** hauberk **10** brigandine *combining form:* **5** hoplo *elbow:* **6** couter **9** cubitiere *face:* **5** visor **6** beaver *flexible:* **4** mail *foot:* **7** sabaton, soleret **8** sabbaton, solleret *forearm:* **8** vambrace *hand:* **8** gauntlet *head:* **6** helmet *horse:* **4** bard **5** barde **6** crinet **7** peytral, peytrel, poitrel **8** chamfron, chanfron, criniere *knee:* **11** genouillere *leg:* **4** jamb **5** jambe **6** greave **7** jambeau *mail:* **4** coif **7** hauberk **8** chausses *neck:* **6** camail *shoulder:* **7** ailette **8** pauldron, pouldron **9** epauliere *skirt:* **6** tonlet *suit:* **7** panoply *thigh:* **4** tace **5** cuish, tasse **6** tasset, tuille **8** flancard **9** flanchard *throat:* **6** gorget

armory 4 dump **5** depot **7** arsenal **8** magazine

armpit 6 axilla **8** underarm *Scottish:* **5** oxter

arms 7 ensigns, warfare **8** weaponry

army 4 host, rout **5** crowd, flock, horde **6** legion, scores **7** militia **9** multitude *combat arm:* **5** armor **8** infantry **9** artillery *commission:* **6** brevet *Fort:* **3** Dix, Lee, Ord **4** Hood, Knox, Polk, Sill **5** Bliss, Bragg, Lewis, Meade, Riley **6** Carson, Eustis, Gordon, Monroe, Rucker **7** Belvoir, Benning, Jackson, Shafter **8** Campbell, Holabird, Huachuca, Monmouth **9** McClellan, McPherson **10** Sam Houston **11** Leavenworth *law enforcer:* **2** MP *mascot:* **4** mule *meal:* **4** chow, mess *mine*

layer: **6** sapper *NCO:* **8** corporal, sergeant *officer:* **5** major **7** captain, colonel, general, warrant **10** lieutenant *post:* **4** base, camp, fort *postal abbreviation:* **3** APO *relating to:* **7** martial **8** military *school:* **3** OCS, OTS **7** academy **9** West Point *store:* **2** PX **10** commissary **12** post exchange *unit:* **5** corps, squad, troop **7** brigade, cavalry, company, platoon **8** division, regiment *vehicle:* **4** jeep, tank **6** Humvee **9** half-track

Arnold's coconspirator 5 André

aroma 4 balm, odor **5** scent, smell, spice **7** bouquet, incense, perfume **9** fragrance, redolence

aromatic 5 balmy, spicy, sweet **6** savory **7** perfumy **8** fragrant, perfumed, redolent **9** ambrosial

around 4 back, near, nigh, over **5** about, again, circa **6** anyhow, extant, nearby, random **7** anywise, through **8** at random, existent, existing, randomly **9** haphazard **10** throughout **11** any which way, haphazardly **13** helter-skelter *prefix:* **4** ambi, amph, peri **5** amphi **6** circum

around-the-clock 8 constant **9** continual, incessant, perpetual **10** continuous **11** unremitting **13** uninterrupted

arouse 4 fire, stir, wake, whet **5** alert, pique, rally, waken **6** awaken, bestir, excite, incite, kindle, work up **7** inflame **9** challenge

arraign 3 tax, try **6** accuse, charge, indict **7** impeach **9** criminate, inculpate **11** incriminate

arrange 4 plan, sort **5** array, chart, order, unify **6** assort, codify, design, devise, lay out, map out, scheme, set out **7** dispose, marshal **8** organize, sequence, tabulate **9** blueprint, harmonize, integrate, methodize **10** categorize, symphonize, synthesize **11** choreograph, orchestrate, systematize

arrangement 5 order, setup **6** layout, lineup, series **8** ordering, sequence **9** structure **11** disposition **12** distribution *combining form:* **4** taxy **5** taxis **6** tactic *of five objects:* **8** quincunx *suffix:* **4** osis

arrant 4 rank **5** gross, total, utter **6** brassy, brazen **7** blatant, flat-out **8** absolute, complete, impudent, infernal, overbold **9** barefaced, downright, out-and-out, shameless, unabashed **10** unblushing

arras 7 drapery **8** tapestry

array 3 lot **4** clad, garb, pomp, show **5** batch, bunch, clump, dress, group, order **6** attire, bundle, clothe, parade **7** apparel, arrange, cluster, display, dispose, garment, marshal, panoply, raiment **8** enclothe, organize, spectrum **11** systematize

arrears 3 due **4** debt **9** liability **12** indebtedness

arrect 6 raised 7 heedful, stand-up, upright 9 advertent, attentive, intentive, observant, regardful 10 straight-up, upstanding

arrest 3 nab 4 bust, halt, jail, stay, stem, stop 5 catch, check, pinch, run in, stall 6 collar, detain, lock up, pickup, pull in, retard, stop up 7 capture, contain, seizure 8 imprison, obstruct, restrain 9 apprehend, detention, interrupt 11 incarcerate 12 apprehension

arresting 6 marked, signal 7 salient 9 affective, appealing, prominent 10 attractive, enchanting, impressive, noticeable, remarkable 11 conspicuous, outstanding

arride 6 divert, please 7 beguile, delight, gladden, gratify 8 pleasure 9 delectate, entertain

arrival 6 advent, coming 7 success 8 entrance, incoming 9 emergence 10 appearance

arrive 4 come, show 5 get in, reach 6 show up, thrive, turn up 7 prosper, succeed 8 flourish

arriviste 7 parvenu, upstart 8 roturier 12 nouveau riche

arrogance 5 pride 6 hubris, hybris, morgue 7 disdain, hauteur 9 loftiness, superbity 11 haughtiness

arrogant 5 cocky, proud, puffy, wiggy 6 lordly, snooty, snotty, stuffy 7 bloated, haughty, pompous 8 cavalier, fastuous, insolent, superior 10 disdainful, peremptory, pontifical 11 domineering, highfalutin, magisterial, overbearing 12 supercilious 13 high-and-mighty, self-important *Scottish:* 7 paughty

arrogate 4 grab, take 5 annex, seize, usurp 6 assume 7 preempt 8 accroach, take over 9 sequester 10 commandeer, confiscate 11 appropriate, expropriate

arrondi 4 bent 5 arced, bowed, round 6 arched, curved 7 rounded 8 arciform 11 curvilinear

arrow *combining form:* 3 tox 4 toxi, toxo 7 hastato *poison:* 4 inée, upas 5 urare, urari 6 antiar, curara, curare, curari, oorali 7 ouabain, woorali, woorari 8 antiarin

arrow-like 6 beloid 7 hastate 8 sagittal 9 sagittate

arrowroot 3 pia 5 araru, tuber 6 ararao 7 coontie, maranta

arroyo 3 gap 4 draw 5 brook, chasm, cleft, clove, creek, gorge, gulch, gully 6 clough, coulee, ravine, stream 7 channel

arsenal 4 dump 5 depot, store 6 armory 8 magazine 10 depository, repository, storehouse

arsenic *symbol:* 2 As

arsonist 5 firer, torch 7 firebug 10 incendiary

art 5 craft, skill, trade 6 métier 7 cunning, finesse, know-how, slyness 8 artifice, foxiness, vocation, wiliness 9 cageyness, canniness, dexterity, expertise 10 adroitness, craftiness, handicraft, profession *combining form:* 4 typy 6 techno *faddish:* 6 kitsch *style:* 2 op 3 pop 6 rococo 7 baroque, Bauhaus, Islamic, optical, surreal 8 abstract, cubistic, romantic 9 arabesque, Byzantine, Christian, classical, dadaistic, realistic 11 Renaissance 12 naturalistic, surrealistic *suffix:* 3 ery 4 ship

Artegal's wife 11 Britomartis

Artemis 5 Diana *birthplace:* 5 Delos *brother:* 6 Apollo *father:* 4 Zeus 7 Jupiter *mother:* 4 Leto 6 Latona *priestess:* 9 Iphigenia

artery 3 way 4 path, road 5 aorta, track 6 avenue, street, vessel 7 carotid, highway 8 coronary 9 boulevard 12 thoroughfare

artful 3 sly 4 foxy, oily, wily 5 suave 6 adroit, astute, crafty, smooth, tricky 7 cunning 8 guileful 9 dexterous, insidious 10 diplomatic

arthropod 3 bee, fly 4 crab, moth 6 beetle, insect, shrimp 7 lobster 8 arachnid, barnacle, chilopod, diplopod, myriapod, myriopod 9 butterfly, centipede, cockroach, millipede 10 crustacean *body segment:* 6 somite, telson 8 metamere *class:* 7 Insecta 8 Symphyla 9 Arachnida, Chilopoda, Crustacea, Diplopoda, Pauropoda *limb segment:* 6 podite 8 podomere

Arthur see **King Arthur**

article 2 an 3 the 4 item 5 essay, paper, point, theme, thing 6 object 7 element 10 particular 11 composition, stipulation

articled 5 bound 10 indentured

articulate 3 say 4 join, oral 5 order, utter, vocal 6 fluent, prolix, relate, sonant, spoken, voiced 7 connect, phonate 8 eloquent 9 enunciate, garrulous, harmonize, integrate, pronounce, talkative 10 coordinate 11 concatenate 12 smooth-spoken

artifice 4 play, ploy, ruse, wile 5 craft, feint, guile, trick 6 deceit, device, gambit 7 cunning, knavery, slyness 8 foxiness, trickery, wiliness 9 adeptness, cageyness, canniness, chicanery, ingenuity, rascality, stratagem 10 adroitness, cleverness, craftiness 11 skulduggery

artificial 4 fake, faux, mock, sham 5 dummy, false, put-on 6 ersatz, forced, unreal 7 assumed, feigned, labored, manmade, pretend 8 affected, spurious 9 contrived, imitation, insincere, simulated, synthetic, unnatural 10 fabricated, factitious, fictitious, substitute

artillery 6 rocket 8 cannonry, howitzer, ordnance, weaponry

artillery plant 11 burning bush

artisan 7 builder, workman 9 carpenter, craftsman

artist 3 ace 4 whiz 5 adept 6 expert, master, wizard, wonder 8 virtuoso 10 first-rater, past master, topnotcher *garb:* 5 smock *knife:* 7 spatula *medium:* 3 oil 5 chalk, paint 6 pastel 7 tempera 8 charcoal 10 watercolor *pigment board:* 7 palette *stand:* 5 easel *workshop:* 6 studio 7 atelier (see also **painter**)

artless 4 free 5 naive 6 simple 7 natural 8 trusting, unartful 9 childlike, ingenuous, unstudied 10 aboveboard, forthright, unaffected, unschooled 12 unartificial, unsuspicious

arty 8 imposing 9 overblown 11 pretentious 12 high-sounding

as 3 for 5 being, since, while 7 because 11 considering

Asa *father:* 6 Abijam 7 Elkanah *grandfather:* 8 Rehoboam *grandmother:* 6 Maacah

____ **as a pin** 4 neat

as a rule 7 usually 8 commonly 9 generally 10 frequently, ordinarily

Ascanius 5 Iulus *father:* 6 Aeneas

ascend 4 lift, rise, soar 5 arise, climb, crest, mount, scale 6 aspire, uprear 7 upclimb 8 escalade, escalate, surmount

ascendancy 8 dominion 9 dominance, masterdom, supremacy 10 domination, prepotency 11 preeminence, sovereignty 13 preponderance

ascendant 6 master 7 regnant 8 ancestor, dominant, forebear 9 paramount, precursor, prevalent, sovereign 10 forefather, forerunner, progenitor 11 overbearing, predecessor, predominant, predominate 12 preponderant, primogenitor

ascension 4 rise 6 rising

ascent 4 rise 5 climb 6 rising 7 raising 9 elevation, uplifting

ascertain 5 learn 7 catch on, find out, unearth 8 discover 9 determine

ascetic 3 nun 4 monk 5 stern, stoic 6 hermit, severe 7 austere, eremite, recluse 8 anchoret 9 abstinent, anchorite, mortified 10 abstemious, astringent, forbearing, restrained 11 disciplined, self-abasing, self-denying *ancient Hebrew:* 6 Essene *Buddhist:* 5 bonze 7 bhikshu *early Christian:* 7 stylite *Hindu:* 4 Yogi 5 fakir, Yogin

Asclepius see **Aesculapius**

ascribe 3 lay 4 cite 5 refer 6 assign, charge, credit, impute 8 accredit 9 attribute

Asenath *husband:* 6 Joseph *son:* 7 Ephraim 8 Manasseh

aseptic 8 retiring 9 shrinking, unaffable, withdrawn 10 restrained 11 unexpansive

asexual 6 agamic 7 agamous *combining form:* 4 agam 5 agamo

as for 2 re 4 in re 7 apropos 8 touching 9 regarding 10 concerning, respecting

as good as 4 nigh 5 about 6 all but, almost, nearly 8 well-nigh 9 just about, nearabout 11 essentially, practically 13 approximately

ash 4 soot 7 cinders, residue 8 clinkers

ashake 6 aquake 7 aquiver, ashiver, quaking 9 quivering, shivering, trembling, tremulous

ashamed 6 abased, abject 7 abashed, hangdog, humbled 8 contrite, penitent 9 chagrined, mortified, repentant 10 humiliated 11 discomfited, embarrassed

ashen 4 gray, pale 5 faded, livid, lurid, waxen 6 doughy, pallid 7 ghostly, macabre 8 blanched, bleached 9 cinereous, colorless 10 corpselike

Asher *daughter:* 5 Serah *father:* 5 Jacob *mother:* 6 Zilpah *son:* 4 Isui 6 Beriah, Ishuah, Jimnah

Ashhur *father:* 6 Hezron *mother:* 5 Abiah

ashiver see **ashake**

Asia *country:* 4 Iran, Iraq, Laos, Oman 5 Burma, China, India, Japan, Nepal, Qatar, Syria, Yemen 6 Bhutan, Cyprus, Israel, Jordan, Kuwait, Russia, Taiwan 7 Armenia, Bahrain, Georgia, Lebanon, Myanmar, Vietnam 8 Cambodia, Malaysia, Maldives, Mongolia, Pakistan, Sri Lanka, Thailand 9 Indonesia, Kampuchea, Singapore 10 Azerbaijan, Bangladesh, Kazakhstan, Kyrgyzstan, North Korea, South Korea, Tajikistan, Uzbekistan 11 Afghanistan, Philippines, Saudi Arabia 12 Turkmenistan *ethnic group:* 3 Han, Jew, Lao, Tai 4 Arab, Kurd, Moor, Shan, Thai, Turk 5 Karen, Khmer, Malay, Tajik, Tamil, Uzbek 6 Burman, Indian, Korean, Lepcha, Manchu, Mongol, Sindhi 7 Baluchi, Bengali, Chinese, Iranian, Persian, Punjabi, Russian, Tibetan 8 Armenian, Assyrian, Japanese, Javanese, Nepalese 9 Dravidian, Indo-Aryan, Pakistani, Sinhalese 10 Circassian, Montagnard, Singhalese, Vietnamese 13 Khalkha Mongol *language:* 3 Lao 4 Urdu 5 Hindi, Malay, Tamil, Uzbek 6 Arabic, Hebrew, Korean, Nepali 7 Bengali, Burmese, Khalkha, Kurdish, Persian, Tibetan, Turkish, Yiddish 8 Armenian, Japanese, Javanese, Mandarin 9 Cambodian 10 Vietnamese 15 Bahasa Indonesia

aside 4 awry 5 apart, askew 6 askant, aslant, aslope 7 askance, slantly 8 excursus, sideways 9 excursion, obliquely, slantways, slantwise 10 digression, discursion, divagation, slantingly 11 parenthesis

aside from 3 bar 4 save 6 bating, except 7 barring, besides 9 excluding, outside of 11 exclusive of

as if *combining form:* 5 quasi

asinine 5 silly 6 absurd, simple 7 fatuous, foolish, puerile, witless 8 mindless 9 brainless 10 irrational, weak-headed

ask 3 beg, bid 4 quiz, seek 5 crave, exact, query 6 appeal, demand, desire, invite 7 beseech, call for, canvass, consult, enquire, entreat, examine, implore, inquire, request, require, solicit 8 question 9 catechize, importune 11 interrogate *Scottish:* 5 speer, speir

askance 4 awry 5 askew 8 cockeyed 9 cock-a-hoop, crookedly, cynically 10 critically, doubtfully, doubtingly 11 skeptically 12 suspiciously 13 distrustfully, mistrustfully

asker 6 beggar, prayer, suitor 9 suppliant 10 petitioner, supplicant 11 supplicator

askew 4 awry 6 askant 7 askance 8 cockeyed 9 cock-a-hoop, crookedly

aslant 5 aside 6 aslope 8 sideways, sidewise 9 obliquely 11 slaunchways *combining form:* 5 plagi 6 plagio

asleep 4 dead, idle, numb 5 inert 6 dozing, numbed 7 defunct, dormant, napping 8 benumbed, deadened, inactive 9 exanimate, senseless, unfeeling 10 insensible, unanimated 11 unconscious 12 anesthetized

as long as 3 for 5 cause, since 6 seeing 7 because, whereas 11 considering

as much as 6 all but, almost 8 well-nigh 11 essentially, practically

asomatous 8 bodiless 10 discarnate, immaterial, unphysical 11 disembodied, incorporeal 13 insubstantial

aspect 4 look, mien, side 5 angle, facet, phase 7 bearing, seeming 10 appearance

asperity 5 rigor 8 acerbity, acrimony, grimness, hardness, hardship, mordancy, tartness 9 harshness, roughness 10 bitterness, difficulty, inclemency, inequality, unevenness 11 vicissitude 12 irregularity, irritability

asperous 5 harsh, rough 6 craggy, jagged, rugged, uneven 7 scraggy, unlevel 8 scabrous, unsmooth

asperse 4 slur 5 libel 6 defame, insult, malign 7 baptize, immerse, slander, traduce 8 christen, sprinkle 9 denigrate 10 calumniate, scandalize

aspersion 4 muck, slam, slur 5 abuse 7 calumny, obloquy, slander 9 invective, stricture 10 detraction, reflection 12 vituperation 13 animadversion

asphalt 7 bitumen 8 blacktop

asphyxiate 5 choke 6 stifle 7 quackle, smother 9 suffocate

aspirant 6 seeker 7 hopeful 9 applicant, candidate

aspiration 3 aim 4 goal 6 desire 8 ambition 9 objective 10 pretension 13 ambitiousness

aspire 3 aim, try 4 long, pant, rise, soar 5 arise, mount 6 ascend, hunger, thirst, uprear

aspiring 7 emulous, wanting, wishful 8 vaulting, yearning 9 ambitious

as regards 2 re 4 in re 7 apropos 8 touching 10 concerning, respecting

ass 4 donk, fool, jerk, moke 5 burro, idiot 6 donkey 8 imbecile 10 nincompoop *female:* 5 jenny *male:* 4 jack *wild Asian:* 5 kiang 6 onager 8 chigetai

assail 4 beat 5 beset, pound, storm 6 attack, buffet, fall on, oppugn, pummel, strike 7 aggress, assault 8 fall upon

assailment 5 onset 6 attack 7 assault, offense 9 offensive, onslaught 10 aggression

Assam silkworm 4 eria

assassin 3 gun 5 bravo 6 gunman, hit man 7 torpedo 8 murderer 9 cutthroat 10 gunslinger, hatchet man, triggerman *of Caesar:* 6 Brutus 7 Cassius *of Garfield:* 7 Guiteau (Charles Julius) *of J.F. Kennedy:* 6 Oswald (Lee Harvey) *of Lincoln:* 5 Booth (John Wilkes) *of Marat:* 6 Corday (Charlotte) *of R.F. Kennedy:* 6 Sirhan (Sirhan)

assassinate 4 cool, do in, kill 6 finish, murder, rub out 7 bump off, execute, put away 8 knock off 9 liquidate

assault 3 mug, war 4 raid 5 beset, fight, onset, set-to, storm 6 assail, attack, fall on, onfall, strike 7 aggress, mugging, offense 8 fall upon, invasion 9 offensive, onslaught 10 aggression, assailment

assay 3 try 4 rate, seek, test 5 offer, value 6 assess, strive, survey 7 attempt, valuate, venture 8 appraise, endeavor, estimate, evaluate, struggle 9 undertake

assemblage 4 ruck 5 crowd, group 6 muster 7 company, turnout 9 gathering 10 collection 11 aggregation 12 congregation

assemble 4 call, form, make, mass, mold 5 amass, build, clump, group, shape 6 gather, muster, summon 7 cluster, collect, convene, convoke, fashion, marshal, produce, round up 8 congress, contrive 9 aggregate, forgather 10 accumulate, congregate 11 manufacture, put together

assembly 4 band, bevy, crew, ruck 5 bunch, covey, crowd, group, party, rally 6 muster, troupe 7 cluster, company, meeting 8 conclave 9 congeries, gathering 10 collection 11 association 12 congregation *American Indian:* 6 powwow *ancient*

Greek: 8 ecclesia *ancient Roman:* 7 comitia *anglo-Saxon:* 4 moot 5 gemot
6 gemote 8 folkmoot, folkmote *ecclesiastical:* 5 synod 10 consistory *Hawaiian:*
3 hui *Irish:* 4 feis *legislative:* 4 diet 6 senate 8 congress 10 parliament *medieval
English:* 7 husting *place:* 4 hall, room
5 agora 10 auditorium *Russian:* 4 duma
witches': 6 sabbat 7 sabbath

assent 3 yes 5 agree 6 accede 7 consent
9 acquiesce, subscribe

assert 4 aver, avow 5 argue, claim, state,
utter, voice 6 adduce, affirm, allege,
avouch, defend, depose, submit
7 advance, contend, declare, express, justify, profess, protest, publish, warrant
8 announce, constate, maintain, proclaim
9 broadcast, predicate, vindicate 10 promulgate 11 disseminate

assertive 4 sure 5 pushy 7 assured, certain, pushing 8 cocksure, emphatic, forceful, positive, sanguine 9 confident, insistent
10 aggressive, resounding 11 affirmative,
self-assured 13 self-confident

assertory 5 pushy 7 pushing 8 militant
10 aggressive

assess 4 deem, levy, rate, scot 5 assay,
exact, judge, put on, set at, value, weigh
6 impose, reckon, survey 7 account, valuate 8 appraise, consider, estimate, evaluate

assessment 3 tax 4 duty, levy 5 stock
6 impost, tariff 8 estimate, judgment
9 appraisal, valuation 10 estimation, evaluation 12 appraisement

asset 6 credit 8 resource 9 advantage
11 distinction *opposite:* 9 liability

assets 5 means, money 6 wealth 7 capital
8 bankroll, property 9 resources, valuables

assiduous 4 busy 7 moiling, operose,
zealous 8 diligent, sedulous, tireless
9 laborious 11 hard-working, industrious
13 indefatigable

assiduously 4 hard 9 earnestly, intensely
10 thoroughly 11 intensively 12 exhaustively 13 painstakingly, unremittingly

assign 3 fix, set 4 cede, deed, give
5 allot, allow, refer 6 charge, convey,
credit, define, impute, remise, settle
7 appoint, ascribe, lay down, mete out, station 8 accredit, allocate, make over, relegate, sign over, transfer 9 admeasure,
apportion, attribute, establish, prescribe
10 pigeonhole

assignation 4 date 5 tryst 9 allotment
10 engagement, rendezvous 11 appointment, get-together

assignee 5 agent, proxy 6 deputy, factor
8 attorney

assignment 3 job 4 duty, task 5 chare,
chore, stint 6 devoir 10 obligation

assimilate 5 adopt, liken, match
6 absorb, equate, imbibe, insorb 7 compare, inhaust, paragon 8 parallel 11 incorporate

assimilation 9 awareness 11 mindfulness, recognition 12 apperception 13 consciousness

assist 3 aid 4 abet, help, lift 5 do for,
stead 6 relief, succor 7 comfort, help out,
secours, support 8 benefact 9 cooperate

assistance 3 aid 4 help, lift 6 relief, succor 7 backing, comfort, secours, subsidy,
support 9 upholding 10 subvention, supporting

assistant 3 aid 4 aide, help 5 aider
6 flunky, helper, lackey, minion, second,
stooge 7 acolyte, ancilla, orderly, striker
8 adjutant, henchman 9 attendant, auxiliary, coadjutor 10 aide-de-camp, coadjutant, lieutenant 12 right-hand man

assistive 6 aidant, aiding 7 helpful 11 serviceable

assize 3 law 4 rule 5 canon, edict
6 decree 7 precept, statute 8 standard
9 ordinance, prescript 10 regulation

associate 3 pal 4 ally, chum, join, link,
mate, yoke 5 buddy, crony, match, merge,
unite 6 cohort, comate, couple, fellow,
friend, hobnob, relate 7 bracket, combine,
compeer, comrade, conjoin, connect, consort, partner 8 confrere, familiar, federate,
intimate 9 affiliate, bedfellow, colleague,
companion, copartner 10 accomplice, amalgamate, compatriot, complement, consociate 11 concomitant, confederate, correlative, counterpart, running mate
12 acquaintance 13 accompaniment,
brother-in-arms, comrade-in-arms

associated *combining form:* 3 sym, syn

associated with *suffix:* 2 ic 4 ical

association 4 axis, bloc, club, hint
5 guild, order, tie-up, union 6 hookup,
league 7 cahoots, circuit, concert, society
8 alliance, congress, overtone, relation,
sodality, teamwork 9 coalition, undertone
10 conference, connection, federation, fellowship, fraternity, suggestion 11 affiliation,
brotherhood, combination, conjunction,
connotation, cooperation, implication, partnership 12 conjointment, organization, relationship, togetherness 13 collaboration

assort 5 class, group, order 7 arrange
8 classify, stratify 9 methodize 10 categorize, pigeonhole 11 systematize

assorted 5 mixed 6 fitted, motley, suited,
varied 7 adapted, matched 8 chowchow
11 conformable, promiscuous 12 conglomerate, multifarious 13 heterogeneous, miscellaneous

assortment 4 olio 6 jumble, medley
7 mélange, variety 8 mishmash, pastiche

9 potpourri **10** hodgepodge, miscellany **11** gallimaufry

assuage **4** calm, ease **5** allay **6** pacify, soothe **7** appease, lighten, mollify, placate, relieve **8** mitigate **9** alleviate **10** conciliate, propitiate

as such **5** per se **13** intrinsically

assumably **6** likely **8** probably **9** doubtless

assume **3** act, don **4** fake, sham, take **5** bluff, feign, get on, posit, put on, seize, usurp **6** affect, draw on, expect, reckon, slip on, strike, take on **7** believe, imagine, preempt, premise, presume, pretend, suppose, suspect **8** accroach, arrogate, shoulder, simulate **9** postulate **10** commandeer, presuppose, understand **11** appropriate, counterfeit

assumed **5** put on **7** feigned **8** affected, delusory, putative, spurious **9** deceptive **10** artificial, factitious

assumption **5** posit **6** thesis **7** premise, surmise **9** apriorism, postulate **10** conjecture **11** supposition

assurance **5** nerve, troth **6** aplomb, parole, pledge, safety, surety **8** audacity, safeness, security, sureness, temerity **9** brashness, certainty, certitude, cockiness, composure, guarantee, hardiness, sangfroid, self-trust **10** brazenness, confidence, conviction, equanimity **11** presumption

assure **5** cinch **6** ensure, insure, secure **7** promise, satisfy **8** convince, persuade

assured **4** cool **6** secure **7** certain, decided **8** clear-cut, composed, definite, sanguine **9** collected, confident, unruffled **10** pronounced, undoubtful **11** unflappable **13** imperturbable, self-confident

assuredness **6** surety **9** certainty, certitude **10** confidence, conviction

Assyria *capital:* **5** Calah **7** Nineveh *city:* **4** Hara, Opis **5** Ashur, Assur, Kalhu **6** Asshur *god:* **3** Sin **4** Asur, Nabu **5** Ashur, Assur, Nusku **6** Asshur, Tammuz **7** Ninurta *goddess:* **6** Ishtar *king:* **3** Pul **6** Sargon **11** Sennacherib, Shalmaneser **12** Ashurbanipal, Assurbanipal *language:* **7** Aramaic *measure:* **4** cane, foot **5** gasab, makuk **6** artaba, gariba **7** mansion *queen:* **9** Semiramis *river:* **6** Tigris *writing:* **9** cuneiform

astatine *symbol:* **2** At

astern **3** aft **4** rear **5** abaft

Asterope *father:* **5** Atlas *mother:* **7** Pleione *sisters:* **8** Pleiades

as to **2** re **4** in re **7** apropos **8** touching **9** regarding **10** concerning, respecting

astonish **5** alarm, amaze **7** astound **8** affright, dumfound, surprise **9** dumbfound **11** flabbergast

astonishing **7** amazing **8** wondrous **9** marvelous, wonderful **10** astounding, miraculous, prodigious, stupendous, surprising **11** spectacular **12** breathtaking

astound **5** amaze **8** astonish, dumfound, surprise **9** dumbfound **11** flabbergast

astounding see **astonishing**

Astraea *father:* **4** Zeus **7** Jupiter *mother:* **6** Themis

astral **6** dreamy, starry **7** exalted, highest, stellar **8** sidereal **9** daydreamy, stellular, top-drawer, unworldly, visionary **10** top-ranking **11** daydreaming **12** otherworldly

astray **4** awry **5** amiss, badly, wrong **6** afield

astricted **5** bound **7** costive **10** obstipated **11** constipated

astringent **4** keen **5** acrid, harsh, sharp, stern, tonic **6** biting, bitter, severe, strict **7** ascetic, austere, caustic, cutting, styptic **8** incisive, roborant **11** contracting **12** constrictive

astrologer **11** Nostradamus

astrological aspect **5** trine **7** sextile **8** quartile **10** opposition **11** conjunction

astronaut **4** Ride (Sally) **5** Glenn (John), Young (John) **6** Aldrin (Edwin), Cooper (Gordon), Lovell (James), Worden (Alfred) **7** Bluford (Guion), Collins (Michael), Gagarin (Yuri), Grissom (Gus), Jemison (Mae), Schirra (Walter), Shepard (Alan), Yegorov (Boris) **8** Stafford (Thomas) **9** Armstrong (Neil), Carpenter (Scott), McAuliffe (Christa) **10** Tereshkova (Valentina)

astronomer *American:* **3** See (Thomas Jefferson) **6** Lowell (Percival) **7** Langley (Samuel), Newcomb (Simon) **8** Tombaugh (Clyde) **9** Pickering (Edward) **11** Schlesinger (Frank) *Austrian:* **13** Schwarzschild (Karl) *Dutch:* **6** Sitter (Willem de) **7** Huygens (Christiaan) *English:* **4** Ryle (Martin), Wren (Christopher) **6** Halley (Edmond), Lovell (Bernard) **7** Lockyer (Joseph), Parsons (William) **8** Herschel (Caroline, John, William) *French:* **6** Picard (Jean) **7** Laplace (Pierre-Simon de), Messier (Charles) *German:* **4** Wolf (Maximilian) **5** Vogel (Hermann) **6** Kepler (Johannes), Muller (Johann), Struve (Otto) *Greek:* **12** Eratosthenes *Italian:* **7** Galilei (Galileo) **12** Schiaparelli (Giovanni) *Persian:* **11** Omar Khayyam *Polish:* **10** Copernicus (Nicolaus) *Swedish:* **7** Celsius (Anders) *Swiss:* **6** Zwicky (Fritz)

astute **3** sly **4** deep, foxy, keen, wily **5** cagey, heady, savvy, sharp **6** argute, artful, crafty, shrewd, tricky **7** cunning, knowing **8** guileful **9** astucious, insidious, sagacious **13** perspicacious

astuteness **3** wit **6** acumen **8** keenness **10** shrewdness **11** discernment, penetration, percipience **12** perspicacity

Astyanax *father:* 6 Hector *mother:* 10 Andromache

asunder 5 apart

as usual 8 wontedly 10 habitually 11 customarily 12 consistently

asweat 5 puggy 8 perspiry 10 perspiring

as well 3 too, yet 4 also, even, just, more 7 besides, exactly 8 likewise, moreover 9 expressly, precisely 11 furthermore 12 additionally

as well as 6 beside, beyond 7 besides 12 over and above

as yet 5 so far 7 earlier, thus far 8 hitherto

asylum 4 home, port 5 cover, haven 6 covert, harbor, refuge 7 retreat, shelter 8 bughouse, loony bin, madhouse, nuthouse, security 9 harborage, sanctuary 10 booby hatch, crazy house, sanatorium 11 institution

asymmetric 6 uneven 7 unequal 8 lopsided 9 irregular 10 off-balance, unbalanced 12 overbalanced

Atalanta *husband:* 8 Melanion *suitor:* 10 Hippomenes

at all 4 ever, once 6 anyway, soever 7 anytime, anywise *Scottish:* 3 ava

ataraxy 8 calmness, coolness 9 composure, sangfroid 10 equanimity

atavism 9 reversion, throwback

ataxia 5 chaos, snarl 6 huddle, muddle 7 clutter 8 disarray, disorder 9 confusion

at close hand 4 near, nigh 6 nearby

atelier 6 studio 7 bottega 8 workshop

Athamas *daughter:* 5 Helle *father:* 6 Aeolus *son:* 7 Phrixos, Phrixus 8 Learchus *wife:* 3 Ino 7 Nephele

Athena, Athene 7 Minerva *attribute:* 3 owl 5 Aegis 7 serpent *father:* 4 Zeus *names:* 4 Alea, Nike 5 Areia 6 Ergane, Hippia, Hygeia, Itonia, Pallas, Polias 8 Apaturia 9 Parthenos, Promachos 10 Chalinitis *shield:* 4 Egis 5 Aegis *statue:* 9 Palladium *temple:* 9 Parthenon

athenaeum 7 library 8 archives

Athens *citadel:* 9 Acropolis *founder:* 7 Cecrops *last king:* 6 Codrus *marketplace:* 5 agora *rival:* 6 Sparta *senate:* 5 boule *temple:* 9 Parthenon

athirst 3 dry 4 avid, keen 5 eager 6 ardent 7 anxious, dried-up 8 appetent 9 impatient 10 dehydrated, desiccated

athlete 4 jock 6 player 7 acrobat, gymnast, tumbler

athlete's foot 8 ringworm

athletic 6 active, brawny, sinewy 8 muscular, vigorous 9 energetic, strenuous *contest:* 4 agon, game 5 match *field:* 4 oval, ring, rink 5 arena, court 7 diamond, stadium 8 gridiron *prize:* 3 cup 5 medal 6 trophy

athletics 5 games 6 sports 8 exercise 10 gymnastics, recreation 12 calisthenics

athwart 4 over 5 cross 6 across, beyond 9 crossways, crosswise 12 transversely

atiptoe 9 expectant, expecting 10 anticipant 12 anticipative, anticipatory

Atlanta's civic center 4 Omni

Atlas *brother:* 10 Prometheus *daughter:* 5 Hyads 6 Hyades 8 Pleiades 10 Atlantides *father:* 7 Iapetus *mother:* 7 Clymene *race:* 5 Titan *wife:* 7 Pleione

at last 7 finally

Atli *slayer:* 6 Gudrun *wife:* 6 Gudrun

atmosphere 3 air 4 aura, mood 6 aether, medium, milieu 7 ambient, climate, feeling, quality 8 ambiance, ambience 9 semblance 11 environment, mise-en-scène 12 surroundings *stratum:* 9 exosphere 10 ionosphere, mesosphere 11 chemosphere, ozonosphere, troposphere 12 stratosphere, thermosphere *sun's:* 12 chromosphere

atmospheric 4 airy 6 aerial 9 pneumatic

atoll 6 island *equatorial area:* 11 Baker Island *Indian Ocean:* 4 Male *Kiribati:* 4 Beru 7 Abaiang, Abemama, Apamama *Marshall Islands:* 4 Ebon, Mili, Ujae 6 Bikini 8 Eniwetok 9 Kwajalein *Northern Cook Islands:* 8 Manahiki *North of Samoa:* 7 Fakaofo *Pacific:* 5 Makin 8 Johnston 10 Butaritari, Palmerston *Tokelau:* 5 Atafu 10 Duke of York *Tuamotu:* 10 Anaa Island 11 Chain Island *Tuvalu:* 8 Funafuti

atom 3 bit, jot 4 iota, mite 5 minim, touch, trace 6 tittle 7 modicum, smidgen 8 particle *charged:* 3 ion 5 anion *group:* 7 radical

atomic particle 3 ion 4 beta, muon, pion 5 alpha, boson, meson 6 baryon, hadron, lepton, proton 7 fermion, hyperon, neutron, nucleon 8 electron, mesotron, neutrino, positron, thermion *hypothetical:* 5 quark 6 parton

atomize 4 ruin 5 smash, wreck 6 rub out 7 destroy, shatter 8 demolish, destruct, dynamite, nebulize 9 devastate, pulverize

at once 3 now 4 away 8 directly, first off, together 9 forthwith, instantly, right away 11 immediately, straightway 12 concurrently, straightaway

atone 3 pay 6 repent 7 expiate, satisfy 10 compensate, recompense

atoner 8 penitent

Atossa *father:* 5 Cyrus *husband:* 6 Darius 7 Smerdes 8 Cambyses *son:* 6 Xerxes

atramentous 3 jet 4 ebon, inky 5 black, ebony, raven, sable 10 pitch-black

at random 5 about 6 anyhow 7 anywise 9 haphazard 11 any which way, haphazardly 13 helter-skelter

Atreus *brother:* 8 Thyestes *father:*
6 Pelops *mother:* 10 Hippodamia *slayer:*
9 Aegisthus *son:* 8 Menelaus 9 Agamemnon 11 Pleisthenes *victim:* 11 Pleisthenes
wife: 6 Aerope

atrocious 4 foul, vile 6 horrid, odious, savage 7 heinous, noisome, obscene 8 shocking 9 desperate, execrable, loathsome,
monstrous, offensive, repulsive, sickening
10 abominable, despicable, disgusting, outrageous, scandalous 12 contemptible

atrocity 8 enormity, savagery 9 brutality
11 heinousness 13 monstrousness

atrophy 7 decline 8 downfall 9 decadence, downgrade 10 degeneracy, devolution 11 declination 12 degeneration
13 deterioration *combining form:* 4 necr
5 necro

attach 3 add, fix, tie 4 bind 5 affix, annex,
rivet 6 adhere, append, fasten

attached 7 sessile

attachment 4 love 6 fealty 7 loyalty
8 adhesion, devotion, fidelity, fondness
9 adherence, affection, constancy 10 allegiance 12 faithfulness

attack 3 fit 4 raid, rush 5 beset, blitz,
drive, fight, foray, onset, sally, siege,
spasm, spell, storm, throe 6 access,
ambush, assail, banzai, battle, charge, fall
on, harass, have at, invade, irrupt, onfall,
savage, sortie, strike, tackle, turn on
7 aggress, assault, besiege, bombard,
offense, seizure 8 fall upon, outbreak, paroxysm 9 beleaguer, incursion, offensive,
onslaught, pugnacity 10 aggression, assailment 11 bellicosity 12 belligerence
13 combativeness *combining form:*
5 lepsy 6 lepsia, lepsis

attacker *combining form:* 6 mastix

attain 3 get, win 4 gain 5 reach, score
6 rack up 7 achieve, realize 10 accomplish

attainment 11 achievement, acquirement,
acquisition, realization

attempt 3 try 4 seek, stab 5 assay,
essay, offer, trial 6 strive 7 venture
8 endeavor, striving, struggle 9 undertake
11 undertaking

attend 3 aid 4 hear, heed, help, mind
5 watch 6 assist, convoy, escort, listen
7 care for, conduct, hearken, oversee
8 chaperon 9 accompany, companion,
supervise 11 consort with

attendant 3 aid 4 help 6 helper, lackey
7 ancilla, doorman, orderly, servant, striker
8 incident 9 ancillary, assistant, satellite
10 bridesmaid, coincident, collateral
11 chamberlain, concomitant 12 accompanying *ancient Roman:* 6 lictor *in court:*
7 bailiff 8 tipstaff

attendants 5 suite, train 7 cortege, retinue 9 entourage

attention 4 heed, mark, note 5 study
6 notice, regard, remark 7 amenity 8 courtesy, sedulity 9 assiduity, awareness, diligence, gallantry 10 absorption, cognizance, observance 11 application,
engrossment, mindfulness, observation,
sensibility 12 deliberation, sedulousness
13 concentration, consciousness, consideration

attention getter 4 ahem 5 gavel

attentive 5 alert, aware 6 arrect, intent
7 heedful, mindful 8 open-eyed 9 advertent, observant, open-eared, regardful
10 interested, thoughtful 11 considerate
13 concentrating

attenuate 3 sap 4 rare, slim, thin 5 blunt,
reedy 6 lessen, rarefy, shrink, slight, stalky,
subtle, twiggy, weaken 7 cripple, deflate,
disable, slender, squinny, subtile, tenuous,
unbrace 8 enfeeble, rarefied, wiredraw
9 dissipate, undermine 10 debilitate

attest 5 argue, swear, vouch 6 affirm, verify 7 bespeak, betoken, certify, point to,
testify, witness 8 announce, indicate
10 asseverate

attestation 5 proof 7 witness 8 evidence
9 testament, testimony 11 testimonial
12 confirmation

attic 4 loft 6 garret 8 cockloft ·

at times 9 sometimes 10 now and then
11 ever and anon, now and again 12 here
and there

attire 4 clad, duds, garb, togs 5 array,
dress 6 clothe, outfit 7 apparel, clothes,
garment, raiment 8 accouter, clothing,
enclothe 11 habiliments

attirement see **clothes**

attitude 4 pose 5 stand 6 stance 7 posture 8 carriage, demeanor, position, positure 11 point of view

attitudinize 4 pose 7 pass for, pass off,
posture 10 masquerade

attorney 5 agent, proxy 6 deputy, factor,
lawyer 7 counsel 8 assignee 9 barrister,
counselor, solicitor 10 counsellor

attract 4 draw, lure, wile 5 charm, court,
tempt 6 allure, appeal, draw in, entice,
invite, seduce 7 beguile, bewitch, enchant,
solicit 8 interest, intrigue, inveigle 9 captivate, fascinate, magnetize

attraction 4 bait, call, draw, lure, pull
5 charm, mecca 6 appeal, liking 8 affinity,
cynosure, sympathy 9 seduction 10 allurement 12 drawing power

attractive 4 cute, fair, sexy 5 bonny,
dishy, siren 6 comely, lovely, luring, pretty
7 Circean, likable 8 alluring, charming,
engaging, enticing, fetching, handsome,
inviting, magnetic, mesmeric, tempting
9 appealing, beauteous, beautiful, beckon-
ing, glamorous, seductive 10 bewitching,

enchanting **11** captivating, fascinating, good-looking, tantalizing **13** prepossessing

attractiveness **5** charm **6** appeal, beauty, glamor

attribute **4** mark **5** refer, trait **6** assign, charge, credit, emblem, impute, symbol, virtue **7** ascribe, earmark, feature, quality **8** accredit, property **9** character

attrition **3** rue **4** ruth, wear **7** penance, remorse **8** abrasion, friction **9** penitence, penitency **10** repentance **12** contriteness

attritional **5** sorry **8** contrite, penitent **9** regretful, repentant **10** apologetic, remorseful **11** penitential

attune **7** balance, conform **9** harmonize, integrate, reconcile **10** coordinate, proportion **11** accommodate

atypical **3** odd **5** queer **7** deviant, strange **8** aberrant, abnormal, peculiar **9** anomalous, deviative, different, irregular, unnatural **11** exceptional, heteroclite **13** preternatural

auberge **3** inn **5** hotel, lodge **6** hostel, tavern **7** hospice **8** hostelry **9** roadhouse **11** caravansary, public house

Auber opera **10** Fra Diavolo

au courant **5** awake, aware **6** au fait, versed **7** abreast, knowing, versant, witting **8** familiar, informed, sentient, up-to-date **9** cognizant, conscious **10** acquainted, conversant **12** contemporary **13** up-to-the-minute

auction *Scottish:* **4** roup

audacious **4** bold, rash **5** brash, brave, saucy **6** brazen, daring **7** valiant **8** fearless, impudent, insolent, intrepid, reckless, unafraid, uncurbed, valorous **9** daredevil, dauntless, foolhardy, shameless, undaunted, venturous **10** courageous, ungoverned, unhampered **11** adventurous, impertinent, temerarious, uninhibited, untrammeled, venturesome **12** contumelious, unrestrained **13** adventuresome

audacity **4** gall **5** brass, nerve **6** mettle, spirit **7** courage **8** temerity **9** assurance, brashness, cockiness, hardihood, hardiness, impudence **10** brazenness

audible **5** aural **9** auricular

audibly **5** aloud

audience **6** public **7** hearing **8** audition **9** clientage, clientele, following **10** spectators

audile **5** aural **8** acoustic

audit **4** scan **5** check, probe **6** review, survey **7** checkup **8** analysis, scrutiny **10** inspection **11** examination **13** investigation, perlustration

audition **7** hearing **8** audience

auditory **4** otic **5** aural **8** acoustic

au fait **4** able **5** right **6** decent, proper, versed **7** abreast, capable, correct, versant **8** becoming, decorous, familiar, informed **9** au courant, befitting, competent, qualified **10** acquainted, conforming, conversant

au fond **8** at bottom **9** basically, in essence **11** essentially **13** fundamentally

Augean stable **3** sty **4** sink **5** Sodom **7** cesspit **8** cesspool

auger *combining form:* **6** trypan **7** trypano

Auge's son **8** Telephus

aught **4** zero **5** zilch **6** cipher **7** nothing **8** goose egg

augment **3** wax **4** hike, rise **5** boost, build, exalt, mount, raise **6** beef up, expand, extend **7** enlarge, magnify, upsurge **8** compound, heighten, increase, manifold, multiply **10** aggrandize

augmentation **4** rise **5** annex, extra, raise **7** adjunct **8** addition, increase **9** accession, accretion, increment **10** complement, enrichment **11** enhancement **13** accompaniment

augur **4** bode, omen **7** betoken, portend, predict, presage, promise, prophet, suggest **8** forebode, forecast, foreshow, foretell, indicate, prophesy, soothsay **9** adumbrate, foretoken, predictor, prefigure **10** forecaster, foreshadow, foreteller, prophesier, vaticinate **11** Nostradamus **13** prognosticate

augury **4** omen **6** boding **7** portent, presage **8** bodement **9** foretoken **10** prognostic

august **5** grand, noble **6** lordly **7** stately **8** baronial, imposing, majestic, princely, splendid **9** grandiose **11** magnificent

auk genus **4** Alca

_____ au lait **4** café

au naturel **3** raw **4** nude **5** naked **6** unclad **8** buff-bare, stripped **9** unclothed, undressed **10** stark-naked

aura **3** air **4** feel, glow, halo, mood **5** aroma **6** nimbus **7** aureole, feeling **8** mystique, radiance **9** emanation, semblance **10** atmosphere

aural **6** audile **7** audible **8** acoustic, auditory **9** auricular

aureate **7** flowery **8** sonorous **9** bombastic, overblown **10** euphuistic, rhetorical **11** declamatory **13** grandiloquent

auricular **5** aural **7** audible

Auriga star **7** Capella

aurora **4** dawn, morn **7** dawning, morning, sunrise **8** cockcrow, daybreak

Aurora **3** Eos *goddess of:* **4** dawn *husband:* **8** Tithonus *son:* **6** Memnon

auslander **5** alien **7** inconnu **8** outcomer, outsider, stranger **9** foreigner

auspex **5** augur **7** prophet **8** foreseer **10** forecaster, foreteller, prophesier, soothsayer **11** Nostradamus

auspices **5** aegis **7** backing **9** patronage **11** sponsorship

auspicious 6 benign, bright, dexter, timely 7 hopeful, timeous 9 favorable, fortunate, opportune, well-timed 10 prosperous, seasonable

Austen novel 4 Emma 10 Persuasion 17 Pride and Prejudice

Auster see Notus

austere 4 bare, dour, grim, hard 5 acrid, bleak, grave, harsh, sharp, stern 6 bitter, severe, simple, somber 7 ascetic, serious 9 stringent, unadorned 10 astringent

Australia *capital:* 8 Canberra *largest city:* 6 Sydney *monetary unit:* 6 dollar

Austria *capital:* 6 Vienna *dynasty:* 8 Habsburg, Hapsburg *monetary unit:* 9 schilling

autarchic 4 free 8 absolute, despotic, dogmatic, separate 9 arbitrary, imperious, sovereign, tyrannous 10 autocratic, autonomous, monocratic, tyrannical 11 independent, self-reliant

authentic 4 real, true 5 pukka, right, solid, sound, valid 6 trusty 7 certain, factual, genuine 8 accurate, bona fide, credible, faithful, reliable 9 simon-pure, undoubted, veritable 10 convincing, dependable, sure-enough 11 indubitable, trustworthy 12 questionless

authenticate 6 verify 7 bear out, confirm, justify, voucher 8 validate 11 corroborate 12 substantiate

author 4 sire 5 maker 6 father, penman, proser, scribe, writer 7 creator, founder 8 inventor, novelist, prosaist 9 architect, generator, patriarch 10 originator *American:* 3 Bly (Robert), Nin (Anaïs), Poe (Edgar Allan) 4 Agee (James), Buck (Pearl), Dana (Richard Henry), Grey (Zane), King (Stephen), Mann (Thomas), Rand (Ayn), Roth (Philip), Shaw (Irwin), Uris (Leon), West (Nathanael) 5 Aiken (Conrad), Alger (Horatio), Barth (John), Crane (Hart, Stephen), Harte (Bret), Oates (Joyce Carol), O'Hara (John), Paine (Thomas), Steel (Danielle), Stone (Irving), Stowe (Harriet Beecher), Turow (Scott), Twain (Mark), Tyler (Anne), White (Edmund, Elwyn Brooks, Theodore Harold), Wolfe (Thomas), Wylie (Elinor) 6 Alcott (Louisa May), Bellow (Saul), Cabell (James Branch), Cather (Willa), Clancy (Tom), Cooper (James Fenimore), Ferber (Edna), Harris (Frank, Joel Chandler), Hersey (John), Holmes (Oliver Wendell), Hughes (Langston), Irving (John, Washington), Jewett (Sarah Orne), Kidder (Tracy), London (Jack), Mailer (Norman), Miller (Arthur, Henry, Joaquin, May), Morley (Christopher), Norris (Frank), Parker (Dorothy), Porter (Katherine Anne, William Sydney), Runyon (Damon), Singer (Isaac Bashevis), Styron (William), Updike (John), Warren (Robert Penn), Wilder (Laura Ingalls, Thornton), Wilson (August, Edmund, Harriet, Lanford), Wister (Owen), Wright (James, Richard) 7 Baldwin (Faith, James), Beattie (Ann), Clemens (Samuel Langhorne), Cozzens (James Gould), Farrell (James Thomas), Gardner (Erle Stanley), Garland (Hamlin), Glasgow (Ellen), Heyward (DuBose), Howells (William Dean), Jarrell (Randall), Johnson (Diane, James), Kerouac (Jack), Lardner (Ring), Malamud (Bernard), Masters (Edgar Lee), Mumford (Lewis), Nabokov (Vladimir), Rexroth (Kenneth), Richter (Conrad), Roberts (Elizabeth Madox, Kenneth), Saroyan (William), Sheehan (Neil), Thoreau (Henry David), Thurber (James), Wallace (Lew), Wharton (Edith) 8 Anderson (Maxwell, Poul, Regina, Sherwood), Caldwell (Erskine), Faulkner (William), Marquand (John Phillips), Melville (Herman), Michener (James), Mitchell (Donald Grant, Margaret, S. Weir), Remarque (Erich Maria), Rinehart (Mary Roberts), Salinger (Jerome David), Sandburg (Carl), Sinclair (Upton), Spillane (Mickey), Stockton (Frank R.) Vonnegut (Kurt) 9 Burroughs (Edgar Rice, John, William Seward), Dos Passos (John), Hawthorne (Nathaniel), Hemingway (Ernest), Isherwood (Christopher), McCullers (Carson), Steinbeck (John), Wodehouse (Pelham Grenville), Woollcott (Alexander) 10 Fitzgerald (F. Scott), Tarkington (Booth) *Australian:* 4 West (Morris Langlo) 5 White (Patrick) 10 Richardson (Henry Handel) *Austrian:* 5 Kafka (Franz) 7 Suttner (Bertha) 10 Schnitzler (Arthur) *Canadian:* 3 Roy (Camille, Gabrielle) 5 Kirby (William) 6 Atwood (Margaret), Davies (Robertson) 7 Leacock (Stephen), Raddall (Thomas), Richler (Mordecai), Service (Robert) 8 Woodcock (George) 9 de la Roche (Mazo), MacLennan (Hugh) *Chinese:* 5 Han Yu *Czech:* 5 Capek (Karel) *Danish:* 4 Rode (Helge), Wied (Gustav) 6 Jensen (Johannes Vilhelm) 7 Holberg (Ludwig) *Dutch:* 6 Vondel (Joost van den) *English:* 4 Amis (Kingsley, Martin), Ford (Ford Madox, John), Lyly (John), Saki, Snow (Charles Percy), Ward (Mrs. Humphry), West (Rebecca) 5 Defoe (Daniel), Doyle (Authur Conan), Eliot (Thomas Stearns), Hardy (Thomas), James (Henry, Phyllis Dorothy), Lewis (Clive Staples, Monk, Wyndham), Lowry (Malcolm), Milne (Alan Alexander), Powys (John Cowper, Llewelyn, Theodore Francis), Reade (Charles), Spark (Muriel), Waugh (Alec, Evelyn), Wells (Charles Jeremiah, Herbert George), White (Terence Hanbury), Woolf (Leonard, Virginia), Young (Arthur, Edward,

Francis Brett) 6 Archer (Jeffrey), Austen (Jane), Belloc (Hilaire), Brontë (Anne, Charlotte, Emily), Bunyan (John), Butler (Samuel), Conrad (Joseph), Graves (Robert), Greene (Graham, Robert), Hilton (James), Hudson (William Henry), Huxley (Aldous), Lytton (Robert Bulwer-), Malory (Thomas), Orwell (George), Potter (Beatrix), Powell (Anthony), Sayers (Dorothy), Sterne (Laurence), Storey (David), Walton (Izaak) 7 Ballard (James Graham), Burgess (Anthony), Dickens (Charles), Durrell (Lawrence), Fleming (Ian), Follett (Ken), Forster (Edward Morgan), Golding (Louis, William), Kipling (Rudyard), Maugham (Robin, William Somerset), Sassoon (Siegfried), Shelley (Mary, Wollstonecraft, Percey Bysshe), Sitwell (Edith, Osbert, Sacheverell), Southey (Robert), Surtees (Robert Smith), Tolkien (John Ronald Reuel), Walpole (Horace, Hugh), Wyndham (John) 8 Christie (Agatha), Forester (Cecil Scott), Koestler (Arthur), Lawrence (David Herbert, Thomas Edward), Macaulay (Rose, Thomas Babington), Meredith (George), Sillitoe (Alan), Smollett (Tobias), Strachey (Lytton), Trollope (Anthony), Zangwill (Israel) 9 De Quincey (Thomas), Du Maurier (Daphne, George), Goldsmith (Oliver), Mansfield (Katherine), Masefield (John), Priestley (John Boynton), Radcliffe (Ann), Thackeray (William Makepeace) 10 Chesterton (Gilbert Keith), Galsworthy (John), Richardson (Dorothy, Samuel) 12 Quiller-Couch (Arthur Thomas) *Finnish:* 7 Waltari (Mika) 9 Sillanpaa (Frans Eemil) *French:* 4 Gide (Andre), Hugo (Victor), Kock (Charles-Paul de), Sade (Marquis de), Sand (George), Zola (Emile) 5 Camus (Albert), Dumas (Alexandre), Sagan (Francoise), Stael (Germaine de), Verne (Jules), Vigny (Alfred-Victor) 6 Balzac (Honoré de), Daudet (Alphonse), France (Anatole), Proust (Marcel), Sartre (Jean-Paul) 7 Cocteau (Jean), Gautier (Leon, Theophile), Malraux (Andre), Mauriac (Claude, Francois), Maurois (Andre), Merimée (Prosper), Rolland (Romain), Romains (Jules), Simenan (Georges) 8 Beauvoir (Simone de), Flaubert (Gustave), Marivaux (Pierre), Rabelais (Francois), Stendhal, Voltaire 9 Giraudoux (Jean) 10 Maupassant (Guy de), Saint-Simon (Duke de) 12 Robbe-Grillet (Alain) *German:* 4 Böll (Heinrich) 5 Grass (Gunter), Hesse (Hermann), Storm (Theodor Woldsen), Tieck (Ludwig), Zweig (Stefan) 6 Toller (Ernst) 7 Fontane (Theodor), Richter (Jean Paul), Wieland (Christoph Martin) 8 Hoffmann (Ernst Theodor Amedeus, Heinrich), Schlegel (August Wilhelm von, Friedrich von, Johann Elias) 9 Hauptmann (Gerhart), Sudermann (Hermann) 10 Wassermann (Jakob) *Greek:* 6 Lucian 11 Kazantzakis (Nikos) *Hungarian:* 5 Jokai (Mor) *Icelandic:* 7 Laxness (Halldor) *Irish:* 5 Joyce (James) 6 Stoker (Bram) 7 Beckett (Samuel), O'Connor (Frank), Russell (George William) 8 O'Faolain (Julia, Sean), Stephens (James) 9 O'Flaherty (Liam) *Italian:* 5 Verga (Giovanni) 6 Silone (Ignazio) 7 Manzoni (Alessandro), Moravia (Alberto) 8 Boccacio (Giovanni) 9 Vittorini (Elio) 10 Pirandello (Luigi), Straparola (Gianfrancesco) *Japanese:* 7 Mishima (Yukio) 8 Kawabata (Yasunari), Murasaki (Shikibu) 9 Yokomitsu (Riichi), Yoshikawa (Eiji) *Lebanese:* 6 Gibran (Khalil) *Norwegian:* 3 Lie (Jonas) 6 Hamsun (Knut), Undset (Sigrid) 8 Bjornson (Bjornstjerne Martinius), Kielland (Alexander Lange) *Norwegian-American:* 7 Rolvaag (Ole Edvart) *Polish:* 7 Reymont (Wladyslau Stanislaw) 8 Zeromski (Stefan) 11 Sienkiewicz (Henryk) *Portuguese:* 6 Pessoa (Fernando) *Roman:* 5 Pliny, Varro (Marcus Terentius) *Russian:* 5 Gorki (Maksim *or* Maxim) 7 Andreev (Leonid Nikoleyevich), Tolstoy (Leo) 8 Turgenev (Ivan), Zamyatin (Yevgeny Ivanovich) 9 Lermontov (Mikhail), Sholokhov (Mikhail) 10 Dostoevsky (Fyodor) 11 Dostoyevsky (Fydor), Yevtushanko (Yevgeny) 12 Solzhenitsyn (Aleksandr) *Scottish:* 4 Lang (Andrew) 5 Scott (Alexander, Walter) 6 Barrie (James M.), Buchan (John) 8 Urquhart (Thomas) 9 Stevenson (Robert Louis) *Spanish:* 6 Baroja (Pio) 7 Alarcon (Pedro Antonio de) 9 Cervantes (Miguel de) *Swedish:* 7 Johnson (Eyvind), Rydberg (Viktor) 8 Lagerlof (Selma) 10 Lagerkvist (Par), Strindberg (August) *Swiss:* 4 Wyss (Johann Rudolf) 6 Frisch (Max) 9 Spitteler (Carl) *Welsh:* 4 Owen (Alun, Daniel, Goronwy, John) 5 Evans (David, Evan), Wynne (Ellis) *Yiddish:* 4 Asch (Sholem)

authoritarian 6 strict 8 dogmatic 9 dictative, stringent 10 oppressive, totalistic 11 dictatorial, doctrinaire, magisterial 12 totalitarian

authoritative 4 sure, true 5 sound 8 accepted, attested, dogmatic, official, orthodox 9 canonical, dictative, ex officio, trustable 10 dependable, ex cathedra, sanctioned 11 cathedratic, dictatorial, doctrinaire, irrefutable, magisterial, trustworthy 12 indisputable

authority 4 rule, sway 6 credit, expert, master, weight 7 command, control, mastery 8 prestige, virtuoso 9 influence 10 domination, governance, government, past master 12 jurisdiction

authorization 5 leave 6 permit 7 consent, go-ahead, mandate 8 sanction 9 allowance, clearance 10 green light, permission, sufferance

authorize 3 let 4 vest 5 allow 6 enable, invest, permit 7 approve, empower, endorse, entitle, license, qualify, warrant 8 accredit, sanction 10 commission 11 countenance

auto see automobile

autobiographer 9 memoirist

autobiography 4 life, vita 5 diary 6 memoir 7 journal 11 confessions

autochthonous 6 native 7 endemic 10 aboriginal, indigenous

autocracy 7 tyranny 9 despotism 12 dictatorship

autocratic 7 haughty 8 absolute, arrogant, despotic 9 arbitrary, tyrannous 10 tyrannical

autodidactic 10 self-taught 12 self-educated

autograph 3 ink 4 sign 9 signature, subscribe 11 John Hancock

autoist 6 driver 8 motorist, operator

Autolycus *daughter:* 8 Anticlea *father:* 6 Hermes 7 Mercury

automate 8 robotize

automatic 8 habitual 9 impulsive, reflexive 10 mechanical, self-acting, unprompted 11 instinctive, involuntary, perfunctory, spontaneous, unmeditated *combining form:* 4 self

automaton 5 golem, robot 7 android, machine

automobile 3 bus, car 5 buggy, coupe, racer, sedan 6 jalopy, tourer 7 flivver, hardtop, machine 8 dragster, motorcar, roadster, runabout *British:* 2 MG 6 Anglia, Austin, Jaguar 7 Bentley, Daimler, Hillman, Sunbeam, Triumph 8 Vauxhall 10 Rolls-Royce 11 Austin-Healy *French:* 5 Simca 7 Citroen, Peugeot, Renault *German:* 3 BMW 7 Porsche 10 Volkswagen 12 Mercedes-Benz *Italian:* 4 Fiat 6 Lancia 7 Ferrari 8 Maserati 9 Alfa-Romeo *Japanese:* 5 Honda, Mazda 6 Datsun, Subaru, Toyota *Korean* 6 Hundai *Swedish:* 4 Saab 5 Volvo

automotive pioneer 4 Benz (Carl Friedrich), Ford (Henry), Olds (Ransom Eli) 5 Evans (Oliver), Roper (Sylvester) 6 Cugnot (Nicholas Joseph), Duryea (Charles E., J. Frank), Lenoir (Etienne), Winton (Alexander) 7 Daimler (Gottlieb), Stanley (Francis, Freelan) 8 Morrison (William)

Autonoe *father:* 6 Cadmus *husband:* 9 Aristaeus *mother:* 8 Harmonia *sister:* 5 Agave *son:* 7 Actaeon

autonomous 4 free 8 separate 9 autarchic, sovereign 11 independent 12 self-governed, uncontrolled

autopsy 8 necropsy 10 postmortem

auto racer 3 Foyt (A. J.) 4 Hill (Graham) 5 Clark (Jim), Petty (Richard), Unser (Al, Bobby) 6 Fangio (Juan) 7 Brabham (Jack), Stewart (Jackie) 8 Andretti (Mario)

autumn casualty 3 DST (Daylight Saving Time) 6 leaves

auxiliary 4 aide 6 helper 7 reserve 8 adjutant, adjuvant 9 accessory, ancillary, assistant, coadjutor 10 additional, collateral, subsidiary 11 appurtenant, subservient 12 contributory 13 complementary, supplementary *verb:* 2 am, do, is 3 are, can, did, had, has, may, was 4 been, does, have, must, were, will 5 could, might, ought, shall, would 6 should

avail 3 use 5 serve 6 profit 7 account, benefit, fitness, service 9 advantage, relevance 10 usefulness 13 applicability

available 8 gettable 9 securable 10 attainable, obtainable, procurable 11 purchasable

avalanche 5 flood, slide 8 mudslide, rockfall 9 landslide, rockslide, snowslide

avarice 5 greed 7 avidity 8 cupidity, rapacity 10 greediness 12 covetousness, graspingness

avenge 5 repay, right 7 pay back, redress, requite 9 retaliate, retribute, vindicate

avengement 7 revenge 8 reprisal, requital, revanche 9 vengeance 11 counterblow, retaliation, retribution

avenue 3 way 4 path, road 5 track 6 artery, street 7 highway 9 boulevard 12 thoroughfare

aver 4 avow 5 state 6 affirm, assert, avouch, depose 7 declare, profess, protest 8 constate, maintain 9 predicate

average 3 par 4 fair, mean, norm, so-so 6 common, median, medium 8 mediocre, middling, moderate, ordinary 11 indifferent 12 intermediate

averagely 4 so-so 6 enough, fairly, rather 8 passably 9 tolerably 10 moderately

avernal 7 hellish, stygian 8 infernal, plutonic 9 cimmerian, plutonian

averse 5 balky, loath 6 afraid 7 uneager 8 backward, hesitant 9 reluctant, resistant, unwilling 10 indisposed 11 disinclined

aversion 4 fear, hate 5 dread 6 hatred, horror 7 allergy, disgust, dislike 8 disfavor, distaste, dyspathy, loathing 9 antipathy, disliking, disrelish, repulsion, revulsion 10 abhorrence, antagonism, repugnance 11 abomination, detestation, displeasure 13 indisposition

aversive 8 ungenial 9 repellent, repugnant 11 uncongenial 12 antipathetic 13 unsympathetic

avert 4 foil, turn, veer, ward 5 check, deter 6 thwart 7 deflect, forfend, obviate, prevent, rule out 8 preclude, stave off 9 forestall, frustrate

avian 8 ornithic

aviary 4 cage 6 volary 8 dovecote, ornithon 9 birdhouse, columbary, dovehouse

aviator 3 ace 5 flier, pilot 6 airman, flyboy, Wright (Orville, Wilbur) 7 birdman, Earhart (Amelia) 9 Lindbergh (Charles) 10 Richthofen (Manfred von) 12 Rickenbacker (Eddie)

avid 4 agog, keen 5 eager 6 ardent, greedy 7 anxious, athirst, craving, thirsty, wanting 8 appetent, covetous, desirous 9 impatient 10 breathless

avidity 5 greed 7 avarice 8 cupidity, rapacity

avoid 4 bilk, duck, shun, snub 5 avert, elude, evade, shirk 6 bypass, divert, escape, eschew 7 obviate, prevent 8 preclude

avoidance 6 escape 7 come-off, elusion, evasion 8 escaping, escapism, eschewal, shunning 9 runaround *combining form:* 4 phob 5 phobo

avouch 3 own 4 aver, avow 5 admit 6 affirm, assert, depose 7 confess, confirm, declare, profess, protest 8 constate 9 predicate 11 acknowledge, corroborate

avow 3 own 4 aver 5 admit, allow, grant, let on, own up 6 affirm, assert, avouch, depose, fess up 7 concede, confess, declare, profess, protest 8 constate, maintain 9 predicate 11 acknowledge

await 4 hope 6 expect 7 count on

awake 4 stir 5 alive, aware, rouse 6 roused 7 aroused 8 sensible, sentient 9 au courant, cognizant, conscious, stirred up

awaken 4 stir, whet 5 alert, rally, rouse 6 arouse, bestir, kindle

awanting 4 sans 5 minus 7 lacking, without

award 4 give, kudo 5 badge, endow, grant, honor, kudos, medal, prize 6 accord, bestow, confer 7 concede, laurels, tribute 8 accolade 9 vouchsafe 10 blue ribbon, decoration 11 distinction *motion picture:* 5 Oscar *mystery novel:* 5 Edgar *record:* 6 Grammy *television:* 4 Emmy *theater:* 4 Tony

aware 5 alert, alive, awake 7 heedful, knowing, mindful, witting 8 informed, sensible, sentient 9 au courant, cognizant, conscious 10 conversant 12 apprehensive

awash 4 full 6 jammed, loaded, packed 7 brimful, crammed, crowded, stuffed 8 brimming 9 chock-full

away 3 far, fro, now, off 4 afar, gone, over 5 apart, aside, forth, hence 7 lacking, missing, omitted, wanting 8 directly, first off, right off 9 forthwith, instantly, therefrom 11 immediately

away from *prefix:* 2 ap 3 aph, apo

awe 4 fear 5 alarm, scare 6 fright, wonder 7 startle, terrify 8 affright, frighten 9 reverence, terrorize 10 veneration, wonderment

aweigh 5 atrip

aweless 4 bold 5 brave 7 valiant 8 fearless, intrepid, unafraid, valorous 9 dauntless, undaunted 10 courageous

awesome 4 eery 5 eerie 6 august, dreary, solemn 7 sublime 8 dreadful, imposing, terrific

awful 7 fearful 8 dreadful, horrible, horrific, shocking, terrible, terrific 9 appalling, frightful 10 formidable

awfully 4 much, very 6 hugely 7 greatly 8 whacking, whopping 9 extremely

awhile *Scottish:* 4 awee

awkward 5 gawky, inept, nerdy, splay 6 clumsy, gauche, wooden 7 gawkish, halting, lumpish, unhandy, unhappy 8 bumbling, bungling, ungainly 9 graceless, hamhanded, ill-chosen, lumbering, maladroit 10 blundering, bunglesome, unskillful 11 heavy-handed, splathering, unfortunate 12 discommoding, embarrassing, incommodious, inconvenient, infelicitous 13 discommodious

awning *ancient Roman:* 8 velarium

awry 5 amiss, askew, badly, wrong 6 afield, askant, astray 7 askance 8 cockeyed 9 cock-a-hoop, crookedly 11 unfavorably *Scottish:* 5 aglee, agley

ax, axe 3 adz, can 4 adze, fire, sack 5 hache 6 bounce 7 boot out, chopper, cleaver, dismiss, hatchet, kick out 8 tomahawk 9 discharge, terminate *blade:* 3 bit *double-headed:* 6 twibil 7 twibill *handle:* 5 helve *ice:* 6 piolet

axiom 3 law 4 rule 5 gnome, maxim, moral 6 dictum, truism 7 brocard, theorem 8 aphorism, apothegm 9 principle 10 principium 11 fundamental

aye 2 OK 3 yea, yep, yes 4 okay 8 all right

Azariah *brother:* 7 Ahimaaz *father:* 4 Obed 5 Zadok 6 Nathan 7 Ahimaaz, Hilkiah, Jeroham, Johanan 8 Hoshaiah, Maaseiah 11 Jehoshaphat *son:* 7 Seraiah

Azimov's forte 5 sci-fi

Aztec *capital:* 12 Tenochtitlan *conqueror:* 6 Cortes, Cortez *emperor:* 9 Montezuma *god:* 4 Xipe 6 Eecatl, Meztli, Tlaloc 9 Xipetotec 11 Xiuhtecutli 12 Quetzalcoatl *hero:* 4 Nata *language:* 7 Nahuatl *temple:* 8 teocalli

B

baa 5 bleat

Babbitt 4 boob 8 boeotian 10 middlebrow, philistine *author:* 5 Lewis (Sinclair)

babblative 5 gabby, talky 6 chatty 9 garrulous, talkative 10 loquacious 11 loose-lipped 12 loose-tongued, multiloquent

babble 3 gab, jaw, yak, yap 4 blab, chat 5 clack, prate, run on 6 burble, drivel, gibber, jabber, patter, piffle, rattle, yammer 7 blabber, blather, chatter, maunder, palaver, prattle, twaddle 8 nonsense 9 gibberish 11 jabberwocky

babbler *Scottish:* 7 blellum

babe 6 infant 7 neonate, newborn 8 bantling

babel 3 din 6 clamor, hubbub, jangle, racket, tumult, uproar 10 hullabaloo, tintamarre 11 pandemonium

baboon. 6 chacma 8 mandrill 9 hamadryas

babushka 8 bandanna, kerchief

baby 3 tot 5 sissy, spoil 6 cocker, coddle, cosset, dote on, infant, pamper 7 bambino, cater to, indulge, neonate, newborn, papoose, toddler 8 bantling, dote upon, nursling, suckling, weakling, weanling 11 mollycoddle *ailment:* 5 colic, croup *baptismal robe:* 7 chrisom *bed:* 4 crib 6 cradle 8 bassinet *bedroom:* 7 nursery *breechcloth:* 6 diaper *cap:* 6 biggin, bonnet *carriage:* 4 pram 5 buggy 8 stroller 12 perambulator *doctor:* 12 pediatrician *food:* 3 pap 4 milk 6 pablum *garment:* 7 rompers *Italian:* 7 bambino *napkin:* 3 bib *nurse:* 4 nana *outfit:* 7 layette *powder:* 4 talc *shoe:* 6 bootee *Spanish:* 4 bebé, nene *unborn:* 5 fetus

baby grand 5 piano

babyhood 7 infancy

babyish 7 puerile 8 childish, immature 9 infantile, infantine

Babylonian 6 lavish 9 luxurious *abode of the dead:* 5 Aralu *capital:* 7 Babylon *chaos:* 4 Apsu *city:* 2 Ur 5 Accad, Akkad 6 Cunaxa, Cuthah *crown prince:* 10 Belshazzar *division:* 5 Accad, Akkad, Sumer *earth mother:* 6 Ishtar *first ruler:* 6 Nimrod *god:* 2 Ea, Zu 3 Anu, Bel, Hea, Sin 4 Adad, Addu, Apsu, Enzu, Irra, Nabu, Nebo 5 Alala, Alalu, Dagan, Enlil, Kingu, Lahmu, Mummu, Ninib, Siris 6 Anshar, Marduk, Namtar, Nannar, Nergal, Ramman, Tammuz 7 Shamash 8 Ningirsu *goddess:* 4 Gula, Nina 5 Aruru, Belit 6 Allatu, Belili, Beltis, Ishtar, Kishar, Lahamu, Ningal, Tiamat 7 Baalath, Damkina *hero:* 5 Adapa, Etana 9 Gilgamesh *king:* 6 Sargon 9 Hammurabi *priest:* 2 en *priestess:* 5 entum *river:* 6 Tigris 9 Euphrates *ruler of the dead:* 6 Nergal *storm god:* 4 Adad, Adda, Addu *sun god:* 3 Bel 7 Shamash *tower:* 5 Babel 8 ziggurat *waters:* 4 Apsu 6 Tiamat *winged dragon:* 6 Tiamat

baccalaureate 6 degree 8 bachelor

bacchanal 4 orgy 5 party 7 debauch 10 saturnalia 11 bacchanalia

bacchanalian 7 drunken, reveler 9 orgiastic

bacchanal's cry 4 evoe 5 evohe

Bacchus 8 Dionysus *attendant:* 6 maenad *father:* 4 Zeus 7 Jupiter *lover:* 5 Venus 9 Aphrodite *mother:* 6 Semele *son:* 7 Priapus *staff:* 7 thyrsus

Bach *birthplace:* 8 Eisenach *composition:* 5 fugue, motet, suite 6 sonata 7 cantata, chorale, partita, prelude, toccata 8 concerto, fantasia, oratorio, sinfonia *deathplace:* 7 Leipzig *musical style:* 7 baroque *religion:* 8 Lutheran

back 3 aid 4 abet, fund, help, hind, rear 5 about, again, dorsa (plural), round, spine, stake 6 around, assist, dorsum, hinder, rachis, recede, remote, retral, uphold 7 endorse, finance, promote, retract, retreat, reverse, sponsor, support 8 advocate, bankroll, champion, frontier, hindmost, rearward, side with 9 in reverse, posterior, retrocede, vertebrae (plural) 10 outlandish, retrograde, round about *ailment:* 7 lumbago 10 rheumatism *combining form:* 2 an 3 ana, not 4 dors, noto 5 dorsi, dorso, notus 6 opisth 7 opistho *of a book:* 5 spine *of an arthropod:* 6 tergum *of an insect:* 5 notum *of the neck:* 4 nape 6 scruff *prefix:* 2 re 4 post 5 retro *relating to:* 6 dorsal

back answer 6 retort 7 riposte 8 comeback, repartee

backbiter 9 slanderer
backbiting 5 abuse 7 calumny, obloquy, scandal, slander 8 libelous 9 invective, maligning, traducing, vilifying 10 calumnious, defamation, defamatory, detracting, detraction, detractive, scandalous, slanderous 12 belittlement, depreciation, vituperation 13 disparagement
backbone 4 grit, guts 5 moxie, nerve, spine, spunk 6 pillar, rachis 8 mainstay 9 fortitude, vertebrae (plural) 12 spinal column
backcountry 4 bush 6 sticks 7 boonies 8 frontier 9 boondocks 10 hinterland
backcourtman 5 guard
back down 4 balk 5 demur, welsh 6 beg off, cry off, recall, recant, renege, resile 7 disavow, retract, stickle 8 withdraw 9 weasel out
backer 5 angel 6 patron, surety 7 sponsor 8 promoter 9 guarantor 10 bankroller, meal ticket
backfire 6 fizzle 8 kick back, miscarry 9 boomerang 11 fall through
background 7 scenery
backhanded 7 devious 8 indirect 9 sarcastic
backing 4 help 5 aegis 7 support 8 auspices 9 patronage 10 assistance 11 sponsorship
backland see backcountry
backlash 5 slack 6 recoil 8 reaction
backlog 5 hoard, stock, store 7 nest egg, reserve 9 inventory, reservoir, stockpile
back of 5 abaft 6 behind
back off see back down
backpack 8 knapsack, packsack, rucksack 9 haversack
backpedal see back down
backset 5 check 7 reverse 8 reversal
backside 4 rear, rump, seat 5 fanny, hiney 6 behind, bottom, heinie 8 buttocks, derriere 9 posterior
backslide 5 lapse 6 return, revert 7 regress, relapse 9 retrovert 10 recidivate
backstabbing 7 calumny, scandal, slander 10 defamation, detraction 12 belittlement, depreciation 13 disparagement
backstairs 6 secret, sordid 7 furtive 10 scandalous
backstop 6 uphold 7 support 8 advocate, champion, side with
back talk 3 lip 4 guff, sass 5 mouth, sauce 9 impudence, insolence
backtrack 7 retrace, retreat, reverse
backward 3 shy 4 dull, slow 5 about, again, loath, round, timid 6 around, averse, demure, modest, retral, stupid 7 bashful, moronic, uneager 8 hesitant, ignorant, inverted, retarded, retiring, retrorse, reversed 9 benighted, diffident, dim-witted, in reverse, reluctant, unwilling 10 behindhand, half-witted, indisposed, retrograde, round about, slow-witted, uncultured 11 disinclined, thickheaded, undeveloped 12 feebleminded, self-effacing, simpleminded, uncultivated 13 unprogressive
backwoods see backcountry
backwoodsman 4 hick, jake 5 yokel 6 rustic 7 bumpkin, hillman 9 hillbilly 10 provincial
bacon *side:* 6 flitch, gammon *slice:* 6 rasher
Bacon, Francis 12 Baron Verulam *work:* 12 Novum Organum
bacteria 5 cocci 7 bacilli, vibrios 8 spirilla *culture medium:* 4 agar *destroyer:* 10 antibiotic
bacterial disease 7 anthrax, leprosy, tetanus 8 syphilis 9 gonorrhea, pneumonia 10 diphtheria
bacteriologist *American:* 6 Enders (John Franklin) 7 Noguchi (Hideyo), Theiler (Max) *British:* 7 Fleming (Alexander) *French:* 5 Widal (Fernand) 7 Nicolle (Charles-Jean-Henri), Pasteur (Louis) *German:* 4 Cohn (Ferdinand Julius), Koch (Robert) 5 Klebs (Edwin) 7 Behring (Emil von), Loffler (Friedrich) 10 Wassermann (August von) *Japanese:* 8 Kitasato (Shibasaburo) *Russian:* 11 Metchnikoff (Elie) *Swiss:* 6 Yersin (Alexandre-Emile-John)
bad 3 ill, low 4 down, evil, foul, null, poor, sour, void 5 amiss, lousy, rough, rowdy, tough, wrong 6 arrant, nocent, putrid, rancid, rotten, sinful, unruly, wicked 7 decayed, froward, harmful, hateful, hurtful, immoral, invalid, naughty, nocuous, noisome, noxious, peccant, spoiled, tainted, unhappy, unsound, vicious 8 damaging, dejected, downcast, inferior, perverse, wretched 9 abhorrent, defective, deficient, depressed, execrable, injurious, loathsome, miserable, obnoxious, offensive, putrefied, reprobate, repulsive, sickening, woebegone 10 decomposed, disgusting, disorderly, dispirited, ill-behaved, indecorous, iniquitous, unpleasant 11 deleterious, detrimental, displeasing, distasteful, distressing, downhearted, intolerable, misbehaving, mischievous, unfavorable 12 disagreeable, disconsolate, insufferable, unacceptable 13 objectionable *combining form:* 3 cac, mal 4 caco *comparative:* 5 worse *prefix:* 3 dys, mis *superlative:* 5 worst
Badebec *husband:* 9 Gargantua *son:* 10 Pantagruel
Baden, for one 3 spa
badge 3 pin 5 award, honor, kudos 6 button, emblem 7 laurels 8 accolade, insignia 10 decoration 11 distinction

badger 3 nag 4 bait, ride 5 brock, chivy, hound 6 heckle, hector 8 balisaur, bullyrag *group of:* 4 cete

Badger State 9 Wisconsin

badinage 6 banter 7 joshing, kidding 8 backchat, repartee, snip-snap 9 cross talk 10 persiflage

badland 4 wild 5 waste 6 barren, desert 8 wildness 10 wilderness

badly 4 awry, illy 5 amiss, wrong 6 afield, astray 7 harshly, roughly 8 severely 9 painfully 10 rigorously 11 unfavorably *combining form:* 3 mal

badman 4 hood, thug 6 bandit, outlaw 7 bandido, hoodlum, villain 8 criminal, hooligan 9 desperado

bad mark 3 gig 7 demerit

bad-tempered 6 cranky, crusty, touchy 8 choleric 9 dyspeptic 10 ill-humored, ill-natured, tempersome 12 cantankerous

Baedeker 5 guide 6 manual 8 handbook 9 guidebook, vade mecum 10 compendium 11 enchiridion

baffle 4 balk, bilk, foil, ruin 5 addle, mix up, stump 6 muddle, puzzle, thwart 7 confuse, flummox, mystify, nonplus 8 befuddle, confound 9 dumbfound, frustrate 10 circumvent, disappoint

bafflement 9 confusion 10 perplexity

bag 3 cop, nab, net 4 grip, hook, land, nail, poke, sack 5 biddy, catch, crone, pouch, purse, seize, steal 6 beldam, collar, secure 7 capture, satchel 8 backpack, knapsack, reticule, suitcase 9 apprehend

bagatelle 6 trifle

baggage 4 gear 5 hussy, tramp, trull, wench 6 wanton 7 effects, luggage, trollop 8 slattern, strumpet

Baghdad *founder:* 6 Mansur *river:* 6 Tigris

bagnio 7 brothel 8 bordello, cathouse 10 bawdy house, whorehouse

Bagnold 4 Enid

bagpipe *part:* 5 drone 7 bourdon, chanter *sound:* 5 skirl

Bahamas' capital 6 Nassau

bail 3 dip 4 bond, lade 5 ladle, scoop 6 surety 8 guaranty, security, warranty 9 guarantee

bailiwick 5 field, realm 6 domain, sphere 7 demesne, terrain 8 district, dominion, province 9 champaign, territory 12 jurisdiction

bait 3 nag 4 lure, ride, toll, trap 5 chivy, decoy, harry, hound, leger, snare, tempt 6 allure, badger, come-on, entice, entrap, harass, heckle, hector, lead on, ledger, molest, pester, seduce 7 torment 8 bullyrag, inveigle 9 persecute 10 allurement, enticement, seducement, temptation 12 inveiglement

bake 4 burn, cook, fire, kiln 5 broil, roast 6 saggar, sagger, scorch 7 scallop, scollop, swelter

baked clay 7 ceramic

baker's dozen 8 thirteen

bakers' yeast 6 leaven

baking 3 hot 5 fiery 6 red-hot, torrid 7 burning 8 broiling, scalding, sizzling, white-hot 9 scorching *chamber:* 4 kiln, oven

baksheesh 3 tip 4 alms 5 favor 6 reward 8 gratuity

Balaam *beast:* 3 ass 6 donkey *father:* 4 Beor

balance 4 rest 5 level, poise 6 adjust, attune, make up, offset, redeem, set off, stasis 7 harmony, remains, remanet, remnant, residue 8 atone for, coolness, leavings, outweigh, residual, residuum, symmetry 9 composure, congruity, equipoise, harmonize, remainder, stability 10 compensate, equanimity, proportion, steadiness 11 consistency, countervail, equilibrium, self-control 12 counterpoise *combining form:* 5 stato

bald 4 bare, nude 5 naked, plain 6 shaven, smooth 8 glabrous, hairless 9 unadorned 11 undecorated, ungarnished 12 unornamented 13 unembellished

baldachin 4 silk 6 canopy, fabric

Balder, Baldur *father:* 4 Odin *mother:* 5 Frigg 6 Frigga *slayer:* 4 Hoth, Loke, Loki 5 Hoder, Hothr *son:* 7 Forsete, Forseti *wife:* 5 Nanna

balderdash 3 rot 4 bosh 5 bilge 6 blague, bushwa 7 eyewash, rubbish 8 claptrap, malarkey, nonsense

baldness 8 alopecia

baldpate 7 widgeon 8 skinhead

balefire 6 beacon

baleful 4 dire, evil 6 malign 7 direful, fateful, malefic, ominous 8 sinister 9 ill-boding, ill-omened 10 maleficent, pernicious 11 apocalyptic, threatening 12 unpropitious

balk 3 gag, jib, shy 4 beam, dash, foil, ruin 5 demur 6 baffle, boggle, refuse, thwart, timber 7 scruple, stickle, stumble 8 hang back 9 frustrate 10 circumvent, disappoint

balky 5 loath 6 averse, ornery 7 froward, restive, wayward 8 contrary, hesitant, perverse 9 reluctant 11 wrongheaded 12 cross-grained

ball 3 orb, wad 5 dance, globe, round 6 sphere 7 rondure 8 conglobe, ensphere 10 conglobate *batted high:* 3 fly *batted straight:* 5 liner *combining form:* 5 globo, spher 6 sphaer, sphero 7 sphaera, sphaero *of thread or yarn:* 4 clew *ornamental:* 6 pom-pom, pompon *tiny:* 7 globule

ballad 3 lay 4 lied, poem, song 7 calypso *rhyme:* 4 ABCB *singer:* 8 minstrel 10 troubadour

ballast 5 poise 6 steady 9 stabilify, stabilize 11 stabilitate

ballerina 6 dancer 7 danseur 8 coryphee, danseuse 9 figurante 11 dancing girl

ballet *costume:* 4 tutu 6 tights 7 leotard *dancer:* 7 danseur 8 coryphee, danseuse, figurant 9 ballerina, figurante *for two:* 9 pas de deux *handrail:* 5 barre *jump:* 4 jeté 8 ballonné 9 entrechat *knee bend:* 4 plié *position:* 6 pointe 8 attitude 9 arabesque *step:* 3 pas 8 glissade *turn:* 6 chaîné 9 pirouette

ball game see at game

balloon sail 9 spinnaker

ball-shaped 7 globoid, globose 8 globular, spheroid 9 globulous, spherical

ball up 4 clew 5 addle 6 fuddle 7 confuse, fluster 8 befuddle, bewilder, distract, throw off

ballyhoo 4 tout 6 herald, hoopla 7 trumpet 9 publicity

balm 4 lull 5 allay, aroma, cream, quiet, salve, scent, spice, still 6 cerate, chrism, settle, soothe 7 bouquet, compose, incense, perfume, unction, unguent 8 ointment 9 fragrance, redolence 11 tranquilize

balmacaan 8 overcoat

balm of Gilead 6 poplar 9 balsam fir 12 balsam poplar

balmy 4 mild, soft 5 bland, faint, spicy, sweet 6 aromal, easing, gentle, insane, savory, smooth 7 foolish, lenient, perfumy 8 aromatic, fragrant, perfumed, pleasant, pleasing, redolent, soothing 9 agreeable, ambrosial

baloney 3 rot 4 bosh, bull, bunk 5 hokum 7 hogwash, rubbish 8 nonsense

balsam poplar 9 tacamahac 10 hackmatack 12 balm of Gilead

Balthazar's gift 5 myrrh

Baltic *native:* 4 Lett 7 Latvian 8 Estonian 10 Lithuanian *state:* 6 Latvia 7 Estonia 9 Lithuania

balustrade 4 rail 7 railing 8 banister

Balzac character 6 Goriot 7 Grandet 9 Birotteau

bamboozle 4 bilk, dupe, fool, gull, hoax 5 trick 6 befool 7 chicane, swindle 8 flimflam, hoodwink 11 hornswoggle

ban 4 tabu 5 taboo 6 enjoin, forbid, outlaw 8 prohibit 9 interdict 11 forbiddance, prohibition 12 interdiction, proscription

Ban *ally:* 6 Arthur *son:* 8 Lancelot

banal 4 flat 5 bland, corny, trite, vapid 6 watery 7 insipid, sapless 8 waterish 9 hackneyed 10 namby-pamby, pedestrian, wishy-washy 11 commonplace

banality 6 cliché, truism 7 bromide 8 prosaism 9 platitude 10 prosaicism, shibboleth 11 commonplace

banana oil 5 hokum

banausic 4 blah, dull, poky 6 dreary, earthy, stodgy 7 humdrum, mundane, sensual, worldly 8 temporal 10 monotonous, pedestrian 13 materialistic

band 4 belt, club, crew, gang, gird, tape 5 bunch, corps, covey, group, party, strap, strip, troop, unite 6 concur, fillet, girdle, league, outfit, ribbon, streak, team up, troupe 7 cluster, combine, company, conjoin 8 begirdle, cincture, coadjute, engirdle, symphony 9 cooperate, orchestra 10 encincture 12 philharmonic *combining form:* 3 zon 4 taen, zono 5 taeni 6 taenio *Mexican:* 8 mariachi *neck:* 6 torque *of flowers:* 7 wreathe *small:* 5 combo

bandage 4 bind 5 dress 6 swathe 7 swaddle

bandanna 8 babushka, kerchief

bandeau 5 strip 6 fillet, ribbon, stripe 9 brassiere

banderilla 4 dart

banderole 4 flag, jack 6 banner, burgee, ensign, pennon 7 pennant 8 streamer

bandicoot 3 rat

bandit 6 badman, outlaw, raider, sacker 7 bandido, brigand, cateran, forager, ravager 8 marauder, pillager 9 cutthroat, desperado, holdup man, plunderer 10 freebooter, highwayman 11 bushwhacker *of India:* 6 dacoit

bandleader 7 maestro 8 choragus 9 conductor

bandolier 4 belt

bandwagon 3 fad 4 chic, mode, rage 5 craze, style, vogue 7 fashion

bandy 4 flip, toss 6 banter 8 exchange 11 interchange

bane 4 ruin 5 venom, virus 6 poison 7 bugaboo, bugbear, undoing 8 downfall 9 contagion, destroyer, ruination 11 destruction

baneful 4 dire 6 deadly 7 fateful, noxious, ominous 9 ill-boding, ill-omened, injurious, pestilent, unhealthy 10 pernicious 11 apocalyptic, pestiferous, threatening 12 pestilential, unpropitious

bang 3 bat, hit, pep, pop, rap 4 bash, beat, belt, blow, boom. clap, kick, push, shot, slam, sock, wham, whop 5 blast, burst, crash, noise, punch, sharp, smack, smash, sound, vigor, whack 6 thrill, wallop 7 surpass 8 smack-dab, squarely, vitality 9 explosion

Bangladesh *capital:* 5 Dacca, Dhaka *monetary unit:* 4 taka

bang-up 5 dandy 7 capital 8 five-star, top-notch, whiz-bang 9 excellent, first-rate 10 first-class 11 first-string

banish 4 oust 5 debar, eject, evict, exile, expel 6 deport, put out, run out 7 cast out, dismiss, exclude, expulse, shut out, turn out 8 displace, drive out, relegate 9 discharge, ostracize, rusticate 10 expatriate 13 excommunicate

banishment 5 exile 9 expulsion, ostracism 10 relegation 11 deportation 12 displacement

Bani's son 3 Uel 5 Amram, Rehum

banister 4 rail 7 railing 10 balustrade

bank 4 heap, hill, mass, pile, save 5 beach, coast, levee, mound, shore, stack, stash 6 invest, mārgin, rely on, rivage, strand 7 build on, count on, deposit, lay away, pyramid, trust in, trust to 8 depend on, lay aside, reckon on, rely upon, salt away, set aside, sock away 10 depend upon, streamside 11 calculate on 12 squirrel away

bank deal 4 loan

bankroll 4 back 5 stake 7 finance 9 grubstake 10 capitalize

bankrupt 4 bare, bust, do in, ruin 5 break, drain, strip, use up, wreck 6 divest, fold up, pauper 7 deplete, deprive, exhaust 9 pauperize 10 impoverish

bankruptcy 4 ruin 7 failure 9 depletion, sterility 10 barrenness, exhaustion

banned 7 illegal, illicit, tabooed 8 enjoined, verboten 9 forbidden 10 prohibited, proscribed

banner 4 flag, jack 6 bang-up, ensign, pennon 7 pendant, pennant 8 champion, five-star, gonfalon, gonfanon, standard, streamer, top-notch 9 banderole, excellent, first-rate, front-rank 10 blue-ribbon, first-class 11 first-string *Roman:* 7 labarum 8 vexillum

bannerol 4 flag, jack 6 ensign, pennon 7 pendant, pennant 8 streamer

banquet 4 feed 5 feast 6 dinner, junket, regale, repast, spread

banquette 4 seat 5 bench, shelf 8 platform

bantam 4 arch, fowl, grig, pert 5 saucy, small 6 little, petite 8 malapert, smallish

banter 3 fun, kid, rag, rib 4 fool, jest, jive, joke, josh, razz 5 chaff, jolly, tease 7 teasing 8 backchat, badinage, chitchat, exchange, repartee, snip-snap 9 small talk 10 persiflage 11 give-and-take

bantling 4 babe, baby 6 infant 7 neonate, newborn

baptize 3 dub 4 call, name 5 title 6 purify 7 asperse, cleanse, immerse 8 christen, sprinkle 9 designate 10 denominate

bar 3 ban, dam, pub, rod, tap 4 bate, café, curb, dive, halt, save, slab, snag, stop 5 block, brake, court, estop, fence, ingot, limit, stick, strip 6 billet, bistro, except, hinder, impede, lounge, saloon, tavern 7 barrier, buvette, cabaret, cantina, confine, delimit, exclude, gin mill, rule out, rummery, rumshop, suspend, taproom 8 alehouse, blockade, count out, drinkery, drunkery, grogshop, lawcourt, obstacle, obstruct, pothouse, prelimit, restrict, traverse, tribunal 9 aside from, barricade, eliminate, excluding, honky-tonk, nightclub, outside of, roadblock, roadhouse 11 exclusive of, obstruction, rathskeller 12 circumscribe, watering hole *fruit:* 4 line 5 olive *iron:* 6 rabble

barb 4 dart 5 shaft *combining form:* 3 onc 4 onch, onci, onco 5 oncho

Barbados *capital:* 10 Bridgetown *monetary unit:* 6 dollar

barbarian 3 Hun 4 Goth, rude, wild 5 brute 6 savage, Vandal 8 Visigoth 9 foreigner, Ostrogoth

barbarism 6 misuse 8 malaprop, slangism, solecism 9 neologism, vulgarism 10 corruption 11 impropriety, malapropism 13 vernacularism, vernacularity

barbarity 7 cruelty 8 atrocity 10 inhumanity

barbarous 4 fell, grim, rude, wild 5 cruel 6 brutal, fierce, Gothic, savage, unholy, vulgar, wicked 7 Hunnish, inhuman, lowbrow, uncivil, ungodly, wolfish 8 backward, fiendish, inhumane, sadistic 9 benighted, ferocious, graceless, heartless, primitive, tasteless, truculent 10 outlandish, outrageous, philistine, unmerciful 11 unchristian, uncivilized 12 uncultivated

Barbary ape 5 magot

Barbary state 5 Tunis 7 Algiers, Morocco, Tripoli

barbate 7 bearded 9 whiskered 11 bewhiskered

barber 6 shaver 7 clipper, cropper, friseur 8 coiffeur 9 coiffeuse 10 haircutter 11 hairdresser, hair stylist

Barber of Seville *author:* 12 Beaumarchais (Pierre-Augustin) *character:* 6 Figaro, Rosina, Rosine 7 Bartolo, Basilio 8 Almaviva, Bartholo *composer:* 7 Rossini (Gioacchino) 9 Paisiello (Giovanni)

barber's itch 8 ringworm

bard 4 muse, poet, scop 5 skald 8 jongleur, minstrel 10 Parnassian, troubadour

bardlet 6 rhymer 8 poetling, verseman 9 poetaster, poeticule, rhymester, versifier 10 versesmith 11 versemonger 12 versificator

Bard of Avon 11 Shakespeare (William)

bare 4 bald, mere, nude, open, show, very, void 5 clear, empty, naked, stark, strip 6 barren, denude, divest, expose, peeled, reveal, unclad, unveil, vacant 7 baldish, denuded, deprive, disrobe, emptied, exhibit, exposed, uncover, unrobed, vacuous 8 bankrupt, denudate, disclose, stripped 9 dismantle, unattired, unclothed, uncovered, undressed *combining form:* 4 gymn, nudi, psil 5 gymno, psilo

barefaced 5 blunt 6 arrant, brassy, brazen 7 blatant 8 impudent, overbold 9 shameless, unabashed 10 unblushing 11 temerarious

barefoot 6 unshod 8 shoeless 9 discalced 10 unsandaled 11 discalceate

bareheaded 7 hatless

barely 4 just 6 hardly, scarce 8 scarcely

bargain 3 buy 4 bond, deal, pact, swap 5 steal, trade, truck 6 barter, dicker, haggle, higgle, palter 7 chaffer, compact, traffic 8 closeout, contract, covenant, exchange, giveaway, huckster 9 agreement, negotiate 10 compromise, convention, loss leader, pennyworth 11 transaction

barge 4 scow 5 clump, stump 6 lumber 7 galumph, stumble

baritone *American:* 5 Gorin (Igor) 6 Milnes (Sherrill), Warren (Leonard) 7 MacNeil (Cornell), Merrill (Robert), Reardon (John), Tibbett (Lawrence) 8 Guarrera (Frank), Warfield (William) *English:* 6 Bailey (Norman) *German:* 4 Prey (Hermann) *Italian:* 5 Gobbi (Tito) 8 Raimondi (Ruggero)

barium *symbol:* 2 Ba

bark 3 arf, yap, yip 4 snap, woof, yelp 5 snarl *combining form:* 6 phello 7 cortico *Scottish:* 4 yaff

barkeeper see **bartender**

barkentine 4 ship

bark remover 4 spud 7 spudder

Barlow epic 9 Columbiad

barman see **bartender**

Barmecidal 8 apparent, illusive, illusory, semblant 10 ostensible

barn 6 stable 10 storehouse *area of:* 4 loft 7 hayloft

barnacle 5 leech 7 sponger 8 hanger-on, parasite 10 freeloader 11 bloodsucker 12 lounge lizard

barnstorm 4 tour 5 pilot 6 travel

Barnum *elephant:* 5 Jumbo *midget:* 8 Tom Thumb *partner:* 6 Bailey

barnyard 4 foul 5 dirty, nasty 6 coarse, filthy, smutty, vulgar 7 obscene, raunchy 8 indecent

baron 4 czar, king 5 mogul 6 tycoon 7 magnate

baronial 5 grand, noble, royal 6 august, lordly 7 stately 8 imposing, majestic 9 grandiose 11 magnificent

baroque 4 gilt, rich 6 florid, ornate, rococo 8 luscious 10 flamboyant, ornamented

Baroque *architect:* 7 Bernini (Gian Lorenzo) 8 Boromini (Francesco) *composer:* 4 Bach (Johann Sebastian, Wilhelm Friedmann) 6 Handel (George Frideric) 9 Scarlatti (Alessandro, Giuseppe) 10 Monteverdi (Claudio)l *painter:* 6 Rubens (Peter Paul) 7 El Greco, Poussin (Nicolas) 8 Carracci (Agustino, Annibale, Lodovico) 9 Velazquez (Diego) 10 Caravaggio *sculptor:* 7 Bernini (Gian Lorenzo), Coustou (Guillaume, Nicholas) 8 Coysevox (Antoine), Girardon (Francois)

bar pin 9 brochette

barrack 6 billet, casern 7 caserne 8 quarters

barracuda 4 fish, spet 5 barry, senet 6 becuna, becune, picuda, sennet 10 guaguanche, guaguancho

barrage 4 hail 5 burst, salvo, storm, surge 6 shower, stream, volley 8 drumfire 9 broadside, cannonade, fusillade 11 bombardment

barrel 3 keg, run, tun 4 butt, cask, much, peck, pipe, rush, whiz 5 fleet, hurry, speed 6 hasten 7 rundlet 8 hogshead 9 great deal *maker:* 6 cooper *part:* 4 hoop 5 stave *stopper:* 4 bung *support:* 6 gantry

barrelhouse 3 zip 4 dive, rush, whiz 5 hurry, joint 6 hasten, hustle 7 hangout 9 honky-tonk

barren 3 dry 4 arid 5 bleak, stark, waste 6 desert, effete, fallow 7 badland, parched, sterile 8 desertic, heirless, impotent, infecund, wild land 9 childless, infertile, unbearing, unfertile, wasteland 10 unfruitful, untillable, wilderness 12 hardscrabble, unproductive

barricade 3 bar 4 stop, wall 5 block, fence 7 barrier, railing 8 blockade 9 blank wall, roadblock *of trees:* 6 abatis

Barrie character 4 John 5 Peter, Tommy, Wendy 7 Michael 8 Crichton 9 Tiger Lily 10 Tinker Bell 11 Captain Hook

barrier see **barricade**

barring 3 but 4 save 6 bating, except, saving 9 aside from, excluding, outside of 11 exclusive of

barrister 6 lawyer 7 counsel 8 attorney

barroom 3 pub 6 lounge, saloon, tavern 7 taproom 8 dramshop, drinkery, groggery, grogshop

bar sinister 4 blot, blur, onus, slur, spot 5 brand, odium, stain 6 stigma 8 black eye

bartender 7 tapster 8 boniface 10 mixologist 12 saloonkeeper

barter 4 swap 5 trade, truck 7 bargain, traffic 8 exchange *Scottish:* 6 niffer

Bartered Bride composer 7 Smetana (Bedrich)

Baruch *father:* 6 Neriah, Zabbai *occupation:* 6 scribe

basal 5 basic 6 bottom, lowest 7 primary, radical 8 simplest 10 bottommost, elementary, nethermost, pedimental, rudimental, underlying 11 fundamental, rudimentary 12 foundational

base 3 bad, bed, fix, low 4 evil, foot, mean, poor, prop, root, seat, ugly, vile 5 build, cheap, dirty, found, lousy, lowly, nadir, plant, set up, sorry, stand, tatty 6 bottom, common, filthy, ground, humble, paltry, scurvy, shoddy, sleazy, sordid, trashy, wicked 7 bedrock, caitiff, footing, ignoble, lowborn, low-down, servile, squalid, support 8 beggarly, buttress, cowardly, pedestal, plebeian, recreant, unwashed, unworthy, wretched 9 construct, dastardly, degrading, establish, framework, loathsome, low-minded, predicate 10 abominable, despicable, foundation, groundwork, substratum, unennobled 11 disgraceful, humiliating, ignominious 12 contemptible, meanspirited, substructure, underpinning

baseball *abbreviation:* 2 AB, AL, BA, BB, BI, CF, DH, DP, ER, FA, HR, IP, LF, LP, NL, RF, SB, SO, SS, WP 3 ERA, HSP, LOB, MVP, PCT, RBI *reputed founder:* 9 Doubleday (Abner) *glove:* 4 mitt *official:* 3 ump 6 umpire *pitch:* 4 drop, heat 5 curve, smoke 6 change, heater, sinker, slider, slurve 7 spitter 8 change-up, fadeaway, fastball, fork ball, knuckler, palm ball, spitball 9 brushback, screwball 12 change of pace, knuckle curve *player:* 6 batter 7 baseman, catcher, fielder, pitcher 9 infielder, shortstop 10 outfielder 11 left fielder 12 right fielder 13 center fielder *practice fly ball:* 5 fungo *term:* 3 bag, bat, box, fan, fly, out, run, tag, tap, tip 4 balk, ball, base, bean, bunt, cage, deck, foul, hook, line, mitt, pill, pole, save, walk 5 alley, apple, bench, bloop, clout, count, drive, error, flare, glove, homer, liner, mound, pop-up, slide, swing 6 assist, clutch, double, dugout, groove, ground, inning, inside, pop fly, pop-out, powder, putout, rubber, runner, single, strike, triple, windup 7 battery, blooper, bullpen, cleanup, diamond, floater, fly ball, home run, infield, manager, outside, pickoff, rhubarb, sidearm, squeeze, stretch 8 baseline, beanball, delivery, foul ball, grounder, keystone, outfield, pinch-hit, rosin bag, southpaw 9 full count, home plate, hot corner, line drive, sacrifice, strikeout, two-bagger 10 double play, frozen rope, ground ball, scratch hit, strike zone 11 knuckleball, pinch hitter, squeeze play, three-bagger 12 Texas leaguer

baseballer 3 Ott (Mel) 4 Bell (George), Cobb (Ty), Cone (David), Dean (Dizzy), Fisk (Carlton), Ford (Whitey), Foxx (Jimmy), Kaat (Jim), Mays (Willie), Rice (Jim), Rose (Pete), Ruth (Babe), Ryan (Nolan) 5 Aaron (Henry), Anson (Cap), Banks (Ernie), Bench (Johnny), Berra (Yogi), Boggs (Wade), Bonds (Barry), Brett (George), Brock (Lou), Carew (Rod), Clark (Will), Davis (Mark), Grove (Lefty), Gwynn (Tony), Henke (Tom), Kiner (Ralph), Maris (Roger), Perez (Tony), Perry (Gaylord), Raines (Tim), Smith (Lee), Spahn (Warren), Staub (Rusty), Tiant (Louis), Viola (Frank), Young (Cy), Yount (Robin) 6 Dawson (Andre), Feller (Bob), Foster (George), Franco (John), Garvey (Steve), Gehrig (Lou), Gibson (Bob, Kirk), Gooden (Dwight), Herzog (Whitey), Hunter (Catfish), Koufax (Sandy), Maddox (Greg), Mantle (Mickey), Morgan (Joe), Murphy (Dale), Murray (Eddie), Musial (Stan), Palmer (Jim), Ripken (Cal), Seaver (Tom), Sutter (Bruce), Sutton (Don), Thomas (Frank), Wagner (Honus) 7 Bagwell (Jeff), Canseco (José), Carlton (Steve), Clemens (Roger), Coleman (Vince), Fingers (Rollie), Hornsby (Roger), Hubbell (Carl), Jackson (Reggie), Johnson (Walter), Justice (David), Puckett (Kirby), Reardon (Jeff), Schmidt (Mike), Speaker (Tris) 8 Anderson (Sparky), Blyleven (Bert), Clemente (Roberto), DiMaggio (Joe), Mitchell (Kevin), Righetti (Dave), Robinson (Brooks, Frank, Jackie), Williams (Ted), Winfield (Dave) 9 Alexander (Grover), Eckersley (Dennis), Henderson (Rickey), Hernandez (Willie), Hershiser (Orel), Killebrew (Harmon), Mattingly (Don) 10 Campanella (Roy), Conigliaro (Tony), Strawberry (Darryl), Valenzuela (Fernando) 11 Yastrzemski (Carl)

baseball team see **American League; National League**

baseboard 7 molding 8 skirting

baseborn 3 low 4 mean 5 lowly 6 humble 7 bastard, ignoble, natural 8 plebeian, spurious, unwashed 11 misbegotten 12 illegitimate

baseless 4 idle, vain 5 empty, false, wrong 9 pointless, senseless, unfounded, untenable 10 gratuitous, groundless, ungrounded 11 uncalled-for, unnecessary, unsupported, unsustained, unwarranted 12 indefensible 13 unjustifiable

basement 6 bottom, ground 10 foundation, groundwork, substratum 12 substructure

base on balls 4 pass, walk

bash 3 bat 4 belt, blow, slam, whop 5 crack, party, smack, smash, whack 6 soiree, wallop 7 blowout, shindig

Bashan *last king:* 2 Og *people:* 7 Rephaim

Bashemath *father:* 7 Ishmael *husband:* 4 Esau *sister:* 8 Nebaioth

bashful 3 coy, shy 5 mousy, timid 6 demure, modest 7 abashed 8 retiring, timorous 9 diffident, recoiling, shrinking, unassured 11 embarrassed, unassertive

basic 4 main 5 basal, chief 6 bottom 7 capital, element, primary, radical 8 rudiment 9 elemental, essential, primitive, principal 10 elementary, substratal, underlying 11 fundamental 12 foundational 13 part and parcel

basically 6 au fond 9 in essence 11 essentially 13 fundamentally

basic point 4 crux, gist 7 essence

basin 3 cwm, dip, sag 4 sink 6 cirque, hollow 7 sinkage 8 sinkhole, washbowl 9 concavity 10 depression *liturgical:* 5 stoup 7 piscina

basis 4 root, seat 5 axiom, heart, right 6 bottom, ground, reason 7 bedrock, essence, footing, grounds, premise, theorem, warrant 9 postulate, principle 10 assumption, foundation, groundwork, substratum 11 fundamental, presumption 12 substructure, underpinning 13 justification

bask 3 sun 4 roll 5 revel 6 wallow, welter 7 indulge, rollick 9 luxuriate

basket 5 frail 6 dosser, gabion 7 pannier *angler's:* 5 creel

basketball *inventor:* 8 Naismith (James) *official:* 6 umpire 7 referee *player:* 5 cager, guard 6 center 7 forward 8 hoopster, swingman 10 point guard *team:* 4 five 7 quintet *term:* 3 gun, jam, key 4 cage, dunk, pass 5 board, lay-up, press, shoot, tip-in 6 freeze, tap-off, tip-off, travel 7 dribble, keyhole, rebound, throw-in, timeout 8 alley-oop, jump ball, slam dunk 9 backboard, backcourt, field goal, free throw 11 ball control

basketballer 3 Bol (Manute) 4 Bird (Larry), Reed (Willis), West (Jerry, Mark) 5 Barry (Rick), Cousy (Bob), Ewing (Patrick), Mikan (George), O'Neal (Shaquille), Price (Mark) 6 Baylor (Elgin), Cowens (Dave), Erving (Julius), Gervin (George), Jordan (Michael), Malone (Jeff, Karl, Moses), McAdoo (Bob), McHale (Kevin), Miller (Reggie), Parish (Robert), Pierce (Ricky), Pippin (Scottie), Skiles (Scott), Thorpe (Otis), Walton (Bill), Worthy (James) 7 Barkley (Charles), Dawkins (Darryl), Edwards (James), Frazier (Walt), Johnson (Magic), Russell (Bill), Rollins (Tree), Wilkins (Dominique) 8 Auerbach (Red), Havlicek (John), Olajuwon (Akeem), Robinson (David), Stockton (John), Williams (Buck) 9 Donaldson (James), Robertson (Oscar) 11 Abdul-Jabbar (Kareem), Chamberlain (Wilt)

Basmath's father 7 Solomon

Basque *cap:* 5 beret *game:* 6 pelota 7 jai alai *mountains:* 8 Pyrenees *province:* 5 Alava 7 Vizcaya 9 Guipuzcoa

bass 6 singer 7 crappie, jewfish, sunfish 8 cabrilla *American:* 5 Hines (Jerome), Ramey (Samuel), Tozzi (Giorgio) 6 Morris (James) 7 Plishka (Paul), Robeson (Paul) 8 Flagello (Ezio) *Bulgarian:* 8 Ghiaurov (Nicolai) *Italian:* 5 Siepi (Cesare) 8 Raimondi (Ruggero) *Russian:* 9 Chaliapin (Fyodor) *Swiss:* 6 Corena (Fernando)

Bassanio's beloved 6 Portia

bassinet 4 pram 9 baby buggy 12 baby carriage, perambulator

bastard 5 cross 6 by-blow, hybrid 7 mongrel 8 baseborn, spurious, whoreson 10 fatherless, unfathered 11 chance child, misbegotten 12 filius populi, illegitimate, natural child 13 filius nullius *combining form:* 4 noth 5 notho

bastardize 4 warp 6 debase 7 corrupt, debauch, deprave, pervert, vitiate 9 brutalize 10 bestialize, demoralize

bastardly 4 mean 12 contemptible

baste 3 wig 4 beat, drub, lash, mill, pelt, rail, whip 5 paste, scold 6 batter, berate, larrup, pummel, stitch, thrash, wallop 7 bawl out, belabor, chew out, clobber, tell off 8 bless out 10 tongue-lash

bastille 4 jail 6 prison

bastinado 3 bat 4 bash, beat, blow 5 crack, pound, smack, smash, stick, whack 6 cudgel, thwack, wallop 8 bludgeon

bastion 7 bulwark, parapet, rampart 10 breastwork

bat 3 bag, bop, bum, gad, hag, jag 4 belt, biff, blow, bust, club, mace, roam, rove, slam, sock, tear, trot, whop, wink 5 baton, biddy, binge, blink, booze, crack, crone, drunk, mooch, smack, spree, witch 6 beldam, bender, cudgel, ramble, rantan, thwack, wander 7 meander, nictate, traipse, twinkle 8 bludgeon 9 chiropter, flying fox, gallivant, nictitate, reremouse, truncheon 10 knobkerrie, shillelagh *combining form:* 8 nycteris *European:* 7 noctule 8 serotine 9 pipistrel 11 pipistrelle *Malaysian:* 6 kalong

batch 3 lot, set 5 array, bunch, clump, group 6 bundle, clutch, parcel 7 cluster

bate 4 omit 6 deduct, except 7 exclude 8 moderate, restrain

bath 3 spa, tub 4 wash 5 hydro, wells 6 shower 7 springs 13 watering place *combining form:* 5 balne 6 balneo *relating to:* 7 balneal

bathe 3 lap, lip, sop, tub 4 bask, lave, soak, soap, wash 5 douse, flush, souse 6 shower

bathetic 5 mushy, soppy, stale, tired, trite 6 cliché 7 clichéd, maudlin, mawkish 9 hackneyed 11 commonplace, sentimental, stereotyped, tear-jerking 13 stereotypical

bathhouse 5 sauna

bathing suit 6 bikini, trunks 7 maillot

bathroom 2 WC 6 toilet 8 lavatory

Bathsheba *father:* 5 Eliam *husband:* 5 David, Uriah *son:* 7 Solomon

bathtub gin 5 hooch 7 bootleg 9 moonshine 11 mountain dew

bating 3 bar, but 4 save 6 except, saving 7 barring 9 aside from, excluding, outside of 11 exclusive of

baton 4 club, mace, wand 5 billy 6 cudgel 7 war club 8 bludgeon 9 billy club, truncheon 10 nightstick

batrachian 4 frog, toad 9 amphibian 10 salientian

batter 4 beat, drub, lame, maim, maul 5 baste, pound, wreck 6 bruise, buffet, bung up, mangle, pummel, thrash, wallop 7 belabor, clobber, contuse, cripple, disable, lambast, shatter 8 lacerate, lambaste, mutilate 9 disfigure

battery 3 lot 4 body 5 array, batch, bunch, clump, group 6 bundle 7 cluster

battery terminal 5 anode 7 cathode

battle 3 tug, war 5 brush, clash, fight 6 action, assail, attack, combat, oppugn, sortie 7 assault, bombard, contend, contest 8 conflict, skirmish 9 encounter, onslaught, scrimmage 10 engagement 11 hostilities *combining form:* 5 machy

battle-ax 6 twibil 7 twibill

Battle Born State 6 Nevada

battle cry 5 motto 9 catchword *Japanese:* 6 banzai

battlement 7 parapet

battlesome 6 brawly 7 scrappy 8 brawling 9 brawlsome 11 quarrelsome

batty 4 nuts 5 crazy, wacky 6 crazed, insane, maniac, screwy 7 cracked 8 deranged 9 bedlamite

bauble 5 curio 6 gewgaw, trifle 7 bibelot, novelty, trinket, whatnot 8 gimcrack 9 objet d'art 10 knickknack

Baucis' husband 8 Philemon

bavardage 6 by-talk 8 chitchat, trifling 9 small talk

Bavaria 6 Bayern *capital:* 6 Munich *city:* 8 Augsburg, Bayreuth, Wurzburg 9 Nurem-

burg *king:* 6 Ludwig *patron saint:* 6 Rupert

bawd 4 drab, moll 5 poule, whore 6 harlot, hooker 8 meretrix 10 prostitute 11 nightwalker 12 streetwalker

bawdy house 4 stew 6 bagnio 7 brothel 8 bordello, cathouse, joyhouse 10 whorehouse 11 parlor house 13 sporting house

bawl 3 cry, sob 4 howl, roar, rout, wail, weep, yell, yowl 5 shout 6 bellow, boohoo, clamor, holler, scream, shriek, squall, yammer 7 blubber, bluster, screech.

bawl out 3 wig 4 lash 5 scold 6 berate 7 chew out, condemn, tell off, upbraid 8 bless out, denounce 10 tongue-lash

bay 3 arm 4 cove, gulf, howl, wail 5 award, badge, bayou, bight, creek, firth, honor, inlet, kudos, quest 6 harbor, slough 7 laurels, ululate 8 accolade 10 decoration 11 distinction *Aegean Sea:* 5 Anzac *Africa:* 6 Walvis *Alaska:* 7 Glacier *Angola:* 5 Bengo, Tiger 6 Tigres *Antarctica:* 3 Ice 8 Amundsen *Arabian Sea:* 4 Qamr 5 Kamar *Argentina:* 6 Blanca *Australia:* 5 Anson, Shark 6 Botany, Sharks 9 Discovery *Baltic:* 4 Hano, Kiel 6 Danzig, Kieler 9 Pomerania 10 Pomeranian, Pommersche *Barents Sea:* 4 Kola 7 Pechora *Beaufort Sea:* 7 Prudhoe 9 Mackenzie *Bismarck Sea:* 5 Kimbe *Brazil:* 9 Guanabara *Bristol Channel:* 10 Carmarthen *California:* 5 Morro 8 Monterey, San Diego 12 San Francisco *Canada:* 5 Fundy *Cape Breton Island:* 4 Mira *Capetown:* 5 Table *Caribbean Sea:* 5 Limon 8 Chetumal *Central America:* 7 Fonseca *China:* 4 Mirs *Crete:* 4 Suda 5 Canea *Cuba:* 4 Broa, Mora, Nipe 10 Guantanamo *Dominican Republic:* 4 Ocoa *East River:* 8 Flushing *Ecuador:* 5 Manta *Egypt:* 6 Abukir 7 Aboukir *Eire:* 4 Clew 7 Brandon *English Channel:* 3 Tor 4 Lyme 5 Seine *Estonia:* 5 Parnu 6 Pyarnu *Europe:* 6 Biscay 11 Aquitanicus *Florida:* 8 Biscayne *Greenland:* 5 Disko 6 Baffin 8 Melville *Gulf of Alaska:* 3 Icy 5 Woman 12 Resurrection *Gulf of Boothia:* 5 Pelly *Gulf of California:* 5 Adair *Gulf of Guinea:* 5 Benin, Bonny 6 Biafra *Gulf of Mexico:* 5 Tampa 6 Mobile 7 Aransas 8 Campeche, Sarasota 9 Matagorda, Pensacola 10 San Antonio, Terrebonne 11 Atchafalaya, Ponce de Leon 12 Apalachicola 13 Corpus Christi *Gulf of St. Lawrence:* 5 Bonne, Gaspé *Hawaii:* 5 Koloa, Lawai *Hong Kong:* 4 Deep *Honshu:* 3 Ise 5 Mutsu, Osaka, Owari, Tokyo 6 Atsuta, Sagami *Hudson River:* 7 New York *Iceland:* 4 Faxa, Huna 8 Faxafloi *Indian Ocean:* 6 Bengal 15 Great Australian *Indonesia:* 4 Bima, Kayo 5 Saleh 8 Humboldt *Irish Sea:*

4 Luce 7 Dundalk *Jamaica:* 4 Long *Japan:*
4 Tosa *Java:* 4 Lada 5 Peper *Java Sea:*
7 Batavia 8 Djakarta *Kara Sea:* 6 Enisei
7 Yenisei *Lake Erie:* 8 Sandusky *Lake
Huron:* 7 Saginaw, Thunder *Lake Michigan:* 5 Green 13 Grand Traverse *Lake
Ontario:* 11 Irondequoit *Lake Superior:*
5 Huron 8 Keweenaw 9 Whitefish *land-
locked:* 5 Lamon *Long Island Sound:*
6 Oyster *Madagascar:* 8 Antongil *Maine:*
5 Casco 7 Machias 9 Penobscot *Marquesas Islands:* 5 Anaho *Maryland-Virginia:*
10 Chesapeake 12 Chincoteague *Massachusetts:* 6 Boston 7 Cape Cod 8 Buzzards, Plymouth *Mediterranean:* 9 Famagusta *Mozambique:* 5 Memba, Pemba
Nantucket Sound: 5 Lewis *New Brunswick:* 13 Passamaquoddy *Newfoundland:*
4 Hare 5 White 7 Fortune *New Guinea:*
3 Oro 5 Berau, Hansa, Milne *New Jersey:*
5 Great 6 Newark 7 Raritan 8 Barnegat
New York: 7 Jamaica *New Zealand:*
5 Hawke 6 Tasman 11 Hauraki Gulf *North
Carolina:* 6 Onslow *North Sea:* 4 Jade
9 Jadebusen *Northwest Territories:*
5 Wager 7 Repulse 8 Franklin 9 Frobisher
Nova Scotia: 8 Cobequid *Oregon:*
4 Coos *Philippines:* 5 Baler, Pilar, Sogod
6 Butuan *Puerto Rico:* 5 Sucia *Quebec:*
6 Ungava *Red Sea:* 4 Foul *Rhode Island:*
12 Narragansett *Russia:* 4 Amur 5 Aniva,
Chaun 6 Ussuri 7 Amurski *Scotland:*
5 Enard *Sea of Japan:* 13 Peter the Great
Solomon Islands: 4 Deep *South Africa:*
5 Algoa, False *South Carolina:* 4 Bull,
Long *South China Sea:* 4 Bias, Datu,
Taya 5 Dasol, Subic, Subig 6 Brunei, Paluan 7 Camranh *Spain:* 5 Cadiz 9 Gibraltar *Spitsbergen:* 5 Cross, Kings *Sri Lanka:*
4 Palk *Strait of Gibraltar:* 7 Tangier
Sumatra: 5 Bajur 10 Koninginne *Sydney:*
6 Botany *Tasmania:* 5 Storm *Texas:*
7 Trinity *Tyrrhenian Sea:* 6 Naples
7 Paestum *Wales:* 9 Carnarvon 10 Caer-
narvon *Washington:* 5 Dabob 6 Skagit
Western Sahara: 8 Rio de Oro *West
Indies:* 5 Coral *White Sea:* 5 Onega *Yellow Sea:* 5 Korea

baygall 3 bog, fen 4 mire, moss, quag,
sump 5 marsh, swamp 6 morass
9 swampland

bayou 3 arm, bay 4 cove, gulf 5 bight,
creek, firth, inlet 6 harbor, slough *Louisiana:* 5 Macon 9 Lafourche 10 Terrebonne
Mississippi: 9 Chickasaw

Bay State 13 Massachusetts

bay window 3 pod, pot 6 paunch 8 potbelly 11 corporation

bazoo 3 boo 4 bird, hiss, hoot, pooh, razz
7 catcall 8 pooh-pooh 9 raspberry
10 Bronx cheer

bazooka's target 4 tank

be 4 go on, hold, live, move 5 abide, exist,
stand 6 endure, obtain, remain 7 breathe,
persist, prevail, subsist 8 continue

beach 4 bank 5 coast, shore, wreck 6 pile
up, strand 8 cast away, lakeside 9 lake-
shore, shipwreck 10 oceanfront *Hawaii:*
7 Waikiki *Massachusetts:* 9 Nantasket
New York: 10 Fire Island

____ **Beach** 5 Dover

beached 7 aground 8 grounded, stranded

beachhead 8 foothold

beachwear see **bathing suit**

beacon 5 flare 6 pharos 7 bonfire 8 balefire 9 watchfire 10 lighthouse

beak 3 neb, nib 4 bill, cape, naze, nose,
peck, pick 5 point, snoot, snout 6 beezer,
pecker 7 sneezer 8 foreland, headland
9 proboscis, schnozzle 10 promontory
combining form: 5 rostr 6 rhamph, rostri,
rostro 7 rhampho 8 rhynchus

beaklike part 7 rostrum

be-all and end-all 3 sum 4 pith, root,
soul, tote 5 stuff, total, whole 6 bottom,
marrow 7 essence 8 entirety, sum total,
totality 9 aggregate, substance 10 rock
bottom 12 quintessence

beam 3 can, ray 4 balk, burn, grin, rear,
seat 5 fanny, gleam, shaft, shine, shoot,
smile 6 behind, bottom, lintel, rafter, timber
7 radiate 8 backside, buttocks, crosstie,
derriere 9 posterior

beaming 6 bright, lucent 7 fulgent, lambent, radiant 8 luminous 9 brilliant, effulgent, refulgent 12 incandescent

bean 3 dry, wax 4 bush, coco, conk,
dome, head, lima, mung, navy, pole, poll,
snap, soya 5 baked, brain, broad, horse,
jelly, pinto 6 belfry, coffee, frijol, kidney,
noddle, noggin, noodle, string 7 frijole,
jumping 9 headpiece 10 stringless *of India:*
3 urd

beano 5 bingo

Bean Town 6 Boston

beany 5 fiery 6 spunky 7 gingery, peppery
8 spirited 10 mettlesome 11 high-hearted
12 high-spirited

bear 2 go 3 act, bow, jag, jam, lug, try
4 born, buck, form, go on, have, head,
hump, lump, make, pack, push, quit, show,
take, tote 5 abide, allow, apply, beget,
birth, breed, bring, brook, bruin, carry,
crowd, crush, defer, ferry, fruit, press, refer,
shape, squab, stand, stick, touch, yield
6 accept, acquit, affect, attend, behave,
convey, convoy, create, demean, deport,
digest, endure, escort, invent, permit,
pocket, relate, seller, set out, squash,
squish, squush, submit, suffer 7 afflict,
comport, concern, condone, conduct,
deliver, display, exhibit, fashion, involve,

pertain, possess, produce, squeeze, stomach, support, sustain, swallow, take off, torment, torture, turn out 8 chaperon, engender, fructify, generate, light out, multiply, parallel, shoulder, stick out, sweat out, tolerate, tough out 9 accompany, acquiesce, appertain, companion, fabricate, procreate, propagate, reproduce, strike out, transport 10 bring forth, correspond 11 consort with, countenance *Alaskan:* 5 polar 6 kodiak *Australian:* 5 koala *combining form:* 4 arct 5 arcto *family:* 7 Ursidae *genus:* 5 Ursus *kind:* 3 sun 5 black, brown, honey, koala, polar, sloth 6 kodiak 7 grizzly 10 spectacled *relating to:* 6 ursine *young:* 3 cub

bearable 7 livable 9 allowable, endurable, tolerable 10 acceptable, admissible, sufferable 11 supportable, sustainable 12 satisfactory

bear cat 5 panda 9 binturong

beard 4 barb, dare, defy, face, fuzz 5 brave, front 6 beaver, goatee 7 galways, outdare, outface, stubble, Vandyke, venture 8 imperial, whiskers 9 burnsides, challenge 11 muttonchops 12 side-whiskers *combining form:* 5 pogon 6 pogono *on grain:* 3 awn *pointed:* 6 goatee 7 Vandyke

bearded 5 hairy 7 barbate, goateed, stubbed, stubbly 8 unshaven 9 whiskered 11 bewhiskered

bear down 5 crush 6 defeat, reduce, subdue 7 conquer 8 vanquish 9 overpower, subjugate

bearer 5 envoy 6 coolie, porter, redcap, skycap 7 bellboy, bellhop, bellman, carrier, courier, drogher 8 cargador, emissary 9 messenger 11 internuncio *combining form:* 3 fer 4 pher, phor 5 phora, phore 6 phorae (plural), phorum

bearing 3 air, set 4 brow, look, mien, port, pose 5 birth, front, poise, stand 6 aspect, stance 7 address, conduct, display, posture 8 attitude, behavior, birthing, carriage, delivery, demeanor, presence 10 childbirth, deportment 11 comportment, parturition *combining form:* 6 ferous, gerous, parous 7 igerous, phorous

bearish 5 waspy 6 cranky, ornery 7 dubious, waspish 8 cankered, vinegary 9 crotchety, declining 10 vinegarish 11 pessimistic 12 cantankerous

bearlike 6 ursine, ursoid 8 ursiform

bear out 6 verify 7 confirm, justify 8 validate 11 corroborate 12 authenticate, substantiate

bear up 4 prop 5 brace, carry 6 uphold 7 bolster, shore up, support, sustain 8 buttress

beast 5 brute 6 animal 7 beastie, critter, varmint 8 behemoth, creature 9 quadruped

combining form: 4 ther 5 thero 6 theria (plural), therio 7 therium

beastly 5 brute, feral 6 animal, brutal, ferine 7 bestial, brutish, swinish

beat 2 do 3 get, gyp, lam, tan, top, wag, win 4 balk, best, bilk, cane, comb, dash, drub, drum, dump, flog, foil, grub, lace, lash, lick, maul, pelt, rake, ruin, trim, wale, wave, welt, whip, whop 5 baste, baton, cheat, cozen, curry, excel, lay on, meter, outdo, paste, pound, pulse, rhyme, scoop, scour, smear, stick, stump, swing, throb, tromp, whisk 6 baffle, batter, better, buffet, chouse, cudgel, diddle, exceed, forage, hammer, larrup, muss up, pummel, rhythm, search, switch, thrash, thwart, waggle, wallop, woggle 7 belabor, buffalo, cadence, cadency, clobber, conquer, defraud, lambast, measure, nonplus, prevail, pulsate, ransack, rough up, rummage, shellac, smother, surpass, triumph, trounce 8 bludgeon, finecomb, flimflam, lambaste, malleate, outshine, outstrip, overcome, rhythmus 9 bastinado, exclusive, frustrate, fustigate, overreach, palpitate, transcend 10 circumvent, disappoint, pistol-whip

beat down 5 crush 6 defeat, reduce, subdue 7 conquer 8 vanquish 9 overpower, subjugate

beating 4 rout 5 lumps 6 defeat, hiding 7 debacle, licking 8 drubbing 9 overthrow, pulsating, thrashing 10 defeasance 11 shellacking 12 vanquishment

beatitude 5 bliss 7 ecstasy, rapture 9 happiness, transport 11 blessedness 12 blissfulness

Beatles 4 John, Paul 5 Ringo 6 George

beau 5 flame, lover, swain 6 steady 7 beloved 8 truelove, young man 9 boyfriend, inamorato 10 sweetheart

Beau Brummel 3 fop 5 dandy 7 coxcomb 8 macaroni 9 exquisite 11 petit-maître 12 lounge lizard

beau ideal 5 model 6 mirror 7 example, pattern 8 ensample, exemplar, paradigm, standard 9 archetype

Beaumarchais' hero 6 Figaro

beauteous 4 fair 5 bonny 6 comely, lovely, pretty 8 handsome 10 attractive 11 good-looking

beautiful 4 fair 5 bonny 6 choice, comely, lovely, pretty, proper, superb 7 elegant, sublime 8 glorious, gorgeous, handsome, pleasing, splendid, stunning 9 exquisite 10 attractive, eye-filling, personable 11 good-looking, resplendent, well-favored 12 eye-appealing *combining form:* 4 call, calo 5 calli, callo

beautiful people 6 jet set 8 smart set

beautify 4 deck, trim 5 adorn, grace, prank 6 bedeck 7 dress up, garnish 8 decorate, ornament, prettify 9 embellish, glamorize

beauty 5 belle, dream, peach, toast 6 eyeful, looker, lovely 7 charmer, dazzler, stunner 8 knockout 9 eye-opener 10 goodlooker *combining form:* 4 cali, calo 5 calli, callo

beaver 5 beard 6 rodent 8 whiskers *family:* 10 Castoridae *genus:* 6 Castor *home:* 5 lodge *young:* 3 kit, pup

Beaver State 6 Oregon

becalm 4 lull 5 allay, quiet, still 6 settle, soothe 7 compose, quieten 11 tranquilize

because 2 as 3 for, now 5 being, since 6 seeing 7 whereas 8 as long as 10 inasmuch as 11 considering

because of 4 over 5 due to 7 owing to, through

Becher's father 7 Ephraim 8 Benjamin

Beckett work 4 Play, Watt 6 Molloy, Murphy 7 Endgame 9 Happy Days 14 Krapp's Last Tape 15 Waiting for Godot

becloud 3 dim, fog 4 blur 5 bedim, befog, muddy 6 darken, puzzle 7 confuse, eclipse, obscure, perplex 8 befuddle 9 obfuscate

become 2 go 3 fit, get, run, wax 4 corrie, grow, rise, soar, suit, turn 5 arise, befit, mount 6 go with 7 enhance, flatter 9 agree with 10 go together *suffix:* 3 ize

becoming 4 nice 5 right 6 decent, proper, seemly 7 correct, fitting 8 decorous, suitable, tasteful 9 befitting 10 attractive, conforming, flattering 11 appropriate, comme il faut *suffix:* 6 escent 7 escence

bed 3 cot 4 base, bunk, flop, rest, seat, twin 5 basis 6 bottom, cradle, double, ground, Murphy, pallet, pile in, retire, roll in, tuck in, turn in 7 bedrock, trundle 8 rollaway 10 foundation, substratum *combining form:* 4 clin 5 clino *of India:* 7 charpai, charpoy

Bedad's son 5 Hadad

bedamn 4 cuss 5 curse, swear 8 execrate 9 imprecate

bedaub 3 dab 5 smarm, smear 6 smudge 7 besmear, plaster

bedaze 4 stun 6 bemuse, benumb 7 petrify, stupefy 8 paralyze

bedazzle 4 daze 5 blind

bedbug 5 cimex 6 chinch 7 cimices (plural)

bedcover 5 quilt 6 afghan, spread 8 coverlet, coverlid 11 counterpane

bedeck 4 trim 5 adorn, prank 6 bedaub 7 bedizen, dress up, garnish 8 beautify, decorate, ornament 9 embellish

Bedeiah's father 4 Bani

bedevil 5 annoy, harry, tease, worry 6 harass, pester, plague 7 hagride, wherret 9 tantalize

bedevilment 7 trouble 8 disorder, vexation 9 confusion

bedfellow 4 ally 9 associate

bedim 3 fog 5 befog, cloud, gloom 6 darken 7 becloud, eclipse, obscure 9 obfuscate

bedlamite 3 mad, nut 4 loon, nuts 5 batty, crazy, loony 6 dement, insane, madman, maniac 7 cracked, lunatic, madling 8 demented, deranged 9 non compos

bedog 3 tag 4 tail 5 trail 6 shadow

bedouin 4 Arab 5 nomad

bedraggled 5 faded, seedy 6 shabby, tagrag 7 rundown 8 decrepit, tattered 10 down-at-heel, threadbare 11 dilapidated

bedridden 4 weak 6 feeble, infirm, laid up, sickly 7 bedfast 8 confined 13 incapacitated

bedrock 4 base, root 5 basis 6 ground 7 footing 10 foundation, groundwork, substratum 12 substructure, underpinning

bedroom 7 boudoir

bedspread 8 coverlet, coverlid 11 counterpane

bed-wetting 8 enuresis

bee *combining form:* 3 api *family:* 6 Apidae 8 Bombidae *food:* 6 nectar *genus:* 4 Apis 5 Osmia 6 Bombus 8 Ceratina 9 Megachile *glue:* 8 propolis *group:* 5 swarm 6 colony *house:* 6 apiary *kind:* 5 drone, mason, queen 6 cuckoo, mining, sewing, worker 8 honeybee, quilting, spelling 9 bumblebee, carpenter 10 leafcutter *nest:* 4 hive, skep *product:* 3 wax 5 honey *relating to:* 5 apian 8 apiarian *study of:* 8 apiology *wax cells:* 9 honeycomb

beechnuts 4 mast

beef 3 arm 4 crab, fuss, miff, thew, tiff, yaup, yawp 5 bitch, bleat, boost, brawl, brawn, force, gripe, might, power, sinew, steam, vigor 6 energy, expand, extend, muscle, squawk, yammer 7 augment, blow off, dispute, enlarge, magnify, quarrel, rhubarb 8 heighten, increase, multiply, squabble, strength 9 bellyache, bickering, strong arm 10 aggrandize, falling-out 11 altercation *cut:* 3 rib 4 loin, rump, side 5 chuck, flank, plate, round, shank 7 brisket, sirloin 10 tenderloin *grade:* 4 good 5 prime 6 choice 7 utility 8 standard 10 commercial *order:* 4 rare 6 medium 8 well-done

beefeater 6 warder, yeoman

beefheaded 4 dull 5 dense 6 stupid 10 numskulled

beefy 5 burly, hefty, husky

Beehive State 4 Utah

beekeeper 8 apiarian, apiarist 12 apiculturist

beekeeping 10 apiculture

Beeliada's father 5 David

beeline 3 nip, zip 4 whiz 5 hurry, speed
6 bullet, hustle, rocket 7 hotfoot 8 highball

Beelzebub 5 devil, fiend, Satan 6 diablo
7 Lucifer, Old Nick, serpent 8 Apollyon
10 Old Scratch 13 Old Gooseberry

beer 3 ale 4 bock, brew 5 draft, lager,
stout, weiss 6 porter 7 pilsner 8 pilsener
cup: 3 mug 4 toby 5 stein 6 flagon, seidel
7 tankard 8 schooner 9 blackjack *drinking
place:* 3 inn, pub 6 saloon, tavern *ingredient:* 4 hops, malt 5 yeast 6 barley *maker:*
6 brewer *mythical inventor:* 9 Gambrinus
plant: 7 brewery *Russian:* 5 kvass *Scottish:* 10 barley-bree, barley-broo *slang:*
4 suds *Tibetan:* 5 chang

beer hall 5 stube 8 alehouse, mughouse

Beeri *daughter:* 6 Judith *son:* 5 Hosea

beet 5 chard 6 mangel, wurzel 7 mangold
family: 9 goosefoot

Beethoven, Ludwig van *birthplace:*
4 Bonn *opera:* 7 Fidelio *overture:*
6 Egmont 7 Leonore 10 Coriolanus, Prometheus *sonata:* 8 Kreutzer, Pastoral
9 Moonlight 10 Pathetique *symphony:*
6 Choral, Eroica 8 Pastoral

beetle 3 jut 4 hang, poke, pout 5 bulge,
pouch 7 project 8 bend over, lean over,
overhang, protrude, stand out, stick out
click: 6 cucuyo, elater 7 firefly 8 cucu-
bano, skipjack *dung:* 6 scarab 9 tumblebug *front wing:* 6 elytra (plural) 7 elytron
fruit-eating: 8 curculio *insect-eating:*
7 ladybug 8 ladybird *kind:* 3 dor 4 bean,
dorr, dung, fire, June, stag 5 click, flour,
grain, tiger, water 6 carpet, chafer, dor bug,
ground, May bug, meloid, museum 7 blister, cadelle, carabid, firefly, goldbug,
goliath, June bug, vedalia 8 ambrosia,
figeater, Japanese, lampyrid, passalid,
pinch bug 9 bombadier, longicorn, potato
bug 10 cockchafer, rhinoceros *order:*
10 Coleoptera *ornamental:* 6 scarab
sacred: 6 scarab *snouted:* 6 weevil 7 billbug 8 curculio 9 wood borer *young:*
4 grub 5 larva 8 wireworm

beetlehead 4 dolt, dope 5 dunce
8 dumbbell

beetleheaded 4 dull 5 dense 6 stupid
10 numskulled

beet soup 6 borsch, borsht 7 borscht

befall 2 go 3 hap 5 break, occur 6 betide,
chance, happen 7 come off, develop, fall
out

befit 4 suit 6 become, go with 9 agree with
10 go together

befitting 3 apt 4 just, meet, nice 5 happy,
right 6 decent, proper, seemly 7 correct
8 becoming, decorous, suitable 10 conforming, felicitous 11 appropriate, comme il
faut *suffix:* 2 ly

befog 3 dim 4 blur 5 bedim, cloud, muddy
6 darken, puzzle 7 becloud, confuse,
eclipse, obscure, perplex, stumble 8 bewilder, confound 9 obfuscate, overcloud
13 metagrobolize

befool 4 dupe, gull, hoax 5 trick 7 chicane
8 hoodwink 9 bamboozle, victimize
11 hornswoggle

before 2 to 3 ere 4 ante, once, then, till,
up to 5 ahead, until 6 facing, sooner, up till
7 ahead of, already, earlier, forward, prior to
8 formerly, previous 9 erstwhile, in
advance, preceding 10 heretofore, previously 11 confronting, in advance of, precedently 12 antecedently *combining form:*
4 fore 6 proter 7 protero *prefix:* 2 ob
3 pre, pro 4 ante

befoul 4 slur 5 dirty, smear 6 defame,
malign 7 blacken, pollute, slander, spatter,
traduce 9 bespatter, denigrate 11 contaminate

befuddle 4 daze 5 addle, mix up 6 ball up
7 confuse, fluster 8 bewilder, distract, throw
off 9 bumfuzzle

befuddlement 3 fog 4 daze, haze, maze
5 mix-up 9 confusion 10 muddlement
11 muddledness

beg 3 ask, nag, sue 4 pray 5 brace,
cadge, crave, plead, press, worry 6 appeal,
call on, demand, invoke, obtest 7 beseech,
besiege, conjure, entreat, implore, request,
solicit 8 petition 9 importune 10 supplicate

begem 5 beset, jewel 7 bejewel, enjewel

beget 4 bear, sire 5 breed 6 father 7 produce 8 generate, multiply 9 procreate,
propagate, reproduce 11 progenerate

begetting *combining form:* 4 gony

beggar 4 hobo 5 asker, tramp 6 bummer,
cadger, pauper, prayer, sponge, suitor
7 moocher, sponger 8 deadbeat 9 schnor-
rer, suppliant 10 down-and-out, freeloader,
panhandler, petitioner, supplicant 11 bindle
stiff, supplicator

beggared 4 flat, poor 5 broke, needy
8 dirt poor, indigent 9 destitute 11 fortuneless, impecunious 12 impoverished

beggarly 4 mean 5 cheap, sorry
6 cheesy, measly, paltry, scurvy, shabby,
trashy 7 pitiful 8 pitiable, wretched
10 despicable, despisable 12 contemptible

Beggar's Opera *music:* 7 Pepusch
(John) *painting:* 7 Hogarth (William) *text:*
3 Gay (John)

beggarweed 6 dodder, spurry 9 knotgrass

beggary 4 need, want 6 penury 7 bumming, cadging, poverty 8 mooching 9 indigence, mendicity, neediness, pauperism
10 mendicancy 11 destitution, panhandling

begin 4 open 5 arise, dig in, enter, found,
set to, start 6 attack, broach, get off,

launch, spring, tackle, take up, tee off
7 break in, jump off, kick off, lead off, prepare, usher in **8** commence, embark on, initiate **9** establish, institute, introduce, originate **10** embark upon, inaugurate

beginner 4 colt, tiro, tyro **6** novice, rookie **8** freshman, neophyte, newcomer **9** novitiate **10** apprentice, tenderfoot

beginning 4 dawn, rise, root **5** alpha, basal, birth, onset, start **6** anlage, origin, outset, primal, setout, source, spring, sprout **7** dawning, genesis, infancy, initial, nascent, opening **8** creation, exordium, outstart, prologue, rudiment, simplest **9** dayspring, elemental, emergence, inception, inceptive, incipient **10** appearance, elementary, incipiency, initiative, initiatory, opening gun, rudimental **11** origination, rudimentary **12** commencement, introductory *combining form:* **3** acr, akr **4** acro, akro, arch *suffix:* **6** escent

begird 3 hem **4** band, belt, ring **5** beset, round **6** circle, girdle **8** cincture, encircle, engirdle, surround **9** encompass **10** encincture

begirdle 4 band, belt **6** engird **8** cincture **10** encincture

begone 4 kite **5** scram **6** decamp, get out **7** buzz off, skiddoo, take off, vamoose **8** clear out, hightail **9** skedaddle

begrime 4 foul, soil **5** dirty **6** besoil, smirch, smooch, smudge, smutch **7** tarnish

begrudge 4 envy

beguile 4 lure, play, wile **5** bluff, fleet, while **6** betray, delude, entice, humbug, illude, jockey, juggle, seduce, take in **7** deceive, exploit, finesse, mislead **8** maneuver **10** manipulate **11** doublecross

beguiling 5 false **8** deluding, delusive, delusory **9** deceiving, deceptive **10** fallacious, misleading

Behan's autobiography 10 Borstal Boy

behave 2 do **3** act **4** bear, go on, move, quit, take, work **5** carry, react **6** acquit, demean, deport, direct, manage **7** comport, conduct, control, disport, operate, perform **8** function

behavior 6 manner **7** bearing, conduct **8** demeanor **10** deportment **11** comportment

behead 4 neck **9** decollate **10** decapitate, guillotine

beheaded noblewoman 4 Grey (Lady Jane) **6** Boleyn (Anne), Howard (Catherine) **10** Antoinette (Marie)

behemoth 5 giant, whale **7** mammoth, monster **9** leviathan

behemothic 4 huge **7** mammoth, titanic **8** colossal, gigantic **9** Herculean, mon-

strous **10** gargantuan, mastodonic **11** elephantine

behest 4 word **5** order **6** charge, demand **7** bidding, command, dictate, mandate, request **9** prompting **10** injunction **12** solicitation

behind 3 can **4** next, rump **5** abaft, after, below, fanny, hiney, infra, later, since **6** back of, bottom, heinie **7** by and by **8** backside, buttocks, derriere, latterly **9** afterward, following, posterior **10** afterwhile **12** subsequently, subsequent to *combining form:* **7** postero *prefix:* **3** met **4** meta, post **5** retro

behindhand 3 lax **4** late **5** lated, slack, tardy **6** in debt, remiss **7** belated, overdue **8** backward, careless, derelict **9** in arrears, negligent **10** delinquent, neglectful, regardless, unpunctual **11** undeveloped **12** disregardful **13** unprogressive

behold 3 see **4** espy, mark, note, view **6** descry, notice **7** discern, observe **11** distinguish *French:* **5** voilà *Latin:* **4** ecce

beholden 7 obliged **8** indebted **9** obligated

beholder 6 viewer **7** watcher, witness **8** by-sitter, looker-on, observer, onlooker **9** bystander, spectator **10** eyewitness

being 2 as **3** for, man **4** body, esse, soul **5** human, since, stuff, thing, wight **6** entity, matter, mortal, nature, object, person, seeing **7** because, essence, texture, whereas **8** as long as, creature, essentia, existent, material **9** actuality, character, existence, personage, something, substance **10** inasmuch as, individual **11** considering, personality **12** essentiality **13** individuality *suffix:* **2** ic **3** ant, ent **4** ical

bejewel 3 gem **5** begem, beset **7** diamond, encrust, spangle **9** bespangle

Bel *father:* **2** Ea *wife:* **5** Belit **6** Beltis

bel ____ 5 canto **6** esprit

Bel ____ 5 Paese

Bela *father:* **4** Beor **8** Benjamin *son:* **3** Ard

belabor 4 beat, drub **5** baste, pound **6** batter, buffet, pummel, thrash, wallop **7** lambast **8** lambaste

Belait 6 Europe

belated 5 dated, passé, tardy **7** antique, archaic, overdue **8** outdated, outmoded **9** out-of-date **10** antiquated, behindhand, oldfangled, unpunctual **12** old-fashioned

belch 4 burp, spew **5** eject, erupt, expel **6** irrupt **8** disgorge, eructate

beldam 3 hag **5** crone **6** virago

beleaguer 4 gnaw **5** annoy, beset, harry, siege, storm, tease, worry **6** harass, invest, pester, plague **7** bedevil, besiege, hagride **8** blockade

belfry 7 clocher 8 carillon 9 bell tower, campanile *dweller:* 3 bat

Belgium *capital:* 8 Brussels *commercial center:* 4 Gent 5 Ghent *horse breed:* 9 Brabançon *language:* 6 French 7 Flemish *monetary unit:* 5 franc *people:* 7 Fleming, Flemish, Walloon *province:* 5 Liège, Namur 7 Antwerp, Brabant, Hainaut, Limburg 8 Flanders 10 Luxembourg *violinist:* 5 Ysaye (Eugene-Auguste)

belie 4 hide, warp 5 color, twist 6 garble 7 conceal, distort, falsify, pervert 8 disguise, disprove, miscolor, misstate, negative 10 contradict, contravene, controvert 12 misrepresent

belief 3 ism 4 idea, mind, view 5 credo, creed, dogma, faith, tenet, trust 6 assent, credit 7 concept, feeling, opinion, precept 8 credence, doctrine, religion, sureness 9 assurance, certainty, certitude, principle, sentiment 10 conviction, persuasion

believable 5 solid 6 likely 7 tenable 8 credible, possible, probable, rational 9 colorable, plausible 10 convincing, creditable, impressive, meaningful, persuasive, presumable, reasonable, satisfying, supposable 11 conceivable, substantial

believe 3 buy 4 deem, feel, hold, take 5 admit, sense, think, trust 6 accept, assume, credit, expect, gather, reckon, repute 7 imagine, suppose, suspect, swallow 8 accredit, consider 10 understand

belittle 5 decry 8 derogate, diminish, discount, minimize, write off 9 criticize, discredit, disparage, dispraise, underrate 10 depreciate, undervalue 11 detract from 13 underestimate

belittlement 4 tale 7 calumny, scandal, slander 10 backbiting, defamation, detraction 12 backstabbing, depreciation 13 disparagement

bell 4 bong, peal, ring, toll 5 chime, knell

bell-bottoms 5 pants 8 trousers

bell cow 4 dean, lead 5 doyen, guide, pilot 6 leader

Bellerophon *father:* 7 Glaucus 8 Poseidon *grandfather:* 8 Sisyphus *horse:* 7 Pegasus *victim:* 7 Chimera

belles lettres 10 literature

belletrist 4 poet 6 author, writer

bellflower 9 campanula

___ **belli** 5 casus

bellicose 7 scrappy, warlike 8 factious, fighting, militant 9 assertive, combative, truculent 10 aggressive, pugnacious, rebellious 11 belligerent, contentious, quarrelsome 12 gladiatorial

belligerence 5 fight 6 attack 9 pugnacity 10 aggression, truculence 13 combativeness

belligerent 3 hot 6 ardent, fierce 7 hostile, scrappy, warlike, warring 8 battling, fighting, invading, militant, ructious 9 attacking, bellicose, combative, truculent 10 aggressive, pugnacious 11 contentious, hot-tempered, quarrelsome 12 antagonistic, gladiatorial

Bellini *opera:* 5 Norma 8 Il Pirata 9 I Puritani 12 La Sonnambula *sleepwalker:* 5 Amina

bell metal 6 bronze

bellow 3 bay, cry, low, moo 4 bark, bawl, roar, rout, wail, yelp 6 clamor 7 bluster

Bellow character 6 Herzog 7 Sammler 9 Henderson 10 Augie March

bell ringer 3 hit, wow 4 bang 5 smash 6 toller 7 success 12 carillonneur

bell ringing 11 campanology

bell-shaped 11 campanulate

bell sound 4 ding, dong, peal, ring, ting, toll 5 clang, knell 6 tinkle

bell tower 6 belfry 7 clocher 8 carillon 9 campanile

___ **bellum** 4 ante, post

bellwether 4 dean, lead 5 doyen, guide, pilot 6 leader

belly 3 gut 5 tummy 6 paunch, venter 7 abdomen, stomach *combining form:* 5 gastr 6 gaster, gastro, ventri, ventro 7 gastero, gastria *Scottish:* 4 wame

bellyache 4 beef, crab, fuss, yaup, yawp 5 bitch, bleat, colic, gripe 6 gripes, squawk, yammer 7 blow off 12 collywobbles

bellyacher 4 crab 5 crank 6 griper, grouch, kicker 7 grouser 8 grumbler 10 complainer, malcontent 11 faultfinder

belly button 5 navel

belong 2 go 3 fit, set 4 suit, vest 5 agree, befit, chime, match, tally 6 accord, become, inhere 7 indwell, pertain 9 appertain, harmonize 10 correspond

belonging *suffix:* 2 an, ar 3 ary, ean, ian, ine

belongings 5 goods 6 estate, things 7 effects 8 chattels, movables 10 possession

beloved 3 pet 4 baby, beau, dear, love 5 flame, honey, lover, sweet 6 steady 7 darling, sweetie 8 blue-eyed, favorite, ladylove, loveling, precious, truelove 9 boyfriend, inamorata, inamorato, sweetling 10 fair-haired, girl friend, heartthrob, sweetheart

below 4 next 5 after, infra, since, under 6 behind, nether 7 beneath 9 following 10 underneath 12 subsequent to *combining form:* 6 infero *prefix:* 3 sub 5 infra

belt 3 bat, bop 4 area, band, bash, biff, blow, gird, loop, ring, sash, slam, slug, sock, whop, zone 5 blast, smack, smash, strap, strip, tie up, tract 6 begird, cestus, circle, engird, girdle, region, wallop 7 baldric, caestus, clobber, stretch 8 begirdle, ceinture, cincture, encircle, engirdle 9 bandoleer, bandolier, territory, waistband 10 cummerbund, encincture *celestial:* 6 zodiac *combining form:* 3 zon 4 żono

belt highway 8 ring road

Belus *brother:* 6 Agenor *daughter:* 4 Dido *father:* 7 Neptune 8 Poseidon *mother:* 5 Libya *son:* 6 Danaus 7 Cepheus, Phineus 8 Aegyptus

belvedere 6 alcove, gazebo, pagoda 11 garden house, summerhouse

bemean 4 sink 5 abase, lower 6 debase, humble 7 degrade 8 cast down 9 humiliate

bemedaled 9 decorated 10 beribboned

bemired 4 miry, oozy 5 muddy 6 claggy, clarty

bemoan 3 rue 4 weep 6 bewail, grieve, lament, regret 7 deplore 8 complain

bemuse 4 daze, stun 5 addle 6 bedaze, benumb, puzzle 7 fluster, perplex, petrify, stupefy 8 paralyze

bemused 4 lost 6 absent 7 faraway 8 distrait 10 abstracted 11 inconscient, preoccupied 12 absentminded

bench 6 settee *church:* 3 pew *outdoor:* 6 exedra *upholstered:* 9 banquette

benchmark 5 gauge 7 measure 8 standard 9 criterion, yardstick 10 touchstone

bend 2 go 3 arc, bow, jut, nod, yaw 4 arch, bias, cave, curl, flex, give, hang, hook, lean, tack, turn 5 angle, apply, break, crook, curve, round, shift, stoop, throw, yield 6 beetle, buckle, devote, direct, double, fold up, inflex 7 address, crumple, dispose, flexure, incline, turning 8 collapse, flection, lean over, overhang 9 curvation, curvature, deviation 10 buckle down, deflection, predispose

bendable 6 pliant, supple 7 elastic, pliable 8 flexible

bender see binge

bending *combining form:* 7 sphingo

___ **bene** 4 nota

beneath 5 below, under *prefix:* 3 hyp, sub 4 hypo 5 infra

___ **Benedict** 4 eggs

benediction 2 OK 4 boon, good, okay 5 favor, grace 6 thanks 7 benefit, benison, godsend 8 approval, blessing 9 advantage 11 approbation 12 thanksgiving

benefact 3 aid 4 abet, help 5 do for, stead 6 assist 7 help out

benefaction 4 alms 7 charity 8 donation, offering 11 beneficence 12 contribution

beneficence see benefaction

beneficial 4 good 5 brave 6 toward, useful 7 helpful 8 favoring, salutary 9 favorable, wholesome 10 propitious 12 advantageous

beneficiary 4 heir 5 donee 6 vassal 7 legatee 9 feudatory *suffix:* 2 ee

beneficiate 5 treat 6 reduce 7 prepare, process

benefit 3 aid 4 boon, gain, good, help, sake 5 avail, build, favor, serve 6 assist, behalf, behoof, better, profit, succor 7 account, advance, further, godsend, improve, promote, relieve, welfare, work for 8 blessing, interest 9 advantage, well-being 10 ameliorate, prosperity 11 benediction 12 contribute to

benevolence 4 boon, gift 5 amity, favor 6 comity 7 largess, present 8 goodwill 10 compliment, friendship, kindliness 12 friendliness

benevolent 3 big 4 good, kind 5 lofty 6 do-good, humane, kindly 7 liberal 8 generous 10 altruistic, beneficent, bighearted, charitable, chivalrous, openhanded 11 considerate, freehearted, magnanimous 12 eleemosynary, greathearted, humanitarian, largehearted 13 compassionate, philanthropic, tenderhearted

benighted 8 backward, ignorant, untaught 9 untutored 10 illiterate, uneducated, uninformed, unlettered, unschooled 11 emptyheaded, know-nothing 12 uninstructed 13 unenlightened, unprogressive

benign 4 kind, mild 6 bright, dexter, gentle, humane, kindly 7 clement 8 gracious, merciful 9 favorable, fortunate 10 auspicious, benevolent, charitable, forbearing, propitious 11 good-hearted

Benin *capital:* 9 Porto Novo *largest city:* 7 Cotonou *monetary unit:* 5 franc

benison 8 blessing 11 benediction

Benjamin *brother:* 6 Joseph *father:* 5 Jacob *mother:* 6 Rachel

bent 3 set 4 bias, gift, head, nose, turn 5 arced, bowed, flair, knack, round 6 arched, curved, genius, intent, talent 7 arrondi, decided, faculty, leaning, rounded, settled, uncinal 8 arciform, decisive, inflexed, penchant, resolute, resolved, tendency, uncinate 9 inclining 10 determined, proclivity, propensity 11 curvilinear, disposition, inclination 12 predilection *combining form:* 4 cyrt 5 ancyl, ankyl, curvi, cyrto 6 anchyl, ancylo, ankylo, campto 7 anchylo

benumb 4 daze, dull, mull, stun 5 blunt 6 bedaze, bemuse, deaden 7 petrify, stupefy 8 paralyze 11 desensitize

benumbed 6 asleep 9 senseless, unfeeling 10 insensible 11 insensitive 12 anesthetized

benzene *combining form:* 4 phen 5 pheno

Beor's son 4 Bela 6 Balaam
bequeath 4 will 5 leave 6 devise, hand on, legate, pass on 8 hand down, transmit
bequest 6 devise, legacy 11 inheritance
berate 3 jaw 4 rail, rate 5 scold 6 revile 7 bawl out, chew out, upbraid 10 tongue-lash, vituperate
berceuse 7 lullaby 10 cradlesong
bereave 3 rob 4 lose, oust 6 divest 7 deprive 10 disinherit, dispossess
bereaved 6 bereft 9 sorrowing 10 distressed
Berechiah's son 9 Zechariah
Bergen's dummy 5 Snerd (Mortimer) 8 McCarthy (Charlie)
Beriah's father 5 Asher 6 Shimei, Shimhi 7 Ephraim
berkelium *symbol:* 2 Bk
Bermuda grass 4 doob
Bernice *brother:* 7 Agrippa *father:* 5 Herod *husband:* 6 Polemo *lover:* 5 Titus 9 Vespasian
berry 4 wort 5 bacca, fruit, grape, whort 6 banana, tomato 7 bramble, currant, madrona, madrone, madrono, whortle 8 allspice *combining form:* 4 cocc 5 cocci, cocco *Latin:* 6 acinus *medicinal:* 5 cubeb
berry-bearing 7 baccate 11 bacciferous
berrylike 7 baccate, coccoid
berth 3 job 4 dock, pier, post, quay, slip, spot 5 jetty, levee, place, wharf 6 billet, office 8 position 9 situation 10 connection 11 appointment
Bertha's son 7 Orlando
beryllium *symbol:* 2 Be
beseech see beg
beset 3 gem, hem 4 gird, ring 5 begem, jewel, storm 6 assail, attack, circle, fall on, girdle, infest, invest, strike 7 aggress, assault, bejewel, besiege, compass, enjewel, environ, overrun 8 blockade, encircle, fall upon, surround 9 beleaguer, encompass, overswarm 10 overspread
besetment 4 pest 6 bother, pester, plague 8 irritant, nuisance 9 annoyance 10 botherment 11 botheration 12 exasperation
besetting 8 dominant, haunting 9 obsessive, principal 10 persistent
beside 2 by 3 bar, but 4 near, nigh, save 5 round 6 beyond, except, nearby, next to 7 barring 8 as well as, opposite 9 alongside, aside from, excluding, outside of 11 exclusive of 12 over and above *prefix:* 2 ep 3 eph, epi, par 4 para
besides 3 bar, but, new, too, yet 4 also, else, more, save, then 5 added, again, along, other 6 as well, beyond, except 7 barring, farther, further 8 as well as, likewise, moreover 9 aside from, excluding, otherwise, outside of 10 additional, in addition 11 exclusive of, furthermore 12 additionally, over and above

besiege 4 trap 5 beset, hem in 6 assail, attack, invest 7 assault 8 blockade, encircle, surround 9 beleaguer, encompass
besmear 3 dab, tar 4 daub, soil 5 smarm, stain, sully, taint 6 bedaub, defile, smudge 7 plaster, tarnish 8 besmirch, discolor
besmirch see besmear
besoil 4 foul 5 dirty, grime 6 smirch, smooch, smudge, smutch 7 begrime, tarnish
besom material 5 twigs
besotted 5 dotty, drunk 8 enamored 9 infatuate 10 infatuated
bespatter 4 slur, spot 5 smear 6 befoul, bespot, defame, malign 7 asperse, blacken, slander, traduce 9 denigrate
bespeak 3 ask 4 book, hire 6 accost, attest, desire 7 address, apply to, betoken, request, reserve, solicit, testify, witness 8 announce, approach, indicate 9 preengage
bespeckle 3 dot 6 pepper 7 freckle, stipple 8 sprinkle
best 3 gem, pip, top 4 beat, down, most, pick 5 cream, elite, excel, model, outdo, pride, prime, prize, worst 6 better, choice, defeat, exceed, flower, master 7 conquer, greater, largest, paragon, pattern, prevail, surpass, triumph 8 exemplar, nonesuch, outshine, outstrip, overcome, primrose 9 nonpareil, transcend 10 bettermost *combining form:* 6 aristo
bestial 5 brute, feral 6 animal, brutal, ferine 7 beastly, brutish, swinish
bestialize 4 warp 6 debase 7 corrupt, debauch, deprave, pervert, vitiate 9 brutalize 10 bastardize, demoralize
bestir 4 wake, whet 5 rally, rouse, waken 6 arouse, awaken, kindle 9 challenge
bestow 3 use 4 bunk, give, pack 5 apply, board, grant, house, lodge, put up, store 6 billet, confer, devote, donate, employ, handle, harbor, lavish 7 exploit, hand out, present, quarter, utilize 8 domicile, exercise, give away 9 entertain, warehouse *Scottish:* 7 propine
bestower 5 donor, giver 7 donator 9 conferrer, presenter
bestrew 3 sow 5 straw 7 disject, scatter 9 broadcast 11 disseminate
bestride 4 back 5 mount 8 straddle, striddle
bet 3 lay, pot, set 4 ante, game, play, risk 5 banco, put on, stake, wager 6 gamble, parlay *racing:* 6 exacta 8 perfecta, quinella, quiniela *taker:* 6 bookie
Betelgeuse 4 star *constellation:* 5 Orion
betel palm 5 areca

bête noire 4 hate 7 bugbear 8 anathema 10 black beast 11 abomination, detestation

bethink 4 cite, mind 6 recall, remind, retain, revive 8 remember 9 recollect, reminisce 10 retrospect

Bethuel *daughter:* 7 Rebekah *father:* 5 Nahor *mother:* 6 Milcah *son:* 5 Laban *uncle:* 7 Abraham

betide 2 go 3 hap 5 break, occur 6 befall, chance, happen 7 come off, develop, fall out

betimes 4 soon 5 early 6 timely 8 oversoon 10 seasonably 11 prematurely

betoken 4 bode, omen 5 argue, augur 6 attest 7 bespeak, portend, presage, promise, testify, witness 8 announce, forebode, foreshow, indicate 9 foretoken 10 foreshadow

betray 4 sell, show, tell, trap 5 bluff, cross, snare, spill, split 6 delude, desert, entrap, evince, humbug, illude, inform, juggle, reveal, take in, turn in, unveil 7 beguile, betoken, blab out, deceive, divulge, ensnare, mislead, sell out, uncover 8 disclose, discover, evidence, give away, indicate, manifest, renegade 10 apostatize 11 collaborate, demonstrate, double-cross

betrayal 7 treason

betrayer 3 rat 4 fink, nark 6 snitch 7 stoolie, tattler, traitor 8 informer, squealer, turncoat 10 talebearer, tattletale 11 stool pigeon

betroth 6 pledge 8 affiance

betrothal 8 espousal 10 engagement

betrothed 6 fiancé 7 engaged, fiancée, pledged 8 intended, plighted, promised, wife-to-be 9 affianced, bride-to-be 10 contracted 11 husband-to-be

better 3 top, win 4 beat, best, good, help, more, most 5 amend, elder, excel, outdo 6 choice, exceed, senior 7 greater, improve, largest, success, surpass, triumph, victory 8 brass hat, higher-up, outshine, outstrip, superior, whip hand 9 advantage, desirable, exceeding, excellent, meliorate, transcend, upper hand 10 ameliorate, preferable, surpassing 11 exceptional, superiority

bettor 7 wagerer

between 5 among, twixt 6 atwixt 7 betwixt *prefix:* 5 inter, intra

betweentimes 11 at intervals

bevel 4 bias 6 biased 7 slanted 8 diagonal, slanting

beverage 3 ade, nog, pop, tea 4 mate, milk, soda 5 cider, cocoa, drink, juice, shake 6 coffee, eggnog, frappe, malted, nectar 7 potable 8 lemonade, libation, potation 9 drinkable, milk shake *alcoholic:* 3 ale, gin, rum 4 beer, grog, mead, wine 5 cider, julep, negus, punch, stout, toddy, vodka 6 bishop, brandy, caudle, cooler, liquor, rickey, shandy, sherry, whisky 7 liqueur, martini, sangria, tequila, whiskey 8 cocktail, highball, sillabub, sillibub, syllabub, vermouth *Australasian:* 4 kava *British:* 5 perry, stout 6 stingo *carbonated:* 4 cola, soda 6 rickey 8 root beer 9 ginger ale *central Asian:* 5 kumys 6 koumis, koumys, kumiss, kumyss 7 koumiss, koumyss *Dutch:* 7 schnaps 8 schnapps *from camel's milk:* 5 kumys 6 koumis, koumys, kumiss, kumyss 7 koumiss, koumyss *from cow's milk:* 5 kefir *Greek:* 4 ouzo 7 oenomel, oinomel, retsina, retzina *Irish:* 5 usque 6 poteen 7 potheen, potteen 8 usquabae, usquebae 10 usquebaugh *medicinal:* 6 elixir *Mexican:* 6 pulque 7 tequila *of the gods:* 6 nectar *Oriental:* 4 sake, saki 6 arrack, samshu *Russian:* 5 kefir, kvass, quass, vodka *Scottish:* 4 yill 6 scotch *South American:* 4 maté 5 yerba *Swedish:* 5 glogg *Turkish:* 4 raki *West Indies:* 3 rum 5 tafia

bevy 4 band, crew 5 bunch, covey, group, party 7 cluster 8 assembly

bewail 4 moan, weep 6 bemoan, grieve 7 deplore

beware 4 heed, mind 5 watch 6 attend, notice 7 look out 8 watch out

bewhiskered 7 barbate, bearded

bewilder 3 fog 4 stun 5 addle, befog, mix up 6 baffle, ball up, fuddle, muddle, puzzle 7 confuse, fluster, perplex, stumble 8 befuddle, confound, distract 9 bumfuzzle 13 metagrobolize

bewitch 3 hex 4 draw, snow, take, wile 5 charm, spell, trick 6 allure, dazzle, voodoo 7 attract, bedevil, enchant, possess 8 demonize, ensorcel, overlook 9 beglamour, captivate, ensorcell, fascinate, magnetize, sorcerize

bewitching 8 alluring, charming, magnetic, mesmeric 9 seductive 10 attractive

bewitchment 5 magic 7 sorcery 8 witchery, wizardry 9 conjuring, magicking 10 necromancy, witchcraft 11 incantation

beyond 3 new, yon 4 else, more, over, past 5 above, added, after, other 6 across, beside, yonder 7 athwart, besides, farther, further, outside, without 8 as well as 9 afterlife, hereafter, otherwise 10 additional, afterworld, otherworld 12 over and above, transversely *combining form:* 6 preter 7 praeter *prefix:* 3 met, par 4 meta, over, para 5 extra, hyper, super, trans, ultra

bias 4 bend, bent, skew 5 angle, bevel, slant 7 beveled, dispose, incline, leaning, slanted 8 diagonal, penchant, slanting 9 inclining, influence, prejudice, viewpoint 10 partiality, predispose, prepossess, proclivity, standpoint 11 disposition, inclination 12 one-sidedness, predilection

biased 6 swayed, warped 7 bigoted, colored, partial, slanted 8 disposed, inclined, one-sided, partisan, slanting 9 jaundiced, unneutral 10 influenced, interested, prejudiced 11 opinionated, predisposed, tendentious 12 prepossessed 13 unindifferent

bibelot 5 curio 6 bauble, gewgaw, trifle 7 novelty, trinket, whatnot 8 gimcrack 9 objet d'art 10 knickknack

Bible *abbreviation:* 2 Ex, Is, Jn, Lk, Mk, Mt, Ps 3 Col, Cor, Dan, Eph, Gal, Gen, Hab, Heb, Hos, Jas, Jer, Jon, Lam, Lev, Mal, Mic, Neh, Num, Pet, Rev, Rom, Sam, Tim, Tit 4 Deut, Ezek, Josh, Judg, Obad, Phil, Prov, Zech, Zeph 5 Chron, Thess 6 Eccles, Philem *Apocrypha book:* 5 Tobit 6 Baruch, Esdras, Esther, Judith 7 Susanna 8 Manasseh, Manasses 9 Maccabees *New Testament book:* 4 Acts, John, Jude, Luke, Mark 5 James, Peter, Titus 6 Romans 7 Hebrews, Matthew, Timothy 8 Philemon 9 Ephesians, Galatians 10 Colossians, Revelation 11 Corinthians, Philippians 13 Thessalonians *Old Testament book:* 3 Job 4 Amos, Ezra, Joel, Ruth 5 Hosea, Jonah, Kings, Micah, Nahum 6 Daniel, Esther, Exodus, Haggai, Isaiah, Joshua, Judges, Psalms, Samuel 7 Ezekiel, Genesis, Malachi, Numbers, Obadiah 8 Habakkuk, Jeremiah, Nehemiah, Proverbs 9 Leviticus, Zechariah, Zephaniah 10 Chronicles 11 Deuteronomy 12 Ecclesiastes, Lamentations 13 Song of Solomon *part:* 4 book 5 verse 7 chapter 9 testament *translator:* 4 Knox (Ronald Arbuthnott) 5 Eliot (John) 6 Jerome, Luther (Martin) 7 Erasmus, Tyndale (William), Zwingli (Huldrych) 8 Wycliffe (John) 9 Coverdale (Miles) *version:* 4 Geez 5 Douay, Itala 6 Coptic, Gothic, Syriac, Targum 7 Vulgate 8 Peshitta 9 Jerusalem, King James, Masoretic, Serampore 10 New English, Septuagint

Biblical *animal:* 4 reem 5 daman 8 behemoth *ascetic order:* 6 Essene *battle:* 7 Jericho *battle site:* 10 Armageddon *charioteer:* 4 Jehu *city, town:* 2 Ai, Ur 3 Ain, Dan, Lod, Luz, Nob 4 Bela, Cana, Gath, Gaza, Nain, Nebo, Tyre, Zoar 5 Bezer, Calno, Derbe, Ekron, Endor, Gerar, Golan, Haifa, Haran, Joppa, Lydda, Ramah, Sidon, Sodom, Tekoa, Zorah 6 Ashdod, Asshur, Beroea, Bethel, Calneh, Dothan, Emmaus, Gadara, Gibeah, Gibeon, Gilgal, Hebron, Kadesh, Lystra, Mizpah, Ophrah, Rimmon, Shiloh, Shunem, Siloan, Smyrna, Tarsus 7 Antioch, Askelon, Baalbec, Bethany, Corinth, Ephesus, Ephraim, Iconium, Jericho, Jezreel, Magdala, Nineveh, Samaria,

Shechem 8 Caesarea, Chorazin, Damascus, Gomorrah, Michmash, Nazareth, Philippi, Tiberias 9 Beersheba, Beth-horon, Bethlehem, Bethsaida, Capernaum, Jerusalem *coin:* (see at Hebrew) *coney:* 5 daman *desert:* 5 Sinai *garden:* 4 Eden 8 Paradise *giant:* 4 Anak, Emim 7 Goliath *giant slayer:* 5 David *hill:* 4 Zion *hunter:* 6 Nimrod *judge:* 3 Eli 4 Ehud, Elon, Jair, Tola 5 Abdon, Ibzan 6 Gideon, Samson, Samuel 7 Deborah, Othniel, Shamgar 8 Jephthah *king:* 2 Og 3 Asa 4 Agag, Ahab, Ahaz, Amon, Bera, Elah, Jehu, Omri, Reba, Saul 5 David, Herod, Hiram, Joash, Joram, Nadab, Pekah, Rezin, Zimri 6 Abijam, Baasha, Birsha, Hoshea, Japhia, Josiah, Jotham, Uzziah 7 Ahaziah, Amaziah, Azariah, Jehoash, Jehoram, Menahem, Shallum, Solomon 8 Hezekiah, Jehoahaz, Jeroboam, Manasseh, Rehoboam, Zedekiah 9 Jehoiakim, Zechariah 10 Jehoiachin 11 Jehoshaphat *land:* 3 Nod, Pul 4 Aram, Elam, Moab, Seba, Seir 5 Judah, Judea, Perea 6 Bashan, Canaan, Goshen, Israel 7 Chaldea, Galilee, Samaria 9 Palestine *land of plenty:* 6 Goshen *measure:* (see at Hebrew) *mountain:* 3 Hor 4 Ebal, Nebo, Peor, Seir 5 Horeb, Sinai, Tabor 6 Abarim, Ararat, Carmel, Gilboa, Gilead, Hermon, Moriah, Olivet, Pisgah 7 Gerizim, Lebanon *name:* 2 Er, Ir, Ur 3 Abi, Asa, Bel, Dan, Eli, Eri, Eve, Gad, Ham, Hen, Hod, Hul, Hur, Ira, Iri, Iru, Job, Lot, Ner, Nun, Ram, Reu, Toi, Uel, Uri, Zur 4 Abel, Adah, Adam, Agag, Ahab, Ahaz, Amon, Aran, Bela, Beor, Boaz, Buzi, Cain, Cush, Dodo, Ebal, Ebed, Eber, Eder, Ehud, Elah, Elam, Elon, Enan, Enos, Eram, Esau, Ezer, Gaal, Gadi, Gera, Guni, Hazo, Heli, Hori, Ibri, Iddo, Igal, Irad, Iram, Ishi, Izri, Jada, Jael, Jair, Jehu, Joab, Joah, Joel, John, Kish, Kore, Lael, Leah, Levi, Lois, Maon, Mark, Mary, Mica, Moab, Moza, Naam, Nebo, Neri, Noah, Obal, Obed, Oded, Ohad, Ohel, Omar, Omri, Onam, Onan, Oreb, Oren, Ozem, Ozni, Paul, Puah, Reba, Rosh, Ruth, Salu, Saph, Sara, Saul, Seth, Shem, Shua, Sodi, Suah, Susi, Tema, Tola, Ucal, Ulam, Uzai, Uzal, Uzzi, Zeeb, Zeri, Ziza, Zuar 5 Aaron, Abiel, Abner, Amasa, Amnon, Amram, Asher, Bedad, Bedan, Beeri, Caleb, Carmi, Chuza, Cozbi, David, Debir, Deuel, Dinah, Eliab, Eliam, Elias, Eliel, Eliud, Emmor, Enoch, Ephah, Ephai, Ephod, Esrom, Ethan, Ezbon, Gaham, Galal, Gazez, Gomer, Hadad, Hagar, Haggi, Haman, Hamul, Hanan, Hanun, Haran, Harum, Heber, Helah, Heleb, Helek, Helon, Hemam, Heman, Herod, Hirah, Hobab, Horam, Hosea, Ibhar, Imlah, Imnah, Isaac, Iscah,

Ishui, Ithra, Ittai, Izhar, Jaasu, Jabal, Jacob, Jahdo, Jakeh, Jalam, Jalon, James, Jamin, Janna, Jared, Jarib, Jeiel, Jerah, Jered, Jesse, Jeush, Jezer, Joash, Jobab, Jogli, Jonah, Jonas, Joram, Jubal, Judah, Judas, Korah, Laban, Lahad, Lahmi, Laish, Libni, Lotan, Mahli, Mahol, Mamre, Maoch, Massa, Merab, Mered, Mesha, Micah, Moses, Mushi, Nabal, Nadab, Nahor, Naomi, Nehum, Nogah, Nohah, Ocram, Onias, Ophir, Orpah, Othni, Palal, Pallu, Palti, Pekah, Peleg, Pelet, Perez, Peter, Puvah, Rahab, Raham, Raphu, Regem, Rekem, Reuel, Rezon, Rizia, Rufus, Sacar, Sallu, Sarah, Segub, Seled, Serah, Sered, Serug, Shama, Shaul, Sheal, Sheba, Shema, Shiza, Shobi, Shuah, Shual, Shuni, Simon, Tahan, Tamar, Tarah, Tebah, Terah, Tibni, Tilon, Timna, Tubal, Uriah, Uriel, Uthai, Uzzah, Zabad, Zabdi, Zabud, Zadok, Zaham, Zebah, Zephi, Zepho, Zerah, Zibia, Zimri, Zohar 6 Abital, Achsah, Ashhur, Balaam, Baruch, Becher, Beriah, Bilhah, Binnui, Canaan, Cheran, Chesed, Daniel, Dathan, Dishan, Dishon, Elasah, Eliada, Elijah, Elisha, Elpaal, Eshban, Eshcol, Esther, Eunice, Gesham, Gideon, Gilead, Ginath, Hanani, Hannah, Hanoch, Hareph, Hebron, Hemdam, Hepher, Hezlon, Hezron, Hodesh, Hoglah, Hophni, Hoshea, Hotham, Hothir, Huldah, Hupham, Hushim, Isaiah, Ishbak, Ishpah, Ishpan, Ishuah, Israel, Ithiel, Ithran, Izliah, Izziah, Jaalam, Jabesh, Jachin, Jahath, Japhia, Jashub, Jehiel, Jehush, Jemuel, Jesher, Jeshua, Jether, Jethro, Jeziel, Jezoar, Joahaz, Joakim, Joanna, Joelah, Joiada, Joktan, Joseph, Joshah, Joshua, Josiah, Jotham, Judith, Kareah, Kemuel, Keziah, Kohath, Laadah, Lamech, Maacah, Maadai, Machir, Mahali, Mahlah, Mahlon, Malcam, Manoah, Martha, Matred, Mattan, Melech, Merari, Midian, Milcah, Miriam, Mirmah, Misham, Naamah, Naaman, Naarah, Nahash, Nahath, Nathan, Nemuel, Nepheg, Neriah, Nimrod, Ochran, Ophrah, Pagiel, Paruah, Pasach, Paseah, Peleth, Penuel, Peresh, Philip, Pilate, Pispah, Pithon, Prisca, Putiel, Raamah, Rachel, Raddai, Ramiah, Ramoth, Raphah, Reaiah, Rechab, Reuben, Rimmon, Rinnah, Rizpah, Rohgah, Salmon, Salome, Samson, Samuel, Shaaph, Shamir, Sharai, Sheber, Shelah, Shemer, Shephi, Shepho, Shilem, Shilhi, Shimea, Shimei, Shimri, Shiphi, Shobab, Shobal, Shoham, Shomer, Shuham, Simeon, Tahash, Tahath, Talmai, Thomas, Tikvah, Tirzah, Tobias, Urijah, Uzziah, Uzziel, Vaniah, Vashni, Vashti, Vophsi, Zaavan, Zabbai, Zaccur, Zalaph, Zebiah, Zephon, Zeresh, Zereth, Zeruah, Zetham, Zibiah, Zichri, Zillah, Zilpah, Zimmah, Zimran, Zippor, Zoheth, Zophah, Zuriel *patriarch:* (see at **Hebrew**) *people:* 6 Kenite, Levite 7 Amorite, Edomite, Elamite, Moabite 9 Israelite *plains:* 4 Maab 5 Mamre 6 Sharon 7 Jericho *plotter:* 5 Haman *poem:* 5 psalm *pool:* 5 Gihon 6 Shelah, Siloam 8 Bethesda *priest:* 3 Eli 4 Levi 5 Aaron, Annas 8 Caiaphas *Promised Land:* 6 Canaan *pronoun:* 2 ye 3 thy 4 thee, thou 5 thine *prophet:* (see **prophet** entry) *Psalmist:* 5 David *punishment:* 7 stoning *queen:* 5 Sheba 6 Esther, Vashti 7 Candace, Jezebel 8 Athaliah *reproach:* 4 raca *river:* 3 Zab 4 Nile 5 Abana, Amon 6 Abanah, Jabbok, Jordan, Kishon *sacred object:* 4 urim 7 thummin *scribe:* 6 Baruch *sea:* 3 Red 4 Dead 7 Galilee *sea monster:* 9 Leviathan *spice:* 5 aloes, myrrh 6 cassia, onycha, stacte 7 calamus 8 cinnamon, galbanum 12 frankincense *spy:* 5 Caleb *temptress:* 3 Eve 7 Delilah *thief:* 8 Barabbas *tree:* 5 cedar *valley:* 4 Baca, Elah 6 Hinnon, Kidron, Shaveh, Siddim *verb ending:* 3 eth *weed:* 4 tare *well:* 3 Ain 4 Esek 6 Jacob's *witch's home:* 5 Endor

bibliography 4 list 7 catalog, history

bibliopole 7 bookman 10 bookdealer, bookseller

bicker 3 row, war 4 spat, tiff 5 argue, clack, fight, scrap 6 argufy, battle, hassle, rattle, ruttle 7 brabble, clatter, clitter, contend, dispute, fall out, quarrel, quibble, shatter, wrangle 8 squabble 9 altercate, caterwaul

bickering 3 row 4 spat 5 run-in 6 hassle 7 dispute, quarrel, wrangle 8 squabble 11 altercation, embroilment

bicycle 4 bike 9 high-riser 11 highwheeler *brake:* 7 caliper, coaster *for two:* 6 tandem *rider:* 6 cycler 7 cyclist *tenspeed:* 10 derailleur

bid 3 ask 4 tell, warn 5 order 6 charge, direct, enjoin, invite, summon 7 command, request 8 instruct

biddable 6 docile 7 amiable, docious 8 amenable, obedient, obliging 9 tractable 11 good-natured

bidding 4 call, word 5 order 6 behest, charge 7 command, dictate, mandate 9 summoning 10 injunction

biddy 3 bag, bat, hag 4 drab, girl, maid, trot 5 crone, witch 6 beldam

bide 4 live, stay, wait 5 dwell, tarry 6 linger, remain, reside 7 hang out 8 continue 11 stick around

bier 10 catafalque

biff 3 bop, hit 4 belt, blow, ding, nail, sock, whop 5 catch, clout, devel, pound, slosh, smack, whack 6 strike, thwack, wallop

bifold see **binary**

bifurcate 4 fork 5 split 6 branch, divide 8 separate 11 dichotomize, dichotomous

bifurcation 4 fork 6 branch 8 division 9 dichotomy 10 separation

big 3 fat 4 arty, bull, full, gone, lion, much, very 5 ample, awash, awful, great, heavy, hefty, husky, large, lofty, major, roomy, sated 6 biggie, bigwig, bumper, clumsy, gravid, hugely, packed, parous 7 awfully, brimful, copious, crammed, crowded, glutted, greatly, hulking, notable, replete, sizable, stuffed, swollen, weighty 8 enceinte, generous, imposing, inflated, material, oversize, pregnant, spacious 9 capacious, chock-full, distended, expectant, expecting, extensive, extremely, important, momentous, overblown, satisfied 10 benevolent, chivalrous, commodious, large-scale, meaningful, voluminous 11 considerate, heavyweight, magnanimous, overflowing, pretentious, significant, substantial 12 considerable, greathearted, high-sounding 13 comprehensive, consequential

Big Bertha's birthplace 5 Essen

Big Dipper *constellation:* 9 Ursa Major *star:* 5 Alcor, Dubhe, Merak, Mizar

bigfoot 4 Omah 9 Sasquatch

biggety 4 bold, wise 5 fresh, nervy, sassy 6 cheeky 7 forward 8 impudent 10 procacious 11 smart-alecky

bighearted 7 liberal 10 openhanded

big house 3 can, jug, pen 4 jail 5 clink 6 lockup, prison 7 slammer 8 hoosegow 11 reformatory 12 penitentiary

bight 3 arm, bay 4 cove, gulf 5 bayou, creek, firth, inlet 6 harbor, slough

bigmouthed 4 loud 10 boisterous

bigness 4 size 9 amplitude, greatness, largeness, magnitude 11 sizableness

bigot 6 maniac, racist, zealot 7 fanatic

bigoted 6 biased, narrow 9 hidebound, illiberal, lily-white 10 brassbound, intolerant, prejudiced, unenlarged 11 smallminded 12 conservative, narrow-minded

big shot 3 VIP 5 celeb, nabob 6 bigwig, fat cat 7 notable 8 big wheel 9 big cheese, celebrity, dignitary 13 high-muck-a-muck

bijouterie 6 jewels 7 jewelry 8 trinkets

bile *combining form:* 4 bili, chol 5 chole, cholo

bilge 4 bunk 5 hooey, trash 6 bushwa 7 hogwash, malarky, rubbish 8 nonsense 10 balderdash

Bilhah's son 3 Dan 8 Naphtali

Bilhan's father 7 Jediael

bilk 3 gyp, shy 4 balk, beat, dash, duck, foil, kite, ruin, shun 5 avoid, cheat, cozen, dodge, elude, evade, shake 6 baffle, chouse, diddle, double, escape, eschew, thwart 7 defraud 8 flimflam 9 frustrate, overreach 10 circumvent, disappoint

bill 3 neb, nib, tab 4 beak, bone, buck, cape, fish, head, naze, oner, peak, skin 5 check, point, score, visor 6 damage, dollar, pecker, poster 7 account, affiche, charges, invoice, ironman, placard, smacker 8 foreland, frogskin, handbill, headland 9 reckoning, smackeroo, statement 10 promontory *five-dollar:* 3 fin *of a bird:* 3 neb, nib 4 beak *one-dollar:* 4 buck *ten-dollar:* 7 sawbuck

billet 3 bar, bed, hut, job, rod 4 post, slab, spot 5 berth, board, house, ingot, lodge, place, put up, stick, strip 6 bestow, canton, harbor, office 7 quarter 8 domicile, position 9 entertain, situation 10 connection 11 appointment

billet-doux 8 mash note 10 love letter

billfold 6 wallet

billiards term 3 cue 4 foot, head, pool, rack, spot 5 break, carom, chalk, masse 6 bridge, cannon, corner, inning, miscue, pocket, string 7 bricole, cue ball, cushion, scratch 8 balkline, cue stick, rotation 9 eight ball 10 object ball

billingsgate 5 abuse 7 obloquy 9 contumely, invective 10 scurrility 12 vituperation

billion *British:* 8 milliard *combining form:* 4 giga

billionth *combining form:* 4 nano

bill of fare 4 menu 7 program 11 carte du jour

bill of lading 7 receipt

Billy Budd's captain 4 Vere

billy club 5 baton 6 cudgel 8 bludgeon 9 truncheon 10 knobkerrie, nightstick

bin 3 box 4 crib, vina 5 frame, pungi, stall 6 hamper, trough 9 container 10 receptacle *for coal:* 6 bunker *for fish:* 5 kench

binary 4 dual 5 duple 6 bifold, double, duplex 7 twofold 9 dualistic

bind 3 tie 4 frap, gird, tape 5 chain, dress, tie up 6 cement, enserf, fetter, ligate 7 bandage, confine, enchain, spancel 8 astringe, enfetter, ligature 9 constrict *bird's wings:* 6 pinion *to secrecy:* 4 tile, tyle *with twigs:* 5 withe

binding *combining form:* 5 desis

binge 3 bat, bum, bun, jag 4 bust, orgy, soak, tear, time, toot 5 blast, booze, drunk, fling, souse, spree 6 bender, ran-tan 7 blowoff, blowout, carouse, debauch, rampage, splurge, wassail 8 carousal, rowdydow 9 bacchanal, brannigan 11 bacchanalia, compotation

bingo 5 beano

Binnui *father:* 7 Henadad *son:* 7 Noadiah

biographer 9 memoirist *American:*
5 Weems (Parson) 6 Parton (James)
7 Freeman (Douglas) 8 Bradford (Gamaliel), Sandburg (Carl) *English:* 6 Aubrey
(John), Morley (John), Walton (Izaak)
7 Boswell (James) 8 Strachey (Lytton)
French: 7 Maurois (Andre) *German:*
6 Ludwig (Emil) *Greek:* 8 Plutarch *Italian:*
6 Vasari (Giorgio) *Roman:* 9 Suetonius

biography 3 bio 4 life, obit 5 diary, story
6 memoir 7 history, journal, letters, profile
8 obituary 11 confessions

biological category 5 class, genus,
order 6 family, phylum 7 species, variety
10 subspecies

bionomics 7 ecology

birchbark 5 canoe

bird *African:* 4 coly, fink, taha, tock
5 paauw 6 barbet, bulbul, jabiru, quelea,
whidah 7 courser, finfoot, marabou, ostrich,
touraco 8 hornbill, oxpecker, parakeet,
umbrette 9 beefeater, broadbill, francolin,
napecrest, trochilus 10 hammerhead, tambourine *antarctic:* 4 skua 7 penguin
10 sheathbill *aquatic:* 3 auk, cob, ern,
mew 4 cobb, coot, duck, erne, gony, gull,
loon, skua, swan, teal, tern 5 booby,
cahow, goose, grebe, murre, rotch, solan
6 fulmar, gannet, hagdon, petrel, puffin,
rotche, scoter, wigeon 7 anhinga, dovekey,
dovekie, finfoot, mallard, moorhen, pelican,
penguin, skimmer, widgeon 8 alcatras,
baldpate, dabchick, murrelet 9 albatross,
cormorant, gallinule, guillemot, kittiwake
10 shearwater, sheathbill *arctic:* 3 auk
4 knot, skua, xema 5 murre, rotch 6 fulmar, jaeger, rotche 7 dovekey, dovekie
9 guillemot *Asian:* 4 kora, myna, ruff,
smew 5 mynah, pewit, pitta 6 chukar,
drongo, dunlin, hoopoe 7 courser, hill tit,
lapwing, peacock, sirgang 8 accentor, dotterel, hornbill, parakeet, tragopan, wheatear
9 brambling, francolin *Australian:* 3 emu
4 kahu, koel, koil, lory 5 arara, galah, pitta
6 drongo, leipoa 7 boobook, bustard, figbird, waybung 8 bellbird, bushlark, cockatoo, lorikeet, lyrebird, manucode, megapode, morepork, parakeet 9 cassowary,
coachwhip, frogmouth, pardalote *blackbird:*
3 ani, daw, pie 4 crow, merl, rook 5 amsel,
merle, ousel, ouzel, raven 6 chough, magpie, thrush 7 grackle, jackdaw, redwing
carrion-eating: 4 aura 5 urubu 6 condor
7 buzzard, vulture *Central American:*
4 guan, ibis 5 booby, macaw 6 barbet, jabiru, toucan 7 bittern, cotinga, jacamar,
quetzal, tinamou 8 curassow, troupial
chimney-nesting: 5 swift *class:* 4 Aves

colony: 5 roost 7 rookery *combining
form:* 5 ornis 6 ornith 7 ornitho 8 ornithes
(plural) *corvine:* (see crow family below)
crocodile: 9 trochilus *crow family:* 3 daw,
jay, kae 4 rook 5 raven 6 chough, corbie,
magpie 7 jackdaw *diving:* 3 auk 4 smew
5 grebe, murre 6 dipper, petrel 8 murrelet
9 guillemot, merganser *European:* 3 mag,
mew, nun 4 clee, darr, gled, mall, merl,
pope, rook, ruff, shag, smew, wren
5 amsel, crake, egret, finch, glede, merle,
ousel, ouzel, pewit, pipit, terek, whaup
6 cuckoo, dunlin, hoopoe, linnet, martin,
merlin, missel, redleg, roller, thrush 7 bustard, jackdaw, kestrel, lapwing, martlet,
ortolan, redwing, ruddock, sparrow, wagtail,
wryneck 8 accentor, blackcap, brantail,
dabchick, dotterel, garganey, nightjar, nuthatch, peesweep, redstart, reedling, starling, throstle, wheatear, whimbrel, whinchat,
woodcock 9 brambling, chaffinch, crossbill,
fieldfare, stonechat 10 chiffchaff, goatsucker, kingfisher 11 lammergeier *extinct:*
3 moa 4 dodo, mamo 8 Diatryma 9 aepyornis, solitaire *fabulous:* 3 roc 5 hansa
6 simurg 7 phoenix, simurgh *fish-eating:*
4 erne *flightless:* 3 emu, moa 4 dodo,
kagu, kiwi, rhea, weka 5 kakapo, ratite,
takahe 7 apteryx, ostrich, penguin, roatelo
8 Diatryma, notornis 9 cassowary *fruit-eating:* 4 coly 6 parrot, toucan *game:* 4 duck,
guan, rail, sora, teal 5 brant, goose, quail,
snipe 6 chukar, grouse, turkey 7 bustard,
mallard, pintail, widgeon 8 baldpate, bobwhite, moorfowl, pheasant, shoveler, tragopan, wildfowl, woodcock 9 merganser, partridge, ptarmigan *ground-dwelling:*
5 colin, quail 6 grouse, peahen, turkey
7 chicken, peacock, peafowl 8 bobwhite,
moorfowl, pheasant 9 partridge, ptarmigan
Hawaiian: 2 io 3 ava, ioa, iwa 4 koae,
mamo, moho, omao *Indian:* 4 baya, kala,
koel, koil 5 sarus, shama 6 argala, bulbul,
homrai, luggar 7 peacock 8 adjutant,
amadavat, tragopan *Jamaican:* 7 vervain
large: 3 emu, moa 4 guan 5 eagle 6 curlew, jabiru, willet 7 bustard, megapod,
ostrich, pelican, seriema 8 curassow, megapode, shoebill *largest:* 7 ostrich *Madagascar:* 6 drongo 7 anhinga, kirombo, roatelo *marsh:* 4 coot, rail, sora 5 crane,
snipe, stilt 8 reedling 9 gallinule *Mexican:*
6 jacana *mythical:* 3 roc 7 phoenix
9 feng-huang, feng-hwang *New Zealand:*
3 ihi, kea, poe, tui 4 huia, kaka, kaki, kiwi,
koko, ruru, titi, weka 6 kakapo 7 apteryx
8 morepork, notornis *nocturnal:* 3 owl
5 cahow, owlet 7 bullbat, dorhawk 8 guacharo, nightjar 9 nighthawk 10 goatsucker
North American: 3 ani, tit 4 coot, pape,
sora, stib, wamp, wren 5 booby, colin,

crane, egret, junco, murre, robin, swift, veery, vireo 6 chebec, darter, dunlin, fulmar, grouse, hagdon, phoebe, towhee, turkey, verdin, willet 7 anhinga, blue jay, catbird, flicker, grackle, tanager 8 bobolink, bobwhite, cardinal, killdeer, nuthatch, thrasher, titmouse, wheatear 9 chickadee, crossbill, nighthawk, partridge, snakebird 10 bufflehead 12 whippoorwill *of Arabian Nights:* 3 roc *of brilliant plumage:* 4 lory, toco, tody 5 macaw, pitta 6 oriole, parrot, toucan, trogon 7 jacamar, kirombo, minivet 8 lorikeet, parakeet, pheasant, tragopan *of omen:* 7 waybird *of peace:* 4 dove *of prey:* 3 owl 4 gled, hawk, kite 5 buteo, eagle, glead, glede, harpy 6 condor, elenet, falcon, osprey, raptor 7 buzzard, goshawk, harrier, kestrel, vulture 8 caracara 9 accipiter 11 lammergeier *passerine:* (see **songbird** below) *razorbilled:* 3 auk *relating to:* 5 avian, avine 8 ornithic *shore:* 3 auk 4 gull, ruff, tern 5 reeve, snipe, stilt 6 avocet, avoset, curlew, dunlin, plover, puffin, willet 7 lapwing, skimmer 8 dotterel, killdeer, redshank, whimbrel, woodcock 9 phalarope, sandpiper, turnstone *small:* 3 tit 4 tody, wren 5 finch, pewee, pipit, serin, sylph, vireo 6 canary, sappho, tomtit, verdin 7 manakin, sparrow 8 titmouse 9 chickadee *songbird:* 3 jay, tit 4 chat, crow, lark, wren 5 finch, mavie, mavis, pipit, robin, shama, veery, vireo 6 bulbul, canary, dipper, linnet, oriole, shrike, thrush 7 catbird, creeper, hill tit, kinglet, redwing, skylark, sparrow, swallow, tanager, titlark, wagtail, warbler, waxwing 8 accentor, amadavat, bobolink, brantail, cardinal, nuthatch, philomel, redstart, starling, thrasher, whinchat, woodlark 9 chickadee, stonechat 10 chiffchaff, flycatcher 11 nightingale *South American:* 3 ara, hia 4 anna, guan, jacu, loro, mitu, rhea, soco, toco, yeni 5 chaja, egret, macaw, potoo, sylph 6 chunga, cracid, jabiru, motmot, sappho, toucan 7 cariama, cotinga, hoatzin, jacamar, limpkin, manakin, seriema, tinamou 8 boatbill, caracara, curassow, guacharo, hoactzin, screamer, tapacolo, tapaculo, terutero, troupial 9 campanero, trumpeter *talking:* 4 myna 5 mynah 6 parrot *tropical:* 3 ani 6 barbet, drongo, motmot, quezal, toucan, trogon 7 cacique, hoatzin, jacamar, manakin, quetzal, sawbill, waxbill 8 guacharo, hoactzin, troupial *turkey-like:* 8 curassow *unfledged:* 4 eyas 5 chick 6 gorlin 8 nestling *wading:* 4 ibis, rail 5 crane, egret, heron, stork 6 godwit, jabiru, jacana 7 bittern, oourlan, limpkin, tattler 8 boatbill, flamingo, shoebill, umbrette 9 spoonbill 10 hammerhead *web-footed:* 3 auk 4 duck, loon, swan 5 goose, murre

6 avocet, avoset, darter, fulmar, gannet, petrel, puffin 7 anhinga, pelican, penguin 8 shoveler 9 albatross, cormorant, guillemot, merganser, razorbill, snakebird 10 shearwater *West Indian:* 3 ani 4 tody

birdbrain 5 dummy, dunce, idiot, moron 7 dullard 8 dullhead, dumbbell 9 ignoramus, simpleton 10 rattlehead 11 featherhead

birdcage *large:* 6 aviary, volary, volery

birdlife 5 ornis 8 avifauna

bird pepper 8 capsicum

birds' eggs *study of:* 6 oology

bird's head *top:* 5 pilea (plural) 6 pileum

birr 3 pep 4 tuck 5 moxie, vigor 6 energy 7 potency 9 hardihood

birth 4 dawn, flow, rise, slip, stem 5 arise, issue, onset, start 6 outset, spring 7 bearing, emanate, genesis, opening, proceed 8 geniture, nascence, nascency, nativity, outstart 9 beginning, originate 10 derive from 12 commencement *combining form:* 4 toky

birth-control leader 6 Sanger (Margaret)

birth flower *April:* 5 daisy *August:* 9 gladiolus *December:* 10 poinsettia *February:* 8 primrose *January:* 9 carnation *July:* 8 sweet pea *June:* 4 rose *March:* 6 violet *May:* 15 lily of the valley *November:* 13 chrysanthemum *October:* 6 dahlia *September:* 5 aster

birthmark 4 mole 5 nevus, point, trait 7 feature 9 character

birthright 6 legacy 8 appanage, heritage 9 heritance, patrimony, privilege 10 perquisite 11 inheritance, prerogative

birthroot 8 trillium

birthstone *April:* 7 diamond 8 sapphire *August:* 7 peridot 8 sardonyx *December:* 6 zircon 9 turquoise *February:* 8 amethyst *January:* 6 garnet *July:* 4 ruby *June:* 5 agate, pearl 11 alexandrite *March:* 6 jasper 10 aquamarine, bloodstone *May:* 7 emerald *November:* 5 topaz *October:* 4 opal 10 tourmaline *September:* 8 sapphire 10 chrysolite

biscuit 3 bun 4 roll, rusk, snap 6 bisque, cookie 7 cracker 8 cracknel, hardtack *Scottish:* 4 bake

bishop *district:* 7 diocese *headdress:* 5 miter, mitre *seat of office:* 3 see *skullcap:* 9 zucchetto *staff:* 7 crosier, crozier *throne:* 8 cathedra

bishopric 3 see 7 diocese

bismuth *symbol:* 2 Bi

bison *European:* 6 wisent 7 aurochs *family:* 7 Bovidae *North American:* 7 buffalo

bistered 4 dark 5 brown, dusky, swart 6 brunet, swarth 7 swarthy 11 darkskinned

bistro 4 café 6 nitery 7 cabaret, hot spot
8 nightery 9 nightclub, night spot 11 discotheque 13 watering place

bit 3 end, jot 4 atom, bite, curb, drop, iota,
mite, time, whet 5 check, minim, scrap,
space, speck, spell, while 6 bridle, hold in,
morsel 7 inhibit, smidgen, stretch 8 fragment, hold back, hold down, molecule,
mouthful, particle, restrain, withhold 9 constrain

bit by bit 9 gradually, piecemeal

bitch goddess 7 success

bite 3 cut, eat, lot 4 burn, chaw, chew,
gnaw, part, tapa 5 bever, chack, champ,
chomp, erode, mug-up, munch, piece,
quota, scour, share, slice, smart, snack,
stang, sting, tooth 6 crunch, morsel, nibble
7 corrode, eat away, partage, portion,
scrunch 8 mouthful 9 allotment, allowance,
masticate

Bithiah's husband 5 Mered

biting 5 crisp, nippy 7 cutting, ingoing,
mordant 8 clear-cut, incisive 9 sarcastic,
trenchant 11 penetrating

bitter 3 bad 4 acid, hard, tart 5 acerb,
acrid, harsh, sharp 6 brutal, picric, rugged,
severe, woeful 7 austere, divided, galling,
hostile, painful 8 grievous, rigorous, virulent
9 alienated, amaroidal, rancorous, vexatious, vitriolic 10 afflictive, disturbing,
unpleasant 11 distasteful, distressing,
intemperate, unpalatable 12 antagonistic,
disagreeable *combining form:* 4 picr
5 picro

bitterness 8 acrimony, asperity

bitterroot 7 dogbane

bitumen 3 tar 5 pitch 7 asphalt, naphtha
8 blacktop

bivalve 4 clam, spat 6 cockle, mussel,
oyster, pholas 7 geoduck, goeduck, mollusk, pandora, piddock, scallop 10 brachio-
pod

bivouac 4 camp 6 encamp, laager,
maroon 10 encampment

bizarre 3 odd 5 antic, queer, weird 7 curious, oddball, strange, unusual 8 peculiar,
singular 9 fantastic, grotesque 10 outlandish

Bizet opera 6 Carmen

blab 3 gab, yak 4 chat, talk, tell 5 rumor
6 babble, betray, gabble, gossip, jabber,
reveal, tattle 7 chatter, divulge, palaver
8 disclose, give away

blabber 3 gab 4 chat 5 clack, drool, prate
6 babble, drivel, gabber, gabble, jabber,
magpie, prater 7 blather, chatter, palaver,
prattle, twaddle 8 jabberer, prattler 9 chatterer 10 chatterbox

blabbermouth 6 gabber, magpie, prater
7 windbag 8 jabberer, prattler 9 bandar-log
10 chatterbox

black 3 jet 4 ebon, foul, inky, noir, onyx
5 bleak, dirty, ebony, nasty, raven, sable,
slate, soily, utter 6 bruise, dismal, dreary,
filthy, gloomy, grubby, impure, pitchy, somber 7 contuse, piceous, squalid, unclean
8 absolute, charcoal, complete, funereal,
outright 9 downright, out-and-out, pitch-
dark 10 depressing, depressive, oppressive 11 atramentous, dispiriting *combining
form:* 3 mel 4 atro, mela, melo 5 melam,
melan 6 melano

blackball 4 veto 7 boycott, exclude
9 ostracize

black bass 7 sunfish 10 priestfish

black beast 4 hate 7 bugbear 8 anathema 9 bête noire 11 abomination, detestation

blackbird see at **bird**

black cohosh 7 bugbane

black crappie 7 sunfish 10 calico bass

black death 6 plague

black diamond 4 coal 8 hematite 9 car-
bonado

blacken 4 slur, soot 5 libel, smear
6 defame, malign, vilify 7 asperse, slander,
traduce 10 calumniate

black eye 4 blot, onus, slur 5 mouse,
odium, stain 6 shiner, stigma 11 bar sinister

blackfish 5 whale 6 bowfin, salmon, tautog 7 galjoen 8 luderick

Black Forest *city:* 10 Baden-Baden
peak: 8 Feldberg *river:* 5 Rhine 6 Danube

black gold 3 oil 9 maldonite, petroleum

blackguard 4 heel 5 knave, rogue 6 rascal 7 lowlife, villain 9 miscreant, scoundrel

blackhead 4 clam 5 sebum 6 comedo,
mussel 9 scaup duck

blackheart 9 sandpiper 12 whortleberry

blackjack 3 oak 6 coerce 7 tankard
9 scaup duck 10 sphalerite

black lead 8 graphite

black letter 6 Gothic 10 Old English

black magic 10 witchcraft

blackmail 6 extort 8 chantage 9 extortion

Black Muslim founder 4 Fard (Wallace) 6 Farrad (Walli)

black out 5 annul, erase, faint, swoon
6 cancel, delete, efface 7 expunge
10 obliterate

blackpoll 7 warbler

Black Prince 6 Edward

Blackshirt 7 fascist

blacksmith 4 fish 6 forger, plover 7 farrier, striker 10 horseshoer

blacktail 6 dassie 11 salmon trout

blackthorn 4 cane, plum 7 pear haw
8 cocktail

black vomit 11 hematemesis, yellow
fever

blackwash 5 libel 6 malign, vilify
7 asperse, slander, traduce 9 denigrate
10 calumniate, scandalize, villainize
black widow 6 spider
bladder 3 sac 4 cyst 5 pouch 6 vesica
7 blister, vacuole 7 vesicae (plural), vesicle
8 vesicula 9 vesiculae (plural) *combining
form:* 3 asc 4 asci, asco, cyst, phys
5 cysto, physo
blah 4 bosh, dull 5 hooey 6 bunkum,
dreary, humbug, stodgy 7 humdrum 8 banausic, nonsense, pishposh, plodding 10 balderdash, monotonous, pedestrian
blamable see blameworthy
blame 3 rap 4 onus 5 fault, guilt, knock
6 accuse 7 censure, condemn
8 denounce, reproach 9 criticize, reprehend, reprobate 10 accusation, denunciate,
imputation 12 condemnation, denunciation,
reprehension *Scottish:* 4 wite, wyte 6 dirdum
blameless 4 good, pure 5 clean 8 innocent, unguilty 9 crimeless, exemplary, faultless, guiltless, lily-white, righteous 10 inculpable
blameworthy 5 amiss 6 guilty, sinful,
unholy 8 culpable, faultful 10 censurable,
delinquent, illaudable, punishable 13 reprehensible, uncommendable
blanch 4 pale 5 quail, start, white, wince
6 bleach, flinch, recoil, shrink, whiten
7 decolor, squinch
blanched 3 wan 4 ashy, pale 5 ashen,
livid, waxen 6 doughy, pallid 9 colorless
Blancheflor's beloved 6 Flores, Floris
bland 4 flat, mild, soft 5 balmy, banal,
suave, vapid 6 gentle, smooth, urbane,
watery 7 insipid, lenient, sapless 8 waterish 10 namby-pamby, wishy-washy
blandish 3 con 4 coax 6 cajole 7 blarney, flatter, wheedle 8 soft-soap
9 sweet-talk
blandishment 3 oil 7 blarney, incense
8 flattery, soft soap 9 adulation
blank 4 skip 5 chasm, empty, utter
6 vacant 7 deadpan 8 absolute, omission
9 downright, out-and-out, oversight 11 preterition 12 inexpressive, unexpressive
blanket 3 cap 5 cover, crown 6 afghan,
stroud 7 overlay 8 overcast 10 overspread
Spanish: 6 sarape, serape
blankness 7 vacancy, vacuity 9 emptiness 11 vacuousness
blare 5 shout 6 scream, shriek
blaring 4 loud 7 roaring 8 piercing
10 stentorian 11 full-mouthed, stentorious
12 earsplitting
blarney 3 con, oil 4 coax 6 cajole
7 incense, wheedle 8 blandish, flattery, soft
soap 9 adulation, sweet-talk 12 blandishment

blasé 5 jaded 7 knowing, worldly 8 mondaine 9 apathetic 11 indifferent, worldly-
wise 12 disenchanted, disentranced,
sophisticate 13 disillusioned, sophisticated
blaspheme 5 abuse, curse, swear
6 revile 7 profane
blasphemous 7 profane 12 sacrilegious
blasphemy 5 abuse 7 cursing, cussing,
shaming 8 swearing 9 befouling, profanity,
sacrilege, violation 10 execration 11 desecration, imprecation, profanation
blast 4 bang, beat, belt, boom, clap, dash,
drub, ruin, slam, slug, toot, wham, whip
5 burst, crack, crash, smash, wreck
6 blight, wallop 7 destroy, lambast 8 lambaste 9 overwhelm
blat 6 cry out 7 exclaim 8 blurt out 9 ejaculate
blatant 4 loud 5 gaudy, overt 6 arrant,
brassy, brazen, flashy, garish, patent, tawdry 7 glaring 8 impudent, overbold, strident
9 barefaced, clamorous, shameless,
unabashed 10 boisterous, unblushing,
vociferant, vociferous 11 loudmouthed
12 obstreperous
blather 4 bosh, rave 5 drool, hokum, prate
6 babble, bunkum, drivel, gabble 7 blabber,
prattle, twaddle 8 nonsense 10 balderdash, double-talk, flapdoodle
blaze 4 glow 5 blare, flame, flare, glare,
shine 7 declare 8 announce, proclaim
10 incandesce 11 scintillate *Scottish:*
3 low 4 lowe
blazes 4 hell 5 abyss, hades, Sheol
6 Tophet 7 Gehenna, inferno 9 perdition
blazing 5 afire, fiery 6 aflame, alight,
ardent, fervid, red-hot 7 burning, fervent,
flaming, flaring, ignited 9 perfervid 10 passionate 11 conflagrant, impassioned
blazing star 8 tritonia 9 colicroot
blazon 5 sound 7 declare, publish
8 announce, proclaim 9 advertise, broadcast 10 annunciate, bruit about, promulgate
bleach 5 white 6 blanch, blench, whiten
7 decolor 8 peroxide
bleak 4 dour, grim, hard 5 harsh 6 dismal,
dreary, gloomy, severe, somber 7 austere
8 funereal 9 stringent 10 depressing,
oppressive 13 disheartening
blear 3 dim 4 blur, dull 5 faint, vague
7 obscure, shadowy, unclear 10 ill-defined,
indistinct
bleary 3 dim 5 all in, faint, spent, vague
6 effete, used up 7 drained, far-gone,
obscure, shadowy, unclear, worn-out
8 depleted 9 exhausted, washed-out 10 ill-
defined, indistinct
bleat 3 baa 4 crab, fuss, yawp 5 gripe
6 squawk, yammer 7 blow off
bleed 4 ooze, seep, weep 5 exude, mulct,

stick, sweat 6 extort, fleece, strain 8 transude

bleeding heart 8 dicentra 11 sympathizer

blemish 3 mar 4 flaw, harm, hurt, scar, vice, wart 5 fault, spoil 6 blotch, damage, defect, impair, injure 7 blister, tarnish, vitiate 8 pockmark 13 disfigurement

blench 5 quail, start, white, wince 6 bleach, flinch, recoil, shrink, whiten 7 decolor, squinch

blend 3 mix 4 fuse, meld 5 alloy, immix, unify, unite 6 commix, fusion 7 amalgam, arrange, combine, mixture 8 coalesce, compound, conflate, immingle, intermix 9 commingle, composite, harmonize, integrate, interfuse 10 amalgamate, commixture, symphonize, synthesize 11 interfusion, orchestrate 12 amalgamation, intermixture

blender setting 4 whip 5 puree

bless 4 laud 5 extol 6 hallow, praise 7 glorify 8 eulogize, sanctify 9 celebrate 10 consecrate, panegyrize

blessed 4 holy 6 sacred 7 saintly 8 hallowed 9 unprofane 10 sanctified 11 consecrated

blessedness 5 bliss 9 beatitude, happiness 12 blissfulness

blessing 2 OK 4 boon, good, okay 5 favor, grace 6 thanks 7 benefit, benison, godsend 8 approval 9 advantage 11 approbation, benediction 12 thanksgiving

blight 3 nip 4 dash, ruin 5 blast 7 disease

blimp 5 fatso, fatty 7 airship 8 zeppelin 9 dirigible

blind 4 daze, dull 5 decoy, drunk, front, shill 6 capper, dazzle 7 eyeless, muddled, shutter 8 bedazzle, unseeing 9 pixilated, shillaber, sightless 10 inebriated, lackluster, lusterless, visionless 11 intoxicated *combining form:* 5 typhl 6 typhlo

blind alley 6 pocket 7 dead end, impasse 8 cul-de-sac

blind god 4 Hoth 5 Cupid, Hoder, Hodur, Hothr

blindworm 6 lizard

blink 3 bat 4 wink 5 flash 7 flicker, nictate, twinkle 9 nictitate

blink at 4 omit 6 forget, ignore, slight 7 connive, neglect 8 discount, overlook 9 disregard

blip 3 box 4 cuff, slap 5 smack, spank 6 buffet, censor, screen 9 expurgate 10 bowdlerize

bliss 4 Zion 6 Canaan, heaven 7 elysium, nirvana 8 empyrean, paradise 9 beatitude, happiness 11 blessedness

blissful 5 happy 6 elated 8 beatific, ecstatic, euphoric 9 contented

blissfulness 7 ecstasy 8 euphoria 9 beatitude, happiness 10 exaltation 11 blessedness

blister 4 bleb, flay 5 blain, bulla, slash 6 canker, scathe, scorch 7 lambast, scarify, scourge, vesicle 8 lambaste, vesicate 9 castigate, excoriate *combining form:* 7 vesicul 8 vesiculo

blithe 3 gay 4 boon 5 jolly, merry, sunny 6 cheery, chirpy, jocund, jovial 7 gleeful 8 cheerful, chirrupy, mirthful, sunbeamy 9 lightsome 12 lighthearted

blithering 4 rank 5 gross, utter 7 blasted 8 absolute, outright, positive 9 downright, out-and-out

blithesome see blithe

blitz 4 raid 7 bombard 10 mass attack 11 bombardment

bloated 5 puffy 6 stuffy 7 pompous 8 arrogant 10 pontifical 11 magisterial 13 self-important

bloc 4 ring 5 party 7 combine, faction 8 alliance 9 coalition 11 combination

block 3 bar, dam, ell 4 clog, fill, plug, stop, wall, wing 5 annex, brake, choke, close 6 cut off, hinder, impede 7 barrier, congest, occlude, stopper 8 obstruct 9 barricade, extension, intercept *iron:* 5 anvil

blockade 3 bar 4 stop, wall 5 beset, siege 6 invest 7 barrier, besiege 9 barricade, beleaguer, blank wall, roadblock

blockbuster 4 bomb

blockhead 4 dolt, dope 5 dunce, idiot, ninny 8 clodpate, dumbbell, numskull 9 simpleton 10 thickskull

blockheaded 4 dumb 5 dense, thick 6 stupid 7 doltish 10 numskulled

block out 5 close, draft 6 screen, shroud, sketch 7 outline, shut off 8 obstruct, skeleton 9 adumbrate 12 characterize

block up 4 clog, plug, stop

bloke 3 guy, man 4 chap, gent 6 fellow 9 gentleman

blond 4 fair 5 light, straw 6 flaxen, golden 7 towhead 8 platinum 9 towheaded

blood 4 gore 6 murder, origin 7 descent, lineage 8 ancestry 10 extraction *cancer of:* 8 leukemia *cell:* 3 red 4 poly 5 white 8 hemocyte, monocyte, platelet 9 corpuscle, leukocyte 10 lymphocyte 11 erythrocyte, granulocyte *clot:* 8 thrombus *clotted:* 4 gore *coloring matter:* 10 hemoglobin *combining form:* 3 hem 4 emia, haem, hema, hemi, hemo 5 aemia, haema, haemo, hemat, hemia 6 haemat, haemia, hemato, sangui 7 haemato 8 sanguini, sanguino *disease:* 6 anemia 8 leukemia 10 hemophilia *factor:* 2 RH *feud:* 8 vendetta *fluid part:* 5 serum 6 plasma *of the gods:* 5 ichor *particle in:* 7 embolus *poisoning:* 6 pyemia 7 toxemia 8 copremia, sapremia 10 septicemia *pressure:* 8 systolic 9 diastolic *relating to:* 5 hemal, hemic 7 hematal *serum:* 6 plasma *study of:* 10 hematology *sugar:* 7 glucose

bloodbath 7 carnage 8 butchery, massacre 9 slaughter

bloodless 4 dull, hard, pale 6 anemic, pallid, watery 8 waterish 9 insensate 10 anesthetic, insensible 11 insensitive

bloodletting 10 phlebotomy 11 venesection

bloodlike 8 hematoid

bloodline 6 family, strain

bloodroot 7 puccoon 8 turmeric 10 tetterwort 11 Indian paint

bloodshed *place of:* 8 aceldama

bloodstained 4 gory 7 imbrued 8 sanguine 10 sanguinary 11 ensanguined, sanguineous

bloodstone 10 chalcedony

bloodsucker 4 tick 5 lamia, leech 6 lizard, sponge 7 sponger, vampire 8 barnacle, hanger on, parasite 10 freeloader 12 lounge lizard

bloodthirsty 8 sanguine 9 homicidal, murdering, murderous 10 sanguinary 11 sanguineous

blood vessel 4 vein 5 aorta 6 artery 7 jugular 9 capillary *combining form:* 3 vas 4 angi, vasi, vaso 5 angio *rupture:* 6 rhexis

bloodwort 6 yarrow 8 centaury 10 herb robert 11 salad burnet

bloody 4 gory, grim 7 imbrued 8 sanguine 9 cutthroat, homicidal, murdering, murderous 10 sanguinary 11 ensanguined, sanguineous 12 slaughterous

bloom 4 blow, glow, posy 5 blush 6 flower 7 blossom, burgeon 10 effloresce

blooper 4 slip, trip 5 boner, break, error, fluff, gaffe, lapse 6 boo-boo, bungle 7 blunder, faux pas, mistake 8 solecism 9 indecorum 11 impropriety

blossom 3 bud 4 blow, glow, open, posy 5 bloom, blush, flush 6 flower, unfold 7 burgeon 10 effloresce

blot 4 blur, onus, slur, smut, spot 5 brand, odium, stain 6 stigma 7 bestain, blemish 8 black eye, discolor 11 bar sinister

blotch 6 macula, macule, mottle 7 splodge, splotch *combining form:* 5 macul 6 maculi, maculo

blot out 5 abate, annul, erase 6 cancel, delete, efface 7 abolish, expunge 9 eradicate, extirpate 10 annihilate, extinguish, obliterate 11 exterminate

blotto see drunk

blouse 5 middy, shirt, smock, tunic 6 basque, guimpe

bloviate 4 rant, rave 5 mouth, orate 7 declaim, soapbox 8 harangue, perorate

blow 3 bop, fan, hit, jar 4 bang, bash, belt, biff, brag, bump, cuff, gasp, gust, huff, jolt, pant, puff, slam, slug, swat, whop, wind 5 bloom, boast, break, crack, pound, prate, punch, shock, slosh, smack, smash, vaunt, waste, whack 6 flower, impact, ruffle, thwack, wallop, winnow 7 blossom, burgeon, consume, fritter, respite 8 breather, knockout, outbloom, squander 9 bastinado, collision, dissipate, gasconade, throw away 10 concussion, effloresce, frivol away, percussion, trifle away 11 rodomontade

blow-by-blow 6 minute 8 detailed, itemized, thorough 9 clocklike 10 particular

blowhard see boaster

blow in 4 come 6 arrive, show up, turn up

blowout 4 bash 6 shindy 7 shindig

blowsy 5 dowdy 6 frowsy, sordid 8 slattern 10 slatternly 13 draggletailed

blow up 4 boil, burn, fume, rage 5 anger, burst, go off 6 seethe 7 bristle, explode 8 boil over, detonate, disprove, dynamite 9 discredit

blowy 4 airy 5 gusty, windy 6 breezy

blubber 3 cry, sob 4 pipe, wail, weep 6 boohoo

bludgeon 3 bat 4 club 5 baton, billy, bully 6 cudgel, hector 7 bluster, war club 8 browbeat, bulldoze, bullyrag 9 bastinado, billy club, strong-arm, truncheon 10 intimidate, nightstick *British:* 4 cosh

blue 3 low, sea 4 down, racy 5 ocean, salty, shady, spicy 6 purple, risqué, wicked 7 profane 8 dejected, downcast, off-color 9 depressed, woebegone 10 dispirited, suggestive 11 downhearted 12 disconsolate *combining form:* 3 ind 4 cyan, indi, indo 5 cyano *dark:* 5 perse 6 indigo *grayish:* 5 merle, slate 7 celeste *greenish:* 4 aqua, bice, cyan, teal 5 beryl 6 cobalt 7 azurite 8 calamine 9 turquoise *moderate:* 5 copen *reddish:* 5 smalt 6 marine, purple, violet 7 cyanine, gentian, lobelia 8 mazarine *sky:* 5 azure 8 cerulean

____ **Blue** 3 Ben

blue blood 5 elite 6 aristo, gentry 7 aristoi 9 gentility, gentleman, patrician 10 aristocrat, upper class 11 aristocracy

bluebonnet 4 Scot 6 parrot 10 cornflower

Blue Boy painter 12 Gainsborough (Thomas)

bluecoat 3 cop 5 bobby 6 copper 8 Dogberry 9 constable, policeman

blue-eyed 8 favorite, precious 10 fairhaired

Bluegrass State 8 Kentucky

Blue Grotto site 5 Capri

bluejacket 6 sailor

blue jeans 6 denims

blue moon 3 age, eon 4 aeon 7 dog's age 8 coon's age, eternity 12 donkey's years

bluenose 4 prig 5 prude 7 puritan 8 comstock 9 Mrs. Grundy, nice Nelly 10 goody-goody

bluenosed 4 prig, prim 6 prissy, stuffy 7 prudish 8 priggish 9 Victorian 10 tight-laced 11 puritanical, straitlaced

blue-pencil 4 edit 6 delete, revise

bluepoint 6 oyster

blueprint 4 cast, plan 5 chart 6 design, devise, scheme, sketch 7 arrange, outline, project 8 game plan, strategy

blue-ribbon 3 top 5 prime 6 Grade A 7 capital 8 five-star, top-notch 9 excellent, first-rate, top-drawer 10 first-class 11 first-string

blues 5 dumps, gloom 7 dismals, sadness 9 dejection 10 depression, melancholy 11 unhappiness 12 mournfulness

bluff 3 act 4 curt, fake, fool, sham 5 blunt, feign, frank, gruff, rough, sharp, trick 6 abrupt, affect, assume, betray, candid, crusty, delude, direct, humbug, illude, snippy 7 beguile, brusque, deceive, mislead, pretend 8 snippety 9 outspoken 10 forthright, no-nonsense 11 counterfeit, double-cross, plainspoken, short-spoken

blunder 4 bull, goof, mess, slip, trip 5 boner, botch, error, fluff, gaffe, gum up, lapse 6 bobble, bollix, bumble, bungle, goof up 7 blooper, louse up, mistake, stumble 8 flounder

blunderbuss 3 gun 7 bungler, firearm

blunt 4 bald, curt, dull, mull, numb 5 bluff, brief, gruff, short 6 abrupt, benumb, crusty, deaden, obtund, obtuse, snippy, snubby, weaken 7 brusque, cripple, disable, disedge, stupefy 8 enfeeble, hebetate, snippety 9 attenuate, undermine 10 debilitate 11 desensitize 12 unstrengthen

blur 3 dim, fog 4 blot, dull, mist, onus, slur, spot 5 befog, blear, brand, cloud, muddy, odium, smear, stain, taint 6 smudge, stigma 7 becloud, besmear, confuse, tarnish 8 besmirch, black eye, discolor 11 bar sinister *In printing:* 6 mackle

blurb 2 ad 4 plug, puff 6 notice 7 puffing, write-up 12 commendation

blurt 4 blat, bolt 6 cry out 7 exclaim 9 ejaculate

blush 4 glow, rose 5 bloom, color, flush, rouge 6 mantle, pinken, redden 7 blossom, crimson, roseate

bluster 4 bawl, huff, rage, roar, rout 5 blast, bully, storm 6 bellow, clamor, hector 7 dragoon 8 bludgeon, browbeat, bulldoze, bullyrag 10 intimidate

blustery 4 wild 5 rough 6 raging, stormy 7 furious 8 stormful 9 turbulent 11 tempestuous

boa 5 scarf, snake

board 4 slab 5 get on, house, lodge, put up, table 6 bestow, billet, embark, harbor 7 emplane, entrain, quarter *artist's:* 7 palette

board game see at **game**

boarding house 7 pension 8 pensione

boardwalk 9 promenade

boast 4 blow, brag, crow, puff 5 exalt, mouth, prate, preen, vaunt 7 bluster, show off, swagger 9 gasconade 11 rodomontade

boaster 6 blower, gascon 7 bragger, vaunter 8 blowhard, braggart, puckfist, rodomont 11 braggadocio, rodomontade

boastful 6 braggy 8 arrogant, braggart, vaunting 9 big-headed, conceited 11 pretentious, rodomontade 12 braggadocian, vainglorious 13 swelled-headed *Scottish:* 6 vaunty

boat 3 ark 4 ship 6 vessel 7 steamer *above-water:* 9 hydrofoil *Arab:* 4 dhow *bottom projection:* 4 keel *British:* 5 coble 6 wherry 7 coracle *Canadian:* 6 bateau *canoe-like:* 7 pirogue *captain:* 7 skipper *cargo:* 3 hoy 4 scow 5 barge 6 wherry 7 drogher, gabbard, gabbart, lighter 8 canaller *Chinese:* 4 junk 6 sampan *dock, basin:* 6 marina *Dutch:* 6 dogger, hooker, schult, schuyt 8 bilander *Egyptian:* 6 sandal 8 dahabeah *Eskimo:* 5 kayak, umiak 6 oomiak 7 bidarka 8 bidarkee *fishing:* 4 dory 5 coble, smack 6 dogger, lugger 7 caravel, coracle, tartana, trawler *flat-bottomed:* 4 dory, keel, punt, scow 5 barge, coble 6 bateau, bugeye 7 lighter, pontoon *French:* 7 caravel *front end of:* 3 bow 4 fore, prow *hide-covered:* 7 coracle *Indian:* 4 doni 5 dhoni 7 masoola *Indonesian:* 4 prao, prau, proa 5 prahu *Irish:* 7 currach, curragh *Italian:* 7 gondola *landing:* 3 LST *Levantine:* 4 saic 6 caique *mail:* 6 packet *Mediterranean:* 6 settee *motor:* 7 cruiser, inboard 8 outboard, runabout *narrow:* 4 punt 5 canoe, scull, shell 7 gondola 8 canaller *Nile river:* 6 sandal 8 dahabeah *on a ship:* 3 gig 5 jolly 6 launch 7 pinnace *Philippine:* 5 banca, casco *pole-propelled:* 4 punt 7 gondola *Polynesian:* 4 pahi *race:* 7 regatta *racing:* 3 gig 5 scull, shell, yacht 6 torpid *rear end of:* 3 aft 5 stern *river:* 4 scow 5 barge, canoe, ferry 6 packet, sampan, wherry *round:* 4 gufa 5 goofa, guffa 6 goofah *rowing:* 4 dory 5 coble, scull, shell, skiff 6 caique, dinghy, randan *sailing:* 4 yawl 5 ketch, skiff, sloop, smack, yacht 6 cutter, lateen, lugger, settee **7** pinnace **8** lateener, schooner *Scandinavian:* **4** pram **5** praam *Scottish:* **5** coble **7** currach, curragh, gabbard, gabbart *scouting:* **7** vedette, vidette *small:* **3** cog **4** dory **5** coble, skiff **6** bugeye, cockle, dinghy **7** coracle, shallop *song:* **9** barcarole **10** barcarolle *three-hulled:* **8** trimaran *three-oared:* **6** randan *towing:* **3** tug *twin-hulled:* **9** catamaran *two-masted:* **4** yawl **5** ketch **8** schooner

boatman **5** poler **6** Charon **7** oarsman, paddler **8** deckhand **9** gondolier

boat-shaped **8** scaphoid **9** cymbiform, navicular *combining form:* **5** scaph **6** scapho *ornament:* **3** nef

boatswain **4** bos'n **5** bosun **6** jaeger **10** tropic bird

Boaz's wife **4** Ruth

bob **3** jig, nod, rap, tap **4** buff, crop, dock **5** bunch, float, gigue **6** weight **7** cluster, nosegay

bobbery **3** row **4** fray **5** brawl, fight, melee **6** affray, fracas, hubbub **7** ruction **10** donnybrook **11** disturbance

bobbin **4** pirn **5** quill, spool **7** spindle

bobble **4** mess **5** botch, gum up **6** bollix, bungle, goof up **7** louse up

bobby **6** copper, peeler **7** officer **9** constable, policeman

bobwhite **5** quail **9** partridge

Boccaccio *beloved:* **9** Fiammetta *tales:* **9** Decameron

bode **4** omen **5** augur **7** betoken, portend, presage, promise **8** foreshow **9** foretoken **10** foreshadow

bodement **4** omen **6** augury **7** portent, presage **9** foretoken **10** prognostic

bodiless **9** asomatous, unfleshly **10** discarnate, immaterial, unphysical **11** disembodied, incorporeal **13** insubstantial

bodily **6** carnal **7** fleshly, sensual, somatic **8** corporal, physical **9** corporeal

body **4** bulk, core, mass, mort, pith, soma **5** array, batch, bunch, clump, group, stiff, stock, torso **6** amount, budget, bundle, burden, corpse, corpus, object, parcel, staple, upshot, volume **7** cadaver, carcass, cluster, corpora (plural), purport, quantum, remains **8** physique, quantity **9** aggregate, substance *combining form:* **4** dema, soma, some, somi (plural) **5** somat, somia, somus **6** somata (plural), somato *suffix:* **2** cy

body cavity **5** cecum, sinus **6** coelom **7** abdomen **8** hemocoel

body check **5** block

bodyguard **9** attendant, protector

body of water **3** bay, sea **4** gulf, lake, pond, pool **5** bight, brook, creek, fiord, firth, fjord, inlet, ocean, river **6** lagoon **7** channel, estuary **9** reservoir

body passage **4** duct, iter, vein **5** canal **6** artery, meatus, vessel **7** trachea

body politic **5** state **6** nation

boeotian **4** boob **7** Babbitt **10** middlebrow, philistine

bog **3** fen **4** mire, quag **5** marsh, swamp **6** morass **8** quagmire **9** swampland *combining form:* **4** helo

Bogart film **6** Sahara **7** Dead End, Sabrina **8** Key Largo **10** Casablanca, High Sierra **11** The Big Sleep **15** The African Queen

bog down **5** delay **6** detain, hang up, retard, slow up **7** set back, slacken **10** decelerate

bogey **5** ghost, shade, spook **6** scarer, spirit, wraith **7** phantom, specter **8** revenant **10** apparition

boggle **3** gag, jib, shy **4** balk, mess **5** botch, demur, gum up, stick **6** bollix, bungle, cobble, goof up, strain **7** louse up, nonplus, scruple, stagger, stickle, stumble **9** dumbfound

bogus **4** fake, sham **5** false, phony, snide **6** forged, pseudo **8** spurious **9** brummagem, imitation, pinchbeck **11** counterfeit

Boheme, La *character:* **4** Mimi **7** Rodolfo *composer:* **7** Puccini (Giacomo) *setting:* **5** Paris

Bohemian **7** beatnik, dropout **8** maverick **9** eccentric **10** iconoclast **13** nonconformist

bohunk **3** oaf **4** gawk, lout, lump **5** klutz **6** lubber, lummox **7** palooka

boil **4** bolt, burn, dash, fume, race, rage, rush, stew **5** anger, churn, fling, poach, shoot **6** blow up, bubble, charge, coddle, pimple, seethe, simmer **7** abscess, bristle, ferment, flare up, pustule, smolder **8** furuncle **9** carbuncle

boil down **8** simplify **10** streamline

boiled *combining form:* **5** cocto

boiler suit **8** coverall

boiling **3** hot **5** fiery **6** baking, red-hot **7** burning **8** scalding, sizzling **9** scorching **10** blistering

boil over **4** burn, fume, rage **5** anger **6** blow up, seethe **7** bristle, flare up

boisterous **5** noisy, rowdy **6** unruly **7** blatant, raucous, riotous **8** rowdyish, strident **9** clamorous, termagant, turbulent **10** disorderly, rollicking, rowdydowdy, tumultuous, vociferant, vociferous **11** loudmouthed, openmouthed **12** obstreperous, rambunctious

Boito opera **11** Mefistofele

bold **4** pert, wise **5** bluff, brave, fresh, nervy, sassy, saucy **6** brazen, cheeky **7** doughty, forward, valiant **8** fearless,

impudent, insolent, intrepid, unafraid
9 audacious, dauntless, undaunted 10 courageous, procacious 11 impertinent, smart-alecky 12 contumelious

boldhearted 5 brave 7 doughty, valiant
8 fearless, intrepid, unafraid 9 audacious, dauntless, undaunted 10 courageous

boldness 4 gall 5 nerve 7 chutzpa
8 audacity, chutzpah, temerity 9 hardihood, impudence, insolence, insolency 10 brazenness, disrespect 12 impertinence

Bolero composer 5 Ravel (Maurice)

Bolivia *capital:* 5 La Paz, Sucre *monetary unit:* 9 boliviano

bollix 4 flub, mess 5 botch, gum up 6 bobble, bungle, fumble, goof up 7 louse up

Bolshevik 3 Red 6 commie 7 comrade
9 communist

bolshevism 9 communism

bolster 4 prop 5 brace, carry 6 bear up, buoy up, upbear, uphold 7 shore up, support, sustain 8 backstop, buttress 9 reinforce, underprop 10 strengthen

bolt 3 fly, run 4 cram, dash, flee, gulp, jump, lash, race, rush, tear 5 chase, rivet, scoot, shoot, skirr, slosh, start 6 charge, cry out, englut, gobble, guzzle, spring 7 exclaim, kingpin, make off, scamper, startle 8 blurt out 9 ejaculate, skedaddle 11 ingurgitate 13 thunderstroke

bomb 3 dud 4 bust, flop 5 blitz, lemon, loser, shell 7 failure 9 cannonade

bombard 4 pelt 5 blitz, shell 6 strike
7 assault 9 cannonade

bombardment 4 hail 5 burst, salvo
6 shower, volley 7 barrage 8 drumfire 9 broadside, cannonade, fusillade

bombardon 4 bass 7 helicon 8 bass tuba

bombast 4 rant 7 fustian 8 rhapsody, rhetoric, tumidity 9 turgidity 11 highfalutin, rodomontade

bombastic 7 aureate, flowery, swollen
8 sonorous 9 overblown 10 euphuistic, rhetorical 11 declamatory 12 magniloquent 13 grandiloquent

bombed 5 drunk 11 intoxicated

bombinate 3 hum 4 buzz 5 drone, strum, thrum 6 bumble

bombshell 8 surprise

bomb shelter 4 abri

bona fide 4 real, true 7 genuine 9 authentic, undoubted, veritable 10 sure-enough 11 indubitable

bona fides 9 good faith, sincerity 11 sincereness

bonanza 4 mine 8 eldorado, Golconda, gold mine, treasury 13 treasure trove

bonbon 5 candy 7 fondant 8 confetti (plural), confetto

bond 3 tie 4 bail, knot, link, pact, yoke
5 nexus 6 surety 7 bargain, compact 8 adhesion, clinging, cohesion, contract, covenant, guaranty, ligament, ligature, security, stickage, sticking, vinculum, warranty 9 adherence, agreement, coherence, guarantee 10 connection, connective, convention 11 transaction *combining form:* 4 desm 5 desmo

bondage 4 yoke 6 thrall 7 helotry, peonage, serfage, serfdom, slavery 9 servility, servitude, thralldom, villenage 11 enslavement, subjugation

bondsman 5 slave 7 chattel 9 mancipium

bone *ankle:* 5 talus 6 tarsus *arm:* 4 ulna
6 radius 7 humerus *back:* 5 spine 8 vertebra 9 vertebrae (plural) *breast:* 7 sternum *calf:* 6 fibula *cavity:* 5 fossa *change into:* 6 ossify *cheek:* 5 malar 6 zygoma *chest:* 3 rib *collar:* 8 clavicle *combining form:* 3 ost 4 osse, ossi, oste 5 osseo, osteo 6 osteon, osteus *face:* 5 malar, nasal 7 frontal 8 temporal *finger:* 7 phalanx 8 phalange *foot:* 6 tarsus 9 calcaneum, calcaneus 10 astragalus, metatarsus *hand:* 10 metacarpus *head:* 5 skull, vomer 7 cranium 8 parietal, sphenoid 9 occipital *heel:* 9 calcaneum, calcaneus *hip:* 5 ilium, pubis 6 pelvis 7 ischium *jaw:* 7 maxilla 8 mandible *kneecap:* 7 patella *Latin:* 2 os 5 ossa (plural) *leg:* 5 femur, tibia 6 fibula 7 patella *lower back:* 6 coccyx, sacrum *middle ear:* 5 anvil, incus 6 hammer, stapes 7 malleus, stirrup *relating to:* 6 osteal *shin:* 5 tibia *shoulder blade:* 7 scapula *small:* 7 ossicle *substance:* 6 ossein *thigh:* 5 femur *toe:* 7 phalanx 8 phalange *U-shaped:* 5 hyoid *wrist:* 6 carpus

bonehead 5 dunce 8 clodpate, numskull
10 thick-skull

bone-like 7 osseous, osteoid

boner see blooper

bone up 4 cram 5 study 6 review

bong 4 bell, peal, ring, toll 5 chime, knell

boniface 8 publican, taverner 9 barkeeper, innholder, innkeeper, saloonist 12 saloonkeeper

bonkers 5 crazy 6 insane

bonny 4 fair 6 comely, lovely, pretty
9 beauteous, beautiful 10 attractive 11 good-looking

bon vivant 7 epicure, gourmet 8 gourmand 10 gastronome 11 gastronomer 12 gastronomist, man-about-town

bon voyage 8 farewell, good trip

bony 4 lank, lean 5 gaunt, lanky, spare
6 skinny 7 angular, scraggy, scrawny 8 rawboned

boo 4 hiss, hoot, razz 5 bazoo 7 catcall
8 cannabis 9 marijuana, raspberry

boob 3 oaf 4 dolt, goof, goon 5 chump, dunce 7 Babbitt, fathead 8 boeotian, dolthead, lunkhead 10 middlebrow, philistine

boo-boo see **blooper**

booby hatch 6 asylum 8 loony bin, madhouse, nuthouse 9 funny farm

booby trap 7 pitfall, springe 8 deadfall, trapfall

boodle 4 bilk, loot, mint 5 booty, cheat, cozen, prize, spoil 6 bundle, chisel, chouse, diddle, packet 7 defraud, fortune, plunder 8 flimflam 10 plunderage

boohoo 3 cry, sob 4 blub, wail, weep 7 blubber

book 4 list, tome 5 album, codex, novel, tract 6 enroll, folder, manual, scroll, volume 7 catalog, edition, leaflet, reserve, writing 8 brochure, hardback, inscribe, pamphlet, schedule, softback, treatise 9 monograph, preengage 10 compendium 11 publication *combining form:* 6 biblio *of hours:* 5 Horae *of psalms:* 7 psalter *of public records:* 5 liber

bookdealer 10 bibliopole 11 bouquiniste

bookie see **bookmaker**

bookish 7 learned 8 academic, literary, pedantic 9 scholarly

bookkeeping term 4 loss 5 asset, audit, check, debit, entry 6 budget, credit, income, ledger, profit 7 account, balance, expense, invoice, voucher 8 discount, interest 9 liability 12 depreciation

bookmaker 6 binder, bookie, editor 7 printer 9 publisher

book of account 6 ledger, record 7 journal 8 register

bookplate 5 label 8 ex libris

bookstall 5 kiosk 9 newsstand

boom 4 bang, clap, slam, wham 5 blast, burst, crack, crash, smash 7 thunder 10 prosperity

boomerang 8 backfire, backlash, kick back 10 bounce back

booming 6 robust 7 roaring, thrifty 8 thriving 10 prospering, prosperous 11 flourishing

boon 4 gift, good 5 favor, jolly, merry 6 blithe, jocund, jovial 7 benefit, festive, gleeful, godsend, largess, present 8 blessing, mirthful 9 advantage 10 blithesome 11 benediction, benevolence

boondocks 6 sticks 8 backland, backwash, frontier 9 backwater, backwoods 10 hinterland 11 backcountry

boor 3 oaf 4 lout 5 chuff, churl, clown, yahoo, yokel 6 lummox, mucker, rustic 7 buffoon, bumpkin, groblan, peasant 10 clodhopper

boorish 4 rude 6 coarse, rugged, vulgar 7 ill-bred, loutish, lowbred, lumpish, uncivil 8 churlish, cloddish, clownish, impolite, lub-berly, swainish 9 graceless, tasteless, unrefined 10 robustious, uncultured, ungracious, unpolished 11 clodhopping, ill-mannered, uncivilized

boost 2 up 3 wax 4 hike, jump, plug, push, rise 5 put up, raise 6 beef up, expand, extend, jack up 7 augment, enlarge, magnify, promote, upgrade 8 heighten, increase, multiply 9 advertise 10 aggrandize 12 breakthrough

boot 2 ax 4 bang, fire, kick, sack, tyro 5 chase, chuck, eject, evict 6 bounce, novice, rookie, thrill 7 dismiss, extrude, kick out 8 beginner, freshman, neophyte, throw out 9 discharge, terminate 10 apprentice, tenderfoot *kind:* 5 kamik, wader 6 arctic, chukka, crakow, gaiter, galosh, golosh, mucluc, mukluk 7 bottine, cothurn, gambado, jodhpur, shoepac 8 balmoral, cothurni (plural), muckluck, overshoe, shoepack 9 cothurnus 10 Wellington *Scottish:* 8 gamashes (plural)

Boötes star 8 Arcturus

booth 5 kiosk, stall, stand

boot hill 8 cemetery 9 graveyard 12 burial ground

bootleg 3 run 5 hooch 7 smuggle 9 moonshine 10 bathtub gin, contraband 11 mountain dew

bootless 4 vain 6 futile 7 useless 8 abortive 9 fruitless 10 profitless, unavailing 11 ineffective, ineffectual 12 unproductive, unprofitable

bootlick 4 fawn 5 cower, toady 6 cringe, grovel, kowtow 7 truckle 9 brownnose 11 apple-polish

bootlicker 4 toad 5 toady 7 spaniel 8 lickspit 9 sycophant, toadeater 11 lickspittle

booty 4 loot, swag 5 prize, spoil 6 boodle 7 plunder 10 plunderage

booze 3 jag 4 grog, swig 5 binge, drink, hooch, sauce, souse, swill 6 bender, guzzle, imbibe, liquor, tipple 7 carouse, spirits, swizzle 8 liquor up 9 aqua vitae, brannigan, firewater

boozehound 4 lush, wino 5 drunk 6 sponge 7 guzzler 8 drunkard 9 inebriate

boozer see **boozehound**

bop 3 bat 4 bash, belt, biff, blow, sock, whop 5 pound, smack

borax 6 tincal

Bordeaux wine *district:* 5 Medoc 6 Graves *grape:* 6 Malbec, Merlot 8 Cabernet *name:* 5 Arsac, Ludon, Macau 6 Moulis 7 Labarde, Margaux, Pomerol 8 Cantenac, Pauillac 9 St. Julien, St. Emilion, St. Estephe, St. Laurent *red:* 6 claret

bordello see **brothel**

border 3 hem, lip, rim 4 abut, brim, edge, join, line 5 bound, brink, flank, frame, march, marge, skirt, touch, verge **6** adjoin, butt on, define, fringe, limbus, margin, trench **7** outline, selvage **8** approach, befringe, boundary, frontier, neighbor, sideline, surround **9** marchland, perimeter, periphery **11** butt against, communicate *embroidered:* **6** orfray **7** orphrey *inlaid:* **8** purfling *raised:* **7** coaming

bordereau 4 note **10** memorandum

bordering 8 abutting, adjacent, touching **9** adjoining **10** approximal, contiguous, juxtaposed **12** conterminous

borderland 5 march **8** frontier **9** marchland

borderline 7 unclear **8** doubtful **9** ambiguous, dubitable, equivocal, uncertain, undecided, unsettled **11** problematic

border line 8 boundary **11** demarcation

border state 8 Delaware, Kentucky, Maryland, Missouri, Virginia

bore 4 gape, gawk, gaze, pall, peer, ream, tire **5** auger, drill, ennui, glare, gloat, prick, punch, stare, weary **6** goggle, wimble **7** fatigue **8** puncture **9** perforate

boreal 3 icy **4** cold, cool **5** chill, gelid **6** arctic, chilly, frosty **7** glacial **8** freezing

Boreas *beloved:* 8 Orithyia *brother:* **5** Notus **8** Hesperus, Zephyrus *father:* **8** Astraeus *mother:* **3** Eos *son:* **5** Zetes **6** Calais

boredom 4 yawn **5** ennui **6** tedium **7** fatigue **8** doldrums **9** weariness

borer *combining form:* 6 trypan **7** trypano

Borgia 6 Alonso, Cesare **7** Rodrigo **8** Lucrezia

boring 4 dull **6** dreary, stodgy, tiring **7** humdrum, irksome, tedious **8** drudging, tiresome **10** monotonous

boring tool 6 trepan

born 3 née **6** inbred **7** built-in **8** inherent **9** intrinsic **10** congenital, deep-seated, ingenerate *combining form:* **3** gen **4** gene **6** genous **7** genetic

borne by the wind 5 eolic **6** aeolic, eolian **7** aeolian

Borodin opera 10 Prince Igor

borough 4 burg, town **5** burgh **7** village **8** township *Scottish:* **5** brugh

bosh see bunkum

bosom 4 soul **5** heart **6** breast

bosomy 5 busty, buxom **6** chesty

boss 4 head **5** chief **6** honcho, leader, master, survey **7** headman, oversee **8** chaperon, hierarch, overlook, superior **9** chieftain, dominator, supervise **11** quarterback, superintend *African:* **5** bwana

bossy 8 imperial **9** imperious, masterful **10** high-handed, imperative, peremptory **11** domineering, magisterial, overbearing

botanist *American:* 4 Gray (Asa) **5** Sears (Paul B.) **6** Bailey (Liberty), Bessey (Charles), Carver (George Washington) **7** Bartram (John), Burbank (Luther) **9** Fairchild (David) *Austrian:* **6** Mendel (Gregor) *British:* **6** Sloane (Sir Hans) *Danish:* **7** Warming (Johannes) *Dutch:* **7** De Vries (Hugo) *French:* **7** Lamarck (Chevalier de) *German:* **4** Cohn (Ferdinand), Mohl (Hugo Von) **5** Sachs (Julius von) *Irish:* **6** Harvey (William) *Scottish:* **5** Brown (Robert) *Swedish:* **8** Linnaeus (Carolus) *Swiss:* **6** Nageli (Karl) **8** Candolle (Augustin)

botany branch 8 algology, bryology, mycology **9** phycology **10** palynology **11** hydroponics, pteridology **12** bacteriology

botch 3 dub **4** blow, flub, mess, muck, muff, mull, muss **5** fluff, gum up, mix-up, spoil **6** bobble, boggle, bollix, bumble, bungle, cobble, foozle, fumble, goof up, mess up, mucker, muddle **7** blunder, louse up **8** bugger up, shambles **9** mishandle, mismanage **10** misconduct

botchy 5 messy **6** sloppy, untidy **8** careless, slapdash, slipshod, slovenly **10** unthorough

both *combining form:* 3 bis *prefix:* **4** ambi, amph **5** amphi

bother 3 bug, irk, vex **4** fret, pest **5** annoy, chafe, upset **6** abrade, flurry, harass, pester, plague, ruffle **7** agitate, disturb, fluster, perturb, provoke, unhinge **8** disquiet, irritant, nuisance **9** annoyance, besetment **10** discompose **11** aggravation **12** exasperation **13** inconvenience

botheration 4 pest **6** pester, plague **8** irritant, nuisance **9** annoyance, besetment **11** aggravation **12** exasperation

Botswana *capital:* 8 Gaborone *monetary unit:* **4** pula

bottle 4 vial **5** ampul, cruet, cruse, flask, phial **6** ampule, carafe, fiasco, flacon, magnum, vessel **8** decanter, jeroboam **9** container *baby's:* **6** nurser

bottle gourd 8 calabash

bottleneck 7 impasse **8** obstruct, paralyze, slowdown, throttle

bottom 3 bed **4** base, foot, seat, sole **5** basal, basic, fanny, found, hiney, nadir **6** behind, breech, heinie, lowest **7** bedrock, essence, footing, primary, rear end **8** backside, buttocks, derriere **9** establish, lowermost, posterior, predicate, underbody, undermost, underside **10** foundation, nethermost, underlying, underneath **11** fundamental **12** foundational, quintessence, substructure, undersurface

bottom dog 4 prey **6** victim **8** casualty

bottomless 4 deep **7** abysmal **8** baseless **9** plumbless, soundless, unfounded

10 fathomless, gratuitous, groundless, ungrounded 11 plummetless, uncalled-for, unwarranted 12 unfathomable

bottommost 6 lowest 9 lowermost, undermost 10 nethermost

bough 4 limb 6 branch

boulevard 3 way 4 path, road 5 track 6 artery, avenue, street 7 highway 12 thoroughfare

boulevardier 7 flaneur, trifler 9 bon vivant 12 man-about-town

bounce 2 ax 3 hop 4 fire, jump, leap, sack 5 bound, vault 6 hurdle, spring 7 boot out, dismiss, kick out, saltate 9 discharge, terminate

bounce back 7 rebound, recover 8 backfire, backlash 9 boomerang

bounce off 5 carom

bouncer 4 goon 7 chucker 8 houseman 9 muscleman, strong arm

bouncy 4 airy 7 buoyant, elastic 8 volatile 9 expansive, resilient 12 effervescent

bound 3 end, hem, hop, rim 4 edge, jump, leap, term 5 limit, skirt, vault, verge 6 border, bounce, define, demark, finite, fringe, hurdle, margin, spring 7 delimit, limited, mark out, measure, saltate 8 articled, confines, surround 9 demarcate, determine 10 delimitate, indentured, limitation 11 apprenticed

boundary 5 ambit 6 limits 7 compass 8 confines, environs, purlieus 9 precincts

bounder 3 cad, cur 6 rotter

boundless 7 endless 8 infinite 9 limitless, unlimited 10 indefinite, unmeasured 11 measureless 12 immeasurable

bounteous 4 free 5 ample 6 plenty 7 copious, liberal 8 abundant, generous, handsome 9 plenteous, plentiful, unsparing 10 freehanded, munificent, openhanded

bountiful see **bounteous**

Bounty captain 5 Bligh (William)

bouquet 4 balm, kudo, posy 5 aroma, scent, spice 7 corsage, garland, incense, nosegay, orchids, perfume 9 fragrance, redolence 10 compliment 11 arrangement, boutonniere

bourgeois 10 philistine 11 middle-class 12 capitalistic

bourgeoisie 11 middle class

bout 4 tour, turn 5 shift, siege, spell, stint, trick

bovine 2 ox 3 cow, yak 4 anoa, bull, calf, gaur, neat, zebu 5 bison, gayal, steer, stirk 6 catalo, cattle, wisent 7 aurochs, banteng, buffalo, bullock, cattalo 8 longhorn *genus:* 3 Bos *sound:* 3 low, moo

bow 3 arc 4 arch, bend, lout, turn 5 angle, crook, curve, defer, round, yield 6 congee, curtsy, salaam, submit 7 flexure, succumb,

turning 8 flection 9 curvation, curvature 10 capitulate 11 buckle under 12 knuckle under

bowdlerize 4 blip 6 censor, screen 9 expurgate

bowed 4 bent 5 arced, bandy, round 6 arched, curved 7 arrondi, rounded 8 arciform 9 bowlegged 11 bandy-legged, curvilinear *combining form:* 3 tox 4 toxi, toxo

bowel 3 gut 4 draw 6 paunch 10 eviscerate, exenterate

bower 5 arbor 7 pergola

bowery 7 skid row 8 skid road

bowfin 7 mudfish

bowl 5 arena, basin, jorum, mazer, stade 6 tureen, vessel 7 stadium 8 coliseum *ornamental:* 5 tazza

bowlegged 5 bandy

bowler 3 hat 5 derby 6 kegler 7 kegeler

Bowl game 3 Sun (El Paso) 4 Rose (Pasadena) 5 Aloha (Honolulu), Gator (Jacksonville), Peach (Atlanta), Pecan (Abilene), Sugar (New Orleans), Super 6 Copper (Tucson), Cotton (Dallas), Fiesta (Tempe), Orange (Miami), Senior (Mobile) 7 Freedom (Anaheim), Holiday (San Diego), Liberty (Memphis) 8 Carquest (Miami), Las Vegas (Las Vegas) 10 Bluebonnet (Houston), California (Fresno) Hall of Fame (Tampa) 12 Independence (Shreveport) 13 Florida Citrus (Orlando)

bowling 7 kegling 8 kegeling *British:* 8 skittles *Italian:* 5 bocce, bocci 6 boccia, boccie *term:* 3 pin 4 hook, lane, spot 5 curve, frame, spare, split 6 gutter, strike, string, turkey 7 duckpin 9 candlepin

bowl over 3 wow 4 stun 5 floor 6 dismay 8 surprise 9 overwhelm 10 disconcert

box 3 bin 4 case, cell, chop, cuff, kist, loge, slap, sock 5 booth, chest, clout, crate, fight, punch, smack, spank, stall, trunk 6 buffet, carton, casket, coffin, encase, hopper, packet, square 7 confine, enclose, package 8 canister 9 container, enclosure, rectangle 10 pigeonhole, receptacle 11 compartment *ancient:* 4 arca *for a document:* 7 hanaper *for ammunition:* 7 caisson *for an official seal:* 7 skippet

boxer 7 fighter, palooka, puncher, slugger 8 pugilist 9 flyweight 11 heavyweight, lightweight 12 bantamweight, middleweight, welterweight 13 featherweight *champ:* 3 Ali (Muhammad) 4 Bowe (Riddick) 5 Bruno (Frank), Lewis (Lennox), Louis (Joe), Moore (Archie), Tyson (Mike) 6 Hearns (Thomas), Holmes (Larry), McCall (Oliver), Moorer (Michael), Seldon (Bruce), Spinks (Leon, Michael), Tunney (Gene), Walker (Mickey) 7 Charles (Ezzard), Corbett (James), Dempsey (Jack), Douglas

(Buster), Foreman (George), Frazier (Joe), Johnson (Jack), Leonard (Sugar Ray), Sharkey (Jack), Walcott (Joe) **8** Marciano (Rocky), Robinson (Sugar Ray), Sullivan (John L.) **9** Armstrong (Henry), Holyfield (Evander), Patterson (Floyd), Schmeling (Max)

boxing 8 pugilism **10** fisticuffs **13** prize-fighting *term:* **2** KO **3** jab, TKO **4** bell, blow, bout, duck, foul, hook, ring, rope, spar **5** break, count, feint, glove, judge, match, parry, punch, round, swing, towel **6** bucket, canvas, corner, sponge **7** low blow, referee **8** heavy bag, knockout, pugilism, speed bag, uppercut **9** knockdown **11** punching bag

boy 3 lad, son **5** gamin, sonny **6** laddie, nipper, shaver **7** gossoon **9** shaveling, stripling, youngster *combining form:* **3** ped **4** paed, paid, pedo **5** paedo, paido *country:* **5** swain *errand:* **5** gofer **8** lobbygow *French:* **6** garçon *Latin:* **4** puer *mischievous:* **6** urchin *small:* **3** tad *Spanish:* **4** niño

boyfriend 4 beau **5** beaux (plural), flame, lover, swain **6** fiancé, steady **7** beloved **8** paramour, truelove **9** inamorato **10** heartthrob, sweetheart

Boy Scout *founder:* **11** Baden-Powell (Robert) *gathering:* **8** jamboree *motto:* **10** be prepared *rank:* **9** Life Scout, Star Scout **10** Eagle Scout, Tenderfoot *unit:* **5** troop **6** patrol

Boys Town *founder:* **8** Flanagan (Edward) *state:* **8** Nebraska

B.P.O.E. member 3 Elk

Brabantio's daughter 9 Desdemona

brabble 3 gab, row **4** chat, spat, tiff **5** clack, scrap **6** bicker, cackle, hassle, jabber **7** chatter, dispute, fall out, palaver, prattle, quarrel, wrangle **8** squabble **9** bickering, brannigan, caterwaul **10** falling-out **11** altercation **12** tittle-tattle

brace 3 beg, duo **4** dyad, gird, pair, pray, prop, stay **5** plead, ready, shore, steel **6** appeal, bear up, column, couple, splent, splint, upbear, uphold **7** beseech, bolster, doublet, entreat, fortify, implore, prepare, refresh, shore up, support, sustain, twosome **8** buttress **9** importune **10** strengthen, supplicate **11** underpinner **12** underpinning **13** underpropping

bracelet 6 bangle **8** wristlet

bracing 5 tonic **9** animating **10** quickening, vitalizing **11** stimulating, stimulative **12** exhilarating, exhilarative, invigorating

bracket 3 wed **4** join, link **5** unite **6** couple, relate **7** collate, combine, compare, conjoin, connect **8** contrast **9** associate

bract 4 leaf **5** glume, palea, palet **6** paleae (plural), spathe **8** phyllary

brad 4 nail

Bradamant *brother:* **7** Rinaldo *husband:* **6** Rogero **8** Ruggiero

Bradbury's forte 5 sci-fi

brag 4 blow, crow, puff **5** boast, mouth, prate, vaunt **9** gasconade **11** rodomontade

braggadocian 8 boastful, braggart, vaunting **11** rodomontade

braggadocio 7 boaster **8** boasting, braggart, bragging **9** cockiness **10** cockalorum

braggart 6 blower **7** boaster, vaunter, windbag **8** blowhard, boastful, fanfaron, puckfist, rodomont, vaunting **11** braggadocio, rodomontade **12** braggadocian

Brahmin 7 egghead **8** highbrow **10** double-dome **12** intellectual

braid 4 plat **5** plait, queue **7** galloon, pigtail **8** soutache **10** intertwine, interweave *gold or silver:* **5** orris *hemp:* **5** tagal

brain 3 wit **4** bean, conk, head, mind **7** concuss **9** intellect **10** gray matter **12** intelligence *bone:* **5** skull **7** cranium *clot:* **10** thrombosis *combining form:* **6** cerebr, enceph **7** cerebri, cerebro **8** cerebell **9** cerebelli, cerebello, encephalo, encephaly **10** encephalia, encephalus *gland:* **6** pineal **9** pituitary *layer:* **4** obex **6** cortex *lobe:* **6** limbic, vermis **7** frontal **8** parietal, temporal **9** occipital *membrane:* **3** pia **4** dura, tela **6** meninx **8** pia mater **9** arachnoid, dura mater *part:* **4** aula, lobe **7** medulla **8** cerebrum, thalamus **9** sensorium, ventricle **10** cerebellum, hemisphere **12** diencephalon *relating to:* **8** cerebral **10** encephalic *ridge:* **4** gyri (plural) **5** gyrus *vertebrate:* **10** encephalon *wave record:* **3** EEG *white matter:* **4** alba

brainchild 7 coinage **9** invention **11** contrivance

brainless 6 simple **7** asinine, foolish, unwitty, witless **8** mindless **9** nitwitted, senseless **10** weak-minded

brainless one 5 ament

brainpower 3 wit **5** sense **9** mentality, mother wit **12** intelligence

brainsick 4 daft **5** batty, crazy **6** crazed, insane **7** cracked, lunatic **8** demented, deranged **9** bedlamite

brainstorm 4 idea **11** inspiration

brainteaser 6 puzzle

brainwashing 10 persuasion

brainwork 7 thought **10** cogitation, reflection **11** cerebration, speculation **12** deliberation

brainy 5 alert, sharp, smart **6** bright, clever **7** knowing **9** brilliant **11** intelligent, quick-witted, ready-witted

brake 3 bar, dam **4** slow, stop **5** block **6** hinder, impede **8** obstruct **10** overslaugh

branch 4 gill, limb, rami (plural) **5** bough, brook, creek, ramus **6** ramify, runnel, stream 7 rivulet *relating to:* 5 ramal 7 ramular

branched 6 ramate, ramose, ramous 8 ramulose, ramulous *combining form:* 7 cladous

brand 4 blot, blur, logo, mark, onus, slur, spot 5 odium, stain 6 stigma 8 black eye, logotype 9 trademark 11 bar sinister

brandish 4 show 5 flash 6 expose, flaunt, parade 7 display, disport, exhibit, show off, trot out

brand-new 4 mint 5 clean, fresh 6 unused 8 pristine 9 untouched 12 spick-and-span

brandy 4 marc 5 pisco, rakia 6 cognac, grappa, kirsch, rakija 7 quetsch 8 armagnac, calvados, slivovic 9 applejack, framboise, mirabelle, slivovitz 11 aquardiente

brannigan 3 row 4 bust 5 binge, fight, spree 6 bender, hassle, ruckus 7 brabble, carouse, dispute, quarrel, wassail, wrangle 10 falling out 11 altercation

brash 4 bold 5 hasty 6 brazen, madcap, uppish, uppity 7 forward, pushful, pushing 8 reckless, tactless 9 ebullient, exuberant, hot-headed, impetuous, impolitic, maladroit, presuming, unpolitic, untactful, vivacious 10 ill-advised, incautious 11 overweening, thoughtless 12 effervescent, high-spirited, presumptuous, undiplomatic 13 inconsiderate, self-asserting, self-assertive

brashness 4 gall 5 brass, cheek, crust, nerve 8 audacity, temerity 9 assurance, hardihood, hardiness 10 confidence, effrontery 11 presumption

brass 4 gall 5 cheek, crust, nerve 9 brashness 10 confidence, effrontery 11 presumption *combining form:* 5 chalc, chalk 6 chalco, chalko

brassbound 5 brash, rigid 6 narrow, uppish, uppity 7 adamant, bigoted, forward, pushful 8 obdurate 9 illiberal, presuming, unbending 10 inexorable, inflexible, intolerant, relentless, unyielding 11 overweening, small-minded 12 narrow-minded, presumptuous, single-minded 13 self-asserting, self-assertive

brass hat 5 elder 6 better, senior 8 higher-up, superior

brass tacks 7 details

brass worker 7 brasier, brazier

brassy see brazen

brat 3 imp

brave 4 bold, dare, defy, face, game, good 5 gutsy, hardy, manly, noble, stout, vivid 6 daring, gritty, heroic, manful, plucky, spunky, useful 7 aweless, benefic, defiant, doughty, gallant, helpful, outdare, outface, valiant, venture 8 colorful, fearless, intrepid, resolute, spirited, stalwart, unafraid, valorous 9 audacious, challenge, dauntless, favorable, soldierly, steadfast, undaunted, unfearful, unfearing 10 beneficial, courageous, propitious, unblenched 11 boldhearted, lionhearted, unblenching, undauntable, unflinching, venturesome 12 advantageous, greathearted, stouthearted, unfrightened

Brave New World author 6 Huxley (Aldous)

bravery 4 grit 5 pluck 6 daring, spirit 7 courage, heroism 8 audacity, boldness 9 fortitude, gallantry 11 intrepidity 12 intrepidness *false:* 7 bravado

brawl 3 row 4 feud, fray, maul, riot, spat, tiff 5 broil, fight, melee, scrap, set-to 6 affray, bicker, dustup, fracas, hassle, mellay, rumble, tussle 7 bobbery, brabble, dispute, quarrel, ruction, scuffle, wrangle 8 dogfight, eruption, rowdydow, slugfest, squabble, struggle, upheaval 9 bickering, caterwaul, commotion, fistfight, imbroglio, scrimmage 10 donnybrook, fisticuffs, free-for-all 11 altercation, disturbance

brawn 4 beef, thew 5 might 6 muscle

brawny 5 beefy, lusty, tough 6 sinewy 8 athletic, muscular, vigorous

bray 4 buck 5 crush 6 powder 9 comminute, pulverize, triturate 12 contriturate

brazen 4 bold, loud 5 gaudy, saucy 6 arrant, brassy, flashy, garish, tawdry, tinsel 7 aeneous, blatant, chintzy, glaring 8 impudent, insolent, overbold 9 audacious, barefaced, shameless, unabashed 10 procacious, unblushing 11 impertinent 12 contumelious, meretricious

Brazil *explorer:* 6 Cabral (Pedro) *largest city:* 8 Sao Paulo *monetary unit:* 8 cruzeiro

breach 3 gap 4 hole, open, rent, rift 5 break, split 6 hiatus, lacuna, offend, schism 7 discord, disrupt, fissure, infract, interim, opening, rupture, violate 8 disunity, division, fracture, infringe, interval, trespass 9 severance, violation 10 alienation, contravene, infraction, separation, transgress 12 estrangement, infringement, interruption 13 contravention, discontinuity, transgression

bread 3 bun 4 feed, food, grub 5 money 6 cocket, living, simnel, viands 7 biscuit, edibles, nurture, support 8 victuals 9 provender 10 livelihood, provisions, sustenance 11 comestibles, maintenance, subsistence *blessed:* 7 eulogia 9 antidoron *bolled:* 4 cush 6 panada *browned:* 5 toast 6 sippet 7 crouton 8 zwieback *combining form:* 4 arto *communion:* 4 azym, host 5 azyme, wafer 9 eucharist *consecrated:* 9 eucharist *cube:* 7 crouton *from heaven:* 5 manna *hard and crisp:* 4 rusk 8 zwieback *ingredient:* 4 meal 5 flour, yeast

6 leaven *Jewish:* **5** matzo **6** hallah, matzoh **7** challah *maker:* **5** baker *relating to:* **6** panary *roll:* **5** bagel *Scottish:* **7** bannock *small piece:* **6** sippet *soup:* **6** panada *spread:* **3** jam **4** oleo **5** jelly **6** butter *unleavened:* **4** azym **5** azyme, matzo **6** matzoh *with fruit and nuts:* **7** stollen

bread and butter 4 keep **6** living **7** support **10** livelihood, sustenance **11** maintenance, subsistence **12** alimentation

breadbasket 7 stomach

breadth 5 range, reach, scope, space, sweep **6** spread **7** compass, expanse, stretch **8** distance, fullness, wideness **9** amplitude, expansion

break 3 gap **4** bust, cave, fail, flee, fold, hole, leak, plow, rent, rift, ruin **5** boner, burst, crack, crash, gaffe, rebut, scape, solve, spell, split, yield **6** befall, betide, breach, chance, convey, decode, demote, escape, fold up, get out, happen, hiatus, lacuna, offend, plow up, reduce, refute, schism, sunder **7** abscond, blooper, come off, come out, confute, crumble, crumple, declass, degrade, demerit, fall out, faux pas, fissure, infract, interim, opening, respite, rupture, shatter, time-out, violate **8** bankrupt, breather, collapse, confound, decipher, disprove, dissolve, fracture, fragment, interval **9** downgrade, interlude, pauperize **10** contravene, controvert, impoverish, transgress **11** communicate, impropriety, interregnum, opportunity, parenthesis **12** intermission, interruption **13** discontinuity

breakable 5 frail **7** fragile **8** delicate, shattery **9** frangible **11** fracturable, shatterable

breakaway 4 prop **10** escarpment, scrummager

breakdown 5 crash, smash, wreck **7** crack-up, debacle, smashup **8** analysis, collapse **10** dissection, resolution

break down 3 rot **4** wilt **5** decay, spoil, taint **6** cave in, digest, molder **7** analyze, crumble, dissect, give out, putrefy, resolve, succumb **9** anatomize, decompose **10** decompound **12** disintegrate

breaker *combining form:* **5** clast **7** clastic

Breakfast at Tiffany's
author 6 Capote (Truman)

breakfront 7 cabinet **8** bookcase

break in 5 train **8** initiate **9** interrupt

breaking up *combining form:* **7** schises (plural), schisis *suffix:* **4** lyse, lyze

breakneck 4 fast **5** fleet, hasty, quick, rapid, swift **6** speedy **10** expeditive, harefooted **11** expeditious

break out 5 erupt **6** escape **7** explode **10** burst forth

breakthrough 4 hike, rise **5** boost **7** advance, upgrade **8** increase

break through 5 burst **6** breach **7** rupture

breakup 8 analysis **10** dissection

break up 4 part **6** divide, sunder **7** disband, disjoin, disrupt, rupture **8** disjoint, disperse, dissever, dissolve, disunite, separate

breast 5 bosom, chest, heart *animal:* **7** brisket *combining form:* **3** maz **4** mast, mazo **5** masto, stern, steth **6** mastia (plural), sterno, stetho

breastbone 7 sternum

breast-feed 5 nurse **6** suckle **7** nourish

breast-shaped 9 mammiform

breastwork 7 bastion, bulwark, parapet, rampart

breath 4 blow, dash, hint **5** break, spell, trace, whiff **6** streak **7** respite, soupçon **9** suspicion **10** suggestion *combining form:* **4** pnea **5** pneum, pnoea **6** pneumo **7** pneumat **8** pneumato

breathe 2 be **4** live, rest, sigh **5** exist **6** exhale, expire, inhale **7** confide, inspire, respire, subsist, whisper

breather 4 rest **5** break, spell **7** respite

breathing *labored:* **7** dyspnea **8** dyspnoea *normal:* **6** eupnea **7** eupnoea *rapid:* **8** polypnea **9** polypnoea

breathing apparatus 10 respirator *underwater:* **5** scuba

breathing orifice 8 blowhole, spiracle

breathless 4 agog, avid, keen **5** close, eager, stivy **6** ardent, stuffy, sultry **7** airless, anxious, athirst, thirsty **8** appetent, stifling **9** impatient **11** suffocating

breathtaking 8 exciting **9** thrilling **11** astonishing

Brecht play 4 Baal **7** Galileo **13** Mother Courage

breech 4 rear, rump **5** fanny **6** behind, bottom **8** backside, buttocks, derriere **9** fundament, posterior

breechclout 9 loincloth

breed 3 ilk **4** bear, grow, kind, sire, type **5** beget, cause, class, hatch, raise **6** father, induce, nature **7** produce, species, variety **8** engender, generate, multiply, muster up **9** character, cultivate, procreate, propagate, reproduce **11** progenerate

breeding 5 grace **6** polish **7** culture **9** gentility **10** refinement **11** cultivation

breeding ground 6 hotbed **8** hothouse **10** forcing bed **12** forcing house

breeze 3 zip **4** snap **5** cinch, waltz **6** zephyr **8** duck soup, kid stuff, pushover **10** child's play

breezy 4 airy **5** blowy, gusty, windy **6** casual, dégagé **7** relaxed, unfussy **8** informal **9** easygoing **11** low-pressure **13** unconstrained

breviary 5 brief 7 epitome 8 abstract, boildown, synopsis 10 conspectus 11 abridgement 12 condensation

breviloquent 4 curt 5 bluff, blunt, brief, gruff, rough, short, terse 6 abrupt, crusty 7 brusque, concise, laconic, summary 8 succinct 11 compendious 13 short and sweet

brevity 8 laconism 9 briefness, shortness, terseness 11 conciseness 12 succinctness

brew 4 loom 6 foment, gather, impend 9 forthcome, potpourri 10 miscellany

Briareus 7 Aegaeon *father:* 6 Uranus *mother:* 2 Ge 4 Gaea

bribe 3 buy, fix, sop 6 buy off, square, suborn 7 corrupt 10 tamper with

bric-a-brac 6 curios

brick 5 block *handler:* 6 hacker *layer:* 5 mason *laying:* 7 masonry *material:* 4 clay, marl *oven:* 4 kiln *pile:* 4 hack *row:* 6 course *sun-dried:* 3 bat 5 adobe *trough for carrying:* 3 hod *wooden:* 3 nog

bridal 7 spousal, wedding 8 marriage, nuptials 9 espousals

bridal wreath 6 spirea

bridewell 4 jail 5 prison

bridge 4 span *kind:* 4 arch, draw, rope 5 swing, truss 7 bascule, covered, natural, pontoon, trestle, viaduct 10 cantilever, suspension *term:* 3 bid 4 book, east, pass, ruff, slam, suit, void, west 5 bonus, dummy, north, raise, south, trick, trump 6 double, renege, rubber 7 auction, finesse, no-trump, overbid 8 contract, jump call, redouble 9 grand slam, overtrick, singleton 10 little slam, undertrick, vulnerable

bridge-like game 5 whist 6 hearts

bridle 3 bit 4 curb, rein 5 check 6 hold in, manage 7 control, inhibit, repress 8 hold back, hold down, restrain, suppress, withhold 9 constrain

brief 4 curt 5 bluff, blunt, gruff, short, terse 6 abrupt, crusty, snippy 7 brusque, concise, epitome, laconic, passing 8 abstract, boildown, breviary, breviate, fleeting, snippety, succinct, synopsis 9 momentary, transient 10 conspectus 11 abridgement, compendiary, compendious 12 breviloquent, condensation 13 short and sweet *combining form:* 5 brevi

brig 4 jail 6 cooler, lockup, prison 7 slammer 8 stockade 9 guardroom

brigand 6 bandit, bummer, looter 7 cateran, forager 8 marauder, pillager 9 plunderer 10 depredator, freebooter

brigandage 7 pillage 11 depredation

bright 4 glad, keen 5 alert, brave, clear, light, lucid, nitid, sharp, shiny, smart, vivid 6 benign, brainy, cheery, clever, colory, dexter, lively, lucent 7 animate, beaming, blazing, flaming, fulgent, glowing, knowing, lam-bent, lighted, radiant 8 animated, cheerful, colorful, gleaming, luminous, lustrous, spirited, sunshiny 9 brilliant, effulgent, favorable, fortunate, refulgent, sparkling, sprightly, vivacious 10 auspicious, glistening, glittering, precocious, propitious, shimmering 11 illuminated, intelligent, quick-witted, ready-witted 12 incandescent 13 scintillating *combining form:* 6 lampro

brighten 5 cheer, shine 6 polish 7 burnish, enliven, furbish, gladden 8 illumine 10 illuminate

brightness 5 éclat 6 luster, reflet 8 radiance, radiancy, splendor 9 luminance 10 brilliance, luminosity *measure of:* 3 lux 4 phot 5 lumen 6 candle 7 candela 10 footcandle

brilliance see brightness

brilliant 4 sage, wise 5 sharp, smart 6 brainy, bright, clever, lucent 7 beaming, fulgent, knowing, lambent, radiant 8 luminous 9 effulgent, refulgent 11 intelligent, quick-witted, ready-witted 12 incandescent 13 knowledgeable

brilliantine 6 pomade

brim 3 hem 4 edge 5 brink, skirt, verge, visor 6 border, fringe, margin 9 perimeter, periphery

brimful see brimming

brimming 3 big 4 full 5 awash 6 filled, jammed, loaded, packed 7 crammed, crowded, replete, stuffed, teeming, welling 8 swelling 9 chock-full

brimstone 6 sulfur *combining form:* 3 thi 4 thio

brine 3 sea 4 deep, main 5 ocean

bring 4 lead, sell 5 fetch 7 convert 8 persuade

bring about 4 make 5 cause 6 draw on, effect, secure 7 produce

bring around 6 induce, prompt 7 win over 8 convince, persuade, talk into 9 argue into 11 prevail upon

bring back 6 recall, return, revive 7 restore 8 retrieve, revivify

bring down 4 drop, fell 5 floor, level 6 ground, tumble 9 prostrate

bring forth 4 bear 7 deliver

bring forward 6 adduce 7 present, produce 9 introduce

bring in 3 get, pay, win 4 earn, gain, make, sell 5 fetch, yield 6 return 7 acquire

bringing *suffix:* 3 fic

bring off 6 effect 8 carry out 10 effectuate 12 carry through

bring out 3 say 4 tell 5 educe, state, utter 7 chime in, declare, deliver

bring together 4 join 5 batch, blend, merge, unify, unite 7 collect, compact, compile 9 integrate 10 synthesize 11 consolidate

bring up 4 halt, moot, rear, stop 5 breed, raise, refer, train 6 advert, allude, broach, draw up, foster, haul up, pull up 7 educate, mention, nourish, nurture 8 point out 9 cultivate, introduce 10 provide for

brink 3 hem 4 brim, edge 5 point, skirt, verge 6 border, fringe, margin 9 perimeter, periphery, threshold

briny 5 salty

brio 3 vim 4 dash, élan, zing 5 oomph, verve 6 esprit, spirit 9 animation

brioche 4 roll

briolette 7 diamond

Briseis' lover 8 Achilles

brisk 4 spry, yare 5 agile, quick, zippy 6 active, adroit, lively, nimble, volant 9 sprightly

bristle 4 boil, burn, fume, rage, seta 5 anger, setae (plural) 6 blow up, chaeta, seethe 7 chaetae (plural), flare up 8 boil over *combining form:* 4 seti 5 chaet 6 chaeta, chaeto 7 chaetae (plural), chaetes, chaetus *Scottish:* 5 birse

British *air force:* 3 RAF *airplane:* 8 Spitfire *bailiff:* 5 reeve *bar:* 3 pub 5 local *bard:* 4 scop *barge:* 6 wherry *bed:* 4 doss *beer:* 6 swipes *boat, ancient:* 7 coracle *boat, fishing:* 5 coble 6 hooker *boy:* 6 nipper *cathedral city:* 3 Ely 4 York 5 Truro 6 Durham, Exeter 7 Lincoln 8 Coventry, Hereford, St. David's 9 Salisbury, Worcester 10 Canterbury, Gloucester *Channel Island:* 4 Sark 6 Jersey 8 Alderney, Guernsey *china:* 5 Spode *coal carrier:* 4 corf *coin, current:* 5 pence (plural), penny 9 halfpenny *coin, old:* 3 bob, ora 5 ackey, angel, crown, groat, noble 6 bawbee, florin, George, guinea, seskin, sovran, tanner, teston 7 angelot, carolus 8 farthing, shilling 9 dandiprat, halfcrown, sovereign 10 threepence *colony, former:* 4 Aden, Cape 5 Adana, Kenya, Malta, Natal 6 Ceylon, Cyprus, Gambia 7 Jamaica, Sarawak 9 Gold Coast, Singapore, Transvaal 10 Basutoland, New Zealand 11 Orange River, Sierra Leone 12 Bechuanaland *conservative party:* 4 Tory *country gentleman:* 6 squire *county:* 4 Kent, York 5 Derby, Devon, Essex, Hants, Salop 6 Dorset, Durham, Oxford, Surrey, Sussex 7 Bedford, Rutland, Suffolk, Warwick 8 Cheshire, Cornwall, Hereford, Hertford, Somerset, Stafford 9 Berkshire, Hampshire, Lancaster, Leicester, Wiltshire, Worcester 10 Cumberland, Gloucester, Shropshire 11 Westmorland *court, local:* 8 hustings *court, medieval:* 4 eyre *cow barn:* 4 byre *dance, ancient:* 6 morris *dandy:* 4 toff *elevator:* 4 lift *farm, small:* 5 croft *field:* 5 croft *flashlight:* 5 torch *football:* 5 rugby *forest:* 5 Arden, weald

8 Sherwood *freeman:* 5 ceorl, churl, thane *game:* 5 darts, rugby 6 soccer 7 cricket *gasoline:* 6 petrol *gun:* 4 Bren, Sten *hat:* 6 bowler *hat, military:* 5 busby *headmaster:* 4 beak *horse:* 5 screw 6 garron *horse dealer:* 5 coper *hunt:* 5 chevy, chivy *hut:* 6 Nissen *idler:* 4 spiv *innkeeper:* 8 publican *jail:* 4 gaol *king, legendary:* 3 Lud 4 Beli, Bran 6 Arthur 7 Artegal, Belinus, Elidure 8 Brannius *laborer:* 5 navvy, prole *landowner:* 6 squire *language, ancient:* 6 Celtic, Cymric 9 Brythonic *lawyer:* 9 barrister, solicitor *legislature:* 10 parliament *letter, old:* 3 wen 5 thorn *liberal party:* 4 Whig *magistrate:* 4 beak *malt liquor:* 6 porter *measure:* 3 ell, pin 4 boll, comb, coom, cran, goad, hand, hide, last, pool, rood, trug, yoke 5 bodge, coomb, digit, float, floor, hutch, jugum, stack, truss 6 bovate, cranne, firkin, oxgang, pottle, runlet, strike, sulung, tierce 7 rundlet, tertian, virgate 8 carucate, chaldron, puncheon 9 kilderkin, shaftment, shathmont 10 barleycorn *molasses:* 7 treacle *news agency:* 7 Reuters *nobleman:* 4 duke, earl, lord, peer 5 baron 6 prince 8 marquess, viscount *nurse:* 6 sister *order:* 6 Garter *ore carrier:* 4 corl *peasant:* 5 churl *peddler:* 7 chapman *people, early:* 4 Celt, Jute, Pict 5 Angle, Iceni, Saxon *poet:* 4 scop *policeman:* 5 bobby 6 copper, peeler *political party:* 4 Tory, Whig 6 Labour *pope:* 8 Adrian IV *pottery:* 5 Spode *prince:* 5 Harry 6 Andrew, Edward 7 Charles, William *princess:* 4 Anne 5 Diana 8 Margaret *printer:* 6 Caxton *prison:* 7 Newgate 8 Dartmoor 13 Tower of London *queen, ancient:* 8 Boadicea *racetrack:* 5 Ascot 10 Epsom Downs *resort:* 4 Bath 7 Margate 8 Brighton 9 Blackpool *rifle:* 7 Enfield *royal house:* 4 York 5 Tudor 6 Stuart 7 Hanover, Windsor 9 Lancaster 11 Plantagenet *royal residence:* 7 Windsor 8 Balmoral 10 Buckingham *school:* 4 Eton 5 Rugby 6 Harrow *school, military:* 9 Sandhurst *seaman:* 6 rating *serf:* 4 esne 6 thrall *solitaire:* 8 patience *spa:* 4 Bath 5 Epsom 6 Buxton 7 Matlock 8 Brighton 10 Cheltenham *stables:* 4 mews *stool pigeon:* 4 nark *streetcar:* 4 tram *tavern:* 3 pub *tax:* 3 VAT 4 geld 6 excise *thicket:* 7 spinney *tinworks:* 8 stannary *tobacco packet:* 5 screw *tourist:* 7 tripper *truck:* 5 lorry *tutor:* 3 don *valley:* 4 dene *wage earner:* 5 prole *weight:* 4 keel 5 stone *woman in the navy:* 4 Wren *wrench:* 7 spanner

British Columbia *capital:* 8 Victoria *largest city:* 9 Vancouver

Britomartis 7 Artemis 8 Dictynna

brittle 5 crisp, short 7 crackly, crumbly, crunchy, friable

broach 3 pin 4 clip, moot 7 bring up, mention 9 introduce, ventilate 10 speak about

broad 4 wide 6 risqué, scopic 7 liberal, radical 8 advanced, extended, off-color, scopious, tolerant 9 expansive, extensive 10 suggestive 11 broad-minded, progressive *combining form:* 4 eury, lati, plat 5 platy

broadcast 3 sow 5 straw, strew 6 blazon 7 bestrew, declare, disject, publish, scatter 8 announce, proclaim, televise, transmit 9 advertise 10 annunciate, bruit about, promulgate 11 blaze abroad, declaration, disseminate, publication 12 announcement, proclamation, promulgation 13 advertisement, pronouncement

broaden 4 open 5 widen 6 expand 9 breadthen, spread out

broadloom 6 carpet

broad-minded 4 wide 7 liberal, radical 8 advanced, tolerant 11 progressive

broadside 4 hail 5 burst, salvo, storm 6 shower, volley 7 barrage 9 cannonade, fusillade 11 bombardment

broadtail 5 sheep 6 parrot 7 karakul, rosella 8 lambskin

Brobdingnagian 4 huge 5 giant 7 Antaean, mammoth, titanic 8 colossal, gigantic 9 cyclopean, monstrous 10 gargantuan

brocade *medieval:* 4 acca

brocaded 6 broché

brocard 4 rule 5 axiom, gnome, maxim, moral 6 dictum, truism 8 aphorism, apothegm

brochette 4 spit 6 skewer

broil 4 bake, burn, cook, fray 5 brawl, fight, grill, roast 6 affray, fracas, scorch 7 bobbery, ruction, swelter 10 donnybrook, free-for-all

broiling 3 hot 5 fiery 6 baking, red-hot, torrid 7 burning 8 scalding, sizzling 9 scorching 10 sweltering

broke 4 flat, poor 5 needy, stony 8 beggared, dirt poor, indigent, strapped 9 destitute

broken-down 5 dingy, seedy, tacky 6 shabby, tagrag 8 decrepit, tattered 10 threadbare 11 dilapidated

brokenhearted 7 crushed 8 dejected 9 depressed

broker 8 mediator 9 go-between, middleman 10 interagent, interceder 11 intercessor 12 entrepreneur, intermediary, intermediate 13 intermediator

bromide 6 cliché, truism 8 banality, prosaism 9 platitude 10 prosaicism, shibboleth 11 commonplace, rubber stamp

bromidic 3 dry 4 arid, dull 5 dusty 7 insipid, tedious 8 weariful 9 dryasdust, wearisome 13 uninteresting

bromine *symbol:* 2 Br

bronco 5 horse 6 cayuse 7 mustang *Australian:* 6 brumby

broncobuster 6 cowboy

Brontë *character:* 9 Catherine, Rochester 10 Heathcliff *novel:* 8 Jane Eyre 16 Wuthering Heights *sisters:* 4 Anne 5 Emily 9 Charlotte

Bronx cheer 3 boo 4 hiss, razz 5 bazoo 7 catcall 9 raspberry

brooch 3 pin 4 clip

brood 3 set, sit 4 mope, seed 5 cover 6 scions 7 despond, progeny 8 children 9 offspring 11 descendants, progeniture *member:* 7 sibling

brook 4 bear, gill, race, rill, take 5 abide, creek, stand 6 arroyo, endure, rillet, runnel, stream, suffer 7 rivulet, stomach, swallow 8 tolerate *Scottish:* 6 burnie

broom 5 besom, brush, shrub, sweep, whisk 7 heather *combining form:* 5 scopi

broth 5 stock 6 brewis 8 bouillon, consomme *Scottish:* 4 bree, broo

brothel 6 bagnio 7 lupanar 8 bordello, cathouse, seraglio 9 call house 10 bawdy house, fancy house 11 parlor house 13 sporting house

brother 3 bub, kin 4 monk 5 friar 7 comrade *French:* 5 frère *Italian:* 3 fra 5 frate 8 fratello *Latin:* 6 frater *relating to:* 9 fraternal *Spanish:* 7 hermano

brotherhood 4 club 5 guild, order, union 6 league 7 society 8 sodality 10 fellowship, fraternity 11 association

brotherly 4 kind 10 cherishing 12 affectionate

Brothers Karamazov 4 Ivan 6 Alexei, Dmitri 10 Smerdyakov

brouhaha 3 din 4 coil, fuss 5 babel 6 clamor, furore, hubbub, hurrah, jangle, racket, ruckus, rumpus, shindy, tumult, uproar 8 foofaraw 9 commotion 10 hullabaloo 11 pandemonium

brow 5 frons, front 8 forehead

browbeat 3 cow 5 bully 6 harass, hector 7 bluster, dragoon 8 bludgeon, bulldoze, bullyrag 10 intimidate

brown 4 dark, sear 5 dusky, toast 6 gloomy, scorch, tanned 7 swarthy *dark:* 5 sepia, umber 9 chocolate *grayish:* 3 dun 6 bister, bistre *light:* 3 tan 4 ecru, fawn 5 beige, hazel, khaki, tawny *moderate:* 4 teak 6 sahara, sienna *reddish:* 3 bay 4 roan 5 henna 6 auburn, russet, sorrel, titian 8 chestnut *yellowish:* 6 bronze, havana 8 bismarck 12 butterscotch

Brown Bomber 5 Louis (Joe)

brown coal 7 lignite

brownie 3 elf, fay 5 fairy, nisse, pixie 6 sprite

Browning poem 8 Prospice 11 Pippa Passes 12 Rabbi Ben Ezra 13 Fra Lippo Lippi, My Last Duchess

brown recluse 6 spider

brownshirt 4 Nazi 12 storm trooper

browse 4 scan, shop 6 go over, peruse 7 dip into, run over 8 glance at, look over 10 glance over, run through 11 flip through, leaf through, riff through, skim through 12 thumb through 13 riffle through

bruise 4 mash, pulp 5 black, crush 6 batter, squash 7 becrush, contuse 8 abrasion, black eye 9 contusion

bruit about 6 blazon 7 declare, publish 8 announce, proclaim 9 advertise, broadcast 10 annunciate, promulgate 11 blaze abroad

bruja 3 hag, hex 5 lamia, witch 9 sorceress 10 witchwoman 11 enchantress

brume 4 film, haze, mist 5 smaze

brummagem 4 fake, sham 5 bogus, false, phony, snide 6 pseudo, tinsel 8 spurious 9 pinchbeck 11 counterfeit

brunet 4 dark 5 dusky, swart 6 swarth 7 swarthy 8 bistered

Brunhild's husband 6 Gunnar 7 Gunther

brush 4 clip, fray, kiss, skim 5 clash, graze, melee, run-in, set-to, shave, sweep 6 affray, glance, mellay, scrape 7 contact 8 skirmish 9 encounter, scrimmage, sideswipe 10 velitation *combining form:* 5 scopi

brusque 4 curt 5 bluff, blunt, brief, gruff, short 6 abrupt, crusty, snippy 8 snippety

brutal 4 hard 5 feral, harsh 6 animal, bitter, ferine, rugged, severe 7 beastly, bestial, swinish 8 rigorous 9 inclement 11 intemperate

brutalize 4 warp 6 debase 7 corrupt, debauch, deprave, pervert, vitiate 10 bastardize, bestialize, demoralize

brute 5 beast, feral 6 animal, ferine 7 beastly, bestial, swinish 8 creature

brutish 3 low 4 base, mean, vile 5 crude, feral 6 animal, coarse, ferine, scurvy 7 beastly, bestial, swinish 11 animalistic

bryophyte 4 moss 9 liverwort

Brythonic see Cymric

bubble 3 lap 4 boil, stir, wash 5 churn, dream, slosh, swash 6 burble, gurgle, seethe, simmer 7 chimera, fantasy, ferment, smolder 8 illusion 9 pipe dream

bubbly 8 effusive 9 champagne, exuberant, sparkling

buccaneer 5 rover 6 pirate, sea dog 7 corsair, sea wolf 8 picaroon, sea rover 9 sea robber 10 freebooter

buck 3 fop, guy, lug, man 4 bear, bill, bray, chap, dude, duel, gent, pack, tote 5 carry, crush, dandy, ferry, fight, horse, pitch, repel, throw 6 combat, convey, dollar, fellow, oppose, powder, resist, unseat 7 contest, coxcomb, dispute, sawbuck, trestle, unhorse 8 sawhorse, traverse 9 comminute, exquisite, gentleman, pulverize, transport, triturate, withstand, workhorse 11 Beau Brummel 12 contriturate

bucket 3 fly, run 4 pail, rush, whiz 5 hurry, speed 6 barrel, hasten, hustle 7 grapple 9 clamshell

Buckeye State 4 Ohio

buckle down 5 apply, set to 6 devote, direct, fall to, jump in, wade in 7 address, pitch in 8 jump into, wade into

buckle under 3 bow 4 cave, give 5 defer, yield 6 submit 7 knuckle, succumb 10 capitulate

Buck novel 12 The Good Earth

buckram 5 stiff 6 wooden 7 stilted 9 cardboard 11 muscle-bound

buck up 5 cheer 6 solace 7 comfort, console, upraise

buckwheat tree 4 titi

bucolic 4 hick, jake 5 rural, yokel 6 rustic 7 bumpkin, country, hayseed, hillman, hoosier, outland 8 agrestic, pastoral 9 chawbacon 10 campestral, out-country, provincial 11 countrified

bud 4 germ, seed 5 chick, child, spark 6 embryo 8 juvenile, young one 9 youngling, youngster *combining form:* 5 blast 6 blasto

Buddha 7 Gautama 10 Siddhartha *Chinese:* 2 Fo *dialogues:* 5 sutra *disciple:* 6 Ananda *Japanese:* 5 Amida, Amita *mother:* 4 Maya *son:* 6 Rahula *teachings:* 6 dharma *wife:* 9 Yasodhara

Buddhism 5 Daijo, Foism, Kegon 7 Lamaism 8 Hinayana, Mahayana

Buddhist *bronze image:* 8 Daibutsu *chant:* 6 mantra *column:* 3 lat *dialogues:* 5 sutra *doctrine:* 7 trikaya *enlightenment:* 6 satori *evil spirit:* 4 Mara *fate:* 5 karma *fertility spirit:* 6 yaksha, yakshi *gateway:* 5 toran 6 torana *god:* 4 deva *hatred:* 4 dosa *hell:* 6 Naraka *language:* 4 Pali *mendicant:* 7 bhikshu *monastery:* 4 tera *monk:* 2 bo 4 lama 5 arhat, bonze, yahan 7 bhikshu, poongee 8 poonghee, poonghie, talapoin *monument, mound:* 5 stupa *novice:* 5 goyin *paradise:* 4 Jodo *religious community:* 6 sangha *sacred city:* 5 Lhasa *saint:* 5 arhat *school:* 5 ritsu *scripture:* 9 Tripitika *sect:* 3 Zen 6 tendai *shrine:* 4 tope 5 stupa 6 dagaba, dagoba 7 chorten *spell:* 6 mantra *spiritual leader:* 4 guru 9 Dalai Lama *state of happiness:*

7 nirvana *temple:* **6** pagoda, vihara *throne:* **5** asana *title:* **7** mahatma *tree of enlightenment:* **2** bo **5** bodhi, pipal *tutelary spirit:* **6** yaksha, yakshi *will to live:* **5** tanha

buddy **3** pal **4** chum **5** crony **6** comate, friend **7** comrade **9** associate, companion **11** running mate

buddy-buddy **4** cozy **5** pally **6** chummy **8** intimate

budgerigar **6** parrot **8** lovebird, parakeet **9** parrakeet

budget **4** body, bulk **5** total **6** amount **7** quantum **8** quantity **9** aggregate

budtime **6** spring **10** springtide

Buenos ___ **5** Aires

buff **3** fan, rub **5** glaze, gloss, shine **6** addict, glance, polish, votary **7** burnish, devotee, furbish, habitué **10** aficionado

buffalo **4** anoa, balk, beat, bilk, dash, foil, ruin **5** bison, stump **6** baffle **7** carabao, nonplus **9** frustrate **10** circumvent, disappoint *Philippines:* **7** tamarao, tamarau, timarou

buffalo grass **5** grama **6** gramma

buffet **3** box **4** beat, blip, chop, cuff, drub, poke, slap, sock **5** clout, pound, punch, smack, spank **6** batter, pummel, thrash, wallop **7** belabor, lambast **8** lambaste

buffoon **4** zany **5** clown **9** harlequin **11** merry-andrew

bug **3** irk, nut, vex **4** fret, gall **5** annoy **6** bother, insect, zealot **7** fanatic, provoke, wiretap **10** enthusiast

bugaboo see **bugbear**

bugbear **4** bogy, fear, ogre **5** bogey **6** goblin **7** problem, specter, spectre **8** anathema, bogeyman **9** bête noire, boogeyman, hobgoblin **10** black beast **11** abomination, detestation

bugle *blare:* **7** tantara *call:* **4** mess, taps **6** sennet, tattoo **7** retreat **8** assembly, reveille

Bugs ___ **4** Baer **5** Bunny

build **3** wax **4** form, make, mold, rise **5** boost, erect, forge, frame, mount, put up, raise, run up, shape **6** expand, uprear **7** augment, enlarge, fashion, habitus, magnify, produce, throw up, upsurge **8** assemble, compound, heighten, increase, multiply, physique **9** construct, fabricate **10** aggrandize **11** manufacture **12** constitution

builder **10** contractor

builder's knot **10** clove hitch

building **3** hut **6** fabric **7** edifice **9** structure *addition:* **3** ell **4** wing **5** annex *compartment:* **3** bay **4** room **6** office *connector:* **9** breezeway *farm:* **4** barn, crib, shed, silo *for apartments:* **8** tenement *for arms:* **7** arsenal *for fodder:* **4** silo *for gambling:*

6 casino *for grain:* **4** silo **7** granary **8** elevator *for horses:* **6** stable *for manufacture:* **4** shop **5** plant **7** factory *for music:* **4** hall **10** auditorium, opera house *for sports:* **3** gym **4** bowl **5** arena **7** stadium **8** coliseum **9** gymnasium **10** hippodrome *material:* **4** iron, wood **5** adobe, brick, glass, steel, stone **6** cement **8** concrete *medieval:* **6** castle *projection:* **3** bay, ell **4** wing **5** annex **6** dormer **7** cornice *round:* **7** rotunda

build up **4** puff **5** erect **9** advertise, construct, establish, publicize **10** press-agent

built-in **6** inborn, inbred, innate **8** inherent **9** essential, ingrained **10** congenital, deepseated, indwelling

bulb **3** bud **4** leek, lily, sego **5** onion, tulip **6** garlic, squill **8** daffodil, hyacinth **9** amaryllis, narcissus *segment:* **5** clove

bulb-like bud **4** corm **5** tuber **7** rhizome

Bulgaria *capital:* **5** Sofia *monetary unit:* **3** lev

bulge **3** jut **4** bump, edge, lump, poke, pout **5** pouch, swell **6** beetle, dilate, expand **7** distend, project **8** handicap, overhang, protrude, stand out, stick out, swelling **9** advantage, allowance, head start, outthrust **10** projection, protrusion **11** protuberate **12** protuberance

bulk **4** body, core, loom, mass **5** total **6** amount, budget, corpus, object, staple, volume **7** bigness, quantum **8** quantity, stand out **9** aggregate, greatness, largeness, magnitude, substance *combining form:* **4** onco **5** oncho

bull **3** big, fat **4** slip, toro, trip **5** boner, buyer, error, fluff, husky, lapse, large **6** bungle **7** blooper, blunder, mistake **8** oversize *combining form:* **4** taur **5** tauri, tauro

bulldoze **3** cow **4** push **5** bully, press, shove **6** hector, hustle, jostle **7** bluster, dragoon **8** bludgeon, browbeat, bullyrag, shoulder **10** intimidate

bullet **3** fly, zip **4** whiz **5** hurry **6** barrel, dumdum, tracer *size:* **7** caliber, calibre

bull fiddle **10** contrabass, double bass

bullfighter **6** torero **7** matador, picador **8** toreador **9** cuadrilla **11** cuadrillero **12** banderillero *famous:* **6** Arruza **8** Belmonte, Joselito, Manolete **10** El Cordobes

bullfighting *arena:* **5** plaza *cheer:* **3** olé *hero:* **6** torero **7** matador **8** toreador *lancer:* **7** picador *red cloth:* **6** muleta *Spanish:* **7** corrida *team:* **9** cuadrilla

bullheaded **6** mulish **8** perverse **9** obstinate, pigheaded **10** headstrong, refractory, self-willed **11** intractable, stiff-necked **12** pertinacious

bullwork **4** moil, toil **5** grind, labor, sweat **6** drudge **7** travail **8** drudgery

bully 3 cow 4 fine, punk 5 meany 6 hector, meanie, menace, pander 7 bluster, dragoon, harrier, torment 8 ballyrag, bludgeon, browbeat, bulldoze, bullyrag, harasser, threaten 9 bulldozer, excellent, first-rate, front-rank, tormenter 10 browbeater, intimidate, macquereau, persecutor 11 antagonizer, intimidator

bullyrag see **bulldoze**

bulwark 4 fend 5 cover, guard 6 defend, screen, secure, shield 7 bastion, parapet, protect, rampart 8 fortress 9 safeguard 10 breastwork, stronghold

bum 3 beg, jag, vag 4 bust, hobo, idle, laze, lazy, loaf, loll, slug 5 binge, cadge, drunk, idler, mooch, tramp 6 bender, dawdle, loafer, loiter, lounge, slouch 7 carouse, drifter, floater, goof off, vagrant, wassail 8 derelict, dolittle, faineant, slugabed, sluggard, vagabond 9 brannigan, do-nothing, goldbrick, lazybones, panhandle 10 street arab

bumbershoot 8 umbrella

bumble 3 hum 4 buzz, muff 5 botch, drone, lurch, strum, thrum 6 bobble, bollix, bungle, fumble, mucker 7 blunder, stumble 9 bombinate

bumbling 5 inept 6 gauche, wooden 7 awkward, halting, unhandy, unhappy 9 ham-handed, maladroit 11 heavy-handed

bummer 6 bandit, beggar, cadger, looter 7 brigand, cateran, forager, moocher 8 marauder, pillager 9 plunderer 10 depredator, freebooter, panhandler

bump 3 hit, jar 4 bang, bust, jolt, knot, knur, lump, slam 5 break, bunch, carom, clash, crash, gnarl, knock, shock 6 demote, impact, jostle, reduce, strike, wallop 7 collide, declass, degrade, demerit, disrate, mudhole, pothole 8 disgrade, pumpknot, swelling 9 chuckhole, collision, downgrade 10 concussion, percussion 12 protuberance

bumpkin 4 hick, jake, rube 6 joskin, rustic 7 bucolic, hayseed, hoosier 9 chawbacon 10 clodhopper, provincial

bump off 4 do in, kill 6 finish, murder 7 execute, put away 9 liquidate 11 assassinate

Bumppo, Natty *alias:* 7 Hawkeye 10 Deerslayer, Pathfinder *creator:* 6 Cooper (James Fenimore)

bumptious 8 arrogant 9 conceited, obtrusive

bumpy 5 jerky, nubby, ridgy, rough 6 bouncy, jouncy 7 jolting

bunch 3 lot, set 4 band, bevy, body, bump, crew, knot, lump, push 5 batch, clump, covey, crowd, group, party 6 bundle, circle, clutch, parcel 7 cluster 8 assembly

bunco steerer 3 gyp 6 con man 7 diddler, sharper 8 swindler 9 defrauder, trickster 12 double-dealer 13 confidence man

bundle 3 lot, pot, set, wad 4 bale, body, mint, pile 5 array, batch, bunch, clump, group, sheaf 6 bindle, boodle, fardel, packet, parcel 7 cluster, fortune *of grain:* 5 sheaf, shock, stook *of hay:* 4 bale, wase *of sticks:* 5 fagot 6 faggot 7 fascine *small:* 8 fascicle

bungle 4 bull, flub, muff, slip, trip 5 boner, botch, error, fluff, gum up, lapse 6 bollix, foozle, goof up 7 blooper, blunder, louse up, mistake

bungler 5 klutz 8 shlemiel 9 blunderer, schlemiel 10 stumblebum 11 blunderbuss

bunglesome 6 clumsy 7 awkward

bunk 3 hut 5 board, hokum, house, lodge, put up 6 bestow, billet, harbor, humbug 7 eyewash, baloney, quarter 8 domicile, nonsense 9 poppycock

bunkum 4 jazz 5 hokum 7 baloney 8 flimflam, nonsense 9 poppycock 10 balderdash

Bunyanesque 4 huge 7 mammoth, titanic 8 colossal, gigantic 9 Herculean, monstrous 10 behemothic, gargantuan, prodigious

Bunyan's ox 4 Babe

buoy 4 prop 6 uphold 7 bolster, support, sustain 9 underprop

buoyancy 10 ebullience, exuberance, exuberancy 13 effervescence

buoyant 4 airy 6 bouncy 7 elastic 8 volatile 9 expansive, resilient 12 effervescent

burble 3 yak 4 chat, wash 5 clack, run on, slosh, swash 6 babble, bubble, gabble, gurgle, rattle, yammer 7 chatter, prattle

burden 3 tax 4 clog, duty, gist, haul, lade, load, onus, task 5 cargo, weigh 6 amount, charge, cumber, lading, lumber, saddle, upshot, weight 7 afflict, freight, oppress, payload, purport 8 encumber, handicap, overload 9 millstone, substance 10 deadweight

burdensome 5 tough 6 taxing 7 exigent, onerous, weighty 8 exacting, grievous 9 demanding 10 oppressive

bureau 5 chest 7 dresser 10 chiffonier

bureaucrat 8 mandarin, official 11 functionary 12 civil servant

burg 6 hamlet, Podunk 7 cowtown, mudhole, village 8 hick town, tank town 11 whistle-stop 12 one-horse town 13 jerkwater town

burgee 4 flag, jack 6 banner, ensign, pennon 7 pendant, pennant 8 standard, streamer

burgeon 4 blow 5 bloom, build, mount, run up 6 expand, flower, sprout 7 augment, blossom, enlarge 8 heighten, increase, multiply, outbloom, snowball 10 effloresce

burghal 4 city 5 urban 9 municipal

burgher 3 cit 5 towny 6 towner 7 citizen, townman 8 townsman

burglar 4 yegg 5 thief 6 robber 7 yegg- man *loot:* 4 swag

burglarize 3 rob 6 burgle 7 ransack 10 housebreak

burgomaster 5 mayor 10 magistrate

Burgundy wine *grape:* 5 Gamay 9 Pinot Noir 10 Chardonnay *red:* 8 Mercu- rey 10 Beaujolais *white:* 5 Rully 6 Chagny 7 Chablis 10 Montrachet 13 Pouilly-Fuissé

burial 4 tomb 5 grave 7 funeral 8 exe- quies 9 interment, obsequies, sepulcher, sepulture 10 entombment, inhumation *box:* 6 casket, coffin *ceremony:* 7 funeral *coffin stand:* 4 bier *mound:* 3 low 6 barrow 7 tumulus *tomb:* 9 mausoleum, sepulcher, sepulchre

burial ground 8 boot hill, cemetery 8 God's acre 9 graveyard 10 necropolis 11 polyandrium 12 memorial park, potter's field *early Christian:* 8 catacomb

burlap 5 gunny 6 fabric 7 bagging, sack- ing 10 wrappering *fiber:* 4 hemp, jute

burlesque 3 ape 4 mock, sham 5 farce, mimic 6 parody 7 imitate, mockery, takeoff 8 travesty 10 caricature

burly 5 beefy, hefty, husky

Burma 7 Myanmar *capital:* 6 Yangon 7 Rangoon

burn 4 bake, beam, bite, boil, char, cook, fire, fume, kiln, melt, rage, sear 5 anger, blaze, broil, chark, creek, flame, flare, gleam, light, parch, roast, scald, shine, singe, smart, smoke, sting, toast 6 blow up, ignite, kindle, scorch, seethe, stream 7 bristle, combust, consume, cremate, flare up, inflame, radiate, smolder, sputter, swel- ter 8 boil over, smoulder 9 carbonize, cau- terize 10 incinerate *Scottish:* 7 scowder 8 scouther

burnable 9 flammable, ignitable 11 com- bustible, inflammable

burned-out 7 worn-out 8 fatigued 9 destroyed, exhausted 10 broken-down 11 debilitated

burning 3 hot 4 dire 5 afire, aglow, fiery 6 ablaze, aflame, alight, ardent, fervid, heated, hectic, red-hot, torrid, urgent 7 blazing, clamant, exigent, fervent, fevered, flaming, flaring, glowing, ignited, instant, lighted 8 broiling, feverish, press- ing, sizzling, white-hot 9 clamorous, scorching 10 imperative, passionate 11 conflagrant, impassioned, importunate 12 incandescent *combining form:* 4 igni *malicious:* 5 arson *relating to:* 5 pyric

burnish 3 rub 4 buff 5 glaze, gloss, shine 6 glance, polish 7 furbish

burnished 5 shiny 6 glossy, sheeny 7 shining 8 gleaming, lustrous, polished 10 glistening

burnsides 5 beard 8 whiskers 10 side- boards 11 dundrearies, muttonchops 12 side-whiskers

burp 5 belch, eruct 8 eructate

burro 3 ass 4 donk 5 donkey 7 jackass

Burroughs' hero 6 Tarzan

burrow 3 den 4 hole, lair, snug 5 couch, hovel, lodge 6 cuddle, nestle, nuzzle 7 snuggle

burst 4 bang, boom, clap, gust, rive, slam, wham 5 blast, crack, crash, erupt, flare, go off, lunge, sally, salvo, smash, storm 6 access, blow up, plunge, shiver, shower, volley 7 barrage, explode, flare-up, rupture, shatter 8 break out, detonate, drumfire, eruption, fragment, mushroom, outbreak, splinter, splitter 9 broadside, cannonade, explosion, fusillade 11 bombardment

bursting 8 erumpent *combining form:* 7 rrhexis, rrhexes (plural)

bury 4 hide, tomb 5 cache, cover, inter, plant, stash 6 coffin, entomb, inhume, screen 7 conceal, lay away, put away, secrete 8 ensconce 9 sepulcher, sepulture

bush 4 rose 5 lilac, shrub, wahoo 6 azalea, cassis, privet 7 currant, weigela 8 backland, backwash, barberry, frontier, hazelnut 9 backwater, backwoods, for- sythia, manzanita, up-country 10 goose- berry, hinterland 11 pussy willow 12 rho- dodendron *combining form:* 5 thamn 6 thamno

bush-league 5 minor 8 mediocre 10 inadequate, second-rate

bushranger 8 woodsman 12 frontiers- man

bushwa 4 bosh 5 hooey 6 bunkum 7 baloney, eyewash 8 malarkey, nonsense 9 poppycock 10 balderdash, flapdoodle

bushwhacker 6 bandit, outlaw, raider, sniper 8 woodsman 9 guerrilla

bushy 5 bosky

business 3 job 4 duty, firm, line, role, work 5 trade 6 affair, custom, matter, office, outfit, racket 7 calling, company, concern, lookout, palaver, pursuit, traffic 8 commerce, function, industry, province 9 patronage 10 employment, enterprise, occupation 13 establishment *expense:* 8 overhead *syndicate:* 6 cartel

businesslike 7 serious 9 efficient, practi- cal 10 purposeful, systematic

businessman 6 dealer, trader, tycoon 7 magnate 8 merchant 9 tradesman 10 trafficker 12 merchandiser

buss 4 kiss, peck 5 smack 6 smooch 8 osculate

bust 3 dud, jag, nab 4 bomb, bump, fail, flop, fold, raid, ruin 5 binge, break, crash, lemon, loser, spree 6 arrest, bender, demote, fold up, pauper, reduce 7 carouse, declass, degrade, demerit, disrate, failure 8 bankrupt, disgrade 9 downgrade, pauperize 10 impoverish

bustard *African:* 7 korhaan 8 knorhaan *genus:* 4 Otis *relating to:* 7 otidine

bustle 3 ado, fly, run 4 flit, fuss, rush, stir, to-do 5 hurry, whirl, whisk 6 clamor, flurry, furore, hassle, hasten, hubbub, hustle, pother, tumult, uproar 7 turmoil 9 commotion, whirlpool, whirlwind 10 hurly-burly

bustling 4 busy 5 brisk, fussy 6 active, lively 7 hopping, humming, popping 9 energetic

busty 5 buxom 6 bosomy, chesty 11 full-bosomed

busy 5 fussy 6 engage, lively, occupy 7 engaged, engross, hopping, humming, immerse, popping, working 8 bustling, employed, hustling, occupied 9 assiduous, intrusive, obtrusive, officious 10 meddlesome 11 impertinent

busybody 5 prier, pryer, snook, snoop 6 butt-in, gossip, rubber 7 meddler, Paul Pry 8 informer, kibitzer, quidnunc 9 pragmatic 10 newsmonger, pragmatist, rubberneck 11 nosey Parker, rumormonger 12 gossipmonger, intermeddler

but 3 bar, yet 4 just, only, save 5 alone 6 bating, except, merely, saving, simply, solely, unless 7 barring, besides, however 8 entirely 9 aside from, excluding, outside of 11 exclusively

butcher 4 slay 9 slaughter

butcher-bird 6 shrike

butcherly 6 bloody, clumsy, savage 10 unskillful

butchery 7 carnage 8 massacre 9 bloodbath, bloodshed, slaughter

Butler, Samuel *novel:* 7 Erewhon 16 The Way of All Flesh *poem:* 8 Hudibras

butt 3 keg, tun 4 abut, cask, dupe, fool, gull, jest, join, joke, line, mark, mock, pipe 5 chump, touch, verge 6 adjoin, barrel, border, jestee, pigeon, sucker, target, victim 7 fall guy, gudgeon, mockery 8 derision, hogshead, neighbor 9 cigarette, pilgarlic 11 communicate, sitting duck 13 laughingstock

butter *artificial:* 4 oleo 9 margarine 13 oleomargarine *Indian:* 3 ghi 4 ghee *piece:* 3 pat *semifluid:* 3 ghi 4 ghee *tree:* 4 shea *tub:* 6 firkin

butterball 5 blimp, fatty 8 dumpling

butterfish 5 coney 6 gunnel

butterfly 5 diana, satyr, zebra 6 copper, morpho 7 admiral, buckeye, kallima, monarch, satyrid, skipper, sulphur, troilus, vanessa, viceroy 8 crescent, grayling, milkweed, victoria 9 aphrodite, metalmark, nymphalid, wood nymph 10 fritillary, hairstreak, parnassius 11 checkerspot, swallowtail *bush:* 8 buddleia *fish:* 6 blenny, chiton 7 gurnard *larva:* 11 caterpillar *lily:* 8 mariposa *order:* 11 Lepidoptera *plant:* 8 oncidium *pupa:* 9 chrysalis *scientist:* 13 lepidopterist

butterlike 8 butyrous 11 butyraceous

butt-in 7 meddler 8 busybody, kibitzer, quidnunc

butt in 6 horn in, meddle 7 intrude, obtrude 8 busybody, chisel in 9 interfere, interlope 10 intertrude, monkey with, tamper with 11 intermeddle

buttinsky see butt-in

buttocks 4 prat, rear, rump, seat, tail 5 fanny, hiney, nates, podex 6 behind, bottom, breech, heinie 7 hind end, hunkers, keester, keister, rear end, tail end 8 backside, derriere, haunches 9 fundament, posterior *combining form:* 3 pyg 4 pyga, pygo 5 pygia 6 procta

button *Japanese:* 7 netsuke

buttonball 8 sycamore

button-down 6 square 8 orthodox, straight 12 conventional

buttonwood 8 sycamore 13 white mangrove

buttress 4 prop, stay 5 brace, shore 6 bear up, column, upbear, uphold 7 bolster, shore up, support, sustain 11 underpinner 12 underpinning 13 underpropping

buxom 5 busty 6 bosomy, chesty 7 shapely, stacked 10 curvaceous 11 full-bosomed, full-figured

buy 3 get 5 bribe 6 obtain, ransom, redeem 7 acquire, bargain, believe 8 closeout, purchase 10 pennyworth, tamper with *Scottish:* 4 coff

buy back 6 redeem

buyer 6 emptor, vendee 8 customer 9 purchaser

buy off 3 fix, sop 5 bribe 10 tamper with

Buzi's son 7 Ezekiel

buzz 3 hum 4 fizz, hiss, whir, whiz 5 drone, rumor, strum, thrum, whirr, whish 6 bumble, fizzle, gossip, report, rumble, sizzle, wheeze, whoosh 7 whisper 8 sibilate 9 bombinate 11 scuttlebutt

by 3 per, via 4 as to, near, nigh, over, with 5 adieu, round 6 beside, nearby, next to, so long 7 good-bye, through 8 farewell 9 alongside 11 according to

by and by 4 anon, next, soon 5 after, infra, later 7 shortly 8 directly, latterly 9 afterward, presently 10 afterwhile 12 subsequently

by and large 7 en masse 8 all in all 9 generally 10 altogether, on the whole

by dint of see by means of

bye-bye 5 adieu 6 so long 7 cheerio 8 farewell, toodle-oo

bygone 3 old 4 dead, late, lost, once, past 5 dated, olden 6 former, whilom 7 antique, archaic, belated, defunct, extinct, old-time, onetime, quondam 8 departed, sometime, vanished 9 erstwhile, out-of-date 10 antiquated, oldfangled 12 old-fashioned

by means of 3 per, via 4 with 7 through

byname 7 moniker 8 nickname 9 sobriquet 10 hypooorism

bypass 5 burke, skirt 6 detour 8 sidestep 10 circumvent

byplace 4 nook 5 niche 6 cranny

by-product 7 spin-off 8 offshoot 9 outgrowth 10 derivative, descendant

Byron work 4 Cain, Lara 5 Beppo 6 Werner 7 Don Juan, Manfred 9 The Giaour 10 The Corsair 12 Childe Harold

bystander 6 viewer 7 watcher, witness 8 beholder, looker-on, observer, onlooker 9 spectator 10 eyewitness

by stealth 7 sub rosa 8 covertly, secretly 9 furtively, privately 13 clandestinely

by virtue of see by means of

by way of see by means of

byword 3 saw 5 adage 6 phrase, saying, slogan 7 proverb 8 nickname 9 sobriquet 10 hypocorism, shibboleth 11 catchphrase

Byzantine 6 daedal, knotty 7 complex, gordian 8 involved 9 elaborate, intricate 11 complicated 12 labyrinthine 13 sophisticated *emperor:* 3 Leo 4 Zeno 5 Basil 6 Bardas, Justin, Phocas 7 Michael, Romanus 9 Heraclius, Justinian 10 Nicephorus, Theodosius *empress:* 3 Zoe 5 Irene 8 Theodora

C

cab 4 hack, taxi

cabal 3 mob 4 camp, clan, plot, ring 5 covin 6 circle, clique, scheme 7 coterie, ingroup 8 intrigue, practice 9 camarilla 10 conspiracy 11 machination

cabaletta 4 aria, song

cabalistic 6 arcane, mystic 8 numinous 9 mysterial, unguessed 10 mysterious, unknowable 11 inscrutable 12 impenetrable 13 unaccountable

caballero 6 knight 8 cavalier, horseman 9 chevalier

cabaret 4 café 6 nitery 7 hot spot 8 nightery 9 nightclub, night spot 10 supper club 11 discotheque 12 watering hole

cabbage 3 nab, nip 4 hook, lift 5 kraut, money, pinch, steal 6 collar 7 purloin 10 greenbacks, sauerkraut 11 appropriate *disease of:* 6 mildew, mosaic 7 root rot, yellows 8 blackleg, club root *family:* 4 cole, kail, kale, rape 5 colza, savoy 6 turnip 7 collard, mustard 8 broccoli, coleseed, colewort, kohlrabi, rutabaga 11 cauliflower

cabbagehead see dunce

cabdriver 4 hack 5 cabby 6 cabbie

cabin 3 cot, hut 4 camp 5 lodge, shack 6 cabana, shanty 7 cottage 9 stateroom

cabin cruiser 4 boat 9 motorboat

cabinet 7 armoire, commode 8 cupboard

cabinetmaker *American:* 5 Eames (Charles), Phyfe (Duncan) 6 Belter (John Henry), Wright (Frank Lloyd) 7 Goddard (John, Stephen, Thomas) 8 McIntire (Samuel), Townsend (Christopher, Edmund, James, Job, John,) *English:* 4 Adam (James, Robert), Hope (Thomas), Kent (William) 6 Morris (William) 8 Sheraton (Thomas) 11 Chippendale (Thomas), Hepplewhite (George) *French:* 6 Boulle (Andre-Charles) 8 Caffieri (Jacques, Jean-Jacques, Philippe), Cressent (Charles) *German:* 10 Weisweiler (Adam)

cable 4 rope, wire 6 stitch

cabriolet 8 carriage

cache 4 bury, hide 5 cover, plant, stash, store 7 conceal, secrete 8 ensconce

cachet 4 rank 5 state 6 status 7 dignity, stature 8 position, prestige, standing 11 consequence

cachinnate 5 laugh

cackle 3 gab, jaw 4 blab, chat 5 clack, run on 6 babble, burble, gabble, gaggle 7 blabber, blatter, chatter, prattle

cacoëthes 5 mania

cacophonic 9 dissonant, immusical, unmusical 10 discordant, inharmonic 11 disharmonic 12 inharmonious, unharmonious 13 disharmonious

cacophonous see cacophonic

cacophony 10 dissonance

cactus 5 dildo, nopal 6 cereus, cholla, mescal, peyote 7 airampo, bisnaga, biznaga, opuntia, saguaro, sahuaro 8 chichipe 11 prickly pear *fruit:* 6 cochal

cad 3 cur 4 heel, lout 5 creep, louse 6 rotter 7 bounder 9 yellow dog

cadaver 4 body, mort 5 stiff 6 corpse 7 carcass, remains

cadaverous 5 gaunt 6 wasted 7 ghastly, ghostly, shadowy 8 skeletal, spectral 9 deathlike, emaciated, ghostlike 10 corpselike

cadence 4 beat 5 meter, pulse, rhyme, swing, throb 6 rhythm 7 measure 8 rhythmus 9 pulsation

cadency see cadence

cadet 4 pimp 5 bully, plebe 6 pander 8 fancy man 10 macquereau

cadge 3 beg, bum 5 mooch 6 sponge 9 panhandle

cadmium *symbol:* 2 Cd

Cadmus *daughter:* 3 Ino 5 Agave 6 Semele 7 Autonoe *father:* 6 Agenor *sister:* 6 Europa *victim:* 6 dragon *wife:* 8 Harmonia

caducity 3 age 6 old age 7 dotardy 10 dotingness, senescence 11 elderliness, senectitude

Caesar *assassin:* 6 Brutus (Marcus Junius) 7 Cassius (Gaius) *battle:* 4 Zela 9 Pharsalus *conquest:* 4 Gaul *eulogist:* 6 Antony (Marc) *message:* 12 veni, vidi, vici *river:* 7 Rubicon *utterance:* 9 et tu Brute *wife:* 7 Pompeia 8 Cornelia 9 Calpurnia

Caesarism 10 absolutism 12 dictatorship

café 5 diner 6 nitery 7 beanery, cabaret, hot spot 8 cookshop, nightery 9 lunchroom, nightclub, night spot 10 coffee shop, supper club 11 discotheque, eating house 12 luncheonette, watering hole 13 watering place

café ___ 6 au lait, filtre

cage 3 hem, mew, pen 4 coop, jail 6 immure, shut in 7 close in, enclose, envelop 8 imprison 11 incarcerate

cagey 3 sly 5 heady 6 argute, astute, shrewd 9 astucious, sagacious 13 perspicacious

cageyness 3 art 5 craft 7 cunning, slyness 8 artifice, foxiness, wiliness 9 canniness 10 artfulness, craftiness

cahoots 5 tie-up 6 hookup 8 alliance 10 connection 11 affiliation, association, combination, conjunction, partnership 12 togetherness

caiman 6 jacare 9 crocodile

Cain *brother:* 4 Abel, Seth *father:* 4 Adam *land:* 3 Nod *mother:* 3 Eve *nephew:* 4 Enos *son:* 5 Enoch *victim:* 4 Abel

Caine Mutiny author 4 Wouk (Herman)

cajole 3 con 4 coax 7 beguile, blarney, wheedle 8 blandish, soft-soap 9 sweet-talk

cake 3 dry, set 4 coat, rime 5 cover, crust 6 harden 7 congeal, encrust, incrust 8 indurate, solidify 10 incrustate *almond:* 8 macaroon *chocolate:* 7 brownie *coffee:* 5 babka 6 kuchen *cornmeal:* 4 pone 8 tortilla *crisp, thin:* 5 wafer *flat:* 5 cooky 6 cookie *oatmeal:* 4 farl 5 farle, scone 7 bannock *of food:* 5 patty 6 pattie *ring-shaped:* 5 donut 6 jumbal, jumble 8 doughnut *rum-soaked:* 4 baba *Scottish:* 4 farl 5 farle, scone *shell-shaped:* 9 madeleine *toasted:* 7 crumpet *topping:* 5 icing 8 frosting, streusel *twisted:* 7 cruller *unleavened:* 8 tortilla *wheat:* 4 puri *without flour:* 5 torte *without shortening:* 6 sponge

Cakes and Ale author 7 Maugham (W. Somserset)

cakewalk 4 romp, rout 5 dance, strut 6 prance 7 runaway

calaboose 4 jail 5 clink, pokey 6 cooler, lockup, prison 8 hoosegow

Calais *brother:* 5 Zetes *father:* 6 Boreas *mother:* 8 Orithyia

calamitous 4 dire 5 fatal 6 woeful 7 fateful, ruinous 8 grievous 10 afflictive, deplorable, disastrous, lamentable 11 cataclysmic, distressing, regrettable, unfortunate 12 catastrophic 13 heartbreaking

calamity 4 ruin, woes 5 wreck 7 tragedy 8 disaster 9 cataclysm 10 affliction 11 catastrophe, tribulation 12 misadventure

Calamity ___ 4 Jane

calamity howler 9 Cassandra, pessimist, worrywart

calcar 4 oven

calcium *symbol:* 2 Ca

calculate 5 count, value 6 assess, cipher, figure, reckon 7 compute 8 appraise, estimate, evaluate 9 ascertain, determine

calculated 7 planned

calculating 3 sly 4 wary, wily 5 chary 6 artful, crafty 7 careful, cunning, guarded

8 cautious, discreet, gingerly, guileful
11 circumspect, considerate
calculating device 6 abacus *ancient Peruvian:* 5 quipo, quipu
calculation 8 figuring 9 ciphering, reckoning 10 arithmetic, estimation 11 computation
calculus *combining form:* 4 lith 5 litho
Caleb *daughter:* 6 Achsah *father:* 6 Hezron 9 Jephunneh *son:* 3 Hur, Iru
Caledonia 8 Scotland
calembour 3 pun 11 paronomasia
calendar 4 card, sked 6 agenda, docket 7 program 8 schedule 9 programma, timetable *abbreviation:* 3 Apr, Aug, Dec, Feb, Fri, Jan, Mar, Mon, Nov, Oct, Sat, Sep, Sun, Tue, Wed 4 Sept 5 Thurs *ecclesiastical:* 4 ordo 8 menology
calenture 4 fire, zeal 5 ardor 6 fervor, hurrah 7 passion 10 enthusiasm
calf *hide:* 3 kip *leather:* 3 elk *meat:* 4 veal *relating to:* 8 vituline *stray:* 4 dogy 5 dogie *unbranded:* 8 maverick
Caliban 5 slave *master:* 8 Prospero *witch-mother:* 7 Sycorax
caliber 5 class, grade, merit, value, worth 6 virtue 7 quality, stature
calibrate 7 measure 9 systemize 11 standardize
California *capital:* 10 Sacramento *college, university:* 3 USC 4 UCLA 5 Biola 8 Stanford 10 Pepperdine 12 San Francisco *colonizer:* 6 Sutter (John Augustus) *fault zone:* 10 San Andreas *largest city:* 10 Los Angeles *motto:* 6 Eureka *nickname:* 11 Golden State *state flower:* 11 golden poppy
californium *symbol:* 2 Cf
caliginous 3 dim 4 dark, dusk 5 dusky, murky 6 gloomy 7 obscure 9 lightless, tenebrous 13 unilluminated
Caligula's mother 9 Agrippina
caliology topic 4 nest
caliph's name 3 Ali 7 Abu Bakr
Calista's seducer 8 Lothario
calisthenics 9 exercises
call 3 bid, cry, dub 4 bawl, draw, hail, hoot, howl, lure, name, note, page, pull, roar, song, term, yell, yowl 5 augur, cause, claim, exact, greet, hallo, hollo, phone, pop in, shout, title, visit 6 accost, appeal, bellow, come by, drop by, drop in, holler, invite, look in, look up, reckon, salute, stop by, stop in, summon 7 address, baptize, convene, convoke, entitle, portend, predict, presage, round up, solicit, summons 8 assemble, christen, estimate, forecast, foretell, occasion, prophesy 9 adumbrate, challenge, designate, necessity, postulate, seduction, telephone 10 allurement, attrac-

tion, denominate, vaticinate, visitation, vociferate 11 approximate, requisition 12 drawing power 13 prognosticate
calla 4 lily
call down 5 chide 6 lesson, monish, rebuke 7 reprove, tick off 8 admonish, reproach 9 reprimand
called 6 yclept 7 ycleped
caller 5 guest 7 visitor 8 visitant
call for 3 ask 5 crave 6 demand 7 require 11 necessitate
call forth 5 evoke 6 elicit 7 conjure
calligrapher 6 penman 7 copyist 9 engrosser
calligraphist see calligrapher
calligraphy 4 hand 6 ductus, script 10 penmanship 11 handwriting
call in 6 summon 7 convene
calling 3 art, job 4 work 5 craft, trade 6 métier 7 mission, pursuit 8 business, lifework, vocation 10 employment, handicraft, occupation, profession
Calliope 4 Muse *father:* 4 Zeus 7 Jupiter *mother:* 9 Mnemosyne *son:* 7 Orpheus
Callisto *lover:* 4 Zeus 7 Jupiter *son:* 5 Arcas
call off 5 scrub 6 cancel
Call of the Wild *author:* 6 London (Jack) *dog:* 4 Buck
call on 5 visit 7 require
callosity 8 hardness 9 thickness
callous 5 stony 8 obdurate 9 heartless, indurated, unfeeling 11 coldhearted, hardhearted, unemotional 12 case-hardened, stonyhearted 13 unsympathetic
callow 3 raw 5 fresh, green, young 6 infant, unripe 7 untried 8 immature, juvenile, unversed, youthful 9 unfledged 10 unseasoned 11 unpracticed 13 inexperienced, unexperienced
call's partner 4 beck
call up 5 draft, evoke 6 summon 8 mobilize
calm 4 cool, easy, hush, lull 5 allay, peace, quiet, relax, salve, still 6 hushed, pacify, placid, poised, sedate, serene, settle, smooth, soothe, stable, steady, stilly 7 appease, assuage, compose, halcyon, mollify, pacific, placate, resting, staunch 8 composed, inactive, peaceful, reposing, tranquil 9 collected, easygoing, impassive, possessed, quiescent, unruffled 10 nonchalant, phlegmatic, untroubled 11 tranquilize, unflappable 12 even-tempered, self-composed 13 imperturbable, self-possessed
calmant 8 quietive, sedative
calmative see calmant
calmness 6 phlegm 7 ataraxy 8 coolness 9 composure, sangfroid 10 equanimity

calumniate 5 libel 6 defame, malign, vilify 7 asperse, slander, traduce 9 denigrate 10 scandalize, villainize

calumnious 8 libelous 9 maligning, traducing, vilifying 10 backbiting, defamatory, detracting, detractive, scandalous, slanderous

calumny 7 scandal, slander 10 backbiting, defamation, detraction, reflection 12 backstabbing, belittlement, depreciation 13 disparagement

Calvados 6 brandy

calvary 5 cross, trial 6 ordeal 10 affliction, visitation 11 tribulation

Calypso *beloved:* 7 Ulysses 8 Odysseus *island:* 6 Ogygia

calyx part 5 sepal

camaraderie 5 cheer 7 jollity 10 affability 11 sociability 12 conviviality, friendliness

camarilla 3 mob 4 camp, clan, ring 5 cabal 6 circle, clique 7 coterie, ingroup

Cambodia 9 Kampuchea *capital:* 9 Phnom penh *monetary unit:* 4 riel

camel *driver:* 6 sarwan *one-humped:* 9 dromedary *two-humped:* 8 Bactrian

camel hair fabric 3 aba

camelopard 7 giraffe

Camelot 6 palace *lord:* 6 Arthur

Camembert 6 cheese

cameraman 6 photog 7 lensman 8 photoist 12 photographer

Cameroon *capital:* 7 Yaounde *largest city:* 6 Douala *monetary unit:* 5 franc

Camilla *father:* 7 Metabus *slayer:* 5 Aruns

Camille's creator 5 Dumas (Alexandre)

camouflage 4 mask 5 cloak 8 disguise 9 dissemble 11 dissimulate

camp 3 cot, hut, mob 4 clan, ring, tent 5 cabal, cabin, lodge, shack 6 circle, clique, shanty 7 bivouac, caboose, coterie, cottage, ingroup 9 camarilla

campaigner 9 candidate

campanile 6 belfry 8 carillon 9 bell tower

campestral 5 rural 6 rustic 7 bucolic, country, outland 8 agrestic, pastoral 10 out-country, provincial 11 countrified

campus see college

Camus work 5 Rebel 6 Plague 8 Caligula, Stranger

can 4 fire 7 dismiss 9 container, discharge 10 receptacle *combining form:* 5 scyph 6 scyphi, scypho

Canaan 4 Zion 5 bliss 6 heaven 7 elysium, nirvana 8 empyrean, paradise *father:* 3 Ham *grandfather:* 4 Noah

Canaanite god 3 Mot 4 Baal 6 Molech, Moloch

Canace *brother:* 8 Macareus *father:* 6 Aeolus

Canada *capital:* 6 Ottawa *college, university:* 6 McGill 8 McMaster 9 Concordia *largest city:* 8 Montreal *monetary unit:* 6 dollar *province:* 6 Quebec 7 Alberta, Ontario 8 Manitoba 10 Nova Scotia 12 New Brunswick, Newfoundland, Saskatchewan *provincial park:* 5 Gaspé 7 Rondeau 9 Garibaldi

Canadian insurgent 4 Riel (Louis)

canaille 3 mob 6 masses, rabble 8 riffraff, unwashed 11 proletariat

canal 4 duct 6 course 7 channel, conduit 8 aqueduct 11 watercourse *Africa:* 4 Suez 8 Ismailia *Belgium:* 6 Albert *Canada:* 7 Welland *Central America:* 6 Panama *China:* 5 Grand 7 Da Yunhe *combining form:* 4 meat 5 meato *Florida:* 10 Saint Lucie *Germany:* 4 Kiel *Greece:* 7 Corinth *Massachusetts:* 7 Cape Cod *Michigan:* 3 Soo *Netherlands:* 8 Noord Zee, North Sea 13 Amsterdam Ship *New York:* 4 Erie 6 Oswego 9 Champlain *Ontario:* 6 Rideau *Thailand:* 6 khlong *Venice:* 5 Grand

canapé spread 4 paté

canard 3 fib, lie 4 tale 5 spoof 7 falsity, untruth 8 untruism 9 falsehood 13 prevarication

canary 4 fink 6 snitch 7 stoolie 8 informer, squealer

Canary Islands 5 Ferro, Lobos, Palma 6 Gomera, Hierro 7 Inferno 8 Graciosa, Tenerife 9 Alegranza, Lanzarote

canary yellow 6 meline

cancel 3 end 4 drop, x out 5 annul, erase, scrub 6 delete, efface, negate, revoke 7 blot out, call off, expunge, redress, rescind, sublate, wipe out 8 black out 9 frustrate, terminate 10 counteract, invalidate, neutralize, obliterate 12 countercheck

cancer 5 tumor 9 carcinoma *combining form:* 6 carcin 7 carcino *treatment:* 5 X rays 7 surgery 9 radiation 12 chemotherapy

cancer-causing 12 carcinogenic *substance:* 10 carcinogen

cancer-like 8 cancroid

candescent 7 glowing 8 dazzling

Candia 5 Crete

candid 4 fair, just, open 5 frank, plain 6 honest 8 unbiased 9 equitable, impartial, objective, uncolored 10 aboveboard, forthright, scrupulous, unreserved 11 openhearted, unconcealed, undisguised 12 undissembled, unprejudiced 13 dispassionate, undissembling

candidate 6 seeker 7 hopeful, nominee, stumper 8 aspirant 9 applicant, dark horse 10 campaigner

Candide *author:* 8 Voltaire *lover:* 9 Cunegonde *tutor:* 8 Pangloss *valet:* 7 Cacambo

candle 6 bougie 8 bayberry *holder:*
6 lampad, sconce 7 menorah, pricket 9 girandole 10 candelabra 11 candelabrum
material: 3 wax 4 wick 6 tallow 7 stearin
8 paraffin *religious:* 6 votive 7 paschal
slender: 5 taper

candlefish 8 eulachon *relative:* 5 smelt

candlelit service 5 vigil

candlepins 7 bowling

candy 5 honey 7 sweeten 9 sugarcoat,
sugar over *kind:* 4 rock 5 fudge, gundy,
lolly, sweet, taffy, toffy 6 bonbon, comfit,
dragée, jujube, nougat, toffee 7 brittle, cara-
mel, fondant, gumdrop, penuche, praline
8 licorice, lollipop, lollypop, marzipan, sour-
ball, taiglach, teiglach 9 chocolate, jelly
bean, nonpareil, sweetmeat 10 confection
12 butterscotch *medicated:* 7 lozenge
9 cough drop

Canea's land 5 Crete

canine 3 dog 4 tyke 5 hound, pooch

Canis Major star 6 Sirius

Canis Minor star 7 Procyon

canker 5 stain 6 debase 7 corrupt,
debauch, deprave, pervert, vitiate 9 animalize 10 bestialize, demoralize

cankered 5 waspy 6 cranky, ornery
7 bearish, waspish 8 vinegary 9 crotchety
10 vinegarish 12 cantankerous, cross-
grained

canker sore 5 ulcer 6 lesion 10 ulcer-
ation

cannabis 3 pot 4 hemp 5 bhang, ganja,
grass 7 hashish 9 marijuana

canned 6 pocket, potted 7 capsule 9 condensed 10 epitomized

Cannery Row author 9 Steinbeck
(John)

cannibalic 4 grim 5 cruel 6 fierce, savage 7 inhuman, wolfish 8 inhumane 9 barbarous, ferocious, truculent

canniness 3 art 5 craft 7 caution, cunning, slyness 8 artifice, foxiness, prudence,
wiliness 9 cageyness, foresight 10 artfulness, craftiness, discretion, precaution,
providence 11 forethought 12 discreetness

cannon 6 pom-pom 8 howitzer, ordnance
9 artillery *part:* 5 chase 6 breech 8 casca-
bel, trunnion *slang:* 6 pistol 10 pickpocket

cannonade 4 bomb, hail 5 blitz, burst,
salvo, shell 6 shower, volley 7 barrage,
bombard 8 drumfire 9 broadside, fusillade
11 bombardment

cannonball 4 dive 5 speed 7 missile

cannoneer 6 gunner

cannon fodder 8 infantry, soldiers

canny 3 sly 4 wise 5 chary, quick, sharp,
slick, smart 6 adroit, clever, frugal, saving
7 cunning, knowing, sparing, thrifty 9 dexterous, ingenious, provident, stewardly

10 economical, unwasteful 11 quick-witted,
sharp-witted 12 nimble-witted

canoe 6 dugout 7 pirogue, piroque
ancient: 7 coracle *Central American:*
6 pitpan *Eskimo:* 5 kayak, umiak
6 oomiak 7 bidarka *Guianan:* 6 corial
Latin American: 5 bungo *Malabar Coast:*
6 ballam *Maori:* 4 waka *Philippine:*
5 banca 6 baroto *Polynesian:* 4 pahi

canon 3 law 4 rule 5 dogma, edict, tenet
6 assize, decree 7 precept, statute
8 decretum, doctrine 9 ordinance 10 regulation

canonical 5 sound 8 accepted, orthodox,
received 10 sanctioned 13 authoritative

canonical hour 4 none, sext 5 lauds,
prime, terce 6 matins, tierce 7 vespers
8 compline

canonicals 9 vestments

can opener 9 church key

canopy 3 sky 5 cover 6 awning 7 marquee, shelter 8 covering 9 baldachin
10 baldachino 11 baldacchino *canvas:*
4 tilt

cant 3 tip 4 heel, lean, list, tilt 5 argot,
idiom, lingo, slang, slant, slope 6 jargon,
patois, patter, speech 7 dialect, diction,
incline, lexicon, palaver, recline 8 language
9 hypocrisy 10 dictionary, pharisaism, sanctimony, Tartuffery, Tartuffism, vernacular,
vocabulary 11 phraseology, terminology
12 pecksniffery

cantaloupe 5 melon 9 muskmelon

cantankerous 4 dour, sour 5 cross,
huffy, waspy 6 cranky, crusty, morose,
ornery 7 bearish, crabbed, prickly, waspish
8 cankered, liverish, petulant, snappish, vinegary 9 crotchety, dyspeptic, irascible, irritable 10 ill-natured, vinegarish 12 cross-
grained

canter 3 bum, vag 4 gait, hobo 5 tramp
7 drifter, vagrant 8 derelict, vagabond
10 street arab 11 bindle stiff

Canterbury *archbishop:* 3 Oda
6 Anselm, Becket (Thomas), Parker (Matthew) 7 Cranmer (Thomas), Dunstan
9 Augustine

Canterbury Tales *author:* 7 Chaucer
(Geoffrey) *inn:* 6 Tabard

canticle 3 ode 4 hymn, song 10 Benedi-
cite, Benedictus, Magnificat 12 Nunc Dimittis

canticles 11 Song of Songs 13 Song of
Solomon

cantilever 6 bridge 7 support

cantillate 4 sing 5 chant 6 recite

cantina 3 bar, pub 6 saloon, tavern 7 barroom, gin mill, rum hole 8 drinkery, groggery, pothouse

canton 6 billet 7 quarter 8 district, division

cantor 5 hazan 6 chazan, hazzan 7 chazzan 9 precentor

canvas 4 duck, sail, tarp, tent 6 awning 8 painting 9 tarpaulin

canvasback 4 duck

canvass 3 con, vet 4 case, drum, moot 5 argue, study 6 debate, drum up, survey 7 agitate, check up, discept, discuss, dispute, examine, inspect, solicit 9 check over, thrash out 10 scrutinize

canyon 5 cajon, chasm, gorge, gulch 6 ravine, valley 10 depression *Colorado River:* 5 Grand *mouth:* 4 abra *Snake river:* 5 Hells

cap 3 cob, top 4 best, pass 5 beret, cover, crest, crown, trump 6 barret, beanie, climax, exceed, top off 7 blanket, overlay, surpass 8 outshine, outstrip, overcast, round off, surmount 9 culminate, finish off, transcend 10 overspread *academic:* 11 mortarboard *brimless:* 3 tam 5 beret, calot 7 calotte *clergyman's:* 5 miter, mitre 7 biretta 9 zucchetto *combining form:* 8 calyptri, calyptro *cone-shaped:* 3 taj *hoodlike:* 4 coif *hunter's:* 7 montero *jester's:* 7 coxcomb 9 cockscomb *Jewish:* 8 yarmulke *knitted:* 5 toque, tuque *military:* 4 kepi *mushroom:* 6 pileus *Muslim:* 3 taj *part:* 4 bill, brim, flap, peak 5 visor 7 earflap *Roman:* 6 pileus *Scottish:* 3 tam 5 mutch 6 bonnet 8 balmoral 9 glengarry 11 tam-o'-shanter *sheepskin:* 6 calpac, kalpak 7 calpack *Turkish:* 6 calpac, kalpak 7 calpack

capability 3 art 5 craft, might, skill 7 ability, cunning, potency 8 adequacy, capacity, efficacy 10 competence, efficiency 13 effectiveness, qualification, qualifiedness

capable 4 able, good 6 au fait, proper, wicked 9 competent, qualified *suffix:* 3 ile 4 able, ible

capacious 4 wide 5 ample, roomy 7 copious 8 abundant, spacious 10 commodious

capacitance *unit of:* 5 farad

capacity 4 bent, gift, rank 5 knack, might, place, state 6 status, talent 7 ability, caliber, faculty, footing, station, stature 8 adequacy, position, standing 9 character, situation 10 capability, competence 13 qualification, qualifiedness *unit of:* 4 gill, peck, pint 5 liter, minim, quart 6 bushel, gallon 8 fluidram 10 fluidounce, milliliter

Capaneus *slayer:* 4 Zeus *wife:* 6 Evadne

caparison 8 clothing 9 adornment

cape 4 beak, bill, head, naze, ness 5 point 8 foreland, headland, pelerine 10 promontory *clergyman's:* 7 mozetta 8 mozzetta *papal:* 5 fanon, orale

Cape *Africa:* 4 Juby, Yubi 5 Blanc 6 Blanco 7 Agulhas *Alaska:* 3 Icy 4 Nome 5 Ocean 11 Krusenstern *Algeria:* 3 Fer *Antarctica:* 3 Ann 4 Dart 5 Adare *Arctic:* 5 North 8 Nordkaap *Asia:* 5 Aniva *Australia:* 5 Byron, Otway, Sandy, Smoky 6 Arnhem 9 Van Diemen *Baffin Island:* 4 Dyer *Black Sea:* 5 Yasun *Borneo:* 4 Datu 6 Datoek *Brazil:* 4 Frio, Raso 5 Norte *California:* 9 Mendocino *Canada:* 5 North *Caribbean:* 8 Honduras *Colombia:* 5 Aguja *Costa Rica:* 5 Velas *Crete:* 5 Plaka *Croatia:* 5 Ploca 6 Planka *Cuba:* 4 Cruz 5 Maisi *Denmark:* 4 Skaw 6 Skagen *Desolación Island:* 5 Pilar 6 Pillar *Djibouti:* 3 Bir *Egypt:* 5 Banas *England:* 8 Bolerium, Lands End *Florida:* 5 Sable 7 Kennedy 9 Canaveral *Greece:* 4 Busa 5 Gallo, Malea, Papas, Vouxa 6 Araxos, Maleas 7 Akritas *Guadalcanal:* 4 West *Guinea:* 5 Verga *Gulf of California:* 5 Lobos *Gulf of Guinea:* 5 Lopez *Gulf of Mexico:* 4 Rojo *Hawaii:* 5 Ka Lae, South 10 South Point 11 Diamond Head *Hispaniola:* 5 Beata *Honshu:* 3 Iro, Oma 5 Inubo, Kyoga, Nyudo *Iceland:* 4 Horn 5 North *Indonesia:* 4 Vals 5 False *Japan:* 4 Esan, Nomo, Sata, Soya 5 Erimo, Kamui *Liberia:* 5 Mount *Libya:* 3 Tin 4 Milh *Long Island Sound:* 10 Throgs Neck *Malay Peninsula:* 5 Bulat 7 Romania *Malaysia:* 4 Piai 5 Sirik *Massachusetts:* 3 Ann, Cod *Mediterranean:* 5 Ajdir *Mexico:* 4 Buey *Morocco:* 3 Sim 4 Guir, Rhir *Namibia:* 4 Fria 5 Cross *Newfoundland:* 4 Pine 5 Bauld *New Jersey:* 3 May *New Zealand:* 4 East 5 Brett, North, South, Table *North Carolina:* 4 Fear 7 Lookout 8 Hatteras *Northwest Territories:* 8 Bathurst *Nova Scotia:* 5 Canso 6 Breton *Oman:* 3 Nus 4 Hadd *Ontario:* 4 Hurd, Rich *Pakistan:* 5 Monze, Muari *Portugal:* 4 Roca *Puerto Rico:* 4 Rojo *Quebec:* 5 Gaspé *Red Sea:* 5 Kasar *Sicily:* 4 Boeo, Faro 7 Lilibeo, Passero, Pelorus *Solomon Islands:* 5 Zelee *Somalia:* 4 Asir 5 Assir, Hafun *South Africa:* 4 Seal 8 Good Hope *South America:* 4 Horn *Spain:* 3 Nao 4 Gata 5 Creus, Penas 9 Trafalgar *Syria:* 5 Basit *Taiwan:* 5 Oluan 7 Garam Bi *Tasmania:* 5 Table *Tierra del Fuego:* 5 Penas *Tunisia:* 5 Blanc *Turkey:* 3 Boz 4 Baba, Ince, Kara, Krio 6 Lectum 8 Bozburun 9 Inceburun, Karaburun *Vancouver Island:* 5 Scott *Virginia:* 5 Henry *Washington:* 5 Alava

Capek *coinage:* 5 robot *play:* 3 R.U.R.

caper 4 dido, lark, romp 5 antic, frisk, prank, shine, trick 6 cavort, frolic, gambol 7 roguery, rollick 8 escapade, mischief

9 capriccio, devilment 10 impishness, she-nanigan, tomfoolery 11 monkeyshine, wag-gishness

Capetown's famous son 5 Smuts (Jan)

capillary 4 tube 6 vessel 8 hairlike 11 blood vessel

capital 3 top 4 cock, fine, main, rank 5 basic, chief, dandy, gross, major, prime, vital 6 assets, famous, wealth 7 glaring 8 cardinal, dominant, five-star, flagrant, top-notch 9 egregious, essential, excellent, first-rate, number one, principal, resources 10 first-class, preeminent, underlying 11 fundamental, outstanding, predominant *Afghanistan:* 5 Kabul *Alberta:* 8 Edmonton *Angola:* 6 Luanda *Antigua:* 7 St. Johns *Armenia:* 7 Yerevan *Assam:* 6 Dispur *Azerbaijan:* 4 Baku *Belize:* 8 Belmopan *Belarus:* 5 Minsk *Bhutan:* 6 Thimbu *Botswana:* 8 Gaborone *Dominica:* 6 Roseau *Equatorial Guinea:* 6 Malabo *Estonia:* 7 Tallinn *Ethiopia:* 10 Addis Ababa *Faeroe Islands:* 9 Thorshavn *Falkland Islands:* 7 Stanley *French Guiana:* 7 Cayenne *Galapagos Islands:* 12 San Cristobal *Georgia, Republic of:* 7 Tbilisi *Ghana:* 5 Accra *Greenland:* 8 Godthaab *Guam:* 5 Agana *Guinea:* 7 Conakry *Kazakhstan:* 7 Alma-Ata *Kiribati:* 6 Tarawa *Kyrgyzstan:* 7 Bishkek *Latvia:* 4 Riga *Lithuania:* 7 Vilnius *Malaysia:* 11 Kuala Lumpur *Manitoba:* 8 Winnipeg *Mauritania:* 10 Nouakchott *Moldova:* 8 Chişinău *Mongolia:* 9 Ulan Bator *Montserrat:* 8 Plymouth *Mozambique:* 6 Maputo *Myanmar:* 6 Yangon *Namibia:* 8 Windhoek *Newfoundland:* 10 Saint Johns *Northern Ireland:* 7 Belfast *Northern Territory:* 6 Darwin *North-West Frontier Province:* 8 Peshawar *Northwest Territories:* 11 Yellowknife *Nova Scotia:* 7 Halifax *Orange Free State:* 12 Bloemfontein *Pakistan:* 9 Islamabad *Papua New Guinea:* 11 Port Moresby *Prince Edward Island:* 13 Charlottetown *Puerto Rico:* 7 San Juan *Queensland:* 8 Brisbane *Réunion:* 10 Saint Denis *Saint Helena:* 9 Jamestown *Saint Lucia:* 8 Castries *Saskatchewan:* 6 Regina *Scotland:* 9 Edinburgh *Seychelles:* 8 Victoria *Shetland:* 7 Lerwick *Sicily:* 7 Palermo *Sierra Leone:* 8 Freetown *Sikkim:* 7 Gangtok *Sind:* 7 Karachi *Slovenia:* 9 Ljubljana *Solomon Islands:* 7 Honiara *South Australia:* 8 Adelaide *South-West Africa:* 8 Windhoek *Suriname:* 10 Paramaribo *Swaziland:* 7 Mbabane *Tahiti:* 7 Papeete *Tajikistan:* 8 Dushanbe *Tasmania:* 6 Hobart *Tibet:* 5 Lhasa *Tirol:* 9 Innsbruck *Tonga:* 9 Nukualofa *Turkmenistan:* 9 Ashkhabad *Ukraine:* 4 Kiev *Uruguay:* 10 Montevideo *Uttar Pradesh:* 7 Lucknow *Uzbekistan:* 8 Tashkent *Victoria:* 9 Melbourne *Vietnam:* 5 Hanoi *Wales:* 7 Cardiff *Western Australia:* 5 Perth *Yukon:* 10 Whitehorse (see also names of individual countries and states)

capitalist 8 investor 9 bourgeois, financier, plutocrat

capitalistic 9 bourgeois

capitalize 3 aid 4 back, fund, help 5 stake 6 assist 7 finance, promote, sponsor, support 8 bankroll 9 grubstake, subsidize

capital sin see deadly sin

Capitol Hill sound 3 aye, nay

capitulate 3 bow 4 cave 5 defer, yield 6 submit 7 knuckle, succumb 11 buckle under 12 knuckle under

capitulation 8 dedition 9 surrender 10 submission

capper 5 blind, decoy, shill, stick 9 shillaber

capriccio 5 caper, fancy, prank 6 whimsy

caprice 3 bee 4 mood, vein, whim 5 crank, fancy, freak, habit, humor, trait, trick 6 foible, maggot, megrim, notion, temper, vagary, whimsy 7 boutade, conceit 8 crotchet 9 mannerism 11 peculiarity 12 whigmaleerie 13 inconsistency

capricious 4 iffy 5 moody 6 chancy, fickle 7 erratic, wayward 8 freakish, ticklish, unstable, variable, volatile, whimsied 9 arbitrary, fluctuant, humorsome, mercurial, uncertain, vagarious, whimsical 10 changeable, inconstant, lubricious 12 effervescent, incalculable 13 temperamental, unpredictable

caprid 4 goat

capsheaf see capstone

capsize 4 keel 5 upset 8 collapse, overturn

capstone 4 acme, apex, peak 6 apogee, climax, summit 8 capsheaf, meridian, pinnacle 11 culmination

capsule 6 canned, pocket, potted 9 condensed 10 epitomized *combining form:* 4 thec 5 theci, theco

capsulize 7 enclose 8 condense

captain 7 skipper 11 four-striper *fictional:* 4 Ahab, Nemo 5 Queeg *historical:* 5 Bligh (William) *pirate:* 4 Kidd (William)

Captains Courageous author 7 Kipling (Rudyard)

caption 6 legend 7 cutline 8 overline 9 underline

captious 5 testy 6 critic, snappy 7 carping, finicky, peevish 8 caviling, contrary, critical, exacting, perverse, petulant, snap-

pish 9 cavillous, demanding, irritable
10 censorious 12 faultfinding, overcritical
13 hypercritical

captivate 4 draw, grip, hold, take, wile
5 charm 6 allure, please 7 attract, bewitch,
delight, enchant, gratify 8 enthrall 9 fascinate, magnetize, mesmerize, spellbind

captivating 8 magnetic 9 appealing,
glamorous, seductive

captive 7 hostage 8 prisoner

captivity 11 confinement 12 imprisonment

capture 3 bag, get, nab 4 nail, take
5 catch, cotch 6 collar, secure 7 prehend

Capuan 4 lush 5 plush 6 deluxe 7 opulent 8 luscious, palatial 9 luxuriant, luxurious, sumptuous 11 upholstered

car 4 auto, heap 5 buggy, coach, coupe,
crate, motor, sedan, wreck 6 hotrod, jalopy,
junker 7 clunker, flivver, hardtop, machine,
phaeton 8 dragster, motorcar, roadster,
runabout 9 limousine 10 automobile, touring car 11 convertible 12 station wagon
(see also **automobile**)

caramel-like 5 chewy

caravansary 3 inn 5 hotel, lodge 6 hostel, tavern 7 auberge, hospice 8 hostelry
9 roadhouse 11 public house

carbohydrate 5 sugar 6 starch 7 glucose, lactose, sucrose 8 fructose, glycogen
9 cellulose, galactose *suffix:* 3 ose

carbon 4 coal, coke, soot 8 graphite,
plumbago 9 lampblack *combining form:*
7 anthrac 8 anthraco

carbonate 6 aerate

carbon compound *suffix:* 2 an 3 ane,
ene, yne 5 ylene

carbon copy 5 ditto 7 replica 9 duplicate, facsimile 11 replication 12 reproduction 13 reduplication

carbonize 4 burn, char

carboxyl *suffix:* 3 oic 4 onic

carbuncle 4 boil 6 pimple 7 abscess,
pustule *combining form:* 7 anthrac
8 anthraco

carcass 4 body, mort 5 stiff 6 corpse,
deader 7 cadaver, remains

carcinoid 5 tumor

carcinoma 5 tumor 6 cancer

card 3 wag, wit 4 menu, sked, zany
5 joker, trump 6 agenda, docket 7 program
8 calendar, comedian, humorist, schedule
9 programma, timetable 11 carte du jour *fortune-telling:* 5 tarot *performer's:* 3 cue
5 idiot *spot:* 3 pip

cardboard 5 stiff 6 unreal, wooden
7 bristol, buckram, stilted 10 unlifelike
11 muscle-bound, stereotyped, unrealistic

card-carrying 7 genuine 11 full-fledged

card game see at **game**

cardiac stimulant 7 ouabain 9 digitalis

cardialgia 9 heartburn

cardinal 5 vital 6 ruling 7 central, pivotal
9 essential 10 overriding, overruling
11 fundamental 12 constitutive

cardinal point 4 east, west 5 north,
south

cardinal suffix 2 ty 4 teen

Cardinal Virtue 7 justice 8 prudence
9 fortitude 10 temperance

care 3 rue, woe 4 dole, fear, heed, mind,
reck, tend, ward 5 alarm, grief, nurse,
pains, serve, trial, trust, watch, worry
6 attend, charge, dismay, effort, mother,
regard, regret, sorrow, strain, stress,
unease, wait on 7 anguish, anxiety, concern, conduct, custody, keeping, running,
tension, trouble 8 disquiet, exertion, handling, interest, suspense, tendance 9 agitation, alertness, attention, curiosity, heartache, misgiving, oversight, vigilance
10 affliction, enthusiasm, foreboding, heartbreak, intendance, management, minister
to, solicitude, uneasiness 11 concernment,
disquietude, disturbance, heedfulness, safekeeping, supervision 12 apprehension,
guardianship, perturbation, watchfulness
13 consciousness, consideration, consternation

careen 4 sway 5 lurch, swing, weave
6 wobble 7 stagger

career 4 race, rush, tear 5 chase, speed
6 course 7 calling 8 vocation

care for 4 like, mind, tend 5 nurse 6 foster

carefree 4 wild 6 breezy 8 feckless, reckless 9 lightsome 10 free-minded, incautious, insouciant 12 happy-go-lucky, lighthearted 13 irresponsible

careful 4 safe, wary 5 chary, exact, fussy
6 intent 7 duteous, dutiful, finical, finicky,
guarded, heedful, precise, prudent, studied
8 accurate, cautious, critical, discreet, gingerly, punctual 9 attentive, observant, provident, religious 10 deliberate, meticulous,
particular, scrupulous 11 calculating, circumspect, considerate, foresighted, painstaking, punctilious 12 conscionable
13 conscientious

carefully 8 gingerly

careless 3 lax 4 rash, wild 5 messy,
slack, unfit 6 botchy, remiss, sloppy,
unneat, untidy 7 raunchy, unkempt 8 derelict, feckless, heedless, reckless, slapdash,
slipshod, slovenly, uncaring 9 forgetful,
incapable, negligent, oblivious, unheeding,
unmindful, unrecking 10 behindhand, delinquent, disheveled, inadequate, incautious,
neglectful, regardless, unthinking, unthorough 11 inadvertent, inattentive, thoughtless, unconcerned, unqualified 12 disregardful, irreflective, unfastidious,
uninterested, unreflective 13 irresponsible

caress 3 pat, pet, toy 4 love, neck 5 dally, flirt 6 cocker, coddle, coquet, cosset, cuddle, dandle, fondle, nuzzle, pamper, stroke, trifle 7 indulge

caressive 7 calming 8 soothing

caretaker 9 custodian

careworn 5 drawn, jaded 6 fagged 7 haggard, pinched 8 troubled, tuckered 9 exhausted 10 distressed

cargo 4 haul, load 6 burden, lading 7 freight, payload

caricature 4 fake, mock, sham 5 farce, phony 6 parody 7 cartoon, lampoon, mockery, takeoff 8 travesty 9 burlesque, clinquant, imitation 10 pasquinade 13 laughingstock

carillon 6 belfry 9 bell tower, campanile

caritas 5 grace, mercy 6 lenity 7 charity 8 clemency

cark 3 ail 4 fret, fuss, stew 5 upset, worry 6 pother 7 trouble 8 distress

Carlsbad feature 6 cavern

Carmen *author:* 7 Mérimée (Prosper) *composer:* 5 Bizet (Georges) *lover:* 7 Don José *toreador:* 9 Escamillo

Carmi *father:* 6 Reuben *son:* 5 Achan

carnage 8 butchery, massacre 9 bloodbath, bloodshed, slaughter

carnal 4 lewd 5 gross 6 animal, bodily, coarse, earthy, vulgar, wanton 7 earthly, fleshly, lustful, mundane, obscene, sensual, somatic, worldly 8 corporal, material, physical, sensuous 9 corporeal 10 lascivious

carnation 4 pink 5 color 6 flower

carnival *attraction:* 4 ride 6 midway 8 sideshow 10 concession *character:* 5 shill 6 barker, hawker 7 grifter, spieler *New Orleans:* 9 Mardi Gras *performer:* 4 geek

carol 4 song 6 ballad *Christmas:* 4 noel

carom 3 dap 4 skim, skip 5 graze 6 glance 8 ricochet

Caron role 4 Gigi, Lili

carotid's relative 5 aorta

carousal 3 bat, jag 4 tear 5 binge, booze, drunk, spree 6 bender 7 blowoff 9 brannigan *Scottish:* 6 splore

carouse 4 hell, riot 5 revel 6 frolic 7 roister, wassail *Scottish:* 4 birl 5 birle

carp 3 nag 4 fuss 5 cavil 6 peck at 7 henpeck

carpe ____ 4 diem

carpenter 3 ant, bee 6 joiner, wright 7 artisan, builder, workman 9 craftsman

carpentry 7 joinery

carper 5 momus 6 critic, Zoilus 7 caviler, knocker 9 aristarch 10 criticizer 11 faultfinder, smellfungus

carpet 3 mat, rug 5 tapis 6 velvet, Wilton 8 Brussels, moquette, Venetian 9 Axminster, broadloom *Afghan:* 5 Herat 6 Herati *Indian:* 4 Agra *Persian:* 4 kali 6 Kerman, Keshan, Kirman, Sarouk *Turkish:* 5 Koula, Ladik 8 Ghiordes

carpet beetle 10 buffalo bug

carpet knight 8 hedonist, sybarite

carping 6 critic, jawing 7 blaming, railing 8 blameful, captious, caviling, critical 9 cavillous, damnatory 10 censorious, upbraiding 11 criticizing, objurgatory, reproachful, reprobating, reprobatory 12 condemnatory, faultfinding, overcritical, reprehending 13 hypercritical

carrageen 7 seaweed 9 Irish moss

carrefour 5 plaza 6 square 10 crossroads

carriage 3 rig 4 pose 6 stance 7 posture, transit, voiture 8 attitude, carrying, positure 9 transport 10 conveyance 12 transporting *American:* 5 buggy 8 dearborn, rockaway 9 buckboard *attendant:* 6 flunky 7 flunkey, footman *baby:* 4 pram 5 buggy 8 stroller 12 perambulator *driver:* 4 hack 5 cabby 8 coachman *folding top:* 6 calash *four-wheeled:* 4 sado, trap 5 buggy, coupe 6 berlin, calash, fiacre, landau, surrey 7 britska, cariole, dos-a-dos, hackney, phaeton 8 barouche, britzska, brougham, carriole, carryall, clarence, dearborn, rockaway, sociable, stanhope, tarantas, victoria 9 buckboard *Indian:* 6 gharri, gharry *Javanese:* 4 sado *man-drawn:* 6 riksha 7 rikisha, rikshaw 10 jinrikisha *Philippine:* 6 calesa 7 calesin 9 carromata *Russian:* 6 drosky, troika 7 droshky 8 tarantas 9 tarantass *stately:* 7 caroche *three-horse:* 6 troika *two-wheeled:* 3 gig 4 shay, trap 5 buggy, sulky 6 calesa, chaise, dennet, hansom, herdic, whisky 7 caleche, calesin, dogcart, tilbury, whiskey 8 curricle 9 cabriolet, carromata *with attendants:* 8 equipage

carriage trade 5 elite 6 flower, gentry 7 quality 9 blue blood, gentility 10 upper class, upper crust 11 aristocracy

carrick bend 4 knot

carrier 5 envoy 6 bearer, porter, vector 7 airline, courier, drogher, vehicle 8 emissary 9 messenger 11 internuncio *combining form:* 4 pher, phor 5 phora, phore 6 phorae (plural), phorum

Carroll character 5 Alice, snark 6 boojum, Hatter 8 Dormouse 9 March Hare 10 Mock Turtle 11 White Rabbit 12 Humpty Dumpty

carrot 4 meed, plum 5 prize 6 reward 7 guerdon, premium 8 dividend

carry 3 act, get, jag, lug 4 bear, buck, have, hump, keep, move, pack, pipe, prop, quit, send, sway, take, tote, waft 5 brace, bring, ferry, fetch, shift, stock, touch 6 acquit, affect, bear up, behave, convey, demean, deport, funnel, remove, siphon, strike, upbear, uphold 7 bolster, channel, comport, conduct, disport, impress, inspire, possess, shore up, support, sustain, traject 8 buttress, transfer, transmit 9 influence, transport

carrying *combining form:* 7 phorous

carrying case 7 holdall

carry off 4 down, kill, slay 6 cut off, finish, lay low, spirit 7 destroy, put away, take off 8 dispatch

carry on 3 run 4 go on, keep, rant, rave 5 act up, cut up, horse 6 direct, hang on, manage, ordain 7 conduct, operate, persist 9 horseplay, persevere

carry out 6 effect, govern, render 7 execute, fulfill 8 bring off, complete, finalize, transact 9 discharge, prosecute 10 administer, effectuate 12 administrate

carry over 8 postpone, transfer

carrytale 5 clack, tabby 6 gossip 8 gossiper, quidnunc 10 newsmonger 12 gossipmonger 13 scandalmonger

carry through 4 last 5 abide 6 effect, endure 7 perdure, persist 8 bring off, continue 10 effectuate

cart 4 dray, haul 5 carry 6 barrow, convey 7 tumbrel, tumbril 8 carriage 9 transport *Indian:* 5 tonga *racing:* 5 sulky

____ **carte** 3 a la

____ **Carte** 5 D'Oyly

carte blanche 3 say 5 power, right, say-so 7 license 8 free hand 9 authority 10 blank check 11 prerogative

carte d'entrée 6 ticket

carte du jour 4 menu

cartel 4 bloc, dare, defy, pool 5 chain, group, stump, trust 7 combine 8 defiance 9 challenge, syndicate 10 consortium

Carthaginian *goddess of the moon:* 5 Tanit 6 Tanith *queen:* 4 Dido 6 Elissa

cartilage 6 tissue 7 gristle *combining form:* 6 chondr 7 chondri, chondro

cartogram 3 map

cartographer *English:* 5 Smith (Willian) *Flemish:* 6 Kremer (Gerhard) 8 Mercator (Gerardus), Ortelius *German:* 13 Waldseemuller (Martin) *Greek:* 7 Ptolemy

cartography 9 mapmaking

cartoonist 4 Capp (Al), Nast (Thomas), Szep 5 Davis (Jim), Gould (Chester), Kelly (Walt), Young (Chic) 6 Addams (Charles), Disney (Walt), Larson (Gary), Schulz (Charles) 7 Mauldin (Bill), Trudeau (Garry) 8 Goldberg (Rube), Groening (Matt), Herblock

cartouche 5 brown, frame 6 shield

cartridge 4 case, tube 5 shell 8 cylinder

cartwheel 4 coin 6 tumble 10 handspring

carve 3 cut 5 sculp, sever, slice, split 6 chisel, cleave, sculpt, sunder 7 dissect 8 dissever 9 sculpture

Casanova 4 wolf 5 Romeo 6 chaser, masher 7 amorist, Don Juan, gallant 8 lothario, paramour 9 ladies' man, philander, womanizer 10 lady-killer 11 philanderer

cascade 5 chute, falls, sault, spout 8 cataract 9 waterfall

case 3 con, pod, vet 4 etui, hull, husk, skin, suit, view 5 cause, event, order, shape, shell, shuck, spook, state, study 6 action, estate, oddity, repair, sample 7 canvass, check up, episode, examine, example, inspect, lawsuit, oddball 8 incident, instance, original, sampling, specimen 9 character, check over, condition, eccentric, situation 10 occurrence, scrutinize 11 eventuality 12 circumstance, illustration *combining form:* 4 thec 5 theca, theci, theco 6 thecae (plural), thecia (plural) 7 thecium *grammatical:* 6 dative 8 ablative, genitive, vocative 9 objective 10 accusative, nominative, possessive

casebearer 5 larva 11 caterpillar

case-hardened 7 callous 10 insensible

case history 6 sample 7 example 8 instance, sampling, specimen 12 illustration

casement 6 window

Casey at the Bat poet 6 Thayer (Ernest Lawrence)

cash 4 coin, jack 5 bread, dough, money 6 mazuma, wampum 7 scratch, shekels 11 legal tender

cashier 2 ax 3 bar, can 4 cast, fire, oust, sack, shed 5 eject, expel, scrap 6 bounce, reject, shelve, slough 7 boot out, discard, dismiss, exclude, kick out 8 abdicate, jettison, pass over, throw out 9 discharge, eliminate, terminate, throw away

cash in 3 die 4 conk, drop 5 croak 6 pop off 7 kick off, succumb 8 check out, pass away

casino attendant 8 croupier

cask 3 keg, tun 4 butt, pipe 6 barrel 8 hogshead

casket 3 box 5 chest 6 coffin

Cassandra 7 seeress 9 doomsayer, pessimist, worrywart 10 prophetess 11 crepehanger *brother:* 7 Helenus *father:* 5 Priam *lover:* 9 Agamemnon *mother:* 6 Hecuba *slayer:* 12 Clytemnestra

casserole 4 dish

Cassiopeia *daughter:* 9 Andromeda *husband:* 7 Cepheus *kingdom:* 8 Ethiopia

Cassio's mistress 6 Bianca

cassock 7 soutane

cast 3 add, aim, hue, lay, sum, tot, way
4 dash, drop, face, fire, foot, form, hint, hurl,
junk, kind, look, mold, plan, shed, sort, tint,
tone, toss, tote, turn, type 5 chart, class,
color, fling, heave, leave, level, pitch, point,
scrap, shade, shape, sling, smack, throw,
tinge, total, touch, trace, train, weird, yield
6 design, devise, direct, figure, launch,
nature, reject, slough, stripe, visage, zero in
7 address, arrange, cashier, discard, dope
out, incline, moulage, project, scatter, soupçon, summate, variety 8 abdicate, disperse, forecast, jettison, prophecy, totalize
9 blueprint, broadcast, character, prevision,
prognosis, suspicion, throw away 10 distribute, expression, intimation, prediction,
suggestion 11 countenance, description,
foretelling 12 conformation 13 configuration

cast about 4 hunt, seek 5 quest 9 ferret
out, search for, search out

cast a spell 3 hex

cast away 4 blow 5 beach, waste, wreck
6 pile up, strand 7 consume, fritter
8 squander 9 dissipate, shipwreck

castaway 5 leper 6 pariah 7 Ishmael, outcast 8 derelict 10 Ishmaelite 11 offscouring, untouchable

cast down 3 bad, low 4 down, sink
5 abase, lower 6 bemean, debase,
demean, humble 7 degrade 8 dejected,
downcast 9 depressed, humiliate, woebegone 10 dispirited 11 crestfallen 12 disconsolate

castigate 3 wig 4 beat, drub, flay, rail,
rate 5 baste, slash 6 berate, pummel, punish, scathe, scorch, thrash 7 belabor, blister, chasten, correct, lambast, scarify,
scourge, upbraid 8 chastise, lambaste, lash
into, penalize 9 excoriate 10 discipline,
tongue-lash

castigation 3 rod 8 punition 10 correction, discipline, punishment
12 chastisement

cast iron 7 spiegel

castle 5 manor, villa 7 chateau, mansion
adjunct: 4 moat *gate:* 10 portcullis *ledge:*
7 rampart *structure:* 6 turret *tower:*
4 keep 6 donjon *wall:* 6 bailey 10 battlement

castle-builder 7 dreamer, utopian 8 idealist 9 ideologue, visionary

cast off 5 fling, let go, loose, untie
6 slough, unmoor 7 unhitch 8 unfasten

Castor *brother:* 6 Pollux 10 Polydeuces
constellation: 6 Gemini *father:* 4 Zeus
9 Tyndareus *mother:* 4 Leda *sister:*
5 Helen *slayer:* 4 Idas

castor oil 9 cathartic, lubricant

cast out 4 oust 5 exile, expel 6 banish,
deport 7 expulse 8 displace 9 ostracize,
transport 10 expatriate

cast overboard 8 jettison

castrate 3 fix 4 geld 5 alter, unman,
unsex 6 neuter 7 unnerve 8 enervate,
mutilate, unstring 9 sterilize 10 emasculate
11 desexualize

castrato singer 9 Farinelli

casual 5 aloof, fluky, light, minor, petty
6 breezy, chance, degage, little, remote
7 offhand, relaxed, trivial, unfussy
8 detached, informal 9 easygoing, extempore, impromptu, impulsive, incurious,
small-beer, uncurious, unplanned, withdrawn 10 accidental, contingent, fortuitous,
improvised, incidental, shoestring 11 indifferent, low-pressure, spontaneous, unconcerned, unimportant 12 uninterested
13 disinterested, insignificant, unconstrained

casualty 4 prey 5 death, fatal 6 mishap,
victim 8 accident, fatality, underdog 9 bottom dog, mischance 12 misadventure

casuistry 7 fallacy, sophism 8 delusion
9 deception, sophistry 12 equivocation,
speciousness, spuriousness 13 deceptiveness

casus ____ 5 belli

cat 4 eyra, lion, lynx, puma, puss 5 felid,
kitty, ounce, pussy 6 bobcat, cougar, feline,
kaffir 7 caracal 12 mountain lion *Alice's:*
5 Dinah *catlike animal:* 5 civet, genet,
zibet 6 zibeth 7 linsang *combining form:*
5 aelur, ailur 6 aeluro, ailuro *disease:*
9 distemper *domestic:* 3 Rex 4 Manx
5 tabby 6 calico 7 Burmese, Persian, Siamese 8 longhair 9 Himalayan, shorthair
10 Abyssinian *extinct:* 10 saber-tooth *fast-
est:* 7 cheetah *female:* 5 queen 7 lioness,
tigress 9 grimalkin *genus:* 5 Felis *grin-
ning:* 8 Cheshire *group:* 7 clowder *male:*
3 gib, tom *relating to:* 6 feline *ring-tailed:*
6 serval *Scottish:* 8 baudrons *sound:*
3 mew 4 hiss, meow, purr, roar 5 miaou,
miaow, miaul 9 caterwaul *spotted:* 4 pard
6 jaguar, margay, ocelot, serval 7 cheetah,
leopard, panther *striped:* 5 tiger *tailless:*
4 Manx *young:* 6 kitten

cataclysm 4 pour, woes 5 flood, spate
6 deluge 7 niagara, torrent, tragedy
8 calamity, cataract, disaster, flooding, overflow 10 inundation 11 catastrophe 12 misadventure

cataclysmic 5 fatal 7 fateful, ruinous
10 calamitous, disastrous 12 catastrophic

catacomb 5 crypt, vault 10 undercroft

catafalque 4 bier

catalog 4 book, list, roll 5 admit, count,
enter, tally 6 enroll, number, roster 7 item-

ize, program 8 inscribe, register, roll call, schedule, syllabus 9 enumerate, introduce, inventory 10 prospectus *of books:* 11 bibliotheca *of goods:* 9 inventory *of saints:* 9 hagiology

catalyst 4 goad, spur 7 impetus, impulse 8 stimulus 9 incentive, stimulant 10 incitation, incitement, motivation

catamaran 4 boat, raft

catamount 4 lynx 6 cougar

cataract 5 chute, falls, flood, sault, spate, spout 6 deluge 7 cascade, niagara, torrent 8 flooding, overflow 9 cataclysm, waterfall 10 inundation

catastrophe 3 woe 7 tragedy 8 calamity, disaster 9 cataclysm 12 misadventure

catastrophic 5 fatal 7 fateful, ruinous 10 calamitous, disastrous 11 cataclysmic

Catawba 4 wine 5 river

catcall 3 boo 4 bird, hiss, hoot, pooh, razz 5 bazoo 8 pooh-pooh 9 raspberry 10 Bronx cheer

catch 3 bag, con, fix, get, hit, nab, net, see, wed 4 ding, dupe, espy, find, fool, grab, grip, gull, hoax, hook, moor, nail, snag, sock, spot, take, trap 5 abash, benet, block, clasp, clout, grasp, hit on, marry, reach, seize, smite, snare, stick, stump, trick, whack 6 accept, anchor, arrest, baffle, clutch, collar, cut off, descry, detect, entrap, fasten, flurry, follow, put out, rattle, secure, snatch, strike, take in, tangle, turn up 7 capture, chicane, confuse, disturb, ensnare, espouse, fluster, grapple, hit upon, nonplus, perplex, prehend 8 confound, contract, entangle, flimflam, hoodwink, meet with, overhaul, overtake 9 apprehend, bamboozle, embarrass, encounter, intercept 10 comprehend, understand 12 come down with

catchall term 3 etc.

Catcher in the Rye *author:* 8 Salinger (Jerome David) *character:* 9 Caulfield (Holden)

catcher's glove 4 mitt

catching 6 taking 10 contagious, infectious 12 communicable

catch on 3 see 4 hear 5 learn 6 tumble 7 find out, unearth 8 discover 9 ascertain, determine

catchphrase see catchword

Catch-22 author 6 Heller (Joseph)

catch up 4 hold 8 enthrall 9 fascinate, mesmerize, spellbind

catchword 5 maxim, motto 6 byword, phrase, slogan 9 battle cry, watchword 10 shibboleth

catchy 6 fitful, spotty, tricky 8 sporadic 9 appealing, desultory, irregular, spasmodic

catechist 7 teacher

catechize 3 ask 4 quiz 5 query 7 examine, inquire 8 question 11 interrogate

catechumen 7 convert, student

categorical 4 sure 6 direct 7 certain, decided, express 8 absolute, clean-cut, clear-cut, definite, explicit, positive, specific, ultimate 9 downright 10 definitive, forthright 11 unambiguous, unequivocal

categorize 3 peg 4 sort 5 class, group 6 assort 7 put down 8 classify, identify, nail down 10 pigeonhole

category 4 tier 5 class, genre, grade, group 6 league 8 grouping 10 pigeonhole

catenation 6 series 10 connection

catercorner 9 slantways, slantwise 10 cornerwise, diagonally 12 slantingways

caterpillar 5 larva 7 cutworm, webworm 8 armyworm, silkworm 10 casebearer *combining form:* 5 campa, eruci

cater to 4 baby 5 humor, spoil 6 cocker, coddle, cosset, cotton, pamper 7 gratify, indulge 11 mollycoddle

caterwaul 3 row 4 howl, meow, spat, tiff 5 miaou, miaow, miaul, scrap 6 bicker 7 brabble, fall out, quarrel, wrangle 8 squabble

catfish see fish

catharsis 9 cleansing, purgation 10 lustration 11 expurgation 12 purification

cathartic 9 castor oil, purgative

Cathay 5 China

cathedral 5 duomo 6 church *passage:* 5 slype

Cather novel 9 A Lost Lady, My Antonia, One of Ours, O Pioneers 12 Lucy Gayheart 13 My Mortal Enemy, Song of the Lark 16 Alexander's Bridge

catholic 6 cosmic, global 7 general, generic 8 eclectic 9 extensive, inclusive, planetary, universal, worldwide 10 ecumenical, large-scale 12 cosmopolitan 13 comprehensive

catholicity 10 liberality 12 universality

catholicon 6 elixir 7 cure-all, nostrum, panacea

catkin 5 ament

catlike 5 catty 6 feline 7 furtive 8 stealthy

catnap 6 siesta, snooze 10 forty winks

Cato *title:* 5 edile 6 aedile, censor, consul 7 praetor, tribune 8 quaestor

Cat on a Hot ___ 7 Tin Roof

cat's-paw 4 pawn, tool 6 puppet, stooge

cattail 4 rush

cattle 4 kine, neat, oxen 5 bovid 6 bovine *breed:* 5 Angus, Devon, Kerry 6 Durham, Jersey, Sussex 7 Brahman, Hariana, Red Poll, Sahiwal 8 Ayrshire, Charbray, Galloway, Guernsey, Hereford, Highland, Holstein, Limousin, Longhorn 9 Charolais, Red Polled, Shorthorn, Simmental 10 Brown

Swiss, Charollais **11** Dutch Belted *call:*
4 sook **6** sookie *castrated:* **5** steer *catching rope:* **5** lasso **6** lariat *combining form:*
4 bovi *cry:* **3** low, moo *dehorn:* **4** poll *disease:* **4** loco **5** bloat **6** garget, nagana
7 anthrax, locoism, measles, murrain
8 blackleg, lumpy jaw, mastitis, staggers
10 rinderpest, Texas fever **11** brucellosis
extinct breed: **9** Teeswater *family:* **7** Bovidae *feed:* **6** fodder **7** farrago *female:*
3 cow *foot:* **4** hoof *genus:* **3** Bos *goddess:*
6 Bubona *grazing land:* **5** range **7** pasture
group: **4** herd **5** drove *herdsman:* **6** cowboy, drover, gaucho **7** vaquero **8** wrangler
10 cowpuncher *hornless:* **5** muley **6** muley *hybrid:* **7** cattalo *identification:*
5 brand *Indian:* **4** dhan *jowl:* **6** dewlap
male: **4** bull *pen:* **6** corral *round up:*
7 wrangle *stable:* **4** barn, byre *steal:*
6 rustle *unbranded:* **8** maverick *wild flight:*
8 stampede *young:* **4** calf *young, motherless:* **5** dogie

catty 4 evil, spry, yare **5** agile, brisk, zippy
6 active, bitchy, feline, lively, nimble, volant,
wicked **7** catlike, furtive, hateful, vicious
8 spiteful, stealthy **9** malicious, rancorous,
sprightly **10** despiteful, malevolent

Caucasian *capital:* **4** Baku **7** Tbilisi,
Yerevan *republic:* **7** Armenia, Georgia
10 Azerbaijan

Caucasus *peak:* **6** Elbrus *people:*
5 Osset

caucho 3 ule **4** hule **6** rubber

caudal *appendage:* **4** tail *combining form:* **2** ur **3** uro

cause 4 call, case, goad, make, root, suit
5 breed, evoke, get up, hatch **6** action,
author, draw on, effect, elicit, induce,
motive, origin, reason, secure, source,
spring, work up **7** creator, impulse, lawsuit,
produce, provoke **8** engender, generate,
muster up, occasion **9** generator, incentive,
necessity **10** antecedent, bring about,
inducement, obligation, originator, prime
mover **11** determinant **13** consideration
combining form: **4** etio **5** aetio, aitio

cause ___ 7 célèbre

caused by *suffix:* **2** ic **4** ical

causerie 3 rap **4** chat, chin, talk, yarn
5 prose

causing *combining form:* **7** facient, factive *suffix:* **3** fic **4** able, ible

caustic 4 keen, tart **5** acerb, acrid, acute,
crisp, harsh, rough, salty, sharp, terse **6** biting, bitter, ironic, severe **7** acerbic, cutting,
mordant, pungent, satiric **8** incisive, scathing, stinging, succinct **9** corrosive, sarcastic, stringent, trenchant **10** mordacious
12 archilochian *solution:* **3** lye

cauterize 4 burn, sear

caution 4 warn **6** caveat **7** warning
8 forewarn, monition, prudence **9** canniness, chariness, foresight **10** admonition,
discretion, precaution, providence **11** commonition, forethought, forewarning **12** discreetness

cautionary 4 wary **6** surety **8** cautious,
monitive, monitory, security **10** admonitory

cautious 4 cozy, safe, wary **5** alert,
cagey, canny, chary **6** shrewd **7** careful,
guarded, politic, prudent **8** discreet, gingerly, scheming, vigilant, watchful **9** judicious, provident **11** calculating, circumspect, considerate, foresighted
13 prethoughtful

cavalcade 6 parade, series **8** sequence
10 procession

cavalier 5 lofty, proud **6** knight **7** haughty
8 arrogant, horseman, insolent, superior
9 caballero **10** disdainful **11** overbearing
12 supercilious **13** high-and-mighty

cavalryman 6 lancer **7** dragoon, trooper
Algerian: **5** spahi **6** spahee *horse:*
5 waler *Prussian:* **4** ulan **5** uhlan *Russian:*
7 cossack *Turkish:* **5** spahi **6** spahee
weapon: **5** lance, saber **7** carbine

cave 3 bow, den **4** bend, drop, give, grot,
lair **5** antre, break, defer, yield **6** fold up,
grotto, hollow, submit **7** crumple, knuckle,
succumb **8** collapse **9** break down
10 capitulate, subterrane **11** buckle under
12 knuckle under, subterranean *combining
form:* **6** speleo *dweller:* **3** bat **4** bear, lion
6 hermit **9** Cro-Magnon **10** troglodite
11 Neanderthal *explorer:* **9** spelunker *formation:* **10** stalactite, stalagmite *France:*
7 Lascaux **10** Rouffignac **13** Gouffre Berger *Iceland:* **7** Singing *Indiana:* **9** Wyandotte *Iraq:* **8** Shanidar *Kentucky:* **7** Mammoth *New Zealand:* **7** Waitomo *rock:*
8 dolomite **9** limestone *South Africa:*
5 Cango *Spain:* **8** Altamira *study of:*
10 speleology

caveat 6 notice **7** caution, warning
8 monition **10** admonition **11** commonition,
forewarning

caveat ___ 6 emptor

cave-dwelling *combining form:* **6** troglo

cavern 6 grotto **10** subterrane **12** subterranean *Capri:* **10** Blue Grotto *combining
form:* **4** antr **5** antro *Montana:* **13** Lewis
and Clark *New Mexico:* **8** Carlsbad *Tennessee:* **10** Cumberland *Virginia:* **5** Luray

cavernous 4 vast **6** gaping, hollow
7 chasmal, yawning **10** commodious, sepulchral **11** reverberant

caviar 3 roe **4** eggs **6** relish *source:*
6 beluga **7** sterlet **8** sturgeon

cavil 4 carp, momi (plural) **7** chicane, quibble

caviler 5 momus 6 carper, critic, Zoilus 7 knocker 9 aristarch 10 criticizer 11 fault-finder, smellfungus

caviling 4 mean 5 fussy, petty, small 6 critic, pickly 7 carping, finicky 8 captious, contrary, critical, exacting, niggling 9 demanding 10 censorious, nitpicking 12 faultfinding, overcritical 13 hairsplitting, hypercritical

cavity 3 pit 4 bore, hole, void 6 boring, hollow 7 vacuity *body:* 5 antra (plural), sinus 6 antrum 8 follicle, hemocoei *combining form:* 3 cel 4 antr, caec, ceci, ceco, cele, celo, coel 5 antro, caeci, caeco, coele, coelo *in a glacier:* 6 moulin

cavort 4 romp 5 caper, cut up, frisk 6 frolic, gambol 7 carry on, rollick 9 horse-play 10 roughhouse 11 horse around

caw 4 yaup, yawp 6 squall, squark, squawk

cay 3 key 4 isle, reef

cayenne 6 pepper *genus:* 8 Capsicum

cayman see calman

Cayuga chief 5 Logan (James)

cease 3 erd 4 halt, quit, stop 5 close 6 desist, ending, finish, period 8 conclude, give over, intermit, knock off, leave off, surcease 9 cessation, terminate 10 conclusion, desistance 11 discontinue, termination

cease-fire 5 truce 9 armistice

ceaseless 7 endless, eternal 8 constant, immortal, unending 9 continual, perpetual, unceasing 10 continuous 11 amaranthine, everlasting, never-ending, unremitting 12 interminable 13 uninterrupted

Cecrops' daughter 5 Herse 8 Aglauros 9 Pandrosos

cecum *combining form:* 5 typhl 6 typhlo

cede 4 deed 5 alien, grant, leave, waive, yield 6 accord, assign, convey, give up, remise, resign 7 abandon, concede 8 alienate, hand over, make over, sign over, transfer 9 surrender, vouchsafe 10 abalienate, relinquish

ceiling *elaborate:* 7 plafond

ceinture 4 belt, sash 6 girdle 8 cincture 9 waistband

Celaeno *father:* 5 Atlas *mother:* 7 Pleione *sisters:* 8 Pleiades

celebrate 4 fete, hymn, keep, laud 5 bless, cry up, extol 6 praise 7 glorify, maffick, magnify, observe 8 eulogize 9 solemnize 10 panegyrize 11 commemorate

celebrated 5 famed, great, noted 6 famous 7 eminent, notable 8 renowned 9 prominent 11 illustrious 13 distinguished

celebration 4 fete, gala 6 fiesta 7 jubilee 8 festival, jamboree

célèbre 5 cause

celebrity 3 VIP 4 fame, hero, lion, name, star 5 éclat 6 renown, repute, worthy 7 big name, mahatma, notable 8 cynosure, immortal, luminary, somebody 9 notoriety, personage, superstar 10 notability, reputation

celerity 4 gait, pace 5 haste, hurry, speed 6 hustle, rustle 8 alacrity, dispatch, legerity, rapidity, velocity 9 briskness, quickness, swiftness 10 expedition, speediness

celery *genus:* 5 Apium *green:* 6 pascal *relative:* 6 carrot 7 parsley, parsnip *white:* 8 blanched *wild:* 8 smallage

celestial 7 blessed, elysian 8 beatific, empyreal, empyrean, ethereal, heavenly, Olympian, supernal 9 unearthly 12 otherworldly, transmundane

celestial body 3 sun 4 moon, star 5 comet 6 meteor, nebula, planet 8 asteroid 9 satellite *hypothetical:* 9 black hole

Celestial Empire 5 China

cell 4 room, zoid 5 cubby, zooid 7 cubicle 11 compartment *blood:* 8 hemocyte *combining form:* 3 cyt 4 cyte, cyto, phag 5 blast, gamet, phage 6 gameto, gonidi 7 gonidio *disease:* 6 cancer *division:* 7 meiosis, mitosis *fertilized egg:* 6 zygote *material:* 3 DNA, RNA 7 protein 9 chromatin, cytoplasm 10 protoplasm *nerve:* 6 neuron *part:* 4 gene 7 nucleus, vacuole 8 ribosome 10 chromosome *reproductive:* 3 egg 4 germ, ovum 5 sperm 6 gamete 8 gonidium

cellist *American:* 4 Rose (Leonard) 6 Lesser (Laurence), Parnas (Leslie) 7 Nelsova (Zara), Parisot (Aldo), Starker (Janos) 8 Schuster (Joseph) *English:* 5 du Pré (Jacqueline) *Russian:* 11 Piatigorsky (Gregor) 12 Rostropovich (Mstislav) *Spanish:* 6 Casals (Pablo)

cellophane 4 wrap 7 wrapper 8 wrapping 9 packaging

celluloid 4 film 7 plastic

cement 4 bind, join 5 unify, unite 6 mortar 8 concrete *combining form:* 4 lith *ingredient:* 4 lime 6 silica 7 alumina 8 magnesia, pozzolan 9 iron oxide, pozzolana

cemetery 8 boneyard, boot hill, catacomb 8 God's acre 9 graveyard 10 churchyard, necropolis 11 polyandrium 12 burial ground, memorial park, potter's field *underground:* 8 catacomb

cense 7 thurify

censer 8 thurible *carrier:* 8 thurifer

censor 4 blip, edit 5 purge 6 cut out, delete, excise, narrow, purify, screen 7 clean up, exscind 8 restrain, restrict 9 expurgate, red-pencil 10 blue-pencil, bowdlerize

censorious 6 critic 7 carping, chiding 8 captious, caviling, critical 9 cavillous, cul-

patory 10 accusatory, condemning, denouncing **11** reproachful **12** condemnatory, denunciatory, faultfinding, overcritical, reprehending **13** hypercritical

censurable 5 amiss, wrong **6** guilty, sinful, unholy **8** blamable, blameful, culpable, doubtful, improper, wrongful **9** incorrect **11** blameworthy **12** inadmissible, questionable, unacceptable **13** demeritorious, discreditable, objectionable, reprehensible

censure 3 rap **4** skin **5** blame, knock, scorn, scout **6** oppose, rebuke, reject, strafe **7** condemn, contemn, disdain, reprove **8** denounce, disallow, reproach **9** criticize, reprehend, reprimand, reprobate **10** denunciate, disapprove, stigmatize

centaur 6 Chiron, Nessus

Centaurus star 4 Beta **5** Alpha

Centennial State 8 Colorado

center 3 hub, mid **4** core, mean, pith, root, seat **5** focus, heart, midst, quick **6** dynamo, inside, medial, median, middle **7** central, essence, halfway, midmost **8** interior, midpoint, omphalos, polestar **9** activator, energizer, stimulant **10** focal point, middlemost **11** equidistant **12** intermediary, intermediate

centerboard 4 keel

centerfold 7 foldout **8** gatefold

centipede 9 arthropod *class:* **9** Chilopoda

central 3 key, mid **4** main, mean **5** basic, chief, focal **6** master, medial, median, middle, ruling, signal **7** leading, pivotal, primary, radical, salient **8** cardinal, dominant, foremost **9** essential, important, paramount **10** overriding, overruling **11** controlling, fundamental, outstanding, predominant, significant **12** all-absorbing, intermediary, intermediate, preponderant

Central African Republic *capital:* **6** Bangui *monetary unit:* **5** franc

Central America *country:* **6** Panama **8** Honduras **9** Costa Rica, Guatemala, Nicaragua **10** El Salvador *ethnic group:* **6** Indian **7** Mestizo, Spanish *language:* **7** Nahuatl, Spanish

centripetal 8 unifying **10** compacting **11** integrative **12** centralizing **13** concentrating, consolidating

centurion 7 officer, soldier **9** commander

century plant *genus:* **5** Agave

cephalalgia 8 headache

cephalopod 5 squid **7** mollusk, octopus **10** cuttlefish

Cepheus *daughter:* **9** Andromeda *kingdom:* **8** Ethiopia *wife:* **10** Cassiopeia

cerate 4 balm **5** cream, salve **6** chrism **7** unction, unguent **8** ointment

cerberus 6 custos, keeper, warden **8** claviger, guardian, watchdog **9** custodian

Cerberus *father:* **6** Typhon *form:* **3** dog *mother:* **7** Echidna

cereal 4 meal, mush **5** gruel **6** farina **7** oatmeal **8** cornmeal, porridge *grass:* **3** rye **4** corn, oats, ragi, rice **5** emmer, maize, spelt, wheat **6** barley, millet **7** sorghum **9** buckwheat *North African:* **8** couscous *Russian:* **5** kasha

cerebral 6 mental **7** psychic **8** highbrow **9** psychical **10** highbrowed **12** intellective, intellectual **13** psychological *combining form:* **5** psych **6** psycho

cerebrate 5 think **6** reason **7** reflect **8** cogitate **9** speculate **10** deliberate

cerebration 7 thought **9** brainwork **10** cogitation, reflection **11** speculation **12** deliberation

ceremonial 3 set **5** fixed, lofty, rigid, stiff **6** august, formal, ritual, solemn **7** courtly, starchy, stately, studied **8** mannered, stylized **10** liturgical **11** ritualistic

ceremonious 6 formal, moving, proper, seemly, solemn **7** stately **8** decorous, imposing, majestic, striking **9** grandiose **10** impressive **12** conventional

ceremony 4 form, rite **6** ritual **7** liturgy, service **9** formality **10** observance *Jewish:* **5** berit, brith **6** berith **8** habdalah, havdalah **10** bar mitzvah, bas mitzvah **11** bath mitzvah *university:* **8** encaenia

Ceres 7 Demeter *daughter:* **10** Persephone, Proserpina, Proserpine *father:* **6** Cronus, Saturn *mother:* **3** Ops **4** Rhea

cerium *symbol:* **2** Ce

certain 3 one, set **4** firm, many, some, sure, true **5** fated, fixed **6** divers, stated, sundry **7** assured, ensured, insured, settled, several, various **8** accurate, cocksure, credible, definite, numerous, positive, provable, reliable, sanguine, surefire, unerring **9** authentic, certified, confident, doubtless, necessary, plausible, unfailing, warranted **10** dependable, guaranteed, inarguable, ineludible, inevasible, inevitable, infallible, returnless, stipulated, undeniable, unevadable, verifiable **11** confirmable, indubitable, ineluctable, inescapable, irrevocable, trustworthy, unalterable, unavoidable, undoubtable, unescapable **12** demonstrable, indefeasible, indisputable, well-grounded **13** establishable, incontestable, predestinated, predetermined, uncontestable

certainty 6 surety **8** firmness, sureness **9** assurance, certitude **10** confidence, conviction, positivism, steadiness **11** assuredness, staunchness **12** absoluteness, definiteness, positiveness

certificate 3 IOU **4** bond, note **6** coupon, notice, ticket **7** diploma, license, receipt, voucher **8** contract, document **9** testimony **10** credential

certifier 6 notary
certify 2 OK 4 aver, avow, okay 5 vouch
6 assert, attest, avouch 7 approve,
endorse, license, profess, warrant, witness
8 accredit, guaranty, notarize, sanction
9 authorize, guarantee 10 commission
Cervantes' hero 10 Don Quixote
cesium *symbol:* 2 Cs
cessation 3 end 4 stop 5 cease, close
6 ending, finish, period 10 conclusion, desistance 11 termination
cesspool 3 den, sty 4 sink 5 Sodom
11 pandemonium 12 Augean stable
Cetus star 4 Mira
cgs unit 3 erg 4 dyne, gram, phot
5 gauss, poise, stilb 6 second, stokes
7 lambert, maxwell, oersted 10 centimeter
Chablis 4 wine 8 Burgundy
Chad *capital:* 8 N'Djamena *monetary
unit:* 5 franc
chafe 3 irk, rub, vex 4 flay, fret, gall, hurt,
peel, skin, wear 5 annoy, erode, graze
6 abrade, bother, damage, impair, injure, ruffle, scrape 7 corrode, inflame, provoke,
scratch 8 exercise, irritate 9 excoriate
chaff 3 fun, kid, rag, rib 4 jest, joke, josh,
razz 5 jolly 6 banter
chaffer 3 beg 4 coax 5 plead 6 dicker,
haggle, higgle, palter 7 bargain 8 huckster
chafing 7 fretful 9 impatient, unpatient
chagrined 5 upset 6 shamed 7 ashamed,
crushed 9 mortified, perturbed 11 discomposed 12 disconcerted
chain 3 row 4 bond, gyve, iron 5 group,
train, trust 6 cartel, catena, fetter, hobble,
series, string, tether 7 combine, manacle,
shackle 8 additive, additory, handcuff,
sequence 9 summative, syndicate 10 cumulative, succession 11 alternation, concatenate, consecution, progression, stereotyped
12 accumulative, conglomerate 13 concat-
enation, stereotypical *adjunct:* 8 sprocket
collar: 6 torque *combining form:* 6 strept
7 strepto *gang:* 6 coffle *ornamental:*
10 chatelaine *ship's:* 3 tye *sound:* 5 clank
chain ___ 3 saw 4 gang, mail 5 smoke,
store 6 letter 8 reaction
Chained Lady 9 Andromeda
chainlike 8 catenate
chain-shaped 10 catenulate
chair 4 seat 5 stool 6 rocker 7 preside
back: 5 splat *bishop's:* 8 cathedra
designer: 5 Eames *portable:* 5 sedan
reclining: 12 chaise longue, chaise lounge
royal: 6 throne *type:* 4 club, easy 6 morris 7 rocking 8 captain's, cogswell 9 reclining 10 ladder-back
chalcedony 4 onyx, sard 5 agate
6 jasper, quartz 9 carnelian 10 bloodstone
11 chrysoprase

chalice 3 ama, cup 5 amula, grail
chalk *combining form:* 4 calc 5 calci,
calco 8 calcareo
chalk out 5 draft 6 sketch 7 outline
8 block out, rough out, skeleton 9 adumbrate 11 skeletonize 12 characterize
chalk up 3 get, win 4 gain, have 5 annex
6 obtain, pick up, secure 7 acquire, procure
challenge 3 try 4 call, dare, defi, defy,
face, stir, wake, whet 5 beard, brave,
claim, demur, doubt, exact, front, rally,
rouse, stump, waken 6 arouse, awaken,
banter, bestir, cartel, demand, kindle, strive
7 calling, dispute, outdare, protest, require,
solicit, venture 8 claiming, defiance, demurral, demurrer, exacting, mistrust, question,
struggle 9 demanding, objection, postulate
10 difficulty, insistence 11 importuning, requisition 12 remonstrance 13 remonstration
challenger 5 rival 8 opponent 9 adversary, contender 10 competitor, contestant
chamber 4 cell, room 5 haven, house
6 harbor, shield 7 cubicle, shelter 9 apartment *combining form:* 6 thalam 7 thal-
amo *in Egyptian tomb:* 6 serdab *underground:* 8 hypogeum
chambered 10 cancellate, cancellous
chamberlain 6 priest 7 officer, servant
9 attendant, treasurer
chameleon 6 lizard
chameleonic 6 fickle 10 changeable,
inconstant
chamois 4 gems 5 gemse 6 shammy
7 leather 8 antelope, ruminant *habitat:*
4 Alps *Old Testament:* 6 aoudad
chamois-like animal 4 ibex 5 goral
6 gooral 7 klipbok 12 klipspringer
champ 3 gum, nip 4 bite, chew, mash,
peck, pick 5 chomp, crush, mouth, munch
6 crunch, mumble, nibble 7 chumble,
scrunch 8 macerate, ruminate 9 masticate
champagne 4 wine 5 color 6 bubbly
bucket: 4 icer *center:* 5 Reims
Champagne *capital:* 6 Troyes
champaign 5 field 6 domain, sphere
7 demesne, terrain 8 dominion, province
9 bailiwick, territory
champignon 6 fungus 8 mushroom
champion 4 arch, back, boss, head
5 chief, dandy, first, prime 6 uphold 7 capital, contend, leading, premier, support, titlist
8 advocate, backstop, exponent, fight for,
foremost, side with, splendid, superior, top-
notch, whiz-bang 9 excellent, expounder,
principal, proponent, supporter 10 blue-ribbon 11 illustrious, outstanding, titleholder
13 distinguished *medieval:* 7 paladin
championing *prefix:* 3 pro
championship 5 crown, title 7 defense,
pennant 8 advocacy

chance 2 go 3 hap, hit, lot, odd 4 bump, fate, luck, meet, risk, shot, show, time 5 break, fluke, fluky, light, occur, wager 6 befall, betide, casual, gamble, happen, hazard 7 come off, fall out, fortune, offhand, opening, outlook, stumble, venture 8 accident, careless, fortuity, heedless, occasion, prospect 9 advantage, adventure, transpire 10 accidental, fortuitous, incidental, likelihood 11 opportunity, possibility, probability *even:* 6 toss-up

chancellor 5 judge 6 priest 7 adviser, officer 8 minister 9 secretary *German:* 6 Brandt (Willy), Erhard (Ludwig), Hitler (Adolf) 7 Schmidt (Helmut) 8 Adenauer (Konrad), Bismarck (Otto)

chancy 4 iffy 5 dicey, fluky, hairy, risky 6 touchy, tricky 7 erratic, unsound 8 perilous, ticklish 9 dangerous, fluctuant, hazardous, uncertain, whimsical 10 capricious, jeopardous, precarious 11 speculative, treacherous 12 incalculable 13 unpredictable

change 3 fix 4 geld, swap, turn, vary 5 alter, shift, sport, trade, unsex 6 avatar, invert, modify, mutate, neuter, reform, revamp, revert, revise, switch 7 commute, convert, inverse, novelty, replace, reverse 8 castrate, exchange, mutation, mutilate, revision, transfer 9 deviation, diversify, permutate, refashion, sterilize, transform, transmute, transpose, variation, variegate 10 aberration, alteration, conversion, divergence, innovation, substitute, transplace 11 desexualize, interchange, permutation, transfigure, vicissitude 12 metamorphose, modification, transmogrify 13 metamorphosis, transmutation *sudden:* 8 peripety 10 peripeteia

changeable 5 fluid 6 fickle, labile, mobile, pliant, shifty 7 movable, mutable, plastic, protean, unfixed 8 moveable, restless, slippery, ticklish, unstable, unsteady, variable, volatile, weathery 9 adaptable, mercurial, uncertain, unsettled 10 capricious, inconstant, lubricious 13 kaleidoscopic, temperamental

change decor 4 redo

changeless 5 fixed 6 steady 7 regular, uniform 8 constant, resolute 9 steadfast 10 invariable

change off 9 alternate

change of heart 8 reversal

change of life 9 menopause 11 climacteric

change of pace 5 pitch, shift

changeover 5 shift 10 alteration, conversion

channel 3 way 4 duct, mean, pass, pipe 5 agent, canal, carry, organ 6 agency, convey, course, funnel, groove, medium, siphon, strait 7 conduct, conduit, passage, vehicle 8 aqueduct, ministry, pipeline, transmit 10 instrument 11 watercourse *Africa-Madagascar:* 10 Mozambique *Atlantic-Nantucket Sound:* 8 Muskeget *Atlantic-North Sea:* 7 English *California:* 12 Santa Barbara *Caribbean-Gulf of Mexico:* 7 Yucatan *combining form:* 3 vas 4 vasi, vaso 5 solen 6 soleno *Ellesmere-Greenland:* 7 Robeson 10 Smith Sound *Ganges:* 5 Hugli 7 Hooghly *Hawaii:* 5 Kaiwi, Kauai *Japan:* 5 Bungo *Long Island:* 13 Rockaway Inlet *Mediterranean:* 5 Malta *Northwest Territories:* 9 M'Clintock *Pakistan:* 4 Nara *Scotland:* 5 Minch *Tierra del Fuego:* 6 Beagle *Tigris-Euphrates:* 11 Shatt al Arab *Virginia:* 12 Hampton Roads *West Indies:* 9 Old Bahama 10 Saint Lucia

channel bass 4 drum 7 redfish

"Chanson ____" 6 Triste

chanson de 5 geste

chant 4 sing, tune 8 vocalize 10 cantillate *Gregorian:* 9 plainsong 12 cantus firmus *Jewish:* 6 Hallel

chanteuse 6 singer 10 cantatrice

chanticleer 4 cock 7 rooster

chaos 4 void 5 snarl 6 ataxia, huddle, muddle 7 anarchy, clutter, misrule 8 disarray, disorder 9 confusion, mobocracy 10 ochlocracy, unruliness 11 lawlessness

Chaos *daughter:* 3 Nox, Nyx 4 Gaea *son:* 6 Erebus

chap 3 guy, man 4 gent 6 fellow 9 gentleman *British:* 5 bloke

chaparral 7 thicket

chaparral bird 10 roadrunner

chaperon 4 boss 5 guide 6 attend, convoy, escort, survey 7 conduct, oversee 9 accompany, companion, supervise 11 consort with, quarterback, superintend

chapfallen see crestfallen

chaplain 5 padre 8 sky pilot

chaplet 5 crown 6 anadem, rosary, wreath 7 coronal, coronet, garland

char 4 burn 9 carbonize

character 3 ilk, rep, VIP 4 case, fame, kind, mark, mind, name, quiz, rank, role, sign, sort, soul, type 5 chief, humor, nabob, place, point, savor, state, trait 6 bigwig, cipher, device, kidney, letter, makeup, mettle, nature, oddity, report, repute, spirit, status, stripe, symbol, temper, virtue, zombie 7 big shot, courage, feature, footing, notable, oddball, persona, quality, station, variety 8 big-timer, capacity, eminence, identity, monogram, original, position, property, standing, uniquity 9 affection, attribute, birthmark, dignitary, eccentric, intellect, reference, situation 10 complexion, notability, reputation, resolution, uniqueness 11 credentials, description, disposition, distinction, personality, temperament, testimonial 13 individualism, individuality *chief:* 4 hero 11 protagonist *defect:* 8 hamartia *suffix:* 3 ery

character assassination 7 calumny, scandal, slander 10 backbiting, defamation, detraction 12 backstabbing, belittlement, depreciation 13 disparagement

characteristic 4 mark, odor, sign, tang 5 badge, point, savor, smack, token, trait 6 flavor, normal, proper, virtue 7 feature, natural, quality, regular, special, typical 8 especial, peculiar, property, specific 9 affection, attribute, birthmark, character, diacritic 10 diagnostic, individual, particular 11 differentia, distinctive, singularity 13 idiosyncratic

characteristic of *suffix:* 2 ic, ly 3 ish, ist 4 ical 5 istic 7 istical

characterize 4 mark 5 draft 6 define, sketch 7 outline, qualify 8 block out, chalk out, describe, identify, rough out, skeleton 9 adumbrate, signalize 11 distinguish, individuate, peculiarize, personalize, singularize, skeletonize 13 differentiate, individualize

characterized by *suffix:* 2 al, ic 3 ful, ial, ous 4 ical

characterless 4 weak 5 sissy 6 futile 7 unmanly 8 childish, impotent 9 infantile, powerless, sissified 10 namby-pamby, panty-waist, wishy-washy

charade 7 pageant 8 disguise, pretense 10 pretension 11 make-believe

chare 3 job 4 duty, task 5 chore, stint 6 devoir 10 assignment

charge 3 ask, bid, fee, lay, tab, tax 4 bill, boil, bolt, care, clog, cost, dash, duty, fill, heap, lade, lash, load, must, need, onus, pack, pile, race, rate, rush, task, tear, tell, toll, warn, word 5 chase, choke, fling, order, ought, place, price, refer, right, shoot, trust, weigh 6 accuse, adjure, assign, behest, burden, credit, cumber, devoir, direct, enjoin, impugn, impute, indict, saddle, tariff, weight 7 arraign, ascribe, bidding, command, conduct, dictate, entrust, expense, impeach, mandate, pervade, request, running, solicit 8 accredit, business, encumber, handling, instruct, permeate, price tag, reproach, saturate 9 attribute, committal, criminate, inculpate, millstone, oversight, penetrate, percolate, reprehend, transfuse 10 commitment, deadweight, impregnate, injunction, intendance, management, obligation 11 impenetrate, incriminate, supervision

chargeable 6 liable 11 responsible

chargeless 4 free 6 gratis 8 costless 10 gratuitous 13 complimentary

charger 5 horse, mount, steed 7 courser 8 war-horse

chariness 7 caution 8 prudence

chariot 5 essed 6 esseda, essede *four-horse:* 8 quadriga *two-horse:* 4 biga

charioteer 5 drive, pilot 6 Auriga, driver

charisma 5 charm 6 allure, appeal, duende, glamor 7 glamour 8 witchery 9 magnetism 10 witchcraft 11 fascination

charitable 4 easy, good 6 benign, humane, kindly 7 clement, helpful, lenient 8 merciful, obliging, tolérant 9 indulgent 10 altruistic, benevolent, forbearing, thoughtful 11 considerate, kindhearted, sympathetic 12 eleemosynary, humanitarian 13 accommodating, philanthropic

charity 4 alms, love 5 amity, grace, mercy 6 lenity 7 caritas 8 altruism, clemency, donation, goodwill, offering 9 affection 10 attachment, humaneness, kindliness 11 benefaction, beneficence, benevolence 12 contribution, friendliness

charivari 5 babel 6 medley 8 serenade, shivaree 10 hodgepodge 11 celebration

charlatan 4 sham 5 bluff, quack 8 imposter 9 quackster 10 mountebank 11 four-flusher, quacksalver 12 saltimbanque

Charlemagne *brother:* 8 Carloman *father:* 5 Pepin *knight:* 4 Ivon, Oton 5 Gerin, Ivory 6 Anseis, Gerard, Gerier, Oliver, Roland, Samson 7 Olivier, paladin 8 douzeper, Engelier 9 Berengier *nephew:* 6 Roland 7 Orlando *sword:* 7 Joyeuse *traitor:* 4 Gano 7 Ganelon

Charles's Wain 9 Big Dipper

charleston 5 dance

Charley's Aunt author 6 Thomas (Brandon)

Charlie Brown creator 6 Schulz (Charles)

Charlie McCarthy 5 dummy 6 stooge *friend:* 5 Snerd (Mortimer) *voice:* 6 Bergen (Edgar)

charm 3 hex 4 draw, juju, luck, lure, rune, take, wile, zemi 5 spell, witch 6 allure, amulet, appeal, enamor, fetish, glamor, mascot, voodoo 7 attract, bewitch, enchant 8 enthrall, entrance, talisman, witchery 9 captivate, ensorcell, fascinate, magnetism, magnetize 10 allurement, attraction, phylactery, witchcraft 11 conjuration, fascination, incantation 12 gratefulness 13 agreeableness

charmed 8 enamored 9 bewitched, enchanted, entranced 10 captivated, fascinated

charmer 4 mage 5 magus 6 magian, wizard 7 warlock 8 conjurer, magician, sorcerer 9 enchanter 11 necromancer

charming 5 siren 7 drawing, winsome 8 adorable, alluring, magnetic 9 glamorous, seductive 10 attracting, attractive, enchanting 11 captivating

Charon 7 boatman 8 ferryman *father:* 6 Erebus *mother:* 3 Nox *river:* 4 Styx

Charpentier opera 6 Louise

charpoy 3 bed, cot

chart 3 map 4 cast, plan, plat, plot 5 graph, table 6 design, devise, scheme 7 arrange, dope out, project 9 blueprint 10 tabulation

charter 3 let 4 deed, hire, rent 5 lease 10 conveyance

Chartreuse 7 liqueur

chary 4 safe, wary 5 canny, loath 6 frugal, saving 7 careful, guarded, sparing, thrifty 8 cautious, discreet, gingerly, hesitant 9 inhibited, provident, reluctant, stewardly 10 economical, restrained, unwasteful 11 calculating, circumspect, considerate, constrained, disinclined

Charybdis 9 whirlpool *rock associated with:* 6 Scylla

chase 3 out, run 4 boil, bolt, dash, game, hunt, lash, prey, race, rush, tear 5 chivy, chuck, eject, evict, fling, shoot, speed, trail 6 career, charge, course, follow, pursue, quarry, venery 7 boot out, dismiss, extrude, hunting, kick out, pursuit 8 throw out

chase away 4 shoo

chaser 4 wolf 6 masher 7 Don Juan 8 Casanova 9 ladies' man, philander, womanizer 10 lady-killer 11 philanderer

chasm 3 gap 4 gulf, skip 5 abysm, abyss, blank, cleft, clove, gorge, gulch, split 6 arroyo, clough, ravine, schism 8 cleavage, omission, overlook 9 oversight 11 preterition 13 pretermission

chasmal 7 yawning 9 cavernous

chassepot 5 rifle

chaste 4 pure 5 clean, moral 6 decent, modest, proper, seemly, vestal, virgin 7 ethical 8 becoming, decorous, maidenly, spotless, virginal, virtuous 9 abstinent, continent, righteous, stainless, undefiled, unsullied 10 immaculate 11 unblemished

chasten 3 try 5 abase 6 humble, punish 7 afflict, correct 8 chastise 9 castigate, humiliate 10 discipline

chastise 4 beat 5 baste 6 pummel, punish, thrash 7 belabor, chasten, correct 9 castigate 10 discipline

chastisement 3 rod 8 punition 10 correction, discipline, punishment 11 castigation

chat 3 gab, jaw, rap, yak, yap 4 blab, chin, gush, talk, yarn 5 clack, prate, prose, run on, visit 6 babble, burble, cackle, confab, dither, gabble, gossip, jabber, parley, patter, rattle, yak-yak, yammer, yatter 7 chatter, clatter, palaver, prattle, smatter, twaddle, twitter 8 causerie, chin-chin, colloque,

colloquy, converse, dialogue, lallygag 9 tête-à-tête, yakety-yak 11 confabulate 12 bibble-babble, conversation, tittle-tattle 13 confabulation

chateau 5 manor, villa 6 castle 7 mansion

chateaubriand 5 steak 10 tenderloin

Chateaubriand novel 4 René 5 Atala 10 Les Natchez

chatelain 6 warden 8 governor 9 castellan

chatelaine 4 hook, wife 5 clasp 8 mistress

chattel 5 slave 7 bondman 8 bondsman 9 bondslave, mancipium

chatter 3 gab, jaw, yak 4 blab, bull, chat 5 clack, prate 6 babble, burble, cackle, gabble, gibber, gossip, jabber, natter, patter, yak-yak, yammer, yatter 7 blabber, blather, blatter, blither, brabble, palaver, prattle 8 chin-chin, chitchat 9 small talk, yakety-yak 12 bibble-babble, gibble-gabble, talkee-talkee, tittle tattle

chatterbox 5 tabby 6 chewet, gabber, gossip, magpie, prater 7 blabber 8 busybody, jabberer, prattler, quidnunc 9 bandarlog, blabmouth, chatterer 10 newsmonger, tattletale 12 blabbermouth 13 scandalmonger

chatty 5 gabby, talky, wordy 9 garrulous, talkative 10 babblative, loquacious 11 loose-lipped 12 loose-tongued, multiloquent 13 multiloquious

chauffeur 5 drive 6 driver 9 transport

chauvinism 8 jingoism 10 partiality, patriotism 11 nationalism

cheap 3 bad, low 4 base, fake, mean, poor, sham, vile 5 petty, phony, sorry, tatty, wrong 6 cheesy, common, flashy, garish, measly, paltry, rotten, scurvy, shabby, shoddy, sleazy, tawdry, trashy, undear 7 chintzy, cut-rate, low-cost, pitiful, popular, reduced 8 beggarly, inferior, pitiable, rubbishy, terrible, trifling, trumpery, uncostly 9 brummagem, low-priced, rubbishly, valueless, worthless 10 despicable, despisable, reasonable, rubbishing 11 inexpensive 12 contemptible, meretricious

cheapen 5 decry, lower 7 devalue 8 mark down, write off 9 devaluate, downgrade, write down 10 depreciate, undervalue

cheap-jack 6 hawker, monger, vendor 7 higgler, packman, peddler 8 huckster, inferior, outcrier 9 worthless

cheapskate 4 skin 5 chuff, miser, stiff 7 niggard 8 muckworm, tightwad 9 skinflint 11 cheeseparer

cheat 3 con, gyp 4 beat, bilk, burn, dupe, fool, gull, hoax, ream, sell, take 5 bunco, cozen, crook, fraud, fudge, hocus, put-on, screw, short, slick 6 befool, boodle, chisel, chouse, con man, deceit, delude, diddle, extort, fleece, humbug, sucker **7** beguile, chicane, deceive, defraud, diddler, hoaxing, mislead, sharper, swindle **8** cozening, flim-flam, swindler, trickery **9** chicanery, deception, defrauder, fourberie, imposture, overreach, trickster **10** dishonesty, hanky-panky **11** double-cross, highbinding **12** double-dealer **13** bamboozlement, confidence man, double-dealing *on a check:* **4** kite

check 2 go **3** bit, tab, try **4** balk, bill, curb, foil, halt, jibe, rein, stay, stem, stop, test, tick **5** agree, cease, prove, score, stall, tally **6** accord, arrest, baffle, bridle, damage, desist, hold in, square, thwart **7** backset, conform, examine, inhibit, obviate, prevent, repress, reverse, setback **8** dovetail, hold back, hold down, preclude, restrain, reversal, suppress, withhold **9** constrain, frustrate, interrupt **10** circumvent, correspond **11** discontinue

checklist 7 catalog **9** catalogue, inventory

checkmate 6 arrest, corner, defeat, thwart **7** counter

check over 3 con, vet **4** view **5** study **6** survey **7** canvass, check up, examine, inspect **10** scrutinize

checkup 7 medical **8** physical **10** inspection **11** examination

cheek 4 face, gall **5** brass, crust, nerve **9** brashness **10** confidence, effrontery **11** presumption *combining form:* **3** mel **4** melo **5** bucco

cheekbone 5 malar

cheeky 4 bold, pert, wise **5** fresh, nervy, sassy, smart **7** forward **8** impudent **11** smart-alecky

cheep 4 chip, peep **5** chirp, tweet **7** chipper, chirrup, chitter, tweedle, twitter

cheer 3 rah **4** root **5** bravo, huzza, nerve, steel **6** buck up, hoorah, hooray, hurrah, hurray, huzzah, solace **7** animate, applaud, comfort, console, hearten, upraise **8** embolden, inspirit **9** encourage, enhearten **10** strengthen *corrida:* **3** olé

cheerful 3 gay **4** airy, glad, rosy **5** chirk, corky, jolly, merry, riant, sunny **6** blithe, bright, chirpy, jaunty, jocund, lively **7** beamish, buoyant, radiant **8** animated, carefree, chirrupy, debonair, sunbeamy **9** lightsome, vivacious **12** lighthearted *Scottish:* **5** cadgy

cheerio 2 by **5** adieu **6** bye-bye, so long **7** good-bye **8** farewell, toodle-oo

cheerless 4 drab **5** bleak **6** dismal, dreary, gloomy, somber **8** funereal **9** dejecting **10** depressing, oppressive, tenebrific **11** dispiriting

cheese 3 pot **4** blue, jack **5** brick, cream, store **6** farmer **7** cottage, process **9** pineapple, smearcase *American:* **8** Longhorn **11** Liederkranz **12** Monterey Jack *Belgian:*

9 Limburger *brown:* **6** mysost **7** gjetost *Canadian:* **3** Oka *combining form:* **3** tyr **4** case, tyro **5** caseo *curdling agent:* **6** rennet, rennin *Danish:* **4** Tybo **5** Esrom **6** Samsoe **7** Havarti *dish:* **6** fondue **7** rarebit, soufflé *Dutch:* **4** Edam **5** Gouda **6** Leyden *English:* **7** cheddar, Stilton **8** Cheshire **10** Lancashire *French:* **4** Brie **7** fromage, Livarot **9** Camembert, reblochon, Roquefort **10** Neufchâtel **11** Pont l'Évêque, Port du Salut *German:* **4** kase **6** Tilsit **7** Munster **8** Muenster, Tilsiter *Greek:* **4** feta **7** kasseri *green:* **7** sapsago *Italian:* **6** Romano **7** fontina, ricotta **8** Bel Paese, Parmesan, pecorino **9** provolone **10** Gorgonzola, mozzarella **12** caciocavallo *lover:* **9** turophile *main ingredient:* **6** casein *Norwegian:* **6** mysost **7** gjetost, primost **9** gammelost, Jarlsberg, taffelost **10** Noekkelost *Oriental:* **4** tofu *protein:* **6** casein *Scottish:* **6** Dunlop, Orkney **7** kebbock, kebbuck *Swedish:* **8** graddost *Swiss:* **6** Saanen **7** Gruyère, sapsago **8** Vacherin **10** Emmentaler **11** Emmenthaler *uncured:* **7** cottage *Welsh:* **10** Caerphilly *whey:* **5** ziger **6** zieger

cheesecloth 5 gauze

cheeselike 6 caseic **7** caseous

cheeseparer 4 skin **5** chuff, miser, stiff **7** niggard **8** muckworm, tightwad **9** skinflint **10** cheapskate

cheeseparing 4 mean **5** cheap, close, tight **6** shabby, stingy **7** miserly **8** grudging **9** illiberal, niggardly, penurious **11** closefisted, tightfisted **12** parsimonious **13** penny-pinching

cheesy 4 mean, poor **5** cheap, tatty **6** common, shoddy, sleazy, trashy **7** caseous **8** rubbishy

chef d'oeuvre 7 classic **9** showpiece **10** magnum opus, masterwork **11** masterpiece, tour de force

Chekhov, Anton *play:* **6** Ivanov **7** Seagull **10** Uncle Vanya **12** Three Sisters **13** Cherry Orchard

chelonian 6 turtle **8** tortoise

chemical *agent:* **8** catalyst *combining form:* **2** is, ol, ox, yl **3** aci, hex, iod, iso, mer, ole, oxa, oxo, oyl, pyr, thi, tri, ure **4** acet, amid, amin, hept, hexa, hydr, iodo, orth, poly, pyro, quin, tetr, thio **5** aceto, amido, amino, hepta, hydro, ortho, quino, tetra, xanth **6** ammino, xantho *combining power:* **7** valence *compound:* **4** acid, base, diol, enol, imid, oxim, salt, tepa, urea **5** amide, amine, diene, ester, imide, imine, indol, orcin, oxime, purin, pyran, salol, tolan, triol **6** alkali, benzin, benzol, diamin, emodin, guanin, halide, hydrid, indole, inulin, ionone, isatin, isolog, isomer, ketone, lactam, maltol, metepa, natron, nitril, pterin, purine, pyrone, pyrrol, quinol, retene, silane, skatol, tannin, tetryl, thiram, thymol, tolane, triene, trimer, uracil, ureide, yttria, zeatin 7 barilla, benzene, benzole, cumarin, diamide, diamine, diazine, diazole, diester, flavone, guanine, heptose, hydride, indamin, indican, indoxyl, isatine, levulin, metamer, monomer, naphtol, nitrile, orcinol, oxazine, phytane, picolin, polyene, polymer, pyrrole, quinoid, quinone, salicin, skatole, steroid, taurine, terpene, thiazin, thiazol, thymine, tolidin, triazin, urethan, uridine, vitamer, xylidin 8 cephalin, cyanamid, disulfid, elaterin, fluorene, furfural, guaiacol, hematein, hexamine, indamine, isologue, kephalin, lichenin, limonene, melamine, naloxone, naphthol, palmitin, phenazin, phosphid, phthalin, picoline, piperine, pristane, quinolin, resorcin, salicine, santonin, siloxáne, sodamide, sorbitol, spermine, squalene, stilbene, strontia, tautomer, thiazine, thiazole, thiophen, thiotepa, thiourea, tolidine, triazine, triazole, triptane, tyramine, urethane, vanillin, warfarin, xanthene, xanthine, xanthone, xylidine, ytterbia, zaratite, zirconia *element:* (see at element) *prefix:* 2 di 3 dia, met 4 meta *quantity:* 4 mole *radical:* 4 acyl, amyl, cyan 5 allyl, butyl, ethyl, tolyl 6 acetyl, formyl, methyl, oxalic, phenyl, propyl, toluyl 7 benzoyl *reaction:* 5 redox *salt:* 5 niter, nitre, urate, ziram 6 haloid, humate, malate, oleate, phytin 7 ferrate, formate, gallate, maleate, pectate, persalt, picrate, tannate, toluate, zincate 8 fumarate, pyruvate, racemate, selenate, silicate, stearate, tartrate, thionate, titanate, valerate, vanadate, xanthate *suffix:* 2 id, il, in, ol, on 3 ane, ase, ate, ein, ene, ide, ile, ine, ite, ium, oic, oin, one, ose, ous, yne 4 eine, idin, itol, oate, olic, onic 5 idine, onium, oside, ylene *warfare agent:* 7 tear gas 8 vesicant 10 mustard gas

chemist 7 analyst 8 druggist 10 apothecary, pharmacist *American:* 4 Urey (Harold) 6 Remsen (Ira), Sumner (James) 7 Onsager (Lars), Pauling (Linus), Seaborg (Glenn) 8 Hoffmann (Roald), Langmuir (Irving), Mulliken (Robert), Richards (Theodore), Woodward (Robert) *Austrian:* 4 Kuhn (Richard) 5 Pregl (Fritz) *British:* 6 Ramsay (William) 8 Smithson (James) *Dutch:* 8 van't Hoff (Jacobus) *English:* 4 Abel (Frederick), Davy (Humphry) 5 Soddy (Frederick) 6 Dalton (John) 7 Faraday (Michael) 9 Priestley (Joseph), Wollaston (William) 10 Williamson (Alexander) *French:* 5 Curie (Irene, Marie, Pierre) 7 Moissan (Henri), Pasteur (Louis) 8 Sabatier (Paul) 9 Lavoisier (Antoine-Laurent) *German:* 5 Haber (Fritz) 6 Bunsen (Robert), Liebig (Justus von), Nernst (Walther),

Wittig (Georg), Wohler (Friedrich) 7 Fischer (Emil, Ernst, Hans), Hofmann (August), Ostwald (Friedrich), Wallach (Otto), Wieland (Heinrich), Windaus (Adolf), Ziegler (Karl) 9 Zsigmondy (Richard) 10 Erlenmeyer (Richard), Staudinger (Hermann) 11 Willstatter (Richard) *Italian:* 5 Natta (Giulio) 8 Avogadro (Amedeo) *Russian:* 7 Semenov (Nikolay) 8 Zelinsky (Nikolay) 9 Mendeleev (Dmitry) *Scottish:* 4 Todd (Alexander) *Swedish:* 8 Svedberg (The, Theodor) *Swiss:* 6 Karrer (Paul), Werner (Alfred) (see also under **Nobel Prize Winner**)

chemist's vessel 4 vial 5 ampul, flask, phial 6 aludel, ampule, beaker, mortar, retort 7 ampoule, matrass 8 bolt head, crucible, cylinder, test tube

chemoreceptor 8 taste bud

cheongsam 5 dress

Cheops 5 Khufu 7 pyramid

Cheran's father 6 Dishon

cherish 4 keep, save 5 guard, nurse, prize, value 6 admire, defend, esteem, foster, harbor, nursle, relish, revere, shield 7 apprize, nourish, nurture, shelter 8 conserve, preserve, treasure, venerate 9 cultivate, delight in, entertain, reverence, safeguard 10 appreciate

Cherokee *chief:* 4 Ross (John) *historian:* 7 Sequoya

cherry *dark:* 4 Bing *family:* 4 rose 8 Rosaceae *genus:* 6 Prunus *hybrid:* 4 Duke *sour:* 7 morello 8 amarelle *sweet:* 4 Bing, gean 7 mazzard, oxheart 9 Bigarreau *wild:* 7 marasca, mazzard 10 maraschino

cherry bomb 11 firecracker

Cherry Orchard author 7 Chekhov (Anton)

cherrystone 4 clam 6 quahog

chersonese 9 peninsula

Chesed *father:* 5 Nahor *wife:* 6 Milcah

chess *champion:* 3 Tal (Mikhail) 4 Euwe (Max) 6 Karpov (Anatoly), Lasker (Emanuel) 7 Fischer (Bobby), Smysolv (Vassily), Spassky (Boris) 8 Alekhine (Alexander), Kasparov (Gary), Steinitz (Wilhelm) 9 Botvinnik (Mikhail), Petrosian (Tigran) 10 Capablanca (Jose) *draw game:* 9 stalemate *goal:* 4 mate 9 checkmate *move:* 6 castle, gambit 10 fianchetto *opening:* 6 gambit *piece:* 4 king, pawn, rook 5 queen 6 bishop, knight *risk:* 6 gambit *term:* 3 net, pin 4 biff, draw, file, fork, mate, rank 5 check 6 attack, castle, gambit, skewer 7 capture, develop, end game 9 checkmate, en passant 10 fianchetto, middle game 11 combination

chest 4 kist 6 breast, bureau, coffer, lowboy, thorax, wangan, wangun 7 dresser, highboy, wanigan **8** treasury, wannigan **9** exchequer **10** chiffonier *combining form:* **5** stern **6** sterno, stetho, thorac **7** thoraci, thoraco

chesterfield 4 sofa **8** overcoat **9** davenport

chestnut 4 tree **5** color, horse **6** cliché, marron **10** brownstone, chinquapin *extract:* **6** tannin *Polynesian:* **4** rata *water:* **4** ling

cheval glass 6 mirror

chevalier 5 noble **6** knight **8** horseman **9** caballero, gentleman

chevron 6 stripe

chew 3 eat, gum **4** bite, chaw, gnaw **5** champ, chomp, chump, crump, munch **6** crunch, devour, mumble, nibble **7** chumble, consume, scrunch **8** ruminate **9** masticate

chewing gum 6 chicle

chew out 3 jaw, wig **5** scold **6** revile **7** bawl out, tell off **10** tongue-lash, vituperate

Chiang ___ 7 Kai-shek

chic 3 cry, fad **4** mode, rage **5** craze, smart, style, swank, swish, vogue **6** furore, modish, trendy, with-it **7** dashing, fashion, stylish **9** exclusive **10** dernier cri **11** fashionable

chicane 4 dupe, fool, gull, hoax, ploy, ruse, wile **5** cavil, feint, fraud, trick **6** befool, gambit **7** quibble **8** artifice, flimflam, hoodwink, maneuver, trickery **9** bamboozle, deception, stratagem, victimize **10** dishonesty, hanky-panky **11** furtiveness, highbinding **13** double-dealing

chicanery 4 plot **5** fraud **8** intrigue, trickery **11** machination

chichi 5 showy, swank **6** dressy, la-di-da **7** splashy **8** affected, overnice, peacocky, précieux, precious **10** flamboyant, peacockish **11** alembicated, overrefined, pretentious **12** orchidaceous, ostentatious

chick 3 kid **5** child **6** moppet, nipper **8** juvenile, young one **9** youngling, youngster

chickadee 8 titmouse *family:* **7** Paridae

chicken 4 fowl, funk **5** sissy **6** coward, craven, funker **7** dastard, gutless, quitter, unmanly **8** cowardly, poltroon **9** spunkless **11** lily-livered, poltroonish, yellowbelly **12** poor-spirited **13** pusillanimous *breed:* **4** Java **6** Ancona, Brahma, Cochin, Lamona, Redcap, Sussex **7** Buckeye, Cornish, Dorking, Holland, Leghorn, Minorca **8** Delaware, Dominick, Langshan **9** Buttercup, Dominique, Orpington, Wyandotte **10** Australorp **11** Jersey Giant, Rock Cornish *castrated:* **5** capon *cooking:* **5** fryer **7** broiler, roaster *disease:* **5** gapes **8** pullorum **11** coccidiosis *female:* **3** hen **6** pullet *genus:* **6** Gallus *male:* **4** cock **7** rooster **8** cockerel *pen:* **4** coop *small:* **6** bantam *sound:* **6** cackle

chicken feed 7 peanuts **8** pittance

chicken pox 9 varicella

chickpea 8 garbanzo

chickweed 4 pink **7** potherb

chicle 3 gum **10** chewing gum

chicory 7 witloof

chide 4 rate **5** scold, sneap **6** berate, lesson, monish, rebuke **7** reprove, tick off, upbraid **8** admonish, call down, reproach **9** reprimand

chiding 3 rap, wig **6** rebuke **7** reproof **8** reproach **9** reprimand **10** admonition **12** admonishment

chief 4 arch, boss, cock, duce, head, jefe, lion, main, star **5** first, major, prime **6** bigwig, führer, honcho, leader, master, potent, primal, ruling, sachem **7** capital, headman, leading, notable, premier, primary, stellar, telling, weighty **8** bigtimer, big wheel, champion, dictator, dominant, eminence, foremost, hierarch, luminary **9** dignitary, dominator, effective, important, momentous, number one, principal, prominent **10** notability, preeminent **11** controlling, outstanding, predominant, significant **13** consequential *combining form:* **4** prot **5** proto *commander:* **4** CINC *prefix:* **4** arch **5** archi *Spanish:* **4** jefe

Chief Justice 3 Jay (John) **4** Taft (William Howard) **5** Chase (Salmon P.), Stone (Harlan), Taney (Roger B.), Waite (Morrison), White (Edward Douglass) **6** Burger (Warren), Fuller (Melville W.), Holmes (Oliver Wendell), Hughes (Charles Evans), Vinson (Frederick M.), Warren (Earl) **8** Marshall (John) **9** Ellsworth (Oliver)

chiefly 6 mainly, mostly **7** largely, overall **9** generally, primarily **11** principally **13** predominantly

chiffchaff 4 bird **7** warbler

chiffonier 5 chest **6** bureau **7** dresser

chigger 4 mite **6** chigoe, red bug

chignon 3 bun **4** knot

chilblain 4 sore **8** swelling **12** inflammation

child 3 kid **5** minor, youth **6** cherub, moppet, nipper, teener **7** dickens **8** innocent, juvenile, runabout, teenager, young one **9** sweetling, youngling, youngster **10** adolescent **11** teenybopper *combining form:* **3** ped **4** paed, paid, pedo **5** paedo, paido, tecno *gifted:* **7** prodigy *homeless:* **4** waif *parentless:* **6** orphan *Scottish:* **5** bairn *spoiled:* **4** brat *young:* **3** tot **4** baby, tike, tyke **6** infant, kiddie **8** bantling, weanling

childish 4 slow **5** naive, silly **6** simple **7** asinine, babyish, fatuous, foolish, kiddish, moronic, puerile **8** arrested, backward,

immature, retarded **9** infantile, infantine
  Scottish: **7** bairnly **8** bairnish
childless 6 barren **7** sterile
childlike 6 docile, filial **7** natural **8** innocent, trustful, trusting **9** ingenuous
child's play 4 snap **5** cinch, setup
  6 breeze, picnic **8** duck soup, kid stuff,
  pushover
Chile *capital:* **8** Santiago *chief export:*
  6 copper *conqueror:* **8** Valdivia (Pedro de)
  monetary unit: **4** peso
Chileab *father:* **5** David *mother:* **7** Abigail
chili con ___ 5 carne
Chilion *father:* **9** Elimelech *mother:*
  5 Naomi
chill 3 icy **4** ague, cold, cool **5** gelid, nippy
  6 arctic, chilly, deject, formal, frigid, frosty
  7 distant, glacial **8** dispirit, freezing,
  reserved, solitary **9** disparage, withdrawn
  10 abstracted, demoralize, discourage, dishearten **11** emotionless, indifferent, standoffish, unemotional **12** uninterested **13** disinterested
chiller 7 shocker **8** thriller
chilly 3 raw **4** cold **5** algid **7** coldish
chilopod 9 centipede
chime 4 bell, bong, peal, ring, toll, tune
  5 knell **6** accord **7** concord, harmony
  9 agreement **10** consonance **11** concordance
chime in 3 say **4** tell **5** state, utter **6** chip
  in **7** break in, declare, deliver **8** bring out,
  throw out **9** interrupt
chimera 5 dream **6** bubble **7** fantasy,
  rainbow **8** illusion, phantasy **9** pipe dream
Chimera *father:* **6** Typhon *mother:*
  7 Echidna *slayer:* **11** Bellerophon
chimerical 6 absurd, unreal **7** fictive, utopian **8** delusive, delusory, fabulous, fanciful, illusory, mythical **9** ambitious, deceptive, fantastic, fictional, imaginary
  10 fictitious **11** pretentious **12** preposterous, suppositious
chiming 7 musical **8** blending, harmonic
  9 consonant, symphonic **10** harmonious
  11 symphonious
chimney 3 lum **4** flue, tube **5** stack
  10 smokestack *corner:* **8** fireside **9** ingle-
  nook *output:* **3** gas **4** fume, soot **5** smoke
chimpanzee 3 ape **6** monkey **7** primate
  10 anthropoid *kin:* **7** gorilla
chin 3 rap **4** chat, talk, yarn **5** prose, visit
  6 mentum **8** causerie, colloque, converse
  combining form: **5** genio, mento
china 6 dishes **7** ceramic **8** crockery
  9 porcelain **11** earthenware *maker:* **3** Bow
  5 Hizen, Imari, Spode **6** Doccia, Sèvres
  7 Bristol, Chelsea, Dresden, Limoges,
  Meissen **8** Caughley, Haviland, Wedgwood

China *capital:* **6** Peking **7** Beijing *largest
  city:* **8** Shanghai *monetary unit:* **4** yuan
  old name: **6** Cathay *province:* **5** Anhui,
  Gansu, Hebei, Henan, Hubei, Hunan, Jilin
  6 Fujian, Shanxi, Yunnan **7** Guizhou,
  Jiangsu, Jiangxi, Qinghai, Shaanxi,
  Sichuan **8** Liaoning, Shandong, Szechwan,
  Zhejiang **9** Guangdong **12** Heilongjiang
  region: **5** Tibet **6** Xizang **10** Nei Monggol
  12 Ningxia Huizu **13** Inner Mongolia, Xin-
  jiang Uygur
china clay 6 kaolin
chinchilla 3 fur **6** rodent
chine 5 crest, ridge **7** hogback
Chinese *administrative unit:* **2** fu
  5 hsien *archway:* **6** pai-lou *aromatic root:*
  7 ginseng *artichoke:* **6** crosne **7** chorogi,
  crosnes **8** knotroot *assembly:* **3** hui *bamboo:* **7** whangee *boat:* **4** junk **6** sampan
  boat-dweller: **3** Tan **5** Tanka *bow:* **6** kowtow *Buddha:* **2** Fo *Buddhism:* **5** Folsm
  cabbage: **6** pechay **7** pakchoi *card game:*
  6 fan tan *cauterizing agent:* **4** moxa *civet:*
  5 rasse *combining form:* **4** Sino **5** Chino
  6 Sinico *conveyance:* **7** pedicab, ricksha
  10 jinrikisha *date:* **6** jujube *deer:* **8** ela-
  phure *dialect:* **2** Wu **4** Amoy **5** Hakka
  6 Swatow **7** Foochow **8** Mandarin **9** Can-
  tonese, Pekingese *dictator:* **10** Mao Tse-
  tung *distance unit:* **2** li *dog:* **4** chow,
  Peke **9** Pekingese *dulcimer:* **7** yang-kin
  8 yang ch'in *dynasty:* **2** Wu **3** Ch'i, Han,
  Sui, Wei, Yin **4** Ch'en, Ch'in, Chou, Hsia
  (first), Ming, Sung, T'ang, Tsin, Yuan
  5 Ch'ing, Liang, Shang **6** Manchu, Mongol,
  Shu Han *fabric:* **5** pekin **6** pongee, tussah
  7 tsatlee **8** shantung *feminine principle:*
  3 yin *festival:* **8** Ch'in Ming *feudal state:*
  3 Wei *figurine:* **5** magot *food:* **6** subgum,
  won ton **7** foo yong *fruit:* **6** lichee, litchi,
  loquat **7** kumquat **8** mandarin *gambling
  game:* **6** fan tan *gazelle:* **6** dzeren, dzeron
  god: **4** joss, Shen **7** Shang-ti, Tien Chu
  gong: **6** tam-tam *grass:* **3** bon *gruel:*
  6 congee *herb:* **5** ramee, ramie **7** ginseng
  idol: **4** joss *jute:* **7** chingma *laborer:*
  6 coolie *legendary emperor:* **7** Huang Ti
  liquid measure: **5** cheng, sheng *liquor:*
  6 samshu *magnolia:* **5** yulan *mandarin's
  residence:* **5** yamen *masculine principle:*
  4 yang *military leader:* **7** warlord *money,
  silver:* **5** sycee *moon guitar:* **6** yue-kin
  8 yueh-ch'in *musical instrument:* **3** kin
  4 ch'in, pi-pa **5** cheng, hsiao **6** yue-kin
  8 yang ch'in, yueh ch'in *nurse:* **4** amah
  official: **4** kuan **8** mandarin *official seal:*
  4 chop *oil:* **4** tung *omelet:* **7** foo yong *ox:*
  4 zebu *pagoda:* **2** ta **3** taa *peony:* **6** mou-
  tan *permit:* **4** chop *porcelain:* **4** chin,
  Ming **7** celadon, Nankeen **8** mandarin *pottery:* **4** Kuan, Ming **5** Chien **7** boccaro,

tz'u-chou *prefecture:* 2 fu *puzzle:* 7 tangram *race:* 9 Mongoloid *religion:* 5 Folsm 6 Taoism 8 Buddhism 12 Confucianism *rice song:* 6 yang ko *sauce:* 3 soy *secret society:* 4 tong *sheep:* 3 sha 5 urial 6 oorial *silkworm:* 6 tussah 7 tussore 9 ailanthus *string money:* 4 tiao *tea:* 5 bohea, congo, hyson 6 congou, oolong 8 souchong *temple:* 2 ta 3 taa 6 pagoda *tree:* 4 tung 6 gingko, ginkgo, loquat, wampee 7 kumquat 8 mandarin *unicorn:* 3 lin *vine:* 5 kudzu 7 yangtao *weight:* 3 fan, fen, tan 4 mace, tael 5 catty, liang, picol, picul

chink 4 rift, rima, rime 5 cleft, clink, crack, split 6 jingle, tingle, tinkle 7 fissure 8 rimation

chinquapin 3 nut 8 chestnut

chintzy 4 loud 5 cheap, gaudy 6 brazen, flashy, garish, tawdry, tinsel 7 blatant, glaring 12 meretricious

chip in 6 kick in 7 break in, chime in, pitch in 9 interrupt, subscribe 10 contribute 11 come through

chipmunk 6 hackee, rodent *family:* 8 squirrel 9 Sciuridae

chipper 3 gay 4 keen, neat, peep, snug, tidy, trig, trim 5 alert, cheep, chirm, chirp, tweet 6 bright, lively 7 animate, chirrup, chitter, orderly, tweedle, twitter 8 animated, spirited 9 shipshape, sprightly, vivacious 11 uncluttered, well-groomed 12 spick-and-span

chirk 3 gay 5 cheer 6 blithe, bright, cheery, chirpy, lively 7 animate, chipper, hearten 8 animated, cheerful, chirrupy, embolden, inspirit, sunbeamy 9 encourage, enhearten, lightsome, sprightly, vivacious 10 strengthen

chirography 4 fist, hand 6 ductus, script 10 penmanship 11 calligraphy, handwriting

chiromancy 9 palmistry

Chiron 7 centaur *father:* 6 Cronus *mother:* 7 Philyra *pupil:* 5 Jason 8 Achilles, Heracles, Hercules 9 Asclepius 11 Aesculapius

chiropody 8 podiatry

chiropractic *founder:* 6 Palmer

chiropter 3 bat

chirp 4 chip, peep 5 cheep, chirm, tweet 7 chipper, chirrup, clutter, tweedle, twitter

chirpy 5 chirk, sunny 6 blithe, cheery 8 cheerful, chirrupy, sunbeamy 9 lightsome

chirrup 4 chip, peep 5 cheep, chirm, chirp, tweet 7 chipper, chitter, tweedle, twitter

chisel 3 gyp 4 beat, bilk 5 carve, cheat, cozen, cut in, sculp 6 butt in, diddle, horn in, sculpt 7 defraud, intrude, obtrude 9 sculpture 10 intertrude

chiselly 3 bad 4 sour 6 rotten 7 unhappy 10 unpleasant 11 displeasing 12 disagreeable

chit 3 kid 4 memo, note 5 chick, child 6 moppet 8 juvenile, notandum, notation, young one 9 youngster 10 memorandum

chitchat 5 clack 6 babble, by-talk, cackle, gabble 7 chatter, prattle 8 trifling 9 bavardage, small talk 12 talkee-talkee, tittle-tattle

chitter 4 chip, peep 5 cheep, chirp, tweet 7 chipper, chirrup, tweedle, twitter

chivalric   see **chivalrous**

chivalrous 3 big 5 lofty, manly, noble 8 generous, knightly 10 benevolent 11 considerate, magnanimous 12 greathearted

chivy, chivvy 3 try 4 bait, ride 5 chase, hound, trail 6 badger, follow, heckle, hector, pursue 7 afflict, torment 8 bullyrag

Chloe 11 shepherdess *beloved:* 7 Daphnis

chlordane 11 insecticide

chloride 4 salt 5 ester 7 muriate

chlorine *symbol:* 2 Cl

Chloris *father:* 7 Amphion *husband:* 6 Neleus 8 Zephyrus *mother:* 5 Niobe *son:* 6 Nestor

chloroform 7 anodyne, solvent 10 anesthetic

choate 4 full 5 whole 6 entire 7 perfect 8 complete, integral

chockablock 4 full 6 jammed, packed 7 brimful, crammed, crowded, jam-full, stuffed 8 bung-full 9 jam-packed

chocolate 3 bar 5 candy, cocoa, color, drink 8 beverage

Chocolate Soldier com-poser 6 Straus (Oscar)

chocolate tree 5 cacao

choice 3 fat, top 4 best, pick, rare 5 cream, elite, pride, prime, prize 6 chosen, culled, dainty, flower, option, picked, rating, select 7 elegant, finding, supreme, verdict 8 decision, delicate, druthers, election, judgment, peerless, selected, superior, volition 9 appraisal, exquisite 8 recherché 9 selection 10 evaluation, preeminent, preference, surpassing 11 alternative, superlative, unsurpassed 12 incomparable, transcendent 13 determination *even:* 6 toss-up

choicy 4 nice 5 fussy, picky 6 choosy 7 finical, finicky 9 finicking 10 fastidious, particular 11 persnickety

choir 6 chorus *area:* 4 loft 7 chancel, gallery *assistant:* 9 succentor *leader:* 6 cantor 8 choragus 9 precentor *member:* 9 chorister *section:* 4 alto, bass 5 tenor 7 soprano *vestment:* 4 gown, robe 5 cotta 8 surplice

choke 4 clog, fill, heap, hush, load, pack, pile, plug, stop 5 block, close, quiet, shusn, still 6 charge, shut up, stifle 7 congest, occlude, quieten, silence, smother, stopper 8 obstruct, strangle, throttle 9 suffocate 10 asphyxiate

choking 8 quashing, stifling 9 quenching, squashing 10 repression, smothering, squelching, strangling 11 suppression

choleric 3 mad 4 waxy 5 angry, fiery, irate, ratty, testy, wroth 6 cranky, heated, ireful, spunky, tetchy, touchy, wrathy 7 carping 8 captious, wrathful 9 indignant, irascible, temperish 11 acrimonious, hot-tempered 12 fault-finding 13 quick-tempered

cholla 6 cactus

chomp 4 bite, chew 5 champ, chump, munch 6 crunch 7 scrunch 8 ruminate 9 masticate

choose 3 opt 4 cull, like, love, mark, pick, take, want, will, wish 5 adopt, elect, favor 6 desire, optate, opt for, please, prefer, select 7 embrace, espouse, pick out 8 handpick 9 single out

choosy 4 nice 5 fussy 7 finical, finicky 8 delicate 9 finicking 10 fastidious, particular, pernickety 11 persnickety

chop 3 box, cut, hew 4 cuff, dice, fell, hack, hash, poke, slap 5 clout, cut up, mince, smack, spank 6 buffet, hackle 8 fragment

chop-chop 4 fast 7 flat-out, hastily, quickly, rapidly 8 full tilt, promptly, speedily 9 posthaste 12 lickety-split

chophouse 10 restaurant

Chopin birthplace: 6 Poland instrument: 5 piano lover: 4 Sand (George)

chord 4 line 5 triad 6 tetrad 9 harmonize sequence: 7 cadence

chore 3 job 4 duty, task 5 stint, trial 6 devoir, effort 8 taskwork 10 assignment 11 tribulation

choreograph 6 direct 7 arrange, compose

choreographer American: 4 Feld (Elliot), Lang (Pearl) 5 Ailey (Alvin), Fosse (Bob), Shawn (Ted), Tharp (Twyla) 6 Fokine (Michel), Graham (Martha), Taylor (Paul), Tetley (Glen) 7 de Mille (Agnes), Massine (Leonide), Robbins (Jerome), Tamiris (Helen), Weidman (Charles) 8 Humphrey (Doris) 10 Balanchine (George), Cunningham (Merce) English: 5 Tudor (Antony) 6 Ashton (Frederick), Weaver (John) 9 MacMillan (Kenneth) French: 6 Béjart (Maurice), Perrot (Jules-Joseph), Petipa (Marius) 7 Noverre (Jean-Georges) German: 5 Jooss (Kurt) Mexi-

can: 5 Limon (José) Russian: 8 Nijinska (Bronislawa)

chorography 3 map 9 mapmaking

chortle 5 laugh, tehee 6 giggle, guffaw, hee-haw, titter 7 chuckle, snicker, sniggle

chorus 4 tune 6 accord 7 concert, concord, harmony 10 consonance

chorus girl 7 chorine

chosen 4 pick 5 elect 6 picked, select 8 selected 9 exclusive

Chou ____ 5 En-Lai

chouse 3 gyp, jig 4 beat, bilk, play, ploy, ruse 5 cheat, cozen, feint, trick 6 diddle, gambit 7 defraud, gimmick, whizzer 8 artifice, flimflam

chow 4 feed, food, grub, meal 6 repast, viands 7 edibles, nurture 8 victuals 9 provender, refection 10 provisions 11 comestibles

chowchow 4 brew, hash, stew 5 mixed 6 jumble, medley, motley, relish, varied 7 mélange 8 assorted, mishmash, preserve 9 potpourri 10 hodgepodge, miscellany 11 promiscuous 12 conglomerate, multifarious 13 heterogeneous, miscellaneous

chowderhead 4 dope 5 dunce, noddy 6 noodle 7 schnook 9 lame-brain

chowhound 7 glutton 8 gourmand

chrism 3 oil 4 balm 5 cream, salve 6 cerate 7 unction, unguent 8 ointment

christen 3 dub 4 call, name, term 5 style, title 7 asperse, baptize, entitle, immerse 8 sprinkle 9 designate 10 denominate

christening 7 baptism

Christian 5 right 6 decent, proper, seemly 8 becoming, decorous 9 befitting, civilized denomination: 6 Mormon, Quaker 7 Baptist 8 Anglican, Catholic, Lutheran 9 Calvinist, Methodist 12 Episcopalian Eastern rite: 5 Uniat 6 Uniate Egyptian: 4 Copt love feast: 5 agape martyr, first: 7 Stephen symbol: 3 IHS 4 rood 5 cross 7 ichthus, ichthys

Christian Science founder 4 Eddy (Mary Baker)

____ Christie 6 Agatha

Christina's World painter 5 Wyeth (Andrew)

Christmas 4 Noel, Xmas, yule 8 Nativity, yuletide symbol: 7 Yule log

Christmas Carol, A author: 7 Dickens (Charles) character: 7 Scrooge, Tiny Tim 8 Cratchit

Christogram 6 Chi-Rho

Christopher Robin creator 5 Milne (Alan Alexander)

chromatic 8 colorful 10 accidental

chromatin thread 7 spireme

chromium symbol: 2 Cr

chromosome component 3 DNA
4 gene 8 telomere 10 centromere, chromo-
mere

chronic 5 usual 6 wonted 7 routine
8 accepted, habitual 9 confirmed, customary 10 accustomed, habituated

chronicle 4 list 5 story 6 annals, record,
relate, report 7 account, history, recital, version 8 describe 9 narration, narrative,
recountal

chronograph 5 watch 9 timepiece

chronometer 5 clock, watch 9 timepiece

chrysalis 4 pupa 8 covering

Chryseis *captor:* 9 Agamemnon *father:*
7 Chryses

Chrysippus *father:* 6 Pelops *slayer:*
6 Atreus 8 Thyestes

chthonian 6 Hadean 8 infernal, plutonic
9 plutonian, Tartarean 10 sulphurous

chubby 5 plump, podgy, pudgy, round,
tubby 6 plumpy, rotund 8 plumpish, roly-
poly 10 roundabout

chuck 4 cast, junk, quit, shed 5 chase,
ditch, eject, evict, scrap 6 desert, reject,
slough 7 abandon, boot out, discard, dismiss, extrude, forsake, kick out 8 jettison,
renounce, throw out 9 throw away, throw
over

chucker 7 bouncer 8 houseman

chuckle 5 laugh, tehee 6 giggle, guffaw,
hee-haw, titter 7 chortle, snicker, sniggle

chucklehead 4 dope 5 dunce, noddy
6 noodle 7 schnook 9 lame-brain

chuff 4 boor, glum, ugly 5 churl, clown,
hunks, miser, nabal, stiff, sulky, surly
6 gloomy, morose, mucker, sullen 7 crabbed, grobian, niggard, scrooge 8 muckworm 9 skinflint 10 clodhopper 12 moneygrubber

chum 3 pal 5 buddy, crony, cully
6 comate, friend 7 comrade 9 associate,
companion 11 running mate

chumble 4 chew 5 champ, chomp, munch
6 crunch 7 scrunch 8 ruminate 9 masticate

chummy 4 cozy 5 close, pally, thick
8 familiar, intimate 10 buddy-buddy, palsy-
walsy 12 confidential

chump 3 oaf, sap 4 boob, butt, chaw,
chew, dolt, dupe, fool, goof, goon, gull,
mark 5 booby, dunce, munch 6 crunch,
pigeon, sucker 7 fall guy, fathead, gudgeon, scrunch 8 dolthead, lunkhead, ruminate 9 masticate

chunk 3 gob, wad 4 clod, hunk, lump
5 clump, hunch 6 nugget

chunky 5 dumpy, squat 6 chubby, rotund,
stocky, stubby, stumpy 8 heavyset, thickset
11 thick-bodied

church 4 cult, fane, kirk, sect 5 creed,
faith 6 temple 7 minster 8 basilica, religion
9 cathedral, communion, spiritual 10 connection, house of God, persuasion, tabernacle 12 denomination 13 house of prayer
adjunct: 6 belfry 7 steeple 9 bell tower
basin: 4 font 5 stoup *bench:* 3 pew *bishop's:* 9 cathedral *Buddhist:* 2 ta 3 taa
6 pagoda *calendar:* 4 ordo *caretaker:*
6 sexton *chapel:* 7 oratory *combining
form:* 7 ecclesi 8 ecclesio *council:*
5 synod *court:* 4 Rota 10 consistory *creed:*
6 Nicene 8 Apostles' *district:* 6 parish
7 diocese *father:* 5 Basil 6 Jerome, Justin,
Origen 7 Clement 8 Ignatius 9 Augustine
10 Chrysostom, Tertullian, theologian *fund-
raiser:* 6 bazaar *governing body:* 5 curia
7 classis 10 consistory *head:* 4 pope
7 pontiff *land:* 5 grebe *law:* 5 canon *member:* 11 communicant *Muslim:* 6 mosque
of a monastery: 7 minster *officer:*
5 elder, vicar 6 beadle, deacon, sexton,
verger, warden 9 presbyter, sacristan *part:*
4 apse, bema, loft, nave 5 aisle, altar, choir
6 vestry 7 chancel, gallery, narthex, steeple
8 sacristy, transept 9 baptistry, sanctuary
10 baptistery, clerestory *porch:* 6 parvis
7 galilee *pulpit:* 4 ambo *reader:* 6 lector
recess: 4 apse *revenue:* 5 tithe *room:*
6 vestry 8 sacristy *Scottish:* 4 kirk *seat
for clergy:* 7 sedilia *service:* 4 mass
6 matins 7 vespers 8 evensong 9 communion *small:* 6 chapel *tribunal:* 4 Rota
vault: 5 crypt

Churchill, Winston *daughter:* 4 Mary
5 Diana, Sarah *father:* 8 Randolph *mother:*
6 Jennie *Order:* 6 Garter *phrase:* 11 Iron
Curtain *son:* 8 Randolph *trademark:*
5 cigar *wife:* 10 Clementine

church key 9 can opener

churchman 6 cleric, divine, parson, priest
8 clerical, minister, preacher, reverend
9 clergyman 12 ecclesiastic

churl 4 boor, clod 5 chuff, clown 6 mucker
7 grobian 10 clodhopper

churlish 4 curt, dour 5 blunt, crude, gruff,
naive, surly 6 coarse, crusty 7 boorish,
brusque, loutish, lowbred 8 cloddish, clownish 10 uncultured, unpolished, unschooled
11 clodhopping, uncivilized 12 discourteous

churn 4 boil, stir 6 bubble, seethe, simmer
7 ferment, smolder *Scottish:* 4 kirn

chute 5 falls, sault, spout 7 cascade
8 cataract 9 waterfall

Chuza's wife 6 Joanna

CIA *predecessor:* 3 OSS

cicatrix 4 scar 13 scarification

Cicero *forte:* 7 oratory *target:* 8 Catiline
10 Mark Antony

Cid 4 epic, hero, play, poem 5 opera *composer:* 8 Massenet (Jules) *meaning:* 4 lord *name:* 4 Díaz (Rodrigo, Rúy) 5 Bivar *playwright:* 9 Corneille (Pierre) *sword:* 6 Colada, Tizona *wife:* 6 Jimena, Ximena

cigar 4 toby 5 breva, stogy 6 concha, corona, Havana, Manila, stogie 7 bouquet, cheroot, culebra, Londres, regalia, trabuco 8 panatela, perfecto, pickwick, puritano 9 belvedere *case:* 7 humidor *color:* 5 claro 6 maduro 8 colorado

cigarette 3 cig, fag 4 butt 5 smoke 6 gasper 10 coffin nail

cigarfish 4 scad

cilium 4 hair, lash 7 eyelash 8 barbicel *combining form:* 7 blephar 8 blepharo

cimmerian 7 avernal, hellish, stygian 8 infernal, plutonic 9 plutonian 11 pandemoniac

cinch 4 snap 5 setup 6 assure, breeze, ensure, insure, picnic, secure 8 duck soup, kid stuff, pushover 10 child's play

cinchona bark extract 7 quinine

cincture 4 band, belt, gird, sash 6 begird, engird, girdle 8 begirdle, engirdle 9 waistband

cinders 3 ash 5 ashes 8 clinkers

cinema 4 film, show 5 flick, movie 7 picture 9 photoplay 11 picture show 13 motion picture, moving picture

cinereous 4 gray 5 ashen

cinnabar 3 ore 7 mineral 9 vermilion *color:* 3 red

cinnamon bark 6 cassia

cinnamon stone 6 garnet 8 essonite

cipher 3 zip 4 zero 5 aught, digit, ought, zilch 6 figure, naught, nobody, nought, number, reckon 7 chiffer, compute, integer, nothing, nullity, numeral, whiffet 8 estimate, goose egg, monogram, whipster 9 calculate, nonentity 11 whole number

ciphering 10 arithmetic 11 calculation, computation

circa 4 near, nigh 5 about 6 around, nearby 7 close on

circadian 5 daily 7 diurnal 9 quotidian

Circe 5 siren 9 sorceress *brother:* 6 Aeetes *father:* 3 Sol 6 Helios *home:* 5 Aeaea *lover:* 7 Ulysses 8 Odysseus *niece:* 5 Medea *son:* 5 Comus 9 Telegonus

Circean 6 luring 8 enticing, fetching, tempting

circinate 6 coiled

circle 3 hem, lot, mob, set 4 camp, clan, gird, gyre, halo, loop, push, ring, roll, turn 5 bunch, cabal, crowd, cycle, group, orbit, range, round, scope, wheel, whorl 6 begird, clique, corona, extent, girdle, gyrate, length, radius, rotary, rotate 7 compass, coterie,

cronies, environ, friends, ingroup, revolve, rondure 8 comrades, encircle, surround 9 camarilla, dimension, encompass, extension, extensity, intimates 10 associates, circumduct, companions 12 acquaintance *bisector:* 8 diameter *colored:* 6 areola, areole *combining form:* 3 gyr 4 cycl, gyro 5 cyclo *graph:* 8 pie chart *luminous:* 4 aura, halo 6 corona, nimbus 7 aureola, aureole *part:* 3 arc 6 sector 8 quadrant *small:* 4 disk 7 annulet 8 roundlet

circlet 4 band, ring 8 bracelet, headband *for head or helmet:* 7 coronal, coronel

circuit 3 way 4 gyre, loop, tour, trip, turn 5 ambit, round, route, wheel, whirl 6 course, league 7 compass, journey, travels 8 gyration, rotation 9 perimeter, periphery, round trip 10 conference, revolution, roundabout 11 association, circulation 13 circumference

circuitous 7 oblique 8 circular, indirect 10 collateral, roundabout

circuit rider 9 clergyman

circular 4 bill 5 flier, flyer, gyral, round 7 annular, cycloid, discoid 8 handbill 10 circuitous *file:* 11 wastebasket *motion:* 4 eddy, gyre, spin 5 whirl 8 gyration, rotation 10 revolution *plate:* 4 disc, dish, disk

circularize 4 poll 9 publicize

circulate 4 flow 5 strew 6 rotate, set off, spread 7 actuate, diffuse, radiate, revolve 8 disperse, exchange, mobilize 9 propagate 10 distribute 11 disseminate, interchange

circulation 4 gyre, turn 5 round, wheel, whirl 7 circuit 8 gyration, rotation 10 revolution

circulator 6 gossip 8 gossiper, quidnunc 9 carrytale 10 newsmonger 11 rumormonger 12 gossipmonger

circumambulate 4 roam, rove 5 drift, mooch, range, stray 6 ramble, wander 7 meander 8 straggle

circumciser 5 mohel

circumcision *Jewish:* 5 Berit, Brith 10 Brith Milah

circumference 3 rim 5 ambit 6 border, bounds, limits, margin 7 circuit, compass 8 boundary, confines 9 perimeter, periphery

circumflex 9 diacritic

circumfuse 7 envelop 8 surround

circumjacent 11 surrounding

circumlocution 8 pleonasm, verbiage 9 tautology, verbality 10 periphrase, redundancy, roundabout 11 periphrasis 13 circumambages

circumnavigate 5 skirt 6 bypass, detour 10 circumvert

circumnavigator 4 Cook (James) 5 Drake (Francis) 8 Magellan (Ferdinand), van Noort (Olivier) 9 Cavendish (Thomas)

circumscribe 3 bar 5 limit 6 fetter, hamper 7 confine, delimit, trammel 8 prelimit, restrict 10 delimitate

circumscribed 5 bound, fixed 6 finite, narrow, strait 7 bounded, cramped, precise 8 definite 11 determinate

circumscription 5 cramp, stint 9 restraint, stricture 10 constraint, limitation 11 confinement, restriction 12 ball and chain 13 constrainment

circumspect 4 safe, wary 5 chary 7 careful, guarded 8 cautious, discreet, gingerly 10 meticulous, scrupulous 11 calculating, considerate, punctilious

circumstance 4 fate, item 5 event, moira, thing 6 detail, factor, kismet 7 destiny, element, episode, portion 8 incident, occasion 9 component, happening 10 occurrence, particular 11 constituent

circumstantial 4 full, nice 5 close, exact 6 minute, strict 7 precise, replete 8 accurate, complete, detailed, itemized, thorough 9 clocklike 10 blow-by-blow, particular

circumvent 4 balk, beat, bilk, dash, dupe, foil, ruin 5 avoid, burke, elude, evade, skirt, trick 6 baffle, befool, bypass, detour, escape, thwart 8 hoodwink, outflank, sidestep 9 frustrate 10 disappoint

circumvolution 4 gyre, turn 5 round, wheel, whirl 7 circuit 8 gyration, rotation 10 revolution 11 circulation

circus 4 ring 5 arena 6 big top, cirque 9 spectacle 12 amphitheater *animal:* 4 bear, flea, lion, seal 5 horse, tiger 8 elephant *attraction:* 5 freak 8 sideshow *owner:* 6 Bailey, Barnum 8 Ringling *performer:* 5 clown, tamer 7 acrobat, athlete, juggler, tumbler 9 aerialist, fire eater *worker:* 7 rouster 10 roustabout

citadel 4 fort 7 redoubt 8 fastness, fortress 10 stronghold *of Carthage:* 5 Bursa, Byrsa *Russian:* 7 kremlin

citation 5 award 6 eulogy, reward 7 guerdon, tribute 8 encomium 9 panegyric 10 salutation

cite 4 name, tell 5 count, offer, quote 6 adduce, allege, number, recall, remind, retain, revive 7 advance, bethink, mention, present, specify 8 instance, remember 9 enumerate, recollect, reminisce 10 retrospect

citizen 5 towny 6 towner 7 burgess, burgher, subject, townman 8 national, townsman

Citizen Kane director 6 Welles (Orson)

citron 4 tree 5 melon 6 yellow

citrus *family:* 3 rue 8 Rutaceae *fruit:* 4 lime 5 lemon 6 citron, orange 7 kumquat, tangelo 8 bergamot, mandarin, shaddock 9 tangerine 10 grapefruit

city 4 burg 5 urban 7 burghal 9 municipal *Alamo:* 10 San Antonio *combining form:* 5 polis *Eternal:* 4 Rome *French:* 5 ville *heavenly:* 4 Sion, Zion *Latin:* 4 urbs *Motor:* 7 Detroit *of Bells:* 10 Strasbourg *of Bridges:* 6 Bruges *of Brotherly Love:* 12 Philadelphia *of David:* 9 Jerusalem *official:* 5 mayor 7 manager 8 alderman 10 councilman *of God:* 6 heaven 8 paradise *of Gold:* 8 Eldorado *of Kings:* 4 Lima *of Lights:* 5 Paris *of Lilies:* 8 Florence *of Masts:* 6 London *of Rams:* 6 Canton *of Refuge:* 6 Medina *of Saints:* 8 Montreal *of Seven Hills:* 4 Rome *of the dead:* 10 Necropolis *of Victory:* 5 Cairo *planner:* 8 urbanist *section:* 4 slum, ward 5 block, plaza 6 barrio, ghetto, square, uptown 8 business, downtown, red-light 11 residential *slicker:* 4 dude *windy:* 7 Chicago

city-state *Greek:* 5 polis 6 poleis (plural)

city, town, village (see also **capital**) *Afghanistan:* 5 Balkh, Farah, Herat, Kushk *Alabama:* 3 Opp 4 Arab, Boaz, Elba 5 Eutaw, Selma 6 Dothan, Mobile 7 Decatur, Florala 8 Prichard 10 Birmingham, Huntsville, Tuscaloosa *Alaska:* 5 Kenai, Sitka 6 Bethel, Kodiak, Valdez 9 Anchorage, Fairbanks, Ketchikan *Albania:* 4 Fier 5 Berat, Korce, Kukes, Vlore *Alberta:* 4 Olds 5 Hanna, Leduc, Taber 7 Calgary 10 Lethbridge *Algeria:* 4 Oran 5 Batna, Blida, Medea, Saida, Setif 6 Annaba, Bechar *Argentina:* 4 Azul, Goya 5 Junin, Lanus, Lujan, Merlo, Salta, Tigre 6 Parana 7 Cordoba, La Plata, Mendoza, Rosario, San Juan, Santa Fe 11 Bahia Blanca *Arizona:* 3 Ajo 4 Eloy, Mesa, Yuma 5 Globe, Tempe 6 Tucson 7 Sun City, Winslow 8 Glendale, Prescott 9 Flagstaff 10 Casa Grande, Scottsdale *Arkansas:* 4 Mena 5 Beebe, Cabot, Earle, Ozark, Wynne 9 Fort Smith, Pine Bluff, Texarkana *Australia:* 3 Ayr 5 Dalby, Dubbo, Unley 8 Randwick 9 Bankstown, Blacktown, Newcastle 10 Kalgoorlie, Parramatta, Sutherland, Wollongong 12 Alice Springs *Austria:* 4 Enns, Graz, Linz, Wels 5 Lienz, Steyr, Traun 8 Salzburg 9 Innsbruck 10 Klagenfurt *Azerbaijan:* 8 Gyandzha *Bangladesh:* 5 Bogra, Pabna 6 Khulna 10 Chittagong *Belarus:* 5 Brest, Gomel, Mazyr, Pinsk 6 Grodno 7 Mogilev, Vitebsk *Belgium:* 3 Ath, Hal, Huy, Mol 4 Amay, Dour, Geel, Genk, Gent, Hoei, Luik, Mons, Vise 5 Aalst, Arlon, Diest, Dison, Eupen, Evere, Ghent, Gilly, Halle, Hamme, Hornu, Ieper, Jette, Jumet, Leuze, Liege, Menen, Namen, Namur, Ronse, Theux, Thuin, Uccle, Ukkel, Wavre, Ypres 6 Bruges 7 Antwerp *Bolivia:*

5 Oruro, Uyuni 9 Santa Cruz 10 Cocha-bamba *Bosnia and Herzegovina:* 5 Bihac, Brcko, Jajce, Tuzla 8 Sarajevo *Botswana:* 4 Maun 5 Kanye *Brazil:* 4 Codo, Para 5 Bahia, Bauru, Belem, Ceara, Natal 6 Campos, Canoas, Caxias, Ilheus, Maceio, Manaus, Olinda, Recife, Santos 7 Aracaju, Caruaru, Goiania, Jundiai, Mari-lia, Niteroi, Pelotas, Sao Luis, Uberaba, Vitoria 8 Campinas, Colatina, Curitiba, Lon-drina, Salvador, Santarem, Sao Paulo, Sorocaba, Teresina 9 Caratinga, Fortaleza, Guarulhos, Rio Grande 10 Guarapuava, Joao Pessoa, Juiz de Fora, Nova Iguacu, Pernambuco, Petropolis, Piracicaba, Santa Maria, Santo Andre, Uberlandia 11 Campo Grande, Caxias do Sul, Ponta Grossa, Porto Alegre 12 Montes Claros, Rio de Janeiro, Teofilo Otoni, Volta Redonda 13 Belo Horizonte, Campina Grande, Duque de Caxias, Florianopolis, Mogi das Cruzes, Riberiao Preto *British Columbia:* 5 Comox 9 Vancouver *Bulgaria:* 3 Lom 4 Ruse 5 Varna, Vidin 6 Burgas 7 Plovdiv 11 Stara Zagora *Burkina Faso:* 13 Bobo Dioulasso *California:* 4 Brea, Galt, Lodi, Ojai 5 Arvin, Azusa, Ceres, Chico, Chino, Dixon, Hemet, Indio, Norco, Ripon, Ukiah, Wasco, Yreka 6 Downey, Encino, Fresno, Oxnard, Pomona, Sonoma 7 Anaheim, Burbank, Compton, Fremont, Hayward, Modesto, Oakland, San Jose, Seaside, Soledad, Van Nuys 8 Berkeley, Glendale, Palo Alto, Pasadena, San Diego, Santa Ana, Stockton, Torrance, Yuba City 9 El Segundo, Hollywood, Long Beach, Menlo Park, Riverside, Sausalito 10 Carmichael, Chowchilla, Chula Vista, Culver City, Los Angeles, Pismo Beach, San Leandro, Santa Clara 11 Bakersfield, Laguna Beach, Pebble Beach, Redwood City, San Cle-mente, Santa Monica 12 Beverly Hills, Mis-sion Viejo, Redondo Beach, San Francisco, Santa Barbara 13 San Bernardino, San Luis Obispo *Cameroon:* 4 Buea, Edea 5 Kribi, Lomie 6 Douala *Canada:* 5 Banff, Edson, Hanna, Leduc, Rouyn 6 Regina 7 Calgary, Halifax, Toronto, Windsor 8 Hamilton, Montreal, Moose Jaw, Victoria, Winnipeg 9 Saint John, Saskatoon, Van-couver 10 Lethbridge, Saint Johns, Sher-brooke, Thunder Bay, Whitehorse 11 Fred-ericton, Yellowknife 12 Peterborough 13 Charlottetown, Trois Rivieres *Central African Republic:* 5 Bouar *Chad:* 4 Sarh *Chile:* 4 Lebu, Lota, Tome 5 Ancud, Angol, Arica, Maipu, Penco, Rengo, Talca 10 Concepcion, Talcahuano, Valparaiso 11 Antofagasta *China:* 4 Amoy, Jian, Luan, Yaan 5 Hefei, Jilin, Jinan, Lhasa, Qinan, Ssuan, Wuhan, Yenan, Yibin, Yumen 6 Andong, Anqing, Anshan, Anshun, Anyang, Beihai, Canton, Datong, Foshan, Fushun, Guilin, Haikou, Handan, Harbin, Hoihao, Jilong, Luzhou, Mukden, Ningbo, Pengbu, Suzhou, Urumqi, Xiamen, Xuzhou, Yanggu, Yichun, Yining, Zhangi, Zhaoan 7 Baoding, Changan, Chengdu, Dandong, Guiyang, Huainan, Jiamusi, Jia-xing, Kaifeng, Kunming, Luoshan, Luoyang, Nanking, Nanning, Shantou, Taiyuan, Wanxian, Weifang, Yizhang 8 Changchi, Changsha, Dangshan, Hangzhou, Han-zhong, Hengyang, Huangshi, Jiangmen, Jiujiang, Kueiyang, Liaoyang, Nanchang, Shanghai, Shangrao, Shaoyang, Tianshui, Zhenjing 9 Changchun, Chenjiang, Chong-qing, Chungking, Huangshih, Zhenjiang 10 Jingdezhen, Laojunmiao 11 Qinhuang-dao, Zhangjiakou *Colombia:* 4 Buga, Cali 5 Bello, Mocoa, Neiva, Ocana, Pasto, Tulua, Tunja 6 Cucuta, Ibague 7 Cienaga, Palmira, Pereira 8 Medellin, Monteria 9 Cartagena, Manizales 10 Santa Marta 11 Bucaramanga 12 Barranquilla *Colorado:* 5 Craig 6 Arvada, Salida 7 Alamosa, Durango, Greeley, La Junta 8 Brighton, Gunnison, Lakewood, Longmont, Loveland, Montrose, Thornton 9 Englewood, Estes Park, Leadville, Littleton, Rocky Ford 10 Broomfield, Castle Rock, Fort Lupton, Fort Morgan, Monte Vista, Northglenn, Wal-senburg, Wheat Ridge 11 Fort Collins 13 Grand Junction *Connecticut:* 5 Byram 6 Bethel, Bolton, Darien, Easton, Granby, Groton, Haddam, Hamden, Moosup, Som-ers, Weston 7 Ansonia, Bethany, Danbury, Enfield, Ledyard, Meriden, Milford, New-town, Niantic, Norwalk, Norwich, Old Lyme, Pomfret, Seymour, Tolland, Windham, Winsted, Wolcott 8 Branford, Cromwell, East Lyme, Guilford, New Haven, Sims-bury, Stamford, Suffield, Westport 9 Dan-ielson, Deep River, East Haven, Ellington, Greenwich, Harwinton, Killingly, Montville, New Canaan, Newington, New London, Pawcatuck, Rocky Hill, Southbury, Thom-aston, Waterbury, Waterford, West Haven 10 Bridgeport, Brookfield, East Granby, East Haddam, Farmington, Gales Ferry, Kensington, Litchfield, New Britain, New Mil-ford, North Haven, Plainville, Ridgefield, Stonington, Terryville, Torrington 11 Bea-con Falls, East Norwalk, East Windsor, Forestville, Glastonbury, Marlborough, Mid-dlefield, Old Saybrook, Southington, Wal-lingford, Willimantic 12 Collinsville, East Hartford, New Fairfield, South Norwalk, South Windsor, West Hartford, Wethers-field, Windsor Locks 13 North Branford, Thompsonville *Croatia:* 4 Pula 5 Sisak, Zadar 6 Rijeka, Zagreb 9 Dubrovnik *Cuba:*

5 Banes, Bauta 7 Holguin 8 Camaguey, Marianao, Matanzas 10 Cienfuegos *Cyprus:* 7 Kyrenia, Larnaca 8 Limassol 9 Famagusta *Czech Republic:* 4 Brno, Cheb 5 Decin, Opava, Pisek, Plzen, Tabor 7 Ostrava *Delaware:* 5 Lewes 7 Seaford 10 Harrington, Wilmington *Denmark:* 5 Arhus, Skive, Vejle 6 Alborg, Odense, Viborg 13 Frederiksberg *Dominican Republic:* 4 Azua, Bani, Moca 5 Cotui, Nagua, Neiba *Ecuador:* 4 Loja 5 Canar, Daule, Manta, Pinas 9 Guayaquil *Egypt:* 4 Giza, Idfu, Isna, Qena 5 Asyut, Benha, Disuq, Girga, Luxor, Minuf, Tahta, Tanta 6 Helwan 7 El Arish, Zagazig 8 Damanhur, Damietta, El Faiyum, Ismailia, Port Said *Eire:* 4 Athy, Birr, Cobh, Naas, Tuam 5 Ennis, Sligo 6 Carlow, Galway, Tralee 7 Dundalk, Kildare, Wexford, Wicklow 8 Kilkenny, Monaghan 9 Castlebar, Killarney, Tipperary, Waterford 10 Balbriggan *England:* 4 Bath, Eton, Hove, Ryde, York 5 Bacup, Brent, Brigg, Colne, Corby, Cowes, Egham, Eling, Esher, Eston, Goole, Leeds, Leigh, Lewes, Luton, Oadby, Poole, Ryton, Wigan 6 Bexley, Bolton, Dudley, Merton, Oldham, Torbay, Warley, Welwyn 7 Bristol, Bromley, Croydon, Hackney, Ipswich, Malvern, Norwich, Salford, Seaford, Walsall 8 Abingdon, Basildon, Brighton, Coventry, Hastings, Hatfield, Havering, Hertford, Lewisham, Plymouth, Wallsend 9 Aylesbury, Blackpool, Islington, Leicester, Liverpool, Sheffield 10 Birkenhead, Canterbury, Colchester, Manchester, Nottingham, Portsmouth, Sunderland 11 Bournemouth, Northampton, Southampton 12 Peterborough, Stoke-on-Trent, West Bromwich 13 Melton Mowbray, Middlesbrough, Southend-on-Sea, Wolverhampton *Estonia:* 5 Parnu, Tartu *Ethiopia:* 5 Aksum, Harar 6 Asmara 8 Dire Dawa *Finland:* 4 Kemi, Oulu, Pori 5 Espoo, Hango, Kotka, Lahti, Rauma, Turku, Vaasa 7 Tampere *Florida:* 4 Leto, Mims, Ojus, Tice 5 Dania, Davie, Largo, Miami, Ocala, Ocoee, Oneco, Tampa 6 DeLand 7 Hialeah, Key West, Orlando 8 Gulfport, Key Largo, Lakeland, Sarasota 9 Boca Raton, Bradenton, Fort Myers, Hollywood, Kissimmee, Palm Beach, Pensacola, Vero Beach 10 Clearwater, Cocoa Beach, Fort Pierce, Miami Beach, Titusville 11 Coral Gables, Gainesville, Key Biscayne, St. Augustine, Winter Haven 12 Apalachicola, Daytona Beach, Ft. Lauderdale, Jacksonville, Pompano Beach, St. Petersburg 13 Chattahoochee *France:* 3 Dax, Pau 4 Agde, Agen, Albi, Ales, Auch, Caen, Gien, Laon, Lyon, Metz, Orly, Reze, Sens, Sete, Vire 5 Arles, Arras, Auray, Auton, Avion, Berck, Blois, Bondy, Brest, Creil, Digne, Dijon, Douai, Dreux, Flers, Gagny, Laval, LePuy, Lille, Lunel, Meaux, Melun, Muret, Nimes, Niort, Noyon, Reims, Revin, Rodez, Rouen, Royan, Tours, Tulle, Vichy, Vitre 6 Amiens, Angers, Calais, Cannes, Evreux, LeMans, Nantes, Nevers, Rennes, Thiers, Toulon 7 Ajaccio, Avignon, Bethune, Bourges, LeHavre, Limoges, Lorient, Lourdes, Orleans, Roubaix 8 Bordeaux, Gentilly, Grenoble, Toulouse 9 Cherbourg, Le Creusot, Marseille, Montreuil 10 Draguignan, Strasbourg, Versailles 11 Montpellier 12 Saint Etienne 13 Aix en Provence *Georgia:* 4 Adel, Alma, Arco 5 Jesup, Macon, McRae 7 Calhoun 8 Americus, Marietta, Savannah, Valdosta 9 Brunswick *Georgia, Republic of:* 6 Batumi 7 Kutaisi, Sukhumi, Tbilisi *Germany:* 3 Aue, Hof, Ulm 4 Gera, Goch, Hamm, Jena, Kehl, Kiel, Koln, Marl, Suhl 5 Aalen, Ahlen, Borna, Bruhl, Calbe, Celle, Duren, Emden, Essen, Forst, Fulda, Furth, Gotha, Greiz, Hagen, Halle, Hanau, Herne, Hurth, Kleve, Lemgo, Lobau, Mainz, Neuss, Peine, Pirna, Riesa, Stade, Thale, Trier, Wesel, Zeitz 6 Aachen, Bremen, Coburg, Dachau, Dessau, Erfurt, Kassel, Lubeck, Munich, Rheydt 7 Cologne, Dresden, Koblenz, Krefeld, Leipzig, Munchen, Munster, Potsdam, Rostock, Zwickau 8 Augsburg, Bayreuth, Chemnitz, Cuxhaven, Dortmund, Duisburg, Hannover, Mannheim, Nurnburg, Wurzburg 9 Bielefeld, Brunswick, Darmstadt, Karlsruhe, Magdeburg, Nuremburg, Oldenburg, Osnabruck, Remscheid, Stuttgart, Wiesbaden, Wuppertal 10 Baden Baden, Dusseldorf, Heidelberg, Oberhausen, Regensburg, Salzgitter 11 Brandenburg, Bremerhaven, Saarbrucken 12 Braunschweig 13 Gelsenkirchen *Ghana:* 2 Wa 4 Axim, Keta, Tema 5 Lawra, Yendi 6 Kumasi *Greece:* 3 Kos 4 Arta 5 Argos, Lamia, Nemea, Volos 6 Sparta 7 Corinth 12 Thessaloniki *Guatemala:* 5 Coban *Guinea:* 4 Labe *Hawaii:* 4 Aiea, Hilo, Laie 5 Kapaa, Lihue, Maili 6 Kailua 7 Kaneohe, Wailuku *Honduras:* 5 Danli *Hong Kong:* 7 Kowloon *Hungary:* 3 Ozd 4 Eger, Gyor, Pecs 5 Abony, Bekes 6 Szeged 7 Miskolc 8 Debrecen *Idaho:* 4 Buhl 5 Nampa 6 Driggs, Dubois, Weiser 7 Gooding, Orofino, Payette, Rexburg 8 Caldwell 9 Blackfoot, Pocatello, Sandpoint, Twin Falls 11 Coeur d' Alene, Grangeville, Saint Maries, Soda Springs 12 Bonners Ferry, Mountain Home, Saint Anthony 13 American Falls *Illinois:* 4 Dupo, Pana 5 Aledo, Alsip, Alton, Carmi, Elgin, Galva, Lacon, Niles, Olney, Pekin, Plano, Posen 6 Albion, Cicero, DeKalb, Galena, Hardin, Joliet,

Macomb, Moline, Paxton, Peoria, Skokie, Toulon, Urbana 7 Chicago, Decatur, Glencoe, Oak Lawn, Oquawka, Tuscola, Watseka, Wheaton 8 Carthage, Evanston, Golconda, Hennepin, Kankakee, La Grange, Monmouth, Rockford, Vandalia, Waukegan 9 Belvidere, Effingham, Galesburg, Park Ridge, Rushville, Yorkville 10 Belleville, Carbondale, Carrollton, Des Plaines, Metropolis, Northbrook, Rock Island 11 Carlinville, Jerseyville, Lindenhurst, McLeansboro, Murphysboro, Shawneetown, Taylorville 12 Edwardsville, Highland Park, Mount Carroll 13 Lawrenceville, Mount Sterling, Pinckneyville *India:* 3 Mau 4 Agra, Ahwa, Bhuj, Durg, Gaya, Kota, Mhow, Puri, Rewa, Tonk, Ziro 5 Adoni, Aimer, Akola, Alwar, Arcot, Arrah, Banda, Barsi, Bidar, Bihar, Churu, Damoh, Delhi, Dewas, Eluru, Gonda, Jalna, Jammu, Karur, Miraj, Morvi, Nasik, Patan, Patna, Poona, Sagar, Satna, Sikar, Simla, Surat, Thana 6 Baroda, Bhopal, Bombay, Guntur, Howrah, Jaipur, Jhansi, Kanpur, Meerut, Mysore, Nagpur, Raipur, Rajkot, Ranchi, Ujjain 7 Aligarh, Asansol, Belgaum, Bikaner, Burdwan, Cuttack, Gauhati, Gwalior, Jodhpur, Kurnool, Lucknow, Madurai, Mathura, Nellore, Patiala, Vellore 8 Alleppey, Amravati, Amritsar, Bareilly, Bhatpara, Calcutta, Dehra Dun, Jabalpur, Jamnagar, Kakinada, Kolhapur, Ludhiana, Malegaon, Sholapur, Srinagar, Varanasi 9 Ahmadabad, Allahabad, Bangalore, Bhagalpur, Bhavnagar, Darbhanga, Gorakhpur, Hyderabad, Jullundur, Kamarhati, Mangalore, Moradabad, Nagercoil, Thanjavur, Tuticorin 10 Ahmadnagar, Chandigarh, Coimbatore, Jamshedpur, Saharanpur, Trivandrum, Ulhashagar, Vijayawada 11 Garden Reach, Muzaffarpur, Rajahmundry 12 Hubli Dharwar, Secunderabad, Shahjahanpur 13 Machilipatnam *Indiana:* 5 Berne, Paoli, Vevay 6 Delphi, Kokomo, Marion, Muncie, Tipton 7 Bedford, Corydon, Elkhart, La Porte, Winamac 8 Bluffton, Kentland 9 Boonville, Cannelton, Fort Wayne, New Albany, Rushville, South Bend, Vincennes 10 Brookville, Brownstown, Crown Point, Evansville, Logansport, Scottsburg, Terre Haute, Valparaiso 11 Greencastle, Noblesville, Shelbyville 12 Connersville, Lawrenceburg, Martinsville *Indonesia:* 4 Pati 5 Bogor, Garut, Kudus, Medan, Tegal, Turen 6 Batang, Kediri, Madiun, Malang, Manado, Padang 7 Bandung 8 Semarang, Surabaja, Tjirebon 9 Palembang, Pontianak, Surakarta 10 Pekalongan 11 Tasikmalaja 12 Bandjarmasin *Iowa:* 4 Adel, Tama 5 Albia, Clive, Onawa, Pella 6 Algona, Cresco, Eldora, Harlan, Keokuk,

Le Mars, Red Oak, Sibley, Waukon 7 Allison, Anamosa, Carroll, Clinton, Corydon, Creston, Decorah, Denison, Dubuque, Elkader, Marengo, Osceola, Ottumwa, Wapello, Waverly 8 Camanche, Chariton, Clarinda, Ida Grove, Mount Ayr, Primghar 9 Davenport, Fort Dodge, Indianola, Keosauqua, Maquoketa, Muscatine, Oskaloosa, Storm Lake, West Union, Winterset 10 Emmetsburg, New Hampton, Rock Rapids, Spirit Lake 11 Cedar Rapids, Estherville, Fort Madison 12 Grundy Center 13 Council Bluffs, Guthrie Center *Iran:* 3 Qum 4 Amul, Arak, Khoi, Sari, Yazd, Yezd 5 Ahwaz, Babol, Rasht 6 Abadan, Meshed, Shiraz, Tabriz 7 Esfahan, Hamadan, Isfahan, Mashhad *Iraq:* 3 Ana, Kut 5 Amara, Basra, Erbil, Hilla, Mosul, Rutba 6 Kirkuk 7 An Najaf *Ireland:* (see *Eire*, above) *Israel:* 5 Afula, Haifa, Holon 8 Nazareth, Ramat Gan 9 Beersheba *Italy:* 4 Acri, Alba, Asti, Atri, Bari, Enna, Este, Fano, Gela, Iesi, Lodi, Lugo, Pisa 5 Adria, Agira, Anzio, Aosta, Arola, Cantu, Capua, Carpi, Crema, Cuneo, Eboli, Fermo, Fondi, Forli, Gaeta, Imola, Ivrea, Lecce, Lecco, Lucca, Massa, Melfi, Menfi, Monza, Padua, Parma, Prato, Siena, Turin 6 Assisi, Foggia, Modena, Naples, Rimini, Venice, Verona 7 Bergamo, Bolzano, Brescia, Catania, Leghorn, Palermo, Pescara, Salerno, Taranto, Trieste 8 Cagliari, La Spezia, Piacenza *Ivory Coast:* 6 Bouake *Jamaica:* 6 May Pen 10 Montego Bay *Japan:* 3 Ina, Ise, Ito, Ota, Tsu, Ube, Uji, Yao 4 Ageo, Ahan, Gifu, Hagi, Himi, Hofu, Iida, Joyo, Kaga, Kobe, Kofu, Kure, Miki, Mito, Naha, Nara, Noda, Oita, Otsu, Saga, Saku, Soka, Tosu, Ueda, Yono 5 Akita, Atami, Beppu, Chiba, Chofu, Daito, Fukui, Hanno, Hyuga, Imari, Itami, Iwaki, Iwata, Izumi, Izumo, Kiryu, Kochi, Kyoto, Minoo, Odate, Ogaki, Okawa, Okaya, Omiya, Omuta, Osaka, Otaru, Oyama, Sabae, Saiki, Sanjo, Suita, Tenri, Urawa, Yaizu, Zushi 6 Akashi, Aomori, Himeji, Kadoma, Kurume, Matsue, Mitaka, Nagano, Nagoya, Numazu, Sasebo, Suzuka, Toyama, Yonago 7 Fukuoka, Hitachi, Ibaraki, Imabari, Iwakuni, Kawagoe, Kodaira, Kushiro, Machida, Matsudo, Morioka, Muroran, Niigata, Niihama, Nobeoka, Obihiro, Odawara, Okayama, Okazaki, Sapporo, Shimizu, Takaoka, Tottori 8 Ashikaga, Fujisawa, Fukuyama, Hachioji, Hakodate, Hirakata, Hirosaki, Ichihara, Ichikawa, Kakogawa, Kamakura, Kanazawa, Kawasaki, Koriyama, Kumagaya, Kumamoto, Maebashi, Miyazaki, Nagasaki, Neyagawa, Onomichi, Shizuoka, Takasaki, Toyonaka, Wakayama, Yamagata, Yokohama, Yokosuka

9 Amagasaki, Asahikawa, Chigasaki, Fukushima, Funabashi, Hachinohe, Hamamatsu, Hiratsuka, Hiroshima, Kagoshima, Kawaguchi, Kishiwada, Koshigaya, Kurashiki, Matsubara, Matsumoto, Matsusaka, Matsuyama, Moriguchi, Musashino, Tachikawa, Takamatsu, Takatsuki, Tokushima, Tomakomai, Toyohashi, Yamaguchi, Yokkaichi 10 Ichinomiya, Ishinomaki, Kitakyushu, Miyakonojo, Takarazuka, Utsunomiya, Yatsushiro 11 Nishinomiya, Shimonoseki 12 Higashiosaka 13 Aizuwakamatsu *Jordan:* 5 Irbid 6 Nablus *Kansas:* 4 Gove, Iola 5 Colby, Hoxie, Lakin, Leoti, Paola, Pratt 6 Atwood, Beloit, Girard, Holton, Larned, Olathe, Salina 7 Abilene, Dighton, Emporia, Garnett, Hugoton, Jetmore, Kinsley, Mankato, Oberlin, Osborne, Wichita 8 Cimarron, Goodland, La Crosse, Sublette, Wakeeney 9 Coldwater, Fort Scott, Great Bend, Oskaloosa 10 Clay Center, Hutchinson 11 Leavenworth, Smith Center, Yates Center 12 Council Grove, Overland Park 13 Medicine Lodge, Sharon Springs *Kazakhstan:* 6 Guryev, Uralsk 8 Balkhash, Chimkent, Dzhambul, Kyzl Orda, Pavlodar 9 Karaganda 10 Aktyubinsk 11 Tselinograd 13 Petropavlovsk, Semipalatinsk *Kentucky:* 4 Inez 5 Cadiz, Hyden, McKee 6 Elkton, Harlan 7 Ashland, Campton, Greenup, Hickman, Hindman, Owenton, Paducah, Stanton 8 Bardwell, Carlisle, Fort Knox, La Grange, Mayfield 9 Bardstown, Covington, Cynthiana, Eddyville, Lexington, Maysville, Owensboro, Pikeville, Pineville, Smithland, Southgate, Vanceburg, Wickliffe 10 Booneville, Frenchburg, Hawesville, Louisville, Whitesburg 11 Beattyville, Brooksville, Burkesville, Hardinsburg, Harrodsburg, Hodgenville, Leitchfield, Morganfield, Mount Olivet, Owingsville, Paintsville, Scottsville, West Liberty 12 Barbourville, Bowling Green, Catlettsburg, Flemingsburg, Hopkinsville, Madisonville, Munfordville, Prestonsburg, Russellville, Salyersville, Taylorsville 13 Elizabethtown, Mount Sterling, Nicholasville, Tompkinsville *Kenya:* 4 Embu 5 Nyeri 6 Kisumu, Nakuru 7 Mombasa *Kyrgyzstan:* 3 Osh 5 Naryn *Laos:* 5 Pakse 11 Savannakhet 12 Luang Prabang *Latvia:* 9 Ventspils 10 Daugavpils *Lebanon:* 5 Sidon, Zahle *Libya:* 4 Homs 5 Derna, Zawia 6 Tobruk 8 Benghazi *Lithuania:* 6 Kaunas 8 Klaipeda *Louisiana:* 4 Jena 5 Amite, Arabi, Houma, Mamou, Norco, Rayne 6 Colfax, Edgard, Gretna, Minden, Ruston 7 Arcadia, Bastrop, Marrero, Oberlin 8 Bogalusa, De Ridder, Metairie, New Roads, Oak Grove, Westwego 9 Abbeville, Chalmette, Coushatta,

Hahnville, Leesville, New Iberia, Opelousas, Port Allen, Thibodaux, Winnfield, Winnsboro 10 Marksville, New Orleans, Plaquemine, Shreveport 11 Farmerville, Franklinton, Lake Charles, Ponchatoula, Ville Platte 12 Natchitoches 13 Napoleonville *Macedonia:* 4 Stip 5 Debar, Ohrid 6 Skopje *Madagascar:* 8 Tamatave 9 Antsirane, Mahajanga 11 Antsiranana 12 Fianarantsoa *Maine:* 4 Milo, Saco 5 Eliot, Orono 6 Auburn, Bangor, Gorham 7 Berwick, Houlton, Kittery, Machias, Rumford 8 Lewiston, Portland, Rockland 9 Bar Harbor, Biddeford, Brunswick, Ellsworth, Kennebunk, Skowhegan, Wiscasset 10 South Paris 11 Millinocket, Presque Isle 13 South Portland *Malawi:* 5 Zomba 8 Blantyre *Malaysia:* 4 Ipoh 5 Gemas, Klang 6 Kelang, Penang, Pinang 11 Johore Bahru *Mali:* 5 Kayes, Mopti, Segou 7 Sikasso *Maryland:* 5 Bowie 6 Denton, Elkton, Towson 8 Bethesda, Landover, Snow Hill 9 Baltimore, Rockville 10 Beltsville, Hagerstown 11 Chestertown, College Park, Leonardtown 12 Havre de Grace, Silver Spring 13 Upper Marlboro *Massachusetts:* 4 Ayer 5 Acton, Athol, Lenox, Salem 6 Agawam, Boston, Dedham, Hadley, Ludlow, Malden, Monson, Natick, Saugus, Woburn 7 Danvers, Duxbury, Holyoke, Hyannis, Medford, Methuen, Needham, Raynham, Seekonk, Swansea, Taunton, Walpole, Waltham, Wareham 8 Brockton, Chicopee, Falmouth, Plymouth, Rockport, Scituate, Somerset, Uxbridge, Yarmouth 9 Attleboro, Braintree, Brookline, Deerfield, Edgartown, Fall River, Fitchburg, Haverhill, Lexington, Southwick, Tewksbury, Westfield, Wilbraham, Worcester 10 Barnstable, Framingham, Gloucester, Greenfield, Leominster, Longmeadow, New Bedford, North Adams, Swampscott, Winchendon 11 Belchertown, Easthampton, Northampton, South Hadley, Springfield 12 Mattapoisett, Provincetown, Turners Falls, West Yarmouth, Williamstown *Mauritania:* 4 Atar 5 Kaedi 6 Dakhla *Mexico:* 4 Leon 5 Ameca, Choix, Tepic 6 Celaya, Colima, Merida, Oaxaca, Puebla, Toluca 7 Durango, Guasave, Morelia, Reynosa, Tampico, Tijuana, Tlalpan, Torreon, Uruapan 8 Chetumal, Coyoacan, Culiacan, Ensenada, Mazatlan, Saltillo, Tuxtepec 9 Fresnillo, Ixtacalco, Monterrey, Queretaro, Salamanca, Tapachula 10 Cuernavaca, Hermosillo, Ixtapalapa, Xochimilco 11 Guadalajara, Nueva Laredo 12 Azcapotzalco 13 Ciudad Obregon, Coatzacoalcos, San Luis Potosi, Veracruz Llave *Michigan:* 3 Mio 4 Alma, Caro, Holt, Novi 5 Ionia, L'Anse, Niles 6 Adrian, Alpena,

Bad Axe, Lapeer, Otsego, Paw Paw 7 Allegan, Corunna, Detroit, Gladwin, Livonia, Midland, Saginaw 8 Ann Arbor, Bessemer, Dearborn, Escabana, Grayling, Hastings, Houghton, Kalkaska, Manistee, Munising, Muskegon, Newberry, Petoskey, Sandusky 9 Big Rapids, Cheboygan, Coldwater, Hillsdale, Kalamazoo, Ludington, Menominee, Ontonagon, Port Huron, Roscommon, Ypsilanti 10 Cassopolis, Charlevoix, Eagle River, Grand Haven, Manistique, West Branch, White Cloud 11 Battle Creek, East Lansing, Grand Rapids, Harrisville, Saint Ignace 12 Crystal Falls, Highland Park, Iron Mountain, Mount Clemens 13 Mount Pleasant *Minnesota:* 3 Ely 4 Mora 5 Anoka, Edina, Osseo 6 Aitkin, Bagley, Benson, Chaska, Duluth, Milaca, New Ulm, Wadena, Waseca, Windom, Winona 7 Bemidji, Glencoe, Hallock, Hibbing, Luverne, Mankato, Red Wing, Slayton, Wabasha, Wheaton 8 Baudette, Brainerd, Elk River, Le Center, Mahnomen, Moorhead, Owatonna, Shakopee 9 Albert Lea, Blue Earth, Caledonia, Crookston, Elbow Lake, Fairbault, Pipestone, Saint Paul, Silver Bay 10 Ortonville, Park Rapids, Saint Cloud, Saint James, Saint Peter, Stillwater, Two Harbors 11 Bloomington, Fergus Falls, Grand Marais, Little Falls, Long Prairie, Mantorville, Minneapolis, Worthington 12 Breckenridge, Detroit Lakes, Granite Falls, Red Lake Falls, Redwood Falls *Mississippi:* 4 Iuka 5 Amory 6 Biloxi, Leland, McComb, Purvis, Sardis, Sumner, Tunica, Tupelo, Vaiden, Winona 7 Belzoni, Brandon, Fayette, Okolona, Quitman, Wiggins 8 Ackerman, Gulfport, Hernando, Lucedale, Meridian, Paulding, Pontotoc, Rosedale, Walthall 9 Greenwood, Indianola, Meadville, New Albany, Pittsboro, Senatobia, Vicksburg, Woodville 10 Batesville, Bay Springs, Booneville, Brookhaven, Clarksdale, Ellisville, Hazlehurst, New Auguste, Pascagoula, Port Gibson, Starkville, Waynesboro 11 Coffeeville, Hattiesburg, Leakesville, Mayersville, Poplarville, Rolling Fork, Water Valley 12 Holly Springs 13 Bay Saint Louis *Missouri:* 3 Ava 4 Linn 5 Eldon, Hayti, Ladue, Rolla 6 Galena, Kahoka, Neosho, Potosi 7 Hermann, Ironton, Kennett, Linneus, Osceola, Palmyra, Sedalia 8 Doniphan, Gallatin, Hannibal 9 Boonville, Camdenton, Cassville, Hartville, Hillsboro, Maryville, Maysville, New Madrid, Pineville, Tuscumbia, Warrenton 10 Kirksville, Marble Hill, Marshfield, Perryville, Saint Louis, Steelville, Unionville, West Plains 11 Keytesville, Poplar Bluff, Saint Joseph, Warrensburg 12 Saint Charles 13 Harrisonville *Mongolia:* 5 Kobdo 6 Darhan 10 Choybalsan *Montana:* 5 Havre, Libby 6 Hardin, Hysham, Polson, Scobey, Wibaux 7 Bozeman, Broadus, Choteau, Cut Bank, Ekalaka, Ryegate, Winnett 8 Billings, Glendive, Missoula, Red Lodge 9 Big Timber, Deer Lodge, Harlowton, Kalispell, Wolf Point 10 Fort Benton, Great Falls, Plentywood 13 Thompson Falls *Montenegro:* 9 Podgorica 10 Podgoritsa *Morocco:* 4 Safi, Taza 5 Nador, Oujda 6 Agadir, Meknes 7 Kenitra 9 Marrakesh 10 Casablanca *Mozambique:* 5 Beira 7 Nampula 9 Quelimane, Quilimane *Myanmar:* 3 Pyu 4 Paan 5 Akyab, Bhamo, Chauk, Katha, Magwe, Minbu, Mogok, Tavoy 7 Bassein 8 Mandalay *Namibia:* 5 Outjo 6 Tsumeb 12 Keetmanshoop *Nebraska:* 3 Ord 5 Cozad, Omaha, Ponca, Tryon, Wahoo 6 Elwood, Gering, McCook, Minden, Mullen, Neligh, Pender, Sidney, Wilber 7 Burwell, Chadron, Fremont, Kearney, Kimball, Osceola, Tekamah 8 Beatrice, Chappell, Fairbury, Hastings, Holdrege, Ogallala, Red Cloud, Schuyler, Tecumseh, Thedford 9 Ainsworth, Benkelman, Broken Bow, Fullerton, Papillion 10 Clay Center, Hartington, Springview, Stockville 11 Grand Island, Hayes Center, North Platte, Plattsmouth *Netherlands:* 3 Ede, Epe, Oss 4 Echt, Tiel, Uden 5 Aalst, Assen, Delft, Emmen, Soest, Vaals, Venlo, Vught, Weert, Weesp, Zeist 6 Arnhem 7 Haarlem, Tilburg, Utrecht 8 Enschede, Nijmegen 9 Apeldoorn, Eindhoven, Groningen, Rotterdam, Zandvoort *Nevada:* 3 Ely 4 Elko, Reno 6 Fallon, Minden, Pioche 7 Tonopah 8 Las Vegas, Lovelock 9 Goldfield, Yerington 10 Winnemucca *New Brunswick:* 5 Minto 9 Dalhousie 10 Edmundston, Richibucto 12 Hopewell Cape, Perth Andover, Saint Andrews *Newfoundland:* 5 Burin 6 Wabana *New Hampshire:* 5 Derry, Keene 6 Exeter, Gorham, Nashua 7 Hanover, Laconia, Ossipee 8 Hinsdale, Seabrook 9 Littleton, Merrimack 10 Portsmouth *New Jersey:* 4 Atco, Lodi 6 Camden, Newark, Nutley, Rahway 7 Bayonne, Clifton, Hoboken, Hohokus, Paramus, Passaic, Raritan, Teaneck 8 Freehold, Metuchen, Paterson, Vauxhall, Woodbury 9 Belvidere, Bridgeton, Glassboro, Lakehurst, Maplewood, Menlo Park, Montclair, Riverside, Toms River 10 Asbury Park, Bloomfield, Cherry Hill, East Orange, Flemington, Hackensack, Mount Holly, Perth Amboy, Piscataway, Plainfield, Somerville, West Orange 11 Mays Landing, South Orange 13 Palisades Park *New Mexico:* 4 Mora, Taos 5 Belen, Hobbs, Raton 6 Clovis, Deming, Grants 7 Roswell,

Socorro **8** Estancia, Los Lunas, Mosquero, Portales **9** Carrizozo, Las Cruces, Lordsburg, Los Alamos, Lovington, Santa Rosa, Tucumcari **10** Alamogordo, Bernalillo, Fort Sumner **11** Albuquerque *New York:* **4** Elma, Ovid **5** Depew, Ilion, Islip, Le Roy, Nyack, Olean, Owego, Utica **6** Attica, Cohoes, Delmar, Elmira, Ithaca, Oneida **7** Batavia, Corning, Geneseo, Katonah, Mineola, Penn Yan, Suffern, Yonkers **8** Bay Shore, Cortland, Herkimer, Hyde Park, Lockport, Mayville, Ossining, Syracuse, Valhalla **9** Greenport, Hempstead, Patchogue, Riverhead, Rochester, Scarsdale, Schoharie **10** Binghamton, Glens Falls, Haverstraw, Huntington, Lackawanna, Lake George, Lake Placid, Mamaroneck, Massapequa, Mount Kisco, Rensselaer, Wampsville, Watervliet **11** Ballston Spa, Canajoharie, Canandaigua, Cheektowaga, Cooperstown, Farmingdale, Hudson Falls, Irondequoit, Plattsburgh, Port Chester, Saint George, Schenectady, Southampton, Watkins Glen, White Plains **12** Lake Pleasant, Little Valley, Poughkeepsie **13** Mechanicville, Port Jefferson *New Zealand:* **4** Hutt, Tawa **5** Levin, Taupo, Waihi **7** Dunedin **8** Auckland **12** Christchurch *Nicaragua:* **4** Leon **5** Boaco, Rivas *Nigeria:* **3** Aba, Ado, Ede, Ife, Iwo, Jos, Owo, Oyo **4** Kano, Ondo **5** Akure, Enugu, Gusau, Okene, Zaria **6** Ibadan, Ilesha, Ilorin, Kaduna, Mushin, Sokoto **7** Onitsha, Oshogbo **8** Abeokuta **9** Maiduguri, Ogbomosho **12** Port Harcourt *North Carolina:* **4** Dunn **5** Ayden, Elkin, Erwin, Oteen, Sylva **6** Burgaw, Dobson, Durham, Lenoir, Manteo, Marion, Shelby, Sparta, Winton **7** Bayboro, Brevard, Edenton, Kinston, New Bern, Newland, Raeford, Roxboro, Sanford, Tarboro **8** Asheboro, Beaufort, Gastonia, Snow Hill **9** Albemarle, Asheville, Charlotte, Currituck, High Point, Louisburg, Lumberton, Morganton, Pittsboro, Southport, Wadesboro, Warrenton, Wentworth **10** Burnsville, Chapel Hill, Gatesville, Greensboro, Hayseville, Laurinburg, Lillington, Lincolnton, Mocksville, Reidsville, Rockingham, Smithfield, Whiteville, Wilkesboro **11** Bakersville, Kenansville, Statesville, Swanquarter, Waynesville, Williamston, Yadkinville, Yanceyville **12** Fayetteville, Hillsborough, Murfreesboro, Robbinsville, Taylorsville, Winston Salem **13** Rutherfordton *North Dakota:* **4** Mott **5** Cando, Fargo, Minot, Rolla **6** Amidon, Ashley, Bowman, Formon, Lakota, Linton, Medora, Mohall **7** La Moure, Langdon **8** Bowbells, McClusky, Wahpeton, Washburn **9** Bottineau, Dickinson, Ellendale, Fessenden, Fort Yates, Hettinger, Williston **10** Carrington,

Devils Lake, Grand Forks **11** Minnewaukan, New Rockford *Northern Ireland:* **5** Derry, Larne, Newry, Omagh **6** Antrim, Armagh **8** Limavady **9** Ballymena, Banbridge, Coleraine, Craigavon, Dungannon, Newcastle **10** Ballymoney **11** Ballycastle, Downpatrick, Enniskillen, Londonderry, Magherafelt **13** Carrickfergus *North Korea:* **5** Haeju, Nampo **6** Wonsan **7** Hamhung, Kaesong, Sinuiju **8** Ch'ongjin, Kimchaek **9** P'yongyang *Norway:* **4** Bodo **5** Hamar, Skien **8** Tromso **9** Stavanger, Trondheim *Nova Scotia:* **5** Digby **6** Pictou **7** Arichat, Baddeck **8** Port Hood **9** Kentville, Lunenburg, Shelburne, Westville **10** Antigonish **11** Guysborough *Ohio:* **4** Kent **5** Akron, Berea, Bryan, Cadiz, Carey, Eaton, Heath, Logan, Niles, Parma, Piqua, Solon, Xenia **6** Canton, Celina, Dayton, Elyria, Euclid, Kenton, Lorain, Marion, Medina, Sidney, Tiffin, Toledo **7** Ashland, Batavia, Bucyrus, Chardon, Findlay, Ironton, Oakwood, Pomeroy, Ravenna, Van Wert, Wauseon, Waverly, Wooster **8** Caldwell, Conneaut, Marietta, Paulding, Sandusky **9** Ashtabula, Cleveland, Coshocton, Mansfield, West Union **10** Cincinnati, Gallipolis, Wapakoneta, Woodsfield, Zanesville **11** Chillicothe, Circleville, Millersburg, Mount Gilead, Painesville, Port Clinton **12** New Lexington, Steubenville **13** Bellefontaine, Cuyahoga Falls, Upper Sandusky *Oklahoma:* **3** Ada **4** Alva, Enid **5** Altus, Atoka, Sayre, Tulsa **6** Arnett, Durant, El Reno, Guymon, Hollis, Idabel, Lawton, Madill, Mangum, Nowata, Okemah, Poteau, Taloga, Vinita, Wewoka **7** Antlers, Ardmore, Cordell, Eufaula, Newkirk, Purcell, Sapulpa, Stigler, Watonga, Waurika **8** Anadarko, Coalgate, Okmulgee, Pawhuska, Sallisaw, Stilwell **9** Chickasha, Claremore, Frederick, McAlester, Tahlequah, Wilburton **10** New Cordell, Stillwater, Tishomingo **11** Holdenville, Pauls Valley **12** Bartlesville *Oman:* **3** Sur **6** Matrah **7** Salalah *Ontario:* **4** Ajax, Wawa, York **6** Barrie, Guelph, Kenora, Minden, Picton, Sarnia, Simcoe **7** Cobourg, Gore Bay, Napanee, Sudbury, Windsor **8** Brampton, Cochrane, Goderich, North Bay, Pembroke, Prescott **9** Brantford, Kitchener, L'Original, Newmarket, Owen Sound, Walkerton **10** Belleville, Brockville, Haileybury, Parry Sound, Thunder Bay **11** Bracebridge, Fort Frances, Mississauga, Orangeville **12** Peterborough, St. Catharines *Oregon:* **4** Moro **5** Canby, Nyssa **6** Condon, Eugene **7** Heppner **8** Coquille, La Grande, Lakeview, Portland, Roseburg **9** Clackamas, Corvallis, Gold Beach, Hood River, Pendleton, The Dalles, Tillamook **10** Grants Pass, Prineville **11** McMinnville

12 Klamath Falls **Pakistan:** 5 Bannu, Bhera, Kasur, Kohat 6 Gujrat, Lahore, Mardan, Multan, Quetta, Sukkur 7 Karachi, Sialkot 8 Lyallpur, Peshawar, Sargodha 9 Hyderabad 10 Bahawalpur, Gujranwala, Rawalpindi **Paraguay:** 3 Ita 4 Yuty 5 Belen, Luque, Pilar **Pennsylvania:** 4 York 5 Avoca, Darby, Muncy, Paoli 6 Easton 7 Altoona, Bedford, Clarion, Hanover, Hershey, Laporte, Latrobe, Reading, Ridgway, Sunbury 8 Carlisle, Edinboro, Hazleton, Montrose, Scranton, Somerset, Tionesta 9 Allentown, Ebensburg, Honesdale, Jim Thorpe, Lancaster, Lewisburg, Lock Haven, Meadville, New Castle, Smethport, Wellsboro 10 Bellefonte, Bloomsburg, Brookville, Carbondale, Clearfield, Gettysburg, Greensburg, Huntingdon, Kittanning, McKeesport, Middleburg, Pittsburgh, Pottsville, Waynesburg 11 Coudersport, Stroudsburg, Tunkhannock, Valley Forge, West Chester, Wilkes Barre 12 Chambersburg, Conshohocken, Philadelphia, State College, Williamsport 13 Hollidaysburg, Kennett Square, New Bloomfield **Peru:** 3 Ica, Ilo 5 Ancon, Cuzco, Jauja, Junin, Lamas, Pisco, Piura, Tacna 6 Callao 8 Arequipa, Chiclayo, Trujillo **Philippines:** 3 Iba 4 Bago, Bais, Boac, Bogo, Cebu, Daet, Jolo, Lipa, Mati 5 Basco, Bulan, Cadiz, Danao, Davao, Digos, Gapan, Gubat, Iriga, Laoag, Ormoc, Silay, Tagum, Vigan 6 Butuan, Iloilo 7 Angeles, Bacolod, Basilan 8 Batangas, Calbayog 9 Zamboanga 13 General Santos **Poland:** 4 Lodz, Nysa, Pila, Zary 5 Brzeg, Bytom, Bytow, Chelm, Gubin, Ilawa, Jaslo, Konin, Kutno, Lomza, Luban, Lubin, Mlawa, Olawa, Opole, Plock, Radom, Rumia, Sanok, Sopot, Tczew, Torun, Tychy, Ursus, Zagan 6 Gdansk, Gdynia, Kielce, Lublin, Poznan, Zabrze 7 Chorzow, Gliwice, Wroclaw 8 Katowice, Szczecin 9 Bialystok, Bydgoszcz, Sosnowiec, Walbrzych 10 Ruda Slaska 11 Czestochowa 12 Bielsko Biala **Portugal:** 4 Faro 5 Braga, Evora 6 Oporto **Prince Edward Island:** 10 Summerside **Puerto Rico:** 5 Ponce 7 Bayamon **Quebec:** 4 Alma 5 Amqui, Anjou, Granb, Laval, Levis, Magog, Percé, Rouyn 6 Ham Sud, Matane, Val d'Or 7 Bedford, Lachute 8 Cap Santé, Joliette, LacBrome, Maniwaki, Montreal, Rimouski, Roberval, Sept Iles, Waterloo 9 Becancour, Cookshire, Iberville, Inverness, La Malbaie, La Prairie, Longueuil, Montmagny, Saint Jean, Tadoussac, Vaudreuil, Vercheres 10 Ayers Cliff, Baie Comeau, Chicoutimi, Huntingdon, Marieville, St. Henedine, St. Julienne, Ville Marie, Yamachiche 11 Beauharnois, Lac

Megantic, L'Assomption, Louiseville, Mont Laurier, Napierville, New Carlisle, Sainte Croix, Saint Pascal 12 Loretteville, Saint Liboire, Saint Raphael 13 Baie Saint Paul, Berthierville, Chateau Richer, Coteau Landing, Drummondville, Papineauville, Riviere du Loup, Sainte Martine, Thetford Mines, Trois Rivieres **Rhode Island:** 7 Newport, Rumford, Warwick 8 Apponaug, Coventry, Cranston, Tiverton, Westerly 9 Hopkinton, Pawtucket 10 Woonsocket 11 West Warwick 12 Narragansett, West Kingston 13 East Greenwich **Romania:** 3 Dej 4 Aiud, Arad, Cluj, Deva, Husi, Iasi 5 Anina, Bacau, Buzau, Carei, Lugoj, Sibiu, Turda 6 Braila, Brasov, Galati, Oradea 7 Craiova 8 Ploiesti 9 Constanta, Timisoara **Russia:** 3 Kem, Ufa 4 Inta, Luga, Okha, Omsk, Orel, Orsk, Perm, Tula, Tura, Zima 5 Aldan, Artem, Chita, Ishim, Kansk, Lysva, Onega, Penza, Pskov, Rzhev, Salsk, Serov, Sochi, Sokol, Tomsk, Tulun, Volsk, Yurga 6 Bratsk, Kaluga, Kovrov, Kurgan, Rostov, Ryazan, Samara, Syzran, Tambov, Tyumen, Vyborg, Yelets 7 Angarsk, Armavir, Barnaul, Bryansk, Irkutsk, Ivanovo, Izhevsk, Kalinin, Kolomna, Lipetsk, Magadan, Nalchik, Norilsk, Rybinsk, Saransk, Saratov, Shakhty, Ulan Ude, Vologda, Yakutsk, Zhdanov 8 Belgorod, Kemerovo, Kostroma, Murmansk, Nakhodka 7 Novorod 8 Orenburg, Smolensk, Taganrog, Vladimir, Voronezh 9 Archangel, Astrakhan, Berezniki, Kiselevsk, Krasnodar, Rubtsovsk, Serpukhov, Stavropol, Syktyvkar, Ulyanovsk, Volgograd, Yaroslavl 10 Cheboksary, Dzerzhinsk, Khabarovsk, Yoshkar Ola 11 Chelyabinsk, Cheremkhovo, Cherepovets, Krasnoyarsk, Makhachkala, Novosibirsk, Prokopyevsk, Sterlitamak, Verkhoyansk, Vladikavkaz, Vladivostok 12 Magnitogorsk, Novokuznetsk, Novomoskovsk, Severodvinsk 13 Yekaterinburg **Saskatchewan:** 8 Moose Jaw 10 Assiniboia **Saudi Arabia:** 4 Jauf, Taif 5 Jidda 6 Medina **Scotland:** 3 Ayr 4 Alva, Caol, Dyce, Oban 5 Alloa, Annan, Beith, Cowie, Cupar, Dalry, Ellon, Kelso, Kelty, Largs, Leven, Nairn, Patna, Troon 6 Dundee 7 Glasgow 8 Aberdeen 9 Inverness **Senegal:** 5 Thies 6 Kaolak 7 Kaolack **Serbia:** 3 Bor, Nis, Pec 4 Ruma 5 Becej, Cacak, Pirot, Sabac, Senta, Vrbas, Vrsac 7 Novi Sad 8 Subotica **Slovakia:** 5 Nitra 6 Kosice 10 Bratislava **Slovenia:** 4 Bled 5 Celje, Koper, Kranj 9 Ljubljana **Somalia:** 3 Eil 5 Afgoi, Alula, Brava, Burao, Obbia 7 Berbera, Kismayu **South Africa:** 5 Brits, Ceres, De Aar, Nigel, Paarl 6 Benoni, Durban 7 Springs 8 Boksburg, Mafeking 9 Germiston, Kimberley, Uitenhage 10 East London 11 Krugersdorp, Vereeniging 12 Johannesburg 13 Port Elizabeth *South Carolina:* 5 Aiken, Cayce, Saxon 6 Saluda, Sumter 7 Bamberg, Gaffney, Laurens, Manning, Pickens 8 Barnwell, Beaufort, Newberry, Rock Hill, Walhalla 9 Abbeville, Allendale, Edgefield, Greenwood, Kingstree, McCormick, Ridgeland, Winnsboro 10 Charleston, Darlington, Greenville, Orangeburg, Walterboro 11 Bishopville, Myrtle Beach, Spartanburg 12 Moncks Corner 13 Bennettsville, Saint Matthews *South Dakota:* 5 Burke, Hayti, Leola, Murdo, Onida, Selby 6 Armour, De Smet, Dupree, Kadoka, Olivet 7 Milbank, Sturgis, Tyndall, Yankton 8 Deadwood, Elk Point, Faulkton, Highmore, Kennebec, Redfield 9 Brookings, Clear Lake, Flandreau, Lake Andes 10 Fort Pierre, Gannvalley, Plankinton, Sioux Falls, Timber Lake 12 Belle Fourche *South Korea:* 3 Iri 4 Yosu 5 Cheju, Masan, Mokpo, Pusan, Suwon, Taegu, Ulson, Wonju 6 Chinju, Chonju, Inchon, Kunsan, Taejon 7 Kwangju *Spain:* 4 Adra, Baza, Elda, Jaca, Jaen, Leon, Loja, Lugo, Olot, Reus, Vich, Vigo 5 Albox, Alcoy, Alora, Baena, Cadiz, Ceuta, Cieza, Ecija, Eibar, Elche, Gijon, Ibiza, Jodar, Lorca, Mahon, Oliva, Osuna, Palma, Ronda, Soria, Ubeda 6 Bilboa, Burgos, Cuenca, Malaga, Murcia, Oviedo 7 Almaden, Almeria, Cordoba, Durango, Granada, Seville, Tarrasa, Vitoria 8 Alicante, La Coruna, Pamplona, Sabadell, Valencia 9 Barcelona, Salamanca, Santander, Saragossa 10 Hospitalet, Valladolid 12 San Sebastion *Sri Lanka:* 5 Galle, Kandy 6 Jaffna 10 Batticaloa *Sudan:* 4 Juba 5 Kodok, Kosti 8 Omdurman *Sweden:* 4 Lund, Umea 5 Boden, Boras, Falun, Gavle, Lulea, Malmo, Nacka, Pitea, Solno, Vaxjo, Visby, Ystad 7 Uppsala 8 Goteborg 9 Jonkoping *Switzerland:* 3 Zug 4 Biel, Chur, Thun 5 Aarau, Arbon, Baden, Basel, Koniz 6 Lugano, Zurich 7 Lucerne 8 Lausanne *Syria:* 4 Hama, Homs 5 Idlib 6 Aleppo 7 Latakia *Tanzania:* 5 Lindi, Mbeya, Tanga 6 Dodoma 8 Zanzibar *Tennessee:* 5 Alcoa, Erwin, Rives 6 Celina, Dunlap, Loudon, Ripley, Selmer 7 Memphis, Waverly 8 Gallatin, Oak Ridge, Rutledge, Tazewell, Wartburg 9 Dandridge, Dyersburg, Hohenwald, Jacksboro, Jonesboro, Knoxville, Lewisburg, Maryville, Pikeville 10 Cookeville, Crossville, Gainesboro, Hartsville, Smithville, Sneedville, Somerville, Waynesboro 11 Blountville, Chattanooga, Clarksville, Greeneville, McMinnville, Rogersville, Sevierville, Shelbyville, Tiptonville 12 Decaturville, Elizabethton, Lawrenceburg, Madisonville, Maynardville,

Murfreesboro *Texas:* 4 Azle, Roby, Vega, Waco 5 Alvin, Anson, Baird, Bowie, Bryan, Clute, Cuero, Emory, Ennis, Freer, Hondo, Marfa, Mexia, Olney, Ozona, Pampa, Pecos, Pharr, Plano, Sealy, Tulia, Vidor, Wylie 6 Belton, Boerne, Bonham, Burnet, Conroe, Dallas, Del Rio, Denton, El Paso, Gilmer, Goliad, Jayton, Lamesa, Laredo, Linden, Lufkin, Menard, Morton, Odessa, Quanah, Sarita, Seguin, Sinton, Tahoka, Tilden, Uvalde 7 Abilene, Anahuac, Bandera, Bastrop, Big Lake, Brenham, Cotulla, Crowell, Dalhart, Denison, Dimmitt, Farwell, Houston, Kaufman, Kountze, Lubbock, Mentone, Mertzon, Midland, Refugio, San Saba, Stanton, Van Horn, Wharton 8 Amarillo, Angleton, Beaumont, Beeville, Cleburne, Eastland, Eldorado, Floydada, Giddings, Glen Rose, Gonzales, Granbury, Groveton, Hemphill, La Grange, Lampasas, Lipscomb, Longview, McKinney, Monahans, Montague, Muleshoe, Pearsall, Perryton, Rockwall, Spearman, Stinnett 9 Arlington, Aspermont, Ballinger, Bellville, Big Spring, Brownwood, Childress, Clarendon, Corsicana, Crosbyton, Eagle Pass, Fort Davis, Fort Worth, Galveston, Groesbeck, Henrietta, Hillsboro, Jacksboro, Kerrville, Levelland, Paint Rock, Palo Pinto, Plainview, San Angelo, Sanderson, San Marcos, Silverton, Woodville 10 Brownfield, Coldspring, Falfurrias, Gatesville, George West, Jourdanton, Kingsville, Port Arthur, Port Lavaca, San Antonio, Sweetwater, Waxahachie 11 Brownsville, Floresville, Goldthwaite, Littlefield, Nacogdoches, Rocksprings, Weatherford 12 Breckenridge, Daingerfield, Fort Stockton, Hebbronville, New Braunfels, Raymondville, San Augustine, Sierra Blanca, Stephenville, Throckmorton, Wichita Falls 13 Brackettville, Corpus Christi, Hallettsville *Thailand:* 3 Nan, Tak 5 Phrae, Roi Et, Surin 8 Songkhla *Tunisia:* 4 Beja, Sfax 5 Gabes, Gafsa 7 Bizerte *Turkey:* 5 Adana, Bursa, Izmir, Konya, Sivas 6 Erzurm, Samsun 7 Kayseri, Malatya 8 Istanbul 9 Eskisehir, Gaziantep 10 Diyarbakir *Turkmenistan:* 8 Nebit Dag *Uganda:* 5 Jinja, Mbale 7 Entebbe *Ukraine:* 4 Lvov, Sumy 5 Lutsk, Rovno 6 Odessa 7 Donetsk, Kharkov, Kherson, Poltava 8 Vinnitsa, Zhitomir 9 Chernigov, Krivoy Rog, Nikolayev 10 Chernovtsy, Kirovograd, Kremenchug, Sevastopol, Simferopol, Zaporozhye *United Arab Emirates:* 5 Ajman, Dubai 7 Sharjah 8 Fujairah 12 Ras al Khaimah *Uruguay:* 4 Melo 5 Minas, Pando, Rocha, Salto *Utah:* 3 Loa 4 Lehi, Moab, Orem 5 Konab, Manti, Nephi, Ogden, Provo 6 Tooele 7 Parowan 8 Duchesne 9 Coalville, Panguitch 10 Castle Dale 11 Saint George *Uzbekistan:* 5 Nukus 6 Kokand 7 Bukhara, Fergana 8 Andizhan, Chirchik, Namangan 9 Samarkand *Venezuela:* 4 Coro 5 Anaco, Cagua 6 Merida 7 Cabimas, Maracay 8 Valencia 9 Maracaibo 12 Barquisimeto, San Cristobal *Vermont:* 5 Barre 7 Chelsea, Newfane, Rutland 8 Winooski 9 Guildhall, North Hero 10 Bennington, Burlington, Middlebury 11 Brattleboro, Saint Albans, St. Johnsbury 12 Bellows Falls *Vietnam:* 3 Hue 4 Vinh 5 Da Lat, Hoi An, My Tho 6 Da Nang 7 Nam Dinh, Qui Nhon 8 Haiphong, Nha Trang *Virginia:* 4 Tabb 5 Luray, Surry 6 Grundy, Saluda 7 Accomac, Boydton, Mathews, New Kent, Norfolk 8 Abingdon, Culpeper, Leesburg, Manassas, Montross, Nottoway, Poquoson, Powhatan, Rustburg, Tazewell 9 Arlington, Clintwood, Courtland, Dinwiddie, Eastville, Farmville, Fincastle, Goochland, Lunenburg, Lynchburg 10 Appomattox, Berryville, Front Royal, Hillsville, Jonesville, King George, Lovingston, Pearlsburg, Portsmouth, Rocky Mount, Wytheville 11 Heathsville, King William, Newport News, Warm Springs 12 Prince George, Spotsylvania, Tappahannock 13 Stanardsville *Wales:* 4 Rhyl 5 Neath, Risca, Tenby, Tywyn 7 Cardiff, Cwmbran, Denbigh, Swansea 8 Aberdare, Bridgend 10 Llangollen *Washington:* 4 Omak 5 Brier, Camas, Kelso, Lacey, Pasco, Selah 6 Asotin, Colfax, Tacoma, Yakima 7 Ephrata, Everett, Pomeroy, Prosser, Seattle, Spokane 8 Bellevue, Chehalis, Colville, Okanogan 9 Cathlamet, Montesano, Ritzville, Snohomish, Wenatchee 10 Bellingham, Coupeville, Ellensburg, Goldendale, Walla Walla, Waterville 11 Port Angeles, Port Orchard 12 Friday Harbor, Port Townsend *West Virginia:* 5 Nitro, Welch 6 Elkins, Hamlin, Hinton, Keyser, Ripley 7 Beckley, Parsons, Weirton 8 Kingwood, Philippi, Wheeling 9 Glenville, Marlinton, Pineville, Wellsburg 10 Buckhannon, Clarksburg, Huntington, Moorefield, Morgantown, Petersburg, Saint Marys, Williamson 11 Grantsville, Harrisville, Martinsburg, Moundsville, Parkersburg 12 Middlebourne, Summersville 13 New Cumberland, Point Pleasant *Wisconsin:* 4 Kiel 5 Ripon, Tomah 6 Antigo, Barron, Durand, Hurley, Oconto, Racine, Wausau 7 Baraboo, Chilton, Crandon, Elkhorn, Hayward, Kenosha, Keshena, Mauston, Merrill, Oshkosh, Shawano, Viraqua, Waupaca, Wautoma 8 Appleton, Green Bay, Kewaunee, La Crosse, Montello, Phillips, Washburn, Waukesha, West Bend 9 Eau Claire, Ellsworth, Fond du Lac, Green Lake, Ladysmith, Manitowoc, Marinette, Menomonie,

Milwaukee, Sheboygan, Shell Lake, Wauwatosa, West Allis, Whitehall 10 Balsam Lake, Darlington, Dodgeville, Eagle River, Grantsburg, Janesville 11 Neillsville, Sturgeon Bay 12 Stevens Point, Whitefish Bay 13 Chippewa Falls *Wyoming:* 4 Lusk 6 Casper, Lander 7 Laramie, Rawlins, Worland 8 Gillette, Kemmerer, Pinedale, Sheridan, Sundance 9 Wheatland 10 Green River 11 Rock Springs, Thermopolis *Yemen:* 5 Taizz 7 Hodeida, Mukalla *Zaire:* 4 Boma 6 Bukavu, Likasi 7 Kananga 9 Kisangani, Mbuji Mayi 10 Lubumbashi *Zambia:* 5 Kabwe, Kitwe, Mansa, Mbala, Mongu, Ndola *Zimbabwe:* 5 Gwelo 6 Umtali 8 Bulawayo

civet 3 cat *African:* 7 nandine *Asian:* 5 zibet 6 zibeth *Chinese:* 5 rasse *East Indian:* 6 musang 9 tangalung *Indian:* 6 bondar *Madagascar:* 5 fossa 8 fanaloka *Malaysian:* 8 mampalon *relative:* 5 genet

civic 6 public 8 national

civil 5 bland, suave 6 polite, public, urbane 7 affable, cordial, courtly, genteel, politic, refined 8 gracious, mannerly, national, obliging, well-bred 9 courteous 10 cultivated, diplomatic 12 well-mannered 13 accommodating

civil court 9 nisi prius

civility 6 comity 7 amenity, decorum 9 etiquette, propriety 10 politeness

civilization 7 culture

civilized 5 bland, suave 6 decent, polite, proper, smooth, urbane 7 refined 8 decorous 9 befitting, Christian 10 conforming 11 comme il faut 13 sophisticated

civil rights *leader:* 4 King (Martin Luther) *organization:* 4 ACLU, CORE 5 NAACP

Civil War *admiral:* 8 Buchanan (Franklin), Farragut (David) *battle:* 6 Shiloh 7 Bull Run 8 Antietam, Manassas 9 Mobile Bay, Nashville, Vicksburg 10 Cold Harbor, Gettysburg 11 Chattanooga, Chickamauga *general:* 3 Lee (Robert E.) 4 Hood (John Bell), Pope (John) 5 Bragg (Braxton), Buell (Don Carlos), Ewell (Richard Stoddart), Grant (Ulysses S.), Meade (George), Sykes (George) 6 Hooker (Joseph) 7 Forrest (Nathan Bedford), Jackson (Thomas "Stonewall"), Sherman (Thomas West, William Tecumseh) 8 Burnside (Ambrose), Johnston (Albert Sidney, Joseph Eggleston), Sheridan (Philip) 9 McClellan (George Brinton), Rosecrans (William), Schofield (John) 10 Beauregard (Pierre) *ship:* 7 Monitor 9 Merrimack

civil wrong 4 tort

Civitas Dei 4 Zion 5 bliss 6 Canaan, heaven 7 elysium, nirvana 8 empyrean, paradise 12 New Jerusalem 13 Abraham's bosom

clabber 5 curds

clack 3 gab, jaw, yak 4 blab, chat 5 prate, sieve, tabby 6 babble, bicker, gabble, gossip, jabber, rattle 7 blabber, chatter, clatter, clitter, palaver, prattle, shatter 8 quidnunc, telltale 9 carrytale, yakety-yak 10 talebearer 11 rumormonger 13 scandalmonger

clad 4 face, garb, side, skin 5 array, dress 6 attire, clothe 7 apparel, garment, raiment, sheathe 8 enclothe

claim 4 call, dibs 5 argue, exact, right, share, stake, title 6 adduce, allege, assert, defend, demand 7 advance, contend, justify, purport, require, solicit, warrant 8 interest, maintain, pretense 9 assertion, challenge, postulate, privilege, vindicate 10 birthright, pretension 11 affirmation, declaration, prerogative, requisition 12 protestation

clairvoyance 3 ESP

clairvoyant 4 seer

clam 5 razor 6 gweduc, quahog 7 bivalve, coquina, geoduck, goeduck, gweduck, mollusk, quahaug, steamer 11 cherrystone *genus:* 3 Mya

clamant 4 dire 6 crying, urgent 7 burning, exigent, instant 8 pressing 9 clamorous 10 imperative 11 importunate

clamber 5 climb, crawl, scale 8 scrabble, scramble, struggle

clamor 3 din 4 bawl, roar, rout, to-do 5 babel, claim, noise, whirl 6 bellow, bustle, debate, demand, hassle, hubbub, jangle, outcry, racket, tumult, uproar, upturn 7 agitate, bluster, dispute, ferment, turmoil 8 upheaval 9 commotion 10 convulsion, hullabaloo, hurly-burly, tintamarre 11 pandemonium

clamorous 4 dire 5 noisy, vocal 6 crying, urgent 7 begging, blatant, burning, clamant, exigent, instant, voluble 8 adjuring, eloquent, pressing, strident 9 imploring 10 articulate, boisterous, imperative, multivocal, vociferant, vociferous 11 importunate, loudmouthed, openmouthed 12 obstreperous

clamp 4 grip, hold, vise 5 clasp, grasp, gripe 6 clench, clinch, clutch, tenure 7 grapple

clamshell 6 bucket 7 grapple

clan 3 mob 4 camp, folk, race, ring, sept 5 cabal, house, stock, tribe 6 circle, clique, family 7 coterie, ingroup, kindred, lineage 9 camarilla *emblem:* 5 totem

clandestine 3 sly 4 foxy 6 artful, covert, secret 7 furtive, illicit 8 hush-hush, stealthy 10 undercover 12 hugger-mugger, illegitimate 13 surreptitious, under-the-table

clang 3 din 4 ding, peal 5 noise 6 jangle

clangorous 5 noisy 7 rackety 8 clattery, noiseful, sonorous 10 uproarious

clap 4 bang, boom, slam, wham 5 blast, burst, crack, crash, smash 7 applaud

claptrap 4 bull 5 hokum 6 bunkum, drivel, humbug 7 baloney, twaddle 8 malarkey, nonsense 10 flapdoodle

Clare Boothe ___ 4 Luce

claret 3 red 4 wine 8 Bordeaux

clarify 5 clean, clear 6 define, purify, settle 7 analyze, cleanse, clear up, explain 8 depurate, simplify 9 break down, delineate, elucidate, formulate 10 illuminate, illustrate 13 straighten out

clarion 4 fair, fine 5 clear, sunny 8 pleasant, rainless, sunshiny 9 cloudless, unclouded 10 undarkened

clarity 4 care 6 nicety 8 accuracy, lucidity 9 clearness, fussiness, limpidity, plainness, precision, propriety 10 exactitude 11 perspicuity 12 articulation, correctitude

clash 3 jar, row, try 4 bump, fray, fret, gall, jolt, riot 5 brawl, broil, brush, crash, grate, melee, scrap, set to, shock, smash 6 action, affray, battle, fracas, impact, jangle, mellay, rumpus, wallop 7 collide, discord 8 conflict, mismatch, skirmish 9 collision, disaccord, encounter, scrimmage 10 concussion, engagement 11 embroilment 12 disharmonize

clasp 3 hug 4 clip, coil, grip, hold, take 5 clamp, grasp, gripe, press, tache 6 clench, clinch, clutch, enfold, tenure 7 embrace, grapple, squeeze 10 chatelaine

class 3 ilk 4 head, hold, kind, mark, part, rank, rate, sort, tier, type 5 allot, brand, caste, color, gauge, genre, genus, grade, grain, group, judge, order, score, stamp, style 6 assess, assign, assort, branch, divide, kidney, league, nature, reckon, regard, stripe 7 account, bracket, caliber, feather, quality, section, species, variety 8 appraise, category, consider, division, evaluate, grouping, separate 10 categorize, pigeonhole 11 description 12 denomination *Hindu:* 5 caste, varna *middle:* 11 bourgeoisie *school:* 6 junior, senior 8 freshman 9 sophomore *scientific:* 5 genus 6 genera (plural) *suffix:* 2 cy *working:* 11 proletariat

classic 3 top 4 fine 5 ideal, model, prime 6 famous 7 capital, typical, vintage 8 champion, superior, top-notch 9 classical, excellent, exemplary 10 magnum opus, masterwork, prototypal 11 chef d'oeuvre, masterpiece, tour de force 12 paradigmatic, prototypical

classification 4 sort, type 5 genre, genus, grade, order 6 family, genera (plural), phylum, rating 7 species 8 category, division, grouping, taxonomy, typology 11 arrangement

classified 6 secret 9 top secret 12 confidential

classify 4 rank, rate, sort 5 grade, group 6 assort 8 evaluate 10 categorize, pigeonhole

classy 2 in 4 tony 5 sharp, swank, swish 6 modish, tonish 7 dashing, stylish 11 fashionable

clatter 3 gab, jaw 4 chat, to-do 5 clack, run on 6 babble, bicker, clamor, dither, hassle, hubbub, pother, rattle, tumult, uproar 7 chatter, clitter, shatter, turmoil 9 commotion 10 hurly-burly *Scottish:* 7 brattle

clattery 5 noisy 7 rackety 8 noiseful, sonorous 10 clangorous, uproarious

Claudia's husband 6 Pilate

Claudio's beloved 4 Hero

Claudius *nephew:* 6 Hamlet *slayer:* 6 Hamlet 9 Agrippina *successor:* 4 Nero

claviger 6 custos, keeper, warden 8 cerberus, guardian, watchdog 9 custodian

claw 3 dig 4 nail, tear 5 chela, grasp, grope, seize, talon, uncus 6 clutch, scrape, ungual, unguis, ungula 7 scratch *combining form:* 4 chel 5 cheli, onych, ungui 6 onycho 8 onychium

clay 3 cob, pug 4 galt, leck, loam, lute, marl 5 argil, brick, earth, gault, loess, ocher, ochre, rabat 6 clunch 8 camstone *baked:* 4 bole, tile 5 adobe, brick *box:* 6 saggar, sagger *brick:* 3 bat *building:* 5 adobe *ceramic:* 10 terra-cotta *combining form:* 3 pel 4 pelo 6 argill 7 argilli, argillo 10 argillaceo *constituent:* 6 silica 7 dickite, nacrite 8 feldspar, silicate 9 kaolinite *friable:* 4 bole *in glass:* 4 tear *made of:* 7 fictile *mold:* 3 dod *porcelain:* 6 kaolin 7 kaoline *red:* 4 bole 8 laterite, sinopite *rock:* 5 shale *slab:* 3 bat *sticky:* 8 gumbotil *tobacco pipe:* 6 dudeen *watery mixture:* 4 slip *white:* 6 kaolin 7 kaoline

clay pigeon 6 target

clean 3 gut 4 dust, fair, pure, swab, tidy, trim, wash, wipe 5 dress, fresh, groom, order, purge, renew, scour, scrub, sweep 6 bright, chaste, decent, modest, neaten, police, purify, spruce, vacuum 7 clarify, freshen, furbish, shining, sinless 8 brighten, depurate, innocent, renovate, spotless, unguilty, unsoiled 9 blameless, crimeless, faultless, guiltless, sparkling, stainless, taintless, undefiled, unsullied, untainted, wholesome 10 immaculate, inculpable 11 recondition, sportsmanly, unblemished 12 spick-and-span, straighten up 13 sportsmanlike *ship's bottom:* 5 bream

clean-cut 7 express 8 definite, explicit, specific 10 definitive 11 categorical, unambiguous

cleaner see **cleanser**

cleanhanded 8 innocent

clean-limbed 4 trim 7 shapely 8 shapeful 10 statuesque, well-turned

cleanse 5 purge, rinse 6 purify, refine 7 clarify, deterge 8 depurate, lustrate, sanitize 9 disinfect, expurgate, sterilize

cleanser 3 lye 4 soap 6 bleach 9 detergent

cleansing 9 catharsis, purgation 10 lustration 11 expurgation 12 purification

Cleante *father:* 8 Harpagon *lover:* 9 Angelique

clear 3 get, net, pay, rid, win 4 bare, earn, fade, fair, fine, gain, leap, lose, make, over, pure, quit, sink, void, well 5 à fond, close, empty, exact, fully, glean, lucid, milky, overt, pay up, plain, quite, repay, solve, stark, sunny, untie, vault 6 acquit, better, gather, hurdle, limpid, lucent, obtain, patent, pay off, pick up, public, secure, settle, simple, square, vacant, vacate, vanish 7 absolve, acquire, clarify, clarion, cleanse, clean up, crystal, defined, evanish, evident, explain, improve, obvious, precise, rule out, satisfy, untwine, utterly, vacuous 8 apparent, definite, distinct, entirely, evanesce, explicit, knowable, luculent, luminous, manifest, overleap, palpable, pellucid, pleasant, rainless, scot-free, sensible, shake off, sunshiny, surmount, tangible, throw-off, unburden, unhidden, univocal, untangle 9 cloudless, disappear, discharge, eliminate, elucidate, evaporate, exculpate, exonerate, extricate, graspable, liquidate, meliorate, negotiate, perfectly, published, stabilize, tralucent, unblurred, unclouded, vindicate 10 accumulate, altogether, ameliorate, completely, disculpate, disentwine, illuminate, illustrate, opalescent, openhanded, seethrough, translucid, undarkened, unentangle, unobscured, unscramble 11 appreciable, conspicuous, disencumber, disentangle, open-and-shut, perceptible, perspicuous, translucent, transparent, unambiguous, unequivocal, unperplexed 12 recognizable, transpicuous, unmistakable 13 apprehensible, uncomplicated

clearance 7 go-ahead 10 green light 13 authorization

clear away 6 remove 7 take out 9 discumber 10 disembroil 12 disembarrass

clear-cut 4 nice 5 crisp, exact, lucid, plain 6 biting, lucent 7 assured, crystal, cutting, decided, express, ingoing, precise 8 definite, distinct, explicit, incisive, luminous, manifest, pellucid, specific 9 trenchant, unblurred, undoubted 10 definitive, pronounced, undisputed 11 categorical, indubitable, penetrating, translucent, transparent, unambiguous 12 transpicuous, unquestioned

clear-eyed 10 discerning

clearheaded 10 perceptive

clear out 4 kite 5 scram 6 begone, decamp, get out 7 skiddoo, take off, vamoose 8 hightail 9 skedaddle

clear-sightedness 3 wit 6 acumen 8 astucity, keenness 10 astuteness, shrewdness 11 discernment, penetration, percipience

clear up 5 solve 6 cipher, unfold 7 clarify, dope out, explain, resolve, unravel 8 decipher, dissolve 9 elucidate, figure out, puzzle out 10 illuminate, illustrate

clearwing 4 moth

cleat 4 bitt 5 cavel, chock, kevel 6 batten 7 bollard, coxcomb, dolphin

cleavage 5 chasm, cleft, split 6 schism

cleave 3 cut, hew, rip 4 chop, join, link, rend, rive, tear 5 carve, cling, sever, slice, split, stick, unite 6 adhere, cohere, divide, sunder 7 combine, conjoin, dissect, divorce 8 dissever, separate 9 associate

cleft 3 gap 4 rift, rima, rime, slit 5 chasm, chink, clove, crack, gorge, gulch, split 6 arroyo, clough, ravine, schism 7 crevice, fissure 8 cleavage, rimation *combining form:* 5 fissi, schiz 6 schizo 7 schisto

clemency 5 grace, mercy 6 lenity 7 caritas, charity 8 fairness, justness, lenience, leniency, mildness 9 endurance, tolerance 10 gentleness, indulgence, sufferance, toleration 11 forbearance 12 mercifulness 13 equitableness

clement 4 easy, kind, mild 6 benign, humane, kindly, tender 7 lenient 8 merciful, tolerant 9 benignant, indulgent 10 benevolent, charitable, forbearing 11 sympathetic 13 compassionate

clench 4 grip, grit, hold 5 clamp, clasp, grasp, gripe 6 clinch, clutch, tenure 7 grapple

Cleopatra *attendant:* 4 Iras 8 Charmian *brother:* 7 Ptolemy *husband:* 7 Ptolemy *killer:* 3 asp *lover:* 6 Antony, Caesar *river:* 4 Nile

Cleopatra's Needle 7 obelisk

clepsydra 9 timepiece 10 water clock

clerestory 7 gallery

clergyman 5 clerk, padre, vicar 6 bishop, cleric, curate, divine, father, parson, pastor, priest, rector 7 dominie, pontiff, prelate 8 chaplain, clerical, minister, ordinary, preacher, pulpiter, reverend, shepherd, sky pilot 9 churchman, predicant, pulpiteer 10 ecclesiast, evangelist, missionary, sermonizer 11 pulpitarian 12 ecclesiastic *American:* 4 Hale (Edward Everett), King (Martin Luther, Thomas Starr) 5 Eliot (John), Stone (Barton Warren), Weems (Parson) 6 Dwight (Timothy), Holmes (John Haynes), Hooker (Thomas), Mather (Cotton, Increase, Richard), Merton (Thomas), Parker (Samuel, Theodore), Powell (Adam Clayton), Taylor (Edward, Graham, Nathaniel William) 7 Beecher (Henry Ward, Lyman), Harvard (John), Russell (Charles Taze) 10 Muhlenberg (Frederick Augustus, Henry Melchior, John Peter Gabriel) *English:* 4 Ward (Nathaniel, Seth, William George) 5 Donne (John), Paley (William), Smith (Henry "Silver-Tonqued," John "The Sebaptist," Sidney) 6 Cotton (John), Fuller (Andrew, Thomas), Taylor (Jeremy, Rowland) 7 Cranmer (Thomas), Parsons (Robert) 8 Kingsley (Charles) *French:* 8 Teilhard (Pierre) 10 Schweitzer (Albert) *home:* 5 manse 6 priory 7 rectory 8 vicarage 9 monastery, parsonage *traveling:* 12 circuit rider

cleric see **clergyman**

clerisy 8 literati 10 illuminati 13 intellectuals

clerk 3 nun 4 monk 5 steno 6 cleric, scribe 7 scholar 8 minister 9 clergyman, secretary 11 salesperson 12 stenographer

clerkish 4 nice 5 fussy, picky 6 choosy 7 finical, finicky 9 finicking, squeamish 10 fastidious, particular

clever 3 apt, sly 4 able, deft, good, racy, slim 5 adept, alert, canny, funny, handy, quick, ready, salty, sharp, slick, smart, witty 6 adroit, brainy, bright, crafty, expert, nimble, pretty, prompt, tricky, wicked 7 amusing, capable, cunning, knowing, piquant, risible, skilled 8 dazzling, fanciful, humorous, masterly, pleasing, skillful 9 allaround, brilliant, competent, deceitful, dexterous, facetious, ingenious, laughable, many-sided, qualified, sparkling, sprightly, versatile, whimsical, workmanly 10 neathanded, proficient 11 coruscating, intelligent, quick-witted, ready-witted, workmanlike 12 entertaining 13 scintillating

cliché 5 stale, trite 6 truism 7 bromide 8 banality, bathetic, prosaism, timeworn 9 hackneyed, platitude 10 prosaicism 11 commonplace, stereotyped 13 stereotypical

click 2 go 4 tick 6 go over, pan out 7 come off, succeed 8 prove out

click beetle 6 elater 8 elaterid

client 6 patron 8 customer

cliff 4 crag 5 bluff, cleve, scarp 7 clogwyn 8 headland, palisade 9 precipice *Scottish:* 5 heuch, heugh

climacteric 4 dire 5 acute 7 crucial 8 critical 9 desperate, menopause 12 change of life

climate 6 medium, milieu 7 ambient 8 ambience 10 atmosphere 11 environment, mise-en-scène 12 surroundings *combining form:* 6 meteor 7 meteoro

climatize 6 harden, season 7 toughen 9 acclimate

climax 3 cap, end 4 acme, apex, peak 5 crown 6 apogee, finish, summit, top off 8 capsheaf, capstone, conclude, meridian, pinnacle, round off 9 culminate, finish off, terminate 11 culmination *in drama:* 10 catastasis

climb 4 shin, upgo 5 mount, scale, speel 6 ascend 7 clamber 8 escalade, escalate

climbing 8 scandent

climbing iron 7 crampon

clinch 3 hug 4 grip, hold 5 clamp, clasp, grasp, gripe, press 6 clutch, enfold, tenure 7 embrace, grapple, squeeze

cling 4 bond 5 stick 6 adhere, cleave, cohere 8 adhesion, cohesion, stickage, sticking 9 adherence, coherence

clingfish 6 remora

clingstone 5 peach

clink 3 can, jug 4 jail, stir 5 pokey 6 cooler, jingle, lockup, tingle, tinkle 7 chinkle, slammer 8 hoosegow 9 calaboose

clinkers 3 ash 5 ashes 7 cinders

clinquant 6 tinsel 10 glittering

Clio see **Muse**

clip 3 cut, mow, pin 4 crop, pare, skin, soak, trim 5 lower, prune, shave, shear, skive, slash, stick 6 broach, brooch, fleece, reduce 7 cut back, cut down 8 mark down 10 overcharge

clique 3 mob, set 4 camp, clan, ring 5 cabal 6 circle 7 coterie, faction, in-group 9 camarilla

cloak 4 cape, face, mask, robe, show, veil, wrap 5 cover, guise 6 facade, joseph, mantle, poncho, screen, shroud, veneer 7 blanket, curtain, dress up, manteau 8 disguise 9 dissemble, semblance 10 camouflage 11 dissimulate *ancient Greek:* 7 chlamys *ancient Roman:* 5 palla, sagum 6 abolla 7 paenula, pallium *Arab:* 3 aba *combining form:* 6 pallio *fur:* 7 pelisse *hooded:* 5 capot 6 capote 7 burnous 8 burnoose, cardinal *Indian:* 5 choga *Jewish:* 6 kittel *liturgical:* 4 cope *monk's:* 8 analabos *Moroccan:* 5 jelab 7 jellaba 8 djellaba *over armor:* 6 tabard 7 surcoat *Spanish:* 4 capa 5 manta *Turkish:* 6 dolman *waterproof:* 6 poncho

clobber 4 belt, slam, slug 5 blast, brain, clout, smash 6 wallop

clochard 3 vag 4 hobo 5 tramp 6 canter 7 drifter, floater, vagrant 8 roadster, vagabond 11 bindle stiff

clock 4 time 9 timepiece 11 chronometer *ship-shaped:* 3 nef *water:* 9 clepsydra

clocklike 4 full 6 minute 7 precise, regular 8 detailed, itemized, thorough 10 blow-by-blow, particular

clockmaker 10 horologist

clockwise 6 deasil, dextro 8 positive 11 right-handed

clod 3 gob, wad 4 boob, dolt, dope, hunk, lump 5 chump, chunk, clump, dummy, dunce, hunch 6 dimwit, nugget 8 dumbbell 9 blockhead, lamebrain

cloddish 7 boorish, ill-bred, loutish 8 churlish, clownish 9 unrefined 10 uncultured, unpolished 11 uncivilized

clodhopper 4 boor, hick, lout, shoe 5 chuff, churl, clown, yokel 6 mucker, rustic 7 bumpkin, grobian, hayseed, hoosier, redneck 9 chawbacon

clog 3 gum, tax, tie 4 curb, fill, lade, load, plug, stop 5 block, choke, close, leash, weigh 6 burden, charge, cumber, fetter, hamper, hobble, hog-tie, lumber, saddle 7 congest, occlude, shackle, stopper, trammel 8 encumber, obstruct 9 cumbrance, entrammel, hindrance, impedance 10 impediment 11 encumbrance

cloister 7 seclude 9 sequester

Cloister and the Hearth *author:* 5 Reade (Charles)

cloistered 7 recluse, secluse 8 hermetic, secluded 9 seclusive 11 sequestered

cloistered one 3 nun 4 monk

Clorinda *beloved:* 7 Tancred *father:* 6 Senapo *guardian:* 6 Arsete *slayer:* 7 Tancred

close 3 end 4 bang, clap, clog, face, fill, firm, halt, hard, meet, near, next, nigh, plug, quit, seal, shut, slam, stop, taut 5 abate, block, cease, choke, debar, dense, front, handy, humid, muggy, solid, stivy, taper, tense, thick, tight 6 almost, chummy, desist, ending, finale, finish, lessen, narrow, nearby, nearly, period, reduce, screen, shroud, silent, sticky, stingy, stuffy, sultry, windup, wrap up 7 airless, compact, congest, crowded, dwindle, exclude, miserly, nearest, occlude, shut off, shut out, stopper 8 abutting, adjacent, block out, complete, conclude, decrease, diminish, familiar, finalize, intimate, nearmost, obstruct, obturate, reserved, reticent, stifling, taciturn, taper off, ultimate, write off 9 adjoining, cessation, compacted, condensed, determine, drain away, encounter, immediate, nearabout, niggardly, penurious, proximate, terminate 10 breathless, compressed, conclusion, consummate, contiguous, contracted, convenient, desistance, near-at-hand 11 constricted, impermeable, neighboring, substantial, suffocating, termination, tight-lipped 12 cheeseparing, confidential, consolidated, impenetrable, parsimonious, tight-mouthed 13 pennypinching *combining form:* 4 pync, sten 5 plesi, pynco, steno 6 plesio

closed *combining form:* 5 clist 6 cleist, clisto, occlus 7 cleisto, occluso

closed-minded 4 deaf 8 unpliant 9 obstinate, pigheaded, unpliable 10 bull-headed, hardheaded, self-willed, unyielding 11 intractable

closefisted 6 stingy 7 miserly 8 clinging, grasping 9 clutching, niggardly, tenacious 13 penny-pinching

close in 3 hem, mew 4 cage, coop 5 fence, hedge 6 corral, immure 7 enclose, envelop

close-knit 8 intimate

close-lipped 6 silent 8 reserved, reticent, taciturn 12 tight-mouthed

closely 4 hard 7 sharply 8 intently, minutely 9 carefully, heedfully, mindfully 11 searchingly 12 meticulously, scrupulously, thoughtfully 13 punctiliously

close match 6 tossup

closemouthed see **close-lipped**

closeness 8 intimacy

close off 6 cut off, enisle, island 7 isolate 8 insulate, separate 9 segregate, sequester

closet 6 hushed, inside, office 7 private 8 academic 11 speculative, theoretical 12 confidential

closing 3 end, lag 4 last, stop 5 final 6 ending, finish, latest, latter, period 8 eventual, hindmost, terminal, ultimate 9 cessation 10 concluding, desistance 11 termination

closure 3 cap, lid 8 fastener 9 cessation *combining form:* 6 clisis 7 cleisis

clot 3 gel, set 4 body, jell 5 array, batch, bunch, clump, group, jelly 6 bundle, gelate 7 battery, cluster, congeal, jellify 8 coagulum, thrombus 9 coagulate 10 gelatinize *combining form:* 6 thromb 7 thrombo

cloth see **fabric**

clothe 3 tog 4 clad, deck, do up, garb, robe 5 array, cloak, drape, dress, endue, equip, tog up 6 attire, bedeck, invest, mantle, outfit, rig out, swathe, tog out 7 apparel, bedrape, costume, dress up, garment, raiment, vesture 8 accouter, enclothe

clothes 3 rig 4 duds, garb, rags, togs 5 array, dress, getup 6 attire, outfit, things 7 apparel, costume, raiment, rigging, toggery, vesture 8 clothing 9 vestments 10 attirement 11 habiliments *basket:* 6 hamper *civilian:* 5 mufti *relating to:* 8 vestiary

clothes moth genus 5 Tinea

clothespress 3 kas 7 armoire 8 wardrobe

clothes tree 8 costumer

cloud 3 dim, fog, tar 4 army, blur, host, rout 5 addle, befog, crowd, flock, gloom, muddy, smear, sully, taint 6 legion, muddle, puzzle, scores, shadow, smudge 7 becloud, besmear, confuse, obscure, perplex, tarnish 8 befuddle, besmirch, discolor, distract, overcast 9 adumbrate, multitude *combining form:* 4 cirr 5 cirrh, cirri, cirro, nepho, nimbo 6 cirrhi, cirrho, nephel 7 nephelo *type:* 6 cirrus, nimbus 7 cumulus, stratus 11 altocumulus, altostratus 12 cirrocumulus, cirrostratus, cumulonimbus, nimbostratus 13 stratocumulus

cloudburst 6 deluge, shower 8 downpour, rainfall

clouded 4 open 5 shady 7 dubious, unclear 8 doubtful 9 ambiguous, equivocal, uncertain, unsettled 11 problematic

cloudless 4 fair, fine 5 clear, sunny 7 clarion 8 pleasant, rainless, sunshiny 10 undarkened

cloud-like mass 6 nebula

cloudy 4 dull, hazy 5 foggy, heavy, misty, mucky, murky, mushy, vague 6 vapory 7 louring 8 lowering, nubilous, overcast, vaporous

clough 3 gap 5 chasm, cleft, clove, gorge, gulch 6 arroyo, ravine

clout 2 in 3 box, hit 4 biff, chop, cuff, ding, drag, nail, poke, pull, slam, slap, slog, slug, sock 5 paste, punch, smack, smite, whack 6 buffet, strike 9 influence

clove 3 gap 5 chasm, cleft, gorge, gulch 6 arroyo, clough, ravine

clove hitch 4 knot

cloven-footed 8 fissiped

clover 5 lotus 6 alsike, ladino, lucern 7 alfalfa, berseem, lucerne, melilot, trefoil 8 four-leaf, shamrock 9 lespedeza *family:* 3 pea *genus:* 9 Trifolium

clown 3 wag 4 boor, fool, hick, jake, mime, rube, zany 5 chuff, churl, cutup, joker 6 jester, mucker, mummer, rustic 7 bucolic, buffoon, bumpkin, farceur, grobian, hayseed, hoosier 8 comedian, jokester 9 harlequin 10 mountebank 11 merryandrew *French:* 7 pierrot *operatic:* 5 buffo *Spanish:* 8 gracioso

clownish 3 row 4 rude, zany 6 clumsy, gauche 7 awkward, boorish, ill-bred, loutish, lumpish, uncouth 8 churlish, cloddish 9 unrefined 10 uncultured, unpolished 11 uncivilized

cloy 4 fill, glut, jade, pall, sate 5 gorge 6 stodge 7 satiate, surfeit

club 3 bat 4 mace 5 baton, billy, guild, order, union 6 bistro, cudgel, league 7 society 8 bludgeon, sodality, sorority 9 truncheon 10 fellowship, fraternity, knobkerrie, nightstick 11 association, brotherhood *Australian:* 5 waddy *college:* 8 sorority 10 fraternity *combining form:* 5 clavi 6 rhopal 7 rhopalo *Irish:* 8 shillala 10 shillelagh *women's:* 7 sorosis

clubfoot 7 talipes

cluck 4 fowl, simp 5 dunce 6 dimwit, nitwit 7 lackwit, pinhead, wantwit 9 dumb bunny 13 featherweight

clue 3 cue 4 hint, post, tell, warn, wind 6 advise, fill in, inform, notify, notion, wise up 7 apprise, inkling 8 acquaint, telltale 10 indication, intimation, suggestion

clump 3 gob, lot, set, wad 4 body, clod, hunk, lump 5 array, barge, batch, bunch, chunk, group, hunch, stump 6 bundle, jumble, lumber, nugget, parcel 7 cluster, clutter, galumph, stumble 10 hodgepodge

clump of grass 4 tuft 6 tuffet

clumsy 5 bulky, gawky, inept, splay 6 gauche, klutzy, wooden 7 awkward, hulking, lumpish, uncouth, unhandy, unhappy 8 bumbling, ungainly, unwieldy 9 graceless, ham-handed, inelegant, lumbering, maladroit 10 bunglesome 11 heavy-handed

clumsy one 3 oaf 4 lout 5 klutz 6 lummox 7 bungler

clunk 4 thud 5 clonk, thump

clunker 4 heap 5 crate, wreck 6 jalopy, junker

cluster 3 lot, set 4 band, bevy, body, crew 5 array, batch, bunch, clump, covey, group, party 6 bundle, clutch, gather, parcel 7 collect, package, round up 8 assemble, assembly, cumulate 9 aggregate, associate 10 accumulate *combining form:* 3 cym, kym 4 cymo, kymo

cluster bean 4 guar

clutch 3 nab, set 4 body, grab, grip, hold, keep, take 5 array, batch, bunch, catch, clamp, clasp, clump, grasp, gripe, group, seize 6 bundle, clench, clinch, harbor, parcel, snatch, tenure 7 cherish, cluster, grapple *Scottish:* 5 cleek 7 claucht, claught

clutter 4 hash, mash, mess, muss, ruck 5 chaos, snarl 6 ataxia, huddle, jumble, jungle, litter, medley, muddle, tumble 7 mélange, rummage, shuffle 8 disarray, disorder, mishmash, scramble 9 confusion, macedoine 10 hodgepodge 12 hugger-mugger

Clydesdale 5 horse

Clymene *father:* 7 Oceanus *husband:* 7 Iapetus *mother:* 6 Tethys *son:* 5 Atlas 10 Epimetheus, Prometheus

Clytemnestra *brother:* 6 Castor, Pollux 10 Polydeuces *daughter:* 7 Electra 9 Iphigenia *father:* 9 Tyndareus *husband:* 9 Agamemnon *lover:* 9 Aegisthus *mother:* 4 Leda *slayer:* 7 Orestes *son:* 7 Orestes *victim:* 9 Agamemnon, Cassandra

Clytie *beloved:* 6 Apollo *form:* 9 sunflower 10 heliotrope

coach 5 stage, train, tutor 6 mentor 8 carriage 10 instructor

coadjutant 3 aid 4 aide 9 assistant 10 aide-de-camp, lieutenant

coadjute 4 band 5 unite 6 concur, league 7 combine, conjoin 9 cooperate

coadjutor see coadjutant

coadunation 5 union 6 merger 7 melding, merging 8 mergence 9 coalition 11 combination, unification 13 consolidation

coagulate 3 dry, gel, set 4 clot, jell 5 jelly 6 curdle, freeze, gelate, harden 7 compact, congeal, jellify, thicken 8 coalesce, concrete, condense, solidify 9 dehydrate 10 gelatinize, inspissate 11 concentrate, consolidate

coal *combining form:* 7 anthrac, carboni 8 anthraco *distillate:* 3 tar *dust:* 4 coom, smut, soot 5 coomb, slack *element:* 6 carbon *fused leavings:* 4 slag 7 clinker *glowing:* 5 ember, gleed *hard:* 10 anthracite *lump:* 3 cob *miner:* 7 collier *region:* 4 Saar *residue:* 4 coke *shaly:* 9 tasmanite *soft:* 6 cannel 10 bituminous

coalesce 3 mix, wed 4 fuse, join, link 5 blend, cling, merge, stick, unite 6 adhere, cleave, mingle, relate 7 bracket, combine, conjoin, connect 9 associate

coalition 4 bloc, ring 5 party, union 6 league, merger 7 combine, faction, melding, merging 8 alliance, mergence 9 anschluss 10 federation 11 coadunation, combination, confederacy, unification 13 confederation, consolidation

coarse 3 low, raw 4 foul, rude 5 caked, cakey, crass, crude, dirty, gross, lumpy, nasty, rough, rowdy, tacky 6 common, filthy, grainy, incult, smutty, vulgar 7 boorish, obscene, raffish, raunchy, uncouth 8 granular, indecent, inexpert, prentice 9 inelegant, roughneck, unrefined, vulgarian 10 uncultured 11 particulate 12 scatological, uncultivated *food:* 6 fodder

coast 4 bank 5 beach, drift, shore, slide 6 strand 8 littoral *of Antarctica:* 4 Knox *of west Africa:* 5 Ivory *swampy:* 7 maremma

coastal 8 littoral

coaster 4 sled

coat 5 layer, plate, tunic 6 blazer, duster, jacket, patina, raglan, reefer, ulster, veneer 7 cutaway, paletot 8 covering, mackinaw, tegument 9 newmarket, redingote 10 integument *animal:* 3 fur 4 hide, pelt, wool 6 pelage *arctic:* 5 parka *fur-lined:* 7 pelisse *glossy:* 5 glacé *kind:* 3 car, pea, top 5 frock 6 trench *Levantine:* 6 caftan *medieval:* 8 gambeson *of arms:* 5 crest 6 blazon, emblem, shield, tabard 7 surcoat 8 blazonry 9 escucheon 10 escutcheon *of egg white:* 5 glair 6 glaire *of gold:* 4 gild, gilt *of mail:* 6 byrnie 7 hauberk *Scottish:*

4 jupe *seaman's:* 5 grego *soldier's:*
5 frock, tunic 6 capote *waterproof:*
7 slicker 10 mackintosh

coating 4 film 5 layer 6 finish, patina,
veneer 7 lacquer 8 covering

coax 3 con, get 4 lure, urge 5 press,
tease, tempt 6 cajole, entice, fleech,
induce, pester, plague 7 blarney, prevail,
wheedle 8 blandish, butter up, inveigle,
persuade, soft-soap 9 importune, sweet
talk *Scottish:* 7 cuittle

cob 3 cap 4 ding, swan 5 excel, horse,
outdo 6 exceed 7 surpass 8 outmatch,
outshine, outstrip

cobalt *symbol:* 2 Co

cobble 4 make, mend, mess 5 botch,
patch, snafu, stone 6 bollix, bungle, foul
up, goof up, mucker, repair 7 confuse,
louse up, screw up, snarl up

cobbler 3 pie 4 fish 5 drink 7 catfish,
pompano 9 shoemaker 10 threadfish

cobbler's form 4 last

cobelligerent 4 ally

cobweb 3 net 4 mesh, toil, trap 8 gossamer 12 entanglement

coccyx 8 tailbone

cochineal 3 dye 6 insect

cochleate 6 spiral 11 shell-shaped

cock 3 tap 4 bank, boss, gate, head, heap,
hill, lord, mass, pile, rick 5 chief, drift,
mound, stack, swank, swell, valve 6 faucet,
honcho, leader, master, spigot 7 headman,
hydrant, pyramid, rooster, swagger 8 hierarch, mountain 9 chieftain, dominator, number one, principal 10 preeminent 11 chanticleer, pontificate

cock-a-doodle-doo 4 blow, brag, crow,
puff 5 boast, mouth, prate, vaunt 9 gasconade 11 rodomontade

cock-a-hoop 4 awry 5 askew 6 askant
7 askance 8 exultant, exulting, jubilant
9 crookedly, triumphal 10 triumphant

Cockaigne 4 Zion 6 heaven, utopia
7 arcadia 8 paradise 9 fairyland, Shangri-la
10 lubberland, wonderland 12 promised
land

cockalorum 8 leapfrog 11 braggadocio

cockamamy 10 incredible, ridiculous

cock-and-bull story 3 fib, lie 6 canard
7 falsity, untruth 9 falsehood 13 prevarication

cockatoo bush 9 blueberry

cockcrow 4 dawn, morn 5 light, sunup
6 aurora 7 dawning, morning, sunrise
8 daybreak, daylight

cocker 4 baby 5 humor, spoil 6 coddle,
cosset, pamper 7 cater to, indulge 11 mollycoddle

cockeyed 4 awry 5 askew, boozy, drunk
6 askant 7 askance, muddled 9 crookedly,

disguised, pixilated, plastered 10 inebriated
11 intoxicated

cockle 4 fret 6 dimple, riffle, ripple

cockleshell 4 boat

cockscomb see **coxcomb**

cocksure 7 certain 8 positive 9 confident

cocktail 5 Bronx, drink, zombi 6 zombie
7 martini, Sazerac, sidecar 8 aperitif, dai-
quiri, pink lady, salty dog, sangrita, sombrero 9 aperitive, appetizer, Manhattan
10 Bloody Mary, Margharita *fruit:* 9 macedoine *gasoline:* 7 Molotov

cocktail lounge 3 bar, pub 6 saloon, tavern 7 barroom, gin mill, taproom 8 groggery, pothouse

Cocktail Party author 5 Eliot (Thomas
Stearns)

coconspirator 7 abettor 9 accessory
10 accomplice 11 confederate

coconut *husk fiber:* 4 coir *meat:* 5 copra

coddle 4 baby 5 humor, spoil 6 cosset,
cotton, pamper 7 cater to, indulge 11 mollycoddle

code 6 cipher 7 encrypt 8 encipher *kind:*
3 zip 4 area 5 Morse, penal *message in:*
10 cryptogram

code word see **communications code
word**

codicil 5 rider 8 addendum, appendix
10 supplement

codswallop 8 nonsense

coefficient 8 coacting, coactive, conjoint,
synergic 10 synergetic 11 cooperative

coelenterate 5 coral 7 hydroid 9 jellyfish
10 sea anemone

coerce 3 cow 4 make, push, urge
5 beset, bully, force 6 compel, menace,
oblige 8 browbeat, bulldoze, threaten
9 blackjack, constrain, terrorize 10 intimidate

coercion 5 force 6 duress, menace, threat
8 menacing 10 compulsion, constraint
11 threatening

coeval see **contemporary**

coexistent see **contemporary**

coffee *alkaloid:* 7 caffein 8 caffeine *bean:*
3 nib *cake:* 6 kuchen *cup:* 9 demitasse
cup holder: 4 zarf *French:* 4 café *grinder:*
4 mill *kind:* 4 drip, java 5 latte, mocha
7 arabica, instant 8 espresso 10 cappuc-
cino *maker:* 6 biggin 10 percolator *pot:*
3 urn

coffee shop 4 café 5 diner 8 snack bar
9 hash house, lunchroom 11 eating house,
greasy spoon 12 luncheonette

coffer 5 chest 8 treasury, war chest
9 exchequer

coffin 3 box 4 kist 6 casket *carrier:*
6 hearse 10 pallbearer *nail:* 9 cigarette
stand: 4 bier 10 catafalque

cogency 5 force, point, punch 7 bearing, concern 8 validity 9 relevance, validness 10 connection, pertinence 13 effectiveness

cogent 5 solid, sound, valid 6 potent 7 telling, weighty 8 forceful, forcible, powerful, puissant 9 justified 10 compelling, convincing, meaningful, persuasive, satisfying 11 influential, significant, well-founded 12 constraining, satisfactory, well-grounded 13 consequential

cogitate 4 plot 5 think 6 devise, reason 7 collude, connive, imagine, reflect 8 conceive, conspire, contrive, envisage, envision, intrigue 9 cerebrate, machinate, scheme out, speculate 10 deliberate

cogitation 7 thought 9 brainwork 10 reflection 11 cerebration, speculation 12 deliberation

cogitative 7 pensive 8 thinking 9 pondering 10 meditative, reflecting, reflective, ruminative, thoughtful 11 speculative 13 contemplative

cognate 4 akin 6 agnate, allied, common 7 connate, general, generic, kindred, related 8 incident 9 universal 10 affiliated, connatural 11 consanguine

cognition 9 knowledge 10 perception *combining form:* 5 gnosy 6 gnosia, gnosis

cognizance 4 heed, mark, note 6 notice, regard, remark 9 attention 10 observance 11 observation

cognizant 5 alive, awake, aware 7 knowing, witting 8 sensible, sentient 9 au courant, conscious 12 apprehensive

cognize 4 know 5 grasp 6 fathom 9 apprehend 10 appreciate, comprehend, understand

cognomen 4 name 5 style, title 7 epithet, moniker 11 appellation, appellative, designation 12 compellation, denomination

cognoscente 5 judge 6 critic, expert 8 aesthete 9 authority 10 dilettante, proficient, specialist 11 connoisseur

cognoscible 8 knowable

cohere 2 go 4 fuse, join 5 agree, blend, check, cling, fit in, merge, stick, unite 6 accord, cleave 7 combine, comport, conform, connect 8 check out, coalesce, dovetail 9 associate 10 correspond

coherence 4 bond 5 cling, union, unity 8 adhesion, clinging, cohesion, stickage, sticking 9 congruity, integrity 10 conformity, solidarity 11 consistency

coherent 7 unified 9 connected 10 consistent

cohesion see coherence

cohort 4 mate 6 fellow 7 partner, sectary 8 adherent, confrere, disciple, follower, henchman, partisan, sectator 9 associate, copartner, satellite, supporter 10 consociate

coif 3 cap 4 hood 6 hairdo 8 skullcap

coiffure 6 hairdo 9 headdress *aid:* 3 net, rat 5 snood

coil 4 curl, fuss, loop, ring, turn, wind 5 helix, twine, twist 6 furore, rotate, ruckus, rumpus, shindy, spiral, tumult, uproar 7 entwine, revolve, shindig, turmoil, wreathe 8 brouhaha, foofaraw 9 commotion, corkscrew *combining form:* 4 spir 5 spiri, spiro

coiled 7 tortile 9 circinate

coin 4 mint *Afghanistan:* 3 pul *Albania:* 3 lek *Algeria:* 5 dinar 7 centime *ancient Greek:* 4 obol *ancient Muslim:* 5 dinar *ancient Roman:* 6 follis 8 denarius *Argentina:* 4 peso 7 centavo *Australia:* 4 cent 6 dollar *Austria:* 8 groschen 9 schilling *Bahamas:* 4 cent 6 dollar *Bahrain:* 4 fils 5 dinar *Barbados:* 4 cent 6 dollar *Belgium:* 5 franc 7 centime *Benin:* 5 franc *Bhutan:* 7 chetrum 8 ngultrum *Bolivia:* 7 centavo *Botswana:* 4 pula 5 thebe *Brazil:* 7 centavo 8 cruzeiro *Bulgaria:* 3 lev 8 stotinka *Burundi:* 5 franc *Cameroon:* 5 franc *Canada:* 4 cent 6 dollar *Cape Verde Islands:* 6 escudo *Chile:* 4 peso 7 centavo *China:* 3 fen 4 jiao, yuan 5 chiao *Columbia:* 4 peso 7 centavo *Costa Rica:* 5 colon *Cuba:* 4 peso 7 centavo *Cyprus:* 4 cent 5 pound *Czech Republic:* 5 haler 6 koruna *defective:* 4 fido *Denmark:* 3 ore 5 krone *Dominican Republic:* 4 peso 7 centavo *Ecuador:* 5 sucre 7 centavo *edge:* 7 milling *Egypt:* 7 piastre 8 millieme *Ethiopia:* 4 cent *European gold:* 5 ducat *Fiji:* 4 cent 6 dollar *Finland:* 5 penni 6 markka *former:* 3 ecu, lek, mil, pie, sol 4 anna, besa, cash, doit, duit, kran, para, pice, real, reis (plural) 5 crown, fanam, litas, mohur, paisa, rupia, shahi, soldo, toman 6 centas, denier, heller, kopeck, macuta, pagoda, tangka 7 santims, sapeque 8 farthing, maravedi, sixpence, skilling 9 half penny, rigsdaler 10 Indian head, reichsmark, threepence 13 reichspfennig *France:* 5 franc 7 centime *Gambia:* 5 butut 6 dalasi *Germany:* 4 mark 7 pfennig *Ghana:* 4 cedi 6 pesewa *Great Britain:* 6 guinea 8 new penny 9 sovereign *Greece:* 6 lepton 7 drachma *Guatemala:* 7 centavo, quetzal *Guinea-Bissau:* 4 peso *Guyana:* 4 cent 6 dollar *Haiti:* 6 gourde 7 centime *Honduras:* 7 centavo, lempira *Hungary:* 6 forint *Iceland:* 5 eyrir, krona *India:* 5 paisa, rupee *Indonesia:* 3 sen 6 rupiah *Iran:* 4 rial *Iraq:* 4 fils 5 dinar *Ireland:* 5 penny 8 farthing *Israel:* 5 agora 6 shekel *Italy:* 4 lira *Jamaica:* 4 cent 6 dollar *Japan:* 3 rin,

sen, yen *Jordan:* 3 fil 5 dinar *Kenya:*
8 shilling *Korea, North:* 3 won 4 chon
Korea, South: 3 won *Kuwait:* 4 fils *large:*
9 cartwheel *Lebanon:* 5 livre 7 piaster,
piastre *Lesotho:* 4 loti *Liberia:* 4 cent
6 dollar *Libya:* 6 dirham *Luxembourg:*
5 franc *Madagascar:* 5 franc *Malawi:*
6 kwacha 7 tambala *Malta:* 4 cent
5 pound *Mauritania:* 7 ouguiya *Mauritius:*
4 cent 5 rupee *Mexico:* 4 peso 7 centavo
Monaco: 5 franc *Morocco:* 6 dirham
Mozambique: 7 metical *Nepal:* 5 paisa,
rupee *Netherlands:* 4 cent 6 florin, gulden
New Zealand: 4 cent 6 dollar *Nicaragua:*
7 centavo, cordoba *Nigeria:* 4 kobo *Norway:* 3 ore 5 krone *old Hungarian:*
5 pengo *old Italian:* 5 scudo *old Swedish:*
8 skilling *Oman:* 4 rial *Pakistan:* 4 pice
5 paisa *Panama:* 6 balboa 9 centesimo
Papua-New Guinea: 4 kina, toea *Paraguay:* 7 centimo, guarani *Peru:* 3 sol
7 centimo *Philippines:* 4 piso 7 sentimo
Poland: 5 grosz, zloty *Portugal:* 6 escudo
7 centavo *Qatar:* 6 dirham *Roman:*
6 aureus, bezant 7 solidus *Romania:* 3 leu
Russia: 5 ruble 6 kopeck *Rwanda:*
5 franc *San Marino:* 4 lira *Saudi Arabia:*
6 halala *Seychelles:* 4 cent 5 rupee *side
of a:* 7 obverse *Sierra Leone:* 4 cent
Singapore: 4 cent 6 dollar *Slovakia:*
5 haler 6 koruna *South Africa:* 4 cent,
rand 10 krugerrand *Spain:* 6 peseta
7 centimo *Sri Lanka:* 4 cent 5 rupee
stamping metal: 8 planchet *Suriname:*
4 cent 6 gulden *Swaziland:* 4 cent 9 lilan-
geni *Sweden:* 3 ore 5 krona *Switzerland:*
5 franc 6 rappen *Syria:* 5 pound *Tanzania:*
8 shilling *Thailand:* 4 baht 6 satang *thick:*
7 piefort 8 piedfort *Tonga:* 6 pa'anga, sen-
iti *Trinidad and Tobago:* 4 cent 6 dollar
Tunisia: 5 dinar *Turkey:* 4 lira 5 kurus
Uganda: 8 shilling *United Arab Emirates:*
6 dirham *United States:* 4 dime 5 penny
6 dollar, nickel 7 quarter 10 half dollar *Uruguay:* 4 peso 9 centesimo *Vatican City:*
4 lira *Venezuela:* 7 bolivar *Western
Samoa:* 4 sene, tala *Zambia:* 5 ngwee
6 kwacha *Zimbabwe:* 4 cent 6 dollar
coinage 9 invention, neologism 10 brainchild 11 contrivance
coincide 4 jibe 5 agree, equal, match,
tally 6 accord, concur 7 concert, concord
9 harmonize 10 correspond
coincident 9 ancillary, attendant, attending, satellite 10 collateral 11 concomitant
12 accompanying
coincidentally 6 at once 8 together
12 concurrently
coin-shaped 8 nummular
___ **colade** 4 piña

colander's cousin 5 sieve 6 sifter
8 strainer
cold 3 icy, raw 4 cool, dead, iced 5 algid,
aloof, bleak, brisk, chill, crisp, drear, frore,
gelid, nippy, polar 6 arctic, biting, chilly,
dismal, frigid, frosty, frozen, gloomy, somber, wintry 7 bracing, cutting, defunct,
extinct, glacial, joyless, nipping, shivery
8 chilling, comatose, deceased, departed,
freezing, heatless, lifeless 9 cheerless,
chillsome, exanimate, inanimate, inhibited,
senseless 10 impersonal, insensible,
oppressive, undersexed 11 dispiriting,
emotionless, inconscious, indifferent, passionless, unconscious, unemotional
12 matter-of-fact, unresponsive 13 unimpassioned, unsympathetic *combining form:*
3 cry, kry 4 cryo, kryo 5 frigo 7 psychro
common: 6 coryza *symptom:* 5 cough,
fever 6 sneeze 7 catarrh
cold ___ 3 war 4 cash, cuts, feet, fish,
pack, room, sore, wave 5 cream, frame,
front, patch, steel, sweat, water 6 turkey
7 storage 8 shoulder
cold-blooded 7 callous 8 hardened,
obdurate 9 heartless, unfeeling 10 hard-
boiled, impersonal 11 emotionless, hardhearted 12 matter-of-fact, stonyhearted
13 unimpassioned
cold box 4 icer
cold feet 4 fear 5 alarm, dread, panic
6 dismay, fright, horror, terror 11 trepidation
13 consternation
coldhearted see cold-blooded
cold-shoulder 3 cut 4 snob, snub
9 ostracize
cold storage 7 latency 8 abeyance, abeyancy, doldrums, dormancy 10 quiescence,
quiescency, suspension 12 intermission,
interruption
cole 4 rape 7 cabbage 8 broccoli, kohlrabi
11 cauliflower
Coleridge poem 9 Kubla Khan 10 Chris-
tabel
Colette character 4 Gigi 5 Cheri
8 Claudine
colewort 4 kale 7 cabbage
colic 5 gripe 9 bellyache 11 stomachache
12 collywobbles
coliseum 4 bowl 5 stade 7 stadium
collapse 2 go 4 bend, cave, drop, fail,
flag, give, tire, wilt 5 break, crash, droop,
smash, weary, wreck, yield 6 cave in, fold
up, peg out, weaken 7 breakup, crack-up,
crumple, debacle, deflate, exhaust, failure,
founder, give out, play out, ruining, shatter,
smashup, succumb, undoing 8 flake out,
languish 9 break-down, cataclysm, ruination 10 disruption 11 catastrophe, destruction 12 disintegrate

collar 3 bag, cop, get, nab, nip 4 hook, lift, nail, take 5 catch, steal 6 corner, secure 7 capture, prehend 8 bottle up 11 appropriate *armor:* 6 gorget *boy's:* 4 Eton *chain:* 4 torc 6 torque *horse:* 7 bargham *jeweled:* 6 carcan 8 carcanet *lace-edged:* 6 rabato, rebato *medieval:* 10 chevesaile *metal:* 4 torc 6 torque *Philippine:* 7 panuelo *pleated:* 4 ruff *wooden:* 4 cang 6 cangue

collarbone 8 clavicle

collate 5 order 7 arrange, bracket, compare 8 assemble, contrast 9 integrate

collateral 3 sub 5 under 6 allied 7 cognate, kindred, oblique, related, subject 8 adjuvant, circular, incident, indirect 9 accessory, ancillary, attendant, attending, auxiliary, dopondont, satellite, secondary, tributary 10 circuitous, coincident, reciprocal, roundabout, subsidiary 11 adminicular, appurtenant, concomitant, subordinate, subservient 12 accompanying, confirmative, confirmatory, contributory, verificatory 13 complementary, corresponding, corroborative, corroboratory

colleague 3 pal 4 aide, chum 5 buddy, crony 6 fellow, helper 7 compeer, partner 8 confrere, co-worker 9 assistant, associate, companion, copartner 10 compatriot, consociate, workfellow

collect 4 draw, make, rank, rein 5 array, group, infer, judge, order, raise 6 deduce, deduct, derive, gather, muster 7 cluster, compile, compose, control, dispose, make out, marshal, round up 8 assemble, conclude, congress, restrain 10 congregate, rendezvous, simmer down

collected 4 calm, cool, easy, smug, sure 5 quiet, still 6 placid, poised, serene 7 assured 8 composed, peaceful, sanguine, tranquil 9 confident, easygoing, possessed, unruffled 10 complacent, nonchalant 11 unflappable 13 imperturbable, self-possessed, self-satisfied

collection 3 ana, kit, lot 4 band, bevy, clan, crew, olio, ruck 5 bunch, clump, crowd, group, hoard, party, trove 6 medley, muster, outfit 7 cluster, company, variety 8 assembly, caboodle 9 aggregate, amassment, colluvies, congeries, gathering 10 assemblage, assortment, cumulation, miscellany 11 aggregation 12 accumulation, congregation 13 agglomeration, armamentarium *miscellaneous:* 4 hash, olio 6 jumble, medley 7 mélange, mixture 8 mishmash, pastiche 9 bric-a-brac, potpourri 10 hodgepodge, salmagundi 11 olla podrida *of anecdotes:* 3 ana *of animals:* 3 zoo 9 menagerie *of artistic works:* 6 museum 7 gallery *of clothes:* 8 ward-

robe *of dried plants:* 9 herbarium *of facts:* 4 data *of literary pieces:* 5 sylva 8 analecta, analects 9 anthology *of proper names:* 11 onomasticon *of reports:* 4 file 7 dossier *of trinkets:* 10 bijouterie *suffix:* 3 ery

collective *association, Russian:* 5 artel *farm, Israeli:* 7 kibbutz *farm, Russian:* 7 kolkhoz

collector *of bird's eggs:* 8 oologist *of books:* 11 bibliophile *of coins:* 11 numismatist *of fares:* 9 conductor *of phonograph records:* 10 discophile *of postcards:* 12 deltiologist *of stamps:* 11 philatelist

colleen 4 girl, lass *country:* 4 Eire, Erin 7 Ireland

college *building:* 3 gym, lab 4 dorm, hall *campus area:* 4 quad 10 quadrangle *class meeting:* 3 lab 7 lecture, seminar 8 tutorial, workshop *degree:* 2 AA, AB, BA, BD, BS, CE, DD, MA, MD, MM, MS 3 BLS, DST, LLB, LLD, MBA, MEd, MFA, MLS, PhD 5 LittD *graduate:* 6 alumna, alumni (plural) 7 alumnae (plural), alumnus *official:* 4 dean 5 prexy 6 bursar, regent 7 proctor, provost, trustee 8 chairman, chaplain, director 9 counselor, librarian, president, registrar *oldest in U.S.:* 7 Harvard *oldest women's in U.S.:* 12 Mount Holyoke *permit for absence:* 5 exeat *relating to:* 8 academic 10 collegiate *social group:* 4 frat 8 sorority 10 fraternity *song:* 9 alma mater *student class:* 4 soph 5 frosh 6 junior, senior 8 freshman 9 sophomore *teacher:* 3 don 4 prof 5 tutor 8 academic 9 professor 10 instructor *term:* 7 quarter, session 8 semester 9 trimester *VIP:* 4 BMOC *woman:* 4 coed

college athletic team *Air Force:* 7 Falcons *Alabama:* 11 Crimson Tide *Arizona:* 8 Wildcats *Arizona State:* 9 Sun Devils *Arkansas:* 10 Razorbacks *Arkansas State:* 7 Indians *Army:* 6 Cadets *Auburn:* 6 Tigers *Baylor:* 5 Bears *Boston College:* 6 Eagles *Boston University:* 8 Terriers *Brigham Young:* 7 Cougars *Brown:* 5 Bears *California:* 11 Golden Bears *Central Michigan:* 9 Chippewas *Cincinnati:* 8 Bearcats *Citadel:* 8 Bulldogs *Clemson:* 6 Tigers *Colgate:* 10 Red Raiders *Colorado:* 9 Buffaloes *Colorado State:* 4 Rams *Columbia:* 5 Lions *Connecticut:* 7 Huskies *Cornell:* 6 Big Red *Dartmouth:* 8 Big Green *Davidson:* 8 Wildcats *Delaware State:* 7 Hornets *Drake:* 8 Bulldogs *Duke:* 10 Blue Devils *Eastern Kentucky:* 8 Colonels *Eastern Michigan:* 6 Eagles *Florida:* 6 Gators *Florida State:* 9 Seminoles *Fresno State:* 8 Bulldogs *Furman:*

8 Palidans *Georgia:* 8 Bulldogs *Georgia Tech:* 13 Yellow Jackets *Harvard:* 7 Crimson *Hawaii:* 15 Rainbow Warriors *Holy Cross:* 9 Crusaders *Houston:* 7 Cougars *Howard:* 6 Bisons *Idaho:* 7 Vandals *Idaho State:* 7 Bengals *Illinois:* 6 Illini *Illinois State:* 8 Redbirds *Indiana:* 8 Hoosiers *Indiana State:* 9 Sycamores *Iowa:* 8 Hawkeyes *Iowa State:* 8 Cyclones *Kansas:* 8 Jayhawks *Kansas State:* 8 Wildcats *Kent State:* 13 Golden Flashes *Kentucky:* 8 Wildcats *Lehigh:* 9 Engineers *Louisiana State:* 6 Tigers *Louisiana Tech:* 8 Bulldogs *Maine:* 10 Black Bears *Maryland:* 5 Terps 9 Terrapins *Massachusetts:* 9 Minutemen *Miami (Florida):* 10 Hurricanes *Miami (Ohio):* 8 Redskins *Michigan:* 10 Wolverines *Michigan State:* 8 Spartans *Minnesota:* 7 Gophers *Mississippi:* 6 Rebels *Mississippi State:* 8 Bulldogs *Missouri:* 6 Tigers *Montana:* 9 Grizzlies *Montana State:* 7 Bobcats *Navy:* 10 Midshipmen *Nebraska:* 11 Cornhuskers *Nevada:* 6 Rebels 8 Wolfpack *New Hampshire:* 8 Wildcats *New Mexico:* 5 Lobos *New Mexico State:* 6 Aggies *North Carolina:* 8 Tar Heels *North Carolina State:* 8 Wolfpack *Northeastern:* 7 Huskies *Northwestern:* 8 Wildcats *Notre Dame:* 13 Fighting Irish *Ohio State:* 8 Buckeyes *Ohio University:* 7 Bobcats *Oklahoma:* 7 Sooners *Oklahoma State:* 7 Cowboys *Oregon:* 5 Ducks *Oregon State:* 7 Beavers *Pennsylvania:* 7 Quakers *Pennsylvania State:* 12 Nittany Lions *Pittsburgh:* 8 Panthers *Princeton:* 6 Tigers *Purdue:* 12 Boilermakers *Rhode Island:* 4 Rams *Rice:* 4 Owls *Rutgers:* 14 Scarlet Knights *San Diego State:* 6 Aztecs *San Jose State:* 8 Spartans *South Carolina:* 9 Gamecocks *South Carolina State:* 8 Bulldogs *Southern California:* 7 Trojans *Southern Illinois:* 7 Salukis *Southern Methodist:* 8 Mustangs *Stanford:* 9 Cardinals *Syracuse:* 9 Orangemen *Temple:* 4 Owls *Tennessee:* 10 Volunteers *Tennessee State:* 6 Tigers *Tennessee Tech:* 12 Golden Eagles *Texas:* 9 Longhorns *Texas A&M:* 6 Aggies *Texas Christian:* 11 Horned Frogs *Texas Southern:* 6 Tigers *Texas Tech:* 10 Red Raiders *Toledo:* 7 Rockets *Tulane:* 9 Green Wave *UCLA:* 6 Bruins *UNLV:* 12 Runnin' Rebels *Utah:* 4 Utes *Utah State:* 6 Aggies *Vanderbilt:* 10 Commodores *Villanova:* 8 Wildcats *Virginia:* 9 Cavaliers *VMI:* 7 Keydets *VPI:* 8 Gobblers *Wake Forest:* 12 Demon Deacons *Washington:* 7 Huskies *Washington State:* 7 Cougars *West Virginia:* 12 Mountaineers *William & Mary:*

5 Tribe *Wisconsin:* 7 Badgers *Wyoming:* 7 Cowboys *Yale:* 4 Elis 8 Bulldogs

collide 3 hit, ram 4 bump 5 carom, clash, crash, smash 6 strike 7 impinge 8 conflict

collision 4 bump, jolt 5 clash, crash, shock, smash, wreck 6 impact, pileup 7 crack-up, smashup 10 concussion, percussion 11 destruction 12 demolishment

collocate 3 set 5 place 7 arrange 8 position

collogue 5 treat 6 advise, confab, confer, huddle, parley, powwow 7 consult 11 confabulate

colloid 3 gel, sol 4 agar 8 hydrogel, hydrosol

colloque 4 chat, chin, talk, yarn 5 visit 8 converse

colloquial 6 patois, vulgar 7 vulgate 8 familiar, informal 10 vernacular

colloquium 7 palaver, seminar 10 conference, rap session

colloquy 4 chat, talk 6 parley 7 palaver, seminar 8 converse, dialogue 10 conference, rap session 12 conversation 13 confabulation

collude 4 plot 6 devise 7 connive 8 cogitate, conspire, contrive, intrigue 9 machinate, scheme out

collusion 10 complicity, connivance

colluvies 4 hash 5 hoard, trove 6 jumble, medley 7 mélange 8 mishmash, pastiche 9 amassment, potpourri 10 assortment, collection, cumulation, hodgepodge, miscellany 11 aggregation 12 accumulation 13 agglomeration

collywobbles 5 colic, gripe 9 bellyache 11 stomachache

Colombia *capital:* 6 Bogota *highest peak:* 9 Cristobal *monetary unit:* 4 peso

Colonel Blimp 10 fuddy-duddy 12 stuffed shirt

colonnade 4 stoa

color 3 dye, hue 4 cast, flag, glow, jack, pink, rose, show, tint, tone 5 belie, blush, flush, paint, rouge, shade, stain, tinct, tinge, twist 6 banner, ensign, mantle, pennon, pinken, redden, stance 7 crimson, distort, falsify, pennant, pigment 8 attitude, disguise, dyestuff, gonfalon, misstate, overdraw, position, standard, streamer, tincture 9 embellish, embroider, oriflamme, overpaint, overstate, semblance 10 exaggerate 12 chromaticity, misrepresent *band:* 5 facia, vitta 6 fascia *combining form:* 5 chrom 6 chromo 7 chromat 8 chromato 9 chromasia *primary:* 3 red 4 blue 6 yellow *relating to:* 9 chromatic *secondary:* 5 green 6 orange, purple *soft:* 6 pastel

Colorado *academy, college:* 5 Regis 10 U.S. Air Force *capital:* 6 Denver *nickname:* 15 Centennial State *park:* 5 Estes *state bird:* 11 lark bunting *state flower:* 9 columbine

colorant 3 dye 5 stain 7 pigment 8 dye-stuff, tincture

coloration *combining form:* 6 chroia, chromy 7 chromia

colored 6 biased, warped 7 bigoted, partial 8 one-sided, partisan 9 jaundiced 10 prejudiced 11 tendentious 12 prepossessed *combining form:* 6 chroic, chrome 7 chromat, chroous 8 chromato

colorful 3 gay 5 gaudy, showy, vivid 6 bright, flashy, florid, garish 7 splashy

coloring 4 face, mask, show 5 front, guise, put-on 6 facade 8 disguise 9 hyperbole, semblance 12 embroidering, exaggeration 13 embellishment, overstatement

coloring matter *combining form:* 5 phyll

colorist 6 tinter

colorless 3 wan 4 ashy, drab, dull, flat, pale 5 ashen, livid, lurid, prosy, waxen, white 6 albino, doughy, pallid 7 insipid, neutral, prosaic 8 abstract, blanched, detached, lifeless, tintless 10 achromatic, impersonal, lackluster, lusterless, pokerfaced 11 unpassioned 13 disinterested, dispassionate, unimaginative *combining form:* 4 leuc, leuk 5 leuco, leuko

colossal 4 huge, vast 7 mammoth, titanic 8 gigantic 9 cyclopean, monstrous 10 behemothic, gargantuan 11 elephantine

Colossus of 6 Rhodes

colporteur 7 apostle 9 missioner 10 evangelist, missionary 12 propagandist

colt 4 tyro 6 novice, rookie 8 beginner, freshman, neophyte, newcomer 9 fledgling, novitiate

coltish 6 elvish, frisky, impish 7 larkish, playful, puckish, waggish 10 frolicsome 11 mischievous

columbary 8 dovecote, pigeonry 9 dovehouse 11 culverhouse, pigeon house

Columbine *beloved:* 9 Harlequin *father:* 9 Pantaloon

columbium *symbol:* 2 Cb

Columbus *birthplace:* 5 Genoa *patron:* 8 Isabella 9 Ferdinand *ship:* 4 Nina 5 Pinta 10 Santa Maria *son:* 5 Diego *starting point:* 5 Palos

column 3 row 4 pier, prop 5 brace, shore 6 pillar 7 support 8 buttress, pilaster 11 underpinner 12 underpinning 13 underpropping *base:* 4 ordo 5 socle 6 plinth 9 stylobate *bulge:* 7 entasis *female figure:* 8 caryatid *male figure:* 5 atlas 7 telamon 8 atlantes (plural) *style:* 5 Doric, Ionic 10 Corinthian *top:* 7 capital 8 chapiter

coma 5 faint, sleep, swoon 6 stupor, torpor 7 languor, slumber, syncope 8 blackout, dullness, hebetude, lethargy 9 lassitude, torpidity

comate 3 pal 4 chum 5 buddy, crony 7 comrade 9 associate, companion 11 running mate

comatose 5 dopey, heavy 6 stupid, torpid 8 sluggish 9 lethargic, senseless 10 insensible, slumberous 11 inconscious, unconscious 12 hebetudinous

comb 4 grub, rake, sift, sort 5 probe, scour 6 forage, search, winnow 7 ransack, rummage 8 finecomb, separate 11 investigate *combining form:* 4 loph 5 lopho 6 pectin 7 pectini

combat 3 war 4 buck, duel 5 fight, repel 6 action, battle, oppose, resist, strife 7 contend, contest, dispute, service 8 traverse 9 withstand

combating *prefix:* 4 anti

combative 7 warlike 8 militant, vigorous 9 agonistic, bellicose, truculent 10 pugnacious 11 belligerent, contentious, quarrelsome 12 gladiatorial

combativeness 5 fight 6 attack 9 pugnacity 10 aggression 11 bellicosity 12 belligerence

combe 4 dale, glen, vale 6 valley

combination 4 bloc, pool, ring 5 party, tie-up, union 6 hookup, merger 7 cahoots, faction, melding, merging 8 alliance, mergence 9 aggregate, coalition 10 connection 11 affiliation, association, coadunation, conjunction, partnership, unification 13 consolidation *combining form:* 4 hapt 5 hapto

combine 3 add, mix, wed 4 band, bloc, fuse, join, link, pool, ring 5 blend, chain, group, merge, party, trust, unify, union, unite 6 cartel, concur, embody, league, mingle, relate 7 bracket, conjoin, connect, faction 8 coadjute, coalesce 9 associate, coalition, commingle, cooperate, integrate, syndicate 10 amalgamate 11 consolidate, incorporate 12 conglomerate *Japanese:* 8 zaibatsu

combined action 7 synergy 8 synergia

combust 4 burn 10 incinerate

combustible 4 edgy, fuel 8 agitable, burnable, skittery, skittish, volatile 9 alarmable, excitable, flammable, ignitable, startlish 11 inflammable *material:* 3 gas, oil 4 coal, peat, wood 6 tinder

come 4 flow, grow, near, show, stem 5 add up, arise, get in, issue, occur, reach, run to, sum to, total 6 amount, arrive, befall, betide, happen, number, show up, spring, turn up 7 advance, develop, emanate, proceed 8 approach, hail from 9 aggregate, originate, transpire 10 derive from *a cropper:* 4 fail, fall *across:* 4 find, meet 8 discover 9 encounter *apart:*

12 disintegrate *at:* 6 attack, attain *away:* 5 leave 6 depart *before:* 7 precede *between:* 9 interfere, interpose *clean:* 7 confess *down from:* 6 alight *forth:* 5 issue 6 appear, emerge *forward:* 9 volunteer *from:* 6 derive, result *into:* 5 enter 7 acquire *near:* 5 verge 8 approach *round:* 5 rally 7 get well, recover *to pass:* 5 occur 6 happen *up:* 5 arise *upon:* 4 find, meet 6 affect, attack 7 afflict 8 discover 9 encounter

comeback 6 retort 7 riposte 8 repartee

come by 3 see 4 call, gain 5 pop in, run in, visit 6 attain, drop in, look in, look up, step in 7 acquire, inherit

comedian 3 wag, wit 4 card, zany 5 comic, droll, joker 6 jester 8 funnyman, humorist, jokester, quipster

comedo 9 blackhead

comedown 4 fall, ruin 5 crash 7 descent, setback 8 collapse

come down with 3 get 5 catch 8 contract

comedy 5 humor 8 drollery 9 drollness, funniness, wittiness 10 comicality 12 humorousness

come in 5 enter, reply 6 answer, rejoin, retort, return 7 ingress, respond 9 penetrate

comely 4 fair, nice 5 bonny, sonsy 6 lovely, pretty, proper, seemly, sonsie 7 correct 8 becoming, decorous, handsome 9 beauteous, beautiful, befitting, civilized 10 attractive 11 good-looking

come off 3 hap 5 break, click, occur 6 befall, betide, go over, happen, pan out 7 develop, succeed 8 prove out

come-off 6 escape 7 elusion, evasion 8 escaping, eschewal, shunning 9 avoidance, runaround

come-on 4 bait, lure, trap 5 cheat, decoy, rogue, snare 6 con man, gypper 8 swindler 9 trickster 10 allurement, enticement, seducement, temptation 11 flimflammer 12 bunco steerer, double-dealer, inveiglement 13 confidence man

come out 4 leak 5 break, debut 6 emerge 9 transpire

come out with 3 say 4 tell 5 state, utter 7 declare, deliver

comestible 6 edible 7 eatable 8 esculent

comestibles 4 feed, food, grub 6 viands 7 edibles 8 victuals 9 provender 10 provisions

come through 6 chip in, kick in 7 pitch in, ride out, survive 9 subscribe 10 contribute

come together 4 meet 7 synapse 8 converge

comeuppance 3 due 5 lumps, merit 6 rights 7 deserts 9 deserving

comfort 3 aid 4 help, lift 5 cheer 6 assist, buck up, relief, solace, succor 7 amenity, condole, console, relieve, secours, support, upraise 8 facility, reassure 10 assistance, sympathize 11 commiserate, convenience

comfortable 4 cozy, easy, homy, snug, soft 5 comfy, cushy, homey 6 loungy 7 content, easeful, pleased, restful, welcome, well-off 8 adequate, homelike, pleasant, pleasing, well-to-do 9 agreeable, competent, satisfied, sufficing, well-fixed 10 gratifying, prosperous, sufficient, well-heeled 11 substantial 12 satisfactory

comforter 4 pouf, puff 5 quilt 9 eiderdown

comfortless 5 harsh 7 uncomfy 12 inconsolable 13 discomforting

comfy 4 cozy, easy, homy, snug, soft 5 cushy, homey 7 easeful 8 homelike 11 comfortable

comic 3 wag, wit 5 antic, droll, funny, joker 6 jester 7 risible 8 comedian, farcical, funnyman, gelastic, humorist, jokester, quipster 9 laughable, ludicrous 10 ridiculing, ridiculous *strip:* 7 funnies

comical 4 zany 5 droll, funny, silly 6 absurd, impish 7 foolish, risible, roguish, waggish 8 farcical, gelastic, sportive 9 laughable, ludicrous 10 ridiculous

coming 4 next 6 advent 7 arrival, ensuing, nearing 9 following 11 approaching *forth:* 7 issuant

comity 5 amity 7 concord, harmony 8 goodwill 10 friendship, kindliness 11 benevolence, camaraderie, comradeship 12 friendliness

comma 4 lull 5 pause 8 interval 9 pausation

command 3 bid, law 4 rule, sway, tell, warn, word 5 canon, might, order, power, skill 6 adjure, behest, charge, compel, direct, enjoin, manage 7 ability, bidding, captain, conduct, control, dictate, knowhow, mandate, mastery, precept, statute 9 authority, constrain, direction, directive, expertise, expertism, ordinance 10 domination, expertness, injunction, mastership 11 instruction 12 jurisdiction *to go:* 4 mush 6 avaunt, begone, giddap *to stop:* 4 whoa 5 avast

commandeer 4 take 5 annex, seize, usurp 6 assume 7 preempt 8 accroach, arrogate 9 sequester 10 confiscate 11 appropriate, expropriate

commander 4 boss, head 6 honcho, leader, master 7 captain, general, headman, officer 8 decurion, hierarch 9 dominator

commandment 3 law 4 rule 5 edict, order 6 decree 7 mitsvah, mitzvah, precept, statute

Commedia dell' ___ 4 Arte

comme il faut 4 nice 5 right 6 decent, proper, seemly 7 correct 8 becoming, decorous 9 befitting 10 conforming

commemorate 4 keep 7 observe 8 monument 9 celebrate, solemnize 11 memorialize 13 monumentalize

commemorative 8 memorial

commence 4 open 5 arise, begin, enter, start 6 launch, take up 7 kick off, lead off 8 embark on 9 originate 10 embark upon, inaugurate

commencement 4 dawn 5 alpha, birth, onset, start 6 outset 7 dawning, genesis, opening 8 outstart 9 beginning

commend 4 hail, laud 5 extol 6 commit, kudize, praise, tender 7 acclaim, applaud, approve, confide, consign, entrust, proffer 8 hand over, relegate, turn over 10 compliment

commendable 6 worthy 8 laudable 9 admirable, deserving, estimable, meritable, praisable 11 meritorious, thankworthy 12 praiseworthy

commensurable see **commensurate**

commensurate 4 even 5 equal 11 symmetrical 12 proportional

comment 4 note 6 notice, remark, review 7 observe 8 critique, reviewal 9 criticism 10 animadvert 11 observation 12 obiter dictum

commerce 5 trade, truck 7 contact, traffic 8 business, congress, dealings, exchange, industry 9 communion 11 interchange, intercourse 13 communication

commercial 2 ad 8 business 10 mercantile 13 advertisement

commie 3 Red 9 Bolshevik, communist

commination 5 curse 7 malison 8 anathema 11 imprecation, malediction

commingle 3 mix 5 immix, merge, unify 8 compound, intermix 9 integrate 10 amalgamate

comminute 4 bray, buck 5 crush 6 powder 9 pulverize, triturate 12 contriturate

commiserable 4 poor 6 rueful 7 piteous, pitiful 8 pathetic, pitiable

commiserate 4 ache, pity 7 feel for 10 sympathize 13 compassionate

commiseration 3 rue 4 pity, ruth 8 sympathy 10 compassion

commission 3 bid 4 name 5 board, order 6 charge, depute, enable, enjoin 7 appoint, command, council, empower, license 8 accredit, delegate, deputize, instruct, nominate 9 authorize, designate

commit 2 do 5 allot 6 assign, invest, ordain 7 commend, confide, consign, entrust, execute, perform, pull off, trustee 8 hand over, relegate, turn over 10 perpetuate

commitment 4 duty, must, need 5 ought 6 charge, devoir 10 obligation

committal see **commitment**

commixture 6 fusion 7 compost 9 composite 11 interfusion

commodious 4 wide 5 ample, roomy 8 spacious 9 capacious

commodities 5 goods, items, wares 6 things 8 articles 9 vendibles 11 merchandise

common 4 flat, park, poor 5 cheap, joint, plaza, prosy, stale, tatty, trite, typic, usual 6 decent, garden, impure, mutual, normal, paltry, shared, shoddy, sleazy, square, trashy 7 defiled, general, generic, natural, prosaic, regular, routine, typical 8 adequate, all right, communal, conjoint, conjunct, déclassé, everyday, familiar, frequent, inferior, low-grade, ordinary 9 customary, pleasance, prevalent, tolerable, universal 10 desecrated, second-rate, sufficient, uneventful, unexciting 11 intermutual, second-class 12 matter-of-fact, satisfactory, second-drawer, unnoteworthy 13 unexceptional, unimpeachable, uninteresting *combining form:* 3 cen 4 caen, ceno, coen 5 caeno, coeno

commonalty 3 mob 5 plebs 6 masses, people, plebes, public, rabble 7 commune 8 populace 9 hoi polloi, multitude, plebeians 11 proletariat, rank and file, third estate

commoners see **commonalty**

commonition 6 caveat 7 caution, warning 11 forewarning

commonplace 5 lowly, tired, trite, usual 6 cliché, normal, truism 7 bromide, clichéd, general, inanity, mundane, natural, prosaic, regular, typical, workday 8 banality, bromidic, chestnut, everyday, ordinary, prosaism, shopworn, timeworn, well-worn, workaday 9 platitude, prevalent, triteness 10 prosaicism, shibboleth, stereotype, threadbare, uneventful 11 stereotyped 12 unnoteworthy 13 stereotypical, unexceptional

common sense 6 wisdom 8 gumption, judgment

Common Sense author 5 Paine (Thomas)

commorancy 4 home 5 abode, house 8 domicile, dwelling 9 residence, residency 10 habitation

commotion 3 din, row 4 coil, flap, fuss, moil, riot, stew, stir, to-do 5 hurly, storm, upset, whirl 6 bustle, clamor, dither, flurry, fracas, furore, hassle, hoopla, hubbub, hurrah, lather, outcry, pother, racket, ruckus, rumpus, shindy, tow-row, tumult, uproar, upturn 7 clatter, ferment, fluster, ruction, shindig, turmoil, whoopla 8 brouhaha, disquiet, foofaraw, rowdydow, upheaval, uprising **9** agitation, confusion **10** convulsion, hullabaloo, hurly-burly, turbulence **11** pandemonium **12** perturbation

commove 5 elate **6** excite **7** inspire **9** stimulate **10** exhilarate

communal 5 joint **6** common, mutual, public, shared **8** conjoint, conjunct **11** intermutual

commune 6 confer **8** commerce, converse, district **10** collective **12** conversation *Israeli:* **7** kibbutz *Russian:* **3** mir **7** kolkhoz

communicable 8 catching **9** expansive, garrulous, talkative **10** contagious, infectious

communicate 4 abut, join, tell **5** touch, verge **6** adjoin, border, butt on, convey, impart, pass on, reveal, signal **7** contact, divulge **8** disclose, neighbor, transmit

communication 4 talk, word **7** contact, message, missive, talking **8** commerce, converse, exchange **9** directive **10** conversing, discussing, discussion **11** interchange, intercourse **12** conversation *means:* **2** TV **4** drum, note **5** media, phone, radio **6** letter, medium, pigeon, speech **9** telegraph, telephone **10** television *system:* **8** language

communications code word 4 Alfa, Echo, Golf, Kilo, Lima, Mike, Papa, Xray, Zulu **5** Bravo, Delta, Hotel, India, Oscar, Romeo, Tango **6** Quebec, Sierra, Victor, Yankee **7** Charlie, Foxtrot, Juliett, Uniform, Whiskey **8** November

communicative 7 voluble **9** expansive, garrulous, talkative **10** loquacious

communion 4 cult, sect **5** creed, faith, truck **6** church **7** contact, traffic **8** commerce, converse, dealings, religion **10** connection, persuasion **11** intercourse **12** denomination *cloth:* **8** corporal *cup:* **3** ama **7** chalice *plate:* **5** paten

communism 8 Leninism **10** bolshevism

Communist 3 red **5** pinko **6** commie **7** comrade, Marxist **8** Leninist **9** Bolshevik, Stalinist **10** Trotskyist

Communist leader *Chinese:* **10** Mao Tse-tung *Russian:* **5** Lenin (Vladimir) **6** Stalin (Joseph) **7** Trotsky (Leon) **10** Khrushchev (Nikita)

community 4 city, town **6** people, public **7** enclave, society **12** neighborhood *ecological:* **10** biocenosis

commute 5 alter **6** change, travel **7** convert **8** exchange, transfer **9** transform, translate, transmute, transpose **10** compensate, substitute **11** interchange, transfigure **12** metamorphose, transmogrify

compact 4 bond, firm, hard **5** close, dense, pithy, thick, tight, unify **6** packed

7 bargain, bunched, crowded **8** compress, condense, contract, covenant **9** agreement, integrate **10** convention **11** concentrate, consolidate, transaction **12** epigrammatic *combining form:* **4** pycn **5** pycno

companion 3 pal **4** chum, fere, mate, twin **5** buddy, crony, match **6** attend, cohort, comate, double, escort, fellow **7** comrade, conduct, consort, partner **8** chaperon, helpmate, helpmeet **9** accompany, associate, colleague, duplicate **10** coordinate, reciprocal **11** concomitant, consort with, running mate **13** accompaniment

companionable 6 social **7** amiable **8** sociable **9** convivial **11** good-natured

companionship 7 company, society **10** fellowship

company 3 mob **4** band, club, crew, firm, gang, pack, ruck, team **5** corps, group, house, party, troop **6** attend, clique, convoy, guests, muster, outfit, troupe **7** concern, conduct, coterie, society, visitor **8** assembly, business, chaperon, visitors **9** companion, gathering **10** assemblage, collection, enterprise, fellowship **11** aggregation, association, camaraderie, comradeship **12** congregation, consociation **13** companionship, establishment

comparable 4 akin, like **5** alike **6** agnate **7** similar, uniform **8** parallel **9** consonant **13** corresponding, undifferenced

comparative 4 near **8** relative **11** approximate *suffix:* **2** er

compare 5 liken, match **6** equate **7** bracket, collate, paragon **8** contrast, parallel **9** correlate **10** assimilate

comparison 6 simile **7** analogy **8** affinity, likeness **9** alikeness, semblance **10** similarity, similitude **11** resemblance

compass 3 get, hem, see, win **4** gain, gird, ring **5** ambit, annex, catch, field, grasp, orbit, range, reach, round, scope, sweep **6** bounds, circle, domain, extent, girdle, limits, obtain, radius, secure, sphere, take in **7** acquire, circuit, environ, procure, purview **8** boundary, confines, encircle, environs, purlieus, surround **9** apprehend, enclosure, extension, perimeter, periphery, precincts **10** comprehend, understand **13** circumference *kind:* **4** gyro **5** solar **8** lensatic, magnetic *stand:* **8** binnacle

compassion 3 rue **4** pity, ruth **5** mercy **7** charity, empathy **8** clemency, humanity, sympathy **10** humaneness **11** benevolence **13** commiseration, fellow feeling

compassionate 4 pity, warm **6** humane, tender **7** clement, feel for **10** responsive **11** commiserate, kindhearted, softhearted, sympathetic, warmhearted

compassionless 5 stony 7 callous 8 obdurate 9 heartless, unfeeling 11 cold-blooded, hardhearted, ironhearted 12 stony-hearted

compass point 2 NE, NW, SE, SW 3 ENE, ESE, NNE, NNW, SSE, SSW, WNW, WSW 4 east, west 5 north, rhumb, south *Scottish:* 4 airt

compatible 6 proper 8 suitable 9 agreeable, congenial, congruous, consonant 10 consistent 11 sympathetic

compatriot 7 compeer 8 confrere 9 associate, colleague

compeer see compatriot

compel 4 hale, make, urge 5 drive, force 6 coerce, impose, oblige 7 concuss, enforce 9 constrain *Scottish:* 3 gar

compellation 4 name 5 nomen, style, title 7 moniker 8 cognomen 11 appellative, designation 12 denomination

compendious 4 curt 5 brief, short 7 compact, concise, laconic, summary 8 succinct 12 breviloquent 13 short and sweet

compendium 5 brief, guide 6 aperçu, digest, manual, précis, sketch, survey 7 pandect, sylloge 8 Baedeker, handbook, overview, syllabus 9 guidebook, vade mecum 10 abridgment, conspectus 11 enchiridion

compensate 3 pay 5 atone, repay 6 make up, offset, redeem, set off 7 balance, guerdon, requite 8 atone for, outweigh 9 indemnify, reimburse 10 counteract, neutralize, recompense, remunerate 11 countervail 12 counterpoise

compensation 6 amends, reward, salary 7 payment, redress 8 reprisal, requital, solatium 9 indemnity, quittance 10 recompense, reparation 11 restitution

compete 3 vie 5 fight, match, rival 6 battle, strive 7 contend, contest, dispute, emulate, tourney 8 rivalize, struggle

competence 5 might 6 enough 7 ability 8 adequacy, capacity 10 capability 11 sufficiency 13 qualification, qualifiedness

competent 4 able 5 adept 6 au fait, decent, enough, proper 7 capable, skilled 8 adequate, masterly 9 qualified, sufficing 10 sufficient 11 comfortable 12 satisfactory

competition 4 game, meet 5 match, rival 6 strife 7 contest, rivalry, warfare 8 concours, conflict, corrival, striving, struggle, tug-of-war 9 emulation, rencontre

competitor 5 rival 8 corrival, opponent 9 adversary 10 antagonist, contestant

compile 4 edit 6 gather, muster, select 7 collect 8 assemble

complacence see complacency

complacency 5 pride 6 egoism 7 conceit, egotism 9 vainglory 10 narcissism

11 amour propre, consequence 13 conceitedness

complacent 4 smug 7 assured 8 egoistic, priggish 9 conceited, confident, egotistic 11 self-assured, self-pleased 13 self-confident, self-contented, self-possessed, self-satisfied

complain 3 nag 4 beef, crab, fuss, kick, wail 5 gripe, grump, whine 6 grouch, grouse, murmur, pester, repine, yammer 7 grizzle, grumble, protest 9 bellyache

complainer 4 crab 5 crank 6 griper, grouch, kicker 7 grouser 8 grumbler, sourpuss 10 malcontent 11 faultfinder

complaint 3 ill 5 gripe 6 malady 7 ailment, disease, protest 8 disorder, sickness, syndrome 9 affection, condition, infirmity

complaisant 4 easy, mild 7 amiable, lenient 8 generous, obliging 9 agreeable, indulgent 11 good-humored, good-natured 12 good-tempered

complement 4 crew 7 pendant 9 correlate 10 enrichment, supplement 11 counterpart, enhancement 12 augmentation 13 accompaniment

complementary *prefix:* 7 counter

complete 3 end 4 done, full, halt 5 close, ended, gross, total, uncut, utter, whole 6 choate, entire, finish, wind up, wrap up 7 achieve, fulfill, perfect, perform, plenary, through 8 absolute, conclude, finished, integral, outright, realized, thorough, totalize, ultimate, undocked, whole-hog 9 concluded, determine, discharge, downright, full-dress, implement, out-and-out, terminate 10 accomplish, consummate, exhaustive, terminated, unabridged 11 uncondensed, unmitigated 13 thoroughgoing, unabbreviated *combining form:* 3 hol, tel 4 holo, tele, telo 5 teleo

completed 4 done, over 5 ended 7 through 8 finished 9 concluded 10 terminated

completion 3 end 6 finish *combining form:* 6 teleut 7 teleuto

complex 5 vague 6 daedal, knotty, system, varied 7 gordian, mixed-up, network, obscure 8 baffling, compound, confused, involved, puzzling 9 Byzantine, composite, confusing, elaborate, intricate 10 mysterious, mystifying, perplexing 11 bewildering, complicated, confounding 12 labyrinthine 13 heterogeneous, sophisticated

complexion 3 hue 4 tint 5 color, humor, tinge 6 makeup, nature, temper 8 tincture 9 character 11 disposition, personality, temperament 13 individualism, individuality

complexionless 4 ashy, pale 5 ashen, livid, lurid, waxen 6 doughy, pallid 8 blanched 9 colorless

compliance 8 docility 9 obedience
10 conformity 11 amenability, resignation
12 acquiescence, tractability
complicate 5 mix up, ravel, snarl, upset
6 jumble, muddle, tangle 7 perplex 8 disorder, entangle 10 disarrange
complicated 4 hard 5 fancy 6 daedal,
knotty 7 complex, gordian 8 abstruse,
involved 9 Byzantine, elaborate, intricate,
recondite 12 labyrinthine 13 sophisticated
complicity 9 collusion 10 connivance
11 involvement
compliment 4 hail, kudo, laud 6 kudize,
praise 7 acclaim, applaud, bouquet, commend, orchids, tribute 8 accolade, encomium 9 laudation, recommend 12 commendation
complimentary 4 free 6 gratis 8 costless 10 chargeless, gratuitous
comply 4 keep, mind, obey 6 follow, submit 7 conform, observe 9 acquiesce
component 4 part 6 factor 7 element
10 ingredient 11 constituent
comport 3 act 4 bear, go on, quit
5 agree, carry, check, fit in, tally 6 accord,
acquit, behave, demean, square 7 conduct
8 dovetail 9 harmonize 10 correspond
comportment 3 air, set 4 mien 5 tenue
7 address, bearing, conduct 8 behavior,
demeanor, presence
compose 4 balm, calm, cool, form, lull,
make, rein 5 allay, quiet, relax, still, verse,
write 6 becalm, create, devise, indite,
invent, make up, settle, solace, soothe
7 collect, comfort, console, contain, control,
dream up, repress, versify 8 comprise, melodize, mitigate, moderate, modulate,
restrain, suppress, tune down 9 originate,
re-collect 10 constitute, simmer down
11 tranquilize *type:* 3 set
composed 4 calm, cool, easy 5 quiet,
staid, still 6 placid, poised, sedate, serene
8 tranquil 9 collected, easygoing, possessed, repressed, unruffled 10 nonchalant, suppressed 11 unflappable
13 imperturbable, self-possessed
composer 4 bard, poet 5 odist 6 author,
lyrist, penman, scorer, writer 7 elegist,
hymnist 8 compiler, essayist, lyricist, melodist, monodist, novelist 9 balladist, dramatist, harmonist, scenarist, songsmith, tunesmith, wordsmith 10 compositor, typesetter
American: 3 Kay (Hershy, Ulysses)
4 Cage (John), Hill (Edward Burlingame,
Jackson), Ives (Charles), Kern (Jerome),
Work (Henry Clay) 5 Arlen (Harold), Bland
(James), Bloch (Ernest), Cohan (George
M.), Dylan (Bob), Friml (Rudolf), Glass
(Philip), Gould (Morton), Grofé (Ferde),
Handy (William Christopher), Loewe (Fred-

erick), Mason (Daniel Gregory, Lowell),
Moore (Douglas), Sousa (John Philip), Still
(William Grant) 6 Barber (Samuel), Berlin
(Irving), Cowell (Henry), Emmett (Daniel),
Foster (Stephen), Hanson (Howard), Harris
(Roy), Joplin (Scott), McKuen (Rod), Morton (Ferdinand Joseph "Jelly Roll"), Oliver
(Joe"King"), Parker (Charlie "Bird," Horatio), Piston (Walter), Porter (Cole), Seeger
(Charles, Pete), Taylor (Deems, James),
Varese (Edgar) 7 Babbitt (Milton), Brubeck
(Dave), Copland (Aaron), Gilbert (Henry F.),
Gilmore (Patrick), Goldman (Edwin), Guthrie (Arlo, Woody), Herbert (Victor), Loesser
(Frank), Maxwell (Elsa), Menotti (Gian-
Carlo), Rodgers (Richard), Romberg (Sigmund), Schuman (Willian), Thomson (Virgil), Tiomkin (Dimitri) 8 Billings (William),
Burleigh (Henry Thacker), Damrosch (Leopold, Walter), Gershwin (George, Ira), Kreisler (Fritz), Sessions (Roger), Sondheim
(Stephen), Spalding (Albert), Williams (Clarence, Bert, Hank, John) 9 Bacharach
(Burt), Bernstein (Elmer, Leonard), Ellington
(Duke), Ledbetter (Huddie "Leadbelly"),
MacDowell (Edward) 10 Blitzstein (Marc),
Gottschalk (Louis Moreau) *Argentinian:*
9 Ginastera (Alberto) *Australian:* 8 Grainger (Percy) *Austrian:* 4 Berg (Alban), Wolf
(Hugo) 5 Haydn (Joseph) 6 Czerny (Karl),
Mahler (Gustav), Mozart (Leopold, Wolfgang Amadeus), Straus (Oscar), Sulzer
(Salomon), Webern (Anton von) 7 Strauss
(Eduard, Johann, Josef, Richard) 8 Bruckner (Anton), Schubert (Franz) 9 Schönberg
(Arnold) *Belgian:* 5 Ysaye (Eugene-
Auguste) *Brazilian:* 10 Villa-Lobos (Heitor)
Czech: 3 Suk (Josef) 6 Dvořák (Antonín)
7 Janáček (Leoš), Kubelik (Jan, Rafael),
Smetana (Bedřich) *Danish:* 7 Nielsen
(Carl) *Dutch:* 9 Sweelinck (Jan) *English:*
4 Arne (Thomas), Byrd (William) 5 Elgar
(Edward William) 6 Delius (Frederick), Morley (Thomas), Tallis (Thomas), Walton (William), Wesley (Charles, Samuel) 7 Britten
(Benjamin), Dowland (John), Gibbons
(Orlando), Purcell (Henry), Weelkes
(Thomas) 8 Sullivan (Arthur) 11 Lloyd
Webber (Andrew) *Finnish:* 8 Palmgren
(Selim), Sibelius (Jean) *Flemish:* 5 Dufay
(Guillaume), Lasso (Orlando di) 6 Lassus
(Orlande de) 8 Willaert (Adriaan) *French:*
4 Indy (Vincent d'), Lalo (Edouard) 5 Auber
(Esprit), Bizet (Georges), Dukas (Paul-
Abraham), Fauré (Gabriel-Urbain), Ibert
(Jacques), Jarre (Maurice), Lully (Jean-
Baptiste), Ravel (Maurice), Satie (Erik),
Widor (Charles-Marie) 6 Boulez (Pierre),
Campra (Andre), Franck (Cesar), Gounod
(Charles-François), Rameau (Jean-Phi-

lippe), Thomas (Ambroise) 7 Berlioz (Hector), Debussy (Claude), Delibes (Leo), Milhaud (Darius), Poulenc (Francis) 8 Chabrier (Emmanuel), Couperin (Francois, Louis), Honegger (Arthur), Massenet (Jules), Messiaen (Olivier) 9 Offenbach (Jacques) *German:* 4 Bach (Carl Philipp, Johann Christian, Johann Christoph, Johann Sebastian, Wilhelm Friedmann, Wilhelm Friedrich), Orff (Carl) 5 Bruch (Max), Gluck (Christoph), Reger (Max), Spohr (Louis), Weber (Carl Maria von), Weill (Kurt) 6 Brahms (Johannes), Handel (George Frideric), Schutz (Heinrich), Vogler (Abt), Wagner (Richard, Siegfried) 7 Hassler (Hans Leo), Richter (Ernst, Franz), Silcher (Friedrich), Strauss (Richard) 8 Schumann (Georg, Robert), Telemann (Georg Philipp) 9 Beethoven (Ludwig van), Buxtehude (Dietrich), Hindemith (Paul), Meyerbeer (Giacomo) 10 Praetorius (Michael) 11 Humperdinck (Engelbert), Mendelssohn (Felix), Stockhausen (Karlheinz) *Hungarian:* 5 Lehar (Franz), Liszt (Franz) 6 Bartok (Bela), Kodaly (Zoltan), Ligeti (Gyorgy) 8 Dohnanyi (Erno) *Italian:* 4 Peri (Jacopo) 5 Boito (Arrigo), Verdi (Giuseppe), Vinci (Leonardo) 6 Busoni (Ferruccio), Viotti (Giovanni), Vitali (Giovanni) 7 Bellini (Vincenzo), Corelli (Arcangelo), Martini (Padre), Puccini (Giacomo), Rossini (Gioacchino), Tartini (Giuseppe), Vivaldi (Antonio) 8 Clementi (Muzio), Gabrieli (Andrea, Giovanni), Mascagni (Pietro), Paganini (Niccolo), Respighi (Ottorino) 9 Cherubini (Luigi), Donizetti (Gaetano), Pergolesi (Giovanni), Scarlatti (Alessandro, Giuseppe), Tommasini (Vincenzo) 10 Boccherini (Luigi), Monteverdi (Claudio), Palestrina (Giovanni da), Ponchielli (Amilcare), Zingarelli (Niccolo) 11 Frescobaldi (Girolamo), Leoncavallo (Ruggero) 12 Dallapiccola (Luigi) *Mexican:* 6 Chavez (Carlos) *Norwegian:* 5 Grieg (Edvard), Olsen (Sparre) *Polish:* 6 Chopin (Frederic) 10 Paderewski (Ignacy), Penderecki (Krzysztof), Wieniawski (Henryk) *Romanian:* 7 Xenakis (Iannis) *Russian:* 6 Glinka (Mikhail) 7 Borodin (Aleksandr) 8 Glazunov (Aleksandr), Scriabin (Aleksandr) 9 Prokofiev (Sergey) 10 Mussorgsky (Modest), Rubinstein (Anton), Stravinsky (Igor), Tcherepnin (Nikolay) 11 Tchaikovsky (Pyotr Ilich) 12 Rachmaninoff (Sergey), Shostakovich (Dmitry) *Spanish:* 5 Falla (Manuel de), Vives (Amadeo) 6 Garcia (Manuel) 7 Albéniz (Isaac) 8 Granados (Enrique), Victoria (Tomas Luis de)

composite 3 mix 6 hybrid 7 amalgam, complex, compost, mixture, montage

8 compound 9 immixture 10 commixture 11 combination 12 amalgamation, intermixture

composition 5 essay, paper, theme 6 design, makeup 7 article, morceau, writing 8 fantasia 9 formation 10 compromise 12 architecture, constitution, construction *choral:* 5 motet *for eight:* 5 octet *for five:* 7 quintet *for four:* 7 quartet *for nine:* 5 nonet *for one:* 4 solo 5 scena *for seven:* 6 septet *for six:* 6 sextet *for three:* 4 trio *for two:* 4 duet 6 duetto *instrumental:* 3 jig 4 reel 5 étude, fugue, gigue, march, rondo, suite 6 sonata 7 caprice, partita, prelude, scherzo 8 allemand, concerto, fantasia, overture, rhapsody, saraband, sinfonia, symphony, tone poem 9 capriccio, sarabande 10 intermezzo *vocal:* 4 aria, lied, mass, song 5 canon, carol, chant, motet, opera, round 6 arioso, ballad, chorus 7 cantata, chanson, chantey, chorale, lullaby, requiem 8 berceuse, madrigal, oratorio 9 barcarole, plainsong, spiritual 12 cantus firmus

compos mentis 4 sane 5 lucid 6 normal

composure 6 phlegm 7 ataraxy 8 calmness, coolness 9 sangfroid 10 equanimity

compound 3 mix 4 join, link 5 admix, alloy, blend, boost, immix, unite 6 commix, couple, expand, extend, fusion, make up, mingle 7 amalgam, augment, bracket, complex, compost, connect, enlarge, magnify, mixture 8 coagment, coalesce, comingle, heighten, increase, intermix, multiply 9 admixture, associate, coadunate, commingle, composite 10 aggrandize, commixture 11 intermingle 12 amalgamation *aromatic:* 7 depside *chemical:* (see at chemical) *combining form:* 5 genin *medicinal:* 7 quassin 8 magnesia *protein:* 7 peptone *sulfur:* 5 thiol 6 sulfid 7 sulfide, sulfone 8 sulfonal, sulfuryl, sulphide, sulphone *volatile:* 8 cymogene

comprehend 3 dig, get, see 4 know 5 catch, grasp 6 accept, embody, fathom, take in 7 cognize, compass, contain, embrace, include, involve, subsume 8 perceive 9 encompass 10 appreciate, understand

comprehendible 5 lucid 8 knowable, luminous 9 graspable 10 fathomable 12 intelligible 13 apprehensible

comprehensible see comprehendible

comprehensive 4 full, wide 5 broad 6 global 7 general, overall 8 sweeping 9 all-around, inclusive 12 encyclopedic

comprehensiveness 5 scope 7 breadth 8 fullness, wideness 9 amplitude

compress 3 jam 4 bear, cram, push 5 crowd, crush, press, stupe 6 shrink, squash, squish **7** bandage, compact, pledget, squeeze **8** condense, contract, laminate **9** constrict **11** concentrate

comprise **4** form, make **6** make up **7** compose, contain, include **10** constitute

compromise **4** mean, pact, risk **5** peril **6** hazard, menace **7** bargain, compact, imperil, jeopard **8** contract, endanger, jeopardy **9** agreement, middle way **10** golden mean, jeopardize **11** composition **12** middle ground

compulsion **4** itch, need, urge **5** drive, force **6** duress **8** coercion, exigency, violence **9** necessity **10** constraint

compulsory **8** required **9** imperious, mandatory **10** imperative, obligatory

compunction **3** rue **4** ruth **5** demur, qualm **6** squeam **7** penance, remorse, scruple **9** attrition, hesitancy, penitence, penitency **10** conscience, contrition, hesitation, repentance **12** contriteness

compunctious **5** sorry **8** contrite, penitent **9** regretful, repentant **10** apologetic, remorseful **11** attritional, penitential

computation **8** figuring **9** ciphering, reckoning **10** arithmetic, estimation **11** calculation

compute **5** total **6** cipher, figure, reckon **8** estimate **9** calculate

computer **6** abacus **7** machine **10** calculator **13** adding machine *data:* **7** readout **8** printout, software *information:* **4** data *instruction:* **5** macro *inventor:* **7** Babbage (Charles) *language:* **5** ALGOL, BASIC, COBOL **7** FORTRAN *operator:* **9** programmer **10** programmer *printer:* **5** laser **9** dot matrix *type:* **6** analog **7** digital

comrade **3** pal **4** ally, chum, mate **5** buddy, crony **6** comate, fellow, frater **7** brother, consort **8** tovarich, tovarish **9** associate, communist, companion

comstock **4** prig **5** prude **6** Grundy **7** puritan **8** bluenose **9** Mrs. Grundy, nice Nelly **10** goody-goody

con **4** anti, bilk, coax, dupe, fool, hoax, scam, view **5** learn, study, trick **6** befool, cajole, gammon, inmate, survey **7** blarney, canvass, chicane, convict, deceive, examine, inspect, opposer, swindle, wheedle **8** blandish, flimflam, hoodwink, jailbird, memorize, opponent, opposure, prisoner, soft soap **9** adversary, bamboozle, check over, oppugnant, sweet-talk **10** antagonism, antagonist, antithesis, opposition, scrutinize **11** contrariety, hornswoggle

concatenate **4** join, link **5** unite **7** connect **9** integrate **10** articulate

concave **6** arched **7** vaulted **8** bowlike **9** depressed *combining form:* **7** coelous

concavity **3** dip, sag **4** bowl, dent, sink **5** basin **6** hollow **7** sinkage **8** sinkhole **10** depression

conceal **4** bury, hide, veil **5** cache, cloak, cover, stash **6** occult, screen **7** secrete **8** ensconce, enshroud, palliate **10** camouflage

concealed **5** privy **6** buried, covert, hidden, secret **7** guarded **8** obscured, shrouded, ulterior **11** clandestine *combining form:* **4** adel **5** adelo

concede **3** own **4** avow **5** admit, allow, award, grant, let on, own up **6** accord, fess up **7** confess **9** vouchsafe **11** acknowledge

conceit **4** idea, whim **5** fancy, freak, humor, image, pride **6** egoism, megrim, notion, vagary, vanity **7** boutade, caprice, concept, egotism, thought **8** crotchet, self-love, smugness, snobbery, vainness **9** self-glory, self-pride, vainglory **10** conception, impression, narcissism, perception, self-esteem **11** amour propre, complacence, complacency, consequence, self-opinion, swelled head **12** apprehension, intellection **13** outrecuidance

conceited **4** vain **6** snobby, snooty **7** pompous, stuck-up **8** snobbish **12** narcissistic, vainglorious

conceitedness **6** vanity **8** self-love, vainness **9** vainglory **10** narcissism, self-esteem **11** amour propre

conceivable **6** likely, mortal **7** earthly **8** possible, probable **9** thinkable **10** imaginable, supposable

conceive **4** form, make **5** beget, fancy, grasp, think **6** accept, assume, expect, follow, gather, ponder, vision **7** believe, compass, feature, imagine, realize, suppose, suspect **8** cogitate, envisage, envision, meditate, ruminate **9** apprehend, speculate, visualize **10** comprehend, excogitate, understand

concentrate **3** fix **4** heap, mass, meet, pile **5** focus, rivet, unify **6** fasten, fixate, gather, shrink **7** collect, compact **8** assemble, compress, condense, contract, converge **9** constrict, integrate **11** consolidate

concentrated **5** fixed, lusty, whole **6** fierce, potent, robust, strong **7** furious, intense **8** vehement **9** exclusive, exquisite, undivided **10** full-bodied, unswerving **12** undistracted

concentrating **8** unifying **10** compacting **11** centripetal, integrative **12** centralizing **13** consolidating

concentration **4** heed **5** study **6** debate **9** attention **11** application **12** deliberation **13** consideration

concept 4 idea 5 image 6 notion 7 conceit, thought 10 impression, perception 12 apprehension, intellection

conception 4 idea 5 image, start 6 notion 7 conceit, thought 9 beginning 10 impression, perception 12 apprehension, intellection

conceptual 5 ideal 8 abstract, notional 9 imaginary, visionary 10 ideational 12 transcendent

concern 4 care, firm, heed 5 doubt, worry 6 affair, gadget, matter, outfit, regard, unease, wonder 7 anxiety, company, dubiety, lookout, palaver 8 business, disquiet, interest, mistrust 9 attention, curiosity, dubiosity, misgiving, occasions, suspicion 10 enterprise, inquietude, skepticism, solicitude, uneasiness 11 carefulness, disquietude, heedfulness, incertitude, uncertainty, uncertitude 12 apprehension 13 consciousness, consideration, establishment

concerned 8 affected, involved 10 implicated, interested

concerning 2 re 4 as to, in re 5 about, anent, as for 7 against, apropos 9 as regards, regarding 10 respecting

concert 4 tune 5 agree 6 accord, chorus, concur, settle 7 arrange, benefit, concord, harmony, recital 8 coincide 9 cooperate, harmonize, negotiate 10 consonance 11 performance

concert hall 5 odeon, odeum 10 auditorium

concession 5 favor 6 gambit 9 allowance, privilege 10 compromise 12 acquiescence

conch 5 shell 6 mussel 7 mollusk

concierge 6 porter, warden 7 doorman, janitor 9 custodian 10 doorkeeper

conciliate 4 calm, ease 5 quiet 6 pacify, soothe 7 appease, assuage, mollify, placate, sweeten 10 propitiate 11 tranquilize

concise 4 curt 5 brief, pithy, short, terse 7 compact, laconic, summary 8 abridged, succinct 9 condensed 10 compressed, contracted 11 compendiary, compendious 12 breviloquent 13 short and sweet

conclude 3 end 4 draw, halt, rule, stop 5 close, infer, judge 6 decide, deduce, deduct, derive, figure, finish, gather, reason, settle, wind up, wrap up 7 collect, resolve 8 complete, ultimate 9 determine, terminate

concluding 4 last 5 final 6 latest, latter 7 closing 8 eventual, hindmost, terminal, ultimate

conclusion 3 end 4 stop 5 cease, close, finis 6 ending, epilog, finale, finish, period, windup 7 closing, closure 8 decision, epilogue, illation, judgment, sequitur 9 cessation, deduction, inference 10 desistance, resolution, settlement 11 termination 13 determination, ratiocination

conclusive 4 last 5 final 6 cogent 7 telling 8 deciding, decisive 10 compelling, convincing, definitive 11 determinant, determinate, irrefutable 12 irrefragable, unanswerable

concoct 3 mix 4 brew, cook 5 frame, hatch 6 cook up, create, devise, invent, make up, vamp up 7 dream up, hatch up 8 conceive, contrive 9 formulate, originate

concomitant 4 mate 6 fellow 7 consort 8 adjuvant, incident 9 accessory, ancillary, associate, attendant, attending, companion, satellite 10 coincident, collateral 12 accompanying 13 accompaniment, supplementary

concord 4 pact, tune 5 agree, chime, unity 6 accord, chorus, concur, treaty 7 concert, harmony, rapport 8 coincide 9 agreement, harmonize 10 consonance, convention

concordance 4 tune 5 chime 6 accord 7 harmony 9 agreement 10 consonance

concordant 8 agreeing 9 congruous 10 harmonious

concourse 6 throng 7 joining, meeting 8 junction 9 gathering 10 concursion, confluence

concrete 3 set 4 join, link 5 beton, solid, unite 6 couple, harden 7 bracket, combine, congeal, connect 8 coalesce, compound, indurate, solidify 9 associate *component:* 4 sand 5 water 6 gravel

concubine 7 hetaera, hetaira, odalisk 8 mistress 9 odalisque

concupiscence 4 lust 6 desire 7 passion 9 eroticism, prurience, pruriency 10 aphrodisia 11 lustfulness 13 lickerishness

concupiscent 3 hot 7 goatish, lustful, satyric 8 prurient 9 lickerish 10 lascivious, libidinous, passionate

concur 4 band, jibe 5 agree, unite 6 accord, league 7 combine, concert, concord, conjoin, go along 8 coadjute, coincide 9 cooperate, harmonize

concurrent 6 coeval 10 coetaneous, coexistent, coexisting, synchronal, synchronic 11 synchronous 12 contemporary, simultaneous

concurrently 6 at once 8 together 12 coincidently

concuss 3 jar 4 rock 5 force, shake, shock 6 coerce, compel, oblige 7 agitate, shotgun 8 convulse 9 constrain

concussion 3 jar 4 bump, jolt 5 clash, clout, crash, shock, smack 6 impact

7 beating, jarring, jolting, shaking 8 pounding 9 buffeting, collision

condemn 3 rap 4 damn, doom 5 blame, decry, knock 7 censure, convict 8 denounce, sentence 9 criticize, proscribe, reprehend, reprobate 10 denunciate

condensation 3 dew 5 brief 7 epitome, summary 8 abstract, boildown, breviary, breviate, synopsis 10 abridgment, conspectus

condense 3 sum 5 sum up 6 digest, reduce, shrink 7 abridge, capsule, compact, shorten, summate 8 boil down, compress, contract 9 capsulize, constrict, epitomize, inventory, summarize, synopsize 10 abbreviate 11 concentrate, consolidate

condescend 5 deign, stoop 6 unbend

condign 3 due, fit 4 fair, just 5 right 7 merited 8 deserved, rightful, suitable 9 requisite 11 appropriate 13 rhadamanthine

condiment 3 soy 4 salt 5 caper, curry, sauce, spice 6 catsup, pepper, relish 7 chutney, ketchup, mustard, paprika, vinegar 8 dressing, turmeric 9 seasoning 10 mayonnaise

condition 2 if 3 ill 4 case, mode 5 order, shape, state, terms 6 estate, fettle, kilter, malady, repair, status 7 ailment, disease, fitness, posture, proviso, strings 8 disorder, sickness, syndrome 9 affection, complaint, essential, exception, infirmity, necessity, provision, requisite, situation 10 limitation, sine qua non 11 requirement, reservation, stipulation 12 prerequisite 13 qualification *suffix:* 2 or, th, ty 3 dom, ery, ice, ile, ion, ism 4 ance, ancy, ence, ency, ment, ness, oses (plural), osis, ship 5 ation

conditional 4 iffy 7 reliant 8 relative 9 dependent, provisory, qualified, tentative, uncertain 10 contingent, restricted 11 provisional 12 provisionary

condolence 3 rue 4 pity, ruth 8 sympathy 10 compassion 13 commiseration

condonable 7 tenable 9 excusable, tolerable 10 acceptable, defensible, vindicable 11 justifiable, warrantable

condone 5 remit 6 excuse, pardon 7 forgive 8 overlook

conduce 4 lead, tend 7 redound 10 contribute

conduct 3 act, run 4 bear, care, head, lead, quit, show 5 guide, pilot, route, steer, tenue, usher 6 acquit, attend, behave, charge, convey, convoy, demean, deport, direct, escort, funnel, handle, keep up, manage, ordain 7 arrange, carry on, channel, company, comport, control, operate, oversee, running, traject 8 behavior, chaperon, handling, shepherd, transmit 9 accompany,

companion, oversight, supervise 10 administer, deportment, intendance, management 11 comportment, supervision

conductor 5 guide 6 copper, escort, leader 7 maestro 8 conveyor, director, motorman 10 bandleader, impresario *American:* 4 Shaw (Robert) 5 Grofé (Ferde), Stock (Frederick August), Szell (George) 6 Levine (James), Maazel (Lorin), Previn (André), Reiner (Fritz), Thomas (Theodore, Michael Tilson), Walter (Bruno) 7 Fiedler (Arthur), Monteux (Pierre), Ormandy (Eugene) 8 Damrosch (Leopold, Walter), Williams (John) 9 Bernstein (Elmer, Leonard), Leinsdorf (Erich), Rodzinski (Artur), Steinberg (William), Stokowski (Leopold) 11 Kostelanetz (Andre), Mitropoulos (Dimitri) *Australian:* 7 Bonynge (Richard) *Austrian:* 4 Bohm (Karl) 6 Mahler (Gustav) 10 von Karajan (Herbert) *Belgian:* 5 Ysaye (Eugene-Auguste) *British:* 5 Solti (Georg) *Canadian:* 9 MacMillan (Ernest) *Czech:* 7 Kubelik (Jan, Rafael) *English:* 4 Wood (Henry) 5 Boult (Adrian) 7 Beecham (Thomas), Malcolm (George), Sargent (Malcolm) 8 Goossens (Eugene) 10 Barbirolli (John) *French:* 5 Munch (Charles) 6 Boulez (Pierre), Pretre (Georges) *German:* 4 Muck (Carl) 5 Spohr (Louis), Weber (Carl Maria von) 9 Klemperer (Otto), Scherchen (Herman) 11 Furtwangler (Wilhelm), Mendelssohn (Felix) *Hungarian:* 5 Seidl (Anton) 7 Nikisch (Arthur), Richter (Hans) *Indian:* 5 Mehta (Zubin) *Italian:* 6 Abbado (Claudio) 9 Toscanini (Arturo) *Japanese:* 5 Ozawa (Seiji) *Mexican:* 6 Chavez (Carlos) *Russian:* 12 Koussevitzky (Serge) *Spanish:* 6 Iturbi (Jose) *Swiss:* 8 Ansermet (Ernest) *stick:* 5 baton *suffix:* 3 eer

conduit 4 duct, main, pipe 5 canal 6 course 7 channel 8 aqueduct, penstock, pipeline 11 watercourse

coney 4 pika 5 hyrax 6 rabbit 10 butterfish

confab 4 chat 5 treat 6 advise, confer, huddle, parley, powwow 7 consult 8 collogue

confabulate see confab

confabulation 3 rap 4 chat, talk 6 parley 8 colloquy, converse, dialogue 10 conference, discussion 12 conversation, deliberation

confection see candy

confederacy 5 union 6 league 8 alliance 9 anschluss, coalition 10 federation

confederate 3 reb 4 ally 5 rebel, unite 6 fellow 7 abettor, partner 8 conspire 9 accessory, associate, colleague 10 accomplice 11 conspirator 12 collaborator 13 coconspirator *admiral:* 6 Semmes *capital:* 8 Richmond *color:* 4 gray *general:* 3 Lee (Robert E.) 4 Hill (Ambrose), Hood (John Bell) 5 Bragg (Braxton), Ewell (Richard Stoddart), Price (Sterling), Smith (Edmund Kirby) 6 Morgan (John Hunt), Stuart (James Ewell Brown) 7 Forrest (Nathan Bedford), Hampton (Wade), Jackson (Thomas Jonathan "Stonewall"), Pickett (George) 8 Johnston (Albert Sidney, Joseph Eggleston) 9 Pemberton (John Clifford) 10 Beauregard (Pierre G. T.), Longstreet (James) *president:* 5 Davis (Jefferson) *soldier:* 9 butternut *spy:* 4 Boyd (Belle) *vice-president:* 8 Stephens (Alexander Hamilton)

confederation see **confederacy**

confer 4 give, meet, talk 5 allot, award, grant, speak, treat 6 accord, advise, bestow, confab, huddle, parley, powwow 7 consult, discuss, present 8 collogue, colloque, converse 10 deliberate 11 confabulate

conference 3 rap 4 loop, talk 5 synod, wheel 6 league, parley, powwow 7 circuit, meeting, palaver, seminar 8 colloquy 9 symposium 10 colloquium, discussion, rap session, round robin, round table 11 association 12 deliberation 13 confabulation

confess 3 own 4 avow, sing 5 admit, allow, grant, let on, own up 6 reveal 7 concede, divulge 8 disclose 11 acknowledge

confession 5 creed 6 avowal 7 peccavi 9 admission, statement 10 disclosure

confidant 4 mate 5 amigo 6 friend 8 familiar, intimate 11 cater-cousin 12 acquaintance

confide 4 tell 6 bestow, commit 7 breathe, commend, consign, entrust, present, whisper 8 hand over, relegate, turn over

confidence 4 gall, hope 5 brass, cheek, faith, nerve, stock, trust 6 aplomb, surety 7 courage 8 reliance, sureness 9 assurance, brashness, certainty, certitude, self-trust 10 conviction, dependence, effrontery, equanimity 11 assuredness *game:* 4 scam 5 bunco, bunko, grift, sting 7 swindle

confidence man 3 gyp 7 diddler, grifter, sharper, sharpie 8 swindler 9 defrauder, trickster 11 bunco artist 12 bunco steerer

confident 4 bold, sure 5 brash, brave, cocky, perky, pushy 6 secure, uppity 7 assured, certain, pushful 8 cocksure, fearless, intrepid, positive, sanguine, trustful, unafraid 9 dauntless, presuming, undaunted 10 brassbound, courageous, undoubtful 11 overweening, self-assured,

self-reliant 12 presumptuous 13 self-assertive, self-possessed

confidential 5 close, privy, thick 6 chummy, closet, hushed, inside, secret 7 private 8 familiar, intimate 9 auricular

configuration 4 cast, form 5 shape 6 figure 7 contour, outline, pattern 12 conformation

confine 3 bar, box, end, mew, pen 4 cage, coop, crib, jail, term 5 bound, cramp, limit, orbit, range, reach, scope, sweep 6 embank, encage, extent, immure, intern, radius 7 delimit, enclose, pinfold, purview 8 bastille, boundary, imprison, localize, prelimit, restrict 9 constrain, periphery 10 delimitate, limitation 11 incarcerate 12 circumscribe 13 circumference

confinement 5 cramp 7 lying-in 8 childbed 9 captivity, restraint 10 constraint 11 restriction 12 accouchement, imprisonment 13 constrainment

confines 6 bounds, limits 7 compass 8 boundary, environs, purlieus 9 precincts

confirm 3 fix, set 4 back 5 check, prove, vouch 6 attest, ratify, uphold, verify 7 bear out, certify, justify, support 8 check out, validate 11 corroborate 12 authenticate, substantiate

confirmation 5 proof 7 witness 8 evidence 9 testament, testimony 11 attestation, testimonial

confirmed 3 set 5 fixed, sworn 7 chronic, settled 8 deep-dyed, definite, habitual, ratified 9 hard-shell 10 accustomed, deep-rooted, deep-seated, entrenched, habituated, inveterate 13 bred-in-the-bone, dyed-in-the-wool

confiscate 4 take 5 annex, seize, usurp 7 escheat, preempt 8 accroach, arrogate 9 sequester 10 commandeer 11 appropriate, expropriate

confiture 3 jam 8 conserve, preserve

conflagrant 5 afire, fiery 6 ablaze, aflame, alight 7 blazing, burning, flaming, flaring, ignited

conflagration 4 fire 5 blaze 7 inferno 9 holocaust

conflict 3 jar, war 4 bout, duel, meet, rift, vary 5 clash, fight 6 battle, combat, differ, jangle, oppose, strife 7 contest, discord, dispute, dissent, meeting, rivalry, warfare 8 argument, concours, disagree, disunity, mismatch, striving, struggle, tug-of-war, variance 9 disaccord, emulation, encounter, rencontre 10 contention, difference, dissension, dissidence 11 competition, controversy 12 disharmonize

conflicting 7 warring 8 clashing, contrary 9 dissonant 10 contending, discordant, discrepant 11 contrariant, incongruent, incongruous, inconsonant 12 antagonistic, antipathetic, disconsonant, incompatible, inconsistent, inharmonious

confluence 7 meeting 8 junction 9 concourse, gathering 10 concursion

conform 3 fit 4 jibe, mind, obey, suit, tune 5 adapt, agree, fit in, yield 6 accord, adjust, attune, comply, follow, square, submit, tailor 7 observe 8 dovetail, quadrate 9 acquiesce, harmonize, integrate, reconcile 10 coordinate, correspond, proportion, tailor-make 11 accommodate 12 reconciliate

conformable 6 fitted, suited 7 adapted, matched 8 assorted, suitable

conformation 4 cast, form 5 shape 6 figure 13 configuration

conforming 4 nice, typy 5 typey 6 decent, proper, seemly 7 uniform 8 becoming, decorous 9 befitting, civilized 11 comme il faut

conformity 7 decorum, harmony 8 affinity, legalism, normalcy 9 coherence, congruity, obedience 10 compliance, submission 11 consistency, resignation 12 acquiescence

confound 3 mix 4 faze, pose, stun 5 abash, befog, evert, mix up, rebut 6 baffle, puzzle, rattle, refute 7 confuse, confute, misdeem, mistake, perplex, stumble, stupefy 8 bewilder, disprove 9 discomfit, dumbfound, embarrass 10 controvert, disconcert, disconfirm 11 misidentify 13 metagrobolize

confounded 4 rank 5 agape, gross, utter 6 aghast, blamed, cursed, cussed, damned 7 blasted, blessed, shocked 8 absolute, dismayed, infernal, outright 9 consarned, dad-burned, execrable, out-and-out 11 dumbfounded, overwhelmed, straightout, unmitigated 13 thunderstruck

confrere see **colleague**

confront 4 defy, face, meet 5 brave 6 accost, breast, oppose 9 challenge, encounter

Confucian way of life: 3 tao

confuse 3 fog, mix 4 blur, faze, mull, pose, warp 5 abash, addle, befog, cloud, dizzy, mix up, muddy, twist, upset, wrest 6 baffle, ball up, bemuse, flurry, foul up, fuddle, garble, jumble, mess up, muddle, puzzle, rattle, wrench 7 agitate, becloud, derange, disrupt, distort, flummox, fluster, misdeem, mislead, mistake, nonplus, perplex, perturb, pervert, snarl up 8 bedazzle, befuddle, bewilder, confound, disorder, disquiet, distract, throw off, unsettle 9 discomfit, embarrass 10 disarrange, discompose, disconcert 11 disorganize, misidentify 12 misrepresent 13 metagrobolize

confused 4 lost 5 muddy, muzzy, vague 7 at a loss, mixed up 9 perplexed 10 bewildered, topsy-turvy 12 disconcerted

confusion 3 din 4 flap, loss, mess, muck, ruin, stew 5 babel, chaos, havoc, mix-up, snafu, snarl 6 ataxia, bedlam, dither, foul-up, hubbub, huddle, jumble, lather, muddle, pother, tumult, unease 7 clutter, turmoil 8 disarray, disorder, misorder, pell-mell 9 abashment, agitation, commotion, ruination 10 hullabaloo, turbulence, uneasiness 11 bedevilment, derangement, destruction, devastation, disturbance, pandemonium 12 discomfiture, discomposure, razzle-dazzle 13 disconcertion, embarrassment

confute 4 deny 5 break, evert, rebut 8 confound, disprove 10 controvert, disconfirm

congé 3 bow 5 adieu 7 good-bye, parting 8 farewell 9 dismissal 11 leave-taking

congeal 3 dry, gel, set 4 cake, clot, curd, jell 5 jelly 6 curdle, gelate, harden 7 jellify, stiffen, thicken 8 concrete, indurate, solidify 9 coagulate 10 gelatinize

congener 3 ilk 4 kind, sort, type 5 class, genus

congenial 4 good, nice 6 amical, social 7 affable, cordial, kindred, welcome 8 amicable, friendly, gracious, pleasant, pleasing, sociable 9 agreeable, congruous, consonant, favorable 10 compatible, consistent, gratifying, harmonious 11 cooperative, pleasurable, sympathetic 13 companionable

congenital 6 inborn, inbred, innate, native 7 connate, natural 8 inherent 9 essential, ingrained, inherited, intrinsic 10 connatural, deep-seated, indigenous, indwelling, unacquired

conger 3 eel 4 pike

congeries 4 ruck 5 group 6 muster 7 company 8 assembly 9 gathering 10 assemblage, collection 11 aggregation 12 congregation

congest 3 jam 4 clog, fill, plug, stop 5 block, choke, close, crowd 7 occlude 8 obstruct

conglobate 4 ball 5 round 6 sphere 8 ensphere

conglomerate 4 heap, mass, pool 5 chain, group, mixed, trust 6 cartel, motley, varied 7 combine 8 assorted, chowchow 9 aggregate, syndicate 11 aggregation, promiscuous 12 multifarious 13 agglomeration, heterogeneous, miscellaneous

conglomeration 5 hoard, trove 9 aggregate, amassment, colluvies 10 collection, cumulation 11 agglomerate, aggregation 12 accumulation

Congo *capital:* 11 Brazzaville *monetary unit:* 5 franc

congratulate 4 laud 6 salute 10 compliment, felicitate

congregate 4 meet, teem 5 raise, swarm 6 gather, muster 7 collect, convene 8 assemble, congress 9 forgather 10 rendezvous

congregation 4 host, mass, ruck 5 crowd, group 6 muster 7 company, meeting 8 assembly, audience 9 gathering 10 assemblage, collection

congress 4 club, diet 5 guild, synod, union 6 gather, league, muster 7 collect, society 8 assemble, assembly 9 forgather 10 congregate, fellowship, fraternity, parliament, rendezvous 11 association, brotherhood, Capitol Hill, legislature

congressman 7 senator 8 delegate 10 legislator 14 representative

congruity 9 agreement, coherence 10 conformity 11 consistency

congruous 3 apt, fit 7 fitting 9 accordant, agreeable, congenial, consonant 10 compatible, concordant, consistent, harmonious 11 appropriate, sympathetic

conjectural 7 reputed 8 putative, supposed 11 suppositive, suppository 12 hypothetical, suppositious 13 suppositional

conjecture 5 fancy, guess, infer 6 assume, theory 7 presume, pretend, suppose, surmise, suspect 9 inference, speculate 11 speculation, supposition

conjoin 3 wed 4 band, knit, link, yoke 5 unite 6 concur, couple, league, relate 7 combine, connect 8 coadjute 9 associate, cooperate

conjoint 6 common, mutual, public, shared 8 coacting, coactive, communal, conjunct, synergic 10 synergetic 11 coefficient, cooperative, intermutual

conjointly 8 mutually, together

conjointment 5 tie-up, union 6 hookup 7 cahoots, wedding 8 alliance 9 coalition 10 connection 11 affiliation, association, combination, conjunction, partnership

conjugal 6 wedded 7 marital, married, nuptial, spousal 8 hymeneal 9 connubial 11 matrimonial

conjugality 7 wedlock 8 marriage 9 matrimony 12 connubiality

conjugate 4 join, link, yoke 5 yoked 6 couple, joined, linked 7 bracket, combine, conjoin, connect, coupled 8 coalesce 9 associate, connected

conjunct 5 joint 6 common, mutual, public, shared 8 communal 11 intermutual

conjunction 2 as, if, or, so 3 and, but, for, nor, tho, yet 4 as if, lest, than, then, when 5 since, tie-up, union, until, while 6 either, hookup, though, unless, whenas, whilst 7 because, neither, wedding, whereas, whether 8 alliance, although, moreover 9 coalition, therefore 10 connection 11 affiliation, association, combination, partnership 12 conjointment

conjuration 4 rune 5 charm, spell, trick 11 incantation, legerdemain

conjure 3 beg 4 pray 5 brace, crave 6 appeal, invoke 7 beseech, entreat, implore 9 importune 10 supplicate

conjurer 4 mage, seer 5 magus 6 magian, shaman, wizard 7 warlock 8 magician, sorcerer 9 enchanter, trickster, voodooist 11 illusionist, necromancer

conjuring 5 magic 7 sorcery 8 witchery, wizardry 10 necromancy, witchcraft 11 bewitchment, enchantment, legerdemain, thaumaturgy

conk 3 die, hit, rap 4 swat 5 knock 7 decease 8 pass away

con man see **confidence man**

connate 4 akin 6 allied, inborn, native 7 kindred, natural, related 8 incident, inherent 9 elemental, essential, inherited, intrinsic 10 affiliated, congenital, deep-seated, indigenous, indwelling, unacquired 11 consanguine

connatural see **connate**

connect 3 tie, wed 4 bind, join, link, yoke 5 marry, unite 6 attach, bridge, couple, fasten, relate 7 combine, conjoin 9 affiliate, associate, interlock

connected with *suffix:* 3 ast 4 aria 5 arium, orial

Connecticut *academy, college, university:* 4 Yale 7 Trinity 8 Hartford, New Haven, Wesleyan 9 Fairfield 10 Bridgeport, Quinnipiac 11 Sacred Heart, Saint Joseph 12 U.S. Coast Guard *capital:* 8 Hartford *nickname:* 11 Nutmeg State 12 Blue Law State, Constitution State *state bird:* 13 American robin *state flower:* 14 mountain laurel

connection 3 job 4 cult, post, seam, sect, spot 5 creed, joint, nexus, tie-in, tie-up, union 6 billet, hookup 7 joining 8 alliance, coupling, junction, juncture, position, religion 9 communion, situation 10 catenation 11 affiliation, appointment, association, combination, conjunction, partnership 12 conjointment, denomination, togetherness

connective 2 or 3 and, nor 6 either 7 neither 8 syndetic 11 conjunction, conjunctive

connivance 9 collusion 10 complicity

connive 4 plot, wink 5 blink 6 devise, wink at 7 blink at, collude 8 cogitate, con-

spire, contrive, intrigue 9 machinate,
scheme out

connoisseur 6 expert 7 epicure, gourmet
8 aesthete, gourmand, highbrow 9 bon
vivant 10 dilettante 11 cognoscente

connotation 4 hint 7 meaning 8 overtone
9 undertone 10 suggestion 11 association,
implication

connote 4 hint, mean 5 imply, spell
6 import, intend 7 add up to, express, signify, suggest 8 intimate 9 insinuate

connubial 6 wedded 7 marital, married,
nuptial, spousal 8 conjugal, hymeneal
11 matrimonial

connubiality 7 wedlock 8 marriage
9 matrimony 11 conjugality

conquer 3 win 4 beat, best, foil, lick,
tame, whip 5 crush 6 defeat, hurdle, master, outwit, reduce, subdue, thwart 7 prevail, triumph 8 bear down, beat down, overcome, override, surmount, vanquish
9 checkmate, overpower, overthrow, overwhelm, subjugate 10 overmaster

conquest 3 win 4 rout 7 routing, subdual,
triumph, victory 9 overthrow

Conrad *character:* 3 Jim 4 Axel, Lena
5 Flora, Kurtz 6 Marlow 7 Almayer
8 MacWhirr, Nostromo *work:* 5 Youth
6 Chance 7 Lord Jim, Typhoon, Victory
8 Nostromo 11 Secret Agent 14 Almayer's
Folly

consanguine 4 akin 6 agnate, allied
7 cognate, connate, kindred, related 8 incident 10 affiliated, connatural

conscience 5 demur, qualm, sense
6 psyche, squeam 7 scruple 11 compunction

conscienceless 6 amoral, shifty, tricky,
unfair 7 devious 12 unprincipled

conscientious 4 fair, just, true 5 exact,
fussy, right 6 honest 7 careful, dutiful,
heedful, upright 8 punctual, studious
9 honorable 10 meticulous, scrupulous
11 painstaking, punctilious 12 conscionable

conscionable see **conscientious**

conscious 5 alive, awake, aware 7 knowing, mindful, witting 8 affected, mannered,
sensible, sentient, vigilant, watchful 9 attentive, au courant, cognizant 10 conversant,
perceptive

consciousness 4 care, heed 6 regard
7 concern 9 awareness 11 carefulness,
needfulness

conscribe, conscript 5 draft 6 enlist,
enroll, muster

consecrate 5 bless 6 anoint, devote, hallow 8 dedicate, sanctify

consecrated 4 holy 6 sacred 7 blessed
8 hallowed 9 unprofane 10 sanctified *oil:*
6 chrism *thing:* 6 sacrum

consecution 3 row 5 chain, order, train
6 sequel, series 8 sequence 10 procession, succession 11 progression

consecutive 4 next 5 after, later 6 serial
7 ensuing, sequent 9 enlarging, following,
succedent 10 increasing, sequential, subsequent, succeeding, successive 11 progressive 12 successional 13 subsequential

consent 3 let, yes 5 agree, allow, leave,
yield 6 accedè, accord, assent, comply,
concur, permit 7 approve 8 sanction
9 acquiesce, agreement, allowance, subscribe 10 permission, sufferance
13 authorization, understanding

consentaneous 5 solid 9 unanimous
11 consentient

consequence 3 end 4 fame, pith, rank
5 event, honor, issue, pride, state 6 cachet,
effect, egoism, import, moment, renown,
repute, result, sequel, status, upshot,
weight 7 conceit, dignity, egotism, outcome, stature 8 position, prestige,
sequence, standing 9 aftermath, magnitude, vainglory 10 importance, narcissism,
reputation 11 aftereffect, amour propre,
complacence, complacency, weightiness
12 significance 13 conceitedness, momentousness

consequent 5 sound 7 logical 8 rational,
sensible 9 following, resulting 10 reasonable 11 intelligent

consequential 3 big 7 weighty 8 material 9 important, momentous 10 meaningful
11 significant, substantial 12 considerable

consequently 2 so 4 ergo, then, thus
5 hence 9 therefore, thereupon 11 accordingly

conservation 4 care 6 saving 7 control,
keeping 8 managing 9 attention, directing,
governing, preserval, salvation 10 cherishing, husbanding, management, protection
11 safekeeping 12 preservation, sustentation

conservative 4 tory, wary 5 chary, right
6 proper 7 diehard, puritan 8 cautious, discreet, moderate, old liner, orthodox, rightist,
standpat 9 temperate, unextreme 10 controlled, reasonable, restrained 11 bitter-
ender, circumspect, reactionary, right-
winger, standpatter, unexcessive

conserve 3 can, jam 4 save 6 keep up
7 support, sustain 8 maintain, preserve
9 confiture

consider 3 eye, see 4 deem, feel, hold,
mind, muse, rate, rule, scan, view 5 fancy,
infer, judge, sense, study, think, weigh
6 admire, credit, esteem, gather, look at,
ponder, reason, reckon, regard 7 account,
believe, bethink, examine, imagine, inspect,
perpend, reflect, respect 8 cogitate, conceive, conclude, gaze upon, look upon, med-

itate, prescind, ruminate, think out **9** speculate, think over **10** excogitate, scrutinize
11 contemplate

considerable 3 big **4** good, tidy **5** hefty,
large, major **6** active, goodly, pretty **7** notable, sizable, weighty **8** material, sensible
9 effective, extensive, important, momentous **10** large-scale, meaningful **11** efficacious, respectable, significant, substantial
13 consequential

considerably 3 far **4** well **5** quite
6 rather **8** somewhat **13** significantly

considerate 3 big **4** kind, safe, wary
5 chary, lofty **6** kindly, polite, tender **7** amiable, careful, guarded **8** cautious, discreet,
generous, gingerly, obliging **9** attentive
10 benevolent, chivalrous, thoughtful
11 calculating, circumspect, complaisant,
magnanimous, sympathetic, warm-hearted
12 greathearted **13** compassionate

consideration 4 heed **5** cause, favor,
mercy, study **6** debate, esteem, motive,
reason, regard, spring **7** account, concern,
respect **9** attention, awareness **10** admiration, estimation, solicitude **11** application,
forbearance, heedfulness, mindfulness
12 deliberation **13** concentration

considered 7 advised, studied, willful
8 designed, prepense, studious **9** voluntary
10 deliberate, thought-out **11** intentional
12 aforethought, premeditated

consign 4 give, send, ship **5** allot, award,
remit, route, yield **6** commit, devote
7 address, commend, confide, entrust, forward **8** dispatch, hand over, relegate, transmit, turn over **9** surrender

consist 2 be, go **3** lie **4** rest **5** abide,
agree, dwell, exist, fit in **6** accord, inhere,
repose, reside **7** comport, conform, consort, subsist **8** dovetail **10** correspond

consistency 7 aptness, concord, fitness,
harmony **8** evenness, felicity, firmness, likeness **9** agreement, coherence, congruity
10 apposition, conformity, consonance, similarity **11** suitability

consistent 4 same, true **8** constant
9 agreeable, congenial, congruous, consonant, unfailing, unvarying **10** compatible,
invariable, unchanging **11** sympathetic

consistently 7 as usual, usually **8** wontedly **10** habitually **11** customarily

console 4 calm **5** cheer, table **6** buck up,
solace **7** animate, cabinet, comfort,
hearten, relieve, upraise **8** inspirit **11** tranquilize

consolidate 3 mix, set **4** fuse **5** blend,
merge, unify, unite **7** compact **8** compress,
condense, solidify **9** integrate **10** amalgamate, strengthen **11** concentrate

consolidation 5 union **6** merger **7** melding, merging **8** mergence **9** coalition

11 coadunation, combination, unification
12 amalgamation

consonance 4 tune **5** chime **6** accord,
chorus **7** concert, concord, harmony
9 agreement **11** concordance

consonant 4 akin, like **5** alike, round
6 agnate, fortis, rotund **7** chiming, musical,
orotund, ringing, similar, uniform, vibrant
8 blending, harmonic, parallel, plangent, resonant, sonorant, sonorous **9** accordant,
agreeable, analogous, congenial, congruous **10** coincident, comparable, compatible,
consistent, harmonious, resounding
11 conformable, sympathetic, symphonious
13 corresponding *kind:* **4** stop, surd
5 nasal, velar **6** atonic, voiced **7** lateral, palatal, spirant **8** alveolar, bilabial, unvoiced
9 fricative, voiceless

consort 4 bear, mate, wife **5** agree,
group, tally **6** accord, attend, convoy, fellow, spouse, square **7** company, comport,
conduct, conform, husband **8** assembly,
chaperon, dovetail **9** accompany, associate, companion, harmonize **10** correspond **11** concomitant **13** accompaniment

consortium 4 club **5** guild, order, union
6 league **7** society **8** congress **10** fellowship, fraternity **11** association

conspectus 5 brief **7** epitome **8** abstract,
boildown, breviary, breviate, synopsis
10 abridgment **12** condensation

conspicuous 5 clear, plain, showy
6 marked, patent, signal **7** blatant, eminent,
evident, obvious, pointed, salient **8** apparent, distinct, flagrant, manifest, striking
9 arresting, arrestive, egregious, prominent
10 celebrated, noticeable, openhanded,
remarkable **11** illustrious, outstanding

conspiracy 4 plan, plot **5** cabal, covin
6 scheme **8** intrigue, sedition **9** treachery
11 machination

conspirator 7 abettor **9** accessory
10 accomplice **11** confederate

conspire 4 plot **5** cabal **6** devise **7** collude, complot, connive **8** cogitate, contrive,
intrigue **9** machinate, scheme out

constancy 6 fealty **7** loyalty **8** adhesion,
fidelity **9** adherence, diligence **10** attachment **12** faithfulness

constant 4 even, fast, same, true **5** fixed,
liege, loyal **6** ardent, dogged, stable,
steady **7** abiding, chronic, endless, equable, lasting, stabile, staunch, uniform
8 clinging, enduring, faithful, unending
9 allegiant, ceaseless, confirmed, continual,
immovable, immutable, obstinate, perpetual, steadfast, unceasing, unfailing, unmovable, unvarying **10** changeless, consistent,
continuous, inflexible, invariable, inveterate,
persistent, persisting, unchanging, unwavering **11** everlasting, inalterable, persever-

ing, unalterable, unremitting **12** interminable, pertinacious, unchangeable, unmodifiable **13** unfluctuating

Constantine *birthplace:* **4** Nish *mother:* **6** Helena *son:* **7** Crispus *victim:* **6** Fausta **7** Crispus *wife:* **6** Fausta

constantly 4 ever **6** always **10** invariably **11** perpetually **12** continuously

constellation 5 group **7** pattern **10** assemblage, collection **11** arrangement *Altar:* **3** Ara *Archer:* **11** Sagittarius *Arrow:* **7** Sagitta *Balance:* **5** Libra *Big Dipper:* **9** Ursa Major *Bird of Paradise:* **4** Apus *Bull:* **6** Taurus *Centaur:* **9** Centaurus *Chained Lady:* **9** Andromeda *Chameleon:* **10** Chamaeleon *Champion:* **7** Perseus *Charioteer:* **6** Auriga *Clock:* **10** Horologium *Colt:* **8** Equuleus *Crab:* **6** Cancer *Crane:* **4** Grus *Cross:* **4** Crux *Crow:* **6** Corvus *Crown:* **6** Corona *Cup:* **6** Crater *Dolphin:* **9** Delphinus *Dove:* **7** Columba *Dragon:* **5** Draco *Eagle:* **6** Aquila *Fishes:* **6** Pisces *Fly:* **5** Musca *Flying Fish:* **6** Volans *Furnace:* **6** Fornax *Graving Tool:* **6** Caelum *Greater Dog:* **10** Canis Major *Hare:* **5** Lepus *Herdsman:* **6** Boötes *Horned Goat:* **11** Capricornus *Hunter:* **5** Orion *Indian:* **5** Indus *Keel:* **6** Carina *Lady in the Chair:* **10** Cassiopeia *Larger Bear:* **9** Ursa Major *Larger Dog:* **10** Canis Major *Lesser Dog:* **10** Canis Minor *Lion:* **3** Leo *Little Dipper:* **9** Ursa Minor *Little Fox:* **9** Vulpecula *Lizard:* **7** Lacerta *Lyre:* **4** Lyra *Mariner's Compass:* **5** Pyxis *Monarch:* **7** Cepheus *Net:* **9** Reticulum *Painter's Easel:* **6** Pictor *Pair of Compasses:* **8** Circinus *Peacock:* **4** Pavo *Pump:* **6** Antlia *Ram:* **5** Aries *Rescuer:* **7** Perseus *River Po:* **8** Eridanus *Sails:* **4** Vela *Scorpion:* **8** Scorpius *Serpent:* **7** Serpens *Serpent Holder:* **9** Ophiuchus *Sextant:* **7** Sextans *Shield:* **6** Scutum *Smaller Bear:* **9** Ursa Minor *Square:* **5** Norma *Stern:* **6** Puppis *Swan:* **6** Cygnus *Table:* **5** Mensa *Toucan:* **6** Tucana *Triangle:* **10** Triangulum *Twins:* **6** Gemini *Unicorn:* **9** Monoceros *Virgin:* **5** Virgo *Water Carrier:* **8** Aquarius *Water Monster:* **5** Hydra *Water Snake:* **6** Hydrus *Whale:* **5** Cetus *Winged Horse:* **7** Pegasus *Wolf:* **5** Lupus

consternate 5 daunt, shake **6** appall, dismay **7** horrify

consternation 4 fear **5** alarm, dread, panic **6** dismay, fright, horror, muddle, terror **9** confusion, trepidity **10** muddlement, perplexity **11** distraction, trepidation **12** bewilderment

constipate 6 stifle **7** trammel **8** stagnate, stultify

constituent 4 part **5** piece, voter **6** factor, member **7** element, portion **8** division, fraction **9** component, principal **10** ingredient

constitute 4 form, make **5** enact, found, set up, start **6** create, embody, make up **7** compose **8** complete, comprise, organize **9** establish, institute

constitution 3 law **4** code **5** build, canon, habit **6** design, makeup, nature **7** habitus **8** physique **9** formation, ordinance, structure **11** composition **12** architecture, construction

Constitution 12 Old Ironsides

constitutional 4 turn, walk **6** inborn, inbred, innate, ramble, stroll **7** built-in, saunter **8** inherent **9** essential, ingrained, intrinsic **10** congenital, deep-seated

Constitution State 11 Connecticut

constitutive 5 vital **8** cardinal **9** essential **11** fundamental

constrain 3 ban, bar, jam, jug **4** bear, curb, deny, hurt, jail, make, pain, push **5** check, crowd, crush, force, press **6** bridle, coerce, compel, enjoin, grieve, hold in, immure, injure, intern, oblige, squash, squish **7** abstain, concuss, confine, deprive, inhibit, refrain, shotgun, squeeze **8** aggrieve, bastille, disallow, distress, hold back, hold down, imprison, restrain, restrict, withhold **11** incarcerate

constraint 4 bond **5** check, cramp, force **6** duress **8** coercion, violence **9** restraint **10** compulsion, repression **11** confinement, restriction, suppression

constrict 4 curb, stop **5** choke, limit, strap **6** hamper, narrow, pucker, shrink **7** confine, inhibit, squeeze, tighten **8** astringe, compress, condense, contract, restrain, strangle, stultify **9** constrain **10** constipate, constringe **11** concentrate **12** circumscribe

constrictor 3 boa **5** snake **6** muscle **8** anaconda **9** sphincter, strangler

construct 4 form, make, rear **5** build, erect, forge, frame, put up, raise, set up **6** devise, uprear **7** build up, fashion, produce **8** assemble **9** establish, fabricate, hammer out **11** put together

construction 6 design, expose, makeup **8** building, exegesis **9** construal, formation **10** exposition **11** composition, explanation, explication **12** architecture, constitution

constructive 7 helpful, virtual **8** implicit **9** practical

construe 7 analyze, explain, expound **8** spell out **9** explicate, interpret, translate

consuetude 3 use **4** wont **5** habit, trick, usage **6** custom, manner, praxis **8** habitude, practice

consult 3 ask **5** refer, treat **6** advise, confab, confer, huddle, parley, powwow

7 counsel, examine 8 collogue, consider 11 confabulate

consume 2 go 3 eat, use 4 down, gulp, meal, raze, ruin, take, wolf 5 crush, drink, eat up, gorge, sew up, shift, spend, swill, use up, waste, wreck 6 absorb, devour, expend, feed on, finish, guzzle, ingest 7 destroy, engross, exhaust, fritter, put away, put down, swallow 8 gobble up, squander 9 dissipate, overwhelm, partake of, polish off, throw away 10 annihilate, extinguish, frivol away, monopolize, run through, trifle away

consumer advocate 5 Nader (Ralph)

consuming 9 absorbing 10 engrossing 12 monopolizing

consummate 3 end 4 able, halt, ripe 5 close, utter 6 finish, gifted, superb, wind up, wrap up 7 perfect, skilled, supreme, trained 8 absolute, complete, conclude, finished, flawless, outright, peerless, positive, talented, ultimate 9 downright, faultless, out-and-out, perfected, practiced, terminate, virtuosic 10 impeccable, inimitable 11 superlative, unmitigated 12 accomplished 13 thoroughgoing, unsurpassable

consumption 2 TB 3 use 5 decay, waste 8 phthisis 11 white plague 12 tuberculosis

contact 3 get 4 abut, meet 5 reach, touch, union 6 accord 7 harmony, oneness, rapport, taction 8 commerce, nearness, relation, tangency, touching 9 closeness, communion, proximity 10 connection, contiguity, fellowship 11 association, contingence, impingement, intercourse, propinquity 13 communication, companionship *combining form:* 4 hapt 5 hapto

contagion 3 pox 4 bane 5 taint, venom, virus 6 miasma, poison 7 disease 9 pollution 10 corruption 13 contamination

contagious 6 catchy, taking 8 catching 10 infectious 12 communicable

contain 4 have, hold, keep, take 5 admit, house, lodge 6 embody, take in 7 collect, compose, control, embrace, include, involve, receive, repress, smother, subsume 8 comprise, restrain 9 encompass 10 comprehend, simmer down 11 accommodate

container 3 bag, bin, box, can, cup, jar, keg, mug, pod, pot, tin, tub, urn, vat 4 cage, case, cask, drum, etui, ewer, pail, sack, silo, tank, vase, vial, well 5 chest, crate, cruet, flask, glass, gourd, phial, pouch 6 basket, bottle, carafe, carton, casket, coffin, cooler, goblet, hamper, hatbox, holder, inkpot, shaker 7 bandbox, capsule, chalice, inkwell, package, pitcher, thermos 8 canister, catchall, decanter, envelope,

hogshead, jerrican, puncheon 10 receptacle *liturgical:* 3 pix, pyx 7 chalice 8 ciborium

containing *suffix:* 2 ic 4 ical

contaminate 4 foul, harm, soil 5 dirty, spoil, stain, taint 6 befoul, debase, defile, infect, injure, poison 7 corrupt, deprave, pervert, pollute, tarnish, vitiate 9 desecrate 10 adulterate

conte 4 tale 5 story 9 narrative

contemn 4 hate 5 abhor, scorn, scout, spurn 7 despise, disdain 8 look down

contemplate 3 aim, eye 4 mean, mull, muse, plan, scan, view 5 study, think, weigh 6 design, intend, look at, ponder 7 examine, inspect, perpend, propose, purpose, reflect 8 consider, gaze upon, look upon, meditate, think out 9 think over 10 excogitate, scrutinize

contemplation 5 study 6 musing 7 thought 8 thinking 9 brainwork, pondering 10 cogitation, meditation, reflection, rumination 11 cerebration, speculation 12 deliberation

contemplative 6 musing 7 pensive 8 thinking, weighing 9 pondering, reasoning 10 cogitative, meditative, reflecting, reflective, ruminative, thoughtful 11 speculative

contemporary 2 up 6 coeval, extant 7 abreast, current, instant, present 8 existent, existing, todayish, up-to-date 9 au courant 10 coetaneous, coexistent, coexisting, coincident, concurrent, present-day, synchronal, synchronic 11 concomitant, synchronous 12 simultaneous 13 up-to-the-minute

contempt 5 scorn, shame 6 hatred, infamy 7 despite, disdain, mockery, sarcasm 8 aversion, defiance, despisal, disfavor, disgrace, dishonor, distaste, ignominy 9 antipathy, contumacy, discredit, disesteem, disrepute 10 opprobrium, repugnance 11 despisement 12 stubbornness 13 disparagement, recalcitrance

contemptible 3 bad, low 4 base, evil, mean, poor, vile 5 cheap, sorry 6 abject, odious, scummy, scurvy, shabby, sordid 7 hateful, ignoble, pitiful 8 beggarly, infamous, inferior, pitiable, shameful 9 abhorrent 10 abominable, despicable, despisable, detestable, disgusting 11 ignominious

contemptible one *suffix:* 3 een, eer

contemptuous 7 haughty 8 arrogant, scornful 10 disdainful 12 supercilious

contend 3 say, tug, vie, war 4 cope, face, meet, tell, urge 5 argue, brawl, claim, fight, rival 6 assert, battle, charge, combat, defend, enjoin, oppose, oppugn, report, resist 7 compete, contest, justify, warrant

8 confront, cope with, maintain 9 encounter, vindicate, withstand

___ **contendere** 4 nolo

content 4 cozy, gist 5 happy 6 at ease 7 appease, gratify, satisfy 9 satisfied, substance 12 significance

contention 3 war 4 feud 6 hurrah, rumpus, strife, thesis 7 discord, dispute, dissent, quarrel, rivalry, wrangle 8 argument, conflict, disunity, squabble, variance 9 disaccord 10 difference, dissension, dissidence 11 altercation, competition, controversy 12 contestation *Scottish:* 5 sturt

contentious 5 fiery 7 carping, froward, peppery, scrappy, warlike 8 captious, caviling, contrary, militant, perverse 9 bellicose, combative, hotheaded, impetuous, litigious, polemical, truculent 10 pugnacious 11 belligerent, quarrelsome 12 disputatious, faultfinding, gladiatorial 13 argumentative, controversial

conterminous 8 abutting, adjacent, touching 9 adjoining, bordering 10 approximal, contiguous, juxtaposed

contest 3 sue, vie 4 bout, buck, duel, feud, fray, game, meet, race, tilt 5 clash, fight, match, repel, rival, trial 6 battle, combat, debate, oppose, resist, strife, strive, trying 7 compete, contend, dispute, rivalry, testing, warfare 8 argument, concours, conflict, endeavor, skirmish, striving, struggle, tug-of-war 9 emulation, encounter, rencontre, withstand 10 engagement, tournament 11 competition *combining form:* 5 machy

contiguity 9 adjacency, confinity, immediacy, proximity 11 propinquity 13 appropinquity

contiguous 4 near, next, nigh 5 close 6 nearby 7 close-by 8 abutting, adjacent, touching 9 adjoining, bordering 10 approximal, juxtaposed, near-at-hand 11 close-at-hand, neighboring 12 conterminous

continence 6 purity, virtue 8 chastity, sobriety 10 abstinence, chasteness, moderation, temperance 13 self-restraint, temperateness

continent 4 Asia, mass, pure 5 sober 6 Africa, chaste, curbed, Europe 7 America, bridled 8 mainland 9 abstinent, Australia, inhibited, temperate 10 abstemious, Antarctica, restrained 11 abstentious 12 North America, South America *lost:* 8 Atlantis

continental pool 3 EEC 12 Common Market

continence 5 touch 7 contact

contingency 4 pass 5 break, event, pinch 6 chance, crisis, strait 8 exigency, juncture, occasion, zero hour 9 emergency

10 crossroads 11 opportunity, possibility 12 turning point

contingent 3 odd 5 fluky 6 casual, chance, likely 7 reliant 8 possible, probable, relative 9 dependent 10 accidental, fortuitous, incidental, unforeseen 11 conditional 13 unanticipated, unforeseeable

continual 6 steady 7 abiding, endless, running, staying 8 constant, enduring, minutely, timeless, unending, unwaning 9 ceaseless, incessant, perpetual, unceasing, unfailing, unvarying 10 continuous, persistent, persisting, relentless, unchanging, unflagging 11 everlasting, unremitting 12 interminable 13 unintermitted, uninterrupted

continually 4 ever 6 always 7 forever, running 8 together 10 constantly 11 incessantly, night and day 12 successively 13 consecutively

continuance 3 run 4 stay 5 delay 6 sequel 8 duration, survival 9 constancy, longevity 10 permanence 11 persistence 12 postponement, prolongation

continuation 3 run 8 duration 9 endurance, extension 11 persistence, protraction 12 prolongation

continue 4 go on, last, ride, stay 5 abide, renew, run on 6 endure, pick up, remain, reopen, resume, retain, take up 7 carry on, outlast, outlive, perdure, persist, prolong, restart, survive 8 maintain, postpone 9 carry over, persevere 10 recommence 12 carry through

continuing 3 old 7 ongoing 8 constant, enduring, lifelong 9 long-lived, perennial 10 inveterate 11 long-lasting

continuity 6 script 8 duration, scenario 9 endurance 11 persistence

continuous see **continual**

continuously see **continually**

contort 3 wry 4 bend, warp, wind 5 curve, gnarl, twist, wring 6 deform, writhe 7 distort, grimace, torture 8 misshape

contortionist 7 acrobat

contour 4 form, line 5 curve, shape 7 outline, profile 9 lineament, lineation 10 figuration, silhouette 11 delineation

contra 5 again 6 facing, toward 7 against, counter, reverse, vis-à-vis 8 antipode, antipole, converse, fronting, opposite 9 vice versa 10 antithesis, conversely, oppositely

contraband 3 hot 5 taboo 6 banned 7 bootleg, illegal, illicit, shut out, smuggle 8 excluded 9 forbidden 10 prohibited, proscribed 11 disapproved

contract 3 get 4 bond, fail, knit, pact, sink, take 5 catch, cause, incur, lease, limit, upset 6 engage, induce, lessen, obtain, reduce, shrink, treaty, weaken 7 abridge, acquire, afflict, bargain, betroth, bring on,

compact, decline, derange, dwindle, wrinkle
8 affiance, compress, condense, covenant,
decrease, diminish, disorder, restrict, sicken
of 9 agreement, betrothal, constrict, indispose, succumb to 10 convention, sicken
with 11 concentrate, transaction 12 come
down with *maritime:* 8 bottomry *part:*
6 clause 7 article, proviso

contraction 3 it's, tic 4 ain't, can't, don't,
flex, isn't, won't 5 aren't, cramp, didn't,
spasm 7 elision 9 reduction, shrinkage
10 abridgment 12 abbreviation *heart's:*
7 systole *poetic:* 3 e'en, e'er, o'er, 'tis
4 ne'er, 'twas 5 'twere, 'twill

contradict 4 deny 5 belie, cross, rebut
6 impugn, negate 7 dispute, gainsay
8 negative, traverse 9 disaffirm 10 contravene

contradiction 6 denial 7 paradox 8 antin-
omy, negation 10 gainsaying

contradictory 7 counter, reverse 8 antipode, antipole, contrary, converse, negat-
ing, opposite 9 antipodal 10 antipodean,
antithesis, nullifying 11 counterpole
12 antagonistic, antithetical 13 counteractive

contraption 3 rig 6 device, gadget
7 machine 11 contrivance

contrariety 3 con 8 opposure 10 antagonism, antithesis, opposition

contrariwise 5 again 9 vice versa
10 conversely, oppositely

contrary 5 balky, polar 6 averse, ornery,
unruly 7 counter, froward, restive, reverse,
wayward 8 antipode, antipole, clashing,
converse, opposite, perverse, recusant,
stubborn 9 antipodal, diametric, dissident,
obstinate, vice versa 10 antipodean, antithesis, conversely, discordant, headstrong,
oppositely, rebellious, refractory 11 conflicting, counterpole, dissentient, intractable,
wrongheaded 12 antagonistic, antipathetic,
antithetical, contumacious, cross-grained,
recalcitrant 13 contradictory, insubordinate,
nonconforming, nonconformist *prefix:* 3 dis
5 retro 6 contra 7 counter

contrast 7 compare 9 diversity 10 comparison, difference, divergence

contravene 4 defy, deny 5 break, cross,
fight, spurn 6 abjure, breach, combat, disown, impugn, negate, offend, oppose,
reject, resist 7 exclude, gainsay, infract, violate 8 disclaim, infringe, negative, traverse
9 disaffirm, repudiate 10 contradict, transgress

contravention 3 sin 4 vice 5 crime
6 breach 7 offense 8 trespass 9 violation
10 infraction 12 infringement 13 transgression

contretemps 4 slip 6 mishap 7 tragedy
9 adversity, mischance 10 misfortune

contribute 3 aid 4 give, help, tend 5 add
to 6 assist, chip in, donate, kick in, submit,
supply 7 augment, conduce, fortify, pitch
in, recruit, redound 9 reinforce, subscribe
10 strengthen, supplement 11 come
through

contribution 4 alms, gift 5 share 7 charity, present 8 donation, offering 11 benefaction, beneficence

contributory 8 adjuvant 9 accessory,
ancillary, auxiliary 10 collateral, subsidiary
11 appurtenant, subservient

contrite 5 sorry 8 penitent 9 regretful,
repentant 10 apologetic, remorseful
11 attritional, penitential 12 compunctious

contriteness see contrition

contrition 3 rue 4 ruth 7 penance,
remorse 9 attrition, penitence, penitency
10 repentance 11 compunction

contrivance 3 art 6 device 7 coinage,
machine 8 artifice 9 apparatus, invention
10 brainchild 11 contraption

contrive 3 rig 4 fake, make, move, plan,
plot 5 fix up, frame 6 cook up, devise, handle, invent, make up, scheme, vamp up,
wangle 7 collude, concoct, connive,
develop, dream up, fashion, hatch up, project, work out 8 cogitate, conspire, intrigue
9 elaborate, fabricate, formulate, machinate, scheme out

contrived 5 hokey 6 forced 7 labored
10 artificial

control 4 curb, rein, rule, sway 5 might,
power, quell 6 adjust, bridle, corner, direct,
govern, handle, manage, master, subdue
7 command, compose, contain, mastery,
repress, smother, strings 8 dominate,
monopoly, regulate, restrain 9 authority,
supervise 10 discipline, domination
12 jurisdiction

controlled 4 tame 8 discreet, moderate
9 temperate, unextreme 10 reasonable,
restrained 11 unexcessive 12 conservative

controversial 7 eristic 9 litigious, polemical 11 contentious 12 disputatious
13 argumentative

controversy 3 row 4 miff, tiff 6 debate,
rumpus, strife 7 dispute, quarrel, wrangle
8 argument, squabble 9 bickering 10 contention, falling-out 11 altercation, embroilment

controvert 4 deny 5 break, rebut
6 oppugn, refute 7 confute 8 confound,
disprove, question 9 challenge 10 disconfirm

contumacious 6 unruly 7 froward 8 contrary, factious, insolent, mutinous, perverse
9 insurgent, seditious 10 rebellious
13 insubordinate

contumacy 7 despite 8 contempt, defiance 12 stubbornness 13 recalcitrance

contumelious 4 bold 5 saucy 6 brazen 7 abusive, scurril 8 impudent, insolent, scurrile 9 audacious, invective, truculent 10 scurrilous, vituperous 11 impertinent, opprobrious 12 vituperative, vituperatory

contumely 4 slap 5 abuse 6 insult 7 affront, despite, obloquy 9 aspersion, indignity, invective, stricture 10 scurrility 12 billingsgate, vituperation 13 animadversion

contuse 5 black 6 bruise, injure

conundrum 3 why 6 enigma, puzzle, riddle 7 mystery, problem 10 puzzlement 13 Chinese puzzle, mystification

convalesce 4 mend 7 improve, recover 10 recuperate

convene 3 sit 4 call, meet, open 6 call in, gather, muster, summon 7 convoke, summons 8 assemble 10 congregate

convenience 4 ease 6 toilet 7 amenity, benefit, comfort

convenient 3 fit 4 good, meet, near, next, nigh 5 close, handy 6 nearby, proper, useful 7 close-by 8 adjacent, suitable 9 immediate 10 accessible, near-at-hand 11 appropriate, close-at-hand

convent 5 abbey 6 friary, priory 7 nunnery 9 monastery, sanctuary

convention 3 law 4 bond, form, pact, rule 5 canon, usage 6 accord, custom, treaty 7 bargain, compact, concord, meeting, precept 8 assembly, contract, covenant, practice 9 agreement, gathering, tradition 10 convenance 11 transaction 13 understanding

conventional 5 trite, usual 6 decent, formal, normal, proper, seemly, solemn, square 7 correct, stately 8 decorous, moderate, ordinary, orthodox, priggish, reliable, straight 9 temperate 10 button-down, ceremonial, dependable, fastidious, restrained, scrupulous 11 ceremonious, commonplace, constrained, responsible, traditional 12 conservative 13 conscientious

conventionalize 5 adapt 7 conform, stylize

converge 4 join, meet 5 focus 8 approach 9 concenter 11 concentrate

conversant 5 awake, aware 6 au fait, versed 7 abreast, knowing, witting 8 familiar, informed, sensible, sentient, up-to-date 9 au courant, cognizant, conscious 10 acquainted, perceptive, percipient 12 apprehending, apprehensive 13 comprehending

conversation 4 chat, talk 6 confab, debate, parley, speech 7 comment, talking 8 causerie, colloquy, dialogue, duologue, repartee, shoptalk 9 cross talk, discourse, tête-à-tête 10 discussion 13 confabulation

conversation piece 6 oddity 9 curiosity

converse 4 chat, chin, talk, yarn 5 polar, speak, visit 6 contra, parley 7 commune, counter, reverse 8 antipode, antipole, colloque, colloquy, contrary, dialogue, opposite 9 antipodal, communion, diametric, discourse 10 antipodean, antithesis 11 counterpole 12 antithetical 13 communication, confabulation, contradictory

conversely 6 contra 8 contrary 9 vice versa 10 contrawise, oppositely 12 contrariwise

conversion 5 shift 6 change 7 novelty, rebirth, turning 8 metanoia, mutation, reversal 9 about-face 10 alteration, changeover, innovation 11 permutation, reclamation 12 modification, regeneration 13 metamorphosis, qualification, transmutation

convert 4 lead, make, move, save, sway 5 alter, bring, forge 6 change, redeem, reform 7 commute, incline 8 persuade 9 proselyte, transform, translate, transmute, transpose 11 proselytize, transfigure 12 metamorphose, transmogrify *Christian:* 10 catechumen

convex 5 bowed, toric 6 arched, curved 7 bulging, gibbous, rounded

convey 3 lug 4 bear, buck, cart, cede, deed, pack, pipe, send, tote 5 bring, carry, ferry 6 assign, funnel, impart, pass on, remise, siphon 7 channel, conduct, consign, project, traject 8 make over, sign over, transfer, transmit 9 put across, transport 11 communicate

conveyance 3 car 4 auto, cart, deed, sled 5 coach, coupe, sedan, stage, wagon 7 charter, trailer, transit, vehicle 8 carriage, carrying 9 transport 10 automobile 12 transporting *public:* 2 el 3 bus, cab 4 taxi, tram 5 plane, train 7 ricksha, trolley 8 airplane, monorail, railroad, rickshaw 9 streetcar 10 jinricksha, jinrikisha

convict 4 find 5 felon, lifer 6 inmate, trusty 7 captive 8 criminal, jailbird, prisoner, sentence 10 malefactor

conviction 4 mind, view 5 creed, faith 6 belief, surety 7 feeling, opinion 8 doctrine, sureness 9 assurance, certainty, certitude, sentiment 10 confidence, persuasion 11 assuredness

convince 3 get 4 draw 6 assure, induce, prompt 7 satisfy, win over 8 persuade, talk into 9 argue into, prevail on 11 bring around, prevail upon

convincing 5 solid, sound, valid 6 cogent, trusty 7 telling 8 credible, faithful 9 authentic 10 persuasive, satisfying 11 trustworthy 12 satisfactory

convivial 3 gay 5 jolly, merry 6 jocund, jovial, lively, social 7 festive 8 sociable 9 vivacious 13 companionable

convocation 5 synod 7 council, meeting 8 assembly 9 gathering 10 assemblage 12 congregation

convoke 3 ask, bid, sit 4 call, meet 6 gather, invite, summon 7 collect, convene, request 8 assemble 10 congregate

convoluted 5 snaky 6 coiled 7 complex, sinuous, winding 8 flexuous, tortuous 9 meandrous 10 meandering, serpentine 11 anfractuous

convoy 4 bear 5 guard, guide, train 6 attend, defend, escort, shield 7 company, conduct, protect 9 accompany, companion, safeguard 11 consort with

convulse 4 rock 5 shake 7 agitate, concuss 8 tetanize

convulsion 3 fit 5 spasm 6 attack, clamor, outcry, tumult, uproar, upturn 7 ferment, quaking, rocking, shaking 8 disaster, laughter, upheaval 9 commotion, trembling

cook 3 fix, fry 4 bake, boil, burn, chef, melt, stew 5 broil, frame, grill, poach, roast, sauté, steam 6 braise, devise, invent, make up, scorch, simmer 7 concoct, dream up, griddle, hatch up, parboil, prepare, swelter 8 barbecue, cocinero, contrive 9 formulate

cooked 4 done *combining form:* 5 cocto *with tomatoes:* 10 cacciatore

cookery 7 cuisine 8 magirics *expert:* 3 Yan (Martin) 4 Chen (Joyce), Kerr (Graham), Puck (Wolfgang), Root (Waverley) 5 Beard (James), Child (Julia), Hines (Duncan), Smith (Jeff) 6 Bocuse (Paul), Carême (Marie Antonin), Farmer (Fannie), Fisher (Mary Frances Kennedy), Franey (Pierre), Waters (Alice) 7 Crocker (Betty), Stewart (Martha) 8 Rombauer (Irma) 9 Claiborne (Craig), Escoffier (Auguste), Prudhomme (Paul) 14 Brillat-Savarin (Anthelme)

cookie 4 cake, snap 7 biscuit, brownie 8 macaroon 10 gingersnap

cooking *appliance:* 4 oven 5 mixer, range, stove 7 blender, toaster 10 rotisserie *Implement:* 3 cup, pan, pot, wok 4 olla 5 ladle, sieve, spoon, whisk 6 frypan, grater, masher, sifter, tureen 7 griddle, skillet, spatula 8 colander 9 eggbeater 10 rolling pin 12 measuring cup *room:* 6 galley 7 kitchen

cool 3 fan, ice 4 calm, cold 5 allay, aloof, chill, frore, gelid, nippy, sober 6 arctic, . chilly, frigid, frosty, offish, placid, serene, stolid 7 assured, collect, compose, control, distant, repress 8 composed, detached, freezing, reserved, restrain, solitary, suppress, tranquil 9 collected, confident, impassive, unruffled, withdrawn 10 nonchalant, phlegmatic, simmer down, unsociable 11 indifferent, standoffish, unflappable

12 happy-go-lucky 13 imperturbable, self-possessed

cooler 3 fan 4 coop, icer, jail 6 lockup, prison 11 refrigerant 12 refrigerator

cooling device 3 fan 4 icer 6 icebox 7 freezer 12 refrigerator

coolness 6 aplomb, phlegm 7 ataraxy 8 calmness 9 composure, sangfroid 10 equanimity

coop 3 hem, mew, pen 4 cage, jail 5 cramp, fence 6 corral, shut in 7 close in, confine, enclose, envelop 9 enclosure

cooperate 5 agree, unite 6 concur, league 7 combine, conjoin, connive 8 coadjute, coincide 11 collaborate

cooperation 8 teamwork

cooperative 8 coacting, coactive, conjoint, synergic 9 concerted 10 synergetic 11 coefficient 13 collaborative, uncompetitive

Cooper hero 11 Natty Bumppo

coordinate 4 mate, tune 5 adapt, atune, match 6 fellow 7 conform, vis-à-vis 9 companion, harmonize, integrate, reconcile 10 proportion, reciprocal 11 accommodate 12 reconciliate

cop 3 nab 4 lift, take 5 filch, pinch, steal, swipe 7 gumshoe, officer, purloin 8 bluecoat 9 patrolman, policeman 11 appropriate

copacetic 4 fine, okay 5 dandy 12 satisfactory

cope 4 arch, bend, face 5 cover, dress, get by, match, notch, vault 6 canopy, handle, make do, manage, mantel, muzzle 8 deal with 9 encounter

copestone 5 crown

copious 4 full, lush, rich 5 ample 6 lavish, plenty 7 liberal, profuse, replete 8 abundant, generous 9 abounding, bounteous, bountiful, exuberant, luxuriant, plenteous, plentiful

Copland work 5 Rodeo

cop-out 6 excuse 7 pretext, retreat

copper 4 cent, coin 5 metal, penny, token 6 cuprum 9 butterfly, policeman *combining form:* 4 cupr 5 chalc, chalk, cupri, cupro 6 chalko *item:* 4 cent 5 penny 6 kettle *sulfate:* 7 vitriol 9 bluestone 11 blue vitriol *symbol:* 2 Cu

copperhead 5 snake, viper 8 squirrel

coppice 4 bosk, wood 5 copse, grove 6 bosque, forest, growth 7 thicket 9 brushwood, underwood

copse see coppice

Copt 8 Egyptian

copula 4 link 5 union 7 coupler

copy 3 ape 4 echo, fake, mock, sham 5 ditto, mimic 6 carbon, ectype, effigy, ersatz, parody, repeat 7 emulate, imitate, replica, takeoff 8 knockoff, likeness, simulate, travesty 9 burlesque, duplicate, facsimile, imitation, replicate, reproduce 10 carbon copy, impression, simulacrum, transcribe 11 counterfeit, counterpart, reduplicate, replication 12 reproduction 13 reduplication

copyist 6 scribe 9 engrosser 10 plagiarist 12 calligrapher 13 calligraphist

copyread 4 edit

coquet 3 toy 4 fool 5 dally, flirt 6 lead on, trifle 11 string along

coquette 4 vamp 5 flirt 11 hummingbird

coquettish 3 coy 4 arch 7 roguish

coral 3 red 4 pink 5 palus, polyp 6 palule 8 skeleton 9 limestone

coral reef 5 atoll *off Australia:* 5 Wreck *world's largest:* 12 Great Barrier

cord 3 tie 4 band, lace, pile, rope, whip, wire, yarn 5 cable, nerve, stack 6 strand, string, tendon, thread 7 amentum *twisted:* 7 torsade

cordage 4 rope 5 ropes 7 rigging *fiber:* 4 bast, eruc, hemp, imbe, jute, pita 5 sisal

Corday's victim 5 Marat (Jean-Paul)

Cordelia *father:* 4 Lear *sister:* 5 Regan 7 Goneril

cordial 4 warm 5 drink, sonsy 6 genial, hearty, tender 7 affable, liqueur, sincere 8 friendly, gracious, sociable 9 congenial, courteous, heartfelt 10 hospitable, responsive 11 sympathetic, warmhearted 12 wholehearted

cordiality 5 ardor, favor 6 warmth 7 amenity 8 approval, sympathy 9 geniality, mutuality, pleasance 10 amiability 12 agreeability, friendliness, pleasantness 13 agreeableness, enjoyableness

cordon 4 lace 5 braid 6 circle, ribbon 7 barrier *blue:* 4 chef, cook 6 ribbon 10 decoration

core 3 hub, nub 4 base, body, bulk, gist, mass, meat, pith, root 5 basis, cadre, focus, heart, midst, quick 6 amount, burden, center, corpus, middle, origin, staple, thrust, upshot 7 purport 8 midpoint 9 substance 10 foundation

corf 3 tub 4 cage 5 truck 6 basket

corium 4 skin 5 cutis, layer 6 dermis

cork 4 bark, plug, seal, stop 5 float 6 bobber 7 stopper, stopple *combining form:* 6 phello

corker 4 lulu 5 dandy, dilly 8 jim-dandy, knockout 9 humdinger 11 crackerjack, lalapalooza

corkscrew 4 coil, curl, wind 5 twine, twist 6 spiral 7 entwine, wreathe

cormorant 4 bird, shag 7 glutton 8 Scottish *norie:* 5 scart

corn 3 zea 4 meal, salt, samp 5 grain, maize 6 clavus, hominy 9 granulate *bread:* 4 pone 7 bannock *Indian:* 3 zea 5 maize

6 mealie *kind:* 3 pop 4 dent 5 flint, flour, sweet 6 Indian *pest:* 5 borer *piece:* 3 cob, ear 5 spike 6 kernel, nubbin

Corncracker State 8 Kentucky

corner 3 box, fix, jam, nab 4 hole, nook, trap, tree 5 angle, catch, coign, niche, seize 6 collar, cranny, dogleg, pickle, plight, recess, scrape 7 capture, dilemma, impasse, trouble 8 bottle up, monopoly 10 bring to bay 11 predicament *combining form:* 4 goni 5 gonio 6 anguli, angulo *of eye:* 7 canthus

cornerstone 4 base 5 basis 7 support 10 foundation, groundwork

cornet 4 cone, horn 5 zinke 8 woodwind 9 cornopean 10 instrument

cornflower 5 bluet 10 bluebonnet, bluebottle

Cornhusker State 8 Nebraska

cornice 3 cap 4 band, eave 5 crown 6 geison 7 molding 8 swanneck *combining form:* 6 geisso

cornmeal 4 masa, samp 5 atole 7 hoecake *mush:* 7 polenta

cornucopia 4 cone, horn 9 abundance 12 horn of plenty

Cornwallis *adversary:* 6 Greene (Nathanael) *surrender site:* 8 Yorktown

corny 5 banal, stale, tired, trite 6 old hat 7 clichéd 8 shopworn 9 hackneyed 10 warmed over 11 commonplace, sentimental, stereotyped

corollary 6 effect, result, sequel, upshot 8 sequence 9 resulting 10 associated, end product, equivalent 11 aftereffect, consequence, precipitate

corona 4 halo 5 cigar, crown, glory 6 circle, rosary, wreath 7 aureola, aureole, circlet, fermata, garland

coronal see **coronet**

coroner 7 crowner, officer 8 examiner

coronet 4 band 5 crown 6 anadem, circle, wreath 7 chaplet, circlet, garland

Coronis *form:* 4 crow *son:* 9 Asclepius 11 Aesculapius

corporal 3 NCO 5 fanon 6 bodily, carnal 7 fleshly, somatic 8 physical

corporate 6 united 7 unified 8 combined 9 aggregate

corporeal 5 hylic, somal 6 bodily, carnal 7 fleshly, somatic 8 material, physical, sensible, tangible 9 objective 10 phenomenal 11 substantial

corps 4 band 5 party, troop 6 outfit, troupe 7 company

corpse 4 body, mort 5 bones, stiff 7 cadaver, carcass, carrion, remains *combining form:* 4 necr 5 necro

corpselike 4 dead 6 deadly 7 deathly, ghastly, ghostly, shadowy 8 deadened, deathful, spectral 10 cadaverous

corpulence 7 fatness, obesity 9 adiposity 10 fleshiness

corpulent 3 fat 5 bulky, gross, heavy, obese, plump, stout 6 fleshy, portly 7 weighty 9 overblown 10 overweight

corpus 4 body, bulk, core, mass 6 oeuvre, staple 9 substance

corpuscle 4 cell 7 hematid 8 hemocyte, monocyte 9 leukocyte 10 lymphocyte 11 erythrocyte, granulocyte

corral 3 hem, mew, pen 4 cage, coop 5 fence, hedge 6 shut in 7 close in, confine, enclose 8 surround 9 enclosure

correct 3 fit, fix 4 done, edit, mend, true 5 amend, emend, exact, right 6 adjust, better, decent, proper, punish, reform, remedy, revise, seemly 7 chasten, improve, perfect, precise, rectify, redress 8 accurate, becoming, chastise, decorous, emendate, flawless, make over, regulate 9 castigate, faultless, veracious, veridical 10 conforming, discipline, impeccable, meticulous, scrupulous 11 comme il faut, punctilious, undistorted 12 conventional *combining form:* 4 orth 5 ortho

correction 3 rod 8 punition 10 discipline, punishment 11 castigation 12 chastisement

corrective 4 cure 6 remedy 8 antidote, remedial 11 counterstep 12 counteragent 13 counteractant, counteractive

correctness 5 order 7 decorum 8 accuracy 9 coherence, congruity, exactness, precision, propriety 10 definitude, exactitude, properness, seemliness 11 orderliness, preciseness 12 decorousness, definiteness

correlate 5 match 6 analog 7 pendant 8 analogue, parallel 10 complement 11 counterpart, countertype 13 correspondent

correlative 2 if, or 3 nor 4 then 6 either 7 neither, related 10 reciprocal 13 corresponding

correspond 4 jibe, suit 5 agree, equal, match, write 6 accord, concur 7 conform, consort 8 dovetail 9 harmonize 11 communicate

correspondence 4 mail 7 letters 8 homogeny, symmetry 9 agreement, congruity 10 conformity 11 consistency *mathematical:* 7 mapping 8 function

correspondent 5 match 6 analog, pen pal, writer 7 fitting 8 analogue, parallel, suitable 9 correlate 11 counterpart, countertype

corresponding 4 akin, like 5 alike 6 agnate 7 similar 8 parallel 9 analogous, consonant 10 comparable *prefix:* 7 counter

correspondingly 2 so 4 also 8 likewise 9 similarly

corrida 9 bullfight *shout:* 3 olé

corridor 4 hall 7 couloir, hallway, passage 10 passageway

corroborate 6 verify 7 bear out, confirm, justify 8 validate 12 authenticate, substantiate

corroborative 7 helping 9 ancillary, assisting, auxiliary 10 collateral, supportive 11 adminicular 12 confirmative, confirmatory, verificatory

corroboratory see corroborative

corrode 3 eat 4 bite, gnaw, rust 5 erode, scour 7 eat away 8 wear away

corrosive 5 acerb 7 acerbic, caustic 9 sarcastic 12 archilochian

corrosiveness 7 sarcasm 8 acerbity 10 causticity

corrugation 4 fold, ruck 5 plica, ridge, rivel 6 crease, furrow, rimple 7 crinkle, wrinkle

corrupt 3 low, rot 4 foul, ruin, turn, warp 5 abase, decay, snide, spoil, stain, taint, venal, wreck 6 abased, befoul, debase, defile, molder, rotten, smirch 7 baneful, crooked, crumble, debauch, degrade, deprave, devious, knavish, noxious, oblique, pervert, putrefy, tarnish, vicious, vitiate 8 bribable, degraded, depraved, infamous, perverse, two-faced 9 animalize, break down, decompose, dishonest, faithless, mercenary, miscreant, nefarious, reprobate, unethical 10 bastardize, degenerate, demoralize, flagitious, inconstant, perfidious, pernicious, unfaithful, unreliable, villainous 11 deleterious, detrimental, treacherous 12 blackguardly, disintegrate, undependable, unprincipled, unscrupulous 13 double-dealing, untrustworthy

corruptible 5 venal 7 buyable 8 bribable 11 purchasable

corruption 4 vice 7 jobbery 8 slangism, solecism 9 barbarism, depravity, vulgarism 10 immorality, wickedness 11 impropriety 13 vernacularism, vernacularity

corsair 5 rover 6 pirate, sea dog 7 sea wolf 8 picaroon, sea rover 9 buccaneer, sea robber 10 freebooter

corset 6 bodice, girdle 7 support

cortex 4 bark, peel, rind 8 peridium *combining form:* 7 cortico

Cortland 5 apple

corundum 4 ruby 5 emery, topaz 7 emerald 8 abrasive, amethyst, sapphire

coruscate 5 flash, gleam, glint 7 glisten, glitter, sparkle 11 scintillate

Corvino's wife 5 Celia

corybantic 3 mad 4 wild 5 rabid 7 frantic, furious 8 frenetic, frenzied 9 delirious

coryphée 6 dancer, hoofer 7 danseur 8 danseuse, figurant 9 ballerina, figurante 10 ballet girl 11 dancing girl

Cosi fan tutte composer 6 Mozart (Wolfgang Amadeus)

cosmetic 4 kohl 5 henna, rouge 6 ceruse, makeup, powder 7 blusher, bronzer, mascara 8 lipgloss, lipstick 9 eye shadow 10 nail polish 11 beautifying, superficial

cosmetologist 10 beautician

cosmic 6 global 8 catholic 9 planetary, universal, worldwide 10 ecumenical 12 cosmopolitan

cosmopolitan 6 cosmic, global, smooth, urbane 8 catholic, cultured, polished 9 civilized, planetary, universal, worldwide 10 cultivated, ecumenical 11 worldly-wise 12 metropolitan 13 sophisticated

cosmos 5 world 6 nature 8 creation, universe

Cossack *army:* 3 Don 4 Ural 5 Kuban 6 voisko *district:* 6 okrugi *land:* 7 Ukraine *leader:* 5 Razin (Stenka) 6 ataman, hetman, Mazepa (Ivan) 7 Bulavin (Kondraty) 8 Pugachev *novel:* 10 Taras Bulba *village:* 8 stanitsa, stanitza

cosset 3 pet 4 baby, love 5 humor, spoil 6 caress, cocker, coddle, cuddle, dandle, fondle, pamper 7 cater to, indulge 11 mollycoddle

cost 3 tab 4 rate, toll 5 price 6 charge, outlay, tariff 7 expense 8 price tag 11 expenditure 12 disbursement *business:* 8 overhead

Costa Rica *capital:* 7 San José *monetary unit:* 5 colon

costermonger 6 hawker 7 peddler 9 barrow boy, barrowman

costive 4 mean 5 bound, close, tight 6 stingy 7 miserly 9 astricted, penurious 10 hardfisted, obstipated 12 cheeseparing, parsimonious

costless 4 free 6 gratis 10 chargeless, gratuitous 13 complimentary

costly 4 dear, high 5 fancy, pricy, steep, stiff 6 pricey 7 premium 8 precious, valuable 9 excessive, expensive, priceless 10 exorbitant, inordinate, invaluable 11 extravagant, inestimable

costume 3 rig 4 garb, mode 5 dress, getup, guise, style 6 outfit, setout 7 fashion, turnout

cot 3 hut 4 camp 5 cabin, lodge, shack 6 shanty 7 cottage *hanging:* 7 hammock *wheeled:* 6 gurney

coterie 3 mob 4 camp, clan, ring 5 cabal 6 circle, clique 7 ingroup 9 camarilla

cottage 3 hut 4 camp 5 cabin, lodge, shack 6 shanty 8 bungalow *Russian:* 5 dacha *Swiss:* 6 chalet

cotton 4 take 5 agree, grasp, toady 6 accept, coddle, kowtow 7 cater to, honey up 8 bootlick, perceive 9 apprehend, harmonize 10 comprehend, fraternize, understand *cleaner:* 3 gin 5 willy 6 linter, willow *cloth:* 4 jean, pima 5 khaki 6 canvas 7 galatea, jaconet, percale, silesia *cloth, Indian:* 5 Surat 6 humhum 7 dhurrie *comb:* 4 card *Egyptian:* 4 maco *fabric:* 3 rep 4 duck, lawn, leno, mull, repp 5 chino, crash, denim, doria, drill, manta, scrim, terry, wigan 6 calico, chintz, dimity, madras, muslin, nankin, sateen, satine 7 batiste, etamine, fustian, nankeen, nanking, organdy 8 drilling, nainsook 9 grenadine 10 seersucker *fabric, lustrous:* 6 sateen, satine *fabric, sheer:* 5 voile *fiber, short:* 4 noil *fuzz remover:* 6 linter *knot:* 3 nep 4 slub *measure:* 3 lea 4 hank, pick, yard 5 count, skein *pad:* 7 pledget *pod:* 4 boll *refuse:* 5 flock 8 grabbots *seed separator:* 3 gin *sheet:* 3 bat 4 batt *thread:* 5 lisle

Cotton State 7 Alabama

cottonwood 5 alamo 6 poplar

cottony 4 soft 5 silky 6 satiny, silken 7 velvety

Coty or Descartes 4 René

couch 3 den, put 4 lair, sink, sofa, word 5 divan, droop, lodge, lower 6 burrow, daybed, phrase 7 depress, express, let down 9 davenport, formulate 12 chesterfield

cougar 3 cat 4 puma 7 panther 9 catamount

cough 6 tussis *drop:* 6 troche 7 lozenge

couloir 4 hall 5 gorge 7 hallway, passage 8 corridor 10 passageway

council 4 diet 5 junta 6 senate 7 cabinet, meeting 8 assembly, conclave, congress, ministry 10 conference, federation 12 consultation *ancient Greek:* 5 boule *church:* 5 synod 10 consistory *medieval English:* 4 moot 5 gemot 6 gemote 7 husting 8 hustings *Muslim:* 5 divan, diwan *Russian:* 4 duma 5 douma 6 soviet *secret:* 5 cabal, junto *Spanish:* 7 cabildo

counsel 4 urge, warn 5 order 6 advice, advise, charge, direct, enjoin, lawyer, prompt 7 suggest 8 admonish, advocate, attorney 9 prescribe, recommend, reprehend 10 advisement *British:* 9 barrister, solicitor

count 3 add, sum, tot 4 hope, look, mean 5 tally, total, weigh 6 bank on, census, expect, figure, import, matter, number, reckon, rely on 7 build on, compute, signify, trust in, trust to 8 bank upon, depend on, estimate, militate, numerate, quantify, reckon on, rely upon 9 calculate, enumerate 10 depend upon 11 calculate on

countenance 3 mug 4 back, cast, face, look, phiz 5 favor, go for 6 accept, visage 7 approve, commend, support 8 advocate, features, hold with 9 approbate, encourage 10 expression *combining form:* 6 prosop 7 prosopo

counter 3 pit, vie 4 anti 5 match, polar 6 oppose 7 adverse, hostile, reverse 8 antipode, antipole, contrary, converse, impeding, opposite 9 antipodal, diametric, hindering, oppugnant 10 antipodean, antithesis 11 obstructive 12 antagonistic, antithetical 13 contradictory

counteract 3 fix 5 annul 6 negate 7 correct, rectify, redress 8 negative 9 cancel out, frustrate 10 neutralize

counteractant 4 cure 6 remedy 8 antidote 10 corrective

counteragent see **counteractant**

counterbalance 6 make up, offset, redeem, set off 7 correct, rectify 8 atone for, outweigh 10 compensate

counterblow 7 revenge 8 avenging, reprisal, requital, revanche 9 vengeance 10 avengement 11 retaliation, retribution

countercheck 5 annul 6 negate 7 redress 8 negative 9 cancel out, frustrate 10 neutralize

counterclockwise 4 levo

counterfeit 3 act, ape, gyp 4 copy, fake, hoax, sham 5 bluff, bogus, dummy, false, feign, fraud, mimic, phony 6 affect, assume, deceit, pseudo 7 feigned, imitate, pretend 8 delusive, delusory, simulate, spurious 9 brummagem, deception, deceptive, imposture, pinchbeck, pretended, simulated 10 fraudulent, misleading, simulacrum *combining form:* 5 pseud 6 pseudo

counterpane 6 spread 8 bedcover, coverlet 9 bedspread

counterpart 4 like 5 equal, match 6 analog 7 vis-à-vis 8 analogue, parallel 9 correlate 10 complement, coordinate, equivalent 13 correspondent

counterpoise 4 trim 6 make up, offset, redeem, set off, stasis, steady 7 balance, ballast 8 atone for, outweigh 9 stabilize 10 compensate 11 equilibrium

counterpole see **opposite**

countersign 4 word 8 password 9 watchword

countertype 5 match 6 analog 8 analogue, parallel 9 correlate 13 correspondent

countervail 4 foil 6 offset, redeem, set off, thwart 7 balance, correct, rectify 8 atone for, outweigh, overcome, surmount 9 frustrate 10 compensate

countless 6 untold 10 innumerous, numberless, unnumbered 11 innumerable

12 unnumberable *combining form:* 4 myri 5 myria, myrio

Count of Monte Cristo 6 Dantes *author:* 5 Dumas (Alexandre)

count out 3 bar 4 bate 5 debar 6 except 7 exclude, rule out, suspend 9 eliminate

countrified 5 rural 6 rustic 7 bucolic 8 agrestic, pastoral 10 campestral, provincial

country 4 home, land, soil 5 rural 6 nation, rustic 7 bucolic, outland 8 agrestic, homeland, pastoral 10 campestral, fatherland, motherland, provincial *dance:* 4 reel *home:* 5 manor, ranch, villa 8 hacienda *music:* 9 bluegrass *road:* 4 lane, path 5 byway

country jake 4 hick, rube 5 clown 6 rustic 7 bumpkin, hayseed 9 hillbilly 10 clodhopper 12 backwoodsman

coup 4 blow, plan 5 d'etat, upset 6 putsch, stroke 8 takeover 9 stratagem

couple 3 duo 4 dyad, join, link, mate, pair, span, team, yoke 5 brace, hitch, marry, unite 6 hook up 7 bracket, combine, conjoin, connect, doublet, harness, twosome 8 coalesce

coupler 4 link, ring 7 shackle *in an organ:* 7 tirasse *railroad:* 7 drawbar

couplet 4 pair 5 twins 7 distich

coupling 4 seam 5 joint, union 7 joining 8 junction, juncture 10 connection

courage 4 grit, guts 5 heart, moxie, pluck, spunk, valor 6 mettle, spirit 7 bravery, heroism 8 audacity, backbone, boldness, firmness, tenacity, valiance, valiancy 9 assurance, fortitude, gallantry 10 resolution 11 doughtiness, intrepidity, persistence 12 fearlessness 13 dauntlessness, determination

courageous 4 bold 5 brave, fiery, stout 6 manful, plucky, spunky, strong 7 doughty, valiant 8 fearless, intrepid, unafraid, valorous 9 audacious, dauntless, tenacious, undaunted 12 high-spirited

courier 5 envoy 6 bearer, legate, nuncio 7 carrier 8 emissary 9 go-between, messenger 11 internuncio

course 3 row, run, way 4 dart, dash, duct, line, path, plan, race, road, rush, tear 5 canal, chain, chase, hurry, orbit, order, range, route, scoot, scope, speed, trend 6 career, design, hasten, hustle, manner, policy, polity, scheme, scurry, sequel, series, sprint, string, system 7 advance, channel, circuit, conduit, passage, pattern, program, regimen, routine, scamper 8 aqueduct, progress, sequence 9 procedure 10 succession 11 progression *combining form:* 4 drom 5 dromo *dinner:* 5 salad 6 entrée 7 dessert 9 blue plate *of study:* 8 syllabus 10 curriculum

courser 4 bird 7 charger 8 huntsman, war-horse

court 3 bar, woo 4 quad, yard 5 charm, judge, spark 6 allure, pursue 7 address, justice, romance 8 tribunal 9 captivate, curtilage, enclosure 10 magistrate, quadrangle, sweetheart *action:* 4 suit 5 trial 6 appeal, assize 7 hearing, inquest, lawsuit 10 proceeding *calendar:* 6 docket *call to:* 7 summons 8 subpoena 11 arraignment *circuit:* 4 eyre *crier's call:* 4 oyes, oyez *decision:* 6 assize 7 finding, verdict 8 judgment *ecclesiastical:* 4 Rota 5 Curia 10 consistory *former English:* 4 leet *Indian:* 6 durbar *kind:* 4 moot 5 civil 6 county, family 7 circuit, customs, federal, supreme 8 chancery, criminal, district, juvenile, kangaroo, superior 9 appellate, municipal 11 territorial *medieval English:* 4 eyre, moot 5 gemot 6 gemote 7 husting 8 hustings *minutes:* 4 acta *of equity:* 8 chancery *officer:* 2 DA 5 clerk, crier, judge 6 puisne 7 bailiff, justice, marshal, sheriff 10 prosecutor *order:* 4 writ 5 arret, edict 6 decree 7 summons 8 mandamus, subpoena *panel:* 4 jury *relating to:* 5 aulic 8 judicial *session:* 6 assize 7 sitting 8 sederunt

courteous 5 civil 6 polite 7 genteel 8 mannerly 9 attentive 10 thoughtful 11 considerate 12 well-mannered

courter 5 wooer 6 suitor

courtesy 5 favor 6 comity 7 amenity, service 8 chivalry, civility, kindness 9 attention, gallantry, geniality 10 affability, cordiality, indulgence 11 courtliness 12 complaisance, dispensation, graciousness 13 attentiveness, consideration

court game see under **game**

courtly 4 prim 5 civil, lofty, preux, stiff 6 august, formal 7 gallant, starchy, stately, stilted, studied 8 gracious, imposing 9 civilized, dignified 11 ceremonious 12 conventional

courtship 4 suit 6 wooing 7 romance *former custom of:* 8 bundling

courtyard 4 quad 5 garth, patio 6 atrium 7 cortile 9 curtilage 10 quadrangle

Cousteau, Jacques *ship:* 7 Calypso *vehicle:* 11 bathysphere

cove 3 arm, bay 4 gulf 5 bayou, bight, creek, firth, inlet 6 harbor, slough

covenant 3 vow 4 bond, pact 5 agree, swear 6 concur, pledge, plight 7 bargain, compact 8 contract 9 agreement 10 convention 11 transaction

cover 3 cap, lid 4 bury, fend, hide, hood, mask, wrap 5 brood, cache, cloak, crown, guard, guise, haven, put-on, stash, track 6 asylum, bush up, canopy, defend, enfold, enwrap, facade, harbor, hiding, refuge, safety, screen, secure, shield, shroud, travel 7 blanket, bulwark, conceal, enclose, envelop, overlay, protect, retreat, secrete, shelter 8 disguise, ensconce, overcast, pass over, security, traverse 9 harborage, safeguard, sanctuary, semblance, superpose 10 false front, masquerade, overspread 11 concealment, superimpose *combining form:* 8 operculi *rooflike:* 6 awning, canopy *the eyes:* 9 blindfold *the face:* 4 mask, veil *the mouth:* 6 muzzle *with asphalt:* 4 pave *with cloth:* 5 drape *with dirt:* 6 bemire, besoil 8 besmirch *with jewels:* 5 begem *with straw:* 6 thatch

coverall 10 boiler suit

covered *combining form:* 5 crypt, krypt 6 crypto, krypto

covered wagon 9 Conestoga

covering *anatomical:* 5 theca, velum 6 tegmen 7 velamen 8 tegument 10 integument *close-fitting:* 6 sheath 9 sheathing *cloth:* 5 sheet *combining form:* 4 cole, derm, steg 5 coleo, derma, stego *flap:* 9 operculum *for a book:* 6 jacket *for a cigar:* 7 wrapper *for a coffin:* 4 pall *for a corpse:* 6 shroud 8 cerement *for a package:* 7 wrapper *for concealment:* 10 camouflage *for food:* 4 cosy, cozy *for soil:* 5 mulch *metal:* 4 mail 5 armor *of a diatom:* 6 lorica *of a plant ovary:* 8 pericarp *of a seed:* 4 aril, case 5 testa *of fruits:* 4 peel, rind *of gloom:* 4 pall *of grain:* 4 hull, husk 5 chaff *shell-like:* 8 carapace *thin:* 4 film 6 patina, veneer *waterproof:* 4 tarp 9 tarpaulin

coverlet 6 spread 8 bedcover 9 bedspread 11 counterpane

covert 5 haven, privy 6 asylum, buried, harbor, hidden, masked, refuge, secret 7 cloaked, furtive, guarded, retreat, shelter, sub-rosa 8 hush-hush, obscured, shrouded, stealthy, ulterior 9 concealed, disguised, harborage, sanctuary 10 dissembled, undercover 11 camouflaged, clandestine 12 hugger-mugger 13 surreptitious, under-the-table

covertly 7 sub rosa 8 in camera, secretly 9 by stealth, furtively, privately 10 stealthily 12 hugger-mugger 13 clandestinely

covet 4 want, wish 5 crave 6 desire 10 desiderate

covetous 4 avid, keen 5 eager, itchy 6 grabby, greedy 7 envious, hoggish, jealous, piggish, selfish, swinish 8 desirous, esurient, grasping, grudging, ravenous 9 rapacious, voracious 10 gluttonous 11 acquisitive

covey 4 band, bevy, crew 5 bunch, group, party 7 cluster 8 assembly

covin 4 plot 5 cabal 6 scheme 8 intrigue 10 conspiracy 11 machination

cow (see also **cattle**) 4 faze, kine (plural), neat 5 abash, bossy, bully, daunt 6 appall, bovine, dismay, hector, rattle 7 bluster, dragoon 8 bludgeon, browbeat, bulldoze, bullyrag 9 discomfit, embarrass, strong-arm 10 disconcert, intimidate *cud:* 5 rumen *French:* 5 vache *hornless:* 5 doddy, muley 6 doddie, mulley 7 pollard *mammary gland:* 5 udder *pasture:* 7 vaccary *pen:* 6 corral *shed:* 4 barn, byre 7 shippen, shippon *Spanish:* 4 vaca *young:* 4 calf 5 stirk 6 heifer

coward 4 baby 6 craven 7 caitiff, chicken, dastard, gutless, milksop, quitter, unmanly 8 poltroon, recreant, weakling 9 fraidy-cat, jellyfish, spunkless 10 scaredy-cat 11 lily-livered, poltroonish, yellowbelly 12 invertebrate, poor-spirited 13 pusillanimous

____ Coward 4 Noel

cowardly 4 vile 6 afraid, craven, yellow 7 caitiff, chicken, fearful, gutless, panicky, unmanly 8 cravenly, poltroon, recreant, timorous 9 dastardly, spunkless, worthless 11 lily-livered, milk-livered, poltroonish 12 fainthearted, poor-spirited, white-livered 13 pusillanimous

cowboy 5 waddy 6 drover, herder, waddie 7 puncher, rancher 8 buckaroo, buckeroo, herdsman, wrangler 9 cattleman 10 cowpuncher 12 broncobuster *contest:* 5 rodeo *legendary:* 9 Pecos Bill *leggings:* 5 chaps *movie:* 3 Mix (Tom) 5 Autry (Gene) 6 Rogers (Roy) 8 Cisco Kid 15 Hopalong Cassidy *rope:* 5 lasso, reata, riata 6 lariat *Spanish-American:* 6 charro, gaucho 7 llanero, vaquero

cower 4 fawn 5 quail, toady, wince 6 blench, cringe, flinch, grovel, kowtow, recoil, shrink 7 honey up, truckle 8 bootlick 9 brownnose 11 apple-polish

cowfish 6 dugong, sea cow 7 grampus, manatee 8 sirenian

cowl 3 cop 4 hood, monk 5 amice 6 almuce 7 capuche

cowpox 8 vaccinia

cowpuncher see cowboy

coxcomb 3 fop 4 buck, dude 5 blood, dandy 8 macaroni 9 exquisite 11 Beau Brummel 12 lounge lizard

coy 3 shy 4 arch 5 timid 6 decent, demure, proper, seemly 7 bashful, playful 8 decorous, retiring, skittish 9 diffident, kittenish, unassured 10 capricious, coquettish 11 mischievous, unassertive 12 self-effacing

Coyote State 11 South Dakota

coypu 6 rodent *fur:* 6 nutria

Cozbi's father 3 Zur

cozen 3 gyp 4 beat, bilk 5 cheat 6 betray, delude, diddle, humbug, illude, take in 7 beguile, deceive, defraud, mislead, sell out, swindle 8 flimflam 11 double-cross

cozy 4 easy, safe, snug, soft 5 comfy, cushy, pally 6 chummy, secure 7 easeful 8 covering, intimate 10 buddy-buddy, palsy-walsy 11 comfortable

crab 4 beef, fuss, yaup, yawp 5 bleat, gripe 6 griper, grouch, kicker, squawk, yammer 7 decapod, grouser, growler 8 arthopod, grumbler 9 bellyache, shellfish 10 bellyacher, complainer, crosspatch, crustacean 11 faultfinder *claw:* 5 chela 6 nipper *combining form:* 6 carcin 7 carcino *constellation:* 6 Cancer *genus:* 3 Uca 6 Birgus 7 Limulus, Pagurus *hermit:* 8 pagurian *kind:* 3 pea 4 blue, king, pine, rock 5 ghost, purse 6 hermit, partan, spider 7 fiddler 9 Dungeness, horseshoe *king, horseshoe:* 7 limulus 8 limuloid *relating to:* 7 cancrid *resembling:* 8 cancroid

crabbed 4 dour, glum 5 blunt, gruff, huffy, sulky, surly, testy 6 cranky, crusty, gloomy, morose, sullen 7 brusque 8 choleric, snappish 9 irascible, irritable, saturnine, splenetic

crabby see crabbed

crab-like 8 cancroid

crabwise 8 sidelong, sideward, sideways 9 laterally

crack 2 go 3 gag, try 4 bang, bash, belt, blow, boom, chap, clap, jape, jest, joke, quip, rent, rift, rima, rime, shot, slam, slap, slit, snap, stab, wham, whop 5 adept, blast, break, burst, chink, cleft, crash, flash, fling, jiffy, smack, smash, split, whack, whirl 6 cranny, decode, expert, master, moment 7 crevice, decrypt, fissure, instant, skilled 8 crevasse, decipher, drollery, interval, masterly, rimation, skillful, superior 9 bastinado, excellent, masterful, witticism 10 interstice, percussion, proficient 11 split second 12 cryptanalyze 13 discontinuity

crackbrain 3 nut 4 kook 5 crank 6 cuckoo 7 lunatic 8 crackpot 9 ding-a-ling, screwball

crackdown 8 quashing 10 repression 11 suppression

cracked 3 mad 4 daft, nuts 5 batty, crazy, daffy 6 crazed, cuckoo, insane, maniac, rimose, rimous, screwy 7 lunatic 8 demented

cracker 5 wafer 7 biscuit, saltine 8 Georgian 9 Floridian

crackerjack 4 lulu 5 adept, dandy, dilly, nifty 6 corker, expert, master 7 skilled 8 jim-dandy, knockout, masterly, skillful 9 humdinger, masterful 10 proficient 11 lalapalooza

crackle 4 snap 7 sparkle 9 crepitate

crackpot 3 nut 4 case, kook, loon
5 crank, loony 6 cuckoo, madman, maniac,
oddity 7 dingbat, lunatic, oddball 9 character, ding-a-ling, eccentric, harebrain, screwball

crack-up 5 crash, smash, wreck 6 pileup
7 debacle, decline, smashup 8 collapse
9 breakdown 13 deterioration

cradlesong 7 lullaby 8 berceuse

craft 3 art, job 5 skill, trade 6 métier
7 calling, cunning, know-how, slyness
8 artifice, foxiness, vocation, wiliness
9 cageyness, canniness, dexterity, expertise 10 adroitness, artfulness, profession
combining form: 6 techno, techny

craftiness 3 art 7 cunning, slyness 8 artifice, foxiness, wiliness 9 cageyness, canniness 10 artfulness

craftsman 5 smith 6 carver, potter,
weaver, wright 7 artisan, builder, jeweler
9 carpenter

crafty 3 sly 4 foxy, keen, wily 5 acute,
sharp 6 adroit, artful, astute, clever, tricky
7 cunning, fawning 8 guileful 9 deceitful,
insidious *Scottish:* 6 sleeky 7 sleekit

cragged 5 harsh, rough 6 jagged, rugged,
uneven 7 scraggy 8 asperous, scabrous,
unsmooth

craggy see **cragged**

cram 3 jam, ram 4 bolt, fill, gulp, heap,
load, pack, tamp, wolf 5 chock, crowd,
crush, drive, force, press, shove, study,
stuff, wedge 6 bone up, englut, gobble,
guzzle, review, squash, thrust 7 jam-pack,
overeat, squeeze 11 ingurgitate

crammed 4 full 5 awash 6 jammed,
loaded, packed 7 brimful, crowded, stuffed
8 brimming 9 chock-full

cramp 5 stint 7 shackle 8 confined
9 restraint, stricture 10 constraint, limitation
11 confinement, restriction 12 incommodious 13 constrainment

cramped 4 tiny 5 close, small, tight 6 little, minute, narrow 8 confined 9 two-by-
four 12 incommodious

cranberry 9 vaccinium *tree:* 7 pembina

crane 4 bird, boom 7 derrick 9 cormorant
10 demoiselle *arm:* 3 jib *genus:* 4 Grus
Indian: 5 sarus *resembling:* 6 gruine
ship's: 5 davit *traveling:* 5 jenny, titan
7 goliath

Crane's hero 12 Henry Fleming

cranium 5 skull

crank 3 bee, nut 4 crab, kook 5 fancy
6 cuckoo, griper, grouch, notion, vagary
7 boutade, caprice, conceit, grouser,
growler, lunatic 8 crackpot, crotchet, grumbler, sourpuss 9 ding-a-ling, harebrain,
screwball 10 bellyacher, crackbrain, crosspatch 11 faultfinder

cranky 4 daft 5 crazy, cross, daffy, ratty,
testy, waspy 6 crazed, cuckoo, insane,
ornery, tetchy, touchy 7 bearish, cracked,
froward, waspish 8 cankered, choleric, contrary, vinegary 9 crotchety, irascible, temperish 10 bad-humored, ill-humored, vinegarish 11 hot-tempered 12 cantankerous,
crackbrained, cross-grained, disagreeable
13 quick-tempered

cranny 4 nook 5 niche 7 byplace

crash 3 din, jar, ram 4 bang, boom, bump,
bust, clap, fail, fold, jolt, slam, wham
5 blast, break, burst, crack, shock, smash,
wreck 6 impact, pileup 7 collide, crack-up,
debacle, smashup 8 accident, collapse
9 breakdown, collision 10 concussion, percussion

crashing 5 gross, utter 7 blasted 8 absolute, infernal, positive 9 downright 10 confounded, consummate

crass 3 raw 4 rude 5 crude, gross, rough
6 coarse, vulgar 7 loutish, uncouth 8 churlish 9 inelegant, unrefined

crate 4 heap 5 wreck 6 jalopy, junker
7 clunker

crater 3 pit 4 hole, pock 6 cavity 7 cal-
dera 10 depression *Hawaiian:* 7 Kilauea

cravat 3 tie 4 band 5 scarf 7 bandage,
necktie

crave 3 ask, beg 4 ache, long, lust, pine,
pray, sigh, want, wish 5 brace, covet, plead
6 appeal, demand, desire, hanker, hunger,
thirst 7 beseech, call for, entreat, implore,
require, suspire 9 importune 10 desiderate,
supplicate 11 necessitate

craven 4 funk 6 coward, funker 7 chicken,
dastard, gutless, quitter, unmanly 8 cowardly, poltroon 9 spunkless 11 lily-livered,
plotroonish, yellowbelly 12 poor-spirited
13 pusillanimous

craving 4 itch, lust, urge 6 desire 7 passion 8 appetite 10 appetition

crawl 4 flow, inch, teem 5 creep, slide,
snail, snake, swarm 6 abound, grovel
9 pullulate

crawling 6 repent 7 reptant

craze 3 fad 4 chic, rage 5 crack, fever,
furor, mania, style, vogue 6 frenzy, furore,
madden 7 derange, fashion, unhinge 8 distract 9 unbalance 10 dernier cri, enthusiasm

craziness 5 folly 7 inanity 8 insanity
9 absurdity, dottiness, silliness 11 foolishness, witlessness 13 senselessness

crazy 3 fey, mad 4 daft, gaga, loco, luny,
nuts, wack 5 balmy, batty, daffy, dotty,
goofy, loony, nutty, silly, wacky, whack
6 absurd, cuckoo, insane, looney, madman,
maniac, screwy, teched, whacky 7 bonkers, cracked, foolish, lunatic, tetched,
touched, unsound 8 crackpot, demented,

deranged **9** bedlamite, possessed, senseless **10** crackbrain, moonstruck, unbalanced **11** harebrained **12** preposterous *British:* **5** potty **6** scatty *Scottish:* **3** wud

crazy house 6 asylum **8** loony bin **9** funny farm **10** booby hatch

cream 3 top **4** balm, beat, best, pick, whip **5** blast, elite, pride, prime, prize, salve **6** cerate, choice, chrism **7** clobber, unction, unguent **8** lambaste, ointment

crease 4 fold, ruck **5** plica, ridge, rivel **6** furrow, rimple **7** crinkle, wrinkle **11** corrugation

create 4 make, sire **5** found, hatch, set up, spawn, start **6** father, parent **7** compose, produce **8** conceive, engender, generate **9** establish, formulate, institute, originate, procreate **10** constitute

creation 5 world **6** cosmos, kosmos, nature **8** megacosm, universe **9** macrocosm **11** macrocosmos

creative 8 original **9** demiurgic, deviceful, ingenious, inventive **10** innovative, innovatory **11** originative **12** innovational

creator 4 sire **5** maker **6** author, father **7** founder **8** inventor **9** architect, generator, patriarch **10** originator

creature 3 man **5** beast, being, brute, human, toady **6** animal, minion, mortal, person **7** critter **8** truckler **9** personage, sycophant *fabled:* **3** elf, imp **4** ogre, puck **5** dwarf, fairy, giant, gnome, troll **6** dragon, goblin, merman, sprite **7** brownie, gremlin, mermaid, monster, unicorn **9** hobgoblin **10** leprechaun; (see also **monster**) *winged:* **4** bird, fowl **8** volatile

credence 5 faith, trust **6** belief, credit **8** reliance **10** confidence

credentials 6 papers **9** character, documents, reference **11** testimonial **13** documentation

credible 5 solid, sound, valid **6** trusty **8** faithful, rational **9** authentic, colorable, plausible **10** believable, convincing, reasonable, satisfying **11** trustworthy **12** satisfactory

credit 3 lay **4** deem, feel **5** asset, faith, honor, refer, sense, think, trust **6** assign, belief, charge, impute, notice, weight **7** ascribe, believe **8** consider, credence, prestige, reliance **9** attribute, authority, influence **10** confidence **11** recognition

creditable 7 reputed **9** colorable, estimable, plausible, reputable **10** believable **11** respectable **13** well-thought-of

credo 5 creed **6** belief **8** ideology

credulous 5 naive **6** unwary **7** dupable **8** gullible, trustful, trusting **9** accepting, believing **12** unsuspecting, unsuspicious **13** unquestioning

creed 4 cult, sect **5** credo, faith **6** belief, church **8** ideology, religion **9** communion **10** connection, persuasion **12** denomination

creek 3 ria **4** gill, race, rill **5** brook **6** arroyo, rillet, runlet, runnel, stream **7** freshet, rivulet **8** brooklet **9** streamlet

creep 4 edge, inch, lurk, slip **5** crawl, glide, shirk, skulk, slide, slink, snake, sneak, steal **6** tiptoe **7** gumshoe, slither, sniggle, wriggle **9** pussyfoot

creeping 6 repent **7** reptant *combining form:* **6** herpet **7** herpeto

crème de la crème 4 best **5** elite **6** gentry **7** aristoi **8** optimacy **9** blue blood, haut monde **10** upper crust **11** aristocracy

Cremona family 6 Amatis

Creon *daughter:* **6** Creusa, Glauce, Glauke *sister:* **7** Jocasta *son:* **6** Haemon *victim:* **8** Antigone

crepehanger 9 Cassandra, pessimist, worrywart

crescendo 4 acme, apex, peak **5** crest **6** apogee, climax, culmen **8** capstone, meridian **11** culmination

crescent-shaped 6 lunate **7** lunated *body or surface:* **8** meniscus *combining form:* **5** selen **6** seleni, seleno

crest 3 cap, top **4** acme, apex, noon, peak, roof **5** arête, chine, crown, ridge **6** apogee, climax, summit, vertex **7** hogback **8** pinnacle, surmount **9** crescendo, fastigium **11** culmination *combining form:* **4** loph **5** lophi, lopho **6** lophio *of a wave:* **8** whitecap

crestfallen 3 low **4** blue, down **8** cast down, dejected, downcast **9** depressed **10** dispirited **11** downhearted **12** disconsolate

Crete *ancient city:* **7** Cnossus, Knossos **8** Phaistos *ancient name:* **6** Candia *capital:* **5** Canea *goddess:* **8** Dictynna **11** Britomartis *guard:* **5** Talos *king:* **5** Minos **9** Idomeneus *maze:* **9** labyrinth *monster:* **8** Minotaur *mountain:* **3** Ida *princess:* **7** Ariadne

cretin 4 fool, zany **5** ament, idiot, moron **6** zombie **7** half-wit **8** imbecile **9** simpleton

Creusa *father:* **5** Priam *husband:* **6** Aeneas *mother:* **6** Hecuba *son:* **3** Ion **8** Ascanius

crevice 4 seam, slit **5** chink, cleft, crack, grike **6** cranny **7** fissure **8** cleavage, crevasse **10** interstice

crew 4 band, bevy, gang, team **5** bunch, covey, group, party **7** cluster, retinue **8** assembly

crib 3 bed, bin, box, hut, key **4** pony, trot, weir **5** cheat, crate, hovel, stall, steal **6** cradle, crèche, manger, pilfer **7** barrier, brothel, purloin 8 bassinet, bedstead, bordello 9 enclosure 10 plagiarism, plagiarize

cricket *period of play:* 7 innings *team:* 6 eleven *term:* 2 on 3 leg, off, rot 4 bowl 5 pitch 6 bowler, wicket, yorker 7 batsman, striker 9 fieldsman *turn at bat:* 4 over

crime 3 sin 4 evil, tort 6 breach, delict, felony 7 misdeed, offense 8 delictum, iniquity 9 diablerie, violation 10 illegality, wrongdoing 11 misdemeanor 13 transgression *instructor:* 5 Fagin

Crimea *capital:* 10 Simferopol *city:* 5 Kerch, Yalta 10 Sevastopol *river:* 4 Alma *sea:* 4 Azov *strait:* 5 Kerch

criminal 4 hood, thug 5 crook, felon 6 outlaw 7 convict, illegal, illicit, lawless, mobster 8 fugitive, gangster, jailbird, offender, unlawful, wrongful 9 racketeer, wrongdoer 10 lawbreaker, malefactor, trespasser 12 illegitimate, transgressor *habitual:* 8 repeater 10 recidivist

criminate 3 tax 6 accuse, charge, indict 7 arraign, impeach 9 inculpate

crimp 3 bar, bit, rub 4 friz, snag 5 check, frizz, screw 6 bridle, hamper, hold in, hurdle, rimple, ruck up, rumple 7 crinkle, crumple, inhibit, scrunch, wrinkle 8 hold back, hold down, mountain, obstacle, restrain, withhold 9 constrain 10 impediment 11 Chinese wall, obstruction

crimple 5 screw 6 ruck up, rumble 7 crinkle, crumple, scrunch, wrinkle

crimson 3 red 4 glow, pink, rose 5 blush, color, flush, rouge 6 mantle, pinken, redden

cringe 4 fawn 5 cower, quail, toady, wince 6 blench, flinch, grovel, kowtow, recoil, shrink, slaver 7 truckle 8 bootlick 11 apple-polish

crinkle 4 fold, ruck 5 crimp, plica, ridge, rivel, screw 6 crease, furrow, rimple, ruck up, rumple 7 crimple, crumple, scrunch 11 corrugation

crinkly 5 crepy 6 crepey

cripple 3 sap 4 lame, maim 5 blunt, palsy 6 disarm, mayhem, weaken 7 disable, dislimb, unbrace 8 enfeeble, mutilate, paralyze 9 attenuate, dismember, prostrate, undermine 10 debilitate, immobilize 12 incapacitate, unstrengthen

cripples' patron saint 5 Giles

crisis 4 pass 5 pinch 6 strait 8 exigency, juncture, zero hour 9 emergency 10 crossroads 11 contingency 12 turning point

crisp 5 short 6 biting 7 brittle, crumbly, crunchy, cutting, friable, ingoing 8 clearcut, incisive 9 trenchant 11 penetrating

crisscross 9 decussate, intersect

criterion 5 gauge 7 measure 8 standard 9 benchmark, yardstick 10 touchstone

critic 5 momus 6 carper, Zoilus 7 carping, caviler, knocker 8 captious, caviling, censurer, quibbler 9 aristarch, belittler, cavillous, muckraker, nitpicker 10 censorious, disparager, mudslinger 11 faultfinder, smellfungus

critical 4 dire 5 acute, fussy 7 carping, crucial, finicky, pivotal, weighty 8 captious, caviling, decisive 9 cavillous, demeaning, desperate, important, momentous 10 belittling, censorious, conclusive, particular 11 climacteric, disparaging, significant 12 faultfinding 13 consequential, determinative *study:* 6 examen 8 exegesis

criticism 5 blame 6 notice, rebuke, review 7 censure, comment, opinion, reproof 8 analysis, critique, diatribe, judgment, reproval, reviewal 9 appraisal 10 assessment, commentary 11 examination, observation

criticize 3 pan, rap 4 carp 5 blame, blast, cavil, cut up, fault, knock, roast, scold 6 rebuke, scathe 7 censure, condemn, reprove 8 badmouth, denounce, lambaste 9 castigate, fustigate, reprehend, reprobate 10 denunciate

criticizer 5 momus 6 carper, Zoilus 7 caviler, knocker 9 aristarch 11 faultfinder

critique see **criticism**

critter 5 beast, brute 6 animal 8 creature

Crius *father:* 6 Uranus *mother:* 4 Gaea *son:* 8 Astraeus

croak 3 die 5 scold 6 grouch, grouse, murmur, mutter 7 grumble, quarrel 8 complain

croaking 5 gruff, husky 6 hoarse

croaky see **croaking**

Croatia *capital:* 6 Zagreb *city:* 5 Split 6 Osijek, Rijeka

crock 3 jar, pot 4 smut, soot 7 disable 8 potsherd 11 earthenware

crocodile 7 reptile *bird:* 6 plover 9 trochilus *Indian:* 6 gavial *relative:* 9 alligator *South American:* 6 caiman, cayman, jacare *Southeast Asian:* 6 muggar, mugger, muggur

Croesus' kingdom 5 Lydia

Cromwell, Oliver *regiment:* 9 Ironsides *son:* 7 Richard *victory site:* 6 Naseby

crone 3 hag 4 drab, trot 5 biddy, witch 6 beldam

Cronus 5 Titan 6 Saturn *daughter:* 4 Hera 6 Hestia 7 Demeter *father:* 6 Uranus *mother:* 4 Gaea *sister:* 4 Rhea 6 Cybele, Tethys *son:* 4 Zeus 5 Hades 7 Jupiter, Neptune 8 Poseidon *wife:* 4 Rhea 6 Cybele

crony 3 pal 4 chum 5 buddy 6 comate 7 comrade 9 associate, companion 11 running mate

crook 3 bow 4 bend 5 curve, round, thief 6 bandit, robber

crooked 5 lying, snaky, snide, venal 6 curved, errant, shifty, zigzag 7 bending, corrupt, curving, devious, winding 8 rambling, ruthless, tortuous, twisting 9 deceitful, dishonest, underhand 10 fraudulent, meandering, serpentine, untruthful 12 unscrupulous 13 double-dealing *combining form:* 5 ancyl, ankyl 6 anchyl, ancylo, ankylo 7 anchylo

crookedly 4 awry 5 askew 6 askant 7 askance 8 cockeyed 9 cock-a-hoop

croon 3 hum, low 4 lull, moan, sing, wail 6 lament, murmur

crooner 4 Cole (Nat "King"), Como (Perry), 6 Crosby (Bing), Martin (Dean), Vallee (Rudy) 7 Sinatra (Frank) 8 Williams (Andy)

crop 3 cut, hew, mow, top 4 chop, clip, pare, snip, trim 5 prune, shave, shear, skive 7 harvest, pollard 8 fruitage, truncate 10 detruncate

cropping 7 harvest, reaping 9 gathering 10 harvesting 11 ingathering

croquet 5 roque

crosier 5 staff

cross 4 deny, mule, over, rood 5 ratty, testy, trial 6 betray, cranky, hybrid, impugn, negate, ordeal, tetchy, touchy 7 athwart, calvary, carping, gainsay, mongrel, sell out 8 captious, choleric, traverse 9 decussate, disaffirm, half blood, half-breed, hybridize, intersect, irascible, temperish 10 affliction, contradict, contravene, interbreed, transverse, visitation 11 tribulation 13 quick-tempered *a river:* 4 ford *bearer:* 8 crucifer *combining form:* 6 stauro *decoration:* 4 Iron 8 Victoria *Egyptian:* 4 ankh *kind:* 3 tau 5 Greek, Latin, papal 6 Celtic, fleury, formée, moline, pommée, potent 7 avellan, botonée, Calvary, Maltese 8 crucifix, fourchée, Lorraine, quadrate 11 patriarchal 12 Saint Andrew's 13 Saint Anthony's *section:* 5 slice *stroke of a letter:* 5 serif

crossbow 8 arbalest, arbalist

crossbreed 4 mule 6 hybrid 7 bastard, mongrel 9 half blood, half-breed, hybridize 10 interbreed

crosscut 9 decussate, intersect

cross-examination 5 grill 8 grilling 11 questioning, third degree 13 interrogation

cross-eye 6 squint 9 esotropia 10 strabismus

crossing 6 thwart 8 traverse 10 transverse 11 transversal

cross out 6 cancel, delete

crosspatch 4 crab 5 crank 6 griper, grouch 7 grouser, growler 8 grumbler, sorehead, sourpuss 10 complainer

crossroads 4 pass 5 pinch 6 crisis, strait 8 exigency, juncture, zero hour 9 carrefour, emergency 11 contingency 12 intersection, turning point *goddess:* 6 Hecate, Hekate, Trivia

cross-shaped 8 cruciate 9 cruciform

crossways 6 across 7 athwart 10 diagonally 12 transversely

crosswise see **crossways**

crotchet 4 whim 5 fancy, freak, quirk 6 megrim, vagary 7 boutade, caprice, conceit 12 eccentricity

crotchety 5 waspy 6 cranky, ornery 7 bearish, waspish 8 cankered, contrary, vinegary 10 vinegarish 12 cantankerous, cross-grained

crouch 4 bend, duck 5 cower, hunch, squat, stoop 6 huddle 10 hunker down 11 scrooch down

crow 4 blow, brag, puff 5 boast, exult, gloat, mouth, prate, vaunt 9 gasconade 11 rodomontade *colony:* 7 rookery *combining form:* 5 corax *cry:* 3 caw *family:* 3 daw, jay 4 rook 5 raven 6 chough, corvid, hoodie, magpie 7 jackdaw 8 Corvidae *genus:* 6 Corvus *Hawaiian:* 5 alala *relating to:* 7 corvine

crowbar 3 pry 5 jimmy, lever 7 gablock 8 gavelock

crowd 3 jam, lot, mob, set 4 army, bear, cram, herd, host, push, rout, ruck 5 bunch, cloud, crush, drove, flock, group, horde, press, serry, shove, swarm, troop 6 circle, gaggle, huddle, legion, rabble, scores, squash, squish, squush, throng 7 cluster, company, squeeze 8 assembly 9 congeries, gathering, multitude 10 assemblage, collection 11 aggregation 12 congregation

crowded 4 full 5 awash, close, dense, thick, tight 6 jammed, loaded, packed 7 brimful, compact, crammed, stuffed 8 brimming, populous 9 chock-full

crow-like 7 corvoid

crown 3 cap, top 4 acme, apex, peak, roof 5 cover, crest, tiara 6 anadem, climax, diadem, laurel, summit, top off, vertex, wreath, zenith 7 chaplet, coronal, coronet, garland, overlay 8 meridian, overcast, pinnacle, round off, surmount 9 culminate, fastigium, finish off 10 overspread 11 culmination *combining form:* 6 corono 7 stephan 8 stephano *Egyptian:* 7 pschent

crucial 4 dire 5 acute, vital 8 critical, decisive 9 desperate, important, necessary 10 imperative 11 climacteric

crucible 4 test 5 trial 6 ordeal 10 affliction 11 tribulation

crucifix 4 rood 5 cross

crucifixion site 7 Calvary 8 Golgotha

crucify 4 kill 5 smite 6 harrow, martyr

7 afflict, agonize, mortify, torment, torture
10 excruciate

crud 3 goo **4** gook, gunk, junk, muck
5 filth, slime, trash **6** debris, sludge **7** rubbish

crude 3 raw **4** foul, poor **5** crass, dirty,
gross, rough **6** coarse, filthy, gauche,
impure, native, ribald, risqué, smutty,
unhewn, vulgar **7** boorish, ill-bred, loutish,
lowbred, obscene, raunchy, uncouth
8 backward, barnyard, cloddish, ignorant,
immature, indecent, inexpert, inferior, prentice, unformed, ungraded, unsorted,
unworked **9** graceless, inelegant, roughhewn, run-of-mine, unrefined, unskilled,
untrained **10** amateurish, unfinished, unpolished **11** clodhopping, ineffective **12** unproficient **13** unenlightened

cruel 4 fell, grim, mean **6** brutal, fierce, savage **7** bestial, brutish, heinous, inhuman,
wolfish **8** inhumane, ruthless **9** atrocious,
barbarous, ferocious, heartless, monstrous,
truculent, unpitying **10** relentless **12** bloodthirsty

cruise 4 sail **6** voyage

cruiser 4 boat **7** warship **9** patrol car,
powerboat

crumb 3 bit, jot **4** iota **5** ounce, scrap,
shred **7** smidgen **8** particle

crumble 3 rot **5** decay, spoil, taint
6 molder **7** putrefy **8** collapse **9** break
down, decompose **12** disintegrate

crumbly 5 crisp, short **7** brittle, crunchy,
friable

crumple 3 wad **4** bend, cave, give
5 break, crimp, screw, yield **6** fold up, rimple, ruck up **7** crinkle, scrunch, wrinkle
8 collapse

crunch 4 chew **5** champ, chomp, chump,
munch **7** chumble **8** ruminate **9** masticate

Crusader *English:* **7** Richard *French:*
6 Philip, Robert **7** Godfrey, Raymond
8 Montfort *German:* **9** Frederick *Norman:*
7 Tancred **8** Bohemund *Preacher:* **7** Bernard **14** Peter the Hermit

crusading 11 evangelical **12** evangelistic

crush 3 jam **4** bear, beat, bray, buck,
cram, dash, mash, pulp, push, ruin
5 crowd, drove, horde, press, quash, quell,
smash, wreck **6** béguin, bruise, defeat,
pestle, powder, quench, reduce, squash,
squish, squush, subdue, throng **7** abolish,
blot out, conquer, contuse, destroy, passion, put down, repress, scrunch, squeeze,
squelch **8** bear down, beat down, demolish, suppress, vanquish **9** comminute, multitude, overpower, pulverize, puppy love,
subjugate, triturate **10** annihilate, extinguish, obliterate **11** infatuation **12** contriturate

crust 4 cake, rime

crustacean 4 crab, flea, scud **5** louse,
prawn **6** isopod, shrimp, slater, sow bug
7 copepod, daphnia, decapod, lobster, pill
bug **8** amphipod, anomuran, barnacle,
crawfish, crayfish, macruran, ostracod,
sand flea **9** arthropod, beach flea, schizopod, shellfish, water flea, wood louse
10 brachyuran, stomatopod, whale louse
11 branchiopod *aggregate of:* **5** krill
appendage: **5** exite **6** endite **7** pleopod
body segment: **6** somite, telson **8** metamere *claw:* **5** chela **6** pincer *covering
substance:* **6** chitin *larva:* **5** alima **8** nauplius *limb segment:* **6** podite **8** podomere

crusty 4 curt, foul, rank **5** bluff, blunt, brief,
dirty, gross, gruff, short, testy **6** abrupt,
coarse, cranky, filthy, snippy **7** brusque,
crabbed, obscene, raunchy, waspish **8** choleric, snippety **9** irascible, irritable, saturnine, splenetic **10** fescennine

crux 3 nub **4** core, gist, meat, pith **6** kernel, thrust **7** purport **9** substance

cry (see also **exclamation**) **3** sob **4** bawl,
blub, call, howl, moan, pule, rage, song,
wail, weep, yaup, yawp, yell, yowl **5** bleat,
craze, groan, hallo, hollo, motto, mourn, ondit, rumor, shout, sniff, trend, vogue, whine,
whoop **6** boohoo, furore, gossip, holler,
lament, report, rumble, scream, snivel,
squawk, squeak, squeal **7** blubber, fashion,
hearsay, screech, ululate, whimper **9** advertise, publicize **10** vociferate **11** scuttlebutt
bacchanals': **4** evoe *calf:* **5** bleat *cat:*
3 mew **4** meow **5** miaou *cattle:* **3** low,
moo *chick:* **4** peep **5** cheep *court:*
4 oyes, oyez *crane:* **5** clang *crow:* **3** caw
dog: **3** arf **4** bark, woof *donkey:* **4** bray
6 hee-haw *duck:* **5** quack *frog:* **5** croak
goat: **5** bleat *goose:* **4** honk **5** clang,
cronk *hen:* **6** cackle *horse:* **5** neigh
6 nicker, whinny **7** whicker *lion:* **4** roar *owl:*
4 hoot *pig:* **4** oink **5** grunt *raven:* **5** croak,
cronk *sheep:* **5** bleat *songbird:* **5** chirp,
tweet *turkey:* **6** gobble

cry down 5 decry **8** belittle, derogate,
diminish **9** disparage **10** depreciate
11 detract from, opprobriate

crying 4 dire **6** urgent **7** burning, clamant,
exigent, heinous **8** pressing, shocking
9 atrocious, clamorous, desperate, monstrous **10** imperative, outrageous, scandalous **11** importunate

cry off 5 welsh **6** renege, resile **7** back
out **8** back down **9** backpedal, backwater

cry out 4 blat, bolt **7** exclaim **9** ejaculate

crypt 4 cave, cell **5** vault **7** chamber
8 catacomb **10** undercroft **11** compartment

cryptanalyze 5 break, crack **6** decode
7 decrypt **8** decipher

cryptic 4 dark 5 murky, vague 6 opaque 7 obscure, unclear 8 abstruse, Delphian 9 enigmatic, tenebrous 10 mysterious, mystifying 12 unfathomable

crystal 5 clear, lucid 6 lucent 8 clear-cut, luminous, pellucid 9 unblurred 11 translucent, transparent 12 transpicuous *combining form:* 5 blast 6 hedron *gazer:* 4 seer

Cry, the Beloved Country *author* 5 Paton (Alan)

cry up 4 laud 5 bless, extol 6 praise 7 glorify, magnify 8 eulogize 9 celebrate 10 panegyrize

Cuba *capital:* 6 Havana *chief export:* 5 sugar *monetary unit:* 4 peso *premier:* 6 Castro (Fidel)

cubbyhole 5 niche 6 recess 7 cubicle

cube 3 die 4 dioo (plural)

cubic meter 5 stere

Cub Scout *rank:* 4 Bear, Wolf 6 Bobcat 7 Webelos *unit:* 3 den 4 pack

Cuchulainn *father:* 3 Lug 4 Lugh *foe:* 4 Medb 5 Maeve *kingdom:* 6 Ulster *mother:* 8 Dechtire *son:* 8 Conlaoch *victim:* 8 Conlaoch *wife:* 4 Emer

cuckoo 3 nut 4 daft, kook 5 crank, crazy, daffy, nutty 6 crazed, insane 7 cracked, lunatic 8 crackpot 9 ding-a-ling, harebrain, screwball 12 crackbrained *bird:* 3 ani

cucumber 4 pepo 6 gerkin 7 gherkin

cuddle 3 pet 4 snug 6 burrow, caress, cosset, dandle, fondle, nestle, nuzzle 7 embrace, snuggle

cuddlesome 8 huggable

cudgel 3 bat 4 cane, club, mace 5 baton, billy 6 paddle 7 war club 8 bludgeon, spontoon 9 billy club, blackjack, truncheon 10 knobkerrie, nightstick

cue 4 clue, hint 6 notion 7 inkling 8 telltale 10 indication, intimation, suggestion

cuff 3 box, hit 4 blip, chop, clip, poke, slap, sock 5 clout, punch, smack, spank 6 buffet, wallop 8 haymaker

cul-de-sac 6 pocket 7 dead end, impasse 10 blind alley

cull 4 pick 5 elect, glean 6 choose, garner, gather, optate, opt for, pick up, prefer, select 7 extract 9 single out

culminate 3 cap 5 crown 6 climax, top off 8 round off 9 finish off

culmination 4 acme, apex, noon, peak 6 apogee, climax, summit 8 meridian, pinnacle 11 ne plus ultra

culpability 4 onus 5 blame, fault, guilt

culpable 5 amiss 6 guilty, sinful, unholy 8 blamable, blameful 10 censurable 11 blameworthy, impeachable 13 demeritorious, reprehensible

cult 4 sect 5 creed, faith 6 church 8 religion 9 communion 10 connection, persuasion 12 denomination *suffix:* 3 ism

cultivable 6 arable 8 tillable

cultivatable see cultivable

cultivate 4 farm, grow, tend, till, work 5 breed, dress, nurse, raise 6 foster, nursle, refine 7 cherish, nourish, nurture, produce 9 propagate

cultivated 6 urbane 7 genteel, refined 8 cultured, polished, well-bred 9 courteous, distingué

cultivation 6 polish 7 culture 8 breeding 10 refinement

culture 5 class 6 polish 8 breeding, elegance, learning, urbanity 9 education, erudition, gentility 10 refinement 11 cultivation, savoir faire 12 civilization 13 enlightenment

cultured 6 urbane 7 erudite, genteel, learned, refined 8 educated, literate, polished, well-bred 9 civilized, distingué 10 cultivated 11 enlightened

culture medium 4 agar

culverhouse 8 dovecote, pigeonry 9 columbary

cumber 3 tax 4 clog, lade, load, task 6 burden, charge, saddle

cumbersome 7 awkward, unhandy 8 cumbrous, unwieldy 9 ponderous

cumbrance 4 clog 6 burden 7 trouble 9 hindrance, impedance 10 impediment

cumbrous see cumbersome

cum ___ salis 5 grano

cumshaw 3 tip 7 largess 8 gratuity 9 lagniappe, pourboire 10 perquisite

cumulate 4 hive 5 amass, lay up, uplay 6 garner, roll up 7 store up 9 stockpile

cumulation 5 hoard, trove 9 amassment, colluvies, stockpile 10 collection 11 aggregation 13 agglomeration

cumulative 5 chain 8 additive, additory 9 summative 10 increasing 11 multiplying

cunning 3 art, sly 4 deep, foxy, keen, wary, wily 5 acute, canny, craft, guile, savvy, sharp, skill, smart 6 adroit, artful, astute, clever, crafty, deceit, tricky 7 finesse, know-how, knowing, slyness 8 artifice, deftness, facility, foxiness, guileful, subtlety, wiliness 9 adeptness, cageyness, canniness, dexterity, dexterous, duplicity, expertise, ingenious, ingenuity, insidious, masterful, sharpness, slickness 10 adroitness, artfulness, cleverness, craftiness, shiftiness, shrewdness, trickiness 12 dissemblance 13 dexterousness, dissimulation, ingeniousness

cup 3 mug 4 toby 5 grail, jorum, stein 6 beaker, seidel 7 chalice, tankard 8 schooner *assayer's:* 5 cupel *combining form:* 5 cotyl, cyath, scyph 6 cotyli, cotylo, cyatho, scyphi, scypho *diamond cutter's:* 3 dop *handle:* 3 ear, lug *holder:* 4 zarf *liturgical:* 3 ama 5 amula, calix 7 chalice

Scottish: 4 tass *small:* 6 noggin 7 canakin, canikin 8 cannikin 9 demitasse
sports: 5 Davis, Ryder 6 Curtis 7 Stanley 8 America's, Wightman *two-handled:* 3 tyg

cupbearer of the gods 4 Hebe 8 Ganymede

cupboard 3 kas 5 ambry, cubby, cuddy 6 buffet, closet, larder, pantry 7 armoire, cabinet 8 credence, credenza 9 sideboard

Cupid 4 Amor, Eros 6 cherub 7 amorino 8 amoretto *beloved:* 6 Psyche *brother:* 7 Anteros *father:* 6 Hermes 7 Mercury *mother:* 5 Venus 9 Aphrodite *title:* 3 Dan

cupidity 4 lust 5 greed 6 desire 7 avarice, avidity, craving, passion 8 rapacity, voracity 9 eagerness 10 greediness 11 infatuation 13 rapaciousness

cupola 4 dome 5 vault 6 turret 7 furnace, lantern, lookout

cup-shaped 8 scyphate

cur 3 cad, dog 4 scum, toad 5 skunk, snake 6 rotter 7 bounder, stinker 8 riffraff, stinkard 9 yellow dog

curative 5 tonic 7 healing 8 remedial, salutary, sanative, sanatory 9 medicinal, remedying, vulnerary, wholesome 10 beneficial, corrective, medicative 11 restorative, therapeutic 12 invigorating

curb 3 bit, tie 4 clog, deny 5 check, leash, tie up 6 bridle, fetter, hamper, hobble, hogtie, hold in 7 abstain, inhibit, refrain, repress, shackle 8 hold back, hold down, restrain, suppress, withhold 9 constrain, entrammel *British:* 4 kerb

curd see **curdle**

curdle 4 clot, sour 5 spoil 7 clabber, thicken 9 coagulate *Scottish:* 6 lapper, lopper

cure 3 age 4 heal 6 physic, remedy 7 restore 8 antidote, medicant, medicine 9 pharmacon 10 corrective, medicament, medication 11 counterstep 12 counteragent 13 counteractant, counteractive *fish:* 6 kipper

cure-all 6 elixir 7 nostrum, panacea 10 catholicon

cureless 8 hopeless 9 incurable, insanable, uncurable 10 impossible 11 immedicable, irreparable 12 irremediable 13 uncorrectable

curio 3 toy 6 bauble, gewgaw, trifle 7 bibelot, trinket, whatnot 9 bric-a-brac, objet d'art, 10 knickknack

curiosity 6 marvel, oddity, rarity, regard, wonder 7 anomaly, concern 8 interest, nonesuch

curious 3 odd 4 nosy 5 nosey, peery, queer, weird 6 prying, quaint, snoopy 7 bizarre, oddball, strange, unusual 8 peculiar, singular 9 inquiring 11 inquisitive, inquisitory, questioning 12 disquisitive 13 inquisitorial, investigative

curium *symbol:* 2 Cm

curl 4 coil, friz, kink, wind 5 frizz, twine, twist 6 spiral 7 entwine, frizzle, ringlet, wreathe 9 corkscrew

curling *match:* 8 bonspiel *period of play:* 3 end *team:* 4 four *term:* 3 tee 4 hack, rink 5 house, stone

curly 5 kinky 6 frizzy

currency 4 cash 5 dough, lucre, money, scrip 11 legal tender *premium:* 4 agio *unit:* (see individual country)

current 3 run 4 eddy, flow, flux, rife, rush, tide 5 drift, flood, spate, tenor, trend 6 extant, modern, stream 7 instant, popular, present, rampant, regnant, topical 8 existent, tendency, up-to-date 9 prevalent 10 present-day, prevailing, widespread 11 fashionable 12 contemporary *air:* 4 gale, gust, wind 5 blast, draft 6 breeze, squall, vortex, zephyr 7 cyclone, indraft, tornado, twister, typhoon, updraft 8 outdraft 9 downdraft, hurricane, whirlwind 10 slipstream *combining form:* 4 rheo *ocean:* 7 riptide 8 undertow 9 maelstrom, whirlpool *unit:* 3 amp 6 ampere 8 abampere 10 statampere

Currier's partner 4 Ives (James)

curry 4 drug, whip 6 thrash 9 overwhelm

curse 4 cuss, damn, oath 5 swear 6 bedamn, plague 7 damning, malison, scourge 8 anathema, cussword, execrate 9 blaspheme, blasphemy, expletive, imprecate, objurgate, profanity, sacrilege, swearword 10 execration, pestilence 11 commination, imprecation, malediction, objurgation, profanation 12 anathematize, denunciation

cursed 6 damned, odious 7 blasted, blessed, doggone, dratted 8 damnable, infernal 9 execrable 10 confounded 13 blankety-blank

cursive 4 easy 6 fluent, smooth 7 flowing, running 10 effortless

cursory 5 brief, hasty, quick, rapid, short 7 hurried, shallow, sketchy 9 depthless 10 uncritical 11 superficial

curt 5 bluff, blunt, brief, gruff, short 6 abrupt, crusty, snippy 7 brusque, concise, laconic, summary 8 snippety, succinct 11 compendiary, compendious 12 breviloquent 13 short and sweet

curtail 3 cut 5 slash 6 lessen, minify 7 abridge, cut back, shorten 8 diminish, retrench 10 abbreviate

curtain 4 drop, veil 5 drape 6 screen 7 barrier *doorway:* 8 portiere *holder:* 3 rod *Indian:* 6 pardah, purdah *rod con-*

cealer: 7 valance *sash:* 7 tieback *stage:* 4 drop 8 backdrop

curtains 3 end 5 death 6 demise 7 decease, drapery

curtilage 4 quad, yard 5 court 9 enclosure 10 courthouse, quadrangle

curvaceous 5 buxom 7 rounded, shapely, stacked 9 Junoesque 13 well-developed

curvation 3 arc, bow 4 arch, bend 5 round

curvature (see curvation) *of the spine:* 8 kyphosis, lordosis 9 scoliosis

curve 3 arc, bow 4 arch, bend, coil, curl, turn, veer, wind 5 crook, round, twist 6 convex, spiral, swerve 7 concave, flexure, rondure, sinuate *of an arch:* 8 extrados, intrados *pitcher's:* 4 hook *plane:* 7 cissoid, cycloid, limaçon 8 parabola, sinusoid, trochoid 9 hyperbola *S-shaped:* 3 ess 4 ogee 7 sigmoid

curved 4 bent 5 arced, bowed, round 6 arched 7 arcuate, arrondi, bending, crooked, embowed, falcate, rounded, twisted 8 arciform, twisting 9 declinate *combining form:* 4 cyrt 5 ancyl, ankyl, curvi, cyrto 6 anchyl, ancylo, ankylo, campto 7 anchylo, clastic *implement:* 6 sickle *molding:* 4 ogee *sword:* 8 scimitar

curvilinear see curved

curvy see curvaceous; curved

Cush *father:* 3 Ham *son:* 6 Nimrod

cushion 3 mat, pad 5 squab 6 absorb, buffer, pillow 7 bolster, hassock, pillion 8 palliate *Indian:* 4 gadi 5 gaddi

cushy 4 cozy, easy, snug, soft 5 comfy 7 easeful 11 comfortable

cusp 3 tip 4 apex, peak 5 point

cuspid 6 canine 8 eyetooth

cuspidate 5 acute, piked, sharp 6 peaked 7 pointed 8 acicular 9 aciculate, acuminate, acuminous

cuss 3 guy, man 4 chap, damn, oath 5 curse, swear 6 bedamn, fellow 8 execrate 9 expletive, imprecate, swearword

cussword 4 oath 5 curse, swear 9 expletive, swearword

custard 4 flan 5 apple, papaw 8 sweetsop

custodian 6 keeper, warden 7 curator, steward 8 cerberus, claviger, guardian, overseer, watchdog 9 caretaker 10 supervisor

custody 4 care, ward 5 trust 6 charge 7 keeping 10 caretaking, management, protection 11 safekeeping, supervision 12 guardianship

custom 3 use 4 want 5 habit, mores (plural), trade, trick, usage 6 manner, praxis, rit-

ual 7 folkway, precept, traffic 8 business, habitude, practice 9 patronage 10 consuetude, tailor-made 11 made-to-order *Latin:* 3 mos

customary 5 usual 6 common, wonted 7 chronic, general, routine 8 accepted, everyday, familiar, frequent, habitual, orthodox, standard 10 accustomed 11 traditional 12 conventional

custom-built 10 tailor-made 11 made-to-order

customer 5 buyer 6 client, patron 7 shopper 8 consumer 9 purchaser *aggregate of:* 9 clientele *frequent:* 7 habitué

customized see custom-built

custom-made see custom-built

cut 3 hew, ilk, lop, mow, saw 4 bite, chop, clip, crop, dice, dock, fell, gash, hack, kind, nick, pare, part, reap, slit, snip, snob, snub, sort, tear, thin, trim, type 5 bevel, carve, ditch, drunk, filet, knife, lathe, lower, mince, notch, piece, prune, quota, sever, share, shave, shear, skive, slash, slice, split, stamp, wound 6 cleave, dilute, divide, fillet, hackle, incise, member, moiety, open up, parcel, pierce, reduce, scythe, sickle, sunder, trench, weaken 7 abridge, curtail, dissect, operate, partage, portion, scissor, section, segment, shorten 8 amputate, dissever, division, lacerate, mark down, retrench, separate 9 allotment, allowance, ostracize 10 abbreviate 11 description, intoxicated 12 cold-shoulder *combining form:* 4 sect, tomy 6 tomous *of beef:* 3 rib 4 loin, rump 5 baron, chine, chuck, flank, plate, roast, round, shank, steak 6 cutlet, saddle 7 brisket, sirloin 8 shoulder 9 aitchbone

cut across 8 transect 9 transcend

cut-and-dried 7 routine

cutaneous 6 dermal

cutaway 4 coat, dive

cut back 4 clip, pare 5 lower, shave, slash 6 reduce 7 abridge, curtail, shorten 8 mark down, retrench 10 abbreviate

cut down 4 clip, pare 5 lower, shave, slash 6 reduce

cute 3 sly 5 sharp 6 clever, dainty, pretty, quaint, shrewd 7 cunning 8 affected 9 ingenious 10 attractive

cut in 6 horn in 7 intrude, obtrude 8 chisel in 10 intertrude

cutlass 5 sword 7 machete

cut off 2 ax 3 axe, lop 4 kill, slay 5 block, catch, scrag 6 enisle, finish, lay low 7 destroy, isolate 8 amputate, dispatch, insulate, separate 9 intercept, segregate, sequester 10 disinherit

cut out 5 usurp 6 delete, excise, exsect,

resect 7 exscind 8 displace, supplant 9 eliminate, extirpate

cutpurse 5 thief 10 pickpocket

cut short 3 bob 4 clip, crop, dock, poll 5 abort, check, shear 7 curtail

cuttable 7 sectile 8 scissile

cutter 4 boat, sled 6 editor, sleigh 7 incisor 9 cutthroat

cutthroat 3 gun 5 bravo 6 gunman, hit man 7 torpedo 8 assassin 10 gunslinger, hatchet man, triggerman

cutting 5 crisp 6 biting 7 ingoing 8 clearcut, incisive, piercing 9 trenchant 11 penetrating *combining form:* 5 cidal *edge:* 5 blade *remark:* 3 dig *tool:* 2 ax 3 adz, axe, hob, saw 4 adze 5 knife, lathe, mower, plane, razor 6 reaper, scythe, shears, sickle 7 hatchet 8 scissors, tomahawk

cutting out *combining form:* 6 ectomy

cuttlefish 7 mollusk 10 cephalopod *ink:* 5 sepia *relative:* 5 squid 7 octopus

cut up 3 pan, rap 4 dice, hash, romp 5 caper, clown, horse, knock, mince 6 cavort, sliver 7 carry on, censure, condemn, show off 8 denounce 9 criticize, horse-play, misbehave, reprehend, reprobate 10 roughhouse

cutup 3 wag 4 zany 5 clown, joker 7 farceur 8 jokester

Cybele 4 Rhea *beloved:* 5 Attis *brother:* 6 Cronus *father:* 6 Uranus *husband:* 6 Cronus *mother:* 2 Ge 4 Gaea *son:* 4 Zeus 7 Jupiter, Neptune 8 Poseidon

cybernetics founder 6 Wiener (Norbert)

cycle 4 bike, loop, ring 5 chain, round, wheel 6 circle, course, series 7 circuit 8 sequence 10 succession, two-wheeler, velocipede

cyclone 7 tornado, twister

cyclopean 4 huge 7 Antaean, mammoth, titanic 8 colossal, gigantic 9 Herculean, monstrous 10 gargantuan 11 elephantine

Cyclops 5 Arges 7 Brontes 8 Steropes 10 Polyphemus

Cycnus *father:* 4 Ares, Mars *slayer:* 8 Hercules

cygnet 4 swan *dam:* 3 pen *sire:* 3 cob

Cygnus *form:* 4 swan *friend:* 7 Phaeton *star:* 5 Deneb

cylinder 4 drum, lock, pipe, tube 5 spool 6 barrel, bobbin, platen, roller

cylindrical 5 tubal 6 terete, tubate 7 tubular 8 tubelike, tuberoid, tubiform, tubulose, tubulous

cyma recta 4 ogee

cymbals *dancer's:* 3 tal 7 crotala

Cymbeline *daughter:* 6 Imogen *son:* 9 Arviragus, Guiderius

Cymric 5 Welsh 6 Celtic 9 Brythonic *bard:* 8 Taliesin *Elysium:* 6 Annwfn *god:* 5 Lludd *of Elysium:* 5 Arawn *of the dead:* 5 Pwyll *of the seas:* 3 Ler 4 Llyr 5 Dylan *of the sky:* 7 Gwydion *of the sun:* 4 Lleu, Llew *of the underworld:* 4 Gwyn *goddess:* 3 Don 9 Arianrhod *magician:* 6 Merlin

Cymry land 5 Wales

cynical 3 wry 6 ironic 8 sardonic

Cynthia 4 Luna, moon 5 Diana 7 Artemis

cyprian 4 jade, slut 5 hussy, tramp 6 wanton 7 jezebel, trollop 8 slattern, strumpet

Cyprus *capital:* 7 Nicosia *language:* 5 Greek 7 Turkish

Cyrano 4 poet 7 duelist *author:* 7 Rostand (Edmond) *feature:* 4 nose

Cyrus *conquest:* 5 Lydia, Media 7 Babylon *daughter:* 6 Atossa *empire:* 7 Persian *father:* 8 Cambyses *son:* 8 Cambyses

Cytherea 5 Venus 9 Aphrodite

czar 4 king 5 baron, mogul 6 prince, tycoon 7 magnate *Russian:* 4 Ivan 5 Basil, Peter 6 Alexis, Feodor, Fyodor 7 Michael, Romanov 8 Nicholas, Romanoff, Theodore 9 Alexander 12 Boris Godunov

czar's wife 7 czarina 8 czaritza

Czech Republic *capital:* 6 Prague *monetary unit:* 6 koruna

D

D.A., e.g. 4 atty
dab 3 hit, pat 4 blow, chit, lump, peck, spot
  5 clout, smear 6 bedaub, blotch, smudge
  7 besmear, plaster, portion, splotch
dabbler 4 tyro 7 amateur 9 smatterer
  10 dilettante, uninitiate 11 abecedarian
dabbling 7 jackleg, shallow 8 ungifted
  9 unskilled 10 amateurish, dilettante, unfinished 11 superficial 12 dilettantish, dilettantist
dabchick 5 grebe 9 hell-diver
Dadaist 3 Arp (Jean), Ray (Man) 4 Ball
  (Hugo) 5 Grosz (George), Tzara (Tristan)
  7 Duchamp (Marcel), Picabia (Francis)
  10 Schwitters (Kurt)
daedal 6 knotty 7 complex, gordian
  8 involved 9 Byzantine, elaborate, intricate
  11 complicated 12 labyrinthine 13 sophisticated
Daedalus 9 architect, artificer *construction:* 9 Labyrinth *father:* 6 Metion *son:*
  6 Icarus *victim:* 5 Talos 6 Perdix
daffy see **daft**
daft 3 mad 4 loco, luny, wild 5 balmy,
  crazy, giddy, potty, silly 6 crazed, cuckoo,
  insane, maniac 7 cracked, foolish, idiotic,
  lunatic, unsound 8 demented, deranged,
  imbecile 9 bedlamite 10 unbalanced
Dag *father:* 7 Delling *horse:* 9 Skinfaksi
  mother: 4 Nott
Dagda *chief god of the:* 5 Gaels, Irish
  daughter: 6 Brigit *instrument:* 4 harp *son:*
  6 Aengus *wife:* 5 Boann
dagger 4 dirk 5 skean, skeen, skene
  6 bodkin 8 stiletto *handle:* 4 hilt *Malay:*
  4 kris *medieval:* 6 anlace
daily 7 diurnal 9 circadian, quotidian
dainty 4 airy, nice, rare 5 fussy, goody,
  light, treat 6 choice, morsel, select, tidbit,
  titbit 7 elegant, finical, finicky 8 delicacy,
  delicate, ethereal, kickshaw, superior
  9 exquisite, finicking, recherché 10 delightful, diaphanous, fastidious, particular, pernickety 11 persnickety
dairy 8 creamery
dais 7 rostrum, terrace 8 platform
daisy 5 oxeye *British:* 10 moonflower
  Scottish: 5 gowan
Daisy Miller author 5 James (Henry)

Daksha's father 6 Brahma
dale 4 glen 6 valley
dally 3 lag, toy 4 drag, fool, idle, play,
  poke 5 delay, flirt, tarry, trail 6 coquet,
  dawdle, frolic, lead on, linger, loiter, put off,
  trifle, wanton 11 string along 13 procrastinate
Dalphon's father 5 Haman
dam 3 bar 4 stay, stem, stop, weir 5 block,
  brake, check, choke 6 hinder, impede
  7 barrier, repress 8 blockade, obstacle,
  obstruct, suppress 10 overslaugh
damage 3 mar 4 blot, harm, hurt, loss,
  ruin 5 abuse, burst, cloud, spoil, wound
  6 deface, impair, injure, injury, scathe
  7 blemish, destroy, marring, tarnish, vitiate
  8 destruct, ill-treat, maltreat, mischief, mistreat, mutilate, sabotage 9 prejudice, vandalism 10 dilapidate, impairment *relating
  to:* 5 noxal
damaging 3 bad 4 evil 6 nocent 7 harmful, hurtful, nocuous 9 injurious 11 deleterious, detrimental, mischievous
dame 4 lady 5 woman 6 beldam, gammer,
  matron 7 dowager, grandam 9 matriarch
Damien's island 7 Molokai
Damkina *husband:* 2 Ea *son:* 6 Marduk
damn 4 cuss, doom, drat, durn 5 curse,
  swear, whoop 7 condemn, doggone 8 execrate, sentence 9 abominate, imprecate,
  objurgate, proscribe 10 vituperate
  12 anathematize
damnable 4 dang, darn 5 gross, utter
  6 blamed, cursed, cussed, odious
  7 blasted, dratted, hateful 8 accursed, infernal, outright 9 abhorrent, dad-burned,
  downright, execrable, out-and-out
  11 unmitigated
damned 4 dang, darn, durn, lost, rank,
  very 5 gross, utter 6 blamed, cursed,
  cussed, dashed, doomed 7 awfully,
  blasted, doggone, dratted, goldarn 8 absolute, accursed, blighted, blinding, complete,
  infernal, outright, whopping 9 dad-blamed,
  downright, execrable, extremely, out-and-
  out, perishing, reprobate 10 confounded,
  dad-blasted 11 straight-out, unmitigated
  13 anathematized, blankety-blank
Damocles' _____ 5 sword

Damon's friend 7 Pythias

damp 3 wet 4 dank, dewy, mist 5 humid, juicy, moist, muggy, musty, rainy, soggy 6 clammy, moisty 7 bedewed, moisten, wettish 8 humidify, humidity, moisture

dampen 4 mute 6 deaden, muffle, sponge, stifle

damsel 3 gal 4 girl, lass, maid, miss 5 missy, wench 6 lassie, maiden, moppet 8 donzella, princess 10 demoiselle

Dan *father:* 5 Jacob *mother:* 6 Bilhah *son:* 6 Hushim

Danaë *father:* 8 Acrisius *lover:* 4 Zeus *son:* 7 Perseus

Danaus *brother:* 8 Aegyptus *daughters:* 8 Danaides *father:* 5 Belus *founder of:* 5 Argos *grandfather:* 7 Neptune 8 Poseidon

dance 3 hop, jig, tap 4 ball, duet, flit, foot, giga, heel, hoof, juba, leap, lope, move, reel, skit, step 5 bamba, brawl, cooch, galop, gigue, hover, lindy, mambo, mixer, polka, rumba, sally, stomp, swing, tread, valse 6 adagio, ballet, bolero, boogie, Boston, cancan, chassé, chi-chi, foot it, formal, frolic, german, hoof it, redowa, rhumba, shimmy 7 beguine, coranto, courant, flicker, flitter, flutter, hoedown, onestep, shuffle 8 Alley Cat, cakewalk, chaconne, cotillon, courante, couranto, fandango, flamenco, galliard, galopade, glissade, hula-hula, rigadoon, rigaudon 9 allemande, jitterbug *art of:* 11 terpsichore 12 choreography *Austrian:* 7 ländler *ballroom:* 5 congo, rumba, tango 6 chacha 7 fox-trot, mazurka, twostep 8 merengue 9 cotillion 10 Charleston *Bohemian:* 5 polka *Brazilian:* 5 samba 6 maxixe 9 bossa nova *chorus:* 5 strut *combining form:* 5 chore 6 choreo, chorio *country:* 3 hay 8 anglaise, hornpipe *couple:* 5 polka *court:* 6 pavane 8 saraband 9 allemande, sarabande *Cuban:* 5 conga 8 habanera *designer:* 13 choreographer *East Indian:* 5 mudra *English:* 6 morris *folk:* 4 hora, kolo 8 hornpipe 10 tarantella, tarantelle *formal:* 4 prom *French:* 5 gavot 7 bourrée, gavotte 8 lanciers 10 carmagnole *garment:* 4 tutu 7 leotard *graceful:* 6 minuet *Haitian:* 4 juba *Hungarian:* 7 Csardas, Czardas *Indian:* 6 nautch *instrument:* 8 castanet *Irish:* 6 fading *Israeli:* 4 hora 5 horah *Italian:* 9 rigoletto 10 tarantella, tarentelle *lively:* 4 reel, trot 6 rhumba 7 bourrée 9 shakedown *modern:* 3 toe *movement:* 4 step 6 minuet 8 glissade 9 allemande, pirouette *1920's:* 10 Charleston *old-time:* 7 hoedown 8 chaconne *Polish:* 5 polka 7 mazurka 8 mazourka *Polynesian:* 4 hula *round:* 5 carol, waltz 6 carole *shoes:* 5 pumps 8 slippers *slip-*

per: 7 toeshoe *slow:* 5 pavan, pavin 6 adagio, pavane *South American:* 7 carioca *Spanish:* 4 jota 6 bolero 7 zapateo 8 cachucha, saraband *springy:* 3 jig *square:* 7 lancers 9 quadrille *stately:* 5 pavan 8 saraband 9 sarabande *step:* 3 pas 4 riff, shag 6 pickup *voluptuous:* 5 belly *woman's:* 6 cancan

dancer 6 hoofer, hopper 7 chorine, clogger, danseur, prancer, stepper 8 coryphée, danseuse, figurant 9 ballerina, chorus boy, chorus man, figurante 10 ballet girl, cakewalker, chorus girl *American:* 4 Feld (Elliot), Lang (Pearl), Tune (Tommy) 5 Kelly (Gene) 6 Duncan (Isadora), Graham (Martha), Taylor (Paul) 7 Astaire (Fred), Bujones (Fernando), de Mille (Agnes), Gregory (Cynthia), Martins (Peter), Massine (Leonide), McBride (Patricia), St. Denis (Ruth), Tamiris (Helen) 8 Kirkland (Gelsey), Villella (Edward) 9 Tallchief (Maria) *ballet:* 6 étoile 7 soliste *Danish:* 8 Tomasson (Helgi) *English:* 5 Somes (Michael), Tudor (Antony) 7 Markova (Alicia) 8 Fonteyne (Margot) *female:* 8 devadasi *French:* 6 Bejart (Maurice), Perrot (Jules-Joseph), Petipa (Marius) *German:* 5 Jooss (Kurt) *Italian:* 5 Grisi (Carlotta) *Javanese:* 7 serimpi *Mexican:* 5 Limón (José) *Russian:* 5 Lifar (Serge) 7 Nureyev (Rudolf), Pavlova (Anna), Ulanova (Galina) 8 Danilova (Aleksandra), Makarova (Natalia), Nijinsky (Vaslav), Vaganova (Agrippina) 9 Karsavina (Tamara), Semyonova (Marina) 11 Baryshnikov (Mikhail) *Scottish:* 7 Shearer (Moira) *sword:* 7 bouffon 8 matachin *Zuni:* 7 shalako

dancing 6 ballet 7 saltant 11 choreography, terpsichore 12 choreography *mania:* 9 tarantism

dandle 3 pet 4 love 6 caress, cosset, cuddle, pamper

dandruff 5 scurf 6 furfur

dandy 3 fop 4 beau, buck, dude, fine, lulu, toff 5 dilly, nifty, peach, swell 6 peachy 7 coxcomb 8 popinjay, terrific 9 excellent, first-rate, humdinger, hunky-dory, marvelous 11 Beau Brummel, crackerjack 12 lounge lizard

dang 4 darn, durn 5 utter 6 cursed, cussed, damned 7 blasted, blessed, dratted, goldarn, regular 8 absolute, outright 9 downright 10 confounded, consummate 11 unmitigated

danger 4 risk 5 peril 6 hazard, menace, plight, threat 7 pitfall 8 distress, jeopardy *signal:* 4 bell 5 alarm, siren 6 redeye, tocsin

dangerous 4 fell 5 dicey, grave, hairy, nasty, risky 6 chancy, scathy, unsafe, unsure, wicked 7 parlous, serious, unsound, vicious 8 grievous, insecure, menacing, perilous 9 hazardous, unhealthy 10 jeopardous, precarious 11 threatening

dangle 4 hang 5 droop, sling, swing 6 depend 7 suspend

Daniel *American pioneer:* 5 Boone *father:* 5 David *mother:* 7 Abigail *statesman:* 7 Webster

Danish *hero:* 5 Ogier *king:* 9 Christian, Frederick *queen:* 9 Margrethe

dank 3 wet 4 damp 5 humid, moist 6 clammy, dampen, moisty 7 dampish, wetness, wettish 8 moisture

Dante *beloved:* 8 Beatrice *birthplace:* 8 Florence *daughter:* 7 Antonia *deathplace:* 7 Ravenna *party:* 6 Guelph 7 Bianchi *patron:* 5 Scala *teacher:* 6 Latini *wife:* 5 Gemma *work:* 7 Inferno 8 Commedia, Convivio 9 Vita Nuova

Dantean division 5 canto

Danton's colleague 5 Marat (Jean-Paul)

Danzig 6 Gdańsk

dap 4 skim, skip 5 carom, graze 6 glance 8 ricochet

Daphne *father:* 5 Ladon 6 Peneus *form:* 10 laurel tree *pursuer:* 6 Apollo 9 Leucippus

Daphnis' lover 5 Chloe

dapper 4 neat, trim 5 natty, sassy 6 jaunty, rakish, spiffy, spruce, sprucy 7 bandbox, doggish, foppish, stylish 8 sparkish 11 well-groomed

dapple 4 spot 5 fleck, patch

dappled 6 dotted, motley 7 flecked, mottled, spotted 8 freckled 9 multihued 10 discolored, multicolor, variegated, versicolor 11 varicolored 12 multicolored, particolored, versicolored

Dardanelles 10 Hellespont

Dardanus *descendants:* 7 Trojans *father:* 4 Zeus 7 Jupiter *mother:* 7 Electra

dare 4 defi, defy, face, risk 5 beard, brave, front, stump 6 brazen, cartel, hazard 7 attempt, outface, venture 8 confront, defiance 9 challenge

daredevil see daring

darer 4 hero 6 risker

daring 4 bold, pert, rash, wild 5 brave, nerve 6 heroic 7 courage, heroism 8 boldness, devilish, fearless, reckless, temerity 9 audacious, daredevil, foolhardy, venturous 10 courageous, jeopardous 11 adventurous, temerarious, venturesome 13 adventuresome

Darius *father:* 9 Hystaspes *son:* 6 Xerxes *wife:* 6 Atossa

Darjeeling 3 tea

dark 3 dim, dun, sad, wan 4 dusk, murk 5 black, blind, brown, cloud, dingy, dusky, mirky, murky, night, shady, sooty, swart,

umber, unlit, vague 6 brunet, cloudy, dismal, gloomy, opaque, somber, sombre, swarth, swarty, wicked 7 aphotic, cryptic, duskish, obscure, rayless, shadowy, stygian, subfusc, sunless, swarthy, unclear 8 abstruse, bistered, Delphian, gloomful, ignorant, mystical, sinister 9 ambiguous, enigmatic, lightless, secretive, tenebrous, unlighted 10 caliginous, indistinct, mysterious, mystifying, pitch-black 11 black-avised 13 unilluminated *combining form:* 3 mel 4 mela, melo 5 melam, melan 6 melano *poetic:* 4 ebon

darken 3 dim, fog 4 dull, dusk, haze, murk 5 bedim, blind, cloud, gloom, lower, shade, sully, umber 6 shadow 7 becloud, benight, blacken, eclipse, embrown, obscure, opacate, tarnish 8 melanize, overcast 9 obfuscate, overcloud 10 overshadow *Scottish:* 5 gloam

dark-haired *female:* 8 brunette *male:* 6 brunet

darkness 4 dusk, mirk, murk 5 black, gloom, night, shade, umbra 6 shadow 7 privacy, secrecy 8 midnight, twilight

dark-skinned 5 dusky, swart 6 brunet, swarth 7 swarthy 8 bistered, melanous 11 black-a-vised

darling 3 pet 4 chou, dear, duck, love, lush 5 deary, ducky, flame, honey, loved, sweet 7 beloved, pigsney, sweetie 8 adorable, favorite, heavenly, precious 9 ambrosial 10 delectable, delightful, fair-haired, honeybunch, sweetheart

darn 4 mend 5 patch, utter 6 blamed, cursed, cussed, damned, repair 7 blasted, doggone 8 infernal, outright 9 downright 10 confounded 11 straight-out 13 blankety-blank

darn it *French:* 3 zut

Darrow client 4 Debs (Eugene), Loeb (Richard) 6 Scopes (John) 7 Leopold (Nathan)

dart 3 fly, jet, run, shy 4 barb, bolt, buzz, flit, leap, sail, scud, skim 5 arrow, bound, fling, hurry, lance, scamp, scoot, shaft, shoot, skirr, spear, speed, spurt 6 glance, hasten, scurry, spring, sprint, squirt 7 javelin, missile, scamper 8 jaculate *barbed:* 10 banderilla

D'Artagnan's friends 5 Athos 6 Aramis 7 Porthos

Dartmouth location 7 Hanover

darts terms 3 leg 4 bust 5 split 6 dosser, double, flight, hockey, treble 8 bull's-eye 10 clock board

Darwin 7 Charles *ship:* 6 Beagle *theory:* 9 evolution

dash 3 nip, pep, run, vim, zip 4 balk, bang, beat, bilk, boil, bolt, brio, élan, foil, hint, hurl, life, pelt, race, ruin, rush, slam, tear, tick, zing 5 ardor, blast, break, chase, crush, drive, fling, oomph, scoot, shoot, smack, speed, spice, style, throw, trace, verve 6 baffle, blight, charge, energy, esprit, hurtle, hyphen, scurry, spirit, sprint, streak, thrust, thwart, trifle 7 bravura, collide, scamper, shatter, soupçon, spatter, splotch 8 confound, tincture 9 animation, bespatter, frustrate 10 circumvent, disappoint, sprinkling, suggestion

dashboard reading 4 fuel 5 speed 7 mileage

dashing 3 gay 4 bold, chic, keen 5 alert, showy, smart, swank, swish 6 bright, dapper, jaunty, lively, modish, swanky, with-it 7 animate, rousing, stylish 8 animated, spirited 9 vivacious 11 fashionable

Das Kapital author 4 Marx (Karl)

dassie 9 blacktail

dastard 4 funk 6 coward, craven, funker 7 chicken, quitter 8 poltroon 11 yellowbelly

dastardly 4 base, mean

data 5 facts, input 8 material 11 information

date 3 age, era, woo 5 court, epoch, tryst 6 cutoff, escort 7 take out 8 deadline 9 accompany 10 engagement, rendezvous 11 anniversary, appointment, assignation *abbreviation:* 4 appt

dated 3 old 5 passé 6 démodé, old hat 7 archaic 8 obsolete, outmoded 10 antiquated 12 old-fashioned 13 unfashionable

Dathan's father 5 Eliab

datum 4 fact

daub 4 blob, blot, spot 5 fleck, paint, smear 6 dapple, smudge, splash 7 besmear, dribble, plaster, spatter, speckle, splotch 9 variegate

daughter *Carter's:* 3 Amy *Cher's:* 8 Chastity *Clinton's:* 7 Chelsea *Cole's:* 7 Natalie *Elizabeth II's:* 4 Anne *Fonda's:* 4 Jane *Ford's (Gerald):* 5 Susan *Garland's:* 12 Liza Minnelli *Johnson's (Lyndon):* 4 Lucy 5 Linda *Kennedy's (John F.):* 8 Caroline *Nixon's:* 5 Julie 6 Tricia *Sinatra's:* 5 Nancy

Daughter of the Moon 7 Nokomis

daunt 3 cow 4 dismay, subdue 7 conquer, horrify, terrify 8 frighten 10 disconcert, discourage, dishearten, intimidate

dauntless 4 bold, game 5 brave 8 fearless, unafraid 9 unfearful, unfearing 10 courageous, invincible 11 indomitable, lionhearted

dauntlessness 4 guts 5 heart, pluck, spunk 6 mettle, spirit 7 cojones, courage 10 resolution

davenport 4 desk, sofa 12 chesterfield

David *commander:* 4 Joab 5 Amasa *companion:* 8 Jonathan *daughter:* 5 Tamar *father:* 5 Jesse *rebuker:*

6 Nathan *scribe:* 7 Seraiah *singer:* 5 Heman *son:* 5 Amnon 7 Absalom, Solomon *wife:* 7 Abigail, Ahinoam 9 Bathsheba

David, for one 4 camp

David Copperfield *author:* 7 Dickens (Charles) *character:* 4 Dora, Heep 5 Agnes, Uriah 6 Barkis, Betsey 7 Creakle 8 Micawber 9 Murdstone, Wickfield 10 Steerforth *nurse:* 8 Peggotty (Clara)

dawdle 3 lag 4 drag, idle, jauk, laze, lazy, loaf, loll, poke 5 dally, delay, tarry, trail 6 linger, loiter, lounge, put off, putter, trifle 7 fritter 8 lallygag, lollygag 13 procrastinate

dawn 4 morn 5 alpha, light, onset, start, sunup 6 aurora, outset 7 genesis, morning, opening, sunrise 8 cockcrow, daybreak, daylight, outstart 9 beginning 11 cockcrowing 12 commencement *goddess:* 3 Eos 6 Aurora *relating to:* 4 eoan

day 3 era, sun 4 time 8 lifetime *abbreviation:* 3 Fri, Mon, Sat, Sun, Thu, Tue, Wed 4 Thur, Tues 5 Thurs *before:* 3 eve *church calendar:* 5 feria *French:* 4 jour *German:* 3 Tag *holy:* 5 feast *hot:* 8 scorcher *hour:* 4 noon *Latin:* 4 dies *Spanish:* 3 dia

day blindness 11 hemeralopia

daybreak 4 dawn, morn 5 sunup 6 aurora 7 dawning, morning, sunrise 8 cockcrow 11 cockcrowing

daydream 4 muse 5 fancy 6 revery, vision 7 fantasy, reverie 8 phantasm, phantasy

days *fourteen:* 9 fortnight *of yore:* 3 eld

daystar 3 Sol, sun 7 phoebus

daze 3 fog 4 haze, stun 5 blind, dizzy 6 bemuse, benumb, dazzle, fuddle, muddle, trance 7 confuse, mystify, petrify, stupefy 8 astonish, bedazzle, befuddle, bewilder, confound, disorder, distract, paralyze 9 dumbfound, overwhelm 10 muddlement 11 muddledness 12 befuddlement

dazed 5 woozy 6 doiled, groggy, punchy 7 witless 8 dithered

___ **d'Azur** 4 Côte

dazzle 5 blind, shine 8 bewilder, outshine

dazzling 6 flashy, garish 7 fulgent, glowing, radiant 9 brilliant 10 candescent

deacon 4 calf 6 cleric, doctor, layman 7 officer 10 adulterate

dead 3 dim 4 cold, dull, flat, gone, late, lost, numb 5 bleak, blind, inert, muted, passé, quiet, slain, utter 6 asleep, buried, bygone, dismal, fallen, lapsed, numbed 7 defunct, disused, exactly, expired, extinct, outworn, tedious 8 benumbed, deceased, departed, inactive, lifeless, obsolete, outmoded 9 apathetic, deathlike, exanimate, inanimate, senseless, unfeeling 10 breathless, corpselike, insensible, insentient, lackluster, lusterless, monotonous, motionless, spiritless, unanimated, unexciting 11 inoperative, insensitive, unconscious 12 anes · thetized, extinguished, unresponsive *Australian:* 4 bung *British:* 5 napoo 6 napooh *combining form:* 4 necr 5 necro

dead duck 5 goner

deaden 4 dull, kill, mull, mute, numb, stun 5 blunt 6 benumb, dampen, muffle, obtund, opiate, stifle 7 mortify, petrify, smother, stupefy 8 paralyze 10 devitalize 11 anesthetize, desensitize

dead end 4 halt 6 pocket 7 impasse 8 cul-de-sac 10 blind alley, bottleneck, standstill

deadened 4 numb 6 asleep, corpsy, numbed 7 deathly 8 benumbed, deathful 9 deathlike, senseless, unfeeling 10 corpselike, insensible 11 insensitive 12 anesthetized

deadfall 4 trap 7 springe 9 booby trap, mousetrap

deadliness 8 fatality 9 lethality, mortality

deadlock 3 tie 4 draw 6 logjam 7 dogfall, impasse 8 standoff, stoppage 9 stalemate 10 standstill

deadly 4 dire 5 fatal, toxic 6 corpsy, lethal, mortal 7 baneful, capital, killing, noxious, ruinous, slaying 8 deathful, lethally, venomous, virulent 9 deathlike, pestilent, poisonous 10 corpselike, pernicious 11 destructive, mortiferous, pestiferous 12 pestilential

deadpan 5 blank, empty 6 vacant 12 inexpressive, unexpressive

dead shot 8 marksman

Dead Souls author 5 Gogol (Nikolay)

dead to rights 9 red-handed

deadweight 3 tax 4 duty, load, onus, task 6 burden, charge 9 millstone

deafen 3 din

deal 4 dole, give, sale 5 allot, serve, shake, share, trade, treat 6 accord, bestow, divide, impart, lot out, parcel, strike 7 bargain, deliver, dish out, dole out, inflict, mete out, portion, scatter, wrestle 8 disburse, dispense, disperse, separate, share out 9 agreement, apportion, negotiate, partition 10 administer, distribute, measure out, portion out 11 transaction 13 understanding *great:* 4 lots 5 loads *out:* 8 dispense 9 apportion 10 administer, distribute *secretly:* 7 trinket *with:* 4 play 5 serve, treat 6 handle

dealer 4 bank 5 agent 6 banker, broker, seller, trader 8 chandler, merchant, operator 9 tradesman 10 negotiator, trafficker 11 businessman, distributer, distributor 12 merchandiser *British:* 6 draper, jobber, mercer 7 chapman *card:* 6 farmer *horse:* 5 coper *women's clothing:* 7 modiste

dealings 5 truck 7 affairs, matters, traffic 8 business, commerce, concerns 11 intercourse

dealing with *suffix:* 2 ic 4 ical

dean 4 head 5 doyen, guide, pilot 6 leader, priest, senior 7 officer 10 bellwether

dear 3 hon, pet 4 fond, high, lamb, love 5 honey, loved, sweet 6 costly, doting, loving, scarce 7 beloved, darling, devoted, lovable, machree, querida, special, tootsie 8 especial, favorite, loveling, lovesome, precious, valuable 9 cherished, expensive, heartfelt, sweetling 10 fair-haired, heartthrob, honeybunch, sweetheart 12 affectionate *French:* 4 cher 5 chère *Irish:* 4 agra *Scottish:* 2 jo

dear one *suffix:* 3 een

dearth 4 lack, want 6 defect, famine 7 absence, default, paucity, poverty 8 scarcity 9 privation, scantness 10 deficiency, meagerness, scantiness *combining form:* 5 penia

death 3 end 4 bane, exit 5 decay, night, sleep 6 demise, ending, expiry 7 decease, parting, passage, passing, quietus, silence 8 biolysis, casualty, curtains, fatality, necrosis, thanatos 9 bloodshed, departure 10 defunction, expiration, extinction, grim reaper 11 dissolution, termination 12 annihilation *after:* 10 posthumous *combining form:* 6 thanat 7 thanato *easy:* 10 euthanasia *music:* 5 dirge, elegy 8 threnody *notice:* 4 obit 8 obituary 9 necrology *of tissue:* 8 gangrene *personification:* 10 grim reaper *portending:* 6 funest *put to:* 3 gas 4 hang, kill, slay 5 choke, lynch 6 murder, stifle 8 strangle, throttle 9 suffocate 11 assassinate, electrocute *rate:* 9 mortality *rites:* 7 funeral

deathless 7 abiding, eternal, lasting, undying 8 immortal 10 persisting 12 imperishable

deathlike see deathly

deathly 5 fatal 6 grisly, lethal, mortal 7 ghastly, haggard, macabre, stygian 8 deadened, gruesome, mortally 9 pestilent 10 cadaverous, corpselike 11 mortiferous 12 pestilential

debacle 4 rout 5 crash, smash, wreck 6 defeat 7 beating, crack-up, failure, licking, smashup 8 collapse, drubbing 9 breakdown, cataclysm, overthrow, trouncing 10 defeasance 11 shellacking 12 vanquishment

debar 4 bate 6 except, forbid, refuse 7 deprive, exclude, prevent, rule out, suspend 8 count out, preclude, prohibit 9 eliminate

debark 4 land

debase 3 mar, rot 4 harm, sink, warp
5 alloy, lower, spoil, stain, stoop, taint
6 bemean, canker, damage, defile,
demean, dilute, dope up, humble, impair,
injure, poison, reduce, vilify, weaken,
worsen 7 corrupt, degrade, deprave,
devalue, pervert, pollute, traduce, vitiate
8 cast down, dishonor 9 animalize, brutalize, humiliate, undermine 10 adulterate,
bastardize, bestialize, degenerate, demoralize 11 contaminate

debatable 4 moot 7 dubious 8 arguable,
doubtful, mootable 9 uncertain 11 problematic 12 questionable

debate 4 fray, heed, moot 5 argue, fight,
plead, rebut, study 6 hassle 7 agitate, canvass, contend, contest, discept, discuss,
dispute, mooting, quarrel, wrangle 8 argument, consider, forensic, question 9 altercate, attention, dialectic, thrash out 10 toss
around 11 application, controversy, disputation 12 deliberation 13 argumentation,
concentration, consideration *art of:* 9 forensics *expert:* 7 eristic *place for:* 5 forum

debauch 4 orgy, undo, warp 5 party
6 seduce 7 corrupt, deprave, pervert, vitiate 9 bacchanal, brutalize 10 bastardize,
bestialize, demoralize, saturnalia 11 bacchanalia

debauched 4 lewd 6 wanton 7 vitiate
8 depraved, vitiated 9 corrupted, dissolute,
lecherous, libertine, perverted 10 lascivious, libidinous, licentious

debilitate 3 sap 5 blunt 6 weaken 7 cripple, disable, unbrace 8 enfeeble 9 attenuate, extenuate, undermine 10 devitalize
12 unstrengthen

debilitated 4 weak 6 feeble, infirm,
sapped 8 burnt-out, decrepit 9 burned-out

debility 7 astheny, disease, malaise
8 asthenia, weakness 9 infirmity 10 feebleness, infirmness, sickliness 11 decrepitude
13 unhealthiness *combining form:*
6 asthen 7 astheno

Debir *kingdom:* 5 Eglon *slayer:* 6 Joshua

debonair 5 suave 6 urbane 8 carefree,
charming, graceful 10 nonchalant 12 lighthearted

Deborah's husband 9 Lappidoth

debris 4 junk, slag 5 offal, trash, waste
6 litter, refuse, rubble, spilth 7 garbage, rubbish 8 detritus, riffraff *rock:* 5 talus 7 eluvium 8 colluvia

debt 3 due, sin 4 evil 5 wrong 6 arrear
7 arrears, default, deficit 9 arrearage,
demurrage, liability 10 obligation, wickedness 11 delinquency *acknowledgment:*
3 IOU 4 bill 5 check

debtless 7 solvent

debunk 6 expose, show up, unmask
7 uncloak, undress 8 discover, unshroud

Debussy's La ____ 3 Mer

debut 7 come out, opening 8 entrance,
premiere 9 beginning 12 introduction

decadence 7 decline 8 downfall 9 downgrade 10 declension, degeneracy, devolution 11 declination, degradation 12 degeneration, dégringolade 13 deterioration

decadent 6 effete 8 overripe 10 degenerate

decalogue verb 5 shalt

Decameron, The *author:* 9 Boccaccio
(Giovanni) *heroine:* 8 Griselda

decamp 2 go 3 fly 4 exit, flee 5 break,
leave, scape, scram 6 begone, escape, get
out, retire 7 abscond, run away, skiddoo,
slip off, take off 8 clear out, hightail, withdraw 9 skedaddle

decanter 6 bottle, carafe

decapitate 4 head, raze, ruin, undo
5 wrack, wreck 6 behead, unmake
7 destroy, unbuild 8 decimate, demolish
9 decollate 10 guillotine

decapod 6 shrimp 7 mollusk 10 crustacean

decathlon champ 6 Jenner (Bruce),
Schenk (Christian), Toomey (Bill), Zmelik
(Robert) 7 Johnson (Rafer), Mathias (Bob)
8 Campbell (Milton), Thompson (Daley)

decay 3 ebb, rot 4 fade, sour, turn, wane
5 spoil, taint, waste 6 blight, curdle, fading,
molder, wither 7 corrupt, crumble, failure,
ferment, moulder, putrefy 8 putresce
9 break down, decompose 11 deteriorate
12 dilapidation, disintegrate, putrefaction
13 deterioration

decayed 3 bad 6 effete, putrid, rotten
7 carious, spoiled 8 decadent, overripe
10 degenerate

decease 3 die 4 fail, pass 5 death, sleep
6 cash in, demise, depart, expire, perish
7 passing, quietus, succumb 8 pass away
9 departure 10 defunction 11 dissolution

deceit 3 gyp 4 hoax, sham 5 fraud, guile
6 humbug 7 chicane, cunning, swindle
8 artifice, flimflam, spoofery, trickery 9 chicanery, duplicity, imposture 12 dissemblance 13 dissimulation, double-dealing

deceitful 3 sly 4 foxy, wily 5 false, lying
6 artful, crafty, fickle, hollow, shifty, sneaky,
tricky 7 cunning, knavish, roguish 8 delusive, delusory, guileful, unhonest 9 dishonest, insidious, insincere, underhand 10 fallacious, mendacious, misleading, untruthful
11 treacherous, underhanded

deceivable 7 dupable 8 gullible

deceive 3 con, fob, fop, fub, lie 4 bilk,
dupe, flam, fool, gaff, gull, hoax, jilt, mock,
wyle 5 blind, bluff, cheat, cozen, dodge,
hocus, spoof, trick 6 baffle, befool, betray,
delude, humbug, illude, juggle, palter, take
in 7 beguile, defraud, mislead, sell out,

two-time **8** flimflam, hoodwink **9** bamboozle, four-flush **11** double-cross **12** misrepresent

deceiving **5** false **8** deluding, delusive, delusory **9** beguiling **10** fallacious, misleading

decelerate **5** delay **6** retard, slow up **7** slacken **8** slow down

decency **7** decorum, dignity, fitness **9** etiquette, propriety **10** seemliness

decent **4** fair, good, just, nice, pure **5** clean, right **6** chaste, common, enough, honest, modest, proper, seemly **7** average, correct, fitting **8** adequate, all right, becoming, decorous, spotless **9** befitting, competent, stainless, sufficing, tolerable, undefiled, unsullied **10** acceptable, conforming, immaculate, sufficient **11** comfortable, comme il faut, presentable, respectable, unblemished **12** satisfactory **13** unexceptional, unimpeachable

deception **3** gyp **4** flam, gaff, gull, hoax, hype, ruse, sham, wile **5** cheat, craft, fraud, guile, magic, put-on, spoof, trick **6** dupery, humbug, mirage **7** chicane, cunning, fallacy, fantasm, knavery, sophism **8** cheating, cozening, flimflam, illusion, intrigue, phantasm, subtlety, trickery, trumpery, wiliness **9** casuistry, chicanery, duplicity, fourberie, imposture, sophistry, treachery **10** artfulness, camouflage, defrauding, dishonesty, hanky-panky, subterfuge **11** dipsy-doodle, highbinding, indirection **12** speciousness, spuriousness **13** double-dealing *Scottish:* **7** blaflum

deceptive **5** false **6** artful, crafty, tricky **7** seeming, trickie **8** deluding, delusory, illusory, specious, trickish **9** beguiling **10** fallacious, misleading

deceptiveness **7** fallacy, sophism **8** delusion **9** casuistry, sophistry **12** equivocation, speciousness, spuriousness

decide **3** opt **4** rule, will **5** judge **6** figure, settle **7** adjudge, resolve **8** conclude **9** determine **10** adjudicate

decided **3** set **4** firm, flat, sure **5** fixed **6** intent **7** assured, certain, obvious, settled **8** clear-cut, cocksure, definite, explicit, positive, resolute, resolved **10** determined, pronounced **11** categorical, established, unequivocal **12** unmistakable

decimate **4** raze, ruin, undo **5** wrack, wreck **6** unmake **7** destroy, unbuild, unframe, wipe out **8** demolish, massacre **9** slaughter **10** annihilate **11** exterminate

decipher **5** break, crack, solve **6** decode, reveal, unfold **7** analyze, decrypt, resolve, unravel **8** unriddle **9** figure out, puzzle out, translate **12** cryptanalyze

decision **4** fiat **6** choice, ruling **7** resolve, verdict **8** firmness, judgment, sentence,

umpirage **9** selection **10** conclusion, resolution, settlement **12** resoluteness **13** determination, purposiveness *rabbinical:* **9** responsum

decisive **3** set **4** bent **6** intent **7** assured, crucial, settled **8** critical, resolute, resolved **9** imperious, masterful **10** determined, imperative, peremptory **11** self-assured **13** self-confident

deck **4** trim **5** adorn, array, dress, equip, floor, prank **6** attire, blazon, clothe **7** apparel, appoint, furnish, garland, garnish **8** accouter, accoutre, beautify, decorate, emblazon, ornament, platform **9** embellish *chief:* **4** bos'n **9** boatswain *high:* **4** poop *lowest:* **5** orlop *out:* **5** fix up, primp, slick, spiff, tog up **6** doll up **7** dress up, gussy up **8** spruce up *part:* **7** scupper

deckhand **3** gob **6** sailor **7** rouster, swabbie

declaim **4** rant, rave **5** mouth, orate, speak, utter **6** recite **7** elocute, inveigh, soapbox **8** bloviate, harangue, perorate

declamatory **7** aureate, flowery **8** sonorous **9** bombastic, high-flown **10** euphuistic, oratorical, rhetorical **12** magniloquent **13** grandiloquent

declaration **4** word **6** avowal, oracle, report **9** broadcast, statement **10** disclosure **12** announcement **13** advertisement, pronouncement

declare **3** say, vow **4** aver, avow, deny, tell, toot, vend, vent **5** sound, state, utter, voice **6** affirm, allege, assert, assure, avouch, blazon, depone, depose, herald, report, reveal **7** chime in, deliver, divulge, express, profess, protest, publish, signify, testify **8** announce, bring out, constate, disclose, indicate, proclaim, throw out **9** advertise, broadcast, predicate, pronounce **10** annunciate, bruit about, promulgate **11** blaze abroad, come out with, disseminate *a saint:* **8** canonize *in cards:* **3** bid **4** meld *invalid:* **5** annul

declare off **5** welsh **6** renege, resile **7** back out **8** back down **9** backpedal, backwater

declass **4** bump, bust **5** break **6** demote, reduce **7** degrade, demerit, disrate **8** disgrade **9** downgrade

déclassé **4** hack, mean, poor **6** common **8** inferior, low-grade **10** second-rate **11** second-class **12** second-drawer

declension **8** downfall **9** decadence, downgrade **10** degeneracy **12** dégringolade

declination **6** ebbing, waning **7** failure **8** downfall **9** decadence, downgrade **10** degeneracy **12** dégringolade

decline **3** dip, ebb, jib, rot, sag, set **4** balk, dive, drop, fade, fail, fall, flag, loss, sink, slip, wane **5** abate, demur, droop, lapse, lower, slide, slope, slump, spurn **6** ebbing, go down, recede, refuse, reject, renege, waning, weaken, worsen **7** abstain, atrophy, descend, descent, dismiss, drop-off, dwindle, failure, falloff, forbear, refrain, relapse, sell-off, sinkage, subside **8** comedown, decrease, downfall, downturn, languish, lowering, toboggan, turn down **9** backslide, decadence, downgrade, downslide, downswing, downtrend, reprobate, repudiate, weakening **10** degeneracy, degenerate, depression, devolution, disapprove, disimprove, falling off, retrograde **11** backsliding, deteriorate **12** degeneration, dégringolade, disintegrate **13** deterioration *combining form:* **4** clin **5** clino

declivitous 6 sloped, tilted, tipped **7** leaning, oblique, pitched, sloping **8** inclined **9** inclining

declivity 3 dip **4** drop, fall **5** slope **7** descent **8** gradient **11** inclination

decode see **decipher**

decollate 4 head **6** behead **10** guillotine

decolor 5 white **6** blanch, bleach, blench, whiten **7** wash out **11** achromatize

decompose 3 rot **4** turn **5** decay, spoil, taint **6** molder **7** analyze, break up, crumble, dissect, putrefy, resolve **8** dissolve **9** anatomize, break down **12** disintegrate

decomposition *combining form:* **4** lyses (plural) **5** lysis

decorate 4 pink, trim **5** adorn, dress, frill, prank **6** bedeck, emboss **7** cornice, dress up, festoon, furnish, garnish, miniate, appliqué **8** beautify, emblazon, ornament **9** embellish *a border:* **6** purfle

decorated 6 ornate **7** adorned, wrought **9** bemedaled **10** beribboned

decoration 2 PH **3** DSC, DSM **4** bays **5** award, badge, honor, kudos, medal **6** boulle, doodad, plaque **7** laurels **8** accolade, fretting, fretwork, ornament, vignette *cutout:* **8** appliqué *furniture:* **4** buhl **8** buhlwork

decorous 3 fit **4** done, good, nice, prim **5** right **6** au fait, comely, decent, proper, seemly **7** correct, elegant, fitting **8** becoming, suitable **9** befitting, civilized, de rigueur **10** conforming **11** appropriate, respectable, well-behaved

decorously 4 well **5** fitly **6** justly, nicely **7** rightly **8** properly **9** correctly, fittingly **11** befittingly

decorousness 5 order **9** propriety **11** orderliness **12** correctitude

decorticate 4 flay, hull, peel, skin **5** scale, scalp, strip **6** denude

decorum 5 order **7** decency, dignity, modesty **9** etiquette, propriety **10** properness,

seemliness **11** correctness, orderliness **12** correctitude, decorousness

decoy 4 bait, lure, toll, trap **5** blind, plant, shill, snare, stick, tempt **6** allure, capper, delude, entice, entrap, lead on, pigeon, seduce **7** deceive, mislead **8** inveigle, trickery **9** deception, shillaber **10** allurement, enticement, seducement, temptation **12** inveiglement

decrease 3 cut, ebb **4** bate, clip, drop, ease, fall, loss, sink, trim, wane **5** abate, allay, close, lower, taper, waste **6** deduct, lessen, rebate, recede, reduce, shrink **7** abridge, atrophy, curtail, cut back, cut down, dwindle, letdown, lighten, peak out, shorten, slacken, subside **8** contract, diminish, downturn, moderate, peter out, retrench, rollback, subtract, taper off **9** alleviate, drain away **10** abbreviate, diminution

decree 3 act, law, set **4** fiat, rule **5** canon, edict, enact, judge, order, tenet, ukase **6** assize, behest, charge, dictum, firman, impose, ordain, ruling **7** adjudge, appoint, bidding, command, dictate, lay down, mandate, precept, statute **8** judgment, sentence **9** directive, enactment, judgement, ordinance, prescribe, prescript **10** adjudicate, injunction, plebiscite, regulation **11** declaration **12** adjudication, announcement, proclamation, promulgation **13** pronouncement *Muslim:* **5** irade

decrepit 3 old **4** aged, lame, weak, worn **5** frail, seedy, tacky, tired **6** creaky, feeble, flimsy, infirm, senile, shabby, sloppy, tagrag, wasted, weakly **7** cast-off, failing, fragile, haggard, run-down, unkempt, unsound **8** slipshod **10** bedraggled, broken-down, down-at-heel, threadbare **13** insubstantial, unsubstantial

decrepitude 7 disease, malaise **8** debility **9** infirmity **10** infirmness, sickliness **13** unhealthiness

decretum 3 law **4** rule **5** canon, edict **6** assize **7** precept, statute **9** ordinance **10** regulation

decry 3 boo **4** slur **5** abuse, lower **6** lessen **7** asperse, censure, condemn, degrade, detract, devalue, run down **8** belittle, denounce, derogate, diminish, discount, mark down, minimize, take away, take from, write off **9** criticize, deprecate, devaluate, disparage, dispraise, downgrade, reprehend, reprobate, underrate, write down **10** depreciate, disapprove, undervalue **11** detract from, opprobriate

decrypt see **decipher**

decumbent 4 flat **5** prone **9** prostrate, reclining

decussate 5 cross **8** crosscut **9** intersect **10** criss-cross, intercross

dedicate 3 vow 6 devote, hallow 10 consecrate

deduce 4 draw, lead 5 infer, judge, trace
6 derive, evolve, gather 7 collect, explain,
extract, make out 8 cogitate, conclude

deduct 4 bate, dock, draw, take 5 abate,
allow, infer, judge 6 derive, gather, remove
7 collect, make out, take off, take out
8 abstract, conclude, discount, knock off,
roll back, subtract, take away

deduction 3 cut 6 rebate 7 dockage
8 decrease, discount, illation, judgment,
sequitur, write-off 9 abatement, decrement,
inference 10 conclusion 13 ratiocination

deductive 7 a priori 8 dogmatic, illative,
reasoned 9 derivable 11 inferential 13 ratiocinative

deed 3 act 4 cede, fact, fait, feat, pact
5 doing, quest, thing, title 6 action, assign,
convey, escrow, remise 7 charter, compact, exploit 8 alienate, contract, covenant,
make over, practice, sign over, transfer
9 adventure 10 abalienate, conveyance,
enterprise 11 achievement, performance,
tour de force *brutal:* 8 atrocity *evil:* 3 sin
11 malefaction

deem 3 say 4 feel, hold, hope, know, tell,
view 5 judge, opine, sense, think 6 credit,
divine, reckon, regard 7 account, adjudge,
believe 8 consider, proclaim 10 conjecture

de-emphasize 8 downplay, play down
9 soft-pedal

deep 3 low, sly 4 foxy, hard, late, rapt,
wily, wise 5 abyss, acute, grave, heavy,
ocean 6 artful, astute, crafty, growly, intent,
middle, occult, orphic, remote, secret,
shrewd, tricky 7 abysmal, complex, cunning, devious, engaged, extreme, intense,
obscure, serious, unmixed 8 absorbed,
abstruse, esoteric, grievous, guileful, hermetic, immersed, involved, profound
9 developed, engrossed, firmament, insidious, intensive, recondite, sagacious, unalloyed, wrapped up 10 acroamatic, bottomless, mysterious, profoundly 11 complicated, preoccupied *combining form:*
5 bathy *pink:* 5 coral

deep-dyed 5 sworn 7 settled 9 confirmed, hard-shell 10 entrenched, inveterate 13 bred-in-the-bone

deepen 4 rise 5 mount, rouse 6 darken
7 enhance, magnify, thicken 8 heighten,
redouble 9 aggravate, intensate, intensify
10 strengthen

deepness 4 drop 5 abyss, depth 10 profundity

deep-rooted see deep-dyed

deep-sea *combining form:* 5 bathy

deep-seated 5 sworn 6 inborn, inbred,
innate 7 connate, settled 8 inherent, pro-

found 9 confirmed, hard-shell, ingrained,
intrinsic 10 congenital, entrenched, indwelling, inveterate 13 bred-in-the-bone, dyed-
in-the-wool

deep water 6 plight 7 dilemma
11 predicament

deer 3 elk, roe 4 buck, musk, stag
5 brown, moose 6 wapiti 7 caribou, venison 8 bobolink 10 camel's hair *Asian:*
4 axis 5 maral 6 chital, sambar, sambur
7 muntjac, sambhar, sambhur 8 muntjak
British: 4 hart *combining form:* 5 cervi
female: 3 doe *female red:* 4 hind *Japanese:* 4 sika *male:* 4 hart 7 roebuck *male
red:* 4 stag 8 staggard, staggart *meat:*
5 jerky 7 venison *path:* 3 run 5 trail *red:*
7 brocket *relating to:* 6 damine 7 cervine
track: 4 slot 5 spoor *young:* 3 kid 4 fawn

Deerslayer *author:* 6 Cooper (James
Fenimore) *character:* 11 Natty Bumppo
12 Chingachgook

deface 3 mar 4 foul, harm, ruin, scar
5 spoil 6 batter, damage, deform, injure,
mangle 7 blemish, distort 8 misshape,
mutilate 9 disfigure, vandalize 10 disfash-
ion, disfeature

de facto 6 really 8 actually 9 genuinely,
veritably

defalcation 4 lack 7 deficit, failing, failure
8 shortage, underage 10 deficiency, inadequacy, negligence, scantiness 13 insufficience, insufficiency

defamation 4 tale 7 calumny, scandal,
slander 10 backbiting 12 backstabbing,
belittlement 13 disparagement

defamatory 8 libelous 9 maligning, traducing, vilifying 10 backbiting, calumnious,
detracting, detractive, scandalous, slanderous

defame 4 foul 5 abase, cloud, libel, smear
6 injure, malign, vilify 7 asperse, blemish,
scandal, slander, traduce 8 dishonor, vili-
pend 9 blackwash, denigrate 10 calumniate, scandalize, villainize

default 4 fail, lack, omit, want 6 dearth,
defect 7 absence, failure, neglect 9 oversight, privation 10 negligence 11 delinquency, dereliction 12 imperfection

defeasance 4 rout 7 beating, debacle,
licking 8 drubbing 9 overthrow 11 shellacking 12 discomfiture, vanquishment

defeat 4 best, down, drub, foil, lick, loss,
rout, ruin, sink, stop, undo, whip 5 check,
crush, outdo, skunk, swamp, waste,
whomp, worst 6 outgun, reduce, subdue
7 beating, conquer, debacle, destroy, failure, licking, nose out, outplay, outvote,
repress, setback, shellac, trounce 8 out-
fight, outtrump, overcome, overvote, vanquish, waterloo 9 downthrow, frustrate,

insuccess, overpower, overthrow, subjugate, thrashing, trouncing, unsuccess 10 nonsuccess 11 shellacking 12 discomfiture, vanquishment

defecate 5 purge, stool 6 purify, refine 7 clarify 9 discharge

defect 3 bug 4 flaw, lack, vice, want 5 botch, error, fault 6 damage, dearth, desert, foible, injury, malady 7 absence, blemish, default, failing, frailty 8 drawback, renounce, weakness 9 infirmity, privation, repudiate 10 apostatize, deficiency, tergiverse 11 shortcoming 12 imperfection, tergiversate *timber:* 4 knot *visual:* 6 myopia, squint 9 amblyopia, hyperopia 10 presbyopia, strabismus 11 hemeralopia

defection 8 apostasy 9 falseness, forsaking, recreancy 10 disloyalty 11 abandonment

defective 3 bad, ill 4 poor, sick 5 amiss, flawy 6 broken, faulty, flawed 7 damaged, lacking, unsound, wanting 8 deranged, impaired 9 corrupted, deficient, imperfect, unhealthy 10 disordered, inaccurate, inadequate, incomplete, uncomplete 12 insufficient *combining form:* 4 atel 5 atelo

defector 3 rat 7 traitor 8 apostate, recreant, renegade, runagate, turncoat 9 turnabout 13 tergiversator

defend 4 back, hold, save 5 argue, claim, cover, fight, guard 6 assert, screen, secure, shield, uphold 7 bulwark, contend, justify, protect, support, warrant 8 advocate, champion, conserve, garrison, maintain, preserve 9 safeguard, vindicate 11 rationalize

defendable see **defensible**

defendant 7 accused, libelee 8 libellee

defender 8 advocate, champion, guardian 9 protector *of people's rights:* 7 tribune

defense 4 egis, fort, ward 5 aegis, alibi, armor, guard 6 answer, excuse, sconce, shield 7 apology, bulwark, rampart, shelter 8 apologia, armament, fastness, fortress, muniment, security 9 safeguard 10 apologetic, protection, stronghold 11 exculpation, explanation 13 justification *organization:* 4 NATO 5 NORAD, SEATO *outer:* 6 tenail 8 tenaille

defenseless 8 helpless 11 unprotected

defensible 7 tenable 9 excusable 10 condonable

defer 3 bow 4 cave, stay, wait 5 adapt, delay, remit, stall, waive, yield 6 accede, adjust, hold up, put off, shelve, submit 7 adjourn, conform, hold off, knuckle, lay over, put over, succumb, suspend 8 hold over, intermit, postpone, prorogue 9 acquiesce 10 capitulate 11 accommodate, buckle under 12 knuckle under 13 procrastinate

deference 5 honor 6 homage 9 obeisance 10 compliance, submission

deferential 5 silky 6 silken 7 duteous, dutiful 9 disarming, regardful 10 respectful, saccharine 11 insinuating, insinuative 12 ingratiating, ingratiatory

defiance 4 dare 5 stump 6 cartel 7 bravado, despite 8 audacity, boldness, contempt, temerity 9 challenge, contumacy, enjoinder, hardihood, impudence, insolence 10 brazenness, effrontery, insurgency, unruliness 12 contrariness, factiousness, stubbornness

deficiency 3 sin 4 lack, want 5 fault, minus 6 dearth 7 absence, blemish, demerit, failing, failure 8 scarcity, shortage, underage 9 privation 10 inadequacy, scantiness 11 defalcation, shortcoming 12 imperfection *combining form:* 5 penia *mental:* 6 idiocy 7 amentia *oxygen:* 8 asphyxia

deficient 3 shy 5 minus, scant, short 6 faulty, flawed, meager, meagre, measly, scanty, scarce 7 bobtail, failing, lacking, unsound, wanting 8 impaired 9 defective, imperfect 10 inadequate, incomplete, uncomplete *combining form:* 6 privic

deficit 4 lack 7 failure 8 shortage, underage 10 inadequacy, scantiness 11 defalcation 13 insufficience, insufficiency

defile 3 tar 4 foul, pass, rape, soil 5 dirty, shame, smear, spoil, stain, sully, taint 6 befoul, debase, ravish 7 besmear, corrupt, outrage, pollute, profane, tarnish, violate 8 besmirch, deflower, discolor, dishonor 9 deflorate, desecrate 11 contaminate

defiled 6 impure 7 unclean 8 profaned 10 desecrated

define 3 fix, hem, rim, set 4 edge, etch, term 5 bound, limit, skirt, verge 6 assign, border 7 clarify, delimit, lay down, mark off, mark out, outline 8 surround 9 delineate, demarcate, prescribe 12 characterize

definite 3 set 4 sure 5 clear, final, fixed, sharp, solid 6 narrow 7 assured, certain, decided, express, limited, precise, settled 8 clean-cut, clear-cut, distinct, explicit, limiting, positive, specific 10 conclusive, determined, forthright, pronounced, restricted 11 categorical, determinate, established, unambiguous, unequivocal 12 unmistakable 13 circumscribed

definiteness 8 accuracy 9 exactness 10 exactitude

definitive 4 last 5 final 7 express 8 absolute, clean-cut, clear-cut, explicit, settling, specific, terminal, ultimate 10 concluding, conclusive 11 categorical, determining, unambiguous

definitiveness see **definiteness**

definitude see definiteness

deflect 4 bend, warp 5 avert, parry, pivot, sheer, wheel, whirl 6 detour, divert, swerve 7 deviate, diverge, hold off, keep off, refract 9 volte-face

deflection 3 yaw 4 bend, tack, turn, veer 5 curve, shift 6 double, swerve 7 bending, turning, veering 8 swerving 9 departure, diversion 10 divergence *combining form:* 7 sphingo

deflorate see deflower

deflower 4 rape 5 force, harry, havoc, spoil 6 defile, devast, devour, ravage, ravish 7 despoil, outrage, violate 8 desolate 9 depredate, desecrate, devastate

Defoe *character:* 6 Crusoe, Friday, Roxana 12 Moll Flanders *heroine:* 4 Moll

deform 3 mar 4 flaw, maim, warp, wind 5 spoil 6 batter, damage, deface, impair, injure, mangle 7 blemish, contort, cripple, distort, torture 8 misshape, mutilate 9 disfigure 10 disarrange

deformity 4 flaw 7 blemish, harelip 8 misshape, ugliness 10 aberration, corruption, impairment 11 abnormality, impropriety 12 irregularity, malformation

____ de France 3 Île

defraud 3 gyp 4 beat, bilk, hoax, take 5 cheat, cozen, mulct, rogue, trick 6 chouse, fleece 7 swindle 8 flimflam 9 bamboozle

deft 4 neat 5 adept, agile, handy, quick 6 adroit, clever, expert, nimble 8 dextrous, skillful 9 dexterous, ingenious 10 neathanded

deftness 7 address, prowess, sleight 9 dexterity, readiness

defunct 4 cold, dead, gone, late, lost 5 inert 6 asleep, bygone 7 extinct 8 deceased, departed, finished, inactive, lifeless, vanished 9 exanimate, inanimate

defy 4 dare, face, gibe, mock 5 beard, brave, flout, front, scorn, spurn, stump 6 cartel, ignore 7 affront, outdare, outface, venture 9 challenge

dégagé 6 breezy, casual 7 relaxed, unfussy 8 informal 9 easygoing 10 unreserved 11 low-pressure 13 unconstrained

degeneracy see degeneration

degenerate 3 rot 4 sink 5 lapse 6 effete, rotten, worsen 7 corrupt, decayed, decline, descend, vicious, vitiate 8 decadent, depraved, infamous, overripe 9 backslide, miscreant, nefarious, unhealthy 10 disimprove, flagitious, villainous

degeneration 7 atrophy, decline 8 downfall, lowering 9 decadence, depravity, downgrade 10 perversion, regression 12 dégringolade, depravedness

degradation 4 fall 7 decline, descent 11 downgrading

degrade 4 bump, bust, sink 5 abase, break, decry, lower 6 bemean, damage, debase, demean, demote, depose, expose, humble, lessen, reduce 7 corrupt, declass, demerit, deprive, detract, disrate, pervert, put down 8 belittle, cast down, derogate, diminish 9 decompose, disparage, humiliate, reduction 12 depolymerize

degree 3 peg 4 heat, rank, rate, rung, step, term, tier 5 grade, honor, notch, order, pitch, point, ratio, scale, shade, stage, stair 6 extent 7 measure, station 8 standing 9 dimension, magnitude 10 proportion *academic:* 2 BA, BS, MA, MD, MS 3 DDS, LLB, LLD, MBA, MFA, PhD *highest:* 8 cum laude 13 magna cum laude, summa cum laude *of combining power:* 7 valence *of height:* 5 grade *of importance:* 7 caliber, calibre *of outward slope:* 5 splay *seeker:* 9 candidate *slight:* 4 hair *suffix:* 2 ty 3 ity 4 ance, ness *utmost:* 4 acme

dégringolade see degeneration

____ de guerre 3 nom

dehydrate 3 dry 4 sear 5 parch 9 desiccate, exsiccate

Delanira *brother:* 8 Meleager *father:* 6 Oeneus *husband:* 8 Heracles, Hercules *mother:* 7 Althaea *victim:* 8 Heracles, Hercules

Deidamia *father:* 9 Lycomedes *husband:* 9 Pirithous *son:* 11 Neoptolemus

delfic 5 godly 6 divine 7 godlike

deification 10 apotheosis

deign 5 stoop 10 condescend

Deiphobus *brother:* 5 Paris 6 Hector *father:* 5 Priam *mother:* 6 Hecuba *wife:* 5 Helen

Deirdre *beloved:* 5 Noisi *father:* 5 Felim

deity 3 god 4 deva 5 numen 6 numina (plural) 7 goddess, godhead, godhood, godling, godship 8 Almighty, divinity 12 supreme being (see also at **Greek; Hindu; Norse; Roman**)

deject 5 chill 8 dispirit 9 disparage 10 demoralize, discourage, dishearten

dejected 3 low, sad 4 blue, down, glum, sunk 6 gloomy, somber, sombre 7 hangdog, humbled, unhappy 8 downcast, wretched 9 cheerless, depressed, woebegone 10 despondent, spiritless 11 crestfallen, downhearted 12 disconsolate

dejection 5 dumps 7 despair 10 melancholy 12 mournfulness

Delaware *capital:* 5 Dover *largest city:* 10 Wilmington *nickname:* 10 First State 12 Blue Hen State, Diamond State *state flower:* 12 peach blossom

delay 3 lag 4 drag, hold, mire, mull, poke, slow 5 check, defer, deter, embog, stall, tarry, trail 6 dawdle, detain, hang up, hinder, hold up, impede, linger, loiter, put off, retard, shelve, slow up **7** adjourn, bog down, hold off, prolong, respite, set back, slacken, suspend **8** hangfire, hesitate, hold over, intermit, obstruct, postpone, prorogue, reprieve, slow down **9** detention, hindrance, lingering **10** decelerate, dillydally, moratorium, suspension **13** procrastinate

delaying 8 dilatory, moratory

delectable 4 lush **5** sapid, tasty, yummy **6** choice, savory **7** darling **8** heavenly, luscious, pleasing **9** ambrosial, delicious, exquisite, toothsome **10** delightful **11** scrumptious

delectation 3 joy **6** relish **7** delight, joyance **8** fruition, pleasure **9** diversion, enjoyment

delegate 4 name, send **5** agent, envoy, proxy **6** assign, charge, commit, depute, deputy **7** appoint, ascribe, consign, empower, entrust **8** deputize, emissary, transfer **9** authorize, catchpole, spokesman **10** commission, mouthpiece **12** representant

delete 4 omit, x out **5** annul, blank, erase, purge **6** cancel, censor, efface, remove **7** blot out, destroy, expunge, wipe out **8** black out, cross out **9** eliminate, eradicate **10** blue-pencil, obliterate

deleterious 3 bad **6** nocent **7** harmful, hurtful, nocuous, ruinous **8** damaging **11** destructive, detrimental, mischievous, prejudicial

deletion 7 erasure **8** omission **10** deficiency

deliberate 4 cool, muse, pore, slow **5** chary, meant, study, think, weigh **6** ponder, reason, regard **7** advised, careful, heedful, laggard, planned, reflect, schemed, studied, unhasty, willful, willing, witting **8** cautious, cogitate, consider, designed, dilatory, intended, measured, meditate, mull over, prepense, ruminate, studious, talk over, turn over, unforced **9** leisurely, meditated, projected, speculate, unhurried, voluntary **10** calculated, considered, purposeful, thought-out **11** circumspect, intentional **12** aforethought, premeditated, unprescribed

deliberately 9 on purpose, purposely **10** purposedly **11** purposively

deliberation 3 rap **4** heed **5** study **6** debate **7** thought **9** brainwork **10** conference, discussion

Delibes *ballet:* **6** Sylvia **8** Coppelia, La Source *opera:* **5** Lakmé

delicacy 4 cate **5** goody, treat **6** caviar, dainty, luxury, morsel, nicety, tidbit, titbit **7** caviare **8** kickshaw **10** daintiness **11** bonne bouche

delicate 4 airy, fine, lacy, mild, nice, rare, soft, weak **5** balmy, frail, fussy, light **6** aerial, choice, dainty, flimsy, gentle, pastel, petite, queasy, select, slight, subtle, tender, touchy, tricky **7** elegant, finical, finicky, fragile, lenient, politic, refined, tactful, tenuous **8** ethereal, feathery, finespun, gossamer, graceful, hairline, shattery, superior, tactical, ticklish **9** breakable, exquisite, finicking, frangible, recherché, sensitive, squeamish **10** diplomatic, fastidious, particular, precarious **11** fracturable, persnickety, shatterable **13** hair-splitting

delicatesse 4 tact **5** poise **7** address **9** diplomacy **11** savoir faire, tactfulness

delicatessen 11 charcuterie

delicious 4 lush **5** sapid, yummy **6** choice, savory **7** darling **8** adorable, heavenly **9** ambrosial, exquisite, palatable, toothsome **10** appetizing, delectable

delight 3 joy **4** glee **5** amuse, bliss, charm, enjoy, exult, glory, mirth, revel **6** arride, divert, please, regale, relish **7** enchant, gladden, gratify, happify, jollity, joyance, rapture, rejoice, triumph **8** enravish, entrance, fruition, hilarity, jubilate, pleasure, savoring **9** delectate, enjoyment, enrapture, entertain **11** contentment, delectation **12** satisfaction *in:* **4** like, love **5** adore, enjoy, savor **6** admire **7** cherish **10** appreciate

delightful 4 lush **5** yummy **6** dreamy, savory **7** darling, elysian **8** adorable, alluring, charming, heavenly, luscious, pleasant, pleasing **9** agreeable, ambrosial **10** attractive, delectable, enchanting, gratifying **11** fascinating, scrumptious

Delilah's victim 6 Samson

delimit 3 bar **5** bound **6** demark **7** confine, mark out, measure **8** restrict **9** demarcate, determine **12** circumscribe

delineate 3 map **4** etch, limn **5** chart, image, trace **6** define, depict, render, survey **7** outline, picture, portray **8** describe **9** interpret, represent

delineation 5 story **7** account, contour, drawing, outline, picture, profile **10** silhouette **11** portraiture, presentment

delinquency 5 lapse **7** default, failure, misdeed, neglect **8** omission **9** oversight **10** misconduct **11** dereliction

delinquent 3 lax **5** slack **6** remiss **8** careless **9** negligent **10** behindhand, regardless **12** disregardful, transgressor

deliquesce 3 run **4** flux, fuse, melt, thaw **5** decay **7** liquefy **8** dissolve **9** decompose, disappear **12** disintegrate

delirious 3 mad **4** wild **5** crazy, manic, rabid **6** crazed, insane, maniac, raving **7** frantic, lunatic **8** confused, demented, deranged, ecstatic, frenetic, frenzied, rambling 9 rapturous, wandering 10 bewildered, corybantic, distracted, irrational 11 overexcited, overwrought 12 unreasonable *Scottish:* 8 brainish

delirium 5 furor 6 fervor, frenzy, ravery 7 ecstasy, jimjams, rapture

delirium ___ 7 tremens

deliver 3 say 4 bail, bear, deal, feed, find, give, hand, save, take, tell, yean 5 bring, pitch, serve, speak, state, throw, utter, whelp 6 convey, redeem, rescue, strike, supply, unbind 7 chime in, consign, declare, inflict, present, provide, release 8 bring out, dispatch, dispense, hand over, liberate, transfer, transmit, turn over 9 surrender 10 administer, bring forth, emancipate 11 come out with

deliverance 6 rescue 7 opinion, release 8 decision 10 liberation 12 disburdening

delivery 5 birth 6 rescue 7 address, bearing 8 shipment 9 rendition 10 childbirth 11 parturition 12 childbearing *combining form:* 4 toky

dell 4 dale 6 dingle, hollow, valley

Delphian 4 dark 5 vatic 6 mantic 7 cryptic, fatidic 8 oracular 9 enigmatic, prophetic, sibylline, vaticinal 10 mystifying 11 apocalyptic, prophetical

delude 5 bluff, trick 6 betray, humbug, juggle, take in 7 beguile, deceive, mislead 8 impose on 11 double-cross

deluge 3 sea, sop, wet 4 gush, pour, soak 5 douse, drown, flood, souse, spate, swamp, whelm 6 drench, engulf 7 niagara, torrent 8 cataract, downpour, flooding, inundate, overcome, overflow, submerge 9 cataclysm, overwhelm 10 cloudburst, inundation

delusion 5 dream, fancy 6 mirage 7 eidolon, fallacy, fantasy, figment, phantom, sophism 8 daydream, phantasm 9 casuistry, deception, sophistry 10 apparition, misleading 11 ignis fatuus 12 equivocation, speciousness, spuriousness 13 deceptiveness, hallucination

delusive 5 false 8 fanciful, illusory, quixotic 9 beguiling, deceiving, deceptive, fantastic, imaginary, visionary 10 chimerical, fallacious, misleading

delusory see **delusive**

deluxe 4 lush 5 plush 6 Capuan, choice 7 elegant, opulent 8 luscious, palatial 9 exquisite, luxuriant, luxurious, recherché, sumptuous 11 upholstered

delve 3 dig, dip 4 hole, mine, void 6 cavity, fathom, hollow, pocket, quarry, vacuum 7 vacancy, vacuity *into:* 4 sift 5 probe 7 explore 8 prospect 11 investigate

delving 5 probe, quest 7 inquest, inquiry, probing 8 research 11 inquisition 13 investigation

demagnetize 6 deperm 7 degauss

demagogue 6 leader 7 inciter 8 agitator, fomenter 9 firebrand 10 instigator 12 rabble-rouser

demand 3 ask, use 4 call, need, take, want 5 claim, crave, exact, force, order 6 compel, direct, elicit, enjoin, expect, insist, oblige 7 call for, request, require, solicit 8 occasion 9 challenge, constrain, postulate 11 requirement, requisition

demanding 5 rigid, stern, tough 6 severe, strict, taxing, trying 7 exigent, onerous, weighty 8 grievous, rigorous 9 stringent 10 burdensome, oppressive

demarcate 5 bound, limit 6 define, set off 7 delimit, mark out, measure 8 separate, set apart 9 determine, segregate 10 delimitate 11 distinguish 12 circumscribe, discriminate 13 differentiate

demarcation 10 border line, separation 11 distinction

demean 3 act 4 bear, go on, mien, quit, sink 5 abase, carry, decry, lower 6 acquit, behave, debase, deport, humble 7 comport, conduct, degrade, detract 8 behavior, belittle, cast down, derogate 9 disparage, humiliate

demeanor 3 air, set 4 mien, port 7 address, bearing, conduct 8 behavior, carriage, portance, presence 10 deportment 11 comportment

demented 3 mad 4 luny 5 crazy, nutty 6 crazed, insane, maniac 7 lunatic, unsound 8 deranged, frenzied 9 delirious 10 hysterical, unbalanced

___ **de mer** 3 mal

demerit 3 sin 4 bump, bust, mark 5 break, fault 6 demote, reduce 7 declass, degrade, disrate 8 disgrade 9 downgrade 10 deficiency 11 shortcoming 12 imperfection

demesne 5 field 6 domain, estate, sphere 7 terrain 8 dominion, province 9 bailiwick, champaign, territory *house:* 5 manor

Demeter see **Ceres**

demigod 8 superman 10 superhuman

demise 3 die 4 drop, pass 5 death, sleep 6 cash in, depart, ending, expire 7 decease, passing, quietus, silence, succumb 8 curtains, pass away 10 defunction, expiration, extinction 11 dissolution 12 annihilation

demit 4 sink 5 couch, droop, lower 6 resign 7 depress, let down 8 abdicate, renounce, withdraw

demiurgic 8 creative, original 9 deviceful, formative, ingenious, inventive 10 innovative, innovatory **11** originative **12** innovational

demobilize **6** dispel **7** break up, disband, scatter **8** disperse, separate **9** discharge, muster out

democratic **7** popular **10** self-ruling **13** self-governing

Democratic party symbol **6** donkey

démodé **5** dated, passé **7** antique, archaic, belated **8** old-timey, outdated **9** out-of-date **12** old-fashioned

demoiselle **5** crane **6** damsel **9** damselfly **10** damselfish **11** earth pillar

demolish **4** raze, ruin, undo **5** crush, level, smash, total, wrack, wreck **6** unmake **7** destroy, unbuild, unframe **8** decimate

demolition bomb **11** blockbuster

demon **3** hag, imp **4** ogre **5** devil, fiend, genie, ghoul, Satan, witch **7** incubus, villain, warlock **9** archfiend *Arabic:* **5** afrit **6** afreet *female:* **5** lamia **7** succuba, succubi (plural) **8** succubae (plural), succubus *Samoan:* **4** aitu *small:* **8** devilkin

demoniac see **demonic**

demonian see **demonic**

demonic **7** satanic **8** devilish, diabolic, fiendish **10** serpentine, unhallowed **11** diabolonian

demonstrate **3** try **4** mark, show, test **5** prove **6** evince, expose, ostend **7** display, exhibit, make out **8** evidence, manifest, proclaim **9** determine, establish

demonstration **4** show **5** proof **7** display **9** spectacle

demonstrative **4** here, open, that, this **7** profuse **8** effusive, outgoing **9** expansive, exuberant, unspoken **10** epideictic, outpouring, unreserved **12** unrestrained **13** unconstrained

demoralize **4** warp **5** chill, unman **6** debase, deject, weaken **7** corrupt, debauch, deprave, pervert, unnerve, vitiate **8** dispirit **9** disparage, undermine **10** bastardize, debilitate, discourage, dishearten

Demosthenes *for one:* **6** orator *oration:* **9** Olynthiac, Philippic

demote **4** bump, bust **5** break, lower **6** reduce **7** declass, degrade, demerit, disrate **8** disgrade **9** downgrade

demulcent **8** soothing **9** softening

demur **3** gag, jib, shy **4** balk **5** qualm, stick, waver **6** boggle, falter, object, oppose, squeam, strain **7** protest, scruple, stickle, stumble **8** aversion, hesitate, question **9** challenge, hesitancy, objection, vacillate **10** conscience, difficulty, hesitation, indecision, reluctance **11** compunction, deprecation, disapproval, remonstrate, uncertainty **12** protestation, remonstrance **13** remonstration, unwillingness

demure **3** coy, mim, shy **4** prim **5** timid **6** modest, silent **7** bashful **8** backward, reserved, reticent, retiring **9** diffident, unassured **11** unassertive

demurral **7** protest **8** question **9** challenge, objection **10** difficulty **12** remonstrance **13** remonstration

demurrer see **demurral**

den **3** sty **4** base, cave, goal, home, lair, room, sink **5** couch, lodge, Sodom, study **6** burrow, cavern, hollow **7** cesspit, dayroom, hideout **8** cesspool, hideaway, playroom, workroom **11** pandemonium **12** Augean stable *rabbit:* **6** warren

denial **2** no **3** nay **7** refusal, refutal **8** disproof, negation, rebuttal **9** rejection **10** abnegation, gainsaying, refutation **11** declination, repudiation **12** disallowance, renouncement, renunciation **13** contradiction, controversion

denigrate **5** libel, sully **6** darken, defame, malign, vilify **7** asperse, slander, traduce **8** belittle, tear down **10** calumniate, scandalize

denims **9** blue jeans

denizen **5** liver **6** native **7** dweller, habitué, haunter, resider **8** habitant, occupant, resident **9** indweller **10** frequenter, inhabitant

Denmark *capital:* **10** Copenhagen *monetary unit:* **5** krone

denominate **3** dub **4** call, name, term **5** style, title **7** baptize, entitle **8** christen

denomination **4** cult, name, sect **5** creed, faith, nomen, style, title **6** church **8** category, cognomen, religion **9** communion **10** persuasion **11** appellative *religious:* **6** Jewish, Muslim **7** Baptist **8** Lutheran **9** Adventist, Episcopal, Mennonite, Methodist **12** Presbyterian **13** Roman Catholic

denotation **4** name, sign **7** meaning **10** signifying

denote **4** mark, name, show **5** spell **6** import, intend **7** add up to, express **8** indicate **9** designate, insinuate, represent

denouement **6** result **7** outcome

denounce **3** rap **4** skin **5** blame, blast, decry, knock **6** accuse, scathe **7** arraign, censure, condemn, redbait, upbraid **9** criticize, reprehend, reprobate **10** denunciate, vituperate **11** incriminate **12** anathematize

de novo **4** anew, over **5** again **6** afresh **8** once more **9** over again

dense **4** dull, dumb **5** close, heavy, massy, solid, thick, tight **6** obtuse, opaque, stupid **7** compact, crammed, crowded, doltish, serried **8** blockish, imporous **9** fatheaded, jam-packed **10** numskulled **11** blockheaded, thickheaded **12** impenetrable

combining form: 4 pycn, pykn 5 pachy, pycno, pykno

dent 4 bash, nick 5 dinge, notch, tooth 6 dimple

dental structures 5 brace 6 bridge 10 bridgework

denticulate 7 serrate, serried 8 saw-edged, saw-tooth, serrated 10 saw-toothed

dentin 6 enamel

denude 4 bare 5 strip 6 divest 7 deprive, disrobe 8 bankrupt, unclothe 9 dismantle

denunciate see denounce

deny 4 curb 5 cross, forgo, rebut 6 disown, eschew, forbid, impugn, negate, refuse, refute, reject, renege 7 abstain, confute, deprive, disavow, forbear, forsake, gainsay, refrain 8 abnegate, disallow, disclaim, forswear, hold back, keep back, negative, renounce, traverse, withhold 9 constrain, disaffirm 10 contradict, contravene, controvert

depart 2 go 3 die 4 exit, flee, pass, quit 5 leave, stray 6 begone, decamp, demise, desert, differ, expire, get off, perish, ramble, recede, retire, set out, skidoo, swerve, wander 7 abandon, abscond, decease, deviate, digress, diverge, excurse, forsake, get away, pull out, skiddoo, succumb 8 divagate, pass away, withdraw

departing 7 good-bye 8 farewell 11 valedictory

department 6 branch, sphere 8 division, province 11 subdivision

departure 4 exit 5 break, death, going 6 egress, exodus, flight 7 exiting, leaving, retreat, turning 8 farewell, offgoing, outgoing, quitting 9 deviation, diversion, egression 10 aberration, decampment, deflection, divergence, setting-out, withdrawal 11 leave-taking *of a ship:* 6 sortie *point:* 7 outport

depend 4 bank, hang, lean, rely, rest, turn 5 count, hinge, sling 6 bank on, dangle, hang on, rely on, turn on 7 build on, count on, hinge on, stand on 8 reckon on 11 calculate on

dependable 4 sure, true 5 loyal, solid, tried 6 secure, steady, trusty 7 certain, staunch 8 accurate, constant, faithful, reliable, surefire 9 authentic, steadfast 11 responsible, trustworthy 12 tried and true 13 authoritative *Scottish:* 6 sicker

dependence 4 hope 5 faith, stock, trust 8 reliance

dependent 3 sub 4 iffy 5 child, under 6 minion, sponge, vassal 7 limited, reliant, relying, sponger see 8 clinging, relative 9 accessory, ancillary, provisory, secondary, tributary, uncertain 10 collateral, contingent, restricted 11 appurtenant, conditional, provisional, subordinate

depict 4 draw, limn 5 image, paint 6 recite, relate, render, report, sketch 7 depaint, express, impaint, narrate, outline, picture, portray, recount 8 describe, emblazon 9 delineate, interpret, represent 12 characterize

depiction 7 picture 9 portrayal 11 portraiture, presentment

deplete 3 sap 4 draw 5 bleed, drain, empty, use up 6 expend, lessen, reduce, weaken 7 consume, disable, draw off, exhaust 8 bankrupt, decrease, diminish, draw down, enfeeble 9 undermine 10 impoverish

depleted 5 all in, spent 6 bleary, effete, used up 7 far-gone, worn-out 8 bankrupt 9 washed-out

deplorable 4 dire 5 awful 6 woeful 8 dolorous, dreadful, grievous, mournful, terrible, wretched 9 sickening 10 afflictive, calamitous, disastrous, horrifying 11 distressing, unfortunate 12 heartrending 13 heartbreaking

deplore 3 rue 4 moan, weep 5 mourn 6 bemoan, bewail, grieve, lament, regret, repent, sorrow 9 deprecate 10 disapprove, sorrow over

____ **de plume** 3 nom

depone 5 swear 6 assert 7 testify

____ **-de-pont** 4 tête

deport 3 act 4 bear, go on, oust, quit 5 carry, exile, expel 6 acquit, banish, behave, demean 7 conduct, expulse 8 displace, relegate 10 expatriate

deportee 2 DP 5 exile 8 expellee

deportment 3 air, set 4 mien, port 5 tenue 7 address, bearing, conduct 8 behavior, carriage, demeanor, presence

depose 4 aver, avow, oust 5 swear 6 affirm, assert, avouch, devest, divest, remove, unmake 7 declare, decrown, profess, protest, testify, uncrown 8 constate, dethrone, discrown, displace, throw out, unthrone 9 disthrone, overthrow, predicate 11 disenthrone

deposit 3 lay, set 4 bank, drop, dump, fund, lees, pawn, stow 5 chest, dregs, lodge, place, put by, store 6 entomb, settle 7 consign, grounds 8 sediment 9 settlings 11 precipitate 13 precipitation *alluvial:* 5 delta *black:* 4 soot *calcium carbonate:* 10 stalactite, stalagmite *containing gold:* 6 placer *eggs:* 5 spawn *geologic:* 7 horizon *glacial:* 4 till 5 drift, esker 7 moraine *loam:* 5 loess *mineral:* 4 lode 10 concretion *muddy:* 6 sludge *sand:* 4 bank 5 beach *sedimentary:* 4 silt *skeletal:* 5 coral *stolen goods:* 5 fence *stream:* 8 alluvium, sediment *tooth:* 6 tartar

deposition 6 burial 7 placing 8 sediment 9 testimony 10 testifying

depository 4 bank, safe 5 attic, store, vault 7 arsenal 8 magazine 10 storehouse *for bones:* 7 ossuary

depot 4 bank, base, dump 5 store 6 armory 7 arsenal, station 8 magazine, terminal, terminus 9 warehouse 10 repository, storehouse 12 station house

deprave 4 warp 6 debase, malign 7 corrupt, debauch, pervert, vitiate 9 brutalize 10 bastardize, bestialize, demoralize

depraved 3 bad 4 evil, ugly, vile 6 putrid, rotten, warped, wicked 7 bestial, corrupt, debased, immoral, twisted, vicious, vitiate 8 degraded, perverse, vitiated 9 corrupted, debauched, miscreant, nefarious, perverted, unhealthy 10 degenerate, flagitious, villainous

depravity 4 vice 8 villainy 10 corruption, immorality, wickedness

deprecate 5 frown 6 object 7 detract 8 derogate, disfavor 9 disesteem 10 disapprove, discommend 12 disapprove of

depreciate 5 abate, abuse, decry, erode, lower 6 lessen, reduce, soften 7 cheapen, devalue, dwindle 8 belittle, decrease, derogate, diminish, discount, mark down, minimize, write off 9 devaluate, disparage, dispraise, downgrade, underrate, write down 10 devalorize, undervalue 11 detract from

depreciation 7 calumny, scandal, slander 8 discount 10 backbiting 12 backstabbing, belittlement 13 disparagement

depreciative 9 slighting 10 derogatory, detracting 11 disparaging, dyslogistic, underrating 12 undervaluing

depreciatory see **depreciative**

depredate 4 sack 5 waste 6 devour, ravage 7 despoil, pillage, plunder 8 desolate, lay waste, prey upon, spoliate 9 desecrate, devastate

depredator 6 looter, raider 7 forager, spoiler 8 marauder 10 freebooter

depress 4 damp, dash, dent, fall, sink 5 chill, couch, demit, droop, lower, slump 6 dampen, deject, dismay, indent, sadden 7 decline, let down, oppress, trouble 8 contrist, dispirit, enfeeble 9 disparage, weigh down 10 discourage, dishearten

depressant 5 black, bleak 6 dismal, dreary, gloomy 9 cheerless 10 oppressive 11 dispiriting

depressed 3 bad, low, sad 4 blue, down, glum, sunk 6 broody, gloomy, glumpy, hollow, lonely, somber 7 hippish, letdown 8 dejected, downcast 9 woebegone 10 dispirited, lugubrious, melancholy, spiritless 11 downhearted, melancholic 12 disconsolate 13 disadvantaged

depressing 3 sad 4 blue 5 black, bleak, chill 6 dismal, dreary, gloomy, somber, triste 7 joyless 8 funereal, mournful 9 sad-

dening 10 melancholy, oppressive 11 melancholic 13 disheartening

depression 3 dip, low, pit, sag 4 drop, hole, sink, vale 5 basin, blues, crash, dumps, gloom, notch, scoop, slump 6 cavity, crater, hollow, pocket, valley 7 cyclone, decline, sadness, sinkage, sinking 8 sinkhole 9 concavity 10 melancholy, stagnation 11 unhappiness 12 mournfulness *anatomical:* 5 fossa, fovea 6 foveae (plural) 7 foveola, foveole 8 foveolae (plural), foveolet *between breasts:* 8 cleavage *geographic:* 7 Qattara *in ridge:* 3 col *in snow:* 8 sitzmark *small:* 4 dent 6 dimple

depressive see **depressant**

deprivation 4 loss 11 bereavement, deprivement, divestiture 13 dispossession

deprive 3 rob 4 bare, lose, oust 5 strip 6 denude, divest 7 bereave, disrobe 8 bankrupt, denudate, disseize 9 dismantle 10 disinherit, dispossess *of brilliancy:* 4 dull 6 deaden *of courage:* 7 unnerve *of sensation:* 6 benumb *of sense and judg-, ment:* 9 inebriate *of virginity:* 8 deflower

deprive of *prefix:* 2 de 3 dis

depth 4 drop 5 abyss 7 lowness 8 deepness 9 acuteness 10 profundity 11 penetration 12 profoundness *combining form:* 4 bath 5 batho, bathy *measure:* 6 fathom *measuring instrument:* 4 gage 5 gauge *of water:* 5 draft 7 draught

depthless 7 cursory, shallow, sketchy 10 uncritical 11 superficial

dept. of ___ 2 ed 3 agr, com, def, int 4 comm 5 labor, state, trans 7 justice

depurate 5 clean 6 purify 7 clarify, cleanse

deputize 8 delegate 10 commission

deputy 5 agent, proxy 6 factor 8 assignee, attorney, delegate 9 catchpole 12 representant *prefix:* 2 co

derange 5 craze, upset 6 frenzy, madden, mess up, sicken 7 disturb, perturb, rummage, unhinge 8 disarray, disorder, distract, unsettle 9 interrupt, unbalance 10 discompose 11 disorganize

deranged 3 mad 5 crazy 6 crazed, insane, maniac 7 cracked, lunatic, unsound 8 demented 9 disturbed 10 disordered, unbalanced

derangement 6 lunacy 7 madness 8 disorder, insanity 9 confusion, unbalance 10 aberration, alienation, insaneness 11 distraction, disturbance, psychopathy, unsoundness

derby 3 hat 4 race, shoe 6 cheese 7 contest 9 horse race 10 field trial

derelict 3 bum, lax, vag 4 hobo, lorn 5 dingy, faded, leper, seedy, slack, tramp 6 pariah, remiss, shabby, unused 7 drifter, floater, Ishmael, outcast, run-down, uncouth, vagrant 8 careless, castaway, deserted, desolate, forsaken, solitary, vagabond 9 abandoned, forgotten, negligent 10 behindhand, delinquent, Ishmaelite, neglectful, regardless, street arab, threadbare, unreliable 11 dilapidated, offscouring, untouchable 12 disregardful, undependable 13 irresponsible, untrustworthy

dereliction 5 fault 7 default, failure, neglect 9 deviation, oversight 11 abandonment, delinquency, shortcoming

deride 4 lout, mock, quiz, razz, twit 5 fleer, rally, scoff, scout, taunt 7 catcall 8 ridicule

de rigueur 4 nice 5 right 6 au fait, decent, proper 7 correct 8 becoming, decorous 11 comme il faut

derision 4 butt, jest, joke, mock 5 sport 6 jestee 7 mockery 9 pilgarlic 13 laughingstock

derisive sound 3 boo 4 hiss

derivable 7 a priori 8 dogmatic, reasoned 9 deducible, deductive

derivation 4 root, well 6 origin, source, whence 7 descent 8 fountain 9 etymology 10 provenance, wellspring 11 provenience

derivative 7 spin-off 8 offshoot 9 by-product, outgrowth, secondary 10 descendant

derive 3 get 4 draw, stem, take 5 adapt, educe, infer, judge 6 deduce, deduct, evolve, gather 7 acquire, collect, emanate, make out, work out 8 arrive at, conclude 9 formulate, originate 10 excogitate

derive from 4 flow, head, rise, stem 5 arise, issue 6 spring 7 emanate, proceed 9 originate

dernier cri 3 cry, fad 4 chic, mode, rage 5 craze, style, vogue 6 furore 7 fashion 8 last word

derogate 5 decry 8 belittle, diminish, minimize, write off 9 disparage, dispraise 10 depreciate 11 detract from, opprobriate

derogatory 5 snide 8 decrying, scornful, spiteful 9 degrading, demeaning, malicious, maligning, slighting, vilifying 10 belittling, calumnious, detracting, disdainful, malevolent, pejorative 11 disparaging, dyslogistic 12 contumelious, depreciative

derout 8 stampede

derrick 5 hoist

derriere 4 beam, rear, seat 5 fanny 6 behind, bottom 7 rear end 8 backside, buttocks 9 posterior

derring-do 5 nerve 7 bravado, bravery, courage

dervish 4 monk 9 mendicant *cap:* 3 taj *In Arabian Nights:* 4 Agib *practice:* 7 dancing, howling 8 whirling *wandering:* 8 calender

descant 3 air, lay 4 aria, hymn, lied, sing, song, tune 5 ditty 6 melody, remark, strain, warble 7 discuss, dissert, measure,

melisma, melodia 8 diapason, dilate on 9 discourse, expatiate, sermonize 10 dilate upon, dissertate 11 observation 12 counterpoint

Descartes' axiom 13 cogito ergo sum

descend 3 rot 4 drop, fall, pass, sink 5 lower, stoop, swoop 6 alight, derive, go down, worsen 7 decline 8 come down 9 originate 10 degenerate, disimprove, retrograde, spring from 11 deteriorate 12 disintegrate *by rope:* 6 rappel

descendant 3 son 5 scion 7 progeny, spin-off 8 offshoot, relative 9 by-product, outgrowth 10 derivative *suffix:* 3 ite

descendants 4 seed 5 brood, issue 7 progeny 8 children 9 offspring, posterity 11 progeniture

descent 3 dip 4 drop, fall 5 birth, blood, slope 6 origin 7 decline, drop-off, incline, lineage, sinking 8 ancestry, comedown, gradient, pedigree, plunging, stooping 9 declivity, downgrade 10 derivation, extraction, plummeting 11 origination 12 discomfiture *airplane:* 8 approach *parachute:* 4 jump 7 bailout

describe 4 limn 5 image, label, state 6 denote, depict, recite, relate, render, report 7 explain, express, mark out, narrate, outline, picture, portray, recount, signify 8 rehearse, vignette 9 chronicle, delineate, interpret, represent 10 illustrate 11 distinguish 12 characterize *grammatically:* 5 parse

description 3 ilk 4 kind, sort, tale, type, yarn 5 story 6 nature 7 account, picture, recital, variety, version 8 anecdote 9 character, chronicle, narrative, portrayal, recountal 10 recounting 11 portraiture, presentment

descry 3 see 4 espy, find, mark, note, spot, view 5 catch, hit on 6 behold, detect, spy out, turn up 7 discern, hit upon, observe 8 discover, meet with, perceive 9 encounter 11 distinguish

Desdemona *father:* 9 Brabantio *husband:* 7 Othello *slanderer:* 4 Iago *slayer:* 7 Othello

desecrate 4 sack 5 waste 6 defile, devour, ravage 7 despoil, pillage, profane 8 spoliate 9 depredate, devastate

desecration 9 blasphemy, sacrilege

desensitize 4 dull, mull, numb 5 blunt 6 benumb, deaden

desert 2 go 3 fly, rat 4 flee, quit, turn, wild 5 chuck, leave, waste 6 barren, betray, decamp, defect, depart, escape, maroon, strand, Tanami 7 abandon, abscond, badland, forsake 8 Karakumy, renounce, wild land, wildness 9 repudiate, throw over, wasteland 10 apostatize, tergiverse, wilderness 12 tergiversate *African:* 6 Libyan,

Sahara 7 Arabian 8 Kalahari *Arizona:*
7 Painted *Asian:* 4 Gobi, Thar 6 Syrian
7 Kara Kum, Qara Qum 8 Kyzyl Kum
10 Great Sandy *basin bottom:* 5 playa
beast: 5 camel 9 dromedary *California:*
6 Mohave, Mojave *clay:* 5 adobe *combining form:* 4 erem 5 eremo *dweller:*
4 Arab 5 nomad 6 Berber, Libyan, Malian,
Nubian 8 Algerian, Egyptian, Maghrebi,
Maghribi, Sudanese 11 Mauritanian *fertile area:* 5 oases (plural), oasis *garb:* 3 aba
hallucination: 6 mirage *region:* 3 erg
Saudi Arabia: 7 An Nafud *Sudan:*
6 Nubian *travel group:* 7 caravan *valley:*
6 bolson *wind:* 7 sirocco

deserted 4 bare, lorn 5 empty 6 barren,
vacant 7 uncouth 8 derelict, desolate, forsaken, solitary 9 abandoned 10 unoccupied 11 uninhabited

deserter 3 rat 4 AWOL 6 bolter 7 runaway 8 apostate, fugitive, renegade, runagate, turncoat

desertion 7 perfidy 8 apostasy 9 falseness, recreancy, treachery 11 abandonment

deserts 3 due 11 comeuppance

deserve 3 get, win 4 earn, gain, rate
5 merit 6 demand

deserved 3 due 4 just 5 right 7 condign,
merited 8 rightful, suitable 9 requisite
11 appropriate 13 rhadamanthine

deserving 3 due 5 lumps, merit 6 rights,
worthy 8 laudable 9 admirable, estimable,
meritable, praisable 11 comeuppance, commendable, meritorious, thankworthy
12 praiseworthy

desexualize 3 fix 4 geld 5 alter, unsex
6 change, neuter 8 castrate, mutilate

desiccate 3 dry 4 fade, sear 5 decay,
drain, dry up, parch, wizen 6 divest, wither
7 deplete, exhaust, shrivel 9 dehydrate
10 devitalize

desiderate 4 want, wish 5 covet, crave
6 choose, desire

design 3 aim 4 cast, draw, form, mean,
mind, plan, plot, will 5 chart, decal, draft,
frame, model, motif 6 animus, create,
device, devise, devote, figure, intend,
intent, invent, lay out, makeup, map out,
motive, scheme, set out, sketch 7 arrange,
diagram, dope out, drawing, execute, fashion, meaning, outline, pattern, prepare, produce, project, propose, purpose, thought,
tracing 8 conation, contrive, creation, game
plan, intrigue, strategy, thinking, volition
9 blueprint, construct, delineate, direction,
formation, intention, invention 10 decoration, figuration, intendment, reflection
11 arrangement, composition, contemplate,
delineation, disposition, machination
12 architecture, constitution, construction,

deliberation *book:* 6 fillet 8 vignette *carpet:*
3 gul 9 medallion *incised:* 8 intaglio *Indonesian:* 5 batik *inlaid:* 6 mosaic *of squares:* 5 check *openwork:* 8 filigree
perforated: 7 stencil *raised:* 8 repoussé
skin: 6 tattoo *textile:* 8 polka dot *velvety:*
8 flocking

designate 3 dub, opt, tap 4 call, make,
name, pick, term 5 allot, elect, label, style,
title 6 assign, choose, denote, depute, finger, induct, select, single 7 appoint, baptize, declare, dictate, earmark, entitle, mete
out, reserve, signify, specify 8 allocate,
christen, identify, stand for 9 apportion,
stipulate 10 decide upon 11 appropriate
12 characterize

designation 4 name 5 nomen, style, title
6 naming 8 cognomen, monicker 9 allotment 10 indicating, pigeonhole 11 appellative, identifying 12 pigeonholing

designed 7 advised, decided, studied
8 prepense, resolved, studious 10 considered, deliberate, determined, thought-out
12 aforethought, premeditated

designedly 9 on purpose, purposely
10 prepensely 11 purposively 12 deliberately 13 intentionally

designless 4 spot 6 random 9 desultory,
haphazard, hit-or-miss, unplanned
12 unconsidered

desirable 6 suited 7 optimal 9 excellent,
expedient

desire 3 aim, ask, yen 4 envy, eros, hope,
itch, like, long, lust, pant, pine, urge, want,
wish 5 covet, crave, enjoy, fancy, greed,
yearn 6 asking, aspire, choice, choose, hanker, hunger, pining, thirst 7 avarice,
bespeak, craving, entreat, impulse, longing,
passion, request, solicit 8 appetite, cupidity, petition, rapacity, striving, yearning
9 appetency, eroticism, hankering, hungering, prurience, pruriency, thirsting 10 aphrodisia, appetition, attraction, preference
11 inclination, lustfulness 13 concupiscence, lickerishness *combining form:*
6 orexia *for liquids:* 6 thirst *restless:*
4 itch

desired 4 true 5 right 6 proper 7 fitting
11 appropriate

desirous 5 itchy 6 grabby, greedy
7 athirst, envious, wishful 8 appetent, covetous, grasping 10 prehensile, solicitous
11 acquisitive

desist 4 halt, quit, stop 5 cease, deval,
yield 6 resign 7 abandon, abstain, forbear,
hold off 8 give over, knock off, leave off,
surcease 10 relinquish 11 discontinue,
refrain from

desistance 3 end 4 stop 5 cease, close
6 ending, finish, period 9 cessation 10 conclusion 11 termination

desk 5 booth, stand, table 7 counter, lectern, roll top 8 lapboard 9 secretary 10 escritoire, secretaire *adjunct:* 8 inkstand, standish *item:* 3 pad 7 blotter, inkwell *library:* 6 carrel 7 carrell *Scottish:* 3 pew

desman 3 fur 4 pelt 6 mammal

___ de soie, French silk 4 peau

desolate 4 bare, dark, lorn, poor, sack 5 black, bleak, drear, empty, murky, stark, waste 6 barren, devoid, devour, dismal, gloomy, ravage, ruined, somber, vacant 7 despoil, joyless, pillage, uncouth 8 bereaved, derelict, deserted, forsaken, funereal, lay waste, lifeless, solitary, spoliate 9 abandoned, cheerless, depredate, desecrate, destitute, devastate, sorrowful 10 acheronian, unoccupied 11 dilapidated, uninhabited 12 inconsolable, unconsolable 13 disheartening

desolation 6 sorrow 7 sadness 9 wasteland 11 abandonment

despair 4 drop 5 yield 6 give up, resign 7 abandon 8 renounce 9 surrender 10 relinquish

despairing 7 cynical, forlorn 8 hopeless 9 depressed, oppressed 10 melancholy 11 atrabilious, melancholic, pessimistic, weighed down 12 misanthropic 13 brokenhearted

desperado 6 badman, bandit, outlaw 7 bandido, convict 8 criminal 10 lawbreaker

desperate 4 dire, rash 5 acute 6 balked, crying, fierce, foiled 7 baffled, crucial, forlorn, furious, heinous, intense, vicious, violent 8 critical, headlong, hopeless, reckless, shocking, terrible, thwarted, vehement 9 atrocious, exquisite, foolhardy, monstrous, outwitted 10 frustrated, outrageous, scandalous 11 climacteric, precipitate, venturesome 12 circumvented, concentrated, overpowering 13 irretrievable, overmastering, uncollectable

despicable 3 low 4 base, mean, ugly, vile 5 cheap, sorry 6 abject, scummy, scurvy, shabby, sordid 7 ignoble 8 beggarly, infamous, wretched 9 loathsome 11 disgraceful, ignominious 12 contemptible

despisable see **despicable**

despise 4 hate, shun, snub 5 abhor, avoid, scorn, scout, spurn 6 detest, eschew, ignore, loathe, reject, slight 7 contemn, disdain 8 execrate, look down, misprize, overlook, renounce 9 abominate, disregard, repudiate

despised one 6 pariah

despisement 4 hate 5 scorn 6 hatred, malice 7 disdain, ill will 8 aversion, contempt, loathing 10 abhorrence 11 detestation, malevolence

despite 3 cut 4 harm, hate, hurt, slap, snub 5 altho, scorn 6 grudge, hatred, injury, insult, malice, rebuff, slight, spleen 7 affront, against, disdain, disgust, dislike, ill will 8 although, aversion, contempt, defiance, disfavor, distaste, loathing, spurning 9 contumacy, contumely, indignity, insolence, in spite of, malignity, rejection 10 abhorrence, incivility, malignancy 11 abomination, detestation, discourtesy, indignation, in the face of, malevolence, repudiation 12 cold shoulder, regardless of, spitefulness, stubbornness 13 disparagement, maliciousness, recalcitrance

despiteful 4 evil 5 catty 6 bitchy, wicked 7 vicious 9 malicious, rancorous 10 malevolent

despoil 4 sack 5 blast, strip, waste, wreck 6 denude, devour, ravage 7 pillage, plunder 8 desolate, spoliate 9 depredate, desecrate, devastate, strip away, wrest away

despoiler 6 looter, ruiner, sacker, vandal 7 defacer, forager, wrecker 8 marauder, pillager, ruinator 9 destroyer, plunderer, spoliator 10 depredator, freebooter

Despoina 8 mistress 10 Persephone *husband:* 5 Hades *realm:* 10 underworld

despond 3 sag 4 mope 5 brood, droop 6 give up 8 languish

despondency 5 blues, dumps, gloom 6 misery, sorrow 7 despair 9 dejection 10 blue devils, depression, melancholy

despondent 3 sad 7 forlorn 8 dejected, downcast, grieving, hopeless, mourning 9 depressed, sorrowful, woebegone 10 dispirited, melancholy 11 discouraged 12 disconsolate, disheartened

despot 4 duce 5 ruler 6 tyrant 7 autarch, emperor 8 autocrat, dictator 9 oppressor, strong man

despotic 8 absolute, tyrannic 9 arbitrary, autarchic, tyrannous 10 autocratic, monocratic, tyrannical

despotism 7 tsarism, tyranny, tzarism 8 autarchy 9 autocracy 10 domination 12 dictatorship

despotize 7 dictate, oppress 8 dominate, domineer, overlord 9 tyrannize

desquamate 4 peel 5 scale 7 peel off 8 flake off, scale off 9 exfoliate

dessert 3 ice, pie 4 cake, flan, fool, tart 5 Betty, bombe, coupe, fruit, grunt, halva, melba, slump, torte 6 afters, cheese, Danish, éclair, frappe, gateau, halvah, hermit, junket, kuchen, mousse, pastry, sorbet, sundae, trifle 7 cassata, cobbler, custard, gelatin, mazarin, parfait, pudding, sabayon, sherbet, spumone, spumoni, strudel 8 Bismarck, flummery, ice cream, marquise, napoleon, pandowdy, streusel, taiglach, teiglach, turnover 9 charlotte, cream puff, petit four, shortcake **10** blancmange, brown Betty, cheesecake, frangipane, marguerite, zabaglione **11** baked Alaska, banana split, gingerbread **12** hasty pudding, zuppa inglese *chilled:* **6** mousse *custard:* **8** zabaione, zabajone *French:* **5** bombe **6** éclair, frappe, gateau, mousse **7** mazarin, parfait, sabayon **8** marquise **9** petit four **10** blancmange, frangipane *frozen:* **5** bombe **7** parfait, sherbet **8** sherbert *German:* **6** kuchen **7** strudel *Italian:* **7** cannoli, cassata, spumone, spumoni **10** zabaglione **12** zuppe inglese *Jewish:* **8** taiglach, teiglach *pastry:* **6** quiche *soft:* **3** pud **7** pudding *Turkish:* **5** halva **6** halvah

destination **3** end, use **6** object **7** purpose **10** appointing

destine **3** fix **4** fate **5** assign, decree, devise, direct, doom to, intend **7** preform **8** dedicate, set aside **9** determine, preordain **10** foreordain **12** predetermine

destiny **3** lot **4** doom, fate, goal **5** moira, weird **6** design, future, intent, kismat, kismet **7** fortune, portion **9** intention, objective **12** circumstance

destitute **4** bare, poor, void **5** empty, needy **6** bereft, devoid **7** drained **8** bankrupt, depleted, dirt poor, divested, indigent, innocent, stripped **9** deficient, exhausted, penurious **10** bankrupted, stone-broke **11** impecunious, necessitous **12** impoverished *of water:* **9** anhydrous

destitute of *prefix:* **2** an *suffix:* **4** less

destitution **4** lack, need, want **6** dearth, penury **7** absence, poverty **9** adversity, indigence, neediness **10** misfortune

destroy **3** zap **4** doom, down, kill, raze, ruin, sack, slay, undo, wipe **5** fordo, havoc, shoot, smash, total, waste, wrack, wreck **6** cut off, finish, foredo, injure, lay low, mangle, quench, ravage, rubble, rub out, unmake **7** abolish, atomize, nullify, pillage, put away, ruinate, shatter, subvert, take off, unbuild, unframe, wipe out **8** carry off, decimate, demolish, dispatch, dissolve, dynamite, fumigate, mutilate, pull down, sabotage, tear down **9** devastate, discreate, dismantle, eradicate, extirpate, pulverize **10** annihilate, counteract, decapitate, extinguish, neutralize **11** exterminate *suffix:* **4** lyse, lyze

destroyer **4** bane, ruin **6** ruiner, tin can, vandal **7** defacer, undoing, warship, wrecker **8** downfall, ruinator **9** despoiler, ruination *combining form:* **4** cide **5** clast **7** clastic, phthora

destroying *combining form:* **5** cidal **7** clastic *prefix:* **3** ant **4** anth, anti

destruction **4** bane, loss, ruin **5** havoc **7** killing, undoing **8** downfall **9** confusion **10** impairment *combining form:* **4** lyses (plural) **5** lysis **6** clasia, clasis

destructive **5** fatal **6** deadly, lethal, mortal **7** baneful, ruinous **8** wrackful, wreckful **9** injurious **10** calamitous, disastrous, shattering **11** deleterious, detrimental

desuetude **3** end **5** cease, close **6** disuse, ending **7** closing, closure, neglect **8** disusage **9** cessation **10** conclusion, suspension **11** abandonment

desultory **6** casual, catchy, fickle, fitful, random, spotty **7** aimless, erratic, vagrant **8** shifting, sporadic, wavering **9** haphazard, hit-or-miss, mercurial, spasmodic, unplanned **10** capricious, designless, digressive, disorderly, inconstant **11** purposeless **12** unconsidered, unmethodical, unsystematic

detach **4** part, wean **5** sever, unfix **6** cut off, sunder, unhang **7** disjoin, divorce **8** abstract, dismount, disunite, separate, uncouple, withdraw **9** disengage, dismantle, dismember **10** disconnect, dissociate **11** disassemble **12** disaffiliate, disassociate

detached **5** alone, aloof, apart **6** casual, remote **7** distant, isolate, neutral, removed **8** abstract, isolated, separate, unbiased **9** colorless, incurious, uncurious, withdrawn **10** impersonal, poker-faced **11** indifferent, unconcerned, unconnected, unpassioned **12** uninterested **13** disinterested, dispassionate, unaccompanied *combining form:* **2** ap **3** aph, apo

detachment **7** divorce, rupture, split up **8** disunion, division **9** partition **10** neutrality, separation **11** dissolution, divorcement **12** unworldliness *combining form:* **5** lyses (plural), lysis

detail **4** item, list, part **5** point, thing **6** assign, relate, report **7** article, element, listing, minutia, program, specify **8** elements, minutiae (plural) **9** enumerate, stipulate **10** brass tacks (plural), particular **11** specificate, specificize **12** circumstance **13** particularize

detailed **4** full **6** minute **7** copious **8** abundant, itemized, thorough **9** clocklike **10** blow-by-blow, exhausting, exhaustive, particular **13** thoroughgoing

detain **3** nab **4** bust, curb, hold, keep, mire **5** check, delay, embog, pinch, run in **6** arrest, hang up, pick up, pull in, retard, slow up **7** bog down, inhibit, keep out, reserve, set back, slacken **8** hold back, keep back, restrain, slow down, withhold **9** apprehend **10** buttonhole, decelerate *in conversation:* **10** buttonhole

detect **4** espy, find, spot **5** catch, hit on **6** descry, turn up **7** discern, hit upon, rectify **8** discover, meet with **9** ascertain, encounter **10** demodulate

detectable 8 sensible, tangible 11 perceptible

detecting device 5 radar, sonar 6 solion 7 antenna, sferics 8 spherics 13 Geiger counter

detection 4 find 6 espial, strike 9 discovery 10 laying open, unearthing *system:* 5 radar, sofar

detective 3 tec 4 dick, G-man 5 roper 6 shamus, sleuth 7 gumshoe, shoofly 8 hawkshaw, informer, Sherlock 9 inspector 12 investigator 13 police officer *fictional:* 4 Chan (Charlie), Moto (Mr.) 5 Dupin (Auguste), Lecoq, Lupin (Arsène), Spade (Sam), Trent (Philip) 6 Carter (Nick), Holmes (Sherlock), Poirot (Hercule), Wimsey (Peter) 7 Charles (Nick, Nora) 11 Father Brown

detective story writer 3 Poe (Edgar Allan) 5 Doyle (Arthur Conan), James (Phyllis Dorothy), Queen (Ellery), Stout (Rex) 6 Parker (Robert), Sayers (Dorothy) 7 Bentley (Edmund Clerihew), Biggers (Earl), Collins (Wilkie), Fleming (Ian), Gardner (Erle Stanley), Hammett (Dashiell) 8 Chandler (Raymond), Christie (Agatha), Gaboriau (Émile), Marquand (John) 10 Chesterton (Gilbert Keith)

detent 3 dog 4 pawl 5 catch, click

detention 3 nab 5 delay, pinch 6 arrest, pickup 10 arrestment, internment 12 apprehension, imprisonment

deter 5 avert, block, debar, scare 6 divert, hinder, impede 7 forfend, inhibit, obviate, prevent, rule out, shut out, ward off 8 dissuade, frighten, obstruct, preclude, restrain, stave off 9 disadvise, forestall, turn aside 10 discourage

deterge 7 cleanse, wash off

detergent 4 soap 6 alkali 8 cleanser 9 cleansing

deteriorate 3 mar, rot 4 fade, fail, flag, sink 5 decay, dwine, spoil 6 impair, lessen, weaken, worsen 7 crumble, decline, descend 8 languish 9 decompose, undermine 10 debilitate, depreciate, disimprove, retrograde

deterioration 4 ruin 5 decay 6 dry rot, ebbing, waning 7 atrophy, decline, erosion, failure, rotting 8 decaying, downfall, spoiling 9 crumbling, decadence, downgrade, lessening 10 debasement, declension, degeneracy, impairment 12 dégringolade

determinant 4 gene, mark 5 agent, cause, trait 6 factor, reason, weight 7 radical 8 occasion 9 attribute, authority, influence 10 antecedent 11 differentia

determinate 4 spot 5 fixed, place 6 cymose, finger, narrow 7 limited, precise, settled 8 constant, definite, diagnose, identify, pinpoint 9 arbitrary, ascertain, immov-

able, immutable, recognize 10 definitive, inflexible, invariable, restricted 11 distinguish, established, inalterable, unalterable 12 unchangeable, unmodifiable 13 circumscribed, diagnosticate

determination 6 fixing 7 purpose, resolve 8 decision, firmness 9 resolving 10 conclusion, settlement 11 decidedness 12 resoluteness 13 purposiveness

determine 3 end, fix, see, set 4 bias, fate, halt, hear, move, rule, show 5 bound, close, drive, impel, learn, limit, prove 6 decide, direct, doom to, figure, finish, induce, ordain, settle, tumble, wind up, wrap up 7 actuate, catch on, control, delimit, destine, dispose, find out, incline, make out, mark out, measure, preform, purpose, resolve, unearth 8 complete, conclude, discover, persuade, regulate, ultimate 9 ascertain, demarcate, establish, preordain, resolve on, terminate 10 delimitate, foreordain, predestine, predispose 11 demonstrate

determined 3 set 4 bent 6 intent 7 decided, earnest, serious, settled 8 decisive, hellbent, resolute, resolved 10 purposeful, unwavering 11 unfaltering 12 unhesitating

detest 4 hate 5 abhor, spurn 6 loathe, reject 7 despise, dislike 8 execrate 9 abominate, repudiate

detestable 4 foul, vile 5 sorry 6 damned, horrid, odious 7 hateful, heinous 9 abhorrent, execrable, loathsome 10 abominable, despicable 12 contemptible

detestation 4 hate 6 hatred, horror 7 bugbear, disgust, dislike 8 anathema, aversion, loathing 9 antipathy, bête noire, repulsion, revulsion 10 abhorrence, black beast, repugnance

dethrone 6 depose, divest, unmake 7 uncrown 8 discrown, displace

detonate 5 burst, go off 6 blow up 7 explode 8 mushroom

detonator 3 cap 4 fuse, fuze 9 explosive 11 blasting cap

detour 5 avoid, skirt 6 bypass 7 deflect 9 deviation, runaround 10 circumvent, roundabout

detract 4 draw 5 decry, libel 6 divert, lessen, reduce 7 slander 8 belittle, decrease, derogate, diminish, discount, minimize, write off 9 disparage, dispraise 10 depreciate

detracting 8 libelous 9 maligning, traducing, vilifying 10 calumnious, defamatory, derogatory, pejorative, scandalous, slanderous 11 disparaging, dyslogistic 12 depreciative, depreciatory

detraction 4 harm, hurt, tale 5 libel, wrong 6 damage, injury 7 calumny, scandal, slander 8 libeling 9 aspersion, injustice, maligning, traducing 10 backbiting, slandering, sycophancy 12 backstabbing, belittlement 13 disparagement

detriment 4 harm, hurt 6 damage, injury 7 marring 8 drawback, handicap, mischief, spoiling 10 disability 12 disadvantage

detrimental 3 bad, ill 4 evil 7 adverse, harmful, hurtful, nocuous 8 damaging, negative 9 injurious 11 deleterious, mischievous, unfavorable

detritus 4 tufa, tuff 5 scree, talus 6 debris

Detroit *county:* 5 Wayne *founder:* 8 Cadillac (Sieur de) *lake:* 4 Erie 10 Saint Clair *sobriquet:* 6 Motown 9 Motor City

de trop 5 extra, spare 6 excess 7 surplus 11 superfluent, superfluous 13 supernumerary

detruncate 3 top 4 crop 7 pollard

Deucalion *father:* 10 Prometheus *kingdom:* 6 Phthia *mother:* 7 Clymene *son:* 6 Hellen *wife:* 6 Pyrrha

Deuel's son 8 Eliasaph

Deutschland über ____ 4 alles

dev, deva 3 god

Devaki's son 7 Krishna

deval 4 halt, quit, stop 5 cease 6 desist 8 give over, knock off, leave off, surcease 11 discontinue

De Valera 5 Eamon

devaluate 5 decry, lower 8 mark down, write off 9 underrate, write down 10 depreciate, undervalue

devaluation 7 atrophy, decline 8 downfall 9 decadence 10 declension, degeneracy

devalue see **depreciate**

devastate 4 sack 6 devour, ravage 7 despoil, pillage 8 desolate, lay waste, overcome, spoliate 9 depredate, desecrate, overpower, overwhelm

devastation 4 loss, ruin 5 havoc 9 confusion

devel 3 hit 4 biff, ding, nail, sock 5 clout, slosh, smite, whack 6 strike

develop 2 go 3 age, get 4 form, gain, grow, ripe 5 break, occur, phase, reach, ripen 6 attain, befall, betide, chance, dilate, enroot, evolve, expand, grow up, happen, lay out, mature, mellow, obtain, open up, thrive, unfold, unfurl 7 achieve, acquire, advance, amplify, burgeon, come off, convert, enlarge, expound, fall out, prepare, promote, prosper, realize 8 flourish, maturate 9 actualize, elaborate, establish, transpire 11 come to light, materialize 13 differentiate *rapidly:* 7 burgeon 8 bourgeon

development 5 phase 6 growth, phasis 7 advance, ongoing 8 ontogeny, progress, upgrowth 9 evolution, expansion, flowering, phylogeny, unfolding 11 elaboration, pro-

gression *combining form:* 5 plasy 6 plasia, plasto *of life:* 10 biogenesis

Devi 7 goddess *consort:* 4 Siva *father:* 7 Himavat *name:* 3 Uma 4 Kali 5 Durga, Gauri 6 Chandi 7 Parvati

deviant 6 off-key 8 aberrant, abnormal, atypical 9 anomalous, divergent, irregular, unnatural, unregular, untypical 11 heteroclite 13 preternatural

deviate 3 err, yaw 4 veer 5 sheer, stray 6 depart, swerve, wander 7 digress, diverge, pervert 9 turn aside 13 sexual pervert

deviation 3 yaw 4 bend, tack, turn 5 error, fault, lapse, shift 6 breach, change, double 7 anomaly, blunder, failing, turning, veering 9 departure, diversion 10 divergence 13 transgression

device 4 play, ploy, tool, type, wile, will 5 feint, motif, motto, shift, trick 6 design, desire, dingus, emblem, figure, gadget, gambit, hickey, motive, resort, scheme, symbol 7 gimmick, machine, pattern, project, utensil 8 artifice, creation, insignia, maneuver, resource 9 apparatus, appliance, attribute, doohickey, expedient, implement, invention, makeshift, mechanism, stratagem 10 instrument, thingumbob 11 contraption, contrivance, inclination *automatic:* 5 servo *baseball:* 11 batting cage *binding:* 5 clamp *combining form:* 4 stat *cooking:* 7 hibachi *electrical:* 8 inverter *electronic:* 7 vocoder *energy changing:* 9 converter, convertor *fastening:* 6 zipper *grasping:* 4 tong *heating:* 8 radiator *hoisting:* 5 lewis 8 lewisson *holding:* 4 vise 5 clamp *in an airplane:* 7 gosport *irrigation:* 6 shaduf 7 shadoof *light-generating:* 7 lampion *literary:* 5 irony *mechanical:* 6 gadget *oil lamp:* 8 pickwick *remote-control:* 6 selsyn 7 synchro *respiratory:* 8 pulmotor *restraining:* 8 holdback *seed-sewing:* 11 broadcaster *ship's:* 7 euphroe *speed of rotation:* 4 tach *stabilizing:* 8 gyrostat *temperature measurement:* 7 thermal *warning:* 5 siren *weighing:* 5 scale, trone *wiretapping:* 3 bug

devil 4 dell, haze, limb 5 annoy, beast, brute, demon, error, fiend, knave, rogue, Satan, scamp, tease 6 Belial, Cloots, diablo, dybbuk, pester, rascal, spirit 7 caitiff, Clootie, dickens, Lucifer, Old Nick, serpent, tempter, torment, villain 8 Apollyon, Mephisto, mischief, scalawag, Succubus 9 Archfiend, Beelzebub, cacodemon, scoundrel, skeezicks 10 blackguard, Old Scratch 11 firecracker, rapscallion 13 Old Gooseberry *combining form:* 6 diabol 7 diabolo

devil-devil 4 rune 5 charm, spell 11 conjuration, incantation

devilfish 3 ray 5 manta 7 octopus
10 cephalopod

devilish 3 bad 4 evil 6 cursed, wicked
7 demonic, extreme, satanic 8 accursed,
damnable, demoniac, demonian, diabolic,
fiendish 9 excessive, execrable, nefarious
10 diabolical, iniquitous, serpentine, unhallowed, villainous 11 diabolonian, excessively

devilkin 3 imp

devil-may-care 3 gay 4 fast, rash, wild
6 rakish, sporty 7 raffish 8 rakehell, reckless

devilment see **deviltry**

devilry see **deviltry**

devil's-bones 4 dice, tats 5 cubes, ivory

deviltry 7 roguery, waggery 8 mischief
9 diablerie 11 roguishness, waggishness
12 sportiveness

devious 3 sly 4 foxy 5 stray 6 artful,
astray, crafty, errant, erring, remote, roving,
secret, shifty, sneaky, tricky, unfair 7 bending, crooked, cunning, curving, erratic,
obscure, removed, retired, winding 8 aberrant, guileful, indirect, lonesome, sneaking,
twisting 9 diverting, underhand, wandering
10 digressing, roundabout

devise 4 cast, form, plan, plot, will 5 chart,
forge, frame, leave, shape 6 cook up, create, design, invent, legacy, legate, make
up, scheme, vamp up 7 arrange, bequest,
collude, concoct, connive, dope out, dream
up, hatch up, project 8 bequeath, cogitate,
collogue, conspire, contrive, discover,
intrigue, property 9 blueprint, determine,
formulate, machinate, scheme for, scheme
out 11 inheritance

devitalize 5 dry up 6 weaken 7 deprive,
destroy 9 desiccate 10 eviscerate

devoid 4 bare 5 empty 6 barren 7 lacking, wanting 8 free from, innocent 9 deficient, destitute

devoir 3 job 4 duty, must, need, task
5 chare, chore, ought, right, stint 6 charge
9 committal 10 assignment, commitment,
obligation

devolution 7 atrophy, decline, passing
8 downfall, receding, transfer 9 conferral,
decadence, recession 10 declension,
degeneracy, regression 12 dégringolade,
retrograding, transference 13 retrogression

devolve 4 pass 8 hand down, transfer

devote 3 try, use, vow 4 bend, damn,
doom, give, turn 5 apply, throw 6 addict,
adjust, attach, bestow, commit, direct,
donate, employ, give up, hallow, strive, take
to, wrap up 7 address, attempt, confide,
consign, entrust, hand out, present, provide, utilize 8 dedicate, endeavor, give
away, sanctify, struggle 9 confirm in, habituate 10 buckle down, consecrate

devoted 4 dear, fond, true 5 loyal
6 ardent, doting, fervid, loving 7 zealous
8 constant, faithful, lovesome 10 thoughtful
12 affectionate *religiously:* 6 oblate

devotee 3 fan 4 buff 5 hound, lover
6 addict, votary 7 admirer, amateur, fancier, habitué 8 follower 9 supporter
10 aficionado, enthusiast *suffix:* 3 ite

devotion 4 love, zeal 5 ardor, piety
6 fealty, fervor, prayer 7 loyalty, passion
8 fidelity, fondness 9 reverence 10 allegiance, attachment, enthusiasm 12 faithfulness *combining form:* 5 latry *religious:*
6 novena

devour 3 eat 4 meal, ruin, sack, take, wolf
5 eat up, enjoy, use up, waste, wreck
6 absorb, engulf, feed on, ingest, ravage,
relish 7 consume, despoil, destroy,
exhaust, feast on, gloat on, pillage, revel in
8 demolish, desolate, dispatch, prey upon,
spoliate, squander 9 delight in, depredate,
desecrate, devastate, dissipate, feast upon,
gloat over, partake of, polish off, rejoice in,
swallow up 10 annihilate

devouring 4 avid 6 greedy 9 voracious
combining form: 6 vorous

devout 4 holy 5 godly, pious 6 ardent, fervid, hearty 7 adoring, fervent, sincere, zealous 8 reverent, revering 9 pietistic, prayerful, religious 10 venerating, worshiping

devoutness 5 piety

dew 3 wet 5 sweat, tears 8 moisture
12 perspiration

dexter 5 right, white 6 benign, bright
9 favorable, fortunate 10 auspicious, propitious

dexterity 3 art 5 craft, skill 7 address,
cunning, know-how, prowess, sleight
8 deftness 9 adeptness, expertise, readiness 10 adroitness, smoothness 12 skillfulness

dexterous 3 sly 4 deft, easy, slim
5 adept, agile, canny, coony, handy
6 adroit, artful, clever, expert, facile, nimble,
smooth 7 cunning, skilled 8 masterly, skillful, sleighty 9 ingenious 10 effortless, neathanded, proficient

diablerie 3 sin 4 evil, tort 5 crime, wrong
7 devilry, roguery, sorcery, waggery 8 deviltry, iniquity, mischief, satanism 9 devilment
10 black magic, wickedness, witchcraft,
wrongdoing 11 roguishness, waggishness
12 sportiveness

diablo 5 devil, fiend, Satan 7 Lucifer, Old
Nick, serpent 8 Apollyon 9 Beelzebub
10 Old Scratch 13 Old Gooseberry

diabolic 4 evil 6 wicked 7 demonic,
satanic 8 demoniac, demonian, devilish,
fiendish 10 serpentine, unhallowed 11 diabolonian

diabolism see diablerie

diacritic 5 breve, haček, tilde 6 macron, proper 7 cedilla 8 dieresis, peculiar 9 diaeresis 10 circumflex, individual 11 distinctive 13 idiosyncratic *Arabic:* 5 hamza 6 hamzah

diadem 5 crown 6 empire 8 headband 11 sovereignty

diagnose 4 spot 5 place 6 finger 8 identify, pinpoint 9 recognize 11 determinate, distinguish

diagnostic 6 proper 8 peculiar 9 diacritic 10 indicating, indicative, individual 11 distinctive 13 idiosyncratic

diagonal 4 bias 5 bevel 6 biased 7 beveled, slanted 8 inclined, slanting 9 slantways

diagonally 8 bendwise 9 slantwise 10 cornerwise 11 catercorner, catty-corner, kitty-corner, slaunchways 12 slantingways

diagram 5 chart, graph 7 isotype 9 represent

dial 3 map, mug, pan 4 face, phiz, puss, tune 6 kisser, visage 7 control 8 features 10 manipulate 11 countenance

dialect 4 cant 5 argot, idiom, koine, lingo, slang 6 jargon, patois, patter, speech, tongue 8 language, localism 10 vernacular 11 regionalism, terminology 13 provincialism *Georgia:* 6 Gullah *London:* 7 cockney

dialectic 5 logic 6 debate 7 mooting 8 forensic 11 disputation 13 argumentation

dialogue 4 chat, talk 6 parley 8 colloquy, converse 12 conversation 13 confabulation

diameter 5 chord 8 bisector 9 thickness

diametric 5 polar 7 counter, opposed, reverse 8 contrary, converse, opposite 9 antipodal 10 antipodean 12 antithetical 13 contradictory

diamond 3 gem 5 stone 6 bright 9 brilliant, sparkling *baseball:* 7 infield *element:* 6 carbon *famous:* 4 Hope, Pitt 5 Sancy 6 Orloff, Regent 8 Braganza, Cullinan, Kohinoor 9 Excelsior 10 Great Mogul *holder:* 3 dop 4 dopp *inferior:* 4 bort 5 boart, bortz *oval:* 9 briolette *playing card:* 7 lozenge *state:* 8 Delaware *surface:* 5 facet

Diana see Artemis

Diana monkey 7 roloway

diapason 3 air, lay 4 tune 5 range, scope 6 melody, strain, warble 7 compass, descant, measure, melisma, melodia 10 tuning fork

diaper 4 didy 5 didie, nappy 6 nappie

diaphanous 5 filmy, gauzy, sheer, vague 6 flimsy 7 tiffany 8 ethereal, gossamer 11 transparent 13 insubstantial

diaphragm 4 stop 9 partition *combining form:* 5 phren 6 phreni, phreno

diarist 1 Gide (André) 5 Frank (Anne), Pepys (Samuel), Scott (Walter) 6 Burney (Fanny) 7 Boswell (James) 8 Robinson (Henry) 10 chronicler, journalist

diary 6 record 7 daybook, diurnal, journal, logbook 8 register 9 chronicle

diaskeuast 6 editor

diastase 6 enzyme

diatribe 6 tirade 7 polemic 8 harangue, jeremiad 9 criticism, philippic

dibs 4 gelt 5 blunt, brass, bread, chips, claim, dough, money, syrup, title 6 dinero, do-re-mi, rights 7 cabbage 8 pretense 10 pretension 11 reservation

dice 4 cast, shed, tats 5 bones, cubes, ivory, scrap 6 reject, slough 7 cashier, checker, discard 8 jettison, throw out 9 throw away 11 devil's-bones *combining form:* 8 astragal 9 astragalo *game:* 5 craps *losing throw:* 7 missout *singular:* 3 die *throw:* 7 boxcars 9 snake eyes

dicer 7 gambler

dichotomize 4 part 5 sever 6 divide, sunder 7 break up, disjoin, dissect 8 disjoint, disunite, separate

dichotomous 9 bifurcate

dichotomy 7 forking 9 bisection, branching, splitting 11 bifurcation

Dickens *birthplace:* 10 Portsmouth *captain:* 6 Cuttle *character:* 3 Pip, Tim 4 Dora, Gamp, Nell 5 Fagin 6 Bumble, Carton, Cuttle, Darnay, Dombey, Oliver 7 Barnaby, Defarge, Manette, Scrooge, Tiny Tim 8 Micawber, Pickwick 9 Bill Sikes, Pecksniff, Uriah Heep 10 Chuzzlewit *hero:* 6 Carton (Sidney) *nationality:* 7 English *pen name:* 3 Boz *villain:* 5 Fagin *work:* 9 Hard Times 10 Bleak House 11 Oliver Twist 12 Barnaby Rudge 15 Tale of Two Cities 16 David Copperfield 17 Great Expectations

dicker 4 deal, swap 6 barter, haggle, higgle, palter 7 bargain, chaffer 8 huckster 11 negotiation

dickey 4 weak 5 gilet, shaky 6 unsure, wobbly 8 insecure, rootless, unstable, wavering 9 fluctuant 10 shirtfront 11 vacillating

dictate 3 bid, say, set 4 lead, rule, tell, word 5 guide, order, speak, utter 6 behest, charge, decree, diktat, direct, enjoin, govern, impose, manage, ordain, recite 7 bidding, command, control, lay down, mandate, read off 8 instruct 9 directive, prescribe 10 injunction 12 prescription

dictative 8 dogmatic 11 doctrinaire, magisterial 13 authoritarian

dictator 4 duce 6 despot, tyrant 7 arbiter 8 martinet 9 oppressor, strong man 10 magistrate *German:* 6 Hitler (Adolf) *Ital-*

ian: 9 Mussolini (Benito) *military:* 8 caudillo *Spanish:* 6 Franco (Francisco)

dictatorial 4 firm 5 bossy, proud, stern 7 haughty 8 absolute, arrogant, despotic, dogmatic 9 arbitrary, imperious, masterful 10 autocratic, imperative, peremptory, tyrannical 11 doctrinaire, domineering, overbearing 12 totalitarian 13 authoritarian, authoritative

dictatorship 7 tyranny 9 autocracy, Caesarism, despotism 10 absolutism

diction 6 phrase 7 wordage, wording 8 parlance, phrasing, verbiage 9 verbalism 11 phraseology *suffix:* 3 ese

dictionary 4 cant 6 jargon 7 lexicon, palaver 8 language, wordbook 10 repository, vocabulary 11 terminology 13 reference book *compiler:* 7 Johnson (Samuel), Webster (Noah) 13 lexicographer *geographical:* 9 gazetteer *of prosody:* 6 gradus *of synonyms:* 8 thesauri (plural) 9 thesaurus

dictum 4 rule 5 axiom, gnome, maxim, moral 6 saying, truism 7 brocard, opinion 8 aphorism, apothegm 9 statement 13 pronouncement

didactic 3 dry 5 moral 6 teachy 7 preachy 8 advisory, sermonic 9 hortative 10 moralizing, preceptive 11 exhortative, sermonizing

diddle 3 gyp 4 beat, bilk, hoax, idle, laze, loaf, loll, take 5 cheat, cozen, drone 6 chouse, dawdle, delude, loiter, lounge 7 defraud 8 lallygag 9 overreach, waste time

diddler 3 gyp 5 cheat 6 con man 7 grifter, sharper 9 defrauder, trickster 12 double-dealer 13 confidence man

dido 3 toy 5 curio, frill 6 bauble, gewgaw, trifle 7 bibelot, trinket, whatnot 8 furbelow, gimcrack 10 knickknack

Dido 6 Elissa *brother:* 9 Pygmalion *city founded by:* 8 Carthage *father:* 5 Belus 6 Mutton *husband:* 7 Acerbas 8 Sichaeus *lover:* 6 Aeneas

Dido and Aeneas composer 7 Purcell (Henry)

die 3 ebb, pip 4 bate, conk, dado, drop, fall, fate, long, mold, pass, stop, wane 5 abate, block, cease, croak, let up, swelt 6 cash in, chance, cop out, demise, depart, expire, kick in, matrix, peg out, perish, pop off, recede 7 decease, ease off, fortune, kick off, pass out, slacken, subside, succumb 8 check out, languish, moderate, pass away, snuff out 9 disappear, grow faint *from hunger:* 6 starve *loaded:* 6 fulham, fullam

____ **die** 4 sine 3 bis in (twice a day), ter in (thrice a day) 6 quater in (four times a day)

die-away 4 limp 7 languid 8 listless 9 enervated 10 languorous, spiritless 11 languishing 13 lackadaisical

diehard 4 tory 5 blimp, fixed, right, white 7 Bourbon, old fogy 8 mossback, old liner, pullback, rightist, royalist, standpat, true blue 9 right wing 10 praetorian 11 bitterender, reactionary, reactionist, right-center, right-winger, standpatter 12 conservative, intransigent 13 reactionarist, stick-in-the-mud

____ **diem** 5 carpe

Dies ____ 4 Irae 7 faustus

diet 4 fast, feed 8 assembly 10 parliament

Diet of ____ 5 Worms 6 Speyer, Spires 8 Augsburg

____ **-dieu** 4 prie

Dieu ____ **, British motto** 10 et mon droit

differ 3 jar 4 vary 5 argue, clash 6 bicker, debate, depart, divide, oppose 7 deviate, discord, dispute, dissent, diverge, quarrel 8 conflict, disagree, squabble 9 disaccord

difference 4 know 5 clash, sever 6 change, effect, strife 7 discern, discord, dissent 8 alterity, conflict, disunity, separate, variance 9 disaccord, extricate, otherness, variation 10 contention, discrepate, dissension, divergency, severalize, unlikeness 11 controversy, discrepancy, distinction, distinguish 12 disagreement, discriminate, dissemblance, modification 13 dissimilarity, dissimilitude *slight:* 5 shade 8 hairline

different 5 other 6 divers, single, sundry, unlike 7 another, distant, diverse, several, special, unalike, unequal, unusual, various 8 discrete, distinct, opposite, peculiar, separate 9 disparate, divergent, otherwise, unsimilar 10 dissimilar, individual, particular 11 distinctive *combining form:* 3 all 4 allo 5 heter 6 hetero 7 diversi

differentiate 4 know 5 sever 7 discern 8 separate 9 extricate 10 comprehend, discrepate, severalize, understand 11 distinguish 12 discriminate

difficult 4 hard 6 uphill 7 arduous, awkward, labored, obscure, operose, problem 8 perverse, puzzling, stubborn, toilsome 9 effortful, hampering, laborious, strenuous 11 problematic *combining form:* 4 mogi *prefix:* 3 dys

difficulty 3 fix, jam 4 beef, nodi (plural) 4 pass, snag 5 cavil, demur, fight, nodus, pinch, rigor 6 bother, hassle, pickle, plight, scrape, strait 7 dilemma, dispute, pitfall, problem, protest, quarrel, trouble 8 asperity, demurral, demurrer, exigency, hardness, hardship, obstacle, quandary, question, squabble 9 bickering, challenge, emergency, objection 10 falling-out, impediment **11** altercation, arduousness, controversy, obstruction, predicament, vicissitude **12** disagreement, remonstrance **13** embarrassment, inconvenience, remonstration

diffidence 7 modesty, reserve **8** distrust **11** bashfulness

diffident 3 coy, shy **5** timid **6** demure, modest **7** bashful **8** hesitant, retiring **9** blenching, flinching, reluctant, shrinking, unassured **11** distrustful, unassertive **12** self-effacing

difform 6 uneven **7** unequal **8** lopsided **10** asymmetric **13** unsymmetrical

diffuse 3 lax **4** full, long **5** loose, slack, strew, windy, wordy **6** casual, expand, extend, lavish, prolix, random, spread **7** copious, lengthy, osmolar, osmotic, perfuse, radiate, scatter, send out, verbose **8** disperse, intersow, permeate **9** broadcast, circulate, desultory, exuberant, interlard, propagate, redundant, scattered, spreading, spread out **10** distribute, long-winded, palaverous, widespread **11** disseminate, intersperse **13** intersprinkle

diffusion 7 osmoses (plural), osmosis **9** broadcast, prolixity, spreading **10** scattering

dig 3 jab, jog, ram, run **4** grub, hole, holk, howk, like, mind, mine, poke, prod, root, sift, sink, site, spud, stab **5** delve, ditch, drive, enjoy, enter, grind, nudge, probe, punch, scoop, spade, stick **6** burrow, drudge, go into, pierce, plunge, quarry, relish, rootle, shovel, thrust, trench, tunnel **7** explore, root out, unearth **8** excavate, look into, prospect **9** delve into, hollow out, penetrate **10** excavation **11** inquire into, investigate *out:* **6** exhume *up:* **7** unearth

digest 2 go **3** sum **4** bear, cook, take **5** abide, brook, stand, sum up **6** aperçu, codify, endure, précis, sketch, survey **7** pandect, stomach, summate, swallow, sylloge **8** compress, condense, nutshell, syllabus, synopsis, tolerate **9** epitomize, inventory, summarize, synopsize **10** abridgment, compendium, comprehend, periodical **11** compilation

digestion *combining form:* **6** pepsia, peptic *good:* **7** eupepsy **8** eupepsia *poor:* **9** dyspepsia

digger 4 plow **5** miner

digit 3 toe **5** thumb **6** cipher, figure, finger, number, pinkie **7** chiffer, integer, numeral **11** whole number *abbreviation:* **2** no. *combining form:* **6** dactyl, digiti **7** dactylo, dactyly **8** dactylia **9** dactylism, dactylous

dignified 4 prim **6** proper **7** stately **8** decorous

dignify 5 erect, exalt, honor **6** uprear **7** ennoble, glorify, sublime **10** aggrandize **11** distinguish

dignitary 3 VIP **4** lion **5** chief, nabob **6** leader **7** notable **8** eminence, luminary **10** notability **13** high-muck-a-muck

dignity 4 rank **5** grace, honor, merit, poise, state, worth **6** cachet, ethics, status, virtue **7** address, decency, decorum, majesty, stature **8** elegance, grandeur, morality, nobility, position, prestige, standing **9** etiquette, grandness, nobleness, propriety **10** augustness, excellence, perfection, seemliness **11** consequence, ethicalness **12** magnificence *suffix:* **3** dom **4** ship

digress 4 roam **5** drift, stray **6** depart, ramble, swerve, wander **7** deviate, diverge, excurse **8** divagate

digression 5 aside **7** episode, excurse **8** drifting, excursus, incident, rambling, straying **9** departure, deviation, wandering **10** deflection, divagation, divergence **11** parenthesis, underaction

dike 4 bank, pond, pool **5** drain, fix up, levee, slick, spiff **6** doll up, dude up **7** barrier, deck out, doll out, dress up, gussy up **8** aboideau, causeway, spruce up **11** watercourse

dilapidate 4 do in, ruin **5** decay, wreck **6** forget, ignore, slight **7** crumble, neglect **8** bankrupt, overlook **9** decompose, disregard, shipwreck **12** disintegrate

dilapidated 5 dingy, faded, seedy, tacky **6** beat-up, marred, shabby, tagrag **7** damaged, decayed, injured, run-down **8** crumbled, impaired **10** broken-down, down-at-heel, threadbare

dilapidation 5 decay, waste **6** debris

dilate 5 swell, widen **6** expand, extend, recite **7** amplify, augment, broaden, descant, discuss, dissert, distend, enlarge, narrate, prolong, recount **8** describe, expanded, increase, lengthen, protract, rehearse **9** discourse, expatiate, sermonize **10** dissertate

dilatory 3 lax **4** slow **5** slack, tardy **6** remiss **7** laggard, unhasty **9** leisurely, negligent, unhurried **10** deliberate, neglectful

dilemma 3 box, fix, jam **4** hole, spot **6** choice, corner, pickle, plight, scrape **7** problem **8** argument, quandary **10** perplexity **11** predicament **12** bewilderment **13** mystification

dilettante 4 tyro **7** amateur, dabbler, jackleg **8** aesthete, dabbling, ungifted **9** smatterer, unskilled **10** amateurish, unfinished, uninitiate **11** abecedarian, cognoscente, connoisseur

dilettantish see **amateurish**

diligence 8 industry **9** assiduity **11** persistence **12** perseverance

diligent 7 operose **8** sedulous **9** assiduous **10** persistent, persisting, unflagging **11** industrious, persevering

dill plant 4 anet

dilly 3 pip **4** lulu **5** dandy, nifty, peach **6** corker, dinger, doozer, pippin, ripper, rouser **8** jim-dandy, knockout **9** humdinger **10** ripsnorter **11** crackerjack, lalapalooza

dillydally see **delay**

dilute 3 cut **4** thin, weak **5** alter, washy **6** debase, modify, temper, watery, weaken **7** liquefy, qualify, reduced **8** deprived, diminish, impaired, moderate, waterish, weakened **9** enfeebled, water down **10** deliquesce **11** adulterated, watered-down **12** impoverished **13** sophisticated

dim 3 fog, mat **4** blur, dark, dead, dull, dusk, fade, flat, haze, hazy, pale **5** befog, blear, blind, cloud, dusky, faint, muddy, murky, muted, vague **6** bleary, darken, gloomy **7** becloud, dislimn, eclipse, low beam, obscure, shadowy, subdued, tarnish, unclear **9** lightless, obfuscate, tenebrous **10** caliginous, ill-defined, indistinct, lackluster, lusterless **12** parking light, undetermined **13** unilluminated

dime novel 4 pulp **7** chiller, shocker **8** dreadful, thriller **10** yellowback **12** bloodcurdler, killer-diller **13** penny dreadful

dimension 4 size **5** scope, trait, width **6** aspect, extent **7** measure, quality **8** life-like **9** magnitude **10** yard lumber **11** proportions

diminish 3 ebb **4** bate, wane **5** abate, abuse, close, decry, peter, taper **6** lessen, minify, reduce, temper **7** abridge, curtail, dwindle, subside **8** belittle, decrease, derogate, minimize, moderate, taper off, write off **9** attenuate, disparage, dispraise, drain away, extenuate **10** depreciate **11** detract from

diminishing 7 calando

diminutive 3 wee **4** tiny **5** small, toony, weeny **6** minute, teensy **9** miniature **10** teeny-weeny **11** lilliputian **12** teensy-weensy

diminutive one *suffix:* **2** el, et, ey, ia (plural), ie **3** cle, ium, kin, ock, ula, ule, uli (plural) **4** ella, ette, illa, ling, ulae (plural), ulum, ulus **5** ellae (plural), illae (plural)

"___ dimittis" 4 nunc

dimmet 4 dusk **7** evening **8** eventide, gloaming, owl-light, twilight **9** nightfall

dimple 4 fret **5** mound **6** cockle, hollow, riffle, ripple **10** depression

dim-sighted 8 purblind **9** half-blind

dimwit 4 simp **5** cluck, dunce **7** pinhead **9** dumb bunny, dumb cluck **13** featherweight

dim-witted 4 dull, slow **7** moronic **8** backward, imbecile, retarded **12** feebleminded, simpleminded

din 3 row **5** babel, chirm, clash, music, noise, sound **6** bedlam, clamor, deafen, hubbub, jangle, racket, rattle, tumult, uproar **7** clangor, clatter, resound **8** blatancy, brouhaha, racketry **9** commotion, stridency **10** hullabaloo, percussion, tintamarre **11** pandemonium **13** clamorousness

Dinah 5 Shore *brother:* **4** Levi **6** Simeon *father:* **5** Jacob *mother:* **4** Leah

dine 3 eat, sup **4** feed

diner 3 bar **4** café **6** eatery **7** counter, hashery **8** snack bar **9** hash house **10** coffee shop, quick-lunch, restaurant **11** eating house, greasy spoon **12** lunch counter, sandwich shop

dinette *ancient Roman:* **5** oecus

ding 3 hit **4** beat, best, damn, sock **5** catch, clang, clout, outdo, outgo, whack **6** better, exceed, strike **7** surpass **8** outmatch, outshine

ding-a-ling 3 nut **4** kook **5** crank **6** cuckoo **7** lunatic **8** crackpot **9** harebrain, screwball **10** crackbrain

dinge 4 dent **5** blues, dumps, gloom **6** batter **7** sadness **9** dejection **10** depression, melancholy **11** unhappiness **12** mournfulness

dinghy 5 yacht **7** rowboat **8** life raft, sailboat

dingle 4 dale, dell **6** ravine, valley **9** storm door **10** passageway

dingus 5 gizmo **6** doodad, gadget, jigger **7** do-funny, thingum **9** doohickey **10** thingumbob **11** thingumajig

dingy 4 dark, drab, dull, mean **5** dirty, dusky, faded, murky, seedy, tacky, tired **6** gloomy, grimed, shabby, smutty, soiled **7** run-down, squalid, sullied **8** smirched **9** tarnished **10** broken-down, discolored, down-at-heel, threadbare **11** dilapidated

dinky 5 minor, small **6** lesser **8** small-fry **9** secondary, small-time **11** minor league **13** insignificant

dinner 4 fete, meal **5** feast **6** entrée, junket, regale, spread **7** banquet **8** festival, luncheon **9** breakfast, collation **10** table d'hôte *coat:* **3** tux **6** tuxedo *course:* **4** meat, soup **6** entrée **7** dessert **9** appetizer *Jewish:* **5** seder **7** sedarim (plural)

"Dinner ___" 7 at Eight

dinosaur 8 theropod **10** allosaurus **11** stegosaurus, triceratops **12** brontosaurus **13** tyrannosaurus

dinosauric 4 huge **7** mammoth **8** colossal, enormous **9** cyclopean, leviathan **10** behemothic, gargantuan, mastodonic **11** elephantine

dint 5 force, might, notch, power, sinew, vigor **6** energy, hollow, virtue **7** drive in, impress, imprint, potency **8** strength **9** puissance **10** impression **11** indentation

diocese 3 see 9 bishopric *Eastern Orthodox:* 7 eparchy *subdivision:* 6 parish

diode 9 rectifier 12 electron tube *type of:* 8 kenotron

Diomedes *city founded by:* 4 Arpi *father:* 4 Ares, Mars 6 Tydeus *foe:* 6 Aeneas, Hector *slayer:* 8 Hercules *victim:* 6 Rhesus

Dione 5 Titan *cult partner:* 4 Zeus *daughter:* 5 Venus 9 Aphrodite *father:* 7 Oceanus *lover:* 4 Zeus *mother:* 6 Tethys

Dionysus see Bacchus

Dionyza's husband 5 Cleon

Dioscuri 5 twins 6 Anaces, Anakes, Castor, Gemini, Pollux *father:* 4 Zeus 9 Tyndareus *mother:* 4 Leda *sister:* 5 Helen

dip 3 sag, set 4 bail, dish, draw, drop, duck, dunk, fall, lade, sink, skew, skid, slip, slue, tilt, veer 5 basin, depth, douse, ladle, lower, pitch, reach, sauce, scoop, sheer, slope, slump, souse, spoon, stoop 6 candle, go down, hollow, plunge, swerve, thrust, tumble 7 decline, delving, descend, descent, explore, falloff, immerse, plummet, sinkage 8 bucket up, decrease, downturn, lowering, nose-dive, sinkhole, submerge, submerse, train off 9 concavity, declivity, downslide, downswing, downtrend, immersion 10 depression, divergence, plunge into 11 inclination *kind:* 4 clam 5 onion 10 blue cheese

diphthong 2 ae, ai, ea, ei, oe, oi, ou, oy 7 digraph 8 ligature

diploma 6 letter 7 charter, writing 8 document

diplomacy 4 tact 5 poise 7 address 10 adroitness, artfulness, settlement 11 delicatesse, savoir faire, tactfulness

diplomatic 4 wily 5 bland 6 artful, astute, crafty, polite, shrewd, smooth 7 politic, tactful 8 delicate, guileful, tactical 9 courteous 12 paleographic

diplomat's office 7 embassy

diplopod 9 millipede

dipper 3 cup 4 bird, grab 5 ladle, scoop 6 bucket, holder 10 bufflehead, water ouzel

dippy 5 crazy, silly, wacky 6 absurd, insane 7 foolish 9 fantastic 11 harebrained 12 preposterous

dipsomania 10 alcoholism

dire 5 acute, awful 6 crying, dismal, urgent, woeful 7 baleful, baneful, burning, clamant, crucial, exigent, extreme, fateful, fearful, instant, ominous, painful 8 critical, dreadful, grievous, horrible, pressing, shocking, sinister, terrible, terrific 9 appalling, cheerless, clamorous, desperate, frightful, ill-boding 10 afflictive, calamitous, deplorable, depressing, imperative, lamentable, oppressing, oppressive 11 apocalyptic, climacteric, distressing, importunate, regretta-

ble, threatening, unfortunate 12 inauspicious, unpropitious 13 heartbreaking

direct 3 aim, bid, due, fix, lay, run, see, set 4 beam, bend, cast, dead, give, head, keep, lead, mark, next, open, show, tell, turn, warn 5 allot, apply, focus, frank, guide, issue, label, level, order, pilot, plain, point, refer, right, route, steer, throw, train 6 assign, candid, charge, custos, define, devote, divert, enjoin, escort, extend, fasten, govern, handle, lineal, linear, manage, ordain, settle, zero in 7 address, carry on, command, conduct, control, genuine, incline, nonstop, operate, oversee, present, preside, primary, project, request, through 8 dispatch, dominate, instruct, man-to-man, point out, regulate, shepherd, straight, unbroken, verbatim 9 determine, effective, firsthand, immediate, literally, literatim, out-and-out, prescribe, proximate 10 administer, buckle down, channelize, contiguous, continuous, explicitly, inevitable, proceeding, straightly, unhampered, unreserved, unswerving 11 categorical, substantive, superscribe, unconcealed, undeviating, undisguised, unequivocal, word for word 12 undissembled 13 undeviatingly, uninterrupted *a helmsman:* 4 conn *proceedings:* 7 preside

direction 3 way 4 east, line, path, role, side, west 5 angle, north, order, point, slant, south, tenor 6 charge, course, design, sphere 7 bearing, channel, command, guiding, outlook, respect 8 guidance, pointing 9 clockwise, viewpoint 10 standpoint *blowing:* 7 leeward 8 windward *combining form:* 5 phoro *court:* 5 order *for Muslims praying:* 5 kibla 6 keblah, kildah *horizontal:* 7 azimuth *main line of:* 4 axis *musical:* (see musical direction) *of a linear arrangement:* 5 grain *square dance:* 4 call *without fixed:* 7 astatic (see also **compass point**)

directive 4 memo, word 5 edict, ukase 6 decree, notice, ruling 7 bidding, message 8 exemplar 10 assignment, injunction, memorandum 11 instruction 13 communication, pronouncement

directly 3 due 4 anon, away, dead, soon 5 right, spang 6 at once 7 by and by, shortly 8 first off, in person, squarely, straight, verbatim 9 forthwith, instanter, instantly, literally, literatim, presently, right away 10 face-to-face, straightly 11 immediately, straight off, straightway, word for word 12 contiguously 13 undeviatingly, unqualifiedly

director 4 head 5 chief 6 leader 7 manager 9 conductor 10 supervisor

directory 4 list, ordo 5 guide, index 8 treatise 11 compilation

direful see fearful; ominous

dirge 4 hymn, song 6 lament 7 epicede, requiem 8 threnody 9 epicedium 11 lamentation *Gaelic:* 8 coronach

dirigible 7 airship 8 zeppelin 9 steerable

dirk 4 stab 5 sword 6 dagger

dirt 4 land, sand, soil, spot 5 earth, filth, fraud, grime, stain 6 gossip, gravel, ground 7 chicane, dry land, squalor 9 chicanery, deception, excrement, fourberie 10 corruption, dishonesty, hanky-panky, terra firma 11 highbinding, uncleanness 13 double-dealing, sharp practice

dirt poor 4 flat 5 broke 8 beggared, indigent 9 destitute, penurious 10 stone-broke 12 impoverished

dirty 3 low, tar 4 foul, smut, soil, wild 5 bawdy, black, dungy, grime, grimy, messy, mucky, muddy, murky, nasty, rough, smear, soily, sooty, stain, sully, taint 6 basely, befoul, begrim, besoil, coarse, dreggy, filthy, grubby, impure, raging, smirch, smooch, smudge, smudgy, smutch, smutty, soiled, sordid, stormy, vulgar 7 abusive, begrime, besmear, clouded, defiled, draggly, dullish, furious, hateful, immoral, obscene, piggish, raunchy, smoochy, smutchy, squalid, sullied, tainted, tarnish, unclean 8 begrimed, besmirch, blustery, discolor, draggled, grievous, indecent, polluted, scroungy, stormful, unchaste 9 uncleanly 10 blustering, scurrilous 11 distressing, regrettable, tempestuous 12 contaminated, contemptible, scatological 13 draggletailed

Dis see Pluto

disability 8 drawback, handicap 9 detriment

disable 3 mar, sap 4 harm, hurt, maim, ruin 5 blunt, spoil, wreck 6 batter, disarm, mangle, weaken 7 cripple, deprive, invalid, unbrace 8 enfeeble, mutilate, paralyze 9 attenuate, prostrate, undermine 10 debilitate, disqualify, immobilize 12 incapacitate, unstrengthen *a racehorse:* 6 nobble

disabuse 4 free 5 amend, emend, purge 7 correct, rectify, redress, release, unblind 8 liberate, undelude 9 disillude, enlighten, undeceive 10 illuminate 11 disillusion

disaccharide 7 lactose, maltose, sucrose

disaccord 3 jar 4 vary 5 clash 6 differ, divide, jangle, strife 7 dissent 8 conflict, disunity, mismatch, variance 10 contention, difference, dissension, dissidence 12 disharmonize

disadvantage 3 bar 4 harm, loss 6 hamper 8 blocking, drawback, handicap, obstacle 9 detriment, hindrance, prejudice 10 impediment, imposition 11 obstruction

disadvantaged 7 lacking 8 deprived 9 depressed

disadvise 5 deter 6 divert 8 dissuade 10 discourage

disaffect 4 wean 5 alien, upset 7 agitate, disturb 8 alienate, diminish, disquiet, disunify, disunite, estrange 10 discompose

disaffection 9 hostility 12 estrangement

disaffirm 4 deny 5 annul, cross 6 impugn, negate 7 gainsay, reverse 8 negative, traverse 9 repudiate 10 contradict, contravene

disagree 4 vary 5 clash 6 differ, divide 7 discord, dissent

disagreeable 3 bad 4 sour 5 waspy, whiny 6 rotten, snappy, twitty, woeful 7 helluva, peevish, pettish, unhappy, waspish 8 annoying, petulant 9 offensive, querulous 10 disturbing, unpleasant 11 displeasing, distressing

disagreement 3 row 4 spat 5 clash 7 discord, dispute, quarrel 8 variance 10 contention, difference, dissension, divergence, unlikeness 11 controversy, discrepancy, incongruity

disallow 4 deny, veto 5 debar 6 disown, refuse, reject 7 disavow, exclude, shut out 8 disclaim, keep back, withhold 9 repudiate

disallowance 6 denial 7 refusal 9 rejection

____ -**disant** 3 soi

disappear 2 go 4 fade 5 clear, leave 6 vanish 7 evanish 8 evanesce 9 evaporate

disappoint 4 balk, beat, bilk, dash, foil, ruin 6 baffle, defeat, thwart 7 let down 9 frustrate 10 circumvent

disappointment 7 failure 9 bringdown 11 frustration

disapproval 4 veto 7 censure, dislike 9 rejection *expression of:* 3 boo 4 hiss, hoot, jeer 7 catcall 9 raspberry 10 Bronx cheer

disapprove 5 blame, decry, frown, pshaw, spurn 6 object, refuse, reject 7 censure, condemn, decline, detract, dislike, dismiss 8 denounce, disfavor, turn down 9 criticize, deprecate, disesteem, disparage, dispraise, reprehend, reprobate, repudiate 10 depreciate, discommend 11 expostulate, remonstrate

disarm 5 charm 6 allure 7 attract, bewitch, cripple, enchant, unsteel, win over 8 paralyze 9 captivate, deprive of, fascinate, prostrate 10 immobilize 12 incapacitate

disarming 5 silky 6 silken 10 saccharine 11 deferential, insinuating, insinuative 12 ingratiating, ingratiatory

disarrange 4 mess 6 jumble, mess up, mislay 7 disturb, replace, rummage 8 disorder, displace, misplace, overturn, unsettle 10 discompose 11 disorganize

disarray 5 chaos, snarl 6 ataxia, huddle, jumble, mess up, muddle, unrobe 7 clutter, derange, disturb, rummage 8 disorder, unsettle 9 confusion 10 discompose 11 disorganize

disassemble 8 dismount, separate, take down, tear down 9 dismantle, dismember, take apart

disassociate 5 unfix 6 detach 8 abstract, uncouple 9 disengage 10 disconnect

disaster 3 woe 4 rock, ruin 6 fiasco, injure, mishap 7 failure, tragedy 8 accident, calamity, casualty, distress, fatality 9 adversity, cataclysm, mischance 10 misfortune 11 catastrophe 12 misadventure

disastrous 4 dire 5 fatal 7 fateful, hapless, ruinous 8 luckless 10 calamitous 11 cataclysmic, destructive, unfortunate 12 catastrophic

disavow 4 deny 6 disown, impugn, negate, recant 8 disclaim, negative 9 repudiate

disband 4 part 5 sever 6 dispel, divide, sunder 7 break up, disjoin, dissect, divorce, scatter 8 disjoint, disperse, dissever, dissolve, disunite, separate 9 dissipate 11 dichotomize

disbelieve 5 doubt, scorn, scout 6 eschew, reject 7 suspect 8 distrust, mistrust, question 9 discredit

disbeliever 5 cynic 7 doubter, sceptic, skeptic

disbelieving 6 show-me 8 aporetic 9 quizzical, skeptical 11 incredulous, questioning

disburden 6 unlade, unload, unship, unstow 7 discard, off-load 8 get rid of, jettison 9 discharge

disburse 3 pay 4 deal, give 5 divvy, spend 6 defray, divide, expend, lay out, lot out, outlay, pay out 7 dole out, fork out 8 dispense, disperse, shell out 9 partition 10 distribute, measure out

disbursement 4 cost 6 outlay 7 expense 11 expenditure

discard 4 cast, drop, dump, junk, oust, shed, waif 5 chuck, ditch, eject, let go, scrap, sluff, spurn 6 desert, reject, slough 7 abandon, cashier, cast off, deep-six, dismiss, forsake, wash out 8 abdicate, get rid of, jettison, lay aside, shuck off, throw out 9 repudiate, throw away

discarnate 8 bodiless 9 asomatous, unfleshly 10 immaterial, unembodied, unphysical 11 disembodied, incorporeal, nonphysical 13 insubstantial

discept 4 moot 5 argue 6 debate 7 agitate, canvass, dispute 9 thrash out 10 toss around

discern 3 see 4 know, note, view 5 sever 6 behold, descry, detect, divine, notice, remark 7 foresee, observe 8 perceive, separate 9 apprehend, ascertain, extricate 10 anticipate, difference, severalize 11 distinguish 13 differentiate

discernible 8 palpable 10 detectable, observable 11 appreciable

discerning 4 sage, wise 5 acute 7 gnostic, knowing 9 clear-eyed, insighted, sagacious 10 insightful, perceptive 11 wise-hearted 13 knowledgeable

discernment 3 wit 6 acumen, reason 8 keenness, sagacity 9 intuition 10 astuteness, shrewdness 11 penetration, percipience 12 perspicacity 13 sagaciousness

discharge 2 ax 3 can, pay, run 4 drop, emit, fire, flow, free, oust, pour, quit, sack, vent, void 5 annul, clear, eject, empty, expel, exude, let go, loose, pay up, quash, rheum, shoot, spare, utter 6 bounce, excuse, exempt, let fly, let off, loosen, outlet, remove, settle, square, unbind, unlade, unload, unship, unstow, vacate 7 absolve, boot out, cashier, deliver, dismiss, exclude, execute, fulfill, give off, kick out, manumit, off-load, release, relieve, removal, replace, satisfy, unchain 8 abrogate, clear off, clear out, dispense, displace, dissolve, emission, get rid of, liberate, separate, set aside, supplant, throw off 9 acquittal, bleach out, disburden, disenroll, eliminate, explosion, expulsion, liquidate, muster out, pour forth, pronounce, send forth, supersede, terminate, unloading, unshackle 10 deactivate, demobilize, disembogue, emancipate, give vent to, inactivate, liberation, separation 11 acquittance, exoneration, fulfillment 13 privilege from *combining form:* 5 rrhea 6 rrhoea 7 rrhagia *concentrated:* 7 barrage *electrical:* 5 spark 6 leader 8 streamer 9 lightning 12 leader stroke *from the body:* 5 egest 7 excrete *simultaneous:* 5 salvo

discinct 3 lax 5 slack 6 remiss 8 careless, derelict 9 negligent 10 behindhand, delinquent, neglectful 12 disregardful

disciple 6 cohort, zealot 7 apostle, fanatic, sectary 8 adherent, follower, henchman, partisan, sectator 9 satellite, supporter 10 enthusiast

disciplinarian 6 ramrod 8 martinet

disciplinary 7 ordered 8 punitive, punitory 9 punishing 11 castigatory

discipline 3 rod 4 curb, lead, whip, will 5 check, drill, guide, spank, teach, train 6 bridle, direct, manage, method, punish, reduce, school, subdue 7 chasten, conduct, control, correct, educate, inhibit, scourge 8 approach, chastise, instruct, overcome, penalize, punition, restrain, training **9** castigate, obedience, subjugate, willpower **10** correction, experience, punishment **11** castigation, self-command, self-control, self-mastery **12** chastisement **13** self-restraint

disclaim 4 deny **5** spurn **6** abjure, disown, recant, refuse, reject **7** disavow, gainsay, retract **8** belittle, disallow, forswear, minimize, renounce, traverse **9** challenge, criticize, deprecate, disparage, repudiate **10** contradict, contravene

disclose 3 own **4** avow, open, tell **5** admit, mouth, spill **6** betray, expose, reveal, unveil **7** blab out, confess, display, divulge, unclose, uncover **8** discover, give away, unclothe **9** make known **11** acknowledge

disclosure 6 exposé **10** confession, revelation **11** divulgation

discolor 3 tar **4** blot, dull, fade, smut, soil **5** smear, stain, sully, taint, tinge **6** defile, motley, streak **7** besmear, bestain, dappled, tarnish **8** besmirch **9** multihued **10** variegated

discoloration 5 stain *combining form:* **6** chroia

discomfit 3 irk, vex **4** faze, foil, rout **5** abash, annoy, upset **6** bother, defeat, rattle, thwart **7** confuse, disturb, perturb **8** confound **9** embarrass

discomfiture 4 rout **5** upset **6** damage, defeat, injury, unease **7** beating, debacle, descent, licking **8** comedown, disquiet, drubbing, prickles **9** abashment, agitation, commotion, confusion, overthrow **10** defeasance, uneasiness **11** frustration, shellacking **12** perturbation, vanquishment **13** embarrassment, inconvenience

discomfort 6 unease **7** malaise, misease **9** annoyance **10** uneasiness **13** embarrassment

discomforting see uncomfortable

discommend 5 frown **6** object **7** censure **8** admonish, disfavor **9** criticize, deprecate, disesteem, reprehend **10** disapprove

discommode 3 irk, vex **5** upset **6** bother, flurry, put out **7** fluster, perturb, trouble **8** put about **9** disoblige **13** inconvenience

discompose 3 irk, vex **5** annoy, harry, upset, worry **6** bother, dismay, flurry, harass, mess up, pester, plague, untune **7** agitate, derange, disturb, fluster, perturb, rummage, unhinge **8** disagree, disarray, disorder, disquiet, unsettle **9** embarrass **10** disarrange **11** disorganize

discomposure 6 unease **9** abashment, agitation, confusion **10** uneasiness **12** perturbation **13** embarrassment

disconcert 4 faze **5** abash, upset **6** puz-

zle, rattle, ruffle **7** break up, confuse, nonplus, perplex **8** bewilder, confound **9** embarrass, frustrate

disconfirm 5 break, evert, rebut **6** refute **7** confute **8** confound, disprove **10** controvert

disconnect 5 sever, unfix **6** detach **8** abstract, separate, uncouple

disconnected 7 muddled **8** inchoate **10** incoherent, incohesive **11** unorganized **12** uncontinuous

disconsolate 3 bad, low, sad **4** cold, down **5** bleak, drear **6** gloomy, somber, woeful **7** doleful, joyless, unhappy **8** dejected, downcast **9** cheerless, depressed, saddening, sorrowful, woebegone **10** depressing, melancholy **11** comfortless, crestfallen, downhearted

discontent 9 dysphoria **10** inquietude, uneasiness

discontented 5 upset **6** uneasy **7** unhappy **8** restless **9** perturbed **11** ungratified, unsatisfied

discontented one see complainer

discontinuance see discontinuation

discontinuation 3 end **5** cease, close **6** ending, finish **7** closing **9** desuetude **10** conclusion, desistance

discontinue 3 end **4** halt, quit, stop **5** cease, sever **6** desist, give up **8** break off, give over, knock off, leave off, surcease **9** terminate

discontinuity 3 gap **4** hole **5** break **6** breach, lacuna **7** opening

discontinuous 7 muddled **8** inchoate, separate **10** incoherent, incohesive **11** unconnected, unorganized

discord 3 jar **4** vary **5** clash **6** differ, divide, enmity, jangle, rancor, strife **7** unpeace **8** conflict, contrast, division, mischief, mismatch, variance **9** animosity, antipathy, collision, hostility, inharmony **10** antagonism, contention, difference, opposition **11** incongruity **12** inconsonance, polarization **13** inconsistency *goddess:* **3** Ate **4** Eris

discordant 5 harsh **7** jarring **8** clashing, contrary **9** immusical, unmixable, unmusical **10** cacophonic, inharmonic **11** cacophonous, conflicting, contrariant, incongruent, incongruous, inconsonant, quarrelsome, uncongenial **12** antagonistic, antipathetic, incompatible, inconsistent, inharmonious, unharmonious

discotheque 4 café, go-go **6** nitery **7** cabaret, hot spot **8** nightery **9** nightclub, night spot **10** supper club **12** watering hole **13** watering place

discount 4 fail, omit, take **5** abuse, decry **6** deduct, forget, ignore, lessen, rebate, slight **7** neglect, take off, take out **8** belittle, derogate, diminish, draw back, knock off, minimize, overlook, overpass, subtract, take away **9** abatement, deduction, reduction, substract, underrate **10** anticipate, depreciate **11** detract from, subtraction

discountenance 4 faze **5** abash, frown **6** object, rattle **7** confuse, reprove **8** confound, reproach **9** deprecate, embarrass **10** put to shame

discourage 3 irk, try, vex **4** damp **5** check, chill, deter, droop, scare, weigh **6** bother, dampen, deject, divert, hinder, lessen **7** afflict, depress, inhibit, prevent, trouble **8** frighten, restrain **10** demoralize

discouraging 5 black, bleak **6** dreary, gloomy **9** deterring, hindering **10** depressing, depressive, oppressive

discourse 3 act **4** play, talk **5** argue, enact, essay, orate, paper, speak, voice **6** expand, memoir, remark, sermon, speech, thesis **7** amplify, article, comment, descant, develop, enlarge, explain, expound, lecture, perform, playact **8** converse, harangue, perorate, rhetoric, speaking, tractate, treatise **9** elaborate, expatiate, monograph, personate, sermonize, utterance **10** commentate, expression, monography **11** impersonate, interchange **12** conversation **13** verbalization *art of:* **8** rhetoric *combining form:* **3** log **4** logo, logy **5** logia, logue *religious:* **6** homily, sermon

discourteous 4 rude **7** ill-bred, incivil, uncivil **8** impolite **10** ungracious, unmannerly **11** ill-mannered, impertinent

discover 3 see **4** espy, find, hear, note, spot, tell **5** learn, mouth, spill **6** betray, debunk, descry, detect, expose, reveal, show up, tumble, unmask **7** catch on, divulge, find out, observe, publish, uncloak, unclose, undress, unearth **8** give away, perceive, proclaim, unshroud **9** advertise, ascertain, determine, encounter, make known

discovery 4 find **5** trove **6** espial, strike **7** finding **8** exposure **9** detection **10** exposition, revelation, unearthing **11** recognition

discredit 4 ruin **5** doubt, odium, shame, shoot **6** blow up, expose, infamy, show up **7** asperse, destroy, explode, obloquy **8** ignominy, puncture, reproach **9** unbelieve **10** opprobrium

discreditable 5 shady **6** shabby, shoddy **8** shameful **10** inglorious **11** ignominious

discreet 4 safe, wary **5** chary, muted, plain **6** modest, simple **7** careful, guarded, prudent, tactful **8** cautious, gingerly, moderate **9** temperate, unadorned, unextreme **10** controlled, reasonable, restrained

11 calculating, circumspect, considerate, inelaborate, unelaborate, unexcessive, unobtrusive **12** conservative, unbeautified **13** unpretentious

discrepancy 8 alterity **9** otherness, variation **10** difference, divergence, divergency, unlikeness

discrepant 7 diverse, varying **8** contrary **9** different, divergent, unmixable **11** conflicting, incongruent, incongruous, inconsonant **12** incompatible, inconsistent

discrete 8 detached, separate **9** countable **13** noncontinuous

discretion 4 tact **5** sense **6** wisdom **7** caution, secrecy **8** delicacy, judgment, prudence, wariness **9** canniness, foresight, restraint **10** providence **11** forethought

discriminate 4 know, note **5** sever **6** remark **7** analyze, compare, make out **8** contrast, perceive, separate **9** extricate **10** difference, severalize **13** differentiate

discriminating 4 wise **6** select **7** careful, prudent **8** eclectic **9** judicious, selective **10** analytical

discrimination 3 wit **5** sense **6** acumen **8** astucity, judgment, keenness **10** astuteness, shrewdness **11** percipience **12** perspicacity

discriminatory 6 biased, unfair, unjust **7** partial **8** partisan **10** prejudiced **11** inequitable **12** prepossessed

disculpate 5 clear **6** acquit **7** absolve **9** exonerate, vindicate

discursion 5 aside **8** excursus **10** divagation **11** parenthesis

discursive 6 chatty, roving **7** roaming **8** rambling **9** desultory *group discussion:* **11** bull session

discuss 4 moot **5** argue, parle, weigh **6** caucus, debate, parley **7** agitate, canvass, descant, expound **8** consider, converse, hash over, talk over **9** elucidate, expatiate, explicate, interpret, talk about, thrash out **10** deliberate, toss around **11** investigate *business:* **8** talk shop *lightly:* **5** bandy *thoroughly:* **7** exhaust

discussion 3 rap **6** confab **8** argument **10** conference **11** ventilation **12** deliberation **13** confabulation

discus thrower 6 Oerter (Al) **10** discobolus **11** Rashchupkin (Viktor)

disdain 5 abhor, pride, scorn, scout **6** morgue **7** contemn, despise, despite, hauteur **8** aversion, contempt, despisal, disprize, look down **9** antipathy, arrogance, insolence, loftiness, superbity **11** despisement, haughtiness

disdainful 5 proud **6** averse, lordly **7** haughty **8** arrogant, cavalier, insolent, scorning, scouting, spurning, superior

9 despising, rejecting 10 contemning
11 overbearing, repudiating 12 antipathetic,
contemptuous, supercilious 13 high and
mighty, unsympathetic

disease 3 bug, ill 4 AIDS 5 virus 6 blight,
malady, scurvy 7 ailment, anthrax, cholera,
derange, endemic, illness, malaise, mycosis, purpura, rickets 8 debility, epidemic,
leukemia, myxedema, paludism, pandemic,
pellagra, rachitis, sickness, syndrome, zoo-
noses (plural), zoonosis 9 affection, black
lung, complaint, condition, infirmity, sclero-
sis 10 alteration, blackwater, bronchitis,
feebleness, impairment, infirmness, rachiti-
des (plural), sickliness 11 decrepitude,
derangement 13 unhealthiness *animal:*
5 mange, surra 8 enzootic, epizooty *blood:*
8 leucemia, leukemia, leukoses (plural),
leukosis *cabbage:* 8 clubroot *cattle:*
6 cowpox 7 murrain, vaccina 8 blackleg,
vaccinia *caused by bacteria:* 11 brucellosis *cereal grass:* 4 smut *children's:*
7 rubella 10 chicken pox *citrus tree:* 8 tris-
teza *classification:* 8 nosology *combining form:* 3 nos 4 noso, path 5 patho
communicable: 12 tuberculosis *dissemi-
nator:* 7 carrier *eye:* 8 glaucoma, trachoma *fish:* 3 ich *foretelling of:* 9 prognosis *hair follicle:* 7 sycoses (plural),
sycosis *heart:* 11 cardiopathy *horse:*
4 clap 5 faroy 6 nagana, spavie, spavin
7 dourine, sarcoid 8 glanders *identification of:* 9 diagnosis *industrial:* 10 byssinosis *infectious:* 4 mono 6 typhus
7 malaria, tetanus, typhoid *liver:* 9 cirrhosis, hepatitis *livestock:* 7 locoism *lung:*
8 phthisic, phthisis 9 pneumonia *lymph
glands:* 6 struma 8 scrofula *metabolic:*
4 gout *nervous system:* 8 kuru *of beets:*
8 heartrot *of mammals:* 10 babesiasis
parasitic: 3 rot *plant:* 4 wilt 5 edema,
scurf 6 blotch 7 frogeye 8 gummosis
poultry: 7 fowlpox *respiratory:* 6 asthma
sheep: 3 gid 7 scrapie 10 bluetongue
skin: 4 acne 5 favus, hives, lupus, mange,
pinta, tinea 6 eczema, tetter 7 leprosy,
pemphix, prurigo, scabies 8 impetigo, kera-
toma, miliaria, pyoderma, ringworm, vitiligo,
xanthoma 9 keratomas (plural), psoriasis,
xanthomas (plural) 10 keratomata (plural),
xanthomata (plural) *suffix:* 3 ses (plural),
sis 4 itis, oses (plural), osis 5 iases (plural), iasis *swine:* 8 bullnose *syphilitic:*
5 tabes *throat:* 5 croup *tropical:* 4 pian
5 sprue 6 carate, dengue 8 psiloses (plural), psilosis *venereal:* 8 syphilis 9 chan-
croid, gonorrhea *viral:* 3 flu 4 noma
5 mumps, polio 6 grippe, rabies, zoster
7 ecthyma, measles, rubella, rubeola, vari-

ola 8 morbilli, psorosis, smallpox 13 poliomyelitis

diseased 6 sickly 7 fevered *combining
form:* 3 cac 4 cace, caco *prefix:* 3 dys
disembark 4 land 6 alight 8 go ashore
disembarrass 3 rid 5 clear, untie
7 relieve, untwine 8 unburden, untangle
9 extricate 10 unentangle
disembodied 9 asomatous, unfleshly
10 immaterial, unphysical 11 incorporeal,
nonphysical 13 insubstantial
disembogue 4 emit, flow, pour, void
6 emerge 7 give off, pour out 9 discharge
disembowel 3 gut 6 paunch, remove
7 exhaust 10 eviscerate, exenterate
disembroil 7 untwine 8 untangle 9 extricate 10 unentangle, unscramble
disemploy 2 ax 3 can 4 drop, fire, sack
5 let go 6 bounce, let out 7 boot out 9 terminate
disenchanted 5 blasé 7 knowing, worldly
8 mondaine 9 world-wise 11 worldly-wise
12 sophisticate 13 sophisticated
disencumber 5 untie 7 lighten, relieve,
untwine 8 free from, untangle 9 alleviate,
extricate 10 unentangle, unscramble
disengage 4 free, undo 5 loose, unfix
6 detach, unbind 7 release, unloose
8 abstract, liberate, uncouple, unfasten,
unloosen 9 extricate
disentangle 4 part 5 sever, untie
6 detach, sunder 7 unravel, untwine 8 separate 9 extricate 10 unscramble
13 straighten out
disenthrall 4 free 5 loose 6 loosen,
unbind 7 manumit, release, unchain 8 liberate 10 emancipate
disenthrone 6 depose, unmake
7 uncrown
disentranced see **disenchanted**
disentwine 5 untie 8 untangle 9 extricate
10 unentangle, unscramble
disesteem see **disfavor**
disfavor 5 frown, odium 6 infamy, object
7 obloquy 8 aversion, bad books, disgrace,
ignominy, mistrust 9 deprecate, detriment
10 opprobrium 13 indisposition
disfigure 3 mar 4 foul 5 spoil 6 deface,
deform, injure, mangle 8 mutilate
disfranchise 7 deprive 8 take away
disgorge 4 barf, spew 5 belch, eject,
empty, eruct, erupt, expel, vomit 6 irrupt,
spit up 7 bring up, throw up, upchuck
disgrace 4 blot, spot 5 brand, odium,
shame, shend, stain 6 infamy, stigma
7 attaint, ill luck, obloquy, stigmas (plural)
8 black eye, contempt, debasing, humbling,
ignominy, stigmata (plural) 9 abasement
10 debasement, misfortune, opprobrium
11 degradation, humiliation

disgraceful 5 shady 6 indign, shabby, shoddy 10 inglorious, unbecoming 11 ignominious 13 unrespectable

disgruntled 4 sore 9 uncontent 10 malcontent 11 uncontented, ungratified 12 malcontented

disguise 4 face, hide, mask, sham, show 5 belie, cloak, color, feign, front, put on 6 affect, assume, facade, garble, veneer 7 charade, conceal, dress up, falsify, obscure, pageant, pretend 8 artifice, coloring, delusion, pretense, simulate 9 deception, obfuscate 10 camouflage, false front, pretension 11 counterfeit, insincerity, make-believe 12 misrepresent, speciousness

disguisement 4 face, mask 5 cloak, color, cover, front 6 facade 8 coloring 10 false front

disgust 5 repel, shock 6 nausea, offend, reluct, revolt, sicken 7 outrage, repulse 8 aversion, nauseate 10 repugnance 13 squeamishness

disgusted 4 sick 5 fed up, tired, weary

disgusting 4 foul, vile 5 nasty 7 noisome 9 loathsome, offensive, repellent, repugnant, repulsive, revolting, sickening *behavior:* 11 beastliness

dish 4 food, stew, tray 5 salmi 6 shelve, tureen 7 platter 8 cup of tea, get rid of, scrapple, set aside *baked:* 7 soufflé *baking:* 7 scallop 12 scallop shell *cheese:* 6 fondue 7 ramekin, rarebit 8 raclette, ramequin *Chinese:* 6 won ton *deep:* 9 casserole *Hungarian:* 7 goulash *Italian:* 7 lasagna, lasagne, ravioli *Japanese:* 7 sashimi, tempura 8 sukiyaki *Mexican:* 5 tamal 6 tamale 7 burrito 11 chimichanga *Middle Eastern:* 8 moussaka *ornamental:* 7 epergne *principal:* 6 entrée *rice:* 7 risotto *rice and meat:* 5 pilaf, pilau, pilaw 6 pilaff *Scottish:* 6 haggis *shallow:* 6 saucer

Dishan's son 2 Uz 4 Aran

disharmonic see **discordant**

disharmonious see **discordant**

disharmonize 3 jar 5 clash 6 jangle 8 conflict, mismatch

disharmony 6 strife 7 discord, unpeace 8 conflict, variance 10 contention, difference, dissension, dissention

dishearten 5 chill 6 deject 7 depress 10 demoralize

disheartening 5 black, bleak 6 dreary, gloomy, somber 8 funereal 10 depressing, depressive, despondent, oppressive 11 pessimistic

dishes 4 ware *clay:* 7 pottery *porcelain:* 5 china

dishevel 5 touse, towse 6 tousel, tousle, touzle

disheveled 5 messy 6 sloppy, untidy 7 raunchy, ruffled, unkempt 8 ill-kempt, slipshod, slovenly, straggly, uncombed 12 unfastidious

dishonest 5 false, lying, snide 6 shifty, tricky 7 corrupt, crooked, devious, furtive, knavish, oblique, roguish 8 cheating, cozening, two-faced 9 deceitful, faithless, insidious, swindling 10 defrauding, fraudulent, mendacious, perfidious, untruthful 13 double-dealing, untrustworthy

dishonesty 5 fraud 7 chicane, roguery 8 trickery 9 chicanery, deception, fourberie 10 hanky-panky 11 highbinding 13 double-dealing, faithlessness

dishonor see **disgrace**

dishonorable see **disgraceful**

Dishon's father 4 Anah

dish out 4 dole, give, hand 6 supply 7 deliver, furnish, provide 8 dispense, hand over, transfer, turn over

disillusioned see **disenchanted**

disimprison 4 free 5 loose 6 unbind 7 manumit, release, unchain 8 liberate 9 unshackle 10 emancipate

disinclination 7 dislike 8 aversion 13 indisposition, unwillingness

disinclined 3 shy 5 loath 6 afraid, averse, shying 7 balking, dubious, uneager 8 backward, boggling, doubtful, hesitant, opposing, sticking 9 objecting, reluctant, resisting, stickling, unwilling, unwishful 10 indisposed, protesting 12 antipathetic 13 unsympathetic

disinfect 7 cleanse 9 sterilize

disingenuous 3 sly 4 foxy, wily 5 false 6 artful, crafty, tricky 7 cunning, devious, feigned, oblique, unfrank 8 guileful, indirect, uncandid 9 insidious, insincere

disinherit 3 rob 4 lose, oust 6 cut off 7 bereave, deprive 9 deprive of, repudiate

disintegrate 3 rot 4 sink, turn 5 break, decay, spoil, taint 6 molder, worsen 7 crumble, decline, descend, putrefy, scatter, shatter 8 separate 9 break down, decompose 10 deliquesce, retrograde *suffix:* 4 lyse, lyze

disintegrating *combining form:* 7 clastic

disintegration *combining form:* 5 lyses (plural), lysis

disinter 5 dig up 6 exhume, unbury 7 unearth 8 exhumate 9 uncharnel

disinterest 6 apathy 8 lethargy 9 lassitude, unconcern 11 insouciance 12 heedlessness, indifference, listlessness 13 unmindfulness

disinterested 4 fair, just 5 aloof 6 casual, remote 7 neutral 8 abstract, detached, negative, unbiased 9 apathetic, colorless, impartial, incurious, withdrawn

10 impersonal, poker-faced 11 indifferent, unconcerned, unpassioned

disjoin 4 part 5 sever 6 divide, sunder, unglue, unlink 7 break up, divorce, unstick 8 separate

disjoint 4 part 5 sever, upset 6 divide, luxate, mess up, muddle, sunder 7 break up, rummage 8 disorder, separate 9 uncombine

disjointed 7 muddled 8 inchoate 10 incoherent, incohesive 11 unconnected, unorganized 12 uncontinuous

disk 4 chip, puck 5 wafer 6 record *metal:* 4 slug *ornamental:* 6 bangle, sequin

dislike 4 hate 6 detest, hatred, resent 8 aversion, distaste 9 prejudice 10 repugnance 11 deprecation, detestation 13 indisposition *object of:* 8 anathema

disliking 8 aversion 13 indisposition

dislimb 4 maim 6 mayhem 7 cripple 8 mutilate

dislimn 3 dim 5 bedim, cloud, gloom 6 darken 7 becloud, obscure 8 overcast 9 adumbrate, obfuscate

dislocate 4 move, ship 5 mix up, shift 6 jumble, remove 7 rummage 8 disorder, transfer

dislodge 5 expel 6 remove 8 drive out

disloyal 5 false 6 untrue 8 recreant 9 alienated, estranged, faithless 10 perfidious, traitorous, unfaithful 11 treacherous

disloyalty 7 falsity, perfidy, treason 9 falseness, treachery 10 infidelity 13 faithlessness

dismal 5 black, bleak 6 dreary, gloomy, somber 8 funereal 10 depressing, depressive, oppressive 13 disheartening

dismantle 4 bare, lift, raze, ruin, undo 5 annul, strip, wrack, wreck 6 denude, divest, recall, repeal, revoke 7 deprive, destroy, rescind, reverse, strip of, unbuild, uncloak 8 bankrupt, decimate, demolish, denudate, dismount, take down, wear down 10 annihilate, do away with

dismay 4 faze, fear 5 abash, alarm, appal, daunt, dread, panic, scare, shake, upset 6 appall, bother, flurry, fright, horror, puzzle, rattle, subdue, terror 7 agitate, fluster, horrify, mystify, nonplus, perplex, perturb, terrify, unhinge 8 affright, bewilder, confound, frighten 9 dumbfound, embarrass 10 discompose 11 consternate, trepidation 12 perturbation 13 consternation

dismayed 5 agape, fazed 6 aghast 7 rattled, shocked 10 confounded 11 dumbfounded, overwhelmed 13 thunderstruck

dismember 4 maim, part 5 sever 6 mangle, mayhem, sunder 7 cripple 8 dismount, mutilate, separate, take down

dismiss 2 ax 3 can, out 4 cast, drop, fire, sack, shed 5 chase, chuck, eject, evict, let go, scoff, scorn, spurn 6 bounce, depose, lay off, let out, refuse, reject, remove, retire, slough, unseat 7 boot out, cashier, contemn, decline, divorce, extrude, kick out, kiss off, put away, suspend, turn off 8 furlough, pooh-pooh, ridicule, throw out, turn away, turn down 9 reprobate, repudiate, terminate

dismissal 5 congé 6 layoff, ouster 7 removal 8 brushoff

dismount 6 alight, detach, get off 7 unhorse 8 separate, take down 10 alight from

Disney 4 Walt 10 cartoonist *character:* 4 Huey 5 Daisy, Dewey, Dumbo, Goofy, Louie, Pluto 6 Donald, Mickey, Minnie *classic:* 8 Fantasia

disobedient 6 unruly 7 naughty, willful 8 contrary 10 headstrong, rebellious 12 contumacious, obstreperous, recalcitrant 13 insubordinate

disoblige 6 offend, put out 7 affront, trouble 8 put about 9 incommode 13 inconvenience

disorder 3 ill 4 riot, turn 5 chaos, mix up, snarl, upset 6 anomie, ataxia, huddle, jumble, malady, mess up, muddle, muss up, rumple, sicken, tumble, tumult 7 ailment, anarchy, clutter, confuse, derange, disease, embroil, illness, misdeed, misrule, rummage, shuffle, turmoil, unhinge 8 disjoint, sickness, syndrome, unhealth, unsettle, upheaval 9 affection, agitation, anarchism, commotion, complaint, condition, confusion, infirmity 10 affliction, convulsion, misconduct, turbulence 11 bedevilment, misdemeanor 13 indisposition *mental:* 8 paranoia

disordered 4 daft 5 crazy 6 crazed, insane 7 cracked, lunatic, muddled 8 demented, deranged, inchoate 9 bedlamite 10 incoherent, incohesive 11 unconnected, unorganized 12 uncontinuous

disorderly 5 rowdy 6 unruly 7 raucous 8 rowdyish 9 termagant, turbulent 10 boisterous, rowdydowdy, tumultuous 11 rumbustious

disorderly house 6 bagnio 7 brothel 8 bordello

disorganize 5 upset 6 jumble, mess up 7 derange 8 unsettle

disoriented 4 lost

disown 4 deny 8 disclaim, renounce 9 repudiate

disparage 5 abuse, chill, decry 6 deject, slight 7 downcry, run down 8 bad mouth, belittle, derogate, minimize, write off 10 demoralize, depreciate 11 detract from

disparagement 4 tale 5 scorn 7 calumny, despite, scandal, slander 8 contempt, despisal 9 aspersion, indignity, stricture **10** backbiting, defamation, detraction, diminution, reflection **11** despisement **12** backstabbing, belittlement, depreciation **13** animadversion

disparate 6 unlike **7** diverse, unalike, unequal, various **9** different, divergent, unsimilar **11** inconsonant **12** incompatible, inconsistent

disparity 8 alterity **9** otherness **10** difference, divergence, divergency, inequality, unevenness, unlikeness

dispassionate 4 calm, cool, fair, just, open **5** aloof, equal, frank **7** neutral **8** abstract, composed, detached, judicial, unbiased **9** colorless, equitable, impartial, uncolored, unruffled **10** aboveboard, impersonal, poker-faced **11** indifferent, unflappable **12** uninfluenced, unprejudiced **13** imperturbable

dispatch 4 kill, send, ship, slay **5** eat up, haste, hurry, remit, route, scrag, speed **6** cut off, devour, finish, hasten, hustle, lay low, rustle **7** address, consign, destroy, forward, killing, message, put away, quicken, take off **8** alacrity, carry off, celerity, get rid of, goodwill, riddance, shipment, transmit **9** diligence, polish off, readiness, swiftness **10** expedition, put to death, speediness **11** promptitude

dispatch boat 5 aviso **6** packet

dispel 4 oust **5** eject **7** crumble, scatter **9** clear away, drive away

dispensable 5 minor **7** trivial **8** needless, unneeded **9** redundant **10** unrequired **11** superfluous, unessential, unimportant, unnecessary **12** nonessential

dispensary 6 clinic

dispensation 5 favor **7** service **8** courtesy, kindness, ordering **9** remission **10** indulgence, management

dispense 3 ply **4** deal, give, hand **5** spare, swing, wield **6** divide, excuse, exempt, handle, let off, let out, supply **7** absolve, deal out, deliver, dish out, dole out, furnish, mete out, portion, prorate, provide, release, relieve **8** deal with, hand over, maneuver, share out, transfer, turn over **9** apportion, discharge, partition **10** administer, distribute, manipulate, measure out, portion out

disperse 3 sow **4** deal **5** spray, strew **6** divide, lot out, spread **7** break up, diffuse, disband, disject, dole out, radiate, scatter **9** circulate, partition, propagate **10** distribute, measure out

dispersion 7 colloid **9** spreading **10** scattering *combining form:* **3** lyo

dispirit 5 chill **6** deject **7** depress **10** demoralize, discourage

dispirited 3 low, sad **4** blue, flat **8** cast down, dejected, downcast, lifeless

9 depressed, woebegone **10** melancholy **11** downhearted

dispiriting 5 black, bleak **6** dreary, gloomy **8** funereal **9** cheerless **10** depressing, depressive, oppressing

displace 4 oust **5** exile, expel, shift, usurp **6** banish, cut out, deport, depose, unmake, winkle **7** expulse, uncrown **8** crowd out, dethrone, redirect, relegate, supplant **9** transport **10** expatriate, substitute

displaced person 2 DP **6** émigré **7** evacuee, refugee **8** fugitive

display 4 open, pomp, show **5** array, flash, offer, shine **6** evince, expose, flaunt, lay out, parade, reveal, setout, spread, unfold, unveil **7** exhibit, fanfare, panoply, showing, show off, trot out, uncover **8** blazonry, brandish, describe, evidence, manifest, unclothe **9** showiness, spectacle **10** exhibiting, exhibition, pretension **11** demonstrate, ostentation **13** demonstration, manifestation

displeasing 3 bad **4** sour **6** rotten, vexing **7** irksome, unhappy **8** annoying **10** bothersome, unpleasant

displeasure 4 pain **5** anger **6** sorrow **8** aversion, vexation **10** uneasiness **11** indignation, unhappiness **13** indisposition

disport 3 act, fun **4** bear, game, go on, play, show **5** amuse, carry, flash **6** acquit, behave, demean, divert, expose, flaunt, parade **7** conduct, exhibit, jollity, pastime, show off, trot out **8** brandish, recreate **9** diversion, entertain, merriment **10** recreation

disposal 5 order **7** dumping, junking **8** bestowal, chucking, jettison, ordering, riddance, sequence **9** clearance, scrapping **10** demolition, destroying, relegation **11** arrangement, demolishing, destruction **12** throwing away, transference

dispose 4 bend, bias **5** array, order **7** arrange, incline, marshal, prepare **8** organize **9** make ready, methodize **11** systematize *of:* **4** sell **5** scrap **6** finish, handle **7** destroy, discard

disposed 4 fain **5** prone, ready **6** minded **7** willing **8** inclined

disposition 4 bent, cast, mood, tone, type, vein **5** being, humor, order, stamp, tenor **6** makeup, nature, temper **7** control, dumping, junking, leaning **8** jettison, ordering, penchant, riddance, sequence, tendency **9** character, direction, inclining, scrapping **10** complexion, management, proclivity, propensity **11** arrangement, controlling, inclination, personality, temperament **12** predilection, throwing away **13** individualism, individuality *favorable:* **8** optimism *unfavorable:* **9** pessimism

dispossess 3 rob 4 lose, oust 5 eject 6 banish, divest 7 bereave, deprive

dispossession 4 loss 6 ouster 9 privation 11 deprivation, deprivement, divestiture

dispraise 5 decry 8 belittle, derogate, diminish, minimize 10 depreciate 11 detract from, opprobriate 12 depreciation

disproportion 8 imparity, mismatch 10 inequality, unevenness

disproportionate 6 uneven 7 unequal 8 lopsided 9 irregular 10 asymmetric, off-balance, unbalanced 12 overbalanced 13 unsymmetrical

disprove 5 break, evert, rebut, shoot 6 blow up, impugn, refute 7 confute, explode 8 confound, negative, overturn, puncture, traverse 9 discredit, overthrow 10 contravene, controvert

disputable 4 moot 7 dubious 8 doubtful 9 uncertain 11 problematic

disputation 6 debate 7 mooting 8 forensic 9 dialectic 11 controversy

dispute 4 buck, duel, miff, moot, tiff 5 argue, doubt, fight, rebut, repel 6 argufy, bicker, combat, debate, hassle, oppose, refute, resist, rumpus, strife 7 agitate, canvass, confute, contend, contest, discuss, quarrel, quibble, wrangle 8 argument, conflict, mistrust, question, squabble, traverse 9 bickering, challenge, thrash out, withstand 10 contention, controvert, falling-out, toss around 11 altercation, controversy, embroilment *Scottish:* 6 threap, threep

disqualified 5 unfit 8 unfitted 9 incapable 10 ineligible, unequipped 11 incompetent

disqualify 3 bar 5 debar 6 except 7 exclude, rule out, suspend 9 deprive of, eliminate, make unfit 12 incapacitate *as judge:* 6 recuse

disquiet 4 care 5 upset, worry 6 bother, flurry, unease, unrest, untune 7 agitate, ailment, anxiety, concern, ferment, fluster, perturb, trouble, turmoil, unhinge 10 discompose, solicitude, uneasiness 11 concernment, restiveness 12 restlessness 13 Sturm und Drang

disquietude 4 care 5 worry 6 unease, unrest 7 ailment, anxiety, concern, ferment, turmoil 9 agitation 10 uneasiness 11 concernment, restiveness 12 restlessness 13 Sturm und Drang

Disraeli, Benjamin *novel:* 7 Tancred

disregard 4 fail, omit 5 belay 6 apathy, forget, ignore, slight 7 blink at, neglect 8 ignoring, lethargy, omission, omitting, overlook, overpass 9 blink away, lassitude, slighting, unconcern 10 forgetting, neglecting 11 insouciance, overlooking

12 heedlessness, indifference, listlessness 13 unmindfulness

disregardful 3 lax 5 slack 6 remiss 8 careless, derelict, heedless 9 negligent 10 behindhand, delinquent, neglectful, regardless

disremember 6 forget

disreputable 4 mean 5 cheap, dingy, faded, seedy, shady, sorry 6 abject, scurvy, shabby, shoddy, sordid 7 run-down 8 beggarly, decrepit, pitiable, shameful 10 bedraggled, down-at-heel, inglorious, threadbare 11 dilapidated, ignominious 12 contemptible

disrepute 5 odium, shame 6 infamy 7 obloquy 8 disgrace, ignominy 10 opprobrium

disrespect 8 boldness 9 hardihood, impudence, insolence, insolency 10 incivility 12 impertinence, insolentness

disrespectful 4 rude 7 ill-bred, incivil, uncivil 8 impolite, impudent 10 ungracious 11 ill-mannered, impertinent

disrobe 4 bare 5 strip 6 denude, divest 7 deprive, strip of, undress 8 bankrupt, denudate, unclothe

disrupt 4 hole, open 5 upset 6 breach, mess up, muddle 7 rummage, rupture 8 disorder, unsettle 10 break apart

dissatisfaction 7 dislike 8 aversion 10 uneasiness

dissatisfactory 3 bad 4 poor 5 amiss, wrong 6 rotten

dissatisfied 5 irked, vexed 7 annoyed 8 bothered 9 uncontent 10 malcontent 11 uncontented 12 discontented, malcontented

dissect 3 cut 4 part 5 carve, probe, sever, slice, split 6 cleave, divide, pierce, sunder 7 analyze, break up, resolve 8 separate 9 anatomize, break down, decompose, penetrate 10 decompound 11 dichotomize

dissection *of animals:* 7 zootomy

dissemblance 5 guile 6 deceit 7 cunning 8 alterity 9 duplicity, otherness 10 difference, divergence, divergency, unlikeness

dissemble 4 mask 5 cloak, feign 7 conceal, dress up 8 disguise 10 camouflage

dissembler 8 pharisee, Tartuffe 9 hypocrite, lip server

disseminate 3 sow 5 straw, strew 6 blazon, spread 7 bestrew, declare, diffuse, publish, radiate, scatter, send out 8 announce, permeate, proclaim 9 advertise, broadcast, circulate, propagate, publicize, spread out 10 annunciate, promulgate 11 blaze abroad

dissension 6 strife 7 discord, quarrel, wrangle 8 argument, conflict, variance 9 bickering 10 contention, difference, quarreling 11 altercation, controversy

dissent 3 shy 4 balk, vary 5 demur
6 boggle, differ, divide, heresy, object,
schism, strife 7 stickle 8 conflict, variance
9 misbelief 10 contention, difference, heterodoxy 11 unorthodoxy 12 nonagreement
13 nonconformism, nonconformity

dissenter 7 heretic, sectary 10 schismatic, separatist 11 misbeliever, schismatist
13 nonconformist

dissertation 6 memoir, thesis 8 tractate,
treatise 9 discourse, monograph, treatment
10 monography

disservice 6 injury 8 mischief

dissever 3 cut 4 part 5 carve, slice, split
6 cleave, divide, sunder 7 divorce 8 separate 11 dichotomize

dissidence 6 heresy, schism, strife 7 discord 8 conflict 9 misbelief 10 contention,
heterodoxy 11 unorthodoxy 13 nonconformism, nonconformity

dissident 7 heretic, sectary 9 differing,
heretical, heterodox, sectarian 10 schismatic, separatist, unorthodox 11 contentious, misbeliever, quarrelsome, schismatist
12 unharmonious 13 nonconformist

dissimilar 6 unlike 7 diverse, unalike,
unequal, various 8 contrary, opposite 9 different, divergent 10 antonymous 12 antithetical 13 contradictory

dissimilarity 8 variance 9 diversity, otherness, severance 10 difference, divergence,
divergency, unlikeness 11 incongruity
12 divarication, inconsonance 13 heterogeneity, inconsistency

dissimulate see dissemble

dissimulation 5 guile 6 deceit, hiding
7 cunning, masking 8 cloaking, feigning,
pretense, shamming 9 duplicity, hypocrisy,
secreting 10 catabolism, concealing, pharisaism, pretending, sanctimony 12 camou-
flaging

dissimulator see dissembler

dissipate 4 blow 5 waste 6 vanish 7 consume, crumble, fritter, scatter 8 evanesce,
fool away, squander 9 evaporate, throw
away 10 frivol away, trifle away 11 blunder
away

dissociate 5 unfix 6 cut off, detach
8 abstract, alienate, estrange, uncouple

dissolute 3 lax 4 fast, wild 5 light, loose,
slack 6 rakish, wanton 7 lawless, raffish,
wayward 9 abandoned, reprobate 10 licentious, profligate 12 unprincipled, unrestrained 13 self-abandoned

dissolution 5 death, decay, sleep
6 demise 7 decease, divorce, passing, quietus, rupture, silence, split-up 8 curtains,
division 10 detachment, profligacy
11 divorcement *combining form:* 3 lys
4 lysi, lyso 5 lyses (plural), lysis

dissolvable 7 soluble

dissolve 3 end 4 flux, fuse, melt, ruin,
thaw, undo, void 5 annul, quash, wrack,
wreck 6 recess, unfold, vacate, vanish
7 adjourn, break up, clear up, destroy, disband, immerse, liquefy, resolve, shatter,
unravel 8 abrogate, decimate, decipher,
demolish, destruct, fade away, get rid of,
liquesce, prorogue, separate 9 decompose,
figure out, lose power, prorogate, puzzle
out, terminate, waste away 10 annihilate,
deliquesce, do away with 13 superimpos-
ing *suffix:* 4 lyse, lyze

dissonance 6 strife 7 discord 8 conflict
9 cacophony 10 contention, difference
11 incongruity

dissonant 4 rude 5 harsh 6 hoarse, rugged 7 grating, jarring, raucous 8 strident
9 immusical, unmixable, unmusical
10 cacophonic, inharmonic 11 cacophonous, conflicting, incongruent, incongruous
12 incompatible, inconsistent, inharmonious

dissuade 5 deter 6 dehort, divert 10 discourage, disincline

distaff 6 female

distance 3 way 4 area, size, ways
5 ambit, orbit, piece, range, reach, route,
scope, space, spell, sweep 6 course,
degree, extent, length, milage, outrun,
radius, spread 7 breadth, compass,
expanse, mileage, outpace, purview,
reserve, spacing, stretch 8 alterity, cold-
ness, interval, outspeed, outstrip 9 amplitude, expansion, extension, otherness
10 difference, divergence, divergency,
remoteness, separation, unlikeness 11 distinction, perspective 12 dissemblance
13 dissimilarity, dissimilitude *angular:* 8 latitude 9 longitude *between levels:* 4 drop
between rails: 4 gage *between supports:*
4 span *from bottom to top:* 6 height *geometric:* 8 altitude *greatest perpendicular:*
6 camber *measuring instrument:* 8 odo-
graph, odometer 9 pedometer, telemeter
11 range finder *minute:* 4 hair *perpendicular:* 5 depth *shortest:* 7 beeline
12 straight line *the wind blows:* 5 fetch

distant 3 far, shy 4 afar, cold, cool
5 aloof, apart 6 far-off, remote 7 diverse,
faraway, haughty, obscure, removed, spacial, spatial, unalike, unequal, various 8 far-
flung, isolated, off-lying, outlying, reserved,
retiring, secluded, solitary 9 different, divergent, separated, unsimilar, withdrawn
10 unsociable 11 out-of-the-way, sequestered, standoffish *combining form:* 3 tel
4 tele, telo

distaste 7 dislike 8 aversion 9 antipathy,
hostility, revulsion 10 abhorrence, repugnance 13 indisposition

distasteful 4 flat 6 bitter, odious 7 galling, insipid, painful 8 grievous, unsavory

9 loathsome, obnoxious, repellent, repugnant, repulsive, savorless, tasteless
10 abominable, afflictive, detestable, flavorless **11** ill-flavored, unpalatable **12** unappetizing

distemper **4** riot **5** mix up, paint **6** choler, muddle **7** anarchy, derange, disease, misrule, rummage **8** disorder **9** anarchism, strangles **10** affliction **11** derangement **13** panleucopenia

distend **5** bloat, swell **6** dilate, expand, extend **7** amplify, augment, enlarge, inflate **8** increase, lengthen **10** stretch out

distill **4** drib, drip, drop, weep **6** infuse, purify **7** dribble, trickle **11** concentrate

distillation apparatus **5** still **7** alembic, limbeck

distinct **4** sole **5** clear, lucid, plain **6** patent, single **7** defined, diverse, evident, express, notable, obvious, special, unusual, various **8** apparent, clear-cut, definite, especial, explicit, manifest, palpable, peculiar, separate, specific **9** different, divergent **10** individual, particular, prescribed **11** categorical, perspicuous, unambiguous, unequivocal *combining form:* **4** idio **5** chori **7** chorist **8** choristo

distinction **4** bays, rank **5** award, badge, class, grade, honor, kudos **6** nicety, renown **7** laurels **8** accolade, alterity, eminence, prestige **9** otherness **10** difference, divergence, divergency, prominence, prominency, unlikeness **11** differentia, preeminence **12** significance **13** dissimilarity

distinctive **6** proper, single, unique **8** peculiar, separate **9** diacritic **10** diagnostic, individual **11** outstanding **13** idiosyncratic

distingué **6** urbane **7** genteel, refined **8** cultured, polished, well-bred **10** cultivated

distinguish **3** see **4** know, mark, note, part, spot, view **5** erect, exalt, honor, place **6** descry, finger, notice, remark, set off **7** dignify, ennoble, glorify, magnify, mark off, observe, pick out, qualify, sublime **8** diagnose, identify, perceive, pinpoint, separate **9** demarcate, extricate, recognize, signalize, single out **10** aggrandize, difference **11** determinate, individuate, singularize **12** characterize **13** diagnosticate, differentiate, individualize

distinguished **5** famed, grand, great **6** famous **7** courtly, eminent, notable, stately **8** imposing, renowned **9** dignified, prominent **10** celebrated, celebrious **11** illustrious

distort **4** bend, warp, wind **5** alter, belie, color, curve, twist, wrest **6** change, deform, garble **7** falsify, pervert, torture **8** miscolor, misshape, misstate **11** misconstrue **12** misinterpret, misrepresent

distortion **8** misshape **9** deformity

distract **5** addle, craze, mix up **6** ball up, frenzy, fuddle, harass, madden **7** confuse, derange, fluster, unhinge **8** befuddle, bewilder, confound, throw off **9** unbalance

distraction **6** lunacy **7** madness **8** insanity **9** amusement, diversion, unbalance **10** insaneness, perplexity **11** derangement, psychopathy **13** entertainment

distrait **4** lost **5** upset **6** absent **7** bemused, faraway, worried **8** harassed, troubled **9** tormented **10** abstracted **11** inattentive, inconscient, preoccupied **12** absentminded

distraught **3** mad **4** daft, nuts **5** crazy, upset **6** addled, crazed, insane **7** cracked, frantic, muddled, worried **8** agitated, confused, demented, deranged, harassed, troubled **9** flustered, perturbed, tormented **10** bewildered, nonplussed

distress **3** ail, irk, try, woe **4** ache, cark, hurt, need, pain, pang, pass, rack **5** agony, annoy, cross, dolor, grief, harry, pinch, rigor, throe, trial, upset, weigh, worry **6** bother, grieve, harass, injure, misery, pester, plague, sorrow, strain, strait, stress, twinge **7** afflict, anguish, exhaust, passion, torment, torture, trouble **8** aggrieve, calamity, exigency, hardship **9** adversity, constrain, suffering **10** affliction, difficulty, heartbreak, misfortune, visitation **11** tribulation, vicissitude *call:* **6** Mayday *signal:* **3** SOS **5** alarm

distressing **4** dire **6** woeful **8** grievous, poignant **10** afflictive, calamitous, deplorable, lamentable **11** regrettable, unfortunate **13** heartbreaking

distribute **3** lot **4** deal, give, mete **5** allot, place, strew **6** assign, assort, bestow, divide, donate, lot out, parcel, ration, spread **7** deal out, deliver, diffuse, dole out, dribble, give out, mete out, portion, present, prorate, radiate, scatter **8** allocate, classify, dispense, position, separate **9** apportion, circulate, partition, propagate, spread out **10** administer, measure out *in a tournament:* **4** seed

distribution **5** order **7** density **8** ordering, sequence **9** allotment, placement **10** scattering **11** arrangement, probability **12** spreading out **13** apportionment

distributor **6** jobber **7** carrier **10** wholesaler

district **4** area **5** tract **6** barrio, parcel, region, sector **7** quarter, section **8** division, locality, precinct, vicinage, vicinity **11** subdivision **12** neighborhood *ecclesiastical:* **5** synod **6** parish **7** diocese *Greek:* **4** deme *Indian:* **6** tahsil *judicial:* **7** circuit *London:* **4** Soho *theater:* **6** rialto *Turkish administrative:* **6** sanjak

distrust 5 doubt 7 suspect 8 wariness 9 suspicion 10 disbelieve

distrustful 4 wary 7 jealous 10 suspicious

distrusting 7 cynical 9 sceptical, skeptical 10 suspicious

disturb 4 faze, move, ship 5 alarm, fease, feaze, feeze, rouse, scare, shift, unset, upset 6 bother, damage, flurry, jumble, meddle, mess up, puzzle, remove, stir up, tamper 7 agitate, break up, derange, destroy, fluster, inquiet, perplex, replace, terrify, trouble, unhinge 8 bewilder, disorder, frighten, transfer, unsettle 9 incommode, interfere 11 intermeddle 13 inconvenience, interfere with

disturbance 6 rumpus, unrest 7 bobbery, cyclone, tornado, unquiet 9 agitating, agitation, commotion, variation 10 alteration 11 derangement 12 diastrophism, interruption *atmospheric:* 5 storm *emotional:* 8 neuroses (plural), neurosis *mental:* 6 frenzy 7 phrensy 8 delirium *oceanic:* 7 tsunami

disunify see **disunite**

disunion 6 strife 7 divorce, rupture, split-up 8 conflict, division, variance 9 partition 10 contention, detachment, difference, separation 11 divorcement

disunite 4 part, wean 5 alien 6 divide, sunder 7 break up, divorce, split up 8 alienate, estrange, separate 9 fall apart, uncombine 11 dichotomize

disunity 6 strife 7 discord 8 conflict, variance 10 alienation, contention, difference

ditch 3 cut, dig, pit 4 cast, foss, junk 5 chuck, fosse, scrap 6 reject, sheuch, sheugh, trench, trough 7 abandon, cashier, discard, dismiss, foxhole 8 jettison, throw out 9 throw away 10 excavation

dither 3 gab, jaw, yak 4 chat, flap, halt, stew 5 clack, jumps, quake, run on, shake, waver 6 babble, cackle, falter, quaver, shakes, shiver, tremor, tumult 7 jitters, shivers, shudder, stagger, tremble, turmoil, twitter, whiffle, willies 8 hesitate 9 agitation, commotion, confusion, vacillate, whim-whams 10 turbulence 12 shilly-shally, wiggle-waggle 13 heebie-jeebies

dithyramb 4 hymn, poem 5 chant

dithyrambic 4 wild 5 fiery 6 ardent, fervid, torrid 7 burning, fervent, flaming 9 perfervid, rhapsodic 10 boisterous, passionate 11 impassioned

ditto 4 copy 6 carbon, repeat 7 replica 9 duplicate, facsimile 10 carbon copy 11 replication 12 reproduction 13 reduplication

ditty 3 lay 4 aria, hymn, lied, song 7 descant

diurnal 5 daily 9 circadian, ephemeral, quotidian

divagate 5 stray 6 depart, ramble, wander 7 digress, diverge, excurse

divan 4 sofa 5 couch 7 council 9 davenport 11 smoking room

diva's solo 4 aria

dive 3 bar, pub 4 dash, dump, hole, jump, leap 5 joint, lunge, pitch, sound 6 gainer, lounge, plunge, saloon, tavern 7 barroom, decline, descend, descent, hangout, taproom 8 submerge 9 belly-flop, honky-tonk, jackknife, roadhouse 10 cannonball, submerging *position:* 4 pike, tuck 8 straight

diver 4 loon *combining form:* 4 dyta 5 dytes

diverge 4 part, vary 5 stray 6 depart, differ, ramble, swerve, wander 7 deflect, deviate, digress, excurse 8 disagree, separate 9 draw apart

divergence 7 parting, turning, variety, varying 8 alterity 9 departure, deviation, differing, otherness 10 aberration, deflection, difference, digression, separation, unlikeness 11 disagreeing, discrepancy, distinction 12 disagreement, dissemblance 13 dissimilarity, dissimilitude

divergent 6 off-key, radial, unlike 7 deviant, distant, unalike, unequal, various 8 aberrant, abnormal, atypical, contrary, opposite 9 anomalous, different, differing, disparate, irregular, radiating, spreading, unnatural, unregular, unsimilar 10 dissimilar 12 antithetical 13 contradictory

divers 4 many, some 6 sundry 7 several, various *combining form:* 4 poly, vari 5 parti, party, vario

diver's disease 5 bends 12 aeroembolism

diverse 6 unlike 7 distant, several, unalike, unequal, various 8 contrary, discrete, distinct, manifold, opposite, separate 9 different, differing, disparate, multifold, multiform, multiplex, unsimilar 10 contrasted, dissimilar 11 contrasting, contrastive 12 multifarious 13 contradictory *meanings:* 8 polysemy

diversion 3 fun 4 play 5 sport 6 levity, relish 7 disport, turning 8 pleasure, sideshow 9 amusement, departure, deviation, enjoyment, frivolity 10 aberration, deflection, recreation 11 delectation, distraction 13 entertainment

diversity 7 variety 8 multeity 10 difference, unlikeness 11 distinction, variousness 12 multiformity, multiplicity 13 dissimilarity

divert 4 turn, veer 5 alter, amuse, deter 6 swerve 7 deflect, deviate, digress 8 dissuade, distract 9 disadvise, disengage, entertain, turn aside **10** discourage *water:* **5** flume

divest 3 rob **4** bare, lose, oust **5** spoil, strip **6** denude **7** bereave, deprive, disrobe, undress **8** bankrupt, denudate, take away **9** dismantle **10** disinherit, dispossess

divide 3 cut **4** chop, deal, fork, part, vary **5** allot, carve, halve, quota, sever, share **6** assign, cleave, differ, lot out, parcel, ration, sector, sunder **7** break up, comport, discord, disjoin, dissect, dissent, divorce, dole out, furcate, portion, prorate, quarter, section, segment, share in, split up **8** allocate, classify, disagree, disburse, disjoint, dispense, disperse, disunite, fraction, graduate, separate **9** apportion, branch out, disaccord, partition, watershed **10** distribute, measure out **11** dichotomize, distinguish *into four parts:* **7** quarter *into three parts:* **7** trisect *into two parts:* **5** halve **6** bisect **9** bifurcate

divided 6 cloven **7** asunder, partite **8** multifid **9** disunited, separated *combining form:* **3** fid **4** sect **5** fissi, schiz **6** fidate, schizo, tomous **7** chorist **8** choristo

dividend 4 meed, plum **5** bonus, prize **6** carrot, return, reward **7** guerdon, premium

divider 6 bunton **7** compass **9** partition

divination 6 augury **7** insight **8** prophecy *by communication with the dead:* **10** necromancy *by dreams:* **11** oneiromancy *by figures:* **8** geomancy *by lots:* **9** sortilege *by numbers:* **10** numerology *by rods:* **7** dowsing **11** rhabdomancy *by stars:* **9** astrology *combining form:* **5** mancy

divine 4 holy **5** clerk, godly, infer **6** cleric, deific, parson, priest, sacred **7** foresee, godlike, preknow, previse, suppose **8** clerical, discover, forefeel, foreknow, minister, preacher, prophesy, reverend **9** apprehend, chthonian, churchman, clergyman, marvelous, prevision, religious, visualize **10** anticipate, conjecture, superhuman, theologian **12** ecclesiastic, extramundane, transmundane **13** superphysical

Divine Comedy author 5 Dante

divining ability, for short 3 ESP

divinity 3 god **5** deity **7** godhead **8** theology *female:* **5** nymph **7** goddess

division 3 cut **4** part, unit **5** class, piece **6** member, moiety, parcel, schism **7** discord, dissent, divorce, parting, portion, rupture, section, segment, split-up **8** category, conflict, district, disunion, disunity, variance **9** disaccord, partition **10** detachment, difference, disharmony, dissidence, dissonance, separation **11** dissolution, divorcement **12** disagreement **13** apportionment *Bible:* **5** verse *book:* **7** chapter *British territorial:*

5 shire *building:* **4** wing *cell:* **7** meiosis, mitosis *city:* **4** ward **7** borough **8** precinct *combining form:* **7** kineses (plural), kinesis *contest:* **4** heat **6** inning, period *corolla:* **5** petal *country:* **5** state **6** canton **8** province **10** department, prefecture *family:* **4** side **6** branch *geologic time:* **5** epoch **6** period *hospital:* **4** ward, wing *into two:* **9** bisection **11** bifurcation, bipartition *mankind:* **4** race *meal:* **6** course *music:* **3** bar **4** line **7** measure **8** movement *opera, play:* **3** act **5** scene *poem:* **5** canto, verse **6** stanza *population:* **7** segment, stratum *race:* **3** lap **4** heat *social:* **5** caste, class, tribe *state:* **6** county, parish *term:* **8** quotient *time:* **3** day, eon **4** week, year **5** month **6** decade, minute, moment, second **7** weekend **9** fortnight *tribal:* **4** clan *word:* **8** syllable *zodiac:* **4** sign

divisive 8 factious

divorce 4 part **5** annul, sever, split **6** cancel, sunder **7** break up, disjoin, dismiss, put away, rupture, split-up, unmarry **8** disjoint, dissever, disunion, disunite, separate **9** disaffect, partition **10** detachment, separation **11** dissolution

divot 4 turf

divulge 4 tell **5** mouth, spill **6** betray, gossip, reveal, tattle **7** blab out **8** disclose, discover, give away, proclaim **13** spill the beans

"Dixie" composer 6 Emmett (Daniel)

___ dixit 4 ipse

dizziness 7 vertigo

dizzy 4 daze **5** addle, dazed, giddy, inane, light, mix up, silly, undue **6** addled, ball up, fuddle, muddle, swimmy **7** asinine, confuse, dazzled, extreme, fatuous, flighty, fluster, foolish, fuddled, muddled, puzzled, reeling, stupefy **8** befuddle, bewilder, confused, heedless, skittish, swimming, throw off, towering, whirling **9** befuddled, confusing, excessive, frivolous **10** bewildered, bird-witted, confounded, distracted, exorbitant, immoderate, inordinate **11** emptyheaded, extravagant, harebrained, light-headed, vertiginous **12** unmeasurable

DNA *component:* 7 adenine, guanine, thymine **8** cytosine **10** nucleotide **11** deoxyribose *segment:* **7** cistron

do 3 act, end, gyp, pay, put, set **4** bear, beat, bilk, cook, fare, feel, go on, halt, play, quit, show, suit, tire, tour, wash, work **5** break, cheat, clean, close, cover, cozen, enact, exert, get by, get on, occur, serve, shift, tonic, track **6** acquit, befall, behave, betide, chance, chouse, commit, demean, deport, diddle, effect, finish, happen, manage, render, travel, wind up, work at, wrap up **7** achieve, approve, arrange, come off, comport, conduct, defraud, develop, execute, exhaust, fall out, furbish, perform, playact, suffice, undergo, wear out **8** carry out, complete, conclude, decorate, flimflam, get along, pass over, traverse **9** determine, discourse, overreach, personate, stagger on, terminate, transpire **11** impersonate **12** stagger along **13** muddle through *away with:* **5** abate **6** banish **7** abolish **8** demolish, dissolve *without:* **5** forgo **6** forego *wrong:* **3** err

doable **8** feasible, possible

docent **7** teacher **8** lecturer, teaching **10** instructor **11** instructive

docile **4** tame **5** tawie **6** pliant **7** pliable **8** amenable, biddable, obedient **9** adaptable, teachable, tractable **10** submissive

dock **4** pier, quay, rump, slip **5** berth, jetty, levee, wharf **6** hangar, lessen, marina, reduce **7** abridge **8** platform *worker:* **6** lumper **9** stevedore **12** longshoreman

docket **4** card, sked **6** agenda **7** program **8** calendar, schedule **9** timetable

doctor **2** MD **3** fix, vet **4** load, mend **5** medic, patch, treat **6** breeze, debase, dope up, medico, repair, revamp **7** dentist, medical, rebuild, scholar, surgeon **8** overhaul **9** clinician, internist, mediciner, physician **10** adulterate, specialist **11** medicine man, recondition, reconstruct *animal:* **3** vet **12** veterinarian *children's:* **12** pediatrician *famous baby care:* **5** Spock (Benjamin) *foot:* **10** podiatrist **11** chiropodist *heart:* **12** cardiologist *slang:* **8** sawbones *teeth:* **7** dentist *women's:* **12** gynecologist

Doctor of the Church **5** Basil **6** Jerome **7** Ambrose, Gregory **9** Augustine **10** Athanasius

doctrinaire **6** dogged, mulish **8** dogmatic, stubborn **9** dictative, obstinate, pigheaded **10** bullheaded **11** dictatorial, magisterial, stiff-necked **12** pertinacious **13** authoritarian, authoritative

doctrine **3** ism **4** doxy **5** axiom, basic, canon, dogma, doxie, tenet **7** plenism **8** teaching **9** principle **11** fundamental, instruction *combining form:* **4** logy **5** logia *legal:* **6** cypres *occult:* **6** cabala, kabala **7** cabbala, kabbala **8** cabbalah, kabbalah *philosophical:* **8** monadism, vitalism *religious:* **8** chiliasm *suffix:* **3** ism

document **5** paper **6** record **8** evidence, monument **9** testimony **11** certificate *travel:* **8** passport

Dodavah's son **7** Eliezer

dodder **8** love vine

doddering **6** doting, senile

dodge **4** duck, jink, jouk, slip **5** avoid, elude, evade, fence, parry, shirk, skirt, slide **6** escape, scheme, weasel **7** evasion, shuffle **8** malinger, sidestep **9** avoidance, expedient, pussyfoot **10** equivocate, tergiverse **12** short circuit, tergiversate

dodger **7** haggler **8** circular, handbill **9** throwaway

Dodger **5** Davis (Tommy) **6** Garvey (Steve), Karros (Eric), Koufax (Sandy), Piazza (Michael), Snider (Duke), Sutton (Don) **8** Newcombe (Don), Robinson (Jackie) **9** Hershiser (Orel) **10** Campanella (Roy) *field:* **7** Ebbetts *manager:* **6** Alston (Walter) **7** Lasorda (Tommy)

dodo **4** boob, dolt **5** dummy, dunce, idiot, moron **6** dimwit, nitwit **8** numskull **9** simpleton

Dodo's son **7** Eleazar, Elhanan

doe **4** deer **6** almond *young:* **3** teg

doer *suffix:* **2** er, or **3** ast, eer, ier, ist **4** ater, ster

doff **5** douse, uncap, unhat **6** remove, unhelm **7** take off

dog **3** cur, pug, pup, tag **4** bird, chap, chow, fice, mutt, peke, puli, stop, tail, tyke **5** boxer, click, feist, frank, hound, lemon, pooch, puppy, spitz, trail **6** Afghan, bawtie, bowwow, briard, canine, collie, detent, poodle, rascal, saluki, shadow, wiener, wretch **7** andiron, Maltese, mastiff, mongrel, pointer, Samoyed, spaniel, terrier, whippet **8** Airedale, inferior, keeshond, papillon, Pekinese, pinscher, spurious, wirehair **9** Chihuahua, dachshund, Dalmation, Great Dane, greyhound, Pekingese, retriever, schnauzer **10** bloodhound, Pomeranian, Weimaraner **11** frankfurter, wienerwurst **12** Newfoundland, Saint Bernard **13** cocker spaniel *Alaskan:* **8** malamute, malemiut, malemute *Australian:* **5** dingo **8** warragal, warrigal *barkless:* **7** basenji *bird:* **6** setter **7** pointer, spaniel **9** retriever *Buster Brown's:* **4** Tige *Charlie Brown's:* **6** Snoopy *combining form:* **3** cyn **4** cyno *Dorothy's:* **4** Toto *Eskimo:* **5** husky *family:* **7** Canidae *FDR's:* **4** Fala *fictional:* **4** Lady **5** Astro, Pluto **6** Big Red **8** McBarker *"Garfield":* **4** Odie *genus:* **5** Canis *Hungarian:* **6** vizsla *hunting:* **4** alan **5** alant, hound **6** alaunt, beagle, borzoi, saluki, setter, Talbot **7** harrier, pointer, redbone **8** elkhound, foxhound **9** wolfhound **10** bloodhound **11** basset hound *Indian:* **5** dhole *L.B.J.'s:* **3** Her *long-bodied:* **9** dachshund *movie:* **4** Asta, Toto **5** Benji **9** Beethoven, Old Yeller, Rin Tin Tin *name:* **4** Fido, Spot **5** Rover **6** Bowser *Nixon's:* **8** Checkers *Odysseus's:* **5** Argos *of Hades:* **8** Cerberus *Orphan Annie's:* **5** Sandy *powerful:* **11** bull mastiff *Roy Rogers's:* **6** Bullet *Russian:* **6** borzoi **7** Samoyed *shaggy-*

coated: 8 komondor *short-legged:*
5 corgi *small:* 3 pom, pug, pup 4 alco,
peke 7 whiffet 8 Pekinese 9 Chihuahua,
Pekingese 10 Pomeranian *space traveler:*
5 Laika *Steinbeck's:* 7 Charley *television:*
4 King 5 Eddie, Tramp 6 Lassie, Murray
8 Wishbone 9 Rin Tin Tin *terrier:* 7 scottie
three-headed: 8 Cerberus *Tibetan:*
9 Lhasa apso *tiny:* 9 Chihuahua *tooth:*
4 fang *tracking:* 10 bloodhound *two-headed:* 6 Orthos *Welsh:* 5 corgi *Wendy's:* 4 Nana *young:* 3 pup 5 puppy,
whelp

dogbane 10 bitterroot

dog days 8 canicule

dogfall 3 tie 4 draw 8 deadlock, standoff
9 stalemate

dogfight 3 row 4 fray 5 brawl, broil,
melee, set-to 6 fracas 7 ruction 10 donny-brook, free-for-all

dogfish 6 bowfin, burbot 8 mud puppy
genus: 7 Squalus

dogged 5 rigid 7 adamant 8 obdurate
9 insistent, steadfast, unbending 10 brass-bound, inexorable, inflexible, persistent, per-sisting, persistive, relentless, unshakable
11 perseverant, persevering, unremitting
12 single-minded 13 perseverative

doggone 4 damn, darn, rank 5 utter
6 damned 7 blasted, blessed, dratted
8 absolute, infernal, outright 9 dad-burned,
out-and-out 10 confounded 11 unmitigated
13 blankety-blank

dogma 5 canon, credo, creed, tenet
6 belief 8 doctrine 10 conviction, persua-sion

dogmatic 7 a priori 8 reasoned 9 deduci-ble, deductive, derivable, dictative, doctrinal
11 dictatorial, doctrinaire, magisterial
13 authoritarian, authoritative

dog-paddle 4 swim

dog's age 3 eon 4 aeon, long 8 blue
moon, eternity 12 donkey's years

Dog Star 6 Sirius

dogwood 5 sumac 6 cornel 8 red osier
9 boobyalla 11 native broom

do in 4 ruin, slay 5 wreck 6 finish, murder
7 execute, exhaust, frazzle, outtire, out-wear, put away, wear out 8 bankrupt,
knock off, knock out 9 liquidate, prostrate,
shipwreck 10 dilapidate 11 assassinate

doing 3 act 6 action *combining form:*
6 praxes (plural), praxia, praxis *good:*
10 beneficent *suffix:* 3 ant, ent

doit 3 bit, jot 4 damn, dram, drop, hoot,
iota, whit 5 whoop 6 trifle 8 particle

doldrums 4 yawn 5 blues, dumps, ennui,
gloom, slump 6 apathy, tedium 7 boredom,
latency 8 abeyance, abeyancy, dormancy
9 dejection 10 depression, inactivity, quies-

cence, quiescency, stagnation 12 indiffer-ence, listlessness

doleful 4 down 7 piteous, pitiful, ruthful
8 cast down, dejected, downcast, grieving,
mournful, mourning, wretched 9 afflicted,
cheerless, depressed, miserable, plaintive,
sorrowful, sorrowing, woebegone 10 dispir-ited, lamentable, lugubrious, melancholy
11 crestfallen, downhearted 12 disconso-late

dole out 4 deal, mete 6 divide, parcel,
ration 7 mete out 8 disburse, dispense, dis-perse, share out 9 apportion, partition
10 administer, distribute

doll 3 Ken 6 Barbie, figure, Kewpie, puppet
10 Betsy Wetsy, Raggedy Ann 11 Rag-gedy Andy *grotesque:* 8 golliwog

dollar 4 bill, buck, oner 8 simoleon

dollop 3 nip, tot 4 dram, drop, jolt, shot,
slug 5 snort 7 snifter 8 toothful

Doll's House, A *author:* 5 Ibsen (Hen-rik) *heroine:* 4 Nora

dolly 4 cart 5 truck 7 stirrer

dolomite 6 marble 9 limestone 10 bitter
spar

dolor 5 agony 6 misery, sorrow 7 anguish,
passion 8 distress 9 suffering

dolorous 4 dire 6 rueful, woeful 7 ruthful
8 grievous, mournful, wretched 9 afflicted,
miserable, plaintive, sorrowful 10 afflictive,
calamitous, deplorable, lamentable, lugubri-ous, melancholy 11 distressing, regrettable
13 heartbreaking

dolphin 5 whale 7 bollard 8 porpoise
9 butterfly *combining form:* 7 delphis

dolt 3 ass, oaf 4 boob, clod, goof 5 booby,
chump, dunce 7 dullard, fathead, jughead,
saphead, schnook 8 dumnkopf, lunkhead,
meathead, numskull 9 blockhead *Scottish:*
4 coof

doltish 4 dull, dumb 5 dense, thick 6 stu-pid 8 blockish, duncical 9 fatheaded
11 blockheaded 12 beetleheaded

domain 4 walk 5 field, realm 6 sphere
7 demesne, terrain 8 dominion, province
9 bailiwick, champaign, territory *nether:*
4 hell *transcendent:* 6 heaven *Turkish:*
6 beylic, beylik

dome 4 roof 7 ceiling 12 snap fastener

domed hut 5 igloo

Domesday Book money 4 oras

domestic 4 home, tame 6 family, native
7 subdued 8 internal, national 9 house-hold, municipal 10 indigenous, submissive

domesticate 4 tame 5 adopt, train
6 master, subdue 10 housebreak, natural-ize 11 familiarize

domicile 3 hut 4 home 5 abode, board,
house, lodge, put up 6 bestow, billet, har-bor 7 quarter 8 dwelling 9 entertain, resi-

dence, residency 10 commorancy, habitation

domiciliate 3 hut 4 bunk, tame 5 board, house, lodge, put up 6 billet, harbor, master, reside 7 quarter

dominance 9 masterdom, supremacy 10 ascendancy, prepotence, prepotency 11 preeminence, sovereignty

dominant 4 main 5 chief, first, major 6 master, ruling 7 capital, leading, regnant, stellar, supreme 8 foremost 9 ascendant, governing, number one, paramount, prevalent, principal, sovereign 10 preeminent, prevailing, surpassing 11 outweighing, overbearing 12 overweighing, preponderant, transcendent 13 overbalancing

dominate 4 rule 5 reign 6 direct, govern, handle, manage, obsess 7 control, overtop, prevail, repress 8 domineer, look down, overarch, overlook, override 9 tower over 10 tower above *at home:* 12 wear the pants

domination 4 sway 5 might, power 7 command, control, mastery, strings 9 authority, masterdom, supremacy 10 ascendancy, prepotence, prepotency, suzerainty 11 preeminence, sovereignty 13 preponderancy

dominator 4 boss, cock, head 5 chief, ruler 6 honcho, leader, master 7 headman 8 hierarch 9 chieftain

domineer 4 rule 5 reign 7 prevail 11 predominate 12 preponderate

domineering 5 bossy 6 lordly 8 arrogant, imperial, insolent 9 imperious, masterful 10 highhanded, imperative, peremptory, tyrannical 11 magisterial

Dominican Republic *capital:* 12 Santo Domingo *island:* 10 Hispaniola *monetary unit:* 4 peso *product:* 5 cocoa, sugar 6 coffee 7 bauxite, tobacco

dominion 3 raj 4 rule, sway 5 field, realm, regna (plural) 6 domain, empery, regnum, sphere 7 demesne, terrain 8 property, province 9 ascendant, bailiwick, champaign, masterdom, ownership, supremacy, territory 10 ascendancy, possession, prepotence, prepotency 11 preeminence, proprietary, sovereignty 13 possessorship

domino 4 mask 5 amice, visor 6 vizard 9 doughface, false face *spot:* 3 pip

don 3 sir 4 lord, pull 5 get on, put on 6 assume, draw on, slip on, strike, take on 7 throw on 8 huddle on

Donalbain *brother:* 7 Malcolm *father:* 6 Duncan

Donar see Thor

donate 4 emit, give, loan 6 bestow, devote, hansel, supply 7 hand out, hand-sel, present 8 give away, transfer 10 contribute

donation 3 aid 4 alms, gift, help 5 grant 7 bequest, charity, handsel, subsidy 8 offering 9 endowment 10 assistance 11 beneficence 12 contribution

donator see donor

Don Camillo 6 priest

Don Carlos *author:* 8 Schiller (Friedrich von) *composer:* 5 Verdi (Giuseppe) *father:* 6 Philip

done 5 all in, ended, right, spent 6 decent, doomed, effete, gone by, proper, used up 7 correct, drained, dressed, far-gone, through, worn-out 8 becoming, complete, decorous, depleted, finished, washed-up 9 befitting, completed, concluded, exhausted, fitted out 10 conforming, terminated *for:* 4 gone, sunk 5 kaput 8 finished *poetic:* 3 o'er

donee 7 grantee 8 receiver 9 appointor, recipient

done in 5 spent 6 effete, used up 7 far-gone, worn-out 8 depleted 9 exhausted, washed-out

Don Giovanni composer 6 Mozart (Wolfgang Amadeus)

Donizetti *hero:* 7 Roberto *opera:* 5 Lucia 10 Anna Bolena, La Favorita 11 Don Pasquale 12 Maria Stuarda

Don Juan 4 rake, wolf 5 Romeo 6 chaser, masher 7 amorist, gallant 8 Casanova, lothario, paramour 9 ladies' man, libertine, philander, womanizer 10 lady-killer, profligate 11 philanderer *drama:* 13 The Stone Guest *home:* 7 Seville *mother:* 4 Inez *poet:* 5 Byron (Lord)

donkey 3 ass 4 fool, jerk 5 burro, idiot 7 jackass 8 imbecile 10 nincompoop *female:* 5 jenny

donkey's years 3 age 4 aeon 7 dog's age 8 blue moon, coon's age, eternity

donkeywork 4 moil, toil 5 grind, labor 6 drudge 7 slavery 8 drudgery, plugging

Donner see Thor

donnybrook 4 fray 5 brawl, fight, melee, set-to 6 affray, fracas 7 bobbery, ruction 10 free-for-all

donor 5 giver 7 donator, granter, grantor 8 bestower 9 conferrer, presenter 11 contributor

do-nothing 3 bum 4 slug 5 idler 6 loafer, slouch 8 dolittle, fainéant, slugabed, sluggard 9 lazybones

Don Quixote *author:* 9 Cervantes (Miguel de) *beloved:* 8 Dulcinea *companion:* 11 Sancho Panza *giant:* 8 windmill *home:* 6 La Mancha *horse:* 9 Rocinante, Rosinante, Rozinante *squire:* 11 Sancho Panza

doodad 5 gizmo 6 dingus, gadget, jigger
7 do-funny, thingum, trinket 9 doohickey,
rigamajig, thingummy 10 thingumbob
11 thingumajig

doodle 3 ass, toy 4 fool, jerk, mess
5 cheat, idiot, ninny 6 donkey, fiddle, potter, puddle, putter, tinker, trifle 7 jackass
8 imbecile, scribble 10 mess around, nincompoop

doohickey see doodad

doom 3 lot 4 damn, fate 5 moira, weird
6 decree, kismet 7 condemn, destine, destiny, portion, preform, tragedy 8 calamity,
disaster, sentence 9 cataclysm, determine,
ordinance, preordain, proscribe 10 foreordain, predestine 11 catastrophe 12 circumstance, last judgment, predetermine

doomful 4 dire 7 baleful, baneful, direful,
ominous, unlucky 9 ill-boding 10 portentous 11 apocalyptic 12 inauspicious,
unpropitious

doomsayer 7 killjoy 9 Cassandra, pessimist 11 crepehanger

____ Doone 5 Lorna

door 3 way 4 adit 5 entry 6 access,
entrée, portal 7 gateway, ingress, opening
8 entrance, entryway 9 admission
10 admittance 11 entranceway *rear:*
7 postern

doorkeeper 6 porter 7 gateman, ostiary

doormat 7 milksop 8 sufferer, weakling
9 jellyfish 10 namby-pamby, pantywaist
11 Milquetoast, mollycoddle

doorway 5 entry 6 portal 8 entrance,
entryway 11 entranceway *column:* 7 tru-
meau 8 trumeaux (plural)

dope 4 drug 5 dunce, noddy 6 doctor, heroin, nitwit, noddle, opiate, sedate 7 cocaine
8 narcotic 9 lamebrain, marijuana 10 dunderhead 11 chowderhead, chucklehead,
preparation 12 spinning bath

doped 4 high 6 stoned, zonked 7 drugged
8 hopped-up, turned on 9 spaced-out
10 tripped out

dope up 4 load 6 debase, doctor, weight
10 adulterate 12 sophisticate

dopey 5 heavy 6 stupid, torpid
7 bemused, fuddled 8 comatose, sluggish
9 lethargic 10 slumberous 12 hebetudinous

dor 6 beetle

Doric Zeus 3 Zan

Doris *brother:* 6 Nereus *daughters:*
7 Nereids *father:* 7 Oceanus *husband:*
6 Nereus

dormancy 7 latency 8 abeyance, dia-
pause, doldrums 10 quiescence, quiescency, suspension 11 cold storage
12 intermission, interruption

dormant 6 drowsy, latent 7 abeyant, lurking, relaxed 8 immobile, inactive, sluggish

9 lethargic, potential, prepatent, quiescent
10 slow-moving 13 unprogressive

dormer 6 window

dorry 4 boat

dorsal 6 aboral 7 abaxial *combining
form:* 6 opisth 7 opistho

____ d'Orsay 4 Quai

dorsum 4 back

Dorus *brother:* 6 Aeolus *father:* 6 Hellen

dose 7 measure, portion 8 quantity
10 proportion

Dos Passos trilogy 3 U.S.A.

dot 4 mark, mote, stud 5 dower, dowry,
point, speck 6 bestud, pepper, period, pimple 7 freckle, speckle, stipple 8 fly-speck,
sprinkle 9 bespeckle 11 intersperse
12 decimal point

dotage 8 senility 11 elderliness, senectitude

dote on 4 like 5 adore, enjoy, fancy 7 idolize, worship

doting 4 dear, fond 5 silly 6 loving, senile
7 asinine, devoted, doddery, fatuous, foolish 8 imbecile, lovesome, overfond 9 doddering 12 affectionate 13 over-indulgent

dotted 6 spotty 8 cribbled, punctate,
stippled *with stars:* 4 semé

dotty 5 crazy, loony, wacky 6 absurd,
insane 7 foolish 8 besotted, enamored
9 eccentric, fantastic, infatuate 10 infatuated, ridiculous 12 feebleminded, preposterous

double 3 dub, shy, yaw 4 bend, bilk, copy,
dual, duck, dupe, fold, mate, shun, tack,
turn, twin 5 avoid, duple, elude, evade,
image, match, shift 6 bifold, binary, clench,
duplex, escape, eschew, paired, ringer,
wraith 7 dualize, enlarge, magnify, two-fold
8 increase 9 companion, deceitful, deviation, dualistic, duplicate, insincere, replicate
10 coordinate, deflection, reciprocal, simulacrum, understudy 12 ambidextrous, hypocritical 13 spitting image *combining form:*
2 di 3 bin 4 dipl, diss 5 diphy, diplo, disso
prefix: 2 bi 3 dis

double agent 3 spy

double-barreled 4 dual 5 duple 6 bifold,
binary, duplex 7 twofold 9 dualistic

double bass 10 bull fiddle

double-cross 4 sell 5 bluff 6 betray,
humbug, illude, juggle, take in 7 beguile,
deceive, mislead, sell out 8 betrayal 9 four-
flush

doubled *combining form:* 3 bis

double dagger 6 diesis

double-dealer 3 gyp 5 cheat 6 con man
7 diddler, sharper 8 swindler 9 defrauder
10 mountebank 11 flimflammer 13 confidence man

double-dealing 5 fraud 7 chicane
8 mala fide, trickery 9 chicanery, deception,

duplicity, fourberie, insincere 10 hanky-panky, left-handed 11 highbinding 12 ambidextrous, hypocritical 13 sharp practice

double-dome 7 Brahmin, egghead 8 highbrow 12 intellectual

double-edged 5 vague 7 obscure, unclear 9 ambiguous, ancipital, equivocal, tenebrous, uncertain

double entendre 9 ambiguity, equivoque 11 amphibology 12 equivocality, equivocation

double-faced 5 vague 7 obscure, unclear 8 mala fide 9 ambiguous, equivocal, insincere, tenebrous, uncertain 10 left-handed 12 ambidextrous, hypocritical

double fold 5 pleat

double meaning see double entendre

double-minded 7 halting 8 hesitant, wavering 10 hesitating, indecisive, irresolute, undecisive 11 vacillating 12 ambidextrous, hypocritical

doublet 3 duo 4 dyad, pair 5 brace 6 couple, jacket 7 twosome

double-talk 4 jazz 5 hokum 6 bunkum, drivel 7 twaddle 8 flimflam, newspeak, nonsense 9 gibberish 10 balderdash 12 gobbledygook

double vision 8 diplopia

doubly *prefix:* 2 bi

doubt 5 qualm 6 wonder 7 concern, dispute, dubiety, misgive, perhaps, suspect, swither 8 distrust, mistrust, question, unbelief 9 challenge, disbelief, dubiosity, suspicion 10 skepticism 11 dubiousness, incertitude, incredulity, uncertainty, uncertitude

doubtable 4 open 7 dubious, suspect 9 ambiguous, equivocal, undecided 10 borderline 11 problematic

doubter 7 skeptic, zetetic 10 headshaker, Pyrrhonian, Pyrrhonist, unbeliever

doubtful 4 hazy, iffy, moot, open 5 fishy, shady, shaky 6 chancy, queasy, uneasy, unsure 7 clouded, dubious, obscure, suspect, unclear 8 arguable, insecure, mootable, unlikely, unstable, wavering 9 ambiguous, debatable, dubitable, equivocal, uncertain, undecided, unsettled 10 borderline, contingent, disputable, hesitating, improbable, impugnable, indecisive, precarious, suspicious, touch-and-go 11 problematic, speculative 12 questionable

doubtfulness 7 concern, dubiety 8 mistrust 9 dubiosity, dubitancy, suspicion 10 skepticism 11 uncertainty, uncertitude

doubting Thomas see doubter

doubtless 4 sure 6 easily, likely 7 certain 8 probably 9 assumably 10 absolutely, definitely, positively, presumably 13 presumptively, unequivocally

doubtlessly 4 well 5 truly 6 easily, indeed, really 8 provenly 10 absolutely, definitely, positively 11 undoubtedly 13 unequivocally

douceur 4 gift 7 present 8 gratuity

dough 4 cash 5 bread, money 8 currency 11 legal tender *cooked in honey:* 8 taiglach, teiglach *inflator:* 5 yeast

doughboy 11 infantryman

doughty 4 able, bold 5 brave, manly 6 plucky, spunky, strong 7 valiant 8 fearless, unafraid 9 dauntless, undaunted

doughy 4 ashy, pale 5 ashen, livid, lurid, waxen 6 pallid 8 blanched 9 colorless

do up 3 fix 4 mend, wrap 5 patch 6 doctor, repair, revamp 7 rebuild 8 overhaul 11 recondition, reconstruct

dour 4 glum, grim, hard, ugly 5 bleak, harsh, rigid, sulky, surly 6 dogged, gloomy, morose, severe, strict, sullen 7 austere, crabbed 8 rigorous 9 saturnine, stringent 10 forbidding, implacable, unyielding

douse 3 bat, bop, dip, out, sop, wet 4 doff, duck, dunk, slop, soak 5 bathe, drown, lower, plash, slosh, swash, throw 6 deluge, drench, put off, put out, quench, remove, splash, splosh 7 immerse, slacken, spatter, splurge, spurtle, take off 8 downpour, splatter, submerge, submerse 9 drenching 10 extinguish

douzeper 4 Ivon, Oton 5 Gerin, Ivory, peers 6 Anseis, Gerard, Gerier, Oliver, Roland, Samson 7 Olivier, paladin 8 Engelier 9 Berengier

dove 6 culver, pigeon 8 pacifist 10 pacificist *call:* 3 coo *genus:* 7 Columba

dovecote 6 aviary 8 pigeonry 9 birdhouse, columbary 11 culver house, pigeon house

dovehouse see dovecote

dovelike 4 mild, pure 6 gentle 7 lovable 9 columbine

dovetail 4 jibe 5 agree, fit in, tally 6 accord, square 8 check out 9 harmonize 10 correspond 13 interlock with

dovish 7 antiwar 8 pacifist 10 pacifistic

dowager 4 dame 6 matron 9 matriarch 10 grande dame

dowdy 4 drab, slut 5 dated, passé, tacky 6 blowsy, bygone, démodé, frowsy, frumpy, old hat, sordid, stodgy 7 archaic, traipse, vintage 8 frumpish, outdated, outmoded, slattern, slovenly 9 out-of-date, unstylish 10 antiquated, slatternly 11 draggle-tail 12 old-fashioned 13 draggletailed *woman:* 5 frump

dowel 3 pin, rod 5 stick

dower 3 dot 5 endow, endue 6 talent 9 crown with, endowment

dowitcher 5 snipe 8 grayback 9 brownback

down 3 bad, fur, ill, low, off, out 4 best, blue, done, drop, fell, flue, fuzz, kilt, lick, lint, pile, sick, slow 5 below, ended, floor, floss, fluff, fully, level, lower, outdo, scrag, slack, throw, under, worst 6 cut off, defeat, fallen, finish, hipped, hurdle, lay low, master, nether 7 conquer, descent, destroy, flatten, for real, handout, swallow, through 8 actively, at hazard, bowl over, carry off, complete, consumed, defeated, dejected, dispatch, feathers, finished, inferior, lay aside, overcome, sluggish, suppress, surmount 9 completed, concluded, depressed, earnestly, earthward, liquidate, processed, seriously, subjacent 10 completely, dispirited, groundward, terminated, vigorously 11 netherwards 12 discomfiture *combining form:* 4 ptil 5 ptilo *prefix:* 2 de 3 cat, hyp, kat 4 cata, cath, cato, hypo, kata

down-and-outer 6 beggar, pauper, wretch

down-at-heel 5 seedy, tacky 6 shabby, tagrag 7 rundown 8 tattered 10 bedraggled, broken down, threadbare 11 dilapidated

downcast 3 bad, low, sad 4 blue, dull, glum, rout, sunk 5 moody, mopey, shaft 6 defeat, droopy, gloomy, hipped, morose 7 beating, debacle, doleful, forlorn, licking 8 dejected, drubbing, listless, soul-sick, troubled 9 depressed, heartsick, heartsore, oppressed, overthrow, woebegone 10 chapfallen, defeasance, despondent, dispirited, distressed, spiritless 11 crestfallen, discouraged, low-spirited 12 disconsolate, disheartened

downcry 5 abuse 8 belittle, derogate, diminish, discount 9 disparage, dispraise 10 depreciate 11 detract from

downfall 4 bane, ruin 7 atrophy, decline, descent, undoing 9 decadence, destroyer, ruination 10 declension, degeneracy, devolution 11 declination, destruction 12 degeneration, dégringolade 13 deterioration

downgrade 4 bump, bust 5 break, decry, lower 6 demote, reduce 7 atrophy, declass, decline, demerit, devalue, disrate 8 mark down, write off 9 decadence, devaluate, write down 10 declension, degeneracy, depreciate, devalorize, devolution, undervalue 12 degeneration, dégringolade 13 deterioration

downhearted see **downcast**

down-in-the-mouth see **downcast**

down payment 7 deposit, earnest

downpour 4 rain 6 deluge 8 rainfall 9 drenching 10 cloudburst

down quilt 5 duvet

downright 4 flat, very 5 gross, plain, utter 8 absolute, complete, positive 9 out-and-

out, up-and-down 10 sure-enough 11 indubitable, unmitigated 13 thoroughgoing

downslide 3 dip, sag 4 drop, slip 5 slump 7 decline, falloff

downstage area 5 apron

downstairs 5 below 8 servants

downswing see **downslide**

down-to-earth 4 hard 5 sober 9 practical, pragmatic, realistic 10 hard-boiled, hardheaded 11 unfantastic 12 matter-of-fact, unidealistic

downtown sign 6 Main St.

downtrend see **downslide**

downtrodden 6 abject, abused 9 oppressed, underfoot 10 maltreated, mistreated, persecuted

downturn see **downslide**

downward 8 debasing 9 declining 10 descending, netherward *combining form:* 4 bath 5 batho

downwardly, downwards see **downward**

downy 4 soft 6 fluffy 8 feathery, soothing *combining form:* 4 hebe *filler:* 5 eider

doxy 3 ism 4 tart 5 creed, wench 6 harlot 7 opinion, trollop 8 doctrine

doyen 4 dean, lead 5 guide, maven, pilot 6 artist, expert, leader, master 8 virtuoso 9 authority 10 bellwether, master-hand, past master, proficient 12 passed master

Doyle's detective 6 Holmes

D'Oyly Carte offering 8 operetta

doze 3 nap 5 sleep 6 catnap, drowse 7 drop off, slumber 9 drowse off

dozy see **drowsy**

DP 6 émigré 7 evacuee, refugee 8 fugitive

drab 3 hag 4 bawd, dowd, dull, flat, slut, trot 5 biddy, bleak, crone, dingy, dowdy, faded, mousy, muddy, murky, prosy, wench, whore, witch 6 beldam, dismal, dreary, harlot, mousey 7 hustler, prosaic, subfusc, traipse 8 desolate, dullness, lifeless, slattern 9 cheerless, colorless 10 lackluster, lusterless, prostitute 11 dispiriting, draggle-tail, fille de joie, nightwalker 12 streetwalker

draconian 5 harsh, rigid 6 strict 8 rigorist, rigorous 9 stringent 10 ironhanded 12 unpermissive

Dracula author 6 Stoker (Bram)

draffy 6 drossy, no-good 7 inutile, nothing 8 unworthy 9 valueless, worthless

draft 3 tap 4 dose, plan, plot, pull, pump, swig 5 check, claim, drink, frame, press, swill, taper 6 call up, demand, design, devise, drench, enroll, induct, potion, scheme, siphon, sketch 7 compose, concoct, current, draught, harness, impress, outline, portion, prepare, project 8 block out, chalk out, contrive, muster in, rough out, skeleton, traction 9 adumbrate, allowance, conscribe, conscript, fabricate, formulate, muster out **11** delineation, skeletonize **12** characterize *avoider:* **6** dodger *of a law:* **4** bill

drag **3** lug, peg, tow, tug **4** hang, haul, poke, puff, pull, swig **5** dally, delay, draft, drain, drink, float, swill, tarry, trail **6** burden, daggle, dawdle, drench, harrow, loiter, put off, schlep, search, strain **7** ransack, sagging, schlepp, skidpan, traipse **8** drooping, friction **9** lag behind, sea anchor **10** conveyance **11** inclination **13** procrastinate *off:* **4** cart

dragging **4** long **7** lengthy, tedious **8** drawn-out, longsome, overlong **9** prolonged **10** protracted **12** long-drawn-out

draggle **5** trail **7** shuffle, traipse **8** besmirch

draggle-tail **4** dowd, drab, slut **5** dowdy **7** traipse **8** slattern

draggletailed **5** dowdy **6** blowsy, frowsy, sordid, untidy **8** slattern, sluttish **10** slatternly

dragnet **5** trawl

dragon **5** beast, Satan **6** wivern **8** basilisk **9** water arum **10** cockatrice *Babylonian:* **6** Tiamat *biblical:* **5** Rahab *Canaanite:* **3** Yam **4** Yamm **5** Lotan *Chinese:* **4** lung *French:* **8** Tarasque *genus:* **5** Draco *Greek:* **5** Ladon **9** Eurythion *horse:* **6** Fafner, Fafnir *slayer:* **4** Baal, Enki, Zeus **5** Indra **6** Cadmus, Marduk, Sigurd, Yahweh **7** Beowulf, Jupiter, Ninurta, Perseus **8** St. George **9** St. Michael **10** St. Margaret *Sumerian:* **3** Kur *two-legged:* **5** wiver **6** wivern, wyvern *Vedic:* **3** Ahi **6** Vritra

dragoon **3** cow **5** bully **6** harass, hector **8** browbeat, bulldoze, bullyrag **9** persecute, strong-arm, terrorize **10** cavalryman, intimidate

drag race entry **6** hot rod

drain **3** tap **4** jade, pump, sink, sump, swig, tire, vent, wear **5** bleed, draft, drink, empty, leech, sewer, swill, use up, weary **6** burden, drench, gutter, siphon, trench **7** conduit, deplete, draw off, exhaust, fatigue **8** bankrupt, draw down, wear down **9** discharge **10** impoverish **11** watercourse *transverse:* **7** culvert

drain away **5** abate, close, taper **6** lessen, reduce **7** dwindle **8** decrease, diminish, taper off

drained **5** all-in, spent **6** bleary, effete, used up **7** far-gone, worn-out **8** depleted **9** exhausted, washed-out

drainpipe **5** spout **9** downspout

drain pit **4** sump

dram **3** bit, nip, tot **4** dash, drop, hoot, iota, jolt, mite, shot, slug, spot, swig **5** crumb, draft, drink, ounce, shred, snort, swill **6** dollop **7** modicum, smidgen, snifter, snorter **8** particle, potation, toothful

drama **4** play **6** boards **7** theater, theatre **8** the stage **10** footlights *award:* **4** Tony *former English:* **6** masque *Japanese:* **3** Noh *main part:* **8** epitasis *musical:* **5** opera **8** operetta *suspenseful:* **11** cliffhanger

dramatic **8** striking, theatral, theatric, thespian **10** histrionic, theatrical *conflict:* **4** agon *scene:* **4** skit

dramatis personae **4** cast

dramatist **10** playwright *American:* **4** Hart (Moss), Inge (William), Rice (Elmer), Uhry (Alfred) **5** Albee (Edward), Mamet (David), Odets (Clifford), Payne (John Howard), Simon (Neil) **6** Miller (Arthur), O'Neill (Eugene), Thomas (Augustus), Wilson (August, Lanford, Robert) **7** Hellman (Lillian), Kaufman (George S.) **8** Anderson (Maxwell, Robert), Sherwood (Robert), Williams (Tennessee) **11** Hammerstein (Oscar), Wasserstein (Wendy) *Austrian:* **10** Schnitzler (Arthur) *Belgian:* **11** Maeterlinck (Maurice) *English:* **3** Fry (Christopher), Gay (John) **4** Rowe (Nicholas), Tate (Nahum) **5** Milne (Alan Alexander), Peele (George), Wilde (Oscar) **6** Coward (Noël), Jonson (Ben), Pinero (Arthur), Pinter (Harold), Steele (Richard), Storey (David) **7** Marlowe (Christopher), Marston (John), Osborne (John), Shaffer (Peter), Webster (John) **8** Congreve (William), Shadwell (Thomas), Stoppard (Tom), Tourneur (Cyril), Vanbrugh (John), Zangwill (Israel) **9** Middleton (Thomas), Wycherley (William) **11** Shakespeare (William) *French:* **5** Camus (Albert), Genet (Jean) **6** Musset (Alfred de), Racine (Jean), Sardou (Victorien), Sartre (Jean-Paul), Scribe (Eugène) **7** Anouilh (Jean), Ionesco (Eugène), Labiche (Eugène-Marin), Molière, Rostand (Edmond) **8** Marivaux (Pierre) **9** Corneille (Pierre), Giraudoux (Jean) **12** Beaumarchais (Pierre-Augustin Caron de) *German:* **5** Weiss (Peter) **6** Brecht (Bertolt), Goethe (Johann Wolfgang von), Kleist (Heinrich von) **8** Schiller (Friedrich von) **9** Hauptmann (Gerhart), Zuckmayer (Carl) *Greek:* **8** Menander **9** Aeschylus, Euripides, Sophocles **12** Aristophanes *Hindu:* **8** Kalidasa *Irish:* **4** Shaw (George Bernard) **5** Behan (Brendan), Yeats (William Butler) **6** O'Casey (Sean) **8** Sheridan (Richard Brinsley) *Italian:* **7** Alfieri (Vittorio), Giacosa (Giuseppe), Goldoni (Carlo) **8** Trissino (Gian Giorgio) *Japanese:* **5** Zeami *Norwegian:* **5** Ibsen (Henrik) **8** Bjornson (Bjornstjerne Martinius) *Roman:* **7** Plautus, Terence *Russian:* **7** Chekhov (Anton) **8** Zamyatin

(Yevgeny) *Spanish:* 4 Vega (Lope de)
8 Quintero (Serafin, Joaquin) 11 Garcia
Lorca (Federico) *Swedish:* 5 Sachs (Nelly)
10 Strindberg (August) *Swiss:* 6 Frisch
(Max)

dramaturge see dramatist
dramaturgic see dramatic
drape 4 roll 5 adorn, cover 6 enfold,
enwrap, sprawl, swathe, wrap up 7 curtain,
swaddle 8 enswathe, envelope, spraddle,
swathe in 11 spread-eagle
drapery 7 curtain 8 hangings
drastic 6 severe 7 extreme, radical 8 rigorous, vigorous 9 purgative
Dravidian language 5 Gondi, Khond,
Malto, Tamil 6 Brahui, Kurukh, Telugu
8 Kanarese 9 Malayalam
draw 3 gut, lug, pen, tap, tie, tow, tug, win
4 call, edge, gain, haul, limn, lure, make,
move, odds, puff, pull, pump, rise, sink,
take, wile 5 alter, angle, bowel, bulge,
charm, draft, drain, educe, evoke, infer,
judge, paint, start, steep, taper, use up
6 allure, appeal, coulee, crayon, deduce,
derive, elicit, entice, extend, gather, indite,
induce, infuse, inhale, paunch, pencil,
prompt, pucker, seduce, siphon, sketch
7 attract, bewitch, collect, deplete, dogfall,
enchant, exhaust, extract, make out, prolong, spin out, stencil, stipple, stretch, vantage, win over 8 bankrupt, conclude, contract, convince, dead heat, deadlock,
elongate, handicap, lengthen, persuade,
protract, standoff 9 advantage, allowance,
argue into, captivate, delineate, drain away,
fascinate, formulate, head start, magnetize,
represent, seduction, stalemate 10 allurement, attraction, disembowel, eviscerate,
exenterate, impoverish, prolongate 11 bring
around *forth:* 5 educe 6 elicit 7 extract
from: 4 milk, pump 5 bleed *the main features of:* 4 etch 6 sketch 7 outline
together: 3 tie 4 join, lace
draw back 5 wince 6 deduct, recede,
recoil, retire 7 retreat, take off, take out
8 discount, knock off, subtract, take away
9 substract
drawback 6 defect, refund 7 trouble
8 handicap 9 detriment, hindrance 10 disability 12 disadvantage 13 inconvenience
draw down 3 get, win 4 earn, gain, make
5 drain, use up 7 acquire, bring in, deplete,
exhaust 8 bankrupt 10 impoverish
drawer 9 draftsman *for money:* 4 till
draw in 3 get 6 induce, prompt 7 win over
8 convince, persuade, talk into 9 argue
into, prevail on 11 bring around, prevail
upon
drawing 4 plan 6 sketch 8 alluring,
charming, magnetic 9 appealing 10 attract-

ing, attractive, bewitching, enchanting
11 captivating, fascinating *combining form:*
4 gram *humorous:* 7 cartoon
drawing power 4 call, lure, pull 6 appeal
9 seduction 10 allurement, attraction
drawing room 5 salon 6 saloon 9 reception
drawn 4 worn 7 haggard, pinched 8 careworn
drawn-out 4 long 7 lengthy 8 dragging,
extended, longsome, overlong 9 prolonged
10 protracted
draw off 3 tap 4 pump 5 bleed, draft,
drain 6 remove, siphon, syphon 8 withdraw
draw on 3 don 5 cause 6 assume, effect,
induce, prompt, secure 7 produce, win over
8 convince, persuade, talk into 9 argue into
10 bring about 11 bring around, prevail
upon
draw out 6 extend, remove 7 extract, prolong, stretch 8 elongate, lengthen, protract
10 prolongate
draw up 4 halt, make, stop 5 draft, frame
7 prepare 9 formulate
dray 4 cart 7 travois 9 stoneboat
dray horse 4 peon 5 slave 6 drudge,
slavey, toiler 11 galley slave
dread 4 fear 5 alarm, panic 6 dismay,
fright, horror, terror 7 anxiety 9 trepidity
11 frightening, trepidation 13 consternation
combining form: 5 phobe 6 phobia, phobic 7 phobous
dreadful 5 awful 6 tragic 7 direful,
extreme, fearful, shocker 8 horrible, horrific, shocking, terrible, terrific 9 appalling,
dime novel, frightful, revolting, unrefined
10 formidable, unpleasant, yellowback
11 frightening
dreadfully 4 very 6 damned 8 horribly
9 extremely 10 strikingly 11 exceedingly
12 surpassingly 13 frighteningly
dreadnought 10 battleship
dream 4 ache, long, lust, moon, pine, sigh
5 crave, fancy, ideal 6 bubble, hanker, hunger, thirst, vision 7 chimera, fantasy, imagine, rainbow, reverie, suspire 8 illusion,
phantasm, phantasy 9 nightmare 10 conceive of *combining form:* 4 onir 5 oneir,
oniro 6 oneiro *god:* 8 Morpheus *interpreter:* 12 oneirocritic
dreamer 6 mystic 7 utopian 8 idealist,
theorist 9 ideologue, visionary 10 Don
Quixote, lotus-eater 11 illusionist 13 castle-builder
dreamlike 5 vague 7 shadowy, surreal
8 nebulous
Dream of Gerontius composer
5 Elgar (Edward)
dream up 5 frame, hatch 6 devise, invent
7 concoct 8 contrive 9 formulate

dreamy 4 hazy, idle 5 ideal, nifty, super, vague 6 astral, divine, groovy, peachy 8 fanciful, glorious, pleasing, romantic 9 marvelous, unworldly, visionary, whimsical 10 delightful, idealistic, indistinct 12 otherworldly

dreary 4 blah, dull, poky 5 black, bleak 6 dismal, gloomy, somber, stodgy 7 forlorn, humdrum 8 banausic, funereal, monotone 10 depressing, depressive, enervating, monotonous, oppressive, pedestrian 11 dispiriting 12 discouraging *Scottish:* 5 dowie

dreck 4 junk 5 offal, swill 6 litter, refuse 7 garbage, rubbish 12 outsweepings

dredge 3 dig 5 scoop 6 deepen, search 8 excavate

dregs 3 mob 4 lees, scum 5 trash 6 masses, rabble 7 deposit, grounds 8 canaille, riffraff, sediment, unwashed 9 settlings 11 precipitate, proletariat 13 precipitation

Dreiser *character:* 5 Clyde 6 Carrie, Sondra 7 Roberta 10 Cowperwood *novel:* 8 The Stoic, The Titan 9 The Genius 12 The Financier 17 An American Tragedy

drench 3 sop, wet 4 drag, dunk, lash, pour, soak, swig, teem, wash 5 douse, draft, drain, drink, drouk, drown, souse, steep, swill 6 deluge, seethe, sodden 7 immerse, overwet, pervade 8 oversoak, saturate, submerge, waterlog 10 impregnate

dress 3 gut, rig, tan 4 bind, clad, deck, doll, duds, garb, gown, sack, tend, till, togs, trim, work 5 adorn, align, array, clean, frock, getup, guise, habit, prank, smock 6 attire, bedeck, clothe, dirndl, enrobe, outfit, sacque, setout, tailor 7 apparel, bandage, bedizen, chemise, clothes, costume, garment, garnish, raiment, turnout 8 beautify, beclothe, clothing, covering, decorate, enclothe, ornament 9 cultivate, embellish, make ready 10 attirement 11 habiliments *a wound:* 7 bandage *designer:* 4 Dior (Christian) 12 Saint-Laurent (Yves) *extravagantly:* 8 overdeck *finically:* 5 primp *hair:* 6 barber *Hawaiian:* 6 muumuu *leather:* 3 taw *line:* 3 hem *mode of:* 5 habit *of the clergy:* 5 cloth *oriental:* 9 cheongsam *South Seas:* 6 sarong *with the beak:* 5 preen *with vulgarity:* 7 bedizen

dress down 4 lash, rail 5 scold 6 berate 7 bawl out, tell off 10 tongue-lash

dresser 5 chest 6 bureau 10 chiffonier 11 flour bolter *gaudy:* 9 butterfly

dressing 5 sauce 6 catsup 7 bandage, catchup, ketchup 8 stuffing *salad:* 6 French 7 Italian, Russian 10 blue cheese

dressing room 8 vestiary *church:* 6 vestry

dressmaker 6 tailor 7 modiste 9 couturier 10 seamstress

dress up 3 tog 4 clad, mask, smug, tart 5 array, cloak, prank, preen, primp, slick, spiff 6 attire, clothe, tog out 7 apparel, deck out, doll out, smarten 8 disguise, enclothe, prettify, trick off, trick out 9 dissemble 10 camouflage 11 dissimulate

dressy 4 chic 6 formal, frilly, ornate 7 elegant, stylish 9 elaborate

Dreyfus' defender 4 Zola (Émile)

drib 4 drop, weep 5 trill 6 gobbet 7 distill, droplet, globule, trickle

dribble 4 blow, drip, drop, weep 5 drool, trill, waste 6 drivel, slaver 7 consume, distill, fritter, slabber, slobber, trickle 8 pittance, salivate, squander 9 throw away 10 frivol away, trifle away 11 blunder away

driblet 4 drop 6 gobbet 7 globule 8 pittance

dried acorns 6 camata 8 camatina

dried brick 5 adobe

dried coconut meat 5 copra

dried grape 6 raisin

dried grass 3 hay

dried meat 5 jerky 7 charqui 8 pemmican

dried orchid tubers 5 salep

dried plum 5 prune

drift 3 bat, gad, run 4 bank, bent, cock, flow, flux, heap, hill, mass, mope, pile, ride, roam, rush, sail, skid, skim, tide, wash 5 amble, coast, creep, dance, float, flood, mosey, mound, range, shock, shoot, slant, slide, spate, stack, stray, tenor, trend 6 bummel, linger, motion, ramble, stream, stroll, upwaft, wander 7 current, leaning, maunder, meander, meaning, purport, pyramid, saunter 8 mountain, movement, penchant, sideslip, tendency 9 deviation, gallivant, inclining, substance 10 partiality, propensity 11 disposition, inclination, progression 12 predilection *languidly:* 5 swoon *of a ship:* 6 leeway *unstratified:* 4 till

drifter 3 bum, vag 4 hobo 5 rover, tramp 6 roamer 7 floater, rambler, vagrant 8 derelict, vagabond, wanderer 9 meanderer 10 street arab, temporizer 12 rolling stone

driftwood 6 jetsam 7 flotsam 8 wreckage

drill 4 bore, skid 5 prick, punch, snail 6 pierce 7 wildcat 8 exercise, practice, practise, puncture, rehearse, sideslip 9 penetrate, perforate 10 discipline *command:* 6 at ease 8 left face 9 about face, attention, right face

drink 3 ade, nip, sea, sip, tea 4 brew, deep, drag, grog, gulp, soak, swig, tope, toss 5 booze, draft, drain, julep, ocean,

quaff, slosh, slurp, sup up, swill, toast
6 absorb, drench, guzzle, imbibe, jigger, liquid, liquor, pledge, potion, sup off, tank up,
tipple **7** potable, spirits, swallow, swizzle
8 aperitif, beverage, libation, liquor up
9 aqua vitae *after-dinner:* **6** frappe *British:*
5 spree *drugged:* **6** mickey *honey:*
4 mead *hot:* **5** toddy **6** saloop *liquor:*
6 booze *mixed:* **3** nog **5** zombi **6** zombie
mixer: **7** swirler *noisily:* **5** slurp *of liquor:*
4 dram, shot **5** snort **8** highball *of the
gods:* **6** nectar *Scottish:* **6** waught *soft:*
7 soda pop *stimulating:* **6** bracer *tall:*
4 fizz (see also **beverage**)

drinkable 6 liquor **7** potable **8** beverage
drinkery 3 bar, pub **4** café **6** lounge,
saloon, tavern **7** barroom, taproom
drinking 8 potation *fountain:* **7** bubbler
horn: **6** rhyton *spree:* **5** binge **6** bender
8 carousal
drip 4 weep **5** trill **7** distill, dribble, spatter,
spurtle, trickle **8** sprinkle
dripping 3 wet **5** runny, soppy **6** soaked,
sodden, soused **7** soaking **8** drenched
9 saturated **11** wringing-wet
drippy 5 mushy, rainy, sappy, sobby,
soupy **6** slushy, sobful **7** drizzly, maudlin,
mawkish **11** sentimental
drive 2 go **3** dig, pep, ram, run, sic, tug
4 auto, bang, dash, élan, goad, herd, moil,
move, prod, push, ride, road, roll, sink,
snap, spin, spur, stab, taxi, toil, tool, trip,
turn, urge **5** burst, chase, defer, force,
getup, grave, guide, impel, labor, lunge,
motor, pilot, pitch, pound, punch, shove,
stamp, steer, stick, surge, tract, vigor,
wheel, whirl **6** attack, coerce, compel, convey, exhort, hammer, plunge, propel, strain,
strike, strive, thrust **7** actuate, impetus,
impress, joyride, operate, produce **8** ambition, mobilize, momentum, navigate, protract, shepherd, vitality **9** chauffeur, excursion, impelling, urge along **10** charioteer,
enterprise, get-up-and-go, initiative *air:*
4 blow *away:* **4** shoo **5** exile, stave
6 aroint *back:* **5** repel **6** defend **7** repulse
close: **8** tailgate *off:* **6** dispel *out:* **8** exor-
cise
drivel 4 blow, bosh **5** drool, Greek, hooey,
prate, waste **6** babble, gabble, jabber,
slaver **7** blabber, blather, consume, dribble,
fritter, prattle, rubbish, slabber, slobber,
twaddle **8** cast away, claptrap, nonsense,
pishposh, salivate, squander **9** gibberish,
throw away **10** double-talk, flapdoodle, frivol away, trifle away **11** blunder away, jabberwocky **12** blatherskite
driveling 4 flat **5** inane, vapid **6** jejune
7 insipid, sapless **9** innocuous **10** namby-
pamby, wishy-washy **12** milk-and-water

driver 5 cabby **6** cabbie, cabman, hackie,
jarvey, mallet, vanman **7** autoist, hackman,
spanker **8** motorist, muleteer, operator
9 chauffeur, dowitcher **10** taskmaster
11 tamping iron **12** automobilist *fast:*
4 jehu *of an elephant:* **6** mahout *Roman:*
10 charioteer *truck:* **8** teamster
driver's light 8 headlamp
driving 6 active, lively **7** dynamic **9** energetic **12** enterprising
drizzle 8 sprinkle
Dr. Jekyll and Mr. ___ 4 Hyde
drogher 6 bearer, porter **7** carrier
drôlerie see drollery
droll 3 odd, wag, wit **5** comic, funny, joker
6 jester **7** comical, risible **8** comedian, farcical, funnyman, gelastic, humorist, humor-
ous, jokester, quipster **9** burlesque, laughable, ludicrous, whimsical **10** puppet show,
ridiculous
drollery 3 gag, yak **4** jape, jest, joke, quip
5 crack, humor **6** comedy **7** waggery
9 funniness, wisecrack, witticism, wittiness
10 comicality **11** comicalness **12** humorousness
drollness see drollery
dromedary 5 camel
drone 3 hum **4** buzz, idle, laze, loaf, loll
5 idler, strum, thrum **6** bumble, dawdle, loiter, lounge **7** bagpipe, male bee **8** parasite
9 bombinate **10** pedal point **12** diddle-dad-
dle
dronish see drony
drony 4 lazy **7** work-shy **8** fainéant, indolent, slothful **9** easygoing, slowgoing
drool 4 guff, rave **5** prate, water **6** babble,
bushwa, drivel, gabble, hot air, saliva,
slaver **7** blabber, blather, dribble, enthuse,
prattle, slabber, slobber, twaddle **8** claptrap, nonsense, rhapsody, salivate **10** balderdash, rhapsodize
droop 3 sag **4** fall, flag, hang, loll, sink,
swag, wilt **5** couch, demit, lower, slump
6 dangle, go down, slouch, weaken
7 decline, depress, let down, subside, trollop **8** languish, pine away **11** deteriorate
droopy 3 bad **4** blue, down **6** gloomy
7 doleful **8** cast down, dejected, downcast
9 depressed **10** dispirited **11** downhearted
drop 3 die, dip, nip, sag, tot **4** down, dram,
drib, dump, fall, fell, fire, iota, jolt, lose,
pass, plop, quit, shot, skid, slip, slot, slug,
thud, weep, wilt **5** cease, crumb, depth,
floor, gutta, lapse, leave, lower, ounce,
pitch, plonk, plump, plunk, scrub, shred,
slide, snort, speck, spend, trill **6** bounce,
cancel, cave in, crouch, curtsy, demise,
depart, expire, fumble, give up, gobbet, go
down, goutte, ground, lay low, peg out,
plunge, pop off, reduce, resign, smitch, top-

ple, tumble, unload, vanish 7 abandon, boot out, call off, decease, decline, deposit, descend, descent, dismiss, distill, dribble, driblet, fall off, forfeit, give out, globule, lose out, pendant, plummet, relapse, smidgen, snifter, spatter, succumb, trickle 8 bowl down, bowl over, break off, collapse, come-down, deepness, defecate, downturn, fall away, keel over, molecule, nose-dive, particle, pass away, toothful 9 backslide, break down, bring down, declivity, disappear, discharge, downslide, downswing, downtrend, knock down, prostrate, reduction, sacrifice, terminate, throw down 10 depository *of liquid:* 5 gutta *saline:* 4 tear

drop in 3 see 4 call 5 visit 6 come by, look up, stop by 8 come over

droplet 4 drib 6 gobbet 7 globule

drop off 3 sag 4 fall, slip 5 slide, slump 8 fall away

dropout's loss 7 diploma

dropsical 5 puffy, tumid, windy 6 turgid 7 swollen 8 inflated 9 flatulent, overblown, tumescent

dropsied see **dropsical**

dropsy 5 edema 7 hydrops 8 anasarca

dross 4 scum, slag 7 schlock 8 impurity

drossy 6 draffy, no-good 7 inutile, nothing 8 unworthy 9 worthless

drought 4 lack 6 dearth 8 scarcity, shortage

droughty 3 dry 4 arid, sere 7 bone-dry, thirsty 9 unwatered, waterless 12 moistureless

drove 4 herd, push 5 crowd, crush, flock, horde, press 6 chisel, squash, throng 9 multitude

drown 3 sop, wet 4 sink, soak, stun 5 douse, flood, souse, swamp, whelm 6 dazzle, deluge, drench, engulf 7 immerse, repress 8 inundate, overcome, overflow, submerge 9 knock over, overpower, overwhelm, prostrate, suffocate, tower over 10 extinguish

drowse 3 nod 4 doze 7 doze off, drop off, slumber

drowsy 4 dozy 6 sleepy, snoozy 7 languid, nodding 8 indolent, slumbery 9 lethargic, somnolent, soporific 10 languorous, slumberous 13 lackadaisical

drub 3 tap 4 beat, flay, lick, trim, whip 5 baste, paste, pound, score, slash, smear, stamp 6 batter, berate, buffet, pummel, scorch, thrash, wallop 7 belabor, blister, censure, scourge, shellac 8 lambaste, lash into 9 castigate, excoriate, overwhelm

drubbing 4 rout 6 defeat 7 beating, debacle, licking 9 overthrow, trouncing 10 defeasance 11 shellacking 12 vanquishment

drudge 4 grub, hack, moil, peon, plod, slog, toil, work 5 grind, labor, slave 6 slavey, toiler 7 grubber, slavery 8 bullwork, hireling, plugging 9 dray horse, mercenary, workhorse 10 donkeywork 11 galley slave

drudgery 4 moil, toil, work 5 grind, labor, sweat 7 travail 8 bullwork, plugging, taskwork 10 donkeywork

drudging 6 boring, tiring 7 irksome, tedious 8 boresome, tiresome 10 monotonous

drug 4 dope, lull 5 sulfa 6 downer, opiate, physic, poison, sulpha 7 generic, stupefy, tetanic 8 biologic, medicine, narcotic, nepenthe, pemoline, relaxant, roborant, sedative, thiazide 9 medicinal 10 medicament, medication 12 pharmaceutic *addict:* 6 junkie *agent:* 4 narc *antibiotic:* 8 neomycin *calming:* 8 sedative *combining form:* 8 pharmaco *experience:* 4 trip *seller:* 10 pharmacist *sleep-inducing:* 8 hypnotic 9 soporific

drugged 4 high 5 doped 6 stoned, zonked 8 hopped-up, turned on 9 spaced-out 10 tripped out

druggist 7 chemist 10 apothecary, pharmacist

drugstore 8 pharmacy 10 apothecary

druid 4 bard 6 priest 7 prophet 8 sorcerer *sacred object:* 3 oak 9 mistletoe

drum 4 cask 5 taber, tabla, tabor 6 atabal, barrel, enlist, gather, summon, tabour, tom-tom, tymbal, tympan 7 canvass, solicit, taboret, taborin, tympani 8 cylinder, taborine, tabourer, tabouret, tympanum *Arab:* 6 atabal *Indian:* 8 mridanga *large:* 4 bass 6 timbal *small:* 5 bongo, tabor 6 tabret 7 taborin, timbrel *string:* 5 snare

drumbeat 3 dub 4 flam, roll, tuck 6 ruffle, tattoo 8 berloque, rataplan

drumfire 4 hail 5 salvo, storm 6 shower, volley 7 barrage 9 broadside, cannonade, fusillade 11 bombardment

drumhead 4 skin 7 summary

drummer 4 Rich (Buddy) 5 Krupa (Gene) 7 swagman 8 weakfish

drum up 6 invent 7 canvass, solicit 9 originate *interest:* 8 ballyhoo

drunk 3 fou, jag, lit, sot 4 bust, lush, soak, tear, wino 5 binge, booze, souse, spree, tight, tipsy 6 bender, blotto, boozer, soused, stewed, stinko, tiddly, zonked 7 crocked, guzzler, pie-eyed, squiffy, stewbum, tippler 8 squiffed 9 brannigan, inebriate 10 boozehound, inebriated 11 intoxicated

drunkard 3 sot 4 lush, soak, wino 5 rummy, stiff, toper 6 bibber, boozer, rumdum, soaker, sponge 7 drammer, fuddler, guzzler, swiller, tippler, tosspot 9 alcoholic, inebriate, juicehead, swillbowl 10 booze-hound 11 dipsomaniac

drunken 5 boozy, tight, tipsy 6 wobbly 7 pie-eyed 8 lurching, unsteady 10 inebriated 11 intoxicated

drupaceous fruit 4 plum 5 peach 6 almond, cherry

Drusilla *brother:* 8 Caligula *father:* 5 Herod 10 Germanicus *husband:* 5 Felix *mother:* 9 Agrippina *sister:* 8 Berenice 9 Agrippina

dry 3 set 4 acid, arid, bare, blot, brut, cake, dull, sear, sere, sour, tart 5 acerb, baked, dusty, empty, harsh, parch, plain, rough, slack, stoic, wizen 6 barren, harden, hoarse, modest, stingy, stolid, thirst, wither 7 acerbic, acetose, athirst, congeal, grating, insipid, jarring, parched, rasping, sapless, shrivel, sterile, tedious, thirsty 8 bromidic, discreet, droughty, indurate, rainless, scariose, scarious, solidify, strident, tearless, teetotal, weariful, withered 9 acidulous, anhydrate, anhydrous, apathetic, dehydrate, desiccate, exsiccate, impassive, juiceless, sugarless, thirsting, unadorned, unwatered, waterless, wearisome 10 dehydrated, desiccated, phlegmatic, stridulous 11 inelaborate, unemotional, ungarnished 12 matter-of-fact, moistureless, unproductive 13 unembellished, unembroidered, uninteresting, unpretentious *biscuit:* 7 cracker 8 hardtack *combining form:* 3 xer 4 xero 5 scler 6 dehydr, sclero 7 dehydro *goods:* 4 wear 6 linens, napery 8 clothing, textiles *out:* 5 sober 8 soberize *period:* 4 sere 6 drouth 7 drought *wine:* 3 sec 4 brut

dryasdust 4 arid, dull 5 dusty 6 pedant 7 insipid, prosaic, tedious 8 bromidic, pedantic, weariful 9 wearisome 10 uninspired 13 uninteresting

dry measure 4 peck, pint 5 quart 6 bushel

Dryope *form:* 5 lotus *husband:* 9 Andraemon *sister:* 4 Iole

dry up 4 wilt 5 mummy, wizen 6 welter, wither 7 mummify, shrivel 8 pipe down 9 desiccate, disappear 10 devitalize

dual 4 twin 5 duple 6 bifold, binary, double, duplex, paired 7 twofold

dualistic 5 duple 6 bifold, binary, double, duplex 7 twofold

dualize 4 dupe 6 double 9 duplicate

dub 4 call, flub, muff, name, term, trim 5 botch, fluff, style, title 6 bobble, boggle, bollix, double, duffer, goof up, thrust 7 baptize, blunder, entitle 8 christen, nickname, rerecord 9 designate 10 denominate

dubiety see **dubiosity**

dubiosity 5 doubt 6 wonder 7 concern 8 mistrust 9 addlement, confusion, suspicion 10 muddlement, skepticism 11 incertitude, uncertainty, uncertitude

dubious 4 moot, open 5 fishy 6 unsure 7 suspect, unclear 8 arguable, doubtful, hesitant, mootable, unlikely, untrusty 9 debatable, dubitable, equivocal, skeptical, trustless, uncertain, undecided 10 disputable, fly-by-night, improbable, unreliable 11 mistrustful, problematic, questioning, unpromising 12 questionable, undependable, undetermined 13 untrustworthy

dubitable 4 open 5 fishy 7 suspect 8 doubtful 9 ambiguous, uncertain, unsettled 10 borderline

duce 6 despot, tyrant 8 dictator 9 Mussolini, oppressor

duck 3 bob, bow, dip, shy 4 bend, bilk, dive, dunk, shun 5 avoid, dodge, douse, elude, evade, fence, parry, shirk, souse, stoop 6 double, escape, eschew, plunge 7 back out, immerse 8 sidestep, submerge, submerse 10 canvasback *Asian:* 5 Pekin 8 mandarin *dabbling:* 7 gadwall, mallard *diving:* 4 smew 7 pochard 9 merganser 10 bufflehead *eggs:* 5 pidan *Eurasian:* 4 smew *European:* 8 garganey, shelduck *genus:* 4 Anas *group:* 4 sord, team 5 brace, flock, skein 6 flight *Hawaiian:* 5 koloa *hunter's screen:* 5 blind *male:* 5 drake *red-wattled:* 7 Muscovy *relating to:* 7 anatine *river:* 4 teal 6 wigeon 7 pintail, widgeon *scaup:* 8 bluebill *sea:* 5 eider, scaup 6 scoter

duckbill 8 platypus 9 monotreme 10 mallangong

duck soup 3 pie 4 snap 5 cinch, setup 6 breeze, picnic 8 kid stuff, pushover 10 child's play

duckweed 6 lemnad

ducky 4 cute, fine 7 darling 8 pleasant, splendid 9 excellent

duct 4 pipe, tube 5 canal 6 course 7 channel, conduit 11 ink fountain, watercourse *anatomical:* 3 vas 4 vasa (plural) *combining form:* 3 vas 4 vasi, vaso

ductile 6 pliant, supple 7 plastic, pliable 8 flexible, moldable 9 adaptable, compliant, malleable, tractable *metal:* 4 wire

ductless gland see **endocrine gland**

ductus 4 fist, hand 6 script 10 penmanship 11 calligraphy, chirography, handwriting

dud 3 bad 4 bomb, bust, fake, flop 5 lemon, loser 7 failure 11 ineffective

dude 3 fop 4 buck 5 blood, dandy 7 coxcomb 8 macaroni 9 exquisite 10 tenderfoot 11 Beau Brummel, petit-maître 12 lounge lizard

dudgeon 4 fury, huff, miff, rage 5 pique, wrath 7 offense, umbrage 10 resentment

duds 4 togs 5 dress 6 attire, things
7 apparel, clothes, raiment 8 clothing
10 attirement 11 habiliments

due 4 debt, fair, good, just, owed 5 lumps,
merit, owing, right 6 direct, earned, lawful,
mature, reward, rights, unpaid 7 arrears,
condign, deserts, exactly, merited, payable,
payment, regular 8 adequate, deserved,
directly, rightful, straight, suitable 9 arrearage, deserving, equitable, liability, requisite,
scheduled, unsettled 10 recompense, satisfying, straightly, sufficient 11 appropriate,
comeuppance, outstanding 12 compensation, indebtedness, satisfaction 13 rhadamanthine, undeviatingly

duel 4 buck 5 fight, repel 6 combat,
oppose, resist 7 contest, dispute 8 conflict,
traverse 9 withstand

duenna 8 chaperon 9 chaperone, governess

duet *dancer's:* 9 pas de deux

due to 4 over 7 through 9 because of

duff 5 slack 7 pudding 8 coal dust, fine
coal

duffer 4 dolt, dope 5 dunce, idiot 6 dimwit
8 dumbbell, numskull 9 blockhead, ignoramus

dugout 4 abri 5 banca, canoe 7 piragua,
pirogue

dukedom 5 duchy

dulcet 5 sweet 7 melodic, tuneful, winning,
winsome 8 engaging, euphonic, luscious,
pleasant, soothing 9 melodious 10 euphonious 11 mellisonant

dulcimer *Chinese:* 7 yang-kin *Hungarian:*
8 cimbalom *Persian:* 6 santir 7 santour

dull 3 bad, dim, dry, dun, mat 4 arid, blah,
blue, blur, dead, down, drab, dumb, fade,
flat, hard, hazy, numb, pale, poky, slow
5 befog, blear, blind, blunt, cloud, dense,
dingy, dusty, heavy, inert, matte, muddy,
murky, muted, prosy, thick 6 benumb,
blurry, boring, cloudy, deaden, dreary,
gloomy, leaden, obtund, obtuse, retard, simple, somber, stodgy, stupid, tiring, weaken
7 becloud, blunted, disedge, doltish, humdrum, insipid, irksome, louring, moronic, muffled, prosaic, stupefy, subfusc, tarnish,
tedious, wash out 8 backward, banausic,
bromidic, cast down, deadened, dejected,
deluster, discolor, downcast, duncical,
enfeeble, hebetate, hopeless, imbecile, lifeless, listless, lowering, monotone, nubilous,
overcast, plodding, retarded, sluggish, weariful 9 bloodless, brainless, colorless,
depressed, dim-witted, dryasdust, insensate, ponderous, unfeeling, wearisome
10 anesthetic, beef-witted, devitalize, dispirited, half-witted, impassible, indistinct, insensible, lackluster, lusterless, monotonous,
numskulled, pedestrian, spiritless 11 blear-

witted, desensitize, downhearted, insensitive, overclouded, thickheaded, thick-witted,
unsharpened 12 disheartened, feebleminded, simpleminded 13 uninteresting
combining form: 5 brady

dullard 5 dummy, dunce, idiot, moron
6 stupid 8 dumbbell 9 ignoramus, simpleton

dulled *combining form:* 5 ambly
6 amblyo

dullness 4 coma 5 sleep 6 apathy, stupor, torpor 7 languor, slumber 8 hebetude,
lethargy, monotony 9 bluntness, dense-
ness, lassitude, stupidity, torpidity
10 drowsiness

duly 8 properly 9 regularly 12 sufficiently

Dumas character 5 Athos 6 Aramis,
Dantes 7 Camille, Porthos 9 D'Artagnan

dumb 3 mum 4 dull, mute 5 dense, quiet,
thick 6 deaden, silent, stupid 7 doltish,
foolish 8 duncical, reticent, taciturn, wordless 9 fatheaded, voiceless 10 numskulled,
speechless, tongue-tied 11 blockheaded,
thick-witted, tight-lipped 12 close-mouthed,
close-tongued, inarticulate, inexpressive,
tight-mouthed, unarticulate, unresponsive

dumbbell see dullard

dumbfound 5 amaze 6 boggle
7 astound, nonplus, stagger 8 astonish,
surprise 11 flabbergast

dumbfounded 5 agape 6 aghast,
amazed 7 shocked 8 confused, dismayed
10 bewildered 11 overwhelmed 13 thunderstruck

dummy 4 dolt, mock, sham 5 dunce,
false, idiot, moron 6 effigy, ersatz, layout,
stooge, stupid, yes-man 7 dullard 8 dullhead, dumbbell, spurious 9 ignoramus, imitation, simpleton, simulated 10 artificial, fictitious, substitute

dump 3 sty 4 cast, drop, junk 5 chuck,
depot, ditch, scrap 6 armory, pigpen, pigsty, plunge 7 arsenal, discard, eyesore
8 jettison, magazine, throw out 9 throw
away

dumpling 5 blimp, fatty 8 quenelle
10 butterball

dumps 5 blues, gloom 7 sadness 9 dejection 10 depression, melancholy, the dismals 11 unhappiness 12 mournfulness

dumpy 5 squat, thick 6 chunky, slummy,
squdgy, stocky, stubby 8 heavyset, thickset
9 shapeless 11 thick-bodied

dun 3 dim 4 dark, dusk, gnaw 5 annoy,
brown, dusky, murky, worry 6 darken,
gloomy, harass, needle, pester, plague,
somber 7 bedevil, hagride, obscure
9 beleaguer, caddis fly, lightless 10 caliginous 12 grayish brown

Duncan's slayer 7 Macbeth

dunce 3 mug, oaf 4 boob, clod, dodo, dolt, dope, fool, goof, jerk, lunk, mutt, poke, simp 5 booby, chump, dummy, idiot, moron, ninny, noddy, prune 6 dimwit, donkey, duffer, nitwit, noodle, stupid, turnip, zombie 7 dullard, fathead, jackass, lackwit, muggins, pinhead, wantwit 8 bonehead, clodpate, clodpoll, dolthead, dullhead, dumbbell, imbecile, ironhead, knothead, lunkhead, numskull 9 birdbrain, blockhead, ignoramus, lamebrain, simpleton, thickhead 10 beetlehead, dunderhead, dunderpate, hammerhead, muddlehead, muttonhead, nincompoop, squarehead, thickskull, woodenhead 11 cabbagehead, chowderhead, chucklehead, knucklehead, pumpkin head 12 featherbrain, scatterbrain 13 featherweight

Dunciad author 4 Pope (Alexander)

duncical 4 dull, dumb 5 dense 6 stupid 7 doltish 8 blockish 9 pinheaded 10 numskulled 11 blockheaded, thickheaded

dunderhead see **dunce**

dunderpate see **dunce**

dundrearies 9 burnsides, sideburns 10 sideboards 11 muttonchops 12 sidewhiskers

dune 5 twine 8 sandbank *area:* 3 erg

dung 4 muck 6 manure, ordure 9 excrement *beetle:* 3 dor 6 scarab 9 tumblebug *combining form:* 4 copr, scat 5 copro, scato

dungaree fabric 5 denim

dungeon 4 cell, jail 5 vault 6 donjon, prison 9 black hole, oubliette

dunghill 6 midden

dungy 4 foul 5 black, dirty, nasty, soily 6 filthy, grubby, sordid 7 squalid, unclean

dunk 3 dip, sop 4 soak 5 douse, souse 7 immerse 8 saturate, submerge, submerse

dunlin 4 stib 9 sandpiper

duo 4 dyad, pair 5 brace 6 couple 7 doublet, twosome

dupe 3 con, job, kid, sap 4 butt, dust, fool, gull, hoax, mark, tool 5 catch, cheat, chump, cozen, patsy, slave, spoof, trick 6 befool, delude, double, outwit, pigeon, puppet, sucker 7 chicane, deceive, defraud, dualize, fall guy, gudgeon, mislead 8 flimflam, hoodwink 9 bamboozle, duplicate, victimize 11 double-cross, hornswoggle

dupery 5 cheat, fraud 7 chicane 9 chicanery, deception 10 dishonesty, hanky-panky 13 double-dealing, sharp practice

duple 4 dual 6 bifold, binary, double, duplex 7 twofold 9 dualistic

duplex see **duple**

duplicate 4 copy, mate, same, twin 5 ditto, equal, match 6 carbon, double, fellow 7 dualize, identic, imitate, replica 9 companion, facsimile, identical, reproduce 10 carbon copy, coordinate, equivalent, reciprocal, tantamount 11 counterpart, replication 12 reproduction *prefix:* 7 counter

duplicitous 6 shifty, sneaky 7 devious 8 guileful, indirect, sneaking 9 underhand 11 underhanded

duplicity 5 guile 6 deceit 7 cunning, perfidy 9 treachery 10 doubleness 12 dissemblance 13 dissimulation, double-dealing, faithlessness

durability 4 wear 11 lastingness

durable 5 stout 6 strong, sturdy 7 lasting 8 enduring 9 diuturnal, perduring, permanent, tenacious

duramen 9 heartwood

durance 9 restraint 11 confinement 12 imprisonment

duration 3 run 4 span, term, time 6 period 9 endurance 10 continuity 11 continuance, lastingness, persistence

duress 5 force 8 coercion, violence 10 compulsion, constraint

Durga see **Devi**

during 3 mid 4 amid, over 5 midst 10 throughout *prefix:* 2 di 3 dia 5 intra

durra 7 sorghum 10 guinea corn 12 Indian millet

durum 5 wheat

dusk 3 dim 4 dark 5 murky 6 darken, gloomy 7 evening, obscure 8 darkness, eventide, glooming, owl-light, twilight 9 lightless, nightfall, tenebrous 10 caliginous 12 semidarkness 13 unilluminated

dusky 3 dim 4 dark 5 black, bleak, drear, murky, swart 6 brunet, dismal, gloomy, opaque, swarth 7 joyless, obscure, swarthy 8 bistered, blackish, desolate, funereal, nubilous 9 ambiguous, cheerless, equivocal, lightless, sibylline, tenebrous 10 acheronion, caliginous, depressing 11 black-a-vised, dark-skinned, double-edged, double-faced 13 unilluminated *combining form:* 4 pheo 5 phaeo

dust 3 row 4 beat, drub, dupe, fool, gull, hoax, lick, sift, whip 5 run-in, trick 6 fracas, hassle, powder, thrash 7 chicane, confuse, dispute, quarrel, shellac 8 flimflam, hoodwink, lambaste, levigate, sprinkle 9 bamboozle, bickering, confusion, overwhelm, powdering 10 besprinkle, falling-out, sprinkling 11 altercation, disturbance, hornswoggle *combining form:* 4 coni 5 conio *Scottish:* 5 stour

dustbowl victim 4 Okie

dustup 3 row 5 run-in 6 fracas, hassle 7 dispute, quarrel 8 argument 9 bickering 10 falling-out 11 altercation

dusty 3 dim, dry 4 arid, dull 5 blowy, stale 6 barren, sordid, stormy 7 clouded, insipid,

powdery, tedious **8** bromidic, weariful
9 dryasdust, miserable, wearisome, worthless **12** contemptible, unproductive, unsat-
isfying **13** uninteresting *Scottish:* **6** stoury
Dutch **7** trouble **8** hot water **9** Afrikaans
commune: **3** Ede *housewife:* **4** frow
scholar: **7** Erasmus *uncle:* **3** oom
dutiful **7** duteous **9** regardful **10** respectful
11 deferential
duty **3** job, tax, use **4** goal, levy, load,
mark, must, need, onus, role, task **5** chare,
chore, ought, stint **6** burden, charge,
devoir, impost, object, office, target, tariff,
weight **7** purpose, respect, service **8** business, function, province **9** committal, millstone, objective **10** assessment, assignment, commitment, deadweight, obligation
Duvalier's land **5** Haiti
dwarf **3** wee **4** runt, tiny **5** gnome, midge,
pygmy, stunt, troll **6** midget, minify, peewee, teensy **7** manikin, minikin **8** suppress,
Tom Thumb **9** miniature **10** diminutive,
homunculus **11** hop-o'-my-thumb, lilliputian
combining form: **3** nan **4** nann, nano
5 nanno *in Snow White:* **3** Doc **5** Dopey,
Happy **6** Grumpy, Sleepy, Sneezy **7** Bashful *Scottish:* **7** blastie
dwarf elder **8** danewort, goutweed
dwarfish **4** tiny **6** midget **7** minikin **9** itsy-
bitsy, itty-bitty, miniature **10** diminutive
11 lilliputian
dwell **3** lie, won **4** bide, live **5** abide, exist
6 inhere, reside **7** consist, hang out
dweller **5** liver **7** denizen, resider **8** habitant, occupant, resident **10** inhabitant
monastic: **4** monk **5** friar **6** oblate *suffix:*
3 ite
dwelling **4** casa, home **5** abode, house
8 domicile **9** residence, residency
10 brownstone, commorancy, habitation
American Indian: **4** tipi **5** hogan, tepee
6 pueblo, teepee, wigwam *clergyman's:*
5 manse **7** rectory **9** parsonage *crude:*
5 shack **6** shanty *Eskimo:* **4** iglu **5** igloo
Hindu: **6** ashram, asrama **7** ashrama *Navaho:* **5** hogan
dwindle **3** ebb **4** fail, wane **5** abate, close,
taper **6** lessen, reduce, shrink, weaken
7 decline, subside **8** decrease, diminish,
taper off **9** attenuate, drain away, extenuate, fall short, waste away
dyad **3** duo **4** pair **5** brace **6** couple
7 doublet, twosome

dye **5** color, stain **6** reddle, ruddle **7** pigment **8** colorant, nigrosin, pyronine, tincture
blue: **4** woad **6** cyanin, indigo **7** cyanine,
indulin **8** indigoid, induline *for hair:*
5 henna *green:* **7** gallein *plant:* **4** chay,
woad **5** chaya, sumac **6** madder *purple:*
6 orchil *red:* **5** eosin **6** eosine, kermes
7 crocein, cudbear, fuchsin, kermess,
magenta **8** alizarin, anchusin, croceine,
fuchsine, rhodamin, safranin **9** cochineal
reddish: **5** henna **8** purpurin *reddish
brown:* **6** orcein *violet:* **7** thionin **8** thio-
nine *yellow:* **8** orpiment *yellowish red:*
7 achiote, annatto
dyed-in-the-wool **5** sworn **7** devoted,
settled **9** confirmed, hard-shell **10** deep-
rooted, deep-seated, entrenched, inveterate
13 bred-in-the-bone
dyeing process **5** batik
dyeleaves **8** inkberry **9** sweetleaf
dye red **6** ruddle
dyer's grape **8** pokeweed
dyer's mulberry **6** fustic
dyestuff see dye
dyewood **6** brasil, brazil, fustet, fustic
dying **8** expiring, moribund
dynamic **4** live **5** alive, lusty, vital **6** active
7 intense, running, working **8** forceful, forcible, vigorous **9** energetic, operative, strenuous **10** functional, red-blooded **11** functioning
dynamite **4** raze, ruin **7** destroy, shatter
8 decimate, demolish, destruct, dissolve
9 dismantle, explosive **10** annihilate *inventor:* **5** Nobel (Alfred)
dynamo **6** peeler **7** hustler, rustler **8** go-
getter, live wire **9** generator **11** self-starter
dysentery **4** flux **6** scours **8** diarrhea
dyslogistic **9** slighting **10** derogatory,
detracting, pejorative **11** disparaging
12 depreciative, depreciatory
dyspathy **7** allergy **8** aversion
dyspepsia **7** pyrosis **9** gastritis, heartburn
11 indigestion
dyspeptic **6** morose **10** ill-humored, ill-natured, tempersome **11** bad-tempered, hot-
tempered, ill-tempered
dysphoria **5** gloom, mopes **7** sadness
9 dejection **10** depression, melancholy
11 unhappiness **12** mournfulness, wretchedness
dysprosium *symbol:* **2** Dy
Dzhugashvili **6** Stalin (Joseph)

E

each 3 all, per 5 every 6 apiece 8 everyone, per caput 9 per capita

eager 3 hot 4 agog, avid, keen 5 itchy, ready 6 ardent, gung ho, heated, hungry, intent, pining, raring 7 anxious, athirst, craving, longing, restive, thirsty, wishful 8 appetent, covetous, desirous, on tiptoe, restless, yearning 9 ambitious, hankering, impatient 10 breathless, solicitous 11 acquisitive 12 enthusiastic

eagerness 4 zeal, zest, zing 5 ardor, gusto 6 fervor 7 avidity 8 alacrity, ambition, fervency, keenness 9 quickness 10 enthusiasm

eagle 4 hawk 9 accipiter *combining form:* 4 aeto 5 aetus *nest:* 4 aery 5 aerie, eyrie *North American:* 4 bald 6 golden 10 bald-headed *sea:* 3 ern 4 erne 6 osprey

eagle-eyed 7 lyncean 12 sharp-sighted

eagre 4 bore, flow, wave 5 flood

ear 4 heed, mark, note 6 notice, regard, remark 7 auricle 8 auricula 9 attention 10 observance 11 observation *bone:* 5 anvil, incus 6 hammer, stapes 7 malleus, stirrup *canal:* 5 scala *combining form:* 2 ot 3 aur, oto 4 auri, otic *doctor:* 9 otologist *inner:* 9 labyrinth *middle:* 8 tympanum *outer:* 5 pinna *part:* 4 drum, lobe 5 canal 6 tragus 7 cochlea *relating to:* 4 otic 5 aural 9 auricular *science:* 7 otology

earache 7 otalgia

eardrum 8 tympanum *combining form:* 6 tympan 7 tympano

____ Earhart 6 Amelia

earl 4 lord, peer 5 noble 8 nobleman 10 aristocrat

earlier 3 ere, yet 4 once 5 as yet, so far 6 before, sooner 7 already, thus far 8 formerly, hitherto, previous 9 erstwhile, preceding 10 beforehand, heretofore, previously *combining form:* 4 fore 6 proter 7 protero

earlier than *prefix:* 3 pre, pro

earliest 5 first, prime 6 maiden 7 initial, pioneer, primary 8 original, primeval, pristine *combining form:* 2 eo

earlike projection 3 lug

Earl of Avon 4 Eden (Anthony)

early 3 old 5 first, prior 6 primal, timely 7 ancient, betimes 8 germinal, original, oversoon, previous, primeval, pristine, untimely 9 preceding, premature, primitive 10 antecedent, antiquated, beforehand, precocious, prevenient, primordial, seasonably 11 precipitant, prematurely *combining form:* 4 pale 5 palae, paleo 6 palaeo, palaio

earn 3 bag, get, net, win 4 gain, make, rate, reap 5 gross, merit, score 6 attain, come by, effect, obtain, secure 7 acquire, bring in, deserve, harvest, procure, realize, receive 8 draw down 9 knock down

earnest 4 busy, pawn, warm, zeal 5 grave, sober, staid, token 6 ardent, pledge, sedate, solemn, somber, warmth 7 serious, sincere, warrant, weighty, zealous 8 diligent, interest, pressing, security, sedulous 9 assiduous, attention, heartfelt 10 enthusiasm, intentness, no-nonsense, passionate, sobersided 11 industrious, perseverant, seriousness 12 enthusiastic, wholehearted

earnestly 4 down, hard 7 for real, soberly 8 actively, dingdong, solemnly 9 intensely, seriously, zealously 10 thoroughly 11 assiduously, intensively 12 exhaustively, thoughtfully 13 painstakingly

earnestness 7 gravity, resolve 8 decision, firmness, sobriety 10 absorption, intentness 11 engrossment, persistence, seriousness 12 deliberation, perseverance 13 concentration, determination

earnings 4 gain 5 lucre 6 income, living, profit, return 8 proceeds

ear shell 7 abalone

earshot 5 sound 7 hearing

earsplitting 4 loud 6 shrill 7 blaring, roaring 8 piercing 10 stentorian 11 fullmouthed, stentorious

earth 3 mud, orb 4 clay, clod, dirt, fill, land, loom, sand, soil, turf, vale 5 glebe, globe, humus, terra, world 6 cosmos, gravel, ground, planet, sphere 7 dry land, subsoil, terrain 8 creation, universe 9 macrocosm 10 terra firma *combining form:* 2 ge 3 geo 6 tellur 7 telluri, telluro *core:* 12 centrosphere *god:* 3 Geb, Keb, Seb 5 Dagan *goddess:* 2 Ge, Ki 4 Erda, Gaea 5 Ceres,

Nintu 6 Kishar 7 Demeter, Nerthus *relating to:* 8 telluric 9 planetary, tellurian 11 terrestrial *satellite:* 4 moon *science:* 7 geology 9 geography *Scottish:* 4 yird 5 yirth

earthenware 4 delf 5 delft 7 biscuit, faience, pottery 8 crockery, majolica 9 stoneware 10 terra-cotta

earthlike 7 terrene 11 terrestrial

earthly 6 carnal, likely, mortal 7 mundane, terrene, worldly 8 material, physical, possible, probable, telluric, temporal 9 corporeal, potential, sublunary, tellurian 10 imaginable 11 conceivable, terrestrial, uncelestial, unspiritual

earthquake 5 seism, shake, shock 6 tremor 7 temblor 8 trembler, tremblor *combining form:* 5 seism 6 seismo *measuring device:* 11 seismograph, seismometer *relating to:* 7 seismic *science:* 10 seismology 11 seismometry

earthwork 4 bank, wall 7 bulwark, rampart 10 embankment 13 fortification

earthworm 7 annelid 9 brandling

earthy 3 low 5 dusty, gross, muddy, sandy 6 clayey 7 mundane, sensual, terrene, worldly 8 banausic, telluric, temporal 9 practical, pragmatic, realistic, sublunary, tellurian 10 hard-boiled, hardheaded 11 terrestrial, uncelestial, unfantastic 12 matter-of-fact 13 materialistic, unsentimental

earwax 7 cerumen

ease 3 aid, lax 4 bate, calm, dull, free, help, rest 5 allay, knock, loose, poise, relax, slack, speed 6 assist, better, deaden, loosen, relief, repose 7 abandon, assuage, calming, fluency, forward, further, improve, inertia, leisure, lighten, mollify, promote, relieve, slacken 8 calmness, deftness, diminish, dispatch, facility, idleness, mitigate, moderate, security, soothing, supinity, thriving 9 abundance, alleviate, disengage, expertise, inertness, passivity, readiness, reduction, untighten, well-being 10 adroitness, ameliorate, artfulness, cleverness, efficiency, expertness, facilitate, inactivity, mitigation, moderation, prosperity, relaxation, smoothness 11 alleviation, naturalness, spontaneity, tranquility 12 skillfulness, tranquillity

easel 5 frame, stand 7 support

easement 6 relief 9 allayment 10 mitigation 11 alleviation 13 mollification

ease off 3 ebb, lax 4 fall, wane 5 abate, let up, loose, relax, slack, unlax 6 loosen, relent, unbend, unwind 7 die away, die down, slacken, subside 8 loosen up, moderate 9 untighten

easily 4 well 6 freely, indeed, simply 7 handily, lightly, readily 8 facilely, smoothly 9 assuredly, certainly, decidedly, doubtless 10 absolutely, definitely, positively 11 competently, dexterously, doubtlessly, efficiently, undoubtedly 12 effortlessly 13 unequivocally *combining form:* 2 eu

east 4 Asia 6 Levant, Orient *German:* 3 ost

Easter 5 Pasch *relating to:* 7 paschal *symbol:* 3 egg 4 lamb 5 bunny 6 rabbit

eastern 8 oriental 9 Levantine *countries:* 6 Orient *name:* 3 Ali 4 Abou *title:* 3 sri

East Indies 9 Indonesia *animal:* 7 tarsier *bark:* 5 niepa *bird:* 4 baya 5 argus *boatman:* 6 serang *civet:* 6 musang *fish:* 5 dorab *fruit:* 6 durian, durion *grass:* 4 kans 5 glaga 6 raggee *herb:* 3 pia 4 chay, sola 6 sesame 7 roselle *monkey:* 7 hanuman 8 entelles *musical instrument:* 4 bina, vina *plant:* 2 da 4 bene, jute, sola, sunn 5 benne, kenaf 6 ambary, sesame 9 patchouli *ship:* 7 patamar 8 pattamar *tree:* 3 nim 4 dhak, neem, poon, toon 5 mahua, niepa, salai, simal, siris 6 banyan, deodar, illupi, sissoo 7 champac, hollong 8 mastwood 10 hursinghar *warrior:* 5 singh *wood:* 3 eng

easy 3 lax 4 calm, cozy, fast, glib, mild, soft, well 5 clear, comfy, cushy, light, loose, naive, plain, royal, suave 6 benign, facile, fluent, kindly, placid, poised, polite, secure, serene, simple, smooth, urbane, wanton 7 amiable, clement, courtly, cursive, evident, flowing, lenient, obvious, relaxed, well-off, whorish 8 apparent, clear-cut, composed, distinct, familiar, graceful, gullible, informal, manifest, merciful, obliging, pleasant, sociable, tolerant, tranquil, trusting, unchaste, well-to-do 9 collected, credulous, forgiving, indulgent, lethargic, possessed, well-fixed 10 charitable, diplomatic, effortless, fleeceable, forbearing, prosperous, successful, uninvolved, well-heeled 11 comfortable, complaisant, good-humored, good-natured, susceptible, sympathetic, unambitious 12 good-tempered 13 compassionate, mollycoddling, self-possessed, uncomplicated, untroublesome

easygoing 3 lax 4 calm, lazy 5 drony 6 breezy, casual, dégagé, folksy, placid, poised, serene 7 affable, offhand, relaxed, unfussy, work-shy 8 carefree, careless, composed, fainéant, flexible, indolent, informal, moderate, slothful, tranquil 9 apathetic, collected, off-handed 10 unaffected, unreserved 11 indifferent, low-pressure, unambitious, unconcerned, uninhibited

12 devil-may-care, happy-go-lucky, self-composed **13** self-possessed, unconstrained

easy mark 3 sap **4** butt, dupe, fool, gull **5** chump **6** pigeon, sucker **7** fall guy **9** soft touch

easy street 8 thriving **9** abundance, well-being **10** prosperity

eat 3 sup **4** bite, chow, dine, gnaw, meal, pick, take, wolf **5** erode, feast, gorge, lunch, mouth, scoff, scour, snack, use up **6** devour, feed on, gobble, ingest, nibble **7** banquet, consume, corrode, exhaust, gorge on, swallow **8** dissolve, wear away **9** breakfast, decompose, partake of, polish off **10** gormandize, nibble away

eatable 6 edible **8** esculent **10** comestible

eater 8 consumer *combining form:* **4** phag, vora, vore **5** estes, phaga, phage **6** phagus

eating *combining form:* **4** phag **5** phago, phagy **6** phagia, vorous **7** phagous

eating place 4 café, mess **5** diner, grill **7** automat, beanery, dinette, tearoom **8** cookshop, messroom, snack bar **9** cafeteria, chophouse, lunchroom **10** coffee shop, restaurant **12** luncheonette

Ebal's father 6 Shobal

ebb 4 fade, fall, tide, wane **5** abate, let up **6** recede, relent **7** decline, die away, die down, ease off, retreat, slacken, subside **8** decrease, diminish, moderate **10** retrograde

Ebed's son 4 Gaal

Eber *father:* **6** Elpaal **7** Shashak *son:* **6** Joktan

Eblis 5 Satan *son:* **3** Tir **4** Awar **5** Dasim **8** Zalambur

ebon, ebony 3 jet **4** inky **5** black, jetty, raven, sable **9** pitch-dark **10** pitch-black **11** atramentous

éboulement 9 avalanche, landslide

ebullience 6 gaiety **7** ferment **8** buoyancy, vitality **9** agitation, animation **10** enthusiasm, excitement, exuberance, exuberancy, liveliness **12** exhilaration **13** effervescence

ebullient 5 brash **7** boiling **8** agitated **9** exuberant, vivacious **12** effervescent, high-spirited

eccentric 3 odd **4** case, coot, kook, quiz **5** crank, freak, kooky, queer, wacky, weird **6** oddity, quirky, zombie **7** bizarre, caution, curious, erratic, heretic, oddball, strange **8** bohemian, crackpot, maverick, original, peculiar, singular **9** anomalous, bee-headed, character, dissenter, fantastic, grotesque, irregular, off-center, quizzical, screwball, unnatural **10** off-balance, unbalanced, uncentered **11** exceptional

12 unconformist **13** exceptionable, idiosyncratic, nonconformist

eccentricity 5 quirk **6** oddity **10** aberration **11** peculiarity, strangeness **12** idiosyncrasy

ecclesiastic 5 clerk **6** cleric, divine, parson **8** clerical, minister, preacher, reverend **9** churchman, clergyman

ecclesiastical 5 papal **6** church **8** churchly, clerical, pastoral, priestly **9** apostolic, canonical, episcopal, prelatial, spiritual, synagogal **10** churchlike, pantheonic, pontifical, rabbinical, sacerdotal, templelike **11** churchmanly, ministerial, patriarchal, synagogical, theological **12** episcopalian, evangelistic, tabernacular

ecdysiast 6 peeler, teaser **8** stripper **10** striptease **11** stripteaser

echelon 3 row **4** file, line, rank, tier **5** queue **6** string **9** formation

echidna 5 bitis, snake, viper **8** anteater

Echidna *father:* **7** Phorcys **8** Chrysaor *mother:* **4** Ceto **10** Callirrhoe *offspring:* **5** Hydra **6** dragon, Orthus, Sphinx **7** Chimera **8** Cerberus, Chimaera

echinoderm 6 urchin **8** starfish

echo 4 ring **5** oread **6** repeat, reverb, second **7** imitate, iterate, reflect, resound, revoice **8** resonate, response **9** reiterate **10** reflection, repetition **11** reverberate **12** repercussion **13** reverberation

echoic 9 imitative **12** onomatopoeic **13** onomatopoetic

Echo's beloved 9 Narcissus

éclat 4 bang, dash, fame, pomp **5** kudos **6** luster, renown, repute **7** acclaim, display **8** applause, standing **9** celebrity, notoriety **10** brilliance, brilliancy, prominence, reputation **11** distinction, ostentation

eclectic 5 broad, fussy, mixed, picky **6** choosy, select, varied **7** derived, diverse, finicky, mingled **8** assorted, catholic, elective **9** inclusive, multiform, selective **10** discerning, fastidious, particular **11** diversified **12** multifarious **13** comprehensive, heterogeneous

eclipse 3 dim **4** murk **5** bedim, cloud, cover, excel, shade **6** darken, exceed, shadow **7** becloud, decline, obscure, surpass **8** downfall **9** adumbrate, overcloud **10** overshadow

eclogue 4 idyl, poem **5** idyll **7** bucolic

ecological 8 bionomic *community:* **5** biome *succession:* **7** subsere

ecology 7 bionomy **9** bionomics *group:* **3** EPA

economic 8 material **10** profitable *doctrine:* **12** laissez-faire *system:* **7** fascism **9** communism, socialism **10** capitalism **11** syndicalism **12** mercantilism

economical 4 mean 5 canny, chary, close, spare 6 frugal, saving, stingy 7 careful, miserly, prudent, sparing, thrifty 8 skimping 9 niggardly, penny-wise, penurious, provident, scrimping, stewardly 10 forehanded, unwasteful 12 cheeseparing 13 penny-pinching

economist *American:* 6 George (Henry), Veblen (Thorstein), Walker (Amasa), Weaver (Robert) 8 Friedman (Milton) 9 Galbraith (John Kenneth), Samuelson (Paul) *Canadian:* 7 Leacock (Stephen) *Dutch:* 9 Tinbergen (Jan) *English:* 4 Mill (John Stuart) 5 Pigou (Arthur) 6 Keynes (John Maynard) 7 Malthus (Thomas Robert), Ricardo (David) *French:* 6 Turgot (Anne-Robert-Jacques), Walras (Léon) 7 Quesnay (François) *German:* 5 Weber (Max) *Scottish:* 5 Smith (Adam) *Swedish:* 6 Myrdal (Gunnar) *Swiss:* 8 Sismondi (Simonde de)

economize 4 save 5 skimp 6 scrimp 7 husband 8 conserve

economy 6 thrift 7 parcity 8 meanness, prudence, skimping 9 frugality, husbandry, parsimony, scrimping 10 discretion, providence, stinginess 11 carefulness, miserliness, thriftiness 13 niggardliness

ecru 5 beige

ecstasy 3 joy 5 bliss 6 frenzy, heaven 7 delight, elation, madness, rapture 8 euphoria, felicity, gladness, paradise, pleasure, rhapsody 9 beatitude, happiness, transport 10 exaltation, joyfulness 11 blessedness, delectation, enchantment, inspiration 12 blissfulness, exhilaration, intoxication 13 seventh heaven

Ecuador *capital:* 5 Quito *monetary unit:* 5 sucre

ecumenical 6 cosmic, global 7 general 8 catholic 9 inclusive, planetary, universal, worldwide 10 heaven-wide 11 all-covering 12 all-including, all-pervading, cosmopolitan 13 comprehensive

ecumenical council 4 Lyon 5 Trent 6 Nicene, Vienne 7 Ephesus, Lateran, Vatican 9 Chalcedon, Constance

eczema 6 tetter 9 malanders 10 mallenders

edacious 8 ravening, ravenous 9 voracious 10 gluttonous

eddo 4 root, taro

eddy 4 purl 5 gurge, surge, swirl, twirl, whirl, whorl 6 swoosh, vortex 8 backwash 9 backwater, maelstrom, whirlpool 10 back stream 11 back current, counterflow, counterflux *combining form:* 4 dino

edema 5 tumor 6 dropsy 8 anasarca, swelling

Eden 6 heaven, utopia 7 arcadia, elysium 8 paradise *river:* 5 Gihon 6 Pishon 8 Hiddekel 9 Euphrates

edentate 5 sloth 8 anteater 9 armadillo, toothless

Ederyn's father 4 Nudd

Edessa's king 5 Abgar

edge 3 cut, end, hem, lip, rim 4 bank, bite, brim, draw, hone, side, whet 5 bound, brink, bulge, ledge, picot, point, ridge, sidle, skirt, start, sting, verge 6 border, fringe, margin, nosing 7 acidity, outline, serrate, sharpen, vantage 8 acerbity, acridity, boundary, emborder, handicap, keenness, surround, thinness 9 acuteness, advantage, allowance, extremity, head start, knife-edge, perimeter, periphery, sharpness, threshold 10 causticity, shrillness, stringency 11 astringency, penetration 12 incisiveness

edged 5 sharp 7 crenate, cutting, vallate

edge in 4 worm 5 foist 9 insinuate 10 infiltrate

edging 3 hem 4 lace 5 braid 6 border, fringe, lacing

edgy 5 nervy, tense 6 touchy, uneasy 7 excited, restive, uptight 8 agitable, restless, skittery, skittish, volatile 9 alarmable, excitable, impatient, irritable, startlish 10 high-strung

edible 7 eatable 8 esculent 9 palatable 10 comestible *root:* 3 oca, yam 4 beet, taro 6 carrot, radish, turnip 7 parsnip 8 rutabaga 11 sweet potato *seed:* 3 nut, pea 4 bean 6 peanut

edibles 4 food, grub 6 viands 7 nurture 8 victuals 9 provender 10 provisions 11 comestibles

edict 3 law 4 bull, fiat, rule 5 canon, order, ukase 6 decree, dictum, ruling 7 command, precept, statute 8 decretum 9 directive, manifesto, ordinance, prescript 10 instrument, regulation 12 proclamation 13 pronouncement *papal:* 4 bull 8 decretal

Edict of ____ 5 Milan 6 Nantes

edifice 4 pile 6 church 8 building, erection 9 structure

edify 5 teach 6 better, illume, uplift 7 educate, elevate, enhance, improve 8 illumine, instruct 9 elucidate, enlighten, irradiate 10 illuminate

edit 3 cut 4 omit 5 adapt, alter, amend, emend 6 delete, redact, refine, review, revise, reword, select 7 compile, correct, rewrite 8 assemble, copyread 9 rearrange

edition 4 copy 5 issue, print 7 reissue, version 8 printing, variorum 10 impression, reprinting 12 reproduction

editor 8 redactor 10 copyreader 11 proofreader

Edomite's ancestor 4 Esau
educate 4 rear 5 brief, teach, train
6 inform, school 7 explain, nurture
8 instruct 9 enlighten 10 discipline
12 indoctrinate
education 7 culture, science, tuition
8 breeding, coaching, guidance, learning, literacy, pedagogy, teaching, training, tutelage, tutorage, tutoring 9 erudition, knowledge, schooling, tutorship 11 instruction, learnedness, scholarship 13 enlightenment
educational 11 informative, informatory, instructive 13 informational, instructional *institution:* 6 school 7 academy, college 9 institute 10 university 12 conservatory
educator 5 tutor 7 teacher 9 professor
10 instructor *American:* 4 Mann (Horace)
6 Conant (James Bryant) 8 McGuffey (William) 10 Washington (Booker T.) *Italian:*
10 Montessori (Maria) *Swiss:* 10 Pestalozzi (Johann Heinrich)
educe 4 drag, draw, gain, milk, pull
5 evoke, wrest, wring 6 derive, elicit, evince, evolve, extort, obtain, secure 7 distill, draw out, extract, procure 10 excogitate
eel 4 worm 5 moray, siren, snake 6 conger, murena 7 hagfish, lamprey, muraena, sniggle 8 wriggler 9 muraenoid *young:*
5 elver
eelboat 5 shuyt
eelpout 6 blenny, burbot 10 muttonfish
eely 6 slippy, wiggly 7 elusive, wriggly
8 slippery, slithery 9 wriggling
eerie 5 scary, weird 6 arcane, crawly, creepy, spooky 7 bizarre, strange, uncanny 9 fantastic, grotesque, unearthly 10 mysterious 11 frightening
efface 4 dele, x out 5 annul, erase 6 cancel, delete 7 blot out, destroy, exclude, expunge, rule out, wipe out 8 black out 9 eliminate, eradicate, extirpate 10 obliterate
effect 3 end 4 make 5 cause, enact, event, fruit, issue, yield 6 create, draw on, induce, invoke, render, result, secure, sequel, upshot 7 achieve, bring on, enforce, fulfill, outcome, perform, procure, produce, realize, turn out 8 bring off, carry out, causatum, conceive, generate, sequence 9 actualize, aftermath, corollary, implement, outgrowth, pursuance
10 accomplish, bring about, conclusion, denouement, end product 11 consequence, development, eventuality, precipitate 12 carry through, ramification, repercussion
effective 4 able 5 sound, valid 6 causal, cogent, direct, potent, useful 7 capable, dynamic, telling, virtual 8 adequate, virtu-

ous 9 competent, efficient, operative
10 compelling, convincing 11 efficacious
effectiveness 5 force, point, power, punch, verve, vigor 7 cogency, potency 8 efficacy, strength, validity 9 validness 10 capability, efficiency 11 performance
effects 5 goods 6 things 8 chattels, movables 10 belongings 11 possessions
effectual 5 sound, valid 6 potent, strong, toothy, useful 8 decisive, powerful, virtuous, workable 9 achieving, efficient
10 conclusive, fulfilling 11 efficacious, influential, practicable 13 accomplishing, authoritative, determinative
effectuate 7 execute, fulfill 8 bring off, carry out 10 accomplish 12 carry through
effeminate 5 sappy, sissy 6 chichi, female, prissy, silken 7 epicene, foppish, unmanly 8 overnice, precious, womanish 9 pansified, sissified 10 old-maidish 12 Miss-Nancyish
effervescence 7 fizzing, foaming 8 bubbling, buoyancy 10 ebullience, ebullition, exuberance, exuberancy
effervescent 3 gay 4 airy 5 brash, jolly 6 bouncy, bubbly, lively 7 boiling, buoyant, elastic, excited, gleeful 8 animated, mirthful, volatile 9 ebullient, expansive, exuberant, hilarious, resilient, sparkling, sprightly, vivacious 12 high-spirited
effete 4 done, sere, soft, weak 5 all in, spent 6 barren, bleary, done in, used up 7 decayed, drained, far-gone, immoral, sterile, worn-out 8 consumed, decadent, decaying, depleted, fatigued, impotent, infecund, overripe 9 declining, dissolute, enfeebled, exhausted, infertile, washed-out 10 degenerate, unfruitful 11 debilitated
efficacious 6 active, potent, strong 8 forceful, forcible, powerful, puissant, virtuous 9 effective, effectual, efficient, operative 10 productive 11 influential
efficacy see effectiveness
efficiency see effectiveness
efficient 4 able 5 adept 6 expert, fitted 7 capable, skilled 8 masterly, skillful, virtuous 9 competent, effective, effectual, qualified 11 efficacious 12 businesslike
effigy 5 dummy, image 7 waxwork 8 likeness, portrait
effloresce 4 blow 5 bloom 6 flower 7 blossom, burgeon 8 outbloom
effluvium 4 odor 5 smell 6 efflux 7 exhaust 9 emanation 10 exhalation
efflux 4 flow 7 outflow 8 effusion 9 emanation
effort 3 job, try 4 task, toil, work 5 chore, essay, force, labor, might, nisus, pains, power, while 6 energy, strain 7 attempt, travail, trouble 8 endeavor, exertion, strug-

gle, taskwork 9 puissance 11 application, elbow grease

effortful 4 hard 5 rough 6 uphill 7 arduous, labored, operose 8 toilsome 9 difficult, laborious, strenuous

effortless 4 easy 5 adept, light, ready, royal 6 expert, facile, fluent, simple, smooth 7 cursive, flowing, running, skilled 8 masterly, skillful 10 proficient 13 untroublesome

effrontery 4 face, gall 5 brass, cheek, nerve 8 audacity, boldness, temerity 9 assurance, brashness, hardihood, impudence, insolence 10 brazenness, confidence 11 presumption 12 impertinence 13 self-assurance

effulgence 4 glow 5 blaze 8 radiance, splendor 10 brightness, brilliance, luminosity

effulgent 5 vivid 6 bright, lucent 7 beaming, lambent, radiant 8 glorious, luminous, splendid 9 brilliant 11 resplendent 12 incandescent

effuse 4 flow, gush, pour, shed 7 emanate, radiate

effusive 5 gushy 6 sloppy, slushy, smarmy 7 cloying, fulsome, gushing, profuse 8 slobbery 9 expansive, exuberant 10 outpouring, slobbering, unreserved 12 unrestrained 13 demonstrative, unconstrained

eft 4 newt 6 triton 10 salamander

egest 4 void 7 excrete 9 discharge

egg 3 ova (plural), sic 4 goad, ovum, prod, seed, spur, urge 5 drive, ovule, pique, prick, rally 6 arouse, excite, exhort, prompt, stir up 7 agitate 9 instigate, stimulate *before maturation:* 6 oocyte *case:* 5 shell 6 ovisac 7 ootheca *combining form:* 2 oo, ov 3 ovi, ovo *dish:* 6 omelet 8 omelette *fertilized:* 6 zygote 7 oosperm, oospore *fish:* 3 roe 6 caviar *French:* 4 oeuf *part:* 4 yelk, yolk 5 glair, shell, white 7 albumen, latebra 10 blastodisc *product:* 3 zoa (plural) 4 zoon *white:* 5 glair 7 albumen *yolk:* 6 yellow 8 vitellus

egghead 7 Brahmin 8 highbrow 10 double-dome 12 intellectual

eggplant 7 brinjal 8 brinjaul 9 aubergine

egg-shaped 4 ooid, oval 5 ovate, ovoid 6 ooidal 7 oviform

eggshell 8 cascaron

Egil's brother 6 Volund

Eglah *husband:* 5 David *son:* 7 Ithream

eglantine 7 dog rose 10 sweetbrier

Eglantine *father:* 5 Pepin *husband:* 9 Valentine

Eglon *king:* 5 Debir *slayer:* 4 Ehud

ego 4 self 6 vanity 7 conceit 10 self-esteem

egocentric 7 pompous, selfish, stuck-up 9 conceited 10 self-loving 11 self-seeking, self-serving 12 megalomaniac, narcissistic, self-absorbed, self-affected, self-centered, self-involved, vainglorious 13 individualist, self-conceited, self-concerned, self-indulgent

egoism 5 pride 6 vanity 7 conceit 9 self-glory, self-pride, vainglory 11 self-opinion 13 self-assurance

egomaniacal 7 selfish 11 self-serving 12 self-absorbed, self-centered, self-exalting, self-involved, vainglorious 13 self-concerned

egotism 5 pride 6 vanity 7 conceit 8 boasting, bragging, self-love, vainness, vaunting 9 arrogance, gasconade, gasconism, self-glory, self-pride, vainglory 10 narcissism, self-esteem 11 megalomania, self-opinion, superiority 12 boastfulness 13 conceitedness

egotistic 5 cocky, proud 7 selfish, stuck-up 8 boastful, inflated, puffed up 9 conceited 11 pretentious, self-serving 12 self-absorbed, self-centered, self-involved 13 self-concerned, self-satisfied

egregious 4 rank 5 gross, stark 6 arrant 7 blatant, capital, glaring, heinous 8 flagrant, infamous, outright, shocking 9 atrocious 10 deplorable, outrageous

egress 4 door, exit 5 issue 6 escape, exodus, outlet 7 doorway, exiting, opening, passage 8 emerging, offgoing 9 departure, emergence 10 setting-out, withdrawal

egression 4 exit 6 exodus 7 exiting 8 offgoing 9 departure 10 setting-out, withdrawal

Egypt *capital:* 5 Cairo *monetary unit:* 5 pound

Egyptian 4 Arab, Copt 6 Coptic 7 African, Arabian *burial jar:* 7 canopic *Christian:* 4 Copt *cross:* 4 ankh *dam:* 4 sudd 5 Aswan *dancing girl:* 4 alme 7 ghawazi (plural) 8 ghawazee (plural) *dynasty:* 5 Saite, Xoite 6 Hyksos, Tanite, Theban 7 Persian, Thinite 8 Memphite 9 Bubastite, Ethiopian 10 Diospolite *god:* chief: 6 Amen-Ra *crocodile-headed:* 5 Sebek *falcon-headed:* 4 Ment 5 Horus, Mentu 6 Sokari 7 Sokaris *ibis-headed:* 5 Thoth 6 Dhouti *jackal-headed:* 6 Anubis *of chaos:* 2 Nu *of creation:* 4 Ptah 5 Phtha *of day:* 5 Horus *of earth:* 3 Geb, Keb, Seb *of evil:* 3 Set 4 Seth 5 Sebek *of life:* 4 Amen, Amon 5 Ammon *of magic:* 5 Thoth 6 Dhouti *of Memphis:* 4 Ptah 5 Phtha 6 Sokari 7 Sokaris *of pleasure:* 3 Bes *of procreation:* 3 Min *of the air:* 3 Shu *of the heavens:*

5 Horus *of the morning sun:* 5 Horus
7 Khepera *of the primeval flood:* 2 Nu *of
the setting sun:* 3 Tem, Tum 4 Atmu *of
the sun:* 2 Ra, Re 6 Amen-Ra *of Thebes:*
4 Amen 6 Khensu, Khonsu *of the underworld:* 6 Osiris *of war:* 4 Ment 5 Mentu
of wisdom: 5 Thoth 6 Dhouti *ram-
headed:* 4 Amen, Amon 5 Ammon,
Khnum 6 Khnemu *snake:* 4 Apep
5 Apepi
goddess:
  cat-headed: 4 Bast 5 Pakht *cow-headed:*
5 Athor 6 Hathor *lioness-headed:* 4 Bast
5 Pakht 6 Sekhet *of arms:* 4 Anta *of fertility:* 4 Isis *of love and mirth:* 5 Athor
6 Hathor *of moisture:* 6 Tefnut *of moth-
erhood:* 4 Apet, Isis *of Thebes:* 3 Mut *of
the dead:* 8 Nephthys *of the heavens:*
3 Nut *of truth and justice:* 4 Maat *queen
of the gods:* 4 Sati *vulture-headed:*
3 Mut 7 Nekhebt 8 Nekhebet
king: (see king entry)
language: 6 Arabic, Coptic *measure:*
3 apt, dra, hen, pik, rob 4 draa, roub
5 ardab, ardeb, cubit, farde, keleh, kilah,
sahme 6 artaba, aurure, feddan, keddah,
robbah 7 choryos, daribah, malouah, rou-
bouh, toumnah 8 kassabah, kharouba
10 dira baladi *month:* 4 Apap, Tybi
5 Payni, Thoth 6 Choiak, Hathor, Mechir,
Mesore, Paophi 7 Pachons 9 Phamenoth,
Pharmuthi *native:* 4 Arab, Copt 5 Nilot
president: 5 Sadat 6 Nasser 7 Mubarak
queen: 9 Cleopatra, Nefertiti *sacred bird:*
4 ibis *season:* 4 Ahet, Pert 5 Shemu
skink: 4 adda *snake symbol:* 6 uraeus
solar disk: 4 Aten *soul:* 2 ba, ka 3 akh
sultan: 7 Saladin *talisman:* 6 scarab
underworld: 4 Aaru, Duat 6 Amenti
weight: 3 kat, oka, oke 4 heml, okia, rotl
5 artal, artel, deben, kerat, okieh, uckia
6 hamlah, kantar 7 quintal *wind:* 7 cham-
sin, khamsin, sirocco 8 khamseen

Ehud's victim 5 Eglon

elder 4 down, duck 8 shoreyer

eidetic 5 vivid 8 lifelike

eidolon 4 icon 5 ghost, ideal, image
7 phantom, specter 8 exemplar, phantasm

eight *combining form:* 3 oct 4 octa, octo
group or: 5 octad, octet 6 octave, ogdoad
7 octette 8 octuplet

eight bells 4 noon

eighth note 6 quaver

Einstein 6 genius *birthplace:* 3 Ulm

einsteinium *symbol:* 2 Es

Eire see Ireland

ejaculate 4 blat, bolt, yell 5 eject, shout
6 cry out 7 exclaim 8 blurt out 10 vociferate

ejaculation see exclamation

eject 3 out 4 boot, bump, fire, oust, rout,
sack, shed, spew 5 belch, chase, chuck,
debar, eruct, erupt, evict, expel, spout,
spurn 6 banish, disbar, irrupt, run off, squirt
7 boot out, discard, dismiss, exclude,
extrude, kick out, rule out, shut out, sputter
8 disgorge, displace, drive off, throw out
9 discharge, ejaculate, eliminate, repudiate
10 dispossess

eke 4 fill 7 squeeze, stretch 10 supplement

elaborate 4 busy 5 fancy 6 daedal,
dressy, evolve, expand, knotty, ornate,
unfold 7 amplify, clarify, comment, complex, develop, discuss, elegant, enlarge,
explain, expound, gordian 8 detailed,
involved, overdone 9 Byzantine, decorated,
interpret, intricate 10 overworked 11 complicated, embellished, overwrought, painstaking 12 labyrinthine

Elah *father:* 4 Uzzi 5 Caleb 6 Baasha
slayer: 5 Zimri *son:* 6 Hoshea

Elaine *father:* 6 Pelles *lover:* 8 Lancelot
9 Launcelot *son:* 7 Galahad

Elam *capital:* 4 Susa 7 Shushan *father:*
4 Shem *king:* 12 Chedorlaomer

élan 3 vim 4 brio, dash, life, zeal, zest,
zing 5 ardor, gusto, oomph, verve, vigor
6 esprit, spirit 7 impetus, potency 9 animation, eagerness 10 enthusiasm

élan vital 4 soul 5 anima 6 animus,
pneuma, psyche, spirit

elapse 2 go 4 flow, pass, slip 5 glide,
slide 6 expire, run out 8 pass away

Elasah's father 6 Pashur 7 Shaphan

elastic 4 airy 5 lithe 6 bouncy, garter, limber, lively, pliant, rubber, supple, whippy
7 buoyant, ductile, pliable, rubbery, soaring,
springy, stretch 8 animated, flexible, moldable, spirited, stretchy, volatile 9 adaptable,
ebullient, expansive, malleable, resilient,
sprightly, vivacious 10 mettlesome, rubber-
like 11 stretchable

elate 4 buoy 5 cheer, exalt, flush, set up
6 excite, uplift 7 cheer up, commove,
delight, gladden, gratify, inspire, overjoy
8 brighten, inspirit, spirit up 9 encourage

elated 4 glad 5 happy 6 jovial 7 excited,
exulted 8 ecstatic, euphoric, exultant, glad-
some, jubilant, turned-on 9 overjoyed
10 enraptured 11 exhilarated, intoxicated

elater 6 beetle 8 skipjack 11 click beetle

Elatha's son 4 Bres

elation 3 joy 4 glee 7 rapture 8 buoyancy,
euphoria 9 happiness, transport 10 exaltation, excitement 12 exhilaration, intoxication

Elbe tributary 4 Eger, Iser

elbow 4 push 5 ancon, joint, nudge, press,
shove 6 hustle, jostle 8 bulldoze *relating
to:* 7 anconal

El Camino ___ 4 Real

elder 5 prior 6 senior 7 ancient, oldster 8 brass hat, higher-up, old-timer, superior 9 presbyter 10 golden-ager 13 senior citizen *French:* 4 aîné 5 aînée

elderliness 3 age 5 years 6 old age 8 caducity 10 senescence 11 senectitude

elderly 3 old 4 aged, gray 5 aging, olden 6 senile 7 ancient 9 declining

eldorado 4 mine 7 bonanza 8 Golconda, gold mine, treasury 13 treasure-house, treasure trove

eldritch 5 eerie, weird 7 uncanny

Eleanor's husband 7 Henry II

Eleazar *brother:* 5 Abihu, Nadab *father:* 4 Dodo 5 Aaron 6 Parosh 8 Abinadab, Phinehas *son:* 8 Phinehas

elect 3 opt 4 cull, like, mark, name, pick, rare, take, vote, will, wish 5 admit, co-opt, judge, saved 6 accept, ballot, choice, choose, chosen, decide, optate, opt for, picked, please, prefer, settle, single, vote in 7 appoint, receive, resolve 8 conclude, destined, nominate, ordained, redeemed 9 delivered, designate, determine, exclusive, single out 10 designated, handpicked, singled out

election 6 choice 7 primary 9 balloting 10 preference 11 alternative

electioneer 5 stump 8 campaign, politick

elective 6 chosen 8 optional 9 voluntary 13 discretionary, nonobligatory

Electra *brother:* 7 Orestes *father:* 5 Atlas 7 Oceanus 9 Agamemnon *husband:* 7 Pylades, Thaumas *mother:* 6 Tethys 7 Pleione 12 Clytemnestra *sister:* 4 Styx 9 Iphigenia *son:* 6 Iasion 8 Dardanus

electric *appliance:* 3 fan 4 iron, oven 5 clock, drier, mixer, range, stove 6 washer 7 blender, freezer, toaster 12 refrigerator *coil:* 5 tesla 8 solenoid *device:* 4 coil, fuse, plug 6 dynamo, magnet, switch 7 battery 8 resistor, rheostat, varistor 9 amplifier, capacitor, condenser, generator, rheotrope 11 transformer *generator:* 6 dynamo *particle:* 3 ion 8 thermion *resistance:* 6 ohmage *unit:* 3 amp, ohm, rel 4 volt, watt 5 farad, henry, joule 6 abvolt, ampere 7 coulomb, faraday 8 kilovolt, kilowatt

electric current 2 AC, DC *combining form:* 5 potam 6 potamo *kind:* 6 direct 11 alternating *power:* 7 wattage *strength:* 8 amperage

electricity 5 juice, spark 7 current 8 voltaism 9 galvanism, lightning 10 enthusiasm, excitement *kind:* 6 static 7 current

electrify 3 jar 4 send, stun 6 excite, thrill 7 enthuse, provoke, stagger, startle

electrode 6 dynode *negative:* 7 cathode *positive:* 5 anode

electron 3 ion 7 polaron 8 negatron *stream:* 10 cathode ray *tube:* 6 triode 7 tetrode 8 dynatron, klystron

Electryon *brother:* 6 Mestor *daughter:* 7 Alcmene *father:* 7 Perseus *mother:* 9 Andromeda *wife:* 5 Anaxo

eleemosynary 6 humane 7 liberal 8 generous 10 altruistic, beneficent, benevolent, charitable, munificent, openhanded 12 humanitarian 13 philanthropic

elegance 4 chic, pomp, tone 5 charm, grace, style, taste 6 beauty, luxury, polish 7 culture, dignity 8 chicness, lushness, poshness, richness, splendor 10 ornateness, refinement 11 cultivation 12 magnificence, tastefulness 13 sumptuousness

elegant 4 chic, fine, posh, rare 5 grand, noble, swank 6 august, choice, classy, dainty, lovely, select, swanky, urbane 7 courtly, genteel, opulent, refined, stately 8 cultured, delicate, finished, graceful, handsome, majestic, polished, superior, tasteful 9 beautiful, exquisite, luxurious, recherché, sumptuous 10 cultivated

elegy 4 poem, song 5 dirge 6 lament, monody 7 epicede 9 epicedium *Hebrew:* 5 kinah

Elektra composer 7 Strauss (Richard)

element 4 item, part 5 basic, facet, metal, piece, point, thing 6 aspect, detail, factor, member, sector 7 article, feature, portion, section 8 division, particle, rudiment 9 component, essential, principle 10 ingredient, particular 11 constituent, fundamental 13 part and parcel *chemical:* 3 tin 4 gold, iron, lead, neon, zinc 5 argon, boron, radon, xenon 6 barium, carbon, cerium, cesium, cobalt, copper, curium, erbium, helium, indium, iodine, nickel, osmium, oxygen, radium, silver, sodium 7 arsenic, bismuth, bromine, cadmium, calcium, fermium, gallium, hafnium, holmium, iridium, krypton, lithium, mercury, niobium, rhenium, rhodium, silicon, sulphur, terbium, thorium, thulium, uranium, yttrium 8 actinium, aluminum, antimony, astatine, chlorine, chromium, europium, fluorine, hydrogen, illinium, lutecium, masurium, nitrogen, nobelium, platinum, polonium, rubidium, samarium, scandium, selenium, tantalum, thallium, titanium, tungsten, vanadium 9 americium, berkelium, beryllium, columbium, germanium, lanthanum, magnesium, manganese, neodymium, neptunium, palladium, plutonium, potassium, ruthenium, strontium, tellurium, virginium, ytterbium, zirconium 10 dysprosium, gadolinium, lawrencium, molybdenum 11 californium, einsteinium, mendelevium, phosphorous 12 praseodymium 13 protoactinium *hypothetical:* 8 coronium

elemental 4 pure 5 basal, basic, crude, prime 6 inborn, innate, primal, simple 7 connate, primary, radical 8 inherent, intimate, simplest 9 beginning, essential, ingrained, intrinsic, primitive 10 deep-seated, primordial, substratal, underlying 14 constitutional

elementary 4 easy 5 basal, basic 6 simple 8 simplest, unsubtle 9 beginning, essential, prefatory, primitive 10 rudimental, substratal, underlying 11 fundamental, preliminary 12 introductory

elemi 5 animé, resin 9 oleoresin

elephant 5 hathi 6 muckna, tusker 9 pachyderm *boy:* 4 Sabu *driver:* 6 mahout *enclosure:* 5 kraal 6 keddah *extinct:* 7 mammoth 8 mastodon *female:* 3 cow *goad:* 5 ankus 7 ankusha *group:* 4 herd *keeper:* 6 mahout *male:* 4 bull *maverick:* 5 rogue *nose:* 5 trunk 9 proboscis *seat:* 6 howdah *sound:* 4 barr 6 bellow 7 trumpet *tooth:* 4 tusk *tusk:* 5 ivory *young:* 4 calf

elephant-headed god 6 Ganesa 7 Ganesha

elephantine 4 huge 6 clumsy 7 awkward, mammoth 8 colossal, enormous, gigantic 9 graceless, maladroit, monstrous, ponderous 10 behemothic, gargantuan, mastodonic, prodigious, ungraceful, uninspired 11 heavy-footed, heavy-handed

elevate 4 lift, rear, rise 5 boost, elate, ensky, erect, exalt, hoist, raise 6 pick up, prefer, take up, uphold, uplift, uprear 7 advance, enhance, glorify, promote, upgrade, upraise 8 heighten 10 exhilarate

elevated 4 high 5 grand, great, lofty, moral, noble 6 aerial, formal, lifted, raised, superb 7 ethical, exalted, stately, sublime, upright, uprisen 8 eloquent, majestic, towering, upheaved, uplifted, upraised, virtuous 9 dignified, grandiose, high-flown, honorable, righteous 10 high-minded, upstanding 13 grandiloquent

elevation 4 hill, rise 5 boost, mount, raise 6 ascent, height 7 advance, raising 8 altitude, highness, mountain 9 acclivity, promotion, upgrading 10 apotheosis, preference, preferment 11 advancement, ennoblement *indication:* 9 bench mark

elevator 4 cage, lift, silo 5 hoist 6 lifter, raiser 7 hoister *maker:* 4 Otis

eleven *combining form:* 5 undec 6 hendec 7 hendeca

elf 3 fay 4 ouph, peri, pixy 5 fairy, nisse, ouphe, pixie 6 goblin, sprite 7 brownie, gremlin 10 leprechaun

elfin 5 child 6 urchin

elfish see elvish

Elgin ____ 7 marbles

Eli 4 Yale *son:* 6 Hophni 8 Phinehas *successor:* 6 Ahitub

Eli ____ 7 Whitney

Eliab *brother:* 5 David *daughter:* 7 Abihail *father:* 5 Helon, Pallu *son:* 6 Abiram, Dathan

Eliada *father:* 5 David *son:* 5 Rezon

Eliakim's father 6 Josiah 7 Hilkiah

Eliam's daughter 9 Bathsheba

Eliasaph's father 4 Lael

Eliashib's father 4 Bani 5 Zattu 8 Elioenai

Eliathah's father 5 Heman

elicit 4 draw, milk 5 bring, cause, educe, evoke, fetch 6 derive, evince, extort 7 extract, provoke 8 bring out 9 call forth

elide 4 fail, omit, pass, skip 6 forget, ignore, slight 7 neglect 8 discount, overlook, suppress 9 disregard

Eliel's father 6 Hebron, Shimhi 7 Shashak

Eliezer's father 5 Harim, Moses 6 Zichri 7 Dodovah

eligible 3 fit 6 fitted, likely, nubile, seemly, suited, worthy 7 capable 8 suitable 9 desirable, qualified, visitable 10 acceptable, preferable 12 marriageable

Elihu ____ 4 Root, Yale

Elijah 5 Elias 7 prophet 8 Tishbite *father:* 5 Harim 7 Jeroham

Elimelech's wife 5 Naomi

eliminate 3 bar 4 bate, oust 5 debar, eject, erase, evict, expel, purge 6 delete, except, remove 7 dismiss, exclude, expunge, obviate, rule out, shut out, suspend, take out 8 count out 9 clear away, freeze out, liquidate

Eliot, George *novel:* 6 Romola 8 Adam Bede 11 Middlemarch, Silas Marner 14 Mill on the Floss

Eliot, T.S. *poem:* 9 Gerontion 12 Ash Wednesday, The Hollow Men, The Waste Land

Eliphal's father 2 Ur

Eliphaz *father:* 4 Esau *mother:* 4 Adah *son:* 5 Teman

Eliphelet's father 5 David 6 Hashum 7 Ahasbai 8 Adonikam

eliquate 4 melt 5 smelt

Elisabeth *husband:* 9 Zacharias *son:* 4 John (the Baptist)

Elisha *father:* 7 Shaphat *servant:* 6 Gehazi

Elishah's father 5 Javan

Elishama's father 5 David 7 Ammihud

Elisheba *brother:* 7 Nahshon *father:* 9 Amminadab *husband:* 5 Aaron *son:* 5 Abihu, Nadab 7 Eleazar, Ithamar

Elishua's father 5 David

Elissa see Dido

elite 3 top 4 best, pick 5 cream, elect, pride, prime, prize 6 choice, flower, gentry, jet set, select 7 aristoi, quality, society 8 optimacy, smart set 9 gentility 10 upper class, upper crust 11 aristocracy

Eliud *father:* 5 Achim *son:* 7 Eleazar

elixir 4 balm, cure 6 potion 7 arcanum, cure-all, nostrum, panacea, therapy 10 catholicon 11 therapeutic

Elizabeth I, name for 6 Oriana

Elizaphan see Elzaphan

elk 4 deer, losh 5 moose 6 sambar, sambur, wapiti

Elkanah *brother:* 5 Assir 8 Abiasaph *father:* 4 Joel 5 Korah 6 Mahath 7 Jeroham *son:* 6 Samuel *wife:* 6 Hannah 8 Peninnah

ell 3 arm 4 wing 5 annex, block 8 addition 9 extension

ellipse 4 oval 5 curve

elliptical 5 brief, ovate, short 7 concise, cryptic, summary 9 condensed, enigmatic

elm 5 wahoo

Elmire's husband 5 Orgon

elocution 7 oratory 8 rhetoric 11 speech-craft

elongate 4 draw 6 extend, string 7 draw out, lengthy, spin out, stretch 8 extended, lengthen, protract, wiredraw 10 lengthened

elongation 9 extension 10 production 11 lengthening, protraction

Elon's father 7 Zebulun

elope 4 flee 6 escape 7 run away

eloquence 5 force, power, vigor 6 fervor, spirit 7 passion 9 facundity 10 expression 12 expressivity, forcefulness

eloquent 4 glib, high, rich 5 lofty, vocal 6 ardent, facund, fervid, fluent, moving, potent 7 fervent, graphic, telling, voluble 8 elevated, forceful, poignant, powerful, pregnant, touching 9 affecting, revealing 10 articulate, expressive, impressive, indicative, meaningful, passionate, persuasive, suggestive 11 impassioned, sententious, significant 12 smooth-spoken 13 silver-tongued

Elpaal's father 9 Shaharaim

Elpalet's father 5 David

else 2 or 3 new 4 more 5 added, fresh, other 7 another, besides, farther, further 9 otherwise 10 additional

elucidate 5 clear, prove 7 clarify, clear up, explain 8 annotate, spell out 9 enlighten, exemplify, interpret 10 illuminate, illustrate

elude 3 fly, shy 4 bilk, duck, flee, foil, shun 5 avoid, dodge, evade 6 baffle, double, escape, eschew, outwit, thwart 9 frustrate 10 circumvate

elusion 6 escape 8 escaping, eschewal, shunning 9 avoidance, runaround

elusive 6 subtle, tricky 7 evasive, phantom 8 baffling, fleeting, fugitive, slippery 10 evanescent, intangible, mysterious 12 imponderable 13 insubstantial

elusory 5 vague 7 evasive 8 nebulous 10 intangible

elvish 5 antic 6 frisky, impish 7 coltish, larkish, playful, puckish, roguish 8 prankish, spiteful 9 kittenish 11 mischievous

elysium 4 Eden, Zion 5 bliss 6 Canaan, heaven 7 nirvana 8 empyrean, paradise 10 Civitas Dei 12 New Jerusalem

elytron 4 wing 5 scale, shard

Elzaphan's father 6 Uzziel 7 Parnach

emaciated 4 bony, lean 5 gaunt 6 skinny, wasted 7 scrawny, starved, wizened 8 skeletal, underfed 10 cadaverous

emaciation 5 tabes 7 atrophy 8 marasmus 10 starvation 11 attenuation

emanate 4 emit, flow, rise, stem 5 arise, birth, exude, issue 6 spring 7 proceed 9 originate 10 derive from

emanation 4 aura, flow 6 efflux 7 outcome 9 effluence 11 consequence

emancipate 4 free 5 loose 6 loosen, unbind 7 manumit, release, unchain 8 liberate, unfetter 9 discharge, unshackle 11 enfranchise

emancipation 7 freedom, release 10 liberation 11 deliverance

emancipator 5 Moses 7 Lincoln (Abraham) 9 deliverer

emasculate 3 wan 4 geld, weak 5 unman 6 soften, weaken 7 unnerve 8 boneless, castrate, enervate, impotent, unstring 9 forceless, spineless 10 devitalize, inadequate 11 ineffective, ineffectual

embalm 5 mummy 7 mummify, perfume 8 preserve

embankment 4 bund, dike, quay 5 levee, mound 7 parados 9 banquette

embargo 5 edict, order 8 blockade, stoppage 10 impediment 11 prohibition

embark 4 open 5 begin, board, enter, set to, start 6 engage, enlist, get off, set out, take up, tee off 7 jump off 8 commence

embarrass 3 vex 4 faze 5 abash, queer, upset 6 bother, flurry, hamper, impede, rattle 7 agitate, chagrin, confuse, flummox, fluster, nonplus, perturb 8 confound, distress 9 discomfit 10 discompose, disconcert

embarrassing 7 awkward 12 discommoding, incommodious, inconvenient 13 discommodious

embarrassment 5 shame 6 strain, unease 7 chagrin 8 distress, vexation 9 abashment, agitation, confusion 10 constraint, difficulty, discomfort, uneasiness 11 humiliation 12 discomfiture, discomposure, perturbation **13** disconcertion, mortification

embassy **5** envoy **8** legation **10** ambassador

embattle **7** fortify, prepare **9** crenelate **10** crenellate

embay **6** shut in **7** shelter **8** encircle, surround

embed **3** fix, set **4** root **5** infix, lodge **7** ingrain **8** entrench

embellish **3** pad **4** deck, gild, trim **5** adorn, array, color, dress, fudge, prank **6** bedeck, blazon, emboss, enrich **7** apparel, dress up, garnish, magnify **8** beautify, decorate, ornament **9** embroider **10** exaggerate

embellishment **7** garnish, melisma, mordent **8** coloring, ornament **9** fioritura, floridity, hyperbole **11** ostentation **12** embroidering, exaggeration **13** ornamentation

ember **3** ash **4** coal **6** cinder

embezzle **4** loot **5** steal **6** pilfer, thieve **8** peculate

embitter **4** sour **7** envenom **8** acerbate **9** acidulate **10** exacerbate

emblaze **5** adorn **6** kindle **9** embellish **10** illuminate

emblazon **4** deck, laud **5** adorn, extol **7** display, glorify **8** inscribe **9** celebrate

emblem **3** bar **4** mace, sign **5** badge, crest, image, token **6** device, symbol **8** insignia, monogram **9** attribute **10** coat of arms **11** adumbration *of mercy:* **8** red cross

embodiment **6** avatar **7** epitome **9** archetype **11** incarnation **13** manifestation

embody **4** fuse, have **5** blend, merge, reify, unify, unite **6** absorb, evince, mirror, take in, typify **7** combine, compose, contain, embrace, exhibit, include, involve, realize, subsume **8** manifest **9** actualize, encompass, epitomize, exemplify, incarnate, integrate, objectify, personify, personize, represent, symbolize **10** amalgamate, assimilate, comprehend, constitute, illustrate **11** consolidate, demonstrate, emblematize, exteriorize, externalize, hypostatize, incorporate, materialize, personalize **12** substantiate

embog **4** mine **5** delay **6** detain, hang up, retard, slow up **7** set back, slacken **8** slow down **10** decelerate

embolden **5** cheer, impel, nerve, steel **6** chance, hazard **7** animate, chirk up, hearten, inspire, venture **8** inspirit **9** encourage, enhearten **10** strengthen

embolus **4** clog, clot

embosom **7** enclose **8** surround

emboss **5** adorn, raise **8** ornament **9** embellish, embroider

embouchure **5** mouth **10** mouthpiece

embowel **3** gut **4** draw **6** paunch **10** eviscerate, exenterate

embrace **3** hug **4** clip, fold, grip, have, hold, lock, wrap **5** admit, adopt, bosom, clasp, cling, cover, press, twine **6** accept, cradle, cuddle, embody, enfold, enwind, fondle, nuzzle, take in, take on, take up **7** cherish, compose, contain, embosom, enclose, entwine, envelop, espouse, include, involve, receive, snuggle, squeeze, subsume, welcome **8** comprise, encircle **9** encompass **10** comprehend **11** accommodate, incorporate

embrangle **7** confuse

embrocation **8** liniment

embroider **3** pad, sew, tat **5** color, couch, fudge **6** emboss, expand, overdo, stitch **7** amplify, build up, distend, enhance, magnify, stretch, tambour **8** decorate, ornament **9** dramatize, elaborate, embellish, overstate **10** aggrandize, exaggerate **11** hyperbolize

embroidery **4** lace **6** edging **7** cutwork, orphery, pinwork **8** couching, smocking, tapestry **10** needlework

embroil **4** mire **6** tangle **7** confuse, involve **8** disorder, distract, entangle **9** implicate

embroilment **4** tiff **6** fracas **7** dispute, quarrel, wrangle **8** squabble **9** bickering **10** falling-out **11** altercation, controversy, involvement **12** entanglement

embryo **3** bud **4** germ, seed **5** fetus, spark **7** nucleus **8** blastula, gastrula *combining form:* **5** blast **6** blasto

emend **4** edit **5** alter, right **6** polish, revise **7** correct, improve, rectify, retouch

emerald **3** gem **5** beryl, green, stone

Emerald Isle **4** Eire, Erin **7** Ireland

emerge **4** flow, loom, rise, show, stem **5** arise, issue **6** appear, derive, spring **7** come out, proceed **9** originate **11** materialize

emergency **3** fix **4** hole, pass, push **5** pinch **6** climax, clutch, crisis, strait **7** squeeze **8** juncture *money:* **5** scrip

Emerson *forte:* **5** essay *friend:* **7** Thoreau (Henry David)

emery **5** board **6** powder **8** abrasive, corundum

Emesh *brother:* **5** Enten *father:* **5** Enlil

émeute **4** riot **6** tumult **8** outbreak, uprising

emigrant **7** pioneer, settler **8** colonist

emigré **2** DP **5** alien, exile **7** evacuee, refugee **8** expellee, fugitive **9** immigrant **10** expatriate

Emilia *husband:* **4** Iago **7** Palamon *slayer:* **4** Iago

eminence **3** VIP **4** fame, note, peak, rise **5** chief, glory, honor, kudos, power, raise

6 bigwig, credit, height, leader, renown, repute, uprise, weight **7** dignity, notable **8** altitude, big-timer, highness, luminary, prestige **9** authority, dignitary, elevation, greatness, influence, loftiness **10** famousness, importance, notability, prepotency, projection, prominency, reputation **11** distinction, superiority

eminent **3** big **4** high **5** famed, great, large, lofty, noble, noted **6** august, famous **7** big-name, big-time, exalted, notable **8** dominant, renowned, towering **9** big league, important, well-known **10** celebrated, celebrious **11** conspicuous, illustrious, outstanding **13** distinguished

eminently **4** very **6** highly **7** notably **9** extremely **10** remarkably, strikingly **11** exceedingly **12** surpassingly **13** exceptionally

emir **5** chief, noble, ruler, title **8** nobleman **9** chieftain

emissary see envoy

emission **4** flow **9** discharge, effluvium, emanation

emit **4** beam, drip, flow, glow, ooze, pour, reek, vent, void **5** expel, exude, issue, loose, utter **6** exhale, expire, let out **7** emanate, excrete, extrude, give off, give out, radiate, release, secrete **8** evacuate, throw off **9** discharge **10** disembogue

emmer **5** grain, spelt, wheat **6** speltz

emmet **3** ant **7** pismire

Emmor's son **7** Shechem

emolliate **6** soften, weaken

emollient **7** lenient **8** lenitive, sedative, soothing

emolument **3** fee, pay **4** hire, wage **6** salary **7** guerdon, stipend **11** pay envelope **12** compensation

emote **3** act **4** gush, rage, rant **5** storm **6** take on **7** carry on, overact

emotion **3** ire, joy **4** fear, glee, hate, love **5** agony, ardor, grief, shame **6** relief, sorrow **7** ardency, despair, disgust, ecstasy, feeling, passion, sadness **8** jealousy, movement, surprise **9** affection, agitation, happiness, sentiment **11** affectivity, sensibility, sensitivity **12** excitability **13** sensitiveness *combining form:* **4** thym **5** thymo **6** thymia

emotional **6** ardent, moving **7** feeling, fervent, soulful **8** sentient, stirring, touching **9** affecting, affective, rhapsodic, sensitive **10** hysterical, passionate, responsive, susceptive **11** rhapsodical, softhearted, susceptible, sympathetic

emotionless **3** icy **4** cold, cool **5** chill, staid **6** frigid, torpid **7** deadpan, distant, glacial **8** reserved **9** apathetic, immovable, impassive, unfeeling **10** impersonal

11 cold-blooded, indifferent **12** matter-of-fact **13** dispassionate, unimpassioned

empathy **4** pity **6** accord, warmth **7** concord, rapport **8** affinity, sympathy **9** communion **10** compassion **12** appreciation, congeniality **13** compatibility, comprehension, fellow feeling, understanding

emperor **4** czar, king, shah, tsar, tzar **5** ruler **6** caesar, kaiser, sultan **7** monarch **8** autocrat, dictator, imperial, padishah **9** sovereign *Japanese:* **6** mikado **7** Akihito **8** Hirohito

emphasis **5** focus, force **6** accent, stress, weight **9** attention **10** insistence **12** accentuation

emphasize **4** mark **5** press **6** accent, assert, charge, play up, stress **7** feature **8** pinpoint **9** highlight, italicize, punctuate, spotlight, underline **10** accentuate, underscore

emphatic **6** marked **7** decided, earnest, pointed **8** accented, forceful, positive, stressed, vigorous **9** assertive, energetic, insistent, insistive **10** aggressive, emphasized, resounding, underlined **11** accentuated, assertative

empire **4** rule, sway **5** power, realm, state **6** domain **7** demesne, kingdom, tsardom, tzardom **8** dominion, province **9** territory *ancient:* (see ancient empire)

Empire State **7** New York

empirical **7** factual **9** experient **12** experiential, experimental **13** observational

emplacement **7** battery, gallery **8** position

employ **3** add, use **4** busy, hire, work **5** apply, avail, exert, put on **6** bestow, devote, engage, handle, obtain, occupy, retain, secure, take on **7** engross, exploit, procure, utilize **8** exercise, practice

employee **4** hand, help **6** worker **7** servant **8** factotum **9** underling *bank:* **5** clerk, guard **6** teller *hotel:* **4** maid **5** clerk **7** bellboy, bellhop, doorman **9** concierge

employer **4** boss, user

employment **3** job, use **4** line, play, post, task, toil, work **5** trade, usage **6** hiring, office, usance **7** calling, mission, purpose, pursuit **8** business, engaging, exercise, exertion, function, handling, position, vocation **9** appliance, operation, situation **10** engagement, exercising, occupation **11** application, disposition, recruitment, utilization **12** exploitation

emporium **4** mall, mart, shop **5** store **6** bazaar, market **11** marketplace

empower **4** vest **5** endow **6** charge, enable, invest **7** entitle, entrust, license **8** accredit, deputize, sanction **9** authorize, privilege **10** commission

empress 5 queen *French:* 7 Eugénie
9 Josephine *Japanese:* 5 Suiko *of India:*
8 Victoria *Russian:* 4 Anna 7 czarina, tsar-
ina, tzarina 9 Catherine, Elizabeth

empressement 6 fervor, warmth 10 cordiality

emprise 4 feat, gest 7 exploit, venture
9 adventure 11 undertaking

emptiness 4 void 6 hunger, vacuum
7 inanity, vacancy, vacuity

emptor 5 buyer 6 vendee 9 purchaser
___ **emptor** 6 caveat

empty 3 rid 4 bare, dumb, dump, flat, idle,
pour, vain, void 5 banal, blank, clear, drain,
inane, petty, silly, stark, vapid 6 barren,
devoid, hollow, jejune, otiose, paltry,
unload, vacant, vacate 7 deadpan, deplete,
drained, exhaust, fatuous, foolish, insipid,
trivial, vacated, vacuous 8 depleted,
deserted, evacuate, forsaken, ignorant,
innocent, nugatory, trifling, unfilled 9 abandoned, destitute, exhausted 10 unoccupied, untenanted 11 godforsaken, ineffectual 12 inexpressive, unexpressive
14 expressionless *combining form:* 3 ken
4 keno *Scottish:* 4 toom

empty-headed 4 rude 5 dizzy, giddy,
silly 6 simple, vacant 7 flighty, vacuous
8 ignorant, skittish, untaught 9 benighted,
brainless, frivolous 10 illiterate, uneducated, unlettered, unschooled 11 harebrained, know-nothing 12 uninstructed
13 rattlebrained

empyreal 4 airy, holy 6 aerial, divine
7 sublime 8 heavenly 9 celestial, spiritual

empyrean 3 sky 4 Zion 5 bliss, ether
6 heaven, welkin 7 elysium, heavens, nirvana 8 heavenly, paradise 9 celestial, firmament 10 civitas Dei 12 New Jerusalem

emu 4 bird, rhea 6 ratite 9 cassowary

emulate 3 ape 4 copy 5 equal, rival
6 outvie 7 compete, imitate 8 rivalize
9 challenge

emulation 6 strife 7 contest, rivalry, warfare 8 conflict, striving, tug-of-war 9 imitation 10 contention 11 competition

emulous 5 vying 6 aiming 7 athirst
8 aspiring, striving, vaulting 9 ambitious
11 competitive

emulsifier 4 soap

enable 3 fit, let 5 allow, ready 6 permit
7 empower, entitle, license, prepare, qualify
8 accredit, sanction 9 authorize, condition
10 commission

enact 2 do 4 make, pass, play 6 decree,
depict, effect, ordain, ratify 7 execute, perform, portray 8 proclaim 9 authorize, discourse, establish, institute, legislate, personate, represent 10 accomplish, bring about,
constitute, effectuate 11 impersonate

enactment 3 law 6 action, assize, decree
7 statute 9 ordinance

enamel 5 email, glaze, gloss, paint

enamored 4 fond 5 dotty 6 loving,
mashed, soft on 7 charmed, devoted, smitten 8 besotted, spoony on 9 bewitched,
enchanted, entranced, infatuate 10 captivated, fascinated, infatuated, spoony over

Enan's son 5 Ahira

encamp 4 tent 6 settle 7 bivouac

encampment 6 laager 7 bivouac, hut-
ment

encase 7 enclose, envelop, sheathe

enceinte 8 pregnant 9 expectant, expecting 10 parturient

enchain 4 bind 6 fetter

enchant 3 hex 4 draw, send, take, wile
5 charm, spell, witch 6 allure, delude,
please, thrill, voodoo 7 attract, bewitch,
delight 9 captivate, ensorcell, fascinate,
magnetize, mesmerize, spellbind

enchanter 4 mage 5 magus 6 wizard
7 charmer, warlock 8 conjurer, magician,
sorcerer 9 voodooist 11 necromancer

enchanting 5 siren 7 sirenic 8 alluring,
charming 9 appealing, glamorous, seductive 10 attractive, bewitching, delectable,
delightful, intriguing 11 captivating, fascinating

enchantment 3 hex 5 charm, magic,
spell 7 sorcery 8 gramarye, witchery, wizardry 9 conjuring, magicking 10 necromancy, witchcraft 11 incantation

enchantress 3 hag, hex 5 bruja, Circe,
lamia, Medea, witch 9 sorceress 10 witchwoman

enchiridion 4 book, text 5 guide 6 manual 8 Baedeker, handbook 9 guidebook,
vade mecum 10 compendium

encincture 4 band, belt, gird 6 begird,
engird, girdle 8 begirdle, engirdle

encipher 4 code

encircle 3 hem 4 band, belt, gird, halo,
hoop, ring 5 girth 6 begird, engird, enlace,
girdle 7 compass, embrace, enclose, environ, wreathe 8 cincture, surround
9 encompass 12 circumscribe

enclose 3 box, hem, mew, pen, rim
4 cage, coop, mure, veil, wall, wrap
5 bound, fence, hedge, limit 6 circle, closet,
corral, encase, enfold, enlock, enwrap,
immure, invest, shroud, shut in 7 compass,
confine, contain, embosom, envelop, environ, harness 8 encircle, enshroud,
ensphere, imprison, insheath, restrict, surround 9 capsulize, encompass 12 circumscribe

enclosed 6 obtect

enclosure 3 box, haw, mew, pen, sty
4 bawn, cage, cell, coop, cote, fold, quad,

tank, trap, wall, weir, yard **5** booly, booth, court, crawl, fence, kench, pound, stall **6** aviary, cancha, corral, cowpen, garden, kennel, paling, prison **7** barrier, cockpit, paddock **8** cincture, cloister, sepiment, stockade **9** cofferdam, courtyard, curtilage **10** quadrangle, sheephouse *African:* **4** boma **5** kraal *elephant:* **6** keddah

encomiast 7 praiser **8** eulogist **10** panegyrist

encomiastic 9 laudative, laudatory, praiseful **11** panegyrical

encomium 4 laud **5** kudos **6** eulogy, praise **7** acclaim, tribute **8** accolade, applause, approval, citation, plaudits **9** laudation, panegyric **10** compliment, salutation **11** acclamation **12** commendation

encompass 3 hem **4** belt, gird, have, ring **5** beset, bound **6** begird, circle, embody, engird, girdle, take in **7** contain, delimit, embrace, enclose, environ, include, involve, subsume **8** encircle, surround **10** comprehend

encore 6 recall, repeat **8** call back **10** repetition

encounter 4 espy, face, find, fray, meet, spot **5** brush, catch, clash, close, fight, front, hit on, run-in, scrap, set-to **6** battle, descry, detect, engage, take on, turn up **7** affront, collide, contest, hit upon, meeting, quarrel **8** argument, conflict, confront, meet with, skirmish **10** contention, velitation

encourage 4 abet, back, push, stir **5** boost, cheer, favor, nerve, pique, rally, serve, steel **6** assist, assure, buck up, excite, foster, incite, induce **7** advance, animate, approve, chirk up, develop, endorse, fortify, forward, further, hearten, improve, prevail, promote, provoke, quicken, support, sustain **8** advocate, embolden, energize, inspirit, reassure, sanction **9** enhearten, galvanize, instigate, patronize, reinforce, stimulate, subsidize **10** invigorate, strengthen **11** countenance

encouragement 4 lift, push **5** boost **7** backing, support

encouraging 4 rosy **6** likely **7** hopeful, roseate **9** promising **10** promiseful **11** rose-colored

encroach 5 poach **6** invade, meddle, trench **7** impinge, intrude **8** entrench, infringe, overstep, trespass **9** interfere, interpose, intervene

encumber 3 tax **4** clog, lade, load **5** beset, block, weigh **6** burden, charge, fetter, hamper, hinder, impede, retard, saddle, weight **7** freight, oppress **8** handicap, obstruct, overload **9** incommode **10** discommode, overburden **13** inconvenience

encumbrance 4 clog, load **6** burden **8** handicap, hardship, mortgage **9** albatross

10 difficulty, impediment **12** disadvantage **13** inconvenience

encyclical 6 letter **7** general **8** circular

encyclopedic 5 broad **7** general **8** complete **9** extensive, inclusive **10** discursive **12** all-embracing, all-inclusive **13** comprehensive

encyclopedist 7 Diderot (Denis)

end 3 aim, bit, tip **4** coda, goal, halt, part, quit, stop, tail, term **5** bound, cease, close, death, finis, limit, piece, scrap **5** teloi (plural), telos **6** expire, finale, finish, object, period, scotch, windup, wrap up **7** abolish, closing, closure, extreme, leaving, lineman, purpose, remnant, residue **8** boundary, complete, conclude, confines, curtains, finality, fragment, particle, surcease, terminal, terminus, ultimate **9** cessation, desuetude, determine, extremity, objective, remainder, terminate **10** borderline, completion, conclusion, desistance, expiration, limitation **11** culmination, discontinue, termination **12** consummation *combining form:* **3** acr, akr, tel **4** acro, akro, tele, telo

endanger 4 risk **5** peril **6** chance, expose, hazard, menace **7** imperil, jeopard, venture **8** jeopardy **10** compromise, jeopardize

endeavor 3 aim, try **4** push, seek, toil, work **5** apply, assay, essay, labor, offer, trial **6** hassle, intend, strain, strive **7** address, attempt, purpose, travail **8** exertion, striving, struggle **9** determine, undertake **11** undertaking

ended 4 done, down, over, past **7** through **8** complete, finished **9** completed **10** terminated

endemic 5 local **6** native **8** home-bred **10** aboriginal, indigenous, native-born

ending 4 stop **5** close **6** finale, finish, period, windup **7** closing **9** cessation **10** conclusion, desistance **11** termination

endive 4 herb **7** witloof **8** escarole

endless 7 eternal, forever, undying **8** constant, immortal, infinite, overlong, unending **9** ceaseless, continual, limitless, perpetual, unbounded, unceasing, unlimited **10** continuous, indefinite, unmeasured **11** amaranthine, everlasting, measureless **12** immeasurable, interminable

endmost 8 farthest, furthest

endocrine gland 5 gonad, ovary **6** pineal, testis, thymus **7** adrenal, thyroid **8** pancreas **9** pituitary **11** parathyroid **12** hypothalamus

endomorphic 6 pyknic

endorse 2 OK **4** okay, sign, visa, visé **5** vouch **6** attest, ratify, second, uphold **7** approve, certify, command, stand by, support, witness **8** accredit, advocate, champion, sanction 9 recommend 12 authenticate

endorsement 2 OK 4 fiat, visa 7 support 8 approval, sanction 9 signature

endow 4 back, fund 5 award, dower, found, grant 6 accord, bestow, confer, donate, enable, enrich, supply 7 empower, enhance, finance, promote, provide, sponsor, support 8 bequeath, heighten, organize 9 crown with, subscribe, subsidize 10 contribute

endowment 4 fund, gift 5 dower, dowry, grant, power, skill 6 talent 7 ability, chantry 8 appanage, dotation

end product 5 issue 6 effect, result, sequel, upshot 7 outcome 8 sequence 9 aftermath 11 aftereffect, consequence

endue 4 vest 5 dower, equip 6 clothe, invest, outfit 7 furnish 8 accouter 9 crown with

endurance 4 wind 5 pluck 7 stamina 8 duration, patience, strength 9 tolerance 10 continuity, toleration 11 persistence 12 continuation, perseverance

endure 2 go 4 bear, bide, last, take, wear 5 abide, allow, brook, stand 6 accept, linger, pocket, suffer 7 outlast, outlive, persist, stomach, sustain, swallow, undergo 8 bear with, continue, tolerate, tough out 9 withstand 12 carry through

enduring 3 old 4 fast, firm, sure 5 solid, sound 6 stable, steady, sturdy 7 abiding, durable, eternal, lasting, staunch 8 lifelong, resolute 9 diuturnal, long-lived, perennial, permanent, steadfast 10 continuing, inveterate, perdurable 11 long-lasting, substantial, unfaltering, unqualified 12 never-failing

Endymion *father:* 8 Aethlius *lover:* 5 Diana 6 Selene

enemy 3 foe 5 rival 7 hostile, invader 8 attacker, emulator, opponent 9 adversary, assailant, combatant, contender 10 antagonist, competitor

energetic 4 spry 5 brisk, fresh, lusty, peppy, vital, zippy 6 active, breezy, lively 7 driving, dynamic, vibrant 8 animated, spirited, tireless, vigorous 9 sprightly, strenuous, vivacious 10 aggressive, red-blooded 12 enterprising 13 indefatigable

energize 3 arm, pep 4 fuel 5 liven 6 actify, enable 7 empower, fortify, sustain 8 activate, activize, vitalize 9 reinforce 10 invigorate, strengthen

energy 2 go 3 pep, vim, zip 4 beef, birr, life, tuck 5 force, might, power, sinew, steam, vigor 6 effort, muscle, spirit 7 potency 8 activity, efficacy, strength 9 hardihood, puissance, toughness 10 mightiness 11 application 12 forcefulness, powerfulness 13 effectiveness, operativeness *excessive:* 7 sthenia *unit:* 3 erg

4 dyne, volt 5 joule 7 quantum 10 horsepower

enervate 3 sap 4 jade, tire 5 unman, weary 6 soften, weaken 7 disable, exhaust, fatigue, unnerve 8 enfeeble, unstring 10 devitalize

enfant terrible 4 limb 5 devil, rogue, scamp 6 rascal 7 villain 8 mischief, scalawag 9 skeezicks 11 rapscallion

enfeeble 3 sap 5 blunt 6 soften, weaken 7 cripple, disable, exhaust, unbrace 8 enervate 9 attenuate, undermine 10 debilitate, devitalize 12 unstrengthen

enfold 3 hug 4 gird, veil, wrap 5 clasp, cover, drape, press 6 encase, enwrap, girdle, invest, shroud, swathe 7 embrace, enclose, envelop, environ, squeeze 8 encircle, enshroud, surround 9 encompass, ensheathe

enforce 5 exact 6 compel, effect, invoke, oblige 7 execute, fulfill 9 discharge, implement, prosecute 10 accomplish, administer

enfranchise 4 free 6 rescue 7 deliver, manumit, release 8 liberate 9 extricate 10 emancipate

engage 3 tie 4 bind, busy, face, grip, hire, meet, mesh, pass, soak 5 fight, imbue, put on, troth 6 absorb, arrest, attack, battle, commit, employ, enlist, occupy, pledge, strike, take on 7 assault, betroth, engross, immerse, involve, promise 8 affiance, enthrall, interact 9 captivate, encounter, fascinate, interlace, interlock, intermesh, interplay, preoccupy, undertake *passage:* 4 book

engaged 4 busy, deep, rapt 6 intent 7 working, wrapped 8 absorbed, employed, immersed, intended, occupied, plighted 9 affianced, betrothed, committed, engrossed, wrapped up 10 contracted 11 preoccupied *person:* 6 fiancé 7 fiancée

engage in 4 wage 5 enter *suffix:* 3 ize

engagement 4 date, word 5 troth, tryst, visit 6 action, battle, hiring, pledge, plight 7 booking, meeting, promise 8 espousal 9 betrothal, interview 10 betrothing, employment, invitation, rendezvous 11 assignation

engaging 5 siren, sweet 6 dulcet 7 winning, winsome 8 magnetic, mesmeric 9 glamorous 10 attractive, bewitching, employment, intriguing 11 fascinating 13 prepossessing

engender 4 stir 5 beget, breed, cause, hatch, rouse 6 arouse, excite, induce, work up 7 develop, produce, provoke, quicken 8 generate, muster up, occasion 9 stimulate

engine 5 motor, turbo 7 turbine 10 locomotive *kind:* 3 gas, jet 5 steam 6 diesel 7 turbine 8 gasoline 9 hydraulic *jet:* 8 turbofan, turbojet *part:* 3 cam, rod 4 gear, plug, pump 5 choke 6 filter, piston, tappet 8 cylinder, manifold, throttle 9 condenser, crankcase 10 carburetor 12 transmission *siege:* 3 ram 12 battering ram *sound:* 4 chug

engineer 4 plan, plot 5 set up, swing 6 devise, driver, manage, scheme, wangle 7 arrange, finagle 8 contrive, intrigue, maneuver 9 machinate, negotiate 10 manipulate, mastermind *kind:* 5 civil 6 mining 8 chemical, sanitary 10 electrical, mechanical 12 aeronautical *military:* 6 sapper

engineers' group *abbreviation:* 4 IEEE

England 6 Albion 7 Britain 9 Britannia 12 Great Britain *capital:* 6 London *monetary unit:* 5 pound

English 7 British *cathedral city:* 3 Ely 4 York 5 Wells 6 Durham, Exeter 7 Lincoln, Norwich 8 Coventry, Hereford 9 Salisbury, Worcester 10 Canterbury, Winchester *coin:* 5 angel, crown, groat, pence 6 florin, guinea, seskin 7 angelet 8 farthing, shilling, sixpence, twopence 9 fourpence, half crown, halfpenny, sovereign 10 threepence *combining form:* 5 Anglo *farm:* 5 croft *forest:* 5 Arden 8 Sherwood *letter:* 3 zed *measure:* 3 ell, pin, rod, tun 4 comb, coom, gill, hand, hide, line, peck, pint, pipe, pole, pool, span, yard, yoke 5 chain, coomb, crane, digit, hutch, jugum, perch, point, truss 6 barrel, bovate, bushel, fathom, firkin, runlet, strike, sulung 7 furlong, quarter, rundlet, virgate 8 carucate, chaldron, hogshead, puncheon, quartern, standard 9 kilderkin 10 barleycorn *military college:* 9 Sandhurst *patron saint:* 6 George *person:* 4 chap 5 bloke 6 Briton *pirate:* 4 Kidd *prince:* 5 Harry 6 Andrew, Edward, Philip 7 Charles, William *princess:* 4 Anne 5 Diana 8 Margaret *professor:* 3 don *royal family:* 7 Windsor *saint:* 7 Dunstan 8 Cuthbert *spa:* 4 Bath *sport:* 5 rugby 7 cricket *tavern:* 3 pub *university:* 5 Leeds 6 Oxford 9 Cambridge *weight:* 3 kip, tod 4 keel 5 barge, fagot, stand, stone, tross 6 firkin, fother, fotmal, pocket 7 quintal 8 quartern

English Channel swimmer 6 Ederle (Gertrude)

englut 4 bolt, cram, gulp, slop, wolf 5 slosh 6 gobble, guzzle 11 ingurgitate

engrave 3 cut, fix 4 etch, root 5 carve, chase, embed, infix, print 6 incise, scrive 7 enchase, impress, imprint, ingrain, insculp, instill 8 entrench, inscribe

engraver 6 chaser, etcher *German:* 5 Dürer (Albrecht) 10 Schongauer (Martin) *Italian:* 8 Raimondi (Marcantonio)

engraving 7 etching, woodcut 8 drypoint, intaglio 9 xylograph *combining form:* 5 glypt 6 glypto

engross 4 bury, busy, fill, grip, hold, soak 5 apply, sew up, write 6 absorb, arrest, engage, indite, occupy, scribe, scroll, take up 7 attract, consume, immerse, involve 8 enscroll, enthrall, inscribe 9 captivate, preoccupy 10 assimilate, monopolize 11 superscribe

engrosser 7 copyist 12 calligrapher 13 calligraphist

engulf 5 drown, flood, swamp, whelm 6 deluge, devour 7 swallow 8 inundate, overflow, submerge 9 overwhelm

enhance 4 lift, rise, suit 5 adorn, exalt, mount, raise, rouse 6 become, deepen 7 augment, elevate, flatter, magnify 8 beautify, heighten, increase, redouble 9 aggravate, embellish, embroider, intensate, intensify 10 exaggerate, strengthen

enhearten 5 cheer, nerve, steel 7 animate, chirk up 8 embolden, inspirit 9 encourage

enigma 3 why 4 crux, knot 5 rebus 6 puzzle, riddle 7 mystery, problem, puzzler, sticker 8 question 9 conundrum 10 closed book, perplexity, puzzlement 12 bewilderment, question mark 13 Chinese puzzle, mystification

enigmatic 4 dark 6 mystic 7 cryptic, obscure 8 Delphian, puzzling 10 mystifying

enisle 6 cut off 7 isolate 8 close off, insulate, separate 9 segregate, sequester

enjoin 3 ban, bid 4 deny, rule, tell, warn 5 order, taboo 6 adjure, advise, charge, decree, direct, forbid, impose, outlaw 7 caution, command, counsel, dictate, inhibit 8 admonish, disallow, forewarn, instruct, prohibit 9 interdict, prescribe

enjoy 3 own 4 fill, have, hold, like, love 5 boast, eat up, fancy, savor 6 occupy, relish, retain 7 command, possess 8 maintain 10 appreciate *a break:* 8 take five

enjoyableness 7 amenity 8 pleasure 9 geniality, pleasance 10 amiability, cordiality 12 agreeability

enjoyment 4 ease, zest 5 gusto, savor 6 relish 7 delight 8 felicity, fruition, pleasure 9 diversion 10 indulgence, recreation, relaxation 11 delectation 12 satisfaction 13 gratification

Enki *consort:* 5 Nintu *son:* 6 Ninsar

enkindle 4 fire 5 light 6 ignite 7 inflame

enlarge 3 wax 4 grow, rise 5 add to, boost, build, mount, widen 6 beef up, expand, extend 7 amplify, augment, develop, greaten, magnify, stretch, upsurge 8 heighten, increase, multiply 9 elaborate, embroider 10 aggrandize, exaggerate

enlargement 4 node 5 tumor 6 growth, nodule 8 addition, increase, swelling 9 accretion, expansion, extension *combining form:* 4 auxe 5 auxae (plural) 6 megaly 7 megalia

enlarging *combining form:* 4 micr 5 micro

enlighten 5 edify, guide, teach, train 6 advise, direct, illume, inform, school, uplift 7 apprise, educate, improve 8 acquaint, illumine, instruct 9 irradiate 10 illuminate

Enlil *father:* 2 An *mother:* 2 Ki *son:* 5 Nanna 6 Nergal, Ninazu *wife:* 6 Ninlil

enlist 4 join 5 enter 6 enroll, join up, muster, sign on, sign up 8 register 9 volunteer

enlistment 5 hitch

enliven 3 pep 4 fire, warm 5 amuse, cheer, pep up, renew, rouse 6 excite, jazz up, vivify 7 animate, inspire, quicken, refresh, restore 8 enspirit, recreate 9 entertain, galvanize, stimulate 10 exhilarate, invigorate, rejuvenate, vivificate

enmesh 4 hook, trap 5 catch 6 draw in, tangle 7 ensnarl, trammel 8 drag into, entangle 9 embrangle, implicate

enmity 4 feud, gall, hate 5 spite 6 animus, hatred, malice, rancor, spleen 7 dislike, ill will 8 aversion, bad blood, loathing 9 animosity, antipathy, hostility, malignity 10 abhorrence, alienation, antagonism, bitterness, malignancy 11 detestation, malevolence 12 disaffection, estrangement, uncordiality

ennoble 5 exalt, honor, raise 6 uplift, uprear 7 dignify, glorify, magnify, sublime 10 aggrandize 11 distinguish

ennui 4 bore, pall, tire, yawn 5 blues, dumps, weary 6 apathy, tedium 7 boredom, fatigue, languor, sadness, satiety, surfeit 8 doldrums 9 dejection, tiredness, weariness 10 depression, melancholy 11 languidness 12 listlessness

Enoch *father:* 4 Cain *son:* 10 Methuselah

Enoch Arden author 8 Tennyson (Alfred)

enormity 7 bigness, outrage 8 atrocity, hugeness, rankness, vastness 9 depravity, flagrancy, graveness, greatness, grossness, immensity, magnitude 11 heinousness, massiveness, seriousness, weightiness 13 atrociousness, monstrousness

enormous 3 big 4 huge, vast 5 great, large 7 immense, mammoth, titanic 8 colossal, gigantic 9 monstrous 10 gargantuan, prodigious, stupendous, tremendous

Enos *father:* 4 Seth *grandfather:* 4 Adam *grandmother:* 3 Eve *uncle:* 4 Abel, Cain

enough 6 fairly, plenty 8 adequacy, adequate, decently, passably 9 abundance, ampleness, averagely, competent, sufficing, tolerably 10 abundantly, acceptably, adequately, admissibly, competence, moderately, sufficient 11 comfortable, sufficiency 12 satisfactory, sufficiently *poetic:* 4 enow

enounce 3 say 5 state, utter 8 proclaim

enrage 3 ire, mad 5 anger 6 madden 7 incense, inflame, steam up, umbrage 9 infuriate

enrapture 5 charm, elate 6 allure, please, ravish, trance 7 attract, enchant, gladden, gratify, rejoice 8 enravish, enthrall, entrance 9 captivate, fascinate, transport

enrich 5 adorn, endow 6 fatten, richen 9 embellish

enroll 4 book, join, list 5 enter 6 enlist, induct, insert, join up, line up, muster, record, sign on, sign up 7 catalog, recruit 8 inscribe, register 11 matriculate

ensconce 4 bury, hide 5 cache, cover, place, plant, stash 6 locate, settle 7 conceal, install, secrete, situate 9 establish

ensemble 5 decor, group, suite, whole 6 outfit 7 costume 9 aggregate

enshroud 4 hide, veil, wrap 5 cloak 6 enfold, enwrap, invest 7 conceal, curtain, enclose, envelop

ensign 4 flag, jack 5 color 6 banner, pennon 7 pennant 8 gonfalon, standard, streamer 9 oriflamme

enslave 4 yoke 5 chain 6 thrall 7 oppress, shackle, subject 8 enthrall 9 subjugate 12 disfranchise

enslavement 4 yoke 6 thrall 7 bondage, helotry, peonage, serfdom, slavery 9 servitude, thralldom, villenage

ensnare 3 bag, net 4 hook, lure, mesh, snag, trap 5 benet, catch, decoy 6 enmesh, entice, entrap, tangle 7 capture, catch up 8 entangle, inveigle

ensnarl 6 enmesh, tangle 7 perplex, trammel 8 entangle 9 embrangle 11 intertangle

ensorcell 3 hex 5 charm, spell, witch 6 voodoo 7 bewitch, enchant

ensorcellment 5 magic 7 sorcery 8 witchery, wizardry 9 conjuring 10 necromancy, witchcraft 11 bewitchment, enchantment, incantation

ensphere 4 ball 5 round 8 conglobe 10 conglobate

ensue 4 stem 5 issue 6 attend, derive, follow, result 7 emanate, proceed, succeed 9 supervene

ensuing 4 next 5 after, later 6 coming 9 following, posterior 10 subsequent 12 postliminary 13 subsequential

ensure 5 cinch 6 secure 7 certify, warrant 9 establish, guarantee

enswathe 4 roll 5 drape 6 enwrap, wrap up 7 envelop, swaddle

entail 6 assign, confer, impose 7 require
8 transmit 11 necessitate

entangle 3 bag 4 clog, mesh, mire, trap
5 benet, catch, ravel, snare, snarl, tie up,
twist 6 ball up, burden, enmesh, entrap, fetter, hamper, impede, muddle 7 capture,
catch up, embroil, ensnare, ensnarl,
involve, perplex, trammel 10 complicate,
intertwine, interweave

entanglement 3 web 4 knot, mesh, toil
6 affair, cobweb 7 contact, liaison
8 intrigue 10 enmeshment 11 association,
embroilment, ensnarement, involvement

Enten *brother:* 5 Emesh *father:* 5 Enlil

entente 6 treaty 8 alliance 9 agreement,
coalition

enter 4 go in, join, list, open, post 5 admit,
begin, probe, put in, set to, start 6 come in,
docket, enlist, enroll, go into, inject, insert,
join up, muster, pierce, record, sign on, sign
up, take up 7 ingress, lead off 8 come into,
commence, embark on, inscribe, register
9 introduce, penetrate 10 embark upon,
inaugurate

enterprise 4 deed, feat, firm, gest, push,
task 5 cause, drive, house, vigor 6 action,
daring, effort, energy, hustle, outfit
7 attempt, company, concern, courage,
exploit, project, pursuit, venture 8 ambition,
boldness, business, campaign, endeavor,
industry, interest, striving, struggle
9 adventure, eagerness 10 enthusiasm,
get-up-and-go, initiative 11 corporation,
speculation, undertaking 12 organization,
self-reliance 13 ambitiousness, establishment, inventiveness

enterprising 4 bold, busy 5 eager
6 active, daring, hungry, lively 7 craving,
dashing, driving, go-ahead, itching, lusting,
pushing, zealous 8 aspiring, diligent, hustling, yearning 9 ambitious, audacious,
energetic, gumptious 10 aggressive
11 adventurous, hard-working, industrious,
up-and-coming, venturesome

entertain 4 host 5 amuse, board, house,
lodge, put up 6 bestow, billet, divert, foster,
harbor, invite, please, regale 7 cherish,
delight, enliven, gladden, gratify, nourish,
receive, rejoice 8 domicile, recreate

entertainer 4 host, mime 5 actor, comic
6 amuser, busker, dancer, singer 7 actress,
trouper 8 comedian, minstrel *female:*
7 actress, diseuse, hostess 10 comedienne

entertainment 4 fete, play, show, skit
5 cheer, revue, sport 6 circus, gaiety, relief
7 banquet, concert, disport, ridotto 8 pleasure 9 amusement, diversion, enjoyment
10 recreation, relaxation 11 dissipation,
distraction

enthrall 4 grip, hold 5 charm 6 absorb,
engage, master, subdue 7 catch up,

enchant, engross, enslave 8 intrigue 9 fascinate, mesmerize, preoccupy, spellbind,
subjugate

enthuse 4 rave, send 5 drool 6 thrill
8 rhapsody 9 electrify 10 rhapsodize

enthusiasm 4 élan, fire, zeal, zest, zing
5 ardor, craze, mania, verve 6 fervor, hurrah, spirit 7 ardency, earnest, passion
8 interest 9 eagerness 10 ebullience

enthusiast 3 bug, fan, nut 4 bear, buff
5 fiend, freak, lover 6 addict, maniac,
votary, zealot 7 devotee, fanatic, habitué
8 partisan 9 extremist, supporter 10 aficionado

enthusiastic 4 gaga, keen 5 eager, nutty,
rabid 6 ardent, gung ho, hearty, hipped, raring 7 devoted, fervent, zealous 8 hopped-
up, obsessed, spirited, vascular 10 passionate

entice 4 bait, coax, lure, toll, wile 5 charm,
decoy, tempt 6 allure, cajole, entrap, lead
on, seduce 8 inveigle, persuade

enticement 4 bait, lure, trap 5 decoy,
snare 6 come-on 10 allurement, seducement, temptation 12 inveiglement

enticer 4 bait, vamp 5 Circe, decoy, siren
7 Lorelei, seducer, taunter, tempter
9 attractor, enchanter, temptress 10 attraction, seductress 11 enchantress, femme
fatale

enticing 5 siren 6 luring 7 circean, likable
8 fetching, inviting, pleasant, pleasing,
tempting, witching 9 beguiling 10 attractive, bewitching, enchanting, intriguing
11 captivating, fascinating

entire 3 all 4 full 5 gross, sound, total,
whole 6 choate, intact, unhurt 7 perfect,
plenary, unified 8 complete, integral, outright, unbroken, unmarred 9 compacted,
undamaged, uninjured 10 integrated, unimpaired 12 concatenated, consolidated *combining form:* 3 hol 4 holo 7 integri

entirely 3 but 4 only, well 5 alone, fully,
quite 6 solely, wholly 7 utterly 9 perfectly
10 altogether, completely, thoroughly
11 exclusively *combining form:* 3 pam,
pan 4 pano

entirety 3 all, sum 5 gross, total, unity,
whole 7 allness, complex, omneity, oneness 8 sum total, totality 9 aggregate,
integrity, plenitude, wholeness 10 everything 12 collectivity, completeness, universality

entitle 3 dub, let 4 call, name, term
5 allow, style 6 enable, permit 7 baptize,
empower, license, qualify 8 christen, headline, nominate 9 authorize, designate
10 denominate

entity 3 ens, sum 4 body, unit 5 being,
stuff, thing, whole 6 matter, object, system
8 existent, integral, material, totality 9 exis-

tence, integrate, something, substance
10 individual

entomb 4 bury 5 inter, inurn 6 inhume,
shrine 8 enshrine 9 sepulcher, sepulture
11 ensepulcher

entombment 6 burial 9 interment, sepulture 10 inhumation

entourage 5 suite, train 7 retinue, toadies
9 courtiers, followers, following, hangers-on,
retainers 10 associates, attendants, syco-
phants

entr'acte 8 interval 9 interlude 12 intermission

entrails 4 guts 5 pluck 6 bowels, tripes,
vitals 7 giblets, innards, insides, inwards,
viscera 8 stuffing 9 internals 10 intestines
combining form: 9 splanchno

entrammel 3 tie 4 clog, curb 5 leash
6 fetter, hamper, hobble, hog-tie 7 shackle

entrance 3 way 4 adit, door, gate
5 charm, entry, foyer, mouth 6 access,
coming, entrée, please, portal, ravish 7 arrival, attract, bewitch, doorway, enchant,
gladden, ingoing, ingress, opening, rejoice
8 aperture, enravish, enthrall, entryway,
incoming, open door 9 admission, captivate, enrapture, fascinate, hypnotize, spellbind, threshold, transport 10 admittance,
ingression 11 penetration

entrant 7 starter 10 competitor, contestant
11 participant

entrap 3 bag, net 4 bait, lure, toll 5 benet,
catch, decoy, snare, tempt 6 allure, entice,
entoil, lead on, seduce, tangle 7 catch up,
ensnare 8 entangle, inveigle

entreat 3 ask, beg, bid 4 coax, pray, urge
5 crave, plead, press 6 appeal, invoke, pester, plague 7 beseech, implore, wheedle
8 blandish 9 importune 10 supplicate

entreaty 4 plea, suit 6 appeal, orison,
prayer 8 petition 11 application, imploration, imprecation 12 supplication

entre ___ 4 nous

entrechat 4 leap

entrée 3 way 4 adit, door 6 access
7 ingress 8 entrance, main dish 9 admission 10 admittance, main course

entrench 3 fix 4 root 5 embed, found,
infix, lodge 6 define, ground, invade, settle
7 confirm, implant, ingrain 8 encroach,
infringe, trespass 9 establish, interfere,
intervene 10 strengthen

entrenched 5 sworn 7 settled 8 deep-
dyed 9 confirmed, hard-shell 10 deep-
rooted, deep-seated, inveterate 13 bred-in-
the-bone, dyed-in-the-wool

entrepôt 9 warehouse 10 storehouse

entrepreneur 6 backer, broker 7 manager 8 mediator, producer, promoter 9 go-
between, middleman, organizer 10 contractor, impresario, interagent, interceder,

undertaker 11 intercessor 12 intermediary,
intermediate 13 administrator, intermediator

entresol 9 mezzanine

entrust 4 bank, give, rely 5 allot, count,
leave 6 assign, charge, commit, confer,
depend, impose, reckon 7 commend, confide, consign, deliver, deposit 8 allocate,
delegate, hand over, relegate, turn over

entry 3 way 4 adit, door 5 debit 6 access,
credit, portal 7 doorway, ingress, opening
9 admission, threshold 10 admittance,
enlistment, enrollment, ingression

entwine 4 coil, curl, lace, wind 5 braid,
twist 6 enmesh, spiral 7 entwist, wreathe
8 entangle 9 corkscrew, interlace 10 inter-
plait, intertwine, interweave

enumerate 4 list, tell 5 count, tally
6 detail, number, recite, relate 7 itemize,
mention, recount, specify, tick off 8 identify
9 inventory 10 specialize 13 particularize

enunciate 3 say 4 show 5 state, utter,
voice 6 affirm, intone, submit 7 advance,
declare, develop, enounce, express, lay
down, outline, phonate 8 announce, modulate, proclaim, vocalize 9 formulate, postulate, pronounce 10 articulate

envelop 3 hem, pen 4 cage, coop, hide,
mask, roll, veil, wrap 5 cloak, drape, fence,
guard, hedge 6 cocoon, corral, enfold,
enwrap, immure, invest, sheath, shield,
shroud, shut in, swathe, wrap up
7 enclose, protect, swaddle 8 enshroud,
enswathe, surround 10 circumfuse

envenom 6 poison 7 corrupt 8 acerbate,
embitter 10 exacerbate

envious 6 greedy 7 jealous, longing
8 appetent, coveting, covetous, desirous,
grasping, grudging, yearning 9 green-eyed,
invidious, resentful 10 begrudging, umbrageous

environ 3 hem 4 gird, ring 5 beset, fence,
limit, round 6 circle, suburb 7 compass,
enclose, envelop 8 encircle, go around, surround 9 encompass

environment 6 medium, milieu 7 ambient, climate, context, element, habitat, setting 8 ambience, backdrop 9 situation
10 atmosphere, background, mise-en-
scène 12 surroundings *combining form:*
2 ec 3 eco, oec 4 oeco, oiko *science:*
7 ecology

environmentalist 6 Carson (Rachel)
9 ecologist

environs 6 bounds, limits 7 compass,
fringes, suburbs 8 boundary, confines,
locality, purlieus, vicinity 9 outskirts, precincts 12 neighborhood, surroundings

envisage 4 view 5 fancy, grasp, image,
think 6 behold, regard, survey, vision 7 feature, foresee, imagine, picture, realize

8 conceive, envision, look upon **9** objectify, visualize

envision 4 view **5** dream, fancy, image, think **7** feature, foresee, imagine, picture, realize **8** conceive, summon up **9** conjure up, visualize

envoy 6 bearer, consul, deputy, legate, nuncio **7** attaché, carrier, courier **8** diplomat, emissary, minister **9** messenger **10** ambassador, councillor **11** internuncio

envy 4 long, want **5** covet, crave, yearn **6** desire, grudge, hanker **8** begrudge, grudging, jealousy **10** resentment **12** covetousness **13** invidiousness

enwrap 4 roll, veil **5** clasp, drape **6** enfold, invest, shroud, swathe **7** enclose, envelop, sheathe, swaddle **8** enshroud, enswathe

enzyme 5 ficin, lyase, renin, urase **6** kinase, ligase, lipase, mutase, papain, pepsin, rennin, urease, zymase **7** amidase, amylase, cyclase, enolase, guanase, hydrase, inulase, isozyme, lactase, maltase, oxidase, pectase, pepsine, plasmin, ptyalin, rennase, sucrase, trypsin, zymogen **8** aldolase, diastase, elastase, esterase, fumarase, lyzozyme, nuclease, protease, steapsin, thrombin, zymogene **9** biogenase, cellulase, invertase **10** amygdalase *combining form:* **3** zym **4** zyme, zymo *suffix:* **2** in **3** ase

eon see aeon

Eos see Aurora

épée 5 sword

epergne 5 stand **11** centerpiece

Ephah *father:* **6** Jahdai *lover:* **5** Caleb

ephelis 7 freckle

ephemeral 5 brief, short **7** passing **8** episodic, fleeting, fugitive, volatile **9** fugacious, momentary, temporary, transient **10** evanescent, short-lived, transitory, unenduring **11** impermanent

Ephialtes 5 giant *brother:* **4** Otus *father:* **6** Aloeus **8** Poseidon *mother:* **9** Iphimedia *slayer:* **6** Apollo

Ephod's son 7 Hanniel

Ephraim *brother:* **8** Manasseh *father:* **6** Joseph *grandfather:* **5** Jacob *mother:* **7** Asenath

Ephratah *husband:* **5** Caleb *son:* **3** Hur

epic 4 epos, poem, saga **5** grand, Iliad **6** Aeneid, heroic **7** Beowulf, Odyssey **8** imposing **9** narrative *suffix:* **2** ad

epicene 5 sissy **6** prissy **7** unmanly **9** pansified, sissified **10** effeminate

epicure 7 glutton, gourmet, ravener **8** gourmand, sybarite **9** bon vivant, high liver **10** gastronome **11** connoisseur, gastronomer **12** gastronomist

epicurean 4 lush **7** sensual **8** luscious, sensuous **9** luxurious **10** voluptuous **12** sensualistic

epidemic 3 flu **4** rash **6** plague **8** outbreak **10** pestilence

epidermis 4 skin **7** cuticle

epigram 4 poem **6** saying

epigrammatic 5 meaty, pithy **7** compact, concise, marrowy, piquant

epigraph 5 motto **11** inscription

epilogue 6 ending, sequel **8** follow-up, postlude **9** afterword **10** conclusion, postscript

Epimetheus *brother:* **10** Prometheus *father:* **7** lapetus *wife:* **7** Pandora

epinard 7 spinach

episode 5 event **8** incident, occasion **9** happening **10** occurrence **12** circumstance

epistaxis 9 nosebleed

epistle 4 note **6** letter **7** missive **13** communication

epitaph 3 R.I.P. **8** hic jacet **11** inscription

epithet 4 name, term **5** title **7** agnomen, moniker **8** cognomen, monicker, nickname **9** sobriquet **11** appellation

epitome 3 sum **5** brief **6** resumé **7** summary **8** abstract, boildown, breviary, breviate, last word, synopsis, ultimate **9** summation, summing-up **10** abridgment, apotheosis, conspectus **12** condensation, quintessence

epitomize 5 sum up **6** digest, embody, mirror, typify **7** outline, summate **8** boil down, condense, nutshell, tabulate **9** capsulize, exemplify, incarnate, inventory, personify, represent, summarize, symbolize, synopsize **10** illustrate **11** emblematize, incorporate

epoch 3 age, day, era **4** date, term, time **6** period **8** interval

equable 4 even, just, same **6** stable, steady **7** orderly, regular, stabile, uniform **8** constant **9** immutable, unvarying **10** equivalent, invariable, methodical, systematic, unchanging **12** unchangeable **13** unfluctuating

equal 3 tie **4** even, fair, just, like, mate, meet, peer, same, twin **5** agree, alike, match, reach, rival **6** accord, amount, equate, even-up **7** emulate, identic, similar, uniform **8** alter ego, parallel **9** duplicate, identical, impartial, measure up, objective **10** competitor, fifty-fifty, tantamount **11** counterpart, symmetrical **12** commensurate, correspond to, proportional, unprejudiced **13** commensurable, corresponding, dispassionate, proportionate *combining form:* **2** is **3** iso **4** equi, pari **5** aequi *French:* **4** égal

equality 3 par **6** equity, parity **7** balance, égalité **8** sameness **10** adequation

Equality State 7 Wyoming

equalize 4 even 5 level 6 square 7 balance

equalizer 6 pistol 8 handicap 10 tying score

equally 6 evenly 8 squarely 10 fifty-fifty 11 impartially

equanimity 5 poise 6 aplomb, phlegm 7 ataraxy, balance 8 calmness, coolness, evenness, serenity 9 assurance, composure, equipoise, placidity, sangfroid 10 confidence, detachment 11 equilibrium, tranquility 12 tranquillity 13 self-assurance

equate 4 even 5 liken, match, treat 6 regard, relate 7 compare, paragon 8 consider, equalize, parallel, similize 9 associate, represent 10 assimilate

equestrian 5 rider 8 horseman

equidistant 3 mid 6 center, medial, median, middle 7 central, halfway, midmost 10 centermost, middlemost

equilibrium 5 poise 6 stasis 7 balance 9 equipoise, steadying 10 steadiness 12 counterpoise 13 stabilization *combining form:* 5 stato

equine 4 colt, mare 5 horse, steed

equip 3 arm, rig 4 gear 5 dress, endow, rig up 6 attire, fit out, outfit, rig out, supply 7 appoint, furnish, prepare, provide, qualify, turn out 8 accouter, accoutre

equipment 3 rig 4 gear 5 traps 6 attire, outfit, tackle, things 7 baggage, fitment 8 fittings, material, materiel, tackling 9 apparatus, machinery, trappings 10 provisions 11 accessories, attachments, habiliments, impedimenta 12 accouterment, accoutrement, provisioning 13 appurtenances, paraphernalia

equitable 4 even, fair, just, same 5 level 6 stable 8 unbiased 9 identical, impartial, objective, uncolored 10 impersonal 12 unprejudiced 13 dispassionate

equity 3 law 7 justice 8 equality, justness

equivalence 3 par 6 parity 8 equality, likeness, sameness 10 adequation 11 correlation

equivalent 4 akin, like, same 5 alike, match 6 agnate 7 identic, obverse, similar 8 parallel 9 analogous, duplicate, identical 10 comparable, reciprocal, substitute, tantamount 11 convertible, correlative, counterpart 12 commensurate 13 corresponding, proportionate

equivocal 4 hazy 5 fishy, vague 7 clouded, dubious, obscure, suspect, unclear 8 doubtful 9 ambiguous, tenebrous, uncertain, undecided 10 ambivalent, borderline, indecisive, indistinct, multivocal, unexplicit 11 problematic 12 disreputable, questionable 13 indeterminate

equivocate 3 fib, lie 5 avoid, cavil, dodge, elude, evade, fence, hedge, parry, skirt 6 escape, eschew, palter, weasel 7 falsify, quibble, shuffle 8 sidestep 9 pussyfoot 10 tergiverse 11 prevaricate 12 tergiversate

equivocation 3 fib, lie 5 lying 6 deceit 7 fallacy, fibbing, hedging, sophism 8 coloring, delusion, haggling 9 ambiguity, casuistry, deception, duplicity, quibbling, sophistry 10 distortion 11 amphibology 12 speciousness, spuriousness 13 deceptiveness, dissimulation, double meaning

equivoque 3 pun 4 quip

era 3 age, day 4 date, term, time 5 epoch, stage 6 period

eradicate 4 dele, raze 5 abate, erase, purge 6 delete, uproot 7 abolish, blot out, destroy, root out, wipe out 8 demolish 9 extirpate, liquidate 10 annihilate, extinguish 11 exterminate

Eran *father:* 9 Shuthelah *grandfather:* 7 Ephraim

erase 4 dele, x out 5 annul, blank 6 cancel, cut out, delete, efface, excise, negate, remove, rub out, scrape 7 abolish, blot out, expunge, nullify, scratch, take out, wipe out 8 black out, blank out, cross off, cross out, disannul, withdraw 9 eliminate, extirpate, sponge out, strike out 10 neutralize, obliterate

Erato see Muse

Erbin *father:* 9 Custennin *nephew:* 6 Arthur *son:* 7 Geraint

erbium *symbol:* 2 Er

ere 6 before

Erebus *daughter:* 3 Day 6 Hemera *father:* 5 Chaos *home:* 5 Hades *sister, wife:* 3 Nox, Nyx *son:* 6 Aether, Charon

Erec et ____ 5 Enide

Erechteus *daughter:* 8 Chthonia *father:* 6 Vulcan 10 Hephaestus *mother:* 2 Ge 4 Gaea *slayer:* 4 Zeus 7 Jupiter

erect 4 form, lift, make, rear 5 build, exalt, forge, frame, hoist, honor, put up, raise, run up, set up, shape, upend 6 create, effect, lifted, make up, raised, uprear 7 build up, compose, dignify, elevate, ennoble, fashion, glorify, magnify, produce, stand-up, sublime, upraise, upright 8 elevated, heighten, standing, upraised, vertical 9 construct, establish, fabricate, hammer out 10 aggrandize, bring about, straight-up, upstanding 11 distinguish, manufacture 13 perpendicular

erection 4 pile 7 edifice 8 building 9 structure

eremite 6 hermit 7 ascetic, recluse

Erewhon 6 utopia *author:* 6 Butler (Samuel)

ergo 2 so 4 then, thus 5 hence 9 therefore, thereupon 11 accordingly 12 consequently

Erichthonius *father:* 8 Dardanus *son:* 4 Tros

Eridanus star 8 Achernar

Erigone *dog:* 5 Maera *father:* 7 Icarius *festival:* 5 Aeora

Erin see **Eire**

Erinyes 6 Alecto, Furies 7 Megaera 9 Eumenides, Tisiphone

Eriphyle *brother:* 8 Adrastus *husband:* 10 Amphiaraus *slayer, son:* 8 Alcmaeon

Eris *brother:* 4 Ares, Mars *daughter:* 3 Ate *fruit:* 5 apple *mother:* 3 Nox, Nyx

Eri's father 3 Gad

ermine 3 fur 5 stoat 6 weasel

erode 3 eat, rub 4 bite, gall, gnaw, rust, wear 5 chafe, decay, grate, graze, scour 6 abrade, rub off, ruffle 7 consume, corrade, corrode, crumble, eat away, rub away 8 wear away 9 scrape off 10 scrape away 11 deteriorate 12 disintegrate

Eroica composer 9 Beethoven (Ludwig van)

Eros see **Cupid**

erotic 4 lewd, sexy 5 bawdy, spicy 6 ardent, carnal, earthy, fervid 7 amative, amatory, amorous, fervent, fleshly, sensual 8 lovesome, prurient, sensuous 9 epicurean, lecherous, lickerish, salacious 10 lascivious, passionate, voluptuous 11 aphrodisiac, impassioned 12 concupiscent

err 3 sin 4 slip, trip 5 lapse, misdo, stray 6 bungle, offend, slip up, wander 7 blunder, deviate, misplay, stumble 8 trespass 10 transgress 12 miscalculate

errand 3 job 4 task 5 chore 7 mission

errand boy 4 page 5 gofer 7 bellboy, bellhop, courier

errant 5 stray 6 roving 7 devious, erratic, naughty, ranging, roaming 8 drifting, fallible, rambling, shifting, straying 9 deviating, itinerant, wandering 10 meandering, unreliable 11 misbehaving, mischievous

erratic 4 iffy, wild 5 queer, stray, wacky, weird 6 chancy 7 bizarre, curving, devious, dubious, oddball, strange, unusual, wayward, winding 8 doubtful, freakish, peculiar, shifting, singular, unstable, variable, volatile, whimsied 9 anomalous, arbitrary, eccentric, fluctuant, irregular, mercurial, uncertain, unnatural, vagarious, wandering, whimsical 10 capricious, changeable, inconstant, meandering, roundabout, undirected 12 incalculable, inconsistent 13 idiosyncratic, unpredictable

erring see **errant**

erroneous 3 off 4 awry 5 amiss, askew, false, wrong 6 untrue 7 unsound 8 mistaken, specious 9 defective, incorrect, misguided 10 inaccurate

error 3 sin 4 bull, flub, muff, slip, trip 5 boner, botch, fault, fluff, lapse 6 boo-boo, bungle, fumble, howler, miscue, slipup 7 blooper, blunder, fallacy, falsity, faux pas, misplay, misstep, mistake, stumble, untruth 8 delusion, illusion, misdoing, screamer 9 falsehood, falseness, indecorum, oversight 10 inaccuracy, misreading 11 impropriety, misjudgment *printing:* 4 typo 6 errata (plural) 7 erratum

ersatz 4 copy, fake, mock, sham 5 dummy, false 8 spurious 9 imitation, simulated, synthetic 10 artificial, factitious, simulacrum, substitute

Erse 5 Irish 6 Celtic, Gaelic 8 Scottish

Er's father 5 Judah

erstwhile 3 old 4 late, once, past 6 before, bygone, former, whilom 7 already, earlier, onetime, quondam 8 formerly, sometime 10 heretofore, previously

eruct 4 burp, emit, spew 5 belch, eject, expel 6 irrupt 8 disgorge

erudite 7 learned 8 lettered, studious, well-read 9 scholarly 10 scholastic

erudition 4 lore 7 culture, letters, science 8 learning, literacy, pedantry 9 education, knowledge 11 bookishness, cultivation, learnedness, scholarship 12 studiousness 13 scholarliness

erupt 3 jet 4 boil, emit, hurl, spew 5 belch, burst, eject, expel, go off, spout, spurt 6 cast up, irrupt 7 cast out, explode 8 break out, detonate, disgorge, throw off, touch off 9 discharge 10 burst forth 11 extravasate

eruption 4 gust, rush 5 burst, flare, sally 6 access 7 flare-up 8 outbreak, outburst 9 commotion, explosion *skin:* 3 zit 4 rash 6 pimple 7 serpigo 8 exanthem

Esau *brother:* 5 Jacob *country:* 4 Edom *descendant:* 7 Edomite *father:* 5 Isaac *father-in-law:* 4 Elon *grandson:* 6 Amalek *mother:* 7 Rebekah *new name:* 4 Edom *son:* 5 Korha, Reuel 7 Eliphaz *wife:* 4 Adah 10 Aholibamah

escalade 5 climb, mount, scale 6 ascend

escalate 4 grow, upgo 5 climb, mount, scale, widen 6 ascend, expand, spread 7 broaden, enlarge, upclimb 8 heighten, increase 9 intensify

escapade 4 lark 5 antic, caper, fling, prank, spree 6 frolic, vagary 7 roguery, rollick 8 mischief

escape 3 fly, lam, shy 4 bilk, duck, flee, flit, jump, miss, shun, skip, skit, slip 5 avoid, break, burke, dodge, elude, evade, shake, skirt 6 bypass, decamp, depart, eschew, flight, outlet, vanish 7 abscond, bail out, come-off, dodging, ducking, duck out, elusion, evasion, get away, make off, release, run away 8 breakout, eschewal, shunning 9 avoidance, bypassing, departure, disappear, runaround 10 circumvent, liberation **11** deliverance, elusiveness, evasiveness **12** sidestepping **13** circumvention *artist:* **7** Houdini (Harry) *narrow:* **9** close call **10** close shave

escargot 5 snail

escarole 6 endive

escarpment 5 cliff, slope

eschar 4 scab **5** crust **6** lesion

eschew 3 shy **4** bilk, duck, shun **5** avoid, elude, evade, forgo **6** double, escape, forego **7** abstain, forbear, refrain **8** forebear **9** sacrifice

eschewal 6 escape, shying **7** come-off, elusion, evasion **8** escaping, shirking, shunning **9** avoidance, runaround

escort 3 see **4** bear, beau, date, lead, show **5** bring, guard, guide, pilot, route, steer **6** attend, convoy, direct, follow, squire **7** company, conduct, gallant, vis-à-vis **8** cavalier, chaperon, shepherd **9** accompany, attendant, boyfriend, companion **11** consort with

escritoire 4 desk **9** secretary **10** secretaire **11** writing desk

escrow 4 bond, deed, fund **7** deposit

esculent 6 edible **7** eatable **10** comestible

escutcheon 6 shield

Eshban's father 6 Dishon

Eshcol *ally:* **7** Abraham *brother:* **4** Aner **5** Mamre

esker 2 os **3** ose **4** kame **5** mound, ridge

Eskimo 3 Ita **4** Yuit **5** Aleut, Inuit *boat:* **5** bidar, kayak, umiak **7** bidarka *boot:* **5** kamik **6** mukluk *dog:* **5** husky **8** malamute *dwelling:* **5** igloo **9** barrabora *outer garment:* **5** parka *sledge:* **7** komatik

esophagus 4 tube **6** gullet, throat **7** pharynx

esoteric 5 inner **6** mystic, occult, orphic, secret **7** private **8** abstruse, hermetic, profound **9** recondite **10** acroamatic **12** confidential

ESP 9 intuition **12** clairvoyance

espadrille 4 shoe **6** sandal

espalier 7 lattice, railing, trellis

esparto 4 alfa **5** grass

especial 4 main **5** chief **7** express, notable, supreme, unusual **8** dominant, singular, specific, uncommon **9** paramount **10** individual, particular, preeminent, surpassing **11** exceptional, predominant **12** preponderant

especially 7 notably **8** in specie, markedly, uniquely **9** eminently, expressly, supremely, unusually **10** peculiarly, remarkably, singularly **12** particularly, preeminently, specifically **13** distinctively, exceptionally

espial 4 find **6** notice, strike **9** detection, discovery **10** unearthing

espionage 6 spying **8** watching **9** sleuthing **11** observation **12** surveillance

espousal 3 aid **5** troth, union **6** mating **7** support **8** adoption, advocacy, approval, ceremony, marriage **9** betrothal, embracing, promotion **10** acceptance, betrothing, engagement **11** betrothment

espouse 3 wed **4** back, mate **5** adopt, catch, marry **6** accept, take on, take up, uphold **7** approve, embrace, support **8** advocate, champion, maintain

esprit 3 vim, wit **4** brio, dash, élan, life, mind, zing **5** humor, oomph, verve **6** acumen, brains, fervor, mettle, morale, spirit **7** courage, loyalty, passion **8** devotion, tenacity **9** acuteness, animation, sharpness **10** brightness, cleverness, enthusiasm, fellowship **11** camaraderie

esprit de corps see **morale**

espy 3 see **4** find, mark, note, spot, view **5** catch, hit on, sight, watch **6** behold, descry, detect, notice, remark, take in, turn up **7** discern, hit upon, make out, observe, witness **8** meet with **9** encounter, recognize **11** distinguish

___ es Salaam 3 Dar

essay 3 try **4** seek, toil, work **5** assay, labor, offer, paper, piece, study, theme, tract, trial **6** hassle, strive, thesis **7** article, attempt, travail, venture **8** endeavor, exertion, striving, struggle, treatise **9** discourse, undertake **10** discussion, exposition **11** composition, explication, undertaking **12** dissertation

essayist *American:* **4** Agee (James), Will (George) **5** Baker (Russell), Cooke (Alistair), Gould (Stephen Jay), White (Elwyn Brooks) **6** Brooks (Cleanth), Fisher (Mary Frances Kennedy), Holmes (Oliver Wendell), Sontag (Susan) **7** Buckley (William Frank), Cousins (Norman), Emerson (Ralph Waldo), Mencken (Henry Louis) **8** Benchley (Robert), Repplier (Agnes) **10** Crèvecoeur (Jean de) *English:* **4** Lamb (Charles) **5** Bacon (Francis), Pater (Walter), Smith (Sydney) **6** Morris (Jan), Ruskin (John), Steele (Richard) **7** Addison (Joseph), Hazlitt (William) *French:* **9** Montaigne (Michel Eyquem de) *Greek:* **8** Xenophon *Scottish:* **7** Carlyle (Thomas)

esse 5 being **9** existence

essence 3 ens, nub **4** body, crux, form, gist, pith, root, soul **5** being, fiber, fibre, stuff **6** aspect, bottom, center, entity, kernel, marrow, nature, nubbin, spirit, timber **7** element, quality, texture **8** property **9** attribute, substance **10** distillate, inwardness, rock bottom, virtuality **12** distillation, significance

essential 4 main, must **5** basal, basic, chief, prime, vital **6** inborn, inbred, innate, needed, primal, wanted **7** capital, connate, element, leading, needful, primary **8** cardinal, foremost, inherent, required, rudiment **9** condition, elemental, intrinsic, necessary, necessity, primitive, principal, requisite, right hand, substance **10** congenital, deepseated, elementary, imperative, sine qua non, substratal, underlying **11** fundamental, necessitous, requirement **12** constitutive, precondition, prerequisite **13** indispensable, part and parcel

essentially **6** almost, au fond, really **8** actually, as good as, as much as, wellnigh **9** basically, virtually **11** practically **13** fundamentally, substantially

essonite **6** garnet **13** cinnamon stone

establish **3** fix, lay, put, set **4** base, make, moor, rest, root, show, stay **5** build, enact, endow, erect, found, infix, place, prove, rivet, set up, start, stick **6** attest, bottom, create, decree, enroot, ground, impose, secure, settle, verify **7** build up, clarify, confirm, implant, instill, make out, provide, set down **8** document, entrench, organize **9** authorize, construct, determine, formulate, hammer out, inculcate, institute, legislate, originate, predicate, prescribe **10** constitute **11** corroborate, demonstrate **12** authenticate, substantiate

establishment **4** firm **5** house **6** outfit **7** company, concern, diehard **8** business, Old Guard **9** institute, workplace **10** enterprise, foundation **11** institution **12** conservative

estate **4** case, farm, form, land, rank **5** acres, caste, class, grade, level, manor, order, place, ranch, shape, state, villa **6** quinta, repair **7** station **8** category, hacienda, mesnalty, position, property, standing **9** condition **10** plantation *feudal:* **4** fief **7** fiefdom *first:* **6** clergy *fourth:* **5** press *Indian:* **5** taluk **6** taluka *manager:* **7** steward **8** executor, guardian *second:* **6** nobles **8** nobility *third:* **7** commons

esteem **5** favor, honor, prize, value **6** admire, credit, liking, regard, revere **7** account, apprize, cherish, idolize, respect, worship **8** approval, consider, treasure, venerate **9** valuation **10** admiration, appreciate, estimation **12** appreciation **13** consideration

ester **6** oleate **7** acetate **8** compound **9** phosphate *suffix:* **4** oate

Esther *cousin:* **8** Mordecai *father:* **7** Abihail *festival:* **5** Purim *Hebrew name:* **8** Hadassah *husband:* **9** Ahasuerus

estimable **4** good **5** noble **6** worthy **7** admired, reputed **8** esteemed, laudable, sterling **9** admirable, deserving, honorable, meritable, praisable, reputable, respected

10 creditable **11** commendable, meritorious, respectable, thankworthy **12** praiseworthy

estimate **3** put, set, sum **4** call, cast, rank, rate **5** assay, count, fancy, guess, infer, judge, place, price, prize, round, set at, stock, value **6** assess, cipher, decide, deduce, figure, rating, reckon, settle, survey **7** adjudge, compute, imagine, suppose, surmise, valuate **8** appraise, discover, evaluate, forecast, judgment, round off, sizing up **9** appraisal, ascertain, calculate, determine, enumerate, reckoning, valuation **10** adjudicate, assessment, conjecture, evaluation, projection **11** approximate, calculation, measurement **12** appraisement

estimation **4** fame **5** favor, honor, stock **6** esteem, regard **7** account, opinion, respect **8** figuring, judgment **9** appraisal, ciphering, reckoning, valuation **10** admiration, arithmetic, assessment, evaluation, impression **11** calculation, computation **12** appraisement **13** consideration

estop **3** bar **7** prevent **8** preclude, prohibit

estrange **4** part, wean **5** alien, sever, split **6** divide, sunder **7** break up, divorce **8** alienate, disunify, disunite, separate **9** disaffect

estrangement **6** schism **7** divorce **8** division **10** alienation, withdrawal **12** disaffection

estreat **4** copy **5** exact **6** record **7** extract **9** duplicate

estuary **5** firth, frith, inlet, mouth **6** estero **10** tidal river

esurient **6** greedy, hungry **9** voracious

étagère **7** cabinet, whatnot

Etats ___ **4** Unis

etch **5** grave **6** define, depict, incise **7** engrave, impress, imprint, outline, picture, portray **8** describe, inscribe, set forth **9** delineate, represent

etcher *American:* **7** Pennell (Joseph) **8** Whistler (James Abbott McNeil) *Dutch:* **9** Rembrandt *French:* **5** Redon (Odilon) **6** Villon (Jacques) *Italian:* **8** Piranesi (Giambattista) *Spanish:* **6** Ribera (José) *Swiss:* **4** Zorn (Anders)

Eteocles *brother:* **9** Polynices *father:* **7** Oedipus *mother:* **7** Jocasta *slayer:* **9** Polynices

eternal **7** ageless, endless, lasting, undying **8** constant, dateless, immortal, infinite, timeless, unending **9** ceaseless, continual, deathless, immutable, permanent, perpetual, unceasing **10** immemorial, intemporal, perdurable, unchanging **11** amaranthine, everlasting, illimitable, inalterable, neverending, sempiternal, unalterable, unremitting **12** interminable

Eternal City 4 Rome

eternally 4 ever 6 always 7 forever 8 evermore 11 forevermore, in perpetuum

eternity 3 age, eon 4 aeon, long 7 dog's age 8 blue moon, coon's age, infinity 9 afterlife 10 eviternity, infinitude, perpetuity 11 endlessness, immortality 12 infiniteness, sempiternity, timelessness

etesian 4 wind 6 annual

Ethan ___ 5 Allen, Brand, Frome

Ethan's father 5 Kishi

Ethbaal's daughter 7 Jezebel

ether 3 air, gas, sky 6 heaven 8 empyrean 10 anesthetic, atmosphere

ethereal 4 aery, airy 5 filmy, light 6 aerial, vapory 7 fragile 8 delicate, empyreal, empyrean, gossamer, heavenly, vaporish, vaporous 9 celestial, vaporlike 13 unsubstantial

ethic 5 ideal, mores, value 6 belief, morals 8 criteria, morality, standard 9 standards 10 moralities, principles

ethical 5 moral, noble 7 upright 8 elevated, virtuous 9 righteous 10 moralistic, principled, upstanding 11 right-minded

Ethiopia 9 Abyssinia *battle site:* 5 Adowa *capital:* 10 Addis Ababa *emperor:* 7 Menalik 8 Selassie 9 Ras Tafari 13 Haile Selassie *language:* 7 Amharic *measure:* 3 tat 4 cubi, kuba 5 derah, messe 6 cabaho, sinjer, sinzer, tanica 7 farsakh, farsang *monetary unit:* 4 birr *region:* 4 Bale, Kefa, Welo 5 Arusi, Gojam, Harer, Shewa, Tigre 6 Gonder, Sidamo, Welega 7 Eritrea 4 Gemu, Gefa 8 Ilubabor

ethnic 5 pagan 6 racial, tribal 7 gentile, heathen, infidel, profane 8 national 9 infidelic 11 unchristian 12 non-Christian

etiolate 4 pale 6 bleach, weaken 9 colorless

etiquette 4 form 5 mores 7 conduct, decency, decorum, dignity, manners 8 behavior, protocol 9 amenities, propriety 10 civilities, convention, deportment, seemliness 11 formalities, proprieties

etna 4 lamp 7 volcano

Etruscan *city, town:* 4 Roma, Veii 5 Caere, Vulci 6 Arezzo 7 Clusium, Felsina, Perugia 8 Volsinii 9 Florentia, Tarquinia, Vetulonia *deity:* 3 Tiv, Uni 4 Turm, Usil 5 Tinia 6 Menfra, Nethun, Trithn 7 Velchan 8 Voltumna *king:* 7 Porsena, Tarquin *kingdom:* 7 Etruria

etui 4 case

etymology 6 origin 7 history, origins

etymon 4 root 5 radix

eucalypt 4 yate

eucalyptus eater 5 koala

Eucharist *container:* 3 pyx *plate:* 5 paten *service:* 4 Mass 9 Communion 11 Lord's Supper *vessel:* 8 ciborium *wafer:* 4 host 8 viaticum

___ Eulenspiegel 4 Till, Tyll

eulogistic 9 approving, laudative, laudatory, praiseful 11 approbatory, encomiastic, panegyrical 12 commendatory 13 complimentary

eulogize 4 hymn, laud 5 bless, cry up, extol 6 belaud, praise 7 applaud, glorify, magnify 8 bepraise 9 celebrate 10 panegyrize

eulogy 5 eloge 6 praise 7 oration, tribute 8 citation, encomium 9 adulation, panegyric 10 salutation 13 glorification

Eumenides see **Erinyes**

Eunice's son 7 Timothy

eunuch 7 gelding 8 castrate, castrato

euphonic 5 sweet 6 dulcet 7 melodic, tuneful 9 melodious 11 mellisonant

euphony 7 harmony

euphoria 4 glee 6 frenzy 7 ecstasy, elation, madness 10 exaltation 12 exhilaration, intoxication

Euphrosyne see **Graces**

euphuistic 7 aureate, flowery, swollen, verbose 8 colorful, elevated, sonorous 9 bombastic, elaborate, overblown 10 rhetorical 11 declamatory 12 magniloquent 13 grandiloquent

eureka 3 aha

Euridice's husband 7 Orpheus

Euripides play 3 Ion 5 Helen, Medea 6 Hecuba 7 Electra, Orestes 8 Alcestis 10 Andromache, Hippolytus 11 Trojan Women

Europa *brother:* 6 Cadmus *father:* 6 Agenor 7 Phoenix *husband:* 8 Asterius *son:* 5 Minos 8 Sarpedon

Europe 9 continent *country:* 4 Eire 5 Italy, Malta, Spain 6 France, Greece, Latvia, Monaco, Norway, Poland, Russia, Sweden, Turkey 7 Albania, Andorra, Armenia, Austria, Belarus, Belgium, Croatia, Denmark, Estonia, Finland, Georgia, Germany, Hungary, Iceland, Ireland, Moldova, Romania, Rumania, Ukraine 8 Bulgaria, Portugal, Slovakia, Slovenia 9 Lithuania, Macedonia, San Marino 10 Azerbaijan, Luxembourg, Yugoslavia 11 Netherlands, Switzerland, Vatican City 13 Czech Republic, Liechtenstein, United Kingdom 17 Bosnia-Herzegovina *ethnic group:* 4 Finn, Lapp, Pole, Serb, Turk, Wend 5 Croat, Czech, Dutch, Greek, Gypsy, Irish, Latin, Swede, Swiss, Welsh 6 Basque, French, German, Magyar, Polish, Scotch, Slovak 7 Bosnian, Catalan, English, Finnish, Fleming, Italian, Russian, Slovene, Spanish, Swedish, Walloon 8 Albanian, Andorran, Armenian, Croatian, Romanian 9 Bulgarian, Hungarian, Ukrainian 10 Macedonian, Monegasque, Phoenician 12 Byelorussian, Scandinavian *language:* 4 Lapp 5 Czech, Dutch, Greek, Irish, Latin, Welsh 6 Basque, Breton, Danish, French, Gaelic, German, Polish, Slovak 7 Catalan, English, Finnish, Flemish, Italian, Maltese, Romansh, Russian, Slovene, Spanish, Swedish, Turkish 8 Albanian, Romanian, Rumanian 9 Bulgarian, Hungarian, Icelandic, Norwegian 10 Macedonian, Portuguese 13 Serbo Croatian *mountain:* 3 Alp 8 Dolomite

europium *symbol:* 2 Eu

Euryale see Gorgon

Eurytus *daughter:* 4 Iole *slayer:* 8 Hercules

Euterpe see Muse

evacuant 6 emetic 8 diuretic, emptying 9 cathartic, purgative

evacuate 4 void 5 clear, empty, expel 6 remove 7 excrete, exhaust 8 withdraw

evacuee 2 DP 6 émigré 7 refugee 8 fugitive

evade 3 fly, shy 4 bilk, duck, flee, foil, shun 5 avoid, dodge, elude, hedge, parry, shirk 6 bypass, double, escape, eschew, outwit, thwart, weasel 7 shuffle 8 sideslip, sidestep, slip away 9 pussyfoot, turn aside 10 circumvent, equivocate, tergiverse 12 tergiversate

Evadne *father:* 5 Iphis *husband:* 8 Capaneus

evaluate 4 rank, rate 5 assay, class, gauge, grade, set at, value 6 assess, ponder, survey 8 appraise, classify, estimate 9 criticize

evaluation 5 stock 6 rating 7 judging 8 decision, estimate, judgment 9 appraisal 10 assessment, estimation 12 appraisement, appreciation, interpreting

Evander *father:* 6 Hermes 7 Mercury *mother:* 8 Carmenta 9 Carmentis *son:* 6 Pallas

evanesce 4 fade 5 clear, empty 6 dispel, vanish 7 scatter 8 disperse, dissolve 9 disappear, dissipate, evaporate 12 disintegrate

evanescent 6 fading, flying 7 cursory, melting, passing 8 fleeting, fugitive, volatile 9 ephemeral, fugacious, momentary, temporary, transient, vanishing 10 dissolving, short-lived, transitory 12 disappearing

evangelical 6 ardent, fervid 7 zealous 8 militant 9 crusading 10 missionary 11 impassioned 13 proselytizing

Evangeline *author:* 10 Longfellow (Henry Wadsworth) *beloved:* 7 Gabriel *home:* 6 Acadia

evangelist 4 John, Luke, Mark 5 Baker (Jim), Moody (Dwight) 6 Graham (Billy), Sunday (Billy), Wesley (John) 7 apostle, Edwards (Jonathan), Falwell (Jerry), Matthew, Roberts (Oral) 9 McPherson (Aimee Semple), missioner, Robertson (Pat) 10 colporteur, missionary, revivalist

evangelistic 9 crusading, reforming 10 missionary

evangelize 6 preach 8 homilize 9 sermonize

evaporate 4 fade 5 clear 6 vanish 7 evanish 8 evanesce, vaporize 9 disappear

evasion 5 dodge 6 escape, excuse 7 come-off, dodgery, dodging, elusion 8 escaping, escapism, eschewal, haggling, shunning 9 avoidance, quibbling, runaround

evasive 3 sly 4 eely 5 dodgy, vague 6 shifty 7 elusive, elusory, sliding, unclear 8 slippery 9 ambiguous, equivocal, shuffling 10 intangible 12 equivocating

eve 4 dusk 5 night 7 sundown

Eve *husband:* 4 Adam *son:* 4 Abel, Cain, Seth

even 3 tie, yet 4 fair, flat, just, same, tied 5 align, equal, exact, flush, grade, level, plane, quite, still, truly 6 as well, equate, honest, indeed, really, smooth, square, stable, steady, verily 7 already, balance, equable, exactly, flatten, pancake, planate, stabile, uniform 8 balanced, constant, equalize, smoothen, so much as, straight, unvaried 9 continual, equitable, expressly, identical, precisely, unvarying 10 absolutely, comparable, consistent, continuous, fifty-fifty, positively, symmetrize, unchanging 11 undeviating 12 unprejudiced 13 fair and square, proportionate, unfluctuating *combining form:* 5 homal 6 homalo

evening 4 dusk 6 soiree, sunset 7 sundown 8 duskness, eventide, gloaming, twilight 9 afternoon, duskiness, nightfall *French:* 4 soir *Italian:* 4 sera *service:* 7 vespers *star:* 5 Venus 6 Hesper, Vesper 8 Hesperus

evenness 7 balance 8 equality, fairness, flatness 10 equanimity, uniformity 11 consistency

event 3 act, hap 4 case, deed, fact, feat, meet 5 issue, match, treat 6 action, affair, chance, effect, result, sequel, upshot 7 contest, delight, episode, exploit, fortune, outcome, product, sequent 8 accident, causatum, fortuity, incident, landmark, milepost, occasion, offshoot 9 aftermath, happening, milestone, outgrowth, resultant 10 occurrence, phenomenon 11 achievement, aftereffect, competition, consequence, eventuality 12 circumstance, happenstance

eventful 4 busy 9 important, momentous

eventual 3 lag 4 last 5 final 6 ending, latest, latter 7 closing, endmost, ensuing

8 hindmost, terminal, ultimate 10 concluding, consequent, inevitable, succeeding

eventuality 4 case 5 issue 6 effect, result, sequel, upshot 7 outcome 9 aftermath 11 aftereffect, consequence, contingency, possibility

eventually 3 yet 7 finally, someday 8 sometime 10 ultimately 13 sooner or later

eventuate 5 occur 6 happen, result

ever 3 too 4 once, over 5 at all, super 6 always, anyway, overly, unduly 7 anytime, anywise, forever, plaguey, usually 8 mortally, overfull, overmuch 9 eternally, extremely, immensely, regularly 10 annoyingly, constantly, consumedly, grievously, invariably 11 excessively, in perpetuum, perpetually 12 consistently, continuously

evergreen 3 fir, ivy, yew 4 ilex, pine, tree 5 cedar, holly, savin 6 laurel, myrtle, spruce 7 conifer, cypress, hemlock, juniper, redwood, sequoia 8 magnolia 9 mistletoe 12 rhododendron

Evergreen State 10 Washington

everlasting 7 endless, eternal, forever, lasting 8 constant, immortal, infinite, termless, unending 9 boundless, ceaseless, continual, limitless, permanent, perpetual, unceasing 10 continuous, perdurable 11 amaranthine, never-ending, unremitting 13 uninterrupted

evermore 6 always 9 eternally 11 in perpetuum

evert 5 upset 9 overthrow

every 3 all 4 each *combining form:* 3 pam, pan 4 pano *suffix:* 2 ly

everybody 3 all 4 each 8 everyone

everyday 5 banal, lowly, plain, usual 6 common 7 mundane, prosaic, routine, workday 8 familiar, frequent, ordinary, workaday 9 customary, plain Jane, quotidian 11 commonplace 12 unremarkable

everyplace see everywhere

everything 3 all *French:* 4 tout *German:* 5 alles

everywhere 7 all over, overall 8 all round, wherever 9 all around 10 far and near, far and wide, high and low, throughout

evict 3 out 4 oust 5 chase, chuck, eject, expel 6 put out 7 boot out, dismiss, extrude, kick out, shut out, turn out 8 dislodge, force out, throw out 10 dispossess

evidence 4 clue, mark, show, sign 5 index, proof, prove, token, trace 6 attest, evince, expose, ostend 7 bespeak, betoken, confirm, display, exhibit, indicia, symptom, testify, witness 8 indicate, manifest, proclaim 9 testament, testimony 10 illustrate, indication 11 attestation, demonstrate, significant, testimonial 12 confirmation

evident 5 clear, overt, plain 6 patent 7 glaring, obvious, visible 8 apparent, distinct, manifest, palpable 9 prominent 10 noticeable, pronounced 11 unambiguous

evidently 9 outwardly, seemingly 10 apparently, officially, ostensibly 11 professedly

evil 3 bad, ill, low, sin 4 base, debt, foul, hard, tort, ugly, vice, vile 5 angry, black, catty, crime, fetid, wrong 6 malice, nocent, putrid, sinful, trying, wicked 7 badness, baleful, baneful, corrupt, devilry, harmful, hateful, hideous, hurtful, immoral, malefic, misdeed, nocuous, obscene, offense, ominous, satanic, unlucky, vicious 8 damaging, damnable, iniquity, satanism, satanity, spiteful, stinking, wrathful 9 atrocious, diablerie, diabolism, difficult, evildoing, execrable, ill-boding, ill-omened, injurious, loathsome, malicious, nefarious, offensive, rancorous, repellent, reprobate, repugnant, repulsive, revolting 10 calamitous, despiteful, disastrous, flagitious, iniquitous, malevolent, misconduct, pernicious, sinfulness, unpleasant, wickedness, wrongdoing 11 deleterious, destructive, detrimental, distasteful, maleficence, mischievous, unfavorable, unfortunate 12 disagreeable, inauspicious *combining form:* 3 mal

evildoer 3 cur 5 crook, felon 6 bad lot, sinner 7 culprit, villain 8 criminal 9 miscreant

evil spirit 3 imp 5 demon, devil, fiend 6 daemon

evince 4 mark, milk, show 5 argue, cause, educe, evoke, prove 6 attest, elicit, expose, extort, ostend 7 bespeak, betoken, confirm, display, exhibit, extract, provoke, signify 8 evidence, indicate, manifest, proclaim 9 stimulate 10 bring about, illustrate 11 demonstrate

evirate 4 geld 8 castrate 10 emasculate

eviscerate 3 gut 4 draw 5 bowel 6 paunch 7 embowel 10 disembowel, exenterate

evocative 6 moving 7 causing, weighty 8 arousing, inducing, pregnant, stirring 9 effecting, producing 10 meaningful, suggestive 11 stimulating

evoke 4 milk, stir 5 educe, raise, rally, rouse, waken 6 arouse, awaken, call up, elicit, evince, excite, extort 7 extract 8 summon up 9 call forth, conjure up, stimulate 11 summon forth

evolution 6 change, growth 8 progress, upgrowth 9 flowering, unfolding 10 biogenesis 11 development, progression

evolve 4 grow 5 educe, get at, ripen 6 change, derive, mature, obtain, open up,

unfold 7 advance, develop 8 progress
9 elaborate 10 excogitate
evulse 4 pull, tear, yank 7 extract
ewe 5 sheep *young:* 6 theave,
ewer 3 jug 4 vase 5 basin 7 pitcher
ex 6 former 7 without
exacerbate 5 annoy 6 worsen
7 envenom, inflame, provoke 8 embitter,
heighten, irritate 9 aggravate, intensify
10 exasperate
exact 4 call, even, levy, nice, same, true,
very 5 claim, force, fussy, gouge, pinch,
put on, right, screw, wrest, wring 6 assess,
coerce, compel, demand, extort, impose,
oblige, proper, square, wrench 7 careful,
correct, extract, precise, require, solicit,
squeeze 8 accurate, punctual, rigorous,
selfsame 9 challenge, constrain, identical,
postulate, shake down 10 meticulous, scrupulous 11 painstaking, punctilious, requisition 12 conscionable 13 conscientious
combining form: 4 orth 5 ortho
exacting 5 fussy, rigid, stern, tough
6 severe, strict, taxing, trying 7 exigent, finicky, onerous, weighty 8 critical, grievous,
rigorous 9 demanding, stringent 10 burdensome, oppressive, particular
exactitude 8 accuracy 9 precision
10 definitude 11 correctness, preciseness
12 definiteness
exactly 3 all 4 bang, even, just 5 quite,
right, sharp, spang, stick 6 as well, in toto,
square, to a tee, wholly 7 totally, utterly
8 all in all, smack-dab, squarely
9 expressly, on the nose, precisely
10 absolutely, accurately, altogether, completely, positively 12 specifically
exaggerate 3 pad 5 color, fudge
6 overdo 7 amplify, magnify, overact,
romance 8 overdraw, overrate 9 embellish,
embroider, overstate 10 overcharge
11 hyperbolize, romanticize
exaggeration 7 romance 8 coloring
9 hyperbole 10 caricature, stretching
11 enlargement, overdrawing 12 embroidering, overcoloring 13 amplification,
embellishment, overstatement
exalt 4 fire, laud, lift 5 boost, elate, erect,
extol, honor, pique, raise 6 deepen, enhalo,
inform, praise, uplift, uprear 7 acclaim, animate, build up, dignify, elevate, enhance,
ennoble, glorify, inspire, magnify, promote,
quicken, sublime, upgrade 8 heighten,
inspirit, pedestal, spirit up, stellify 9 encourage, intensify, stimulate 10 aggrandize
11 apotheosize, distinguish
exaltation 3 joy 5 bliss 6 praise 7 delight,
ecstasy, elation, rapture 8 euphoria, rhapsody 9 extolment, laudation, upgrading,
uplifting 10 apotheosis 11 deification,

delectation 12 exhilaration, intoxication
13 dignification, glorification
exalted 4 high 5 first, grand, lofty, noble
6 astral, august, superb 7 eminent, highest,
leading, sublime 8 elevated, foremost
9 number one, prominent, top-drawer
10 top-ranking 11 high-ranking, illustrious,
outstanding
examination 4 oral, quiz, scan, test, view
5 assay, audit, trial 6 review, survey
7 autopsy, canvass, checkup, hearing,
inquest, inquiry, sifting, testing 8 analysis,
quizzing, scanning, scrutiny 9 breakdown,
check-over, diagnosis, winnowing 10 dissection, inspection 11 questioning 13 cate-
chization, investigation, perlustration *kind:*
4 oral 5 final 7 medical, midterm 8 physical *of accounts:* 5 audit *of a corpse:*
7 autopsy
examine 3 ask, con, try, vet 4 pump, quiz,
scan, sift, test, view 5 audit, check, grill,
probe, prove, query, study 6 go over, look
at, peruse, survey 7 canvass, check up,
inquire, inspect, observe 8 check out, look
into, look over, overhaul, question 9 catechize, check over 10 scrutinize 11 contemplate, interrogate, investigate *eggs:* 6 candle
examiner 6 censor, critic, tester 7 auditor,
coroner 9 inspector
examining tool *combining form:*
5 scope
example 4 case 5 ideal, model 6 mirror,
sample 7 pattern, problem 8 ensample,
exemplar, instance, paradigm, sampling,
specimen, standard 9 archetype 11 case
history 12 illustration
exanimate 4 dead 8 lifeless 10 spiritless
exasperate 3 get, irk 4 gall, huff, rile, roil
5 peeve, pique 6 nettle, work up 7 agitate
8 irritate 9 aggravate
exasperation 4 pest 6 bother, pester,
plague, pother 8 irritant, nuisance, vexation
9 annoyance, besetment 10 botherment,
irritation, resentment 11 aggravation, botheration, displeasure
ex cathedra 8 official 9 ex officio
13 authoritative
excavate 3 dig 4 grub 5 scoop, spade
6 dig out, shovel 7 unearth 8 gouge out,
scoop out 9 hollow out, quarry out, scrape
out
excavation 3 dig, pit 4 hole, mine
5 stope 6 trench
exceed 3 top 4 beat, best, dare, pass
5 break, excel, outdo 6 better, overdo
7 outstep, overrun, presume, surpass, venture 8 outreach, outshine, outstrip, outweigh, overstep 9 overreach, transcend
exceedingly 4 very 6 hugely 7 notably,
parlous, vitally 9 extremely 10 remarkably,

strikingly **12** surpassingly **13** exceptionally *prefix:* **3** pre **5** ultra

excel 3 top **4** beat, best **5** outdo, shine **6** better, exceed **7** surpass **8** outclass, outshine, outstrip **9** transcend

excellence 5 arête, class, merit, value, worth **6** virtue **7** quality **8** fineness, goodness, niceness **10** perfection, superbness **11** distinction, superiority

excellent 3 top **4** brag, fine, good **5** bully, dandy, nobby, noble, prime, royal, smart **6** bang-up, banner, famous, Grade A, proper, superb, tip-top **7** capital, classic, premium, quality, supreme **8** champion, five-star, splendid, stunning, superior, terrific, top-notch, whiz-bang **9** classical, first-rate, front-rank, high-class, high-grade, marvelous, number one, sovereign **10** blue-ribbon, first-class **11** exceptional, first-string, magnificent, sensational, superlative, unsurpassed **12** incomparable

except 3 bar, but, yet **4** bate, kick, omit, only, save **5** debar **6** bating, beside, exempt, object, reject, saving, unless **7** barring, besides, exclude, however, outside, protest, rule out, suspend **8** count out, pass over **9** apart from, aside from, eliminate, excluding, outside of **11** exclusive of, expostulate, remonstrate

exception 5 demur **7** dissent **9** exclusion, objection

exceptionable 8 unwanted **9** unwelcome **10** ill-favored **11** undesirable **12** inadmissible, unacceptable **13** objectionable

exceptional 4 rare **6** scarce, unique **7** notable, premium, special, strange, unusual **8** distinct, singular, superior, uncommon, unwonted **9** excellent, marvelous, wonderful **10** infrequent, noteworthy, phenomenal, remarkable, unordinary **11** outstanding, uncustomary, unthinkable **12** unimaginable **13** extraordinary

exceptionally 4 very **6** hugely **7** notably, parlous, vitally **9** extremely, unusually **10** especially, remarkably, strikingly **11** exceedingly, marvelously, wonderfully **12** particularly, phenomenally, stupendously, surpassingly

excerpt 4 cite, cull, pick **5** glean, quote **6** choose, select, single **7** extract, pick out

excess 3 fat **4** plus **5** extra, flood, spare **6** de trop **7** overage, surfeit, surplus **8** overflow, overkill, overmuch, overplus, plethora **9** boundless, indulgent, limitless, overboard, overdoing, overspill, overstock, profusion, redundant, unbounded **10** immoderacy, indulgence, oversupply, Saturnalia, surplusage **11** dissipation, overbalance, overmeasure, prodigality, superfluent, superfluity, superfluous, unessential **12** extravagance, immoderation, intemperance **13** overabundance, supernumerary

excessive 4 over **5** dizzy, steep, stiff, super, undue **6** too-too **7** extreme, skyhigh **8** overmuch, prodigal, towering **10** dissipated, exorbitant, immoderate, inordinate, untempered **11** extravagant, intemperate, overweening **12** supernatural, unmeasurable, unrestrained **13** overindulgent *combining form:* **4** poly *prefix:* **3** sur

excessively 3 too **4** ever, over **6** overly, unduly **7** parlous **8** overfull, overmuch **9** extremely, immensely **12** inordinately *prefix:* **5** hyper

exchange 4 swap **5** bandy, trade, truck **6** barter, change, market, switch **7** bargain, commute, pay back, replace, traffic **8** displace **10** substitute **11** reciprocate *premium:* **4** agio

exchequer 5 chest **6** coffer **8** treasury, war chest

excise 3 tax **4** toll **5** elide, slash **6** cut off, cut out, delete, exsect, remove, resect **7** exscind, root out **8** amputate **9** eradicate, expurgate, extirpate, strike out

excision 3 cut **7** erasure, removal, surgery **9** resection **11** destruction, extirpation

excitable 4 edgy **6** touchy **8** agitable, skittery, skittish, unstable, volatile **9** alarmable, mercurial, startlish **10** high-strung **11** combustible **13** temperamental

excite 4 fire, move, spur, stir **5** elate, pique, prime, rouse, set up, waken **6** appeal, arouse, stir up, thrill, turn on **7** agitate, attract, commove, disturb, innerve, inspire, perturb, provoke, quicken **8** charge up, disquiet, energize, interest, intrigue, motivate, spirit up, touch off **9** fascinate, galvanize, impassion, innervate, stimulate **10** discompose, exhilarate

excited 3 hot **4** avid **5** eager **6** hectic **7** fevered, frantic **8** aflutter

excitement 3 ado **4** stir **6** furore, warmth **8** delirium, hysteria **9** commotion **11** disturbance, pandemonium

exclaim 4 blat, bolt, roar **5** snort **6** cry out **8** blurt out, burst out **9** ejaculate

exclamation 2 ah, ai, ay, ha, hi, ho, lo, oh, ow, so **3** aah, aha, bah, boo, cry, eek, feh, fie, gee, hah, hey, hic, huh, och, oho, ooh, pah, tsk, tut, ugh, wow, yeh **4** ahem, alas, damn, dang, darn, drat, egad, gosh, heck, hell, oops, ouch, phew, pish, posh, rats, whew, yell, yipe **5** alack, bravo, faugh, golly, humph, pshaw, shout **6** clamor, hurrah, indeed, phooey, shucks **7** doggone, gee whiz, hosanna, jeepers, whoopee **9** expletive **12** interjection *of disgust:* **3** bah, feh, ugh **5** yecch **6** phooey *of dismay:* **4** oh no *of pain:* **2** ow **4** ouch *of relief:* **4** phew *of sorrow:* **4** alas **5** alack

of surprise: 2 ah, oh 3 aha, oho, wow *of triumph:* 3 hah
(see also **interjection**)

exclude 3 ban, bar 4 bate 5 block, debar, estop 6 banish, disbar, except, put out 7 keep out, lock out, obviate, prevent, rule out, shut out, suspend, ward off 8 close out, count out, preclude, prohibit 9 blackball, blacklist, eliminate, ostracize *prefix:* 3 dis

excluding 3 bar, but 4 less, save 6 bating, except, saving 7 barring, besides 9 outside of 11 exclusive of

exclusive 4 chic, lone, only, pick, sole, tony 5 aloof, elect, elite, scoop, smart, swank, swish, whole 6 chosen, cliquy, picked, select, single, with-it 7 barring, dashing, high-hat, stylish 8 clannish, cliquish, limiting, selected, snobbish, unshared 9 debarring, excluding, preferred, undivided 10 individual, limitative, privileged, unswerving 11 fashionable, prohibitive, restrictive, standoffish 12 aristocratic, concentrated, undistracted

exclusively 3 but 4 only 5 alone 6 solely, wholly 8 entirely 10 completely 12 particularly

excogitate 4 mind 5 educe, study, weigh 6 derive, evolve, invent, ponder 7 develop, perpend, think up 8 consider, contrive, think out 9 think over 11 contemplate

excommunicate 8 unchurch

excoriate 3 rub 4 flay, fret, gall 5 chafe, slash 6 abrade, scathe, scorch 7 blister, scarify, scourge 8 lambaste, lash into 9 castigate

excorticate 4 peel, skin 5 scale, strip

excrement 4 dirt 5 feces 6 ordure, refuse *combining form:* 4 copr, scat 5 copro, scato *of animals:* 4 dung, muck 6 manure *of sea birds:* 5 guano

excrescence 4 wart 6 pimple 7 process 9 outgrowth, processus

excruciate 3 try 4 hurt, pain, rack 5 wound, wring 6 harrow, martyr 7 afflict, agonize, crucify, inflame, torment, torture 8 convulse, irritate

excruciating 5 acute, sharp 7 extreme, racking, rending, tearing 8 piercing, shooting, stabbing 9 agonizing, consuming, harrowing, torturing, torturous 10 tormenting

exculpate 4 free 5 clear, remit 6 acquit, excuse, let off, pardon 7 absolve, amnesty, condone, explain, forgive, justify 9 exonerate, vindicate 11 rationalize

excurse 5 stray 6 depart, ramble, wander 7 digress, diverge 8 divagate

excursion 4 ride, tour, trek, trip, walk 5 aside, jaunt, paseo, sally, tramp 6 cruise, junket, outing, safari 7 circuit, journey 9 round trip 10 digression, divagation,

expedition, one-way trip, roundabout 11 parenthesis 12 pleasure trip

excusable 6 venial 7 tenable 10 condonable, defensible, forgivable, pardonable, remittable, vindicable 11 justifiable

excuse 4 plea 5 alibi, clear, remit, shift, spare 6 acquit, cop-out, exempt, let off, pardon, reason, wink at 7 absolve, apology, condone, defense, explain, forgive, justify, pretext, regrets, relieve, stopgap 8 dispense, overlook, palliate, pass over, shrug off 9 discharge, exculpate, exonerate, extenuate, gloss over, makeshift, vindicate, whitewash 10 substitute 11 explanation, rationalize 13 justification

execrable 3 bad, low 4 base, foul, vile 6 cursed, cussed, damned 7 blasted, heinous 8 accursed, damnable, horrific, infernal 9 atrocious, loathsome, monstrous, repulsive, revolting 10 confounded, despicable, detestable, horrifying, nauseating

execrate 3 ban 4 cuss, damn, hate 5 abhor, curse, swear 6 bedamn, detest, loathe, revile 7 accurse, censure, condemn, reprove 8 denounce 9 abominate, imprecate, objurgate, reprehend, reprobate 12 anathematize

execute 2 do 3 act 4 do in, hang, kill, slay 5 cause, lynch, purge 6 finish, gibbet, govern, handle, murder, render 7 achieve, bump off, conduct, fulfill, perform, put away 8 carry out, complete, dispatch, knock off, transact 9 discharge, eliminate, implement, liquidate 10 administer, bring about, put through 11 assassinate 12 administrate

execution 6 murder 7 facture, garrote, hanging 8 garrotte 9 beheading 11 performance

executioner 6 hanger 7 hangman, headman 8 headsman

executive 4 dean 6 leader 7 manager, officer 8 director, governor, higher-up, official 9 president 10 supervisor 11 businessman 12 entrepreneur 13 administrator, businesswoman

executor 4 doer 5 agent 9 performer

exegesis 6 exposé 9 construal 10 exposition 11 explanation, explication 12 construction

exemplar 4 soul 5 ideal, model 6 mirror 7 example, pattern 8 ensample, exponent, paradigm, standard 9 archetype, prototype 12 illustration

exemplary 4 good, pure 5 ideal, model 6 worthy 7 classic, typical 8 innocent, laudable, virtuous 9 admirable, blameless, classical, guiltless, righteous 10 inculpable, prototypal, unblamable 11 commendable 12 paradigmatic, praiseworthy, prototypical

exemplify 4 cite 5 quote 6 embody, mirror, typify 7 clarify, clear up 8 spell out

9 enlighten, epitomize, personify, represent, symbolize **10** illuminate, illustrate **11** demonstrate, emblematize

exempt 4 free **5** spare **6** except, excuse, let off **7** absolve, relieve **8** dispense **9** discharge *combining form:* **6** immuno

exemption 7 freedom, release **8** immunity, impunity **9** discharge, exception

exenterate 3 gut **4** draw **5** bowel **6** paunch **7** embowel **10** disembowel, eviscerate

exercise 3 irk, ply, use, vex **4** fret, gall **5** annoy, apply, chafe, drill, exert, sit-up, sport, study, throw, train, wield **6** abrade, action, bestow, bother, employ, foster, handle, lesson, pushup, put out **7** develop, exploit, improve, prepare, problem, provoke, utilize, workout **8** activity, drilling, exertion, movement, practice, rehearse **9** athletics, condition, cultivate, operation **10** employment **11** application **12** calisthenics

exert 3 ply, use **5** apply, throw, wield **6** employ, put out, strain **8** exercise

exertion 3 use **4** toil, work **5** labor, pains, trial, while **6** effort, strain **7** trouble **8** activity, exercise, striving, struggle **9** operation **10** employment, exercising **11** application, elbow grease

exfoliate 4 peel **5** scale **8** flake off **10** desquamate

exhalation 6 breath **7** halitus **9** breathing, effluvium, emanation **10** expiration

exhale 4 blow, emit **6** expire, let out **7** breathe **10** breathe out, outbreathe

exhaust 3 fag, sap **4** do in, draw, tire **5** drain, eat up, spend, use up **6** devour, dispel, expend, finish, overdo, run out, tucker, wash up, weaken **7** consume, deplete, frazzle, outtire, outwear, overply, scatter, wear out **8** bankrupt, disperse, draw down, enfeeble, knock out, overwork **9** dissipate, overdrive, overexert, prostrate **10** debilitate, impoverish, overextend, run through

exhausted 4 beat, dead, done, limp, weak **5** all in, spent, tired **6** bleary, effete, used up **7** drained, far-gone, run-down, worn-out **8** consumed, depleted, dog-tired **9** washed-out

exhaustion 7 fatigue **8** collapse **9** lassitude, tiredness, weariness **11** prostration

exhaustive 5 total **6** all-out **7** radical **8** complete, profound, sweeping, thorough, whole-hog **9** full-blown, full-dress, full-scale, intensive, out-and-out **13** comprehensive, thoroughgoing

exhibit 3 air **4** fair, look, mark, show **5** flash, sight **6** evince, expose, flaunt, ostend, parade **7** display, disport, show off, trot out **8** brandish, evidence, manifest, proclaim, showcase **10** exposition, illustrate **11** demonstrate

exhibition 4 fair, show **5** sight **7** display, pageant, showing **8** offering **9** spectacle **10** exposition **12** presentation **13** demonstration, manifestation

exhilarate 4 buoy, lift **5** boost, cheer, elate, exalt, pep up, set up **6** excite, thrill, uplift **7** animate, commove, delight, enliven, gladden, inspire **8** inspirit, spirit up, vitalize **9** stimulate **10** invigorate

exhilaration 6 firing, gaiety, uplift **7** ecstasy, elation **8** euphoria, gladness **9** animation, elevation **10** exaltation, excitation, excitement, quickening **11** enlivenment, inspiration, stimulation **12** invigoration, vitalization, vivification **13** galvanization

exhort 3 sic **4** goad, prod, spur, urge **5** egg on, plead, prick **6** insist, prompt, propel **8** admonish, call upon **9** stimulate

exhume 3 dig **5** dig up **6** unbury **7** unearth **8** disinter **9** disembalm, disentomb, disinhume, uncharnel

exigency 3 fix, jam **4** need, pass, want **5** pinch, rigor **6** crisis, demand, duress, pickle, scrape, strait **7** dilemma **8** coercion, hardship, juncture, pressure, zero hour **9** necessity **10** compulsion, constraint, crossroads, difficulty, insistence **11** requirement, vicissitude **12** turning point

exigent 5 acute, tough, vital **6** crying, taxing **7** burning, clamant, instant, onerous, weighty **8** exacting, grievous, menacing, pressing **9** clamorous, demanding, insistent, necessary **10** burdensome, imperative, oppressive **11** importunate, threatening

exiguous 4 poor, thin, tiny **5** scant, skimp, small, spare **6** little, meager, narrow, scanty, scrimp, skimpy, slight, sparse **7** limited, scrimpy, slender, tenuous **8** confined **10** diminutive, restricted, straitened

exile 4 oust **5** expel **6** banish, deport, emigré **7** cast out, expulse, outcast, refugee **8** diaspora, displace, drive out, evacuate, expellee, unperson **9** exclusion, expulsion, extradite, migration, nonperson, ostracism, ostracize, transport **10** banishment, dispersion, dispossess, expatriate, relegation, scattering **11** deportation, extradition **12** displacement, expatriation *place of:* **7** Siberia

exist 2 am, be, is **3** are, lie **4** live, move **5** dwell **6** inhere, reside **7** breathe, consist, subsist

existence 3 ens **4** esse, life **5** being, thing **6** entity **7** reality **8** perseity **9** actuality, something **13** individuality *combining form:* **3** ont **4** onto

existent 4 real 5 alive, being, thing
6 actual, around, entity, living 7 instant,
present 8 todayish 10 present-day 12 contemporary

existentialist writer 5 Buber (Martin),
Camus (Albert) 6 Marcel (Gabriel-Honoré),
Sartre (Jean-Paul) 7 Jaspers (Karl) 9 Hei-
degger (Martin) 11 Kierkegaard (Søren)

existing 5 alive, being, ontic 6 around,
extant, living *from birth:* 6 innate 10 congenital *Latin:* 6 in esse

exit 2 go 4 door, gate, move, quit 5 going,
leave 6 depart, egress, exodus, get off, outlet, portal, retire 7 doorway, get away 8 offgoing, withdraw 9 departure, egression
10 setting-out, withdrawal

exode 5 farce 8 travesty

exodus 4 exit 6 egress, flight 7 exiting
8 offgoing 9 departure, egression, migration 10 emigration, setting-out, withdrawal

Exodus author 4 Uris (Leon)

exonerate 4 free 5 clear 6 acquit, excuse
7 absolve 9 disburden, exculpate, vindicate
10 disculpate

exorbitant 5 dizzy, undue 7 extreme
8 exacting, overmuch, towering 9 excessive, overboard 10 immoderate, inordinate,
outrageous
11 extravagant, unwarranted 12 preposterous, unmeasurable

exordium 5 proem 7 preface, prelude
8 foreword, overture, preamble, prologue
9 prelusion 11 preliminary 12 introduction,
prolegomenon

exotic 5 alien 7 foreign, strange, unusual
8 alluring, enticing, imported, romantic 9 different, glamorous 10 introduced, mysterious, romanesque 11 fascinating

expand 3 wax 4 grow, open, rise 5 boost,
built, mount, swell, widen 6 beef up, detail,
dilate, fan out, spread, unfold 7 amplify,
augment, bolster, develop, distend, enlarge,
inflate, magnify, prolong, stretch, upsurge
8 escalate, heighten, increase, multiply,
mushroom, protract 9 discourse, elaborate,
expatiate, explicate, outspread 10 aggrandize, outstretch

expanse 4 area, room 5 field, ocean,
orbit, range, reach, scope, space, sweep,
tract 6 domain, extent, sphere, spread
7 breadth, compass, stretch 8 distance
9 amplitude, immensity, magnitude, territory

expansion 5 space 6 growth, spread
7 breadth, stretch 8 distance, increase
9 amplitude 11 enlargement

expansive 3 big 4 airy, free, wide
5 ample, broad, great, gushy, large
6 bouncy, lavish, scopic 7 buoyant, elastic,
liberal 8 effusive, extended, generous, outgoing, scopious, volatile 9 resilient 10 gregarious, openhanded, unreserved 11 extro-

verted 12 communicable, effervescent,
unrestrained 13 communicative, demonstrative, unconstrained

expatiate 6 ramble, recite, relate, wander
7 descant, discuss, dissert, recount 8 dilate
on, rehearse 9 discourse, sermonize
10 dilate upon, dissertate

expatriate 4 oust 6 banish, deport, emigré 8 displace, expellee, relegate 9 transport

expect 4 feel, hope, look, take 5 await,
sense, think 6 assume, divine, gather
7 believe, count on, foresee, imagine, presume, suppose 8 foreknow 9 apprehend,
count upon 10 anticipate, presuppose

expectant 3 big 5 alert, eager, heavy
6 gravid, parous 7 atiptoe, hopeful 8 childing, enceinte, open-eyed, pregnant, watchful 10 parturient 11 openmouthed 12 anticipative, anticipatory

expectation 4 hope 6 design, motive
8 prospect

expectorate 4 spit

expediency 4 step 5 order, shift
6 design, resort, tactic 7 aptness, fitness,
measure, stopgap 8 meetness, recourse,
resource, strategy 9 makeshift, propriety,
rightness, surrogate 10 substitute 11 suitability 12 appositeness, suitableness

expedient 3 fit 4 wise 5 dodge, means,
shift 6 agency, medium, refuge, resort,
timely, useful 7 fitting, politic, prudent, stopgap 8 feasible, possible, recourse,
resource, suitable, tactical 9 advisable, judicious, makeshift, opportune, practical, well-
timed 10 beneficial, convenient, instrument,
profitable, seasonable, substitute 11 appropriate, practicable, utilitarian 12 advantageous

expedite 3 hie 4 send 5 hurry, issue,
speed 6 hasten 7 quicken 8 dispatch
10 accelerate, facilitate

expedition 4 trek, trip 5 haste, hurry,
speed 6 hustle, rustle 7 entrada, journey,
travels 8 alacrity, campaign, celerity, dispatch, goodwill 9 excursion, readiness,
swiftness 10 speediness 11 promptitude,
punctuality

expeditious 4 fast 5 fleet, hasty, quick,
rapid, ready, swift 6 prompt, speedy
9 breakneck, effective, effectual, efficient
10 harefooted 11 efficacious

expeditiousness 5 haste, hurry, speed
6 hustle, rustle 8 celerity, dispatch 9 swiftness

expel 4 oust, spew 5 belch, eject, eruct,
erupt, evict, exile 6 banish, deport, disbar,
irrupt 7 blow off, blow out, cast out, drum
out, exhaust, expulse, kick out, read out,
turn out 8 disgorge, displace 9 ejaculate,

eliminate, transport **10** expatriate *prefix:* **3** dis

expellee 6 emigré

expend 2 go **3** pay **4** blow, give **5** spend, use up, waste **6** finish, lay out, outlay, wash up **7** consume, exhaust, fork out **8** disburse, dispense, shell out **10** distribute, run through

expenditure 4 cost **6** outlay **12** disbursement

expense 4 cost, loss, toll **5** price **6** charge, outlay **7** forfeit **8** overhead **9** decrement, sacrifice **10** forfeiture **11** deprivation **12** disbursement

expensive 4 dear, high **6** costly **9** big-ticket **10** high-priced, immoderate **12** uneconomical

experience 3 see **4** feel, have, know, live, meet, view **5** savor, skill, taste, trial **6** accept, behold, ordeal, suffer, survey, wisdom **7** know-how, receive, sustain, undergo **8** intimacy, practice **9** encounter, go through **10** background, inwardness **11** familiarity, observation, savoir faire **12** acquaintance *anew:* **6** relive *combining form:* **7** empirio **8** empirico

experienced 3 old, vet **4** wise **6** versed **7** old-line, old-time, skilled, veteran, worldly **8** broken in, seasoned, skillful **9** practical, practiced, qualified, underwent **10** proficient **12** accomplished

experiential see empirical

experiment 3 try **4** test **5** probe, study, trial, try on, weigh **6** search, try out **7** analyze, test out **8** analysis, research, trial run **10** scrutinize **11** examination, investigate **13** investigation, trial and error *combining form:* **7** empirio **8** empirico

experimental 4 test **5** trial **9** empirical, temporary, tentative **11** preliminary, preparatory, provisional **13** developmental

experimentation 4 test **5** trial **8** trial run **13** trial and error

expert 3 ace, pro, wiz **4** deft, whiz **5** adept, crack, doyen, maven, mavin, swell **6** adroit, artist, master, mayvin, wizard **7** artiste, skilled, trained **8** masterly, schooled, skillful, virtuoso **9** authority, dexterous, masterful **10** master-hand, past master, proficient, specialist **11** crackerjack **12** passed master, professional *suffix:* **5** ician

expertise 3 art **5** craft, knack, savvy, skill **7** ability, command, cunning, finesse, know-how, mastery **9** dexterity, quickness, readiness **10** adroitness, cleverness, competence, mastership **12** skillfulness **13** ingeniousness

expertness 5 knack, skill **7** ability, command, know-how, mastery **8** facility **10** mastership

expiate 3 pay **5** amend, atone, avert **6** remedy **7** correct, rectify, redress

expiation 9 atonement

expiatory 7 atoning, lustral **9** purgative **10** lustratory **11** purgatorial **12** propitiatory **13** expurgatorial

expiration 3 end **5** death **10** exhalation **11** termination

expire 2 go **3** die **4** conk, pass **5** lapse **6** demise, depart, elapse, exhale, perish, run out **7** decease **8** pass away **10** breathe out, outbreathe

explain 4 undo **5** clear, gloss, gloze, solve **6** acquit, define **7** absolve, account, analyze, clarify, clear up, condone, justify, resolve, unravel **8** annotate, construe, decipher, footnote, spell out, unriddle, untangle **9** break down, elucidate, exculpate, exonerate, interpret, vindicate **10** illuminate, illustrate, unscramble **11** disentangle, rationalize

explain away 7 account, justify **11** rationalize

explanation 3 key **6** excuse, motive, reason **7** account, example, grounds, meaning **8** exegesis **9** construal, rationale **12** unscrambling **13** enlightenment

explanatory 8 exegetic **10** discursive **12** enlightening, illuminating, illustrative, interpretive **13** demonstrative

expletive 4 cuss, oath **5** curse, swear **8** cussword **9** swearword (see also **exclamation**)

explicate 6 unfold **7** amplify, develop, explain, expound **8** construe, spell out **9** interpret

explication 8 exegesis **9** construal **11** development, enlargement

explicative 8 exegetic **10** scholastic **12** interpretive

exploit 4 open, sure **5** clear, exact, lucid, overt, plain **7** certain, correct, obvious, precise **8** accurate, clean-cut, clear-cut, definite, distinct, specific **10** definitive **11** categorical, perspicuous, unambiguous, unequivocal

explode 3 pop **4** fire **5** blast, burst, erupt, go off, shoot **6** blow up **7** deflate **8** break out, detonate, disprove, dynamite, mushroom, puncture **9** discharge, discredit **10** burst forth

exploit 3 act, job, use **4** blow, coup, deed, feat, gest, play, skin, soak, work **5** abuse, apply, bleed, stick, stunt **6** bestow, effort, employ, fleece, handle, jockey, parlay, stroke **7** beguile, emprise, finesse, utilize, venture **8** exercise, impose on, maneuver **9** adventure, cultivate **10** enterprise, impose upon, manipulate **11** achievement, performance, tour de force

explore 3 try 4 feel, sift, test 5 probe 6 burrow, go into, quarry, search 7 dig into, examine 8 look into, prospect, question 9 delve into, inquisite 11 inquire into, investigate

explorer *African:* 3 Cam, Cão (Diogo) 4 Park (Mungo) 5 Grant (James), Laird (Macgregor), Speke (John Hanning) 6 Akeley (Carl, Mary), Burton (Richard), Lander (John, Richard) 7 Covilhã (Pero da), Stanley (Henry) 8 Covilhão (Pero da) 10 Clapperton (Hugh) 11 Livingstone (David) *American:* 4 Byrd (Richard), Hall (Charles Francis), Kane (Elisha Kent), Pike (Zebulon) 5 Clark (William), Lewis (Meriwether), Peary (Robert) 6 Henson (Matthew), Powell (John Wesley), Wilkes (Charles) 7 Frémont (John Charles) *Antarctic:* 4 Byrd (Richard), Cook (Frederick), Ross (James Clark) 5 Fuchs (Vivian), Ronne (Finn), Scott (Robert Falcon) 6 Palmer (Nathaniel), Rymill (John Riddoch), Wilkes (Charles) 7 Weddell (James), Wilkins (George) 8 Amundsen (Roald), d'Urville (Dumont) 9 Ellsworth (Lincoln) 10 Shackleton (Ernest) *Arctic:* 3 Rae (John) 4 Byrd (Richard), Cook (Frederick) 5 Davis (John), Peary (Robert) 6 Baffin (William), Bering (Vitus), Henson (Matthew), Hudson (Henry), Nansen (Fridtjof), Nobile (Umberto) 7 Barents (Willem), Bennett (Floyd), Wilkins (George), Wrangel (Ferdinand von) 8 Amundsen (Roald) 9 Mackenzie (Alexander), MacMillan (Donald) 10 Stefansson (Vilhjalmur) *Australian:* 7 Wilkins (George) *Austrian:* 9 Weyprecht (Carl) *British:* 12 Younghusband (Francis) *Canadian:* 9 Mackenzie (Alexander) 10 Stefansson (Vilhjalmur) *Danish:* 9 Rasmussen (Knud) *Dutch:* 6 Tasman (Abel Janszoon) *English:* 4 Cook (James) 5 Drake (Francis), Scott (Robert Falcon), Smith (John) 6 Baffin (William), Burton (Richard), Hudson (Henry) 7 Raleigh (Walter), Stanley (Henry) 9 Vancouver (George) 10 Shackleton (Ernest) *French:* 7 Cartier (Jacques), La Salle (Sieur de), Nicolet (Jean) 8 Cousteau (Jacques) 9 Champlain (Samuel de), La Perouse (Comte de), Marquette (Jacques) *French Canadian:* 6 Joliet (Louis) 7 Jolliet (Louis) 9 Iberville (Sieur d') *German:* 6 Peters (Carl) 7 Humboldt (Alexander von) *Italian:* 5 Cabot (John) 6 Nobile (Umberto) *New Zealand:* 7 Hillary (Edmund) *Norwegian:* 6 Nansen (Fridtjof) 8 Amundsen (Roald), Sverdrup (Otto) 9 Heyerdahl (Thor) *Portuguese:* 6 Cabral (Pedro) 8 Magellan (Ferdinand) *Scottish:* 3 Rae (John) 4 Park (Mungo), Ross (James Clark) 7 Thomson (Joseph) 11 Livingstone (David) *Spanish:* 6 Balboa (Vasco Núñez de), Cortés (Hernando), de Soto (Hernando), Pinzon (Martin Alonso) 7 Mendoza (Pedro de), Pizarro (Francisco) 8 Bastidas (Rodrigo de), Coronado (Francisco de) 11 Ponce de León (Juan)

explosion 3 pop, pow 4 bang, gust 5 blast, burst, sally 6 access 7 flare-up 8 outburst 10 detonation

explosive 3 TNT 4 bomb, mine 5 nitro, troty 6 amatol, petard, powder 7 ammonal, cordite, dunnite, grenade, lyddite 8 cheddite, dynamite, fulminic, melinite 9 fulminate 10 detonative 13 nitroglycerin *device:* 3 cap 4 bomb, mine 5 shell 6 petard 7 grenade 8 firework *display:* 9 fireworks *expert:* 5 Maxim (Hudson) *sound:* 3 pop, pow 4 bang, boom

exponent 6 backer 7 booster 8 advocate, champion, defender, partisan, promoter, upholder 9 supporter

expose 3 air 4 bare, open, risk, show 5 flash, peril, strip 6 debunk, flaunt, hazard, parade, reveal, show up, unfold, unmask, unveil 7 display, disport, exhibit, imperil, jeopard, lay open, publish, show off, subject, trot out, uncloak, uncover, undress 8 brandish, disclose, discover, endanger, jeopardy, muckrake, unclothe, unshroud 9 advertise, broadcast

exposé 10 revelation

exposed 4 bare, open 5 naked, prone 6 liable, likely, peeled 7 denuded, evident, menaced, subject, visible 8 apparent, manifest, revealed, stripped, unhidden 9 obnoxious, sensitive, uncovered 10 threatened 11 susceptible, unconcealed

exposition 4 fair, show 7 display, exhibit 8 analysis, exegesis 9 construal, discourse, statement 10 discussion, exhibition 11 delineation

expository 8 critical, exegetic 11 explanative, explanatory 12 interpretive

expostulate 4 kick 5 argue, fight 6 combat, debate, except, object, oppose, resist 7 discuss, dispute, protest 11 remonstrate

exposure 4 risk 5 peril 6 danger 8 jeopardy, openness 9 liability 12 helplessness, susceptivity 13 vulnerability

expound 5 state, teach 7 clarify, comment, explain, express, lecture, present 8 construe, describe, spell out 9 delineate, discourse, exemplify, explicate, interpret 10 illustrate

expounder 7 teacher 8 advocate, champion 9 proponent, supporter

express 3 air, put, say, set 4 give, mean, tell, vent, word 5 couch, crush, frame, spell, state 6 broach, convey, denote, impart, import, intend, phrase, voiced 7 add up to, connote, declare, signify, special, uttered 8 announce, clean-cut, clear-cut, definite, disclose, especial, explicit, intended, proclaim, put about, specific **9** circulate, enunciate, formulate, out-and-out, pronounce, ventilate **10** definitive, individual, particular **11** categorical, communicate, intentional, unambiguous, unqualified *gratitude:* **5** thank *regret:* **9** apologize

expression 4 cast, face, form, look, mien, show, sign, vent, word **5** idiom, issue, motto, token, voice **6** clause, phrase, symbol, visage **7** gesture **8** locution, reminder **9** eloquence, facundity, statement, utterance, verbalism, vividness **10** embodiment, indication, reflection **11** countenance, graphicness, observation **13** demonstration, manifestation *combining form:* **4** logy **5** logia *facial:* **4** grin, phiz **5** frown, scowl, smile, wince **7** grimace *of assent:* **3** aye, nod, yea, yes **4** okay **6** placet **9** exequator *of sorrow:* **4** alas, tear *trite:* **6** cliché **7** bromide **8** banality *witty:* **4** quip **8** atticism

expressionless 4 dead, dull **5** blank, empty, stony **6** stolid, vacant, wooden **7** deadpan, vacuous **9** impassive **10** lackluster **11** inscrutable

expressive 4 rich **5** vivid **6** facund, lively, poetic **7** graphic **8** eloquent, emphatic, pregnant, senseful, spirited **9** pictorial, revealing **10** meaningful, revelatory **11** sententious, significant

expressly 4 even, just **6** as well, namely **8** in specie

expressway 4 road **7** freeway, highway, parkway **8** turnpike

expropriate 4 take **5** annex, seize **7** preempt **8** accroach **9** sequester **10** commandeer, confiscate, dispossess

expulse 4 oust **5** eject **6** banish, deport **7** cast out **8** displace, relegate **9** transport

expulsion 5 exile **7** ousting, removal **8** ejection **9** ostracism **10** banishment, driving out, forcing out, relegation **11** deportation **12** displacement

expunge 4 dele, drop, omit, x out **5** annul, erase **6** cancel, delete, efface **7** blot out, destroy, discard, exclude, wipe out **8** black out **9** eradicate **10** annihilate, obliterate

expurgate 4 blip **5** purge **6** censor, purify, screen **7** cleanse **10** bowdlerize

expurgation 9 catharsis, cleansing

exquisite 3 fop **4** buck, dude, nice, rare **5** acute, blood, dandy **6** choice, dainty, fierce, select, superb **7** coxcomb, elegant, extreme, furious, intense, vicious, violent **8** delicate, finished, flawless, macaroni, superior, terrible, vehement **9** desperate, errorless, faultless, recherché **10** consummate, immaculate, impeccable

exsanguine 6 anemic **9** bloodless

exsect 6 cut out, excise

exsiccate 3 dry **4** sear **5** parch

exsuccuous 3 dry **4** sere **7** sapless **8** withered

extant 5 alive, being **6** actual, around, living **7** current, present **8** todayish **9** immediate **10** present-day **12** contemporary

extemporaneous 4 snap **6** casual **7** offhand **8** informal **9** impromptu, impulsive, unstudied **10** improvised, unprepared **11** unrehearsed **12** unthought-out

extempore see extemporaneous

extemporize 3 act **5** ad-lib **7** dash off, toss off **8** knock off **9** improvise **11** improvisate

extend 2 go **3** eke, run **4** draw, give, grow, make, open, pose, span, vary **5** allot, award, boost, grant, offer, range, reach **6** accord, attain, beef up, bestow, confer, donate, fan out, spread, tender, unfold **7** advance, amplify, augment, draw out, enlarge, hold out, magnify, present, proceed, proffer, project, prolong, spin out, stretch **8** allocate, continue, elongate, heighten, increase, lengthen, multiply, protract **9** outspread **10** aggrandize, outstretch, prolongate

extended *combining form:* **3** meg **4** mego **5** megal **6** megalo

extension 3 arm, ell **4** area, size, wing **5** ambit, annex, block, orbit, range, reach, scope, sweep **6** radius, spread **7** compass, purview, stretch **8** increase **9** magnitude **10** continuing, drawing out, elongation, production, stretch-out **11** enlargement, lengthening, prolongment, protraction **12** augmentation, continuation, prolongation, spreading out

extensity 5 ambit, orbit, range, reach, scope, sweep **6** radius **7** compass, purview

extensive 3 big **4** vast, wide **5** broad, hefty, large, major **6** scopic **7** blanket, general, immense, sizable **8** scopious, spacious **9** boundless, wholesale **10** large-scale **11** far-reaching, wide-ranging **12** considerable, far-spreading

extent 4 size, tune, writ **5** ambit, field, orbit, order, range, reach, scope, sweep, width **6** amount, degree, domain, matter, radius, sphere **7** breadth, compass, measure, purview **8** province, vicinity **9** magnitude **10** dimensions, proportion

extenuate 4 thin **5** white **6** temper, veneer, whiten **7** explain, justify, qualify, varnish **8** palliate, wiredraw **9** apologize, gloss over, gloze over, sugarcoat, whitewash **10** blanch over **11** rationalize

exterior 4 over **5** ectal, outer **6** facade **7** outmost, outside, outward, surface **8** external **9** outermost

exterminate 4 kill 5 abate 6 uproot 7 abolish, blot out, root out, wipe out 8 massacre 9 finish off, slaughter 10 annihilate, extinguish

external 3 out 4 over 5 ectal, outer 7 outmost, outside, outward 9 outermost 10 peripheral 11 superficial *combining form:* 3 ect 4 ecto

externalize 6 embody 8 manifest 9 incarnate, objectify, personify 12 substantiate

extinct 4 cold, dead, gone, late, lost 5 passé 6 asleep, bygone, fallen 7 archaic, defunct, disused, outworn 8 deceased, departed, lifeless, obsolete, outmoded, perished, vanished 9 collapsed 10 antiquated, overthrown, superseded, unanimated 11 disappeared, nonexistent 12 old-fashioned *combining form:* 4 necr 5 necro

extinction 5 death 11 destruction 12 annihilation, obliteration

extinguish 3 out 5 abate, check, crush, douse, erase, quash, quell 6 put out, quench, squash, stifle, uproot 7 abolish, blot out, blow out, destroy, expunge, put down, root out, smother, wipe out 8 suppress 9 eradicate 10 annihilate, obliterate

extirpate 4 raze 5 erase 6 cut out, efface, excise, resect, uproot 7 abolish, blot out, destroy, expunge, kill off, root out, wipe out 8 demolish 10 annihilate

extol 4 hymn, laud 5 bless, cry up, exalt 6 praise 7 applaud, commend, elevate, glorify, magnify 8 eulogize 9 celebrate 10 panegyrize

extort 3 get 4 milk, skin 5 bleed, cheat, educe, evoke, exact, force, gouge, pinch, screw, wrest, wring 6 coerce, compel, demand, elicit, evince, fleece, obtain, secure, wrench 7 squeeze 9 blackmail, shake down

extortion 8 chantage, exaction 9 blackmail

extra 3 odd 4 more, over 5 added, spare 6 de trop, rarely 7 surplus 8 markedly 9 lagniappe, unusually 10 additional, especially, noticeably, uncommonly 11 superfluent, superfluous 12 considerably, particularly, supplemental 13 supernumerary, supplementary *prefix:* 5 hyper, super

extract 3 dig, pry 4 cull, draw, milk, pull, tear, yank 5 educe, evoke, glean, wring 6 avulse, eke out, elicit, evince, evulse, garner, gather, pick up 7 abridge, distill, excerpt, scratch, shorten, squeeze 8 condense

extraction 5 birth, blood 6 origin 7 descent, essence, lineage 8 ancestry, pedigree 9 parentage

extraneous 5 alien, outer 6 exotic 7 foreign 9 pointless, unrelated 10 accidental, immaterial, inapposite, incidental, irrelative, irrelevant 11 impertinent, unessential 12 adventitious, inapplicable 13 inappropriate

extraordinary 3 odd 4 rare 6 unique 7 amazing, notable, unusual 8 singular, terrific, uncommon, unwonted 9 wonderful 10 noteworthy, remarkable, stupendous, tremendous 11 exceptional, unthinkable

extravagance 5 frill, luxus, waste 6 luxury 7 amenity 8 squander, unthrift 9 overdoing 10 lavishness 11 prodigality, superfluity 12 wastefulness

extravagant 4 wild 5 crazy, dizzy, outré, silly, undue 6 absurd, lavish 7 bizarre, foolish, profuse 8 prodigal, towering, wasteful 9 fantastic, ludicrous 10 immoderate, inordinate, profligate, ridiculous, unbalanced 11 exaggerated, implausible, nonsensical 12 preposterous, unmeasurable, unrestrained

extreme 3 top 4 deep, dire, last, peak, wild 5 crest, crown, dizzy, final, limit, rabid, ultra, undue 6 ardent, climax, excess, height, moving, summit, utmost 7 ceiling, drastic, fanatic, intense, maximum, outmost, radical, violent 8 farthest, furthest, pinnacle, remotest, towering, ultraist 9 desperate, excessive, outermost, uttermost 10 immoderate, inordinate, outlandish 11 culmination, furthermost, inordinancy, intolerable, unwarranted 12 consummation, revolutional, unmeasurable, unreasonable 13 revolutionary *degree:* 3 nth

extremely 3 too 4 ever, over, very 6 mighty 7 parlous 8 overfull, overmuch 11 exceedingly

extremist 5 rabid, ultra 7 fanatic, radical 12 revolutional 13 revolutionary

extremity 3 arm, end, leg, tip 4 acme, apex, foot, hand, tail 5 limit, verge 6 apogee, vertex, zenith 8 terminal, terminus *combining form:* 3 acr, akr 4 acro, akro

extricate 4 free 5 clear, loose, sever, untie 6 detach, rescue 7 deliver, discern, release, resolve, unravel, untwine 8 abstract, untangle 9 clear away, disburden, discumber, disengage 10 discrepate, disembroil, disentwine, disinvolve, severalize, unentangle, unscramble 11 disemburden, disencumber, disentangle, distinguish 12 disembarrass

extrinsic 5 alien, outer 6 gained 7 foreign, outside, outward 8 acquired, external 10 accidental, extraneous

extrude 3 out 4 spew 5 chase, chuck, eject, evict 7 boot out, dismiss, kick out, project 8 throw out

exuberance 4 life, zest 5 ardor 6 spirit 7 abandon, gayness 8 buoyancy 10 friskiness, liveliness 11 zestfulness 13 sprightliness

exuberant 3 gay 4 glad, lush, rank
5 brash, happy 6 ardent, fecund, lavish,
lively 7 diffuse, fertile, opulent, profuse, riotous, zestful 8 fruitful, prodigal, prolific, spirited 9 ebullient, profusive, sprightly, vivacious 10 frolicsome, passionate
12 effervescent, high-spirited

exude 4 emit, ooze, seep, weep 5 bleed,
sweat 6 strain 7 emanate, secrete, trickle
8 perspire 9 discharge, percolate

exult 4 brag, crow 5 boast, gloat, glory
7 delight, rejoice, show off, triumph 8 jubilate 9 celebrate

exultant 4 glad 5 happy 6 elated, joyous
7 flushed 8 jubilant 9 cock-a-hoop, overjoyed, rejoicing, triumphal 10 cock-a-
whoop, delighting

exultation 3 joy 7 delight, rapture, triumph
8 gloating 9 jubilance, rejoicing 10 jubilation

exuviate 4 molt, shed, slip 5 moult
6 slough

eye 3 orb, tab 4 gape, gaze, lamp, look,
loop, mind, ring, tail, view 5 grasp, optic,
sight, stare, watch 6 behold, belief, goggle,
look at, ocular, oculus, peeper, regard, seeing, size up, staple, vision, winker 7 blinker,
feeling, opinion 8 attitude, consider, gaze
upon, judgment, look upon, position, scrutiny, thinking 9 sentiment, viewpoint
10 conception, conclusion, conviction, persuasion, rubberneck, scrutinize 11 contemplate 12 surveillance *combining form:*
3 ope, opy 4 ocul, opia, opto 5 oculo
8 ophthalm 9 ophthalma, ophthalmo
10 ophthalmia, ophthalmus *defect:* 6 myopia 9 hyperopia 10 emmetropia, presbyopia 11 astigmatism *disease:* 8 cataract,
glaucoma, trachoma *doctor:* 7 oculist
11 optometrist *opening:* 5 pupil *part:*
4 iris, lens, uvea 5 pupil 6 cornea, retina,
sclera *relating to:* 5 optic 7 optical *socket:*
5 orbit *Spanish:* 3 ojo

eyeball 3 see 4 ogle 6 look at 7 examine,
observe

eye-catching 6 marked, signal 7 pointed,
salient 9 prominent 10 noticeable, remarkable 11 conspicuous

eyedropper 7 pipette

eyeful 6 beauty, looker, lovely 7 stunner
8 knockout

eyeglass 4 lens 5 lense 7 monocle

eyeglasses 5 specs 6 lenses 7 lorgnon
8 pince-nez 9 lorgnette

eyelash 6 cilium

eyelid 8 palpebra 9 palpebrae (plural)
combining form: 7 blephar 8 blepharo

eyepiece 4 lens 6 ocular

eye-popping 8 exciting, stirring 9 thrilling
10 exhilarant 11 astonishing 12 exhilarative

eyesore 4 mess 5 sight 6 defect, fright
7 blemish, desight 11 monstrosity

eyespot 7 disease, ocellus

eyetooth 6 canine

eyewash 3 rot 5 bilge, hooey 6 bunkum
7 twaddle 8 malarkey, nonsense

eyewitness 6 viewer 7 watcher
8 beholder, by-sitter, looker-on, observer,
onlooker 9 bystander, spectator

eye worm 3 loa

eyrie   see aerie

Ezbon's father 3 Gad

Ezekiel's father 4 Buzi

Ezer's father 6 Jeshua 7 Ephraim

F

Fabian 4 Shaw (George Bernard) 8 cautious 9 socialist

fable 4 myth, tale 5 story 6 legend 7 fiction, figment 8 allegory, apologue *animal:* 8 bestiary

fabric 3 rep, web 4 repp 5 cloth, fiber, grain 7 texture 8 building, material, shirting 9 structure *coarse:* 5 crash, gunny 6 burlap, linsey, ratiné 7 cheviot, hopsack 8 homespun, osnaburg *corded:* 3 rep 4 repp 5 piqué 6 calico, moreen, poplin 7 pinwale 8 corduroy, paduasoy 9 bengaline *cotton:* 4 jean, leno 5 baize, chino, drill, scrim, swiss, wigan 6 chintz, dimity, faille, madras, muslin 7 etamine, galatea, gingham, nankeen, percale, silesia, ticking 8 chambray, dungaree, nainsook, osnaburg, tarlatan *cotton and linen:* 4 huck 7 fustian 9 huckaback *crepe:* 8 marocain *dealer:* 6 draper, mercer *durable:* 4 huck, jean 5 chino, denim, drill 6 frieze, moreen 7 lasting, ticking 8 cretonne, dungaree, osnaburg *embroidered:* 9 baldachin, baldaquin 10 baldachino 11 baldacchino *finishing process:* 8 lustring 9 mercerize 10 causterize *flag material:* 7 bunting *glazed:* 6 chintz 7 cambric, holland *knitted:* 6 tricot 10 balbriggan *linen:* 7 cambric, lockram *looped:* 6 bouclé *lustrous:* 4 silk 5 moiré, satin, surah 7 silesia, taffeta 12 brilliantine *metallic:* 4 lamé *net:* 5 tulle 8 bobbinet, illusion *openwork:* 4 lace 8 fillgree *ornamental:* 4 lace 5 braid 6 ribbon 7 bunting *pebbly-surface:* 6 armure 8 barathea *pile-surface:* 5 panne, plush, terry 6 velour, velvet 7 bolivia, duvetyn, velours 8 chenille, moleskin, velveret 9 velveteen *plaid:* 6 tartan *printed:* 5 batik, toile 6 calico, chintz, damask 7 allover, challis, dornick, pintado 8 cretonne, jacquard 11 toile de jouy *raised pattern:* 7 brocade 10 brocatelle *satin weave:* 5 panne *sheer:* 4 lawn 5 gauze, ninon, swiss, voile 6 barege, dimity, tissue 7 batiste, chiffon, cypress, organdy, organza, tiffany 8 tarlatan *silk:* 4 acca, fuji 5 pekin 6 cendal, chappe, pongee, samite, sendal 7 alamode, foulard, grogram, schappe 8 paduasoy, sarcenet, sarsenet, shantung 9 bombazine *striped:* 3 aba 4 abba 5 abaya,

pekin 7 galatea, ticking 8 algerine 10 algerienne *synthetic:* 5 ninon, nylon, Orlon, rayon 6 Dacron *twill:* 4 jean 5 chino, drill, serge 7 foulard, galatea, nankeen, silesia, ticking 8 dungaree, shalloon 9 bombazine 10 broadcloth *unfinished:* 6 greige *waterproof:* 7 oilskin *wool:* 5 baize, loden, tweed 6 caddis, camlet, duffel, duffle, melton, merino, wadmad, wadmel, wadmol, witney, woolen 7 caddice, delaine, whitney, woollen 8 algerine, mackinaw, prunella 9 cassimera 10 algerienne *wool, poor quality:* 5 mungo 6 shoddy *wool mixture:* 5 tammy 6 saxony, wincey, winsey 7 drugget, ratteen 8 moquette, shalloon, zibeline *woven:* 4 weft 7 textile

fabricate 4 form, make 5 build, frame, shape 6 devise, invent, make up 7 concoct, fashion, produce, turn out 8 assemble, contrive 9 construct 11 manufacture

fabrication 3 fib, lie 4 opus, work 6 deceit 7 fiction, figment, product, untruth 9 falsehood

fabulist *French:* 10 La Fontaine (Jean de) *Greek:* 4 Esop 5 Aesop *Indian:* 6 Bidpai, Pilpai, Pilpay *Roman:* 8 Phaedrus *Russian:* 6 Krylov (Ivan)

fabulous 7 amazing 8 mythical 9 legendary, wonderful 10 astounding, exorbitant, fictitious, incredible, inordinate, outrageous, prodigious, stupendous 11 astonishing, extravagant 12 mythological *animal:* 6 dragon 7 centaur, unicorn *bird:* 3 roc 6 simurg 7 simurgh *serpent:* 8 basilisk 10 cockatrice

facade 4 face, mask, show 5 color, front, guise, put-on 6 veneer 8 disguise, pretense

face 3 mow, mug, top 4 cast, clad, dare, defy, gall, gaze, look, mask, meet, moue, phiz, pout, show, side, skin, veil 5 await, beard, brass, brave, cheek, cloak, close, cover, fight, front, frown, glare, guise, lower, mouth, nerve, paint, scowl, stare, watch 6 accost, border, brazen, breast, engage, expect, glower, makeup, mazard, muzzle, oppose, resist, take on, visage 7 affront, contend, grimace, outdare, seeming, sheathe, showing, venture 8 confront, dis-

guise, features, mouthing, war paint
9 brashness, challenge, encounter, semblance, withstand 10 appearance, confidence, effrontery, expression, false front, lineaments, maquillage, masquerade, simulacrum 11 countenance, physiognomy

facet 4 hand, side 5 angle, bezel, front, phase 6 aspect

facetious 5 comic, droll, funny, jolly, merry, witty 6 blithe, jocose, jocund, joking, jovial 7 comical, jesting, jocular 8 humorous 9 laughable, ludicrous 12 wisecracking

face-to-face 7 vis-à-vis

facile 4 able, deft, easy, glib 5 light, quick, royal 6 adroit, expert, fluent, simple, smooth 7 cursory, shallow, voluble 9 dexterous 10 effortless, uncritical

facilitate 3 aid 4 ease, help 6 assist 8 expedite

facility 3 aid, wit 4 bent, ease, tact, turn 5 poise, skill 7 abandon, address, amenity, comfort, fitting, leaning 8 aptitude 9 advantage, dexterity, lightness, readiness 10 smoothness 11 convenience, spontaneity 13 accommodation

facing 5 front, panel 6 before, contra, toward, veneer 7 against, vis-à-vis 8 covering, opposite, paneling 11 over against *down:* 5 prone *up:* 6 supine

facsimile 4 copy 5 ditto 6 carbon 7 replica 9 duplicate, imitation 10 carbon copy 11 replication 12 reproduction

fact 5 datum, event, truth 6 detail 7 episode, reality 8 incident 9 actuality, happening 10 observable, occurrence, particular, phenomenon 11 genuineness 12 authenticity, circumstance

faction 4 bloc, camp, part, ring, sect, side, wing 5 junto, party 7 combine 8 offshoot 11 combination

factious 7 warring 8 fighting 9 alienated, estranged, insurgent, seditious 10 contending 11 belligerent, contentious, disaffected, quarrelsome 13 insubordinate

factitious 4 sham 5 false 6 forced 7 assumed, feigned, man-made, shammed 8 affected 9 pretended, simulated, synthetic 10 artificial 13 counterfeited

____**facto** 4 ipso

factor 3 aid 4 doer, gene 5 agent, cause, maker, means, proxy 6 agency, deputy, helper 7 bailiff, element, steward 8 adjutant, assignee, attorney 9 assistant, coadjutor, component, consignee, majordomo, seneschal 10 antecedent, ingredient, instrument 11 determinant

factory 4 mill, shop 5 plant, works

factual 4 hard, true 5 valid 7 certain, genuine 8 absolute, positive 9 authentic, undoubted, veritable

faculty 4 bent, bump, gift, nose, turn 5 flair, knack, power 6 genius, talent 7 aptness, leaning 8 aptitude, capacity, function, instinct, penchant, property 12 predilection

facund 4 rich 8 eloquent, pregnant 10 expressive, meaningful 11 sententious, significant

fad 3 cry 4 chic, mode, rage, whim 5 craze, fancy, style, trend, vogue 6 furore, vagary, whimsy 7 caprice, conceit, fashion 10 dernier cri

fade 3 die, dim, ebb 4 dull, flag, melt, pale, thin 5 abate, clear, muddy 6 lessen, rarefy, vanish, weaken, wither 7 decline, dwindle, evanish, tarnish 8 diminish, dissolve, evanesce, languish, moderate 9 attenuate, disappear, evaporate 10 deliquesce 11 deteriorate

Faerie Queen, The *author:* 7 Spenser (Edmund) *character:* 3 Ate, Una 4 Alma 5 Guyon, Talus 6 Abessa, Amavia, Amoret, Arthur, Cambel, Duessa, Palmer 7 Artegal, Corceca, Fidessa, Maleger, Sansloy 8 Calidore, Florimel, Fradubio, Gloriana, Lucifera, Orgoglio, Satyrane 9 Archimago, Britomart 11 Britomartis

Fafner, Fafnir *brother:* 5 Regin 6 Fasolt, Reginn *father:* 8 Hreidmar *form:* 6 dragon *slayer:* 6 Sigurd 9 Siegfried *victim:* 6 Fasolt 8 Hreidmar

fag 4 flag, tire 5 smoke, weary 6 drudge, tucker 7 exhaust, frazzle, outtire, outwear, servant, wear out 8 knock out 9 cigarette, prostrate

fag end 4 butt 7 remnant 8 last part

fail 3 ebb, end 4 bomb, bust, flag, fold, jade, lose, miss, omit, sink, slip, wane 5 break, close, crash, drain, flunk, short 6 falter, finish, forget, ignore, lessen, run out, shrink, slight, weaken, worsen 7 blink at, bust out, decline, default, deplete, dwindle, exhaust, flummox, founder, gazette, give out, neglect, wash out 8 bankrupt, decrease, diminish, discount, languish, miscarry, overlook, overpass 9 blink away, disregard, terminate 10 impoverish 11 deteriorate

failing 3 shy 4 vice 5 fault, scant, short 6 foible, scanty, scarce 7 frailty 8 weakness 9 deficient 10 deficiency, inadequate 12 imperfection, insufficient, unsufficient

failure 3 dud 4 bomb, bust, flop, hash, lack, miss 5 botch, fault, lemon, loser 6 dearth, defeat, ebbing, fiasco, fizzle, laxity, muddle, outage, waning 7 absence, debacle, decline, default, deficit, neglect, paucity, washout 8 collapse, flagging, poorness, scarcity, shortage, underage, weakness 9 insuccess, oversight, slackness, unconcern, unsuccess 10 bankruptcy, deficiency, exhaustion, inadequacy, meagerness, negligence, nonsuccess, remissness, scantiness, skimpiness **11** declination, defalcation, delinquency, dereliction, inferiority, miscarriage, shortcoming **12** debilitation, enfeeblement, imperfection, indifference **13** deterioration, insufficience, insufficiency, might-have-been

fain 4 glad **5** eager, prone, ready **6** minded **7** willing **8** desirous, disposed, inclined **11** predisposed

faint 3 dim, low, wan **4** coma, mild, pale, soft, swim, thin, weak **5** balmy, bland, blear, dusty, fuzzy, small, swoon, vague **6** bleary, feeble, gentle, hushed, smooth **7** blurred, grayout, languid, lenient, muffled, obscure, pass out, shadowy, stifled, syncope, unclear, vertigo **8** black out, listless **9** dizziness, inaudible, undefined **10** ill-defined, indistinct, undistinct

fair 4 calm, even, fine, just, mean, mild, pure, sane, show, so-so **5** balmy, blond, clean, clear, equal, light, right, ruddy, sunny, tawny **6** bazaar, blonde, candid, chaste, comely, common, dainty, decent, honest, lawful, lovely, medium, placid, pretty, square **7** average, clarion, clement, exhibit **8** balanced, carnival, charming, delicate, detached, festival, handsome, mediocre, middling, moderate, ordinary, pleasant, rainless, rational, straight, sunshine, sunshiny, tranquil, unbiased **9** beauteous, beautiful, cloudless, equitable, exquisite, impartial, objective, unclouded, uncolored **10** attractive, enchanting, exhibition, exposition, impersonal, open-minded, reasonable, sunshining, undarkened **11** good-looking, indifferent, nonpartisan, sportsmanly **12** intermediate, unprejudiced **13** disinterested, dispassionate, sportsmanlike, undistinctive, unthreatening

fair-haired 3 pet **4** dear **5** blond, loved **6** blonde **7** beloved, darling **8** blue-eyed, favorite, precious

fairness 6 equity **12** impartiality

fairy 3 elf, imp **4** pixy, puck **5** dwarf, elfin, gnome, nisse, pixie **6** goblin, kobold, sprite **7** banshee, brownie, gremlin **10** leprechaun *king:* **6** Oberon *palace:* **4** shee **5** sidhe *queen:* **3** Mab **7** Titania *shoemaker:* **10** leprechaun

fairy tale *author:* **5** Grimm (Jacob, Wilhelm), Wilde (Oscar) **8** Andersen (Hans Christian), Perrault (Charles) *character:* **6** Gretel, Hansel **8** Rapunzel **9** Snow White **10** Cinderella, Goldilocks

faith 4 cult, hope, sect **5** creed, stock, troth, trust **6** belief, church, credit, dogmas, tenets **8** credence, reliance, religion **9** communion, doctrines **10** confidence, connection, dependence, persuasion **12** denomination *article of:* **5** tenet **9** credendum

faithful 4 fast, firm, just, true **5** exact, liege, loyal, pious, right, tried **6** ardent, loving, steady, strict, trusty **7** binding, devoted, staunch **8** constant, credible, reliable, resolute, trueblue **9** allegiant, authentic, steadfast, veracious, veridical **10** convincing, dependable **11** trustworthy, undistorted **12** affectionate **13** conscientious, dyed-in-the-wool

faithfulness 5 ardor, piety **6** fealty **7** loyalty **8** adhesion, devotion, fidelity **9** adherence, constancy **10** allegiance, attachment

faithless 5 false **6** fickle, untrue **7** erratic, unloyal **8** disloyal, recreant, unstable, wavering **9** changeful **10** capricious, changeable, inconstant, perfidious, traitorous **11** fluctuating, treacherous

faithlessness 7 falsity, perfidy, treason **8** betrayal **9** treachery **10** disloyalty, infidelity

fake 3 act, gyp **4** hoax, mock, sell, sham **5** bluff, bogus, false, feign, fraud, phony, put on, snide, spoof **6** affect, assume, doctor, forged, framed, humbug, pseudo **7** falsify, pretend **8** impostor, invented, simulate, spurious **9** brummagem, charlatan, concocted, fabricate, imitation, imposture, pinchbeck, pretended, pretender, simulated **10** fabricated, fictitious, fraudulent, simulation **11** counterfeit *combining form:* **5** pseud **6** pseudo

fakir 7 ascetic **9** mendicant

falcon 4 hawk **5** hobby, saker **6** lanner, luggar, merlin **7** kestrel **9** peregrine *male:* **4** jack **6** musket, tassel, tercel **7** sakeret, tiercel **8** lanneret *mature:* **7** haggard, passage *young:* **4** eyas **5** eyess **8** brancher

falcon-headed god see at **Egyptian**

falconry 7 hawking *equipment:* **4** bell, hood, jess, lure **5** bewet, bewit **7** creance *procedure:* **3** imp **4** cope, seel

fall 3 dip, ebb, sag **4** drag, drip, drop, flop, plop, sink, skid, slip, trip, wane **5** abate, beset, crash, droop, lapse, let up, lower, pitch, plonk, plunk, slide, slump, storm, trail, yield **6** assail, attack, dangle, give up, go down, lessen, plunge, relent, sprawl, strike, submit, topple, tumble **7** aggress, assault, cascade, decline, descend, descent, die away, die down, drop off, ease off, go under, plummet, relapse, slacken, stumble, subside, succumb, wipeout **8** decrease, diminish, downcome, downfall, keel over, moderate, nose-dive **9** declivity, surrender

fallacious 3 mad **6** untrue **7** invalid **8** deluding, delusive, delusory **9** beguiling, deceiving, deceptive, illogical, sophistic **10** irrational, misleading, reasonless, unreasoned **11** nonrational **12** unreasonable

fallacy 4 idol 5 error, idola (plural) 6 idolum 7 elusion, evasion, falsity, quibble, sophism, untruth 8 delusion 9 casuistry, deception, falsehood, falseness, quibbling, sophistry 12 equivocation, misconstrual, speciousness, spuriousness 13 deceptiveness, erroneousness, misconception

fall back 6 recede, retire 7 relapse, retract, retreat 8 withdraw 9 retrocede 10 retrograde

fall behind 3 lag

fall flat 4 fail 5 flunk 7 bust out, flummox, wash out

fall guy 3 sap 4 butt, dupe, fish, fool, goat, gull 5 chump, patsy 6 pigeon, sucker 7 gudgeon 9 scapegoat 11 whipping boy

falling-out 3 row 4 beef, feud 5 run-in 6 hassle 7 dispute, quarrel 9 bickering 11 altercation, controversy

falloff 3 dip, sag 4 drop, slip 5 slump 7 decline 8 downturn 9 downslide, downswing, downtrend

fall out 2 go 3 row 4 spat, tiff 5 break, occur, scrap 6 betide, bicker, chance, happen, result 7 brabble, come off, develop, quarrel, wrangle 8 disagree, squabble

false 4 fake, mock, sham 5 bogus, dummy, hokey, lying, phony, snide, wrong 6 ersatz, hollow, pseudo, untrue 7 crooked, devious, seeming, unloyal, unsound 8 apostate, apparent, deluding, delusive, delusory, disloyal, recreant, renegade, specious, spurious 9 beguiling, brummagem, deceitful, deceiving, deceptive, dishonest, distorted, erroneous, faithless, illogical, imitation, incorrect, pinchbeck, simulated 10 artificial, fictitious, fraudulent, inaccurate, mendacious, misleading, ostensible, perfidious, substitute, traitorous, unfaithful, untruthful 11 backsliding, counterfeit, treacherous *combining form:* 5 pseud 6 pseudo

false face 4 mask 5 visor 6 domino, vizard

false front 4 face, mask, show, veil 5 cloak, cover 6 facade 8 disguise 10 masquerade

falsehood 3 fib, lie 4 sham, tale 5 error, fraud, story 6 canard, deceit, fakery 7 fallacy, falsity, fibbery, untruth 8 feigning, pretense, untruism 9 mendacity 10 unveracity 11 fabrication 13 dissimulation, erroneousness, prevarication, truthlessness

falseness 5 error 7 fallacy, perfidy, untruth 8 apostasy 9 defection, desertion, recreancy 10 disloyalty, infidelity

false teeth 7 denture 8 dentures

falsify 3 fib, lie 4 cook, deny, fake, warp 5 alter, belie, color, fudge, twist 6 change, doctor, garble, palter 7 contort, distort, pervert 8 miscolor, misstate, traverse 10 contradict, contravene, equivocate 11 prevaricate 12 misrepresent

falsity 3 fib, lie 4 sham, tale 5 bluff, error, story 6 canard 7 perfidy, untruth 8 untruism 9 falsehood, hypocrisy 10 disloyalty, infidelity 11 fabrication, insincerity 12 uncandidness 13 erroneousness, faithlessness, prevarication

Falstaff *companion:* 3 Nym 4 Peto 6 Pistol 8 Bardolph *composer:* 5 Verdi *creator:* 11 Shakespeare (William) *play:* 7 Henry IV *prince:* 3 Hal *tavern:* 9 Boar's Head

Falstaffian 3 fat 6 coarse, jovial 8 boastful, humorous 9 dissolute

falter 4 halt, limp 5 lurch, quail, quake, shake, waver 6 blench, dither, flinch, quaver, recoil, shrink, topple, wobble 7 shudder, stagger, stumble, tremble, whiffle 8 hesitate, tick over 9 vacillate 12 shilly-shally

fame 4 note 5 éclat, glory, honor 6 renown, report, repute 7 acclaim 8 applause, eminence 9 celebrity, character, greatness, notoriety 10 prominence, reputation 11 acclamation, distinction, preeminence, recognition

famed 5 great, noted 7 eminent, notable 8 renowned 9 prominent 10 celebrated, celebrious 11 illustrious 13 distinguished

familiar 2 up 4 boon, cozy, easy, mate, snug 5 amigo, aware, close, fresh, thick 6 au fait, chummy, common, friend, genial, versed, wonted 7 abreast, affable, cordial, forward, mindful, prosaic, versant 8 amicable, everyday, frequent, friendly, gracious, habitual, informed, intimate, sociable 9 au courant, cognizant, confidant, conscious, customary, intrusive, obtrusive, officious 10 accustomed, acquainted, conversant, neighborly 11 cater-cousin, comfortable, commonplace, impertinent

familiarity 8 intimacy 9 awareness, cognition, knowledge 10 experience, inwardness 12 acquaintance 13 comprehension, understanding

familiarize 3 use 4 wont 5 adapt, inure 6 adjust, season 8 accustom, acquaint 9 condition, habituate

family 3 kin 4 clan, folk, home, line, race 5 brood, folks, house, issue, stirp, stock, tribe 6 ménage, strain 7 dynasty, kindred, lineage, progeny 8 domestic 9 bloodline, household, offspring *branch:* 6 stirps *lineage:* 4 tree 6 stemma 8 pedigree 9 genealogy

famished 6 hungry 7 starved 8 ravenous, starving

famous 3 top 5 great, noted 7 capital, eminent, leading, notable, popular 8 fivestar, renowned, superior, topnotch 9 estimable, excellent, first-rate, honorable, noto-

rious, prominent, reputable, well-known
10 celebrated, celebrious, first-class
11 first-string, illustrious, prestigious,
redoubtable, respectable 13 distinguished,
well-thought-of

fan 4 blow, buff, open, wind 5 hound, lover
6 addict, expand, extend, rooter, ruffle,
spread, unfold, votary, winnow 7 admirer,
amateur, devotee, habitué 8 follower 9 outspread 10 aficionado, enthusiast, outstretch *combining form:* 5 rhipi 6 rhipid
7 rhipido 8 flabelli *horseracing:* 7 turfman
India: 5 punka 6 punkah *movie:* 7 cineast

fanatic 3 bug, nut 5 bigot, fiend, freak,
rabid, ultra 6 maniac, zealot 7 extreme,
radical 8 ultraist 9 extremist 10 monoma-
niac 12 revolutional 13 revolutionary, revolutionist

fancier 6 votary 7 admirer, amateur, devotee

fanciful 5 false, wrong 6 absurd, unreal
7 bizarre, fictive, shadowy, strange 8 fabulous, illusory, imagined, mythical, notional,
romantic 9 fantastic, fictional, grotesque,
imaginary, legendary 10 apocryphal, chimerical, fictitious 11 unrealistic 12 preposterous

fancy 3 bee, fad 4 idea, like, mind, whim,
will 5 dream, fable, freak, humor, image,
think 6 liking, megrim, mirage, notion,
vagary, vision, whimsy 7 approve, boutade,
caprice, chimera, conceit, concept,
endorse, feature, fiction, figment, imagine,
realize, whimsey 8 conceive, crotchet, daydream, delusion, envisage, envision, illusion, phantasm, phantasy, pleasure, sanction, velleity 9 capriccio, elaborate,
intricate, invention, nightmare, visualize
10 conception 11 complicated, envisioning,
fabrication, fata morgana, imagination, inclination 12 contrariness, envisagement, per-
verseness 13 hallucination, irrationality

fan dancer 4 Rand (Sally)

fandango 4 ball 5 dance

fanfare 4 pomp, show 5 array, shine
6 parade 7 display, panoply 8 flourish
trumpet: 6 tucket

fanlike 7 plaited, plicate

fanny 4 seat 5 hiney 6 behind, bottom,
heinie 7 hind end 8 backside, buttocks,
derriere 9 posterior

fanon 5 cloth, orale 7 maniple 8 corporal

fan palm 7 talipot 8 palmetto

fantasize 7 imagine 8 daydream

fantastic 3 odd 4 wild 5 crazy, loony,
queer, silly, wacky 6 absurd, adroit, clever,
insane, mortal, unreal 7 bizarre, fictive, foolish, massive, strange 8 cracking, delusive,
delusory, fanciful, illusory, romantic, singular, towering 9 deceptive, eccentric, fictional, grotesque, imaginary, ingenious,

monstrous, unearthly, whimsical 10 capricious, chimerical, fictitious, incredible, irrational, misleading, monumental, prodigious,
ridiculous, stupendous, tremendous
11 extravagant, implausible, nonsensical
12 preposterous, suppositious, unbelievable, unreasonable

fantasy 4 whim 5 dream, freak 6 bubble,
vagary, vision, whimsy 7 caprice, chimera,
rainbow, whimsey 8 daydream, illusion,
phantasm 9 imagining, nightmare, pipe
dream 10 bizarrerie, conceiving 11 envisioning, imagination 12 grotesquerie

Fantine's daughter 7 Cosette

far 4 deep, long, well 5 quite 6 rather,
remote 7 distant, removed 8 off-lying, outlying, somewhat 12 considerably *combining form:* 3 tel 4 tele, telo

far and away 4 just, very 5 quite 6 by
odds 9 by all odds, decidedly, doubtless
10 absolutely, by long odds, definitely, positively 11 by a long shot, undoubtedly

far and near 7 all over, overall 8 all round
9 all around 10 everyplace, everywhere,
throughout

far and wide see far and near

faraway 4 lost 6 absent, dreamy, remote
7 bemused, distant, removed 8 distrait,
heedless, off-lying, outlying 9 oblivious,
unheeding, unmindful 10 abstracted, star-
gazing 11 inconscient, preoccupied
12 absentminded, disregardful

farce 4 mock, sham 7 mockery 8 travesty
9 burlesque 10 caricature

farceur 3 wag 4 zany 5 clown, cutup,
joker 8 jokester

farcical 5 comic, droll, funny 6 absurd
7 risible 8 gelastic 9 laughable, ludicrous
10 outrageous, ridiculous 11 extravagant
12 preposterous

fare 2 do, go 3 hie, way 4 diet, food, pass,
path, rate, wend 5 get by, get on, shift,
track 6 manage, push on, repair, travel
7 advance, journey, proceed 8 get along,
progress 12 stagger along

farewell 2 by 3 ave, bye 5 adieu, adios,
aloha, congé 6 bye-bye, so long 7 good-
bye, parting 9 bon voyage, departing
11 leave-taking, valedictory

farfetched 5 queer 6 forced 7 bizarre,
erratic, labored, strange 8 strained
9 eccentric, fantastic, grotesque, recherché

far-flung 6 remote 7 distant, removed
8 off-lying, outlying

farinaceous 5 mealy 7 starchy *food:*
4 meal 5 flour, salep 6 cereal 7 pudding,
tapioca

farm 4 till 5 croft, ranch 6 grange, rancho
7 hennery 8 estancia, hacienda, hatchery,
steading 9 cultivate, farmstead *building:*
4 barn, shed, silo *Dutch:* 6 bowery *Israeli*

collective: 7 kibbutz *Russian:* 7 kolkhoz, sovkhoz

farmer 6 grower, tiller, yeoman 7 granger, planter, rancher 8 ranchero, ranchman 13 agriculturist *Israeli:* 6 halutz *Russian:* 5 kulak *South African:* 4 Boer *tenant:* 6 cotter 7 cottier, crofter 12 sharecropper

farming 7 tillage 8 agronomy 9 geoponics, husbandry 11 agriculture, cultivation, hydroponics

faro 5 monte *bet:* 7 sleeper *card:* 4 case, hock, soda

Faroes whirlwind 2 oe

far-off 6 remote 7 distant, removed 8 outlying

farrier 5 smith 10 blacksmith

farsighted 9 hyperopic, sagacious 10 presbyopic

farther 3 now 4 else, more 5 added, fresh 6 beyond, longer, yonder 10 additional

farthest 6 utmost 7 endmost, extreme, outmost 9 outermost, uttermost

fascinate 4 draw, grip, hold, sway, take, wile 5 charm, touch 6 absorb, affect, allure, appeal, engage, excite, occupy, please, strike 7 attract, bewitch, catch up, delight, enchant, engross, gladden, impress, rejoice 8 enthrall, entrance, interest, intrigue 9 captivate, enrapture, influence, magnetize, mesmerize, preoccupy, spellbind

fascination 5 charm 6 allure, appeal, glamor 7 glamour 8 charisma, witchery 9 magnetism 10 witchcraft 11 enchantment

Fascist 4 Nazi 6 Hitler (Adolph) 9 Mussolini (Benito)

fashion 3 cry, fad, ton, way 4 chic, form, make, mode, mold, plan, plot, rage, tone, vein, wise, wont 5 build, craft, craze, drift, erect, forge, frame, habit, modus, sculp, shape, style, thing, trend, usage, vogue 6 create, custom, design, devise, furore, manner, method, sculpt, system 7 produce, turn out 8 contrive, practice, tendency 9 bandwagon, construct, fabricate, technique 10 convention, dernier cri

fashionable 4 chic, tony 5 smart, swank, swish 6 modish, with-it 7 a la mode, current, dashing, popular, stylish 9 exclusive, prevalent 13 up-to-the-minute

fashion designer *American:* 4 Head (Edith) 5 Beene (Geoffrey), Blass (Bill), Dache (Lilly), Ellis (Perry), Karan (Donna), Klein (Anne, Calvin) 6 Lauren (Ralph), Mackie (Bob) 7 Galanos (James), Halston, Mizrahi (Isaac) 8 Hilfiger (Tommy) 9 Claiborne (Liz), de la Renta (Oscar), Gernreich (Rudi) *Anglo-French:* 5 Worth (Charles) *French:* 4 Dior (Christian) 6 Chanel (Coco) 6 Ungaro (Emanuel) 7 Montana (Claude) 8 Givenchy (Hubert) 9 Lagerfeld

(Karl) 12 Saint-Laurent (Yves) *Italian:* 5 Pucci (Emilio) 6 Armani (Giorgio) 7 Cassini (Oleg), Versace (Gianni)

fast 3 gay, lax, set 4 diet, easy, firm, hard, held, keen, lewd, soon, sure, true, wild 5 alert, apace, bawdy, brisk, fixed, fleet, hasty, liege, light, loose, loyal, quick, rapid, slack, stuck, swift, tight, wingy 6 active, ardent, firmly, lively, presto, pronto, raking, rakish, secure, snappy, speedy, sporty, stable, starve, strong, wanton, wedged 7 fixedly, flat-out, fleetly, hastily, lustful, quickly, raffish, rapidly, riotous, satyric, solidly, staunch, swiftly, tightly, whorish 8 careless, chop-chop, constant, faithful, full tilt, heedless, indecent, promptly, rakehell, resolute, speedily, unchaste 9 breakneck, immovable, lecherous, libertine, lickerish, posthaste, salacious, tenacious 10 expeditive, harefooted, lascivious, libidinous, licentious, stationary 11 expeditious, incontinent 12 devil-may-care, inextricable, lickety-split 13 expeditiously

fasten 3 bar, bed, fix, gib, peg, pin, put, set, tie 4 bind, hank, hasp, hook, join, lash, link, lock, moor, seal, turn, weld 5 affix, apply, catch, clamp, clasp, cling, embed, focus, hitch, infix, latch, lodge, reeve, rivet, screw, stake, stick, strap, train, unite, wedge 6 adhere, anchor, attach, bundle, button, cleave, cohere, devote, direct, fixate, secure, settle, staple, zipper 7 address, connect, implant, mortise 9 concenter, establish 11 concentrate

fastener 3 pin 4 frog, snap, tack 5 catch, rivet 6 button, needle, staple, toggle 10 clothespin

fastidious 4 nice 5 fussy 6 choosy, dainty 7 choosey, finical, finicky 8 critical, exacting 9 demanding, finicking, squeamish 10 particular, pernickety 11 persnickety 13 hypercritical

fastness 4 fort 5 guard 6 adytum, castle 7 citadel, defense, redoubt, retreat, sanctum, shelter 10 protection, stronghold

fast-talking 4 glib

fat 3 big, oil, top 4 best, bull, deep, flab, lard, pick, rich, suet, wide 5 beefy, broad, bulky, burly, cream, dumpy, elite, great, gross, heavy, husky, large, lipid, obese, pride, prime, pudgy, pursy, round, squat, stout, thick, tubby 6 brawny, choice, chunky, excess, fleshy, flower, grease, portly, rotund, stocky, stubby, tallow 7 adipose, blubber, fertile, orotund, paunchy, pinguid, porcine, ringing, surfeit, surplus, vibrant, wealthy, weighty 8 blubbery, heavyset, overflow, overkill, overmuch, overplus, oversize, plethora, resonant, sonorant, sonorous, thickset 9 consonant, corpulent, overblown 10 full-bodied, overweight, potbellied, productive, prosperous, resounding 11 superfluity, upholstered 13 overabundance *combining form:* 3 lip 4 adip, lipo, sebi, sebo 5 adipo, lipar, steat 6 liparo, steato

fatal 5 death 6 deadly, doomed, lethal, malign, mortal 7 baleful, baneful, deathly, malefic, ruinous, unlucky 8 casualty, sinister 9 pestilent 10 calamitous, disastrous, ill-starred, maleficent, pernicious 11 cataclysmic, mortiferous 12 catastrophic, pestilential

fatality 5 death 9 virulence 10 deadliness, malignancy 11 noxiousness

fata morgana 6 mirage

fate 3 end, lot 4 doom 5 issue, karma, moira, weird 6 chance, doom to, effect, ending, kismet, result, upshot 7 destine, destiny, fortune, outcome, portion, preform 9 determine, preordain 10 foreordain, predestine 12 circumstance, predetermine 13 inevitability

fateful 5 acute 7 crucial, ominous, ruinous 8 critical, decisive 9 ill-boding, important, momentous 10 calamitous, conclusive, disastrous 11 apocalyptic, cataclysmic, significant, threatening 12 catastrophic, inauspicious, unpropitious 13 determinative

Fates see at **Greek; Norse; Roman**

fathead 3 oaf 4 boob, dolt, goof 5 booby, chump, dunce

fatheaded 5 dense, thick 6 stupid 10 numskulled

father 2 pa 3 dad, get, pop 4 dada, make, papa, père, sire 5 beget, breed, daddy, hatch, maker, motor, mover, padre, pappy, pater, poppa, spawn 6 author, create, parent, priest 7 builder, creator, founder, produce 8 engender, generate, inventor, producer, promoter 9 architect, generator, initiator, organizer, originate, patriarch, procreate, supporter 10 encourager, ingenerate, introducer, originator, prime mover 11 inaugurator, progenerate, promulgator *combining form:* 4 patr 5 patri, patro *of his country:* 6 Cicero 10 Washington (George) *of history:* 9 Herodotus *of medicine:* 11 Hippocrates *of modern surgery:* 4 Paré (Ambroise) *of the symphony:* 5 Haydn (Joseph) *of waters:* 11 Mississippi

Father Brown creator 10 Chesterton (Gilbert Keith)

fatherland 4 home, soil 7 country

fatherless 7 bastard, natural 8 baseborn, spurious 11 misbegotten 12 illegitimate

Father Time's implement 6 scythe

fathom 4 have, know 5 grasp, plumb, probe, savvy, sound 6 pierce 7 cognize 8 perceive 9 apprehend, penetrate, plumb-

line, recognize 10 appreciate, comprehend, understand

fathomless 7 abysmal

fatidic 8 Delphian, oracular 9 prophetic, sibylline, vaticinal 11 prophetical

fatigue 3 irk, vex 4 jade, tire, wear 5 annoy, drain, ennui, spend, weary 6 bother, tucker, weaken 7 deplete, disable, exhaust, languor, wear out 8 weakness, wear down 9 faintness, lassitude, tiredness, weariness 10 debilitate, enervation, exhaustion, feebleness 12 debilitation, listlessness

Fatima *father:* 8 Mohammed, Muhammad *husband:* 9 Bluebeard *step-brother:* 3 Ali

fatness 7 obesity 9 adiposity 10 corpulence

fatten 5 plump 6 batten, enrich 7 plumpen, stouten, thicken

fatty 4 oily 5 blimp, lardy, pudge, suety 6 greasy 7 adipose 8 blubbery, dumpling, potbelly, roly-poly, strapper, unctuous 10 butterball, oleaginous, overweight *combining form:* 3 lip 4 adip, lipo 5 adipo, lipar 6 liparo

fatuous 4 dumb, fond 5 inane, silly 6 absurd, simple, stupid 7 asinine, foolish, idiotic, moronic, unwitty, witless 8 besotted, imbecile 9 brainless, insensate 10 infatuated, weak-headed, weak-minded 11 sheepheaded

faucet 3 tap 4 bung, cock, gate 5 spile, valve 6 spigot 7 bibcock, hydrant, petcock 8 stopcock

Faulkner *character:* 5 Caddy, Jason 7 Candace, Quentin 8 Benjamin *family:* 7 Compson *novel:* 8 Sartoris 9 Sanctuary, The Hamlet 11 As I Lay Dying 13 Light in August

fault 3 nag, sin 4 carp, flaw, flub, lack, onus, slip, vice 5 blame, crime, error 6 defect, foible 7 blemish, blunder, demerit, failing, frailty, mistake, offense 8 weakness 9 infirmity, liability 10 deficiency 11 culpability, shortcoming 12 imperfection 13 answerability, transgression

faultfinder 4 crab 5 grump, momus 6 critic, grouch, Zoilus

faultfinding 6 critic 8 captious, critical 9 cavillous 10 censorious, particular, pernickety 12 overcritical 13 hypercritical

faultless 4 pure 5 clean, whole 6 entire, intact 7 correct, perfect 8 flawless, innocent, unguilty 9 blameless, exquisite 10 immaculate, impeccable, inculpable 13 unimpeachable

faulty 4 sick 5 amiss, wrong 6 flawed, marred 7 damaged, defaced, inexact 8 fallible, specious 9 blemished, defective, deficient, erroneous, imperfect, imprecise, incorrect, uncorrect 10 disfigured, fallacious, inaccurate, inadequate, incomplete *prefix:* 3 dys

Faunus *grandfather:* 6 Saturn *son:* 4 Acis 7 Latinus

Faust *author:* 6 Goethe (Johann von) 7 Marlowe (Christopher) *beloved:* 8 Gretchen *composer:* 6 Gounod (Charles)

faux pas 4 slip 5 boner, break, error, gaffe 6 boo-boo, bungle, howler 7 blooper, blunder, misstep, mistake, stumble 8 pratfall, screamer, solecism 9 indecorum, oversight 11 impropriety, misjudgment 12 indiscretion

favor 2 OK 3 aid, for, pro 4 back, boon, gift, help, okay 5 prize, value 6 accept, esteem, oblige, pamper, regard 7 account, approve, backing, endorse, forward, indulge, largess, present, respect, service, support 8 advocate, approval, blessing, courtesy, goodwill, hold with, kindness, resemble, sanction, simulate 9 approbate, encourage, patronage 10 admiration, appreciate, assistance, estimation, indulgence 11 accommodate, approbation, benediction, benevolence, convenience, cooperation, countenance 12 dispensation 13 consideration, encouragement

favorable 4 good, kind, nice 5 brave, happy, lucky, white 6 benign, bright, dexter, kindly, timely, toward, useful 7 benefic, helpful, timeous, welcome 8 cheering, grateful, pleasant, pleasing, salutary 9 approving, benignant, fortunate, healthful, laudatory, opportune, praiseful, promising, well-timed, wholesome 10 auspicious, beneficial, gratifying, propitious, prosperous, reassuring 11 approbative, approbatory, encouraging, pleasureful 12 advantageous, commendatory, providential, well-disposed 13 complimentary

favoring 4 good 5 brave 6 toward, useful 7 benefic, helpful 10 beneficial, propitious 12 advantageous *prefix:* 3 pro

favorite 3 pet 4 dear 5 loved 6 adored, prized 7 admired, beloved, darling, popular, revered 8 blue-eyed, esteemed, laudable, pleasant, precious 9 cherished, preferred, treasured, well-liked 10 fair-haired

favoritism 4 bias 8 cronyism, nepotism 9 prejudice

fawn 3 bow, woo 4 cave, coax, deer 5 abase, court, cower, crawl, defer, toady, yield 6 cajole, cotton, cringe, debase, demean, grovel, invite, kowtow, slaver, submit 7 flatter, honey up, truckle, wheedle 8 blandish, bootlick 10 ingratiate 11 apple-polish

fawning 4 mean 6 abject, humble, smarmy 7 ignoble, servile, slavish 8 toadyish, toadyism 9 adulatory, compliant, flun-kyish, groveling, kowtowing, parasitic, spineless, sycophant, truckling 10 flattering, obsequious, submissive 11 bootlicking, deferential, subservient, sycophantic 12 mealy-mouthed, sycophantish

fay 3 elf 5 fairy, nisse, pixie 6 sprite 7 brownie

faze 3 vex 5 abash, annoy, daunt, worry 6 appall, bother, dismay, muddle, puzzle, rattle 7 confuse, horrify, mystify, nonplus, perplex 8 confound, irritate 9 discomfit, dumbfound, embarrass 10 disconcert

FBI director 5 Freeh (Louis) 6 Hoover (John Edgar)

fealty 5 ardor, faith, truth 7 loyalty, support 8 devotion, fidelity, trueness 10 allegiance 11 devotedness 12 faithfulness

fear 3 awe 4 funk 5 alarm, angst, dread, panic, scare, worry 6 dismay, esteem, fright, horror, phobia, terror 7 anxiety, concern, respect 8 cold feet, disquiet, timidity 9 agitation, cowardice, misgiving, reverence, trepidity 10 foreboding 11 disquietude, trepidation 12 apprehension, cowardliness, discomposure, perturbation, presentiment, timorousness *combining form:* 4 phob 5 phobe, phobo 6 phobia, phobic 7 phobous *of animals:* 9 zoophobia *of being buried alive:* 11 taphephobia *of cats:* 12 aelurophobia, allurophobia *of crowds:* 11 ochlophobia *of darkness:* 11 nyctophobia *of dirt:* 10 mysophobia *of fire:* 10 pyrophobia *of heights:* 10 acrophobia *of men:* 11 androphobia *of new things:* 9 neophobia *of open areas:* 11 agoraphobia *of pain:* 10 algophobia *of strangers:* 10 xenophobia *of thunder:* 12 brontophobia *of water:* 11 hydrophobia *of women:* 10 gynophobia

fearful 4 dire, grim 5 awful, lurid, scary, timid 6 afraid, aghast, grisly, malign, scared, uneasy 7 alarmed, anxious, ghastly, jittery, macabre, nervous, panicky, sublime, worried 8 aflutter, agitated, alarming, dreadful, gruesome, horrible, horrific, shocking, sinister, terrible, terrific, timorous 9 appalling, concerned, disturbed, frightful, perturbed, terrified 10 disquieted, formidable, frightened, horrendous, solicitous, terrifying, tremendous 11 discomposed, frightening, redoubtable 12 apprehensive

fearless 4 bold, game, sure 5 brave 6 daring 7 assured 8 intrepid, sanguine, unafraid 9 audacious, confident, dauntless 10 courageous 11 lionhearted

feasible 6 doable, likely, viable 8 possible, workable 9 practical 11 practicable

feast 3 eat 4 dine, meal 6 dinner, regale, repast, spread 7 banquet 8 potlatch *Hawaiian:* 4 luau *Scottish:* 3 foy

Feast of Lights 8 Hanukkah
Feast of Lots 5 Purim
Feast of Tabernacles 7 Sukkoth
Feast of Weeks 8 Shabuoth
feat 3 act 4 deed, gest 5 geste, stunt, trick 6 action 7 emprise, exploit, venture 9 adventure 10 enterprise 11 achievement, tour de force
feather 3 ilk 4 down, kind, sort, type 5 breed, order, pinna, plume, quill 6 fledge, fletch, pinion 7 species, variety *combining form:* 4 pinn, pter, ptil 5 penni, penno, pinni, ptero, ptile, *kind:* 4 down 5 penna, remex 6 covert 7 contour, plumule, rectrix, tectrix, tertial 8 scapular, tertiary *part:* 3 web 4 barb, vane 5 shaft 7 barbule 8 barbicel
featherbrained 5 dizzy, giddy, silly 7 flighty 8 skittish 9 frivolous 11 emptyheaded, hare-brained 13 rattlebrained
feathered 7 pennate, plumose 8 pennated
feather-like 7 pinnate, plumate 8 pinnated
feathers 7 plumage
featherweight 4 simp 5 dunce, light 6 dimwit, nitwit 7 lackwit, pinhead, unheavy, wantwit
feature 4 item, mark 5 fancy, image, point, savor, think, trait 6 aspect, detail, factor, play up, stress, virtue, vision 7 article, element, imagine, quality, realize 8 conceive, envisage, envision, property 9 affection, attribute, birthmark, character, component, emphasize, italicize, underline, visualize 10 ingredient, particular, underscore 11 constituent
febrile 5 fiery 7 fevered, pyretic 8 feverish
feces 4 dung 5 waste 7 excreta 9 excrement *combining form:* 4 copr, scat 5 copro, scato
feckless 4 wild 6 remiss 7 fustian, useless 8 careless, heedless, uncaring 9 shiftless, uncareful, unheeding, unrecking, worthless 10 incautious, unpurposed, unreliable, unthinking 11 inadvertent, meaningless, purposeless, thoughtless 12 irreflective, undependable, unreflective 13 irresponsible, lackadaisical, untrustworthy
fecund 4 rich 7 fertile 8 childing, fruitful, prolific, spawning 10 productive 11 proliferant
fecundity 9 eloquence, fertility 10 expression 11 prodigality, profuseness, prolificacy 12 expressivity, fruitfulness, productivity
Federalist writer 3 Jay (John) 7 Madison (James) 8 Hamilton (Alexander)
federation 5 union 6 league 8 alliance 9 coalition 11 association, confederacy
fedora 3 hat

fed up 4 sick 5 bored, tired, weary 9 disgusted
fee 3 pay, tax 4 cost, dues, hire, wage 5 price 6 charge, salary 7 expense, payment, stipend, tuition 8 retainer 9 emolument 10 recompense *minting:* 8 brassage 10 seignorage 11 seigniorage *wharf:* 7 quayage
feeble 4 puny, weak 5 frail 6 ailing, flimsy, infirm, senile, sickly, weakly 7 doddery, fragile, sapless, tenuous 8 decrepit 9 doddering 13 insubstantial
feebleminded 4 dull, slow 7 moronic 8 backward, imbecile, retarded 9 dim-witted 10 half-witted, slow-witted 12 simpleminded
feebleness 7 disease, malaise 8 debility 9 infirmity 10 infirmness, sickliness 11 decrepitude
feed 3 eat 4 find, food, give, grub, hand, meal 5 feast, graze 6 devour, fatten, fodder, ingest, repast, supply, viands 7 banquet, consume, deliver, dish out, edibles, furnish, nourish, nurture, provide, sustain 8 dispense, hand over, victuals 9 partake of, provender, refection 10 provisions *combining form:* 4 phag 5 phago
feed the kitty 4 ante
feel 3 air, paw 4 aura, deem, hold, know, mood 5 grope, guess, savor, sense, sound, taste, think, touch 6 assume, credit, endure, finger, fumble, handle, notice, suffer 7 believe, explore, grabble, observe, palpate, presume, suppose, surmise, suspect, undergo 8 consider, perceive 9 semblance, tactility
feeler 4 palp, test 5 probe, query 6 palpus 7 antenna, inquiry 10 intimation, prospectus 12 trial balloon
feeling 3 air 4 aura, mind, mood, vein, view 5 humor, sense, touch 6 belief, morale, notion, temper 7 emotion, opinion, outlook, passion, sensate 8 attitude, passible, reaction, sentient 9 affection, emotional, semblance, sensation, sensitive, sentiment 10 atmosphere, conviction, persuasion 11 affectivity, emotionable, palpability, sensibility, sensitivity, tangibility *combining form:* 5 pathy 6 pathic
feign 3 act 4 fake, sham 5 bluff, put on 6 affect, assume 7 connive, pretend 8 simulate 11 counterfeit
feint 3 jig 4 fake, hoax, play, ploy, ruse, sham, wile 5 trick 6 gambit 7 whizzer 8 maneuver 9 stratagem *fencing:* 5 appel 4 deke *hockey:* 4 deke
feldspar 6 albite 8 andesine, sanidine 9 anorthite, moonstone 10 microcline, orthoclase 11 labradorite, plagioclase *clay:* 6 kaolin
felicitate 6 salute 7 commend 10 compliment 12 congratulate

felicitous 3 apt, fit 4 just, meet 5 happy
6 proper, timely 7 apropos, fitting 8 apposite, suitable 9 well-timed 10 applicable,
seasonable 11 appropriate

feline 3 cat, tom 4 lion, lynx, pard, puma,
puss 5 catty, felid, pussy, tiger 6 bobcat,
cougar, jaguar, margay, ocelot, tomcat
7 catlike, cheetah, furtive, leonine, leopard,
lioness, panther, tigress, wildcat 8 pussycat, stealthy *hybrid:* 5 liger, tigon 6 tiglon

fell 3 cut, fur, hew 4 chop, down, drop,
grim, hide, kill, pelt, raze, skin, ugly 5 cruel,
floor, grave, level, major 6 deadly, fierce,
ground, jacket, lay low, savage, tumble
7 fearful, flatten, inhuman, mow down, serious, wolfish 8 bowl down, bowl over, grievous, horrible, horrific, inhumane 9 barbarous, bring down, dangerous, ferocious,
knock down, knock over, prostrate, shoot
down, throw down, truculent

Fellini film 8 Amarcord, Casanova, La
Strada 9 Satyricon 11 La Dolce Vita

fellow 2 he 3 boy, bub, guy, joe, lad, man
4 bozo, buck, chap, gent, mate, peer, twin
5 bloke, match 6 codger, cohort, double,
hombre, person 7 consort, partner 8 confrere 9 associate, companion, copartner,
duplicate, gentleman 10 consociate, coordinate, reciprocal 11 concomitant 12 contemporary *prefix:* 2 co

fellowship 4 club 5 guild, order, union
6 league 7 company, society 8 alliance,
sodality 10 fraternity 11 association, brotherhood, camaraderie 13 companionship

felon 8 criminal, offender 10 lawbreaker,
malefactor

felt hat 6 fedora

female 4 girl 5 woman 7 womanly 8 feminine, womanish *combining form:* 3 gyn
4 gyne, gyno, gyny 5 gynec, gyneo, thely
6 gynaec, gynaeo, gyneco, gynous
7 gynaeco *suffix:* 3 ess, ine 4 ette, trix

femme fatale 5 siren 7 Lorelei 9 temptress 10 seductress

fen 3 bog 4 mire, quag 5 marsh, swamp
6 morass, slough 7 baygall 8 quagmire

fence 3 bar, hem, mew, pen 4 cage, duck,
mure, stop, wall, weir 5 block, dodge,
hedge, parry, shirk 6 corral, immure, paling
7 barrier, enclose, railing 8 blockade, palisade, sidestep, stockade 9 barricade, roadblock 12 circumscribe

fencer 7 duelist, épéeist 8 foilsman
9 swordsman

fencing 9 swordplay *attack:* 5 lunge
6 thrust 7 reprise, riposte *defense:* 5 parry
movement: 4 volt *ploy:* 5 appel *position:*
5 prime, sixte, terce 6 octave, quarte,
quinte, tierce 7 seconde, septime *term:*
4 jury 5 forte, lunge, piste 6 flèche, foible,
pointe, touché 7 sabreur, stop cut, stop-hit

11 corps-à-corps *touch:* 3 cut, hit 5 punto
weapon: 4 épée, foil 5 blade, guard,
saber, sabre 6 pommel

fend 4 ward 5 avert, avoid, cover, guard,
parry, rebut, repel 6 defend, rebuff, resist,
screen, secure, shield 7 bulwark, deflect,
hold off, keep off, protect, repulse, ward off
8 stave off 9 safeguard

fender 5 guard 6 buffer, shield 8 mud-
guard

Fenrir *chain:* 8 Gleipnir *father:* 4 Loki
form: 4 wolf *mother:* 9 Angerboda
10 Angerbotha *slayer:* 5 Vidar 6 Vithar *victim:* 4 Odin

feral 4 wild 5 brute 6 animal, brutal, ferine,
fierce, savage 7 beastly, bestial, brutish,
inhuman, swinish, untamed, vicious 8 barbaric 9 barbarous, ferocious

Ferber novel 5 Giant, So Big 8 Cimarron,
Show Boat, The Girls 9 Ice Palace

Ferber or Millay 4 Edna

Ferdinand *beloved:* 7 Miranda *father:*
6 Alonso

Ferdinand, King *conquest:* 7 Granada
daughter: 6 Joanna *wife:* 8 Germaine,
Isabella

ferment 4 boil, stir 5 churn 6 bubble,
clamor, foment, leaven, outcry, seethe, simmer, tumult, unrest, upturn 7 agitate, ailment, smolder, turmoil 8 disquiet, upheaval
9 commotion 10 convulsion, inquietude
11 disquietude, restiveness 12 restlessness

fermentation 7 zymosis

fern 4 tree 5 brake, holly, royal 6 Boston
7 bracken, woodsia 8 polypody 10 maidenhair, spleenwort *combining form:* 6 pterid,
pteris 7 pterido *leaf:* 5 frond

ferocious 4 fell, grim 5 brute, cruel, feral
6 brutal, fierce, savage 7 bestial, inhuman,
vicious, violent, wolfish 8 inhumane, ravening, ravenous 9 barbarous, rapacious, truculent 10 implacable, relentless 12 bloodthirsty

ferret out 4 hunt, seek 5 learn, probe,
quest 6 elicit 7 extract 8 discover 9 ascertain, cast about, determine, search for,
search out

Ferrex's brother 6 Porrex

ferrule 3 cap, tip 4 band, knob

ferry 3 lug 4 bear, buck, pack, tote 5 carry
6 convey 9 transport

ferryman of Hades 6 Charon

fertile 4 lush, rich 6 fecund 7 bearing,
copious 8 abundant, childing, creative, fruitful, pregnant, prolific, spawning, yielding
9 bountiful, ingenious, inventive, luxuriant,
plenteous, producing 10 productive 11 proliferant

fertilize 6 enrich 9 pollenate, pollinate
10 impregnate, inseminate

fertilizer 4 dung, marl 5 guano 6 manure 7 compost

ferule 3 rod 5 ruler, stick 6 switch

fervent 3 hot 4 keen 5 eager, fiery 6 ardent, devout, hearty 7 blazing, burning, earnest, glowing, intense, sincere 8 vehement 9 heartfelt, perfervid 10 hot-blooded, passionate 11 impassioned 12 enthusiastic, wholehearted

fervor 4 fire, zeal 5 ardor 6 hurrah, warmth 7 passion 9 calenture, sincerity, vehemence 10 devoutness, enthusiasm, heartiness 11 earnestness

fess up 3 own 4 avow 5 admit, allow, grant, let on, own up 7 concede, confess 11 acknowledge

fester 3 rot 5 ulcer 6 rankle 7 influme, putrefy 8 ulcerate 9 suppurate

festina ___ 5 lente

festival 4 fair, fete, gala 5 feast, gaudy 6 fiesta 8 carnival 9 festivity 11 celebration

festive 3 gay 4 gala 5 jolly, merry 6 blithe, jocund, jovial, joyous 7 gleeful 8 mirthful 10 blithesome 12 lighthearted

festivity 5 revel 6 gaiety 7 jollity, revelry, whoopee 8 reveling 9 merriment, revelment 11 celebration, merrymaking

fetch 4 sell 5 bring 7 bring in

fetching 6 luring 7 Circean 8 alluring, enticing, tempting

fete 4 fair 5 party 6 bazaar 8 festival 9 entertain 11 celebration

fetid 4 foul, rank 6 putrid, rancid, smelly 7 rankish, reeking 8 mephitic, stinking 10 malodorous

fetish 4 idol, juju, luck, zemi 5 charm, mania, thing 6 amulet, mascot 7 periapt 8 fixation, gris-gris, penchant, talisman 9 obsession 10 phylactery

fetter 3 tie 4 clog, curb 5 leash 6 hamper, hobble, hog-tie 7 manacle, shackle, trammel 8 handcuff, restrain 9 entrammel

fettle 4 trim 5 order, shape 6 kilter, repair 7 fitness 9 condition

feud 3 row 5 run-in 6 combat, fracas 7 contest, dispute, quarrel 8 argument, squabble, vendetta 9 bickering 10 falling-out 11 altercation, controversy

feudal *estate:* 4 feod, feud, fief *jurisdiction:* 3 soc 4 soke *laborer:* 4 serf *lord:* 5 liege 8 suzerain *service:* 5 avera *status:* 9 vassalage *tax:* 7 tallage *tenant:* 6 vassal 7 homager, socager, sokeman, vavasor 8 vavasour *tenure of land:* 6 socage *tribute:* 6 heriot

fever 4 ague, fire 6 dengue 7 ferment, pyrexia 9 calenture *combining form:* 5 febri, pyret 6 pyreto *recurrent:* 6 sextan 7 malaria, quartan, quintan, tertian

feverish 3 hot 5 fiery 6 fervid, heated, hectic 7 burning, excited, febrile, flushed,

furious, pyretic 8 febrific, frenzied, inflamed 10 passionate 11 overwrought

fever tree 7 blue gum

few 4 rare 6 scarce, seldom, smatch 7 handful, smatter, spatter 8 sporadic, uncommon 10 infrequent, occasional, scattering, smattering, spattering, sprinkling, unfrequent *combining form:* 4 olig 5 oligo, pauci

___**-fi** 2 hi 3 sci

fiat 5 edict, order 6 decree 7 command 8 sanction 11 endorsement 12 proclamation

fib 3 lie 4 tale 5 story 6 canard, palter 7 falsify, falsity, untruth 9 falsehood, mendacity 10 equivocate 11 evasiveness, prevaricate 13 prevarication

fiber 3 web 4 noil, pita 5 grain, istle 6 fabric, strand, thread 7 texture *basketry:* 5 istle *brain:* 4 pons *coarse:* 4 adad, jute 8 piassava *coconut husk:* 4 coir, kyar *combining form:* 2 in 3 ino 4 fibr 5 fibro *knot:* 3 nep *rope:* 5 sisal 8 henequen *silky:* 5 kapok *small:* 6 fibril *substructure:* 7 micelle, spongin *synthetic:* 5 nylon, rayon, saran, vinal *woody:* 4 bast *woollike:* 7 lanital

fibrous 4 ropy, wiry 6 sinewy 7 stringy 8 muscular

fibula 5 clasp 7 leg bone

fickle 7 flighty, moonish 8 ticklish, unstable, variable, volatile 9 mercurial 10 capricious, changeable, inconstant, lubricious, unfaithful, unreliable 12 undependable 13 temperamental

fiction 4 tale, yarn 5 fable, story 6 deceit 7 fantasy, figment 9 fish story, invention, narrative 10 concoction 11 fabrication

fictional 5 false, phony 6 unreal 7 fictive 8 fanciful, illusory 9 fantastic, imaginary 10 chimerical, fictitious 12 supposititious

fictitious 4 fake, mock, sham 5 false 6 ersatz, made-up, unreal, untrue 7 assumed, created, fictive 8 cooked-up, fanciful, illusory, invented 9 concocted, fantastic, fashioned, fictional, imaginary, simulated, trumped-up 10 artificial, chimerical, fabricated 12 supposititious *combining form:* 5 pseud 6 pseudo

fiddle 4 fool, mess, play 6 dabble, doodle, fidget, handle, monkey, potter, puddle, putter, tinker, trifle, violin 10 mess around

fiddle-faddle 4 bosh 5 fudge, hooey 6 bunkum, piffle 8 nonsense, pishposh 10 flapdoodle

Fidelio *composer:* 9 Beethoven (Ludwig van) *hero:* 9 Florestan *heroine:* 7 Leonora

___ **fidelis** 6 semper

fidelity 5 ardor, piety 6 fealty 7 loyalty 8 adhesion, devotion 9 adherence, constancy 10 allegiance, attachment 11 reli-

figure 283

ability, staunchness 12 faithfulness
13 dependability, steadfastness

fidget 4 play 6 fiddle, jitter, trifle 7 twiddle

fidgety 5 fussy, jumpy, nervy 6 goosey,
spooky 7 jittery, nervous, restive, twitchy
8 restless, twittery 9 unrestful 10 high-
strung

field 4 area, walk 5 milpa 6 domain, meadow, region, sphere 7 demesne, terrain
8 dominion, precinct, province 9 bailiwick,
champaign, territory 10 department *combining form:* 4 agro

fieldbird 6 plover

field crop 3 hay 5 grain 6 cotton

field deity 3 Pan 4 Faun 5 Fauna

field glasses 10 binoculars

field hand 4 hoer 5 sower 6 picker
7 laborer, planter

Fielding novel 6 Amelia 8 Tom Jones
13 Joseph Andrews

field marshal *Austrian:* 8 Radetzky
(Joseph) *British:* 6 Napier (Robert), Raglan (Baron), Wavell (Archibald), Wilson
(Henry) 7 Roberts (Frederick) 8 Wolseley
(Garnet) 9 Kitchener (Horatio) 10 Montgomery (Bernard) *French:* 4 Foch (Ferdinand) 6 Joffre (Joseph-Jacques-Cesaire),
Pétain (Philippe) *German:* 6 Keitel (Wilhelm), Paulus (Friedrich), Rommel (Erwin),
Rupert (Prince) 9 Mackensen (August von),
Rundstedt (Karl von), Waldersee (Alfred
von) 10 Kesselring (Albert) *Japanese:*
8 Sugiyama (Gen) *Prussian:* 6 Moltke
(Helmuth von) *Russian:* 7 Kutuzov (Mikhail), Suvorov (Aleksandr) 8 Potemkin (Grigory)

field mouse 4 vole

Field of Blood 8 Aceldama

field officer 5 major 7 colonel

field rat 5 metad

fiend 3 bug, nut 5 bigot, demon, devil,
freak, Satan 6 diablo, maniac, zealot
7 fanatic, Lucifer, Old Nick, serpent 8 Apollyon, succubus 9 Beelzebub 10 enthusiast,
Old Scratch 13 Old Gooseberry

fiendish 5 cruel 6 malign, savage, wicked
7 baleful, demonic, hellish, inhuman,
malefic, satanic, vicious 8 demoniac,
demonian, devilish, diabolic, infernal, sinister 9 barbarous, ferocious, malicious,
malignant

fierce 4 fell, grim, wild 5 cruel 6 brutal,
savage 7 brutish, enraged, furious, inhuman, intense, vicious, violent, wolfish
8 inhumane, maddened, pitiless, ruthless,
terrible, tigerish, vehement 9 barbarous,
bellicose, desperate, ferocious, merciless,
truculent 10 aggressive, cannibalic, infuriated, pugnacious 11 belligerent

fiery 3 hot 5 afire 6 ablaze, aflame,
ardent, fervid, fierce, heated, red-hot,
spunky, torrid 7 blaring, blazing, burning,
febrile, fervent, fevered, flaming, flaring,
gingery, igneous, ignited, intense, peppery
8 broiling, feverish, inflamed, scalding, sizzling, spirited, vehement, white-hot 9 hotheaded, perfervid, scorching 10 mettlesome, passionate 11 conflagrant,
impassioned 12 high-spirited

fifteen *combining form:* 8 pentadec
9 pentadeca

fifth *combining form:* 5 quint 6 quinti

fig *genus:* 5 Ficus *sacred:* 5 pipal *variety:*
5 eleme, elemi 6 Smyrna

fight 3 row, tug, war 4 beef, bout, buck,
duel, feud, fray, spat, tiff 5 brawl, broil,
clash, joust, melee, repel, scrap, words
6 affray, attack, battle, bicker, combat,
debate, fracas, hassle, oppose, oppugn,
resist, strive, tussle 7 contend, contest, crusade, dispute, quarrel, scuffle, wrangle,
wrestle 8 skirmish, slugfest, squabble,
struggle, traverse 9 bickering, pugnacity,
withstand 10 aggression, donnybrook
11 altercation 12 belligerence, disagreement 13 combativeness *combining form:*
5 machy

fighter 2 GI 4 swad 5 boxer 7 soldier,
warrior 8 pugilist, scrapper 9 man-at-arms

fighter plane 3 MiG, Roc 4 Zero 5 Sabre
6 Fokker, Hawker, Mirage, Voodoo 7 Corsair, Harrier, Stealth 8 Spitfire

fighting fish 5 betta

figment 5 dream, fable, fancy 6 bubble
7 chimera, fiction 8 daydream, illusion
9 invention 11 fabrication

figurant 6 dancer, hoofer 7 danseur
8 coryphée

figuration 4 line 5 shape 7 contour, outline, profile 8 allegory 9 lineament, lineation, symbolism 10 silhouette 11 delineation

figure 3 add, sum, tot 4 cast, foot, form,
rule, tote 5 build, count, digit, frame, motif,
shape, total 6 cipher, decide, design,
device, motive, number, reckon, settle, symbol 7 chiffer, compute, integer, numeral,
outline, pattern, resolve, summate 8 conclude, estimate, physique, totalize 9 calculate, character, determine, enumerate
11 whole number 12 conformation 13 configuration *geometric:* 4 cone, cube
5 rhomb 6 circle, isogon, square 7 decagon, ellipse, hexagon, nonagon, octagon,
polygon, rhombus 8 pentacle, pentagon,
rhomboid, tetragon, triangle 9 rectangle
10 hexahedron, octahedron
11 icosahedron 12 dodecahedron, rhombo-
hedron 13 quadrilateral *human:* 4 nude
5 atlas 7 telamon 8 caryatid *ornamental:*
6 statue 8 gargoyle

figure of speech 5 trope 6 aporia, simile
7 imagery, litotes 8 metaphor, metonymy
10 synecdoche

figure out 4 dope 5 crack, solve
6 decode, unfold 7 clear up, resolve,
unravel 8 decipher, unriddle, untangle
9 puzzle out 10 unscramble 11 disentangle

figure skating *jump:* 4 axel, loop, lutz
5 split 6 rocker 7 bracket, counter, salchow
11 spreadeagle *spin:* 3 sit 5 camel

Fiji *capital:* 4 Suva *monetary unit:* 6 dollar

filch 3 nim, nip, rob 4 lift 5 pinch, steal,
swipe 6 pilfer, snitch 7 purloin

file 3 row 4 line, rank, rasp, tier 5 queue
6 string 7 dossier, echelon

fill 3 gob, jam, jug 4 brim, clog, cloy, cram,
glut, heap, jade, load, meet, pack, pall, pile,
plug, sate, stop 5 block, choke, close,
gorge 6 answer, bumper, charge, stodge
7 congest, engorge, occlude, satiate, satisfy, stopper, surfeit *interstices:* 3 pug
4 calk 5 chink, putty

filled 4 full 5 sated 7 replete 9 saturated

fillet 4 band, orle, tape 5 snood, strip 6 ribbon, stripe 7 bandeau, banding 8 headband *anatomical:* 9 lemniscus *architectural:* 6 cimbia, listel, reglet, taenia
combining form: 4 taen 5 taeni 6 taenio
meat: 10 tenderloin

fill-in 3 sub 7 stand-in 9 alternate, surrogate 10 substitute 11 locum tenens, pinch
hitter, replacement, succedaneum

fill in 4 clew, clue, post, tell, warn
6 advise, inform, insert, notify, wise up
7 apprise, throw in 8 acquaint 9 insinuate,
interject, interpose, introduce 11 intercalate, interpolate

film 4 cine, haze, mist, show, skin, veil
5 brume, flick, layer, movie, smaze 6 patina 7 picture 8 pellicle 9 celluloid, photoplay 10 cinematize 11 picture show
13 motion picture, moving picture

filmy 4 fine, hazy 5 gauzy, misty, sheer,
wispy 6 cloudy, dainty, flimsy 7 tiffany
8 delicate, gossamer 10 diaphanous
11 transparent

filter 4 sift 5 leach, sieve 6 purify, refine,
screen, strain 8 filtrate 9 percolate

filth 4 dirt, dung, gore 6 ordure 7 squalor
9 obscenity *combining form:* 4 copr
5 copro

filthy 4 foul, vile 5 black, dirty, dungy,
gross, mucky, nasty, soily 6 coarse,
grubby, impure, ribald, sloppy, smutty, sordid, vulgar 7 obscene, raunchy, squalid,
unclean 8 indecent 9 loathsome, offensive,
repulsive, revolting, uncleanly, verminous
12 scatological

filthy lucre 4 cash, loot, pelf 5 dough,
money 8 currency 11 legal tender

fin 4 anal 5 pinna 6 caudal, dorsal, pelvic
7 acantha, flipper, ventral 8 pectoral

finagle 5 cheat, trick 6 wangle 7 deceive,
snaffle, swindle 8 engineer, maneuver
9 machinate

final 3 lag 4 last 6 ending, latest, latter
7 closing 8 crowning, decisive, eventual,
hindmost, terminal, ultimate 9 finishing
10 concluding, conclusive, definitive
11 terminating

finale 3 end 5 close, finis 6 climax, ending, finish, payoff, windup 7 closing
9 cessation 10 conclusion, denouement
11 culmination, termination

finalize 3 end 5 close 6 finish, wind up
8 conclude, solidify 9 terminate 10 consummate

finance 4 back, bank, fund 5 endow,
stake 7 promote, revenue, sponsor, support 8 bankroll 9 grubstake, patronize, subsidize 10 capitalize, underwrite

financial 6 fiscal, pocket 8 business, economic, monetary 9 pecuniary 10 commercial *plan:* 6 budget *statement:* 12 balance
sheet

financier *American:* 4 Hill (James
Jerome), Ryan (Thomas Fortune), Sage
(Russell) 5 Baker (George Fisher), Eaton
(Cyrus), Field (Cyrus West), Gould (Jay),
Grace (William Russell), Green (Hetty)
6 Boesky (Ivan), Girard (Stephen), Mellon
(Andrew), Morgan (John Pierpont, Junius
Spencer), Morris (Robert), Rogers (Henry
Huttleston), Yerkes (Charles Tyson) 7 Pea-
body (George) 10 Vanderbilt (Cornelius,
William) *British:* 6 Rhodes (Cecil)
7 Gresham (Thomas) *French:* 6 Necker
(Jacques) *German:* 7 Schacht (Hjalmar)
10 Rothschild (Amschel, Jakob, Karl,
Mayer, Nathan, Salomon)

finch 4 pape 5 junco, serin, zebra 6 linnet,
siskin, towhee 7 bunting, chewink, redpoll
8 grosbeak, longspur

find 4 espy, give, hand, note, spot 5 catch,
dig up, hit on, sight, solve 6 descry, detect,
espial, locate, strike, supply, turn up 7 discern, dish out, furnish, hit upon, provide,
scare up 8 discover, dispense, hand over,
meet with, transfer, treasure, turn over
9 detection, discovery, encounter
10 unearthing 13 treasure trove

find out 3 see 4 hear 5 learn 6 tumble
7 catch on, unearth 8 discover 9 ascertain,
determine

fine 3 tax, top 4 fair, levy, nice 5 bonny,
clear, dandy, mulct, sheer, sunny
6 amerce, choice, minute, sconce, subtle
7 capital, clarion, damages, elegant, forfeit,
penalty, powdery, refined 8 delicate, five-
star, hairline, penalize, pleasant, rainless,
splendid, sunshiny, superior, top-notch

9 beautiful, cloudless, enjoyable, excellent, first-rate, unclouded **10** amercement, assessment, first-class, impalpable, pulverized, reparation, undarkened **11** first-string **13** hairsplitting

finery 5 frill **6** gewgaw, tawdry **7** apparel, bravery, clothes, gaudery, regalia **8** foofaraw, frippery, ornament, trimming, war paint **9** full dress **10** Sunday best

finesse 3 art **4** play **5** skill **6** jockey, outwit **7** beguile, cunning, exploit **8** maneuver, subtlety **9** dexterity **10** manipulate

Fingal's Cave island 6 Staffa

finger 3 paw, tap, toy **4** feel, make, name, spot **5** digit, index, pinky, place, strum, touch **6** handle, medius, pilfer, pinkie **7** appoint, palpate **8** diagnose, identify, nominate, pinpoint **9** designate, determine, recognize **11** distinguish **13** diagnosticate *bone:* **7** phalanx **9** phalanges (plural) *combining form:* **6** dactyl, digiti **7** dactylo, dactyly **8** dactylia **9** dactylism, dactylous *cymbal:* **8** castanet

fingernail *combining form:* **4** onyx **7** onychia **8** onychium *crescent:* **6** lunule

fingerprint 4 arch, loop **5** whorl

finicky 4 nice **5** fussy **6** choosy, dainty, prissy **7** choosey **9** squeamish **10** fastidious, particular, pernickety **11** persnickety

finish 3 die, end **4** cool, do in, down, halt, kill, slay, stop **5** cease, close, glaze, scrag, spend, use up **6** cut off, ending, expend, finale, murder, polish, wash up, windup, wrap up **7** closing, consume, destroy, execute, exhaust, put away, surface, take off **8** carry off, complete, conclude, dispatch, finalize, knock off, terminus, ultimate **9** cessation, determine, liquidate, terminate **10** attainment, conclusion, desistance, run through **11** achievement, acquirement, acquisition, assassinate, termination *dull:* **3** mat **4** matt **5** matte *second:* **5** place *third:* **4** show

finished 4 done, down, over, ripe **5** ended, suave **6** closed, smooth, urbane **7** done for, refined, through **8** complete, washed-up **9** completed, concluded, perfected, virtuosic **10** consummate, terminated **12** accomplished

finish off 3 cap **5** crown **6** climax, top off **8** round off **9** culminate.

finite 5 bound **7** bounded, defined, limited **9** definable **10** restricted

Finland *capital:* **8** Helsinki *monetary unit:* **6** markka

Finlandia composer 8 Sibelius (Jean)

Finnish *bath:* **5** sauna *combining form:* **5** Fenno *epic:* **8** Kalevala *god:* **6** Jumala

fin's double 7 tenspot

fir 7 conifer **9** evergreen *genus:* **5** Abies

fire 2 ax **3** can, pep, vim, zip **4** bake, burn, cast, dash, drop, hurl, kiln, sack, stir, toss, zeal, zest, zing **5** ardor, blaze, drive, exalt, flame, flare, fling, glare, gusto, heave, ingle, light, loose, pitch, rouse, salvo, shoot, sling, spark, throw, torch, verve, vigor **6** arouse, bounce, energy, excite, fervor, hurrah, ignite, inform, kindle, launch, spirit, thrill **7** animate, boot out, burnout, dismiss, enliven, enthuse, inferno, inflame, inspire, kick out, passion, provoke **8** enkindle, heighten **9** calenture, discharge, holocaust, intensify, terminate **10** enthusiasm, heartiness, liveliness **13** conflagration *combining form:* **3** pyr **4** igni, pyro *god:* **4** Agni, Loki **6** Vulcan **10** Hephaestus

firearm see gun

firebrand 7 hothead, hotspur **8** agitator

firebug 5 torch **8** arsonist **10** incendiary, pyromaniac

firecracker 5 squib **9** explosive **10** cherry bomb, noisemaker

firedog 7 andiron

firedrake 6 dragon

firefly 7 glowfly **12** lightning bug

fire opal 7 girasol

fireplace 5 ingle *equipment:* **6** fender, screen **7** andiron, fireset *part:* **3** hob **6** hearth, mantel

fireplug 7 hydrant

fire up 5 rouse **6** excite, ignite, incite, kindle **7** enflame, enliven, inflame, inspire, provoke **8** enkindle **9** intensify

firework 4 gerb **5** gerbe **6** fizgig, petard, rocket **8** sparkler **10** tourbillon **11** pyrotechnic, tourbillion *cluster:* **9** girandole

firm 3 set **4** fast, hard, sure **5** exact, fixed, house, rigid, solid, sound, stiff, tight, tough **6** outfit, secure, stable, stated, steady, stolid, strong, sturdy **7** abiding, adamant, certain, company, concern, confirm, fixedly, settled, solidly, staunch, tightly, unmoved **8** business, constant, definite, enduring, faithful, resolute, specific **9** inelastic, steadfast, tenacious **10** determined, enterprise, inflexible, stipulated, unwavering, unyielding **11** established, steadfastly, substantial, unfaltering, unqualified **12** never-failing **13** establishment

firmament 3 sky **6** welkin **7** heavens **8** empyrean

firmness 7 resolve **8** decision, security, solidity, strength, tenacity **9** constancy, soundness, stability **10** resolution, stableness, steadiness **11** decidedness **12** resoluteness **13** determination, purposiveness

first 4 arch, head **5** alpha, chief, least, prime **6** maiden, primal **7** eminent, highest, initial, leading, pioneer, premier, primary, supreme **8** champion, dominant, earliest, foremost, headmost, original, smallest

9 inaugural, initially, paramount, principal, slightest, sovereign 10 aboriginal, preeminent, primordial *combining form:* 4 prot 5 proto

firstborn 4 heir 5 eigne 6 eldest

first-class 3 top 4 A-one, fine 5 prime 6 tip-top 7 capital 8 five-star, superior, topnotch 9 excellent, top-drawer

first fruits 7 annates

firsthand 6 direct 7 primary 9 immediate

first man in space 7 Gagarin (Yury)

first-rate see **first-class**

first showing 8 premiere

First State 8 Delaware

first-string see **first-class**

firth 3 arm, bay 4 cove, gulf 5 inlet 6 harbor, slough 7 estuary

fiscal 6 pocket 8 monetary 9 financial

fish 3 net, sap 4 butt, cast, dupe, fool, gill, hint 5 angle, chump, seine, trawl, troll 6 sucker 7 fall guy, gillnet, gudgeon, sniggle *angler:* 7 lophiid 9 goosefish *aquarium:* 4 barb 5 betta, danio, guppy, limia, platy, tetra 6 mollie 7 cichlid, gourami, rasbora 8 goldfish 9 angelfish *basket:* 5 creel *catfish:* 4 wels 5 dorad 6 madtom 7 candiru 8 bullhead, bullpout, hornpout, stonecat *cod:* 4 cusk, hake, ling 5 torsk 6 burbot, tomcod 7 pollack, pollock *combining form:* 6 ichthy 7 ichthyo, ichthys *croaker:* 4 drum 7 corbina 8 kingfish, seatrout, weakfish 10 squeteague, squiteague *eellike:* 5 moray 6 conger 7 hagfish, lamprey *eggs:* 3 roe 5 spawn *electric:* 4 raad 7 torpedo 9 stargazer *extinct:* 10 coelacanth *flatfish:* 3 dab 4 butt, dace, sole 5 bream, brill, fluke 6 plaice, turbot 7 halibut 8 flounder *food:* 3 cod, eel, ide 4 bass, carp, cero, hake, ling, scup, shad, sole, tuna 5 jurel, perch, scrod, skate, smelt, trout 6 bonito, caviar, kipper, mullet, plaice, pompon, salmon, tautog, weever, wrasse 7 alewife, catfish, cavalla, escolar, grouper, haddock, halibut, herring, morwong, pollack, pollock, pompano, pompoon, sardine, sea carp, snapper, tautaug 8 brisling, crevalle, flounder, mackerel 9 barracuda *game:* 4 bass, pike, tuna 5 perch, trout 6 grilse, marlin, salmon, tarpon 8 pickerel 9 swordfish *grunt:* 5 sargo 7 pigfish, tomtate 8 porkfish 10 bluestripe *herring:* 4 shad, sild 5 sprat 7 alewife, sardine 8 brisling, pilchard *kind:* 3 ray 4 bass, cero, chub, dory, goby, jack, opah, pike, rudd, scup, tuna 5 balao, bream, cisco, loach, perch, porgy, sargo, shark, skate, smelt, snook, tench, tunny, wahoo 6 anabas, blenny, bonito, dorado, marlin, minnow, mullet, permit, puffer, remora, sauger, splake, sucker, tarpon, tautog, warsaw, wrasse 7 anchovy, boxfish, buffalo, cabe-

zon, capelin, cavalla, chimera, cowfish, crappie, dolphin, grunion, haddock, hogfish, jewfish, mojarra, muddler, mudfish, oarfish, opaleye, piranha, pupfish, sardine, sawfish, sculpin, snapper, sunfish, tilapia, vendace, whiting 8 albacore, blowfish, bluefish, bluegill, bonefish, burrfish, chimaera, filefish, gambusia, grayling, halfbeak, ladyfish, lookdown, lumpfish, lungfish, mackerel, menhaden, moonfish, pickerel, pipefish, rockfish, sailfish, seahorse, skipjack, stingray, sturgeon, tilefish, topsmelt, warmouth, wolffish 9 amberjack, barracuda, greenling, jacksmelt, killifish, mummichog, pilotfish, spadefish, swordfish, topminnow, trunkfish, whitebait, whitefish 10 butterfish, flying fish, lizardfish, needlefish, parrotfish, silverside, tripletail, yellowtail 11 harvestfish, muskellunge, pumpkinseed, stickleback, triggerfish 12 schoolmaster *luminescent:* 9 viperfish 10 midshipman 11 hatchetfish, lanternfish *minnow:* 4 carp, chub, dace 6 shiner *pan:* 5 bream, perch, trout 7 crappie, sunfish 8 bluegill, rock bass 11 pumpkinseed *porgy:* 4 scup 7 pinfish 8 jolthead 10 sheepshead *relating to:* 7 piscine 8 ichthyic *rockfish:* 8 bocaccio, lionfish, rosefish 11 chilipepper *salmon:* 3 dog 4 chum, coho 6 sebago 7 chinook, sockeye *spear:* 3 gig 7 harpoon, trident *stew:* 8 cioppino, matelote 13 bouillabaisse *trap:* 3 dam 4 weir 6 eelpot 9 fishgarth *trout:* 5 charr 7 oquassa, rainbow 9 cutthroat 11 Dolly Varden *voracious:* 6 caribe 7 piranha *young:* 3 fry 4 parr 5 larva, smolt 6 alevin, grilse

fisherman 6 angler 8 piscator

fish hawk 6 osprey

fishhook 5 drail *adjunct:* 5 snell *part:* 4 barb 5 shank

fishing area 7 piscary

fishing line 4 trot 7 boulter, setline 8 longline, trotline *float:* 3 bob 5 quill 6 dobber *leader:* 5 snell

fishing lure 3 fly 4 herl

fishing net 5 seine, trawl

fishlike mammal 3 orc 5 whale 7 dolphin 8 porpoise

fish owl 6 ketupa

fishwife 5 harpy, scold, shrew, vixen 6 amazon, ogress, virago 9 termagant, Xanthippe

fishy 4 cold, dull 7 dubious, suspect 8 doubtful 9 ambiguous, doubtable, dubitable, equivocal, uncertain 10 suspicious

fission element 7 uranium 9 plutonium

fissure 3 gap 4 gash, hole, rent, rift, rima, rime 5 break, chasm, chink, cleft, crack, split 6 breach, schism 7 crevice, opening, rupture 8 crevasse, fracture, rimation

fist 3 job 4 grip, hand 5 grasp, index 6 clench, clutch, ductus, effort, handle, script 7 attempt 10 penmanship 11 calligraphy, chirography, handwriting

fisticuffs 4 ring 6 boxing 8 pugilism 13 prizefighting

fit 2 go 3 apt, set 4 good, hale, jibe, just, meet, sane, suit, turn, well 5 adapt, agree, frame, happy, joint, ready, right, sound, spasm, spell, tally, throe 6 access, accord, adjust, attack, become, belong, decent, go with, make up, proper, seemly, square, tailor, useful 7 capable, conform, healthy, prepare, qualify, seizure, tantrum 8 apoplexy, assemble, decorous, dovetail, eligible, paroxysm, quadrate, rightful, suitable 9 agree with, befitting, congruous, consonant, harmonize, reconcile, wholesome 10 applicable, convenient, correspond, felicitous, go together, tailor-make, well-liking 11 accommodate, appropriate *suffix:* 4 able, ible

fitful 6 catchy, random, spotty 8 periodic, sporadic, unstable, variable 9 desultory, haphazard, hit-or-miss, irregular, recurrent, spasmodic 10 capricious, changeable, inconstant 11 interrupted

fitness 3 use 4 trim 5 order, shape 6 fettle, kilter, repair 7 account, aptness, service, utility 8 capacity, justness, meetness 9 advantage, condition, propriety, relevance, rightness, soundness 10 expediency, usefulness 11 eligibility, suitability 12 appositeness, suitableness 13 applicability

fit out 3 arm, rig 4 gear 5 equip 6 outfit 7 appoint, furnish, turn out 8 accouter, accoutre

fitting 3 apt 4 just, meet, true 5 happy 6 proper, seemly 7 adjunct, apropos, desired, germane 8 apposite, relevant, suitable 9 accessory, accordant, befitting, pertinent 10 applicable, attachment, concordant, felicitous, harmonious 11 appropriate

fit together 4 join, mesh 5 unite 6 hook up 7 connect 8 dovetail

Fitzgerald novel 13 The Last Tycoon 14 The Great Gatsby

five *combining form:* 3 pen 4 pent 5 penta 6 quinqu 7 quinque *group of:* 6 pentad 7 quintet *of trumps:* 5 pedro

five-dollar bill 3 fin

fivefold 7 quinary 8 quintuple

Five Nations 8 Iroquois *member:* 7 Cayugas, Mohawks, Oneidas, Senecas 9 Onondagas

five-sided figure 8 pentagon

five-year period 6 luster, lustre 7 lustrum

fix 3 buy, jam, lay, put, set, sop 4 do up, geld, make, mend, moor, root, spot, work 5 alter, bribe, catch, embed, focus, lodge, patch, place, ready, rivet, solve, stick, unsex 6 adjust, anchor, attach, buy off, change, corner, doctor, fasten, make up, neuter, pickle, plight, repair, revamp, scrape, secure, settle, square, steady, tune up 7 appoint, arrange, dilemma, ingrain, instill, prepare, rebuild, resolve, specify, work out 8 castrate, entrench, mutilate, overhaul, regulate, renovate 9 concenter, establish, stabilize, sterilize 10 tamper with 11 concentrate, desexualize, predicament, recondition, reconstruct

fixation 5 craze, mania, thing 9 obsession 11 fascination, infatuation

____ **fixe** 4 idée

fixed 3 pat, set 4 fast, firm, sure 5 tight, whole 6 frozen, narrow, secure, stable, stated, steady 7 abiding, certain, limited, precise, settled 8 constant, definite, enduring, immobile, immotile, immotive, resolute 9 exclusive, immovable, immutable, permanent, steadfast, tenacious, undivided, unmovable 10 inflexible, invariable, restricted, stationary, stipulated, unswerving, unwavering 11 determinate, inalterable, irremovable, unalterable, unfaltering, unqualified 12 concentrated, never-failing, unchangeable, undistracted, unmodifiable 13 circumscribed *combining form:* 6 aplano

fix up 5 equip, primp, slick, spiff 6 devise, doll up, supply 7 deck out, doll out, dress up, furnish, gussy up 8 contrive, spruce up 9 smarten up 11 accommodate

fizzle 4 fail, hiss 6 fiasco 7 failure, sputter

fjord *Baffin Island:* 9 Admiralty *Denmark:* 3 Ise, Lim 5 Lamme *Iceland:* 4 Axar, Eyja 5 Horna, Skaga, Vopna *Norway:* 3 Tys 4 Bokn, Nord, Salt, Stor, Tana, Vest 5 Lakse, Ranen, Sogne 9 Stavanger, Trondheim *Spitsbergen:* 3 Ice *Svalbard:* 4 Stor

flabbergast 5 amaze, shock 7 astound 8 astonish, surprise 9 dumbfound, overwhelm

flabby see flaccid

flaccid 4 limp, soft, weak 6 feeble, flabby, flimsy, floppy, sleazy 8 weakened, yielding

flag 3 ebb, sag 4 fade, fail, jack, sign, swag, tire, wane, wilt 5 abate, color, droop 6 banner, burgee, colors, ensign, fanion, guidon, motion, pencel, pennon, signal, weaken 7 decline, gesture, pendant, pennant 8 banneral, gonfalon, gonfanon, languish, penoncel, standard, streamer, tricolor 9 banderole, oriflamme, pennoncel, signalize 10 Jolly Roger 11 deteriorate

flagellate 4 flog, hide, lash, whip 5 whale 6 stripe, switch, thrash 7 scourge

flagellum 4 whip 5 shoot 6 runner, stolon 7 scourge

flagitious 6 rotten, sinful, wicked 7 corrupt, vicious 8 criminal, depraved, infamous, perverse, shameful 9 miscreant, nefarious 10 degenerate, scandalous, villainous 11 disgraceful

flagon 3 cup, mug 5 stoup 7 tankard

flagpole 4 mast 5 staff *rope:* 7 halyard

flagrant 3 bad 4 bold, rank 5 gross 6 wanton 7 capital, glaring, heinous, obvious 8 striking 9 atrocious, egregious, monstrous 10 outrageous 11 conspicuous

flagstone 5 shale, slate

flag-waver 7 patriot 10 patrioteer 12 superpatriot

flail 4 beat, flog, skin, whip 6 strike, thrash, thresh 7 scourge

flair 4 bent, bump, gift, head, turn 5 knack 6 genius, talent 7 aptness, faculty 8 aptitude

flake 3 bit 4 chip, peel, rack, snow, tray 5 fleck, scale 6 lamina 8 fragment

flake off 4 peel 5 scale 9 exfoliate 10 desquamate

flamboyant 4 rich 5 showy, swank 6 chichi, florid, ornate, rococo 7 baroque, splashy 8 luscious, peacocky 10 peacockish 11 pretentious 12 orchidaceous, ostentatious

flame 4 beau, dear, fire, glow, love 5 ardor, blare, blaze, flare, flash, glare, honey, light, lover 7 beloved, darling, sweetie 8 ladylove, loveling, truelove 9 boyfriend, inamorata, inamorato 10 girlfriend

flamen 6 priest

flamenco 5 dance, gypsy, music

flaming 5 afire, fiery, flamy 6 ablaze, aflame, alight, ardent, flambé, red-hot 7 blazing, burning, fervent, flaring, ignited 8 white-hot 10 hot-blooded, passionate 11 conflagrant, impassioned

flammable 8 burnable 9 ignitable 11 combustible

flammable liquid 3 oil 6 acetyl 7 acetone, alcohol 8 gasoline, kerosene 10 turpentine

Flanders *capital:* 5 Lille *language:* 7 Flemish

flannelflower 7 mullein

flap 3 tab 4 clap, fold, leaf, stew 6 crisis, dither, lather, pother, tongue, tumult 7 aileron, flutter, turmoil 9 agitation, commotion, confusion

flapdoodle 4 bosh 5 fudge 6 bunkum 7 rubbish 8 malarkey, nonsense 9 poppycock 12 blatherskite, fiddle-faddle

flapjack 7 hotcake, pancake 11 griddle cake

flare 4 glow 5 blaze, burst, flame, flash, torch 6 signal 7 flicker 8 eruption, outbreak, outburst

flare-up 4 gust 5 burst, sally 6 access 8 eruption, outburst 9 explosion

flaring 5 afire, fiery 6 ablaze, aflame, alight 7 blazing, burning, flaming, ignited 11 conflagrant

flash 3 ray 4 beam, burn, glow, show 5 blare, blaze, blink, crack, flame, flare, glare, gleam, glint, jiffy, shake, shine, spark 6 dazzle, expose, flaunt, glance, minute, moment, parade, quiver, second 7 display, disport, exhibit, flicker, glimmer, glisten, glitter, instant, radiate, shimmer, show off, spangle, sparkle, trot out, twinkle 8 brandish 9 breathing, coruscate 10 incandesce 11 coruscation, scintillate, split second 13 scintillation

flashy 4 loud 5 gaudy, showy 6 brazen, florid, garish, ornate, tawdry, tinsel 7 blatant, chintzy, glaring 9 sparkling 10 flamboyant, glittering 12 meretricious

flask 5 frame 6 bottle, fiasco, flacon 7 ampulla, canteen, costrel

flat 3 dim, mat 4 dead, drab, dull, even, poor 5 banal, bland, blind, broke, flush, inane, level, muted, needy, plane, prone, prosy, rooms, stale, stony, suite, vapid 6 jejune, planar, rental, smooth 7 insipid, planate, prosaic, sapless 8 dirt poor, lifeless, lodgings, strapped, tenement, unsavory 9 apartment, colorless, decumbent, destitute, downright, innocuous, penurious, prostrate, reclining, recumbent, savorless, tasteless 10 flavorless, lackluster, lusterless, monotonous, namby-pamby, procumbent, stone-broke

flatfish see at **fish**

flatland 4 mesa, moor 5 plain 6 steppe, tundra 7 plateau 9 tableland

flat-out 4 fast, rank 5 apace, utter 6 damned 7 blasted, goldarn, hastily, quickly, rapidly, swiftly 8 absolute, outright, speedily 9 out-and-out, posthaste 11 straight-out, unmitigated 12 lickety-split 13 expeditiously

flatten 3 lay 4 down, even, fell, flat 5 floor, flush, level, plane 6 deject, ground, lay low, smooth 7 depress, mow down 8 smoothen 9 bring down, knock down, prostrate

flattened at the poles 6 oblate

flatter 4 coax, suit 5 toady 6 become, cajole, praise 7 blarney, enhance, gratify, wheedle 8 blandish, bootlick, inveigle

flattery 3 oil 4 laud 6 praise 7 blarney, fawning, incense 8 cajolery, soft soap, toadying 9 adulation, laudation, truckling 10 sycophancy 11 bootlicking, compliments 12 blandishment, ingratiation

flatulent 4 vain 5 empty, gassy, tumid, windy 6 hollow, turgid 8 dropsied, inflated 9 dropsical, overblown, tumescent

Flaubert *heroine:* 4 Emma *novel:*
8 Salammbo 12 Madame Bovary

flaunt 4 show, wave 5 flash, flout, vaunt
6 expose, parade 7 display, disport, exhibit,
flutter, show off, trot out 8 brandish, flourish

flavor 4 tang, zest 5 sapor, savor, smack,
taste, tinge 6 relish, season 8 sapidity

flavorless 4 drab, flat 5 stale 7 insipid
8 unsavory 9 tasteless 11 distasteful,
unpalatable

flavorsome 5 sapid, tasty 6 savory
9 aperitive, flavorful, palatable, relishing,
toothsome 10 appetizing 11 good-tasting

flaw 3 gap, rip 4 rent, tear, vice 5 crack,
fault 6 breach, defect 7 blemish, fissure
12 imperfection

flawed 4 sick 5 amiss 6 faulty, marred
7 damaged, spoiled 8 impaired 9 defective, imperfect

flawless 4 pure 5 ideal, model, sound,
whole 6 entire, intact 7 perfect 8 absolute,
unbroken, unmarred 9 errorless, exquisite,
faultless, fleckless, undamaged 10 immaculate, impeccable, unimpaired 11 note-perfect, unblemished 12 indefectible

flax 5 linen *fiber:* 3 tow 4 harl 5 harle
6 strick *prepare:* 3 ret 4 card 5 dress
6 hackle, scutch *refuse:* 5 hards, hurds

flaxen 5 blond, straw 6 blonde, golden

flay 4 skin 5 slash 6 assail, attack, berate,
scathe, scorch 7 blister, censure, scarify,
scourge 8 lambaste, lash into 9 castigate,
excoriate 10 tongue-lash

flea 5 pulex 6 chigoe, jigger 7 chigger
water: 7 daphnid

Fleance's father 6 Banquo

fleckless 7 perfect 8 absolute, flawless,
unflawed 10 impeccable 11 note-perfect

flection 3 bow 4 bend, turn 5 angle
7 flexure, turning

Fledermaus, Die 3 bat *character:*
5 Adele, Falke, Frank 6 Alfred 9 Rosalinde
10 Eisenstein *composer:* 7 Strauss
(Johann)

fledgling 4 boot, colt, tyro 6 novice,
rookie 8 beginner, freshman, neophyte,
newcomer 10 apprentice

flee 3 fly, lam, run 4 bolt, scat, shun, skip
5 break, elude, scape, scoot, scram, skirr
6 decamp, escape 7 abscond, make off,
scamper, scarper 9 skedaddle

fleece 3 web 4 bilk, clip, milk, rook, skin,
soak, wool 5 bleed, cheat, cozen, mulct,
shear, stick, sweat 6 extort, hustle
7 defraud, despoil, plunder, swindle
10 overcharge

fleeceable 4 easy 5 naive 8 gullible
11 susceptible

fleecy 5 hairy 6 pilose, woolly 7 hirsute,
pileous 9 whiskered

fleer 4 gibe, gird, jeer, jest, mock 5 flout,
laugh, scoff, sneer, taunt 6 quip at 7 scout
at 8 fugitive

fleet 3 fly, run 4 fast, flit, navy, sail, spry,
wile, wing 5 agile, brisk, hasty, hurry, quick,
rapid, speed, sweep, swift, while 6 armada,
hasten, hustle, nimble, rocket, speedy
7 beguile 8 flotilla 9 breakneck 10 evanescent, expeditive, harefooted 11 expeditious

fleeting 5 brief 7 passing 8 fugitive, volatile 9 ephemeral, fugacious, momentary,
transient 10 evanescent, short-lived, transitory

Fleming, Ian *hero:* 9 James Bond *novel:*
4 Dr. No 10 Goldfinger 11 Thunderball
12 Casino Royale

fleshly 3 lay 6 animal, bodily, carnal 7 profane, secular, sensual, somatic 8 corporal,
physical, sensuous, temporal 9 corporeal,
epicurean, luxurious, sybaritic 10 voluptuous

fleshy 3 fat 5 beefy, gross, heavy, obese,
plump, stout 6 portly 7 porcine, sarcous,
weighty 9 corpulent 10 overweight *fruit:*
4 pome 5 bacca, berry, drupe

Fletcher's partner 8 Beaumont (Francis)

fleur--de-- ____ 3 lis, lys

flex 4 bend 5 tense 7 pliancy, tension

flexible 5 withy 6 docile, floppy, limber, pliant, supple, whippy 7 elastic, pliable,
springy, stretch, willowy 8 amenable,
stretchy, yielding 9 resilient, tractable
10 manageable

flexuous 5 snaky 7 sinuous, winding
8 tortuous 9 meandrous 10 circuitous, convoluted, meandering, serpentine 11 anfractuous

flick 3 hit 4 blow, cine, film, show 5 movie
6 strike 7 picture 9 photoplay 11 picture
show 13 motion picture, moving picture

flicker 4 flit 5 blink, dance, flash, gleam,
glint, hover, waver 7 flitter, flutter, glitter,
sparkle, twinkle

flickering 7 lambent 8 unsteady

flier 3 ace 5 pilot 6 airman, fly-boy 7 aviator, birdman 8 aviatrix

flight 3 lam 4 rout, slip 5 floor, story
6 escape 7 getaway 8 breakout, escaping
10 escapement

flighty 5 dizzy, giddy, silly, swift 7 foolish
8 freakish, skittish, unstable, volatile 9 frivolous, mercurial, transient 10 capricious,
changeable, inconstant 11 empty-headed,
harebrained 13 irresponsible, rattlebrained

flimflam 3 gyp 4 beat, bilk, dupe, fake,
fool, gull, hoax, jazz, sell, sham 5 cheat,
cozen, fraud, freak, hokum, trick 6 befool,
chouse, deceit, diddle, drivel, hot air, humbug, pigeon, trifle 7 chicane, deceive,
defraud, eyewash, swindle 8 hoodwink,
nonsense 9 bamboozle, deception, impos-

ture, moonshine, overreach 10 balderdash, double-talk 11 hornswoggle

flimflammer 3 gyp 4 skin 5 cheat 6 con man 7 diddler, sharper 8 swindler 9 defrauder 12 double-dealer

flimsy 4 limp, thin, weak 5 filmy, frail, gauzy, sheer 6 feeble, flabby, floppy, infirm, sleazy, slight, slimsy, weakly 7 flaccid, fragile, rickety, slimpsy, tiffany, unsound 8 decrepit, delicate, gossamer 10 diaphanous, improbable, incredible 11 implausible, transparent 12 unbelievable, unconvincing

flinch 5 quail, start, wince 6 blanch, blench, recede, recoil, shrink 7 retreat, squinch 8 withdraw

fling 2 go 3 pop, try 4 boil, bolt, cast, dash, emit, fire, gibe, hurl, lash, orgy, race, rush, shot, slap, stab, tear, toss 5 binge, chase, crack, dance, heave, pitch, shoot, sling, spree, throw, whack, whirl 6 charge, launch 7 discard, rampage, sarcasm, splurge 9 disregard, overthrow

flip 3 tap 4 blow, flap, glib, pert, riff 5 drink, flick 6 riffle 8 flippant 10 somersault 11 smart-alecky

flippancy 6 levity 8 archness, pertness 9 cockiness, freshness, frivolity, lightness, sauciness 10 cheekiness, impishness, volatility 11 flightiness, playfulness, roguishness

flippant 4 flip, glib, pert

flip through 4 scan 6 browse 7 dip into, run over 8 glance at 10 glance over

flirt 3 toy 4 dart, flip, flit, fool, minx, ogle, play, toss, vamp 5 dally, flick 6 coquet, lead on, trifle, wanton 8 coquette

flit 3 fly, run, zip 4 dart, pass, rush, sail, scud, whiz, wing 5 dance, fleet, flick, float, hover, hurry, scoot, speed, sweep 6 dartle, hasten 7 flicker, flutter

flitter 3 bit 5 dance, flake, hover 7 flicker, flutter, skitter

float 3 bob, fly 4 buoy, cork, dart, hang, raft, ride, sail, scud, skim, waft, wash 5 drift, drink, flood, hover, poise, shoot, skirr 8 levitate 9 negotiate

floater 3 bum, vag 4 hobo, raft 5 tramp 6 boomer 7 drifter, vagrant 8 derelict, vagabond

floating 5 loose 6 adrift, afloat, natant 7 buoyant, movable 8 moveable, shifting

flocculent 6 woolly

flock 3 mob 4 army, bevy, herd, host, pack, rout 5 bunch, cloud, covey, crowd, drove, group 6 flight, legion, scores, volary 9 multitude 11 aggregation *of mallards:* 4 sute

flog 3 tan 4 beat, cane, hide, lash, whip 5 birch, flail, knout, tawse, whale 6 larrup,

stripe, switch, thrash 7 exhaust, scourge 10 flagellate

flood 4 bore, flow, flux, pour, rush, tide 5 drift, drown, eager, eagre, spate, swamp, whelm 6 deluge, engulf, stream 7 current, freshet, niagara, torrent 8 cataract, flooding, inundate, overflow, submerge 9 cataclysm, overwhelm 10 inundation, outgushing, outpouring

floor 4 down, drop, fell 5 level, story 6 defeat, ground, lay low 7 flatten, silence 8 audience, bowl down, bowl over 9 bring down, knock down

flop 3 dud 4 bomb, bust, fail, fall, flap 5 lemon, loser 6 fizzle 7 failure

floppy 4 limp 5 loose 6 flabby, flimsy, sleazy 7 flaccid 8 flexible

flora 6 plants 10 vegetation

flora and fauna 5 biota

Florence *bridge:* 12 Ponte Vecchio *cathedral:* 5 Duomo *family:* 6 Medici *gallery:* 6 Uffizi *museum:* 8 Bargello *palace:* 5 Pitti *river:* 4 Arno

florid 4 rich 5 flush, gaudy, ruddy, showy 6 ornate, rococo 7 aureate, baroque, flowery, flushed, glowing 8 figurate, luscious, rubicund, sanguine, sonorous 9 bombastic, overblown 10 euphuistic, flamboyant, rhetorical 11 declamatory, full-blooded 12 magniloquent 13 grandiloquent

Florida *capital:* 11 Tallahassee *college, university:* 4 Nova 5 Barry 6 Eckerd 7 Stetson *discoverer:* 11 Ponce de Leon (Juan) *Key:* 4 Long, Vaca, West 5 Largo 7 Big Pine 9 Sugarloaf *largest city:* 12 Jacksonville *motto:* 12 In God We Trust *nickname:* 13 Sunshine State *state bird:* 11 mockingbird *state flower:* 13 orange blossom

florilegium 3 ana 4 posy 5 album 7 garland, omnibus 8 analects 9 anthology 10 miscellany

Florimel's husband 7 Marinel

florist's milieu 10 greenhouse

floss 3 fur 4 down, flue, fuzz, lint, pile 5 fluff

flotilla 5 fleet

Flotow opera 5 Indra 6 L'Ombre, Martha

flotsam 6 jetsam 8 wreckage 9 driftwood

flounce 5 fling, frill, mince, strut 6 prance, ruffle, sashay 8 flounder, struggle

flounder 5 fling, labor, lurch 6 muddle, wallow 7 blunder, stumble 8 flatfish, struggle

flour 4 atta, bolt, meal, mill 5 grind 6 pinole, powder 9 pulverize *beetle:* 6 weevil

flourish 3 wax 4 brag, grow, wave 5 adorn, bloom, boast, score, swing 6 arrive, flower, stroke, thrive 7 blossom, develop, fanfare, make out, prosper, succeed 8 brandish, curlicue, decorate, ornament 9 grace note

flout 4 gibe, gird, jeer, jest, mock 5 fleer, scoff, scorn, sneer, taunt 6 deride, insult, quip at 7 jeering, mockery 9 disregard

flow 3 run 4 emit, flux, gush, hang, head, pour, rill, rise, roll, rush, stem, teem, tide, void, well 5 arise, crawl, drift, flood, issue, spate, surge, swarm 6 abound, course, gurgle, onrush, ripple, series, sluice, spring, stream 7 cascade, current, emanate, give off, indraft, outflow, proceed 8 fountain, inundate, sequence 9 discharge, originate, pullulate 10 continuity, derive from, disembogue, inundation, menstruate, succession 11 continuance, progression 12 continuation, menstruation *combining form:* 4 rheo 5 rrhea 6 rrhoea 7 rrhagia

flower 3 top 4 best, blow, pick, posy 5 bloom, cream, elite, pride, prime, prize 6 choice, gentry 7 aristoi, blossom, burgeon, develop, fleuron, quality, society 8 optimacy, outbloom 9 gentility 10 effloresce, upper class, upper crust 11 aristocracy 13 inflorescence *buttonhole:* 11 boutonniere *cluster:* 4 cyme 5 spike, umbel 6 corymb, floret, raceme, spadix, thyrse 7 panicle 8 spikelet 9 capitulum, dichasium, glomerule 11 monochasium, polychasium 13 inflorescence *combining form:* 4 anth 5 antho, anthy, flori 6 anthes, anthus 7 anthous, florous *cup:* 5 calyx *garden:* 4 iris, lily, pink, rose 5 aster, canna, daisy, pansy, peony, phlox, poppy, tulip 6 azalia, cosmos, crocus, dahlia, orchid, violet 7 jonquil, petunia 8 camellia, daffodil, gardenia, geranium, gloxinia, hyacinth, larkspur, marigold, primrose 9 carnation, gladiolus, narcissus 10 delphinium, heliotrope 13 chrysanthemum *opening:* 8 anthesis *part:* 5 bract, calyx, ovary, ovule, petal, sepal, style 6 anther, pistil, spathe, stamen, stigma 7 corolla, nectary, pedicel, petiole 8 calyptra, filament, gynecium, peduncle, perianth *spike:* 5 ament 6 catkin, spadix *stalk:* 7 pedicel 8 peduncle *type:* 3 ray 4 disk 6 annual, simple 9 composite, perennial *wild:* 4 flag 5 bluet, daisy, gilia, vetch 6 lupine 7 anemone, arbutus, cowslip, gentian, vervain 8 bluebell, hepatica, trillium 9 buttercup, columbine, dandelion, saxifrage 10 cinquefoil 11 lady slipper 12 lady's slipper

flower arranging 7 ikebana

flowering 6 growth 8 progress, upgrowth 9 evolution, unfolding 10 evolvement 11 development, florescence, progression

flowerless plant 4 fern, moss 6 fungus, lichen 9 liverwort

flower-shaped ornament 7 fleuron

flowery 5 wordy 6 florid, ornate 7 aureate, swollen, verbose 8 sonorous 9 bombastic, overblown 10 euphuistic, rhetorical 11 declamatory 12 magniloquent 13 grandiloquent

Flowery Kingdom 5 China

flowing 4 easy 5 fluid 6 afflux, fluent, smooth 7 copious, cursive, running, streamy 8 freeform 10 effortless *back:* 6 reflux 8 refluent *in:* 6 influx 8 influent *together:* 7 conflux 9 confluent

flow regulator 5 valve

flub 4 mess, muff 5 boner, botch, error, fluff 6 bollix, bungle, goof up 7 blunder, louse up

fluctuate 4 sway, wave 5 swing, waver 8 undulate 9 oscillate, vacillate 10 irresolute

flue 3 fur 4 down, fuzz, lint, pile 5 floss, fluff 7 channel, dragnet, feather, fishnet, passage

fluent 4 easy, free, glib 5 fluid, vocal 6 facile, liquid, smooth 7 cursive, flowing, running, voluble 8 eloquent 9 talkative 10 articulate, effortless, loquacious 12 smooth-spoken

fluff 3 fur 4 bull, down, flub, flue, fuzz, lint, mess, muff, pile, slip, trip 5 boner, botch, error, floss, lapse 6 bollix, bungle, goof up 7 blooper, blunder, louse up, mistake

fluid 4 free 5 lymph, water 6 liquid, mobile 7 mutable, protean 8 unstable, unsteady, variable, weathery 9 changeful, unsettled 10 changeable *combining form:* 4 sero *excessive:* 5 edema

fluid pressure record 8 kymogram

fluky 3 odd 6 casual, chance 8 unsteady 9 uncertain 10 accidental, capricious, contingent, fortuitous, incidental

flume 5 chute 6 sluice, stream 7 channel

flummox 4 fail 7 confuse, perplex 8 confound 9 embarrass 10 disconcert

flunky 5 toady 7 footman, servant, steward

flurry 3 ado 4 fuss, gust, stir 5 haste, upset, whirl 6 bother, bustle, furore, pother, scurry 7 agitate, confuse, disturb, fluster, perturb, turmoil, unhinge 8 disquiet 9 agitation, confusion, whirlpool, whirlwind 10 discompose, excitement, turbulence

flush 3 lay 4 even, flat, glow, pink, rich, rose 5 bloom, blush, color, level, plane, rouge, ruddy 6 florid, mantle, pinken, redden, smooth 7 blossom, crimson, flatten, flushed, glowing, moneyed, opulent, planate, wealthy 8 abundant, affluent, rubicund, sanguine, smoothen 11 full-blooded

fluster 5 addle, dizzy, shake, upset 6 ball up, bother, flurry, fuddle, muddle, puzzle, rattle, ruffle 7 agitate, confuse, disturb, mystify, nonplus, perplex, perturb, unhinge 8 befuddle, bewilder, confound, disquiet, distract 10 discompose

flute 4 fife, roll 5 pleat 6 goffer, groove 7 chamfer, channel, flutist, piccolo, shuttle 8 recorder 9 wineglass *combining form:* 3 aul 4 aulo *player:* 5 piper 7 flutist 8 flautist

flutist *American:* 5 Baker (Julius), Baron (Samuel) 7 Robison (Paula) 8 Zukerman (Eugenia) *British:* 6 Galway (James) *French:* 6 Rampal (Jean-Pierre)

flutter 4 beat, flap, flit 5 dance, hover, quake, shake, throb 6 flurry, quaver, quiver, wobble 7 flicker, flitter, pulsate, tremble, vibrate 8 disorder 9 agitation, confusion, palpitate, vibration 11 fluctuation, oscillation

flux 3 run 4 flow, fuse, melt, rush, thaw, tide 5 drift, flood, spate 6 scours, stream 7 current, flowing, liquefy, outflow 8 diarrhea, dissolve, liquesce 9 dysentery 10 deliquesce

fly 3 run, zip 4 bolt, dart, dash, flee, flit, lure, rush, sail, scud, skip, soar, whiz, wing 5 break, fleet, float, glide, hover, hurry, pilot, scape, scoot, shoot, skirr, speed, sweep, whish, whisk 6 aviate, decamp, escape, flight, hasten, hustle 7 abscond, airlift, flutter, hotfoot, make off, scamper 8 highball 9 skedaddle *combining form:* 3 myi 4 myia, myio 5 musci *insect:* 4 gnat, zimb 5 fruit, midge 6 botfly, gadfly, mayfly, tsetse 7 deerfly, sandfly, tachina 8 blackfly, dipteron, horsefly, housefly, mosquito, tachinid 10 bluebottle *larva:* 3 bot 4 bott 6 maggot

fly-by-night 6 unsure 7 dubious 8 untrusty 9 trustless 10 unreliable 12 questionable, undependable 13 untrustworthy

flycatcher 4 tody

flying 5 aloft, brief 6 volant 7 soaring 8 airborne, volitant

Flying Dutchman *composer:* 6 Wagner (Richard) *heroine:* 5 Senta

flying fish 7 gurnard

flying fox 3 bat 6 kalong 8 fruit bat

flying horse 7 Pegasus 10 hippogriff

flying island 6 Laputa

flying lemur 6 colugo

flying mammal 3 bat

flying saucer 3 UFO

fly in the ointment 5 catch

foam 4 head, scud, scum, suds 5 froth, spume, yeast 6 lather

fob 4 seal 5 chain 6 pocket, ribbon 8 ornament

fob off 5 foist 6 palm on, put off 7 palm off

focus 3 fix, hub, put 4 meet, seat 5 heart, rivet 6 center, fasten, fixate 8 converge, polestar 9 concenter 11 concentrate, nerve center

fodder 4 feed, food 6 forage, silage 9 provender *crop:* 3 hay, oat, rye 4 corn 5 maize, vetch, wheat 6 barley, clover, millet 7 alfalfa, sorghum 9 broad bean *storage structure:* 4 silo *store:* 6 ensile

foe 5 enemy, rival 8 opponent 9 adversary 10 antagonist

fog 3 dim 4 blur, daze, haze, mist, murk 5 addle, bedim, brume, cloud, muddy, vapor 6 darken, muddle, puzzle 7 becloud, confuse, eclipse, mystify, obscure, perplex, pogonip 8 bewilder, distract 9 obfuscate, overcloud 10 muddlement 11 muddledness 12 befuddlement, bewilderment

foggy 4 hazy 5 misty, murky, soupy, vague 7 brumous, muddled, obscure, tenuous 8 confused, vaporous

foghorn 8 diaphone

fogy 6 square 7 diehard 8 mossback, standpat 10 back number, fuddy-duddy 12 antediluvian, conservative, mid-Victorian 13 stick-in-the-mud

fogyish 4 tory 5 right 7 die-hard, old-line 8 orthodox 9 out-of-date 10 antiquated 11 reactionary 12 conservative, old-fashioned

foible 5 fault 7 failing, frailty 8 weakness 11 shortcoming 12 imperfection

foil 4 balk, beat, bilk, curb, dash, faze 5 sword 6 baffle, defeat, rattle, thwart, tissue 7 buffalo, repulse 8 restrain 9 discomfit, embarrass, frustrate 10 circumvent, disappoint, disconcert

foist 3 fob 4 dupe, gull, hoax, wish, worm 5 cheat, trick 6 delude, edge in, fob off, impose, palm on, work in 7 beguile, deceive, defraud, inflict, mislead, palm off, pass off, swindle, work off 8 hoodwink 9 bamboozle, insinuate, overreach 10 infiltrate

fold 3 lap, pen, ply 4 bend, bust, coat, fail, leaf, ruck, tuck 5 break, crash, drape, flock, layer, plait, pleat, plica, purse, ridge, rivel 6 crease, cuttle, double, furrow, pucker, rimple 7 confine, crinkle, crumple, embrace, entwine, envelop, flexure, overlap, plicate, wrinkle 8 surround 9 plication 11 corrugation *combining form:* 5 ptych 6 ptycho, valvul 7 valvulo *skin:* 4 ruga 5 plica, rugae (plural) 6 dewlap, plicae (plural)

folder 4 file 5 cover 6 binder 8 circular

foliage 6 growth, leaves 7 leafage, verdure 9 greenness 10 vegetation

folk 4 clan, race 5 house, laity, stock, tribe 6 family, people 7 kindred, lineage 9 relatives

folklore 4 myth 6 belief, custom, legend, mythos 9 mythology, tradition 12 superstition

folksinger 4 Baez (Joan), Ives (Burl) 5 Dylan (Bob), Niles (John Jacob), White (Josh) 6 Seeger (Pete) 7 Chapman (Tracy), Guthrie (Arlo, Woody) 9 Ledbetter (Huddie)

folktale 7 märchen

follow 3 ape, dog, see, spy, tag 4 copy, hunt, keep, mind, obey, seek, tail, take 5 after, catch, chase, chivy, ensue, grasp, hound, trace, track, trail 6 accept, attend, comply, convoy, pursue, search, shadow, take in 7 conform, imitate, observe, replace, succeed 8 displace, exercise, postdate, practice, supplant 9 accompany, apprehend, supersede, supervene 10 comprehend, understand

follower 3 fan 5 freak, toady 6 addict, cohort, patron, sequel, votary 7 devotee, groupie, habitué, sectary, sequent, trailer 8 adherent, advocate, disciple, faithful, hanger-on, henchman, myrmidon, parasite, partisan, sectator, tagalong 9 dependent, satellite, supporter, sycophant 10 aficionado 11 lickspittle *of Theodore Roosevelt:* 9 Bull Moose *suffix:* 3 ite

following 4 next 5 after, below, since, suite, train 6 behind, public 7 ensuing, retinue, sequent 8 audience 9 clientage, clientele, entourage 10 sequential, subsequent, succeeding, successive 12 subsequent to

follow-up 6 sequel

folly 4 whim 6 lunacy, vanity 7 fatuity, foolery, inanity, madness 8 insanity, nonsense 9 absurdity, craziness, dottiness, silliness, stupidity 10 imprudence, indulgence 11 foolishness, wittlessness

foment 3 set 4 abet, brew, goad, spur 5 nurse, raise, rouse, set on 6 arouse, excite, foster, incite, stir up, whip up 7 agitate, ferment, nurture, provoke 9 cultivate, encourage, instigate

Fomorian one-eyed giant 5 Balor

fond 4 dear, warm 5 basis, silly 6 doting, loving, tender, upbeat 7 devoted, foolish 8 enamored, lonesome, romantic, sanguine 9 indulgent 10 groundwork, infatuated, optimistic, responsive 11 sentimental, sympathetic 12 affectionate

fondle 3 hug, pet 4 love 5 clasp 6 caress, cosset, dandle 7 embrace

fondness 4 love 5 taste 6 liking, relish 8 appetite, devotion, soft spot 9 affection 10 attachment, partiality, propensity 11 inclination 12 predilection

fondness for *combining form:* 5 phily 6 philia *suffix:* 4 itis

fond of *combining form:* 4 phil 5 phile, philo 6 philic 7 philous

food 3 pap 4 bite, chow, diet, fare, grub, meal, meat 5 bread, manna, scoff 6 fodder, viands, vivres 7 aliment, edibles, nurture, pabulum 8 delicacy, victuals 9 nutriment, provender 10 provisions, sustenance 11 comestibles, nourishment *combining form:* 4 sito 6 phagia *craving for:* 7 bulimia *divine:* 8 ambrosia *element:* 5 sugar 6 starch 7 mineral, protein, vitamin 12 carbohydrate *from heaven:* 5 manna *lover:* 7 epicure, gourmet 8 gourmand *provision:* 4 mess 6 ration 7 serving *scarcity:* 6 famine *waste:* 4 orts 7 garbage

foofaraw 4 coil, fuss 6 furore, hurrah, ruckus, rumpus, shindy 8 brouhaha 9 commotion

fool 3 ass, fun, kid, rag, rib, sap, toy 4 blow, butt, dolt, dope, dupe, fish, gull, hoax, jerk, jest, joke, josh, mark, poop, razz, simp, wolf, zany 5 amble, ament, chump, clown, comic, dally, dummy, dunce, flirt, goose, idiot, jolly, loser, moron, ninny, noddy, patsy, schmo, silly, trick, waste 6 banter, befool, butt in, coquet, cretin, cuckoo, dimwit, donkey, doodle, horn in, jester, lead on, loiter, madman, meddle, monkey, motley, nincom, nitwit, pigeon, schmoe, simple, stooge, stupid, sucker, trifle, victim, wanton 7 asshead, buffoon, chicane, consume, deceive, fall guy, foolish, fritter, gudgeon, half-wit, jackass, natural, pinhead, saphead, schmuck, tomfool 8 busybody, comedian, dumbbell, easy mark, flimflam, hoodwink, imbecile, lunkhead, mooncalf, numskull, pushover, softhead, squander, underwit, womanize 9 bamboozle, birdbrain, blockhead, dissipate, interfere, interlope, philander, simpleton, throw away 10 frivol away, instrument, mess around, monkey with, nincompoop, play around, tamper with, trifle away 11 featherhead, hornswoggle, merry-andrew, ninnyhammer, rattlebrain, string along 12 featherbrain, scatterbrain 13 laughingstock

foolhardy 4 rash 6 daring 8 headlong, reckless 9 audacious, daredevil, impetuous, venturous 11 adventurous, precipitate, temerarious, venturesome 13 adventuresome

foolish 3 mad 4 daft, fond, rash, zany 5 batty, crazy, dippy, dizzy, dotty, goofy, inane, jerky, loony, loopy, sappy, silly, wacky 6 absurd, insane, simple, stupid, unwise 7 asinine, doltish, fatuous, idiotic, lunatic, moronic, offbeat, unwitty, witless 8 headless, reckless 9 brainless, fantastic, half-baked, imbecilic, laughable, ludicrous, senseless, unearthly 10 half-cocked, half-witted, idleheaded, irrational, ridiculous, unorthodox, weak-headed, weak-minded 11 harebrained, nonsensical

foolishness 4 bull, bunk 5 folly 6 lunacy 7 fatuity, inanity, waggery 8 drollery, insanity, nonsense, unwisdom 9 absurdity 10 imprudence 12 indiscretion 13 senselessness

fool's gold 6 pyrite

foot 3 add, sum, tot 4 base, cast, pace, step, tote, walk 5 dance, nadir, total, tread, troop 6 bottom, figure, hoof it, prance, tootsy 7 summate, tootsie, traipse 8 ambulate, totalize *ailment:* 4 corn 6 bunion, callus *animal:* 3 pad, paw 4 hoof 7 fetlock, flipper, pastern, trotter *bones of:* 5 talus, tarsi (plural) 6 cuboid, tarsal, tarsus 7 phalanx 9 calcaneus, cuneiform, navicular, phalanges (plural) 10 metatarsal *combining form:* 3 ped, pod, pus 4 pede, pedi, pedo, poda, pode, podo 5 podia 6 podium *doctor:* 10 podiatrist 11 chiropodist *metric:* 4 iamb 5 arsis 6 dactyl, thesis 7 anapest, pyrrhic, spondee, trochee *part:* 3 toe 4 arch, ball, claw, nail 5 ankle, digit, talon 6 hallux, instep

football 5 rugby 6 rugger, soccer 7 pigskin *field:* 8 gridiron *foul:* 7 holding, offside 8 clipping 12 interference *official:* 6 umpire 7 referee 8 linesman 9 back judge, line judge 10 field judge *play:* 4 dive, trap 5 sneak, sweep 6 option, screen 7 audible, counter, handoff, rollout, runback 8 dropback 9 crossbuck, off-tackle 10 buttonhook *player position:* 3 end 4 back 5 guard 6 center, safety, tackle 7 flanker, lineman, wideout 8 fullback, halfback, slotback, split end, tailback, tight end, wingback 9 noseguard 10 cornerback, linebacker, nose tackle 11 quarterback 12 defensive end, wide receiver *scoring:* 6 safety · 9 field goal, touchdown 10 conversion *starting play:* 7 kickoff *team:* 6 eleven *term:* 4 down, kick, pass, punt, rush, snap 5 blitz, block, squad 6 fumble, huddle, onside, option, safety, spiral 7 end zone, handoff, kickoff, offside, pigskin, quarter, spinner, yardage 8 clipping, crossbar, goal line, goalpost, gridiron, halftime 9 backfield, defensive, field goal, intercept, offensive, placekick, scrimmage, touchback, touchdown 11 broken field 12 interception

footballer 4 Kemp (Jack), Moon (Warren), Rice (Jerry) 5 Allen (Marcus), Baugh (Sammy), Berry (Raymond), Brown (Jim), Ditka (Mike), Elway (John), Jones (Bert, Deacon), Kelly (Jim), Kosar (Bernie), Shula (Don), Simms (Phil), Smith (Emmitt), Starr (Bart), Swann (Lynn), Young (Steve) 6 Aikman (Troy), Blanda (George), Butkus (Dick), Carter (Ki-Jana), Csonka (Larry), Dawson (Len), Graham (Otto), Grange (Red), Greene (Joe), Jaeger (Jeff), Marino (Dan), Namath (Joe), Payton (Walter), Rypien (Mark), Sayers (Gale), Thorpe (Jim), Tittle (Y. A.), Unitas (Johnny), Walker (Herschel) 7 Bledsoe (Drew), Dorsett (Tony), Esiason (Boomer), Gifford (Frank), Hornung (Paul), Luckman (Sid), Montana (Joe), Riggins (John), Sanders (Barry, Deion), Simpson (O. J.) , Stabler (Ken), Thurman (Thomas) 8 Anderson (Ottis), Bradshaw (Terry), Nagurski (Bronko), Plunkett (Jim), Staubach (Roger) 9 Dickerson (Eric), Jurgensen (Sonny), Hostetler (Jeff), Tarkenton (Fran)

footed *combining form:* 3 ped, pod 6 podous

footfall 4 step 5 tread

footing 4 base, rank, seat, term 5 basis, place, state 6 bottom, ground, status 7 bedrock, seating, station, warrant 8 basement, capacity, position 9 character, situation 10 foundation, groundwork, substratum

footless 6 apodal

foot lever 5 pedal 7 treadle

footlike 6 pedate 8 pediform

footpad 6 robber 10 highwayman

footprint 3 pug 4 sign, step 5 spoor, trace, track, tract 7 pugmark, vestige *fossil:* 7 ichnite 9 ichnolite

footslog 4 plod, slop, toil 6 stodge, trudge 8 plunther

footstep 5 spoor, track, tract 7 vestige

footstone 6 ledger 8 monument 11 grave marker

footstool 7 hassock, ottoman

fop 4 buck, dude 5 blade, blood, dandy, spark, sport, swell 6 masher 7 coxcomb, gallant 8 cavalier, macaroni, popinjay 9 exquisite 10 ladies' man, lady-killer 11 Beau Brummel, petit-maître 12 fashion plate, lounge lizard, man-about-town

for *prefix:* 3 pro

forage 4 beat, comb, grub, raid, rake 5 scour 6 browse, fodder, ravage, search 7 ransack, rummage 8 finecomb, scrounge 9 pasturage; (see also **fodder**)

forager 6 raider, sacker 8 marauder, ravisher

foray 4 raid 5 harry 6 attack, harass, inroad, invade, maraud, sortie 7 overrun, pillage 8 invasion 9 incursion, irruption

forbear 4 curb, keep, shun 5 avoid, cease, evade, forgo, spare 6 bridle, desist, endure, escape, eschew, forego, suffer 7 abstain, decline, inhibit, refrain 8 restrain, tolerate, withhold 9 sacrifice

forbearance 5 grace, mercy 6 lenity 7 charity 8 clemency, lenience, leniency,

mildness, patience 9 restraint, tolerance
10 abstinence, toleration

forbearing 4 easy, mild 6 gentle 7 clement, lenient, patient 8 merciful, tolerant
9 indulgent 10 charitable, thoughtful
11 considerate

Forbes hero 8 Tremaine (Johnny)

forbid 3 ban, bar 4 curb, deny, halt, stop, veto 5 block, check, debar, estop, taboo 6 enjoin, hinder, impede, outlaw, refuse 7 exclude, inhibit, obviate, prevent, rule out, shut out 8 obstruct, preclude, prohibit, restrain 9 interdict, proscribe

forbidden 5 taboo 6 banned 8 verboten
10 prohibited

Forbidden City 5 Lhasa

force 2 od 3 arm, jam, vim, vis 4 beef, cram, make, move, odyl, push, rape 5 cause, drive, exact, foist, impel, karma, might, odyle, order, pains, point, power, press, punch, sinew, speed, spoil, vigor, visit, wreak, wreck, wrest 6 coerce, compel, defile, demand, duress, effort, energy, enjoin, extort, impose, inject, legion, muscle, oblige, ravish, strain, stress 7 cogency, command, concuss, headway, impetus, inflict, outrage, potency, require, sandbag, shotgun, tension, trouble, violate 8 coercion, deflower, manpower, momentum, obligate, occasion, pressure, shoehorn, strength, validity, velocity, violence 9 constrain, deflorate, exertions, intensity, puissance, strong arm, validness, vehemence 10 compulsion, constraint *apart:* 5 wedge *unit:* 4 dyne

forced 5 rigid, stiff 6 wooden 7 labored 9 contrived, fatiguing, unnatural 10 artificial, compulsory, exhausting, factitious, farfetched, inflexible 11 involuntary

forceful 6 cogent, mighty, potent, virile 7 dynamic, telling 8 emphatic, forcible, powerful, puissant, vigorous 9 assertive, effective, energetic, insistent 10 compelling, resounding 12 constraining

forceless 4 weak 5 wimpy 6 feeble 8 impotent 10 emasculate, inadequate 11 ineffective, ineffectual, slack-spined 12 invertebrate

force out see **expel**

forcible 6 mighty, potent 7 intense, violent 8 coercive, emphatic, militant, powerful, puissant, vehement 9 assertive 10 aggressive

Ford's folly 5 Edsel

for each 3 per

forearm bone 4 ulna 6 radius

forebear 8 ancestor 9 ascendant 10 progenitor 11 antecedents 12 primogenitor

forebode 4 omen 5 augur 7 betoken, portend, predict, presage, promise 8 foretell

foreboding 4 omen 5 dread 6 augury 7 anxiety, portent, presage, warning 9 prenotion 10 prediction, prognostic 11 premonition, presagement 12 presentiment

forecast 5 augur, guess, infer, weird 6 gather 7 foresee, portend, predict, presage, surmise 8 conclude, foreshow, foretell, prophecy, soothsay 9 adumbrate, prevision, prognosis 10 conjecture, prediction, vaticinate 13 prognosticate

forecaster 4 seer 5 augur 6 auspex, oracle 7 prophet 8 haruspex 9 predictor 10 prophesier 11 Nostradamus 13 meteorologist

foreclose 3 bar 5 debar 6 cut off, hinder 7 prevent 8 preclude

forefather see **forebear**

forefeel 6 divine 7 preknow, previse 9 apprehend, prevision, visualize

forefinger 5 index

forefront 8 vanguard

foregoer 7 example 8 ancestor 9 precursor, prototype 10 antecedent, antecessor 11 predecessor

foregoing 4 past 5 prior 8 anterior, previous 9 precedent, preceding 10 antecedent

forehanded 7 prudent, thrifty

forehead 4 brow 5 frons, front 8 sinciput 9 sincipita (plural) *combining form:* 6 fronto *ornamental spot:* 5 tilak

foreign 5 alien 6 exotic 7 strange 9 extrinsic, obnoxious, repellent, repugnant 10 accidental, extraneous, immaterial, inapposite, irrelative, irrelevant 11 distasteful, impertinent, incongruous, inconsonant 12 adventitious, inapplicable, incompatible, inconsistent 13 inappropriate *combining form:* 3 xen 4 xeno

foreigner 5 alien 7 inconnu 8 outsider, stranger

foreknow 6 divine 7 previse 8 conclude 9 apprehend, prevision, visualize 10 anticipate

foreland 4 beak, bill, cape, head, naze 5 point 8 headland 10 promontory

forelock 5 bangs, quiff 8 linchpin, split pin 9 cotter pin

foreman 4 boss 5 chief 6 gaffer, ganger, honcho, leader 7 captain, headman, manager, overman, steward 8 overseer 10 supervisor

foremost 4 arch, head, main 5 chief, first, front 7 initial, leading, premier, supreme 8 champion, headmost 9 inaugural, principal 10 preeminent

forenoon 4 morn 7 morning

forensics 6 debate 7 mooting 11 disputation 13 argumentation

foreordain 4 fate 6 doom to 7 destine, preform 9 determine 10 predestine 12 predestinate, predetermine

forerun 4 pace 6 herald 7 precede, predate, presage 8 announce, antecede, antedate 9 harbinger 10 anticipate, foreshadow

forerunner 4 mark, omen, sign 5 model, token 6 augury, author, herald 7 example, pattern, pioneer, portent, presage, symptom, warning 8 ancestor, exemplar 9 announcer, harbinger, initiator, messenger, precursor, prototype 10 antecedent, antecessor, originator, prognostic 11 anticipator, predecessor 12 announcement

foresee 4 espy 6 descry, divine 7 discern, predict, preknow, presage, previse 8 perceive, prophesy 9 apprehend, prevision, visualize 10 anticipate 13 prognosticate

foreseer 5 augur 6 auspex, oracle 7 diviner, prophet 8 haruspex 9 predictor 10 prophesier, soothsayer 11 Nostradamus

foreshadow 4 bode, hint, omen 5 augur 7 betoken, portend, presage, promise 9 adumbrate, prefigure 11 prefigurate

foresight 6 vision 7 caution 8 prudence, sagacity 9 canniness 10 discretion, perception, precaution, prescience, providence 11 discernment 12 clairvoyance

forest 4 bosk, wood 5 copse, grove, weald, woods 6 timber 7 coppice, thicket, woodlot 8 wildwood, woodland 10 timberland, wilderness *combining form:* 3 hyl 4 hylo *deity:* 5 dryad 6 sylvan 8 Sylvanus *English:* 5 Arden 8 Sherwood *opening:* 5 glade *relating to:* 6 sylvan *subarctic:* 5 taiga *tropical:* 5 selva 6 jungle

forestall 4 ward 5 avert, deter 7 obviate, prevent, rule out 8 preclude, stave off 10 anticipate

Forester *hero:* 10 Hornblower (Horatio) *novel:* 12 African Queen

foretell 4 bode, call, warn 5 augur 6 divine, reveal 7 declare, divulge, portend, predict, presage, promise 8 announce, disclose, proclaim, prophesy, soothsay 9 adumbrate, apprehend, prefigure 10 anticipate, vaticinate 13 prognosticate

foreteller see **foreseer**

forethought 5 sense 7 caution 8 gumption, judgment, prudence 9 canniness, foresight 10 discretion, precaution, providence 12 deliberation, discreetness 13 premeditation

foretime 4 past, yore 9 yesterday 10 yesteryear

foretoken 4 bode, hint, mark, note, omen, sign 5 augur, badge 6 augury, boding, herald, ostent, shadow 7 inkling, portend, portent, presage, promise, symptom, warning 8 bodement, forecast 9 harbinger, precursor 10 indication, intimation

forever 3 aye 4 ever 6 always 7 endless, eternal 8 eternity, evermore 9 endlessly, eternally 11 ceaselessly, continually, everlasting, incessantly, in perpetuum, perpetually, unceasingly 13 everlastingly

forewarning 6 caveat 7 caution 8 monition 10 admonition 11 commonition

foreword 5 proem 7 preface, prelude 8 exordium, overture, preamble, prologue 9 prelusion 12 introduction, prolegomenon

for example 2 as, e.g. 6 such as

for fear that 4 lest

forfeit 4 drop, fine, lose 5 mulct 7 penalty 9 sacrifice 10 amercement

forfend 4 ward 5 avert, deter 6 secure 7 obviate, prevent, protect, rule out, ward off 8 preclude, preserve, stave off

forge 4 beat, copy, make, mold 5 build, pound, shape 6 smithy 7 advance, fashion, imitate, produce, turn out 8 bloomery, progress 9 construct, fabricate 11 counterfeit, manufacture, put together

forget 4 fail, omit 5 fluff 6 blow up, ignore, slight, unknow 7 blink at, neglect, unlearn 8 discount, overlook 9 blink away, disregard 11 disremember 12 misrecollect

forgetful 3 lax 5 slack 6 absent, remiss 7 bemused 8 careless, heedless 9 negligent, oblivious, unwitting 10 abstracted, neglectful 11 inattentive, thoughtless 12 absentminded

forgetfulness 5 lethe 7 amnesia 8 oblivion

forgivable 6 venial 10 pardonable

forgive 5 remit 6 excuse, pardon, slight 7 absolve, condone, neglect 8 overlook

forgo 5 leave, waive 6 eschew, give up, resign 7 abandon, forbear 8 abdicate, abnegate, renounce 9 sacrifice, surrender 10 relinquish

fork 6 bisect, branch, crotch 7 utensil *prong:* 4 tine

fork out 3 pay 5 spend

forlorn 4 vain 5 alone 6 bereft, futile, lonely 7 cynical 8 deserted, desolate, forsaken, helpless, homeless, hopeless, lonesome, solitary, wretched 9 abandoned, depressed, desperate, destitute, fruitless, miserable, oppressed 10 bedraggled, despairing, despondent, desponding, disordered, friendless 11 defenseless, pessimistic 12 disconsolate

form 3 law, way 4 body, cast, make, mode, mold, plan, plot, rite, rule 5 build, canon, forge, found, frame, habit, image, model, shape, style, usage 6 create, custom, design, devise, figure, invent, make up, manner, method, ritual, scheme, system **7** acquire, anatomy, compose, contour, decorum, develop, economy, fashion, liturgy, outline, precept, process, produce, profile, project, turn out **8** ceremony, comprise, organism, organize, practice, skeleton **9** construct, establish, etiquette, fabricate, formality, framework, procedure, propriety, structure **10** ceremonial, constitute, convenance, convention, proceeding, regulation, silhouette **11** manufacture **13** configuration *combining form:* **3** gen **4** gene **5** morph, plasm, plast **6** morpha, morphi (plural) **6** morpho, plasma **7** morphae (plural), morphic **8** morphism **9** morphosis *suffix:* **2** fy **3** ify

formal 3 set **4** prim **5** exact, rigid, stiff **6** dressy, proper, seemly, solemn **7** distant, nominal, orderly, precise, regular, stately, titular **8** decorous, reserved, so-called **9** essential, unbending **10** ceremonial, methodical, systematic **11** ceremonious, syntactical **12** constitutive, conventional

formality 4 form, rite **6** ritual **7** liturgy, service **8** ceremony, insignia **10** ceremonial, convenance, convention, observance

format 4 plan, size **5** shape, style **6** makeup

formation 4 form, rank **6** design, makeup **9** structure **10** production **11** arrangement, composition, development **12** architecture, construction

formative material *combining form:* **5** plasm **6** plasma

former 3 old **4** late, once, past **5** maker, prior **6** bygone, shaper, whilom **7** creator, earlier, onetime, quondam **8** anterior, previous, sometime **9** erstwhile, precedent, preceding **10** antecedent *combining form:* **6** proter **7** protero

formerly 4 erst, once **6** before, whilom **7** already, earlier **9** erstwhile **10** heretofore, previously

formidable 4 hard **5** awful, tough **6** uphill **7** arduous, fearful, labored **8** alarming, dreadful, horrific, shocking, terrible, terrific, toilsome **9** appalling, difficult, effortful, frightful, laborious, strenuous

formless 3 raw **4** rude **5** crude, rough, vague **7** chaotic, obscure, unclear **8** inchoate, unshaped **9** amorphous, shapeless, undefined, unordered **10** immaterial, indefinite, indistinct **11** unorganized

Formosa 6 Taiwan *capital:* **6** Taipei

formulate 3 put **4** make, word **5** couch, draft, frame, hatch **6** cook up, devise, draw up, invent, make up, phrase, vamp up **7** concoct, dream up, express, hatch up, prepare **8** contrive

forsake 4 quit **5** avoid, chuck, leave, spurn **6** defect, depart, desert, reject,

resign **7** abandon **8** abdicate, renounce **9** throw over

forsaken 4 lorn **7** uncouth **8** derelict, deserted, desolate, solitary **9** abandoned

forsaker 8 apostate

Forseti *father:* **6** Balder *palace:* **7** Glitnir

forswear 4 deny **5** unsay **6** abjure, recall, recant, reject **7** perjure, retract **8** palinode, renounce, take back, withdraw

fort 6 castle **7** bastion, bulwark, citadel, redoubt **8** fastness, fortress, martello **10** stronghold *Baltimore:* **7** McHenry *California:* **3** Ord *New Jersey:* **3** Dix *New York:* **7** Niagara, Stanwix **8** Schuyler **11** Ticonderoga *Ontario:* **9** Frontenac *San Antonio:* **8** The Alamo *South Carolina:* **6** Sumter *Spanish:* **7** alcazar **8** presidio

forte 3 bag **5** thing **6** medium, métier, oyster **7** ability **8** ableness, eminency, long suit, strength **10** competence, efficiency, strong suit **11** strong point

forth 2 on **3** out **4** alee **5** ahead, along **6** onward **7** forward

forthcoming 6 future **7** affable, awaited **8** approach, expected, imminent, sociable **11** anticipated, approaching **12** approachable

for the most part 9 generally **10** on the whole

for the time being 6 pro tem **10** pro tempore

forthright 4 open **5** frank, plain **6** candid, direct, single **7** frankly **10** aboveboard **11** openhearted, undisguised, unvarnished

forthwith 3 now **4** away **5** short **6** at once, sudden **7** asudden **8** abruptly, directly, suddenly **9** instanter, instantly, right away, thereupon **11** immediately, straightway **12** straightaway

fortification 4 boma, moat, wall **5** agger, redan **6** abatis, glacis, sangar, sungar **7** barrier, parapet, rampart, ravelin, redoubt **8** barbican, enceinte, palisade **9** barricade, earthwork **10** breastwork *part:* **7** salient

fortify 3 arm **4** gird, stir **5** brace, rally, ready, renew, rouse, steel **6** arouse **7** bulwark, prepare, protect, rampart, refresh, restore **8** energize, palisade **9** encourage **10** invigorate, strengthen

fortitude 4 grit, guts, pith, sand **5** nerve, pluck, spunk, valor **6** bottom, mettle, spirit **7** bravery, courage, stamina **8** backbone, boldness, strength, tenacity, valiancy **9** constancy, endurance **10** resolution **11** intrepidity **12** fearlessness, perseverance, resoluteness, valorousness **13** dauntlessness, determination

fortress see **fort**

fortuitous 3 odd **5** fluky **6** casual, chance **10** accidental, contingent, incidental

fortuity 3 hap 4 luck 6 chance 8 accident

Fortuna 5 Tyche *symbol:* 5 wheel 6 rudder

fortunate 4 good, well 5 happy, lucky, white 6 benign, bright, dexter 9 favorable 10 auspicious, propitious 12 providential

Fortunate Islands 8 Canaries

fortune 3 lot, pot, wad 4 doom, fate, luck, mint, pile 5 worth 6 boodle, bundle, chance, hazard, packet, riches, wealth 7 destiny, portion, success 8 property 9 luckiness, resources, substance

fortune-teller 4 seer 7 palmist; (see also foreteller)

fortune-telling see divination

forty winks 3 nap 6 catnap, dog nap, siesta, snooze

forward 2 on, to 3 aid 4 abet, alee, ante, back, bold, help, pert, send, ship, wise 5 ahead, along, brash, eager, fresh, nervy, ready, relay, remit, route, sassy, saucy, serve, smart, ultra 6 cheeky, foster, hasten, onward, uphold, uppish, uppity 7 address, advance, anxious, consign, extreme, further, promote, pushful, pushing, radical, support 8 advanced, champion, dispatch, impudent, previous, transmit 9 encourage, in advance, presuming 11 overweening, precedently, smart-alecky 12 antecedently, presumptuous 13 self-asserting, self-assertive *prefix:* 4 ante

For Whom the Bell Tolls *author:* 9 Hemingway (Ernest) *character:* 5 Maria, Pablo, Pilar 6 Jordan

foss, fosse 4 moat 5 canal, ditch 6 trench

fossa 3 pit 6 cavity 10 depression

fossil 4 fogy 5 amber 6 square 7 antique 8 calamite, conodont, mossback 10 antiquated, fuddy-duddy 12 antediluvian, mid-Victorian 13 stick-in-the-mud *combining form:* 4 lite, lith, lyte, necr 5 necro, oryct 6 orycto *fuel:* 3 oil 4 coal, peat 9 petroleum

foster 4 back, help, rear, warm 5 favor, house, lodge, nurse, serve 6 assist, harbor, nursle, oblige, uphold 7 advance, cherish, forward, further, nourish, nurture, promote, shelter, support, sustain 8 champion 9 cultivate, encourage, entertain

foul 4 base, soil, vile 5 black, block, dirty, fetid, grime, muddy, nasty, soily 6 besoil, coarse, defile, filthy,. grubby, horrid, impure, odious, putrid, rotten, smirch, smooch, smudge, smutch, smutty, vulgar, wicked 7 abusive, begrime, noisome, obscene, pollute, profane, raunchy, squalid, tarnish, unclean 8 dishonor, feculent, indecent, obstruct, polluted, stinking 9 dangerous, desecrate, entangled, loathsome, obnox-ious, offensive, repellent, repugnant, repulsive, revolting, uncleanly 10 detestable, disgusting, malodorous 11 contaminate 12 scatological

foul play 5 blood 6 murder 7 killing 8 homicide, violence 12 manslaughter

found 4 base, cast, rear, rest, stay 5 begin, erect, raise, set up, start 6 bottom, create 7 fashion, support, sustain 8 commence, initiate, organize 9 establish, institute, originate, predicate

foundation 3 bed 4 base, rest, sill 5 basis 6 bottom 7 bedrock, footing, roadbed, support, warrant 9 endowment 10 substratum 11 institution 12 organization, substructure, underpinning

foundational 5 basic 6 bottom 7 primary 10 underlying 11 fundamental

founder 4 fail, sink, sire 5 wreck 6 author, damage, go down 7 creator 8 collapse, inventor, submerge, submerse 9 architect, generator, patriarch 10 originator

fountain 3 jet 4 head, root 6 origin, source, spring, whence 8 wellhead 9 inception, reservoir 10 wellspring *nymph:* 6 Egeria

four 6 tetrad 7 quartet 10 quaternion *bagger:* 5 homer 7 homerun *combining form:* 4 tetr 5 quadr, tetra 6 quadri, quadru, quater, tessar 7 tessara, tessera *gills:* 4 pint *hundred:* 5 elite 10 upper crust *inches:* 4 hand *pecks:* 6 bushel *quarts:* 6 gallon

fourberie 5 fraud 7 chicane 8 trickery 9 chicanery, deception 10 dishonesty, hanky-panky

four-flush 5 bluff 6 betray, delude, humbug, juggle, take in 7 beguile, deceive 11 double cross

four-footed animal 8 tetrapod 9 quadruped

Four Horsemen 3 War 5 Death 6 Famine 10 Pestilence

four-in-hand 3 tie 7 necktie

fourpence 5 groat

four-poster 3 bed

fourscore 6 eighty

four-sided figure 6 square 7 rhombus 9 rectangle

foursquare 7 solidly 8 quadrate 9 quadratic 10 forthright 11 quadratical 12 forthrightly

fourteen pounds 5 stone

fourth 7 quarter 8 quadrant, quartern *combining form:* 5 quadr, quart 6 quadri, quadru 7 tetarto

fowl 3 hen 4 bird, cock 5 chick, poult 6 Bantam, pullet 7 chicken, rooster; (see also **chicken; poultry**)

fox 4 fool 5 trick 6 baffle, outwit 7 confuse, Reynard 8 bewilder 9 dissemble *female:*

5 vixen *kind:* 6 corsac, corsak, fennec *Scottish:* 3 tod *young:* 3 cub

foxglove 7 mullein 8 pokeweed 9 fairy bell 10 fingerroot

fox grape 9 muscadine

foxiness 3 art 5 craft 7 cunning 8 artifice 10 cleverness

foxlike 7 vulpine

foxy 3 sly 4 deep, wily 6 artful, astute, clever, crafty, shrewd, tricky 7 cunning 8 guileful 9 deceitful, dishonest, insidious

foyer 5 lobby 8 anteroom, entrance 9 vestibule

fracas 3 row 4 feud 5 brawl, broil, fight, melee, run-in, set-to 6 affray, hassle 7 dispute, quarrel, ruction 8 squabble 9 bickering 10 donnybrook 11 altercation

fraction 3 bit, cut 4 part 5 piece, scrap 6 divide, little 7 portion, section 8 fragment

fractious 4 wild 5 cross, huffy, waspy 6 unruly 7 fretful, peevish, pettish, waspish 8 contrary, indocile, petulant, snappish 9 irritable 10 refractory 11 indomitable, intractable, quarrelsome 12 recalcitrant, ungovernable, unmanageable

fracturable 7 fragile 8 delicate, shattery 9 breakable

fracture 4 rent, rift, tear 5 break, cleft, crack, split 6 breach, schism 7 rupture, violate *combining form:* 7 rrhexis

Fra Diavolo composer 5 Auber (Esprit)

fragile 4 fine, thin, weak 5 crisp, frail, short 6 feeble, flimsy, infirm, slight, weakly 7 brittle, crumbly, crunchy, friable, slender, tenuous, unsound 8 decrepit, delicate, shattery

fragment 3 ace, bit, end, jot 4 atom, chip, iota, part, rive 5 burst, crumb, flake, grain, minim, piece, scrap, shard, sherd, shive, shred, smash, spall 6 morsel, shiver, sliver 7 flinder, shatter 8 particle, splinter, splitter 11 splinterize

fragmentary 4 part 6 broken 7 partial 10 fractional, incomplete 12 disorganized

fragrance 4 balm, odor 5 aroma, scent, smell, spice 7 bouquet, incense, perfume 9 redolence

fragrant 5 balmy, spicy, sweet 6 aromal, savory 7 perfumy 8 aromatic, perfumed, redolent 9 ambrosial, delicious

frail 4 puny, slim, thin, weak 5 petty 6 feeble, flimsy, infirm, sickly, slight, weakly 7 fragile, slender, tenuous, unsound 8 decrepit, delicate, shattery 9 breakable, frangible 11 fracturable, shatterable

frailty 3 sin 4 vice 5 fault 6 foible 7 failing 8 weakness 9 infirmity 11 tenuousness 12 imperfection

frame 4 body, form, make, mold, plan, sash 5 build, cause, draft, easel, erect, forge, shape, state, utter 6 cook up, deckle, devise, draw up, figure, invent, make up, system, vamp up 7 arrange, chassis, concoct, dream up, fashion, hatch up, imagine, prepare, produce 8 casement, conceive, contrive, regulate 9 cartouche, construct, fabricate, formulate *part:* 4 sill, stud 5 joist, plate

framework 4 rack 7 trestle 8 cribbing, cribwork, scaffold, skeleton, studding, studwork, trussing 9 structure *of crossed strips:* 7 lattice, trellis

France *ancient name:* 4 Gaul 6 Gallia *capital:* 5 Paris *combining form:* 5 Gallo *historic province:* 4 Foix 5 Anjou, Aunis, Beam, Berry, Maine 6 Alsace, Artois, Marche, Poitou 7 Gascony, Guyenne, Picardy 8 Auvergne, Brittany, Burgundy, Dauphine, Flanders, Limousin, Lorraine, Lyonnais, Normandy, Provence, Touraine 9 Angoumois, Champagne, Languedoc, Nivernais, Orleanais, Saintonge, Venaissin 10 Roussillon 11 Bourbonnais, Ile de France 12 Franche Comte *monetary unit:* 5 franc

Francesca's lover 5 Paolo

franchise 4 vote 6 ballot 8 suffrage 9 exemption

frangible 7 brittle, fragile 8 delicate, shattery 9 breakable

frank 3 dog 4 fair, free, just, open 5 bluff, blunt, naive, plain 6 brazen, candid, direct, honest, hot dog, simple, single, wiener 7 natural, sincere, upright 8 man-to-man, unbiased 9 barefaced, impartial, ingenuous, outspoken 10 forthright, scrupulous, single-eyed, unmannered, unreserved 11 openhearted, plainspoken, unconcealed, undisguised, uninhibited, unvarnished, wienerwurst

Frankenstein author 7 Shelley (Mary)

frankfurter 3 dog 6 hot dog, wiener 11 wienerwurst

Frankie's lover 6 Johnny

Frankish hero 6 Roland

Franklin *birthplace:* 6 Boston *invention:* 5 stove 8 bifocals *pen name:* 11 Poor Richard

frankness 6 candor 8 openness

frantic 3 mad 4 wild 5 rabid 6 insane 7 extreme, furious, violent 8 deranged, feverish, frenetic, frenzied 9 delirious, desperate 10 distraught

fraternal society 4 Elks 5 Moose 6 Eagles, Masons 10 Hibernians, Odd Fellows

fraternity 4 club 5 guild, order, union 6 league 7 company 10 fellowship 11 association, brotherhood 13 brotherliness

fraud 4 fake, hoax, sell, sham 5 cheat, faker, phony, trick 6 deceit, dupery, duping, humbug 7 chicane, defraud, swindle 8 impostor, trickery 9 chicanery, deception, fourberie, imposture, pretender, trickster 10 hanky-panky 11 bamboozling, highbinding, hoodwinking 13 bamboozlement, double-dealing, sharp practice

fraudulence 6 deceit 8 quackery, trickery 9 chicanery, deception, fourberie, phoniness 10 dishonesty

fraudulent 4 fake 5 false 7 crooked 8 cheating, guileful, quackish 9 deceitful, deceiving, deceptive, dishonest 10 fallacious

fray 3 row 4 fret 5 brawl, broil, brush, clash, fight, melee 6 combat, debate, strife, tumult 7 discord, dispute, quarrel, ruction, scuffle 8 skirmish 9 commotion, scrimmage 10 contention, dissension, donnybrook

frayed 4 worn 6 ragged 7 shreddy 10 threadbare

frazzle 4 fray, wear 5 upset 6 tucker 7 exhaust, outtire, outwear, wear out 8 knock out 9 prostrate

freak 3 bug, nut 4 whim 5 fancy, fiend, lusus 6 maniac, megrim, oddity, rarity, vagary, whimsy, zealot 7 anomaly, boutade, caprice, chimera, conceit, fanatic, monster, whimsey 8 crotchet, misshape, mutation, rara avis 9 androgyne, curiosity 10 aberration, enthusiast 11 abnormality, miscreation, monstrosity 12 malformation, whimsicality

freckle 3 dot 4 spot 7 ephelis, lentigo, speckle, stipple

free 3 lax, rid 4 open 5 clear, loose, round, unmew, unpen, untie, vocal 6 acquit, detach, exempt, gratis, loosen, ransom, redeem, rescue, unbind, uncurb, unpaid, untied, vagile 7 absolve, deliver, liberal, manumit, release, unbound, unchain, unclasp, unleash, unloose 8 autarkic, costless, detached, generous, handsome, liberate, released, separate, sui juris, unburden, unfasten, unloosen, untether 9 autarchic, bounteous, bountiful, delivered, discharge, disengage, exculpate, exonerate, extricate, liberated, outspoken, sovereign, unchained, unchecked, unshackle, unsparing 10 autonomous, chargeless, democratic, emancipate, gratuitous, heart-whole, munificent, openhanded, self-ruling, unconfined, unenslaved, unfettered, unshackled 11 affranchise, disencumber, disentangle, disenthrall, disimprison, emancipated, enfranchise, independent, untrammeled 12 enfranchised, unregimented, unrestrained, unrestricted 13 complimentary, self-directing, self-governing, unconstrained, unrecompensed, unremunerated

freebie 4 gift, pass 7 present 8 giveaway

freebooter 5 rover 6 bandit, bummer, pirate, raider, sea dog 7 brigand, cateran, corsair, forager, sea wolf 8 marauder, picaroon, pillager

freedom 4 ease 5 right, scope, sweep 7 compass, liberty, license, release 8 facility, immunity, latitude, vagility 9 exemption, privilege 10 generosity 11 magnanimity, prerogative 12 emancipation, independence

free-for-all 4 fray 5 brawl, broil, fight, melee, spree 6 affray, fracas 7 ruction 10 donnybrook

freehanded 7 liberal 8 generous 9 bounteous, bountiful, unsparing 10 munificent, openhanded

freeloader 5 leech 6 sponge 8 barnacle, hanger-on, parasite 12 lounge lizard

freeman 4 carl 5 carle, churl, thane, thegn 6 yeoman 7 burgess, burgher, citizen

Free State 8 Maryland

free ticket 4 pass 11 Annie Oakley

freezing 3 icy 4 cold 5 chill, gelid, nippy 6 arctic, chilly, frigid, frosty 7 glacial, shivery *combining form:* 3 cry 4 cryo, kryo

freight 4 haul, load 5 cargo 6 burden, charge, lading 7 payload 9 transport

French *article:* 2 la, le, un 3 les, une *attendant:* 9 concierge *back:* 3 dos *bed:* 3 lit 6 couche *boy:* 6 garçon *brother:* 5 frère *cap:* 5 beret *cardinal:* 7 Mazarin (Jules) 9 Richelieu (Duc de) *castle:* 7 château *cathedral city:* 4 Albi 5 Paris, Reims, Rouen 6 Amiens, Nantes, Rheims 8 Chartres *clergyman:* 4 abbé, curé, père *combining form:* 5 Gallo 6 Franco *conjunction:* 2 et, ou 4 mais *couturier:* 4 Dior (Christian) 5 Patou (Jean) 6 Chanel (Coco) 7 Balmain (Pierre) 8 Givenchy (Hubert) 9 Courrèges (Andre), St. Laurent (Yves) *daughter:* 5 fille *day:* 5 jeudi, lundi, mardi 6 samedi 8 dimanche, mercredi, vendredi *dear:* 4 cher *department head:* 7 prefect *direction:* 3 est, sud 4 nord 5 ouest *down with:* 4 a bas *dream:* 4 rêve *drink:* 5 boire *dynasty:* 5 Capet 6 Valois 7 Bourbon *egg:* 4 oeuf *emblem:* 10 fleur-de-lis *empress:* 7 Eugénie 9 Joséphine *evening:* 4 soir *exclamation:* 3 zut 4 eheu, hein 9 sacrebleu *farewell:* 5 adieu 8 au revoir *father:* 4 père *forest:* 7 Argonne, Belleau *friend:* 3 ami 4 amie *game:* 3 jeu 4 jeux (plural) *God:* 4 dieu *good:* 3 bon *hat:* 7 chapeau *here:* 3 ici *income:* 5 rente *king:* 3 roi *language:* 9 Provençal *month:* 3 mai 4 août, juin, mars, mois 5 avril 7 février, janvier, juillet *mother:* 4 mère *national anthem:* 12 Marseillaise *opera:* 5 Faust, Lakmé, Manon, Thaïs 6 Carmen, Mignon 7 Werther *pancake:* 5 crêpe *pastry:* 6 éclair 8 napoleon *patron saint:* 5 Denis *policeman:* 4 flic 8 gendarme *porcelain:* 6 Sèvres 7 Limoges *preposition:* 2 de 3 par, sur 4 avec, dans, pour, sans, sous *pretty:* 4 joli 5 jolie *prison:* 8 Bastille *pronoun:* 2 il, je, te, tu, un 3 eux, ils, mes, moi, toi, une 4 elle, nous, vous *Protestant:* 6 Calvin 8 Huguenot *pupil:* 5 élève *queen:* 5 reine *rabbit:* 5 lapin *railroad station:* 4 gare *resort:* 3 Pau 4 Nice 5 Vichy 6 Cannes, Menton 7 Antibes 8 Biarritz *resort area:* 7 Riviera *restaurant:* 6 bistro *revolutionist:* 5 Marat (Jean-Paul) 6 Danton (Georges-Jacques) *Revolution party:* 7 Gironde, Jacobin 8 Mountain *Revolution song:* 5 Caira *saint:* 4 Joan 6 Martin *school:* 5 école, lycée *sea:* 3 mer *season:* 3 été 5 hiver 7 automne 9 printemps *servant:* 5 valet *shop:* 8 boutique *shrine:* 7 Lourdes *singer:* 4 Piaf (Edith) 8 chanteur 9 chanteuse *sister:* 5 soeur *small:* 5 petit 6 petite *soldier:* 5 poilu 6 soldat, Zouave 8 chasseur *son:* 4 fils *star:* 6 étoile *state:* 4 état *stock exchange:* 6 bourse *street:* 3 rue *subway:* 5 metro *there!:* 5 voilà *too much:* 4 trop *very:* 4 très *waiter:* 6 garçon *wartime capital:* 5 Vichy *water:* 3 eau *well:* 4 bien *wineshop:* 6 bistro *wood:* 4 bois *yesterday:* 4 hier

frenetic 3 mad 4 wild 5 crazy, rabid 6 hectic 7 frantic, furious, violent 8 frenzied 9 delirious

frenzied see frenetic

frenzy 3 mad 4 amok, fury, rage 5 amuck, craze, furor, mania 6 madden 7 derange, madness, unhinge 8 delirium, distract, insanity 9 unbalance *of a bull elephant:* 4 must 5 musth

frequency unit 5 hertz 7 fresnel

frequent 5 haunt, often, usual, visit 6 affect, attend, common, infest, resort 7 hang out, overrun 8 everyday, familiar, habitual 9 customary 10 hang around

frequenter 7 denizen, habitué, haunter

fresh 3 new, raw 4 anew, bold, else, more, pert, pure, rude, wise 5 added, alive, brisk, crude, green, naive, nervy, novel, other, renew, sassy, saucy, smart, sweet, vital, vivid, young 6 bright, callow, cheeky, lively, modern, recent, unused 7 another, artless, farther, forward, further, natural, uncouth, untried 8 gleaming, impudent, neoteric, original, striking, unversed, virginal, youthful 9 new-sprung, sparkling, unspoiled 10 additional, glistening, newfangled, unseasoned 11 impertinent, modernistic, smart-

alecky, unpracticed 12 invigorating, new-fashioned 13 inexperienced

freshet 5 flood, spate

freshman 4 colt, tyro 5 frosh, plebe 6 novice, rookie 8 beginner, neophyte, newcomer 9 novitiate 10 apprentice, tenderfoot

fret 3 irk, nag, rub, vex 4 cark, fray, fume, fuss, gall, gnaw, mope, stew, wear 5 annoy, brood, chafe, grate, ravel, worry 6 abrade, bother, cockle, dimple, dither, harass, nettle, plague, pother, rankle, riffle, ruffle 7 agitate, corrode, disturb, provoke, roughen, torment 8 exercise, irritate 9 excoriate 10 irritation

fretful 5 angry, cross, huffy, waspy 7 carping, chafing, peevish, pettish, waspish 8 captious, caviling, contrary, critical, perverse, petulant, restless, snappish 9 fractious, impatient, irascible, irritable, querulous, unpatient 12 faultfinding

Frey *father:* 5 Njord 6 Njorth *sister:* 5 Freya *wife:* 4 Gerd 5 Gerda, Gerth

Freya *brother:* 4 Frey *father:* 5 Njord 6 Njorth *husband:* 4 Odin

friable 5 crisp, mealy, short 7 crumbly, crunchy

fribble 5 dizzy, giddy, light 7 flighty, trifler 8 trifling 9 frivolous 11 harebrained, light-headed

friction 7 discord, rubbing 8 abrasion 9 attrition 10 disharmony, dissension, resistance 12 disagreement

friction match 5 vesta 7 lucifer 8 locofoco

Friday's rescuer 6 Crusoe (Robinson)

friend 3 aid, pal 4 ally, chum, mate 5 buddy, crony, matey, serve 7 comrade, partner 8 alter ego, compadre, familiar, intimate, playmate, sidekick 9 associate, colleague, companion, confidant 10 confidante 11 cater-cousin 12 acquaintance *French:* 3 ami 4 amie *Scottish:* 3 eme *Spanish:* 5 amiga, amigo

Friend 6 Quaker *founder:* 3 Fox (George)

friendly 5 close, pally 6 amical, chummy, loving 7 affable, amiable, cordial, devoted 8 amicable, amicably, familiar, intimate, sociable 9 congenial, favorable, receptive 10 harmonious, hospitable 11 sympathetic 12 affectionate, well-disposed

Friendly Islands 5 Tonga

friends 4 kith

friendship 5 amity 6 accord, comity, fusion, league 7 concord, empathy, harmony 8 affinity, alliance, goodwill 9 coalition 10 attraction, consonance, federation, kindliness 11 benevolence

frigate bird 3 ioa, iwa 8 alcatras *genus:* 7 Fregata

Frigga, Frigg *husband:* 4 Odin *son:* 6 Balder

fright 3 awe 4 fear, mess 5 alarm, dread, panic, scare, shock 6 dismay, horror, terror 7 eyesore, startle, terrify 9 terrorize, trepidity 11 trepidation

frighten 3 awe, cow 4 faze 5 alarm, daunt, scare, shock, unman, upset 6 affray, appall, dismay 7 agitate, astound, horrify, perturb, startle, terrify, unnerve 8 affright, browbeat, bulldoze, disquiet 9 terrorize 10 demoralize, discompose, disconcert, intimidate

frightful 4 grim 5 awful, scary 6 horrid 7 fearful, ghastly, hideous 8 alarming, dreadful, fearsome, horrible, horrific, shocking, terrible, terrific 9 appalling 10 formidable, horrendous

frigid 3 icy 4 cold, cool, dull 5 bleak, chill 6 arctic, chilly, frosty 7 glacial, hostile, insipid 8 freezing 9 inhibited 10 undersexed 11 emotionless, indifferent, passionless, unemotional 12 unresponsive

frill 3 air 5 jabot, luxus, ruche 6 luxury, ruffle 7 amenity, flounce, ruching 8 furbelow 11 affectation, superfluity 12 extravagance

fringe 3 hem, rim 4 brim 5 bound, brink, skirt, verge 6 border, define, edging, margin 7 fimbria 8 surround, trimming 9 perimeter, periphery

frippery 6 finery 7 bravery, regalia 8 trumpery 9 full dress 10 Sunday best 11 ostentation

frisk 4 leap, romp, skip 5 caper, dance 6 cavort, curvet, frolic, gambol, search 7 disport, rollick 9 shake down

frisky 3 gay 5 antic 6 feisty, lively 7 larkish, playful, waggish 8 gamesome, prankish, sportive 9 kittenish 10 frolicsome

fritter 4 blow 5 shred, spend, waste 7 consume 8 cast away, diminish, disperse, fool away, fragment, squander 9 dissipate, throw away 10 trifle away

frivolity 3 fun 4 game, jest, play 5 sport 6 levity, toying 8 dallying, flirting, nonsense, trifling 9 flippancy, lightness 10 coquetting 11 flightiness

frivolous 3 gay 5 dizzy, giddy, light, silly 6 toyish 7 flighty, playful, shallow, trivial 8 carefree, careless, heedless 10 bird-witted, unprofound 11 empty-headed, harebrained, superficial 13 rattlebrained

frog 4 toad 5 ranid 6 anuran 9 amphibian 10 batrachian *combining form:* 4 rani 7 batrach 8 batracho 9 batrachus *family:* 7 Ranidae *genus:* 4 Rana *kind:* 4 hyla 6 peeper 8 bullfrog, tree toad *larva:* 7 tadpole *relating to:* 6 ranine

frogmouth 8 morepork

frolic 3 fun, gay 4 hell, lark, riot, romp 5 caper, dance, frisk, merry, party, prank, revel, sport, spree, trick 6 cavort, didoes,

gaiety, gambol, prance, shines 7 carouse, disport, roister, rollick, wassail 9 merriment 10 shenanigan, tomfoolery

frolicsome 3 gay 5 antic 6 frisky, impish 7 coltish, playful, roguish, waggish 8 sportive 9 sprightly 10 rollicking 11 mischievous

from *French, Portuguese, Spanish:* 2 de *German:* 3 von *Italian:* 2 da *Scottish:* 4 frae

frondeur 5 rebel 6 anarch 8 mutineer, revolter 9 anarchist, dissident, insurgent 10 malcontent

front 3 bow, van 4 brow, dare, defy, face, fore, look, mask, meet, prow, show, veil 5 beard, blind, brave, close, color, put-on 6 accost, before, facade, facing 7 forward, outdare, outface, venture 8 anterior, coloring, disguise, forehead 9 challenge, encounter 10 appearance, figurehead 11 countenance *combining form:* 6 antero *prefix:* 3 pro

frontier 4 back, bush 5 march 6 border, remote, sticks 8 backland, backwash, boundary 9 backwater, backwoods, bordering, marchland, unsettled, up-country 10 borderland, hinterland, outlandish 11 backcountry, exploratory 12 conterminous

frontiersman 5 Boone (Daniel), Clark (George Rogers, William) 6 Carson (Kit) 7 pioneer, settler 8 Crockett (Davy) 10 bushranger

fronton game 7 jai alai

front-rank 5 prime 6 Grade A 8 five-star, superior, top-notch 9 excellent, first-rate, top-drawer 10 blue-ribbon, first-class 11 first-string

frontward 8 anterior

frost 4 hoar 6 freeze *combining form:* 4 crym 5 crymo

frostfish 5 smelt 6 tomcod

frost heave 5 pingo

frosting 5 icing 7 topping

frosty 3 icy 4 cold, cool, rimy 5 chill, gelid, hoary, nippy, rimed 6 chilly, frigid 7 glacial, shivery 8 freezing, reserved 10 unfriendly

froth 4 barm, foam, scum, suds, vent 5 spume, yeast 6 lather, levity 9 flippancy, frivolity, lightness

froward 5 balky, cross 6 ornery 7 peevish, restive 8 contrary, perverse, petulant 10 refractory 11 disobedient

frown 4 pout, sulk 5 glare, gloom, lower, scowl 6 glower, object 7 grimace 8 disfavor 9 deprecate, disesteem 10 disapprove

frowsy 3 lax 4 mean, rank 5 dowdy, funky, fusty, musty, slack, stale 6 blowsy, remiss, shabby, smelly, sordid 7 noisome, reeking, squalid, unkempt 8 slattern, slovenly, stinking **9** negligent **10** disheveled, disordered, malodorous, neglectful, slatternly **13** draggletailed

frozen 4 hard **5** fixed, frore, gelid, rigid, stiff **6** chilly, frigid **7** chilled **8** benumbed, immobile **9** congealed, impassive, petrified **10** mechanical, unyielding **12** refrigerated

frugal 4 mean, wary **5** canny, chary, spare **6** saving, scanty, Scotch **7** careful, prudent, sparing, thrifty **8** discreet, stinting **9** scrimping, stewardly **10** conserving, economical, meticulous, preserving, unwasteful **12** cheeseparing, parsimonious **13** pennypinching

frugality 6 thrift **7** economy **8** prudence **9** husbandry **10** providence **11** thriftiness

fruit 5 issue, young **6** result **7** progeny **9** offspring *citrus:* **4** lime **5** lemon **6** citron, orange, pomelo **7** kumquat, tangelo **8** bergamot, mandarin, shaddock **9** tangerine **10** calamondin, grapefruit *combining form:* **4** carp **5** carpo **6** carpia (plural), carpic, carpus, fructi **7** carpium, carpous *decay:* **4** blet *dried:* **5** prune **6** raisin *drink:* **3** ade **5** juice, punch *fleshy:* **7** syconia (plural) **8** syconium *hard-shelled:* **3** nut **4** seed **5** gourd **7** coconut *residue:* **4** marc **6** pomace *seed:* **3** pip *study of:* **8** pomology **9** carpology *subtropical:* **3** fig **4** date, lime **5** lemon, olive **6** citron, orange **7** avocado, kumquat **9** tangerine **10** grapefruit *sugar:* **7** glucose **8** fructose, levulose *temperate zone:* **4** pear, plum, sloe **5** apple, grape, melon, peach, prune **6** casaba, cherry, loquat, quince **7** apricot, azarole, currant **8** dewberry **9** blueberry, cranberry, muskmelon, nectarine, raspberry **10** blackberry, gooseberry, loganberry, strawberry **11** boysenberry, huckleberry, pomegranate *tropical:* **5** guava, mango **6** ajowan, banana, papaya **7** acerola **8** breadnut, rambutan, tamarind **9** cherimoya, persimmon, pineapple **10** calamondin, mangosteen *type:* **3** nut **4** pepo, pome **5** berry, drupe **6** achene, legume, loment, samara **7** capsule, cypsela, silicle, silique, utricle **11** hesperidium *undeveloped:* **6** nubbin *woody:* **8** xylocarp

fruit basket 8 calathos, calathus

fruitful 4 rich **6** fecund **7** fertile **8** abundant, breeding, childing, prolific, spawning **9** abounding, plenteous, plentiful **10** productive **11** proliferant, propagating, reproducing

fruition 3 joy **7** delight, joyance **8** pleasure **9** enjoyment **10** attainment, conclusion **11** achievement, delectation, fulfillment, realization

fruitless 4 vain **6** barren, foiled, futile **7** sterile, useless **8** abortive, thwarted

9 infertile **10** unavailing **11** ineffective, ineffectual, infructuous, unavailable **12** unproductive, unprofitable

frumpy 4 drab, dull **5** dowdy, tacky **6** stodgy **8** outmoded **9** out-of-date, unstylish

frustrate 3 bar **4** balk, beat, bilk, dash, foil, halt, lick, null, ruin, vain **5** annul, block, check, cross, elude **6** arrest, baffle, blight, cancel, defeat, forbid, hinder, impede, outwit, thwart **7** buffalo, conquer, inhibit, nullify, prevent, redress **8** confound, negative, obstruct, overcome, preclude, prohibit **9** cancel out, checkmate, forestall, interrupt **10** circumvent, counteract, disappoint, neutralize

fry 5 sauté **6** sizzle

frying pan 6 spider **7** griddle, skillet

fuddle 5 mix up **6** ball up, jumble, muddle, tipple **7** confuse, fluster, stupefy **8** bewilder, distract, throw off **10** intoxicate

fuddy-duddy 4 fogy **5** Blimp, fussy **6** fogram, fossil, square **7** fusspot **8** mossback, outdated **10** fuss-budget **12** antediluvian, Colonel Blimp, mid-Victorian, stuffed shirt **13** stick-in-the-mud

fudge 3 pad **4** blur, bosh, fake **5** cheat, color, dodge, hedge, hooey, welsh **6** bunkum **7** distort, hogwash, magnify, traddle **8** contrive, nonsense, overdraw **9** embellish, embroider, overpaint, overstate, poppycock **10** exaggerate, overcharge

fuel 3 gas, oil **4** coal, coke, food, peat, wood **5** stoke **6** petrol **7** support **8** charcoal, gasoline, hypergol, kerosene **9** petroleum, stimulate **13** reinforcement

fugacious 6 flying **7** passing **8** fleeting, volatile **9** ephemeral, momentary, transient **10** evanescent, short-lived, transitory

fugitive 2 DP **5** exile **6** emigré, outlaw **7** evacuee, lamster, passing, refugee, runaway **8** deserter, fleeting, vagabond, volatile **9** ephemeral, momentary, transient **10** evanescent, perishable, short-lived, transitory

fugue master 4 Bach (Johann Sebastian)

Führer, der 6 Hitler (Adolf)

fulfill 4 fill, meet **6** answer, effect, finish **7** achieve, execute, perform, satisfy **8** complete **9** discharge, implement **10** accomplish, effectuate

fulgent 6 bright **7** beaming, radiant, shining **8** luminous **9** brilliant

full 3 big **5** awash, jaded, plumb, round, sated, total, whole **6** choate, entire, gorged, jammed, loaded, minute, packed **7** brimful, copious, crammed, crowded, glutted, orotund, perfect, replete, satiate, stuffed, teem-

ing 8 brimming, complete, detailed, integral, itemized, satiated, thorough
9 abounding, clocklike, jam-packed, plentiful, surfeited

full-blooded 4 rich 5 flush, ruddy
6 ardent, florid 7 flushed, genuine, glowing
8 forceful, pedigree, purebred, rubicund,
sanguine 9 impelling, pedigreed, pureblood
12 thoroughbred

full bloom 8 anthesis

full-blown 4 lush, ripe 5 adult, total 6 all-out, mature 7 grown-up, matured, ripened
9 unlimited 12 totalitarian

full-bodied 5 lusty, stout 6 potent, robust,
strong 9 corpulent 11 substantial

full-bosomed 5 busty, buxom 6 chesty

full dress 6 finery 7 bravery, regalia
8 frippery 10 Sunday best

full-figured 6 zaftig, zoftig

full-fledged 4 ripe 5 adult, grown
6 mature 7 genuine, grown-up, matured,
ripened 12 card-carrying

full-grown 4 ripe 5 adult 6 mature
7 matured, ripened

fullness 5 scope 6 plenty 7 breadth, satiety 9 abundance, amplitude, repletion
10 perfection 12 completeness

full of *suffix:* 3 ose, ous 4 ious

full-scale 5 total 6 all-out 8 complete
9 unlimited 12 totalitarian

full tilt 4 fast 7 flat-out, hastily, quickly,
rapidly, swiftly 8 speedily 9 posthaste
12 lickety-split 13 expeditiously

fulsome 3 fat 4 full, glib, oily 5 bland,
plump, slick, soapy, suave 6 lavish, sating,
smarmy, smooth 7 buttery, canting, cloying, copious, profuse 8 abundant, unctious,
unctuous 9 bombastic, excessive, exuberant, repulsive, satiating, sickening, wheedling 10 disgusting, flattering, nauseating,
oleaginous 11 extravagant, oily-tongued,
pharisaical 12 honey-mouthed, honey-tongued, hypocritical, ingratiating, magniloquent, mealy-mouthed, pecksniffian

Fulton's steamboat 8 Clermont

fumble 3 paw 4 feel, flub, mess, muff
5 botch, error, grope 6 bobble, bollix, bungle, goof up, muddle, mumble, murmur, mutter 7 blunder, louse up, misplay, swallow
8 flounder

fume 4 boil, burn, odor, rage, reek, snit,
stew 5 anger, smoke, sweat, tizzy, vapor
6 blow up, seethe, swivet 7 bristle, flare up
8 boil over 10 exhalation

fun 3 gag, kid, rag, rib 4 fool, game, glee,
jest, joke, josh, play, razz 5 jolly, mirth,
sport 6 banter, gaiety 7 disport, jollity,
teasing, whoopee 8 hilarity, mischief, ridicule 9 amusement, diversion, high jinks,
horseplay, jocundity, joviality, merriment

10 blitheness, pleasantry, recreation
13 entertainment

function 2 do, go 3 act, job, run, use
4 duty, goal, mark, role, take, task, work
5 power, react, serve 6 affair, behave,
object, office, target 7 concern, faculty,
operate, perform, purpose, service 8 activity, behavior, business, ceremony, occasion, province 9 objective, officiate, operation *suffix:* 2 cy 3 ure *trigonometric:*
4 sine 6 cosine, secant 7 tangent 8 cosecant 9 cotangent

functional 5 handy, utile 6 useful 7 working 9 practical 11 practicable, serviceable,
utilitarian 12 occupational

functioning 4 live 5 alive 6 active
7 dynamic 9 operative

fund 4 pool 5 endow, stock, store 6 supply
7 capital, finance, reserve 9 inventory, subsidize 10 accumulate

fundament 4 beam, rear, rump, seat
6 behind, bottom 8 backside, buttocks, derriere 9 posterior 10 foundation

fundamental 3 law 4 pure 5 axiom,
basal, basic, prime, vital 6 bottom, factor,
primal 7 needful, primary, radical, theorem
8 cardinal, dominant 9 component, essential, formative, important, necessary, paramount, primitive, principal, principle, requisite 10 elementary, primordial, principium,
substratal, underlying 11 constituent, irreducible 12 constitutive, foundational

fundamentalist 4 tory 5 right 7 diehard
8 old liner, standpat 11 bitter-ender, right-winger, standpatter 12 conservative

fundamental nature 7 essence

fund-raiser 6 dinner 8 telethon

funeral 6 burial *car:* 6 hearse *director:*
9 mortician 10 undertaker *oration:*
6 eulogy 8 encomium 9 panegyric *procession:* 6 exequy 7 cortege *service:*
7 requiem 9 obsequies *song:* 5 dirge,
elegy 7 epicede 8 threnody 9 epicedium

funereal 4 back 5 bleak, grave 6 dismal,
dreary, gloomy, solemn, somber 8 mournful 10 depressing, depressive, lugubrious,
oppressive 13 disheartening

fungus 4 cepe, mold, rust, smut 5 ergot,
morel, yeast 6 agaric, bolete, mildew
7 amanita, truffle 8 mushroom, polypore,
puffball 9 earthstar, stinkhorn, toadstool
10 champignon 11 chanterelle *combining
form:* 3 myc 4 myco 5 myces, mycet
6 mycete, myceto 7 mycetes *part:* 3 cap
4 gill, umbo 5 ascus, gleba, hypha, stipe,
volva 7 annulus, cortina 8 basidium, conidium, mycelium

fungus disease 3 rot 4 mold, rust, scab,
smut 5 ergot, tinea 6 blight, mildew, thrush

7 mycosis 8 lumpy jaw, ringworm 12 athlete's foot *suffix:* 4 oses (plural), osis

funk 4 odor, rage, reek 5 dread, panic, smell, stink 6 coward, craven, flinch, stench 7 chicken, dastard, quitter, shirker 8 poltroon 11 yellowbelly

funky 4 foul, rank 5 musty, stale 6 frowsy, smelly 7 noisome, panicky, reeking 8 stinking 10 malodorous

funnel 4 pipe 5 carry, widen 6 convey, narrow, siphon 7 conduct, traject 8 transmit

funny 3 odd 4 zany 5 antic, comic, droll, fishy, queer 6 sneaky 7 amusing, bizarre, comical, jocular, risible, strange 8 farcical, gelastic, humorous 9 facetious, fantastic, grotesque, laughable, ludicrous 10 ridiculous 11 underhanded

funnyman 3 wag, wit 5 comic, droll, joker 6 jester 8 comedian, humorist, jokester, quipster

fur 4 down, fell, flue, hide, lint, pelt, pile, skin 5 floss, fluff, stole 6 jacket, pelage, peltry *kind:* 3 fox 4 mink, seal 5 fitch, otter, sable 6 ermine, fisher, marten, nutria, tanuki 7 raccoon 10 chinchilla *lamb:* 6 galyak, mouton 7 caracul, karakul, krimmer 9 broadtail *medieval:* 4 vair 7 miniver

furbish 3 rub 4 buff 5 glaze, gloss, shine 6 glance, polish, revive 7 burnish 8 renovate

Furies 6 Alecto 7 Erinyes, Megaera 9 Eumenides, Tisiphone

furious 3 mad 4 wild 5 angry, dirty, hasty, irate, rabid, rough, upset 6 crazed, fierce, insane, maniac, raging, stormy 7 enraged, excited, extreme, fanatic, frantic, intense, violent 8 blustery, demented, feverish, frenetic, frenzied, furibund, incensed, maddened, provoked, terrible, vehement, vigorous, wrathful 9 desperate, energetic, excessive, exquisite, fanatical, impetuous, turbulent 10 bewildered, blustering, boisterous, corybantic, distracted, hysterical, infuriated, inordinate, irrational

furl 4 curl, fold, roll, wrap 5 cover 6 enfold 7 wrinkle

furnace 4 kiln, oven 5 forge, stove 6 heater 7 smelter 8 bloomery, tryworks 11 incinerator *part:* 4 port, vent 5 bocca 6 trompe, tuyere *tender:* 6 stoker

furnish 3 arm, rig 4 feed, gear, give, hand, lend 5 array, dower, endow, endue, equip, mount, yield 6 afford, clothe, fit out, outfit, supply 7 apparel, appoint, deliver, provide, turn out 8 accouter, dispense, hand over, transfer, turn over 10 contribute

furnishings 4 gear 5 decor 9 equipment, trappings

furniture 8 equipage, hardware 9 equipment 10 furnishing *shoddy:* 5 borax *style:* 4 Adam 6 Empire 8 Colonial, Sheraton 9 Queen Anne 11 chinoiserie, Chippendale, Hepplewhite

furniture designer *American:* 5 Phyfe (Duncan) 7 Goddard (John, Stephen, Thomas), Haldane (William) *British:* 6 Morris (William) 7 Gibbons (Grinling), Shearer (Thomas) 8 Sheraton (Thomas) 11 Chippendale (Thomas), Hepplewhite (George) *French:* 5 Marot (Daniel) 6 Boulle (André-Charles) *Scottish:* 4 Adam (James, Robert)

furor 3 ado, cry, fad 4 chic, coil, fury, mode, rage, stir, to-do 5 craze, mania, style, vogue, whirl 6 bustle, flurry, frenzy, pother, ruckus, rumpus, uproar 7 fashion, madness, shindig 8 foofaraw 9 commotion, whirlpool, whirlwind 10 dernier cri

furore 4 stir 5 craze 6 uproar 11 controversy

furrow 3 rut 4 fold, plow, ruck 5 plica, ridge, rivel, stria, sulci (plural) 6 cleave, course, crease, groove, rimple, striae (plural), sulcus, trench 7 channel, crinkle, wrinkle 11 corrugation

furrowed 6 rugose 7 sulcate 8 sulcated, wrinkled 10 corrugated

further 3 new 4 abet, also, else, help, more, then 5 added, again, fresh, serve 6 beyond 7 advance, besides, forward, promote 8 engender, generate, moreover 9 encourage, propagate 10 additional, in addition 12 additionally

furthermore 3 and, too, yea, yet 4 also 5 along 6 as well, withal 7 besides 8 likewise, moreover

furthermost 7 extreme 8 farthest, remotest

furthest 6 utmost 7 extreme, outmost 9 outermost, uttermost

furtive 3 sly 4 foxy, wary, wily 5 catty 6 artful, covert, crafty, feline, masked, secret, shifty, sneaky, stolen, tricky 7 catlike, cloaked, cunning, sub-rosa 8 cautious, guileful, hush-hush, scheming, stealthy 9 disguised, insidious 11 calculating, circumspect, clandestine 12 hugger-mugger 13 surreptitious, under-the-table *look:* 4 peek, peep

furuncle 4 boil 7 abscess

fury 3 ire, mad 4 rage 5 anger, wrath 6 frenzy 7 madness, passion 8 acerbity, acrimony, afflatus, asperity, violence 9 vehemence 11 indignation

furze 4 whin 5 gorse *genus:* 4 Ulex 7 Genista

fuse 3 mix, run 4 flux, frit, meld, melt, thaw, weld 5 blend, merge, smelt, unify, unite 6 anneal, mingle, solder 7 compact, liquefy 8 dissolve, intermix, liquesce 9 integrate 10 amalgamate, deliquesce, interblend 11 consolidate, incorporate

fusillade 4 hail 5 burst, salvo 6 shower, volley 7 barrage 8 drumfire 9 broadside 11 bombardment

fusion 5 alloy, blend, union 6 merger 7 amalgam, mixture 8 compound 9 admixture, coalition, immixture, synthesis *combining form:* 3 zyg 4 zygo

fuss 3 ado, nag, row 4 cark, coil, crab, flap, fret, kick, miff, stew, stir, to-do, wail, yaup 5 annoy, bleat, fight, gripe, haste, hurry, speed, upset, whine, whirl, worry 6 bother, bustle, carp at, flurry, hassle, hurrah, murmur, peck at, pother, putter, racket, repine, ruckus, rumpus, shindy, squawk, yammer 7 agitate, dispute, fluster, henpeck, protest, quarrel, shindig 8 complain 9 bickering, commotion, complaint, objection, whirlpool, whirlwind 11 controversy 12 perturbation

fussbudget 5 crank 8 stickler 10 fuddy-duddy 12 precisionist 13 perfectionist

fussy 4 nice 5 exact, picky 6 dainty, lively, ornate 7 careful, fidgety, finical, finicky, fretful, heedful 8 bustling, hustling 9 finicking, irritable, querulous, squeamish 10 fastidious, meticulous, particular, pernickety, scrupulous 11 painstaking, persnickety, punctilious 13 conscientious

fustian 4 rant 7 bombast, pompous, useless 8 feckless, rhapsody, rhetoric 9 worthless 10 unpurposed 11 exaggerated, highfalutin, meaningless, purposeless

fusty 4 rank 5 close, dated, fetid, moldy, musty, passé, stale 6 bygone, filthy, old hat, putrid, rancid, sloppy, smelly 7 archaic, noisome, squalid, unkempt 8 outdated 10 antiquated, disheveled, malodorous 12 old-fashioned

futile 4 idle, vain 5 empty 6 hollow, otiose 7 useless 8 abortive, bootless, hopeless, nugatory 9 frivolous, fruitless, worthless 10 inadequate, unavailing 11 ineffective, ineffectual, inefficient 12 insufficient, unprevailing, unproductive, unsuccessful

future 4 to-be 5 later 6 offing 7 by-and-by 9 afterward, hereafter 10 subsequent

Futurism *founder:* 9 Marinetti (Filippo Tommaso) *painter:* 5 Balla (Giacomo), Carra (Carlo) 7 Russolo (Luigi) 8 Boccioni (Umberto), Severini (Gino) *sculptor:* 8 Boccioni (Umberto)

fuzz 3 nap 4 blur, down, flue, lint, pile 5 floss, fluff

fuzzy 3 dim 5 faint, vague 6 bleary, blurry, frizzy 7 blurred, muddled, obscure, shadowy, unclear 8 confused 9 undefined 10 ill-defined, incoherent, indefinite, indistinct 12 inconclusive

fylfot 8 swastika

G

Gaal's father 4 Ebed
gab see gabble
gabbard 4 scow, ship 5 barge 7 lighter
gabber 6 magpie, prater 7 blabber 8 jabberer, prattler 9 bandar-log, blabmouth, chatterer 10 chatterbox
gabble 3 gab, jaw, yak 4 chat, talk 5 olaok, drool, prate 6 drivel, gibber, gossip, jabber 7 blabber, blather, chatter, palaver, prattle, twaddle 9 yakety-yak
gabby 5 talky 6 chatty 9 garrulous, talkative 10 babblative, loquacious 11 loose-lipped 12 loose-tongued
gaberdine 4 coat, suit 5 cloth, cover, smock 7 garment
gable 4 wall 8 pediment *ornament:* 6 finial
Gabon *capital:* 10 Libreville *monetary unit:* 5 franc
gad 3 bat 4 band, roam, rope, rove 5 mooch, range, stray 6 ramble, wander 7 maunder, traipse 9 gallivant
Gad *brother:* 5 Asher *father:* 5 Jacob *mother:* 6 Zilpah *son:* 3 Eri 5 Ezbon, Haggi
gadfly 4 pest 6 bother, critic
gadget 4 tool 5 gizmo 6 device, dingus, doodad, hickey, jigger, widget 7 concern, dofunny, gimmick, utensil 9 apparatus, appliance, doohickey, rigamajig 11 contraption, thingamajig, thingumajig
Gadi's son 7 Menahem
gadwall 4 duck
Gaea 2 Ge *husband:* 6 Uranus *offspring:* 6 Giants, Titans, Typhon, Uranus 7 Erinyes 8 Cyclopes *parent:* 5 Chaos
Gaelic 4 Erse 5 Irish 6 Celtic 8 Scottish *god:* 3 Ler 5 Dagda *hero:* 5 Oisin 6 Ossian 11 Finn MacCool *king:* 9 Conchobar, Conchobor *language:* 4 Manx *poem:* 7 aisling *poet:* 4 bard, fili 6 Ossian *queen:* 4 Medb *soldier:* 4 kern 6 Fenian *spirit:* 7 banshee *tale:* 4 tain
gaff 3 fix 4 hoax, hook, spar, spur 5 abuse, fraud, trick 6 clamor, fleece, outcry, uproar 7 gimmick
gaffe 5 boner, break 7 blooper, faux pas 8 solecism 9 indecorum 11 impropriety
gag 3 jib, shy 4 balk, hoax, jape, jest, joke, keck, quip, ruse, wile 5 choke, crack, demur, heave, retch, sally, stick, trick 6 boggle, muzzle, strain 9 wisecrack, witticism
gage 6 pledge 8 security; (see also gauge)
Gaham *father:* 5 Nahor *mother:* 6 Reumah
Gaheris *brother:* 6 Gareth, Gawain *father:* 3 Lot *mother:* 8 Margawse, Morgause *uncle:* 6 Arthur *victim:* 8 Margawse, Morgause
gaiety 3 joy 4 glee 5 mirth, revel 7 jollity, revelry, whoopee 8 gladness, hilarity, radiance, reveling, vivacity 9 animation, festivity, geniality, happiness, merriment, revelment 10 liveliness 11 merrymaking
gain 3 get, net, win 4 earn, have, land, make, mend, reap 5 annex, clear, lucre, reach, score 6 attain, look up, obtain, perk up, pick up, profit, rack up, return, secure 7 achieve, acquire, bring in, clean up, improve, procure, realize 8 draw down, earnings, proceeds, windfall 9 knock down 10 accomplish
gainful 4 good, rich 6 paying 8 fruitful 9 lucrative 10 productive, profitable, satisfying, well-paying, worthwhile
gainly 8 graceful, pleasing
gainsay 4 deny 5 cross, fight 6 combat, impugn, negate, oppose, resist 7 dispute, subvert 8 disprove, negative, traverse 9 disaffirm, withstand 10 contradict, contravene, controvert
Gainsborough painting 7 Blue Boy
gait 3 run 4 lope, pace, rate, step, trot, walk 5 speed, strut 6 canter, gallop
gaiter 4 boot, shoe 8 overshoe
gala 3 gay 4 fair, fete 5 merry, party 6 festal, lively 7 festive 8 festival 9 festivity 11 celebration
Galahad *father:* 8 Lancelot 9 Launcelot *mother:* 6 Elaine *quest:* 9 Holy Grail
Galatea *father:* 6 Nereus *husband:* 9 Pygmalion *lover:* 4 Acis *mother:* 5 Doris
galaxy 6 nebula 8 Milky Way
Galba *predecessor:* 4 Nero *successor:* 4 Otho
gale 4 blow, gust, wind 5 blast, storm 6 squall 7 tempest 8 outburst 9 hurricane
Galen's forte 8 medicine

galilee 5 porch 6 chapel 7 portico
Galilee *town:* 4 Cana 7 Gergesa 8 Nazareth, Tiberias 9 Bethsaida, Capernaum
Galileo's birthplace 4 Pisa
gall 3 get, irk, rub, vex 4 face, fray, fret, rile, roil, wear 5 annoy, brass, chafe, cheek, chide, erode, grate, graze, harry, nerve, scurr, worry 6 abrade, bother, burn up, harass, ruffle, scrape 7 conceit, corrade, disturb, frazzle, inflame, provoke, scratch, torment 8 exercise, irritate 9 aggravate, arrogance, brashness, excoriate 10 confidence, effrontery *combining form:* 4 chol 5 chole, cholo
gallant 3 fop 4 beau, bold, buck, dude, game 5 blade, blood, brave, dandy, lover, manly, preux, Romeo, suave, swain, wooer 6 heroic, manful, suitor, urbane 7 amorist, courtly, coxcomb, Don Juan, stately 8 Casanova, gracious, lothario, paramour 9 dauntless, exquisite
gallantry 5 poise, valor 6 mettle, spirit 7 amenity, bravery, courage, heroism, prowess, suavity 8 courtesy, urbanity, valiance, valiancy 9 attention 10 resolution
gallery 5 porch 6 arcade, loggia, museum, piazza 7 balcony, passage, portico, veranda 8 audience, corridor 9 colonnade, promenade *ancient Greek:* 4 stoa
galley 4 boat, ship, tray 5 cuddy, proof 6 bireme 7 dromond, galliot, kitchen, trireme, unireme 9 cookhouse
Gallic 6 French
gallimaufry 4 hash, olio 6 jumble, medley 7 mélange, mixture 8 pastiche 9 potpourri 10 assortment, hodgepodge, miscellany, salmagundi
gallinaceous bird 3 hen 5 quail 6 grouse, turkey 7 chicken, hoatzin 8 curassow, megapode, pheasant 9 partridge
gallivant 3 bat, gad 4 roam, rove 5 mooch, range, stray 6 ramble, travel, wander 7 meander, traipse
gallows 5 frame 6 gibbet 7 hanging, potence *bird:* 7 villain 8 criminal
galore 7 aplenty, profuse 8 abundant 9 plentiful
galosh 4 boot, shoe 6 arctic 8 overshoe
Galsworthy work 7 Justice 14 The Forsyte Saga
galvanize 4 coat, move 5 pique, prime 6 arouse, excite 7 innerve, provoke, quicken 8 activate, energize, motivate, vitalize 9 innervate, stimulate
gam 3 leg, pod 5 visit
Gambia *capital:* 6 Banjul *monetary unit:* 6 dalasi
gambit 3 jig 4 move, play, ploy, ruse 5 trick 6 device 7 gimmick, whizzer 8 artifice, maneuver 9 stratagem

gamble 3 bet, lay, set 4 game, play, risk 5 put on, stake, wager 6 chance, hazard 7 venture 9 speculate
gambler 5 dicer, shark, sharp 6 bettor, player 7 sharper 8 gamester 10 speculator
gambling place 4 Reno 5 Vegas 6 casino 8 Las Vegas 10 Monte Carlo 12 Atlantic City
gambol 3 hop 4 lark, leap, romp 5 bound, caper, frisk, revel 6 cavort, frolic, spring 7 roister, rollick
Gambrinus' invention 4 beer
game 3 bet, fun, lay, set 4 bold, jest, joke, lark, play, prey 5 brave, chase, put on, sport, stake, trick, wager 6 gamble, quarry, spunky 7 contest, pastime, valiant, willing 8 fearless, intrepid, resolute, unafraid, valorous 9 amusement, dauntless, diversion, undaunted 10 courageous *ball:* 3 tut 4 golf, polo, pool 5 fives, rogue, rugby 6 hockey, pelota, soccer, squash, tennis 7 cricket, croquet, jai alai 8 baseball, football, handball, hardball, lacrosse, racquets, rounders, softball 9 billiards 10 basketball, volleyball 11 racquetball *Basque:* 6 pelota 7 jai alai *bird:* 5 quail 6 chukar, turkey 7 bustard 8 bobwhite, pheasant 9 partridge *board:* 5 chess, darts, salta 7 pachisi, reversi, squails 8 checkers 9 crokinole 10 backgammon *card:* 3 gin, loo, nap, pam, war 4 brag, faro, fish, skat, solo 5 monte, omber, ombre, pitch, poker, rummy, stuss, whist 6 Boston, bridge, casino, écarté, euchre, fan-tan, hearts, piquet 7 auction, bezique, canasta, cassino, cooncan, muggins, old maid, primero, reversi, setback 8 baccarat, Canfield, conquian, cribbage, Michigan, napoleon, pinochle 9 blackjack, matrimony, Newmarket, solitaire, twenty-one, vingt-et-un 11 chemin de fer *child's:* 3 tag 5 potsy 8 leapfrog, peekaboo 9 hopscotch *confidence:* 4 scam 5 bunco, bunko, sting *court:* 5 roque 6 pelota, squash, tennis 7 jai alai 8 handball, racquets 9 badminton 10 basketball, volleyball *electric:* 7 pinball *English:* 5 kails, rugby 7 cricket, loggats, loggets 8 draughts *Irish:* 6 hurley 7 hurling *of chance:* 4 faro, keno 5 beano, bingo, boule, craps, lotto, rondo 6 fan-tan, hazard, policy, raffle 7 lottery, rondeau 8 crack-loo, roulette 9 crackaloo *parlor:* 5 jacks 8 charades *racket:* 5 bandy 6 squash, tennis 8 lacrosse, racquets 9 badminton 11 racquetball, table tennis *roulette-like:* 5 boule *rule maker:* 5 Hoyle *string:* 10 cat's cradle *table:* 4 pool 5 craps 7 mah-jong, snooker 8 dominoes, mah-jongg, roulette 9 bagatelle, billiards 11 table tennis *word:* 5 rebus 6 crambo,

ghosts 7 anagram, hangman 8 acrostic, charades 9 crossword, logogriph

game plan 6 design, scheme 7 project 8 strategy 9 blueprint

gamete 3 egg 4 ovum 5 sperm 8 oosphere

gamin 3 imp, tad 6 monkey, urchin

gamine 6 hoyden, tomboy

gaming cubes 4 dice

gammadion 8 swastika

gammon 3 ham 4 dupe, fool 5 bacon, feign 6 delude, humbug 7 deceive, pretend

gamut 4 note 5 range, scale 6 extent, series

gamy 4 olid, rank 5 fetid, funky 6 plucky, smelly, sordid, stinky, strong 7 noisome, reeking 10 malodorous

gander 4 fool, look 5 goose 6 glance 9 simpleton

Gandhi 5 Rajiv 6 Indira 7 Mahatma

ganef 5 thief 6 rascal

Ganesa, Ganesh · *father:* 4 Siva 5 Shiva *head:* 8 elephant *mother:* 7 Parvati

gang 3 mob, set 4 band, crew, pack, team 5 group, horde 6 clique, outfit

gangling 4 bony 5 gaunt, lanky, rangy 6 skinny 7 spindly 9 spindling

ganglion 5 tumor 7 nucleus

gangly see gangling

gangrene 3 rot 5 decay 7 mortify 8 necrosis

gangster 4 goon, hood, thug 5 rough, thief, tough 6 bandit, gunman 7 mafioso, mobster 8 criminal 9 cutthroat *girl friend:* 4 moll

gangway 4 hall 5 aisle 7 passage 8 corridor

gannet 4 bird, ibis 5 solan

ganoid fish 3 gar 6 beluga, bowfin 8 sturgeon

Ganymede *abductor:* 4 Zeus 7 Jupiter *brother:* 4 Ilus *father:* 4 Tros *function:* 9 cupbearer

gaol 4 jail 6 prison

gap 3 col 4 hole, lull, pass, slit, slot 5 break, chasm, chink, cleft, clove, crack, gorge, gulch, pause 6 arroyo, breach, clough, cranny, hiatus, lacuna, ravine 7 caesura, crevice, fissure, interim, opening, orifice, rupture 8 aperture, cleavage, division, fracture, interval 10 separation 12 intermission, interruption 13 discontinuity

gape 3 eye, yaw 4 bore, gawk, gaze, look, ogle, peer, yawn 5 glare, gloat, stare 6 goggle 10 rubberneck

gaping 4 open 7 chasmal, yawning 9 cavernous

gar 4 fish, pike 8 billfish 10 needlefish

Garand 5 rifle

garb 4 clad 5 array, dress, getup, style 6 attire, clothe, outfit 7 apparel, garment, raiment 8 enclothe

garbage 4 junk, orts, slop 5 dregs, filth, offal, trash, waste 6 debris, kelter, litter, refuse, rubble, sewage 7 rubbish 8 riffraff *heap:* 6 midden

garble 4 sift, warp 5 belie, color, twist 6 jumble, mangle 7 becloud, distort, falsify, obscure, pervert 8 miscolor, misstate, mutilate 9 obfuscate 12 misrepresent

garçon 3 boy 6 waiter 7 servant

garden 3 hoe 4 Eden, farm, hall, park, plot, till, yard 5 grove, tract 8 rosarium 9 cultivate 11 commonplace *shelter:* 5 arbor 6 arbour

Garden City 7 Chicago

gardener 7 yardman 9 topiarist

garden house 6 alcove, gazebo, pagoda 9 belvedere

Garden State 9 New Jersey

garden tool 3 hoe 4 claw, fork, rake 5 mower, spade 6 pruner, scythe, sickle, trowel, weeder 8 clippers

Gareth *brother:* 6 Gawain 7 Gaheris *father:* 3 Lot *mother:* 8 Margawse, Morgause *slayer:* 8 Lancelot 9 Launcelot *uncle:* 6 Arthur *wife:* 6 Liones

Gargamelle's son 9 Gargantua

Gargantua *abbey:* 7 Theleme *author:* 8 Rabelais (François) *father:* 12 Grandgousier *first word:* 5 drink *mother:* 10 Gargamelle *son:* 10 Pantagruel

gargantuan see gigantic

Garibaldi follower 8 redshirt

garish 4 loud 5 gaudy, showy 6 brazen, flashy, tawdry, tinsel 7 blatant, chintzy, glaring 12 meretricious

garland 3 ana, lei 4 band, posy 5 album, crown 6 anadem, wreath 7 chaplet, coronal, coronet, omnibus 8 analects 9 anthology 10 miscellany 11 florilegium

garlic 4 moly, ramp 5 clove 6 ramson

garment 4 cape, clad, coat, garb, gear, gown, robe, vest 5 array, cloak, dress, frock, habit, shirt, skirt, talar, tunic 6 attire, blouse, clothe 7 apparel, chemise, raiment 8 clothing, enclothe, vestment, wearable 10 habiliment *Afghan:* 6 postin 7 posteen 8 poshteen *African:* 6 kaross 7 dashiki *Arab:* 3 aba 4 haik *British:* 4 brat 10 mackintosh *Burmese:* 6 tamein *clergy's:* 3 alb 4 cope 7 cassock, soutane 8 vestment *close-fitting:* 6 girdle, tights 7 leotard *for sleeping:* 6 pajama 7 nightie 9 nightgown *Greek:* 5 tunic 6 chiton, peplos, tribon 7 chlamys 8 himation *Hindu:* 4 sari 5 saree *hooded:* 7 jellaba 8 djellaba *Japanese:* 6 kimono *lace:* 10 chemisette *Malay:* 6 sarong *men's:* 3 tie 4 vest 5 pants, shirt, socks 6 jacket, slacks

7 drawers 8 trousers *Muslim:* 4 izar *outer:*
4 cape, coat, robe, wrap 5 cloak, parka,
shawl, smock, stole, wamus 6 capote,
jacket, kimono, poncho, sarong, ulster,
wammus 7 overall, paletot, pelisse, surtout,
sweater, topcoat, zamarra 8 overcoat, pinafore, pullover, scapular 9 coveralls, gaberdine, polonaise *patchwork:* 5 cento 7 khir-
kah *Polynesian:* 5 pareu 8 lavelava *rain:*
6 poncho 7 oilskin, slicker *Roman:* 4 toga
5 stola, tunic *Scottish:* 4 jupe, kilt 7 sporran *sleeveless:* 3 aba 4 cape 6 mantle,
tabard *trim:* 7 falbala *Turkish:* 6 dolman
women's: 4 gown 5 dress, skirt 6 blouse,
vestee 7 blouson, nightie, partlet 8 negligee, peignoir, pelerine

garner 4 cull, hive, reap 5 amass, glean,
hoard, lay up, store, uplay 6 gather, pick
up, roll up 7 extract, granary, harvest, store
up 8 cumulate, ingather 9 stockpile
10 accumulate

garnet 5 jewel, stone 6 pyrope 8 essonite
black: 8 melanite *red:* 9 almandite

garnish 4 deck, trim 5 adorn, prank
6 bedeck 7 dress up 8 beautify, decorate,
ornament 9 embellish

garret 4 loft, room 5 attic, solar 6 sollar,
soller 7 mansard 8 cockloft

garrison 4 fort, post 6 occupy 7 station
10 stronghold

garrote 4 kill 5 choke 7 execute 8 strangle, throttle 9 execution

garrulous see gabby

garter 4 band, belt 5 snake 7 elastic
9 supporter

garth 3 dam 4 weir, yard 5 close

gas 4 fuel, fume 5 steam, vapor 6 petrol
8 gasoline 9 petroleum *atmospheric:*
4 neon 5 argon, oxide, ozone, xenon
6 helium, oxygen 7 krypton, methane
8 hydrogen, nitrogen *combining form:*
3 aer 4 mano 5 pneum 6 pneumo 7 pneumat 8 pneumato *flammable:* 6 butane,
ethane, ethyne 7 methane, propane, pro-
pene 8 ethylene *inert:* 4 neon 5 argon,
radon, xenon 6 helium 7 krypton *intestinal:*
6 flatus *mine:* 8 firedamp 9 blackdamp,
chokedamp *oxygen:* 5 ozone *toxic:*
5 sarin 6 arsine, ketene 7 mustard, stibine,
yperite 8 phosphin

gasconade 4 brag 7 bravado 8 boasting

gash 3 cut 4 slit 5 carve, slash, slice, split,
wound 6 incise, pierce

gasket 4 band, line, ring, seal 6 sealer

gasoline 4 fuel 6 petrol *rating:* 6 octane

gasp 4 blow, huff, pant, puff 5 heave

Gaspar *companion:* 8 Melchior 9 Balthazar *gift:* 12 frankincense

gassy 5 windy 8 inflated, vaporous

gastronome 7 epicure, gourmet 8 aesthete, gourmand 9 bon vivant

gastronomer, gastronomist see gastronome

gastropod 4 slug 5 cowry, murex, snail,
whelk 6 cowrie, limpet, volute 7 abalone,
mollusk 8 pteropod

gat 3 gun 6 pistol 7 channel, passage

gate 3 tap, way 4 cock, door, exit 5 hatch,
valve 6 faucet, portal, spigot, wicket
7 hydrant, opening, petcock 8 stopcock
9 turnstile

gatefold 6 insert 7 foldout

Gates of Hercules 9 Gibraltar

gateway 4 arch, door 5 pylon, toran
6 portal, torana 8 entrance

gather 4 brew, cull, draw, heap, herd,
loom, mass, meet, pick, pile, reap, take
5 amass, bunch, flock, glean, group, horde,
infer, judge, pluck, raise, shirr, stack, think,
troop 6 assume, deduce, deduct, derive,
expect, garner, impend, muster, pick up,
take in 7 believe, cluster, collect, extract,
harvest, imagine, make out, round up, suppose, suspect 8 assemble, conclude, congress 9 aggregate, forthcome 10 accumulate, congregate, rendezvous, understand

gathering 4 bevy, crew, gang, mass, ruck
5 bunch, crowd, crush, flock, group, horde,
party, press, swarm 6 klatch, muster
7 company, harvest, klatsch, meeting, reaping, reunion, turnout 8 assembly, cropping,
junction 9 concourse, congeries 10 assemblage, collection, concursion, confluence,
harvesting 11 aggregation 12 congregation
combining form: 4 fest

Gath's giant 7 Goliath

gauche 5 crude, inept 6 clumsy, wooden
7 awkward, halting, unhappy 8 bumbling
9 ham-handed, maladroit

gaucho 6 cowboy 8 herdsman *weapon:*
4 bola 7 machete

Gaudeamus ____ 6 igitur

gaudy 4 loud 5 crude, feast, gross, showy
6 brazen, coarse, flashy, garish, tawdry, tinsel, vulgar 7 blatant, chintzy, glaring 8 festival 9 tasteless 12 meretricious, ostentatious

gauge 5 judge, meter, scale 7 measure
8 estimate, standard 9 benchmark, criterion, yardstick 10 touchstone

Gauguin's island home 6 Tahiti

Gaul 4 Celt 6 France 9 Frenchman

Gaulish 6 French *combining form:*
5 Gallo *god:* 4 Esus 7 Taranis *goddess:*
8 Belisama *priest:* 5 druid

gaunt 4 bony, lank, lean 5 lanky, spare
6 skinny, wasted 7 angular, scraggy,
scrawny 8 rawboned, skeletal 9 emaciated
10 cadaverous

gauntlet 4 dare, test 5 glove 6 cestus,
ordeal 9 challenge

Gautama 6 Buddha 10 Siddhartha
mother: 4 Maya *son:* 6 Rahula *wife:*
9 Yasodhara

gauze 4 film, haze, leno, mist 5 cloth,
crepe, lisse, tulle 6 fabric, tissue 7 bandage, chiffon 11 cheesecloth

gauzy 5 filmy, sheer 6 flimsy 7 tiffany
8 gossamer 10 diaphanous 11 transparent

gavel 6 hammer, mallet

gavial 7 reptile 9 crocodile

gavotte 5 dance

Gawain *brother:* 6 Gareth 7 Gaheris
father: 3 Lot *mother:* 8 Margawse, Morgause *slayer:* 8 Lancelot 9 Launcelot
uncle: 6 Arthur *victim:* 6 Uwayne 7 Lamerok 9 Pellinore

gawk 3 oaf 4 bore, gape, gaze, lout, lump,
peer 5 glare, gloat, klutz, looby, stare

gawky 5 splay 6 clumsy, gauche 7 awkward, lumpish 8 ungainly 9 lumbering

gay 4 glad, keen, wild 5 alert, bonny,
brash, brave, happy, jolly, merry, queer,
riant, vivid 6 blithe, bright, colory, festal,
frisky, jocund, jovial, lively, rakish, sporty
7 animate, festive, forward, gleeful, playful,
pushful, raffish, uranian 8 animated, colorful, mirthful, rakehell, spirited, sportive
9 confident, homophile, presuming,
sprightly, vivacious 10 blithesome, brassbound, frolicsome, homoerotic, homosexual

____ **Gay** 4 John 5 Enola

Gaza victor 7 Allenby (Edmund)

gaze 3 eye, see 4 bore, gape, gawk, leer,
look, ogle, peer, pore, scan, view 5 glare,
gloat, stare, watch 6 goggle, look at
7 observe 8 consider, look upon

gazebo 6 alcove, pagoda 8 pavilion 9 belvedere 11 garden house, summerhouse

gazelle 3 ahu, goa 4 admi, cora, dama,
kudu, mohr, oryx 5 ariel, mhorr 6 dorcus
7 chikara, corinne 8 antelope

gazette 5 paper 6 record 7 courant, journal 9 newspaper

gazetteer 5 atlas, guide

Gazez's father 5 Caleb

Ge see Gaea

gear 3 arm, cam, cog, rig 5 dress, equip,
goods, stuff 6 fit out, outfit, tackle, things
7 apparel, appoint, furnish, rigging, turn out
8 accouter, accoutre, cogwheel, materiel,
property, tackling 9 apparatus, equipment,
machinery 10 belongings 11 accessories,
habiliments, possessions 13 accouterments, accoutrements, paraphernalia

Geats *king:* 7 Hygelac *prince:* 7 Beowulf

Geb *daughter:* 4 Isis 8 Nephthys *father:*
3 Shu *mother:* 6 Tefnut *sister:* 3 Nut *son:*
3 Set 6 Osiris *wife:* 3 Nut

gecko 6 lizard

Gedaliah *father:* 6 Ahikam 7 Pashhur
8 Jeduthun *slayer:* 7 Ishmael

Gehenna 3 pit 4 hell 5 abyss, hades,
Sheol 6 Tophet 7 inferno 9 perdition
10 underworld 11 netherworld

geisha wear 6 kimono

gel 3 dry, set 4 clot, jell 5 jelly 6 gelate
7 congeal, jellify 9 coagulate

gelatin 4 agar 5 jelly 7 sericin

geld 3 fix 4 spay 5 alter, unsex 6 change,
neuter 8 castrate, mutilate 9 sterilize
10 emasculate 11 desexualize

gelid 3 icy 4 cold, cool 5 chill, nippy 6 arctic, chilly, frosty 7 glacial 8 freezing

gem 3 jet 4 jade, onyx, opal, ruby, sard
5 agate, amber, beryl, coral, jewel, pearl,
stone, topaz 6 amulet, garnet, jasper,
scarab, sphene, spinel, zircon 7 bejewel,
cat's-eye, citrine, diamond, emerald,
enjewel, peridot 8 amethyst, diopside, fluorite, intaglio, obsidian, sapphire, sardonyx,
tigereye 9 carnelian, danburite, moonstone,
phenakite, scapolite, spodumene, turquoise
10 aquamarine, cordierite, tourmaline
11 alexandrite, chrysoberyl, chrysoprase,
lapis lazuli, masterpiece *blue:* 6 zircon
8 sapphire 9 turquoise 10 aquamarine
11 lapis lazuli *carved:* 8 intaglio *changeable:* 9 chatoyant *cut:* 7 navette
8 baguette, cabochon, marquise 9 brilliant
face: 5 facet *green:* 4 jade 7 emerald,
peridot, smaragd 10 chrysolite 11 chrysoprase *red:* 4 ruby, sard 6 garnet, pyrope,
spinel 9 carnelian *support:* 7 setting
weight: 5 carat *yellow:* 5 amber, topaz
6 sphene 7 citrine

Gemariah *brother:* 6 Ahikam *father:*
7 Hilkiah, Shaphan

Gemini star 6 Castor, Pollux

gemmule 3 bud 8 antelope

gemsbok 4 oryx

Gem State 5 Idaho

gemütlich see genial

gendarme 7 soldier 9 policeman

gender 3 sex 4 kind, male, sort, type
5 class 6 female, neuter

genealogy 6 stemma 7 descent, history,
lineage 8 pedigree 10 family tree

general 4 wide 5 broad, typic, usual
6 common, global, normal, public, vulgar
7 generic, natural, overall, regular, routine,
typical 8 everyday, sweeping 9 all-around,
inclusive, prevalent, universal 11 commonplace 12 run-of-the-mill 13 comprehensive
American: 3 Lee (Robert E.) 4 Pike (Zebulon), Wood (Leonard) 5 Clark (Mark, William), Grant (Ulysses S.), Meade (George),
Scott (Charles, Hugh, Winfield), Smith
(Andrew Jackson, Giles, Holland, Morgan,
Samuel, Walter, Bedell), Stark (John),
Worth (William) 6 Abrams (Creighton),
Custer (George Armstrong), Kearny (Philip,
Stephen), Patton (George S.), Porter (Fitz-

John), Powell (Colin), Slocum (Henry), Spaatz (Carl), Taylor (Maxwell, Richard, Zachary) **7** Bradley (Omar), Fremont (John Charles), Houston (Samuel), Jackson (Andrew, Thomas "Stonewall"), Lejeune (John), Ridgway (Matthew B.), Sherman (William Tecumseh), Twining (Nathaniel), Wallace (Lewis), Wheeler (Joseph) **8** Burnside (Ambrose), Goethals (George Washington), Marshall (George), Mitchell (Billy), Pershing (John J.), Sheridan (Philip), Stilwell (Joseph) **9** MacArthur (Arthur, Douglas), McClellan (George), Rosecrans (William), Schofield (John), Wilkinson (James) **10** Eisenhower (Dwight David), Vandegrift (Alexander), Wainwright (Jonathan) **11** Schwarzkopf (Norman) *American Revolutionary:* **4** Knox (Henry), Ward (Artemas) **5** Gates (Horatio), Wayne ("Mad Anthony") **6** de Kalb (Baron), Greene (Nathanael), Morgan (Daniel), Putnam (Israel, Rufus) **8** Moultrie (William), Sullivan (John) **10** Washington (George) *Austrian:* **11** Wallenstein (Albrecht von) *British:* **4** Gage (Thomas), Howe (William) **5** Clive (Robert), Monck (George), Wolfe (James) **6** Rupert (Prince) **7** Amherst (Jeffrey), Wingate (Orde Charles, Reginald) **8** Burgoyne (John), Cromwell (Oliver) **10** Abercromby (Ralph, Robert), Cornwallis (Charles), Wellington (Duke of) *Carthaginian:* **8** Hamilcar, Hannibal **9** Hasdrubal *Chinese:* **3** Yen (Hsishan) **4** Feng (Kuo-chang, Yü-hsiang) **5** Chang (Tso-lin) *combining form:* **3** cen, pan **4** caen, ceno, coen, pano **5** caeno, coeno *Confederate:* **3** Lee (Robert E.) **4** Hill (Ambrose), Hood (John Bell) **5** Bragg (Braxton), Ewell (Richard Stoddart), Price (Sterling), Smith (Edmund Kirby) **6** Morgan (John Hunt), Stuart (Jeb) **7** Forrest (Nathan Bedford), Hampton (Wade), Jackson (Thomas "Stonewall"), Pickett (George) **8** Johnston (Albert Sidney, Joseph Eggleston) **9** Pemberton (John) **10** Beauregard (Pierre G. T.), Longstreet (James) *French:* **4** Foch (Ferdinand) **6** Moreau (Victor), Petain (Philippe) **7** Lefebre (Pierre), Weygand (Maxime) **8** de Gaulle (Charles), Montcalm (Marquis de), Saint-Cyr (Laurent de Gouvion-) **9** Frontenac (Comte de) **10** Rochambeau (Comte de) *German:* **4** Jodl (Alfred) **6** Kleist (Paul Ludwig von) **10** Ludendorff (Erich) *Greek:* **6** Nicias **9** Miltiades **10** Alcibiades **12** Themistocles *Japanese:* **4** Tojo (Hideki) **5** Koiso (Kuniaki) **6** Yasuda (Yoshisada) **8** Yamagata (Aritomo) **9** Yamashita (Tomoyuki) *Mexican:* **9** Santa Anna (Antonio Lopez de) *Prussian:* **11** Scharnhorst (Gerhard von) *Roman:* **5** Sulla (Lucius Corne-

lius) **6** Caesar (Julius), Fabius (Quintus), Marius (Gaius), Pompey (the Great), Scipio (Gnaeus Cornelius, Publius Cornelius) **7** Regulus (Marcus Atilius), Ricimer (Flavius) **8** Agricola (Gnaeus Julius), Lucullus (Lucius Licinius), Stilicho (Flavius) **9** Marcellus (Marcus Claudius), Sertorius (Quintus) **10** Theodosius (the Great) **11** Cincinnatus (Lucius Quinctius) *Russian:* **7** Wrangel (Pyotr), Zhdanov (Andrey) **9** Yeremenko (Andrey) *Spanish:* **4** Alba (Duke of), Alva (Duke of) **6** Franco (Francisco) *Swedish:* **7** Wrangel (Karl Gustav)

general assembly 6 plenum

generalize 5 infer, widen **6** extend, induce, spread

generally 6 mainly, mostly **7** as a rule, chiefly, en masse, largely, overall, usually **8** all in all, commonly **9** primarily **10** altogether, by and large, by ordinary, frequently, on the whole, ordinarily **11** principally **13** predominantly

generate 4 bear, make, sire **5** beget, breed, cause, get up, hatch, spawn **6** create, father, induce, parent, whip up, work up **7** develop, produce, provoke **8** engender, multiply, muster up **9** originate, procreate, propagate, reproduce **10** bring about

generic 6 common **7** general **9** universal

____ generis 3 sui

generosity 7 charity, largess **8** largesse **10** liberality

generous 3 big **4** free, kind **5** ample, lofty, noble **6** kindly, lavish, plenty **7** copious, helpful, liberal, profuse **8** abundant, handsome **9** bounteous, bountiful, plenteous, plentiful, unselfish, unsparing **10** altruistic, benevolent, bighearted, charitable, chivalrous, freehanded, munificent, openhanded, thoughtful, ungrudging **11** considerate, kindhearted, magnanimous

genesis 4 dawn **5** alpha, birth, start **6** origin, outset, setout **7** dawning, opening **8** outstart **9** beginning **12** commencement

genetic 10 hereditary *material:* **3** DNA, RNA **7** cistron **9** chromatid **10** chromosome *term:* **8** synapsis **9** backcross

genial 4 warm **5** jolly, merry **6** benign, blithe, gentle, jocund, jovial, kindly **7** affable, amiable, cordial **8** amicable, cheerful, friendly, gracious, sociable **9** congenial **10** neighborly

genie 4 jinn **5** afrit, jinni **6** afreet, spirit, yaksha

genitor 6 father, parent **7** creator

geniture 5 birth **8** nativity

genius 4 bent, bump, gift, head, turn **5** flair, knack **6** brains, talent, wizard **7** aptness, faculty **9** ingenuity, intellect **10** creativity **12** intelligence **13** inventiveness

Genoa's liberator 5 Doria (Andrea)
genre 3 ilk 4 kind, sort, type 5 class, style
7 species 8 category
gens 4 clan 5 group 6 family, people
Genseric's subjects 7 Vandals
genteel 4 nice, prig, prim 5 civil, noble
6 la-di-da, polite, prissy, stuffy, too-too,
urbane 7 elegant, mincing, prudish, refined,
stilted, stylish 8 affected, cultured, graceful,
knightly, ladylike, mannerly, polished, precious, priggish, well-bred 9 courteous, distingué, Victorian 10 chivalrous, cultivated,
tight-laced 11 fashionable, gentlemanly,
pretentious, well-behaved 12 aristocratic,
well-mannered 13 straightlaced
gentile 3 goy 4 Arya 5 Aryan
gentility 5 elite 6 flower, gentry 7 aristoi,
quality, society 8 breeding, optimacy
10 upper class, upper crust 11 aristocracy
gentle 4 calm, easy, kind, meek, mild, soft,
tame 5 balmy, bland, faint, quiet, tamed
6 benign, genial, kindly, mellow, placid,
serene, smooth, tender 7 affable, amiable,
lenient 8 delicate, peaceful, pleasant, pleasing, soothing, tranquil 9 agreeable 11 softhearted, sympathetic, warmhearted
13 compassionate *creature:* 4 lamb
gentleman 6 aristo, fellow, mister 8 cavalier 9 blue blood, chevalier, patrician
10 aristocrat *English:* 6 milord *French:*
8 monsieur *Hindu:* 4 babu *Spanish:* 3 don
5 senor
gentleman friend 4 beau 5 swain
gentry 4 rank 5 elite 6 flower 7 aristoi,
quality, society 8 optimacy 9 gentility
10 upper class, upper crust 11 aristocracy
genu 4 knee 5 joint
Genubath's father 5 Hadad
genuflect 5 kneel 6 kowtow
genuine 4 hard, real, true, very 5 plain,
pucka, pukka 6 actual, dinkum, honest
7 factual, natural, sincere 8 absolute, bona
fide, positive, trueborn 9 authentic,
undoubted, unfeigned, veritable 10 heart-
whole, sure-enough, unaffected
genus 4 kind, mode, sort, type 5 class,
group, order 8 category
geode 6 cavity, nodule
geographer *American:* 10 Huntington
(Ellsworth) *Flemish:* 8 Mercator (Gerardus)
German: 6 Ratzel (Friedrich) *Greek:*
6 Strabo 7 Ptolemy
geologic *period:* 5 azoic 6 Eocene
7 Miocene, Permian 8 Cambrian, Ceno-
zoic, Devonian, Jurassic, Mesozoic, Plio-
cene, Silurian, Triassic 9 Oligocene, Paleo-
cene, Paleozoic 10 Cretaceous, Ordovician
13 Mississippian, Pennsylvanian *study:*
4 rock 5 earth 6 fossil
geometer 6 Euclid

geometric *coordinate:* 8 abscissa *curve:*
3 arc 6 spiral 7 cissoid, ellipse, evolute
8 parabola *solid:* 4 cone, cube 5 prism
7 pyramid 8 spheroid, spherule *surface:*
5 nappe, torus 6 toroid
geometric figure 4 cone, cube 5 prism,
rhomb 6 circle, oblong, sphere, square
7 ellipse, hexagon, octagon, polygon, pyramid, rhombus 8 cylinder, heptagon, pentagon, rhomboid, spheroid, triangle 9 rectangle *combining form:* 5 hedra (plural)
6 hedron
geometry letters 3 Q.E.D.
geophagy 4 pica
Georgia *capital:* 7 Atlanta *college, university:* 4 Tift 5 Clark, Emory, Paine
founder: 10 Oglethorpe (James) *nickname:* 10 Peach State
Gera *father:* 4 Bela *grandfather:* 8 Benjamin *son:* 4 Ehud 6 Shimei
Geraint's wife 4 Enid
Gerda's husband 4 Frey
germ 3 bud, bug 4 seed 5 spark, spore,
virus 6 embryo 7 microbe, nucleus 9 bacterium *cell:* 3 egg 4 ovum 5 sperm
German 4 Goth 6 Teuton *article:* 3 das,
der, des, die *bomber:* 5 Gotha, Stuka
child: 4 kind *coin:* 4 mark 5 taler 6 thaler
7 pfennig *empire:* 5 reich *head:* 4 kopf
highway: 8 autobahn *leader:* 6 führer, kaiser *measles:* 7 rubella *mister:* 4 herr *no:*
4 nein *nobleman:* 6 Junker *pronoun:*
2 du, er, es 3 ich, sie, wir *rifle:* 6 Mauser
weight: 3 lot 5 pfund, stein 8 vierling
woman: 4 frau 8 fräulein
germane 5 ad rem 7 apropos, related
8 apposite, material, pointful, relevant
9 pertinent 10 applicable
Germany 11 Deutschland *capital:* 6 Berlin *monetary unit:* 4 mark
germinate 3 bud 6 evolve, sprout
Gerontion poet 5 Eliot (Thomas Stearns)
Gershom, Gershon *father:* 4 Levi *son:*
5 Libni 6 Shimei
Gershwin 3 Ira 6 George *opera:*
12 Porgy and Bess
Gertrude *husband:* 8 Claudius *son:*
6 Hamlet
Gervaise's daughter 4 Nana
Geryon *dog:* 6 Orthus *father:* 8 Chrysaor
mother: 10 Callirrhoe *slayer:* 8 Hercules
Gesham's father 5 Jahdai
gest, geste 4 deed, feat 7 emprise,
exploit, venture 9 adventure 10 enterprise
Gestapo chief 7 Himmler (Heinrich)
gesticulate 6 motion 7 gesture
gesture 3 act, nod 4 flag, sign 5 token
6 motion, salute, signal 8 reminder 9 signalize 10 expression, indication *graceful:*
9 beau geste

get 3 bag, fix, win 4 beat, come, draw, earn, gain, gall, grow, have, land, move, rile, sire, sway, turn 5 annex, breed, catch, educe, evoke, learn, peeve, reach, ready, touch, upset 6 accept, affect, arrive, attain, become, bother, burn up, collar, elicit, extort, father, induce, make up, master, obtain, pick up, secure, show up, turn up 7 acquire, bring in, capture, chalk up, compass, disturb, extract, impress, nonplus, perturb, prehend, prepare, procure, realize, receive, win over 8 contract, convince, distress, draw down, irritate, memorize, persuade, sicken of, talk into 9 aggravate, argue into, influence, knock down, prevail on, procreate 10 exasperate, sicken with 11 bring around, prevail upon, progenerate 12 come down with

get around 5 evade

get away see get out

getaway 3 lam 4 slip 6 escape, flight 8 breakout, escaping 10 escapement

get back 6 recoup, regain 7 recover, recruit 8 retrieve 9 repossess

get by 4 fare 5 shift 6 manage

get off 2 go 4 exit, open, quit 5 begin, leave, start 6 depart, launch, retire 7 jump off, kick off, pull out 8 commence *prefix:* 2 de

get out 2 go 4 exit, kite, leak 5 break, issue, leave, scram, split 6 begone, decamp, depart, egress, escape 7 publish, skiddoo, take off 8 clear out, hightail 9 skedaddle

Gettysburg general 3 Lee (Robert E.) 5 Meade (George)

get up 4 rise 5 arise, breed, cause, hatch, mount, stand 6 induce, uprise 7 pile out, produce, roll out, turn out 8 engender, generate, muster up, occasion, upspring 12 rise and shine

getup 2 go 3 pep, rig 4 bang, push, snap, togs 5 dress, drive, guise, punch, vigor 6 outfit, setout 7 costume 8 vitality

get-up-and-go 3 pep 4 bang, push, snap 5 drive, punch, vigor 8 ambition, vitality 10 enterprise, initiative

gewgaw 3 toy 5 curio 6 bauble, trifle 7 bibelot, novelty, trinket, whatnot 8 gimcrack 9 objet d'art 10 knickknack

geyser 5 spurt 6 spring 11 Old Faithful

Ghana *capital:* 5 Accra *monetary unit:* 4 cedi

ghastly 3 wan 4 grim, pale 5 awful 6 grisly, horrid, shadow 7 hideous, macabre 8 dreadful, gruesome, horrible, nauseant, shocking, spectral, terrible 9 appalling, deathlike, frightful, ghostlike, sickening 10 cadaverous, corpselike, disgustful, disgusting, horrifying, nauseating, terrifying 11 frightening

ghee 3 fat 6 butter

gherkin 6 pickle 8 cucumber

ghetto 4 slum

ghost 5 shade, spook 6 shadow, spirit, wraith 7 phantom, specter 8 phantasm 10 apparition 11 poltergeist

ghostlike see ghostly

ghostly 5 eerie, scary 6 spooky 7 shadowy 8 spectral 9 deathlike 10 cadaverous, corpselike

ghoul 4 ogre 5 fiend 7 monster

GI 7 fighter, soldier, warrior 9 man-at-arms 10 serviceman

giant 4 huge, ogre, Otus 5 gross, Gyges, Hymir, jumbo, titan, troll, whale 6 Cottus, Typhon 7 Aloadae (plural), Antaeus, Cyclops, mammoth, monster, titanic 8 behemoth, Briareus, colossal, colossus, gigantic, Orgoglio 9 cyclopean, Enceladus, Ephialtes, Gargantua, Herculean, leviathan, monstrous, polypheme 10 behemothic, gargantuan *armadillo:* 4 tatu 5 tatou *biblical:* 4 Anak 7 Goliath *cactus:* 7 saguaro *clam:* 8 tridacna *grass:* 5 otate *killer:* 4 Jack 5 David *one-eyed:* 5 Arges 7 Cyclops 10 Polyphemus *100-armed:* 9 Enceladus *100-eyed:* 5 Argus *perch:* 5 begti, bekti 6 cockup *rime-cold:* 4 Ymer, Ymir *sea god:* 5 Aegir

Giant author 5 Ferber (Edna)

gibber 5 prate 6 babble, drivel, gabble, jabber, yammer 7 blather, chatter, prattle

gibberish 5 Greek 6 babble, bunkum, drivel, gabble, jabber 7 blabber, blather, mummery, palaver, prattle, twaddle 8 claptrap, nonsense 10 double-talk, hocus-pocus, mumbo jumbo 11 abracadabra, jabberwocky 12 gobbledygook

gibbet 4 hang 5 noose, scrag 7 gallows, turn off 8 string up

gibbon 3 ape, lar 6 monkey 7 primate, siamang 10 anthropoid

gibbous 6 convex, humped 7 rounded, swollen 10 humpbacked

gibe 4 gird, jeer, jest, mock, quip 5 fleer, flout, gleek, scoff, sneer 6 quip at 7 scout at 8 ridicule

Gibraltar *colony of:* 12 Great Britain *conqueror:* 5 Tarik, Tariq *country:* 5 Spain *opposite:* 5 Ceuta

Giddalti *father:* 5 Heman *occupation:* 6 singer

giddy 5 dizzy, light, silly 6 swimmy, volage, yeasty 7 flighty, fribble 8 skittish, swimming 9 fribbling, frivolous 10 birdwitted, hoity-toity 11 empty-headed, harebrained, light-headed, vertiginous 13 rattlebrained

____ **Gide** 5 André

Gideon *father:* 5 Joash *servant:* 5 Purah *son:* 9 Abimelech

Gideoni's son 6 Abidan

gift 3 set, tip 4 alms, bent, boon, bump, head, turn 5 award, favor, flair, grant, knack 6 genius, legacy, reward, talent 7 aptness, cumshaw, faculty, handout, largess, present, subsidy 8 bestowal, donation, gratuity, offering 9 lagniappe 11 benefaction, benevolence 12 contribution, presentation

gig 3 jab, job 4 boat, fool, goad, prod 5 annoy, rotor, spear 6 chaise, harass 7 demerit, provoke

gigantic 3 big 4 huge, vast 5 giant, large 7 hulking, immense, mammoth 8 colossal, enormous 9 cyclopean, monstrous 10 gargantuan, prodigious, stupendous 11 elephantine

giggle 5 laugh, tehee 6 guffaw, hee-haw, teehee, titter 7 chortle, chuckle, snicker, snigger

Gilbert and Sullivan opera 8 Iolanthe, Patience 9 Ruddigore, The Mikado 11 H.M.S. Pinafore, Princess Ida, The Sorcerer, Trial by Jury 12 The Grand Duke 13 The Gondoliers

Gil Blas author 6 Lesage (Alain-René)

gild 5 adorn, cover, tinge 7 overlay 8 brighten 9 embellish

Gilda's father 9 Rigoletto

Gilead *father:* 6 Machir *grandfather:* 8 Manasseh *son:* 8 Jephthah

Gilgamesh 4 epic *companion:* 6 Eabani, Engidu, Enkidu *home:* 5 Erech *mother:* 6 Ninsun *victim:* 7 Humbaba

gill 4 race 5 brook, creek 6 runnel, stream, wattle 7 rivulet *relating to:* 9 branchial

gilly flower 4 pink 9 clove pink

gilt 3 hog, pig, sow 4 gold 5 swine 6 gilded, golden

gimlet 4 tool 5 drink 6 pierce 7 gum tree 8 eucalypt 10 eucalyptus *ingredient:* 3 gin 9 lime juice

gimmick 4 ploy, ruse, wile 5 feint, gizmo, trick 6 gadget, gambit, jigger, widget 7 concern, whizzer 8 artifice, maneuver 9 stratagem

gimpy 4 lame 7 limping 8 crippled

gin 3 net 4 sloe, trap 5 catch, rummy, snare 6 liquor 7 springe 8 Hollands

Ginath's son 5 Tibni

ginger 3 fig, pep, vim 4 herb, stir 5 liven, spice, vigor 6 mettle, revive, spirit *cookie:* 4 snap

gingerly 4 safe, wary 5 chary 7 careful, guarded 8 cautious, discreet 11 calculating, circumspect, considerate

gingery 5 beany, fiery 6 spunky 7 peppery 8 spirited 10 mettlesome 11 high-hearted 12 high-spirited

gingham 5 cloth 6 fabric

gingiva 3 gum

ginseng 4 herb, root

Gioconda, La 8 Mona Lisa *composer:* 10 Ponchielli (Amilcare) *painter:* 7 da Vinci (Leonardo)

giraffe 3 car 5 piano 8 ruminant 10 camelopard

girandole 6 mirror 7 earring, pendant 11 candelabrum

girasol 4 opal 8 fire opal 9 artichoke

gird 3 hem 4 band, belt, gibe, jeer, jest, ring, wrap 5 beset, brace, fleer, flout, ready, round, scoff, sneer, steel 6 circle, quip at 7 bolster, forearm, fortify, prepare, scout at, shore up, wreathe 8 begirdle, buttress, cincture, encircle, engirdle, surround 9 encompass, reinforce 10 encincture, strengthen

girdle 3 hem 4 band, bark, belt, ring, sash 5 beset, round 6 begird, cestus, circle, engird 8 ceinture, cincture, encircle, surround 9 encompass, waistband 10 encincture *combining form:* 3 zon 4 zono 6 pleura *of Aphrodite:* 6 cestus 7 caestus

girl Friday 9 secretary

girth 4 band, belt, bind, size 5 brace, cinch, strap 6 girdle 7 measure 8 cincture, encircle 10 dimensions 13 circumference

gist 3 nub 3 core, meat, pith 5 sense, short 6 burden, matter, thrust, upshot 7 bearing 9 substance

gitano 5 gypsy

give 3 air, lot, pay 4 bend, cave, deal, fail, feed, find, hand, pose, sell, vend, vent 5 allot, allow, apply, award, break, grant, issue, offer, spend, throw, yield 6 accord, afford, assign, befall, bestow, betide, chance, confer, devote, direct, donate, expend, extend, fold up, happen, lay out, lot out, market, outlay, relent, render, strike, supply, tender, weaken 7 address, crumple, deliver, dish out, dole out, express, fall out, fork out, furnish, hand out, hold out, inflict, mete out, present, produce, proffer, provide, slacken 8 allocate, collapse, disburse, dispense, disperse, give away, hand over, shell out, transfer, turn over 9 admeasure, apportion, ventilate 10 buckle down, contribute, distribute

give away 4 tell 5 grant, mouth, spill 6 bestow, betray, devote, donate, reveal 7 blab out, divulge, hand out, present, unclose 8 disclose, discover

give back 4 echo 6 refund, retire, return 7 replace, restore, retreat 8 withdraw 9 reinstate

give in 5 yield 6 relent 7 indulge, succumb 9 surrender

give off 4 emit, flow, pour, vent, void 5 issue 7 release 8 throw off 9 discharge

give out 4 deal, dole, drop, emit, fail, mete, vent, wilt 5 issue 6 cave in, peg out, run out 7 release, succumb 8 collapse, throw off 9 break down

giver 5 donor 7 donator 8 bestower 9 conferrer, presenter

give up 4 cede, quit, sell 5 forgo, leave, waive, yield 6 forego, resign, vacate 7 abandon, despair, despond 8 abdicate, hand over 9 surrender 10 relinquish

gizmo see gadget

glabrous 4 bald 6 shaven, smooth 8 hairless 9 beardless 12 smooth-shaven

glacial 3 icy 4 cold 5 chill, gelid, nippy 6 arctic, chilly, frigid, frosty 8 freezing

glacier 3 ice 6 ice cap 8 ice sheet *Alaska:* 4 Muir, Taku 6 Bering *Antarctica:* 9 Beardmore *deposit:* 4 kame 5 esker 6 placer 7 moraine 8 diluvium *fissure:* 8 crevasse *fragment:* 4 berg 7 iceberg *hill:* 7 drumlin *Karakoram:* 5 Biafo 7 Baltoro *New Zealand:* 6 Tasman *pinnacle:* 5 serac

glad 4 fain 5 happy, jolly, merry 6 blithe, bright, cheery, genial, jocund, jovial, joyful, joyous 7 beaming, gleeful, pleased, radiant, tickled 8 cheerful, mirthful, pleasant, rejoiced 9 delighted, gratified 11 exhilarated 12 lighthearted

gladden 5 cheer, elate 6 arride, please 7 delight, gratify, happify, rejoice 8 pleasure

glade 5 grove, marsh 8 clearing

gladiator 7 battler, fighter 9 combatant *Roman:* 9 retiarius

gladly 4 fain, lief

gladness 3 joy 4 glee 5 bliss, cheer, mirth 7 jollity, joyance 9 happiness 10 joyfulness

gladstone 3 bag

glamorous 5 siren 8 alluring, charming, magnetic 9 seductive 10 attractive, bewitching, enchanting 11 captivating, fascinating

glamour 5 charm, magic 6 allure, appeal 8 charisma, witchery 9 magnetism 10 witchcraft 11 fascination

glance 3 rub 4 buff, kiss, peek, peep, skim, skip 5 brush, carom, flash, glaze, gleam, glime, glint, gloss, graze, shave, shine, touch 6 bounce, careen, polish, scrape 7 burnish, contact, furbish, glimmer, glimpse, glisten, glitter, shimmer, sparkle, twinkle 8 ricochet 9 coruscate *sinister:* 4 leer

gland 5 gonad, liver, organ 6 thymus 7 adrenal, mammary, thyroid 8 exocrine, pancreas, prostate 9 endocrine, pituitary 11 parathyroid *secretion:* 7 hormone *sex:* 5 gonad *swelling:* 4 bubo

glare 4 bore, gape, gawk, gaze, glow, peer 5 blaze, flame, flash, frown, gleam, gloat,

lower, scowl, stare 6 dazzle, glower, goggle 7 glisten, glitter

glaring 4 loud, rank 5 gaudy, plain, vivid 6 brazen, flashy, garish, tawdry, tinsel 7 blatant, capital, chintzy 8 flagrant 9 egregious, obtrusive 10 noticeable 11 conspicuous, outstanding

Glasgow's patron saint 5 Mingo 9 Kentigern

glass 4 lens, pane 5 image, lense, prism 6 mirror 7 reflect 9 barometer, telescope *combining form:* 4 hyal, vitr 5 hyalo, vitro *container:* 3 jar 6 beaker, bottle *decorative:* 7 schmelz 8 schmelze *drinking:* 3 mug 4 pony 5 stein 6 goblet, jigger, rummer, seidel 7 snifter, tumbler 8 schooner *gem:* 5 paste 6 strass *magnifying:* 5 loupe *milky:* 7 opaline *volcanic:* 7 perlite 8 obsidian

glasses 5 specs 6 shades 7 goggles 10 spectacles

glass-like 6 vitric 8 vitreous

glassmaker 6 blower 7 glazier, Tiffany (Louis Comfort)

glassmaking *oven:* 4 lehr *tool:* 5 ponty 6 pontil 8 blowpipe

Glaucus *father:* 5 Minos 8 Sisyphus *mother:* 6 Merope 8 Pasiphae *son:* 11 Bellerophon

glaze 3 rub 4 buff, coat 5 glint, gloss, sheen, shine 6 enamel, glance, luster, polish 7 burnish, furbish

gleam 3 ray 4 beam, glow 5 flash, glint, sheen, shine 6 glance 7 glimmer, glisten, glitter, radiate, shimmer, sparkle, twinkle 8 radiance 11 coruscation, scintillate 13 scintillation

gleaming 5 shiny 6 glossy, sheeny 7 shining 8 lustrous, polished 9 burnished 10 glistening

glean 4 cull, reap 6 garner, gather, pick up 7 extract

glede 4 kite 6 osprey

glee 3 joy 5 mirth 6 gaiety, levity 7 delight, jollity 8 hilarity, pleasure 9 enjoyment, jocundity, joviality, merriment

gleeful 3 gay 4 boon 5 jolly, merry 6 blithe, jocund, jovial 8 mirthful 10 blithesome

glen 4 dale, vale 6 dingle, valley *deep:* 5 gorge 6 ravine *Scottish:* 5 heuch, heugh

glib 4 easy 5 slick 6 facile, fluent, smooth 7 voluble 8 eloquent, flippant, vocative, well-hung 9 talkative 10 articulate

glide 3 fly 4 flow, sail, skim, slip, soar 5 creep, float, mouse, skate, skulk, slick, slide, slink, sneak, steal 7 gumshoe, slither 8 glissade, volplane 9 pussyfoot

glimmer 4 glow 5 flash, gleam, glint 6 glance 7 glisten, glitter, shimmer, sparkle,

twinkle 9 coruscate 11 coruscation
13 scintillation

glimpse 4 look, peek, peep 5 stime
6 glance

glint 5 flash, glaze, gleam, gloss, sheen,
shine 6 glance, luster, polish 7 glimmer,
glisten, glitter, shimmer, sparkle, twinkle
9 coruscate 11 coruscation 13 scintillation

glissade 4 skim, slip 5 glide, slick, slide
7 slither

glisten 5 flash, gleam, glint, shine
6 glance 7 glimmer, glitter, shimmer, sparkle, twinkle 9 coruscate 11 coruscation

glitter 5 flash, gleam, glint, shine 6 glance
7 glimmer, glisten, shimmer, spangle, sparkle, twinkle 9 bespangle, coruscate 11 coruscation 13 scintillation

glittering 5 gaudy, showy 7 shining 9 brilliant, clinquant, sparkling

gloaming 3 eve 4 dusk 7 evening
8 eventide, owl-light, twilight 9 nightfall

gloat 4 bore, gape, gawk, gaze, peer
5 exult, glare, stare 6 goggle

global 5 grand 6 cosmic 7 general, overall
8 all-round, catholic 9 inclusive, planetary,
universal, worldwide

globe 3 orb 4 ball 5 earth, round, world
6 planet, sphere 7 rondure *half:* 10 hemisphere

globule 4 bead, drib, drip, drop 6 gobbet
7 driblet, droplet 8 spherule

gloom 3 dim 4 dusk, murk 5 bedim, blues,
cloud, dumps, frown, lower, scowl
6 darken, glower 7 becloud, obscure, sadness 8 darkness, overcast 9 adumbrate,
dejection 10 depression, melancholy, overshadow, the dismals 11 unhappiness
12 mournfulness

gloomy 3 dim, dun, sad 4 cold, dark,
dour, drab, dull, glum, ugly 5 black, bleak,
drear, dusky, morne, murky, muzzy, sulky,
surly 6 dismal, dreary, morose, solemn,
somber, sullen 7 crabbed, joyless, obscure,
stygian, unhappy 8 dejected, desolate,
downcast, funereal, mournful 9 cheerless,
depressed, lightless, mirthless, oppressed,
saturnine, tenebrous, woebegone 10 acheronian, acherontic, caliginous, depressant,
depressing, depressive, despondent, lugubrious, melancholy, oppressive, tenebrific
11 dispiriting, pessimistic 12 disconsolate,
discouraging

glorify 4 hymn, laud 5 bless, cry up, erect,
exalt, extol, honor 6 praise, uprear 7 dignify, ennoble, magnify, sublime 8 eulogize
9 celebrate 10 aggrandize, panegyrize

glorious 5 grand, great, noble, proud
6 divine, groovy, superb 7 radiant, sublime
8 gorgeous, lustrous, majestic, splendid,
stunning 9 beautiful, brilliant, effulgent,

hunky-dory, marvelous, ravishing
11 magnificent, resplendent, splendorous

glory 4 fame, halo 5 exult, honor 6 praise,
renown 7 acclaim, aureole, delight, triumph
8 eminence, jubilate, splendor 9 greatness
11 distinction 12 magnificence

gloss 4 buff 5 glaze, glint, sheen, shine
6 enamel, glance, luster, polish 7 burnish,
furbish, varnish 8 annotate 9 sleekness,
slickness

glossary 6 clavis 7 lexicon

gloss over 5 white 6 veneer, whiten
7 falsify, varnish 8 palliate 9 extenuate,
sugarcoat, whitewash 12 misrepresent

glossy 5 shiny, sleek 6 sheeny, sleeky,
smarmy 7 shining 8 gleaming, lustrous,
polished 9 burnished 10 glistening *fabric:*
4 silk 5 satin *paint:* 6 enamel

glove 4 mitt 5 cover 6 mitten, sheath
8 gauntlet

glow 4 pink, rose 5 blare, blaze, bloom,
blush, color, flame, flare, flush, glare,
rouge, shine 6 mantle, pinken, redden
7 blossom, crimson, foxfire

glower 4 gaze 5 frown, gloom, scowl,
stare

glowing 3 hot 5 fiery, flush, ruddy, shiny
6 ardent, fervid, florid, heated 7 blazing,
burning, candent, fervent, flaming, flushed,
radiant 8 dazzling, rubicund, sanguine
10 candescent, hot-blooded, passionate
11 full-blooded, impassioned 12 enthusiastic

gloze over see **gloss over**

Gluck opera 5 Orfeo 6 Armide 7 Alceste

glucose 5 sugar

glue 3 fix 4 join 5 epoxy, paste, stick
6 adhere, attach, cement 8 adhesive, mucilage

gluey 5 gooey, gummy 6 cloggy, sticky,
stodgy 8 adhesive

glum 4 dour 5 moody, sulky, surly
6 gloomy, morose, silent, sullen 7 crabbed
8 taciturn 9 depressed, oppressed, saturnine

glut 4 clog, cloy, cram, fill, jade, pall, sate
5 feast, gorge, stuff 6 stodge 7 satiate,
surfeit

glutinous 4 ropy 5 gluey, gummy 6 sticky
7 viscous

glutton 3 hog, pig 5 gulch 8 gourmand
9 chowhound

gluttonous 7 hoggish, piggish 8 edacious, ravening, ravenous 9 indulgent,
rapacious, voracious 11 intemperate

gluttony 7 edacity 8 gulosity

G-man 3 fed

gnarl 4 bend, knot 5 snarl, twist 6 deform
7 contort, distort

gnash 4 bite 5 grind

gnat 3 fly 4 pest 6 insect

gnaw 3 eat 4 bite, chew 5 annoy, erode, harry, scour, tease, worry 6 harass, nibble, pester, plague 7 bedevil, consume, corrode, eat away, hagride 8 wear away

gnome 3 elf, saw 4 rule 5 axiom, dwarf, maxim, moral, troll 6 dictum, goblin, sprite, truism 7 brocard 8 aphorism, apothegm

gnostic 4 sage, wise 6 sophic 7 knowing 9 insighted, sagacious 10 discerning, insightful, perceptive 13 knowledgeable

go 3 act, die, fit, fly, hie, pep, run, set, try 4 bear, bout, exit, fare, flee, give, jibe, like, move, pass, quit, shot, wend, work 5 abide, agree, apply, brook, drive, enjoy, event, fit in, fling, leave, occur, range, recur, refer, siege, spell, stint, vigor, whirl 6 accord, become, belong, decamp, demise, depart, elapse, endure, energy, escape, expire, extend, get off, happen, pan out, pop off, push on, repair, resort, retire, thrive, travel 7 abscond, advance, come off, conform, crumble, decease, episode, get away, journey, potency, proceed, prosper, pull out, push off, succeed, success, succumb, take off 8 collapse, flourish, function, incident, occasion, pass away, run along, shove off, tolerate, vitality, withdraw 9 happening, hardihood 10 correspond, get-up-and-go, occurrence *against:* 5 fight 6 oppose *ahead:* 4 lead 7 precede, proceed 8 continue, progress *along:* 5 agree 6 concur *around:* 5 avoid 7 compass 10 circumvent *at:* 6 attack 8 approach *away:* 3 off 4 exit, quit, scat, shoo 5 leave, scram 6 depart, retire *back:* 6 recede, return, revert 7 regress, retreat *back on:* 6 betray, renege 7 abandon *back over:* 6 review 7 retrace *before:* 4 lead 7 precede 8 antedate *beyond:* 6 exceed 7 surpass *forward:* 7 advance, proceed 8 continue, progress *in:* 5 enter 7 ingress 9 penetrate *out:* 4 date, exit 5 leave 6 egress *Scottish:* 3 gae *through:* 3 cut 6 endure 7 undergo 9 penetrate 10 experience *together:* 3 fit 4 suit 5 agree, befit 6 become 9 agree with, harmonize *with:* 4 date, suit 5 befit 6 escort 9 accompany

goad 3 egg, sic 4 prod, spur 5 drive, egg on, impel, prick 6 exhort, needle, prompt, propel 7 impetus, impulse 8 catalyst, stimulus 9 impulsion, incentive, stimulant

go-ahead 4 okay 9 clearance, gumptious 10 green light 11 up-and-coming 12 enterprising 13 authorization

goal 3 aim, end, use 4 duty, mark 6 object, target 7 purpose 8 ambition, function 9 objective, quaesitum

goat 3 kid, ram 5 billy, nanny, patsy 6 alpaca, angora, caprid, nubian 7 fall guy 8 cashmere 9 scapegoat *combining form:*

5 capri *female:* 3 doe 5 nanny *flesh:* 6 chevon *genus:* 5 Capra *Himalayan:* 4 tahr, thar *male:* 4 buck 5 billy *wild:* 4 ibex 7 markhor

goat antelope 5 goral, serow 7 chamois

goatee 5 beard 7 Vandyke

goatfish 6 mullet

goatish 3 hot 4 lewd 7 caprine, hircine, lustful, satyric 8 prurient 9 lickerish 10 lascivious, libidinous, passionate 12 concupiscent

goat-man deity 3 Pan

goat nut 6 jojoba

goatsfoot 8 goutweed

goatskin 9 chevrette

gob 3 wad 4 clod, hunk, lump, mass 5 chunk, mouth 6 nugget

gobbet 4 drip, drop 7 driblet, droplet, globule

gobble 4 bolt, cram, gulp, slop, wolf 5 slosh 6 englut, guzzle 11 ingurgitate

gobbledygook see gibberish

go-between 5 agent, envoy 6 broker 8 attorney, emissary, mediator 9 middleman 10 arbitrator, interagent, interceder, matchmaker, negotiator 11 intercessor 12 entrepreneur, intermediary, intermediate 13 intermediator

goblet 5 glass 6 vessel

goblin 3 elf, fay 4 bhut, bogy 5 bogie, bogle, fairy, gnome, pooka 6 booger, sprite 7 brownie 8 barghest, bogeyman

gobs 4 heap, wads 5 loads, reams, scads 6 oodles 8 slathers 10 quantities

god 4 idol 5 deity 7 creator 8 Almighty, divinity, immortal *combining form:* 3 the 4 theo *false:* 4 baal *French:* 4 dieu *Latin:* 4 deus *Spanish:* 4 dios; (see specific entries (as Greek; Roman) for names of specific gods and goddesses)

God Bless America composer 6 Berlin (Irving)

goddess 4 idol 5 deity 8 divinity, immortal *Latin:* 3 dea; (see note at god)

godfather 3 don 4 capo 7 sponsor

God-fearing 5 pious 6 devout 8 reverent 9 religious

godforsaken 6 dismal 7 pitiful 8 desolate, pitiable, wretched 9 miserable, neglected 11 unfortunate

Godiva's husband 7 Leofric

godless 6 wicked 7 impious, infidel 8 agnostic 9 atheistic 11 irreligious, unreligious

godlike 6 deific, divine 8 deifical, immortal

godly 4 holy 5 pious 6 deific, devout, divine 7 angelic, saintly 9 pietistic, prayerful, religious

go down 3 dip, sag, set 4 drop, fall, fold, sink 5 droop, pitch, slump 6 cave in, plunge, submit, topple, tumble 7 crumple, decline, descend, founder, go under, succumb **8** collapse, keel over, submerge, submerge **9** surrender

God's acre 8 cemetery **9** graveyard **10** churchyard, necropolis **11** polyandrium **12** burial ground, memorial park, potter's field **13** burying ground

godsend 4 boon, good **7** benefit **8** blessing **9** advantage **11** benediction

Goethe work 5 Faust **6** Egmont, Stella **7** Clavigo **10** Prometheus

goffer 5 crimp, flute, plait

go-getter 6 dynamo, peeler **7** hustler, rustler **8** live wire **11** self-starter

goggle 3 eye **4** bore, gape, gawk, gaze, look, ogle, peer **5** glare, gloat, stare

goggles 5 specs **7** glasses **8** blinkers **10** spectacles

Gogol novel 9 Dead Souls **10** Taras Bulba

Gog's land 5 Magog

goiter 6 struma **8** swelling

gola 4 cyma **7** granary **9** storeroom, warehouse

Golconda see gold mine

gold 4 gilt **5** aurum, metal, money **6** riches, wealth, yellow **7** bullion, element **8** treasure *bar:* **5** ingot *combining form:* **4** auri, auro **5** chrys **6** chryso *fool's:* **6** pyrite *heraldic:* **2** or *imitation:* **6** ormolu *measure:* **5** carat, karat *Spanish:* **3** oro *symbol:* **2** Au

goldbrick 3 bum **4** idle, laze, lazy, loaf, loll **6** dawdle, loiter, lounge **7** shirker, slacker, slinker

Gold Bug author 3 Poe (Edgar Allan)

gold cloth 4 lamé

gold-covered 4 gilt

golden 4 gilt, rich **5** blond, straw **6** blonde, flaxen, gilded, liquid, mellow, yellow **7** aureate, aureous, honeyed **8** Hyblaean

golden-ager 5 elder **6** senior **7** ancient, oldster **8** old-timer **13** senior citizen

golden apple 3 bel **6** tomato **7** hog plum

golden-apples guardian 5 Ithun **6** Ithunn

golden bough 9 mistletoe

Golden Boy playwright 5 Odets (Clifford)

golden-crowned accentor 8 ovenbird

goldeneye 4 duck **8** lacewing **9** merrywing

Golden Fleece seeker 5 Jason **8** Argonaut

Golden Hind captain 5 Drake (Francis)

Golden Horde 6 Tatars **7** Mongols

golden horse 8 palomino

golden shiner 4 dace

Golden State 10 California

golden wolf 6 chanco

goldfinch 8 graypate **12** yellowhammer

gold mine 7 bonanza **8** El Dorado, Golconda, treasury **13** treasure-house, treasure trove

golem 4 dolt **5** robot **7** machine **9** automaton, blockhead

golf *assistant:* **5** caddy **6** caddie *award:* **8** Ryder Cup **9** Curtis Cup, Walker Cup *club:* **4** iron, wood **5** baffy, cleek, spoon, wedge **6** driver, mashie, putter **7** brassie, niblick, pitcher **9** metal wood, sand wedge *club part:* **3** toe **4** face, grip, head, heel, neck, sole **5** hosel, shaft **6** socket *course:* **5** links *hazard:* **4** trap **6** bunker **8** sand trap *mound:* **3** tee *score:* **3** ace, par **5** bogey, bogie, eagle **6** birdie **9** albatross *stroke:* **4** baff, chip, draw, fade, hook, putt **5** drive, pitch, shank, slice **6** sclaff *target:* **3** cup, par, pin **4** flag **5** green **7** fairway *term:* **3** lie **4** ball, club, fore, hole, loft **5** divot, rough, round, swing **6** course, hazard, marker, stance, stroke **8** approach, foursome, handicap **9** backswing, downswing, flagstick **10** Vardon grip

golfer 8 linksman *man:* **3** Els (Ernie) **4** Daly (John), Ford (Doug), Kite (Tom), Lyle (Sandy), Mize (Larry), Tway (Bob) **5** Boros (Julius), Faldo (Nick), Floyd (Ray), Grady (Wayne), Green (Hubert), Hagen (Walter), Hogan (Ben), Jones (Bobby), Irwin (Hale), North (Andy), Pavin (Corey), Price (Nick), Shute (Denny), Snead (Sam) **6** Casper (Billy), Graham (David), Janzen (Lee), Langer (Bernhard), Miller (Johnny), Nelson (Byron, Larry), Norman (Greg), Ouimet (Francis), Palmer (Arnold), Player (Gary), Sluman (Jeff), Sutton (Hal), Vardon (Harry), Watson (Tom) **7** Azinger (Paul), Couples (Fred), Guldahl (Ralph), Mayfair (Billy), Sarazen (Gene), Simpson (Scott), Stewart (Payne), Strange (Curtis), Trevino (Lee), Woosnam (Ian), Zoollor (Fuzzy) **8** Crenshaw (Ben), Nicklaus (Jack), Olazabal (José), Weiskopf (Tom), Rodriquez (Chi Chi) **9** Elkington (Steve) **10** Middlecoff (Cary) **11** Ballesteros (Seve) *woman:* **4** Berg (Patty), King (Betsy) **5** Baker (Kathy), Lopez (Nancy), Rawls (Betsy), Stacy (Hollis), Suggs (Louise) **6** Alcott (Amy), Carner (Joanne), Daniel (Beth), Davies (Laura), Geddes (Jane), Mallon (Meg), Merten (Lauri), Wright (Mickey) **7** Bradley (Pat), Mochrie (Dottie), Sheehan (Patty) **8** Zaharias (Babe) **9** Sorenstam (Annika), Whitworth (Kathy) **10** Stephenson (Jan)

Goliath 5 giant **10** Philistine *deathplace:* **4** Elah *home:* **4** Gath *slayer:* **5** David

Gomer *father:* **7** Diblaim *husband:* **5** Hosea

gonad 5 gland, ovary **6** testis

gondola 3 car **4** boat **5** chair

gone 4 away, dead, left, lost 6 absent, gravid, parous 7 defunct, extinct, lacking, missing, omitted, wanting 8 childing, departed, enceinte, pregnant, vanished

gonef see ganef

Goneril *father:* 4 Lear *husband:* 6 Albany *sister:* 5 Regan 8 Cordelia *victim:* 5 Regan

Gone with the Wind *author:* 8 Mitchell (Margaret) *character:* 6 Ashley 7 Melanie 11 Rhett Butler 13 Scarlett O'Hara *plantation:* 4 Tara

gonfalon 4 flag 6 banner, ensign 7 pendant, pennant 8 standard 9 banderole

goo 4 crud, gook, goop, guck, gunk, muck

goober 3 nut 6 peanut

good 3 apt, fit 4 able, boon, just, meet, nice, pure 5 brave, right, sound, whole 6 adroit, au fait, clever, cogent, common, decent, humane, intact, kindly, proper, seemly, toward, useful 7 benefic, benefit, capable, fitting, gainful, godsend, healthy, helpful, welcome, welfare 8 adequate, all right, blessing, decorous, flawless, hygienic, innocent, interest, pleasant, pleasing, salutary, sensible, skillful, straight, unmarred, virtuous 9 advantage, agreeable, blameless, competent, congenial, exemplary, favorable, guiltless, healthful, incorrupt, justified, lily-white, lucrative, qualified, righteous, tolerable, undamaged, untainted, well-being, wholesome, workmanly 10 acceptable, altruistic, beneficial, benevolent, charitable, gratifying, inculpable, profitable, propitious, prosperity, salubrious, sufficient, unblamable, unimpaired, worthwhile 11 appropriate, benediction, considerate, pleasurable, pleasureful, respectable, unblemished, uncorrupted, well-behaved, well-founded, workmanlike 12 advantageous, considerable, eleemosynary, humanitarian, remunerative, salutiferous, satisfactory, well-grounded 13 philanthropic *combining form:* 2 eu 5 agath 6 agatho *French:* 3 bon *German:* 3 gut *Spanish:* 5 bueno

good-bye 4 ta-ta 5 adieu, congé 6 so long 7 cheerio, parting 8 farewell, toodle-oo 9 departing 11 leave-taking, valedictory *French:* 5 adieu *German:* 8 lebe wohl *Japanese:* 8 sayonara *Spanish:* 5 adios

Good Earth author 4 Buck (Pearl)

good-for-nothing 6 drafty, drossy, no-good, waster 7 fustian, inutile, nothing, rounder, useless, wastrel 8 feckless, unworthy 9 valueless, worthless 10 ne'er-do-well, profligate, scapegrace, unpurposed 11 meaningless, purposeless

good-humored see good-natured

good-looking 4 fair 6 comely, lovely, pretty 8 handsome 9 beauteous, beautiful 10 attractive

goodly 5 ample, large 6 comely, pretty 8 handsome 9 excellent 12 considerable

good-natured 4 easy, mild 6 genial, jovial 7 amiable, lenient 8 cheerful, obliging 9 gemütlich 10 altruistic, benevolent, charitable 11 complaisant

goodness 5 honor, merit 6 purity, virtue 7 honesty, probity 8 chastity, morality 9 integrity, rectitude, rightness 11 benevolence, uprightness 13 righteousness

goods 4 gear, line 5 stock, wares 7 effects 8 chattels, movables 9 vendibles 10 belongings 11 commodities, merchandise, possessions *smuggled:* 10 contraband *stolen:* 4 loot 5 booty 6 spoils *thrown overboard:* 5 lagan, ligan 6 jetsam

good-tasting 5 sapid, tasty 6 savory 8 tasteful 9 palatable, relishing, toothsome 10 appetizing, flavorsome

goodwill 5 amity, favor 6 comity 7 charity, rapport 8 alacrity, altruism, dispatch, kindness, sympathy 9 readiness, tolerance 10 expedition, friendship, generosity, kindliness 11 benevolence, helpfulness, promptitude 12 friendliness

goody 5 candy, treat 6 bonbon, dainty, morsel, tidbit, titbit 8 delicacy, kickshaw

goody-goody 4 prig 5 prude 6 Grundy 7 puritan 8 bluenose, comstock 9 Mrs. Grundy, nice Nelly

gooey 5 gluey, gummy, mushy, sappy, sobby, soupy 6 cloggy, drippy, slushy, sticky, stodgy 7 maudlin 8 adhesive 11 sentimental

goof 3 err 4 boob, dolt, mess 5 booby, botch, chump, dunce, gum up 6 bobble, bollix, bungle 7 blunder, fathead, louse up 8 dolthead, lunkhead

go off 4 blow 5 burst 7 explode 8 detonate

goofy 5 crazy, silly 6 stupid 7 foolish

gook 3 rot 4 crud, goop, gunk, muck 5 bilge, gumbo, hooey, trash 6 drivel

go on 3 act 4 bear, quit 5 carry 6 acquit, behave, demean, deport, hang on 7 carry on, comport, conduct, persist 8 continue 9 persevere

goon 3 sap 4 boob, dolt, dope, thug 7 hoodlum

gooney 9 albatross

goop 4 gook, gunk, muck 5 gumbo

goose 4 bird, dolt, poke 5 solan 9 simpleton *cry:* 4 honk, yang *genus:* 5 Anser *Hawaiian:* 4 nene *male:* 6 gander *relating to:* 8 anserine *snow:* 4 chen, wavy

5 wavey *wild:* 5 brant 7 graylag, greylag 8 barnacle, bernicle *young:* 7 gosling

goose egg 4 zero 5 aught, ought, zilch 6 cipher, naught, nought 7 nothing

gooseflesh 5 bumps 7 pimples

gopher 6 marmot, rodent 8 squirrel, tortoise

Gopher State 9 Minnesota

Gordian knot cutter 9 Alexander

Gordius' son 5 Midas

gore 4 stab, tush, tusk 5 blood, slime, wound 6 pierce

gorge 3 gap 4 cloy, fill, glut, jade, pall, sate 5 chasm, cleft, clove, flume, gulch, stuff 6 arroyo, clough, devour, gobble, guzzle, ravine, stodge 7 couloir, overeat, satiate, surfeit 11 overindulge *Arizona:* 11 Grand Canyon *China:* 7 Yangtze *Colorado:* 5 Royal

gorgeous 5 grand, plush, proud 6 lavish, lovely, pretty, superb 7 opulent, sublime 8 glorious, splendid 9 beautiful, luxurious, sumptuous 10 impressive 11 magnificent, resplendent, splendorous

Gorgon 6 Medusa, Stheno 7 Euryale *father:* 7 Phorcus, Phorcys *mother:* 4 Ceto *sentinel:* 4 Enyo 5 Deino 6 Graeae, Graiae 8 Pephredo

gorilla 3 ape 6 monkey 7 primate 10 anthropoid

Gorki drama 14 The Lower Depths

gorse 5 furze 7 juniper

gory 6 bloody 7 imbrued 8 sanguine 10 sanguinary 11 ensanguined, sanguineous 12 bloodstained

gospel 5 truth 6 truism 8 doctrine, teaching

gossamer 3 web 5 filmy, gauzy, sheer 6 flimsy 7 tiffany 10 diaphanous 11 transparent

gossip 3 cry 4 blab, buzz, chat, dirt, talk 5 clack, on-dit, prate, rumor, sieve, tabby 6 babble, claver, report, rumble, tattle 7 chatter, hearsay, prattle, rumorer 8 bigmouth, busybody, informer, quidnunc, telltale 9 carrytale, grapevine 10 circulator, mumblenews, newsmonger, talebearer 11 rumormonger, scandalizer, scuttlebutt

Gotham 7 New York

Gothic 4 rude, wild 5 crude 6 brutal, coarse, Hunnic, savage 7 Hunnish 8 barbaric 9 barbarian, barbarous 11 uncivilized

Gouda 6 cheese

gouge 3 con, dig 4 tool 5 cheat, exact, pinch, screw, wrest, wring 6 extort, wrench 7 squeeze, swindle 9 shake down 10 overcharge

goulash 4 stew 6 jumble, medley 8 mishmash

go under 4 fall, sink 6 go down, submit 7 founder, succumb 8 submerge, submerse 9 surrender

Gounod work 5 Faust 8 Ave Maria

gourd 4 pepo 5 fruit, melon 6 bottle, vessel 7 pumpkin 8 calabash, cucurbit *instrument:* 6 maraca

gourmand see glutton; gourmet

gourmet 7 epicure 9 bon vivant 10 gastronome 11 gastronomer 12 gastronomist

gout 4 blob, clot 5 spurt 6 splash 7 podagra 8 swelling

govern 3 run 4 head, lead, rule, sway 5 guide, reign, steer 6 direct, handle, manage, master, render 7 command, conduct, control, execute, oversee 8 carry out, dominate, overrule, regulate, shepherd 9 supervise 10 administer

governess 4 nana 5 nanny, nurse 6 duenna, nannie 8 mistress 9 nursemaid

government 4 rule 5 power 6 polity, regime 7 conduct, control, regency, regimen, tyranny 8 guidance, monarchy, republic 9 authority, autocracy, democracy, direction, hierarchy, oligarchy 10 management 11 aristocracy 12 dictatorship, organization *autocratic:* 7 czarism 9 despotism 10 absolutism 12 dictatorship *by a few:* 9 oligarchy *by eight:* 8 octarchy *by one:* 8 monarchy *by three:* 8 triarchy 11 triumvirate *by women:* 8 gynarchy *combining form:* 5 archy, cracy 6 ocracy *official:* 6 consul, syndic 8 diplomat 10 bureaucrat *relating to:* 9 political *science:* 8 politics *without:* 7 anarchy

government agency 2 VA 3 CIA, FAA, FBI, FCC, FDA, FHA, GAO, GPO, HUD, ICC, NBS, NRC, TVA 4 FEPC, NASA

governor 3 bey 4 head, lord 5 chief, nabob, pilot, ruler 6 leader, rector, regent 7 captain, manager, viceroy 8 director, official 9 executive, regulator 10 commandant, controller, magistrate *Chinese:* 6 tuchun *of a fort:* 7 alcaide 9 castellan, chatelain *Persian:* 6 satrap *Turkish:* 8 hospodar

gown 4 robe, toga 5 dress, frock, habit, tunic 6 banian, banyan, camise, clothe, kimono, mantua 7 cassock, chemise, garment 8 peignoir *hospital:* 6 johnny

goy 7 gentile

grab 3 hog, nab 4 nail, take 5 catch, clasp, grasp, seize 6 clutch, snatch, tackle 7 grapple

grabby 5 itchy 6 greedy 8 covetous, desirous, grasping 10 prehensile 11 acquisitive

grace 4 ease 5 adorn, charm, favor, mercy 6 lenity, polish, prayer, thanks, virtue 7 caritas, charity, dignify, dignity 8 blessing, clemency, easiness, elegance, goodness, kindness, leniency, petition **9** embellish **10** indulgence, invocation, suppleness **11** benediction, forbearance **12** thanksgiving

graceful 4 airy, deft, easy **6** featly, gainly, smooth, urbane **7** elegant, flowing, genteel, refined **8** debonair, polished

graceless 4 wild **5** inept **6** vulgar **7** awkward, unhappy **8** barbaric **9** barbarian, barbarous, ill-chosen, tasteless **10** outlandish **11** unfortunate **12** infelicitous

Graces 6 Aglaia (brilliance), Charis, Thalia (bloom) **8** Charites (plural) **10** Euphrosyne (joy) *mother:* **5** Aegle

gracious 4 easy, kind, mild **5** preux **6** benign, clubby, genial, kindly **7** affable, amiable, cordial, courtly, gallant, starchy, stately **8** mannered, obliging, outgoing, sociable **9** benignant, bonhomous, congenial, courteous

grackle 3 jaw **7** jackdaw **9** blackbird

gradation 4 step. **5** range, shade **6** ablaut, change, degree, nuance, series **8** position **9** variation **10** difference, divergence

grade 3 peg **4** lean, rank, rate, rung, sort, step, tier, tilt **5** class, group, notch, order, slant, slope, stage **6** assort, degree, estate, league **7** arrange, caliber, incline, leaning, quality **8** appraise, category, classify, evaluate, grouping

Grade A 3 top **4** fine **5** prime **7** capital **8** five-star, superior, top-notch **9** excellent, first-rate, top-drawer **10** first-class

gradient 4 lean, ramp, tilt **5** slant, slope **7** incline, leaning **11** inclination *combining form:* **5** cline **6** clinal

gradine 4 seat, step **5** shelf **6** chisel

gradually 8 bit by bit **9** piecemeal **10** step by step

graduate *female:* 6 alumna **7** alumnae (plural) *male:* **6** alumni (plural) **7** alumnus

Graeae, Graiae 4 Enyo **5** Deino **8** Pephredo *father:* **7** Phorcus, Phorcys *mother:* **4** Ceto *sisters:* **7** Gorgons

graft 4 join, mend **5** crime, scion, unite **6** attach, boodle, fasten, inarch **7** implant, topwork

grail 3 cup **7** chalice, platter

grain 3 bit, jot, rye **4** corn, iota, meal, mite, oats, rice **5** crumb, fiber, maize, speck, trace, wheat **6** barley, cereal, tittle **7** granule, smidgen, sorghum, texture **8** molecule, particle *bundle:* **4** bale **5** sheaf *chute:* **6** hopper *ear:* **5** spica, spike *elevator:* **4** silo *mixture:* **6** fodder *row:* **5** swath **7** windrow

grainy 6 coarse **8** granular

grammarian *Roman:* 7 Donatus (Aelius)

grammatical case 6 dative **8** ablative, genitive, locative, vocative **9** objective **10** accusative, nominative, possessive, subjective

grampus 5 whale **8** cetacean, scorpion **9** blackfish

Granada *building:* 8 Alhambra *citadel:* **8** Alcazaba *last Moorish king:* **7** Boabdil

granary 3 bin **4** gola, silo **10** repository, storehouse

grand 4 epic, huge **5** gaudy, lofty, noble, royal, showy **6** august, flashy, garish, lavish, lordly, ornate, superb **7** exalted, stately, sublime **8** baronial, elevated, gorgeous, imposing, magnific, majestic, princely, splendid, towering **9** luxurious, sumptuous **10** impressive, monumental, prodigious, stupendous, tremendous **11** magnificent **12** ostentatious

Grand Canyon *explorer:* 6 Powell (John Wesley) *state:* **7** Arizona

grande dame 6 matron **7** dowager **9** matriarch

grandee 5 pasha **6** bashaw **8** nobleman

grandeur 4 pomp **7** dignity, majesty **8** nobility, splendor, vastness **9** greatness, largeness, loftiness, nobleness, sublimity **10** augustness **11** stateliness **12** magnificence

grand inquisitor *Spanish:* 10 Torquemada (Tomas de)

grandiose 4 epic, vast **5** lofty, noble, royal, showy **6** august, cosmic, lordly **7** stately, utopian **8** imposing, majestic, princely **9** ambitious, visionary **11** magnificent, pretentious **12** ostentatious

grandmother *Russian:* 8 babushka *Scottish:* **6** gudame

grange 4 farm **5** lodge **9** farmhouse

granite 4 rock **6** aplite

Granite State 12 New Hampshire

grant 3 aid, own **4** alms, avow, cede, dole, gift, give **5** admit, allow, award, let on, own up, yield **6** accord, bestow, confer, donate, fess up, permit **7** charity, concede, confess, entitle, handout, present, subsidy **8** bequeath, donation **9** vouchsafe **10** assistance, relinquish, subvention **11** acknowledge, benefaction **12** contribution **13** appropriation

granular 5 rough, sandy **6** coarse, grainy

granule 4 pill, spot **5** grain **6** pellet **8** particle

grape 3 fox, uva **4** Bual **5** Gamay, Pinot **6** Arinto, Burger, Gentil, Merlot, muscat **7** Albillo, Aligote, Barbera, Catawba, Concord, Furmint, Niagara, sultana **8** Aleatico, Cabernet, Charbono, Delaware, Friularo, Grenache, Isabella, labrusca, malvasia, muscadel, Nebbiolo, Riesling, Semillon, Sylvaner, Thompson, Traminer, vinifera,

Viognier 9 Chasselas, Lambrusco, Malvoisie, muscadine, Pinot Gris, Pinot Noir, Sauvignon, Trebbiano, zinfandel 10 Grignolino, muscadelle, Pinot Blanc, Verdicchio 11 Chenin Blanc, Mavrodaphne, Petite Sirah, scuppernong *disease:* 4 esca *dried:* 6 raisin *drink:* 4 wine *pulp:* 4 rape 6 pomace *residue:* 4 marc

grapefruit 6 pomelo

Grapes of Wrath *author:* 9 Steinbeck (John) *family:* 4 Joad *people:* 5 Okies

grapevine 4 buzz, talk 5 on-dit, rumor 6 gossip, report, rumble 7 hearsay

graph 3 map 5 chart 6 sketch 7 diagram, outline 8 nomogram

graphic 5 clear, lucid, vivid 6 cogent, visual 7 precise, telling 8 clear-cut, definite, explicit, incisive, pictoric, striking 9 pictorial, realistic 10 compelling

graphite 4 lead 6 carbon 8 plumbago

grapnel 4 hook 6 anchor

grapple 3 nab 4 grab, grip, hold, take 5 catch, clamp, clasp, grasp, gripe, seize 6 bucket, clench, clinch, clutch, snatch, tenure, tussle 7 scuffle, wrestle

grasp 3 dig, see 4 grip, have, hent, hold, know, take 5 catch, clamp, clasp, gripe 6 accept, clench, clinch, clutch, fathom, follow, take in, tenure 7 cognize, compass, grapple 8 envisage, perceive 9 apprehend 10 appreciate, comprehend, understand

graspable 5 lucid 8 knowable 10 fathomable 12 intelligible 13 apprehensible

grasping 4 avid 5 itchy 6 grabby, greedy 8 covetous, desirous 9 extorting 10 prehensile 11 acquisitive

grass 3 pot, sod, tea 4 lawn, reed, turf, weed 6 moocah, redtop 7 herbage, panicum, pasture 8 cannabis, Mary Jane 9 cocksfoot, marijuana *African:* 6 imphee *annual:* 6 darnel 8 teosinte *Asian:* 7 vetiver, whangee *Australian:* 8 spinifex *beach:* 6 marram *cereal:* 3 oat, rye 4 milo, teff 5 kafir, maize, proso, wheat 6 kaffir, millet, sorgho 7 sorghum 8 feterita, triticum *clump:* 4 tuft 7 tussock *combining form:* 6 gramin 7 gramini *dried:* 3 hay *European:* 7 Bermuda, timothy *fiber:* 4 flax *forage:* 7 setaria *fragrant:* 10 citronella *giant:* 5 otate *Mexican:* 7 zacaton *pasture:* 5 Bahia, grama *perennial:* 5 muhly 6 fescue, quitch, zoysia 7 esparto, galleta *prairie:* 8 bluestem *second growth:* 5 rowen *tropical:* 5 cogon 6 bamboo

grasshopper 4 grig 6 locust 7 katydid

grassland 3 lea 5 field 6 meadow 7 pasture, prairie *African:* 4 veld 5 veldt *flat:* 7 savanna 8 savannah *South American:* 5 pampa

grate 3 get, jar 4 bark, fray, gall, rasp, rile, skin 5 chafe, peeve, pique, scuff 6 abrade, burn up, nettle, scrape 7 provoke, scratch 8 irritate 9 aggravate

grateful 4 good 7 obliged, pleased, welcome 8 beholden, pleasant, renewing, solacing, thankful 9 agreeable, congenial, consoling, delicious, favorable, gratified

Gratiano *brother:* 9 Brabantio *friend:* 7 Antonio 8 Bassanio *niece:* 9 Desdemona *wife:* 7 Nerissa

gratify 4 baby, feed, sate 5 favor, feast, humor 6 arride, coddle, oblige, pamper, pander, please 7 appease, cater to, content, delight, gladden, happify, indulge, satisfy

grating 3 dry 4 grid, rasp 5 grill, harsh, rough 6 grille, hoarse 7 jarring, rasping, raucous 8 gridiron, strident 10 stridulent

gratis 4 free 8 costless 10 chargeless, gratuitous 13 complimentary

gratuitous 4 free 6 gratis, wanton 7 unasked, willing 8 baseless, costless 9 unfounded, voluntary 10 bottomless, chargeless, groundless, reasonless, ungrounded 11 uncalled-for, unwarranted 12 indefensible, supererogant 13 complimentary

gratuity 3 fee, tip 4 alms, gift, perk 5 bonus 6 reward 7 cumshaw, douceur, largess 8 donation, offering 9 baksheesh, lagniappe, pourboire 10 perquisite 11 benefaction 12 contribution

grave 3 pit, sad 4 dire, etch, fell, grim, tomb, ugly 5 awful, crypt, drive, fatal, heavy, major, pound, sober, staid, stamp, vault 6 burial, deadly, hammer, incise, sedate, severe, solemn, somber 7 austere, earnest, ghastly, impress, killing, ossuary, serious, weighty 8 catacomb, dreadful, grievous, horrible, terrible 9 dangerous, mausoleum, murderous, ponderous, saturnine, sepulcher, sepulture *marker:* 5 stela, stele 6 ledger 8 memorial, monument 9 footstone, headstone, tombstone 11 sarcophagus *mound:* 6 barrow 7 tumulus *robber:* 5 ghoul

gravel 4 dirt, grit, sand *ridge:* 5 esker

graven image 4 idol

graver 5 burin 8 sculptor

graveyard 8 boot hill, cemetery, God's acre 10 necropolis 11 polyandrium 12 burial ground, memorial park, potter's field 13 burying ground

gravid 6 parous 8 childing, enceinte, pregnant 9 expectant, expecting 10 parturient

gravity 6 weight 7 dignity 8 sobriety 9 heaviness, solemnity 10 importance, somberness 11 seriousness

gravy 5 juice, sauce 8 dressing, windfall *French:* 3 jus

gray 3 ash, old 4 aged, ashy, blah, drab, dull 5 ashen, bleak, color, hoary, slate, slaty, taupe **6** dismal, gloomy, leaden **7** elderly, grizzly, neutral **8** cinerous, gunmetal, overcast **9** colorless *brownish:* **7** fuscous *combining form:* **4** poli **5** glauc, polio **6** glauco

gray dawn 4 zinc

gray duck 7 gadwall, mallard, pintail

grayfish 7 pollack

gray matter 3 wit **4** head, mind, obex **5** brain **9** intellect

graze 3 dop, rub **4** feed, gall, harm, hurt, kiss, skim, skip, wear **5** brush, carom, chafe, erode, shave, wound **6** abrade, bruise, glance, injure, ruffle **7** contuse, corrade, pasture **8** ricochet

grease 3 fat, oil **4** lard, soil **5** smear **6** smooth **7** lanolin **9** lubricant, lubricate *combining form:* **4** sebi, sebo

greasy 4 oily **5** fatty, slick **6** slippy **7** pinguid **8** slippery, slithery, unctuous **10** lubricious, oleaginous

greasy spoon 4 café **5** diner **7** beanery, hashery **9** hash house, lunchroom **10** coffee shop

great 3 big, fat **4** bull, huge, vast **5** famed, grand, husky, large **6** famous, heroic **7** eminent, extreme, immense, notable, supreme, titanic **8** enormous, oversize, renowned **9** excellent, fantastic, important, prominent, wonderful **10** celebrated, celebrious, surpassing **11** illustrious, magnificent, superlative **13** distinguished *combining form:* **3** meg **4** mega **5** megal **6** megalo

Great Bear 9 Big Dipper, Ursa Major

Great Britain see England

Great Commoner, the 4 Pitt (William)

Great Emancipator, the 7 Lincoln (Abraham)

greater 4 more, over **6** better, higher, larger **8** superior **9** overlying **11** superjacent

greatest 4 best, most **6** utmost **7** largest, noblest, supreme *amount:* **7** maximum

Great Expectations author: **7** Dickens (Charles) *character:* **3** Pip **5** Biddy **7** Estella, Jaggers **8** Havisham, Magwitch

greathearted 3 big **5** brave, lofty, manly **6** heroic **7** gallant **8** fearless, generous **10** benevolent, chivalrous, courageous **11** considerate, magnanimous

Great Lake 4 Erie **5** Huron **7** Ontario **8** Michigan, Superior *acronym:* **5** HOMES

Great Lake State 8 Michigan

grebe 4 bird, fowl **8** dabchick, didapper

Greece capital: **6** Athens *monetary unit:* **7** drachma

greed 7 avarice, avidity **8** cupidity, gluttony, rapacity, voracity **12** ravenousness

greedy 5 itchy **6** grabby **7** miserly, selfish **8** covetous, desirous, esurient, grasping **10** avaricious, gluttonous **11** acquisitive

Greek 6 babble, drivel, jabber **7** Achaean **8** Hellenic, nonsense **9** gibberish *alien resident:* **5** metic *assembly:* **5** agora, boule *coin:* **4** obol **5** hecte **6** lepton, stater *column:* **5** Doric, Ionic **10** Corinthian *contest:* **4** agon *counselor:* **6** Nestor *cup:* **5** kylix *dictator:* **7** Metaxas (Ioannis) *dragon:* **9** Eurythion *drink:* **4** ouzo *epic:* **5** Iliad **7** Odyssey *Fates:* **6** Clotho, Moirae **7** Atropos **8** Lachesis

god:

chief: **4** Zeus *messenger:* **6** Hermes *of agriculture:* **6** Cronus *of death:* **8** Thanatos *of fire:* **10** Hephaestus *of healing:* **9** Asclepius *of love:* **4** Eros *of marriage:* **5** Hymen *of physicians:* **6** Hermes *of the sea:* **6** Triton **7** Oceanus **8** Poseidon *of the sun:* **6** Helios *of the underworld:* **5** Pluto *of the wind:* **5** Eurus, Notus **6** Aeolus, Boreas **8** Zephyrus *of war:* **4** Ares *of wine:* **8** Dionysus *of woods:* **3** Pan

goddess:

of agriculture: **7** Demeter *of beauty:* **9** Aphrodite *of dawn:* **3** Eos *of discord:* **4** Eris *of flowers:* **7** Chloris *of harvests:* **4** Rhea *of hunting:* **7** Artemis *of justice:* **7** Astraea *of love:* **9** Aphrodite *of marriage:* **4** Hera *of night:* **3** Nyx *of peace:* **5** Irene *of retribution:* **7** Nemesis *of ruin:* **3** Ate *of the earth:* **2** Ge **4** Gaea, Gaia *of the moon:* **6** Hecate, Hekate, Selena, Selene **7** Artemis, Astarte *of the seasons:* **5** Horae *of the underworld:* **6** Hecate, Hekate *of vengeance:* **7** Nemesis *of victory:* **4** Nike *of wisdom:* **4** Athena *of witchcraft:* **6** Hecate, Hekate *of womanhood:* **4** Hera *of youth:* **4** Hebe

hero: **4** Aias, Ajax **5** Jason **7** Theseus **8** Achilles, Argonaut, Heracles, Hercules, Odysseus **9** Achilleus *historian:* **8** Xenophon **9** Herodotus **10** Thucydides *lawgiver:* **5** Draco, Solon *leader:* **9** Agamemnon *letter:* **2** mu, nu, pi, xi **3** chi, eta, phi, psi, rho, tau **4** beta, iota, zeta **5** alpha, delta, gamma, kappa, omega, sigma, theta **6** lambda **7** epsilon, omicron, upsilon *magistrate:* **6** archon *marketplace:* **5** agora *measure:* **3** ona, pik **4** bema **5** cados, chous, digit, maris, pygon, xylon **6** acaena, bachel, barile, cotula, dichas, gramme, hemina, koilon, pechys, pelame, schene **7** amphora, cyathos, diaulos, hekteus, stadion, stadium, stremma **8** condylos, daktylos, dekapode, dolichos, medimnos, metretes, palaiste, plethron,

spithame, stathmos 9 oxybaphon *porch:*
4 stoa *sandwich:* 4 gyro *shield:* 5 pelta
soldier: 7 hoplite *theater:* 5 odeon,
odeum *underworld:* 5 Hades *war cry:*
5 alala *warrior:* 4 Ajax 7 Ulysses 8 Achilles, Diomedes, Odysseus 9 Agamemnon,
Palamedes *weight:* 3 mna, oka 4 mina
5 litra, livre 6 diobol, kantar, obolus, stater
7 chalcon, chalque, drachma 8 diobolon,
talanton *wine:* 7 retsina, retzina

green 3 raw 5 alive, fresh, plaza, virid,
young 6 callow, common, infant, square,
unripe 7 celadon, emerald, untried, verdant
8 immature, juvenile, pistache, unversed,
youthful 9 unfledged 10 unseasoned
11 unpracticed 13 inexperienced *bluish:*
8 glaucous *combining form:* 4 verd
5 chlor, verdo 6 chloro *grayish:* 5 olive
yellowish: 7 luteous 10 chartreuse

greenbacks 4 cash, jack 5 bread, dough,
money 6 wampum 7 scratch 8 currency
11 legal tender

green-eyed 7 envious, envying, jealous
9 invidious *monster:* 8 jealousy

greenfish 7 opaleye, pollack

greenfly 5 aphid

greengage 4 plum

greenhead 3 fly 5 scaup 7 mallard

greenheart 4 tree 7 bebeeru

greenhorn 4 hick, jake, rube, tyro 5 clown
6 novice, rustic 7 bumpkin, hayseed 9 hillbilly 10 clodhopper, provincial 12 backwoodsman

greenhouse 12 conservatory

Greenland *capital:* 7 Godthab 8 Godthaab *discoverer:* 10 Eric the Red *native:*
3 Ita *settlement:* 4 Etah

green light 2 OK 7 go-ahead 9 clearance
13 authorization

Green Mansions *author:* 6 Hudson
(William Henry) *character:* 4 Rima

green monkey 6 guenon

Green Mountain State 7 Vermont

greenness 5 youth 6 spring 7 puberty,
rawness 8 verdancy, viridity 9 freshness,
youthhood 10 callowness, juvenility, pubescence, springtide, springtime 11 adolescence 12 inexperience, youthfulness

green osier 7 dogwood

green plover 7 lapwing

green poppy 8 foxglove

greenroom 6 lounge

greenstone 7 diabase, diorite 8 nephrite

greet 3 cry 4 hail 6 accost, call to, salute
7 address, receive, welcome

greeting 3 ave, bow 4 hail 5 aloha, hello
6 salute 7 address, welcome 9 reception
10 salutation

gregarious 6 social 8 friendly, outgoing,
sociable

gremlin 3 elf, imp 5 gnome 6 sprite

grenade 4 bomb 5 shell 7 missile
9 explosive

grenadier 4 fish 7 rattail, soldier

grenadine 4 pink, yarn 5 syrup 9 carnation

Grendel's slayer 7 Beowulf

Gretchen's lover 5 Faust

Grey's forte 7 Western

grid 5 grate 7 grating, network

griddle 3 pan 5 grill

griddle cake 7 pancake 8 flapjack

gridiron 5 field, grill 7 grating, network

grief 3 rue, woe 4 care 5 dolor, tears
6 regret, sorrow 7 anguish, chagrin, emotion, sadness, trouble 8 distress, hardship
9 bemoaning, bewailing, deploring, heartache, lamenting, suffering 10 affliction,
heartbreak 11 lamentation

Grieg work 8 Peer Gynt

grievance 5 cross, rigor, trial, wrong
6 burden, injury 8 hardship 9 complaint,
injustice 10 affliction 11 tribulation

grieve 3 cry, rue 4 bear, hurt, keen, moan,
pain, wail, weep 5 mourn 6 bemoan,
bewail, endure, injure, lament, sorrow, suffer 7 deplore 8 distress 9 constrain

grievous 3 sad 4 dire, fell, sore, ugly
5 grave, major, tough 6 bitter, taxing, woeful 7 exigent, galling, onerous, painful, serious, weighty 8 exacting 9 dangerous,
demanding 10 afflictive, burdensome,
calamitous, deplorable, lamentable, oppressive 11 distasteful, distressing, regrettable,
unfortunate, unpalatable

grill 3 vex 4 cook, grid 5 broil, grate
7 afflict, griddle, torment 8 gridiron, question 11 third degree 12 cross-examine
13 interrogation

grilse 4 fish 6 salmon

grim 3 set 4 cold, dour, fell, firm, hard
5 angry, bleak, cruel, fixed, harsh, lurid,
rigid, stern 6 dogged, fierce, grisly, mortal,
savage, severe 7 adamant, austere, certain, ghastly, hideous, inhuman, macabre,
ominous, wolfish 8 gruesome, horrible, inhumane, obdurate, resolute, ruthless, stubborn, terrible 9 barbarous, ferocious, loathsome, merciless, offensive, repugnant,
repulsive, revolting, stringent, truculent
10 determined, forbidding, foreboding, horrifying, implacable, inevitable, inexorable,
inflexible, ironfisted, off-putting, relentless,
terrifying, unyielding, vindictive 11 unflinching, unforgiving

grimace 3 mop, mow, mug 4 face, moue
5 mouth, smirk, sneer 6 deform 7 contort,
distort

grimalkin 3 cat, hag 6 feline

grime 4 dirt, foul, soil 5 dirty, sully 6 besoil, smirch, smooch, smudge, smutch 7 tarnish

grim reaper 5 death

grin 4 beam 5 fleer, risus, smile, smirk

grind 3 rut, vex 4 chew, grub, mill, moil, pace, plod, rote, slog, toil, work 5 crush, gnash, grate, labor, slave, sweat 6 crunch, drudge, groove, kibble 7 routine, travail 8 bullwork, drudgery, plugging 9 treadmill 10 donkeywork

grinder 4 hero 5 molar, stone, tooth 8 sandwich 9 submarine

grinding 5 harsh 6 severe 7 grating, wearing *stone:* 4 mano 6 muller, pestle

grip 4 hold, take, vice 5 clamp, clasp, grasp, seize 6 clench, clinch, clutch, duress, handle, tenure, valise 7 catch up, grapple 8 coercion, enthrall, handfast, handhold 9 fascinate, mesmerize, restraint, spellbind 10 constraint

gripe 4 beef, crab, fuss, hold, kick, yaup, yawp 5 bitch, bleat, brawl, clamp, clasp, croak, grasp 6 clench, clinch, clutch, grouch, grouse, murmur, mutter, squawk, take on, tenure, yammer 7 blow off, grapple, grumble 8 complain 9 bellyache

griper see **grumbler**

grippe 3 flu 7 disease 9 influenza

gripper 4 clip, hand, vice 5 clamp, clasp, tongs 6 pliers

gris-gris 5 charm, spell 6 amulet 8 talisman 11 incantation

grisly 4 grim 5 eerie, lurid, weird 6 horrid 7 ghastly, hideous, macabre, uncanny 8 gruesome, horrible, terrible 10 horrifying, terrifying

grist 3 lot 5 grain, stint 6 output 8 quantity

gristle 9 cartilage

grit 4 dirt, guts, sand, soil 5 earth, moxie, nerve, spunk 6 gravel 7 courage 8 backbone 9 fortitude

gritty 4 game 5 brave, dirty, sandy 6 plucky, soiled 8 resolute

groan 4 moan, rasp 5 creak, grate

grocery 5 store 11 supermarket *Spanish:* 6 bodega

grog 3 rum 5 booze, drink, hooch, juice 6 liquor, tipple 7 alcohol, spirits

groggy 4 logy, weak 5 dazed, foggy, tired 6 sleepy 7 muddled 8 sluggish

groin 4 fold 6 crotch, inguen *combining form:* 6 inguin 7 inguino

groom 4 comb, tidy 5 brush, clean, curry, ready, shave 6 neaten, polish, refine, toilet 7 prepare, servant 8 benedict 9 attendant 11 horsekeeper *Chinese:* 5 mafoo *Indian:* 4 syce

groove 3 rut 4 nurl, pace, rote, slot 5 canal, flute, glyph, grind, stria 6 fuller, fur-row, gutter, hollow 7 chamfer, channel, routine

grope 3 pry 4 feel, poke, root, test 5 probe 6 fumble, handle, search 7 examine, explore, grabble 8 scrabble

grosbeak 4 bird 5 finch 8 haw finch

gross 3 all, big, fat, raw, sum 4 foul, mass, rank, rude 5 brute, crass, crude, heavy, obese, rough, stout, total, utter, whole 6 animal, carnal, coarse, damned, entire, fleshy, portly, smutty, vulgar 7 capital, extreme, glaring, obscene, perfect, porcine, sensual, uncouth, weighty 8 absolute, barn-yard, complete, entirety, flagrant, improper, material, outright, physical, sensible, sum total, tangible, totality 9 aggregate, corpo-real, corpulent, downright, egregious, exces-sive, inelegant, loathsome, objective, offen-sive, out-and-out, repulsive, revolting, unrefined 10 exorbitant, immoderate

grotesque 5 antic, comic, droll, eerie, weird 6 rococo 7 baroque, bizarre, comi-cal, extreme, uncanny 9 fantastic, ludicrous

grotto 4 cave, hole 5 crypt, vault 6 cavern *Capri:* 4 Blue

grouch 4 crab, sulk 5 crank, croak, grump, scold 6 griper, grouse, kicker, mur-mur, mutter 7 crabber, grouser, growler, grumble 8 grumbler, sorehead, sourpuss 10 bellyacher, complainer, crosspatch, mal-content 11 faultfinder

ground 3 bed, why 4 base, dirt, down, drop, fell, land, rest, root, seat, soil, stay, test 5 basis, cause, earth, floor, level, proof, trial 6 bottom, reason, whyfor 7 bed-rock, dry land, flatten, footing, mow down, support, sustain 8 argument, basement, but-tress, evidence 9 bring down, establish, knock down, predicate, testimony, throw down, wherefore 10 antecedent, founda-tion, substratum, terra firma *combining form:* 2 ge 3 geo, ped 4 pedo 5 chame 6 chamae

grounded 7 beached 8 stranded

groundhog 6 marmot 9 woodchuck

groundless 4 idle 5 false 8 baseless 9 unfounded 10 bottomless, gratuitous, ungrounded 11 uncalled-for, unwarranted

groundwork 3 bed 4 base, root 5 basis 6 bottom 7 bedrock, footing, support 8 basement 10 foundation, substratum 12 substruction, substructure, underpinning

group 3 lot, set 4 band, bevy, body, clot, club, crew, gang, mess, pool, push, ruck, sect, sort, team, tier 5 array, batch, bunch, chain, class, clump, covey, crowd, grade, horde, party, place, squad, suite, trust 6 adjust, assort, bundle, cartel, circle, clique, clutch, gather, huddle, league, mus-ter, parcel, passel 7 arrange, battery, brigade, cluster, collect, combine, company, coterie, council, dispose, echelon, platoon, round up 8 assemble, assembly, category, classify, ensemble, organize 9 congeries, gathering, harmonize, syndicate 10 assemblage, categorize, collection *of angels:* 4 host *of ants:* 6 colony *of badgers:* 4 cete *of bears:* 6 sleuth *of bees:* 4 hive 5 grist, swarm *of birds:* 6 flight, volery *of boars:* 7 sounder *of cats:* 7 clowder, clutter *of cattle:* 5 drove *of chicks:* 5 brood 6 clutch *of clams:* 3 bed *of cranes:* 5 sedge, siege *of crows:* 6 murder *of ducks:* 5 brace *of eight:* 5 octet *of elephants:* 4 herd *of elks:* 4 gang *of fish:* 5 shoal 6 school *of five:* 5 quint 6 pentad 7 quinary, quintet *of four:* 6 tetrad 7 quartet *of foxes:* 5 leash, skulk *of geese:* 5 flock, skein 6 gaggle *of gnats:* 5 cloud, horde *of goats:* 4 trip 5 tribe *of goldfinches:* 5 charm *of gorillas:* 4 band *of greyhounds:* 5 leash *of grouse:* 5 covey *of hares:* 4 down, husk *of hawks:* 4 cast *of hounds:* 3 cry 4 mute, pack *of kangaroos:* 3 mob 5 troop *of kittens:* 6 kendle, kindle *of larks:* 10 exaltation *of leopards:* 4 leap *of lions:* 5 pride *of locusts:* 6 plague *of monkeys:* 5 troop *of mules:* 4 span *of nightingales:* 5 watch *of nine:* 5 nonet *of oysters:* 3 bed *of partridges:* 5 covey *of peacocks:* 6 muster *of pheasants:* 3 nye 4 nest, nide *of plovers:* 4 wing 12 congregation *of quail:* 4 bevy 5 covey *of seals:* 3 pod 5 patch *of seven:* 6 pleiad, septet *of sheep:* 5 drove, flock *of six:* 5 hexad 6 hexade, sextet *of swans:* 4 bevy *of swine:* 7 sounder *of teals:* 6 spring *of three:* 4 trio 5 triad 7 ternary, trinity, triplet *of toads:* 4 knot *of vipers:* 4 nest *of whales:* 3 gam, pod *of wolves:* 4 pack *suffix:* 2 ad, et 3 ome 4 some

grouper 4 fish 8 rockfish 10 tripletail

grouse 5 croak, gripe, quail, scold 6 gorhen, grouch, murmur, mutter 7 gorcock, greyhen, grumble 8 complain, pheasant 9 blackcock, ptarmigan 10 whitebelly 12 capercaillie *extinct:* 8 heath hen *red:* 8 moorfowl *strut:* 3 lak

grouser see grumbler

grout 4 lees 5 dregs 6 cement, mortar 7 grounds, plaster 8 concrete

grove 3 bed 4 holt, wood 5 copse, hurst 7 boscage, coppice, orchard, thicket *suffix:* 3 eta (plural) 4 etum

grovel 4 fawn 5 cower, toady 6 cringe, kowtow, wallow 7 honey up, truckle 8 bootlick 9 brownnose 11 apple-polish

grow 3 age, get, run, wax 4 come, rear, rise, tend, turn 5 breed, nurse, raise, ripen, swell 6 become, expand, foster, mature,

mellow, sprout, thrive 7 care for, develop, enlarge, gestate, nurture, produce 8 escalate, increase, maturate, mushroom 9 cultivate, propagate

growing 8 crescive, vegetive 10 vegetative

growl 3 grr 4 roll 5 snarl 6 mutter, rumble 7 grumble 8 complain 9 complaint

growler 3 can 4 crab, floe 5 crank, grump 6 griper, grouch 7 grouser, iceberg, pitcher 8 grumbler, sorehead, sourpuss 9 container 10 bellyacher

grow old 3 age 5 ripen 6 mature

growth 4 rise 5 swell, tumor 7 merisis 8 increase, progress, swelling 9 accretion, evolution, expansion, flowering, unfolding 10 evolvement 11 development, enlargement, progression *malignant:* 6 cancer *skin:* 3 wen 4 corn, mole, wart 6 bunion, keloid

grub 3 dig 4 beat, chow, comb, feed, food, hack, plod, poke, rake, root, slog, toil 5 grind, larva, scour, slave, spade, stump 6 burrow, drudge, forage, search, shovel, slavey, uproot, viands 7 edibles, grubber, nurture, ransack, rummage 8 excavate, finecomb, hireling, victuals 9 mercenary, provender

grubby 4 foul 5 black, dirty, grimy, nasty, soily 6 filthy, impure 7 squalid, unclean

grubstake 4 back 7 finance 8 bankroll

grudge 4 deny, envy 5 spite 6 injury, malice, refuse, spleen 7 despite, ill will 9 grievance, injustice, malignity 10 malignancy 11 malevolence 12 spitefulness

gruel 5 atole 8 porridge *Scottish:* 6 crowdy

gruesome see grisly

gruff 4 curt, dour, sour 5 bluff, blunt, husky, short, surly 6 abrupt, croaky, crusty, fierce, hoarse, morose, snippy, sullen 7 bearish, boorish, brusque, crabbed 8 churlish, croaking, snippety 9 saturnine

grumble 4 beef, crab, fuss, kick, moan, roll 5 bitch, brawl, croak, gripe, groan, growl, scold, snarl, whine 6 grouch, grouse, holler, murmur, mutter, repine, rumble, squawk 8 complain 9 bellyache

grumbler 4 crab 6 grouch 7 grouser, growler 8 sorehead 10 bellyacher, complainer, crosspatch, malcontent 11 faultfinder

grump 3 pet 4 crab, pout, sulk 5 crank 6 griper, grouch, kicker 7 growler 8 grumbler, sorehead, sourpuss 10 bellyacher

grumpy 5 moody, surly 6 crabby, cranky

guacharo 7 oilbird

Guam *capital:* 5 Agana *native:* 8 Chamorro

guanaco 5 llama 6 alpaca *kin:* 5 camel

guarantee, guaranty 3 vow 4 bail, bond, oath, seal, word 5 token, vouch 6 assure, ensure, insure, pledge, surety 7 certify, earnest, promise, warrant 8 security, warranty 9 assurance 11 undertaking

guarantor 5 angel 6 backer, patron, surety 7 sponsor 8 backer-up 11 underwriter

guard 4 fend, keep, mind, tend, ward 5 aegis, armor, cover, watch 6 attend, convoy, defend, escort, jailer, keeper, patrol, picket, screen, secure, sentry, shield, warden, warder 7 bulwark, conduct, defense, lookout, protect, turnkey 8 armament, chaperon, security, sentinel, shepherd, watchdog, watchman 9 accompany, patrolman, protector 10 protection

guarded 4 safe, wary 5 chary, privy 6 buried, covert, hidden 7 careful 8 cautious, discreet, gingerly, obscured, shrouded, ulterior 9 concealed 11 calculating, circumspect, considerate

guardhouse 4 brig 6 prison

guardian 6 custos, keeper, parent, patron, warden 7 sponsor 8 cerberus, claviger, watchdog 9 custodian, protector

guardianship 4 care, ward 5 trust 7 custody, keeping, tuition 11 safekeeping

guava 4 inga, tree 5 fruit

gudgeon 3 pin 4 fish 5 pivot 6 socket

Gudrun *brother:* 6 Gunnar 7 Gunther *father:* 5 Hetel *husband:* 4 Atli 5 Etzel 6 Sigurd 9 Siegfried

guerrilla 7 fighter, patriot, soldier 8 partisan 9 irregular 11 bushwhacker *Greek:* 6 klepht

guess 4 call, shot, stab 5 fancy, infer, think 6 deduce, reason, reckon 7 predict, presume, pretend, suppose, surmise 8 estimate 9 speculate 10 conjecture

guest 6 caller, lodger, patron, roomer 7 visitor

guff 3 jaw, lip 4 sass 5 hokum, hooey, mouth, sauce, trash 6 bunkum 7 hogwash 8 back talk, claptrap, malarkey, nonsense 9 poppycock 10 balderdash

guffaw 5 laugh, tehee 6 giggle, hee-haw, titter 7 chortle, chuckle, snicker, sniggle

guidance 7 auspice, conduct, control 9 direction 10 leadership, management

guide 3 see 4 airt, clue, dean, lead, show 5 airth, doyen, pilot, route, steer, teach, usher 6 beacon, convoy, direct, escort, leader, manage, manual, vector 7 conduct, control, marshal 8 Baedeker, chaperon, contrive, director, engineer, handbook, maneuver, navigate, shepherd 9 accompany, conductor, lead pilot, vade mecum 10 bellwether, compendium 11 enchiridion

guidebook 6 manual 8 Baedeker, handbook 9 itinerary, vade mecum 10 compendium 11 enchiridion

guided missile 3 ABM 4 Hawk, ICBM, IRBM, Nike, Thor, Zuni 5 Atlas, drone, Snark, Titan 6 Bomarc, Falcon 7 Bullpup, Polaris, Terrier 8 Redstone 9 Minuteman 10 Sidewinder

Guiderius *brother:* 9 Arviragus *father:* 9 Cymbeline

Guido's scale 2 fa, la, mi, re, ut 3 Ela, sol

guild 4 club 5 order, union 6 cartel, league 7 society 8 sodality 10 fellowship, fraternity 11 association, brotherhood *medieval:* 5 Hansa, Hanse

guile 4 wile 5 craft, fraud 6 deceit 7 cunning 9 duplicity 12 dissemblance

guileful 3 sly 4 deep, foxy, wily 6 artful, astute, crafty, shifty, sneaky, tricky 7 cunning, devious 8 indirect, sneaking 9 insidious, underhand 11 duplicitous, underhanded

guileless 5 naive 6 honest 7 artless, natural 8 unartful 9 ingenuous, unstudied, untutored

guillemot 3 auk 5 murre

guillotine 6 behead 9 decollate 10 decapitate

guilt 3 sin 4 onus 5 blame, crime, fault, shame 7 offense, remorse 11 culpability

guiltless 4 good, pure 5 clean 8 innocent, unguilty, virtuous 9 blameless, crimeless, exemplary, faultless, righteous 10 inculpable, unblamable

guilty 5 amiss 6 nocent, sinful, unholy, wicked 7 ashamed 8 blamable, blameful, culpable, indicted 9 impeached 10 answerable, censurable 11 accountable, blameworthy, responsible 12 incriminated

guinea fowl *genus:* 6 Numida *young:* 4 keet

guinea pig 4 cavy 6 rodent *genus:* 5 Cavia

Guinevere *husband:* 6 Arthur *lover:* 8 Lancelot 9 Launcelot

guise 3 hue, rig 4 face, mask, show 5 cloak, color, cover, dress, getup 6 facade, outfit, setout 7 costume 8 coloring 9 semblance 10 appearance

guitar *part:* 3 nut, peg 4 fret, neck 5 brace 6 bridge, string 7 peghead *player:* 7 plucker 8 strummer *small:* 3 uke 7 ukulele *soprano:* 5 tiple *tool:* 4 pick 8 plectrum

guitarist *American:* 9 Parkening (Christopher) *Australian:* 8 Williams (John) *British:* 5 Bream (Julian) *Italian:* 7 Ghiglia (Oscar) *Spanish:* 5 Yepes (Narciso) 6 Romero (Celedonio) 7 Segovia (Andrés)

guitarlike instrument 3 uke 4 lute, vina 5 banjo, sitar 6 sancho 7 bandore, pandora, samisen, ukulele

gulch 3 gap 5 chasm, cleft, clove, gorge, gully 6 arroyo, canyon, clough, ravine

gulf 3 arm, bay, pit 4 cave, cove, eddy, well 5 abysm, abyss, bayou, bight, chasm, firth, gulch, inlet, shaft 6 cavity, harbor, hollow, ravine, slough 8 crevasse *Adriatic Sea:* 6 Venice *Aegean Sea:* 7 Saronic 8 Salonika *Africa:* 6 Guinea *Arabian Sea:* 4 Oman 7 Persian *Arctic Ocean:* 2 Ob *Australia:* 9 Van Diemen 11 Carpentaria *Baltic Sea:* 4 Riga 6 Danzig, Gdansk 7 Bothnia, Finland *Bering Sea:* 6 Anadyr *Canada:* 13 Saint Lawrence *Caribbean Sea:* 8 Honduras 9 Venezuela *Central America:* 6 Panama 7 Fonseca *Djibouti:* 6 Tajura 8 Tadjoura *Europe:* 7 Bothnia, Gascony 8 Gascogne *Greece:* 7 Corinth, Lepanto *Indian Ocean:* 4 Aden *Ionian Sea:* 4 Arta 7 Taranto *Iran:* 4 Arabian *Italy:* 5 Genoa *Mediterranean Sea:* 5 Sidra, Tunis 8 Valencia 10 Khalij Surt 11 Syrtis Major *Mexico:* 10 California *New Guinea:* 5 Papua 7 McCluer *New Zealand:* 7 Hauraki *North America:* 6 Alaska, Mexico *Northwest Territories:* 7 Boothia 8 Amundsen 9 Queen Maud *Philippines:* 4 Asid 5 Davao, Leyte, Panay, Ragay *Red Sea:* 4 Suez 5 Aqaba 11 Aelaniticus *Russia:* 8 Sakhalin *Solomon Sea:* 4 Huon, Kula 5 Vella *South China Sea:* 4 Siam 6 Tonkin 8 Lingayen, Thailand *Tyrrhenion Sea:* 7 Paestum *Yellow Sea:* 2 Bo, Po 6 Chihli

Gulf State 5 Texas 7 Alabama, Florida 9 Louisiana 11 Mississippi

gull 3 mew, sap 4 bird, dupe, fish, fool, hoax 5 chump 6 befool, fleece, pigeon, sucker 7 chicane, fall guy, gudgeon, saphead 8 flimflam, hoodwink 9 bamboozle 11 hornswoggle *relating to:* 6 larine, laroid

gullet 3 maw 4 tube 6 dewlap, ravine, throat 7 channel 9 esophagus

gullible 4 easy 5 naive 9 credulous 10 fleeceable 11 susceptible

Gulliver's Travels *author:* 5 Swift (Jonathan) *land:* 6 Laputa 8 Lilliput 11 Brobdingnag *people:* 6 Yahoos

gully 5 gorge, gulch 6 arroyo, hollow, ravine, valley 7 couloir

gulp 4 bolt, cram, glut, slop, swig, wolf 5 slosh, stuff, swill 6 devour, englut, gobble, guzzle 7 swallow 11 ingurgitate

gum 4 chew, kino 5 botch, cheat, nyssa, stick, tuart 6 bobble, bollix, bungle, chicle, gluten, goof up, mucker, tupelo 7 bilsted, exudate, gingiva, louse up 8 adhesive, mucilage 9 sapodilla 10 eucalyptus *kind:* 6 acacia, Arabic, balata, bubble 7 chewing, dextrin *resin:* 5 myrrh 7 gamboge 8 ammoniac, galbanum, scammony 9 asafetida 12 frankincense

gummy 5 gooey 6 cloggy, sticky, stodgy 7 viscous 8 adhesive

gumption 5 sense 6 wisdom 8 judgment, sagacity 9 good sense 10 astuteness, enterprise, horse sense, shrewdness 11 common sense

gums 3 ula 8 gingivae

gumshoe 3 cop, tec 4 dick, fuzz, heat, lurk, slip 5 creep, shirk, skulk, slink, sneak, snoop, steal 6 peeler, sleuth 7 officer 8 flatfoot, hawkshaw, Sherlock 9 detective, policeman, pussyfoot 12 investigator

gun 3 gat, rod 5 rifle 6 cannon, heater, mortar, musket, pistol, weapon 7 bazooka, carbine, firearm 8 howitzer, revolver 9 derringer *antiaircraft:* 6 ack-ack, Bofors *big-game:* 4 roer *British:* 4 sten *French:* 8 arquebus *German:* 5 Luger *mount:* 6 turret *part:* 3 pin 4 bolt, bore, butt, lock 5 sight, stock 6 barrel, breech, hammer, muzzle, safety 7 chamber, trigger 8 cylinder, magazine 9 buttstock

gunfire 4 shot 5 salvo 6 ack-ack, strafe, volley 7 barrage 9 fusillade

gung ho 4 keen 7 zealous 12 enthusiastic

Guni's father 8 Naphtali

gunk 3 goo 4 crud, gook, goop, muck

gunman 5 bravo 6 hit man 7 torpedo 8 assassin 9 cutthroat

Gunnar *brother-in-law:* 6 Sigurd *father:* 5 Hetel *sister:* 6 Gudrun *wife:* 8 Brynhild

gunnel 6 blenny 10 butterfish

gunner 7 shooter 8 marksman, rifleman 9 cannoneer 12 artilleryman

Gunther *sister:* 7 Gutrune 9 Kriemhild *slayer:* 5 Hagen *uncle:* 5 Hagen *wife:* 8 Brunhild 9 Brynhilde 11 Brunnehilde

guppy 4 fish 6 minnow

gurgle 3 lap 4 wash 5 slosh, swash 6 bubble, burble

Gurkha knife 5 kukri

gurney 3 cot 9 stretcher

guru 5 guide 6 mentor 7 teacher

gush 4 flow, pour, roll, teem 5 flood, flush, issue, spout, spurt, surge 6 sluice, spring, stream 7 emanate

gusset 4 fold 5 armor, pleat 6 insert

gust 4 gale, puff, waft, wind 5 blast, burst, draft, sally, whiff 6 access, breeze, squall 7 bluster, flare-up 8 eruption, outburst

gusto 4 élan, zeal, zest 5 ardor, heart, taste 6 fervor, palate, relish, spirit 7 delight, passion 8 pleasure 9 enjoyment 10 enthusiasm 11 delectation

gut 4 draw 5 belly, bowel, clean, dress, inner 6 paunch 7 embowel, passage, stomach 8 interior, internal, intimate, visceral 9 viscerous 10 disembowel, eviscerate, exenterate

Gutenberg *city:* 5 Mainz *invention:* 11 movable type *partner:* 4 Fust (Johann)

gutless 6 coward, craven 7 chicken, unmanly 8 cowardly 9 spunkless 11 lily-livered, poltroonish 13 pusillanimous

guts 4 grit 5 moxie, nerve, pluck, spunk 6 mettle, spirit, tripes 7 courage, innards, insides, viscera 8 backbone, entrails, stuffing 9 fortitude, internals 10 resolution

gutsy 4 bold 5 brave, manly 6 manful, plucky, spunky 7 valiant 8 intrepid 9 unfearful 10 courageous

gutter 5 ditch, gully 6 furrow, groove, trench, trough 7 channel

guttural 4 deep 5 harsh, rough, velar 7 palatal, rasping, throaty

Guyana *capital:* 10 Georgetown *monetary unit:* 6 dollar

guzzle 4 bolt, cram, gulp, slop, soak, swig, wolf 5 booze, drink, slosh, swill 6 englut, gobble, imbibe, tank up, tipple 7 swizzle

Gwendolen's husband 7 Locrine

gymnast 7 acrobat, athlete, tumbler *American:* 5 Rigby (Cathy) 6 Conner (Bart), Retton (Mary Lou), Thomas (Kurt) *Romanian:* 8 Comaneci (Nadia) *Russian:* 3 Kim (Nelly) 6 Korbut (Olga)

gymnastics 5 sport 8 exercise, tumbling 9 athletics 10 acrobatics 12 calisthenics *apparatus:* 3 bar 4 beam, buck, ring, rope 5 horse *feat:* 3 kip 4 flip 5 vault 6 tumble 9 handstand, headstand 10 handspring, headspring, somersault

gyp 4 beat, bilk, fake, hoax, sell 5 cheat, cozen, fraud, phony, spoof 6 chisel, chouse, con man, diddle, humbug, rip off 7 defraud, diddler, sharper, swindle 8 swindler 9 defrauder, imposture, overreach, trickster 10 mountebank 11 flimflammer 12 double-dealer

gypsum 4 yeso 8 selenite 9 alabaster

gypsy 4 caló 5 caird, nomad 6 roamer, Romany 7 tzigane, zingana, zingano 8 Bohemian, wanderer *Spanish:* 6 gitano

gyrate 4 roll, spin, turn 5 twirl, whirl 6 circle, rotate 7 revolve 9 pirouette, whirligig

gyration 4 turn 5 round, wheel, whirl 7 circuit 8 rotation 10 revolution 11 circulation

gyre 4 ring, spin 5 twirl, whirl 6 rotate, spiral, vortex 7 revolve 10 revolution

gyro 8 sandwich 9 gyroscope

gyve 4 bond, iron 5 chain 6 fetter 7 shackle

H

H 4 high 5 aitch 7 hundred

habeus corpus 4 writ

habilimented 4 clad 7 clothed

habilitate 5 dress 6 clothe

habit 3 rut, set, use, way 4 bent, form, mode, rote, turn, wont 5 build, dress, style, trick, usage 6 clothe, custom, groove, manner, praxis 7 carcass, contour, fashion, habitus, outline, pattern, routine 8 behavior, physique, practice, tendency 9 addiction, framework 10 consuetude, convention, proclivity 11 disposition, inclination *riding:* 6 joseph 8 jodhpurs *wearer:* 3 nun 5 rider

habitant 5 liver 7 denizen, dweller, resider 8 occupant, resident 9 indweller

habitat 4 home, site 5 abode, haunt, range 6 locale 7 station 8 locality 9 territory 11 environment 12 surroundings *combining form:* 2 ec 3 eco, oec 4 oeco

habitation 3 pad 4 digs, flat, home, nest, nook, roof, seat 5 abode, astre, haunt, haven, house, place, roost 6 colony, hearth 7 housing, lodging 8 domicile, dwelling, fireside, lodgment, peopling, quarters, rooftree, tenement 9 apartment, homeplace, homestead, occupancy, residence, residency

habitual 6 addict, inborn, native, steady, wonted 7 chronic, regular, routine 8 accepted, addicted, constant, frequent 9 automatic, confirmed, continual, customary, ingrained 10 accustomed, inveterate, persistent 11 established, instinctive, involuntary

habituate 3 use 4 bear, wont 5 enure, inure 6 addict, adjust, devote, endure, season, take to 7 support 8 accustom, devote to, tolerate 9 condition, confirm in 11 familiarize

habitué 3 fan 4 buff, user 5 hound, lover 6 addict, patron, votary 7 denizen, devotee, haunter 8 customer 10 frequenter

Hacaliah, Hachaliah *son:* 8 Nehemiah

hacienda 4 farm 5 ranch 6 estate 10 plantation

hack 3 cab, cut, hew, old, try 4 chip, chop, dull, fell, gash, grub, jade, mean, nick, poor, taxi, trim, turn 5 cabby, cough, frame, grind, horse, notch, petty, shape, slash, slave, stale, tired, trite, usual 6 cabbie, cli-

ché, common, drudge, haggle, lackey, mangle, slavey 7 clichéd, grating, grubber, machine, outworn, plodder, potboil, servant, taxicab, trivial 8 déclassé, hireling, inferior, low grade, mediocre, ordinary, outmoded, timeworn, well-worn 9 cabdriver, mercenary, potboiler 10 second-rate, uninspired 11 commonplace

hackneyed 4 worn 5 stale, stock, tired, trite 6 cliché 7 archaic, clichéd, worn-out 8 bathetic, everyday, obsolete, outmoded, timeworn, well-worn 9 moth-eaten, out-of-date, quotidian 10 antiquated 11 commonplace

Hadad *father:* 5 Bedad 7 Ishmael *victim:* 6 Midian

Hadadezer *father:* 5 Rehob *kingdom:* 5 Zobah

hades 3 pit 4 hell 5 Sheol 6 Tophet 7 Abaddon, Avernus, Gehenna, inferno 8 Tartarus 9 barathrum, perdition 10 underworld 11 netherworld, Pandemonium *Babylonian:* 5 Aralu *god:* 3 Dis 5 Orcus, Pluto *guard:* 8 Cerberus *lake:* 7 Avernus *river:* 4 Styx 5 Lethe 7 Acheron, Cocytus 10 Phlegethon

hafnium *symbol:* 2 Hf

hag 3 hex 4 drab, trot 5 biddy, bruja, crone, harpy, lamia, shrew, vixen, witch 6 beldam, gorgon, virago 7 grandam 8 battle-ax, fishwife, harridan, slattern 9 sorceress 10 witchwoman 11 enchantress

Hagar's son 7 Ishmael

Hagen *father:* 8 Alberich *nephew:* 7 Gunther *slayer:* 9 Kriemhild *victim:* 9 Siegfried

haggard 3 wan 4 lank, lean, pale, worn 5 ashen, drawn, faded, gaunt, spare, tired 6 fagged, pallid, skinny 7 angular, pinched, scraggy, scrawny, wearied 8 careworn, fatigued, harrowed, worn-down 9 exhausted

Haggard novel 3 She

Haggi's father 3 Gad

Haggith *husband:* 5 David *son:* 8 Adonijah

haggle 4 deal, hack 5 cavil, slash, trade 6 barter, bicker, dicker, hackle, palter 7 bargain, chaffer, dispute, quibble, stickle, wrangle 8 huckster, squabble 10 horse-trade

hagiography subject 5 saint
hail 4 ahoy 5 greet, hallo, salvo, shout, storm 6 accost, call to, hallow, holler, kudize, praise, salute, shower, volley 7 acclaim, address, applaud, barrage, call out, commend 8 come from, drumfire 9 broadside, cannonade, fusillade, originate, recommend 10 salutation 11 bombardment
Haile Selassie *nation ruled:* 8 Ethiopia
hair 3 ace, bit, jot 4 hint, mite, wool 5 pilus, trace 6 nicety, trifle 7 whisker 8 fraction, particle *animal:* 3 fur 4 mane, pelt 8 vibrissa 9 vibrissae (plural) *braid of:* 5 queue 7 pigtail *clip:* 8 barrette *coarse:* 7 bristle *combining form:* 3 pil 4 coma, pili, pilo 5 chaet, crini, thrix, trich 6 chaeta, chaeto, tricha, trichi, tricho, trichy 7 chaetae (plural), chaetes, chaetus, trichia 8 trichous *covering of:* 3 wig *facial:* 5 beard 6 goatee 8 mustache, whiskers 9 moustache, sideburns 11 muttonchops *fine:* 6 lanugo *front:* 4 bang *head of:* 9 chevelure *instrument:* 4 comb *knot of:* 3 bun 6 tangle *lock of:* 4 curl 5 tress 7 cowlick *loose roll:* 4 pouf 5 pouff 6 pouffe *matted:* 4 shag *ornament:* 7 topknot *preparation:* 6 pomade 12 brilliantine *relating to:* 8 hirsutal *root:* 6 fibril *set:* 4 perm *stiff:* 4 seta 5 setae (plural) *style:* 9 pompadour *tangled:* 7 elflock *tuft of:* 7 fetlock *unruly:* 3 mop 7 cowlick *without:* 4 bald
haircutter 6 barber 7 friseur
hairdo 4 perm 7 chignon 8 bouffant
hairdresser 6 barber 7 friseur 10 beautician 13 cosmetologist
hair-raising 4 eery 5 eerie 9 thrilling 10 terrifying
hairsplitter 8 quibbler
hairstyle 2 DA 4 Afro 5 bangs 7 beehive, crew cut, pageboy 8 bouffont, coiffure, ducktail, ponytail
hairy 5 bushy, crude, downy, furry, fuzzy, harsh, nappy, risky, rough 6 chancy, craggy, fleecy, fluffy, jagged, lanate, pilose, rugged, shaggy, tufted, uneven, wicked, woolly 7 bristly, hirsute, pileous, scraggy, unshorn, unsound, villous 8 asperous, perilous, scabrous, strigose, unsmooth 9 dangerous, hazardous, pubescent, tomentose, unhealthy, whiskered 10 jeopardous, unpleasant 11 frightening, treacherous *combining form:* 4 dasy, hebe
Haiti *capital:* 12 Port au Prince *export:* 6 coffee 7 bauxite *island:* 10 Hispaniola *location:* 10 West Indies *monetary unit:* 6 gourde *ruler:* 8 Duvalier
Hajji Baba creator 6 Morier (James Justinian)
hake 5 gadid 7 codling, whiting *relative:* 3 cod

halcyon 4 calm 5 happy, quiet, still 6 golden, hushed, placid, serene, stilly 8 affluent 10 kingfisher, prosperous, untroubled
Halcyone *father:* 6 Aeolus *husband:* 4 Ceyx
hale 3 fit, tug 4 draw, pull, sane, well 5 husky, right, sound, stout 6 robust 7 healthy, summons 9 strapping, wholesome
Hale character 5 Nolan (Philip)
haleness 6 health
Haley (Alex) epic 5 Roots
half *prefix:* 3 sam 4 demi, hemi, semi
half-assed 7 lacking, wanting 9 defective, deficient 10 inadequate, incomplete, uncomplete
half-breed 4 mule 5 cross 6 hybrid 7 bastard, mestizo, mongrel, mulatto 8 mixblood
halfhearted 5 tepid 8 lukewarm
half-moon 7 scalare 8 demilune 9 blue perch
halfway 3 mid 6 almost, center, medial, median, middle 7 midmost, partial 8 amenably 9 partially 10 centermost, middlemost, more or less 11 equidistant
half-wit 4 dolt, fool, zany 5 ament, idiot, moron 6 cretin 7 natural 8 imbecile 9 blockhead, simpleton
half-witted 4 dull, slow 5 silly 7 foolish, moronic 8 backward, imbecile, retarded 9 senseless 12 feebleminded, simpleminded
hall 4 dorm 5 foyer, lobby, lycea (plural) 6 lyceum 7 couloir, passage 8 building, corridor 9 dormitory 10 auditorium, living room, passageway 12 entrance room *ancient Roman:* 5 oecus *exhibition:* 5 salon *Salvation Army:* 7 citadel
Halley's ___ 5 comet
Hallohesh's son 7 Shallum
hallow 5 bless 6 devote, revere 8 dedicate, sanctify, venerate 10 consecrate
hallucination 6 mirage, wraith 7 fantasy, phantom 8 delusion, illusion, phantasm 11 fata morgana, ignis fatuus
hallucinogen 3 LSD 9 mescaline 10 psilocybin 11 scopolamine
halo 4 aura 5 nimbi (plural) 6 corona, gloria, nimbus 7 aureole 8 encircle, gloriole *combining form:* 7 stephan 8 stephano
halogen 6 iodine 7 bromine 8 astatine, chlorine, fluorine
halt 3 end 4 lame, limp, quit, stay, stop 5 cease, check, close, hitch, lapse, stall, waver 6 arrest, desist, dither, draw up, falter, finish, haul up, hobble, pull up, wind up, wrap up 7 bring up, fetch up, stagger, suspend, whiffle 8 complete, conclude, give over, hesitate, knock off, leave off, sur-

cease, ultimate 9 determine, interrupt, terminate, vacillate 11 discontinue

ham 4 hock 5 emote, thigh 7 buttock, overact 8 overplay, strutter 13 exhibitionist

Ham *brother:* 4 Shem 7 Japheth *father:* 4 Noah *son:* 4 Cush, Phut 6 Canaan 7 Mizraim

Haman's father 10 Hammedatha

hamartiology subject 3 sin

Hamilcar *conquest:* 5 Spain *home:* 8 Carthage *son:* 8 Hannibal *surname:* 5 Barca

hamlet 5 moray 7 grouper, village *Irish, Scottish:* 7 clachan

Hamlet *author:* 11 Shakespeare (William) *beloved:* 7 Ophelia *castle:* 8 Elsinore *country:* 7 Denmark *friend:* 7 Horatio *mother:* 8 Gertrude *slayer:* 7 Laertes *uncle:* 8 Claudius *victim:* 7 Laertes 8 Claudius, Polonius

Hamlet, The *author:* 8 Faulkner (William) *family:* 6 Snopes

Hammedatha's son 5 Haman

hammer 4 beat, cock, drub, form, maul, peen, pein, pelt, toil 5 drive, erect, gavel, grave, labor, pound, set up, shape, stamp, swage, thump 6 batter, mallet, pummel, sledge, thrash, wallop 7 belabor, build up, fashion, foliate, impress, malleus, planish, trippet 8 lambaste, malleate *type:* 3 air 4 claw 6 sledge 8 ball peen 9 pneumatic

hammerhead 3 bat 5 dunce, shark, stork 8 clodpate, numskull 9 hog sucker 10 thickskull

Hammoleketh's brother 6 Gilead

hamper 3 bar, bin, rub, tie 4 balk, clog, curb, foil, snag 5 block, check, crimp, leash, limit, tie up 6 baffle, basket, cumber, fetter, hinder, hobble, hog-tie, hurdle, impede, lumber, retard, thwart 7 disrupt, inhibit, shackle, trammel 8 encumber, handicap, obstacle, obstruct, restrain, restrict 9 discomfit, embarrass, entrammel, frustrate

hamstring 6 hinder, impair, tendon 7 cripple, disable

Hamul's father 5 Perez 6 Pharez

Hamutal *father:* 8 Jeremiah *husband:* 6 Josiah *son:* 8 Jehoahaz, Zedekiah

Hanameel *cousin:* 8 Jeremiah *father:* 7 Shallum

Hanani *brother:* 8 Nehemiah *father:* 5 Heman, Immer *son:* 4 Jehu

Hananiah *father:* 4 Azur 5 Azzur, Bebai, Heman 7 Shashak 10 Zerubbabel *son:* 8 Jeshaiah, Pelatiah, Zedekiah

Hanan's father 4 Azel 6 Zaccur 7 Maachah, Shashak 8 Igdaliah

hand 3 aid 4 buck, feed, find, fist, furl, give, help, lift, pass, side 5 angle, facet, index, manus, phase, reach, skill, touch

6 aspect, assist, ductus, inning, pledge, relief, script, succor, supply, worker 7 ability, comfort, concern, conduct, deliver, dish out, laborer, provide, secours, support, workman 8 dispense, employee, interest, transfer, turn over 9 direction, operative, signature 10 assistance, penmanship, roustabout, workingman 11 calligraphy, chirography *clenched:* 4 fist *combining form:* 4 chir 5 cheir, chiro, palmi 6 cheiro, palmat 7 palmati *counting zero:* 8 baccarat *covering:* 5 glove 6 mitten *declarer's:* 7 laydown *down:* 8 bequeath *gestures:* 5 mudra *make:* 5 craft *on hip:* 6 akimbo *part:* 4 palm 5 thumb 6 finger *poker:* 5 flush 8 straight 9 full house *protector:* 5 glove 8 gauntlet

handbag 5 purse 8 reticule

handbill 5 flier, flyer 6 dodger, poster 7 affiche, leaflet, placard 8 circular

handbook 5 guide 6 manual 8 Baedeker 9 vade mecum 10 compendium 11 enchiridion *religious:* 9 catechism

handcuff 7 manacle 8 restrain *British:* 7 darbies (plural)

hand down 6 pass on 8 bequeath, transmit

Handel *aria:* 5 Largo *birthplace:* 5 Halle (Germany) *opera:* 4 Nero 5 Serse 6 Almira, Xerxes 7 Rodrigo 8 Berenice 9 Agrippina *oratorio:* 4 Saul 6 Esther, Joshua, Samson 7 Messiah 8 Jephthah

handicap 4 edge, load, odds 5 bulge, start 6 burden 8 drawback 9 advantage, allowance, detriment, head start 10 disability 11 encumbrance 12 disadvantage

handicraft 3 art 5 trade 6 métier 7 calling 8 vocation 10 profession

handkerchief 5 hanky 6 hankie 7 bandana 8 bandanna, mouchoir

handle 3 aim, ear, lay, paw, ply, run, try, use 4 ansa, bail, feel, grip, haft, knob, knop, name, play, take, test, wave, work 5 apply, guide, level, nomen, point, serve, shake, style, swing, title, touch, treat, wield 6 bestow, byname, byword, direct, employ, finger, govern, manage 7 act upon, conduct, control, exploit, moniker, operate, palpate, trade in, utilize 8 brandish, cognomen, deal with, dispense, dominate, doorknob, exercise, flourish, maneuver, nickname *scythe:* 5 snath 6 snathe

handle-shaped 6 ansate

handling 4 care 6 charge 7 conduct, running 9 oversight 10 intendance, management 11 supervision

hand out 4 give 6 bestow, devote, donate 7 present 8 give away 10 administer

hand over 4 cede, feed, find, give 5 leave, waive, yield 6 commit, give up, resign, supply 7 abandon, commend, con-

fide, consign, deliver, entrust, provide
8 dispense, relegate, transfer 9 deliver up,
surrender 10 relinquish

handrail 8 banister

handsome 3 apt 4 chic, fair, free
5 ample, noble, smart, sonsy 6 adroit,
august, comely, lovely, modish, pretty, sonsie 7 dashing, liberal, sizable, stately, stylish 8 generous, majestic 9 beauteous,
beautiful, bounteous, bountiful, unsparing
10 attractive, munificent, openhanded
11 fashionable, good-looking

handspring 6 tumble *lateral:* 9 cartwheel

handwriting 6 ductus, script 8 longhand
10 manuscript, penmanship 11 calligraphy,
chirography *bad:* 10 cacography *study of:*
10 graphology

handy 4 deft 5 adept, utile 6 adroit,
clever, nearby, nimble, useful, wieldy
7 close-by 8 adjacent, skillful 9 adaptable,
dexterous, practical 10 beneficial, convenient, functional 11 practicable

handyman 6 jumper 8 factotum

hang 3 art, fix, jut, lop, pin, sag 4 hook,
idle, lean, loll, pend, rest 5 await, cling,
craft, drape, droop, float, hover, knack,
lynch, noose, pause, poise, scrag, skill,
sling, slope, stick, swing, trail, trick
6 adhere, attach, dangle, depend, gibbet,
impend, loiter, tack up, turn on 7 execute
back: 3 lag *loosely:* 3 sag 6 dangle

hangbird 6 oriole

hangdog 5 cowed 6 guilty 7 ashamed,
pitiful 8 dejected

hanger-on 5 leech 6 sponge, sucker
7 sponger 8 barnacle, follower, parasite
9 bystander, spectator, sycophant 10 freeloader 11 bloodsucker 12 lounge lizard

hanging 7 pendent, pensile 9 declivity,
pendulant, pendulous, suspended

Hanging Gardens 7 Babylon

hangings 5 arras 6 drapes 7 drapery
8 curtains, tapestry

hangout 4 dive 5 haunt, joint 6 resort
7 purlieu 9 honky-tonk 10 rendezvous
11 barrelhouse 12 watering hole

hang up 4 mire 5 delay, embog 6 detain,
retard 7 achieve, bog down, set back,
slacken 8 slow down 10 decelerate

hank 4 coil, loop, ring

hanker 3 yen 4 ache, long, lust, pine,
sigh, wish 5 covet, crave, yearn 6 desire,
hunger, thirst

hanky-panky 5 fraud 7 chicane 8 trickery 9 chicanery, deception, fourberie
11 highbinding 13 double-dealing, sharp
practice

Hannah *husband:* 7 Elkanah *son:*
6 Samuel

Hannibal *defeat:* 4 Zama *father:* 8 Hamilcar *home:* 8 Carthage *surname:* 5 Barca
vanquisher: 6 Scipio *victory:* 6 Cannae

Hanniel's father 4 Ulla 5 Ephod

Hanoch's father 6 Midian, Reuben

hansa, hanse 5 guild 6 league 11 association

Hans Brinker author 5 Dodge (Mary
Mapes)

Hanseatic League City 6 Bremen,
Lubeck, Wismar 7 Cologne, Hamburg,
Rostock

Hansen's disease 7 leprosy

Hanun's father 6 Nahash

haphazard 5 about 6 anyhow, around,
chance, random 7 aimless, anywise, unaimed 8 accident, at random, careless,
casually, randomly, slipshod 9 aimlessly,
desultory, hit-or-miss, irregular, unplanned
10 accidental, carelessly, designless
11 any which way, unorganized 12 accidentally, unconsidered, unsystematic
13 helter-skelter

hapless 4 poor 6 woeful 7 unhappy,
unlucky 8 ill-fated, untoward, wretched
9 miserable 10 ill-starred 11 star-crossed,
unfortunate 12 infelicitous, misfortunate

happen 2 do, go 3 hit 4 bump, come, fall,
give, luck, meet, pass, rise 5 break, light,
occur 6 befall, betide, chance, drop in, tumble, turn up 7 come off, develop, fall out,
stumble, turn out 8 bechance 9 transpire
again: 5 recur *together:* 6 concur

happening 5 event, thing 7 episode
8 incident, occasion 10 occurrence 12 circumstance

happiness 3 joy 4 glee 5 bliss, cheer,
mirth 6 gaiety 7 content, delight, jollity
8 felicity, gladness, pleasure 9 beatitude,
enjoyment 11 delectation 12 satisfaction

happy 3 apt, fit, pat 4 glad, just, meet,
nice, well 5 lucky, right 6 casual, cogent,
joyful, joyous, proper, timely, upbeat 7 content, correct, fitting, pleased, telling
8 friendly, pleasant, suitable 9 befitting,
congenial, contented, effective, effectual,
efficient, favorable, fortunate, opportune,
satisfied, well-timed 10 accidental, convincing, felicitous, fortuitous, harmonious, incidental, propitious, prosperous, seasonable
11 appropriate, efficacious 12 lighthearted

happy-go-lucky 4 cool, easy 6 blithe,
casual 8 carefree, careless, cheerful, debonair, feckless, heedless, reckless 9 easygoing, lightsome 10 free-minded, insouciant,
nonchalant 11 unconcerned 12 devil-may-
care, light-hearted 13 lackadaisical

hara-kiri 7 seppuku, suicide 8 felo-de-se
10 self-murder 12 self-violence 13 self-
slaughter

Haran *brother:* 7 Abraham *daughter:*
5 Iscah 6 Milcah *father:* 5 Terah 6 Shimei
son: 3 Lot

harangue 4 rant, rave 5 mouth, orate
6 tirade 7 declaim, lecture, oration, soapbox 8 bloviate, diatribe, jeremiad, perorate
9 philippic 11 declamation

harass 3 irk, try, vex 4 bait, gnaw, pain,
raid, ride 5 annoy, chivy, devil, foray, harry,
hound, tease, worry 6 badger, hassle,
heckle, hector, maraud, pester, plague, rat-
ten, strain, stress 7 bedevil, dragoon,
exhaust, fatigue, hagride, torment, trouble
8 bullyrag, distress 9 beleaguer

harasser 5 bully 6 hector 7 harrier, hassler 9 bulldozer 10 browbeater 11 intimidator

harassment 6 irking, vexing 8 vexation
9 annoyance, bothering, provoking 10 irritation 11 aggravation, disturbance, provocation 12 exasperation, perturbation

harbinger 4 omen, sign 6 herald, symbol
7 apostle, forerun, portent, presage
8 announce, foreshow, outrider 9 precursor
10 forerunner, indication 11 preindicate

harbor 3 arm, bay, hut 4 bunk, camp,
cove, gulf, hide, live, port, roof, room
5 bight, board, cabin, cover, firth, guard,
haven, house, inlet, lodge, nurse, put up,
roost 6 asylum, bestow, billet, covert,
encamp, foster, refuge, screen, shield, take
in 7 chamber, cherish, conceal, contain,
nurture, protect, quarter, retreat, seaport,
secrete, shelter 8 domicile 9 anchorage,
entertain, safeguard, sanctuary 11 accommodate *fee:* 7 keelage *Greece:* 5 Aulis
Guam: 4 Apra *Hawaii:* 5 Pearl *Ireland:*
4 Cork *Long Island Sound:* 8 New Haven
Massachusetts: 4 Lynn 9 Annisquam
New Jersey: 9 Little Egg *Solomon:* 4 Viru
Washington: 5 Grays

hard 3 bad, set 4 dark, deep, dour, dull,
fast, firm, grim, iron, near, nigh 5 amiss,
badly, bleak, close, crisp, cruel, fixed,
harsh, heavy, horny, madly, rocky, rough,
sharp, sober, solid, stark, tight, tough, vivid
6 actual, ardent, bitter, brazen, brutal,
coarse, firmly, flinty, keenly, knotty, meanly,
nearby, packed, rugged, severe, sorely,
sticky, strict, strong, thorny, tiring, trying,
unjust, uphill, wildly 7 angrily, arduous, austere, binding, briskly, callous, closely, compact, complex, cruelly, durable, factual, fixedly, genuine, glaring, harshly, hostile,
intense, irksome, labored, largely, obscure,
onerous, operous, petrous, precise,
roughly, rowdily, serious, sharply, slavish,
solidly, tightly, tiredly, toilful, violent, wearing 8 absolute, actively, bitterly, brutally,
concrete, definite, dingdong, exacting,

fiercely, forcibly, frugally, granitic, grievous,
grinding, indurate, intently, involved, mightily, petrosal, pitiless, positive, profound, reliable, rigorous, savagely, scabrous,
severely, shabbily, snapplly, stormily, strident, strongly, tempered, terrible, toilsome,
unfairly, urgently, wearying 9 alcoholic,
arduously, austerely, awkwardly, bloodless,
compacted, demanding, difficile, difficult,
earnestly, effortful, fatiguing, furiously,
inclement, indurated, insensate, intensely,
intensive, intricate, laborious, massively,
merciless, offensive, onerously, painfully,
pointedly, practical, pragmatic, punishing,
realistic, resentful, resistant, searching, seriously, shameless, sprightly, straining, strenuous, stringent, unfeeling, unhandily,
unsparing, viciously, violently, wearisome
10 adamantine, anesthetic, animatedly,
bothersome, burdensome, compressed,
cumbrously, exhausting, forbidding, forcefully, formidable, frenziedly, gruelingly,
impassible, insensible, oppressive, perplexing, powerfully, rigorously, spiritedly, spirituous, sure-enough, thoroughly, toilsomely,
unpleasant, unwieldily, unyielding, vigorously 11 assiduously, at close hand, complicated, difficultly, distressing, down-to-earth,
exuberantly, ferociously, frantically, inequitable, insensitive, intemperate, intensively,
intractable, laboriously, ponderously, rancor-
ously, resentfully, searchingly, steadfastly,
strenuously, troublesome, turbulently,
unfantastic, unfavorable, unpalatable, unrelenting, unremitting, vivaciously 12 back-
breaking, blood-and-guts, boisterously, bur-
densomely, concentrated, consolidated,
cumbersomely, exhaustingly, exhaustively,
incorrigible, intoxicating, matter-of-fact,
meticulously, might and main, relentlessly,
tumultuously *combining form:* 5 scler,
stere 6 sclero, stereo *to please:* 7 finicky

hard-boiled 5 crude, rough, sober, stiff,
tough 6 coarse 7 callous 8 obdurate, seasoned 9 heartless, practical, pragmatic,
realistic, unfeeling 11 coldhearted, down-
to-earth, unemotional, unfantastic, worldly-
wise 12 matter-of-fact, stonyhearted, unidealistic 13 sophisticated, unsympathetic

harden 3 dry, set 4 cake, firm 5 adapt,
enure, inure, steel 6 adjust, anneal, callus,
freeze, ossify, season, temper 7 calcify, callous, compact, conform, congeal, densify,
lithify, petrify, stiffen, toughen 8 accustom,
concrete, indurate, sclerose, solidify 9 acclimate, climatize, fossilize, habituate
10 strengthen

hardfisted 4 mean 5 close, tight, tough
6 stingy, strong 7 save-all 9 niggardly
11 tough-minded 13 penny-pinching

hardheaded 5 sober 6 mulish 7 willful 8 perverse, stubborn 9 obstinate, practical, pragmatic, realistic 10 self-willed 11 down-to-earth, intractable, unfantastic 12 matter-of-fact, pertinacious, unidealistic

hardhearted see **hard-boiled**

hardihood 3 pep 4 birr, grit, guts, sand, tuck 5 moxie, nerve, pluck, vigor 6 energy 7 potency 8 audacity, boldness, temerity 9 assurance, brashness, cockiness, fortitude, impudence, insolence, insolency 10 brazenness, disrespect, robustness

hardly ever 6 little, rarely, seldom 7 unoften 12 infrequently, unfrequently

hardness 5 rigor 8 adamancy, asperity, obduracy, severity 9 callosity 10 difficulty, inclemency

hardscrabble 6 barren 8 marginal 9 infertile, unbearing, unfertile 12 impoverished, unproductive

hardship 4 toil 5 peril, rigor, trial 6 danger, hazard 7 travail 8 asperity, distress, drudgery 9 adversity, mischance, privation, suffering 10 affliction, difficulty, discomfort, misfortune 11 tribulation

Hard Times author 7 Dickens (Charles)

hardy 4 bold 5 brave, tough 6 brazen, daring, robust, rugged, strong 8 resolute 9 audacious

Hardy *character:* 3 Sue 4 Alec, Clym, Jude, Tess 5 Angel 8 Arabella, Eustacia, Henchard *setting:* 6 Wessex

hare 3 wat 4 fool 6 rabbit 7 leporid 8 leporine *Belgian:* 8 leporide *combining form:* 3 lag 4 lago *female:* 3 doe *genus:* 5 Lepus *male:* 4 buck *relating to:* 7 leporid 8 leporine *young:* 7 leveret

harebrained 5 balmy, crazy, dizzy, giddy, loony, silly, wacky 6 absurd, insane 7 flighty, foolish 8 skittish 9 frivolous 11 empty-headed 12 preposterous

harefooted 4 fast 5 fleet, hasty, quick, rapid, swift 6 speedy 9 breakneck 10 expeditive 11 expeditious

harem 6 serail, zenana 8 seraglio *concubine:* 3 oda 4 odah 7 odalisk 9 odalisque *room:* 3 óda 4 odah

Hareph's father 5 Caleb

Harhaiah's son 6 Uzziel

hark 4 hear, heed, mind, note 6 attend, listen, notice

harlequin 4 zany 5 clown 6 mottle 7 buffoon

Harlequin *beloved:* 9 Columbine *rival:* 7 Pierrot

harm 3 mar, sap 4 hurt, ruin 5 abuse, spoil 6 damage, ill-use, impair, injure, injury, misuse, molest 7 blemish, marring, outrage, tarnish, vitiate 8 maltreat, mischief, mistreat, sabotage 9 incommode, mischance, prejudice, undermine 10 dilapidate, discommode, disservice, impairment, misfortune 11 banefulness, noxiousness

harmful 3 bad, ill 4 evil 5 risky, toxic 6 malign, nocent, unsafe 7 baleful, baneful, hurtful, malefic, nocuous, noisome, noxious 8 damaging 9 dangerous, hazardous, injurious, malignant, unhealthy 10 pernicious 11 deleterious, detrimental, mischievous, prejudicial, troublesome, unhealthful, unwholesome 12 insalubrious

harmless 4 safe 6 unhurt 8 innocent, nontoxic 9 innocuous, innoxious 11 inobnoxious, inoffensive, unoffending, unoffensive

Harmonia *daughter:* 3 Ino 5 Agave 6 Semele 7 Autonoe *father:* 4 Ares, Mars *husband:* 6 Cadmus *mother:* 5 Venus 9 Aphrodite *son:* 9 Polydorus

harmonious 4 calm 5 sweet 6 amical, dulcet, irenic 7 chiming, chordal, musical, pacific, silvery, tuneful 8 amicable, blending, canorous, coactive, empathic, friendly, peaceful, pleasing, sonorous 9 accordant, agreeable, congenial, congruous, consonant, simpatico, symphonic 10 compatible, concinnate, concordant, empathetic, polyphonic, satisfying 11 cooperative, mellifluous, mellisonant, symmetrical, sympathetic 12 contrapuntal

harmonize 2 go 3 fit 4 jibe, tune 5 adapt, agree, blend, coapt, fit in, match, tally, unify, unite 6 accord, adjust, attune, concur, relate, square 7 arrange, concert, concord, conform 8 coincide, dovetail 9 cooperate, correlate, integrate, reconcile 10 coordinate, correspond, proportion, synthesize 11 accommodate, orchestrate 12 reconciliate

harmony 4 tune 5 chime, grace, peace, unity 6 accord, chorus, melody, unison 7 balance, concert, concord, dignity, empathy, kinship, oneness, rapport 8 affinity, diapason, elegance, sonority, symmetry 9 agreement, congruity, integrity, polyphony 10 accordance, coaptation, concinnity, conformity, consonance, musicality, proportion 11 concordance, concurrence, conformance, consistency, integration, tunefulness 12 articulation, togetherness *lack of:* 7 discord *of movement:* 8 eurythmy

Harnepher's father 6 Zophah

harness 4 gear, leaf, yoke 5 armor, hitch 6 couple, tackle 7 utilize 8 clothing 9 equipment *part:* 3 bit 4 rein 5 girth, trace 6 collar 7 blinder, crupper 9 bellyband, breeching, checkrein 12 breast collar *ring:* 6 terret, territ

harp 4 lyre 9 harmonica *Irish:* 8 clarsach

harpsichord 7 cembalo 8 clavecin

harpsichordist *American:* 6 Fuller (Albert, David), Kipnis (Igor), Newman (Anthony) 7 Marlowe (Sylvia), Pinkham (Daniel), Valenti (Fernando) 11 Kirkpatrick (Ralph) *English:* 7 Malcolm (George) *German:* 7 Richter (Karl) 9 Leonhardt (Gustav) *Italian:* 7 Sgrizzi (Luciano) *Polish:* 9 Landowska (Wanda)

harpy 5 leech, scold, shrew, vixen 6 amazon, ogress, virago 8 fishwife, swindler 9 termagant, Xanthippe

Harpy 5 Aello 7 Celaeno, Ocypete *father:* 7 Thaumas *mother:* 7 Electra *sister:* 4 Iris

harrier 3 dog 4 hawk 5 bully 6 hector, runner 8 harasser 9 bulldozer 10 browbeater 11 intimidator

harrow 3 try 4 bait, fret, rack 5 devil, tease, wring 6 badger, heckle, hector, martyr, needle, pester 7 afflict, agonize, bedevil, crucify, torment, torture 8 irritate 9 tantalize 10 excruciate

harry 3 irk 4 gnaw, raid, sack 5 annoy, foray, havoc, tease, upset, worry 6 attack, badger, harass, maraud, pester, plague, ravage, worrit 7 assault, bedevil, despoil, disturb, hagride, perturb, pillage, torment 8 desolate, irritate, spoliate, vexation 9 beleaguer, depredate

harsh 3 dry, raw 4 dour, grim, sour, tart 5 acerb, acrid, bleak, crude, cruel, gruff, loose, rough, rusty, sharp, stark, stern, tangy 6 biting, bitter, brassy, brutal, coarse, craggy, gruffy, hoarse, jagged, rugged, severe, shaggy, shrill, uneven 7 acerbic, austere, blaring, bristly, burning, grating, jarring, mordant, pungent, rasping, raucous, scraggy, squawky, squeaky, stubbly, uncomfy, unlevel 8 asperous, exacting, granular, grinding, jangling, piercing, rigorous, scabrous, scraggly, scraping, scratchy, strident, unsmooth 9 amaroidal, dissonant, inclement, stringent, unmusical 10 astringent, discordant, irritating, stridulent, stridulous

hart 4 stag 7 red deer *mate:* 4 hind

Hart, Moss *autobiography:* 6 Act One *collaborator:* 7 Kaufman (George S.)

hartebeest 4 tora 5 bubal 6 lelwel 7 bubalis 8 antelope *family:* 7 Bovidae

Hartford *college:* 7 Trinity *economic activity:* 9 insurance

Harumaph's son 7 Jedaiah

Harum's son 7 Aharhel

haruspex 5 augur 7 prophet 8 foreseer 9 predictor 10 forecaster, foreteller, prophesier, soothsayer 11 Nostradamus

harvest 2 in 3 bin 4 crop, hide, reap 5 amass, cache, hoard, stash, yield 6 garner, gather 7 bearing, collect, reaping, store up, storing, vintage 8 assemble, cropping, fruitage, ingather, squirrel, stow away 9 garnering, gathering 10 accumulate *bug:* 4 mite 7 chigger *fly:* 6 cicada *former festival:* 6 Lammas *goddess:* 3 Ops

harvester *grain:* 6 header *of grapes:* 8 vintager

Harvey 5 pooka 6 rabbit *author:* 5 Chase (Mary)

Hasadiah's father 10 Zerubbabel

hash 4 chop, mess, mull, muss, stew 5 botch, mince, mix-up 6 jumble, jungle, litter, medley, mess-up, muddle, review, tumble 7 clutter, mélange, mixture, rummage 8 botchery, consider, scramble, shambles 9 patchwork, talk about 10 assortment, hodgepodge, miscellany 11 gallimaufry

Hashabiah's father 6 Kemuel 8 Jeduthun

Hashabniah's son 7 Hattush

hashish 5 bhang, ganja 6 charas 8 cannabis, narcotic *plant:* 4 hemp

Hashubah's father 10 Zerubbabel

hasp 6 fasten 8 fastener

Hassenuah's son 8 Hodaviah

hassle 3 row, try 4 beef, miff, spar, to-do 5 argue, brawl, cavil, essay, fight, run-in, trial, whirl 6 argufy, bicker, clamor, hubbub, pother, tumult, uproar 7 attempt, dispute, quarrel, quibble, rhubarb, turmoil, wrangle 8 endeavor, squabble, striving, struggle 9 bickering, commotion 10 hurly-burly 11 altercation, controversy

hassock 4 gadi, pouf 5 gaddi 7 cushion, ottoman 9 footstool

haste 3 run 4 dash, pace, rush 5 drive, hurry, speed 6 barrel, bucket, bustle, flurry, hustle, rocket, rustle 7 beeline, hotfoot 8 celerity, dispatch, fastness, highball, rapidity, velocity 9 fleetness, quickness, swiftness 10 expedition, nimbleness, speediness 11 hurriedness, impetuosity 12 precipitance, precipitancy 13 impetuousness, impulsiveness, precipitation

hasten 3 fly, run 4 flit, rush 5 fleet, hurry, speed 6 barrel, hustle, step up, urge on 7 hotfoot, quicken, shake up, speed up, swiften 10 accelerate

hasty 4 fast, rash 5 agile, brash, brisk, eager, fleet, quick, rapid, swift 6 abrupt, brashy, madcap, nimble, speedy, sudden 7 cursory, hurried, rushing 8 headlong, reckless, slambang, slapdash 9 breakneck, hotheaded, impatient, impetuous, irritable, quickened 10 expeditive, harefooted, ill-advised, incautious, mad-brained 11 expeditious, precipitant, precipitate, precipitous, subitaneous, thoughtless

hat 5 derby, tuque 6 cloche, fedora, panama, topper 7 bicorne, chapeau, haircap, homburg, porkpie, stetson, tricorn 8 som-

brero, tricorne **9** headpiece **11** chapeau
bras *ancient Greek:* **7** petasus *brimless:*
7 pillbox *close-fitting:* **5** toque, tuque
6 toquet, turban *cone-shaped:* **3** fez *felt:*
5 derby **6** bowler, trilby *fur:* **5** busby *hel-
metlike:* **4** topi **5** topee *lightweight:*
6 panama *maker:* **8** milliner *military:*
5 shako **6** shacko *Muslim:* **6** turban **7** tar-
bush **8** tarboosh *Near East:* **3** fez *sheepskin:* **6** calpac, kalpak **7** calpack *soft:*
5 toque *straw:* **6** boater, panama, sailor
7 bangkok **8** sombrero *sun:* **5** terai *tall:*
9 stovepipe *wide-brimmed:* **9** sou'wester
11 southwester *woman's:* **4** coif **5** beret

hatch 4 door, line, make, sire **5** breed,
brood, cause, cover, frame, get up, spawn
6 cook up, create, devise, father, induce,
invent, make up, parent, stroke, vamp up,
work up **7** concoct, dream up, produce,
provoke **8** contrive, engender, generate,
incubate, occasion **9** floodgate, formulate,
originate, procreate **11** compartment

hatchet 8 dispatch, tomahawk

hatchet man 3 gun **6** critic, killer **7** torpedo **8** assassin **9** cutthroat **10** highbinder

hate 5 abhor, gripe, scorn, spite **6** animus,
bother, detest, horror, loathe, rancor, resent
7 bugbear, contemn, despise, disdain, disgust, dislike, ill will, trouble **8** anathema,
aversion, distaste, execrate, irritant, loathing, nuisance **9** animosity, antipathy, bête
noire, deprecate, grievance, hostility, repulsion, revulsion **10** abhorrence, black beast,
disapprove, repugnance **11** abomination,
detestation

hateful 4 evil, foul, mean, vile **5** catty,
nasty **6** bitchy, bitter, horrid, malign, odious, scurvy **7** vicious **8** accursed, annoying, damnable, infamous **9** abhorrent,
execrable, malicious, obnoxious, repellent,
repulsive, resentful **10** abominable, despicable, despiteful, detestable, ill-natured,
malevolent **11** acrimonious, blasphemous,
distasteful, distressing, opprobrious, uncongenial, unspeakable **12** contemptible
13 reprehensible

Hatfield vs. ____ 5 McCoy

Hathath's father 7 Othniel

hatred 5 odium, spite **6** animus, enmity,
rancor **7** dislike **8** aversion, loathing **9** animosity, antipathy, hostility, repulsion, revulsion **10** abhorrence, repugnance **11** abomination, detestation, malevolence
combining form: **3** mis **4** miso *of mankind:* **11** misanthropy *of marriage:*
8 misogamy *of women:* **8** misogyny

hats 9 millinery

Hattush's father 8 Shemaiah **10** Hashabniah

hauberk 5 armor **9** chain mail, habergeon

haughtiness 5 pride **6** morgue **7** disdain,
hauteur **9** arrogance, insolence, superbity

haughty 5 aloof, lofty, proud **6** lordly,
sniffy **7** distant **8** arrogant, cavalier,
detached, insolent, parvenue, reserved,
scornful, sniffish, superior, toplofty **9** egotistic **10** disdainful **11** indifferent, overbearing
12 contemptuous, supercilious

haul 2 go **3** lug, tow, tug **4** cart, come,
drag, draw, lift, load, move, pull, take
5 boost, cargo, hoist, raise, shift **6** burden,
lading, remove **7** elevate, freight, payload
with a tackle: **5** bouse, bowse

haul up 4 stop **5** hoise, hoist *with a rope:*
5 trice

haunches 4 beam, rump, tail **7** hind end,
hunkers, rear end **8** backside, buttocks
9 fundament, posterior

haunt 4 home, howf, site **5** ghost, howff,
range, shade **6** affect, linger, molest,
resort, shadow, spirit, wraith **7** habitat,
hang out, phantom, purlieu, specter, trouble
8 frequent, locality, phantasm **10** apparition, hang around, rendezvous **12** watering
hole

haunter 7 denizen, habitué **10** frequenter

hautbois 4 oboe

hauteur see haughtiness

haut monde 5 elite **6** gentry **7** quality,
society, who's who **8** optimacy **9** blue
blood **10** patriciate **11** aristocracy **13** carriage trade

have 3 buy, eat, fix, get, let, own, see, sop,
use, win **4** bear, fool, gain, hire, hold, keep,
know, land, lead, must, need, pass, show,
take, undo, wear **5** admit, allow, annex,
beget, bribe, carry, cheat, drink, enjoy,
grasp, leave, smoke, trick **6** accept, buy
off, convey, defeat, embody, fathom,
obtain, outfox, outwit, permit, pick up,
retain, square, suborn, suffer, take in
7 achieve, acquire, carry on, chalk up, cherish, cognize, compass, compose, contain,
control, embrace, execute, exhibit, include,
involve, outplay, perform, possess, procure,
receive, subsume, support, sustain,
undergo **8** comprise, dominate, engage in,
exercise, manifest, outreach, outslick, outsmart **9** apprehend, bamboozle, encompass, out-jockey, overreach, partake of
10 appreciate, categorize, comprehend,
experience

haven 4 port, roof **5** cover, house, roads
6 asylum, covert, harbor, refuge, riding,
shield **7** chamber, retreat, shelter **9** anchorage, harborage, roadstead, sanctuary

haversack 3 bag **4** case **8** backpack

havoc 4 loss, ruin, sack **5** waste **6** ravage
7 despoil, destroy, pillage **8** calamity, desolate, lay waste, ravaging, spoliate **9** cata-

clysm, confusion, depredate, desecrate, devastate, pillaging, ruination, vandalism 10 despoiling 11 catastrophe, destruction, devastation

haw 4 tree, yard 5 berry, fruit, shrub

Hawaii *author:* 8 Michener (James A.) *capital:* 8 Honolulu *discoverer:* 4 Cook (Captain James) *highest point:* 8 Mauna Kea *island:* 4 Maui, Oahu 5 Kauai, Lanai 6 Niihau 7 Molokai 9 Kahoolawe *nickname:* 10 Aloha State *state bird:* 4 nene *state flower:* 11 red hibiscus

Hawaiian *dance:* 4 hula *duck:* 5 koloa *feast:* 4 luau *food:* 3 poi *god:* 2 Ku 4 Kane, Lono 5 Wakea 7 Kanaloa *goddess:* 4 Pele *goose:* 4 nene *instrument:* 3 uke 7 ukulele *lava:* 2 aa *neckwear:* 3 lei *nonnative:* 8 malihini *resident:* 8 kamaaina *thrush:* 4 omao

hawk 4 vend 5 buteo 6 monger, osprey, peddle 7 goshawk, haggard 8 caracara, huckster, roughleg 9 accipiter *Hawaiian:* 2 io *young:* 4 eyas

hawker 6 coster, monger, pedlar, pedler, vendor 7 packman, peddler 8 falconer, pitchman

hawk-eyed 7 lyncean 12 sharp-sighted

Hawkeye State 4 Iowa

Hawthorne *birthplace:* 5 Salem *novel:* 13 The Marble Faun 16 The Scarlet Letter

hay-building machine 5 baler

Haydn oratorio 10 The Seasons 11 The Creation

hay fever 10 pollenosis, pollinosis *cause:* 6 pollen 7 ragweed

haymaker 3 box 4 chop, cuff, poke, sock 5 clout, punch, smack 6 buffet

hayseed see hick

haywire 4 amok 5 amuck, crazy 8 confused 10 broken-down, out of order

hazard 3 bet 4 luck, risk 5 peril, wager 6 chance, danger, gamble, menace 7 fortune, imperil, venture 8 accident, endanger, jeopardy

hazardous 5 hairy, risky 6 chancy, wicked 7 unsound 8 aleatory 9 dangerous, unhealthy

haze 3 dim, fog 4 film, mist, murk, smog 5 befog, bloom, brume, cloud, dream, fog up, smoke, vapor 6 stupor, trance 7 becloud, obscure, reverie 8 overcast 9 mistiness, murkiness, overcloud, smokiness 10 bemusement, cloudiness, muddlement 11 muddledness 12 befuddlement

hazel 3 nut 6 muffin 7 filbert 8 noisette

Hazo *father:* 5 Nahor *mother:* 6 Milcah

hazy 3 dim 5 filmy, foggy, misty, murky, mushy, smoky, vague 6 cloudy, dreamy, vapory 7 bemused, blurred, clouded, nebular, obscure, tranced, unclear 8 nebulous,

vaporous 9 stuporous, uncertain 10 indefinite, indistinct

head 2 go 3 aim, top, wit 4 arch, bent, bill, boss, bump, cape, cast, cock, flow, gift, john, make, mind, naze, neck, pate, poll, rise, stem, text, turn 5 arise, brain, caput, chief, crown, first, flair, front, issue, knack, level, motif, point, poise, privy, scalp, skull, start, theme, topic, train 6 climax, crisis, direct, genius, honcho, johnny, leader, master, matter, mazard, motive, noddle, noggin, noodle, scolex, sconce, set out, talent, toilet, zero in 7 address, aptness, cranium, emanate, faculty, incline, latrine, leading, premier, proceed, subject, surpass, take off 8 argument, brainpan, champion, coiffure, director, foreland, foremost, hierarch, lavatory, light out 9 capitulum, chieftain, decollate, dominator, originate, principal, strike out 10 decapitate, derive from, gray matter, guillotine, individual, promontory 11 convenience, water closet *area:* 5 crown 6 temple *back part:* 7 occiput *bone:* 5 skull 7 cranium 8 parietal *combining form:* 5 crani 6 cephal, cranio 7 cephalo 8 cephalic 9 cephalous *covering:* 3 cap, hat 8 kercheif *flower:* 6 arnica, button *monastery:* 4 dean 5 abbot 8 superior *nunnery:* 4 dame 6 abbess 8 superior *of hair:* 6 fleece *relating to:* 8 cephalic *shaving of:* 7 tonsure *skin:* 5 scalp *tapeworm's:* 6 scolex *top:* 4 pate 5 crown

headache 6 megrim 7 problem 8 migraine 11 cephalalgia

headband 7 bandeau *ancient Greek:* 6 taenia 7 taeniae (plural)

headdress *bishop's:* 5 miter, mitre *medieval:* 5 barbe *military:* 5 busby, shako 6 helmet *nobleman's:* 7 coronet *prelate's:* 9 zucchetto *priest's:* 7 biretta *royal:* 5 crown, tiara 6 diadem *Spanish women's:* 8 mantilla *women's:* 6 bonnet; (see also hat)

headland 4 beak, bill, cape, naze, ness 5 point 10 promontory

headline 6 banner 7 feature 8 screamer

headlong 4 rash 5 hasty 6 abrupt, daring, rashly, sudden 7 hurried, rushing 8 gadarene, reckless 9 daredevil, foolhardy, impetuous 10 heedlessly, recklessly 11 precipitant, precipitate, precipitous, subitaneous

headmaster 9 principal

headshaker 7 skeptic, zetetic 9 pessimist 10 Pyrrhonian, Pyrrhonist

head-shaped 7 globose 8 capitate

head start 4 draw, edge, odds 5 bulge 7 vantage 8 handicap 9 advantage, allowance

headstone 6 ledger 8 monument 11 grave marker

headstrong 6 mulish 7 willful 8 stubborn
9 obstinate 10 refractory, self-willed
11 stiff-necked

heady 4 rash 5 cagey, giddy, smart
6 argute, astute, clever, shrewd 7 violent,
willful 9 astucious, impetuous, sagacious
11 exhilarated, intoxicated 12 intoxicating

heal 4 cure, mend, scab 6 cement, remedy

healer *combining form:* 7 iatrist

healing 8 curative, remedial, sanative, sanatory 9 vulnerary, wholesome 11 restorative *combining form:* 5 iatro, iatry
7 iatrics *goddess of:* 3 Eir

health 7 stamina 8 euphoria, haleness,
tonicity, vitality 9 soundness, well-being,
wholeness *club:* 3 spa

healthful 4 good 6 aiding 8 curative,
hygienic, remedial, salutary, sanative
9 wholesome 10 beneficial, corrective, miti-
gative, profitable, salubrious 11 alleviative,
restorative

healthy 3 fit 4 good, hale, iron, rosy, safe,
sane, spry, well 5 agile, lusty, right, ruddy,
sound, tough, whole 6 robust, rugged,
strong, sturdy, vegete, viable 7 chipper,
massive 8 blooming, hygienic, positive, rubicund, salutary, stalwart, thriving, vigorous
9 desirable, wholesome 10 beneficial, prosperous, salubrious, well-liking 11 flourishing, uninjurious *Scottish:* 5 gawsy 6 gaw-
sie

heap 3 lot 4 bank, cock, cord, dump, fill,
gobs, hill, load, lump, mass, much, pack,
pile, rick, scad 5 amass, bunch, choke,
clump, crate, drift, group, loads, mound,
shock, stack, wreck 6 barrel, charge,
gather, jalopy, junker, lumber, oodles
7 clunker, collect, deposit, jillion, million
8 assemble, cumulate, mountain, slathers,
thousand, trillion 9 congeries, gathering,
great deal, stockpile 10 accumulate, cumulation, quantities *combining form:* 5 cumul
6 cumuli, cumulo *combustible:* 4 pyre *of
dead bodies:* 7 carnage

hearing 4 test 5 sound, trial 6 parley, try-
out 7 earshot, meeting 8 audience, audition 9 interview 10 conference, discussion
combining form: 4 acou 5 acouo, audio
6 acusia 7 acousia *distance:* 7 earshot

hearken 6 attend, listen

hearsay 3 cry 4 buzz, talk 5 on-dit, rumor
6 gossip, report, rumble 7 account
9 grapevine 11 scuttlebutt

heart 3 hub 4 core, guts, love, mood, pith,
root, seat, soul, zest 5 ardor, bosom, focus,
gusto, pluck, quick, spunk, taste 6 breast,
center, mettle, palate, relish, spirit 7 courage 8 feelings, polestar 9 character
10 affections, compassion, conscience,
enthusiasm, focal point *combining form:*
5 cardi 6 cardia, cardio 7 cardium *contrac-*

tion: 7 systole *dilation:* 8 diastole *part:*
6 atrium, septum 9 ventricle

heartache 3 rue, woe 4 care, pang
5 grief 6 regret, sorrow 7 anguish 10 affliction, cardialgia

heartbeat 5 pulse, throb 9 pulsation *irregular:* 8 arythmia

heartbreak 3 rue, woe 4 bale, care
5 agony, grief 6 regret, sorrow 7 anguish,
torment 10 affliction

heartbreaking 4 dire 8 grievous
10 afflictive, calamitous, deplorable, lamentable 11 regrettable, unfortunate

heartburn 7 pyrosis 10 cardialgia

hearten 4 stir 5 cheer, nerve, rally, rouse,
steel 6 arouse 7 animate, chirk up, enliven
8 energize, inspirit 9 encourage

heartfelt 4 deep, true 6 honest 7 earnest,
genuine, sincere 8 bona fide, profound
9 unfeigned 11 whole-souled

heartleaf 6 ginger

heartless 5 cruel 7 callous 8 obdurate
9 unfeeling 10 hard-boiled 11 unemotional
13 unsympathetic

Heart of Dixie 7 Alabama

heartrending see **heartbreaking**

heartsease 5 pansy, viola 6 violet
9 smartweed

heart-shaped 7 cordate

heartsick 4 blue, down 8 cast down,
dejected, downcast 9 depressed 10 dispirited 12 disconsolate

heartthrob 4 love 5 flame, honey, sweet
7 beloved, darling, passion 10 sweetheart

heartwood 7 duramen

hearty 4 deep, warm 5 ample 6 jovial,
sailor 7 profuse, sincere 8 abundant, profound, vehement 9 approving, exuberant,
flavorful, unfeigned 10 full-bodied, responsive 11 whole-souled 12 enthusiastic

heat 3 hot 4 cook, move, warm 6 excite,
simmer, warmth 7 caloric, convect, furnace, hotness, inflame 8 pyrolyze *combining form:* 3 pyr 4 pyro 5 therm 6 calori,
thermo, thermy 7 thermia *measuring
device:* 11 colorimeter, thermometer *quantity:* 3 BTU

heated 3 hot, mad 4 warm, waxy 5 angry,
fiery, irate, wroth 6 ardent, baking, fervid,
fierce, hectic, ireful, steamy, wrathy 7 boiling, burning, fevered 8 brolling, feverish,
scalding, sizzling, wrathful 9 indignant,
scorching 11 acrimonious

heater 5 stove 7 furnace 8 radiator

heathbird 7 gray hen 9 blackcock
11 black grouse

heathen 5 pagan 6 ethnic 7 foreign, gentile, infidel, profane, strange 8 paganish,
paganist 9 infidelic 10 unfamiliar

heat-producing 9 calorific

heave 3 gag 4 blow, cast, fire, gasp, huff, hurl, keck, pant, puff, rock, roll, toss 5 fling, labor, pitch, retch, sling, throw, vomit

heaven 3 God 4 Zion 5 bliss, glory 6 Canaan, utopia 7 arcadia, ecstasy, elysium, nirvana, rapture 8 empyrean, eternity, paradise, rhapsody 9 Cockaigne, hereafter, Shangri-la 10 afterworld, Civitas Del, lubberland, wonderland 11 immortality, kingdom come 12 New Jerusalem, promised land 13 Abraham's bosom

heavenly 4 lush 5 yummy 6 divine, sacred 7 blessed, darling 8 adorable, empyreal, empyrean, luscious 9 ambrosial, celestial, delicious 10 delectable, delightful, enchanting 11 exceedingly, scrumptious

heavenly body see **celestial body**

heavy 3 big, fat 4 deep, drab, dull, gone, hard, loud, rich 5 acute, bulky, dopey, grave, gross, hefty, inert, obese, steep, stout, tough 6 clayey, cloggy, cloudy, clumsy, coarse, drowsy, fleshy, gravid, leaden, occult, orphic, parous, portly, secret, severe, sleepy, stupid, torpid 7 arduous, awkward, doleful, intense, labored, louring, massive, porcine, serious, unhandy, villain, weighty 8 abstruse, burdened, childing, comatose, cumbrous, enceinte, esoteric, grievous, hermetic, inactive, lowering, nubilous, overcast, pregnant, profound, sluggish, toilsome, unwieldy 9 corpulent, difficult, effortful, expectant, expecting, laborious, lethargic, lumbering, ponderous, recondite, strenuous 10 acroamatic, afflictive, burdensome, cumbersome, encumbered, formidable, lumbersome, oppressive, overweight, parturient, slumberous *combining form:* 4 bary, hadr 5 gravi, hadro

heavy-handed 5 inept 6 gauche, wooden 7 awkward, halting, unhappy 8 bumbling 9 maladroit, ponderous 10 uninspired

heavyhearted 3 sad 5 sorry 7 unhappy 8 mournful, saddened 10 dispirited, melancholy

heavyset 5 dumpy, thick 6 chunky, squdgy, stocky, stubby, stumpy 11 thickbodied

heavyweight 3 VIP 4 lion 5 chief 6 big boy, leader 7 notable 8 big-timer

Hebe *father:* 4 Zeus 7 Jupiter *husband:* 8 Hercules *mother:* 4 Hera, Juno *successor:* 8 Ganymede

Heber *father:* 6 Beriah *grandfather:* 5 Asher *mother:* 4 Jael

hebetude 4 coma 5 sleep 6 stupor, torpor 7 languor, slumber 8 dullness, lethargy 9 torpidity

hebetudinous 5 dopey, heavy 6 stupid, torpid 8 comatose, sluggish 9 lethargic

Hebrew *bushel:* 4 epha 5 ephah *coin:* 4 beka, gera, mina, mite 5 bekah, gerah, maneh 6 lepton, shekel *festival:* 5 Pesah, Purim, Seder 6 Pesach, Succos, Sukkos 7 Hanukah, Sukkoth 8 Chanukah, Hanukhah, Hanukkah, Lag b'Omer, Passover, Shabuoth 9 Chanukhah, Chanukkah, Tishah-b'Ab, Yom Kippur 11 Rosh Hashana 12 Simchas Torah *God:* 2 El 5 Eloah, Yahwe 6 Adonai, Elohim, Yahweh 7 Jehovah *instrument:* 4 Asor 5 nabla, nebel *judge:* 6 Gideon *lawgiver:* 5 Moses *letter:* (see at **alphabet**) *measure:* 3 cor, hin, kab, log 4 bath, omer, seah, span 5 cubit, ephah, homer 6 finger 11 handbreadth *month:* 2 Ab 4 Adar, Elul, Iyar 5 Nisan, Sivan, Tebet 6 Kislev, Shebat, Tammuz, Tishri 6 Veadar (in leap year) 7 Heshvan *patriarch:* 3 Dan, Gad 4 Cain, Levi, Seth 5 Asher, David, Isaac, Jacob, Judah 6 Joseph, Reuben, Simeon 7 Abraham, Zebulun 8 Benjamin, Issachar, Naphtali *sacred city:* 5 Safad, Safed 6 Hebron 8 Tiberias 9 Jerusalem; (see also **Jewish**)

Hebron's father 6 Kohath

Hecate *father:* 6 Perses *mother:* 7 Asteria

heckle 3 nag 4 bait, faze, gibe, ride 5 chivy, hound, tease, worry 6 badger, harass, hector, molest, needle, plague, rattle 7 torment 8 bullyrag

hectic 3 red 6 fervid 7 burning, fevered, flushed 8 feverish, habitual, restless 10 persistent

hector 3 cow 4 bait, ride 5 bully, chivy, hound 6 badger 7 dragoon, harrier, swagger 8 bludgeon, braggart, browbeat, bulldoze, bullyrag, harasser

Hector *brother:* 5 Paris 7 Helenus, Troilus 9 Deiphobus, Polydorus *father:* 5 Priam *mother:* 6 Hecuba *sister:* 6 Creusa 8 Polyxena 9 Cassandra *slayer:* 8 Achilles *victim:* 9 Patroclus *wife:* 10 Andromache

Hecuba *daughter:* 6 Creusa 8 Polyxena 9 Cassandra *father:* 5 Dymas *husband:* 5 Priam *son:* 5 Paris 6 Hector 7 Helenus, Troilus 9 Deiphobus, Polydorus *victim:* 11 Polymnestor

hedge 3 mew, pen 4 cage, coop, mure, trim 5 evade, fence, guard 6 corral, hinder, immure, weasel 7 enclose, protect, shuffle 8 encircle, restrict, roadside, sidestep

hedonist 4 rake 7 epicure, gourmet 8 gourmand, sybarite 9 bon vivant, debauchee, epicurean, libertine 10 voluptuary

heebie-jeebies 5 jumps 6 dither, shakes 7 jitters, shivers

heed 3 see 4 care, hark, mark, mind, note, obey 5 study, watch 6 attend, beware, debate, listen, notice, regard, remark 7 concern, hearing, hearken, observe, respect 8 audience, consider, interest 9 attention, awareness 10 cognizance, observance 11 application, carefulness, mindfulness

heedful 5 alert, exact, fussy 6 arrect 7 careful 8 punctual 9 advertent, attentive, intentive, observant, observing 10 meticulous, scrupulous, thoughtful 11 observative, painstaking, punctilious 12 conscionable 13 conscientious

heedless 8 uncaring 9 oblivious, unmindful, unrecking 10 unthinking 11 inadvertent, inattentive, unobservant 12 unreflective

heedlessness 6 apathy 8 lethargy 9 disregard, lassitude, unconcern 11 disinterest, insouciance 12 indifference

hee-haw 4 bray 5 laugh 6 giggle, guffaw, titter 7 chortle, chuckle, snicker

heel 3 run, tip 4 cant, hock, lean, list, rest, tilt 5 knave, rogue, slant, slope 6 rascal 7 balance, incline, lowlife, recline, remains, remanet, remnant, residue, villain 8 leavings, residual, residuum 9 miscreant, remainder, scoundrel 10 blackguard *bones:* 8 calcanea, calcanei

heft 4 lift 5 hoist, raise, weigh 6 weight 9 heaviness

hefty 3 big 5 beefy, burly, husky, large, major 6 mighty, rugged 7 massive, sizable 8 abundant, imposing, powerful 9 extensive, good-sized, plentiful, ponderous

Heidi *author:* 5 Spyri (Johanna) *setting:* 4 Alps

height 4 apex, rise 6 climax, summit, zenith 7 stature 8 altitude, highness, pinnacle, tallness 9 elevation, loftiness *combining form:* 3 acr, akr 4 acro, akro, hyps 5 hypsi, hypso

heighten 3 wax 4 lift, rise 5 boost, build, mount, raise, rouse 6 better, deepen, expand, extend 7 amplify, augment, elevate, enhance, enlarge, improve, magnify, sharpen, upsurge 8 compound, increase, multiply, redouble 9 aggravate, highlight, intensate, intensify 10 aggrandize

heinous 6 crying 8 shocking 9 desperate, execrable 10 abominable, outrageous

heinousness 8 atrocity, enormity

heir 3 son 5 heres 6 haeres 7 heredes (plural), heritor 8 haeredes (plural) 9 inheritor, successor *joint:* 8 parcener

Hel, Hela *father:* 4 Loki *hall:* 7 Niflhel 8 Niflheim *mother:* 9 Angerboda

Helah's husband 5 Ashur 6 Ashhur

Heleb's father 6 Baanah

Helek's father 6 Gilead

Helenus *brother:* 5 Paris 6 Hector 7 Troilus 9 Deiphobus, Polydorus *father:* 5 Priam *mother:* 6 Hecuba *sister:*

6 Creusa 8 Polyxena 9 Cassandra *wife:* 10 Andromache

helical 6 spiral

helicopter 7 chopper 10 whirlybird *armed:* 7 gunship

Helios 6 Apollo *daughter:* 5 Circe 8 Pasiphae *father:* 8 Hyperion *mother:* 5 Theia *sister:* 3 Eos 6 Aurora, Selene *son:* 8 Phaethon

heliotrope 10 bloodstone

Heli's daughter 4 Mary

helium *symbol:* 2 He

hell see hades

Hellen *father:* 9 Deucalion *mother:* 6 Pyrrha *son:* 5 Dorus 6 Aeolus, Xuthus

hellhole 8 dystopia

hellish 7 avernal, stygian 8 infernal, plutonic 9 cimmerian, plutonian 11 pandemoniac

helm 5 steer

helmet 3 cap 5 salet 6 barbut, casque, morion, salade, sallet 7 morrion 8 burgonet, headgear *medieval:* 5 armet 6 heaume, sallet 7 basinet *part:* 7 ventail 8 aventail *sun:* 4 topi 5 topee

helmet-shaped 7 galeate

Heloise *husband:* 7 Abelard *son:* 9 Astrolabe

Helon's son 5 Eliab

helotry 4 yoke 6 thrall 7 bondage, peonage, serfdom 9 servitude, thralldom, villenage 11 enslavement

help 3 aid, use 4 abet, ally, back, cure, hand, lift, mend 5 amend, avail, avoid, boost, do for, serve, stead 6 assist, better, fail in, profit, relief, remedy, second, succor, uphold 7 advance, ancilla, benefit, bestead, bolster, comfort, forward, further, improve, prevent, promote, relieve, secours, service, striker, support 8 befriend, benefact, champion, minister, mitigate, palliate 9 alleviate, assistant, attendant, extricate, meliorate 10 ameliorate, assistance, facilitate 11 cooperation *forward:* 7 further *hired:* 5 labor

helper 3 aid 4 aide 6 deputy, server 7 ancilla, servant 8 employee 9 assistant, associate, attendant, auxiliary 10 apprentice, benefactor 11 subordinate

helpful 4 good 5 brave 6 aidant, aidful, aiding, toward, usable 7 benefic 8 favoring, salutary 9 assistive, effective, favorable, practical 10 beneficial, profitable, propitious 11 encouraging, serviceable 12 advantageous, constructive

helping 7 portion 8 friendly 9 auxiliary

helpless 4 weak 6 feeble, futile 7 forlorn 8 desolate, forsaken, impotent 9 abandoned 10 bewildered 11 unprotected

helter-skelter 6 anyhow, around, random 7 anywise, flighty, hotfoot, turmoil 8 at random, pellmell, randomly **9** haphazard, hit-or-miss **11** any which way, haphazardly, hurry-scurry, impetuously, precipitate

helve 4 haft **6** handle

Helvetian 5 Swiss

hem 3 pen, rim **4** brim, cage, edge, gird, ring, seam, shut **5** beset, bound, brink, fence, hedge, round, skirt, verge **6** begird, border, circle, corral, define, edging, fringe, girdle, immure, margin, stitch **7** close in, enclose, envelop, selvage, shorten **8** encircle, surround **9** encompass, perimeter, periphery *turned-back:* **4** cuff

Hemam's father 5 Lotan

Heman *father:* 4 Joel *grandfather:* **6** Samuel

hematite 3 ore **10** bloodstone **12** black diamond

Hemdam's father 6 Dishon

Hemingway work 9 In Our Time **14** A Moveable Feast **15** A Farewell to Arms, The Sun Also Rises **16** To Have and Have Not **18** Islands in the Stream, The Old Man and the Sea **19** For Whom the Bell Tolls **21** The Snows of Kilimanjaro

hemlock 4 herb, tree **6** conium

hemophiliac 7 bleeder

hemp 3 kef, kif **4** kaif, keef, kief **8** cannabis *fiber:* **5** oakum *kind:* **4** aloe

hemplike 4 towy

hen *broody:* 6 sitter *coop:* **5** cavie *spayed:* **7** poulard **8** poularde *young:* **6** pullet

hence 2 so **4** away, ergo, thus **5** since **9** therefore, thereupon **11** accordingly **12** consequently

henceforth 9 from now on, hereafter

henceforward see henceforth

henchman 6 cohort, lackey, minion, stooge **7** sectary **8** adherent, disciple, follower, partisan, retainer, sectator **9** attendant, supporter

Hengist *brother:* 5 Horsa *kingdom:* **4** Kent *people:* **5** Jutes

Henley poem 8 Invictus

henpeck 3 nag **4** fuss **6** carp at

henpecked 8 uxorious

Henry II *adversary:* 6 Becket (Thomas à) *son:* **7** Richard *surname:* **5** Anjou **11** Plantagenet *wife:* **7** Eleanor

Henry IV *surname:* 9 Lancaster *victim:* **7** Richard

Henry VIII *daughter:* 9 Elizabeth *son:* **6** Edward *surname:* **5** Tudor *victim:* **4** Anne **9** Catherine **10** Thomas More *wife:* **4** Anne, Jane **9** Catherine

Hen's father 9 Zephaniah

hepatic, hepatica 9 liverwort

Hephaestus 6 Vulcan *father:* **4** Zeus **7** Jupiter *mother:* **4** Hera, Juno *wife:* **6** Charis

Hepher's father 5 Ashur **6** Ashhur, Gilead

Hephzibah *husband:* 8 Hezekiah *son:* **8** Manasseh

Hera 4 Juno *father:* **6** Cronus, Saturn *husband:* **4** Zeus **7** Jupiter *messenger:* **4** Iris *mother:* **4** Rhea

Heracles, Hercules *beloved:* 4 Iole *brother:* **8** Iphicles *charioteer:* **6** Iolaus *father:* **4** Zeus **7** Jupiter *mother:* **7** Alcmene *son:* **6** Hyllus *victim:* **5** Hydra, Ladon **6** Geryon, Megara, Orthus **10** Nemean lion *wife:* **4** Hebe **6** Megara **8** Deianira

herald 4 hail, tout **5** crier, greet **6** signal **7** courier, forerun, precede, presage, trumpet **8** announce, ballyhoo, foreshow, outrider **9** announcer, harbinger, messenger, precursor, publicize, spokesman **10** forerunner, foreshadow **11** preindicate

heraldic *animal:* 7 gardant *border:* **4** orle *cross:* **6** fitchy, fleury, formée **7** fitchée **8** fourchée *design:* **5** giron, gyron **6** manche **7** saltier, saltire, sautoir **8** sautoire, tressour, tressure *term:* **4** ente, paty, pily **6** pattée **7** passant

heraldry 6 armory **9** pageantry *term:* **4** vert **6** moline, pommée, sejant **7** nombril, purpure, sejeant, statant

herb 4 forb, leek, mint, sage, wort **5** chive **6** allium, endive, garlic, pusley, pussly **7** campion, caraway, comfrey, gerbera, puccoon, pussley, spinach, spinage, tobacco **8** angelica, brassica, cilantro, costmary, deerweed, erigeron, gerardia, gromwell, hawkweed, marjoram, plantain, polygony, purslane, tithonia **9** buckwheat, clintonia, nemophila *African:* **7** freesia, tritoma *annual:* **4** dill, flax, okra **5** blite **6** crambe **7** bugseed, clarkia, clivers, sandbur, tampala, waxweed **8** ouphrasy, sandburr, tidytips **9** bush basil **10** calliopsis *aquatic:* **6** elodea **7** nelumbo **8** hornwort *aromatic:* **4** nard **5** basil, clary, thyme **6** catnip **7** catmint, chervil, monarda, oregano **8** origanum, woodruff **9** spikenard *Asian:* **7** perilla, skirret **8** chickpea *biennial:* **11** blazing star *bitter:* **9** chamomile *bulb:* **5** onion *composite:* **8** knapweed **9** centaurea **10** bitterweed **11** bur marigold *cultivated:* **7** parsley *East Indian:* **8** pachouli, turmeric **9** patchouli, patchouly *Eurasian:* **6** mullen, squill **7** mullein *European:* **5** paris **6** axseed, betony **7** parsnip, salsify **8** earthnut, fleawort, lungwort, mandrake, oxtongue, rapeseed, samphire, snowdrop, wormwood **9** birthwort **13** Christmas rose *evergreen:* **5** galax *fragrant:* **6** cicely **7** pinesap **10** basil thyme **12** balm of Gilead *garlic:* **6** ramson *genus:* **7** solanum *Japanese:* **3** udo *leafless:* **9** broomrape *marjoram:* 6 origan *medicinal:* 6 borage, eringo, eryngo, hyssop 7 allheal, sanicle 8 blueball, camomile, centaury 9 chamomile *Mexican:* 4 chia 8 tuberose *mythical:* 4 moly *ornamental:* 8 dianthus *perennial:* 4 geum, sego 5 avens, camas, orpin, tansy 6 arnica, asarum, bennet, burnet, camass, fennel, henbit, lovage, madder, orpine, pyrola, yarrow 7 bistort, boneset, bugbane, chicory, cicoree, cudweed, dittany, dogbane, genseng, ginseng, jonquil, milfoil, pinweed, primula, quamash, redroot, rhubarb, shortia, succory, witloof 8 agrimony, boltonia, calamint, chiccory, dicentra, dropwort, eggplant, eremurus, feverfew, finochio, fireweed, gaywings, harebell, hepatica, honewort, licorice, mayapple, nutgrass, nutsedge, pokeroot, pokeweed, primrose, roseroot, sainfoin, selfheal, shinleaf, soapwort, stokesia, tarragon, toadflax, valerian 9 bloodwort, finocchio, squawroot *poisonous:* 6 conium 7 aconite, hemlock, henbane 8 veratrum *prickly:* 8 acanthus *purple:* 12 checkerbloom *Rocky mountain:* 10 bitterroot *salad:* 7 lettuce *seaside:* 8 saltwort *small-flowered:* 11 baby's breath *South African:* 12 Cape marigold *South American:* 3 oca *summer-blooming:* 11 bunchflower *tall:* 4 hemp *tropical:* 6 crinum 7 begonia, episcia, petunia 8 abelmosk, capsicum, cardamom, cardamon, cardamum *twining:* 8 lovevine *weedy:* 7 ragweed *wild garlic:* 4 moly *woody:* 8 bedstraw *yellow:* 9 celandine *yellow-rayed:* 9 calendula

herbicide 6 diquat, diuron 7 dalapon, monuron 8 picloram, simazine

Herculean 4 huge, vast 5 giant 7 immense, mammoth, titanic 8 colossal, enormous, gigantic 10 superhuman

Hercules see Heracles

herd 3 mob, run 4 lead 5 drive, drove, flock 6 gather 9 associate *sheep:* 6 hirsel

here and there 6 passim 7 at times 9 sometimes 11 irregularly

hereditary 9 ancestral

heredity unit 4 gene

heresy 5 error 6 schism 7 dissent, fallacy, impiety 9 defection, misbelief 10 dissidence, heterodoxy, infidelity, radicalism 11 revisionism, unorthodoxy 13 nonconformism, nonconformity

heretic 7 infidel, sectary 8 apostate, defector, recreant, recusant, renegade 9 dissenter, dissident, innovator 10 iconoclast, schismatic, separatist, unbeliever 11 misbeliever, revisionist, schismatist 12 deviationist 13 nonconformist

heretical 7 infidel 8 apostate 9 differing, dissident, heterodox, miscreant, sectarian 10 dissenting, dissentive, schismatic, unor-

thodox 11 disagreeing, dissentient, revisionist, unbelieving 12 misbelieving 13 nonconformist

heritage 6 legacy 9 patrimony, tradition 10 birthright

Hermes 7 Mercury *attribute:* 7 petasos, petasus, talaria 8 caduceus *father:* 4 Zeus 7 Jupiter *mother:* 4 Maia *winged cap:* 7 petasos, petasus *winged shoes:* 7 talaria

hermetic 4 deep 5 heavy 6 occult, secret 7 recluse, secluse 8 abstruse, airtight, profound, secluded 9 alchemist, recondite, seclusive 10 cloistered 11 sequestered

Hermia *beloved:* 8 Lysander *father:* 5 Egeus

Hermione *father:* 8 Menelaus *husband:* 7 Orestes, Pyrrhus 11 Neoptolemus *mother:* 5 Helen

hermit 5 loner 7 eremite, recluse 8 solitary 9 anchorite

hermitage 8 hideaway 9 monastery

hernia 6 breach 7 rupture 10 protrusion *combining form:* 4 cele *of the bladder:* 9 cystocele *support:* 5 truss *type:* 6 cystic, hiatal 7 femoral 9 umbilical 10 incisional

hero 6 knight 7 demigod, paladin 8 champion 11 protagonist *American:* 6 Bunyan (Paul) 8 Superman *Babylonian:* 9 Gilgamesh *Celtic-French:* 7 Tristam, Tristan 8 Tristram *Crusades:* 7 Tancred 8 Tancredi *English:* 6 Arthur 7 Beowulf 9 Robin Hood *French:* 6 Roland 11 Charlemagne *German:* 5 Etzel 9 Siegfried *Greek:* 4 Ajax 5 Jason 7 Perseus, Ulysses 8 Achilles, Heracles, Hercules, Odysseus *Hebrew:* 5 David 6 Samson *Irish:* 9 Cuchullin 10 Cuchullain *Italian:* 7 Orlando *Roman:* 7 Romulus 8 Horatius *Scandinavian:* 6 Sigurd *Scottish:* 5 Bruce (Robert) 6 Rob Roy *Spanish:* 5 El Cid *Spartan:* 8 Leonidas *Trojan:* 6 Aeneas, Hector

Herod *daughter:* 6 Salome *father:* 7 Antipas 9 Antipater *kingdom:* 5 Judea 6 Judaea *mother:* 6 Cyprus *son:* 5 Herod (Antipas) 6 Joseph 7 Pheroas 9 Phasaelus

Herodias *daughter:* 6 Salome *father:* 11 Aristobulus *husband:* 5 Herod (Antipas)

heroic 4 bold, huge 5 brave 6 mighty 7 extreme, radical, valiant 8 colossal, enormous, fearless, gigantic, intrepid, unafraid, valorous 9 cyclopean, dauntless, Herculean, undaunted 10 courageous

heroin 4 skag 5 horse, smack 8 narcotic 11 diamorphine

heroism 5 valor 6 spirit 7 bravery, courage, prowess 8 boldness, chivalry, nobility, valiance, valiancy **9** gallantry **11** intrepidity **12** fearlessness, valorousness

Hero's love **7** Leander

herring **8** brisling *smoked:* **7** bloater *young:* **4** brit **5** britt

Herse *father:* **7** Cecrops *sister:* **8** Aglauros *son:* **8** Cephalus

Hersey *novel:* **7** The Wall **13** A Bell for Adano *town:* **5** Adano

Hesione *brother:* **5** Priam *father:* **8** Laomedon *husband:* **7** Telamon *rescuer:* **8** Heracles, Hercules *son:* **6** Teucer

hesitant **3** shy **5** chary, loath **6** afraid, averse, wobbly **7** halting, uneager **8** backward **9** faltering, tentative, uncertain, unwilling **10** indisposed, irresolute **11** disinclined, vacillating, vacillatory **12** wiggle-waggle

hesitate **4** balk, halt **5** delay, demur, pause, stall, stick, swing, waver **6** boggle, dawdle, dither, falter, mammer **7** scruple, stagger, stammer, stickle, stutter, whiffle **8** hang back **9** temporize **10** dillydally **12** shilly-shally, wiggle-waggle **13** procrastinate

Hesperia **5** Italy, Spain **9** butterfly

Hesperides **5** Aegle **8** Erytheia, Hesperis

Hesperus **5** Venus **11** evening star *father:* **8** Astraeus *mother:* **3** Eos

Hesse novel **6** Demian **11** Steppenwolf **12** Magister Ludi

Hestia **5** Vesta *father:* **6** Cronus, Saturn *mother:* **4** Rhea

heterodox **9** dissident, heretical, sectarian **10** schismatic **13** nonconformist

heterodoxy **6** heresy, schism **7** dissent **9** misbelief **10** dissidence **13** nonconformism, nonconformity

heterogeneous **5** mixed **6** motley, varied **8** assorted, chowchow **9** disparate **12** conglomerate

hew **3** cut **4** chop, fell **5** stick **6** adhere **7** conform, cut down

hex **3** hag **4** jinx **5** bruja, charm, lamia, queer, spell, witch **6** hoodoo, voodoo, whammy **7** bewitch, enchant **9** ensorcell, sorceress **10** Indian sign, witchwoman **11** enchantment, enchantress

heyday **4** acme **5** prime **6** spring

Hezekiah *father:* **4** Ahaz **7** Neariah *mother:* **3** Abi *son:* **8** Manasseh *wife:* **9** Hephzibah

Hezion *grandson:* **8** Benhadad *son:* **8** Tabrimon **9** Tabrimmon

Hezron's father **5** Perez **6** Pharez, Reuben

hiatus **3** gap **5** break **6** breech, lacuna **7** interim **8** aperture, interval **12** interruption

Hiawatha *author:* **10** Longfellow (Henry Wadsworth) *grandmother:* **7** Nokomis

mother: **7** Wenonah *tribe:* **6** Ojibwa **7** Ojibway *wife:* **9** Minnehaha

Hibernia **4** Eire, Erin **7** Ireland

hick **4** jake, rube **5** yokel **6** rustic **7** bucolic, bumpkin, country, hayseed **8** cornball, ruralist, ruralite **10** clodhopper, provincial

hick town **4** burg **6** Podunk **7** mudhole **11** whistlestop

hidden **5** privy **6** buried, covert, secret **7** guarded, obscure **8** obscured, shrouded, ulterior **9** concealed **11** undisclosed *combining form:* **5** crypt, krypt **6** crypto, krypto

hide **3** fur **4** bury, coat, fell, flog, lash, life, lurk, mask, pelt, skin, veil, whip **5** cache, cloak, cover, inter, lodge, plant, shade, stash **6** entomb, harbor, jacket, lather, mantle, occult, screen, shield, shroud, stripe, thrash **7** conceal, cover up, curtain, leather, obscure, retreat, scourge, seclude, secrete, shelter, veiling **8** ensconce **10** flagellate *combining form:* **4** derm **5** derma **6** dermia, dermis **9** dermatous

hideaway **3** den **4** lair **6** refuge **7** retreat **8** secluded **9** concealed

hideous **4** ugly **5** lurid, nasty **6** grisly, horrid **7** ghastly, hateful, macabre **8** gruesome, horrible, shocking, terrible, uncomely **9** dismaying, frightful, loathsome, ludicrous, monstrous, offensive, repellent, repugnant, repulsive, revolting, unsightly **10** disgusting, horrifying, ill-favored, ill-looking, terrifying

hideout **3** den **4** lair **5** haven **6** covert, refuge **7** retreat, shelter **9** hermitage, sanctuary

hiding place **5** cache, cover **6** covert, refuge **7** retreat

hie **2** go **4** fare, pass, wend **6** hasten, push on, repair, travel **7** journey, proceed ·

hiemal **6** wintry

hierarch **4** boss, cock, head **5** chief **6** honcho, leader, master **7** headman **9** chieftain

hieratic **8** priestal, priestly **9** priestish **10** priestlike, sacerdotal **12** sacerdotical

high **3** big, gay **4** acme, dear, loud, olid, rank, rick, tall, thin **5** acute, doped, drunk, fetid, grand, grave, knoll, large, lofty, noble, sharp **6** aerial, argute, bright, costly, elated, florid, height, piping, putrid, raised, rancid, remote, richly, shrill, smelly, stoned, strong, treble, whiffy, zonked **7** ancient, drugged, eminent, extreme, intense, keyed up, reeking, serious, soaring, supreme, violent **8** abstruse, arrogant, cheerful, critical, edifying, elevated, eloquent, exciting, gigantic, hopped-up, long past, nidorous, piercing, powerful, stinking, towering, turned on, vehement, wrathful **9** ambitious, climactic, excellent, expensive, imperious, important, intensive, luxurious, prominent, spaced-out 10 boisterous, malodorous, pronounced, tripped out 11 anti-cyclone, extravagant, intoxicated *combining form:* 4 alti

high-and-mighty 5 proud 6 lordly 8 arrogant, cavalier, insolent, superior 9 imperious 10 disdainful 11 overbearing 12 supercilious

highball 3 fly, run 4 rush, whiz 5 hurry, speed 6 barrel, hustle 7 hotfoot

highbinding 5 fraud 7 chicane 8 trickery 9 chicanery, deception, fourberie 10 dishonesty, hanky-panky 11 skulduggery

highboy 5 chest 6 bureau

highbrow 4 snob 7 Brahmin, egghead 8 cerebral 10 doubledome 12 intellectual

highest 3 top 5 chief 6 apical, astral, upmost 7 exalted, supreme, topmost 9 top-drawer, uppermost 10 top-ranking *point:* 4 acme, apex 5 crest 6 summit, zenith 8 pinnacle

highfalutin 4 rant 6 florid 7 aureate, bombast, flowery, fustian, pompous 8 rhapsody, rhetoric 9 bombastic 10 oratorical, rhetorical 11 declamatory, pretentious

high-handed 5 bossy 8 imperial 9 arbitrary, imperious, masterful 10 imperative, peremptory 11 domineering, magisterial, overbearing

high-hat 4 snub 5 potty 6 snobby, snooty 8 snobbish 12 aristocratic

high jinks 5 revel 7 fooling, revelry, wassail, whoopee, whoopla, whoop-up 9 horseplay, revelment, rowdiness, whoop-de-do 10 roughhouse, skylarking 12 roughhousing

highlight 6 stress 7 feature 9 emphasize

high-minded 5 moral, noble 8 elevated

high-muck-a-muck 3 VIP 5 nabob 6 big boy, bigwig 7 big shot, mugwump, notable

high-pitched 6 shrill 7 shrieky 8 agitated

high-principled 5 noble 6 worthy 8 sterling 9 estimable, honorable

high roller 7 gambler, spender, wastrel 8 prodigal, unthrift 10 profligate 11 scattergood, spendthrift, waste-thrift

high sign 3 nod, tip 4 wink 5 alarm 6 signal, tipoff 7 warning

high-sounding 3 big 4 arty 7 pompous 9 overblown 10 arty-crafty 11 pretentious

high-spirited 5 beany, brash, fiery, jolly, merry 6 joyful, lively, spunky 7 gingery, gleeful, peppery 8 mirthful 9 ebullient, exuberant, vivacious 10 mettlesome 12 effervescent, lighthearted

high-strung 4 taut 5 jumpy, tense, tight 6 goosey, spooky 7 fidgety, jittery, nervous, uptight 8 twittery 9 excitable, unrelaxed

hightail 3 run 4 kite 5 scram 6 begone, decamp, get out 7 skiddoo, take off 8 clear out 9 skedaddle

highway 4 path, pike, road 5 track 6 artery, avenue, street 8 turnpike 9 boulevard 12 thoroughfare *German:* 8 autobahn *Italian:* 10 autostrada

Highwayman author 5 Noyes (Alfred)

hike 2 up 3 wax 4 jump, rise, rove, trek, walk 5 boost, march, put up, raise, tramp, tromp 6 jack up, ramble, stroll, trapes, travel, wander 7 explore, journey, traipse, upgrade 8 backpack, footslog, increase 9 walkabout 12 breakthrough

hilarious 5 funny, merry 8 humorous, mirthful

hilarity 4 glee 5 cheer, mirth 6 gaiety 8 jocosity, laughter 9 merriment 12 cheerfulness

Hilkiah *father:* 4 Amzi 5 Hosah *son:* 7 Eliakim 8 Gemariah, Jeremiah

hill 3 kop 4 bank, bump, cock, heap, knob, pile, rick 5 butte, drift, mound, ridge, shock, slope, stack 6 cuesta, height 7 hummock, incline 8 mountain 9 elevation, monadnock *African veld:* 5 kopje *Charlestown:* 6 Bunker *craggy:* 3 tor *Cuba:* 7 San Juan *D.C.:* 7 Capitol *elongate:* 7 drumlin *high:* 5 mount *level-topped:* 4 mesa 5 butte *of stratified drift:* 4 kame *rounded:* 5 swell *sand:* 4 dune *small:* 5 knoll, kopje, mound 6 koppie *surrounded by ice:* 7 nunatak

hillbilly 4 rube 5 yokel 6 rustic 7 bucolic, bumpkin, hayseed 10 clodhopper 12 backwoodsman

hillock 5 knoll, mound *British:* 4 toft

hillside 5 slope *Scottish:* 4 brae

Himavat's daughter 4 Devi

hind 3 doe 4 back, deer, rear 5 after 6 retral, rustic 7 bailiff, grouper 9 posterior *mate:* 4 hart

hind end 4 beam, rear, rump, tail 7 hunkers 8 backside, buttocks, haunches 9 fundament, posterior

hinder 3 bar, dam, let 4 back, balk, clog, curb, mire, rear 5 after, block, brake, check, deter, embog 6 arrest, baffle, burden, cumber, fetter, hamper, hog-tie, impede, lumber, retard, retral, thwart, tramel 7 inhibit, manacle, shackle, tramell, trammel 8 blockade, handicap, obstruct, restrain 9 entrammel, frustrate, hamstring, interrupt 10 overslaugh

hindmost 3 lag 4 back, last, rear 5 after, final 6 latter, retral 7 closing 8 eventual, terminal, ultimate 9 posterior 10 concluding

hindquarters 8 haunches

hindrance 4 clog 5 block 8 drawback, obstacle 10 impediment

Hindu *age:* 4 yuga *ascetic:* 4 yogi *caste (varna):* 5 Sudra 6 Vaisya 7 Brahman 9 Kshatriya *class:* 5 caste, varna *dancing*

girl: 8 devadesi *demon:* 4 Rahu
6 Ravana *essence:* 5 atman *force:*
5 karma *garment:* 4 sari 5 saree *god:*
3 dev 4 deva *goddess:* 4 devi *goddess
of beauty:* 7 Lakshmi *goddess of
destruction:* 4 Kali *god of fire:* 4 Agni
god of love: 4 Kama *god of the heavens:*
7 Krishna *god of war:* 6 Skanda 10 Karttikeya *god of wisdom:* 6 Ganesa, Ganesh
hell: 4 Naraka *holy man:* 5 sadhu 6 sad-
dhu *leader:* 6 Gandhi (Mahatma) *lowest
caste:* 5 Sudra *lute:* 5 sitar *marriage:*
9 gandharva *nobleman:* 4 raja 5 rajah
precept: 5 sutra, sutta *prince:* 4 raja
5 rajah 8 maharaja 9 maharajah *queen:*
4 rani 5 ranee 8 maharani 9 maharanee
sacred thread: 7 upavita *salvation:* 7 nirvana *scripture:* 12 Bhagavad Gita *social
group:* 5 caste, varna *teacher:* 4 guru
term of respect: 5 sahib *treatise:*
9 Upanishad *twice-born:* 6 Vaisya 7 Brahman 9 Kshatriya
hinge 4 pawl 5 joint, mount 12 turning
point *kind:* 4 butt 5 piano 10 hook-and-
eye
hint 3 beg, cue, key, tip 4 cast, clue, coax,
dash, fish, hair, lick, seek, sign, vein
5 angle, imply, plead, point, press, shade,
smack, smell, spice, taint, taste, tinge,
touch, trace, twang, whiff 6 advice, aiming,
breath, notion, shadow, smatch, strain,
streak, tipoff, trifle 7 connote, inkling,
pointer, presage, solicit, soupçon, suggest,
vestige, whisper 8 indicate, innuendo, intimate, overtone, particle, pointing, telltale,
tincture 9 adumbrate, direction, importune,
insinuate, prefigure, prompting, scintilla, suspicion, undertone 10 assistance, foreshadow, indication, intimation, sprinkling,
suggestion 11 adumbration, association,
connotation, forewarning, implication, insinuation
hinterland 4 bush 6 sticks 8 backwash,
frontier, interior 9 backwater, backwoods,
up-country 10 background, wilderness
11 back-country
hip 4 coxa 6 haunch, huckle *bone:* 5 ilium,
pubis 6 pelvis 7 ischium *cattle:* 5 thurl
combining form: 5 ischi 6 ischio *disorder:*
8 sciatica
hippie 8 bohemian, longhair
Hippocratic ___ 4 oath
Hippodamia *father:* 8 Oenomaus *husband:* 6 Pelops 9 Pirithous 10 Peirithous
son: 6 Atreus 8 Thyestes
Hippolytus *father:* 7 Theseus *mother:*
7 Antiope 9 Hippolyte *stepmother:*
7 Phaedra
Hippomenes'wife 8 Atalanta
Hirah's friend 5 Judah
hire 3 fee, let, pay 4 book, rent, wage

5 lease, put on, wages 6 employ, engage,
salary, sublet, take on 7 charter, recruit
hireling 4 grub, hack 6 drudge, slavey
7 grubber 9 mercenary
hirsute 5 hairy 6 fleecy, pilose, shaggy,
woolly 7 pileous 9 whiskered
Hispania 5 Spain 6 Iberia
hiss 3 boo 4 bird, buzz, fizz, hoot, pooh,
sizz, whiz 5 bazoo, swish, whish, woosh
6 fizzle, sizzle, wheeze, whoosh 7 catcall,
whisper, whistle 8 pooh-pooh, sibilate
9 raspberry
historian 8 annalist 10 chronicler *American:* 4 Webb (Charles Richard) 5 Adams
(Brooks, Charles Kendall, Hannah, Henry,
Herbert Baxter), Beard (Charles, Mary),
Foote (Shelby) 6 Durant (Ariel, Will),
Malone (Dumas), Miller (Perry), Muzzey
(David), Nevins (Allen), Sarton (George
Alfred), Sparks (Jared), Turner (Frederick
Jackson) 7 Morison (Samuel Eliot), Park-
man (Francis), Ridpath (John Clark), Tuch-
man (Barbara), Woodson (Carter G.)
8 Channing (Edward), Commager (Henry
Steele), Prescott (William H.), Robinson
(James Harvey) 11 Schlesinger (Arthur
Meier) *English:* 4 Bede (Venerable), Stow
(John), Ward (Adolphus) 5 Acton (Lord),
Grote (George), Wells (Herbert George)
6 Camden (William), Gibbon (Edward),
Namier (Lewis Bernstein), Stubbs (William)
7 Hakluyt (Richard), Raleigh (Walter), Toyn-
bee (Arnold), Whewell (William) 8 Geoffrey
(of Monmouth), Macaulay (Thomas Babington) 9 Holinshed (Raphael), Trevelyan
(George) *French:* 5 Renan (Joseph-
Ernest), Taine (Hippolyte-Adolphe) 6 Guizot (Francois-Pierre-Guillaume), Thiers
(Louis-Adolphe), Volney (Comte de)
8 Hanotaux (Gabriel), Michelet (Jules) *German:* 5 Ranke (Leopold von) 7 Mommsen
(Theodor), Niebuhr (Barthold Georg)
8 Spengler (Oswald) *Greek:* 8 Polybius,
Xenophon 9 Dionysius, Herodotus 10 Thucydides *Italian:* 5 Croce (Benedetto)
9 Salvemini (Gaetano) *Jewish:* 8 Josephus (Flavius) *Roman:* 4 Livy 7 Sallust,
Tacitus (Cornelius) 9 Suetonius *Scottish:*
7 Carlyle (Thomas) 9 Robertson (William)
Swiss: 6 Müller (Johannes von) *Welsh:*
7 Nennius
historical period 3 age, era 5 epoch
7 ancient 8 medieval
history 4 epic, saga, tale 5 diary, story
6 annals, memoir, report 7 account, journal, recital, version 8 relation 9 chronicle,
narrative
histrionic 5 actor 6 staged 8 dramatic,
theatral, thespian 10 theatrical 11 dramaturgic

hit 3 bop, rap, wow 4 bang, bash, bean, biff, blow, bump, bunt, butt, conk, cuff, ding, fill, fist, lick, luck, meet, slap, slog, slug, sock, swat, swot, wipe 5 clout, knock, light, occur, pound, skelp, smash, smite, swipe, whack 6 affect, attack, buffet, chance, happen, stress, strike, stroke, thwack, tumble 7 censure, stumble 8 bludgeon 9 collision, emphasize *baseball:* 5 homer, liner 6 double, single, triple 7 home run 9 line drive *golf ball:* 5 shank

hitch 4 jerk, lift, limp, yoke 5 thumb 6 couple, hobble 7 harness 8 stoppage 10 impediment 11 obstruction 12 entanglement

Hitchcock forte 8 suspense

hitchhike 5 thumb

hither 4 here 6 nearer 11 to this place

hitherto 3 yet 4 here, once 5 as yet, prior, so far 6 before 7 earlier, thus far 8 formerly, previous 10 heretofore, previously

Hitler *follower:* 4 Nazi *title:* 6 Führer 7 Fuehrer *wife:* 5 Braun (Eva)

hit man 3 gun 5 bravo 7 torpedo 8 assassin, gangster 9 cutthroat 10 gunslinger

hit-or-miss 6 chance, random 7 aimless, unaimed 9 desultory, haphazard, irregular, unplanned 10 designless 12 unconsidered

hive 5 amass, lay up, uplay 6 apiary, garner, roll up 7 store up 8 cumulate 9 stockpile 10 accumulate

hoar 4 rime 5 frost

hoard 4 save 5 lay by, lay up, stash, stock, store, trove 6 garner 7 backlog, nest egg, reserve 8 squirrel, treasure 9 amassment, colluvies, inventory, reservoir, stockpile 10 accumulate, collection, cumulation 11 aggregation 12 accumulation

hoarder 5 miser

hoarfrost 4 rime

hoarse 3 dry 5 gruff, harsh, husky, rough, thick 6 croaky, rasped 7 grating, jarring, rasping, raucous, throaty 8 croaking, guttural, strident 10 discordant, stridulent, stridulous *Scottish:* 5 roupy 6 roupet

hoary 3 old 4 aged 5 stale, trite 6 age-old, remote 7 ancient, antique 8 Noachian, timeworn 9 canescent, hackneyed, venerable 12 antideluvian

hoax 3 gyp 4 dupe, fake, fool, gull, sell 5 fraud, phony, put-on, spoof, trick 6 befool, delude, humbug, take in 7 chicane, mislead 8 flimflam, hoodwink 9 bamboozle, imposture, mare's nest, victimize 11 hornswoggle

hob 4 nail 6 ferret, leader

Hobab *brother-in-law:* 5 Moses *father:* 5 Reuel

Hobbit creator 7 Tolkien (John Ronald Reuel)

hobble 3 tie 4 clog, curb, halt, limp 5 hitch, leash 6 fetter, hamper, hog-tie, impede 7 cripple, trammel 8 obstruct 9 entrammel

hobby 7 pastime 9 avocation, diversion

hobgoblin 5 bogey 7 bugaboo

hobnail 4 stud

hobo 3 bum, vag 5 tramp 7 drifter, floater, swagman, vagrant 8 derelict, vagabond 10 street arab

hock 4 knee, pawn 6 pledge 8 mortgage 9 hamstring 11 impignorate

hockey 6 shinny 7 shinney *arena:* 4 rink *cup:* 7 Stanley *implement:* 4 puck 5 stick *official:* 7 referee 8 linesman *player:* 3 Orr (Bobby), Roy (Patrick) 4 Bure (Pavel), Fuhr (Grant), Howe (Gordie), Hull (Bobby, Brett), Jagr (Jaromir), wing 5 Bossy (Mike), Bucyk (John), Hasek (Dominik), Kurri (Jari), Maruk (Dennis), Shore (Eddie), Shutt (Steve) 6 center, Clarke (Bobby), Coffey (Paul), Dionne (Marcel), Dryden (Ken), goalie, Harvey (Doug), Juneau (Joe), Leetch (Brian), Mikita (Stan), Morenz (Howie), Parent (Bernie), Potvin (Denis), Recchi (Mark), Savard (Denis), Sundin (Mats) 7 Belfour (Ed), Bourque (Ray), Brodeur (Martin), Chelios (Chris), Fedorov (Sergei), forward, Francis (Ron), Gretzky (Wayne), Lafleur (Guy), Lemieux (Claude, Mario), Lindros (Eric), Messier (Mark), Mogilny (Alexander), Richard (Maurice), Selanne (Teemu), Stastny (Peter), Yzerman (Steve) 8 Beliveau (Jean), Esposito (Phil, Tony), Nicholls (Bernie), pointman, Trottier (Bryan), Ysebaert (Paul) 9 Hawerchuk (Dale) 10 Carbonneau (Guy), defenseman, goalkeeper *stick:* 5 caman (Scottish, Irish), camog (Irish) 7 cammock (Scottish) *team:* 4 Jets 5 Blues, Kings, Stars 6 Bruins, Devils, Flames, Flyers, Oilers, Sabres, Sharks 7 Canucks, Rangers, Whalers 8 Capitals, Panthers, Penguins, Red Wings, Senators 9 Canadiens, Islanders, Lightning, Nordiques 10 Black Hawks, Maple Leafs, North Stars 11 Mighty Ducks *term:* 3 box 4 cage, goal, puck, rink 5 bandy, bench, check, icing, stick 6 charge, crease, shinny 7 face-off, off-side 8 blue line 9 backcheck, body-check 10 center line, penalty box *variation of:* 9 broomball

hod 4 tray 6 trough 7 scuttle 11 coal scuttle

Hodaviah's father 8 Elioenai 9 Hassenuah

Hoder, Hoth *brother:* 6 Balder *slayer:* 4 Vali *victim:* 6 Balder

Hodesh's husband 9 Shaharaim

hodgepodge 4 hash 6 jumble, medley 7 mélange, mixture 8 eclectic, mishmash

9 patchwork, potpourri **10** hotchpotch, miscellany **11** gallimaufry

Hod's father 6 Zophah

hoe 4 till **9** cultivate

hog 3 pig, sow **4** boar **5** roach, swine **8** boshvark *family:* **6** Suidae *female:* **3** sow **4** gilt *genus:* **3** Sus *red:* **5** duroc *young:* **5** shoat, shote

hogback 5 chine, crest, ridge

Hoglah's father 10 Zelophehad

Hogni's victim 6 Sigurd

hogshead 3 keg, tun **4** butt, cask, pipe **6** barrel

hog-tie 4 clog, curb **5** leash **6** fetter, hamper, hobble **7** shackle, trammel **9** entrammel

hogwash 4 slop **5** bilge, hokum, hooey, swill **8** nonsense **9** poppycock

hoi polloi 3 mob **4** scum **5** dregs, trash **6** masses, rabble **8** populace, riffraff **9** multitude **11** proletariat

hoist 4 lift, rear, rise **5** boost, raise, winch **6** pick up, take up, uphold, uplift, uprear **7** derrick, elevate, upraise **8** windlass

hoity-toity 5 dizzy, giddy, silly **7** flighty, pompous **8** skittish **9** frivolous **11** harebrained, thoughtless **13** rattlebrained

hokum 4 bosh, jazz **5** hooey **8** flimflam, malarkey, nonsense **9** poppycock **11** foolishness

hold 3 fix, own **4** bear, deem, feel, grab, grip, halt, have, keep, last, stay, stop **5** apply, carry, clamp, clasp, cling, delay, enjoy, grasp, gripe, judge, limit, pause, poise, sense, think, value **6** accept, arrest, clench, clinch, clutch, credit, detain, esteem, harbor, prison, regard, retain, steady, tenure **7** believe, catch up, comport, contain, convene, convoke, custody, fermata, grapple, keep out, possess, reserve, support, sustain **8** conceive, consider, enthrall, keep back, maintain, preserve, purchase, restrict **9** fascinate, handclasp, mesmerize, spellbind *as precious:* **8** treasure *close:* **6** cuddle *dear:* **7** cherish *from proceeding:* **4** stay *in check:* **7** repress *in common:* **5** share *out:* **4** last **6** endure *together:* **4** bond **5** clamp **6** fasten *wrestling:* **8** headlock, scissors

hold back 3 bit **4** curb, deny, keep **5** check **6** bridle, detain, retain **7** abstain, inhibit, keep out, refrain, reserve **8** restrain **9** constrain

hold in 3 bit **4** curb **5** check **6** bridle **7** inhibit **8** restrain **9** constrain **10** keep silent

hold off 4 stay **5** defer, delay, rebut, remit, repel **6** rebuff, shelve **7** abstain, adjourn, repulse, suspend **8** hesitate, postpone, prorogue **9** withstand

hold up 4 halt, lift, stay **5** check, defer, delay, raise, remit, waive **6** put off **7** prevail, support, suspend, sustain **8** postpone, prorogue

hole 3 box, den, fix, gap, jam, pit **4** cave, cove, flaw, open, rent, rift, spot, vent, void **5** break, fault, niche **6** breach, burrow, cavity, corner, cranny, eyelet, hiatus, lacuna, outlet, pickle, pierce, plight, scrape, vacuum **7** dilemma, disrupt, fissure, opening, orifice, rupture, vacancy, vacuity **8** aperture **9** perforate **10** excavation, interstice **11** perforation

hole in one 3 ace

holiday 5 leave **6** May Day **7** festive, Flag Day **8** Arbor Day, carefree, vacation **9** Halloween **10** Father's Day, Mother's Day **12** All Saints' Day, Groundhog Day **13** St. Patrick's Day, Valentine's Day *Alaska:* **10** Seward's Day *British:* **9** Boxing Day *Canadian:* **11** Dominion Day, Victoria Day *Federal:* **8** Labor Day, New Year's **9** Christmas **11** Veterans Day **12** Armistice Day, Thanksgiving *Hawaii:* **8** Kuhio Day **13** Kamehameha Day *Jewish:* **8** Passover *Maryland:* **12** Defender's Day *Newfoundland:* **12** Discovery Day, St. George's Day **13** Orangemen's Day *Rhode Island:* **10** Victory Day *Texas:* **13** San Jacinto Day *Utah:* **10** Pioneer Day

holiness 5 piety **8** devotion, divinity, sanctity **12** consecration, spirituality

Holland see Netherlands

holler 3 cry **4** call, yell **5** gripe, shout **6** outcry **7** grumble **8** complain **9** complaint **10** vociferate

hollow 3 dip, sag **4** idle, sink, vain, void **5** basin, empty, false, notch, womby **6** cavity, dingle, otiose, ravine, sunken **7** channel, concave, echoing, sinkage, vacuity **8** complete, nugatory, resonant, sinkhole, sounding, thorough **9** cavernous, concavity, deceitful **10** depression, resounding, sepulchral *out:* **3** dig, gut **4** mine **5** gouge **8** excavate

holly 4 tree **5** shrub *genus:* **4** Ilex

holocaust 4 fire **7** inferno **9** sacrifice **11** destruction **13** conflagration

Holofernes' slayer 6 Judith

holy 3 god **5** pious **6** adored, devout, divine, sacred **7** angelic, awesome, blessed, revered, saintly **8** hallowed, priestly **9** glorified, pietistic, prayerful, religious, sanctuary, spiritual, unprofane, venerated, worshiped **10** reverenced, sanctified **11** consecrated, frightening *bread:* **7** eulogia **9** antidoron *combining form:* **4** hagi, hier **5** hagio, hiero *communion:* **9** eucharist *oil:* **6** chrism *person:* **5** saint **6** zaddik **8** zaddikim (plural) *Spirit:* **9** Paraclete *vessel:* **7** chalice **8** ciborium

holy place 6 shrine 7 sanctum 9 sanctuary 10 sanctorium

Holy Roman Emperor 4 Karl, Otho, Otto 5 Adolf, Franz, Henry, Louis 6 Albert, Arnulf, Conrad, Joseph, Lothar, Ludwig, Philip, Rudolf, Rupert, Wenzel 7 Charles, Francis, Leopold, Lothair 8 Heinrich 9 Ferdinand, Frederick, Friedrich, Sigismund 10 Maximilian

Holy Writ 4 Book 5 Bible 9 Scripture

homage 5 honor 7 respect, tribute 9 deference, obeisance, reverence

home 4 land, site, soil 5 abode, haunt, house, local, range 6 family, native 7 country, habitat, housing 8 domestic, domicile, dwelling, internal, locality, location, national 9 household, intestine, municipal, residence, residency 10 commoracy, fatherland, focal point, habitation, motherland 12 headquarters 13 mother country *country:* 7 cottage 8 bungalow

homely 3 dry 4 ugly 5 plain 6 direct, kindly, modest, simple 8 familiar, intimate, unpretty 10 unalluring, unhandsome 11 commonplace, inelaborate, unbeauteous, unbeautiful, unelaborate, ungarnished 12 unattractive, unornamented 13 plain-featured, unpretentious

Homer epic 5 Iliad 7 Odyssey

homesickness 9 nostalgia

homespun 6 folksy 9 practical 13 unpretentious

Home, Sweet Home *music:* 6 Bishop (Henry) *words:* 5 Payne (John Howard)

homicidal 6 bloody 8 sanguine 9 murdering, murderous 10 sanguinary 11 sanguineous 12 bloodthirsty

homicide 5 blood 6 killer, murder, slayer 7 killing 8 foul play, murderer 9 manslayer 12 manslaughter

homilize 6 preach

homily 6 sermon 7 lecture 9 discourse 10 admonition

homogeneous 4 like, same 7 similar, uniform 10 comparable, compatible, consistent, equivalent *combining form:* 2 is 3 hol, iso 4 holo

Homo sapiens 3 man 5 flesh 7 mankind 8 humanity 9 humankind, mortality

homunculus 4 runt 5 dwarf, midge, pygmy 6 midget, peewee 7 manikin 8 Tom Thumb 11 hop-o'-my-thumb, lilliputian

honcho 4 boss, cock, head 5 chief 6 leader, master 7 headman 8 hierarch 9 chieftain

Honduras *capital:* 11 Tegucigalpa *monetary unit:* 7 lempira *neighbor:* 9 Guatemala, Nicaragua 10 El Salvador *product:* 6 coffee 7 bananas

hone 4 edge, whet 7 sharpen

honest 4 open, real, true 5 frank, plain, right 6 candid, humble, simple 7 genuine, sincere, upright 8 innocent, reliable, truthful 9 objective, reputable, unfeigned, veracious 10 forthright, heart-whole, legitimate, scrupulous, unaffected 11 undesigning 12 praiseworthy, undissembled 13 conscientious, dispassionate, unimpeachable

honesty 6 virtue 7 probity 8 goodness, justness 9 integrity, rectitude, sincerity 11 uprightness 12 incorruption, truthfulness

honey *combining form:* 4 meli, mell 5 melli *drink:* 4 mead

honey badger 5 ratel

honey bear 8 kinkajou

honeybee genus 4 Apis

honeyberry 5 genip

honey bread 5 carob

honey buzzard 4 hawk, kite, pern

honeydew 5 melon

honeyed 6 golden, liquid, mellow 8 Hyblaean 9 sweetened 11 mellifluent, mellifluous

honeysuckle 8 rewa-rewa 9 columbine 11 swamp azalea 13 pinxter flower

Hong Kong's capital 8 Victoria

honky-tonk 4 dive 5 joint 7 hangout 11 barrelhouse

honor 4 bays, fete, kudo 5 adorn, asset, award, badge, erect, exalt, glory, kudos, medal, mense 6 esteem, homage, praise, regard, trophy, uprear 7 dignify, ennoble, glorify, laurels, magnify, respect, sublime, worship 8 accolade, approval, carry out, devotion 9 adoration, adulation, deference, integrity, obeisance, privilege, recognize, reverence 10 admiration, aggrandize, blue ribbon, compliment, decoration, reputation, veneration 11 distinction, distinguish, recognition 12 incorruption

honorable 4 just, true 5 right 6 august, worthy 7 ethical, upright 8 reverend, sterling 9 dignified 10 scrupulous, worshipful 11 illustrious 13 conscientious

hood 4 cowl, hide 5 cover 6 bonnet, helmet 7 bashlyk, blinder, capouch, capuche 8 covering *clergyman's:* 6 almuce

hoodlum 4 thug 7 mobster, ruffian 8 plug-ugly 9 strong arm

hoodwink 4 dupe, fool, gull, hoax 5 blind, trick 6 befool 7 chicane 8 flimflam 9 bamboozle 10 impose 11 hornswoggle

hooey 4 bosh, bunk 5 bilge 6 bunkum 7 baloney 8 claptrap, malarkey, nonsense

hoof 4 boot, foot, kick, pace, walk 5 eject, troop 6 unguis, ungula 7 traipse, trample, ungulae (plural) 8 ambulate, throw out *cloven:* 5 cloot

hoofer 6 dancer 7 danseur 8 coryphée, danseuse, figurant 9 ballerina, figurante

hooflike 6 ungual

hook 3 ear, nab, nim, nip 4 flag, gore, lift 5 catch, curve, hitch, pinch, steal 6 anchor, fasten, pilfer, scythe, secure, sickle 7 cabbage, hamulus 8 crotchet *a fish:* 4 gaff, snag *combining form:* 3 onc 4 onch, onci, onco 5 oncho *for a watch:* 10 chatelaine

hooklike 7 falcate 8 unciform *part:* 5 uncus 7 hamulus

hookup 7 cahoots, circuit 8 alliance 10 connection 11 affiliation, association, combination, conjunction, partnership

hooky 7 truancy 8 truantry

hooligan see **hoodlum**

hoop 4 band, ring 5 clasp 6 circle 7 circlet, enclose 8 surround 10 finger ring

Hoosier State 7 Indiana

hoot 3 boo, jot 4 bird, damn, hiss, iota, jeer, whit 5 bazoo, ounce, scrap, shout, whoop 7 catcall, modicum 8 particle, poohpooh 9 raspberry

hooter 3 owl 5 owlet

hop 3 run 4 ball, jump, leap, skip, tend, trip 5 bound, dance, serve, vault 6 bounce, hurdle, spring, wait on 7 rebound, saltate, skitter 8 jump over

hope 4 look 5 await, faith, stock, trust 6 aspire, desire, expect 7 count on, promise 8 reliance 9 count upon 10 confidence *loss of:* 7 despair

hopeful 4 easy, fond, rosy 5 happy, sunny 6 bright, cheery, golden, hoping, likely, secure, seeker, upbeat 7 assured, budding, content, halcyon, roseate 8 aspirant, cheerful, cheering, sanguine 9 applicant, candidate, confident, expectant, promising, satisfied 10 auspicious, optimistic, propitious 11 encouraging, rose-colored, undisturbed, up-and-coming 12 advantageous, anticipative, Pollyannaish

hopeless 4 glum, vain 6 futile, gloomy, morose 7 forlorn 8 downcast 9 desperate, incurable, insanable, insoluble, uncurable 10 despairing, despondent, desponding, impossible 11 immedicable, ineffectual, irreparable 12 incorrigible, irredeemable, irremediable 13 uncorrectable

hoper 8 optimist 9 Pollyanna

Hophni *brother:* 8 Phinehas *son:* 3 Eli

hopped-up 4 high 6 stoned, zonked 7 drugged

hopper 3 box 4 frog, hare, toad 5 bunny, chute 6 rabbit 7 cricket

___ **Hopper** 5 Hedda

hopping 4 busy 5 fussy 6 lively

Horae 4 Dike 6 Eirene 7 Eunomia

Horam *kingdom:* 5 Gezer *slayer:* 6 Joshua

horde 4 army, push 5 crowd, crush, drove, press, swarm 6 squash, throng 9 multitude

hordeolum 3 sty

Hori's son 7 Shaphat

horizon 3 ken 4 goal, zone 5 limit, range, reach 7 purview, skyline 8 prospect

horizontal 4 flat 7 general, overall

hormone 5 kinin 6 estrin 7 estriol, estrone, gastrin, insulin, relaxin 8 autacoid, estrogen, glucagon, kallidin, secretin *female:* 8 estrogen *insect:* 7 ecdyson 8 ecdysone *pituitary:* 8 oxytocin *sex:* 6 prolan

horn 4 gore, toot 5 cornu, drink, glory, power, pride 6 antler, claxon, klaxon, shofar, tootle 7 cuckold 10 cornucopia, projection *ancient Greek:* 5 rhyta (plural) 6 rhyton *animal:* 6 antler *combining form:* 4 cera 5 ceras, cerus, corne 6 corneo *signal:* 6 typhon

___ **Hornblower** 7 Horatio

horn in 4 fool 6 meddle 7 intrude, obtrude 8 busybody 9 interfere, interlope 10 intertrude, monkey with, tamper with

hornlike 8 ceratoid, corneous 10 keratinous

horn-shaped 7 cornute 8 cornuted

hornswoggle 4 dupe, fool, gull, hoax 6 befool, pigeon 7 chicane 8 flimflam, hoodwink 9 bamboozle

horny 4 hard 7 callous 8 keratoid

horrible 4 grim 5 awful, lurid, nasty 6 grisly 7 fearful, ghastly, hateful, hellish, hideous 8 dreadful, gruesome, shocking, terrible 9 abhorrent, appalling, frightful, loathsome, obnoxious, offensive, repellent, repugnant, repulsive, revolting 10 disgusting, terrifying

horrid see **horrible**

horrific 5 awful 7 fearful 8 dreadful, shocking, terrible 9 appalling, frightful 10 formidable

horrify 5 daunt, shake, shock 6 appall, dismay

horrifying 4 grim 5 lurid 6 grisly 7 ghastly, hideous 8 gruesome, terrible

horror 4 fear, hate, pain 5 alarm, dread, panic, shock, throe 6 dismay, fright, hatred, wrench 8 aversion, distress, loathing 9 repulsion, revulsion, trepidity 10 abhorrence, repugnance 11 abomination, detestation, trepidation

Horsa's brother 7 Hengist

hors d'oeuvre 4 whet 7 zakuska 9 antipasto, appetizer

horse 3 kid 4 buck, roam 5 act up, bronc, cut up, pacer, steed 6 bayard, bronco, brumby, equine, padnag 7 broncho, carry on, cavalry, palfrey, sawbuck, trestle, trotter 8 footrope, jackstay, palomino, skewbald, stallion, traveler *Asian:* 6 tarpan *Australian-bred:* 5 waler *battle:* 7 charger *breed:* 6 Morgan 7 Arabian, Belgian, Iceland 8 Shetland 9 Percheron 10 Lippizaner 12 Thoroughbred *collar:* 7 brecham, brechan *collar part:* 4 hame *combining form:* 4 hipp 5 hippo 6 hippus *covering:* 8 trapping *draft:* 10 clydesdale *extinct:* 8 eohippus *farm:* 6 dobbin *female:* 4 mare 5 filly *foot part:* 7 pastern *gait:* 4 trot 6 canter, gallop *gear:* 3 bit 4 rein 6 saddle 7 harness 9 checkrein *leg joint:* 7 fetlock *leg part:* 6 gaskin 7 gambrel *male:* 4 colt 8 stallion *mark:* 5 blaze *naturalized:* 7 mustang *nervous:* 5 shier, shyer *of the movies:* 6 Flicka, Silver 7 Trigger 8 Champion 11 Black Beauty *race:* 5 derby 6 mudder 8 Affirmed, Citation 9 Preakness 11 Seattle Slew, Secretariat 13 Belmont Stakes, Kentucky Derby *rump:* 7 crupper *saddle:* 9 Appaloosa *small:* 6 garron, jennet *spotted:* 5 Pinto 7 piebald *tan:* 8 palomino *thoroughbred:* 8 hot-blood *war:* 8 destrier *wild:* 7 mustang

horseman 6 cowboy, knight 7 vaquero 8 cavalier 9 caballero, chevalier 10 equestrian

horsemanship 6 manege 10 equitation

horse opera 5 oater 7 western

horseplay 5 act up, cut up 7 carry on, fooling 8 clowning 9 high jinks, rowdiness 10 buffoonery, roughhouse, skylarking 12 roughhousing

horseshoer 6 smithy 10 blacksmith

horticulturist 7 Burbank (Luther)

Horus *brother:* 6 Anubis *father:* 6 Osiris *mother:* 4 Isis *victim:* 4 Seth

hose 4 tube 5 water 8 stocking

Hosea's father 5 Beeri

Hoshaiah's son 7 Azariah 8 Jezaniah

Hoshea *father:* 3 Nun 4 Elah 7 Azaziah *victim:* 5 Pekah

hospice see hostel

hospitable 6 social 7 cordial 8 friendly 9 convivial 10 gregarious 11 cooperative

hospital 6 clinic 7 lazaret 9 infirmary *attendant:* 7 orderly *ship's:* 7 sickbay

Hospitallers' island 5 Malta 6 Rhodes

host 4 army 5 cloud, crowd, emcee, flock 6 angels, legion, myriad, scores 7 compere 8 assemble 9 innkeeper, multitude

hostage 4 pawn 5 token 6 pledge, surety 7 earnest 8 guaranty, security 9 guarantee

hostel 3 inn 5 lodge 6 tavern, travel 7 auberge 9 roadhouse 11 caravansary, public house

hostile 3 dim, ill 4 dour, sour 5 enemy 6 bitter, fierce 7 adverse, opposed, warlike 8 contrary, inimical, militant, opposite, virulent 9 bellicose, rancorous, vitriolic 10 inimicable, pugnacious, unfriendly 11 belligerent, competitive, contentious, disaffected, unfavorable 12 antagonistic, disapproving 13 argumentative

hostility 6 animus, enmity, rancor 9 antipathy 10 antagonism

hot 5 eager, fiery, fresh, nifty, super 6 ardent, baking, banned, biting, groovy, heated, hectic, raging, stolen, sultry, torrid, tropic, unsafe, urgent 7 boiling, burning, febrile, fevered, goatish, lustful, peppery, pungent, satyric, summery, sweltry, violent, zealous 8 broiling, feverish, feverous, glorious, prurient, scalding, sizzling, tropical, vehement 9 lecherous, lickerish, marvelous, scorching 10 blistering, contraband, lascivious, libidinous, passionate, sweltering 11 radioactive 12 concupiscent

hot air 4 bosh 6 bunkum 7 blather, twaddle 8 flimflam, malarkey, nonsense 9 poppycock 10 double-talk

hot-blooded 5 fiery 6 ardent 7 blazing, burning, fervent, flaming 9 excitable 10 passionate 11 impassioned 12 high-spirited

hotchpotch see hodgepodge

hot dog 5 frank 6 weenie, weiner, wiener, wienie 7 show-off 11 frankfurter, wienerwurst

hotel 3 inn, spa 5 lodge 6 boatel, tavern 7 auberge, hospice, pension 8 motor inn 9 roadhouse 11 caravansary, public house 12 lodging house, rooming house 13 boardinghouse *chain:* 5 Hyatt 6 Hilton, Westin 8 Marriott, Radisson, Sheraton, Stouffer 9 Ramada Inn 10 Holiday Inn 11 Four Seasons *inferior:* 7 fleabag

Hoth see Hoder

Hotham's father 5 Heber

hotheaded 4 rash 5 brash, fiery, hasty 6 madcap 8 reckless 9 impetuous

Hothir's father 5 Heman

hot spot 4 café 6 nitery 7 cabaret 8 nightery 9 nightclub 10 supper club 11 discotheque 12 watering hole 13 watering place

hot springs 7 thermae

hot-tempered 5 ratty, testy 6 cranky, tetchy, touchy 7 peppery 8 choleric 9 dyspeptic, irascible 10 passionate

hot water 3 box, fix, jam 4 hole 5 Dutch 6 corner, pickle 7 dilemma, trouble 8 quagmire 10 difficulty 11 predicament

____ Houdini 5 Harry

hound 3 dog, fan 4 bait, buff, ride, tyke 5 chivy, lover 6 addict, badger, bowwow, canine, heckle, hector, votary 7 devotee, dogfish, habitué 8 bullyrag 10 aficionado *Russian:* 6 borzoi

house 3 hut, ken 4 casa, clan, firm, folk, home, race, roof, shed 5 abode, board, dwell, folks, haven, hotel, lodge, put up, stock, tribe 6 bestow, biggin, billet, casino, encase, family, harbor, ménage, outfit, shield 7 château, company, concern, contain, cottage, enclose, kindred, lineage, man-

sion, quarter, saltbox, shelter, theater
8 audience, business, domicile, dwelling,
messuage **9** caparison, entertain, residence, residency *clergyman's:* **5** manse
7 rectory **9** parsonage *country:* **5** manor
7 cottage **8** bungalow *dog:* **6** kennel *earth:*
5 adobe *Eskimo:* **5** igloo *lower:* **8** assembly *mean:* **5** hovel *of prostitution:* **4** crib
6 bagnio **7** brothel **8** bordello *religious:*
5 abbey **6** priory **7** convent, nunnery
9 monastery *room in a:* **7** chamber *rooming:* **5** lodge *Russian:* **5** dacha *small:*
5 shack *Spanish:* **4** casa *women's (Muslim):* **5** harem

housebreak 3 rob **4** tame **5** rifle **6** subdue **7** ransack **9** knock over **10** burglarize

household 4 home **5** folks **6** common,
family, ménage **8** domestic, familiar *combining form:* **2** ec **3** eco, oec **4** oeco, oiko
gods (Roman): **5** lares **7** penates

house of God see **house of worship**

house of prayer see **house of worship**

house of worship 5 abbey, stupa
6 bethel, chapel, church, pagoda, shrine,
temple **7** chantry, minster, oratory **8** basilica **9** cathedral, sanctuary **10** tabernacle
11 conventicle *Aztec:* **6** teopan **8** teocalli
Jewish: **7** synagog **9** synagogue *Muslim:*
6 masjid, mosque, musjid

housewife 5 hussy **8** hausfrau

housing 4 case **7** shelter **9** enclosure
run-down: **4** slum

hovel 3 hut, sty **5** hutch, shack **6** burrow,
pigpen, pigsty, shanty **10** tabernacle

hover 4 flit, hang **5** cower, dance, float,
poise **7** flicker, flitter, flutter **9** hang about

howbeit 3 yet **4** when **5** still, while
6 much as, though, withal **7** whereas
8 after all, although **11** nonetheless, still
and all **12** nevertheless

however 3 but, yet **4** only, save **5** still
6 except, though, withal **8** after all,
although **9** per contra **11** nonetheless, still
and all

howl 3 bay, cry, yip **4** bark, keen, riot, wail,
weep, yell, yelp **5** quest **6** scream, squall,
squawl, squeal **7** blubber, protest, ululate,
whimper **9** caterwaul, complaint **11** oscillation **12** sidesplitter

hoyden 6 gamine, tomboy

Hreidmar's son 5 Regin **6** Fafnir,
Reginn

Hrimfaxi's rider 4 Nott

H-shaped 5 zygal

hub 4 band, bell, nave, seat **5** focus, heart
6 barrel, center **8** polestar **9** master tap
10 focal point **11** nerve center *opposite:*
3 rim

hubbub 3 din **4** stir, to-do **5** babel, whirl
6 clamor, hassle, jangle, pother, racket, rumpus, tumult, uproar **7** turmoil **8** brouhaha

9 commotion **10** hullabaloo, hurly-burly, tintamarre **11** disturbance, pandemonium

hubristic 4 vain **5** proud **7** haughty
8 arrogant, cavalier, insolent, superior
10 disdainful **11** overbearing **12** supercilious **13** high-and-mighty

Huckleberry Finn *author:* **5** Twain
(Mark) *character:* **3** Jim, Tom *river:*
11 Mississippi

huckster 4 hawk, vend **5** adman **6** dicker,
haggle, hawker, higgle, monger, palter, peddle, vendor **7** bargain, chaffer, higgler, packman, peddler **8** outcrier

huddle 3 don **4** lump **5** bunch, chaos,
crowd, get on, hunch, put on, snarl, throw,
treat **6** advise, assume, ataxia, confab, confer, crouch, draw on, jumble, parley, powwow, slip on **7** clutter, consult, cover up,
meeting **8** assemble, colloque, disarray, disorder **9** confusion **10** conference, discussion **11** confabulate, scrooch down

Hudson's ship 8 Half Moon

hue 4 cast, tint, tone **5** color, shade,
shape, tinge **6** aspect, outcry **10** complexion

huff 4 blow, gasp, pant, rant, rile, roil, snap
5 annoy, grate, heave, peeve, pique, storm
6 nettle, put out **7** bluster, dudgeon,
flounce, inflame, inflate, offense, provoke,
umbrage **8** irritate **10** resentment

huffy 5 proud, waspy **6** touchy **7** fretful,
haughty, peevish, pettish, waspish **8** arrogant, cavalier, insolent, petulant, snappish,
superior **9** fractious, irritable, querulous
10 disdainful **11** overbearing **12** supercilious **13** high-and-mighty

hug 5 clasp, crowd, press **6** clutch, cuddle,
enfold **7** cherish, embosom, embrace,
squeeze **10** felicitate **12** congratulate

huge 4 vast **5** bulky, giant, grand, great,
jumbo, large, lusty, massy, Titan **6** heroic,
mighty, untold **7** Antaean, immense, mammoth, massive, monster, outsize, titanic,
whaling **8** colossal, enormous, gigantic,
oversize, pythonic, towering, whacking,
whopping **9** cyclopean, extensive, gigan-
tean, Herculean, leviathan, monstrous, planetary, unbounded, walloping **10** behemothic, dinosauric, gargantuan, mastodonic,
monumental, prodigious, tremendous,
unfathomed **11** Bunyanesque, elephantine,
gigantesque, magnificent, mountainous

hugeness 8 enormity **9** immensity, magnitude

hugger-mugger 4 hash, hush, mash
6 covert, jumble, jungle, litter, muddle,
secret, tumble **7** clutter, furtive, jumbled,
rummage, secrecy, silence, sub-rosa **8** covertly, hush-hush, in camera, scramble,
secretly **9** by stealth, confusion, furtively,
privately **10** mumbo jumbo, secretness,

stealthily, undercover **11** clandestine
13 clandestinely

Hugo, Victor *character:* **6** Javert **7** Cosette, Fantine, Valjean **9** Esmeralda, Quasimodo

Huguenot leader **5** Condé (Prince de)
6 Adrets (Baron des), Mornay (Philippe)

Huguenots composer **9** Meyerbeer (Giacomo)

Huldah's husband **7** Shallum

hulk **4** loom, ship

hull **3** pod **4** bark, case, peel, rind, skin
5 chaff, shell, shuck **6** casing **8** covering
9 cartridge **11** decorticate

hullabaloo **3** din **5** babel **6** clamor, hubbub, jangle, racket, tumult, uproar **8** ballyhoo **10** tintamarre **11** pandemonium

Hul's father **4** Aram

hum **4** buzz, moan, purr, sing, zing
5 drone **6** bumble, melody, murmur
7 vibrate

human **4** body, life, soul **5** being, party, wight **6** mortal, person **7** hominid, mankind **8** creature, hominine, hominoid **9** enigmatic, personage **10** anthropoid, ethnologic, individual **12** ethnological *being:*
6 mortal, person **7** primate *combining form:* **7** anthrop **8** anthropo *race:* **7** mankind

humane **4** good, kind, mild **6** gentle, kindly **8** merciful **10** altruistic, benevolent, charitable **11** kindhearted, soft-hearted
12 eleemosynary **13** compassionate, philanthropic

humanitarian **4** good **10** altruistic, benevolent, charitable **12** eleemosynary **13** philanthropic

humanity **3** man, men **5** flesh **6** people
7 mankind **9** mortality **10** compassion
11 benevolence, Homo sapiens

Humbaba's slayer **9** Gilgamesh

humble **3** low **4** base, mean, meek, sink
5 abase, abash, lower, lowly, quiet
6 bemean, debase, demean, modest, simple **7** chagrin, degrade, ignoble, lowborn, lowbred, mortify, subdued **8** baseborn, cast down, plebeian, resigned, unwashed
9 compliant, discomfit, embarrass, humiliate **10** submissive, unassuming, unennobled
11 acquiescent, unobtrusive **13** insignificant, unpretentious

humbug **3** gyp, rot **4** bosh, fake, hoax, sell, sham **5** bluff, faker, fraud, hokum, phony, spoof **6** betray, bunkum, cajole, delude, drivel, illude, juggle, piffle, take in **7** beguile, deceive, mislead **8** flimflam, impostor, malarkey, nonsense, quackery
9 hypocrite, imposture, pretender **10** balderdash

humdinger **5** dandy, doozy, nifty, peach
8 jim-dandy **11** crackerjack

humdrum **4** blah, dull **6** dreary, stodgy
7 prosaic **8** banausic, monotone, monotony, plodding, workaday **10** monotonous, pedestrian

humid **4** damp, dank **5** close, moist, mucky, muggy, soggy **6** clammy, sodden, sticky, stuffy, sultry **8** stifling, vaporous
10 oppressive, sweltering

humiliate **4** sink **5** abase, lower, shame
6 bemean, debase, demean, humble **7** chagrin, degrade, mortify **8** belittle, cast down, disgrace

humming **4** busy **5** brisk, fussy **6** lively
7 hopping, popping **8** bustling, hustling

hummingbird **5** sylph **6** sappho **7** vervain **9** thorntail, trochilus *genus:* **6** Sappho

humor **3** bee, wit **4** baby, mind, mood, tone, vein, whim **5** fancy, freak, spoil
6 banter, cocker, coddle, comedy, cosset, cotton, esprit, joking, levity, makeup, megrim, nature, pamper, strain, temper, vagary **7** boutade, caprice, cater to, conceit, gratify, gruntle, indulge, jesting, kidding **8** chaffing, chitchat, crotchet, drollery, jocosity, repartee **9** character, drollness, flippancy, funniness, jocundity, lightness, wittiness **10** comicality, complexion, jocularity, jocundness, pleasantry

humorist **3** Ade, wag, wit **4** card, Nash (Ogden), Shaw (Henry Wheeler), Ward (Artemus, Edward), zany **5** Adams (Franklin Pierce), Allen (Fred), clown, comic, cutup, droll, Dunne (Finley Peter), joker, Twain (Mark), White (Elwyn Brooks)
6 Browne (Charles Farrar), gagman, jester, kidder, Rogers (Will), Runyon (Damon), Thorpe (Thomas Bangs) **7** buffoon, Burgess (Gelett), Clemens (Samuel Langhorne), gagster, Hubbard (Kin), Marquis (Don), punster, Thurber (James) **8** Aleichem (Shalom), banterer, Benchley (Robert), comedian, funnyman, jokester, Perelman (Sidney Joseph), quipster **9** jokesmith, prankster **11** merry-andrew *Canadian:*
7 Leacock (Stephen)

humorous **5** funny, witty **6** jocose **7** jocular, waggish, wagsome **9** facetious

humpback **5** whale **8** kyphosis

humpbacked **7** gibbous

Humperdinck opera **15** Hansel und Gretel

humus **3** mor **4** mull, soil

hunch **3** gob, wad **4** arch, clod, lump, push, rear **5** chunk, clump, crook, fudge, shove, squat **6** crouch, curl up, huddle, jostle, nugget **11** scrooch down

Hunchback of Notre Dame **9** Quasimodo *author:* **4** Hugo (Victor)

hundred *combining form:* **4** hect
5 centi, hecto **6** hecato **7** hecaton

hundredth *combining form:* 5 centi
Hungary *capital:* 8 Budapest *dog:* 4 puli
ethnic group: 6 Magyar *monetary unit:*
6 forint *national hero:* 5 Arpad *wine:*
5 tokay
hunger 3 yen 4 ache, long, lust, pine, sigh
5 crave, yearn 6 famine, famish, hanker,
thirst 7 craving
hungry 4 avid, poor 6 barren 7 starved
8 famished, ravenous, starving, underfed
hunk 3 gob, wad 4 clod, lump 5 chunk,
clump, piece 6 nugget
hunker down 5 squat
Hunnish 4 rude, wild 6 Gothic, savage
7 uncivil 9 barbarian, barbarous 11 uncivilized 12 uncultivated
hunt 3 dog, gun, run 4 hawk, kill, prey,
rout, seek 5 chase, drive, hound, quest,
shoot, snare, stalk, start, track 6 battue,
course, dig out, ferret, pursue, rabbit, safari,
shikar 7 capture, explore, rummage 9 cast
about, ferret out, search for, search out
birds: 4 fowl *illegally:* 5 poach
hunter 5 jager, yager 6 chaser, jaeger,
nimrod 7 stalker 8 chasseur, predator *biblical:* 6 Nimrod *cap:* 5 terai 7 montero
constellation: 5 Orion *cry:* 6 yoicks 7 tallyho *horn:* 5 bugle *mythological:* 5 Orion
7 Actaeon
hunting 5 chase 6 venery 7 angling, fishing, gunning, hawking 8 coursing, falconry
9 predatory 10 predacious *bird:* 6 falcon
call: 7 recheat *cry:* 4 toho 7 tallyho, tantivy *dog:* 4 alan 5 alant, hound 6 alaunt,
basset, beagle, borzoi, setter 7 pointer,
spaniel *expedition:* 6 safari
huntress 5 Diana 7 Artemis 8 Atalanta
Hupham's father 8 Benjamin
Hur *grandson:* 8 Bezaleel *son:*
8 Rephaiah
hurdle 3 bar, hop, lop, rub 4 down, jump,
leap, lick, over, snag 5 bound, clear, throw,
vault 6 bounce, hamper, master, spring
7 barrier, conquer, saltate 8 mountain,
obstacle, overcome, overleap, surmount,
traverse 9 negotiate 10 impediment
11 obstruction
hurl 4 cast, fire, rush, toss 5 drive, fling,
heave, pitch, sling, throw, whirl 6 launch,
thrust 8 catapult *stones:* 8 lapidate
hurly-burly 4 to-do 5 melee, whirl
6 clamor, hassle, hubbub, pother, tumult,
uproar 7 turmoil 8 confused 9 commotion,
confusion
hurrah 4 coil, fire, fuss, romp, to-do, zeal
ardor, cheer, scold, spree, tease 6 fervor,
furore, harass, ruckus, rumpus, shindy,
uproar 7 dispute, fanfare, passion 8 argument, raillery 9 calenture, commotion
10 contention, enthusiasm 11 controversy

hurricane 5 storm 7 tornado, typhoon
8 williwaw 9 whirlwind 13 tropical storm
tropical: 7 typhoon
hurried 4 fast 5 hasty 6 abrupt, sudden
7 rushing 8 headlong 9 impetuous
10 tumultuous 11 precipitant, precipitate,
precipitous, subitaneous
hurry 3 fly, hie, jog, peg, run, zip 4 flit,
pelt, post, rock, rush, skin, trot, whiz 5 dig
in, fleet, haste, scoot, scour, skelp, skirr,
skite, smoke, speed, stave, whirl, whish,
whisk, whizz 6 barrel, breeze, bucket, bullet, bustle, hasten, hustle, rocket, rustle,
step up, tumult, whirry 7 beeline, hotfoot,
quicken, scutter, scuttle, shake up, skelter,
swiften 8 celerity, dispatch, expedite, highball 9 bowl along, commotion, swiftness
10 accelerate, expedition, speediness
hurt 3 mar 4 ache, harm, pain, ruin
5 abuse, check, smart, spoil, wound, wrong
6 damage, grieve, hamper, impair, injure,
injury, misuse, offend, suffer, weaken
7 afflict, blemish, damaged, outrage, tarnish, vitiate, wounded 8 aggrieve, distress,
mischief, mistreat 9 constrain, detriment,
prejudice, resentful, suffering 10 resentment
hurtful 4 evil, sore 6 aching 7 algetic,
harmful, nocuous, painful 8 damaging
9 injurious 10 afflictive 11 deleterious, detrimental, mischievous, prejudicial 12 preju-
dicious
hurtle 4 rush 5 crash, fling, shoot, throw
6 clater 8 catapult 9 collision
husband 3 man 4 lord, mate, save
6 manage, mister, spouse 7 consort,
hoarder 8 benedict, conserve, helpmate,
helpmeet 9 other half 10 bridegroom
husbandry 6 thrift 7 economy, farming
8 prudence 9 frugality 10 management,
providence 11 agriculture, thriftiness
12 conservation
hush 4 calm, lull 5 burke, quell, quiet,
shush, still, whist 6 shut up, silent, stifle,
stilly, whisht 7 mollify, secrecy, silence
8 choke off, suppress 9 cessation, noiseless, soundless, stillness 10 secretness
12 hugger-mugger 13 hugger-muggery,
secretiveness
hush-hush 6 covert, secret 7 secrecy,
silence, sub rosa 10 censorship, secretness, undercover 11 clandestine, suppression 12 confidential, hugger-mugger
13 hole-and-corner, hugger-muggery,
secretiveness, surreptitious, under-the-table
Hushim *father:* 3 Dan *husband:* 9 Shaharaim
husk 3 pod 4 case, peel, skin 5 bract,
carob, hoose, shell, shuck, strip *combining
form:* 4 lepo 7 siliqui

husky 3 big, fat 4 bull 5 beefy, burly, empty, great, gruff, hefty, large, stout 6 brawny, croaky, hoarse, mighty, robust, strong, sturdy 8 croaking, gigantic, muscular, oversize, powerful, rattling, stalwart 9 Herculean, strapping, well-built 10 membranous 11 Bunyanesque

hustle 3 fly, rob, run 4 earn, move, push, rush, work 5 cheat, elbow, haste, hurry, press, shove, speed 6 gather, hasten 7 hotfoot, swindle 8 bulldoze, celerity, dispatch, shoulder 9 swiftness

hustler 4 bawd, doer, drab, moll 5 whore 6 dynamo, harlot, hooker, hummer, peeler, vendor 8 call girl, go-getter, live wire, new broom 9 humdinger 10 powerhouse, prostitute 11 self-starter 12 streetwalker

hustling 4 busy 5 fussy 6 lively 7 hopping, humming, popping 9 energetic

hut 3 cot 4 camp, crib, room, shed 5 cabin, dacha, house, hovel, hutch, jacal, lodge, roost, shack 6 bestow, billet, cabana, chalet, harbor, lean-to, shanty 7 cottage, edifice, quarter 8 building, domicile *American Indian:* 6 wikiup 7 wickiup, wickyup *Russian:* 4 isba, izba *shepherd's:* 5 sheal, shiel 8 shealing, shieling

hutch 3 bin 4 cage 5 shack 6 locker, shanty

Huxley novel 11 Crome Yellow 13 Brave New World, Eyeless in Gaza

Hyacinthus *father:* 7 Amyclas *slayer:* 6 Apollo

hybrid 4 mule 5 cross 7 bastard, incross, mixture, mongrel 8 outcross 9 composite, crossbred, half blood, half-breed, loanblend 10 crossbreed 11 combination

hybridize 5 cross 9 cross-mate 10 crossbreed, interbreed, intercross

Hydra *father:* 6 Typhon *mother:* 7 Echidna *slayer:* 8 Heracles, Hercules

hydrant 3 tap 4 cock, gate 5 valve 6 faucet, spigot 7 petcock 8 fireplug, stopcock

hydraulic device 3 ram 4 jack, lift, pump 5 brake, press 8 elevator

hydrocarbon 5 xylol 6 ethane, indene, xylene *liquid:* 6 octane 7 retinol, styrene 8 menthene *suffix:* 5 ylene

hydroid 5 polyp 6 medusa, obelia 9 jellyfish, millepore

hydrometer scale 4 Brix 5 Baumé

hydrophobia 5 lyssa 6 rabies

hydroponics 11 aquiculture, tank farming

Hygeia 5 Salus *father:* 9 Asclepius 11 Aesculapius *goddess of:* 6 health

hygienic 4 good 7 healthy 8 salutary, sanitary 9 healthful, wholesome 10 salubrious

Hyllus' father 8 Heracles, Hercules

hymeneal 6 wedded 7 marital, married, nuptial, spousal 8 conjugal 9 connubial 11 matrimonial

hymn 3 lay 4 aria, laud, lied, sing, song 5 bless, carol, chant, cry up, ditty, extol, paean, trill, troll 6 choral, intone, praise, warble 7 chorale, descant, glorify, gradual, magnify 8 antiphon, canticle, doxology, eulogize 10 panegyrize

hyperbole 8 coloring 12 embroidering, exaggeration 13 embellishment, overstatement

hyperbolic function 4 cosh, coth, csch, sech, sinh, tanh

hypercritical 7 carping 8 captious, caviling 9 cavillous 10 censorious 12 faultfinding

Hyperion *daughter:* 3 Eos 6 Aurora, Selene *father:* 6 Uranus *mother:* 2 Ge 4 Gaea *son:* 4 Helios *wife:* 5 Theia

hypnotic 6 opiate, sleepy 8 mesmeric, somnific 9 somnolent, soporific 10 somnorific 11 somniferous

hypnotize 5 charm 6 trance 8 entrance 9 mesmerize, spellbind

hypocorism 6 byname, byword 8 nickname 9 sobriquet

hypocrisy 4 cant, sham 6 humbug 7 pietism 8 glibness, quackery 9 casuistry 10 pharisaism, sanctimony, Tartuffery, Tartuffism 11 charlatanry, insincerity, religiosity 12 pecksniffery, unctuousness

hypocrite 4 sham 5 actor, faker, fraud, phony, poser, quack 6 humbug, phoney, poseur 7 bluffer, pietist, Tartufe 8 deceiver, impostor, pharisee, Tartuffe 9 charlatan, lip server, pretender 10 dissembler 11 fourflusher, masquerader 12 dissimulator

hypocritical 4 glib, oily 5 bland, false 6 smooth 7 canting 8 affected, janiform, malafide, specious, unctuous 9 casuistic, insincere, pharisaic, pietistic, religiose 10 goody-goody, left-handed, moralistic 11 dissembling, double-faced 12 ambidextrous, double-minded, mealymouthed, pecksniffian, smooth-spoken 13 double-dealing, doublehearted, double-tongued, sanctimonious, self-righteous, smooth-tongued

hypothesis 6 theory 8 supposal 11 supposition

hypothetical 5 ideal 7 assumed, reputed 8 abstract, doubtful, putative, supposed 11 conditional, conjectural, implication, problematic, suppositive, suppository 12 supposititious, transcendent 13 suppositional

Hypsipyle's father 5 Thoas

hyrax 4 cony 5 coney

hysterical fear 5 panic

I

Iago *general:* 7 Othello *victim:* 6 Cassio, Emilia 7 Othello 9 Desdemona *wife:* 6 Emilia

Iapetus *father:* 6 Uranus *mother:* 2 Ge 4 Gaea *son:* 5 Atlas 9 Menoetius 10 Epimetheus, Prometheus *wife:* 7 Clymene

Iasion *brother:* 8 Dardanus *father:* 4 Zeus 7 Jupiter *lover:* 5 Ceres 7 Demeter *mother:* 7 Electra *son:* 6 Plutus

ibex 3 tur 4 tahr 8 wild goat *family:* 7 Bovidae *genus:* 5 Capra

Ibhar's father 5 David

ibis-headed god 5 Thoth

Ibneiah's father 7 Jeroham

Ibnijah's son 5 Reuel

Ibri's father 7 Jaaziah

Ibsen *character:* 3 Ase 4 Nora 5 Brand, Hedda 7 Solness 8 Peer Gynt *country:* 6 Norway *play:* 6 Ghosts 8 Peer Gynt 11 A Doll's House, Hedda Gabler, Little Eyolf, Rosmersholm, The Wild Duck

Icarius *brother:* 9 Tyndareus *daughter:* 7 Erigone 8 Penelope *mother:* 10 Gorgophone

Icarus'father 8 Daedalus

ice 4 rime, sish 5 chill, frost, glace 6 freeze *area:* 4 rink *combining form:* 6 glacio 8 crystall 9 crystallo *floating:* 4 berg, floe *glacial:* 5 serac *hanging:* 6 icicle *on rock:* 7 verglas *pinnacle:* 5 serac

ice cream 7 spumone, spumoni, tortoni *dish:* 4 soda 6 frappe, sundae

iced 5 glacé 6 glazed

ice field 7 glacier

ice game 6 hockey 7 curling

ice house 4 iglu 5 igloo

Iceland *capital:* 9 Reykjavik *monetary unit:* 5 krona

Icelandic *epic:* 4 Edda *hero:* 7 Grettir

Ichabod *father:* 8 Phinehas *grandfather:* 3 Eli

Ichabod Crane's beloved 8 Caterina

icing 7 topping 8 frosting

icky 4 vile 5 nasty 6 sticky 7 noisome 8 horrible 9 loathsome, offensive, repellent, revolting, sickening 10 disgusting

icon 5 image

icy 4 cold 5 chill, gelid 6 arctic, chilly, frigid, frosty 7 glacial 8 chilling, freezing 11 emotionless, indifferent, unemotional

Idaho *capital:* 5 Boise *nickname:* 8 Gem State *state flower:* 7 syringa

Idas *brother:* 7 Lynceus *father:* 8 Aphareus *slayer:* 4 Zeus *victim:* 6 Castor *wife:* 8 Marpessa

Iddo *father:* 9 Zechariah *grandson:* 9 Zechariah *son:* 8 Ahinadab

idea 4 view, whim 5 fancy, guess, image 6 belief, notion, theory, vagary, whimsy 7 caprice, conceit, concept, fantasy, feeling, figment, inkling, opinion, subject, surmise, thought 8 judgment, reaction 9 sentiment, suspicion 10 assumption, brainstorm, conception, conclusion, conjecture, conviction, estimation, hypothesis, impression, perception, persuasion, reflection 11 inspiration

ideal 4 goal, very 5 jewel, model 6 mirror 7 classic, example, paragon, pattern, perfect, phoenix, typical, utopian 8 abstract, ensample, exemplar, flawless, nonesuch, notional, paradigm, standard 9 archetype, classical, exemplary, imaginary, nonpareil, visionary 10 archetypal, conceptual, ideational, prototypal 11 theoretical

idealist 7 dreamer, quixote, utopian 9 ideologue, visionary 13 castle-builder

idealistic 6 starry 7 utopian 8 poetical, quixotic, romantic 9 visionary 10 starry-eyed 11 impractical, unrealistic

idée ___ 4 fixe

identical 3 one 4 like, same, self, very 5 alike, equal, exact 8 selfsame

identification *abbreviation:* 2 ID *mark:* 5 brand, label

identify 3 tag 4 find, mark, name, spot 5 brand, place 6 finger, select 7 make out, pick out 8 diagnose, pinpoint 9 determine, establish, recognize

ideology 3 ism 4 view 5 credo, creed 7 outlook 10 philosophy

idiocy 5 folly 7 amentia, fatuity 9 stupidity

idiosyncratic 3 odd 5 queer, weird 6 proper 7 curious, erratic, oddball, strange 8 peculiar, singular 9 diacritic, eccentric 10 diagnostic, individual 11 distinctive

idiot 3 ass 4 fool, jerk, simp, zany 5 ament, dummy, dunce, moron, ninny, schmo 6 cretin, donkey, jester, motley, schmoe, stupid 7 dullard, half-wit, jackass, natural, tomfool 8 dullhead, dumbbell, imbe-

cile, numskull **9** ignoramus, simpleton
10 nincompoop

idiotic 4 daft **6** stupid **7** foolish, moronic
9 senseless

idle 3 bum **4** laze, lazy, loaf, loll, rest, vain
5 amble, daily, drone, empty, inert, mooch,
mosey, quiet, relax, sit by, tarry **6** asleep,
dawdle, diddle, futile, hollow, linger, loiter,
lounge, otiose, potter, repose, sleepy, stroll,
unused, vacant **7** aimless, passive, saunter, sit back, useless **8** inactive, indolent,
nugatory, slothful

idleness 4 laze **5** sloth **6** acedia, slouch
8 flânerie, laziness **9** indolence **12** slothfulness

idler 3 bum **4** slug **5** drone **6** loafer,
slouch **8** dolittle, fainéant, slugabed, sluggard **9** do-nothing, lazybones

Idmon *daughter:* **7** Arachne *father:*
6 Apollo *mother:* **6** Cyrene

idol 3 god **4** hero, icon **5** image *Chinese:*
4 joss

idolatry 7 baalism, worship **9** adoration
11 idolization

idolize 5 adore **6** admire, dote on, revere
7 worship **8** dote upon, venerate

Idylls of the King *author:* **8** Tennyson
(Alfred) *character:* **4** Enid **6** Arthur, Elaine,
Gareth, Merlin, Vivien **7** Geraint, Lynette
8 Lancelot

iffy 5 dicey **6** chancy **7** erratic **8** doubtful
9 fluctuant, uncertain, whimsical **10** capricious **12** incalculable **13** unpredictable

Igal's father 6 Nathan **8** Shemaiah

Igdaliah's son 5 Hanan

igneous rock 4 lava **5** magma **6** basalt,
gabbro, pumice, scoria **7** diabase, granite
8 obsidian, porphyry

ignis fatuus 6 mirage **8** delusion, illusion,
phantasm **12** will-o'-the-wisp **13** hallucination

ignitable 8 burnable **9** flammable **11** combustible, inflammable

ignite 4 fire **5** light **6** excite, kindle
7 inflame **8** enkindle

ignited 3 lit **5** afire, fiery **6** ablaze, aflame,
alight **7** blazing, burning, flaming, flaring,
lighted

ignoble 3 low **4** base, mean, poor, vile
5 lowly, plain **6** abject, coarse, common,
homely, humble, modest, scurvy, simple,
sordid, vulgar **7** lowborn, peasant, popular,
servile **8** baseborn, inferior, ordinary, plebeian, shameful, unwashed, wretched
10 despicable, inglorious, unennobled
11 disgraceful **12** dishonorable

ignominious 5 shady **6** shabby, shoddy
8 shameful **10** inglorious **11** disgraceful
12 dishonorable, disreputable **13** discreditable, unrespectable

ignominy 5 odium, scorn, shame
6 infamy **7** chagrin, despite, disdain, obloquy **8** contempt, disgrace, dishonor **9** discredit, disesteem, disrepute **10** opprobrium
13 mortification

ignoramus 4 dolt, fool **5** dummy, dunce,
idiot, moron **6** nitwit, stupid **7** dullard
8 dullhead, dumbbell **9** simpleton

ignorance 7 naiveté, rawness **8** darkness
9 greenness, innocence, inscience, nescience **10** callowness, illiteracy, simple-
ness, simplicity **11** unawareness, uncouth-
ness, witlessness

ignorant 3 raw **4** rude **5** crude, green,
gross, naive **6** callow, simple, stupid **7** lowbrow, unaware, uncouth **8** backward, nes-
cient, untaught **9** benighted, ingenuous,
oblivious, unknowing, untutored, unwitting
10 illiterate, uncultured, uneducated, unfamiliar, uninformed, unlettered, unschooled
11 empty-headed, incognizant, know-
nothing **12** inconversant, unacquainted,
uninstructed

ignore 3 cut **4** fail, omit, snub **5** avoid,
evade **6** forget, slight **7** blink at, neglect
8 discount, overlook, overpass **9** blink
away, disregard

Igraine, Ygerne *husband:* **5** Uther
7 Gorlois *son:* **6** Arthur

iguana 6 lizard **7** tuatara

ilex 5 holly **7** holm oak

Iliad 4 epic *author:* **5** Homer *character:*
4 Ajax **5** Helen, Paris, Priam **6** Aeneas,
Hector **8** Achilles, Diomedes, Odysseus
9 Agamemnon, Patroclus *city:* **4** Troy

Ilion, Ilium 4 Troy

ilk 4 kind, sort, type **5** breed, class **6** family, kidney, nature, stripe **7** variety

ill 3 bad **4** down, evil, rude, sick **5** amiss
6 malady, nocent **7** ailment, disease, harmful, hostile, hurtful, ill-bred, nocuous, noxious, uncivil **8** damaging, disorder, feverish,
feverous, impolite, inimical, nauseous, sickness, syndrome **9** affection, complaint, condition, infirmity, injurious

ill-adapted 5 inapt, unfit **6** unmeet
8 unfitted, unsuited **9** ill-suited **10** unsuitable **13** inappropriate

ill-advised 4 rash **5** brash, hasty **6** madcap, unwise **8** reckless **9** hotheaded, ill-
judged, impolitic, imprudent **10** incautious,
indiscreet, mad-brained **11** inadvisable,
inexpedient, injudicious, thoughtless, unadvisable, unexpedient **13** inconsiderate

ill-boding 4 dire **7** baleful, baneful, fateful,
ominous, unlucky **9** ill-omened **11** apocalyptic **12** inauspicious, unpropitious

ill-bred 4 rude **6** rugged **7** boorish, incivil,
loutish, lowbred, uncivil **8** churlish, cloddish, impolite **9** unrefined **10** uncultured,
ungracious, unpolished **11** disgracious, ill-

mannered, impertinent, uncivilized **12** discourteous **13** disrespectful

ill-defined 3 dim **5** blear, faint, fuzzy, vague **6** bleary **7** shadowy, unclear **9** undefined **10** indistinct

illegal 3 hot **6** banned **7** illicit, lawless **8** criminal, nonlegal, outlawed, unlawful, wrongful **9** felonious, forbidden, irregular **10** actionable, contraband, prohibited, proscribed, unlicensed **11** interdicted, unwarranted **12** illegitimate, unauthorized *act:* **5** crime **6** felony *scheme:* **4** scam

illegible 5 faint **7** obscure, unclear **10** indistinct, unreadable

illegitimacy 8 bastardy **10** illegality **11** bar sinister, illicitness **12** unlawfulness

illegitimate 6 by-blow **7** bastard, bootleg, illegal, illicit, lawless, natural **8** baseborn, criminal, spurious, unlawful, wrongful

ill-fated 7 hapless, unhappy, unlucky **8** luckless, untoward **11** star-crossed, unfortunate **12** misfortunate

ill health 7 cachexy **8** cachexia

ill-humored 5 cross **6** cranky **7** peevish **8** choleric **9** dyspeptic **10** tempersome **11** bad-tempered, hot-tempered

illiberal 4 mean **5** petty, rigid, small **6** biased, little, narrow, paltry, stingy **7** bigoted, insular, partial **8** grudging, one-sided, partisan, rigorous **9** hidebound, jaundiced, parochial, stringent **10** brassbound, intolerant, prejudiced, provincial, unenlarged, ungenerous **11** opinionated, small-minded **12** narrow-minded, uncharitable

illicit 7 bootleg, illegal, lawless **8** criminal, unlawful, wrongful **12** illegitimate

illimitable 7 endless, eternal **8** infinite **9** boundless **10** perdurable **11** measureless, sempiternal **12** immeasurable, interminable

Illinois *capital:* **11** Springfield *college, university:* **5** Barat **6** De Paul **7** Wheaton **12** Northwestern *largest city:* **7** Chicago *nickname:* **11** Sucker State **12** Prairie State *state bird:* **8** cardinal *state flower:* **6** violet

illiterate 4 rude **8** ignorant, untaught **9** benighted, unlearned, untutored **10** analphabet, uncultured, uneducated, unlettered

ill-kempt 5 messy **6** sloppy, unneat, untidy **8** careless, slipshod, slovenly, uncombed **10** disheveled

ill-mannered 4 rude **7** incivil, uncivil **8** impolite **10** ungracious **11** disgracious, impertinent **12** discourteous **13** disrespectful

ill-natured 5 cross, nasty, surly **6** crabby **8** choleric **9** dyspeptic **10** tempersome **11** bad-tempered, hot-tempered

illness 6 malady **7** ailment, disease **8** cachexia, disorder, sickness, unhealth **9** infirmity **10** affliction **13** indisposition *mental:* **8** dementia

illogical 3 mad **5** false **6** absurd **7** invalid, unsound **8** specious **9** plausible, senseless, sophistic **10** fallacious, irrational, reasonless, unreasoned **11** meaningless, nonrational **12** unreasonable, unscientific

ill-starred 6 malign **7** baleful, bodeful, fateful, hapless, malefic, ominous, unhappy, unlucky **8** luckless, sinister, untoward **10** foreboding, portentous **11** starcrossed, unfavorable, unfortunate, unpromising **12** misfortunate, unpropitious

ill-suited 5 inapt, unfit **6** unmeet **8** unfitted **10** unsuitable **13** inappropriate

ill-tempered 4 sour **5** cross, huffy, surly **6** crabby, grumpy **7** crabbed, grouchy, peevish, waspish **8** choleric, petulant, shrewish, snappish, vixenish **9** dyspeptic, fractious, irritable, querulous

ill-timed 5 inept **8** improper, mistimed, unseemly, untimely **10** malapropos, unbecoming, unsuitable **11** inopportune, unbefitting **12** unseasonable **13** inappropriate

ill-treat 5 abuse, harry **6** harass, misuse, molest **7** outrage **8** aggrieve, maltreat, mistreat

illude 4 bilk **5** bluff, cheat, elude **6** betray, delude, humbug, juggle, take in **7** beguile, deceive, mislead **11** double-cross

illume 5 edify, light **6** uplift **7** improve, lighten **8** illumine **9** enlighten, irradiate

illuminate 4 fire **5** clear, edify, exalt, gloss, light **6** better, define, finish, ignite, kindle, mature, polish, refine, uplift **7** clarify, clear up, ennoble, explain, expound, express, improve, lighten, perfect **8** brighten, construe **9** dramatize, elucidate, enlighten, highlight, interpret, irradiate, spotlight

illuminati 7 clerisy **8** literati **13** intellectuals

illumination 8 lighting *unit of:* **3** lux **4** phot **5** lumen **6** candle **7** candela **10** footcandle

illumine see **Illuminate**

illusion 5 dream **6** bubble, mirage **7** chimera, fantasy, rainbow, seeming **8** delusion, phantasm, phantasy **9** invention, pipe dream, semblance **10** appearance **11** ignis fatuus **12** will-o'-the-wisp **13** hallucination

illusionist 8 conjurer, magician **9** trickster

illusive 5 false **6** unreal **7** seeming **8** apparent

illusory 6 unreal **7** fictive, seeming **8** apparent, delusive, delusory, fanciful, illusive, semblant **9** deceptive, fantastic, fictional, imaginary, visionary **10** Barmecidal, chimerical, fictitious, misleading, ostensible

illustrate 4 mark, show **5** clear **6** embody, evince, expose, mirror, ostend, reveal, typify, vivify **7** clarify, clear up, display, enliven, exhibit, explain, expound, picture **8** disclose, discover, evidence, instance, manifest, proclaim **9** elucidate, epitomize, exemplify

illustration 4 case **6** sample **7** example, problem **8** ensample, instance, sampling, specimen

illustrative 7 graphic **8** pictoric **9** pictorial **12** iconographic

illustrator *American:* **5** Flagg (James Montgomery), Wyeth (Newell Convers) **7** Burgess (Gelett) **8** Rockwell (Norman) **9** Remington (Frederic) *English:* **6** Potter (Beatrix) **7** Tenniel (John) **9** Beardsley (Aubrey), du Maurier (George) *French:* **4** Doré (Gustave) *German:* **5** Dürer (Albrecht)

illustrious 5 famed, great, lofty, noted **6** famous, signal **7** eminent, exalted, notable, sublime **8** glorious, renowned, splendid, striking **9** prominent **10** celebrated, celebrious **11** conspicuous, outstanding, resplendent **13** distinguished

illustriousness 6 renown **8** eminence, prestige **10** prominence, prominency **11** distinction, preeminence

ill will 5 spite, venom **6** animus, grudge, malice, rancor, spleen **7** despite **9** hostility, malignity **10** malignancy **11** malevolence **12** spitefulness **13** maliciousness

Ilus *father:* **4** Tros *grandson:* **5** Priam *mother:* **10** Callirrhoe *son:* **8** Laomedon

image 4 copy, form, icon, idea, idol, limn **5** equal, fancy, glass, match, split, think **6** depict, double, effigy, mirror, notion, recept, render, ringer, vision **7** conceit, concept, fantasm, feature, imagine, picture, portray, realize, reflect, thought **8** conceive, describe, envisage, envision, likeness, phantasm, portrait **9** delineate, interpret, represent, semblance, visualize **10** conception, equivalent, impression, perception, simulacrum *Polynesian:* **4** tiki *Semitic:* **6** teraph **8** teraphim (plural)

imaginary 5 ideal **6** unreal **7** fancied, fictive, shadowy **8** abstract, chimeric, fanciful, illusory, imagined, notional, quixotic, spectral, visional **9** fantastic, fictional, figmental, visionary **10** chimerical, fictitious, phantasmal, phantasmic **11** imaginative **12** apparitional, hypothetical, supposititious **13** hallucinatory, unsubstantial

imagination 5 fancy **7** fantasy **8** phantasy **9** invention **10** creativity **11** inspiration **13** inventiveness, visualization

imagine 5 take **6** dream, fancy, guess, image, think **6** assume, expect, gather, vision **7** believe, feature, picture, realize, suppose, suspect **8** conceive, envisage,

envision **9** fabricate, visualize **10** conjecture, understand

imbecile 3 ass **4** dolt, dull, fool, jerk, slow, zany **5** ament, idiot, moron, ninny **6** cretin, donkey **7** half-wit, jackass, moronic, natural, tomfool **8** backward, retarded **9** dimwitted, simpleton **10** half-witted, nincompoop, slow-witted **12** feebleminded, simpleminded

imbibe 3 sip **4** soak, swig, toss **5** booze, drink, quaff, sup up, swill **6** absorb, guzzle, insorb, sup off, tank up, tipple **7** inhaust, swallow, swizzle **8** liquor up **10** assimilate

imbricate 3 lap **4** ride **7** overlap, overlie, shingle **8** override

imbroglio 3 row **4** miff, spat **7** dispute, quarrel **8** squabble **9** bickering **10** falling-out **11** altercation, embroilment **12** disagreement

imbue 3 dye **4** soak **5** steep, tinge **6** infuse, invest, leaven **7** ingrain, suffuse **8** permeate, saturate **9** inoculate **10** impregnate

imitate 3 ape **4** copy, echo, mime, mock **5** mimic **6** parody **7** emulate, take off **8** travesty **9** burlesque, duplicate, replicate, reproduce **11** reduplicate *combining form:* **3** mim **4** mimo

imitation 4 copy, fake, mock, sham **5** dummy, false, phony **6** ersatz **7** forgery, replica **8** likeness, spurious **9** duplicate, semblance, simulated **10** artificial, simulacrum, simulation, substitute **11** counterfeit, counterpart **12** reproduction *suffix:* **3** een **4** ette

imitative 5 apish **6** echoic **7** parodic, slavish **9** emulative **12** onomatopoeic **13** onomatopoetic

Imlah's son 7 Micaiah

immaculate 4 pure **5** clean **6** chaste, decent, modest **7** cleanly, perfect **8** flawless, innocent, spotless, unsoiled **9** errorless, exquisite, faultless, stainless, taintless, undefiled, unsullied **10** impeccable **11** unblemished

immaterial 4 airy **6** aerial **7** foreign, ghostly, psychic, shadowy **8** bodiless, ethereal, heavenly, unbodied **9** asomatous, celestial, disbodied, spiritual, unearthly, unfleshly, unworldly **10** discarnate, extraneous, impalpable, inapposite, insensible, intangible, irrelative, irrelevant, subjective, unembodied, unmaterial, unphysical **11** disembodied, impertinent, incorporeal, nonmaterial, nonphysical **12** apparitional, imponderable, inapplicable, metaphysical, supernatural **13** insubstantial, unsubstantial

immature 3 raw **5** green, vealy, young **6** callow, infant, unripe **7** babyish, puerile **8** childish, juvenile, youthful **9** infantile,

infantine, premature, unfledged 10 precocious 11 undeveloped

immaturity 6 nonage

immeasurable 7 endless 8 infinite
9 boundless, limitless, unbounded, unlimited 10 indefinite, unmeasured 11 illimitable, inestimable, measureless, uncountable
12 incalculable, unmeasurable, unreckonable

immediate 4 near, next, nigh 5 close
6 direct, nearby, urgent 7 instant, primary
9 first-hand, proximate 10 near-at-hand
11 hair-trigger 12 straightaway 13 instantaneous

immediately 3 now, PDQ 4 anon, away,
soon, stat 6 at once, presto, pronto
7 shortly 8 directly, hereupon 9 forthwith,
instanter, instantly, right away 11 straight
way

immense 4 huge, vast 5 great, large
6 mighty 7 titanic 8 colossal, enormous,
gigantic 9 monstrous 10 prodigious, tremendous

immensely 3 too 4 ever, over, very
6 overly, unduly 8 overfull, overmuch
9 extremely 11 exceedingly, excessively
12 inordinately

immensity 8 enormity, hugeness, vastness 9 magnitude 12 enormousness

immerse 3 dip 4 bury, busy, duck, dunk,
sink, soak 5 bathe, douse, embed, souse
6 absorb, engage, occupy, plunge
7 asperse, baptize, engross, include
8 christen, saturate, sprinkle, submerge,
submerse

immigrant 6 emigré *Israeli:* 6 halutz
7 chalutz 8 halutzim (plural) 9 chalutzim
(plural) *Japanese:* 5 issei

imminent 5 loury 6 coming, likely, lowery
7 brewing, louring, nearing, ominous, pending 8 alarming, lowering, menacing, mina-
tory, possible, probable, sinister, upcoming
9 gathering, impending, proximate 10 inevasible, inevitable 11 approaching, ineluctable,
inescapable, overhanging, threatening,
unavoidable, unescapable

immobile 3 set 5 fixed, inert, still 6 frozen, stable, static 8 immotile, immotive,
stagnant, unmoving 9 immovable, steadfast, unmovable 10 motionless, stationary
11 irremovable

immobilize 6 disarm 7 cripple, disable
8 paralyze 9 prostrate 12 incapacitate

immoderate 5 dizzy, undue 7 extreme
8 towering 9 boundless, excessive, voracious 10 exorbitant, inordinate, untempered
11 extravagant, intemperate 12 unmeasurable, unreasonable, unrestrained
13 overindulgent

immoderation 6 excess 12 intemperance

immodest 4 bold, lewd 5 brash, gross
6 brazen 8 boastful, indecent, unchaste

immolate 4 kill 7 destroy 8 abnegate
9 sacrifice, victimize

immoral 3 bad 4 evil 5 dirty, loose, wrong
6 impure, sinful, wanton, wicked 7 corrupt,
unclean, vicious 8 depraved, indecent,
unchaste 9 dissolute, reprobate, uncleanly
10 iniquitous, licentious

immorality 4 vice 9 depravity 10 corruption, unchastity, wickedness

immortal 6 divine 7 abiding, endless, eternal, undying 8 enduring, timeless, unending 9 ceaseless, deathless, perpetual
11 amaranthine, everlasting, never-ending,
sempiternal 12 imperishable

immotile 5 fixed 8 immobile, immotive
9 immovable, steadfast, unmovable 11 irremovable

immovable 3 pat, set 4 fast, firm 5 fixed,
rigid, stuck 6 rooted, stable 7 adamant
8 constant, immobile, immotile, immotive,
obdurate, unmoving 9 immutable, impassive, steadfast, unmovable 10 inflexible,
invariable, stationary, unyielding

immunity 7 freedom 8 impunity 9 exemption

immunizer 7 vaccine 8 antibody

immure 3 hem, jug, pen 4 cage, coop, jail,
mure, wall 5 fence, hedge 6 corral, intern
7 confine, enclose 8 bastille, cloister,
imprison 9 constrain 11 incarcerate

immutable 4 firm 5 fixed 7 eternal 8 constant 9 immovable, unmovable 10 inflexible, invariable, unchanging 11 inalterable,
unalterable 12 unchangeable, unmodifiable

Imnah *father:* 5 Asher *son:* 4 Kore

Imogen *father:* 9 Cymbeline *husband:*
9 Posthumus

imp 3 elf 4 brat, ouph, puck 5 cutup,
demon, devil, gamin, gnome, pixie, scamp,
troll 6 goblin, kobold, monkey, sprite, urchin
7 gremlin 9 hobgoblin

impact 3 hit, jar, rap 4 blow, bump, jolt,
rock, slam, slap 5 brunt, clash, crash,
crowd, pound, punch, quake, shake, shock,
smash 6 bounce, buffet, jounce, quiver,
strike, stroke, tremor, wallop 7 appulse,
congest, impulse, meeting, smiting, tremble
9 collision, encounter 10 concussion, percussion

impair 3 mar, sap 4 harm, hurt 5 spoil
6 damage, debase, injure, lessen, weaken
7 blemish, cripple, tarnish, vitiate 8 enfeeble 9 prejudice, undermine

impaired 6 flawed, marred 7 damaged,
spoiled 9 afflicted *prefix:* 3 dys

impala 7 rooibok 8 antelope

impale 4 spit, stab 5 lance, prick, punch,
spear, spike 6 pierce, skewer, skiver

8 puncture, transfix **9** perforate **11** transpierce

impart 4 give, lend, tell **5** break, grant, share, yield **6** bestow, convey, pass on **8** disclose, transmit **11** communicate *knowledge:* **5** teach **6** inform **7** educate **8** instruct

impartial 4 even, fair, just **5** equal **7** neutral **8** unbiased **9** equitable, objective, uncolored **12** unprejudiced **13** disinterested, dispassionate

impasse 3 box, fix, jam **4** hole **6** corner, pickle, plight, pocket, scrape **7** dead end, dilemma **8** cul-de-sac, deadlock **9** stalemate **10** blind alley **11** predicament

impassioned 4 deep, warm **5** fiery, gushy, mushy **6** ardent, fervid, fierce, red-hot, torrid **7** blazing, burning, fervent, flaming, furious, glowing, gushing, intense, maudlin, violent, zealous **8** eloquent, feverish, profound, romantic, vehement, white-hot **9** perfervid **10** hot-blooded, overheated, passionate **11** dithyrambic, sentimental **12** melodramatic **13** overemotional

impassive 3 dry **4** calm, cold, cool **5** stoic **6** bovine, placid, stolid, wooden **7** callous **8** composed, hardened, reserved, reticent, taciturn **9** apathetic, collected, heartless, inanimate, indurated **10** insensible, insentient, motionless, phlegmatic, spiritless **11** cold-blooded, coldhearted, emotionless, inexcitable, insensitive, passionless, unconcerned, unemotional, unexcitable, unflappable **12** inexpressive, matter-of-fact, unexpressive, unresponsive **13** dispassionate, imperturbable, unimpressible, unsusceptible

impassivity 6 apathy, phlegm **8** stoicism **9** stolidity **13** insensibility

impatient 3 hot **4** agog, avid, edgy, keen **5** eager, harsh, hasty, itchy **6** abrupt, ardent **7** anxious, athirst, chafing, fidgety, fretful, nervous, thirsty **8** appetent, headlong, restless **9** demanding, impetuous, irascible, irritable

impeach 3 tax **6** accuse, charge, indict **7** arraign, censure **9** criminate, inculpate **11** incriminate

impeccable 4 nice **5** clean, exact, right **7** correct, perfect, precise **8** absolute, accurate, flawless, unerring, unflawed **9** errorless, exquisite, faultless, fleckless **10** immaculate, infallible **12** indefectible

impecunious 4 poor **5** needy **8** dirt poor, indigent **9** destitute, penniless, penurious **11** necessitous **12** impoverished, unprosperous

impecuniousness 4 need, want **6** penury **7** poverty **8** poorness **9** indigence, neediness, privation **11** destitution

impedance 4 clog **9** cumbrance, hindrance **10** impediment **11** encumbrance

impede 3 bar, bog, dam **4** clog, faze **5** block, brake, check, debar **6** hinder, hold up, rattle **8** obstruct **9** discomfit, embarrass

impediment 3 bar, rub **4** clog, snag **5** block, hitch **6** hamper, hurdle **8** obstacle **9** cumbrance, hindrance **10** difficulty **11** encumbrance, obstruction

impel 4 good, move, spur, urge **5** drive, force **6** compel, foment, incite, propel **7** actuate, inspire **8** mobilize, motivate **9** constrain, instigate, stimulate

impend 4 brew, hang, loom **6** gather, menace **8** approach, overhang **9** forthcome

impenetrable 4 firm, hard **5** dense, solid **6** arcane, mystic **8** numinous **9** mysterial, unguessed **10** cabalistic, impassable, impervious, mysterious, unknowable **11** impermeable, imperviable, inscrutable, substantial, ungraspable **12** incognizable, unfathomable

imperative 4 need, rule **5** acute, basic, bossy, guide, harsh, order, stern **6** crying, urgent **7** bidding, burning, claimed, clamant, command, crucial, exacted, exigent, instant **8** critical, demanded, imperial, ordering, pressing, required **9** clamorous, essential, imperious, insistent, mandatory, masterful, necessary, necessity **10** commanding, compulsory, high-handed, obligatory, peremptory **11** domineering, fundamental, importunate, magisterial, necessitous, overbearing **12** compulsatory, prerequisite

imperceptible 5 faint, vague **6** slight **7** obscure, trivial **8** fugitive **9** ephemeral, invisible, momentary **10** evanescent, impalpable, indistinct, insensible, intangible, unapparent **12** imponderable, unnoticeable, unobservable **13** inappreciable, inconspicuous, indiscernible, insignificant, unappreciable, undiscernible, unperceivable

imperceptive 7 cursory, shallow **8** slapdash **11** superficial, unobservant **12** impercipient, undiscerning, unperceiving, unperceptive

imperfect 4 sick **5** amiss **6** faulty, flawed, second **9** defective **10** defeasible, inadequate, incomplete, unfinished

imperfection 3 sin **4** flaw **5** fault **6** defect, foible **7** blemish, demerit, failing, frailty **8** weakness **10** deficiency **11** shortcoming

imperial 5 bossy, regal, royal **6** kingly **7** haughty **8** majestic **9** grandiose, imperious, masterful, sovereign **10** high-handed, imperative, peremptory **11** domineering, magisterial, overbearing

imperil 4 risk **6** hazard, menace **7** jeopard, venture **8** endanger, jeopardy, threaten **10** compromise, jeopardize

imperious 5 bossy 6 lordly, strict, urgent 7 haughty 8 absolute, arrogant, despotic, dominant, imperial, required 9 arbitrary, mandatory, masterful, stringent 10 commanding, compulsory, high-handed, imperative, obligatory, oppressive, peremptory, tyrannical 11 dictatorial, domineering, heavy-handed, magisterial, overbearing

impermanent 7 passing 8 fleeting, fugitive, unstable 9 ephemeral, fugacious, momentary, temporary, tentative, transient 10 evanescent, short-lived, transitory

impersonal 4 cold, fair 5 equal 7 neutral 8 abstract, detached, unbiased 9 colorless, equitable, impartial, objective, uncolored 10 poker-faced 11 cold-blooded, emotionless, unpassioned 12 matter-of-fact, unprejudiced 13 disinterested, dispassionate, unimpassioned

impersonator 4 mime 5 actor, mimic 6 mummer, player 7 actress, trouper 8 thespian 9 performer, playactor 13 impressionist

impertinence 4 sass 8 audacity, boldness 9 hardihood, impudence, insolence, insolency, unfitness 10 disrespect, incivility 11 irrelevance 12 insolentness

impertinent 4 bold, busy, nosy, pert, rude 5 brash, fresh, sassy, saucy 6 brazen, prying 7 foreign, ill-bred, uncivil 8 arrogant, impolite, impudent, insolent, meddling 9 audacious, intrusive, obtrusive, offensive, officious 10 extraneous, immaterial, inapposite, irrelative, irrelevant, meddlesome, procacious, ungracious 11 ill-mannered, inquisitive, interfering, uncalled-for 12 contumelious, discourteous, inapplicable, presumptuous 13 disrespectful

imperturbability 6 phlegm 7 ataraxy 8 calmness, coolness 9 composure, sangfroid 10 equanimity

imperturbable 4 calm, cool, smug 6 placid, serene 7 unmoved 8 composed, tranquil 9 collected, impassive, unruffled, untouched 10 complacent, nonchalant, phlegmatic, unaffected 11 unflappable 13 self-satisfied

impervious 5 tight 8 hardened 10 impassable 11 impermeable, imperviable 12 impenetrable, unpierceable

impetuous 3 hot 4 rash 5 eager, fiery, hasty 6 abrupt, ardent, fervid, sudden 7 furious, hurried, restive, rushing, violent 8 headlong, vehement 9 hotheaded, impulsive 10 passionate 11 impassioned, precipitant, precipitate, precipitous, spontaneous

impetus 4 good, spur 5 force 7 impulse 8 catalyst, momentum, stimulus 9 incentive, stimulant 10 incitation, incitement, motivation

impious 6 sinful, unholy, wicked 7 froward, godless, profane, ungodly, wayward 8 contrary, indevout, perverse, undevout 9 atheistic, unduteous, undutiful 10 irreverent, scandalous, unfaithful, unhallowed 11 disobedient, irreligious, wrongheaded 12 iconoclastic, sacrilegious

impish 4 arch, pert 5 elfin, fresh, giddy, saucy 6 casual, elfish, elvish 7 coltish, offhand, playful, puckish, roguish, waggish 8 flippant, pixieish, sportive 10 frolicsome 11 free and easy, mischievous

impishness 7 devilry, roguery, waggery 8 deviltry, mischief 9 devilment 11 roguishness, waggishness 12 sportiveness

implacable 4 grim 6 mortal 8 ruthless 9 merciless 10 inexorable, ironfisted, relentless, unyielding 11 unflinching, unrelenting 12 unappeasable

implant 4 root 5 embed, imbue, infix, inset 6 enroot, infuse, leaven 7 impress, ingrain, inspire, instill, pervade 8 permeate, saturate 9 inculcate, inoculate, insinuate, introduce, penetrate 10 impregnate, inseminate 11 impenetrate

implausible 4 thin, weak 5 fishy, thick 6 flimsy 7 dubious, suspect, tenuous 8 doubtful, puzzling 10 improbable, incredible 11 problematic 12 unconvincing

implement 4 tool 6 device, effect, gadget, invoke 7 enforce, execute, fulfill, perform, realize, utensil 8 complete 9 actualize, apparatus, appliance 10 accomplish, instrument, supplement 11 contraption, contrivance *cleaning:* 3 mop 5 broom, brush 6 vacuum 7 sweeper 10 whiskbroom *cutting:* 5 knife, mower, razor 6 scythe, shears, sickle 8 scissors *digging:* 5 spade 6 shovel *drawing:* 3 pen 6 eraser, pencil 7 compass 8 charcoal, template *eating:* 4 fork 5 knife, spoon *engraving:* 5 burin 6 graver *farm:* 4 disc, dish, plow 6 dibber, harrow, seeder, tiller 8 gangplow, reaphook *fireplace:* 5 tongs 7 andiron *fishing:* 3 rod 4 hook 7 harpoon, trident *garden:* 3 hoe 4 rake 6 trowel *grooming:* 4 comb 5 brush 8 tweezers 10 toothbrush *kind:* 3 die, saw 4 file 5 brace, clamp, drill, punch, tongs 6 chisel, hammer, pliers, reamer, sander, wrench 7 hacksaw, scraper 9 blowtorch 11 screwdriver *kitchen:* 3 pan, pot 4 mold 5 mixer 6 kettle, mortar, pestle 7 blender, skillet, spatula *logging:* 4 pevy 5 peavy, peevy 6 peavey 8 cant hook *measuring:* 4 gage, rule 5 gauge, ruler, scale 7 caliper, divider, trammel, T-square 10 micrometer, protractor *stone:* 5 burin 6 colith 7 neolith 9 paleolith

implicate 4 mire 5 imply 6 affect, tangle

7 concern, embroil, implied, include, involve **8** implicit **11** incriminate

Implication 4 hint **8** overtone **9** inference, undertone **10** suggestion **11** association, connotation

implicit 4 real **5** tacit **6** unsaid **7** genuine, implied, virtual **8** absolute, complete, inferred, unspoken **9** potential, practical, unuttered **10** undeclared, understood **11** unexpressed, unqualified

implied 5 tacit **6** unsaid **8** implicit, inferred, unspoken, wordless **9** unuttered **10** undeclared, understood

imploration 4 plea, suit **6** appeal, orison, prayer **8** entreaty, petition **11** application, imprecation **12** supplication

implore 3 ask, beg **4** coax, pray **5** crave, plead **6** appeal **7** beseech, conjure, entreat **9** importune **10** supplicate

imply 4 hint **5** point **7** connote, include, suggest **8** indicate, intimate **9** insinuate

impolite 4 rude **5** crude, rough **7** ill-bred, incivil, uncivil **10** ungracious, unmannerly, unpolished **11** disgracious, ill-mannered, uncourteous **12** discourteous **13** disrespectful

impolitic 5 brash **6** unwise **8** tactless **9** ill-judged, imprudent, maladroit, unpolitic, untactful **10** ill-advised, indiscreet **11** inadvisable, inexpedient, injudicious, unadvisable, unexpedient **12** undiplomatic

import 4 mean, pith **5** count, sense, spell, value, weigh, worth **6** convey, denote, design, intend, intent, matter, moment, object, stress, weight **7** add up to, concern, connote, express, meaning, message, purport, purpose, signify **8** emphasis, indicate **9** magnitude, objective, substance **10** importance, intendment **11** acceptation, consequence, weightiness **12** significance, significancy

importance 4 mark, note, pith **5** value, worth **6** import, moment, weight **7** account, gravity **8** eminence, priority, salience, standing **9** magnitude, substance **10** notability, prominence, reputation, worthiness **11** consequence, distinction, seriousness, weightiness **12** significance

important 3 big **5** grave, great, noted, puffy, wiggy **6** famous, marked, potent, stuffy, urgent, worthy **7** big-time, bloated, crucial, eminent, fateful, notable, pompous, salient, serious, telling, unusual, weighty **8** arrogant, eventful, material, powerful, topnotch, valuable **9** effective, essential, firstrate, front-page, memorable, momentous, ponderous, prominent **10** first-class, impressive, meaningful, noteworthy, noticeable, pontifical, remarkable, worthwhile **11** conspicuous, distinctive, exceptional,

magisterial, outstanding, significant, substantial **12** considerable **13** consequential, distinguished

importune 3 beg **4** pray, urge **5** annoy, crave, plead, worry **6** appeal, invoke **7** beseech, entreat, implore, solicit, trouble **10** supplicate

impose 3 fob, set, use **4** lade, levy, wish **5** abuse, exact, foist, order, put on, visit, wreak, wreck **6** assess, burden, charge, compel, create, decree, demand, enjoin, fob off, oblige, ordain, saddle **7** command, dictate, exploit, force on, inflict, intrude, lay down, obtrude, palm off, presume, put upon, require **8** encroach, generate, infringe, trespass **9** constrain, force upon

imposing 3 big **4** arty **5** grand, noble, regal, royal **6** august, moving **7** stately **8** baronial, imperial, majestic, princely **9** grandiose, overblown **10** arty-crafty, commanding, impressive **11** magnificent, pretentious **12** high-sounding

imposition 3 tax **4** duty, fine, levy **6** burden **7** penalty **9** deception

impossible 6 absurd **8** cureless, hopeless **9** incurable, insanable, uncurable **10** infeasible, unfeasible, unworkable **11** immedicable, impractical, irreparable, unthinkable **12** inexecutable, irrealizable, irremediable, unacceptable, unattainable, unobtainable, unrealizable, unreasonable

impost 3 tax **4** duty, levy **6** tariff, weight **7** tribute **10** assessment

imposter 4 fake **5** cheat, faker, fraud, mimic, phony, quack **6** humbug **7** bluffer, shammer, shyster **8** beguiler, deceiver, imitator **9** charlatan, hypocrite, misleader, pretender, trickster **10** dissembler, mountebank **11** four-flusher, pettifogger

imposture 3 gyp **4** copy, fake, flam, hoax, ploy, ruse, sell, sham, wile **5** cheat, feint, fraud, phony, put-on, spoof, trick **6** deceit, gambit, humbug **7** forgery, sleight, swindle **8** artifice, flimflam, maneuver, pretense **9** deception, falsehood, imitation, mare's nest, stratagem **10** pretension **11** counterfeit, fabrication, make-believe

impotent 4 weak **5** frail **6** barren, effete, feeble **7** sterile **8** boneless, crippled, disabled, helpless, infecund **9** enfeebled, forceless, infertile, powerless, spineless **10** emasculate, inadequate, unfruitful **11** ineffective, ineffectual, slack-spined **12** invertebrate

impoverish 4 bust, draw, ruin **5** break, drain, use up **6** beggar, fold up, pauper **7** deplete, exhaust **8** bankrupt, draw down **9** pauperize

impoverished 4 poor **5** needy **6** scanty **8** bankrupt, beggared, indigent **9** destitute, penurious **10** stone-broke **11** impecunious

impoverishment 4 need, want 6 penury 7 poverty 8 poorness 9 indigence, neediness, privation 11 destitution

impracticable 6 unwise 7 awkward, useless 8 unusable 9 imprudent 10 impossible, infeasible, unfeasible, unworkable

impractical 5 viewy 7 useless 8 quixotic, romantic, unusable 9 visionary 10 idealistic, impossible, infeasible, ivory-tower, starry-eyed, unfeasible, unworkable 11 theoretical, unrealistic

imprecation 4 oath, plea, suit 5 curse 6 appeal, orison, prayer 7 cursing, cussing, malison 8 anathema, entreaty, petition, swearing 9 blasphemy, profanity

impregnable 4 safe 6 secure 7 guarded 8 defended, shielded 9 protected 10 invincible, unbeatable 11 indomitable

impregnate 3 sop 4 soak 5 imbue, souse, steep 6 charge, drench, infuse, leaven, seethe, sodden 7 pervade 8 permeate, saturate, waterlog 9 fertilize, inoculate, penetrate, percolate, transfuse 10 inseminate

impresario 5 agent, Carte, Hurok (Sol) 7 manager 9 Diaghilev (Sergei) 10 D'Oyly Carte (Richard)

impress 3 fix, get, set 4 etch, mark, move, seal, sway 5 brand, carry, drive, exert, force, grave, infix, pique, pound, print, stamp, touch 6 affect, effect, excite, hammer, strike, thrill 7 engrave, enthuse, implant, imprint, ingrain, inspire, provoke 8 inscribe 9 electrify, establish, galvanize, inculcate, influence, stimulate

impression 4 dent, dint, idea, mark, sign 5 image, print, shock, stamp, trace, track 6 hollow, impact, notion 7 conceit, concept, edition, impress, imprint, reissue, thought, vestige 8 printing, reaction

impressionable 7 plastic, sensile 8 sensible, sentient 9 sensitive 10 affectable, responsive, susceptive 11 impressible, susceptible 13 influenceable

impressionist *composer:* 5 Ravel (Maurice) 7 Debussy (Claude) *mimic:* 6 Little (Rich) *painter:* 5 Degas (Edgar), Manet (Edouard), Monet (Claude) 6 Renoir (Pierre-Auguste), Sisley (Alfred) 7 Cassatt (Mary) 8 Pissarro (Camilla); (see also **postimpressionist**)

impressive 5 grand, noble 6 august, lavish, moving, superb 7 notable 8 gorgeous, imposing, majestic, poignant, splendid, striking, touching 9 affecting, arresting, grandiose, luxurious, sumptuous

imprimatur 7 license 8 approval, sanction

imprint 4 etch, mark 5 press, stamp 7 engrave, impress 8 inscribe 10 impression

imprison 3 jug 4 cage, curb, jail 5 check, limit 6 detain, immure, intern 7 confine, enclose 8 bastille, restrain, restrict 9 constrain 11 incarcerate 12 circumscribe

impromptu 7 offhand 9 extempore, makeshift, unstudied 10 improvised 11 extemporary, unrehearsed 13 autoschediasm, improvisation

improper 5 amiss, crude, fresh, inapt, inept, outré, rough, sassy, unapt, undue, unfit, wrong 6 gauche, unmeet 7 illicit, ungodly, unhappy 8 ill-timed, indecent, informal, tactless, uncomely, unseemly, untimely, untoward 9 incorrect, unfitting 10 inaccurate, inapposite, indecorous, indelicate, malapropos, malodorous, unbecoming, undecorous, unsuitable 11 impertinent, unbefitting 12 illegitimate, inadmissible, inapplicable, infelicitous, intempestive, unseasonable 13 inappropriate, unceremonious *prefix:* 3 mis

impropriety 5 boner, break, error, gaffe 7 blooper, faux pas 8 slangism, solecism 9 barbarism, indecorum, vulgarism 10 corruption, inelegance, unmeetness 12 unseemliness, untowardness 13 incorrectness

improve 4 edit, gain, help, mend 5 amend, edify, emend, rally, rub up 6 better, enrich, illume, look up, perk up, refine, reform, remedy, revise, revive, uplift 7 advance, augment, benefit, correct, develop, enhance, enlarge, perfect, recover, rectify, upgrade 8 illumine, increase, progress 9 cultivate, enlighten, intensify, irradiate, meliorate 10 ameliorate, convalesce, illuminate, recuperate, strengthen

improvident 6 lavish 7 profuse 8 careless, heedless, prodigal, reckless, unthrift, wasteful 9 imprudent, negligent, unthrifty 10 profligate, thriftless 11 extravagant, spendthrift 12 uneconomical

improvise 5 ad-lib 6 devise, invent 7 concoct 8 contrive 11 extemporize

improvised 7 offhand 9 extempore, impromptu, unstudied 11 extemporary, unrehearsed

imprudent 4 rash 6 unwary, unwise 7 foolish 8 reckless 10 ill-advised, incautious, indiscreet 11 inadvisable, inexpedient, injudicious, unadvisable, unexpedient 12 shortsighted

impudence 4 gall 8 audacity, boldness 9 arrogance, hardihood, insolence, insolency 10 disrespect, effrontery 11 presumption 12 impertinence, insolentness

impudent 4 bold, flip, pert, wise 5 brash, fresh, lippy, nervy, sassy, saucy, smart 6 arrant, brassy, brazen, cheeky 7 blatant, forward 8 flippant, insolent, overbold

9 audacious, barefaced, shameless, unabashed 10 procacious, unblushing 11 brazenfaced, impertinent, smart-alecky 12 contumelious 13 disrespectful

impugn 4 deny 5 cross, fight 6 assail, attack, negate, oppose, resist 7 gainsay 8 negative, traverse 9 disaffirm 10 contradict, contravene

impugnable 5 fishy, shady 7 suspect 8 doubtful 9 doubtable, equivocal, uncertain 10 borderline, suspicious 11 problematic

impulse 3 ate 4 goad, lust, push, spur, urge, whim 5 drive, force 6 impact, motive, thrust, whimsy 7 impetus, passion, whimsey 8 catalyst, excitant, stimulus 9 actuation, impulsion, incentive, stimulant 10 incitation, incitement, motivation 11 instigation

impulsive 5 hasty 6 abrupt, sudden 8 headlong, will-less 9 automatic, impetuous 10 unprompted 11 instinctive, involuntary, precipitate, spontaneous, unmeditated

impure 3 raw 4 foul, lewd, vile 5 black, crude, dirty, gross, mixed, nasty, soily 6 carnal, common, filthy, grubby, native, unholy 7 bastard, defiled, immoral, lustful, obscene, scarlet, sensual, squalid, unclean 8 immodest, indecent, polluted, profaned, prurient, unchaste, ungraded, unsorted 9 run-of-mine, uncleanly, unrefined 10 desecrated, indecorous, lascivious, unhallowed 11 adulterated

impute 3 lay 4 give, hint 5 refer 6 accuse, adduce, assign, charge, credit, impart, indict 7 ascribe 8 accredit, intimate 9 attribute

inability 9 inaptness, ineptness 10 inadequacy, inaptitude, incapacity, inefficacy, ineptitude 11 inadeptness 12 incapability, incompetence, inefficiency

inaccessible 3 far 6 closed, far-off, remote 7 distant, faraway 8 abstruse, esoteric 11 out-of-the-way, ungetatable, unreachable 12 unattainable, unobtainable

in accordance with 5 as per 10 pursuant to

inaccurate 5 false, wrong 6 faulty, untrue 7 inexact, unsound 8 specious 9 defective, erroneous, incorrect

inaction 5 drift 8 idleness, lethargy 9 indolence, inertness, slackness, torpidity 10 inactivity, quiescence 12 inactiveness, slothfulness

inactive 4 dead, idle, slow 5 inert, quiet, slack, still 6 asleep, latent, sleepy, static, supine, torpid 7 abeyant, dormant, jobless, passive 8 indolent, ossified, slothful, sluggish 9 do-nothing, lethargic, lymphatic, quiescent, sedentary, unworking 10 disengaged, motionless, unemployed, unoccupied

in addition 4 also, then 5 again 7 besides, further 8 moreover 12 additionally

inadequacy 4 lack 7 deficit, failure 8 shortage, underage 9 inability 10 deficiency, incapacity, inefficacy, scantiness 11 defalcation 12 incapability, incompetence 13 insufficience, insufficiency

inadequate 3 shy 4 weak 5 scant, short 6 meager, scanty, scarce, skimpy 7 failing, lacking, scrimpy, wanting 8 boneless, impotent 9 defective, deficient, forceless, spineless 10 emasculate, incomplete, uncomplete 11 ineffective, ineffectual, slack-spined 12 insufficient

inadmissible 5 inapt, inept, unapt 8 ill-timed, improper, unseemly, unwanted 9 unwelcome 10 ill-favored, malapropos, unbecoming 11 undesirable 12 unacceptable

inadvertent 8 careless, feckless, heedless, uncaring 9 negligent, undevised, unheeding, unplanned, unrecking, unthought 10 undesigned, unintended 13 unintentional

inadvisable 4 rash 6 unwise 7 foolish 8 careless 9 foolhardy, impolitic, imprudent, pointless 10 ill-advised, incautious, indiscreet, unsensible 11 harebrained, inexpedient, undesirable, unexpedient 13 inappropriate

inalterable 5 fixed 8 constant 9 immovable, immutable, steadfast, unmovable 10 inflexible, invariable 12 unchangeable, unmodifiable

inamorata 5 flame, honey, lover, woman 6 steady 7 beloved, sweetie 8 ladylove, mistress, paramour, truelove 10 girl friend, sweetheart

inamorato 4 beau 5 flame, lover 6 steady 7 beloved 8 truelove 9 boyfriend 10 sweetheart

inane 4 flat, idle, vain 5 blank, empty, silly, vapid 6 hollow, jejune, vacant 7 asinine, fatuous, foolish, idiotic, insipid, sapless, shallow, vacuous 8 mindless, trifling 9 driveling, frivolous, innocuous, pointless, senseless

inanimate 4 cold, dead, dull, late 5 inert 6 asleep 7 defunct, extinct 8 deceased, departed, lifeless 9 exanimate, insensate, senseless, unfeeling 10 insensible, insentient

inanity 5 folly 7 vacuity 8 insanity, unwisdom, vapidity 9 absurdity, craziness, dottiness, emptiness, frivolity, silliness 10 hollowness, triviality 11 foolishness, shallowness, witlessness 13 senselessness

inappreciable 6 meager, scanty, skimpy 7 scrimpy 10 impalpable, inadequate, insensible, intangible, unapparent 12 imponderable, insufficient, unobservable

inappropriate 5 inapt, inept, undue, unfit 6 clumsy, unmeet 8 ill-timed, improper, unfitted, unseemly, unsuited, untimely 9 ill-suited 10 ill-adapted, indecorous, malapropos, unbecoming, unsuitable 11 inconsonant, unbefitting 12 unseasonable

inapt 4 flat 5 banal, undue, unfit 6 clumsy, gauche, jejune, unmeet 7 awkward, inadept, insipid, unhandy 8 ill-timed, improper, inexpert, unfacile, unfitted, unsuited, untimely 9 ill-suited, maladroit, unfitting 10 amateurish, ill-adapted, inadequate, malapropos, unskillful, unsuitable

in arrears 6 behind 10 behindhand

inarticulate 4 dumb, mute 5 tacit 6 silent, unsaid 7 blurred, halting, implied, unvocal 8 implicit, inferred, mumbling, unspoken, wordless 9 faltering, stammered, unuttered, voiceless 10 hesitating, incoherent, indistinct, maundering, speechless, stammering, tongue-tied, undeclared 11 unexpressed

inasmuch as 2 as 3 for, now 5 since 7 because, whereas 8 as long as 11 considering

inattentive 3 lax 5 bored 6 ennuyé, remiss 8 careless, distrait, heedless 9 forgetful, negligent, unheeding, unmindful 10 abstracted, distracted, distraught, unnoticing, unthinking, unwatchful 11 inobservant, thoughtless, unobservant, unobserving

inaugural 5 first 7 initial, leading 8 foremost, headmost 9 induction 10 initiation 11 investiture 12 installation

inaugurate 4 open 5 begin, enter, set up, start 6 get off, induct, invest, launch 7 install, instate, jump off, kick off, usher in 8 commence, dedicate, initiate 9 institute, introduce, originate 10 consecrate

inauspicious 3 bad 4 dire, evil 7 adverse, baleful, baneful, fateful, ominous, unlucky 8 sinister 9 ill-boding, ill-omened 11 threatening 12 unpropitious

inborn 6 inbred, innate, native 7 connate, natural 8 inherent 9 essential, ingrained, inherited, intrinsic 10 congenital, connatural, deep-seated, hereditary, indigenous, indwelling, unacquired

inbred 6 inborn, innate 7 connate 8 inherent 9 ingrained, intrinsic 10 congenital, deep-seated, indwelling

inca *beverage:* 5 chica *capital:* 5 Cusco, Cuzco *conqueror:* 7 Pizarro (Francisco) *god:* 4 Inti 9 Viracocha 10 Pachacamac *half-breed:* 5 Cholo *language:* 8 Quechuan *priest:* 3 umu *record:* 5 quipu *ruler:* 9 Atahualpa, Pachacuti *sacred object:* 5 huaca 8 apacheta *socioeconomic unit:* 5 ayllu

incalculable 4 iffy, vast 6 chancy, untold 7 erratic 8 enormous, infinite 9 boundless, countless, fluctuant, limitless, uncertain, whimsical 10 capricious, unmeasured, unnumbered 11 illimitable, inestimable, innumerable, measureless, uncountable 12 immeasurable, unmeasurable

in camera 7 sub rosa 8 covertly, secretly 9 by stealth, furtively, privately 10 stealthily 12 hugger-mugger 13 clandestinely

incandescent 3 hot 5 lucid 6 ardent, bright, lucent 7 beaming, fulgent, glowing, lambent, radiant 8 luminous 9 brilliant, effulgent, refulgent

incantation 4 rune 5 chant, charm, magic, spell 7 sorcery 8 witchery, wizardry 9 conjuring, magicking 10 necromancy, witchcraft 11 bewitchment, conjuration, enchantment *Buddhist, Hindu:* 6 mantra

incapable 5 inept, unfit 6 unable 8 inexpert, unexpert, unfitted 9 unskilled 10 ineligible, unequipped, unskillful 11 incompetent

incapacitate 6 disarm 7 cripple, disable 8 paralyze 9 disenable, prostrate 10 disqualify, immobilize

incapacity 9 inability 10 inadequacy, inefficacy 12 incapability, incompetence

incarcerate 3 jug 4 jail 6 immure, intern 7 confine, enclose 8 bastille, imprison 9 constrain

incarnadine 3 red 4 ruby 5 ruddy 6 redden, rubify, rubric, ruddle

incarnate 5 utter 6 embody 8 embodied, manifest 9 actualize, objectify, personify, personize 11 exteriorize, externalize, materialize, personalize, unspeakable 12 substantiate

incarnation 6 avatar 7 avatara 10 embodiment *Of Christ:* 7 kenosis

incautious 4 bold, rash, wild 5 brash, hasty 6 madcap, unwary 7 unalert 8 carefree, careless, feckless, heedless, reckless 9 hotheaded, impetuous, impolitic, imprudent, negligent, uncareful, unguarded, unmindful 10 ill-advised, indiscreet, madbrained, neglectful, regardless, unvigilant, unwatchful 11 injudicious, thoughtless 13 inconsiderate, irresponsible

incendiary 5 torch 7 exciter, firebug 8 agitator, arsonist 10 pyromaniac 12 inflammatory

incense 3 ire, mad, oil 4 balm, burn 5 anger, aroma, scent, spice 6 arouse, enrage, homage, incite, madden *vessel:* 6 censer 8 thurible

incentive 4 goad, spur 5 spark 6 motive 7 impetus, impulse 8 catalyst, stimulus 9 stimulant 10 incitation, incitement, inducement, motivation 11 provocation, stimulative 13 encouragement

inception 4 root, well 5 start 6 origin, source, whence 8 fountain 9 beginning 10 derivation, initiation, provenance, wellspring 11 provenience 12 commencement

inceptive 7 initial, nascent 9 beginning, incipient 10 initiative, initiatory 12 introductory

incertitude 5 doubt 6 wonder 7 concern, dubiety 8 mistrust 9 dubiosity, suspicion 10 indecision, skepticism 11 uncertainty

incessant 6 steady 7 endless, eternal 8 constant, timeless 9 ceaseless, continual, perpetual, unceasing 10 continuous 11 everlasting, unremitting 12 interminable

inchoate 7 muddled 8 formless, unformed, unshaped 9 amorphous, expectant, incipient, potential, shapeless 10 contingent, disjointed, disordered, incoherent, incohesive, incomplete 11 imperfected, unconnected, unorganized 12 disconnected, uncontinuous 13 discontinuous

incident 4 akin 5 event 6 agnate, allied 7 cognate, connate, episode, kindred, related 8 accident, external, occasion 9 ancillary, attendant, attending, happening, satellite 10 affiliated, collateral, connatural, occurrence 11 concomitant, consanguine 12 accompanying, circumstance

incidental 3 odd 5 fluky 6 casual, chance 8 episodic 9 accessory 10 accidental, contingent, digressive, fortuitous 11 subordinate 12 nonessential

incidentally 6 obiter 8 by the bye, by the way, casually 9 in passing 12 accidentally, fortuitously

incipient 7 initial, nascent 8 inchoate 9 beginning, inceptive 10 commencing, initiative, initiatory 12 introductory

incise 3 cut 4 etch, gash, kerf, slit 5 grave, slash, slice 6 pierce 7 engrave

incisive 4 keen, tart 5 acerb, acute, crisp, sharp, terse 6 biting 7 acerbic, caustic, concise, cutting, ingoing, laconic, mordant 8 clear-cut, drilling, piercing, scathing, slashing, succinct 9 sarcastic, trenchant 11 penetrating

incite 3 egg, set 4 abet, goad, prod, spur, urge 5 raise, rouse, set on 6 arouse, compel, excite, exhort, foment, motive, set off, stir up, whip up 7 actuate, agitate, forward, further, inflame, promote, provoke, solicit, trigger 8 motivate 9 encourage, instigate, stimulate

incitement see **incentive**

inclement 3 raw 4 hard 5 harsh, rough 6 bitter, brutal, rugged, severe, stormy 8 rigorous 10 unmerciful 11 intemperate

inclination 3 bow, nod 4 bent, bias, lean, love, mind, tilt, will 5 fancy, grade, slant, slope, taste 6 ascent, desire, liking 7 descent, incline, leaning 8 affinity, appetite, fondness, gradient, penchant, pleasure, soft spot, tendency, velleity, weakness 9 affection 10 attachment, proclivity, propensity 11 disposition 12 predilection *rate of:* 8 gradient

incline 3 aim, lay, tip 4 bend, bias, cant, cast, hade, heel, lean, list, look, move, sway, tend, tilt, turn 5 drive, grade, impel, level, point, slant, slide, slope, train 6 affect, direct, induce, prompt, zero in 7 address, deflect, dispose, leaning 8 gradient, persuade 9 influence, prejudice *combining form:* 4 clin 5 clino

inclined 3 apt 4 fain, wont 5 given, prone, raked, ready 6 biased, graded, liable, likely, minded, sloped, tilted, tipped 7 dipping, leaning, oblique, pitched, sloping, tilting, willing 8 diagonal, disposed, pitching 9 declivate 11 declivitous, predisposed *way:* 4 ramp

include 4 have, hold 5 admit, bound, cover 6 embody, enfold, number, take in 7 confine, contain, embrace, enclose, involve, receive, subsume 8 comprise, encircle 9 encompass 10 comprehend

inclusive 6 global 7 general, overall 8 sweeping 9 all-around, enclosing 12 encompassing, encyclopedic 13 comprehensive

incognizant 7 unaware 8 ignorant 9 oblivious, unknowing, unwitting 10 unfamiliar, uninformed 12 inconversant, unacquainted, uninstructed

incoherent 5 loose 6 broken, raving 7 muddled 8 inchoate 9 illogical 10 discordant, disjointed, disordered, incohesive, maundering, tongue-tied 11 incongruous, inconsonant, nonadhesive, unconnected, unorganized 12 disconnected, inarticulate, incompatible, inconsequent, inconsistent, inharmonious, uncontinuous 13 discontinuous

incombustible 7 apyrous 12 nonflammable

income 4 gain, take 6 profit, return 7 annuity, comings, produce, revenue 8 interest, proceeds, receipts 9 emolument

incommode 3 irk, vex 5 annoy, block 6 bother, hinder, impede, molest, plague, put out 7 disturb, trouble 8 disquiet, obstruct, put about 9 disoblige 13 inconvenience

incommodious 5 cramp 7 awkward, cramped, squeezy 8 confined 12 discommoding, embarrassing, inconvenient

incommunicable 8 reserved, taciturn 9 ineffable, withdrawn 10 restrained, untellable 11 constrained, indefinable, inenarrable, unspeakable, unutterable 12 noncommittal 13 indescribable, inexpressible, undescribable, unexpressible

incomparable 7 supreme **8** peerless, towering, ultimate **9** matchless **10** preeminent, surpassing **11** unequalable, unmatchable **12** transcendent **13** unsurpassable

incompatible 7 adverse, counter **8** contrary, opposite **9** antipodal, dissonant, unmixable **10** antipodean, discordant, discrepant **11** conflicting, disagreeing, incongruent, incongruous, inconsonant, unadaptable **12** antagonistic, antipathetic, antithetical, disconsonant, inconsistent, inharmonious **13** contradictory, inconformable, unconformable, unsympathetic

incompetence 9 inability, unfitness **10** disability, inadequacy, incapacity, inefficacy **12** incapability **13** insufficiency

incompetent 5 inept, unfit **8** helpless, inexpert, unexpert, unfitted **9** incapable, unskilled **10** ineligible, unequipped, unskillful **11** inefficient, unqualified **12** disqualified, insufficient *legally:* **12** inadmissible

incomplete 4 part **5** bitty, short **6** broken **7** lacking, partial, scrappy, sketchy, wanting **8** immature **9** composite, defective, deficient **10** fractional, inadequate, incoherent, uncomplete, unfinished **11** fragmentary, imperfected **12** insufficient

incompliant 5 rigid, stiff **6** mulish **8** perverse, stubborn **9** impliable, obstinate, pigheaded, resistant, unbending **10** bullheaded, headstrong, inflexible, self-willed, unflexible, unyielding **11** immalleable, intractable **12** pertinacious

incomprehensible 7 cryptic, obscure, unclear **8** abstruse **9** enigmatic **10** fathomless, mysterious, mystifying, unknowable, unreadable **11** inscrutable, ungraspable **12** impenetrable, incognizable, unfathomable, unimaginable, unsearchable **13** imperceptible, inconceivable

inconceivable 4 thin, weak **6** flimsy **10** improbable, incredible, unknowable **11** implausible, incogitable, unthinkable **12** insupposable, unbelievable, unconvincing, unimaginable

in conclusion 6 lastly **7** finally

inconclusive 4 open **9** uncertain, undecided, unsettled **10** incomplete, indecisive, indefinite, unfinished **11** ineffective

incongruous 5 alien **6** absurd **7** bizarre, foreign **9** dissonant, fantastic, grotesque, unmixable **10** discordant, discrepant, extraneous **11** conflicting, inconsonant **12** disconsonant, incompatible, inconsistent, inharmonious

inconscient 4 lost **6** absent **7** bemused, faraway **8** distrait, mindless **10** abstracted **11** preoccupied **12** absentminded

inconsequential 5 petty, small **6** measly, paltry **7** trivial **8** picayune, trifling **10** irrelevant, picayunish

inconsiderable 4 puny **5** light, minor, petty, small **6** casual, little, meager, paltry, peanut, scanty, skimpy **7** scrimpy, trivial **8** picayune, trifling **9** small-beer **10** inadequate, negligible, shoestring **11** unimportant **12** inconsequent, insufficient, unconsidered **13** inappreciable, insignificant

inconsiderate 4 rash **5** brash, hasty, sharp, short **6** madcap, unkind **8** careless, heedless, reckless **9** hotheaded **10** illadvised, incautious, ungracious **11** precipitate, thoughtless

inconsistent 6 fickle **8** ticklish, unstable **9** dissonant, mercurial, uncertain, unmixable **10** capricious, changeable, discordant, discrepant, inconstant, lubricious **11** conflicting, incongruent, incongruous, inconsonant **12** disconsonant, incompatible, inharmonious **13** contradictory, inconformable

inconsolable 7 forlorn **8** dejected, desolate **9** heartsick **11** comfortless, heartbroken **12** disconsolate

inconspicuous 5 vague **7** obscure **10** indistinct, unemphatic **11** unobtrusive **12** unnoticeable

inconstant 5 false, light **6** fickle, shifty, untrue **7** elusive, erratic, mutable, protean, vagrant, variant, wayward **8** disloyal, slippery, ticklish, unstable, unsteady, variable, volatile, wavering **9** changeful, faithless, frivolous, mercurial, uncertain, unsettled **10** capricious, changeable, irresolute, lubricious, perfidious, traitorous, unreliable **11** chameleonic, light-minded, treacherous, vacillating **12** inconsistent, shilly-shally, undependable **13** temperamental

incontestable 4 sure **7** certain **8** positive **9** undoubted **10** undeniable **11** indubitable, irrefutable, unequivocal **12** indisputable

incontinent 4 fast, lewd **7** lustful, satyric **9** lecherous, libertine, salacious **10** lascivious, libidinous, licentious **12** unrestrained

incontrovertible 4 sure **7** certain **8** positive **10** inarguable, undeniable **11** indubitable, unequivocal **12** indisputable, undisputable **13** incontestable, uncontestable

inconvenience 3 try **4** fuss, stew **5** annoy, trial **6** bother, meddle, pother, put out **7** disturb, trouble **8** handicap, put about **9** aggravate, annoyance, disoblige, incommode, interfere **10** discomfort, discommode, discompose, exasperate **11** aggravation, awkwardness, intermeddle **12** disadvantage, discomfiture, exasperation **13** embarrassment

inconvenient 7 awkward, unhandy **8** annoying **10** bothersome, unsuitable **11** detrimental, inexpedient, inopportune, pestiferous, prejudicial, troublesome **12** discommoding, embarrassing, incommodious, unreasonable **13** discommodious

incorporate 3 mix 4 fuse, join 5 blend, merge, unite 6 absorb, embody, imbibe, insorb, mingle 7 combine, inhaust 9 integrate 10 assimilate

incorporeal 4 airy 8 bodiless 9 asomatous, spiritual 10 discarnate, immaterial, unembodied, unphysical 11 disembodied, nonmaterial, nonphysical 12 metaphysical 13 unsubstantial

incorrect 5 false, wrong 6 faulty, untrue 7 unsound 8 improper, specious 9 erroneous, imprecise 10 inaccurate, unbecoming *combining form:* 3 cac 4 caco *prefix:* 3 mis

increase 2 up 3 add, rev, wax 4 gain, grow, hike, jump, plus, push, rise, soup, teem 5 boost, build, mount, put up, raise, run up, swarm, swell 6 accrue, amount, beef up, dilate, expand, extend, gather, growth, jack up, markup 7 advance, amplify, augment, burgeon, distend, enhance, enlarge, inflate, magnify, prolong, pyramid, upgrade, upsurge 8 addition, compound, elongate, escalate, flourish, heighten, lengthen, manifold, multiply, protract, snowball 9 accession, accretion, aggravate, expansion, extension, increment, intensify, pullulate, reinforce 10 accelerate, accumulate, aggrandize, appreciate, strengthen 11 enlargement 12 augmentation, breakthrough 13 amplification *Scottish:* 3 eke *suddenly:* 4 zoom

increasing 8 crescent, crescive

incredible 4 thin, weak 5 thick 6 absurd, flimsy 8 unlikely 9 cockamamy, untenable 10 cockamamie, impossible, improbable, outlandish, ridiculous 11 implausible, incogitable, unthinkable 12 insupposable, preposterous, unbelievable, unconvincing, unimaginable 13 inconceivable

incredulity 7 unfaith 8 unbelief 9 disbelief

incredulous 4 wary 6 show-me 7 dubious 8 aporetic, doubting, hesitant 9 faithless, quizzical, skeptical, uncertain 10 suspicious 11 distrustful, distrusting, mistrustful, questioning, unbelieving, unconvinced, unsatisfied 12 disbelieving

increment 4 gain, rise 5 raise 6 growth 8 addition, increase 9 accession, accretion 11 enlargement 12 augmentation

incriminate 6 accuse, charge, indict 7 arraign, impeach, involve 9 implicate, inculpate

incrustation 4 rime, scab 5 scale 6 plaque, tartar

incubus 4 onus 5 demon 6 burden 9 nightmare 10 evil spirit

inculcate 5 infix, teach 6 impart, infuse 7 educate, implant, impress, instill 8 instruct 10 inseminate 11 communicate

inculpable 4 good, pure 5 clean 8 innocent, unguilty, virtuous 9 blameless, crimeless, exemplary, faultless, guiltless, righteous

incumbent 7 binding, leaning 8 occupant 9 overlying 12 superimposed

incur 3 get 6 induce 7 acquire, bring on 8 contract 9 encounter

incurable 8 cureless, hopeless 9 insanable 10 impossible 11 immedicable, irreparable 12 irremediable 13 irretrievable, uncorrectable, unrecoverable

incursion 4 raid 5 foray 6 attack, inroad 7 assault 8 invasion 9 irruption

incus 4 bone 5 anvil

indebted 7 obliged 8 beholden 9 dutybound, obligated 10 honor-bound

indebtedness 3 due 4 debt 7 arrears, failure 8 beholden 9 arrearage, liability 10 bankruptcy, insolvency, nonpayment, obligation 11 delinquency

indecent 4 foul, racy 5 dirty, gross, nasty 6 coarse, filthy, impure, risqué, smutty, vulgar 7 immoral, obscene, raunchy, ungodly 8 immodest, improper, off-color, unseemly, untoward 10 indecorous, indelicate, malodorous, ridiculous, scurrilous, unbecoming, undecorous 12 scatological

indecision 5 doubt 8 to-and-fro, wavering 9 hesitancy 10 hesitation 11 uncertainty, vacillation 12 irresolution, shilly-shally

indecisive 4 open 5 shaky, vague 7 dubious, halting, unclear, unfixed 8 doubtful, hesitant, wavering 9 equivocal, faltering, tentative, uncertain, undecided, unsettled 10 borderline, hesitating, indistinct, irresolute 11 problematic, vacillating

indecorous 4 rude 5 gross, loose, rough, unfit 6 coarse, vulgar 7 uncivil, ungodly 8 immodest, impolite, improper, indecent, shameful, unlawful, unseemly, untoward 9 incorrect, inelegant, irregular, offensive, tasteless, unfitting 10 indelicate, malodorous, ridiculous, unbecoming 11 ill-mannered, unbefitting, undignified 12 discourteous 13 inappropriate

indecorum 5 boner, break, gaffe 7 blooper, faux pas 8 solecism 10 inelegance, unmeetness 11 impropriety

indeed 3 nay, yea 4 even, well 5 truly 6 easily, really, verily 7 in truth 8 forsooth, honestly 9 assuredly, certainly 10 admittedly, positively, undeniably 11 doubtlessly, undoubtedly

indefatigable 6 dogged 7 patient 8 diligent, sedulous, stubborn, tireless, untiring, vigorous 9 assiduous, energetic, steadfast, strenuous, tenacious, weariless 10 determined, persistent, relentless, unflagging, unwavering, unwearying 11 painstaking, persevering, unfaltering, unflinching, unrelenting, unwearable 13 inexhaustible

indefensible 9 untenable 10 inexpiable 11 inexcusable 12 unforgivable, unpardonable 13 unjustifiable

indefinable 5 vague 9 ineffable, uncertain 10 untellable 11 inenarrable, unspeakable, unutterable 13 indescribable, indeterminate, inexpressible, undescribable, unexpressible

indefinite 4 wide 5 broad, loose, vague 7 endless, general, inexact, obscure, unclear, unfixed 8 infinite 9 ambiguous, boundless, imprecise, limitless, unbounded, uncertain, undefined, unlimited 10 indistinct, inexplicit, unmeasured, unspecific 11 measureless 12 immeasurable, inconclusive 13 indeterminate *article:* 2 an *pronoun:* 3 all, any, few 4 each, many, most, none, some 6 anyone, nobody 7 anybody, several, someone 8 everyone, somebody 9 everybody

indehiscent fruit 3 nut 4 pepo 5 akene, berry, grain, grape, melon 6 achene, loment, samara, squash 7 pumpkin 8 cucumber 9 caryopsis 10 schizocarp

indelible 4 fast 5 fixed 7 lasting 8 enduring 9 permanent 10 inerasable, unerasable 12 ineffaceable, ineradicable, inexpungible, inextirpable, uneradicable 13 undestroyable

indelicate 3 raw 4 lewd, rude 5 crude, gross, rough 6 callow, coarse, wanton 7 uncouth, ungodly 8 impolite, improper, indecent, tactless, unseemly, untoward 9 unrefined 10 indecorous, malodorous, unbecoming

indemnify 3 pay 5 repay 7 requite 9 reimburse 10 compensate, recompense, remunerate

indemnity 6 amends 7 amnesty, redress 8 reprisal, security 9 exemption, quittance 10 protection, recompense, reparation 11 restitution 12 compensation

indentation 3 bay 4 dent, nick 5 notch, print, stamp 6 recess 7 impress, imprint

indenture 4 nick 5 notch 11 indentation

indentured 5 bound 8 articled 11 apprenticed

independent 4 free 6 closed 8 autarkic, separate 9 autarchic, sovereign 10 autonomous 11 self-reliant 12 self-centered 13 self-contained, self-sufficing, self-supported, self-sustained *combining form:* 4 self

indescribable 9 ineffable 10 untellable 11 indefinable, inenarrable, unspeakable, unutterable 13 inexpressible, unexpressible

indestructible 7 durable, lasting, undying 8 enduring, immortal 9 deathless, immutable, indelible, permanent, perpetual

10 changeless, inviolable, quenchless 11 unalterable 12 imperishable, ineradicable, inextirpable, irrefragable, unchangeable, unperishable, unquenchable 13 incorruptible, irrefrangible, undestroyable

indeterminate 5 vague 7 inexact, unfixed 9 uncertain, unlimited 10 indefinite, indistinct

index 4 list, mark, sign 5 table, token 7 catalog, indices (plural), indicia, symptom 8 evidence 9 catalogue

India *bread:* 7 chapati 8 chapatti *butter:* 3 ghi 4 ghee *capital:* 8 New Delhi *caste:* 5 Sudra 6 Vaisya 7 Brahman 9 Kshatriya *female dancer:* 8 bayadere *groom:* 4 syce *harem:* 6 zenana *lady:* 4 bibi 5 begum 8 mem-sahib *language:* 4 Urdu 5 Hindu, Tamil 6 Telugu 7 Bengali, Kannada, Marathi, Punjabi 8 Assamese, Gujarati, Kashmiri 9 Malayalam 10 Hindustani, Rajasthani *largest city:* 6 Bombay *monetary unit:* 5 rupee *nurse:* 4 amah, ayah *official:* 5 dewan, diwan *outcast:* 6 pariah *prime minister:* 5 Nehru (Jawaharlal) 6 Gandhi (Indira, Rajiv) *prince:* 4 raja, rana 5 rajah 8 maharaja 9 maharajah *princess:* 4 rani 5 begum, ranee *scholar:* 6 pandit, pundit *servant:* 4 maty *screen:* 6 purdah *seal, stamp:* 4 chop *soldier:* 4 peon 5 sepoy *teacher:* 4 guru *viceroy:* 5 nabob, nawab *weight unit:* 3 ser 4 cash, dhan, pank, pice, powe, rati, tank, tola 5 adpao, fanam, hubba, masha, maund, pally, pouah, ratti 6 dhurra, pagoda, pollam 7 chinnam, chittak

Indian, American *baby:* 7 papoose *ball game:* 8 lacrosse *carrier:* 7 travois *Central and South American:* 2 Ge 3 Ona 4 Cuna, Inca, Maya 5 Arara, Aztec, Carib, Huave, Olmec, Yagua 6 Arawak, Aymara, Jivaro, Omagua, Toltec, Yahgan 7 Chibcha, Quechua, Zapotec 8 Tarascan 10 Araucanian 11 Tupi-Guarani *colonists' greeting to Indian friend:* 5 netop *drink:* 6 chicha *food:* 4 samp 5 maize 8 pemmican *game:* 6 chunky 7 chunkey *home:* 5 hogan, lodge, tepee 6 pueblo, teepee, wigwam 7 wickiup *leader:* 4 Popé 6 Wovoka 7 Cochise, Osceola, Pontiac, Sequoya 8 Geronimo, Hiawatha, Powhatan, Tecumseh 9 Massasoit 10 Crazy Horse 11 Cornplanter, Sitting Bull *money:* 5 sewan 6 wampum *North American:* 3 Oto, Sac, Ute 4 Cree, Crow, Hopi, Hupa, Iowa, Otoe, Pima, Pomo, Sauk, Taos, Yuma 5 Aleut, Caddo, Creek, Haida, Huron, Kansa, Kiowa, Maidu, Miami, Modoc, Omaha, Osage, Sioux 6 Apache, Cayuga, Dakota, Lenape, Mandan, Micmac, Mohawk, Munsee, Navaho, Navajo, Nootka, Ojibwa, Oneida, Paiute, Pawnee,

Pueblo, Quapaw, Seneca, Siwash **7** Arapaho, Arikara, Bannock, Chilkat, Chinook, Choctaw, Dakotah, Esselen, Klamath, Kutenai, Mohican, Naskapi, Natchez, Ojibway, Pontiac, Shawnee, Tlingit **8** Cherokee, Cheyenne, Chippewa, Comanche, Delaware, Illinois, Iroquois, Kickapoo, Kwakiutl, Nez Percé, Onondaga, Powhatan, Seminole, Shoshoni **9** Blackfoot, Chickasaw, Menominee, Tsimshian, Tuscarora, Wampanoag, Winnebago `10` Assiniboin, Chiricahua, Gros Ventre, Potawatomi **11** Massachuset, Narraganset *pipe:* **7** calumet *spirit:* **5** totem **7** kachina

Indiana *college, university:* **6** De Pauw, Marion, Purdue **9** Ball State, Notre Dame *nickname:* **12** Hoosier State *state bird:* **8** cardinal *state flower:* **5** peony

indicate 3 say **4** bode, hint, mark, mean, read, show **5** argue, augur, imply, point, prove **6** attest, denote, evince, import, record, reveal **7** bespeak, betoken, connote, display, exhibit, express, presage, signify, suggest, testify, witness **8** announce, disclose, evidence, intimate, manifest, register **9** designate **10** illustrate **11** demonstrate

indication 3 cue **4** clue, hint, mark, omen, sign, type, wind **5** index, proof, token, trace **6** notion, signal, symbol **7** gesture, indicia, inkling, reading, symptom **8** evidence, reminder, telltale **9** testimony **10** expression, intimation, suggestion **11** significant **13** manifestation, prefiguration

indicative 8 denotive, evincive, indicial, symbolic **9** testatory **10** denotative, evidential, exhibitive, expressive, suggestive **11** designative, symptomatic **13** demonstrative

indicia 4 fact, mark, sign **5** index, token **7** symptom **8** evidence **9** criterion

indict 6 accuse, charge **7** arraign, impeach **9** criminate, inculpate **11** incriminate

indifference 6 apathy **8** lethargy **9** aloofness, disregard, lassitude, unconcern **10** negligence **11** disinterest, insouciance **12** carelessness, heedlessness **13** unmindfulness

indifferent 3 icy **4** cold, cool, fair, mean, numb, so-so **5** aloof, blasé, chill, equal, stoic **6** casual, frigid, medium, remote **7** average, fairish, glacial, neutral, off-hand, unmoved **8** by-the-way, careless, detached, heedless, inferior, listless, mediocre, middling, moderate, passable, unbiased, uncaring **9** apathetic, equitable, impartial, impassive, incurious, negligent, objective, uncurious, unmindful, withdrawn **10** impersonal, insensible, nonchalant, regardless, unaffected, unsociable **11** unconcerned, unemotional, unobserving

12 unimpressive, uninterested, unprejudiced **13** disinterested, dispassionate

indigence 4 lack, need, want **6** penury **7** poverty **9** neediness, privation **11** destitution

indigenous 6 inborn, innate, native **7** connote, endemic, natural **8** inherent **9** inherited **10** aboriginal, congenital, connatural, unacquired **13** autochthonous

indigent 4 poor **5** needy **6** beggar, pauper **8** dirt poor **9** destitute, penniless, penurious **11** impecunious, necessitous **12** impoverished

indigestion 9 dyspepsia

indignant 3 mad **5** angry, irate, wroth **6** heated, wrathy, wrothy **7** annoyed **8** incensed, wrathful, wrothful **9** irritated, resentful

indignation 3 ire, mad **4** fury, rage **5** anger, wrath **10** resentment

indignity 3 cut **4** slap **5** wrong **6** injury, insult, slight **7** affront, despite, outrage **9** contumely, grievance, injustice **13** disparagement

indigo 4 anil, blue

indigo bird 5 finch **7** bunting

indigo plant 4 anil

Indira Gandhi's father 5 Nehru

indirect 6 errant, shifty, sneaky **7** crooked, devious, oblique, sinuous, vagrant, winding **8** circular, guileful, sneaking, tortuous, twisting **9** deceitful, dishonest, underhand, wandering **10** circuitous, collateral, meandering, roundabout, serpentine **11** duplicitous, underhanded

indiscreet 6 unwary, unwise **9** ill-judged, impolitic, imprudent, untactful **10** ill-advised, incautious **11** injudicious **13** inconsiderate

indiscretion 4 slip **5** folly **9** incaution **10** imprudence, unwariness

indiscriminate 4 spot, wide **5** broad, mixed **6** motley, random, varied **7** aimless, jumbled, mingled, shallow **8** assorted, chowchow, confused, sweeping **9** desultory, extensive, haphazard, hit-or-miss, unplanned, wholesale **10** designless, uncritical **11** promiscuous, purposeless, superficial **12** conglomerate, multifarious, unconsidered

indispensable 5 basic, vital **6** needed **7** exigent, needful **8** cardinal **9** essential, necessary, requisite **10** imperative **11** fundamental

indisposed 3 ill, low **4** mean, sick **5** loath **6** afraid, ailing, averse, offish, poorly, sickly, unwell **7** hostile, underly, uneager **8** backward, hesitant, inimical, off-color **9** reluctant, unwilling, unwishful **11** disinclined

indisposition 6 malady **7** ailment, dislike, illness, malaise **8** aversion, bad books, dis-

favor, disorder, distaste, sickness, unhealth
9 disliking, disrelish, infirmity 10 affliction,
reluctance 11 displeasure

indisputable 4 real, sure, true 6 actual
7 certain, evident 8 positive, unfabled
9 veridical 10 undeniable 11 indubitable,
irrefutable, unequivocal 12 irrefragable
13 incontestable, uncontestable

indistinct 3 dim 4 hazy 5 faint, misty,
vague 6 bleary, cloudy 7 blurred, inexact,
obscure, shadowy, unclear 8 confused
9 uncertain, undefined 10 ill-defined, indefinite 12 undetermined 13 indeterminate

indistinguishable 4 same 5 equal
7 identic 9 duplicate, identical 10 equivalent, tantamount

indite 3 pen 5 write 6 scribe 7 compose,
engross 8 inscribe

individual 3 one 4 body, lone, self, sole,
soul, unit 5 being, human, party, stuff, thing
6 entity, matter, mortal, object, person,
proper, single 7 several, special 8 creature, especial, existent, material, peculiar,
personal, separate, singular, solitary, specific 9 diacritic, existence, personage,
something, substance 10 diagnostic, individual, particular, respective 11 distinctive
13 idiosyncratic *combining form:* 4 idio

individualist 10 egocentric

individuality 4 self 5 seity, unity
6 makeup, nature, temper 7 ipseity, oneness, selfdom 8 identity, selfhood, selfness
9 character 10 complexion, difference, singleness, uniqueness, unlikeness 11 disposition, personality, singularity, temperament
12 independence, separateness, singularness

individualize 4 mark 7 qualify, specify
9 signalize 11 distinguish, singularize
12 characterize 13 particularize

Indochina country 4 Laos 5 Burma
7 Vietnam 8 Cambodia, Thailand

indoctrinate 5 teach, tutor 7 educate
8 instruct

indolence 4 laze 5 sloth 6 slouch 7 inertia, languor 8 idleness, laziness 10 inactivity 12 slothfulness, sluggishness

indolent 4 idle, lazy 5 drony 7 work-shy
8 fainéant, inactive, slothful, sluggish
9 easygoing, slowgoing

indomitable 4 wild 6 dogged, unruly
7 staunch 8 indocile, resolute, stubborn
9 fractious, steadfast 10 impassable, invincible, unbeatable 11 impregnable, insuperable, intractable 12 inexpugnable, invulnerable, pertinacious, recalcitrant, unassailable,
undefeatable, ungovernable, unmanageable 13 unconquerable, undisciplined

Indonesia *capital:* 7 Jakarta 8 Djakarta
monetary unit: 6 rupiah *president:*
7 Suharto

indubitable 4 flat, real, sure, true
7 assured, certain, evident, genuine 8 bona
fide, positive 9 authentic, downright,
undoubted, up-and-down, veritable 10 inarguable, sure-enough, undeniable 11 irrefutable 12 indisputable, irrefragable
13 incontestable, uncontestable

induce 3 get 4 abet, draw, lead, move,
sway, urge 5 breed, cause, get up, hatch,
impel, infer, tempt 6 arouse, draw in, draw
on, effect, elicit, incite, prompt, work up
7 actuate, inspire, procure, produce, win
over 8 activate, conclude, convince, engender, generate, motivate, muster up, occasion, oversway, persuade, talk into 9 argue
into, encourage, influence, prevail on

inducement 4 bait, lure 6 motive 9 incen-
tivo 10 enticement 13 consideration

induct 4 lead 6 enroll, invest 7 conduct,
install, instate 8 initiate 9 introduce

inductance unit 5 henry 6 henrys (plural) 7 henries (plural)

induction 8 entrance 9 accession, inaugural, inference 10 initiation 11 investiture
12 inauguration, installation, introduction

inductive 8 Baconian, epagogic 9 inducible, prefatial, prefatory, preludial, prelusive
11 a posteriori, prefatorial, preliminary, preparative, preparatory 12 introductory

indulge 3 pet 4 baby, bask, roll 5 favor,
humor, revel, spoil 6 cocker, coddle, cosset, oblige, pamper, please, regale, wallow,
welter 7 cater to, delight, gratify, rollick, satisfy 9 luxuriate 11 mollycoddle

indulgence 5 favor 6 liking, luxury 7 service 8 clemency, courtesy, fondness, kindness, lenience, leniency, mildness 9 benignity, tolerance 10 benignancy, benignness,
gentleness, kindliness, toleration 11 forbearance 12 dispensation, mercifulness
13 gratification

indulgence seller 5 Tezel (Johann)
6 Tetzel (Johann)

indulgent 4 easy, kind, mild 6 benign,
kindly 7 clement, lenient 8 excusing, merciful, tolerant 9 benignant, compliant, condoning, cosseting, forgiving, pampering, pardoning 10 charitable, forbearing,
permissive

indurate 3 dry, set 4 cake 5 inure
6 harden 7 confirm, congeal 8 concrete,
hardened, solidify, stubborn 9 unfeeling

industrialist 6 tycoon 7 magnate

industrious 4 busy, live 6 active
7 dynamic, operose, zealous 8 diligent, sedulous 9 assiduous

industry 4 work 5 labor, trade 7 traffic
8 business, commerce 9 diligence

inebriant 5 booze, drink 6 liquor 7 alcohol, spirits 9 aqua vitae 10 intoxicant

inebriate 3 sot 4 lush, soak 5 drunk, toper 6 bibber, boozer 7 tippler, tosspot 8 drunkard

inebriated 5 drunk, tight, tipsy 7 muddled 9 disguised, pixilated 11 intoxicated

inedible 7 baneful, insipid, noxious 9 poisonous, uneatable 10 inesculent 11 unwholesome 12 indigestible, unappetizing

ineffable 4 holy 5 ideal, taboo 6 divine, sacred 8 abstract, empyreal, empyrean, ethereal, heavenly 9 celestial, spiritual 10 untellable 11 indefinable, inenarrable, unspeakable, unutterable 12 transcendent 13 indescribable, inexpressible, undescribable, unexpressible

ineffaceable 9 indelible 10 inerasable, unerasable 12 ineradicable, inexpungible, inextirpable, uneradicable

ineffective 4 vain, weak 6 futile 7 useless 8 abortive, boneless, bootless, impotent, inferior 9 forceless, fruitless, incapable, spineless, worthless 10 emasculate, inadequate, unavailing 11 incompetent, ineffectual, inefficient, slack-spined, unavailable 12 invertebrate, unproductive 13 inefficacious

ineffectiveness 9 inability 10 inadequacy, incapacity, inefficacy 12 incapability, incompetence

ineffectual see **ineffective**

ineffectualness see **ineffectiveness**

inefficacious see **ineffective**

inefficacy see **ineffectiveness**

inefficient 5 inept 8 careless, inexpert, slipshod, slovenly, unexpert, unfitted 9 incapable, unskilled, untrained 10 unprepared, unskillful 11 incompetent, ineffective, ineffectual, unqualified 12 insufficient 13 inefficacious, unworkmanlike

inelaborate 5 plain 6 modest, simple 11 undecorated, ungarnished 12 unbeautified 13 unembellished, unembroidered, unpretentious

inelastic 5 rigid, stiff 9 impliable, unbending 10 inflexible, unflexible, unyielding 11 immalleable, incompliant

inelegant 3 raw 4 rude 5 crass, crude, gross, rough 6 coarse, vulgar 7 awkward, uncouth 9 graceless, unrefined

ineligible 5 unfit 8 unfitted, unworthy 9 incapable 10 unequipped 11 incompetent, unqualified 12 disqualified

ineluctable 4 sure 5 fated 6 doomed 7 certain 9 necessary 10 ineludible, inevasible, inevitable, returnless, unevadable 11 ineluctable, inescapable, unavoidable, unescapable

ineludible 7 certain 9 necessary 10 inevasible, inevitable, returnless, unevadable 11 ineluctable, unavoidable, unescapable

inept 4 dull 5 inapt, unapt, undue, unfit 6 clumsy, gauche, wooden 7 awkward, foolish, halting, inadept, unhandy, unhappy 8 bumbling, bungling, ill-timed, improper, inexpert, unexpert, unfacile, unseemly 9 graceless, ham-handed, ill-chosen, incapable, lumbering, maladroit, unskilled 10 inadequate, malapropos, unskillful, unsuitable 11 incompetent, inefficient, undexterous, unfortunate

inequality 8 asperity, imparity, rugosity 9 disparity, roughness 10 cragginess, jaggedness, ruggedness, unevenness 12 irregularity, variableness 13 disproportion

inequitable 3 bad 5 undue, wrong 6 unfair, unjust 8 wrongful 9 arbitrary, inequable, unmerited 10 high-handed, oppressive, undeserved 11 unequitable, unrighteous

inequity 5 wrong 9 injustice 10 unfairness, unjustness

inerasable 9 indelible 12 ineffaceable, ineradicable, inexpungible, inextirpable, uneradicable

inert 4 dead, idle 5 quiet, still 6 asleep, sleepy, stolid 7 neutral, passive 8 immobile, impotent, inactive, indolent, lifeless, sluggish 9 apathetic, impassive, inanimate, lethargic, powerless 10 motionless, phlegmatic

inert gas 4 neon 5 argon, radon, xenon 6 helium 7 krypton 8 nitrogen, noble gas 13 carbon dioxide *suffix:* 2 on

inescapable see **inevitable**

inescapably see **inevitably**

inesculent 8 inedible 9 uneatable

in essence 6 au fond 7 morally 9 basically, virtually 11 essentially, practically 13 fundamentally

inessential see **unessential**

inestimable 6 costly 8 precious, valuable 9 priceless 10 invaluable, unmeasured 11 measureless, uncountable 12 immeasurable, incalculable, unmeasurable, unreckonable

inevitable 4 sure 5 fated 7 certain, decided, settled 8 destined 9 necessary 10 ineludible, inevasible, inexorable, inflexible, returnless, unevadable 11 ineluctable, inescapable, unavoidable, unescapable 12 foreordained, ineliminable 13 unpreventable

inevitably 8 perforce 10 helplessly, willynilly 11 inescapably, unavoidably, whether or no

inexcusable 8 blamable 9 untenable 10 censurable, inexpiable 11 blameworthy, intolerable, unallowable 12 criticizable, indefensible, unforgivable, unpardonable

13 impermissible, reprehensible, unjustifiable

inexhaustible 8 tireless, untiring 9 unfailing, wearless 10 unflagging, unwearying 11 unweariable 13 indefatigable

in existence 6 extant

inexorable 5 rigid 6 dogged, strict 7 adamant 8 immobile, obdurate, resolute 9 immovable, unbending 10 inflexible, relentless, unyielding 11 unrelenting 12 single-minded

inexpensive 3 low 5 cheap 6 frugal, undear 7 low-cost, popular 8 uncostly 9 low-priced 10 reasonable

inexperience 7 naiveté, rawness 8 verdancy 9 freshness, greenness, ignorance 10 callowness 13 unfamiliarity

inexperienced 3 row 5 fresh, green, inept, naive, young 6 callow 7 untried 8 ignorant, immature, inexpert, prentice, unversed 9 incapable, unskilled, untrained 10 amateurish, unfamiliar, unseasoned 11 unpracticed 12 unacquainted, unconversant

inexpert see **inexperienced**

inexplicable 3 odd 7 strange, uncanny 8 peculiar 9 ambiguous, enigmatic 10 mysterious, unsolvable 11 inscrutable, undefinable 12 unfathomable 13 indescribable, inexplainable, unaccountable, unexplainable

inexpressible 8 nameless 9 ineffable 10 untellable 11 indefinable, inenarrable, unspeakable, unutterable 13 indescribable

inexpressive 4 dull 5 blank, empty 6 vacant, wooden 7 deadpan

inexpugnable 5 fixed 6 stable 10 invincible, unbeatable 11 impregnable, indomitable, unopposable 12 invulnerable, irresistible, unassailable, undefeatable 13 unconquerable

inextricable 8 involved 9 insoluble, intricate, unsoluble 10 insolvable, unsolvable

infallible 4 sure 5 exact 7 certain, correct, perfect 8 flawless, inerrant, surefire, unerring 9 faultless, inerrable, unfailing 10 impeccable 11 indubitable 12 undeceivable

infamous 4 base, evil, vile 5 sorry 6 odious, rotten, scurvy 7 corrupt, hateful, heinous, vicious 8 ill-famed, perverse, shameful 9 abhorrent, atrocious, miscreant, nefarious, notorious, unhealthy 10 abominable, degenerate, despicable, detestable, flagitious, iniquitous, scandalous, villainous 11 disgraceful, ignominious, opprobrious 12 contemptible, disreputable

infamy 5 odium, shame 7 obloquy 8 disgrace, dishonor, ignominy 9 discredit, disesteem, disrepute, notoriety 10 opprobrium 13 notoriousness

infancy 6 nonage 8 babyhood, minority 9 childhood, juniority 10 immaturity, infanthood, juvenility

infant 4 babe, baby 5 child, green, minor, young 6 callow, unripe 7 neonate, newborn, toddler 8 bantling, immature, juvenile, nursling, youthful 9 unfledged *bed:* 4 crib 6 cradle 8 bassinet *food:* 3 pap 4 milk *room:* 7 nursery

infantile 7 babyish, puerile 8 childish, immature

infantryman 7 dogface 8 doughboy 11 foot soldier *Algerian:* 6 Zouave

infatuated 3 mad 5 dotty, silly 7 foolish 8 besotted, enamored, obsessed 9 bewitched 10 captivated, enraptured

infatuation 4 rage 5 ardor, craze, crush, folly 6 beguin 7 passion 8 devotion 9 obsession 11 fascination

in favor of 3 for, pro 4 with 10 impossible, unworkable 11 impractical 12 irrealizable, unattainable, unrealizable 13 impracticable

infect 5 taint 6 defile, infest, poison 7 pollute 11 contaminate

infection 6 plague, sepses (plural), sepsis 7 disease, illness *fungous:* 8 mycetoma *skin:* 6 herpes

infectious 5 toxic 6 taking 7 miasmic, noxious 8 catching, mephitic, virulent 9 pestilent, poisonous, vitiating 10 contagious, corrupting 11 sympathetic 12 communicable, pestilential 13 contaminating

infecund 6 barren, effete 7 sterile 8 impotent 9 infertile 10 unfruitful

infelicitous 5 inapt, inept, unapt 6 gauche 7 awkward, unhappy 9 defective, graceless, ill-chosen, imperfect, inapropos 10 deplorable, malapropos 11 regrettable, unfortunate 13 inappropriate

infer 4 draw, hint, make 5 glean, guess, judge, think 6 bestow, confer, deduce, deduct, derive, gather, induce, reason, reckon 7 collect, inflict, make out, surmise 8 conclude, construe

inference 5 guess 7 surmise 8 guessing, illation, judgment, sequitur 9 deduction, reckoning 10 assumption, conclusion, conjecture, derivation 11 presumption, supposition

inferior 3 bad, low 4 base, cull, fair, hack, mean, poor, punk, puny 5 cheap, lousy, lower, minor, petty, scrub, sorry, under 6 common, deputy, feeble, heeler, impure, junior, lesser, minion, nether, no-good, paltry, puisne, satrap, shoddy, sleazy, tawdry, tinpot, vassal 7 average, subject, unequal 8 adherent, declassé, disciple, follower, hanger-on, henchman, hireling, low-grade, mediocre, middling, ordinary, retainer, unworthy, wretched 9 attendant, auxiliary, no-account, satellite, secondary, subaltern, subjacent, sycophant, underling, valueless, worthless 10 inadequate, second-rate *prefix:* 3 sub 4 demi 5 infra

inferior one *suffix:* 3 een 4 ling 5 aster

infernal 6 Hadean 7 avernal, hellish, satanic, stygian 8 chthonic, damnable, demoniac, devilish, diabolic, fiendish, plutonic 9 chthonian, plutonian, Tartarean 10 diabolical, sulphurous

inferno 3 pit 4 fire, hell 5 abyss, hades, Sheol 6 blazes, Tophet 7 Gehenna 9 holocaust, perdition 11 netherworld

Inferno *division:* 5 canto *poet:* 5 Dante *verse form:* 9 terza rima

infertile 6 barren, effete 7 drained, sterile 8 depleted, impotent, infecund 9 exhausted, unbearing, unfertile 10 unfruitful 12 hardscrabble, impoverished, unproductive

infest 4 teem 5 annoy, beset, crawl, harry, haunt, swarm, worry 6 abound, harass, pester, plague 7 overrun 8 parasite 9 overswarm 10 overspread, parasitize

infidel 5 pagan 6 ethnic 7 gentile, heathen, profane, skeptic 9 infidelic 10 unbeliever

infidelity 7 falsity, perfidy, treason 9 falseness, treachery 10 disloyalty, fickleness 11 inconstancy 13 faithlessness

infiltrate 4 leak, seep, worm 5 foist 6 edge in, work in 9 insinuate

infinite 4 vast 7 endless, eternal, immense 9 boundless, countless, limitless, perpetual, unbounded, unlimited 10 indefinite, perdurable, unmeasured 11 everlasting, illimitable, measureless, sempiternal 12 immeasurable

infirm 4 lame, weak 5 anile, frail 6 ailing, feeble, flimsy, senile, weakly 7 fragile, unsound 8 decrepit 10 irresolute 11 debilitated, vacillating 13 unsubstantial

infirmity 3 ill 5 decay 6 foible, malady 7 ailment, disease, failing, frailty, illness, malaise 8 debility, disorder, sickness, syndrome, unhealth, weakness 9 affection, complaint, condition, weakening 10 affliction, feebleness, infirmness, sickliness 11 unwellness 12 debilitation, diseasedness, enfeeblement 13 indisposition, unhealthiness

infix 4 root 5 embed, lodge 6 insert 7 implant, impress, ingrain, instill 8 entrench 9 inculcate 10 inseminate

inflame 3 get 4 fire, gall, good, heat, rile, roil, stir 5 grate, light, rouse 6 arouse, burn up, enrage, excite, ignite, kindle, madden, put out, redden 7 incense, provoke 8 enkindle, irritate 9 aggravate, intensify 10 exasperate

inflammable 5 fiery 6 ardent 8 burnable 9 excitable, ignitable, irascible, irritable 11 combustible

inflammation 4 gout, sore 5 felon 6 quinsy 7 catarrh, coxitis, gonitis, rickets 8 adenitis, cystitis, neuritis, pleurisy, rachitis, swelling 9 arthritis, chilblain, gastritis, phlebitis 10 combustion 12 encephalitis 13 conflagration, poliomyelitis *ear:* 6 otitis *eye:* 6 iritis 7 pinkeye 9 keratitis *horse:* 6 thrush 7 fistula, quittor 8 poll evil *intestines:* 7 ileitis 9 enteritis *suffix:* 4 itis

inflammatory 8 exciting, incitive 9 seditious 10 incendiary 11 instigative, provocative, seditionary 13 revolutionary

inflate 4 fill 5 bloat, elate, swell 6 dilate, expand, tumefy 7 amplify, distend

inflated 5 showy, tumid, windy, wordy 6 elated, prolix, turgid 7 aureate, bloated, diffuse, flowery, fustian, pompous, ranting, swollen, verbose 8 bladdery, dropsied 9 bombastic, distended, dropsical, flatulent, overblown, tumescent 10 rhetorical 11 exaggerated, pretentious, rhapsodical

inflection 4 bend, tone 5 curve 6 accent, timbre 8 tonality 9 accidence 10 intonation 11 enunciation 12 articulation 13 pronunciation

inflexible 3 set 4 grim, hard, iron 5 fixed, rigid, stiff, tough 6 dogged, strict 7 adamant, settled 8 constant, granitic, hard-line, immobile, ironclad, obdurate, rigorous, stubborn 9 immovable, immutable, impliable, inelastic, obstinate, rockbound, steadfast, unbending, unmovable 10 adamantine, brassbound, changeless, implacable, inexorable, invariable, invincible, relentless, rockribbed, unbendable, unchanging, unswayable, unyielding 11 unalterable, uncompliant, unrelenting 12 single-minded, unchangeable, unmodifiable 13 dyed-in-the-wool

inflict 4 deal, give 5 visit, wreak, wreck 6 expose, impose, strike 7 force on, subject

inflow 6 influx, inpour, inrush 9 influxion

influence 4 move, pull, sway 5 alter, bribe, carry, clout, force, impel, lobby, touch 6 affect, compel, credit, induce, modify, moment, strike, weight 7 command, control, impress, inspire, mastery 8 dominion, eminence, militate, persuade, prestige 9 authority, dominance

influenceable 8 suasible, swayable 9 acceptant, acceptive, receptive 10 responsive 11 persuadable, persuasible

influential 6 potent 8 powerful 9 effective, important

influx 6 inflow, inpour, inrush 7 illapse 8 increase 9 accession, inpouring 11 debouchment 12 augmentation

inform 3 rat 4 blab, clew, clue, fire, post, talk, tell, warn 5 endow, endue, exalt, imbue, peach, teach, train 6 advise, betray, fill in, infuse, leaven, notify, preach, snitch, squeak, squeal, tattle, turn in, wise up 7 animate, apprise, arrange, caution, educate, inspire 8 acquaint, forewarn, give away, instruct, permeate 9 advertise, enlighten 10 illuminate 11 familiarize

informal 6 breezy, casual, dégagé, simple 7 natural, private, relaxed, special, unfussy 8 familiar 9 easygoing, irregular 10 colloquial, unofficial

information 4 data (plural), fact, lore, news, word 5 datum 6 advice, notice, wisdom 7 science, tidings 9 complaint, knowledge, speerings 11 instruction 12 intelligenoo *second hand:* 7 hearsay *suffix:* 3 ana 4 iana

information bureau *abbreviation:* 4 USIA, USIS

informative 8 edifying 9 educative 11 educational, elucidative, explanatory, informatory, instructive 12 enlightening, illuminating 13 informational, instructional

informed 2 up 3 hip 4 wise 5 aware 6 au fait, posted, versed 7 abreast, knowing, versant 8 apprised, educated, familiar 9 au courant 10 acquainted, conversant, cultivated 11 enlightened, intelligent

informer 3 rat, spy 4 fink 5 stool 6 canary, gossip, snitch 7 stoolie, tattler, tipster 8 betrayer, busybody, squawker, squealer, telltale 10 talebearer, tattletale 11 stool pigeon

infra 4 next 5 after, below, later, under 6 behind, within 7 beneath

infract 5 break 6 breach, offend 7 violate 8 infringe 10 contravene, transgress

infraction 3 sin 4 slip 5 crime, error, lapse 6 breach 7 faux pas, offense 8 trespass 9 intrusion, violation 12 encroachment, infringement 13 contravention, transgression

infrastructure 4 base, root 5 basis 6 bottom, ground 7 bedrock, footing 10 foundation, groundwork, substratum 12 substructure, underpinning

infrequent 3 few, odd 4 rare 5 scant, stray 6 meager, scanty, scarce, seldom, sparse 7 limited, unusual 8 isolated, sporadic, uncommon, unwonted 9 scattered, spasmodic 10 occasional 11 exceptional

infringe 5 break 6 breach, defeat, impose, invade, offend, refute 7 confute, infract, intrude, obtrude, presume, violate 8 encroach, entrench, trespass 10 contravene, transgress

infuriate 3 ire, mad 5 anger 6 enrage, madden 7 incense, steam up, umbrage

infuse 4 fill, fire 5 imbue, steep 6 inform, invest, leaven 7 animate, diffuse, implant, ingrain, inspire, instill, pervade, suffuse, suggest 8 intersow, permeate, saturate 9 inoulcate, inoculate, insinuate, interfuse, interlard, introduce 10 impregnate 11 intersperse 12 indoctrinate 13 intersprinkle

ingenious 3 sly 4 slim 5 acute, canny, sharp, smart 6 adroit, clever, crafty 7 cunning 8 creative, original 9 demiurgic, deviceful, inventive 11 intelligent, originative, resourceful 12 innovational

ingenuous 4 open 5 naive 6 simple, unwary 7 artless, natural, unaware 8 innocent, unartful 9 childlike, guileless, unstudied 10 unaffected, unschooled 12 unartificial

Inge play 6 Picnic 7 Bus Stop

ingest 3 eat 4 meal, take 6 absorb, devour, feed on, take in 7 consume, swallow

inglorious 5 shady 6 shabby, shoddy 8 shameful 11 disgraceful, ignominious 12 dishonorable, disreputable 13 discreditable, unrespectable

ingot 3 bar, rod 4 slap 5 stick, strip 6 billet

ingrained 7 built-in, chronic 8 inherent 10 congenital, deep-rooted, deep-seated, indwelling, inveterate

ingratiating 5 silky 6 silken 8 pleasing 9 adulatory 10 flattering, saccharine 11 deferential, sycophantic

ingredient 6 factor 7 element 9 component 11 constituent

ingress 3 way 4 adit, door, go in 5 enter, entry 6 access, come in, entrée 8 entrance 9 admission, penetrate 10 admittance

ingurgitate 4 bolt, cram, gulp, slop, wolf 5 slosh, stuff, swill 6 devour, englut, gobble, guzzle 7 swallow

inhabit 4 live 5 abide, dwell 6 occupy, people, settle, tenant 8 populate

inhabitant 5 liver 6 inmate, native 7 citizen, denizen, dweller, resider 8 indigene, resident 9 aborigine 10 autochthon *foreign:* 5 alien *indigenous:* 6 native 9 aborigine *suffix:* 3 ese, ite, ote

inhale 7 breathe, consume, respire 9 breathe in

inharmonious 6 atonal 7 jarring 9 cat-and-dog, differing, dissonant, immusical, unmusical 10 cacophonic, discordant 11 conflicting, conflictive, disagreeing, quarrelsome, uncongenial 12 antagonistic

inhere 3 lie 5 dwell, exist 6 belong, reside 7 consist

inherent 4 born 5 basic 6 inborn, innate, normal 7 built-in, connate, infixed, natural, regular, typical 8 immanent, peculiar 9 elemental, essential, ingrained, intrinsic 10 congenital, deep-seated, elementary, individual, indwelling, ingenerate

inherit 7 possess, receive, succeed

inheritance 6 devise, legacy 7 bequest 8 heritage 9 patrimony 10 birthright, entailment 13 primogeniture

inherited 6 innate, native 7 connate, natural 10 congenital, connatural, indigenous

inheritor 4 heir 7 heretor, heritor, legatee *female:* 7 heiress 8 heretrix, heritrix 10 heretrices (plural), heritrices (plural)

inhibit 3 ban 4 curb, ward 5 avert, check, taboo 6 bridle, enjoin, forbid, hinder, hold in, outlaw, reduce, retard 7 prevent, repress 8 diminish, hold back, hold down, prohibit, restrain, suppress, withhold 9 constrain

inhibited 4 cold 6 frigid 9 repressed 11 passionless 12 unresponsive

inhibition 3 ban, bar 6 hangup 9 restraint 10 impediment

inhuman 4 cold, fell 5 cruel 6 brutal, fierce, malign, savage 7 beastly, bestial, brutish, wolfish 8 devilish, fiendish, nonhuman 9 barbarous, ferocious, malicious, malignant, truculent 10 cannibalic, diabolical, impersonal, implacable, mechanical

inhumane 4 fell, grim 5 cruel 6 brutal, fierce, savage 7 wolfish 9 barbarous, ferocious, truculent

inhumation 6 burial 9 interment, sepulture 10 entombment

inhume 4 bury, tomb 5 inter, plant 6 entomb 7 lay away, put away 9 sepulcher, sepulture

inimical 3 ill 7 adverse, harmful, hostile 10 unfriendly 11 unfavorable

iniquitous 3 bad 4 evil 5 wrong 6 sinful, unjust, wicked 7 immoral, vicious 9 nefarious, reprobate

iniquity 3 sin 4 evil, tort 5 crime, wrong 9 diablerie, injustice 10 wickedness, wrongdoing

initial 5 basic, early, first, prime 6 letter, maiden 7 leading, nascent, opening, pioneer, primary 8 earliest, foremost, germinal, headmost, monogram, original 9 beginning, embryonic, incipient

initiate 4 open 5 admit, begin, enter, set up, start 6 enroll, get off, induct, invest, launch, take in, take up 7 install, kick off, usher in 8 commence 9 originate 10 inaugurate

initiation 7 baptism 9 admission, beginning, induction 10 admittance 11 origination 12 commencement, introduction

initiative 4 push 6 energy 8 ambition, aptitude, gumption 9 beginning 10 enterprise, get-up-and-go

injudicious 6 unwise 9 ill-judged, impolitic, imprudent 10 ill-advised, indiscreet 11 inexpedient

injunction 4 word 5 order 6 behest, charge 7 bidding, command, dictate, mandate 9 direction 11 prohibition

injure 3 mar 4 foul, harm, hurt, maim, pain 5 spoil, wound, wrong 6 batter, blight, bruise, damage, deface, deform, foul up, grieve, impair, mangle, offend, weaken 7 afflict, blemish, contort, cripple, disable, distort, louse up, tarnish, torment, torture, vitiate 8 aggrieve, disserve, distress, maltreat, mutilate 9 bespatter, constrain, disfigure, prejudice 12 incapacitate

injurious 3 bad 4 evil 6 nocent 7 abusive, harmful, hurtful 8 damaging 9 offensive 10 defamatory 11 detrimental

injury 3 bad, ill 4 evil, harm, hurt, loss, pain, pang, ruin 5 agony, wound, wrong 6 damage, trauma 7 outrage 8 distress, mischief 9 detriment, grievance, injustice

injustice 4 harm, hurt, ruin, tort 5 crime, wrong 6 breach, damage, injury 7 outrage 8 inequity, mischief, trespass, villainy 9 grievance, violation 10 favoritism, partiality, unfairness, wrongdoing

ink 4 sign 9 autograph, signature, subscribe

inkling 3 cue 4 clue, hint, idea, wind 6 notion 8 telltale 10 intimation, suggestion

ink or rubber 5 India

inky 3 jet 4 ebon 5 black, ebony, jetty, raven, sable 9 cimmerian, pitch-dark 10 pitch-black 11 atramentous

inlaid 5 piqué

Inland Empire 8 Illinois

inlet 3 arm, bay, cay, ria, voe 4 cove, gulf 5 bayou, bight, creek, fiord, firth, fjord, sound 6 harbor, slough, strait 7 estuary *Admiralties:* 4 Kali *Adriatic Sea:* 5 Vlorë *Aegean Sea:* 7 Saronic 12 Gulf of Aegina *Africa:* 6 Walvis 12 Gulf of Guinea *Alaska:* 4 Cook 5 Cross, Taiya 7 Glacier 8 Chilkoot *Aleutians:* 5 Holtz, Nazan *Angola:* 5 Bengo, Tiger 6 Tigres *Antarctica:* 3 Ice 7 McMurdo 8 Amundsen 10 Shackleton *Arabian Sea:* 4 Qamr 5 Kamar *Arctic Ocean:* 8 Gulf of Ob *Australia:* 4 King 6 Botany 9 Discovery 10 Broad Sound 13 Van Diemen Gulf *Baffin Bay:* 8 Melville *Baffin Island:* 9 Admiralty *Baltic Sea:* 4 Hano 6 Danzig, Gdansk 9 Pomerania 10 Gulf of Riga, Pomeranian *Barents Sea:* 4 Kola 7 Pechora *Beaufort Sea:* 7 Prudhoe 9 Mackenzie *Bering Sea:* 12 Gulf of Anadyr *Bismarck Sea:* 5 Kimbe *Brazil:* 9 Guanabara *Bristol Channel:* 10 Carmarthen *California:* 5 Morro 8 Monterey, San Diego 12 San Francisco *Canada:* 5 Fundy

9 Howe Sound *Cape Breton Island:*
4 Mira *Caribbean Sea:* 5 Limon 8 Chetumal, Honduras 9 Venezuela *Central America:* 7 Fonseca *Chile:* 5 Otway *China-Korea:* 8 Huang Hai, Hwang Hai 9 Yellow Sea *Crete:* 4 Suda 5 Canea *Denmark:* 3 Ise *Djibouti:* 6 Tajura 8 Tadjoura *East River:* 8 Flushing *Ecuador:* 5 Manta *Eire:* 4 Clew 7 Brandon *English Channel:* 3 Tor 5 Seine 8 Plymouth *Florida:* 8 Biscayne 10 Saint Lucie 11 Indian River *France-Spain:* 6 Biscay 13 Gulf of Gascony *Georgia:* 8 Altamaha *Greece:* 13 Gulf of Corinth, Gulf of Lepanto *Greenland:* 6 Baffin *Gulf of Alaska:* 3 Icy 5 Woman 12 Resurrection *Gulf of Mexico:* 5 Tampa 6 Mobile 7 Aransas 8 Sarasota, Suwannee 9 Matagorda, Pensacola 10 San Antonio, Terrebonne 11 Atchafalaya, Mississippi, Ponce de Leon 12 Apalachicola 13 Corpus Christi *Gulf of St. Lawrence:* 5 Bonne, Gaspé *Hawaii:* 11 Pearl Harbor *Honshu:* 3 Ise 5 Osaka, Owari, Tokyo 6 Atsuta *Hudson Bay:* 7 Repulse *Hudson River:* 7 New York *Iceland:* 4 Axar, Eyja, Huna 5 Horna, Skaga, Vopna 8 Hunafloi *Indonesia:* 4 Bima 5 Saleh *Ionian Sea:* 7 Taranto *Irish Sea:* 4 Luce 7 Dundalk *Italy:* 11 Gulf of Genoa 14 Lagoon of Venice *Japan:* 4 Tosa *Java:* 4 Lada 5 Peper *Java Sea:* 7 Batavia 8 Djakarta *Kara Sea:* 6 Enisei 7 Yenisei *Labrador:* 8 Hamilton *Lake Erie:* 8 Put-in-Bay, Sandusky *Lake Huron:* 7 Saginaw, Thunder *Lake Michigan:* 5 Green 13 Grand Traverse *Lake Ontario:* 11 Irondequoit *Lake Superior:* 5 Huron 8 Keweenaw 9 Whitefish *Long Island:* 8 Rockaway *Long Island Sound:* 6 Oyster 8 New Haven *Madagascar:* 8 Antongil *Maine:* 5 Casco 7 Machias 9 Penobscot 12 Damariscotta *Maryland-Virginia:* 10 Chesapeake *Massachusetts:* 8 Buzzards, Plymouth 9 Annisquam *Massachusetts Bay:* 10 Lynn Harbor *Mediterranean Sea:* 8 Valencia 9 Famagusta 10 Khalij Surt 11 Gulf of Sidra, Gulf of Tunis, Syrtis Major *Mozambique:* 5 Memba, Pemba *Nantucket Sound:* 5 Lewis *New Brunswick:* 13 Passamaquoddy *Newfoundland:* 4 Hare 5 White 7 Fortune *New Guinea:* 3 Oro 5 Berau, Hansa 11 McCluer Gulf *New Jersey:* 5 Great 7 Raritan 8 Barnegat 9 Little Egg *New York:* 7 Jamaica *New Zealand:* 5 Hawke 6 Tasman *North Carolina:* 7 Roanoke 9 Albemarle *Northern Ireland:* 12 Belfast Lough *North Sea:* 4 Lyse 9 Hardanger *Northwest Territories:* 5 Wager 8 Bathurst, Franklin 9 Frobisher 12 Prince Albert *Norway:* 3 Tys 4 Bokn,

Tana 5 Lakse, Sogne *Norwegian Sea:* 4 Nord, Salt, Stor, Vest 5 Ranen 8 Scoresby 9 Trondheim *Ontario:* 4 Owen *Oregon:* 4 Coos *Philippines:* 5 Baler, Pilar, Sogod 6 Butuan 9 Davao Gulf, Leyte Gulf, Panay Gulf *Puget Sound:* 4 Carr, Case *Quebec:* 6 Ungava *Red Sea:* 4 Foul *Rhode Island:* 12 Narragansett 13 Sakonnet River *Russia:* 5 Chaun 8 Sakhalin, White Sea 12 Sea of Okhotsk *Santo Cruz Islands:* 8 Basilisk *Sea of Japan:* 13 Peter the Great *Solomon Islands:* 4 Deep 8 Huon Gulf *South Africa:* 5 Table *South Carolina:* 4 Bull *South China Sea:* 4 Bias, Datu, Siam, Taya 5 Dasol, Subic, Subig 6 Brunei, Paluan 7 Camranh 8 Lingayen, Thailand *Spain:* 5 Cadiz *Spitsbergen:* 3 Ice 4 Bell 5 Kings *Strait of Gibraltar:* 7 Tangier *Sumatra:* 5 Bajur 10 Koninginne *Tasmania:* 5 Storm *Tyrrhenian Sea:* 6 Naples 7 Paestum 13 Gulf of Salerno *Wales:* 5 Burry *Washington:* 5 Dabob 6 Skagit 11 Grays Harbor

inmate 7 convict 8 occupant, prisoner 10 inhabitant

inmost part 4 core, pith 5 heart 6 center, depths, kernel, marrow 7 nucleus

inn 5 fonda, hotel, house, lodge, motel 6 hostel, posada, tavern 7 auberge, hospice 8 hostelry, wayhouse 9 roadhouse 11 caravansary, public house 13 boardinghouse *German:* 8 gasthaus *Turkish:* 6 imaret

innards 4 guts 6 tripes 7 viscera 8 entrails, stuffing

innate see **inherent**

inner 3 gut 5 close, focal 6 hidden, inside, inward, middle, secret 7 central, nuclear, private 8 familiar, interior, internal, personal, visceral 9 concealed, essential *combining form:* 3 ent 4 ento

innervate 4 move 5 pique, rouse 7 provoke, quicken 9 galvanize

Innisfail 4 Eire, Erin 7 Ireland

innkeeper 4 host 8 boniface, hosteler, publican

innocence 6 purity 7 naiveté 8 chastity 9 ignorance, silliness 10 simplicity 11 artlessness, sinlessness, unawareness

innocent 4 free, good, pure, void 5 clean, empty, legal, licit, naive, white 6 candid, chaste, devoid, lawful, simple 7 artless, natural, unaware 8 harmless, ignorant, unguilty, virtuous 9 blameless, childlike, crimeless, destitute, exemplary, faultless, guileless, guiltless, ingenuous, innocuous, permitted, righteous, stainless, unstained, unstudied, unsullied, untainted 10 inculpable, legitimate, tenderfoot, unaffected, unblamable, unschooled **11** inobnoxious, inoffensive, unoffending, unoffensive, white-handed **12** simpleminded, unartificial, unsuspecting

innocuous **4** flat **5** banal, bland **6** jejune, pallid **7** insipid, sapless **8** harmless **9** driveling **10** namby-pamby **11** inoffensive, unoffending, unoffensive **13** insignificant

innovation **6** change **7** novelty, wrinkle **11** vicissitude

innovative **3** new **5** novel **8** creative, original **9** demiurgic, deviceful, inventive

innovator **5** maker **7** builder **8** original, producer **9** architect, developer **10** originator

innuendo **4** clue, hint, slur **8** allusion **10** intimation **11** implication, insinuation

innumerable **4** many **6** legion, myriad, untold **9** countless, uncounted **10** numberless

Ino *brother:* **9** Polydorus *father:* **6** Cadmus *grandfather:* **6** Agenor *husband:* **7** Athamas *mother:* **8** Harmonia *sister:* **5** Agave **6** Semele **7** Autonoe *son:* **8** Learchus, Palaemon **10** Melicertes

inobtrusive **5** quiet, tasty **7** subdued **8** tasteful **10** restrained

inoculate **5** admit, enter, imbue, steep **6** infuse, leaven **7** implant, suffuse

inoffensive **8** harmless **9** innocuous, peaceable

inopportune **8** ill-timed, mistimed, untimely

inordinate **5** dizzy, extra, undue **6** wanton **7** extreme, surplus **8** towering **9** excessive **10** disorderly, exorbitant, gratuitous, immoderate, irrational, untempered **11** extravagant, intemperate, superfluous, uncalled-for **12** unmeasurable, unreasonable, unrestrained **13** extraordinary

in passing **6** obiter **8** by the bye, by the way **12** incidentally

in perpetuum **4** ever **6** always **7** forever **8** evermore **9** eternally **11** forevermore

inquest **5** probe **6** search **7** delving, inquiry, probing **8** research **11** examination **13** investigation

inquietude **6** unrest **7** ailment, anxiety, ferment, turmoil **10** uneasiness **11** restiveness **12** restlessness **13** Sturm und Drang

inquire **3** ask **4** seek **5** query, study **6** search **7** examine **8** question **9** catechize **10** scrutinize **11** interrogate, investigate

inquiry **5** audit, check, probe, query, quest **7** delving, hearing, probing **8** question, research, scrutiny **11** catechizing, examination, questioning **13** investigation

inquisition **4** hunt **5** probe, quest **6** search **7** delving, inquiry, probing **8** grilling, research **11** examination **13** investigation

inquisitive **4** nosy **5** peery **6** prying, snoopy **7** curious **11** questioning

inquisitor *Spanish:* **10** Torquemada (Tomas de)

in re **4** as to **5** about, as for **7** apropos **9** as regards, regarding **10** as respects, concerning, respecting

in respect to see **in re**

inroad **4** raid **5** foray **6** invade **7** overrun **8** invasion **9** incursion, irruption, overswarm **12** encroachment

ins and outs **5** ropes **6** quirks **7** details **8** minutiae, oddities **11** incidentals, particulars **13** peculiarities, ramifications

insane **3** mad, off **4** daft, nuts **5** crazy, daffy, dotty, loony, manic, nutsy, nutty, rocky, silly, wacky, wrong **6** absurd, crazed, cuckoo, maniac, screwy, teched **7** cracked, foolish, lunatic, strange, tetched, touched, unsound, witless **8** demented, deranged, fanciful, mindless **9** bedlamite, brainsick, eccentric, fantastic, imaginary, visionary **10** bewildered, disordered, distracted, distraught, irrational, reasonless, ridiculous, unbalanced **11** harebrained, impractical, unrealistic **12** crackbrained, preposterous, unreasonable

insane asylum **6** bedlam **8** loony bin, madhouse, nuthouse **9** funny farm **10** booby hatch, sanatorium, sanitarium

insanity **5** folly, mania **6** dotage, frenzy, lunacy **7** madness **8** delirium, delusion, dementia, hysteria, illusion **9** acromania, craziness, dottiness, silliness, unbalance **10** aberration, alienation **11** derangement, distraction, fatuousness, foolishness, psychopathy, witlessness **13** hallucination, senselessness

insatiable **6** crying, greedy, urgent **7** exigent **8** pressing, yearning **9** clamorous, demanding, voracious **10** quenchless **11** importunate **12** unappeasable, unquenchable

inscribe **4** book, etch, list **5** enter, print, write **6** enroll **7** catalog, engrave, engross, impress, imprint **8** enscroll

inscription **5** title **6** legend **7** epigram, epitaph, heading **8** epigraph **10** enrollment

inscrutable **6** arcane, mystic, secret **8** numinous **9** mysterial, unguessed **10** cabalistic, mysterious, unknowable **12** impenetrable, unfathomable

insect **3** bee, bug, fly **6** beetle *adult:* **5** imago *antenna:* **4** palp **6** feeler *butterfly:* (see **butterfly** entry) *combining form:* **5** entom **6** entomo *covering:* **6** chitin *immature:* **4** grub, pupa **5** larva, nymph **6** larvae (plural), maggot **8** wriggler **9** chrysalis **11** caterpillar *kind:* **3** ant

4 flea, moth, wasp **5** aphid, scale **6** bedbug, beefly, beetle, cicada, earwig, hornet, mantid, mantis, mayfly **7** ant lion, cricket, firefly, June bug, katydid, ladybug, termite **8** honeybee, horsefly, housefly, lacewing, mosquito, stinkbug **9** bumblebee, butterfly, damselfly, dragonfly **10** silverfish, springtail **11** grasshopper **12** walkingstick *luminous:* **7** firefly **8** glowworm *molt:* **7** ecdysis *moth:* **4** luna **6** sphinx **8** Cecropia **10** Polyphemus *multi-legged:* **8** diplopod **9** centipede, millepede, millipede *part:* **4** palp **5** cerci (plural) **6** cercus, labium, labrum, ocelli (plural), thorax **7** antenna, maxilla, ocellus **8** antennae (plural), mandible, maxillae (plural) **9** proboscis, spiracles **10** ovipositor **11** exoskeleton *pest:* **4** flea, lice (plural), mite **5** louse, midge, scale **7** blowfly, termite **8** horsefly, housefly, mealybug **9** cockroach, gypsy moth **10** boll weevil, Hessian fly, silverfish *science:* **10** entomology *winged:* **5** alate *wingless:* **4** flea, lice (plural) **5** louse **8** firebrat **10** silverfish **11** bristletail

insecticide 3 DDT **5** mirex, naled **6** endrin, ronnel **7** lindane, phorate **8** carbaryl, dieldrin, rotenone **9** chlordane

insecure 4 weak **5** shaky **6** dickey, infirm, unsafe, unsure, wobbly **8** hesitant, rootless, unstable, wavering **9** fluctuant, unassured, uncertain **11** questioning, unconfident

inseminate 7 implant, instill **9** fertilize **10** impregnate

insensate 4 dull, hard **5** rocky, silly **6** simple **7** fatuous, foolish, witless **8** mindless **9** bloodless, brainless, nitwitted, unfeeling **10** anesthetic, unanimated **11** sheepheaded

insensibility 4 coma **6** apathy, phlegm, torpor **8** lethargy, stoicism **12** indifference

insensible 4 cold, dead, dull, hard, numb, rapt **5** blunt, rocky, stoic **6** asleep, intent, numbed, obtuse, stolid **7** brutish, callous **8** absorbed, benumbed, comatose, deadened, hardened, obdurate **9** apathetic, bloodless, engrossed, impassive, unfeeling **10** anesthetic, phlegmatic, unapparent **11** unconscious **12** anesthetized

insensitive 4 dead, dull, hard, numb **5** aloof, rocky **6** asleep, numbed **8** benumbed, deadened **9** bloodless, unfeeling **10** anesthetic, impossible **11** indifferent, unconcerned **12** anesthetized, unresponsive **13** insusceptible, unimpressible, unsusceptible

insert 5 admit, enter, infix, inlay, inlet, inset **6** fill in **7** implant, obtrude, throw in **9** interpose **11** intercalate, interpolate

in short 7 briefly, tersely **9** concisely **10** succinctly **11** laconically

inside 5 inner **6** closet, hushed, inward, within **7** private **8** interior **11** withindoors **12** confidential *combining form:* **3** end **4** endo

insidious 3 sly **4** deep, foxy, wily **6** artful, astute, crafty, subtle, tricky **7** cunning, gradual **8** guileful **9** deceitful **10** fraudulent **11** treacherous

insight 6 wisdom **8** sagacity, sageness, sapience **9** intuition **10** anschauung **11** discernment, penetration **13** intuitiveness, sagaciousness, understanding

insightful 4 sage, wise **6** sophic **7** gnostic, knowing **9** sagacious **10** discerning, perceptive **11** penetrating **13** knowledgeable

insignia 4 mark, sign **5** badge **6** emblem **8** brassard **10** decoration

insignificant 4 puny **5** dinky, light, minor, petty, small **6** casual, lesser, little, paltry **7** trivial **8** inferior, small-fry, trifling **9** pointless, secondary, senseless, small-beer, small-time, unmeaning **10** shoestring **11** meaningless, minor-league, unimportant

insincere 5 false, lying **6** double, shifty, tricky **7** feigned **8** mala fide, slippery **9** deceitful, deceptive, dishonest **10** lefthanded, mendacious, untruthful **11** doublefaced **12** hypocritical

insinuate 4 hint, worm **5** foist, imply **6** allude, edge in, fill in, impugn, impute, insert, work in **7** ascribe, connote, implant, instill, suggest, throw in **9** introduce

insipid 3 dry **4** arid, dull, flat, mild, pale, soft, tame, thin, weak **5** banal, bland, dusty, plain, vapid **6** feeble, jejune, slight, swashy, watery **7** mundane, prosaic, sapless, subdued, tedious, tenuous **8** bromidic, lifeless, ordinary, unsavory, waterish, weariful **9** driveling, dryasdust, innocuous, pointless, savorless, tasteless, wearisome **10** flavorless, monotonous, namby-pamby, spiritless, wishy-washy **11** commonplace

insistent 4 dire **6** crying, dogged, urgent **7** burning, clamant **8** emphatic, forceful, pressing **9** assertive, clamorous, obtrusive **10** imperative, resounding **11** persevering

insolence 5 nerve **6** insult **8** audacity, boldness, contempt, rudeness **9** arrogance, hardihood, impudence **10** brazenness, disrespect, effrontery **11** haughtiness, presumption **12** impertinence

insolent 4 bold, pert, rude **5** lofty, proud, saucy **6** brazen **7** defiant, haughty, uncivil **8** arrogant, cavalier, impolite, impudent, superior **9** audacious **10** disdainful, imperative, peremptory, procacious, ungracious **11** dictatorial, impertinent, magisterial, overbearing **12** contumelious, discourteous, supercilious **13** high-and-mighty

insouciance 6 apathy 8 lethargy 9 disregard, lassitude, unconcern 11 disinterest 12 heedlessness, indifference, listlessness

insouciant 8 carefree, heedless 9 lightsome 10 free-minded 11 indifferent, unconcerned 12 happy-go-lucky, lighthearted

inspect 3 con, vet 4 view 5 check, study 6 notice, review, survey 7 canvass, check up, examine, observe 8 question 9 catechize, check over 10 scrutinize

inspiration 4 muse 6 animus, genius, vision 8 afflatus 9 brainwave, influence 10 brainstorm 13 enlightenment

inspire 3 get 4 fire, move, stir, sway 5 carry, elate, endow, endue, exalt, imbue, set up, touch 6 affect, excite, foment, incite, inhale, strike 7 animate, commove, enliven, impress, quicken 8 motivate, spirit up 9 breathe in, encourage, influence, stimulate 10 exhilarate

instability 9 shakiness 10 insecurity 11 inconstancy, unfixedness 12 unsteadiness 13 changeability, unsettledness

install 4 seat, vest 5 chair 6 induct, invest, settle 8 ensconce, enthrone, initiate 9 establish

instance 4 case, cite, item, name 5 proof 6 detail, ground, reason, sample 7 example, mention, request, specify 8 exponent, sampling, specimen 9 exemplify 10 illustrate, particular, suggestion 11 case history, instigation 12 illustration

instant 4 dire, time, wink 5 crack, flash, jiffy, point, shake, trice, while 6 minute, moment, second, urgent 7 current, exigent, present, twinkle 8 existent, juncture, occasion, pressing, todayish 9 immediate, insistent, twinkling 10 imperative, present-day

instantaneous 4 fast 5 quick, rapid 9 immediate, momentary 10 transitory 11 hair-trigger

instanter 3 now 4 away 5 right 6 at once 8 directly, first off 9 forthwith, right away 11 immediately

instantly 3 now 4 away 5 right 6 at once 8 directly, first off 9 forthwith, right away 10 pressingly

instead 4 else 6 in lieu, rather 11 alternately 13 alternatively

instigate 3 set 4 abet, fire, goad, hint, move, plan, plot, prod, spur, urge 5 impel, raise, set on 6 excite, foment, incite, scheme, stir up, whip up 7 provoke, suggest 8 motivate 9 stimulate

instill 5 imbue, infix 6 impart, infuse 7 implant 9 inculcate, introduce

instinctive 6 innate, normal 7 natural, regular, typical 8 inherent, visceral, will-less 9 automatic, intuitive, unlearned 10 congenital, unprompted, unreasoned 11 involuntary, spontaneous, unmeditated

institute 3 law 4 rule 5 begin, edict, found, set up, start 6 decree, launch, ordain 7 precept, usher in 8 decretum, initiate, organize 9 establish, introduce, ordinance, originate 10 inaugurate 12 organization

institution 4 rite 5 habit 6 custom 7 fixture 9 enactment 10 foundation 13 establishment *kind:* 6 school 7 academy, college 8 hospital 10 university

instruct 3 bid 4 lead, show, tell, warn 5 coach, drill, guide, order, pilot, steer, teach, train, tutor 6 assign, charge, define, direct, enjoin, inform, school 7 apprise, command, counsel, educate 8 acquaint, engineer 9 prescribe 10 discipline

instruction 6 advice, lesson 7 precept 8 teaching, training, tutelage 9 catechism, education, schooling 10 directions *place of:* 6 school 7 academe

instructive 8 didactic 10 moralistic, moralizing 11 educational

instrument 4 deed, gear, mean, tool 5 agent, means, organ 6 agency, device, medium, tackle 7 channel, utensil, vehicle 8 ministry 9 appliance, machinery 13 paraphernalia *aircraft:* 3 aba 5 radar, radio 7 compass 8 yawmeter 9 altimeter, gyroscope 10 altazimuth, tachometer 11 transponder *calculating:* 6 abacus 8 computer 9 slide rule *combining form:* 4 labe, stat 5 meter *graphic:* 6 camera 8 otoscope 9 telescope 10 binoculars, microscope 11 fluoroscope, stethoscope, stroboscope 12 bronchoscope, oscilloscope, spectrograph, spectroscope *measuring:* 5 clock, gauge, radar, scale, sonar 7 alidade, ammeter, balance, caliper, sextant, transit 8 quadrant 9 altimeter, astrolabe, barometer, bolometer, manometer, pedometer, sonometer, voltmeter 10 anemometer, fathometer, hydrometer, hygrometer, micrometer, radiometer, radiosonde, spirometer, tachometer, theodolite 11 chronometer, lie detector, range finder, seismograph, speedometer, thermometer 12 electroscope, galvanometer, oscillograph, oscilloscope 13 Geiger counter, potentiometer *medical:* 5 curet 6 lancet, plexor, trocar 7 curette, forceps, probang, specula (plural), tenacula (plural) 9 tenaculum *radiation-producing:* 5 laser, maser; (see also **implement; musical instrument; tool**)

instrumental 6 useful 7 helpful 9 conducive 11 serviceable

instrumentality 5 agent, force, means, might, organ, power 6 agency, energy, medium 7 channel, vehicle 8 ministry

insubordinate 5 rebel 6 unruly 7 riotous 8 factious, mutinous 9 seditious 10 headstrong, rebellious, refractory 11 disaffected, disobedient, dissentious, intractable, uncompliant, uncomplying 12 contuma-cious, recalcitrant, ungovernable

insubstantial 4 airy, puny, weak 5 frail 6 feeble, flimsy 7 fragile, tenuous, unsound 8 bodiless, decrepit 9 imaginary, unfleshly 10 intangible, unembodied 11 disembodied 12 apparitional

insufferable 7 painful 10 unbearable 11 distressing, intolerable

insufficiency 4 lack 7 failure, paucity, poverty 8 scarcity, shortage, underage 9 inability 10 inadequacy, scantiness, scarceness 11 defalcation

insufficient 3 shy 5 scant, short, unfit 6 scanty, scarce 7 failing, lacking, unequal, wanting 9 defective 10 inadequate, incomplete

insular 5 local 6 narrow 7 limited 8 confined, detached, islander, isolated, regional, secluded 9 illiberal, insulated, parochial, sectarian, sectional, small-town 10 prejudiced, provincial, restricted

insulate 6 cut off, enisle, island 7 isolate 8 close off 9 segregate, sequester

insult 4 gibe, gird, jeer, mock, rump, slap, slur 5 abase, abuse, fleer, flout, scoff, scorn, shame, sneer, taunt 6 debase, deride, humble, offend, revile 7 affront, degrade, despite, disdain, obloquy, offense, outrage 8 contempt, disgrace, ignominy, ridicule 9 contumely, humiliate, insolence 10 opprobrium 12 unpleasantry, vituperation

insurance 8 guaranty, warranty 10 protection *agency:* 7 actuary 8 adjuster 11 underwriter *term:* 6 policy 7 annuity 8 coverage 9 bordereau 11 beneficiary

insure 5 cinch, guard 6 assure, shield 7 protect 9 safeguard 10 underwrite

insurgent 5 rebel 6 anarch 8 factious, frondeur, mutineer, mutinous, revolter 9 anarchist, seditious 10 rebellious 12 contumacious 13 insubordinate

insurrection 6 mutiny, revolt 8 uprising 9 rebellion

insurrectionist 5 rebel 6 anarch 8 frondeur, mutineer, revolter 10 malcontent

insusceptible 6 immune 9 impassive, unfeeling 10 insentient 12 unresponsive

intact 5 sound, whole 6 entire, maiden, unhurt, virgin 7 perfect 8 complete, flawless, unbroken, unmarred, virginal 9 undamaged, uninjured, untouched 10 unimpaired

intangible 4 airy, rare, thin 5 vague 6 aerial, slight 8 aeriform, ethereal 10 immaterial, impalpable, unapparent 11 incorporeal

integer 5 digit 6 figure, number 7 chiffer, numeral 11 whole number

integral 3 sum 4 full 5 whole 6 choate, entire, entity, system 7 inbuilt, perfect 8 complete, inherent, totality 9 component, composite 11 constituent

integrate 3 mix, sum 4 fuse, join, link, tune 5 blend, merge, unify, unite, whole 6 attune, embody, entity, system 7 arrange, combine, compact, conform, conjoin 8 coalesce, organize, totality 9 harmonize, reconcile 10 articulate, coordinate, proportion, symphonize, synthesize 11 desegregate

integrity 5 honor 7 honesty, probity 9 constancy, soundness, wholeness 10 entireness, honestness, perfection 12 absoluteness, completeness, incorruption 13 honorableness

integument 4 coat 5 testa 7 coating, cuticle 8 covering, envelope 10 investment *combining form:* 4 derm, scyt 5 derma, scyto 6 dermia, dermis 9 dermatous

intellect 3 wit 4 mind, nous 5 brain 6 genius, pundit, reason 7 egghead, thinker 9 intuition, mentality 12 intelligence 13 comprehension, understanding

intellectual 5 brain 6 brainy, mental 7 Brahmin, egghead, psychic 8 highbrow, longhair 9 reasoning 10 double-dome, highbrowed, reflective

intelligence 3 wit 4 mind, news, word 5 brain, sense 6 acumen, advice, brains, notice, reason, wisdom 7 tidings 8 judgment, learning, sagacity 9 knowledge, mentality, mother wit, speerings 10 brainpower, shrewdness

intelligent 4 keen, wise 5 acute, alert, aware, sharp, smart, sound 6 adroit, astute, brainy, bright, clever, shrewd 7 cunning, knowing, logical 8 rational, sensible 9 brilliant, ingenious, sagacious 10 reasonable 11 quick-witted, ready-witted 13 knowledgeable, perspicacious

intelligentsia 7 clerisy 8 literati, vanguard 10 avant-garde, illuminati

intelligible 5 clear, lucid, plain 8 luminous 10 conceptual 13 supersensible, suprasensuous

intemperance 6 excess 10 debauchery 11 drunkenness 12 immoderation

intemperate 4 hard 5 harsh 6 bitter, brutal, rugged, severe 7 drunken, extreme, violent 8 bibulous, rigorous 9 bibacious, crapulous, excessive, inclement 10 gluttonous, immoderate, inordinate 12 unrestrained 13 overindulgent

intend 3 aim, try 4 mean, plan, plot 5 essay, spell 6 assign, denote, design, import, scheme, strive 7 add up to, attempt, connote, destine, express, propose, purpose, signify 8 endeavor 9 designate

intended 6 fiancé 7 engaged, fiancée 8 proposed 9 affianced, betrothed

intense 3 hot 4 deep, hard, keen 5 acute, great, vivid 6 ardent, fervid, fierce, severe, strong 7 extreme, fervent, furious, serious, vicious, violent, zealous 8 enhanced, powerful, profound, stressed, terrible, vehement 9 assiduous, desperate, excessive, exquisite 10 aggravated, emphasized, heightened 11 accentuated 12 concentrated

intensify 4 rise 5 exalt, mount, rouse 6 accent, deepen, stress 7 enhance, sharpen 8 heighten, increase, redouble 9 aggravate, emphasize 10 accentuate, aggrandize 11 concentrate

intensity 5 depth 6 energy, fervor 7 passion 8 fervency, loudness

intensive 5 eager 7 zealous 10 exhaustive 12 concentrated *pronoun:* 6 itself, myself 7 herself, himself 8 yourself 9 ourselves 10 themselves, yourselves

intent 3 aim, set 4 deep, plan, rapt, will 5 eager, fixed, sense 6 animus, design, import 7 decided, earnest, engaged, meaning, minding, purport, purpose, riveted, settled, wrapped 8 absorbed, conation, decisive, diligent, immersed, resolute, resolved, sedulous, volition, watching 9 engrossed, wrapped up 10 determined

intention 3 aim, end 4 goal, hope, plan, wish 6 animus, design, desire, object, scheme 7 meaning, purpose

intentional 5 meant 7 advised, studied, willful, willing, witting 8 designed, proposed, purposed, unforced 9 designful, voluntary 10 considered, deliberate 12 premeditated, unprescribed

intentionally 9 on purpose, purposely

inter 4 bury, tomb 5 plant 6 entomb, inhume 7 lay away, put away 9 sepulcher, sepulture

interact 4 join 5 merge, unite 7 combine 9 cooperate 11 collaborate

interbreed 5 cross 9 cross-mate, hybridize

intercede 6 step in 7 mediate 9 arbitrate, interpose, intervene

intercept 4 curb, grab, stop, take 5 block, catch, check, seize 6 cut off, hinder 9 forestall, interrupt

intercessor 6 broker 8 advocate, mediator 9 go-between, middleman 12 entrepreneur

interconnect 4 join 5 blend, unite 10 anastomose, inosculate

intercourse 5 truck 7 contact, dealing, traffic 8 business, commerce, converse 9 communion 10 connection 12 conversation 13 communication

intercross 9 decussate, hybridize

interdict 3 ban 4 veto 5 taboo 6 enjoin, forbid, outlaw 8 prohibit 9 proscribe

interest 4 care, good, lure, pull 5 claim, pique, share, snare, stake, tempt 6 appeal, arouse, behalf, excite, regard 7 attract, benefit, concern, passion, welfare 9 advantage, attention, curiosity, fascinate, tantalize, titillate, well-being 10 absorption, enthusiasm, excitement, prosperity

interested 4 rapt 6 caring 7 partial 8 partisan

interfere 3 bar 4 balk, foil, fool 5 block 6 baffle, butt in, hamper, hinder, horn in, impede, meddle, step in, tamper, thwart 7 intrude, mediate, trouble 8 busybody, obstruct 9 frustrate, incommode, intervene 10 discommode, monkey with, tamper with

interim 3 gap 5 break 6 acting, breach, hiatus, lacuna, pro tem, supply 8 meantime 9 temporary 10 pro tempore

interior 3 gut 5 belly, bosom, heart, inner 6 center, inland, inside, inward, within 8 visceral 9 viscerous

interject 6 fill in 7 throw in 9 introduce

interjection *agreement:* 6 righto 7 right on *attention-getter:* 3 hey 4 ahem, psst 5 heigh *calling pigs:* 5 sooey *cheer:* 3 rah 6 hooray, hurrah, hurray *contempt:* 3 poh 4 pooh 5 pshaw *disappointment:* 4 rats 6 shucks *disapproval:* 3 fie *disbelief:* 2 aw 3 huh *disgust:* 3 bah, pah, ugh 4 pugh, rats 5 faugh, nerts, yecch 6 phooey *dismay:* 2 oy 4 oh no *dismissal:* 3 git *farewell:* 4 by-by, ciao 6 bye-bye, so long *gratitude:* 8 gramercy *greeting:* 2 hi 4 ciao 5 aloha, hello *hesitation:* 2 er, um *in golf:* 4 fore *in hunting:* 6 yoicks *in marching:* 3 hup *joy:* 4 whee 6 hooray, hurrah, hurray, yippee 7 whoopee *mild apology:* 4 oops 5 woops 6 whoops *mild oath:* 3 gad, gor 4 darn, drat, egad, geez, gosh, heck, jeez 5 egads, golly, zooks 6 cracky, jiminy, zounds 7 begorra, begorry, gee whiz, jeepers, jimminy 8 gadzooks, gee whizz 13 gee whillikers, gee whillikins *of warning:* 8 gardyloo *O.K.:* 5 wilco *pain:* 2 ow 4 ouch, yipe 5 yipes *peace:* 6 shalom, sholom *regret:* 4 alas 5 alack 8 lackadaisy *relief:* 4 phew *request:* 7 prithee *silence:* 2 sh 3 shh *sneeze:* 5 achoo 6 atchoo 7 kerchoo *sorrow:* 4 alas 5 alack 8 lackaday *stop:* 4 whoa *surprise:* 2 ah, ho, lo, oh 3 aha, huh, oho, wow 4 gosh, oops, yipe 5 blimy, yipes, zowie 6 blimey *to a horse:* 4 whoa 6 giddap *toast:* 5 salud, skoal 6 cheers, prosit 7 l'chayim *triumph:* 3 aha, hah 6 eureka; (see also **exclamation**)

interlace 3 mix 5 braid, twine, weave 9 alternate, interlock 10 intertwine, interweave 11 intersperse

interlard 3 mix 6 mingle 7 diffuse

interlope 4 fool 6 butt in, horn in, meddle
7 intrude 8 busybody 9 interfere 10 monkey with, tamper with 11 intermeddle

interlude 4 lull, rest 5 break, idyll, pause,
spell 7 episode, respite 8 breather, entr'acte, interval, meantime 9 meanwhile

intermediary 3 mid 4 mean 5 agent,
organ 6 agency, broker, center, medium,
middle 7 central, channel, vehicle 8 mediator, ministry 9 go-between, middleman
10 interagent

intermediate 3 mid 4 fair, mean, so-so
6 broker, center, medium, middle, step in
7 average, between, central, fairish 8 middling 9 go-between, middleman 11 intervening 12 entrepreneur *combining form:*
3 mes 4 medi, meso 5 medio

intermediator 6 broker 9 go-between,
middleman 12 entrepreneur

interment 6 burial 9 sepulture 10 inhumation

interminable 7 endless, eternal, lasting
8 constant, infinite, unending 9 boundless,
ceaseless, continual, limitless, permanent,
perpetual, unceasing, unlimited 10 continuous 11 everlasting

intermission 4 rest, stop 5 break, pause
6 recess 7 latency, respite 8 abeyance,
abeyancy, doldrums, dormancy, interval
10 quiescence, quiescency, suspension
11 cold storage, parenthesis 12 interruption

intermit 4 stay 5 check, defer, delay
6 arrest, hold up, put off 7 hold off, suspend 8 hold over, postpone, prorogue
9 interrupt

intermittent 6 broken, cyclic, fitful, serial
7 checked, iterant 8 arrested, cyclical, metrical, periodic, rhythmic, seasonal, sporadic
9 alternate, iterative, recurrent, recurring,
spasmodic 10 alternated, isochronal, occasional, periodical, rhythmical 11 interrupted,
isochronous

intermix 6 mingle 8 comingle, immingle
9 commingle 11 intermingle

intermixture 5 blend 7 amalgam
12 amalgamation 13 miscegenation

intern 3 jug 4 jail 6 immure 7 confine,
impound, trainee 8 bastille, imprison
9 constrain

internal 3 gut 4 home 5 inner 6 inward,
native 7 private 8 domestic, inherent, interior, visceral 9 intrinsic, viscerous 10 subjective *prefix:* 5 intra

internal organs 4 guts 6 vitals 7 viscera
8 entrails

international organization 2 UN
3 FAO, IAM, ICJ, IFC, ILO, ITO, ITU, OAS,
WHO, WMO 4 IAAF, IABA, IAEA, IARU,
IATA, ICAO, IFIP, IMCO, NATO 5 ICFTU,
SEATO 6 UNESCO, UNICEF

internuncio 5 envoy 6 bearer 7 carrier,
courier 8 emissary 9 messenger

interpolate 3 add 5 admit, annex, enter
6 append, fill in, insert 7 throw in 8 superadd 9 introduce 11 intercalate

interpose 4 cast, push, toss 5 shove,
throw 6 butt in, fill in, insert, meddle, step
in, thrust 7 intrude, mediate, obtrude, throw
in 8 moderate 9 arbitrate, insinuate, intercede, interfere, intervene, introduce, negotiate

interpret 4 limn 5 gloss, image 6 decode,
depict, render 7 comment, explain,
expound, picture, portray 8 annotate, construe, describe, spell out 9 delineate, exemplify, explicate, represent 10 commentate

interpretation 7 meaning, reading, version 8 exegesis 9 construal, rendering
11 explanation, translation

interpretive 8 exegetic 10 expository
11 explanatory, explicatory 12 expositional

interregnum 5 break 8 interval

interrogate 3 ask 4 quiz 5 grill, query
7 examine, inquire 8 question 9 catechize

interrupt 4 halt, stay, stop 5 break, check,
cut in, defer, put in, stall 6 arrest, chip in
7 break in, chime in, disturb, suspend
8 postpone 9 intercept

interruption 3 gap 4 rent, rift 5 break,
pause, split 6 breach, hiatus, lacuna 7 caesura, latency

intersect 4 meet 5 cross 8 crosscut, traverse 9 decussate 10 crisscross

intersection 8 crossing, junction
10 crossroads

intersperse 7 diffuse, scatter

interval 3 gap 4 lull 5 break, comma,
pause, space 6 breach, hiatus, lacuna
7 caesura, interim, respite 9 pausation
11 parenthesis *music:* 4 rest

intervene 4 part 5 sever 6 divide, step in
7 mediate 8 separate 9 intercede, interpose

interweave 3 mix 4 fuse, join, link
5 blend 9 associate

intestinal fortitude 4 grit, guts, sand
5 nerve, pluck, spunk 6 mettle, spirit
7 courage 8 backbone 10 resolution

intestine 3 gut 4 tube 5 bowel, canal
6 inward, viscus 7 viscera (plural) *combining form:* 3 col 4 coli, colo 5 enter
6 entero *part:* 5 cecum, colon, ileum 6 rectum 7 jejunum 8 duodenum

in the same place 6 ibidem

intimacy 7 liberty 9 closeness 10 experience 11 familiarity 12 acquaintance

intimate 3 gut 4 cozy, fond, hint, next
5 amigo, close, crony, imply, inner, pally,
privy, thick 6 attest, chummy, friend,
impart, loving, notify, secret, sexual
7 bespeak, betoken, comrade, connote,

devoted, nearest, suggest 8 announce, familiar, inherent, visceral 9 close-knit, companion, confidant, elemental, essential, ingrained, insinuate, intrinsic, viscerous 10 deep-seated, indwelling 11 cater-cousin 12 acquaintance, confidential

intimation 3 cue 4 clue, hint, wind 5 shade, tinge, trace 6 breath, shadow, strain, streak 7 inkling 8 telltale 10 suggestion

intimidate 3 awe, cow 4 bait, ride 5 abash, alarm, bully, chivy, daunt, deter, force, hound, scare 6 badger, coerce, compel, hector, oblige 7 bluster, buffalo, dragoon, overawe, terrify 8 bludgeon, browbeat, bulldoze, bullyrag, dispirit, disquiet, frighten 9 constrain, strong-arm, terrorize

intolerant 5 irate, upset 6 averse, narrow, stuffy 7 bigoted, waspish 8 dogmatic, obdurate, outraged, snappish, worked up 9 fractious, hidebound, illiberal, impatient, irritable 10 brassbound, disdainful, inflexible, prejudiced, unenlarged 11 smallminded, unindulgent 12 antipathetic, contemptuous, narrow-minded, unforbearing 13 unsympathetic

intonation 4 tone 5 chant 6 accent 10 recitation

in toto 3 all 4 just 5 quite, stick 6 wholly 7 exactly, utterly 10 altogether

intoxicant 5 booze, drink 6 liquor 7 alcohol, spirits 9 aqua vitae

intoxicated 3 cut, wet 4 high 5 blind, dopey, drunk, fried, loopy, soppy, stiff, tight, tipsy 6 elated, looped, rum-dum, sloppy, sodden, soshed, stewed, stoned, tanked, zonked 7 drunken, excited, maudlin, muddled, slopped, sozzled, unsober 8 cockeyed, polluted, squiffed, turned-on 9 inebrious 11 alcoholized, exhilarated

intoxication 7 elation 8 euphoria 11 drunkenness, inebriation

intractable 4 wild 6 mulish, unruly 7 willful 8 indocile, mutinous, obdurate, perverse, stubborn 9 fractious, obstinate 10 bullheaded, headstrong, refractory, selfwilled, unyielding 11 unteachable 12 pertinacious, recalcitrant, ungovernable 13 undisciplined

intransigent 5 tough 7 willful 8 stubborn 9 obstinate, unpliable 10 self-willed, unyielding 12 pertinacious

intrepid 4 bold 5 brave, hardy 6 daring, heroic 7 gallant, valiant 8 fearless, resolute, unafraid, valorous 9 audacious, dauntless, undaunted 10 courageous

intricate 4 hard 5 fancy 6 daedal, knotty 7 arduous, complex, gordian 8 involved 9 Byzantine, difficult, elaborate 11 complicated 12 labyrinthine 13 sophisticated

intrigue 4 plot 5 amour, cabal, covin 6 affair, appeal, devise, excite, scheme 7 attract, beguile, collude, connive, liaison 8 cogitate, conspire, contrive, interest, practice 9 fascinate, machinate, scheme out 10 conspiracy 11 machination

intrinsic see inherent

intrinsically 5 per se 6 as such

introduce 4 lead, moot 5 admit, begin, enter, found, set up, usher 6 broach, fill in, insert, launch, unveil, work in 7 bring up, implant, install, instill, pioneer, precede, preface, present, throw in, usher in 8 acquaint, initiate, innovate, organize 9 establish, insinuate, institute, interject, interpose, originate

introduction 5 debut, proem 7 introit, preface, prelude 8 entrance, exordium, foreword, overture, preamble, prologue, protases (plural), protasis 9 prelusion 12 prolegomenon

introductory 7 initial, nascent 8 proemial 9 beginning, prefatial, prefatory, preludial, prelusive 11 prefatorial, preliminary, preparative

intrude 5 cut in 6 bother, butt in, horn in, impose, invade, meddle, muscle, pester 7 disturb, presume 8 chisel in, encroach, entrench, infringe, trespass 9 interfere, interlope, interpose

intrusive 4 busy 7 curious 9 butting in, officious 10 meddlesome 11 impertinent 13 polypragmatic

in truth 6 indeed, really, verily 8 actually

intuition 7 insight 8 instinct 10 anschauung, sixth sense 11 second sight

inundate 5 drown, flood, swamp, whelm 6 deluge, engulf 8 overflow, submerge 9 overwhelm

inundation 4 pour 5 flood, spate 6 deluge 7 niagara, torrent 8 cataract, flooding, overflow 9 cataclysm

inure 3 use 4 wont 5 steel, train 6 harden, season 7 toughen 8 accustom 9 habituate 10 discipline 11 familiarize

inutile 6 draffy, drossy, no-good 7 nothing 8 unworthy 9 valueless, worthless

invade 4 loot, raid 5 foray 6 ravage 7 assault, overrun, pillage, plunder 8 encroach, entrench, infringe, permeate, trespass 9 overswarm 11 impenetrate

invalid 3 bad, mad 4 null, void 6 infirm, sickly 9 illogical, sophistic 10 fallacious, irrational, reasonless, unreasoned 11 nonrational, null and void 12 unreasonable

invalidate 4 undo 5 abate, annul, quash 6 offset 7 abolish, nullify 8 negative 9 discredit 10 circumduct, counteract, neutralize

invaluable 6 costly 8 precious 9 priceless 11 inestimable

invariable 4 same 5 fixed 6 steady 7 uniform 8 constant 9 continual, immovable, immutable, unfailing, unmovable, unvarying 10 consistent, inflexible, unchanging 11 inalterable, unalterable 12 unchangeable, unmodifiable

invariably 4 ever 6 always 7 forever 10 constantly 11 continually, perpetually

invasion 4 raid 5 foray 6 attack, inroad 9 incursion, intrusion, irruption, offensive 12 encroachment, entrenchment

invective 5 abuse 6 tirade 7 abusive, obloquy 8 diatribe, jeremiad, scurrile 9 contumely, damnatory, philippic, truculent 10 censorious, scurrility, scurrilous, vituperous 11 opprobrious, reproachful 12 billingsgate, condemnatory, contumelious, denunciatory, vituperation, vituperative, vituperatory

inveigh 4 kick, rail 6 except, object 7 protest 9 fulminate 11 expostulate, remonstrate

inveigle 4 bait, coax, lure, toll 5 decoy, snare, tempt 6 allure, cajole, entice, entrap, lead on, seduce 8 persuade

invent 4 coin, mint 5 frame 6 cook up, create, design, devise, make up, patent, vamp up 7 concoct, dream up, fashion, hatch up, pioneer 8 conceive, contrive, discover, engineer, envision 9 fabricate, formulate, originate

invention 7 coinage, fiction 8 creation 10 brainchild, concoction, innovation 11 contrivance, origination

inventive 7 fertile, teeming 8 creative, fruitful, original 9 demiurgic, deviceful, ingenious 10 innovative, innovatory, productive

inventor 4 sire 5 maker 6 author, father 7 creator, founder 8 engineer, original 9 architect, generator, innovator, patriarch 10 discoverer, introducer, originator *air brake:* 12 Westinghouse (George) *air conditioning:* 7 Carrier (Willis) *automobile:* 7 Daimler (Gottlieb) *ballpoint pen:* 4 Loud (John) *barbed wire:* 7 Glidden (Joseph Farwell) *barometer:* 10 Torricelli (Evangelista) *bifocal lens:* 8 Franklin (Benjamin) *camera:* 7 Eastman (George) *cash register:* 5 Ritty (James) *cotton gin:* 7 Whitney (Eli) *cylinder lock:* 4 Yale (Linus) *dirigible:* 8 Zeppelin (Ferdinand von) *dynamite:* 5 Nobel (Alfred) *electric battery:* 5 Volta (Alessandro) *electric fan:* 7 Wheeler (George) *electric organ:* 7 Hammond (Laurens) *electric razor:* 6 Schick (Jacob) *electric stove:* 7 Hadaway *elevator:* 4 Otis (Elisha) *fountain pen:* 8 Waterman (Lewis) *friction match:* 6 Walker (John) *gyrocompass:* 6 Sperry (Elmer) *helicopter:* 8 Sikorsky (Igor) *hot-air balloon:* 11 Montgolfier (Jacques, Joseph) *incandescent lamp:* 6 Edison (Thomas Alva) *induction motor:* 5 Tesla (Nikola) *lawn mower:* 5 Hills *Linotype:* 12 Mergenthaler (Ottmar) *logarithm:* 6 Napier (John) *machine gun:* 7 Gatling (Richard) *microphone:* 8 Berliner (Emile) *movable type:* 9 Gutenberg (Johannes) *parachute:* 9 Blanchard (Jean-Pierre) *pendulum clock:* 7 Huygens (Christiaan) *phonograph:* 6 Edison (Thomas Alva) *photography:* 6 Niepce (Joseph), Talbot (William Henry) 8 Daguerre (Louis) *piano:* 10 Cristofori (Bartolomeo) *radio:* 7 Marconi (Guglielmo) *reaper:* 9 McCormick (Cyrus) *revolver:* 4 Colt (Samuel) *rocket engine:* 7 Goddard (Robert) *safety pin:* 4 Hunt (Walter) *safety razor:* 8 Gillette (King Camp) *sewing machine:* 4 Howe (Elias) *sleeping car:* 7 Pullman (George) *spinning jenny:* 10 Hargreaves (James) *steamboat:* 5 Fitch (John) 6 Fulton (Robert), Miller (Patrick), Rumsey (James) 8 Jouffroy (Claude de) *steam engine:* 4 Watt (James) *steam locomotive:* 10 Stephenson (George) *stethoscope:* 7 Laennec (Rene) *submarine:* 7 Holland (John Philip) *tank:* 7 Swinton (Ernest) *telegraph:* 5 Morse (Samuel F. B.) *telephone:* 4 Bell (Alexander Graham) *telescope:* 10 Lippershey (Hans) *television:* 5 Baird (John) 6 Nipkow (Paul) 8 Zworykin (Vladimir) 10 Farnsworth (Philo) *torpedo:* 9 Whitehead (Robert) *vulcanized rubber:* 8 Goodyear (Charles) *writing for the blind:* 7 Braille (Louis) *zipper:* 6 Judson (Whitcomb)

inventory 3 sum 4 fund, list 5 hoard, stock, store, sum up, tally 6 digest, record, supply, survey 7 account, backlog, catalog, itemize, nest egg, reserve, specify, summary, summate 8 condense, nutshell, register, tabulate 9 checklist, enumerate, epitomize, reservoir, stockpile, summarize, synopsize

inverse 4 turn 6 change, revert 7 reverse 8 contrary, opposite 9 transpose 10 transplace *prefix:* 2 ob

inversion 4 turn 7 reverse, turning 8 reversal 9 about-face, turnabout, volteface 11 changeabout, reversement

invert 4 flip, turn 6 change 7 reverse, uranian, uranist 8 turn over 9 transpose 10 homosexual, transplace

invertebrate 4 weak 5 sissy 7 doormat, milksop 8 boneless, impotent, weakling 9 forceless, jellyfish, spineless 10 emasculate, inadequate, namby-pamby, pantywaist 11 ineffective, ineffectual, Milquetoast, mollycoddle, slack-spined *kind:* 4 worm 6 insect, sponge 7 mollusk 8 arachnid 12 coelenterate

invest 4 gird, veil, wrap 5 adorn, array, beset, dress, endow, endue, imbue, steep 6 clothe, confer, enfold, enwrap, induct, infuse, leaven, ordain, shroud 7 besiege, empower, enclose, envelop, ingrain, install, instate, suffuse

investigate 3 pry 4 poke, sift 5 probe, study 6 go into, search 7 dig into, examine, explore, inquire 8 look into, muckrake, prospect, research 9 delve into 10 scrutinize 11 inquire into

investigation 5 probe, quest 6 survey 7 delving, inquest, inquiry, probing 8 research, sounding 9 surveying 11 inquisition

investigator 4 dick 6 sleuth 7 gumshoe 8 hawkshaw, sherlock 9 detective

investiture 5 siege 8 blockage 9 inaugural, induction 10 initiation 12 inauguration, installation

inveterate 3 old, set 5 fixed, sworn 6 rooted 7 abiding, chronic, settled 8 deep-dyed, enduring, habitual, hardened, lifelong 9 confirmed, hard-shell, ingrained, long-lived, perennial 10 continuing, deep-rooted, deep-seated, entrenched, persistent, persisting 11 established

Invictus author 6 Henley (William Ernest)

invidious 6 bitter, odious 7 envious, envying, hateful, jealous 8 libelous 9 abhorrent, green-eyed, injurious, malignant, maligning, obnoxious, repellent, repugnant, revulsive, vilifying 10 abominable, calumnious, defamatory, detestable, detracting, detractive, detractory, scandalous, slanderous

invigorate 4 stir, zest 5 brace, cheer, rally, renew, rouse 7 animate, enliven, fortify, refresh, restore 8 energize, vitalize 9 reinforce, stimulate 10 exhilarate, rejuvenate, strengthen

in vino ___ 7 veritas

inviolable 4 holy, pure 6 chaste, divine, sacred 7 blessed 8 hallowed 9 undefiled 10 sacrosanct 11 consecrated 13 incorruptible

Invisible Man, The *author:* 5 Wells (Herbert George)

Invisible Man author 7 Ellison (Ralph)

invitation 4 call, lure 7 bidding, proffer, request 8 entreaty, proposal, stimulus 9 incentive 10 attraction, suggestion 11 proposition

invite 3 ask, bid 4 call, lure 5 tempt 6 allure, call in, entice, summon 7 request, solicit

invoice 3 tab 4 bill 5 score 7 account 9 reckoning, statement

invoke 3 beg 4 pray 5 crave, plead 6 appeal, effect 7 beseech, enforce, entreat, implore 9 implement, importune 10 supplicate

involuntary 6 forced, reflex 8 will-less 9 automatic, impulsive, unwitting 10 compulsory, unintended, unprompted 11 instinctive, spontaneous, unmeditated 13 unintentional

involve 4 mire 6 embody, engage, entail, take in, tangle 7 concern, contain, embrace, embroil, include, subsume 8 comprise, entangle 9 encompass, implicate 10 complicate, comprehend

involved 6 daedal, knotty 7 complex, gordian, muddled 8 affected, confused, enmeshed 9 Byzantine, concerned, elaborate, entangled, intricate 10 implicated, interested 11 complicated 12 labyrinthine

invulnerable 10 invincible, unbeatable 11 impregnable, indomitable

inward 5 entad, inner 6 inside, mental 8 interior, internal 9 innermore, intestine, spiritual

inwards 4 guts 6 inside, tripes, within 7 innards, insides, viscera 8 entrails, interior 9 internals

Io *father:* 7 Inachus *guard:* 5 Argus *son:* 7 Epaphus

iodine source 4 kelp

Iolcus king 5 Aeson 6 Pelias

Iole *captor:* 8 Heracles, Hercules *father:* 7 Eurytus *husband:* 6 Hyllus

Ion 6 ligand *kind:* 5 anion 6 cation 8 thermion *suffix:* 3 ium 5 onium

Ion *father:* 6 Apollo *mother:* 6 Creusa *stepfather:* 6 Xuthus

Ionesco play 5 Chairs (The) 10 Rhinoceros (The) 11 Bald Soprano (The)

iota 3 bit, jot, ray 4 atom, mite, whit 5 crumb, grain, ounce, speck 6 tittle 7 smidgen 8 molecule, particle

IOU 4 debt *part:* 3 owe, you

Iowa *capital:* 9 Des Moines *college, university:* 3 Coe 5 Dordt, Drake, Loras *nickname:* 12 Hawkeye State *state bird:* 9 goldfinch *state flower:* 8 wild rose

Iphicles *brother:* 8 Heracles, Hercules *mother:* 7 Alcmene *son:* 6 Iolaus

Iphigenia *brother:* 7 Orestes *father:* 9 Agamemnon *mother:* 12 Clytemnestra *sister:* 7 Electra

Iphis' daughter 6 Evadne

Iran *capital:* 6 Tehran 7 Teheran *monetary unit:* 4 rial *oil center:* 6 Abadan

Iranian 7 Persian *language:* 5 Farsi 7 Kurdish, Persian *non-Persian people:* 5 Kurds *parliament:* 6 Majlis *sect:* 4 Shia 5 Sunni *sect member:* 6 Shiite 7 Sunnite *title:* 4 shah

Iraq *capital:* 7 Baghdad *monetary unit:* 5 dinar

irascible 5 cross, huffy, irate, ratty, surly, testy 6 cranky, ireful, snappy, tetchy, touchy 7 bristly, peevish, peppery 8 choleric, petulant, snappish 9 fractious, impatient, irritable, querulous, temperish 10 passionate 11 belligerent, hot-tempered 12 cantankerous 13 quick-tempered

Ira's father 6 Ikkesh

irate 3 mad 4 waxy 5 angry, wroth 6 ireful, wrathy, wrothy 7 enraged, furious 8 choleric, incensed, provoked, wrathful

ire 3 mad 4 fury, rage 5 anger, wrath 6 enrage, madden, temper 7 incense, steam up, umbrage 9 infuriate 10 exasperate 11 indignation 12 exasperation

Ireland 4 Eire, Erin 5 Ierne 8 Hibernia 9 Innisfail *capital:* 6 Dublin *monetary unit:* 5 pound

Irene 3 Pax *father:* 4 Zeus 7 Jupiter *mother:* 6 Themis

irenic 4 calm 7 pacific 8 pacifist, peaceful 9 peaceable 10 nonviolent 12 conciliatory, pacificatory

Iris *father:* 7 Thaumas *mother:* 7 Electra

Irish 4 Erse 6 Celtic, Gaelic *accent:* 6 brogue *battle cry:* 3 abu 4 aboo *cattle:* 5 Kerry *clan:* 4 sept *combining form:* 7 Hiberno *coronation stone:* 7 Lia Fail *cudgel:* 9 shillalah 10 shillelagh *death spirit:* 7 banshee *dirge:* 8 ullagone *dog:* 6 setter 7 terrier *elf:* 10 leprechaun *exclamation:* 3 aru 5 arrah *festival:* 4 feis *flag color:* 5 green, white 6 orange *flower:* 8 shamrock *girl:* 4 lass 6 lassie 7 colleen *goblin:* 5 pooka *god:* 3 Ler 5 Dagda 6 Aengus *goddess:* 4 Badb, Bodb 6 Brigit 8 Morrigan *harp:* 8 clarsach *hero:* 9 Cuchulain, Cuchullin 11 Chuchulainn *heroine:* 7 Deirdre *king:* 9 Brian Boru *lake:* 5 lough *language:* 6 Gaelic *legislature:* 4 Dail *militant force:* 3 IRA *nationalist:* 7 Parnell (Charles) 8 O'Connell (Daniel) *nationalist society:* 8 Sinn Fein *noble:* 6 flaith *patron saint:* 7 Patrick *theater:* 5 Abbey *writing system:* 4 ogam 5 ogham; (see also **Gaelic; Celtic**)

Irish moss 7 seaweed 9 carrageen

irk 3 try, vex 4 fret, gall, pain 5 anger, annoy, peeve, pique, upset 6 abrade, bother, harass, nettle, ruffle, strain, stress 7 provoke, trouble 8 distress, exercise, irritate 10 exasperate

Irma ___ 7 La Douce

iron 4 hard 5 gyves, press 6 ferrum, fetter, strong 7 adamant, manacle, shackle 8 handcuff, obdurate 9 unbending 10 adamantine, brassbound, inexorable, inflexible, relentless, unyielding *combining form:* 5 ferri, ferro, sider 6 sidero *German:* 5 eisen *relating to:* 6 ferric 7 ferrous *symbol:* 2 Fe *wrought:* 5 mitis

ironbound 5 harsh, rough 6 craggy, jagged, rugged, uneven 7 scraggy 8 asperous, scabrous, unsmooth

Iron City 10 Pittsburgh

ironclad 5 fixed 8 constant 9 immovable, immutable 10 inflexible, invariable 11 inalterable, unalterable 12 unchangeable

ironhanded 5 rigid 6 strict 8 rigorist, rigorous 9 draconian, stringent 12 unpermissive

ironhearted 5 stony 7 callous 8 hardened, obdurate 9 heartless, unfeeling 10 hard-boiled 11 cold-blooded 13 unsympathetic

ironic 3 wry 6 biting 7 caustic, cutting, cynical, mordant, satiric 8 sardonic 9 sarcastic, trenchant

iron ore 8 goethite, hematite, limonite, siderite, taconite 9 magnetite

Iron Pants 6 Patton (George)

irons 5 bonds, gyves 6 chains 7 fetters 8 manacles, shackles

Iroquois tribe 6 Cayuga, Mohawk, Oneida, Seneca 8 Onondaga

irradiate 5 edify 6 illume, uplift 7 improve 8 illumine 9 enlighten 10 illuminate

irrational 3 mad 5 crazy 6 absurd, insane 7 invalid 8 demented 9 illogical, senseless, sophistic 10 fallacious, reasonless, ridiculous, unreasoned 11 nonrational 12 unreasonable

irrefutable 4 sure 7 certain 8 positive 10 conclusive, inarguable 11 indubitable 12 indisputable 13 incontestable, uncontestable

irregular 3 odd 5 queer 6 fitful, off-key, patchy, random, spotty, uneven, unique 7 aimless, deviant, devious, erratic, strange, unaimed, unequal 8 aberrant, abnormal, atypical, informal, lopsided, partisan, peculiar, singular, sporadic, unstable, unsteady, variable 9 anomalous, desultory, divergent, eccentric, guerrilla, haphazard, hit-or-miss, spasmodic, unnatural, unregular, unsettled 10 asymmetric, changeable, designless, inconstant, off-balance, unbalanced, unofficial 11 exceptional, purposeless 12 overbalanced, unconsidered, unsystematic *combining form:* 4 anom 5 anomo 6 anomal 7 anomali, anomalo

irregularity 7 anomaly 8 asperity, disorder 9 roughness 10 inequality, unevenness

irrelevant 7 foreign 9 unrelated 10 extraneous, immaterial, inapposite, irrelative 11 impertinent, inessential, unessential, unimportant 12 inapplicable 13 insignificant

irreligious 5 pagan 6 amoral, unholy 7 godless, impious, profane, ungodly,

unmoral 8 indevout, undevout 11 blasphemous 12 sacrilegious

irreparable 8 cureless, hopeless 9 incurable, insanable, uncurable 10 impossible
11 immedicable 12 irredeemable,
irremediable 13 irreclaimable, irrecover-
able, irretrievable, uncorrectable, unrecoverable

irreproachable 4 good, pure 8 flawless,
innocent, spotless, virtuous 9 blameless,
errorless, exemplary, exquisite, faultless,
guiltless, righteous 10 immaculate, impeccable, inculpable, unblamable

irresolute 6 fickle, unsure, wobbly 7 halting 8 doubtful, hesitant, unstable, wavering
9 faltering, tentative, uncertain, undecided
10 changeable, inconstant 11 fluctuating,
vacillating, vacillatory 12 wiggle-waggle

irresponsible 4 wild 8 carefree, careless,
feckless, reckless 9 uncareful 10 incautious, unreliable 12 unanswerable, undependable 13 unaccountable, untrustworthy

irreverent 6 unholy 7 impious, profane,
ungodly 10 unhallowed

irrevocable 4 firm 5 final 9 immutable
11 unalterable 12 irreversible, unchangeable, unmodifiable, unrepealable 13 non-
reversible

irrigation ditch 5 flume 6 sluice 7 ace-
quia

irritability 6 choler 9 petulance 11 fretful-
ness *abnormal:* 8 erethism

irritable 4 edgy 5 cross, huffy, raspy,
techy, testy, waspy, whiny 6 cranky,
ornery, snappy, tetchy, touchy, twitty 7 fretful, peevish, pettish, prickly, raspish, waspish 8 choleric, petulant, prickish, snappish
9 fractious, impatient, irascible, querulent,
querulous, splenetic 12 cantankerous, disagreeable, querulential

irritant 4 pest 6 bother, pester, plague
8 nuisance 9 annoyance, besetment
10 botherment 11 botheration 12 exasperation

irritate 3 get, irk, rub, try, vex 4 fret, gall,
goad, huff, rile, roil 5 anger, annoy, chafe,
grate, peeve, pique, spite 6 abrade,
badger, bother, burn up, harass, hector,
madden, needle, nettle, offend, put out, ruffle 7 affront, inflame, provoke 8 acerbate
9 aggravate, stimulate 10 exacerbate,
exasperate

irritated 5 irate, testy 7 fretful, peevish
8 choleric 9 impatient, irascible 11 hot-tempered

irritation 4 itch, rash, sore 5 uredo
9 annoyance 10 excitation

irrupt 4 spew 5 belch, eject, eruct, expel
7 intrude 8 disgorge

irruption 4 raid 5 foray 6 inroad 8 invasion 9 incursion

I.R.S. employee 4 acct 10 accountant

Iru's father 5 Caleb

Isaac *father:* 7 Abraham *mother:* 5 Sarah
son: 4 Esau 5 Jacob *wife:* 7 Rebekah

Isabella *brother:* 7 Claudio *husband:*
9 Vincentio

Isabella I *country:* 5 Spain *home:* 7 Castile *husband:* 9 Ferdinand

Isaiah's father 4 Amoz

Iscah *brother:* 3 Lot *father:* 5 Haran *sister:* 6 Milcah

Iseult, Isolde *beloved:* 7 Tristan *husband:* 4 Mark

Ishbak *father:* 7 Abraham *mother:*
7 Keturah

Ishbosheth's father 4 Saul

Ishi *father:* 6 Appaim *son:* 6 Zoheth

Ishmael 6 pariah 7 outcast 8 castaway,
derelict, outsider 11 offscouring, untouchable *father:* 4 Azel 7 Abraham, Pashhur
9 Jehonanan, Nethaniah *mother:* 5 Hagar
son: 5 Massa 8 Zebadiah

Ishmaiah's father 7 Obadiah

Ishpah's father 6 Beriah

Ishpan's father 7 Shashak

Ishtar *brother:* 7 Shamash *father:* 3 Anu,
Sin *lover:* 6 Tammuz

Ishuah's father 5 Asher

Ishui's father 4 Saul 5 Asher

Isis *brother:* 6 Osiris *father:* 3 Geb *husband:* 6 Osiris *mother:* 3 Nut *son:* 4 Sept
5 Horus

Islam *adherent:* 6 Moslem, Muslim
founder: 8 Mohammed, Muhammad *god:*
5 Allah *priest:* 4 imam *scriptures:*
5 Koran; (see also Muslim)

island 3 ait, cay, key 4 holm, isle 5 atoll,
islet 6 cut off, enisle, skerry 7 crannog, iso-
late 8 close off, insulate, separate 9 segre-
gate, sequester *Admiralty group:*
5 Manus *Adriatic Sea:* 3 Vis 4 Brac, Cres,
Hvar 5 Brach, Ciovo, Mljet, Solta 6 Lesina,
Pharus *Aegean Sea:* 4 Scio 5 Chios,
Khios, Samos, Thira 6 Ikaria, Lemnos, Les-
bos, Limnos 7 Nikaria 8 Mitilini, Mytilene,
Santorin 10 Sakis-Adasi, Susam-Adasi
Alaska: 4 Adak, Atka, Attu, Kulu 6 Wran-
gell *Aleutian group:* 3 Rat 4 Adak, Akun,
Attu 5 Amlia, Kiska, Umnak 6 Kanaga,
Tanaga, Unimak 8 Amchitka, Unalaska
American Samoa: 3 Ofu, Tau 4 Rose
6 Swains *Andaman Sea:* 4 Mali 5 Tavoy
Antarctica: 5 Scott, Young *Apostle group:*
3 Oak 4 Long, Sand 5 Outer 8 Madeline,
Michigan, Stockton *Arafura Sea:* 5 Dolak
Arctic Archipelago: 6 Baffin 8 Victoria
Arctic Ocean: 5 Senja *Australian:*
5 Cocos 8 Tasmania *Azores:* 4 Pico
5 Corvo, Faial *Bahamas:* 3 Cat, Rum
4 Long 5 Abaco, Exuma 6 Andros, Inagua
7 Acklins, Crooked 8 Watlings 9 Eleuthera,

Mayaguana 11 San Salvador *Bahrain:*
5 Sitra 8 Muharraq *Balearic group:*
5 Ibiza 7 Majorca, Menorca, Minorca
8 Mallorca *Baltic Sea:* 4 Moon, Muhu
5 Faron, Mukhu, Rugen, Worms 6 Vormsi
7 Gotland 8 Bornholm, Gothland, Gottland
Barents Sea: 4 Bear *Bay of Biscay:* 2 Re
Bay of Naples: 5 Capri *Bay of Panama:*
4 Naos *Bering Sea:* 5 Medny 7 Nunivak
10 Big Diomede 13 Little Diomede *Bismarck Archipelago:* 5 Lihir 10 New Britain *Bristol Channel:* 5 Lundy *Buzzards
Bay:* 9 Cuttyhunk *Canadian:* 5 Banks,
Devon 6 Baffin 8 Bathurst, Melville, Somerset, Victoria 9 Anticosti, Ellesmere
10 Cape Breton 11 Axel Heiberg, Southampton 12 Newfoundland, Prince Edward
Canaries: 6 Gomera 7 La Palma 8 Tenerife 9 Lanzarote *Cape Verde:* 4 Fogo,
Maio, Mayo 5 Brava, Rombo *Caribbean
Sea:* 4 Cuba 5 Aruba, Utila, Vache
6 Tobago 7 Antigua, Curaçao, Jamaica
8 Barbados, Dominica, Trinidad 10 Guadeloupe, Martinique, Puerto Rico; (see also
Virgin group) *Carolines:* 5 Sorol 6 Pon-
ape 9 Ascension *Chagos Archipelago:*
11 Diego Garcia *Channel group:* 4 Herm,
Sark 5 Lihou, Sercq 6 Jersey 8 Guernsey
Chesapeake Bay: 4 Deal, Kent 5 Smith,
Watts *Chukchi Sea:* 6 Herald *Comoro
group:* 7 Mayotte *Congo River:* 4 Bamu
Cook group: 4 Atiu 5 Mauke *Croatia:*
3 Krk, Pag, Rab 5 Susak, Unije *Cyclades:*
3 Ios, Kea, Nio 4 Ceos, Keos, Milo
5 Delos, Melos, Milos, Naxos, Paros, Siros,
Syros 6 Andros, Dhilos 7 Amorgos, Cyth-
nos, Kithnos, Kythnos, Mykonos *Denmark:*
3 Als, Fyn, Mon 4 Aero, Fano, Moen, Mors
5 Alsen, Funen, Moers, Samso 8 Bornholm
13 Fanum Fortunae *D'Entrecasteaux
group:* 8 Kaluwawa 9 Fergusson *Dodecanese group:* 3 Coo, Cos, Kos 4 Caso,
Lero, Simi, Syme 5 Kasos, Leros, Lipso,
Lisso, Patmo, Telos 6 Calino, Lipsos,
Nisiro, Patmos 7 Calimno, Nisiros, Nisyros
8 Kalymnos *East River:* 5 Ward's 7 Welfare 9 Roosevelt *England's:* 7 Britian
9 Britannia 12 Great Britain *English Channel:* 5 Wight *Faeroes:* 4 Vago 5 Bordo,
Sando *Fiji:* 4 Koro 5 Mango, Vatoa *Florida Keys:* 4 Long, Vaca, West 5 Largo
7 Big Pine 9 Matecumbe, Sugarloaf *Fox
group:* 5 Umnak 6 Akutan, Unimak
8 Unalaska *French:* 7 Corsica 12 New
Caledonia *French Polynesia:* 4 Rapa,
Reao, Ua Pu 5 Ua Pau *Frisian group:*
3 Rom 4 Föhr, Sylt 5 Amrum, Juist, Man-
do, Texel 6 Borkum 7 Ameland 8 Lange-
eoog, Pellworm, Vlieland 9 Helgoland, Nor-
derney *Futunas:* 5 Alofi *Galápagos:*
5 Pinta 7 Chatham, Isabela 8 Abingdon

10 Albermarle *Georgia:* 5 Tybee *Germany:*
4 Fohr 7 Fehmarn 9 Helgoland 10 Heligo-
land *Greater Antilles:* 4 Cuba 7 Jamaica
10 Hispaniola, Puerto Rico *Greece:* 4 Milo,
Rodi 5 Creta, Crete, Hydra, Idhra, Kriti,
Rodos, Tenos, Tinos 6 Euboea, Evvoia,
Hydrea, Rhodes, Rhodus 9 Negropont
10 Negroponte *Grenadines:* 5 Union *Gulf
of Alaska:* 6 Kodiak *Gulf of Bothnia:*
5 Karlö *Gulf of Carpentaria:* 5 Maria
6 Groote 7 Eylandt *Gulf of Guinea:* 7 Sao
Tomé 8 Principe, Sao Thomé 11 Saint
Thomas *Gulf of Mexico:* 3 Cat 5 Lobos
Gulf of Panama: 3 Rey *Gulf of St. Law-
rence:* 5 Brion *Gulf of Thailand:* 3 Kut
5 Samui *Haiti:* 6 Gonave *Hawaii:* 4 Maui,
Oahu 5 Kauai, Lanai 6 Niihau 7 Molokai
9 Kahoolawe *Hudson Bay:* 5 Coats *Indian
Ocean:* 4 Mahé, Nias 5 Heard, Pemba
7 La Dique, Praslin, Réunion 8 Sri Lanka,
Zanzibar 9 Mauritius 10 Madagascar *Indo-
nesia:* 4 Bali, Biak, Java, Maja, Muna,
Nias, Rhio, Riau, Roma, Roti, Savu, Sawu
5 Batam, Boano, Buton, Djawa, Japen,
Lakor, Moena, Riouw, Rotti, Rupat, Sawoe,
Solor, Sumba, Wetar, Wokam 6 Butung,
Flores, Jappen, Lombok, Madura, Padang,
Roepat, Romang, Soemba 7 Celebes,
Madoera, Sumatra, Sumbawa 8 Boetoeng,
Soembawa, Sulawesi 10 Bandanaira,
Banda Neira, Sandalwood *Inner Hebrides:*
4 Coll, Eigg, Iona, Jura, Muck, Mull, Skye
5 Canna, Gigha, Islay, Tiree, Tyree *Ionian
group:* 5 Corfu, Paxos, Zante 6 Cerigo,
Ithaca, Leukas, Levkas 10 Santa Maura
Iran: 5 Shahi *Ireland:* 4 Aran *Irish Sea:*
3 Man *Italy:* 4 Elba 6 Sicily 8 Sardinia
Japan: 3 Iki, Uku 4 Naru, Yezo 5 Awaji,
Fukae, Fukue, Hondo, Shodo 6 Honshu,
Kyushu 7 Shikoku 8 Hokkaido 10 Sho-
doshima *Java Sea:* 4 Laut *Kiribati:*
6 Tarawa *Kuril group:* 4 Urup 5 Ketoi,
Matua 6 Iturup 7 Etorofu, Matsuwa
8 Kunashir 9 Kunashiri *Lake Champlain:*
5 Grand *Lake Erie:* 9 North Bass, South
Bass 10 Middle Bass *Lake Huron:*
8 Drummond 10 Manitoulin *Lake Michigan:*
3 Hog 4 High 6 Beaver *Lake Ontario:*
5 Wolfe *Lake Superior:* 4 Sand 6 Royale
7 Manitou *Lake Winnipeg:* 5 Hecla *largest:* 9 Greenland *Leeward group:* 5 Nevis
7 Antigua, Barbuda, Redonda 8 Anguilla,
Sombrero 10 Montserrat, Saint Kitts 13 St.
Christopher *legendary:* 7 Cipango *Lesser
Sundas:* 4 Alor 5 Ombai *Leti group:*
3 Moa 5 Lakor *Line group:* 5 Flint 6 Malden, Vostok 7 Fanning, Palmyra 8 Starbuck 9 Christmas *Long Island Sound:*
4 City, Hart 5 Goose, Harts *Loyalty group:*
3 Uea 4 Lifu, Maré, Uvea 5 Lifou *Malay
Archipelago:* 5 Kisar, Larat, Timor 6 Bor-

neo **9** New Guinea *Malaysia:* **6** Penang, Pinang **13** Prince of Wales *Malta:* **4** Gozo *Marianas:* **4** Maug, Rota **5** Pagan **6** Saipan *Marquesas group:* **4** Eiào, Ua Pu **6** Hatutu, Hiva Oa, Ua Huka **7** Tahuata **8** Fatu Hiva, Nuku Hiva *Marshall group:* **5** Wotho, Wotje **8** Eniwetok **9** Kwajalein *Massachusetts:* **9** Nantucket *Mediterranean Sea:* **4** Elba **5** Corfu, Crete, Malta **6** Cyprus, Euboea, Rhodes, Sicily **7** Corsica **8** Sardinia *Midway group:* **4** Sand **7** Eastern *Moluccas:* **4** Buru **5** Ambon, Ceram, Seram **6** Boeroe *Mozambique channel:* **10** Juan de Nova *Myanmar:* **5** Daung, Kadan, Lanbi *Narragansett Bay:* **5** Rhode **8** Prudence **9** Aquidneck, Conanicut *Netherlands:* **5** Texel **7** Ameland **8** Vlieland *Netherlands Antilles:* **7** Curaçao *New York:* **4** Fire, Long **9** Gardiners, Roosevelt *New York Bay:* **5** Ellis **6** Staten **7** Liberty **9** Governors, Manhattan *New Zealand:* **5** South, White **7** Chatham, Stewart **8** D'Urville *Niagara River:* **4** Goat *Nile River:* **4** Argo, Roda, Ruda **5** Rhoda **6** Rawdah **11** Elephantine *North Channel:* **3** Mew *Northern Cook group:* **7** Penrhyn **8** Manihiki **9** Tongareva *North Pacific:* **4** Wake *Northwest Territories:* **5** Banks, Bylot, Devon **8** Bathurst, Melville **9** Ellesmere **10** Cornwallis, Resolution **13** Prince of Wales *Norwegian:* **8** Jan Mayen *Norwegian Sea:* **5** Donna, Smola, Vikna *Nova Scotia:* **5** Sable **10** Cape Breton *off Alaska:* **4** Dall **5** Kayak *off Albania:* **5** Sazan **6** Saseno *off Australia:* **4** Dunk *off Belize:* **9** Ambergris *off Brazil:* **4** Apeu **5** Rocas *off British Columbia:* **4** King, Pitt **9** Vancouver *off Cape Cod:* **8** Muskeget **9** Nantucket *off Chile:* **5** Guafo, Mocha *off China:* **4** Amoy **5** Ma-tsu **6** Hainan, Quemoy, Taiwan *off Crete:* **3** Dia *off Ecuador:* **4** Puna *off England:* **3** Man **5** Wight **6** Walney *off Florida:* **3** Dog **4** Pine **6** Amelia **7** Pelican, Sanibel **9** Anastasia *off France:* **2** If *off French Guiana:* **6** Devil's *off Georgia:* **10** Cumberland **11** Saint Simons *off Germany:* **4** Sylt *off Greenland:* **5** Disko *off Guinea:* **5** Tombo *off Hispaniola:* **5** Beata *off Honduras:* **5** Tigre *off Iceland:* **7** Surtsey *off India:* **5** Sagar *off Ireland:* **4** Tory **5** Clare, Clear *off Kenya:* **4** Lamu *off Long Island:* **7** Fishers *off Louisiana:* **5** Marsh *off Maine:* **4** Deer, Orrs **5** Swans **8** Monhegan **11** Mount Desert *off Malay Peninsula:* **6** Phuket **9** Singapore *off Maryland:* **10** Assateague *off Massachusetts:* **4** Plum **7** Naushon *off Mexico:* **7** Cozumel *off Mississippi:* **4** Horn, Ship *off Mozambique:* **3** Ibo *off New Brunswick:* **10** Campobello *off Newfoundland:* **4** Bell *off Nige-*ria:* **5** Lagos *off North Carolina:* **5** Bodie *off Norway:* **5** Bomlo, Froya, Hitra, Sotra, Stord, Vardo **8** Hitteren *off Panama:* **5** Coiba **6** Parida *off Poland:* **5** Wolin **6** Wollin *off Puerto Rico:* **4** Crab **7** Culebra, Vieques *off Rhode Island:* **5** Block *off Scotland:* **4** Bute **5** Arran *off South Carolina:* **5** North **6** Parris **10** Hilton Head *off Sri Lanka:* **5** Delft *off Staten Island:* **7** Hoffman *off Sumatra:* **2** We **3** Weh *off Sweden:* **5** Graso, Oland, Vaddo *off Syria:* **5** Arvad, Arwad, Rouad **6** Aradus *off Tanzania:* **5** Mafia, Pemba *off Tasmania:* **5** Bruni, Bruny *off Tunisia:* **5** Jerba **6** Djerba, Meninx *off Venezuela:* **5** Aruba **7** Bonaire **8** Buen Aire *off Virginia:* **5** Wreck *off Wales:* **5** Caldy **6** Caldey *Okinawa group:* **4** Kume *Orkneys:* **3** Hoy *Outer Hebrides:* **5** Barra, Scarp *Palmer Archipelago:* **6** Anvers **7** Antwerp, Brabant *Pearl Harbor:* **4** Ford *Persian Gulf:* **4** Qeys **5** Kharg, Khark *Philippines:* **4** Buad, Cebu, Fuga, Ilin, Poro, Sulu **5** Balut, Batan, Bohol, Coron, Daram, Leyte, Luzon, Panay, Samal, Samar, Sugbu, Talim, Ticao, Verde **6** Negros **7** Masbate, Mindoro, Palawan, Paragua **8** Limasawa, Mindanao **10** Corregidor *Phoenix group:* **4** Hull, Mary **6** Birnie, Canton **9** Enderbury *Puerto Rico:* **4** Mona *Quebec:* **4** Alma *Queen Charlotte group:* **7** Moresby *Red Sea:* **5** Tiran, Zugur, Zuqar *Russia:* **7** Wrangel *Ryukyu group:* **7** Okinawa *St. Lawrence River:* **4** Hare **5** Jesus **8** Montreal *San Francisco Bay:* **5** Angel *Santa Cruz:* **5** Anuda, Ndeni **6** Cherry *Sea of Japan:* **4** Sado **5** Rebun *Sea of Marmara:* **4** Avsa *second largest:* **9** New Guinea *Senegal:* **5** Gorée *Seychelles:* **4** Mahé **7** La Digue, Praslin *Shetland archipelago:* **4** Unst, Yell **5** Foula *Shumagin group:* **4** Unga *Sierra Leone:* **5** Tasso *Society group:* **5** Eimeo, Tahaa, Tahao, Taiti **6** Moorea, Tahiti **8** Otaheite *Solomon group:* **4** Buka, Gizo, Savo **7** Malaita **11** Guadalcanal **12** Bougainville *South Atlantic:* **5** Gough **6** Gough's **11** Saint Helena *South Korea:* **5** Cheju *South of Tokyo:* **3** Iwo **7** Iwo Jima, Naka Iwo *South Orkneys:* **10** Coronation *South Pacific:* **3** Hiu **4** Niue **5** Raoul **6** Savage, Sunday **7** Norfolk **8** Pitcairn *Spitsbergen archipelago:* **4** Edge *Strait of Hormuz:* **5** Qeshm, Qishm *Sulu Archipelago:* **4** Jolo **5** Lapac *Svalbard:* **4** Hope *Sverdrup:* **11** Axel Heiberg **12** Amund Ringnes *Swedish:* **3** Ven **4** Hven **5** Hveen, Orust *Tanzania:* **8** Zanzibar *Texas:* **5** Padre *Thames River:* **7** Sheppey *third largest:* **6** Borneo *Tierra del Fuego:* **5** Hoste *Tonga:* **3** Eua, Foa **4** Uiha **5** Haano *Treasury group:* **4** Mono

Truk group: 3 Tol 4 Haru, Moen, Udot, Uman 5 Fefan *Tuamotu Archipelago:* 4 Anaa 5 Chain *Turkish:* 5 Imroz 6 Imbros *Tuvalu:* 7 Nanumea 9 Nukufetau *Tyrrhenian Sea:* 6 Ischia 11 Montecristo *Vanuatu:* 3 Api, Epi, Oba 4 Aoba, Gaua, Tana, Vate 5 Efate, Maewo, Tanna *Venezuelan:* 5 Patos 9 La Tortuga *Virgin group, American:* 9 Saint John 10 Saint Croix 11 Saint Thomas *Virgin group, British:* 5 Peter 6 Norman 7 Anegada, Tortola 11 Jost Van Dyke *volcanic:* 5 Tofua 7 Iwo Jima *Wales:* 8 Anglesea, Anglesey, Holyhead *Weddell Sea:* 4 Ross 6 Hearst *Western Samoa:* 5 Upolu 6 Savaii *West Indies:* 4 Mona, Saba, Salt 5 Nevis, Peter, Saona 6 Tobago, Tortue 7 Grenada, Tortuga 8 Trinidad 9 Santa Cruz 10 Concepción, Hispaniola, Montserrat, Saint Croix; (see also **Bahamas; Greater Antilles; Leeward group; Virgin group; Windward group**) *West of England:* 7 Ireland *West Pacific:* 5 Dyaul, Fauro, Ocean 6 Banaba, Marcus 7 Iwo Jima, Kita Iwo 9 Minami Iwo *Windward group:* 10 Martinique *with former penitentiary:* 8 Alcatraz

island group *Alaska:* 3 Rat 8 Aleutian, Pribilof 9 Andreanof, Catherine *Aleutians:* 4 Near *American Samoa:* 5 Manua *Arabian Sea:* 9 Laccadive *Arctic Archipelago:* 8 Sverdrup *Arctic Ocean:* 8 Svalbard 12 Novaya Zemlya *Bahamas:* 5 Berry, Exuma 6 Bimini *Banda Sea:* 5 Damar *Bangladesh:* 5 Hatia, Hatya *Bay of Bengal:* 7 Andaman, Nicobar *between England and France:* 7 Channel *Bismarck Archipelago:* 4 Feni 5 Tabar, Tanga *Bismarck Sea:* 4 Vitu *British:* 7 Bermuda *Caribbean Sea:* 4 Swan 5 Pearl 6 Cayman, Perlas, Pigeon 8 Pichones 10 Grenadines, West Indies *Carolines:* 3 Uap, Yap 4 Truk 5 Nomoi 7 Hogoleu *Central Pacific Ocean:* 4 Line 5 Samoa, Union 6 Danger, Midway 7 Phoenix, Tokelau 8 Manihiki 9 Polynesia 12 Northern Cook *Coral Sea:* 4 Huon *Cuba:* 8 Camaguey *East of Philippines:* 10 Micronesia *East Siberian Sea:* 4 Bear 8 Medvezhi *Ecuador:* 5 Colon 9 Galápagos *England:* 5 Farne *Fiji:* 3 Lau 7 Eastern *Formosa Strait:* 4 Hoko 6 Peng hu 10 Pescadores *French:* 5 Salut 6 Safety 9 Kerguelen *French Polynesia:* 3 Low 6 Tubuai 7 Austral, Paumotu, Société, Society, Tuamotu 9 Marquesas, Touamotou *Germany:* 8 Halligen *Greece:* 6 Aegean, Ionian 8 Cyclades 10 Dodecanese 11 Dodecanesus *Hudson Bay:* 7 Belcher *Indian Ocean:* 7 Aldabra *Indonesia:* 4 Asia, Batu, Pagi, Sula 5 Babar, Batoe, Pagai, Pageh, Penju, Spice, Wakde 6 Maluku *Ireland:* 4 Aran *Japan:* 5 Osumi *largest:* 5 Malay 8 Malaysia *Lesser Antilles:* 8 Windward *Malay Archipelago:* 5 Sunda 6 Soenda *Mediterranean Sea:* 8 Baleares, Balearic *Moluccas:* 3 Kai, Kei, Obi 4 Leti 5 Banda, Letti 8 Tanimbar 9 Timorlaut *New Caledonia:* 7 Loyalty 9 Loyalties *North of Australia:* 9 Melanesia *North of British Isles:* 5 Faroe 7 Faeroes *North off Fiji:* 5 Hoorn 6 Futuna *North of Madagascar:* 7 Aldabra 8 Farquhar *North of New Caledonia:* 5 Belep *North of New Guinea:* 8 Bismarck 9 Admiralty 11 Admiralties *Northwest Territories:* 5 Parry *off Alaska:* 3 Fox *off Alaska Peninsula:* 8 Shumagin *off Cape Cod:* 9 Elizabeth *off eastern Asia:* 5 Kuril 6 Kurile *off England:* 6 Scilly *off Florida:* 11 Dry Tortugas *off Guinea:* 3 Los 4 Loos *off Honduras:* 5 Bahia *off Morocco:* 7 Madeira *off New Guinea:* 3 Aru 4 Aroe *off Nicaragua:* 4 Corn *off northern Africa:* 6 Canary 8 Canaries *off northern Australia:* 6 Wessel 7 Dampier *off Sicily:* 5 Egadi 8 Aegadian *Outer Hebrides:* 4 Uist *Pago Pago's:* 13 American Samoa *Papua New Guinea:* 5 Green *Persian Gulf:* 4 Tunb *Philippines:* 4 Cuyo 5 Tapul 6 Lubang 7 Basilan, Bisayas, Visayan *Portuguese:* 6 Azores *Quebec:* 8 Magdalen 9 Madeleine *Ryukyus:* 5 Amami *St. Lawrence River:* 8 Thousand *Sea of Japan:* 3 Oki *Sea of Marmara:* 5 Kizil 7 Princes 11 Kizil Adalar *South Atlantic Ocean:* 8 Falkland, Malvinas *South China Sea:* 6 Hirata 7 Paracel, Spratly *South of New Zealand:* 8 Auckland *South Pacific:* 11 Austronesia *Sulu Sea:* 7 Cagayan 9 Cagayanes *Tonga:* 5 Vavau *Tyrrhenian Sea:* 5 Ponza *Venezuelan:* 4 Aves, Bird 9 Los Roques *West Europe:* 12 British Isles *West Indies:* 6 Virgin 10 Guadeloupe *West of French Polynesia:* 4 Cook *West of Scotland:* 7 Western 8 Hebrides *West Pacific Ocean:* 4 Duff 5 Bonin, Mapia, Palau, Pelew 7 Ladrone, Mariana, Solomon, Vanuatu 8 Marshall, Treasury 9 Ogasawara 10 Saint David

island nation *Atlantic Ocean:* 9 Cape Verde *Indian Ocean:* 8 Malagasy, Malgache, Sri Lanka 10 Madagascar, Seychelles *Mediterranean Sea:* 6 Cyprus *Mozambique Channel:* 6 Comoro 7 Comores *off southern China:* 6 Taiwan *south of Greenland:* 7 Iceland *West Indies:* 4 Cuba 7 Jamaica 8 Barbados 10 Saint Lucia *West Pacific Ocean:* 5 Nauru *Windward group:* 8 Dominica

island province 12 Prince Edward

island state 6 Hawaii

isle see **island**

Ismene *brother:* 9 Polynices *father:* 7 Oedipus *mother:* 7 Jocasta *sister:* 8 Antigone *uncle:* 5 Creon

isochronous 8 periodic 9 alternate, recurrent, recurring 10 periodical 12 intermittent

isolate 5 alone, apart 6 cut off, detach, enisle, island, remove 7 removed, seclude 8 block off, close off, detached, insulate, pinpoint, separate 9 segregate, sequester 13 unaccompanied

Isolde see Iseult

Israel 4 Zion 5 Jacob 6 Canaan 9 Palestine *capital:* 9 Jerusalem *district:* 5 Haifa 7 Central, Tel Aviv 8 Northern, Southern 9 Jerusalem *legislature:* 7 Knesset *monetary unit:* 6 shekel

Israelite see Hebrew; Jewish

Issachar *father:* 5 Jacob *mother:* 4 Leah

issue 4 emit, flow, gush, pour, rise, seed, stem, vent 5 arise, birth, brood, child, topic 6 effect, emerge, get out, put out, result, scions, sequel, source, spring 7 descent, edition, emanate, give off, give out, outcome, problem, proceed, progeny, publish, release, subject 8 bulletin, causatum, children, question, throw off 9 offspring, originate, posterity 10 derive from, distribute, end product 11 consequence, descendants, eventuality, progeniture

Istanbul *ancient name:* 9 Byzantium *business section:* 6 Galata *country:* 6 Turkey *foreign quarter:* 4 Pera 7 Beyoglu *park:* 8 Seraglio *residential section:* 7 Uskudar

isthmus *Africa-Asia:* 4 Suez *Greece:* 7 Corinth *North America-South America:* 6 Panama

Italian *article:* 2 il, la 3 gli *automobile:* 4 Fiat *cathedral:* 5 duomo *condiment:* 6 tamara *dialect:* 6 Tuscan 8 Sicilian *dictator:* 9 Mussolini (Benito) *family:* 4 Este 5 Cenci, Savoy 6 Borgia, Medici, Orsini, Pepoli, Sforza 7 Colonna, Gonzaga, Spinola 8 Visconti *fascist:* 10 Blackshirt *game:* 4 mora 5 bocce, bocci, morra 6 boccie *gentleman:* 3 ser 6 signor 7 signore *highway:* 10 autostrada *lady:* 5 donna 7 signora 9 signorina *magistrate:* 7 podesta *opera house:* 7 La Scala *patriot:* 6 Cavour (Conte di), Rienzo (Cola di) 7 Mazzini (Giuseppe) 9 Garibaldi (Giuseppe) *reformer:* 10 Savonarola (Girolamo) *resort:* 4 Lido 5 Abano, Capri 7 Locarno 8 Sorrento *road:* 6 strada *sausage:* 6 salami *soup:* 10 minestrone

square: 6 piazza *street:* 3 via 5 corso *weight:* 5 libra, oncia

Italy *capital:* 4 Rome *monetary unit:* 4 lira

itch 4 ache, long, lust, pine, sigh, stew, urge 5 crave, yearn 6 desire, hanker, hunger, seethe, thirst 7 craving, longing, passion 8 appetite, pruritus 9 eroticism, hankering, prurience, pruriency 10 aphrodisia, appetition 11 lustfulness 13 concupiscence, lickerishness *combining form:* 4 psor 5 psoro

itching 8 pruritus 10 avaricious

itchy 5 jumpy 6 grabby, greedy 7 restive 8 covetous, desirous, grasping, prurient 10 prehensile 11 acquisitive

item 3 bit, too 4 also, more, well 5 along, entry, point, scrap, thing, topic 6 detail, matter 7 account, article, besides, element, feature, product 8 clipping, likewise, moreover 9 commodity 10 particular

itemize 4 list 5 count, tally 6 number 7 catalog, specify 8 document, spell out 9 catalogue, enumerate, inventory 10 specialize 13 particularize

iterate 5 renew, resay 6 repeat 7 reprise 10 ingeminate

Ithaca king 8 Odysseus

Ithamar's father 5 Aaron

Ithiel's father 7 Jesaiah

Ithra *son:* 5 Amasa *wife:* 7 Abigail

Ithran's father 6 Dishon, Zophah

Ithream *father:* 5 David *mother:* 5 Eglah

Ithunn's husband 5 Brage, Bragi

itinerant 6 moving, roving 7 migrant, nomadic, ranging, roaming, vagrant 8 ambulant, rambling, shifting, traveler, vagabond, wanderer 9 transient, unsettled, wandering, wayfaring 10 ambulatory 11 perambulant, peripatetic

Ittai's father 5 Ribai

Ivanhoe *author:* 5 Scott (Walter) *character:* 5 Isaac 6 Cedric, Rowena, Ulrica 7 Rebecca, Wilfred 9 Robin Hood

Ivory Coast 11 Cote d'Ivoire *capital:* 7 Abidjan *monetary unit:* 5 franc

ivory-tower 6 dreamy 8 escapist 11 impractical, unpractical, unrealistic 12 nonrealistic

Ixion *descendant:* 7 Centaur *father:* 8 Phlegyas

Izhar's father 6 Ashhur, Kohath

Izliah's father 6 Elpaal

Izrahiah's father 4 Uzzi

Izri's father 8 Jeduthun

Izziah's father 6 Parosh

J

jaal goat 4 ibex
Jaazaniah's father 4 Azur 5 Azzur
7 Shaphan 8 Jeremiah
jab 3 dig, hit, jog 4 poke, prod, stab
5 nudge, prick, punch 8 puncture
Jabal *brother:* 5 Jubal *father:* 6 Lamech
mother: 4 Adah
jabber 3 gab, jaw, yak 4 chat 5 clack,
Greek 6 babble, drivel, gabble, gibber
7 blabber, chatter, palaver, prattle 8 nonsense 9 gibberish 11 jabberwocky
jabberer 6 gabber, gossip, magpie, prater
7 blabber 8 prattler 9 bandar-log, blabmouth, chatterer 10 chatterbox 12 blabbermouth
Jabberwocky author 7 Carroll (Lewis)
Jabesh's son 7 Shallum
jabot 4 fall 5 frill 6 ruffle
jacamar 4 bird
jacare 6 caiman 9 crocodile
___ jacet 3 hic
Jachin's father 6 Simeon
jack 2 up 3 tar 4 card, flag, hike, jump, lift,
salt 5 boost, color, knave, put up, raise
6 banner, ensign, pennon, sailor, seaman
7 mariner, pendant, pennant 8 bannerol,
increase, standard, streamer 9 sailorman,
tarpaulin
jackal god 5 Apuat 6 Anubis
jackanapes 3 ape 6 monkey 7 coxcomb
jackass 4 dolt, donk, fool, jerk 5 burro,
idiot 6 donkey 8 imbecile 10 nincompoop
jackass deer 3 kob 8 antelope
jackdaw 4 bird 7 grackle 9 blackbird
jacket 3 fur 4 coat, Eton, fell, hide, pelt,
skin 5 grego, parka, wamus 6 anorak,
blazer, bolero, dolman, jerkin, reefer, wammus, wampus 7 cassock, doublet, peacoat,
spencer 8 camisole 10 roundabout
armored: 5 acton 7 hauberk 9 habergeon
cowboy's: 8 chaqueta *Scottish:* 4 jupe
sleeveless: 4 vest 6 bolero, jerkin
9 waistcoat
jackhammer 5 drill 9 rock drill
jackknife 4 dive 6 barlow *game:*
11 mumblety-peg
jackleg lawyer 7 shyster 11 pettifogger
jack-of-all-trades 6 tinker 8 handyman
Jack of clubs 3 pam

jack-o'-lantern 7 pumpkin
jackpot 4 pool 5 award, kitty 7 bonanza
8 windfall 9 pot of gold
jackrabbit 4 hare
Jack's companion 4 Jill
jackstay 3 bar, rod 4 rope 5 horse 7 rigging, support
Jacob *brother:* 4 Esau *daughter:*
5 Dinah *father:* 5 Isaac *father-in-law:*
5 Laban *mother:* 7 Rebekah *new name:*
6 Israel *son:* 3 Dan, Gad 4 Levi 5 Asher,
Judah 6 Joseph, Reuben, Simeon 7 Zebulun 8 Benjamin, Issachar, Naphtali *variant:*
5 James *wife:* 4 Leah 6 Rachel
Jacob's rod 8 asphodel
jade 3 fag, gem 4 cloy, fill, glut, minx, pall,
sate, slut, snip, tire, wear 5 drain, gorge,
hussy, jewel, stone, tramp, weary, wench
6 stodge, wanton 7 fatigue, jezebel, satiate,
surfeit, trollop 8 malapert, saucebox, slattern, strumpet, wear down
jaded 4 full, worn 5 sated, tired, weary
6 gorged 7 glutted, satiate, wearied, worn-
out 8 fatigued, satiated, worn down 9 surfeited
jaeger 4 bird, skua 6 hunter 8 huntsman,
rifleman 9 boatswain
Jael *husband:* 5 Heber *victim:* 6 Sisera
jag 3 bum, dag, tab 4 barb, bolt, bust,
soak, tear 5 binge, booze, drunk, notch,
prick, souse, spell, spree 6 bender, thrill
7 portion 8 quantity
jagged 5 erose, harsh, rough, sharp
6 craggy, hackly, rugged, uneven
7 scraggy, unlevel 8 asperous, scabrous,
unsmooth
___ Jagger 4 Mick
Jaggers' ward 3 Pip
Jahaziah, Jahzeiah *father:* 6 Tikvah
Jahaziel's father 9 Zechariah
Jahzeel, Jahziel *father:* 8 Naphtali
jai alai 6 pelota *basket:* 5 cesta *court:*
6 cancha 7 fronton
jail 3 can, jug, pen 4 coop, gaol, keep,
poky, stir 6 cooler, immure, intern, lockup,
prison 7 confine, freezer, slammer 8 bastille, hoosegow, imprison, rock pile, stockade 9 bridewell, constrain, guardroom
11 incarcerate, reformatory 12 penitentiary

jailbird 3 con 5 loser 7 convict 8 prisoner

jailer 5 guard, screw 6 keeper, warden 7 turnkey

Jair *father:* 5 Segub *grandfather:* 6 Hezron *son:* 7 Elhanan 8 Mordecai

Jakeh's son 4 Agur

jakes 5 privy 8 outhouse 9 backhouse

Jalam *father:* 4 Esau *mother:* 9 Oholibama

jalopy 3 car, dog 4 auto, heap 5 crate, wreck 6 junker 7 clunker 10 automobile

jalousie 5 blind 6 window 7 shutter

jam 3 fix, ram 4 bear, bind, cram, push, tamp 5 crowd, crush, jelly, press, stuff 6 plight, scrape, squash, squish, squush 7 dilemma, squeeze 8 bar-le-duc, conserve, preserve 9 confiture, marmalade 11 predicament

Jamaica *capital:* 8 Kingston *monetary unit:* 6 dollar

Jamaican *export:* 3 rum *hair style:* 10 dreadlocks *music:* 3 ska 6 reggae *nationalist:* 6 Garvey (Marcus)

James *brother:* 4 John 5 Jesus, Joses *cousin:* 5 Jesus *father:* 7 Zebedee 8 Alphaeus *mother:* 4 Mary 6 Salome

James novel 10 Confidence 11 Daisy Miller, The American 12 The Europeans 13 The Bostonians, The Golden Bowl, The Tragic Muse

Jamin's father 6 Simeon

Jammy and ___ 7 Kashmir

Jane Eyre *author:* 6 Brontë (Charlotte) *lover:* 9 Rochester

jangle 3 din, jar 4 ring 5 babel, clash 6 clamor, hubbub, racket, tumult, uproar 7 discord 8 conflict, mismatch 9 disaccord 10 hullabaloo, tintamarre 11 pandemonium 12 disharmonize

jangling 5 harsh 7 grating 9 dissonant 10 discordant

janitor 6 porter 7 charman 9 caretaker, custodian 10 doorkeeper

japan 7 varnish

Japan 5 Nihon 6 Nippon *capital:* 5 Tokyo *monetary unit:* 3 yen

Japanese *aborigine:* 4 Ainu *apricot:* 3 ume *baron:* 6 daimio, daimyo *battle cry:* 6 banzai *Buddha:* 5 Amida, Amita *coin:* 2 bu 3 rin, sen, yen 4 oban 5 koban, obang 6 kobang *court:* 5 dairi *dancing girl:* 6 geisha *dish:* 5 kombu 7 tempura 8 sukiyaki, teriyaki *drink:* 4 sake, saki *emperor:* 6 Mikado 7 Akihito 8 Hirohito *festival:* 3 Bon *fish:* 3 ayu, tai 4 fugu *garment:* 5 haori 6 kimono *god:* 4 kami 5 Ebisu, Hotei 7 Daikoku, Jurojin 8 Bishamon *goddess:* 6 Benten 9 Amaterasu *governor:* 6 shogun *grill:* 7 hibachi *instrument:* 4 koto 7 samisen *martial art:* 4 judo 6 karate 7 jujitsu, jujutsu *measure:*

2 bu, go, jo, mo, ri, se, to 3 boo, cho, ken, rin, sho, sun, tan 4 hiro, koku 5 shaku, tsubo *monastery:* 4 tera *money:* 3 sen, yen *persimmon:* 4 kaki *plum:* 6 loquat *poem:* 5 haiku, hokku, tanka 6 haikai *pottery:* 7 Satsuma *radish:* 6 daikon *religion:* 6 Shinto 8 Buddhism 9 Shintoism *rice wine:* 4 sake, saki *robe:* 6 kimono *samurai clan:* 5 Taira 8 Minamoto *servant:* 6 geisha *ship:* 4 maru *song:* 3 uta *suicide:* 7 seppuku 8 hara-kiri, hari-kari, kamikaze *sword:* 5 catan 6 cattan, katana *theater:* 2 No 6 Kabuki *tidal wave:* 7 tsunami *tree:* 4 kiri, kozo, sugi 5 akeki, kiaki 6 hinoki, keyaki *vehicle:* 7 ricksha 8 rickshaw *warrior:* 7 samurai *weight:* 2 mo 3 fun, kin, rin, shi 4 kwan, niyo 5 momme 8 hiyak-kin, hiyaku-me *wrestling:* 4 sumo *writing:* 4 kana 8 hiragana, katakana *zither:* 4 koto

Japanese-American 5 Issei, Kibei, Nisei *second generation:* 6 Sansei

jape 3 gag 4 fool, jeer, jest, joke, mock, quip 5 crack, taunt 7 waggery 8 drollery 9 wisecrack, witticism

Japheth *brother:* 3 Ham 4 Shem *father:* 4 Noah *son:* 5 Gomer, Javan, Madai, Magog, Tiras, Tubal 7 Meshech

Japhia's father 5 David

jar 4 bump, ewer, jolt, olla, vase 5 clash, crash, cruse, quake, shake, shock, smash, upset 6 impact, jangle, jounce, tinaja, tremor 7 discord, terrine, tremble, vibrate 8 conflict, gallipot, mismatch 9 collision, container, disaccord, vibration 10 concussion 12 disharmonize *ancient:* 6 hydria, krater 7 amphora 8 lecythus, lekythos, lekythus *Egyptian:* 7 canopic *long-necked:* 6 goglet *Mexican:* 6 pinata *Philippine:* 5 banga

jardiniere 3 pot, urn 4 vase 5 stand 7 garnish 9 flowerpot

Jared *father:* 10 Mahalaleel *son:* 5 Enoch

jargon 4 cant 5 argot, idiom, lingo, slang 6 patois, patter, pidgin 7 chatter, dialect, lexicon, palaver, twitter 8 language 9 gibberish 10 dictionary, vernacular, vocabulary 11 terminology *lawyer's:* 8 legalese

jarl 4 earl 5 chief, noble 8 nobleman

jarring 3 dry 5 harsh, rough 6 hoarse 7 grating, rasping, raucous 8 strident 9 dissonant 10 discordant, stridulent, stridulous

Jashub's father 4 Bani 8 Issachar

jasmine 4 vine 5 shrub 6 flower 7 perfume

Jason *father:* 5 Aeson *helper:* 5 Medea *lover:* 6 Creusa, Glauce, Glauke *quest:* 12 Golden Fleece *ship:* 4 Argo *shipmate:* 8 Argonaut *teacher:* 6 Chiron 7 Cheiron *uncle:* 6 Pelias *wife:* 5 Medea

jasper 6 morlop, quartz 10 chalcedony

jaundice 4 bias 7 disease, icterus 9 prejudice *combining form:* 5 icter 6 ictero *Scottish:* 7 gulsach

jaunt 4 perk, ride, trip 5 sally 6 junket, outing, ramble 7 journey, joyride 9 excursion

jaunty 4 airy 5 light, perky 7 perkish 8 debonair 9 sprightly 10 nonchalant

java 6 coffee

Java almond 7 talisay

Java cotton 5 kapok

Java jute 5 kenaf

Javanese *carriage:* 4 sado *civet:* 5 rasse *Instrument:* 5 saron 6 bonang, gender 7 gamelan *measure:* 4 paal *skunk:* 6 teledu *tree:* 4 upas 7 gondang *village:* 4 desa 5 dessa

Javan squirrel 8 jelerang

Java plum 5 jaman 6 jambul 7 jambool

javelin 5 lance, shaft, spear 6 weapon 7 assagai, assegai, harpoon

Javert's prey 7 Valjean

jaw 3 gab, wig, yak 4 chat, rail, rate, talk 5 baste, clack, prate, scold 6 babble, berate, gabble 7 chatter, prattle, upbraid 9 yakety-yak 10 tongue-lash *kind:* 5 glass *relating to:* 7 gnathal, gnathic

jawbone 7 maxilla 8 mandible

jawbreaker 5 candy

jay 4 bird, hick, jake, rube 5 clown, dandy 6 rustic 7 bumpkin, hayseed 9 greenhorn

Jayhawker 6 Kansan, outlaw 9 guerrilla *State:* 6 Kansas

jazz 4 guff, jive 5 bebop, swing 6 boogie 7 ragtime 8 malarkey, nonsense *up:* 7 enliven 10 popularize

jealous 5 green 7 envious, envying 8 doubting 9 demanding, green-eyed, invidious 10 possessive, possessory, suspicious 11 distrustful, mistrustful

Jecoliah's Son 6 Uzziah

Jediael's father 8 Benjamin

Jedidah *husband:* 4 Amon *son:* 6 Josiah

jeer 4 gibe, gird, jest, jibe, mock 5 fleer, flout, scoff, sneer, taunt 6 deride, quip at 7 scout at 8 ridicule

Jeeves *creator:* 9 Wodehouse (Pelham Grenville) *employer:* 7 Wooster (Bertie) *position:* 5 valet 6 butler

Jefferson *home:* 10 Monticello *state:* 8 Virginia

Jehiel *father:* 4 Elam 8 Hachmoni 11 Jehoshaphat *son:* 7 Obadiah 10 Shechaniah

Jehizkiah's father 7 Shallum

Jehoaddan's Son 7 Amaziah

Jehoahaz *brother:* 9 Jehoiakim *father:* 4 Jehu 6 Josiah 7 Jehoram *mother:* 7 Hamutal *son:* 5 Joash 7 Jehoash

Jehohanan *father:* 5 Bebai 6 Tobiah 8 Eliashib *son:* 7 Ishmael

Jehoiada *father:* 6 Paseah 7 Benaiah *son:* 7 Benaiah *wife:* 9 Jehosheba

Jehoiakim *father:* 6 Josiah *mother:* 7 Zebidah *son:* 10 Jehoiachin

Jehoram *brother:* 7 Ahaziah *father:* 4 Ahab 11 Jehoshaphat *kingdom:* 5 Judah *slayer:* 4 Jehu *wife:* 8 Athaliah

Jehoshaphat *father:* 3 Asa 6 Ahilud, Nimshi, Paruah *father-in-law:* 4 Ahab *son:* 4 Jehu 7 Jehoram *wife:* 8 Athaliah

Jehosheba *father:* 7 Jehoram *husband:* 8 Jehoiada *sister:* 7 Ahaziah *son:* 5 Joash

Jehovah 3 God 5 Yahwe 6 Adonai, Elohim, Yahweh

Jehozabad's father 8 Obededom

Jehozadak see Jozadak

Jehu 6 driver *father:* 6 Hanani 11 Jehoshaphat *grandfather:* 6 Nimshi *son:* 8 Jehoahaz *victim:* 5 Joram 7 Jehoram

Jehudijah's husband 5 Mered

Jehush *father:* 4 Esau 5 Eshek 6 Bilhan, Shimei 8 Rehoboam *mother:* 10 Oholibamah

jejune 4 dull, flat 5 banal, bland, inane, trite, vapid 7 insipid, sapless, tenuous 9 innocuous 10 namby-pamby 12 milk-and-water

Jekyll's alter ego 4 Hyde

jell 3 set 4 clot 6 gelate 7 congeal, pectize, thicken 9 coagulate 10 gelatinize

jelly 3 gel, set 4 clot, pulp 5 aspic 6 gelate, pectin, spread 7 congeal, gelatin, pectize, thicken 9 coagulate 10 gelatinize

jellyfish 3 sop 4 baby 5 sissy 6 medusa 7 acaleph, doormat, medusan, milksop 8 medusoid, weakling 10 pantywaist 11 Milquetoast, mollycoddle 12 invertebrate

Jemimah's father 3 Job

Jemuel's father 6 Simeon

jennet 3 ass 5 hinny, horse 6 donkey

jeopardize 4 risk 5 peril 6 expose, hazard, menace 7 imperil 8 endanger 10 compromise

jeopardy 4 risk 5 peril 6 danger, hazard, menace 7 imperil 8 endanger, exposure 9 liability 10 compromise

Jephthah's father 6 Gilead

Jephunneh's son 5 Caleb

jeremiad 6 lament, tirade 8 diatribe, harangue 9 complaint, philippic

Jeremiah *daughter:* 7 Hamutal *father:* 8 Hilkiath 10 Habaziniah *scribe:* 6 Baruch *son:* 8 Jaazniah

Jericho's conqueror 6 Joshua

Jerimoth *daughter:* 8 Mahalath *father:* 5 David

Jerioth's husband 5 Caleb

jerk 3 ass, lug, tic 4 fool, nerd, snap, yank
5 idiot, lurch, ninny, throw, wrest, wring
6 twitch, wrench 7 flounce, jackass, tomfool 9 vellicate 10 nincompoop

jerked beef 7 charqui

jerkin 4 coat 6 jacket 9 gyrfalcon

jerky 4 meat 5 inane, wagon 7 charqui,
foolish, jolting 8 saccadic

Jeroboam *father:* 5 Joash, Nebat *foe:*
6 Abijam 8 Rehoboam *mother:* 6 Zeruah
son: 5 Nadab 9 Zechariah

Jerome's Bible 7 Vulgate

jersey 3 cow 5 shirt 6 tricot 7 sweater
8 pullover 10 undershirt

Jerusalem 4 Sion, Zion 5 Salem 8 Holy
City *hill:* 4 Sion, Zion 6 Moriah *market:*
4 souk *mosque:* 4 Omar *pool:* 6 Siloam
8 Bethesda

Jerusalem artichoke 5 tuber 7 girasol
8 girasole 9 sunflower

Jerusalem thorn 5 shrub 6 retama
7 catechu 9 horsebean

Jerusha *father:* 5 Zadok *husband:*
6 Uzziah *son:* 6 Jotham

Jeshaiah *father:* 7 Athalia 8 Hananiah,
Jeduthun, Rehabiah *son:* 6 Ithiel

Jeshua *father:* 7 Jozadek *son:* 4 Ezer

jess 5 strap

Jesse *daughter:* 7 Abigail, Zeruiah *father:*
4 Obed *grandfather:* 4 Boaz *son:*
4 Ozem 5 David, Eliab, Elihu 6 Raddai
7 Shammah 8 Abinadab, Nethanel *young-
est son:* 5 David

Jessica *father:* 7 Shylock *husband:*
7 Lorenzo

jest 3 fun, gag, kid, rag, rib 4 butt, game,
gibe, gird, jape, jeer, joke, josh, mock, play,
quip, razz 5 chaff, crack, fleer, flout, scoff,
sneer, sport 6 banter, quip at 7 mockery,
scout at, waggery 8 derision, drollery, ridicule 9 pilgarlic, wisecrack, witticism
13 laughing stock

jester 3 wag, wit 4 fool 5 clown, comic,
droll, idiot, joker 6 motley 8 comedian, funnyman, humorist, jokester, quipster

Jesuit's founder 6 Loyola, Ignatius

jet 4 ebon, inky 5 black, ebony, plane,
raven, sable, sprit, spurt 6 engine, splurt,
squirt 8 airplane, fountain 9 pitch-dark

Jether *father:* 4 Ezra 6 Gideon, Zophah
son: 5 Amasa

Jethro *daughter:* 8 Zipporah *son-in-law:*
5 Moses

jetsam 7 flotsam 8 wreckage 9 driftwood

jettison 4 cast, dump, junk, shed 5 scrap
6 reject, slough 7 cashier, discard, dumping, junking 8 abdicate, disposal, riddance
9 scrapping, throw away 10 discarding

jetty 4 dock, ebon, inky, pier, quay, slip
5 berth, black, ebony, groin, levee, raven,
sable, wharf 9 pitch-dark 10 pitch-block

Jew 6 Essene, Semite 8 Judahite 9 Israelite

jewel 3 gem 5 adorn, begem, beset, bijou,
ideal, stone 7 paragon, phoenix 8 nonesuch, ornament 9 nonpareil; (see also
gem)

jeweler 8 lapidary, lapidist *famous:* 7 Tiffany (Charles Lewis)

jewelry 10 bijouterie *artificial:* 5 glass,
paste 6 strass 7 costume *piece:* 3 pin
4 ring 6 brooch 7 earring 8 bracelet, lava-
lier, necklace, tieclasp 9 lavaliere *set:*
6 parure

Jewish *bread:* 5 matzo 6 matzoh, matzos
8 afikomen *ceremony:* 5 berit, brith 6 berith 10 bar mitzvah *combining form:*
5 Judeo 6 Judaeo *doctrine:* 6 Mishna
7 Mishnah *liturgy:* 6 maarib, maariv, min-
hah 7 minchah 9 shaharith *New Year:*
11 Rosh Hashana *organization:* 8 Hadassah 9 B'nai B'rith *pioneer:* 6 halutz 7 chalutz *prayer book:* 6 mahzor, siddur
7 machzor *sabbath:* 8 Saturday *scripture:*
6 Talmud *synagogue:* 4 shul 5 schul
teacher: 5 rabbi 6 Hillel; (see also
Hebrew)

jezebel 4 jade, slut 5 hussy, tramp, trull,
wench 6 wanton 7 trollop 8 slattern,
strumpet

Jezebel *father:* 7 Ethbaal *home:* 5 Sidon
husband: 4 Ahab *slayer:* 4 Jehu *victim:*
6 Naboth

Jezer's father 8 Naphtali

Jezreel's father 5 Hosea

jib 3 gag, shy 4 balk, sail 5 demur, stick

jibe 2 go 5 agree, fit in, tally 6 accord,
square 7 conform 8 dovetail 9 harmonize
10 correspond

jiffy 5 crack, flash, hurry, shake, trice
6 minute, moment, second 7 instant
9 breathing 11 split second

jig 4 hook, play, ploy, ruse, wile 5 dance,
feint, trick 6 device, gambit 7 gimmick

jigger 3 cup 4 boat, mast 5 gizmo, glass
6 dingus, doodad, gadget, widget 7 concern, dofunny, gimmick, thingum 9 doohickey, shot glass

jiggle 5 shake 9 oscillate

jigsaw 4 tool 6 puzzle

jihad 3 war 6 strife 7 crusade, holy war
8 campaign

jilt 6 reject 7 abandon, cast off, discard

jim-dandy 5 nifty 8 knockout 9 humdinger

jimmy 3 bar, pry 4 open 5 lever 7 crowbar

jingle 4 ring, song 5 chime, chink, clink,
verse 6 tinkle 7 chinkle

jinn 5 afrit, genie 6 afreet, spirit, yaksha

jinx 3 hex 5 charm, curse, spell 6 hoodoo,
voodoo, whammy 7 evil eye

jitters 5 jumps, panic 6 dither, nerves, shakes 7 shivers, willies 9 whim-whams 13 heebie-jeebies

jittery 5 jumpy, nervy 6 goosey, spooky 7 fidgety, nervous 9 unrestful 10 high-strung

jive 3 kid 4 jazz, talk 5 dance, music, swing 6 jargon

Joab *brother:* 6 Asahel 7 Abishai *father:* 7 Seraiah, Zeruiah *slayer:* 7 Benaiah *uncle:* 5 David *victim:* 5 Abner, Amasa

Joah *father:* 5 Asaph 6 Joahaz, Zimmah 8 Obededon *son:* 4 Eden

Joanna's husband 5 Chuza

Joan of Arc *birthplace:* 7 Domremy *epithet:* 7 Pucelle 13 Maid of Orleans *victory:* 7 Orleans

Joan's husband 5 Darby

Joash *father:* 4 Ahab 7 Ahaziah 8 Jehoahaz *son:* 6 Gideon 7 Amaziah 8 Jeroboam *victim:* 9 Zechariah

job 4 dupe, duty, fool, gull, hoax, line, post, spot, task, work 5 berth, chare, chore, place, stint, trade 6 befool, billet, devoir, effort, office, pigeon 7 calling, chicane, posting, pursuit 8 business, flimflam, position, sinecure, taskwork, vocation 9 bamboozle, situation, victimize 10 assignment, connection, employment, engagement, occupation, profession 11 appointment

Job *daughter:* 6 Keziah 7 Jemimah *father:* 8 Issachar *friend:* 6 Bildad, Zophar 7 Eliphaz *home:* 2 Uz

Jobab's father 5 Zerah 6 Joktan 9 Shaharaim

jobber 6 trader 10 contractor, wholesaler

job-training program 4 CETA

Jocasta *daughter:* 6 Ismene 8 Antigone *husband:* 5 Laius 7 Oedipus *son:* 7 Oedipus 8 Eteocles 9 Polynices

Jochebed *brother:* 6 Kohath *father:* 4 Levi *husband:* 5 Amram

jock 7 athlete

jockey 4 play 5 rider, trick 7 beguile, exploit, finesse 8 maneuver 10 manipulate *famous:* 5 Baeza (Braulio) 6 Arcaro (Eddie), Murphy (Isaac), Pincay (Laffit) 7 Cauthen (Steve), Cordero (Angel), Hartack (Bill), Longden (Johnny) 8 McHargue (Darrel), Turcotte (Ron) 9 Shoemaker (Willie)

jocular 3 gay 5 comic, jolly, merry, silly, witty 6 blithe, jocose, jovial 7 comical, playful 8 cheerful, humorous, sportive 9 facetious

jocularity 4 glee 5 mirth 7 jollity 8 hilarity 9 jocundity, joviality, merriment

jocund 3 gay 5 jolly, merry 6 blithe, jovial 7 festive, gleeful, playful 8 mirthful, sportive 10 blithesome 12 lighthearted

Joel *brother:* 6 Nathan *father:* 4 Nebo 5 Ladan 6 Samuel, Zichri 7 Azariah, Pedaiah, Pethuel *son:* 5 Heman

jog 3 dig, jab, run 4 lope, poke, prod, trot 5 nudge, punch, shake 6 remind

jogger 6 layboy, runner

joggle 5 dowel, joint, notch, shake 6 jostle

Johanan *father:* 6 Josiah, Kareah, Tobiah 8 Eliashib, Elioenai, Hakkatan *son:* 7 Azariah

john 2 WC 4 head 5 privy 6 toilet 7 latrine 8 lavatory 11 convenience, water closet

John *father:* 5 Accos, Simon 10 Mattathias *son:* 5 Peter 9 Eupolemus 10 Mattathias; (see also **John the Baptist; John the Evangelist**)

John *Irish:* 4 Sean

John Hancock 9 autograph, signature

Johnson's biographer 7 Boswell (James)

John the Baptist *father:* 9 Zacharias *mother:* 9 Elisabeth

John the Evangelist *brother:* 5 James *father:* 7 Zebedee *mother:* 6 Salome

join 3 fay, mix, tie, wed 4 abut, ally, bind, bond, fuse, knot, line, link, mate, weld, yoke 5 affix, blend, march, marry, merge, piece, touch, unify, unite, verge 6 attach, border, butt on, couple, enlist, enroll, fasten, relate, sign up, splice 7 bracket, combine, connect 8 coagment, coalesce, compound, concrete, neighbor 9 associate, coadunate, conjugate, integrate

joint 3 ell, hip, tie 4 butt, crux, dive, knee, link, seam 5 ankle, elbow, hinge, scarf, union, wrist 6 common, mutual, public, shared, suture 7 hangout, knuckle, shiplap 8 abutment, communal, conjunct, coupling, junction, juncture, shoulder 9 honky-tonk 10 connection *combining form:* 5 arthr 6 arthro, condyl 7 condylo *disease:* 9 arthritis 10 rheumatism *prefix:* 2 co

join up 5 enter 6 enlist, enroll, muster, sign up

joist 4 beam, stud 6 timber 7 sleeper, support

joke 3 fun, gag, kid, pun, rag, rib, wit, yak 4 butt, dido, fool, game, jape, jest, josh, mock, play, quip, razz 5 antic, caper, crack, humor, jolly, prank, sally, sport 6 banter, jestee, parody 7 mockery, sarcasm, waggery 8 badinage, derision, drôlerie, drollery, one-liner, repartee 9 burlesque, pilgarlic, wisecrack, witticism 10 caricature 11 monkeyshine 13 laughing stock *stale:* 8 chestnut

joker 3 wag, wit 4 card, zany 5 clown, comic, cutup, droll 6 gagman, jester 7 farceur 8 comedian, funnyman, humorist, quipster

Jokshan *father:* 7 Abraham *mother:*
7 Keturah *son:* 5 Dedan, Sheba

Joktan *brother:* 5 Peleg *father:* 4 Eber
son: 4 Obal 5 Ophir

jollity 3 fun 4 glee, play, romp 5 cheer,
mirth, revel, sport 6 frolic, gaiety, gambol
7 disport, revelry, rollick, whoopee 8 hilarity, reveling 9 festivity, jocundity, joviality,
merriment, revelment 10 blitheness, jocularity 11 merrymaking

jolly 3 fun, gay, kid, rag, rib 4 glad, jest,
josh, razz 5 chaff, merry 6 banter, blithe,
jocund, jovial 7 festive, gleeful, jocular, playful, roguish, waggish 8 mirthful, sportive
10 blithesome, frolicsome

Jolly Roger 4 flag 6 ensign *user:*
6 pirate

jolt 3 jar, nip, tot 4 blow, bump, dram, drop,
shot, slug 5 clash, crash, knock, shake,
shock, snort 6 impact, jounce 7 snifter,
startle 8 toothful 9 collision

Jonadab *cousin:* 5 Amnon *father:*
6 Rechab 7 Shimeah *uncle:* 5 David

Jonah 4 jinx 7 prophet *father:* 7 Amittai
son: 5 Peter, Simon *swallower:* 5 whale

Jonathan *brother:* 7 Johanan *father:*
4 Jada, Saul 6 Joiada, Kareah, Uzziah
7 Absolom, Shimeah 8 Abiathar 10 Mattathias *friend:* 5 David

Jones, John Paul *ship:* 15 Bonhomme
Richard *victim:* 7 Serapis

jongleur 4 bard 6 singer 8 minstrel
10 troubadour

jonquil 8 daffodil 9 narcissus

Jonson play 6 The Fox 7 Epicene, Volpone

Joplin creation 3 rag

Joram *brother:* 7 Ahaziah *father:* 3 Toi
4 Ahab 11 Jehoshaphat *slayer:* 4 Jehu
son: 7 Ahaziah

Jordan *capital:* 5 Amman *king:* 7 Hussein *monetary unit:* 5 dinar

jorum 3 cup, jug 4 bowl

Joseph *brother:* (see Jacob, son) *buyer:*
8 Potiphar *father:* 5 Asaph, Jacob 9 Zacharias 10 Mattathias *mother:* 6 Rachel *son:*
5 Jesus 7 Ephraim 8 Manasseh *wife:*
4 Mary 7 Asenath

Joseph's coat 6 coleus 7 tampala

josh 3 fun, guy, kid, rag, rib 4 jest, joke,
razz 5 chaff, jolly, tease 6 banter

Joshua's father 3 Nun

Joshua tree 5 yucca

Josiah *father:* 4 Amon 9 Zephaniah
mother: 7 Jedidah *son:* 8 Jehoahaz
9 Jehoiakim

joss 4 idol 5 image

Jo's sister 3 Amy, Meg 4 Beth

jostle 3 jar, jog 4 push 5 elbow, press,
shove 6 hustle 8 bulldoze, shoulder

jot 3 bit 4 atom, iota, whit 5 grain, minim,
speck 6 tittle 7 modicum, smidgen, smid-
gin 8 particle, smidgeon

jot down 4 note 5 write

Jotham *father:* 6 Gideon, Jahdai, Uzziah
mother: 8 Jerushah

joule component 3 erg

jounce 3 jar, jog 4 bump, jolt 5 shock
6 impact, wallop 9 collision 10 concussion

journal 3 log 5 diary, organ, paper 6 record, review 7 gazette 8 magazine 9 newspaper 10 periodical

journalist 3 Bly (Nellie) 4 Drew (Eliza-
beth), Pyle (Ernie), Reed (John), Will
(George F.) 5 Baker (Russell), Cooke (Alis-
tair), Evans (Rowland), Hersh (Seymour),
Novak (Robert), Rowan (Carl), Royko
(Mike), Smith (Hedrick), Stone (I. F.), Szulc
(Tad), Wolfe (Tom) 6 Bierce (Ambrose),
Broder (David), Ephron (Nora), Greene
(Bob), Kennan (George), Koppel (Ted),
Lehrer (Jim), Moyers (Bill), Murrow (Edward
R.), Reston (James), Runyon (Damon),
Safire (William), Shirer (William L.), Thomas
(Helen, Lowell), Zenger (John Peter)
7 Breslin (Jimmy), Cousins (Norman),
Greeley (Horace), Gunther (John), McGrory
(Mary), Mencken (H. L.), Pearson (Drew),
St. Johns (Adela Rogers), Tarbell (Ida), Tril-
lin (Calvin), Wallace (Mike), Walters (Bar-
bara) 8 Amanpour (Christiane), Anderson
(Jack, Terry), Atkinson (Brooks), Brinkley
(David), Garrison (William Lloyd), Lippmann
(Walter), Pulitzer (Joseph), Salinger
(Pierre), Steffens (Lincoln), Thompson
(Dorothy, Hunter), Winchell (Walter), Wood-
ward (Bob) 9 Bernstein (Carl), Donaldson
(Sam), Frederick (Pauline), Hohenberg
(John), Salisbury (Harrison), Watterson
(Henry)

journey 2 go 3 hie 4 eyre, fare, pass,
tour, trek, trip, wend 5 jaunt, sally 6 cruise,
junket, push on, repair, safari, travel, voyage 7 odyssey, proceed, travels 8 progress 9 excursion 10 expedition, pilgrimage
route: 9 itinerary *stage:* 3 leg

joust 4 tilt 5 fight 6 combat 10 tournament
arena: 8 tiltyard

Jove see Jupiter

jovial see jocular

jowl 3 jaw 5 cheek 6 dewlap, wattle
8 mandible

joy 4 glee 5 bliss, mirth 6 gaiety 7 delight,
ecstasy, elation, rapture 8 fruition, gladness, pleasure 9 enjoyment 11 delectation

Joyce, James *birthplace:* 6 Dublin *character:* 5 Bloom (Leopold), Bloom (Molly)
7 Dedalus (Stephen) *work:* 6 Exiles 7 Ulysses 9 Dubliners 13 Finnegans Wake

joyful see joyous

joyous 3 gay 4 glad 5 happy, merry
7 buoyant, festive, gleeful 8 ecstatic, mirthful 9 delighted, rapturous 12 lighthearted

Jozabad's father 6 Jeshua 7 Pashhur

Jozacar *mother:* 8 Shimeath *victim:*
5 Joash

Jozadak's son 6 Jeshua

Jubal *father:* 6 Lamech *mother:* 4 Adah

jubilant 6 elated 8 exultant, exulting
9 cock-a-hoop, triumphal 10 cock-a-whoop,
triumphant

jubilate 5 exult, glory 7 delight, triumph

Judah *brother:* (see **Jacob,** son) *father:*
5 Jacob *king:* 3 Asa 4 Ahaz, Amon
5 Joash 6 Abijam, Josiah, Jotham, Uzziah
7 Ahaziah, Amaziah, Jehoram 8 Hezekiah,
Jehoahaz, Manasseh, Rehoboam, Zedekiah 9 Jehoiakim 10 Jehoiachin
11 Jehoshaphat *mother:* 4 Leah *son:* 2 Er
4 Onan 6 Shelah

Judas 7 traitor *father:* 5 Simon 7 Chalphi
10 Mattathias *replacement:* 8 Matthias *suicide place:* 8 Aceldama, Akeldama

judge 3 put, ref, try, ump 4 call, draw,
make, rule, test 5 check, court, infer
6 critic, decide, deduce, derive, gather,
jurist, reckon, settle, umpire 7 arbiter, collect, justice, make out, referee 8 conclude,
critique, doomster, estimate, mediator, sentence 9 arbitrate, criticize, determine
10 adjudicate, arbitrator, chancellor, magistrate, negotiator, reconciler 11 approximate, conciliator 12 intermediary *Athenian:*
6 dicast 7 heliast *bench:* 4 banc *chamber:*
6 camera *gown:* 4 robe, toga *in Hades:*
5 Minos 6 Aeacus 12 Rhadamanthys *mallet:* 5 gavel *Muslim:* 4 cadi 5 mufti

judgment 4 doom 5 award, sense, stock,
taste 6 acumen, ruling, wisdom 7 insight,
opinion, verdict 8 decision, estimate, gumption, illation, sagacity, sequitur 9 appraisal,
criticism, deduction, good sense, inference
10 assessment, astuteness, conclusion, discretion, estimation, evaluation, horse
sense, shrewdness 11 common sense,
discernment 12 appraisement, perspicacity
13 determination, ratiocination

Judgment Day 8 doomsday

____**judicata** 3 res

judicial 8 critical 10 judgmental *assembly:*
5 court *document:* 4 writ

judicious 4 fair, sage, sane, wise 7 prudent, sapient 8 rational, sensible 9 equitable, judgmatic, objective, sagacious 10 reasonable 13 dispassionate

Judith *father:* 5 Beeri *home:* 8 Bethulia
husband: 4 Esau *victim:* 10 Holofernes

Judy's husband 5 Punch

jug 3 jar, pen 4 coop, ewer, jail, toby
5 gotch 6 cooler, immure, intern, lockup,
prison, urceus 7 confine, pitcher 8 bastille,

demijohn, imprison 9 constrain 11 incarcerate

jug band instrument 5 kazoo 6 bottle
7 washtub 9 stovepipe, washboard

Juggernaut's temple 4 Puri

juggle 5 bluff 6 betray, delude, humbug,
illude, take in 7 beguile, deceive, mislead,
shuffle

juice 3 sap 4 fuel, must, stum 5 cider, fluid
7 essence, vinegar 8 vitality 10 succulence
11 electricity *combining form:* 3 opo
4 chyl 5 chyli, chylo *fermented:* 4 wine
5 cider *Scottish:* 4 broo

juicy 4 racy 7 piquant 9 succulent

juju 4 luck, zemi 5 charm 6 amulet, fetish,
mascot 7 periapt 8 talisman 10 phylactery

jujube 3 ber 7 gumdrop, lozenge

julep 5 drink

Julian's epithet 8 Apostate

Juliet *betrothed:* 5 Paris *father:* 7 Capulet *lover:* 5 Romeo

July 14 11 Bastille Day

jumble 3 mix, pie 4 hash, mess, olio
5 mix up, shake, snafu 6 foul up, litter,
medley, mess up, muddle, muss up 7 clutter, confuse, derange, disturb, rummage,
shuffle, snarl up 8 disorder, mishmash,
pastiche, scramble 9 patchwork, potpourri
10 assortment, disarrange, miscellany, salmagundi 11 disorganize, gallimaufry

jumbo 4 huge 5 giant 6 mighty 7 mammoth 8 colossal, enormous, gigantic
9 cyclopean 10 prodigious 11 elephantine

jump 3 hop, lop 4 bolt, hike, jink, leap,
loup 5 boost, bound, lunge, put up, raise,
vault 6 bounce, hurdle, jack up, pounce,
spring 7 saltate, startle 8 increase

jumper 5 dress, shirt, smock 6 blouse,
jacket

jumping 7 saltant

jumping frog county 9 Calaveras

jump over 8 leapfrog

jumps 6 dither, shakes 7 jitters, shivers,
willies 9 whim-whams 13 heebie-jeebies

jumpy see **jittery**

junction 4 seam 5 joint, union 6 suture
7 joining, meeting 8 coupling 9 concourse,
gathering 10 concursion, confluence, connection

juncture 4 pass, seam 5 joint, pinch,
point, union 6 crisis, moment, strait
7 instant, joining 8 coupling, exigency, zero
hour 9 emergency 10 connection, crossroads 11 contingency 12 turning point

june bug 6 beetle

jungle 3 web 4 hash, knot, mash, maze,
mesh 5 skein, snarl 6 jumble, litter,
morass, muddle, tangle 7 clutter, mizmaze,
rummage 8 mishmash, scramble 9 labyrinth

Jungle, The *author:* 8 Sinclair (Upton) *locale:* 7 Chicago

Jungle Books, The *author:* 7 Kipling (Rudyard) *character:* 6 Mowgli *python:* 3 Kaa

juniper 4 cade, tree 5 cedar, larch, retem, savin

junk 4 boat, cast, dope, drug 5 offal, scrap, trash, waste 6 debris, kelter, litter, refuse, reject, slough 7 cashier, discard, garbage, rubbish, wash out 8 jettison, throw out 9 narcotics, throw away

junker 4 heap 5 crate, noble, wreck 6 jalopy 10 aristocrat

junket 4 trip 5 jaunt, sally 6 outing, picnic 9 excursion 10 roundabout

junkyard 4 dump

Juno *bird:* 7 peacock *epithet:* 6 Moneta; (see also **Hera**)

Junoesque 5 curvy 7 rounded 9 curvesome 10 curvaceous 11 curvilinear 13 well-developed

junta 5 group 7 council 9 committee 10 government

junto 5 cabal, group 7 coterie, faction

Jupiter 4 Jove, Zeus *angel:* 7 Zadkiel *cupbearer:* 8 Ganymede *daughter:* 5 Venus 7 Minerva *epithet:* 6 Fidius, Fulgur, Stator, Tonans 7 Pluvius *father:* 6 Saturn *lover:* 2 Io 6 Europa 8 Callisto *mother:* 3 Ops *satellite:* 2 Io 6 Europa 8 Callisto, Ganymede *son:* 5 Arcas 6 Castor, Pollux *temple:* 7 Capitol *wife:* 4 Juno

Jurgen *author:* 6 Cabell (James Branch) *trade:* 10 pawnbroker

juridical 5 legal 8 juristic

jurisdiction 3 law, see 4 sway 5 might, power, range, reach, scope, venue 6 county, domain, parish, sphere 7 command, compass, control, diocese, mastery 8 dominion, province 9 authority, bailiwick, territory 10 domination *suffix:* 3 dom

jurisprudence 3 law

jury 5 panel 9 committee *decision:* 7 verdict

just 3 all, apt, due, fit 4 even, fair, good, meet, only, true 5 equal, happy, legal, quite, right, sharp 6 as well, barely, cogent, hardly, honest, in toto, merely, proper, scarce, simply, square, wholly 7 condign, exactly, fitting, merited, totally, upright, utterly 8 all in all, deserved, faithful, rightful, scarcely, squarely, suitable, unbiased 9 befitting, equitable, expressly, honorable, impartial, justified, objective, precisely, requisite, uncolored, veracious, veridical 10 accurately, altogether, completely, felicitous, legitimate, scrupulous 11 appropriate, undistorted, well-founded 12 unprejudiced, well-grounded 13 conscientious, dispassionate, rhadamanthine

justice 3 law 5 court, judge 6 equity 7 honesty 8 evenness, fairness 10 magistrate 12 impartiality

justification 6 excuse, reason 7 account, apology, defense 8 apologia 9 rationale 10 apologetic 11 explanation

justify 5 argue, claim 6 assert, defend, excuse, uphold, verify 7 account, bear out, confirm, contend, explain, support, warrant 8 maintain, validate 9 vindicate 11 corroborate, explain away, rationalize 12 authenticate, substantiate

justly 4 well 5 fitly 6 nicely 7 rightly 8 decently, properly 9 correctly, fittingly 10 decorously 11 befittingly

jut 4 hang, poke, pout 5 bulge, jetty, pouch 6 beetle 7 project 8 bend over, lean over, overhang, protrude, stand out, stick out 9 outthrust 10 projection, protrusion 12 protuberance

jute 5 gunny 6 burlap 7 sacking *Indian:* 4 desi

Juvenal's forte 6 satire

juvenile 3 kid 5 child, green, young, youth 6 callow, infant, moppet, unripe 8 immature, young one, youthful 9 unfledged, youngling, youngster 11 undeveloped

juvenility 5 youth 7 puberty 9 greenness, youthhood 10 pubescence, springtide, springtime 11 adolescence 12 youthfulness

juxtaposed 8 abutting, adjacent, touching 9 adjoining, bordering 10 approximal, contiguous 12 conterminous

K

kabob 7 shaslik 8 shashlik 9 shashlick
kaddish 6 cantor, prayer
kady 3 hat 5 derby
Kafka, Franz *character:* 4 Olga
 5 Samsa (Gregor) 6 Joseph (K.) *novel:*
 7 Amerika 8 The Trial 9 The Castle
kaiser 5 ruler 7 emperor, monarch 9 sovereign
kaka 6 parrot
kakariki 6 lizard 8 parakeet
kakatoe 6 parrot 8 cockatoo
kale 4 cole 7 cabbage, collard 8 borecole,
 colewort
kaleidoscopic 7 diverse, various 8 colorful 10 variegated
Kali *aspect:* 5 Durga 7 Parvati *husband:*
 4 Siva 5 Shiva
kalium 9 potassium
kalong 3 bat 8 fruit bat
Kama *god of:* 4 love *mount:* 6 parrot
 7 sparrow *wife:* 4 Rati
kambal 5 shawl 7 blanket
kamik 4 boot
kamikaze 7 suicide 8 airplane, suicidal
kampong 6 hamlet 7 village
Kampuchea see **Cambodia**
kangaroo 4 euro 6 leaper 7 bettong, wallaby 8 boongary, wallaroo 9 marsupial
 10 macropodid *herd:* 3 mob *male:*
 6 boomer *young:* 4 joey
kangaroo bear 5 koala
kangaroo rat 7 potoroo
kans 5 grass 6 glagah
Kansas *capital:* 6 Topeka *college:*
 5 Tabor *fort:* 5 Riley *largest city:* 7 Wichita *nickname:* 14 Jayhawker State,
 Sunflower State *prison:* 11 Leavenworth
kaolin 4 clay
kapelle 5 choir 9 orchestra
kaput 6 ruined 7 done for 8 defeated,
 finished 9 destroyed
karakul 5 sheep
karakurt 6 spider 9 black wolf
Kareah's son 7 Johanan 8 Jonathan
karma 4 aura 5 force, power 6 spirit
kaross 3 rug 7 garment
kasha 4 mush 5 grain
katabasis 7 retreat 9 troparion
Katharina *father:* 8 Baptista *suitor:*
 9 Petruchio

Katrina's suitor 9 Brom Bones 12 Ichabod Crane
katydid 6 insect 11 grasshopper
katzenjammer 6 clamor, nausea 8 hang-
 over, headache
kava 3 awa 5 shrub 6 pepper
kayak 4 boat 5 canoe
kayo 8 knockout
Kazantzakis hero 5 Zorba
kea 6 parrot
Keats poem 5 Lamia 8 Endymion, Hyperion, Isabella, To Autumn 11 Ode to Psyche
kedge 6 anchor
keel 4 boat, drop, fall, ship 5 barge, pitch,
 ridge, slump, upset 6 carina, go down,
 plunge, topple, tumble 7 capsize 8 overturn 11 centerboard
keelbird 3 ani
keen 4 agog, avid, wail, yowl 5 acute,
 alert, eager, honed, nutty, sharp, smart
 6 ardent, bewail, clever, fervid, gung ho,
 lively, shrewd 7 animate, anxious, athirst,
 fervent, thirsty, whetted, zealous 8 animated, appetent, spirited 9 impatient, perfervid, sensitive, sprightly, unblunted, vivacious 10 breathless, perceptive,
 razor-sharp 11 penetrating, penetrative,
 quick-witted, sharp-witted 12 enthusiastic,
 quick-sighted, sharp-sighted
keenness 3 wit 4 edge 6 acumen
 9 sharpness 10 astuteness, shrewdness
 11 discernment, penetration, percipience
 12 incisiveness, perspicacity
keep 3 own, pen 4 curb, fend, have, hold,
 jail, mind, obey, save 5 carry, check, stock
 6 bridle, comply, detain, direct, follow, hold
 in, living, lockup, manage, ordain, prison,
 retain 7 abstain, alimony, carry on, conduct, conform, control, forbear, inhibit,
 observe, operate, possess, refrain, reserve,
 support 8 conserve, hold back, hold down,
 maintain, preserve, restrain, withhold 9 celebrate, constrain, solemnize 10 livelihood,
 sustenance 11 commemorate, maintenance, subsistence
keep back 3 dam 4 deny, hold, save
 6 detain, refuse, retain, retard 7 reserve
 8 disallow, withhold
keeper 5 guard 6 custos, pastor, warden

7 curator 8 cerberus, claviger, guardian, watchdog 9 constable, custodian

keeping 4 care, ward 5 trust 6 charge, saving 7 custody 9 salvation 10 caretaking 12 conservation, guardianship

keep on 7 persist 8 continue 9 persevere

keep out 3 bar 4 hold 5 debar 6 detain, retain 7 reserve 8 hold back, withhold

keepsake 5 relic, token 6 trophy 7 memento 8 giftbook, memorial, reminder, souvenir 11 remembrance 12 remembrancer

keep up 7 sustain 8 continue, maintain, preserve

keeve 3 tub, vat 4 kier 5 basin

kef 4 hemp 7 languor, tobacco 10 dreaminess 12 tranquillity

keg 3 tun 4 butt, cask, pipe 6 barrel 7 barrico 8 hogshead

kegler 6 bowler

keister, keester 7 satchel 8 buttocks, suitcase

keitloa 5 rhino

keloid 4 scar

kelp 3 ash 4 agar, alga 5 varec 7 seaweed

Kemuel *father:* 5 Nahor *mother:* 6 Milcah *son:* 9 Hashabiah

ken 4 view 5 grasp, range, reach, scope, sight 7 horizon, purview 10 perception

kenaf 4 hemp, jute 6 ambari 8 hibiscus

kench 3 bin 9 enclosure

Kenilworth author 5 Scott (Walter)

kennel 3 den 4 pack 5 drain, house, sewer 6 gutter 7 confine, shelter 9 enclosure

keno 4 game *similar to:* 5 beano, bingo, lotto

Kentucky *capital:* 9 Frankfort *largest city:* 10 Louisville *nickname:* 14 Bluegrass State *state bird:* 8 cardinal *state flower:* 9 goldenrod

Kentucky bluegrass 3 poa

Kenya *capital:* 7 Nairobi *monetary unit:* 8 shilling

kepi 3 cap

kerchief 6 hankie 8 babushka, bandanna, headrail, kaffiyeh *Scottish:* 5 curch

kerf 3 cut 4 slit 5 notch 6 groove

kermis 4 fair 8 carnival, festival

kernel 3 nub, nut 4 core, crux, gist, meat, pith, seed 5 grain 6 matter, nubbin, upshot 7 nucleus 9 substance *combining form:* 4 cary, kary 5 caryo, karyo

Kerouac novel 6 Big Sur 9 On the Road

kestrel 4 bird, hawk 6 falcon, fanner 9 windhover

ketch 4 boat 8 sailboat

ketone 5 irone 7 acetone, camphor, muscone 8 acridone, butanone, civetone

kettle 3 pot, vat 6 vessel 7 caldron, marmite, pothole 8 cauldron, flambeau

kettledrum 5 naker, party 6 timbal, tymbal *Arabian:* 6 atabal

Keturah's husband 7 Abraham

kevel 5 cleat, staff 6 cudgel, hammer, timber 7 bollard

key 3 cay 4 isle, reef, tone 5 islet, pitch, vital 6 clavis, cotter, island, legend, opener, samara, spline, ticket 7 central, digital 8 critical, passport, password, solution, tonality 9 important 10 open sesame *combining form:* 5 clavi, clavo, cleid 6 cleido *notch:* 4 ward

keyboard 6 manual 7 clavier 8 pedalier 10 claviature

key fruit 6 samara

key man 9 locksmith

keynote 4 tone 5 theme, tonic 7 feature

keynoter 6 orator 7 speaker

Keystone State 12 Pennsylvania

Keziah's father 3 Job

khaki 5 cloth, color 7 uniform

khamsin 4 wind

khan 5 chief, ruler 9 chieftain, sovereign

khedive 5 ruler 7 viceroy

Khomeini, e.g. 4 imam

Ki *brother, consort:* 2 An *mother:* 5 Nammu *son:* 5 Enlil

kiang 3 ass

kibble 4 meal 5 grain, grind

kibbutz 4 farm 7 commune 10 collective, settlement

kibe 4 chap 5 crack 9 chilblain

kibitzer 5 prier, pryer, snoop 6 butt-in 7 meddler 8 busybody, observer, quidnunc 9 spectator 10 pragmatist, rubberneck

kick 4 bang, boot, fuss, punt, wail 5 whine 6 except, murmur, object, repine, thrill, wallop 7 grumble, protest 8 complain 11 expostulate, remonstrate

kicker 4 crab 5 crank 6 griper, grouch, punter 7 growler 8 grumbler, sorehead, sourpuss 10 complainer

kick off 4 open 5 begin, start 6 launch 8 commence, embark on, initiate 10 embark upon, inaugurate

kick out 2 ax 4 drop, fire, sack 5 chase, chuck, eject, evict 6 bounce 7 boot out, cashier, dismiss, extrude 8 throw out 9 discharge

kickshaw 3 toy 5 goody, treat 6 bauble, dainty, morsel, tidbit, titbit, trifle 8 delicacy

kid 3 bud, fun, guy, rag, rib 4 dupe, fool, gull, hoax, jest, joke, josh, razz 5 child, jolly, trick, youth 6 banter, befool, moppet 8 flimflam, hoodwink, juvenile, young one 9 bamboozle, youngling, youngster

kidnap 6 abduct, waylay 8 shanghai 10 spirit away

kidney 5 gland, organ *combining form:* 4 reni, reno 5 nephr 6 nephro 7 nephron, nephros *Scottish:* 4 neer

kidney-shaped 8 reniform

kielbasa 7 sausage

kier 3 vat

kilderkin 3 keg 4 cask 6 barrel

killm 3 mat, rug 6 carpet

kill 3 zap 4 bane, down, hang, slay, veto 5 croak, scrag, shoot 6 cut off, finish, lay low, murder, poison, stifle 7 butcher, destroy, execute, garrote, put away, take off 8 carry off, dispatch, immolate, massacre, negative, strangle 9 non-placet, sacrifice, slaughter 10 annihilate 11 assassinate, exterminate

killer 6 gunman, hit man, slayer 7 torpedo 8 assassin, homicide, murderer *combining form:* 4 cide 6 ctonus

killer whale 4 orca 7 grampus

killing 5 blood 6 murder 8 foul play, homicide 9 slaughter 12 manslaughter *combining form:* 5 cidal *of a race:* 8 genocide *of bacteria:* 11 bactericide *of brother:* 10 fratricide *of father:* 9 parricide, patricide *of king:* 8 regicide *of mother:* 9 matricide *of self:* 7 suicide *of sister:* 10 sororicide

Kilmer poem 5 Trees

kiln 4 bake, burn, fire, oast, oven 7 furnace

kilt 5 skirt 7 filabeg, filibeg 8 fillebeg *fabric:* 5 plaid 6 tartan

kilter 4 trim 5 order, shape 6 fettle, repair 7 fitness 9 condition

kimono 4 gown, robe *sash:* 3 obi

kin 3 sib 4 clan, folk, race, sept 5 stock, tribe 6 family 7 kindred, lineage, related 8 kinsfolk, relation, relative 9 cousinage

kind 3 ilk, way 4 good, mild, sort, type, warm 5 breed, class, genre, genus, order 6 benign, gender, genial, gentle, humane, kidney, nature, stripe, tender 7 affable, amiable, clement, cordial, feather, lenient, species, variety 8 merciful, obliging, tolerant 9 benignant, character 10 altruistic, benevolent, charitable, forbearing, propitious, responsive 11 complaisant, considerate, description, good-hearted, good-humored, good-natured, openhearted, sympathetic, warmhearted 12 eleemosynary, good-tempered, humanitarian 13 compassionate, philanthropic

kindle 4 fire, move, stir, wake, whet 5 light, rally, rouse, waken 6 arouse, awaken, bestir, excite, foment, ignite, incite 7 inflame, provoke 9 challenge, instigate, stimulate

kindliness 5 amity 6 comity 8 goodwill 10 friendship 11 benevolence 12 friendliness

kindly 4 well 6 benign 7 benefic 8 friendly, gracious 9 attentive, benignant, heedfully 10 generously, neighborly 11 considerate, good-hearted 12 thoughtfully 13 considerately

kindness 5 favor 7 service 8 clemency, courtesy, goodwill, sympathy 10 indulgence 11 benevolence 12 dispensation

kindred 3 sib 4 akin, clan, folk, race, sept 5 house, stock, tribe 6 agnate, allied, family 7 cognate, connate, lineage, related 8 incident 10 affiliated, connatural 11 consanguine

king 3 rex 4 czar, tsar 5 baron, mogul, ruler 6 tycoon 7 magnate, monarch 9 sovereign *Albanian:* 3 Zog 7 William *Assyrian:* 6 Sargon 11 Sennacherib, Shalmaneser *Babylonian:* 6 Sargon 9 Hammurabi 10 Belshazzar *Belgian:* 6 Albert 7 Leopold 8 Baudouin *Bohemian:* 9 Wenceslas 10 Wenceslaus *Damascus:* 8 Benhadad *Danish:* 4 Abel, Eric, Germ, Hans, John, Olaf 5 Sweyn 6 Canute, Harold, Magnus 8 Nicholas, Waldemar 9 Christian, Frederick 11 Christopher *Dutch:* 7 William *Egyptian:* 3 Tut 4 Pepi, Seti 5 Khufu, Menes, Necho 6 Cheops, Ramses 7 Harmhab, Osorkon, Psamtik, Ptolemy 8 Ikhnaton, Thothmes, Thutmose 9 Amenhotep, Sesostris 11 Tutankhamen *English:* 4 John 5 Henry, James 6 Alfred, Canute, Edmund, Edward, Egbert, George, Harold 7 Charles, Richard, Stephen, William 8 Ethelred 9 Athelstan, Ethelbald, Ethelbert *French:* 3 Odo, roi 4 John 5 Henry, Louis, Pepin, Raoul 6 Philip, Robert, Rudolf 7 Charles, Francis, Lothair 9 Hugh Capet 11 Charlemagne *German:* 4 Karl 5 Louis 6 Lothar, Ludwig 7 Charles, Lothair *Greek (modern):* 4 Paul 6 George 9 Alexander 11 Constantine *Hawaiian:* 10 Kamehameha *Hungarian:* 6 Attila *Indian:* 4 raja 5 rajah *Irish:* 9 Brain Boru *Italian:* 7 Humbert *Jordanian:* 5 Talal 7 Hussein 8 Abdullah *Judah:* (see at Judah) *Judean:* 5 Herod *Lydian:* 5 Gyges 7 Croesus 8 Alyattes *Norwegian:* 4 Eric, Erik, Inge, Olaf 5 Sweyn 6 Haakon, Harald, Harold, Magnus, Sigurd, Sverre *Ostrogothic:* 9 Theodoric *Persian:* 5 Cyrus 6 Darius, Xerxes *Portuguese:* 4 John 5 Henry, Louis, Peter 6 Carlos, Edward, Manuel, Sancho 7 Alfonso 9 Ferdinand, Sebastian *Prussian:* 7 Wilhelm, William 9 Frederick, Friedrich *relating to:* 5 regal, royal *Saudi Arabian:* 4 Saud 6 Faisal 9 Abdul-Aziz *Scottish:* 4 John 5 David, Edgar, James 6 Duncan 7 Macbeth, Malcolm, William 9 Alexander, Donalbane 10 David Bruce 11 Robert Bruce *Spanish:* 3 rey 5 Louis 6 Philip 7 Alfonso,

Amadeus, Charles 9 Ferdinand 10 Juan Carlos *Spartan:* 8 Leonidas *Swedish:* 4 Eric, John 5 Oscar 6 Birger, Gustav, Haakon, Magnus 7 Charles 8 Gustavus, Waldemar 9 Frederick, Sigismund, Sten Sture *Visigothic:* 6 Alaric

King Arthur *birthplace:* 8 Tintagel *chronicler:* 8 Geoffrey *court site:* 7 Camelot 8 Caerleon *deathplace:* 6 Camlan *father:* 5 Uther *father-in-law:* 9 Laodogant, Leodegran 11 Leodegrance *foster father:* 5 Ector *jester:* 7 Dagonet *knight:* 3 Kay 4 Bors 5 Balan, Balin 6 Gareth, Gawain, Modred 7 Galahad, Geraint, Lamerok, Mordred, Tristan 8 Bedivere, Lancelot, Parsifal, Percival, Tristram 9 Percivale *lance:* 3 Ron *last abode:* 6 Avalon *last name:* 9 Pendragon *magician:* 6 Merlin *mother:* 6 Ygerne 7 Igraine *nephew:* 6 Gareth, Modred 7 Mordred *queen:* 9 Guinevere *shield:* 7 Pridwin *sister:* 7 Morgain 11 Morgan le Fay *slayer:* 6 Modred 7 Mordred *son:* 6 Modred 7 Mordred *steward:* 3 Kay *sword:* 9 Excalibur *victim:* 6 Modred 7 Mordred *wife:* 9 Guinevere

king crab 7 limulus

kingdom 5 realm 6 domain, empire 7 demesne

kingfish 4 cero 7 croaker, whiting 8 mulloway

kingfisher 4 bird 6 alcedo, dacelo 7 halcyon 10 kookaburra

kingly 5 regal, royal 6 lordly, regnal 8 imperial, majestic, powerful, puissant 9 imperious, masterful, monarchal, sovereign 10 monarchial 11 monarchical

King Philip 9 Metacomet

Kingsley play 7 Dead End 10 Men in White

Kingu *consort:* 6 Tiamat *slayer:* 6 Marduk

kink 4 bend, curl, turn, whim 5 cramp, crick, quirk, snarl, twist 6 buckle, tangle 12 imperfection

kinky 3 odd 5 outré, ultra, weird 6 far-out 7 bizarre, crooked, deviant, strange, twisted 10 outlandish

kiosk 5 booth 8 pavilion 9 newsstand 11 summerhouse

kip 3 bed 4 hide, pelt, skin 5 sleep

Kipling, Rudyard *trio:* 3 rag 4 bone 10 hank of hair *work:* 3 Kim, 6 L'Envoi 8 Gunga Din, Mandalay 10 Fuzzy Wuzzy 11 Recessional 13 Soldiers Three, The Jungle Book

kirsch 6 brandy

kirtle 4 coat, gown 5 dress, tunic

Kish *father:* 3 Ner 4 Abdi 5 Abiel, Jeiel 6 Jehiel *son:* 4 Saul

kismet 3 lot 4 doom, fate 5 moira, weird 7 destiny, portion 12 circumstance

kiss 4 buss, peck, skim 5 brush, graze, shave, smack 6 glance, smooch 8 osculate

kisser 4 face 5 mouth

Kiss sculptor 5 Rodin (Auguste)

kit 3 bag, box, set 6 outfit 7 package 9 container 10 collection

kitchen 6 galley 7 cuisine 8 scullery *appliance:* (see at **appliance**) *boss:* 4 chef; (see also **cooking**)

kite 4 bird, hawk, sail 5 scram 6 begone, decamp, get out 7 skiddoo, take off 8 clear out, hightail 9 skedaddle

kith 7 friends, kindred 9 neighbors

kittenish 3 coy 6 elvish, frisky, impish 7 coltish, larkish, playful, roguish 8 prankish 10 frolicsome 11 mischievous

kitty 3 cat, pot 4 pool 6 feline, stakes 7 jackpot

kiwi 4 bird 5 fruit 7 apteryx

kleptomaniac 5 thief 10 shoplifter

klutz 3 oaf 4 gawk, lout, lump 5 looby 6 lubber, lummox 7 lobster, palooka 9 schlemiel

knack 3 set 4 bent, gift, hang, head, nose, turn 5 skill, swing, trick 6 genius, talent 7 ability, aptness, command, know-how, mastery 8 facility 9 dexterity, expertise, expertism 10 expertness, mastership

knapsack 3 bag 4 case, pack 8 backpack, packsack, rucksack 9 haversack

knave 4 heel, jack 5 rogue, scamp 6 rascal, varlet 7 lowlife, villain 8 coistrel 9 miscreant, scoundrel 10 blackguard

knavery 5 fraud 8 mischief, trickery, villainy 9 rascality

knavish 5 lying 6 shifty 7 roguish 8 unhonest 9 deceitful, dishonest 10 mendacious, untruthful

knee 4 genu 5 joint *armor:* 6 poleyn *bend:* 5 kneel 9 genuflect *bone:* 7 patella

kneeler 5 stool 7 cushion 8 prie-dieu

knell 4 bong, peal, ring, toll 5 chime 6 summon 7 warning

knickknack 3 toy 4 dido 5 curio, virtu 6 bauble, gadget, gewgaw, trifle 7 bibelot, novelty, trinket, whatnot 8 gimcrack, souvenir 9 bric-a-brac, objet d'art 11 rattletraps

knife 3 cut, ulu 4 bolo, shiv, stab 5 blade, bowie, corer, gouge, panga, slice, sword 6 barong, colter, coutel, cutter, dagger, kuttar, parang, sickle 7 cleaver, couteau, machete, whittle 8 yataghan *case:* 6 sheath *maker:* 6 cutler 7 grinder *surgical:* 6 catlin 7 catling, scalpel 8 bistoury

knifelike 5 acute, sharp 8 piercing, shooting, stabbing

knight 3 dub, sir 5 eques 6 ritter 8 cavalier, chessman, horseman 9 caballero, chevalier *code:* 8 chivalry *competition:* 7 listing, tilting 8 jousting 10 tournament *flag:* 6 pennon 8 gonfalon, gonfanon *legendary:* 8 douzeper *servant:* 4 page 5 valet 6 squire *title:* 3 sir *wife:* 4 lady

knighthood 8 chivalry

knightly 5 brave, noble 7 gallant 10 chivalrous

Knight of the Round Table see King Arthur

Knight of the Rueful Countenance 10 Don Quixote

knit 4 bind, heal, join, mend, purl 5 plait, unite, weave 6 cement, stitch 7 conjoin, crochet, wrinkle 8 contract 10 intertwine

knitting 9 handiwork *material:* 4 yarn *stitch:* 3 rib 4 purl 6 garter 11 stockinette *tool:* 6 needle

knob 3 bun, bur, nub 4 bump, burr, dial, hill, lump, node, peak, umbo 5 bulge, gnarl, knoll, mound 6 button, finial, handle, nubble, pommel 7 hillock 12 protuberance *combining form:* 3 tyl 4 tylo 6 condyl 7 condylo

knobkerrie 3 bat 4 club, mace 5 billy 6 cudgel 7 war club 8 bludgeon 9 billy club, truncheon

knock 3 bob, hit, rap, tap 4 blow, bump, lick, skin, swat, tunk, wipe 5 blame, clout, pound, swipe, thump 7 censure, condemn 8 denounce 9 criticize, reprehend, reprobate 10 denunciate

knock down 3 get, win 4 drop, earn, fell, gain, make 5 floor, level 6 ground, lay low 7 acquire, bring in, flatten 8 bowl over

knocker 5 momus 6 carper, critic, Zoilus 7 caviler 9 aristarch 10 criticizer 11 faultfinder

knock off 4 do in, halt, quit, stop, take 5 cease 6 deduct, desist, finish, murder 7 execute, put away, take off, take out 8 discount, draw back, give over, leave off, subtract, surcease, take away 9 liquidate, substract 11 assassinate, discontinue

knockout 2 K.O. 4 kayo 5 dandy, peach 6 beauty, eyeful, looker, lovely 7 stunner 8 jim-dandy 9 humdinger 11 crackerjack

knock over 3 rob 4 down, drop, fell, loot 5 floor, rifle, upset, whelm 6 ground, lay low, topple 7 flatten, overset, plunder, ransack, stick up, tip over 8 bowl down, overcome, overturn 9 bring down, overpower, overthrow, overwhelm, prostrate

knoll 4 hill, knob 5 mound 7 hillock

knot 3 bow, tie, web 4 bond, bump, burr, link, loop, lump, maze, mesh, node, snag, yoke 5 bunch, gnarl, hitch, nexus, skein, snarl 6 jungle, morass, tangle 7 mizmaze 8 ligament, ligature, vinculum 9 labyrinth *in fiber:* 3 nep *kind:* 4 bend, loop, slip 5 hitch, honda 6 granny, splice, square 7 bowline

knotty 4 hard 5 rough, tough 6 daedal, rugged, sticky, uphill 7 complex, gordian, twisted 8 involved, terrible 9 Byzantine, difficult, effortful, elaborate, intricate 10 formidable 11 complicated 12 labyrinthine

knout 4 flog, lash, whip

know 3 see, wot 4 feel 5 grasp, savor, sever, taste 6 fathom, intuit, suffer 7 cognize, discern, realize, sustain, undergo 8 separate 9 apprehend, extricate, recognize 10 apperceive, appreciate, comprehend, difference, discrepate, experience, severalize, understand *Scottish:* 3 ken

knowable 5 lucid 8 luminous 9 graspable 10 cognizable, fathomable 11 cognoscible 12 intelligible 13 apprehensible

know-how 3 art 5 craft, knack, skill 7 ability, command, cunning, mastery 9 dexterity, expertise, expertism 10 adroitness, expertness, mastership

knowing 3 hep, hip 4 gash, sage, wise 5 alive, awake, aware, blasé, canny, quick, sharp, slick, smart 6 brainy, bright, clever, sophic 7 gnostic, witting, worldly 8 mondaine, sensible, sentient 9 brilliant, cognizant, conscious, insighted, observant, sagacious, world-wise 10 conversant, discerning, insightful, perceptive 11 intelligent, quick-witted, ready-witted, sharp-witted, worldly-wise 12 apprehensive, disenchanted, disentranced, nimble-witted, sophisticate 13 disillusioned, sophisticated *combining form:* 7 gnostic 9 gnostical

know-it-all 6 smarty 7 wise guy 8 wiseacre, wisehead 10 smart aleck 11 smartypants, wisecracker, wisenheimer

knowledge 3 ken 4 data, lore, news 5 facts 6 wisdom 7 science 8 evidence, learning 9 cognition, education, erudition 10 cognizance 11 information, scholarship 12 intelligence 13 enlightenment *combining form:* 5 gnosy, sophy 6 gnosia, gnosis *from meditation:* 5 jnana *lack of:* 9 ignorance *mystical:* 6 gnosis *suffix:* 3 ics *systematized:* 7 science *universal:* 8 pansophy 9 pantology

knowledgeable 4 sage, wise 5 sharp, smart 6 brainy, bright, clever, sophic 7 gnostic, knowing 9 brilliant, insighted, sagacious 10 discerning, insightful, perceptive 11 intelligent, quick-witted, ready-witted

know-nothing 4 dolt, dope, rude 5 dummy, dunce, idiot 6 dimwit 7 lackwit, pinhead, wantwit 8 ignorant, untaught 9 benighted, ignoramus, untutored 10 illiterate, uneducated, unlettered 11 empty-headed

knuckle 5 joint *combining form:* 6 condyl 7 condylo

knucklehead 5 dunce 8 clodpate, numskull 10 thickskull

knuckle under 3 bow 4 cave 5 defer, yield 6 submit 7 succumb 10 capitulate

knurl 4 bead, knob, knot 5 ridge

K.O. 4 kayo 8 knockout

koan 7 paradox

kobold 5 gnome 6 goblin, spirit, sprite

Kohath *father:* 4 Levi *sister:* 8 Jochebed *son:* 5 Izhar

Kohinoor 7 diamond

kohlrabi 6 turnip 7 cabbage

kokoon 3 gnu

kola 3 nut 7 extract

Kolaiah's son 4 Ahab

komatik 4 sled 6 sledge

kook 3 nut 5 crank 6 cuckoo 7 lunatic 8 crackpot 9 ding-a-ling, harebrain, screwball 10 crackbrain

kopeck 4 coin *one hundred:* 5 ruble

Korah *father:* 4 Esau 7 Eliphaz *mother:* 10 Oholibamah

Koran *chapter:* 4 sura *revealer of:* 7 Gabriel *scholar:* 5 ulama, ulema

Korea see North Korea; South Korea

Korean *dynasty:* 2 Yi *national dish:* 6 kimchi

kosher 3 fit 4 pure 5 clean 6 proper 7 genuine 10 legitimate

Koussevitzky 5 Serge 6 Sergei 9 conductor

kowtow 4 fawn 5 cower, toady 6 cringe, grovel 7 honey up, truckle 8 bootlick 11 apple-polish

kraal 3 hut, pen 6 corral 8 manyatta 9 enclosure

krater 6 vessel *ovoid:* 6 kelebe

Kriemhild *brother:* 7 Gunther *husband:* 5 Etzel 6 Attila 9 Siegfried *slayer:* 10 Hildebrand *victim:* 5 Hagen

kris 6 dagger

Krishna *avatar of:* 6 Vishnu *brother:* 8 Balarama *father:* 8 Vasudeva *mother:* 6 Devaki *uncle:* 5 Kansa *victim:* 5 Kansa

Krupp works site 5 Essen

krypton *symbol:* 2 Kr

kudize 4 hail 6 praise 7 acclaim, applaud, commend 9 recommend 10 compliment

kudo 7 bouquet, orchids 10 compliment

kudos 4 bays 5 award, badge, glory, honor 6 praise, renown 7 laurels 8 accolade, eminence, prestige 10 decoration, prominence, prominency 11 distinction

kudu 8 antelope

kukri 5 sword

kumquat 5 fruit *kin:* 6 orange

kusu 5 mouse

kuttar 6 dagger

kvass 4 beer

kylin 7 unicorn

kylix 3 cup 7 chalice

kyphosis 8 humpback 9 hunchback

L

Laadah *father:* 6 Shelah *grandfather:* 5 Judah

laager 4 camp, tent 6 encamp 7 bivouac

Laban *daughter:* 4 Leah 6 Rachel *father:* 7 Bethuel *grandfather:* 5 Nahor *sister:* 7 Rebekah

label 3 tag 4 band, mark 6 marker, ticket 8 classify *adhesive:* 7 sticker

labium 3 lip

labor 3 tug 4 moil, task, toil, work 5 drive, grind 6 strain, strive 7 slavery, travail 8 bullwork, drudgery, endeavor, slogging, struggle 10 birth pangs, childbirth, donkey-work 12 childbearing *group:* 3 AFL, CIO 5 ILGWU, union *leader:* 5 Hoffa (Jimmy), Lewis (John L.), Meany (George) 6 Chavez (Cesar) 7 Gompers (Samuel), Reuther (Walter) 8 Randolph (Asa Philip)

laboratory *device:* 4 etna 5 flask 6 beaker, mortar, pestle, retort 7 pipette 8 crucible, test tube 12 Bunsen burner

laborer 3 man 4 hand, peon 5 hunky, navvy 6 bohunk, toiler, worker 7 workman 8 workhand 9 operative 10 roustabout, workingman *Mexican:* 7 bracero *Oriental:* 5 cooly 6 coolie

laborious 4 hard 5 heavy 6 uphill 7 arduous, labored, onerous, operose 8 toilsome 9 difficult, effortful, strenuous 10 burdensome

La Brea 4 pits 7 tar pits *fossil:* 10 sabertooth

labyrinth 3 web 4 knot, maze, mesh 5 skein, snarl 6 jungle, morass, tangle 7 mizmaze *builder:* 8 Daedalus *monster:* 8 Minotaur

labyrinthine 6 daedal, knotty 7 complex, gordian 8 involved, tortuous 9 Byzantine, elaborate, intricate 11 complicated

lace 3 net, tat, tie 4 beat, cord, lash, trim 5 adorn, braid, frill, liven, plait, twine 6 defeat, fabric, fasten, ribbon, string, thrash, thread 7 entwine, tatting 8 decorate, openwork 9 embroider 10 embroidery, intertwine, shoestring 11 needlepoint *edge:* 5 picot *ground:* 6 réseau *into:* 5 abuse 6 attack 7 condemn *kind:* 6 bobbin 7 Alençon, guipure, Maltese, Mechlin 8 Argentan, Brussels, Venetian 9 Chantilly

10 colberteen, colbertine 11 needlepoint 12 Valenciennes *make:* 3 tat *pattern:* 5 toilé

Lacedaemon 6 Sparta

lacerate 3 cut, rip 4 rend, tear 5 wound 6 mangle, pierce

lachrymose 3 sad 5 teary, weepy 7 tearful, weeping 8 mournful

lack 4 need, want 6 dearth, defect 7 absence, default, deficit, failure, require 8 shortage, underage 9 privation 10 deficiency, inadequacy, scantiness

lackadaisical 4 idle, lazy, limp 7 dieaway, languid, passive 8 fainéant, indolent, listless, romantic, slothful 9 enervated, incurious 10 languorous, spiritless

lacking 3 shy 4 away, gone, sans 5 minus, short 6 absent, devoid 7 missing, omitted, wanting, without 8 awanting 9 defective, deficient 10 inadequate, incomplete, uncomplete 12 insufficient

lackluster 3 dim, mat 4 dead, drab, dull, flat 5 blind, muted, prosy, rusty 6 leaden 7 prosaic 8 lifeless 9 colorless, tarnished

Laconian 7 Spartan *king:* 5 Lelex, Myles

laconic 4 curt 5 brief, pithy, short, terse 7 brusque, concise 8 succinct 11 compendiary, compendious 12 breviloquent

lacquer 5 gloss 6 finish 7 shellac, varnish

lacquered metalware 4 tole

lacrosse *team:* 3 ten

lactate 4 salt 5 ester 7 secrete

lacteal 5 milky

lacuna 3 gap 5 break 6 breach, hiatus 7 interim 8 interval 12 interruption

lad 3 boy, son, tad 5 youth 6 shaver 9 shaveling, stripling *Scottish:* 6 callan 7 callant

ladder 3 run 5 scale 6 series *adjunct:* 4 rung 6 rundle

ladderlike 6 scalar 11 scalariform

lade 3 dip, tax 4 ball, clog, load, pack, ship, stow 5 ladle, scoop, weigh 6 burden, charge, cumber, saddle, weight 8 encumber

lading 4 haul, load 5 cargo 6 burden 7 freight, payload

ladle 3 dip 4 bail, lade 5 scoop, spoon 6 dipper

Ladon 6 dragon *father:* 7 Phorcus, Phorcys *mother:* 4 Ceto *slayer:* 8 Heracles,
Hercules

lady *French:* 4 dame *Italian:* 5 donna
7 signora *Muslim:* 5 begum *Spanish:*
4 doña 6 senora

lady ___ 4 crab, fern, luck, palm 5 chair,
tulip 6 beetle, friend, killer 7 cracker
9 bountiful

ladybird 6 beetle 7 pintail

ladybug 6 beetle *Australian:* 7 vedalia

Lady Chatterley's Lover *author:*
8 Lawrence (David Herbert) *character:*
6 Connie 7 Mellors 9 Constance

Lady of the Lake, The 5 Ellen, Nimue
6 Vivien *author:* 5 Scott (Walter)

Lady Windermere's Fan *author:*
5 Wilde (Oscar)

Laertes *father:* 8 Acrisius, Polonius *sister:*
7 Ophelia *son:* 7 Ulysses 8 Odysseus
wife: 8 Anticlea

La Fontaine's forte 5 fable

lag 4 drag, last, poke, slow, stay, tire
5 dally, delay, final, tarry, trail 6 dawdle,
deport, latest, latter, loiter, put off, retard
7 closing, slacken 8 eventual, hindmost, terminal, ultimate 10 concluding

lager 4 beer

laggard 4 slow 6 loafer, remiss 7 dawdler,
unhasty 8 comatose, dawdling, delaying,
dilatory, lingerer, loiterer, slowpoke, sluggish 9 apathetic, impassive, lazybones, leisurely, lethargic, loitering, slow coach,
straggler, unhurried 10 deliberate, phlegmatic

La Gioconda *composer:* 10 Ponchielli
(Amilcare) *painter:* 7 da Vinci (Leonardo)

lagniappe 3 tip 4 perk 7 cumshaw, largess, palm oil 8 gratuity 9 pourboire
10 perquisite

lagomorph 4 hare, pika 6 rabbit

lagoon 4 pond, pool 5 liman, sound
7 channel

___ **La Guardia** 8 Fiorello

Lahmi *brother:* 7 Goliath *slayer:*
7 Elhanan

laic 6 layman

lair 3 den 4 cave 5 couch, haunt, lodge
6 burrow 7 hideout, retreat 8 hideaway

Laius *father:* 8 Labdacus *slayer, son:*
7 Oedipus *wife:* 7 Jocasta

lake 3 sea 4 loch, mere, pond, pool
5 lough 6 lagoon *Adriatic:* 6 Varano
Alberta: 6 Louise *Algeria:* 5 Hodna *Alps:*
6 Annecy *Arizona-Nevada:* 4 Mead *Armenia:* 5 Sevan 6 Gokcha, Sevang 9 Lychni-
tis *Aswan's:* 6 Nasser *Australia:* 4 Eyre
5 Carey, Cowan, Frome, Wells 6 Barlee
7 Amadeus, Everard, Torrens 8 Gairdner
Austria: 5 Atter, Traun 6 Kammer 8 Atter-
see 9 Kammersee *Bolivia:* 5 Poopo *Botswana:* 5 Ngami *British Columbia:* 4 Pitt
5 Atlin *California:* 4 Mono, Tule 5 Clear,
Eagle, Honey *Cambodia:* 8 Tonle Sap
Canada: 4 Dyke 8 Manitoba *central
Africa:* 4 Kivu 5 Mweru 6 Albert *Central
America:* 5 Guija *central Europe:*
5 Leman 6 Geneva, Lugano 7 Ceresio
8 Bodensee 9 Constance *central North
America:* 5 Rainy *Chile:* 4 Laja 5 Ranco
China: 6 Poyang 8 Dongting *Colorado:*
5 Grand *combining form:* 4 limn 5 limni,
limno 6 limnia (plural) 7 limnion *Connecticut:* 6 Bantam 7 Gardner 8 Highland
10 Candlewood, Pocotopaug *Denmark:*
5 Esrum *east Africa:* 6 Rudolf 7 Turkana
east Asia: 6 Khanka 7 Xingkai 8 Hsingkai
east central Africa: 8 Victoria 10 Tangan-
yika *east China:* 3 Tai 5 Dalai, Hulun
Ethiopia: 4 Tana, Zwai 5 Abaya, Shala,
Shamo, Tsana 8 Stefanie 9 Chew Bahir
Finland: 5 Inari *Florida:* 5 Worth
10 Okeechobee *Germany:* 5 Ammer,
Chiem 8 Ammersee, Chiemsee *Ghana:*
5 Volta *Great:* 4 Erie 5 Huron 7 Ontario
8 Michigan, Superior *Greece:* 5 Bolbe,
Volvi *Guatemala:* 7 Atitlan *Honduras:*
5 Yojoa *Honshu:* 3 Omi 4 Biwa, Suwa,
Yodo *Hungary:* 7 Balaton 10 Plattensee
Idaho: 4 Waha 5 Grays 6 Priest 11 Coeur
d'Alene, Pend Oreille *India:* 3 Dal 5 Wular
6 Chilka *Indonesia:* 4 Poso, Toba
5 Ranau *Iowa:* 5 Storm *Iran:* 5 Niriz,
Shahi, Urmia 8 Matianus, Urumiyeh
9 Bakhtigan *Ireland:* 3 Gur, Ree 4 Conn,
Derg, Mask 5 Allen, Arrow, Leane *Israel:*
12 Bahr Tabariya, Sea of Galilee *Israel-Jor-
dan:* 7 Dead Sea *Italy:* 4 Como, Iseo,
Nemi 5 Garda 6 Albano 7 Bolsena, Perugia 8 Maggiore 9 Trasimene *Japan:*
4 Imba 8 Imbanuma *Kazakhstan:*
7 Balqash 8 Balkhash *largest inland:*
10 Caspian Sea *Louisiana:* 4 Soda
5 Black, White 9 Catahoula 13 Pontchar-
train *Maine:* 3 Big 6 Sebago 9 Moose-
head *Mali:* 4 Debo *Manitoba:* 4 Gods
5 Cedar, Moose 8 Winnipeg *Mexico:*
7 Chapala *Michigan:* 4 Burt *Minnesota:*
3 Red 4 Cass, Gull, Swan 5 Leech
6 Itasca 9 Mille Lacs 10 Minnetonka, of the
Woods 11 Lac qui Parle *Minnesota-Wis-
consin:* 5 Pepin *Mongolian:* 3 Har 5 Har
Us, Khara 8 Khara Usu *Montana:* 8 Medicine *mountain:* 4 tarn *Myanmar:* 4 Inle
Nevada: 4 Ruby 7 Pyramid *New Hampshire:* 4 Echo 5 Squam 7 Sunapee
13 Winnipesaukee *New Jersey:* 5 Union
New York: 4 Long 5 Chazy, Keuka
6 Cayuga, George, Oneida, Otsego,
Owasco, Placid, Seneca 7 Crooked, Sara-
nac 8 Onondaga, Saratoga 10 Chautau-
qua 11 Canandaigua, Skaneateles *New*

Zealand: 4 Ohau 5 Hawea, Taupo
6 Pukaki, Wanaka 8 Wakatipu *Nicaragua:*
7 Managua *North Africa:* 4 Chad *North
America:* 9 Champlain *Northern Ireland:*
5 Neagh *Northwest Territories:* 4 Gras
5 Baker, Garry, Pelly 9 Great Bear
10 Great Slave *Norway:* 5 Mjosa *Nova
Scotia:* 7 Bras d'Or *Ontario:* 4 Rice, Seul
5 Trout *Oregon:* 5 Abert 6 Crater 7 Malheur, Wallowa *Paraguay:* 4 Ypoá *Peru:*
5 Junin 13 Chinchaycocha *Philippines:*
4 Bato, Taal 5 Lanao 6 Bombon *Poland:*
5 Mamry, Mauer *Quebec:* 5 Minto, Payne
Russia: 3 Seg 5 Chany, Ilmen, Lacha,
Onega 6 Ladoga 7 Rybinsk 10 Eltonskoye
11 Ladozhskoye *saline:* 5 chott, shott *Saskatchewan:* 4 Cree 5 Ronge *Scotland:*
3 Ard, Awe 4 Doon, Earn, Ness, Olch,
Shin, Sloy 5 Leven, Lochy, Maree, Morar,
Shiel 6 Lomond *Siberia:* 6 Baikal, Baykal
South Africa: 4 Kosi *South America:*
5 Merin, Mirim 8 Titicaca *South Carolina:*
11 Wateree Pond *South Dakota:* 5 Andes
southeast Africa: 5 Nyasa 6 Nyassa
southern United States: 5 Caddo *south-
west Europe:* 5 Ohrid 7 Okhrida *Sudan:*
2 No *Sweden:* 5 Asnen, Roxen 8 Siljan,
Vetter 7 Malaren, Vattern *Switzerland:*
3 Zug 4 Biel, Joux 5 Zuger 6 Bieler,
Bienne, Brienz, Samen, Samer, Zurich
7 Lucerne, Lungern 8 Brienzer, Zuricher
9 Neuchatel, Zurichsee *Tadzhikistan:*
7 Karakul *Tanzania:* 5 Rukwa *Tibet:* 4 Na-
mu 6 Nam Tso, Tengri *Turkey:* 2 Ak
3 Tuz, Van 4 Bafa, Nice 5 Iznik, Sugla
6 Nicaea *Uganda:* 5 Kyoga *Utah:* 6 Powell, Sevier 9 Great Salt *volcanic:* 8 Ilo-
pango *Wales:* 4 Bala *Washington:*
4 Omak 5 Moses 6 Chelan 9 Wenatchee
western China: 4 Ai-pi 6 Ebinur *western
United States:* 4 Bear 5 Tahoe *Wisconsin:* 5 Green 9 Winnebago *Yellowstone
National Park:* 5 Heart, Lewis 8 Shoshone
Zaire: 5 Tumba *Zambia:* 9 Bangweolo,
Bangweulu
lake duck 7 mallard
lake herring 5 cisco
Lake poet 7 Southey (Robert) 9 Coleridge (Samuel Taylor) 10 Wordsworth (William)
lakes *central North America:* 5 Great
Connecticut: 4 Twin *Egypt:* 5 Balah
Maine: 8 Rangeley *New Hampshire:*
11 Connecticut *New York:* 6 Finger *Saskatchewan:* 5 Quill *Twin:* 8 Washinee
9 Washining *Wisconsin:* 4 Four
Lakmé *aria:* 8 Bell Song *composer:*
7 Delibes (Leo)
Lakshmi *husband:* 6 Vishnu *son:*
4 Kama
lalapalooza 5 beaut

lam 3 hit 4 beat, drub, pelt, slip 5 paste,
pound 6 batter, escape, flight, hammer,
pummel, thrash, wallop 7 getaway
8 breakout, escaping 10 escapement
La Mancha's knight 10 Don Quixote
lamb 4 cade, dupe, yean 5 sheep 6 cosset 8 yeanling *leg of:* 5 gigot
lambaste 3 pan 4 beat, drub, flay, lick,
pelt, slam, slap, trim, whip 5 paste, pound,
roast, scold, score, slash, smear 6 assail,
attack, berate, hammer, pummel, scathe,
scorch, thrash, wallop 7 blister, censure,
clobber, reprove, scarify, scourge, shellac,
smother 8 denounce, harangue, lash into,
squabash 9 castigate, criticize, excoriate
10 tongue-lash
lambent 6 bright, lucent 7 beaming, glowing, radiant 8 luminous, lustrous 9 brilliant,
effulgent, refulgent 12 incandescent
lamblike 4 meek 5 ovine 6 gentle
lamb of God 8 Agnus Dei
Lamb's pseudonym 4 Elia
lame 3 ill 4 halt, limp, sick, weak 6 feeble,
sickly 7 cripple, halting, hipshot, limping
8 crippled, disabled 13 incapacitated
lamebrain 3 oaf 4 dope 5 dunce, noddy,
stupe 6 noodle 7 schnook 8 dumbhead
10 dunderhead
Lamech *daughter:* 6 Naamah *father:*
9 Methusael 10 Methuselah *son:* 4 Noah
5 Jabal, Jubal 9 Tubalcain *wife:* 4 Adah
6 Zillah
lament 3 cry, rue 4 keen, moan, pine, pity,
sigh, wail, weep 5 dirge, elegy, mourn
6 bemoan, bewail, grieve, plaint, regret,
repent, repine 7 deplore, despair, elegize
8 jeremiad 9 complaint
lamentable 3 sad 4 dire 6 rueful, woeful
7 doleful, pitiful 8 dolesome, dolorous,
grievous, mournful 9 plaintive, sorrowful
10 afflictive, calamitous, deplorable, lugubrious, melancholy 11 distressing, regrettable, unfortunate 13 heartbreaking
Lamerok *father:* 9 Pellinore *lover:* 8 Margawse *slayer:* 6 Gawain
lamia 3 hag, hex 5 bruja, witch 9 sorceress 10 witchwoman 11 enchantress
Lamia *country:* 5 Libya *form:* 7 serpent
lover: 4 Zeus
lamina 5 blade, flake, layer, plate
lamp 3 arc, eye, orb 4 bulb, davy 5 klieg,
light, torch 6 ocular, oculus, peeper, winker
7 lantern 10 candelabra 11 candelabrum
floor: 8 torchère *hanging:* 10 chandelier
lampblack 4 soot 6 carbon
Lampetia *father:* 6 Apollo, Helios *husband:* 9 Asclepius *mother:* 6 Neaera *sister:* 9 Phaethusa
lampoon 4 mock 5 squib 6 satire 7 pasquil 8 ridicule, satirize 10 pasquinade
lamprey 3 eel

lanai 5 porch 7 terrace, veranda

lanate 5 hairy 6 woolly

lance 3 cut 4 spit 5 blade, spear, spike 6 impale, pierce, skewer, skiver, weapon 7 javelin 8 transfix 11 transpierce

Lancelot, Launcelot *father:* 3 Ban *lover:* 6 Elaine 9 Guinevere *son:* 7 Galahad *victim:* 6 Gawain

lancer *Prussian:* 4 ulan 5 uhlan

land 3 get, win 4 dirt, gain, have, home, soil 5 acres, annex, catch, earth, light, manor, perch, roost, shore, terra, tract 6 alight, debark, estate, ground, obtain, pick up, quinta, secure, settle 7 acquire, acreage, country, procure, set down, sit down 8 plottage 9 disembark, touch down 10 terra firma 13 mother country *alluvial:* 5 delta *along a river:* 5 carse 7 bottoms *area:* 7 terrain, terrene *barren:* 5 waste 6 desert *combining form:* 3 geo 4 chor, gaea 5 choro *cultivated:* 4 farm 5 tilth 7 tillage *for grazing:* 3 lea, ley 5 range 6 meadow 7 pasture *high:* 4 hill, mesa 7 plateau 8 mountain *level:* 4 mesa 5 plain 7 plateau *low:* 4 vale 6 valley 9 intervale *measure:* 3 rod 4 acre 7 centare 8 centiare *open:* 5 field, plain *piece:* 3 lot 6 estate, parcel *reclaimed:* 6 polder *relating to:* 8 agrarian *sloping:* 6 cuesta *strip:* 7 isthmus *wet:* 3 bog, fen 4 moor 5 marsh, swamp 6 marish 7 maremma

land east of Eden 3 Nod

landing place of the Ark 6 Ararat

landlord 6 lessor

landmark 5 bound, cairn 9 milestone

Land of Cakes 8 Scotland

Land of Enchantment 9 New Mexico

Land of Lakes 8 Michigan

Land of Lincoln 8 Illinois

Land of Milk and Honey 6 Israel

land of Nod 5 sleep

Land of Opportunity 8 Arkansas

Land of Plenty 6 Goshen

Land of the Midnight Sun 6 Norway

Land of the Rising Sun 5 Japan

landowner 6 squire, yeoman *Anglo-Saxon:* 5 thane, thegn *Dutch:* 7 patroon *Scottish:* 5 laird

landscape 5 scene 7 picture, scenery 8 painting *gardener:* 9 topiarist

lane 3 way 4 path, road 5 aisle, alley, byway, track 6 street 7 loaning, pathway 8 footpath 10 passageway

Langobard see Lombard

lang syne 4 past, yore 8 foretime 9 yesterday 10 yesteryear

language 4 cant 5 argot, idiom, lingo, prose, slang 6 jargon, patois, speech, tongue 7 dialect, lexicon, palaver 10 dictionary, vernacular, vocabulary 11 terminol-

ogy *ambiguous:* 6 jargon 8 newspeak 10 double-talk *ancient:* 5 Greek, Latin 6 Hebrew 8 Sanskrit *artificial:* 2 Ro 3 Ido 7 Volapük 9 Esperanto *classical:* 5 Greek, Latin *combining form:* 5 gloss, glott 6 glosso, glotto *expert:* 8 linguist *informal:* 5 lingo, slang *meaningless:* 9 gibberish *mixed:* 6 pidgin *pretentious:* 6 hot air 7 bombast 8 claptrap *regional:* 7 dialect *relating to:* 10 linguistic *Romance:* 6 French 7 Catalan, Italian, Spanish 8 Romanian, Rumanian 10 Portuguese *secret:* 4 cant, code 5 argot *structure:* 6 syntax 7 grammar *suffix:* 3 ese *written:* 5 prose

languid 4 limp, slow, weak 5 inert 6 supine, torpid 7 die-away 8 comatose, inactive, listless, slothful, sluggish 9 apathetic, enervated, impassive, lethargic 10 languorous, phlegmatic, spiritless 11 languishing 13 lackadaisical

languishing 4 limp 6 pining 7 die-away, languid, longing 8 fainéant, indolent, listless, weakened, yearning 9 enervated, enfeebled 10 languorous, spiritless 11 debilitated 13 lackadaisical

languor 3 kef, kif 4 coma 5 blues, dumps, ennui, sleep 6 stupor, tedium, torpor 7 fatigue, slumber 8 doldrums, dullness, hebetude, lethargy 9 lassitude, torpidity, weariness 10 depression, exhaustion

languorous 3 lax 4 limp, slow 5 loose, slack 7 die-away, laggard, languid, passive, relaxed 8 dilatory, fainéant, indolent, indulged, listless, pampered, slothful 9 enervated, leisurely 10 spiritless 11 languishing 13 lackadaisical

lank 4 bony, lean 5 gaunt, lanky, spare 6 gangly, skinny 7 angular, scraggy, scrawny 8 gangling, rawboned 10 attenuated, extenuated

lanyard 4 cord, line, rope

Laocoon *city:* 4 Troy *killer:* 7 serpent

Laodamia *father:* 7 Acastus *husband:* 11 Protesilaus

Laomedon *daughter:* 7 Hesione *father:* 4 Ilus *kingdom:* 4 Troy *mother:* 8 Eurydice *slayer:* 8 Heracles, Hercules *son:* 5 Priam 8 Tithonus

Laos *capital:* 9 Vientiane *monetary unit:* 3 kip

lap 3 lip, sip 4 lave, ride, wash 5 bathe, slosh, swash 6 bubble, burble, gurgle 7 overlie, shingle 8 override 9 imbricate

lapidary 6 cutter 7 jeweler 8 engraver, polisher

lapideous 5 stony

lapillus 4 lava 6 cinder

lapin 6 rabbit

Lapiths *foes:* 8 centaurs *king:* 5 Ixion

lappet 4 flap, fold, moth 5 lapel 6 infula
Lappidoth's wife 7 Deborah
Lapsang 3 tea
lapse 3 err, sin 4 bull, slip, trip, vice 5 boner, crime, error, fluff, slide 6 breach, bungle, foible, recede, return, revert 7 blooper, blunder, decline, descend, failing, frailty, mistake, offense, subside 8 trespass 9 backslide, decadence, recession, violation 10 apostatize, declension, degenerate, devolution, recidivate, regression, retrograde 11 backsliding, deteriorate 12 degeneration 13 deterioration, retrogression, transgression
Laputan 6 absurd 9 visionary
lar 3 god 6 gibbon, spirit
larboard 4 left, port
larcenist 4 prig 5 thief 6 nimmer, robber 7 burglar, filcher, stealer 8 pilferer 9 purloiner
larceny 4 lift 5 pinch, steal, theft 7 looting, robbery 8 burglary, stealage, stealing, thievery, thieving 10 purloining *kind:* 5 grand, petty
lard 3 fat 6 fatten, grease 10 shortening
larder 6 pantry
large 3 big, fat 4 bull, huge, vast 5 ample, bulky, grand, great, hefty, husky, jumbo, major 6 goodly 7 extreme, immense, mammoth, massive, outsize, sizable 8 colossal, enormous, gigantic, oversize 9 excessive, extensive, monstrous 10 exorbitant, immoderate, inordinate, large-scale, monumental, prodigious, stupendous, tremendous, voluminous 11 extravagant *combining form:* 3 meg 4 macr, mega 5 macro, megal 6 megalo
largess 3 tip 4 boon, gift, perk 5 favor 7 cumshaw, present 8 gratuity 9 lagniappe, pourboire 10 perquisite 11 benevolence
lariat 4 rope 5 lasso, noose, reata, riata *part:* 5 honda, hondo *user:* 6 cowboy, drover 10 cowpuncher
lark 4 bird, dido 5 antic, caper, prank, shine, trick 6 frolic 7 rollick 8 carousal, escapade 10 shenanigan, tomfoolery 11 monkeyshine
larrup 4 beat, drub, dust, flog, hide, lash, lick, whip 5 mop up, whale 6 lather, stripe, thrash 7 clobber, scourge, shellac 8 lambaste 9 overwhelm 10 flagellate
larva 3 bot 4 grub, worm 5 eruca 6 dobson, maggot 7 atrocha 8 cercaria, hornworm, mealworm 10 case bearer, helgramite 11 caterpillar 12 hellgrammite *amphibian:* 7 tadpole *crustacean:* 4 zoea *flatworm:* 5 redia *free-swimming:* 7 planula *mollusk:* 7 veliger *moth:* 8 leafworm *tapeworm:* 6 measle

larynx 8 voice box
lasagna 5 pasta 7 noodles
lascivious 3 hot 4 fast, lewd 5 gross 6 coarse, wanton 7 goatish, lustful, obscene, satyric 8 prurient 9 lecherous, libertine, lickerish, salacious 10 libidinous, licentious, passionate 11 incontinent 12 concupiscent
lash 3 jaw, wag 4 beat, bind, boil, bolt, dash, flay, flog, hide, pour, race, rush, tear, teem, wave, whip 5 baste, chase, fling, scold, shoot, slash, whale 6 charge, drench, lather, scathe, scorch, stripe, switch, thrash, waggle, woggle 7 bawl out, blister, chew out, scarify, scourge, tell off, upbraid 8 lambaste 9 castigate, excoriate 10 flagellate
lassitude 5 blues, dumps, ennui, sleep 6 apathy, stupor, tedium, torpor 7 fatigue, languor, slumber 8 doldrums, dullness, hebetude, lethargy 9 disregard, impotence, tiredness, torpidity, unconcern, weariness 10 depression, exhaustion, torpidness 11 disinterest, insouciance 12 heedlessness, indifference, listlessness
lasso see lariat
last 3 end, lag 5 abide, final 6 endure, latest, latter, utmost 7 closing, dernier, extreme, perdure, persist 8 continue, eventual, furthest, hindmost, rearmost, remotest, terminal, ultimate 9 outermost, umpteenth, uttermost 10 bottommost, concluding 11 terminating *next to:* 6 penult 11 penultimate
last extremity 9 bitter end
lasting 3 old 6 stable 7 abiding, durable, endless, eternal 8 enduring, lifelong 9 continual, diuturnal, incessant, indelible, perduring, perennial, permanent, unceasing 10 continuing, continuous, perdurable, persisting
Last of the Goths 8 Roderick
Last of the Mohicans, The 5 Uncas *author:* 6 Cooper (James Fenimore) *character:* 4 Cora 5 Alice, Magua, Uncas 11 Natty Bumppo 12 Chingachgook
Last of the Saxons 6 Harold
Last Supper, The *painter:* 7 da Vinci (Leonardo)
Las Vegas district 5 Strip
latch 4 bolt 5 catch 6 fasten 8 fastener *British:* 5 sneck
latchet 4 lace 5 strap, thong
late 3 new, old 4 cold, dead, once, past 5 tardy 6 asleep, bygone, former, modern, recent, whilom 7 belated, defunct, extinct, onetime, overdue, quondam 8 deceased, departed, lifeless, sometime
Late George Apley, The *author:* 8 Marquand (John P.)

latent 4 idle 5 inert 6 hidden, unripe
7 abeyant, dormant, lurking 8 immature,
inactive 9 concealed, potential, prepatent,
quiescent, unmatured *combining form:*
5 crypt, krypt 6 crypto, krypto

later 4 anon, next, soon 5 after, infra
6 behind 7 by and by, ensuing 8 latterly,
tomorrow 9 afterward, posterior 10 afterwhile, subsequent 12 postliminary, subsequently 13 subsequential

lateral 4 pass, side 8 sideways

laterally 8 crabwise, sideling, sidelong,
sideward, sideways, sidewise

latest 3 lag 4 last 5 final 6 latter, newest
7 closing 8 eventual, hindmost, rearmost,
terminal, ultimate 10 concluding

latex 5 paint 8 emulsion *product:*
6 balata, chicle, rubber

lath 4 slat 5 stave, stick, strip 8 forepole

lather 4 flap, flog, foam, hide, lash, moil,
soap, stew, suds, whip 5 froth, spume,
storm, yeast 6 bustle, clamor, dither, hassle, hubbub, pother, stripe, thrash, tumult
7 scourge, turmoil, whoopla 8 rowdydow
9 agitation, commotion, confusion

Latin 5 Roman 7 Italian 8 Hispanic *after:*
4 post *always:* 6 semper *and:* 2 et *before:*
4 ante, prae *book:* 5 liber *boy:* 4 puer
bronze: 3 aes *brother:* 6 frater *but:*
3 sed *day:* 4 dies *dog:* 5 canis *foot:*
3 pes *force:* 3 vis *friend:* 6 amicus *god:*
4 deus *goddess:* 3 dea *grammarian:*
7 Donatus *hand:* 5 manus *is:* 3 est *law:*
3 ius, jus, lex *light:* 3 lux *peace:* 3 pax *pronoun:* 2 tu 3 ego, nos, vos *road:* 3 via
4 iter *see:* 4 vide *that is:* 5 id est *thing:*
3 res *this:* 3 hic, hoc 4 haec *thus:* 3 sic
war: 6 bellum *wife:* 4 uxor *woman:* 6 fem-
ina *year:* 5 annus

Latin-American *country:* 4 Cuba, Peru
5 Chile 6 Belize, Brazil, Guyana, Mexico,
Panama 7 Bolivia, Ecuador, Uruguay
8 Colombia, Honduras, Paraguay 9 Argentina, Costa Rica, Guatemala, Nicaragua
10 El Salvador *revolutionary:* 6 Castro
(Fidel) 7 Bolivar (Simon), Guevara (Ché)

Latinus *daughter:* 7 Lavinia *father:*
6 Faunus 8 Odysseus *son-in-law:*
6 Aeneas *wife:* 5 Amata

latitude 4 play, room 5 scope, space
6 leeway, margin 7 freedom 9 elbowroom

latke 7 pancake 11 griddle cake

Latona 4 Leto *daughter:* 5 Diana 7 Artemis *father:* 5 Coeus *mother:* 6 Phoebe
son: 6 Apollo

Latter-day Saint 6 Mormon

lattice 4 grid 5 grate 7 grating, trellis

Latvia *capital:* 4 Riga

Latvian 4 Lett *coin:* 7 santims *measure:*
4 stof 5 faden, kanne, stoff, stoof, vedro
6 kulmet, sagene, versta 8 krouchka

laud 4 hymn 5 adore, bless, cry up, extol
6 admire, praise, revere 7 flatter, glorify,
magnify, worship 8 eulogize, venerate
9 celebrate, reverence 10 panegyrize

laudable 6 worthy 9 admirable, deserving,
estimable, meritable, praisable 11 commendable, meritorious, thankworthy
12 praiseworthy

laugh 3 yuk 4 beam, crow, grin, ha-ha,
roar 5 smile, smirk, snort, tehee, whoop
6 cackle, giggle, guffaw, hee-haw, simper,
titter 7 chortle, chuckle, snicker, sniggle
10 cachinnate

laughable 4 rich 5 comic, droll, funny,
witty 6 jocose 7 amusing, comical, jocular,
mocking, risible 8 derisive, derisory, farcical, gelastic, humorous 9 diverting, facetious, ludicrous 10 ridiculous 12 entertaining

laughing 5 riant 8 derisive

laughingstock 4 butt, fool, jest, joke,
mark, mock 5 sport 6 jestee, target
7 mockery 8 derision 9 pilgarlic

launch 4 cast, fire, hurl, open, toss
5 begin, fling, heave, pitch, set up, sling,
start, throw 6 get off 7 jump off, kick off,
usher in 8 commence, embark on, initiate
9 institute, introduce, originate 10 inaugurate

launching 7 lift-off, takeoff 8 blast-off

launder 4 wash 5 clean 7 cleanse

Laura's lover 8 Petrarch

laurels 4 bays 5 award, badge, honor,
kudos 8 accolade 10 decoration 11 distinction

laurel tree nymph 6 Daphne

lava 2 aa 4 rock, slag 5 magma 6 latite,
scoria 8 andesite, trachyte *cooled:*
8 pahoehoe *fragment:* 8 lapillus *stream:*
4 flow 6 coulee

lavalava 5 cloth, skirt

lavaliere 7 pendant 8 necklace

lavatory 2 WC 3 loo 4 head, john
5 basin, privy 6 johnny, toilet 7 latrine
8 bathroom, washroom 11 convenience,
water closet

lave 3 lap, lip 4 pour, wash 5 bathe

Lavinia *father:* 7 Latinus *husband:*
6 Aeneas *mother:* 5 Amata

Lavinium's founder 6 Aeneas

lavish 4 free, lush 5 grand, spend, waste
7 opulent, profuse, riotous 8 gorgeous,
prodigal, splendid, squander 9 exuberant,
luxuriant, luxurious, profusive, sumptuous

law 3 act, lex 4 bill, code, doom, rule
5 axiom, canon, edict, nomos, Torah
6 assize, custom, decree, equity 7 command, dictate, justice, mandate, precept,
statute, theorem 8 decretum, exigency
9 enactment, institute, necessity, ordinance,
prescript, principle 10 principium, regulation

11 commandment, fundamental 12 constitution, prescription *body of:* 4 code 7 pandect 12 constitution *combining form:* 4 nomy *degree:* 3 LLB, LLD *expert:* 5 judge 6 jurist 7 justice *practitioner:* 6 lawyer 7 counsel 8 attorney *relating to:* 5 jural, legal 7 canonic 8 forensic, juristic 9 judiciary *violation of:* 3 sin 4 tort 5 crime, malum 6 felony

lawbreaker 5 felon 6 sinner 8 criminal, offender, scofflaw, violator 10 malefactor

lawcourt 3 bar 8 tribunal

lawful 3 due 5 legal, licit 7 condign 8 bona fide, innocent, rightful 9 allowable 10 legitimate

lawgiver 5 Moses, solon 10 legislator

lawlessness 4 riot 5 chaos 6 strife 7 anarchy, discord 8 conflict, variance 9 mobocracy 10 ochlocracy

lawman 7 marshal, officer, sheriff 9 policeman

Law of Moses 5 Torah 10 Pentateuch

Lawrence novel 8 Kangaroo 9 Aaron's Rod 10 The Rainbow 11 Women in Love 13 Sons and Lovers

Lawrence of ____ 6 Arabia

lawrencium *symbol:* 2 Lr

lawsuit 4 case 5 cause 6 action 10 litigation

lawyer 6 jurist, legist 7 counsel, pleader 8 advocate, attorney 9 barrister, counselor, solicitor 10 mouthpiece 12 jurisconsult, jurisprudent 13 attorney-at-law *dishonest:* 7 shyster 11 pettifogger *fictional:* 10 Perry Mason *French:* 6 avocat *Indian:* 5 vakil 6 vakeel

lawyers' patron saint 4 Ives

lax 4 ease, easy, open 5 loose, slack 6 loosen, remiss 7 ease off, lenient, slacken 8 careless, derelict 9 forgetful, negligent, oblivious, unmindful, untighten 10 behindhand, delinquent, neglectful, regardless 12 disregardful

lay 3 aim, air, bet, fix, put, set 4 aria, cast, cite, even, game, hymn, lied, play, song, tune, turn 5 ditty, flush, level, offer, place, plane, point, put on, refer, stake, stick, train, wager 6 adduce, allege, assign, ballad, charge, credit, direct, expose, gamble, impute, melody, settle, smooth, spread, strain, warble, zero in 7 address, advance, ascribe, descant, flatten, incline, measure, melisma, melodia, present, profane, secular, subject, uncover 8 accredit, diapason, smoothen, temporal, unsacred 9 attribute, establish

lay aside 4 cast, save, shed 5 chuck, ditch, put by, scrap 6 reject, slough 7 discard, neglect 8 jettison, salt away 9 throw away

lay by 4 save 5 amass, hoard, store 7 deposit 8 salt away

lay down 3 set 4 cede 5 leave, waive, yield 6 assign, decree, define, give up, impose, ordain, resign 7 abandon, dictate 8 hand over 9 establish, prescribe, surrender 10 relinquish

lay eggs 5 spawn 8 oviposit

layer 3 hen, ply 4 coat, film, seam, tier 5 paver, sheet 6 folium, lamina, veneer 7 coating, provine, stratum 8 laminate, membrane, sandwich, stratify *combining form:* 5 cline, lamin, ptych 6 lamell, lamino, ptycho, strati 7 lamelli *inner:* 6 lining *of odds:* 6 bookie 9 bookmaker *of skin:* 6 dermis 9 epidermis *outer:* 4 skin 6 veneer

lay for 6 ambush, waylay 8 surprise

lay in see lay by

lay low 4 down, fell, hide, kill, slay 5 floor, level, scrag 6 cut off, finish, ground 7 destroy, flatten, mow down, put away, take off 8 bowl down, bowl over, dispatch 9 knock down, knock over, throw down

layman 4 laic 7 secular

lay off 4 halt, quit, stop 5 avoid, cease 7 dismiss, measure 9 disemploy 11 discontinue

lay open 4 bare, show 6 expose, reveal 7 uncover

lay out 3 pay 4 give, plan 5 spend 6 design, expend, map out, outlay, set out 7 arrange, fork out 8 disburse, shell out

lay waste 4 ruin 6 ravage 7 destroy 8 desolate 9 devastate

lazar 5 leper

Lazarus' sister 4 Mary 6 Martha

laze 3 bum 4 idle, lazy, loaf, loll 5 sloth 6 dawdle, loiter, lounge, slouch 7 goof off 8 idleness, laziness, malinger 9 goldbrick, indolence

laziness 5 sloth 6 slouch 8 idleness 9 indolence

lazy 3 bum, lax 4 idle, loaf, loll 5 drony, inert, slack 6 dawdle, loiter, lounge, remiss, supine, torpid 7 goof off, languid, passive, work-shy 8 comatose, fainéant, inactive, indolent, listless, slothful, sluggish, trifling 9 easygoing, goldbrick, lethargic, negligent, shiftless, slowgoing

Lazy Susan 4 tray 9 turntable

lea 6 fallow, meadow 7 pasture 8 unplowed 9 grassland

leach 4 suck 7 draw out 9 lixiviate, percolate 11 bloodsucker

lead 3 get, see 4 dean, head, move, show, star 5 bring, doyen, guide, metal, pilot, route, steer, usher 6 bullet, ceruse, direct, escort, induce, leader 7 captain, conduct, convert, plumbum, precede, preface, prevail 8 graphite, persuade, shepherd 9 intro-

duce 10 bellwether *combining form:*
5 plumb 6 molybd, plumbo 7 molybdo *ore:*
6 galena 8 galenite 9 anglesite, cerrusite
oxide: 6 sinter *sounding:* 7 plummet
symbol: 2 Pb

lead astray 4 undo 6 delude, entice,
seduce 7 corrupt, deceive, degrade, pervert

leaden 3 dun 4 drab, dull, flat, gray
5 heavy, inert 8 dragging, lifeless, sluggish
9 plumbeous

leader 4 boss, cock, dean, duce, head,
lead, lion, lord 5 chief, doyen, guide, pilot
6 bigwig, herald, honcho, master, rector
7 captain, foreman, general, headman, manager, notable 8 big-timer, big wheel, chairman, director, eminence, hierarch, luminary, superior 9 chieftain, commander,
conductor, dignitary, dominator, harbinger,
pacemaker, precursor, president, principal,
straw boss 10 bellwether, chairwoman,
forerunner, notability, pacesetter 11 chairperson *authoritarian:* 10 Big Brother *combining form:* 4 arch *Cossack:* 6 ataman,
hetman *German:* 6 führer 7 fuehrer *Japanese:* 6 shogun *military:* 7 admiral, general, warlord 9 commander 12 field marshal *Muslim:* 4 caid 5 calif 6 caliph,
mollah, mullah *national:* 7 premier 9 president 12 chief of state *religious:* 4 pope
5 rabbi 6 bishop, priest 7 prelate 8 hierarch

leading 4 arch, head, main 5 chief, first,
noted 6 famous 7 initial, popular, premier
8 champion, foremost, headmost 9 inaugural, notorious, principal, prominent, well-
known

lead on 3 toy 4 bait, fool, lure, toll 5 dally,
decoy, flirt, tempt 6 allure, coquet, entice,
entrap, seduce, trifle, wanton 8 inveigle
11 string along

leaf 4 foil, olla, page, scan 5 blade, bract,
folio, frond, petal, scale, sepal 6 browse,
spathe 7 dip into, run over 8 glance at
10 glance over, run through 11 flip through,
riff through, skim through 12 thumb through
13 riffle through *aperture:* 5 stoma *axis:*
6 rachis *combining form:* 5 phyll 6 phylla
(plural), phyllo 7 phyllum *edge:* 9 crenation
lily: 3 pad *part:* 4 lobe, vein 5 blade,
costa, stoma 7 petiole, stipule, tendril *pine:*
6 needle *scale:* 8 ramentum *vein:* 5 costa

leafage 7 foliage, umbrage, verdure

leaflet 5 pinna, sheet, tract 6 folder 8 circular, pamphlet

leafy 4 lush 5 green 7 foliate, foliose,
folious 8 foliated, laminate

league 4 band, bond, club, loop, tier
5 class, grade, group, guild, order, union,
unite, wheel 6 concur 7 circuit, combine,
conjoin, society 8 alliance, category, coad-

jute, division, grouping, sodality
9 anschluss, coalition, cooperate 10 conference, federation, fellowship, fraternity,
pigeonhole 11 association, brotherhood,
confederacy 13 confederation

Leah *daughter:* 5 Dinah *father:* 5 Laban
husband: 5 Jacob *sister:* 6 Rachel *son:*
4 Levi 5 Judah 6 Reuben, Simeon 7 Zebulun 8 Issachar

leak 3 out 4 drip, ooze, seep 5 bilge,
break, crack 6 escape, get out 7 come out

leaky 6 porose, porous

lean 3 jut, tip 4 bend, bony, cant, hang,
heel, lank, list, look, slim, tend, thin, tilt,
turn, worn 5 curve, gaunt, grade, lanky,
sheer, slant, slope, spare 6 beetle, divert,
meager, skinny, slight, wasted 7 angular,
deflect, haggard, incline, pinched, recline,
scraggy, scrawny, slender, stringy, wizened
8 bend over, gradient, overhang, rawboned,
spare-set 10 cadaverous

Leander's beloved 4 Hero

Leandre *beloved:* 7 Lucinde *father:*
7 Geronte

Leaning Tower site 4 Pisa

lean-to 3 hut 5 shack 7 shelter

leap 3 hop, lop 4 buck, jump, loup, over,
rise, soar 5 arise, bound, caper, clear,
mount, vault 6 ascend, bounce, gambol,
hurdle, spring 7 saltate 8 capriole, surmount *ballet:* 4 jeté 6 entrechat *by a
horse:* 7 gambade, gambado 9 ballotade

leaping light 3 arc

Lear *daughter:* 5 Regan 7 Goneril 8 Cordelia *servant:* 4 Kent

learn 3 con, get, see 4 find, hear 5 study
6 master, peruse, pick up, tumble 7 catch
on, find out, realize, unearth 8 discover,
memorize 9 ascertain, determine

learned 4 sage, wise 6 astute 7 bookish,
erudite 8 abstruse, academic, cultured,
educated, esoteric, pedantic, polymath
9 recondite, scholarly 10 cultivated, scholastic

learner 5 pupil 7 scholar, student, trainee
10 apprentice

learning 4 lore 6 wisdom 7 science
8 booklore, pedantry 9 education, erudition,
knowledge 11 scholarship *man of:* 7 egghead, scholar, teacher 9 professor 12 intellectual

lease 3 let 4 hire, rent 7 charter 8 contract

leash 3 tie 4 bind, clog, cord, curb, rope
5 strap 6 fetter, hamper, hobble, hog-tie,
tether 7 shackle, trammel 9 entrammel
hawk's: 4 lune

leather 3 tan 4 hide, skin, whip 6 thrash
kind: 3 kid, kip, oak 4 alum, bock, buff,
calf, napa, ooze, roan 5 aluta, basil, crown,
grain, japan, mocha, strap, suede, whang
6 castor, comber, latigo, levant, oxhide, pat-

ent, roller, saddle, skiver **7** buffalo, cane-
pin, carding, chamois, hemlock, morocco,
ostrich, peccary, rutland, saffian **8** cape-
skin, cheverel, cordovan, cordwain, shagreen *maker:* **5** tawer **6** tanner **7** tannery
piece: **4** rand, welt **5** strap, thong, trank
prepare: **3** sam, tan, taw **4** mull **5** curry,
sammy *soft:* **5** aluta, mocha, suede
8 cabretta
Leatherneck **6** marine
Leatherstocking Tales, The *author:*
6 Cooper (James Fenimore) *title:* **10** The
Prairie **11** The Pioneers **13** The Deerslayer, The Pathfinder
leave **2** go **3** let **4** cede, drop, exit, have,
quit, will **5** allot, allow, scram, waive, yield
6 assent, assign, commit, decamp, depart,
desert, devise, escape, get off, give up, legate, maroon, permit, resign, retire, strand,
suffer, vacate **7** abandon, confide, consent,
consign, entrust, forsake, get away, holiday, pull out **8** bequeath, emigrate, hand
over, sanction, vacation, withdraw **9** allowance, apportion, surrender, terminate
10 permission, relinquish, sufferance
13 authorization
leaved **7** foliate, foliose, folious **8** foliated
leaven **5** imbue, steep, yeast **6** infuse,
invest, temper, vivify **7** enliven, ingrain,
qualify, quicken, suffuse **8** moderate
9 inoculate
leavening agent **5** yeast **12** baking powder
leave of absence **5** exeat **8** furlough
leave off **4** halt, quit, stop **5** cease
6 desist **8** give over, knock off, surcease
11 discontinue
leave out **4** omit, skip **5** elide **7** exclude
Leaves of Grass author **7** Whitman
(Walt)
leavings **4** heel, junk, lees, orts, rest
5 dregs, scrap **7** balance, remains, remanet, remnant, residue, rubbish **8** discards,
portions, residual, residuum **9** fragments,
remainder
Lebanon *capital:* **6** Beirut *monetary unit:*
5 pound
lecher **4** rake, roué **9** debauchee, libertine
lecherous **4** fast, lewd **7** goatish, lustful,
satyric **9** libertine, salacious **10** lascivious,
libidinous, licentious **11** incontinent
lectern **4** desk **5** stand
lecture **4** talk **5** scold, speak **6** preach,
sermon, speech **7** address, oration, prelect
8 briefing **9** discourse **10** allocution
lecturer **6** docent, orator, reader
7 speaker, teacher **9** professor **10** praelec-
tor
Leda *daughter:* **5** Helen **12** Clytemnestra
father: **8** Thestius *husband:* **9** Tyndareus
lover: **4** swan, Zeus *son:* **6** Castor, Pollux

ledge **4** berm, lode, sill **5** berme, ridge,
shelf
ledger **4** book **6** record **8** monument
9 footstone, headstone, tombstone
10 gravestone **11** grave marker
lee **5** haven **6** harbor **7** shelter
leech **4** worm **6** sponge, sucker **7** sponger
8 barnacle, hanger-on, parasite **10** freeloader **11** bloodsucker **12** lounge lizard
Leeds' river **4** Aire
leer **4** look, ogle **5** empty, fleer, smirk,
sneer **6** glance **7** grimace
leery **4** wary **8** doubtful **10** suspicious
11 distrustful
lees **5** draff, dregs **6** dunder, refuse
7 deposit, grounds, vinasse **8** leavings, sediment **9** settlings **11** precipitate
leeward **8** downwind
leeway **4** play, room **5** scope, space
6 margin **8** latitude **9** elbowroom
left **4** port **8** larboard
left-handed **8** southpaw
left-hand page **5** verso
leftovers see **leavings**
leftward **4** levo **5** aport, laevo **8** levogyre
10 levogyrate *go:* **3** haw
leg **3** gam, run **4** gamb, limb, walk
5 gambe, shank **6** gammon **7** support
8 cabriole **9** appendage, drumstick *bone:*
4 shin **5** femur, tibia **6** fibula **7** patella *part:*
4 calf, crus, foot, knee, shin **5** ankle, thigh
6 cnemis
legacy **4** gift **6** devise **7** bequest **8** heritage **9** heritance, patrimony **10** birthright
11 inheritance
legal **5** licit **6** lawful **7** juridic **8** innocent
9 juridical **10** legitimate *matter:* **3** res
4 case, suit *order:* **4** writ **7** summons
8 subpoena *party:* **6** suitor **8** litigant
9 defendant, plaintiff *restraint:* **8** estoppel
legal aid group **4** ACLU
legal tender **4** cash **5** money **6** dollar
8 currency
legate **4** will **5** envoy, leave **6** deputy,
devise **8** bequeath, delegate, emissary,
governor **10** ambassador
legatee **4** heir **9** inheritor
legend **4** lore, myth, saga **5** fable, story
6 mythos, mythus **7** caption, fiction **8** folklore **9** mythology, tradition
legendary **6** fabled, mythic **7** fabular
8 fabulous, mythical **12** mythological
legerdemain **5** magic **8** trickery **9** conjuring
legging **5** chaps **6** puttee **7** gambade,
gambado **11** spatterdash **12** antigropelos
leghorn **4** fowl **5** straw **7** chicken
legible **5** clear **8** distinct, readable
legion **4** army, host, many, rout **5** cloud,
crowd, flock **6** scores, sundry **7** various
8 numerous, populous **9** multitude

legislate 5 enact
legislation 3 act, law 4 bill 7 statute
legislator 3 rep 5 solon 6 deputy 7 senator 8 lawgiver, lawmaker 9 statesman 10 politician 11 congressman
legislature 4 diet 5 house, junta 6 senate 7 council 8 assembly, congress 10 parliament *Communist:* 6 soviet 9 politburo, presidium *czarist Russian:* 4 duma *Danish:* 9 Folketing *Finnish:* 9 Eduskunta *German:* 9 Bundesrat, Bundestag *Iceland:* 7 Althing *Israel:* 7 Knesset *Norway:* 8 Storting *one-house:* 10 unicameral *Poland:* 4 Sejm *Spain:* 6 Cortes *Sweden:* 7 Riksdag *two-house:* 9 bicameral
legitimate 4 fair, just, true 5 legal, licit, sound, usual, valid 6 cogent, lawful, normal 7 natural, regular, typical 8 innocent, rightful 9 customary 10 recognized
leg of lamb 5 gigot
Legree type 6 tyrant
legume 3 pea, pod, soy 4 bean, guar, seed, soya 5 pulse 6 lentil 7 soybean 9 bird's-foot, vegetable
leg up 5 boost
lei 6 wreath 7 garland 8 necklace
Leibnitz's invention 8 calculus
Leif Ericson *discovery:* 7 Vinland *father:* 4 Eric
leisure 4 ease, rest, time 6 casual, repose 10 relaxation 12 requiescence
leisurely 3 lax 4 easy, slow 5 slack 7 delayed, laggard, relaxed, restful, unhasty 8 dilatory 9 slackened, unhurried
leitmotiv 5 theme 6 motive
lemma 5 bract, theme 7 premise, theorem
lemon 3 dud 4 bomb, bust, flop 5 fruit, loser 7 failure
lemur 4 maki, vari 5 indri, locis, potto 6 aye-aye, colugo, macaco 7 half-ape, tarsier 9 babacoote
lend 4 give, loan 5 allow, grant 6 oblige 7 advance, furnish 11 accommodate
length 4 term 5 orbit, range, reach, realm, scope 6 radius 7 compass, purview, stretch, yardage 8 distance, panorama
lengthen 4 draw 6 expand, extend 7 draw out, prolong, spin out, stretch 8 elongate, increase, protract 10 prolongate *Scottish:* 3 eke
lengthy 4 long 8 dragging, drawn-out, elongate, extended, longsome, overlong 9 elongated, prolonged 10 protracted
leniency 5 mercy 8 clemency 9 tolerance 10 indulgence, toleration 11 forbearance
lenient 3 lax 4 easy, kind, mild, soft 5 balmy, bland, faint 6 benign, gentle, kindly, smooth, tender 7 amiable, clement 8 excusing, humoring, merciful, obliging, spoiling, tolerant 9 benignant, condoning, forgiving, indulgent, indulging, pampering, pardoning 10 charitable, forbearing
lenity 5 grace, mercy 7 caritas, charity 8 clemency 10 humaneness, tenderness
lens 5 glass 6 lentil 8 meniscus *kind:* 5 toric 6 convex 7 bifocal, concave 8 trifocal
lentigo 5 nevus 7 freckle
lentil 4 lens, seed 6 legume
Leofric's wife 6 Godiva
Leoncavallo opera 9 Pagliacci
leonine 8 lionlike
Leonora *alias:* 7 Fidelio *husband:* 9 Florestan
leopard 3 cat 7 panther *relating to:* 7 pardine
Leo star 7 Regulus
leper 6 pariah 7 Ishmael, outcast 8 castaway, derelict 10 Ishmaelite 11 untouchable
Leper King 7 Baldwin
Leper Priest 6 Damien
lepers' hospital 9 lazaretto
lepers' island 7 Molokai
lepidopter 4 moth 6 insect 9 butterfly
Leporello's master 11 Don Giovanni
leprechaun 3 elf 5 fairy 6 sprite *trade:* 8 cobbling
Lesage hero 7 Gil Blas
Lesbos poet 6 Sappho 7 Alcaeus
lesion 3 cut 4 flaw, sore 5 ulcer, wound 6 injury 10 impairment
Lesotho *capital:* 6 Maseru *monetary unit:* 4 loti
lessen 4 clip, crop, ease, thin, wane 5 abate, close, drain, lower, taper 6 dilute, minify, reduce, shrink, weaken 7 abridge, assuage, curtail, dwindle, lighten, relieve 8 amputate, decrease, diminish, minimize, mitigate, taper off, truncate 9 attenuate
lessening 5 letup 8 decrease, slowdown 9 abatement
lesser 3 low 5 dinky, lower, minor, small, under 6 nether 8 inferior, small-fry 9 secondary, small-time, subjacent 11 minor-league 13 insignificant
lesson 4 text 5 chide, moral, study 6 monish, rebuke 7 lecture, reading, reprove, tick off 8 admonish, call down, exercise, reproach 9 reprimand 11 instruction
lessor 6 bailor 8 landlady, landlord
let 4 have, hire, rent 5 allow, grant, lease, leave 6 permit, suffer 7 approve, certify, charter, concede, endorse, license 8 accredit, sanction 9 authorize
letdown 5 slump 7 decline 10 depression
let go 4 emit, fire, free 6 unhand 7 dismiss, release 9 discharge
lethal 5 fatal 6 deadly, mortal, poison 7 deathly 9 pestilent, poisonous

lethargic 4 dull, idle, slow 5 dopey, heavy, inert 6 stolid, stupid, supine, torpid 7 dormant, laggard, languid, passive 8 comatose, dilatory, inactive, listless, sluggish 9 apathetic, impassive 10 languorous, phlegmatic, slumberous, spiritless 12 hebetudinous 13 lackadaisical

lethargy 4 coma 5 sleep, sloth 6 apathy, phlegm, stupor, torpor 7 inertia, languor, slumber 8 dullness, hebetude, idleness, laziness 9 disregard, inanition, indolence, inertness, lassitude, torpidity, unconcern 10 inactivity, supineness, torpidness 11 disinterest, impassivity, insouciance, passiveness

lethe 8 oblivion 13 forgetfulness

let in 5 admit

Leto see Latona

let off 5 spare 6 excuse, exempt 7 absolve, relieve 8 dispense 9 discharge

let on 3 own 4 avow, tell 5 admit, allow, grant, own up, spill 6 betray, fess up, reveal, unveil 7 concede, confess, divulge, uncover 8 disclose, give away

letter 2 ar, ef, el, em, en, ex 3 bee, cee, cue, dee, ess, gee, jay, kay, pee, tee, vee, wye, zed, zee 4 line, mail, memo, note, rune 5 aitch, print, vowel 6 report, screed, symbol 7 epistle, message, missive 8 dispatch, inscribe 9 consonant *airmail:* 8 aerogram *Anglo-Saxon:* (see **Anglo-Saxon**) *Arabic:* (see alphabet) *Greek:* (see alphabet) *Hebrew:* (see alphabet) *kind:* 5 chain, roman 6 italic, uncial 8 Dear John *large:* 7 capital 9 majuscule, upper case *small:* 9 lower case, miniscule

lettuce 3 cos 4 Bibb, head 6 Boston 7 iceberg, romaine, Simpson 10 butterweed

let up 3 ebb 4 fall, wane 5 abate 6 relent 7 die away, die down, ease off, slacken

letup 5 break 7 respite 9 reduction

Levant, Levantine 7 eastern

levee 4 dike, dock, pier, quay, slip 5 berth, jetty, wharf 10 embankment

level 3 aim, lay, par 4 akin, cast, down, drop, even, fell, flat, like, raze, same, tier, true, turn 5 alike, equal, floor, flush, plane, point, train 6 direct, ground, smooth, zero in 7 address, aligned, flatten, incline, mow down, planate, regular, similar, uniform 8 parallel, smoothen 9 bring down

lever 3 bar, lam, pry 4 jack 5 helve, jimmy, peavy, prize 6 peavey, tappet 7 crowbar

leverage 5 power 9 influence

leveret 4 hare

Levi *father:* 5 Jacob *mother:* 4 Leah *son:* 6 Kohath, Merari 7 Gershon

leviathan 4 huge 5 giant, titan, whale 7 immense, mammoth, monster 8 behemoth, enormous, gigantic 9 cyclopean 10 gargantuan 11 elephantine

Leviathan author 6 Hobbes (Thomas)

levitate 4 lift, rise 5 float 7 suspend

levity 5 folly, humor 8 buoyancy 9 absurdity, flippancy, frivolity, lightness, silliness

levy 3 set, tax 4 duty 5 exact, lay on, place, put on, wrest, wring 6 assess, charge, impose, impost, tariff 10 assessment

lewd 4 base, fast 5 bawdy, gross 6 coarse 7 lustful, obscene, satyric, whorish 8 improper, indecent 9 lecherous, libertine, salacious 10 indelicate, lascivious, libidinous, licentious 11 incontinent

Lewis and Clark interpreter 9 Sacagawea, Sacajawea

Lewis novel 7 Babbitt 9 Dodsworth 10 Arrowsmith, Main Street 11 Elmer Gantry

lexicographer 8 compiler *American:* 6 Porter (Noah) 7 Webster (Noah) 9 Worcester (Joseph) *English:* 4 Wyld (Henry) 6 Fowler (Francis, Henry), Murray (James), Onions (Charles) 7 Craigie (William), Johnson (Samuel) *French:* 6 Littré (Paul-Emile) 8 Larousse (Pierre)

lexicon 4 cant 6 jargon 7 palaver 8 language, wordbook 9 word-hoard, word-stock 10 dictionary, vocabulary 11 onomasticon, terminology

liable 3 apt 4 open, tied 5 bound, given, prone 6 likely 7 exposed, subject 8 amenable, beatable, inclined, vincible 9 obnoxious, sensitive 10 answerable, assailable, attackable, chargeable, penetrable, vulnerable 11 accountable, conquerable, responsible, susceptible

liaison 4 bond 5 amour 6 affair 7 affaire 8 intrigue 12 relationship

liar 6 fibber 7 Ananias, fibster 8 fabulist, perjurer 9 falsifier 12 prevaricator *female:* 8 Sapphira

libation 5 drink 6 liquid 7 potable 8 beverage, potation

libel 6 defame, malign, vilify 7 asperse, calumny, slander, traduce 8 tear down, travesty 9 burlesque, denigrate 10 calumniate, caricature, scandalize

libelous 8 debasing 9 invidious, maligning, traducing, vilifying 10 backbiting, calumnious, defamatory, derogative, detracting, detractive, detractory, malevolent, pejorative, scandalous, slanderous

liberal 4 free, open, wide 5 ample, broad 6 lavish, plenty 7 copious, lenient, profuse, radical 8 abundant, advanced, generous, handsome, prodigal, tolerant 9 bounteous, bountiful, exuberant, indulgent, plenteous, plentiful, unsparing 10 benevolent, bighearted, charitable, forbearing, freehanded, munificent, openhanded

liberate 4 free 5 loose, remit 6 detach, loosen, unbind, unhook 7 manumit, release, unchain 8 untangle 9 discharge, unshackle 10 emancipate 12 disembarrass

liberator 7 messiah *of Argentina:* 9 San Martin (Jose de) *of Chile:* 8 O'Higgins (Bernardo) *of Ecuador:* 5 Sucre (Antonio Jose de) *of Scotland:* 5 Bruce (Robert the) *of South America:* 7 Bolivar (Simon)

Liberia *capital:* 8 Monrovia *monetary unit:* 6 dollar

Liberian *language:* 3 Kwa *native:* 3 Kru, Vai 4 Gola, Toma 5 Bassa, Grebo 6 Kruman

libertine 4 fast, lewd, rake, roué 7 lustful, satyric 9 debauchee, lecherous, salacious 10 lascivious, libidinous, licentious

liberty 5 leave 7 freedom, license 8 autonomy, delivery 10 liberation 12 emancipation, independence

libidinous 3 hot 4 fast, lewd 5 gross 6 coarse 7 goatish, lustful, obscene, satyric 8 prurient 9 lecherous, libertine, lickerish, salacious 10 lascivious, licentious, passionate 11 incontinent 12 concupiscent

Libni *father:* 5 Mahli 7 Gershon *grandfather:* 4 Levi

librarian 5 Dewey (Melvil)

library 7 archive 9 athenaeum 11 bibliotheca, reading room *desk:* 6 carrel

Libya *capital:* 7 Tripoli *chief export:* 3 oil *largest city:* 7 Tripoli *monetary unit:* 5 dinar *father:* 7 Epaphus *son:* 5 Belus 6 Agenor

license 3 let 5 allow, leave 6 enable, laxity, permit, suffer 7 certify, empower, freedom, liberty 8 accredit, passport, sanction, variance 9 authorize, looseness, slackness

licentious 3 lax 4 fast, lewd 5 loose, randy 6 amoral, animal, carnal 7 corrupt, fleshly, immoral, lustful, relaxed, satyric, sensual, unmoral 8 depraved, scabrous 9 abandoned, debauched, dissolute, lecherous, libertine, oversexed, reprobate, salacious 10 lascivious, libidinous, profligate 11 incontinent 12 unprincipled

lichen 4 moss 6 archil, litmus 7 oakmoss *genus:* 5 Usnea

licit 5 legal 6 lawful 8 approved, innocent, licensed 10 authorized, legitimate, sanctioned

lick 3 hit, lap, rap 4 beat, cast, dash, down, drub, flog, hint, swat, whip, wipe 5 knock, smack, smear, swipe, taste, throw, tinge, touch, trace, whiff 6 hurdle, master, thrash, tongue 7 clobber, conquer, shellac, smother 8 lambaste, overcome, surmount 9 overwhelm

lickerish see libidinous

lickety-split 4 fast 5 apace 7 flat out, hastily, quickly, rapidly, swiftly 8 speedily 9 posthaste 13 expeditiously

licorice 4 root 5 candy *pill:* 6 cachou

lid 3 cap, top 5 cover 8 covering *moss:* 9 operculum

lie 3 fib 4 flam, myth, rest, tale 5 dwell, exist, fable, libel, story 6 canard, delude, inhere, palter, repose, reside 7 beguile, consist, deceive, distort, falsify, falsity, forgery, lie down, mislead, perjure, perjury, recline, untruth 8 misguide, misstate, nontruth, untruism 9 falsehood, fish story, mendacity, misinform 10 dishonesty, distortion, equivocate, exaggerate, inaccuracy, inveracity, stretch out, taradiddle 11 fraudulence, misinstruct, prevaricate 12 misstatement, song and dance

Liebestraum composer 5 Liszt (Franz)

lied 4 aria, hymn, song 5 ditty 7 descant

lie down 4 rest 6 repose 7 recline 10 stretch out

lief 4 fain 6 freely, gladly 9 willingly

liege 4 true 5 loyal 6 ardent, vassal 7 staunch 8 constant, faithful, resolute 9 steadfast

lien 5 claim 6 charge 8 interest, mortgage

lieu 5 place, stead

lieutenant 3 aid 4 aide, zany 7 officer 9 assistant, coadjutor 10 aide-de-camp, coadjutant

life 3 bio, man, vim 4 body, brio, dash, élan, soul, zing 5 being, blood, human, oomph, verve 6 energy, esprit, memoir, mortal, person, spirit 8 creature, vitality 9 animation, biography, existence, personage 13 autobiography *animal:* 5 fauna *animal and plant:* 5 biota *combining form:* 2 bi 3 bia, bio 4 blum, bius 5 biont 6 bioses (plural), biosis, biotic *plant:* 5 flora *relating to:* 5 vital 8 biologic 10 biological *science:* 7 biology

life jacket 7 Mae West

lifeless 4 cold, dead, drab, dull, flat, late 5 amort, inert, prosy 6 asleep, torpid 7 defunct, extinct, prosaic 8 deceased, departed 9 colorless, exanimate, inanimate 10 lackluster, lusterless

lifelike 6 verist 8 accurate, veristic 9 realistic

life of ____ 5 Riley 8 the party

Life with Father author 3 Day (Clarence)

lift 2 up 3 aid, nip 4 doff, hand, heft, help, hook, jack, rear, rise, soar 5 arise, exalt, filch, heave, hoist, mount, pinch, raise, shrug, steal, surge, swipe, theft, tower 6 ascend, aspire, assist, pick up, pilfer, recall, relief, repeal, revoke, rocket, snitch, succor, take up, uphold, uprear 7 comfort, elevate, larceny, magnify, purloin, rescind, reverse, secours, support, upraise **8** levitate, stealage, stealing, thievery

lift-off 6 launch **7** takeoff **9** launching

ligament 3 tie **4** band, bond, knot, link, yoke **5** nexus **8** ligature, vinculum

ligature see **ligament**

Ligeia author 3 Poe (Edgar Allan)

light 3 gay, hit **4** airy, bump, dawn, deft, easy, fair, fast, fire, lamp, land, luck, meet, morn, neon, soft **5** blond, dizzy, flash, giddy, loose, minor, perch, petty, roost, royal, small, sunny, torch **6** aurora, beacon, bright, candle, casual, chance, facile, flimsy, fluffy, happen, ignite, illume, kindle, little, meager, settle, simple, slight, smooth, strobe, swimmy, tumble, wanton **7** downing, flighty, inflame, lantern, lighten, morning, set down, sit down, slender, stumble, sunrise, trivial, unheavy, whorish **8** cheerful, cockcrow, daybreak, daylight, enkindle, illumine, luminous, skittish, swimming, trifling, unchaste **9** frivolous, small-beer, touch down **10** bird-witted, chandelier, effortless, illuminate *combining form:* **4** luci, phos, phot **5** lumin, photo **6** lumini, lumino *measure:* **3** lux **4** phot **5** lumen **6** candle **7** candela *refractor:* **5** prism *relating to:* **6** photic *ring:* **4** halo **6** corona **7** aureola, aureole *science:* **6** optics **7** photics *source:* **3** sun **4** lamp

light-emitting *suffix:* **6** escent

lighten 4 dawn, ease, fade, thin **5** allay **6** bleach, dilute, illume **7** assuage, mollify, relieve **8** brighten, illumine, mitigate **9** alleviate, attenuate, extenuate **10** illuminate

light-headed 5 dizzy, giddy **6** swimmy **7** flighty **8** swimming **9** frivolous **10** bird-witted **11** vertiginous

lighthearted 3 gay **4** glad **5** happy, jolly, merry **6** blithe, jocund, jovial, joyful, joyous, lively **7** buoyant, festive, gleeful **8** carefree, cheerful, mirthful, spirited, volatile **9** expansive, resilient, sprightly, vivacious **10** blithesome, free-minded, insouciant **12** effervescent, happy-go-lucky, high-spirited

lighthouse 5 guide, phare **6** beacon, pharos **7** warning **8** guidance **9** direction

lightless 3 dim **4** dark, dusk **5** dusky, murky **6** gloomy **7** obscure **9** tenebrous **10** caliginous **11** unillumined

lightness 6 gaiety, levity **8** buoyancy, vivacity **9** flippancy, frivolity **10** elasticity, liveliness, resiliency, volatility **11** flightiness **12** cheerfulness **13** effervescence, expansiveness

lightning bug 7 firefly

lignite 4 coal **9** brown coal

likable 6 genial **8** friendly, pleasant, pleasing **10** attractive

like 2 as **3** dig **4** akin, same, such, will, wish **5** close, elect, enjoy, equal, match **6** admire, agnate, allied, choose, esteem, please, prefer, regard, relish, select **7** approve, cognate, endorse, kindred, related, respect, similar, uniform **8** parallel, selfsame, suchlike **9** analogous, consonant, identical **10** appreciate, comparable, comprehend, equivalent, resembling *combining form:* **3** sym, syn **4** home **5** homeo, homoe, homoi **6** homoeo, homoio *suffix:* **2** ar, ic, ly **3** ine, ish, oid **4** eous, ical **5** oidal

likelihood 6 chance **11** probability

likely 3 apt **4** rosy **5** given, prone **6** liable, mortal **7** earthly, hopeful, roseate **8** inclined, possible, probable, probably **9** assumably, doubtless, promising **10** presumably, promiseful

liken 5 match **6** equate **7** compare, paragon **8** parallel **10** assimilate

likeness 4 copy, twin **5** image **6** effigy, simile **7** analogy, picture, replica **8** affinity, equality, identity, sameness **9** agreement, facsimile, semblance **10** comparison, conformity, photograph, similarity, similitude, uniformity **11** equivalence, parallelism, resemblance

likewise 2 so **3** and, too **4** also, more **5** along **6** as well, withal **7** besides **8** moreover **9** similarly **11** furthermore

liking 4 lust, mind, will **5** fancy, gusto, taste **8** affinity, appetite, fondness, penchant, pleasure, soft spot, velleity, weakness **11** inclination **12** predilection *combining form:* **4** phil **5** phile **6** philic **7** philous

Lilith *husband:* **4** Adam *successor:* **3** Eve

lilliputian 3 wee **4** runt, tiny **5** dwarf, midge, pygmy, teeny, weeny **6** midget, minute, peewee, teensy, teenty **7** manikin **8** Tom Thumb **10** diminutive, homunculus, teeny-weeny **12** teensy-weensy

lilt 3 air **4** sing, song, tune **5** swing

lily 3 pad **4** aloe, ixia, sego **5** calla, tiger, white, yucca **6** flower **7** leopard **8** mariposa *combining form:* **6** crinus

Lily ____ 4 Pons

lily of France 10 fleur-de-lis

lily-livered 6 coward, craven **7** chicken, gutless, unmanly **8** cowardly **9** spunkless **11** poltroonish **12** poor-spirited **13** pusillanimous

lily-white 4 good, pure **8** innocent, virtuous **9** blameless, exemplary, guiltless, righteous **10** inculpable

lima 4 bean, seed **7** mollusk

liman 3 bay **6** lagoon **7** estuary

limb 3 arm, fin, leg **4** twig, wing **5** bough, devil, rogue, scamp, shoot, spray, sprig **6** branch, member, rascal, switch **7** villain **8** mischief, scalawag **9** appendage

limber 5 agile, lithe, loose 6 pliant, supple 7 elastic, lissome, plastic, pliable, springy 8 flexible 9 lithesome, resilient

limbo 5 dance 6 prison 8 oblivion

lime 5 color, fruit, green 6 citrus

limen 9 threshold

limerick 4 poem 5 verse 8 fishhook
writer: 4 Lear (Edward)

limestone 4 malm, tufa 5 chalk 6 marble, oolite, oolith 7 coquina

lime tree 4 teil 6 linden

limit 3 bar, end, fix, rim, set 4 brim, curb, edge, term 5 brink, check, pinch, quota, verge 6 assign, border, curfew, define, hinder, lessen, margin, narrow 7 appoint, extreme, mark out, measure 8 contract, deadline, restrain, restrict 9 constrict, demarcate, determine, extremity, prescribe

limitless 4 vast 8 infinite, termless 9 unbounded 10 indefinite, unmeasured 11 innumerable, undrainable 12 immeasurable, incalculable, unfathomable 13 inexhaustible

limn 4 draw 5 image 6 depict, render, sketch 7 picture, portray 8 describe 9 delineate, interpret, represent

Limoges product 9 porcelain

limp 3 lax 4 halt, lame, wilt 5 hitch, loose, slack 6 falter, flabby, floppy, hobble, muddle, sleazy, supple, toddle, totter, waddle, wobble 7 die-away, flaccid, languid, relaxed, shuffle, stagger, stumble 9 enervated 10 languorous, spiritless

limpid 4 pure 5 clear, lucid 10 see-through 11 translucent, transparent

limping 4 halt, lame 5 gimpy 8 lameness 12 claudication

Lincoln *assassin:* 5 Booth (John Wilkes) *biographer:* 7 Masters (Edgar Lee) 8 Sandburg (Carl) *debater:* 7 Douglas (Stephen) *law partner:* 7 Herndon (William) *mother:* 5 Nancy (Hanks) *nickname:* 9 Honest Abe 12 Railsplitter *photographer:* 5 Brady (Mathew) *secretary of state:* 6 Seward (William) *secretary of war:* 7 Stanton (Edwin) *wife:* 8 Mary Todd

line 3 job, pad, ray, row, way 4 abut, file, join, path, rank, road, rope, tier, work 5 align, array, goods, march, order, queue, range, route, touch, train, verge, wares 6 adjoin, border, butt on, column, course, policy, polity, series, string 7 arrange, calling, contour, echelon, marshal, passage, profile, program, pursuit 8 business, neighbor, ordinate, sequence 9 procedure, vendibles 10 employment, figuration, occupation, silhouette, succession *curved:* 3 arc *mathematical:* 6 vector *metrical:* 5 verse 6 verset 8 versicle *weather map:* 6 isobar

lineage 4 clan, folk, race 5 birth, blood, house, stock, tribe 6 family, origin, stirps 7 descent, kindred 8 ancestry, pedigree

lineal 6 direct 10 hereditary

lineament 7 contour, feature, outline, profile 10 figuration, silhouette

lineation see **lineament**

lined 5 ruled 7 lineate, striate, striped 8 lineated, streaked, wrinkled

linen 4 lawn 5 cloth, toile 6 byssus, damask, dowlas, fabric, forfar, napery, sheets 7 batiste, bedding, cambric, Holland, taffeta 8 cretonne, lingerie *fiber:* 3 tow 4 line *source:* 4 flax

liner 4 ship 6 insert, vessel

Linet, Lynette *brother:* 6 Liones *husband:* 6 Gareth

linger 3 lag 4 bide, drag, mope, poke, stay, wait 5 abide, amble, dally, delay, drift, mosey, tarry 6 bummel, dawdle, loiter, put off, remain, stroll 11 stick around

lingerie 6 undies 9 underwear

lingo 4 cant 5 argot, slang 6 jargon, patois, patter 7 dialect 10 vernacular

linguist 8 polyglot 11 philologist

linguistics 9 philology

liniment 3 oil 6 lotion 8 ablution, ointment

lining 6 facing, insert 8 wainscot *combining form:* 6 pleura

link 3 tie 4 bond, join, knot, yoke 5 nexus, unite 6 couple, relate 7 combine, conjoin, connect 8 catenate, vinculum 9 associate, conjugate

linksman 6 golfer

linnet 5 finch

lint 3 fur 4 down, flue, fuzz, pile 5 floss, fluff 7 charpie 9 ravelings

lion 3 cat, VIP 4 king, puma 5 chief 6 big boy, cougar, leader 7 notable 8 bigtimer, eminence, luminary 9 carnivore *group:* 5 pride *young:* 3 cub

lioness headed goddess 3 Mut 6 Sekhet

lionhearted 4 bold 5 brave 7 valiant 8 fearless, intrepid, unafraid, valorous 9 dauntless 10 courageous

lionlike 7 leonine

lion monkey 7 tamarin 8 leoncito, marmoset

Lion of Judah 13 Haile Selassie

lip 3 rim 4 brim, buss, edge, kiss, lave, peck, wash 5 bathe, smack 6 labium, labrum, margin, smooch 8 osculate *relating to:* 6 labial

lipid 3 fat, wax

lipped 7 labiate 9 bilabiate

lip server 8 pharisee, Tartuffe 9 hypocrite

liquefy 3 run 4 flux, fuse, melt, thaw, thin 6 soften 8 dissolve

liqueur 4 ouzo, raki 5 crème, noyau
6 kummel 7 cordial, curaçao, ratafia, roso-
lio, sloe gin 8 absinthe, anisette, prunelle
10 chartreuse, pousse-café

liquid 5 drink, fluid, sauce, water 6 golden,
lotion, mellow, watery 7 honeyed 8 beverage, emulsion, Hyblaean 11 mellifluent,
mellifluous *aromatic:* 7 eugenol 8 terpinol
container: 3 cup, jug, mug 4 vial 5 glass
6 bottle, goblet 7 pitcher, tumbler *corrosive:* 5 oleum *flammable:* 3 gas, oil
5 ether, furan 6 butane, toluol 7 alcohol,
dioxine, ligroin, toluene 8 furfuran, gasoline, ligroine, propenol, pyridine *measure:*
2 cc, ml, oz, pt, qt 3 cup, gal 4 pint 5 liter,
ounce, quart 6 gallon *medicinal:* 8 liniment, ointment *oily:* 5 fusel 6 octane *resinous:* 6 tallol *scented:* 7 cologne, perfume
thick: 5 sirup, syrup 8 molasses *volatile:*
6 hexane 7 naphtha, pentane 8 isoprene,
phenetol

liquidate 3 pay 4 cool, do in, quit 5 clear,
pay up, purge 6 murder, remove, settle,
square 7 satisfy 8 amortize, clear off

liquor 4 grog 5 booze, drink 7 alcohol,
potable, spirits 8 beverage, potation
9 aqua vitae, drinkable, firewater, inebriant,
moonshine 10 intoxicant *add:* 4 lace
5 spike *homemade:* 9 moonshine 10 bathtub gin *inferior:* 5 hooch, smoke 6 rotgut
kind: 3 gin, rum, rye 5 vodka 6 brandy,
geneva, scotch 7 bourbon, whiskey 8 vermouth *malt:* 3 ale 4 beer 5 stout *measure:*
4 dram *Mexican:* 5 sotol 6 mescal
7 tequila *Oriental:* 4 sake, saki 6 arrack,
samshu

liquor cabinet 10 cellarette

lissome 5 agile, lithe 6 limber, supple
8 flexible

list 3 tip 4 book, cant, file, heel, lean,
menu, note, post, roll, tilt 5 count, index,
slant, slope 6 agenda, detail, enroll, record,
roster 7 catalog, incline, itemize, recline,
specify, tick off 8 glossary, inscribe, numerate, register, roll call, schedule, tabulate
9 chronicle, enumerate, inventory 10 specialize 13 particularize

listen 4 hark, hear, heed, note 6 attend,
harken 8 overhear 9 eavesdrop

listeners 8 audience

listless 4 dull, limp 6 drowsy, sleepy
7 die-away, languid 9 apathetic, enervated
10 languorous 11 languishing 13 lackada-
sical

listlessness 6 apathy 8 doldrums, lethargy 9 disregard, lassitude, unconcern
11 disinterest, insouciance 12 indifference

litany 4 list 5 chant 6 ektene, prayer
7 synapte 8 rogation

literal 5 exact 7 precise 8 verbatim
11 word-for-word

literally 6 direct 8 verbatim 11 word for
word

literary 7 bookish, erudite, learned 8 lettered, well-read

literary style *suffix:* 3 ese

literary work 4 book, opus, play, poem
5 cento, drama, essay, novel 10 short story

literature 4 kind 5 prose 6 poetry 7 fiction 10 nonfiction

lithe 4 lean, slim, thin 5 agile, spare 6 lis-
som, slight, supple, svelte 7 lissome, slender 8 graceful

lithium *symbol:* 2 Li

lithographer 4 Ives (James Merritt)
7 Currier (Nathaniel) *French:* 5 Redon
(Odilon)

Lithuanian 4 Balt 6 Baltic *capital:* 7 Vilnius *coin:* 6 centas

litigant 4 suer 6 suitor

litigation 4 case, suit 6 action 7 lawsuit

litter 3 bed 4 hash, junk 5 offal, trash,
waste, young 6 basket, debris, jumble, jungle, muddle, refuse, tumble 7 garbage, rubbish, rummage, shuffle 8 mishmash, scramble 9 offspring, stretcher

little 3 set, wee 4 mean, puny, tiny
5 borne, light, minor, petty, short, small
6 bantam, casual, minute, monkey, narrow,
paltry, petite, rarely, seldom 7 bigoted, limited, niggard, selfish, trivial, unoften 8 smallish 9 hidebound, illiberal, niggardly, secondary, small-beer 10 collateral, diminutive,
fortuitous, hardly ever, incidental, provincial,
shoestring, subsidiary 11 unimportant

Little Bighorn victor 11 Sitting Bull

little by little 8 inchmeal 9 gradually,
piecemeal

Little Corporal 8 Napoleon

Little Dipper *constellation:* 9 Ursa
Minor *star:* 5 North 7 Polaris

little finger or toe 7 minimus

Little Minister *author:* 6 Barrie (James)
character: 5 Gavin 6 Babbie 7 Dishart

little one *suffix:* 2 el, et, ey 2 ia (plural),
ie 3 cle, ium, kin, ock, ula, ule, uli (plural)
4 ella, ette, illa, ling, ulae (plural), ulum,
ulus 5 ellae (plural), illae (plural)

Little Women *author:* 6 Alcott (Louisa
May) *character:* 2 Jo 3 Amy, Meg 4 Beth
surname: 5 March

liturgy 4 form, rite 7 service 8 ceremony
9 formality 10 ceremonial, observance

livable 4 cosy, snug 5 homey 6 viable
8 bearable, homelike 9 endurable

live 2 be, is 3 are 4 fare 5 abide, dwell,
exist, green, vital 6 reside 7 breathe,
dynamic, hang out, running, subsist, working

livelihood 3 art, fee, job, pay 4 keep, wage 5 bread, craft, trade 6 living, salary 7 alimony, stipend, support 9 emolument 10 handicraft, profession, sustenance 11 maintenance, subsistence

liveliness 4 brio, élan 5 verve 6 spirit 8 vibrance, vibrancy, vitality, vivacity

lively 3 gay 4 busy, fast, keen, pert, spry, yare 5 agile, alert, brisk, catty, fussy, jazzy, jolly, merry, peppy, zippy 6 active, blithe, bright, brisky, chirpy, frisky, jocund, nimble 7 animate, buoyant, chipper, dashing, driving, elastic, gleeful, hopping, humming, popping, rousing 8 animated, bustling, cheerful, chirping, chirrupy, hustling, mirthful, spirited, volatile 9 cock-a-hoop, energetic, expansive, hilarious, resilient, sprightly, vivacious

liven 5 cheer 6 vivify 7 animate, quicken

live oak 6 encina

liver 4 fole 5 hepar 7 denizen 8 habitant, occupant, resident 9 indweller 10 inhabitant *combining form:* 5 hepat 6 hepato *disease:* 9 cirrhosis, hepatitis *lobster's:* 8 tomalley

liverwort 8 hepatica 9 bryophyte

livestock 6 cattle 7 animals

live wire 6 dynamo, peeler 7 hustler, rustler 8 go-getter 11 self-starter

livid 3 wan 4 ashy, pale 5 ashen, dusky, lurid, murky, waxen 6 doughy, gloomy, grisly, pallid, sultry 8 blanched 9 colorless

living 4 keep, salt 5 bread, vital 6 active, around, extant, zoetic 7 alimony, animate, dynamic, support 8 animated, existent 9 operative 10 livelihood, sustenance *combining form:* 3 ont 4 onto, vivi

living being 8 creature *combining form:* 2 zo 3 ont, zoa (plural), zoo 4 onto, zoon

living room 6 parlor 7 parlour 10 lebensraum

lizard 3 dab, eft, uma 4 adda, gila, newt, seps, uran 5 agama, anole, gecko, skink, teiid, tokay, varan, waral 6 dragon, goanna, iguana, moloch, worral, worrel 7 cheecha, monitor, reptile 8 basilisk, lacertid, slowworm, whiptail 9 alligator, blindworm, chameleon, crocodile 10 chuckwalla, salamander *combining form:* 4 saur 5 saura, sauro 6 sauria (plural) *genus:* 3 Uta 5 Agama 6 Ameiva, Anolis 7 Lacerta

llama 6 alpaca 7 guanaco *country:* 4 Peru *habitat:* 5 Andes

Lloyd's business 9 insurance

lo 4 hark, look

load 3 tax 4 bale, bear, care, cram, drag, duty, fill, glut, haul, lade, onus, pack, pile, task 5 cargo, carry, choke, drain, flood, gorge, laden, swamp, weigh 6 burden, charge, convey, cumber, debase, doctor, dope up, lading, parcel, saddle, weight 7 freight, surfeit 8 encumber, pressure, shipment 9 liability, millstone, transport

loaded 4 full 7 brimful 8 brimming 9 chock-full

loaf 3 bum 4 idle, laze, lazy 6 dawdle 9 goldbrick

loafer 3 bum 4 shoe, slug 5 idler 6 slouch 8 deadbeat, dolittle, fainéant, slugabed, sluggard 9 do-nothing, lazybones

loam 4 dirt, sand, silt, soil 7 topsoil *deposit:* 5 loess

loan 4 lend 5 prest 7 advance, imprest

loan shark 6 lender, usurer 7 Shylock 11 moneylender

loath 6 afraid, averse 7 uneager 8 hesitant 9 reluctant, unwilling 10 indisposed

loathe 4 hate 5 abhor, spurn 6 detest, refuse, reject 7 decline, despise 8 execrate 9 abominate, repudiate

loathsome 4 foul, ugly, vile 5 nasty 7 hateful, hideous 8 horrible 9 invidious, obnoxious, offensive, repellent, repugnant, repulsive, revolting 10 disgusting

lob 3 hit 4 shot, step, toss, vein 5 stair, throw

lobby 4 hall 5 foyer 8 anteroom 9 vestibule

lobe 4 flap 7 lobulus

lobo 4 wolf 10 timber wolf

lobster 10 crustacean *African:* 12 Cape crawfish *claw:* 5 chela 6 pincer *female:* 3 hen *male:* 4 cock *trap:* 3 pot 5 creel

local 6 native 7 endemic, insular, topical *combining form:* 3 top 4 topo

locale 4 area, site 5 place, scene, venue 6 region 8 district, vicinage, vicinity 11 mise-en-scène 12 neighborhood

locality 4 area, belt, home, seat, site, zone 5 field, haunt, range, tract 6 domain, region, sector, sphere 7 habitat, section 8 district, province, vicinage 9 bailiwick, territory 12 neighborhood

localize 8 pinpoint

locate 3 spy 4 espy, find, site, spot 5 place, trace 6 settle 7 situate, station, uncover 8 discover, pinpoint, position 9 establish

locating device 5 lidar, radar, sonar

location 4 area, site, spot 5 locus, place, point, scene, where 7 habitat

loch 3 bay 4 lake

lock 3 fix 4 bolt, curl, hank, tuft 5 click, latch, tress 6 bundle, fasten, secure 7 ringlet 8 fastening

Locke's tabula ____ 4 rasa

lockjaw 7 tetanus, trismus

Locksley Hall author 8 Tennyson (Alfred)

lockup 3 jug, pen 4 coop, jail 6 cooler, prison

loco 3 mad 5 crazy 6 insane

locomotive 5 cheer, dolly, train 6 engine 7 movable 8 moveable 9 camelback *small:* 5 dinky 6 dinkey *type:* 5 steam 6 diesel 8 electric

Locrine *daughter:* 7 Sabrina *father:* 4 Brut 6 Brutus *lover:* 9 Estrildis *wife:* 9 Gwendolen

locum tenens 3 sub 6 fill-in 7 stand-in 9 alternate, surrogate 10 substitute 11 pinch hitter, replacement, succedaneum

locust 5 carob 6 cicada, insect 11 grasshopper

locust bird 5 stork 7 grackle

locution 4 word 6 phrase 10 expression

lode 4 lead, vein 7 deposit

lodestar 5 guide 6 leader

lodestone 6 magnet 9 magnetite

lodge 3 cot, den, fix, hut, inn 4 camp, club, hold, lair, root, take 5 admit, board, cabin, couch, embed, hotel, house, infix, motel, put up, shack 6 accept, bestow, billet, burrow, harbor, hostel, shanty, tavern 7 auberge, contain, cottage, hospice, ingrain, quarter, receive 8 domicile, entrench, hostelry 9 entertain, roadhouse 11 accommodate, caravansary, public house

lodger 5 guest 6 renter, roomer, tenant

loess 4 loam 7 deposit

loft 3 bin 5 attic, raise 6 garret

loftiness 5 pride 6 height, morgue 7 disdain, hauteur, stature 9 arrogance, superbity

lofty 3 big 4 airy, epic, high, tall 5 grand, noble, proud 6 aerial, august, raised, superb 7 exalted, haughty, soaring, spiring, stately, sublime, topless, utopian 8 arrogant, cavalier, elevated, eloquent, generous, imposing, insolent, majestic, superior, towering 9 ambitious, grandiose, magnified, visionary 10 benevolent, chivalrous, disdainful 11 aggrandized, considerate, magnanimous, overbearing, pretentious, skyscraping 12 greathearted, supercilious

log 4 book, note, wood 5 diary, stick 6 record, timber 7 journal *mover:* 7 cantdog

logarithm inventor 6 Napier (John)

loge 3 box 5 booth, stall 9 enclosure

logger 9 lumberman 10 lumberjack, woodcutter *legendary:* 10 Paul Bunyan

loggerhead 6 shrike, turtle

loggia 6 arcade 7 balcony, gallery

logic 6 reason 9 reasoning *specious:* 7 sophism 9 sophistry

logical 4 sane 5 clear, lucid, sound, valid 6 cogent, subtle 7 telling 8 analytic, sensible 10 compelling, convincing, reasonable

logjam 7 impasse 8 blockage, deadlock, stoppage

logo 4 mark 5 brand 9 trademark

logograph 6 puzzle 7 anagram

logroll 4 birl

logrolling contest 5 roleo

logy 4 dull, slow 5 dopey, heavy 6 drowsy, groggy, torpid 8 listless, sluggish

Lohengrin *composer:* 6 Wagner (Richard) *father:* 8 Parsifal, Parzival *wife:* 4 Elsa

loincloth *African:* 5 pagne *Hindu:* 5 dhoti, dhuti 6 dhooti *Indian:* 5 lungi 6 lungyi

Loire, city on the 5 Blois, Tours 6 Nantes 7 Orléans

Lois *daughter:* 6 Eunice *grandson:* 7 Timothy

loiter 3 bum, lag 4 drag, idle, laze, lazy, loaf, poke 5 dally, delay, tarry, trail 6 dawdle, diddle, lounge, put off

Loki *father:* 8 Farbauti *mother:* 3 Nal 6 Laufey *offspring:* 3 Hel 4 Hela 6 Fenris 7 Midgard *slayer:* 8 Heimdall *victim:* 6 Balder *wife:* 5 Sigyn 9 Angurboda

Lolita author 7 Nabokov (Vladimir)

loll 3 bum 4 idle, laze, lazy 5 droop, slump, tarry 6 dawdle, diddle, slouch

Lollards' leader 8 Wycliffe (John)

lombard 6 cannon

Lombard king 5 Cleph 6 Alboin, Audoin 7 Aistulf, Aripert, Authari 9 Liudprand

London *borough:* 5 Brent 6 Barnet, Bexley, Ealing, Harrow, Sutton 7 Barking, Bromley, Chelsea, Croydon, Enfield, Hackney, Lambeth 8 Haringey, Havering, Hounslow, Lewisham 9 Greenwich, Islington, Redbridge 10 Kensington 11 Westminster *cathedral:* 7 St. Paul's *clock:* 6 Big Ben *district:* 4 Soho 5 Acton 7 Chelsea, Mayfair *gallery:* 4 Tate *policeman:* 5 bobby *prison:* 7 Newgate *river:* 6 Thames *square:* 9 Leicester, Trafalgar *street:* 4 Bond 5 Fleet 6 Strand 7 Downing 9 Whitehall 10 Piccadilly *subway:* 4 tube

London novel 9 White Fang 10 Martin Eden, The Sea Wolf 11 The Iron Heel 16 The Call of the Wild

lone 4 only, sole, solo 5 alone 6 single, unique 8 deserted, forsaken, isolated, secluded, separate, singular, solitary

lonely 4 lorn 5 alone 7 forlorn 8 deserted, homesick, lonesome, solitary

loneness 8 solitude 9 isolation

loner 6 hermit 7 outcast, recluse 8 outsider, solitary

Lone Ranger, The *creator:* 7 Striker (Fran) *companion:* 5 Tonto *horse:* 6 Silver *trademark:* 4 mask 12 silver bullet

lonesome see lonely

Lone Star State 5 Texas

long 3 age, aim, yen 4 ache, aeon, itch, lust, miss, pine, sigh, want 5 crave, dream, wordy, yearn 6 aspire, hanker, hunger, prolix, thirst 7 diffuse, dog's age, lengthy, suspire, verbose **8** blue moon, coon's age, dragging, drawn-out, eternity, extended **9** diffusive, extensive **10** protracted

long dozen 8 thirteen

long-drawn-out 7 lengthy **8** dragging **10** protracted

Longfellow poem 8 Christus, Hiawatha, Hyperion, Kavanagh **10** Evangeline **11** My Lost Youth **12** A Psalm of Life

long for 4 ache, pine, want **5** covet, crave, yearn

longing 3 yen **4** wish **6** desire, thirst **7** craving **8** appetite

Long, Long Ago composer 5 Bayly (Thomas)

longshoreman 9 stevedore

long-suffering 7 patient **8** humility, meekness, patience **9** lowliness **11** forbearance, patientness, resignation, subduedness

long suit 5 forte **6** medium, métier, oyster **8** eminency, strength **9** specialty **10** specialism

long-winded 5 wordy **6** prolix **7** diffuse, lasting, lengthy, verbose **9** redundant **10** palaverous

loo 6 toilet

look 3 air, mug, see **4** cast, face, gape, gawk, heed, hope, lean, leer, mien, mind, note, ogle, peek, peep, peer, seem, show, spot, tend, view **5** await, front, glare, gloat, sight, slant, sound, stare, watch **6** appear, aspect, attend, beware, divine, expect, eyeful, glance, glower, goggle, notice, regard, squint, survey, visage **7** count on, display, exhibit, express, glimpse, incline, observe, seeming **8** forecast, foretell, indicate, manifest **9** count upon **10** appearance, expression, rubberneck **11** countenance, physiognomy

look after 4 tend **6** attend **7** care for

look at 3 eye, see **4** ogle, view **6** behold **7** examine

look back 6 recall, review **7** reflect **8** remember **9** reminisce

look down 5 abhor, scorn, scout **7** contemn, despise, disdain, overtop **8** dominate, outstare **9** tower over **10** tower above

looker 6 beauty, eyeful, lovely **8** knockout

looker-on 6 viewer **7** watcher, witness **8** beholder, by-sitter, observer **9** bystander, spectator **10** eyewitness

look for 4 seek **5** await

looking glass 6 mirror

look into 5 study **7** examine, inspect **11** investigate

look out 4 mind **6** beware

lookout 4 ward **5** guard, scape, vigil, vista, watch **6** affair, cupola, picket, sentry **7** concern, palaver **8** business, prospect,

sentinel, watchman **9** crow's nest, firetower, occasions, vigilance **10** observance, watchtower **9** widow's walk **11** observation, observatory, perspective **12** surveillance

loom 4 brew, bulk, hulk, near, rear, show **5** tower **6** appear, come on, emerge, gather, impend, make up, weaver **8** approach, stand out, threaten **9** forthcome *part:* **3** lam **4** caam **5** easer **6** heddle **7** harness, shuttle, treadle, trundle

loon 3 nut **4** bird **5** grebe

loony 3 nut **5** batty, crazy, silly, wacky **6** absurd, dement, insane, madman, maniac **7** foolish, lunatic, madling **9** bedlamite, non compos **10** Tom o' Bedlam **11** harebrained **12** preposterous

loony bin 6 asylum **8** madhouse, nuthouse **9** funny farm **10** booby hatch, crazy house

loop 3 arc, eye **4** ansa, arch, bend, coil, curl, gird, knot, ring **5** beset, curve, noose, picot, wheel **6** begird, circle, girdle, league, staple, wreath **7** circlet, circuit, compass **8** encircle, surround **9** encompass **13** circumference

looped 5 drunk **11** intoxicated

loophole 3 out **6** outlet **7** opening

loose 3 lax **4** bate, ease, easy, fast, fire, free, limp, undo, vent **5** abate, clear, let up, light, relax, shoot, slack, unbar, unfix, unpin, untie **6** flabby, remiss, unbind, unbolt, undone, unglue, unhook, unlace, unlash, unlock, unsnap, wanton **7** ease off, flaccid, manumit, relaxed, release, slacken, unchain, unclasp, unhitch, unlatch, unleash, unscrew, unstick, unstrap, whorish **8** detached, liberate, mitigate, reckless, separate, unbuckle, unbutton, unchaste, unfasten **9** alleviate, desultory, discharge, disengage, negligent, take out on, unbandage, untighten **10** capricious, disjointed, emancipate, incoherent, inconstant, unattached, unconfined, unfastened **11** disenthrall, extravagant, nonadhesive, unconnected **12** disconnected, unrestrained

loose end 6 detail **8** fragment

loose-fitting 5 baggy **6** droopy

loose-lipped see **loquacious**

loosen 3 lax **4** ease, free **5** relax, slack, untie **6** unbind **7** ease off, manumit, release, slacken, unchain **8** liberate, unbuckle, unfasten **9** discharge **10** emancipate

loosen up 5 relax **6** unbend, unwind **7** ease off

loot 3 rob **4** sack, swag **5** booty, dough, lucre, money, prize, rifle, spoil **6** boodle **7** pillage, plunder, ransack, relieve, seizure, stick up **9** knock over **10** plunderage **11** filthy lucre

looter 5 thief 6 reaver, riever 8 marauder, pillager, ravisher

lop 3 cut 4 chop, clip, jump, leap, trim 5 bound, droop, slump, vault 6 bounce, hurdle, slouch, spring 7 pendent, saltate 8 truncate

lope 3 jog, run 4 gait, romp, skip, trip 6 spring, sprint 7 skitter

lopsided 6 uneven 7 crooked, difform, unequal 8 top-heavy, unsteady 9 irregular 10 asymmetric, off-balance, unbalanced 13 unsymmetrical

loquacious 5 gabby, talky, wordy 6 chatty, prolix 7 verbose 9 jabbering, talkative 10 babblative 11 loose-lipped 12 loose-tongued, multiloquent 13 over-talkative

lord 2 Mr. 3 man, sir 4 boss, cock, earl, peer 5 noble, put on, swank, swell 6 affect, master, mister 7 husband, overawe, peacock, pretend, swagger 8 governor, nobleman, overbear 9 tyrannize *feudal:* 5 liege 8 seigneur, suzerain *Muslim:* 6 sayyid

Lord High Executioner 4 Koko

Lord Jim author 6 Conrad (Joseph)

lordly 5 grand, noble, proud 6 august, puffed, uppity 7 haughty, swollen 8 affected, arrogant, cavalier, imposing, insolent, magnific, majestic, princely, snobbish, superior 9 egotistic, grandiose 10 disdainful 11 dictatorial, magisterial, magnificent, overbearing 12 supercilious 13 authoritarian, high-and-mighty

Lord of the Flies author 7 Golding (William)

Lord's Prayer 9 Our Father 11 Paternoster

lore 4 myth, saga, tale 5 fable 6 custom, legend, mythos, wisdom 7 folkway, science 9 knowledge, mythology, tradition 11 information 12 old wives' tale, superstition

Lorelei 5 siren 9 temptress 10 seductress 11 femme fatale *poet:* 5 Heine (Heinrich) *river:* 5 Rhine *victim:* 6 sailor 7 mariner

Lorenzo's beloved 7 Jessica

lorgnette 8 eyeglass 10 opera glass

Lorna Doone author: 9 Blackmore (Richard) *hero:* 4 Ridd (John)

___-Lorraine 6 Alsace

lose 3 rid, rob 4 drop, fail, fall, miss, oust, slip, tine, tyne 5 clear, shake, yield 6 divest, give up, mislay 7 bereave, decline, deprive, forfeit, regress, succumb 8 misplace, shake off, throw off, unburden 9 sacrifice, surrender

lose feathers 4 molt

loser 3 dud 4 bomb, bust, flop 5 lemon 7 also-ran, convict, failure 8 jailbird

loss 4 leak, ruin 5 havoc, waste 6 damage, defeat, injury 7 failure, forfeit 8 decrease 9 confusion, mislaying, priva-tion, ruination, sacrifice 10 divestment, forfeiture, misplacing 11 bereavement, deprivation, deprivement, destruction

lost 4 dead, gone 6 absent, astray, bygone, damned, doomed, hidden, musing, passed, ruined 7 bemused, defunct, extinct, faraway, lacking, mislaid, missing 8 absorbed, departed, distrait, vanished 9 condemned, daydreamy, graceless 10 abstracted 11 inconscient, irrevocable, preoccupied, unconscious, unconverted 12 absentminded, incorrigible, irredeemable, irreformable, unregenerate

Lost Horizon *author:* 6 Hilton (James) *land:* 9 Shangri-La

lot 3 cut, ilk, set 4 bite, body, doom, fate, give, heap, kind, lump, mass, much, part, peck, plat, push, sort, type, yard 5 allow, array, batch, block, breed, bunch, clump, crowd, field, group, moira, patch, quota, share, slice, tract, weird 6 assign, barrel, bundle, circle, clutch, decree, kidney, kismet, parcel, stripe 7 cluster, destiny, feather, fortune, mete out, partage, portion, species 8 allocate, clearing, frontage 9 admeasure, aggregate, allowance, apportion, character, great deal

Lot *father:* 5 Haran *sister:* 5 Iscah 6 Milcah *son:* 4 Moab 5 Ammon *uncle:* 7 Abraham

Lotan's father 4 Seir

lothario 5 Romeo 7 amorist, Don Juan, gallant 8 Casanova, paramour

Loti, Pierre 5 Viaud (Louis-Marie-Julien)

lotion 3 oil 4 balm 8 ablution, liniment, ointment

lottery 6 raffle 7 drawing 11 sweepstakes

lotus-eater 7 dreamer

loud 5 gaudy, harsh, noisy, showy 6 brassy, brazen, flashy, garish, hoarse, tawdry, tinsel, vulgar 7 blaring, blatant, booming, chintzy, glaring, pealing, raucous, ringing, roaring 8 piercing, resonant, sonorous, strident 9 deafening, obnoxious, obtrusive, offensive 10 bigmouthed, resounding, stentorian, stertorous, thunderous 11 ear-piercing, full-mouthed, fulminating, stentorious 12 ear-splitting

loudmouth 7 stentor 8 blowhard, braggart

loudspeaker 6 woofer 7 tweeter

Louise composer 11 Charpentier (Gustave)

Louisiana *capital:* 10 Baton Rouge *county:* 6 parish *largest city:* 10 New Orleans *nickname:* 11 Creole State 12 Pelican State *state flower:* 8 magnolia *university:* 3 LSU 6 Tulane 9 Grambling

lounge 3 bar, bum, lie, pub, tap 4 idle, laze, lazy, loaf, loll, sofa 5 dally, drift, slack

6 dawdle, loiter, saloon 7 barroom, buvette, lie down, recline, taproom

lounge lizard 3 fop 4 buck, dude 5 blood, dandy, leech 6 sponge, sucker 7 coxcomb, sponger 8 barnacle, hanger-on, macaroni, parasite 9 exquisite 10 free-loader 11 Beau Brummel, bloodsucker, petit-maître

Lourdes saint 10 Bernadette

louse 3 cur, dog, rat 4 snot, toad 5 aphid, skunk, snake 6 cootie, psylla, slater, wretch 7 stinker *egg:* 3 nit

louse up 4 mess, ruin 5 botch 6 bobble, bollix, bungle, mucker

lout 3 oaf 4 boor, dolt, gawk, hick, lump, mock, quiz, razz, rube, twit 5 churl, klutz, looby, rally, scout, taunt, yokel 6 deride, galoot, lubber, lummox, rustic 7 bumpkin, hayseed, lobster, palooka, peasant 8 ridicule, stinkard 10 clodhopper

Louvre masterpiece 8 Mona Lisa 11 Venus de Milo

lovable 4 dear 6 genial 7 winning, winsome 8 adorable, alluring, charming, engaging, fetching, pleasing 9 appealing, endearing, ravishing, seductive 10 attractive, bewitching, enchanting, entrancing 11 captivating, enthralling

love 3 pet 4 dear, like, lust, zeal 5 adore, amour, ardor, crush, Cupid, deify, exalt, fancy, honey, piety, prize, sweet, value 6 admire, affair, caress, cosset, cuddle, dandle, desire, enamor, fealty, fervor, fondle, liking, regard, revere 7 ardency, cherish, darling, emotion, idolize, loyalty, passion, romance, worship 8 devotion, fidelity, fondness, idolatry, treasure, venerate, yearning 9 adoration, affection, delight in, sentiment, sweetling 10 allegiance, appreciate, attachment, enthusiasm, honeybunch, sweetheart 11 amorousness, infatuation *combining form:* 5 phily 6 philia *French:* 5 amour *Italian:* 5 amore

love apple 6 tomato

lovebird 6 budgie, parrot 10 budgerigar

love feast 5 agape

love god 4 Amor, Eros, Kama 5 Bhaga, Cupid

love goddess 5 Athor, Freya, Venus 6 Hathor, Inanna, Ishtar 7 Astarte 9 Aphrodite, Ashtoreth

love letter 8 mash note 9 valentine 10 billet-doux

lovely 4 fair, rare 5 sweet 6 beauty, dainty, eyeful, looker, pretty 7 stunner 8 alluring, charming, delicate, engaging, graceful, handsome, knockout 9 beauteous, beautiful, exquisite 10 attractive, bewitching, delectable, delightful, enchanting, entrancing 11 captivating, good-looking

love-potion 7 philter, philtre 11 aphrodisiac

lover 3 fan, man 4 beau, buff 5 flame, hound, leman, Romeo 6 addict, master, steady, votary 7 amorist, devotee, Don Juan, gallant, habitué 8 fancy man, lothario, mistress, paramour 9 boyfriend, inamorata, inamorato 10 aficionado, girl friend *of beauty:* 7 esthete 8 aesthete *of books:* 11 bibliophile

love song 5 canso 6 ballad, serena 8 serenade

love story 7 romance

love token 4 ring 6 amoret

loving 4 dear, fond, kind 6 ardent, erotic, tender 7 amatory, amorous, bound up, cordial, devoted, fervent 8 attached, enamored, faithful 9 attentive 10 benevolent, infatuated, passionate, solicitous 11 considerate, impassioned, warmhearted 12 affectionate *combining form:* 4 phil 5 phile, philo 6 phillic 7 philous

low 3 bad, cut, moo, raw 4 base, blue, deep, down, flat, mean, neap, poor, rude, vile, weak 5 brief, broke, cheap, crass, crude, dizzy, faint, gross, needy, rough, short, under 6 abject, ailing, coarse, fallen, humble, lesser, nether, offish, poorly, scurvy, sickly, sordid, undear, unwell, vulgar, woeful 7 cut-rate, ignoble, nominal, popular, reduced, scrubby, scruffy, servile, slashed, uncouth, underly 8 atypical, baseborn, beggared, cast down, dejected, dirt poor, downcast, feverish, indigent, inferior, mediocre, moderate, off-color, plebeian, uncostly, unwashed, wretched 9 declining, depressed, destitute, inelegant, miserable, penurious, subjacent, subnormal, woebegone 10 despicable, economical, indisposed, marked down, reasonable, spiritless, subaverage, unennobled 11 crestfallen, downhearted

lowbred 7 boorish, loutish 8 churlish, cloddish, lubberly 9 unrefined 10 unpolished 11 uncivilized

low-cost 5 cheap 6 undear 7 popular 10 affordable, reasonable 11 inexpensive

low-down 4 base, mean, ugly, vile 6 scurvy 7 ignoble, servile 8 wretched 10 despicable

lowdown 4 dope 5 facts 11 information

lower 3 cut 4 clip, drop, fall, pare, peer, rail, sink 5 abase, abate, couch, decry, demit, droop, frown, gloom, scowl, shave, slash, stare, under 6 bemean, debase, demean, demote, humble, lesser, menace, nether, reduce 7 cut back, cut down, deflate, degrade, demerit, depress, descend, detrude, devalue, let down 8 cast down, inferior, mark down, overcast, submerge, threaten, write off 9 devaluate, downgrade, humiliate, subjacent *combining form:* 4 bath, cato 5 batho *prefix:* 5 infra

Lower Depths author 5 Gorki, Gorky (Maksim)

lowest 5 least 6 bottom 7 deepest 9 undermost 10 bottommost, nethermost, rock-bottom

lowest point 5 nadir 6 trough *on earth:* 7 Dead Sea

low-grade 4 hack, mean, poor 6 common 8 declassé, inferior 10 second-rate 11 second-class 12 second-drawer

low-key 4 soft 5 sober 7 subdued 8 softened 9 toned down

lowland 4 flat, vale 6 valley 7 bottoms *Scottish:* 6 lallan 7 lalland

Lowlander 4 Scot 8 Scotsman

lowlife 4 heel, worm 5 knave, rogue 6 mucker, no-good, rascal, wretch 7 villain 8 wormling 9 miscreant, scoundrel 10 blackguard

lowly 4 base, mean, meek 6 humble, modest 7 ignoble, mundane, prosaic, servile, workday 8 baseborn, everyday, obeisant, plebeian, retiring, unwashed, workaday

low-pitched 4 bass

low-pressure 6 casual, degagé 7 relaxed, unfussy 8 informal 9 easygoing 10 unreserved 13 unconstrained

low-priced 5 cheap 6 undear 7 popular 8 uncostly 10 reasonable 11 inexpensive

low-spirited 4 blue, down 8 dejected, downcast 9 depressed, heartsore, woebegone

low tide 3 ebb 4 neap

loyal 4 firm, true 5 liege 6 ardent, trusty 7 devoted, staunch 8 constant, faithful, resolute 9 allegiant, steadfast

loyalist 4 Tory 7 patriot

loyalty 5 ardor, truth 6 fealty 8 adhesion, devotion, fidelity, trueness 9 adherence, constancy 10 allegiance, attachment 12 faithfulness

lozenge 4 pill 5 candy 6 tablet, troche 7 diamond, rhombus, tabella 8 pastille

LSD 4 acid *user:* 8 acidhead

lubricate 3 oil 6 grease 7 moisten

lubricious 4 lewd 5 slick 6 fickle, greasy, slippy, wanton 8 slippery, slithery, ticklish, unstable, variable, volatile 9 lecherous, salacious, uncertain 10 changeable, inconstant 13 temperamental

lucent 5 clear 6 bright 7 beaming, crystal, radiant, shining 8 clear-cut, luminous, pellucid 9 brilliant, unblurred 11 unambiguous

Lucia di Lammermoor *composer:* 9 Donizetti (Gaetano)

lucid 4 sane 5 clear, right 6 bright, normal 7 beaming, crystal, lambent, radiant 8 all there, clear-cut, knowable 9 brilliant, efful-gent, graspable, refulgent, unblurred 10 fathomable 11 transparent, unambiguous 12 compos mentis, incandescent, intelligible, transpicuous 13 apprehensible

lucidity 3 wit 4 mind 6 reason, sanity, senses 7 clarity 8 saneness 9 clearness, plainness, soundness 12 distinctness, explicitness

Lucifer 5 devil, fiend, Satan 6 diablo 7 Old Nick, serpent 8 Apollyon 9 Beelzebub 10 Old Scratch 13 Old Gooseberry

Lucinde *beloved:* 7 Leandre 9 Clitandre *father:* 7 Geronte 10 Sganarelle

luck 3 hap, hit, lot 4 bump, juju, meet, weal, zemi 5 break, charm, fluke, light 6 amulet, chance, fetish, happen, hazard, kismet, mascot, tumble 7 fortune, godsend, periapt, stumble 8 accident, fortuity, occasion, talisman, windfall 9 advantage 10 phylactery 11 opportunity 13 fortunateness *token:* 5 charm 6 amulet, clover, mascot 8 talisman 9 horseshoe

luckless 7 hapless, unhappy 8 ill-fated, untoward, wretched 9 miserable 10 ill-starred 11 star-crossed, unfortunate 12 misfortunate

lucky 4 well 5 happy 6 benign 9 favorable, fortunate 10 auspicious, beneficial, felicitous, profitable, propitious 12 advantageous, providential *Scottish:* 5 canny

lucrative 4 good 6 paying 7 gainful 10 productive, profitable, well-paying, worthwhile 11 moneymaking 12 advantageous

Lucrezia ____ 6 Borgia

ludicrous 5 antic, awful, comic, droll, funny, silly 6 absurd 7 bizarre, comical, foolish, risible 8 farcical, gelastic 9 fantastic, grotesque, laughable

Lud's town 6 London

lug 3 box, tow 4 bear, buck, drag, draw, haul, jerk, pack, pull, snap, tote, worm, yank 5 carry, ferry, shlep 6 convey, schlep, twitch 9 transport, vellicate

luggage 4 bags 7 baggage 9 suitcases

lugubrious 3 sad 4 dour, glum 5 black, bleak 6 dismal, dreary, gloomy, morose, rueful, somber, sullen, woeful 7 doleful, joyless 8 dolesome, mournful 9 cheerless, plaintive, saturnine, sorrowful 10 depressant, depressing, lamentable, melancholy, oppressing, oppressive 11 dispiriting

lukewarm 4 cool 5 tepid 8 hesitant 9 uncertain, undecided 10 indecisive, irresolute, irresolved, unresolved, wishy-washy 11 halfhearted, uncommitted

lull 3 ebb 4 balm, calm, hush, wane 5 abate, allay, comma, let up, pause, quiet, still 6 becalm, settle, soothe, temper 7 compose, die away, die down, ease off, qualify, slacken, subside 8 abeyance, interval, moderate **9** pausation **10** quiescence **11** tranquilize

lullaby 4 song **8** berceuse **10** cradlesong *Scottish:* **5** baloo, balow

lumber 3 tax **4** clog, lade, load, logs, plod, slog, wood **5** barge, clump, stump, weigh **6** burden, charge, saddle, timber, trudge

lumberjack see **logger**

Lumber State 5 Maine

luminance 10 brightness

luminary 3 big, sun, VIP **4** lion, name, star **5** light, nabob **6** leader **7** big name, notable **8** big-timer, eminence, somebody **9** celebrity **10** notability **12** leading light

luminous 5 clear, lucid **6** bright, lucent **7** beaming, crystal, fulgent, lambent, radiant, shining **8** clear-cut, knowable, pellucid **9** brilliant, effulgent, graspable, refulgent, unblurred **10** fathomable **11** translucent, transparent **12** incandescent

lummox 3 oaf **4** boor, gawk, lout **5** klutz, looby **7** lobster, palooka

lump 3 bit, gob, lot, oaf, wad **4** bear, blob, bulk, chip, clod, clot, gawk, heap, hunk, knot, lout, mass, much, peck, pile, welt **5** abide, batch, block, brook, bulge, bunch, chunk, crumb, hunch, klutz, looby, piece, scrap, stand, wedge **6** barrel, digest, endure, lubber, morsel, nugget **7** lobster, palooka, portion, stomach, swallow **8** swelling **12** protuberance

lumpy 3 raw **4** rude **5** crude, rough **8** clumpish, unformed **9** roughhewn, undressed

lunacy 5 folly, mania **7** fatuity, foolery, inanity, madness **8** delirium, insanity **9** absurdity, asininity, craziness, silliness, stupidity, unbalance **10** aberration, alienation, ineptitude, insaneness **11** derangement, distraction, foolishness, psychopathy, witlessness **13** senselessness

lunar *dark area:* **4** mare **5** maria (plural) *valley:* **4** rill **5** rille

lunatic 3 mad, nut **4** kook, loon **5** crank, crazy, loony, raver, wacky **6** absurd, crazed, cuckoo, dement, insane, madman, maniac, psycho **7** cracked, foolish, madling, unsound **8** crackpot, demented, demoniac, deranged, paranoid **9** bedlamite, ding-a-ling, energumen, fantastic, harebrain, neuropath, non compos, screwball **10** crackbrain, Tom o' Bedlam

lunch 4 meal, nosh **5** snack **6** tiffin

luncheonette, lunchroom 4 café **6** eatery **7** beanery **8** snack bar **9** cafeteria **10** coffee shop **11** eating house **12** sandwich shop

lune 5 leash

lung 5 organ **8** breather *combining form:* **5** pneum, pulmo **6** pneumo, pulmon **7** pul-

moni, pulmono *disease:* **9** emphysema, pneumonia **12** tuberculosis

lunge 4 dive, stab **5** burst, drive, pitch **6** thrust

lunkhead 3 oaf **4** boob, dolt, goof **5** booby, chump, dunce

lupine 6 fierce **7** wolfish **10** bluebonnet

lurch 3 bob, yaw **4** bent, jerk, reel, rock, roll, snap, swag, sway, tilt, toss, wave, yank **5** swing, waver, weave, whirl **6** bumble, careen, falter, plunge, seesaw, swerve, teeter, tilter, topple, totter, twitch, wallow, wobble **7** blunder, leaning, stagger, stumble **8** flounder, penchant, tendency

lure 3 bag **4** bait, call, draw, fake, pull, rope, toll, trap, wile **5** blind, catch, charm, decoy, tempt, train, trick **6** ambush, appeal, cajole, come-on, draw in, draw on, entice, entrap, invite, lead on, seduce, suck-in **7** attract, beguile, bewitch, capture, con game, enchant, ensnare, gimmick, wheedle **8** blandish, delusion, illusion, inveigle **9** captivate, fascinate, incentive, seduction, siren song **10** attraction, camouflage, enticement, inducement, seducement, temptation *fishing:* **3** fly **4** herl, worm **5** spoon **6** minnow **8** bucktail

lurid 3 wan **4** ashy, grim, pale **5** ashen, livid, waxen **6** doughy, malign, sultry **7** baleful, ghastly, hideous, macabre, malefic, tabloid **8** blanched, gruesome, horrible, sinister, terrible **9** colorless **10** horrifying, maleficent, terrifying **11** sensational

lurk 4 hide, slip **5** creep, skulk, slide, slink, sneak, steal **7** gumshoe **9** pussyfoot

luscious 4 rare, rich **5** sapid, tasty, yummy **6** Capuan, choice, deluxe, florid, ornate, rococo, savory **7** baroque, darling, opulent, piquant, sensual **8** adorable, heavenly, palatial, sensuous **9** ambrosial, epicurean, exquisite, palatable **10** appetizing, delectable, delightful, flamboyant, flavorsome **11** distinctive, scrumptious, upholstered

lush 3 sot **4** rich **5** drunk, yummy **6** bibber, boozer, Capuan, deluxe **7** opulent, profuse, riotous, sensual, tippler **8** adorable, drunkard, heavenly, palatial, prodigal, sensuous **9** ambrosial, delicious, epicurean, exuberant, inebriate, luxuriant, luxurious, profusive, sumptuous **10** boozehound, delectable, delightful, voluptuous

Lusitania 4 ship **5** liner **8** Portugal

lust 3 rut, yen **4** ache, heat, itch, long, pine, urge, wish **5** crave, letch, yearn **6** desire, fervor, hanker, hunger, libido, thirst **7** craving, lechery, passion **8** appetite, coveting, cupidity, priapism, salacity, satyrism, yearning **9** carnality, eroticism, lubricity, prurience, pruriency **10** aphrodi-

sia, appetition, excitement, satyriasis
11 nymphomania 13 concupiscence, lecherousness

luster 4 glow 5 glaze, gleam, glint, gloss,
sheen, shine 6 polish 8 radiance 9 after-
glow 10 brightness, brilliance, brilliancy,
effulgence, luminosity, refulgence 11 can-
descence, iridescence, opalescence

lusterless 3 dim, mat, wan 4 dead, drab,
dull, flat 5 blind, faded, muted, prosy 7 prosaic

lustful 3 hot 4 fast, lewd 5 rutty 7 burning, goatish, itching, ruttish, satyric 8 prurient 9 lecherous, libertine, lickerish, salacious 10 hot-blooded, lascivious, libidinous,
licentious, passionate 11 incontinent
12 concupiscent

lustrate 5 purge 6 purify 7 cleanse

lustration 9 catharsis, cleansing

lustrous 5 nitid, shiny 6 bright, gleamy,
glossy, sheeny 7 fulgent, lambent, radiant,
shining 8 gleaming, glinting, polished, splendid 9 brilliant, burnished, effulgent, refulgent, sparkling 10 glimmering, glistening
11 resplendent 12 incandescent

lusty 4 hale, huge, vast 5 hardy, vital
6 mighty, potent, robust, strong 7 dynamic,
healthy, immense, massive 8 enormous,
vigorous, whacking, whopping 9 energetic,
strenuous 10 full-bodied, prodigious, red-
blooded, tremendous

lusus 5 freak 7 monster 8 abortion
11 miscreation, monstrosity

lute 4 clay, ring, seal 6 cement 7 bandora,
bandore 10 chitarrone, instrument *Arabic:*
3 oud *Greco-Roman:* 7 pandura 8 pan-
doura *Oriental:* 3 tar *Russian:* 7 bandura
Spanish: 8 banduria *two-necked:* 7 theorbo

lutenist 4 Mace (Denis, Thomas) 5 Bream
(Julian) 6 Gallot (Antoine, Jacques, Henry
Francois), Mouton (Charles), Radolt (Won-
zel Ludwig von) 7 Bakfark (Balint), Dowland (John, Robert), Gautier (Jacques,

Pierre), Perrine 8 Capirola (Vincenzo),
Gaultier (Denis, Ennemond)

Lutetia 5 Paris

luxuriant 4 lush, posh, rank, rich 5 plush
6 Capuan, fecund, lavish 7 fertile, opulent,
profuse, riotous 8 fruitful, luscious, palatial,
prodigal, prolific 9 exuberant, sumptuous

luxuriate 4 bask, love, riot, roll 5 eat up,
enjoy, feast, revel 6 overdo, wallow, welter
7 indulge, rollick 11 overindulge

luxurious 4 lush, posh, rich 5 awful,
fancy, grand, plush, showy 6 Capuan,
costly, deluxe, lavish, palace, plushy
7 opulent, sensual, stately 8 imposing,
majestic, palatial, splendid 9 elaborate, epicurean, expensive, grandiose 10 impressive 11 extravagant, languishing, magnificent *situation:* 7 fat city 10 bed of roses,
easy street

luxury 5 frill 6 dainty 7 amenity, comfort
8 delicacy 10 redundancy 11 superfluity
12 extravagance 13 embellishment

Lycaon *daughter:* 8 Callisto *father:*
8 Pelasgus *mother:* 8 Meliboea

Lycidas author 6 Milton (John)

Lycomedes *daughter:* 8 Deidamia *victim:* 7 Theseus

Lycus *brother:* 7 Nycteus *father:* 7 Pandion *slayer:* 6 Zethus 7 Amphion *wife:*
5 Dirce

Lydian *king:* 5 Gyges 7 Croesus 8 Alyattes *queen:* 7 Omphale

lye 7 caustic 8 lixivium

Lynceus *brother:* 4 Idas *father:*
8 Aphareus

lynch 4 hang 6 murder

Lynette see Line

lynx 3 cat 6 bobcat 7 caracal 9 catamount

Lyra star 4 Vega

lyre 4 harp 6 kissar 10 instrument

lyric 3 ode 4 odic, poem 5 melic 6 poetic
7 melodic, musical

lyric drama 5 opera

Lysander's beloved 6 Hermia

M

Maacah *father:* 5 Nahor 6 Talmai
7 Absalom *husband:* 5 David 6 Jehiel,
Machir 8 Rehoboam *son:* 5 Hanan 6 Abijam, Achish 7 Absalom 10 Shephatiah

Maaseiah *father:* 6 Jotham 7 Shallum
son: 7 Azariah 8 Zedekiah 9 Zephaniah

macabre 4 grim 5 lurid 6 deadly, grisly,
horrid 7 deathly, ghastly, ghostly, hideous
8 gruesome, horrible, terrible 9 deathlike,
ghostlike 10 horrifying, unpleasant

macaque 6 monkey, rhesus

macaroni 3 fop 4 buck, dude 5 dandy
7 coxcomb

Macbeth *character:* 4 Ross 5 Angus
6 Hecate, Lennox 7 Fleance *slayer:*
7 Macduff *successor:* 7 Malcolm *title:*
5 thane *victim:* 6 Banquo, Duncan

mace 3 bat, rod 4 beat, bilk, club 5 baton,
billy, staff 6 cudgel, strike 8 bludgeon
9 billy club 10 knobkerrie, nightstick

Macedonia *capital:* 5 Pella 6 Skopje
king: 6 Philip 9 Alexander *last king:*
7 Perseus

machete 4 bolo 5 knife 6 guitar

Machiavelli work 9 The Prince 11 The
Mandrake

machinate 4 plot 6 devise, scheme, wangle 7 collude, connive, finagle 8 cogitate,
conspire, contrive, engineer, intrigue,
maneuver 9 scheme out

machine 3 car 4 auto 5 buggy, golem,
motor, robot 6 device 7 autocar, fashion,
vehicle 8 motorcar 9 automaton 10 automobile, conveyance 11 standardize
component: 3 cam 4 belt, gear, seal
5 brake, chain, screw, shaft 6 clutch, spring
7 linkage 8 coupling *excavating:* 7 backhoe *humanlike:* 5 robot *laboratory:*
10 centrifuge

machine-gun 6 strafe

machine gun inventor 7 Gatling (Richard)

machinery 4 gear, tool 5 agent, means,
organ, works 6 agency, device, gadget,
medium, outfit, tackle 7 channel, utensil,
vehicle 8 matériel, tackling 9 apparatus,
appliance, equipment, implement 10 instrument 11 contraption, contrivance

Machir's father 6 Ammiel 8 Manasseh

Macher Picchu resident 4 Inca

mackle 4 blur

macrocosm 5 world 6 cosmos, nature
8 creation, universe

McTeague author 6 Norris (Frank)

mad 3 ire 4 daft, fury, rage, rash, sore,
waxy, wild 5 anger, angry, crazy, irate,
irked, loony, rabid, wacky, wrath, wroth
6 absurd, enrage, heated, insane, ireful
7 cracked, enraged, foolish, frantic, furious,
incense, invalid, lunatic, steam up,
umbrage 8 choleric, demented, deranged,
frenetic, frenzied, offended, outraged,
worked up, wrathful 9 affronted, delirious,
fantastic, hilarious, illogical, indignant, infuriate, senseless, sophistic 10 corybantic,
exasperate, fallacious, irrational, reasonless, unbalanced

Madagascar *capital:* 10 Tananarive
12 Antananarivo *export:* 5 sugar 6 cloves,
coffee 7 vanilla *monetary unit:* 5 franc

Madame Bovary 4 Emma *author:*
8 Flaubert (Gustave)

Madame Butterfly *character:* 9 Cho-Cho-San, Cio-Cio-San, Pinkerton, Sharpless *composer:* 7 Puccini (Giacomo)

madcap 4 rash 5 brash, hasty 8 reckless
9 hotheaded 10 ill-advised, incautious
11 thoughtless 13 inconsiderate

Mad Cavalier 6 Rupert (Prince)

madden 3 ire 5 anger, craze 6 enrage,
frenzy 7 derange, incense, possess, shatter, steam up, umbrage, unhinge 8 distract
9 infuriate, unbalance

Madeira *capital:* 7 Funchal *export:*
4 wine 5 sugar 7 bananas

made-to-order 6 custom 10 customized
11 custom-built

madhouse 5 chaos 6 asylum, bedlam
8 loony bin 9 funny farm 10 booby hatch

madman 3 ass, nut 4 bawd, fool, jerk,
loon 5 idiot, loony, ninny 6 dement, donkey, maniac, psycho 7 jackass, lunatic
8 imbecile 9 bedlamite, non compos
10 nincompoop, Tom o' Bedlam

madness 4 rage 6 lunacy, rabies
7 ecstasy 8 insanity 9 unbalance 10 aberration, alienation, enthusiasm 11 derangement, distraction, psychopathy

Madonna initials 3 BVM

Madras 9 Tamil Nadu *founder:* 3 Day (Francis)

Madrid museum 5 Prado

madrigal 4 glee, poem, song 8 part-song

madrigalist *Dutch:* 8 Arcadelt (Jacques) *English:* 4 Byrd (William) 6 Morley (Thomas), Wilbye (John) 7 Tomkins (Thomas), Weelkes (Thomas) *Flemish:* 8 Willaert (Adriaan) *Italian:* 5 Festa (Costanzo) 7 Landini (Francesco) 8 Marenzio (Luca) 10 Monteverdi (Claudio)

maelstrom 4 eddy, fury 5 storm, whirl 6 vortex 7 turmoil 9 commotion, confusion, whirlpool

maestro see conductor

magazine 4 dump, Life, Time 5 cache, daily, depot, organ, store 6 annual, armory, digest, review, weekly 7 arsenal, gazette, journal, McCall's, monthly, Playboy, Redbook, TV Guide 8 biweekly 9 bimonthly, newspaper, quarterly, warehouse, Woman's Day 10 depository, lumber room, periodical, repository, semiweekly, storehouse 11 publication 12 Family Circle 13 Reader's Digest

maggot 4 grub, whim 5 fancy, freak, humor, larva 6 notion, vagary 7 boutade, caprice, conceit

Magi 6 Gaspar 8 Melchior 9 Balthazar *gift:* 4 gold 5 myrrh 12 frankincense

magian 6 mystic, witchy, wizard 7 charmer, warlock 8 conjurer, sorcerer, wizardly 9 enchanter, sorcerous 11 necromancer, necromantic 12 thaumaturgic

magic 5 charm, wicca 6 augury, mystic, witchy 7 alchemy, bewitch, conjury, devilry, gramary, sorcery 8 deviltry, divining, exorcism, gramarye, satanism, witchery, witching, wizardly, wizardry 9 conjuring, diablerie, diabolism, marvelous, occultism, sorcerous, sortilege, voodooism 10 mumbo jumbo, necromancy, prodigious, remarkable, stupendous, witchcraft 11 abracadabra, bewitchment, enchantment, incantation, legerdemain, necromantic, soothsaying, thaumaturgy 12 thaumaturgic, unbelievable

magical 6 mystic, witchy 8 wizardly 9 sorcerous 10 bewitching 11 necromantic 12 thaumaturgic

Magic Flute composer 6 Mozart (Wolfgang Amadeus)

magician 4 seer 5 brujo, witch 6 medium, shaman, voodoo, wizard 7 augurer, charmer, diviner, Houdini, prophet, warlock 8 conjurer, exorcist, satanist, sorcerer 9 archimage, diabolist, enchanter, exorciser, invocator, trickster, voodooist 10 soothsayer 11 illusionist, medicine man,

necromancer, thaumaturge *Arthurian:* 6 Merlin

magicking 7 sorcery 8 witchery, wizardry 9 conjuring 10 necromancy, witchcraft 11 bewitchment, enchantment, thaumaturgy

Magic Mountain, The *author:* 4 Mann (Thomas) *character:* 7 Castorp

magisterial 5 bossy, puffy, wiggy 6 lordly, stuffy 7 bloated, pompous 8 arrogant, dogmatic, insolent 9 dictative, imperious, important, masterful 10 disdainful, high-handed, imperative, peremptory, pontifical 11 doctrinaire, domineering, overbearing 12 supercilious 13 authoritarian, authoritative, self-important

Magister Ludi author 5 Hesse (Hermann)

magistrate 5 court, judge 7 bencher, justice 8 official *ancient Greek:* 5 ephor 6 archon *ancient Roman:* 5 edile 6 aedile, pretor 7 duumvir, praetor, questor 8 quaestor *Italian:* 7 podesta *Scottish:* 6 bailie *Venice (former):* 4 doge

Magna Carta *king:* 4 John *place signed:* 9 Runnymede

magnanimous 3 big 5 great, lofty, noble 7 liberal 8 generous, knightly, princely 9 forgiving, unselfish 10 altruistic, benevolent, chivalrous, highminded 11 nobleminded

magnate 4 czar, king, lion, name, peer 5 baron, mogul, nabob 6 biggie, big gun, fat cat, figure, prince, tycoon 8 big-timer, nobleman 9 personage, plutocrat

magnesium *symbol:* 2 Mg

magnet 8 terrella 9 lodestone

magnetic 7 drawing 8 alluring 9 appealing, arresting, seductive 10 attracting, attractive, bewitching, enchanting 11 captivating, charismatic, fascinating 12 irresistible *substance:* 4 iron 7 ferrite

magnetism 5 charm 6 allure, appeal, glamor 7 glamour 8 charisma, witchery 10 witchcraft 11 fascination

magnetize 4 draw, lure, take, wile 5 charm 6 allure 7 attract, bewitch, enchant 9 captivate, fascinate

magnification unit 8 diameter

magnificence 8 grandeur, splendor 13 sumptuousness

magnificent 5 grand, noble, proud 6 august, lordly, superb 7 opulent, stately, sublime 8 glorious, gorgeous, imposing, majestic, princely, splendid, standout 9 brilliant, grandiose, inspiring, luxurious, sumptuous 11 extravagant, outstanding, resplendent, splendorous, superlative 13 splendiferous

magnifier 4 lens *jeweler's:* 5 loupe

magnify 3 pad 4 hymn, laud, rise 5 add to, bless, boost, color, cry up, erect, exalt, extol, fudge, honor, mount, rouse, swell 6 beef up, deepen, dilate, expand, extend, praise, uprear 7 amplify, augment, distend, enhance, enlarge, ennoble, glorify, inflate, sublime 8 eulogize, heighten, increase, maximize, multiply, overdraw, overplay, redouble 9 aggravate, celebrate, embellish, embroider, intensate, intensify, overpaint, overstate 10 aggrandize, exaggerate, overcharge, overstress, panegyrize 13 overemphasize

magnifying *combining form:* 4 micr 5 micro

magniloquent 7 aureate, flowery, swollen 8 sonorous 9 bombastic, overblown 10 euphuistic, rhetorical 11 declamatory

magnitude 4 pith, size, tune 5 order, range 6 extent, import, matter, moment, number, volume, weight 7 bigness, caliber, measure, quality 8 enormity, hugeness, loudness, quantity, vastness, vicinity 9 greatness, immensity, largeness 10 dimensions, importance, proportion 11 consequence, sizableness, weightiness

Magnolia State 11 Mississippi

magnum opus 7 classic 10 masterwork 11 chef d'oeuvre, masterpiece, tour de force

Magog's king 3 Gog

magpie 4 bird, crow 6 gabber, prater 7 blabber 8 jabberer, prattler 9 bandar-log, blabmouth, chatterer 10 chatterbox, piping crow 12 blabbermouth 13 miscellaneous

maguey 5 agave, fiber 7 cantala *relative:* 4 aloe

magus 6 wizard 7 charmer, warlock 8 conjurer, sorcerer 9 enchanter 11 necromancer

Magyar 9 Hungarian

Mahalath *father:* 7 Ishmael 8 Jerimoth *husband:* 4 Esau 8 Rehoboam

mah-jongg piece 4 tile

Mahli, Mahali *brother:* 5 Mushi *father:* 6 Merari

Mahlon *father:* 9 Elimelech *mother:* 5 Naomi *wife:* 4 Ruth

Mahol's son 5 Darda, Heman 6 Calcol

Maia *father:* 5 Atlas *mother:* 7 Pleione *sisters:* 8 Pleiades *son:* 6 Hermes 7 Mercury

maid 3 gal 4 girl, lass, miss 5 biddy, bonne, missy, wench 6 damsel, lassie, virgin 7 servant 8 charlady, domestic, factotum 9 charwoman, hired girl 10 au pair girl, handmaiden *lady's:* 7 abigail

maiden 3 gal 4 burd, girl, lass, miss 5 first, fresh, missy, prime, wench 6 burdie, damsel, intact, lassie, unused, virgin 7 damosel, damozel, initial, pioneer, primary,

untaken, untried 8 earliest, original, virginal 10 old-maidish, spinsterly 11 husbandless, spinsterish 12 undeflowered *combining form:* 7 parthen 8 partheno *Muslim:* 5 houri *Norse mythological:* 6 valkyr 8 valkyrie, walkyrie

maidenhair tree 6 gingko, ginkgo

maidenhead 5 hymen 6 purity 9 freshness, virginity

maidenhood 9 virginity

maiden lady 7 old maid 8 spinster 10 spinstress

Maid of Astolat 6 Elaine

Maid of Orleans, The 4 Joan 7 Pucelle *author:* 8 Schiller (Friedrich von)

____ mail 3 air 5 chain

maim 4 maul 5 break 6 batter, bung up, mangle, mayhem 7 cripple, disable, dislimb 8 massacre, mutilate, paralyze 9 disfigure, dismember, hamstring

main 3 big, sea 4 blue, deep, head, line, star, very 5 brine, chief, drink, great, major, ocean, sheer, vital 7 capital, high sea, leading, stellar 8 cardinal, foremost 9 essential, paramount, principal 10 preeminent, prevailing 11 controlling, fundamental, outstanding, predominant

Maine *capital:* 7 Augusta *college:* 5 Bates, Colby 7 Bowdoin *highest point:* 10 Mt. Katahdin *largest town:* 8 Portland *motto:* 6 dirigo 7 I direct *nickname:* 11 Lumber State 13 Pine Tree State

mainstay 3 key 4 prop 5 brace, staff 6 crutch, pillar, sinews 7 standby, support 8 backbone, buttress, upholder 9 supporter, sustainer

Main Street author 5 Lewis (Sinclair)

maintain 4 aver, avow, save 5 argue, claim, guard, right 6 affirm, assert, avouch, back up, defend, insist, keep up, manage, stress, uphold 7 care for, carry on, contend, correct, declare, husband, justify, persist, profess, protect, protest, rectify, support, warrant 8 continue, preserve 9 cultivate, emphasize, vindicate 10 provide for

maintenance 4 care, keep, salt 5 bread 6 living, upkeep 7 alimony, support 10 livelihood 11 subsistence 12 alimentation *worker:* 7 janitor 9 custodian

maize 4 milo 10 Indian corn

majestic 5 grand, noble, regal, royal 6 august, kingly, lordly 7 courtly, stately 8 elevated, imperial, imposing, kinglike, magnific, princely 9 dignified, grandiose, monarchal, sovereign 10 monarchial 11 ceremonious, magnificent, monarchical

major 3 big 4 fell, main, star, ugly 5 chief, grave, hefty, large 6 better, higher, larger 7 capital, greater, serious, sizable, stellar 8 grievous, superior 9 dangerous, extensive, principal **10** large-scale, preeminent **11** outstanding, predominant **12** considerable

Major Barbara author **4** Shaw (George Bernard)

majority **4** edge **6** margin

make **3** act, eat, fit, fix, get, lay, net, run, set, tap, win **4** bear, brew, draw, earn, form, gain, head, mold, name, reap, sire **5** begin, build, catch, cause, clear, draft, enact, equal, erect, force, forge, frame, hatch, infer, judge, reach, ready, shape, spawn, start, write **6** attain, behave, coerce, compel, create, deduce, deduct, derive, draw on, draw up, effect, extend, father, finger, gather, intend, oblige, ordain, output, parent, secure, seduce, set out **7** achieve, acquire, appoint, bring in, clean up, collect, compose, concuss, count as, destine, fashion, harvest, perform, prepare, proceed, produce, serve as, shotgun, stretch, take off **8** assemble, break for, comprise, conclude, drag down, draw down, generate, initiate, light out, nominate, traverse **9** constrain, construct, designate, establish, fabricate, formulate, knock down, originate, procreate, strike out **10** bring about, constitute **11** manufacture, put together *amends:* **5** atone *a metallic sound:* **5** chink, clang *a mistake:* **3** err **4** goof *ashen:* **6** blanch *a statement:* **7** expound *a witty remark:* **4** jest *bare:* **5** strip **6** denude *believe:* **7** pretend *certain:* **6** assure **8** convince *cheerful:* **6** solace *coins:* **4** mint *different:* **6** change *fast:* **3** fix **4** gird **6** secure *hair curly:* **5** crimp **6** buckle *happy:* **5** bless **6** please **7** satisfy *holy:* **6** hallow *inoperative:* **5** annul *into a law:* **5** enact *known:* **3** air **6** expose, reveal, spread **7** declare, divulge, uncover **8** announce, disclose, proclaim *less severe:* **6** weaken **8** mitigate **9** attenuate *manifest:* **7** explain *melodious:* **6** attune *merry:* **5** cheer *numb:* **4** daze, stun *presentable:* **5** groom *quiet:* **4** calm **5** allay, quell **6** pacify **7** appease *ready beforehand:* **7** prepare *red:* **5** flush *rigid:* **5** brace **7** stiffen *sacred:* **8** sanctify *slick:* **3** oil **9** lubricate *small:* **8** belittle *smaller:* **8** compress *strong:* **7** fortify *suffix:* **2** en, fy **3** ify *suitable:* **5** adapt *supremely happy:* **7** beatify *unclean:* **4** soil *understandable:* **7** clarify *useful:* **7** utilize *use of:* **6** employ *vigorous:* **8** energize

make-believe **7** charade, feigned, fiction, pageant **8** disguise, pretense **9** insincere, pretender **10** pretension

make off **2** go **3** fly; run **4** bolt, flee, quit, skip **5** leave, scoot, skirr **6** decamp, depart, escape, retire **7** abscond, run away, scamper **8** withdraw **9** skedaddle

make out **2** go **3** dig, see **4** draw, show **5** catch, grasp, infer, judge, prove, score **6** accept, arrive, deduce, deduct, derive, follow, gather, take in, thrive **7** collect, compass, discern, prosper, succeed **8** conclude, flourish, get along **9** apprehend, determine, establish, interpret **10** comprehend, understand **11** demonstrate

make over **4** cede, deed **5** alien **6** assign, convey, reform, remise **7** remodel **8** alienate, renovate, transfer **10** abalienate

makeshift **6** refuge, resort **7** stopgap **8** recourse, resource **9** expedient, temporary **10** expediency, substitute **11** provisional **13** rough-and-ready

make similar to *suffix:* **2** fy **3** ify

make up **3** fit, fix, get, mix, pay, sue, woo **4** fuse, meld, rise **5** atone, blend, court, frame, merge, ready, spark **6** decide, derise, gather, invent, mingle, offset, pursue, redeem, set off, settle **7** address, advance, arrange, balance, compile, compose, concoct, prepare, replace, reprint **8** approach, atone for, compound, comprise, contrive, intermix, outweigh **9** formulate, improvise, interfuse **10** compensate

makeup **3** lie **4** cast, face, form, mold, plan, vein **5** fiber, grain, humor, paint, setup, shape, stamp, style **6** design, nature, powder, stripe, temper **7** fiction **8** ordering, war paint **9** blackface, character, formation **10** complexion, maquillage **11** arrangement, composition, disposition, grease paint, personality, replacement, temperament **12** architecture, compensation, constitution, construction, organization *eye:* **4** kohl **7** mascara *facial:* **5** rouge **6** powder

maladroit **5** brash, inept **6** clumsy, gauche **7** awkward, halting, unhandy **8** bumbling, bungling, tactless **9** hamhanded, impolitic, lumbering, stumbling, unpolitic, unskilled, untactful **10** blundering, left-handed, ungraceful **11** floundering, heavy-handed **12** undiplomatic

malady **3** ill **7** ailment, disease, illness **8** disorder, sickness, syndrome **9** affection, complaint, condition, infirmity **10** affliction *suffix:* **4** itis

malaise **7** disease **8** debility **9** infirmity **10** feebleness, infirmness, sickliness **11** decrepitude **13** unhealthiness

Malaprop creator **8** Sheridan (Richard Brinsley)

malapropos **5** inapt, undue **8** ill-timed, improper, mistimed, unseemly, untimely **10** unsuitable **11** ill-seasoned, inopportune, unbefitting **12** unseasonable, unseasonably **13** inappropriate, inopportunely

malaria **6** miasma **8** paludism *transmitter:* **8** mosquito

malarkey 4 guff 5 hooey 6 bunkum, bushwa 7 hogwash, twaddle 8 nonsense 9 poppycock 10 balderdash 12 blatherskite

Malawi *capital:* 8 Lilongwe *export:* 3 tea 7 tobacco *largest city:* 8 Blantyre *monetary unit:* 6 kwacha

Malaysia *capital:* 11 Kuala Lumpur *export:* 3 tin 6 rubber, timber 7 palm oil

Malchiel *father:* 6 Beriah *grandfather:* 5 Asher

Malchijah, Malchiah *father:* 5 Harim 6 Parosh, Rechab

Malchishua's father 4 Saul

malcontent 5 crank, rebel 6 anarch, griper, grouch, kicker, únruly 7 growler 8 factious, frondeur, grumbler, mutineer, mutinous, restless, revolter, sorehead 9 alienated, anarchist, estranged, insurgent, seditious 10 bellyacher, complainer, rebellious 11 disaffected, disgruntled, disobedient, faultfinder, ungratified 12 contumacious, dissatisfied, ungovernable

mal de ___ 3 mer

Maldives capital 4 Male

maldonite 9 black gold

male 3 tom 5 fella, manly 6 manful, virile 7 manlike 9 masculine, staminate *combining form:* 4 andr 5 andro *dark-haired:* 6 brunet

malediction 5 curse 7 malison 8 anathema

malefactor 5 felon, knave, rogue 6 rascal, sinner 8 criminal, evildoer, offender 9 miscreant, scoundrel, wrongdoer 10 blackguard, lawbreaker

malefic see malicious

malevolence 5 spite 6 grudge, malice, spleen 7 despite, ill will 9 hostility, malignity 10 abhorrence, antagonism 11 abomination, detestation 12 spitefulness 13 maliciousness

malevolent 4 evil 6 bitchy, malign, wicked 7 baleful, hateful, hurtful, vicious 8 sinister, spiteful 9 injurious, malicious, malignant 10 despiteful

malfunction 6 glitch

Mali *capital:* 6 Bamako *monetary unit:* 5 franc *product:* 4 fish 6 cotton 7 peanuts

malice 4 bane, bile, hate 5 spite, venom 6 animus, enmity, grudge, hatred, poison, spleen 7 despite, ill will, umbrage 8 meanness 9 animosity, antipathy 10 bitterness, resentment 11 hatefulness, malevolence 12 spitefulness 13 invidiousness

malicious 4 evil, mean 5 catty, green, nasty, petty 6 bitchy, wicked, witchy 7 baneful, hateful, heinous, jealous, spitish 8 spiteful, venomous, virulent 9 green-eyed, poisonous, poison-pen, rancorous 10 despiteful, malevolent

maliciousness see malevolence

malign 4 evil, slur, soil 5 decry, libel, smear, stain, sully, taint 6 befoul, defame, defile, revile, smirch, vilify, wicked 7 asperse, baleful, baneful, blacken, detract, hateful, hostile, noxious, pollute, slander, spatter, tarnish, traduce, vicious 8 backbite, besmirch, derogate, inimical, sinister, spiteful, tear down, virulent 9 bespatter, denigrate, disparage, injurious, rancorous 10 calumniate, depreciate, despiteful, maleficent, malevolent, pernicious, scandalize, villainize, vituperate 11 deleterious, detrimental, opprobriate 12 antagonistic, antipathetic

malignant 4 evil 6 wicked 7 baleful, hateful, vicious 8 devilish, fiendish, spiteful 9 injurious, rancorous 10 despiteful, diabolical, malevolent

malison 5 curse 8 anathema 11 commination, imprecation, malediction

mall 4 lane 5 alley 6 mallet 9 concourse, esplanade, promenade 10 passageway 11 median strip

malleable 6 pliant, supple 7 ductile, plastic

malleate 4 beat 5 pound 6 hammer

mallet 6 hammer, strike

Mallothi's father 5 Heman

Malluch's father 4 Bani 5 Harim

malodorous 4 foul, gamy, high, olid, rank, vile 5 fetid, fuggy, funky, fusty, musty, nasty, reeky, rough, stale 6 frowsy, putrid, rancid, rotten, smelly, stinky, strong, whiffy 7 decayed, noisome, noxious, reeking, spoiled, stenchy, tainted, ungodly 8 improper, indecent, mephitic, polluted, stinking, unseemly, untoward 9 offensive, poisonous, stenchful 10 decomposed, indelicate, nauseating, unbecoming 11 ill-smelling 12 pestilential

Malta *capital:* 8 Valletta *monetary unit:* 4 lira 5 pound *product:* 8 textiles

Maltese Falcon, The *author:* 7 Hammett (Dashiell) *detective:* 5 Spade (Sam)

maltreat 5 abuse 6 ill-use, misuse 7 outrage 8 disserve

mammal 3 ass 5 camel, daman, hippo, hyrax 6 alpaca, colugo, dassie 7 bearcat, primate 8 elephant 12 hippopotamus *African:* 5 okapi, zebra, zoril 7 zorilla, zorille, zorillo 8 aardvark, aardwolf *aquatic:* 5 yapok 6 desman, dugong, narwal, yapock 7 cowfish, manatee, narwhal, platypi (plural) 8 cetacean, narwhale, platypus, porpoise, sirenian 10 platypuses (plural) *arboreal:* 5 lemur 6 cuscus 7 opossum 8 kinkajou, lemuroid *Australian:* 5 coala, koala 8 kangaroo *burrowing:* 8 moldwarp, starnose, suricate *carnivorous:* 3 cat, dog, fox **4** bear, lion, mink, seal, wolf **5** genet, hyena, otter, panda, pekan, ratel, sable, tiger **6** badger, grison, marten, racoon, teledu, walrus **7** dasyure, genette, linsang, polecat, raccoon **8** carcajou, mongoose, mungoose *catlike:* **5** civet *doglike:* **6** jackal *extinct:* **6** quagga **8** mastodon, stegodon *feline:* **4** lion **5** tiger, tigon **6** tiglon **7** leopard, lioness, tigress *flying:* **3** bat *gnawing:* **3** rat **6** beaver, rodent **7** leporid **8** squirrel *goatlike:* **4** tahr **5** takin *harelike:* **5** hyrax **7** hyraces (plural), hyraxes (plural) **8** hyracoid *hoofed:* **2** ox **3** cow, pig **4** deer, goat, owse, oxen (plural) **5** camel, owsen (plural), sheep, tapir **6** alpaca, ovibos **7** peccary **8** ruminant, ungulate **12** hippopotamus *horned:* **4** goat *insect-eating:* **4** mole **5** shrew **6** tanrec, tenrec **8** hedgehog *long-necked:* **7** giraffe *marine:* **3** orc **4** orca **6** walrus **7** dolphin, grampus *marsupial:* **9** bandicoot *nocturnal:* **6** wombat *raccoon-like:* **8** cacomixl *ruminant:* **4** deer **5** llama, moose, sheep **6** vicuña **7** vicugna *small:* **4** pika **8** hedgehog, hedgepig *South American:* **7** guanaco *toothless:* **5** sloth **8** edentate, pangolin **9** armadillo *tropical:* **5** coati *unweaned:* **8** suckling *with flippers:* **8** pinniped *wolflike:* **5** hyena **6** hyaena

mammoth **4** huge **5** giant, whale **7** monster **8** colossal, enormous, gigantic **9** leviathan, monstrous **10** behemothic, gargantuan, mastodonic **11** elephantine

Mamre's brother **4** Aner **6** Eshcol

man **2** he, Mr. **3** boy, guy **4** body, buck, chap, cuss, gent, lord, soul **5** being, brace, flesh, lover, skate **6** fellow, galoot, mister, mortal, person, police, vassal **7** bruiser, fortify, husband, John Law, officer **8** bluecoat, creature, humanity, paramour **9** boyfriend, humankind, mortality, personage **10** individual **11** Homo sapiens *brass:* **5** Talos, Talus *castrated:* **6** eunuch *combining form:* **4** andr **5** andro, homin **6** homini *eccentric:* **6** codger, geezer *French:* **5** homme *Italian:* **4** uomo *Latin:* **3** vir **4** homo *Spanish:* **6** hombre *Yiddish:* **6** mensch *young:* **3** boy, lad **8** springal **9** springald, stripling

manage **2** do **3** run **4** fare, keep **5** get by, get on, guide, shift **6** afford, direct, effect, govern, handle, ordain **7** achieve, carry on, conduct, control, execute, husband, operate, steward, succeed **8** carry out, contrive, dominate, engineer, get along, work upon **9** cultivate, stagger on, supervise **10** accomplish, administer, adulterate, bring about **11** superintend **12** riding school, stagger along **13** muddle through

management **4** care **6** charge **7** conduct, running **8** handling, intrigue **9** oversight **10** conducting, intendance **11** supervising, supervision

manager **4** exec **6** gerent **7** handler, officer **8** director, official, producer **9** conductor, executive **10** impresario, supervisor **13** administrator *museum:* **7** curator *suffix:* **3** eer

Manahath's father **6** Shobal

Man and Superman author **4** Shaw (George Bernard)

Manassas battle **7** Bull Run

Manasseh, Manasses *brother:* **7** Ephraim *father:* **6** Hashum, Joseph **8** Hezekiah **10** Pahathmoab *grandfather:* **5** Jacob *grandson:* **6** Gilead *mother:* **7** Asenath *son:* **6** Machir

man-at-arms **2** GI **7** fighter, soldier, warrior **10** serviceman **11** fighting man

mancipium **5** slave **7** bondman, chattel **8** bondsman **9** bondslave

Mandalay author **7** Kipling (Rudyard)

mandarin **4** duck, tree **5** elder **6** orange **8** official **9** tangerine **10** bureaucrat

mandate **4** fiat, word **5** edict, order, ukase **6** behest, charge, decree **7** bidding, command, dictate **9** authority **10** imperative, injunction **13** authorization

mandatory **6** forced **7** binding, needful **8** required **9** de rigueur, essential, imperious, necessary, requisite **10** commanding, compelling, compulsory, imperative **11** involuntary **12** irremissible **13** indispensable

mandible **3** jaw

Manette's daughter **5** Lucie

maneuver **3** jig, ply **4** move, plan, play, plot, ploy, step **5** feint, swing, trick, wield **6** design, device, gambit, handle, jockey, scheme, tactic, wangle **7** beguile, exploit, finagle, finesse, gimmick, measure **8** artifice, demarche, dispense, engineer, exercise, intrigue, movement, navigate **9** machinate, procedure, stratagem **10** manipulate, proceeding, subterfuge **11** contrivance, machination **12** manipulation

maneuvering room **8** latitude

Man for All Seasons, A *author:* **4** Bolt (Robert) *subject:* **4** More (Thomas)

manful see manly

manganese *ore:* **10** pyrolusite *symbol:* **2** Mn

manger **4** rack **6** cratch, trough

mangle **3** mar **4** hack, iron, maul **5** press **6** batter, damage, deface, deform, impair, injure, padder **7** butcher, contort, distort **9** disfigure

mangy **5** seedy **6** shabby, sleazy, tagrag **7** scruffy, squalid **8** decrepit, tattered **9** moth-eaten **10** down-at-heel

manhandle 4 maul 5 abuse 6 batter 7 rough up 8 maltreat, mistreat 10 knock about, roughhouse, slap around

Manhattan *purchaser:* 6 Minuit (Peter) *school:* 9 Juilliard *university:* 8 Columbia

mania 4 rage 5 craze, fancy, thing 6 fetish, hangup 7 madness, passion 8 fixation, idée fixe, insanity 9 cacoëthes, fixed idea, obsession 10 compulsion, enthusiasm 11 fascination, infatuation

maniac 3 bug, mad, nut 4 loon, wild 5 bigot, crazy, fiend, freak, loony, rabid 6 crazed, dement, insane, madman, raging, zealot 7 berserk, cracked, fanatic, frantic, furious, lunatic, madling, ranting, unsound, violent 8 demented, deranged, frenetic, frenzied 9 bedlamite, delirious, non compos 10 enthusiast

manifest 4 mark, show, told, vent 5 clear, overt, plain, shown, utter, voice 6 appear, embody, evince, expose, ostend, patent 7 display, evident, evinced, exhibit, express, obvious 8 apparent, distinct, divulged, evidence, palpable, proclaim, revealed 9 disclosed, evidenced, incarnate, objectify, personify, personize, prominent 10 illustrate, indication, noticeable 11 demonstrate, exteriorize, externalize, materialize, personalize, unambiguous

manifestation 4 show 7 display 8 epiphany 10 revelation *combining form:* 5 phany

manifold 5 boost 6 beef up, expand 7 augment, diverse, enlarge, magnify 8 compound, increase, multiply, numerous 9 aggregate, multiform, multiplex 10 aggrandize, multiphase 11 diversiform, polymorphic 12 multifarious, multivarious

manikin 4 puny, runt 5 dwarf, midge, pygmy 6 midget, peewee 8 Tom Thumb 10 diminutive, homunculus

Manila *founder:* 7 Legazpi (Miguel Lopez de) *victor:* 5 Dewey (George)

manipulate 3 ply, rig, use 4 play 5 swing, wield 6 direct, doctor, handle, jockey, juggle, manage 7 beguile, conduct, control, exploit, finesse 8 dispense, engineer, maneuver 9 machinate 10 tamper with

Manitoba *capital:* 8 Winnipeg *university:* 7 Brandon 13 Saint Boniface

mankind 5 flesh, human 6 humans, people 8 humanity 9 mortality 11 homo sapiens

manlike 4 male 6 virile 8 hominoid, humanoid 9 masculine 10 anthropoid

manly 4 bold, male 5 brave 6 virile 7 gallant, valiant 8 fearless, intrepid, unafraid, valorous 9 dauntless, masculine, undaunted 10 courageous

man-made 9 synthetic 10 artificial, factitious *object:* 8 artefact, artifact

Mann character 7 Castorp 10 Felix Krull

manner 3 use, way 4 form, kind, mien, mode, sort, tone, turn, vein, wise, wont 5 habit, modus, mores, style, trick, usage 6 custom, method, system 7 bearing, fashion, p's and q's quomodo 8 behavior, decorums, demeanor, habitude, practice, protocol 9 amenities, etiquette, technique 10 civilities, consuetude, deportment, elegancies 11 affectation, formalities, peculiarity, proprieties 12 affectedness, idiosyncrasy *combining form:* 4 wise *suffix:* 2 ic, ly 4 ical

mannered 6 cutesy 8 affected 9 conscious 13 self-conscious

mannerism 4 airs, lugs, pose 7 oddness 9 prettyism, queerness 10 preciosity 11 affectation, peculiarity, singularity 12 eccentricity, idiosyncrasy 13 artificiality

mannerless 4 rude 7 ill-bred, uncivil 8 impolite 11 disgracious 12 discourteous 13 disrespectful

mannerly 5 civil 6 polite 7 civilly, genteel 8 politely 9 courteous 10 respectful 12 respectfully

Manoah's son 6 Samson

Manon composer 8 Massenet (Jules)

Manon Lescaut *author:* 7 Prevost (Abbé) *composer:* 7 Puccini (Giacomo)

manor 4 land 5 acres, villa 6 castle, estate, quinta 7 château 12 landed estate

manservant 5 valet 6 butler

mansion 4 hall 5 house, villa 6 castle, estate 7 château

manslaughter 5 blood 6 murder 7 bump-off, killing 8 foul play, homicide

manslayer 6 killer 8 homicide, murderer

mantic 7 fatidic 8 Delphian, oracular 9 sibylline, vaticinal 11 prophetical

mantle 4 glow, pink, robe, rose 5 blush, cloak, color, cover, flush, rouge 6 pinken, redden 7 crimson *combining form:* 7 chlamyd 8 chlamydo

Manto *father:* 8 Tiresias *husband:* 7 Rhacius *son:* 6 Mopsus

man-to-man 4 open 5 frank 6 candid 10 unreserved 11 openhearted, unconcealed, undisguised, unvarnished 12 undissembled

mantra 2 om 4 hymn 5 chant 6 prayer 11 incantation

manual 4 text 5 guide 6 primer 7 primary 8 Baedeker, handbook, hornbook, textbook 9 guidebook, vade mecum 10 compendium 11 abecedarium, enchiridion *religious:* 9 catechism *worker:* 7 laborer

manufactory 4 mill 5 plant, works

manufacture 4 form, make, mold 5 forge, frame, shape 6 create, invent 7 fashion, produce 8 creation 9 fabricate 10 production 11 put together

manumit 4 free 5 loose 6 loosen, unbind 7 release, set free, unchain 8 liberate 9 discharge, unshackle 10 emancipate

manure 4 dung 6 ordure 7 excreta 9 excrement 10 fertilizer

manuscript 4 hand *ancient:* 5 codex 7 codices (plural) *red part:* 6 rubric

Man Without a Country, The *author:* 4 Hale (Edward Everett) *character:* 5 Nolan

many 4 much 5 monie 6 divers, legion, myriad, sundry 7 copious, diverse, several, various 8 abundant, manifold, multiple, numerous, populous 9 abounding, bounteous, bountiful, countless, multitude, plentiful 10 multiplied, voluminous 12 multifarious, multiplicate, multitudinal 13 multitudinous *combining form:* 4 poly 5 multi, pluri

Maon's father 7 Shammai

Mao's successor 3 Hua (Kuo-feng)

map 4 plan, plat 5 chart, draft, graph 6 design, lay out, set out, sketch, survey 7 arrange, diagram, drawing, explore, outline, picture, tracing 9 cartogram, delineate *collection:* 5 atlas *line:* 6 isohel 7 contour, isobath, isogone, isogram, isogriv, isohyet, isotach 8 isarithm, isocheim, isochime, isogloss, isogonal, isogonic, isograph, isopleth, isotherm *maker:* 12 cartographer *making:* 11 cartography, chorography

map projection 5 Bonne, conic 6 Albers 8 gnomonic, Mercator 9 Mollweide, polyconic 10 sinusoidal 12 orthographic 13 stereographic

maquillage 4 face 5 paint 6 makeup 8 war paint

mar 4 flaw, harm, hurt, ruin, scar, warp 5 spoil, wreck 6 bruise, damage, deface, deform, impair, injure, injury 7 blemish, scratch, tarnish, vitiate 9 prejudice *the countryside:* 6 litter

marabou 4 silk 5 stork 12 adjutant bird

Marat *colleague:* 6 Danton (Georges) *slayer:* 6 Corday (Charlotte)

maraud 4 raid 5 foray, harry 6 harass

marauder 6 bandit, bummer, looter, pirate, raider, sacker 7 brigand, cateran, forager, ravager, spoiler, wrecker 8 pillager, ravisher 9 buccaneer, desperado, despoiler, plunderer, spoliator 10 depredator, freebooter

marble 3 mib, mig 4 immy, migg 5 aggie, rance 6 blotch, miggle, mottle, streak 7 cipolin, glassie, steelie

Marble Faun, The *author:* 9 Hawthorne (Nathaniel) *character:* 5 Hilda 6 Kenyon, Miriam 9 Donatello *setting:* 4 Rome

marblehearted 5 stony 7 callous 8 hardened, obdurate 9 heartless, unfeeling 10 hard-boiled 11 cold-blooded 13 unsympathetic

marcelled hair 4 wavy

march 2 go 3 hem, rim 4 abut, jibe, join, line, move 5 agree, check, fit in, get on, skirt, sling, stalk, tally, touch, verge 6 accord, adjoin, border, butt on, course, extend, fringe, parade, square, stride, travel 7 advance, headway, ongoing, proceed 8 anabasis, boundary, dovetail, frontier, get along, neighbor, outlands, parallel, progress, traverse 9 periphery, provinces, territory 10 borderland, correspond 11 advancement

March *date:* 4 ides *sisters:* 2 Jo 3 Amy, Meg 4 Beth

March Hare creator 7 Carroll (Lewis)

March King 5 Sousa (John Philip)

Mardi Gras 8 carnival 10 Fat Tuesday *city:* 10 New Orleans

Marduk, Merodach *city:* 7 Babylon *consort:* 8 Zarpanit 9 Sarpanitu *father:* 2 Ea *victim:* 5 Kingu

mare 3 sea 5 horse 6 equine

Mareshah's son 6 Hebron

mare's nest 3 din 4 hoax, sell 5 babel, cheat, fraud, put on, spoof 6 clamor, hubbub, humbug, racket, uproar 7 swindle 8 flimflam 9 imposture 10 hullabaloo

margarine 4 oleo

margin 3 hem, rim 4 abut, brim, edge, join, line, play, room, side 5 bound, brink, frame, scope, shore, skirt, touch, verge 6 border, fringe, leeway 7 connect, minimum, outline, selvage 8 latitude, neighbor, surround, trimming 9 elbowroom, perimeter, periphery *of shortcoming:* 6 leeway *tiny:* 4 hair

Marguerite's lover 5 Faust

Maria ___ 5 Elena 7 Stuarda

Marianas *discoverer:* 8 Magellan (Ferdinand) *island:* 4 Rota 5 Pagan 6 Guguan, Saipan, Tinian 7 Agrihan, Aguijan

marijuana 3 boo, pot 4 hash, hemp, weed 5 grass, joint 6 moocah, reefer 7 hashish 8 cannabis

marina 4 dock 5 basin 8 boatyard 9 esplanade, promenade

marine 5 naval 6 dipsey, dipsie, gyrene 7 abyssal, aquatic, bathyal, benthic, deep-sea, fluvial, neritic, oceanic, pelagic 8 bathybic, nautical, seagoing, seamanly 9 bathysmal, seafaring, thalassic 10 fluviatile, lacustrine, oceangoing, seamanlike 12 hydrographic, navigational 13 oceanographic *crustacean:* 8 barnacle *deposit:* 5 coral *plant:* 4 alga, kelp 7 seaweed

mariner 3 gob, tar 4 jack, salt 6 rating, sailor, sea dog, seaman 7 jack-tar, old salt, swabbie 8 seafarer 9 sailorman, shellback, tarpaulin 10 bluejacket

marionette 6 puppet 10 bufflehead

marital 6 wedded 7 married, nuptial, spousal 8 conjugal, hymeneal 9 connubial

maritime 7 oceanic 8 nautical 9 thalassic 12 navigational

mark 3 aim, jot, map, sap, say, see, use 4 butt, cull, dupe, duty, fish, fool, goal, gull, heed, logo, look, note, pick, read, show, sign, type, view 5 bound, brand, chart, chump, elect, grade, index, label, limit, stamp, token, trait 6 assign, attend, behold, choose, denote, emblem, evince, lay off, lay out, notice, object, optate, opt for, ostend, pigeon, prefer, rating, record, regard, select, sucker, symbol, target, victim, virtue 7 bespeak, betoken, delimit, destine, discern, exhibit, fall guy, feature, gudgeon, indicia, initial, measure, observe, pick out, purpose, qualify, quality, scratch, signify, symptom 8 ambition, evidence, function, indicate, logotype, manifest, perceive, proclaim, property, register 9 affection, attention, attribute, character, demarcate, designate, determine, objective, quaesitum, signalize, single out 10 importance, indication 11 differentia, distinction, distinguish 12 characterize *a tree:* 5 blaze *by cutting:* 4 nick 5 notch 6 scribe *distinctive:* 7 indicia 8 indicium *identifying:* 6 signet *low-water:* 5 datum *musical notation:* 6 corona 7 fermata *of insertion:* 5 caret *of omission:* 8 ellipsis 10 apostrophe *over a vowel:* 5 breve 6 accent, macron *over n:* 5 tilde *punctuation:* 4 dash 5 colon, comma 6 hyphen, period 9 semicolon *skate:* 4 cusp *time:* 5 count *under a letter:* 7 cedilla *with welts:* 4 wale

Mark *cousin:* 8 Barnabas *mother:* 4 Mary

mark down 3 cut 4 clip, pare 5 decry, lower, shave, slash 6 reduce 7 cut back, devalue 8 write off 9 devaluate 10 depreciate, underprize, undervalue

marked 5 noted 6 signal 7 pointed, salient 8 striking 9 arresting, prominent 10 noticeable, remarkable 11 conspicuous, outstanding 12 considerable 13 distinguished *man:* 4 Cain

market 4 give, sell, shop, vend 5 cheap, store 6 outlet, retail, tryste 8 showroom 9 traffic in, wholesale 11 merchandise *kind:* 4 flea 5 money, stock

marketable 3 fit 4 good 5 sound 7 selling 8 vendible 9 wholesome 10 commercial

marketplace 4 souk 5 agora, bazar 6 bazaar, rialto

marksman 4 shot 7 deadeye, shooter

marl 4 clay 5 earth 9 fertilize

marlin 9 spearfish

Marlowe play 8 Edward II 9 Dr. Faustus 11 Tamburlaine 13 The Jew of Malta

marmalade fruit 6 orange, quince

marmot 10 prairie dog

Marpessa *abductor:* 4 Idas *father:* 6 Evenus

Marquand character 4 Gray, Moto 5 Apley, Wayde 6 Pulham 7 Goodwin

Marquis *cat:* 9 Mehitabel *cockroach:* 5 Archy

marriage 5 match, union 6 bridal 7 nuptial, spousal, wedding, wedlock 8 espousal, monogamy, nuptials, polygamy, polygyny 9 espousals, matrimony 11 conjugality 12 connubiality *combining form:* 4 gamy 6 gamous *notice:* 5 banns *outside a group:* 7 exogamy *second:* 6 bigamy, digamy *within a group:* 8 endogamy

marriageable 6 nubile

marriage broker 9 go-between 10 matchmaker *Jewish:* 8 shadchan

marriage portion 3 dot 5 dower, dowry

marrow 4 core, meat, pith, soul 5 heart, stuff 6 bottom, kernel 7 essence 9 substance 10 virtuality 12 essentiality, quintessence

marry 3 tie, wed 4 join, link, mate, wive, yoke 5 catch, hitch 6 couple, relate, splice, spouse 7 combine, conjoin, espouse, husband 9 associate, conjugate

Mars 6 planet *combining form:* 4 areo *moon:* 6 Deimos, Phobos *relating to:* 7 martian; (see also **Ares**)

Marseillaise composer 13 Rouget de Lisle (Claude-Joseph)

marsh 3 bog, fen 4 mire, ooze, quag 5 bayou, glade, swail, swale, swamp 6 maskeg, morass, muskeg, slough 7 baygall, wetland 8 moorland, quagmire 9 swampland *combining form:* 4 helo 6 paludi

marshal 5 array, guide, order, rally, space, usher 6 direct, escort, muster 7 arrange, dispose, officer 8 mobilize, organize, shepherd 9 methodize 10 distribute

marshland see **marsh**

marshlight 7 spunkie 11 ignis fatuus

Martha *brother:* 7 Lazarus *sister:* 4 Mary

martial 7 warlike 8 militant, military, spirited 9 bellicose, combative 10 aggressive, mettlesome, pugnacious 11 belligerent

Martial's forte 7 epigram

Martin Chuzzlewit author 7 Dickens (Charles)

Martinique *capital:* 12 Fort-de-France *discoverer:* 8 Columbus (Christopher)

martyr 4 Paul, rack 5 Agnes, Alban, James, Peter, saint, wring 6 George, harrow, Justin 7 afflict, agonize, crucify, Cyprian, Stephen, torment, torture 8 Ignatius,

Lawrence, Polycarp, sufferer 9 Joan of Arc, Sebastian 10 excruciate *Protestant:* 6 Ridley (Nicholas) 7 Cranmer (Thomas), Latimer (Hugh)

marvel 6 wonder 7 miracle, portent, prodigy, stunner 9 horehound, sensation 10 phenomenon 12 astonishment

marvelous 5 awing, nifty, super, swell 6 divine, dreamy, groovy, peachy 7 amazing, awesome, ripping 8 glorious, pleasant, striking, stunning, superior, terrific, wondrous 9 agreeable, enjoyable, excellent, hunky-dory, rewarding, wonderful 10 astounding, incredible, phenomenal, prodigious, satisfying, staggering, stupendous, surprising 11 astonishing, bewildering, confounding, exceptional, pleasurable, sensational, spectacular 12 awe-inspiring, supernatural, unimaginable 13 extraordinary, inconceivable

Marx, Karl *book:* 10 Das Kapital *collaborator:* 6 Engels (Friedrich)

Marx brother 5 Chico, Harpo, Zeppo 7 Groucho

Mary *husband:* 6 Clopas, Joseph 8 Alphaeus *kinswoman:* 9 Elisabeth *son:* 4 Mark 5 James, Jesus, Joses

Maryland *academy, university:* 7 U.S. Naval 11 Towson State 12 Johns Hopkins *capital:* 9 Annapolis *largest city:* 9 Baltimore *nickname:* 12 Cockade State, Old Line State

mascot 4 juju, luck, zemi 5 charm 6 amulet, bat boy, fetish 7 periapt 8 talisman 10 phylactery

masculine 4 male 5 manly 6 manful, robust, virile 7 manlike 9 unwomanly *combining form:* 4 andr 5 andro

masculinity 8 machismo, virility 9 manliness

mash 4 mess, pulp 6 accost, bruise, jumble, jungle, litter, muddle, suitor, tumble 7 clutter, rummage 8 scramble 10 sweetheart 12 hugger-mugger

masher 4 wolf 5 flirt 6 chaser 7 Don Juan 8 Casanova 9 ladies' man, philander, womanizer 10 lady-killer 11 philanderer

mash note 10 billet-doux, love letter

mask 4 blur, face, pose, sham, show, veil 5 block, cloak, color, cover, front, guard, guise, put-on, visor 6 aspect, defend, domino, facade, fakery, flavor, screen, shield, veneer, visard, vizard 7 dress up, frisket, muffler, posture, pretext, protect, secrete, seeming, veiling 8 coloring, disguise, pretense 9 dissemble, doughface, false face, safeguard, semblance 10 appearance, camouflage, false front, simulation 11 affectation, dissembling, dissimulate 12 disguisement 13 dissimulation

masonry 9 brickwork, stonework *in a frame:* 7 nogging

masquerade 4 face, pose, show, veil 5 cloak, color, cover, front 6 facade, pass as 7 pass for, pass off, posture 8 disguise 10 camouflage 12 attitudinize

mass 3 lot, sum, wad 4 bank, body, bulk, clot, core, glob, heap, hill, lump, much, pack, peck, pile 5 clump, group, mound, shock, stack, total, whole 6 corpus, nugget, object, staple, volume 7 expanse, globule, pyramid, wadding 8 assemble, mountain 9 aggregate, great deal, magnitude, stockpile, substance 10 generality 11 aggregation, proletariat 12 conglomerate *combining form:* 4 onco 5 oncho *confused:* 7 clutter 9 imbroglio *for departed:* 7 requiem *ice:* 4 calf, floe *indefinite:* 3 gob *jumbled:* 8 pell-mell, scramble *metal:* 5 ingot *muddy:* 6 sludge *of hair:* 3 mop *of individuals:* 5 crowd, horde, swarm 13 agglomeration *part:* 6 proper 8 ordinary *rock:* 4 dome *rounded:* 4 knob *suffix:* 3 ium, ome *swollen:* 4 cere *tight:* 4 knot

Massachusetts *capital:* 6 Boston *college, university:* 3 MIT 5 Clark, Curry, Smith, Tufts 6 Babson, Boston 7 Amherst, Harvard 8 Brandeis, Williams 9 Hampshire, Holy Cross, Merrimack, Radcliffe, Wellesley 11 Springfield 12 Mount Holyoke, Northeastern *highest point:* 10 Mt. Greylock *nickname:* 8 Bay State 9 Old Colony *state bird:* 9 chickadee

massacre 4 kill 6 mangle, murder, pogrom 8 butchery, decimate, genocide, mangling, mutilate 9 bloodbath, bloodshed, slaughter 10 annihilate, blood purge, decimation 11 exterminate, internecion

massage 3 rub 5 knead 7 rubdown

Massa's father 7 Ishmael

Massenet opera 5 Le Cid, Manon, Sapho, Thais 7 Werther

massive 4 huge, vast 5 bulky, giant, grand, heavy, hefty, hulky, jumbo, large, solid 6 mighty, mortal 7 compact, hulking, immense, mammoth, notable, weighty 8 colossal, cracking, cumbrous, enormous, gigantic, towering 9 fantastic, monstrous, ponderous 10 cumbersome, monumental, prodigious, stupendous, tremendous 11 elephantine, mountainous

master 3 get 4 best, boss, cock, down, guru, head, lick, rule, tame, whiz 5 adept, bwana, chief, crack, learn, lover, marse, ruler, sahib, swami, throw, tutor 6 artist, direct, domine, expert, genius, govern, honcho, hurdle, leader, pick up, ruling, savant, subdue, victor, wizard 7 artiste, captain, conquer, headman, maestro, overman, padrone, prevail, rabboni, regnant, skilled, subduer, triumph **8** defeater, dominant, dominate, employer, fancy man, governor, hierarch, overcome, overlord, overseer, paramour, regulate, skillful, superior, surmount, virtuoso **9** ascendant, authority, boyfriend, chieftain, conqueror, dominator, paramount, prevalent, principal, sovereign **10** proficient, subjugator, vanquisher **11** controlling, crackerjack, domesticate, domesticize, domiciliate, overbearing, predominant, predominate *combining form:* **4** arch

masterdom 8 dominion **9** ascendant, dominance, supremacy **10** ascendancy, domination, prepotence, prepotency **11** preeminence, sovereignty

masterful 4 deft **5** adept, bossy, crack **6** adroit, expert **7** skilled, supreme **8** absolute, despotic, dogmatic, imperial, skillful, vigorous **9** arbitrary, dexterous, dictative, energetic, imperious **10** autocratic, highhanded, imperative, peremptory, preeminent, proficient, self-willed, tyrannical **11** crackerjack, dictatorial, doctrinaire, domineering, magisterial, overbearing, superlative **12** transcendent **13** authoritarian, authoritative, high-and-mighty

masterly 5 adept, crack **6** expert **7** skilled, supreme **8** skillful **10** preeminent, proficient **11** crackerjack, superlative **12** transcendent

Master of Ballantrae 6 Durrie *author:* **9** Stevenson (Robert Louis)

masterpiece 7 classic **9** objet d'art **10** magnum opus **11** chef d'oeuvre, tour de force

mastery 4 sway **5** knack, might, power, skill **7** ability, command, control, know-how **8** dominion **9** authority, expertise, expertism **10** ascendancy, domination, expertness **11** superiority **12** jurisdiction

masticate 4 chew, pulp **5** champ, chomp, chump, crush, munch, smash **6** bruise, crunch, squash **7** chumble, pulpify, scrunch **8** macerate, ruminate **9** break down

mastodonic see **mammoth**

mast support 4 bibb

mat 3 dim, rug **4** dead, dull, felt, flat, shag **5** blind, doily, muted **6** carpet **10** lackluster, lusterless

matador 6 torero **8** toreador **11** bullfighter *adjunct:* **6** muleta *move:* **4** pase **5** faena **8** veronica

Mata Hari 3 spy

match 3 con, pit, tie, vie **4** anti, bout, game, like, meet, suit, twin **5** adapt, array, equal, event, liken, rival, touch **6** amount, double, equate, fellow, oppose **7** compare, compeer, counter, opposer, paragon, play off, stack up **8** analogue, approach, opponent, parallel **9** adversary, companion, cor-

relate, duplicate, encounter, measure up, oppugnant, partake of **10** antagonist, assimilate, complement, coordinate, engagement, equivalent, reciprocal, supplement **11** counterpart, countertype **12** correspond to **13** correspondent, harmonize with *a bet:* **3** see *friction:* **5** fusee, fuzee **7** lucifer **8** locofoco

matchless 4 only **5** alone **6** unique **9** unequaled, unrivaled **10** inimitable **11** unparagoned **12** incomparable, unparalleled

matchmaker see **marriage broker**

mate 3 pal, tie, wed **4** chum, pair, peer, twin **5** amigo, breed, buddy, equal, hitch, marry, parti, sosie **6** cohort, couple, double, fellow, friend, helper, splice, spouse **7** compeer, consort, partner **8** alter ego, confrere, familiar **9** associate, companion, confidant, copartner, duplicate, procreate **10** complement, crossbreed, equivalent, reciprocal **11** cater-cousin, concomitant **12** acquaintance **13** accompaniment

maté 3 tea **5** holly **8** beverage

material 3 big **4** real, true **5** ad rem, being, cloth, gross, stuff, tapis, thing, vital **6** actual, animal, bodily, carnal, entity, fabric, matter, object **7** apropos, earthly, element, fleshly, germane, sensual, weighty, worldly **8** apposite, cardinal, palpable, physical, pointful, relevant, sensible, tangible **9** apparatus, component, corporeal, equipment, essential, important, machinery, momentous, objective, pertinent, substance **10** applicable, individual, ingredient, meaningful, phenomenal **11** applicative, applicatory, appreciable, constituent, fundamental, perceptible, significant, substantial **12** considerable **13** consequential *building:* **5** adobe, brick **7** plywood, shingle **8** concrete *cementing:* **7** plaster *combining form:* **3** hyl **4** hylo *combustible:* **8** kindling *cushioning:* **4** foam *glutinous:* **7** gelatin *hard:* **7** carbide *hard covering:* **6** stucco *indecent:* **4** smut *insulating:* **7** lagging **10** fiberglass *leftover:* **5** waste **7** rubbish *petrified:* **8** gemstone

materialistic 6 carnal, earthy **7** earthly, mundane, profane, secular, sensual, worldly

materialize 4 loom, rise, show **5** issue, reify **6** appear, embody, emerge, entify, show up, spring, typify **8** manifest **9** incarnate, objectify, personify, personize, take shape **10** pragmatize **11** exteriorize, hypostatize **12** substantiate

matériel 4 gear **6** outfit, tackle **8** tackling **9** apparatus, equipment, machinery **11** habiliments **13** accouterments, accoutrements, paraphernalia

maternal 6 mother **8** motherly

maternally related 5 enate
mathematician *American:* 5 Wiles
(Andrew) 6 Peirce (Charles S.), Veblen
(Oswald), Wiener (Norbert) *British:*
6 Stokes (George) *Dutch:* 7 Huygens
(Christiaan) *English:* 6 Newton (Isaac),
Taylor (Brook), Turing (Alan), Wallis (John)
7 Pearson (Karl), Russell (Bertrand)
9 Whitehead (Alfred North, Henry) *French:*
5 Borel (Emile), Comte (Auguste), Viète
(François) 6 Galois (Evariste), Pascal (Blaise), Picard (Charles-Emile) 7 Fourier
(Jean-Baptiste), Laplace (Marquis de), Vernier (Pierre) 8 Painlevé (Paul), Poincaré
(Jules-Henri) 9 Descartes (René) *German:*
5 Gauss (Carl), Wolff (Freiherr von)
6 Staudt (Karl von) 7 Riemann (Georg)
11 Weierstrass (Karl) *Greek:* 6 Euclid
10 Archimedes, Pythagoras *Italian:* 8 Vol-
terra (Vito) 10 Torricelli (Evangelista) *Norwegian:* 7 Stormer (Fredrik) *Russian:*
11 Lobachevsky (Nikolay) *Scottish:* 4 Tait
(Peter) 6 Napier (John) 8 Stirling (James)
Swiss: 5 Sturm (Jacques) 7 Steiner
(Jakob)
mathematics *branch:* 7 algebra 8 calculus, geometry 10 arithmetic 12 trigonome-
try *proven statement in:* 7 theorem
___ **Mather** 6 Cotton 7 Richard
8 Increase
Matred *daughter:* 9 Mehetabel *father:*
7 Mezahab *son-in-law:* 5 Hadar
matriarch 4 dame 6 mother 7 dowager
10 grande dame 13 materfamilias
matrimonial 6 bridal, wedded 7 marital,
married, nuptial, spousal 8 conjugal, hymeneal 9 connubial 11 epithalamic
matrimony 7 wedlock 8 marriage 11 conjugality 12 connubiality
matrix 3 die 6 cradle, gangue, strike
10 groundmass, truth table
matron 4 dame 7 dowager 10 grande
dame, parlormaid
Mattaniah *father:* 4 Bani, Elam, Mica
5 Asaph, Heman, Zattu 6 Josiah
10 Pahathmoab *grandson:* 5 Hanan *son:*
6 Zaccur 8 Shemaiah
Mattatha *father:* 6 Nathan *grandfather:*
5 David
Mattathias *father:* 5 Simon 6 Ananos
7 Absalom, Boethus 10 Theophilus *son:*
8 Josephus
matter 3 pus 4 body, core, gist, head,
mail, mean, meat, pith, text, to-do, tune
5 being, cause, count, motif, order, point,
range, sense, stuff, theme, thing, topic,
value, weigh, worry 6 affair, amount, burden, entity, extent, import, motive, object,
source, upshot 7 concern, signify, subject
8 argument, business, material, vicinity
9 grievance, magnitude, substance, suppu-

rate 10 individual 11 constituent, predicament 12 circumstance *added to book:*
8 addendum, appendix *coloring:* 3 dye
6 indigo 7 pigment 8 tinction 10 indigo
blue *combining form:* 3 hyl 4 hylo
decayed organic: 4 duff *diffused:*
5 vapor *in dispute:* 5 issue *inferior:*
5 trash *waste:* 5 dross 6 sewage
7 excreta *white:* 4 alba *worthless:* 4 slag
7 garbage
matter-of-fact 3 dry 4 cold 5 prose,
prosy, sober, sound, stoic 6 earthy, stolid
7 prosaic, prosing 9 apathetic, impassive,
objective, practical, pragmatic, realistic
10 hard-boiled, hardheaded, impersonal,
phlegmatic, unaffected 11 cold-blooded,
commonplace, down-to-earth, emotionless
12 unidealistic 13 unimpassioned, unsentimental
Matthew's father 8 Alphaeus
Mattithiah's father 4 Nebo 7 Shallum
8 Jeduthun
mattress 3 pad 4 sack *case:* 4 tick *fabric:*
7 ticking *straw:* 6 pallet
mature 3 age, due 4 grow, ripe, wane
5 adult, grown, olden, owing, ready, ripen,
round 6 flower, grow up, mellow, season,
unpaid 7 advance, blossom, decline,
develop, grown-up, outgrow, overdue,
payable, ripened 8 progress 9 developed,
full-blown, full-grown *combining form:*
3 tel 4 tele, telo
maudlin 5 mushy, silly 6 addled, slushy,
sticky 7 fuddled, mawkish, muddled
8 bathetic, confused, romantic 9 befuddled
11 sentimental, tear-jerking
Maugham character 4 Kear, Liza
5 Carey, Rosie, Sadie 7 Mildred 8 Crad-
dock 10 Strickland
maul 3 paw, row 4 bang, bash, club, fray,
lash, mace, whip 5 abuse, brawl, broil, flail,
melee, pound, set-to 6 batter, beetle, buffet, fracas, hammer, injure, molest, sledge
7 rough up, ruction 8 dogfight, maltreat
9 manhandle 10 donnybrook
Mauna ___ 3 Loa
maunder 3 bat, gad 5 drift, mooch, range
6 ramble 9 gallivant
Mauritania *capital:* 10 Nouakchott *monetary unit:* 7 ouguiya
Mauritius *capital:* 9 Port Louis *export:*
5 sugar *monetary unit:* 5 rupee
Maurois biographee 4 Hugo (Victor),
Sand (George) 5 Byron (Lord), Dumas
(Alexandre) 6 Proust (Marcel) 7 Shelley
(Percy Bysshe) 8 Disraeli (Benjamin)
mauve 6 purple, violet
maven, mavin 5 adept 6 expert, master
8 virtuoso 9 authority 10 past master, proficient 12 professional

maverick 5 stray 8 bohemian, unmarked 9 unbranded 13 nonconformist

maw 4 crop 7 stomach 9 poppy seed

mawkish 4 flat 5 banal, mushy 6 slushy, sticky 7 cloying, maudlin 8 bathetic, romantic 9 sickening 10 lovey-dovey, nauseating 11 sentimental, tear-jerking

maxilla 3 jaw 4 bone

maxim 3 law 4 rule 5 axiom, gnome, large, moral, motto 6 dictum, saying, truism 7 brocard, precept, proverb, theorem 8 aphorism, apothegm 9 platitude, prescript 11 commonplace

maximal 3 top 6 utmost 7 highest, topmost 8 greatest

maximize 7 magnify 8 overplay 10 overstress 13 overemphasize

maximum 3 top 6 utmost 7 highest, largest, supreme, topmost 8 extremum, greatest

may 5 shrub 6 spirea 8 hawthorn

maybe 7 perhaps 8 possible, possibly 9 perchance 10 indecision 11 uncertainty

Mayflower *document:* 7 Compact *passengers:* 8 pilgrims

mayhem 4 maim 7 cripple, dislimb 8 mutilate 9 dismember

mayor 11 burgomaster *Chicago (former):* 5 Daley (Richard) *New York (former):* 9 La Guardia (Fiorello) *Spanish:* 7 alcalde

Mayor of Casterbridge, The *author:* 5 Hardy (Thomas) *character:* 8 Henchard

maze 3 web 4 knot, mesh 5 skein, snarl 6 jungle, morass, tangle 7 confuse 8 bewilder, mishmash 9 labyrinth 10 hodgepodge, miscellany 11 gordian knot

MD 3 doc 6 doctor, medico 7 medical 8 sawbones 9 mediciner, physician

meadow 3 lea, ley 9 grassland *low-lying:* 5 haugh

meadow beauty 9 deer grass

meadow bird 8 bobolink

meadow chicken 8 sora rail

meadow hen 4 coot, rail 7 bittern

meadowlark 4 bird 5 acorn

meadow mushroom 6 agaric

meadow sorrel 4 dock

meager 4 bare, bony, lank, lean, mere, poor, thin 5 gaunt, lanky, scant, short, skimp, spare 6 lenten, scanty, scrimp, shabby, skimpy, skinny, slight, sparse 7 angular, minimum, scraggy, scrawny, scrimpy 8 exiguous, inferior, rawboned, scrimpit 9 deficient, miserable 10 inadequate 12 insufficient

meal 3 eat 4 chow, fare, feed, grub, take 5 board, feast, lunch, salep, snack, table 6 brunch, devour, dinner, farina, feed on, ingest, picnic, repast, spread, supper 7 consume, nooning 8 victuals 9 breakfast, collation, partake of, refection *army:* 4 mess

mealy 6 spotty, uneven 8 farinose 9 pollinose 11 farinaceous

mean 3 aim, low, mid, par, set, way 4 base, fair, hack, hint, mode, name, norm, pile, plan, poor, sick, so-so, ugly, want, wish 5 agent, borne, cheap, count, cruel, imply, lousy, lowly, mingy, organ, pesky, purse, rough, small, spell, tatty, tight, tough, weigh 6 agency, ailing, attest, center, common, denote, design, desire, donsie, estate, humble, import, intend, little, manner, matter, medial, medium, method, middle, narrow, offish, ornery, paltry, pocket, poorly, rugged, scrimy, scummy, scurvy, shabby, shoddy, sickly, sleazy, stingy, system, trashy, unwell, wealth, wicked 7 add up to, ashamed, average, betoken, capital, central, channel, connote, express, fairish, fashion, fortune, ignoble, limited, lowborn, miserly, nest egg, niggard, pitiful, propose, purpose, savings, scrimpy, signify, suggest, underly, vehicle 8 baseborn, beggarly, count for, déclassé, indicate, inferior, intimate, kindless, low-grade, mediocre, middling, ministry, moderate, off-color, ordinary, pitiable, plebeian, rubbishy, unwashed 9 apparatus, bastardly, designate, difficult, equipment, low-minded, machinery, niggardly, penurious, troublous, vexatious 10 despicable, despisable, formidable, indisposed, instrument, second-rate, unennobled 11 closefisted, contemplate, indifferent, ineffectual, second-class, tightfisted, troublesome 12 contemptible, intermediary, intermediate, narrow-fisted, second-drawer

meander 4 roam, rove, turn, wind 5 drift, range, snake, stray, twist 6 ramble 7 traipse 8 vagabond 9 gallivant, labyrinth

meandering 5 snaky 7 sinuous, winding 8 flexuous, tortuous 10 convoluted, serpentine 11 anfractuous

meandrous see meandering

meaning 3 aim 4 hint, plan 5 drift, force, point, sense, tenor, value 6 animus, design, effect, import, intent, object, syntax 7 essence, message, purport, purpose 9 intention, substance 10 definition, denotation, intendment, intimation, suggestion 11 acceptation, connotation, implication, significant 12 significance, significancy 13 signification, understanding

meaningful 4 rich 6 facund 7 weighty 8 eloquent, material, pregnant 9 important, momentous 10 expressive 11 sententious, significant, substantial 12 considerable 13 consequential

meaningless 5 blank, empty 6 vacant 7 fustian 10 unpurposed 13 insignificant

meanings *diverse:* 8 polysemy *study of:* 9 semantics

means 5 funds, money 6 agency, assets 7 quomodo 8 finances 9 apparatus, equipment, resources 10 instrument 11 wherewithal

meantime 8 interval

measly 4 poor, puny 5 petty 6 paltry 7 trivial 8 blighted, inferior, niggling, picayune, piddling, trifling 10 picayunish 12 pettifogging

measure 4 beat, bill, deal, meed, move, part, size, step, test, tune 5 bound, dance, gauge, index, limit, meter, metre, quota, rhyme, scale, share, shift, swing, weigh 6 amount, bounds, degree, effort, extent, figure, govern, melody, ration, reckon, resort, rhythm, size up, strain, survey 7 cadence, cadency, caliper, compute, delimit, mark out, melodia, portion, project, quantum, stopgap 8 calliper, estimate, indicate, maneuver, proposal, regulate, resource, rhythmus, standard 9 allotment, allowance, benchmark, calculate, calibrate, criterion, demarcate, determine, expedient, magnitude, makeshift, procedure, yardstick 10 delimitate, dimensions, indication, moderation, proceeding, proportion, temperance, touchstone 11 denominator, proposition 13 apportionment *area:* 4 acre 7 hectare 9 square rod 10 square foot, square inch, square mile, square yard 11 square meter *arrow weight:* 8 shilling *butter:* 4 span *capacity:* 4 gill, peck, pint 5 liter, minim, quart 6 bushel, gallon 8 fluidram 10 cubic meter, fluidounce, milliliter *cloth:* 3 ell *combining form:* 6 metric 8 metrical *depth:* 5 plumb, sound *electrical:* 7 coulomb *Hebrew:* (see at Hebrew) *horse height:* 4 hand *interstellar space:* 6 parsec *length:* 3 rod 4 foot, inch, mile, yard 5 cubit (ancient), meter 9 kilometer 10 centimeter *liquid:* 4 pint 5 pipet, quart 6 gallon 7 pipette *metrical foot:* 8 monopody *mixed drinks:* 6 jigger *of advantage:* 4 lead *of comparison:* 8 standard *out:* 5 batch *paper:* 4 ream *printer's:* 2 em, en 4 pica 5 point *radioactive decay:* 8 halflife *rotation:* 5 angle *silk size:* 8 drammage *Spanish dry:* 5 fanga 6 fanega *strength of solution:* 7 titrate *surface:* 3 are *thermodynamic:* 7 entropy 8 enthalpy *volume:* 9 cubic foot, cubic inch, cubic yard 10 cubic meter

Measure for Measure *character:* 6 Angelo, Juliet 7 Claudio, Mariana 8 Isabella 9 Vincentio *setting:* 6 Vienna

measurement 4 area 6 degree 8 capacity, quantity 9 dimension 11 mensuration *rain:* 8 udometry *weight:* 6 metage

measure up 3 tie 4 meet 5 equal, match, rival, touch

measuring *combining form:* 5 metry *device for liquid:* 7 venturi *rod:* 8 dipstick *stick:* 8 yardwand *tube:* 5 buret 7 burette

meat 4 core, food, gist, pith, pork, veal 5 flesh, jerky, sense, short, steak 6 burden, matter, thrust, upshot 7 charqui, edibles, nurture 8 victuals 9 foodstuff, provender, substance 10 provisions 11 comestibles *broiled:* 8 barbecue, grillade *broth:* 8 bouillon *cake:* 6 burger *cured:* 7 biltong *cut:* 3 rib 4 loin, rump 5 chuck, flank, plate, round, shank 7 brisket, sirloin 8 rib roast 9 club steak, rump roast, short loin, short ribs 10 blade roast, flank steak, round steak, T-bone steak 11 arm pot roast 12 boneless neck, pinbone steak, sirloin steak 13 blade rib roast, crosscut shank *dealer:* 7 butcher *deer:* 7 venison *dried:* 5 jerky *fastening pin:* 6 skewer *holding rod:* 4 spit *juices:* 5 gravy *minced:* 7 rissole *packer:* 5 Swift 6 Armour *raw:* 6 gobbet *roasting shop:* 10 rotisserie *rounded mass of:* 9 croquette *seasoned:* 7 sausage 8 pastrami, pastromi *sheep:* 6 mutton *side:* 8 sowbelly *skewered:* 5 kabab, kabob, kebob *slice:* 6 cutlet, rasher *small portion:* 6 collop *tough part:* 7 gristle

meat-eating 11 carnivorous

meathead 3 oaf 4 gawk, lout, lump 5 klutz, looby 6 lubber 7 palooka

Mebd *husband:* 6 Ailill *victim:* 10 Cuchulainn

Mecca *country:* 11 Saudi Arabia *pilgrimage:* 4 hadj, hajj *port:* 5 Jidda *shrine:* 5 Caaba, Kaaba

mechanic 7 artisan 9 automatic, machinist 10 uninspired

mechanism 4 gear 5 ratch, slide, steer 6 cutoff, infeed, rachet 7 ratchet 8 rackwork, signaler 9 apparatus *bookbinder's:* 7 gripper *card game:* 7 holdout *clutch:* 8 throwout *dam:* 7 tripper *fastening:* 5 catch *firearm:* 7 ejector, gunlock *guiding:* 5 apron *part:* 7 trippet *printing:* 8 elevator *raising:* 4 lift *timepiece:* 7 setting

meddle 3 pry 4 fool, nose 5 snoop 6 butt in, dabble, horn in, invade, kibitz, monkey, putter, tamper, tinker 7 intrude, obtrude 8 busybody, trespass 9 interfere, interlope, intervene 10 mess around, monkey with, tamper with

meddlesome 4 busy 9 intrusive, obtrusive, officious 11 impertinent 13 polypragmatic

Medea *brother:* 8 Absyrtus *father:* 6 Aeëtes *husband:* 5 Jason 6 Aegeus *son:* 6 Medeus *victim:* 6 Creusa, Glauce, Glauke

medial 3 mid 4 fair, mean 6 center, middle 7 average, central, fairish, halfway, midmost **8** middling, moderate **10** centermost, middlemost **11** equidistant, indifferent **12** intermediary, intermediate

median see **medial**

mediate 6 convey, liaise, step in **9** intercede, interfere, interpose, intervene

mediator 5 judge **6** broker **7** arbiter **9** go-between, middleman **10** interagent, interceder, peacemaker **11** intercessor

medical 3 doc **6** doctor **9** physician *instrument:* **11** cardiograph, stethoscope

medical treatment *combining form:* **5** iatry **6** iatric **7** iatrics **8** iatrical

medicament 4 cure **6** physic, remedy **9** pharmacon *inert:* **7** placebo

medication see **medicament**

medicinal 4 drug **8** biologic, salutary, sanative **12** pharmaceutic *extract:* **10** belladonna

medicine 4 cure **5** bromo **6** physic, remedy **7** anodyne, nostrum **8** busulfan, poultice **9** pharmacon **11** antipyretic, magical rite **12** magical power *ball:* **4** pill *bottle:* **4** vial *branch:* **7** surgery **8** posology **9** pathology **10** bariatrics, geriatrics, gynecology, obstetrics, pediatrics *cathartic:* **8** evacuant **9** purgative *combining form:* **5** iatro **8** pharmaco *quantity of:* **4** dose **6** dosage *shell:* **7** capsule *soothing:* **7** nervine **8** lenitive, sedative

medicine man 6 doctor, kahuna, shaman

medieval *guild:* **5** Hanse *military unit:* **5** lance *study:* **5** logic **6** trivia (plural) **7** grammar, trivium **8** rhetoric

mediocre 3 bad **4** fair, hack, mean, poor, so-so **6** common **7** average, fairish **8** inferior, middling, moderate, ordinary, passable **10** bush-league **11** commonplace

meditate 4 muse, roll **6** intend, ponder **7** purpose, revolve **8** consider, mull over, ruminate, turn over **9** reflect on **10** deliberate **11** contemplate

meditator 4 yogi **5** yogin

Mediterranean 11 Mare Nostrum **12** Mare Internum *coastal region:* **7** Riviera *eastern shores:* **6** Levant *island:* (see at **island**) *vessel:* **5** setee **6** settee *wind:* **6** solano **7** mistral, sirocco

medium 3 par **4** fair, mean, so-so **5** agent, forte, organ, radio **6** agency, métier, milieu, normal, oyster, vulgar **7** ambient, average, channel, climate, fairish, neutral, popular, vehicle **8** ambience, eminency, long suit, middling, ministry, moderate, passable, standard **9** go-between, run-of-mine, tolerable **10** atmosphere, compromise, instrument, middle-rate, strong suit, television **11** clairvoyant, environment *nutrient:* **7** culture *of exchange:* **5** money *of radio transmission:* **3** air **7** airwave

medley 4 brew, olio **6** jumble **7** mélange **8** pastiche **9** pasticcio, patchwork, potpourri **10** assortment, hodgepodge, miscellany **11** gallimaufry

Medusa 6 Gorgon *father:* **7** Phorcus, Phorcys *mother:* **4** Ceto *offspring:* **7** Pegasus **8** Chrysaor *sister:* **6** Stheno **7** Euryale *slayer:* **7** Perseus

meed 3 due **4** part, plum **5** merit, prize, quota, share **6** amount, carrot, desert, ration, reward **7** guerdon, measure, portion, premium, quantum **8** dividend **9** allotment, allowance **12** recompensing, satisfaction **13** apportionment

meek 4 mild, tame, weak **5** lowly **6** gentle, humble, modest **7** lenient, patient **8** moderate, tolerant **10** forbearing, submissive, unassuming **13** long-suffering

meerschaum 4 pipe **6** gravel **9** sepiolite

meet 3 apt, fit, hit, sit, tie **4** bump, espy, face, fair, fill, find, good, join, just, luck, open, spot **5** brave, catch, clash, close, cross, equal, event, focus, front, greet, happy, hit on, light, match, right, rival, touch, unite **6** accost, answer, chance, descry, detect, engage, happen, oppose, proper, salute, settle, suffer, take on, tumble, turn up, tussle, useful **7** affront, collide, contest, convene, fitting, fulfill, grapple, hit upon, satisfy, stumble, sustain, undergo, wrestle **8** approach, assemble, come upon, concours, conflict, confront, converge, cope with, suitable **9** concenter, conformed, encounter, equitable, impinge on, measure up, rencontre **10** applicable, congregate, convenient, experience, felicitous, provide for, reconciled **11** appropriate, competition *a bet:* **3** see *a need:* **7** suffice *athletic:* **8** gymkhana *by appointment:* **10** rendezvous

meeting 4 moot, talk **5** tryst **6** parley, powwow **7** contest, session **8** assembly, conclave, concours, conflict, congress, junction **9** concourse, encounter, gathering, rencontre **10** concursion, conference, confluence **11** competition **12** intersection *Anglo-Saxon:* **5** gemot **6** gemote *place:* **5** forum *spiritual:* **6** séance

Mefistofele composer 5 Boito (Arrigo)

Megaera see **Erinyes**

megaphone 7 address **8** bullhorn **10** mouthpiece

Megara *father:* **5** Creon *husband:* **8** Heracles, Hercules *king:* **5** Nisus

megillah 5 story **6** scroll **7** account

megrim 4 urge, whim **5** fancy, freak, humor, whiff **6** whimsy **7** boutade, caprice, conceit, impulse, vertigo **8** crotchet, migraine **9** dizziness

Mehetabel *husband:* **5** Hadar *mother:* **6** Matred *son:* **7** Delaiah

Mehitabel 3 cat *creator:* 7 Marquis (Don) *friend:* 5 Archy

Mein Kampf author 6 Hitler (Adolf)

meiosis 7 litotes 12 cell division

Meistersinger 4 Folz (Hans) 5 Sachs (Hans)

melancholic 3 sad 6 triste 7 joyless 8 mournful 9 depressed, saddening 10 depressing

melancholy 3 sad 5 blues, dumps, ennui, gloom, sorry 6 dismal, dreary, gloomy, misery, rueful, somber, tedium, triste, woeful 7 boredom, despair, dismals, doleful, joyless, moanful, pensive, sadness, sighful, unhappy, wailful 8 dejected, dolesome, dolorous, funereal, mournful, saddened, sombrous 9 dejection, plaintive, saddening, sorrowful 10 afflicting, depressing, depression, disturbing, lachrymose, lamentable, lugubrious, perturbing, reflective, thoughtful 11 desperation, disquieting, unhappiness 12 discomposing, heavyhearted, mournfulness, wretchedness 13 miserableness

mélange see **medley**

Melanippe's son 6 Aeolus

Melanippus *father:* 7 Theseus *slayer:* 10 Amphiaraus *victim:* 6 Tydeus

Melchior *companion:* 6 Gaspar 9 Balthazar *gift:* 4 gold

Melchizedek's kingdom 5 Salem

meld 3 mix 4 fuse 5 blend, merge 6 mingle 8 compound 9 interfuse 10 amalgamate, interblend 11 intermingle

Meleager *beloved:* 8 Atalanta *father:* 6 Oeneus *mother:* 7 Althaea *victim:* 4 boar

Melech's father 5 Micah

melee 3 row 4 fray, hash, riot, stew 5 brawl, broil, brush, clash, fight 6 affray, fracas, jumble, ruckus 7 ruction, scuffle 8 dogfight, mishmash, pastiche, skirmish 9 potpourri, scrimmage 10 donnybrook, free-for-all, hodgepodge, miscellany

Melicertes *father:* 7 Athamas *mother:* 3 Ino

meliorate 4 help 5 amend 6 better, soften 7 improve

Mélisande's lover 7 Pelleas

melisma 3 air, lay 4 song, tune 6 strain, warble 7 cadenza, descant, measure 8 diapason

mellifluous 5 sweet 6 dulcet, golden, liquid, smooth 7 honeyed, silvery 8 euphonic, Hyblaean, resonant 9 accordant 13 golden-tongued, silver-tongued

mellisonant 5 sweet 6 dulcet 7 tuneful 8 euphonic 10 euphonious

mellow 3 age 4 aged 5 ripen 6 genial, golden, grow up, liquid, mature 7 develop, honeyed, matured, ripened

melodic 5 sweet, tuned 6 dulcet 7 musical, songful, tuneful 8 canorous 10 euphonious

melodious 5 lyric, sweet, tuned 6 dulcet 7 musical, songful, tuneful 8 euphonic, soundful 9 cantabile

melody 3 air, lay 4 sing, song, tune 5 canto 6 lyrics, strain, warble 7 descant, measure 8 bel canto, diapason, vocalize 11 tunefulness

melon 4 pepo 5 gourd, mango 6 casaba, papaya 7 cassaba 8 honeydew 10 cantaloupe

Melpomene see **Muse**

melt 3 rin, run 4 bake, burn, cook, flux, fuse, thaw, warm 5 blend, broil, roast, sweat 6 scorch, soften, spleen 7 liquefy, liquify, swelter 8 dissolve, liquesce, perspire, unfreeze 9 disappear 10 deliquesce *down:* 6 render *together:* 4 fuse

Melville *character:* 3 Pip 4 Ahab, Toby 5 Bembo, Chase 6 Cereno, Jermin, Pierre 7 Fayaway, Ishmael 8 Bartleby, Queequeg, Starbuck *novel:* 4 Omoo 5 Mardi, Typee 6 Pierre 7 Redburn 8 Moby Dick 11 White Jacket

member 3 cut 4 part 5 penis, piece 6 clause, moiety, parcel 7 portion, section, segment 8 division *architectural:* 3 fan 7 cornice *armed forces:* 5 cadet 6 airman, Marine, sailor 7 soldier *chivalry order:* 6 knight *combining form:* 3 mer 4 crat, mere 5 ocrat *gang:* 7 mobster 8 henchman 10 hatchet man *Girl Scout:* 7 brownie, Cadette *household:* 8 familiar *legislative:* 7 senator *mendicant order:* 5 friar 9 Dominican *middle class:* 7 burgher *monastic order:* 4 monk 5 friar 6 hermit *Parliament:* 2 MP *political party:* 4 Tory, Whig 7 Liberal 8 Democrat, Laborite 9 Communist, Socialist 10 Republican 12 Conservative *secret society:* 7 DeMolay, tongman 8 Klansman, Ku Kluxer *senior male:* 5 doyen *service club:* 4 Lion 8 Kiwanian, Rotarian *structural:* 4 arch *suffix:* 2 ad, id *triangular:* 5 gable

membrane 6 pleura 7 pleurae (plural) *bodily:* 6 serosa 7 serosae (plural) *brain:* 3 pia *combining form:* 3 vel 5 chori, hymen 6 chorio, hymeno, mening, myring 7 meningi, meningo, myringo *diffusion through:* 7 osmosis *dividing:* 5 septa (plural) 6 septum *ear:* 8 tympanum *enclosing:* 8 indusium *thin:* 6 lamina 7 lamella, laminae (plural) 8 lamellae (plural) *wing:* 8 patagium

memento 5 relic, token, trace 6 shadow, trophy 7 vestige 8 keepsake, reminder, souvenir 11 remembrance 12 remembrancer

Memnon *father:* 8 Tithonus *mother:* 3 Eos 6 Aurora *slayer:* 8 Achilles

memoir 3 bio 4 life 6 record, report, thesis 8 anecdote, tractate, treatise 9 biography, discourse, monograph 10 monography 11 confessions, remembrance 12 disquisition, dissertation, recollection, reminiscence 13 autobiography

memoirist 7 Boswell 10 biographer

memorable 6 rubric 9 deathless, momentous, red-letter 10 impressive, noteworthy, remembered 11 significant 13 distinguished

memorandum 4 chit, note 5 diary 6 letter, minute, notice 7 epistle, message, missive, tickler 8 dispatch, notation, reminder 9 directive 12 announcement

memorial 4 note 5 relic, token, trace 6 record, trophy 7 relique 8 keepsake, monument, reminder, souvenir 10 dedicatory, enshrining 11 celebrative, remembrance 12 consecrative, remembrancer 13 commemoration, commemorative, commemoratory *mound:* 4 carn 5 cairn

memorial park 8 cemetery, God's acre 9 graveyard 10 necropolis 11 polyandrium 12 burial ground, potter's field 13 burying ground

memorize 3 con, get 5 learn, study 8 remember

memory 4 mind 6 recall 8 mind's eye, souvenir 9 anamnesis, awareness, retention 10 cognizance, reflection 11 remembrance 12 recollection, reminiscence 13 concentration, consciousness, retentiveness, retrospection *assisting:* 8 mnemonic *combining form:* 4 mnem 5 mnemo 6 mnesia *loss:* 7 amnesia

menace 4 loom, risk 5 alarm, lower, peril, scare 6 danger, hazard, threat 7 imperil, jeopard, torment 8 endanger, frighten, jeopardy, threaten 10 jeopardize

ménage 5 folks, house 6 family 8 quarters 9 household 12 housekeeping

Menahem *father:* 4 Gadi *son:* 8 Pekahiah *victim:* 7 Shallum

mend 3 fix, sew 4 cure, darn, do up, gain, heal, vamp 5 patch, ready, renew 6 bushel, cobble, doctor, look up, perk up, reform, remedy, repair, revamp 7 correct, improve, patch up, rebuild, rectify, redress, restore, service 8 overhaul, renovate 9 condition, refurbish 10 ameliorate, convalesce, recuperate, rejuvenate 11 recondition, reconstruct

mendacious 5 false, lying, wrong 6 shifty 7 fibbing, knavish, roguish 8 unhonest 9 deceitful, dishonest, paltering 10 untruthful 12 equivocating 13 prevaricating

mendacity 7 dodging, fibbery, hedging 8 boggling, caviling, shifting 9 falsehood, quibbling 12 equivocation, sidestepping 13 truthlessness

mendelevium *symbol:* 2 Md

mendicancy 7 beggary, bumming, cadging 8 mooching, sponging 11 panhandling

mendicant 5 friar 6 beggar 7 begging

Mending Wall author 5 Frost (Robert)

Menelaus *brother:* 9 Agamemnon *father:* 6 Atreus *kingdom:* 6 Sparta *mother:* 6 Aerope *wife:* 5 Helen

menial 5 lowly 6 humble 7 servile, slavish 8 obeisant 10 obsequious 11 subservient

Men in White author 8 Kingsley (Sidney)

Menlo Park inventor 6 Edison (Thomas Alva)

menopause 11 climacteric 12 change of life

Menotti, Gian Carlo *character:* 5 Amahl *opera:* 9 The Consul, The Medium 12 The Telephone

men's store 12 haberdashery

mental 5 inner 6 genial 7 psychic 8 thinking 9 reasoning, spiritual 10 immaterial, telepathic 11 ideological, intelligent 12 intellective, intellectual 13 psychological *faculty:* 6 memory

mentality 3 wit 5 sense 6 brains 7 outlook 9 mother wit 10 brainpower 12 intelligence

mention 4 cite, name, note 5 quote, refer 6 advert, allude, detail 7 refer to, specify 8 instance 9 designate, reference 10 denominate

mentor 5 coach 7 teacher

Mentor's pupil 10 Telemachus

menu 4 card, diet 5 carte 7 regimen 10 bill of fare 11 carte du jour *item:* 4 soup 5 salad 6 entrée 7 dessert 9 appetizer

Mephibosheth *father:* 4 Saul 8 Jonathan *mother:* 6 Rizpah

Mephistophelian 7 satanic 8 devilish, diabolic

mephitic 4 olid 5 fetid, funky, musty 6 poison, smelly 7 noisome, noxious, reeking, stenchy 8 stinking, toxicant, venomous, virulent 9 poisonous 10 malodorous

Merab *father:* 4 Saul *husband:* 6 Adriel

Meraioth *father:* 6 Ahitub 8 Zerahiah *son:* 5 Zadok

Merari *brother:* 6 Kohath 7 Gershon *daughter:* 6 Judith *father:* 4 Levi *son:* 5 Mahli, Mushi

mercenary 4 grub, hack 5 venal 6 drudge, slavey 7 corrupt, grubber, soldier 8 hireling

merchandise 4 line, sell 5 cargo, goods, stock, trade, wares 6 deal in, job lot, market, retail 7 effects, staples, traffic 9 publicize, vendibles 11 commodities

merchandiser 9 tradesman 11 businessman

merchant 5 buyer 6 dealer, jobber, seller, trader, vender, vendor 7 peddler 8 purveyor, retailer 9 tradesman 10 specialist, trafficker, wholesaler 11 businessman, storekeeper *guild:* 5 hansa, hanse *Hindu:* 6 banian, banyan *League:* 9 Hanseatic *ship:* 5 oiler 6 argosy, coaler, galiot, packet, tanker, trader 7 collier, galliot, steamer 8 Indiaman 9 freighter *wine:* 7 vintner

Merchant of Venice 7 Antonio *character:* 6 Portia 7 Jessica, Lorenzo, Nerissa, Shylock 8 Bassanio

merciful 4 easy, kind 6 benign, humane, kindly 7 clement, lenient, sparing 8 tolerant 9 condoning, forgiving, indulgent, pardoning 10 charitable, forbearing 11 softhearted 13 compassionate

merciless 4 grim 5 cruel, harsh 6 mortal, savage, wanton 9 cutthroat, ferocious, unpitying 10 gratuitous, implacable, ironfisted, unyielding 11 uncalled-for, unflinching, unrelenting 12 unappeasable

mercurial 6 adroit, clever, fickle, mobile 7 buoyant, cunning, elastic, movable 8 ticklish, unstable, variable, volatile 9 expansive, ingenious, resilient, sprightly 10 capricious, changeable, inconstant, lubricious 12 effervescent 13 temperamental

mercury 5 azoth 9 poison ivy 11 quicksilver *ore:* 8 cinnabar *symbol:* 2 Hg

Mercury 6 planet; (see also **Hermes**)

Mercutio *friend:* 5 Romeo *slayer:* 6 Tybalt

mercy 4 pity, ruth 5 grace 6 lenity 7 caritas, charity 8 clemency, goodwill, kindness, leniency 9 benignity, tolerance 10 compassion, generosity, kindliness 11 benevolence, forbearance 13 commiseration *petition for:* 5 kyrie 8 miserere

mere 3 fen 4 bare, lake, pool, pure, very 5 marsh 9 undiluted

Mered's father 5 Ezrah

merely 3 but 4 just, only 5 quite 6 simply, wholly

Meremoth's father 4 Bani 5 Uriah

meretricious 4 loud 5 gaudy 6 brazen, flashy, garish, tawdry, tinsel 7 blatant, chintzy, glaring 8 delusive, delusory 9 deceptive, insincere 10 misleading

merganser 4 duck, smew

merge 3 mix 4 fuse, join 5 blend, unify, unite 6 mingle 7 combine 8 coalesce, compound 9 commingle, interfuse 10 amalgamate, interblend 11 consolidate, intermingle

mergence   see **merging**

merger 5 union 9 coalition 11 coaduna- tion, combination, unification 12 amalgam- ation 13 consolidation

merging 5 union 9 coalition 11 coaduna- tion, combination, unification 13 consolida- tion

meridian 4 acme, apex, peak 6 apogee, climax, comble, summit, zenith 8 pinnacle

merit 3 due 4 earn, rate 5 arete, award, lumps, repay, value, worth 6 reward, rights, virtue 7 caliber, deserts, deserve, entitle, justify, quality, requite, stature, warrant 9 deserving 10 excellence, excellency, per- fection, recompense

meritable   see **meritorious**

merited 3 due 4 just 5 right 7 condign 8 deserved, rightful, suitable 9 requisite 11 appropriate 13 rhadamanthine

meritorious 6 worthy 8 laudable 9 admi- rable, deserving, estimable, honorable, praisable 11 commendable, thankworthy 12 praiseworthy

merlin 6 falcon 10 pigeon hawk

mermaid 7 manatee 8 sirenian 11 sire- nomelus

Merodach   see **Marduk**

Merope *father:* 5 Atlas 8 Oenopion *hus- band:* 7 Polybus 8 Sisyphus 11 Cres- phontes *lover:* 5 Orion *mother:* 7 Pleione *sisters:* 8 Pleiades *son:* 7 Aepytus, Glau- cus

merriment 4 glee 5 mirth, revel 6 gaiety 7 jollity, revelry, whoopee 8 hilarity, revel- ing 9 festivity, jocundity, joviality 10 jocu- larity, jubilation 13 entertainment

merry 3 gay, mad 4 boon, gean, glad, high, wild 5 happy, jolly, riant, sharp 6 blithe, jocund, jovial, joyful, joyous, lively 7 festive, gleeful, intense 8 animated, cheerful, gleesome, laughing, mirthful 9 hilarious, sprightly, vivacious 10 blithe- some 12 lighthearted 13 unconstrained

merry-andrew 4 zany 5 clown 7 buffoon 9 harlequin 10 mountebank

merrymaking 5 party, revel 6 gaiety 7 jollity, revelry, whoopee 8 pleasure 9 enjoyment, festivity, revelment 10 indul- gence 12 conviviality

Merry Widow composer 5 Lehar (Franz)

Merry Wives of Windsor, The *charac- ter:* 3 Nym 4 Ford, Page 5 Caius 6 Fen- ton, Pistol 7 Slender 8 Falstaff

mesa 5 bench 7 plateau 9 cartouche, tableland

mescal 5 agave 6 cactus, liquor, maguey

mesh 3 net, web 4 knot, maze, nett 5 skein, snarl 6 accord, engagé, jungle, morass, tangle 7 mizmaze, netting, network 8 entangle 9 harmonize, interlock, labyrinth 10 coordinate

Mesha *father:* 9 Shaharaim *kingdom:* 4 Moab *mother:* 6 Hodesh

Meshech's father 7 Japheth

meshuggaas 4 guff 6 drivel 7 twaddle 8 claptrap, nonsense 9 poppycock 10 balderdash

Meshullam *father:* 4 Bani 5 Zadok 9 Berechiah, Besodeiah 10 Shephatiah, Zerubbabel 12 Meshillemith *son:* 5 Sallu 7 Hilkiah

Meshullemeth *husband:* 8 Manasseh *son:* 4 Amon

mesmeric 5 siren 7 drawing 8 alluring, charming 9 glamorous 10 attractive, bewitching, enchanting 11 captivating

mesmerize 4 grip, hold 7 catch up 8 enthrall, entrance 9 fascinate, hypnotize, spellbind

Mesopotamia *civilization:* 7 Assyria 9 Babylonia *river:* 6 Tigris 9 Euphrates

mess 4 hash, mull, play 5 botch, catch, gum up, mix up, snafu, wreck 6 bobble, bollix, bungle, dabble, doodle, fiddle, fright, goof up, jumble, muddle, potter, puddle, putter, tinker, trifle 7 bitch up, confuse, desight, eyesore, louse up 8 botchery, disarray, dishevel, disorder, shambles, wreckage 9 confusion 10 disarrange, hodgepodge, miscellany 11 monstrosity *up:* 5 touse 6 tousle, touzle, untidy

message 4 note, word 5 sense 6 import, letter, report 7 epistle, evangel, meaning, mission, purport 8 dispatch, telegram 9 directive, telegraph 10 communiqué, intendment, memorandum 11 acceptation 12 significance 13 communication, signification

Messalina's husband 8 Claudius

mess around 4 fool, idle, wolf 5 flirt 6 butt in, dabble, dawdle, doodle, fiddle, horn in, meddle, potter, puddle, putter, tinker 7 intrude 8 busybody, womanize 9 associate, interfere, interlope, manhandle, philander 10 monkey with, tamper with

messenger 4 post 5 envoy 6 herald 7 apostle, courier 8 emissary 9 character, go-between 11 internuncio 12 intermediary *God's:* 5 angel *of the gods:* 6 Hermes 7 Mercury *Turkish:* 6 chiaus, chouse

Messiah composer 6 Handel (George Frideric)

messy 5 dirty, grimy 6 botchy, sloppy, unneat, untidy 7 raunchy, unkempt 8 careless, ill-kempt, slapdash, slipshod, slovenly 10 disheveled, unthorough 12 unfastidious *abode:* 3 sty

Mestor *father:* 7 Perseus *mother:* 9 Andromeda

metal 4 gold 5 steel, sword 6 bronze *alloy:* (see alloy) *casting mold:* 5 ingot *corrosion:* 4 rust *design:* 7 chasing *dross:* 4 slag *drum:* 8 canister *fittings:* 5 brass *in mass:* 7 bullion *layer:* 7 plating *lump:* 6 nugget *magnetic:* 4 iron *piece:* 4 slug *refuse:* 6 scoria *sheath:* 5 armor *substance:* 5 alloy *surface scum:* 5 dross *thin:* 4 foil, leaf 5 plate *type:* 7 quadrat *unite:* 6 solder *worker:* 5 smith 10 blacksmith

metallic element 3 tin 4 gold, iron, lead, zinc 6 barium, cobalt, copper, nickel, radium, silver, sodium 7 arsenic, bismuth, lithium, mercury, uranium 8 aluminum, platinum, tungsten, vanadium 9 magnesium, manganese, potassium, strontium 10 molybdenum

metamere 6 somite 7 segment

metamorphic *rock:* 5 slate 6 gneiss, marble, schist 9 quartzite, soapstone

metamorphose 3 age 5 ripen 6 change, mature 7 commute, convert, develop 9 transform, translate, transmute 11 transfigure 12 transmogrify

metamorphosis 6 change 8 changing *combining form:* 3 ody

Metamorphosis author 5 Kafka (Franz)

metanoia 7 rebirth 10 conversion

metaphor 5 trope 6 simile 7 analogy 8 allegory 10 comparison, similitude

metaphorical compound 7 kenning

metaphysical 8 bodiless, numinous, superior 9 unearthly, unfleshly 10 discarnate, immaterial, superhuman, suprahuman 12 supermundane, supernatural, supramundane, supranatural, transcendent 13 preternatural *poet:* 5 Donne (John) 7 Crashaw (Richard), Herbert (George), Marvell (Andrew)

mete 4 deal, dole, give 5 allot 6 parcel 7 portion 8 allocate, dispense 9 apportion

meteor 8 fireball 12 shooting star *exploding:* 5 bolis 6 bolide *shower:* 5 Lyrid 6 Leonid, Taurid 7 Aquarid, Geminid, Orionid, Perseid 10 Quadrantid *suffix:* 2 id

meteorite 8 aerolite, aerolith 10 siderolite

meter 4 beat, scan 5 rhyme, swing 6 rhythm 7 cadence, cadency, measure, versify

metheglin 4 mead 8 beverage *ingredient:* 5 honey

method 3 way 4 form, line, mode, modi (plural), plan, wise 5 means, modus, order, style, track 6 course, design, manner, schema, scheme, system 7 fashion, formula, pattern, process, routine, technic, wrinkle 8 practice 9 procedure, technique 11 orderliness 13 modus operandi *careful:* 8 strategy *of employing troops:* 6 tactic *of procedure:* 2 MO 4 game

methodical 5 exact 7 careful, orderly, precise, regular 9 organized 10 scrupulous, systematic 12 systematized

Methuselah *father:* 5 Enoch *grandson:* 4 Noah *son:* 6 Lamech

Methushael *father:* 8 Mehujael *son:* 6 Lamech

meticulous 4 neat 5 exact, fussy, picky 6 strict 7 careful, finicky, heedful 8 punctual, thorough 10 pernickety 11 microscopic, painstaking 12 conscionable

métier 3 art 4 mode 5 craft, forte, trade 7 calling 8 business, eminency, long suit, vocation 10 handicraft, profession, strong suit

metrical foot 4 iamb 5 iambi (plural), ionic, paeon 6 cretic, dactyl, iambic, iambus 7 anapest, pyrrhic, spondee, triseme, trochee 8 bacchius, choriamb, spondaic, tribrach, trochaic

metric unit *area:* 7 centare, deciare, hectare *capacity:* 5 liter 9 decaliter, deciliter, kiloliter 10 centiliter, hectoliter, milliliter *length:* 5 meter 9 decameter, decimeter, kilometer 10 centimeter, hectometer, millimeter, myriameter *mass and weight:* 4 gram 7 quintal 8 decagram, decigram, kilogram 9 centigram, hectogram, metric ton, milligram *volume:* 5 stere 9 decastere, decistere

metropolis 4 city 7 capital 13 mother country

metropolitan 5 urban 6 urbane 10 archbishop

mettle 4 guts 5 heart, pluck, spunk 6 spirit, temper 7 cojones, courage 10 resolution 12 spiritedness 13 dauntlessness

mettlesome 4 edgy 5 beany, fiery 6 spunky 7 gingery, peppery 8 skittish, spirited 9 excitable, startlish 10 high-strung 11 high-hearted 12 high-spirited

mew 3 hem, pen 4 cage, coop, gull, molt, mure 5 fence 6 corral, immure, shut in 7 enclose 8 hideaway

mewl 4 meow 5 whine 7 whimper

Mexico *aborigine:* 4 Maya 5 Aztec *coin:* 7 centavo *conqueror:* 6 Cortes, Cortez (Hernan, Hernando) *crop:* 5 sisal *emperor:* 10 Maximilian *estate:* 8 hacienda *ethnic group:* 6 Indian 7 Mestizo *export:* 6 coffee, cotton, sulfur 9 petroleum *food:* 4 masa, taco 5 chili, salsa 6 tamale 7 burrito, panocha, penuche, tostada 8 frijoles, tortilla 9 enchilada, guacamole 10 quesadilla 11 chimichanga *house:* 5 jacal *language:* 7 Spanish *liquor:* 7 tequila *monetary unit:* 4 peso *oil enterprise:* 5 PEMEX *reformer:* 6 Juarez (Benito) *revolutionist:* 5 Villa (Pancho) 6 Zapata (Emiliano) 8 Carranza (Venustiano) *stimulant:* 6 mescal

mezzanine 5 story 7 balcony 8 entresol

mezzo-soprano *American:* 5 Elias (Rosalind), Horne (Marilyn), Jones (Sissieretta) 6 Bumbry (Grace) 7 Verrett (Shirley) 8 Troyanos (Tatiana), von Stade (Frederica) *Austrian:* 6 Ludwig (Christa) *English:* 5 Baker (Janet) *Italian:* 8 Cossotto (Fiorenza)

Miami *bowl:* 6 Orange *chief:* 12 Little Turtle *county:* 4 Dade *stadium:* 9 Joe Robbie *team:* 4 Heat 7 Marlins 8 Dolphins, Panthers

miasma 4 smog

mib 5 agate 6 marble

mica 4 talc 7 biotite 8 silicate 9 muscovite

Mica *father:* 6 Zichri 12 Mephibosheth *grandfather:* 8 Jonathan

Micah *father:* 9 Meribbaal *son:* 5 Abdon

Micaiah *father:* 5 Imlah, Uriel 8 Gemariah *grandfather:* 7 Absalom *husband:* 8 Rehoboam *mother:* 5 Tamar *son:* 6 Abijah, Achbor

Michelangelo *painting:* 10 Holy Family 12 Last Judgment *statue:* 5 David, Moses, Pietà 7 Bacchus

Michener novel 5 Space, Texas 6 Hawaii, Poland 8 Caravans, Sayonara 9 The Source 10 Centennial, Chesapeake 11 The Covenant, The Drifters 16 The Fires of Spring 18 The Bridges of Toko-ri

Michigan *capital:* 7 Lansing *college:* 4 Alma *highest point:* 9 Mt. Curwood *largest city:* 7 Detroit *nickname:* 9 Lake State 14 Wolverine State *state bird:* 5 robin *state flower:* 12 apple blossom

microfilm sheet 5 fiche

Micronesia *political division:* 4 Guam 5 Nauru 6 Tuvalu 8 Kiribati

microorganism 4 germ 5 virus 6 aerobe 7 bacilli (plural), microbe 8 bacillus, bacteria (plural), pathogen, protozoa (plural) 9 bacterium, protozoan

microphone 3 bug 4 mike *shield:* 4 gobo

microscope 7 magnify 9 magnifier 10 instrument *part:* 5 stage 6 mirror 8 eyepiece 9 objective

microscopic 4 tiny 5 small 6 minute

midday 4 noon, sext 8 noontide, noontime

middle 4 core, mean 5 mesne, waist 6 center, medial, median 7 central, halfway 8 interior 10 centermost 11 equidistant, intervening 12 intermediary, intermediate *combining form:* 3 mes 4 medi, meso 5 medio, mesio

Middle America country 4 Cuba 5 Haiti 6 Mexico, Panama 8 Honduras 9 Costa Rica, Guatemala, Nicaragua 10 El Salvador

Middle Atlantic State 7 New York 9 New Jersey 12 Pennsylvania

middlebrow 4 boob 7 Babbitt 10 philistine

middle class 11 bourgeoisie

middle-class 9 bourgeois

middle ear *bone:* 5 incus 6 stapes 7 malleus *membrane:* 7 eardrum 8 tympanum

Middle East country 4 Iran, Iraq, Oman 5 Egypt, Qatar, Sudan, Syria, Yemen 6 Cyprus, Israel, Jordan, Kuwait, Turkey 7 Bahrain, Lebanon 11 Saudi Arabia

Middle Kingdom 5 China

middleman 6 broker 7 bailiff 8 mediator 9 go-between 10 interagent, interceder 11 intercessor 12 entrepreneur, intermediary, intermediate 13 intermediator

Middlemarch author 5 Eliot (George)

middle-of-the-road 8 moderate 9 softshell

middling 4 fair, mean, poor, so-so 6 fairly, flitch, medium, rather 7 average, fairish 8 inferior, mediocre, moderate 10 moderately, second-rate 11 indifferent 12 intermediate

midge 3 fly 4 runt 5 dwarf, pygmy 6 peewee 7 manikin 8 mannikin, Tom Thumb 10 homunculus 11 lilliputian *larva:* 9 bloodworm

midget 3 wee 4 runt, tiny 5 dwarf, pygmy, teeny 6 peewee, punkie, teensy 7 manikin 8 dwarfish, mannikin, Tom Thumb 9 miniature 10 diminutive, homunculus 11 hop-o'-my-thumb, lilliputian

Midian *father:* 7 Abraham *mother:* 7 Keturah

mid-Victorian 4 fogy, prig 5 prude 6 fogram, fossil, square 7 puritan 8 bluenose, mossback 9 Mrs. Grundy 10 antiquated, fuddy-duddy, goody-goody 12 old-fashioned 13 stick-in-the-mud

midwife 10 accoucheur *Scottish:* 5 howdy 6 howdie

mien 3 air, set 4 look, port 6 aspect, manner 7 address, bearing, seeming 8 demeanor, presence 9 mannerism 10 appearance, deportment, expression 11 comportment

miff 3 fit 4 beef, spat 5 pique, run-in 7 dispute, dudgeon, offense, quarrel, rhubarb, umbrage 8 squabble 10 conniption, falling-out, resentment 11 altercation

mig 6 marble

might 3 arm 4 beef, sway, thew 5 brawn, force, means, power, sinew 6 energy, muscle 7 ability, command, control, mastery, potency, strings 8 capacity, strength 9 authority, lustiness, resources, strong arm 10 capability, competence, domination 12 forcefulness, jurisdiction, powerfulness, vigorousness 13 energeticness

mighty 4 high, huge, very 5 grand, great 6 august, heroic, hugely, moving, potent, strong, wieldy 7 eminent, immense, massive, notable, violent 8 enormous, forceful, forcible, gigantic, imposing, powerful, puissant, rattling, renowned, whacking, whopping 9 efficient, extremely, strenuous 10 impressive, monumental, prodigious, tremendous 11 efficacious, exceedingly, illustrious 12 surpassingly 13 extraordinary *combining form:* 3 din 4 dein, dino 5 deino

Mignon composer 6 Thomas (Ambroise)

mignonette 4 herb 6 reseda

migrant 5 mover, nomad 6 mobile 7 drifter 8 traveler, wanderer

migrate 4 move, roam, rove, trek 5 drift, range, shift 6 wander 8 nomadize, transfer

migration 6 moving 8 diaspora, movement *of professionals:* 10 brain drain

migratory 5 nomad 6 errant, mobile, moving, roving 7 nomadic, ranging 9 wandering

Milan *family:* 6 Sforza 8 Visconti *opera house:* 7 La Scala

Milcah *brother:* 3 Lot *father:* 5 Haran 10 Zelophehad *husband:* 5 Nahor *son:* 7 Bethuel

mild 4 calm, easy, meek, soft, tame 5 balmy, bland, faint 6 benign, choice, dainty, docile, gentle, smooth 7 amiable, clement, lenient, subdued 8 delicate, moderate, obeisant, obliging 9 benignant, exquisite, temperate 10 forbearing, submissive

mildew 4 mold 6 fungus, growth

___ **mile** 7 statute 8 nautical

mileage recorder 8 odometer

milepost 5 event 6 marker 8 occasion

milestone 5 event 8 landmark, occasion

milieu 6 medium 7 ambient, climate, setting 8 ambience 10 atmosphere 11 environment, mise-en-scéne 12 surroundings

militant 5 pushy 7 fighter, martial, pushful, pushing, scrappy, warlike 8 fighting 9 assertive, assertory, bellicose, combative, truculent 10 aggressive, pugnacious 11 belligerent, contentious, quarrelsome 12 gladiatorial 13 self-assertive

military 5 troop 6 forces 7 martial, warlike 9 soldierly 10 jingoistic, servicemen 11 armed forces, soldierlike 12 chauvinistic, warmongering *alliance:* 4 NATO *base:* 4 camp, fort, post 5 depot, field 6 billet 8 barracks, garrison, quarters 10 encampment *officer:* 5 major 7 captain, colonel, general 9 brigadier 10 lieutenant *prisoner:* 3 POW *school:* 3 OCS, OTS 4 ROTC, USMA 9 West Point *sector:* 10 combat zone 11 battlefront *store:* 2 BX, PX

10 commissary *storehouse:* **5** depot, étape **6** armory **7** arsenal *supplies:* **8** matériel, ordnance *unit:* **5** corps, squad, troop **7** company, platoon **8** division, regiment **9** battalion **11** battle group *vehicle:* **4** jeep, tank **9** half-track

militate **4** tell **5** count, weigh

milk **4** draw, pump, rook, suck **5** bleed, drain, educe, empty, evoke, exact, mulct, nurse, stick, sweat, wring **6** elicit, evince, extort, fleece, suckle **7** exhaust, exploit, extract *coagulated:* **4** curd *combining form:* **4** lact **5** lacti, lacto **6** galact **7** galacto *curdled:* **5** leben **7** clabber *fermented:* **5** kefir, kumys **6** kumiss, kumyss, yogurt **7** koumiss, matzoon, yoghurt *liquid part:* **4** whey *store:* **5** dairy *sugar:* **7** lactose

milk shake **6** frappe **7** frosted

milksop **4** baby **5** sissy **6** coward **7** doormat **8** weakling **9** jellyfish **10** effeminate, namby-pamby, pantywaist **11** Milquetoast, mollycoddle

milky **4** meek, mild, tame **5** white **6** chalky, gentle **7** lacteal, lactean **8** timorous

Milky Way *combining form:* **6** galact **7** galacto

mill **4** beat, slug **5** dress, fight, plant, quem, shape, works **6** finish, thrash **7** factory, machine **11** manufactory

Miller, Arthur *film:* **10** The Misfits *play:* **9** All My Sons **11** The Crucible **12** After the Fall **16** Death of a Salesman **18** A View From the Bridge *salesman:* **5** Loman (Willy)

mill fever **10** byssinosis

million *combining form:* **3** meg **4** mega

millionth *combining form:* **4** micr **5** micro

Mill on the Floss author **5** Eliot (George)

millstone **3** tax **4** duty, load, onus, task **6** burden, charge, weight **9** buhrstone **10** affliction, deadweight

Milne bear **4** Pooh

Milquetoast, Caspar *creator:* **7** Webster (Harold Tucker); (see also **milksop**)

Miltiades' victory **8** Marathon

Milton work **5** Comus **7** Lycidas **8** L'Allegro **12** Areopagitica, Paradise Lost

mime **3** act **5** actor **6** act out, player **7** trouper **8** thespian **9** performer, playactor, represent **12** impersonator *famous:* **7** Marceau (Marcel)

mimic **2** do **3** act, ape **4** copy, mock, play **5** actor, enact **6** hit off, mummer, parody, parrot, player **7** copycat, imitate, perform, take off, trouper **8** simulate, thespian, travesty **9** burlesque, imitation, pantomime,

performer, personate, playactor **11** impersonate **12** impersonator

mimicry **4** echo, mock **5** apery **6** parody **9** imitation **10** caricature

mince **3** cut **4** chop, hash **5** cut up, strut **6** finick, sashay **7** finnick **8** moderate, restrain **9** euphemize

mincing **4** nice **5** fussy **6** dainty, la-di-da, too-too **7** finical, finicky, genteel, stilted **8** affected, delicate **9** squeamish **10** fastidious, particular, pernickety **11** persnickety

mind **3** eye, see, wit **4** care, espy, keep, look, mood, nous, obey, soul, tend, tone, vein, view, will, wish, wits **5** brain, fancy, humor, power, study, watch, weigh, worry **6** attend, behold, belief, beware, brains, comply, descry, desire, follow, govern, liking, memory, notice, ponder, psyche, reason, sanity, senses, spirit, strain, temper **7** care for, conform, discern, dislike, faculty, feeling, look out, observe, opinion, oversee, perpend, purpose **8** consider, function, lucidity, perceive, pleasure, remember, saneness, think out, villeity, watch out **9** intellect, intention, mentality, sentiment, soundness, supervise, think over **10** brainpower, conviction, discipline, excogitate, gray matter, persuasion **11** disposition, inclination, superintend, temperament **12** intelligence, recollection **13** consciousness *combining form:* **3** noo **5** menti, phren, psych **6** phreni, phreno, psycho

mindful **5** alert, alive, awake, aware **7** knowing **8** sensible, vigilant **9** attentive, au courant, cognizant, conscious, observant, observing, regardful **10** conversant **12** apprehensive **13** conscientious

mindless **3** mad **4** nuts **5** nutsy, silly **6** insane, maniac, simple, stupid **7** asinine, foolish, lunatic **9** nitwitted **10** unthinking **11** sheepheaded **13** unintelligent

mine **3** dig, pit, sap **4** lode, vein, well, work **5** delve, drill, scoop **6** burrow, quarry, spring **7** bonanza, extract **8** eldorado, excavate, Golconda, treasury **10** excavation, wellspring **13** treasure-house, treasure trove *coal:* **8** colliery *French:* **4** à moi **6** le mien

mine gas **9** blackdamp, chokedamp

miner **6** digger, pitman **7** collier

mineral **5** beryl, topaz, trona **6** augite, barite, garnet, iolite, pinite, rutile, sphene, spinel, sulfur, zircon **7** apatite, azurite, bornite, calcite, citrine, coesite, cyanite, jadeite, kernite, kunzite, olivine, zeolite **8** boracite, cinnabar, dolomite, epsomite, fayalite, feldspar, fluorite, hematite, lazulite, lazurite, siderite, sodalite, stibnite, triplite, wellsite **9** aragonite, celestite, cerussite, danburite, fosterite, kaolinite, lawsonite, magnetite, malachite, muscovite, phenakite, scapolite, tridymite, turquoise, wulfenite **10** chalcedony, orthoclase, pyrrhotite, tourmaline **11** alexandrite, chrysoberyl, melanterite **12** brazilianite, chalcopyrite, tincalconite **13** rhodochrosite *combining form:* **3** ine, ite **4** lite, lith, lyte, xene **5** oryct **6** orycto *flaky:* **4** mica *greasy:* **4** talc **10** serpentine *hard:* **6** spinel **7** diamond **8** corundum *iridescent:* **4** opal *nonmetallic:* **5** boron **6** gypsum, halite **8** asbestos, graphite *shiny:* **4** gold **6** galena, pyrite, silver *soft:* **4** talc **6** gypsum **8** graphite *transparent:* **6** quartz

mineral water 7 seltzer

Minerva see Athena

mingle 3 mix **4** meld **5** merge **6** commix, make up **7** combine, concoct **8** intermix **9** socialize

mingy 4 mean **5** tight **6** stingy **7** scrimpy **8** ungiving **9** niggardly, penurious **11** closefisted

miniature 3 wee **4** copy, tiny **5** model, small, teeny, weeny **6** little, minute, teensy **8** portrait **9** itty-bitty **10** diminutive, small-scale, teeny-weeny **11** lilliputian **12** illumination

minify 5 dwarf **6** lessen, shrink **7** abridge, curtail **8** diminish

minim 3 jot **4** atom, iota **5** grain, speck **6** minute, smitch **7** modicum, smidgen **8** particle *music:* **8** half note, half rest

minimal 5 basic **6** lowest **8** littlest, smallest **9** slightest

minimize 5 decry, dwarf **6** reduce **7** run down **8** belittle, derogate, discount **9** disparage, dispraise **10** depreciate **11** detract from

minimum 3 dab, jot **4** hair, iota, whit **5** least, speck **6** lowest, margin **7** smidgen **8** particle, pittance, smallest

minion 4 idol, toad **6** yes-man **7** darling, spaniel **8** creature, favorite, truckler **9** sycophant, toadeater, underling **10** bootlicker **11** lickspittle, subordinate

minister 4 tend **5** agent, clerk, serve **6** cleric, curate, divine, parson **8** clerical, preacher, reverend **9** churchman, clergyman **10** ambassador **12** ecclesiastic *of state:* **10** chancellor

minister plenipotentiary 5 envoy

ministry 4 mean **5** agent, organ **6** agency, clergy, medium **7** channel, vehicle **10** instrument

Minnehaha's husband 8 Hiawatha

Minnesota *capital:* **6** St. Paul *nickname:* **11** Gopher State **14** North Star State *state bird:* **10** common loon

minor 4 fair **5** dinky, light, lower, petty, small, youth **6** casual, infant, lesser, little, medium, slight **7** average, trivial **8** inferior,

mediocre, piddling, small-fry, trifling **9** dependent, secondary, small-beer, small-time **10** bush-league, second-rate, shoe-string **11** indifferent, unimportant **12** unnoticeable **13** insignificant

minority 6 nonage **7** infancy **10** immaturity

minor-league 5 dinky, small **6** lesser **8** small-fry **9** secondary, small-time **11** unimportant

Minos *daughter:* **7** Ariadne, Phaedra *father:* **4** Zeus **7** Jupiter *kingdom:* **5** Crete *monster:* **8** Minotaur *mother:* **6** Europa *son:* **9** Androgeos *wife:* **8** Pasiphaë

Minotaur *father:* **4** bull *home:* **9** labyrinth *mother:* **8** Pasiphaë *slayer:* **7** Theseus

minstrel 4 bard, wait **6** harper, singer **7** gleeman **8** jongleur **9** balladist **10** troubadour *end man:* **7** Mr. Bones, Mr. Tambo *instrument:* **4** lute **10** tambourine

mint 3 pot, wad **4** coin, pile **6** boodle, bundle, intact, packet, unused **7** fire-new, fortune, perfect, span-new **8** brand-new, lavender, original, spang-new, unmarred **9** blue curls, bugleweed, spearmint **10** peppermint **11** spanking-new **12** spick-and-span

Minuit's purchase 9 Manhattan

minus 4 less, sans **7** lacking, wanting, without **8** awanting, subtract **10** deficiency

minute 3 jot, wee **4** full, tiny **5** crack, flash, jiffy, light, petty, shake, small, teeny, weeny **6** little, moment, second, teensy, tittle **7** careful, instant, precise, trivial **8** detailed, itemized, thorough, trifling **9** breathing, clocklike, itty-bitty, small-beer **10** blow-by-blow, meticulous, particular, scrupulous, teeny-weeny **11** lilliputian, punctilious, split second, unimportant **13** infinitesimal, insignificant

minutes 6 record **7** summary

minutiae 5 ropes **6** trivia **7** details **9** small beer **10** ins and outs, triviality **11** particulars, small change **13** small potatoes

miracle 4 feat **6** marvel, wonder **7** portent, prodigy, stunner **9** sensation **10** phenomenon

miraculous 7 amazing, strange **8** superior **9** marvelous, unearthly, wonderful **10** astounding, prodigious, staggering, superhuman, suprahuman **11** astonishing, spectacular **12** supermundane, supernatural, supramundane, supranatural **13** preternatural

mirage 8 delusion, illusion, phantasm **11** fata morgana, ignis fatuus **13** hallucination

Miranda *father:* **8** Prospero *lover:* **9** Ferdinand

mire 3 bog, fen, mud 4 muck, ooze, quag, sink, soil, trap 5 cling, delay, embog, marsh, slush, stick, swamp 6 cleave, detain, enmesh, entrap, hang up, morass, retard, slow up, tangle 7 baygall, bog down, embroil, ensnare, involve, set back, slacken 8 entangle, slow down 9 implicate

Miriam's brother 5 Aaron, Moses

mirror 5 glass, ideal, image, model 6 embody, typify 7 example, pattern, reflect 8 ensample, exemplar, paradigm, speculum, standard 9 archetype, beau ideal, body forth, epitomize, exemplify, personify, pier glass, reflector, represent, symbolize 10 illustrate 11 cheval glass, emblematize 12 looking glass *sight:* 5 image *signalling:* 5 helio 10 heliograph, heliotrope

mirth 3 fun, joy 4 glee 5 cheer 6 gaiety, levity 7 jollity 8 gladness, hilarity 9 frivolity, happiness, jocundity, joviality, merriment, rejoicing 10 jocularity, joyfulness 12 cheerfulness

mirthful 3 gay 5 jolly, merry, riant 6 blithe, jocund, jovial 7 festive 10 blithesome 12 lighthearted

miry 4 oozy 5 boggy, muddy

misadventure 4 bull, slip, woes 5 boner, error, lapse 6 howler, mishap 7 blunder, faux pas, tragedy 8 accident, calamity, casualty, disaster 9 cataclysm 11 catastrophe

misanthropic 7 cynical 8 reserved, solitary 9 reclusive 10 antisocial 11 standoffish

misappropriate 5 steal 8 embezzle

misbegotten 7 bastard, natural 8 baseborn, deformed, spurious 10 fatherless, unfathered 12 contemptible, illegitimate

misbehaving 3 bad 7 naughty

misbehavior 8 rudeness 10 misconduct, wrongdoing

miscalculate 3 err 8 discount, miscount, misgauge, overlook 9 disregard, overprize, overvalue 10 underprize, undervalue

miscarry 4 fail, flop 5 abort

miscellaneous 3 odd 4 many 5 mixed 6 divers, motley, sundry, varied 7 diverse, jumbled, mingled 8 assorted, chowchow, unsorted 9 different, disparate, divergent, scrambled 10 commingled, unassorted 12 conglomerate 13 heterogeneous

miscellany 3 ana 4 brew, hash, olio, posy, stew 5 album, melee, salad 6 jumble, medley, motley, muddle 7 garland, mélange, mixture, omnibus 8 analects, chowchow, mixed bag, pastiche, porridge 9 anthology, colluvies, congeries, pasticcio, patchwork, potpourri 10 assortment, cumulation, hodgepodge, hotchpotch, salmagundi 11 aggregation, combination, florilegium, gallimaufry, odds and ends, olla podrida, smorgasbord

mischance 6 mishap 7 tragedy 8 accident, casualty 9 adversity 10 misfortune 11 contretemps

mischief 3 ill 4 evil, harm, hurt, limb, ruin 5 devil, prank, rogue, scamp 6 damage, injury, rascal, strife 7 devilry, discord, dissent, outrage, roguery, trouble, villain, waggery 8 conflict, deviltry, division, hardship, scalawag, variance 9 devilment, diablerie, disaccord, skeezicks 10 contention, difference, difficulty, dissension 11 rapscallion, roguishness, waggishness 12 sportiveness

mischief-maker 3 imp 4 puck 5 devil, knave, rogue, scamp 6 rascal 7 villain 8 scalawag 9 prankster, trickster 11 rapscallion

mischievous 3 bad, ill, paw, sly 4 evil, foxy 5 antic, risky 6 artful, impish, irking, tricky, vexing, wicked 7 harmful, hurtful, irksome, larkish, naughty, playful, puckish, roguish, tricksy, waggish 8 annoying, damaging, prankish, sportive 9 bothering, injurious 10 bothersome, frolicsome, ill-behaved

mischievousness 4 evil, harm, hurt 6 injury 7 devilry, roguery, teasing, waggery 8 annoying, deviltry 9 devilment, diablerie, pestering

miscolor 4 warp 5 belie, twist 6 garble 7 distort, falsify, pervert 12 misrepresent

misconduct 10 wrongdoing 11 impropriety, malfeasance, misbehavior 12 malversation

miscreant 4 heel 5 knave, rogue 6 rascal, wretch 7 corrupt, heretic, infidel, lowlife, vicious, villain 8 depraved, infamous, perverse 9 heretical, nefarious, scoundrel, unhealthy 10 blackguard, degenerate, flagitious, unbeliever, villainous

miscue 4 miss, slip, trip 5 error, fluff, lapse 6 slipup 7 blooper, blunder, mistake

misdeed 3 sin 5 crime, wrong 7 offense 13 transgression

misdoubt 4 fear 5 dread 7 suspect 8 distrust 9 apprehend, suspicion

mise-en-scène 3 set 4 site 6 locale, medium, milieu 7 ambient, climate, setting 8 ambience, stage set 10 atmosphere 11 environment 12 stage setting, surroundings

miser 3 hog, pig 4 skin 5 chuff, hunks, nabal, piker, stiff 7 glutton, niggard, scrooge 8 muckworm, tightwad 9 skinflint 10 cheapskate

miserable 6 dolent, rueful, woeful 7 doleful, forlorn, piteous, pitiful, ruthful 8 dolorous, hopeless, shameful, wretched 9 afflicted, sorrowful, worthless 10 despairing, despondent, melancholy 12 contemptible 13 discreditable

Miserables, Les *author:* 4 Hugo (Victor) *character:* 6 Javert 7 Cosette, Fantine, Valjean

miserly 4 mean 5 close, tight 6 abject, greedy, sordid, stingy 7 ignoble 8 covetous, grasping, stingily 9 penurious, scrimping 10 avaricious 11 closefisted, tightfisted 12 cheeseparing, parsimonious 13 penny-pinching

misery 3 woe 5 agony, dolor, grief 6 sorrow 7 anguish, passion, sadness, squalor 8 calamity, distress 9 adversity, dejection, privation, suffering 10 affliction, depression, desolation, melancholy 11 despondency, unhappiness 12 wretchedness

misfortune 3 woe 4 harm 5 cross, trial 7 tragedy, trouble 8 accident, calamity, casualty, disaster 9 adversity, cataclysm 10 affliction, visitation 11 catastrophe, contretemps, tribulation *Scottish:* 6 dirdum

misgiving 4 fear 5 doubt, qualm 7 anxiety, presage 8 distrust 9 prenotion, suspicion 11 premonition 12 apprehension, presentiment

misguided 5 wrong 9 erroneous 10 ill-advised

Mishael *brother:* 8 Elzaphan *cousin:* 5 Aaron *father:* 6 Uzziel

Misham's father 6 Elpaal

mishandle 5 abuse 7 pervert, rough up 10 knock about, prostitute, roughhouse, slap around

mishap 7 tragedy 8 accident, casualty 9 adversity 11 contretemps

mishmash 6 jumble, jungle, litter, medley, muddle, tumble 7 clutter, mélange, mixture, rummage 8 pastiche, scramble 9 pasticcio, patchwork, potpourri 10 hodgepodge, hotchpotch

misidentify 7 confuse 8 confound

misinterpret 3 err 7 misread

mislay 4 lose

mislead 3 lie 4 dupe, fool, lure 5 bluff, cheat, tempt 6 betray, delude, entice, illude, juggle, seduce, take in 7 beguile, deceive 8 hoodwink, inveigle 11 double-cross

misleading 5 false, wrong 8 delusive, delusory, specious 9 deceitful, deceiving, deceptive 10 fallacious, inaccurate 11 casuistical, sophistical

mismatch 3 jar 5 clash 6 jangle 7 discord 8 conflict 9 disaccord 12 disharmonize

misplace 4 lose

misrepresent 3 lie 4 gild, mask, warp 5 belie, cloak, color, dress, feign, gloss, twist, wrest 6 garble, palter, weasel, wrench 7 confuse, deceive, distort, falsify, pervert, varnish 8 disguise, simulate 9 dissemble, embellish, embroider 10 camouflage, equivocate 11 counterfeit, prevaricate

misrepresentation 3 fib, lie 4 tale 5 story 6 canard 7 falsity, untruth 8 untruism 9 falsehood

miss 3 err, gal 4 fail, girl, maid, omit 5 avoid, wench 6 damsel, escape, forget, ignore, lassie, maiden, slight 7 failure, neglect 8 discount, overlook 9 disregard

Missa Solemnis com-poser 9 Beethoven (Ludwig van)

misshape 4 warp, wind 6 deform 7 contort, distort, torture 9 deformity 10 distortion 12 malformation

missile 4 bolt, dart 5 arrow, shell, spear 6 bullet, rocket 10 cannonball, projectile *underwater:* 7 torpedo; (see also **guided missile**)

mission 4 goal, task 5 trade 6 errand 7 calling, embassy, purpose 8 business, legation, lifework, ministry, vocation

missionary 5 agent 7 apostle 8 emissary, promoter 10 colporteur, evangelist, revivalist 12 propagandist

Mississippi *capital:* 7 Jackson *highest point:* 9 Woodall Mt. *motto:* 14 By Valor and Arms *nickname:* 10 Bayou State 13 Magnolia State *state flower:* 8 magnolia *university:* 12 Jackson State

missive 4 memo, note 6 letter 7 epistle

Miss Julie author 10 Strindberg (August)

Miss Lonelyhearts author 4 West (Nathanael)

Miss-Nancyish 5 sissy 6 prissy 7 epicene, unmanly 9 pansified, sissified 10 effeminate

Missouri *capital:* 13 Jefferson City *college:* 5 Avila, Drury *nickname:* 11 Show Me State 12 Bullion State *state flower:* 9 hawthorne

misstate 4 warp 5 belie, color, twist 6 garble 7 distort, falsify, pervert

misstatement 3 fib, lie 4 tale 7 falsity, untruth 8 untruism 9 falsehood 10 taradiddle 13 prevarication

misstep 4 bull, slip 5 boner, error, fluff, lapse 6 slipup 7 blooper, blunder, faux pas

mist 3 dim, fog 4 blur, film, haze, murk 5 befog, brume, cloud, smaze 7 becloud, obscure 9 overcloud

mistake 3 err 4 bull, slip, trip 5 addle, boner, error, fluff, folly, lapse 6 boo-boo, bungle, jumble, lapsus, muddle, slight, slipup, tumble 7 blooper, blunder, confuse, neglect 8 confound, omission, omitting 9 confusion, slighting 10 inaccuracy, neglecting

mister 3 man, sir 4 lord 7 husband
French: 8 monsieur *German:* 4 herr *Italian:* 6 signor *Spanish:* 5 señor
Mister Roberts author 6 Heggen
(Thomas)
mistreat 5 abuse 6 ill-use 7 outrage
mistress 4 amie 5 lover, woman 6 harlot
7 bedmate, hetaira 8 dulcinea, ladylove,
paramour 9 concubine, courtesan, inamorata, kept woman 10 chatelaine, girl friend
of Charles II: 4 Gwyn (Nell) 8 Villiers (Barbara) *of Edward III:* 7 Perrers (Alice) *of
Henry II (England):* 8 Clifford (Rosamund)
of Henry II (France): 9 de Poiters (Diane)
of Louis XV: 9 Pompadour (Madame de)
mistrust 5 alarm, doubt, scare 6 appall,
dismay, wonder 7 concern, dispute, dubiety, foresee, surmise, suspect 8 frighten,
question 9 apprehend, challenge, dubiosity, suspicion 10 anticipate, foreboding,
skepticism 11 incertitude, uncertainty,
uncertitude 12 apprehension, presentiment
mistrustful 7 jealous 10 suspicious
misty 3 dim 4 hazy 5 foggy, mushy,
vague 6 cloudy, vapory 7 obscure, unclear
8 confused, vaporous 10 indistinct
misunderstanding 7 quarrel 9 imbroglio
12 disagreement
misuse 5 abuse 7 outrage, pervert 8 illtreat, maltreat 10 prostitute *of a word:*
8 malaprop
mite 3 bit, jot 4 atom, iota 5 grain, minim,
ounce, speck 6 acarid, minute, tittle 7 chigger, modicum, smidgen 8 molecule, particle, smidgeon *combining form:* 4 acar
5 acari, acaro *family:* 8 oribatid
mitigate 4 ease 5 abate, allay, relax,
slake 6 lessen, soften, temper 7 assuage,
lighten, mollify, relieve 8 palliate 9 alleviate, meliorate
mitigation 4 ease 6 relief 8 easement
10 moderation, palliation 11 alleviation
mitosis 12 cell division, karyokinesis
stage: 8 anaphase, prophase 9 metaphase, telophase
mix 4 fuse, join, link, lump, meld, stir
5 blend, braid, merge, unite 6 blunge,
fusion, jumble, make up, mingle, tangle,
work in 7 amalgam, combine, concoct, confuse, conjoin 8 coalesce, comingle, compound, confound, immingle 9 associate,
commingle, interflow, interfuse 10 amalgamate, crossbreed, inosculate, interblend
11 interfusion, intermingle, misidentify
12 amalgamation
mixable 8 miscible
mixed 6 impure, motley, varied 8 chowchow 9 irregular 11 promiscuous 12 conglomerate, multifarious 13 heterogeneous,
miscellaneous

mixed bag 4 olio 5 salad 6 jumble, medley 8 pastiche 10 assortment, hodgepodge, miscellany 11 gallimaufry
mixed-blooded person 7 mestizo,
mulatto 8 octoroon 9 half-breed
mixologist 6 barman 7 tapster 9 barkeeper, bartender
mixture 4 brew, hash, olio 5 alloy, blend
6 fusion, medley 7 amalgam, compost, farrago, mélange 8 compound, mishmash,
solution 9 composite, potpourri 10 concoction, confection 11 interfusion 12 amalgamation
mix up 5 addle, dizzy 6 fuddle, jumble,
muddle, tumble 7 confuse, derange, disrupt, fluster, misdeem, mistake 8 befuddle,
bewilder, confound, disarray, disjoint, disorder, distract 9 distemper 10 disarrange,
discompose 11 disorganize, misidentify
mix-up 4 hash, mess, mull, muss 5 blend,
botch, melee 6 fusion, muddle, tangle
8 botchery, compound, shambles 9 composite, confusion 11 interfusion
mizmaze 3 web 4 knot, mesh 5 skein,
snarl 6 jungle, morass, tangle 9 confusion,
labyrinth 12 bewilderment
mks unit 3 lux, ohm 4 mole, volt, watt
5 farad, henry, hertz, joule, lumen, meter,
metre, tesla, weber 6 ampere, kelvin, newton, pascal, second 7 candela, coulomb,
siemens 8 kilogram
Mnemosyne 6 Memory *daughters:*
5 Muses *father:* 6 Uranus *lover:* 4 Zeus
mother: 2 Ge 4 Gaea
Moabite *city:* 3 Kir *god:* 7 Chemosh *king:*
5 Eglon, Mesha
Moab's father 3 Lot
moan 4 weep 5 groan 6 bewail, grieve,
lament 7 deplore 8 complain
mob 3 set 4 camp, clan, gang, herd, push,
ring, riot, rout, scum 5 cabal, crowd, crush,
dregs, horde, posse, press, swarm, trash
6 circle, clique, masses, rabble, throng
7 coterie, ingroup 8 canaille, riffraff,
unwashed 9 camarilla 11 proletariat
mobile 5 fluid 6 liquid, moving 7 migrant,
movable, protean 8 moveable, unstable,
unsteady, variable, weathery 9 all-around,
changeful, many-sided, mercurial, migrative, migratory, unsettled 10 capricious,
changeable, inconstant 11 migratorial
mobile phone area 4 cell
mobilize 5 drive, impel, rally 6 muster,
propel, set off 7 actuate, marshal 8 activate, assemble, organize 9 circulate
Moby Dick 5 whale *author:* 8 Melville
(Herman) *character:* 3 Pip 6 Daggoo, Parsee 7 Ishmael 8 Queequeg, Starbuck,
Tashtego *pursuer:* 4 Ahab *ship:*
6 Pequod

moccasin 3 pac 6 loafer 7 slipper 8 larri-
gan

mock 3 ape 4 butt, copy, defy, fake, gibe,
jape, jeer, jest, joke, lout, quiz, razz, sham,
twit 5 bogus, dummy, false, farce, feign,
mimic, phony, quasi, rally, scout, sneer,
sport, taunt 6 affect, assume, betray,
delude, deride, ersatz, humbug, illude,
jester, juggle, parody, pseudo 7 beguile, buffoon, deceive, imitate, mislead, sell out,
take off 8 derision, ridicule, simulate, so-
called, spurious, travesty 9 burlesque, disregard, imitation, pilgarlic, simulated
10 artificial, caricature, fictitious, substitute
11 counterfeit, double-cross 13 laughingstock

mockery 4 butt, jest, joke, sham 5 farce,
sport 6 japery, jester, parody, satire 7 takeoff 8 derision, ridicule, travesty 9 burlesque, imitation, pilgarlic 10 caricature
13 laughingstock

mocking 8 derisive, sardonic

mode 3 cry, fad, way 4 chic, rage, vein,
wise 5 craze, state, style, vogue 6 custom,
furore, manner, method, status, system
7 fashion, posture 9 condition, situation,
technique 10 convention, dernier cri

model 4 copy, type, very 5 dummy, frame,
gauge, ideal, shape 6 design, effigy,
emblem, mirror, mockup, symbol 7 classic,
epitome, example, fashion, imitate, manikin,
paragon, pattern, perfect, replica, typical
8 ensample, exemplar, flawless, mannikin,
nonesuch, paradigm, standard 9 archetype, beau ideal, blueprint, classical, criterion, exemplary, miniature, nonpareil
10 apotheosis, embodiment, prototypal,
touchstone 11 commendable 12 indefectible, paradigmatic, prototypical, quintessence, reproduction *combining form:*
3 typ 4 typo *preliminary:* 8 maquette

moderate 3 ebb 4 calm, cool, even, fair,
fall, mean, mild, slow, soft, so-so, wane
5 abate, bland, let up, small, sober 6 gentle, lessen, medium, paltry, reduce, relent,
slight, soften, steady, subdue, temper
7 average, chasten, control, cushion, die
away, die down, ease off, equable, fairish,
lighten, qualify, relieve, slacken, subside,
trivial 8 attemper, constant, decrease,
diminish, discreet, mediocre, middling, piddling, restrain, trifling 9 alleviate, constrain,
soft-shell, temperate, unextreme
10 abstemious, controlled, middle-road,
reasonable, restrained 11 indifferent, unexcessive 12 conservative 13 unimpassioned

moderation 7 control, measure
9 restraint 10 abstinence, limitation, temperance 13 temperateness

moderator 5 judge 7 arbiter 8 chairman,
examiner, governor, mediator 10 peacemaker 11 chairperson

modern 3 new 4 late 5 fresh, novel 6 latter, recent 7 current 8 neoteric, up-to-date
9 new-sprung, prevalent 10 coincident,
concurrent, newfangled, present-day, prevailing 11 concomitant 12 contemporary,
new-fashioned *combining form:* 2 ne
3 neo

modernize 5 renew 6 update 7 refresh,
restore 8 renovate 9 refurbish 10 rejuvenate

modest 3 coy, dry, shy 4 meek, nice,
prim, pure 5 clean, lowly, plain, timid
6 chaste, decent, demure, humble, prissy,
proper, seemly, silent, simple, stuffy
7 bashful, prudish 8 decorous, discreet,
moderate, priggish, reserved, reticent, retiring, spotless 9 diffident, stainless, temperate, unassured, undefiled, unsullied
10 immaculate, reasonable, unassuming,
unboastful 11 inelaborate, puritanical,
straitlaced, unassertive, unblemished, unelaborate, unpresuming, withdrawing
12 self-effacing, unornamented, unpretend-
ing 13 unembellished, unembroidered,
unpretentious

Modest Proposal author 5 Swift (Jonathan)

modesty 7 decency, pudency, reserve
8 chastity, humility, pudicity, timidity 10 diffidence

modicum 3 bit, jot 4 atom, iota, whit
5 grain, minim, ounce, scrap 7 soupçon
8 particle

modify 4 turn, vary 5 alter, amend
6 change, mutate, temper 7 qualify 8 mitigate, moderate, restrain 9 refashion

modish 4 chic 5 smart, swank 6 with-it
7 dashing 9 exclusive 11 fashionable

Modred, Mordred *father:* 6 Arthur
mother: 8 Margawse *slayer, victim:*
6 Arthur

modulate 4 sing 6 intone, temper
8 restrain

modus 3 way 4 wise 5 means 6 manner,
method, system 7 fashion 9 technique

modus ____ 7 vivendi 8 operandi

mogul 4 czar, king, lord 5 baron, nabob,
ruler 6 prince, tycoon 7 magnate

Mohammed see Muhammad

Mohawk chief 5 Brant (Joseph) 8 Hiawatha

Mohican chief 5 Uncas

moiety 3 cut 4 half, part 5 piece 6 member, parcel 7 element, portion, section, segment 8 division 9 component

moil 3 tug 4 grub, to-do, work 5 churn,
drive, grind, labor, swirl 6 bustle, clamor,

drudge, hubbub, lather, strain, strive, uproar 7 chaffer, ruction, slavery, travail, trouble, wrangle 8 drudgery, plugging, rowdydow, slogging 9 commotion, confusion 10 hurly-burly, turbulence

moira 3 lot 4 doom, fate 5 weird 6 kismet 7 destiny, portion 12 circumstance

moist 3 wet 4 damp, dank, dewy 5 gooey, humid, mushy, sappy, soggy, soupy 6 drippy, slushy, steamy, sticky, watery 7 dampish, maudlin, tearful, wettish

moisten 3 wet 6 dampen 8 humidify, saturate

moisture 5 vapor 11 tearfulness 13 precipitation *combining form:* 4 hygr 5 hygro

moistureless 3 dry 4 arid, sere 7 bone-dry, parched, thirsty 8 droughty 9 unwatered 10 desiccated

molar 5 tooth 7 grinder *combining form:* 3 myl 4 mylo

molasses 7 treacle 8 theriaca 10 blackstrap

mold 3 die, hug, lot 4 cast, form, kind, make, soil, sort, type 5 adapt, build, class, erect, forge, frame, knead, shape, stamp 6 design, fungus, growth, nature 7 fashion, pattern 8 template 9 character, construct 11 description, put together *combining form:* 5 plasm, plast, plasy 6 plases (plural), plasia, plasis, plasma

moldable 6 pliant, supple 7 ductile, fictile, plastic, pliable 9 adaptable, malleable

molder 3 rot 4 turn 5 decay, spoil, taint, waste 7 crumble, putrefy 9 break down, decompose 11 deteriorate 12 disintegrate

molding 4 bead, cove, gula, list, reed, tore 5 angle, congé, ogive, talon, thumb 6 baston, nebulé, reglet 7 annulet, beading, cornice, reeding 8 cincture 9 baseboard *compound:* 4 beak, ogie 8 cymatium 9 cyma recta 10 serpentine 11 cyma reversa *edge:* 5 arris *flat:* 4 band, face 5 bevel, splay 6 fascia, fillet, listel, regula 7 chamfer *simple curve:* 4 roll 5 flute, ovolo, torus 6 scotia 8 astragal

moldy 5 dated, fusty, musty, passé 6 bygone, old hat, rococo 7 ancient, archaic 8 mildewed, outdated 9 crumbling, moth-eaten 10 antiquated 12 old-fashioned

mole 4 pier, quay 5 jetty, nevus 6 burrow, tunnel 9 birthmark 10 breakwater *combining form:* 5 talpi

molecule 3 bit, jot 4 atom, iota 5 minim, ounce, speck 7 modicum 8 fraction, fragment, particle

molest 3 vex 4 bait, raid 5 annoy, harry, tease 6 bother, harass, heckle, pester 7 disturb, torment, trouble 9 persecute

Moll Flanders author 5 Defoe (Daniel)

mollify 4 calm, ease 5 allay, relax 6 pacify, soften, soothe, temper 7 appease, assuage, lighten, placate, relieve, sweeten 8 mitigate 9 alleviate 10 ameliorate, conciliate, propitiate

mollusk 6 chiton *bivalve:* 4 clam 6 bankia, cockle, mussel, oyster, teredo 7 geoduck, scallop 8 shipworm *cephalopod:* 5 squid 7 octopus 8 argonaut, nautilus 10 cuttlefish *part:* 6 mantle, radula, siphon *tooth shell:* 9 dentalium *univalve:* 4 slug 5 conch, cowry, murex, snail, whelk 6 cowrie, limpet, triton 7 abalone 10 nudibranch, periwinkle

mollusk-like 8 limacine

Molly ___ 7 Maguire, Pitcher

mollycoddle 4 baby 5 humor, sissy, spoil 6 cocker, cosset, pamper 7 cater to, doormat, indulge, milksop, protect 8 weakling 9 jellyfish 10 goody-goody, pantywaist 11 Milquetoast 12 invertebrate

molt 4 cast, shed, slip 6 change, slough 7 discard, ecdysis 8 exuviate

molted covering 7 exuviae

molten 6 heated, melted 7 glowing

molten rock 4 lava 5 magma

molybdenum *symbol:* 2 Mo

moment 4 pith, time 5 crack, flash, jiffy, point, shake, while 6 import, minute, second, weight 7 instant 8 juncture, occasion 9 breathing, magnitude 10 importance 11 consequence, split second, weightiness 12 significance 13 consideration

momentary 5 brief, quick, short 8 fleeting, fugitive, volatile 9 ephemeral, fugacious, transient 10 evanescent, short-lived, transitory 11 impermanent

momentous 3 big 5 grave 7 epochal, fateful, serious, weighty 8 eventful, material 9 important 10 meaningful 11 significant, substantial 12 considerable 13 consequential

momentousness 4 pith 6 import, weight 9 magnitude 10 importance 11 consequence, weightiness 12 significance

momus 6 carper, critic, Zoilus 7 caviler, knocker 9 aristarch 10 criticizer 11 faultfinder, smellfungus

Monaco *casino:* 10 Monte Carlo *prince:* 6 Ranier *princess (former):* 5 Grace

monad 3 one 4 atom, unit 8 zoospore

Mona Lisa 10 La Gioconda *painter:* 7 da Vinci (Leonardo)

monarch 4 czar, king, raja, tsar, tzar 5 queen, rajah, ruler 6 kaiser, prince 7 emperor 9 potentate, sovereign

monarchical 5 regal, royal 6 kingly 8 imperial, kinglike, majestic 9 sovereign

monarch's daughter 8 princess *Portuguese, Spanish:* 7 infanta

monarch's son 6 prince *French:* 7 dauphin *Portuguese, Spanish:* 7 infante

monastery 5 abbey 6 friary, priory 7 convent, nunnery *Buddhist:* 8 lamasery *Eastern Orthodox:* 5 laura *head:* 5 abbot, prior 7 hegumen

___ Mondrian 4 Piet

monetary 6 fiscal, pocket 9 financial, pecuniary 10 numismatic

monetary rate 7 millage

monetary unit see at individual countries

money 4 bill, cash, coin, gelt, loot, pelf, swag 5 bread, chips, dough, funds, lucre, moola, rhino, rocks 6 boodle, change, dinero, mammon, mazuma, moolah, riches, specie, wampum, wealth 7 cabbage, capital, coinage, lettuce, needful, scratch, stipend 8 bankroll, currency, finances, treasure 9 resources 10 greenbacks 11 filthy lucre, legal tender

moneyed 4 rich 7 opulent, wealthy 8 affluent 10 well-heeled

moneygrubber 4 skin 5 chuff, miser, nabal, stiff 7 niggard, scrooge 8 muckworm 9 skinflint 10 cheapskate

moneymaking 6 paying 7 gainful 9 lucrative 10 profitable, well-paying, worthwhile 12 advantageous, remunerative

monger 4 hawk, rend 6 dealer, hawker, peddle, spread, trader, vendor 7 higgler, packman, peddler 8 huckster, outcrier

Mongol conqueror 9 Tamerlane 10 Kublai Khan 11 Genghis Khan, Tamburlaine

mongrel 3 cur 4 mule, mutt 5 cross 6 hybrid 7 bastard 9 crossbred, half blood, half-breed 10 crossbreed

monish 5 chide 6 rebuke 7 reprove, tick off 8 call down, reproach 9 reprimand

monition 6 caveat 7 caution, warning 11 forewarning

monitor 4 test 5 check, watch 7 adviser, observe 8 reminder 9 counselor *lizard:* 7 varanid

Monitor *designer:* 8 Ericsson (John) *opponent:* 8 Virginia 9 Merrimack

monitory 7 warning 8 advisory 10 cautionary, cautioning, counseling 11 admonishing

monk 5 friar 7 brother 8 monastic 9 anchorite *Buddhist:* 4 lama 5 bonze *Eastern Orthodox:* 7 caloyer *Hindu:* 8 sannyasi *Roman Catholic:* 9 Dominican 10 Cistercian, Franciscan *room:* 4 cell *shaven crown:* 7 tonsure *title:* 3 dom, fra 5 padre

monkey 3 imp, sap 4 dupe, fool, gull, mark 5 cebid, gamin, small 6 bantam, butt in, ceboid, horn in, little, meddle, petite, simian, sucker, tamper, urchin, victim 7 fall guy 8 busybody, easy mark, smallish 9 interfere, interlope 10 tamper with 11 intermeddle *combining form:* 6 pithec 7 pitheco *New World:* 4 saki, titi 5 sajou 6 howler, spider, uakari, woolly 7 sapajou, tamarin 8 capuchin, marmoset, squirrel 11 douroucouli *Old World:* 4 douc, mona 5 Diana, drill, patas 6 grivet, guenon, langur, rhesus, vervet 7 colobus, hanuman, macaque 8 entellus, mandrill, mangabey, talapoin, wanderoo 9 proboscis 10 Barbary ape

monkeyshine 4 dido, lark 5 antic, caper, prank, trick 6 frolic 10 shenanigan, tomfoolery

monocratic 8 absolute, despotic 9 arbitrary, autarchic, tyrannous 10 autocratic, tyrannical

monogram 6 cipher, sketch 7 outline 8 initials

monograph 5 study 6 memoir, thesis 8 tractate, treatise 9 discourse 12 disquisition, dissertation

monopolize 3 hog 5 sew up 6 absorb, corner, manage 7 consume, control, engross

monopoly 5 trust 6 cartel, corner 7 control 9 ownership, syndicate 10 consortium 11 exclusivity

monotonous 4 blah, dull, poky, same 6 dreary, stodgy 7 humdrum, uniform 8 banausic, unvaried 10 pedestrian 11 repetitious

monotony 6 tedium 7 humdrum 8 flatness, sameness 10 uniformity

monster 4 huge, ogre 5 demon, devil, fiend, freak, giant, lusus, teras, whale 6 ogress 7 mammoth, titanic 8 abortion, behemoth, colossal, enormous, giantess, gigantic 9 hellhound, leviathan, manticore 10 behemothic, gargantuan 11 elephantine, miscreation *biblical:* 5 Rehab 8 Behemoth 9 Leviathan *combining form:* 4 pagi (plural) 5 pagus, terat 6 terato *female:* 6 Gorgon, Medusa, Scylla *fire-breathing:* 6 dragon, Typhon 7 Chimera 8 Chimaera *fowl-dragon:* 10 cockatrice *French:* 8 Tarasque *horse-fish:* 11 hippocampus *hundred-armed:* 9 Enceladus *hundred-eyed:* 5 Argus *hundred-handed:* 8 Briareus *lion-eagle:* 7 griffin *serpent-headed:* 6 gorgon *study of:* 10 teratology *three-bodied:* 6 Geryon *three-headed dog:* 5 Cerberus *two-headed dog:* 6 Orthos *water:* 6 kraken, nicker *winged dragon:* 6 wivern, wyvern *woman-bird:* 5 Harpy *woman-lion:* 6 Sphinx *woman-serpent:* 7 Echidna; (see also dragon)

___ monster 4 Gila

monstrosity 4 mess 5 freak, lusus, sight
6 fright 7 desight, eyesore 8 abortion
11 miscreation

monstrous 3 big 4 huge, rank, vast
5 awful, large 6 crying, mighty, mortal
7 glaring, heinous, hideous, immense, mammoth, massive, titanic 8 colossal, cracking,
deformed, dreadful, enormous, gigantic, horrible, infamous, shocking, towering 9 atrocious, desperate, fantastic, malformed,
unnatural 10 flagitious, gargantuan, impressive, monumental, outrageous, prodigious,
scandalous, stupendous, tremendous
11 elephantine, magnificent

Montagues'enemies 8 Capulets

Montaigne's forte 5 essay

Montana *capital:* 6 Helena *highest point:*
11 Granite Peak *largest town:* 8 Billings
nickname: 13 Mountain State, Treasure
State *state flower:* 10 bitterroot

Monteverdi opera 5 Orfeo 7 Arianna

Montezuma *conqueror:* 6 Cortes, Cortez
(Hernan, Hernando) *people:* 6 Aztecs
revenge: 8 diarrhea

month *combining form:* 4 meno *current:*
7 instant *following:* 7 proximo *Hindu:*
3 Pus 4 Asin, Jeth, Magh 5 Aghan, Chait,
Sawan 6 Asargh, Bhadon, Kartik, Phagun
7 Baisakh *Jewish:* 2 Ab 4 Adar, Elul, Iyar
5 Nisan, Sivan, Tebet 6 Kislev, Shebat,
Tammuz, Tishri 7 Heshvan *Muslim:*
4 Rabi 5 Rajab, Safar 6 Jumada, Sha 'ban
7 Ramadan, Shawwal 8 Muharram
9 Dhu'l-Hijja, Dhu'l-Qa'dah *preceding:*
6 ultimo

Montmartre church 10 Sacré Coeur

monument 5 relic, stela, stupa 6 ledger,
record 7 chaitya, example, memento, tribute 8 archives, cenotaph, document,
memorial 9 footstone, headstone, tombstone 10 gravestone 11 commemorate,
grave marker, memorialize, testimonial *prehistoric:* 6 dolmen, menhir 8 cromlech,
megalith

monumental 4 huge, vast 6 mighty, mortal 7 immense, mammoth, massive
8 cracking, enormous, gigantic, towering
9 fantastic, monstrous 10 prodigious, stupendous, tremendous 11 inestimable,
mountainous 12 overwhelming

moocah 3 pot 5 grass 8 cannabis 9 marijuana

mooch 3 bat, beg 4 roam, rove 5 amble,
cadge, drift, range, slink, sneak, steal, stray
6 ramble, sponge, wander 7 meander,
saunter 8 straggle

mooching 7 beggary, bumming, cadging
9 mendicity 10 mendicancy 11 panhandling

mood 3 air 4 aura, feel, mind, tone, vein,
whim 5 humor 6 aspect, spirit, strain, tem-

per, timbre 7 caprice, emotion, feeling
8 ambiance, ambience 9 character, semblance 10 atmosphere 11 disposition, personality, temperament

moody 3 sad 4 glum 5 sulky 6 fickle,
gloomy, grumpy 7 pensive 8 unstable
9 humorsome, mercurial, whimsical
10 capricious, inconstant 13 temperamental

moon 4 gape 5 dream 6 dawdle 9 satellite *combining form:* 5 selen 6 seleni,
seleno *dark area:* 4 mare 5 maria (plural)
god: 3 Sin 5 Nanna 6 Meztli *goddess:*
4 Luna 5 Diana, Tanit 6 Hecate, Hekate,
Selena, Selene, Tanith 7 Artemis, Astarte;
(see also *satellite*)

Moon and Sixpence author
7 Maugham (W. Somerset)

mooncalf 4 dolt, fool 5 idiot, ninny 6 doodle, madman 7 jackass, tomfool 8 imbecile

Moon River composer 7 Mancini
(Henry)

moonshine 4 bosh, jake 5 hokum
6 bunkum, humbug 7 bootleg, eyewash
8 homebrew, malarkey, nonsense 10 balderdash, bathtub gin, flapdoodle 11 mountain dew 12 blatherskite

Moonstone, The *author:* 7 Collins
(Wilkie) *detective:* 4 Cuff

moor 3 bog, fen 4 fell 5 berth, catch
6 anchor, Berber, fasten, Muslim, secure
8 Moroccan *fictional:* 7 Othello

moose 6 cervid *female:* 3 cow *male:*
4 bull *relative:* 3 elk 4 deer

moot 5 argue, plead 6 broach, debate
7 agitate, bring up, canvass, discept, discuss, dispute, dubious, suggest, suspect
8 arguable, disputed, doubtful 9 debatable,
introduce, thrash out, uncertain, unsettled,
ventilate 10 disputable, toss around
11 problematic 12 questionable 13 controversial

mooting 6 debate 8 forensic 9 dialectic
11 disputation 13 argumentation

mop 3 mug 4 swab, wipe 5 mouth 7 grimace, shellac, trounce

mope 4 ache, pout, sulk 5 ample, brood,
drift, grump, mosey 6 bummel, dawdle,
grieve, linger, stroll 7 despond, saunter

mopes 5 blues, dumps 7 dismals, sadness 8 dolefuls 10 depression, melancholy
11 unhappiness 12 mournfulness

mopey 3 low 4 blue, down 6 droopy
8 cast down, dejected, downcast
9 depressed 10 dispirited, spiritless

moppet 3 bud, kid, tot 4 chit, tyke 5 chick,
child, youth 8 juvenile, young one 9 youngster

mop up 4 beat, drub, dust, lick, whip
6 absorb, garner 7 shellac, trounce 8 lambaste 9 overwhelm

moral 4 good, just, pure, rule 5 axiom, gnome, maxim, noble, right 6 chaste, decent, dictum, honest, proper, teachy, truism 7 brocard, ethical, preachy, upright 8 aphorism, apothegm, didactic, elevated, sermonic, virtuous 9 honorable, righteous 10 high-minded, principled, scrupulous 11 right-minded, sermonizing 13 conscientious

morale 4 mood 5 vigor 6 esprit, spirit 9 assurance 10 confidence 13 esprit de corps

moralistic 5 noble 7 ethical 8 didactic, virtuous 9 righteous 10 principled 11 right-minded

morality 5 ethic, mores 6 virtue 7 probity 8 goodness 9 rectitude, rightness 11 saintliness, uprightness 13 righteousness

moralize 6 preach 7 lecture 9 preachify, sermonize 11 pontificate

morals 5 mores 6 ethics 9 standards

morass 3 bog, fen, web 4 knot, maze, mesh, mire, quag 5 marsh, skein, snarl, swamp 6 jungle, tangle 7 mizmaze 8 quagmire

moratorium 3 ban 5 delay 8 suspense 10 suspension

moray 3 eel

morbid 4 dark, sick 5 moody 6 gloomy, grisly, morose, sickly, sullen 7 unsound 8 diseased, gruesome 9 saturnine, unhealthy 11 melancholic, unwholesome 12 pathological

mordacious see mordant

mordancy 7 acidity 8 acerbity, acridity, acrimony, asperity, pungency 10 causticity, trenchancy

mordant 4 keen 5 salty, sharp 6 biting 7 burning, caustic, pungent 8 incisive, scathing 9 sarcastic, trenchant

Mordecai *cousin:* 6 Esther *father:* 4 Jair *mother:* 6 Esther

more 3 new, too 4 also, else, plus 5 added, again, along, extra, fresh, older, other 6 as well, better, nearer, withal 7 another, besides, farther, further, greater 8 likewise, moreover 10 additional *combining form:* 4 pleo, plio 5 pleio

More book 6 Utopia

moreover 3 and, too, yet 4 also, then 6 as well, withal 7 besides, further 8 likewise 11 furthermore 12 additionally

morepork 3 owl 9 frogmouth

mores 6 ethics, habits 7 customs, manners 8 decorums, folkways, morality 9 amenities, etiquette 10 civilities 11 proprieties

Morgana's brother 6 Arthur

morgue 5 pride 7 disdain, hauteur 8 mortuary 9 arrogance, loftiness, superbity 11 haughtiness

moribund 5 dying, going 6 fading 7 dormant 8 decaying, expiring 10 regressing 13 deteriorating

Mormon Church *administrative unit:* 4 ward 5 stake *founder:* 5 Smith (Joseph) *leader:* 5 Young (Brigham) *priest:* 5 elder

Mormon State 4 Utah

morn see morning

morne 4 cold 5 black, bleak 6 dismal, gloomy 8 desolate 9 cheerless 10 depressant, depressing, depressive

morning 4 dawn 5 light, sunup 6 aurora 7 dawning, sunrise 8 cockcrow, daybreak, daylight, forenoon *moisture:* 3 dew 8 dewdrops *song:* 6 aubade

Morocco *capital:* 5 Rabat *largest city:* 10 Casablanca *monetary unit:* 6 dirham

moron 4 fool, zany 5 ament, dummy, dunce, idiot 6 cretin, stupid 7 dullard, half-wit 8 dullhead, dumbbell, imbecile 9 ignoramus, simpleton

moronic 4 dull 6 simple, stupid 7 brutish 8 backward, imbecile, retarded 9 dim-witted 10 half-witted, slow-witted 12 feebleminded, simpleminded

morose 4 dour, glum, sick, sour, ugly 5 gruff, sulky, surly, testy 6 cranky, crusty, gloomy, morbid, sickly, sullen 7 crabbed, unhappy 8 choleric 9 irascible, saturnine, splenetic 10 ill-humored

Morpheus *father:* 6 Hypnos *god of:* 5 sleep

Morse code *dash:* 3 dah *dot:* 3 dit

morsel 3 bit 4 bite, tapa 5 crumb, goody, mug-up, piece, scrap, snack, taste, treat 6 dainty, tidbit, titbit 8 delicacy, fragment, kickshaw, mouthful 11 bonne bouche

mortal 3 man 4 body, grim, weak 5 awful, being, fatal, frail, human, party 6 deadly, finite, lethal, person 7 deathly, earthly, extreme, fleshly, massive, tedious 8 creature, hominine, possible, probable, ruthless, temporal, towering 9 fantastic, merciless, monstrous, personage, pestilent 10 implacable, individual, ironfisted, monumental, prodigious, relentless, stupendous, tremendous, unyielding 11 conceivable, mortiferous, unflinching, unrelenting 12 overpowering, pestilential, unappeasable

mortality 5 flesh 7 mankind 8 fatality, humanity 9 humankind, lethality 10 deadliness

mortally 4 very 7 awfully, fatally, vitally 8 terribly 9 extremely, intensely 10 dreadfully, grievously 11 exceedingly

Morte d'Arthur author 6 Malory (Thomas)

mortgage 4 hock, pawn 6 pledge 10 obligation

mortician 8 embalmer 10 undertaker

mortiferous 5 fatal 6 deadly, lethal, mortal 7 deathly 9 pestilent 12 pestilential

mortified 5 stern 6 severe, shamed 7 ascetic, ashamed, austere 9 chagrined

mortuary 8 tumulary 10 sepulchral 11 funeral home

mosaic 5 inlay 7 chimera 8 terrazzo 9 composite, patchwork 12 tessellation *piece:* 6 smalto 7 tessera 8 tesserae (plural)

Moscow *citadel:* 7 Kremlin *resident:* 9 Muscovite

Moses *brother:* 5 Aaron *brother-in-law:* 5 Hobab *deathplace:* 4 Nebo *father-in-law:* 6 Jethro *sister:* 6 Miriam *son:* 7 Eliezer, Gershom *spy:* 5 Caleb *successor:* 6 Joshua *wife:* 8 Zipporah

mosey 4 mope 5 amble, drift 6 bummel, linger, ramble, stroll, wander 7 saunter

Moslem see Muslim

mosque 6 masjid *niche:* 6 mihrab *prayer caller:* 7 muezzin *pulpit:* 6 mimbar *turret:* 7 minaret

mosquito 5 culex 7 culicid 8 culicine *genus:* 5 Aëdes, Culex 9 Anopheles

moss 9 bryophyte *kind:* 4 peat 8 sphagnum *part:* 4 seta 7 capsule, rhizoid *study of:* 8 bryology

mossback 4 fogy, hick 5 yokel 6 fogram, fossil, rustic, square 7 bumpkin, hayseed 9 hillbilly 10 clodhopper, fuddy-duddy, provincial 12 antediluvian, backwoodsman, mid-Victorian 13 stick-in-the-mud

most 3 too 4 best, much, nigh, very 5 about, chief, super 6 all but, better, nearly, utmost 7 greater, highest, largest, maximum 8 greatest, majority, mightily, mortally, well-nigh 9 eminently, extremely, principal 10 remarkably 11 exceedingly, practically 12 surpassingly 13 approximately

mostly 6 mainly 7 chiefly, largely, overall, usually 9 generally, primarily 11 principally 13 predominantly

mote 3 dot 4 hill 5 point, speck 6 barrow, height 7 tumulus 8 flyspeck, particle

moth 6 tineid 7 tineoid 8 bombycid *immature:* 5 larva 6 larvae (plural) 11 caterpillar *kind:* 4 luna 7 codling, tussock 8 Cecropia, silkworm 9 browntail *order:* 11 Lepidoptera

moth-eaten 4 worn 5 dated, dingy, faded, moldy, passé, seedy 6 bygone, old hat, patchy, rococo, shabby, tagrag 7 archaic, raggedy, run-down, unkempt 8 decrepit, outdated, outmoded, tattered 10 antiquated, down-at-heel, threadbare 11 dilapidated

mother 2 ma 3 dam, mom 4 mama, root 5 fount, mamma, mammy, mater, momma, mommy, mummy, nurse, serve 6 mammie, origin, source, wait on 7 care for, nurture, produce, rootage 9 prototype, rootstock 10 minister to, provenance, wellspring *combining form:* 4 matr 5 matri, matro

mother country 4 home, land, soil 8 homeland 10 fatherland

Mother Courage author 6 Brecht (Bertolt)

mother-of-pearl 5 nacre

Mother of Presidents 8 Virginia

Mother of the Gods 3 Ops 4 Rhea

motif 4 head, text 5 point, theme, topic 6 design, device, figure, matter 7 pattern, subject 8 argument 13 subject matter

motion 4 flag, move, sign, stir, sway 5 swing 6 signal 7 gesture 8 carriage, movement, proposal, stirring, wavering 9 agitation, signalize 10 suggestion 11 application, fluctuation, oscillation *combining form:* 3 cin, kin 4 cino, kine, kino, moto 5 cinet, kinet, phoro 6 cineto, kineto, praxia, praxis 7 cinesia, kinesia

motionless 5 fixed, inert, rigid, still 6 static 8 becalmed, immobile, immotile, immotive, stagnant, unmoving 9 immovable, sedentary, steadfast, unmovable 10 stationary, stock-still, stone-still

motion picture see movie

motivate 4 move 5 impel, pique, rouse 6 excite, incite, induce 7 innerve, inspire, provoke, quicken 9 galvanize, influence, innervate, stimulate

motivation 4 spur 5 drive 7 impetus, impulse 8 catalyst, stimulus 9 incentive, stimulant 10 incitation, incitement 11 instigation

motive 3 aim, end 4 good, head, spur, text 5 cause, point, theme, topic 6 design, device, figure, intent, matter, object, reason, spring 7 impulse, pattern, purpose, subject 8 argument, stimulus 9 incentive, intention 10 incitement, inducement

motley 4 fool 5 idiot, mixed, salad 6 jester, jumble, medley, varied 7 dappled, diverse, mottled, piebald 8 assorted, chow-chow, discolor, pastiche 9 colluvies, multi-hued 10 assortment, hodgepodge, miscellany, multicolor, variegated, versicolor 11 gallimaufry, promiscuous, varicolored 12 conglomerate, multicolored, multifarious, parti-colored, versicolored 13 heterogeneous, miscellaneous *combining form:* 5 parti, party

motor 3 car 4 auto, ride, tool 5 buggy, drive, pilot, wheel 6 engine 7 autocar, machine 10 automobile

motorbike 5 moped

motorboat 7 cruiser, inboard 8 outboard, runabout 12 cabin cruiser

motorcar 4 auto 5 buggy 10 automobile

motorcycle 7 chopper 8 minibike 9 trail bike *adjunct:* 7 sidecar

motorist 6 driver 7 autoist 8 operator 12 automobilist

Motown 7 Detroit

mottle 4 spot 6 blotch, marble 7 splotch

motto 3 cry 5 adage, axiom, maxim 6 byword, saying, slogan, war cry 7 precept 8 aphorism 9 battle cry, catchword, watchword 10 shibboleth 11 catchphrase, rallying cry

moue 3 mow, mug 4 face, pout 5 mouth 7 grimace 8 mouthing

mound 4 bank, cock, heap, hill, hump, mass, pile 5 cairn, drift, shock, stack 6 barrow, tumuli (plural) 7 bulwark, hillock, rampart, tumulus 8 mountain 9 elevation 10 embankment *Buddhist:* 5 stupa *burial, Eastern Europe:* 6 kurgan *burial, Peruvian:* 5 huaca *of detritus:* 4 kame *of sand:* 4 dune *of stones:* 5 cairn *Polynesian:* 3 ahu *prehistoric:* 4 terp *Scottish:* 5 toman

mound-like 7 tumular

mount 2 up 3 alp, wax 4 back, hill, lift, peak, pony, rise, show, soar, upgo 5 arise, build, climb, frame, horse, put on, rouse, scale, stage, steed, stuff 6 ascend, aspire, deepen, expand, uprear 7 advance, augment, enhance, enlarge, magnify, produce, support, upclimb, upsurge 8 bestride, escalade, escalate, heighten, increase, multiply, redouble 9 aggravate, intensate, intensify 10 promontory

mountain 3 alp, lot 4 bank, dome, heap, hill, hulk, lump, mass, mesa, much, peak, peck, pile, slew 5 bluff, butte, drift, mound, shock, stack 6 hurdle, sierra 8 obstacle 10 impediment 11 obstruction *Alaska:* 4 Bona 6 Denali 7 Foraker, Sanford 8 Wrangell *Alberta:* 6 Castle 10 Eisenhower *Alps' highest:* 5 Blanc *Angola's highest:* 4 Moco *Antarctica:* 4 Mohl 7 Gardner 9 Elizabeth 12 Vinson Massif *Appalachians:* 10 Kittatinny *Argentina:* 9 Aconcagua *Australia:* 4 Ziel 5 Bruce 6 Cradle 9 Kosciusko *beyond the:* 10 tramontane 11 transalpine *biblical:* 5 Horeb, Tabor 6 Hermon 8 Har Tavor *Black Hills:* 10 Harney Peak *Bolivia:* 6 Sorata 8 Illimani *Borneo:* 8 Kinabalu, Kinabulu *California:* 5 Guyot 7 Palomar, Whitney 8 Tuolumne 10 Buena Vista, Sonora Peak, Stanislaus *China:* 4 Emei, Song *Colorado:* 9 Pikes Peak 13 Purgatory Peak *combining form:* 3 ore, oro 4 oreo *Connecticut's highest:* 8 Frissell *Costa Rica:* 6 Blanco 14 Chirripó Grande *Cyprus' highest:* 7 Olympus, Troodos *depression:* 3 col *Dominican Republic:* 6 Duarte 8 Trujillo *Egypt:* 4 Musa 5 Sinai *Fiji:* 8 Victoria 9 Tomaniivi *foot:* 8 piedmont *Gabon:* 8 Iboundji *Georgia:* 8 Springer 10 Oglethorpe *Germany:* 7 Zollern 11 Fichtelberg *Greece:* 3 Ida 5 Athos, Levka 7 Helicon 9 Parnassus, Psiloriti 10 Pendelikon, Pentelicus *Greenland:* 9 Gunnbjørn *Himalayas:* 10 Kula Kangri *India:* 5 Japvo *Indonesia:* 4 Lawu 5 Kwoka, Lawoe, Raung 6 Raoeng *Israel:* 5 Meron 6 Carmel *Ivory Coast:* 5 Nimba *Japan:* 4 Fuji 5 Iwate 7 Fujisan 8 Fujiyama 9 Iwate-yama 10 Fuji-no-Yama *Java:* 5 Liman *Jordan:* 3 Hor 5 Hārūn *Malaysia:* 5 Ophir, Tahan 6 Ledang *Mediterranean entrance:* 5 Calpe 15 Rock of Gibraltar *New York:* 4 Bear *North America's highest:* 6 Denali 8 McKinley *Oman:* 4 Sham *Pakistan:* 9 Tirich Mir *Papua New Guinea:* 7 Wilhelm *Pennine Alps:* 4 Rosa *Philippines:* 3 Apo, Iba 4 Labo 5 Silay *ridge:* 4 spur 5 arête, crest 7 sawbuck *Romania:* 11 Moldoveanul *South America:* 7 Roraima *South Dakota:* 10 Custer Peak *Syria:* 4 Druz 5 Druze, Duruz *Tanzania:* 11 Kilimanjaro *Tasmania's highest:* 4 Ossa *Tennessee:* 7 Jumpoff, Lookout 11 Chimney Tops 13 Clingmans Dome *Togo:* 4 Agou *Vermont:* 11 Glastenbury *Vietnam:* 8 Ngoo Linh *West Africa:* 8 Cameroon *western hemisphere's highest:* 9 Aconcagua *world's highest:* 7 Everest; (see also peak)

mountain chain *Asia:* 8 Tien Shan *Greece:* 4 Oeta *Turkey:* 6 Taurus

mountain climbing *equipment:* 2 ax 3 axe, nut 5 piton 7 crampon 9 carabiner *maneuver:* 6 rappel 10 rappelling

mountain dew see moonshine

mountain formation 7 orogeny 9 orogenesy 10 orogenesis

mountain group *Germany:* 4 Harz *Idaho:* 10 Clearwater *New York:* 8 Catskill 10 Adirondack *Sinai:* 9 Gebel Musa *Slovakia:* 5 Tatra, Tatry 9 High Tatra *South Dakota-Wyoming:* 10 Black Hills *Utah:* 5 La Sal *Washington:* 7 Olympic *Zimbabwe:* 11 Matopo Hills 12 Matoppo Hills

mountainous 4 huge, vast 6 mighty 7 immense, mammoth, massive 8 enormous, gigantic 10 monumental, prodigious

mountain pass *Afghanistan-Pakistan:* 6 Khyber *Alps:* 5 Gries *California:* 4 Muir 6 Sonora *China-Myanmar:* 5 Namni *Colorado:* 3 Ute 5 Mosca, Muddy, Music, Raton *Europe:* 8 Moravian *Greece:* 5 Rupel *Hindu Kush Mts.:* 5 Dorah, Durah *Pakistan:* 5 Bolan, Gomal, Gumal *Sierra Nevada:* 4 Mono *Switzerland:* 5 Furka, Gemmi 7 Grimsel 8 Lötschen *Tunisia:*

4 Faïd *Ukrainian:* 5 Uzhok *Wyoming:*
5 Union
mountain range *Alaska:* 6 Brooks
7 Chugach 8 Wrangell *Alaska-Canada:*
10 Saint Elias *Algeria:* 3 Zab *Alps:*
8 Bavarian *ancient Edom:* 4 Seir *Antarctica:* 9 Ellsworth *Appalachian:* 4 Bald,
Blue 5 Green 6 Unicoi 10 Great Smoky
12 Great Smokies *Arizona:* 8 Maricopa
10 Chiricahua *Australia:* 7 Darling 10 Macpherson *Brazil:* 5 Organ *California:*
4 Inyo 6 Nevada 7 Klamath 10 San
Gabriel 13 San Bernardino *Canada:*
10 Laurentian *central Asia:* 9 Hindu Kush
11 Paropamisus *China:* 5 Helan *Colorado:*
7 San Juan *Czech Republic-Slovakia:*
11 West Beskids *England:* 12 Pennine
Chain *Ethiopia:* 4 Gugu *Eurasia:* 8 Caucasus *Europe:* 4 Jura 8 Pyrenees *France:*
6 Vosges 8 Cévennes *Germany:* 4 Rhön
13 Thüringer Wald *Greece:* 6 Othris, Othrys, Pindus 7 Olympus 8 Taygetus *Hawaii:*
7 Waianae *Himalayas:* 8 Anapurna
9 Annapurna *Idaho:* 5 Lemhi 7 Wasatch
India: 7 Vindhya 12 Eastern Ghats, Western Ghats *Indonesia:* 5 Maoke *Iran:*
6 Elburz *Iran-Turkmenistan:* 8 Kopet Dag
Ireland: 7 Wicklow *Italy:* 9 Apennines
Kazakhstan-Russia: 4 Ural *Kyrgyzstan:*
4 Alai *McKinley's:* 6 Alaska *Massachusetts:* 6 Hoosac *Mexico:* 11 Sierra Madre
Minnesota: 6 Mesabi *New Hampshire:*
12 Presidential *New Jersey:* 6 Ramapo
New Zealand: 12 Southern Alps *North
Carolina:* 5 Black *Northern Ireland:*
6 Mourne *Pakistan:* 8 Sulaiman *Papua
New Guinea:* 6 Albert 11 Owen Stanley
Philippines: 11 Sierra Madre *Rockies:*
11 Medicine Bow *Russia:* 8 Barguzin,
Stanovoi *Scandinavia:* 5 Kölen 6 Kjølen
Slovakia-Poland: 11 East Beskids *South
Africa:* 9 Nieuwveld 10 Kwathlamba,
Quathlamba 11 Drakensberg *South Asia:*
5 Ladak 6 Ladakh *Spain:* 6 Morena,
Toledo 8 Maladeta 10 Cantabrian *United
States:* 7 Cascade 8 Gallatin, Ouachita
Utah: 5 Uinta *Venezuela:* 6 Mérida *Wales:*
8 Cambrian *Washington:* 6 Chelan *Wyoming:* 5 Teton 11 Sierra Madre *Yosemite
National Park:* 9 Cathedral
mountains *Algeria:* 6 Hoggar 7 Ahaggar
England: 8 Cumbrian *Idaho:* 10 Clearwater *New Hampshire:* 5 White *New York:*
8 Catskill 10 Adirondack *Pennsylvania:*
6 Pocono *Slovakia:* 5 Tatra, Tatry 9 High
Tatra *study of:* 7 orology *Sudan:* 4 Nuba
Utah: 5 La Sal *Washington:* 7 Olympic
western North America: 11 Coast
Ranges
mountain sickness 4 veta 7 soroche

Mountain State 7 Montana 12 West Virginia
mountain system *Asia:* 5 Altai 8 Himalaya 9 Himalayas *Europe:* 4 Alps 10 Carpathian *Iran:* 6 Zagros *North Africa:*
5 Atlas *North America:* 5 Rocky 7 Rockies 11 Appalachian 12 Appalachians *Scotland:* 9 Grampians 13 Grampian Hills
South America: 5 Andes
mountebank 3 gyp 5 cheat, quack 6 con
man 7 diddler, sharper 8 swindler 9 charlatan, defrauder, pretender, quackster
11 flimflammer, quacksalver 12 doubledealer, saltimbanque 13 confidence man
Mount St. Helens 7 volcano
mourn 3 rue 6 bemoan, bewail, grieve,
lament, sorrow 7 protest
mournful 3 sad 4 dire 5 sorry 6 dismal,
rueful, somber, triste, woeful 7 doleful, joyless, unhappy 8 dolesome, dolorous, funereal, grievous, saddened 9 plaintive, saddening, sorrowful 10 afflictive, calamitous,
deplorable, depressing, dispirited, lamentable, lugubrious, melancholy 11 distressing,
melancholic, regrettable, unfortunate
12 heavyhearted
mournfulness 5 blues, dumps, gloom
7 sadness 9 dejection 10 depression, melancholy, the dismals 11 unhappiness
Mourning Becomes Electra *author:*
6 O'Neill (Eugene)
mourning period *Jewish:* 5 shiva
6 shibah, shivah
mourning symbol 7 armband
mouse 3 pry 4 hunt, nose, poke, slip
5 creep, glide, slide, snoop, steal 6 shiner
7 explore, saunter 8 black eye, busybody
combining form: 2 my 3 myo, mys
mouth 3 eat, gab, gob, mop, mow, yap
4 blow, brag, crow, face, guff, moue, puff,
rail, rant, rave, sass, talk, tell, trap 5 boast,
orate, prate, sauce, speak, spill, vaunt,
voice 6 betray, mumble, palate, recite,
reveal, tongue 7 blab out, declaim, divulge,
grimace, soapbox, speaker, unclose
8 back talk, bloviate, disclose, discover,
entrance, give away, harangue, perorate
9 gasconade, impudence, pronounce,
spokesman 10 embouchure, volubility
11 rodomontade, spokeswoman
12 embouchement, spokesperson *combining form:* 3 ori, oro 4 stom 5 stoma,
stome, stomi, stomo, stomy 6 stomat, stomia, stomum 7 stomata, stomate, stomato,
stomous 9 stomatous
mouthing 3 mow, mug 4 face 7 grimace
mouthlike opening 5 stoma 7 stomata
(plural)
mouthpiece 7 speaker 9 spokesman
11 spokeswoman 12 spokesperson

mouthward 4 orad
mouth-watering 5 sapid, tasty 6 savory, toothy 8 tasteful 9 aperitive, delicious, palatable, relishing 10 appetizing 11 good-tasting
mouthy 5 talky 9 bombastic, garrulous, talkative
movable 5 loose 6 mobile, motile, moving, roving 8 unstable, unsteady 10 changeable 11 unsteadfast
movables 5 goods 7 effects 8 chattels 10 belongings
move 2 go 3 act, hum 4 bear, blow, exit, goad, go on, lead, live, spur, step, stir, sway, turn, void 5 bring, budge, carry, drive, exist, get on, impel, leave, march, pique, rouse, shift, start, touch 6 acquit, affect, behave, convey, demean, depart, deport, excite, get off, incite, induce, kindle, motion, prompt, propel 7 actuate, advance, agitate, animate, breathe, comport, conduct, convert, disturb, get away, impress, innerve, inspire, measure, migrate, proceed, propose, provoke, pull out, replace, request, suggest, take off 8 activate, dislodge, displace, evacuate, get along, maneuver, mobilize, motivate, persuade, progress, relocate, resettle, stirring, supplant, transfer, transmit, withdraw 9 dislocate, galvanize, influence, innervate, instigate, stimulate, supersede, transport 10 proceeding
movement 3 act 4 deed, stir, time 5 tempo, trend 6 action, motion, rhythm 8 activity, dynamism, liveness, maneuver, stirring, tendency *away:* 6 exodus *combining form:* 3 cin, kin 4 cino, kine, kino 5 cinet, kinet 6 cineto, kineto 7 cinesia, kinesia *music:* 4 moto *reflex:* 5 taxis *stimulated:* 7 kinesis
movie 4 cine, film, show 5 flick 6 cinema 7 picture 9 photoplay 11 picture show 13 motion picture, moving picture *combining form:* 4 cine *cowboy:* 5 oater 7 western *short:* 4 clip 8 newsreel
movie director *American:* 2 Oz (Frank) 3 Lee (Spike), Ray (Nicholas) 4 Coen (Joel), Ford (John), Wise (Robert) 5 Allen (Woody), Capra (Frank), Cukor (George), Demme (Jonathan), Hawks (Howard), Kazan (Elia), Lucas (George), Roach (Hal), Stone (Oliver), Vidor (King), Wyler (William), Zwick (Ed) 6 Altman (Robert), Beatty (Warren), Burton (Tim), Curtiz (Michael), Gibson (Mel), Howard (Ron), Huston (John), Welles (Orson), Wilder (Billy) 7 Cameron (James), Coppola (Francis Ford), Costner (Kevin), De Mille (Cecil B.), Fleming (Victor), Kubrick (Stanley), Nichols (Mike), Pollack (Sidney), Redford (Robert),

Stevens (George), Sturges (Preston) 8 Eastwood (Clint), Flaherty (Robert), Griffith (David Wark), Levinson (Barry), Lubitsch (Ernst), Marshall (Penny), Minnelli (Vincente), Scorsese (Martin), Zemeckis (Robert) 9 Hitchcock (Alfred), Preminger (Otto), Spielberg (Steven), Sternberg (Josef von), Streisand (Barbra), Tarantino (Quentin), Zinnemann (Fred) 10 Heckerling (Amy) *Australian:* 4 Weir (Peter) 6 Noonan (Chris) 9 Armstrong (Gillian), Beresford (Bruce) *Austrian:* 4 Lang (Fritz) 8 Stroheim (Erich von) *British:* 4 Lean (David) 5 Ivory (James), Scott (Ridley) 6 Figgis (Mike), Frears (Stephen), Jordan (Neil), Newell (Mike), Parker (Alan), Powell (Michael) 7 Branagh (Kenneth), Forsyth (Bill), Gilliam (Terry) 10 Richardson (Tony) 11 Schlesinger (John) *Chinese:* 3 Lee (Ang) 5 Zhang (Yimou) *French:* 4 Tati (Jacques) 5 Malle (Louis) 6 Godard (Jean-Luc), Renoir (Jean), Rohmer (Eric) 8 Truffaut (François) *German:* 6 Herzog (Werner) 10 Fassbinder (Rainer) 11 Riefenstahl (Leni) *Italian:* 5 Leone (Sergio) 6 De Sica (Vittorio) 7 Fellini (Federico) 8 Pasolini (Pier Paolo), Visconti (Luchino) 9 Antonioni (Michelangelo) 10 Bertolucci (Bernardo), Rossellini (Roberto), Wertmuller (Lina), Zeffirelli (Franco) *Japanese:* 8 Kurosawa (Akira) *New Zealand:* 7 Campion (Jane) *Polish* 7 Holland (Agnieszka) *Russian:* 10 Eisenstein (Sergei) *Spanish:* 6 Buñuel (Luis) 9 Almodovar (Pedro) *Swedish:* 7 Bergman (Ingmar) 10 Zetterling (Mai)
movie producer *American:* 5 Mayer (Louis B.), Roach (Hal) 6 Kramer (Stanley), Warner (Jack L.), Welles (Orson), Zanuck (Darryl, Richard) 7 De Mille (Cecil B.), Goldwyn (Samuel), Sennett (Mack) 8 Griffith (David Wark), Selznick (David O.) *Austrian:* 9 Reinhardt (Max) *French:* 6 Renoir (Jean)
moving 5 astir 6 mobile 7 emotive, rousing 8 arousing, exciting, gripping, pathetic, poignant, rallying, stirring, touching, unstable, unsteady 9 actuating, affecting, affective, awakening, emotional, provoking, transient 10 ambulatory, impressive 11 stimulating, unsteadfast
moving picture see **movie**
moving stairs 9 escalator
mow 3 cut, mop, mug 4 bank, clip, cock, crop, down, drop, face, fell, heap, hill, kill, moue, pile, rick, rout 5 drift, floor, level, mouth, shock, smash, stack 6 ground 7 grimace 8 bowl down, bowl over, mouthing 9 bring down, knock down, throw down
moxie 2 go 3 pep 4 birr, grit, guts, tuck 5 heart, nerve, pluck, spunk, vigor

6 energy, mettle, spirit 7 cojones, courage, potency 8 backbone 9 fortitude, hardihood 10 resolution 13 dauntlessness

Mozart *birthplace:* 8 Salzburg *cataloger:* 6 Köchel (Ludwig) *deathplace:* 6 Vienna *opera:* 8 Idomeneo 10 Magic Flute 11 Don Giovanni 12 Cosi fan Tutte

MP's prey 4 AWOL 8 deserter

Mr. Moto star 5 Lorre (Peter)

Mrs. Grundy 4 prig 5 prude 7 puritan 8 bluenose, comstock 9 nice Nelly 10 goody-goody

much 3 lot, oft 4 good, heap, long, lots, lump, many, mass, most, nigh, pack, peck, pile, scad, very 5 about, often 6 all but, almost, highly, hugely, nearly, plenty 7 greatly, notably 8 abundant, lashings, ofttimes, well-nigh 9 eminently, extremely, great deal, multitude 10 frequently, oftentimes, repeatedly *combining form:* 4 poly 5 multi

Much Ado About Nothing *character:* 4 Hero 7 Claudio, Don John 8 Beatrice, Benedick

much as 4 when 5 while 6 albeit, though 7 howbeit, whereas 8 although

muck 3 goo 4 crap, dirt, dung, gook, goop, grub, gunk, junk, mess, mire, murk, plod, slog, slum, soil, toil 5 dirty, filth, grime, grind, gumbo, muddy, offal, slave, slime, swill, trash, waste 6 debris, drudge, litter, manure, refuse, sludge, smirch, smooch, smudge, smutch 7 garbage, rubbish

muckamuck 3 VIP 5 nabob 6 bigwig 7 big shot, notable 8 somebody 9 dignitary 10 notability

mucker 3 cad, oaf 4 boor, punk, worm 5 botch, chuff, churl, clown, gum up, rough, rowdy, tough, yahoo 6 bobble, bollix, bungle, no-good, wretch 7 bitch up, blunder, grobian, louse up, lowlife, ruffian, toughie 8 bullyboy, wormling 9 roughneck 10 clodhopper

mucky 4 foul 5 black, dirty, dungy, humid, messy, muddy, muggy, murky, nasty, soggy 6 cloudy, filthy, grubby, sordid, sticky, sultry 7 clouded, squalid, unclean

mucous 5 slimy 6 viscid

mucronate 5 acute, piked, sharp 6 peaked 7 pointed 8 acicular 9 aciculate, acuminate, acuminous, cuspidate

mucus 9 secretion

mud 4 dirt, mire, ooze, rile, roil 5 dregs, slime 6 depths, sludge *combining form:* 3 pel 4 pelo

muddle 3 mix 4 blow, daze, hash, limp, mess, muck, mull, muss, rile, roil 5 addle, botch, mix up, muddy, ravel, snarl, waste 6 ataxia, drivel, foul up, fuddle, fumble, huddle, jumble, jungle, litter, mess up, mumble,

murmur, muss up, mutter, tangle, tumble 7 clutter, confuse, fluster, fritter, perplex, rummage, shuffle, snarl up, stumble, stupefy, swallow 8 befuddle, bewilder, botchery, cast away, confound, disarray, disorder, distract, entangle, mishmash, scramble, shambles, squander, throw off, unsettle 9 confusion, throw away 10 complicate, disarrange, discompose, frivol away, trifle away 11 blunder away, disorganize

muddled 5 drunk, tight, tipsy, vague 6 cloudy 7 mixed-up 8 inchoate 9 disguised, pixilated 10 disjointed, disordered, incoherent, incohesive, inebriated 11 intoxicated, unconnected, unorganized 12 disconnected, uncontinuous 13 discontinuous

muddlehead 4 dolt 5 dunce, idiot, moron 6 dimwit 7 fathead 8 dumbbell 9 blockhead, simpleton 11 chowderhead

muddle through 2 do 4 fare 5 get by, get on, shift 6 manage 8 get along 9 stagger on 12 stagger along

muddy 3 dim, fog 4 base, blur, drab, dull, fade, foul, miry, oozy, pale, rile, roil, soil 5 befog, black, cloud, dirty, dungy, grime, murky, riley, roily, soily 6 cloudy, gloomy, sordid, turbid 7 becloud, begrime, bemired, confuse, squalid, subfusc, tarnish, unclean, unclear 8 confused 9 uncleanly

mudfish 6 bowfin

mud hen 4 coot, rail

muezzin's faith 5 Islam

muff 4 blow, flub 5 botch, error, fluff 6 bobble, bollix, bungle, fumble, goof up 7 louse up

muffle 4 dull, mute, veil 5 shush 6 dampen, deaden, lessen, shroud, soften, stifle, subdue, wrap up 7 envelop, repress, silence, smother, squelch 8 bundle up, strangle, suppress, tone down 10 overspread

muffler 4 mask, veil 5 cloak, cover, guise, scarf 6 facade, veneer 8 disguise 10 masquerade 12 disguisement

muffler mangler 3 rut 7 pothole 9 chuckhole

mug 3 cup, mop, mow 4 boob, dolt, dope, face, fool, moue, phiz, punk, puss, thug, toby 5 dunce, grail, idiot, mouth, rough, rowdy, stein, stoup, tough 6 dimwit, mucker, seidel, visage 7 assault, chalice, grimace, ruffian, tankard 8 bullyboy, dumbbell, features, mouthing, numskull, plugugly, schooner 9 blockhead, ignoramus, roughneck 11 countenance

mugger 4 thug 9 assailant, assaulter

muggy 4 damp 5 humid, moist, mucky, soggy 6 moisty, sticky, sultry 7 dampish, wettish

Muhammad, Mohammed *adopted son:* 3 Ali *birthplace:* 5 Mecca *camel:* 5 Kaswa *daughter:* 6 Fatima *deathplace:* 6 Medina *deity:* 5 Allah *father:* 8 Abdallah, Abdullah *father-in-law:* 7 Abu Bakr *flight:* 6 hegira, hejira *follower:* 6 Moslem, Muslim *horse:* 5 Buraq 7 Alborak *religion:* 5 Islam *son:* 7 Ibrahim *son-in-law:* 3 Ali *successor:* 5 calif 6 caliph 7 Abu Bakr *tribe:* 7 Koreish *uncle:* 8 Abu Talib *wife:* 5 Aisha 6 Ayesha 7 Khadija

mulct 4 fine, milk, rook 5 bleed, cheat, stick, sweat 6 amerce, fleece 7 deceive, defraud, forfeit, penalty, swindle 8 penalize 10 amercement

mule 5 cross 6 hybrid 7 bastard, mongrel 9 crossbred, half blood, half-breed 10 crossbreed

muleheaded see **mulish**

mulish 5 balky 6 unruly 8 perverse, stubborn 9 obstinate, pigheaded 10 bullheaded, headstrong, inflexible, refractory, self-willed, unyielding 11 stiff-necked, wrongheaded

mull 4 hash, mess, muse, muss, numb, poke, roll, stir 5 addle, blunt, botch, dally, delay, mix-up, tarry, think 6 ball up, bemuse, benumb, dawdle, deaden, fuddle, linger, loiter, mess-up, muddle, ponder, put off 7 confuse, crumble 8 befuddle, bewilder, botchery, cogitate, consider, distract, meditate, ruminate, shambles, throw off, turn over 9 pulverize 10 deliberate, dillydally 11 desensitize 13 procrastinate

mulligrubs 4 sulk 5 blues, dumps, gloom, mumps, pouts 6 grumps 7 sullens 9 dejection 10 depression, melancholy

multicolored 4 pied 6 motley 7 dappled 8 discolor 10 variegated, versicolor

multifarious 4 many 5 mixed 6 legion, motley, sundry, varied 7 diverse, various 8 assorted, chowchow, manifold, numerous, populous 10 voluminous 11 diversiform, promiscuous 12 conglomerate 13 heterogeneous, miscellaneous

multiform 7 diverse 8 manifold 11 diversiform 12 multifarious, multivarious

multiformity 7 variety 8 multeity 9 diversity 11 diverseness, variousness 12 multiplicity

multihued see **multicolored**

multilateral 9 many-sided

multiloquent 5 gabby, talky 6 chatty 9 garrulous, talkative 10 babblative, loquacious 11 loose-lipped 12 loose-tongued

multiplex see **multiform**

multiplicity 3 lot 4 mass, much, peck 6 barrel 7 variety 8 multeity 9 diversity, great deal 11 diverseness, variousness

multiply 3 wax 4 bear, rise 5 beget, boost, breed, build, mount 6 beef up, expand, extend, spread 7 amplify, augment, enlarge, magnify, produce, upsurge 8 generate, heighten, increase 9 procreate, propagate, reproduce 10 aggrandize

multitude 3 mob 4 army, host, many, rout 5 cloud, crowd, crush, drove, flock, horde, press, swarm 6 legion, oodles, public, scores, squash, throng 7 numbers

multitudinal see **multitudinous**

multitudinous 4 many 6 legion, myriad, sundry 7 various 8 manifold, numerous, populous 9 countless 10 innumerous, numberless, voluminous 11 innumerable 12 multifarious

multivocal 7 blatant 8 strident 9 clamorous, equivocal 10 boisterous, vociferant, vociferous 11 loudmouthed, openmouthed 12 obstreperous

mum 4 dumb, mute 5 still 6 silent 7 silence 8 wordless 10 speechless

mumble 4 chew 5 mouth, rumor 6 muddle, murmur, mutter 7 maunder, swallow, whisper 9 undertone 11 susurration

mumbo jumbo 7 mummery 9 gibberish 10 hocus pocus 11 abracadabra

mummer 4 mime 5 actor, mimic 6 player 7 trouper 8 thespian 9 performer, playactor 12 impersonator

mummery 6 acting 9 gibberish, hypocrisy 10 hocus pocus, mumbo jumbo 11 abracadabra

mummify 4 wilt 5 dry up, wizen 6 welter, wither 7 shrivel

mumpish 4 dour, ugly 5 sulky, surly 6 morose, sullen 9 saturnine

munch 3 eat 4 bite, chew 5 champ, chomp, chump 6 crunch 7 chumble, scrunch 8 ruminate 9 masticate

mundane 5 lowly 6 cosmic, earthy 7 earthly, prosaic, sensual, terrene, workday, worldly 8 banausic, everyday, telluric, workaday 9 sublunary, tellurian 11 commonplace, terrestrial, uncelestial 13 materialistic

municipal 4 city, home 5 urban 6 native 7 burghal 8 domestic, internal, national 9 intestine

munificent 4 free 6 lavish 7 liberal 8 generous, handsome 9 bounteous, bountiful, unsparing 10 freehanded, openhanded

munitions maker 5 Krupp

muralist 4 Sert (José María) 6 Benton (Thomas Hart), Giotto, Orozco (José Clemente), Rivera (Diego) 7 La Farge (John) 9 Siqueiras (David) 12 Michelangelo 16 Puvis de Chavannes (Pierre-Cecile); (See also **painter**)

murder 4 cool, do in, hang, kill, slay 5 abate, blood, lynch, scrag 6 finish, mangle, rub out 7 abolish, blot out, destroy, execute, garrote, killing, put away, root out, smother 8 foul play, homicide, knock off, strangle, uncreate 9 eradicate, liquidate, slaughter 10 annihilate, asphyxiate, decapitate, extinguish, guillotine 11 assassinate, electrocute, exterminate 12 manslaughter *brother:* 10 fratricide *father:* 9 patricide *king:* 8 regicide *mother:* 9 matricide *parent:* 9 parricide *sister:* 10 sororicide

murderer 6 killer, slayer 7 butcher 8 assassin, homicide 9 manslayer 11 slaughterer

Murder in the Cathedral *author:* 5 Eliot (Thomas Stearns) *character:* 5 Henry 7 Beckett

murderous 6 brutal 9 ferocious 11 devastating 12 bloodthirsty

mure 3 pen 4 cage, wall 5 fence, hedge 6 shut in, thrust 7 close in, enclose, envelop, squeeze

murk 3 dim, fog 4 foul, haze, mist, soil 5 bedim, cloud, dirty, gloom, grime, muddy 6 besoil, darken, smirch, smudge 7 becloud, begrime, obscure, tarnish 8 darkness 9 obfuscate

murky 3 dim, dun 4 dark, drab, dull, dusk, foul 5 black, dirty, dusky, foggy, misty, muddy, nasty, roily 6 cloudy, filthy, gloomy, grubby, opaque, somber, sordid, turbid 7 obscure, squalid, subfusc, unclean 8 nubilous 9 ambiguous, equivocal, sibylline, tenebrous 10 caliginous

murmur 3 cry, hum 4 buzz, fuss, kick, purr, talk, wail 5 croak, drone, rumor, scold, whine 6 fumble, gossip, grouch, grouse, muddle, mumble, mutter, repine, report, rumble 7 grumble, hearsay, swallow, whisper 8 complain 9 grapevine, grumbling, undertone 11 scuttlebutt, susurration

muscle 4 beef, thew 5 brawn, force, might, power, sinew 6 energy 7 potency 8 strength 9 necessity, strong arm *arm:* 6 biceps 7 triceps *back:* 9 trapezius *calf:* 6 soleus *chest:* 10 pectoralis *combining form:* 2 ei (plural) 3 eus, mya 6 muscul, myaria (plural) 7 musculo *jaw:* 8 masseter *kind:* 6 flexor, tensor 7 dilator, evertor, levator, rotator 8 abductor, adductor, extensor *loin:* 5 psoas *neck:* 8 platysma *shoulder:* 7 deltoid 10 deltoideus *study of:* 7 myology *thigh:* 8 gracilis 9 sartorius

muscle-bound 5 rigid, stiff 6 wooden 7 buckram, stilted 9 cardboard

muscular 4 ropy, wiry 5 beefy, burly, husky, stout 6 brawny, mighty, robust, sinewy, strong, sturdy, supple 7 fibrous, stringy, well-set 8 athletic, forceful, powerful, stalwart, vigorous, well-knit 9 Herculean, well-built

muse 4 bard, poet 5 study, think 6 ponder, trance 7 reflect, reverie 8 cogi-

tate, meditate, mull over, ruminate, turn over 10 deliberate, excogitate 11 contemplate

Muse *father:* 4 Zeus 7 Jupiter *mother:* 9 Mnemosyne *of astronomy:* 6 Urania *of choral song:* 11 Terpsichore *of comedy:* 6 Thalia *of dancing:* 11 Terpsichore *of epic poetry:* 8 Calliope *of history:* 4 Clio *of love poetry:* 5 Erato *of lyric poetry:* 5 Erato *of music:* 7 Euterpe *of pastoral poetry:* 6 Thalia *of sacred poetry:* 8 Polymnia 10 Polyhymnia *of tragedy:* 9 Melpomene

museum 5 salon 7 exhibit, gallery 8 atheneum 10 collection, repository 11 pinacotheka

Mushi's father 6 Merari

mushroom 4 grow 5 burst, go off 6 blow up, expand, spread 7 explode 8 detonate *combining form:* 3 myc 4 myco 5 mycet 6 myceto *edible:* 5 morel 10 champignon 11 chanterelle *kind:* 6 agaric, bolete 7 inky cap, russula *part:* 3 cap 4 gill, ring 5 stipe, volva 6 pileus 7 annulus 8 mycelium *poisonous:* 7 amanita 8 death cup 9 toadstool

mushy 4 hazy, soft, weak 5 foggy, misty, pappy, pulpy, vague 6 cloudy, quaggy, spongy, sticky, vapory 7 blurred, maudlin, mawkish, pulpous, squashy, squishy, squushy 8 bathetic, effusive, romantic, sluggish, squelchy, vaporous 10 lovey-dovey 11 sentimental, tear-jerking

music *abbreviation:* 2 ff, mf, mp, pp, sf 3 sfz *bass staff lines:* 5 GBDFA *bass staff spaces:* 4 ACEG *characteristic phrase:* 9 leitmotif, leitmotiv *chord:* 5 tonic 8 dominant 9 augmented 10 diminished *embellishment:* 3 run 4 turn 5 trill 7 cadenza, mordent, roulade 8 arpeggio, flourish 9 grace note *for eight:* 5 octet *for five:* 7 quintet *for four:* 7 quartet *for nine:* 5 nonet *for one:* 4 solo *for seven:* 6 septet *for six:* 6 sextet *for three:* 4 trio *for two:* 3 duo 4 duet *god:* 6 Apollo *hall:* 7 cabaret, theater *instrumental form:* 3 jig 4 jazz, reel 5 étude, fugue, gigue, march, polka, rondo, suite, swing, waltz 6 minuet, pavane, sonata 7 bourrée, gavotte, mazurka, prelude, ragtime, toccata 8 chaconne, concerto, courante, fantasia, galliard, nocturne, overture, rhapsody, ricercar, saraband, serenade, symphony, tone poem 9 allemande, polonaise 11 rock and roll *medley:* 4 olio *morning:* 6 aubade *Muse:* 7 Euterpe *night:* 8 nocturne, serenade *note:* 4 half 5 breve, minim, neume, whole 6 eighth 7 quarter 9 sixteenth *patron saint:* 7 Cecilia *period:* 6 Modern, Rococo 7 Baroque 8 Medieval, Romantic 9 Classical *reformer:* 5 Guido (of Arezzo) *symbol:*

3 bar, key 4 clef, flat, note, rest, slur, turn 5 sharp, staff 7 fermata, mordent 9 alla breve 10 accidental *treble staff lines:* 5 EGBDF *treble staff spaces:* 4 FACE *vocal form:* 3 air 4 aria,.hymn, lied, mass, song 5 canon, chant, motet, opera, round 6 anthem, ballad 7 cantata, chanson, chorale 8 cavatina, madrigal, operetta, oratorio, serenade 9 cabaletta

musical 4 show 5 revue 6 turned 7 chiming, lyrical, melodic, songful, tuneful 8 blending, harmonic 9 consonant, melodious, symphonic 10 harmonious 11 symphonious

musical composition 4 aria, hymn, opus, solo 5 étude, fugue, motet, opera, psalm, rondo, suite 6 anthem, ballad, sonata, verset 7 cantata, chanson, chorale, prelude, requiem, toccata 8 concerto, madrigal, nocturne, operetta, oratorio, postlude, serenade, sonatina, symphony 9 bagatelle, cabaletta, interlude, toccatina 10 intermezzo

musical direction *accented:* 7 marcato 8 sforzato 9 sforzando *airy:* 7 sfogato *all:* 5 tutti *as written:* 3 sta *bold:* 6 audace *brisk:* 4 vivo 6 vivace 7 allegro, animato *connected:* 6 legato *detached:* 8 spiccato, staccato *dignified:* 8 maestoso *disconnected:* 8 staccato *dying away:* 7 calando *emotional:* 12 appassionato *emphatic:* 7 marcato *evenly:* 10 egualmente *excited:* 7 agitato 9 spiritoso *fast:* 4 vite, vivo 5 tosto 6 presto, veloce, vivace 7 allegro 10 tostamente *faster:* 7 stretto 11 accelerando *fluctuating tempo:* 6 rubato *forcefully:* 7 furioso *freely:* 9 ad libitum *gay:* 7 giocoso *gentle:* 5 dolce 7 amabile, amoroso 9 affettuso *graceful:* 6 adagio 8 grazioso *half:* 5 mezzo *heavy:* 7 pesante *held firmly:* 6 tenuto *hurried:* 7 agitato *joyous:* 7 giocoso *less:* 4 meno *little:* 4 poco *little by little:* 9 poco a poco *lively:* 4 vite 6 vivace 7 allegro, animato, giocoso 9 capriccio *loud:* 5 forte *louder:* 9 crescendo *lovingly:* 7 amabile, amoroso *majestic:* 8 maestoso *moderate:* 7 andante 8 moderato *moderately loud:* 2 mf 10 mezzo forte *moderately soft:* 2 mp 10 mezzo piano *muted:* 5 sorda, sordo *passionless:* 6 freddo *plaintive:* 7 dolente 8 doloroso *playful:* 7 giocoso 10 scherzando *plucked:* 9 pizzicato *quick:* 4 vite, vivo 5 tosto 6 presto, veloce, vivace 7 allegro 10 tostamente *quickening:* 11 affrettando *repeat:* 2 DC 3 bis 6 da capo *sad:* 7 dolente 8 doloroso *separate:* 6 divisi *showily:* 10 brilliante *silent:* 5 tacet *singing:* 9 cantabile *sliding:* 9 glissando *slow:* 5 grave, largo, tardo 6 adagio 7 andante 9 larghetto *slowing:*

3 rit 6 ritard 10 ritardando 11 rallentando *smooth:* 5 dolce 6 legato 8 grazioso *soft:* 5 dolce, piano *softening:* 10 diminuendo 11 decrescendo *solemn:* 5 grave *sorrowful:* 7 dolente 8 doloroso *spirited:* 4 vivo 6 audace, vivace 7 animato 9 spiritoso *stately:* 7 pomposo 8 maestoso *strong:* 5 forte *sustained:* 6 tenuto 9 sostenuto *sweet:* 5 dolce *tender:* 7 amabile, amoroso 10 affettuoso *together:* 4 a due *tranquil:* 7 calmato *very fast:* 11 prestissimo *very loud:* 2 ff 10 fortissimo *very soft:* 2 pp 10 pianissimo

musical drama 5 opera 8 operetta 9 singspiel

musical group 4 band, trio 5 choir, combo 6 chorus 7 quartet 8 ensemble, glee club, symphony 9 orchestra

musical instrument *African:* 5 mbira, sansa, zanza 7 kalimba, marimba *ancient:* 4 lyre, rote 5 crwth, rotte, shawm 6 cither, syrinx, trigon 7 cithara, mandola, pandura, panpipe, serpent, sistrum, theorbo *Arabic:* 3 oud 6 atabal *bagpipe:* 7 musette, pibroch *biblical:* 4 asor, harp, horn, pipe 5 flute 6 cymbal, sabeca, tabret 7 timbrel, trumpet 8 psaltery *brass:* 4 horn, tuba 5 bugle 6 cornet 7 althorn, clarion, helicon, saxhorn, trumpet 8 trombone 10 French horn *Chinese:* 3 kin *Indian:* 4 vina 5 sarod, sitar, veena *Japanese:* 4 biwa, koto 7 samisen *keyboard:* 5 organ, piano 6 spinet 7 celesta, cembalo, clavier 8 calliope, melodeon, virginal 9 accordion 10 clavichord, concertina, pianoforte 11 harpsichord *medieval:* 4 lute 5 naker, rebab, rebec, shawm, tabor 6 citole 7 cow horn, gittern, mandola, panpipe 8 cornetto, doucaine, dulcimer, gemshorn, hornpipe, Jew's harp, oliphant, recorder 9 monochord, rommelpot 10 clavichord, hurdygurdy *percussion:* 4 bell, drum 5 guiro, piano 6 cymbal, maraca 7 marimba, timbrel, tympani 8 bass drum, castanet, triangle 9 snare drum, xylophone 10 kettledrum, tambourine, vibraphone *Persian:* 6 santir *pipe:* 6 syrinx 7 bagpipe, musette, panpipe 9 cornemuse *reed:* 4 oboe 7 bassoon 8 clarinet 9 harmonica, saxophone 11 English horn *Renaissance:* 4 viol 5 regal, shawm 6 curtal, lirone, spinet 7 bagpipe, bandora, cittern, rackett, sackbut, serpent, theorbo, vihuela, violone 8 crumhorn, penorcon, recorder, virginal 9 angelique, cornamuse, orpharion, pandurina 10 bassanello, chitarrone, colascione 11 harpsichord *Russian:* 9 balalaika *stringed:* 3 oud 4 asor, harp, lute, lyre, vina, viol 5 banjo, cello, piano, rebec, sitar, viola 6 fiddle, guitar, violin, zither 7 bandora, cittern, gittern, kantele, pandura, ukulele

8 autoharp, dulcimer, mandolin 10 contrabass, double bass 11 harpsichord, vio-
loncello *suffix:* 3 ina, ine *toy:* 5 kazoo
7 ocarina *two-necked:* 7 theorbo *woodwind:* 4 oboe 5 flute 7 bassoon, piccolo
9 flageolet, saxophone 11 English horn

musical interval 5 fifth, major, minor,
sixth, third 6 ditone, fourth, octave, second
7 perfect, seventh, tritone

musical syllable 2 do, fa, la, mi, re, si, ti,
ut 3 Ela, sol *Guido's:* 2 ut 3 Ela

musician 4 bard 5 piper 6 player 7 jazz-
man 8 minstrel, virtuoso 9 performer

muskeg 3 bog, fen 4 mire, quag 5 marsh,
swamp 6 slough 7 baygall

musket 5 fusil 6 dragon 7 dragoon 9 flint-
lock, matchlock 12 muzzleloader *medieval:*
8 culverin

Musketeer 5 Athos 6 Aramis 7 Porthos
author: 5 Dumas (Alexandre) *friend:*
9 d'Artagnan

muskmelon 10 cantaloupe

Muslim, Moslem *ascetic:* 4 Sufi 5 fakir
7 dervish 8 marabout *Bible:* 5 Koran *body
of scholars:* 5 ulema *branch:* 4 Shia
5 Sunni *caller to prayer:* 7 muezzin *call to
prayer:* 4 adan, azan *cap:* 3 taj *creed:*
6 Kelima 7 Kalimah *devil:* 5 Eblis *festival:*
3 Eed 6 Bairam *garment:* 4 izar 5 ihram
6 chador *god:* 5 Allah *holy city:* 5 Mecca
6 Medina *holy war:* 5 jahad, jehad, jihad
judge: 4 cadi *lawyer:* 5 mufti *marriage:*
4 mota, muta *mendicant:* 5 fakir *monastery:* 5 ribat 7 khankah *month:* (see at
month) *month of fasting:* 7 Ramadan
mosque: 6 masjid *mystic:* 4 Sufi *nonbe-
liever:* 5 Kafir 6 Kaffir *nymph:* 5 houri *pilgrim:* 4 haji 5 hadji, hajji *pilgrimage:*
3 haj 4 hadj, hajj *priest:* 4 imam *prophet:*
8 Mohammed, Muhammad *religion:*
5 Islam *saint:* 3 pir 6 santon *saint's tomb:*
3 pir *shrine:* 5 Caaba, Kaaba 6 Kaabah
student: 5 softa *teacher:* 4 alim 5 mulla
6 mullah *temple:* 6 mosque *title:* 3 aga
4 agha, emir, said 5 calif, emeer, sayid
6 caliph *tradition:* 5 sunna 6 sunnah; (see
also **mosque; Muhammad**)

muss 4 mess 5 botch, mix-up, upset
6 jumble, mess-up, muddle, rumple 7 disrupt, rummage, wrinkle 8 botchery, disarray, dishevel, disorder, shambles 10 disarrange 11 disorganize

mussel 5 naiad *genus:* 4 Unio 7 Mytilus
8 Anodonta *larva:* 9 blackhead

Mussolini, Benito 7 Fascist 8 dictator
title: 4 Duce (Il)

mussy 5 messy 6 sloppy, sloven, unneat,
untidy 7 unkempt 8 ill-kempt, slobbery,
slovenly 10 disheveled

must 4 duty, have, need, want 5 ought
6 charge, devoir, should 9 committal, condi-

tion, essential, necessity, requisite 10 commitment, obligation, sine qua non
11 requirement 12 precondition, prerequisite

muster 4 call, roll 5 breed, cause, crowd,
enter, get up, group, hatch, raise, rally
6 enlist, enroll, gather, induce, invoke, join
up, number, roster, sample, sign on, sign
up, summon, work up 7 collect, company,
convene, develop, include, marshal, produce 8 assemble, assembly, comprise,
congress, engender, generate, mobilize,
occasion, organize 9 congeries, forgather,
gathering, inventory 10 accumulate,
assemblage, collection, congregate, rendezvous 11 aggregation, examination
12 accumulation, congregation

muster out 8 separate 9 discharge
10 demobilize

musty 4 dull, rank, sour 5 dirty, fetid,
funky, moldy, stale, tired, trite 6 frowsy, old
hat, smelly, whiffy 7 noisome, spoiled,
squalid 8 shopworn, timeworn 10 antiquated, malodorous, threadbare

Mut *husband:* 4 Amen, Amon *son:*
5 Chons 6 Chonsu, Khonsu

mutable 5 fluid 6 fickle, mobile, shifty
7 protean 8 slippery, unstable, unsteady,
variable, wavering, weathery 9 changeful,
mercurial, uncertain, unsettled 10 capricious, changeable, inconstant 11 fluctuating, vacillating 12 inconsistent

mutate 4 turn, vary 5 alter 6 change,
modify 7 commute 9 refashion, transform,
transmute, transpose 11 transfigure
12 metamorphize, metamorphose, transmogrify

mutation 4 turn 6 change 7 novelty
9 variation 10 alteration, innovation
11 vicissitude 12 modification

mute 3 mum 4 dumb 6 dampen, deaden,
muffle, reduce, silent, soften, stifle
8 silencer, wordless 9 voiceless
10 speechless 12 inarticulate, unarticulate

muted 3 dim, mat 4 dead, dull, flat 5 blind
6 silent 10 lackluster, lusterless, speechless

mutedly 6 weakly 7 faintly 9 sotto voce

mutilate 3 mar 4 geld, hurt, maim 5 alter,
spoil, unsex 6 change, damage, deface,
injure, mangle, mayhem, neuter 7 cripple,
dislimb 8 castrate 9 disfigure, dismember,
sterilize 11 desexualize

mutineer 5 rebel 6 anarch 8 frondeur,
revolter 9 anarchist, insurgent 10 malcontent

mutinous 6 unruly 8 factious 9 insurgent,
seditious, turbulent 10 rebellious 12 contumacious 13 insubordinate

mutiny 5 rebel 6 revolt 9 insurrect, rebellion 11 rise against 12 insurrection

mutt 3 cur, dog 4 boob, dolt, dope
5 dunce, idiot 6 dimwit 7 mongrel 8 dumbbell, numskull 9 blockhead, ignoramus
Mutt and ____ 4 Jeff
mutter 5 croak, growl, rumor, scold 6 fumble, grouch, grouse, muddle, mumble, murmur 7 grumble, swallow, whisper 9 undertone 11 susurration
muttonchops 9 burnsides, sideburns
10 sideboards 11 dundrearies 12 side-
whiskers
muttonhead 3 oaf 5 dunce, idiot 8 clodpate, numskull 9 blockhead 10 thickskull
mutual 5 joint 6 common, public, shared,
united 7 related 8 communal, conjoint, conjunct 9 connected 10 associated, reciprocal, respective *prefix:* 2 co 5 inter
muzzle 3 gag, mug 4 face, nose, phiz
5 snout 6 nuzzle, visage 8 features,
restrain 11 countenance
My Antonia author 6 Cather (Willa)
My Last Duchess author 8 Browning
(Robert)
My Lost Youth author 10 Longfellow
(Henry Wadsworth)
myrmecology subject 3 ant
myrmidon 8 follower, hireling, retainer
9 attendant, underling 11 subordinate
Myron's statue 10 Discobolus
Myrrha's son 6 Adonis
mysterious 6 arcane, mystic, occult,
secret 7 cryptic, obscure, strange
8 abstruse, esoteric, numinous 9 ambiguous, enigmatic, equivocal, recondite,
unguessed 10 cabalistic, unknowable
11 enigmatical, inscrutable, ungraspable
12 impenetrable, incognizable, inexplicable,
unexaminable, unfathomable 13 unaccountable

mystery 5 poser 6 enigma, puzzle, riddle,
secret 7 arcanum, problem, stumper
9 conundrum 10 closed book, perplexity,
puzzlement 13 Chinese puzzle, mystification *story:* 8 whodunit
mystic 4 seer 5 magic, vague 6 arcane,
magian, occult, secret, witchy 7 magical,
obscure 8 anagogic, esoteric, numinous,
quixotic, telestic, wizardly 9 enigmatic, mysterial, sorcerous, unguessed 10 cabalistic,
mysterious, unknowable 11 inscrutable,
necromantic 12 impenetrable, thaumaturgic
13 unaccountable
mystical 4 deep, holy 6 covert, divine,
orphic, sacred, secret 7 cryptic, furtive,
sub-rosa 8 anagogic, hush-hush, orphical,
profound, stealthy, telestic 9 spiritual
10 miraculous, symbolical 11 clandestine
12 hugger-mugger, supernatural, supranatural 13 hole-and-corner
mysticism 8 cabalism, quietism
mystify 6 puzzle 7 confuse, perplex
8 befuddle, bewilder 9 obfuscate
mystifying 4 dark 7 cryptic 8 Delphian
9 enigmatic
myth 4 lore, saga, tale 5 fable, story 6 legend 7 fiction, figment, parable 8 allegory,
apologue, creation, folklore 9 invention, tradition 11 fabrication
mythical 6 unreal 7 created, fictive 8 fabulous, fanciful, invented 9 fantastic, fictional, imaginary, legendary, visionary
10 fictitious 12 mythological
mythological see **mythical**
mythologist 5 Tylor (Edward) 6 Frazer
(James) 5 Müller (Friedrich Max)
9 Euhemerus 10 Malinowski (Bronislaw)
mythology see **myth**

N

Naamah *brother:* 9 Tubalcain *father:*
6 Lamech *husband:* 7 Solomon *mother:*
6 Zillah *son:* 8 Rehoboam

Naaman *disease:* 7 leprosy *father:*
4 Bela *grandfather:* 8 Benjamin *healer:*
6 Elisha

Naam's father 5 Caleb

Naarah's husband 6 Ashhur

nab 3 nip 4 hook, nail, take 5 catch, pinch,
run in, seize, steal 6 arrest, clutch, collar,
detain, pickup, pull in, snatch 7 capture,
grapple 9 apprehend

nabal 5 chuff, hunks, miser, stiff 7 niggard,
scrooge 8 muckworm, tightwad 9 skinflint
12 moneygrubber

Nabal's wife 7 Abigail

nabob 6 biggie, bigwig, fat cat 7 notable
8 big chief, eminence 9 dignitary 10 notability

Nabokov novel 3 Ada 4 Pnin 6 Lolita,
The Eye 7 Despair, The Gift 8 Mashenka,
Pale Fire, The Event 10 The Defense, The
Exploit

nacre 13 mother-of-pearl

nada 7 nullity, vacuity 8 nihility 11 nothingness 12 nonexistence

Nadab *brother:* 4 Kish 5 Abihu *father:*
5 Aaron, Jeiel 6 Gibeon 8 Jeroboam
mother: 6 Maacah 8 Elisheba *slayer:*
6 Baasha

nadir 4 base, foot 6 bottom *opposite:*
6 zenith

nag 3 egg, irk, vex 4 bait, carp, fuss, goad,
jade, prod, ride, urge 5 annoy, chivy, harry,
hound, tease, worry 6 badger, bother, carp
at, harass, heckle, hector, needle, peck at,
pester, plague 7 henpeck, torment
8 harangue, irritate

Nahash's daughter 7 Abigail, Zeruiah

Nahath *father:* 5 Reuel *grandfather:*
7 Elkanah

Nahor *brother:* 5 Haran 7 Abraham *concubine:* 6 Reumah *father:* 5 Serug, Terah
grandson: 7 Abraham *son:* 5 Terah
7 Bethuel *wife:* 6 Milcah

Nahshon *brother-in-law:* 5 Aaron *father:*
9 Amminadab *grandson:* 4 Boaz *sister:*
8 Elisheba *son:* 6 Salmon

naiad 5 nymph

naif 7 ingenue

nail 3 bag, get 4 brad, spad, stud, tack,
trap 5 catch, clone, spike, sprig 6 collar,
secure, tacket, unguis, ungula 7 capture,
prehend, ungulae (plural) 8 sparable *combining form:* 4 helo, onyx 5 onych, ungui
6 onycho 7 onychia 8 onychium

naive 4 easy 5 fresh 6 simple 7 artless,
natural 8 gullible, innocent, original, unartful
9 ingenuous, unstudied 10 fleeceable,
unaffected, unschooled 11 susceptible

naked 3 raw 4 bald, bare, mere, nude,
open, pure 5 clear, sheer 6 meager,
peeled, scanty, simple, unclad 7 denuded,
evident, exposed, obvious, unarmed 8 buff-
bare, garbless, manifest, palpable,
revealed, stripped 9 au naturel, colorless,
destitute, disclosed, unclothed, uncolored,
uncovered, undressed 10 discovered *combining form:* 4 gymn, nudi 5 gymno

Naked and the Dead author 6 Mailer
(Norman)

namby-pamby 3 sop 4 baby, flat
5 banal, bland, inane, sissy 6 jejune 7 doormat, insipid, milksop, sapless 8 weakling
9 driveling, innocuous, jellyfish 10 pantywaist, wishy-washy 11 Milquetoast, mollycoddle 12 milk-and-water 13 characterless

name 3 dub, nom, tab, tag, tap 4 call, cite,
clan, make, race, term 5 alias, label,
nomen, quote, state, style, title 6 byword,
family, finger, handle, report, repute, rubric,
ticket 7 appoint, baptize, declare, entitle,
epithet, mention, moniker, notable, publish,
specify 8 announce, christen, cognomen,
identify, instance, luminary, monicker, nominate, somebody 9 advertise, celebrity,
character, designate, incognito, pseudonym, recognize, sobriquet, stipulate
10 denominate, hypocorism, nom de plume,
notability, reputation 11 appellation, appellative, designation *ancient Rome:* 7 agnomen 8 prenomen *assumed:* 5 alias
9 sobriquet *combining form:* 4 onym
7 onomato *family:* 8 cognomen *fictitious:*
9 pseudonym *giver:* 6 eponym

namely 5 to wit 8 scilicet 9 expressly,
specially, videlicet 10 especially 12 particularly, specifically *abbreviation:* 3 viz

nana 5 nurse 9 nursemaid 11 nurserymaid

Nana *author:* 4 Zola (Emile) *mother:* 8 Gervaise

Nanna *brother:* 6 Nergal, Ninazu *father:* 5 Enlil *husband:* 6 Balder *mother:* 6 Ninlil *son:* 3 Utu *wife:* 6 Ningal

nanny see nana

Naomi 4 Mara *daughter-in-law:* 4 Ruth 5 Orpah *husband:* 9 Elimelech *meaning:* 8 pleasant *son:* 6 Mahlon 7 Chilion

nap 3 nod 4 doze, rest, shag 5 break, cover, let up, pause, relax, sleep, unlax 6 drowse, siesta, snooze 7 respite 10 forty winks

nape 6 scruff

Naphish's father 7 Ishmael

Naphtali *brother:* 3 Dan *father:* 5 Jacob *mother:* 6 Bilhah *son:* 4 Guni 5 Jezer 7 Jahzeel, Jahziel, Shallum

naphtha 7 solvent 9 petroleum

napkin 5 cloth, doily, towel 9 handcloth

napoleon 4 boot 6 pastry 8 card game 9 solitaire *bid:* 7 blucher 10 wellington

Napoleon *adversary:* 6 Nelson (Horatio) 7 Kutuzov (Mikhail) 10 Wellington (Duke of) *birthplace:* 7 Ajaccio (Corsica) *brother:* 5 Louis 6 Jerome, Joseph, Lucien *brother-in-law:* 5 Murat (Joachim) *deathplace:* 8 St. Helena *defeat:* 7 Leipzig 8 Waterloo 9 Trafalgar *father:* 5 Carlo *island of exile:* 4 Elba 8 St. Helena *marshal:* 3 Ney (Michel) 5 Murat (Joachim), Soult (Nicolas-Jean) 6 Suchet *nickname:* 14 Little Corporal *sister:* 5 Maria 8 Carlotta, Carolina *victory:* 3 Ulm 4 Jena, Lodi 5 Ligny 6 Abukir, Arcole, Wagram 7 Bautzen, Dresden, Marengo 8 Borodino 10 Austerlitz *wife:* 9 Josephine 11 Marie Louise

narcissism 6 vanity 7 conceit 8 self-love, vainness 9 vainglory 10 self-esteem 11 amour propre, self-conceit 13 conceitedness

narcissistic 4 vain 7 stuck-up 8 conceity 9 conceited 12 vainglorious 13 self-conceited

Narcissus *father:* 9 Cephissus *mother:* 7 Liriope *rejected admirer:* 4 Echo

narcotic 3 hop 4 dope, drug, junk 5 opium 6 heroin, opiate 7 anodyne, cocaine, hashish 8 hasheesh, hypnotic, morphine, nepenthe, somnific 9 somnolent, soporific 10 somnorific 11 somniferous, soporifical *peddler:* 6 dealer, pusher

nark 3 rat 4 fink 5 peach, stool 6 canary, inform, snitch, squeak, squeal 7 tipster 8 betrayer, informer, squeaker, squealer 10 talebearer 11 stool pigeon

narrate 4 tell, yarn 5 state, story 6 detail, dilate, recite, relate, report 7 descant, recount 8 describe, rehearse 9 discourse

narrative 4 epic, myth, saga, tale, yarn 5 fable, story 6 legend, report 7 account, history, recital, version 8 anecdote 9 chronicle *medieval French:* 5 roman 7 romance *prose:* 5 novel 7 novella

narrow 3 set 4 mean 5 close, fixed, limit, small, taper, tense 6 lessen, little, meager, paltry, strait 7 bigoted, limited, precise 8 contract, decrease, definite, obdurate, straiten 9 confining, constrict, hidebound, illiberal 10 brassbound, constringe, inexorable, inflexible, intolerant, restricted

narrowly 6 barely 8 scarcely

narrow-minded 5 petty 7 bigoted, shallow 9 hidebound, illiberal 10 brassbound, intolerant, provincial, unenlarged

nasal 6 rhinal, twangy 9 nosepiece *combining form:* 4 rhin 5 rhino

nascency 5 birth 6 origin

nascent 7 initial 9 beginning, inceptive, incipient 10 initiative, initiatory 12 introductory

Naseby victor 7 Fairfax (Thomas) 8 Cromwell (Oliver)

nasicorn 10 rhinoceros

nasty 4 evil, foul, icky, mean, vile 5 black, cheap, dirty, gross, snide, soily 6 coarse, filthy, grubby, horrid, impure, malign, oafish, ribald, smutty, tawdry, vulgar, wicked 7 hateful, ill-bred, obscene, raunchy, spitish, squalid, unclean, vicious 8 improper, indecent, spiteful, unseemly 9 loathsome, malicious, malignant, offensive, repugnant, repulsive, uncleanly, vexatious 10 disgusting, disturbing, indecorous, indelicate, malevolent

natant 8 swimming

Nathan *father:* 4 Bani 5 Attai, David *son:* 5 Zabad

national 4 home 5 civic, civil 6 public 7 citizen, subject 8 domestic, internal 9 intestine, municipal

National Basketball Association *Atlanta:* 5 Hawks *Boston:* 7 Celtics *Charlotte:* 7 Hornets *Chicago:* 5 Bulls *Cleveland:* 9 Cavaliers *Dallas:* 9 Mavericks *Denver:* 7 Nuggets *Detroit:* 7 Pistons *Golden State:* 8 Warriors *Houston:* 7 Rockets *Indiana:* 6 Pacers *Los Angeles:* 6 Lakers 8 Clippers *Miami:* 4 Heat *Milwaukee:* 5 Bucks *Minnesota:* 12 Timberwolves *New Jersey:* 4 Nets *New York:* 6 Knicks *Orlando:* 5 Magic *Phoenix:* 4 Suns *Portland:* 12 Trail Blazers *Sacramento:* 5 Kings *San Antonio:* 5 Spurs *Seattle:* 11 SuperSonics *Toronto:* 7 Raptors *Utah:* 4 Jazz *Vancouver:* 9 Grizzlies *Washington:* 7 Bullets

National Football League *Arizona:* 9 Cardinals *Atlanta:* 7 Falcons *Buffalo:*

5 Bills *Carolina:* 8 Panthers *Chicago:*
5 Bears *Cincinnati:* 7 Bengals *Cleveland:*
6 Browns *Dallas:* 7 Cowboys *Denver:*
7 Broncos *Detroit:* 5 Lions *Green Bay:*
7 Packers *Houston:* 6 Oilers *Indianapolis:*
5 Colts *Jacksonville:* 7 Jaguars *Kansas*
City: 6 Chiefs *Los Angeles:* 7 Raiders
Miami: 8 Dolphins *Minnesota:* 7 Vikings
New England: 8 Patriots *New Orleans:*
6 Saints *New York:* 4 Jets 6 Giants *Phila-*
delphia: 6 Eagles *Phoenix:* 9 Cardinals
Pittsburgh: 8 Steelers *St. Louis:* 4 Rams
San Diego: 8 Chargers *Seattle:* 8 Sea-
hawks *Tampa Bay:* 4 Bucs *Washington:*
8 Redskins
national historical park *Alaska:*
5 Sitka *Idaho:* 8 Nez Percé *Kentucky-*
Tennessee: 13 Cumberland Gap
Maryland-West Virginia: 12 Harpers Ferry
Massachusetts: 9 Minute Man *New York:*
8 Saratoga
National Hockey League *Anaheim:*
11 Mighty Ducks *Boston:* 6 Bruins *Buffalo:*
6 Sabres *Calgary:* 6 Flames *Chicago:*
10 Black Hawks *Colorado:* 9 Avalanche
Dallas: 5 Stars *Detroit:* 8 Red Wings
Edmonton: 6 Oilers *Florida:* 8 Panthers
Hartford: 7 Whalers *Los Angeles:*
5 Kings *Montreal:* 9 Canadiens *New Jer-*
sey: 6 Devils *New York:* 7 Rangers
9 Islanders *Ottawa:* 8 Senators *Philadel-*
phia: 6 Flyers *Pittsburgh:* 8 Penguins *St.*
Louis: 5 Blues *San Jose:* 6 Sharks
Tampa Bay: 9 Lightning *Toronto:*
10 Maple Leafs *Vancouver:* 7 Canucks
Washington: 8 Capitals *Winnipeg:* 4 Jets
nationalism 10 patriotism *excessive:*
8 jingoism 10 chauvinism
National League *Atlanta:* 6 Braves *Chi-*
cago: 4 Cubs *Cincinnati:* 4 Reds *Colo-*
rado: 7 Rockies *Florida:* 7 Marlins *Hous-*
ton: 6 Astros *Los Angeles:* 7 Dodgers
Montreal: 5 Expos *New York:* 4 Mets *Phil-*
adelphia: 8 Phillies *Pittsburgh:* 7 Pirates
St. Louis: 9 Cardinals *San Diego:*
6 Padres *San Francisco:* 6 Giants
national military park *Alabama:*
13 Horseshoe Bend *Arkansas:* 8 Pea
Ridge *Mississippi:* 9 Vicksburg
Pennsylvania: 10 Gettysburg *South*
Carolina: 13 Kings Mountain *Tennessee:*
6 Shiloh
national monument *Alabama:* 11 Russell Cave *Alaska:* 9 Aniakchak *Arizona:*
5 Tonto 6 Navajo 7 Saguaro, Wupatki
8 Tuzigoot 10 Chiricahua, Pipe Spring,
Tumacacori 11 Hohokam Pima 12 Sunset
Crater, Walnut Canyon *California:* 8 Ca-
brillo, Lava Beds 9 Muir Woods, Pinnacles
10 Joshua Tree 11 Death Valley *Colorado:*

10 Yucca House *Colorado-Utah:* 8 Dinosaur 9 Hovenweep *Florida:* 12 Fort
Matanzas 13 Fort Jefferson *Georgia:*
8 Ocmulgee 11 Fort Pulaski 13 Fort Frederica *Iowa:* 12 Effigy Mounds *Louisiana:*
12 Poverty Point *Maryland:* 11 Fort
McHenry *Minnesota:* 9 Pipestone
12 Grand Portage *Nebraska:* 9 Homestead 11 Scotts Bluff *New Mexico:*
5 Pecos 7 El Morro 9 Bandelier, El Mal-
pais, Fort Union 10 Aztec Ruins, White
Sands *New York:* 11 Fort Stanwix
13 Castle Clinton *South Carolina:* 10 Fort
Sumter 13 Congaree Swamp *South*
Dakota: 9 Jewel Cave *Utah:* 11 Cedar
Breaks 13 Rainbow Bridge *Wyoming:*
11 Devils Tower, Fossil Butte
national park *Alaska:* 6 Denali, Katmai
9 Lake Clark 10 Glacier Bay 11 Kenai
Fjords, Kobuk Valley *Angola:* 4 Iona,
Mupa *Arizona:* 11 Grand Canyon *Arkan-*
sas: 10 Hot Springs *Botswana:* 5 Chobe
California: 7 Redwood, Sequoia
8 Yosemite 11 King's Canyon *Chad:*
5 Manda *Colombia:* 5 Uraba *Colorado:*
9 Mesa Verde 13 Rocky Mountain *eastern*
Africa: 10 Mount Kenya *Florida:* 8 Biscayne 10 Everglades *Hawaii:* 9 Haleakala
India: 4 Kanha *Japan:* 5 Nikko *Kentucky:*
11 Mammoth Cave *Kenya:* 4 Meru
5 Tsavo 10 Royal Tsavo *Lake Superior:*
10 Isle Royale *Maine:* 6 Acadia *Malaysia:*
8 Kinabalu *Minnesota:* 9 Voyageurs *Mon-*
tana: 7 Glacier *Nevada:* 10 Great Basin
Oregon: 10 Crater Lake *Poland:* 5 Ojcow,
Tatra *South Africa:* 6 Kruger *South*
Dakota: 8 Badlands, Wind Cave *Sri Lanka:*
4 Yala *Sweden:* 5 Sarek *Tanzania:*
5 Ruaha 9 Serengeti *Texas:* 7 Big Bend
Utah: 4 Zion 6 Arches 11 Bryce Canyon,
Canyonlands, Capitol Reef *Virginia:*
10 Shenandoah *Washington:* 7 Olympic
12 Mount Rainier 13 North Cascades *Wyo-*
ming: 10 Grand Teton *Wyoming-Idaho-*
Montana: 11 Yellowstone *Zambia:*
5 Kafue *Zimbabwe:* 13 Rhodes Inyanga,
Victoria Falls
native 3 raw 4 home, wild 5 crude, local
6 impure, inborn, innate, normal, simple
7 connate, endemic, indigen, natural
8 agrarian, agrestal, domestic, indigene,
inherent, internal, national, ungraded,
unsorted 9 inherited, intestine, municipal
10 aboriginal, congenital, connatural, indigenous, unacquired, unaffected *Acadian Loui-*
siana: 5 Cajun *China:* 3 Han 9 Celestial
India: 5 sepoy *Japan:* 9 Nipponese *Lon-*
don: 7 Cockney *New England:* 4 Yank
6 Yankee *New York:* 13 Knickerbocker *suf-*
fix: 2 er 3 ese, ier, ite, ote, yer

Native Son author 6 Wright (Richard)
Nativity 4 noel, Xmas, yule 5 birth 8 yuletide 9 Christmas
natty 4 jimp 5 doggy, jimpy, sassy, smart 6 dapper, spiffy, spruce, sprucy 7 bandbox, doggish 11 well-groomed
natural 4 easy, feeb, fool, open, wild, zany 5 ament, frank, idiot, moron, naive, plain, typic, usual, white 6 candid, common, cretin, folksy, inborn, innate, native, normal, rustic, simple 7 artless, bastard, connate, general, genuine, half-wit, regular, sincere, typical 8 agrarian, agrestal, baseborn, homespun, ignorant, imbecile, inherent, innocent, spurious, unartful 9 blackjack, childlike, guileless, impulsive, ingenuous, ingrained, inherited, prevalent, primitive, simpleton, unfeigned, unlabored, unstudied, untutored, unworldly 10 congenital, fatherless, indigenous, legitimate, provincial, unacquired, unaffected, unfathered, unschooled 11 commonplace, instinctive, misbegotten, spontaneous, undesigning
naturalist *American:* 4 Muir (John) 5 Hyatt (Alpheus) 7 Audubon (John James), Verrill (Addison, Alpheus) *English:* 3 Ray (John) 5 White (Gilbert) 6 Darwin (Charles) 7 Wallace (Alfred) 10 Williamson (William) *French:* 5 Fabre (Jean-Henri) 7 Lamarck (Chevalier de), Réaumur (René-Antoine) *Scottish:* 6 Wilson (Alexander) 10 Richardson (John)
nature 3 ilk, way 4 kind, sort, type 5 being, humor, shape, world 6 cosmos, figure, kidney, kosmos, makeup, stripe, temper 7 anatomy, essence, texture, variety 8 creation, essentia, megacosm, universe 9 character, framework, macrocosm, normality 10 complexion 11 description, disposition, macrocosmos, personality, temperament 12 essentiality
naught 3 nil 4 zero 5 zilch 6 cipher, ruined 7 nothing 8 goose egg 11 nonexistent, nothingness 12 nonexistence
naughty 3 bad, paw 4 evil 5 rowdy 6 unruly, wicked 7 froward, wayward, willful 8 contrary, perverse 9 ruffianly 10 disorderly, headstrong, ill-behaved, indecorous, refractory 11 disobedient, intractable, misbehaving, mischievous 12 obstreperous, recalcitrant, ungovernable
nauseate 5 abhor, repel 6 loathe, reluct, revolt, sicken 7 disgust, repulse
nauseated 4 sick 6 queasy, queazy 7 carsick 9 squeamish
nauseating 4 foul, icky 5 nasty 7 noisome 9 loathsome, offensive, repugnant, repulsive, sickening
nauseous see **nauseated**
Nausicaa *father:* 8 Alcinous *mother:* 5 Arete

nautical 5 naval 6 marine 7 oceanic 8 maritime 12 navigational *instrument:* 3 aba 7 compass, pelorus, sextant
Navajo *dwelling:* 5 hogan
naval hero 5 Jones (John Paul), Perry (Matthew, Oliver Hazard) 8 Farragut (David, George), Lawrence (James)
nave 3 hub
navel 6 middle 7 nombril 9 umbilicus 11 belly button *combining form:* 6 omphal 7 omphalo
navigate 4 move, sail, walk 5 pilot, steer
navigation 6 voyage 7 passage 8 piloting, seacraft, shipping
navigational system 5 loran 6 shoran 7 teleran
navigator 5 flyer, pilot 6 airman 7 copilot *Danish:* 6 Bering (Vitus) *Dutch:* 6 Tasman (Abel) 7 Barents (Willem) *English:* 4 Cook (Captain James) 5 Cabot (John, Sebastian), Drake (Francis) 6 Hudson (Henry) 7 Gilbert (Humphrey), Raleigh (Walter) 9 Vancouver (George) *French:* 7 Cartier (Jacques) 9 La Perouse (Comte de) *Italian:* 6 Caboto (Giovanni) 8 Columbus (Christopher), Vespucci (Amerigo) 9 Verrazano (Giovanni) *Norwegian:* 4 Eric (the Red) 8 Ericsson 12 Leif Eriksson *Portuguese:* 4 Dias (Bartolomeu, Dinis) 6 Cabral (Pedro Alvars), da Gama (Vasco) 8 Magellan (Ferdinand) *Spanish:* 9 Fernandez (Juan)
navy 5 fleet
Nazi 9 Hitlerite 10 brownshirt *admiral:* 6 Dönitz (Karl), Raeder (Erich) 7 Doenitz (Karl) *air force:* 9 Luftwaffe *armed forces:* 9 Wehrmacht *collaborator:* 5 Laval (Pierre) 8 Quisling (Vidkun) *concentration camp:* 6 Belsen, Dachau 9 Auschwitz 10 Buchenwald, Nordhausen *field marshal:* 5 Model (Walter) 6 Keitel (Wilhelm), Paulus (Friedrich), Rommel (Erwin) 9 Rundstedt (Karl von) 10 Kesselring (Albert) *greeting:* 4 Heil *leader:* 3 Ley (Robert) 4 Hess (Rudolf), Röhm (Ernst) 5 Roehm (Ernst) 6 Führer, Göring (Hermann), Hitler (Adolph) 7 Fuehrer, Goering (Hermann), Himmler (Heinrich) 8 Goebbels (Joseph), Heydrich (Reinhard) 9 Rosenberg (Alfred) *police:* 2 SS 7 Gestapo *propagandist:* 8 Goebbels (Joseph) *submarine:* 5 U-boat *surrender signer:* 4 Jodl (Alfred) 6 Keitel (Wilhelm) *symbol:* 6 fylfot 8 swastika *tactic:* 10 blitzkrieg *tank:* 6 panzer
NCO 3 cpl, sgt 8 corporal, sergeant
neap 4 tide
near 2 by 4 nigh 5 about, circa, close, round 6 almost, around, beside, narrow, stingy 7 close by, closely, close on 8 adjacent, approach, stingily 9 immediate, proximate, thriftily 10 intimately 11 approximate, at close hand, closefisted *combining form:*

5 juxta *prefix:* **2** ad, ep **3** eph, epi **4** peri, pros **5** plesi **6** plesio

nearby **4** nigh **5** about, aside, circa, close, handy, round **6** around, beside **7** closeby, close on, vicinal **8** adjacent **9** immediate, proximate **10** contiguous, convenient **11** neighboring

nearest **4** next **8** proximal

nearsighted **6** myopic

neat **3** net **4** deft, nice, prim, pure, snug, tidy, trig, trim **5** clean, clear, exact, kempt, plain **6** adroit, clever, dainty, dapper, spruce, sprucy **7** chipper, correct, finicky, orderly, precise, primsie, regular, unmixed **8** accurate, spotless, straight **9** ingenious, shipshape, undiluted **10** fastidious, gratifying, immaculate, methodical, systematic **11** uncluttered, well-groomed **12** spick-and-span **13** unadulterated

neb **3** ear, nib, tip **4** beak, bill, nose **6** pecker

Nebaioth *brother:* **5** Kedar *father:* **7** Ishmael

Nebraska *capital:* **7** Lincoln *college, university:* **4** Dana **5** Doane **9** Creighton *Indian:* **4** Otoe *largest city:* **5** Omaha *state flower:* **9** goldenrod

nebula **6** galaxy

nebulous **4** hazy **6** turbid **7** clouded **10** indistinct

necessary **5** vital **6** needed **7** certain **8** cardinal, inerrant, integral, unerring **9** essential, important, inerrable, mandatory, momentous, requisite **10** compelling, compulsory, imperative, ineludible, inevasible, inevitable, obligatory, unevadable **11** fundamental, ineluctable, inescapable, significant, unavoidable, unescapable **12** constraining, prerequisite **13** indispensable

necessitate **3** ask **4** take **5** crave **6** compel, demand **7** call for, require **9** constrain, force into

necessitous see needy

necessity **4** call, must, need **5** cause **6** duress **7** poverty **8** coercion, exigency, occasion **9** condition, essential, requisite **10** compulsion, constraint, obligation, sine qua non **11** needfulness, requirement **12** precondition, prerequisite **13** requisiteness

neck **3** pet **4** kiss **5** beard **6** behead, cervix, collet, fondle, smooch, strait **7** embrace **8** gorgerin **9** decollate **10** decapitate, guillotine *back of:* **4** nape **5** nucha **6** scruff *ornament:* **6** gorget, torque

necklace **4** band **5** chain **6** locket **7** rivière **8** carcanet

neckpiece **3** boa **5** scarf

necktie **5** ascot **6** cravat **10** four-in-hand *adjunct:* **6** tiepin **8** tie clasp

necrology **4** obit **8** obituary

necromancy **5** magic **7** sorcery **8** witchery, wizardry **9** conjuring, magicking **10** witchcraft **11** bewitchment, enchantment, thaumaturgy

necropolis **8** boneyard, boot hill, cemetery, God's acre **9** graveyard **12** burial ground

necropsy **7** autopsy **10** postmortem

need **3** use **4** call, duty, have, lack, long, must, pine, want, wish **5** claim, covet, crave, drive, exact, ought, yearn **6** charge, demand, desire, devoir, hanker, hunger, penury, thirst **7** deficit, poverty, require **8** exaction, exigency, occasion, poorness, shortage **9** committal, indigence, necessity, privation, requisite **10** commitment, compulsion, deficiency, dependence, obligation **11** destitution, requirement

neediness **4** want **6** penury **7** poverty **9** indigence, privation **11** destitution

needle **3** dun **5** annoy, tease, worry **6** harass, pester, plague **7** bedevil, hagride, obelisk, pricker, syringe *blunt:* **6** bodkin *case:* **4** etui *combining form:* **3** acu *hole:* **3** eye

needlefish **3** gar

needlelike **7** styloid **8** belonoid *part:* **7** acicula

needlepoint lace **7** alençon

needle-shaped **6** acuate **7** acerose, acerous, aciform

needlework **6** sewing **7** crochet, sampler, seaming, tatting **8** knitting **10** crocheting, embroidery

needy **4** poor **6** hard up **8** dirt poor, indigent, strapped **9** destitute, penniless, penurious **11** impecunious, necessitous **12** impoverished, unprosperous

ne'er-do-well **6** bad lot, no-good, waster **7** rounder, wastrel **9** shiftless **10** profligate, scapegrace **11** incompetent

nefarious **4** rank **5** gross **6** putrid, rotten **7** corrupt, glaring, heinous **8** flagrant, infamous, perverse **9** miscreant, monstrous **10** degenerate, detestable, outrageous, villainous

negate **4** deny, undo, void **5** abate, annul, cross, quash **6** impugn **7** abolish, gainsay, nullify, redress, vitiate **8** negative, traverse **9** cancel out, disaffirm, frustrate **10** annihilate, contradict, contravene, counteract, invalidate, neutralize **12** countercheck

negative **2** no **3** nix **4** deny, kill, veto **5** annul, cross, minus **6** impugn **7** adverse, gainsay, nullify, redress, refusal **8** abrogate, disprove, traverse **9** cancel out, disaffirm, frustrate, non-placet **10** contradict, contravene, counteract, invalidate, neutralize **11** detrimental, unfavorable *battery terminal:* **5** anode *ion:* **5** anion *Scottish:* **3** nae *sign:* **5** minus

neglect 4 fail, miss, omit, pass 5 elide, scant, scorn, shirk 6 forget, ignore, pass by, reject, slight 7 blink at, default, disdain, dismiss, failure 8 brush off, discount, omission, overleap, overlook, overpass, pass over, shrug off, slur over 9 blink away, disregard, oversight, pretermit, shrug away 10 brush aside, slough over

neglectful see negligent

negligee 4 gown 8 camisole 9 nightgown

negligent 3 lax 5 slack 6 remiss 7 offhand 8 careless, derelict, discinct, heedless, slipshod, slovenly 9 incurious, unheedful, unstudied 10 behindhand, delinquent, regardless, unthinking 11 inadvertent, inattentive, indifferent, thoughtless, unconcerned 12 disregardful 13 inconsiderate

negligible 4 slim 5 small 6 remote, slight 7 outside, slender 8 trifling

negotiate 4 leap, over 5 agree, clear, vault 6 adjust, handle, hurdle, manage, settle 7 arrange, bargain, compose, concert, conduct 8 complete, contract, covenant, overleap, surmount, transact 10 accomplish

Nehemiah's father 5 Azbuk 9 Hachaliah

Nehushta *father:* 8 Elnathan *husband:* 9 Jehoiakim *son:* 10 Jehoiachin

neigh 6 nicker, whinny 7 snicker, snigger

neighbor 4 abut, join, line 5 march, touch, verge 6 adjoin, border, butt on, corner 8 border on

neighborhood 4 area, tune 5 order, range 6 extent, matter 8 district, locality, vicinage, vicinity 9 magnitude, proximity

neighborly 6 social 7 cordial 8 amicable, friendly, gracious, sociable 10 gregarious, hospitable 11 cooperative

nematode 4 worm 7 eelworm 9 roundworm

Nemean predator 4 lion

neon 3 gas *symbol:* 2 Ne

neonate see newborn

neophyte see newcomer

Neoptolemus 7 Pyrrhus *father:* 8 Achilles *slayer:* 7 Orestes *victim:* 5 Priam *wife:* 8 Hermione

Nepal *capital:* 8 Katmandu 9 Kathmandu *forest land:* 5 Terai *monetary unit:* 5 rupee

nepenthe 6 opiate 7 anodyne 8 narcotic

Nepheg *brother:* 5 Korah 6 Zichri *father:* 5 David, Izhar

Nephele *daughter:* 5 Helle *husband:* 7 Athamas *son:* 7 Phrixos, Phrixus

Nephthys *brother, husband:* 3 Set 4 Seth

Neptune 6 planet *satellite:* 6 Nereid, Triton; (see also **Poseidon**)

Ner *father:* 5 Abiel, Jeiel *son:* 5 Abner

Nereides 6 Thetis 7 Galatea 10 Amphitrite *father:* 6 Nereus *mother:* 5 Doris

Nereus *daughters:* 8 Nereides *emblem:* 7 trident *father:* 6 Pontus *mother:* 2 Ge 4 Gaea *wife:* 5 Doris

Nergal *brother:* 5 Nanna 6 Ninazu *father:* 5 Enlil *mother:* 6 Ninlil

Neriah *father:* 8 Maaseiah *son:* 6 Baruch 7 Seraiah

Nerissa's husband 8 Gratiano

Nero *birthplace:* 4 Rome *mother:* 9 Agrippina *successor:* 5 Galba *tutor:* 6 Seneca *victim:* 5 Lucan 6 Seneca 7 Octavia, Poppaea 9 Agrippina *wife:* 7 Octavia, Poppaea

Nero Wolfe creator 5 Stout (Rex)

nerve 4 face, gall, grit, guts, sand, vein 5 brass, cheek, cheer, crust, heart, moxie, spunk, steel 6 daring 7 animate, chirk up, hearten, sciatic, stamina 8 audacity, backbone, boldness, embolden, inspirit, strength, temerity 9 assurance, brashness, encourage, enhearten, fortitude, hardihood, hardiness 10 confidence, effrontery, strengthen 11 presumption *cell:* 6 neuron *cell group:* 7 ganglia (plural) 8 ganglion *combining form:* 4 neur 5 neura, neuro *cranial:* 4 vagi (plural) 5 optic, vagus 8 abducens *ending:* 8 receptor *lesion:* 8 neuritis

nerve center 3 hub 4 seat 5 focus, heart 8 polestar 10 focal point

nervous 4 edgy 5 jerky, jumpy, timid 6 feisty, goosey, spooky 7 fidgety, fretful, jittery, uptight, waspish 8 aflutter, agitated, critical, forcible, skittery, skittish, snappish, spirited, twittery, unsteady, volatile 9 difficult, excitable, irritable, querulous, unrestful 10 high-strung 12 apprehensive

nervy 4 bold, edgy, pert, wise 5 brash, fresh, jerky, jumpy, sassy, smart, tense 6 cheeky, goosey, spooky, uneasy 7 fidgety, forward, jittery, restive, twitchy, uptight 8 impudent, intrepid, twittery 9 excitable, unrestful 10 high-strung 11 smart-alecky

ness 4 cape 8 headland 10 promontory

Nessus' victim 8 Heracles, Hercules

nest 3 den 4 aery, home, lair, nidi (plural) 5 aerie, eyrie, nidus 6 nidify 7 hangout, shelter 8 smuggery 11 aggregation *eagle's:* 4 aery 5 aerie, eyrie *wasp's:* 8 vespiary

nest egg 5 hoard, stock, store 7 backlog, reserve 9 inventory, reservoir, stockpile

nestle 4 snug 5 house 6 burrow, cuddle, nuzzle 7 shelter, snuggle

Nestor *father:* 6 Neleus *kingdom:* 5 Pylos

net 4 gain, gist, make, mesh, pure 5 basic, catch, clear, seine, tulle, yield 6 maline 7 clean up, essence, malines *combining form:* 5 dicty 6 dictyo *conical:* 5 trawl *fishing:* 5 seine *hair:* 5 snood

Nethanel *brother:* 5 David *father:* 5 Jesse 7 Pashhur 8 Obededom *son:* 8 Shemaiah

Nethaniah's father 5 Asaph 6 Jehudi 7 Ishmael

nether 3 low 5 lower, under 6 lesser 8 inferior 9 subjacent

Netherlands *capital:* 9 Amsterdam *de facto capital:* 8 The Hague *monetary unit:* 6 florin, gulden 7 guilder *patron saint:* 10 Willibrord *piano city:* 3 Ede

netherworld 3 pit 4 hell 5 abyss, hades, Sheol 6 blazes 7 inferno 9 perdition 11 Pandemonium

netlike 9 reticular 10 reticulate

nettle 3 get, vex 4 huff, rile, roil 5 peeve, pique, upset 6 incite, put out, stir up 7 agitate, disturb, perturb, provoke 8 irritate 10 discompose, exasperate

nettle rash 5 hives 9 urticaria

nettlesome 5 spiny 6 thorny 7 prickly 9 irritable 10 irritating

network 3 web 4 mesh 8 gridiron 9 reticulum *anatomical:* 4 rete 5 retia (plural)

neurotic 6 phobic 7 nervous 8 unstable 9 obsessive 10 compulsive

neuter 3 fix 4 geld 5 alter, unsex 6 change, worker 7 sexless 8 castrate, mutilate 9 sterilize 11 desexualize 12 intransitive

neutral 4 calm, cool, easy 5 aloof 6 normal 7 hueless, relaxed 8 abstract, clinical, composed, detached, middling, unbiased 9 collected, colorless, impartial 10 achromatic, impersonal, nonchalant, pokerfaced 11 indifferent, unpassioned 13 disinterested, dispassionate

neutralize 5 annul 6 defeat, negate, offset, subdue 7 balance, conquer, nullify, redress 8 abrogate, negative, overcome, override, overrule 9 cancel out, frustrate 10 compensate, counteract, invalidate 11 countervail 12 countercheck, counterpoise

Nevada *capital:* 10 Carson City *largest city:* 8 Las Vegas *nickname:* 11 Silver State 14 Sagebrush State *state flower:* 9 sagebrush

névé 4 firn, snow

never-ending 7 endless, eternal 8 immortal 9 ceaseless 11 amaranthine, everlasting

never-failing 4 firm, sure 6 steady 7 abiding 8 enduring 9 steadfast 11 unfaltering, unqualified 12 wholehearted 13 unquestioning

nevertheless 3 but, yet 5 still 6 though, withal 7 howbeit, however 8 after all 11 still and all

nevus 4 mole 9 birthmark

new 5 fresh, novel 6 afresh, lately, modern, of late, recent 7 another, revived, strange 8 neoteric, pristine 9 first-hand, recreated, refreshed, renovated 10 additional, unfamiliar 11 modernistic, regenerated 12 unaccustomed 13 reinvigorated *combining form:* 2 ne 3 cen, neo, nov 4 caen, ceno, novo 5 caeno *word:* 7 coinage, neology 9 neologism

newcomer 4 colt, tyro 6 novice, rookie 8 beginner, chechako, freshman, neophyte 9 immigrant, novitiate 10 apprentice, tenderfoot

New Deal agency 3 CCC, NRA, TVA, WPA

Newfoundland *capital:* 10 Saint Johns *discoverer:* 5 Cabot (John) *part:* 8 Labrador

new gas 4 neon

New Hampshire *capital:* 7 Concord *college:* 9 Dartmouth 10 Keene State 12 Saint Anselms *highest point:* 12 Mt. Washington *largest city:* 10 Manchester *motto:* 13 Live Free or Die *nickname:* 12 Granite State *state bird:* 11 purple finch *state flower:* 11 purple lilac

New Jersey *capital:* 7 Trenton *college, university:* 4 Drew 6 Upsala 7 Rutgers 9 Princeton, Seton Hall 10 Bloomfield 11 Saint Peters *largest city:* 6 Newark *nickname:* 11 Garden State *state bird:* 9 goldfinch *state flower:* 6 violet

New Mexico *capital:* 7 Santa Fe *largest city:* 11 Albuquerque *state bird:* 10 roadrunner *state flower:* 5 yucca

news 4 dope, poop, word 5 rumor 6 advice, gossip, report, tattle 7 lowdown, tidings 9 knowledge, speerings 11 information, scuttlebutt 12 announcement, intelligence *agency:* 2 AP 3 UPI 4 Tass 7 Reuters

newspaper 5 daily, organ 6 review 7 journal, tabloid 8 magazine 10 periodical *publisher:* 6 Hearst (William Randolph)

newt 3 eft 6 triton *green:* 5 ebbet

New Testament see at Bible

New York *academy, college, (university):* 3 RPI 4 Iona, Pace, SUNY 5 Keuka, Kings, Nyack, Pratt, Siena, Utica 6 CW Post, Elmira, Hunter, Ithaca, Marist, Queens, Vassar 7 Adelphi, Colgate, Cornell, Fordham, Hofstra, Niagara, St. Johns,

Yeshiva 8 Brooklyn, Canisius, Columbia, Hamilton, Hartwick, Skidmore, Syracuse 9 Juilliard, Manhattan, St. Francis, St. Josephs, West Point 10 Long Island 13 Sarah Lawrence, St. Bonaventure *capital:* 6 Albany *motto:* 9 Excelsior 10 Ever Upward *nickname:* 11 Empire State *state flower:* 4 rose

New York City 6 Gotham *borough:* 5 Bronx 6 Queens 8 Brooklyn, Richmond 9 Manhattan

New Zealand *capital:* 10 Wellington *discoverer:* 6 Tasman (Abel) *monetary unit:* 6 dollar *parrot:* 3 kea

next 4 then 5 after, below, infra, later, since 6 behind, coming, second 7 by and by, closest, ensuing 8 latterly 9 afterward, following, proximate 10 afterwhile, contiguous, succeeding

nexus 3 tie 4 bond, knot, link, yoke 8 ligament, ligature, vinculum 10 connection

Nez Percé chief 6 Joseph

niagara 5 flood, spate 6 deluge 7 torrent 8 cataract, flooding, overflow 9 cataclysm 10 inundation

nib 4 beak, bill 5 tooth 6 pecker 8 pen point

nibble 4 bite, gnaw, peck, pick

Nicanor's father 9 Patroclus

Nicaragua *capital:* 7 Managua *monetary unit:* 7 cordoba *neighbor:* 8 Honduras 9 Costa Rica

nice 4 fine, good, mild, neat, rare, sage, wise 5 exact, fussy, picky, right, rigid 6 benign, chaste, choosy, comely, dainty, decent, proper, queasy, seemly, strict, subtle 7 affable, careful, clement, correct, finical, finicky, fitting, precise, refined, welcome 8 accurate, becoming, clerkish, decorous, delicate, finespun, hairline, picksome, pleasant, pleasing, precieux, precious, rigorous, suitable, virtuous 9 agreeable, befitting, congenial, enjoyable, exquisite, favorable, finicking, judicious 10 attractive, conforming, delightful, discerning, fastidious, gratifying, meticulous, oldmaidish, particular, pernickety, personable, scrupulous

niche 4 nook 5 place 6 cranny, crater, nestle, recess 7 byplace, secrete

Nicholas Nickleby author 7 Dickens (Charles)

nick 4 deny, hack 5 cut in, notch, score, snipe 6 charge, record 9 indenture 11 indentation

nickname 3 tag 5 label, style 6 byword, handle 7 epithet, miscall, moniker 8 cognomen 9 sobriquet 10 hypocorism

Nicomede *conquest:* 10 Cappodocia *dramatist:* 9 Corneille (Pierre) *half-brother:* 6 Attale *stepmother:* 7 Arsinoë

nictate 3 bat 4 wink 5 blink 7 twinkle

nictitate see **nictate**

nifty 4 cool, keen, neat 5 adept, dandy, dilly, handy, peach, smart, super, swell 6 clever, corker, groovy, peachy 7 stylish 8 jim-dandy, knockout, splendid, terrific

Niger *capital:* 6 Niamey *export:* 7 uranium *monetary unit:* 5 franc

Nigeria *capital:* 5 Lagos *monetary unit:* 5 naira *people:* 3 Ibo 4 Igbo *product:* 3 tin 4 coal 5 cocoa 6 rubber

niggard 5 miser

niggardly 5 close, tight 6 scanty, stingy 7 miserly 9 penurious 11 closefisted, tightfisted 12 cheeseparing, parsimonious 13 penny-pinching

niggling 5 petty 6 measly, paltry, peanut 8 picayune, piddling, trifling 10 picayunish

nigh 2 by 4 near 5 about, circa, close, round 6 all but, almost, around, beside, nearby, nearly 7 close on 8 approach 9 immediate, proximate 10 near-at-hand 11 approximate, at close hand, practically

night blindness 10 nyctalopia

nightfall 3 eve 4 dusk, even 6 sunset 7 evening, sundown 8 eventide, gloaming, owl-light, twilight

nighthawk 6 petrel 7 bullbat 10 goatsucker *Australian:* 8 morepork

nightingale 6 thrush

nightjar 5 potoo 10 goatsucker

nightly 9 nocturnal

nightmare 5 dream, fancy, worry 6 vision 7 fantasy, incubus 8 daydream, phantasm, phantasy, succubus 12 apprehension

nightshade 7 henbane 10 belladonna *weedy:* 11 bittersweet

nightstick 3 bat 4 club, mace 5 baton, billy 6 cudgel 8 bludgeon 9 billy club, truncheon

Nike *father:* 6 Pallas *mother:* 4 Styx

nil 4 zero 6 naught, nought 7 nothing 11 nonexistent

Nile 6 Al-Bahr *dam:* 6 Makwar 9 Aswan High 10 Gebel Aulia *explorer:* 5 Baker (Sir Samuel), Bruce (James), Grant (James Augustus), Speke (John Hanning) *queen:* 4 Cleo 9 Cleopatra *section:* 4 Abai, Abay 5 Abbai

nilgai 8 antelope, blue bull

nimble 3 yar 4 deft, spry, yare 5 agile, alert, brisk, catty, fleet, handy, light, quick, zippy 6 active, adroit, brisky, clever, limber, lively 8 vigilant, watchful 9 dexterous, lightsome, sprightly, wide-awake

nimble-witted 3 hep 4 wise 5 canny, quick, sharp, slick, smart 7 knowing

Nimrod 6 hunter *father:* 4 Cush

Ninazu *brother:* 5 Nanna 6 Nergal *father:* 5 Enlil *mother:* 6 Ninlil

nincompoop 3 ass 4 fool, jerk 5 idiot, ninny 6 donkey 7 jackass, tomfool 8 imbecile 9 simpleton

nine 12 baseball team *combining form:* 3 non 4 nona 5 ennea *goddesses:* 5 Muses *group:* 6 ennead *inches:* 4 span *instruments:* 5 nonet

nine day devotion 6 novena

Nine Worlds 3 Hel 6 Asgard 7 Alfheim, Midgard 8 Niflheim, Vanaheim 10 Jotunnheim 12 Muspellsheim 13 Svartalfaheim

ninny see nincompoop

Ninsun's son 9 Gilgamesh

ninth *combining form:* 3 non 4 nona

Nintu *consort:* 4 Enki *son:* 6 Ninsar

Ninurta *father:* 5 Enlil *victim:* 3 Kur

Ninus *father:* 5 Belus *wife:* 9 Semiramis

Niobe *brother:* 6 Pelops *father:* 8 Tantalus *husband:* 7 Amphion *sister-in-law:* 5 Aedon

nip 3 bit, dig, hop, nab 4 balk, dart, dash, dram, drop, hook, jolt, jump, lift, nail, peck, shot, slug, soak, swig 5 blast, booze, check, chill, clamp, drink, hurry, pinch, sever, snort, steal, swill 6 arrest, blight, guzzle, imbibe, snatch, tank up, thwart, tipple 7 cabbage, snifter, swizzle 8 compress, cutpurse, liquor up, piquancy, toothful 9 frustrate 10 pickpocket

nipper 3 bud, kid 4 rack 5 chick, child 6 cunner, moppet 8 brakeman, juvenile, young one 9 youngling, youngster

nipping 3 icy 4 cold, cool 5 chill, sharp 6 arctic, chilly, frosty 7 caustic, glacial, shivery 8 freezing

nipple 3 pap 4 teat 8 mammilla *combining form:* 4 mast 5 masto 6 papill 7 papillo

nipple-shaped 9 mammiform

Nippon 5 Japan

nippy see nipping

nirvana 4 Zion 5 bliss, dream 6 Canaan, heaven 7 elysium 8 empyrean, oblivion, paradise 10 Civitas Dei 12 New Jerusalem

nisse 3 elf, fay 5 fairy, pixie 6 kobold, sprite 7 brownie

Nisus *betrayer, daughter:* 6 Scylla *father:* 7 Pandion

nitid 6 bright, glossy 8 lustrous

nitrogen 5 azote *combining form:* 2 az 3 azo

nitwit 4 dope, simp 5 cluck, dunce 7 pinhead 9 dumb bunny, dumb cluck, simpleton

nix 2 no 3 nay 4 kill, nope, veto 6 naught, nought 7 nothing 8 negative

Njord, Njorth *daughter:* 5 Freya *son:* 4 Frey *wife:* 6 Skadhi, Skathi

no 3 nae, nay, nix 6 denial *combining form:* 5 nulli

no-account see no-good

Noachian 3 old 4 aged 5 hoary 6 age-old 7 ancient, antique 8 timeworn 9 venerable 12 antediluvian

Noah *father:* 6 Lamech 10 Zelophehad *grandson:* 4 Aram 6 Canaan *great grandson:* 3 Hul *landing place:* 6 Ararat *son:* 3 Ham 4 Shem 6 Canaan 7 Japheth

Nobel Prize Winner

chemistry:

1901: 8 van't Hoff (Jacobus) *1902:* 7 Fischer (Emil) *1903:* 9 Arrhenius (Svante) *1904:* 6 Ramsay (William) *1905:* 9 von Baeyer (Adolph) *1906:* 7 Moissan (Henri) *1907:* 7 Buchner (Eduard) *1908:* 10 Rutherford (Ernest) *1909:* 7 Ostwald (Wilhelm) *1910:* 7 Wallach (Otto) *1911:* 5 Curie (Marie) *1912:* 8 Grignard (François), Sabatier (Paul) *1913:* 6 Werner (Alfred) *1914:* 8 Richards (Theodore) *1915:* 11 Willstatter (Richard) *1918:* 5 Haber (Fritz) *1920:* 6 Nernst (Walther) *1921:* 5 Soddy (Frederick) *1922:* 5 Aston (Francis) *1923:* 5 Pregl (Fritz) *1925:* 9 Zsigmondy (Richard) *1926:* 8 Svedberg (Theodor) *1927:* 7 Wieland (Heinrich) *1928:* 7 Windaus (Adolf) *1929:* 6 Harden (Athur) 12 Euler-Chelpin (Hans) *1930:* 7 Fischer (Hans) *1931:* 5 Bosch (Carl) 7 Bergius (Friedrich) *1932:* 8 Langmuir (Irving) *1934:* 4 Urey (Harold) *1935:* 11 Joliot-Curie (Frederic, Irene) *1936:* 5 Debye (Peter) *1937:* 6 Karrer (Paul) 7 Haworth (Walter) *1938:* 4 Kuhn (Richard) *1939:* 7 Ruzicka (Leopold) 9 Butenandt (Adolph) *1943:* 6 Hevesy (Georg von) *1944:* 4 Hahn (Otto) *1945:* 8 Virtanen (Artturi) *1946:* 6 Sumner (James) 7 Stanley (Wendell) 8 Northrup (John) *1947:* 8 Robinson (Robert) *1948:* 8 Tiselius (Arne) *1949:* 7 Giauque (William) *1950:* 5 Alder (Kurt), Diels (Otto) *1951:* 7 Seaborg (Glenn) 8 McMillan (Edwin) *1952:* 5 Synge (Richard) 6 Martin (Archer) *1953:* 10 Staudinger (Hermann) *1954:* 7 Pauling (Linus) *1955:* 10 du Vigneaud (Vincent) *1956:* 7 Semenov (Nikolay) 11 Hinshelwood (Cyril) *1957:* 4 Todd (Alexander) *1958:* 6 Sanger (Frederick) *1959:* 9 Heyrovsky (Jaroslav) *1960:* 5 Libby (Willard) *1961:* 6 Calvin (Melvin) *1962:* 6 Perutz (Max) 7 Kendrew (John) *1963:* 5 Natta (Giulio) 7 Ziegler (Karl) *1964:* 7 Hodgkin (Dorothy) 8 Woodward (Robert) *1965:* 8 Mulliken (Robert) *1967:* 5 Eigen (Manfred) 6 Porter (George) 7 Norrish (Ronald) *1968:* 7 Onsager (Lars) *1969:* 6 Barton (Derek), Hassel (Odd) *1970:* 6 Leloir (Luis) *1971:* 8 Herzberg (Gerhard) *1972:* 5 Moore (Stanford), Stein (William) 8 Anfinsen (Christian) *1973:* 7 Fischer (Ernst) 9 Wilkinson

(Geoffrey) *1974:* 5 Flory (Paul) *1975:* 6 Prelog (Vladimir) 9 Cornforth (John) *1976:* 8 Lipscomb (William) *1977:* 9 Prigogine (Ilya) *1978:* 8 Mitchell (Peter) *1979:* 5 Brown (Herbert) 6 Wittig (Georg) *1980:* 4 Berg (Paul) 6 Sanger (Frederick) 7 Gilbert (Walter) *1981:* 5 Fukui (Kenichi) 8 Hoffmann (Roald) *1982:* 4 Klug (Aaron) *1983:* 5 Taube (Henry) *1984:* 10 Merrifield (R. Bruce) *1985:* 5 Karle (Jerome) 8 Hauptman (Herbert) *1986:* 3 Lee (Yuan) 7 Polanyi (John) 10 Herschbach (Dudley) *1987:* 4 Cram (Donald), Lehn (Jean-Marie) 8 Pedersen (Charles) *1988:* 5 Huber (Robert) 6 Michel (Hartmut) 11 Deisenhofer (Johann) *1989:* 4 Cech (Thomas) 6 Altman (Sidney) *1990:* 5 Corey (Elias) *1991:* 5 Ernst (Richard) *1992:* 6 Marcus (Rudolph) *1993:* 5 Smith (Michael) 6 Mullis (Kary) *1994:* 4 Olah (George) *1995:* 6 Molina (Mario) 7 Crutzen (Paul), Rowland (F. Sherwood)

economics:
1969: 6 Frisch (Ragnar) 9 Tinbergen (Jan) *1970:* 9 Samuelson (Paul) *1971:* 7 Kuznets (Simon) *1972:* 5 Arrow (Kenneth), Hicks (John) *1973:* 8 Leontief (Wassily) *1974:* 5 Hayek (Friedrich von) 6 Myrdal (Gunnar) *1975:* 8 Koopmans (Tjalling) 11 Kantorovich (Leonid) *1976:* 8 Friedman (Milton) *1977:* 5 Meade (James), Ohlin (Bertil) *1978:* 5 Simon (Herbert) *1979:* 5 Lewis (Arthur) 7 Schultz (Theodore) *1980:* 5 Klein (Lawrence) *1981:* 5 Tobin (James) *1982:* 7 Stigler (George) *1983:* 6 Debreu (Gerard) *1984:* 5 Stone (Richard) *1985:* 10 Modigliani (Franco) *1986:* 8 Buchanan (James) *1987:* 5 Solow (Robert) *1988:* 6 Allais (Maurice) *1989:* 8 Haavelmo (Trygve) *1990:* 6 Miller (Merton), Sharpe (William) 9 Markowitz (Harry) *1991:* 5 Coase (Ronald) *1992:* 6 Becker (Gary) *1993:* 5 Fogel (Robert), North (Douglass) *1994:* 4 Nash (John) 6 Selten (Reinhard) 8 Harsanyi (John) *1995:* 5 Lucas (Robert)

literature:
1901: 9 Prudhomme (Sully) *1902:* 7 Mommsen (Theodor) *1903:* 8 Bjornson (Bjornstjerne) *1904:* 7 Mistral (Frederic) 9 Echegaray (Jose) *1905:* 11 Sienkiewicz (Henryk) *1906:* 8 Carducci (Giosue) *1907:* 7 Kipling (Rudyard) *1908:* 6 Eucken (Rudolf) *1909:* 8 Lagerlof (Selma) *1910:* 8 von Heyse (Paul) *1911:* 11 Maeterlinck (Maurice) *1912:* 9 Hauptmann (Gerhart) *1913:* 6 Tagore (Rabindranath) *1915:* 7 Rolland (Romain) *1916:* 13 von Heidenstam (Verner) *1917:* 9 Gjellerup (Karl) 11 Pontoppidan (Henrik) *1919:* 9 Spitteler (Carl) *1920:* 6 Hamsun (Knut) *1921:*

6 France (Anatole) *1922:* 9 Benavente (Jacinto) *1923:* 5 Yeats (William Butler) *1924:* 7 Reymont (Wladyslaw) *1925:* 4 Shaw (George Bernard) *1926:* 7 Deledda (Grazia) *1927:* 7 Bergson (Henri) *1928:* 6 Undset (Sigrid) *1929:* 4 Mann (Thomas) *1930:* 5 Lewis (Sinclair) *1931:* 9 Karlfeldt (Erik Axel) *1932:* 10 Galsworthy (John) *1933:* 5 Bunin (Ivan) *1934:* 10 Pirandello (Luigi) *1936:* 6 O'Neill (Eugene) *1937:* 12 Martin du Gard (Roger) *1938:* 4 Buck (Pearl) *1939:* 9 Sillanpaa (Frans Eemil) *1944:* 6 Jensen (Johannes) *1945:* 7 Mistral (Gabriela) *1946:* 5 Hesse (Hermann) *1947:* 4 Gide (Andre) *1948:* 5 Eliot (Thomas Stearns) *1949:* 8 Faulkner (William) *1950:* 7 Russell (Bertrand) *1951:* 10 Lagerkvist (Par Fabian) *1952:* 7 Mauriac (Francois) *1953:* 9 Churchill (Winston) *1954:* 9 Hemingway (Ernest) *1955:* 7 Laxness (Halldor) *1956:* 7 Jimenez (Juan Ramon) *1957:* 5 Camus (Albert) *1958:* 9 Pasternak (Boris) *1959:* 9 Quasimodo (Salvatore) *1960:* 5 Perse (Saint-John) *1961:* 6 Andric (Ivo) *1962:* 9 Steinbeck (John) *1963:* 7 Seferis (George) *1964:* 6 Sartre (Jean-Paul) *1965:* 9 Sholokhov (Mikhail) *1966:* 5 Agnon (Shmuel Yosef), Sachs (Nelly) *1967:* 8 Asturias (Miguel Angel) *1968:* 8 Kawabata (Yasunari) *1969:* 7 Beckett (Samuel) *1970:* 12 Solzhenitsyn (Alexander) *1971:* 6 Neruda (Pablo) *1972:* 4 Böll (Heinrich) *1973:* 5 White (Patrick) *1974:* 7 Johnson (Eyvind) 9 Martinson (Edmund) *1975:* 7 Montale (Eugenio) *1976:* 6 Bellow (Saul) *1977:* 10 Aleixandre (Vicente) *1978:* 6 Singer (Isaac Bashevis) *1979:* 6 Elytis (Odysseus) *1980:* 6 Milosz (Czeslaw) *1981:* 7 Canetti (Elias) *1982:* 13 Garcia Marquez (Gabriel) *1983:* 7 Golding (William) *1984:* 7 Siefert (Jaroslav) *1985:* 5 Simon (Claude) *1986:* 7 Soyinka (Wole) *1987:* 7 Brodsky (Joseph) *1988:* 7 Mahfouz (Naguib) *1989:* 4 Cela (Camilo Jose) *1990:* 3 Paz (Octavio) *1991:* 8 Gordimer (Nadine) *1992:* 7 Walcott (Derek) *1993:* 8 Morrison (Toni) *1994:* 2 Oe (Kenzaburo) *1995:* 6 Heaney (Seamus)

peace:
1901: 5 Passy (Frederic) 6 Dunant (Jean-Henri) *1902:* 5 Gobat (Charles Albert) 8 Ducommun (Elie) *1903:* 6 Cremer (William) *1905:* 10 von Suttner (Bertha) *1906:* 9 Roosevelt (Theodore) *1907:* 6 Moneta (Ernesto) 7 Renault (Louis) *1908:* 5 Bajer (Fredrik) 9 Arnoldson (Klas Pontus) *1909:* 9 Beernaert (Auguste) 13 d'Estournelles (Paul) *1911:* 5 Asser (Tobias), Fried (Alfred) *1912:* 4 Root (Elihu) *1913:* 10 La Fontaine (Henri) *1919:* 6 Wilson (Wood-

row) *1920:* 9 Bourgeois (Leon) *1921:*
5 Lange (Christian Louis) 8 Branting (Karl
Hjalmar) *1922:* 6 Nansen (Fridtjof) *1925:*
5 Dawes (Charles) 11 Chamberlain (Austen) *1926:* 6 Briand (Aristide)
10 Stresemann (Gustav) *1927:* 6 Quidde
(Ludwig) 7 Buisson (Ferdinand) *1929:*
7 Kellogg (Frank) *1930:* 9 Soderblom
(Nathan) *1931:* 6 Addams (Jane), Butler
(Nicholas) *1933:* 6 Angell (Norman) *1934:*
9 Henderson (Arthur) *1935:* 9 Ossietzky
(Carl von) *1936:* 13 Saavedra Lamas
(Carlos) *1937:* 5 Cecil (Robert) *1945:*
4 Hull (Cordell) *1946:* 4 Mott (John)
5 Balch (Emily Greene) *1949:* 3 Orr (John
Boyd) *1950:* 6 Bunche (Ralph) *1951:*
7 Jouhaux (Leon) *1952:* 10 Schweitzer
(Albert) *1953:* 8 Marshall (George) *1957:*
7 Pearson (Lester) *1958:* 4 Pire (Dominique Georges) *1959:* 9 Noel-Baker
(Philip) *1960:* 7 Luthuli (Albert John) *1961:*
12 Hammarskjold (Dag) *1962:* 7 Pauling
(Linus) *1964:* 4 King (Martin Luther) *1968:*
6 Cassin (Rene) *1970:* 7 Borlaug (Norman) *1971:* 6 Brandt (Willy) *1973:* 8 Le
Duc Tho 9 Kissinger (Henry) *1974:*
4 Sato (Eisaku) 8 MacBride (Sean) *1975:*
8 Sakharov (Andrey) *1976:* 8 Corrigan
(Mairead), Williams (Betty) *1978:* 5 Begin
(Menachem), Sadat (Anwar el-) *1979:*
12 Mother Teresa *1980:* 8 Esquivel
(Adolfo Perez) *1982:* 6 Myrdal (Alva)
12 Garcia Robles (Alfonso) *1983:*
6 Walesa (Lech) *1984:* 4 Tutu (Desmond)
1986: 6 Wiesel (Elie) *1987:* 12 Arias Sanchez (Oscar) *1989:* 9 Dalai Lama *1990:*
9 Gorbachev (Mikhail) *1991:* 13 Aung San
Suu Kyi *1992:* 6 Menchu (Rigoberta) *1993:*
7 de Klerk (Frederik), Mandela (Nelson)
1994: 5 Peres (Shimon), Rabin (Yitzhak)
6 Arafat (Yasir) *1995:* 7 Rotblat (Joseph)
physics:
1901: 8 Roentgen (Wilhelm) *1902:* 6 Zeeman (Pieter) 7 Lorentz (Hendrik Antoon)
1903: 5 Curie (Marie, Pierre) 9 Becquerel
(Antoine-Henri) *1904:* 8 Rayleigh (Lord)
1905: 6 Lenard (Philipp) *1906:* 7 Thomson (Joseph John) *1907:* 9 Michelson
(Albert) *1908:* 8 Lippmann (Gabriel) *1909:*
5 Braun (Karl) 7 Marconi (Guglielmo)
1910: 11 van der Waals (Johannes) *1911:*
4 Wien (Wilhelm) *1912:* 5 Dalen (Nils)
1914: 7 von Laue (Max) *1915:* 5 Bragg
(Wilham) *1917:* 6 Barkla (Charles) *1918:*
6 Planck (Max) *1919:* 5 Stark (Johannes)
1920: 9 Guillaume (Charles) *1921:* 8 Einstein (Albert) *1922:* 4 Bohr (Niels) *1923:*
8 Millikan (Robert) *1924:* 8 Siegbahn
(Karl) *1925:* 5 Hertz (Gustav) 6 Franck
(James) *1926:* 6 Perrin (Jean-Baptiste)
1927: 6 Wilson (Charles) 7 Compton

(Arthur) *1928:* 10 Richardson (Owen)
1929: 7 Broglie (Louis-Victor de) *1930:*
5 Raman (Chandrasekhara) *1932:* 10 Heisenberg (Werner) *1933:* 5 Dirac (Paul)
11 Schrodinger (Erwin) *1935:* 8 Chadwick
(James) *1936:* 4 Hess (Victor) 8 Anderson (Carl) *1937:* 7 Thomson (George)
8 Davisson (Clinton) *1938:* 5 Fermi
(Enrico) *1939:* 8 Lawrence (Ernest) *1943:*
5 Stern (Otto) *1944:* 4 Rabi (Isidor Isaac)
1945: 5 Pauli (Wolfgang) *1946:* 8 Bridgman (Percy) *1947:* 8 Appleton (Edward)
1948: 8 Blackett (Patrick) *1949:*
6 Yukawa (Hideki) *1950:* 6 Powell (Cecil)
1951: 6 Walton (Ernest) 9 Cockcroft
(John) *1952:* 5 Bloch (Felix) 7 Purcell
(Edward) *1953:* 7 Zernike (Frits) *1954:*
4 Born (Max) 5 Bothe (Walther) *1955:*
4 Lamb (Willis) 5 Kusch (Polykarp) *1956:*
7 Bardeen (John) 8 Brattain (Walter),
Shockley (William) *1957:* 3 Lee (Tsung
Dao) 4 Yang (Chen Ning) *1958:* 4 Tamm
(Igor) 5 Frank (Ilya) 9 Cherenkov (Pavel)
1959: 5 Segre (Emilio) 11 Chamberlain
(Owen) *1960:* 6 Glaser (Donald) *1961:*
9 Mossbauer (Rudolf) 10 Hofstadter (Robert) *1962:* 6 Landau (Lev) *1963:* 5 Mayer
(Maria) 6 Jensen (J. Hans), Wigner
(Eugene) *1964:* 5 Basov (Nikolay)
6 Townes (Charles) 9 Prochorov (Alexander) *1965:* 7 Feynman (Richard)
8 Tomonaga (Sin-itiro) 9 Schwinger (Julian) *1966:* 7 Kastler (Alfred) *1967:*
5 Bethe (Hans) *1968:* 7 Alvarez (Luis)
1969: 8 Gell-Mann (Murray) *1970:* 4 Néel
(Louis) 6 Alfven (Hannes) *1971:* 5 Gabor
(Dennis) *1972:* 6 Cooper (Leon) 7 Bardeen (John) 10 Schrieffer (John) *1973:*
5 Esaki (Leo) 7 Giaever (Ivar) 9 Josephson (Brian) *1974:* 4 Ryle (Martin) 6 Hewish (Antony) *1975:* 4 Bohr (Aage) 9 Mottelson (Ben), Rainwater (L. James) *1976:*
4 Ting (Samuel) 7 Richter (Burton) *1977:*
4 Mott (Nevill) 8 Anderson (Philip), Van
Vleck (John) *1978:* 6 Wilson (Robert)
7 Kapitsa (Pyotr), Penzias (Arno) *1979:*
5 Salam (Abdus) 7 Glashow (Sheldon)
8 Weinberg (Steven) *1980:* 5 Fitch (Val)
6 Cronin (James) *1981:* 8 Schawlow
(Arthur), Siegbahn (Kai) 11 Bloembergen
(Nicholaas) *1982:* 6 Wilson (Kenneth)
1983: 6 Fowler (William) 13 Chandrasekhar (Subrahmanyan) *1984:* 6 Rubbia
(Carlo) 11 van der Meere (Simon) *1985:*
8 Klitzing (Klaus von) *1986:* 5 Ruska
(Ernst) 6 Binnig (Gerd), Rohrer (Heinrich)
1987: 6 Müller (K. Alex) 7 Bednorz (J.
Georg) *1988:* 8 Lederman (Leon),
Schwartz (Melvin) 11 Steinberger (Jack)
1989: 4 Paul (Wolfgang) 6 Ramsey (Norman) 7 Dehmelt (Hans) *1990:* 6 Taylor

(Richard) 7 Kendall (Henry) 8 Friedman (Jerome) *1991:* 8 De Gennes (Pierre-Gilles) *1992:* 7 Charpak (Georges) *1993:* 5 Hulse (Russell) 6 Taylor (Joseph) *1994:* 5 Shull (Clifford) 10 Brockhouse (Bertram) *1995:* 4 Perl (Martin) 6 Reines (Frederick)

physiology or medicine:
1901: 10 von Behring (Emil) *1902:* 4 Ross (Ronald) *1903:* 6 Finsen (Niels) *1904:* 6 Pavlov (Ivan) *1905:* 4 Koch (Robert) *1906:* 5 Golgi (Camillo) 11 Ramon y Cajal (Santiago) *1907:* 7 Laveran (Charles) *1908:* 7 Ehrlich (Paul) 11 Metchnikoff (Elie) *1909:* 6 Kocher (Emil) *1910:* 6 Kossel (Albrecht) *1911:* 10 Gullstrand (Allvar) *1912:* 6 Carrel (Alexis) *1913:* 6 Richet (Charles) *1914:* 6 Barany (Robert) *1919:* 6 Bordet (Jules) *1920:* 5 Krogh (August) *1922:* 4 Hill (Archibald) 8 Meyerhof (Otto) *1923:* 7 Banting (Frederick), Macleod (John) *1924:* 9 Einthoven (Willem) *1926:* 7 Fibiger (Johannes) *1927:* 13 Wagner-Jauregg (Julius) *1928:* 7 Nicolle (Charles) *1929:* 7 Eijkman (Christiaan), Hopkins (Frederick) *1930:* 11 Landsteiner (Karl) *1931:* 7 Warburg (Otto) *1932:* 6 Adrian (Edgar) 11 Sherrington (Charles) *1933:* 6 Morgan (Thomas) *1934:* 5 Minot (George) 6 Murphy (William) 7 Whipple (George) *1935:* 7 Spemann (Hans) *1936:* 4 Dale (Henry) 5 Loewi (Otto) *1937:* 12 Szent-Gyorgyi (Albert) *1938:* 7 Heymans (Corneille) *1939:* 6 Domagk (Gerhard) *1943:* 3 Dam (Henrik) 5 Doisy (Edward) *1944:* 6 Gasser (Herbert) 8 Erlanger (Joseph) *1945:* 5 Chain (Ernst) 6 Florey (Howard) 7 Fleming (Alexander) *1946:* 6 Muller (Hermann) *1947:* 4 Cori (Carl, Gerty) 7 Houssay (Bernardo) *1948:* 7 Mueller (Paul) *1949:* 4 Hess (Walter) 5 Moniz (Antonio) *1950:* 5 Hench (Philip) 7 Kendall (Edward) 10 Reichstein (Tadeus) *1951:* 7 Theiler (Max) *1952:* 7 Waksman (Selman) *1953:* 5 Krebs (Hans) 7 Lipmann (Fritz) *1954:* 6 Enders (John), Weller (Thomas) 7 Robbins (Frederick) *1955:* 8 Theorell (Hugo) *1956:* 8 Cournand (Andre), Richards (Dickinson) 9 Forssmann (Werner) *1957:* 5 Bovet (Daniel) *1958:* 5 Tatum (Edward) 6 Beadle (George) 9 Lederberg (Joshua) *1959:* 5 Ochoa (Severo) 8 Kornberg (Arthur) *1960:* 6 Burnet (Macfarlane) 7 Medawar (Peter) *1961:* 5 Bekesy (Georg von) *1962:* 5 Crick (Francis) 6 Watson (James) 7 Wilkins (Maurice) *1963:* 6 Eccles (John), Huxley (Andrew) 7 Hodgkin (Alan) *1964:* 5 Bloch (Konrad), Lynen (Feodor) *1965:* 5 Jacob (Francois), Monod (Jacques) 5 Lwoff (Andre) *1966:* 4 Rous (Francis) 7 Huggins (Charles) *1967:* 4 Wald (George) 6 Granit (Ragnar) 8 Hartline (H. Keffer) *1968:* 6 Holley (Robert) 7 Khorana (H. Gobind) 9 Nirenberg (Marshall) *1969:* 5 Luria (Salvador) 7 Hershey (Alfred) 8 Delbruck (Max) *1970:* 4 Katz (Bernard) 7 Axelrod (Julius) 8 Von Euler (Ulf) *1971:* 10 Sutherland (Earl) *1972:* 6 Porter (Rodney) 7 Edelman (Gerald) *1973:* 6 Frisch (Karl von), Lorenz (Konrad) 9 Tinbergen (Nikolaas) *1974:* 4 Duve (Christian) 6 Claude (Albert), Palade (George) *1975:* 5 Temin (Howard) 8 Dulbecco (Renato) 9 Baltimore (David) *1976:* 8 Blumberg (Baruch), Gajdusek (D. Carleton) *1977:* 5 Yalow (Rosalyn) 7 Schally (Andrew) 9 Guillemin (Roger) *1978:* 5 Arber (Werner), Smith (Hamilton) 7 Nathans (Daniel) *1979:* 7 Cormack (Allan) 10 Hounsfield (Godfrey) *1980:* 5 Snell (George) 7 Dausset (Jean) 10 Benacerraf (Baruj) *1981:* 5 Hubel (David) 6 Sperry (Roger), Wiesel (Torsten) *1982:* 4 Vane (John) 9 Bergstrom (Sune) 10 Samuelsson (Bengt) *1983:* 10 McClintock (Barbara) *1984:* 5 Jerne (Niels) 7 Koehler (Georges) 8 Milstein (Cesar) *1985:* 5 Brown (Michael) 9 Goldstein (Joseph) *1986:* 5 Cohen (Stanley) 14 Levi-Montalcini (Rita) *1987:* 8 Tonegawa (Susumu) *1988:* 5 Black (James), Elion (Gertrude) 9 Hitchings (George) *1989:* 6 Bishop (J. Michael), Varmus (Harold) *1990:* 6 Murray (Joseph), Thomas (E. Donnall) *1991:* 5 Neher (Erwin) 7 Sakmann (Bert) *1992:* 5 Krebs (Edwin) 7 Fischer (Edmond) *1993:* 5 Sharp (Phillip) 7 Roberts (Richard) *1994:* 6 Gilman (Alfred) 7 Rodbell (Martin) *1995:* 5 Lewis (Edward) 9 Wieschaus (Eric) 15 Nüsslein-Volhard (Christiane)

Nobel's invention 8 dynamite
nobility 7 peerage, royalty 8 eminence, noblesse 11 aristocracy, superiority
noble 4 peer 5 grand, lofty, moral 6 august, lordly, worthy 7 eminent, ethical, stately 8 baronial, elevated, heroical, highborn, highbred, imposing, magnific, majestic, princely, sterling, virtuous, wellborn 9 estimable, excellent, grandiose, honorable, righteous 10 high-minded, impressive, moralistic, principled 11 illustrious, magnificent, outstanding, right-minded 12 aristocratic
nobleman 4 duke, peer 5 baron 6 prince 7 baronet 8 principe *British:* 4 earl 8 viscount *European:* 7 marquis 8 marquess *French:* 5 comte 7 vicomte *German:* 4 Graf 8 burgrave, margrave 9 landgrave *Indian:* 6 sardar, sirdar 8 maharaja *Italian:* 8 marchese *Japanese (former):* 6 daimio,

daimyo *Scandinavian:* 4 jarl *Spanish:* 7 hidalgo

noblewoman 4 lady 7 baronne, duchess, peeress 8 baroness, countess, princess *European:* 8 marquise *Italian:* 8 marchesa

nobody 4 none, zero 5 no man, no one, zilch 6 cipher 7 nothing, nullity, whiffet 8 whipster 9 nonentity

nocturnal 5 night 7 nightly 10 night piece

nocuous 3 bad, ill 6 nocent 7 harmful, hurtful 8 damaging 9 injurious 11 deleterious, detrimental, mischievous

nodding 4 dozy 6 drowsy, sleepy, snoozy 8 slumbery 9 pendulous, somnolent, soporific 10 slumberous

noddle 4 bean, head, poll 6 noggin 9 headpiece

noddy 4 dope, fool, jack, tern 5 dunce, stupe 6 fulmar, noodle 7 schnook 8 dumbhead 9 lamebrain, razorbill, simpleton

node 4 knob 5 point 11 predicament 12 entanglement, protuberance

nog 3 ale, peg, pin 5 block

Nogah's father 5 David

noggin 4 bean, head, pate, poll 6 noddle, noodle

no-good 4 worm 6 bad lot, draffy, drossy, mucker, waster, wretch 7 inutile, lowlife, nothing, rounder, wastrel 8 unworthy, wormling 9 no-account, valueless, worthless 10 ne'er-do-well, profligate, scapegrace

Nohah's father 8 Benjamin

noise 3 din 4 blab, talk 5 babel, rumor, sound 6 clamor, gossip, hubbub, racket, ruckus, rumpus, tattle, uproar 7 ruction, sonance, stridor 8 resonant 11 pandemonium *explosive:* 6 report

noiseless 4 hush 5 quiet, still, whist 6 silent, stilly

noisemaker 4 horn 6 rattle 7 clapper

noisette 5 hazel

noisome 4 foul, rank, vile 5 dirty, fetid, funky, fusty, musty, nasty 6 filthy, horrid, putrid, rancid, sickly 7 harmful, noxious, squalid 8 nidorous, stinking 9 offensive, repulsive, revolting, sickening, unhealthy 10 disgusting, insalutary, malodorous, nauseating, unsalutary 11 destructive, distasteful, unhealthful 12 insalubrious

noisy 4 loud 7 blatant, clamant, rackety, squeaky 8 clattery, overloud, sonorous, strident 9 clamorous, turbulent 10 boisterous, clangorous, strepitous, tumultuous, uproarious, vociferous 12 obstreperous

nomad 6 roving *Arabic:* 6 beduin 7 bedouin

nomadic 6 roving 7 vagrant 8 vagabond 9 itinerant, itinerate, wandering, wayfaring

11 perambulant, peripatetic 13 perambulatory

nom de plume see pen name

nomen 4 name, noun 5 style, title 7 moniker 11 appellation, appellative, designation

nomenclature 4 list, name 7 catalog 9 designate 11 appellation, designation, terminology

nominal 5 rated 6 formal 7 alleged, seeming, titular 8 apparent, so-called, trifling 9 pretended, professed 10 ostensible 11 approximate 12 substantival 13 insignificant

nominate 3 tap 4 call, name 5 offer 6 tender 7 appoint, name off, present, proffer, propose, purpose

nonage 7 infancy 8 minority 10 immaturity

nonchalant 4 cool, easy, glad 5 light 6 casual, smooth 8 careless, cheerful, composed 9 collected, unruffled 10 effortless 11 unflappable 12 lighthearted 13 imperturbable

noncleric 4 laic 6 layman

nonclerical 3 lay

nonclerics 5 laity

noncommittal 7 neutral 8 reserved 10 restrained

nonconformist 5 rebel 6 hippie 7 beatnik, heretic, sectary 8 bohemian, maverick 9 dissenter, dissident, heretical, heterodox, sectarian 10 schismatic, separatist, unorthodox 11 misbeliever, schismatist

nonconformity 6 heresy, schism 7 dissent 9 misbelief 10 dissidence, heterodoxy 11 unorthodoxy 13 individualism

nonentity 4 zero 5 aught, zilch 6 cipher, nobody 7 nothing, nullity, sad sack, whiffet 8 small fry, unperson, whipster 9 obscurity, rushlight, small beer

nonesuch 5 ideal, jewel 7 paragon 9 matchless, nonpareil, unequaled, unrivaled

nonetheless 3 yet 5 still 6 though, withal 7 howbeit, however 8 after all 11 still and all

nonexistence 4 nada 7 nullity, vacuity 8 nihility 11 nothingness

nonflammable 7 apyrous 13 incombustible

nonfunctional 7 useless 8 unusable 10 unworkable 11 impractical 13 impracticable, unserviceable

non-Hawaiian 5 haole

non-Jew 3 goy 5 goyim (plural) 7 gentile

nonmilitary 8 civilian

non-Muslim 6 giaour

no-nonsense 5 grave, sober, staid 6 sedate, solemn, somber 7 earnest, serious, weighty 10 sobersided

nonpareil see nonesuch

nonpartisan 4 fair, just 9 equitable, impartial, objective, uncolored 11 indifferent 12 unprejudiced 13 undistinctive

nonplus 4 balk, beat, faze 5 stick, stump, throw 6 baffle, boggle, flurry, muddle, puzzle, rattle, stymie, thwart 7 buffalo, confuse, dilemma, fluster, mystify, perplex, stagger 8 confound, overcome, paralyze, quandary 9 dumbfound, frustrate

nonprofessional 3 lay 4 laic, tyro 7 amateur, dabbler 9 smatterer 10 dilettante 11 abecedarian

nonrational 3 mad 7 invalid 9 illogical, sophistic 10 fallacious, reasonless, unreasoned 12 unreasonable

nonreactive 5 inert

nonreligious 3 lay 7 godless, profane, secular 8 temporal

nonresistant 7 passive 8 resigned, yielding 10 submissive 11 acquiescent

nonsense 3 rot 4 blah, bosh, bull, bunk, crap, gook, guff, jazz, punk, tosh 5 bilge, drool, folly, fudge, Greek, hokum, hooey, trash 6 babble, blague, bunkum, bushwa, drivel, hot air, humbug, jabber, piffle 7 baloney, blather, eyewash, flubdub, foolery, fooling, hogwash, inanity, rubbish, trifles, twaddle 8 buncombe, claptrap, falderal, falderol, flimflam, malarkey, pishposh, slipslop, tommyrot, trumpery 9 gibberish, moonshine, poppycock 10 applesauce, balderdash, double-talk, flapdoodle, meshuggaas, tomfoolery 11 jabberwocky, whangdoodle, windbaggery 12 blatherskite, fiddle-faddle, fiddlesticks, flummadiddle 13 horsefeathers *British:* 10 codswallop

nonsensical 5 inane 6 absurd 7 foolish 9 unmeaning 12 preposterous

nonsuccess 6 defeat 7 failure

nonviolent 6 irenic 7 pacific 8 pacifist, peaceful 9 peaceable 12 pacificatory

noodle 4 bean, dope, head, poll 5 chump, dunce, ninny, noddy, stupe 6 noggin 7 schnook 8 dumbhead 9 blockhead, lamebrain, simpleton 10 dunderhead

nook 4 cove, hole 5 niche 6 alcove, corner, cranny, recess 7 byplace 9 cubbyhole

Noon Wine author 6 Porter (Katherine Anne)

noose 3 tie 4 bond, hang 5 lasso, scrag, snare 6 entrap, gibbet, secure 7 turn off 8 string up

Nordhoff's partner 4 Hall (James)

norm 3 par 4 mean, type 5 maxim, model 6 median 7 average, pattern

Norma *composer:* 7 Bellini (Vincenzo) *librettist:* 6 Romani (Felice)

normal 4 mean, sane 5 lucid, right, typic, usual 6 common 7 average, general, natural, regular, typical 8 all there, ordinary, standard 9 customary, prevalent 11 commonplace 12 compos mentis

Normandy's capital 5 Rouen

Norns 5 fates, Skuld, Urdur 9 Verthandi

Norris novel 4 Blix 6 The Pit 8 McTeague 10 The Octopus

Norse *abode of the dead:* 8 Niflheim *alphabet:* 5 Runic *archer:* 4 Egil *bard:* 5 scald, skald *chieftain:* 4 jarl, Rolf 5 Rollo *demon:* 4 Mara, Surt 5 Surtr *dragon:* 6 Fafnir 8 Nithhogg *epic:* 4 Edda *explorer:* 4 Erik 8 Ericsson, Eriksson *first man:* 3 Ask 4 Askr *first woman:* 5 Embla *giant:* 4 Egil, Wade, Wate, Ymer, Ymir 5 Aegir, Egill, Hymir, Jotun, Mimir 6 Fafnir, Jotunn *giantess:* 4 Egia, Norn, Nott *god:* 2 As, Ve 3 Asa, Ass 4 Surt, Vali, Vili 5 Aesir (plural), Surtr, Vanir (plural) 6 Hoenir, Vithar 7 Vitharr *blind:* 4 Hoth 5 Hoder, Hodur, Hothr *chief:* 4 Odin 5 Othin, Wodan, Woden, Wotan *guardian:* 7 Heimdal 8 Heimdall 9 Heimdallr *messenger:* 6 Hermod 7 Hermodr *of beauty:* 5 Baldr 6 Balder, Baldur *of evil:* 4 Loke, Loki *of fertility:* 4 Frey 5 Freyr *of justice:* 7 Forsete, Forseti *of light:* 3 Dag *of peace:* 5 Baldr 6 Balder, Baldur *of poetry:* 5 Brage, Bragi *of the hunt:* 3 Ull 4 Ullr *of the seas:* 5 Njord 6 Njoerd, Njorth 4 Hler 5 Aegir, Gymir *of the sky:* 4 Odin 5 Othin *of thunder:* 4 Thor 5 Donar *of war:* 3 Tiu, Tiw, Tyr, Zio, Ziu *wolf:* 6 Fenrir *goddess:* 3 dis 4 Saga 5 disir (plural) 7 Asynjur *of fate:* 3 Urd 4 Norn, Urth, Wyrd 5 Skuld 9 Verthandi *of healing:* 3 Eir *of love:* 5 Freya *of marriage:* 5 Frigg 6 Frigga *of night:* 4 Natt, Nott *of storms:* 3 Ran *of the earth:* 5 Joerd, Jorth *of the moon:* 5 Nanna *of the sea:* 3 Ran *of the sky:* 5 Frigg 6 Frigga *of the underworld:* 3 Hel 4 Hela *of youth:* 4 Idun 5 Ithun 6 Ithunn *gods' abode:* 6 Asgard *hall of heroes:* 8 Valhalla *king:* 4 Atli, Olaf *nobleman:* 4 jarl *patron saint:* 4 Olaf *poem:* 4 rune *poet:* 5 scald, skald *rainbow bridge:* 7 Bifrost *sea serpent:* 4 Wade, Wate 6 kraken 7 Midgard *smith:* 6 Völund *tale:* 4 saga *toast:* 5 skoal *watchdog:* 4 Garm 5 Garmr *world's destruction:* 8 Ragnarok *world tree:* 8 Ygdrasil 10 Yggdrasill

north *combining form:* 4 arct 5 arcto

North African *country:* 5 Egypt, Libya 7 Algeria, Morocco, Tunisia *fruit:* 3 fig 4 date *garment:* 4 haik *grass:* 4 alfa 7 esparto *jackal:* 4 dieb *language:* 6 Arabic, Berber *Muslim sect:* 6 Sanusi 7 Senussi *people:* 6 Berber, Hamite 7 bedouin *seaport:* 4 Oran, Sfax 6 Annaba 7 Tangier 10 Casablanca

North America *country:* 4 Cuba 5 Haiti 6 Canada, Mexico, Panama 7 Bahamas, Grenada, Jamaica 8 Dominica, Honduras 9 Costa Rica, Guatemala, Nicaragua 10 El Salvador, Saint Lucia 12 United States *ethnic group:* 5 Negro 6 Indian 7 Mestizo, Spanish *language:* 6 Creole, French 7 English, Nahuatl, Spanish

North Carolina *capital:* 7 Raleigh *college, university:* 4 Duke, Elon 8 Davidson 10 Wake Forest *largest city:* 9 Charlotte *nickname:* 12 Tar Heel State *state bird:* 8 cardinal *state flower:* 7 dogwood

North Dakota *capital:* 8 Bismarck *largest town:* 5 Fargo *nickname:* 10 Sioux State

northern 4 pike 6 boreal 11 hyperborean

northern limit of the world 5 Thule

North Korea *capital:* 9 Pyongyang *monetary unit:* 3 won

North Star State 9 Minnesota

Northwest Passage author 7 Roberts (Kenneth)

Northwest Territories *capital:* 11 Yellowknife *district:* 8 Franklin, Keewatin 9 Mackenzie

north wind see at wind

Norway *capital:* 4 Oslo *inlet:* 5 fiord, fjord *monetary unit:* 5 krone *patron saint:* 4 Olaf *plateau region:* 5 fjeld

Norwegian *goblin:* 5 nisse *language:* 5 Norse 6 Bokmal 7 Bokmaal, Nynorsk, Riksmal 8 Landsmal, Riksmaal 9 Landsmaal

nose 3 pry 4 beak, bent, bump, gift, head, poke 5 aroma, flair, knack, prier, pryer, scent, smell, sniff, snift, snoop, snoot, snout, snuff 6 butt-in, genius, muzzle, nuzzle, pecker, talent 7 aptness, faculty, meddler, Paul Pry, smeller, sneezer 8 busybody, kibitzer, quidnunc, smell out 9 olfaction, proboscis, schnozzle *combining form:* 3 nas 4 nasi, naso 5 rhina, rhine 6 rhinus, rrhine *kind:* 3 pug 5 Roman 8 aquiline *lengthener:* 3 lie *opening:* 7 nostril

nosebleed 6 yarrow 9 epistaxis

nose-dive 3 dip 4 drop, fall, skid 6 plunge, tumble 7 plummet

nosegay 4 posy 7 bouquet

nosey see nosy

nosh 5 snack

Nostradamus 5 augur 6 auspex 7 prophet 8 foreseer, haruspex 9 predictor 10 forecaster, foreteller, prophesier

Nostromo author 6 Conrad (Joseph)

nostrum 6 elixir 7 cure-all, panacea

nosy 5 peery 6 prying, snoopy 7 curious 9 intrusive 11 inquisitive, inquisitory

not *prefix:* 2 an, il, im, in, ir, un 3 ant, dis, non 4 anth, anti

notability 3 VIP 4 lion, name 5 celeb, chief 6 leader 7 big name, big shot 8 bigtimer, eminence, luminary, somebody 9 celebrity, dignitary

notable 3 big, VIP 4 czar, king, lion, name, star 5 baron, celeb, chief, famed, great, light, mogul, nabob, nawob, power 6 big boy, biggie, big gun, bigwig, famous, fat cat, figure, leader, prince, rubric 7 big name, big shot, eminent, magnate, mugwump, pooh-bah 8 big chief, big noise, bigtimer, big wheel, eminence, great gun, luminary, renowned, somebody, striking 9 big cheese, celebrity, character, dignitary, important, muckamuck, personage, prominent, red-letter 10 celebrated, celebrious, noteworthy 11 conspicuous, heavyweight, illustrious, personality 13 distinguished, high-muck-a-muck

notarize 7 certify 8 validate

notch 3 cut, gap, peg 4 gash, mark, nick, nock, rung, step 5 cleft, grade, score, stage 6 degree, indent, record 7 scratch 8 incision, undercut 9 indenture 10 depression 11 indentation

note 3 cry, jot, see 4 call, chit, heed, mark, memo, mood, odor, show, song, tone, view 5 motif, smell, sound, tenor 6 descry, letter, regard, remark 7 comment, discern, element, epistle, jotting, missive, observe 8 annotate, eminence, indicate, perceive, reminder 9 attention, knowledge 10 cognizance, commentary, memorandum, observance, reputation 11 distinction, distinguish, information, observation 12 obiter dictum

notebook 3 log 5 diary 6 cahier 7 journal

noted 6 famous 7 eminent, leading, popular 9 prominent, well-known

noteworthy 6 patent, rubric 7 evident, notable 8 manifest, nameable 9 memorable, prominent, red-letter 10 noticeable, observable, remarkable 11 conspicuous, exceptional, outstanding 12 considerable 13 extraordinary

nothing 3 nil, nix 4 zero 5 aught, nihil, ought, zilch 6 cipher, draffy, drossy, naught, nobody, no-good, nought, trifle 7 inutile, nullity, whiffet 8 goose egg, unworthy, whipster 9 bagatelle, no-account, nonentity, valueless, worthless *French:* 4 rien *German:* 6 nichts *Latin:* 5 nihil *Spanish:* 4 nada

nothingness 4 nada, void 5 death 6 vacuum 7 nullity, vacuity 8 nihility 9 emptiness 12 nonexistence

notice 2 ad 3 see 4 care, espy, heed, mark, memo 5 favor, grasp, greet, refer, sense, sight 6 advert, descry, regard, remark, review 7 comment, concern, discern, observe, respect, thought 8 civility, critique, perceive, reviewal 9 attention, criticism, directive, recognize 10 book review, cognizance, evaluation, memorandum, observance 11 acknowledge, distinguish, information, observation 12 announcement

noticeable 6 marked, patent, signal 7 evident, obvious, pointed, salient 8 manifest, striking 9 arresting, arrestive, prominent 10 noteworthy 11 conspicuous, eye-catching, outstanding, sensational, significant, spectacular

notify 4 clew, clue, post, tell, warn 6 advise, fill in, inform, reveal, signal, wise up 7 apprise, declare, divulge, publish 8 acquaint, announce, disclose, discover, proclaim 9 broadcast 10 promulgate

notion 4 clue, hint, idea, term, whim 5 fancy, freak, humor, image 6 maggot, phrase 7 boutade, caprice, conceit, concept, inkling, thought 8 crotchet, telltale 9 knowledge 10 impression, knickknack 12 apprehension 13 understanding

notional 5 ideal 6 unreal 7 fancied, shadowy 8 fanciful, imagined 9 crotchety, imaginary, visionary, whimsical 10 conceptual 11 theoretical

notorious 5 noted 6 famous 7 leading, popular 8 ill-famed, infamous 9 prominent, well-known

Nott's horse 8 Hrimfaxi

Notus 6 Auster *brother:* 5 Eurus 6 Boreas 8 Zephyrus *father:* 6 Aeolus 8 Astraeus *mother:* 3 Eos

noun 4 name 7 nominal 11 substantive *inflectional form:* 4 case *suffix:* 2 et, ia, ic 3 ent, ery, ier, ing, ion, ist 4 ence *verbal:* 6 gerund

nourish 4 rear 5 nurse, raise 6 foster, nursle, suckle 7 bring up, build up, nurture, support 8 maintain 9 cultivate 10 breastfeed, provide for, strengthen

nourishment 3 pap 4 food, keep 6 living 7 aliment, pabulum, support 8 nutrient 10 sustenance 11 maintenance

____**nous** 5 entre

nouveau riche 7 parvenu, upstart 8 roturier 9 arriviste

Nova Scotia *capital:* 7 Halifax *original name:* 6 Acadia, Acadie

novel 3 new, odd 5 fresh 6 modern, recent, unique 7 special, strange, unusual 8 neoteric, original, peculiar, singular, uncommon 9 different, new-sprung 10 newfangled, unfamiliar 11 modernistic 12 new-fashioned

novelty 5 curio, sport 6 bauble, change, gewgaw, trifle 7 bibelot, newness, trinket, whatnot 8 gimcrack, mutation 9 objet d'art 10 innovation, knickknack

novice 3 cub 4 boot, colt, punk, tyro 6 greeny, rookie 7 amateur, learner, recruit, student, trainee 8 beginner, freshman, inexpert, neophyte, newcomer, prentice 9 fledgling, greenhorn, novitiate, postulant 10 apprentice, tenderfoot

Novum Organum author 5 Bacon (Francis)

now 2 as 3 for 4 away 5 since, today 6 at once, hereat, seeing 7 anymore, because, present, whereas 8 as long as, directly, existing, first off, up-to-date 9 forthwith, instanter, instantly, presently, right away, sometimes 10 inasmuch as 11 considering, immediately, straightway

now and again 7 at times, betimes 9 sometimes

now and then see now and again

Nox, Nyx *brother:* 6 Erebus *daughter:* 3 Day 4 Eris 5 Light *father:* 5 Chaos *husband:* 6 Erebus *son:* 6 Charon, Hypnos 8 Thanatos

noxious 5 fetid 6 deadly, putrid, sickly 7 baneful, noisome 8 stinking 9 pestilent, unhealthy 10 insalutary, unsalutary 11 distasteful, pestiferous, unhealthful, unwholesome

nozzle 5 eject, spray 9 nose about

nuance 4 dash 5 shade, tinge, touch 6 nicety 7 soupçon 8 subtlety 9 gradation, suspicion 10 refinement, suggestion

nub 4 core, crux, gist, knob, lump, meat, pith 5 point, short 6 kernel, upshot 9 substance 12 protuberance

Nubian 8 Cushitic

nucha 4 nape

nuclear agency 3 AEC, NRC

nuclear particle 5 meson 6 proton 7 neutron

nucleus 3 bud 4 core, germ, head, kern, ring, seed 5 focus, spark 6 embryo *material:* 8 karyotin

Nudd's son 6 Edeym

nude 3 raw 4 bald, bare 5 naked, stark 6 peeled, unclad 7 unrobed 8 buff-bare, stripped 9 au naturel, unattired, unclothed, uncovered, undressed 10 dishabille, stark-naked 11 garmentless

nudge 3 dig, jab, jog, toe 4 near, poke, prod 5 punch 9 ease along

nugatory 4 idle, vain 5 empty 6 hollow, otiose 7 invalid 9 worthless

nugget 3 gob, wad 4 clod, hunk, lump 5 chunk, clump, hunch

nuisance 4 harm, pest 6 bother, injury, pester, plague 7 nudnick 8 irritant, pesterer

9 besetment **10** botherment **11** botheration **12** exasperation

null 3 bad, nil **4** knur, void, zero **5** annul, empty, knurl **7** destroy, expunge, invalid, useless **9** worthless **10** obliterate **11** ineffective, ineffectual, nonexistent **13** inefficacious, insignificant

nullify 4 undo **5** abate, annul, limit, quash **6** efface, negate, offset **7** abolish, confine, vitiate **8** abrogate, restrict **10** annihilate, compensate, counteract, invalidate, neutralize **11** countervail

nullity 4 nada, zero **5** zilch **6** cipher, nobody **7** nothing, vacuity, whiffet **8** whipster **9** annulment, nonentity **11** nothingness **12** nonexistence

numb 4 dead, dull, mull **5** aloof, blunt, chill, frost **6** asleep, casual, deaden, freeze, remote **8** comatose, deadened, detached **9** incurious, insensate, senseless, stupefied, uncurious, unfeeling **10** insensible, insentient **11** desensitize, indifferent, insensitive, unconcerned, unconscious **12** anesthetized, desensitized, uninterested

number 5 add up, count, digit, run to, sum to, tally, total **6** amount, cipher, come to, figure **7** chiffer, include, integer, numeral, numeric, ordinal, run into, several, sum into **8** cardinal, numerate, paginate **9** aggregate, enumerate *added to another:* **6** augend *combining form:* **7** arithmo *large indeterminate:* **7** zillion *resulting from division:* **8** quotient *resulting from multiplication:* **7** product *resulting from subtraction:* **10** difference *science:* **11** mathematics *whole:* **7** integer

number one 4 main **5** chief, major **6** Grade A **7** capital, stellar **8** dominant, five-star, foremost, superior **9** excellent, first-rate, front-rank, numero uno, top-drawer **10** blue-ribbon, first-class, preeminent **11** first-string, outstanding, predominant

numbness 6 stupor *combining form:* **4** narc **5** narco

numeral 5 digit **6** cipher, figure, number **7** chiffer, integer **11** whole number

numerate 4 list, tale, tell **5** count, tally **6** number **7** tick off

numerous 3 big **4** many **5** great, large **6** legion, sundry **7** several, umpteen, various **8** populous **9** plentiful **10** voluminous **12** multifarious, multitudinal **13** multitudinous

Numitor *brother:* **7** Amulius *daughter:* **9** Rea Silvia **10** Rhea Silvia *grandson:* **5** Remus **7** Romulus

numskull 4 dolt **5** dunce **8** bonehead, clodpate **9** blockhead, thickhead

numskulled 5 dense, thick **6** stupid **9** fatheaded **10** beefheaded **11** blockheaded, thickheaded, thick-witted

nunnery 7 convent **10** sisterhood *head:* **8** superior

Nun's son 6 Joshua

nuptial 6 bridal, wedded **7** marital, married, spousal, wedding **8** conjugal, hymeneal **9** connubial, espousals **11** matrimonial

nurse 4 feed, nana, rear, suck **5** humor, nanny, serve **6** attend, foster, mother, pamper, suckle, wait on **7** advance, care for, cherish, educate, forward, further, indulge, nourish, nurture, promote **9** cultivate **10** minister to *children's:* **5** nanny **6** nannie *English:* **11** Nightingale (Florence) *Indian:* **4** ayah *Oriental:* **3** ama **4** amah

nursemaid 4 nana **5** nanny **6** minder, nannie, sitter **9** governess **10** babysitter *Indian:* **4** ayah *Oriental:* **3** ama **4** amah

nursery 6 crèche **7** brooder

nurture 4 feed, food, grub, rear **5** nurse, raise, train **6** cradle, foster, nursle, school, uphold, viands **7** bolster, bring up, cherish, edibles, educate, nourish, support, sustain **8** tutelage, victuals **9** cultivate, provender **10** discipline, provisions, upbringing **11** comestibles

nut 2 en **3** bug **4** kook, loon **5** acorn, bigot, crank, fiend, freak, issue, loony, pecan, tryma **6** almond, cashew, cuckoo, dement, madman, maniac, zealot **7** fanatic, filbert, hickory, lunatic, madling, problem, trymata (plural) **8** crackpot, question **9** bedlamite, ding-a-ling, harebrain, macadamia, non compos, pistachio, screwball **10** crackbrain, enthusiast, Tom o' Bedlam *combining form:* **4** cary, kary **5** caryo, karyo *European shrub:* **7** filbert *of a violin bow:* **4** frog, heel

Nut *consort:* **3** Geb, Keb *daughter:* **4** Isis **8** Nephthys *son:* **2** Ra **6** Osiris

nuthouse 6 asylum **8** loony bin **9** funny farm **10** booby hatch

Nutmeg State 11 Connecticut

nutria 5 coypu

nutriment 3 pap **4** food, keep **5** bread **6** living **7** pabulum, support **10** livelihood, sustenance **11** maintenance, subsistence

nutrition *study of:* **8** sitology

nutritious 9 healthful, wholesome **10** nourishing

nuts 3 mad **4** daft, wild **5** batty, crazy, wacky **6** insane, screwy **7** cracked **8** demented **10** unbalanced

nutshell 3 sum **5** sum up **6** digest **7** summate **8** condense **9** epitomize, inventory, summarize, synopsize

nutty see **nuts**

nuzzle 4 push, root, snug 5 nudge 6 burrow, cuddle, nestle, snudge, thrust 7 snoozle, snuggle

Nycteus *brother:* 5 Lycus *daughter:* 7 Antiope

nymph 5 deity, larva 6 maiden *changed into a bear:* 8 Callisto *changed into a*

laurel: 6 Daphne *changed into a rock:* 4 Echo *mountain:* 5 oread *of Muslim paradise:* 5 houri *sea:* 6 Nereid 7 Calypso *water:* 5 naiad 6 undine *wood:* 5 dryad

Nym's crony 8 Falstaff

Nyx see Nox

oaf 2 ox 3 dub 4 boob, bull, clod, dolt, gawk, goof, goon, hulk, lout, lump, slob 5 beast, booby, brute, chump, clown, dunce, klutz, looby 6 bohunk, galoot, lubber, lummox, slouch 7 bruiser, fathead, gorilla, lobster, lumpkin, palooka 8 bonehead, dolthead, lunkhead, meathead 9 blockhead, blunderer, lamebrain, simpleton

oak 4 tree, wood 9 broadleaf *African:* 7 turtosa *family:* 8 Fagaceae *fruit:* 5 acorn *genus:* 7 Quercus *kind:* 3 bur, pin, red 4 bear, cork, holm, ilex, live 5 black, holly, roble, white 6 barren, cerris, encina 7 durmast, English, moss-cup, valonia 9 blackjack *Mexican:* 8 chaparro *young:* 7 oakling 8 flittern

oar 3 row 4 pole, pull 5 rower, scull 6 paddle 7 paddler *part:* 4 loom, palm 5 blade, shaft 6 button, collar *pin:* 5 thole

oarsman 3 bow 5 rower 6 stroke 7 sculler *director:* 3 cox 8 coxswain

oasis 3 spa 4 wadi, wady 6 refuge, relief *ancient:* 4 Merv *Egypt:* 4 Siwa 5 Gafsa 6 Dakhla 7 Farafra 8 Ammonium *Libya:* 5 Mizda, Sebha 6 Sabhah 7 Gadames 8 Ghudamis *Niger:* 5 Bilma *Saudi Arabia:* 5 Hofuf, Taima 7 Al-Hufuf

oat 5 grain, grass 6 cereal *genus:* 5 Avena *Scottish:* 3 ait

oater 7 western 10 horse opera

oath 3 vow 4 cuss 5 curse, swear 6 pledge 8 cussword 9 expletive, profanity, swearword 11 affirmation *mild:* 3 gee 4 darn, drat, gosh 5 by gor, golly

oatmeal 6 burgoo 8 porridge *Scottish:* 8 drammock

Obadiah *father:* 4 Azel 6 Jehiel 8 Izrahiah, Shemaiah *son:* 8 Ishmaiah

obdurate 4 firm, hard 5 harsh, rigid, rough 6 dogged, mulish, rugged 7 adamant, cal-

lous 8 stubborn 9 heartless, immovable, unbending, unfeeling 10 brassbound, hardboiled, inexorable, inflexible, relentless, unyielding 11 coldhearted, hardhearted, stiff-necked, unemotional 12 stonyhearted 13 unsympathetic

obeah 5 charm, magic

Obed *father:* 4 Boaz 6 Ephlal 8 Shemaiah *mother:* 4 Ruth *son:* 5 Jesse 7 Azariah

Obededom's father 8 Jeduthun

obedient 5 loyal 6 docile 7 duteous, dutiful, slavish 8 amenable, biddable, obeisant, yielding 9 compliant, sheeplike, tractable 10 law-abiding, submissive 11 acquiescent, subservient

obeisance 3 bow 5 congé, honor, kotow 6 curtsy, fealty, homage, kowtow, salaam 7 gesture, loyalty 9 deference, reverence 10 allegiance

Oberon *messenger:* 4 Puck *wife:* 7 Titania

Oberto composer 5 Verdi (Giuseppe)

obese 3 fat 5 gross, heavy, plump, pudgy, stout 6 fleshy, portly 7 porcine 9 corpulent 10 overweight 11 upholstered

obey 3 bow 4 heed, keep, mind 5 agree, defer, yield 6 accede, assent, comply, follow, regard, submit 7 conform, fulfill, observe, satisfy 8 carry out 9 acquiesce

obfuscate 3 dim 4 murk 5 befog, cloud, gloom 6 darken, shadow 7 becloud, confuse, obscure 8 overcast 9 adumbrate

obi 4 sash

obiter dictum 4 note 6 remark 7 comment 10 commentary 11 observation

obituary 9 necrology

object 3 aim, end, jib, use 4 balk, body, bulk, duty, goal, item, kick, mark, mass, rail, rant, rave, view 5 being, demur, frown, spurn, storm, stuff, thing 6 boggle, doodad, entity, except, gadget, matter, target, volume 7 article, dissent, protest, purpose, stickle 8 complain, disfavor, function, material 9 challenge, criticize, deprecate, disesteem, objective, substance 10 disapprove, discommend, individual

objection 5 demur 7 protest 8 demurral, demurrer, question 9 challenge, exception 10 difficulty 12 remonstrance 13 remonstration

objectionable 4 vile 5 unfit 8 unwanted 9 abhorrent, invidious, loathsome, obnoxious, offensive, repellent, repugnant, repulsive, revolting, unwelcome 10 censurable, ill-favored, unpleasant, unsuitable 11 distasteful, undesirable 12 disagreeable

objective 3 aim, end, use 4 duty, fair, goal, mark 5 gross, outer 6 object, target 7 outside, outward, purpose 8 ambition, external, function, material, physical, sensible, tangible, unbiased 9 corporeal, equitable, impartial, quaesitum, uncolored 10 impersonal, phenomenal 11 substantial 12 unprejudiced 13 dispassionate

objet d'art 5 curio, vertu (plural), virtu (plural) 6 bauble, gewgaw, trifle 7 bibelot, novelty, trinket, whatnot 8 gimcrack 10 knickknack

objurgate 4 damn 5 curse, decry 7 censure, reprove 8 execrate 9 castigate 12 anathematize

oblate 4 monk 5 offer

oblation 6 corban, korban 8 offering 9 sacrifice 12 presentation

obligated 5 bound 8 beholden, indebted

obligation 3 vow 4 call, debt, duty, must, need, oath, part 5 cause, ought, place 6 burden, charge, devoir, pledge 7 promise 8 business, contract, occasion 9 arrearage, committal, liability, necessity, restraint 10 commitment, compulsion, constraint 11 requirement 12 indebtedness

obligatory 7 binding 8 required 9 imperious, mandatory 10 compulsory, imperative

oblige 3 aid 4 help, make 5 avail, favor, force 6 assist, coerce, compel, please, profit 7 benefit, concuss, gratify, shotgun 9 constrain 10 contribute 11 accommodate

obliged 5 bound 8 beholden, grateful, indebted, thankful

obliging 4 easy, kind, mild 5 civil 7 amiable, lenient 11 complaisant, good-humored, good-natured 12 good-tempered

oblique 6 sloped, tilted, tipped 7 leaning, pitched, sloping, tilting 8 circular, inclined, indirect, pitching 9 inclining

obliterate 4 raze, x out 5 erase 6 cancel, delete, efface 7 blot out, expunge, wipe out 8 black out, cross out 10 annihilate

oblivion 5 lethe, limbo 6 pardon 7 amnesty, nirvana 13 forgetfulness, obliviousness

oblivious 7 unaware 8 absorbed, ignorant 9 forgetful, unknowing, unmindful, unwitting 10 unfamiliar, uninformed 11 incognizant, unconscious

oblong 4 oval 7 ellipse 9 elongated, rectangle 11 rectangular

obloquy 4 slam, slur 5 abuse, odium, shame 6 infamy 7 calumny, censure 8 disgrace, dishonor, ignominy 9 aspersion, contumely, discredit, disesteem, disrepute, invective, stricture 10 opprobrium, reflection, scurrility 12 billingsgate, vituperation

obnoxious 4 open, vile 5 prone 6 liable, odious 7 exposed, hateful, subject 9 abhorrent, invidious, offensive, repellent, repugnant, revulsive, sickening 10 disgusting

oboe 4 reed 7 hautboy 8 hautbois, woodwind *oriental:* 6 surnai, surnay

obscene 4 foul, lewd, rank, vile 5 bawdy, crude, dirty, gross, lurid, nasty 6 coarse, crusty, earthy, filthy, impure, ribald, risqué, smutty, sultry, vulgar 7 hideous, noisome, profane, raunchy 8 barnyard, horrible, indecent, scabrous 9 offensive, repellent, repugnant, salacious, sickening 10 disgusting, fescennine, lascivious, nauseating, scurrilous 11 foulmouthed, unprintable 12 pornographic, scatological

obscure 3 dim, far, fog, odd 4 blur, dark, dusk, fuzz, haze, hide, mask, mist, murk, veil 5 bedim, befog, belie, blear, blind, cloak, close, cloud, cover, dusky, faint, gloom, lowly, minor, murky, shade, shady, vague 6 bemask, bleary, cloudy, darken, dim out, far-off, gloomy, hidden, humble, mystic, opaque, remote, screen, secret, shadow, shroud 7 becloud, clouded, conceal, cryptic, devious, dislimn, distant, eclipse, falsify, removed, retired, shadowy, unclear, unfamed, unknown, unnoted 8 abstruse, Delphian, disguise, esoteric, lonesome, mystical, nameless, nubilous, overcast, puzzling, secluded, solitary 9 adumbrate, ambiguous, difficult, enigmatic, equivocal, illegible, lightless, obfuscate, overcloud, sibylline, tenebrous, uncertain, undefined, unheard-of 10 caliginous, camouflage, fuliginous, ill-defined, indecisive, indefinite, indistinct, mysterious, overshadow, umbrageous, unemphatic, unexplicit, unrenowned 11 double-edged, double-faced, inscrutable, out-of-the-way, sequestered, unimportant 12 inaccessible, inconclusive, inexplicable, misrepresent, uncelebrated, unfathomable, unnoticeable 13 inconspicuous, unilluminated

obsequies 5 rites 7 funeral

obsequious 6 menial 7 dutiful, fawning, servile, slavish 8 obedient, obeisant, toadying 9 parasitic 10 submissive 11 deferential, subservient, sycophantic

observance 4 heed, mark, note, rite 6 notice, regard, remark, ritual 7 liturgy, service 8 ceremony 9 attention, formality 10 ceremonial, cognizance 11 observation

observant 5 alert, awake, aware 6 arrect 7 heedful, mindful 8 watchful 9 advertent, attentive, regardful 10 thoughtful

observation 4 heed, mark, note 6 notice, regard, remark 7 comment 9 attention 10 cognizance, commentary 12 obiter dictum

observatory 5 tower 7 lookout, outlook 8 overlook *famous:* 4 Lick 6 Wilson, Yerkes 7 Palomar *instrument:* 9 telescope

observe 3 see 4 espy, keep, look, mark, mind, note, obey, twig, view 5 sight, study, watch 6 behold, comply, follow, notice, remark, revere 7 comment, conform, discern 8 perceive, venerate 9 celebrate, reverence, solemnize 10 animadvert, commentate 11 commemorate

obsessed 4 held 5 beset, queer 6 dogged, hipped 7 gripped, haunted, plagued 8 harassed, overcome, troubled 9 bedeviled, bewitched, dominated, hagridden, possessed 12 prepossessed

obsession 5 craze, mania, thing 6 fetish, hang-up 8 fixation 13 preoccupation

obsolete 3 old 4 dead 5 passé 6 démodé, old hat 7 worn-out 8 old-timey, outmoded, time-worn 10 superseded 12 old-fashioned

obstacle 3 bar, dam, rub 4 bump, clog, snag, wall 5 block, catch, crimp, hitch 6 hamper, hurdle 7 barrier 8 handicap, hardship, mountain, traverse 9 hindrance 10 difficulty, impediment 11 Chinese wall, encumbrance, obstruction, vicissitude

obstinate 4 deaf 5 balky, muley, stiff, tough 6 dogged, mulish, unruly 7 crabbed, staunch, willful 8 contrary, obdurate, perverse, renitent, resolute, stubborn, unpliant 9 pigheaded, resistant, steadfast, unbudging, unpliable 10 bullheaded, hardheaded, headstrong, inexorable, inflexible, muleheaded, refractory, self-willed, unyielding 11 incompliant, intractable, opinionated, stiff-necked, wrongheaded 12 closedminded, intransigent, pertinacious, pervicacious, recalcitrant

obstreperous 4 loud 5 noisy 6 unruly 7 blatant 8 strident 9 clamorous 10 boisterous, multivocal, vociferant, vociferous 11 disobedient, loudmouthed, openmouthed

obstruct 3 bar, dam, gag 4 clog, fill, plug, stop 5 block, brake, choke, close 6 hinder, impede, screen, shroud 7 congest, occlude, shut off, shut out, stopper, trammel 8 block out 10 bottleneck, overslaugh

obstruction 3 bar, dam, rub 4 snag 5 hitch 6 hamper, hurdle 8 mountain, obstacle 9 hindrance 10 impediment

obtain 3 buy, eke, get, win 4 earn, gain, have, reap 5 annex, reach 6 pick up, secure 7 acquire, chalk up, procure 8 purchase

obtrude 5 cut in 6 butt in, horn in, impose 7 presume 8 chisel in, infringe

obtrusive 4 busy 5 pushy 7 forward 9 bumptious, officious 10 meddlesome 11 impertinent

obtuse 4 dull, mild 5 blunt, dense, thick 6 stupid

obverse 4 face, side 5 front 10 complement

obviate 4 ward 5 avert, deter 7 forfend, prevent, rule out 8 preclude, stave off 9 forestall, interfere, interpose, intervene

obvious 5 clear, overt, plain 6 patent 7 blatant, evident, glaring 8 apparent, distinct, manifest, palpable 10 plain as day 11 conspicuous, unambiguous, unequivocal

oca 5 tuber 6 sorrel

____**O'Casey, dramatist** 4 Sean

occasion 3 use 4 call, need, shot, show, time 5 basis, break, breed, cause, event, hatch, right, thing, while 6 chance, demand, excuse, ground, induce, look-in, moment, reason, squeak, work up 7 episode, instant, opening, produce, provoke, warrant 8 engender, generate, incident, milepost, muster up 9 happening, milestone, necessity 10 antecedent, foundation, obligation, occurrence 11 determinant, opportunity 12 circumstance 13 justification

occasional 3 few, odd 4 rare 6 casual, random, scarce, seldom 8 sporadic, uncommon 10 incidental, infrequent, unfrequent

Occidental 7 Western 9 Westerner

occlude 4 clog, fill, plug, stop 5 block, choke, close 7 congest, stopper 8 obstruct

occult 4 bury, deep, hide 5 cache, eerie, heavy, magic, stash, weird 6 arcane, orphic, screen, secret, voodoo 7 conceal, secrete 8 abstruse, ensconce, esoteric, hermetic, mystical, profound 9 recondite, unearthly 10 acroamatic, cabalistic, mysterious 12 supernatural *ability:* 3 ESP *combining form:* 5 crypt, krypt 6 crypto, krypto

occupant 5 liver 6 inmate, tenant 7 denizen, dweller, resider 8 habitant, resident 9 indweller 10 inhabitant *suffix:* 3 ite

occupation 3 job 4 line, work 5 trade

6 career, métier 7 calling, pursuit 8 business 9 occupancy, residence 10 employment, habitation, settlement

occupy 3 use 4 busy, fill, hold 5 seize 6 engage, people, tenant 7 engross, immerse, inhabit 8 populate

occur 3 hap 4 pass 6 befall, betide, chance, happen, strike 7 come off, develop, fall out 9 transpire

occurrence 2 go 3 hap 4 pass 5 event, state, thing 7 episode 8 exigency, incident, juncture, occasion 9 adventure, condition, emergency, happening, situation *extraordinary:* 7 miracle *unexpected:* 8 surprise 9 bombshell

ocean 3 sea 4 blue, deep, main 5 brine, drink 6 Arctic, Indian 7 Pacific 8 Atlantic 9 Antarctic *movement:* 4 tide, wave

Oceania *country:* 4 Fiji 8 Kiribati 9 Australia 10 New Zealand 12 Western Samoa *ethnic group:* 6 Fijian, Indian, Papuan, Samoan 7 British 10 Melanesian, Polynesian 11 Micronesian *language:* 5 Hindi, Maori 6 Fijian, Papuan, Pidgin, Samoan 7 English 10 Melanesian

oceanic 6 marine 7 pelagic 8 maritime 9 thalassic

Ocean State 11 Rhode Island

Oceanus *daughter:* 5 Doris 7 Oceanid 8 Eurynome *father:* 6 Uranus *mother:* 2 Ge 4 Gaea *sister:* 6 Tethys *son:* 6 Peneus 7 Alpheus *wife:* 6 Tethys

ocellus 3 eye 7 eyespot

ocelot 3 cat 7 wildcat

octave 4 cask, note 5 eight, scale 6 eighth

Octavia *brother:* 8 Augustus *grandson:* 8 Caligula *husband:* 4 Nero 6 Antony

octopus 7 mollusk 9 devilfish 10 cephalopod *arm:* 8 tentacle *genus:* 7 Polypus *kin:* 5 squid 10 cuttlefish

ocular 3 eye, orb 4 lamp 5 optic 6 oculus, peeper, visual, winker 7 optical, seeable, visible 8 viewable, visional

"Odalisque" painter 6 Ingres (Jean-Auguste-Dominique) 7 Matisse (Henri)

odd 4 lone, only, rare 5 extra, fluky, queer, rummy, weird 6 casual, chance, single, uneven 7 curious, erratic, oddball, strange, unusual 8 peculiar, singular, unpaired 9 eccentric, unmatched 13 idiosyncratic *combining form:* 5 azygo

oddball 4 case, quiz 5 queer, weird 6 oddity, weirdo, zombie 7 bizarre, curious, strange 8 original, peculiar 9 character, eccentric 10 outlandish 13 idiosyncratic

oddity 4 case, quiz 5 quirk 8 original 9 character, curiosity, eccentric 12 idiosyncrasy

odd job 5 chore

odds and ends 4 olio 5 melee 6 jumble, medley, motley, scraps 7 mélange, mixture 8 oddments, sundries 9 etceteras, leftovers, potpourri 10 assortment, hodgepodge, miscellany

ode 4 hymn, poem 5 lyric, psalm, verse *part:* 5 epode 7 strophe 11 antistrophe

Oded's son 7 Azariah

Odets play 9 Golden Boy 10 Night Music 12 Awake and Sing, Paradise Lost 14 The Country Girl 15 Waiting for Lefty

odeum 4 hall 7 theater

Odin *brother:* 2 Ve 4 Vili *daughter-in-law:* 5 Nanna *father:* 3 Bor *hall:* 8 Valhalla *horse:* 8 Sleipnir *maiden:* 8 Valkyrie *mansion:* 9 Gladsheim *mother:* 6 Bestla *raven:* 5 Hugin, Munin *ring:* 8 Draupnir *ship:* 7 Naglfar 11 Skidbladnir *son:* 3 Tyr 4 Thor, Vali 6 Balder *spear:* 7 Gungnir *sword:* 4 Gram *throne:* 10 Hlidskjalf 11 Hlithskjalf *wife:* 4 Fria, Rind 5 Frigg 6 Frigga *wolf:* 4 Geri 5 Freki

odious 4 foul, vile 6 horrid 7 hateful 8 hateable 9 abhorrent, invidious 10 abominable, despicable, detestable

odium 4 blot, blur, hate, onus, slur, spot 5 brand, shame, stain 6 hatred, infamy, stigma 7 obloquy 8 black eye, disgrace, dishonor, ignominy 9 discredit, disesteem, disrepute 10 opprobrium 11 bar sinister

odontalgia 9 toothache

odor 4 funk 5 aroma, scent, smell *combining form:* 3 osm 4 osma, osmo *offensive:* 5 stink 6 stench

odorous 5 heady, sweet 6 smelly, strong 7 pungent, reeking, scented 8 aromatic, fragrant, redolent, smelling

Odysseus 7 Ulysses *dog:* 5 Argos *enchantress:* 5 Circe *father:* 7 Laertes *friend:* 6 Mentor *harasser:* 8 Poseidon *herb:* 4 moly *kingdom:* 6 Ithaca *mother:* 8 Anticlea *son:* 9 Telegonus 10 Telemachus *swineherd:* 7 Eumaeus *voyage:* 7 odyssey *wife:* 8 Penelope

Odyssey author 5 Homer

Oedipus *brother-in-law:* 5 Creon *daughter:* 6 Ismene 8 Antigone *father:* 5 Laius *foster father:* 7 Polybus *foster mother:* 8 Periboea *kingdom:* 6 Thebes *mother:* 7 Jocasta *son:* 8 Eteocles 9 Polynices 10 Polyneices *victim:* 5 Laius *wife:* 7 Jocasta

Oeneus *kingdom:* 7 Calydon *son:* 8 Meleager *wife:* 7 Althaea

oenochoe 3 jug 7 pitcher *relative:* 4 olpe

Oenomaus *charioteer:* 8 Myrtilus *daughter:* 10 Hippodamia *kingdom:* 4 Pisa *slayer:* 6 Pelops

Oenone *husband:* 5 Paris *rival:* 5 Helen

oeuvre 4 work 6 corpus, output

of *French:* 2 de *German:* 3 aus, von

offal 4 junk 5 trash, waste 6 debris, litter, refuse, spilth 7 carrion, garbage, rubbish 9 sweepings *fish:* 5 gurry

off-balance 6 uneven 7 unequal 8 lopsided 9 irregular 10 asymmetric 13 unsymmetrical

off-center 9 eccentric

off-color 3 low 4 blue, mean, racy 5 broad, salty, shady, spicy 6 ailing, poorly, purple, risqué, sickly, unwell, wicked 7 underly 10 indisposed, suggestive

offend 3 sin, vex 4 gall, hurt, miff 5 break, pique, shock, sting, upset, wound 6 appall, breach, excite, insult, nettle 7 affront, disturb, horrify, infract, mortify, outrage, provoke, violate 8 aggrieve, distress, infringe, irritate, trespass 9 disoblige, displease

offender 5 felon 6 sinner 8 criminal, violator 10 lawbreaker, malefactor

offense 3 fit, pet, sin 4 huff, miff, tort 5 anger, crime, onset, pique, scene, tizzy 6 attack, catfit, delict, felony, insult, onfall 7 affront, assault, dudgeon, flare-up, misdeed, tantrum, umbrage 8 delictum, outburst 9 explosion, indignity, offensive, onslaught 10 aggression, assailment, conniption, resentment 11 displeasure, indignation, misdemeanor

offensive 3 bad 4 evil, foul, grim, icky, rank, vile 5 awful, lurid, nasty, onset 6 attack, grisly, horrid, odious, onfall 7 assault, beastly, fulsome, ghastly, hideous, noisome, obscene 8 dreadful, gruesome, horrible, shocking, terrible, unsavory 9 abhorrent, appalling, atrocious, frightful, loathsome, onslaught, repellent, repugnant, repulsive, revolting, sickening 10 abominable, aggression, assailment, detestable, disgusting, nauseating, ungrateful, unpleasant 11 uncongenial, unpalatable, unwholesome 12 disagreeable, unappetizing 13 objectionable

offer 3 bid, lay, try 4 cite, give, pose, seek, show 5 assay, essay 6 adduce, allege, extend, strive, tender 7 advance, attempt, display, exhibit, hold out, present, proffer, propose 8 endeavor, proposal, struggle

offering 4 alms, gift 6 corban, korban, victim 7 charity, present 8 donation, oblation 9 sacrifice 11 benefaction, beneficence 12 contribution

offhand 6 casual 8 informal 9 extempore, impromptu, unstudied 10 improvised 11 extemporary, unrehearsed

office 3 job 4 duty, post, role, spot 5 berth, place 6 billet 7 station 8 business, function, position, province 9 situation 10 connection 11 appointment *head:*

4 boss 7 manager *machine:* 6 copier 9 stenotype 10 calculator, typewriter *seeker:* 9 candidate 10 politician *suffix:* 2 cy 3 ate, dom, ure 4 ship *worker:* 5 clerk, steno 6 typist 9 secretary 10 bookkeeper 12 stenographer

officer 3 cop 4 exec 6 noncom, police 7 John Law, manager 8 official 9 executive *abbreviation:* 2 Lt. 3 Adm., Col., Ens., Gen., Maj. 4 Capt., Cmdr. 5 Comdr., Lieut. *army:* 5 major 7 captain, colonel, general 10 lieutenant *British:* 9 brigadier *court:* 7 bailiff *king's:* 11 chamberlain *law-enforcement:* 3 cop 6 deputy, police 7 marshal, sheriff 9 constable, patrolman, policeman *naval:* 4 mate 6 ensign 7 admiral, captain 9 commander, commodore 10 lieutenant *noncommissioned:* 5 sarge 8 corporal, sergeant *petty:* 5 bosun, chief 6 yeoman 7 teleman 9 boatswain *prison:* 5 guard 6 warden

official 4 exec 7 cleared, manager, officer 8 approved, endorsed 9 canonical, cathedral, certified, executive, ex officio 10 authorized, ex cathedra, sanctioned 13 administrator, authoritative *city or town:* 5 mayor 8 alderman 9 selectman 10 councilman *diplomatic:* 5 envoy 6 consul 7 attaché 10 ambassador *governmental:* 6 syndic *parish:* 6 beadle *sports:* 3 ref, ump 6 umpire 7 referee 8 linesman *university:* 4 dean 6 bursar 7 provost 9 registrar 10 chancellor

officious 4 busy 9 intrusive, obtrusive 10 meddlesome 11 impertinent 13 polypragmatic

offing 6 future 7 by-and-by 9 aftertime, afterward, hereafter 10 background

offscouring 5 filth, leper 6 pariah, refuse 7 Ishmael, outcast 8 castaway, derelict 10 Ishmaelite 11 untouchable

offset 4 stop 5 check 6 contra, make up, redeem, set off 7 balance 8 atone for, outweigh 10 compensate 11 countervail

offshoot 5 scion 6 branch 7 spin-off 9 by-product, outgrowth 10 derivative, descendant

offspring 3 kid, son 4 seed 5 brood, hatch, issue, scion, spawn, swarm, young 7 produce, product, progeny 8 children 9 posterity 10 descendant 11 progeniture *combining form:* 3 gen, ped 4 geno, paed, paid, pedo 5 paedo, paido, proli

Of Human Bondage *author:* 7 Maugham (W. Somerset)

Of Mice and Men *author:* 9 Steinbeck (John) *character:* 6 George, Lennie

ogee 3 ess 4 arch 5 curve 7 molding

Ogier the ___ 4 Dane

ogive 4 arch

ogle 3 eye 4 gape, gaze, leer, look 5 stare
6 goggle 10 rubberneck

ogre 5 beast, bogey, demon, giant
6 booger 7 bugbear, monster 8 bogeyman
9 boogeyman *Algonquian:* 7 windigo

ogress 5 harpy, scold, shrew, vixen
6 amazon, virago 8 fishwife 9 termagant,
Xanthippe

Ohio *capital:* 8 Columbus *college, university:* 5 Akron, Hiram, Miami 6 Dayton
7 Antioch, Denison, Oberlin 8 Defiance,
Ursuline 9 Kent State *largest city:* 9 Cleveland *nickname:* 12 Buckeye State *state
bird:* 8 cardinal

Oholibamah *father:* 4 Anah *husband:*
4 Esau

oil 3 fat, gas 4 balm, fuel, lube, oleo
5 oleum 6 anoint, grease 7 blarney,
incense, lanolin 8 flattery, soft soap 9 adulation, lubricant, lubricate, petroleum *combining form:* 3 ole 4 eleo, olei, oleo
5 elaeo, elaio *consecrated:* 6 chrism *fragrant:* 5 attar 6 neroli *fuel:* 3 gas 8 gasoline, kerosene, kerosine *relating to:* 5 oleic
ship: 6 tanker *source:* 5 olive, shale *well:*
6 gusher

Oil! author 8 Sinclair (Upton)

oilbird 8 guacharo

oily 5 fatty, slick, soapy, suave 6 greasy,
smarmy, smooth 7 fulsome 8 unctious,
unctuous 10 oleaginous

ointment 4 balm, nard 5 cream, salve
6 cerate, chrism, lotion 7 unction, unguent
8 calamine, dressing, liniment 9 demulcent,
emollient 11 embrocation

OK, okay 3 aye, yea, yes 5 favor
6 agreed 7 approve, certify, endorse
8 accredit, all right, approval, blessing,
sanction

Okinawa capital 4 Naha

Oklahoma *city:* 3 Ada 4 Enid 5 Tulsa
nickname: 11 Sooner State *state flower:*
9 mistletoe *university:* 11 Oral Roberts

okra 4 soup 5 bendy, gumbo 8 hibiscus

old 4 aged, late, once, past 5 dated, hoary,
passé, solid, stale 6 bygone, démodé, former, steady, versed, whilom 7 ancient,
antique, archaic, elderly, lasting, onetime,
overage, quondam, skilled, staying, veteran
8 enduring, lifelong, Noachian, outmoded,
seasoned, sometime, timeworn 9 erstwhile,
long-lived, perennial, perpetual, practical,
practiced, primitive, venerable 10 antiquated, continuing, inveterate *Scottish:*
4 auld

old age 10 feebleness, senescence
11 decrepitude, elderliness, senectitude
combining form: 6 geront, presby 7 ge-

ronto, presbyo *relating to:* 6 senile 8 ge-
rontal, gerontic 9 geriatric

Old Bailey 5 court

Old Colony State 13 Massachusetts

Old Curiosity Shop author 7 Dickens
(Charles)

Old Dominion State 8 Virginia

Old English letter see Anglo-Saxon,
letter

Old Faithful 6 geyser

old-fashioned 4 aged 5 dated, dowdy,
drink, fusty, moldy, mossy, passé
6 bygone, crusty, démodé, old hat, quaint,
rococo, stodgy 7 ancient, antique, archaic,
belated, demoded, disused, fogyish, outworn, vintage 8 cocktail, obsolete, outdated, outmoded, unmodern 9 discarded,
moss-grown, moth-eaten, out-of-date,
Victorian 10 antiquated, fuddy-duddy,
moss-backed

old hand 3 vet 7 veteran 9 longtimer

old hat 5 dated, stale, tired, trite 6 cliché,
démodé 7 antique, archaic, clichéd, old-
time, vintage 8 shopworn, timeworn, well-
worn 9 hackneyed, out-of-date 10 antiquated, oldfangled, threadbare

Old Ironsides 12 Constitution *poet:*
6 Holmes (Oliver Wendell)

old liner 4 tory 5 right 7 diehard 8 rightist, standpat 11 bitter-ender, right-winger,
standpatter 12 conservative

Old Line State 8 Maryland

old maid 7 fusspot 8 spinster

Old North State 13 North Carolina

Old Rough and Ready 6 Taylor (Zachary)

Olds' car 3 Reo

Old Scratch 5 devil, fiend, Satan 7 Lucifer, Old Nick, serpent 8 Apollyon 9 Beelzebub

old-time 5 dated 6 bygone, old hat,
versed 7 antique, archaic, skilled, veteran,
vintage 8 seasoned 9 practical, practiced
10 antiquated 11 experienced

old-timer 3 vet 5 elder 6 senior
7 ancient, old hand, oldster, veteran
10 golden-ager

old womanish 5 anile

Old World 6 Europe

oleaginous see oily

oleaster 5 olive 9 olive tree

olecranon 9 funny bone

oleo 9 margarine

oleoresin 10 turpentine

oleum 3 oil

olfaction 5 sense, smell 7 osmesis
8 smelling

olid 4 rank 5 fetid, funky 6 putrid, rancid,
smelly 7 stenchy 8 mephitic, stinking
10 malodorous

olio 4 brew, hash, stew 6 medley 7 mélange, mixture 8 mishmash 9 potpourri 10 assortment, hodgepodge, miscellany 11 olla podrida

olive *genus:* 4 Olea *stuffing:* 7 pimento 8 pimiento

Oliver Twist *author:* 7 Dickens (Charles) *character:* 5 Bates, Fagin, Nancy, Sikes 6 Bumble 7 Dawkins 12 Artful Dodger

olla podrida see olio

Ollie's pal 4 Stan

Olympian 3 god 5 lofty 7 athlete, exalted 8 majestic 10 competitor

Olympics 5 games 6 sports 9 athletics *place of origin:* 6 Athens *symbol:* 5 flame, torch

Oman *capital:* 6 Masqat, Muscat *monetary unit:* 4 rial

Omar 4 poet 7 Khayyém *country:* 6 Persia *father:* 7 Eliphaz *poem:* 8 Rubáiyát

omega 3 end 6 ending, letter *kin:* 3 zee

omelet 4 eggs *kind:* 7 foo yong, Spanish, western

omen 4 bode, sign 5 augur, token 6 augury, boding 7 auspice, betoken, portend, portent, presage, promise, warning 8 bodement, forebode, foreshow 9 foretoken 10 foreshadow, prognostic

ominous 4 dire, dour, evil, grim 6 dismal, malign 7 baleful, baneful, direful, doomful, fateful, hostile, malefic, unlucky 8 lowering, menacing, sinister 9 ill-boding, ill-omened 10 forbidding, maleficent, portentous, unfriendly 11 apocalyptic, threatening 12 inauspicious, inhospitable, unpropitious

omission 3 cut, gap 4 skip, slip 5 blank, break, chasm, error, lapse 6 hiatus, lacuna 8 eclipsis, ellipsis, overlook 9 exclusion *mark:* 5 caret 8 ellipsis 10 apostrophe

omit 3 cut 4 dele, drop, fail, skip 5 elide 6 cancel, delete, except, forget, ignore, slight 7 blink at, neglect 8 discount, leave out, overlook, overpass

Omni and Cobo 6 arenas

omnibus 3 ana 4 posy 5 album 7 garland, vehicle 8 analects 9 anthology 10 miscellany 11 florilegium *horse-drawn:* 10 shillibeer

omnipotent 3 god 5 deity 6 divine 7 godlike 8 almighty 9 unlimited 11 all-powerful

omnipresent 7 allover, endless 8 infinite, unending 9 boundless, limitless, universal 10 ubiquitous 12 immeasurable

omniscient 4 wise 7 learned 10 all-knowing

omnium-gatherum see olio

Omphale *domain:* 5 Lydia *slave:* 8 Heracles, Hercules

omphalos 5 navel 9 umbilicus 10 focal point

Omri's father 4 Imri 6 Becher 7 Michael

on 4 atop, over, upon, with 5 about, above, along, forth 7 forward

onager 5 kiang 8 catapult

Onan's father 5 Judah

once 3 odd 4 ever, late, past 5 at all 6 anyway, before, bygone, former, whilom 7 already, anywise, earlier, onetime, quondam 8 formerly, sometime *Scottish:* 4 anes 5 yince

once-over 6 glance, survey 10 inspection 11 examination

one 3 wed 4 join, link, lone, only, sole, unit 5 monad, unite 6 number, relate, single, unique, united 7 connect, numeral 8 coagment, coalesce, separate, singular, solitary 9 associate, coadunate, undivided 10 individual, particular *combining form:* 3 mon 4 heno, mono *French:* 2 un 3 une *German:* 3 ein 4 eine *prefix:* 3 uni *Scottish:* 2 ae 3 ane, yae *Spanish:* 2 un 3 uno

one and a half *combining form:* 6 sesqui

one-eyed giant 7 Cyclops 10 Polyphemus

one-handed god 3 Tiu, Tyr

one-horse town 4 burg 6 Podunk 7 mudhole 11 whistle-stop

one hundred 6 centum *years:* 7 century

O'Neill, Eugene *heroine:* 4 Anna, Nina *play:* 3 Ile 4 Gold 11 The Hairy Ape 12 Ah Wilderness, Anna Christie, Emperor Jones 13 Marco Millions 15 The Iceman Cometh 16 Strange Interlude, The Great God Brown

oneiric 6 dreamy 8 anagogic

oneness 5 unity 7 allness, unicity 8 entirety, identity, sameness, totality, uniquity 9 wholeness 10 entireness, singleness, uniqueness 11 singularity 12 completeness, selfsameness, singularness 13 identicalness, individuality

onerous 4 hard 5 heavy, hefty, tough 6 taxing, trying, unruly 7 arduous, driving, exigent, weighty 8 exacting, grievous, toilsome, unwieldy 9 demanding, difficult, laborious, ponderous 10 burdensome, cumbersome, oppressive 11 heavy-headed

oneself *combining form:* 3 aut 4 auto

one-sided 6 biased, unfair, unjust, warped 7 bigoted, colored, partial 8 lopsided, partisan, weighted 9 jaundiced 10 prejudiced

onetime 4 late, once, past 6 bygone, former, whilom 7 quondam 8 formerly 9 erstwhile

on hand 4 here 7 present

Onias' son 5 Simon

onion 4 bulb 5 cibol 7 shallot 8 eschalot *bulb:* 3 set *genus:* 6 Allium *kin:* 4 leek 6 garlic *kind:* 3 red 5 green 7 Bermuda,

Danvers, Spanish *roll:* 5 bialy *young:*
8 scallion

only 3 but, one, yet 4 just, lone, mere,
save, sole, solo 5 alone 6 except, merely,
simply, single, solely, unique 7 however
8 entirely, peerless, separate, singular, solitary 9 matchless, unequaled, unmatched

onomasticon 7 lexicon 8 wordbook

onomatopoeic 5 mimic 6 echoic
7 mimetic, mimical 9 emulative, imitative
10 simulative

onomatopoetic see onomatopoeic

onrush see onslaught

onset 4 dawn 5 birth, start 6 attack, onfall,
origin, outset, setout 7 assault, dawning,
offense, opening 8 outstart 9 beginning,
offensive, onslaught 10 aggression, assailment 12 commencement

onslaught 5 onset 6 attack, onfall, onrush
7 assault, offense 9 offensive 10 aggression, assailment

Ontario *capital:* 7 Toronto *university:*
4 York 5 Brock, Trent 8 McMaster

on the other hand 3 but 7 however

on the whole 7 en masse 8 all in all
9 generally 10 altogether, by and large

onto 4 atop

onus 3 tax 4 blot, blur, duty, load, slur,
spot, task 5 blame, brand, fault, guilt,
odium, stain 6 burden, charge, stigma,
weight 8 black eye 9 millstone 10 deadweight

onward 4 alee, away 5 ahead, along, forth
7 forward

onyx 3 jet 4 inky 5 black, ebony, jetty,
raven, sable 9 pitch-dark 10 chalcedony,
pitchblack 11 atramentous

oodles 4 gobs, heap, slew, tons 5 loads,
scads 7 jillion 10 quantities

ooid 4 oval 5 ovate, ovoid 7 oviform

oolong 3 tea

oomph 3 vim 4 brio, dash, élan, gimp, life,
push 5 drive, verve, vigor 6 esprit, pizazz,
spirit 7 pizzazz 8 strength, vitality 9 animation

ooze 3 mud 4 leak, seep, weep 5 bleed,
exude, marsh, slime, sweat 6 strain
7 secrete 8 transude

opah 4 fish 5 cravo

opal 3 gem 5 glass, jewel, stone 7 girasol,
hyalite 8 girasole 9 cacholong

opaque 4 dark, dull 5 dense, vague
6 cloudy, stupid 7 obscure, unclear 8 nubilous

OPEC nation 4 Iran, Iraq 5 Gabon,
Libya, Qatar 6 Kuwait 7 Algeria, Ecuador,
Nigeria 9 Indonesia, Venezuela 11 Saudi
Arabia

open 3 cut, tap 4 ajar, bare, free, gash,
hole, meet, undo, wide 5 agape, begin,
break, clear, cover, frank, naked, overt,
plain, prone, slash, start, swell, untie 6 billow, breach, broach, candid, dilate, expand,
expose, extend, fan out, gaping, get off,
launch, liable, mantle, patent, peeled,
pierce, public, reveal, spread, unbolt,
unfold, unlock, unseal, unshut, unstop,
unveil, unwrap, usable 7 convene,
denuded, jump off, kick off, outdoor, outside, release, ringent, rupture, subject,
unblock, unclose, uncover, unlatch, without,
yawning 8 commence, disclose, doubtful,
embark on, initiate, outdoors, patulous,
stripped, unbarred, unbolted, unclench,
unclosed, unclothe, unlocked, unsealed
9 agreeable, ambiguous, available, dehis-
cent, dubitable, equivocal, obnoxious, operative, outspread, perforate, reachable,
securable, sensitive, uncertain, uncovered,
undecided, unimpeded, unsettled
10 accessible, attainable, embark upon,
employable, inaugurate, indecisive, obtainable, out-of-doors, outstretch, overspread,
unfastened 11 practicable, problematic,
susceptible, unconcealed, undisguised,
unvarnished 12 undissembled, unobstructed, unrestricted *poetic:* 3 ope
slightly: 4 ajar

open-air 7 outdoor, outside 8 alfresco
9 out-of-door 10 hypaethral

open-and-shut 5 clear, plain 6 patent
7 evident, obvious 8 apparent, distinct,
manifest

openhanded 4 free 5 clear, plain 6 patent 7 evident, liberal, obvious 8 apparent,
distinct, generous 9 bounteous, bountiful,
unsparing 10 bighearted, munificent

openhearted 4 kind, warm 5 frank, plain
6 candid

opening 2 os 3 gap, ora (plural) 4 dawn,
door, gate, hole, pass, pore, rift, rima, shot,
show, slit, slot, time, vent 5 birth, break,
chasm, chink, cleft, crack, debut, mouth,
onset, start, stoma 6 breach, chance, eyelet, lacuna, look-in, outlet, outset, setout,
squeak 7 crevice, dawning, fissure, orifice,
pinhole, ventage 8 aperture, crevasse,
débouché, occasion, outstart, overture
9 beginning 11 opportunity *bodily:* 4 pore
5 hilum, hilus 7 foramen, orifice, ostiole
8 fenestra *combining form:* 4 pora, pore,
pyle 5 stoma, stome, stomi, stomy, trema
6 stomia, stomum 7 stomata (plural), stomate, tremata (plural) *ship's:* 5 hatch
8 hatchway, porthole

openmouthed 5 agape 6 amazed, gaping 7 blatant 8 strident 9 clamorous
10 boisterous, multivocal, vociferant, vociferous

open sesame 3 key 6 ticket 8 passport,
password

opera 7 musical *comic:* 5 buffa 6 bouffe *glasses:* 9 lorgnette *kind:* 4 soap 5 comic, grand, horse, space *part:* 3 act 4 aria 5 scena *solo:* 4 aria *star:* 4 diva 10 prima donna *text:* 8 libretto (see also individual titles and composers)

operate 2 go 3 act, cut, ply, run, use 4 keep, play, take, work 5 drive, pilot, react, steer, wield 6 behave, direct, handle, manage, open up, ordain 7 carry on, conduct, control, perform 8 function, maneuver 10 manipulate

operation 3 use 4 play 6 action 7 surgery 8 exercise, exertion, function 9 appliance, procedure 10 employment, exercising

operative 4 hand, live, open 5 agent, alive 6 active, usable, worker 7 dynamic, laborer, running, working, workman 8 mechanic, workhand 9 Pinkerton

operator 5 agent 6 doctor, driver 7 autoist, surgeon 8 motorist 9 conductor *suffix:* 3 ist 4 ster

operculum 3 lid 4 flap

operetta composer 5 Lehar (Franz), Suppe (Franz von) 6 Straus (Oscar) 7 Herbert (Victor), Romberg (Sigmund), Strauss (Johann) 8 Sullivan (Arthur) 9 Offenbach (Jacques)

operose 4 busy, hard 5 tough 6 severe 7 arduous 8 diligent, sedulous, toilsome 9 assiduous, difficult, effortful, laborious

Ophelia *beloved:* 6 Hamlet *brother:* 7 Laertes *father:* 8 Polonius

ophidian 5 snake 9 snakelike

Ophir's father 6 Joktan

opiate 4 dope, drug 6 deaden, sleepy 7 anodyne 8 hypnotic, narcotic, nepenthe, somnific 9 soporific 10 somnorific

opine 4 deem, hold, view 5 judge, think 6 accept, regard 7 believe, suppose

opinion 3 eye 4 idea, mind, view 5 tenet, think 6 belief, notion, theory 7 feeling, thought 8 attitude, estimate, judgment, reaction 9 sentiment 10 assumption, conclusion, conjecture, conviction, estimation, impression, persuasion 11 speculation, supposition *express an:* 4 vote 5 judge 9 criticize

opium 4 dope, drug 8 narcotic *derivative:* 6 heroin 7 codeine, meconin, narcein 8 laudanum, morphine, narceine 9 narcotine, paregoric *prepared:* 6 chandu *source:* 5 poppy

opossum 9 marsupial *kin:* 8 kangaroo

oppidan 8 townsman

opponent 3 con, foe 4 anti 5 enemy, match, rival 7 nemesis, opposer 9 adversary, assailant, combatant, oppugnant 10 antagonist, competitor 12 counteragent

opportune 3 fit 5 happy 6 timely 7 timeous 9 favorable, well-timed 10 auspicious, felicitous, propitious, prosperous 11 appropriate

opportunity 4 hope, pass, room, shot, show, time, turn 5 break, space, spell 6 chance, look-in, prayer, relief, squeak 7 opening 8 juncture, occasion

oppose 3 pit, vie 4 buck, duel, face 5 array, beard, fight, match, repel 6 combat, differ, object, refute, repugn, resist 7 contest, counter, dispute, play off 8 confront, contrast, traverse 9 withstand 10 contradict

opposite 2 to 4 foil 5 polar 6 contra, facing, unlike 7 antonym, counter, inverse, obverse, opposed, reverse, unlike 8 antipode, antipole, contrary, contrast, converse, separate 9 antipodal, diametric, different, divergent, unrelated, unsimilar 10 antipodean, antithesis, antonymous, dissimilar 11 contrasting, counterpole, independent, unconnected 12 antagonistic, antithetical, counterpoint 13 contradictory *combining form:* 7 enantio *French:* 8 en face de *prefix:* 2 ob 3 dis 5 retro 6 contra 7 counter

opposition 3 con 8 defiance 9 animosity, hostility 10 antagonism, antithesis, resistance 11 contrariety

oppress 5 harry, wrong 6 burden, harass, sadden, subdue 7 afflict, conquer, depress, outrage, torment, torture, trouble 8 aggrieve, distress, overcome 9 overthrow, persecute, subjugate

oppressive 4 hard 5 black, bleak, harsh, heavy, tough 6 dismal, gloomy, severe, somber, taxing 7 exigent, onerous, weighty 8 exacting, grievous 9 demanding 10 burdensome, depressing 11 dispiriting 12 discouraging 13 disheartening

oppressive force 4 onus, yoke 6 burden, weight 10 juggernaut

oppressor 6 despot, tyrant 8 dictator 9 strong man

opprobrious 7 abusive 8 ill-famed, infamous, scurrile 9 invective, notorious, truculent 10 scurrilous, vituperous 12 contumelious, vituperative, vituperatory

opprobrium 5 abuse, odium, scorn, shame 6 infamy 7 obloquy 8 disgrace, dishonor, ignominy 9 discredit, disesteem, disrepute 10 scurrility 12 vituperation

oppugn 3 tug, war 5 fight 6 battle 7 contend

Ops 4 Rhea *consort:* 6 Cronus, Saturn *daughter:* 5 Ceres 7 Demeter

opt 4 cull, mark, pick, take 5 elect 6 choose, decide, prefer, select 9 single out

optical 6 ocular, visual 8 visional *instrument:* 4 lens 5 glass, scope 7 transit

9 magnifier, optometer, periscope, telescope **10** microscope

optimist **5** hoper **7** dreamer **8** idealist, micawber **9** Pollyanna **10** positivist

optimistic **4** fond, rosy **5** merry, sunny **6** bright, hoping, upbeat **7** assured, hopeful **8** cheerful, sanguine **9** confident **12** Pollyannaish

option **5** right **6** choice **8** election **9** privilege, selection **10** preference **11** alternative, prerogative

optional **4** free **8** elective **9** voluntary **11** alternative, facultative **13** discretionary *item:* **5** add-on

opulence **6** plenty, riches, wealth **9** affluence

opulent **4** lush, rich **5** plush, showy, swank **6** Capuan, deluxe, lavish **7** elegant, moneyed, profuse, wealthy **8** affluent, luscious, palatial, prodigal **9** exuberant, luxuriant, luxurious, profusive, sumptuous

opuntia **6** cactus

or **4** else, gold **6** golden, yellow **9** otherwise

oracle **4** sage, seer **6** medium, vision **8** prophecy **10** apocalypse, revelation *site:* **6** Claros, Delphi, Didyma, Dodona **9** Epidaurus

oracular **5** vatic **6** mantic **7** fatidic **8** Delphian **9** prophetic, sibylline, vaticinal

oral **4** told **5** vocal **6** sonant, spoken, verbal, voiced **7** related, uttered **8** narrated, viva voce **9** recounted, unwritten

orange **5** color, fruit **6** citrus **8** jacinthe *brownish:* **6** Titian *deep:* **11** bittersweet *genus:* **6** Citrus *kin:* **9** tangerine **10** grapefruit *kind:* **4** sour **5** blood, chino, navel, Osage, sweet **7** Seville **8** bergamot, mandarin, Valencia *seed:* **3** pip *skin:* **4** rind

orangutan **3** ape **4** mias **5** pongo

orate **4** rant, rave **5** mouth, speak, spiel **7** bombast, declaim, elocute, soapbox **8** blah-blah, bloviate, harangue, perorate **9** sermonize, speechify **11** rodomontade

oration **6** sermon, speech **7** address **9** discourse *funeral:* **6** eulogy

orator **7** demagog, speaker **9** demagogue *American:* **4** Clay (Henry) **5** Bryan (William Jennings), Henry (Patrick) **7** Calhoun (John C.), Douglas (Stephen), Webster (Daniel) *British:* **5** Burke (Edmund) **8** Disraeli (Benjamin) **9** Churchill (Winston), Gladstone (William) *French:* **8** Mirabeau (Comte de) *Greek:* **5** Corax **8** Pericles **11** Demosthenes *Roman:* **6** Cicero

oratory **6** chapel **8** rhetoric **9** elocution, eloquence **11** speechcraft

orb **3** eye **4** ball, lamp **5** globe, round **6** circle, ocular, oculus, peeper, sphere, winker

orbit **4** path **5** ambit, range, reach, scope, sweep, track **6** extent, radius *farthest point:* **5** apsis **6** apogee **8** aphelion *nearest point:* **5** apsis **7** perigee **10** pericenter, perihelion

orchard **5** copse **6** garden **8** arbustum **10** plantation

orchestra **4** band **5** combo, group **7** gamelan **8** ensemble, symphony **12** philharmonic *leader:* **9** conductor *section:* **5** brass **6** string **8** woodwind **10** percussion

orchestrate **5** blend, score, unify **7** arrange **9** harmonize, integrate **10** symphonize, synthesize

orchid **6** flower *kind:* **5** faham, vanda **7** calypso, pogonia **8** cattleya, oncidium **9** cymbidium **11** cypripedium *petal:* **3** lip **8** labellum *product:* **5** faham, salep *tuber:* **5** salep

Orcus see Hades

ordain **4** keep **5** order **6** decree, direct, impose, manage **7** carry on, command, conduct, dictate, lay down, operate **9** prescribe

ordeal **5** cross, trial **7** calvary **8** crucible **10** affliction, visitation **11** tribulation

order **3** bid, fix, ilk, row, set **4** case, club, fiat, gear, kind, line, plan, rank, rule, sort, tell, trim, tune, type, warn, word **5** align, array, breed, chain, edict, genus, grace, grade, guild, range, right, shape, train, union **6** adjust, behest, branch, charge, codify, decree, direct, enjoin, estate, extent, fettle, kidney, kilter, league, line up, matter, method, nature, police, repair, sequel, series, settle, status, stripe, system **7** aptness, arrange, arrayal, bidding, bracket, command, decorum, dictate, dispose, feather, fitness, mandate, marshal, pattern, probity, routine, society **8** approach, organize, regiment, regulate, sequence, sodality, tidiness, vicinity **9** allotment, amendment, arrayment, closeness, condition, following, integrity, magnitude, methodize, propriety, proration, proximity, rectitude, rightness, routinize **10** adjustment, allocation, correction, expediency, fellowship, fraternity, injunction, permission, pigeonhole, procession, properness, seemliness, streamline, succession, timeliness **11** alternation, arrangement, association, brotherhood, collocation, consecution, correctness, description, disposition, hierarchize, orderliness, progression, suitability, systematize *good:* **6** eutaxy *lack of:* **5** chaos **6** ataxia **7** anarchy, clutter **9** confusion **11** pandemonium *of business:* **6** agenda, docket *of preference:* **8** priority

orderly **4** aide, neat, snug, tidy, trig, trim **5** alike, exact **6** batman, formal **7** chipper, correct, precise, regular, uniform **8** accu-

rate, methodic, picked up 9 shipshape
10 methodical, systematic 11 uncluttered,
well-groomed 12 businesslike

ordinal 4 book 6 number *suffix:* 2 nd, st,
th 3 eth

ordinance 3 law 4 fiat, rule 5 canon,
edict 6 decree 7 precept, statute 8 decretum 9 prescript 10 capitulary, regulation

ordinary 4 so-so 5 banal, plain, trite,
usual 6 common, normal 7 mundane, natural, prosaic, regular, routine 8 everyday,
familiar, frequent, workaday 9 customary,
plain Jane, quotidian 10 uneventful
11 commonplace 12 unnoteworthy

ordnance 4 guns 6 cannon 7 weapons
8 supplies 9 artillery 10 ammunition

ordure 9 excrement *combining form:*
4 copr, scat 5 copro, scato

ore 4 gold, rock 5 metal 6 copper, silver
7 mineral 8 platinum *analysis:* 5 assay
deposit: 4 lode, vein *excavation:* 5 stope
iron: 5 ocher 8 goethite, hematite, limonite
lead: 6 galena *process:* 8 leaching, smelt-
ing *refuse:* 4 slag 5 dross, matte 6 scoria
smelted: 6 speiss 7 regulus

oread 5 nymph

Oreb's slayer 6 Gideon

Oregon *capital:* 5 Salem *largest city:*
8 Portland *nickname:* 11 Beaver State,
Sunset State 12 Webfoot State

Orel's river 3 Oka

Orestes *father:* 9 Agamemnon *friend:*
7 Pylades *mother:* 12 Clytemnestra *sister:*
7 Electra 9 Iphigenia *victim:* 9 Aegisthus
12 Clytemnestra *wife:* 8 Hermione

organ 5 agent, means 6 agency, medium,
review 7 channel, journal, vehicle 8 magazine, ministry 9 newspaper 10 instrument,
periodical *ancient:* 6 syrinx 9 hydraulus
barrel: 10 hurdy-gurdy *bodily:* 3 ear, eye
4 lung, nose 5 gland, heart, liver 6 kidney,
larynx, spleen, tongue, tonsil, viscus
9 intestine *combining form:* 6 viscer 7 vis-
ceri, viscero *mouth:* 9 harmonica *part:*
4 pipe, reed, stop 5 pedal, valve 6 blower
7 console, tremolo 8 keyboard, pedalier
9 wind chest *reed:* 8 melodeon 9 harmo-
nium *stop:* 4 oboe, sext 5 gamba, quint,
viola 6 dolcan, dulcet 7 bassoon, celesta,
melodia, subbass, tertian 8 carillon, dul-
ciana, gemshorn *tactile:* 6 feeler 8 tentacle

organ cactus 7 saguaro

organism 4 unit 5 being, biont, plant
6 animal *disease-producing:* 4 germ
5 virus 7 microbe 8 pathogen 9 bacterium
single-celled: 5 monad 6 amoeba 9 protozoan *suffix:* 5 acean

organist *American:* 3 Fox (Virgil)
5 Biggs (E. Power) 6 Newman (Anthony)
Danish: 9 Buxtehude (Dietrich) *Dutch:*

9 Sweelinck (Jan) *English:* 6 Wesley
(Samuel) 7 Gibbons (Christopher, Edward,
Ellis, Orlando) *French:* 5 Widor (Charles)
6 Franck (Cesar) 8 Messiaen (Olivier)
10 Schweitzer (Albert) *German:* 4 Bach
(Carl Philipp, Johann Christian, Johann
Christoph, Johann Sebastian, Wilhelm Frie-
demann, Wilhelm Friedrech) 6 Walcha
(Helmut) 7 Richter (Anton, Ernst, Ferdi-
nand, Johann, Karl) *Italian:* 7 Germani
(Fernando) 8 Gabrieli (Andrea, Giovanni)

organization 4 body, club, unit 5 group,
guild, setup 6 agency 11 arrangement,
association *college:* 4 frat 8 sorority
10 fraternity *criminal:* 4 gang 5 Mafia *fraternal:* (see fraternal society) *government:* (see government agency) *lack of:*
5 chaos *political:* 4 bloc 5 party 7 appa-
rat, machine

organize 4 form 5 array, found, order,
rally, set up, start 6 create, muster
7 arrange, dispose, marshal 8 mobilize
9 construct, establish, institute, integrate,
methodize, systemize 10 constitute, coordinate 11 put together

orgy 3 bat 4 romp, soak, tear 5 binge,
fling, party, revel, spree 6 ran-tan 7 blowoff, carouse, debauch, rampage, splurge,
wassail 8 carousal 9 bacchanal 10 saturnalia 11 bacchanalia

oriel 3 bay 6 window

orient 5 adapt, pearl, sheen 6 adjust, luster 8 acquaint 11 accommodate

Orient 4 Asia, East 7 Far East

Oriental 5 Asian 7 Asiatic, Chinese, Eastern 8 Japanese *chieftain:* 4 khan *coin:*
3 sen, yen *dish:* 5 pilaf *drink:* 3 tea
4 sake, tuba 6 arrack *inn:* 4 khan 5 serai
11 caravansary 12 caravanserai *litter:*
4 kago 5 dooly 6 doolie 9 palanquin *market:* 3 suq 4 souk 6 bazaar *nana:* 4 amah
prince: 4 raja *ruler:* 4 khan, raja, shah
5 calif, nawab, rajah 6 caliph, sultan *storm:*
7 monsoon *taxi:* 7 ricksha 8 rickshaw
10 jinrikisha *title:* 4 raja 5 rajah *weight:*
4 tael 5 catty, liang *worker:* 6 coolie

orifice see opening

oriflamme 4 flag 5 color 6 banner, pennon 7 pendant, pennant 8 banneroi, gonfalon, standard, streamer

origin 4 root, seed, well 5 birth, blood,
start 6 source, whence 7 descent, genesis,
lineage 8 ancestry, fountain, nascence, nascency, pedigree 9 beginning, inception,
maternity, parentage, paternity 10 derivation, extraction, provenance, wellspring
combining form: 4 geny *of a word:*
9 etymology

original 3 new 4 case, quiz 5 first, model,
novel, prime 6 maiden, mother, native, oddity, unique, zombie 7 initial, oddball, pat-

tern, pioneer, primary 8 creative, earliest, inventor 9 archetype, character, demiurgic, deviceful, eccentric, ingenious, innovator, inventive, precedent, precursor, primitive, prototype, underived 10 archetypal, forerunner, innovative, innovatory, introducer *prefix:* 4 arch 5 arche, archi

originate 4 coin, flow, make, open, rise, sire, stem 5 arise, begin, birth, breed, hatch, issue, set up, spawn, start 6 create, father, launch, parent, spring 7 emanate, proceed, produce, usher in 8 come from, commence, generate, hail from, initiate, stem from 9 institute, introduce, procreate 10 derive from, inaugurate, spring from

originator 4 sire 5 maker 6 author, father 7 creator, founder 8 inventor 9 architect, generator, innovator, patriarch 10 introducer

oriole 4 bird 8 troupial *European:* 6 loriot *genus:* 7 Icterus *golden:* 5 pirol 6 loriot *kind:* 6 golden 7 orchard 8 Bullock's 9 Baltimore

Orion 6 hunter 13 constellation *beloved:* 3 Eos *belt:* 7 Ellwand *father:* 7 Hyrieus 8 Poseidon *slayer:* 5 Diana 7 Artemis *star:* 5 Rigel 9 Bellatrix 10 Betelgeuse

orison 4 plea, suit 6 appeal, prayer 8 entreaty, petition 11 application, imploration, imprecation 12 supplication

Orithyia *lover:* 6 Boreas *son:* 5 Zetes 6 Calais

Orlando author 5 Woolf (Virginia)

Orlando Furioso author 7 Ariosto (Ludovico)

Orleans heroine 9 Joan of Arc

orlop 4 deck

ornament 3 gem 4 bead, deck, trim 5 adorn, jewel, prank 6 bedeck, enrich, finial, tassel 7 dress up, garnish, jewelry, pendant, whatnot 8 beautify, decorate, filigree 9 embellish, embroider, lavaliere 10 lavaliere *architectural:* 7 crocket 10 ball-flower *Christmas tree:* 4 bulb 5 angel 6 tinsel *lip:* 6 labret *shoulder:* 7 epaulet

ornate 4 lush, rich 5 fancy, showy 6 florid, frilly, gilded, rococo 7 aureate, baroque, labored, opulent 8 luscious, overdone 9 elaborate, luxuriant, luxurious, sumptuous 10 flamboyant, overworked

ornery 4 mean 5 balky, nasty, waspy 6 cranky 7 bearish, froward, restive, waspish, wayward 8 cankered, contrary, perverse, stubborn, vinegary 9 crotchety 10 vinegarish 11 wrongheaded 12 cantankerous, cross-grained

ornithic 5 avian

ornithologist *American:* 4 Bond (James) 7 Audubon (John James), Bartram (William) *English:* 5 Gould (John) *Scottish:* 6 Wilson (Alexander)

ornithon 6 aviary

orotund 4 full, loud 5 round 7 aureate, flowery, ringing, vibrant 8 plangent, resonant, sonorant, sonorous 9 bombastic, consonant 10 euphuistic, oratorical, resounding, rhetorical, stentorian 11 declamatory 12 magniloquent 13 grandiloquent

Orpah *husband:* 7 Chilion *sister-in-law:* 4 Ruth

orphan 4 lost, waif 5 alone, Annie 6 bereft 7 cast-off, ignored 8 forsaken, slighted, solitary 9 abandoned, foundling, neglected 10 parentless, unparented

Orpheus *father:* 6 Apollo 7 Oeagrus *home:* 6 Thrace *instrument:* 4 lyre *mother:* 8 Calliope *wife:* 8 Euridice

ort 3 bit 5 scrap 6 morsel 7 leaving, remnant 8 leftover

orthodox 4 good, tory 5 right, sound 6 proper, square 7 correct, die-hard, fogyish, oldline 8 accepted, admitted, approved, official, received, standard, straight 9 canonical, customary 10 buttondown, recognized, sanctioned 11 reactionary, traditional 12 acknowledged, conservative, conventional 13 authoritative

orthography 8 spelling

ortolan 4 sora 7 bunting 8 bobolink

Orwell novel 10 Animal Farm

oryx 7 gemsbok 8 antelope

os 4 bone 5 esker, mouth 7 orifice

oscillate 4 sway, vary 5 squeg, swing, waver 7 vibrate 9 fluctuate, pendulate

osculate 3 lip 4 buss, kiss, peck 5 smack

osier 3 rod 6 willow 7 dogwood

Osiris *brother:* 3 Set 4 Seth *crown:* 4 atef *father:* 3 Geb, Keb, Seb *mother:* 3 Nut *scribe:* 5 Thoth *sister:* 4 Isis *slayer:* 3 Set 4 Seth *son:* 5 Horus 6 Anubis *wife:* 4 Isis

osmium *symbol:* 2 Os

osmosis 4 flow 9 diffusion 10 absorption 12 assimilation

osprey 4 hawk 8 fish hawk

Ossa and ___ 6 Pelion

osseous 4 bony

ossicle 4 bone 5 incus 6 stapes 7 malleus

ossify 3 set 6 harden

ossuary 3 urn 4 tomb 5 vault

ostensible 7 alleged, seeming 8 apparent, illusive, illusory, semblant, so-called, supposed 9 pretended, professed, purported

ostentation 4 show 7 display 9 showiness

ostentatious 4 loud 5 gaudy, showy, swank 6 chichi 7 splashy 8 peacocky 10 flamboyant, peacockish 11 pretentious

ostiole 4 pore 5 mouth 7 orifice 8 aperture

ostracism 5 exile 9 expulsion 10 banishment, relegation 11 deportation 12 displacement

ostracize 3 cut 4 oust, snob, snub 5 exile, expel 6 banish, deport 7 cast out, expulse 8 displace, throw out 9 blackball 10 expatriate 12 cold-shoulder

ostrich *female:* 3 hen *genus:* 8 Struthio *male:* 4 cock

Ostrogoth king 9 Theodoric

otalgia 7 earache

Otello composer 5 Verdi (Giuseppe) 7 Rossini (Gioacchino)

o temporal o ___! 5 mores

Othello *ensign:* 4 Iago *lieutenant:* 6 Cassio *victim, wife:* 9 Desdemona

other *combining form:* 3 all 4 allo 5 heter 6 hetero

others 4 rest 9 remainder *and:* 4 et al 6 et alii

Othniel *brother:* 5 Caleb *father:* 5 Kenaz *wife:* 6 Achsah

Othni's father 8 Shemaiah

otic 5 aural 8 auditory 9 auricular

otiose 4 idle, lazy, vain 5 empty 6 futile, hollow 7 surplus, useless 8 nugatory 11 inexcusable, purposeless, superfluous 13 supernumerary

Otis 7 bustard

Ottawa chief 7 Pontiac

otter *genus:* 5 Lutra 7 Enhydra

ottoman 4 seat 5 couch 9 footstool

Ottoman 4 Turk 7 Turkish *ruler:* 5 Osman 8 Suleyman

Otus 5 giant *brother:* 9 Ephialtes *father:* 6 Aloeus 8 Poseidon *mother:* 9 Iphimedia *slayer:* 6 Apollo

ouch 2 ow 3 cry 5 bezel, jewel 6 brooch, buckle 7 setting 8 bracelet, necklace 11 exclamation

ounce 3 cat 4 atom, doit, dram, drop 5 crumb, grain, minim, shred 6 weight 7 leopard, measure, smidgen 8 particle

ouph 3 elf

our *French:* 5 notre *German:* 5 unser *Italian:* 6 nostra

Our Town author 6 Wilder (Thornton)

oust 3 bar, rob 4 lose 5 eject, evict, expel 6 banish, deport, remove 7 bereave, cast out, deprive, expulse, kick out 8 displace, relegate 9 ostracize, transport 10 disinherit, dispossess

out 4 away, free, leak, show 5 break, chase, chuck, douse, eject, evict, forth, loose 6 absent, quench 7 dismiss, extrude, showing 9 transpire 10 extinguish *of control:* 4 wild 7 chaotic *of gas:* 5 tired 9 exhausted *of line:* 4 awry, rude 5 askew, fresh *of place:* 13 inappropriate *of sorts:* 5 cross 7 grouchy, peevish 9 irritable *of the ordinary:* 3 odd 7 strange, unusual

outage 7 failure 8 blackout 12 interruption

out-and-out 5 gross, sheer, utter 7 perfect 8 absolute, complete, positive 10 consummate 13 thoroughgoing

outback 4 bush 10 wilderness

outboard 5 motor

outbreak 4 dawn, rash 5 burst, flare, onset 6 plague, revolt 8 epidemic, eruption 9 beginning 12 commencement

outbreathe 6 exhale, expire

outburst 4 gale, gust, tiff 5 flare, sally, scene, storm 6 access, fantod, frenzy, tirade 7 flare-up, rapture, tantrum, torrent 8 eruption 9 explosion

outcast 4 hobo 5 exile, leper, tramp 6 pariah 7 Ishmael, vagrant 8 castaway, derelict, vagabond 9 reprobate 10 expatriate, Ishmaelite 11 offscouring, untouchable *Japanese:* 3 eta

outclass 4 best 5 excel 7 surpass

outcome 4 fate 5 event, issue 6 effect, result, sequel, upshot 8 causatum 9 aftermath 11 aftereffect, consequence

outcrop 4 rock 5 ledge 6 basset

outcry 4 yell 5 shout 6 clamor, tumult, upturn 7 ferment 8 upheaval 9 commotion

outdare 4 defy, face 5 beard, brave, front 7 venture 9 challenge

outdated see out-of-date

outdo 3 top 4 beat, best, down 5 excel, trump, worst 6 better, defeat, exceed 7 surpass, upstage 9 transcend

outdoor 7 open-air 8 alfresco 10 hypaethral

outer 5 ectad, ectal 6 remote 7 surface 8 exterior, external 9 extrinsic 10 extraneous 11 superficial

outermost 4 last 5 final 7 extreme 8 farthest, furthest, remotest

outfit 3 arm, kit, rig 4 band, firm, gear 5 corps, dress, equip, getup, guise, house, party, troop 6 tackle, troupe 7 appoint, company, concern, costume, furnish 8 accouter, accoutre, business, ensemble, materiel, tackling 9 apparatus, equipment, machinery 10 enterprise 11 habiliments 12 organization 13 accouterments, accoutrements, establishment, paraphernalia

outflow 4 flux 6 efflux 8 drainage, effluent

outfox see outwit

outgrowth 4 tuft 5 child, issue, shoot 6 branch, effect, member, result 7 process, product, spin-off 8 offshoot, swelling 9 byproduct, offspring, processus 10 derivative, descendant 11 aftereffect, consequence, enlargement, excrescence, excrescency

outhouse 5 jakes, privy 7 latrine

outing 4 trip 5 jaunt, sally 6 junket, picnic 9 excursion 10 roundabout

outland 5 rural 6 rustic 7 bucolic, country 8 agrestic, pastoral 10 campestral, provincial 11 countrified

outlandish 3 odd 4 back, wild 5 alien, kinky, queer, ultra, weird 6 remote, vulgar 7 bizarre, curious, extreme, foreign, strange, uncouth, unusual 8 barbaric, frontier, peculiar, singular 9 barbarian, barbarous, graceless, monstrous, tasteless, unsettled 10 unorthodox 11 extravagant

outlaw 3 ban 5 taboo 6 badman, bandit, enjoin, forbid, gunman 7 inhibit 8 criminal, prohibit, renegade 9 desperado, interdict

outlay 4 cost, give 5 spend 6 expend 7 expense 8 disburse 11 expenditure 12 disbursement

outlet 4 exit, hole, shop, vent 5 store 6 egress, escape 7 opening, orifice, release 8 aperture, showroom

outline 3 hem, map, rim 4 edge, form, limn, plan 5 bound, chart, draft, shape, skirt, trace 6 border, figure, fringe, margin, projet, sketch 7 contour, profile 8 skeleton, surround, syllabus 9 adumbrate 10 figuration, silhouette 11 skeletonize

outlive 7 survive

outlook 4 side, view 5 angle, scape, scene, sight, slant, vista 8 prospect 9 direction, viewpoint 10 standpoint 11 observatory, perspective, point of view

outlying 3 far 6 far-off, remote 7 distant, faraway, removed 8 far-flung

outmoded see out-of-date

out-of-date 3 old 5 dowdy, passé, tacky 6 démodé, frumpy, stodgy 7 antique, archaic, oldtime, vintage 8 frumpish 9 unstylish 10 antiquated 12 old-fashioned

out-of-the-way 5 aside 6 remote, secret 7 devious, obscure, removed, retired 8 lonesome

outpouring 4 flow, gush 8 effusion, outburst

output 4 crop, gain, take 5 yield 6 profit 7 harvest, produce, product 10 production

outrage 4 harm, hurt, rape, ruin 5 abuse, anger, force, spoil, wrong 6 defile, ill-use, injury, insult, misuse, offend, ravish 7 affront, oppress, violate 8 aggrieve, deflower, ill-treat, maltreat, mischief, mistreat

outrageous 5 awful, gross 6 crying, horrid, unholy, wicked 7 beastly, ghastly, obscene, ungodly 8 dreadful, flagrant, horrible, shocking, terrible 9 desperate 10 abominable, impossible 11 intolerable, unchristian, uncivilized 12 unreasonable

outré 5 kinky, ultra 7 bizarre, strange

outrigger 4 prao, prau, proa 5 canoe, prahu

outright 3 all 5 gross, total, utter, whole 6 entire 7 perfect 8 absolute, complete,

positive 10 consummate 11 unmitigated 13 thoroughgoing

outrun 4 beat 6 exceed 7 surpass

outset 4 dawn 5 birth, start 7 dawning, opening 9 beginning 12 commencement

outshine see outdo

outside 3 bar, but, off, top 4 open, over, past, save, slim 5 after, alien, small 6 beyond, except, remove, saving, slight, utmost 7 foreign, maximal, maximum, open-air, slender, topmost 8 alfresco, exterior, external 9 apart from, excluding 10 hypaethral, negligible 11 exclusive of
prefix: 2 ec, ex 3 ect, exo 5 extra, extro

outsider 5 alien 7 inconnu 8 stranger 9 foreigner

outsmart see outwit

outspoken 4 free, open 5 bluff, blunt, frank, plain, round, vocal 6 candid, direct 8 explicit, strident 10 forthright, pointblank

outspread 4 open 6 expand, extend, unfold

outstanding 3 due 4 main, star 5 chief, major, noted 6 marked, mature, signal, superb, unpaid 7 capital, notable, overdue, payable, salient, stellar 8 dominant 9 arrestive, principal, prominent, unsettled 10 noticeable, preeminent, remarkable 11 conspicuous, magnificent, predominant, superlative

outstart 4 dawn 5 birth, onset 7 dawning, opening 9 beginning 12 commencement

outstrip 3 top 4 beat, best, lose, pass 5 excel 6 better, exceed 7 surpass 8 distance

outsweepings 4 junk 5 trash, waste 6 debris, litter, refuse 7 garbage, rubbish

outward 4 over 5 ectad, ectal, overt 7 visible 8 apparent, exterior, external 10 ostensible 11 superficial

outweigh 6 make up, offset, redeem, set off 7 balance 8 atone for, overbear 10 compensate 11 countervail, overbalance

outwit 3 fox 4 dupe, foil, gull, have, hoax, undo 5 trick 6 befool 8 hoodwink 9 bamboozle, frustrate, overreach

outworn see out-of-date

ouzel 4 bird 6 thrush 9 blackbird

oval 4 ooid 5 track 7 ellipse 8 elliptic 9 egg-shaped 11 ellipsoidal

ovation 6 homage, praise 8 applause

oven 4 kiln, lehr, oast 5 range, stove 6 calcar

over 2 by, on 3 mid, off, too 4 amid, anew, atop, away, done, leap, past, upon, with 5 about, above, again, aloft, clear, cross, due to, ended, extra, midst, round, vault 6 across, afresh, around, beyond, de novo, during, higher, hurdle, unduly 7 athwart, greater, outside, outward, owing to, through

8 exterior, external, finished, once more, superior, surmount 9 because of, extremely, immensely, negotiate 10 throughout 11 excessively, superjacent 12 inordinately, transversely *French:* 3 sur *German:* 4 über *prefix:* 2 ep 3 eph, epi, sur 5 extra, hyper, super, supra *Spanish:* 5 sobre

overabundance 6 excess 7 surfeit, surplus 8 plethora 10 surplusage 11 superfluity

overact 3 ham, mug 4 rant 5 emote, spout

overage see overabundance

overall 6 global, mainly, mostly 7 chiefly, general, largely 8 sweeping 9 generally, inclusive, primarily 10 high and low, far and wide 11 principally 13 comprehensive, predominantly

overalls 5 pants 8 trousers

over and above 6 beside, beyond 7 besides 8 as well as

over and over 3 oft 4 much 5 often 8 ofttimes 10 frequently, oftentimes, repeatedly

overbearing 5 bossy, proud 6 lordly, master 7 haughty, pompous, regnant 8 absolute, arrogant, cavalier, despotic, dominant, imperial, insolent, superior 9 ascendant, imperious, masterful, paramount, prevalent, sovereign 10 autocratic, disdainful, highhanded, imperative, peremptory, tyrannical 11 magisterial, predominant, predominate 12 preponderant, supercilious 13 high-and-mighty

overblown 3 big, fat 4 arty 5 gross, heavy, obese, stout, tumid, windy 6 fleshy, portly, turgid 7 aureate, flowery, porcine 8 dropsied, imposing, inflated, sonorous 9 bombastic, corpulent, dropsical, flatulent, tumescent 10 arty-crafty, euphuistic, oratorical, rhetorical 11 declamatory, exaggerated, pretentious 12 high-sounding, magniloquent 13 grandiloquent

overbold 6 arrant, brassy, brazen 7 blatant 8 impudent 9 barefaced, shameless, unabashed 10 unblushing 11 brazenfaced

overcast 3 cap, dim 4 dull, gray, hazy 5 cloud, cover, crown, dirty, heavy 6 cloudy, darken, shadow, sullen 7 becloud, blanket, louring, obscure 8 brooding, lowering, nubilous 9 adumbrate 10 oppressive

overcharge 3 gyp, pad 4 clip, skin, soak 5 gauge, stick 6 fleece 7 magnify 9 embellish

overcoat 6 capote, raglan, ulster 7 paletot, surtout 9 balmacaan, inverness 12 chesterfield

overcome 3 win 4 beat, best, down, lick 5 drown, throw, whelm 6 defeat, hurdle, master 7 conquer, outlive, prevail, triumph 8 surmount 9 prostrate *by grief:* 8 dejected, downcast 10 dispirited 12 disconsolate 13 broken-hearted

overconfident 5 brash, cocky 6 uppity 7 pushful 9 presuming 10 brassbound 12 presumptuous

overdo 7 exhaust, fatigue 10 exaggerate

overdue 4 late 5 lated, owing, tardy 6 mature, unpaid 7 belated, payable 9 unsettled 10 behindhand, unpunctual 11 outstanding

overemphasize 7 magnify 10 exaggerate

overflow 4 brim, pour, slop, teem 5 drown, flood, slosh, spate, spill, swamp, whelm 6 deluge, engulf, excess 7 cascade, niagara, surfeit, surplus, torrent 8 cataract, flooding, inundate, plethora, spillage, submerge 9 cataclysm 10 inundation, surplusage 11 superfluity

overflowing 4 rife 5 alive, awash 7 replete, teeming 8 thronged 13 superabundant

overgrown 4 lush, rank 5 braky, copsy, dense, thick 6 brushy, jungly 7 brambly 8 thickety 9 thicketed

overhang 3 jut 4 poke, pout 5 bulge, jetty, pouch 6 beetle 7 project 8 protrude

overhaul 3 fix 4 do up, mend, take 5 catch, patch 6 doctor, repair, revamp 7 rebuild 8 renovate 11 recondition, reconstruct

overhead 5 above, aloft 7 expense

overindulgence 6 excess 8 gluttony 12 immoderation, intemperance

overindulgent 9 excessive 10 immoderate, inordinate, untempered 11 intemperate 12 unrestrained

overkill 6 excess 7 surfeit, surplus 8 plethora 10 surplusage 11 superfluity

overlap 7 shingle 9 imbricate

overlay 3 cap 4 coat 5 cover, crown 6 veneer 7 blanket 8 covering

overload 4 glut 6 excess 7 surfeit

overlook 4 boss, fail, omit, skip 5 blank, chasm 6 forget, ignore, slight, survey 7 blink at, condone, neglect 8 chaperon, discount, dominate, omission 9 blink away, chaperone, disregard, supervise 10 tower above

overlord 5 chief, ruler 8 suzerain 9 chieftain

overpass 4 fail, omit 6 bridge, forget, ignore 7 blink at, neglect 8 discount 9 blink away, disregard

overplay 6 accent 7 magnify, point up, stretch 8 maximize 9 dramatize 10 accentuate, exaggerate 11 hyperbolize

overpower 4 rout 5 crush, drown, whelm 6 defeat, master, reduce, subdue 7 conquer 8 bear down, vanquish 9 prostrate, subjugate

overreach 3 gyp 4 beat, bilk, undo 5 cheat, cozen 6 chouse, diddle, outfox, outwit 7 defraud 8 flimflam, outslick, outsmart 11 outmaneuver

override 3 lap 4 veto 7 nullify, shingle 9 imbricate

overriding 7 central, pivotal, primary 8 cardinal 9 principal

overrule 4 sway, veto 5 reign 6 govern

overrun 4 beat, drub, lick, raid, trim, whip 5 beset, foray, smear, spill, swarm 6 exceed, infest, inroad, invade, thrash 7 outstep, surpass 8 lambaste

overseas 5 alien 6 abroad, exotic 7 foreign, strange 11 transmarine, ultramarine

oversee 3 run 4 boss 5 watch 6 survey 8 chaperon 9 chaperone, supervise 11 quarterback, superintend

overseer 4 boss, head 5 chief 7 foreman, manager 8 chaperon 9 chaperone 10 supervisor

overshadow 3 dim 4 haze 5 cloud, cover 6 darken 7 becloud, obscure 9 adumbrate

overshoe 4 boot 6 arctic, galosh, patten, rubber

oversight 4 care, skip 5 aegis, blank, chasm, check, error, guard 6 charge 7 conduct, control, custody, default, failure, keeping, mistake, neglect, running 8 handling, omission, tutelage 10 ciceronage, intendance, management 11 chaperonage

overslaugh 3 bar, dam 5 block, brake 6 hinder, impede 8 obstruct

oversoon 5 early 7 betimes 8 previous, untimely 9 premature 11 prematurely

overspread 3 cap 5 beset, cover, crown 6 infest 7 blanket

overstate 3 pad 5 color, fudge 7 magnify 9 embellish, embroider 10 exaggerate

overstep 6 exceed 7 surpass 8 infringe, trespass 10 transgress

overstock 6 excess 7 surplus 9 remainder 10 surplusage

overstress 7 magnify 8 maximize 10 exaggerate

overswarm 4 raid 5 beset, foray 6 infest, inroad, invade

overt 4 open 6 patent 7 obvious, outward, visible 8 apparent, manifest

overtake 4 pass

over there 3 yon 6 yonder

overthrow 4 down, fell, oust, rout, ruin 5 purge, upset 6 defeat, depose, remove, topple, tumble, unseat 7 beating, conquer, debacle, destroy, licking, unhorse

8 dethrone, downcast, drubbing 9 liquidate, trouncing 10 defeasance 11 shellacking 12 vanquishment

overtone 4 hint 8 harmonic 10 suggestion 11 association, connotation, implication

overture 3 bid 5 proem 6 tender 7 advance, preface, prelude 8 approach, exordium, foreword, preamble, prologue, proposal 9 prelusion 11 proposition 12 introduction, prolegomenon

overturn 3 tip 4 coup, down 5 upend, upset 6 keel up, topple, tumble 7 capsize, shake-up, unhorse 9 prostrate 10 revolution

overweening 5 brash 6 uppish, uppity 7 forward, pushful 8 arrogant 10 immoderate 12 presumptuous 13 self-assertive

overweight 3 fat 5 gross, heavy, obese, stout 6 fleshy, portly 9 corpulent

overwhelm 4 beat, bury, drub, lick, ruin, sink, trim, whip 5 crush, drown, flood, floor, lower, smear, swamp, upset, wreck 6 deluge, engulf, thrash 7 destroy, disturb, shatter, shellac, smother 8 inundate, submerge 9 devastate, downgrade, dumbfound, prostrate 10 demoralize 11 subordinate

overwhelmed 5 agape 6 aghast 7 stunned 13 thunderstruck

overword 6 burden 7 refrain

Ovid work 5 Fasti 7 Tristia 8 Heroides 13 Metamorphoses

oviform 4 ooid, oval 5 ovate 6 ooidal 9 egg-shaped

ovine 5 sheep 9 sheeplike

ovoid see oviform

ovule 3 egg *fertilized:* 4 seed

ovum 3 egg 6 gamete 7 egg cell

owing 3 due 6 mature, unpaid 7 overdue, payable 9 unsettled

owing to 4 over 7 through 9 because of

owl *Australian:* 7 boobook 8 morepork *cry:* 4 hoot *genus:* 4 Otus *kind:* 3 elf 4 barn, gray, lulu 5 eagle, gnome, madge, pygmy, snowy 6 barred, horned 7 sawwhet, screech 9 long-eared 10 short-eared 11 great horned *resembling:* 8 strigine *snowy:* 7 harfang

Owl and Pussycat author 4 Lear (Edward)

own 4 avow, have, hold 5 admit, allow, enjoy, grant, let on 6 fess up, retain 7 concede, confess, possess 11 acknowledge

owner 4 lord 8 landlady, landlord 9 possessor 10 proprietor

ownership 4 hand 5 title 8 dominion, property 10 possession 11 proprietary *perpetual:* 8 mortmain

ox 3 yak 4 anoa, buff, gaur, musk, zebu 5 bison, gayal, steer 6 bovine, ovibos 7 banteng, bantery, brahman, buffalo *Asian:*

4 zebu *attachment:* 4 yoke *combining form:* 4 bovi *extinct:* 4 urus 7 aurochs *family:* 7 Bovidae *relating to:* 6 bovine *Scottish:* 4 nowt, owse *wild:* 4 anoa, gaur 7 banteng 8 saladang, seladang

oxeye 5 daisy 6 flower

oxford 4 shoe 5 cloth, sheep

oxide *calcium:* 4 lime 9 quicklime *ferric:* 4 rust *sodium:* 4 soda

oxidize 4 rust

oxygen 3 air, gas 5 ozone 7 element *discoverer:* 9 Lavoisier *form:* 5 ozone *liquid:* 3 lox

oyster 5 forte 6 medium 7 bivalve, mollusk *bed:* 4 park 6 claire, cultch *combining form:* 5 ostre 6 ostrei, ostreo *eggs:* 5 spawn *genus:* 6 Ostrea 11 Crassostrea *Long Island:* 9 bluepoint *product:* 5 pearl *shell:* 4 test 5 shuck *young:* 4 spat

oysterbird 5 tirma 10 sanderling

oysterfish 6 tautog

oyster grass 4 kelp 10 sea lettuce

Oz *creator:* 4 Baum (Frank) *inhabitant:* 8 Munchkin

Ozark State 8 Missouri

Ozem *brother:* 5 David *father:* 5 Jesse 9 Jerahmeel

Ozni's father 3 Gad

Ozymandias author 7 Shelley (Percy Bysshe)

P

pabulum 4 food 7 aliment 8 nutrient 9 nutriment 10 sustenance 11 nourishment

pace 3 rut 4 gait, hoof, rate, step, time, walk 5 grind, speed, tempo, tread, troop 6 timing 7 example, fluency, forerun, precede, proceed, routine, traipse 8 ambulate, antecede, celerity, rapidity, regulate, velocity 9 quickness, rapidness, swiftness, treadmill

pachyderm 8 elephant

pacific 4 calm, meek, mild 6 gentle, irenic, placid, serene 8 dovelike, peaceful, tranquil 9 appeasing, peaceable

Pacificator, Great 4 Clay (Henry)

Pacific Ocean discoverer 6 Balboa (Vasco Nunez de)

pacifist 4 dove 6 irenic 8 appeaser, peaceful 9 peaceable 10 nonviolent, satyagrahi 11 peacemonger

pacify 4 calm, ease, lull 5 allay, quiet, still 6 settle, soften, soothe, subdue, temper 7 appease, assuage, mollify, placate

pack 3 jam, lot, lug, mob, ram, wad 4 bear, cram, fill, heap, load, lump, mass, much, pile, stow, tamp, tote 5 carry, choke, crowd, ferry, group, store, stuff, troop 6 barrel, bestow, bundle, charge, convey, depart 7 compact 8 compress 9 container

pack animal 3 ass 4 mule 5 burro, camel, horse, llama 6 donkey 7 jackass, sumpter 13 beast of burden

packed 4 full 5 awash 7 brimful, crowded, stuffed 8 brimming 9 chock-full

packet 3 pot, wad 4 boat, mint, pile 6 boodle, bundle, parcel 7 fortune

pact 4 bond 6 treaty 7 bargain, concord 8 alliance, covenant 9 agreement

pad 3 mat, wad 5 fudge, guard, quilt, stuff 6 muffle, shield, tablet, trudge 7 bolster, cushion, magnify, stretch 8 overdraw 9 embellish, embroider, overpaint, overstate 10 exaggerate, overcharge

paddle 3 fin, oar, row 4 pull 5 spank 6 dabble, thrash 7 flipper

pagan 7 gentile, heathen, infidel, profane 8 idolator 9 infidelic 10 unbeliever *god:* 4 idol

page 4 book, call, leaf 5 folio, sheet 6 locate, summon 7 writing *left-hand:* 5 verso *reverse:* 5 verso *right-hand:* 5 recto

pageant 4 sham, show 7 charade 8 disguise, pretense 9 spectacle 10 exhibition

Pagiel's father 5 Ocran 6 Ochran

Pagliacci *character:* 5 Canio, Nedda, Tonio 6 Silvio *composer:* 11 Leoncavallo (Ruggero)

pagoda 2 ta 3 taa 6 alcove, gazebo, temple 9 belvedere 11 garden house, summerhouse

pail 6 bucket, piggin

pain 3 ail, irk, try 4 ache, care, hurt, pang 5 agony, cramp, grief, throe, upset, wound

6 effort, grieve, harass, harrow, injure, stitch, stress, twinge 7 afflict, agonize, anguish, crucify, provoke, torment, torture, travail, trouble 8 aggrieve, convulse, distress, lacerate 9 suffering 10 affliction, discomfort, excruciate *abdominal:* 5 colic *back:* 7 lumbago *combining form:* 3 alg 4 agra, algo, noci 5 agrae (plural), algia, algic 6 odynia, odynic *ear:* 6 otalgy 7 otalgia *intensity unit:* 3 dol *muscular:* 7 myalgia

painful 3 raw 4 sore 5 acute, sharp 6 aching, bitter 7 algetic, galling, hurting, irksome, racking 8 annoying, grievous, piercing, shooting, stabbing, stinging, unsavory 9 agonizing, harrowing, torturous, upsetting, vexatious 10 afflictive, tormenting

painkiller 6 opiate 7 anodyne 8 morphine, narcotic 9 analgesic 10 anesthetic

painstaking 5 exact, fussy 7 careful, heedful 8 diligent, exacting, punctual 9 laborious 10 meticulous, scrupulous 11 punctilious

paint 4 coat, daub, face, limn 5 color, japan, stain 6 depict, fresco, makeup 7 portray 9 delineate, represent 10 maquillage

painter 6 artist *American:* 4 Haas (Richard), West (Benjamin), Wood (Grant) 5 Abbey (Edwin Austin), Henri (Robert), Hicks (Edward), Homer (Winslow), Johns (Jasper), Kroll (Leon), Marin (John), Moses (Grandma), Peale (Anna, Charles Willson, James, Raphaelle, Rembrant, Sarah, Titian), Ryder (Albert), Shahn (Ben), Sloan (Eric, John), Weber (Max), Wyeth (Andrew, Jamie, Newell Convers) 6 Benton (Thomas Hart), Catlin (George), Copley (John Singleton), Eakins (Thomas), Hassam (Childe), Hopper (Edward), Inness (George), Leutze (Emanuel), Martin (Agnes, Homer), Rivers (Larry), Rothko (Mark), Stella (Frank), Stuart (Gilbert), Tanguy (Yves), Thorpe (Thomas), Warhol (Andy) 7 Allston (Washington), Bellows (George), Cassatt (Mary), La Farge (John), O'Keeffe (Georgia), Parrish (Maxfield), Pollock (Jackson), Sargent (John Singer), Sheeler (Charles), Tiffany (Louis Comfort), Tworkov (Jack), Wiggins (Carleton) 8 Melchers (Gari), Rockwell (Norman), Sullivan (Patrick), Trumbull (John), Whistler (James Abbott McNeil) 9 Feininger (Lyonel), Remington (Frederic), Twachtman (John Henry), Vanderlyn (John) 10 Motherwell (Robert), Whittredge (Thomas) 12 Lichtenstein (Roy) *Austrian:* 9 Kokoschka (Oskar) *Belgian:* 6 Campin (Robert) 8 Magritte (René) *Canadian:* 4 Kane (Paul) 6 Harris (Lawren), Watson (Homer) 7 Jackson (Alexander Young),

Thomson (Tom) 9 MacDonald (James Edward Hervey) *Chinese:* 4 Wu Li 6 Ma Yüan 7 Wang Wei 8 Yen Li-pen *Dutch:* 4 Hals (Franz), Lely (Peter), Maas (Nicolas) 5 Bosch (Hieronymus), Steen (Jan) 6 Potter (Paul) 7 de Hooch (Pieter), de Witte (Emanuel de), Hobbema (Meindert), van Gogh (Vincent), Vermeer (Jan) 8 Mondrian (Piet), Ruisdael (Jacob van), Ruysdael (Salomon), Terborch (Gerard) 9 Rembrandt, Wouwerman (Philips) 11 Terbrugghen (Hendrik) *English:* 4 John (Augustus), Lear (Edward) 5 Bacon (Francis), Blake (William), Brown (Ford Madox), Lewis (Wyndham), Watts (George) 6 Romney (George), Turner (Joseph Mallord William), Wilson (Richard) 7 Hogarth (William), Kneller (Godfrey), Millais (John), Raeburn (Henry) 8 Lawrence (Thomas), Reynolds (Joshua), Rossetti (Dante Gabriel) 9 Constable (John), Nicholson (Ben, William) 12 Gainsborough (Thomas) *Flemish:* 4 Goes (Hugo van der) 6 Rubens (Peter Paul), Weyden (Rogier van der) 7 Memling (Hams), Teniers (David), Van Dyck (Anthony), Van Eyck (Hubert, Jan) 8 Breughel, Brueghel (Abraham, Ambrose, Jan, Pieter) *French:* 4 Doré (Gustave), Dufy (Raoul) 5 Corot (Camille), David (Jacques-Louis), Degas (Edgar), Léger (Fernand), Manet (Édouard), Monet (Claude), Puvis (Pierre), Redon (Odilon), Vouet (Simon) 6 Braque (Georges), Breton (André), Claude (of Lorrain), Clouet (François, Jean) Gerome (Jean-Léon), Greuze (Jean-Baptiste), Ingres (Jean-Auguste-Dominique), Le Brun (Charles), Le Nain (Antoine, Louis, Mathieu), Millet (Jean-François), Renoir (Pierre-Auguste), Seurat (Georges), Sisley (Alfred), Tanguy (Yves), Vernet (Carle, Horace, Joseph) 7 Bonheur (Rosa), Bonnard (Pierre), Cézanne (Paul), Chardin (Jean-Baptiste), Courbet (Gustave), Daumier (Honore), Duchamp (Gaston, Marcel), Gauguin (Paul), Matisse (Henri), Morisot (Berthe), Poussin (Nicolas), Rouault (Georges), Utrillo (Maurice), Watteau (Antoine) 8 Dubuffet (Jean), Pissarro (Camille), Rousseau (Henri, Theodore), Vlaminck (Maurice de), Vuillard (Edouard) 9 Delacroix (Eugène), Fragonard (Jean-Honoré), Géricault (Théodore), Laurencin (Marie) 10 Meissonier (Jean-Louis) 11 Le Corbusier *German:* 5 Dürer (Albrecht), Ernst (Max), Grosz (George), Nolde (Emil) 6 Müller (Friedrich "Maler") 7 Cranach (Lucas), Holbein (Hans), Lochner (Stefan), Schwind (Moritz von), Zoffany (Johann) 8 Kirchner (Ernst), Kollwitz (Käthe) 9 Grünewald (Matthias), Kandinsky (Wassily) 10 Schongauer (Martin), Wohlgemuth (Michael) *Greek:*

6 Zeuxis 7 Apelles 10 Polygnotus *Irish:*
5 Yeats (Jack, John Butler) *Italian:* 4 Reni
(Guido), Rosa (Salvator), Tura (Cosme)
5 Campi (Antonio, Bernardino, Giulio, Vin-
cenzo), Lippi (Fra Filippo, Filippino, Lor-
enzo), Piero (della Francesca, di Cosimo),
Sarto (Andrea del) 6 Cosimo (Agnolo di,
Piero di), Giotto, Romano (Giulio), Sodoma
(Il), Titian, Vasari (Giorgio) 7 Bellini (Gen-
tile, Giovanni, Jacopo), Chirico (Giorgio
De), Cimabue, da Vinci (Leonardo), Fiesole
(Giovanni da), Martini (Simone), Orcagna,
Peruzzi (Baldassare), Raphael, Tiepolo
(Giovanni), Uccello (Paolo), Zuccari (Tad-
deo) 8 Del Sarto (Andrea), Fabriano (Gen-
tile da), Giordano (Luca), Mantegna
(Andrea), Masaccio, Montagna (Bartolom-
meo), Perugino, Pontorno (Jacopo da),
Severini (Gino), Veronese (Paolo), Vivarini
(Alvise, Antonio, Bartolomeo) 9 Carpaccio
(Vittore), Correggio, Francesca (Piero della)
10 Caravaggio, Modigliani (Amedeo),
Signorelli (Luca), Tintoretto, Verrocchio
(Andrea del), Zuccarelli (Francesco)
11 Ghirlandajo (Domenico) 12 Michelan-
gelo, Parmigianino *Japanese:* 5 Korin
6 Sesshu *Lithuanian:* 7 Soutine (Chaim)
Mexican: 6 Orozco (Jose), Rivera (Diego),
Tamayo (Rufino) 9 Siqueiros (David) *Nor-
wegian:* 5 Munch (Edvard) *Russian:*
7 Chagall (Marc), Roerich (Nikolay) 9 Kan-
dinsky (Wassily) *Scottish:* 6 Ramsay
(Allan) 7 Nasmyth (Alexander), Raeburn
(Henry) *Spanish:* 4 Dali (Salvador), Goya
(Francisco), Gris (Juan), Miro (Joan), Sert
(José Maria) 6 Ribera (José), Rincon
(Antonio del), Tapies (Antonio) 7 El Greco,
Herrera (Francisco de), Murillo (Bartolomé
Esteban), Picasso (Pablo), Zuloaga (Igna-
cio) 8 Zurbaran (Francisco de) 9 Velaz-
quez (Diego) *Swedish:* 4 Zorn (Anders)
6 Roslin (Alexander) *Swiss:* 4 Klee (Paul),
Witz (Konrad)

painting 3 oil 7 acrylic, picture 10 watercolor *circular:* 5 tondo *combining form:*
6 chromy *one-color:* 8 monotint 10 mono-
chrome *plaster:* 5 secco 6 fresco *style:*
6 cubism, Gothic, pop art, rococo
7 baroque, Bauhaus, dadaism, fauvism,
realism 8 Barbizon, futurism 9 Byzantine,
geometric, mannerism 10 avant-garde,
classicism, surrealism 11 romanticism
13 expressionism, impressionism *technique:* 3 oil 6 fresco, gouche, pastel
7 polymer, tempera 9 encaustic 10 watercolor *tool:* 5 brush, easel, knife, paint
6 canvas 7 palette *wall:* 5 mural

pair 3 duo, two 4 dyad, join, mate, span,
team, yoke 5 brace, match, unite 6 couple
7 doublet, twosome 8 geminate

Pakistan *capital:* 9 Islamabad *largest
city:* 7 Karachi *monetary unit:* 5 rupee
province: 4 Sind 6 Punjab 11 Baluchistan
pal 4 chum, mate 5 buddy, crony
6 comate, friend 7 comrade, partner
9 associate, companion 11 confederate
paladin see douzeper
Palal's father 4 Uzai
Palamedes *brother:* 6 Sforza 8 Achilles
father: 8 Nauplius *slayer:* 7 Corinda, Ulysses 8 Odysseus
palatable 5 sapid, tasty, yummy 6 savory,
toothy 8 luscious, pleasing, saporous,
savorous, tasteful, tempting 9 aperitive,
delicious, relishing, saporific, savorsome,
toothsome 10 appetizing, delightful, flavorsome
palate 4 zest 5 gusto, heart, taste 6 relish
palatial 4 lush, rich 5 large, noble, plush
6 Capuan, deluxe, ornate 7 opulent, stately
8 luscious, splendid 9 luxuriant, luxurious,
sumptuous 10 impressive 11 magnificent,
upholstered
palaver 3 gas, yak 4 blab, cant, chat, guff,
tack 5 clack 6 affair, babble, hot air, jargon, parley 7 chatter, concern, lexicon,
lookout, prattle, seminar 8 business, colloquy, dialogue 10 colloquium, conference,
discussion, rap session 12 conversation
palaverous 5 windy, wordy 6 prolix 7 diffuse, verbose 9 redundant 10 long-winded
pale 3 dim, wan 4 ashy, dull, fade, gray,
sick, weak 5 ashen, faint, fence, inane,
livid, lurid, muddy, pasty, stake, waxen,
white 6 anemic, blanch, chalky, doughy,
feeble, jejune, pallid, picket, sallow, sickly,
watery, whiten 7 ghastly, insipid, tarnish,
waxlike 8 blanched, encircle, waterish,
whitened 9 bloodless, colorless, deathlike
paleness 6 pallor
palinode 5 unsay 6 abjure, recall, recant
7 retract 8 forswear, take back, withdraw
10 retraction 11 recantation
pall 4 bore, cloy, glut, jade, sate, tire
5 cloak, drape, ennui, gorge, weary 6 canopy, clothe, mantle, stodge 7 disgust, satiate, surfeit 8 covering 11 counterpane
palladium *symbol:* 2 Pd
Pallas *brother:* 6 Aegeus *father:* 7 Pandion *slayer:* 7 Theseus *wife:* 4 Styx; (see
also Athena)
palliate 4 ease, hide, mask 5 cloak, cover,
glass, gloze, salve 6 excuse, lessen,
soften, temper, veneer, whiten 7 conceal,
condone, cover up, lighten, qualify, varnish
8 disguise, mitigate, moderate, prettify
9 alleviate, dissemble, extenuate, glass
over, gloze over, sugarcoat, whitewash
pallid 3 wan 4 ashy, dull 5 ashen, waxen
6 anemic, doughy, watery 8 blanched,
waterish 9 bloodless, colorless

Pallu *father:* 6 Reuben *son:* 5 Eliab
pally 4 cozy 6 chummy 8 intimate
palm 3 tip 4 hide 5 bribe, merus, prize
6 thenar 7 conceal *beverage:* 4 nipa
5 assai *fiber:* 4 bass, bast 6 gomuti 7 bassine 8 piassava *fruit:* 4 date 7 coconut
11 coquilla nut *kind:* 3 fan, wax 4 coco,
date, doom, hemp, nipa, sago 5 areca,
assai, betel, datil, ivory, royal, tucum
6 gomuti, grigri, grugru, jupati, raffia, rattan
7 cabbage, feather, palmyra, talipot 8 carnauba, palmetto, piassava 12 Washingtonia *leaf:* 4 olla 5 frond *starch:* 4 sago
vine: 6 rattan
palmer 7 pilgrim
Palmetto State 13 South Carolina
palm lily 2 ti
palm off 5 foist 7 deceive
Palmyra's queen 7 Zenobia
palooka 3 oaf 4 gawk, lout, lump 5 klutz
6 lubber, lummox
palpable 4 sure 5 clear, plain 6 patent
7 certain, evident, obvious, seeming, tactile
8 apparent, distinct, manifest, positive, striking, tangible 9 arresting 10 noticeable
11 perceptible, unequivocal
palpate 4 feel 5 touch 6 finger, handle
palpitate 4 beat 5 pulse, throb 6 quiver
7 flutter, pulsate 12 pitter-patter
palter 3 fib, lie 5 evade, fence 6 haggle,
parley 7 bargain, chaffer, falsify 10 equivocate 11 prevaricate
Palti *father:* 5 Laish, Raphu *wife:*
6 Michal
Paltiel's father 5 Azzan
paltry 3 low, set 4 base, mean, poor,
puny, vile 5 borne, cheap, petty, small,
tatty, trash 6 common, little, measly, narrow, shabby, shoddy, sleazy, slight, trashy
7 limited, low-down, pitiful, rubbish, trivial
8 beggarly, inferior, picayune, piddling, rubbishy, trifling 9 worthless 10 despicable,
picayunish 11 ineffectual, Mickey Mouse,
unimportant 13 insignificant
paludous place 5 marsh
Pamela author 10 Richardson (Samuel)
pamper 3 pet 4 baby 5 humor, spoil
6 caress, cocker, coddle, cosset, cuddle,
dandle, fondle, regale, tickle 7 cater to,
cherish, gratify, indulge 11 mollycoddle
Irish: 6 cosher
pamphlet 5 tract 6 folder 7 booklet, leaflet 8 brochure 10 broadsheet
pan 3 rap 5 basin, blame, cut up, knock,
trash 6 attack 7 censure, condemn
8 denounce, ridicule 9 criticize, reprehend
Pan 5 Inuus 6 Faunus *father:* 6 Hermes
invention: 6 syrinx *lower part:* 4 goat
mother: 8 Penelope *pipe:* 6 syrinx *seat of
worship:* 7 Arcadia *son:* 7 Silenus

panacea 4 cure 6 elixir, relief, remedy
7 cure-all, nostrum 10 catholicon
Panacea's father 9 Asclepius 11 Aesculapius
pancake 8 flapjack, slapjack *French:*
5 crepe *Jewish:* 5 latke 6 blintz 7 blintze
Russian: 5 blini
Pandarus 6 archer 8 procuror *father:*
6 Lycaon *slayer:* 8 Diomedes
pandect 4 code 6 aperçu, digest, précis,
sketch, survey 8 syllabus 10 compendium
pandemoniac 7 avernal, hellish, riotous,
stygian 8 infernal, plutonic 9 cimmerian,
plutonian
pandemonium 3 din 4 hell, sink 5 babel,
Sodom 6 clamor, hubbub, jangle, racket,
tumult, uproar 7 cesspit 8 cesspool, disorder 9 confusion 10 hullabaloo, tintamarre
pander 4 pimp 5 bully, cadet, cater
8 fancy man, procurer 9 procuress
Pandion *daughter:* 6 Procne 9 Philomela
son: 6 Pallas
Pandora *creator:* 10 Hephaestus *husband:* 10 Epimetheus
pandurina 4 lute
panegyric 6 eulogy, praise 7 tribute
8 citation, encomium 9 laudation 10 salutation
panegyrical 9 laudative, laudatory, praiseful 10 eulogistic 11 encomiastic
panegyrize 4 hymn, laud 5 bless, cry up,
extol 6 praise 7 glorify, magnify 8 eulogize
9 celebrate
panel 4 gore, jury 5 board, label 6 hurdle
pan-fry 5 sauté
pang 4 ache, pain, stab 5 agony, prick,
spasm, throe 6 stitch, twinge 7 anguish,
torment
Pangloss' pupil 7 Candide
panhandler 6 beggar
panic 4 fear, wild 5 alarm, dread, scare
6 dismay, frenzy, fright, horror, terror 8 cold
feet, frighten, hysteria, stampede 11 trepidation 13 consternation
panoply 4 pomp, show 5 armor, array,
shine 6 parade 7 display, fanfare
panorama 4 view 5 orbit, range, reach,
scene, scope, sweep, vista 6 extent, radius
7 compass, purview 9 cyclorama
pan out 5 click 6 go over 7 come off, succeed
pant 3 aim 4 blow, gasp, gulp, huff, long,
puff, wind, wish 5 chuff, heave, throb,
yearn 6 aspire, desire, hunger, thirst,
wheeze 7 pulsate 9 palpitate
Pantagruel 5 giant *companion:* 7 Panurge *father:* 9 Gargantua *mother:* 7 Badebec
Pantaloon's daughter 9 Columbine
Panthea's husband 9 Abradatus

pantomime 6 ballet, dancer 7 charade
12 harlequinade

pantry 6 closet, larder 7 buttery

pants 5 jeans 6 slacks 7 drawers
8 britches, knickers, trousers

pantywaist 5 sissy 7 doormat, milksop

Panurge's companion 10 Pantagruel

Paolo's lover 9 Francesca

pap 4 food, mash, pulp, slop 5 paste, trash
7 aliment, garbage, rubbish 9 nutriment
10 sustenance 11 nourishment

papal 8 pontific 9 apostolic 10 pontifical
cape: 5 fanon, orale *court:* 5 Curia
decree: 8 decretal *envoy:* 6 nuncio
8 ablegate *letter:* 4 bull 10 encyclical

paper 4 card 5 essay, sheet, theme 6 letter, report 7 article, nominal 8 clerical, document 9 monograph, newspaper, wallpaper
10 memorandum 11 composition, publication 12 dissertation *arrangement:*
3 pad 6 tablet *coarse:* 9 newsprint *collection:* 4 file 7 dossier *combining form:*
6 papyro *copying:* 6 carbon *currency:*
5 scrip *measure:* 4 page, ream 5 quire,
sheet *roll:* 6 scroll *scrap:* 4 chad *size:*
3 cap 4 demi, demy 5 atlas, crown, folio,
legal, royal, sexto, sixmo 6 octavo, quarto
7 emperor 8 elephant, foolscap, imperial
10 typewriter *stiff:* 9 cardboard, wallboard
12 Bristol board *strong:* 5 kraft 6 manila
thin: 4 bank 6 pelure, tissue 9 onionskin
transparent: 8 glassine *writing:* 3 rag
6 vellum 9 parchment

paper folding *Japanese:* 7 origami

paphian 6 erotic, wanton

pappy 3 dad 4 soft 5 mushy 6 father,
spongy 7 pulpous, squashy, squishy,
squushy 8 squelchy, yielding 9 succulent

par 4 mean, norm 5 equal 6 median
7 average 8 equality, sameness, standard

parable 4 myth, tale 5 fable, story 8 allegory

parachute 7 bailout, skydive 8 paradrop
part: 5 riser 6 canopy 7 harness, ripcord

paraclete 6 helper 8 advocate, consoler
9 comforter 10 Holy Spirit 11 intercessor

parade 4 brag, pomp, show 5 array,
boast, flash, march, shine, strut 6 expose,
flaunt, reveal 7 declare, display, disport,
divulge, exhibit, fanfare, listing, marshal,
panoply, publish, recital, show off, trot out
8 brandish, disclose, movement, proclaim
9 advertise, cavalcade, formation, pageantry, promenade 10 exhibition, masquerade

paradigm 5 ideal, model 6 mirror 7 example, pattern 8 ensample, exemplar, standard 9 archetype, beau ideal, prototype

paradise 4 Eden, Zion 5 bliss 6 Canaan,
heaven, utopia 7 arcadia, elysium, nirvana
8 empyrean 9 Cockaigne, fairyland, Shan-

gri-la 10 Civitas Dei, lubberland, wonderland 12 New Jerusalem, promised land

Paradise Lost author 6 Milton (John)

paragon 3 gem 4 love, pick, tops
5 champ, cream, ideal, jewel, liken, match,
model, peach, trump 6 beauty, equate,
lovely 7 compare, epitome, pattern, phoenix 8 champion, exemplar, last word, nonesuch, parallel, ultimate 9 archetype, beau
ideal, nonpareil 10 apotheosis, assimilate

Paraguay *capital:* 8 Asuncion *monetary
unit:* 7 guarani

parallel 4 akin, even, like 5 align, alike,
along, equal, liken, match 6 agnate, double, equate, line up 7 compare, similar, uniform 8 analogue 9 analogous, collimate,
collocate, consonant, correlate, duplicate
10 assimilate, comparable, comparison, correspond, equivalent, similarity 11 counterpart, countertype, duplication, resemblance
13 correspondent, corresponding

parallelogram 5 rhomb 6 oblong, square
7 rhombus 8 rhomboid 9 rectangle

paralysis 5 palsy 9 impotence *combining form:* 5 lyses, lysis, plegy 6 plegia

paralyze 4 daze, maim, stun 5 close,
daunt 6 appall, bemuse, benumb, deaden,
disarm, dismay, weaken 7 astound, cripple,
destroy, disable, horrify, nonplus, petrify,
prevent, stupefy, unnerve 8 demolish,
enfeeble, knock out, shut down 9 prostrate
11 flabbergast 12 incapacitate

paramount 5 above, chief 6 master
7 capital, regnant, supreme 8 cardinal,
crowning, dominant, headmost, superior
9 sovereign, uppermost 10 commanding,
preeminent

paramour 5 lover, Romeo 6 master
7 amorist, Don Juan, gallant 8 Casanova,
fancy man, lothario, mistress 9 boyfriend,
inamorata, inamorato 10 girl friend

parapet 4 wall 7 bastion, bulwark, rampart
10 battlement, breastwork *part:* 6 merlon

paraphernalia 4 gear 6 outfit, tackle
8 materiel, tackling 9 apparatus, equipment, machinery, materials, trappings
11 furnishings, habiliments 13 accouterments, accoutrements, appurtenances

paraphrase 6 reword 7 restate, version
9 rendering, summarize, translate 10 transcribe 11 restatement, translation

parasite 4 laze 5 idler, leech, toady
6 infest, sponge, sucker 7 sponger 8 barnacle, deadbeat, ectozoan, entozoan,
hanger-on 9 dependent, sycophant
10 freeloader, smell-feast 11 bloodsucker

parasitic 7 fawning 8 cowering, cringing,
sponging, toadying, toadyish 9 groveling,
kowtowing, leechlike, truckling 11 bootlicking, freeloading, sycophantic

___ **paratus** 6 semper

paravane 5 otter

parboil 4 stew 5 sweat 6 seethe, simmer

Parcae 5 Fates *name:* 4 Nona 5 Morta 6 Decuma

parcel 3 box, cut, lot 4 body, clot, deal, mete, pack, part, plot, wrap 5 allot, array, batch, bunch, clump, group, piece, quota, share, tract 6 assign, bundle, clutch, divide, member, moiety, packet, ration 7 cluster, package, portion, prorate, section, segment 8 allocate, disburse, disperse, division, fragment 9 apportion 10 distribute

parch 3 dry 4 burn, sear 5 roast, toast 6 scorch 7 shrivel 9 dehydrate, desiccate, exsiccate

parchment 5 paper 6 vellum 8 document

pardon 4 free 5 remit, spare 6 accept, excuse 7 absolve, amnesty, condone, forgive, justify, release 8 liberate, reprieve, tolerate 9 acquittal, exculpate, indemnity, remission 10 absolution, indulgence 11 exculpation, exoneration, forgiveness, vindication

pardonable 6 venial 9 excusable

pare 3 cut 4 clip, crop, flay, peel, skin, trim 5 lower, prune, scalp, shave, shear, skive, slash, strip 6 reduce, remove 7 curtail, cut back, cut down, whittle 8 diminish

parent 4 make, sire 5 cause, hatch, spawn 6 author, create, father, mother, origin 7 forbear, produce 8 ancestor, begetter, forebear, generate 9 originate, procreate 10 forefather, progenitor

parenthetically 6 obiter 8 by the bye, by the way 9 in passing

parentless 6 orphan 8 orphaned

par excellence 4 fine 5 prime 6 famous 7 classic 8 champion, superior 9 classical, number one 10 first-class 12 preeminently

pariah 5 leper 7 Ishmael, outcast 8 castaway, déclassé, derelict 10 Ishmaelite 11 offscouring, untouchable *Japanese:* 3 eta

Paris *beloved:* 5 Helen *betrothed:* 6 Juliet *father:* 5 Priam *mother:* 6 Hecuba *slayer:* 11 Philoctetes *wife:* 6 Oenone

Paris *ancient name:* 7 Lutetia *avenue:* 13 Champs-Elysées *basilica:* 10 Sacré Coeur *cathedral:* 9 Notre Dame *city hall:* 12 Hôtel de Ville *college:* 8 Sorbonne *garden:* 9 Tuileries 10 Luxembourg *island:* 11 Île de la Cité *museum:* 4 Army 5 Cluny 6 Louvre *palace:* 6 Louvre 7 Bourbon *patron saint:* 9 Geneviève *racecourse:* 7 Auteuil *river:* 5 Seine *section:* 8 Left Bank 9 Right Bank 10 Montmartre 12 Latin Quarter *stock exchange:* 6 Bourse *subway:* 5 Metro *tower:* 6 Eiffel

Parisina *author:* 5 Byron (Lord) *husband:* 3 Azo *lover:* 4 Hugo *slayer:* 3 Azo

parity 7 analogy 8 equality, likeness, nearness, sameness 9 closeness 10 adequation, similarity, similitude 11 equivalence

parka 6 anorak, jacket 8 pullover

park designer 4 Vaux (Calvert) 6 Paxton (Joseph) 7 Alphand (Jean), Olmsted (Frederick Law)

parlance 4 talk 5 idiom 6 phrase, speech 7 diction, wordage, wording 8 phrasing, verbiage 9 verbalism 11 phraseology

parley 3 bet, use 4 chat, talk 5 speak, treat 6 advise, confab, confer, huddle, powwow 7 consult, discuss, meeting, utilize 8 collogue, colloquy, converse, dialogue 9 discourse 10 conference, converse in, discussion, rap session 11 confabulate 12 conversation 13 confabulation

parliament see legislature

parlor 5 salon

parlous 4 very 5 hairy, risky 6 chancy, damned, mighty, wicked 7 greatly 8 critical 9 dangerous, extremely, hazardous 11 exceedingly, excessively

Parnassian 4 poet

parochial 5 petty 6 narrow 7 bigoted, insular 9 sectarian, small-town 10 provincial

parody 3 ape, rib 4 mock 5 mimic, spoof 6 satire, send-up 7 imitate, takeoff 8 ridicule, spoofery, travesty 9 burlesque, imitation 10 caricature

paronomasia 3 pun 9 calembour

parous 6 gravid 8 childing, enceinte, pregnant 9 expectant, expecting

parrot 4 copy, echo 5 mimic, polly 6 repeat 7 chatter, imitate *kind:* 3 ara, kea 4 jako, kaka, lory 5 macaw 6 Amazon, budgie, kakapo 8 cockatoo, lorikeet, lovebird, parakeet 9 cockatiel, parrakeet 10 budgerigar

parrot fever 11 psittacosis

parrot fish 4 loro 5 lauia 6 scarid

parry 4 duck, fend, ward 5 avert, avoid, block, dodge, evade, fence, shirk 7 deflect, prevent 8 preclude, sidestep 9 forestall

Parsifal *composer:* 6 Wagner (Richard) *magician:* 8 Klingsor *quest:* 5 grail *son:* 9 Lohengrin *temptress:* 6 Kundry

parsimonious 4 mean 5 cheap, close, tight 6 frugal, stingy 7 miserly 9 niggardly, penurious 11 closefisted, tightfisted 12 cheese-paring 13 penny-pinching

parson 5 clerk 6 cleric, divine, rector 8 clerical, minister, preacher, reverend 9 churchman, clergyman 12 ecclesiastic

parsonage 5 manse

parson bird 3 poe, tui 4 koko

part 3 bit, cut, lot 4 bite, chip, duty, meed, role, side, some, spot, unit 5 allot, chunk, organ, piece, place, quota, scrap, sever, share, slice 6 behalf, cleave, detach, detail, divide, member, moiety, office, ration, region, sector, sunder 7 break up, disjoin, dissect, element, measure, portion, quality, quantum, quarter, section, segment 8 dissever, district, disunite, division, fraction, fragment, function, separate 9 allotment, allowance, component *combining form:* 3 mer 4 mere, mero, mery, toma, tome, tomy 5 meric, meris, parti 6 merous

partake 5 share 6 accept 7 receive 11 participate

Parthenon *sculptor:* 7 Phidias *site:* 9 Acropolis

partial 6 biased, unfair, warped 7 colored, half-way 8 one-sided 9 jaundiced 10 fractional, incomplete, prejudiced 11 fragmentary, predilected, predisposed *prefix:* 4 demi, semi

partiality 4 bent, bias 7 leaning 8 penchant, tendency 9 inclining, prejudice 10 chauvinism 11 inclination 12 one-sidedness, predilection

participant 4 aide 5 actor 6 fellow, helper, sharer 7 sharing 8 confrere 9 colleague

participate 5 share 7 partake

particle 3 ace, bit, dot, jot, ray 4 atom, damn, doit, dram, drop, hoot, iota, mite, mote, snap, spot, whit 5 atomy, crumb, fleck, grain, minim, ounce, scrap, shred, speck, whoop 6 morsel, smidge, smitch, tittle 7 dribbet, granule, modicum, smidgen 8 fragment 9 scintilla *atomic:* 3 ion 5 anion 6 cation *combining form:* 5 plast *elementary:* 3 psi, tau 4 kaon, muon, pion 5 boson, meson 6 baryon, hadron, lambda, lepton, photon, proton 7 fermion, hyperon, neutron, nucleon, upsilon 8 electron, mesotron, neutrino, positron *hypothetical:* 5 gluon, quark 6 parton 8 graviton *suffix:* 2 id *virus:* 6 virion *with negative charge:* 8 electron *with positive charge:* 6 proton 8 positron

motley 7 piebald 8 skewbald 9 multihued 10 variegated

particular 3 one 4 full, item, lone, nice, only, sole 5 fussy, picky, point, thing 6 dainty, detail, minute, single, unique 7 careful, correct, element, finical, finicky, precise, several, special, unusual 8 accurate, detailed, distinct, especial, exacting, itemized, separate, solitary, specific, thorough 9 clocklike, finicking 10 blow-by-blow, fastidious, individual, meticulous, pernickety, respective, scrupulous, speciality 11 appropriate, persnickety, punctilious

particularize 4 list 6 detail 7 itemize, specify 8 separate 9 enumerate, inventory, stipulate 11 specificate 13 individualize

parting 4 last 5 adieu, congé, final 7 good-bye 8 farewell 10 divergence, separation 11 leave-taking, valedictory

partisan 5 blind 6 backer, biased, cohort, warped 7 colored, devoted, devotee, die-hard, fanatic, patriot, sectary 8 adherent, advocate, champion, disciple, follower, henchman, one-sided, sectator, stalwart, upholder 9 factional, guerrilla, irregular, jaundiced, satellite, sectarian, supporter *combining form:* 4 crat 5 ocrat

partition 4 deal, wall 6 divide, lot out, screen 7 divorce, dole out, portion, rupture, section, split-up 8 disburse, dispense, disperse, division 9 severance 10 detachment, distribute, measure out, separation

partner 4 ally, chum, mate, wife 5 buddy, crony 6 cohort, fellow 7 comrade, husband 8 confrere, sidekick 9 assistant, associate, bedfellow, colleague, companion 10 accomplice, consociate 11 confederate *prefix:* 2 co

partnership 4 firm 5 tie-up 6 hookup 7 cahoots, company 8 alliance 11 association, combination, conjunction 12 consociation, togetherness 13 participation

parturient 6 gravid, parous 8 childing, enceinte, pregnant 9 expecting

parturition 5 birth 7 bearing 8 delivery 10 childbirth 12 childbearing *combining form:* 4 toky

party 4 ball, band, bevy, bloc, body, crew, fete, orgy, ring, side 5 actor, being, bunch, cabal, corps, covey, group, human, revel, troop, union 6 fiesta, mortal, outfit, person, sharer, social, soiree, troupe 7 carouse, cluster, combine, company, debauch, faction, shindig 8 alliance, assembly, carousal, creature, litigant, wingding 9 bacchanal, coalition, gathering, personage 10 detachment, individual, saturnalia 11 bacchanalia, celebration, combination, participant *food:* 4 cake 6 canapé 8 crudités, ice cream 11 hors d'oeuvre

parvenu 7 upstart 8 roturier 9 arriviste 12 nouveau riche

Pasha or Baba 3 Ali

Pashhur *father:* 5 Immer 8 Malchiah *son:* 8 Gedaliah

Pasiphaë *daughter:* 7 Ariadne, Phaedra *husband:* 5 Minos *son:* 8 Minotaur

pass 2 go 3 die, end, hap, hie, jog, top 4 beat, buck, fare, give, hand, omit, pose, wend 5 cease, lapse, occur, outdo, reach, relay, spend, while 6 crisis, demise, depart, elapse, exceed, expire, forget, hand on, happen, ignore, perish, permit, push on, repair, roll on, slight, slip by, strait, travel 7 approve, blink at, come off, decease, develop, devolve, journey, neglect, proceed, succumb 8 bequeath, exigency, fade away, fork over, hand down, juncture, outmatch, outshine, outstrip, overlook, peter out, transmit 9 blink away, disregard, emergency, terminate, transcend, transpire, while away **Afghanistan:** 5 Murgh **Afghanistan-Pakistan:** 6 Khyber **Alaska:** 5 White **Alps:** 3 col 5 Cenis, Loibl 7 Brenner, Ljubelj, Simplon 9 St. Bernard **California:** 5 Cajon **China-India:** 9 Karakoram **Colorado:** 3 Ute **into law:** 5 enact **Pakistan:** 5 Kilik **Russian:** 12 Caspian Gates **Tennessee:** 10 Cumberland **Turkey:** 13 Cilician Gates **Wyoming:** 5 South

passable 4 open 9 navigable, reachable, tolerable, unblocked 10 accessible, attainable, negotiable, travelable

passably 4 so-so 6 enough, fairly, rather 9 averagely, tolerably 10 moderately

passage 3 way 4 exit, fare, hall, line, path, road, text 5 route, shift 6 access, arcade, avenue, course, egress, strait, trajet, travel, tunnel, voyage 7 areaway, channel, couloir, excerpt, hallway, journey, traject, transit 8 corridor, transfer, traverse 9 enactment, quotation 10 transition, traversing 11 transmittal 12 transference, transmission 13 transmittance **air:** 7 windway **arched:** 6 arcade **Atlantic-Pacific:** 9 Northwest **combining form:** 4 meat, pora 5 meato **money:** 4 fare **roofed:** 6 arcade 9 breezeway **to water's edge:** 4 ghat

Passage to India author 7 Forster (Edward Morgan)

pass away 2 go 3 die 4 drop 6 cash in, demise, depart, elapse, expire, perish 7 decease, succumb

pass by 4 fail, omit 6 forget, ignore 7 neglect 8 overlook 9 disregard

passé 4 dead 5 dated 6 démodé, old hat 7 belated, demoded, disused, extinct, outworn 8 obsolete, outdated, outmoded 9 out-of-date 10 antiquated, superseded 12 old-fashioned 13 superannuated

passed master 5 maven, mavin 6 artist, expert, wizard 7 artiste 8 virtuoso 9 authority

passel 4 body, clot 5 array, batch, bunch, clump, group 6 bundle 7 battery, cluster

passenger 4 fare 8 traveler, wayfarer **hidden:** 8 stowaway **vessel:** 5 liner 7 steamer

passerine bird see bird, *songbird*

passing 5 death, sleep 6 demise 7 cursory, decease, elusory 8 fleeting, illusive, illusory 9 ephemeral, fugacious, momentary, transient 10 evanescent, short-lived, transitory

passion 3 ire 4 fire, fury, heat, itch, love, lust, rage, urge, zeal 5 agony, amour, anger, ardor, crush, dolor 6 béguin, desire, fervor, hurrah, misery, temper 7 craving, ecstasy, emotion, feeling, panting, rapture 8 appetite, devotion, distress, lyricism, outbreak, outburst 9 affection, calenture, eagerness, eroticism, prurience, pruriency, sentiment, suffering, transport 10 aphrodisia, appetition, dedication, enthusiasm, heartthrob, sensuality 11 affectivity, amorousness, infatuation, lustfulness 12 sensuousness 13 concupiscence, lickerishness

passionate 3 hot 5 fiery, testy 6 ardent, fervid, steamy, sultry 7 amorous, blazing, burning, excited, fervent, flaming, glowing, goatish, lustful, peppery, satyric 8 headlong, prurient, vehement 9 impetuous, irascible, lickerish, quickened, steamed up 10 hot-blooded, lascivious, libidinous, stimulated 11 high-powered, hot-tempered, precipitate 12 concupiscent, high-pressure, unrestrained 13 quick-tempered

passive 4 idle 5 inert, quiet, stoic 6 asleep, docile, latent, sleepy, stolid 7 bearing, patient 8 enduring, inactive, resigned, yielding 9 apathetic, compliant, lethargic, quiescent, tractable 10 nonviolent, phlegmatic, submissive 11 acquiescent, unresistant

pass on 3 die 6 convey, depart, expire, impart 7 decease 8 transmit 11 communicate

pass out 5 faint, swoon

pass over 4 fail, omit, pass 6 forget, ignore 7 neglect 8 overlook 9 disregard

Passover 5 Pasch **bread:** 4 azym 5 azyme, matzo 6 matzoh **meal:** 5 seder

past 2 by 3 ago, old 4 gone, late, once, yore 5 above, after, prior 6 beyond, bygone, former, gone-by, whilom 7 onetime, outside, present, quondam, without 8 anterior, foretime, lang syne, previous, sometime 9 antiquity, erstwhile, foregoing, precedent, preceding, yesterday 10 antecedent, yesteryear **combining form:** 6 preter 7 praeter **prefix:** 5 retro

pasta 5 dough, paste **kind:** 4 ziti 7 gnocchi, lasagna, pastina, ravioli 8 alfabeto, linguine, linguini, macaroni, rigatoni, tortelli 9 canneloni, quadrucci, spaghetti 10 malfattini, tagliolini, tortellini, vermicelli 11 cappelletti, stricchetti 12 paglia e fieno

paste 4 beat, drub, glue 5 dough, pound, stick, stuff 6 attach, batter, buffet, cement, pummel, spread, thrash, wallop 7 belabor 8 adhesive, lambaste, material

Pasternak hero 7 Zhivago

pasticcio see **pastiche**

pastiche 6 medley 7 mélange 8 mish-mash 9 potpourri 10 assortment, hodge-podge, hotchpotch, miscellany 11 gallimau-fry

pastime 4 game 5 hobby, sport 9 amuse-ment, diversion 10 recreation 13 entertain-ment

past master see **passed master**

pastoral 5 rural 6 rustic 7 bucolic, coun-try, idyllic, outland 8 agrarian, agrestic, innocent 10 campestral, out-country, pro-vincial

pastor's assistant 6 curate

pastry 3 bun, pie 4 baba, cake, flan, tart 5 torte 6 cornet, Danish, éclair, gâteau, kolach, pirogi, strata, torten (plural) 7 baklava, beignet, bouchée, dariole, fritter, gâteaux (plural), kolacky, palmier, savarin, strudel, tartlet 8 napoleon, papillon, piroshki, turnover, vacherin 9 barquette, cream puff, gugelhupf, kugelhupf, made-leine, petit four, vol-au-vent 10 cheesecake 11 profiterole 12 millefeuille *kind:* 4 filo, puff 5 choux, flaky 6 phyllo *shell:* 7 tim-bale 8 meringue

pasty 5 gluey 6 chalky, pallid, sickly

patch 3 bit, fix 4 do up, mend 5 cover, scrap 6 doctor, emblem, repair, revamp

patchwork 4 hash, olio, stew 5 salad 6 jumble 8 mishmash 10 hodgepodge, hotchpotch, miscellany, salmagundi

patchy 6 spotty, uneven 9 irregular

pate 4 head, poll 5 brain, crown 6 noddle, noggin, noodle

pâté de ____ 8 foie gras

patella 7 kneecap, kneepan

patent 4 open, rank 5 clear, gross, plain 7 evident, glaring, license, obvious 8 appar-ent, distinct, flagrant, manifest, palpable, unclosed 9 privilege, prominent

paternal 8 fatherly

path 3 way 4 fare, lane, line, road, walk 5 byway, route, track, trail 6 artery, avenue, course, street 7 highway, passage 9 boul-evard 12 thoroughfare

pathetic 3 sad 4 poor 6 moving, rueful 7 piteous, pitiful 8 pitiable 9 affecting

Pathfinder *author:* 6 Cooper (James Fenimore) *hero:* 6 Bumppo (Natty)

pathogen 4 germ 5 virus 6 fungus 9 bac-terium

pathological condition *suffix:* 2 ia

pathos 4 pity 9 poignance, poignancy

pathway 5 track, trail 6 course

patience 4 cool 9 composure, endurance, passivity, suffering, tolerance 10 equanim-ity, submission, sufferance, toleration 11 forbearance, longanimity, passiveness, resignation, self-control 13 long-suffering

patient 4 case, meek 6 patron 8 enduring 9 admitting, undaunted 11 susceptible 13 long-suffering *man:* 3 Job

patina 4 film 6 finish 7 surface 10 colora-tion

patio 5 court 7 terrace 9 courtyard

patois 4 cant 5 argot, lingo, slang 6 jar-gon 7 dialect 10 colloquial, vernacular

patriarch 4 sire 5 maker 6 author, father, gaffer 7 creator, founder 8 inventor 9 architect, generator, graybeard 10 origi-nator *biblical:* 5 David, Isaac, Jacob 7 Abraham

patrician 6 aristo 9 blue blood, gentleman 10 aristocrat

patriciate 5 elite 6 flower, gentry 7 aristoi, quality 8 optimacy 9 blue blood, gentility 10 upper crust 11 aristocracy

patrimony 6 legacy 8 heritage 9 heri-tance 10 birthright 11 inheritance

patriot 8 loyalist, partisan 9 flag-waver, guerrilla, irregular 11 nationalist *overzeal-ous:* 5 jingo 8 jingoist 10 chauvinist

Patroclus *friend:* 8 Achilles *slayer:* 6 Hector

patrol 5 scout, watch 7 protect

patrolman 3 cop 6 police 7 John Law, officer

patrol wagon 10 Black Maria

patron 5 angel 6 avowry, backer, client, surety 7 sponsor 8 backer-up, customer

patronage 5 aegis, trade 6 custom 7 backing, subsidy, traffic 8 auspices, busi-ness, cronyism 9 clientage, clientele 10 protection 11 benefaction, sponsorship 12 guardianship 13 pork-barreling

patronize 3 use 5 deign, favor 7 protect, support 8 frequent 10 condescend

patron saint *of beggars, cripples:* 5 Giles *of children:* 8 Nicholas *of England:* 6 George *of fishermen:* 5 Peter *of France:* 5 Denis *of Ireland:* 7 Patrick *of lawyers:* 4 Ives *of musicians:* 7 Cecilia *of Norway:* 4 Olaf *of physicians:* 4 Luke *of sailors:* 4 Elmo 8 Nicholas *of Scotland:* 6 Andrew *of shoemakers:* 7 Crispin *of Spain:* 5 James 8 Santiago *of Wales:* 5 David *of winegrowers:* 7 Vin-cent *of workers:* 6 Joseph

patsy 3 sap 4 dupe, fool, goat, gull, mark 5 chump 6 pigeon, sucker, victim 7 fall guy 9 scapegoat 11 whipping boy

patter 3 jaw, yak 4 cant, chat 5 argot, clack, lingo, prate, slang 6 babble, gabble, jargon, patois 7 chatter, dialect, prattle 9 yakety-yak 10 vernacular

pattern 4 plan 5 ideal, model, motif, order 6 design, device, figure, method, mirror, motive, system 7 example 8 ensample, exemplar, original, paradigm, standard, template 11 arrangement, orderliness

paucity 4 lack 6 dearth 7 fewness, poverty 8 scarcity 10 scarceness 13 insufficiency

Paulina's husband 7 Camillo 9 Antigonus

____ **Paulo** 3 São

Paul the Apostle *birthplace:* 6 Tarsus *companion:* 5 Silas, Titus 7 Artemas, Timothy 8 Barnabas *original name:* 4 Saul *place of conversion:* 8 Damascus *prosecutor:* 9 Tertullus *teacher:* 8 Gamaliel *tribe:* 8 Benjamin

paunch 3 pod 4 draw 5 belly, bowel, tummy 6 venter 7 abdomen, embowel, stomach 8 potbelly 9 bay window

pauper 4 bust, ruin 5 break 6 beggar 7 almsman, have-not, lazarus 8 bankrupt, indigent 10 down-and-out, impoverish

pauperism 4 need, want 6 penury 7 beggary, poverty 9 indigence, neediness 11 destitution

pause 3 gap 4 halt, hush, lull, stop, wait 5 break, comma, lapse, letup 6 hiatus, recess 7 caesura, respite 8 interval 9 cessation, interlude 10 hesitation, suspension 12 intermission, interruption

pave 3 lay, tar 5 cover, floor 7 overlie, surface 8 blacktop

pavement 6 tarmac 7 macadam 8 concrete, flagging, sidewalk

paw 4 feel, foot, hand 5 touch 6 finger, handle 7 palpate

pawn 4 hock, tool 5 token 6 pledge, puppet, stooge 7 earnest, warrant 8 impledge

Pax see Irene

Pax 3 Dei 6 Romana 10 Brittanica

pay 3 fee 4 give, hire, quit, wage 5 clear, remit, spend, yield 6 defray, expend, lay out, outlay, pony up, render, return, salary, settle, square, tender 7 bring in, cough up, fork out, guerdon, requite, satisfy, stipend 8 clear off, disburse, pungle up, shell out 9 discharge, emolument, indemnify, liquidate, plunk down, reimburse 10 compensate, recompense, remunerate

payable 3 due 5 owing 6 mature, unpaid 7 overdue 9 unsettled 11 outstanding

payload 4 haul 5 cargo 6 burden, lading 7 freight

payment 3 fee, tax 4 duty 6 return 7 premium 12 compensation

payoff 3 fix 5 bribe 6 climax, profit, reward 8 decisive 11 retribution

PDQ 6 at once 8 directly, right off 9 forthwith, instanter, instantly, right away 11 immediately, straightway

pea 6 legume

peace 3 pax 4 calm, ease, rest 5 amity, order, quiet 6 repose 7 concord, harmony 8 serenity 11 tranquility 12 tranquillity

peaceable 6 irenic 7 amiable, pacific 8 amicable, friendly, pacifist 10 neighborly, nonviolent 11 complaisant 12 pacificatory

peaceful 4 cool 6 irenic, placid, steady 7 equable, pacific 8 composed, constant, pacifist 9 collected, unruffled 10 nonviolent

pause: 5 truce

peacemaker 8 appeaser, mediator, placater 10 arbitrator, negotiator 11 pacificator

peace officer 3 cop 6 police 7 John Law, officer 9 patrolman, policeman

peach 3 rat 4 blab 5 dandy, nifty 6 betray, inform, snitch, squeak, squeal 8 jim-dandy 9 freestone, humdinger, nectarine 10 clingstone 11 crackerjack

Peach State 7 Georgia

peachy 4 fine, nice 6 divine 8 glorious 9 excellent, hunky-dory, marvelous

peacockish 5 showy, swank 6 chichi 7 splashy 10 flamboyant 11 pretentious

peacock-like 8 pavonine

peak 3 alp, top 4 acme, apex, bill, roof 5 abate, crest, crown, mount, visor 6 apogee, lessen, rebate, recede, summit, vertex, zenith 7 dwindle 8 capsheaf, capstone, decrease, diminish, meridian, mountain, pinnacle, taper off *Adirondack:* 9 Whiteface *Africa's highest:* 4 Kibo *Alaska-Canada:* 12 Mt. Saint Elias *Andes:* 4 Ruiz 5 Torrá *Apennines:* 5 Amaro *Argentina:* 4 Azul 5 Negra, Payún *Bavaria:* 5 Arber *Berkshires:* 10 Mt. Greylock *Black Hills:* 10 Mt. Rushmore *Bolivia:* 5 Cuzco, Tahua, Ubina 6 Sajama *Borneo:* 4 Raja *California:* 6 Sonora 7 Palomar 8 Half Dome, Mt. Shasta 9 Excelsior *California's highest:* 9 Mt. Whitney *Canada:* 5 Keele *Canaries:* 5 Teide 8 Tenerife *Carpathian:* 4 Rysy *Catskill:* 5 Mt. Vly 8 Mt. Pisgah *Caucasus:* 5 Ushba 6 Elbrus *Chile:* 4 Mayo, Pili 5 Paine, Pular *Colombia:* 4 Tama 5 Neiva *Colorado:* 3 Ute 5 Pikes 9 Purgatory *combining form:* 3 acr, akr 4 acro, akro *Cuba:* 8 Turquino *Ecuador:* 10 Chimborazo *England:* 11 Scafell Pike *Ethiopia:* 4 Guna 5 Holla *France:* 5 Pilat *French Guiana:* 5 Amana *Georgia:* 16 Springer Mountain *Glacier National Park:* 8 Kootenai *Greece:* 6 Mt. Ossa 6 Pelion *Himalayas:* 3 Api 5 Kamet 7 Lhotse I 8 Lhotse II 10 Gasherbrum *Honshū:* 4 Yari 10 Yarigatake *Idaho:* 13 Mt. Pend Oreille *Iran:* 8 Damavand *Japan:* 4 Sobo 5 Oyama 7 Sobozan *Java:* 6 Slamet *Jordan:* 8 Mt. Gilead *Karakoram Range:*

10 Masherbrum *Karakoram Range's highest:* 7 Dapsang 12 Godwin Austen *Maine:* 10 Mt. Katahdin 10 Saddleback *Montana:* 8 Gallatin *Nevada:* 5 Mt. Ely. *Newfoundland:* 9 Gros Morne *New Hampshire:* 11 Mt. Monadnock *New Zealand:* 5 Mt. Una 6 Mt. Cook 7 Aorangi 10 Mt. Aspiring *Oahu:* 5 Kaala *Oregon:* 6 Mt. Hood *Papua New Guinea:* 10 Mt. Victoria *Pennine Alps:* 10 Matterhorn, Mont Cervin *Philippines:* 4 High *Pyrenees:* 11 de Vignemale *Russia's highest:* 6 Elbrus *Scotland:* 8 Ben Nevis *Spain:* 5 Yelmo 8 Mulhacén *Switzerland:* 3 Dom 4 Dôle, Tôdi 5 Eiger, Mönch 6 La Dôle, Rusein 7 Pilatus 8 Jungfrau *U.S.S.R.'s highest:* 9 Communism *Utah:* 5 Kings *Venezuela:* 7 Mt. Icutú *Vermont:* 8 Haystack, Stratton 10 Mt. Ascutney 11 Mt. Mansfield *Washington:* 9 Mt. Olympus, Mt. Rainier 13 Mt. Saint Helens *White Mts.:* 12 Mt. Washington *Wyoming:* 10 Grand Teton 11 Elk Mountain *Yukon:* 4 King 7 Mt. Logan

peaked 3 wan 4 pale, sick 5 acute, drawn, piked, sharp 6 sickly 7 pointed 8 acicular 9 aciculate, acuminate, acuminous, cuspidate

peal 4 bell, bong, ring, toll 5 chime, knell

peanut 4 mani, puny 5 petty, small 6 goober, measly, paltry 8 earthnut, picayune

pear 4 Bosc 5 Anjou, Hardy 6 Comice, Garber, Seckel 7 Kieffer, LeConte 8 Bartlett *cider:* 5 perry

Pearl Mosque site 4 Agra

Pearl of the Pacific 4 Guam

pearly 8 nacreous

pear-shaped 8 pyriform

peasant 4 boor, carl, hick, kern, peon, serf 5 churl, knave, yokel 6 rustic 7 bumpkin, hayseed, redneck, villein 9 hillbilly *Arab:* 6 fellah *Latin-American:* 9 campesino *Russian:* 5 mujik 6 moujik, muzhik, muzjik

peccary 7 tayassu 8 javelina

peck 3 lip, lot, nag 4 beak, buss, fuss, kiss, much 5 smack 6 carp at, smooch 7 henpeck 8 osculate 9 great deal

pecker 3 neb, nib 4 beak, bill, nose 5 snoot, snout 9 proboscis

peculate 8 embezzle

peculiar 3 odd 5 queer, weird 6 proper, unique 7 bizarre, curious, oddball, strange, unusual 8 singular 9 diacritic, eccentric 10 diagnostic, individual 11 distinctive

peculiarity 4 mark 5 savor, trait 7 feature, quality 8 property 9 affection, attribute, character

pecuniary 6 fiscal 8 monetary 9 financial

pedagogue 5 tutor 7 teacher 12 schoolmaster

Pedaiah *brother:* 9 Shealtiel *father:* 6 Parosh 7 Kolaiah *grandson:* 9 Jehoiakim *son:* 4 Joed, Joel

pedal digit 3 toe

pedantic 3 dry 4 arid, dull 5 booky 7 bookish, donnish, erudite, inkhorn, learned 8 academic, didactic 9 dryasdust, schoolish 10 scholastic 11 book-learned

peddle 4 hawk, push, sell, vend 5 shove 6 monger 8 huckster

peddler 6 hawker, monger, pusher, vendor 7 chapman, higgler, packman, roadman 8 huckster, mongerer, outcrier 9 cheapjack, cheap-john, piepoudre 10 colporteur 12 costermonger

pedestal part 4 base, dado 6 plinth 7 surbase

pedestrian 4 blah, dull 5 banal, heavy, inane 6 dreary, jejune, stodgy 7 humdrum, prosaic 8 banausic, monotone, plodding, truistic 10 monotonous, wishy-washy 11 commonplace 13 unimaginative

pedigree 5 blood 6 origin, stemma 7 descent, lineage 8 ancestry, purebred 9 genealogy, pureblood 10 extraction, family tree

peduncle 4 stem

peek 6 glance 7 glimpse

peel 4 bark, pare, skin 5 flake, scale, strip 8 flake off 9 exfoliate 10 desquamate 11 decorticate, excorticate

peeled 4 bare, open 5 naked 7 denuded, exposed 8 stripped 9 uncovered

peep 3 pip, spy 4 chip, look, ogle, peer 5 cheep, chirp, stare, tweet 6 glance, peek in, squeak 7 chipper, chirrup, chitter, glimpse, look-see, peek out, tweedle, twitter 8 look-over, oeillade

peeping tom 5 snoop 6 peeper, voyeur 7 prowler, snooper

peer 3 eye, pry 4 bore, gape, gawk, gaze, lord 5 equal, glare, gloat, noble, snoop, stare 6 goggle, squint 9 associate *British:* 4 duke, earl 5 baron 7 marquis 8 viscount *highest:* 4 duke *lowest:* 5 baron

Peer Gynt *author:* 5 Ibsen (Henrik) *beloved:* 7 Solveig *composer:* 5 Grieg (Edvard) *mother:* 3 Ase

peerless 4 only 5 alone 6 unique 8 dominant 9 matchless, nonpareil, paramount, sovereign, unequaled, unmatched, unrivaled 11 unparagoned 12 unparalleled

peeve 3 get, irk 4 miff, rile, roil 5 pique 6 nettle, put out 7 disturb, provoke 8 irritate 9 aggravate 10 exasperate

peevish 5 huffy, waspy 7 carping, fretful, pettish, waspish 8 captious, caviling, critical, petulant, snappish 9 fractious, irritable

peewee 4 runt, tiny 5 dwarf, midge, pygmy 6 midget 7 manikin, minikin 8 dwarfish,

Tom Thumb **9** miniature **10** diminutive, homunculus **11** lilliputian

Peewee or Della **5** Reese

peg **3** pin **4** plod, plug **5** dowel, prong, stake, throw **6** attach **8** identify

Pegasus **5** horse, steed *rider:* **11** Bellerophon

Pekah *father:* **8** Remaliah *slayer:* **6** Hoshea *victim:* **8** Pekahiah

Pekahiah *father:* **7** Menahem *slayer:* **5** Pekah

Pelatiah's father **4** Ishi **7** Benaiah **8** Hananiah

Peleg *father:* **4** Eber *son:* **3** Reu

Peleus *brother:* **7** Telamon *father:* **6** Aeacus *half brother:* **6** Phocus *son:* **8** Achilles *victim:* **8** Eurytion *wife:* **6** Thetis

pelf **5** money, rhino, stuff **7** needful

Pelias *country:* **6** Iolcus *father:* **8** Poseidon *half brother:* **5** Aeson *son:* **7** Acastus

Pelican State **9** Louisiana

Pelion and ___ **4** Ossa

Pelleas *beloved:* **9** Mélisande *brother, slayer:* **6** Golaud

Pelles *daughter:* **6** Elaine *grandson:* **7** Galahad

pellet **3** wad **4** ball, dung, shot **5** bolus **6** bullet

Pellinore *slayer:* **6** Gawain *son:* **5** Torre **6** Dornar **7** Lamerok **8** Percival **9** Agglovale

pell-mell **5** chaos, snarl **6** ataxia, huddle, muddle, rashly **7** clutter, hotfoot **8** disarray, disorder, headlong, stampede **9** confusion, hurriedly **10** carelessly, heedlessly **11** hurry-scurry, impetuously **12** indiscreetly **13** helter-skelter, incontinently

pellucid **5** clear, sheer **6** limpid, lucent **7** crystal **8** clear-cut, luminous **9** unblurred **10** see-through **11** crystalline, translucent

Pelops *father:* **8** Tantalus *son:* **6** Atreus **8** Pittheus, Thyestes *wife:* **10** Hippodamia

pelota see jai alai

pelt **3** fly, fur **4** beat, drub, fell, hide, rush, skin, whop **5** fleet, haste, hurry, pound, scoot **6** batter, hammer, jacket, pummel, thrash, wallop **7** beeline, belabor, hotfoot

pen **3** hem, mew **4** cage, coop, crib, jail, yard **5** fence, hedge **6** cooler, corral, kennel, prison, shut in, stylus **7** close in, enclose

penalize **4** fine **5** judge, mulct **6** amerce, punish **7** chasten, condemn, correct **8** chastise **9** castigate **10** discipline

penalty **4** fine, loss **5** mulct **7** forfeit **10** amercement

penance **3** rue **4** ruth **7** remorse **9** atonement, attrition, penitence, penitency **10** contrition, repentance **11** compunction

penchant **4** bent **7** leaning **8** tendency **9** inclining **10** proclivity, propensity **11** disposition, inclination **12** predilection

pendant **4** flag, jack **5** color **6** banner, ensign, pennon **7** pennant **8** bannerol, standard, streamer **9** correlate **10** complement

pendent **7** hanging, pensile **9** pendulant, pendulous, suspended, undecided, unsettled **12** undetermined

pending **6** during **9** undecided, unsettled **12** undetermined

___ Pendragon **5** Uther

pendulous **6** wobbly **7** hanging, pendent, pensile **8** wavering **9** faltering, suspended, tentative **10** hesitating **11** vacillating

Penelope *father:* **7** Icarius *father-in-law:* **7** Laertes *husband:* **7** Ulysses **8** Odysseus *mother:* **8** Periboea *son:* **10** Telemachus *suitor:* **7** Agelaus

penetrable **6** porose, porous **8** pervious **9** permeable

penetrate **3** jab **4** bore, go in, stab **5** break, drill, drive, enter, knife, prick **6** charge, come in, insert, invade, pierce **7** ingress, pervade **8** encroach, permeate, puncture, saturate, trespass **9** insinuate, introduce, percolate, perforate, transfuse **10** impregnate

penetrating **4** keen **5** acute, crisp, sharp **6** astute, biting, shrewd **7** cutting, ingoing **8** clear-cut, incisive **9** trenchant **11** quick-witted, sharp-witted **12** quick-sighted, sharp-sighted

Peneus *daughter:* **6** Daphne *father:* **7** Oceanus *mother:* **6** Tethys

Peninnah's husband **7** Elkanah

peninsula **4** neck **10** chersonese *Alaska:* **5** Kenai **6** Seward *Australia:* **6** Tasman *Barents Sea:* **5** Kanin *British colony:* **9** Gibraltar *Canada:* **8** Labrador *Cape Cod:* **9** Race Point **12** Monomoy Point *Chile:* **5** Swett *Costa Rica:* **3** Osa *Denmark:* **7** Jutland *eastern United States:* **8** Delmarva *Estonia:* **5** Sorve *Florida:* **8** Pinellas **9** Canaveral *France:* **5** Glens *Greece:* **4** Acte **10** Chalcidice **11** Peloponnese **12** Peloponnesus *Guam:* **5** Orote *Hong Kong:* **7** Kowloon *Honshū:* **3** Izu **5** Miura *Massachusetts:* **7** Cape Ann, Cape Cod *Mexico:* **7** Yucatan **14** Baja California *Michigan:* **8** Keweenaw *Middle East:* **5** Sinai *New Guinea:* **4** Huon *New Jersey:* **9** Sandy Hook *New Zealand:* **5** Banks, Mahia *Northern Territory:* **4** Gove *Northwest Territories:* **4** Hall **7** Boothia **8** Melville *Ontario:* **5** Bruce *Persian Gulf:* **9** Ras Tanura **13** Ras at Tannurah *Quebec:* **5** Gaspé *Russia:* **4** Kola **5** Taman, Yamal **6** Kolski, Taimyr **9** Kamchatka *Scotland:*

7 Cantyre, Kintyre *South Australia:* 4 Eyre
5 Yorke 6 Yorkes *southeast Asia:*
5 Malay 9 Indochina 12 Farther India
southeastern Europe: 6 Balkan *south-
western Asia:* 6 Arabia 7 Arabian *south-
western Europe:* 7 Iberian *Texas:* 9 Matagorda *Tierra del Fuego:* 5 Mitre *Turkey:*
8 Anatolia 9 Asia Minor *Ukraine:* 5 Kerch
Wales: 5 Gower, Lleyn *Washington:*
7 Olympic *west Africa:* 11 Sierra Leone
Wisconsin: 4 Door

Peninsular State 7 Florida

penis 7 phallus

penitence 3 rue 4 ruth 5 grief, qualm
6 regret, sorrow 7 anguish, penance,
remorse, sadness, scruple 8 distress, humbling 10 contrition, debasement, repentance 11 compunction, degradation, humiliation, self-reproof 12 contriteness,
self-reproach

penitent 5 sorry 8 contrite 9 regretful,
repentant 10 apologetic, remorseful

penitentiary see prison

penman 5 clerk 6 author, scribe, writer
12 calligrapher 13 calligraphist

penmanship 4 hand 6 ductus, script
7 writing 11 calligraphy, chirography, handwriting

pen name 6 anonym 9 pseudonym
10 nom de plume *Addison (Joseph):*
4 Clio *Arouet (François-Marie):* 8 Voltaire
Beyle (Marie-Henri): 12 George Orwell *Brontë (Anne):*
9 Acton Bell *Brontë (Charlotte):* 10 Currer
Bell *Brontë (Emily):* 9 Ellis Bell *Clemens
(Samuel):* 9 Mark Twain *Dickens
(Charles):* 3 Boz *Dodgson (Charles
Lutwidge):* 12 Lewis Carroll *Dupin
(Amandine-Aurore):* 10 George Sand
Evans (Mary Ann): 11 George Eliot *Faust
(Frederick):* 8 Max Brand *Franklin (Ben-
jamin):* 11 Poor Richard *Geisel (Theo-
dore):* 7 Dr. Seuss *Glidden (Frederick):*
9 Luke Short *Lamb (Charles):* 4 Elia
Munro (Hector Hugh): 4 Saki *Poquelin
(Jean-Baptiste):* 7 Molière *Porter (William
Sidney):* 6 O. Henry *Ramé (Maria Louise):*
5 Ouida *Russell (George):* 2 AE *Thibault
(Jacques-Anatole-François):* 13 Anatole
France *Viaud (Louis-Marie-Julien):*
10 Pierre Loti

pennant 4 flag, jack 5 color 6 banner,
ensign, pennon 7 pendant 8 standard,
streamer 9 banderole

penniless 4 poor 5 broke 8 bankrupt
11 impecunious

pennilessness see penury

pennon 4 flag, jack 5 color 6 banner,
ensign 8 bannerol, gonfalon, gonfanon
9 banderole, oriflamme

Pennsylvania *battlefield:* 10 Gettysburg
capital: 10 Harrisburg *college, university:*
5 Gratz, Thiel 6 Drexel, Lehigh, Temple
7 La Salle 8 Alliance, Bryn Mawr, Bucknell
9 Dickinson, Lafayette, St. Joseph's, Villanova 10 Pittsburgh, Swarthmore *nickname:*
13 Keystone State *state bird:* 12 ruffed
grouse *state flower:* 14 mountain laurel

penny pincher 5 miser, piker, stiff 7 niggard 8 tightwad 9 skinflint 10 cheapskate
11 cheeseparer 12 moneygrubber

penny-pinching 5 close, tight 6 stingy
7 miserly 9 niggardly, penurious 11 closefisted, tightfisted 12 cheeseparing, parsimonious

pensile 7 hanging, pendent 9 pendulant,
pendulous, suspended

pensioner 7 retiree 8 retirant

pensive 3 sad 4 blue 6 musing 7 wistful
8 absorbed, saddened, thinking 9 pondering, withdrawn 10 abstracted, cogitative,
meditative, melancholy, reflecting, reflective, ruminating, ruminative, thoughtful
11 preoccupied, speculative 13 contemplative

Pentateuch 5 Torah 6 Exodus 7 Genesis, Numbers 9 Leviticus 11 Deuteronomy

Penthesilea *queen of:* 7 Amazons
slayer: 8 Achilles

Pentheus *grandfather:* 6 Cadmus *king
of:* 6 Thebes *mother:* 5 Agave

Penuel *father:* 3 Hur 7 Shashak *grandfather:* 5 Judah

penumbra 5 shade 6 shadow 7 umbrage

penurious 4 poor 5 close, needy, tight
6 stingy 7 miserly 8 beggared, dirt poor,
indigent 9 destitute, niggardly 10 avaricious 11 closefisted, impecunious, necessitous, tightfisted 12 cheeseparing, impoverished, parsimonious 13 penny-pinching

penury 4 need, want 7 poverty 8 poorness 9 indigence, neediness, privation
11 destitution

peon 4 serf 5 slave 6 drudge, slavey,
toiler 7 laborer, peasant 9 dray horse,
workhorse 11 galley slave *Anglo-Saxon:*
4 esne

peonage 4 yoke 6 thrall 7 bondage, helotry, serfdom, slavery 9 servitude, thralldom, villenage 11 enslavement

people 3 kin, men 4 folk 5 plebs
6 occupy, plebes, public, tenant 7 inhabit,
society 8 populace, populate 9 commonage, commoners, common men, community, plebeians 10 commonalty 11 inhabi-
tants, rank and file, third estate *combining
form:* 4 demo, ethn 5 ethno

pep 2 go 3 vim 4 dash, push 5 getup,
punch, verve, vigor 6 energy, starch
7 potency 8 vitality 9 animation, hardihood
10 get-up-and-go, liveliness

pepo 5 gourd, melon 6 squash 7 pumpkin 8 cucumber

pepper 3 dot 5 chili, speck 7 cayenne, freckle, paprika, pimento, speckle, stipple 8 capsicum, pimiento, sprinkle 9 bespeckle

peppery 4 keen, racy 5 alert, cross, fiery, spicy, zesty 6 cranky, lively, snappy, spunky 7 gingery, piquant, pungent 8 choleric, poignant, spirited 9 irascible, temperish 10 mettlesome, passionate 11 highhearted, hot-tempered 12 highspirited 13 quick-tempered

peppy 4 keen 5 alert 6 bright, lively 7 animate 8 animated, spirited 9 sprightly, vivacious

Pepys' journal 5 Diary

Pequod *cabin boy:* 3 Pip *captain:* 4 Ahab *harpooner:* 6 Daggoo 8 Queequeg, Tashtego *mate:* 8 Starbuck

Pequot sachem 5 Uncas

per 2 by 3 via 4 with 7 by way of, through 8 by dint of 9 by means of

perambulate 4 walk 6 stroll 8 traverse 9 promenade

per capita 3 all 4 each 5 aside 6 apiece

perceive 3 see 4 espy, feel, know, mark, mind, note, take 5 grasp, seize, sense 6 behold, descry, detect, divine, notice 7 discern, observe, realize 8 identify 9 apprehend, recognize 10 comprehend, understand

perceptible 5 clear, lucid 6 signal 8 palpable, sensible, tangible 10 cognizable, detectable, noticeable, observable 11 appreciable, conspicuous, discernible, perspicuous 12 recognizable

perception 4 idea 5 image 6 acumen, notion 7 conceit, concept, insight, thought 9 cognition 10 impression

perceptive 4 keen, sage, wise 5 acute, aware, sharp 6 sophic 7 gnostic, knowing 9 insighted, sagacious, sensitive 10 discerning, insightful, prehensile, prehensive, responsive

perch 3 bar, set 4 land 5 light, roost 6 alight, settle 7 set down, sit down, station

perchance 5 maybe 7 perhaps 8 possibly

percipience 3 wit 6 acumen 8 keenness 10 astuteness, shrewdness 11 discernment, penetration 12 perspicacity

percolate 4 ooze, seep, sift 5 exude 6 charge, filter, strain 7 pervade 8 permeate, saturate, transude 9 penetrate, transfuse 10 impregnate 11 impenetrate

percussion 3 jar 4 bump, jolt 5 clash, crash, shock 6 impact 9 collision 10 concussion *instrument:* (see at **musical instrument**)

Perdita *father:* 7 Leontes *mother:* 8 Hermione

perdition 3 pit 4 hell 5 abyss, hades 7 Gehenna, inferno 9 barathrum, damnation 10 underworld 11 netherworld, Pandemonium

Père Goriot author 6 Balzac (Honoré)

peregrination 4 trek, trip 7 journey, travels 10 expedition

peremptory 5 bossy, fixed 7 certain, decided 8 absolute, decisive, imperial, positive 9 imperious, masterful, obstinate 10 high-handed, imperative 11 domineering, magisterial, overbearing

perennial 3 old 7 durable 8 enduring, lifelong 9 continual, long-lived, permanent, perpetual, unceasing 10 continuing, inveterate, perdurable 11 long-lasting

Perez *brother:* 5 Zerah *father:* 5 Judah *mother:* 5 Tamar

perfect 3 fit 4 full, pure, rank, very 5 exact, gross, ideal, model, right, round, sheer, sleek, slick, sound, utter, whole 6 choate, entire, expert, intact, needed, polish, proper, refine, simple, smooth 7 express, precise, unmixed 8 absolute, complete, finished, flawless, integral, masterly, outright, positive, required, suitable, unbroken, unflawed 9 downright, excellent, fleckless, masterful, requisite, unalloyed, undamaged, undiluted, uninjured 10 consummate, impeccable, unimpaired

perfection 5 arête, ideal, merit 6 virtue 7 paragon, quality 9 integrity, wholeness 10 entireness, excellence, excellency 12 completeness

perfidious 5 false, venal 6 untrue 7 unloyal 8 disloyal, recreant 9 alienated, deceitful, dishonest, estranged, faithless, mercenary 10 traitorous, unfaithful 11 treacherous

perfidiousness see **perfidy**

perfidy 6 deceit 7 falsity, sellout, treason 8 betrayal, foul play 9 falseness, treachery 10 disloyalty, infidelity 13 faithlessness

perforate 3 pit 4 bore 5 drill, drive, prick, probe, punch 6 pierce 8 puncture 9 penetrate

perform 2 do 3 act, end 4 play, take, work 5 enact, react 6 behave, effect, finish, wind up 7 achieve, execute, fulfill, operate, playact 8 bring off, complete, function 9 discourse, implement, personate 10 accomplish, perpetrate

peformance 3 act 4 deed, feat, show, work 5 stunt 6 acting, action 7 concert, exploit, matinee 8 behavior, efficacy 9 discharge, execution 10 efficiency 11 fulfillment 12 presentation

performer 4 doer, mime 5 actor, mimic 6 mummer, player, worker 7 actress, artiste, trouper 8 thespian 9 playactor 12 impersonator *suffix:* 3 ant, ent

perfume 4 balm 5 aroma, cense, scent, smell, spice 6 sachet 7 bouquet, incense, odorize 9 aromatize, fragrance, redolence *source:* 4 musk 5 attar, myrrh, orris 6 chypre 8 bergamot

perfumer 6 Chanel (Coco)

perfunctory 4 cool 5 stock, usual 6 wooden 7 cursory, routine, unaware 8 careless, standard 9 automatic 10 impersonal, mechanical 11 indifferent, involuntary, superficial, unconcerned 12 uninterested

pergola 5 arbor, bower

perhaps 5 maybe 6 theory 7 suppose 8 feasibly, possibly 9 perchance 10 conjecture, imaginably 11 conceivably, speculation

periapt 4 juju, luck, zemi 5 charm 6 amulet, fetish, mascot 8 talisman 10 phylactery

Pericles *father:* 10 Xanthippus *mistress:* 7 Aspasia *mother:* 8 Agariste

peril 4 risk 6 danger, hazard, menace 7 jeopard 8 endanger, exposure, jeopardy, openness 9 liability 10 compromise, jeopardize, subjection 12 endangerment

perilous 5 hairy, risky, shaky 6 chancy, touchy, wicked 7 tottery, unsound 8 delicate, dreadful, ticklish, unstable, unsteady 9 dangerous, desperate, hazardous, unhealthy 10 jeopardous 11 treacherous

____ Perilous 5 Siege

perimeter 3 hem, rim 4 brim, edge 5 ambit, brink, skirt, verge 6 border, fringe, margin 7 circuit, compass 8 boundary 9 periphery 13 circumference

period 3 age, end, era 4 days, span, stop, term, time 5 close, epoch 6 ending, season 7 closing, closure 8 duration 9 cessation 10 conclusion, generation 11 termination

periodical 5 organ 6 review 7 journal 8 magazine 9 alternate, newspaper, recurrent, recurring 10 isochronal 11 isochronous 12 intermittent

Peri opera 5 Dafne 8 Euridice

peripatetic 6 roving 7 nomadic, vagrant 8 ambulant, vagabond 9 itinerant, itinerate, wandering, wayfaring 11 perambulant

periphery see perimeter

periphrasis see pleonasm

perish 3 die, end 4 pass 5 cease 6 demise, depart, expire, vanish 7 decease, decline, go under, succumb 8 collapse, pass away 9 disappear

perjure 3 lie 5 trick 6 delude 7 deceive, mislead 8 forswear 10 equivocate 11 prevaricate

perk 4 gain, mend 6 look up 7 freshen, improve, smarten 9 percolate 10 ameliorate, convalesce, perquisite, recuperate

permanent 5 fixed 6 stable 7 abiding, durable, lasting 8 constant, enduring 9 continual, diuturnal, perduring, perennial 10 invariable, perdurable 12 imperishable

permeable 6 porose, porous 8 passable, pervious 10 penetrable

permeate 4 fill, soak 5 imbue, steep 6 charge, drench, imbrue, infuse, invade 7 diffuse, ingrain, pervade, suffuse 8 saturate 9 interfuse, penetrate, percolate, transfuse 10 impregnate, infiltrate 11 impenetrate

permissible 7 allowed 8 approved, bearable, endorsed 9 allowable, permitted, tolerable, tolerated 10 acceptable, admissible, authorized, sanctioned 11 unforbidden 12 unprohibited

permission 5 leave 6 permit 7 consent, license 8 approval, sanction 9 allowance 10 acceptance, sufferance 11 approbation, endorsement 12 acquiescence 13 authorization

permit 3 let 4 have 5 admit, allow, grant, leave 6 suffer 7 consent 8 sanction, tolerate 9 allowance, authorize 10 permission, sufferance 13 authorization

permitted 5 licit

permutation 5 sport 6 change 7 novelty 10 alteration, innovation 11 vicissitude 12 modification

pernicious 3 bad 4 evil 5 fatal, swart, toxic 6 deadly, lethal, malign, mortal, wicked 7 baleful, baneful, harmful, hurtful, killing, malefic, miasmic, noxious, ruinous 8 damaging, sinister, venomous, virulent 9 malignant, miasmatic, pestilent, poisonous 10 maleficent 11 deleterious, destructive, detrimental, devastating

Pernod flavor 5 anise 8 licorice

perorate 4 rant, rave 5 mouth 7 declaim, soapbox 8 bloviate, harangue

perpend 4 mind 5 study, weigh 6 ponder 8 consider, think out 9 think over 10 excogitate 11 contemplate

perpendicular 5 plumb 7 stand-up, upright 8 straight, vertical 10 straight-up

perpetrate 2 do 4 pull 5 wreak 6 commit, effect 7 inflict, execute, perform

perpetual 7 endless, eternal 8 constant, unending 9 ceaseless, continual, incessant, perennial, unceasing 10 continuous 11 everlasting, unremitting 12 interminable

perpetuate 4 keep 6 secure 7 bolster, support, sustain 8 conserve, eternize, maintain, preserve 10 eternalize 11 immortalize

perplex 4 balk, pose 5 amaze, befog, ravel, snarl 6 baffle, bemuse, muddle, puzzle, tangle, thwart 7 astound, confuse, ensnarl, mystify, nonplus, perturb, stumble 8 astonish, bewilder, confound, entangle,

surprise 10 complicate, discompose
11 intertangle

perquisite 3 tip 5 right 6 income 7 cumshaw, largess 8 appanage, gratuity
9 lagniappe, pourboire, privilege 10 birthright 11 prerogative

per se 5 alone 6 as such, solely 8 in itself

persecute 4 bait, rack, ride 5 harry,
hound, worry, wrong 6 harass, heckle,
molest 7 afflict, dragoon, oppress, outrage,
torment, torture 8 aggrieve

Persephone 4 Kore 10 Proserpina *father:*
4 Zeus 7 Jupiter *husband:* 5 Hades, Pluto
mother: 5 Ceres 7 Demeter

Perseus *father:* 4 Zeus 7 Jupiter *grandfather:* 8 Acrisius *mother:* 5 Danaë *victim:*
6 Medusa 8 Acrisius *wife:* 9 Andromeda

perseverance 8 tenacity 9 diligence,
endurance 11 persistence 13 steadfastness

persevere see persist

persevering see persistent

Persian *fairy:* 4 peri *fire worshiper:*
5 Parsi 6 Parsee *governor:* 6 satrap *mystic:* 4 sufi *poet:* 5 Hafez 8 Firdausi, Firdawsī 11 Omar Khayyam *prophet:*
9 Zoroaster *robe:* 6 caftan *sacred books:*
6 Avesta *sun-god:* 7 Mithras *title:* 4 shah
writing: 9 cuneiform

persiflage 6 banter 8 backchat, badinage,
raillery, repartee, snip-snap

persist 4 go on, last 5 abide 6 endure,
hang on, linger, obtain 7 carry on, perdure,
prevail 8 continue 9 persevere 12 carry
through

persistence 3 run 6 course 8 duration
9 endurance 10 continuity 11 continuance
12 continuation *combining form:* 6 stasia,
stasis

persistent 6 dogged 7 archaic 8 enduring
9 insistent, primitive, steadfast, tenacious,
unevolved 10 determined, relentless,
unshakable 11 perseverant, persevering,
undeveloped, unremitting 13 perseverative

persnickety 4 nice 5 fussy, picky
6 choosy 7 finicky 8 clerkish 10 fastidious

person 3 guy, man, one 4 body, chap,
coot, life, self, soul 5 being, human, stick
6 entity, fellow, galoot, mortal 8 creature,
specimen 10 individual *admirable:*
6 mensch *ambitious:* 8 go-getter 10 upand-comer *betrothed:* 6 fiancé 7 fiancée
clumsy: 5 klutz 6 kludge *combining form:*
6 prosop 7 prosopo *contemptible:* 3 cad
4 heel 5 knave 6 varlet *distinguished:*
3 VIP 5 great *dressy:* 12 clotheshorse
eighty-year-old: 12 octogenarian *energetic:* 10 ball of fire *guilty:* 7 culprit *meek:*
7 nebbish *ninety-year-old:* 12 nonagenarian *non-Jewish:* 3 goy 7 gentile *of mixed
ancestry:* 5 métis 7 mestizo, mulatto

8 octoroon *one-hundred-year-old:*
11 centenarian *rude:* 4 boor *rural:* 4 hick
sixty-year-old: 12 sexagenarian *virtuous:*
6 zaddik 7 tzaddik *wealthy:* 3 nob
5 nabob

personable 6 comely 7 shapely 8 charming, handsome 10 attractive 11 good-looking

personage 3 VIP 4 body, life, soul
5 being, chief, human, nabob 6 bigwig, mortal 7 big shot, notable 8 creature, eminence, somebody 9 dignitary 10 individual,
notability 11 personality

personal 3 own 5 privy 7 private, special
8 peculiar 10 individual, particular *combining form:* 4 idio

personal effects 5 goods, stuff, traps
6 things, tricks 10 belongings 11 possessions

personality 3 ego, VIP 5 chief, humor,
nabob, seity 6 makeup, nature, temper
7 big shot, ipseity, notable, selfdom 8 eminence, identity, selfhood, selfness, somebody 9 character, dignitary, personage
10 complexion, notability 11 disposition,
singularity, temperament 13 individualism,
individuality

personate 2 do 3 act 4 play 5 enact
6 embody, mirror, typify 7 perform, playact
9 discourse, epitomize, exemplify, personify, represent 10 illustrate 11 emblematize

personify 6 embody, mirror, typify 8 manifest 9 body forth, epitomize, exemplify,
incarnate, objectify, represent, symbolize
10 illustrate 11 emblematize, exteriorize,
externalize, materialize, personalize,
reincarnate 12 substantiate

perspective 5 scape, vista 7 lockout, outlook 8 prospect 9 viewpoint

perspicacious 4 keen 5 cagey, heady
6 argute, astute, shrewd 9 astucious, sagacious 10 perceptive 11 penetrating, sharpwitted 12 quick-sighted, sharp-sighted

perspicacity 3 wit 6 acumen 8 astucity,
keenness 10 astuteness, shrewdness
11 discernment, penetration, percipience

perspicuity 7 clarity 8 lucidity 9 clearness, limpidity, plainness 12 explicitness

perspicuous 5 clear, lucid 6 lucent
7 crystal 8 clear-cut, luculent, luminous, pellucid 9 unblurred 11 unambiguous

perspiration 4 work 5 sweat 9 exudation
abnormal: 8 hidrosis

perspire 5 sweat 7 swelter

persuadable 8 amenable, exorable,
suasible, swayable 9 acceptant, acceptive,
receptive

persuade 3 win 4 coax, draw, lead, move,
sway 5 bring, touch 6 affect, assure,
entice, induce, prompt, reason 7 convert,

entreat, impress, satisfy, win over 8 convince, talk into 9 argue into, prevail on 11 bring around, prevail upon

persuasible　see persuadable

persuasion 3 ilk, lot 4 bias, cast, cult, mind, mold, sect, sort, type, view 5 class, creed, faith, order 6 belief, church, nature 7 feeling, opinion 8 religion 9 character, communion, prejudice, sentiment 10 cajolement, connection, conviction, partiality 11 affiliation, description 12 denomination

Persuasion author 6 Austen (Jane)

pert 4 arch, bold, keen, rude, wise 5 alert, fresh, nervy, sassy, saucy, smart 6 bantam, brazen, bright, cheeky, daring, lively 7 animate, forward 8 animated, impudent, spirited 9 audacious, sprightly, vivacious 11 smart-alecky 13 disrespectful

pertain 4 join, vest 5 apply 6 bear on, belong, relate 7 combine, concern, connect 8 bear upon 9 associate

pertaining to　*suffix:* 2 al, an, ar, ic 3 ean, ese, ial, ile, ine, ist, ory 4 ical 5 ative, istic 6 itious 7 istical

pertinacious 6 dogged, mulish 7 willful 8 perverse, stubborn 9 obstinate, tenacious 10 bullheaded, headstrong, inflexible, refractory, self-willed, unshakable, unyielding

pertinent 3 apt, fit 5 ad rem 7 apropos, germane 8 apposite, material, pointful, relevant 10 applicable, pertaining 11 applicative, applicatory, appropriate

perturb 5 upset, worry 6 bother, dismay, flurry 7 agitate, disturb, fluster, trouble 8 disquiet, unsettle 10 discompose, disconcert

Peru　*capital:* 4 Lima *conqueror:* 7 Pizarro (Francisco) *monetary unit:* 3 sol

peruse 4 read, scan 5 study 6 survey 7 examine

pervade 4 fill 5 bathe, imbue 6 charge 8 permeate, saturate 9 penetrate, percolate, transfuse 10 impregnate 11 impenetrate

perverse 5 balky 6 cranky, mulish, ornery, putrid, rotten 7 corrupt, froward, restive, vicious, wayward 8 contrary, depraved, stubborn 9 irritable, miscreant, nefarious, obstinate, unhealthy 10 degenerate, headstrong, refractory, self-willed, unyielding, villainous 11 stiff-necked, wrongheaded 12 cross-grained, pertinacious, unreasonable

pervert 4 ruin, skew, warp 5 abuse, belie, color, twist 6 debase, garble, misuse 7 corrupt, debauch, deprave, distort, falsify, outrage 8 ill-treat, maltreat, misapply, miscolor, misstate, mistreat 9 animalize, brutalize, misemploy, mishandle 10 bastardize, bestialize, demoralize, misimprove, prostitute 12 misrepresent

pervious 6 porose, porous 9 permeable 10 penetrable

pesky 4 mean, ugly 8 annoying 9 troublous, vexatious 10 bothersome 11 troublesome

pessimist 5 cynic 7 killjoy 9 Cassandra, defeatist, doomsayer, worrywart 10 fussbudget 11 crepehanger, misanthrope

pessimistic 6 gloomy 7 cynical 10 despairing

pest 4 bane 5 worry 6 bother, pester, plague, vermin 7 heckler, nudnick, trouble 8 badgerer, irritant, nuisance, vexation 9 annoyance, besetment, tormentor

pester 4 ride 5 annoy, devil, harry, tease, worry 6 badger, bother, harass, plague 7 bedevil, hagride, torment 8 irritant, nuisance 9 annoyance, beleaguer, besetment, tantalize 10 botherment 11 botheration

pesticide 3 DDT 7 biocide 9 fungicide, germicide, vermicide 11 bactericide, insecticide, microbicide, rodenticide

pestiferous 6 deadly 7 baneful, noxious 9 pestilent 10 pernicious 12 pestilential

pestilence 5 curse 6 plague 7 scourge

pestilential 5 fatal 6 deadly, lethal, mortal, vexing 7 baneful, deathly, noxious 9 pestilent 10 irritating, pernicious 11 mortiferous

pestle 4 mano 5 pilum 6 muller *vessel:* 6 mortar

pet 3 hug 4 dear, love, pout, sulk 5 grump, loved 6 caress, cosset, cuddle, dandle, fondle, stroke 7 beloved, cherish, darling, embrace, indulge 8 blue-eyed, favorite

petcock 3 tap 4 gate 5 valve 6 faucet, spigot 7 hydrant 8 stopcock

peter 4 fade, fail 5 abate, cease 6 lessen, rebate, recede 7 dwindle 8 decrease, diminish, taper off 9 drain away

Peter Pan　*author:* 6 Barrie (James) *character:* 4 John 5 Wendy 7 Michael 9 Tiger Lily 10 Tinker Bell *dog:* 4 Nana *pirate:* 4 Hook, Smee

Peter the Apostle　*brother:* 6 Andrew *father:* 5 Jonah *original name:* 5 Simon

Peter the Great　*father:* 6 Alexis *wife:* 7 Eudoxia 9 Catherine

Pethuel's son 4 Joel

petite 3 wee 5 dwarf, small 6 bantam, little, monkey 8 smallish 9 miniature 10 diminutive 11 lilliputian

petition 3 ask, beg, sue 4 plea, pray, suit 5 plead, sue to 6 appeal, orison, prayer, sue for 7 beseech, entreat, implore, request 8 entreaty 10 supplicate 11 application, imploration, imprecation 12 supplication

Petrarch's beloved 5 Laura
Petrified Forest author 8 Sherwood (Robert)
petrify 4 daze, numb, stun 5 alarm 6 appall, bedaze, bemuse, benumb, dismay 7 horrify, startle, stupefy, terrify 8 frighten, paralyze
Petruchio's wife 9 Katharina, Katharine
pettifogger 6 lawyer 7 shyster 10 bush lawyer 13 jackleg lawyer
pettish see petulant
petty 4 base, mean, puny 5 light, minor, small 6 casual, little, measly, paltry, peanut 7 pimping, trivial, unvital 8 childish, niggling, peddling, picayune, piddling, piffling, trifling 9 frivolous, hair-drawn, small-beer 10 irrelevant, negligible, picayunish, shoe-string, ungenerous 11 impertinent, Mickey Mouse, unimportant
petty officer 6 noncom, yeoman
petulant 5 cross, huffy, sulky, testy, waspy 7 fretful, grouchy, peevish, pettish, waspish 8 snappish 9 fractious, irascible, irritable, querulous
peyote 6 cactus, mescal *drug:* 9 mescaline
Phaedra *father:* 5 Minos *husband:* 7 Theseus *mother:* 8 Pasiphaë *sister:* 7 Ariadne *stepson:* 10 Hippolytus
Phaëthon's father 6 Helios 7 Phoebus
phantasm 4 dream, fancy, ghost, shade 6 mirage, shadow, spirit, vision 7 eidolon, fantasy, fiction, specter 8 daydream, delusion, illusion, revenant, spectrum 9 invention, nightmare 10 apparition 11 fabrication, ignis fatuus 13 hallucination
phantom 5 ghost, shade 6 eidola (plural), shadow, spirit 7 eidolon, specter 8 phantasm, revenant, spectrum 10 apparition
Phanuel's daughter 4 Anna
pharaoh 3 Tut 4 Seti 6 Ahmose, Ramses 7 Harmhab 8 Ikhnaton, Thutmose 9 Amenhotep, Merneptah 11 Tutankhamen
pharisaism 4 cant 9 hypocrisy 10 sanctimony, Tartuffery, Tartuffism 12 pecksniffery
pharisee 8 Tartuffe 9 hypocrite, lip server 10 dissembler 12 dissimulator
pharmacist 8 druggist 10 apothecary *British:* 7 chemist
pharos 6 beacon 10 lighthouse
Pharsalus, battle of *vanquished:* 6 Pompey *victor:* 6 Caesar (Julius)
phase 4 hand, look, side, view 5 angle, color, facet, state 6 aspect 7 posture 8 position 9 condition, semblance, situation, viewpoint 10 appearance, complexion
PhD exam 5 orals
pheasant 5 argus, monal 8 tragopan
Phebe's husband 7 Silvius

Phèdre author 6 Racine (Jean)
phenomenal 4 rare 5 gross 6 unique 7 unusual 8 material, physical, sensible, singular, tangible, unwonted 9 corporeal, objective 10 remarkable 11 exceptional, substantial, unthinkable 13 extraordinary
phenomenon 4 fact 5 event 6 marvel, wonder 7 anomaly, miracle, paradox, portent, prodigy, reality, stunner 9 actuality, sensation 10 experience, uniqueness 11 peculiarity, singularity, unusualness
philander 4 wolf 5 chase, dally, flirt 6 chaser, masher, pursue, trifle 7 Don Juan 8 Casanova, womanize 9 ladies' man, womanizer 10 fool around, lady-killer, mess around, play around 11 philanderer
philanthropic 4 good 6 giving, humane 8 donating 10 altruistic, benevolent, bighearted, charitable, freehanded 11 civic-minded, freehearted, kindhearted, magnanimous, openhearted 12 contributing, eleemosynary, greathearted, humanitarian
philanthropist *American:* 6 Girard (Stephen) 7 Cornell (Ezra) 8 Carnegie (Andrew) 9 Rosenwald (Julius) 11 Rockefeller (John Davison) *English:* 11 Wilberforce (William) *Swedish:* 5 Nobel (Alfred)
Philemon's wife 6 Baucis
philharmonic 4 band 8 symphony 9 orchestra
Philip of Macedonia *father:* 7 Amyntas *son:* 9 Alexander
philippic 6 tirade 8 diatribe, harangue, jeremiad
Philippics author 6 Cicero
Philippines *capital:* 6 Manila *discoverer:* 8 Magellan (Ferdinand) *hero:* 5 Rizal (Jose) *language:* 7 Spanish, Tagalog, Visayan 8 Filipino *liberator:* 9 MacArthur (Douglas) *monetary unit:* 4 peso *president:* 6 Marcos (Ferdinand), Aquino (Corazon)
Philippi victor 6 Antony (Marc) 8 Octavian
Philip the Tetrarch *father:* 5 Herod *mother:* 9 Cleopatra
philistine 4 boob, boor, lout 5 clown 7 Babbitt 8 boeotian 9 barbarian, bourgeois, vulgarian 10 capitalist, middlebrow 11 materialist
Philistine *champion:* 7 Goliath *city:* 4 Gath, Gaza 5 Ekron 6 Ashdod 8 Ashkelon *foe:* 5 David 6 Samson *god:* 5 Dagon
Philoctetes *father:* 5 Poeas *victim:* 5 Paris
Philomela 11 nightingale *father:* 7 Pandion *ravisher:* 6 Tereus *sister:* 6 Procne
philosopher *American:* 5 Adler (Mortimer), James (Henry, William), Quine (Willard), Royce (Josiah) 6 Langer (Susanne)

7 Marcuse (Herbert) 9 Santayana (George) *Arab:* 8 Avicenna *British:* 7 Russell (Bertrand) 12 Wittgenstein (Ludwig) *Chinese:* 6 Lao-tsu 7 Mencius, Tai Chen 9 Confucius *Danish:* 11 Kierkegaard (Soren) *Dutch:* 7 Spinoza (Baruch) *English:* 4 Mill (John Stuart), More (Henry, Thomas) 5 Bacon (Francis), Locke (John), Moore (George), Occam (William) 6 Hobbes (Thomas), Ockham (William) 7 Bentham (Jeremy), Russell (Bertrand), Spencer (Herbert), Whewell (William) 9 Whitehead (Alfred North) *Finnish:* 11 Westermarck (Edward) *French:* 5 Comte (Auguste), Taine (Hippolyte) 6 Pascal (Blaise), Sartre (Jean-Paul), Valery (Paul) 7 Abelard (Peter) 8 Maritain (Jacques), Rousseau (Jean-Jacques), Teilhard (Pierre) 9 Descartes (Rene) 10 Saint-Simon (Comte de), Schweitzer (Albert) *German:* 4 Kant (Immanuel), Marx (Karl) 5 Hegel (Georg Wilhelm Friedrich), Wolff (Christian von) 6 Fichte (Immanuel, Johann), Herder (Johann von) 7 Jaspers (Karl), Leibniz (Gottfried) 8 Spengler (Oswald) 9 Heidegger (Martin), Nietzsche (Friedrich), Schelling (Friedrich von) 12 Schopenhauer (Arthur) 14 Albertus Magnus *Greek:* 4 Zeno 5 Plato, Timon 6 Thales 7 Gorgias, Proclus 8 Diogenes, Epicurus, Longinus, Socrates 9 Aristotle 10 Anaxagoras, Democritus, Empedocles, Heraclitus, Parmenides, Protagorus, Pythagorus, Xenocrates, Xenophanes 11 Anaximander 12 Theophrastus *Indian:* 13 Gautama Buddha *Irish:* 8 Berkeley (George) *Italian:* 6 Ficino (Marsilio) *Jewish:* 5 Buber (Martin), Philo 12 Philo Judaeus *Roman:* 6 Seneca (Lucias Annaeus) 8 Boethius (Anicius), Plotinus 9 Lucretius *Scottish:* 4 Hume (David), Mill (James), Reid (Thomas) 7 Stewart (Dugald) *Spanish:* 6 Suarez (Francisco) 13 Ortega y Gasset (Jose) *Swedish:* 10 Swedenborg (Emanuel)

philosophers' stone 6 elixir

philosophical 4 calm 8 composed, rational 9 temperate

philosophy 3 tao 4 yoga 5 deism 7 dualism, inquiry, wholism 8 stoicism 10 empiricism, pragmatism 12 Cartesianism

Phineas *beloved:* 9 Andromeda *tormentors:* 7 Harpies *wife:* 9 Cleopatra

Phinehas *father:* 3 Eli 7 Eleazar *grandfather:* 5 Aaron

phlegm 6 apathy 7 ataraxy 8 calmness, coolness, stoicism 9 composure, sangfroid, stolidity, unconcern 10 equanimity 11 impassivity, nonchalance

phlegmatic 3 dry 4 calm, dull 5 aloof, stoic 6 stolid 8 sluggish 9 apathetic, impassive, incurious, lethargic 11 indifferent, unconcerned

Phlegyas *daughter:* 7 Coronis *father:* 4 Ares, Mars *son:* 5 Ixion

phobia see fear

Phobos 4 moon 9 satellite *brother:* 6 Deimos *father:* 4 Ares, Mars

Phocus *father:* 6 Aeacus 8 Ornytion *half brother:* 6 Peleus 7 Telamon *mother:* 8 Psamathe *slayer:* 6 Peleus 7 Telamon *wife:* 7 Antiope

Phoebe 5 Diana 7 Artemis *daughter:* 4 Leto *father:* 9 Leucippus *mother:* 2 Ge 4 Gaea

phoebus 3 sun 7 daystar

Phoebus see Apollo

Phoenician *city:* 4 Acre, Tyre 5 Sidon *colony:* 8 Carthage *god:* 4 Baal 6 Eshmun *goddess:* 6 Baltis 7 Astarte

Phoenix 4 bird *brother:* 5 Cilix *pupil:* 8 Achilles *sister:* 6 Europa *team:* 4 Suns

phony 4 fake, hoax, sham 5 bogus, cheat, faker, false, fraud, put-on, snide, spoof 6 humbug, pseudo 7 swindle 8 impostor, spurious 9 brummagen, charlatan, imposture, pinchbeck, pretender 11 counterfeit

photograph 3 mug, pic 4 film, snap 5 kodak, shoot 6 glossy 7 filmize, picture, tintype 8 cinemize, likeness, snapshot 9 snapshoot *three dimensional:* 8 hologram

photographer 8 camerist, photoist 9 cameraman 10 shutterbug 11 snapshooter *famous:* 3 Ray (Man) 4 Capa (Robert), Haas (Ernst), Hine (Lewis), Riis (Jacob) 5 Adams (Ansel), Arbus (Diane), Atget (Eugene), Brady (Mathew), Evans (Frederick, Walker), Horst (Horst Peter), Karsh (Yousuf), Lange (Dorothea), Model (Lisette), Parks (Gordon), Smith (W. Eugene), Weber (Bruce), White (Clarence, Minor) 6 Abbott (Berenice), Avedon (Richard), Beaton (Cecil), Brandt (Bill), Coburn (Alvin), Curtis (Edward S.), Newton (Helmut), Porter (Eliot), Rowell (Galen), Siegel (Eliot), Strand (Paul), Talbot (William Henry Fox), Weegee, Weston (Brett, Edward) 7 Brassaï, Cameron (Julia Margaret), Emerson (Peter), Jackson (William Henry), Kertész (Andre), Salomon (Erich), Siskind (Aaron), Snowdon (Earl of), Thomson (John), Watkins (Carleton) 8 Callahan (Harry), Cosindas (Marie), Daguerre (Louis-Jacques-Mande), Kasebier (Gertrude), Scavullo (Francesco), Steichen (Edward), Steinert (Otto) 9 Caponigro (Paul), Feininger (Andreas, T. Lux), Leibovitz (Annie), Meyrowitz (Joel), O'Sullivan (Timothy), Rejlander (Oscar), Rothstein (Arthur), Stieglitz (Alfred), Winogrand (Garry) 10 Cunningham (Imogen), Heartfield (John), Moholy-Nagy (Laszlo) 11 Bourke-White (Margaret), Eisenstaedt (Alfred) 12 Mapplethorpe (Robert) 14 Cartier-Bresson (Henri)

photographic 5 exact, vivid 7 graphic 8 accurate, detailed 9 pictorial 11 picturesque *solution:* 4 hypo 5 fixer, toner 7 reducer 9 developer

phrase 3 put 4 term, word 5 couch, idiom 6 byword, slogan 7 diction, express, styling, wordage, wording 8 locution, parlance, verbiage 9 catchword, formulate, verbalism, watchword 10 expression, shibboleth

Phrixus *father:* 7 Athamus *mother:* 7 Nephele *sister:* 5 Helle *wife:* 9 Chalciope

Phrontis *brother:* 5 Argus, Melas 9 Cytisorus *father:* 7 Phrixus *mother:* 9 Chalciope

Phrygian *god:* 3 Men 4 Atys 5 Attis *goddess:* 6 Cybele *king:* 5 Midas 7 Gordius

phthisis 2 TB 11 consumption, white plague 12 tuberculosis

phylactery 4 juju, luck, zemi 5 charm 6 amulet, fetish, mascot 7 periapt 8 talisman

physic 4 cure, heal 5 purge 6 remedy 7 relieve 8 medicant, medicine 9 cathartic, purgative 10 medicament, medication

physical 5 brute, gross, lusty 6 bodily, carnal 7 fleshly, natural, somatic 8 corporal, material, sensible, tangible, visceral 9 corporeal, elemental, objective 10 elementary, phenomenal 11 substantial

physician 2 MD 3 doc 5 medic 6 doctor, medico 7 medical, surgeon 9 mediciner 10 specialist 12 practitioner *American:* 4 Rush (Benjamin), Salk (Jonas) 5 Minot (George), Spock (Benjamin), Still (Andrew) 6 Jarvik (Robert), Murphy (John), Weller (Thomas) 7 Huggins (Charles), Robbins (Frederick), Theiler (Max) 8 Richards (Dickinson) 9 Sternberg (George Miller) *Arab:* 8 Avicenna *Austrian:* 6 Mesmer (Anton) *Canadian:* 5 Osler (William) *combining form:* 5 iatro 7 iatrist *English:* 4 Ross (Ronald) 6 Harvey (William), Jenner (Edward, William), Willis (Thomas) 8 Sydenham (Thomas) *French:* 5 Widal (Fernand) 7 Laveran (Charles) 10 Schweitzer (Albert) *German:* 7 Sylvius (Franciscus) *Greek:* 5 Galen 11 Hippocrates *Italian:* 7 Galvani (Luigi) *slang:* 8 sawbones *South African:* 7 Barnard (Christaan) *Swiss:* 10 Paracelsus; (see also **Nobel Prize Winner,** *physiology or medicine;* surgeon)

physicist *American:* 4 Rabi (Isidor Isaac), Ting (Samuel) 5 Fermi (Enrico), Gibbs (J. Willard), Kusch (Polykarp), Mayer (Maria-Goeppert), Pauli (Wolfgang), Pupin (Michael), Segre (Emilio), Smyth (Henry Dewolf), Stern (Otto) 6 Teller (Edward), Townes (Charles), Wigner (Eugene) 7 Goddard (Robert), Purcell (Edward) 8 Einstein (Albert), Gell-Mann (Murray), McMillan (Edwin), Millikan (Clark, Robert), Mulliken (Robert), Shockley (William), Van Allen (James) 9 Michelson (Albert), Schwinger (Julian) 11 Oppenheimer (J. Robert) *Austrian:* 4 Mach (Ernst) 7 Doppler (Christian) 11 Schrodinger (Erwin) *British:* 6 Stokes (George) 7 Tyndall (John) 8 Thompson (Benjamin, Silvanus) *Chinese:* 4 Yang (Chen Ning) *Danish:* 4 Bohr (Aage, Niels) *Dutch:* 6 Zeeman (Pieter) 7 Huygens (Christian), Lorentz (Hendrik), Zernike (Frits) 11 Van der Waals (Johannes) *English:* 4 Snow (Charles Percy) 5 Jeans (James), Joule (James) 6 Dalton (John), Kelvin (Baron), Newton (Isaac), Powell (Cecil) 7 Faraday (Michael), Hodgkin (Dorothy), Thomson (George, Joseph, William) 8 Rayleigh (Lord), Robinson (Robert) 9 Wollaston (William) 10 Richardson (Owen), Rutherford (Ernest), Wheatstone (Charles) *French:* 4 Néel (Louis) 5 Arago (François) 6 Ampere (Andre-Marie), Perrin (Jean-Baptiste) 7 Coulomb (Charles-Augustin de), Kastler (Alfred), Reaumur (Rene-Antoine de) 8 Lippmann (Gabriel) *German:* 3 Ohm (Georg) 4 Laue (Max von), Wien (Wilhelm) 5 Hertz (Gustav, Heinrich), Stark (Johannes) 6 Jensen (Hans), Lenard (Philipp), Nernst (Walther), Planck (Max) 7 Meitner (Lise) 8 Roentgen (Wilhelm) 9 Helmholtz (Hermann von), Kirchhoff (Gustav), Mossbauer (Rudolf) 10 Fahrenheit (Daniel), Hofstadter (Robert) *Indian:* 5 Raman (Chandrasekhara) *Irish:* 6 Walton (Ernest) *Italian:* 5 Rossi (Bruno), Volta (Alessandro) 7 Galileo, Galvani (Luigi) 10 Torricelli (Evangelista) *Japanese:* 6 Yukawa (Hideki) 8 Tomonaga (Shin'ichirō) *Mexican:* 8 Vallarta (Manuel) *Russian:* 4 Tamm (Igor) 5 Landau (Lev) 9 Prokhorov (Aleksandr) *Scottish:* 4 Tait (Peter) 6 Wilson (Charles) 7 Maxwell (James Clerk) *Swedish:* 7 Rydberg (Johannes) 8 Angstrom (Anders), Siegbahn (Kai, Karl) *Swiss:* 6 Zwicky (Fritz) 7 Piccard (Auguste); (see also **Nobel Prize Winner,** *physics*)

physiologist *English:* 8 Starling (Ernest) *German:* 5 Weber (Ernst), Wundt (Wilhelm) 7 Schwann (Theodor) 9 Helmholtz (Hermann von) *Italian:* 11 Spallanzani (Lazzaro); (see also **Nobel Prize Winner,** *physiology or medicine*)

physique 4 body, form 5 build, frame, habit, shape 6 figure 7 anatomy, habitus 9 structure 12 constitution 13 configuration

pianist *American:* 4 Nero (Peter), Wild (Earl) 5 Arrau (Claudio), Davis (Anthony), Janis (Byron), Tatum (Art), Watts (Andre) 6 Duchin (Peter), Joplin (Scott), Serkin (Peter, Rudolf), Waller (Fats) 7 Cliburn (Van), Istomin (Eugene), Ohlsson (Garrick), Perahia (Murray), Winston (George) 8 Graffman (Gary), Grainger (Percy), Horowitz (Vladimir), Pennario (Leonard) 10 Johannesen (Grant), Rubinstein (Arthur) *Austrian:* 6 Czerny (Karl) 8 Schnabel (Artur) 9 Rosenthal (Moriz) *Bulgarian:* 11 Weissenberg (Alexis) *Cuban:* 5 Bolet (Jorge) *English:* 4 Hess (Myra) 5 Katin (Peter), Ogdon (John) 6 Curzon (Clifford) *Finnish:* 8 Palmgren (Selim) *French:* 6 Cortot (Alfred-Denis) 7 Cziffra (Gyorgy) 9 Entremont (Philippe) 10 Saint-Saens (Camille) *German:* 5 Bülow (Hans von) 6 Kempff (Wilhelm) 8 Schumann (Clara, Robert) 9 Gieseking (Walter) *Hungarian:* 5 Liszt (Franz) 6 Vasary (Tamas) *Italian:* 6 Busoni (Ferruccio) 8 Clementi (Muzio) *Polish:* 6 Chopin (Frederic) 7 Hofmann (Josef) 9 Landowska (Wanda) 10 Paderewski (Ignacy) *Russian:* 6 Berman (Lazar), Gilels (Emil) 7 Richter (Sviatoslav) 8 Pachmann (Vladimir von) 9 Ashkenazy (Vladimir), Prokofiev (Sergey) 10 Rubinstein (Anton) 12 Rachmaninoff (Sergey) *Spanish:* 6 Iturbi (Jose) 8 Granados (Enrique) 10 de Larrocha (Alicia) *Swiss:* 4 Anda (Geza)

piano 5 grand 6 softly, spinet 7 quietly, upright *builder:* 5 Knabe (William), Stein (Johann), Zumpe (Johann) 7 Baldwin (Dwight) 8 Steinway (Henry) 9 Bechstein (Friedrich) 10 Chickering (Jonas), Cristofori (Bartolomeo), Silbermann (Johann) *inventor:* 10 Cristofori (Bartolomeo) *key:* 7 digital *pedal:* 6 damper 7 celeste

Piazza Tales author 8 Melville (Herman)

picaroon 5 rogue, rover, thief 6 pirate, sea dog 7 brigand, corsair, sea wolf 8 sea rover 9 buccaneer, sea robber 10 freebooter

picayune *see* piddling

Piccini's rival 5 Gluck (Christoph)

pick 3 top 4 beak, best, cull, gaff, mark, take 5 elect, elite, pluck, pride, prime, prize 6 choice, choose, chosen, optate, opt for, prefer, select 8 plectrum, selected 9 exclusive, single out

picket 3 peg 4 pale, post, ward 5 guard, stake, watch 6 sentry, tether 7 lookout 8 palisade, sentinel, watchman

pick handle 5 helve

pickle 3 fix, jam 4 dill, spot 5 brine, souse 6 capers, corner, plight, scrape 7 dilemma, gherkin, trouble 8 marinate 11 predicament

pickpocket 5 thief 8 cutpurse 11 purse cutter *slang:* 3 dip

pick up 3 get 4 cull, gain, land, lift, rear 5 annex, glean, hoist, learn, pinch, raise, renew, run in 6 arrest, detain, garner, gather, master, obtain, pull in, reopen, resume, uphold, uplift, uprear 7 acquire, compass, elevate, extract, procure, restart, upraise 8 continue 9 apprehend 10 recommence

pickup 5 truck 6 arrest 9 detention 10 arrestment, hitchhiker 11 arrestation, improvement 12 acceleration, apprehension

picky 4 nice 5 fussy 6 choosy, dainty 7 finical, finicky 9 finicking 10 fastidious, particular 11 persnickety

picnic 4 snap 5 cinch 6 breeze, outing *beach:* 8 clambake

picture 4 cine, copy, draw, film, idea, limn, show 5 flick, image, movie, photo, pinup, print 6 depict, render 7 drawing, portray, tableau 8 describe, painting, portrait 9 delineate, depiction, interpret, photoplay, portrayal, represent 10 simulacrum 11 delineation, description, portraiture, presentment 13 spitting image *stand:* 5 easel

picture show 4 cine, film 5 flick, movie 9 photoplay

piddling 4 puny 5 petty 6 measly, paltry 7 trivial 8 niggling, trifling 11 Mickey Mouse

pie 4 flan, tart 5 pasty 6 affair, pastry 7 cobbler 8 business, crustade, turnover

piece 3 cut 4 part 6 member, moiety, parcel 7 portion, section, segment 8 division, fraction, fragment

pièce de résistance 8 main dish 9 showpiece 11 centerpiece, chef d'oeuvre, masterpiece

piecemeal 7 gradual 8 bit by bit 9 gradually 10 step-by-step

pie chart 5 graph 11 circle graph

pier 4 dock, quay, slip 5 berth, jetty, levee, wharf 6 column, pillar 8 pilaster *architectural:* 4 anta

pierce 3 cut 4 bore, gash, gore, slit, stab 5 slash, slice, spear 6 incise, riddle, skewer 8 transfix 9 penetrate, perforate 10 run through

piercing 4 high, keen, loud, thin 5 acute, sharp 6 argute, piping, shrill, treble 7 blaring, roaring 8 shooting, stabbing 9 knifelike 10 stentorian 12 earsplitting *tool:* 3 awl

piety 5 ardor 6 fealty, fervor 7 loyalty 8 devotion, fidelity, holiness, sanctity 9 godliness, reverence 10 allegiance, devoutness 12 faithfulness

piffle 4 bosh 5 hooey 6 bunkum 7 twaddle 8 malarkey, nonsense, pishposh 10 balderdash, flapdoodle 12 blatherskite

pig 3 hog 5 swine 6 farrow, porker 7 casting, glutton *breed:* 5 Duroc 8 Tamworth 9 Berkshire, Hampshire, Yorkshire *combining form:* 3 hyo 7 choerus *female:* 3 sow 4 gilt *feral:* 9 razorback *litter:* 6 farrow *male:* 4 boar 6 barrow *meat:* 3 ham 4 pork 5 bacon 7 sausage 8 chitlins 9 chitlings 12 chitterlings *wild:* 7 peccary, warthog 8 babirusa 9 babirussa *young:* 4 gilt 5 shoat 6 farrow, piglet

pigeon 3 sap 4 dupe, fool, gull, hoax, mark 5 chump, decoy 6 culver, sucker 7 fall guy, gudgeon 8 flimflam, hoodwink 9 bamboozle, victimize 11 hornswoggle *genus:* 7 Columba *house:* 4 cote, loft *kind:* 4 barb, rock 5 homer 6 pouter, roller 7 carrier, crowned, dragoon, fantail, jacobin, tumbler 8 carneaux *relative:* 4 dove *young:* 5 squab

pigeonhole 4 slot, sort, tier 5 class, cubby, grade, group, niche 6 assort, league 7 catalog, cubicle 8 category, classify, grouping 9 cubbyhole 10 categorize

pigeon pea 3 dal 4 dhal, herb

piggish 6 greedy 7 selfish, swinish 10 gluttonous

pigheaded 6 mulish 7 willful 8 perverse, stubborn 9 obstinate 10 headstrong, self-willed, unyielding 11 intractable, stiff-necked

pigment 3 dye 5 color, paint, stain 8 colorant, dyestuff, tincture *black:* 9 lampblack *blue:* 4 cyan 5 azure, smalt 6 indigo 7 cyanine 8 cerulean 9 verdigris 11 ultramarine *brown:* 5 sepia *umber:* 6 bister, sienna *combining form:* 5 chrom 6 chromo *dark:* 7 melanin *green:* 7 celadon 8 viridian 10 biliverdin *orange:* 7 realgar 8 carotene *red:* 4 lake *minium:* 7 carmine, crimson, pimento, scarlet, sinopia 8 lycopene 9 bilirubin, vermilion 10 vermillion *toxic:* 8 gossypol *yellow:* 5 ocher, ochre 6 flavin, lutein 7 flavine, xanthin 8 luteolin, massicot

pigpen 3 sty 4 dump, mess

pigsty see **pigpen**

piker 3 bum, vag 5 miser, stiff 7 drifter, floater, niggard, vagrant 8 roadster, tightwad, vagabond 9 skinflint 10 cheapskate 11 cheeseparer 12 moneygrubber, penny pincher

pilaster 4 anta, pier 6 column, pillar

Pildash *father:* 5 Nahor *mother:* 6 Milcah

pile 3 fur, lot, mow, nap, pot, wad 4 bank, cock, down, fill, flue, fuzz, heap, hill, lint, load, lump, mass, mint, much, pack, peck, pyre, rick 5 choke, drift, floss, fluff, hoard, mound, shock, stack 6 barrel, barrow, boodle, bundle, charge, jumble, packet 7 edifice, fortune, haycock, hayrick, pyramid, tumulus, windrow 8 erection, haystack, mountain 9 aggregate, amassment, great deal, structure 10 assemblage, collection 11 aggregation, glomeration 12 accumulation

pileous 5 hairy 6 fleecy, pilose, woolly 7 hirsute 9 whiskered

pileup 5 crash, smash 7 crack-up, smashup 8 accident 9 collision

pilfer 3 rob 4 lift 5 filch, pinch, steal, swipe 6 finger, snitch, thieve 7 purloin 11 appropriate

pilferer 4 prig 5 thief 6 nimmer 7 filcher, stealer 8 larcener 9 larcenist

pilgarlic 4 butt 5 sport 6 jestee 8 baldhead 13 laughingstock

pilgrim 5 hadji, hajji 6 palmer 8 traveler, wanderer, wayfarer *famous:* 5 Alden (John) 6 Carver (John) 8 Bradford (William), Brewster (William)

pilgrimage 4 hadj, hajj, trip 7 journey

Pilgrims' Interpreter 7 Squanto

Pilgrim's Progress 8 allegory *author:* 6 Bunyan (John) *hero:* 9 Christian

pill 4 ball 5 bolus 6 pellet, pilule 7 capsule

pillage 3 nab 4 lift, loot, sack 5 filch, pinch, steal, swipe, usurp, waste 6 devour, maraud, pilfer, ravage, thieve 7 despoil, plunder, purloin 8 arrogate, desolate, spoliate 9 depredate, desecrate, devastate 10 confiscate 11 appropriate

pillager 6 looter, raider, sacker 7 forager, ravager, spoiler 8 marauder, ravisher 9 plunderer 10 freebooter

pillar 4 pier, post, prop 5 pylon, shaft, stela, stele 6 column, stelae (plural) 7 obelisk 8 backbone, mainstay, pedestal, pilaster *combining form:* 4 cion, styl 5 ciono, style, stylo 6 stelic, stylar

Pillar of Hercules 5 Abila, Abyla, Calpe

pillow 3 pad 7 bolster, cushion

pilose see **pileous**

pilot 3 ace 4 auto, dean, lead, show, tool 5 doyen, drive, flier, guide, motor, route, steer, wheel 6 airman, direct, escort, flyboy, leader 7 aviator, birdman, conduct 8 aviatrix, helmsman, shepherd

pimp 6 pander 8 fancy man, procurer

pimple 3 dot, zit 4 boil, spot, stud 6 papule 7 abscess, pustule, speckle 8 furuncle, sprinkle 9 carbuncle

pin 3 fid, peg 4 clip 5 affix, dowel, stake, thole 6 broach, brooch, cotter, fasten, secure

pinch 3 nab, nip 4 lift 5 exact, filch, gouge, run in, screw, skimp, spare, steal, stint, swipe, theft, tweak, wrest, wring 7 larceny, squeeze 8 exigency, juncture, stealing, thievery, thieving, zero hour 9 apprehend, detention, emergency, shake down 10 arrestment, crossroads, purloining

pinchbeck 4 fake, sham 5 bogus, false, phony, snide 6 pseudo 8 spurious 9 brummagen 11 counterfeit

pinch hitter 3 sub 6 fill-in 7 stand-in 9 alternate, surrogate 10 substitute 11 locum tenens, replacement, succedaneum

Pindar *home:* 6 Thebes *poems:* 4 odes

pine 4 ache, fret, long, mope, sigh 5 brood, crave, dream, yearn 6 grieve, hanker, hunger, lament, repine, thirst 7 agonize

Pine Tree State 5 Maine

pinguid 3 fat

pinhead 4 fool, simp 5 dense, dunce 6 dimwit, nitwit, stupid 7 doltish, lackwit, wantwit

Pinkerton 6 shamus 9 detective, operative 10 private eye

pinnacle 3 top 4 acme, apex, peak 5 crest, crown 6 apogee, climax, summit, zenith 8 capsheaf, meridian 11 culmination *of a glacier:* 5 serac

pinniped 4 seal 6 walrus

Pinocchio author 7 Collodi (Carlo) 9 Lorenzini (Carlo)

pinochle *card:* 3 ace, ten 4 jack, king, nine 5 queen *term:* 4 meld 5 widow 7 auction *two-handed:* 7 goulash

pinpoint 4 spot 5 exact, place 6 finger 7 precise 8 diagnose, identify 9 recognize 11 determinate, distinguish 13 diagnosticate

pinto 4 pied 5 overo, paint 7 painted, piebald, tobiano 8 skewbald

pint-size 3 wee 4 tiny 5 teeny, weeny 6 midget, pocket, teensy 9 miniature 10 diminutive, pocket-size

pioneer 5 first, prime 6 maiden 7 initial, primary, settler 8 colonist, earliest, original *famous:* 5 Boone (Daniel), Bowie (Jim), Clark (William), Lewis (Meriwether) 6 Carson (Kit), Colter (John) 7 Bridger (Jim), Chapman (John), Fremont (John C.), Whitman (Marcus) 8 Crockett (Davy)

pious 4 holy 5 godly 6 devout 8 priestly 9 pietistic, prayerful, religious

pip 3 dot 4 blip, peep, root, seed, spot 5 image, speck

pipe 3 keg, tun 4 butt, cask 5 carry 6 barrel, convey, funnel, siphon 7 channel, conduct, conduit, traject 8 hogshead *ceremonial:* 7 calumet *combining form:* 3 aul 4 aulo 5 solen 6 siphon, soleno 7 siphono *part:* 4 bowl, stem

pipe down 5 dry up, quiet 6 dumb up, shut up

pipe dream 6 bubble 7 chimera, fantasy, rainbow 8 illusion, phantasy

pipeline 7 channel, conduit 8 supplier 10 connection

piquant 4 racy, tart 5 spicy, zesty 6 biting, snappy 7 peppery, pungent 8 poignant 9 sparkling 10 appetizing

pique 3 irk 4 huff, miff, move, rile, roil 5 annoy, peeve, plume, preen, pride, rouse, snuff 6 excite, irking, nettle, put out 7 dudgeon, innerve, offense, provoke, quicken, umbrage 8 irritate, motivate, vexation 9 aggravate, annoyance, galvanize, innervate, stimulate 10 exasperate, irritation, resentment

piranha 6 caribe

pirate 5 rover 6 looter, raider, robber, sea dog 7 brigand, corsair, sea wolf 8 marauder, picaroon, pillager, sea rover 9 buccaneer, plunderer, privateer, sea robber 10 freebooter *Celtic:* 5 Fomor 8 Fomorian *flag:* 10 Jolly Roger *French:* 7 Lafite (Jean), Lafitte (Jean) *Scottish:* 4 Kidd (William)

Pirithous' wife 10 Hippodamia

pirogue 5 canoe

pirouette 4 gyre, spin 5 twirl, whirl 6 gyrate 9 whirligig

piscator 6 angler 9 fisherman

pismire 3 ant

pistol 7 handgun 8 revolver 9 derringer *case:* 7 holster

pit 3 vie 4 hell, hole 5 abyss, chasm, hades, match 6 cavity, oppose 7 counter, Gehenna, inferno, play off 9 barathrum, perdition 10 underworld 11 netherworld, Pandemonium

Pit and the Pendulum author 3 Poe (Edgar Allan)

pitch 3 dip, yaw 4 cant, cast, dive, drop, fall, fire, hurl, rock, roll, swag, tilt, tone, toss 5 burst, drive, fling, heave, lunge, lurch, sling, slump, spiel, throw 6 go down, launch, plunge, seesaw, tilter, topple, tumble, unseat 7 buck off, unhorse 8 keel over 12 song and dance

pitch-black see pitch-dark

pitch-dark 3 jet 4 ebon, inky 5 black, ebony, jetty, raven, sable 11 atramentous

pitched 6 sloped, tilted, tipped 7 leaning, oblique, sloping, tilting 8 inclined 9 inclining

pitcher 4 ewer, olla, toby 5 cruse 7 creamer *area:* 5 mound *handle:* 3 ear 4 ansa

pitch in 5 begin, set to, start 6 chip in, fall to, jump in, kick in 8 commence, jump into, start off 9 subscribe 10 buckle down, contribute 11 come through

piteous 4 poor 6 rueful, ruined 7 pitiful 8 pathetic, pitiable 12 commiserable

pitfall 4 lure, risk, trap 5 peril, snare 6 danger, hazard 7 springe 8 deadfall, trapfall 9 booby trap, mousetrap 12 entanglement

pith 3 nub 4 core, gist, meat, pulp, root, soul 5 focus, heart 6 center, import, kernel, marrow, matter, upshot, weight 7 essence, nucleus 9 magnitude, substance 10 importance 11 consequence, weightiness 12 essentiality, significance

Pithon's father 5 Micah

pithy 4 curt 5 brief, crisp, meaty, short, terse 7 compact, concise, marrowy 8 succinct 12 epigrammatic 13 short and sweet

pitiable see **pitiful**

pitiful 3 sad 4 poor 5 cheap, sorry 6 rueful, scummy, scurvy, shabby, woeful 7 forlorn, piteous 8 beggarly, pathetic, pitiable, wretched 9 miserable, sorrowful 10 despicable, despisable 12 commiserable, contemptible, heartrending

pitiless 5 cruel, stony 6 brutal, savage 8 inhumane, ruthless 9 barbarous, cutthroat, heartless, merciless, unfeeling, unpitying 10 relentless, unmerciful 11 coldhearted, hardhearted, ironhearted 12 stonyhearted 13 marblehearted

pittance 3 bit 4 mite 5 scrap, trace 6 trifle 7 dribble, driblet, smidgen

pity 3 rue 4 ache, ruth 5 mercy 7 feel for 8 clemency, sympathy 10 compassion 11 commiserate 13 commiseration

pivot 4 turn, veer, whip 5 avert, sheer, swing, wheel, whirl 6 divert, swivel 7 deflect

pivotal 3 key 5 vital 6 ruling 7 central, crucial 8 cardinal 9 essential 10 overriding

pixie 3 elf, fay 5 antic, devil, fairy, nisse, rogue, scamp 6 elvish, impish, rascal, sprite 7 brownie, coltish, playful, puckish 8 prankish, scalawag, slyboots 9 skeezicks

pixieish 5 antic 6 elvish, frisky, impish 7 playful, puckish 9 kittenish, pixilated 11 mischievous

pixilated 5 drunk 6 elvish, pranky, stoned 7 larkish, muddled, playful, puckish, roguish, waggish 9 disguised 10 frolicsome, inebriated 11 intoxicated

Pizarro *city founded:* 4 Lima *conquest:* 4 Peru *victims:* 5 Incas

placard 4 bill, post 6 poster 7 affiche 8 handbill

placate 4 calm 6 pacify, soothe 7 appease, assuage, comfort, mollify, sweeten 10 conciliate, propitiate 11 tranquilize

place 3 fix, job, lay, put, set 4 area, call, lieu, loci (plural), post, rank, site, spot, zone 5 berth, judge, locus, point, posit, state, stick, tract, where 6 billet, finger, office, reckon, region, settle, status 7 deposit, footing, install, situate, station 8 capacity, diagnose, district, estimate, identify, locality, location, pinpoint, position, standing, vicinity 9 character, establish, recognize *com-*

bining form: 3 top 4 chor, loco, topo, topy 5 choro *of ease:* 10 bed of roses *of sin:* 5 Sodom *suffix:* 3 ary, ery, ory 4 aria (plural), oria (plural) 5 arium, orium

place-name 7 toponym

placid 4 calm, easy, mild 5 quiet, still 6 hushed, irenic, poised, serene, stilly 7 halcyon 8 composed, peaceful, tranquil 9 collected, easygoing, unruffled 10 unagitated, untroubled 12 self-composed 13 imperturbable, self-possessed

plague 3 vex 4 bane, fret, gnaw, pest, rash 5 annoy, beset, curse, harry, hound, tease, worry 6 bother, harass, hassle, hector, pester 7 afflict, bedevil, disease, hagride, scourge, torment, trouble 8 epidemic, invasion, irritant, nuisance, outbreak 9 annoyance, beleaguer, besetment 10 affliction, black death, botherment, pestilence 11 botheration, infestation

plain 3 dry, lea 4 bald, bare, moor, neat, open, pure 5 campo, clear, frank, heath, llano, stark, usual, veldt 6 candid, homely, modest, pampas, patent, severe, simple, steppe, tundra 7 austere, evident, obvious, prairie, routine, savanna, Spartan, unmixed 8 apparent, discreet, distinct, everyday, homespun, manifest, ordinary, palpable, savannah, straight, uncomely, unpretty, workaday 9 inelegant, quotidian, unadorned, undiluted 10 unaffected, unalluring, unhandsome

plainclothesman 4 dick 6 sleuth 7 gumshoe 8 hawkshaw, Sherlock 9 detective 12 investigator

plain Jane 5 usual 7 routine 8 everyday, ordinary, workaday 9 quotidian 12 unremarkable

plainness 7 clarity 8 lucidity 9 clearness, limpidity

plainsong 5 chant 12 cantus firmus

plainspoken 4 open 6 candid, direct 10 forthright 11 undisguised, unvarnished

plaintive 3 sad 6 rueful, woeful 7 doleful, elegiac, piteous, pitiful 8 dolesome, dolorous, mournful 9 sorrowful 10 lamentable, lugubrious, melancholy

plait 4 fold 5 braid, weave 7 pigtail 10 intertwine

plan 3 aim, map, way 4 cast, mean, plot 5 chart, draft, frame, order 6 animus, budget, design, devise, intend, intent, lay out, map out, method, policy, projet, scheme, set out, sketch, system 7 arrange, concert, meaning, outline, pattern, program, project, propose, purpose, regimen, work out 8 conspire, contrive, engineer, organize, platform, schedule, strategy, think out 9 blueprint, calculate, figure out, formulate, intention 10 intendment

plane 3 jet, lay 4 even, flat 5 flush, level 6 smooth 7 flatten 8 aircraft, airliner, smoothen

plane surface 4 area

planet 4 Mars 5 Earth, Pluto, Venus 6 Saturn, Uranus 7 Jupiter, Mercury, Neptune *brightest:* 5 Venus *closest to sun:* 7 Mercury *farthest from sun:* 5 Pluto *largest:* 7 Jupiter *path:* 5 orbit *red:* 4 Mars *ringed:* 6 Saturn *satellite:* 4 moon *shadow:* 5 umbra *small:* 8 asteroid *smallest:* 7 Mercury

planetary 6 global 7 immense 8 colossal, enormous 9 universal, worldwide

plangent 5 round 6 rotund 7 orotund, ringing, vibrant 8 resonant, sonorant, sonorous 9 consonant 10 resounding

plank 4 slab 5 board 6 lumber, timber 7 deposit, support

plant 3 fix, pot, set, sow 4 bury, grow, hide, mill, root, seed, tomb 5 cache, cover, imbed, inter, place, put in, stash, works 6 entomb, inhume, occult, screen 7 conceal, factory, lay away, put away, secrete 8 colonize, populate 9 cultivate *African:* 4 aloe 6 acacia 8 stapelia *angiosperm:* 5 dicot 7 monocot *aquatic:* 4 reed 5 lotus, sedge 7 awlwort, cattail, fanwort, papyrus 8 duckweed, eelgrass, hornwort, pondweed 9 water lily 10 watercress 11 bladderwort 12 pickerelweed *Australian:* 6 mallee 7 banksia 8 blackboy 10 eucalyptus *body:* 4 stem 7 thallus *bract:* 5 glume 8 phyllary *bulbous:* 4 lily 5 camas, onion, tulip 7 jonquil 8 hyacinth 9 narcissus *cactus:* 5 nopal 6 cereus, mescal 7 opuntia, saguaro 11 prickly pear *carnivorous:* 6 sundew 10 butterwort 12 pitcher plant 13 Venus's-flytrap *cell layer:* 5 suber 7 phellem *climbing:* 3 ivy 4 vine 5 betel, liana, vetch 6 bryony, derris, smilax 7 creeper, jasmine 8 bignonia, fumitory, moonseed, scammony, wisteria 12 morning glory *coloring agent:* 8 carotene 11 chlorophyll, xanthophyll *combining form:* 4 phyt 5 chore, cocci (plural), oecia (plural), phyta (plural), phyte, phyto *conebearing:* 3 fir, yew 4 pine 5 cedar, cycad 6 gingko, ginkgo, spruce 7 conifer, cypress, redwood 10 arborvitae, gymnosperm *desert:* 4 aloe 5 agave 6 cactus, cholla 8 mesquite, ocotillo 9 paloverde 11 brittlebush, Welwitschia *disease:* 3 rot 4 gall, mold, rust, scab, smut, wilt 5 ergot 6 blight, mildew, mosaic 7 blister 8 clubroot 9 black spot 10 black heart *epiphyte:* 6 orchid 8 air plant 9 bromeliad 11 Spanish moss *evergreen:* 3 fir 4 pine 6 spruce 7 lycopod 8 boxberry, clubmoss 9 bearberry 11 wintergreen 12 partridge pea *extinct:* 8 calamite *fern:* 5 royal 6 Boston 7 bracken 8 polypody, staghorn 10 cliffbrake, maidenhair *flowerless:* 4 alga, fern, kelp, moss 5 algae (plural), fungi (plural) 6 fungus, lichen 7 seaweed 8 clubmoss 9 bryophyte, equisetum, horsetail, liverwort *fluid:* 3 gum, sap 4 milk 5 latex, resin *garden:* 4 iris, ixia, lily, pink, rose 5 aster, calla, canna, daisy, oxlip, pansy, peony, phlox, stock, tulip 6 betony, cosmos, crocus, dahlia, lupine, malope, oxalis, salvia, violet, zinnia 7 anemone, begonia, bluecap, cowslip, fuchsia, gentian, jonquil, lobelia, petunia, statice, verbena 8 bluebell, cyclamen, daffodil, foxglove, gardenia, geranium, hyacinth, larkspur, marigold, primrose, sweet pea 9 amaryllis, campanula, carnation, cineraria, gladiolus, hollyhock, ligularia, narcissus, pimpernel, portulaca, saxifrage, sunflower 10 delphinium, marguerite, mignonette, nasturtium, snapdragon 11 forget-me-not 12 rhododendron, sweet william 13 bleeding heart, chrysanthemum *gland:* 7 nectary *grain:* 3 oat, rye 4 corn, rice 5 maize, wheat 6 barley, millet 9 buckwheat *hallucinogenic:* 4 hemp 6 mescal 8 cannabis 9 marihuana, marijuana *herb:* 4 balm, mint, sage 5 basil, calla, tansy, thyme 6 catnip, cicely, fennel 7 bitters, boneset, caraway, figwort, ginseng, parsley, saffron, vanilla 8 geranium, lavender, marjoram, rosemary, valerian 9 calendula, celandine, cineraria, coriander, horehound, portulaca, spearmint, spikenard 10 elecampane, pennyroyal *largest:* 7 sequoia *life:* 5 flora *marine:* 4 kelp 5 fucus 7 seaweed 10 sea lettuce *marsh:* 4 reed 5 carex, sedge 7 bogbean, bulrush, calamus, cattail 8 red maple, sphagnum 11 loosestrife *medicinal:* 4 aloe, sage 5 poppy, senna, tansy 6 catnip, fennel, garlic, ipecac, nettle 7 aconite, boneset, camphor, hemlock, henbane, juniper, lobelia, mustard, parsley 8 camomile, cinchona, licorice, pilewort, wormwood 9 asafetida, chamomile, dandelion, monkshood 10 peppermint 11 assafoetida *microscopic:* 4 mold 6 diatom 7 euglena 8 bacteria (plural) 9 bacterium *mushroom:* 5 morel 7 amanita 10 champignon 11 chanterelle *oldest:* 11 bristlecone *onion-like:* 4 leek 5 chive 7 shallot 8 scallion *opening:* 5 stoma 7 stomata (plural) *parasitic:* 6 dodder, fungus 9 mistletoe 10 beechdrops *part:* 3 bud, nut, sap 4 bark, bulb, cell, cone, corm, leaf, pome, root, seed, stem, wood 5 drupe, fruit, grain, spore, thorn, tuber, xylem 6 catkin, flower, nectar, phloem, raceme 7 rhizome 8 lenticel 9 cellulose, cotyledon 11 chlorophyll, chloroplast 13 inflorescence *pest:* 5 aphid, scale 6 chafer, thrips, weevil 7 cutworm 8 fruit fly, wireworm 9 gypsy moth 10 can-

kerworm, leafhopper, phylloxera **11** codling
moth *poisonous:* **4** poke, upas **5** sumac
6 castor, croton, datura **7** amantia, cassava, cowbane, henbane, lobelia, tobacco
8 foxglove, larkspur, locoweed, mayapple,
oleander, pokeweed **9** baneberry, monkshood **10** belladonna, jimsonweed, manchineel, nightshade *product:* **3** dye, tar
4 cork, drug, food, rope **5** fiber, paper,
resin, rosin **6** lumber, rubber **7** alcohol, perfume, tobacco **10** turpentine *saprophytic:*
5 fungi (plural) **6** fungus **10** Indian pipe
shrub: **3** box **5** broom, furze, lilac, sumac
6 azalea, datura, hyssop, privet, spirea
7 begonia, dogwood, spiraea **8** hawthorn,
magnolia, oleander, plumbago, viburnum
9 forsythia *succulent:* **5** agave **6** cactus
10 bitterroot *suffix:* **2** ad **4** ales (plural)
5 aceae (plural), ineae (plural) *support:*
7 trellis *thorny:* **4** rose **5** briar **6** cactus,
nettle, teasel, teazel, teazle **7** caltrop, thistle **8** cockspur **9** cocklebur *tissue:* **5** xylem
6 phloem **7** cambium, medulla **8** meristem
unit of structure: **6** telome *wild flower:*
4 ramp **5** bluet, calla, daisy **6** adonis,
lupine **7** arbutus, cowslip, gentian **8** fireweed, hepatica, toadflax, trillium **9** bloodroot, buttercup, campanula, columbine,
dandelion, goldenrod *young:* **5** scion,
shoot **6** sprout **7** cutting **8** seedling
plantlike **7** phytoid
plant louse **5** aphid
plaster **3** dab **4** coat, daub, sham **5** cover,
gesso, salve, smear **6** bedaub, mortar, remedy, smudge, soothe, stucco
plastic **4** soft **5** vinyl **6** pliant, supple
7 ductile, organic, pliable **8** creative, flexible, moldable **9** adaptable, formative, malleable **10** sculptural
plat **3** lot, map **4** plan **5** chart, floor, tract
6 parcel **7** surface **8** platform
plate **4** base, coat, disc, dish, disk, tile
5 layer, paten, scute, slice **6** fascia, lamina,
plaque **7** lamella, overlay *kind:* **4** blue,
home
plateau **4** mesa **5** table **6** upland **9** altiplano, tableland *arid:* **4** puna *barren:*
5 field **6** paramo *dry:* **5** karoo **6** karroo
platform **3** map **4** bank, base, dais, deck,
plan **5** forum, ledge, shelf, stage **6** design,
podium, pulpit, scheme **7** balcony, pattern,
rostrum **9** banquette **11** declaration *temporary:* **7** staging **8** scaffold *wooden:*
9 boardwalk
platinum *symbol:* **2** Pt
platitude **6** cliché, truism **7** bromide
8 banality, prosaism **10** prosaicism, shibboleth
Plato *father:* **7** Ariston *literary form:*
6 dialog **8** dialogue *original name:*
10 Aristocles *school:* **7** Academy *work:*

3 Ion **4** Meno **5** Crito, Lysis **6** Laches,
Phaedo **7** Apology, Gorgias **8** Phaedrus,
Republic **9** Charmides, Symposium
platoon **3** lot, set **4** team, unit **5** array,
batch, bunch, clump, group, squad **6** parcel
7 battery, cluster **8** division **9** formation
platter **6** salver **8** trencher
platypus **8** duckbill
plaudits **5** kudos **6** praise **7** acclaim
8 applause, encomium **11** acclamation,
approbation
plausible **8** credible **10** believable, creditable
play **3** act, bet, fun, use **4** game, jest, joke,
ploy, romp, room, take, wile **5** dally, drama,
enact, feint, flirt, scope, serve, sport, stake,
treat, trick, wager **6** cavort, comedy,
device, fiddle, fidget, frolic, gambit, gamble,
gambol, handle, jockey, leeway, margin, trifle **7** beguile, delight, disport, exploit,
finesse, gimmick, perform, roister, rollick,
twiddle **8** artifice, latitude, maneuver, pleasure, recreate **9** amusement, dalliance, discourse, diversion, elbowroom, enjoyment,
pantomime, personate, stratagem
10 manipulate, recreation *kind:* **5** farce,
opera **6** comedy **7** musical, tragedy **8** oneacter, operetta **9** melodrama, pantomime
part: **3** act **5** exode, scene **8** epilogue,
prologue
playact **2** do **7** perform **9** discourse, personate **11** impersonate
playboy **4** roué
play down **4** mute **6** soften **9** soft-pedal
11 deemphasize
player **4** mime **5** actor, mimic **6** mummer
7 actress, trouper **8** thespian **9** performer
11 participant **12** impersonator
playful **3** gay **5** antic, jolly, merry, pixie
6 blithe, elvish, frisky, impish, jocund, joking, jovial, lively, pranky, wicked **7** coltish,
dashing, gleeful, jocular, larking, larkish,
puckish, roguish, waggish **8** gamesome,
humorous, mirthful, pixieish, playsome,
prankful, prankish, sportive **9** kittenish, pixilated, sprightly, whimsical **10** frolicsome,
rollicking **11** mischievous **12** lighthearted
play off **3** pit, vie **5** match **6** oppose
7 counter
play on words **3** pun
play up **6** stress **7** feature **9** emphasize,
italicize, underline **10** underscore
playwright **6** author, writer **9** dramatist
10 dramatizer, dramaturge
plaza **5** green **6** common, square **9** carrefour **11** marketplace
plea **4** suit **5** alibi **6** appeal, excuse, orison,
prayer **7** apology, pretext, request
8 entreaty, overture, petition **11** application,
imploration, imprecation **12** supplication
defendant's: **4** nolo **6** guilty **9** not guilty

plead 3 beg, sue 4 pray 5 brace, crave
6 appeal 7 beseech, entreat, implore
9 importune 10 supplicate

pleasant 4 fair, fine, glad, good, nice
5 clear, sunny, sweet, tasty 6 cheery,
genial, joyful, joyous, pretty 7 amiable, clarion, likable, welcome 8 amicable, charming, cheerful, cheering, engaging, gracious,
grateful, likeable, pleasing, sunshine, sunshiny, tasteful 9 agreeable, appealing,
cloudless, congenial, convivial, enjoyable,
favorable, unclouded 10 delightful, gratifying, undarkened *and unpleasant:* 11 bittersweet

pleasantry 3 fun 4 jest, joke 6 banter
10 jocularity

please 4 like, suit, will, wish 5 agree,
amuse, elate, elect, enjoy 6 arride, choose,
tickle 7 content, delight, gladden, gratify,
happify, indulge, satisfy 9 delectate, titillate

pleasing 4 good, nice 5 nifty 6 comely,
pretty, seemly 7 welcome, winning
8 charming, grateful, suitable 9 agreeable,
congenial, favorable, palatable 10 attractive, delectable, delightful, enchanting, gratifying 11 pleasurable 12 satisfactory

pleasingly plump 6 zaftig, zoftig

pleasurable see **pleasing**

pleasure 3 fun, joy 4 will 5 bliss, fancy,
mirth 6 arride, liking, relish 7 delight, gladden, gratify, happify, joyance 8 felicity, fruition, gladness, hedonism, velleity 9 amusement, delectate, diversion, enjoyment,
happiness, merriment

pleasuremonger 8 hedonist, sybarite

pleat 4 fold 5 crimp 6 crease 7 flounce

pleated 7 plicate

plebeian 3 low 4 base, mean 5 lowly
6 coarse, common, homely, humble, vulgar
7 ignoble, ill-bred, lowborn 8 baseborn,
everyday, ordinary, unwashed

plebeians see **populace**

plectrum 4 pick

pledge 3 row 4 bail, bond, gage, hock,
oath, pass, pawn, seal, word 5 drink,
swear, toast, token 6 engage, plight, surety
7 earnest, hostage, promise, warrant
8 contract, covenant, guaranty, mortgage,
security, warranty 9 assurance, certainty,
guarantee, undertake 11 impignorate

pledget 3 wad 8 compress

Pleiades 4 Maia 6 Merope 7 Alcyone,
Celaeno, Electra, Sterope, Taygeta 8 Asterope *brightest star:* 7 Alcyone

plenteous see **plentiful**

plentiful 4 full, rich 5 ample 6 bumper,
galore, plenty 7 copious, fertile, fulsome,
liberal, opulent, profuse, teeming 8 abundant, affluent, bursting, fruitful, generous,
prolific, swarming, swimming 9 abounding,
bounteous, bountiful, plenteous, unstinted

plenty 3 lot 4 heap, much, pack, peck, pile
5 ample 7 copious, liberal 8 abundant,
generous, mountain, opulence 9 abundance, bounteous, bountiful, great deal,
plenteous, plentiful 10 cornucopia

pleonasm 8 verbiage 9 tautology, verbality 10 periphrase, redundancy, roundabout
11 periphrasis 13 circumambages

plethora 4 glut 5 flood 6 deluge, excess
7 surfeit, surplus 8 fullness, overflow, overkill, overmuch, overplus 9 repletion 10 surplusage 11 superfluity 13 overabundance

plexus 4 rete 7 network

pliable see **pliant**

pliant 4 limp, soft 5 lithe 6 limber, supple
7 ductile, plastic, tensile, willowy 8 flexible,
moldable, workable, yielding 9 adaptable,
compliant, malleable, tractable 11 manipula-
ble 13 manipulatable

plica 4 fold, ruck 5 ridge, rivel 6 crease,
furrow, rimple 7 crinkle, wrinkle 11 corrugation

plight 3 box, fix, jam, vow 4 hole, spot,
word 5 swear 6 corner, engage, pickle,
pledge, scrape 7 betroth, dilemma, promise
8 covenant, quandary 9 betrothal 10 difficulty, engagement 11 predicament

plighted 7 engaged 8 intended 9 affianced, betrothed 10 contracted

plod 4 grub, slog, slop, toil 5 grind, slave,
tramp, tromp 6 drudge, stodge, trudge
7 trample 8 footslog, plunther

plot 4 plan 5 cabal, covin, tract 6 design,
devise, parcel, scheme 7 collude, compact,
connive, diagram, outline 8 cogitate, conspire, contrive, engineer, intrigue, practice,
scenario 9 collusion, conniving, machinate,
scheme out 10 complicity, connivance, conspiracy 11 machination

plover 4 bird 5 pewit, stilt 7 lapwing
8 dotterel, killdeer *relative:* 9 sandpiper,
turnstone

plow 3 dig 4 till, turn 5 break 6 furrow,
trench 8 turn over 9 cultivate *part:*
4 beam, frog 5 share 8 landside 9 mold-
board

ploy 4 ruse, scam, wile 5 feint, trick
6 device, gambit 7 gimmick 8 artifice,
maneuver 9 stratagem

pluck 3 tug 4 grit, guts, pick, pull 5 cheek,
heart, nerve, spunk 6 daring, mettle,
snatch, spirit, tweeze 7 bravery, cojones,
courage 8 gameness 10 resolution

plucky 4 bold, game 5 brave 6 feisty,
spunky 7 doughty 8 fearless 9 dauntless,
unfearing 10 courageous 11 undauntable

plug 3 tap 4 bung, clog, cork, fill, pack,
puff, push, stop, tout 5 block, blurb, boost,
choke, close, spile 7 congest, occlude, promote, puffing, stopper, stopple, tampion,
tompion, write-up 8 obstruct 9 advertise

plug-ugly 3 mug 4 thug 5 rowdy, tough, yahoo 6 mucker 7 ruffian 8 bullyboy 9 roughneck

plum 5 prize 6 reward 7 guerdon, premium 8 dividend *dried:* 5 prune *kind:* 4 Agen 6 Damson, Duarte 7 bullace 8 Hortulan, Salicina 9 Green Gage, myrobalan *spiny:* 10 blackthorn

plumage 8 feathers *early:* 4 down

plumb 5 delve, probe, sound 6 fathom 7 explore, plummet 8 absolute, vertical 10 straight-up 13 perpendicular

plume 5 pique, preen, pride 7 feather 8 aigrette

plummet 3 dip 4 drop, fall, sink, skid 5 crash 6 plunge, tumble 7 decline, descend 8 collapse, decrease, nose-dive 11 precipitate

plump 3 fat 5 buxom, podgy, pudgy, round, stout, tubby 6 chubby, fleshy, portly, rotund 8 roly-poly 10 roundabout

plunder 3 rob 4 loot, swag 5 booty, prize, rifle, spoil 6 boodle 7 despoil, pillage, ransack, relieve, stick up 9 knock over

plunderage 4 loot, swag 5 booty, prize, spoil 6 boodle

plunderer 6 looter, raider, sacker 7 forager, ravager 8 marauder, pillager, ravisher 9 despoiler 10 freebooter

plunge 3 dig, dip, ram, run 4 dive, drop, fall, rush, sink, skid, stab 5 burst, douse, drive, lunge, pitch, slump, stick 6 charge, go down, thrust, topple, tumble 7 immerse, plummet 8 keel over, nose-dive, submerge

plus 4 more, over 5 asset, boost, build 6 beef up, excess, expand 7 augment, enlarge, magnify, overage, surplus 8 compound, increase 9 overstock 10 oversupply

plush 4 posh 6 Capuan, deluxe 7 opulent 8 luscious, palatial 9 luxuriant, luxurious, sumptuous 11 upholstered

Pluto 3 Dis 5 Hades *brother:* 4 Zeus 7 Jupiter, Neptune 8 Poseidon *father:* 6 Cronus, Saturn *mother:* 3 Ops 4 Rhea *wife:* 10 Persephone, Proserpina

plutonic 6 Hadean 7 avernal, hellish, stygian 8 chthonic, infernal 9 chthonian, cimmerian, Tartarean 10 sulphurous 11 pandemoniac

plutonium *symbol:* 2 Pu

Plutus *father:* 6 lasion *god of:* 6 riches, wealth *mother:* 5 Ceres 7 Demeter

ply 4 bend, fold 5 exert, layer, swing, throw, wield 6 handle, put out 7 belabor 8 dispense, exercise, maneuver 9 importune 10 manipulate

pneuma 4 soul 5 anima 6 animus, psyche, spirit 9 élan vital 10 vital force

pneumatic 4 airy 6 aerial 11 atmospheric

Pocahontas *father:* 8 Powhatan *husband:* 5 Rolfe (John)

pock 3 pit 4 hole, spot 6 pimple 7 pustule

pocket 3 bag, nab, wee 4 hook, lift, sack, tiny 5 filch, pinch, pouch, purse, steal, swipe, weeny 6 accept, cavity 7 capsule, conceal, dead end, impasse, swallow 8 abstract, bear with, cul-de-sac, dwarfish, monetary, pint-size, tolerate, tough out 9 condensed, financial, itsy-bitsy, miniature, pecuniary 10 blind alley, diminutive *billiards:* 4 pool

pocket money 6 change 9 petty cash 11 small change

pocket-size 4 tiny 6 midget, minute, peewee 8 dwarfish, pint-size 9 itsy-bitsy, miniature 10 diminutive

pod 3 bag, gam, sac 4 boll, case, hull, husk, skin 5 shell, shuck 6 cocoon, paunch, school 7 capsule, silique 8 potbelly, seedcase 9 bay window 11 corporation *combining form:* 7 siliqui *plant:* 3 pea 4 bean, okra 5 chili, gumbo 6 cassia, cowpea, legume, lentil, peanut, pepper 8 capsicum, mesquite, milkweed 9 lespedeza

pod-bearing tree 5 carob 6 locust 7 catalpa

podiatry 9 chiropody

Poe, Edgar Allan *detective:* 5 Dupin *poem:* 6 Lenore 7 Israfel, To Helen, Ulalume 8 Eldorado, For Annie, The Raven 10 Annabel Lee *tale:* 6 Ligeia, Shadow 7 Morella, Silence 10 The Gold Bug

poem 3 ode 4 epic, epos, idyl, rime, rune, song 5 ditty, elegy, epode, idyll, lyric, rhyme, verse 6 ballad, epopee, jingle, rondel, sonnet 7 rondeau 8 limerick, madrigal *closing:* 5 envoi, envoy *combining form:* 5 stich *division:* 4 foot, line 5 canto, epode, stich, verse 6 stanza 7 refrain 8 epilogue, prologue *Japanese:* 5 haiku, tanka *of eight lines:* 6 octave 7 triolet *of four lines:* 8 quatrain *of fourteen lines:* 6 sonnet *of three lines:* 7 triplet *pastoral:* 7 eclogue, georgic *short:* 5 ditty 7 epigram

poet 4 bard, muse, scop 5 odist, skald 6 lyrist 7 elegist 8 idyllist, lyricist, satirist 9 balladist, sonneteer, sonnetist 10 Parnassian *American:* 3 Poe (Edgar Allan) 4 Dove (Rita), Hass (Robert), Nash (Ogden), Read (Thomas), Tabb (John Banister), Tate (Allen) 5 Auden (Wystan Hugh), Benét (Stephen Vincent), Crane (Hart), Field (Eugene), Frost (Robert), Guest (Edgar), Moore (Marianne), Plath (Sylvia), Pound (Ezra), Riley (James Whitcomb), Wylie (Elinor) 6 Barlow (Joel), Bryant (William Cullen), Ciardi (John), Dunbar (Paul), Kilmer (Joyce), Lanier (Sidney), Lowell (Amy, James Russell, Robert), Millay (Edna St. Vincent), Ransom (John Crowe), Seeger (Alan), Strand (Mark), Taylor (Edward),

Warren (Robert Penn), Wilbur (Richard) 7 Emerson (Ralph Waldo), Jeffers (Robinson), Lindsay (Vachel), Markham (Edwin), Merrill (James), Nemerov (Howard), Roethke (Theodore), Shapiro (Karl), Stevens (Wallace), Whitman (Walt) 8 Cummings (Edward Estlin), Ginsberg (Allen), MacLeish (Archibald), Robinson (Edwin Arlington), Teasdale (Sara), Whittier (John Greenleaf), Williams (Charles Kenneth, William Carlos) 9 Dickinson (Emily), Santayana (George) 10 Bradstreet (Anne), Longfellow (Henry Wadsworth) 12 Wigglesworth (Michael) *Anglo-Saxon:* 7 Caedmon, Cynwulf 8 Cynewulf *Arab:* 5 Jarir *Australian:* 8 Paterson (Andrew Barton) *Belgian:* 11 Maeterlinck (Maurice) *Canadian:* 5 Pratt (Edwin John) 7 Roberts (Charles G. D.) *Chinese:* 4 Li Po, Tu Fu *Danish:* 5 Ewald (Johannes) *English:* 3 Gay (John) 4 Gray (Thomas), Owen (Wilfred), Pope (Alexander), Rowe (Nicholas), Tate (Nahum), Wyat (Thomas) 5 Blake (William), Byron (Lord), Donne (John), Eliot (Thomas Stearns), Noyes (Alfred), Wilde (Oscar), Wyatt (Thomas), Young (Edward) 6 Arnold (Matthew), Brooke (Rupert), Cowper (William), Dryden (John), Graves (Robert), Milton (John), Savage (Richard), Sidney (Philip), Surrey (Earl of), Symons (Arthur), Waller (Edmund), Warton (Thomas), Watson (William), Wotton (Henry) 7 Chaucer (Geoffrey), Herrick (Robert), Hopkins (Gerard Manley), Housman (Alfred Edward), Layamon, Patmore (Coventry), Quarles (Francis), Shelley (Percy Bysshe), Skelton (John), Southey (Robert), Spender (Stephen), Spenser (Edmund) 8 Betjeman (John), Browning (Elizabeth, Robert), Langland (William), Lovelace (Richard), Meredith (George), Rossetti (Christina, Dante Gabriel), Suckling (John), Tennyson (Alfred Lord), Thompson (Francis) 9 Coleridge (Samuel Taylor), Swinburne (Algernon) 10 Wordsworth (William) 11 Shakespeare (William) *Finnish:* 8 Runeberg (Johan Ludvig) *French:* 5 Marot (Clement) 6 Musset (Alfred de), Valery (Paul), Villon (François) 7 Bourget (Paul), Chenier (Andre de, Marie-Joseph), Gautier (Theophile), Rimbaud (Arthur), Ronsard (Pierre de) 8 Malherbe (François de), Mallarmé (Stephane), Verlaine (Paul) 9 Lamartine (Alphonse de) 10 Baudelaire (Charles) 11 Apollinaire (Guillaume) *German:* 5 Heine (Heinrich), Rilke (Rainer Maria), Storm (Theodor Woldsen) 6 Goethe (Johann Wolfgang von), Uhland (Ludwig) 7 Walther, Wolfram 8 Schiller (Friedrich von) 9 Klopstock (Friedrich Gottlieb) *Greek:* 5 Arion, Homer 6 Erinna, Hesiod, Pindar, Sappho 7 Agathon, Thespis 8 Anacreon 9 Simonides 10 Apollonius, Theocritus *Hindu:* 5 Naidu (Sarojini) 6 Tagore (Rabindranath) 8 Kalidasa *Hungarian:* 6 Zrinyi (Miklos) *Irish:* 5 Moore (Thomas), Synge (John Millington), Wolfe (Charles), Yeats (William Butler) 8 Stephens (James) *Italian:* 4 Rosa (Salvator), Vida (Marco) 5 Dante, Tasso (Torquato) 7 Ariosto (Ludovico), Manzoni (Alessandro), Montale (Eugenio) 8 Leopardi (Giacomo), Petrarch 9 D'Annunzio (Gabriele), Marinetti (Filippo Tommaso), Ungaretti (Giuseppe) *medieval:* 8 minstrel, trouvère, trouveur 10 troubadour *nonsense:* 4 Lear (Edward) *Norwegian:* 8 Björnson (Bjornstjerne), Welhaven (Johan) 9 Wergeland (Henrik) *Persian:* 4 Sadi 5 Attar, Hafiz 11 Omar Khayyam *Roman:* 4 Ovid 6 Horace, Vergil, Virgil 7 Juvenal, Statius 8 Catullus, Tibullus 9 Lucretius *Russian:* 7 Pushkin (Aleksandr), Yesenin (Sergey) 9 Kheraskov (Mikhail), Pasternak (Boris) *Scottish:* 4 Hogg (James), Muir (Edwin) 5 Burns (Robert), Scott (Alexander, Walter) 6 Ramsay (Allan) 7 Thomson (James) *Spanish:* 7 Jimenez (Juan Ramon) 11 Garcia Lorca (Federico) *Swedish:* 5 Sachs (Nelly) 6 Tegner (Esaias) 8 Snoilsky (Carl Johan) 9 Karlfeldt (Erik Axel) *Swiss:* 5 Amiel (Henri Frederic) 9 Spitteler (Carl) *Welsh:* 6 Thomas (Dylan) 7 Aneurin, Watkins (Vernon)

poetaster 6 rhymer, verser 7 bardlet 8 bardling, verseman 9 rhymester, versifier

poetic 5 lyric 6 bardic, dreamy 8 romantic

poetic contraction   see at **contraction**

poet laureate 3 Pye (Henry) 4 Rowe (Nicholas), Tate (Nahum) 6 Austin (Alfred), Cibber (Colley), Dryden (John), Hughes (Ted), Jonson (Ben) 7 Bridges (Robert), Southey (Robert) 8 Betjeman (John), Davenant (William), Day-Lewis (Cecil), Shadwell (Thomas), Tennyson (Alfred Lord) 9 Masefield (John), Whitehead (William) 10 Wordsworth (William)

Pogo creator 9 Walt Kelly

poignancy 6 pathos

poignant 4 keen, racy 5 acute, sharp, spicy, zesty 6 moving, snappy, urgent 7 cutting, peppery, piquant, pungent 8 incisive, piercing, touching 9 affecting 10 impressive

point 3 aim, awn, bit, dot, jag, nib, tip 4 apex, barb, beak, bill, cape, cast, cusp, edge, head, hint, item, mite, mote, naze, site, snag, spot, tine, turn 5 brink, force, imply, level, locus, motif, place, prong, punch, refer, speck, spike, steer, theme, topic, trace, verge 6 allude, detail, direct,

matter, moment, motive, tip-off, zero in
7 address, article, cogency, element, feature, instant, station, subject, suggest
8 argument, flyspeck, foreland, headland, indicate, juncture, location, particle, position, validity 9 birthmark, character, punctuate, situation, threshold, validness 10 particular, promontory 12 significance

Point Counter Point author 6 Huxley (Aldous)

pointed 5 acute, peaky, piked, sharp
6 marked, peaked, signal 7 salient 8 acicular, striking 9 aciculate, acuminate, acuminous, arresting, cuspidate, mucronate, prominent

pointer 3 dog, tip 4 dial, hint 5 arrow, steer 6 tip-off 9 indicator

pointillist 6 Seurat (Georges)

point of view 5 angle 7 outlook 11 perspective

point out 8 indicate

poise 4 hang, tact 5 float, grace, hover
6 aplomb, stasis, steady 7 address, balance, ballast, dignity 8 calmness, elegance, serenity 9 assurance, diplomacy, equipoise, stability, stabilize 10 confidence 11 delicatesse, equilibrium, savoir faire, stabilitate, tactfulness, tranquility

poised 4 calm, easy 6 placid, serene
8 composed, tranquil 9 collected, easygoing, possessed 13 self-possessed

poison 4 bane, harm, loco, warp 5 stain, taint, toxic, toxin, venom, virus 6 debase, infect, toxine, toxoid 7 botulin, cacodyl, corrupt, debauch, deprave, destroy, envenom, pervert, vitiate 8 mephitic, toxicant, venenate, venomous, virulent 9 contagion
10 corruption, demoralize 13 contamination *arrow:* 4 inée, upas 5 urare, urari 6 antiar, curara, curare, curari, curure, oorali 7 ouabain, woorali, woorari 8 antiarin *combining form:* 3 tox 4 toxi, toxo 5 toxic 6 toxico

poisoning *food:* 8 botulism *lead:*
8 plumbism

poisonous 5 fatal, toxic 6 deadly, lethal, mortal 7 baneful, miasmal, miasmic, nocuous, noxious, toxical 8 mephitic, toxicant, venenous, venomous, virulent 9 miasmatic, pestilent 10 nauseating, pernicious *alkaloid:* 8 nicotine 10 strychnine *element:*
7 arsenic

poke 3 box, dig, hit, jab, jog, jut, lag, pry
4 chop, cuff, dolt, dope, drag, nose, pout, prod, push, sock, stab, stir 5 bulge, chump, clout, dally, delay, dunce, idiot, moron, mouse, nudge, punch, rouse, shove, smack, snoop, spank, tarry, trail 6 arouse, awaken, beetle, buffet, cowboy, dawdle, dimwit, loiter, pierce, put off, putter, thrust 7 project 8 busybody

poker *bet total:* 3 pot *form:* 4 stud
8 baseball *hand:* 4 pair 5 flush 8 straight
9 full house 10 royal flush 13 straight flush
stake: 4 ante *term:* 3 see 4 call, draw, open 5 raise *token:* 4 chip

poker-faced 5 grave, sober, staid
6 sedate, solemn, somber 7 earnest, neutral, serious

poky 4 blah, dull 6 dreary, stodgy 7 humdrum 8 banausic, monotone 10 monotonous

Poland *capital:* 6 Warsaw *labor leader:*
6 Walesa (Lech) *monetary unit:* 5 zloty

polar 8 opposite

pole 4 punt, spar 5 shaft, stick, stilt *Indian:*
5 totem *Scottish:* 5 caber

polecat 5 fitch, skunk 7 fitchet

polestar 3 hub 4 seat 5 focus, guide, heart 6 center 10 focal point 11 nerve center

policeman 3 cop 4 fuzz, heat 5 bobby
6 copper, peeler 7 gumshoe, John Law, officer, trooper 8 bluecoat, Dogberry, flatfoot, gendarme 9 constable, patrolman
12 peace officer *Italian:* 11 carabiniere
Parisian: 4 flic 8 gendarme *Spanish:*
10 carabinero *Turkish:* 6 kavass 7 zaptiah, zaptieh

policy 3 wit 4 line 6 course, govern, wisdom 7 program 8 sagacity 9 procedure

polio vaccine developer 4 Salk (Jonas) 5 Sabin (Albert)

polish 3 rub, wax 4 buff 5 glaze, glint, gloss, round, sheen, shine, sleek, slick
6 glance, luster, pumice, refine, smooth
7 brush up, burnish, culture, perfect, touch up 8 breeding, brighten 10 refinement

Polish *dumpling:* 7 pierogi *patriot:* 9 Kosciusko (Thaddeus) *pope:* 8 John Paul *sausage:* 8 kielbasa *soldier:* 7 Pulaski (Casimir)

polish off 5 eat up, shift, swill 6 devour, punish 7 consume, put away 8 dispatch

polite 5 civil 7 courtly, genteel 8 mannerly
9 attentive, courteous 10 thoughtful
11 considerate 12 well-mannered

politeness 8 chivalry, civility, courtesy

politic 4 wise 7 cunning, prudent, tactful
8 delicate, tactical 9 advisable, expedient, judicious 10 diplomatic 11 worldly-wise

political *association:* 4 bund *meeting:*
6 caucus *party:* 3 GOP 9 Communist, Socialist 10 Democratic, Republican *system:* 7 fascism 9 communism, democracy, socialism

politics *conservative:* 8 rightism *liberal:*
7 leftism

poll 4 clip, crop, head, nape 5 shear 6 noddle, noggin, noodle, survey 7 canvass

pollack, pollock 6 saithe 8 bluefish, coalfish

pollard 3 top 4 crop 8 truncate 10 detruncate

pollen-producing organ 6 stamen

pollex 5 thumb

polliwog 7 tadpole

polltaker 6 Gallup

pollute 4 foul, soil 5 dirty, taint 6 befoul, defile 7 corrupt, profane 11 contaminate

pollution 4 smog 8 impurity 10 defilement

Pollux 10 Polydeuces *brother:* 6 Castor *father:* 4 Zeus *mother:* 4 Leda *sister:* 5 Helen 12 Clytemnestra

Pollyanna 8 optimist 10 daydreamer *author:* 6 Porter (Eleanor)

Pollyannaish 8 cheerful, sanguine 10 optimistic

Polonius *daughter:* 7 Ophelia *slayer:* 6 Hamlet *son:* 7 Laertes

poltergeist 5 ghost 6 spirit

poltroon 4 funk 6 coward, craven, funker 7 dastard, gutless, quitter, unmanly 8 cowardly 9 spunkless 11 lily-livered, yellowbelly

Polyclitus statue 4 Hera

Polydorus *father:* 5 Priam 6 Cadmus *mother:* 6 Hecuba 8 Harmonia *slayer:* 8 Achilles 10 Polymestor 11 Polymnestor

polygon *eight-sided:* 7 octagon *five-sided:* 8 pentagon *four-sided:* 8 tetragon *nine-sided:* 7 nonagon *seven-sided:* 8 heptagon *six-sided:* 7 hexagon *ten-sided:* 7 decagon *three-sided:* 8 triangle *twelve-sided:* 9 dodecagon

Polyhymnia 4 Muse *invention:* 4 lyre

Polynesian 5 Maori 6 Samoan, Tongan 8 Hawaiian, Tahitian 9 Marquesan

Polynices *brother:* 8 Eteocles *father:* 7 Oedipus *mother:* 7 Jocasta *wife:* 5 Argia 6 Argeia

polyp 5 zooid 7 hydroid *freshwater:* 5 hydra

Polyphemus 7 cyclops *beloved:* 7 Galatea *father:* 8 Poseidon *victim:* 4 Acis

pome 4 pear 5 apple 6 quince 8 hawthorn

pommel 4 knob 6 finial

pomp 4 form, show 5 array, shine 6 parade, ritual 7 display, fanfare, liturgy, panoply 8 ceremony, splendor 9 formality

pompano 4 fish 6 permit 8 carangid 10 butterfish

Pompeii's volcano 8 Vesuvius

pom-pom 4 ball, tuft

pompous 4 vain 5 proud, puffy, wiggy 6 stuffy 7 aureate, bloated, flowery, stilted, stuck-up 8 arrogant, sonorous 9 bombastic, important, overblown 10 egocentric, euphuistic, hoity-toity, pontifical, rhetorical 11 declamatory, highfalutin, magisterial, pretentious

pond 4 mere 5 stank 6 lagoon, salina *combining form:* 4 limn 5 limni, limno

ponder 4 mind, mull, muse 5 brood, study, think, weigh 6 reason 7 perpend, reflect, revolve 8 appraise, cogitate, consider, evaluate, meditate, mull over, muse over, ruminate, think out, turn over 9 speculate, think over 10 deliberate, excogitate 11 contemplate

ponderous 4 dull 5 heavy, hefty, stiff, vapid 6 dreary, stodgy, stuffy, wooden 7 buckram, humdrum, massive, onerous, stilted, weighty 8 plodding, unwieldy 10 burdensome, cumbersome, oppressive

poniard 6 dagger

Ponocrates' pupil 9 Gargantua

Ponte Vecchio *city:* 8 Florence *river:* 4 Arno

Pontiac's tribe 6 Ottawa

pontiff 4 pope 6 bishop

pontifical 5 puffy, wiggy 6 stuffy 7 bloated, pompous 8 arrogant, dogmatic 9 episcopal, important 11 magisterial

pony 4 crib, trot 5 horse 6 cayuse *breed:* 6 Exmoor 8 Shetland

Pooh creator 5 Milne (Alan Alexander)

pooh-pooh 3 boo 4 bird, hiss, hoot, razz 5 bazoo 7 catcall, dismiss, kiss off 9 raspberry

pool 3 pot, pul 4 mere 5 chain, group, kitty, trust 6 cartel, lagoon, laguna, puddle 7 combine, jackpot 9 syndicate *player:* 7 Mosconi (Willie) 13 Minnesota Fats

poor 3 bad, low 4 base, flat, hack, mean, punk 5 amiss, broke, cheap, needy, scant, skimp, spare, stony, tatty, wrong 6 common, crummy, humble, meager, paltry, rotten, rueful, scanty, scrimp, shoddy, skimpy, sleazy, sparse, trashy 7 piteous, pitiful, scrawny, scrimpy, squalid, trivial 8 bankrupt, beggared, beggarly, déclassé, exiguous, indigent, inferior, low-grade, pathetic, pitiable, rubbishy, strapped 9 deficient, destitute, insolvent, moneyless, penceless, penniless, penurious, unmoneyed 10 bankrupted, down-and-out, pauperized, second-rate, stone-broke 11 fortuneless, impecunious, indifferent, necessitous, second-class, unfavorable *combining form:* 3 mal

poorly 3 low 4 mean 6 ailing, offish, sickly, unwell 8 off-color 10 indisposed 11 undesirably 13 ineffectively

pop 3 dad, dot, gun, hit, try 4 dada, dart, ding, jump, papa, shot, slap, slog, sock, soda, stab, swat 5 break, catch, crack, daddy, drink, fling, shoot, smite, whack, whirl 6 attack, effort, father, strike 7 assault, attempt, explode, instant 8 backfire *in:* 3 see 4 call 5 visit 6 by, look up, stop by 8 come over

pop artist 5 Blake (Peter) 6 Warhol (Andy) 7 Hockney (David), Indiana (Robert) 9 Oldenburg (Claes), Wesselman (Tom) 12 Lichtenstein (Roy)

pope 3 Leo 4 John, Mark, Paul, Pius 5 Caius, Conon, Donus, Felix, Gaius, Lando, Linus, Peter, Soter, Urban 6 Adrian, Agatho, Fabian, Julius, Lucius, Martin, Sixtus, Victor 7 Anterus, Clement, Damasus, Gregory, Hadrian, Hyginus, Marinus, Paschal, Pontian, Romanus, Sergius, Stephen, Zosimus 8 Agapetus, Anicetus, Benedict, Boniface, Calixtus, Eugenius, Eusebius, Formosis, Gelasius, Hilarius, Honorius, Innocent, John Paul, Liberius, Nicholas, Pelagius, Siricius, Theodore, Vigilius, Vitalian 9 Adeodatus, Alexander, Anacletus, Callistus, Celestine, Cornelius, Densdedit, Dionysius, Eutychian, Evaristus, Hormisdas, Marcellus, Miltiades, Severinus, Silverius, Silvester, Sisinnius, Sylvester, Symmachus, Valentine, Zacharias 10 Anastasius, Melchiades, Sabinianus, Simplicius, Zephyrinus 11 Christopher, Constantine, Eleutherius, Eutychianus, Marcellinus, Telesphorus

Pope poem 10 The Dunciad 12 An Essay on Man 16 The Rape of the Lock

Popeye *accessory:* 4 pipe *baby:* 8 Sweet Pea *energizer:* 7 spinach *friend:* 5 Wimpy 8 Olive Oyl *occupation:* 6 sailor *rival:* 5 Bluto

poplar 5 abele, alamo, aspen 9 tulip tree 10 cottonwood 12 balm of Gilead *North American:* 6 balsam

Poppaea's husband 4 Nero

poppycock 3 rot 4 bosh, guff 5 bilge, hokum 6 bunkum 8 malarkey, nonsense 10 balderdash 12 blatherskite, fiddle-faddle

populace 5 plebs 6 masses, people, plebes 9 commonage, commoners, common men, plebeians 10 commonalty 11 rank and file, third estate *combining form:* 3 dem 4 demo

popular 4 rife 5 cheap, noted 6 famous, public, ruling, vulgar 7 current, favored, general, leading, rampant, regnant 8 approved, favorite 9 notorious, preferred, prevalent, prominent, well-known, well-liked 10 democratic, prevailing, widespread

populate 6 occupy, people, tenant 7 inhabit

populous 7 crowded 8 numerous

Poratha's father 5 Haman

porcelain *Chinese:* 9 Lowestoft *English:* 3 Bow 5 Derby, Spode 6 Minton 7 Bristol, Chelsea 8 Caughley, Wedgwood *French:* 6 Sèvres 7 Limoges *German:* 7 Dresden, Meissen *ingredient:* 6 kaolin 8 petuntse *Italian:* 6 Doccia *Japanese:* 5 Imari

porch 5 lanai 7 galilee, passage, veranda 8 verandah

porcine see portly

porcupine 5 porky, prick 7 echidna 8 hedgehog

porgy 4 scup 6 sparid 7 margate, pinfish 8 menhaden

Porgy and Bess composer 8 Gershwin (George)

Porgy author 7 Heyward (Dubose)

Po River *cities:* 5 Milan, Padua, Turin 6 Verona 7 Brescia

pork 3 ham, pig 5 bacon, swine 8 sowbelly *cut:* 3 ham 4 jowl, loin, side 7 fatback 8 forefoot, hind foot, spare rib 9 picnic ham 10 Boston butt

pork-barreling 9 patronage

pornographic 7 obscene

porous 5 leaky 6 leachy 8 pervious 9 permeable 10 cancellate, cancellous, penetrable 13 insubstantial

porridge 4 stew 5 brose, salad 6 crowdy, sowans, sowens 7 crowdie

port 3 air, set 4 goal, mien 5 cover, haven 6 asylum, covert, harbor, refuge, riding 7 address, bearing, retreat, shelter 8 demeanor, larboard, presence 9 anchorage, harborage, roadstead, sanctuary 10 deportment 11 comportment, destination; (see also seaport)

portable 5 handy 6 mobile, wieldy

portal 4 door, gate 5 entry 7 doorway 8 entrance, entryway 11 entranceway

portcullis 3 bar 4 shut 7 grating, lattice

portend 4 bode, omen 5 augur 7 betoken, predict, presage, promise, signify 8 forebode, forecast, foreshow, foretell, indicate, prophesy 9 adumbrate, foretoken 10 foreshadow, vaticinate

portent 4 omen, sign 6 augury, boding, marvel, wonder 7 miracle, presage, prodigy, stunner 8 bodement 9 foretoken, sensation

portentous 7 pompous, weighty 8 inflated 9 marvelous 10 prodigious

porter 5 carry, hamal 6 bearer, hamaul, hammal, redcap 7 carrier, drogher 9 transport 10 doorkeeper *airport:* 6 skycap

Portia *husband:* 6 Brutus 8 Bassanio *maid:* 7 Nerissa

portion 3 cut, lot 4 bite, doom, fate, meed, part 5 dower, endow, moira, piece, quota, share, slice, weird 6 divide, kismet, member, moiety, parcel 7 deal out, destiny, dole out, measure, mete out, partage, prorate, quantum, segment 8 dispense, division *largest:* 10 lion's share *unused:* 8 leftover

portly 3 fat 5 heavy, obese, stout 6 fleshy 7 weighty 8 imposing 9 corpulent, overblown 10 overweight

portmanteau 9 gladstone 12 traveling bag

portrait 4 bust 5 image 6 double, ringer, statue 7 picture 10 similitude, simulacrum

portray 4 limn 5 cameo, enact, image 6 depict, render 7 picture 8 describe 9 delineate, interpret, represent

portrayal 7 picture 9 depiction 11 delineation, description, presentment

Portugal 9 Lusitania *capital:* 6 Lisbon *coin:* 7 centavo *export:* 4 cork, wine 8 textiles *monetary unit:* 6 escudo *premier:* 7 Salazar (Antonio de)

pose 3 ask, dog, put, sit 4 airs, fake, give, lugs, sham 5 befog, feign, offer, query, strut 6 baffle, extend, pass as, prefer, puzzle, stance, tender 7 confuse, hold out, pass for, pass off, peacock, perplex, present, pretend, profess, proffer, propone, purport, show off, stumble, suggest 8 attitude, bewilder, carriage, confound, pretense, propound, question 9 mannerism 10 grandstand, masquerade, pretension 11 affectation, proposition 12 attitudinize

Poseidon 7 Neptune *brother:* 4 Zeus 5 Hades, Pluto 7 Jupiter *consort:* 4 Tyro 6 Medusa 7 Demeter *father:* 6 Cronus *mother:* 4 Rhea *offspring:* 7 Pegasus *son:* 5 Orion 6 Neleus, Pelias 7 Antaeus 10 Polyphemus *weapon:* 7 trident *wife:* 10 Amphitrite

posh 4 chic, tony 5 smart, swank 7 à la mode 9 exclusive 11 fashionable

posit 6 assume, thesis 7 premise, presume 9 apriorism 10 assumption, presuppose 11 presumption

position 3 job 4 rank, side, site, spot, view 5 angle, berth, color, locus, place, point, situs, slant, stand, state, where 6 belief, billet, cachet, locate, office, stance, status 7 dignity, emplace, footing, stature 8 attitude, capacity, judgment, prestige, standing 9 character, viewpoint 10 standpoint *troops:* 6 deploy

positive 4 firm, hard, rank, sure 5 clear, gross, sound, utter 6 actual 7 assured, certain, decided, express, factual, genuine, perfect 8 absolute, cocksure, complete, definite, emphatic, explicit, forceful, forcible, outright, specific 9 clockwise, confident, doubtless, downright, energetic, practical 10 consummate, inarguable, reasonable, sure-enough, undeniable 11 categorical, indubitable, irrefutable, right-handed, unambiguous, undoubtable, unequivocal, unmitigated 12 indisputable, irrebuttable, undisputable, unmistakable

possess 3 own 4 bear, have, hold, keep 5 carry, enjoy 6 retain

possessed 4 calm, easy 6 placid, serene 8 tranquil

possession 8 property 9 ownership 11 proprietary

possessive 7 jealous

possessive pronoun see at **pronoun**

possibility 2 if 9 potential 11 contingency

possible 6 latent, likely, mortal, viable 7 dormant, earthly 9 expedient, potential

possibly 5 maybe 7 perhaps 9 perchance

post 3 job, set 4 clew, clue, mail, spot, tell, warn 5 berth, place 6 advise, billet, fill in, inform, notify, office, wise up 7 apprise, placard, station 8 acquaint

poster 4 bill, sign 6 banner, notice 7 affiche, placard 8 handbill 9 billboard, broadside, signboard 12 announcement 13 advertisement

posterior 4 back, hind, rear, rump, seat, tail 5 after, later 6 behind, hinder, retral 7 ensuing, rear end, tail end 8 backside, buttocks, hindmost, rearward 10 subsequent 13 subsequential

posterity 4 seed 5 brood, issue 6 scions 7 progeny 8 children 9 offspring 11 descendants, progeniture

posthaste 4 fast 5 fleet, quick, rapid, swift 6 speedy 7 flat-out, fleetly, quickly, rapidly, swiftly 8 full tilt, speedily 9 breakneck 10 harefooted 11 expeditious 12 lickety-split

postimpressionist painter 6 Seurat (Georges) 7 Cezanne (Paul), Gauguin (Paul), Van Gogh (Vincent)

postmortem 7 autopsy 8 necropsy

postpone 5 defer, delay 6 hold up, put off, shelve 7 hold off, lay over, suspend 8 hold over, prorogue, reprieve 9 carry over

postulate 4 aver, call 5 claim, exact 6 affirm, assert, assume, demand, thesis 7 premise, presume, require, solicit 9 apriorism, challenge 10 assumption, presuppose 11 presumption, requisition, supposition

posture 3 sit 4 mien, mode 5 state 6 manner, stance, status 7 bearing, pass for, pass off 8 attitude, carriage 9 condition, situation 10 deportment, masquerade 12 attitudinize

posy 3 ana 5 album, bloom 6 flower 7 blossom, bouquet, corsage, garland, nosegay, omnibus 8 analects 9 anthology 10 miscellany 11 florilegium

pot 3 bet, wad 4 ante, mint, olla, pile, weed 5 grass, kitty, stake, wager 6 boodle, bundle 7 fortune 8 cannabis 9 marihuana, marijuana, sideswipe *small:* 6 pipkin

potable 4 pure 5 clean, drink, fresh 6 liquor 8 beverage 9 drinkable

potassium 6 kalium *ore:* 6 sylvin 7 sylvine, sylvite

potato 3 yam 4 spud 5 praty, tater 6 murphy *bud:* 3 eye *cooked strips of:* 11 French fries

potbelly 5 stove 6 paunch 9 bay window

potency 3 pep 4 birr, tuck 5 force, might, power, sinew, vigor 6 energy, muscle, virtue 8 strength 9 hardihood, puissance 10 capability 13 effectiveness

potent 5 lusty 6 mighty, robust, strong, virile 8 forceful, forcible, powerful

potential 6 latent, likely 7 abeyant, dormant, lurking 8 possible, probable 9 plausible, prepatent, quiescent 10 imaginable 11 conceivable, possibility

pother 3 ado 4 cark, flap, fret, fuss, stew, stir, to-do 5 furor, whirl, worry 6 bustle, clamor, flurry, furore, hassle, hubbub, tumult, uproar 7 turmoil 9 agitation, annoyance, commotion, confusion, whirlpool, whirlwind 10 hurly-burly, turbulence

potion 7 philter, philtre

Potiphar's slave 6 Joseph

Potiphera *daughter:* 7 Asenath *son-in-law:* 6 Joseph

potpourri 4 hash, olio 6 medley 7 mélange 8 mishmash, pastiche 9 patchwork 10 assortment, hodgepodge, miscellany, salmagundi

potshot 3 cut, dig 4 gibe, jeer 5 crack 6 insult 9 aspersion, criticism, sideswipe

potter 4 mess 6 doodle, fiddle, puddle 10 mess around *English:* 8 Wedgwood (Josiah)

Potter, Beatrix *creation:* 11 Peter Rabbit

potter's field 8 cemetery, God's acre 9 graveyard

pottery, glazed 5 delft

pouch 3 bag, jut, sac 4 sack 5 bulge, burse 6 beetle, pocket 7 project, saccule 8 overhang, protrude, sacculus, stand out *bodily:* 5 bursa

pouf 5 quilt 9 comforter

poultice 7 plaster 8 compress, dressing 9 cataplasm

poultry 4 fowl *type:* 4 duck, swan 5 goose, quail 6 grouse, pigeon, turkey 7 chicken, ostrich, peacock 8 pheasant 9 partridge

pounce 5 swoop, talon 6 emboss, powder

pound 3 bat 4 bang, bash, beat, belt, biff, blow, drub, pelt, slam, sock 5 crack, drive, grave, smack, stamp 6 batter, buffet, hammer, pummel, thrash, wallop 7 belabor, impress 8 malleate

pound and sponge 5 cakes

pour 3 run 4 beat, emit, flow, gush, lash, rain, rill, roll, rush, teem, void 5 flood, issue, skink, spate, surge, swarm 6 decant, deluge, drench, sluice, spring, stream 7 cascade, give off, niagara, proceed, torrent 8 cataract, flooding, inundate, overflow *forth:* 6 effuse

pourboire 3 tip 7 cumshaw, largess 8 gratuity 9 lagniappe 10 perquisite

pout 3 pet 4 moue, sulk 5 bulge, grump 7 project 8 overhang, protrude

poverty 4 need, want 6 penury 7 beggary, borasca 8 poorness, scarcity 9 indigence, indigency, necessity, neediness, pauperism, privation, suffering 10 mendicancy, scarceness 11 destitution 13 destituteness, insufficience, insufficiency, pennilessness *combining form:* 5 penia

poverty-stricken see **penurious**

POW camp *German:* 6 stalag

powder 4 bray, buck, dust, talc 5 crush 6 talcum 8 sprinkle 9 comminute, pulverize, triturate 10 besprinkle 12 contriturate *medicinal:* 7 lupulin

power 3 arm, vis 4 dint, sway 5 force, might, right, sinew, steam, vigor, vires (plural) 6 energy, muscle, talent, virtue, weight 7 ability, command, control, dynamis, faculty, mastery, potence, potency, voltage 8 aptitude, capacity, dominion, dynamism, function, imperium, prestige, strength 9 authority, direction, dominance, endowment, influence, masterdom, privilege, puissance, strong arm, supremacy 10 ascendancy, birthright, capability, competence, domination, management 11 prerogative, sovereignty, superiority 12 jurisdiction, potentiality 13 effectiveness *combining form:* 5 dynam 6 dynamo *in Hindu philosophy:* 4 maya *reduction:* 8 brownout *sacred:* 4 kami *unit of:* 4 watt

powerful 4 able 5 great 6 mighty, potent, strong, wieldy 7 capable, dynamic, weighty 8 almighty, dominant, forcible, puissant, vigorous 9 competent, effective, effectual, efficient, energetic, strenuous 10 convincing, invincible 11 efficacious, influential 13 authoritative

powerless 4 weak 5 inert, unfit 6 feeble, infirm, supine 7 passive 8 decrepit, impotent, inactive, nugatory 9 incapable 11 incompetent, ineffective

powwow 4 chat, talk 5 treat 6 advise, confab, confer, huddle, parley 7 consult, meeting 8 collogue 10 conference 11 confabulate

poyou 6 peludo 9 armadillo

practicable 4 open 5 handy, utile 6 useful 9 operative 10 functional

practical 5 handy, sober, utile 6 usable, useful, versed 7 old-time, skilled, veteran 8 banausic, implicit, seasoned, sensible 9 pragmatic, realistic 10 functional, hard-boiled, hardheaded 11 down-to-earth, experienced, serviceable 12 businesslike

practically 4 most, much, nigh 5 about 6 all but, almost, nearly 8 as good as, as much as, well-nigh 9 in essence

practice 3 use, way 4 form, mode, plot, wont 5 cabal, covin, drill, habit, trick, usage 6 custom, follow, manner, method, pursue, repeat, scheme, system, usance 7 execute, fulfill, iterate, perform, process, utility 8 drilling, exercise, habitude, intrigue, rehearse 9 procedure 10 conspiracy, convenance, convention, proceeding *suffix:* 2 cy 3 ery, ics, ism

practitioner *combining form:* 4 path *suffix:* 5 ician

pragmatic 9 practical, realistic 10 hardboiled, hardheaded, unromantic 11 down-to-earth

pragmatist 7 realist

prairie antelope 9 pronghorn

prairie apple 9 breadroot

prairie berry 9 trompillo

prairie chicken 6 grouse

prairie hen 11 clapper rail

prairie potato 9 breadroot

prairie wolf 6 coyote

praise 4 hail, hymn, laud 5 bless, cry up, erect, exalt, extol, honor, psalm, roose 6 anthem, belaud, extoll, kudize, uprear 7 acclaim, adulate, applaud, commend, dignify, enhance, ennoble, flatter, glorify, hosanna, magnify, plaudit, puffery, resound, sublime 8 eulogize, heighten, proclaim, psalmody 9 celebrate, intensify, recommend 10 aggrandize, compliment, panegyrize *expression of:* 8 accolade 9 encomium

praiseworthy 7 palmary 8 laudable 9 admirable, deserving, estimable, meritable 11 commendable, meritorious

prance 4 step 5 strut, tread 6 curvet, foot it, hoof it, jaunce, sashay 8 cakewalk

prank 4 deck, lark, play, trim, whim 5 adorn, antic, caper, fancy, fix up, freak, spiff, sport, trick 6 bedeck, didoes, doll up, frolic, gambol, levity, shines, vagary, wheeze, whimsy 7 caprice, conceit, deck out, doll out, dress up, fooling, garnish, gussy up, rollick 8 beautify, decorate, escapade, ornament, spruce up 9 capriccio, embellish, frivolity, high jinks, horseplay, lightness, rowdiness, smarten up 10 roughhouse, shenanigan, skylarking, tomfoolery 11 monkeyshine *Scottish:* 6 shavie

prate 3 gab, jaw, yak 4 blab, blow, brag, chat, crow, puff, yack 5 boast, clack, drool, mouth, vaunt 6 babble, drivel, gabble, jabber, waffle, yabber 7 blabber, blather, chatter, palaver, twaddle, twattle 9 gasconade, yakety-yak 11 rodomontade

prater 6 magpie 9 bandar-log, blabmouth 10 chatterbox 12 blabbermouth

prattle see **prate**

prattler see **prater**

prawn 6 shrimp 8 crevette 13 Norway lobster

praxis 3 use 4 wont 5 habit, trick, usage 6 custom, manner 8 habitude 10 consuetude

Praxiteles statue 6 Hermes 8 The Satyr

pray 3 beg 5 brace, crave, daven, doven, plead 6 appeal 7 beseech, entreat, implore 8 meditate 10 supplicate

prayer 4 plea, suit 6 appeal, beggar, litany, orison, suitor 7 angelus, begging, complin, worship 8 blessing, compline, entreaty, petition, pleading 9 adoration, imploring, suppliant 10 beseeching, supplicant 11 application, imploration, imprecation, supplicator 12 supplication *beads:* 6 rosary *ending:* 4 amen *for the dead:* 7 requiem *Jewish:* 7 kaddish, kiddush 9 kaddishim (plural) *period:* 6 novena 7 triduum *shawl:* 6 tallis, tallit 7 tallith

prayer book 6 missal 8 breviary *Jewish:* 6 mahzor, siddur 7 machzor

prayerful 4 holy 5 godly, pious 6 devout

praying figure 5 orant

preach 7 address, lecture 8 advocate, homilize, moralize 9 sermonize 10 evangelize

preacher 6 cleric, divine, parson 7 evangel 8 clerical, homilist, minister, reverend 9 churchman, clergyman 10 evangelist 12 ecclesiastic

preacher bird 5 vireo

preaching friar 9 Dominican

preamble 5 proem 8 exordium, foreword, overture, prologue 12 introduction, prolegomenon

precarious 4 iffy 5 risky 6 touchy, tricky 7 dubious 8 delicate, doubtful, insecure, ticklish, unstable 9 sensitive, uncertain

precaution 8 prudence 9 foresight, safeguard 10 providence 11 forethought

precede 4 lead, pace, rank 5 forgo, usher 6 forego, herald 7 forerun, outrank 8 announce, antedate 9 introduce

precedence 8 priority

precedent 4 past 5 prior 6 former 7 example 8 anterior 9 foregoing

preceding 4 past 5 prior 6 before, former 7 ahead of, prior to 8 anterior, hitherto 9 erstwhile 10 heretofore 11 in advance of *prefix:* 4 ante

precept 3 law 4 rule 5 axiom, canon, dogma, edict, tenet 6 behest, decree 7 bidding, statute 8 decretum, doctrine 9 ordinance, principle 10 injunction, regulation 11 fundamental

preceptive 8 didactic 9 mandatory

preceptor 5 tutor 7 teacher 9 principal 10 headmaster

precinct 6 domain, region, sector, sphere 7 quarter, section 8 district, dominion, province 9 bailiwick, territory

precious 3 pet 4 dear, nice, rare, rich 5 fussy, loved, picky, showy 6 artful, chichi, choice, choosy, costly, la-di-da 7 beloved, darling, finicky, genteel, studied 8 affected, blue-eyed, favorite, overnice, prizable, valuable 9 exquisite, priceless, prizeable, recherché 10 fair-haired, fastidious, invaluable, particular

precipitancy 4 rush 5 haste 9 hastiness 10 suddenness 11 hurriedness

precipitant 5 hasty 6 abrupt, sudden 7 hurried, rushing 8 headlong 9 impetuous

precipitate 4 lees 5 dregs, event, hasty, issue, sheer, steep 6 abrupt, effect, madcap, result, sequel, sudden, upshot 7 arduous, deposit, grounds, hurried, rushing 8 headlong, sediment 9 aftermath, breakneck, hotheaded, impatient, impetuous, impulsive, overhasty, settlings 10 headstrong, refractory, unexpected, unforeseen 11 aftereffect, consequence, subitaneous

precipitation 4 hail, lees, rain, rush, snow 5 dregs, haste, sleet 7 deposit, grounds 8 sediment 9 hastiness, settlings 11 hurriedness

precipitous 5 hasty, sheer, steep 6 abrupt, sudden 7 hurried, rushing 8 headlong

précis 6 aperçu, digest, sketch, survey 7 pandect, sylloge 8 syllabus 10 compendium

precise 4 nice, prim, very 5 exact, fixed, right, rigid 6 narrow, prissy, proper, stuffy 7 correct, genteel, limited, missish, prudish 8 accurate, definite, priggish, rigorous, specific 9 clocklike, stringent 10 particular

preciseness see precision

precision 4 care, heed 6 timing 8 accuracy 9 exactness 10 definitude, exactitude 11 carefulness, correctness

preclude 4 quit, stop, ward 5 avert, cease, deter 7 forfend, obviate, rule out 8 stave off 9 forestall 11 discontinue

precondition 4 must 9 essential, necessity, requisite 10 sine qua non 11 requirement

precursor 6 herald 8 foregoer 9 harbinger, prototype 10 antecedent, forerunner

predate 7 forerun 8 antecede

predatory 9 rapacious, raptorial, vulturine, vulturous

predecessor 7 forbear 8 ancestor, forebear, foregoer 9 prototype 10 antecedent, forerunner

predestine see preordain

predetermine see preordain

predeterminism 8 fatalism

predicament 3 box, fix, jam 4 hole, pass, soup, spot 5 Dutch, pinch, rigor, state 6 corner, pickle, plight, scrape, strait 7 dilemma, impasse, posture, trouble 8 asperity, exigency, hardness, hardship, hot water, juncture, quagmire 9 condition, deep water, emergency, situation 10 difficulty

predicate 4 aver, avow, base, rest, stay 5 found 6 affirm, assert, avouch, depose, ground 7 declare, profess, protest 9 establish

predict 5 augur, guess, infer, judge 7 forbode, foresee, portend, suppose, surmise 8 conclude, forebode, forecast, forefeel, foreshow, foretell, prophesy, soothsay 9 adumbrate 10 conjecture, vaticinate 13 prognosticate

predictor 4 seer 5 augur, weird 6 auspex 7 prophet 8 foreseer, haruspex 10 forecaster, foreteller, prophesier, soothsayer 11 Nostradamus

predilection 4 bent 7 leaning 8 penchant, tendency 9 inclining 10 proclivity, propensity

predispose 4 bend, bias, sway 6 strike 7 incline

predisposed 4 fain 5 prone, ready 7 willing 8 inclined

predisposition 4 bent 7 leaning 8 penchant, tendency 9 inclining 10 proclivity, propensity

predominant 4 main 5 chief, major 6 master 7 capital, general, primary 9 number one, paramount, principal, sovereign 11 outstanding, overbearing

predominate 4 rule 5 reign 6 master 7 regnant 9 ascendant, paramount, prevalent, sovereign 11 overbearing

preeminence 6 renown 7 primacy 8 dominion 9 masterdom, supremacy 10 ascendancy, domination 11 distinction, superiority

preeminent 4 main 5 chief, major 7 capital, stellar, supreme 8 dominant, towering, ultimate 9 number one, principal 10 surpassing 11 outstanding, unequalable, unmatchable 12 incomparable, transcendent *prefix:* 4 arch

preempt 4 take 5 annex, seize, usurp 6 assume 8 accroach, arrogate 9 sequester 10 commandeer, confiscate 11 appropriate, expropriate

preen 5 plume, pride, primp

preface 4 lead 5 proem, usher 6 prolog 8 exordium, foreword, overture, preamble, prologue 9 introduce 12 introduction

prefatory 8 proemial 9 inductive, preludial 12 introductory

prefer 3 put 4 cull, mark, pick, pose, take 5 elect 6 choose, optate, opt for, select

preference 6 choice, option 8 druthers, election 9 elevation, prelation, promotion, selection, upgrading 10 partiality

prefigure 4 hint 9 adumbrate 10 foreshadow

pregnancy 6 cyesis 9 fertility, gestation, gravidity

pregnant 4 rich 5 heavy 6 facund, gravid, parous 7 weighty 8 childing, eloquent, enceinte 9 expecting, momentous 10 expressive, meaningful, parturient 11 sententious

prehend 3 bag, get 4 nail, take 5 catch 6 collar, secure 7 capture

prehensile 6 grabby, greedy 8 covetous, desirous, grasping 11 acquisitive

preindicate 6 herald 7 forerun, presage 8 announce, foreshow 9 harbinger

prejudice 3 mar 4 bend, bias, harm, hurt, skew 5 angle, slant, spoil 6 damage, impair, injure, racism, sexism 7 bigotry, blemish, dispose, incline, leaning, tarnish, vitiate 9 influence 10 partiality 12 one-sidedness, partisanship

prejudicial 3 bad 4 evil 7 harmful, nocuous 8 damaging 9 injurious 11 deleterious, detrimental, mischievous

preknow 3 see 6 divine 7 foresee 8 forefeel 9 apprehend, visualize 10 anticipate

preliminary 5 basic 7 fitting 8 proemial, readying 9 elemental, inductive 11 fundamental 12 introductory

preliterate 9 primitive

prelude 5 proem 8 exordium, foreword, overture, prologue 12 introduction, prolegomenon

premature 5 early 8 oversoon, untimely 9 overearly

premeditated 7 advised, studied 8 designed, studious 10 considered, deliberate, thought-out

premier 4 arch, head 5 chief, first 7 leading 8 champion, foremost 9 principal

premise 5 posit 6 assume, thesis 9 apriorism, postulate 10 assumption 11 postulation, supposition

premium 4 agio, meed, plum 5 prize 6 carrot, reward 7 guerdon 8 buckshee, dividend, superior 11 exceptional

premonition 9 misgiving 10 foreboding 12 apprehension

preoccupied 4 deep, lost, rapt 6 absent, intent 7 bemused, engaged, faraway, wrapped 8 distrait, immersed 9 engrossed, forgetful, wrapped up 10 abstracted 11 inconscient 12 absentminded

preordain 4 fate 6 doom to 7 destine 9 determine 10 predestine 11 foredestine

preparation 7 fitness 8 training 9 readiness 11 compounding

preparatory 9 preludial, prelusive 11 prefatorial, preliminary

prepare 3 fit, fix, get 4 busk, gird, make 5 brace, dower, draft, endow, endue, equip, frame, prime, ready, steel, train 6 draw up, make up, outfit, supply 7 confect, dispose, fortify, furnish, provide 9 formulate 10 strengthen *for publication:* 4 edit 6 redact *leather:* 5 curry

prepared 3 set 5 ready

preponderance 8 dominion 9 ascendant, masterdom, supremacy 10 ascendancy, domination

preponderant 8 dominant, superior 9 paramount, sovereign 11 overbearing

preponderate 4 rule 5 reign 8 domineer

preposition 2 at, by, in, of, on, to, up 3 but, cum, ere, for, off, out, per, via 4 amid, down, from, into, like, onto, over, save, thru, till, unto, upon, with 5 about, above, after, along, among, anent, below, circa, since, tween, twixt, under, until 6 aboard, across, amidst, around, before, behind, beside, beyond, contra, except, gainst, inside, mongst, toward, versus, within 7 against, amongst, athwart, beneath, besides, between, betwixt, despite, outside, through, towards, without 10 throughout, underneath

prepossess 4 bias 5 imbue 6 absorb, engage, occupy 7 engross, immerse, involve 9 influence, prejudice, preoccupy

prepossessing 10 attractive

preposterous 4 wild 5 crazy, loony, silly, wacky 6 absurd, insane 7 foolish 9 fantastic 10 irrational 11 extravagant, harebrained 12 unreasonable

preposterousness 5 folly 8 insanity 9 absurdity

prerequisite 4 must 9 condition, essential, necessary, necessity 10 imperative, sine qua non 11 necessitous, requirement

prerogative 5 right 8 appanage, immunity 9 exemption, privilege 10 birthright, perquisite

presage 4 bode, omen 5 augur 6 augury, boding, herald 7 bespeak, betoken, forerun, portend, portent, predict, promise 8 announce, bodement, forebode, forecast, foreshow, foretell, indicate, prophesy, soothsay 9 adumbrate, foretoken, harbinger, misgiving, prenotion 10 foreboding, foreshadow, prognostic, vaticinate 12 apprehensive 13 prognosticate

presbyter 5 elder 6 priest

prescience 9 foresight

prescribe 3 fix, set 6 assign, choose, decide, decree, define, impose, ordain, select, settle 7 dictate, lay down, pick out 9 determine

prescript 3 law 4 rule 5 edict 6 decree 8 decretum 9 institute, ordinance 10 regulation

prescription 3 law 4 rule 5 edict 6 decree 8 decretum 9 institute, ordinance

presence 3 air 4 look, mien, port 6 aspect 7 address, bearing, seeming 8 demeanor

present 3 aim, lay, now 4 boon, cast, cite, gift, give, head, past, pose, show 5 favor, level, offer, point, today, train 6 adduce, allege, bestow, devote, direct, donate, extant, extend, modern, tender 7 address, advance, hand out, hold out, instant, largess, proffer 8 acquaint, nowadays, today-ish, up-to-date 9 introduce 12 contemporary, newfashioned

presentable 3 fit 6 decent, proper 9 befitting 11 appropriate

presentiment see **premonition**

presently 3 now 4 anon, soon 5 today 7 by and by 8 nowadays

preservation 4 care, ward 5 guard 6 saving, shield 7 defense, keeping 9 safeguard 10 husbanding 11 conservancy, safekeeping

preserve 3 can, jam 4 save 6 keep up, pickle 7 sustain 8 maintain 9 confiture

preside 3 run 4 head, keep 5 chair 6 direct, handle, manage, ordain 7 carry on, conduct, control, operate, oversee

president *United States:* 4 Bush (George), Ford (Gerald R.), Polk (James K.), Taft (William H.) 5 Adams (John, John Quincy), Grant (Ulysses S.), Hayes (Rutherford B.), Nixon (Richard M.), Tyler (John) 6 Arthur (Chester A.), Carter (Jimmy), Hoover (Herbert), Monroe (James), Pierce (Franklin), Reagan (Ronald), Taylor (Zachary), Truman (Harry S.), Wilson (Woodrow) 7 Clinton (Bill), Harding (Warren), Jackson (Andrew), Johnson (Andrew, Lyndon) Kennedy (John F.), Lincoln (Abraham), Madison (James) 8 Buchanan (James), Coolidge (Calvin), Fillmore (Millard), Garfield (James), Harrison (Benjamin, William H.), McKinley (William), Van Buren (Martin) 9 Cleveland (Grover), Jefferson (Thomas), Roosevelt (Franklin D., Theodore) 10 Eisenhower (Dwight D.), Washington (George)

press 3 hug, jam, ram 4 bear, cram, iron, mass, move, pack, pile, push, rice, tamp 5 clasp, crowd, crush, drive, drove, elbow, force, horde, impel, shove, stuff 6 enfold, gather, goffer, hustle, jostle, propel, sadden, sinter, squash, squish, squush, throng, thrust 7 collect, embrace, gauffer, imprint,

squeeze, squelch, squoosh 8 assemble, bulldoze, shoulder 9 constrain, multitude, weigh down 10 congregate

pressing 4 dire 5 acute 6 direct, urgent 7 clamant, crucial, exigent, instant 8 critical 9 clamorous, immediate, insistent 10 imperative 11 importunate

pressure 4 push, rush 5 drive, impel 6 strain, stress 7 tension 9 overpress *combining form:* 4 tono 5 piezo *instrument:* 9 barometer *unit:* 3 bar 5 barye

prestige 4 rank, sway 5 power, state 6 cachet, credit, renown, status, weight 7 dignity, stature 8 eminence, position, standing 9 authority, influence 10 prominence, prominency 11 consequence, distinction

prestigious 5 famed, great 7 eminent, notable 8 renowned 9 prominent 10 celebrated 13 distinguished

presto 4 fast 7 flat-out, hastily, quickly, rapidly 8 chop-chop, full tilt 9 posthaste 12 lickety-split 13 expeditiously

presumably 6 likely 9 doubtless

presume 5 guess, opine, posit, think 6 impose, reason 7 intrude, obtrude, suppose, surmise 8 infringe 9 postulate 10 conjecture

presuming see **presumptuous**

presumption 4 face, gall 5 brass, cheek, nerve, posit 6 thesis 9 apriorism, brashness, postulate 10 confidence, effrontery

presumptuous 4 smug 5 brash, lofty 6 uppish, uppity 7 forward, pushful, pushing 9 confident 10 brassbound, complacent 11 inexcusable, overweening, self-assured

presuppose 5 guess, infer, judge, posit, think 6 assume, deduce, expect, gather, reckon 7 believe, imagine, surmise, suspect 9 postulate

presupposition 5 guess, posit 6 belief, thesis 7 surmise 8 judgment 9 apriorism, inference, judgement, postulate 10 conjecture

pretend 3 act 4 fake, sham 5 bluff, feign, guess, put on, think 6 affect, assume, delude 7 beguile, deceive, mislead, profess, purport, suppose, surmise 8 simulate

pretender 4 fake 5 faker, fraud, phony 6 humbug 8 impostor

pretense 3 air 4 face, fake, mask, sham 5 claim, cloak, color, cover, fraud, guise, title 6 deceit, facade, humbug 7 charade, pageant 8 coloring, disguise 9 deception, imposture, mannerism 10 false front, masquerade 11 affectation, make-believe

pretension 5 claim, title 7 charade, pageant 8 disguise 11 make-believe 13 ambitiousness

pretentious 3 big 4 arty 5 lofty, put-on, showy, swank, tumid 6 chichi, la-di-da, too-too, turgid 7 aureate, feigned, flowery, genteel, mincing, pompier, splashy, stilted, utopian 8 affected, imposing, inflated, peacocky 9 bombastic, grandiose, overblown, visionary 10 arty-crafty, euphuistic, flamboyant, peacockish, rhetorical 12 high-sounding, magniloquent *speech:* 7 bombast

preternatural 7 deviant 8 aberrant, abnormal, atypical, numinous, superior 9 anomalous, deviative, unearthly, untypical 10 miraculous, superhuman, suprahuman 11 heteroclite 12 supermundane, supra-mundane

pretext 4 mask 5 alibi, cloak, cover, front, guise 6 excuse 8 pretense

pretty 4 cute, fair, good, some 5 bonny, ducky 6 adroit, bonnie, clever, comely, fairly, incony, kind of, lovely, rather, seemly, sort of, wicked 7 cunning, darling, dollish 8 handsome, skillful, somewhat 9 beauteous, beautiful 10 attractive, moderately, more or less 11 good-looking

prevail 4 beat, rule 5 reign 6 affect, master 7 conquer, impress, triumph 8 dominate, domineer, overcome, override

prevailing see **prevalent**

prevalent 4 rife 5 usual 6 common, master, normal, ruling, wonted 7 general, natural, popular, rampant, regnant, regular, typical 8 dominant 9 ascendant, customary; paramount, sovereign 10 accustomed, widespread 11 commonplace

prevaricate 3 fib, lie 6 palter 7 falsify 12 misrepresent

prevarication 3 fib, lie 4 tale 5 lying, story 6 canard 7 falsity 9 falsehood

prevaricator 4 liar 6 fibber 7 Ananias, fibster 8 perjurer 9 falsifier 11 storyteller

prevent 3 bar, dam 4 balk, foil, ward 5 avert, block, check, debar, deter 6 arrest, baffle, forbid, hinder, impede, thwart 7 forfend, inhibit, obviate, rule out, shut out 8 obstruct, prohibit, stave off 9 forestall, frustrate, interdict, interrupt 10 anticipate *access:* 9 barricade

previous 4 fore, past 5 prior 6 before, former 7 earlier, forward 8 anterior, oversoon 9 foregoing, in advance, overearly 10 antecedent, beforehand

previously 4 once 6 before 7 already, earlier, priorly 8 formerly 9 erstwhile 10 heretofore

prey 4 game 5 chase 6 quarry, victim 8 casualty, underdog 9 bottom dog

Priam *daughter:* 6 Creusa 8 Polyxena 9 Cassandra *father:* 8 Laomedon *grandfather:* 4 Ilus *kingdom:* 4 Troy *slayer:* 7 Pyrrhus 11 Neoptolemus *son:* 5 Paris

6 Hector, Lycaon 7 Helenus, Troilus 9 Deiphobus, Polydorus *wife:* 6 Arisbe, Hecuba

Priapus *father:* 7 Bacchus 8 Dionysus *mother:* 5 Venus 9 Aphrodite

price 3 tab 4 cost, rate, toll 6 charge, tariff 7 expense

priceless 6 costly, valued 8 precious, valuable 9 cherished, treasured 10 invaluable

prick 3 cut, jab, sic 4 bore, goad, hole, prod, slit, spur, stab, urge 5 drill, egg on, enter, pique, punch, rowel, slash, sting, thorn 6 excite, exhort, prompt, propel 8 puncture 9 perforate, stimulate

prickly 5 burry, spiny 6 nettly, thorny, tingly, twitty 7 brambly, fretful, peevish, pettish, waspish 8 annoying, petulant, snappish 9 fractious, irritable 10 bothersome, nettlesome

pride 3 fat, top 4 best, brag, crow, face, pick 5 boast, cream, elite, pique, plume, preen, scorn, vaunt 6 choice, egoism, flower, morgue 7 bighead, conceit, dignity, disdain, egotism, hauteur 8 contempt, smugness, vainness 9 arrogance, cockiness, gasconade, insolence, loftiness, self-glory, self-trust, superbity, vainglory 10 felicitate, self-esteem, self-regard 11 amour propre, haughtiness, self-opinion, self-respect 12 congratulate, snobbishness 13 condescension, self-assurance

Pride and Prejudice author 6 Austen (Jane)

prier 5 snoop 6 butt-in 7 meddler, Paul Pry 8 busybody, quidnunc 10 rubberneck

priest 9 clergyman 10 chancellor 11 chamberlain *ancient Roman:* 6 fecial, fetial, flamen 8 pontifex *Buddhist:* 4 lama *Celtic:* 5 druid *French:* 4 abbé, curé *Indian:* 6 shaman *military:* 5 padre 8 chaplain *Muslim:* 4 imam *of Bacchus:* 6 maenad 9 bacchante

priestly 8 hieratic 10 sacerdotal 12 sacerdotical

prig 5 prude, thief 6 Grundy, nimmer, stuffy, wowser 7 filcher, genteel, prudish, puritan, stealer 8 bluenose, comstock, larcener, pilferer 9 larcenist, Mrs. Grundy, nice Nelly, purloiner, Victorian 10 goody-goody, tight-laced 11 puritanical, straitlaced

priggish 4 smug 6 stuffy 7 genteel, prudish 9 Victorian 10 complacent, self-loving, tight-laced 11 puritanical, self-pleased, straitlaced 13 self-contented, self-esteeming, self-righteous, self-satisfied

prim 4 neat, nice, snug, tidy 5 rigid, stiff 6 formal, proper, stuffy, wooden 7 chipper, correct, genteel, missish, orderly, precise, prudish 8 decorous, straight 9 bluenosed, shipshape, Victorian 10 ceremonial, tight-laced 11 ceremonious, puritanical, straitlaced, uncluttered, well-groomed **12** conventional

prima facie 11 self-evident

primary 4 main **5** basal, basic, chief, first **6** bottom, direct **7** initial, pioneer, radical **8** earliest, original **9** firsthand, immediate, underived **10** underlying **11** fundamental **12** foundational, underivative *combining form:* **4** prot **5** proto *prefix:* **4** arch **5** archi

primate 3 ape, man **5** human **6** monkey **7** gorilla **10** anthropoid, chimpanzee, human being **11** Homo sapiens *nocturnal:* **7** tarsier *small:* **6** galago

prime 3 top **4** best, fine, morn, move, pick **5** cream, elite, first, sunup, youth **6** aurora, choice, excite, famous, spring **7** capital, initial, morning, provoke, quicken, sunrise **8** cockcrow, daybreak, earliest, motivate, original, superior **9** dayspring, excellent, first-rate, galvanize, stimulate, underived **10** first-class, juvenility, springtide **11** adolescence

primer 4 book **6** reader **8** hornbook

primeval 10 aboriginal; (see also **primordial**)

primitive 5 basic, early **7** archaic **8** original **9** barbarian, elemental, essential, underived, unevolved **10** elementary, persistent, substratal, underlying **11** fundamental, nonliterate, preliterate, uncivilized, undeveloped **12** uncultivated *combining form:* **4** pale **5** palae, paleo **6** archae, archeo, palaeo, palaio **7** archaeo *prefix:* **4** arch **5** arche, archi

primogenitor 7 forbear **8** ancestor, forebear **9** ascendant **10** forefather

primordial 5 early, first **8** earliest, original **10** elementary **11** fundamental, undeveloped

primordium 6 anlage, origin **9** beginning

primp 5 fix up, preen, slick, spiff **6** doll up **7** deck out, doll out, dress up, gussy up

prince *Anglo-Saxon:* **8** atheling *Arab:* **4** emir **5** emeer *Austrian:* **8** archduke *Ethiopian:* **3** ras *Indian:* **4** raja **5** rajah *Muslim:* **4** amir **5** ameer *of demons:* **9** Beelzebub *of Monaco:* **7** Rainier *of the church:* **8** cardinal *of Wales:* **7** Charles

Prince and the Pauper author 5 Twain (Mark)

Prince Edward Island *capital:* **13** Charlottetown *discoverer:* **7** Cartier (Jacques)

Prince Igor composer 7 Borodin (Aleksandr)

princely 5 grand, noble, royal **6** august, lordly **8** baronial, imposing **9** grandiose **11** magnificent

princess *mythical:* **3** Ino *of Monaco:* **5** Grace

principal 4 arch, head, main, star **5** chief, first, major **7** capital, leading, premier, pri-

mary, stellar **8** champion, dominant, foremost **10** preeminent **11** outstanding, predominant *combining form:* **4** prot **5** proto *prefix:* **4** arch **5** archi

principium 3 law **5** axiom, basis **7** element, theorem **10** foundation **11** fundamental

principle 3 law **4** form, rule **5** axiom, basis, canon, tenet, usage **6** ground **7** precept, theorem **8** polestar **10** convention, foundation **11** fundamental

principled 5 moral, noble **7** ethical **8** virtuous **9** righteous **10** moralistic

print 4 type **5** litho, stamp, write **7** engrave, impress, publish, typeset **10** impression *style:* **5** roman **6** italic **7** cursive

printer *English:* **6** Caxton (William) *Italian:* **6** Bodoni (Giambattista) **8** Manutius (Aldus)

printers' mark see proofreaders' mark

printer's receptacle 7 hellbox

printing 7 edition, reissue **10** impression *measure:* **2** em, en **4** pica **5** agate **6** cicero *plate:* **6** stereo **7** linecut *process:* **4** roto **7** gravure *style:* **6** gothic

prior see previous

priority 5 order **8** ordering **9** supremacy **10** ascendancy, precedence

prison 3 pen **4** jail, keep **6** cooler, lockup **7** bastile, dungeon, slammer **8** bastille, stockade **11** reformatory **12** penitentiary *California:* **10** San Quentin *former:* **8** Alcatraz, Sing-Sing *New York:* **6** Attica **12** Rikers Island *Northern Ireland:* **4** Maze *resident:* **6** inmate **7** convict **8** jailbird

prissy 6 stuffy **7** epicene, finicky, genteel, missish, prudish, unmanly **9** pansified, sissified, squeamish, Victorian **10** effeminate, fastidious, tight-laced **11** puritanical, straitlaced **12** Miss-Nancyish

pristine 4 pure **8** earliest, original

privacy 7 secrecy **9** seclusion

private 6 closet, hidden, hushed, inside, secret **7** soldier **8** discreet, personal **9** concealed **10** closed-door **12** confidential

private detective see detective

privately 7 sub rosa **8** covertly, in camera, secretly **9** by stealth **10** stealthily

privation 4 lack, loss, need, want **6** dearth, defect, losing, misery, penury **7** absence, default, poverty **8** distress, poorness **9** indigence, mislaying, neediness, suffering **10** misplacing **11** deprivement, divestiture

privilege 4 boon **5** favor, right **8** appanage **9** allowance **10** birthright, concession, perquisite **11** prerogative *popegranted:* **6** indult

privy 2 WC **4** head, john **5** jakes **6** buried, covert, hidden, johnny, toilet **7** latrine **8** lavatory, obscured, outhouse, personal, shrouded, stealthy, ulterior 9 backhouse, concealed 11 convenience, water closet

prize 3 pry, top 4 best, loot, meed, pick, plum, swag 5 award, booty, cream, elite, jimmy, lever, spoil, value 6 boodle, carrot, choice, esteem, reward, trophy 7 cherish, guerdon, jackpot, plunder, premium 8 dividend, treasure 10 appreciate, plunderage 11 outstanding

prizefighting 8 pugilism 10 fisticuffs

pro 3 for, vet, wiz 4 whiz, with 5 adept, doyen 6 expert, master 9 authority, in favor of 10 master-hand

probable 6 likely 7 seeming 8 apparent, rational 10 reasonable

probe 3 ask 4 quiz, sift 5 query, quest, scout 6 go into 7 delving, dig into, examine, explore, feel out, inquest, inquire, inquiry 8 look into, research, sound out 9 catechize, delve into 11 inquire into, inquisition, interrogate, investigate, reconnoiter 13 investigation

probity 6 virtue 7 honesty 8 goodness 9 integrity, rectitude, rightness 11 uprightness

problem 3 nut 5 issue 6 enigma, puzzle 7 bugaboo, bugbear, dilemma, example, mystery

problematic 4 moot, open 7 dubious, suspect 8 arguable, doubtful, mootable 9 ambiguous, debatable, dubitable, uncertain, unsettled 10 disputable, indecisive, precarious 12 questionable

proboscis 4 beak, nose 5 snoot, snout 7 smeller

procedure 4 line, move, step 6 course, method, policy, polity 7 measure, program 8 demarche, maneuver

proceed 2 go 3 hie 4 fare, flow, head, move, pass, rise, stem, wend 5 arise, get on, issue, march, segue 6 push on, repair, spring, travel 7 advance, emanate, journey 8 get along, progress 9 originate 10 derive from

proceedings 8 goings-on *recorded:* 4 acta

proceeds 4 gain 5 lucre 6 profit, return 8 earnings

process 3 way 4 mode, wise 5 modus 6 manner, method, system 7 fashion, recycle, routine 9 operation, outgrowth, technique *combining form:* 4 typy *suffix:* 2 al, th 3 ing, ism, sis 4 ance, ence, esis, osis 7 ization

procession 5 order 6 parade, series 8 sequence 9 cavalcade 11 consecution *combining form:* 4 cade

proclaim 4 mark, show, vent 5 bruit, utter, voice 6 blazon, evince, herald, ostend 7 clarion, declare, exhibit, publish 8 announce, evidence, manifest, promulge

9 advertise, broadcast, ventilate 10 annunciate, bruit about, illustrate, promulgate 11 blaze abroad, demonstrate

proclivity see **penchant**

Procne *father:* 7 Pandion *husband:* 6 Tereus *sister:* 9 Philomela *son:* 4 Itys

procrastinate 3 lag 4 drag, poke, stay 5 dally, defer, delay, tarry 6 dawdle, linger, loiter, put off 7 prolong, suspend 8 postpone

procreate 4 bear, make, sire 5 beget, breed, hatch, spawn 6 father, mother, parent 7 produce 8 engender, generate, multiply 9 originate, propagate, reproduce

Procris' husband and slayer 8 Cephalus

Procrustean ___ 3 bed

proctor 9 supervise 10 supervisor

procure 3 get 4 draw, gain, have, land 5 annex 6 draw in, draw on, induce, obtain, pick up 7 acquire, compass, win over

prod 3 dig, jab, jog, sic 4 goad, poke, spur, urge 5 egg on, nudge, pique, prick, punch 6 excite, exhort 9 stimulate

prodigal 4 lush 6 lavish, waster 7 opulent, profuse, riotous, spender, wastrel 8 unthrift 9 exuberant, luxuriant, profusive 10 high roller, profligate, squanderer 11 scattergood, spendthrift, wastethrift

prodigious 4 huge, vast 6 mighty, mortal 7 amazing, immense, mammoth, massive 8 colossal, cracking, enormous, gigantic, towering 9 fantastic, marvelous, monstrous, wonderful 10 astounding, miraculous, monumental, staggering, stupendous, surprising

produce 4 bear, form, give, grow, make, show, sire 5 beget, breed, build, cause, erect, frame, get up, hatch, mount, put on, raise, spawn, stage, yield 6 create, draw on, effect, father, output, parent, secure, work up 7 deliver, fashion, outturn, turn out 8 engender, generate, multiply, muster up 9 construct, cultivate, fabricate, originate, procreate, propagate 10 bring about 11 manufacture, put together *combining form:* 3 fer, gen 4 gene 5 genic 6 genous 7 genetic

product 5 fruit, yield 6 effect, output, result 7 harvest, outcome, outturn, turnout 8 multiple, offshoot 9 handiwork, outgrowth 11 consequence *combining form:* 3 ade, ine, ite

production 5 fruit, yield 6 output 7 outturn, turnout *combining form:* 4 geny, gony 7 genesia, poiesis 8 fication

productive 4 rich 6 fecund 7 fertile 8 childing, fruitful, prolific, spawning 11 proliferant

proem see **prologue**

profane 3 lay 4 foul 5 dirty, nasty, pagan 6 coarse, ethnic, filthy, smutty, unholy, vulgar 7 earthly, gentile, heathen, impious, infidel, mundane, obscene, raunchy, secular, ungodly, worldly 8 indecent, temporal, unsacred 9 infidelic 10 irreverent, unhallowed 11 blasphemous, terrestrial 12 sacrilegious 13 irreverential

profanity 4 oath 5 curse 7 cursing, cussing 8 swearing 9 blasphemy 10 execration 11 imprecation

profess 4 aver, avow 6 affirm, assert, avouch, depose 7 declare, protest, purport 8 constate 9 predicate

profession 3 art, job 5 craft, trade 6 career, métier 7 calling 8 vocation 10 handicraft *suffix:* 4 ship

professional 3 pro 4 paid, whiz 5 adept 6 artist, expert, master 7 artiste 8 virtuoso 9 authority 10 past master, proficient

professor 3 don 7 teacher

proffer 4 give, pose 5 offer 6 extend, tender 7 hold out, present 8 proposal 10 invitation, suggestion 11 proposition

proficiency 5 march, skill 7 advance, headway, ongoing 8 anabasis, progress 9 adeptness

proficient 4 able, whiz 5 adept, crack 6 artist, expert, master 7 artiste, capable, drilled, skilled 8 finished, masterly, skillful, virtuoso 9 authority, competent, effective, effectual, efficient, exercised, masterful, practiced, qualified 10 checked-out, consummate, past master 11 crackerjack, experienced 12 accomplished, professional

profile 4 line 7 contour, outline 9 lineament, lineation 10 figuration, silhouette

profit 3 net 4 gain, take 5 avail, lucre, serve, yield 6 output, return 7 benefit, cleanup, killing, outturn, product, receipt, turnout, work for 8 cleaning, earnings, proceeds

profitable 6 paying 7 gainful 9 lucrative 10 well-paying, worthwhile 11 moneymaking 12 advantageous, remunerative

profligate 6 bad lot, no-good, waster 7 rounder, spender, wastrel 8 prodigal, unthrift, wasteful 9 abandoned, dissolute, reprobate 10 high roller, licentious, ne'er-do-well, scapegrace, squanderer 11 scattergood, spendthrift, wastethrift

profound 3 low 4 deep, hard, wise 5 heavy 6 occult, orphic, secret 7 abysmal, intense 8 abstruse, esoteric, hermetic 9 intensive

profoundness 5 abyss, depth 8 deepness 10 profundity

profundity see **profoundness**

profuse 4 lush 6 lavish 7 copious, liberal, opulent, riotous, teeming 8 abundant, generous, prodigal, swarming 9 abounding,

bounteous, bountiful, excessive, exuberant, luxuriant 10 immoderate, munificent

profusive see **profuse**

progenitor 4 sire 8 ancestor, forebear 9 ascendant 10 forefather

progeny see **posterity**

prognosis 4 cast 5 weird 8 forecast, prophecy 9 prevision 10 prediction 11 foretelling

prognostic 4 omen, sign 6 augury, boding 7 portent, presage 8 bodement 9 foretoken

prognosticate see **predict**

program 4 bill, card, line, plan, sked 5 slate 6 agenda, course, docket, policy, polity 8 calendar, schedule 9 procedure, timetable 10 bill of fare *theater:* 8 playbill

progress 2 go 4 fare, grow, move 5 get on, march 6 course, growth 7 advance, headway, ongoing, passage, proceed, promote 8 anabasis, get along, upgrowth 9 evolution, flowering, unfolding 10 evolvement 11 advancement, development, proficiency *planned:* 7 telesis

progressing 5 afoot 8 under way

progression 3 row 5 chain, order, train 6 course, growth, sequel, series 7 advance 8 sequence, upgrowth 9 evolution, flowering, unfolding 10 evolvement, succession 11 alternation, consecution, development

progressive 4 wide 5 broad 7 liberal, radical 8 advanced, stepwise, tolerant

prohibit 3 ban, bar 5 taboo 6 enjoin, forbid, outlaw 7 inhibit 9 interdict

prohibited 5 taboo 6 banned 7 illegal, illicit 8 verboten 9 forbidden

project 3 jut, see 4 cast, feat, gest, plan, poke, pout 5 bulge, chart, image, pouch, thing, think 6 affair, beetle, design, devise, extend, intend, matter, scheme, vision 7 arrange, concern, diagram, dope out, emprise, exploit, feature, imagine, prolong, propose, purpose, venture 8 business, conceive, envisage, envision, game plan, lengthen, overhang, protrude, stand out, stick out, strategy 9 adventure, blueprint, delineate, visualize 10 enterprise 11 proposition, undertaking *trivial:* 10 boondoggle

projecting 7 salient

projection 3 jut 4 bump, hook, knob, spur 5 bulge, bunch, ledge, point, spine 8 eminence, forecast, salience, swelling 9 extension, outthrust 10 prominence, protrusion

projet 4 plan 5 draft

proletariat 3 mob 4 mass 6 rabble 7 workers 8 canaille, laborers

prolific 4 rich 6 fecund 7 fertile 8 breeding, childing, fruitful, spawning, swarming 9 abounding 10 generating, productive 11 propagating, reproducing 12 reproductive

prolix 5 windy, wordy 7 diffuse, irksome, tedious, verbose 8 tiresome 9 prolonged, redundant, wearisome 10 long-winded, palaverous, protracted

prolixity 9 verbalism, verbosity, windiness, wordiness 11 verboseness

prologue 5 proem 7 preface, prelude 8 exordium, foreword, overture, preamble 9 prelusion 12 introduction, prolegomenon

prolong 4 draw, last 6 endure, extend 7 draw out, persist, spin out, stretch 8 continue, elongate, lengthen, protract

prolonged 4 long 7 lengthy 8 dragging, drawn-out, longsome, overlong 10 protracted

promenade 4 deck, walk 5 dance 6 parade, stroll 7 balcony, gallery 9 boardwalk

Prometheus *brother:* 5 Atlas 9 Menoetius 10 Epimetheus *creation:* 3 man *father:* 7 Iapetus *gift to man:* 4 fire *mother:* 7 Clymene *rescuer:* 8 Heracles, Hercules

prominence 6 renown 8 eminence, prestige, salience 10 importance, projection 11 distinction *combining form:* 8 tubercul 9 tuberculo

prominent 5 famed, great, noted 6 famous, marked, signal 7 eminent, leading, notable, popular, salient 8 renowned, striking 9 arresting, arrestive, notorious, well-known 10 celebrated, celebrious, noticeable, remarkable 11 conspicuous, illustrious, outstanding 13 distinguished *person:* 3 VIP 6 bigwig 7 grandee

promiscuous 5 mixed 6 motley, random, varied 7 aimless 8 assorted, chowchow 9 desultory, haphazard, hit-or-miss, irregular, unplanned 10 designless 11 purposeless

promise 3 vow 4 bode, oath, omen, pass, pawn, word 5 agree, augur, swear, token 6 accede, assent, assure, engage, ensure, insure, pledge, plight 7 bargain, betoken, compact, consent, earnest, portend, presage, warrant 8 contract, covenant, forebode, foreshow, security 9 assurance, foretoken, guarantee, undertake

promised land 4 Zion 6 Canaan, heaven, utopia 7 arcadia 8 paradise 9 cockaigne, fairyland, shangri-la 10 lubberland, wonderland

promising 4 rosy 6 likely 7 hopeful, roseate 11 encouraging, rose-colored

promissory note 3 IOU

promontory 4 beak, bill, cape, head, naze, peak 5 point 8 foreland, headland

promote 3 aid, cry 4 help, plug, puff, push 5 boost, serve 6 foster, impart, prefer 7 advance, build up, elevate, forward, fur-

ther, upgrade 8 ballyhoo 9 advertise, encourage, publicize 10 press-agent

promoter 5 agent

promotion 7 advance, buildup, puffery 9 elevation, prelation, publicity, upgrading 10 preference, preferment 11 advancement, advertising 13 advertisement

prompt 3 apt, cue, get, sic 4 draw, fast, goad, prod, spur, urge 5 alert, egg on, prick, quick, rapid, ready, swift 6 exhort, induce, propel, speedy, timely 7 win over 8 convince, persuade, punctual, talk into

promulgate 4 toot 5 sound 7 declare, publish 8 announce, proclaim 9 advertise, broadcast 10 annunciate 11 disseminate

prone 3 apt 4 fain, flat, open 5 given, level, ready 6 liable, likely, minded, supine 7 exposed, subject, willing 8 disposed, inclined, resupine 9 decumbent, obnoxious, prostrate, reclining, recumbent, sensitive 11 predisposed, susceptible

prong 3 nib 4 fang, fork, stab, tine 5 point

pronghorn 6 cabree 8 antelope

pronoun *archaic:* 2 ye 3 thy 4 thou 5 thine *demonstrative:* 4 that, this 5 these, those *indefinite:* 3 all, any, few, one 4 both, each, none, some 5 no one, other 6 anyone, either, nobody 7 another, anybody, neither, nothing, someone 8 anything, somebody 9 everybody, something 10 everything *personal:* 2 he, it, my, we 3 her, him, his, its, our, she, you 4 hers, mine, ours, them, they, your 5 their, yours 6 theirs *possessive:* 2 my 3 her, his, its, our 4 hers, mine, ours, your 5 their, yours 6 theirs *reflexive:* 6 itself, myself 7 herself, himself, oneself, ourself 8 yourself 9 ourselves 10 themselves, yourselves *relative:* 3 who 4 that, what, whom 5 which, whose, whoso 6 whomso 7 whoever 8 whatever, whomever 9 whichever, whosoever 10 whatsoever, whomsoever 11 whichsoever

pronounce 3 say 5 speak, utter 6 recite 7 declare, phonate 9 enunciate 10 articulate

pronounced 7 assured, decided 8 clearcut, definite

pronouncement 9 statement 11 declaration, publication 12 proclamation, promulgation

pronto 4 fast 6 at once 7 quickly 8 promptly 9 posthaste 11 immediately

pronunciation 6 speech 9 utterance *distinctive:* 4 burr 5 drawl, twang 6 accent *study:* 8 orthoepy 9 phonetics

proof 4 test 6 galley 8 argument, evidence 9 testament, testimony 10 impression 11 attestation 12 confirmation

proofreaders' mark 3 cap, rom 4 dele, ital, stet 5 caret

prop 3 leg 4 stay 5 brace, carry, shore 6 bear up, buoy up, column, upbear, uphold 7 bolster, shore up, support, sustain 8 buttress 12 underpinning

propaganda 4 hype 8 agitprop 9 publicity

propagandist 7 apostle 9 missioner 10 colporteur, evangelist, missionary

propagate 4 bear, grow 5 beget, breed, raise, strew 6 spread 7 diffuse, produce, radiate 8 disperse, generate, multiply 9 circulate, cultivate, procreate, reproduce 10 distribute 11 disseminate

propel 4 goad, move, prod, push, spur, urge 5 drive, egg on, impel, power, prick, shove 6 exhort, prompt, thrust 7 actuate

propellant 4 fuel, spur 7 impetus, impulse 8 catalyst, stimulus 9 incentive, stimulant 10 incitation, motivation 11 provocative

propeller 3 fan, oar 5 screw 6 paddle

propensity see penchant

proper 3 apt, due, fit 4 able, good, just, meet, nice, prig, prim, true 5 exact, happy, right 6 au fait, comely, decent, prissy, stuffy, useful 7 capable, correct, desired, fitting, genteel, missish, precise, prudish 8 accurate, becoming, decorous, peculiar, priggish, rightful, rigorous, suitable 9 befitting, competent, diacritic, qualified 10 applicable, conforming, convenient, diagnostic, felicitous, individual 11 appropriate, comme il faut, distinctive, puritanical, straitlaced *combining form:* 4 orth 5 ortho

property 4 land, mark 5 trait, worth 6 estate, realty, riches, virtue, wealth 7 feature, fortune, quality 8 dominion 9 affection, attribute, character, ownership, resources, substance 10 possession, real estate *conveyor:* 7 alienor *private:* 8 peculium *recipient:* 7 alienee *seller:* 7 Realtor *transfer:* 8 alienate

prophecy 4 cast 5 weird 6 oracle, vision 8 forecast 9 prevision, prognosis 10 apocalypse, prediction, revelation 11 foretelling

prophesier 4 seer 5 augur 6 auspex 7 prophet 8 foreseer, haruspex 9 predictor 10 forecaster, foreteller 11 Nostradamus

prophesy 5 augur 7 portend, predict, presage 8 forecast, foretell, soothsay 9 adumbrate 10 vaticinate 13 prognosticate

prophet 4 seer 5 augur 6 auspex, oracle 7 seeress 8 foreseer, haruspex 9 predictor 10 forecaster, foreteller, prophesier, soothsayer 11 Nostradamus *Arthurian:* 6 Merlin *Major:* 6 Daniel, Isaiah 7 Ezekiel 8 Jeremiah *Minor:* 4 Amos, Joel 5 Hosea, Jonah, Micah, Nahum 6 Haggai 7 Malachi, Obadiah 8 Habakkuk 9 Zechariah, Zephaniah

prophetess 4 Anna 5 Sibyl 6 Huldah, Miriam 7 Deborah, Noadiah 9 Cassandra

prophetic 5 vatic 6 mantic, mystic 7 fatidic, strange, vatical 8 Delphian, oracular 9 sibylline, vaticinal 10 mysterious, revelatory 11 apocalyptic, prophetical

propinquity 7 kinship 8 nearness 9 closeness, immediacy, proximity 10 contiguity

propitiate 5 adapt, atone 6 adjust, pacify 7 appease, assuage, conform, content, mediate, mollify, placate, satisfy, sweeten 9 intercede, reconcile 10 conciliate

propitiatory 7 lustral 9 expiative, expiatory, purgative

propitious 4 good, rosy 5 brave, white 6 benign, bright, dexter, timely, toward, useful 7 benefic, helpful, timeous 8 favoring 9 favorable, fortunate, opportune, well-timed 10 auspicious, beneficial, prosperous, seasonable 12 advantageous

proponent 6 backer 8 advocate, champion 9 expounder, supporter

proportion 4 rate, size, tune 5 ratio, scale 6 attune, degree, extent 7 balance, conform, harmony, measure, prorate 8 symmetry

proportional 5 equal 7 in scale 8 relative 9 dependent 10 contingent, reciprocal 11 correlative, symmetrical 12 commensurate 13 commensurable, corresponding

proposal 3 bid 4 idea, plan 6 motion, scheme 7 outline, proffer, project 10 invitation, suggestion 11 proposition *final:* 9 ultimatum

propose 3 aim, ask, put 4 mean, plan, pose 5 offer 6 design, intend, prefer, submit, tender 7 move for, present, purpose, request, solicit, suggest 8 nominate, propound, theorize 11 contemplate

proposition 3 put 4 pose 5 lemma, offer 6 prefer, thesis 7 premise, proffer, propose, suggest, theorem 8 proposal, propound 10 invitation, suggestion

propound 3 put 4 pose 6 prefer 7 propone, propose, suggest 11 proposition

proprietor 5 owner 6 holder 9 possessor

propriety 5 order 6 manner 7 aptness, decency, decorum, dignity, fitness 8 meetness 9 etiquette, rightness 10 expediency, propeness, seemliness 11 correctness, orderliness, suitability 12 appositeness, correctitude, decorousness, suitableness

propulsion 4 fuel, push 5 drive, power

prorate 5 allot, divvy, quota, share 6 divide, parcel, ration 7 portion 9 apportion

prorogate see prorogue

prorogue 4 rise, stay 5 defer, delay, remit 6 hold up, put off, recess, shelve 7 adjourn,

hold off **8** dissolve, hold over, postpone
9 prorogate, terminate

prosaic 4 drab, dull, flat **5** lowly, prose,
prosy **6** actual, boring, common **7** factual,
irksome, literal, mundane, tedious, workday
8 everyday, lifeless, ordinary, workaday
9 colorless, practical **10** lackluster, lusterless, uneventful **11** commonplace

proscenium 5 stage **9** forestage **10** fore-
ground

proscribe 3 ban **4** damn, doom **7** condemn **8** prohibit, sentence

proscription 3 ban **5** taboo **11** forbiddance, prohibition **12** interdiction

prosecute 3 sue **5** press **6** charge, indict

prosecutor 2 DA **6** lawyer **7** accuser
public: **6** fiscal

proselyte 7 convert, recruit **8** neophyte

____ **prosequi 5** nolle

prospect 4 mine, sift **5** probe, scape,
vista **6** go into **7** dig into, explore, lookout,
outlook **8** look into **9** candidate

prosper 3 dow **4** boom **5** score, yield
6 arrive, thrive **7** augment, make out, produce, succeed, turn out **8** flourish, increase

prosperity 4 boom, ease **6** growth,
riches, wealth **7** arrival, benefit, success,
welfare **8** interest, thriving **9** abundance,
advantage, affluence, expansion, inflation,
well-being **10** easy street **12** flying colors

Prospero *daughter:* **7** Miranda *servant:*
5 Ariel *slave:* **7** Caliban

prosperous 4 easy, rich, well **5** happy,
lucky, lusty, palmy **6** robust, strong, timely
7 booming, halcyon, opulent, roaring, thrifty,
timeous, wealthy, well-off **8** affluent, thriving, well-to-do **9** desirable, favorable, fortunate, opportune, well-fixed, well-timed
10 auspicious, convenient, felicitous, propitious, seasonable, successful, well-heeled
11 appropriate, comfortable, flourishing,
substantial

prostitute 4 bawd, doxy, drab, moll
5 abuse, madam, poule, quean, whore
6 callet, debase, harlot, hooker, misuse,
pickup, tomato, wanton **7** cocotte, corrupt,
cruiser, Cyprian, debauch, deprave, hustler,
joy girl, Paphian, vitiate **8** call girl, meretrix,
misapply, strumpet **9** cocodette, misemploy, mishandle, party girl **10** misimprove,
street girl **11** fille de joie, nightwalker
12 camp follower, streetwalker *reformed:*
8 Magdalen

prostitution 8 harlotry, whoredom
10 social evil **13** streetwalking *house of:*
7 brothel **8** bordello

prostrate 4 down, drop, fell, flat, poop
5 floor, level, prone, whelm **6** disarm,
ground, lay low, tucker **7** cripple, disable,
exhaust, frazzle, outtire, outwear, wear out

8 knock out, overcome, paralyze **9** decumbent, knock over, overpower, overwhelm,
reclining, recumbent, throw down

protagonist 4 hero, star **5** actor **6** leader
8 advocate, champion **9** spokesman

protean 5 fluid **6** mobile **7** mutable
8 unstable, unsteady, variable, weathery
9 changeful, unsettled **10** changeable

protect 4 fend, save **5** cover, guard
6 defend, harbor, screen, secure, shield
7 bulwark, shelter **8** conserve, preserve
9 safeguard

protected 4 safe **6** immune

protection 3 pad **4** ward **5** aegis, armor,
bribe, graft, guard **6** safety, shield
7 defense, squeeze **8** armament, security
9 extortion, safeguard, shakedown

protector 5 armor, guard **6** patron, shield
7 tutelar **8** guardian

protégé 4 ward **5** pupil **7** student

protein 4 zein **5** actin, opsin **6** avidin,
enzyme, fibrin, globin **7** albumin, elastin,
fibroin, histone, keratin, legumin, sericin
8 creatine, globulin, glutelin, prolamin, prota-
min, proteose, vitellin *complex:* **6** mucoid
derivative: **7** peptone *poisonous:* **5** abrin,
ricin *source:* **4** eggs, fish, meat, milk
6 cheese

pro tem 6 acting, supply **7** interim **9** ad
interim, temporary **10** pro tempore

protest 4 aver, avow, kick **5** demur, fight
6 affirm, assert, avouch, combat, depose,
except, object, oppose, picket, resist
7 declare, profess **8** constate, demurral,
demurrer **9** challenge, objection

Protestant 5 Amish **6** Mormon, Quaker,
Shaker **7** Baptist, Lollard, Pilgrim, Puritan
8 Anglican, Lutheran, Moravian **9** Adventist, Mennonite, Methodist, Unitarian
12 Episcopalian, Presbyterian *Bohemian:*
7 Hussite *dissenter:* **7** sectary *French:*
8 Huguenot *martyr:* (see at martyr)

prototypal see prototypical

prototype 5 model **8** ancestor, foregoer,
original **9** archetype, precursor **10** antecedent, antecessor, forerunner, protoplast
11 predecessor

prototypical 5 ideal, model **7** classic
9 classical, exemplary **10** archetypal

protozoan 4 cell **5** ameba **6** amoeba
7 arcella, ciliate, stentor **10** flagellate, para-
mecium

protract see prolong

protrude 3 jut **4** poke, pout **5** bulge,
pouch **6** beetle **7** project **8** overhang,
stand out, stick out

protrusion 3 jut, nub **4** bump, hump
5 bulge **8** eminence, swelling **9** outthrust
10 projection **12** protuberance

protuberance see protrusion

protuberate see protrude

proud 4 vain 5 huffy, lofty, noble, wiggy 6 lordly, stuffy, superb 7 bloated, haughty, pompous, stuck-up, sublime 8 arrogant, cavalier, glorious, gorgeous, insolent, misproud, orgulous, scornful, splendid, superior, toplofty 9 conceited, hubristic, imperious, important, masterful 10 disdainful, dismissive, high-handed 11 domineering, magnificent, overbearing, pretentious, resplendent, splendorous, toploftical 12 contemptuous, narcissistic, ostentatious, proudhearted, supercilious

prove 3 try 4 show, test 5 argue, check 6 attest, verify 7 bespeak, betoken, confirm, examine, make out 8 document, indicate 9 determine, establish 11 corroborate, demonstrate 12 substantiate

provenance 4 root, well 6 origin, source, whence 8 fountain 9 inception 10 derivation, wellspring 11 provenience

provender see provisions

provenience see provenance

proverb 3 saw 4 word 5 adage, axiom, maxim 6 byword, saying

provide 4 feed, give, hand 5 cater, endow, equip 6 afford, supply 7 deliver, furnish, support 8 dispense, hand over, maintain

provided 2 if 6 if only 8 equipped

providence 6 thrift 7 caution, economy 8 prudence 9 canniness, foresight, frugality, husbandry 10 discretion, precaution 11 forethought, thriftiness 12 discreetness

provident 5 canny, chary 6 frugal, saving, Scotch 7 sparing, thrifty 9 stewardly 10 economical, unwasteful

providential 4 kind, well 5 happy, lucky 6 kindly 9 benignant, fortunate

province 4 area, duty, role, walk, work 5 field 6 domain, office, sphere 7 calling, demesne, pursuit, terrain 8 business, district, dominion, function 9 bailiwick, champaign, territory 10 department *Greek:* 4 nome 8 nomarchy

provincial 4 hick, jake, rube 5 clown, local, rural 6 rustic 7 bigoted, bucolic, bumpkin, country, hayseed, insular, outland, peasant 8 agrestic, pastoral 9 hidebound, parochial, sectarian, small-town 10 campestral, out-country 11 countrified

provision 4 term 6 clause 7 proviso, strings 9 condition 11 reservation, stipulation

provisional 4 iffy 7 stopgap 9 dependent, makeshift, provisory, temporary, tentative 10 contingent 11 conditional 13 rough-and-ready

provisions 4 feed, food, grub 6 viands 7 edibles, nurture 8 supplies, victuals 9 provender 11 comestibles *dealer:* 8 chandler

proviso see provision

provocation 6 irking, vexing 8 vexation 9 annoyance, bothering, provoking 10 harassment

provocative 4 goad, push, spur 7 impetus, impulse 8 stimulus 9 incentive 10 incitation, incitement, motivation 11 challenging

provoke 3 bug, get, irk, vex 4 abet, fire, fret, gall, move, rile, roil, stir, wake, whet 5 anger, annoy, breed, cause, chafe, exalt, get up, grate, hatch, pique, prime, raise, rally, rouse, set on, upset, waken 6 abrade, arouse, awaken, bestir, bother, excite, foment, harass, incite, induce, inform, insult, kindle, madden, put out, ruffle, stir up, thrill, whip up 7 animate, build up, enthuse, incense, inflame, innerve, inspire, outrage, perturb, produce, quicken 8 engender, exercise, generate, irritate, motivate, muster up, occasion, titivate 9 aggravate, challenge, electrify, galvanize, innervate, instigate, stimulate, titillate

provost 4 head 6 keeper 7 marshal 8 director 13 administrator

prow 3 bow 4 beak, stem 5 front

prowess 5 skill, valor 7 address, heroism, sleight 8 deftness, valiance, valiancy 9 dexterity, gallantry, readiness 10 adroitness 12 valorousness 13 dexterousness

prowl 4 hunt, pace, roam 5 creep 6 wander

proximate 4 near, next, nigh, rude 5 close, rough 6 nearby 8 imminent 9 immediate, impending 10 near-at-hand

proximity 8 nearness, vicinity 9 adjacency, closeness, immediacy 10 contiguity 11 propinquity 12 togetherness

proxy 5 agent, power 6 deputy, factor 8 assignee, attorney 9 authority

prude 4 prig 6 Grundy 7 old fogy, old maid, Puritan 8 bluenose, comstock 9 Mrs. Grundy, nice Nelly 10 fuddy-duddy, fussbudget, goody-goody, spoilsport, wet blanket 12 stuffed shirt

prudence 3 wit 6 acumen, thrift, wisdom 7 caution, economy, insight 8 astucity, keenness, sagacity, sageness, sapience 9 canniness, chariness, foresight, frugality, husbandry 10 astuteness, discretion, expediency, precaution, providence, shrewdness 11 calculation, forethought, penetration, percipience, thriftiness 12 discreetness, perspicacity

prudent 4 sage, sane, wary, wise 5 canny, chary 7 politic, sapient 8 cautious, sensible, tactical 9 advisable, expedient, judicious

prudish 4 prim 5 stern 6 prissy, proper, severe, strict, stuffy 7 austere, genteel 8 priggish 9 Victorian 11 puritanical, strait-laced

prune 3 cut, lop 4 clip, crop, dolt, dope, pare, plum, thin, trim 5 brash, chump, dunce, fruit, idiot, moron, shave, shear, skive

prurience 4 itch, lust 6 desire 7 passion 9 eroticism 11 lustfulness 13 concupiscence

prurient 3 hot 4 lewd 5 bawdy 6 erotic 7 goatish, lustful, satyric, sensual 9 lickerish 10 lascivious, libidinous, passionate 12 concupiscent

pruritic 5 itchy

Prussian *aristocrat:* 6 Junker 12 Hohenzollern *prime minister:* 8 Bismarck (Otto von) *ruler:* 7 Wilhelm 9 Frederick

pry 4 lift, nose, open, peek, poke, rear, turn 5 hoist, jimmy, lever, mouse, prize, raise, snoop, twist 6 divide, pick up, take up, uphold, uplift, uprear 7 crowbar, disjoin, elevate, upraise 8 busybody, separate

psalm 3 ode 4 hymn, laud, poem, song 5 cry up, extol 6 praise 7 glorify, magnify 8 eulogize 9 celebrate *book:* 7 psalter *selection:* 6 hallel *word:* 5 selah

psalmist 4 poet 5 Asaph, David 6 cantor

pseudo 4 fake, mock, sham 5 bogus, false, phony, snide, wrong 8 spurious 9 brummagem, pinchbeck 11 counterfeit

pseudonym 5 alias 6 ananym, anonym 7 pen name 9 incognito, stage name 10 nom de plume 11 nom de guerre; (see also **pen name**)

psyche 4 mind, soul 5 anima 6 animus, pneuma, spirit 9 élan vital 10 vital force *part:* 2 id 3 ego 8 superego

Psyche's beloved 4 Eros 5 Cupid

psychiatrist 6 shrink *American:* 9 Menninger (Karl) *Austrian:* 5 Adler (Alfred) *Swiss:* 4 Jung (Carl) 9 Rorschach (Hermann)

psychic 6 mental 7 sensile 8 cerebral, sensible, sentient 9 sensitive, spiritual 10 responsive, susceptive, telepathic 11 impressible, susceptible 12 intellective, intellectual, supersensory 13 psychological *American:* 5 Cayce (Edgar) *power:* 3 ESP

psychoanalyst 5 Freud (Sigmund), Fromm (Erich) 6 Horney (Karen)

psychological 6 mental 7 psychic 8 cerebral 9 psychical 12 intellective, intellectual

psychologist 6 shrink *American:* 3 May (Rollo) 5 James (William) 6 Rogers (Carl), Terman (Lewis), Watson (John), Yerkes (Robert) 7 Skinner (Burrhus Frederic)

8 Brothers (Joyce) 9 Thorndike (Edward Lee) *English:* 4 Ward (James) 8 Spearman (Charles), Tichener (Edward) *German:* 5 Wundt (Wilhelm) 6 Muller (Georg), Stumpf (Carl) 10 Wertheimer (Max) *Swiss:* 4 Jung (Carl) 6 Piaget (Jean)

psychopathy 6 lunacy 7 madness 8 insanity 9 unbalance 10 aberration, alienation, insaneness 11 derangement, distraction

psychotic 3 mad 5 crazy 6 insane 8 schizoid

ptarmigan 6 grouse

ptomaine 6 poison

pub 3 bar, inn 6 tavern 7 barroom, rummery, taproom 8 drinkery, groggery, grogshop

puberty 5 youth 6 spring 9 greenness, youthhood 10 juvenility, pubescence, springtide, springtime 11 adolescence *combining form:* 4 hebe

public 4 open 5 civic, civil, joint, state, suite, urban 6 common, mutual, people, shared, vulgar 7 general, popular, society 8 audience, communal, conjoint, conjunct, national, open-door 9 clientage, clientele, community, following, hangers-on, municipal, prevalent, universal 10 accessible, government, widespread 11 intermutual

publican 8 boniface, taverner 9 barkeeper, collector, innholder, innkeeper, saloonist 12 saloonkeeper, tax collector

publication 4 book 5 paper 7 journal 8 magazine, pamphlet 9 broadcast, newspaper 10 periodical 11 declaration *list:* 12 bibliography

public house 3 inn 5 hotel, lodge 6 hostel, tavern 7 auberge, hospice 8 hostelry 9 road-house 11 caravansary

publicity 4 hype, plug, puff 5 blurb 6 hoopla 7 buildup, puffery, réclame, write-up 8 ballyhoo, hard sell 9 promotion 11 advertising 12 announcement

publicize 3 cry 4 hype, plug, puff, push, tout 5 boost, bruit, extol 7 advance, build up, promote, trumpet 8 announce, headline, skywrite 9 advertise, broadcast 10 press-agent, promulgate 11 circularize 12 propagandize

publish 3 air 4 toot, vent 5 issue, print, utter 6 broach, get out, market, put out 7 declare, express, produce 8 announce, bring out, proclaim 9 advertise, broadcast, ventilate 10 annunciate, distribute, promulgate 11 blaze abroad, disseminate

publisher 6 editor 7 printer 10 journalist

Puccini, Giacomo *heroine:* 4 Mimi *opera:* 5 Edgar, Tosca 7 Le Villi 8 La Bohème, Turandot 12 Manon Lescaut, Suor Angelica

puck 3 elf, imp 4 disk 5 fairy 6 spirit, sprite 9 hobgoblin, prankster

pucker 4 fold 5 purse 6 cockle 7 wrinkle 8 contract

puckish 5 antic 6 impish, wicked 7 larkish, playful, roguish, waggish 8 prankish, sportive 11 mischievous

Puck's master 6 Oberon

pudding 4 duff 6 burgoo 7 custard, dessert, tapioca *baked:* 10 brown Betty

pudgy 5 plump, round, squab, tubby 6 chubby, plumpy, rotund, squdgy, stumpy 8 plumpish, roly-poly 10 roundabout

pueblo 4 town 7 village 8 dwelling *ceremonial room:* 4 kiva

puerile 6 boyish 7 babyish 8 childish, immature

Puerto Rico *capital:* 7 San Juan *discoverer:* 8 Columbus (Christopher)

puff 3 cry 4 blow, brag, crow, drag, draw, gasp, huff, pant, plug, pouf, pull, push 5 blurb, boast, boost, heave, mouth, prate, quilt, vaunt 6 praise 7 build up, puffing, write-up 8 inhaling 9 advertise, comforter, gasconade, laudation, publicize

puffer 8 blowfish 9 globefish

puffery 7 buildup 9 promotion, publicity 11 advertising 12 press-agentry

puffin 4 bird 9 sea parrot 10 shearwater

puff up 5 bloat, swell 7 inflate

puffy 5 wiggy 6 stuffy 7 bloated, pompous 8 arrogant 9 important 10 pontifical 11 magisterial 13 self-important

pug 3 bun, dog 4 nose 5 boxer, track 9 footprint

pugilism 4 ring 6 boxing 10 fisticuffs 13 prizefighting

pugilist 5 boxer 7 fighter

pugnacious 5 pushy 7 defiant, pushing, scrappy, warlike 8 brawling, militant 9 bellicose, combative, truculent 10 rebellious 11 belligerent, contentious, quarrelsome

pugnacity 5 fight 6 attack 10 aggression 12 belligerence 13 combativeness

puisne 5 judge, later 6 junior 9 associate

puissance 4 sway 5 clout, force, might, power, sinew, vigor 6 energy, muscle, virtue 7 potency 8 strength 9 influence

puissant 6 mighty, potent, ruling, strong 8 forceful, forcible, powerful 10 commanding

pukka 4 real, true 5 right 7 genuine 8 bona fide 9 authentic, simon-pure

pule 3 cry 5 whine 7 whimper

Pulitzer Prize winner, fiction *1918:* 5 Poole (Ernest) *1919:* 10 Tarkington (Booth) *1921:* 7 Wharton (Edith) *1922:* 10 Tarkington (Booth) *1923:* 6 Cather (Willa) *1924:* 6 Wilson (Margaret) *1925:* 6 Ferber (Edna) *1926:* 5 Lewis (Sinclair) *1927:* 9 Bromfield (Louis) *1928:* 6 Wilder (Thornton) *1929:* 8 Peterkin (Julia) *1930:* 7 La Farge (Oliver) *1931:* 6 Barnes (Margaret) *1932:* 4 Buck (Pearl) *1933:* 9 Stribling (Thomas Sigismund) *1934:* 6 Miller (Caroline) *1935:* 7 Johnson (Josephine) *1936:* 5 Davis (Harold) *1937:* 8 Mitchell (Margaret) *1938:* 8 Marquand (John) *1939:* 8 Rawlings (Marjorie Kinnan) *1940:* 9 Steinbeck (John) *1942:* 7 Glasgow (Ellen) *1943:* 8 Sinclair (Upton) *1944:* 6 Flavin (Martin) *1945:* 6 Hersey (John) *1947:* 6 Warren (Robert Penn) *1948:* 8 Michener (James) *1949:* 7 Cozzens (James Gould) *1950:* 7 Guthrie (Alfred Bertram) *1951:* 7 Richter (Conrad) *1952:* 4 Wouk (Herman) *1953:* 9 Hemingway (Ernest) *1955:* 8 Faulkner (William) *1956:* 6 Kantor (MacKinlay) *1958:* 4 Agee (James) *1959:* 6 Taylor (Robert Lewis) *1960:* 5 Drury (Allen) *1961:* 3 Lee (Harper) *1962:* 7 O'Connor (Edwin) *1963:* 8 Faulkner (William) *1965:* 4 Grau (Shirley Ann) *1966:* 6 Porter (Katherine Anne) *1967:* 7 Malamud (Bernard) *1968:* 6 Styron (William) *1969:* 7 Momaday (N. Scott) *1970:* 8 Stafford (Jean) *1972:* 7 Stegner (Wallace) *1973:* 5 Welty (Eudora) *1975:* 6 Shaara (Michael) *1976:* 6 Bellow (Saul) *1978:* 9 McPherson (James Alan) *1979:* 7 Cheever (John) *1980:* 6 Mailer (Norman) *1981:* 5 Toole (John Kennedy) *1982:* 6 Updike (John) *1983:* 6 Walker (Alice) *1984:* 7 Kennedy (William) *1985:* 5 Lurie (Alison) *1986:* 8 McMurtry (Larry) *1987:* 6 Taylor (Peter) *1988:* 8 Morrison (Toni) *1989:* 5 Tyler (Anne) *1990:* 8 Hijuelos (Oscar) *1991:* 6 Updike (John) *1992:* 6 Smiley (Jane) *1993:* 6 Butler (Robert Olen) *1994:* 6 Proulx (E. Annie) *1995:* 7 Shields (Carol)

pull 3 don, get, lug, oar, row, tow, tug, win 4 drag, draw, gain, haul, have, jerk, land, lure, puff, push, tear, yank 5 clout, drive, heave, impel, put on, shove 6 appeal, assume, commit, evulse, obtain, paddle, pick up, secure, strain, strike, take on, wrench 7 chalk up, extract, procure 9 influence, seduction 10 allurement, attraction, perpetrate, persuasion 12 drawing power

pull down 4 raze, ruin 5 wreck 7 destroy 8 decimate, demolish, destruct, tear down 9 dismantle 10 annihilate

pullet 3 hen

pulley 5 wheel 6 sheave *watch's:* 5 fusee, fuzee

pull in 3 bit, nab 4 curb 5 check, pinch, run in 6 arrest, bridle, detain, hold in, pick up 7 inhibit 8 hold back, hold down, restrain

pulling 8 traction *cable for:* 7 towline

Pullman 3 car 7 sleeper

pull out 4 exit, quit 5 leave, pluck 6 depart, get off, retire 7 retreat, take off 8 shove off, withdraw

pull through 7 recover, ride out, survive

pullulate 4 flow, teem 5 crawl, swarm 6 abound

pull up 4 halt, stop 6 draw up, haul up

pulp 4 mash, pith 5 crush 6 bruise, squash 7 bagasse, becrush

pulpit 4 ambo 7 lectern 8 ministry, platform *Muslim:* 6 minbar

pulsate 4 beat, drum, pump, roar 5 pound, throb, thrum 7 vibrate 9 fluctuate, oscillate, palpitate

pulse 4 beat 5 throb 6 rhythm *combining form:* 6 crotic 7 sphygmo *relating to:* 8 sphygmic

pulverize 4 beat, bray, buck, mill, mull, ruin 5 crush, flour, grate, grind, smash, wreck 6 abrade, crunch, powder, rub out 7 atomize, break up, crumble, destroy, shatter, smatter 8 decimate, demolish, destruct, dynamite, fragment, levigate, splinter, tear down 9 comminute, micronize, triturate 11 fragmentize 12 contriturate

puma 3 cat 6 cougar

pumice 5 glass, stone

pummel 4 beat, drub, pelt 5 pound 6 batter, buffet, hammer, thrash, wallop 7 belabor

pump 3 tap 4 draw, shoe 5 draft, drain 6 siphon 7 draw off, syringe

pumpernickel 3 rye 5 bread

pumpkin 4 pepo 5 fruit 6 cushaw, squash 12 jack-o'-lantern

pun 4 joke 9 calembour, equivoque 11 paronomasia

punch 3 box, dig, hit, jab, jog, pep 4 bang, bore, cuff, poke, prod, push, slap, snap, sock, stab 5 clout, drill, drive, force, getup, nudge, paste, point, prick, smack, vigor 6 buffet, starch, strike 7 cogency 8 puncture, uppercut, validity, vitality 9 perforate, validness 13 effectiveness

punch bowl 8 monteith

puncheon 4 tool 5 stamp

puncher 5 boxer 6 cowboy

Punch's wife 4 Judy

punctilious 4 nice 5 exact, fussy 6 formal 7 careful, heedful 8 punctual 9 observant 10 meticulous, scrupulous 11 painstaking

punctual 5 exact, fussy, quick, ready 6 prompt, timely 7 careful, heedful 10 meticulous

punctuate 4 mark 5 point 6 divide 8 separate

punctuation mark 4 dash 5 brace, colon, comma 6 hyphen, parens, period 7 bracket, virgule 8 diagonal, ellipsis 9 semicolon 10 apostrophe 11 parenthesis

puncture 3 jab 4 bore, hole, stab 5 drill, prick, punch, shoot 6 blow up, riddle 7 explode 8 disprove 9 discredit, perforate 11 perforation *surgical:* 8 centesis

pundit 4 sage 5 swami 6 critic 7 teacher

pungency 4 tang, zest 8 piquancy

pungent 3 hot 4 keen, racy, rich, salt 5 acute, salty, sharp, spicy, tangy, zesty 6 biting, bitter, snappy 7 cutting, peppery, piquant 8 exciting, incisive, poignant 9 trenchant 11 provocative, stimulating

punish 3 fix 4 fine, whip 5 mulct, shift, swill 6 amerce, avenge 7 chasten, consume, correct, put away, put down, reprove, revenge, scourge, torture 8 chastise, lambaste, penalize 9 castigate, criticize, polish off 10 discipline

punishment 3 rod 4 fine 5 mulct 7 penalty, reproof, revenge 8 punition 9 criticism 10 amercement, avengement, correction, discipline 11 castigation 12 chastisement *Scottish:* 6 dirdum

punitive 5 penal 8 punitory 9 punishing 11 castigating 12 correctional, disciplinary

punk 4 bosh, colt, hood, thug 5 rough, rowdy, tough, yahoo 6 bunkum, hot air, mucker, novice, rookie 7 baloney, hogwash, hoodlum, ruffian, toughie 8 beginner, bullyboy, claptrap, neophyte, newcomer, nonsense 9 fledgling, novitiate, roughneck 10 apprentice, balderdash

punt 4 boat, kick

puny 4 weak 5 frail, petty 6 feeble, infirm, measly, paltry, sickly, weakly 7 fragile, trivial, unsound 8 decrepit, niggling, picayune, piddling, trifling 10 picayunish

pupa 9 chrysalid, chrysalis

pupil 5 cadet, tutee 7 learner, scholar, student 8 disciple *French:* 5 élève

puppet 4 doll, dupe, pawn, tool 5 slave 6 stooge 7 cat's-paw

puppy 3 dog 5 whelp

Purcell opera 13 Dido and Aeneas

purchase 3 buy 4 take 6 obtain 7 acquire 11 acquisition

purchaser 4 user 5 buyer 6 client, emptor, patron, vendee 7 shopper 8 consumer, customer

pure 4 good, neat 5 clean, fresh, gross, plain, sheer, total, utter 6 chaste, decent, modest, simple 7 blasted, blessed, classic, genuine, perfect, plenary, sinless, unmixed 8 absolute, complete, infernal, innocent, spotless, straight, virtuous 9 authentic, blameless, exemplary, guiltless, inviolate, out-and-out, righteous, stainless, unalloyed,

undefiled, undiluted, unsullied **10** confounded, immaculate, inculpable, unblamable, unblighted, unprofaned **11** unblemished, unmitigated, unqualified **13** unadulterated
purebred 8 pedigree **9** pedigreed **10** registered **11** full-blooded **12** thoroughbred
puree 4 soup **5** paste
purely 3 all **4** just **5** quite **6** in toto, wholly **7** exactly, totally, utterly **8** all in all **10** altogether
purfle 4 trim **6** border **8** decorate, ornament
purgation 9 catharsis, cleansing **10** lustration
purgative 5 jalap **7** lustral **9** cathartic, expiatory
purge 3 rid **4** oust **5** clear, debar, eject, erase, expel **6** purify, remove **7** absolve, cleanse, dismiss, exclude, expunge, shut out, wipe out **8** disabuse, lustrate, undelude **9** eliminate, expurgate, liquidate, undeceive **11** exterminate
purification 5 grace **7** rebirth **9** atonement, catharsis, cleansing, expiation, purgation, salvation **10** absolution, lustration, redemption **11** expurgation, forgiveness **12** regeneration *sacrament:* **7** baptism
purify 5 atone, clean, purge, remit **6** filter, refine **7** absolve, baptize, clarify, cleanse, expiate **8** depurate, lustrate **9** elutriate, expurgate
Purim 11 Feast of Lots
purist 7 diehard, Puritan **8** Atticist **9** precisian **10** classicist **11** bitter-ender **12** conservative, precisionist
puritan 4 prig **5** prude **6** Grundy **8** bluenose, comstock **9** Mrs. Grundy, nice Nelly
puritanical 4 prim **6** narrow, prissy, strict, stuffy **7** bigoted, genteel, prudish **8** priggish, rigorous **9** blue-nosed, hidebound, illiberal, victorian **10** intolerant, tight-laced **11** straitlaced **12** narrow-minded
purity 8 chastity **9** innocence
purl 4 eddy, knit **5** gurge, swirl, whirl, whorl **6** stitch, swoosh **9** whirlpool
purlieu 5 haunt **6** resort **7** hangout
purlieus 6 bounds, limits **7** compass, suburbs **8** boundary, confines, environs **9** outskirts, precincts
purloin 5 filch, pinch, steal, swipe **6** pilfer, rip off, snitch, thieve **7** cabbage **11** appropriate
purloiner 4 prig **5** thief **6** nimmer **7** filcher, stealer **8** larcener, pilferer **9** larcenist
purple 4 blue, plum, racy **5** broad, grape, lilac, mauve, regal, salty, shady, spicy **6** florid, maroon, murrey, orchid, risqué, turgid, violet, wicked **7** flowery, pompous,

stilted **8** lavender, off-color **9** bombastic, high-flown, overblown **10** oratorical, rhetorical, suggestive
Purple Heart 5 award, medal
purport 4 core, gist, meat, pith **5** drift, sense, tenor **6** burden, matter, thrust, upshot **7** meaning, message **9** substance **10** intendment **11** acceptation, connotation, implication **12** significance, significancy
purported 7 alleged, reputed, rumored **8** academic, so-called, supposed **9** pretended, professed, suspected **10** ostensible, postulated **11** presupposed, speculative
purpose 3 aim, use **4** duty, goal, mark, mean, plan **5** point **6** animus, decide, design, intend, intent, object, ponder, target **7** meaning, mission, resolve **8** ambition, conclude, consider, function, meditate, proposal **9** determine, direction, intention, objective **10** aspiration, intendment
purposeless 6 random **7** aimless, fustian, unaimed, useless **8** feckless **9** desultory, haphazard, hit-or-miss, irregular, senseless, unhelpful, unplanned, worthless **10** designless, unpurposed **11** meaningless, nonsensical, purportless **12** unprofitable
purposely 9 expressly **10** designedly, explicitly, prepensely **12** deliberately **13** intentionally
purr 3 hum **6** murmur
purse 3 bag, sum **4** knit **5** money, pouch, prize **6** pucker, wallet **7** handbag **9** clutch bag **10** pocketbook, prize money *Scottish:* **7** sporran
pursual 5 chase, quest **6** search **7** pursuit
pursue 3 woo **4** hunt, seek **5** chase, chivy, court, hound, spark, stalk, track, trail **6** badger, follow **7** address, oppress, persist **8** make up to **9** persecute, persevere
pursuit 3 job **4** hunt, line, work **5** chase, quest **6** racket, search **7** calling, seeking **8** business, reaching **9** following, obtaining **10** employment, occupation
pursy see portly
purvey 6 obtain, supply **7** provide
purview 3 ken **5** ambit, orbit, range, reach, scope, sweep **6** extent, radius **7** compass
pus 6 fester *combining form:* **2** py **3** pyo
push 3 dig, jam, lot, pep, ram, set **4** bang, bear, bump, butt, goad, move, plug, prod, snap, spur **5** boost, build, bunch, crowd, crush, drive, drove, elbow, force, getup, group, horde, hunch, impel, nudge, press, punch, shove, vigor **6** beef up, circle, expand, hustle, jostle, launch, peddle, propel, squash, squish, squush, starch, throng,

thrust **8** ambition, bulldoze, compound, increase, oversell, pressure, shoulder, stimulus, vitality **9** advertise, incentive **10** aggrandize, enterprise, get-up-and-go, incitation, incitement, initiative

push around 4 bait, ride **5** bully, chivy, hound **6** badger, heckle, hector **8** bullyrag

pushful 5 brash **6** uppish, uppity **7** assured, forward, pushing **8** imposing, militant **9** assertive, assertory, confident, intrusive, obtruding, obtrusive, officious, presuming **10** aggressive **11** overweening **12** presumptuous **13** self-asserting, self-assertive

Pushkin *novel:* **12** Eugene Onegin *play:* **12** Boris Godunov

push off 2 go **4** exit, quit **5** leave **6** depart, get off **7** get away, pull out **8** withdraw

push on 2 go **3** hie **4** fare, pass, wend **6** repair, travel **7** journey, proceed

pushover 3 pie **4** snap **5** cinch, setup **6** breeze, picnic **8** duck soup, kid stuff **10** child's play

pushy see **pushful**

pusillanimous 6 coward, craven **7** chicken, gutless, unmanly **8** cowardly, poltroon **9** spunkless **11** lily-livered, poltroonish

puss 3 cat, kid, mug **4** face **5** child **6** kisser, kitten, moppet, nipper, visage **8** juvenile

pussyfoot 4 lurk, slip **5** creep, dodge, evade, glide, hedge, skulk, slide, slink, sneak, steal **6** weasel **7** gumshoe, shuffle **8** sidestep **10** equivocate, tergiverse **12** tergiversate

pustule 4 boil, wart **5** whelk **6** pimple **7** abscess **8** furuncle **9** carbuncle

put 3 air, fix, lay, set **4** call, give, levy, pose, turn, vent, word **5** couch, exact, focus, judge, place, rivet, state, stick **6** assess, fasten, fixate, impose, phrase, prefer, reckon, render, return, settle **7** express, propose, replace, restore, suggest **8** estimate, give back, propound **9** concenter

putative 7 reputed **8** supposed **11** conjectural, suppositive, suppository **12** hypothetical

put away 4 bury, do in, kill, slay, stow **5** inter, plant, scrag, swill **6** cut off, entomb, finish, inhume, lay low, murder, punish **7** bump off, consume, destroy, dismiss, divorce, execute, reposit, take off, unmarry **8** carry off, dispatch, knock off **9** liquidate

put back 6 demote, return **7** replace, restore **8** give back **9** reinstate

put by 4 save **5** lay in, lay up **7** lay away **8** lay aside, salt away

put down 4 bump, bust **5** break, crush, quash, quell, shift, swill **6** demote, humble, punish, quench, squash, subdue **7** consume, declass, degrade, demerit, disrate, put away **8** disgrade, suppress **9** downgrade

put in 3 sow **4** seed **5** plant **6** insert

put off 5 delay, elude, repel **7** suspend **8** dissuade, postpone **9** frustrate **10** disconcert

put on 3 act, don, kid **4** fake, hire, pose, sham, show **5** bluff, feign, get on, mount, stage **6** affect, assume, draw on, employ, engage, slip on, strike, take on **7** mislead

put-on 3 act **4** face, fake, mask, sell, sham, show **5** cheat, cloak, cover, faked, guise, phony, posed, spoof **6** deceit, facade, parody **7** assumed, feigned **8** affected, disguise, mannered, spurious **9** deception, imposture **10** artificial, false front, masquerade

put on the block 4 sell

put out 3 ply, vex **4** gall, rile, roil **5** annoy, douse, exert, grate, issue, throw, wield **6** burn up, quench **7** inflame, publish, trouble **8** exercise, irritate **9** aggravate, disoblige, displease, incommode **10** discommode, dissatisfy, exasperate, extinguish **13** inconvenience

putrefy 3 rot **4** turn **5** decay, spoil, taint **6** molder **7** crumble **9** break down, decompose **12** disintegrate

putrid 3 bad **4** foul, high, olid **5** fetid **6** rancid, rotten, smelly, whiffy **7** corrupt, decayed, noisome, reeking, spoiled, vicious **8** depraved, nidorous, perverse **9** nefarious **10** malodorous *combining form:* **4** sapr **5** sapro

putter 4 club, mess **6** dawdle, doodle, fiddle, golfer, puddle, tinker **10** boondoggle

putting area 5 green

put together 4 form, join, make **5** build, erect, frame, shape, unite **7** fashion, produce **9** construct, fabricate

putty 3 mud **4** clay **6** cement

put up 3 can, hut **4** bunk, hike, jump, make, rear **5** board, boost, build, erect, forge, house, lodge, raise, set up, shape **6** bestow, billet, harbor, jack up, uprear **7** elevate, quarter **8** domicile, escalate, increase **9** construct *with:* **4** bear **5** stand **6** endure **8** tolerate

puzzle 3 why **4** foil, pose **5** addle, amaze, befog, poser, rebus, upset **6** baffle, enigma, fuddle, muddle, riddle **7** anagram, confuse, disturb, mystery, mystify, nonplus, perplex, problem, stumble **8** acrostic, befuddle, bewilder, confound, distract **9** conundrum, crossword, dumbfound, frustrate **10** closed book, disconcert, puzzlement **11** brainteaser *Chinese:* **7** tangram

puzzle out 5 break, solve 6 cipher, unfold 7 clear up, dope out, unravel 8 decipher, unriddle 9 figure out

Pygmalion *father:* 5 Belus *playwright:* 4 Shaw (George Bernard) *sister:* 4 Dido *statue, beloved:* 7 Galatea *victim:* 8 Sichaeus

pygmy 4 runt, tiny 5 dwarf, midge 6 midget, peewee 7 manikin, minikin 8 dwarfish, Tom Thumb 10 diminutive, homunculus, pocket-size 11 lilliputian

Pylades *companion:* 7 Orestes *father:* 9 Strophius *wife:* 7 Electra

pylon 4 post 5 tower 7 gateway

Pym's creator 3 Poe (Edgar Allan)

Pynchon novel 15 Gravity's Rainbow

pyramid 4 bank, heap, hill, mass, pile, tomb 5 drift, mound, stack 7 windrow *builder:* 5 Khufu 6 Cheops

Pyramus' beloved 6 Thisbe

pyre 4 heap, pile

pyromaniac 8 arsonist

pyrosis 9 heartburn

pyrotechnics 9 fireworks

Pyrrha's husband 9 Deucalion

Pyrrhonian 7 doubter, skeptic, zetetic 10 unbeliever

Pyrrhus *kingdom:* 6 Epirus *victory:* 7 Asculum; (see also **Neoptolemus**)

Pythias' friend 5 Damon

python 3 boa 5 snake

pyx 3 box 4 case 5 chest 6 coffer, vessel

Qatar's capital 4 Doha

Q.E.D. word 4 erat, quod

q.t., on the 8 in secret, secretly

qua 2 as 4 bird 5 heron

quack 3 cry 4 honk, sham 7 shammer 9 charlatan, pretender, quackster, simulator 10 mountebank 12 saltimbanque *combining form:* 5 pseud 6 pseudo

quad see quadrangle

quadra 5 frame 6 border, fillet, listel, plinth

quadragenarian 8 fortyish

quadrangle 4 yard 5 court 6 figure, square 9 courtyard, curtilage, enclosure

quadrant 6 fourth 10 instrument

quadratic 6 square 10 foursquare

quadriga 7 chariot

quadrille 5 dance, ombre 8 card game

quadrillion *combining form:* 4 peta

quadrillionth *combining form:* 5 femto

quadrivium subject 5 music 8 geometry 9 astronomy 10 arithmetic

quaestor 5 judge 8 official 9 paymaster, treasurer 10 prosecutor

quaff 3 sip 4 toss 5 drink, sup up 6 imbibe, sup off 7 swallow

quagga 3 ass

quaggy 4 soft 5 boggy, mushy, pappy, pulpy 6 spongy 7 squashy, squishy, squushy 8 squelchy, yielding

quagmire 3 bog, box, fen, fix, jam 4 hole, mire 5 marsh, swamp 6 corner, morass, pickle, plight, scrape, slough 7 dilemma 9 marshland 11 predicament

quahog 4 clam 11 cherrystone

quail 4 bird 5 colin, cower, wince 6 blanch, blench, cringe, flinch, recoil, shrink 7 massena, shudder, squinch, tremble 8 bobwhite *flock of:* 4 bevy *young:* 7 cheeper 8 squealer

quaint 3 odd 5 droll, funny, queer 7 antique, archaic, curious, oddball, strange, unusual 8 peculiar, singular 9 eccentric, laughable, whimsical 10 antiquated

quake 3 jar 5 shake, shock, waver 6 dither, quaver, quiver, shiver, tremor 7 shudder, temblor, tremble, twitter, vibrate 8 trembler, tremblor 9 fluctuate

Quaker 6 Friend 9 broadbrim *city:* 12 Philadelphia *colonizer:* 4 Penn (William) *founder:* 3 Fox (George) *gray:* 5 acier *poet:* 6 Barton (Bernard) 8 Whittier (John Greenleaf) *state:* 12 Pennsylvania

qualification 5 might 7 ability 8 adequacy, aptitude, capacity 10 capability, competence

qualified 3 fit 4 able, good 5 fixed, tried 6 au fait, proper, proved, tested 7 capable, limited, partial, quizzed, trained 8 definite, eligible, examined, modified, reserved 9 competent 10 catechized, determined, instructed, restricted 11 conditional, disciplined

qualify 4 mark 6 assign, impute, soften 7 ascribe, certify, entitle, license, prepare 8 moderate 9 attribute, authorize

quality 4 fine, mark, rank 5 arete, class, elite, grade, merit, place, prime, savor, state, trait, value, worth 6 factor, flower, gentry, Grade A, status, virtue 7 aristoi, caliber, element, feature, footing, society, station, stature 8 capacity, five-star, position, property, standing, superior 9 affection, attribute, blue blood, character, excellent, first-rate, gentility, parameter, situation 10 blue-ribbon, excellence, first-class, patriciate, perfection, superbness *essential:* 8 suchness *suffix:* 2 cy, ty 3 ice, ity 4 ance, ancy, ence, ency, hood, ness, ship

qualm 5 demur, doubt 6 squeam, unease 7 scruple 8 mistrust 9 agitation, misgiving, objection, suspicion 10 conscience, foreboding, impatience, insecurity, reluctance, uneasiness 11 compunction, nervousness, uncertainty 12 apprehension, perturbation, presentiment, remonstrance 13 unwillingness

qualmish 5 queer 6 queasy 9 nauseated

quandary 3 fix, jam 6 pickle, plight, scrape 7 dilemma 11 predicament

quantity 4 body, bulk, dose, unit 5 total 6 amount, budget, degree 9 aggregate *fixed:* 8 constant *small:* 3 bit, jot, ray 4 atom, dram, drop, iota, mite, whit 5 grain, scrap, shred, speck 7 modicum, smidgen

Quantrill's ___ 7 raiders

quantum 3 sum 4 body, bulk, meed, part 5 quota, share, total 6 amount, budget, ration 7 measure, portion 9 aggregate, allotment, allowance 13 apportionment *of radiant energy:* 6 photon *of vibrational energy:* 6 phonon *theory originator:* 6 Planck (Max)

quarantine 6 cut off 7 isolate 9 interdict, isolation

quarrel 3 row, war 4 beef, bolt, bump, dust, feud, fray, fuss, miff, spat, tiff, tile, vary 5 argue, arrow, brawl, broil, clash, fight, melee, run-in, scrap, set-to, words 6 affray, battle, bicker, chisel, differ, divide, dustup, fracas, hassle, ruckus, rumpus, squall, strife, thwart 7 bobbery, brabble, cast out, collide, contend, diamond, discord, dispute, dissent, fall out, rhubarb, ruction, scuffle, wrangle 8 catfight, conflict, squabble, to-and-fro, variance 9 altercate, bickering, brannigan, caterwaul, disaccord, imbroglio, scrimmage 10 contention, difference, difficulty, dissension, donnybrook, falling-out, free-for-all 11 altercation, battle royal, controversy, embroilment 12 disagreement

quarrelsome 6 brawly 7 adverse, counter, crabbed, hostile, scrappy, warlike 8 brawling, cankered, inimical, militant, ructious 9 bellicose, brawlsome, combative, irascible, irritable, rancorous, truculent 10 battlesome, pugnacious 11 belligerent, contentious 12 disputatious 13 argumentative

quarry 3 pit 4 game, mine, prey 5 chase, delve, pluck 6 victim 7 lozenge

quart 6 fourth *four:* 6 gallon *metric:* 5 liter, litre

quarter 3 hut 4 area, bunk, part 5 board, house, lodge, put up 6 barrio, billet, canton, fourth, harbor, sector 7 barrack, section 8 district, division, domicile, locality, precinct, quadrant 9 entertain 11 domiciliate *circle:* 8 quadrant *note:* 8 crotchet *pint:* 4 gill *ship's:* 6 fo'c'sle 10 forecastle *year, Scottish:* 5 raith

quarterback 4 boss 6 survey 7 oversee 9 supervise 10 footballer

quartet 4 four 6 tetrad 7 quatuor 8 foursome 10 quadruplet, quaternion

quartz 4 onyx, sard 5 agate, smoky 6 jasper, rubace 7 citrine, rubasse, sardius 8 amethyst, sardonyx, sunstone 9 cairngorm, carnelian 10 chalcedony

quash 4 undo, void 5 abate, annul, crush, quell 6 negate, quench, stifle, vacate 7 abolish, nullify, put down, repress, smother, squelch, vitiate 8 abrogate, dissolve, strangle, suppress 9 discharge

quasi 6 almost 7 seeming, virtual

Quasimodo 9 hunchback *creator:* 4 Hugo (Victor) *occupation:* 10 bell ringer *residence:* 9 Notre Dame

quat 3 sty 4 beat, boil 6 squash 7 upstart

quaver 5 quake, shake, waver 6 dither, falter, shiver, tremor 7 shudder, tremble, twitter 8 hesitate 9 vacillate

quawk 5 heron 10 night heron

quay 4 dock, pier, slip 5 berth, jetty, levee, wharf

quean 4 bawd 5 wench, whore 6 harlot 7 hustler 8 meretrix 10 prostitute

queasy 4 open 5 fishy, queer, shady 6 qualmy 7 dubious 8 doubtful, qualmish 9 ambiguous, doubtable, nauseated, squeamish

Quebec *college, university:* 5 Laval, Lévis 6 McGill 9 Concordia *largest city:* 8 Montreal *peninsula:* 5 Gaspé *vehicle:* 7 caleche

queen 4 card 6 regina 7 goddess, monarch 8 chessman 9 sovereign *Austria-Hungary:* 12 Maria Theresa *Belgian:* 6 Astrid *Danish:* 8 Margaret, Margrete *Egyptian:* 9 Cleopatra 10 Hatshepsut *English:* 4 Anne, Mary 8 Victoria 9 Elizabeth *French and English:* 7 Eleanor *Netherlands:* 7 Beatrix, Juliana 10 Wilhelmina *of heaven:* 4 Mary, moon 7 Astarte *of Isles:* 6 Albion *of Ithaca:* 8 Penelope *of Navarre:* 8 Margaret *of Scots:* 4 Mary *of Sheba:* 6 Balkis *of the Adriatic:* 6 Venice

of the Antilles: 4 Cuba *of the East:*
7 Zenobia *of the fairies:* 3 Mab 7 Titania
of the gods: 4 Hera, Juno, Sati *of the Nile:*
9 Cleopatra *of the North:* 9 Edinburgh *of the underworld:* 3 Hel 4 Hela 10 Persephone, Proserpina *Spanish:* 8 Isabella
Swedish: 9 Christina
Queen Anne's Lace 6 carrot
Queen of Spades *author:* 7 Pushkin
(Aleksandr) *composer:* 11 Tchaikovsky
(Pyotr)
Queensland *capital:* 8 Brisbane
explorer: 4 Cook (Captain James)
Queeg's command 5 Caine
queer 5 droll, funny, weird 6 qualmy,
queasy 7 bizarre, curious, dubious, oddball, strange, unusual 8 doubtful,
obsessed, peculiar, qualmish, singular
9 eccentric, laughable, squeamish 10 outlandish
quell 5 crush, quash 6 quench, squash
7 conquer, put down 8 overcome, suppress, vanquish 9 subjugate 10 extinguish
Quemoy's neighbor 4 Amoy
quench 3 end, out 4 raze, ruin, sate
5 allay, crush, douse, quash, quell, slake,
wreck 6 lessen, put out, reduce, squash
7 appease, assuage, content, destroy, gratify, lighten, put down, relieve, satiate, satisfy, shatter 8 decimate, decrease, demolish, destruct, diminish, mitigate, suppress
9 alleviate, terminate 10 extinguish
quenelle 8 meatball 9 forcemeat
quern 4 mill
querulous 5 huffy, waspy 6 crying 7 fretful, peevish, pettish, wailing, waspish, weeping 8 petulant, snappish 9 bemoaning,
deploring, fractious, irritable, lamenting
10 blubbering, whimpering
query 3 ask 4 quiz 7 concern, dubiety,
examine, inquire, inquiry 8 mistrust, question 9 catechize, dubiosity, dubitancy, suspicion 10 skepticism 11 interrogate, questioning, uncertainty, uncertitude
13 interrogation, interrogatory
quest 3 bay 4 howl, hunt, seek, wail
5 probe 6 search 7 delving, inquiry, probing, pursual, pursuit, seeking, ululate 8 pursuing, research 9 cast about, ferret out,
pursuance, search for, search out 11 inquisition
question 3 ask, nut 4 poll, quiz 5 demur,
doubt, issue, query 7 debrief, dispute,
examine, inquire, inquiry, problem, protest,
suspect 8 demurral, demurrer, mistrust
9 catechize, challenge, objection 10 difficulty, puzzle over 11 interrogate, wonder
about 12 hesitate over, remonstrance
13 interrogation, interrogatory
questionable 4 moot 5 vague 6 unsure
7 dubious, obscure 8 arguable, doubtful,

mootable, unlikely, untrusty 9 debatable,
equivocal, refutable, trustless, uncertain
10 disputable, fly-by-night, improbable,
unreliable 11 problematic 12 undependable
questioning 5 query 6 show-me 7 curious, inquiry 8 aporetic 9 inquiring, quizzical, skeptical 11 incredulous, inquisitive,
unbelieving 12 disbelieving, disquisitive
13 interrogation, interrogatory, investigative
quetzal 4 bird, coin 6 trogon
queue 3 row 4 file, line, rank, tier 5 braid
quibble 4 carp 5 argue, cavil 6 argufy,
bicker, hassle 7 chicane, dispute, wrangle
8 pettifog, squabble 9 criticize
quick 3 apt 4 able, core, deft, fast, keen,
pith, root, wise 5 acute, agile, apace, brisk,
canny, fleet, hasty, heart, rapid, ready,
sharp, slick, smart, swift 6 abrupt, adroit,
center, clever, nimble, prompt, speedy, sudden 7 capable, flat-out, hastily, knowing,
rapidly, swiftly 8 speedily 9 breakneck,
competent, dexterous, effective, effectual,
impetuous, posthaste 10 expeditive, harefooted 11 expeditious, intelligent, quick-witted, sharp-witted 12 lickety-split, nimblewitted 13 expeditiously *combining form:*
3 oxy 5 tachy
quick bread 6 muffin 7 biscuit
quicken 4 goad, move, spur, stir, wake
5 hurry, liven, pique, rouse, speed
6 arouse, awaken, excite, hasten, induce,
step up, vivify 7 actuate, animate, enliven,
innerve, provoke, shake up, swiften 8 activate, energize, motivate, vitalize 9 galvanize, innervate, stimulate 10 accelerate,
exhilarate, invigorate, vivificate
quickness 4 gait, pace 5 speed 8 celerity, legerity, rapidity, velocity 9 rapidness,
swiftness
quicksand 3 bog 4 mire, syrt 6 syrtis
quicksilver 7 mercury 9 mercurial
quick-tempered 5 cross, ratty 6 cranky
7 peppery 8 choleric 9 irascible 10 passionate
quick-witted 3 apt, hep 4 keen, wise
5 acute, alert, canny, ready, sharp, slick,
smart, witty 6 brainy, bright, clever, prompt
7 knowing 8 humorous 9 brilliant, facetious
11 intelligent, penetrating, penetrative
quid 3 cut, wad 4 chew 5 pound 9 sovereign
quiddity 6 trifle 7 essence, quibble
quidnunc see **rumormonger**
quiescent 4 calm 5 quiet, still 6 hushed,
latent, placid, stilly 7 abeyant, dormant, halcyon, lurking 10 untroubled
quiet 4 calm, hush, idle, lull, stop 5 abate,
allay, inert, plain, shush, still, tasty, whist
6 asleep, becalm, homely, hushed, lessen,

placid, settle, shut up, silent, simple, sleepy, soothe, stilly, subdue 7 compose, halcyon, hushful, passive, silence, subdued 8 choke off, decrease, inactive, tasteful 9 cessation, noiseless, soundless, stillness 10 restrained, untroubled 11 inobtrusive, termination, tranquilize, unobtrusive

quietus 5 death, sleep 6 demise 7 decease, passing, silence 8 curtains 10 inactivity

quill 3 pen 5 spine, spool 6 bobbin 7 feather 8 plectrum

quill pig 9 porcupine

quilt 4 pouf, puff 8 bedcover 9 bedspread, comforter, eiderdown 11 counterpane *design:* 8 trapunto

quink 5 brant, goose

quintessence 4 meat, pith, soul 5 stuff 6 bottom, marrow 7 epitome 8 last word, ultimate 9 substance 12 essentiality

quintessential 4 pith, soul 5 ideal, model, stuff 6 bottom, marrow 7 classic, essence, typical 9 classical, exemplary, substance 10 archetypal, prototypal 12 prototypical

quintillion *combining form:* 3 exa

quintillionth *combining form:* 4 atto

quintuple 8 fivefold

quintuplets *famous:* 6 Dionne

quip 3 gag 4 gibe, gird, jape, jeer, jest, joke 5 crack, fleer, flout, sally, scoff, sneer 8 drollery 9 wisecrack, witticism

quipster 3 wag, wit 5 comic, droll, joker 6 jester 8 comedian, funnyman, humorist, jokester

quirk 4 bend, quip 5 crook 6 groove, retort 7 channel 9 mannerism 11 peculiarity

quirt 4 whip

quisling 7 traitor 8 turncoat

quit 3 act, pay 4 bear, drop, exit, halt, stop 5 carry, cease, chuck, clear, leave, pay up 6 behave, demean, depart, deport, desert, desist, get off, resign, retire, secede, settle, square 7 abandon, comport, conduct, forsake, get away, satisfy, take off 8 clear off, give over, knock off, leave off, renounce, surcease, withdraw 9 discharge, liquidate, surrender, terminate, throw over 10 relinquish 11 discontinue

quite 3 all, far 4 just, well 5 fully, in all 6 in toto, purely, rather, wholly 7 all told, exactly, totally, utterly 8 all in all, cleverly,

entirely, somewhat 9 perfectly 10 altogether, completely, thoroughly

quittance 6 amends 7 redress 8 reprisal 9 indemnity 10 recompense, reparation 11 restitution 12 compensation

quitter 4 funk 6 coward, craven, funker 7 chicken 8 poltroon 11 yellowbelly

quiver 4 beat 5 flash, gleam, glint, pulse, quake, shake, throb 6 dither, glance, shiver, tremor 7 glimmer, glisten, glitter, pulsate, shimmer, shudder, sparkle, tremble, twinkle, twitter 9 palpitate

quiverleaf 5 aspen

quiver tree 4 aloe

Quixote see Don Quixote

quixotic 8 fanciful, illusory, romantic 9 fantastic, visionary 10 chimerical, idealistic 11 impractical

quiz 3 ask 4 lout, mock, razz, twit 5 query, rally, scout, taunt 6 deride, oddity, zombie 7 examine, inquire, oddball 8 original, question, ridicule 9 catechize, character, eccentric 11 interrogate

quizzical 6 show-me 7 curious, probing 8 aporetic 9 searching, skeptical 11 incredulous, inquisitive, questioning, unbelieving 12 disbelieving

quizzing glass 7 monocle

quodlibet 6 debate, medley 8 fantasia, question

quoin 5 angle, facet, wedge 6 corner 7 lozenge 8 keystone, voussoir

quoit 4 ring, rope 5 cover 6 circle

quoits 4 game *peg:* 3 hob

quondam 3 old 4 late, once, past 6 bygone, former, whilom 7 onetime 8 sometime 9 erstwhile

quorum 7 council 8 majority

quota 3 cut, lot 4 bite, meed, part 5 share, slice 6 divide, parcel, ration 7 measure, partage, portion, prorate, quantum 9 allotment, allowance, apportion

quotation 3 bid 5 offer, price 7 excerpt, passage

quotation mark *French:* 9 guillemet

quote 4 cite, list, mark 5 refer 6 adduce, notice, set off 7 excerpt

quotidian 5 daily, plain, usual 7 diurnal, routine 8 everyday, ordinary, workaday 9 circadian 12 unremarkable

Quo Vadis *author:* 11 Sienkiewicz (Henryk) *character:* 4 Nero 5 Lygia, Peter 8 Vinicius 9 Petronius

R

Ra *son:* 6 Khonsu *wife:* 3 Mut
Raamah *father:* 4 Cush *son:* 5 Dedan, Sheba
Rabbi Ben Ezra author 8 Browning (Robert)
rabbit 4 cony 5 bunny, coney, lapin *castrated:* 5 lapin *female:* 3 doe *fictional:* 5 Fiver, Hazel, Mopsy, Peter 6 Flopsy, Harvey 7 Thumper 8 Crusader, Ricochet 9 Bugs Bunny 10 Cottontail 11 Easter Bunny *food:* 5 salad 6 carrot 7 lettuce
rabbitlike 8 leporine
rabble 3 mob 4 many, raff, rout, scum 5 dregs, scurf, trash 6 masses, people, polloi, public, ragtag 7 doggery 8 canaille, populace, riffraff, unwashed, varietry 9 hoi polloi, other half, tag and rag 10 commonalty, roughscuff 11 bourgeoisie, proletariat, rank and file
rabble-rouser 9 demagogue
Rabelais character 9 Gargantua 10 Pantagruel
rabid 3 mad 4 keen, wild 5 crazy, ultra 6 crazed, insane 7 extreme, fanatic, frantic, furious, radical, zealous 8 demented, deranged, frenetic, frenzied, obsessed, ultraist 9 delirious, extremist 10 corybantic 12 enthusiastic
rabies 5 lyssa 11 hydrophobia
raccoon 5 panda 10 cacomistle *relative:* 5 coati 10 coatimundi
race 4 boil, bolt, clan, dash, drag, folk, gill, lash, rush, tear, type 5 breed, brook, chase, creek, fling, house, shoot, speed, stock, tribe 6 career, charge, course, endure, family, nation, people, runnel, stream 7 culture, kindred, lineage, Negroid, rivulet, running, variety 8 marathon 9 Caucasian, Mongoloid *auto:* 5 rally 6 rallye 9 grand prix *combining form:* 3 gen 4 geno, phyl 5 ethno, phylo
racecourse 4 oval, turf 5 track *combining form:* 4 drom 5 drome, dromo
racehorse *champion:* 5 Kelso 6 Forego 7 Man O' War 8 Affirmed, Citation 9 Riva Ridge 10 War Admiral 11 Forward Pass, Seattle Slew, Secretariat 12 Native Dancer
Rachel *father:* 5 Laban *husband:* 5 Jacob *servant:* 6 Bilhah *sister:* 4 Leah *son:* 6 Joseph 8 Benjamin

rachis 4 back 5 spine 8 backbone 9 vertebrae
rachitic 5 shaky 6 wobbly 7 rackety, rickety ·10 rattletrap
rachitis 7 rickets
____ Rachmaninoff 6 Sergei
racing enthusiast 8 railbird
rack 3 try 4 pain 5 frame, wring 6 harrow, martyr 7 afflict, agonize, crucify, oppress, sawbuck, torment, torture 8 distress, sawhorse 9 persecute 10 excruciate
racket 3 din 5 babel 6 clamor, hubbub, jangle, tumult, uproar 8 brouhaha 10 hullabaloo 11 pandemonium
rack up 3 win 4 gain 5 reach, score 6 attain 7 achieve, realize 10 accomplish
raconteur 11 storyteller
racy 4 blue 5 broad, fiery, salty, shady, spicy, zesty 6 purple, risqué, snappy, wicked 7 gingery, peppery, piquant, pungent 8 off-color, spirited 10 suggestive
Radames' beloved 4 Aïda
radar image 4 blip
Raddai *brother:* 5 David *father:* 5 Jesse
radiance 5 glory 8 splendor
radiant 4 glad 6 bright, cheery, lucent 7 beaming, fulgent, lambent 8 cheerful, luminous 9 brilliant, effulgent, refulgent 12 incandescent
radiate 4 beam, burn 5 gleam, shine, strew 6 spread 7 diffuse, diverge 8 disperse 9 circulate, eradicate, propagate
radiation unit 3 rem, rep 8 roentgen
radiator 6 cooler, heater 11 transmitter
radical 4 acyl, root 5 basal, basic, pinko, rabid, rebel, ultra, vital 6 bottom 7 extreme, fanatic, primary 8 advanced, agitator, cardinal, inherent, nihilist, reformer, tolerant, ultraist 9 anarchist, essential, extremist, insurgent, intrinsic 10 separatist, subversive, underlying 11 broad-minded, fundamental, out-and-outer, progressive, reactionary 12 foundational, revolutional, secessionist 13 revolutionary *combining form:* 2 yl 3 oyl 5 ylene *mathematical:* 4 surd
radicle 4 root 5 radix 9 hypocotyl
radio 8 wireless *frequency range:* 8 waveband
radioactive debris 7 fallout

radium *symbol:* 2 Ra

radius 5 ambit, orbit, range, reach, scope, sweep 6 extent 7 compass, purview 9 extension

radix 4 base, root 6 etymon, source

radon 5 niton 6 thoron 7 actinon *symbol:* 2 Rn

raffish 4 fast, wild 6 sporty 8 rakehell 12 devil-may-care

raffle 4 game 6 refuse 7 lottery, rubbish, serrate 8 riffraff

raft 3 lot, mat 4 slew 5 balsa, float

rafter 4 beam, bird 10 flycatcher

rag 3 fun, jaw, kid, rib 4 fool, jive, joke, josh, rail, rant, razz 5 baste, jolly, scold, tease 9 newspaper

ragamuffin 3 bum 4 hobo, waif 5 tramp 6 loafer, orphan 7 ragshag, vagrant, wastrel 8 vagabond 9 scarecrow

rage 3 cry, fad, ire, mad 4 boil, burn, chic, fume, fury, mode, rant, whim 5 anger, craze, fancy, freak, mania, style, upset, vogue, wrath 6 blow up, frenzy, furore, seethe, vagary 7 bristle, caprice, conceit, fashion, flare up 8 acerbity, acrimony, asperity, boil over, crotchet, hysteria 9 agitation 10 dernier cri 11 indignation

ragged 4 rent, torn 5 dingy, faded, seedy 6 frayed, shabby 7 patched, shreddy, worn-out 8 battered, frazzled, tattered 10 threadbare 11 dilapidated

raging 4 wild 5 dirty, rough 6 stormy 7 furious 8 blustery 9 turbulent 10 blustering 11 tempestuous

rags 5 dress 6 attire, shreds, things 7 apparel, clothes, raiment, ribbons, tatters 8 clothing 10 attirement 11 habiliments, odds and ends

ragtag see **rabble**

ragwort 7 senecio 10 butterweed

Rahab *husband:* 6 Salmon *son:* 4 Boaz

raid 3 rob 4 loot, sack 5 foray, harry, onset, rifle, waste 6 harass, inroad, invade, maraud, pirate, ravage 7 assault, despoil, overrun, plunder 8 invasion, picaroon, spoliate 9 devastate, incursion, irruption, onslaught, overswarm

raider 6 looter, pirate, sacker 7 forager, ravager, spoiler 8 marauder, picaroon, pillager, ravisher 9 plunderer 10 freebooter 11 bushwhacker

rail 3 jaw 4 rate 5 scold 6 berate, revile 7 bawl out, upbraid 8 banister 10 balustrade, tongue-lash, vituperate

rail bird 4 sora

railing 8 banister 10 balustrade *part:* 8 baluster

raillery 6 satire 10 lampoonery 13 satiricalness

railroad 5 frame 9 iron horse *car:* 5 coach, diner, stock 6 hopper 7 caboose,

gondola, Pullman *engine:* 10 locomotive *station:* 5 depot *underground:* 6 subway *worker:* 6 porter 7 fireman 8 brakeman, engineer 9 conductor 10 dispatcher 11 gandy dancer

raiment 4 clad, duds, garb, togs 5 array, dress 6 attire, clothe, things 7 apparel, clothes, garment 8 clothing, enclothe 10 attirement 11 habiliments

rain 6 mizzle, shower 7 drizzle 8 downpour *combining form:* 4 hyet 5 hyeto, ombro, pluvi 6 pluvia, pluvio *fine:* 6 serein

rainbow 3 arc 4 iris 5 gamut 7 fantasy 8 illusion, phantasy 9 pipe dream *bridge:* 7 Bifrost *chaser:* 9 visionary *combining form:* 4 irid 5 irido *goddess:* 4 Iris

rainbow fish 5 guppy, trout 6 wrasse

raincoat 3 mac 4 mack 6 poncho 7 slicker 10 mackintosh

rain gauge 8 udometer

rain leader 9 downspout

rain tree 9 monkeypod

raise 2 up 4 abet, ante, grow, hike, jack, jump, lift, pump, rear 5 boost, breed, build, erect, exalt, hoist, put up 6 foment, gather, incite, jack up, muster, pick up, stir up, take up, upbear, uphold, uplift, uprear, whip up 7 bring up, collect, elevate, enhance, inflate, produce, provoke 8 addition, assemble, congress, heighten, increase 9 accession, accretion, construct, cultivate, forgather, increment, instigate, propagate, resurrect 10 congregate, rendezvous 12 augmentation *nap:* 5 tease *spirits:* 5 elate

raisin 7 sultana

raison d' ___ 4 être

raja 4 king 5 chief, ruler 6 prince 9 dignitary

rake 3 cad 4 beat, comb, grub, roué, tool 5 angle, scour, slope 6 forage, rascal, search 7 coxcomb, playboy, ransack, rummage 8 finecomb 9 implement, libertine 10 profligate 11 inclination

rakehell 4 fast, wild 6 rascal, sporty 7 raffish 8 rascally 9 dissolute, libertine 10 licentious, profligate 12 devil-may-care

rake's look 4 ogle

Rake's Progress engraver 7 Hogarth (William)

rakish see **rakehell**

rally 4 fire, lout, mock, quiz, race, razz, stir, twit, wake, whet 5 harry, renew, rouse, scout, taunt, tease, waken, worry 6 arouse, awaken, bestir, deride, harass, kindle, muster, perk up, pick up 7 brace up, enliven, marshal, recover, refresh, restore 8 mobilize, organize, ridicule 9 challenge, come round, tantalize 10 invigorate

rallying cry 5 motto 6 slogan

ram 5 Aries, crash, drive, sheep, stick, stuff 6 plunge, strike, thrust 7 jam-pack, warship

Rama's wife 4 Sita

ramble 3 gad 4 roam, rove, turn, walk 5 drift, range, stray 6 depart, sprawl, stroll, wander 7 digress, diverge, excurse, meander, saunter, traipse 8 divagate, straggle 9 gallivant

rambunctious 5 rowdy 6 unruly 7 raucous 8 rowdyish 9 termagant, turbulent 10 boisterous, rowdydowdy, tumultuous

ramification 6 branch 8 offshoot 9 branching, outgrowth 11 consequence

Ramona author 7 Jackson (Helen Hunt)

ramose 8 branched

ramp 5 apron, climb, storm 6 easing

rampage 4 orgy 5 binge, fling, spree 6 uproar 7 splurge, turmoil

rampageous 4 wild 6 unruly 7 riotous

rampant 4 rank, rife 6 ruling 7 current, popular, regnant 9 excessive, prevalent 10 immoderate, inordinate, widespread

rampart 7 bastion, bulwark, parapet 10 breastwork

ramshackle 7 rickety 10 dissipated 11 dilapidated

ram's mate 3 ewe

ranch 8 estancia, hacienda *worker:* 6 cowboy, gaucho 7 cowgirl, cowhand, cowpoke 10 cowpuncher

rancid 4 high, olid 5 fetid 6 putrid, smelly, whiffy 7 noisome, reeking 8 nidorous 10 malodorous

rancor 6 animus, enmity 9 animosity, antipathy, hostility, virulence 10 antagonism, bitterness

rancorous 4 evil 6 bitter, malign, wicked 7 hateful, hostile, vicious 8 spiteful, virulent 9 malicious, malignant, vitriolic 10 despiteful, malevolent 12 antagonistic

Rand, Ayn *novel:* 6 Anthem 12 Fountainhead 13 Atlas Shrugged

random 4 spot 7 aimless, anywise, unaimed 8 slapdash 9 desultory, haphazard, hit-or-miss, irregular, unplanned 10 accidental, contingent, designless, fortuitous, incidental, objectless 11 any which way, haphazardly, promiscuous, purposeless

randy 4 lewd 7 lustful, satyric 9 lecherous, libertine 10 lascivious, libidinous, licentious 11 incontinent

range 3 ken, row, run 4 area, bias, home, line, roam, rove, site, sort, span, tune, vary 5 align, ambit, drift, field, gamut, haunt, orbit, order, reach, realm, scope, space, stray, sweep, width 6 assort, circle, differ, domain, extend, extent, length, line up, matter, radius, ramble, sphere, spread, wander 7 compass, dispose, earshot, expanse, eyeshot, habitat, horizon, meander, purview, stretch 8 confines, locality, panorama, prov-

ince, straggle, vicinity 9 fluctuate, gallivant, magnitude, territory

range finder 9 telemeter 10 tachymeter

rangy 5 lanky 6 gangly 7 spindly 8 gangling

rani's mate 4 raja 5 rajah

rank 3 row 4 file, foul, line, lush, olid, rate, sort, tier 5 class, dirty, fetid, funky, grade, gross, grown, humid, order, place, queue, state, utter 6 assort, cachet, coarse, estate, filthy, lavish, putrid, rancid, smelly, smutty, status, string, vulgar 7 arrange, capital, dignity, echelon, footing, glaring, noisome, obscene, peerage, perfect, precede, profuse, rampant, raunchy, reeking, station, stature 8 absolute, capacity, classify, complete, evaluate, flagrant, gentrice, indecent, outright, position, positive, prestige, standing, stinking 9 character, downright, egregious, exuberant, loathsome, luxuriant, overgrown, repulsive, situation 10 consummate, malodorous, noticeable 11 consequence, conspicuous, outstanding, unmitigated *honorary:* 8 brevetcy *suffix:* 2 cy

rank and file 5 plebs 6 people, plebes 8 populace 9 commonage, commoners, common men, plebeians 10 commonalty 11 third estate

rankle 3 irk, vex 5 annoy 6 bother, fester, harass, obsess, plague 7 torment 8 irritate 9 aggravate 10 exasperate

ransack 3 rob 4 beat, comb, grub, loot, rake 5 rifle, scour 6 forage, search 7 plunder, relieve, rummage, stick up 8 finecomb

Ran's husband 5 Aegir

ransom 3 buy 4 free 6 redeem, regain 7 recover, release 8 liberate, retrieve

rant 3 jaw, rag 4 huff, rage, rail, rate, rave 5 mouth, orate, scold 6 berate 7 bawl out, bluster, bombast, declaim, fustian, soapbox 8 bloviate, harangue, perorate, rhetoric 10 vituperate 11 rodomontade

ranula 4 cyst

rap 3 bob, hit, wig 4 chat, chin, lick, skin, swat, talk, tunk, wipe, yarn 5 blame, knock, prose, swipe 6 rebuke 7 censure, chiding, condemn, reproof 8 causerie, denounce, reproach 9 criticize, reprehend, reprimand, reprobate 10 admonition, conference, denunciate, discussion

rapacious 6 fierce 8 ravening, ravenous 9 predative, predatory, raptorial, vulturine, vulturish, vulturous 10 gluttonous 11 predatorial

rapacity 5 greed 6 demand 7 avarice, avidity 8 cupidity, exaction, voracity

rape 4 cole, ruin 5 spoil 6 defile, ravage, ravish 7 debauch, despoil, outrage, plunder, seizure, violate 9 violation 10 spoliation

Rape of the Lock *author:* 4 Pope (Alexander) *heroine:* 7 Belinda

Raphael *birthplace:* 6 Urbino (Italy) *subject:* 7 Madonna *teacher:* 8 Perugino

rapid 4 fast 5 agile, brisk, fleet, hasty, quick, swift 6 nimble, speedy 7 hurried 9 breakneck, quickened 10 expeditive 11 expeditious

rapidity 4 gait, pace 5 speed 8 celerity, velocity 9 quickness, swiftness

rapids 6 dalles 10 whitewater

rapine 7 pillage, plunder 10 spoliation

Rappaccini's Daughter 8 Beatrice *author:* 9 Hawthorne (Nathaniel)

rapport 5 unity 7 concord, harmony

rapscallion see **rascal**

rap session 6 confab, parley 7 palaver 8 colloquy 10 colloquium, conference, discussion

rapt 4 deep 6 intent 7 engaged 8 absorbed, immersed 9 engrossed, wrapped up 11 preoccupied

raptorial see **rapacious**

rapture 6 heaven 7 ecstasy 8 rhapsody 9 transport 13 seventh heaven

rara ____ 4 avis

rare 3 few 4 fine, thin 6 choice, dainty, scarce, seldom, select, subtle, unique 7 elegant, subtile, tenuous, unusual 8 delicate, singular, sporadic, superior, uncommon, unwonted 9 attenuate, exquisite, recherché 10 attenuated, infrequent, occasional, unfrequent, unordinary 11 exceptional 13 extraordinary

rarefied 4 thin 6 subtle 7 subtile, tenuous 9 attenuate 10 attenuated

rarefy 4 thin 9 attenuate

rarely 5 extra 6 little, seldom 7 unoften 9 extremely, unusually 10 hardly ever

raring 4 agog, avid, keen 5 eager 6 ardent 7 anxious, athirst, thirsty 9 impatient 10 breathless

rarity 6 oddity 7 fewness 8 scarcity

rascal 5 devil, knave, rogue, scamp 7 lowlife, skellum, villain 8 mischief, scalawag 9 miscreant, scoundrel, skeezicks 10 blackguard 11 rapscallion *Irish:* 8 spalpeen

rash 5 hasty, silly 6 abrupt, daring, madcap, plague, sudden, unwary, unwise 7 foolish 8 careless, epidemic, headlong, heedless, outbreak, reckless 9 audacious, daredevil, foolhardy, hotheaded, impetuous, imprudent, impulsive, unadvised, venturous 10 ill-advised, incautious, incogitant, indiscreet, mad-brained, unthinking 11 adventurous, injudicious, precipitate, precipitous, temerarious, thoughtless, venturesome 12 unconsidered 13 adventuresome, inconsiderate

rasp 4 file 5 grate 6 scrape, wheeze 7 scratch

raspberry 3 boo 4 bird, hiss, hoot, pooh, razz 5 bazoo 7 catcall 8 pooh-pooh

raspy 3 dry 5 harsh, rough 6 hoarse, snappy 7 grating, jarring, peevish, pettish, raucous 8 petulant, prickish, snappish 9 irritable

rat 3 pad 4 fink, heel, scab 5 louse 6 defect, desert, inform, rodent, snitch, squeak, squeal 7 caitiff, stoolie 8 apostate, defector, informer, recreant, renegade, renounce, runagate, squealer, turncoat 9 bandicoot, repudiate, turnabout 10 apostatize, tergiverse 11 stool pigeon *female:* 3 doe

rate 3 tab 4 cost, earn, rail, rank 5 assay, class, grade, merit, price, scale, scold, set at, value 6 assess, berate, charge, degree, revile, survey, tariff 7 apprize, bawl out, chew out, deserve, upbraid, valuate 8 appraise, classify, estimate, evaluate, price tag 10 proportion, tongue-lash

rather 5 quite 6 enough, fairly, in lieu, kind of, pretty, sort of 7 instead 8 passably, somewhat 9 averagely, tolerably 10 moderately, more or less 11 alternately 12 considerably 13 alternatively

ratify 5 enact 7 approve, confirm, endorse, license 8 accredit, sanction, validate

rating 4 mark, rank 5 grade 6 rebuke 8 standing

ratio 5 scale 7 percent 8 quotient 10 proportion

ratiocination 8 judgment, sequitur 9 inference, reasoning 10 conclusion

ration 4 dole, meed, part 5 allot, quota, share 6 assign, divide, parcel 7 measure, mete out, prorate, quantum 8 allocate, division 9 allotment, allowance 10 assignment 13 apportionment

rational 4 calm, cool, sane 5 lucid, sober, sound 6 normal, stable 7 logical, prudent 8 sensible 9 judicious 10 consequent, reasonable 11 circumspect, intelligent, levelheaded

rationale 6 reason 11 explanation 13 justification

rationalize 7 explain, justify 10 account for

rattail 4 file, fish, mule 5 spoon 6 cactus, fescue 8 tapering 9 grenadier

rattan 4 cane, palm, stem

rattle 3 gab, jaw, yak 4 chat, faze 5 abash, addle, clack, run on, upset 6 babble, gabble 7 chatter, clatter, confuse, disturb, perplex 8 bewilder, confound, distract 9 discomfit, embarrass

rattlebrained 5 dizzy, giddy, silly 7 flighty 8 skittish 9 frivolous 11 empty-headed

rattling 4 very 6 damned, mighty 7 parlous 8 snapping, spanking, whacking, whopping 9 extremely 11 exceedingly

ratty 5 cross, testy 6 cranky, shabby, tetchy, touchy 7 peppery, unkempt 8 choleric 9 irascible, temperish

raucous 3 dry 5 gruff, harsh, rough, rowdy 6 hoarse, unruly 7 brusque, grating, jarring, squawky 8 rowdyish, strident 9 termagant, turbulent 10 boisterous, disorderly, rowdydowdy, stridulent, stridulous, tumultuous 11 rumbustious

raunchy 4 foul 5 dirty, messy, nasty 6 coarse, filthy, sloppy, smutty, unneat, untidy, vulgar 7 obscene, unkempt 8 ill-kempt, indecent, slipshod, slovenly 10 disheveled

ravage 3 rob 4 loot, raze, ruin, sack 5 crush, harry, havoc, spoil, strip, waste, wreck 6 devast, devour, invade 7 despoil, destroy, overrun, pillage, plunder, ransack, scourge 8 deflower, demolish, desolate, encroach, spoliate, trespass 9 depredate, desecrate, devastate, overpower, overthrow, overwhelm

rave 4 rant 5 drool, mouth, orate 7 declaim, enthuse, soapbox 8 bloviate, harangue, perorate, rhapsody 10 rhapsodize

ravel 5 snarl 6 muddle, tangle 7 perplex 8 entangle 10 complicate

ravelings 4 lint

Ravel work 6 Bolero

raven 3 jet 4 bird, ebon, inky, prey 5 black, ebony, jetty, sable 7 despoil, plunder 9 pitch-dark 10 pitch-black *combining form:* 5 corax *relating to:* 7 corvine

Raven, The *author:* 3 Poe (Edgar Allan) *refrain:* 9 Nevermore

ravenous 6 hungry 7 starved 8 edacious, famished, starving 9 rapacious, voracious

ravine 3 cut, gap 4 gulf, pass 5 abyss, chasm, cleft, clove, gorge, gulch, gully, notch 6 arroyo, canyon, clough, coulee, defile, gutter, nullah 7 crevice, fissure 8 barranca, barranco, crevasse *Mt. Washington's:* 9 Tuckerman

ravish 3 rob 4 rape 5 spoil 6 defile 7 despoil, outrage, pillage, violate 8 deflower, entrance, overcome 9 deflorate, enrapture, transport

raw 4 nude, rude 5 crass, crude, fresh, green, gross, naked, rough, young 6 callow, coarse, impure, native, unclad, unhewn, unripe, vulgar 7 uncouth, untried 8 buff-bare, stripped, uncooked, unformed, ungraded, unsorted, untaught, unversed 9 au naturel, inelegant, roughhewn, run-of-mine, unclothed, undressed, unmatured, unrefined, untutored 10 stark-naked, unfin-

ished, unpolished, unseasoned 11 unfashioned, unpracticed 13 inexperienced

rawboned 4 bony, lank, lean 5 gaunt, lanky, spare 6 skinny 7 angular, scraggy, scrawny

ray 4 beam, beta 5 alpha, gamma, gleam, light, manta, shaft, shine, shoot, skate, trace 6 radius, streak 7 radiate, sawfish, torpedo 8 particle 9 irradiate, radiation

raze 4 ruin, undo 5 wrack, wreck 6 unmake 7 destroy, unbuild, unframe 8 decimate, demolish

razor 3 cut 5 shave

razz 3 kid, rag, rib 4 fool, jest, joke, josh, lout, mock, quiz, twit 5 jolly, rally, scout, taunt 6 banter, deride, heckle 8 ridicule; (see also **raspberry**)

RBI 11 run batted in

re 4 as to 5 as for 7 apropos 9 as regards, regarding 10 as respects, concerning, respecting 13 with respect to

reach 2 go 3 get, ken, run, win 4 buck, come, gain, hand, make, move, pass, show, sway 5 ambit, get at, get in, orbit, range, scope, score, sweep, touch 6 affect, arrive, attain, extend, extent, rack up, radius, show up, turn up 7 achieve, compass, contact, horizon, purview, realize, stretch 8 approach 9 extension, influence 10 accomplish

react 6 behave 7 respond

_____ reaction 5 chain 7 nuclear 8 chemical

reactionary 4 fogy, tory 5 blimp, right 7 diehard, fogyish, old-line, radical 8 mossback, orthodox, rightist, royalist 11 bitterender, right-winger, standpatter 12 conservative

reactionist see **reactionary**

reactivate 5 renew 6 revive 8 rekindle, renovate, retrieve, revivify 9 resurrect 10 revitalize 11 resuscitate

read 3 say 4 mark, scan, show 5 proof 6 peruse, record 7 dictate 8 indicate, register *inability to:* 8 dyslexia

readable 7 legible

reader 6 lector, primer 8 bookworm 9 anthology

readily 4 well 6 easily, freely 7 lightly 12 effortlessly

readiness 4 ease 5 skill 7 address, fluency, prowess, sleight 8 alacrity, dispatch, facility, goodwill 9 dexterity, eloquence 10 expedition, volubility 11 promptitude

reading 7 version 9 rendition

readjust 6 modify 7 reorder 8 reorient 9 rearrange, reshuffle 10 reorganize 11 reconstruct, reorientate

ready 3 apt, fit, fix, get, set 4 fain, gird, live, make, prep, ripe 5 adept, brace, prime, prone, psych, quick, steel **6** active, expert, make up, minded, primed, prompt **7** dynamic, fortify, prepare, skilled, willing **8** adjusted, disposed, imminent, inclined, masterly, prepared, skillful **9** qualified **10** proficient, strengthen **11** predisposed

real 4 true **5** being, pucka, pukka, sound, valid **6** actual, honest **7** certain, genuine, sincere **8** bona fide, existing **9** authentic, necessary, undoubted, unfeigned, veridical **10** undeniable **12** indisputable

realism 6 verism **7** verismo

realistic 4 hard, sane **5** sober, sound **6** astute, earthy, shrewd **8** lifelike, rational, sensible, veristic **9** practical, pragmatic **10** hard-boiled, hardheaded, reasonable, unromantic **11** down-to-earth, nonacademic, pragmatical, utilitarian **12** matter-of-fact **13** unsentimental

reality 4 fact **5** truth

realize 3 win **4** gain **5** fancy, image, reach, score, think **6** attain, rack up, vision **7** achieve, feature, imagine **8** conceive, envisage, envision **10** accomplish

realm 5 orbit, range, scope, sweep **6** empire, extent, radius **7** compass, purview *suffix:* **3** dom

reanimation 7 rebirth, revival **10** renascence, resurgence **11** renaissance **12** risorgimento

reap 5 glean **6** garner, gather, thresh **7** harvest **8** ingather

rear 4 back, hind, lift, ramp, rump, seat, tail **5** after, breed, build, erect, fanny, hoist, nurse, put up, raise, set up **6** behind, bottom, foster, hinder, pick up, retral, take up, uphold, uplift **7** bring up, elevate, hind end, nurture, upraise **8** backside, buttocks, hindmost **9** construct, posterior

rear end 4 rump, seat, tail **5** fanny **6** behind, bottom **8** backside, buttocks, derriere

rearmost 4 last **5** final **6** latest, latter **7** closing **8** eventual, terminal, ultimate **10** concluding

rearrange see readjust

rearward 4 back **9** posterior

Rea Silvia, Rhea Silvia *father:* **7** Numitor *son:* **5** Remus **7** Romulus

reason 3 why, wit **4** mind, nous **5** cause, infer, proof, think **6** ground, motive, sanity, senses, spring, whyfor **7** account, reflect **8** argument, cogitate, logicize, lucidity, occasion, persuade, saneness **9** cerebrate, inference, intellect, rationale, soundness, speculate, wherefore **10** antecedent, deliberate **11** determinant, explanation **13** consideration, justification, ratiocination, understanding

reasonable 3 low **5** cheap, sound **6** modest, undear **7** logical, low-cost, popular **8** discreet, moderate, rational, sensible, uncostly **9** low-priced, temperate, unextreme **10** affordable, consequent, controlled, restrained **11** inexpensive, intelligent

reasoning 5 logic

reasonless 3 mad **4** daft **5** crazy **6** crazed, insane **7** cracked, invalid, lunatic **8** demented, deranged **9** bedlamite, illogical, sophistic **10** fallacious, irrational **11** nonrational

rebate 5 taper **6** lessen, reduce, refund **7** dwindle **8** decrease, diminish, discount, taper off **9** abatement, deduction, drain away, reduction **11** subtraction

Rebecca *beloved:* **7** Ivanhoe *father:* **5** Isaac

Rebekah *brother:* **5** Laban *father:* **7** Bethuel *husband:* **5** Isaac *nurse:* **7** Deborah *son:* **4** Esau **5** Jacob

rebel 6 anarch, mutiny, revolt, rise up **7** radical **8** attacker, debunker, frondeur, mutineer, opponent, revolter, ultraist **9** adversary, anarchist, assailant, extremist, insurgent, insurrect **10** antagonist, iconoclast, malcontent **11** rise against **13** revolutionary, revolutionist

rebellion 6 mutiny, revolt **8** sedition **10** revolution **12** insurrection

rebellious 8 mutinous **9** alienated, estranged, insurgent **11** disaffected **13** insubordinate

rebirth 7 revival **8** metanoia **10** conversion, renascence, resurgence **11** reanimation, renaissance **12** resurrection, risorgimento

rebound 7 recover **8** ricochet, snap back

rebuff 5 repel **6** reject **7** fend off, hold off, keep off, repulse, ward off **8** stave off

rebuke 3 rap, wig **5** chide, scold, scorn **6** earful, lesson, monish **7** chiding, lecture, reproof, reprove, tick off **8** admonish, call down, reproach, scolding **9** reprimand, talking-to **10** admonition **12** admonishment, dressing down **13** tongue-lashing

rebut 5 break, evert, repel **6** refute **7** confute, fend off, hold off, keep off, repulse, ward off **8** confound, disprove, stave off **10** controvert, disconfirm

recalcitrant 4 wild **6** unruly **8** opposing, stubborn, untoward **9** fractious, obstinate, resisting **11** indomitable, intractable

recall 4 cite, lift, stir **5** educe, evoke, renew, rouse, unsay, waken **6** abjure, arouse, awaken, elicit, memory, remind, repeal, retain, revive, revoke **7** bethink, extract, rescind, restore, retract, reverse **8** forswear, palinode, remember, take back, withdraw **9** anamnesis, dismantle, recollect, reinstate, reminisce **10** retrospect **12** recollection, reminiscence

recant 5 unsay 6 abjure 7 retract 8 forswear, palinode, take back, withdraw
recap 4 tire 7 retread
recapitulate 5 sum up, unite 9 summarize
recapitulation 3 sum 5 sum-up 6 précis,
resumé 7 epitome, summary 9 summing-
up
recede 3 ebb 4 back 5 abate, close, taper
6 depart, lessen, reduce, retire 7 dwindle,
regress, retract, retreat 8 decrease, diminish, fall back, withdraw 9 drain away
10 retrograde, retrogress
receipts 6 income 7 revenue
receive 4 take 5 admit 6 take in
received 5 sound 8 accepted, orthodox
9 canonical 10 sanctioned 13 authoritative
receiver 5 donee, fence 9 treasurer
recent 3 new 4 late 5 fresh, novel 6 latest, modern 8 neoteric 9 new-sprung
10 newfangled 11 modernistic 12 new-
fashioned *combining form:* 2 ne 3 cen,
neo 4 caen, cene, ceno 5 caeno
receptacle 5 torus 6 cupule 8 placenta
9 container 10 repository *laundry:* 6 hamper *narrow:* 6 trough
receptive 4 open 8 amenable, friendly,
suasible, swayable 9 acceptant 10 accessible, open-minded, responsive 11 persuadable, persuasible, suggestible, sympathetic
recess 4 nook 5 niche 6 alcove 7 adjourn
8 dissolve, prorogue 9 prorogate, terminate
Recessional author 7 Kipling (Rudyard)
recessive 8 retiring 9 withdrawn
recherché 3 new 4 rare 5 fresh, novel
6 choice, dainty, exotic, select 7 elegant,
unusual 8 delicate, original, superior,
uncommon
recidivate 5 lapse 7 relapse 9 backslide
recipe 7 formula 12 prescription
reciprocal 4 mate, twin 5 match 6 double, fellow 9 companion, duplicate 10 coordinate *combining form:* 6 allelo *prefix:*
5 inter
reciprocate 5 repay 6 retort, return
7 requite 8 exchange, serve out 9 retaliate
10 compensate, recompense 11 interchange
recital 5 story 9 discourse, narration,
recountal 10 recounting 11 description
combining form: 3 log 5 logue
recite 4 tell 5 chant, count, state 6 number, relate, report 7 narrate, recount
8 describe, rehearse 9 enumerate
reckless 4 rash, wild 5 brash, hasty
6 daring, madcap 7 carefree 9 audacious,
daredevil, desperate, foolhardy, hotheaded,
uncareful, venturous 10 ill-advised, incautious, mad-brained 11 adventurous, temerarious, venturesome 13 adventuresome,
inconsiderate, irresponsible

reckon 3 add, put, sum 4 call, cast, deem,
foot, view 5 count, guess, judge, lot on,
place, total 6 bank on, cipher, figure, number, regard, rely on 7 account, build on,
compute, count on, lot upon, surmise, trust
in, trust to 8 bank upon, consider, depend
on, estimate, rely upon 9 calculate, enumerate 10 conjecture, depend upon
11 approximate, calculate on
reckoning 3 tab 4 bill 5 score 7 account,
invoice 8 figuring 9 ciphering, statement
10 arithmetic, estimation 11 calculation,
computation
reclaim 7 recover, restore 9 restitute
10 rejuvenate 11 recondition, reconstruct
12 rehabilitate
recline 3 lie, tip 4 cant, heel, lean, list,
rest, tilt 5 slant, slope 6 lounge, repose
7 lie down 10 stretch out
reclining 4 flat 5 prone 9 decumbent,
prostrate, recumbent 10 procumbent
recluse 6 hermit 7 eremite 8 cenobite,
hermetic, secluded, solitary 9 anchorite,
seclusive 10 cloistered 11 sequestered
female: 7 ancress 9 anchoress
reclusive 8 eremitic, reserved, solitary
10 antisocial 11 standoffish 12 misanthropic
recognition 6 credit 9 awareness
10 cognizance *combining form:* 5 gnosy
6 gnosia, gnosis
recognize 4 know, note, spot 5 admit,
agree, place 6 finger, notice, recall, remark
7 observe 8 diagnose, identify, pinpoint,
remember 11 acknowledge, determinate,
distinguish
recoil 3 shy 4 balk, duck 5 dodge, quail,
quake, shake, start, stick, waver, wince
6 blanch, blench, falter, flinch, shrink,
swerve 7 shudder, squinch, stickle, tremble
8 hesitate, reel back
recollect 4 cite, stir 5 rally, rouse, waken
6 arouse, awaken, recall, remind, retain,
revive 7 bethink 8 remember 9 reminisce
10 retrospect
recollection 6 memory, recall 9 anamnesis 11 remembrance 12 reminiscence
recommence 5 renew 6 pick up, reopen,
resume, take up 7 restart 8 continue
recommend 4 hail, tout 6 advise, commit, kudize, praise 7 acclaim, applaud, consign, counsel, entrust 8 advocate 10 compliment
recommendation 6 advice 8 approval
9 character, reference 11 credentials,
endorsement, testimonial
recompense 3 pay 5 award, grant, repay
6 accord, amends, offset, return, reward
7 balance, redress, requite 8 reprisal
9 indemnify, indemnity, quittance, reimburse, retaliate, vouchsafe 10 compensate,

remunerate, reparation 11 reciprocate, restitution

reconcile 3 fit 4 suit, tune 5 adapt 6 adjust, attune, square, tailor 7 conform 8 quadrate 9 harmonize, integrate 10 coordinate, proportion 11 accommodate

recondite 4 dark, deep, hard 5 heavy, runic 6 mystic, occult, orphic, secret 7 cryptic, learned, obscure 8 abstruse, academic, anagogic, esoteric, hermetic, mystical, pedantic, profound 9 difficult, enigmatic, scholarly, sibylline 10 cabalistic

recondition 3 fix 4 do up, mend 5 patch 6 doctor, repair, revamp 7 rebuild, reclaim, restore 8 overhaul 9 restitute 10 rejuvenate 12 rehabilitate

reconnoiter 5 probe, scout

reconsider 5 amend 6 review, revise 7 correct, draw off, rethink, re-treat, reweigh, sleep on 9 reexamine, think over 10 reevaluate

reconstruct 3 fix 4 do up, mend 5 patch 6 doctor, repair, retool, revamp 7 rebuild, reclaim, reorder, restore 8 overhaul, readjust, reorient 9 rearrange, reshuffle, restitute 10 rejuvenate, reorganize 12 rehabilitate

record 3 say 4 date, disc, mark, read, show 5 enrol 6 annals, enroll 7 archive, journal 8 archives, document, register 9 chronicle *combining form:* 4 gram 5 graph *of a meeting:* 7 minutes *of past events:* 7 history *of proceedings:* 4 acta *ship's:* 3 log 7 logbook

recorder 5 flute

record player 5 phono 9 turntable 10 phonograph

recount 4 tell 5 state 6 recite, relate, report 7 narrate 8 describe, rehearse

recoup 6 regain 7 get back, recruit 8 retrieve 9 repossess

recourse 5 shift 6 refuge, resort 7 stopgap 9 expedient, makeshift 10 expediency

recover 4 heal, mend 5 rally, renew, rewin 6 offset, perk up, redeem, regain, resume, retake, revive 7 balance, get back, improve, rebound, reclaim, recruit, refresh, restore 8 reoccupy, retrieve, snap back 9 come round, reacquire, recapture, repossess, restitute 10 bounce back, compensate, convalesce, recuperate, rejuvenate 12 rehabilitate

recreant 3 rat 5 false 6 coward, untrue 7 unloyal 8 apostate, defector, disloyal, renegade, turncoat 9 faithless, turnabout 10 perfidious, traitorous, unfaithful

recreate 4 play 5 amuse, renew, sport 6 divert 7 disport, refresh, restore 9 entertain

recreation 3 fun 4 ease, play 5 mirth, sport 6 frolic, repose 7 disport, leisure, rollick 9 amusement, diversion 13 entertainment

recrudesce 5 react, recur, renew 6 return, revert, revive 7 reoccur

recruit 4 hire, mend 5 raise, renew 6 enlist, muster, novice, recoup, regain, repair, rookie 7 draftee, get back, rebuild, recover, refresh, restore 8 beginner, enlistee, freshman, neophyte, newcomer, renovate, retrieve 9 fledgling, novitiate, repossess 10 apprentice, tenderfoot

rectifier 4 tube 5 diode 8 detector

rectify 4 mend 5 amend, emend, right 6 repair 7 correct, rebuild

rectitude 6 virtue 7 honesty, probity 8 goodness, justness, morality 9 rightness 11 uprightness 13 righteousness

rector 6 pastor 9 clergyman 10 headmaster

rectory 5 manse 9 parsonage

recumbent 4 flat 5 prone 9 prostrate, reclining

recuperate 4 gain, mend 6 look up, perk up 7 improve 10 convalesce

recur 6 repair, repeat, resort, return, revert 7 iterate 8 turn back 9 reiterate 10 recrudesce

recurrent see recurring

recurring 8 periodic 9 alternate 10 isochronal, periodical 11 isochronous 12 intermittent *combining form:* 6 ennial

red 4 laky, puce, ruby 5 gules, ocher, rouge, ruddy 6 bloody, cerise, florid, wanton 7 carmine, flushed, glowing, oxblood, radical, rubious, scarlet, stammel, vermeil 8 flagrant, sanguine 9 carnation *combining form:* 4 rhod 5 pyrrh, pyrro, rhodo 6 erythr, pyrrho 7 erythro

Red 6 commie 9 Bolshevik, Communist

redact 4 edit 5 frame 6 revise 7 compose

Red and the Black author 8 Stendhal

red ape 9 orangutan

red arsenic 7 realgar

red-backed parrot 7 grassie

red-backed sandpiper 6 dunlin 10 blackheart

Red Badge of Courage *author:* 5 Crane (Stephen) *hero:* 7 Fleming (Henry)

red-bellied snipe 9 dowitcher

red benjamin 9 birthroot

redbird 8 cardinal 13 summer tanager

redbird cactus 7 jewbush

red blindness 10 protanopia

red blood cell 11 erythrocyte

red-blooded 5 lusty, vital 7 dynamic 8 vigorous 9 energetic, strenuous

redbreast 4 knot 5 robin

red-breasted snipe 9 dowitcher

redbuck 6 impala

Redburn author 8 Melville (Herman)

red carp 8 goldfish

red chalk 4 bole 6 ruddle

red cobalt 9 erythrite

red copper ore 7 cuprite

Red Cross *founder:* 6 Barton (Clara)
  Knight: 6 George

red currant 4 goya

redden 3 rud 4 glow, pink, rose, ruby
  5 blush, color, flush, rouge, ruddy 6 mantle,
  pinken, rubify, rubric, ruddle 7 crimson
  11 incarnadine

red dog 5 dhole, flour 8 card game

redecorate 9 refurbish

redeem 3 buy 4 free 5 loose 6 make up,
  offset, ransom, set off, unbind 7 balance,
  manumit, release, unchain 8 atone for, liberate, outweigh 10 compensate

redeemer 6 savior 7 messiah, saviour

redemption 6 ransom 7 release 9 atonement, expiation, salvation 11 deliverance

redeye 4 rudd 7 whiskey 8 rock bass,
  warmouth 10 copperhead

redfish 4 drum 6 salmon 11 channel bass

red grouper 5 negre

red grouse 8 moorbird, moorfowl, moor
  game

red hickory 6 pignut 9 mockernut

red hind 7 graysby 8 cabrilla

red-hot 2 up 5 fiery 6 ardent, fervid
  7 abreast, blazing, boiling, burning, flaming,
  glowing 8 scalding, sizzling, up-to-date
  9 au courant, scorching 10 blistering, passionate, sweltering 11 impassioned

red hot cattail 8 chenille

red Indian paint 9 bloodroot

red ink 7 deficit

red inkberry 8 pokeweed

red ironbark 5 mugga 8 eucalypt

red iron ore 8 hematite

red lauan 8 tanguile

red lead 6 minium

red lead ore 8 crocoite

red-legged crow 6 chough

red-legged plover 9 turnstone

red-letter 6 rubric 7 notable 8 nameable
  9 memorable 10 noteworthy, observable

red-light district 5 levee, stews 10 tenderloin

red mite 7 chigger

red-neck 4 hick, rube 5 yokel 6 rustic
  7 bumpkin, hayseed, peasant 9 hillbilly
  10 provincial 12 backwoodsman

red-necked gazelle 5 addra

redo 5 renew 6 revamp 7 remodel, restyle
  8 refinish, renovate 9 reproduce, restyling
  10 redecorate, repetition

red ocher 4 bole

redolence 4 balm 5 aroma, scent, spice
  7 bouquet, incense, perfume 9 fragrance

redolent 5 balmy, spicy, sweet 6 aromal,
  savory 7 perfumy 8 aromatic, fragrant, per-

fumed 9 ambrosial, remindful 11 reminis-
  cent

redouble 4 rise 5 mount, rouse 6 deepen
  7 enhance, magnify 8 heighten 9 intensify

redoubt 4 fort 7 citadel 8 fastness, fortress 10 stronghold

redoubtable 5 awful, famed, great
  6 famous 7 eminent, fearful 8 dreadful,
  horrible, horrific, renowned, shocking, terrible 9 appalling, frightful, prominent 10 celebrated 11 illustrious 13 distinguished

redound 6 accrue 7 conduce 10 contribute

red pine 4 rimu 10 Douglas fir

Red Planet 4 Mars

redpoll 6 linnet

redraft 6 revamp, review, revise, rework
  7 restyle, revisal, rewrite 8 rescript, revision, work over 9 recension

redrawer 6 winder

redress 5 annul, venge 6 amends,
  avenge, negate 7 revenge 8 negative,
  reprisal 9 balancing, cancel out, frustrate,
  indemnity, quittance, vengeance, vindicate
  10 counteract, neutralize, offsetting, recompense, reparation 11 restitution, retaliation
  12 compensation, countercheck

red roe 5 coral

redroot 7 alkanet, pigweed

red sable 8 kolinsky

red silk cotton 5 simal

red silver ore 9 proustite 11 pyrargyrite

red snapper 6 rasher

red sorrel 7 roselle

red squirrel 9 chickaree

red-stalk aster 6 cocash

reduce 3 cut 4 bate, clip, diet, pare, slow
  5 abate, break, crush, lower, shave, slash,
  taper 6 debase, defeat, demote, humble,
  lessen, rebate, recede, subdue, weaken
  7 conquer, cripple, curtail, cut back, cut
  down, declass, deflate, degrade, demerit,
  disable, disrate, dwindle 8 bear down, beat
  down, decrease, diminish, discount, disgrade, enfeeble, mark down, roll back, slim
  down, step down, taper off, unweight, vanquish 9 downgrade, drain away, humiliate,
  overpower, scale down, subjugate, undermine 10 depreciate, slenderize

reductio ad _____ 8 absurdum

reduction 6 rebate 7 cutback, cutdown
  8 discount, markdown 9 abatement
  11 downgrading *combining form:* 5 lyses
  (plural), lysis

redundancy 8 pleonasm, tumidity, verbiage 9 inflation, prolixity, tautology, turgidity
  10 flatulence, periphrase, roundabout
  11 periphrasis, superfluity

redundant 5 extra, spare, windy, wordy
  6 prolix 7 diffuse, surplus, verbose 9 iterat-
  ing 10 long-winded, palaverous 11 reiterat-

ing, repetitious, superfluous **13** supernumerary

red vitriol 9 bieberite, colcothar

redware 7 boccaro

red whelk 6 buckie

redwing 7 gadwall

redwing blackbird 6 maizer

redwood 5 rohun **7** amboyna, sequoia **8** mahogany **10** Scotch pine

reed 4 pipe **5** arrow *weaver's:* **4** slay, sley **6** sleigh

reedy 4 slim, thin **6** slight, stalky, twiggy **7** slender, squinny, tenuous **9** attenuate

reef 4 lode, vein **7** bioherm

reek 4 funk **5** smell, stink **6** stench

reeking 4 rank **5** fetid, funky, fusty **6** putrid, rancid, smelly **7** noisome **10** malodorous

reel 3 bob **4** spin, sway, swim, turn **5** lurch, swing, waver, weave, whirl **6** careen, falter, teeter, topple, totter, wobble **7** stagger, stumble **8** titubate

reestablish 5 renew **6** recall, revive **7** restore **9** reinstate **11** reintroduce

reevaluate 6 review **7** rethink, re-treat, reweigh **9** think over **10** reconsider

reeve 4 ruff **6** thread **8** official **10** magistrate

reexamine see **reevaluate**

refashion 4 turn, vary **5** alter **6** change, modify

refection 4 feed, meal **6** repast

refectory 10 dining hall

refer 4 cite, name **5** apply, quote **6** advert, advise, allude, assign, charge, credit, hand in, impute, insert, submit **7** ascribe, bring up, mention, specify **8** accredit, instance, point out **9** attribute

referee 3 ump **5** judge **6** umpire **7** adjudge, arbiter **9** arbitrate **10** adjudicate, arbitrator

reference book 5 atlas **6** manual **7** almanac **10** dictionary **12** encyclopedia

reference guide 5 index

referendum 4 poll

refine 6 polish, smooth **7** improve, perfect

refined 4 nice **6** subtle, urbane **7** genteel **8** cultured, debonair, delicate, finespun, polished, précieux, well-bred **9** distingué **10** cultivated

refinement 5 couth, grace **6** finish, polish **7** culture, dignity, suavity **8** breeding, civility, courtesy, elegance, urbanity **10** politeness **11** cultivation

reflect 4 echo **5** glass, image, study, think, weigh **6** mirror, ponder, reason **7** sparkle **8** cogitate **9** cerebrate **10** deliberate

reflecting 7 pensive **8** lustrous **10** cogitative, meditative, ruminative, thoughtful *light:* **8** relucent *suffix:* **6** escent

reflective 7 pensive **8** thinking **9** pondering **10** cogitative, meditative, ruminative, thoughtful

reflux 6 ebbing **9** condenser, returning

reform 5 amend, emend **7** correct, improve

Reformation leader 4 Knox (John) **6** Calvin (John), Luther (Martin) **7** Zwingli (Huldrych)

reformatory 3 pen **4** jail **6** cooler, lockup, prison **7** borstal **8** stockade **12** penitentiary

refractory 6 mulish **8** perverse, stubborn **9** obstinate **10** bullheaded, headstrong, self-willed, unyielding **11** intractable, stiff-necked

refrain 4 curb, deny, halt, keep, stop **5** check **6** arrest, chorus **7** forbear, inhibit **8** hold back, withhold **9** interrupt

refresh 4 rest **5** amuse, renew **6** divert, update, vivify **7** animate, enliven, quicken, restore **8** recreate, renovate **9** modernize, stimulate **10** rejuvenate

refresher 5 drink, tonic **6** bracer **9** stimulant

refrigerant 3 ice **5** freon **7** ammonia, cooling **13** carbon dioxide

refrigerator 6 fridge, icebox **9** condenser

refuge 4 port **5** cover, haven, shift **6** asylum, covert, harbor, resort, shield **7** hideout, retreat, shelter, stopgap **8** hideaway, immunity, recourse, resource **9** expedient, harborage, makeshift, sanctuary

refugee 2 DP **5** exile **6** emigré **7** evacuee **8** emigrant, fugitive **10** expatriate

refulgent 6 bright **7** beaming, radiant **8** luminous **9** brilliant

refund 5 repay **6** rebate **9** reimburse, repayment

refurbish 5 renew **6** update **7** restore, retouch **8** renovate **9** modernize **10** rejuvenate

refuse 3 jib **4** deny, dump, junk, nill **5** dreck, offal, spurn, swill, trash, waste **6** debris, kelter, litter, lumber, reject, scraps, spilth **7** decline, dismiss, garbage, rubbish **8** disallow, dustheap, keep back, riffraff, turn down, withhold **9** reprobate, repudiate, sweepings **10** disapprove

refutation 8 disproof, elenchus

refute 5 break, evert, rebut **8** confound, disprove **10** controvert, disconfirm

regain 6 recoup **7** get back, recover, recruit **8** reassume, reoccupy, retrieve **9** repossess *possession:* **7** replevy **8** replevin

regal 6 august, kingly **7** queenly, stately, sublime **8** glorious, imposing, kinglike, majestic, princely, splendid **9** monarchal, sovereign **10** monarchial **11** magnificent, monarchical, resplendent

regale 5 feast 6 dinner, spread 7 banquet

regalia 5 cigar 6 finery 8 frippery 9 full dress

Regan *father:* 4 Lear *husband:* 8 Cornwall *sister:* 7 Goneril 8 Cordelia

regard 4 care, deem, heed, mark, note, rate, view 5 assay, favor, honor, value 6 admire, assess, esteem, homage, notice, reckon, remark 7 account, concern, prizing, respect, valuing 8 approval, consider, estimate, interest 9 attention, curiosity, deference 10 admiration, cherishing, cognizance, estimation, observance, solicitude 11 approbation, carefulness, heedfulness, observation 12 appreciation, satisfaction 13 consciousness, consideration *as perfect:* 8 idealize

regardful 6 arrect 7 duteous 9 advertent, attentive, intentive, observant, observing

regarding 4 as to, in re 5 about, anent 6 anenst 7 apropos 10 as respects 13 with respect to

regatta 4 race 6 fabric 7 liberty

regenerate 6 reform, revive 9 reproduce

regent 5 ruler 8 governor 9 professor

regicide's victim 4 king

regimen 4 rule 9 governing 10 government

region 4 area, belt, part, walk, zone 5 field, tract 6 domain, sector, sphere 7 demesne, terrain 8 province, vicinity 9 bailiwick, territory 12 neighborhood *elevated:* 8 highland

regional 5 areal, local 9 localized 10 provincial

register 3 say 4 list, mark, read, roll, show 6 enroll, record 7 catalog 8 indicate

regnant 4 rife 6 master, ruling 7 current, popular 9 paramount, prevalent, sovereign 10 prevailing, widespread

regress 6 revert 9 throw back

regret 3 rue, woe 4 care 5 demur, grief, mourn, qualm 6 bemoan, bewail, grieve, lament, repent, sorrow 7 anguish, apology, deplore, scruple 9 deprecate, heartache, penitence 10 affliction, contrition, disapprove, heartbreak 11 compunction

regretful 5 sorry 8 contrite, penitent 9 repentant 10 apologetic 11 attritional, penitential

regrettable 4 dire 6 woeful 8 grievous 10 afflictive, calamitous 11 distressing, unfortunate 13 heartbreaking

regular 3 set 4 even 5 fixed, gross, typic, usual, utter 6 common, normal, steady 7 equable, general, natural, orderly, perfect, settled, typical, uniform 8 absolute, complete, constant, methodic, ordinary, outright, positive 9 clocklike, customary, downright, prevalent 10 consummate, methodical, systematic 11 commonplace, unmitigated 12 run-of-the-mill

regulate 3 fix 5 order 6 adjust, temper, tune up 7 arrange 8 organize 9 methodize 11 systematize

regulation 3 law 4 rule 5 canon, edict 6 curfew, decree 7 precept, statute 8 decretum 9 ordinance, prescript

regulator 8 governor

Rehabiah *father:* 7 Eliezer *grandfather:* 5 Moses

rehabilitate 7 reclaim, recover, restore 11 recondition

rehearse 5 drill, state 6 recite, relate, report 7 iterate, narrate, recount 8 describe, exercise, practice 10 run through

Rehoboam *father:* 7 Solomon *kingdom:* 5 Judah 6 Israel *mother:* 6 Naamah

reign 4 king, rule, sway 6 govern 7 prevail 8 dominate, domineer, overrule 11 predominate 12 preponderate

reimburse 3 pay 5 repay 7 balance, requite 9 indemnify 10 compensate, remunerate

rein 4 cool 7 collect, compose, control, repress, smother 8 restrain, suppress

reinforce 4 prop 5 super 6 pillar 7 augment, bolster, enlarge, fortify, sustain 8 buttress, energize, increase, multiply 10 invigorate, strengthen

reinstate 5 renew 6 recall, return, revive 7 put back, replace, restore 8 give back 11 reestablish

reintroduce 5 renew 6 recall, revive 7 restore 11 reestablish

reinvestment 8 plowback

reiterate 5 renew, resay 6 repeat 7 reprise

reject 4 cast, jilt, junk, shed 5 debar, scrap, spurn 6 rebuff, refuse, slough 7 cashier, decline, discard, dismiss, exclude, shut out 8 jettison, throw out, turn down 9 eliminate, reprobate, repudiate, throw away 10 disapprove

rejoice 3 joy 5 exult, glory 7 gladden

rejoin 5 reply 6 answer, come in, retort 7 respond

rejoinder 5 reply 6 answer, retort, return 7 respond 8 antiphon, response

rejuvenate 5 renew 7 reclaim, recover, refresh, restore 9 modernize, refurbish 11 recondition, reconstruct

Rekem's father 6 Hebron

rekindle 5 renew 6 revive 8 renovate, retrieve, revivify 9 resurrect 10 reactivate, revitalize 11 resuscitate

relate 4 join, link, tell, yoke 5 apply, unite 6 assign, bear on, couple, credit, depict, detail, impute, render, report 7 connect, divulge, express, itemize, pertain, recount **8** bear upon, describe, disclose **9** appertain, pronounce

related 4 akin **5** alike **6** agnate, allied **7** cognate, connate, germane, kindred **8** incident **9** analogous, identical, pertinent **10** connatural **11** consanguine *by marriage:* **7** affined

relating to *suffix:* **2** al, an, ar, ic **3** ean, ese, ial, ile, ine, ist, ory **4** ical **5** ative, istic **6** itious **7** istical

relation 3 kin **7** kinsman **9** kinswoman *on father's side:* **6** agnate *on mother's side:* **5** enate

relative 2 ma, pa **3** kin, mom, sib, sis, son **4** aunt, mama, nana, papa, sibb **5** madre, mamma, mammy, momma, niece, pappy, pater, poppa, uncle **6** agnate, cousin, father, mother, nephew, parent, sister **7** brother, cognate, kinsman, sibling **8** daughter, grandson **9** dependent, kinswoman **10** contingent, grandchild **11** approximate, conditional, grandfather, grandmother, grandparent **13** granddaughter

relatives 7 kinfolk **8** kinfolks

relax 4 ease, loll, rest **5** loose, slack **6** lollop, loosen, lounge, rest up, unbend, unwind **7** ease off, slacken **8** loosen up **9** untighten

relaxation 4 ease, rest **6** repose **7** leisure **9** amusement **11** assuagement **12** requiescence

relaxed 4 mild, soft **5** loose, slack **6** breezy, casual, dégagé, gentle **7** lenient, sinuous, unfussy **8** flexuous, informal **9** easygoing **10** unreserved **11** low-pressure

release 4 emit, free, vent **5** issue, loose, unfix, yield **6** acquit, loosen, pardon, ransom, resign, unbind, uncage, uncoil **7** give off, give out, manumit, unchain, unleash **8** liberate, throw off, unfetter, untether **9** discharge, exculpate, exonerate, surrender, take out on, unshackle **10** emancipate *conditional:* **6** parole

relegate 5 exile, expel, refer **6** banish, charge, commit, credit, deport **7** commend, confide, consign, entrust, expulse **8** accredit, displace, hand over, turn over

relent 3 ebb **4** fall, wane **5** abate, let up **7** die away, die down, ease off, slacken, subside **8** moderate

relentless 4 grim **5** cruel, rigid **6** dogged, fierce, mortal, strict **7** adamant, inhuman **8** obdurate, rigorous **9** ferocious, stringent, unbending **10** implacable, inexorable, inflexible, ironfisted, unyielding **11** unflinching **12** unappeasable

relevant 3 apt, fit **5** ad rem **6** allied, proper **7** apropos, cognate, fitting, ger-

mane, weighty **8** apposite, material, pointful, suitable **9** allowable, important, pertinent **10** admissible, applicable **11** applicative, applicatory, appropriate

reliable 4 safe **5** sound, tried, valid **6** cogent, proven, secure, trusty **7** certain, telling **8** accurate, apposite, attested, inerrant, unerring, verified **9** authentic, confirmed, validated **10** dependable **11** trustworthy **12** tried and true

reliance 4 hope **5** faith, stock, trust

relic 5 token, trace **6** shadow, trophy **7** memento, vestige **8** keepsake, memorial, reminder, souvenir **11** remembrance

relict 5 widow **8** residual

relief 3 aid **4** ease, hand, help, lift **6** assist, succor **7** comfort, secours, support **8** easement **9** allayment, softening **10** assistance, lightening, mitigation **11** alleviation, appeasement, assuagement

relieve 3 aid, rob, sub **4** ease, help, loot **5** allay, quiet, rifle, spare, spell **6** excuse, exempt, fill in, lessen, let off, reduce, soften, solace, soothe, subdue, supply, temper **7** absolve, appease, assuage, benefit, comfort, console, lighten, mollify, plunder, qualify, ransack, stick up, subvene **8** decrease, diminish, dispense, mitigate, moderate, palliate, take over **9** alleviate, discharge

religion 4 cult, sect **5** creed, faith **6** belief, church

religious 3 nun **4** holy, just, monk, true **5** godly, moral, noble, pious **6** devout, priest, sister, votary **7** ethical, staunch, upright, votress **8** faithful, monastic, votaress, votarist **9** pietistic, prayerful, steadfast *foot-washing ceremony:* **6** maundy *offering:* **8** oblation *order member:* **5** friar **8** cenobite

relinquish 4 cast, cede, quit, shed **5** forgo, leave, waive, yield **6** desert, forego, give up, resign **7** abandon, discard, forbear, forsake, lay down, throw up **8** abdicate, abnegate, hand over, lay aside, renounce **9** sacrifice, surrender

relish 4 like, tang, zest **5** enjoy, flair, gusto, heart, sapor, savor, smack, taste **6** admire, flavor, liking, loving, palate **7** leaning **8** enjoying, penchant, pleasure, sapidity **9** delight in, diversion, enjoyment, prejudice **10** appreciate, propensity **11** delectation

relucent 7 radiant, shining **10** reflecting

reluctant 3 shy **4** wary **5** chary, loath **6** afraid, averse **7** uneager **8** backward, cautious **9** unwilling **10** indisposed *prophet:* **5** Jonah

rely on 5 trust **7** count on **8** depend on

remain 4 bide, stay, wait **5** abide, tarry **6** linger **7** survive **11** stick around

remainder 6 excess 7 balance, residue, surplus 8 leavings, leftover, residual, residuum

remains 4 body, mort 5 stiff 6 corpse, debris, fossil 7 balance, cadaver, carcass, residue 8 leavings, residual, residuum

remark 3 see 4 heed, note 5 glass 6 notice, postil, saying 7 comment, discern, mention, observe 8 exegesis, perceive, scholium 9 assertion, attention, statement, utterance 10 animadvert, annotation, cognizance, commentary, commentate, exposition 11 observation *in a play:* 5 aside *witty:* 7 epigram

remarkable 4 rare 6 signal, unique 7 salient, strange, unusual, weighty 8 peculiar, singular, striking, uncommon, unwonted 9 arresting, arrestive, important, momentous, prominent 10 unordinary 11 conspicuous, exceptional, outstanding, significant, uncustomary 13 extraordinary

_____ **Remarque** 5 Erich (Maria)

remedial 6 curing 7 healing 8 curative, sanative, sanatory 9 vulnerary 11 restorative

remedy 4 cure, drug, heal 6 elixir, physic 7 cure-all, nostrum, panacea 8 antidote, biologic, medicant, medicine, specific 9 medicinal, pharmacon 10 corrective, medicament, medication 11 counterstep

remember 4 cite 5 educe, evoke 6 elicit, recall, relive, retain 9 recollect 10 retrospect

remembrance 4 gift 5 favor, relic, token 6 memory, recall, trophy 7 memento, present 8 keepsake, memorial, souvenir 9 anamnesis 12 recollection

remind 3 jog 4 warn 5 alert 6 advise, prompt 8 admonish

reminder 4 hint, memo, note, sign 5 relic, token 6 notice, trophy 7 gesture, memento, warning 8 keepsake, memorial, souvenir 10 admonition, expression, indication, intimation, memorandum, suggestion

reminisce see **remember**

reminiscence 6 memory, recall 9 anamnesis 12 recollection

remise 4 cede, deed 5 alien 6 assign, convey 8 alienate, make over, sign over, transfer

remiss 3 lax 4 lazy 5 slack 8 careless, derelict, fainéant, indolent, slothful 9 negligent 10 behindhand, delinquent, neglectful, regardless 12 disregardful

remit 4 send, ship, stay 5 defer, delay, route 6 excuse, hold up, pardon, put off, shelve 7 address, condone, consign, forgive, forward, hold off 8 dispatch, postpone

remnant 4 heel, rest 7 balance, oddment, residue 8 leavings, residual, residuum

remodel 6 revamp 11 reconstruct

remonstrance 5 demur 7 protest 8 demurral, demurrer, question 9 challenge, objection

remonstrate 4 kick 5 fight 6 combat, except, object, oppose, resist 7 protest 9 withstand

remonstration see **remonstrance**

remora 4 clog, drag 11 shark sucker, sucking fish

remorse 3 rue 6 regret 7 penance 9 attrition, penitence, penitency 10 contrition, repentance 11 compunction 12 contriteness

remorseful see **regretful**

remorsefulness see **remorse**

remote 3 far, off 4 back, slim 5 aloof, small 6 casual, far-off, secret, slight 7 devious, distant, faraway, obscure, outside, retired, slender 8 detached, far-flung, frontier, lonesome, off-lying, outlying, ulterior 9 incurious, uncurious, unsettled, withdrawn 10 negligible, outlandish 11 indifferent, out-of-the-way, unconcerned 12 uninterested *combining form:* 3 tel 4 dist, pale, tele 5 disto, palea, paleo 6 palaeo, palaio

remotest 6 utmost 7 extreme, outmost 9 outermost, uttermost 11 furthermost

remove 4 doff, ship, skim 5 douse, erase, purge, shift 6 efface, put off, unseat 7 blot out, cast off, disturb, expunge, extract, take off, take out 8 dislodge, displace, displant, evacuate, take away, throw off, transfer, withdraw 9 clear away, dislocate, eliminate, eradicate, extirpate, liquidate 10 obliterate 11 exterminate *from office:* 6 depose *hair:* 8 depilate *prefix:* 2 de *surgically:* 6 resect

removed 3 far 5 alone, aloof, apart 6 far-off, secret 7 devious, distant, faraway, isolate, obscure 8 detached, far-flung, isolated, lonesome, off-lying, outlying

remunerate 3 pay 5 award, grant, repay 6 accord 7 guerdon, requite 9 indemnify, reimburse, vouchsafe 10 recompense

remunerative 6 paying 7 gainful 9 lucrative 10 profitable, well-paying, worthwhile 11 moneymaking 12 advantageous

Remus *brother:* 7 Romulus *father:* 4 Mars *mother:* 10 Rhea Silvia *slayer:* 7 Romulus

renaissance see **rebirth**

renal 7 nephric

rend 3 rip 4 rive, tear 5 split 6 cleave, divide

render 3 put 4 limn, turn 5 image 6 depict, govern, return 7 execute, picture, portray 8 carry out, describe 9 delineate, interpret, represent, translate, transpose 10 administer 12 administrate *suffix:* 2 en

rendering 7 version 10 paraphrase 11 restatement, translation

rendezvous 4 date 5 haunt, raise, tryst 6 gather, muster, resort 7 collect, hangout, purlieu 8 assemble, congress 9 forgather 10 congregate, engagement 11 appointment, assignation

rendition 7 reading, version 11 translation

renegade 3 rat 5 rebel 7 heretic 8 apostate, defector, deserter, forsaker, recreant, turncoat 9 abandoner, insurgent, turnabout 10 iconoclast, schismatic 13 tergiversator

renege 5 welsh 6 cry off, resile 7 back off, back out 8 back down 9 backpedal

renew 4 mend 5 fresh, resay 6 pick up, recall, reform, reopen, repair, repeat, resume, revise, revive, take up, update 7 correct, freshen, iterate, rebuild, rectify, refresh, remodel, reprise, restart, restore 8 continue, make over, rekindle, retrieve, revivify 9 modernize, refurbish, reinstate, reiterate, resurrect 10 ingeminate, reactivate, recommence, rejuvenate, revitalize 11 reestablish, reintroduce

rennet 8 abomasum

renounce 3 rat 4 quit, turn 5 chuck, demit 6 defect, desert, resign 7 abandon, forsake 8 abdicate, disclaim 9 repudiate, throw over 10 apostatize, tergiverse

renovate 5 clean 6 revive 7 cleanse, refresh, restore 8 rekindle, retrieve, revivify 9 modernize, refurbish, resurrect 10 revitalize

renown 4 fame 5 éclat, kudos 6 repute 8 eminence, prestige 9 celebrity, notoriety 10 prominence, prominency, reputation 11 distinction, preeminence

renowned 5 famed, great 6 famous, lauded, signal 7 eminent, notable, praised 8 extolled 9 acclaimed, prominent 10 celebrated, celebrious 11 illustrious, outstanding 13 distinguished

rent 3 let 4 hire, rift, torn 5 break, lease, split 6 breach, schism, sublet 7 charter, fissure, mangled, rupture 8 fracture, sublease

rental 4 flat 5 rooms, suite 8 lodgings, tenement 9 apartment

renter 6 lessee

renunciation 6 denial 8 forgoing, yielding 9 eschewing, sacrifice, surrender 10 abjurement, forbearing, self-denial 11 forswearing

reopen 5 renew 6 pick up, resume, take up 7 restart 8 continue 10 recommence

reorder 6 retool 7 permute 8 readjust 9 rearrange, reshuffle 11 reconstruct 12 reconstitute

reorganization 7 shake-up 8 overturn, turnover

reorganize 6 retool 7 rebuild, refound 8 readjust, renovate, resettle 9 rearrange, reshuffle 10 regenerate 11 reconstruct, reestablish 12 reconstitute

reorient 6 retool 8 readjust 9 rearrange, reshuffle

repair 3 fix, hie, run 4 case, do up, fare, mend, pass, trim, turn, wend 5 apply, order, patch, recur, refer, shape 6 doctor, estate, fettle, kilter, push on, resort, revamp, travel 7 fitness, journey, proceed, rebuild, service 8 overhaul 11 recondition

reparation 6 amends, reward 7 redress 8 requital 9 atonement, indemnity, quittance 10 adjustment, recompense, settlement

repartee 3 wit 5 humor, irony 6 banter, retort, satire 7 riposte, sarcasm 8 backchat, badinage, comeback, response, snip-snap 9 rejoinder 10 back answer, persiflage

repast 4 feed, meal 9 refection

repay 5 award 6 accord, offset 7 balance, requite 9 indemnify, reimburse 10 compensate, recompense, remunerate

repeal 4 lift, void 6 recall, revoke 7 rescind, reverse 9 dismantle

repeat 4 copy, echo, harp, ring 5 chime, ditto, quote, recap, recur, renew, rerun, resay 6 parrot, recite, rehash, relate, retell, return 7 imitate, iterate, recount, restate 8 hash over, rehearse 9 duplicate, reiterate 12 recapitulate

repeater 7 firearm 10 recidivist

repeating 7 iterant

repel 4 buck 5 fight, rebut 6 combat, oppose, rebuff, reluct, resist, revolt, sicken 7 contest, disgust, dispute, fend off, hold off, keep off, ward off 8 nauseate, stave off

repellent 4 foul, vile 5 nasty 7 noisome 8 aversive, kindless, ungenial 9 invidious, loathsome, obnoxious, offensive, revolting, revulsive 10 disgusting 11 uncongenial

repent 3 rue 6 regret 7 deplore

repentance 3 rue 4 ruth 7 remorse 9 penitency 10 contrition 11 compunction 12 contriteness

repentant see **regretful**

repetition 4 copy 7 recital 8 iterance 9 rehearsal

rephrase 6 reword 7 restate

repine 4 fret, fuss, kick, wail 6 murmur 8 complain 10 discontent

replace 5 renew, shift 6 change, recoup, regain, return 7 put back, recover, restore 8 give back, retrieve, supplant, take back 9 reinstate, restitute, supersede

replacement 3 sub 6 fill-in 7 stand-in 9 alternate, surrogate 10 substitute 11 locum tenens, pinch hitter, succedaneum

replenish 5 refit, renew, stock 7 restore

replete 4 full, rife 5 alive, awash 6 jammed, loaded 7 brimful, crammed, crowded, stuffed, teeming 8 brimming, swarming, thronged 9 abounding, chock-full 11 overflowing

replica 4 copy 5 ditto 6 carbon 9 duplicate, facsimile 10 carbon copy

replicate 4 copy

reply 6 answer, come in, rejoin, retort, return 7 respond 8 response 9 rejoinder

report 3 cry 4 buzz, chat, dirt, fame, name, news, talk, word 5 brief, on-dit, rumor, state, story 6 advice, canard, gossip, impart, murmur, notice, recite, relate, review, rumble, speech, tattle 7 account, chatter, comment, hearsay, history, narrate, prating, recount, scandal, tidings, version 8 advisory, bulletin, chitchat, describe, rehearse 9 character, chronicle, grapevine, narrative, small talk, statement

reporter 7 newsman 10 journalist *inexperienced:* 3 cub

repose 3 lie 4 rest 7 leisure, lie down, recline, renewal 10 relaxation, stretch out 11 refreshment, restoration 12 requiescence

repository 5 depot, store 7 arsenal 8 magazine 10 storehouse

repossess see **regain**

reprehend 3 rap 4 rate, skin 5 blame, chide, knock, scold 6 berate, rebuke 7 censure, condemn, upbraid 8 admonish, denounce 9 criticize 10 denunciate

reprehensible 5 amiss 6 guilty, sinful, unholy 8 blameful 11 blameworthy 13 demeritorious

represent 4 body, copy, limn, mean, show 5 draft, image 6 denote, depict, embody, mirror, relate, render, sketch, typify 7 display, exhibit, express, imitate, narrate, outline, picture, portray, realize, signify, suggest 8 describe 9 body forth, delineate, epitomize, exemplify, interpret, personate, personify, symbolize 10 illustrate, substitute 11 emblematize, impersonate, personalize

representation 6 symbol 7 picture 8 likeness 9 portrayal 11 portraiture

representative 4 case 5 agent, envoy, ideal, model, typal, typic 6 deputy, sample 7 classic, example, typical 8 delegate, emissary, instance, monotype, sampling, specimen 9 catchpole, classical, exemplary 10 archetypal, prototypal 11 case history 12 illustrative, prototypical

repress 4 cool 5 shush 6 muffle 7 collect, compose, control, smother, squelch 8 restrain

repression 4 curb 5 check 7 choking, control, subdual 8 crushing, quashing, quelling, stifling 9 clampdown, crackdown, quenching, restraint, squashing 10 smothering

reprieve 7 respite

reprimand 3 rap, wig 5 chide 6 lesson, monish, rebuke 7 chiding, tick off 8 admonish, call down 10 admonition 12 admonishment

reprisal 6 amends 7 redress, revenge 8 avenging, revanche 9 indemnity, quittance, vengeance 10 avengement, recompense 11 counterblow, retaliation, retribution

reprise 5 renew, resay 7 iterate 9 reiterate

reproach 3 rap, wig 5 blame, chide, taunt 6 lesson, monish, rebuke 7 censure, chiding, upbraid 8 admonish, call down 9 discredit 10 admonition 12 admonishment

reprobate 3 bad, rap 4 evil, heel, skin 5 blame, knock, spurn, wrong 6 refuse, reject, sinful, wicked 7 censure, condemn, decline, dismiss, immoral, lowlife, vicious, villain 8 denounce, roperipe, turn down 9 abandoned, criticize, dissolute, miscreant, scoundrel 10 blackguard, disapprove, iniquitous, licentious 12 unprincipled

reproduce 4 bear, copy 5 beget, breed 7 imitate 8 generate, multiply 9 duplicate, procreate, propagate 11 reduplicate

reproduction see **replica**

reproductive cell 3 egg 4 ovum 5 sperm, spore 6 gamete 7 agamete

reproof 3 rap, wig 6 rebuke 7 chiding 8 scolding 10 admonition 12 admonishment

reprove 4 warn 5 blame, chide, scold 6 lesson, monish, punish, rebuke 7 censure, chasten, correct, counsel, tick off 8 admonish, call down, lambaste 9 criticize

reptile 5 snake 6 caiman, cayman, gavial, lizard, turtle 7 tuatara 8 hatteria, tortoise 9 crocodile, sphenodon *combining form:* 6 herpet 7 herpeto *extinct:* 8 dinosaur

republic 5 state 6 nation *Africa:* 4 Chad, Mali, Togo 5 Benin, Congo, Egypt, Gabon, Ghana, Kenya, Niger, Sudan, Zaire 6 Angola, Gambia, Guinea, Malawi, Rwanda, Uganda, Zambia 7 Algeria, Burundi, Comoros, Liberia, Namibia, Senegal, Somalia, Tunisia 8 Botswana, Cameroon, Djibouti, Tanzania 9 Cape Verde 10 Ivory Coast, Madagascar, Mauritania, Mozambique 11 Sierra Leone 12 Guinea-Bissau *Asia:* 4 Iran, Iraq, Laos 5 China, India, Syria, Yemen 6 Turkey 7 Vietnam 8 Maldives, Mongolia, Pakistan, Sri Lanka 9 Indonesia, Singapore 10 Bangladesh, North Korea, South Korea 11 Philippines *Central America:* 4 Cuba 5 Haiti 6 Panama 7 Ecuador 8 Honduras 9 Costa Rica, Guatemala, Nicaragua *Europe:* 5 Italy 6 France, Greece, Poland 7 Albania, Austria, Finland, Germany, Hungary, Iceland, Ireland, Romania, Rumania 8 Bulgaria,

Portugal 9 San Marino *Pacific:* 5 Nauru
8 Kiribati *South America:* 4 Peru 5 Chile
6 Brazil, Guyana 7 Bolivia, Uruguay
8 Colombia, Paraguay 9 Argentina, Venezuela

Republican Party 3 GOP *mascot:*
8 elephant

Republic author 5 Plato

repudiate 4 deny 5 spurn 6 defect,
desert, disown, refuse, reject 7 abandon,
decline, disavow, discard, dismiss, forsake
8 disallow, disclaim, renounce, turn down
10 apostatize, disapprove, tergiverse

repugnance 4 hate 6 hatred, horror
8 aversion, loathing 11 abomination, detestation

repugnant 4 foul, vile 5 alien, nasty
6 creepy, horrid 7 foreign, noisome 8 aversive, gruesome 9 abhorrent, extrinsic, invidious, loathsome, obnoxious, offensive,
repulsive, revolting, revulsive 10 disgusting

repulse 5 rebut 6 rebuff, reluct, revolt,
sicken 7 disgust, fend off, hold off, keep
off, ward off 8 nauseate, stave off

repulsion see **repugnance**

repulsive see **repugnant**

reputation 4 fame, name 5 éclat 6 credit,
renown, weight 8 prestige 9 authority,
celebrity, character, influence, notoriety

reputed 8 putative, supposed 9 estimable
10 creditable 11 conjectural, respectable,
suppositive 12 hypothetical, suppositious

request 3 ask, sue 4 pray 5 apply
6 appeal, desire, invite 7 solicit 8 entreaty,
petition

Requiem for a Nun author 8 Faulkner
(William)

requin 5 shark 8 cub shark, man-eater

require 3 ask 4 call, lack, need, take, want
5 claim, crave, exact 6 demand 7 call for,
solicit 11 necessitate

required 6 needed 9 mandatory 10 compulsory, obligatory 12 compulsatory

requirement 4 must, need, want
6 demand 9 condition, essential, necessity
10 sine qua non

requisite 3 due 4 just, must 5 right
6 needed 7 condign, merited, needful
8 deserved, rightful, suitable 9 condition,
essential, necessity 10 sine qua non
11 appropriate 12 precondition

requisition 4 call 5 claim, exact
6 demand 7 solicit 9 challenge, postulate

requital 7 revenge 8 avenging, revanche
9 vengeance 10 avengement 11 counterblow, retaliation, retribution

requite 3 pay 5 repay 6 return 7 content,
revenge, satisfy 9 indemnify, reimburse
10 compensate 11 reciprocate

reredos 6 screen 7 brazier 9 partition

rescind 4 lift 6 recall, repeal, revoke
7 reverse

rescue 4 free, save 6 ransom, redeem,
regain 7 deliver, manumit, recover, release
8 conserve, liberate, preserve, retrieve
9 extricate 10 emancipate 11 disentangle
12 disembarrass

research 5 probe, quest 7 delving,
inquest, inquiry, probing 11 inquisition
13 investigation

resect 6 cut out, excise 9 extirpate

resemblance 6 simile 7 analogy 8 affinity, likeness, parallel 9 alikeness 10 comparison, similarity, similitude

resemble 5 favor 8 look like, simulate

resembling *combining form:* 4 form
5 iform *suffix:* 2 ar 3 ful 4 eous, itic

resentful 4 sore 6 bitter, piqued, sullen
7 envious, jealous 9 grudgeful

resentment 4 huff, miff 5 pique, spite
6 animus, malice, rancor 7 dudgeon, ill will,
offense, umbrage 9 animosity, antipathy,
malignity 10 antagonism, malignancy

reservation 5 terms 7 proviso, strings

reserve 4 book, fund, hold, keep 5 hoard,
stock, store 6 detain, engage, retain, supply 7 backlog, bespeak, keep out, nest egg
8 contract, hold back, keep back, withhold
9 inventory, preengage, stockpile

reserved 3 shy 5 aloof, close 6 formal,
modest, offish, silent 7 bashful, distant, limited 8 eremitic, modified, reticent, solitary,
taciturn 9 diffident, qualified, reclusive, withdrawn 10 antisocial, unsociable 11 ceremonious, close-lipped, constrained,
standoffish, tight-lipped 12 closemouthed

reservoir 5 hoard, stock, store 7 backlog,
nest egg 9 inventory, stockpile

reside 3 lie 4 live 5 dwell, exist 6 endure,
inhere, occupy, people, tenant 7 consist,
hang out, inhabit 8 continue, domicile

residence 4 home 5 abode, house
8 domicile, dwelling 9 occupancy 10 commorancy, habitation, occupation, settlement
11 inhabitancy 12 inhabitation

resident 5 liver 7 denizen, dweller 8 habitant, occupant 9 indweller 10 inhabitant

residential area 5 exurb 6 suburb
7 exurbia 8 suburbia

resident of *suffix:* 2 er 3 ese, ier, ite, yer

residual 4 heel 7 balance, remains, remanet, remnant 8 leavings 9 remainder

residue 3 ash 4 heel 7 balance, remains,
remanet, remnant 8 bone char, leavings
9 bone black, remainder 11 animal black
from honey: 7 slumgum *metallic:* 4 slag
mineral: 4 calx

resign 4 cede, drop, quit 5 demit, leave,
waive, yield 6 give up, submit 7 abandon
8 abdicate, hand over, renounce 9 surrender, terminate 10 relinquish

resignation 7 modesty 8 meekness, patience 9 lowliness 10 compliance, conformity, humbleness 11 forbearance, longanimity, patientness 12 acquiescence

resigned 7 passive 8 yielding 10 submissive 11 acquiescent, unresistant, unresisting

resile 6 recede, recoil 7 rebound, retract, retreat

resilient 4 airy 6 bouncy, supple, whippy 7 buoyant, elastic, springy, stretch 8 flexible, stretchy, volatile 9 expansive

resin 4 balm 5 copal, damar, roset 6 dammar 7 acrylic, copaiba *aromatic:* 6 balsam, mastic 8 sandarac *fossil:* 8 retinite *fragrant:* 4 tolu 5 elemi 6 storax, styrax 7 ladanum 8 labdanum, olibanum *gum:* 4 kino 5 myrrh 7 benzoin 8 bdellium *medicinal:* 6 guaiac 8 guaiacum *of an insect:* 3 lac *synthetic:* 8 phenolic *used by bees:* 8 propolis

resist 4 balk, buck, defy, duel, foil, stem 5 check, fight, repel 6 assail, attack, baffle, combat, hinder, impugn, oppose, thwart 7 assault, contest, counter, dispute, gainsay 8 obstruct, traverse 9 frustrate, withstand 10 contradict, contravene

resistance unit 3 ohm

resistor 8 rheostat

resolute 3 set 4 bent, fast, true 5 loyal 6 ardent, intent, steady 7 decided, settled, staunch 8 constant, decisive, faithful, stubborn 9 allegiant, obstinate, steadfast 10 determined 12 pertinacious

resolution 4 guts 5 heart, pluck, spunk 6 mettle, spirit 7 courage 8 analysis, decision, firmness 11 decidedness 13 dauntlessness, determination, purposiveness

resolve 3 fix, rid 4 rule, work 5 break, clear, purge 6 decide, dispel, figure, settle, unfold 7 analyze, clear up, dissect, unravel, work out 8 conclude, decipher, decision, disabuse, disperse, firmness, unriddle 9 anatomize, breakdown, decompose, determine, dissipate, puzzle out 11 decidedness 13 determination, purposiveness

resonant 3 fat 4 deep, full, loud, rich 5 noisy, round 6 mellow, rotund 7 beating, booming, orotund, pulsing, ringing 8 enhanced, plangent, powerful, profound, sonorous, sounding, strident 9 pulsating, thrilling, throbbing 10 clangorous, heightened, stentorian, thundering, thunderous 11 intensified 13 reverberating

resort 2 go 3 den, inn, spa, use 4 nest, turn 5 apply, haunt, haven, hotel, lodge, recur, refer, shift 6 affect, devote, direct, employ, harbor, refuge 7 address, hang out, purlieu, retreat, riviera, stopgap, utilize 8 frequent, recourse 9 expedient, makeshift 10 substitute *beach:* 4 lido

resound 4 echo, hymn, laud 5 bless, cry up, extol 6 praise 7 glorify, magnify 9 celebrate

resounding 5 round 6 rotund 7 orotund, reboant, vibrant 8 emphatic, forceful, plangent, sonorant, sonorous 9 assertive, consonant

resource 3 way 4 hope, mode, step 5 dodge, means, shift 6 device, lash-up, manner, method, refuge, relief, string, system 7 fashion, measure, stopgap 8 artifice, creation 9 expedient, invention, makeshift, stratagem, surrogate

resources 5 means, worth 6 assets, riches, wealth 7 capital, fortune 8 property 9 substance

respect 3 awe 4 fear 5 favor, honor 6 admire, devoir, esteem, regard, revere 7 account, worship 8 consider, venerate 9 adoration, reverence 10 admiration, estimation, veneration 13 consideration

respectable 4 done, good, nice 5 right 6 comely, decent, proper, worthy 7 correct, reputed 8 adequate, all right, becoming, decorous 9 befitting 10 conforming, sufficient 11 appropriate 12 satisfactory 13 well-thought-of

respectful 5 civil 6 polite 7 duteous 8 gracious, obeisant, reverent 9 attentive, courteous 10 venerating 11 deferential, reverential

respecting 4 as to, in re 5 about 7 apropos 9 as regards

respire 7 breathe

respite 3 ten 4 blow, ease, lull 5 break, pause, spell 6 breath, recess 7 leisure 8 breather, reprieve 12 intermission

resplendent 5 proud 6 superb 7 blazing, flaming, glowing, sublime 8 glorious, gorgeous

respond 3 act 5 react, reply 6 answer, behave, come in, rejoin, retort, return 8 antiphon

response 5 reply 6 answer, retort, return 8 antiphon 9 rejoinder *involuntary:* 6 reflex 7 tropism

responsibility 4 duty, onus 6 burden, charge

responsible 6 liable 10 answerable, dependable 11 accountable

responsive 4 warm 6 tender 7 sensile 8 replying, sensible, sentient, suasible, swayable 9 acceptant, answering 11 impressible, kindhearted, persuadable, persuasible, softhearted, susceptible, sympathetic

rest 3 bed, lie, nap, nod, sit 4 base, calm, doze, ease, hang, heel, loaf, loll, lull, seat, stay 5 basis, count, found, hinge, let up, lie by, pause, peace, quiet, relax, sleep, spell, unlax 6 bottom, depend, ease up, excess, ground, lay off, lounge, repose, snooze, unbend 7 balance, breathe, ease off, footing, leisure, let down, lie down, recline, remains, remanet, remnant, seating, silence, slacken, slumber, surplus 8 interval, leavings, overplus, serenity, slack off, vacation 9 deferring, establish, placidity, predicate, remainder, stillness

restate 6 reword 8 rephrase 9 translate 10 paraphrase

restatement 7 version 9 rendering 10 paraphrase 11 translation

restaurant 4 café 5 diner 6 eatery 7 beanery, tearoom, teashop 8 teahouse 9 brasserie, cafeteria 10 coffee shop 11 coffeehouse *price:* 8 a la carte, prix fixe 10 table d'hôte *worker:* 4 chef, cook 6 busboy, waiter 7 maître d' 8 waitress 10 dishwasher, headwaiter 12 maître d'hôtel

___ **Restaurant** 6 Alice's

restful 6 placid 7 easeful, relaxed 8 tranquil

restitute 6 return 7 reclaim, recover, replace 8 take back 10 rejuvenate 11 recondition, reconstruct 12 rehabilitate

restitution 6 amends 7 redress 8 reprisal 9 indemnity, quittance 10 recompense

restive 4 edgy 5 balky, nervy, tense 6 ornery, uneasy 7 fidgety, froward, uptight, wayward 8 contrary, perverse

restiveness 7 ferment, turmoil 8 disquiet 10 inquietude 11 disquietude

restless 5 itchy, jumpy 6 fitful, fretty, uneasy 7 fidgety, fretful, jittery, nervous, unquiet 8 agitated, fretsome, troubled 9 disturbed, perturbed, spasmodic, unsettled

restlessness see **restiveness**

restorative 5 tonic 6 curing 7 healing 8 remedial, roborant, sanatory 9 remedying, vulnerary, wholesome 10 astringent

restore 4 cure, heal, save, stir 5 amend, rally, renew, right, rouse 6 arouse, better, recall, recoup, redeem, reform, regain, remedy, repair, return, revise, revive, update 7 correct, get back, improve, put back, reclaim, recover, recruit, rectify, refresh, replace 8 give back, renovate, retrieve, revivify, take back 9 modernize, refurbish, reinstate 10 rejuvenate 11 recondition, reconstruct, reestablish, reintroduce 12 rehabilitate

restrain 3 bit, gag 4 cool, curb, keep, rein, stop 5 block, check, cramp, crimp, leash 6 arrest, bridle, coarct, halter, hamper, hinder, hold in, impede, muzzle, pull in, temper 7 collect, compose, control, forbear, harness, inhibit, prevent, repress, smother 8 hold back, hold down, moderate, modu-

late, obstruct, suppress, underact, withhold *trade:* 7 embargo

restrained 5 quiet, tasty 7 aseptic, subdued 8 discreet, moderate, retiring, tasteful 9 shrinking, temperate, unaffable, unextreme, withdrawn 10 controlled, reasonable

restraint 5 cramp 7 durance, embargo 8 pullback 11 confinement *legal:* 5 estop

restrict 3 bar, tie 4 bind 5 limit 6 shrink 7 confine, delimit 8 prelimit 10 delimitate 12 circumscribe *a will:* 6 entail

restriction 4 curb 5 brake, check, cramp, limit, stint 7 control 10 constraint 11 confinement

restyle 6 redraw, revamp, revise, rework 7 redraft, rewrite 8 work over

result 3 end 5 close, ensue, issue 6 answer, effect, finish, sequel, upshot 7 outcome, product 8 sequence, solution 9 aftermath 10 conclusion, production 11 aftereffect, consequence, eventuality, termination *incidental:* 7 spinoff *suffix:* 7 ization

resume 4 go on 5 renew 6 keep up, pick up, recoup, regain, reopen, retake, take up 7 carry on, reclaim, recover 8 continue, reoccupy, retrieve 10 recommence

resumé 5 sum-up 7 epitome, summary 9 summation, summing-up

resurgence 7 rebirth, revival 11 reanimation 12 risorgimento

resurrect 5 raise, renew 6 revive 8 rekindle, renovate, retrieve, revivify 10 reactivate, revitalize

resurrection 7 rebirth, revival 10 renascence 11 renaissance 12 reviviscence, risorgimento

resuscitate see **resurrect**

retail 4 sell 6 market 11 merchandise

retain 3 own 4 have, hold, keep 7 possess, reserve 8 continue, hold back, keep back, preserve, remember, withhold

retainer 3 fee 6 lackey, minion 7 servant 8 employee, follower 9 dependent

retaliate 5 repay 6 avenge, punish 7 requite, revenge 10 recompense 11 reciprocate

retaliation see **reprisal**

retaliatory *prefix:* 7 counter

retard 4 balk, clog, mire 5 delay, embog, stunt 6 baffle, detain, fetter, hamper, hang up, hinder, impede, lessen, reduce, slow up 7 bog down, inhibit, set back, slacken 8 decrease, restrain, slow down 10 decelerate

retarded 3 dim 4 dull, dumb, slow 6 opaque, simple, stupid 7 moronic 8 backward, imbecile 9 dim-witted 10 half-witted, slow-witted 11 exceptional

retch 3 gag 4 keck 5 heave, vomit

retention 6 memory 7 holding, keeping, storage

reticent see reserved

reticulate 6 meshed, netted 10 cancellate

retinue 4 band 5 suite, train 7 company, cortege 9 entourage, following

retire 2 go 3 bed 4 drop, exit, quit 5 leave, yield 6 depart, get off, recede, resign, turn in, vacate 7 abandon, dismiss, get away, pension, retreat, take off 8 fall back, give back, run along, withdraw 9 discharge, surrender, terminate 10 pension off, relinquish 12 superannuate

retired person 7 emerita 8 emeritus

retirement allowance 7 pension

retiring 3 shy 5 timid 6 demure, modest 7 aseptic, bashful, rabbity 8 backward, reserved 9 diffident, unaffable, unassured, withdrawn 10 restrained 11 unassertive

retool 7 reequip, reorder 8 readjust, reorient 9 rearrange, reshuffle 10 reorganize

retort 3 gag, mot 4 jape, jest, joke, quip, snap 5 crack, repay, reply, sally 6 answer, come in, rejoin, return 7 respond, revenge, riposte 8 antiphon, comeback, repartee, reprisal, response 9 rejoinder

retract 4 back 5 unsay 6 abjure, disown, recall, recant, recede, revoke 7 exclude, rescind, rule out, suspend, unswear 8 fall back, forswear, palinode, take back, withdraw

retral 4 back, hind, rear 5 after 6 hinder 8 backward, hindmost 9 posterior 10 retrograde

retread 4 tire 5 recap

retreat 2 go 3 den, fly 4 back, flee, port, quit 5 cover, haven, leave, quail 6 asylum, bow out, covert, decamp, depart, escape, harbor, recede, recoil, refuge, shrink, vacate 7 abandon, back out, pull out, shelter 8 back down, crawfish, evacuate, fall back, give back, hightail, withdraw 9 climb down, harborage, sanctuary *religious:* 5 asram 6 ashram

retrench 3 cut 4 omit 5 slash 6 delete, excise, lessen, reduce 7 abridge, curtail, cut back, shorten 9 economize

retribution 3 pay 6 return 7 revenge 8 avenging, reprisal, requital, revanche 9 vengeance 10 avengement, punishment, recompense 11 counterblow *goddess of:* 3 Ate 4 Fury 7 Nemesis

retrieve 5 renew 6 recall, recoup, regain, rescue, revive 7 get back, recover, recruit, salvage 8 rekindle, renovate, revivify 9 repossess, resurrect 10 reactivate, revitalize

retrograde 4 back, sink 5 lapse 6 invert, recede, retral, revert, worsen 7 decline, descend, inverse, relapse, retreat, reverse 8 backward, decadent, fall back, inverted, rearward 9 backslide 10 degenerate, disimprove 11 deteriorate 12 disintegrate, recapitulate

retrogress see revert

retrospect 4 cite 6 recall, remind, review, revive 7 bethink 8 remember, revision 9 reminisce 10 afterlight 13 reexamination

retrospective 6 review 8 backward 10 exhibition

return 3 lob, pay 4 gain, give 5 lucre, react, recur, renew, repay, reply, yield 6 advert, answer, bestow, come in, profit, rebate, regain, rejoin, render, retort, revert, rotate 7 bring in, put back, rebound, recover, reentry, reflect, replace, reprise, requite, respond, restore, revenue, reverse, revolve 8 antiphon, comeback, earnings, feedback, give back, proceeds, response, take back, turn back 9 reinstate, rejoinder, repayment, repercuss, restitute, retaliate, reversion 10 recompense, recrudesce, recurrence 11 reciprocate 12 reappearance, reoccurrence

Return of the Native *author:* 5 Hardy (Thomas) *character:* 4 Clym 8 Eustacia

Reuben *brother:* 6 Joseph *father:* 5 Jacob *mother:* 4 Leah *son:* 5 Carmi 6 Hanoch, Hezron, Phallu

Reuel *father:* 4 Esau 7 Ibnijah *mother:* 8 Basemath *son:* 5 Zerah 6 Mizzah, Nahath 7 Shammah 8 Eliasaph *son-in-law:* 5 Moses

revamp 5 patch, renew 6 redraw, repair, rework 7 rebuild, redraft, restyle, rewrite 8 make over, overhaul, renovate 11 recondition, reconstruct

reveal 3 bid, rat 4 avow, bare, blab, leak, open, show, talk, tell, vent 5 admit, break, let on, mouth, peach, spill 6 betray, expose, impart, squeak, unmask, unveil 7 bespeak, blab out, breathe, confess, declare, display, divulge, exhibit, give out, publish, unbosom, unclose, uncover, whisper 8 announce, decipher, disclose, discover, give away, unclothe 9 broadcast, uncurtain 11 acknowledge, communicate

revel 4 bask, hell, orgy, riot, roll 5 feast, gloat, spree 6 frolic, gaiety, wallow, welter 7 carouse, delight, indulge, jollity, roister, rollick, royster, wassail, whoopee, whoopla, whoop-up 8 carnival, festival 9 celebrate, festivity, high jinks, luxuriate, merriment, whoop-de-do 10 skylarking 11 merrymaking

revelation 4 tora 5 torah 6 oracle 8 epiphany, prophecy 9 discovery 10 apocalypse, disclosure 13 manifestation

reveler 8 bacchant, carouser 10 merrymaker

revelry 6 gaiety 7 jollity, wassail, whoopee, whoopla, whoop-up 8 carousal 9 festivity, high jinks, merriment, whoop-de-do 10 skylarking 11 merrymaking

revenant 5 ghost, shade 6 shadow, spirit, wraith 7 phantom, specter 8 phantasm 9 recurring 10 apparition

revenge 6 defend 7 justify, redress 8 reprisal, requital 9 vindicate 11 counterblow, retaliation, retribution

revenue 2 in 4 rent 5 gains, wages, yield 6 income, profit, return, salary 7 comings 8 earnings, interest, proceeds, receipts

reverberant 6 hollow 7 reboant 8 resonant

reverberate 4 echo, ring 5 repel 7 rebound, reflect, resound

revere 4 love 5 adore, enjoy, exalt, honor, prize, value 6 admire, esteem, hallow, regard 7 cherish, magnify, respect, worship 8 treasure, venerate 10 appreciate

revered 9 venerable

reverence 3 awe 4 fear 5 adore, dread, honor, piety 6 fealty, homage 7 loyalty, worship 8 devotion, venerate 9 deference, obeisance, solemnity *gesture of:* 3 bow 8 kneeling 11 genuflexion 12 genuflection

reverend 3 sri 4 holy 5 abbot, clerk 6 clergy, cleric, divine, parson, sacred 8 clerical, minister, preacher 9 churchman, clergyman, monsignor, venerable 11 patriarchal 12 ecclesiastic

reverent 6 devout 7 dutiful 10 respectful

reverie 4 muse 5 dream, study 6 musing, trance, vision 7 fantasy, thought 8 daydream, dreaming 10 absorption, brown study, meditation 11 abstraction, daydreaming

reversal 4 turn 5 check 6 change, switch 7 backset, setback, turning 8 backfire 9 about-face, inversion, turnabout, volte-face

reverse 4 lift, turn 5 annul, check, polar, shift, verso 6 change, contra, defeat, invert, recall, repeal, revoke 7 backset, capsize, counter, rescind, set back, subvert 8 antipode, antipole, backward, contrary, converse, disaster, exchange, opposite, overrule, overturn, transfer 9 about-face, antipodal, backwards, diametric, dismantle, overthrow, transpose, turnabout, volte-face 10 antipodean, antithesis, misfortune, right-about, transplace *prefix:* 2 de, ob 3 dis, dys

reversion 4 turn 5 lapse 6 return 7 atavism, escheat, relapse 9 about-face, throwback, turnabout, volte-face 10 right-about 11 backsliding, changeabout

revert 4 turn 5 lapse, react, recur 6 change, return 7 decline, escheat,

inverse, regress, relapse 8 turn back 9 backslide, throw back, transpose 10 degenerate, recrudesce, retrograde, retrogress, transplace

revetment 7 sodwork 9 barricade 10 embankment

review 4 edit, scan 5 audit, organ, recap, study 6 notice, parade, revise, survey 7 account, brushup, checkup, comment, journal, recense, redraft, rethink, re-treat, revisal, reweigh 8 analysis, critique, magazine, rescript, revision, scrutiny 9 checkover, criticism, criticize, recension, reexamine, think over 10 afterlight, inspection, periodical, reconsider, reevaluate, reflection, retrospect 11 examination 13 reexamination, retrospection, second thought

revile 4 hate, rail, rate 5 abuse, libel, scold 6 berate, defame, malign, vilify 7 asperse, bawl out, chew out, slander, traduce, upbraid 8 backbite, disgrace, execrate, reproach 9 blaspheme 10 calumniate, tongue-lash, vituperate

revise 4 edit 5 alter, amend, emend 6 change, polish, redact, redraw, reform, revamp, review, rework, update 7 correct, improve, perfect, recense, redraft, restyle, rewrite, upgrade 8 overhaul, rescript, work over 9 recension 10 blue-pencil, reorganize

revitalize see **revive**

revival 7 rebirth, renewal 8 wakening 10 renascence, resurgence 11 reanimation, renaissance, restoration 12 regeneration, rejuvenation, reproduction, resurrection, reviviscence, risorgimento 13 recrudescence, resuscitation

revive 4 wake 5 rally, renew, rouse 6 arouse, exhume, recall 7 bethink, enliven, freshen, quicken, refresh, respire, restore 8 activate, energize, reawaken, rekindle, remember, renovate, retrieve, revivify, vitalize 9 galvanize, reanimate, recollect, refreshen, reinstate, resurrect, stimulate 10 reactivate, recuperate, regenerate, rejuvenate, revitalize 11 reestablish, reintroduce, resuscitate 12 reinvigorate

revivify see **revive**

revoke 4 lift, void 5 adeem, annul, erase 6 abjure, cancel, recall, recant, remind, renege, repeal 7 abolish, expunge, nullify, rescind, retract, reverse 8 abrogate, forswear 10 invalidate 11 countermand

revolt 4 defy, riot 5 rebel, repel 6 mutiny, offend, oppose, reluct, resist, sicken, uprise, uproar 7 boycott, disgust, repulse 8 mutineer, nauseate, overturn, renounce, sedition, uprising 9 insurrect, overthrow, rebellion 11 rise against, turn against 12 insurrection

revolter 5 rebel 6 anarch 8 frondeur, mutineer 9 anarchist, insurgent 10 malcontent

revolting 4 foul, ugly, vile 5 nasty 6 horrid 7 hideous, noisome 8 shocking 9 loathsome, offensive, repellent, repugnant, repulsive 10 disgusting, nauseating

revolution 4 gyre, reel, riot, roll, spin, turn 5 cycle, round, twirl, wheel, whirl 6 change 7 circuit, shake-up 8 disorder, gyration, overturn, rotation, sedition, turnover, uprising 9 overthrow, pirouette, rebellion

revolutionary 5 rabid, rebel, ultra 7 extreme, fanatic, radical 8 mutineer, rotating, ultraist 9 extremist, insurgent 10 malcontent *American:* 4 Reed (John) 5 Shays (Daniel) *French:* 5 Marat (Jean-Paul) 8 Mirabeau (Comte de) 11 Robespierre (Maximilien) *Irish:* 4 Tone (Wolfe) *Mexican:* 5 Villa (Pancho) 6 Zapata (Emiliano) *Russian:* 5 Kirov (Sergey) 7 Trotsky (Leon) 8 Kerensky (Aleksandr) 9 Kropotkin (Pyotr)

revolutionist see **revolutionary**

revolutionize 5 alter 6 change, modify, recast, redraw, reform, revamp, revise 7 remodel, restyle 8 overturn 9 overthrow, refashion, transform 11 transfigure 12 metamorphose

revolve 4 birl, chaw, gyre, muse, roll, spin, turn 5 orbit, round, wheel, whirl 6 circle, gyrate, ponder, rotate 7 agitate, circuit 8 consider, gyration, meditate, mull over, rotation, ruminate, turn over

revolver 3 gat, gun, rod 6 pistol 7 firearm, handgun

revulsion 4 hate 6 hatred, horror 8 aversion, loathing 9 repulsion 10 abhorrence, repugnance 11 abomination, detestation

reward 4 meed, plum 5 bonus, booty, crown, medal, prize 6 bounty, carrot, trophy 7 guerdon, premium 8 dividend, requital 10 compensate, honorarium, recompense, remunerate 12 compensation, remuneration

reword see **restate**

rework 6 redraw, revamp, revise 7 redraft, restyle, rewrite

rewrite see **revise**

Reynard the ___ 3 Fox

Rezon's father 6 Eliada

rhadamanthine 3 due 4 just 5 right 7 condign, merited 8 deserved, rightful, suitable 9 requisite 11 appropriate

Rhadamanthus 5 judge *brother:* 5 Minos *father:* 4 Zeus 7 Jupiter *mother:* 6 Europa

rhapsodic 8 ecstatic, effusive 9 emotional

Rhea 3 Ops *daughter:* 4 Hera, Juno 5 Ceres, Vesta 6 Hestia 7 Demeter *father:* 6 Uranus *husband:* 6 Cronus, Saturn *mother:* 2 Ge 4 Gaea *son:* 4 Zeus

5 Hades, Pluto 7 Jupiter, Neptune 8 Poseidon

Rheingold, Das *character:* 4 Loki 5 Freya, Wotan 6 Fafner, Fasolt 8 Alberich *composer:* 6 Wagner (Richard)

rheostat 6 dimmer 8 resistor

rhesus 6 monkey 7 macaque

rhetoric 4 rant 6 speech 7 bombast, fustian, oratory 8 rhapsody 9 discourse, elocution, eloquence, verbosity 11 highfalutin, rodomontade, speechcraft 13 lexiphanicism *term:* 6 aporia, ecbole, simile 7 epandos, litotes 8 metaphor 10 apostrophe, digression 12 alliteration, onomatopoeia

rhetorical 4 glib 5 gassy, grand, showy, tumid, vocal, windy 6 florid, fluent, mouthy, ornate, purple, turgid 7 aureate, flowery, orotund, pompous, stilted, swollen 8 eloquent, forensic, imposing, inflated, overdone, sonorous, swelling 9 bombastic, grandiose, high-flown, overblown, turnescent 10 articulate, euphuistic, figurative, flamboyant, oratorical 11 declamatory, embellished, exaggerated, highfalutin, overwrought, pretentious 12 high-sounding, magniloquent, orchidaceous, ostentatious 13 grandiloquent

rhetorician 6 orator, writer 7 speaker *Roman:* 11 Quintillian

Rhine River *city:* 4 Bonn, Köln 5 Mainz 7 Cologne 8 Mannheim 9 Weisbaden 10 Dusseldorf *golden ring:* 9 Rheingold, Rhinegold *nymph:* 7 Lorelei *tributary:* 3 Aar, Ill, Lek 4 Aare, Lahn, Main, Ruhr, Waal

rhinoceros 5 badak 6 borele 7 keitloa, upeygan 8 nasicorn *feature:* 4 horn *relative of:* 5 tapir

rhizome 4 root, stem 5 shoot 6 branch

Rhode Island *capital:* 10 Providence *college, university:* 5 Brown 6 Bryant 10 Providence 11 Salve Regina *founder:* 8 Williams (Roger) *nickname:* 10 Ocean State 11 Little Rhody *state flower:* 6 violet

Rhodesia see **Zimbabwe**

rhombus 7 diamond, lozenge 13 parallelogram

rhonchus 5 snore

Rhone River *lake:* 6 Geneva *mountain:* 4 Jura *town:* 4 Lyon 5 Arles 6 Geneva *tributary:* 5 Isère, Saône

rhubarb 3 row 4 beef 5 plant, run-in, set-to 7 dispute, quarrel, yawweed 8 pieplant 9 bickering 11 altercation, controversy

rhyme 4 beat, poem, rune, song 5 agree, check, meter, poesy, swing, verse 6 accord, cohere, poetry, rhythm 7 cadence, cadency, comport, conform, consist, consort, measure 8 dovetail, rhythmus 10 correspond

rhymer 4 bard, poet 5 rimer 7 bardlet 8 bardling, poetling, rimester, verseman 9 poetaster, poeticule, versifier 11 verse-monger

rhymester see rhymer

rhythm 4 beat, lilt, time 5 meter, pulse, swing, tempo 6 accent 7 cadence, cadency, measure 8 movement, sequence

rhythmic 6 poetic 7 pulsing, regular 8 cadenced, measured, metrical 9 cadential, pulsating

rialto 4 mart 6 market 8 district, exchange

riant 3 gay 4 boon 5 jolly, merry 6 blithe, bright, jocund, jovial 7 festive, gleeful, smiling 8 cheerful, laughing, mirthful

riata 4 rope 5 lasso 6 lariat

rib 3 fun, kid, rag 4 band, bone, dike, fool, jest, joke, josh, purl, razz, stay, wale 5 chaff, costa, ridge, tease 6 banter, costae (plural), lierne *combining form:* 4 cost 5 costi, costo, pleur 6 pleuri, pleuro *relating to:* 6 costal 7 costate

ribald 5 devil, rogue, scamp 6 coarse, rascal, risqué, vulgar 7 obscene 8 indecent, mischief, scalawag, slyboots 9 skeezicks 10 irreverent 11 rapscallion

ribbon 3 bow 4 band, tape 5 braid, reins, shred, strip 6 cordon, fillet, stripe, tatter 7 bandeau, banding, binding 8 fragment, tressure 9 banderole *combining form:* 4 taen 5 taeni 6 taenio

rice 4 boro, paga, twig 5 arroz, bigas, canin, macan 6 branch 7 risotto *boiled with meat:* 5 pilaf, pilau *combining form:* 4 oryz 5 oryzi, oryzo *cooked with meat:* 7 risotto 9 jambalaya *drink:* 4 saki 7 pangasi *field:* 3 cut 4 padi 5 paddy, sawah *husk:* 5 lemma, shood, shude *long-stemmed:* 4 aman *mountain:* 5 smilo *short-stemmed:* 3 aus

rich 3 fat 4 dear, easy, high, lush, oofy, warm 5 ample, flush, heavy, meaty, plump, round, sweet, vivid 6 absurd, costly, creamy, daedal, facund, fecund, florid, fruity, hearty, mellow, monied, ornate, potent, rococo, sating, superb 7 amusing, baroque, cloying, copious, fertile, filling, moneyed, opulent, orotund, pinguid, wealthy, well-off 8 abundant, affluent, childing, eloquent, fruitful, well-to-do 9 abounding, bountiful, elaborate, laughable, luxuriant, oversweet, plentiful, satiating, sumptuous, well-fixed 10 expressive, flamboyant, meaningful, productive, prosperous, well-heeled 11 comfortable *person:* 5 Midas, nabob 7 Croesus 9 plutocrat

Richardson work 6 Pamela 8 Clarissa 15 Clarissa Harlowe

Richelieu's successor 7 Mazarin

riches 4 gold, pelf, weal 5 booty, lucre, worth 6 mammon, wealth 7 fortune 8 opulence, property, treasure 9 resources *demon of:* 6 Mammon

rick 3 mow 4 bank, cock, heap, hill, pile, ruck 5 drift, shock, stack

rickety 4 weak 5 shaky 6 feeble, senile, wobbly 7 unsound 8 rachitic, unstable, unsteady 10 ramshackle, rattletrap

ricochet 3 dap 4 skim, skip 5 bound, carom, graze 6 bounce, glance, recoil 7 rebound

rid 4 free, lose, quit, shed 5 clear, empty 6 remove, uproot 7 abolish, deliver, release, relieve 8 liberate, shake off, throw off, unburden 11 disencumber

riddle 3 pan, why 4 crux, sift 5 griph, rebus 6 enigma, pierce, puzzle, screen 7 griphus, mystery, perplex, problem 8 permeate, separate 9 conundrum, penetrate, perforate 10 puzzlement

ride 2 go 3 rib 4 auto, bait, last, lift, sail, spin, tour, trip, turn 5 chivy, coast, drift, drive, float, glide, hound, motor, tease 6 badger, banter, canter, gallop, harass, heckle, hector 7 journey, oppress, overlap, overlie, shingle, survive, torment, torture 8 bullyrag, carousel, ridicule 9 carrousel, excursion, imbricate, persecute

ride out 7 outlast, weather

rider 6 clause, cowboy, jockey, knight 7 codicil 8 addendum, addition, appendix, horseman, reinsman 9 amendment 10 equestrian, supplement

ridge 3 rib, top 4 bank, brow, fold, hill, keel, reef, roll, ruck, seam, spur, wave 5 arris, chine, costa, crest, knurl, ledge, plica, quill, rivel, spine 6 crease, divide, furrow, rideau, rimple, saddle, summit 7 annulet, breaker, costula, crinkle, hogback, hummock, wrinkle 8 headland, shoulder 9 razorback 11 corrugation *gravelly:* 5 esker *on the skin:* 4 welt *sharp:* 7 hogback

ridicule 3 guy, pan 4 gibe, haze, jape, jeer, lout, mock, quiz, razz, ride, twit 5 chaff, flout, mimic, rally, roast, scoff, scout, sneer, squib, taunt 6 deride, satire 7 lampoon, mockery, pillory, sarcasm & derision, raillery, satirize, travesty 9 burlesque 10 caricature *god of:* 5 Momus *object of:* 4 butt 13 laughingstock

ridiculous 5 antic, comic, dotty, droll, funny, rough, silly 6 absurd, insane 7 amusing, bizarre, comical, foolish, mocking, risible, ungodly 8 derisive, derisory, farcical, gelastic, improper, indecent, unseemly 9 cockamamy, fantastic, grotesque, laughable, ludicrous 10 indeco-

rous, irrational, outrageous, unbecoming
12 preposterous

riding *academy:* 6 manège *costume:*
5 habit *pants:* 8 jodhpurs *whip:* 4 crop
5 quirt

Rienzi composer 6 Wagner (Richard)

rife 4 full, rank 5 alive, ariot 6 active, filled,
strong 7 current, popular, rampant, reg-
nant, replete, teeming 8 abundant, manifest, numerous, swarming, thronged
9 abounding, plentiful, prevalent 10 prevailing, widespread 11 overflowing

riff 4 scan, skim 6 browse

riffle 4 fret, scan, skim, wave 5 rapid,
shoal 6 browse, cockle, dimple, ripple
7 dip into, run over, shuffle 8 glance at
10 glance over, run through 11 flip through,
leaf through, skim through 12 thumb
through

riffraff 3 mob 4 junk, mass, scum 5 dregs,
offal, trash, waste 6 debris, kelter, litter,
rabble, refuse, tagrag 7 garbage, rubbish
8 canaille, unwashed 11 proletariat

rifle 3 arm, gun, rob 4 loot 5 piece, steal,
yager 6 furrow, groove, jaeger, weapon
7 carbine, despoil, firearm, pillage, plunder,
ransack, relieve 9 chassepot *accessory:*
6 ramrod *kind:* 6 Garand, Mauser
7 Enfield 8 Browning 9 Remington
10 Winchester 11 Springfield *pin:* 4 tige

rift 3 gap 4 flaw, rent, rima, rime, rive
5 break, chasm, chink, cleft, crack, split
6 breach, cleave, divide, hiatus, schism
7 blemish, fissure, opening, rupture 8 crevasse, division, fracture, interval, rimation

rig 3 arm, fit, fix 4 gear, hoax, wind
5 dress, equip, getup, guise, trick 6 fit out,
outfit, setout, tackle 7 appoint, arrange,
costume, derrick, furnish, turn out 8 accouter, accoutre, carriage, equipage 9 apparatus, equipment

rigadoon 5 dance

rigamarole see **rigmarole**

rigging 3 net 4 duds, gear, togs 5 dress,
lines, ropes 6 attire, chains, tackle, things
7 apparel, clothes, raiment 8 clothing

right 3 apt, due, fit, ius, jus, now 4 away,
bang, dead, done, fair, good, hale, jura (plural), just, nice, real, sane, tory, true, very,
well 5 amend, amply, claim, clear, droit,
emend, exact, fully, happy, legal, lucid,
quite, sharp, sound, spang, title, whole 6 at
once, comely, common, decent, dexter,
direct, equity, highly, honest, lawful, normal,
patent, proper, square, strict 7 condign,
correct, diehard, exactly, fitting, fogyish,
freedom, genuine, healthy, liberty, license,
merited, notably, old-line, parlous, precise,
rectify, redress, utterly 8 accurate, adequate, all there, appanage, becoming, bona

fide, decorous, deserved, directly, easement, entirely, faithful, first off, interest, old
liner, orthodox, properly, rigorous, smack-
dab, squarely, standpat, straight, suffrage,
suitable, suitably, usufruct 9 authentic,
authority, befitting, equitable, extremely, fittingly, forthwith, franchise, honorable,
instanter, perfectly, precisely, privilege, propriety, requisite, simon-pure, tolerable,
undoubted, veracious, veridical, veritable,
wholesome 10 acceptable, acceptably,
accurately, adequately, altogether, applicable, becomingly, completely, concession,
felicitous, perquisite, properness, remarkably, scrupulous, straightly, sufficient, sure-
enough, well-liking 11 appropriate, bitter-
ender, comme il faut, correctness,
exceedingly, immediately, indubitable, prerogative, reactionary, standpatter, undistorted 12 compos mentis, conservative
combining form: 4 orth, rect 5 dextr,
ortho, recti 6 dextro *feudal:* 4 soke *legal:*
5 droit 8 usufruct *royal:* 6 regale 7 regalia
(plural)

right away 3 now 6 at once 8 directly,
first off, straight 9 forthwith, instanter,
instantly 11 immediately, straightway

righteous 4 good, holy, just, pure 5 godly,
moral, noble, pious 6 devout, worthy 7 ethical, sinless, upright 8 innocent, virtuous
9 blameless, equitable, exemplary, guiltless
10 inculpable, moralistic, principled

righteousness 6 equity, virtue 7 justice,
probity 8 goodness, holiness, justness,
morality 9 rectitude 11 uprightness

rightful 3 apt, due, fit 4 fair, just, true
5 legal 6 honest, lawful, proper 7 condign,
fitting, merited 8 deserved, suitable 9 befitting, equitable, impartial, requisite 10 applicable, legitimate 11 appropriate

right-handed 7 dextral 8 dextrous
9 clockwise, dexterous

right-hand page 5 recto

rightist 4 tory 7 diehard 8 old liner, standpat 11 bitter-ender, reactionary, right-winger, standpatter 12 conservative

right-minded 5 moral, noble 7 ethical
8 virtuous 10 moralistic, principled

Rights of Man author 5 Paine
(Thomas)

rigid 3 set 4 firm, hard, taut 5 fixed, solid,
stein, stiff, tough 6 formal, severe, strait,
strict 7 adamant, austere, buckram, hard-
set 8 hard-line, ironclad, obdurate, rigorist,
rigorous 9 draconian, immovable, impliable,
inelastic, stringent, unbending 10 adamantine, inexorable, inflexible, ironhanded,
motionless, relentless, unflexible, unyielding
11 immalleable

rigidity 5 frost 6 turgor 7 buckram 8 hardness, turgency 9 stiffness *muscular:* 8 myotonia

rigmarole 6 ramble 8 nonsense 9 procedure 10 balderdash

Rigoletto *composer:* 5 Verdi (Giuseppe) *daughter:* 5 Gilda

rigor 5 trial 7 cruelty 8 asperity, hardness, hardship, severity 9 austerity, harshness, roughness, sharpness, sternness 10 affliction, difficulty, exactitude, strictness, visitation 11 tribulation, vicissitude 13 inflexibility

rigorous 4 hard, nice 5 exact, harsh, right, rigid, rough, stern, stiff 6 bitter, brutal, proper, rugged, severe, strait, strict 7 ascetic, correct, drastic, onerous, precise 8 accurate, exacting 9 draconian, inclement, stringent 10 burdensome, inexorable, inflexible, ironhanded, oppressive

rile 3 mud, vex 4 roil 5 anger, annoy, grate, muddy, peeve, pique, upset 6 muddle, nettle, put out 7 agitate, disturb, inflame, provoke 8 irritate 9 aggravate

rim 3 hem, lip 4 bank, boss, brim, edge, ring 5 bezel, bezil, bound, brink, skirt, verge 6 border, flange, fringe, margin, shield 7 annulus, horizon, outline 8 boundary, surround 9 perimeter, periphery *of a basket:* 4 hoop *of a cask:* 5 chime, chine *of an insect's wing:* 6 termen *of a spoked wheel:* 5 felly 6 felloe *of a volcanic crater:* 5 somma

rima 5 rift 5 chink, cleft, crack, split 7 fissure 8 aperture

rime 3 ice 4 cake, rift 5 chink, cleft, crack, crust, frost, split 7 encrust, fissure, incrust 10 incrustate 12 incrustation

Rimmon's son 6 Baanah, Rechab

rimple 4 fold, ruck 5 crimp, plica, ridge, rivel, screw 6 crease, furrow, ruck up, rumple 7 crimple, crinkle, crumple, scrunch, wrinkle 11 corrugation

Rinaldo *beloved:* 8 Angelica *cousin:* 7 Orlando *father:* 5 Aymon *horse:* 6 Bayard *mother:* 3 Aya *sister:* 10 Bradamante *uncle:* 11 Charlemagne

rind 4 bark, husk, peel, skin 5 crust *of roast pork:* 9 crackling

ring 3 bee, eye, hem, mob, rim 4 bail, band, bell, bloc, bong, camp, clan, cric, ding, dirl, echo, gird, gyre, hoop, loop, peal, toll 5 anlet, arena, bague, bezel, cabal, chime, clang, cycle, group, knell, knoll, party, rigol, round, sound 6 begird, boxing, circle, clique, collar, collet, dindle, famble, girdle, staple 7 annulus, clangor, combine, compass, coterie, faction, ferrule, grommet, ingroup, resound, vibrate 8 bracelet, cincture, encircle, pugilism, surround 9 camarilla, coalition, encompass 11 combination, reverberate *around sun or moon:* 5 broch

6 corona *combining form:* 3 gyr 4 cycl, gyro 5 cyclo *curtain:* 3 eye *for a compass:* 6 gimbal *for a lampshade:* 4 harp 7 gallery *harness:* 3 dee 6 button, largo, terret, territ *heraldic:* 7 annulet *in a hinge:* 7 gudgeon *of chain:* 4 link 7 belcher *of color:* 8 stocking *of dots around a coin:* 8 graining *of leaves or flowers:* 6 wreath 7 garland *of light:* 4 halo 5 glory 6 corona, nimbus 7 aureole 8 halation *of Odin:* 8 draupnir *of rope or metal:* 4 hank 6 becket 7 garland, grommet, snotter, thimble *of two hoops:* 5 gemel 6 gemmel, gimmal *on a key, pocket watch or scissors handle:* 3 bow *on an archery target:* 4 sous 5 souse *relating to:* 7 annular *rubber, for a fruit jar:* 4 lute *used as a valve or diaphragm:* 5 wafer *used for securing a bird:* 6 vervel *used to enclose deer:* 7 tinchel *wedding:* 4 band

Ring and the Book author 8 Browning (Robert)

ringed 8 annulate, circular 9 encircled 10 surrounded

ringer 4 fake, spit 5 image 6 double 7 picture 8 impostor, portrait 9 direct hit 10 simulacrum 13 spitting image

ringing 5 round 6 bright, fervid, jangle, rotund 7 clangor, orotund, vibrant 8 decisive, plangent, resonant, sonorant, sonorous 9 consonant 10 resounding

ringleader 4 boss 5 chief 6 honcho 10 instigator, mastermind

ringlet 4 curl, lock 5 tress 7 tendril

rinse 4 lave, wash 5 douse, swill 6 douche, sluice 7 cleanse *the mouth:* 6 gargle

riot 4 hell, howl 5 brawl, melee, revel, smash, spree 6 attack, bedlam, clamor, émeute, excess, frolic, jumble, scream, tumult, uproar 7 anarchy, carouse, debauch, dispute, misrule, quarrel, revelry, roister, wassail 8 carousal, disorder, uprising 9 anarchism, commotion, distemper, sensation 10 donnybrook 11 disturbance

riotous 4 loud, lush, wild 5 noisy 6 lavish, stormy, wanton 7 bacchic, opulent, profuse, roaring 8 bacchian, prodigal 9 exuberant, luxuriant, profusive 10 boisterous 11 saturnalian 12 unrestrained

rip 3 cut 4 rend, rent, rive, spit, tear 5 shred, slash, split 6 attack, cleave, sunder 7 sputter 8 lacerate, splutter

ripe 3 fit 4 aged, late 5 adult, grown, ready 6 mature, mellow, timely 7 grown-up, matured, overdue 8 complete, finished 9 developed, full-blown, full-grown, perfected, virtuosic, well-timed 10 consummate, seasonable 11 full-fledged

ripen 3 age 4 grow 6 better, grow up, mature, mellow, season 7 develop, enhance, improve, perfect 8 heighten, maturate 9 intensify

ripening early 4 rath 5 rathe 8 rareripe

riposte 5 reply 6 retort, return, thrust 8 comeback, repartee 10 back answer 13 counterattack

ripping 4 fine 5 grand, nifty, super, swell 6 divine, peachy 7 capital 8 glorious, splendid, terrific 9 admirable, excellent, marvelous, wonderful 10 remarkable 11 sensational

ripple 3 cut, lap 4 curl, fret, riff, wave 5 acker 6 cockle, dimple, lipper, popple, riffle, rimple 7 crinkle, wrinkle

rip-roaring 5 noisy 6 lively 8 exciting 9 hilarious 10 boisterous, uproarious

ripsnorter 5 dandy 8 jim-dandy 9 humdinger 11 crackerjack

riptide 8 undertow

Rip Van Winkle *author:* 6 Irving (Washington) *dog:* 4 Wolf

rise 2 up 3 wax 4 come, flow, grow, head, hike, lift, rear, soar, stem, well 5 awake, begin, boost, build, climb, get up, issue, mount, occur, raise, rebel, rouse, scale, sit up, stand, start, surge, swell, tower 6 ascend, ascent, aspire, awaken, befall, betide, chance, deepen, emerge, expand, growth, happen, recess, revolt, spring, thrive, uprear 7 adjourn, advance, augment, bristle, develop, elevate, emanate, enhance, enlarge, fall out, magnify, pile out, proceed, prosper, roll out, stand up, succeed, surface, turn out, upgrade, upstand, upsurge 8 addition, dissolve, eminence, heighten, increase, levitate, multiply, prorogue, redouble, upspring 9 accession, accretion, aggravate, ascension, increment, intensate, intensify, originate, prorogate, terminate, transpire 10 derive from *above:* 8 surmount *abruptly:* 9 skyrocket *again:* 7 resurge 9 resurrect *against:* 5 rebel 6 mutiny, revolt 9 insurrect *and fall:* 4 tide 5 heave 6 welter *and shine:* 5 get up 7 pile out, roll out, turn out *gradually:* 4 loom *swiftly:* 4 boil, boom 6 spring *up:* 4 fume, rear, well 5 rebel, swell, tower 6 ascend, revolt 9 insurrect

Rise of Silas Lapham author 7 Howells (William Dean)

riser 4 step

risible 5 comic, droll, funny 7 comical 8 farcical, gelastic 9 laughable, ludicrous 10 ridiculous

risk 4 dare, defy, face, luck, meet 5 beard, brave, peril, stake, wager 6 chance, danger, gamble, hazard, menace 7 fortune, imperil, jeopard, venture 8 accident, confront, endanger, exposure, jeopardy, openness 9 adventure, encounter, liability 10 compromise, jeopardize

risky 4 bold 5 hairy 6 chancy, daring, touchy, wicked 7 parlous, unsound 8 delicate, perilous, ticklish 9 dangerous, hazardous, sensitive, unhealthy 10 jeopardous, precarious 11 speculative, treacherous

risqué 3 raw 4 blue, foul, lewd, racy, sexy 5 broad, crude, dirty, gross, salty, shady, spicy 6 coarse, daring, earthy, purple, ribald, vulgar, wicked 7 naughty, obscene, raunchy 8 indecent, off-color, scabrous 9 audacious, inelegant, salacious, unrefined 10 indecorous, indelicate, suggestive

rite 4 cult, form 6 fetish, honors, office 7 liturgy, mystery, service 8 ceremony, hierurgy, occasion 9 formality, ordinance, procedure, sacrament, solemnity 10 ceremonial, initiation, observance 11 celebration, sacramental *aborigine:* 4 bora *American Indian:* 8 huskanaw 11 huskanawing *Buddhist:* 6 pansil *funeral:* 6 exequy 7 obsequy 8 exequies *Hindu:* 4 puja 5 pooja, sradh 6 poojah, sradha 7 sraddha *Jewish:* 4 bris 5 berith, briss, brith 6 berith 7 tashlik 8 tashlich 12 circumcision *Mayan:* 3 kex *of initiation or purification:* 7 baptism *of knighthood:* 8 accolade *of prophecy:* 6 augury *of recognition of merit:* 8 accolade; (see also **sacrament**)

ritual see rite

ritzy 6 modish 7 elegant, haughty 8 snobbish 9 expensive, luxurious 11 fashionable 12 ostentatious

rival 3 tie, try, vie 4 even, meet, peer, side 5 equal, fight, match, touch 6 amount, strive 7 attempt, compete, contend, contest, emulate, entrant, feuding 8 approach, emulator, opponent, rivalize, struggle 9 adversary, competing, contender, measure up, partake of 10 antagonist, competitor, contending, contestant 11 comparative, competition *prefix:* 3 ant 4 anth, anti

rivalry 6 strife 7 contest, warfare 8 conflict, jealousy, striving, tug-of-war 9 emulation 11 competition

rive 3 hew, rip 4 chop, plow, rend, tear 5 burst, sever, smash, split 6 cleave, divide, pierce, shiver, sunder, thrust 7 shatter 8 fracture, fragment, lacerate, separate, splinter, splitter 11 splinterize

river *Africa:* 4 Bomu 5 Congo, Mbomu, Zaire 6 Atbara 7 Aruwimi, Atbarah, Zambesi, Zambeze, Zambezi 9 Astaboras *Alabama:* 5 Coosa 6 Mobile 7 Conecuh, Perdido 9 Tombigbee 10 Tallapoosa *Alaska:* 5 Kobuk 6 Copper, Noatak, Tanana 7 Koyukuk, Susitna 9 Kuskokwim *Albania:* 4 Drin 5 Drini *Argentina:* 5 Negro 6 Paraná 7 Matanza *arm:* 6 branch 9 tributary *Asia:* 3 Ili 4 Amur, Oxus 5 Indus 6 Jayhun, Sutlej 7 Oedanes 8 Amu Darya 9 Dyardanes 11 Brahmaputra *Australia:*

4 Daly 5 Roper, Yarra 6 Barwon, Culgoa, Dawson, DeGrey, Murray 7 Darling, Fitzroy, Lachlan 8 Victoria 10 Yarra Yarra *Austria:* 4 Enns *bank:* 5 levee *Belgium:* 5 Rupel, Senne, Weser 6 Dender, Dindar, Ourthe 8 Visurgis *Bolivia:* 4 Beni 5 Abuná 6 Mamoré *Borneo:* 5 Kajan *bottom:* 3 bed *Brazil:* 3 Ica 4 Pará, Paru 5 Negro, Xingu 6 Paraná 7 Madeira, Tapajós, Tapajoz *British Columbia:* 6 Skeena 10 Bella Coola *California:* 3 Eel, Pit 4 Kern, Yuba 6 Merced 7 Feather, Salinas, Trinity 8 Tuolumne 9 Mokelumne 10 Sacramento, Stanislaus *Cambodia:* 8 Tonle Sap *Canada:* 3 Bow 4 Back 5 Moose, Peace 6 Beaver, Fraser, Nelson, Ottawa 8 Gatineau, Saguenay 9 Athabasca, Great Fish, Mackenzie, Richelieu 11 Assiniboine *Carolinas:* 7 Catawba *central Africa:* 6 Ubangi *central Asia:* 5 Orhon 6 Gandak, Orkhon 8 Syr Darya *central Canada:* 5 Slave *central Europe:* 4 Eger, Elbe, Labe, Ohře 5 Albis 6 Danube *central United States:* 3 Fox 5 Grand 6 Neosho, Platte, Wabash 8 Keya Paha, Missouri, Niobrara 9 Tennessee, Verdigris 10 Republican, Saint Croix 11 Mississippi *channel:* 6 alveus *Chile:* 3 Loa 5 Itata, Maule 6 Bío-Bío 8 Valdivia *China:* 2 Si, Xi, Zi 3 Bei, Hun, Wei 4 Dong 5 Baihe, Huang, Hwang, Tarim 6 Yellow 7 Kashgar, Yangtze *China-North Korea:* 4 Yalu *Colombia:* 4 Tomo 6 Atrato 9 Magdalena *Colorado:* 5 Yampa 8 Gunnison *combining form:* 5 fluvi, potam 6 fluvio, potamo *Connecticut:* 6 Thames 7 Niantic, Shepaug 9 Naugatuck 10 Farmington, Housatonic, Quinnipiac 11 Willimantic *crossing:* 4 ford *current:* 4 eddy 6 rapids *Czech Republic:* 4 Iser 6 Jizera, Moldau, Vltava *dam:* 4 weir *Denmark:* 4 Stor *dried bed:* 4 wadi 5 waddy *drowned:* 7 estuary *East Africa:* 4 Juba 5 Tsavo 6 Songwe *East Asia:* 4 Yalu 5 Amnok 7 Oryokko *eastern United States:* 7 Potomac *Ecuador:* 4 Napo 10 Esmeraldas *England:* 3 Esk, Exe, Nen, Ure 4 Aire, Avon, Eden, Nene, Ouse, Tees, Tyne, Wear, Yare 5 Swale, Trent 6 Mersey, Ribble, Thames *Ethiopia:* 3 Omo 4 Baro, Dawa *Europe:* 4 Oder 5 Saale 6 Danube, Ticino *Florida:* 6 Indian 9 Kissimmee 10 Saint Johns 12 Apalachicola *France:* 3 Ain, Lot, Var 4 Aire, Aude, Cher, Eure, Gers, Loir, Oise, Orne, Saar, Tam, Yser 5 Adour, Aisne, Drôme, Indre, Isère, Loire, Marne, Saare, Sâone, Seine, Somme, Yonne 6 Allier, Ariège, Scarpe, Vienne 7 Durance, Garonne, La Riège 8 Charente, Dordogne *Georgia:* 6 Etowah, Oconee 8 Altamaha, Ocmulgee 13 Chattahoochee *Germany:* 3 Ems, Rur 4 Eder, Eger, Elbe, Isar, Main, Rems, Ruhr 5 Hunte, Lippe, Rhine, Spree, Werra, Weser 6 Neckar *Germany-Poland:* 4 Oder *Ghana:* 5 Volta *god:* 7 Alpheus, Inachus 8 Achelous *Greece:* 3 Iri 4 Arta 5 Lerna, Lerne 7 Alpheus, Eurotas 8 Achelous 9 Arakhthos *hazard:* 4 snag 6 rapids 7 Lorelei *Honduras:* 4 Ulúa 5 Aguán 6 Patuca *Iberian:* 5 Douro, Duero *Idaho:* 5 Lemhi *Illinois:* 8 Mackinaw *India:* 4 Sind 5 Sindh, Tapti 6 Chenab, Jhelum, Kaveri, Kistna 7 Cauvery, Krishna 8 Acesines, Godavari *Indian subcontinent:* 5 Ganga 6 Ganges *inlet:* 5 bayou 6 slough *Iran:* 3 Kor 4 Mand, Mund 5 Kārūn 8 Safīd Rud, Sefīd Rud *Ireland:* 3 Lee 4 Deel, Erne, Suir 5 Boyne, Clare, Foyle 6 Barrow, Liffey 7 Shannon *Italy:* 2 Po 4 Adda, Arno, Liri, Nera 5 Adige, Arnus, Etsch, Liris, Oglio, Padus, Piave, Tiber 6 Ollius, Rapido, Tevere, Trebia 7 Athesis, Rubicon, Secchia, Tiberis, Trebbia 8 Rubicone, Volturno *Kansas:* 6 Pawnee *Kazakhstan-Russia:* 4 Ural 5 Tobol 6 Irtysh *Kenya:* 4 Athi, Tana *Kubla Khan's:* 4 Alph *land:* 4 holm 5 carse, flats 7 bottoms *Latvia:* 2 Aa 5 Gauja *Latvia-Lithuania:* 7 Lielupe *Lebanon:* 6 Litani *Little Rock's:* 8 Arkansas *living in:* 9 rheophile *living on the bank of:* 8 riparian *longest:* 4 Nile *Louisiana:* 11 Atchafalaya *Maine:* 8 Kennebec 9 Aroostook, Penobscot *Malaysia:* 9 Trengganu 10 Terengganu *Maryland:* 8 Monocacy, Patapsco, Patuxent 9 Nanticoke *Massachusetts:* 7 Charles, Taunton 9 Westfield 10 Housatonic *Mexico:* 6 Pánuco, Sonora 7 Tabasco 8 Grijalva *Michigan:* 4 Cass 5 Flint, Huron 7 Detroit, Saginaw 8 Manistee, Muskegon 9 Cheboygan, Kalamazoo 10 Michigamme, Shiawassee *Mississippi:* 5 Pearl, Yazoo 10 Pascagoula *Moldova-Ukraine:* 8 Dneister *Missouri:* 5 Osage *Montgomery's:* 7 Alabama *mouth:* 4 lade 5 delta *Myanmar (Burma):* 4 Pegu 8 Chindwin, Irrawady *Nebraska:* 4 Loup 6 Nemaha, Platte 7 Elkhorn *Netherlands:* 4 Waal 5 Issel, Yssel 6 Ijssel 7 Vahalis *New England:* 4 Saco 6 Nashua 9 Merrimack 10 Blackstone 11 Connecticut 12 Androscoggin *New Jersey:* 6 Rahway 7 Passaic, Raritan 8 Tuckahoe *New York:* 4 East 5 Tioga 6 Hudson, Mohawk, Oneida, Oswego, Seneca 7 Chemung, Niagara 8 Chenango, Cohocton 9 Conhocton *New Zealand:* 7 Waikato *Nicaragua:* 4 Coco 7 Segovia *Nigeria:* 5 Benin *North Carolina:* 3 Haw, Tar 5 Neuse 6 Chowan 8 Alamance *northeast North America:* 13 Saint Lawrence *northeast United States:* 4 Ohio 6 Hoosic 7 Genesee, Hocking 8 Delaware,

Mahoning 9 Allegheny 11 Monongahela, Susquehanna *Northern Ireland:* 4 Bann 6 Mourne *North Korea:* 5 Daido 7 Taedong *northwest North America:* 5 Yukon *northwest United States:* 5 Snake 7 Klamath 8 Columbia 11 Pend Oreille *Norway:* 4 Tana, Teno *nymph:* 4 nais 5 naiad *obstruction:* 4 snag *of fire:* 9 Phlegeton *of forgetfulness:* 5 Lethe *of ice:* 7 glacier *of woe:* 7 Acheron *Ohio:* 5 Miami 8 Cuyahoga, Sandusky 9 Muskingum 10 Tuscarawas *Oklahoma:* 8 Cimarron *Oregon:* 5 Rogue 6 Owyhee 7 Malheur 8 McKenzie 9 Clackamas, Deschutes 10 Willamette *Panama:* 5 Tuira 7 Chagres *Papua New Guinea:* 3 Fly 5 Sepik *Paraguay:* 3 Apa 9 Pilcomayo *Pennsylvania:* 6 Lehigh 10 Schuylkill *Peru:* 5 Rímac, Santa 7 Marañón 8 Apurímac, Huallaga, Urubamba *Philippines:* 4 Abra, Agno 5 Pasig 7 Cagayan 8 Cotabato, Mindanao, Pampanga *Poland:* 3 San 7 Vistula *Portugal:* 4 Sado 7 Mondego *relating to:* 7 fluvial, potamic 9 fluminose, fluminous *Rhode Island:* 7 Seekonk 8 Sakonnet 10 Providence *Romania:* 5 Arges *Russia:* 2 Ob, Om 3 Don, Oka, Ufa, Usa 4 Kama, Kara, Lena, Msta, Neva, Sura, Svir 5 Onega, Terek, Volga 6 Anadyr, Angara, Belaya, Kolima, Kolyma, Ussuri, Vyatka 7 Dnieper, Pechora, Yenisei, Yenisey 8 Barguzin, Kostroma, Voronezh, Vychegda *Russia-Ukraine:* 6 Donets *sacred:* 5 Ganga 6 Ganges *São Paulo's:* 5 Tietê *Scotland:* 3 Dee, Don, Esk, Tay 4 Doon, Nith, Spey, Tyne 5 Afton, Annan, Clyde, Forth, Tweed 6 Teviot 7 Deveron 8 Findhorn *Shanghai's:* 7 Huang-p'u, Hwang Pu *Sicily:* 5 Salso 6 Simeto *siren:* 7 Lorelei *Slovakia:* 3 Vag, Vah 4 Gran, Hron, Waag 5 Garam, Nitra 6 Neutra, Nyitra *South Africa:* 4 Vaal 6 Orange *South America:* 3 Apa 6 Amazon 8 Amazonas, Orellana, Paraguay 9 Pilcomayo *South Carolina:* 6 Saluda, Santee 7 Wateree 8 Congaree *South Dakota:* 3 Bad *southeast Africa:* 7 Limpopo 9 Crocodile *southeast Asia:* 6 Dza-chu, Mekong 7 Salween 8 Lants'ang *southeast United States:* 6 Pee Dee 7 Noxubee, Washita 8 Escambia, Ouachita, Suwannee 10 Okanoxubee *southern United States:* 6 Sabine *South Korea:* 3 Kŭm *southwest Asia:* 5 Dijla 6 Jordan, Tigris 8 Hiddekel 9 Euphrates *southwest United States:* 4 Gila, Zuni 5 Pecos 8 Colorado *Spain:* 4 Ebro 6 Aragon 12 Guadalquivir *Sweden:* 4 Göta 5 Kalix *Switzerland:* 3 Aar 4 Aare 5 Reuss *Syria:* 6 Khabur 7 Orontes *Tasmania:* 4 Huon *Tbilisi's:* 4 Kura *Texas:*

5 Llano 6 Brazos, Nueces 7 San Saba, Trinity 9 Guadalupe *Texas-Mexico:* 8 Rio Bravo 9 Rio Grande *tidal:* 7 estuary *Tokyo's:* 6 Sumida *Turkey:* 4 Aras 5 Araks 6 Seihun, Seyhan *Ukrainian:* 3 Bug 4 Alma *underworld:* 4 Styx 5 Lethe 7 Acheron, Cocytus 10 Phlegethon *Uruguay:* 5 Negro *Utah:* 5 Uinta, Weber 6 Jordan, Sevier *valley:* 6 strath *Venezuela:* 5 Apure, Caura 6 Caroní 7 Orinoco *Vermont:* 3 Mad 5 Onion, White 8 Winooski *Virginia:* 3 Dan 5 James 7 Rapidan 9 Nansemond 10 Appomattox, Shenandoah 12 Chickahominy, Rappahannock *walling:* 7 Cocytus *Wales:* 4 Dyfi 5 Clwyd, Dovey, Teifi *Washington:* 6 Skagit, Yakima 9 Klickitat, Snohomish, Wenatchee *West Africa:* 5 Niger 6 Gambia 7 Senegal *western North America:* 8 Columbia, Flathead *western United States:* 7 Laramie 11 Yellowstone *West Virginia:* 7 Kanawha *Wisconsin:* 8 Kickapoo 9 Menominee *Wyoming:* 8 Shoshone 10 Gros Ventre 11 Medicine Bow

____ **Rivera, Painter** 5 Diego

river duck 4 teal 6 wigeon 7 mallard, widgeon 9 greenwing

river horse 5 hippo 12 hippopotamus

riverine 7 potamic

rivet 3 fix 4 bolt, brad, stud 5 affix 6 attach, fasten 8 fastener

rivulet 3 run 4 burn, gill, race, rill 5 bache, bayou, bourn, brook, creek 6 runlet, runnel, stream 7 channel 9 streamlet

Rizpah *father:* 4 Aiah *lover:* 4 Saul *son:* 6 Armoni 12 Mephibosheth

roach 4 fish, rock, spot 6 braise

road 3 way 4 fare, lane, line, path 5 drive, going, route, track 6 artery, avenue, career, causey, course, street 7 highway, journey, passage 8 causeway, chaussée, crossway, highroad, pavement, speedway, turnpike 9 boulevard 12 thoroughfare *along a cliff:* 8 corniche *around a city:* 6 bypass 7 beltway *bend:* 7 hairpin *edge:* 4 berm 8 shoulder *French:* 6 chemin *in or to a mine:* 4 bord 5 board 8 footrill *Irish:* 6 boreen 8 beallach *machine:* 4 harl 5 paver 6 grader 9 bulldozer *narrow (in England):* 4 loke 6 drang, drong 8 driftway *of stones:* 7 telford *raised:* 5 agger *Roman:* 3 via 4 iter *Scottish:* 4 brae 8 beallach *side:* 5 biway 6 branch 8 shunpike *Spanish:* 6 camino *surface:* 3 tar 6 bricks, gravel, stones 7 macadam 8 concrete, pavement *temporary:* 7 shoofly *zigzag:* 10 switchback

roadblock 7 barrier 8 blockade 9 barricade

road book 3 map 5 atlas 9 gazetteer, itinerary

roadhouse 3 inn 5 hotel, lodge 6 hostel, tavern 7 auberge, hospice 8 hostelry 11 caravansary

roadman 6 hawker, monger, vendor 7 drummer, higgler, packman, peddler 8 huckster, mongerer, salesman 9 canvasser

roadrunner 6 cuckoo 7 paisano

road rut 7 pothole 9 chuckhole

roam 3 bat, gad, run 4 rove, walk 5 drift, prowl, range, stray 6 ramble, stroll, travel, wander 7 meander 8 gadabout, straggle, vagabond 9 gallivant

roamer 5 gipsy, gypsy, nomad, rover 6 gadder, walker 7 drifter, rambler 8 gadabout, stroller, traveler, vagabond, wanderer 9 meanderer 12 peregrinator, rolling stone

roar 3 cry, din 4 bawl, bell, boom, bray, howl, rout, yell 5 laugh, shout 6 bellow, clamor, outcry, scream, shriek 7 bluster, rebound, ululate 9 repercuss 10 vociferate 11 reverberate *bullring:* 3 olé *low:* 5 brool *of a boar:* 5 fream *of the surf:* 3 rut 4 rote

roast 4 bake, cook, flay, melt, razz, roti 5 broil, parch, score, slash 6 scathe, scorch 7 blister, lambast, swelter, torrefy, torrify 8 lambaste, lash into, ridicule 9 castigate, excoriate

rob 3 cop, mug 4 fake, flap, lift, loot, lose, nick, oust, pelf, roll, sack, take 5 bribe, cheat, filch, harry, heist, pinch, pluck, reave, rifle, spoil, steal, touch 6 burgle, divest, hijack, hold up, hustle, pilfer, pirate, ravage, ravish, snatch, snitch, thieve 7 bereave, defraud, deprive, despoil, pillage, plunder, purloin, ransack, relieve, stick up, swindle 8 jackroll 9 knock over, strong-arm 10 burglarize

robber 4 yegg 5 crook, thief 6 bandit, catman, pirate, rifler 7 brigand, footpad, heister, ladrone, raffles, reifier 8 hightoby, hijacker, swindler 9 holdup man 10 cat burglar, highwayman, sandbagger, stickup man 12 housebreaker *grave:* 5 ghoul *Irish:* 8 woodkern *murderous (in India and Burma):* 6 dacoit *of pedestrians:* 3 pad 7 footpad *on high seas:* 6 pirate

robbery 3 job 5 heist, theft 6 holdup, piracy 7 larceny, stickup 8 banditry *Scottish:* 4 reif

robe 3 aba 4 mant, wrap 5 cloak, cover, habit 6 caftan, clothe, mantle, revest 7 becloak, costume, garment, manteau 8 clothing, covering, dalmatic, vestment *ancient Greek tragedian's:* 5 syrma *baptismal:* 7 chrisom *bishop's:* 6 chimer 7 chimere *coronation:* 8 colobium *Eastern Orthodox:* 10 sticharion *Indian:* 4 jama 6 khalat, khilat *Jewish:* 6 kittel *knight's:* 6 cyclas *Latin:* 5 stola *loose:* 5 camis,

camus 6 kimona *Mexican:* 5 manga *monarch's:* 7 pluvial *of Roman emperors:* 6 purple *of tartan:* 7 arisaid *Turkish:* 6 dolman *woman's:* 5 cymar, simar, symar

Robinson Crusoe author 5 Defoe (Daniel)

robot 5 golem 7 android, machine 8 automata (plural) 9 automaton

Rob Roy author 5 Scott (Walter)

robust 4 hale, hard, iron, rude 5 hardy, lusty, sound, stout, wally 6 browny, hearty, potent, rugged, sinewy, strong 7 booming, healthy, roaring, thrifty, valiant 8 athletic, muscular, thriving, vigorous 9 strapping 10 boisterous, full-bodied, prospering, prosperous 11 flourishing 12 concentrated

robustious 6 rugged 7 boorish, ill-bred, loutish, lumpish 8 churlish, clownish, lubberly 9 unrefined 10 unpolished

rock 3 fly, zip 4 bill, crag, oner, reel, roll, rush, slip, sway, toss 5 boner, error, fluff, geode, heave, hurry, pitch, quake, shake, speed, swing 6 barrel, bullet, bungle, dollar, gangue, hustle, miscue, rocket, slipup, totter 7 agitate, blooper, blunder, boulder, breccia, concuss, hotfoot, misstep, tremble 8 astonish, convulse, undulate 9 oscillate *basaltic:* 5 wacke *cavity:* 3 vug 4 vugg, vugh *combining form:* 4 lite, lith, lyte, petr, saxi 5 clast, petri, petro, phyre *decomposed:* 6 gossan *fissile:* 5 shale *foliated:* 8 phyllite *formation:* 4 sial 5 nappe 6 pluton 7 rimrock, terrane 8 isocline, syncline *fragment:* 8 xenolith *fragmental:* 8 psephite *granular:* 6 norite *igneous:* 4 lava, sial, sima 6 basalt, dunite, gabbro, ophite, pumice 7 diabase, diorite, felsite, granite, greisen, picrite, sienite, syenite 8 eruptive, felstone, obsidian, porphyry, trachyte, traprock 9 tachylyte 10 travertine *layer:* 8 regolith 10 mantlerock *mass:* 5 scree 9 batholith *metamorphic:* 5 slate 6 gneiss, marble, schist 8 eclogite, ganister, mylonite 9 quartzite, soapstone *molten:* 4 lava *protruding:* 5 scaur *sedimentary:* 4 clay, coal 5 chalk, chert, coral, flint, shale 6 pelite 8 mudstone, psammite 9 limestone, sandstone, siltstone *silicate:* 8 hornfels *siliceous:* 9 buhrstone *soft:* 7 tripoli *suffix:* 3 ite *volcanic:* 4 tuff 5 trass 6 basalt, taxite, terras 8 pumicate, rhyolite, tephrite

rock badger 4 cony 5 coney, hyrax

rock bass 6 redeye 8 cabrilla

rock bottom 4 pith, root, soul 5 stuff 6 lowest, marrow 7 essence 8 cheapest 9 lowermost, substance, undermost 10 nethermost

rockbound 5 rigid 7 adamant 8 obdurate 9 unbending 10 inexorable, inflexible, unyielding 12 single-minded

rocker 6 cradle 7 shoofly

rocket 3 fly, zip 4 soar, whiz 5 arise, haste, hurry, mount, smoke, surge, tower, whish 6 ascend, bullet 7 missile, shoot up 8 firework, starship *engineer:* 8 Von Braun (Wernher) *landing:* 7 reentry 10 splashdown *launcher:* 7 bazooka *launching:* 7 liftoff 8 blastoff

rocketry *father of:* 7 Goddard (Robert)

rockfish 5 reina, viuva 6 gopher, rasher, tambor 7 corsair, garrupa, grouper 8 bocaccio

____ Rockne 5 Knute

rock-ribbed see rockbound

rockweed 4 tang 5 fucus 7 seatang, seaweed

rocky 4 dull, hard, weak 5 dizzy, reefy, shaky, stony 6 stoney, tricky, wobbly 7 petrean 8 bouldery, obdurate, ticklish, unstable, unsteady 9 bloodless, difficult, insensate, rockbound, steadfast 11 insensitive

rocky hill 3 tor

rococo 4 arty 6 florid, ornate 7 baroque 8 luscious 9 fantastic 10 flamboyant

rod 3 bar, gad, guy 4 bolt, came, cane, good, pole, scob, slab, ward 5 ingot, lytta, osier, perch, power, spoke, staff, stick, strip 6 billet, broach, carbon, etalon, pistol, raddle, skewer, switch, toggle 7 baculus, crowbar, scepter, spindle 8 punition, revolver 9 authority 10 correction, discipline, oppression, punishment 11 castigation 12 chastisement *bundle of:* 6 fasces *combining form:* 5 rhabd 6 rhabdo *glassmaking:* 5 punty

rodent 3 rat 4 cavy, cony, degu, hard, mole, paca, pika, utia, vole 5 cavie, coney, coypu, gundi, hutia, jutia, lerot, mouse, zokor 6 agouti, agouty, beaver, biting, cururo, gerbil, gopher, jerboa, marmot, murine, nutria, rabbit 7 chincha, hamster, lemming, leveret, muskrat 8 abrocome, capibara, capybara, chipmunk, cricetid, dormouse, gerbille, leporide, pacarana, sewellel, squirrel, tuco tuco, viscacha, vizcacha, water rat 9 guinea pig, porcupine 10 chinchilla, field mouse, prairie dog, springhare 11 kangaroo rat, meadow mouse, pocket mouse 12 pocket gopher *aquatic:* 5 coypu 6 beaver, coypou, nutria 7 muskrat 8 musquash *burrowing:* 6 gerbil, gopher 7 hamster 8 gerbille, viscacha, vizcacha *Eurasian:* 6 suslik *family:* 5 murid 6 murine 7 Muridae, sciurid 9 Sciuridae 10 Cricetidae 12 Octodontidae *furry:* 10 chinchilla *genus:* 3 Mus 5 Lepus *relating to:* 8 rosorial *South American:* 4 mara

rodeo 7 contest, roundup 9 enclosure 10 exhibition 11 competition *animal:* 5 horse, steer 10 Brahma bull *event:* 10 calf roping 11 bulldogging 12 bronco riding *performer:* 5 clown 6 cowboy

____ Rodin 7 Auguste

rodomontade 4 blow, brag, crow, puff, rant 5 boast, mouth, prate, pride, vaunt 6 blower, braggy, vanity 7 bluster, boaster, bombast, bragger, fustian, vaunter 8 blowhard, boastful, boasting, braggart, bragging, puckfist, rhapsody, rhetoric, vaunting 9 gasconade, vainglory 11 braggadocio

Rodomonte *beloved:* 8 Doralice *slayer:* 8 Ruggiero

Rodrigo Diaz de Bivar 5 el Cid

rod-shaped 7 virgate 8 bacillar, rhabdoid 9 bacillary, virgulate

roe 2 ra 3 ova, pea 4 deer, eggs, hart, hind 5 coral, spawn 6 caviar 7 caviare

Roentgen's discovery 4 X ray

rogation 3 law 6 decree, litany, prayer 7 inquiry 8 petition, proposal 12 supplication

____ Rogers 3 Roy 4 Will

rogue 3 boy, guy, gyp, imp 4 heel, kite 5 cheat, crank, devil, gipsy, gypsy, hempy, knave, scamp 6 beggar, canter, chiaus, coquin, harlot, rascal 7 cheater, culprit, erratic, lowlife, sharper, villain 8 mischief, picaroon, scalawag, swindler 9 defrauder, miscreant, scoundrel, skeezicks, trickster 10 blackguard, delinquent, mountebank 11 rapscallion *relating to:* 10 picaresque

roguery 5 fraud 7 devilry, waggery 8 deviltry, mischief, trickery 9 devilment, diablerie 11 waggishness 12 sportiveness

roguish 3 coy, sly 4 arch 5 antic, lying 6 impish, pranky, shifty, wicked 7 knavish, larkish, playful 8 espiègle, prankful, prankish 11 mischievous

roil 3 mud, vex 4 foul, rile 5 annoy, dirty, grate, muddy, peeve 6 befoul, burn up, muddle, nettle 7 blunder, disturb, inflame, polluto, provoke, turmoil 8 irritato 9 aggravate 10 exasperate 11 contaminate

roily 5 muddy, riley 6 turbid

roister 4 hell, riot 5 revel, spree 6 frolic 7 carouse, wassail

Roland 7 Orlando *beloved:* 4 Aude *betrayer:* 4 Gano 7 Ganelon *friend:* 6 Oliver 7 Olivier *horn:* 7 Olivant *sword:* 8 Durandal, Durendal *uncle:* 11 Charlemagne

role 3 bit 4 duty, face, look, part, show 5 guise 6 aspect, office 7 seeming 8 business, clothing, function, province 9 character, semblance 10 appearance

roll 3 bun, gad, rob 4 bask, bolt, bunn, clew, coil, file, flow, furl, gush, gyre, list, muse, pour, roam, rock, rota, rove, toss, turn, wind, wrap 5 drape, drift, growl, heave, pitch, range, revel, stray, surge, troll 6 bundle, circle, enwrap, goggle, grovel, gyrate, muster, ponder, ramble, roster, rotate, rumble, scroll, stream, swathe, wallow, wander, welter, whelve, wintle, wrap up 7 biscuit, brioche, catalog, envelop, grumble, indulge, revolve, rissole, rollick, swaddle, trundle 8 enswathe, involute, meditate, mull over, register, ruminate, schedule, turn over *of coins:* 7 rouleau *sweet:* 8 schnecke

roll about 6 wallow, welter

roll back 5 lower 6 reduce 7 repulse

roll call 4 list 6 roster 7 catalog 8 register, schedule

rolled 8 obvolute *backward:* 8 revolute *together:* 9 convolute

roller 4 wave 5 finer, inker, winch 6 caster, fascia, rowlet 7 breaker, carrier 8 cylinder

roller derby round 3 jam

rollick 4 bask, lark, play, roll, romp 5 caper, frisk, revel, sport 6 cavort, frolic, gambol, wallow, welter 7 indulge 8 escapade

rollicking 3 gay 4 glad, wild 5 antic, happy, merry 6 jovial, joyful, joyous, lively 7 playful 8 cheerful 9 hilarious, sprightly 10 frolicsome 12 lighthearted

rolling stock 4 cars 6 trucks 7 coaches, engines 8 cabooses, Pullmans, sleepers, trailers 11 locomotives

rolling stone 5 rover 6 roamer 7 drifter, rambler 8 wanderer 9 meanderer

roll up 4 furl 10 accumulate

roly-poly see rotund

Roman 5 brave, Latin, papal 7 Italian *amphitheater:* 9 Colosseum *assembly:* 5 forum 6 senate 7 comitia *building:* 5 Forum 6 Circus 8 basilica, Pantheon *clan:* 4 gens *comedy writer:* 7 Plautus (Titus), Terence *conspirator:* 6 Brutus (Marcus Junius) 7 Cassius (Gaius) 8 Catiline *date:* 4 Ides 7 calends, kalends *emperors:* 4 Nero, Otho 5 Galba (Servius Sulpicius), Nerva (Marcus Cocceius), Titus, Verus (Lucius Aurelius) 6 Julian, Trajan 7 Hadrian, Maximus (Magnus Clemens, Marcus Clodius, Petronius), Severus (Lucius Septimius) 8 Augustus, Caligula, Claudius, Commodus (Lucius Aelius), Domitian, Tiberius, Valerian 9 Caracalla, Vespasian 10 Diocletian, Theodosius 11 Constantine, Valentinian *entrance hall:* 5 atria (plural) 6 atrium *epic:* 6 Aeneid *epigrammatist:* 7 Martial *family:* 7 Gracchi *Fates:* 4 Nona 5 Morta 6 Decuma, Parcae *founder:* 5 Remus 7 Romulus *fountain:* 5 Trevi *garment:* 4 toga 5 palla, sagum, stola, stole, tunic *general:* 5 Sulla (Lucius Cornelius), Titus 6 Antony (Marc), Marius (Gaius), Scipio (Publius Cornelius) 8 Agricola (Gnaeus Julius)

god: 4 deus *blind:* 6 Plutus *chief:* 4 Jove 7 Jupiter *messenger:* 7 Mercury *of agriculture:* 6 Saturn *of animals:* 6 Faunus *of death:* 4 Mors *of dreams:* 8 Morpheus *of fire:* 6 Vulcan *of gates and doors:* 5 Janus *of healing:* 11 Aesculapius *of heaven:* 6 Uranus *of households:* 5 Lares 7 Penates *of love:* 4 Amor 5 Cupid *of medicine:* 11 Aesculapius *of mirth:* 5 Comus *of regeneration:* 7 Priapus *of sleep:* 6 Somnus *of the sea:* 6 Pontus 7 Neptune, Proteus *of the sun:* 3 Sol 6 Apollo *of the underworld:* 3 Dis 5 Orcus, Pluto 8 Dispater *of the wind:* 5 Eurus, Notus 6 Aeolus, Aquilo, Auster, Boreas 8 Favonius, Zephyrus *of war:* 4 Mars 8 Quirinus *of wealth:* 6 Plutus *of wine:* 7 Bacchus *of woods:* 6 Faunus *two-faced:* 5 Janus

goddess: 3 dea *of agriculture:* 5 Ceres *of beauty:* 5 Venus *of dawn:* 6 Aurora *of flowers:* 5 Flora *of handicrafts:* 7 Minerva *of harvests:* 3 Ops *of health:* 7 Minerva *of hope:* 4 Spes *of hunting:* 5 Diana *of justice:* 7 Astraea *of love:* 5 Venus *of marriage:* 4 Juno *of night:* 3 Nox *of peace:* 3 Pax *of springs:* 7 Juturna *of strife:* 9 Discordia *of the earth:* 6 Tellus *of the hearth:* 5 Vesta *of the moon:* 4 Luna *of the sea:* 10 Amphitrite *of the underworld:* 10 Proserpina *of victory:* 6 Vacuna *of war:* 7 Bellona *of wisdom:* 7 Minerva *of womanhood:* 4 Juno *greeting:* 3 ave *helmet:* 5 galea 6 cassis *hero:* 6 Caesar (Julius) 11 Cincinnatus (Lucius Quinctius) *hill:* 7 Caelian, Viminal 8 Aventine, Palatine, Quirinal 9 Esquiline 10 Capitoline *historian:* 4 Livy 5 Nepos (Cornelius) *king:* 7 Romulus, Servius, Tullius 12 Ancus Martius 13 Numa Pompilius *military formation:* 3 ala 6 alares (plural) 7 phalanx *military unit:* 6 cohort, legion 7 maniple *officer:* 9 centurion *official:* 5 augur, edile 6 aedile, censor, consul, lictor 7 praetor, prefect, tribune 8 irenarch, quaestor *people:* 5 Laeti 6 populi (plural) 7 populus, Sabines 8 plebians 9 plebeians 10 patricians *philosopher:* 4 Cato (Marcus Porcius) 6 Seneca (Lucius Annaeus) *physician:* 11 Aesculapius *port:* 5 Ostia *procurator:* 6 Pilate (Pontius) *racecourse:* 6 circus *road:* 4 iter *slave:* 9 Spartacus *statesman:* 4 Cato (Marcus Porcius) 5 Pliny 6 Caesar (Julius), Cicero (Marcus Tullius), Seneca (Lucius Annaeus) 7 Agrippa (Marcus Vipsanius) 8 Augustus, Maecenas (Gaius) *symbol of authority:* 6 fasces

roman à ___ 4 clef
romance 3 woo 4 gest, love, tale 5 amour, court, fable, fancy, feign, geste, novel, story 6 affair 7 fantasy, fiction 8 stardust 10 love affair
Romance language 6 French 7 Catalan, Italian, Spanish 8 Romanian, Rumanian 9 Provençal 10 Portuguese
Romania *capital:* 9 Bucharest *monetary unit:* 3 leu
romantic 4 wild 5 ideal, mushy 6 ardent, dreamy, exotic, gothic, poetic, slushy, sticky, unreal 7 maudlin, mawkish, strange 8 bathetic, fabulous, fanciful, invented, quixotic 9 fantastic, imaginary, visionary 10 idealistic, lovey-dovey 11 extravagant, sentimental
Romany 5 gipsy, gypsy
Romeo 7 amorist, Don Juan, gallant 8 Casanova, lothario, paramour *beloved:* 6 Juliet *enemy:* 6 Tybalt *father:* 8 Montague *friend:* 8 Mercutio
Rommel, Erwin *nickname:* 9 Desert Fox
romp 4 play, roil, rout 5 caper, frisk 6 cavort, frolic, gambol, hoyden 7 courant, gammock, rollick, runaway, skylark
Romulus *brother:* 5 Remus *father:* 4 Mars *mother:* 10 Rhea Silvia *victim:* 5 Remus
rondure 3 orb 4 ball 5 globe, round 6 circle, sphere
rood 5 cross 8 crucifix
roof 3 hip, top 4 apex, deck, dome, flat, peak 5 cover, crest, crown, haven, house 6 cupola, harbor, palate, shield, summit, vertex 7 chamber, mansard, shelter 8 covering, housetop 9 fastigium *automobile:* 8 fastback *false:* 7 cricket *material:* 3 tar, tin 4 tile 5 paper, slate, straw, terne 6 copper, gravel, thatch 8 shingles *of a cavern:* 4 dome *of the mouth:* 6 palate *part:* 3 hip 4 eave 7 cricket *peak:* 3 hip *structure:* 9 penthouse *type:* 5 gable 6 cupola 7 gambrel, mansard 9 butterfly 10 jerkinhead *vaulted:* 4 dome
roofer 5 tiler
rook 4 bird, crow, milk 5 bleed, cheat, mulct, raven, steal, stick, sweat 6 castle, fleece 7 defraud, swindle
rookery 5 roost 8 building
rookie 4 colt, tyro 6 novice 7 recruit, trainee 8 beginner, freshman, neophyte, newcomer 9 novitiate 10 apprentice, tenderfoot
room 3 den, hut 4 aula, cell, hall, play, rein, seat, sway 5 board, divan, house, lodge, place, put up, range, roost, salon, scope, space, study 6 billet, camera, harbor, leeway, margin, reside, studio 7 boudoir, cabinet, chamber, cubicle, expanse, gallery, lodging 8 domicile, latitude 9 apartment, clearance *ancient Roman:* 5 atria (plural), oecus 6 atrium 7 fumaria 8 aedicule *eating:* 4 nook 7 cenacle, kitchen 9 refectory *food storage:* 6 larder, pantry *for paintings:* 7 gallery *for small meetings:* 7 seminar *in a monastery:* 4 cell 6 lavabo 8 locutory 9 refectory 11 calefactory *in a prison:* 4 cell 7 dungeon *in a tower:* 6 belfry *next to dining room:* 7 servery *on a ship:* 5 cabin 6 galley *public:* 7 theater *round:* 7 rotunda
room and board 7 lodging 8 lodgment
roomer 5 guest 6 lodger, tenant 7 boarder
roomy 4 wide 5 ample, broad, large, spacy 7 spacial 8 spacious 9 capacious 10 commodious
Roosevelt, F.D. *birthplace:* 8 Hyde Park *dog:* 4 Fala *message:* 12 fireside chat *mother:* 4 Sara *predecessor:* 6 Hoover (Herbert) *program:* 7 New Deal *successor:* 6 Truman (Harry) *wife:* 7 Eleanor
roost 3 hut, sit 4 land, nest, room 5 board, house, light, lodge, perch, put up 6 alight, billet, garret, harbor, settle 7 dovecot, lodging, quarter, set down, sit down 8 domicile, dovecote 9 touch down
rooster 4 cock 5 capon, gallo 8 gamecock 11 chanticleer
root 3 dig, fix 4 base, bulb, core, grub, moot, pith, soul, stem, well 5 basis, cheer, embed, grout, heart, infix, lodge, plant, quick, radix, shout, stuff, tuber 6 bottom, center, etymon, ground, marrow, origin, rise to, settle, source 7 applaud, bedrock, essence, footing, ingrain, radical, support 8 entrench, fountain, radicate, wellhead 9 beginning, establish, inception, substance 10 derivation, foundation *aromatic:* 7 ginseng *combining form:* 4 rhiz 5 rhiza, rhizo 6 rhizae (plural), rrhiza 7 rrhizae (plural) *edible:* 3 oca, oka, roi, yam 4 beet, eddo 6 carrot, ginger, radish, turnip 7 parsnip 8 rutabaga, tuckahoe *fragrant:* 4 khus 5 orris 6 cuscus, kuskus 7 vetiver 8 khuskhus *main:* 7 taproot *medicinal:* 5 jalap 7 ginseng, zedoary *relating to:* 7 radical *starch:* 4 arum *tropical:* 4 taro *word:* 6 etymon *yielding red dye:* 4 chay, choy 5 chaya, choya 6 madder
rootlet 7 radicel, radicle, rhizoid
root out 4 grub, stub 6 evulse 7 abolish, blot out, destroy, wipe out 8 demolish 9 eradicate, extirpate 10 annihilate, deracinate, extinguish 11 exterminate
Roots author 5 Haley (Alex)
rope 3 gad, guy, tie, toe 4 bind, cord, hemp, line, stay 5 belay, bight, brace,

cable, chord, hoose, lasso, longe, riata,
sheet, widdy 6 becket, binder, fasten, halter, hawser, lariat, shroud, strand, string,
tether 7 aweband, binding, bobstay, halyard, lashing, marline, outhaul, painter, towline 8 backstay, buntline, downhaul, inveigle, jackstay, lifeline, prolonge *loop:*
7 cringle *maker:* 8 strander *mooring:*
6 hawser *of flowers:* 3 lei *saving:* 8 lifeline *ship's:* 4 vang 6 parral, parrel, ratlin
7 laniard, lanyard, marline, marling, ratline,
swifter 8 rattling

ropedancer 7 acrobat 11 funambulist

rope off 6 cordon

ropes 8 minutiae 10 ins and outs, proce-
dures, techniques

ropy 4 wiry 6 sinewy 7 fibrous, stringy
8 muscular

roque 7 croquet

rorqual 5 whale 7 finback

Rosalind's beloved 7 Orlando

rosary 5 beads 7 chaplet, garland 8 beadroll

rose 4 glow, pink 5 blush, color, flush,
rouge 6 mantle, pinken, redden 7 crimson
10 erysipelas *Chinese:* 8 Cherokee *combining form:* 4 rhod 5 rhodo, roseo *cotton:* 7 cudweed *feature:* 5 thorn *kind:*
4 moss 5 Peace, Vogue 6 Circus, damask
7 Fashion, Granada, Iceberg, New Dawn,
Pascali, Tiffany 8 Rubaiyat 9 Floradora,
Montezuma, polyantha, Tropicana 10 Flori-
bunda 11 grandiflora, Mount Shasta
12 Crimson Glory, Paul's Scarlet, Red Pinocchio 13 Golden Showers 14 Queen Elizabeth *wild:* 8 eglatere

roseate 3 red 4 pink 6 blushy, bright,
florid, likely 7 auroral, flushed, healthy,
hopeful 8 aurorean, blooming, blushful,
blushing, cheerful, rubicand 9 favorable,
promising 10 optimistic, promiseful

rose-colored see roseate

rosemary 4 mint 8 costmary 9 rosmarine

Rosenkavalier composer 7 Strauss
(Richard)

rose of ___ 6 Sharon

rose oil 5 attar

Rose Tattoo author 8 Williams (Tennessee)

rosette 7 cockade 8 ornament

Rosh's father 8 Benjamin

Rosinante's master 7 Quixote (Don)

Rosmersholm author 5 Ibsen (Henrik)

___ Rossetti 5 Dante 9 Christina
12 Dante Gabriel *work:* 8 Sing-Song
11 Annus Domini, Seek and Find, Sister
Helen 12 Beata Beatrix 14 The House of
Life

Rossini opera 6 Otello 8 Tancredi
11 William Tell

Rostand hero 6 Cyrano

roster 4 list, roll, rota 5 slate 6 muster,
scroll 7 catalog 8 beadroll, register, roll
call, schedule 10 muster roll

rostrum 4 beak, dais 5 snout 6 pulpit
7 lectern, tribune 8 platform 9 proboscis

rosy see roseate

rot 3 ret 4 bosh, bull, crap, sink, turn, warp
5 bilge, chaff, decay, hooey, spoil, stain,
taint, trash 6 banter, debase, fester,
molder, worsen 7 corrode, corrupt, crumble, debauch, decline, deprave, descend,
hogwash, pervert, putrefy, rubbish, vitiate
8 nonsense 9 animalize, break down,
decompose, poppycock 10 bestialize,
degenerate, demoralize, disimprove, retrograde 11 deteriorate 12 disintegrate
13 decomposition

rotary 6 circle 8 gyratory, spinning

rotate 4 gyre, pass, roll, spin, turn 5 pivot,
twirl, wheel 6 circle, follow, gyrate 7 pre-
cess, relieve, revolve, succeed, trundle
8 exchange, rotiform, windmill 9 alternate
10 circumduct 11 interchange *a log:* 4 birl

rotation 4 gyre, turn 5 round, wheel, whirl
7 circuit, turning 8 gyration 10 revolution

rote 4 list, pace 5 grind, learn 6 course,
custom, groove, memory, repeat, system
7 routine 8 practice 9 automatic, treadmill
10 memorizing, repetition 12 memorization

rotten 2 up 3 bad, bum 4 foul, poor, punk,
sour 5 amiss, fetid, nasty, wrong 6 crappy,
putrid 7 carrion, corrupt, decayed, spoiled,
tainted, touched, unhappy, unsound,
vicious 8 chiselly, depraved, perverse,
unstable 9 nefarious, offensive, putrified,
unhealthy 10 abominable, decomposed,
degenerate, flagitious, putrescent, under-
mined, unpleasant, villainous 11 displeasing 12 disagreeable 13 disintegrated *combining form:* 4 sapr 5 sapro

rotter 3 cad, cur 7 bounder, shirker,
slacker 9 yellow dog 10 blackguard

rotund 3 fat 5 beefy, buxom, dumpy,
obese, plump, podgy, pudgy, round, squat,
stout, thick, tubby 6 chubby, chunky,
plumpy, spuddy, stocky, stubby 7 paunchy,
ringing, vibrant 8 heavyset, plangent,
plumpish, resonant, roly-poly, sonorant,
sonorous, thickset 9 consonant, spherical
10 potbellied, resounding, roundabout

rouge 3 red 4 glow, pink, rose 5 blush,
color, flush 6 mantle, pinken, redden
7 crimson

rough 3 bad, dry, raw 4 curt, firm, hard,
punk, rude, wild 5 bluff, blunt, brief, brute,
bumpy, crass, crude, draft, gross, gruff,
hairy, harsh, heavy, raspy, rowdy, short,
solid, tight, tough, uncut, yahoo 6 abrupt,
broken, brushy, burred, choppy, coarse,

craggy, crusty, hispid, hoarse, jagged, knotty, mucker, raging, rugged, severe, sketch, stormy, trying, uneven, unhewn, vulgar 7 arduous, boorish, brusque, cragged, furious, grating, jarring, operose, outline, rasping, raucous, ruffian, scraggy, toughie, tricksy, uncivil, uncouth, ungodly, unlevel, violent 8 asperous, block out, blustery, bullyboy, chalk out, churlish, impolite, improper, indecent, scabrous, skeleton, stormful, unformed, unseemly, unsmooth 9 adumbrate, difficult, imperfect, inclement, inelegant, ironbound, laborious, manhandle, mishandle, proximate, strenuous, turbulent, undressed, unrefined 10 blustering, boisterous, formidable, indecorous, indelicate, knock about, malodorous, ridiculous, slap around, stridulent, stridulous, tumultuous, unbecoming, undecorous, unfinished, ungracious, unpolished 11 approximate, short-spoken, skeletonize, tempestuous, unfashioned 12 characterize, discourteous *combining form:* 6 trachy

roughhewn 4 rude 5 crude, plain, rough 8 unformed, unworked 9 undressed 10 unfinished, unpolished 11 unfashioned 12 uncultivated

roughhouse 7 fooling, rough up 9 high jinks, horseplay, manhandle, mishandle, rowdiness 10 knock about, skylarking, slap around

roughneck   see **ruffian**

roughness 7 crudity 8 acrimony, asperity 10 inequality, unevenness 12 irregularity

rough out 5 draft 6 sketch 7 outline 8 block out, chalk out, skeleton 9 adumbrate 11 skeletonize 12 characterize

rough up 9 manhandle, mishandle 10 knock about, roughhouse, slap around

round 2 by 3 arc, bow, hem, orb 4 arch, back, ball, bend, bent, bold, fast, free, full, gird, gyre, most, near, nigh, over, rich, ring, tour, turn 5 about, again, ample, arced, bowed, brisk, crook, curve, cycle, globe, harsh, large, orbed, plain, plump, podgy, pudgy, sleek, slick, tubby, vocal, wheel, whirl 6 all but, almost, arched, around, begird, beside, chubby, circle, curved, girdle, mellow, nearby, nearly, plumpy, polish, refine, rotund, smooth, sphere 7 annular, arrondi, bulbous, circuit, compass, orotund, perfect, ringing, rondure, spheric, through, vibrant 8 arciform, as good as, backward, circular, complete, conglobe, encircle, ensphere, finished, globular, gyration, plangent, plumpish, resonant, roly-poly, rotation, sonorant, sonorous, surround, vigorous, well-nigh 9 consonant, curvation, curvature, encompass, in reverse, just about, orbicular, outspoken, spherical 10 conglo-

bate, free-spoken, resounding, revolution, throughout 11 circulation, curvilinear, cylindrical *combining form:* 5 globo, troch, ventr 6 trocho, ventri, ventro *prefix:* 4 peri

roundabout 4 tour 5 jaunt, plump, tubby 6 chubby, detour, junket, outing, plumpy, rotary, rotund 7 circuit, curving, oblique, winding 8 circular, indirect, pleonasm, plumpish, roly-poly, verbiage 9 excursion, runaround, tautology, verbality 10 circuitous, collateral, meandering, periphrase 11 periphrasis

rounded 4 bent 5 arced, bowed, curvy, round 6 arched, convex, curved, mellow 7 arrondi, gibbous 8 arciform, complete, sonorous 9 curvesome, Junoesque, perfected 10 curvaceous 11 approximate, curvilinear 13 well-developed

rounder 4 rake, roué 6 bad lot, no-good, waster 7 wastrel 10 ne'er-do-well, profligate, scapegrace

roundly 4 most, well 5 about, à fond, fully, quite 6 all but, almost, nearly, wholly 7 bluntly, sharply, smartly, utterly 8 as good as, bitterly, candidly, entirely, promptly, well-nigh 9 just about, perfectly 10 altogether, completely, scathingly

round off 3 cap 5 crown 6 climax, top off 9 culminate, finish off

round robin 6 letter, series 7 protest 8 petition, sequence 10 tournament

round trip 4 tour 7 circuit 9 excursion

round up 5 group 6 gather 7 cluster, collect 8 assemble

rouse 4 call, move, rise, stir, wake, whet 5 alarm, awake, mount, pique, rally, waken 6 awaken, bestir, deepen, excite, foment, incite, kindle, revive, vivify 7 agitate, animate, disturb, enhance, enliven, innerve, magnify, provoke, quicken 8 heighten, motivate, redouble 9 aggravate, challenge, galvanize, innervate, instigate, intensate, intensify, stimulate

rousing 3 gay 4 keen 5 alert, brisk, peppy 6 bright, lively 7 animate, dashing 8 animated, exciting, spirited, stirring 9 inspiring, sprightly 10 exhilarant, eye-popping 11 stimulating, superlative 12 exhilarating, exhilarative, intoxicating

Rousseau work 5 Émile

roust 4 move, stir 5 pique, rouse 6 excite 7 innerve, provoke, quicken 8 motivate 9 galvanize, stimulate

roustabout 4 hand 6 worker 7 laborer, workman 8 deckhand, floorman, workhand 9 operative 10 workingman

rout 3 mob 4 army, bawl, beat, drub, dust, fuss, herd, host, lick, mass, roar, romp, root, whip 5 chase, cloud, crowd, dregs, drive, eject, expel, flock, trash 6 bellow, clamor, defeat, dig out, dispel, flight, hunt up, legion, number, rabble, scores, soiree, throng, wallop **7** beating, bluster, clobber, conquer, debacle, hunt out, licking, rummage, runaway, shellac, warming **8** cakewalk, drubbing, hunt down, lambaste, riffraff, stampede, walkaway, walkover **9** clean up on, hoi polloi, multitude, other half, overthrow, reception **10** defeasance, demoralize **11** proletariat

route 3 way **4** lead, line, path, road, send, ship, show **5** guide, pilot, remit, steer, track, trail **6** course, direct, divert, escort **7** address, channel, circuit, conduct, consign, forward, highway, journey, passage **8** dispatch, shepherd, transmit **9** direction, itinerary

routine 3 act, bit, rut **4** pace, rote **5** drill, grind, habit, plain, usual **6** course, groove, wonted **7** chronic, regular **8** accepted, everyday, habitual, ordinary, standard, workaday **9** customary, plain Jane, quotidian, treadmill **10** accustomed **11** commonplace **12** unremarkable

rove 3 gad **4** move, roam **5** drift, prowl, range, stray **6** ramble, wander **7** meander, traipse **8** vagabond **9** gallivant

rover 3 gad **5** stray **6** gadder, pirate, roamer, sea dog **7** corsair, drifter, floater, rambler, sea wolf **8** gadabout, picaroon, runabout, traveler, wanderer **9** buccaneer, itinerant, meanderer, sea robber **10** freebooter **11** peripatetic **12** rolling stone

roving 6 errant, mobile **7** nomadic, roaming, vagrant **8** rambling, vagabond **9** itinerant, itinerate, wandering, wayfaring **10** discursive **11** perambulant, peripatetic

row 3 oar **4** beef, file, fray, fuss, line, list, pull, punt, rank, sail, scud, spat, tier, tiff **5** align, brawl, broil, chain, fight, melee, mouth, order, queue, run-in, scrap, scull, set-to, swath, train **6** affray, bicker, clamor, fracas, paddle, propel, sequel, series, string **7** brabble, dispute, echelon, quarrel, rhubarb, wrangle **8** argument, sequence, squabble **9** bickering, caterwaul, commotion **10** falling-out, succession **11** altercation, consecution, disturbance, progression

rowdy 4 punk, rude **5** rough, tough, yahoo **6** mucker, unruly, vulgar **7** hoodlum, raffish, raucous, ruffian, toughie **8** bullyboy, stubborn **9** roughneck, turbulent **10** boisterous, disorderly, tumultuous **11** rumbustious

Rowena *father:* **7** Hengist *guardian:* **6** Cedric *husband:* **7** Ivanhoe **9** Vortigern

Roxana *husband:* **9** Alexander *rival:* **7** Statira

royal 3 top **4** easy **5** grand, light, noble, prime, regal **6** august, facile, kingly, lordly, simple, smooth, superb **7** stately **8** baronial, champion, tive-star, glorious, imperial, imposing, kinglike, majestic, princely, splendid, superior **9** classical, excellent, frontrank, grandiose, monarchal, number one, sovereign **10** effortless, monarchial **11** magnificent, monarchical

royalist 4 Tory **5** blimp, white **7** Bourbon, diehard **8** Cavalier **11** reactionary

rub 3 bar, irk, vex **4** buff, fret, gall, rasp, rile, snag, wear, wipe **5** annoy, chafe, crimp, erode, glaze, gloss, grate, graze, grind, peeve, scour, scrub, shine **6** abrade, bother, glance, hamper, hurdle, nettle, polish, ruffle, scrape, smooth, stroke **7** burnish, corrade, furbish, massage, provoke **8** irritate, obstacle, traverse **9** aggravate, excoriate, hindrance **10** difficulty, exasperate, impediment **11** obstruction

Rubaiyat author 11 Omar Khayyam

rubber 4 nose **5** snoop **6** butt-in, eraser **7** Paul Pry, trouble **8** busybody, quidnunc **9** whetstone **10** caoutchouc, misfortune **11** nosey Parker **12** intermeddler *basis:* **5** latex *hard:* **7** ebonite *synthetic:* **8** neoprene *tree:* **5** Hevea **7** manihot

Rubber City 5 Akron (Ohio)

rubberneck 3 eye **4** gape, gaze, look, ogle **5** prier, pryer, snoop, stare **6** butt-in, goggle **7** meddler, tourist, tripper **8** busybody, kibitzer, quidnunc, sight-see **9** buttinsky, sightseer **10** pragmatist **12** intermeddler

rubbish 3 pap, rot **4** bosh, crap, junk, slop **5** bilge, dreck, dross, hooey, offal, trash, waste, wrack **6** debris, kelter, litter, pablum, refuse, rubble **7** garbage, hogwash **8** nonsense, tommyrot **9** poppycock, sweepings **11** foolishness

rubbishy 4 base, mean, poor **5** cheap, tatty **6** common, paltry, shoddy, sleazy, trashy **9** worthless

rube 4 boor, hick **5** yahoo **6** rustic **7** bucolic, bumpkin, hayseed, redneck **9** hillbilly **10** clodhopper, provincial **12** backwoodsman

rubicund 3 red **5** flush, ruddy **6** florid **7** flushed, glowing **8** sanguine **11** full-blooded

rubidium *symbol:* **2** Rb

rub out 4 do in, kill, raze, ruin **5** smash, wreck **6** finish, murder **7** bump off, destroy, put away, shatter **8** decimate, demolish, destruct, knock off **9** liquidate **10** annihilate, extinguish, obliterate **11** assassinate

rubric 3 rud **4** name, ruby **5** canon, class, nomen, ruddy, style, title **6** redden, rubify, ruddle **7** concept, notable **8** category, cognomen, nameáble **9** memorable, red-letter **10** noteworthy, observable **11** appellation, appellative, designation, incarnadine **12** compellation, denomination

ruck 3 mob 4 fold, heap, mass, pile 5 crimp, crowd, group, plica, ridge, rivel, screw 6 crease, furrow, jumble, muster, pucker, rimple, rumple 7 company, crimple, crinkle, crumple, scrunch, wrinkle 9 congeries, gathering, multitude 10 assemblage, collection, generality 11 aggregation, corrugation

rucksack 4 pack 8 backpack

ruckus 3 row 4 coil, fuss, to-do 5 brawl, broil, melee, scrap 6 fracas, furore, hassle, rumpus, shindy, uproar 7 dispute, quarrel, shindig, wrangle 8 squabble 9 bickering, commotion, confusion 10 falling-out 11 altercation, controversy, disturbance

ruction see ruckus

ruddle see redden

ruddy 3 red 4 rosy, ruby 5 flush, vivid 6 blowsy, florid, lively, redden, rubify, rubric 7 bronzed, flushed, glowing 8 blooming, rubicund, sanguine 11 full-blooded, incarnadine

rude 3 ill, raw 4 curt, wild 5 bluff, crass, crude, fresh, green, gross, gruff, harsh, lumpy, rough, surly 6 abrupt, bitter, callow, clumsy, coarse, crusty, Gothic, ribald, rugged, savage, simple, stormy, unhewn, vulgar 7 angular, boorish, brusque, crabbed, Hunnish, ill-bred, incivil, inexact, loutish, natural, uncivil, uncouth 8 arrogant, barbaric, churlish, clownish, ignorant, impolite, impudent, inexpert, insolent, inurbane, tactless, unformed, unlicked, unsubtle, untaught, unversed, unworked 9 barbarian, barbarous, benighted, dissonant, elemental, imperfect, imprecise, incondite, inelegant, intrusive, makeshift, primitive, proximate, rough-hewn, truculent, turbulent, undressed, unfleshed, unrefined, unwrought 10 cacophonic, discordant, illiterate, immoderate, mannerless, meddlesome, uncultured, uneducated, unfinished, ungracious, unhandsome, unlettered, unmannered, unmannerly, unpolished, unschooled 11 approximate, cacophonous, disgracious, disharmonic, empty-headed, ill-mannered, impertinent, know-nothing, rudimentary, uncalled-for, uncivilized, uncourteous, unfashioned, unmitigated, unpracticed, unprocessed 12 discourteous, inharmonious, unconversant, uncultivated, unharmonious, uninstructed 13 disrespectful

rudiment 5 basic 6 anlage 7 element, vestige 9 beginning, essential 11 fundamental

rudimentary 5 basal, basic 7 initial 8 simplest 9 beginning, elemental, vestigial 10 elementary 11 fundamental, undeveloped *prefix:* 3 pro

rue 3 woe 4 care, pity, ruth 5 dolor, grief, mourn 6 bewail, grieve, lament, regret, repent, sorrow 7 anguish, deplore, penance, remorse 8 sympathy 9 heartache, penitence, penitency 10 affliction, compassion, contrition, heartbreak, repentance 11 compunction 12 contriteness

rueful 3 sad 4 poor 5 sorry 6 dolent, woeful 7 doleful, piteous, pitiful, ruthful 8 contrite, dolesome, dolorous, hopeless, mournful, pathetic, penitent, pitiable, wretched 9 afflicted, depressed, miserable, oppressed, plaintive, sorrowful 10 despairing, despondent, lamentable, lugubrious, melancholy 11 weighed down

ruff 5 frill, perch 6 collar, fringe, pigeon, ruffle 9 sandpiper 11 pumpkinseed *female:* 5 reeve

ruffian 4 hood, punk, thug 5 bully, rough, rowdy, tough, yahoo 6 brutal, coarse, mucker 7 gorilla, hoodlum, toughie 8 bullyboy, hooligan 9 roughneck, strong arm

ruffle 3 bug, fan, irk, rub, vex 4 blow, fret, gall, wear, wind 5 annoy, chafe, erode, frill, graze, jabot, pleat, ruche 6 abrade, bother, gather, nettle, ripple, winnow 7 agitate, corrade, dispute, disturb, provoke, stiffen, trouble, wrinkle 8 dishevel, disorder, distract, drumbeat, exercise, furbelow, irritate, skirmish 10 disarrange, discompose

Rufus' father 5 Simon

rug 3 mat 4 wrap 5 cover 6 carpet, runner 7 blanket, laprobe 8 covering *kind:* 3 rag, rya 6 dhurry, hooked 7 braided, flokati, Persian 8 Aubusson, Oriental 10 Savonnerie

rugby *formation:* 5 scrum 9 scrummage *goal:* 7 dropped, penalty *period:* 4 half *player:* 6 center, hooker, winger 8 standoff 9 scrum half *scoring:* 3 try 4 goal 10 conversion *team:* 7 fifteen *term:* 4 heel 5 match 7 convert, dribble, hand off, knock on 9 fair catch *time-out:* 8 stoppage *version:* 5 union 6 league

rugged 3 dry 4 hard, rude, wild 5 burly, hardy, harsh, heavy, husky, rough, stern, tough 6 bitter, brawny, brutal, coarse, craggy, hoarse, jagged, knotty, robust, severe, strong, sturdy, uneven 7 arduous, austere, boorish, grating, ill-bred, jarring, loutish, lumpish, operose, rasping, raucous, scraggy, unlevel 8 asperous, churlish, clownish, lubberly, muscular, rigorous, scabrous, stalwart, unsmooth, vigorous 9 difficult, inclement, laborious, strenuous, unrefined, weathered 10 formidable, robustious, stridulent, stridulous, unpolished 11 intemperate

Ruggiero *guardian:* 7 Atlante *sister:* 7 Marfisa *slayer:* 11 Tisaphernes *wife:* 10 Bradamante

ruin 4 balk, bane, beat, bilk, bust, dash, do in, doom, draw, fall, foil, harm, hurt, loss, maim, raze, sack, undo 5 break, decay, drain, havoc, spoil, use up, waste, wrack, wreck 6 baffle, beggar, blight, damage, debase, deface, devour, fold up, impair, injury, mangle, pauper, ravage, reduce, thwart, unmake 7 atrophy, break up, corrupt, decline, deplete, despoil, destroy, exhaust, outrage, pillage, unbuild, undoing, unframe, vitiate, wipe out, wrecker 8 bankrupt, calamity, clean out, collapse, decimate, demolish, desolate, dishonor, downfall, draw down, mischief, mutilate, spoliate 9 confusion, crumbling, decadence, depredate, desecrate, destroyer, devastate, disfigure, disrepair, downgrade, frustrate, overthrow, pauperize 10 circumvent, declension, degeneracy, degenerate, devolution, dilapidate, disappoint, impoverish 11 destruction, devastation, dissolution 12 degeneration 13 deterioration

ruination 4 bane, loss 5 havoc 7 undoing 8 downfall 9 confusion, destroyer 11 destruction, devastation

ruinous 5 fatal 7 fateful 8 wrackful, wreckful 10 calamitous, disastrous, pernicious, shattering 11 cataclysmic, destructive 12 annihilative, catastrophic

rule 3 law 4 lead, sway 5 axiom, bylaw, canon, edict, gnome, guide, habit, infer, judge, maxim, moral, order, reign 6 assize, course, custom, decide, decree, deduce, dictum, direct, figure, gather, govern, manage, method, regime, settle, truism 7 brocard, command, control, decorum, precept, preside, prevail, regency, regimen, resolve, statute 8 aphorism, apothegm, conclude, decretum, doctrine, dominate, domineer, dominion, overrule 9 authority, determine, etiquette, influence, ordinance, principle, procedure, propriety 10 regulation 11 fundamental *absolute:* 8 autarchy *by a god:* 8 thearchy, theonomy *combining form:* 4 nomy 5 archy

Rule Britannia composer 4 Arne (Thomas)

rule out 3 bar 4 bate, ward 5 avert, debar, deter 6 except, forbid, refuse 7 exclude, forfend, obviate, prevent, scratch, suspend 8 count out, preclude, prohibit, stave off 9 eliminate, forestall

ruler 4 king, lord 5 queen 6 archon, dynast, ferule, gerent, prince, regent, satrap, sultan 7 emperor, monarch, viceroy 8 governor, hierarch, oligarch, pentarch, princess, theocrat 9 dominator, imperator, matriarch, patriarch, potentate, sovereign 12 straightedge *absolute:* 6 despot, tyrant 8 autocrat, dictator, omniarch, overlord *Arab:* 4 amir, emir 5 emeer, sheik 6 sharif, sheikh, sherif, sultan *Asian:* 4 khan *Byzantine Empire:* 6 exarch *combining form:* 4 arch *Egyptian:* 7 pharaoh *family:* 7 dynasty *Iranian:* 4 shah *one of four:* 8 tetrarch *one of seven:* 8 heptarch *one of three:* 7 triarch 8 triumvir *Persian:* 6 satrap *Russian:* 4 czar, tsar, tzar *Turkish:* 3 bey, dey

ruling 3 law 4 rife 5 chief, edict, ukase 6 decree 7 central, current, pivotal, popular, rampant, regnant, statute 8 cardinal, decision 9 directive, prevalent 10 overriding, prevailing, widespread 11 predominant

Rumania see **Romania**

rumble 3 cry 4 boom, buzz, clap, peal, roar, roll, talk 5 blast, burst, crack, crash, growl, ondit, rumor 6 gossip, murmur, report, uproar 7 hearsay, quarrel, resound, thunder 9 complaint, grapevine 11 disturbance, scuttlebutt

ruminant 3 cow, yak 4 deer, goat, tahr 5 bison, camel, goral, llama, okapi, serow, sheep, takin 6 alpaca, cattle, musk ox, vicuña 7 buffalo, chamois, chewing, giraffe, guanaco 8 antelope *stomach:* 5 rumen 6 omasum 8 abomasum 9 reticulum

ruminate 4 chew, mull, muse, roll 5 champ, chomp, chump, munch, think, weigh 6 crunch, ponder 7 chumble, reflect, revolve, scrunch 8 cogitate, consider, meditate, mull over, turn over 9 masticate 10 deliberate, excogitate 11 contemplate

ruminative 7 pensive 8 thinking 9 pondering 10 cogitative, meditative, reflecting, reflective, thoughtful 11 speculative 13 contemplative

rummage 4 beat, comb, fish, grub, hash, mash, poke, rake, rout, seek 5 mix up, scour 6 dig out, forage, hunt up, jumble, jungle, litter, mess up, muddle, search, spy out, tumble 7 clutter, disrupt, disturb, examine, hunt out, ransack 8 disarray, disorder, finecomb, hunt down, mishmash, scramble 9 ferret out, patchwork, potpourri, search out 10 collection, disarrange, discompose, hotchpotch, miscellany, scrutinize 11 disorganize

rummy 3 odd 4 lush 5 drunk, queer 6 boozer, lusher 7 bizarre, curious, guzzler, oddball, strange, swiller, tippler 8 drunkard, peculiar, singular 9 eccentric, inebriate 10 boozehound

rumor 4 blab, buzz, talk, word 5 on-dit, story 6 gossip, mumble, murmur, mutter, report, rumble, tattle 7 hearsay, tidings, whisper 9 grapevine, undertone 11 scuttlebutt, susurration

rumormonger 5 tabby 6 gossip 8 gossiper, quidnunc, telltale 9 carrytale 10 talebearer

rump 4 beam, hind, rear 5 fanny 6 behind, bottom 7 rear end 8 backside, buttocks, derriere, haunches 9 posterior *combining form:* 3 pyg 4 pyga, pygo 5 pygal, pygia

rumple 4 fold, muss 5 crimp, screw 6 tousle 7 crimple, crinkle, scrunch, wrinkle

rumpus see ruckus

run 2 go 3 act, dig, fly, get, ram, set, use, wax 4 bolt, come, dart, dash, flee, flit, flow, flux, fuse, gill, grow, hare, herd, hunt, keep, line, make, melt, move, pour, race, rush, shin, sink, skip, stab, tear, thaw, trip, turn, vary, work 5 apply, blend, brook, chase, creek, drift, drive, fleet, haste, hurry, range, reach, recur, refer, scoot, skirr, speed, stick, swing, tenor, trend 6 become, bustle, career, course, direct, escape, extend, gallop, govern, handle, hustle, manage, ordain, plunge, repair, resort, runnel, scorch, scurry, sprint, stream, thrust 7 bearing, bootleg, carry on, conduct, current, hotfoot, liquefy, make off, operate, proceed, retreat, rivulet, scamper, scuttle, smuggle, stretch 8 dissolve, duration, function, highball, liquesce, tendency, traverse 9 direction, endurance, skedaddle 10 continuity, contraband, deliquesce 11 continuance, persistence 12 continuation, prolongation

run across 4 meet 8 discover 9 encounter

runagate 3 rat, vag 4 hobo 5 tramp 7 drifter, floater, vagrant 8 apostate, defector, fugitive, recreant, renegade, roadster, turncoat, vagabond, wanderer 9 turnabout

run along 2 go 4 exit, quit 5 leave 6 depart, get off 7 pull out, take off 8 shove off

runaround 6 detour, escape 7 come off, elusion, evasion 8 escaping, eschewal, shunning 9 avoidance 10 roundabout

run away 4 bolt, flee 5 elope 6 desert, escape 7 abscond 8 stampede

runaway 8 decisive, deserter, fugitive

run down 3 hit 4 stop 5 decry, trace 6 pursue 7 downcry 8 belittle, derogate, diminish 9 disparage, dispraise 10 depreciate 11 detract from, opprobriate

run-down 5 dingy, seedy, tacky, tired 6 shabby, tagrag 8 decrepit, tattered, untended 9 exhausted, neglected 10 broken-down, down-at-heel, uncared-for 11 dilapidated

rune 4 poem, song 5 charm, ogham, poesy, rhyme, spell, verse 6 poetry 11 conjuration, incantation

rung 4 step 5 grade, notch, spoke, stage, stair, tread 6 degree, handle 10 crosspiece

run in 3 nab 4 bust 5 pinch, visit 6 arrest, come by, detain, drop by, look up, pick up, stop by 9 apprehend

run-in 3 row 4 tiff 5 brush, fight, set-to 6 hassle 7 dispute, quarrel, rhubarb 8 skirmish 9 bickering, encounter 10 falling-out, velitation 11 altercation

run into 4 meet 6 become 9 encounter

runnel see rivulet

runner 3 rug 5 agent, blade, miler, racer 6 carpet, stolon 8 operator, sprinter 9 messenger

running 4 care, easy, live, race 5 alive 6 active, charge, fluent, linear, smooth 7 conduct, cursive, dynamic, flowing, working 8 handling, roadwork, together 9 operative, oversight 10 continuous, effortless, intendance, management 11 continually, functioning, night and day, supervision 12 continuously, successively 13 consecutively *combining form:* 4 drom 5 dromo 7 dromous

running mate 3 pal 4 chum 5 buddy, crony 7 comrade 9 associate, companion

run-of-the-mill 4 fair, mean 5 typic, usual 6 common, medium, normal 7 average, general, natural, regular, typical 8 mediocre, middling, moderate, ordinary, uncommon 9 prevalent 11 commonplace, indifferent 12 intermediate 13 unexceptional

run on 3 gab, jaw, yak 4 chat, talk 5 clack 6 babble, gabble, rattle 7 chatter, prattle 8 continue

run out 4 fail, flow, oust 5 exile, expel 6 banish, deport, elapse, expire 7 cast out, give out 8 complete, displace 9 ostracize, transport

run over 5 spill 6 exceed, repeat 7 examine 8 overbrim, overfill, overflow, rehearse

runt 5 dwarf, midge, pygmy 6 midget, peewee 7 manikin 8 Tom Thumb 10 homunculus 11 hop-o'-my-thumb, lilliputian

run through 2 go 4 scan 5 spend, use up 6 browse, expend, finish, pierce 7 consume, dip into, examine, exhaust 8 glance at, rehearse, transfix 10 glance over

runty 4 puny 5 small 7 stunted 8 dwarfish 10 diminutive, undersized 12 contemptible

run up 3 wax 4 rise 5 build, erect, mount 6 expand 7 augment, enlarge 8 increase, multiply, snowball 9 construct 10 accumulate

runway 4 path 5 strip, track, trail 6 bridge 7 channel 8 airstrip, platform

rupture 4 hole, open, part, rend, rent, rift, rive 5 break, burst, sever, split 6 breach, cleave, divide, hernia, schism, sunder 7 blowout, break up, disjoin, disrupt, dissect, divorce, fissure, parting, split-up 8 disunion, disunite, division, fracture, separate 9 partition 10 detachment, separation 11 dissolution, divorcement *combining form:* 7 rrhexes (plural), rrhexis

R.U.R. *author:* 5 Čapek (Karel) *character:* 5 robot

rural 6 rustic, simple 7 bucolic, country, idyllic, natural, outland 8 agrestic, arcadian, pastoral, villatic 10 campestral, out-country, provincial 11 countrified

ruse 3 jig 4 hoax, ploy, wile 5 dodge, feint, fraud, trick 6 deceit, gambit 7 gimmick 8 artifice, maneuver, trickery 9 stratagem 10 subterfuge

rush 3 fly, run 4 boil, bolt, dart, dash, flit, flow, flux, lash, race, scud, tear, tide, whiz 5 break, chase, drift, fleet, fling, flood, haste, hurry, onset, sally, scoot, shoot, spate, speed, surge 6 attack, barrel, bustle, career, charge, course, hasten, hurtle, irrupt, plunge, stream 7 assault, cattail, current 8 stampede, vanquish 9 hastiness, overpower 11 hurriedness 12 precipitance, precipitancy 13 precipitation

rushing 5 hasty 6 abrupt, sudden 7 hurried 8 headlong 9 impetuous 11 precipitant, precipitate, precipitous, subitaneous

Russian *family:* 7 Romanov 9 Stroganov *monk:* 8 Rasputin *peasant:* 5 kulak, mujik 6 moujik, muzhik, muzjik *ruler:* (see czar) *saint:* 15 Alexander Nevsky *villa:* 5 dacha

rustic 3 jay, yap 4 hick, jake, rube, rude 5 churl, clown, plain, rough, rural, swain, yokel 6 farmer, joskin, simple, sturdy, sylvan, woodsy 7 artless, bucolic, bumpkin, country, granger, hayseed, hillman, hoosier, outland, peasant, plowboy, plowman, redneck, uncouth 8 agrestic, mossback, pastoral 9 chawbacon, greenhorn, hillbilly 10 campestral, clodhopper, countryman, exurbanite, husbandman, out-country, provincial 11 countrified, country jake, mountaineer 12 backwoodsman

rustle 5 haste, hurry, speed, steal, swish 6 forage, hustle, swoosh 7 crinkle 8 celerity, dispatch, susurrus 9 swiftness 10 expedition, speediness

rustler 5 thief 6 dynamo, peeler 7 hustler 8 go-getter, live wire 11 self-starter

Rustum's son and victim 6 Sohrab

rusty 3 dry 4 slow 5 harsh, hoary, inept, rough 6 hoarse, rugged 7 grating, jarring, rasping, raucous, restive 8 outmoded, strident 10 discolored

rut 4 heat, pace, rote 5 grind, track 6 estrus, furrow, groove 7 channel, routine 9 treadmill

rutabaga 5 swede 6 turnip

ruth 3 rue 4 pity 5 grief, mercy 6 regret, sorrow 7 penance, remorse, sadness 8 distress, sympathy 9 attrition, penitence, penitency 10 compassion, contrition, repentance 11 compunction

Ruth *husband:* 4 Boaz 6 Mahlon *mother-in-law:* 5 Naomi *son:* 4 Obed

ruthenium *symbol:* 2 Ru

ruthful 6 dolent, rueful, tender, woeful 7 doleful, pitiful 8 dolorous, wretched 9 afflicted, miserable, sorrowful

ruthless 4 grim 5 cruel 6 mortal, savage 8 pitiless 9 ferocious, merciless, unsparing 10 implacable, ironfisted, relentless, unyielding 11 unflinching, unrelenting 12 unappeasable

ruttish 3 hot 5 rutty 7 goatish, lustful, satyric 9 lickerish, salacious 10 lascivious, libidinous 12 concupiscent

Rwanda *capital:* 6 Kigali *monetary unit:* 5 franc

S

Sabatini novel 11 Scaramouche 12 Captain Blood
sabbatical 4 rest 5 leave
saber 5 sword
sabertooth 3 cat 5 tiger
sable 3 jet 4 dark, ebon, inky '5 black, dusky, ebony, jetty, murky, raven 6 gloomy, mammal, somber 9 pitch-dark 10 pitch-black
sabot 4 clog, shoe
sabotage 5 block, wreck 6 damage, hamper, hinder, injury 7 break up, destroy, subvert 8 obstruct, wreckage, wrecking 9 frustrate, undermine 10 impairment, subversion 11 undermining 12 subversivism
Sabra *father:* 7 Ptolemy *husband, rescuer:* 8 St. George *son:* 3 Guy 5 David 9 Alexander
Sabrina *father:* 7 Locrine *mother:* 9 Estrildis
sac 4 cyst 5 pouch
Sacar *father:* 8 Obededom *son:* 5 Ahiam
saccharine 5 sweet 6 sugary, syrupy 7 candied, cloying, honeyed, sugared 9 disarming, oversweet 11 deferential, sugarcoated 12 ingratiating
sacerdotal 8 priestly 9 religious 10 priestlike 11 ministerial
sachem 4 boss 5 chief 6 leader
sachet 3 bag 6 powder 7 perfume
sack 2 ax 3 bag, bed 4 base, drop, fire, raid, ship, wine 5 expel, pouch, strip, waste 6 bounce, devour, forage, pocket, ravage 7 boot out, cashier, despoil, dismiss, kick out, pillage 8 desolate, spoliate 9 container, depredate, desecrate, devastate, terminate
sackbut 8 trombone
sacque 6 jacket
sacrament 4 rite, sign 6 symbol 7 baptism, penance 8 ceremony 9 eucharist, matrimony 10 holy orders 12 confirmation
sacrarium 6 chapel, shrine 7 oratory, piscina 8 sacristy 9 sanctuary
sacred 4 holy 5 godly 6 immune 7 angelic, blessed, guarded, saintly 8 defended, hallowed, numinous 9 cherished, inviolate, spiritual, unprofane 10 inviolable, sacrosanct, sanctified 11 consecrated, sacramental *combining form:*

4 hagi, hier, sacr 5 hagio, hiero, sacro *monkey:* 6 baboon, rhesus 7 hanuman *place:* 7 sanctum *weed:* 7 vervain
sacrifice 4 cede, drop, give, lose 5 forgo, yield 6 devote, donate, eschew, martyr, victim 7 forbear, forfeit, offer up 8 dedicate, hecatomb, immolate, oblation, offering
sacrilege 7 impiety, offense 9 blasphemy, violation 11 desecration, irreverence, profanation
sacrilegious 7 impious, profane, ungodly 10 irreverent 11 blasphemous, irreligious
sacristan 6 sexton
sacristy 6 vestry
sacrosanct 6 sacred 8 esteemed, regarded 9 inviolate, respected 10 inviolable
sad 4 blue, down 5 drear, dumpy, sorry 6 dismal, dreary, gloomy, morose, triste, woeful 7 doleful, dumpish, joyless, piteous, pitiful, unhappy 8 dejected, desolate, dolorous, downbeat, downcast, grieving, mournful, pathetic, pitiable, saddened, tristful 9 depressed, mirthless, sorrowful, woebegone 10 afflicting, depressing, dispirited, lamentable, melancholy 11 melancholic 12 heavyhearted
sadden 7 depress, oppress 9 weigh down
saddle 3 tax 4 lade, load, task 5 weigh 6 burden, charge, cumber, hamper, impede, impose, weight 7 aparejo, inflict 8 encumber, restrict *adjunct:* 7 stirrup *covering:* 7 mochila *part:* 6 cantle, pommel 8 tapadera, tapadero *strap:* 5 cinch, girth 6 latigo 7 harness
sadness 3 woe 4 funk 5 blues, dinge, downs, dumps, gloom, grief, mopes 6 misery, sorrow 7 anguish, dismals, megrims 8 doldrums, dolefuls, glumness, mourning 9 dejection, dysphoria, moodiness 10 blue devils, depression, desolation, melancholy 11 despondency, forlornness, melancholia, unhappiness 12 downcastness, hopelessness, listlessness, mournfulness 13 sorrowfulness
safari 4 hunt, trek, trip 7 caravan 10 expedition
safe 4 wary 5 chary 6 intact, secure, unhurt 7 careful, guarded, healthy 8 cautious, defended, discreet, gingerly, guard-

ing, harmless, innocent, riskless, shielded, unharmed 9 innocuous, protected, sheltered, shielding, uninjured, unscathed, wholesome 10 inviolable, protecting, scatheless, sheltering 11 calculating, circumspect, considerate, impregnable, inoffensive, uninjurious 12 invulnerable, safeguarding, unassailable, unthreatened

safety 5 cover 7 defense, shelter 8 security 9 assurance 10 protection 13 inviolability *org.:* 4 OSHA

sag 3 dip 4 bend, drop, flag, flap, flop, sink, slip, swag, wilt 5 basin, droop, slide, slump 6 dangle, hollow, slouch 7 decline, drop off, falloff, sinkage, sinking 8 downturn, fall away, settling, sinkhole 9 concavity, downslide, downswing, downtrend 10 depression

saga 4 edda, epic, tale 5 story 6 legend 9 narrative

sagacious 4 sage, wise 5 cagey, heady, smart 6 argute, astute, clever, shrewd 7 gnostic, knowing, prudent, sapient 8 critical 9 astucious, far-seeing, insighted, judicious 10 discerning, insightful, perceptive 11 intelligent 13 knowledgeable, perspicacious

sagacity 5 grasp 6 wisdom 7 insight 8 prudence, sageness, sapience, wiseness 10 perception 11 discernment, penetration, sensitivity 13 comprehension, judiciousness, understanding

sagamore 5 chief 6 sachem

sage 4 mint, sane, wise 5 acute 6 expert, master, nestor, savant, sophic 7 gnostic, knowing, learned, probing, prudent, sapient, scholar, wise man 8 polymath, profound, sensible 9 insighted, judgmatic, judicious, sagacious 10 discerning, insightful, perceptive 11 penetrating, philosophic 13 knowledgeable *Hindu:* 5 rishi 6 pandit 7 mahatma

Sagebrush State 6 Nevada

sage cock 6 grouse

Sage of ____ *Chelsea:* 7 Carlyle (Thomas) *Concord:* 7 Emerson (Ralph Waldo) *Emporia:* 5 White (William Allen) *Ferney:* 8 Voltaire *Monticello:* 9 Jefferson (Thomas) *Pylos:* 6 Nestor

sagging 8 swayback

Sagittarius 6 archer 7 centaur 13 constellation

saguaro 6 cactus

saharan 3 dry 4 arid, sere 6 barren 8 deserted

sail 3 fly 4 boat, dart, flit, scud, skim, wing 5 fleet, float, mizen, shoot, skirr, sweep, yacht 6 cruise, mizzen 7 spencer 9 spinnaker *triangular:* 3 jib 6 genoa

sailboat 4 bark, yawl 5 ketch, skiff, sloop 8 skipjack

sailing vessel 4 bark, brig, saic 5 xebec 6 barque 7 frigate, galleon 8 schooner 10 barkentine, brigantine

sailor 3 tar 4 jack, salt 5 jacky 6 seaman, swabby 7 jack-tar, mariner, swabbie, yachter 8 seafarer, shipmate 9 tarpaulin, yachtsman 10 bluejacket *British:* 5 limey *fictional:* 6 Sinbad *patron saint:* 4 Elmo *song:* 6 chanty 7 chantey 9 barcarole

saint *biography:* 11 hagiography *list:* 9 hagiology; (see also **patron saint**)

Saint, the 12 Simon Templar *creator:* 9 Charteris (Leslie)

Saint Anthony's cross 3 tau

Saint Elmo's Fire 9 corposant

Saint Joan author 4 Shaw (George Bernard)

Saint John's bread 5 carob

saintly 4 holy 5 godly, pious 6 devout, seraph, worthy 7 angelic, upright 8 seraphic, virtuous 9 righteous

Saint Paul's Church (London) *designer:* 4 Wren (Christopher)

Saint Peter's Basilica *architect:* 7 Bernini (Gian Lorenzo) 12 Michelangelo *sculpture:* 5 Pietà

Saint Vitus' dance 6 chorea

sake 3 end 4 good 5 drink 7 purpose

salaam 3 bow 8 greeting

salacious 4 fast, lewd 7 lustful, satyric 9 lecherous, libertine 10 lascivious, libidinous, licentious 11 incontinent

salad 4 brew, hash, stew, toss 5 chef's 6 Caesar 7 mélange *item:* 3 egg 4 bean, cuke, herb 5 cress, fruit, olive, onion 6 carrot, celery, cheese, endive, pepper, potato, radish, tomato 7 anchovy, cabbage, crouton, lettuce, parsley, spinach 8 chick-pea, coleslaw, cucumber, garbanzo, mushroom, scallion 10 watercress 11 cauliflower

salamander 3 eft 4 newt 8 mudpuppy, waterdog *Mexican:* 7 axolotl

salient 6 marked, moving, signal 7 obvious, weighty 8 striking 9 arresting, arrestive, important, intrusive, obtrusive, pertinent, prominent 10 impressive, noticeable, pronounced, remarkable 11 conspicuous, outstanding, significant

saline 4 salt 5 briny, salty 8 brackish 10 saliferous

saliva 4 spit 5 water 6 slaver, sputum 7 spittle

salivate 5 drool 6 drivel, slaver 7 dribble, slabber, slobber

____ Salk 5 Jonas

sallow 3 wan 4 pale 6 willow, yellow

sally 3 gag 4 gust, jape, jest, joke, quip 5 burst, crack, jaunt 6 junket, outing 7 flare-up 8 drollery, eruption, outburst 9 excursion, explosion, wisecrack, witticism

salmagundi see **hodgepodge**

salmon 4 parr, pink 5 smolt 6 grilse
7 essling, geelbec, sockeye 9 brandling
female: 4 raun *male:* 6 kipper *smoked:*
3 lox

Salmon *father:* 3 Hur 7 Nahshon *grandfather:* 5 Caleb *son:* 4 Boaz

Salmoneus *brother:* 7 Athamas 8 Sisyphus *daughter:* 4 Tyro *father:* 6 Aeolus
mother: 7 Enarete

Salome *composer:* 7 Strauss (Richard)
father: 5 Herod *husband:* 6 Philip 7 Zebedee 11 Aristobulus *mother:* 8 Herodias
son: 4 John 5 James

salon 4 hall, shop 5 suite 6 parlor 9 apartment, reception

saloon 3 bar 4 hall 6 tavern 7 barroom,
cantina, gallery, taproom 8 drinkery

salt 3 tar 4 jack, keep, NaCl 5 brine, salty
6 sailor, saline, seaman 7 jack-tar, mariner
8 salinize 9 sailorman, tarpaulin 10 saliferous

salt away 4 save 5 lay by, lay in, lay up,
put by 8 lay aside

saltpeter 5 niter, nitre

saltworks 6 salina 7 saltern

salty 4 blue, racy 5 briny, broad, shady,
spicy 6 purple, risqué, saline, wicked
7 caustic, mordant 8 brackish, off-color,
scathing 9 trenchant 10 mordacious, saliferous, suggestive

salubrious 4 good 7 bracing, healthy
8 hygienic, salutary 9 healthful, wholesome
11 stimulating 12 invigorating

Salus see Hygeia

Salu's son 5 Zimri

salutation 2 hi 4 hail 5 hello 7 Dear Sir
8 greeting *Arab:* 6 salaam *French:* 5 salut
German: 4 heil *Hawaiian:* 5 aloha *Italian:*
4 ciao *Latin:* 3 ave *Spanish:* 4 hola

salute 4 hail, heil 5 greet 6 accost, call to
7 address 8 greeting

salvage 4 save 6 ransom, redeem, regain,
rescue 7 deliver, reclaim, recover
8 retrieve

salvation 6 saving 7 keeping 9 preserval
11 conservancy, safekeeping 12 conservation, preservation, sustentation

Salvation Army founder 5 Booth (General William)

salve 3 aid 4 balm 5 cream 6 cerate,
chrism, remedy 7 unction, unguent 8 ointment 9 emollient, lubricant

salver 4 tray

salvo 4 hail 5 burst, spray, storm
6 shower, volley 7 barrage, tribute
9 broadside, cannonade, discharge, fusillade 11 bombardment, testimonial
12 appreciation

samaritan 6 helper 8 welldoer 10 benefactor

same 4 idem, like, very 5 equal, exact
7 coequal, identic, similar 8 constant
9 duplicate, identical, unfailing, unvarying
10 comparable, consistent, equivalent,
invariable, tantamount, unchanging

Samoa's capital 4 Apia 8 Pago Pago

samovar 3 urn

sampan 4 boat 5 skiff

sample 4 case, part, sign, unit 5 piece,
taste 7 element, example, portion, segment
8 fragment, instance, sampling, specimen
10 indication, individual 11 case history,
constituent 12 illustration

Samson *betrayer:* 7 Delilah *birthplace:*
5 Zorah *deathplace:* 4 Gaza *father:*
6 Manoah *tribe:* 3 Dan

Samson Agonistes author 6 Milton
(John)

Samuel *father:* 7 Elkanah *grandson:*
5 Heman *mother:* 6 Hannah

samurai 7 soldier, warrior *code:*
7 bushido

San Antonio *team:* 5 Spurs *landmark:*
5 Alamo

sanctify 5 bless 6 hallow 10 consecrate

sanctimonious 5 false 7 canting
9 deceiving, pharisaic 11 pharisaical
12 hypocritical, pecksniffian 13 self-righteous

sanction 2 OK 4 fiat, okay 5 leave 6 permit, ratify 7 approve, certify, consent,
endorse, license, support 8 accredit,
approval 9 allowance, authorize 10 commission, permission, sufferance 11 approbation, endorsement 12 confirmation, ratifi-
cation 13 authorization, encouragement

sanctity 8 holiness 9 godliness 11 saintliness, uprightness 13 righteousness

sanctuary 4 port 5 bamah, cover, haven,
oasis 6 asylum, covert, harbor, refuge,
shrine 7 retreat, sanctum, shelter 9 harborage, holy place

sanctum 6 shrine 9 holy place, sanctuary

sandal 4 zori 8 huarache, huaracho
winged: 7 talaria (plural)

sandbar 4 reef, spit 7 tombolo

sand hill 4 dune

sandpiper 4 knot, ruff, stib 5 reeve, terek
6 dunlin, teeter

sandstone deposit 6 flysch

sandwich 3 BLT, sub 4 club 5 hoagy
6 hoagie 7 grinder 9 submarine *combining form:* 6 burger *shop:* 4 deli

sandy 6 beachy, gritty 7 arenose, arenous
8 sabulose, sabulous

sane 3 fit 4 good, hale, sage, well, wise
5 lucid, right, sober, sound 6 cogent, normal 7 healthy, logical, prudent, sapient
8 all there, balanced, oriented, rational,
sensible 9 judgmatic, judicious, wholesome
10 compelling, convincing, reasonable,

well-liking 11 levelheaded 12 compos mentis

San Francisco *hill:* 3 Nob 7 Russian *tower:* 4 Coit

sangfroid 6 phlegm 7 ataraxy 9 aloofness, composure, unconcern 10 equanimity 11 self-control 12 indifference

sanguinary 4 gory 6 bloody 7 imbrued 9 homicidal, murdering, murderous 12 bloodstained, bloodthirsty

sanguine 4 gory 5 flush, ruddy 6 bloody, florid, secure, upbeat 7 assured, flushed, glowing, hopeful, imbrued 8 rubicund 9 confident, expectant, homicidal, murdering, murderous 10 optimistic, undoubtful 11 full-blooded, self-assured 12 bloodstained, bloodthirsty, Pollyannaish, undespairing 13 self-confident

sanitary 5 clean 8 hygienic 9 healthful

sanity 3 wit 4 mind 6 reason, senses 8 lucidity, saneness 9 soundness 12 intelligence 13 comprehension

Sanskrit 5 Indic 8 language *dialect:* 4 Pali *epic:* 8 Ramayana *school:* 3 tol *Scripture:* 4 Veda

Santa Lucia composer 5 Denza (Luigi)

sap 4 dupe, fool, gull, mark, ruin 5 blunt, chump, drain, wreck 6 pigeon, sucker, weaken 7 cripple, deplete, destroy, disable, exhaust, fall guy, saphead, unbrace 8 enervate, enfeeble, knock out 9 attenuate, schlemiel, undermine 10 debilitate

Saph's slayer 8 Sibbecai

sapid 5 tasty 6 savory 8 saporous 9 aperitive, palatable, relishing, toothsome 10 appetizing, flavorsome

sapience *see* **sagacity**

sapient *see* **sagacious**

sapling 4 tree 5 youth

Sapphira *coconspirator, husband:* 7 Ananias

Sappho *forte:* 6 poetry *island:* 6 Lesbos

sappy 5 crazy, loony, mushy, silly, soupy 6 absurd, drippy, insane, slushy, sticky 7 foolish, maudlin, mawkish 8 bathetic 11 harebrained, sentimental

Saracen 4 Arab 6 Muslim *hero:* 9 Rodomonte

Sarah *husband:* 7 Abraham *maid:* 5 Hagar *son:* 5 Isaac

sarcasm 3 wit 4 gibe, jest 5 humor, irony, scorn 6 rancor, satire 7 mockery 8 acerbity, acrimony, mordancy, raillery, repartee, ridicule, sneering 9 invective, sharpness 10 causticity, lampooning 13 corrosiveness *writer:* 7 ironist

sarcastic 3 dry 4 tart 5 acerb, sharp 6 biting, ironic 7 acerbic, caustic, cutting, cynical, jeering, mocking, mordant, pungent, satiric 8 incisive, sardonic, scathing, scornful, stinging 9 corrosive, trenchant

sarcophagus 4 tomb 6 coffin

sardine 4 sild 7 herring 8 pilchard

Sardinia's capital 8 Cagliari

sardonic 3 wry 6 ironic 7 caustic, cynical, jeering, mocking, satiric 8 derisive, scornful, sneering 9 corrosive, sarcastic, saturnine 10 disdainful 12 contemptuous

sarong 5 skirt 7 garment

Sarpedon *brother:* 5 Minos 12 Rhadamanthus *father:* 4 Zeus 7 Jupiter *mother:* 6 Europa 8 Laodamia

Sartor ____ 8 Resartus

Sartre work 4 Kean 6 Nausea 7 The Wall 8 The Flies 10 Baudelaire, Saint Genet

sash 4 belt 6 girdle 8 ceinture, cincture 9 waistband

sashay 4 perk 5 mince, strut 6 prance 7 flounce, swagger

Saskatchewan's capital 6 Regina

sass 4 guff 5 cheek, mouth, sauce 8 back talk, saucebox 9 insolence, sassiness 12 impertinence

sassafras 3 tea 6 saloop

sassy 4 bold, pert, wise 5 doggy, fresh, lippy, natty, nervy, smart 6 brazen, cheeky, dapper, spiffy, spruce, sprucy 7 bandbox, doggish, forward 8 impudent, malapert, sparkish 9 audacious, unabashed 11 smart-alecky, well-groomed

Satan 5 beast, demon, deuce, devil, fiend, viper 6 diablo 7 Lucifer, Old Nick, serpent, villain 8 Apollyon, devil-god, renegade, succubus 9 archfiend, Beelzebub 10 Old Scratch 13 Old Gooseberry

satanic 4 evil 6 wicked 7 demonic 8 demoniac, demonian, devilish, diabolic, fiendish 9 saturnine 10 serpentine, unhallowed 11 diabolonian

satanism 9 diabolism

satchel 3 bag 4 case 5 pouch 6 valise

sate 4 cloy, fill, glut, jade, pall 5 gorge, stuff 6 stodge 7 overeat, satiate, surfeit 8 overfill 9 overstuff

satellite 4 moon 6 cohort, minion 7 sectary, sputnik 8 adherent, disciple, favorite, follower, henchman, incident, partisan, sectator 9 ancillary, attendant, attending, supporter *of Jupiter:* 2 Io 6 Europa 8 Callisto, Ganymede *of Mars:* 6 Deimos, Phobos *of Neptune:* 6 Nereid, Triton *of Saturn:* 4 Rhea 5 Dione, Janus, Mimas, Titan 6 Phoebe, Tethys 7 Iapetus 8 Hyperion 9 Enceladus *of Uranus:* 5 Ariel 6 Oberon 7 Miranda, Titania, Umbriel

satiate *see* **sate**

satire 5 irony, spoof, squib 6 banter, parody 7 mockery, pasquil, takeoff 8 chaffing, raillery, ridicule, spoofery, travesty 10 causticity, lampoonery, pasquinade, persiflage

satiric 6 ironic 7 caustic, mocking 8 chaffing, farcical, ironical, spoofing 9 bantering, parodying 10 lampooning, ridiculing

satirist *English:* 5 Swift (Jonathan) 7 Marston (John) *French:* 8 Rabelais (François), Voltaire *Greek:* 8 Menippus *Roman:* 6 Horace 7 Juvenal, Persius 9 Petronius

satirize 4 mock 5 spoof 6 parody 7 cartoon, censure, lampoon 8 ridicule

satisfaction 6 amends 8 pleasure 9 atonement 10 attainment 11 contentment, fulfillment, restitution 13 gratification

satisfactory 2 OK 4 fair, good, okay 5 solid, sound, valid 6 cogent, decent, enough 8 adequate, all right, passable 9 competent, sufficing, tolerable 10 acceptable, convincing, sufficient 11 comfortable 13 unexceptional

satisfy 3 pay 4 fill, meet, quit, sate, suit 5 clear, humor, pay up, serve 6 answer, assure, induce, pacify, please, settle, square 7 appease, content, fulfill, gladden, gratify, indulge, placate, satiate, suffice, win over 8 clear off, convince, inveigle, persuade, pleasure 9 conform to 10 comply with

satrap 5 ruler 7 viceroy 8 governor, henchman 11 subordinate

saturate 3 sop, wet 4 soak, wash 5 bathe, imbue, madid, probe, souse, steep 6 charge, douche, drench, infuse, pierce, soaked, sodden, soused 7 instill, pervade, soaking, sopping, suffuse 8 drenched, dripping, permeate, waterlog 9 inoculate, penetrate, percolate, transfuse

Saturn see Cronus

saturnalia 4 orgy 5 party 7 debauch 9 bacchanal 11 bacchanalia

saturnine 4 dark, dour, glum, ugly 5 grave, staid, sulky, surly 6 gloomy, moping, morose, silent, solemn, somber, sullen 7 crabbed, serious 8 funereal, reserved, taciturn

satyric 4 lewd 5 horny, randy 7 goatish, lustful 8 prurient 9 lecherous, libertine, lickerish, salacious 10 lascivious, libidinous, licentious, passionate 12 concupiscent

sauce 4 guff, sass 5 mouth 6 relish 7 topping 8 back talk, pertness 9 condiment, impudence *kind:* 3 soy 4 hard, lear, mole 5 bercy, chili, curry, dashi, gravy, melba, pesto, salsa 6 catsup, chivry, Mornay, panada, Robert, tartar, tomato 7 catchup, chutnee, chutney, ketchup, marengo, Newburg, piquant, soubise, supreme, tartare, velouté 8 béchamel, duxelles, marinara, matelote, noisette, normande, normandy, poivrade, poulette, ravigote, remolade 9 bearnaise, lyonnaise, mariniere, remou-

lade 10 bordelaise, Provençale 11 hollandaise, vinaigrette

saucy see sassy

Saudi Arabia *capital:* 6 Riyadh *monetary unit:* 5 riyal

Saul *concubine:* 6 Rizpah *cousin:* 5 Abner *daughter:* 5 Merab 6 Michal *father:* 4 Kish *son:* 8 Jonathan *su[r]* *r:* 5 David *uncle:* 3 Ner *wife:* 7 Ahino[..]

saunter 4 mope, roam, rove, walk 5 amble, drift, mosey, tarry 6 bummel, linger, loiter, ramble, stroll, wander 7 meander 8 ambulate

sausage 5 wurst 6 banger, kishka, kishke, salami, Vienna, wiener 7 baloney, bologna, boloney, chorizo, saveloy 8 cervelat, chaurice, drisheen, kielbasa, pemmican 9 bratwurst, frankfort, frankfurt, pepperoni, Thuringer 10 knackwurst, knockwurst, liverwurst, mortadella 11 frankforter, frankfurter

sausage-shaped 10 botuliform

savage 4 fell, grim, rude, wild 5 brute, cruel, feral, harsh, rabid, rough 6 bloody, brutal, fierce, Gothic, Hunnic, rugged 7 bestial, brutish, Hunnish, inhuman, untamed, vicious, wolfish 8 barbaric, inhumane, primeval, ravenous, unbroken 9 barbarian, barbarous, butcherly, ferocious, heartless, murderous, primitive, rapacious, truculent, unsubdued, voracious 10 implacable, relentless 11 coldhearted, uncivilized, unharnessed, unrelenting 12 bloodthirsty, uncontrolled, uncultivated, unsocialized

savanna 5 plain 9 grassland

savant 4 sage 7 scholar, wise man

save 3 bar, but, yet 4 bank, keep, only, Stow 5 cache, guard, hoard, lay by, lay in, lay up, put by, set by, skimp, spare 6 bating, defend, except, keep up, manage, rescue, saving, scrimp, shield, unless 7 barring, besides, collect, deliver, deposit, however, husband, lay away, protect, reclaim, reserve, salvage, store up, sustain, unchain 8 conserve, lay aside, maintain, preserve, salt away, squirrel 9 aside from, economize, excluding, safeguard, stash away, stockpile, unshackle 10 accumulate 11 exclusive of

saving 3 but 6 beside, except 7 barring, besides, sparing, thrifty 9 aside from, except for, excluding, preserval, provident, salvation, stewardly 10 economical, husbanding, unwasteful 11 conservancy, safekeeping 12 conservation, preservation, sustentation

savoir faire 4 tact 5 grace, poise, taste 6 aplomb 7 address, dignity, manners 8 elegance 9 blaséness, diplomacy 10 confidence, experience, refinement 11 delicatesse, tactfulness 13 self-assurance

savor 4 feel, know, mark, tong 5 sapor, scent, smack, smell, taste, tinge, trait 6 flavor, relish, virtue 7 feature, quality 8 property, sapidity 9 affection, attribute, character 10 experience

savory 5 balmy, sapid, spicy, sweet, tasty 6 aromal 7 flavory, gustful, perfumy 8 aromatic, fragrant, perfumed, pleasing, redolent, tempting 9 ambrosial, aperitive, palatable, relishing, toothsome 10 appetizing, flaversome

saw 3 hew 4 word 5 adage 6 byword, saying 7 proverb

____ **saw** 3 bow, jig, pit, rip 4 band, buck, buzz, fret, hack, whip 5 chain, crown, saber 6 coping, scroll 7 compass, keyhole 8 circular, crosscut

sawbuck 5 horse 6 tenner 7 trestle 9 workhorse

sawhorse see **sawbuck**

saw-toothed 7 serrate, serried 8 serrated 11 denticulate

Saxon *serf:* 4 esne *warrior:* 5 thane

say 4 aver, avow, cite, give, mark, most, much, nigh, read, show, talk, tell 5 about, mouth, quote, speak, state, utter, voice 6 affirm, almost, assert, nearly, recite, record, remark, repeat 7 breathe, chime in, comment, declare, deliver, express, phonate, protest 8 announce, bring out, decision, indicate, proclaim, register, throw out 9 authority, enunciate, just about, pronounce 10 animadvert, articulate

saying 3 mot 4 word 5 adage, axiom, maxim 6 byword, dictum, truism 7 proverb

scab 5 crust 6 eschar 13 strikebreaker

scabbard 6 sheath

scabby 4 mean 5 scaly 7 blotchy 10 scurrilous

scabrous 5 downy, harsh, rough, scaly 6 craggy, jagged, knobby, knotty, rugged, scabby, scurfy, thorny, uneven 7 bristly, prickly, scraggy, unlevel 8 asperous, unsmooth

scads 3 lot 4 gobs, heap, much, slew, wads 5 loads, reams 6 oodles 7 jillion, million, umpteen, zillion 8 slathers, thousand, trillion 9 great deal, multitude 10 quantities

scaffold 5 stage 7 staging 8 platform

Scala, La *city:* 5 Milan *production:* 5 opera

scalawag see **scamp**

scald 4 bard, boil, burn, poet 6 scorch

scale 4 peel, rate, skin, upgo 5 climb, flake, gauge, mount, ratio, scute, strip 6 ascend, degree, scutum, squama 7 chip off, measure 8 escalade, escalate, flake off, spall off 9 exfoliate 10 desquamate, proportion 11 decorticate, excorticate *auxiliary:* 7 vernier *earthquake:* 7 Richter *temperature:* 6 Kelvin 7 Celsius 10 centigrade, Fahrenheit

scallion 4 leek 5 onion 7 shallot

scalp 4 skin 5 cheat 6 trophy

scalpel 5 knife 7 dissect

scamp 5 devil, joker, pixie, rogue 6 rascal, ribald 7 villain 8 mischief, scalawag, slyboots 9 prankster, skeezicks 11 rapscallion

scamper 3 fly, run 4 bolt, dash, flee, scud, shin, skip 5 scoot, shoot, skirr 6 scurry, sprint 7 dash off, make off, rush off, scuddle, scuttle, tear off, whip off, whiz off 8 hurry off, light out 9 hasten off, hurry away, skedaddle, speed away

scan 3 eye 4 view 5 audit 6 browse, review, survey 7 perusal, run over 8 analysis, glance at, scrutiny 9 check-over 10 glance over, inspection, run through 11 examination, flip through, leaf through, observation, riff through, skim through 12 thumb through

scandal 4 tale 7 calumny 8 reproach 9 aspersion, discredit, disrepute 10 backbiting, defamation, detraction

scandalize 4 slur 5 libel, shock, smear 6 defame, malign 7 asperse, slander 9 denigrate 10 calumniate

scandalmonger 5 tabby 6 gossip 8 gossiper, quidnunc, telltale 9 backbiter, carrytale, muckraker 10 talebearer

scandalous 7 heinous 8 libelous, shocking 9 atrocious, desperate, maligning, monstrous, traducing, vilifying 10 backbiting, calumnious, defamatory, detracting, detractive, outrageous, slanderous

Scandinavia 6 Norway, Sweden 7 Denmark, Finland, Iceland

Scandinavian see **Norse**

scant 4 poor 5 chary, close, short, skimp, spare, stint, tight 6 meager, meagre, scarce, scrimp, skimpy, sparse 7 scrimpy, wanting 8 exiguous 9 deficient 10 inadequate 12 insufficient

scantiness 4 lack 6 dearth 7 deficit, failure, paucity, poverty 8 scarcity, shortage, sparsity, underage 10 deficiency, inadequacy, scarceness, sparseness 11 defalcation 13 insufficience, insufficiency

scanty see **scant**

scapegoat 4 mark 5 patsy 6 target, victim 7 fall guy 11 whipping boy

Scapin 5 rogue, valet *author:* 7 Molière *employer:* 7 Léandre

scar 3 cut, mar 4 flaw, scab 5 score 6 damage, deface, defect, keloid 7 blemish, blister, scratch 8 cicatrix, pockmark 9 cicatrize, disfigure 13 disfigurement *on a seed:* 5 hilum

scarab 6 beetle

scaramouch see **scamp**

scarce 3 few, shy 4 just, rare 5 scant, short 6 barely, hardly, scanty, seldom 7 failing, wanting 8 sporadic, uncommon 9 curtailed, deficient, shortened, truncated 10 inadequate, infrequent, occasional 12 insufficient

scarceness see **scantiness**

scarcity see **scantiness**

scare 3 awe 5 alarm, panic, spook 6 freeze, fright 7 horrify, petrify, shake up, startle, terrify 8 affright, frighten, paralyze 9 terrorize

scarf 3 boa 5 ascot, fichu, nubia, plaid, shawl, stole 8 babushka, liripipe *Latin-American:* 6 tapalo *long:* 6 rebozo

Scarlet Letter, The *author:* 9 Hawthorne (Nathaniel) *character:* 5 Pearl, Roger 6 Arthur, Hester

Scarlet Pimpernel author 5 Orczy (Baroness Emmuska)

Scarlett's home 4 Tara

scary 6 afraid, aghast, spooky 7 anxious, fearful 8 spookish 9 terrified 10 frightened

scat 4 flee, jazz 5 scoot, scram 7 singing

scathe 4 flay 5 slash 6 scorch 7 blister, scarify, scourge 8 lambaste, lash into 9 castigate, excoriate

scathing 5 salty 6 brutal 7 burning, caustic, mordant, searing 9 scorching, trenchant 10 mordacious, sulphurous

scatological 4 foul 5 dirty, nasty 6 coarse, filthy, smutty, vulgar 7 obscene, raunchy 8 indecent

scatter 3 sow 4 cast, part, shed 5 sever, straw, strew 6 dispel, divide, splash 7 bestrew, break up, disband, discard, disject, diverge, spatter 8 dispense, disperse, separate, splatter, sprinkle 9 broadcast, dissipate 10 besprinkle, distribute 11 disseminate

scatterbrained 5 dizzy, giddy, silly 7 flighty, foolish 9 frivolous

scavenge 5 clean 7 cleanse, collect, extract, salvage

scavenger 5 hyena 7 vulture

scenario 4 plot 6 script 7 outline 10 screenplay

scene 3 set 4 site, spot, view 5 arena, field, place, sight, vista 6 locale, milieu, sphere 7 compass, culture, outlook, setting, tableau 8 backdrop, hangings, locality, location, stage set 10 background 11 environment, mise-en-scène 12 stage setting

scenery 3 set 5 decor, props 7 setting 8 stage set 9 furniture 10 properties 11 furnishings, mise-en-scène 12 stage setting

scent 4 balm, nose, odor 5 aroma, smell, sniff, snuff, spice, whiff 7 bouquet, essence, incense, odorize, perfume 9 aromatize, fragrance, redolence

scepter 4 mace 5 baton, staff 11 sovereignty

schedule 4 list, roll, sked, time 5 chart, slate, table 6 agenda, docket, record, roster 7 catalog, program 8 calendar, register, roll call 9 catalogue, timetable

scheme 4 plan, plot 5 cabal, order 6 design, device, devise 7 collude, connive, project 8 cogitate, conspire, contrive, game plan, intrigue, ordering, practice, proposal, strategy 9 blueprint, expedient, machinate 10 conspiracy 11 arrangement, contrivance, machination

schism 4 rent, rift 5 break, chasm, cleft, split 6 breach, heresy 7 dissent, fissure, rupture 8 cleavage, division, fracture 10 dissidence, divergence, heterodoxy, separation 11 unorthodoxy 12 estrangement

schizoid 5 split

schlemiel 4 fool 7 bungler 10 ne'er-do-well

schlepp 3 lug 4 drag, haul, jerk

schmaltzy 5 showy 6 florid 11 sentimental

schnoz 4 beak, nose

scholar 4 sage 5 pupil 6 savant 7 bookman, student, wise man 8 literati (plural), polymath 10 classicist *Hindu:* 6 pundit *Muslim:* 5 ulama, ulema

scholarly 7 erudite, learned, trained 8 educated, studious 10 scholastic 12 intellectual

scholarship 7 science 8 learning 9 education, erudition, knowledge 11 eruditeness, learnedness

scholastic 5 booky 6 versed 7 bookish, erudite, learned 8 academic, lettered, literary, pedantic 9 scholarly 10 conversant 11 book-learned, quodlibetic *life:* 8 academia

school 3 gam, pad 4 lead, show 5 guide, shoal, teach, train 6 direct, inform, manage 7 academy, advance, college, control, educate 8 instruct 9 cultivate 10 discipline *French:* 6 école, lycée *grounds:* 6 campus *Jewish:* 5 heder 7 yeshiva 8 yeshivah *judo:* 4 dojo *organization:* 3 PTA, PTO *religious:* 8 seminary *term:* 7 quarter 8 semester

schoolbook 4 text 6 primer, reader 7 speller

School for Scandal author 8 Sheridan (Richard Brinsley)

schooner 4 ship 5 stein, stoup 6 goblet, seidel 7 tumbler

science 4 lore 6 wisdom 8 learning 9 education, erudition, knowledge 11 information, scholarship *combining form:* 4 logy 5 logia, sophy *of agriculture:* 8 agronomy *of animals:* 7 zoology *of armorial bearings:* 8 heraldry *of criminal punishment:* 8 penology *of environment:* 7 ecology *of fermentation:* 8 zymology *of government:* 8 politics *of health:* 7 hygiene 9 hygienics *of heredity:* 8 genetics *of human behavior:* 10 psychology *of lawmaking:* 8 nomology *of measuring time:* 8 horology 10 chronology 11 chronometry *of motion:* 8 kinetics *of mountains:* 7 orology *of nutrition:* 8 sitology *of plants:* 6 botany *of projectiles:* 10 ballistics *of soils:* 8 agrology *of the earth:* 7 geology *of time:* 10 chronology 11 chronometry *of tumors:* 8 oncology *suffix:* 3 ics

scientific classification 8 taxonomy

sci-fi writer 3 Lem (Stanislaw) 4 Pohl (Frederick) 5 Clark (Arthur), Niven (Larry), Verne (Jules), Wells (Herbert George) 6 Aldiss (Brian), Asimov (Isaac), Bishop (Michael), Butler (Octavia), Delany (Samuel), Le Guin (Ursula), Miller (Walter) 7 Ballard (James Graham), Ellison (Harlan), Herbert (Frank), Van Vogt (Alfred Elton), Zelazny (Roger) 8 Anderson (Poul), Bradbury (Ray), Heinlein (Robert), Sturgeon (Theodore) 10 Silverberg (Robert)

scimitar 5 saber, sword

scintilla 3 jot 4 iota 5 trace 8 particle

scintillate 5 flash, gleam, glint 6 glance 7 glimmer, glisten, glitter, shimmer, sparkle, twinkle 9 coruscate

scoff 3 boo 4 gibe, jeer, jest, mock, twit 5 fleer, flout, rally, scorn, sneer, taunt 6 deride, quip at 7 contemn, despise, disdain, scout at 8 pooh-pooh, ridicule

scold 3 jaw, rag, wig 4 chew, lash, rail, rant, rate 5 baste, blame, brace, chide, croak, grill, grunt, harpy, hound, shrew, vixen 6 amazon, berate, grouch, grouse, harass, murmur, mutter, ogress, rebuke, revile, tongue, virago 7 bawl out, blister, censure, chew out, grumble, reprove, tell off, upbraid 8 admonish, denounce, execrate, fishwife, lambaste, objurate, reproach 9 criticize, dress down, excoriate, reprehend, reprimand, reprobate, termagant, Xanthippe 10 tongue-lash, vituperate

sconce 4 head, poll 5 cover 6 noggin, noodle, screen 7 shelter 11 candlestick

scoop 3 dig, dip 4 bail, beat, grub, lade, lift 5 gouge, ladle, spade 6 dig out, gather, pick up, shovel 8 excavate 9 exclusive

scoot 3 fly, run, zip 4 bolt, dash, flee, rush, shin, skip 5 fleet, hurry, scram, skirr 6 barrel, bustle, hasten, hustle, scurry, sprint 7 beeline, make off, scamper 8 highball 9 skedaddle

scope 4 area, play, room 5 ambit, orbit, range, reach, sweep 6 extent, leeway, margin, radius 7 breadth, compass, purview 8 fullness, latitude, wideness 9 amplitude, elbowroom, extension

Scopes trial lawyer 5 Bryan (William Jennings) 6 Darrow (Clarence)

scorch 4 bake, burn, cook, flay, melt, sear 5 broil, roast, slash 6 scathe, seethe, simmer 7 blister, scarify, scourge, swelter 8 lambaste, lash into 9 castigate, excoriate

score 3 cut, tab, win 4 bill, flay, gain, gash, goal, line, mark, nick, slit 5 cleft, notch, reach, slash, tally, total 6 arrive, attain, furrow, groove, grudge, rack up, record, scathe, scorch, scotch, thrive 7 account, achieve, invoice, make out, prosper, realize, ream out, scarify, scourge, scratch, succeed 8 flourish, lambaste, lash into 9 castigate, excoriate, reckoning, serration, statement 10 accomplish

scorn 4 gibe, jeer, mock, pooh 5 abhor, flout, scoff, scout, taunt 6 gibing 7 contemn, despise, despite, disdain, jeering, mockery 8 contempt, derision, despisal, flouting, look down, ridicule, scoffing, taunting 11 despisement 13 disparagement

Scorpius star 7 Antares

Scotch cocktail 6 Rob Roy

Scotch fiddle 4 itch, scab

scoter 7 sea coot, sea duck

Scotland's capital 9 Edinburgh

Scott, Sir Walter *novel:* 6 Rob Roy 7 Ivanhoe, Waverly 8 The Abbot 9 Woodstock 10 Kenilworth 11 Redgauntlet, The Talisman *poem:* 7 Marmion

___ **Scott case** 4 Dred

Scottish *cap:* 11 tam-o'-shanter *child:* 5 bairn *hero:* 5 Bruce (Robert) 7 Wallace (William) *hill:* 4 brae *landowner:* 5 laird *outlaw:* 6 Rob Roy *patron saint:* 6 Andrew *plaid:* 6 tartan *pudding:* 6 haggis *spirit:* 5 kelpy 6 kelpie *trousers:* 5 trews

scoundrel see **scamp**

scour 3 eat, fan, fly 4 beat, bite, comb, find, flit, flux, gnaw, grub, rake, rout, seek 5 erode, fleet, hurry, range, rifle, scrub, smoke, speed 6 bullet, forage, rocket, search 7 beeline, corrode, eat away, look for, ransack, rummage 8 finecomb, highball, wear away 9 ferret out 13 fine-tooth comb

scourge 3 hit 4 flay, flog, hide, lash, sack, whip, whop 5 curse, flail, knout, slash, waste, whale 6 lather, plague, ravage, scathe, scorch, stripe, thrash 7 blister, despoil, pillage, scarify 8 desolate, lambaste, lash into, spoliate 9 castigate, depre-

date, desecrate, devastate, excoriate
10 flagellate, pestilence

Scourge of God 6 Attila

scouting group 3 BSA, GSA

scow 3 hoy 5 barge 6 garvey 7 lighter

scowl 5 frown, glare, gloom, lower
6 glower

scrabble 6 scrawl 7 clamber, scratch
8 scramble, scribble, squiggle

scraggy 4 bony, lank, lean 5 gaunt,
harsh, lanky, rough, spare 6 jagged, rugged, skinny, uneven 7 angular, dwarfed,
scrawny, scrubby, spindly, stunted, unlevel
8 asperous, gangling, rawboned, scabrous,
skeletal 9 spindling, undersize

scram 4 kite 6 begone, decamp, get out
7 skiddoo, take off 8 clear out, hightail
9 skedaddle

scramble 4 hash 6 jumble, jungle, litter,
muddle, ramble, scurry, sprawl, tumble
7 clamber, clutter, rummage, scuttle, shuffle
8 mishmash, scrabble, straggle

scrap 3 bit, end, jot, ort, row 4 cast, chip,
dump, fray, junk, shed, spat, tiff, whit
5 brawl, broil, crumb, fight, set-to, shred,
speck, waste, whoop 6 affray, bicker, fracas, reject, slough, smitch, tittle 7 bobbery,
brabble, cashier, cutting, discard, fall out,
quarrel, scuffle, wrangle 8 fragment, jettison, leftover, particle, squabble, throw out
9 caterwaul, scrappage, throw away

scrape 3 fix, jam, rub 4 hole, rasp, spot
5 chafe, get by, grate, graze, grind, pinch,
screw, scuff, shave, skimp, spare, stint
6 abrade, corner, pickle, plight, scrimp
7 dilemma, scratch, trouble 8 get along,
struggle 11 predicament

scrappy 6 brawly 7 warlike 8 brawling,
militant 9 bellicose, brawlsome, combative,
truculent 10 battlesome, pugnacious
11 belligerent, contentious, quarrelsome

scratch 4 claw, rake, rasp 5 grate, score
6 scotch, scrape, scrawl 8 scrabble, scribble, squiggle

scrawl 6 doodle 7 scratch 8 inscribe,
scrabble, scribble, squiggle

scrawny 4 bony, lank, lean 5 gaunt,
lanky, spare 6 skinny 7 angular, scraggy
8 rawboned

scream 3 cry, yip 4 howl, riot, roar, wail,
yell, yowl 5 blare, shout 6 bellow, screak,
shriek, shrill, squeak, squeal 7 grumble,
protest, screech 8 complain 9 caterwaul

screech 4 hoot 6 pierce, screak, scream,
shriek, shrill, squeal

screen 4 blip, bury, fend, hide, sift, sort
5 cache, cloak, close, cover, guard, shade,
sieve, stash 6 censor, choose, defend,
embosk, riddle, secure, select, shadow,
shield, shroud 7 bulwark, conceal, cover
up, extract, pick out, protect, seclude,

secrete, shut off, shut out, sort out,
umbrage, wall off 8 blindage, block out,
disguise, ensconce, obstruct, separate
9 expurgate, filter out, inumbrate, safeguard, winnow out 10 bowdlerize, camouflage *Japanese:* 5 shoji

screw 5 crimp, exact, gouge, pinch, skimp,
spare, stint, wrest, wring 6 extort, rimple,
ruck up, rumple, scrape, scrimp, skinch,
wrench 7 crimple, crinkle, crumple,
scrunch, squeeze, wrinkle 8 thumbkin
9 shake down

screwy 3 mad 4 daft, nuts 5 wacky
6 insane 7 cracked, lunatic, unsound
10 unbalanced

scribble 5 write 6 scrawl, scribe 7 jot
down, scratch 8 scrabble, squiggle

scribe 5 clerk, write 6 author, writer
7 copyist 9 secretary

scrimmage 4 fray 5 brawl, broil, brush,
clash, fight, melee, set-to 6 affray, fracas,
mellay 7 scuffle 8 skirmish 10 donnybrook, free-for-all

scrimp 4 save 5 stint 6 save up, scrape
9 economize

script 4 hand, text 10 penmanship 11 calligraphy, chirography, handwriting

scrivener 6 notary, scribe, writer 7 copyist

scrooge 5 miser 7 niggard 8 muckworm,
tightwad 9 skinflint 10 cheapskate
12 moneygrubber

scrub 3 rub 4 buff, drop, wash 5 brush,
scour 6 cancel, mallee, maquis, polish
7 call off, cleanse 8 inferior 9 chaparral,
secondary, subaltern, underling 11 subordinate

scruff 4 nape, neck

scruffy 5 seedy, tacky 6 shabby, tagrag
7 run-down, scrubby 8 tattered 10 downat-heel, threadbare

scrumptious 5 yummy 8 adorable, heavenly, luscious 9 ambrosial, delicious
10 delectable, delightful

scruple 3 bit, jot 4 atom, balk, fret, iota
5 demur, grain, qualm, scrap, shred, worry
7 modicum 8 particle, question 9 faltering,
hesitancy 11 compunction

scrupulous 4 just, true 5 exact, fussy,
right 6 honest, strict 7 careful, heedful,
upright 8 critical, punctual 9 honorable
10 fair-minded, fastidious, meticulous,
upstanding 11 painstaking, punctilious
12 conscionable 13 conscientious

scrutinize 3 eye 4 comb, scan 5 audit,
probe, study, watch 6 peruse, survey
7 analyze, canvass, check up, dig into, dissect, examine, eyeball, inspect 8 consider,
look over, pore over 9 check over 11 contemplate, perlustrate

scrutiny 3 eye 4 scan 5 audit, watch
6 look-in, review, survey 7 look-see 8 anal-

ysis, eagle eye, lookover **9** check-over **10** inspection **11** examination **12** surveillance **13** perlustration

scuba diver 7 frogman **8** aquanaut

scuff 6 scrape **7** scratch, shamble, shuffle

scuffle 3 row **4** cuff, fray **5** brawl, broil, fight, scrap, set-to **6** affray, fracas, shovel, tussle **7** bobbery, grapple, shamble, shuffle, wrestle

scull 3 oar, row **4** boat **6** propel

sculpt 5 carve **6** chisel

sculptor *American:* **4** Gabo (Naum), Taft (Lorado) **5** Andre (Carl), Pratt (Bela), Segal (George), Smith (David), Story (William) **6** Aitkin (Robert), Calder (Alexander), French (Daniel Chester), Powers (Hiram), Zorach (William) **7** Borglum (Gutzon), Noguchi (Isamu) **8** Lachaise (Gaston), Lipchitz (Jacques), Nadelman (Elie), Nevelson (Louise) **9** Bourgeois (Louise), Mestrovic (Ivan), Remington (Frederic) **12** Saint-Gaudens (Augustus) *Czech:* **6** Stursa (Jan) *Danish:* **11** Thorvaldsen (Bertel), Thorwaldsen (Bertel) *Dutch:* **6** Sluter (Claus) *English:* **5** Moore (Henry), Watts (George) **7** Epstein (Jacob), Flaxman (John) **8** Hepworth (Barbara) *French:* **3** Arp (Hans, Jean) **4** Bloc (Andre) **5** Rodin (Auguste) **6** Dubois (Paul), Houdon (Jean-Antoine) **7** Maillol (Aristide), Pevsner (Antoine) **9** Bartholdi (Frederic-Auguste), Roubillac (Louis-François) *Greek:* **5** Myron **7** Phidias **10** Polyclitus, Praxiteles **11** Polycleitus *Italian:* **5** Leoni (Leone), Salvi (Niccolò, Nicola) **6** Canova (Antonio), Pisano (Andrea, Nino), Robbia (Andrea, Giovanni, Girolamo, Luca della) **7** Bernini (Gian Lorenzo), Cellini (Benvenuto), da Vinci (Leonardo), Orcagna, Quercia (Jacopo della) **8** Ghiberti (Lorenzo), Vittoria (Alessandro) **9** Donatello, Sansovino (Jacopo) **10** Verrocchio (Andrea del) **12** Michelangelo *Rhodian:* **9** Polydorus *Romanian:* **8** Brancusi (Constantin) *Russian:* **7** Zadkine (Ossip) *Swedish:* **6** Milles (Carl) *Swiss:* **10** Giacometti (Alberto)

scum 3 cur, mob **5** dregs, dross, skunk, snake, trash **6** masses, rabble, refuse **7** stinker **8** canaille, riffraff, unwashed

scummy 3 low **4** base, mean, vile **5** cheap, sorry **6** scurvy, shabby **8** beggarly, pitiable **10** despicable, despisable **12** contemptible

scurrilous 4 foul **5** dirty, gross, nasty **6** coarse, filthy, smutty, vulgar **7** abusive, obscene, raunchy **8** indecent **9** insulting, invective, offending, offensive, outraging, truculent **10** outrageous, vituperous **11** opprobrious **12** blackguardly, contumelious, vituperative, vituperatory

scurry 3 fly, run **4** dart, dash, shin, tear **5** scoot, shoot **6** sprint **7** scamper, scuffle, scutter, scuttle, skelter

scurvy see **scummy**

scut 4 tail

scuttlebutt 4 buzz, talk **5** on-dit, rumor **6** gossip, report, rumble **7** hearsay **9** grapevine

Scylla 4 rock *father:* **5** Nisus *lover:* **5** Minos; (see also **Charybdis**)

scythe handle 5 snath **6** snathe

sea 4 blue, deep, main **5** brine, briny, drink, ocean *Antarctica:* **4** Ross **5** Davis **7** Weddell **8** Amundsen *Arctic:* **4** Kara **7** Chukchi **8** Beaufort, Karskoye **9** Chuckchee, Norwegian **11** Chukotskoye **12** East Siberian *Asia-Europe:* **5** Black *Asia Minor:* **7** Icarian *Atlantic:* **5** North **7** Weddell **9** Caribbean *Australia-Indonesia:* **7** Arafura *Balkan Peninsula-Italy:* **8** Adriatic *Bay of Bengal:* **7** Andaman *China-Korea:* **5** Huang, Hwang **6** Yellow *combining form:* **3** mer **4** mari **5** pelag **6** pelago **7** thalass **8** thalasso *Corsica-Italy:* **10** Tyrrhenian *Denmark-Norway:* **8** Skagerak **9** Skagerrak *Denmark-Sweden:* **8** Kattegat *England-Ireland:* **5** Irish *Fiji:* **4** Koro *France-Italy:* **8** Ligurian *Greece:* **5** Crete *Greece-Italy:* **6** Ionian *Greece-Turkey:* **6** Aegean **8** Thracian *Honshu:* **6** Sagami *Indian Ocean:* **4** Savu, Sawu **5** Timor **7** Arabian *Indonesia:* **4** Bali **6** Flores *inland:* **3** Red **4** Aral **7** Caspian *Japan:* **3** Iyo, Suo **6** Inland *largest island:* **7** Caspian *Malay Archipelago:* **5** Banda *Mexico:* **6** Cortes *Netherlands:* **6** Wadden *North Atlantic:* **8** Sargasso *Northern Europe:* **6** Baltic, Ostsee **8** Suevicum **10** Baltiskoye *North Pacific:* **6** Bering *Novaya Zemlya-Svalbard:* **7** Barents *off Scotland:* **8** Hebrides *off Sweden:* **5** Aland *Pacific:* **4** Java **5** China, Coral **6** Maluku **7** Celebes, Eastern, Molucca, Solomon **9** East China, Moluksche **10** South China *Philippine:* **4** Sulu *Russia:* **5** White **7** Okhotsk *Russia-Ukraine:* **4** Azov **9** Azovskoye *South Pacific:* **4** Ross **6** Tasman **8** Amundsen *Turkey:* **7** Marmara **9** Propontis *West Pacific:* **5** Ceram, Japan **8** Bismarck **10** Philippine

sea anemone 7 actinia

seabird see **bird**, *aquatic*

sea channel 6 strait **7** euripus

sea coot 6 scoter **9** guillemot

sea cucumber 7 trepang **11** holothurian

sea dog see **sailor**

sea duck 5 eider, scaup **6** scoter **9** merganser

sea eagle 3 ern **4** erne **6** osprey

seafood dish 4 clam, crab, tuna **5** scrod **6** oyster, shrimp **7** lobster, scallop

seagoing 8 maritime, nautical

seal 5 sigil, stamp 6 cachet, signet
7 sticker *bearded:* 6 makluk *eared:*
5 otary *female:* 3 cow 5 matka *herd:*
3 pod 5 patch *male:* 8 seecatch *young:*
3 pup

sealant 4 lute 6 luting

sea lily 7 crinoid

seallike 7 phocine

seam 4 bond 5 joint, union 7 joining
8 coupling, junction, juncture 10 connection

seaman see **sailor**

sea monster 3 Orc *legendary:* 6 kraken

seamount *flat-topped:* 5 guyot

seamy 5 dirty, rough, seedy 6 sordid
12 disreputable

séance 7 meeting, session, sitting *holder:*
6 medium

seaport *Adriatic:* 5 Split 6 Spljet *Aegean:*
5 Vathy *Alaska:* 9 Anchorage *Albania:*
5 Vlona, Vlorë *Algeria:* 4 Bona, Oran
5 Arzew 6 Annaba 9 Arsenaria, Cherchell,
Shershell *Angola:* 6 Lobito 7 Cabinda
8 Benguela 9 Mocamedes *Argentina:*
7 La Plata *Australia:* 4 Eden 5 Bowen
8 Brisbane, Wallaroo 10 Wollongong
Azores: 5 Horta *Balearic:* 5 Ibiza *Baltic:*
5 Visby *Belgium:* 6 Ostend *Benin:*
6 Kotonu 7 Cotonou *Black Sea:* 6 Odessa
Bosnia and Herzegovina: 4 Omis *Brazil:*
3 Rio 4 Para 5 Bahia, Belem, Natal
6 Recife, Santos 8 Salvador 10 Pernambuco 11 Pôrto Alegre, São Salvador
12 Rio de Janeiro *Bulgaria:* 5 Varna *Cameroon:* 5 Campo, Duala, Kampo, Kribi
Canaries: 8 Arrecife *Celebes:* 7 Makasar
8 Macassar, Makassar *Chile:* 4 Lebu, Lota
5 Ancud, Arica 8 Coquimbo 10 Valparaiso
China: 4 Amoy 6 Lushun, Xiamen *Colombia:* 6 Lorica 9 Cartagena *Corsica:*
5 Calvi *Costa Rica:* 10 Puntarenas *Cri-
mean:* 10 Sevastopol *Croatia:* 4 Senj
5 Zadar 9 Dubrovnik *Cuba:* 5 Banes
Cyprus: 7 Limasol 8 Limassol 9 Famagusta *Delaware:* 5 Lewes *Denmark:*
5 Arhus, Ronne, Vejle 6 Aarhus, Alborg
7 Aalborg 8 Elsinore *Djibouti:* 4 Obok
5 Obock 6 Tajura 8 Tadjoura *Ecuador:*
5 Manta 9 Guayaquil *Egypt:* 4 Said 8 Al
Qusayr, Al Quseir, El Qoseir 10 Alexandria
England: 10 Portsmouth *Equatorial
Guinea:* 4 Bata *Eritrea:* 4 Aseb *Estonia:*
5 Parnu 6 Pyarnu 7 Tallinn *Ethiopia:*
4 Zula *Finland:* 3 Abo 4 Kemi, Oulu, Pori,
Vasa 5 Hango, Kotka, Rauma, Turku,
Vaasa 8 Uleaborg 10 Bjorneborg *Florida:*
5 Miami, Tampa 8 Pensacola 12 Apalachicola, Jacksonville *France:* 4 Meze, Nice
5 Havre, Nizza 6 Calais, Cannes, Toulon
7 Dunkirk, Le Havre, Lorient 8 Bordeaux,
Boulogne 9 Cherbourg, Dunkerque, Mar-

seille 10 Marseilles *French Polynesia:*
7 Papeete *Georgia:* 9 Brunswick *Georgia,
Republic of:* 4 Poti *Germany:* 4 Kiel
5 Bremen, Emden, Husum 6 Wismar
8 Cuxhaven 11 Bremerhaven
13 Wilhelmshaven *Ghana:* 4 Keta 6 Kwitta
Greece: 4 Kimi, Kyme 5 Pylos, Syros,
Volos 7 Piraeus 8 Peiraeus *Guatemala:*
7 San José 10 Livingston *Gulf of Aden:*
5 Alula *Haiti:* 5 Cayes 8 Aux Cayes *Honduras:* 8 Trujillo *India:* 3 Goa 4 Puri
5 Marud 6 Old Goa 9 Jagannath 10 Juggernaut *Ionian:* 5 Corfu *Iran:* 4 Jask
7 Bushehr, Bushire *Iraq:* 5 Basra *Ireland:*
4 Cork 5 Sligo 6 Dingle, Tralee 10 Balbriggan *Israel:* 4 Acre, Akko, Elat, Yafa
5 Accho, Eilat, Elath, Haifa, Jaffa, Joppa
9 Ptolemais, Sycaminum *Italy:* 4 Bari
5 Anzio, Gaeta, Genoa, Pizzo, Trani
6 Naples, Pesaro, Venice 7 Leghorn,
Rapallo, Salerno, Taranto, Trieste, Venedig
8 Sorrento 10 Senigallia *Ivory Coast:*
4 Tabu 5 Tabou *Jamaica:* 10 Montego
Bay *Japan:* 5 Kochi, Rumoi, Ujina, Uraga
6 Sasebo 7 Fukuoka 8 Nagasaki, Yokohama *Java:* 5 Tegal, Tuban 8 Samarang,
Semarang, Surabaja, Tjirebon *Jordan:*
5 Akaba, Aqaba, Elath 6 Aelana *Latvia:*
4 Riga 9 Ventspils *Lebanon:* 5 Saida
7 Tripoli *Libya:* 4 Homs 5 Khoms
6 Tobruk *Lithuania:* 5 Memel 8 Klaipeda
Madagascar: 8 Tamatave *Maine:* 7 Belfast 8 Portland *Malaysia:* 4 Miri, Weld
5 Pekan 6 Melaka, Pinang 7 Malacca
10 George Town *Massachusetts:* 9 Fall
River *Mauritius:* 5 Louis *Mediterranean:*
4 Gaza, Oran, Said 5 Genoa, Haifa, Jaffa
6 Bayrut, Beirut 7 Algiers, Bizerte, Catania,
Tripoli 8 Benghazi 9 Barcelona 10 Alexandria, Marseilles *Mexico:* 8 Acapulco, Veracruz *Minorca:* 5 Mahon *Moluccas:*
5 Ambon *Montenegro:* 5 Kotov *Morocco:*
3 Sla 4 Safi, Sale 5 Ceuta, Saffi 6 Agadir
7 Larache, Tangier 10 Casablanca *Mozambique:* 5 Beira, Pemba 6 Amelia, Xai Xai
11 Porto Amelia *New Hampshire:* 10 Portsmouth *New Zealand:* 8 Auckland *Nicaragua:* 5 Brito *Nigeria:* 8 Harcourt *Niger
mouth:* 5 Bonny *North Korea:* 4 Yuki
5 Unggi *Norway:* 4 Bodo, Moss 5 Vadso
6 Tromso 9 Stavanger, Trondheim, Trond-
hjem 11 Fredrikstad *Oman:* 3 Sur 5 Sohar
6 Matrah *Pakistan:* 5 Pasni *Panay:* 6 Iloilo
Papua New Guinea: 3 Lea *Peru:* 3 Ilo
4 Eten 5 Paita, Pisco *Philippines:* 4 Cebu
5 Davao, Laoag 6 Aparri, Cavite, Iloilo,
Manila 7 Legaspi 8 Tacloban 9 Zamboanga *Poland:* 6 Gdynia 7 Gdingen,
Stettin 8 Szczecin *Portugal:* 4 Faro
5 Lagos 6 Oporto 7 Funchal 9 Lacobriga
Puerto Rico: 5 Ponce *Russia:* 3 Kem

5 Anapa, Sochi 6 Vyborg 11 Kaliningrad, Vladivostok *Ryukyu:* 4 Naha, Nawa *Sakhalin Island:* 8 Korsakov *Saudi Arabia:* 4 Wejh 5 Jidda, Qatif, Yanbu, Yenbo 6 Juddah 7 Djeddah *Scotland:* 3 Ayr 4 Oban 5 Alloa, Largs, Leven 6 Dundee *Sicily:* 5 Avola 7 Messina, Palermo 8 Syracuse *Slovenia:* 5 Kopar, Koper, Piran *Somalia:* 7 Berbera, Kismayu 9 Chisimaio *South Africa:* 6 Durban 8 Cape Town, Kaapstad *South Carolina:* 10 Charleston *South Korea:* 5 Mason, Mokpo 6 Inch'on, Jinsen 7 Masampo 8 Chemulpo *Spain:* 4 Adra, Noya, Vigo 5 Cadiz, Gadir, Gijon, Marin 6 Abdera 8 Alicante 9 Cartagena, Las Palmas *Sri Lanka:* 10 Batticaloa *Sumatra:* 6 Padang *Sweden:* 4 Umea 5 Gavle, Lulea, Malmo, Pitea, Ystad 8 Göteborg 10 Gothenburg *Tanzania:* 5 Lindi, Tanga *Thailand:* 4 Trat 8 Bang Phra *Tunisia:* 4 Sfax 5 Gabes 7 Bizerte, Safaqis *Turkey:* 4 Rize 5 Coruh, Sinop 6 Coroch *Ukraine:* 7 Kherson *U.S. Virgin Islands:* 8 St. Thomas *Vanuatu:* 4 Vila *Vietnam:* 6 Da Nang 7 Tourane 8 Haiphong, Nha Trang *Virginia:* 10 Portsmouth *Yemen:* 5 Mocha, Mokha 7 Hodeida; (see also **seaport capital**)

seaport capital 4 Aden, Apia, Lomé, Suva 5 Accra, Adana, Alger, Dakar, Lagos 6 Banjul, Belize, Bissão, Bissau, Boston, Dublin, Eblana, Havana, Juneau, Kuwait, Lisbon, Maputo, Masqat, Muscat, Roseau 7 Algiers, Batavia, Colombo, Icosium, Jakarta, Moresby, San Juan 8 Al-Jazā'ir, Al-Kuwait, Bathurst, Castries, Djakarta, Freetown, Hamilton, Helsinki, Honolulu, Kingston, La Habana, Monrovia, Valletta 9 Annapolis, Mogadishu, Nukualofa, Porto-Novo, Reykjavík, Singapore 10 Bridgetown, Daressalem, Libreville, Mogadiscio, Paramaribo 11 Dar es Salaam, Port of Spain 12 Port-au-Prince

sear 3 dry 5 parch 6 burn up, scorch, sizzle 7 shrivel 9 cauterize, dehydrate, desiccate, exsiccate

search 4 beat, comb, grub, hunt, peer, rake, scan, seek 5 check, delve, frisk, quest, rifle, scour, study 6 ferret, forage, pry out 7 examine, hunting, inspect, manhunt, pursual, pursuit, ransack, rummage, run down, seeking 8 finecomb, look over, pursuing, scavenge, scout out, skirmish 9 cast about, ferret out, pursuance, scrimmage, shake down 10 scrutinize 11 scout around 13 fine-tooth comb *for gold:* 7 fossick

sea robber 5 rover 6 pirate 7 corsair 8 picaroon 9 buccaneer 10 freebooter

sea rover see **sea robber**

seasickness 8 mal de mer 9 naupathia

season 3 fit 4 fall, salt, term, time 5 spice, steel, train 6 autumn, harden, pepper, period, school, spring, summer, winter 7 prepare, toughen 8 marinade, marinate 9 acclimate, climatize 10 case harden, discipline 11 acclimatize

seasonable 3 apt 6 timely 7 apropos, timeous 8 relevant 9 favorable, opportune, pertinent, well-timed 10 auspicious, convenient, propitious, prosperous 11 appropriate

seasoning 4 herb, sage, salt 5 spice 6 fennel, garlic, pepper 7 cayenne, mustard, paprika 9 condiment

seat 3 bed, hub, put, sit 4 base, beam, rest 5 basis, focus, heart, place, usher 6 behind, bottom, center, settee 7 footing, fulcrum 8 backside, basement, buttocks, derriere, polestar 9 establish, fundament, posterior 10 focal point, foundation, groundwork 11 nerve center *church:* 3 pew *on a camel or elephant:* 6 howdah *upholstered:* 9 banquette

sea urchin 7 echinus 8 echinoid

seaweed 4 agar, alga, kelp 5 dulse 6 murlin 7 henware 9 carrageen 11 badderlocks *brown:* 6 fucoid 8 gulfweed, rockweed, sargasso *edible:* 4 ulva 7 redware *purple:* 9 carrageen, Irish moss

Sea Wolf, The *author:* 6 London (Jack) *captain:* 10 Wolf Larsen *ship:* 5 Ghost

Sebastian *brother:* 6 Alonso *sister:* 5 Viola

secede 4 quit 5 leave 8 withdraw

seclude 4 hide 6 closet, immure, retire, screen 7 confine, enclose, isolate, shut off 8 cloister, separate, withdraw 9 sequester

seclusion 7 privacy 8 solitude 9 aloneness, isolation 10 detachment, retirement, separation, withdrawal 11 privateness 12 separateness

second 3 aid 4 abet, back, wink 5 flash, jiffy, trice 6 assist, minute, moment 7 endorse, instant, support 9 twinkling *combining form:* 4 deut 5 deuto 6 deuter 7 deutero

secondary 3 sub 5 dinky, minor, scrub, small, under 6 lesser 7 derived, subject 8 borrowed, derivate, inferior, small-fry 9 accessory, dependent, resultant, smalltime, subaltern, tributary, underling 10 collateral, consequent, derivative, secondhand, subsequent 11 minor-league, subordinate, subservient *prefix:* 3 sub

second-class 4 hack, mean, poor 6 common 8 déclassé, inferior, low-grade

secondhand 4 used, worn 7 derived 8 borrowed

second-rate see **second-class**

second-string 3 sub 10 substitute

secrecy 4 hush 7 silence, stealth 8 hush-hush 10 censorship, covertness, subterfuge 11 concealment, furtiveness

secret 4 deep 5 heavy, sneak 6 covert, hidden, occult, orphic, remote 7 devious, furtive, obscure, removed, retired, sub-rosa 8 abstruse, esoteric, hermetic, hush-hush, lonesome, mystical, profound, screened, stealthy, unavowed 9 concealed, recondite 10 acroamatic, classified, restricted, undeclared, undercover 11 clandestine, out-of-the-way, underhanded 12 confidential, hugger-mugger 13 surreptitious, under-the-table *combining form:* 5 crypt, krypt 6 crypto, krypto

secret agent 3 spy 8 emissary

secretaire 4 desk 10 escritoire

secretary 4 desk 5 clerk 6 scribe 10 amanuensis, escritoire *king's:* 10 chancellor

secrete 4 bury, hide 5 cache, cover, exude, plant, stash 6 screen 7 conceal, deposit 8 ensconce, withhold

secretly 7 sub rosa 8 covertly 9 furtively 10 stealthily

secret society 3 KKK 4 Poro, tong 5 Mafia 7 camorra 10 Ku Klux Klan

sect 4 cult 5 creed, faith 6 church 8 religion 9 communion 10 connection, persuasion 12 denomination

sectarian 5 local 7 insular 8 splinter 9 dissident, heretical, heterodox, parochial, small-town 10 provincial, schismatic, unorthodox 13 nonconformist

sectary 5 bigot, rebel 6 cohort, hippie 7 beatnik, heretic, liberal, radical 8 adherent, bohemian, disciple, follower, henchman, maverick, partisan, sectator 9 dissenter, dissident, satellite, supporter, Young Turk 10 schismatic, separatist 11 misbeliever, schismatist 13 nonconformist, revolutionary

section 3 cut 4 area, belt, part, zone 5 field, piece, slice, split, tract 6 divide, member, moiety, parcel, region, sector, sphere 7 break up, portion, quarter, segment 8 district, division, locality, precinct, separate, vicinity 9 territory 11 subdivision *combining form:* 4 tome, tomy

sector 7 quarter, section 8 district, precinct

secular 3 lay 7 profane 8 temporal, unsacred 11 nonclerical 12 nonreligious

secure 3 bag, fix, get, set 4 bind, fast, fend, firm, gain, have, iron, land, lock, make, moor, nail, safe, sure, take 5 annex, catch, cause, chock, cinch, clamp, cover, fixed, guard, rivet, solid, sound, tight, tried 6 anchor, assure, cement, clinch, collar,

defend, draw on, effect, ensure, fasten, insure, obtain, pick up, pinion, pledge, screen, shield, stable, strong, trusty 7 acquire, assured, bulwark, capture, chalk up, prehend, procure, produce, protect, settled, staunch, tie down 8 balanced, reliable, riskless, sanguine 9 confident, safeguard, tenacious 10 batten down, bring about, dependable, underwrite, undoubtful 11 established, self-assured, trustworthy 12 tried and true 13 self-confident

security 4 bail, bond, pawn, ward 5 aegis, armor, guard, token 6 pledge, safety, shield, surety 7 defense, earnest, warrant 8 armament, firmness, guaranty, safeness, strength, warranty 9 assurance, guarantee, safeguard, soundness, stability 10 protection, stableness, steadiness 13 certification

sedan 3 car 4 auto, limo 10 automobile

sedate 4 calm 5 grave, sober, staid 6 placid, proper, seemly, serene, solemn, somber 7 earnest, serious, weighty 8 composed, decorous, tranquil 9 collected, dignified, unruffled 10 no-nonsense, sobersided 13 dispassionate, imperturbable

sedative 4 balm 7 calmant 8 barbital, hyoscine, pacifier, quietive 9 calmative 10 depressant 11 barbiturate 12 sleeping pill, tranquilizer

sedentary 4 lazy 7 settled 8 inactive 10 stationary

sediment 4 lees, silt, slag 5 draff, dregs, dross 6 scoria 7 bottoms, deposit, grounds, heeltap 9 recrement, settlings 11 precipitate 13 precipitation *layer:* 5 varve

sedition 4 coup 6 action, mutiny, putsch, revolt, strike 7 protest, treason 8 uprising 9 coup d'etat, rebellion 10 alienation, revolution 12 disaffection, estrangement, insurrection

seditious 7 lawless, violent 8 disloyal, factious, mutinous 9 alienated, dissident, faithless, insurgent 10 perfidious, rebellious, traitorous 11 disaffected, treacherous

seduce 4 bait, coax, lure, rape, ruin, undo 5 decoy, tease, tempt, train 6 allure, betray, delude, entice, entrap, lead on, ravish 7 corrupt, debauch, deceive, degrade, enslave, mislead, pervert, violate 8 deflower, entrance, inveigle 9 overpower, overwhelm

seducer 7 Don Juan 8 lothario

seduction 4 call, draw, lure, pull, rape, ruin 6 appeal 9 siren song, violation 10 allurement, attraction, corruption, perversion, ravishment, seducement, temptation 11 deflowering

seductive 5 siren 7 drawing, vampish 8 alluring, magnetic 9 desirable 10 attract-

ing, attractive, bewitching, enchanting
11 captivating, fascinating, provocative

seductress 5 siren **7** Lorelei **9** temptress
11 femme fatale

sedulous 4 busy **6** active **7** operose
8 diligent, hustling **9** assiduous **10** persistent **11** industrious, persevering, unremitting

see 4 call, date, espy, gape, gaze, have,
hear, know, lead, look, mark, mind, note,
peek, peep, peer, scan, show, take, twig,
vide, view **5** catch, fancy, glare, grasp,
guide, learn, pilot, pop in, probe, route,
sight, stare, steer, study, think, visit, watch,
weigh **6** accept, attend, behold, come by,
descry, direct, divine, drop by, drop in,
escort, follow, go with, look in, look up,
notice, pierce, ponder, remark, step in, stop
by, stop in, suffer, take in, tumble, vision
7 catch on, conduct, discern, examine, feature, find out, foresee, glimpse, imagine,
·inspect, look out, make out, observe, preknow, previse, realize, sustain, take out,
undergo, unearth **8** appraise, come over,
conceive, consider, discover, envisage,
envision, forefeel, foreknow, perceive,
shepherd, watch out **9** accompany, apprehend, ascertain, determine, penetrate, prevision, recognize, visualize **10** anticipate,
comprehend, experience, scrutinize, understand **11** distinguish **12** discriminate

seed 3 bud, sow **4** core, germ **5** brood,
image, issue, ovule, plant, put in, spark
6 embryo, kernel, notion, scions **7** conceit,
concept, nucleus, progeny **8** children, rudiment **9** offspring, posterity **10** conception,
impression **11** progenitors, progeniture
aromatic: **6** fennel *coating:* **5** testa **6** tes-
tae (plural) *combining form:* **3** gon
4 cocc, gono, spor **5** cocci, cocco, sperm,
spori, sporo **6** sperma, spermi, spermo
7 spermae (plural), spermat **8** spermato
covering: **4** aril *medicinal:* **7** ignatia *of a
bean:* **7** haricot *of an herb:* **3** pea, soy
4 soya **7** soybean *of a vine:* **6** peanut
palm tree: **6** jarina *poisonous:* **10** castor
bean *prickly:* **6** bonduc *vessel:* **3** pod
5 fruit, pyxis **7** pyxides, pyxidia (plural), silicle, siliqua **8** pyxidium, sillique

seedcase 3 pod

seedy 5 dingy, faded, messy, tired
6 droopy, shabby, untidy, wilted **7** run-
down, sagging, unkempt, wilting **8** decrepit,
drooping, flagging, slovenly, tattered
9 neglected, overgrown **10** bedraggled,
down-at-heel, threadbare

seek 3 dig, try **4** fish, hunt, nose, root
5 assay, delve, essay, mouse, offer, quest,
sniff **6** strive **7** attempt, bird-dog
8 endeavor, smell out, struggle **9** cast

about, ferret out, search for, search out,
undertake

seem 4 hint, look **5** imply, sound **6** appear
7 suggest **8** intimate, resemble **9** insinuate

seeming *combining form:* **5** quasi

seemly 4 nice **5** right **6** decent, proper
7 correct **8** becoming, decorous, pleasing
9 befitting, congenial, congruous, consonant **10** compatible, conforming, consistent
11 comme il faut

seep 4 drip, flow, leak, ooze, weep
5 bleed, exude, sweat **6** strain **8** transude

seer 5 augur **6** auspex **7** prophet **8** foreseer, haruspex **9** predictor **10** forecaster,
foreteller **11** Nostradamus

seesaw 3 yaw **4** cant, lean, list, rock, roll,
swag, sway, tilt, toss **5** lurch, pitch **6** teeter, tilter **7** bascule, incline

seethe 3 sop **4** boil, burn, fret, fume, rage,
soak, stew, stir, teem **5** anger, churn,
erupt, souse, steam, steep, swarm
6 abound, blow up, bubble, drench, simmer, sizzle, sodden **7** bristle, ferment, flare
up, parboil **8** boil over, overflow, saturate,
waterlog **10** bubble over, impregnate

see-through 5 clear **6** limpid **8** pellucid
11 translucent, transparent

segment 3 cut **4** part **5** piece **6** divide,
member, moiety, parcel, set off **7** isolate,
portion, seclude, section **8** division, separate **10** categorize

sego 4 lily

segregate 6 choose, cut off, enisle,
island, select, single **7** isolate **8** close off,
insulate, separate **9** sequester **10** disconnect

segregation 9 apartheid, isolation, seclusion **10** jim crowism, separation, separatism **12** separateness **13** ghettoization

Segub's father 4 Hiel **6** Hezron

seidel 3 cup, mug **5** stein, stoup

seine 3 net **5** trawl

seismologist 7 Richter (Charles)

seize 3 nab **4** grab, take **5** annex, catch,
grasp, usurp **6** abduct, arrest, clutch, kidnap, occupy, secure, snap at, snatch, strike
7 afflict, capture, grapple, impound, preempt **8** accroach, arrogate, carry off, overtake, take over **9** apprehend, latch onto,
sequester, spirit off **10** commandeer, confiscate, fasten onto, spirit away **11** appropriate, expropriate

seizure 3 fit **4** turn **5** spell, throe
6 access, attack, taking **9** breakdown
10 convulsion

seldom 3 few **4** rare **6** hardly, little, rarely,
scarce **7** unoften **8** scarcely, sporadic,
uncommon **10** hardly ever, infrequent,
occasional **11** irregularly **12** infrequently,
occasionally, sporadically

select 3 top 4 best, cull, fine, mark, pick, rare, take 5 elect, elite 6 choice, choose, chosen, culled, dainty, optate, opt for, picked, prefer, single 7 elegant, favored 8 blue-chip, delicate, eclectic, screened, superior 9 exclusive, exquisite, preferred, recherché, single out, weeded out 11 winnowed out

selection 5 draft 6 acumen, choice, option 7 culling, excerpt, insight, picking 8 choosing, drafting, election 10 preference 11 alternative, discernment

selective 5 fussy, picky 6 choosy 7 choosey, finicky 8 eclectic 10 particular, scrupulous

Seled's father 5 Nadab

Selene 4 Luna 6 Hecate 7 Artemis *beloved:* 8 Endymion *brother:* 6 Helios *father:* 8 Hyperion *mother:* 4 Thea

selenium *symbol:* 2 Se

self 3 ego *combining form:* 3 aut 4 auto

self-acting 9 automatic

self-assertive 4 bold, sure 6 uppish, uppity 7 forward, pushful, pushing 8 cocksure, militant 9 audacious, intrusive, obtrusive, officious, presuming 10 aggressive, meddlesome 11 impertinent, overweening 12 presumptuous

self-assurance 6 aplomb 8 coolness 9 composure, sangfroid, self-trust 10 confidence, equanimity 13 collectedness

self-assured 4 smug 6 secure 8 sanguine 9 confident 10 undoubtful

self-complacent 4 smug 8 priggish

self-composed 4 calm, easy 6 placid, poised, serene 8 tranquil 9 collected, possessed

self-confidence 6 aplomb, hutzpa 7 chutzpa, hutzpah 8 chutzpah, sureness 9 assurance, cockiness, self-trust 12 sanguineness 13 self-assurance

self-confident 5 cocky, janty 6 jaunty, secure 7 assured, cockish 8 sanguine 10 undoubtful

self-conscious 4 prim 5 stiff 6 formal, uneasy 7 anxious, flaunty, stilted 8 affected, mannered 9 ill at ease 10 artificial 12 ostentatious

self-control 4 will 7 balance, dignity, reserve 9 stability, willpower 10 constraint, discipline

self-defense 4 judo 6 aikido, karate 7 jujitsu, jujutsu

self-destruction 7 suicide 8 felo-de-se, hara-kiri

self-discipline 4 will 9 willpower

self-effacing 3 shy 5 timid 6 modest 7 bashful, rabbity 8 backward, retiring 9 diffident, unassured 11 unassertive

self-esteem 5 pride 6 vanity 7 conceit 10 narcissism 11 amour propre

self-evident 5 clear, plain 7 obvious 8 manifest 10 prima facie 12 unmistakable

self-explanatory 5 clear, plain 7 evident, obvious 8 manifest

self-governing 7 popular 10 autonomous, democratic

self-importance 5 pride 6 egoism 7 conceit, egotism 9 arrogance, pomposity, vainglory

self-important 5 puffy, wiggy 6 stuffy 7 bloated, pompous 8 arrogant 10 pontifical 11 magisterial

self-indulgent 9 sybaritic 10 hedonistic, sybaritish 11 sybaritical

self-interest 6 egoism

selfish 6 stingy 7 hoggish, hoglike 8 egoistic 9 egotistic 10 egocentric 11 egomaniacal

self-love 6 vanity 7 conceit, narcism 8 vainness 9 vainglory 10 narcissism 11 amour propre 13 conceitedness

self-possessed 4 calm, easy 5 aloof 6 placid, poised, serene 8 composed, reserved, tranquil 9 collected, easygoing

self-proclaimed 9 soi-disant 10 self-styled

Self-Reliance author 7 Emerson (Ralph Waldo)

self-respect 5 pride 11 amour propre

self-righteous 7 canting 9 pharisaic 11 pharisaical 12 hypocritical, pecksniffian 13 sanctimonious

self-sacrificing 6 kindly 8 generous, selfless 9 unselfish 10 charitable 13 philanthropic

self-satisfied 4 smug 8 priggish 10 complacent

self-seeking 7 selfish 8 egoistic, selfhood 9 egotistic 10 egocentric 11 egomaniacal

self-service *combining form:* 5 teria

self-serving see **self-seeking**

self-starter 6 dynamo, peeler 7 hustler, rustler 8 go-getter, live wire

self-styled 5 quasi 7 would be 8 so-called 9 self-given, soi-disant

self-taught 12 autodidactic

sell 3 net 4 draw, hawk, mart, sale, vend 5 bring, fetch, trade, yield 6 barter, betray, deal in, market, peddle, retail, return 7 auction, bring in, command, realize, traffic 8 exchange

sell out 4 dump, move 5 cross 6 betray, delude, humbug, take in, unload 7 beguile, deceive, mislead 8 close out 9 four-flush, sacrifice 11 double-cross

selvage 4 edge

semblance 3 air 4 aura, face, feel, look, mask, mood, pose, show, veil 5 front, guise 6 aspect, facade, simile, veneer 7 analogy, feeling, seeming, showing 8 affinity, disguise, likeness 9 alikeness 10 appearance, atmosphere, comparison, false front, masquerade, similarity, similitude, simulacrum **11** resemblance

Semele *father:* **6** Cadmus *mother:* **8** Harmonia *sister:* **3** Ino **5** Agave **7** Autonoe *son:* **7** Bacchus **8** Dionysus

semi **4** demi, half, hemi **6** partly **7** partial

seminar **8** colloquy **10** colloquium, conference

Seminole chief **7** Osceola

Semiramis *husband:* **5** Ninus *kingdom:* **7** Babylon

Semite **3** Jew **4** Arab **6** Hebrew **7** Maobite **8** Assyrian **9** Canaanite **10** Babylonian, Phoenician

Senapo *daughter:* **8** Clorinda *kingdom:* **8** Ethiopia

senate **7** council **8** assembly **11** legislature

senator **5** solon **8** lawmaker **10** legislator

send **4** mail, post, rush, ship **5** relay, remit, route **6** assign, commit, export, launch, thrill **7** address, advance, airmail, consign, enthuse, forward, mission, traject **8** allocate, delegate, dispatch, expedite, transmit **9** electrify *back:* **6** remand *forth:* **4** emit **7** emanate

senectitude see **senescence**

Senegal *capital:* **5** Dakar *monetary unit:* **5** franc

senescence **6** old age **8** caducity **11** elderliness, senectitude

senile **3** old **4** aged, weak **5** aging **6** doting, feeble **7** ancient, doddery **8** decrepit, doddered **9** doddering, enfeebled, senescent, shattered

senility **6** dotage **7** decline **8** caducity **10** senescence

senior **5** doyen, elder, older **6** better **7** ancient, doyenne, oldster **8** brass hat, higher-up, old-timer, superior **10** goldenager

Sennacherib *domain:* **7** Assyria *father:* **6** Sargon *kingdom:* **7** Assyria *slayer, son:* **8** Sharezer **11** Adrammelech

sensation **4** bomb **5** sense **6** marvel, wonder **7** feeling, miracle, portent, prodigy, stunner **8** response **9** bombshell **10** impression, perception, phenomenon **11** sensibility, sensitivity **13** consciousness, sensitiveness *combining form:* **8** esthesio **9** aesthesio

sensational **3** hot **5** boffo, juicy, livid, lurid, smash **6** coarse, divine, groovy, marked, signal, sultry, vulgar **7** colored, piquant, pointed, pungent, rousing, salient, sensory, sensual, tabloid **8** crashing, glorious, slambang, smashing, stunning **9** arresting, hunky-dory, marvelous, prominent, sensatory, sensitive, sensorial, super-

fine **10** impressive, noticeable, remarkable **11** conspicuous, extravagant, outstanding

sense **3** wit **4** core, deem, feel, gist, hold, know, meat, pith **5** focus, short, smell, think **7** believe, feeling, meaning, message, nucleus, purport, realize **8** consider, gumption, judgment, perceive, prudence **9** awareness, foresight, mentality, mother wit, substance **10** anticipate, brainpower, cognizance, discretion, intendment **11** acceptation, discernment, penetration, recognition **12** appreciation, intelligence, significance, significancy **13** comprehension, consciousness, signification, understanding *sixth:* **3** ESP

Sense and Sensibility author **6** Austen (Jane)

senseless **4** cold, dead, numb, surd **5** silly **6** asleep, numbed, simple, wooden **7** foolish, trivial, unaware, unwitty, witless **8** benumbed, comatose, deadened, mindless **9** brainless

senselessness **5** folly **7** inanity **8** insanity **9** absurdity, craziness, dottiness, silliness, stupidity **11** foolishness, witlessness **12** illogicality

sense organ **3** ear, eye **4** nose, skin **6** tongue

sensibility **5** heart, sense **7** emotion, feeling, insight **8** keenness **9** affection, sensation **11** discernment, penetration, sensitivity

sensible **4** good, sage, sane, wise **5** alive, awake, aware, gross, smart, solid, sound **6** noting, patent, seeing **7** evident, knowing, logical, obvious, prudent, sapient, sizable, witting **8** concrete, imaginal, manifest, material, palpable, physical, rational, sentient, tangible **9** au courant, cognizant, conscious, corporeal, judgmatic, judicious, objective, observing, remarking, sensitive, weighable **10** consequent, conversant, detectable, observable, perceiving, perceptual, phenomenal, reasonable, responsive

sensitive **4** keen, open, sore **5** acute, aware, prone, sharp, tense **6** liable, seeing, touchy, tricky **7** exposed, feeling, knowing, nervous, psychic, sensile, sensory, sensual, subject **8** affected, delicate, disposed, inclined, sensible, sentient, ticklish, unstable **9** cognizant, conscious, emotional, impressed, irritable, obnoxious, sensatory, sensorial **10** high-strung, influenced, insultable, perceiving, perceptive, precarious, responsive, susceptive, umbrageous **11** emotionable, impressible, predisposed, sensational, susceptible **13** understanding

sensitive plant **6** minosa *family:* **3** pea

sensual **4** lush **6** animal, carnal, earthy **7** fleshly, mundane, sensory, worldly **8** banausic, luscious, sensuous, temporal **9** epicurean, luxurious, sensatory, sensitive, sensorial **10** voluptuous **11** irreligious, sensational, unspiritual **13** materialistic

sensuous 4 lush **6** carnal, fleshy **7** bacchic, fleshly, sensual **8** luscious **9** dionysiac, Dionysian, epicurean, luxurious, sybaritic **10** hedonistic, voluptuous **12** sensualistic **13** self-indulgent

sentence 4 damn, doom, rule **5** blame, judge **6** devote, ordain, punish **7** adjudge, condemn **8** denounce, penalize **9** proscribe **10** adjudicate

sententious 4 rich **5** crisp, pithy, terse **6** facund **7** concise, piquant **8** eloquent, pregnant **10** aphoristic, expressive, meaningful **11** significant

sentiment 3 eye **4** bias, mind, view **6** belief **7** emotion, feeling, leaning, opinion, passion, posture **8** penchant, position, tendency **9** affection, inclining, sensation **10** conception, conviction, partiality, persuasion, propensity **11** affectivity, disposition, inclination **12** emotionalism

sentimental 4 soft **5** gooey, gushy, inane, moist, mushy, sappy, sobby, soupy, sweet, vapid **6** dreamy, drippy, jejune, loving, slushy, sobful, sticky, sugary, syrupy, tender **7** gushing, insipid, maudlin, mawkish **8** bathetic, effusive, romantic, schmalzy **9** misty-eyed, nostalgic, rosewater **10** lovey-dovey, moonstruck, namby-pamby, passionate, saccharine, soft-boiled, sugar-candy **11** tear-jerking **12** affectionate **13** demonstrative

sentimentalist 5 softy **6** softie

sentimentality 4 mush **7** schmalz **8** schmaltz

sentinel see **sentry**

sentry 4 ward **5** guard, watch **6** picket **7** lookout, outpost **8** sentinel, watchman

separate 3 one **4** comb, free, know, lone, only, part, sift, solo, sort **5** apart, halve, ravel, sever, split **6** cut off, detach, dispel, divide, enisle, island, single, sunder, unglue, unique, unjoin, unknit, unlink, winnow **7** break up, discern, disjoin, dislink, dispart, dissect, diverse, divorce, isolate, quarter, rupture, scatter, several, split up, unravel, various **8** alienate, autarkic, close off, detached, diffract, discrete, disjoint, disperse, dissever, dissolve, distinct, disunify, disunite, estrange, insulate, peculiar, solitary, splinter, uncouple, unmingle, unsolder **9** autarchic, different, discharge, disengage, disrelate, extricate, muster out, segregate, sequester, sovereign, uncombine **10** autonomous, demobilize, difference, discrepate, disengaged, disgregate, dissociate, particular, severalize **11** compartment, dichotomize, disassemble, discontinue, distinctive, distinguish, independent **12** disaggregate,

disconnected, discriminate **13** differentiate

flax: **7** hatchel *into filaments:* **6** sleave

separation 6 schism **7** breakup, divorce, parting, rupture, split-up **8** disunion, disunity, division, shedding **9** apartheid, dichotomy, dispersal, partition **10** detachment, diffluence, diremption, dissection, separatism, trichotomy **11** disjointure, disjunction, disrelation, dissolution, divorcement, segregation **12** dissociation **13** disconnection, sequestration

separatism 9 apartheid **11** segregation

separatist 7 heretic, sectary **9** dissenter, dissident **10** schismatic **11** misbeliever, schismatist **13** nonconformist

sepia 3 ink **4** gray **5** brown

sepulcher 4 bury, tomb **5** grave, inter, plant **6** burial, entomb, inhume **7** lay away, put away

sequel 3 end, row **5** chain, close, issue, order, train **6** effect, ending, finish, result, series, upshot **7** closing, outcome **8** causatum, epilogue, sequence **9** aftermath, finishing **10** succession **11** aftereffect, alternation, consecution, consequence, development, eventuality, progression, termination **12** continuation

sequence 3 row **5** chain, issue, order, train **6** effect, result, sequel, series, upshot **7** outcome **8** disposal, grouping, ordering **9** aftermath, cavalcade, placement **10** procession, succession **11** aftereffect, alternation, arrangement, consecution, disposition, eventuality, progression **12** distribution

sequential 6 serial **9** succedent **10** succeeding, successive **11** consecutive **12** successional

sequester 4 hide, take **5** annex, seize **6** attach, cut off, enisle, island **7** impound, isolate, preempt, seclude, secrete **8** accroach, arrogate, cloister, close off, insulate, separate **9** segregate **10** commandeer, confiscate, dispossess **11** appropriate, expropriate

seraglio 5 harem **6** bagnio **7** brothel, lupanar **8** bordello

Serah's father 5 Asher

Seraiah *brother:* **6** Baruch **7** Othniel *father:* **5** Asiel, Kenaz **7** Hilkiah **9** Tanhumeth *grandson:* **4** Jehu **6** Jeshua *son:* **4** Joab **7** Jozadak **9** Joshibiah

seraphic 4 pure **7** angelic, sublime

sere 3 dry **4** arid **5** parch **7** bone-dry, thirsty **8** droughty **9** unwatered, waterless **12** moistureless

Sered's father 7 Zebulun

serene 4 calm, easy **5** quiet, still **6** placid, poised **7** resting **8** composed, tranquil

serf 4 esne, peon **5** churl, helot, slave **6** thrall **7** villein *freeborn:* **7** colonus

series 3 row, run, set 4 tier 5 chain, group, scale, train 6 catena, column, parade, sequel, string 8 category, sequence 9 cavalcade, gradation 10 procession, succession 11 alternation, consecution, continuance, progression 12 continuation

serious 4 fell, grim, hard, ugly 5 grave, heavy, major, sober, staid, stern, tough 6 intent, sedate, severe, solemn, somber, steady 7 arduous, austere, earnest, intense, operose, pensive, unfunny, weighty 8 grievous, menacing, resolute, sobering 9 dangerous, difficult, humorless, important, laborious, strenuous, unamusing 10 determined, formidable, meditative, nononsense, poker-faced, purposeful, reflective, sobersided, thoughtful, unhumorous 11 significant, steady-going, threatening 12 businesslike 13 contemplative

sermon 6 homily, preach, tirade 7 lecture 8 harangue 9 preaching 10 preachment 11 exhortation

sermonize 6 preach 7 descant, discuss, dissert 8 dilate on, homilize, moralize 9 discourse, expatiate, preachify 10 dilate upon, dissertate, evangelize

serpent 5 devil, fiend, Satan, snake 6 dipsas *combining form:* 4 ophi 5 ophio, ophis *fabled:* 8 basilisk *mythical:* 10 cockatrice *sound:* 4 hiss

serpentine 5 snaky 7 crooked, demonic, devious, satanic, sinuous, winding 8 demoniac, demonian, devilish, diabolic, fiendish, flexuous, tortuous 9 meandrous, snakelike 10 convoluted, meandering

serrated 6 scored 7 notched, serried, toothed 8 indented, saw-edged, sawtooth 10 saw-toothed 11 denticulate

Serug *father:* 3 Reu *son:* 5 Nahor

servant 4 maid 5 valet 6 butler, menial 7 famulus, footman 8 domestic, handmaid, houseboy, houseman, servitor 9 attendant 11 chamberlain, chambermaid *India:* 4 syce *kitchen:* 8 scullion *Wodehouse:* 6 Jeeves

serve 3 act, fit, use 4 make, play, suit, take, work 5 avail, nurse, put in, spend, treat 6 foster, handle, mother, profit, wait on 7 advance, benefit, care for, forward, further, promote, satisfy, service, suffice, undergo, work for 8 deal with, function, minister 9 advantage, encourage, officiate 10 minister to

service 3 use 4 duty, rite 5 avail, cater, favor 6 action, combat, ritual 7 account, fitness, liturgy 8 ceremony, courtesy, fighting, kindness 9 advantage, formality, relevance 10 active duty, ceremonial, indulgence, observance, usefulness 12 dispensation 13 applicability

servile 3 low 4 base, mean, ugly, vile 6 abject, menial, scurvy, sordid 7 ignoble, passive, slavish, toadish 8 obedient, obeisant 9 groveling 10 despicable, obsequious, submissive 11 bootlicking, subservient, unresisting

servility 4 yoke 7 bondage, helotry, peonage, serfage, serfdom, slavery 9 servitude, thralldom 11 enslavement

serving 6 dollop 7 portion

sesame 3 til *grass:* 4 gama *seed:* 8 gingelly

session 6 assize 7 meeting, sitting *combining form:* 4 fest

set 3 aim, dry, fit, fix, gel, kit, lay, lot, put 4 firm, jell, park, sink 5 affix, array, batch, brood, bunch, crowd, fixed, group, place, put on, ready, rigid, scene, sited, stick 6 anchor, belong, circle, clique, gelate, go down, harden, impose, placed, rooted, secure, stated 7 arrange, certain, cluster, congeal, decided, deposit, descend, dictate, emplace, express, faction, install, jellify, lay down, limited, located, prepare, scenery, situate, specify, station, valuate 8 appraise, ensconce, estimate, evaluate, fastened, grouping, prepared, resolute, resolved, situated, solidify, specific 9 confirmed, designate, establish, prescribe, specified, stipulate, tenacious, unbending 10 assortment, determined, entrenched, gelatinize, inflexible, positioned, prescribed, stipulated, unyielding 11 established, mise-en-scène *a gem:* 6 collet *right:* 7 redress

set apart 7 isolate, seclude 8 dedicate

set aside 4 void 5 annul 8 overrule

set back 4 mire 5 delay, embog 6 detain, hang up, retard, slow up

setback 5 check 6 defeat, rebuff 7 reverse 8 comedown, obstacle, reversal 9 hindrance 10 impediment, regression

set down 4 land 5 light, perch, roost 6 alight, record 9 establish, touch down

set fire to 4 burn 6 ignite 7 emblaze, inflame

set free 7 manumit, unloose 8 liberate, unloosen, untangle 10 emancipate

Seth *brother:* 4 Abel, Cain *father:* 4 Adam *mother:* 3 Eve *son:* 4 Enos

set off 5 start 7 actuate, balance 8 activate, atone for, outweigh 9 circulate 10 compensate 11 countervail 12 counterpoise

set out 4 head, plan 5 start, state 6 design, intend 7 arrange, present, take off 9 undertake

Set's victim 6 Osiris

setting 5 scene 7 scenery 11 mise-en-scène *for a stone:* 4 ouch

settle 3 fix, lay, pay, put 4 calm, land, lull 5 allay, clear, light, pay up, perch, place, quiet, roost, stick, still 6 alight, becalm, clinch, decide, soothe, square, wind up 7 arrange, clean up, compose, concert, install, resolve, satisfy, set down, sit down 8 clear off, colonize, conclude, ensconce 9 determine, discharge, establish, negotiate, reconcile, touch down 11 tranquilize

settlement 7 quietus, village 8 decision 9 agreement 10 conclusion, habitation, resolution 13 determination *Israeli:* 6 moshav

settler 7 pioneer 8 colonist 9 colonizer

set-to 3 row 4 fray 5 brawl, broil, brush, fight, run-in, scrap 6 affray, fracas, hassle 7 bobbery, dispute, quarrel, rhubarb, scuffle 8 skirmish 9 bickering, encounter 10 falling-out, velitation 11 altercation

set up 4 blow, open, rear 5 elate, erect, found, put up, raise, stand, start, treat 6 create, excite, launch 7 build up, commove, inspire, start up, usher in 8 generate, initiate, organize, spirit up 9 construct, establish, hammer out, institute, introduce, originate

seven *combining form:* 4 hept, sept 5 hepta, septi *group of:* 6 heptad 8 hebdomad

seventeenth century 8 seicento

sever 3 cut 4 chop, part 5 carve, slice, split 6 cleave, divide, sunder 7 break up, dissect, divorce 8 disjoint, separate

severe 3 raw 4 dear, dour, grim, hard, sore 5 acute, bleak, grave, harsh, heavy, rigid, sharp, smart, sober, stern, tough 6 bitter, brutal, crimpy, rugged, savage, stormy, strict, wintry 7 arduous, ascetic, austere, drastic, extreme, hostile, intense, onerous, painful, serious, weighty 8 blustery, exacting, rigorous, toilsome 9 difficult, effortful, inclement, laborious, mortified, strenuous, stringent 10 astringent, blistering, blustering, forbidding, inflexible, ironwilled, oppressive, unpleasant, unyielding 11 disciplined, heavy-handed, intemperate, restrictive 12 disagreeable, inhospitable

sew 4 darn, mend, seam 5 baste 6 needle, stitch, suture

sewing *aid:* 7 thimble *case:* 4 etui *kit:* 5 hussy 9 housewife

sewing-machine inventor 4 Howe (Elias)

sexless 6 neuter 7 epicene

sex manual 9 Kama-sutra

sexton 9 custodian, sacristan

sexual *combining form:* 3 gam, gon 4 gamo, gono

sexual desire 4 eros

sexy 4 blue, racy 5 broad, salty, shady, spicy 6 erotic, purple, risqué 8 off-color 10 suggestive

Sganarelle *brother:* 6 Ariste *daughter:* 7 Lucinde *ward:* 7 Leonore 8 Isabelle *wife:* 7 Martine

Shaaph *father:* 5 Caleb 6 Jahdai *mother:* 6 Maacah

shabby 4 bare, mean, poor 5 cheap, dingy, dowdy, faded, mangy, ratty, seedy, shady, sorry, tacky, tired 6 ruined, scummy, scurvy, shoddy, sleazy, sordid, tagrag 7 outworn, rickety, ruinous, rundown, scrubby, scruffy, squalid, worn-out, wrecked 8 beggarly, decaying, decrepit, desolate, dog-eared, pitiable, shameful, slipshod, tattered 9 abandoned, miserable, moth-eaten, neglected, worm-eaten 10 bedraggled, broken-down, despicable, despisable, disfigured, down-at-heel, inglorious, ramshackle, threadbare 11 dilapidated, disgraceful, ignominious 12 contemptible, deteriorated, dishonorable, disreputable 13 deteriorating, discreditable, unrespectable

shack 3 cot, hut 4 camp 5 cabin, hovel, lodge 6 shanty 7 cottage

shackle 3 tie 4 clog, curb, gyve, lash, rope 5 bilbo, bonds, chain, gyves, irons, leash, strap 6 anklet, chains, collar, fetter, hamper, hobble, hog-tie, pinion, secure 7 enchain, fetters, garrote, leg-iron, manacle, trammel 8 bracelet, handcuff 9 entrammel

shad 4 fish 7 clupeid, herring

shade 3 hue 4 cast, hint, tint, tone, veil 5 bogey, color, cover, ghost, spice, tinge, trace, umbra 6 awning, nuance, screen, shadow, spirit, streak 7 dimness, phantom, shelter, soupçon, specter, umbrage 8 darkness, penumbra, phantasm, tincture 9 blackness, gradation, intensity, inumbrate, obscurity, suspicion, variation 10 apparition, difference, saturation, suggestion 11 adumbration, distinction, obscuration

shadow 3 dim, dog, tag 4 haze, hint, tail 5 bedim, bedog, cloud, relic, shade, shady, smack, tinge, touch, trace, trail, umbra 6 breath, screen, shaded, spirit, wraith 7 becloud, eidolon, memento, obscure, phantom, predict, specter, suggest, umbrage, umbrous, vestige 8 forecast, foretell, overcast, penumbra, phantasm, revenant, shadowed, tincture 9 adumbrate, inumbrate, overcloud, prefigure, suspicion 10 apparition, intimation, suggestion, umbrageous 11 adumbration, prefigurate *combining form:* 3 sci 4 scia, scio, skia

shadowbox 4 spar

shadowy 3 dim 4 dark 5 faint, vague
7 ghostly 8 adumbral 10 indistinct

shady 4 blue, dark, racy 5 bosky, broad,
dusky, fishy, salty, spicy 6 purple, risqué,
shabby, shoddy, wicked 7 clouded, shadowy, suspect, úmbrous 8 doubtful, off-
color, screened, shadowed, shameful
9 equivocal, sheltered, uncertain, undecided 10 impugnable, indecisive, inglorious, suggestive, suspicious, umbrageous
11 disgraceful, ignominious 12 dishonorable, disreputable 13 discreditable *spot:*
4 glen

shaft 3 cut, jab, ray, rod 4 axle, barb,
beam, dart, pole, stem 5 arrow, lance,
shoot, spear 6 thrust 7 chimney, potshot
8 short end *of a vehicle:* 5 thill

shag 3 mat, nap, rug 5 chase, fetch
7 thicket 9 cormorant

shaggy 5 bushy, rough 7 thrummy,
unkempt

shake 3 jar, jog, rid 4 deal, flit, jerk, jolt,
lose, rock, roil, slip, whip 5 avoid, churn,
clear, crack, daunt, elude, flash, jiffy, quail,
quake, shock, trill, upset, waver, worry
6 appall, bother, bounce, dismay, dither,
escape, jiggle, joggle, jostle, jounce, minute, moment, outwit, quaver, quiver, rattle,
ruffle, second, shimmy, shiver, stir up,
tremor, wiggle 7 agitate, chatter, commove,
concuss, disturb, flicker, flitter, flutter, horrify, instant, perturb, shudder, stagger, temblor, tremble, twitter, unnerve, vibrate
8 convulse, disorder, disquiet, throw off,
tremblor, unburden, unsettle, unstring
9 breathing, fluctuate, oscillate, palpitate
10 discompose, earthquake 11 consternate, split second

shake down 5 frisk, gouge, pinch, screw,
wrest, wring 6 extort, search, wrench
7 squeeze

Shakespeare, William *mother:* 9 Mary
Arden *play:* 6 Hamlet, Henry V 7 Henry
IV, Henry VI, Macbeth, Othello 8 King
John, King Lear, Pericles 9 Cymbeline,
Henry VIII, Richard II 10 Coriolanus, Rich-
ard III, The Tempest 11 As You Like It
12 Julius Caesar, Twelfth Night *theater:*
5 Globe *wife:* 12 Anne Hathaway

Shakespearean actor 4 Kean
(Edmund) 5 Evans (Maurice) 7 Branagh
(Kenneth), Garrick (David), Gielgud (John),
Olivier (Laurence) 8 Ashcroft (Peggy),
Macready (William), Redgrave (Michael),
Scofield (Paul) 10 Richardson (Ralph)

shaky 4 weak 6 aquake, ashake, dickey,
infirm, unsure, wobbly 7 aquiver, dubious,
quaking, quivery, rackety, rickety, suspect,
tottery, trembly, unclear, unsound 8 doubtful, insecure, rachitic, rootless, unstable,
unsteady, wavering 9 fluctuant, quivering,

tottering, trembling, tremorous, tremulous,
uncertain, unsettled 10 indecisive, precarious, rattletrap 11 problematic, vacillating

shale 4 rock 5 slate

shallot 4 herb, tube 5 onion 8 eschalot

shallow 4 idle, vain 5 empty, petty, shoal
6 hollow, paltry 7 cursory, flighty, sketchy,
surface, trivial 8 trifling 9 depthless
10 bird-witted, shallowish, uncritical
11 superficial

shallows 6 lagoon

Shallum *father:* 5 Shaul, Zadok
6 Jabesh, Josiah, Sismai, Tikvah 8 Col-
hozeh, Naphtali 9 Hallohesh *mother:*
6 Bilhah *nephew:* 8 Jeremiah *slayer:*
7 Menahem *son:* 6 Mibsam 7 Hilkiah
8 Maaseiah *victim:* 9 Zechariah

shalom 5 peace 8 farewell, greeting

sham 3 act, ape, lie 4 cant, copy, fake,
hoax, mock, sell 5 bluff, bogus, cheat,
dummy, false, farce, feign, phony, put on,
snide, spoof 6 affect, assume, create,
deceit, ersatz, facade, fakery, invent,
pseudo 7 assumed, feigned, imitate, mislead, mockery, plaster, pretend 8 affected,
flimflam, simulate, so-called, spurious, travesty 9 brummagem, burlesque, deception,
hypocrisy, imitation, imposture, pinchbeck,
simulated, synthetic 10 artificial, caricature,
false front, fictitious, pharisaism, sanctimony, substitute, Tartuffery, Tartuffism
11 adulterated, counterfeit, make believe
12 pecksniffery *combining form:* 5 pseud
6 pseudo

Shamariah see **Shemariah**

Shama's father 6 Hotham

Shamash 6 sun-god *father:* 3 Sin *sister:*
6 Ishtar *wife:* 2 Ai 3 Aya

shamble see **shuffle**

shambles 4 mess 5 botch, mix-up
6 mess-up, muddle 8 botchery, wreckage
9 confusion

shame 5 abash, guilt, odium 6 infamy
7 chagrin, obloquy 8 disgrace, dishonor,
ignominy 9 discredit, disesteem, disrepute
10 opprobrium 11 self-reproof 12 self-
reproach 13 embarrassment, mortification

shameless 4 bold, lewd 6 arrant, brassy,
brazen, cheeky 7 blatant 8 immodest,
impudent, overbold 9 abandoned, audacious, bald-faced, barefaced, dissolute,
unabashed 10 high-handed, outrageous,
profligate, unblushing 11 brazenfaced, disgraceful 12 presumptuous

Shamgar's father 5 Anath

Shamir's father 5 Micah

Shammah *brother:* 5 David *father:*
4 Agee 5 Jesse, Reuel *grandfather:*
4 Esau 7 Ishmael *son:* 7 Jonadab 8 Jonathan

Shammai's father 4 Onam 5 Ezrah, Rekem

Shammua *father:* 5 David, Galal 6 Bilgah, Zaccur *mother:* 9 Bathsheba *son:* 4 Abda

Shamsherai's father 7 Jeroham

shanghai 6 abduct, kidnap

Shangri-la 4 Zion 6 heaven, utopia 7 arcadia 8 paradise 9 Cockaigne, fairyland 10 lubberland, wonderland 12 promised land

shank 3 leg 4 shin, stem 5 stalk, tibia

shanty 3 cot, hut 4 camp 5 cabin, hovel, lodge, shack 7 cottage

shape 3 fit 4 case, cast, form, look, make, mold, plan, trim 5 build, forge, frame, order, state, whack 6 aspect, devise, estate, fettle, figure, kilter, repair, tailor, work up 7 fashion, fitness 8 assemble 9 condition, construct, fabricate, semblance 10 appearance 12 conformation 13 configuration *combining form:* 5 morph 6 morpho

shapeable 4 soft 6 pliant 7 ductile

shapeless 8 formless, inchoate, unformed 9 amorphous, unshapely

shapely 4 trim 5 buxom 6 comely 7 regular, rounded 8 balanced, clean-cut 9 Junoesque 10 curvaceous, statuesque, well-turned 11 clean-limbed, full-figured, symmetrical 12 proportioned

Shaphan *grandson:* 8 Gedaliah *son:* 6 Ahikam 8 Gemariah 9 Jaazaniah

Shaphat *father:* 4 Hori 5 Adlai 8 Shemaiah *son:* 6 Elisha

Sharai's father 4 Bani

share 3 cut, lot 4 bite, meed, part 5 claim, quota, slice, stake 6 assign, divide, parcel, quotum, ration 7 deal out, dole out, give out, measure, mete out, partage, partake, portion, prorate, quantum, rake-off 8 dispense, interest, quotient 9 allotment, allowance, apportion 10 commission, experience, percentage, proportion 11 participate 13 apportionment

shared 5 joint 6 common, mutual, public 8 communal, conjoint, conjunct *prefix:* 2 co

Sharezer *father, victim:* 11 Sennacherib

shark 5 cheat 8 swindler *kind:* 4 blue, gata, haye, mako, sand, tope 5 nurse, tiger, whale, white 7 basking, dogfish, leopard 8 mackerel, maneater, thresher 9 porbeagle 10 great white, hammerhead *skin:* 8 shagreen

sharp 3 hep, sly 4 acid, cute, fast, high, keen, sour, thin, tony, trig, wise 5 acrid, acute, alert, blunt, canny, harsh, honed, peaky, piked, quick, short, slick, smart, swank, swish 6 adroit, argute, biting, bitter, brainy, bright, clever, nimble, peaked, piping, severe, shrewd, shrill, snappy, tonish, treble 7 austere, caustic, dashing, exactly,

intense, knowing, odorous, pointed, prickly, stylish, whetted 8 acicular, drilling, incisive, original, piercing, shooting, stabbing, stinging, virulent 9 aciculate, acuminate, acuminous, agonizing, amaroidal, brilliant, cuspidate, ingenious, knifelike, precisely, sensitive, unblunted, unethical, vitriolic 10 accurately, astringent, paralyzing, perceptive, ungracious 11 acrimonious, double-edged, intelligent, penetrating, penetrative, quick-witted, ready-witted, resourceful, suffocating, thoughtless 12 excruciating, nimble-witted, quick-sighted 13 inconsiderate, strong-scented, unceremonious *combining form:* 3 oxy 5 acuto

sharp-edged 8 cultrate

sharpen 4 edge, file, hone, whet 5 dress, grind, strop 6 stroke

sharper 3 gyp 5 cheat 6 con man 7 diddler 8 swindler 9 defrauder, trickster 10 mountebank 12 double-dealer

sharpie see **sharper**

sharpness 4 edge 6 acumen 8 acrimony, keenness 12 incisiveness

sharpshooter 8 marksman

sharp-sighted 4 keen 5 acute 7 lyncean 8 hawk-eyed, lynx-eyed 9 eagle-eyed 11 penetrating, penetrative, quick-witted

sharp-witted 3 hep 4 keen, wise 5 acute, canny, quick, slick, smart 6 shrewd 7 knowing 10 discerning 11 intelligent

Shashai's father 4 Bani

Shashak's father 6 Elpaal

shatter 4 dash, raze, rend, rive, ruin, snap 5 break, burst, clack, crack, crash, crush, shoot, smash, split, wrack, wreck 6 bicker, crunch, rattle, shiver 7 clatter, clitter, destroy 8 decimate, demolish, destruct, fragment, splinter, splitter 9 pulverize 10 annihilate 11 fragmentize, splinterize 12 disintegrate

shatterable 5 frail 7 fragile 8 delicate, shattery 9 breakable, frangible 11 fracturable

Shaul's father 6 Simeon

shave 3 cut 4 clip, crop, kiss, pare, skim, trim 5 brush, graze, lower, prune, shear, shred, skive, slash 6 glance, reduce, scrape, sliver 7 cut back, cut down, shingle, tonsure, whittle 8 mark down

shaveling 3 boy, lad, son, tad 6 laddie 9 stripling

shaver 3 boy, lad 5 child, razor 6 barber 9 youngster

shawl 4 maud, wrap 5 cloak, manta 6 chadar, chador, sarape, serape 7 blanket, tallith

shawm's descendant 4 oboe

Shawnee chief 8 Tecumseh 9 Cornstalk

Shaw play 6 Geneva 7 Candida 9 Pygmalion, Saint Joan 11 Misalliance 12 Major Barbara

sheaf 6 bundle 7 cluster

Sheal's father 4 Bani

Shealtiel *father:* 4 Neri 8 Jeconiah *son:* 10 Zerubbabel

shear 3 cut, mow 4 barb, clip, crop, pare, snip, trim 5 prune, shave, skive 6 barber 8 manicure

Shearjashub's father 6 Isaiah

shears 8 scissors

shearwater 4 bird 6 hagdon, haglet 7 skimmer

sheath 4 case, skin 5 cover 8 scabbard *combining form:* 4 cole 5 coleo, theca

sheathe 4 case, clad, face, side, skin, wrap 5 cover, panel 6 encase, jacket 7 envelop 8 surround

Sheba *father:* 6 Bichri *queen:* 6 Balkis

shebang 3 hut 6 affair 8 business

Sheber *father:* 5 Caleb *mother:* 6 Maacah

Shebuel *father:* 5 Heman 7 Gershom *grandfather:* 5 Moses

Shecaniah *father:* 6 Jehiel 8 Jehaziel *son:* 7 Hattush 8 Shemaiah *son-in-law:* 6 Tobiah

Shechem's father 5 Hamor 6 Gilead 8 Shemidah

shed 3 hut 4 abri, cast, doff, drop, junk, molt, slip 5 scrap 6 divest, lean-to, reject, slough 7 cashier, cast off, discard, ecdysis, take off 8 exuviate, jettison, throw out 9 throw away

Shedeur's son 6 Elizur

sheen 5 glaze, glint, gloss, shine 6 finish, luster, polish 9 shininess

sheeny see shiny

sheep 5 dumba, ovine *Australian:* 7 jumbuck *breed:* 5 Tunis 6 Dorper, Dorset, Merino, Navajo, No-Tail, Oxford, Panama, Romney 7 Cheviot, Colbred, Karakul, Lincoln, Ryeland, Suffolk 8 Columbia, Cotswold, Polwarth 9 Hampshire, Leicester, Montadale, Southdown 10 Corriedale, Debouillet 11 Rambouillet *coat:* 4 wool 6 fleece *disease:* 3 gid 5 braxy 6 sturdy *female:* 3 ewe *male:* 3 ram 6 wether *meat:* 6 mutton *relating to:* 5 ovine *Scottish:* 9 blackface *skin:* 4 slat *sound:* 5 bleat *tender of:* 8 shepherd *wild:* 3 sha 5 urial 6 aoudad, argali, bharal, nahoor, oorial 7 bighorn, mouflon 8 moufflon *young:* 3 teg 4 hogg, lamb

sheepish 4 meek 5 timid 7 abashed, bashful 9 diffident 11 embarrassed

sheepskin 4 roan 5 basil 6 mouton 7 diploma 9 parchment *prepare:* 3 taw

sheer 3 dip 4 airy, pure, skew, slue, thin, turn, veer, whip 5 avert, filmy, gauzy, pivot,

steep, utter, wheel, whirl 6 abrupt, arrant, divert, flimsy, simple, swerve 7 chiffon, deflect, perfect, unmixed 8 absolute, complete, gossamer, outright 9 out-and-out, unalloyed, undiluted 10 diaphanous, see through 11 precipitate, precipitous, transparent, unmitigated

sheet 4 leaf, page, sail 5 cover, linen, paper 9 newspaper *combining form:* 6 pallio

sheet ___ 3 ice 4 film 5 glass, metal, music 6 anchor

Shehariah's father 7 Jeroham

Shelah *father:* 5 Judah 8 Arphaxad *son:* 4 Eber

Shelemiah *father:* 5 Cushi 6 Abdeel, Binnui 8 Hananiah *son:* 5 Jucal 6 Irijah 8 Hananiah

Sheleph's father 6 Joktan

Shelesh's father 5 Helem

shelf 4 bank, edge, reef, sill 5 ledge, shoal 6 gradin, mantel 7 gradine 8 sandbank

shell 3 pod 4 boat, bomb, case, hull, husk, rake, skin 5 blitz, conch, shuck 6 pepper 7 bombard, capsule, grenade, mollusk 9 cannonade, cartridge *combining form:* 5 conch 6 concho, ostrac 7 ostraca, ostraco *defective:* 3 dud *explosive:* 4 bomb *layer:* 5 nacre *ornamental:* 5 cowry 6 cowrie *study:* 10 conchology

shellac 4 beat, drub, lick, rout, trim, whip 5 resin, smear 6 defeat, thrash 7 smother, trounce 8 lambaste, vanquish

Shelley *elegy:* 7 Adonais *poem:* 7 Alastor 8 Queen Mab, The Cloud 10 Ozymandias, To a Skylark

shellfish 4 clam, crab 5 conch, cowry, prawn 6 cockle, limpet, mussel, oyster, triton 7 abalone, lobster, mollusk, scallop 8 barnacle 10 crustacean

shell out 3 pay 4 give 5 spend 6 expend, outlay 8 disburse

shell-shaped 6 spiral 9 cochleate

Shelomi's son 6 Ahihud

Shelomith *father:* 5 Dibri, Izhar 8 Rehoboam 9 Josiphiah 10 Zerubbabel *mother:* 6 Maacah

shelter 3 den, hut, lee 4 abri, cote, fold, hide, port, roof, shed, tent 5 arbor, benab, bower, cloak, cover, haven, house, shack, tower 6 asylum, burrow, covert, defend, harbor, refuge, shield 7 chamber, defense, foxhole, hideout, hospice, housing, lodging, pergola, pillbox, protect, retreat 8 hideaway, security 9 dwellings, harborage, hermitage, hidey-hole, sanctuary 10 quarterage, retirement *for a car:* 6 garage *for aircraft:* 6 hangar *for cows:* 4 barn, byre *toward:* 4 alee

shelve 4 dish, drop, stay, tilt 5 defer, delay, stock, waive 6 give up, hold up, put

off **7** hold off **8** hold over, postpone, prorogue
Shem *brother:* **3** Ham **7** Japheth *father:*
4 Noah
Shemaiah *father:* **4** Joel **7** Delaiah
8 Adonikam, Nethanel, Obededom **9** Elizaphan, Shecaniah *son:* **5** Uriah **6** Urijah
7 Delaiah, Obadiah
Shemariah's father **4** Bani **5** Harim
8 Rehoboam
Shema's father **4** Joel **6** Hebron
Shemer's father **5** Mahli
Shemida's father **6** Gilead
Shemuel's father **4** Tola **7** Ammihud
shenanigan **4** game, lark, play, ploy,
ruse, wile **5** antic, caper, prank, stunt, trick
6 device, didoes, frolic, shines **7** fast one,
gimmick, whizzer **8** goings-on, maneuver
9 stratagem **10** tomfoolery **11** legerdemain,
monkeyshine
Shenazzar's father **8** Jeconiah
10 Jehoiachin
Sheol see hades
Shephatiah *father:* **5** David **6** Maacah,
Mattan **11** Jehoshaphat *mother:* **6** Abital
shepherd **3** see **4** lead, show, tend
5 guide, pilot, route, steer, watch **6** direct,
escort, leader **7** conduct **8** guardian *dog:*
6 Collie *stick:* **4** kent **5** crook, staff
Shephi, Shepho *father:* **6** Shobal
Sheridan play **7** Pizarro **9** The Critic,
The Rivals
sheriff **6** lawman **7** marshal, officer *aide:*
6 deputy
Sherlock Holmes **6** sleuth **7** gumshoe
8 hawkshaw **9** detective **12** investigator
creator: **5** Doyle (Arthur Conan) *sidekick:*
6 Watson
sherry **4** fino, wine **7** oloroso **11** amontil-
lado
Sherwood play **13** Idiot's Delight, The
Road to Rome **14** The Petrified Forest,
Waterloo Bridge
Sheshai's father **4** Anak
Shoshan's servant **5** Jarha
shibboleth **3** tag **6** byword, cliché,
phrase, slogan, truism **7** bromide **8** banality, password, prosaism **9** catchword, platitude, watchword **10** prosaicism **11** catchphrase
shield **4** fend, roof, ward **5** aegis, armor,
cover, guard, haven, house **6** defend, harbor, screen, secure **7** buckler, bulwark, protect, shelter **8** defilade **9** safeguard
10 escutcheon *band:* **4** fess *bullfighter's:*
9 burladero *combining form:* **4** scut
5 aspid, scuti **6** aspido *large:* **5** pavis
6 pavise *light:* **5** targe *part:* **4** boss, umbo
7 bordure *Roman:* **6** scutum **7** clipeus,
testudo
shield-like **7** peltate, scutate **9** scutiform

shift **3** yaw **4** bend, bout, move, stir, tack,
time, tour, turn, vary **5** alter, budge, get by,
get on, spell, stint, trick **6** change, make
do, manage, remove, swerve **7** disturb,
replace, shuffle **8** get along, relocate,
transfer **9** deviation, dislocate **10** alteration,
changeover, conversion, deflection, transition
shiftless **4** lazy
shifty **5** cagey, lying, shady **6** crafty,
sneaky, tricky **7** cunning, devious, dodging,
elusive, evasive, furtive, knavish, mutable,
roguish **8** guileful, indirect, slippery, sneaking, unhonest, unstable, unsteady, variable
9 collusive, conniving, deceitful, dishonest,
insidious, shuffling, uncertain, underhand
10 changeable, fraudulent, inconstant, mendacious, untruthful **11** duplicitous, treacherous, underhanded **12** equivocating **13** pre-
varicative, prevaricatory
Shilem's father **8** Naphtali
Shilhi *daughter:* **6** Azubah *grandson:*
11 Jehoshaphat
shill **5** blind, decoy, stick **6** capper
shilling **3** bob
shilly-shally **4** halt **5** waver **6** dither, falter, wobbly **7** halting, stagger, whiffle
8 hesitate, to-and-fro, wavering **9** faltering,
hesitancy, vacillate, whiffling **10** hesitating,
hesitation, indecision **11** vacillating, vacillation, vacillatory **12** irresolution
Shilshah's father **6** Zophah
Shimea *brother:* **5** David *father:* **5** David,
Jesse *son:* **7** Jonadab **8** Jonathan
Shimeam's father **7** Mikloth
Shimei *brother:* **8** Conaniah, Cononiah
10 Zerubbabel *father:* **4** Bani, Gera, Kish
6 Hashum, Jahath **7** Gershon **8** Jeduthun
grandfather: **4** Levi
Shimeon's father **5** Harim
shimmer **5** flash, gleam, glint, spark
7 glimmor, glisten, glitter, spangle, sparkle,
twinkle **8** blinking, sparking **9** coruscate
11 coruscation, scintillate **13** scintillation
shimmy **5** dance, shake **7** chemise,
vibrate
Shimrath's father **6** Shimei
Shimri's father **5** Hosah **8** Shemaiah
9 Elizaphan
Shimrith's son **9** Jehozabad
Shimron's father **8** Issachar
shin **3** run **4** dash **5** scoot, tibia **6** scurry,
sprint **7** scamper
shindig **4** ball, bash, coil, fête, gala, to-do
5 dance, party **6** affair, furore, ruckus, rumpus, shindy, uproar **7** shebang **8** foofaraw
9 commotion
shine **3** ray, rub **4** beam, buff, burn, glow,
pomp, show **5** array, flare, flash, glare,
glaze, gleam, glint, gloss, sheen **6** finish,
glance, luster, parade, polish **7** burnish, dis-

play, fanfare, furbish, glimmer, glisten, panoply, radiate, sparkle, twinkle 9 luminesce 10 incandesce

shiner 4 fish 8 black eye, cyprinid

Shinto gods 4 kami

shiny 6 glossy, sheeny 7 fulgent 8 gleaming, lustrous, polished 9 burnished 10 glistening

ship 4 boat, move, send 5 remit, route, shift 6 direct, export, remove 7 address, consign, disturb, forward, freight 8 dispatch, transfer, transmit *ancient:* 5 knorr 6 galley 7 galleon, trireme *attendant:* 7 steward *beam:* 7 carling, keelson *berth:* 4 dock, slip *boat:* 6 dinghy *body:* 4 hull *cabin:* 9 stateroom *commercial:* 5 liner, oiler 6 argosy, tanker, trader 9 freighter *crew member:* 4 hand, mate 5 bosun 6 purser, sailor *deck:* 4 boat, main, poop 5 orlop 6 bridge 10 forecastle *fishing:* 6 lugger 7 trawler *fleet:* 6 armada *floor:* 4 deck *front:* 3 bow 4 prow, stem 8 cutwater *holster:* 4 boom 5 davit 7 capstan *kitchen:* 6 galley *left side:* 4 port 8 larboard *merchant:* (see **commercial**) *military:* 6 cutter, PT boat 7 carrier, cruiser 9 destroyer, submarine *officer:* 4 mate 5 bosun 6 purser 7 captain, steward *of the desert:* 5 camel *part:* 3 bow 4 beam, deck, helm, hold, hull, keel, mast, stem 5 bilge, hatch, stern 6 bridge, rudder 7 scupper *partition:* 7 bulwark 8 bulkhead *personnel:* 4 crew *platform:* 9 crow's nest, gangboard, gangplank *post:* 4 mast 7 bollard *prison:* 4 brig *projection:* 7 sponson *rear:* 5 stern *record:* 3 log *right side:* 9 starboard *room:* 4 brig 5 cabin 6 galley *rope:* 4 line 7 halyard *sailing:* 4 brig, dhow, prao, prau, proa, yawl 5 ketch, prahu, sloop, xebec 6 chebec, lugger 7 caravel, galleon 8 bilander, schooner *spar:* 6 bumkin *steerer:* 4 helm 6 tiller *storage area:* 4 hold *submersible:* 9 submarine 11 bathyscaphe *to the rear of:* 3 aft 5 abaft 6 astern *valve:* 7 seacock *window:* 4 port 8 porthole

Shiphi's father 5 Allon

Shiphtan's son 6 Kemuel

shipment 5 cargo 8 delivery

Ship of Fools author 6 Porter (Katherine Anne)

ships *group of:* 4 navy 5 fleet, flota 6 armada 8 flotilla

shipshape 4 neat, snug, tidy, trig, trim 7 chipper, orderly 11 spic-and-span, uncluttered, well-groomed 12 spick-and-span

shire 5 horse 6 county 8 district

shirk 4 duck, lurk, shun, slip 5 creep, dodge, fence, parry, skulk, slink, sneak, steal 6 bypass, eschew 8 sidestep

shirker see **slacker**

shirt 4 sark 6 camisa, camise, jersey 7 garment 8 guernsey, pullover *armored:* 6 byrnie *hair:* 6 cilice *kind:* 3 tee 4 polo 5 dress, sport *Scottish:* 4 jupe

shirty 3 mad 4 waxy 5 angry, irate, wroth 6 heated, ireful, wrathy 8 choleric, wrathful

Shiva, Siva *consort:* 3 Uma 4 Devi, Kali 5 Durga, Gauri 6 Ambika, Chandi 7 Parvati 9 Haimavati *son:* 6 Ganesa, Skanda 7 Ganesha 10 Karttikeya

shiver 4 rive 5 burst, quake, shake, smash 6 dither, quaver, quiver, tremor 7 shatter, shudder, tremble, twitter 8 fragment, splinter, splitter 11 splinterize

Shiza's son 5 Adina

shoal 3 bar 4 bank, hook, reef, spit 7 barrier, sandbar, shallow, tombolo 8 sandbank, sand reef, seamount 9 coral reef 11 barrier reef, superficial

Shobab *father:* 5 Caleb, David *mother:* 6 Azubah 9 Bathsheba

Shobal's father 3 Hur 4 Seir

Shobi's father 6 Nahash

shock 3 jar 4 bank, bump, cock, hill, jolt, pile, rick 5 clash, crash, floor, mound, quake, shake, smash, stack 6 appall, impact, insult, offend, sicken, trauma, tremor 7 astound, disgust, horrify, outrage, pyramid, shake up, startle, temblor 8 astonish, knock out, nauseate, surprise, tremblor 9 collision, electrify, stockpile 10 concussion, earthquake, percussion, scandalize, traumatism 11 prostration 12 stupefaction

shock absorber 6 spring 7 dashpot, snubber

shocking 5 awful, lurid 6 crying, horrid 7 burning, direful, fearful, glaring, heinous 8 dreadful, horrible, horrific, shameful, terrible 9 appalling, atrocious, desperate, frightful, monstrous 10 formidable, outrageous, scandalous 11 disgraceful, unspeakable

shoddy 4 base, mean, poor 5 cheap, dingy, seedy, shady, tacky, tatty 6 common, paltry, shabby, sleazy, trashy 7 rundown, scruffy 8 rubbishy, shameful 9 makeshift, scambling 10 broken-down, down-at-heel, inglorious 11 dilapidated, disgraceful, ignominious 12 dishonorable, disreputable 13 discreditable

shoe 3 bal, pac 4 boot, clog, geta, mule, pump 5 gilly, plate, sabot, tegua, wedge 6 brogan, brogue, buskin, crakow, gaiter, galosh, gillie, loafer, oxford, patten, sandal 7 chopine, ghillie, slipper, sneaker 8 balmoral, moccasin, platform, plimsoll 9 brodequin, pampootie, spectator 10 clodhopper, espadrille *accessory:* 4 horn, tree 6 polish *armored:* 8 solleret *athlete's:* 7 sneaker *form:* 4 last, tree *kind:* 8 elevator, open-toed **10** high-heeled *part:* **3** tip, toe **4** arch, heel, lace, lift, sole, vamp **5** shank, upper **6** box toe, collar, foxing, insole, lining, throat, tongue **7** counter, outsole **8** backstay *protective:* **6** galosh, rubber *Roman:* **6** caliga, sandal *shiner:* **6** polish **9** bootblack *wooden:* **5** sabot **7** chopine

shoelace tip 5 aglet **6** aiglet

shoeless 6 unshod **8** barefoot

shoemaker 5 soler **7** cobbler, crispin *patron saint:* **7** Crispin *Scottish:* **6** souter

Shogun author 7 Clavell (James)

Shoham's father 7 Jaaziah

Shomer *father:* **5** Heber *son:* **9** Jehozabad

shoo-in 9 sure thing

shoot 3 bud, fly, gun, ray **4** beam, bolt, dart, dash, fire, lash, race, raze, ruin, rush, sail, scud, skim, spew, tear **5** blast, chase, fling, float, loose, photo, shaft, skirr, snipe, spurt, wrack, wreck **6** branch, charge **7** destroy, explode, project, shatter **8** decimate, demolish, destruct, disprove, puncture **9** discharge, discredit **10** annihilate, photograph *combining form:* **5** blast, thall **6** blasto, thalli, thallo

shooting 5 acute, sharp **7** gunplay **8** piercing, stabbing **9** knifelike

shooting star 6 meteor **8** fireball

shoot up 4 soar **6** rocket **9** skyrocket

shop 4 hunt **5** store **6** market, outlet **8** boutique, emporium, showroom

shoplift 3 bag, cop **4** palm **5** pinch, steal, swipe **6** pilfer, rip off, snitch

shop owner 3 cit **8** merchant, retailer **10** proprietor

shopworn 5 stale, tired, trite **6** cliché **7** clichéd **8** overused **9** hackneyed **10** overworked **13** stereotypical

shore 4 bank, prop, stay **5** beach, brace, brink, carry, coast **6** bear up, column, rivage, strand, upbear, uphold **7** bolster, support, sustain **8** buttress, littoral, seacoast **9** coastland, coastline, riverbank, riverside, waterside **10** embankment, waterfront **11** underpinner **12** underpinning

shorebird see at **bird**

short 3 shy **4** core, curt, gist, meat, pith **5** aback, bluff, blunt, brief, crisp, dumpy, gruff, scant, sharp, skimp, spare, squat, stint, terse, thick **6** abrupt, amount, burden, chunky, crusty, low-set, meager, scanty, scarce, skimpy, snippy, sparse, stubby, sudden, thrust, upshot **7** asudden, brittle, brusque, compact, concise, crumbly, crunchy, curtate, failing, fragile, friable, lacking, laconic, needing, pointed, purport, scrimpy, slender, squatty, summary, unaware, wanting **8** abridged, abruptly, delicate, exiguous, lessened, snippety, suc-

cinct, suddenly, thickset, unawares **9** curtailed, decreased, decurtate, deficient, forthwith, irascible **10** diminished, inadequate, ungracious **11** abbreviated, compendiary, compendious **12** breviloquent, insufficient, unexpectedly, unsufficient **13** inconsiderate, unceremonious *combining form:* **5** brevi **6** brachy

shortage 4 lack **5** pinch **6** dearth **7** deficit, failure **8** underage **10** deficiency, inadequacy, scantiness *in container:* **6** ullage

shortcoming 3 sin **5** fault **7** demerit **10** deficiency **12** imperfection

shortcut 6 bypass, cutoff

shorten 3 bob, cut **4** clip, dock **5** elide, slash **6** lessen, reduce, shrink **7** abridge, bobtail, curtail, cut back, excerpt **8** compress, condense, contract, decrease, diminish, minimize, retrench, truncate **10** abbreviate

shorthand 11 stenography *method:* **5** Gregg **6** Pitman

shorthanded 7 wanting **11** undermanned **12** understaffed

shortly 4 anon, soon **6** pronto **7** briefly, by and by, in brief, quickly, tersely **8** directly **9** concisely, presently **10** succinctly **11** laconically

shortness 7 brevity

shortsighted 6 myopic

short-spoken 4 curt **5** bluff, blunt, brief, gruff **6** abrupt, crusty, snippy **7** brusque **8** snippety

short-tempered 5 testy **6** touchy **9** irascible

Shoshoni chief 8 Washakie **9** Pocatello

shot 2 go **3** nip, pop, try **4** dram, drop, jolt, show, slug, stab, time **5** break, carom, crack, fling, snort, whack, whirl **6** chance **7** snifter **8** occasion, toothful **11** opportunity

shoulder 4 edge, push, side **5** elbow, press, shove **6** axilla, hustle, jostle **8** bulldoze *bone:* **7** scapula **8** clavicle *combining form:* **2** om **3** omo *covering:* **6** tippet **8** scapular *muscle:* **7** deltoid *relating to:* **7** humeral **8** scapular

shoulder blade 7 scapula

shout 3 cry **4** bark, bawl, bray, call, howl, roar, yell **5** blare, whoop **6** bellow, clamor, holler, scream, shriek **7** exclaim **10** vociferate

shove 3 dig, jab, jam **4** cram, poke, prod, push **5** drive, elbow, press **6** hustle, jostle, peddle, propel, thrust **8** bulldoze, shoulder

shovel 3 dig **4** grub **5** scoop, scuff, spade **6** dig out **7** scuffle, shamble, shuffle **8** excavate

shoveler 4 duck **9** broadbill

shovelhead 7 catfish

shove off 2 go 4 exit, quit 5 leave
6 depart, get off 7 pull out, take off 8 run
along

show 3 air, get, say, see 4 cine, come,
fair, film, lead, look, loom, mark, pomp,
read 5 array, flash, flick, front, get in,
guide, mount, movie, offer, pilot, prove,
revue, sport, stage, steer, vaunt 6 appear,
arrive, blazon, chance, direct, emerge,
escort, evince, expose, flaunt, lay out, look-
in, ostend, parade, record, reveal, set out,
submit, turn up, unveil 7 conduct, display,
disport, divulge, exhibit, fanfare, make out,
panoply, picture, present, produce, proffer,
project, seeming, trot out 8 brandish, disclose, evidence, flourish, indicate, manifest,
occasion, proclaim, register, shepherd
9 determine, establish, photoplay, represent, semblance, spectacle 10 appearance, exhibition, exposition, illustrate, simulacrum 11 demonstrate, materialize,
opportunity, performance 13 demonstration, motion picture, moving picture

Show Boat *author:* 6 Ferber (Edna)
composer: 4 Kern (Jerome)

showcase 7 exhibit, vitrine

shower 3 tub 4 hail, rain, wash 5 bathe,
burst, party, salvo, spray, storm 7 barrage,
shatter, spatter 8 downpour, rainfall
9 broadside, cannonade, fusillade 10 cloudburst 11 bombardment

showman 8 producer *famous:* 4 Cody
(William Frederick) 6 Barnum (Phineas
Taylor)

Show Me State 8 Missouri

show off 4 brag 5 boast, flash 6 expose,
flaunt, parade 7 display, disport, exhibit,
swagger, trot out 8 brandish

showoff 3 ham 6 hotdog 7 hotshot
13 exhibitionist

showpiece 3 gem 5 jewel, prize 11 chef
d'oeuvre, masterpiece

show up 3 get 4 come 5 get in, reach
6 arrive, debunk, expose, turn up, unmask
7 uncloak, undress 8 discover, unshroud
9 discredit 10 invalidate

showy 3 gay 4 arty, loud 5 gaudy, jazzy,
swank 6 chichi, flashy, garish, ornate,
sporty, tawdry 7 opulent, splashy 8 gorgeous, overdone, peacocky 9 luxurious,
sumptuous 10 flamboyant, peacockish
11 overwrought, pretentious, resplendent,
sensational 12 meretricious, orchidaceous,
ostentatious

shrapnel 8 fragment 10 projectile

shred 3 bit, dag, rag 4 iota 5 crumb,
grate, ounce, scrap, shave, speck 6 silver
7 modicum, smidgen 8 fragment, particle

shrew 5 harpy, scold, vixen, witch 6 amazon, ogress, rodent, virago 8 fishwife, she-
devil, spitfire 9 termagant, Xanthippe

shrewd 3 sly 4 cagy, foxy, keen, tidy, wise
5 acute, cagey, canny, heady, sharp, slick,
smart 6 argute, astute, clever, crafty, polite,
smooth 7 knowing, probing, prudent
8 piercing, sensible 9 astucious, ingenious,
judicious, sagacious 10 farsighted 11 foresighted, intelligent, penetrating, quick-witted
13 perspicacious

shriek 3 cry 4 yell 5 blare, shout
6 screak, scream, shrill, squawk, squeal
7 screech

shrill 4 high, keen, thin 5 acute, sharp
6 argute, piping, scream, shriek, squeal,
treble 7 screech 8 piercing, strident

shrimp 4 runt 5 prawn 6 peanut 10 crustacean *combining form:* 5 caris

shrine 3 box 4 tomb 5 altar 6 temple
7 sanctum 9 holy place, reliquary, sanctuary 10 sanctorium *Buddhist:* 5 stupa
6 dagoba

shrink 3 shy 4 fail, funk, wane 5 cower,
demur, quail, slink, start, wince 6 blanch,
blench, boggle, cringe, crouch, flinch, huddle, recede, recoil, retire, weaken, wither
7 dwindle, retreat, scruple, squinch 8 compress, condense, contract, draw back, withdraw 9 constrict, fall short, shrivel up,
waste away 11 concentrate

shrinking 3 shy 5 timid 7 aseptic 8 retiring 9 unaffable, withdrawn 10 restrained
11 unexpansive

shrive 4 free 5 purge 6 pardon 7 confess

shrivel 4 wilt 5 dry up, parch, wizen
6 welter, wither

Shropshire Lad author 8 Houseman
(Alfred Edward)

shroud 3 lop 4 hide, veil, wrap 5 cloak,
close, cover, shade 6 enfold, enwrap,
invest, screen 7 enclose, envelop, shut off,
shut out 8 block out, cerement, obstruct
9 cerecloth

shrouded 5 privy 6 buried, covert, hidden
7 guarded 8 obscured, ulterior 9 concealed

shrub 3 lop 4 bush 5 elder, erica, hazel,
plant, prune 6 cercis, muskit, privet.
7 arboret, dyeweed, guayule 8 barberry,
bluewood, boxthorn, inkberry, ironweed,
rosebush 9 bearberry 10 bladdernut *Asian:*
4 bago 5 ramee, ramie 6 kerria 8 cara-
gana, japonica 10 beauty bush *climbing:*
7 jasmine *combining form:* 5 thamn
6 thamno *desert:* 5 retem 6 alhagi
7 ephedra *dwarf:* 6 bonsai *East Indian:*
3 aal 4 sunn *European:* 4 cade 8 wood-
bind, woodbine *evergreen:* 3 box, kat, yew
4 ilex, khat, titi 5 furze, heath, holly, pyxie,
savin, taxus, thuja, thuya, toyon, yapon
6 kalmia, laurel, myrtle, nandin, protea,
sabine, savine, yaupon 7 boxwood,
heather, jasmine, juniper, rosebay 8 lamb-
kill, oleander, rosemary, tamarisk *flowering:*

5 lilac, ribes, tiara, wahoo 6 azalea, daphne, laurel, myrtle, spirea, wicopy 7 chamise, chamiso, fuchsia, mahonia, maybush, rhodora, spiraea, weigela 8 magnolia, mezereon, mezereum, nineback, oleander, oleaster, shadblow, shadbush, snowball, snowbell, snowbush, tornillo, viburnum, wistaria, wisteria *fragrant:* 4 mint, sage 5 thyme 8 rosemary 10 basil thyme *genus:* 4 Inga, Itea 7 Solanum 8 Euonymus *hardwood:* 6 cornel *Mexican:* 8 ocotillo *ornamental:* 6 privet 7 deutzia, jetbead, syringa, woodwax 9 bluebeard *pasture:* 8 cowberry *prickly:* 4 whin 5 briar, chico, furze, gorse 7 bramble, rhamnus 8 hawthorn, mesquite 9 buckthorn *South American:* 4 coca 7 rhatany *thicket:* 6 maquis 7 macchia 9 chaparral *tropical:* 4 kava 5 guava, henna 7 camelia, lantana 8 buddleia, camellia, gardenia 10 frangipani *West Indian:* 4 anil 7 acerola

shrug 6 jacket 7 gesture *off:* 5 evade 8 minimize

Shua *father:* 5 Heber *son-in-law:* 5 Judah

Shuah *father:* 7 Abraham *mother:* 7 Keturah

Shual's father 6 Zophah

shuck 3 pod 4 case, cast, hull, husk, junk, peel, shed, skin 5 chuck, ditch, scrap, shell, strip 6 reject, slough 7 discard 8 jettison 11 decorticate

shudder 5 quake, shake 6 dither, gyrate, quaver, quiver, shimmy, shiver, tremor 7 frisson, tremble, twitter

shuffle 4 hash, limp, mash 5 dodge, evade, hedge, scuff 6 jumble, jungle, litter, mess up, muddle, shovel, tumble, weasel 7 clutter, disrupt, disturb, rummage, shamble, stumble 8 disarray, disorder, mishmash, sidestep 9 dislocate, pussyfoot 10 disarrange, discompose, equivocate, tergiverse 11 disorganize 12 tergiversate

Shuham's father 3 Dan

shun 3 shy 4 duck, snub 5 avoid, elude, evade 6 double, escape, eschew, refuse, reject 7 decline, disdain

Shuni's father 3 Gad

shunt 4 move, turn 5 avert, shift 6 change, divert, switch 7 deflect, head off, shuttle 8 transfer 9 sidetrack

shush 4 hush 5 quiet, still 6 muffle, shut up 7 repress, silence, squelch 8 choke off, strangle, suppress

shut 4 lock, seal 5 close 6 fasten 7 confine 10 batten down *loudly:* 4 slam

Shute, Nevil *novel:* 7 Marazan 9 Pied Piper 10 On the Beach 11 So Disdained

Shuthelah's father 7 Ephraim

shut in 3 hem, pen 4 cage, coop, mure, wall 5 fence 6 immure 7 close in, confine, enclose, envelop 8 imprison

shut-in 7 invalid 12 convalescent

shut out 3 bar 5 close 6 screen, shroud 7 exclude 8 obstruct

shutter 5 blind 6 screen

shuttle 5 shunt 6 bobbin 9 alternate

shuttlecock 4 bird 6 birdie

shut up 3 gag 4 hush 5 dry up, quiet, shush, still 6 dumb up 7 dummy up, silence 8 choke off, pipe down 9 quiet down

shy 3 coy, gag, jib, pot 4 balk, bilk, duck, meek, shun, wary 5 avoid, chary, demur, elude, evade, loath, quail, scant, short, timid 6 afraid, averse, blench, boggle, demure, double, escape, eschew, modest, recoil, scanty, scarce, shrink 7 bashful, failing, fearful, lacking, nervous, potshot, rabbity, scruple, stickle, stumble, uneager, wanting 8 backward, cautious, hesitant, inturned, reserved, retiring, sheepish, skittish, timorous 9 conscious, deficient, diffident, introvert, reluctant, sideswipe, unassured, unwilling 10 backhanded, inadequate, indisposed, shamefaced, suspicious 11 circumspect, disinclined, introverted, unassertive 12 apprehensive, insufficient, introversive, self-effacing, unsufficient 13 self-conscious

Shylock 6 usurer 9 loan shark *daughter:* 7 Jessica

shyster 11 pettifogger

Siam see Thailand

Siamese coin see coin, *Thailand*

sib 3 kin 4 akin 6 sister 7 brother, kindred, related 8 relative

Sibbecai's victim 4 Saph

Sibelius composition 9 Finlandia

Siberian *antelope:* 5 saiga *dog:* 5 husky *gulf:* 2 Ob *native:* 5 Tatar, Yakut 6 Tartar 9 Mongolian *plain:* 6 steppe *storm:* 5 buran *tent:* 4 yurt

sibilate 4 buzz, fizz, hiss, whiz 5 swish, whisk 6 fizzle, sizzle, wheeze 7 whisper

sibling 6 sister 7 brother

sibyl 4 seer 7 prophet 10 prophetess 13 fortune-teller

sic 2 so 4 abet, goad, prod, spur, thus, urge 5 egg on, favor, prick 6 exhort, prompt, propel 7 agitate 8 catalyze, inspirit 9 instigate

Sicilian *secret organization:* 5 Mafia *volcano:* 4 Etna

Sicily's capital 7 Palermo

sick 3 ill 4 down, mean, weak 5 amiss, fed up, funny, lousy, peaky, rocky, tired, weary 6 ailing, faulty, flawed, laid up, morbid, morose, peaked, rotten, unwell, wobbly 7 fevered 8 confined, diseased 9 defective, disgusted, imperfect, tottering, unhealthy 10 disordered, indisposed 11 debilitated

sicken 5 repel, upset 6 reluct, revolt 7 derange, disgust, repulse, unhinge 8 disorder, nauseate, unsettle

sickle 5 blade, mower 8 crescent

sickly 3 ill, low 4 down, mean, puny, weak 5 pecky 6 ailing, morbid, morose, offish, peaked, poorly, unwell 7 noisome, noxious, underly 8 diseased, off-color 9 unhealthy 10 indisposed, insalutary, unsalutary 11 unhealthful, unwholesome 12 insalubrious

sickness 3 ill 6 malady 7 ailment, disease, illness 8 disorder, syndrome, unhealth 9 affection, complaint, condition, infirmity 10 affliction, unwellness 12 diseasedness 13 indisposition, unhealthiness

sic transit gloria ___ 5 mundi

side 4 clad, face, hand, part, skin 5 angle, facet, flank, phase, slant, stand 6 aspect, sector, stance 7 outlook, posture, sheathe 8 attitude, position 9 direction, viewpoint 10 standpoint 11 disposition *combining form:* 5 later, pleur 6 lateri, latero, pleuri, pleuro *sheltered:* 3 lee

sideboard 5 table 6 buffet 8 credence *for wine:* 8 cellaret 10 cellarette

sideboards see **sideburns**

sideburns 9 burnsides 10 sideboards 11 dundrearies, muttonchops

side by side 8 together *combining form:* 3 par 4 para

sidekick 3 pal 7 partner 9 assistant, companion

sidereal 6 astral, starry 7 stellar

side road 5 byway 8 bystreet, shunpike

sidestep 4 duck 5 avoid, burke, dodge, evade, fence, hedge, parry, shirk, skirt 6 bypass, weasel 9 pussyfoot 10 circumvent, equivocate 12 tergiversate

sidetrack 5 shunt 6 divert, switch

sidewalk 6 paving 7 walkway 8 pavement 9 banquette

sidewhiskers see **sideburns**

side with 4 back 6 uphold 7 support 8 advocate, backstop, champion

sidle 4 ease, edge, slip 7 saunter

siege 4 bout 5 spell 6 attack 7 seizure 9 onslaught

Siegfried *mother:* 9 Sieglinde *slayer:* 5 Hagen *sword:* 7 Balmung *vulnerable spot:* 4 back 8 shoulder *wife:* 9 Kriemhild

Sienkiewicz novel 8 Quo Vadis

sierra 4 fish 5 range

Sierra ___ 5 Ancha, Leone, Madre 6 Blanca, Nevada

siesta 3 nap 5 sleep 6 catnap, dog nap, snooze 10 forty winks

sieve 4 sift 5 clack, tabby 6 gossip, screen 8 colander, gossiper, quidnunc, strainer 10 talebearer

Sif's husband 4 Thor

sift 4 bolt, comb, cull, sort 5 probe, sieve 6 filter, go into, screen, winnow 7 dig into, explore 8 filtrate, look into, prospect, separate 9 delve into 11 inquire into, investigate

sigh 3 sob 4 ache, blow, gasp, howl, long, lust, moan, pant, pine, roar 5 crave, dream, groan, sough, whine 6 exhale, hanker, hunger, murmur, thirst, wheeze 7 breathe, respire, suspire, whisper, whistle

sight 3 aim, eye, spy 4 espy, look, mess, view 5 scene 6 fright, seeing, vision 7 eyesore, outlook 11 monstrosity *combining form:* 4 opsy 5 opsia, opsis *relating to:* 5 optic 6 ocular, visual 7 optical

sightseer 7 tourist 10 rubberneck

sign 3 cue, ink 4 flag, hint, mark, omen, show 5 index, proof, token, trace 6 motion, signal, symbol 7 earmark, endorse, exhibit, gesture, indicia, initial, symptom, vestige, warning 8 evidence, exponent, reminder 9 autograph, character, indicator, subscribe 10 expression, indication, suggestion 11 attestation 13 gesticulation, symbolization *commercial:* 4 neon *directional:* 5 arrow *of the zodiac:* (see **zodiac sign**)

signal 3 cue 4 flag 5 alarm, alert, siren 6 beckon, famous, marked, motion, tocsin, wigwag 7 eminent, gesture, salient 8 high sign, movement, peculiar, renowned, striking 9 arresting, arrestive, prominent 10 individual, noticeable, remarkable 11 conspicuous, distinctive, illustrious, outstanding *distress:* 3 SOS 6 Mayday

signature 3 ink 4 name, sign 9 autograph, subscribe 11 John Hancock *flourish:* 6 paraph

signet 4 ring, seal 5 stamp

significance 4 pith 5 merit, sense 6 credit, import, moment, virtue, weight 7 meaning, message, purport 8 prestige 9 authority, influence, magnitude 10 excellence, importance, intendment, perfection 11 acceptation, consequence, weightiness

significant 3 big 4 rich 5 sound, valid 6 cogent, facund 7 telling, weighty 8 eloquent, forceful, material, powerful 9 important, momentous 10 compelling, convincing, expressive, meaningful 11 sententious, substantial 12 considerable 13 consequential

signification 4 gist 5 sense 6 import 7 essence, meaning, message, purport 8 implying 9 substance 10 intendment 11 acceptation, implication 12 construction 13 understanding

signify 4 bear, mean, show **5** carry, count, spell, weigh **6** convey, denote, import, intend, matter **7** add up to, bespeak, connote, express, purport

sign over 4 cede, deed **5** alien **6** assign, remise **8** alienate, make over, transfer **10** abalienate

sign up 4 join **5** enrol, enter **6** enlist, enroll, join up, muster

Sigurd *horse:* **5** Grani *slayer:* **5** Hogni *victim:* **6** Fafnir *wife:* **6** Gudrun

Sigyn's husband 4 Loki

silage 6 fodder

silence 3 gag **4** calm, dumb, hush, lull, mute **5** death, quash, quell, quiet, shush, sleep, still **6** dampen, deaden, demise, muffle, muzzle, shut up, squash **7** decease, passing, quietus, secrecy, squelch **8** choke off, curtains, hush-hush, quietude, suppress **9** quietness, stillness

silent 3 mum **4** dumb, hush, mute **5** close, muted, quiet, still, tacit, whist **6** curbed, stilly **7** checked, hushful **8** reserved, reticent, taciturn, unspoken, unvoiced, wordless **9** inhibited, noiseless, secretive, soundless, unuttered, voiceless **10** incoherent, restrained, speechless, tongue-tied, unsociable **11** close-lipped, shut-mouthed, tight-lipped, unexpressed **12** closemouthed, close-tongued, inarticulate, tight-mouthed

silhouette 4 line **6** shadow **7** contour, outline, profile **9** lineament, lineation **10** figuration **11** delineation

silicon *symbol:* **2** Si

silk 5 fiber, honan **7** foulard **8** sarcenet, sarsenet *fabric:* **4** gros **5** caffa, ninon, Pekin, satin, surah, tulle **6** cendal, mantua, pongee, samite, sendal, tussah **7** taffeta, tussore *factory:* **8** filature *hat:* **6** topper *maker:* **4** worm **7** thrower *raw:* **5** grège **6** greige *source:* **6** ooooon *waste:* **4** noil **5** floss *wild:* **6** tussah **7** tussore *yarn:* **4** tram

silkworm 3 eri **6** bombyx, tussah **7** tussore **8** bombycid

sill 5 bench, ledge, shelf **9** threshold

silliness 5 folly **7** inanity **8** insanity **9** absurdity, craziness, dottiness **11** foolishness, witlessness **12** illogicality **13** senselessness

silly 3 off **4** daft **5** crazy, daffy, dizzy, empty, funny, giddy, loony, sappy, wacky **6** absurd, insane, simple, unwise **7** asinine, fatuous, flighty, foolish, unwitty, vacuous, witless **8** ignorant **9** fantastic, nitwitted, senseless **10** bird-witted, irrational, weak-headed, weak-minded **11** empty-headed, harebrained, light-headed, sheep-headed **12** preposterous, unreasonable **13** rattle-brained, unintelligent

silt 4 scum, soil **5** dregs **7** deposit, residue **8** sediment

silver 4 coin **5** money, shiny **6** argent, dulcet **7** bullion, element **8** argentum, flatware, lustrous, sterling **9** argentine, tableware *relating to:* **5** lunar **8** argentic **9** argentine, argentous *symbol:* **2** Ag

silverfish 6 insect, tarpon

silver fox 5 caama

silversmith 6 Revere (Paul)

silver-tongued 4 glib **7** voluble **8** eloquent

silvery 6 argent **7** frosted, shining **9** argentate, argentine, argentous, brilliant **10** glittering, shimmering

Silvia's beloved 9 Valentine

Simeon *father:* **5** Jacob *mother:* **4** Leah *son:* **4** Ohad **6** Nemuel

simian 3 ape **6** monkey **10** anthropoid

similar 4 akin, like **5** alike **6** agnate **7** uniform **8** parallel, suchlike **9** analogous, consonant **10** comparable, reciprocal **11** correlative **13** complementary, corresponding *combining form:* **3** hol, hom **4** holo, home, homo **5** homeo, homoe, homoi **6** homoeo, homoio

similarity 6 simile **7** analogy **8** affinity, likeness, parallel **9** alikeness, closeness, collation, semblance **10** comparison, similitude, synonymity **11** association, coincidence, correlation, resemblance

similarly 2 so **4** also **8** likewise

simile 7 analogy **8** affinity, likeness, metaphor **9** alikeness, semblance **10** comparison, similarity, similitude **11** resemblance *word:* **2** as **4** like

similitude 4 copy **6** double, simile **7** analogy, replica **8** affinity, likeness, metaphor **9** alikeness, semblance **10** comparison, similarity **11** resemblance

simmer 4 boil, stew, stir **5** churn **6** bubble, seethe **7** ferment, parboil, smolder

simmer down 4 cool **7** collect, compose, control, repress, smother, subside **8** restrain, suppress **9** quiet down, re-collect

Simon *brother:* **5** Jesus **6** Andrew *father:* **5** Jonah *new name:* **5** Peter *son:* **5** Judas, Rufus **9** Alexander

Simon ___ 5 Magus **6** Legree **8** of Cyrene **9** the Zealot

Simon Maccabeus *father:* **10** Mattathias *nickname:* **6** Thassi *slayer:* **7** Ptolemy

simp 5 dunce **6** dimwit, nitwit **7** lackwit, pinhead, wantwit **13** featherweight

simper 5 smirk

simple 4 dull, dumb, dupe, easy, mere, pure, slow, soft **5** crass, dense, dopey, light, naive, plain, royal, sheer, silly, stark

6 doting, facile, modest, smooth, spoony, stupid 7 artless, asinine, fatuous, foolish, idiotic, moronic, natural, perfect, unmixed, unwitty, witless 8 absolute, backward, childish, discreet, gullible, ignorant, imbecile, mindless, retarded, trusting, unartful, untaught 9 brainless, childlike, credulous, dim-witted, ingenuous, nitwitted, senseless, unalloyed, unstudied 10 effortless, half-witted, illiterate, slow-witted, unaffected, uneducated, unschooled, weak-headed, weak-minded 11 fundamental, inelaborate, sheepheaded, undecorated, unelaborate, unmitigated, unqualified 12 feebleminded, unartificial, unbeautified, uncompounded, unornamented 13 inexperienced, unadulterated, unintelligent, unpretentious, untroublesome *combining form:* 3 apl 4 aplo, hapl 5 haplo

simpleminded 4 dull, slow 6 stupid 7 moronic 8 imbecile, retarded 9 dim-witted 10 half-witted, slow-witted

simpleton 4 dolt, fool, zany 5 ament, dummy, dunce, idiot, moron 6 cretin, stupid 7 bungler, dullard, half-wit, natural 8 dullhead, dumbbell, imbecile 9 ignoramus

simplify 6 reduce 7 abridge, clarify, clean up, cut down, shorten 8 boil down 10 disinvolve, streamline, unscramble 11 disentangle 13 straighten out

simply 3 but 4 just, only 6 merely

simulacrum 4 copy, face, show, spit 5 guise, image 6 double, ersatz, ringer 7 picture, seeming, showing 8 portrait 9 imitation, semblance 10 appearance 13 spitting image

simulate 3 act, ape 4 copy, fake, pose, sham 5 bluff, favor, feign, mimic, put on 6 affect, assume 7 imitate, play-act, pretend 8 resemble 11 counterfeit

simulated 4 fake, mock, sham 5 dummy, false, phony 6 ersatz 8 spurious 9 imitation 10 artificial, fictitious, substitute

simultaneous 6 coeval 8 agreeing 10 coetaneous, coexistent, coexisting, coinciding, concurrent, concurring, synchronal, synchronic 11 synchronous 12 contemporary

simultaneously 6 at once 8 together 12 coincidently, concurrently

sin 3 err 4 debt, evil, tort 5 crime, fault, wrong 6 offend 7 demerit 8 hamartia, iniquity, trespass 9 diablerie 10 deficiency, transgress, wickedness, wrongdoing 11 shortcoming 12 imperfection *deadly:* 4 envy, lust 5 anger, pride, sloth 8 gluttony 12 covetousness

Sin 7 moon-god *daughter:* 6 Ishtar *son:* 7 Shamash *wife:* 6 Ningal

since 2 as 3 for 4 next 5 after, below 6 behind, seeing 7 because, whereas 8 as

long as 9 following 10 inasmuch as 11 considering 12 subsequent to *Scottish:* 4 syne

sincere 4 dear, open, real, true 5 frank, meant, plain 6 actual, candid, devout, hearty, honest 7 genuine, serious 8 bona fide, faithful, heartful, truthful 9 authentic, heartfelt, unfeigned 10 aboveboard, forthright, heart-whole, unaffected 11 undesigning, whole-souled 12 frankhearted, undissembled, wholehearted 13 unpretentious

sincerity 6 candor 8 goodwill 9 bona fides, good faith 11 earnestness

sinecure 4 snap 5 cinch

sine qua non 4 must 9 condition, essential, necessity, requisite 11 requirement 12 precondition, prerequisite

sinew 5 force, might, power 6 energy, muscle, tendon 7 potency 8 strength

sinewy 4 ropy, wiry 5 tough 6 brawny, strong, sturdy 7 fibrous, stringy 8 athletic, muscular 9 tenacious

sinful 3 bad, low 4 base, evil, vile 5 amiss, wrong 6 guilty, unholy, wicked 7 immoral, peccant, vicious 8 blamable, blameful, culpable, damnable, shameful 9 reprobate 10 censurable, iniquitous 11 blameworthy, disgraceful 13 demeritorious, reprehensible

sing 3 hum 4 hymn, lilt, lull, tune 5 carol, chant, croon, yodel 6 intone, warble 7 confess, descant, lullaby 8 serenade, vocalize 10 cantillate

singe 4 burn, char 6 scorch

singer 4 alto, bass 5 tenor 6 cantor 7 crooner, soloist, songman, soprano 8 baritone, choirboy, songster, vocalist 9 balladeer, balladier, chorister *cabaret:* 11 chansonnier *female:* 9 chanteuse, chantress 10 cantatrice *opera:* 4 diva 5 buffa, buffo *religious:* 6 cantor

singing *exercise:* 7 solfège *group:* 4 duet, trio 5 choir 6 chorus 7 quartet *voice:* 4 alto, bass 5 tenor 7 soprano 8 baritone 9 contralto 12 mezzo-soprano

single 3 hit, one 4 free, lone, only, open, sole 5 frank, plain, unwed 6 candid, maiden, screen, unique, virgin 7 base hit, special 8 celibate, distinct, especial, separate, singular, solitary, specific, unshared 9 exclusive, unmarried 10 individual, particular, spouseless, unattached, unfettered *combining form:* 3 apl, mon 4 aplo, hapl, mono 5 haplo *prefix:* 3 uni

single-minded 4 open 5 frank, plain, rigid 6 candid 7 adamant, bigoted, diehard 8 obdurate 9 unbending 10 brassbound, inexorable, inflexible, relentless, unyielding

single out 4 cull, mark, pick, take 5 elect 6 choose, optate, opt for, prefer, select

singular 3 odd 4 lone, only, rare, sole, solo 5 alone, queer, weird 6 unique 7 bizarre, certain, curious, oddball, strange, unusual 8 definite, discrete, peculiar, solitary, uncommon, unwonted 9 exclusive 10 individual, outlandish, particular, respective, unexampled, unordinary 11 exceptional 13 extraordinary

singularity 5 seity, unity 7 ipseity, oneness, selfdom 8 identity, selfhood, selfness 10 singleness 11 personality 13 individualism, individuality, particularity

singularize 4 mark 7 qualify 9 signalize 11 distinguish, individuate 12 characterize 13 individualize

sinister 4 dark, dire, evil 6 malign 7 baleful, doomful, fateful, malefic, ominous 8 lowering, menacing 9 ill-boding, ill-omened, malicious 10 maleficent, portentous 11 apocalyptic, threatening 12 inauspicious, unpropitious

sink 3 dip, pit, ram, rot, run, sag, set, sty 4 dive, pool, stab 5 abase, basin, demit, drive, droop, lower, slump, Sodom, stoop 6 bemean, debase, demean, go down, hollow, humble, plunge, thrust, worsen 7 cesspit, decline, degrade, depress, descend, founder, go under, let down, subside, torpedo 8 cast down, cesspool, hellhole, submerge, submerse 9 concavity, humiliate 10 degenerate, depression, disimprove, retrograde 11 deteriorate, pandemonium 12 Augean stable, disintegrate

sinker 4 drop 5 pitch 6 weight

sinkhole 3 dip, sag 5 basin 6 hollow 8 cesspool 9 concavity 10 depression

sinless 4 pure 8 innocent

Sinn ____ 4 Fein

sinuous 4 wavy 5 shaky 7 twisted, winding 8 flexuous, tortuous 9 meandrous 10 convoluted, meandering, serpentine 11 anfractuous, snake-shaped

sinus 6 cavity, hollow, recess

Sioux 6 Dakota *chief:* 8 Red Cloud 10 Crazy Horse 11 Sitting Bull *people:* 3 Ofo 4 Crow 6 Biloxi, Tutelo 7 Catawba, Hidatsa 9 Winnebago

sip 4 toss 5 drink, quaff, sup up, taste 6 imbibe, sup off 7 swallow

siphon 3 tap 4 draw, pipe, pump 5 carry, draft, drain 6 convoy, funnel 7 channel, conduct, draw off, traject 8 transmit

sir 4 lord 5 title 6 knight, mister 9 gentleman

sire 4 lord 5 beget, breed, hatch, maker, spawn 6 author, create, father, parent 7 creator, founder, produce 8 generate, inventor 9 architect, generator, originate, patriarch, procreate 10 originator 11 progenerate

siren 4 vamp 7 charmer, drawing, enticer, Lorelei 8 alluring, magnetic 9 seductive, temptress 10 attracting, attractive, bewitching, enchanting, seductress 11 captivating, fascinating, femme fatale *of silent screen:* 4 Bara (Theda)

Siren 5 Ligea 8 Leucosia 10 Parthenope *German:* 7 Lorelei

sirenian 6 dugong, sea cow 7 manatee

siren song 4 bait, lure, trap 5 decoy, snare 6 come-on 10 allurement, enticement, seducement, temptation

sissy 4 baby 6 prissy 7 doormat, epicene, milksop, unmanly 8 weakling 9 jellyfish 10 effeminate, pantywaist 11 Milquetoast, mollycoddle

sister 3 nun 4 girl 7 sibling 8 relative

Sister Carrie author 7 Dreiser (Theodore)

sisterly 7 sororal

Sisyphus *brother:* 7 Athamas 9 Salmoneus *father:* 6 Aeolus *mother:* 7 Enarete *son:* 7 Glaucus

sit 4 meet, open, pose, rest, seat 5 brood, cover, perch, squat 6 settle 7 convene, install, posture 8 ensconce

Sita *abductor:* 6 Ravana *husband, rescuer:* 4 Rama

sitarist 7 Shankar (Ravi)

sit down 4 land 5 light, perch, roost 6 alight, settle 9 touch down

site 3 dig 4 home, spot 5 haunt, locus, place, point, range, scene, where 6 locale 7 habitat, station 8 locality, location, position

sit-in 7 protest

sitting 6 séance 7 session *prolonged:* 8 sederunt

Sitting Bull's tribe 5 Sioux

sitting duck 4 butt, mark 6 target

situate 3 put, set 4 site 5 place 6 locate 8 position

situation 3 job 4 mode, post, rank, site, spot 5 berth, locus, place, point, state, where 6 billet, office, status 7 bargain, footing, posture, station 8 location, position, standing 9 condition

situs 5 place

Siva see Shiva

six *combining form:* 3 hex, sex 4 hexa, sexi 5 sexti *group of:* 5 hexad 6 hexade, sestet, sextet 7 sestole, sextole 8 sestolet, sextette 9 sextuplet *on a die:* 4 sice *relating to:* 6 senary

sixfold 9 sextuplex

six-shooter 3 gun 6 pistol 8 revolver

sixth sense 3 ESP

sizable 3 big 4 good 5 hefty, large, major 8 sensible 9 extensive 10 giant-sized, large-scale 11 respectable 12 considerable

size 4 area, body, bulk, mass 5 width
6 extent, height, length, spread, volume
7 bigness, breadth, expanse, measure,
stretch 9 amplitude, dimension, extension,
greatness, largeness, magnitude 10 dimensions, proportion 11 measurement

sizzle 3 fry 4 buzz, fizz, hiss, sear, whiz
5 swish, whish 6 wheeze, whoosh 8 sibilate

sizzling 3 hot 5 fiery 6 baking, red-hot,
torrid 7 burning 8 broiling, scalding, white-
hot 9 scorching

skald 4 bard, poet

Skanda 6 war-god *brother:* 6 Ganesa
7 Ganesha *father:* 4 Siva 5 Shiva

skate 4 fish, skid 5 glide, slide 6 fellow
blade: 6 runner *kind:* 6 figure, hockey

skating site 3 ice 4 rink

skedaddle 3 fly, run 4 bolt, flee, kite, skip
5 scoot, scram, screw, skirr, split 6 begone,
cut out, decamp, get out 7 make off,
scamper, skiddoo, take off, vamoose
8 clear out, hightail

skeleton 5 bones, draft, frame 6 sketch
7 diagram, outline 9 framework *marine:*
5 coral, shell

skeptic 5 cynic 7 doubter, scoffer, zetetic
8 agnostic 10 headshaker, Pyrrhonian, Pyrrhonist, questioner, unbeliever 11 disbeliever

skeptical 6 show-me 7 cynical 8 aporetic,
doubtful, doubting 9 quizzical 10 dissenting, suspicious 11 incredulous, mistrustful,
questioning, unbelieving 12 disbelieving,
freethinking

skepticism 5 doubt, qualm 6 wonder
7 concern, dubiety 8 mistrust 9 dubiosity,
suspicion 11 incertitude, uncertainty

skerry 4 isle, reef

sketch 4 draw, line, plot 5 draft, trace
7 aperpçu 6 depict, design, detail, lay out,
map out, précis, survey 7 develop, diagram, outline, pandect, sylloge 8 block out,
chalk out, rough out, skeleton, syllabus
9 adumbrate, blueprint, delineate 10 compendium 11 skeletonize 12 characterize
13 diagrammatize

sketchy 5 rough 7 cursory, shallow
8 skeletal 9 depthless 11 superficial

skew 3 dip 4 bias, skid, slip, slue, veer
5 angle, sheer, slant, slide 6 swerve 8 train
off

skewer 3 rod 4 spit 5 lance, spear, spike
6 impale, skiver 8 transfix 9 brochette
11 transpierce

ski 5 glide, slide *lift:* 4 J-bar, T-bar 5 chair
7 gondola

skid 3 dip 4 drop, fall, skew, slue, veer
5 sheer, slide 6 plunge, tumble 7 plummet,
spinout 8 nose-dive

skid row 4 slum 6 bowery

skier *American:* 3 Moe (Tommy) 4 Kidd
(Billy) 5 Mahre (Phil) 7 Johnson (Bill) *Aus-
trian:* 6 Proell (Annemarie) 7 Klammer
(Franz), Schranz (Karl) *expert:* 6 kanone
French: 5 Killy (Jean-Claude) *Italian:*
5 Tomba (Alberto) 6 Theoni (Gustavo)
Swedish: 8 Stenmark (Ingemar)

skiff 4 boat 7 rowboat

skiing *area:* 3 run 5 slope *cross-country:*
7 touring *event:* 6 schuss, slalom 8 down-
hill 11 giant slalom *horse-drawn:* 9 skijor-
ing *kind:* 6 Alpine, Nordic *position:* 7 vor-
lage *technique:* 6 wedeln 8 snowplow,
traverse *turn:* 7 christy 8 christie

skill 3 art 5 craft, knack 7 ability, address,
command, cunning, know-how, mastery,
prowess, sleight 8 deftness 9 dexterity,
expertise, expertism, readiness 10 adroitness, expertness, mastership 13 dexterousness *combining form:* 6 techno,
techny *suffix:* 3 ics 4 ship

skillet 3 pan 6 frypan, spider 9 frying pan

skillful 4 deft, good 5 adept, crack
6 adroit, clever, daedal, expert, master,
pretty, wicked 7 learned, skilled, versant
8 masterly 9 masterful, workmanly 10 proficient, well-versed 11 crackerjack, workmanlike

skim 3 dap, fly 4 dart, kiss, sail, scud, skip
5 brush, carom, float, graze, shave, shoot,
skirr 6 glance 8 ricochet

skimpy 3 shy 4 poor 5 scant, short, spare
6 meager, scanty, scarce, scrimp, sparse
7 failing, scrimpy, wanting 8 exiguous
9 deficient 10 inadequate 12 insufficient

skim through 4 scan 6 browse 8 glance
at 10 glance over

skin 3 fur, gyp, pod, rap 4 clad, clip, face,
fell, hide, pare, peel, pelt, rind, side, soak
5 blame, cheat, cover, fleet, haste, hurry,
knock, miser, nabal, scale, stick, stiff, strip
6 barrel, bucket, bullet, con man, fleece,
hasten, hustle, sheath, slough 7 beeline,
censure, condemn, diddler, grifter, niggard,
scrooge, sharper, sheathe 8 denounce,
highball, swindler, tightwad 9 criticize,
defrauder, dermatous, excoriate, reprehend, reprobate, sheathing 10 cheapskate,
denunciate, overcharge 11 cheeseparer,
decorticate, excorticate, flimflammer *animal:*
4 coat, hide, pelt 6 hackle, peltry *bird:*
7 pteryla *combining form:* 3 cut 4 cuti,
derm, scyt 5 derma, dermo, dermy, scyto
6 dermat, dermia, dermis 7 cutaneo, der-
mata (plural), dermato, epiderm 8 epidermo
depression: 6 dimple *disease:* 4 acne
5 hives, mange 6 eczema 10 dermatitis
dry: 5 scurf *fold:* 5 plica *layer:* 5 derma
6 corium, dermis 7 corneum, cuticle 9 epi-

dermis *opening:* 4 pore *protuberance:* 4 mole, wart 6 pimple *rabbit:* 5 coney *relating to:* 6 dermal 9 cuticular, epidermal *seal:* 5 sculp *spot:* 7 freckle *tumor:* 3 wen

skinflint 5 chuff, miser, nabal 7 niggard 8 muckworm, tightwad 10 cheapskate 11 cheeseparer

skink 4 soup 6 lizard

skinny 4 bony, lank, lean 5 gaunt, lanky, spare, weedy 6 twiggy 7 angular, scraggy, scrawny 8 rawboned, skeletal 9 emaciated

Skin of Our Teeth author 6 Wilder (Thornton)

skip 3 dap, fly, hop, run 4 bolt, flee, jump, leap, lope, skim, trip 5 blank, bound, caper, carom, chasm, frisk, graze, scoot, skirr 6 bounce, cavort, curvet, gambol, glance, spring 7 make off, scamper, skitter 8 omission, overlook, ricochet 9 oversight, skedaddle 10 hippety-hop

skipjack 3 fop 4 fish 6 beetle 8 sailboat

skipper 6 leader 7 captain 9 commander

skirl 6 scream, shriek

skirmish 4 fray 5 brush, clash, melee, run-in, set-to 6 affray, ambush, attack, melay 7 assault 9 encounter, scrimmage 10 velitation

skirr 3 fly, run 4 bolt, dart, flee, sail, scud, skim, skip 5 float, scoot, shoot 7 make off, scamper 9 skedaddle

skirt 3 hem, rim 4 brim, duck, edge, skip 5 avoid, bound, brink, burke, dodge, elude, evade, hedge, verge 6 border, bypass, define, detour, escape, fringe, ignore, margin 7 garment 8 sidestep, surround 9 perimeter, periphery 10 circumvent, equivocate *ballet:* 4 tutu *feature:* 3 hem 4 slit *long:* 4 maxi *Scottish:* 4 kilt *short:* 4 mini *style:* 5 A-line

skit 3 act 4 jibe 5 caper, taunt 6 parody, shtick, sketch 7 schtick 9 burlesque

skitter 3 hop 4 lope, skip, trip 6 spring

skittery see **skitterish**

skittish 4 edgy 5 dizzy, giddy 7 flighty, nervous, restive 8 agitable, unstable, volatile 9 alarmable, excitable, frivolous, startlish 10 capricious, unreliable

skivvies 9 underwear

skoal 5 drink, toast

skua 4 bird 6 jaeger

skulduggery 8 foul play, trickery

skulk 4 lurk, slip 5 creep, shirk, slink, sneak, steal 7 gumshoe 9 pussyfoot

skull 4 bone, head, mind 5 brain 7 cranium 8 brainpan 9 braincase *back of:* 7 occiput *bone:* 5 vomer 6 zygoma 7 ethmoid, frontal 8 parietal, sphenoid, temporal *jawless:* 9 calvarium *joint:* 6 suture *part:* 3 jaw 5 inion 6 basion

skullcap 5 calot 6 beanie, pileus 7 calotte 8 yarmulke 9 calvarium, zucchetto

skunk 3 cur, dog 4 beat, drub, lick, scum, snot, toad, whip 5 snake 6 thrash 7 polecat, shellac 8 conopate, lambaste 9 overwhelm *genus:* 8 Mephitis

sky 5 azure 6 heaven, welkin 7 heavens 8 empyrean 9 firmament *combining form:* 4 uran 5 urano *sky-blue:* 5 azure 8 cerulean 9 caerulean

sky chief 5 pilot

skylarking 5 revel 7 fooling, revelry, wassail, whoopee, whoopla, whoop-up 9 high jinks, horseplay, revelment, rowdiness, whoop-de-do 10 roughhouse 12 roughhousing

skylight 6 window

skyline 7 horizon

sky pilot 5 padre 6 cleric, divine, parson 8 chaplain, clerical, minister, preacher 9 churchman, clergyman 12 ecclesiastic

skyrocket 4 rise, soar 5 climb 7 shoot up 8 upspring

sky sighting 3 UFO

slab 3 bar, rod 4 tile 5 ingot, slice, stick, strip 6 billet

slabber 5 drool 6 drivel, slaver 7 dribble 8 salivate

slack 3 lax, off 4 down, ease, lazy, slow, soft, weak 5 inert, loose, relax 6 feeble, infirm, loosen, remiss, slow-up 7 ease off, laggard, passive, relaxed 8 careless, derelict, dilatory, fainéant, inactive, indolent, slothful, slowdown, sluggish, stagnant, unsteady 9 leisurely, lethargic, negligent, untighten

slacken 3 ebb, lax 4 ease, fall, mire, wane 5 abate, delay, embog, let up, loose, relax 6 detain, hang up, loosen, relent, retard, slow up 7 bog down, die away, die down, ease off, set back, subside 8 moderate, slow down 9 untighten 10 decelerate

slacker 5 idler 6 loafer 7 shirker, slinker 8 slugabed, sluggard 9 goldbrick

slag 4 lava 5 dross 6 cinder, debris, scoria

slake 5 allay 6 deaden, quench 7 crumble, hydrate, satisfy

slam 3 bat, dig, hit, jab, rap 4 bang, bash, beat, belt, blow, boom, clap, ding, drub, flay, mace, slug, slur, swat, wham 5 blast, burst, crack, crash, fling, knock, pound, slash, slate, smack, smash, swipe, whack 6 batter, cudgel, hammer, scathe, strike, thwack, wallop 7 clobber, obloquy, potshot, scourge 8 lambaste, lash into 9 aspersion, bastinado, castigate, stricture

slammer 3 jug, pen 4 jail 6 cooler, prison

slander 4 hurt, slur, tale 5 belie, libel, smear 6 assail, attack, damage, defame, injure, malign 7 asperse, calumny, scandal, traduce 8 muckrake, roorback, strumpet, tear down 9 black wash, denigrate 10 backbiting, calumniate, defamation, detraction, muckraking 11 mud-slinging 12 back-stabbing, belittlement, depreciation 13 disparagement

slang 4 cant 5 argot, lingo 6 jargon, patois, patter 7 dialect 10 vernacular

slant 3 aim, tip 4 bank, bend, bias, cant, heel, lean, list, side, skew, tilt, veer, warp 5 angle, aside, bevel, color, focus, grade, point, slope, splay, train, twist 6 aslope, direct, orient, swerve 7 decline, descend, deviate, distort, diverge, incline, leaning, outlook, recline 8 gradient, sideways, sidewise 9 direction, influence, obliquely, prejudice, viewpoint 10 standpoint 11 concentrate, inclination 12 predilection *combining form:* 4 clin 5 clino

slap 3 box, hit, pop, try 4 bash, blip, chop, cuff, drub, flay, poke, shot, slam, stab, swat, wham 5 clout, crack, fling, punch, score, slash, smack, spank, whack, whirl 6 buffet, insult, scathe, strike 7 affront, despite, scourge 8 haymaker, lambaste, lash into 9 castigate, contumely, indignity

slapdash 5 messy 6 botchy, random, sloppy, untidy 7 aimless 8 careless, slipshod, slovenly 9 desultory, haphazard, hit-or-miss, irregular 10 designless, unthorough

slaphappy 7 foolish 8 carefree, reckless 10 punch-drunk

slash 3 cut 4 clip, flay, gash, hack, pare, slit 5 lower, shave, slice 6 hackle, haggle, incise, pierce, reduce, scathe, scorch 7 abridge, blister, curtail, cut back, cut down, scarify, scourge, shorten 8 lambaste, lash into, mark down, retrench 9 castigate, excoriate 10 abbreviate

slasher 5 knife, razor, sword 9 swordsman 12 swashbuckler

slat 4 lath 5 board, stave, strip 6 louver 7 airfoil 9 sheepskin

slate 4 gray, list, rock, tile 6 record, tablet, ticket 7 shingle 8 schedule 9 designate

slaughter 4 kill, maim, slay 6 mangle, murder 7 butcher, carnage, torture, wipe out 8 butchery, decimate, hecatomb, massacre, mutilate 9 bloodbath, bloodshed 10 annihilate 11 destruction, exterminate 12 annihilation

slaughterhouse 8 abattoir

Slav 4 Pole, Serb, Sorb, Wend 5 Croat, Czech 6 Bulgar, Slovak 7 Russian, Serbian, Slovene 8 Bohemian, Croatian, Moravian 9 Bulgarian, Ruthenian, Ukrainian

slave 4 grub, help, peon, plod, serf, slog, toil 5 grind, helot 6 drudge, menial, thrall, toiler, vassal 7 bondman, chattel, servant 8 bondsman 9 dray horse, mancipium,

workhorse *feudal:* 4 serf *harem:* 9 odalisque *liberated:* 8 freedman *Muslim:* 8 Mameluke *Spartan:* 5 helot

slave driver 6 tyrant 8 martinet, rawhider 10 taskmaster 11 Simon Legree

slaver 4 fawn, spit 5 cower, drool, toady, water 6 cringe, drivel, grovel, kowtow, saliva 7 dribble, honey up, slabber, slobber, spittle, truckle 8 bootlick, salivate

slavery 4 moil, toil, work, yoke 5 grind, labor 6 drudge, thrall 7 bondage, helotry, peonage, serfdom 8 bullwork, drudgery, plugging 9 servitude, thralldom, villenage 10 donkeywork

Slavic apostle 5 Cyril 9 Methodius

slavish 3 low 4 hard, tame 5 apish, heavy, rough 6 knotty, menial, rugged 7 operose, servile, subdued 8 obeisant, wretched 9 difficult, emulative, imitative, laborious, miserable, spineless, strenuous 10 formidable, obsequious, uninspired, unoriginal 11 subservient

slay 4 do in, down, kill 6 cut off, finish, lay low, murder 7 butcher, destroy, execute, put away 8 dispatch, knock off 9 liquidate, slaughter 11 assassinate

slayer 4 bane 6 killer 8 homicide, murderer

sleazy 3 low 4 mean, thin 5 cheap, dingy, seedy, tacky, tatty 6 cheesy, common, flabby, flimsy, floppy, paltry, shabby, shoddy, slight, trashy 7 flaccid, run-down, tenuous 9 gossamery 10 broken-down, down-at-heel 11 dilapidated 12 disreputable

sled 4 luge, pung 6 sleigh 7 coaster, travois 8 toboggan *Russian:* 6 troika

sled dog 5 husky 8 malamute

sledge 6 hammer, sleigh *Eskimo:* 7 komatik

sleek 4 oily 5 round, slick 6 glassy, glossy, polish, refine, smarmy, smooth 7 perfect 8 lustrous, polished 10 glistening

sleep 3 nap 4 coma, doze, rest 5 death, relax, sopor 6 demise, repose, siesta, snooze, torpor 7 decease, languor, passing, quietus, shut-eye, silence, slumber 8 dullness, hebetude, lethargy 9 lassitude, torpidity 10 defunction, torpidness 11 dissolution, slumberland *bringer:* 7 sandman *combining form:* 4 hypn, narc 5 hypno, narco, somni *god:* 6 Hypnos, Hypnus, Somnus

sleeper 4 beam 7 Pullman, support 8 dormeuse, long shot

sleeping 4 abed 7 dormant 8 comatose *disease:* 10 narcolepsy

sleeplessness 8 insomnia

sleepwalker 12 somnambulist

sleepy 4 dozy 5 dazed, dopey, inert, quiet 6 drowsy, opiate, snoozy, torpid 7 nodding, passive, poppled, yawning **8** comatose, hypnotic, inactive, listless, narcotic, oscitant, sleeping, sluggish, slumbery, somnific **9** heavy-eyed, lethargic, somnolent, soporific **10** nepenthean, slumbering, slumberous, somnorific **11** somniferous

sleigh 4 pung, sled **6** sledge

sleight 4 play, ploy, ruse, wile **5** skill, trick **6** device **7** address, gimmick, prowess **8** artifice, deftness, maneuver **9** dexterity, readiness, stratagem **10** adroitness **13** dexterousness

sleight of hand 5 magic, trick **9** dexterity **11** legerdemain

slender 4 lean, slim, thin, trim **5** lithe, reedy, scant, short, small **6** remote, scanty, scarce, skinny, slight, stalky, svelte, twiggy **7** outside, spindly, squinny, tenuous, wanting **8** slimmish **9** attenuate, deficient **10** inadequate, negligible **12** insufficient

sleuth 3 tec **4** dick **7** gumshoe **8** hawkshaw, Sherlock **9** detective **10** private eye **12** investigator

slice 3 cut, lot **4** bite, gash, part, slit **5** carve, quota, sever, share, slash, split **6** cleave, incise, pierce, sunder **7** dissect, partage, portion, segment **8** dissever **9** allotment, allowance

slick 4 oily, slip, wise **5** canny, fix up, glide, quick, round, sharp, sleek, slide, smart, soapy, spiff **6** doll up, glossy, greasy, polish, refine, slippy, smarmy, smooth **7** deck out, doll out, dress up, fulsome, gussy up, knowing, perfect, slither **8** glissade, slippery, slithery, spruce up, unctious, unctuous **10** lubricious, oleaginous **11** quick-witted, sharp-witted

slicker 4 dude **6** gypper **7** cheater, diddler, oilskin, sharper **8** raincoat, swindler **9** defrauder, trickster **11** flimflammer

slide 3 dip, sag **4** drop, fall, flow, lurk, move, skid, slip **5** chute, coast, crawl, creep, drift, glide, shift, shirk, skate, skulk, slick, slink, slump, sneak, spill, steal **6** stream, tumble **7** decline, drop off, fall off, slither **8** downturn, fall away, glissade **9** downswing, downtrend

slight 4 fail, omit, skip, slim, thin **5** flout, reedy, scoff, small **6** flimsy, forget, ignore, remote, sleazy, stalky, subtle, twiggy **7** blink at, contemn, despise, neglect, outside, slender, squinny, tenuous **8** delicate, discount, overlook, overpass, smallish **9** attenuate, blink away, disregard, gossamery, pint-sized **10** negligible

slim 4 thin **5** canny, lithe, reedy, small **6** adroit, clever, narrow, remote, skinny, slight, stalky, svelte, twiggy **7** cunning, lissome, outside, slender, squinny, tenuous **9** attenuate, dexterous, ingenious, lithesome **10** negligible

slim down 4 diet **6** reduce **10** slenderize

slime 3 mud **4** muck, ooze, scum, slum **6** sludge *combining form:* **3** myx **4** myxa, myxo

slimy 4 oozy, vile **7** viscous

sling 4 cast, fire, hang, hurl, sock, toss **5** fling, heave, march, pitch, stalk, throw **6** dangle, depend, launch, stride **7** suspend **8** catapult

slink 4 lurk **5** creep, shirk, skulk, slide, sneak, steal **6** weasel **7** gumshoe, sneaker **8** sneaksby **9** pussyfoot

slip 3 dip, lam, sag **4** bull, dock, drop, fall, lose, lurk, molt, pier, quay, shed, sink, skid, trip **5** berth, boner, crash, creep, erode, error, fluff, glide, jetty, lapse, levee, mouse, shake, shirk, skulk, slick, slide, slink, slump, sneak, steal, wharf **6** bungle, escape, flight, go down, slough, soften, topple **7** blooper, blunder, decline, drop off, fall off, faux pas, getaway, gumshoe, mistake, plummet, slither **8** breakout, downturn, escaping, exuviate, fall away, glissade, nose-dive, prolapse, throw off **9** downslide, downswing, downtrend, pussyfoot

slipper 4 mule, shoe **5** brake, romeo, scuff **6** juliet, sandal **8** babouche, pantofle

slippery 3 icy **4** eely, oily **5** slick **6** greasy, lubric, shifty **7** mutable **8** slithery, unstable, unsteady, variable **9** uncertain **10** changeable, inconstant, lubricious

slipshod 5 messy, tacky **6** botchy, faulty, shabby, shoddy, sloppy, tagrag, unneat, untidy **7** inexact, raunchy, scrubby, scruffy, unkempt **8** careless, fouled-up, ill-kempt, messed-up, slapdash, slovenly, tattered **9** botched-up, haphazard, imperfect, neglected, negligent, slaphappy **10** bedraggled, disheveled, down-at-heel, inaccurate

slipup 5 boner, error, fluff, lapse **6** bungle, miscue **7** blooper, blunder, mistake **9** oversight

slit 3 cut **4** gash, rent, tear **5** slash, slice **6** incise, pierce **7** opening **8** roulette

slither 4 lurk, slip **5** creep, glide, prowl, sidle, slick, slide, slink, snake, sneak, steal **8** glissade, undulate

slithery 5 slick **6** greasy, slippy **8** slippery **10** lubricious

sliver 5 carve, shave, shred, slice **6** haggle **8** splinter

slob 4 boor, clod **6** sloven

slobber 4 gush **5** drool **6** drivel, slaver **7** dribble, slabber **8** salivate

sloe 4 plum **10** blackthorn

slog 3 hit **4** ding, grub, plod, slop, sock, toil **5** catch, clout, grind, slave, smite, whack **6** drudge, stodge, strike, trudge **8** plunther

slogan 4 word **5** idiom, motto **6** byword, phrase **8** locution **9** catchword, watchword **10** expression, shibboleth **11** catchphrase

sloop 4 boat, dray 8 longboat, sailboat

slop 3 mud, pap 4 bolt, cram, food, gulp, plod, slog, toil, wolf 5 douse, plash, slosh, spill, squab, swash 6 englut, gobble, guzzle, pablum, splash, splosh, stodge, trudge 7 rubbish, spatter, splurge, spurtle 8 footslog, plunther, splatter 11 ingurgitate

slope 3 tip 4 bend, cant, heel, lean, list, rise, skew, swag, sway, tilt 5 grade, pitch, scarp, slant 6 ascent, escarp, glacis 7 descent, incline, leaning, recline, versant 8 gradient 9 acclivity, declivity, deviation, obliquity 10 deflection 11 inclination, obliqueness *combining form:* 5 cline 6 clinal

sloppy 4 poor, soft 5 drunk, gushy, messy 6 botchy, clumsy, unneat, untidy 7 awkward, gushing, muddled, unkempt 8 careless, effusive, ill-kempt, mediocre, slapdash, slipshod, slobbery, slovenly 9 disguised, pixilated 10 amateurish, disheveled, inebriated, slobbering, unthorough 11 intoxicated

slosh 3 bat, lap 4 bang, bash, belt, blow, bolt, cram, dash, gulp, gush, roar, rush, slam, slop, wash, wolf 5 churn, crack, douse, plash, pound, smack, swash, whirl 6 babble, bubble, burble, englut, gobble, gurgle, guzzle, ripple, splash, wallop 7 spatter, splurge, spurtle 8 splatter 9 bespatter 11 ingurgitate

slot 5 niche, notch, track, trail 6 groove, keyway 7 keyhole, opening, passage . 10 pigeonhole

sloth 4 laze 6 acedia, apathy, idling, lazing, slouch 7 languor, loafing 8 idleness, laziness, lethargy 9 faineancy, heaviness, indolence, lassitude, torpidity 10 ergophobia 11 inattention, languidness 12 heedlessness, listlessness, slothfulness, sluggishness 13 shiftlessness *three-toed:* 2 ai *two-toed:* 4 unav

slothful 4 idle, lazy 5 drony 7 work-shy 8 fainéant, indolent 9 easygoing, slowgoing

slouch 3 bum, hat, lop, oaf, sag 4 bend, gawk, laze, lean, loaf, loll, lout, lump, slug, wilt 5 droop, idler, klutz, looby, sloth, slump, stoop 6 loafer, lounge, lubber 7 saunter, shamble, shuffle, trollop 8 dolittle, fainéant, idleness, laziness, meathead, slugabed, sluggard 9 do-nothing, indolence, lazybones 12 slothfulness, sluggishness

slough 3 arm, bay, bog, fen, mud 4 cast, cove, gulf, junk, mire, molt, shed, slip, sump 5 bayou, firth, inlet, marsh, scrap, swamp 6 harbor, morass, reject 7 cashier, discard 8 exuviate, jettison, quagmire, throw out 9 marshland, swampland, throw away

sloven 5 messy 6 sloppy, untidy 7 unkempt 8 careless, ill-kempt, slipshod, uncombed 10 disheveled

slow 3 low, off 4 down, dull, late, poky 5 brake, rusty, slack, tardy 6 leaden, retard, simple, steady, stupid 7 halting, laggard, lagging, limited, reduced, unhasty 8 backward, crawling, dawdling, delaying, dilatory, dragging, flagging, measured, plodding, retarded, sluggish, stagnant 9 dim-witted, leisurely, snaillike, unhasting, unhurried 10 deliberate, half-witted, snailpaced, straggling, unhurrying

slowpoke 5 snail 6 lagger 7 dawdler, laggard 8 lingerer, loiterer 9 slow coach, straggler

sludge 3 mud 4 mire, muck, ooze, slob 5 slime 8 sediment

slue 3 dip 4 skew, turn, veer 5 sheer 6 swerve 8 train off

sluff 7 discard

slug 3 bum, hit, nip, tot 4 belt, dram, drop, jolt, shot, slam 5 blast, idler, larva, smash, snail, snort 6 loafer, slouch, sloven, wallop 7 clobber, slacker, snifter 8 dolittle, fainéant, toothful 9 do-nothing, lazybones *genus:* 5 Limax

sluggard 3 bum 5 idler 6 loafer, slouch 7 dawdler, laggard, lie-abed, shirker 8 dolittle, fainéant, slowpoke, slugabed 9 do-nothing, goldbrick, lazybones, slow coach 10 sleepyhead

slugger 5 boxer 6 batter, hitter

sluggish 3 off 4 down, lazy, logy, slow 5 dopey, heavy, slack, stiff 6 bovine, draggy, leaden, stupid, torpid 7 costive, lumpish 8 comatose, dragging, slothful 9 apathetic, lethargic, stupified 10 slumberous 12 hebetudinous

sluice 4 flow, gush, pour, roll, soak, wash 5 douse, flush, surge 6 drench, stream

slum 4 dump 6 ghetto 7 skid row

slumber 4 coma, doze 5 sleep 6 drowse, stupor, torpor 7 languor 8 dullness, hebetude, lethargy 9 lassitude, torpidity

slumberous see **sleepy**

slump 3 dip, lop, sag 4 drop, fall, flag, loll, slip 5 droop, pitch, slide 6 cave in, go down, plunge, slouch, topple, tumble 7 decline, drop off, falloff, trollop 8 collapse, downturn, fall away, keel over 9 downslide, downswing, downtrend, recession 10 depression, stagnation

slur 4 blot, blur, lisp, onus, slam, spot 5 brand, odium, smear, stain 6 befoul, defame, insult, malign, slight, stigma 7 blacken, obloquy, traduce 8 black eye, tear down 9 aspersion, bespatter, denigrate, stricture 10 calumniate

slurp 4 suck 5 lap up, slosh, smack, swill 6 guzzle 8 wolf down

slush 3 mud 4 mire, muck, snow 5 grout 6 drivel

sly 4 deep, foxy, lurk, slim, wily 5 cagey, canny, creep, shady, skulk, slick, slide, slink, smart, sneak, steal 6 adroit, artful, astute, clever, covert, crafty, shifty, smooth, sneaky, subtle, tricky 7 crooked, cunning, devious, furtive, gumshoe, slanter, unfrank, vulpine 8 guileful, scheming, slippery, stealthy 9 designing, dexterous, dishonest, ingenious, insidious, masterful, predatory, subdolous, underhand 11 calculating, clandestine, underhanded 12 disingenuous, unscrupulous 13 Machiavellian

slyboots see scamp

slyness 3 art 5 craft 7 cunning 8 artifice, foxiness, wiliness 9 cageyness, canniness 10 artfulness, craftiness

smack 3 bat, bop, box, lip 4 bash, belt, biff, blip, blow, buss, chop, cuff, dash, hint, kiss, lick, peck, reek, slap, sock, tang 5 clout, crack, punch, sapor, savor, smash, smell, spank, stink, taste, tinge, trace 6 buffet, flavor, relish, smooch 7 soupçon, suggest 8 osculate, resemble, sapidity, tincture 9 suspicion 10 sprinkling

small 3 off, set, wee 4 mean, mini, puny, slim, tiny 5 borne, dinky, light, micro, minor, petty, short 6 bantam, lesser, little, minute, monkey, narrow, paltry, petite, remote, slight 7 cramped, limited, outside, slender, trivial 8 picayune, piddling, pint-size, trifling 9 miniature, minuscule, secondary, two-by-four 10 diminutive, negligible, picayunish, undersized 11 ineffectual, minor-league, unimportant 12 inconsequent 13 insignificant *amount:* see particle *combining form:* 4 lept, micr, mini, olig, parv 5 lepto, oligo, parvi, parvo

small fry 4 kids 8 children

small-minded 4 mean 6 narrow 7 bigoted 9 hidebound, illiberal 10 brassbound, intolerant, unenlarged

smallness *abnormal:* 6 nanism 8 dwarfism

small one *suffix:* 2 el, et, ey, ia (plural), ie 3 cle, ium, kin, ock, ula, ule, uli (plural) 4 ella, ette, illa, ling, ulae (plural), ulum, ulus 5 ellae (plural), illae (plural)

smallpox 7 variola

small talk 6 babble, banter 7 chatter, prattle 8 babbling, badinage, chitchat, repartee, trifling 9 bavardage, prattling

smalt 4 blue 5 glass

smarmy 4 oily 5 sleek, slick, soapy 6 glassy, glossy, sleeky 7 fulsome 8 polished, unctious, unctuous 10 oleaginous

smart 3 hep 4 ache, bite, bold, burn, chic, hurt, pain, pert, trig, wise 5 alert, canny, fresh, nervy, prick, quick, sassy, saucy, sharp, slick, sting, swank, swish 6 brainy, bright, cheeky, clever, dapper, modish, shrewd, spruce, suffer, tingle, with-it 7 dashing, knowing, stylish 8 impudent 9 brilliant, exclusive, sprightly 11 fashionable, intelligent, quick-witted, ready-witted, sharp-witted

smart aleck 7 show-off, wise guy 8 wiseacre 9 know-it-all 11 wisecracker, wisenheimer 12 grandstander 13 exhibitionist

smart-alecky 4 wise 5 fresh, nervy, sassy 6 cheeky 8 impudent 9 bold-faced 10 procacious

smarten 5 fix up, primp, slick, spiff 6 doll up, spruce 7 deck out, doll out, dress up, gussy up 8 spruce up

smart set 3 ton 5 elite 6 bon ton 7 aristoi, society, who's who 10 blue bloods, upper crust 11 aristocracy, Four Hundred

smash 3 hit, jar, wow 4 bang, bash, belt, blow, boom, bump, clap, jolt, raze, rive, ruin, slam, slug, sock, wham, whop 5 blast, burst, clash, crack, crash, shock, whack, wreck 6 impact, pileup, shiver, wallop 7 clobber, crack-up, debacle, destroy, shatter, smashup 8 collapse, decimate, demolish, destruct, fragment, knockout, splinter, splitter, tear down 9 bastinado, breakdown, collision, sensation, succès fou 10 annihilate, bell ringer, percussion 11 splinterize

smashup 5 crash, wreck 6 pileup 7 crack-up, debacle 8 collapse 9 breakdown

smattering 3 few 7 handful 10 sprinkling

smear 3 dab, rub, tar 4 beat, coat, daub, drub, foil, lick, slur, soil, trim, whip 5 cover, smarm, stain, sully, taint 6 bedaub, befoul, defame, defile, malign, smirch, smudge, spread, thrash 7 asperse, blacken, overlay, plaster, repulse, shellac, slander, smother, tarnish 8 besmirch, discolor, lambaste 9 bespatter, denigrate, frustrate 10 calumniate, overspread

smell 4 funk, hint, nose, odor, reek 5 aroma, scent, sense, smack, sniff, snuff, stink, trace, whiff 6 detect, stench 7 soupçon 8 tincture 9 fragrance, redolence, suspicion 10 intimation, suggestion *combining form:* 3 osm 4 osma, osmo

smell, sense of 9 olfaction, osphresis

smelly 4 olid, rank 5 fetid, funky, reeky 6 foetid, putrid, rancid, stinky 7 noisome, reeking, stenchy 8 stinking 10 malodorous

smelt 4 flux, slag 6 reduce, refine, speise, speiss, tomcod 7 scorify 8 sparling 9 sand borer, sand lance, whitebait, sand lance

smidgen see particle

smile 4 beam, grin 6 simper

smirch see smudge

smirk 4 grin, leer 5 fleer, sneer 6 simper

smitch see particle

smite 3 bat, hit, try 4 belt, dash, ding, slog, sock 5 catch, clout, whack 6 harrow, martyr, strike 7 afflict, agonize, clobber, crucify, torment, torture 10 excruciate

smithereens 6 pieces 9 fragments, particles

smitten 6 mashed, soft on 8 enamored, spoony on 10 spoony over

smoke 4 cure, floc, fume 8 fumigate 9 cigarette

smoking material 3 pot 4 hash 5 cigar, joint 6 reefer 7 hashish, tobacco 9 cigarette, cigarillo, marihuana, marijuana

smolder 4 boil, stir 5 burst, churn, erupt 6 bubble, seethe, simmer 7 explode, ferment 9 fulminate

smooch 3 lip 4 buss, foul, kiss, peck, soil 5 dirty, grime, smack 6 besoil, smirch, smudge, smutch 7 begrime, tarnish 8 osculate

smooth 3 lay 4 bald, easy, even, fair, flat, mild, soft 5 balmy, bland, faint, flush, level, light, plane, preen, round, royal, sleek, slick, suave 6 evenly, facile, flatly, fluent, gentle, glossy, polish, polite, refine, simple, sleeky, trowel, urbane, velure 7 courtly, cursive, flatten, flowing, jagless, lenient, perfect, planate, running 8 glabrate, glabrous, hairless, soothing, unbroken, waveless 9 agreeable, civilized, courteous, uniformly 10 effortless, rippleless, unwrinkled *combining form:* 3 lio 4 leio, liss 5 lisso

smoothen 3 lay 4 even 5 flush, level, plane 7 flatten

smooth-spoken 5 vocal 6 fluent 8 eloquent 10 articulate

smorgasbord 4 hash 6 jumble, medley 7 mélange 8 mishmash, pastiche 9 potpourri 10 hodgepodge, miscellany 11 gallimaufry

smother 4 beat, cool, cork, drub, lick, rein, trim, whip 5 choke, quash, quell, smear 6 hush up, muffle, quench, stifle, thrash 7 clobber, collect, compose, control, quackle, repress, shellac, squelch 8 lambaste, restrain, suppress 9 suffocate 10 asphyxiate

smudge 3 dab 4 daub, foul, soil 5 dirty, grime, smear, stain, sully, taint 6 bedaub, besoil, blotch, defile, smirch 7 begrime, besmear, plaster, splotch, tarnish 8 besmirch

smug 4 tidy 5 slick 6 spruce 8 priggish 10 complacent 11 self-pleased 13 self-contented, self-satisfied

smuggle 3 run 7 bootleg 10 contraband

smut 4 blot, soil 5 dirty, smear, stain, taint 6 defile 7 bestain 8 besmirch, discolor

smutty 4 foul 5 dirty, nasty 6 coarse, filthy, vulgar 7 obscene, raunchy 8 indecent 12 scatological

Smyrna 5 Izmir

snack 3 tea 4 bite, nosh, tapa 5 mug-up 6 morsel 9 collation 11 refreshment

snaffle 3 bit

snag 3 bar, rub 4 clog, curb, drag 5 brake, crimp 6 hamper, hold-up, hurdle 8 obstacle, traverse 10 impediment 11 obstruction

snail 8 escargot, ramshorn, slowpoke 9 band shell

snake 3 boa, cur, dog 4 scum, snot, toad 5 crawl, creep, prick, skunk, slide 6 python 7 serpent, slither 8 anaconda, ophidian, undulate *combining form:* 4 ophi 5 ophio, ophis *poisonous:* 3 asp 4 habu 5 adder, cobra, coral, krait, mamba, viper 6 elapid, taipan 7 rattler 8 cerastes, pit viper, ringhals 10 bushmaster, copperhead, fer-de-lance 11 cottonmouth 13 water moccasin *South African:* 5 aboma

snakebird 6 darter 7 anhinga

snake crane 7 cariama

snake-eater 7 markhor 8 mongoose 13 secretary bird

snakelike 7 anguine 8 ophidian

snakeroot 7 bugbane 10 wild ginger 11 blazing star

snakeweed 7 bistort 13 poison hemlock

snakewood 9 nux vomica 10 frangipani

snaky 7 sinuous, winding 8 flexuous, tortuous 9 meandrous 10 convoluted, meandering, serpentine 11 anfractuous

snap 3 bit, jot, lug, pep, pie 4 bang, bark, dram, drop, hoot, iota, jerk, push, yank 5 cinch, drive, getup, grain, lurch, punch, setup, vigor 6 breeze, picnic, starch, twitch 7 crackle, modicum 8 duck soup, fragment, kid stuff, particle, pushover, sinecure, vitality 9 soft touch, vellicate 10 child's play

snap back 7 rebound, recover

snape 5 taper

snappy 4 fast, racy, tony, trig 5 fleet, hasty, huffy, quick, rapid, raspy, ready, sharp, smart, spicy, swank, swift, swish, zesty 6 lively, prompt, speedy, twitty 7 dashing, peppery, piquant, pungent, raspish, stylish 8 animated, petulant, poignant, prickish 9 breakneck, fractious, irritable, vivacious 10 harefooted 11 expeditious

snare 4 bait, lure, trap 5 catch, decoy, tempt 6 come-on, enmesh, entrap, seduce, tangle 7 catch up, chicane, ensnarl, involve, springe, trammel 8 entangle 9 chicanery, deception, embrangle 10 allurement, enticement, entrapment, seducement, temptation 12 inveiglement

snarl 3 jam, web 4 bark, gnar, knot, maze, mesh, muck 5 chaos, gnarr, ravel, skein, swarm 6 ataxia, huddle, jungle, morass, muddle, tangle 7 clutter, mizmaze, perplex 8 disarray, disorder, entangle, mishmash 9 confusion, intricacy, labyrinth 10 complexity, complicate **11** intertangle **12** complication, entanglement **13** intricateness

snatch 3 nab **4** grab, jerk, nail, take, yank **5** catch, cotch, nip up, seize **6** clutch, whip up, wrench **7** grapple

sneak 3 cur, sly **4** heel, lurk, slip, toad, worm **5** crawl, creep, glide, knave, louse, prowl, shirk, skulk, skunk, slide, slink, steal **6** covert, secret, tiptoe, weasel **7** furtive, gumshoe, hangdog, reptile, slither, smuggle, sub-rosa **8** hush-hush, slyboots, stealthy **9** pussyfoot, scoundrel **10** blackguard, undercover **11** clandestine

sneaky 6 shifty **7** devious **8** guileful, indirect **9** underhand **11** duplicitous, underhanded

sneer 4 gibe, gird, grin, jest, pish **5** fleer, flout, scoff, smile, smirk **6** quip at **7** detract, scout at **8** belittle **9** disparage, underrate

snicker 5 laugh, tehee **6** giggle, guffaw, hee-haw, titter **7** chortle, chuckle

snide 4 fake, sham **5** bogus, false, phony **6** pseudo **7** corrupt, crooked **8** spurious **9** brummagem, dishonest, pinchbeck **11** counterfeit

sniff 4 nose **5** scent, smell

snifter 3 nip, tot **4** dram, drop, jolt, shot, slug **5** snort **8** toothful

snippety see **snippy**

snippy 4 curt **5** bluff, blunt, brief, gruff, short **6** abrupt, crusty **7** brusque

snit 3 fit **4** flap, fume, huff, stew **5** panic, pique, sweat, tizzy **6** dither, frenzy, swivet, taking **7** seizure **10** conniption

snitch 3 cop, nip, rat **4** beak, hook, lift, tell **5** filch, peach, pinch, steal, swipe **6** inform, squeal, tattle **7** purloin, tattler, tipster **8** betrayer, informer, squealer **11** stool pigeon

snob 5 toady **6** poseur **7** high-hat, parvenu, sneerer, tinhorn, upstart **8** popinjay **9** sycophant

snobbish 5 aloof, potty, ritzy **6** remote, snooty, snotty, uppish, uppity **7** haughty, high-hat, pompous **9** high-flown **10** hoity-toity **11** patronizing, pretentious **12** supercilious **13** condescending

snook 5 cobia **6** robalo **12** sergeant fish

snoop 3 pry, spy **4** mess, nose, peek, peep, peer, poke **5** mouse, prier, pryer, stare **6** butt-in, meddle **7** intrude, meddler, Paul Pry **8** busybody, quidnunc **9** detective, inspector, interfere **10** rubberneck

snooper 3 spy **7** meddler **9** detective, inspector **12** investigator

snoopy 4 nosy **5** peery **6** prying **7** curious **11** inquisitive, inquisitory **13** inquisitorial

snoot see **snout**

snooty see **snobbish**

snooze 3 nap **5** dover **6** catnap, dog nap, siesta **10** forty winks

snore 8 rhonchus

snort 3 nip, tot **4** dram, drop, jolt, shot, slug **7** snifter **8** toothful

snot 3 cur, dog, pig, rat, sod **4** puke, scum, toad **5** knave, louse, rogue, skunk, snake **6** wretch **7** high-hat, lowlife, reptile, stinker, villain **8** stinkard **9** scoundrel, stinkaroo

snout 4 beak, nose **6** pecker **7** smeller *combining form:* **6** rhynch **7** rhyncho **8** rhynchus

snow *combining form:* **4** chio **5** chion **6** chiono *glacial:* **4** firn, névé *melted:* **5** slush *pellet:* **7** graupel *ridge:* **8** sastruga, zastruga

snow apple 8 mushroom

snowball 3 wax **4** rise **5** build, mount, run up **6** expand **7** augment, upsurge **8** increase, multiply

snowberry 6 blolly

snowbird 9 fieldfare, ivory gull

Snow-Bound author 8 Whittier (John Greenleaf)

snow eater 7 chinook

snow finch 9 brambling

snow goose 4 wavy **5** wavey

snow grouse 9 ptarmigan

snowlike 7 niveous

snowstorm 8 blizzard

snub 3 cut **5** spite, swank **6** slight **7** high-hat, put down **9** ostracize **12** cold-shoulder

snuff 4 kill, nose, odor **5** aroma, pinch, scent, smell, sniff **6** rappee **8** maccaboy

snug 4 cosy, cozy, easy, neat, soft, tidy, trig, trim **5** comfy, cushy **6** burrow, cuddle, nestle, nuzzle **7** chipper, croodle, easeful, orderly **9** shipshape **11** comfortable

snuggle 5 spoon **6** burrow, cuddle, curl up, huddle, nestle, nuzzle

so 3 sae **4** also, ergo, much, then, thus, very **5** hence **6** thusly **7** awfully, parlous **8** likewise **9** extremely, similarly, therefore, thereupon **11** accordingly, exceedingly **12** consequently

soak 3 wet **4** clip, lush, skin, swig **5** douse, drink, imbue, souse, steep **6** boozer, drench, fleece, infuse, seethe **7** guzzler, immerse, insteep, overwet **8** bedrench, drunkard, permeate, saturate, submerge **9** penetrate **10** impregnate, overcharge *flax:* **3** ret

soap 4 suds **7** flatter *hard:* **7** castile *ingredient:* **3** lye

soapbox 4 rant, rave **5** mouth, orate **7** declaim **8** bloviate, harangue, perorate

soaproot 8 sand lily

soapstone 8 steatite

soapwood 8 wild pear

soapwort 7 cowherd **11** bouncing Bet

soar 2 up 3 fly 4 lift, rise 5 arise, climb, mount, shoot 6 ascend, aspire, rocket, uprear 7 shoot up 9 skyrocket

sob 3 cry 4 blub, wail, weep 6 boohoo 7 blubber

sober 4 calm, cool, hard, soft 5 grave, staid 6 low-key, placid, proper, sedate, serene, solemn 7 earnest, serious, subdued, weighty 8 composed, decorous, forgoing, low-keyed, moderate, rational, reserved, softened, tranquil 9 abstinent, collected, continent, eschewing, inhibited, practical, pragmatic, realistic, temperate, toned down 10 abnegating, abstaining, abstemious, controlled, forbearing, hardboiled, hardheaded, no-nonsense, reasonable, refraining, restrained 11 abstentious, constrained, disciplined, down-to-earth 12 matter-of-fact, unidealistic 13 imperturbable, self-possessed, unimpassioned

sobriety 7 gravity 9 soberness 10 abstinence, continence, sedateness, temperance 11 seriousness

sobriquet 6 byname, byword 8 nickname 10 hypocorism

so-called 6 formal 7 alleged, nominal, titular 8 supposed 9 pretended, professed, purported 10 ostensible

soccer *cup:* 5 World *official:* 7 referee 8 linesman *player:* 6 booter, goalie, kicker, winger 7 forward, link man, striker, sweeper 8 defender, fullback, halfback 10 goalkeeper *player of renown:* 4 Pele *term:* 3 net 4 boot, chip, kick, trap 6 corner, header, tackle, volley 7 dribble, kickoff, throw-in 8 back-heel, free kick, goal kick, goal line 9 touchline 10 center spot, corner flag, corner kick 11 dropped ball, halfway line, penalty kick, penalty spot

sociable 5 close 6 genial 7 cordial 8 familiar, gracious, intimate 9 congenial, convivial 10 gregarious 11 good-natured

social 6 genial 7 amusing, cordial 8 friendly, gracious, pleasant 9 convivial 10 gregarious, hospitable 11 pleasurable 12 entertaining 13 companionable *class:* 5 caste

Social Contract author 8 Rousseau (Jean-Jacques)

socialist *American:* 4 Debs (Eugene) 6 Ripley (George), Thomas (Norman) *English:* 4 Webb (Sidney) 6 Morris (William) *French:* 7 Viviani (René) *German:* 4 Marx (Karl) 6 Engels (Friedrich) 9 Luxemburg (Rosa) 10 Liebknecht (Wilhelm)

socialize 3 mix 5 party 6 mingle 9 associate

social worker 4 Riis (Jacob), Wald (Lillian D.) 6 Addams (Jane) 7 Alinsky (Saul D.), Lathrop (Julia C.)

society 4 club 5 elite, guild, order, union 6 flower, gentry, league, masses, people, public 7 aristoi, company, quality, who's who 8 populace, sodality 9 community 10 fellowship, fraternity, patriciate, upper class, upper crust 11 aristocracy, association, brotherhood 13 companionship *girl:* 3 deb 9 debutante *high:* 9 beau monde, haut monde

Society Islands *capital:* 7 Papeete *discoverer:* 7 Queirós (Pedro Fernandes de)

sociologist *American:* 4 Ward (Lester Frank) 5 Balch (Emily Green), Whyte (William H.) 6 Du Bois (William Edward Burghardt), Sumner (William Graham) 7 Johnson (Charles Spurgeon), Riesman (David) *English:* 7 Spencer (Herbert) *French:* 8 Durkheim (Emile) *German:* 5 Weber (Max) *Italian:* 6 Pareto (Vilfredo) *Swedish:* 6 Myrdal (Alva, Gunnar)

sock 3 bop, box, hit 4 bash, belt, blow, chop, cuff, ding, slap, slog 5 clout, punch, smack, smash, whack 6 argyle, buffet, strike, thwack 8 stocking

socks 4 hose 7 hosiery

Socrates *birthplace:* 6 Athens *poison:* 7 hemlock *pupil:* 5 Plato *wife:* 8 Xantippe

sodality 4 club 5 guild, order, union 6 league 7 society 10 fellowship, fraternity 11 association, brotherhood

sodden 3 wet 4 soak 5 soppy, souse, steep 6 drench, seethe, soaked, soused 7 soaking, sopping 8 drenched, dripping, saturate, waterlog 9 saturated 11 wringing-wet

Sodi's son 7 Gaddiel

sodium 7 natrium *symbol:* 2 Na

Sodom and _____ 8 Gomorrah

sofa 5 couch, divan 7 ottoman 9 banquette

Sofia native 6 Bulgar 9 Bulgarian

soft 4 cozy, easy, mild, snug 5 balmy, bland, comfy, cushy, downy, faint, mushy, pappy, pulpy, silky, silly, sleek, sober, wooly 6 doughy, flabby, fleshy, gentle, low-key, pliant, quaggy, satiny, silken, simple, smooth, spongy, spoony, tender, woolly 7 cottony, easeful, fatuous, foolish, lenient, pillowy, pliable, pulpous, squashy, squishy, subdued, velvety, witless 8 cushiony, formless, low-keyed, moderate, squelchy, woollike, workable, yielding 9 malleable, temperate, toned down 10 weak-headed, weak-minded 11 comfortable 12 compressible

soft-cover 9 paperback

soft hail 7 graupel

softhearted 4 warm 6 tender 10 responsive 11 sympathetic 13 compassionate

soft palate 5 velum

soft-pedal 6 dampen, hush up, muffle, subdue 7 conceal, cushion, silence 8 disguise, play down, suppress, tone down, tune down 11 de-emphasize

soft-soap 3 con 4 coax 6 cajole 7 blarney, flatter, wheedle 8 blandish 9 sweet-talk

Sohrab and Rustum author 6 Arnold (Matthew)

soil 3 mud, tar 4 daub, dirt, foul, home, land, loam, mess, muck, murk 5 crock, dirty, earth, glebe, grime, muddy, smear, stain, sully, taint 6 bedaub, defile, ground, smirch, smooch, smudge, smutch 7 begrime, besmear, country, drabble, draggle, dry land, pedocal, pollute, regosol, tarnish 8 bedabble, besmirch, discolor, homeland, laterite, lithosol, pedalfer, planosol, rendzina, sierozem, solonets, solonetz 10 fatherland, motherland, terra firma 11 contaminate **aggregate:** 3 ped **clay:** 5 gault **combining form:** 2 ge 3 geo, ped 4 agro, pedo **dark:** 9 chernozem **deposit:** 5 loess 7 eluvium **infertile:** 6 podsol, podzol **layer:** 4 gley, sola (plural) 5 solum **prairie:** 8 brunizem **rich:** 6 hotbed **soft:** 4 mool **tropical:** 7 latosol

sojourn 4 stay, stop 5 abide, tarry, visit 6 linger 7 layover 8 stopover 9 tarriance

Sol 3 sun 7 daystar, phoebus **horse:** 4 Eous 5 Ethon 9 Erythreos; (see also **Helios**)

solace 5 cheer 6 buck up 7 comfort, console, upraise

solar disk 4 Aten

solarium 7 sunroom

solder 4 weld 5 braze

soldier 2 GI 4 swad 5 perdu 6 perdue 7 dogface, fighter, pandoor, pandour, pikeman, private, trooper, warrior 8 doughboy, fusileer, fusilier, partisan, rifleman 9 free lance, guerrilla, man-at-arms, mercenary 10 carabineer, serviceman 11 condottiere, fighting man, infantryman **ancient Greece:** 7 hoplite, peltast **British:** 5 Tommy 7 redcoat **cavalry:** 6 hussar 8 chasseur **Celtic:** 4 kern 5 kerne **Confederate:** 3 reb **French:** 5 poilu 6 Zouave **German:** 5 jerry **Greek:** 6 evzone 7 palikar **India:** 5 jawan, sowar 7 jemadar, jemidar **irregular:** 8 guerilla 9 guerrilla **Prussian:** 4 ulan 5 uhlan **Turkish:** 8 janizary 9 janissary

sole 3 one 4 lone, only 5 alone, unwed 6 bottom, single, unique 8 separate, singular, unshared 9 exclusive

solecism 5 boner, break, gaffe 7 blooper, faux pas 8 slangism 9 indecorum, vulgarism 11 impropriety

solemn 4 full 5 grand, grave, sober, staid 6 august, formal, sedate, somber 7 earnest, plenary, serious, stately, weighty 8 majestic 10 ceremonial, impressive, no-nonsense, sobersided 11 ceremonious, magnificent

solemnize 4 keep 5 honor 7 dignify, observe 8 venerate 9 celebrate 11 commemorate

solicit 3 ask, beg 4 call, drum, tout, turn 5 apply, claim, exact, refer 6 demand, desire, drum up, resort 7 beseech, bespeak, canvass, implore, request, require 9 challenge, postulate 11 requisition

solicitous 4 avid, keen 5 eager 6 ardent, raring 7 anxious, athirst, thirsty 8 appetent 9 impatient

solicitude 4 care, heed 5 qualm, worry 6 regard, unease 7 anxiety, concern, scruple 8 disquiet 9 attention 10 uneasiness 11 compunction, concernment 12 presentiment, watchfulness 13 consideration

solid 4 firm, hard 5 sound 6 cogent, firmly, hardly, secure, square, stable 7 telling 9 compacted, unanimous 10 convincing

solidarity 5 union, unity 6 esprit, fixity 7 oneness 8 cohesion, firmness 9 integrity 10 singleness 12 cohesiveness, togetherness 13 esprit de corps, undividedness

solidify 3 dry, set 4 cake 6 harden 7 congeal 8 compress, concrete, contract, indurate

solitary 3 one 4 lone, lorn, only 5 alone, aloof 6 hermit, lonely, offish, single, unique 7 distant, recluse, uncouth 8 derelict, deserted, desolate, eremitic, forsaken, lonesome, reserved, separate, singular 9 abandoned, reclusive, withdrawn 10 antisocial, insociable, particular, unattended, unexampled, unsociable 11 standoffish 12 misanthropic, unrepeatable 13 companionless, unaccompanied

solitude 8 loneness 9 aloneness, isolation, seclusion 10 detachment, loneliness, quarantine, retirement, withdrawal 11 confinement 12 lonesomeness, separateness

solo 4 lone 5 alone

Solomon **brother:** 8 Adonijah **daughter:** 7 Taphath 8 Basemath **father:** 5 David **kingdom:** 6 Israel **mother:** 9 Bathsheba **son, successor:** 8 Rehoboam **victim:** 4 Joab 8 Adonijah

Solomon Islands' capital 7 Honiara

solution 6 answer, result **salt:** 6 saline

solve 3 fix 4 work 5 break 6 decide, settle, unfold 7 clear up, dope out, explain, unravel, work out 8 construe, decipher, unpuzzle, unriddle 9 determine, elucidate, enlighten, figure out, interpret, puzzle out

Somalia **capital:** 9 Mogadishu **monetary unit:** 8 shilling

somatic 6 bodily, carnal 7 fleshly 8 corporal, physical 9 corporeal

somber 3 dim 4 dark, dusk 5 black, bleak, dusky, grave, murky, staid 6 dismal, dreary, gloomy, sedate, solemn 7 earnest, obscure, serious, weighty 8 funereal 9 lightless, tenebrous 10 caliginous, depressing, depressive, no-nonsense, sobersided, tenebrific 11 dispiriting

sommelier's offering 4 wine

somniferous see sleepy

somnolent see sleepy

Somnus *brother:* 4 Mors *god of:* 5 sleep *mother:* 3 Nox

song 3 air, cry, lay 4 aria, call, glee, hymn, lied, note 5 ditty, lyric, paean, piece, poesy, rhyme, verse 6 ballad, melody, poetry 7 calypso, chanson, descant 8 alleluia, cavatina *biblical:* 8 canticle *boat:* 9 barcarole 10 barcarolle *combining form:* 4 melo *French:* 7 chanson *funeral:* 5 dirge *German:* 4 lied 6 lieder (plural) *lamentation:* 8 threnode, threnody *medieval:* 8 sirvente *morning:* 6 aubade *of joy:* 5 paean *operatic:* 4 aria 8 cavatina 9 cabaletta *Portuguese:* 4 fado *sacred:* 5 psalm *sailor's:* 6 chanty 7 chantey, shantey *short:* 8 canzonet *wedding:* 8 hymeneal

song and dance 5 pitch, spiel

songbird see at bird

Song of Myself author 7 Whitman (Walt)

Song of Solomon 9 Canticles

songwriter 8 composer, lyricist

Sonja ___ 5 Henie

Sonnambula composer 7 Bellini (Vincenzo)

sonnet *developer:* 8 Petrarch *part:* 5 octet 6 octave, sestet

Son of the Middle Border author 7 Garland (Hamlin)

sonorous 5 noisy, round 6 rotund 7 aureate, flowery, orotund, rackety, ringing, vibrant 8 clattery, noiseful, plangent, resonant, voiceful 9 bombastic, consonant, overblown 10 euphuistic, oratorical, resounding, rhetorical, uproarious 11 declamatory 12 magniloquent 13 grandiloquent

soon 6 any day

Sooner State 8 Oklahoma

soothe 3 pat 4 balm, calm, hush, lull 5 allay, salve, still 6 becalm, pacify, settle, subdue 7 comfort, compose, console, massage, mollify, placate 11 tranquilize

soothsay 5 augur 7 portend, predict, presage 8 forecast, foretell, prophesy 9 abumbrate 13 prognosticate

soothsayer 5 augur 6 auspex 7 prophet 8 foreseer, haruspex 9 predictor 10 forecaster, foreteller, prophesier *ancient Roman:* 6 auspex 8 haruspex *blind:* 8 Tiresias; (see also **prophet**)

sop 3 buy, fix, wet 4 have, soak 5 bribe, douse, drown, sissy, souse, steep 6 buy off, deluge, drench, seethe, sodden, square 7 doormat, douceur 8 gratuity, saturate, waterlog, weakling 10 namby-pamby, pantywaist, tamper with 11 Milquetoast, mollycoddle

Sopater's father 7 Pyrrhus

sophic 4 sage, wise 7 gnostic, knowing 9 insighted, sagacious 10 discerning, insightful, perceptive 13 knowledgeable

sophism see sophistry

sophisticate 6 debase 10 adulterate 11 disillusion

sophisticated 5 adult, blasé, bored, couth, jaded, salty, suave 6 daedal, knotty, mature, smooth, svelte, urbane 7 complex, cynical, gordian, knowing, worldly 8 involved, mondaine, schooled, seasoned, well-bred 9 Byzantine, elaborate, intricate, practiced, skeptical, world-wise 10 world-weary 11 experienced, worldly wise 12 cosmopolitan, disenchanted, disentranced, labyrinthine 13 disillusioned

sophistry 7 fallacy 8 delusion 9 ambiguity, casuistry, deception 12 equivocation, speciousness, spuriousness 13 deceptiveness

Sophocles play 4 Ajax 7 Electra 8 Antigone 10 Oedipus Rex

Sophonisba *brother:* 8 Hannibal *father:* 9 Hasdrubal *husband:* 6 Syphax

soporiferous 6 opiate 8 hypnotic, narcotic, somnific 9 somnolent 10 somnorific 12 somnifacient

soporific 4 dozy 6 drowsy, opiate, sleepy, snoozy 7 calming, nodding, numbing 8 hypnotic, narcotic, sedative, slumbery 9 deadening, somnolent 10 anesthetic, quietening, slumberous 11 somniferous 12 somnifacient 13 tranquilizing

soprano *American:* 4 Pons (Lily) 5 Costa (Mary), Gluck (Alma), Moffo (Anna), Moore (Grace), Price (Leontyne), Sills (Beverly) 6 Arroyo (Martina), Battle (Kathleen), Callas (Maria), Curtin (Phyllis), Donath (Helen), Farrar (Geraldine), Garden (Mary), Munsel (Patrice), Norman (Jessye), Peters (Roberta), Piazza (Marguerite), Resnik (Regina) 7 Farrell (Eileen), Kirsten (Dorothy), Stevens (Rise), Traubel (Helen) 8 Ponselle (Rosa) *Australian:* 5 Melba (Nellie) 10 Sutherland (Joan) *Austrian:* 7 Rysanek (Leonie) 8 Sembrich (Marcella) *Canadian:* 7 Stratas (Teresa) *French:* 7 Crespin (Regine) *German:* 6 Leider (Frida) 7 Lehmann (Lilli, Lotte) 11 Schwarzkopf (Elisabeth) *Italian:* 5 Freni

(Mirella), Grisi (Giuditta, Giulia), Patti (Adelina) **6** Scotto (Renata) **7** Tebaldi (Renata) **10** Tetrazzini (Luisa) **11** Ricciarelli (Katia) *Mexican:* **8** Cruz-Romo (Gilda) *Norwegian:* **8** Flagstad (Kirsten) *Romanian:* **8** Cotrubas (Ileana) *Spanish:* **7** Caballe (Montserrat) **8** Berganza (Teresa) **12** de los Angeles (Victoria) *Swedish:* **4** Lind (Jenny) **7** Nilsson (Birgit); (see also **mezzosoprano**)

sorcerer 4 mage **5** magus **6** wizard **7** charmer, warlock **8** conjurer, conjuror, magician **9** enchanter, voodooist **11** necromancer

sorceress 3 hag, hex **5** bruja, Circe, lamia, witch **10** witchwoman

sorcery 5 magic **8** diablery, witchery, witching, wizardry **9** conjuring **10** necromancy, witchcraft **11** bewitchment, enchantment, incantation, thaumaturgy *African:* **3** obe, obi **4** obia **5** obeah

sordid 3 low **4** base, foul, mean, vile **5** black, dirty, dowdy, nasty, seamy **6** blowsy, filthy, frowsy, grubby, impure, scurvy, sodden **7** ignoble, low-down, servile, squalid, unclean **8** slattern, wretched **9** uncleanly **10** despicable, slatternly

sore 5 angry, vexed **6** aching, bitter **7** algetic, chancre, hurtful, hurting, painful **9** rancorous, resentful **10** afflictive

sorehead 4 crab **6** griper, grouch **7** grouser, growler **8** grumbler, sourpuss **10** complainer, malcontent

sorrel 4 dock **7** roselle

sorrow 3 rue, sob, woe **4** care, moan **5** agony, dolor, grief, groan, mourn **6** grieve, misery, regret **7** anguish, remorse, sadness **8** distress, grieving, mourning **9** dejection, heartache, suffering **10** affliction, depression, heartbreak, melancholy **11** lamentation, unhappiness **12** mournfulness, wretchedness

sorrowful 6 dolent, rueful, tragic, triste, woeful **7** doleful, ruthful **8** dolesome, dolorous, mournful, tragical, tristful, wretched **9** afflicted, miserable, plaintive **10** lamentable, lugubrious, melancholy

sorry 3 bad, sad **4** mean, poor **5** cheap **6** cheesy, paltry, scummy, scurvy, shabby, shoddy **7** scruffy, unhappy **8** beggarly, contrite, mournful, penitent, pitiable, saddened, trifling, wretched **9** miserable, regretful, repentant **10** apologetic, despicable, despisable, inadequate, melancholy, remorseful **11** attritional, disgraceful, penitential **12** compunctious, contemptible, heavyhearted

sort 3 ilk, lot, set **4** body, comb, cull, kind, pick, sift, type **5** array, batch, class, group, order, suite **6** choose, clutch, parcel, riddle, screen, select, stripe, winnow **7** battery,

catalog, species, unravel, variety **8** classify, separate **9** catalogue, character **10** categorize, pigeonhole

sortie 5 sally

sortilege 7 sorcery **8** witchery **10** divination

so-so 4 fair **6** enough, fairly, medium, rather, subpar **7** average, fairish **8** mediocre, middling, moderate, passable, passably, somewhat **9** averagely, tolerably **10** moderately **11** indifferent **12** run-of-the-mill

sot 4 lush **5** drunk **6** bibber, boozer **7** guzzler, tippler **8** drunkard **9** inebriate **10** boozehound

sotto voce 3 low **5** aside **6** softly, weakly **7** faintly, mutedly, quietly **9** muffledly, privately **11** mutteringly

souchong 3 tea

sough 4 sigh **7** suspire

soul 4 life, pith **5** anima, being, bosom, heart, human, stuff, wight **6** animus, bottom, breast, marrow, mortal, person, pneuma, psyche, spirit **7** essence **8** creature, noumenon, vitality **9** élan vital, personage, substance **10** conscience, individual, virtuality, vital force **11** personality **12** essentiality, quintessence *combining form:* **4** thym **5** psych, thymo **6** psycho

soul singer 5 Baker (Anita), Brown (James), Flack (Roberta) **6** Sledge (Percy) **7** Charles (Ray), Pickett (Wilson), Redding (Otis) **8** Franklin (Aretha)

sound 3 fit **4** firm, hale, look, ping, sane, seem, well **5** audio, exact, music, noise, plumb, probe, right, sober, solid, valid, whole **6** appear, cogent, fathom, intact, secure, stable, unhurt **7** correct, declare, earshot, feel out, healthy, hearing, logical, perfect, precise, publish, sonance, sonancy, telling **8** accepted, accurate, announce, flawless, orthodox, proclaim, rational, received, sensible, unbroken, unmarred **9** advertise, broadcast, canonical, errorless, faultless, resonance, undamaged, uninjured, vibration, wholesome **10** annunciate, consequent, convincing, impeccable, promulgate, reasonable, sanctioned, satisfying, unimpaired **11** disseminate, intelligent, right-minded, soberminded, unblemished, well-founded **12** satisfactory, well-grounded **13** authoritative, reverberation *combining form:* **3** son **4** phon, soni, sono **5** audio, audit, phone, phony **6** audito, phonia *high-pitched:* **4** ping, ting *of a horn:* **7** tantara *of disapproval:* **7** catcall *pleasant:* **7** euphony *quality:* **6** timbre *repeating:* **7** ratatat **8** rataplan *resounding:* **8** resonant *ringing in ears:* **8** tinnitus *rustling:* **8** froufrou *sci-*

ence: 6 sonics 7 phonics *throaty:* 8 guttural

Sound *Alaska:* 5 Cross *Antarctica:* 7 McMurdo *Australia:* 4 King 5 Broad *Bahamas:* 5 Exuma *Canada:* 4 Howe 6 Nansen *Connecticut-New York:* 10 Long Island *English Channel:* 8 Plymouth *Georgia:* 8 Altamaha *Greenland:* 5 Smith *Gulf of Mexico:* 8 Suwannee 11 Mississippi *Massachusetts:* 8 Vineyard 9 Nantucket *New England:* 11 Block Island *North Carolina:* 4 Core 5 Bogue 7 Pamlico, Roanoke 9 Albemarle, Currituck *Northwest Territories:* 4 Peel 8 Melville 9 Lancaster 12 Prince Albert *Norwegian Sea:* 8 Scoresby *Ontario:* 4 Owen *Scotland:* 3 Hoy 4 Jura, Mull 5 Inner *Spitsbergen:* 4 Bell *Washington:* 5 Puget

Sound and the Fury, The *author:* 8 Faulkner (William) *character:* 5 Benjy, Caddy, Jason 7 Quentin *family:* 7 Compson

soundness 3 wit 4 mind 6 health, reason, sanity, senses 8 lucidity, security, strength 9 stability

sound off 7 speak up 8 speak out

soup *beet:* 6 borsch 7 borscht *bowl:* 6 tureen *clear:* 5 broth 8 bouillon, consommé, julienne *cold:* 8 gazpacho 11 vichyssoise *curry:* 12 mulligatawny *okra:* 5 gumbo *seafood:* 7 chowder *thick:* 5 gumbo, puree 6 bisque, burgoo *vegetable:* 10 minestrone

soupçon see **particle**

soupy 5 mushy, sobby 6 drippy, slushy, sticky 7 maudlin, mawkish 11 sentimental, tear-jerking

sour 3 bad, dry 4 acid, keen, tart 5 acerb, acrid, sharp, tangy 6 acidic, bitter, rotten, turned 7 acerbic, acetose, unhappy 8 acescent, vinegary 9 acidulous, fermented

sourness 7 acidity 8 acerbity 10 discontent

sourpuss 4 crab 5 crank 6 griper, grouch, kicker 7 grouser, killjoy 8 sorehead 10 complainer

south *combining form:* 3 not 4 noto 5 austr 6 austro *French:* 3 sud

South Africa *capital:* 8 Cape Town, Pretoria 12 Bloemfontein *colonizer:* 9 Pretorius (Andries, Marthinus) *enclave:* 7 Leso-tho *grassland:* 4 veld *largest city:* 12 Johannesburg *monetary unit:* 4 rand *settlers:* 5 Boers

South America *country:* 4 Peru 5 Chile 6 Brazil, Guyana 7 Bolivia, Ecuador, Surinam, Uruguay 8 Colombia, Paraguay, Suriname 9 Argentina, Venezuela *ethnic group:* 5 Negro 6 Aymara, Creole, Indian 7 Mestizo, Mulatto, Quechua, Spanish 10 Amerindian, Portuguese *language:* 6 Aymara 7 Guarani, Quechua, Spanish 10 Portuguese

South Carolina *capital:* 8 Columbia *college, university:* 5 Coker 6 Furman 7 Clemson *nickname:* 13 Palmetto State *state flower:* 13 yellow jasmine

South Dakota *capital:* 6 Pierre *largest town:* 10 Sioux Falls *nickname:* 11 Coyote State 13 Sunshine State

southerly 7 austral

South Korea *capital:* 5 Seoul *monetary unit:* 3 won

South-West Africa 7 Namibia *capital:* 8 Windhoek

south wind see at **wind**

souvenir 5 relic, token 6 trophy 7 memento 8 keepsake, memorial, reminder 11 remembrance 12 remembrancer

sovereign 4 fine, free 5 regal, royal 6 kingly, master, regent 7 capital, guiding, highest, padshah, regnant 8 autarkic, champion, dominant, five-star, kinglike, loftiest, majestic, padishah, separate 9 ascendant, autarchic, classical, directing, excellent, monarchal, number one, paramount, prevalent 10 autonomous, blue-ribbon, commanding, first-class, monarchial 11 independent, monarchical, overbearing, predominant, predominate 12 preponderant, self-governed

soviet 7 council 9 committee

sow 4 seed, toss 5 drill, fling, plant, put in, straw, strew 7 bestrew, disject, scatter 9 broadcast 11 disseminate *combining form:* 3 hyo 7 choerus

spa 5 baths, hydro, wells 6 resort, waters 7 springs 13 watering place *Czech:* 6 Bilina 8 Karlsbad *English:* 4 Bath 6 Buxton 9 Harrogate *French:* 3 Dax 5 Évian *German:* 3 Ems 5 Baden 6 Bad Ems 9 Kissingen

space 4 area, room 6 cavity, spread 7 breadth, expanse, stretch 8 distance, interval, universe 9 amplitude, expansion

spaced-out 4 high 5 doped 6 stoned, zonked 7 drugged 8 hopped-up, turned on

spacious 3 big 4 vast, wide 5 ample, great, large, roomy 7 immense 8 enormous, extended 9 boundless, expansive, extensive

spade 3 dig 4 grub 5 scoop 6 dig out, shovel 8 excavate

Spade, Sam 9 detective *creator:* 7 Hammett (Dashiell)

Spain *ancient name:* 8 Hispania *capital:* 6 Madrid *former leader:* 6 Franco (Francisco) *monetary unit:* 6 peseta

spall 4 chip 5 flake 8 fragment

span 4 term, time 8 duration, interval

spangle 4 trim 5 adorn, flash, gleam 7 glimmer, glisten, glitter, shimmer, sparkle, twinkle 8 decorate, ornament 9 coruscate 11 scintillate

Spaniard 9 Castilian

Spanish *combining form:* 7 Hispano *folksong:* 6 tonada *hero:* 5 El Cid 8 Palmerin *penal settlement:* 8 presidio *saint:* 7 Dominic 8 Ignatius *title:* 5 señor 6 señora 8 señorita *wine:* 4 sack

Spanish fly 9 cantharis

spank 3 box 4 blip, cuff, slap, sock 5 clout, punch, smack 6 buffet

spar 3 box 5 stall 7 dispute, wrangle 8 longeron *ship's:* 4 yard 6 bumkin, sprite 7 boomkin, jibboom, spright, yardarm 8 bowsprit

spare 4 bony, lank, lean, poor, save 5 extra, gaunt, lanky, lay by, lay in, lay up, pinch, put by, scant, screw, short, skimp, stint 6 de trop, excess, excuse, exempt, let off, meager, scanty, scrape, scrimp, skimpy, skinny 7 absolve, angular, lay away, relieve, scraggy, scrawny, scrimpy, surplus 8 dispense, exiguous, lay aside, rawboned, salt away 9 discharge 11 superfluent, superfluous

sparing 4 wary 5 canny, chary, tight 6 frugal, saving, Scotch, stingy 7 thrifty 8 ungiving 9 provident, stewardly 10 economical, unwasteful 11 tightfisted 12 parsimonious

spark 3 bud, woo 4 beau, germ, seed 5 court, lover, swain, wooer 6 embryo, incite, suitor 7 gallant 8 activate

sparker 5 swain, wooer 6 suitor

sparkle 5 flash, gleam, glint 6 glance 7 glimmer, glisten, glitter, shimmer, twinkle 9 coruscate 11 coruscation, scintillate 13 scintillation

sparkling 6 lively 8 animated 9 brilliant 12 effervescent

sparling 5 smelt

sparse 4 poor, rare 5 scant, skimp 6 meager, scanty, scarce, scrimp, skimpy 7 scrimpy 8 exiguous, sporadic, uncommon 9 dispersed, scattered 10 infrequent, occasional

Sparta 10 Lacedaemon *country:* 7 Laconia *hero, king:* 8 Leonidas *opponent:* 6 Athens

Spartacus *author:* 4 Fast (Howard) *slayer:* 7 Crassus

spasm 3 fit, tic 4 pang 5 burst, crick, throe *muscular:* 6 clonus

spasmodic 6 catchy, fitful, spotty 8 sporadic, spurtive 9 desultory

spat 3 row 4 beef, miff, tiff 5 fight, scrap 6 bicker, hassle 7 brabble, dispute, fall out, quarrel, wrangle 8 squabble 9 bickering, brannigan, caterwaul 10 falling-out 11 altercation

spate 4 flow, flux, pour, rain, rush, tide 5 drift, flood, river, spurt 6 deluge, series, stream 7 current, torrent 8 cataract, flooding, overflow 9 cataclysm 10 inundation

spatter 3 few 4 slop, slur, spit, spot 5 douse, plash, slosh, smear, swash 6 befoul, bespot, defame, malign, smatch, sparge, splash, splosh 7 asperse, blacken, handful, splurge, spurtle, traduce 9 denigrate 10 scattering, smattering, sprinkling

spawn 4 make, sire 5 hatch 6 create, father, parent 7 produce 8 generate 9 originate, procreate

speak 4 talk, tell 5 blurt, drawl, mouth, orate, shout, spout, utter, voice 6 assert, convey, intone, mumble, murmur, mutter, parley 7 address, declaim, declare, descant, lecture, phonate, prelect, whisper 8 converse, dilate on, intonate, perorate, splutter, vocalize 9 discourse, expatiate, verbalize *confusedly:* 8 splutter *for:* 7 testify *hesitantly:* 7 stammer

speaker 9 spokesman 10 mouthpiece

spear 4 bore, pike, ream, spit 5 drill, gouge, lance, spike, stick 6 impale, pierce, skewer, skiver 7 fishgig, harpoon, leister, trident 8 transfix 9 penetrate 11 transpierce

special 4 rare 6 unique 7 express 8 peculiar, uncommon 9 earmarked 10 designated, particular 11 distinctive, exceptional

specialist *suffix:* 5 ician

specialize 4 list 7 itemize 9 enumerate, inventory 13 particularize

species 4 kind, sort, type 5 breed, class, order

specific 3 set 6 strict 7 express, limited 8 clean-cut, clear-cut, definite, especial, explicit, reserved 10 individual, particular 11 categorical, unambiguous

specify 3 fix, set 4 cite, list, name 5 limit 6 detail, settle 7 itemize, mention, pin down, precise 8 instance 9 condition, determine, enumerate, establish, inventory, stipulate 13 particularize

specimen 4 case, sort, type 6 sample 7 example, neotype, variety 8 instance, sampling 12 illustration *animal or plant:* 8 holotype *typical:* 8 topotype

specious 4 idle, vain 5 empty, false, wrong 6 hollow, untrue 7 seeming, unsound 8 apparent, nugatory 9 beguiling, colorable, erroneous, illogical, incorrect, plausible 10 inaccurate

speciousness 7 fallacy, sophism 8 delusion 9 casuistry, deception, sophistry 12 equivocation

speck 3 bit, dot, jot 4 atom, iota, mite, mote, tick 5 crumb, grain, point 6 pepper, smitch 7 freckle, stipple 8 molecule, particle, pinpoint, sprinkle

speckle 3 dot 4 spot, stud 5 flake, fleck 6 dapple, pepper, pimple 7 stipple 8 sprinkle

spectacle 4 show 7 display, pageant 10 exhibition 13 demonstration *combining form:* 4 cade

spectacular 5 stagy 7 amazing 8 dramatic, striking, wondrous 9 marvelous, thrilling, wonderful 10 astounding, eye-popping, histrionic, miraculous, prodigious, staggering, stupendous, theatrical 11 astonishing, sensational

spectator 4 seer 5 gazer 6 viewer 7 watcher, witness 8 beholder, observer, onlooker 9 bystander, perceiver 10 eyewitness

Spectator, The *author:* 6 Steele (Richard) 7 Addison (Joseph)

specter 5 ghost, shade, umbra 6 shadow, spirit 7 eidolon, phantom 8 phantasm, revenant 10 apparition

spectral 6 ghosty, spooky 7 ghastly, ghostly, phantom, shadowy 9 deathlike, ghostlike, unearthly 10 cadaverous, corpselike, shadowlike 11 disembodied, phantomlike

spectrum 5 bogey, ghost, shade 6 spirit 7 eidolon 8 phantasm, revenant 10 apparition

speculate 5 study, think, weigh 6 reason, review 7 reflect 8 cogitate, theorize 9 cerebrate 10 deliberate, excogitate

speculation 6 review, theory 7 perhaps, suppose, thought 8 studying, weighing 9 brainwork 10 conjecture

speculative 5 pensy 6 closet, musing 7 curious, pensive 8 academic, thinking 9 inquiring 10 reflecting, ruminating, thoughtful 11 questioning, theoretical

Spedding biographee 5 Bacon (Francis)

speech 4 talk 5 idiom, voice 6 debate, parley, tongue 7 address, dialect, lecture, monolog, oration, voicing 8 harangue, language, parlance, speaking, uttering 9 discourse, monologue, utterance 10 allocution, expressing, expression, vernacular, vocalizing 11 declamation 12 articulation, vocalization 13 verbalization *defect:* 4 lisp 7 stutter

speechcraft 7 oratory 8 rhetoric 9 elocution

speechless 3 mum 4 dumb, mute 6 silent 7 aphonic

speed 3 aid, fly, rev, run, zip 4 clip, ease, gait, pace, race, rush, tear, whiz 5 chase, haste, hurry, tempo, woosh 6 barrel, bucket, burn up, career, course, goad on, hasten, hustle, rustle, smooth, spur on, step up, whoosh 7 quicken, swiften 8 alacrity, celerity, dispatch, expedite, fastness, highball, legerity, rapidity, velocity 9 fleetness, quickness, rapidness, swiftness 10 accelerate, cannonball, expedition, facilitate

speedy 4 fast 5 agile, brisk, fleet, hasty, quick, rapid, ready, swift 6 nimble, prompt, raking 8 hasteful 9 breakneck 10 harefooted 11 expeditious

spell 2 go 3 bit, fix, hex 4 bout, time, tour, turn 5 charm, shift, stint, throe, trick, while 6 access, attack, period, streak, voodoo 7 bewitch, enchant, relieve, seizure, stretch 9 ensorcell 11 conjuration, incantation

spellbind 4 grip, hold 5 charm 7 catch up 8 enthrall 9 fascinate, mesmerize

spelling 11 orthography *bad:* 10 cacography

spell out 7 explain, expound 8 construe 9 explicate, interpret

spend 3 pay 4 blow, drop, give, pass 5 use up, waste 6 lay out, outlay 7 consume, exhaust, fork out, hand out, splurge 8 disburse, shell out, squander 9 dissipate, throw away, while away 10 contribute, run through *wisely:* 7 husband

spender 6 waster 7 wastrel 8 prodigal, unthrift 10 high roller, profligate, squanderer 11 scattergood, wastethrift

spendthrift see **spender**

spent 5 all in 6 bleary, effete, used up 7 drained, far-gone, worn-out 8 depleted 9 exhausted, washed-out

spew 4 gush 5 belch, eject, eruct, erupt, expel, flood, vomit 6 irrupt, spit up 7 bring up, throw up, upchuck 8 disgorge

sphagnum 4 moss

sphere 3 orb 4 ball, walk 5 field, globe, realm, round 6 circle, domain 7 demesne, rondure, terrain 8 conglobe, dominion, province 9 bailiwick, champaign, territory 10 conglobate 12 jurisdiction

spherical 5 round 6 global 7 globate, globose, globous 8 globated, globular 9 orbicular *combining form:* 5 globo

Sphinx *builder:* 6 Khafre *father:* 6 Typhon *head:* 3 man, ram 4 hawk 5 woman *mother:* 7 Echidna *query:* 6 riddle *site:* 4 Giza 6 Thebes

spice 4 balm, cast, dash, hint, lick 5 aroma, clove, scent, smack, smell, taste, tinge, touch, trace 6 ginger, nutmeg 7 bouquet, incense, perfume 8 cinnamon 9 fragrance, redolence

Spice Islands 8 Moluccas

spick-and-span 3 new 4 mint, neat, snug, tidy, trig, trim 5 clean, fresh 6 spruce 7 chipper, orderly 8 brand-new 9 shipshape 11 uncluttered, well-groomed

spicy 4 blue, racy 5 broad, fiery, salty, shady, sweet, zesty 6 aromal, purple, risqué, savory, snappy, wicked 7 gingery, peppery, perfumy, piquant, pungent, scented, zestful 8 aromatic, fragrant, offcolor, perfumed, poignant, redolent, spirited 9 ambrosial 10 suggestive 12 high spirited 13 sophisticated

spider 6 frypan 7 araneid, skillet 8 arachnid 9 frying pan 10 black widow *combining form:* 6 arachn 7 arachno

spider monkey 7 sapajou

spiel 4 line 5 pitch 12 song and dance

spieler 6 gypper 7 cheater, diddler, grifter, sharper, slicker 8 swindler 9 defrauder 11 flimflammer 12 double-dealer

spigot 3 tap 4 cock, gate 5 valve 6 faucet 7 hydrant, petcock 8 stopcock

spike 5 lance, piton, spear 6 impale, skewer, skiver 8 transfix 11 transpierce

spile 4 bung 5 spout 8 forepole

spill 4 drip, drop, slop, tell 5 mouth, spray, squab 6 betray, reveal, splash 7 blab out, divulge, dribble, overrun, run over, spatter 8 disclose, discover, give away, overfill, overflow, well over

Spillane detective 10 Mike Hammer

spin 4 gyre, reel, ride, swim, turn 5 dizzy, drive, giddy, mix up, swirl, twirl, wheel, whirl 6 gyrate, muddle, rotate 7 fluster, revolve, vibrate 9 oscillate, pendulate, pirouette, whirligig *a log:* 4 birl *out:* 4 draw 6 extend 7 prolong, stretch 8 elongate, lengthen, protract 10 prolongate

spinal column 6 rachis *curvature:* 7 lordoma 8 lordosis *part:* 8 vertebra; (see also spine)

spindle 3 pin, rod 5 newel 6 rachis

spindly 5 lanky, rangy 6 gangly

spine 4 back 6 rachis 8 backbone 9 vertebrae

spineless 4 weak 8 impotent 9 weakkneed 10 emasculate, inadequate, weakwilled 11 ineffective, ineffectual 12 invertebrate

spin-off 8 offshoot 9 by-product, outgrowth 10 derivative, descendant

——— **Spinoza** 6 Baruch

spinster 7 old maid 10 maiden lady

spiny 6 thorny 7 prickly 8 echinate 10 nettlesome

spiral 4 coil, curl, wind 5 helix, twine, twist 7 entwine, helical, helices (plural), wreathe 8 gyroidal, volution 9 cochleate, corkscrew

combining form: 3 gyr 4 gyro 5 helic 6 helico

spire 4 coil, curl 5 twist, whorl 6 sprout 7 steeple 8 pinnacle 9 germinate

spirit 3 pep, vim, zip 4 brio, dash, élan, gimp, grog, guts, life, mood, snap, soul, tone, zeal, zing 5 anima, ardor, drive, force, heart, might, moxie, oomph, pluck, power, shade, spunk, umbra, verve, vigor 6 animus, daimon, energy, esprit, fervor, ginger, mettle, morale, pneuma, psyche, shadow, starch, temper, timbre, wraith 7 cojones, courage, eidolon, passion, phantom, specter, spectre 8 phantasm, revenant, strength, vitality 9 animation, briskness, character, élan vital, substance 10 apparition, enthusiasm, get-up-and-go, liveliness, resolution, vital force 13 dauntlessness *away:* 6 abduct, kidnap, snatch *combining form:* 4 thym 5 psych, thymo 6 psycho, thymia 7 pneumat 8 pneumato *evil:* 5 afrit, demon 6 afreet 7 erlking, shaitan, sheitan *female:* 5 nymph 7 banshee, banshie, nymphet *good:* 7 eudemon 8 eudaemon *Hopi:* 7 kachina, katcina *Persian:* 4 peri

spirited 3 hot 4 avid, bold, game, keen 5 alert, beany, brave, eager, fiery, nervy, peppy, sharp 6 ardent, bright, gritty, lively, plucky, spunky 7 animate, chipper, fervent, gingery, peppery, valiant, zealous 8 animated, cheerful, fearless, intrepid, resolute 9 audacious, dauntless, sprightly, vivacious 10 courageous, mettlesome, passionate 11 high-hearted 12 enthusiastic

spirits 5 booze, drink 6 liquor, tipple 9 aqua vitae, firewater *low:* 5 blues 8 doldrums 10 blue devils, melancholy

spiritual 4 high 5 lofty 6 church, mental, sacred 7 saintly 8 bodiless, cerebral, churchly, elevated, mystical, numinous, platonic 9 unfleshly 10 discarnate, highminded, immaterial, unphysical 11 disembodied, incorporeal, nonmaterial, nonphysical 12 metaphysical, supernatural, supramundane

spiritualist 6 mystic

spit 5 lance, spear 6 impale, saliva, skewer, skiver, slaver, sputum 7 spatter, sputter 8 splutter, transfix 9 brochette 11 expectorate

spite 6 grudge, malice, rancor, spleen 7 ill will, revenge 9 vengeance 10 malignancy 11 malevolence 12 vengefulness 13 maliciousness

spiteful 4 evil 5 catty 6 malign, wicked 7 cattish, hostile, vicious 9 malicious, malignant, rancorous 10 malevolent, vindictive 12 antagonistic

Spitta biographee 4 Bach (Johann Sebastian)

spitting image 4 twin 6 double, ringer 7 picture 8 portrait 10 simulacrum

spittoon 8 cuspidor

splash 3 sop, wet 4 slop, soak 5 douse, drown, slosh, spray, swash, throw 6 dabble, drench, squirt 7 spatter, splurge, spurtle 8 sprinkle

splatter 4 slop 5 douse, plash, slosh, swash 6 splosh 7 splurge, spurtle

spleen see spite

splendor 4 pomp 5 adorn, glory, value, worth 6 beauty 8 grandeur 10 brilliancy, excellence 12 magnificence

splice 3 tie 4 join, mate 5 unite

splinter 4 rive 5 burst, smash, spall, spale 6 shiver 7 shatter 8 fragment

split 3 cut, rip 4 part, rend, rent, rift, rima, rime, rive, tear 5 break, carve, chasm, chink, cleft, crack, sever, slice 6 breach, cleave, cloven, divide, schism, sunder 7 break up, disjoin, dissect, divorce, fissate, fission, fissure, rupture 8 cleavage, dissever, fracture, rimation, separate 10 alienating, estranging 11 dichotomize *combining form:* 5 schiz 6 schizo 7 schisto

splotch 4 blob, blot, spot 5 fleck, stain 6 bespot, dapple, marble, motley, mottle 9 harlequin, variegate

splurge 4 orgy, slop 5 binge, douse, fling, plash, slosh, spree, swash 6 splash, splosh 7 rampage, spatter, spurtle 8 splatter 12 extravagance

spoil 3 mar, rot 4 baby, grab, harm, haul, hurt, loot, rape, ruin, sack, swag, take, turn 5 booty, decay, favor, force, humor, louse, prize, queer, snafu, taint, waste, wreck 6 boodle, cocker, coddle, cosset, damage, defile, impair, injure, molder, oblige, pamper, ravage, ravish 7 blemish, cater to, crumble, destroy, indulge, outrage, pillage, plunder, putrefy, tarnish, violate, vitiate 8 deflower, demolish, desolate, pickings, spoliate 9 break down, decompose, deflorate, depredate, desecrate, devastate 10 plunderage, spoliation 11 acquisition, mollycoddle

spoilsport 7 killjoy

spoke 3 bar, rod 5 chock, stake 8 baluster 11 obstruction

sponge 5 leech, mooch 7 moocher 8 parasite 10 freeloader *material:* 8 mesoglea *opening:* 6 oscula (plural), oscule 7 osculum, ostiole

sponger 5 leech 7 moocher 8 parasite 10 freeloader

spongy 4 soft 5 mushy, pappy, pulpy 6 quaggy 7 pulpous, squashy, squishy 8 squelchy, yielding

sponsor 5 angel 6 backer, patron, surety 8 advocate, backer-up, champion, Maece-nas, mainstay, promoter, upholder 9 guarantor, preferrer, supporter 10 benefactor

sponsorship 4 egis 5 aegis 7 backing 8 auspices 9 patronage

spontaneous 7 natural, offhand 8 unforced 9 automatic, extempore, impromptu, impulsive, unstudied 10 improvised, unprompted 11 instinctive, unmeditated 13 unconstrained

spontoon 3 bat 4 club, mace 5 baton, billy 6 cudgel 8 bludgeon 9 billy club, truncheon 10 nightstick

spoof 4 dupe, fake, fool, hoax, sell, sham 5 cheat, farce, phony, put-on, trick 6 befool, deceit, parody, send-up 7 chicane, takeoff 8 flimflam, hoodwink 9 bamboozle, deception, imposture 11 hornswoggle

spook 3 spy 5 agent, alarm, ghost, scare 6 fright 7 specter, startle, terrify 8 affright, frighten 9 terrorize 10 ghostwrite 13 undercover man

spooky 5 eerie, jumpy, nervy, weird 6 goosey 7 fidgety, jittery, nervous, ominous, uncanny 8 twittery 9 unearthly, unrestful 10 high-strung

spool 4 wind 6 bobbin, holder

spoon 3 pet, woo 4 neck 5 court, ladle, scoop 7 scraper

spoonbill 8 shoveler 9 ruddy duck 10 paddlefish

Spoon River Poet 7 Masters (Edgar Lee)

spoony 5 silly 6 simple 7 fatuous, foolish, unwitty, witless 10 weak-headed, weak-minded 11 sheepheaded *over/on:* 6 mashed 7 smitten 8 enamored

spoor 4 step 5 track, tract 7 vestige 8 footstep 9 footprint

sporadic 3 few 4 rare 6 catchy, fitful, scarce, seldom, single, spotty 8 separate, uncommon 9 desultory, irregular, spasmodic 10 infrequent, occasional, unfrequent

sport 3 fun 4 game, jest, joke, mock, play 6 frolic, racing, trifle 7 mockery, show off 9 diversion, high jinks, horseplay, pilgarlic 10 recreation *indoor:* 6 boxing, hockey, squash 7 bowling 8 handball 9 wrestling 10 acrobatics, basketball, gymnastics 11 racquetball, table tennis *Olympic:* 4 judo 6 boxing, diving, hockey, rowing 7 archery, cycling, fencing, shot put 8 canoeing, football, high jump, long jump, marathon, shooting, swimming, yachting 9 decathlon, pole vault, water polo, wrestling 10 basketball, gymnastics, pentathlon, triple jump, volleyball 11 discus throw, hammer throw 12 javelin throw, steeplechase 13 weightlifting *water:* 6 diving, rowing 7 sailing, surfing 8 canoeing, swimming, yachting *winter:* 6 hockey, skiing 7 curling, lugeing, skating 8 biathlon, sledding 10 ski jumping 11 bobsledding, tobogganing

sporting house 6 bagnio 7 brothel 8 bordello, seraglio

sportive 5 antic 6 frisky, impish 7 larkish, playful, roguish, waggish 8 gamesome 10 frolicsome 11 mischievous

sportiveness 7 devilry, roguery, waggery 8 deviltry, mischief 9 devilment

spot 3 fix, jam, job, nip, see 4 drop, espy, find, iota, mite, onus, post, site, slug, whit 5 brand, catch, fleck, hit on, locus, place, point, speck 6 blotch, corner, dapple, descry, detect, dollop, finger, macula, mottle, office, pickle, pimple, plight, random, scrape, stigma, turn up 7 aimless, dilemma, freckle, hit upon, smidgen, spatter, speckle, splotch, station, unaimed 8 diagnose, flyspeck, identify, location, maculate, meet with, particle, pinpoint, position 9 bespatter, encounter, haphazard, hit-or-miss, irregular, recognize, situation, unplanned 10 connection, designless 11 determinate, distinguish, predicament *combining form:* 5 macul 6 maculi, maculo

spotless 4 pure 5 clean 6 chaste, decent, modest 7 cleanly 8 hygienic, sanitary, unsoiled 9 undefiled, unsullied 10 immaculate 11 unblemished

spotted eagle ray 6 obispo

spouse 4 mate, wife 5 hubby 7 consort, husband

spout 5 chute, falls, sault 6 nozzle 7 cascade 8 cataract 9 waterfall

sprain 4 pull, tear, turn 5 break, throw, twist 6 wrench 7 stretch 8 fracture 9 dislocate

sprawl 4 loll 5 drape, slump 6 extend, lounge, ramble, slouch, spread 7 stretch 8 scramble, straddle, straggle 11 spread-eagle

spray 3 fog 4 hose 7 aerosol 8 atomizer, fumigate, nebulize

spread 3 jam, lay, set, sow 4 deal, oleo, open, pâté, push 5 feast, jelly, noise, space, splay, strew, sweep 6 butter, dinner, expand, extend, fan out, pass on, peddle, regale, retail, unfold 7 banquet, breadth, diffuse, expanse, overrun, perfuse, pervade, radiate, scatter, slather, stretch, suffuse 8 bedcover, coverlet, dispense, disperse, distance, mushroom, permeate, transmit 9 amplitude, broadcast, circulate, diffusion, dissipate, expansion, extension, profusion, propagate 10 distribute, outstretch 11 communicate, counterpane, disseminate, enlargement *on:* 5 apply

spree 3 bat, jag 4 bust, hell, orgy, riot, tear 5 binge, fling, revel 6 bender, frolic, rantan

7 carouse, rampage, roister, splurge, wassail 8 carousal

sprig 4 brad, heir 5 dowel, scion 6 figure 7 pintail 9 ruddy duck

sprightly 3 gay 4 keen, yare 5 agile, alert, antic, brisk, perky, sharp, smart, zippy 6 active, breezy, brisky, clever, frisky, lively, nimble, volant 7 animate, coltish, playful, pungent 8 animated, spirited, sportive 9 vivacious 10 frolicsome, keen-witted, rollicking, unpedantic 11 quick-witted 13 scintillating

spring 3 hop, lop 4 bolt, come, flow, head, jump, leap, loom, lope, rise, root, skip, stem, trip, well 5 arise, begin, birth, bound, cause, fount, hatch, issue, start, vault, youth 6 appear, arrive, bounce, emerge, geyser, hurdle, motive, origin, reason, source, tittup, uncoil, updive, vernal 7 budtime, come out, emanate, impetus, proceed, puberty, rebound, saltate, skitter, startle 8 come from, commence, excitant, fountain, stimulus, wellhead 9 greenness, originate, stimulant, youthhood 10 derive from, incitement, juvenility 12 fountainhead, youthfulness *back:* 6 resile *combining form:* 4 cren 5 creno

springe 5 noose, snare 7 pitfall 8 deadfall, trapfall 9 booby trap, mousetrap

springlike 6 vernal

springy 6 supple, whippy 7 elastic, stretch 8 flexible, stretchy 9 recoiling, resilient 10 rebounding

sprinkle 3 dot 4 dust, spot 5 shake, speck, strew 6 pepper, powder, sparge 7 asperse, drizzle, freckle, scatter, speckle, stipple 9 bespeckle

sprint 3 run 4 dash, shin 5 scoot 6 scurry 7 scamper

sprite 3 elf, fay 5 fairy, nisse, pixie 7 brownie *water:* 5 kelpy 6 kelpie

spritz 3 jet 5 spurt 6 squirt

sprout 3 bud 4 grow 5 scion, shoot 6 ratoon, sucker 8 offshoot 9 germinate *combining form:* 4 clad 5 blast, clado 6 blasto, blasty 7 blastic

spruce 4 trim 5 natty, sassy 6 dapper, spiffy 11 well-groomed *up:* 5 slick, spiff 6 doll up 7 deck out, gussy up

spry 4 yare 5 agile, brisk, quick, ready, sound, zippy 6 active, brisky, lively, nimble, prompt, robust, volant 7 healthy 8 vigorous 9 energetic

spud 6 potato 8 spade lug

____ spumante 4 asti

spume 4 foam, suds 5 froth, yeast 6 lather

spunk 4 grit, guts, sand 5 heart, moxie, nerve, pluck 6 mettle, spirit 7 cojones, courage 8 backbone 9 fortitude 10 doggedness, resolution 13 dauntlessness

spunky 4 bold 5 beany, brave, fiery, gutsy
6 plucky 7 doughty, gingery, peppery
8 fearless, spirited 9 dauntless, unfearing
10 courageous, mettlesome 11 high-
hearted, undauntable 12 high-spirited

spur 3 sic 4 goad, prod, stir, urge 5 egg
on, favor, prick, rally, rouse, rowel
6 arouse, awaken, exhort, prompt, propel
7 impetus, impulse 8 catalyst, excitant,
stimulus 9 actuation, incentive, instigate,
stimulant 10 activation, incitation, incitement, motivation 11 countenance

spurious 4 fake, mock, sham 5 bogus,
dummy, false, phony, put-on, snide
6 ersatz, pseudo, unreal 7 assumed, bastard, feigned, pretend 8 affected, baseborn
9 brummagem, imitation, pinchbeck, pretended, simulated, ungenuine 10 apocryphal, artificial, substitute 11 counterfeit,
make-believe, misbegotten, unauthentic
12 illegitimate *combining form:* 4 noth
5 notho, pseud 6 pseudo

spurn 5 flout, scoff, scorn, scout, sneer
6 refuse, reject 7 conspue, contemn,
decline, despise, disdain, dismiss 8 turn
down 9 reprobate, repudiate 10 disapprove

spurt 3 jet 5 spout, surge 6 spritz, sprout,
squirt

sputter 3 pop 4 fizz, hiss, rage, rant, rave,
spit 6 gibber, jabber 7 bluster, crackle

spy 5 agent, scout, snoop, spook 6 beagle,
sleuth 7 gumshoe 8 informer, saboteur
9 detective 12 investigator 13 undercover
man *name:* 4 Boyd (Belle), Hari (Mata)
5 André (John)

Spy, The *author:* 6 Cooper (James Fenimore)

spying 9 espionage

Spyri's heroine 5 Heidi

squab 5 couch 6 pigeon 7 cushion

squabble see spat

squalid 3 low 4 base, foul, mean, ugly,
vile 5 black, dingy, dirty, nasty, seedy, soily
6 filthy, frowzy, grubby, impure, scurvy,
shabby, shoddy, sleazy, sloppy 7 ignoble,
low-down, run-down, scrubby, unclean,
unkempt 8 slipshod, slovenly, wretched
10 broken-down, despicable, disheveled,
slatternly 11 dilapidated 12 disreputable

squall 3 caw, yap, yip 4 bark, bawl, beef,
feud, howl, roar, wail, yaup, yawp, yell,
yelp, yowl 5 brawl, croak, fight, shout
6 bellow, hassle, shriek, squeal 7 dispute,
quarrel, screech 9 bickering 10 falling-out
11 altercation

squander 4 blow 5 waste 7 consume,
fritter 8 fool away, unthrift 9 dissipate,
overdoing, throw away 10 frivol away, lavishness, trifle away 11 prodigality, prodigalize 12 extravagance, extravagancy, wastefulness

squanderer see spender

square 3 fit, fix, pay, sop 4 bang, boxy,
even, fair, fogy, have, jibe, just, quit, suit
5 adapt, agree, bribe, clear, equal, exact, fit
in, green, pay up, plaza, right, sharp, spang
6 accord, adjust, buy off, common, fogram,
fossil, settle, tailor 7 balance, boxlike, conform, exactly, satisfy 8 check out, clear off,
coincide, dovetail, mossback, orthodox,
quadrate, smack-dab, straight, unbiased
9 discharge, equitable, harmonize, impartial, liquidate, objective, precisely, quadratic, reconcile 10 accurately, button-
down, correspond, fuddy-duddy
12 conventional 13 stick-in-the-mud

squash 3 jam 4 cram, mash, pepo, pulp
5 crush, gourd, press, quell 7 put down,
squeeze, squelch, squidge 8 suppress
10 annihilate, extinguish *variety:* 5 acorn
6 cushaw, cymlin, Sibley, turban 7 cymling,
dunkard, Hubbard, scallop 8 cymbling, pat-
typan, zucchini 9 butternut, cocozelle,
crookneck 10 Marblehead

squat 5 dumpy, hunch, stoop, thick
6 chunky, crouch, hunker, stocky, stubby
8 heavyset, thickset 10 hunker down
11 thick-bodied

squawfish 4 chub 8 cyprinid

squawk 3 caw, yap, yip 4 beef, crab, fuss,
yaup, yawp 5 bitch, bleat, gripe 6 yammer
7 protest 8 complain

squeak 3 rat 4 pipe, shot, show, talk, time
5 grate, peach 6 change, inform, look-in,
scream, snitch 7 opening, screech 8 occasion 11 opportunity

squeal 3 rat, yip 4 howl, rasp, talk, yell,
yowl 5 bitch, bleat, creak, grate, gripe,
peach 6 inform, screak, scream, shriek,
shrill, snitch, squawk 7 screech 8 complain

squealer 4 fink 6 canary, snitch 7 ratfink,
tipster 8 betrayer, informer 10 talebearer
11 stool pigeon

squeamish 5 dizzy, fussy, queer, shaky,
upset 6 dainty, qualmy, queasy 7 finical,
finicky 8 nauseous 9 finicking, nauseated,
unsettled 10 fastidious, particular, pernickety 11 persnickety, vertiginous

squeamishness 6 nausea

squeeze 3 hug, jam 4 bear, cram, push
5 clasp, crowd, crush, exact, gouge, juice,
pinch, press, screw, wrest, wring 6 eke out,
enfold, extort, squash, squish, squush,
wrench 7 embrace, extract, scratch 8 compress, contract 9 shake down

squelch 5 shush 6 muffle, squash,
squish, stifle 7 repress, squidge 8 strangle,
suppress

squib 4 fire 6 filler 7 lampoon 8 scribble,
shoot off 9 detonator

squid 7 calamar, mollusk 8 calamary
10 cephalopod *kin:* 7 octopus 10 cuttlefish

squiggle 4 worm 6 scrawl, writhe
7 scratch 8 scrabble, scribble

squinch 5 quail, start, wince 6 blanch,
blench, recoil, shrink

squint 4 bent 5 trend 10 hagioscope, strabismus

squire 5 judge, lover 6 escort, lawyer
7 gallant 9 accompany

squirm 4 toss, worm 6 wiggle, writhe
7 agonize, wriggle

squirrel 5 hoard, stash *African:* 5 xerus
red: 9 chickaree

squirrel-like 8 sciuroid

squirt 3 jet, pup 4 pour 5 puppy, sprat,
spray, sprit, spurt, surge, twerp 6 splurt,
spritz, stream 7 spatter

squish 3 jam 4 bear, push 5 crush, press
7 squeeze, squelch

squishy 4 soft 5 pulpy 6 quaggy, spongy
7 pulpous 8 squelchy

Sri Lanka *capital:* 7 Colombo *export:*
3 tea 6 rubber *former name:* 6 Ceylon
monetary unit: 5 rupee

SRO 7 sellout

SS chief 7 Himmler (Heinrich)

S-shaped 7 sigmoid 9 sigmoidal

stab 2 go 3 dig, pop, ram, run, try 4 dirk,
poke, shot, sink, slap 5 crack, drive, fling,
prick, prong, punch, spear, stick, whack,
whirl 6 dagger, pierce, plunge, thrust
7 bayonet, poniard 8 puncture, stiletto

Stabat ___ 5 Mater

stabile 6 steady 9 sculpture 10 stationary

stabilize 3 fix, set 4 prop 5 poise 6 fixate,
secure, settle, steady 7 balance, ballast,
support, sustain

stable 3 set 4 even, fast, firm, safe, sure
5 fixed, solid, sound 6 poised, secure,
steady, strong, sturdy 7 lasting, staunch,
uniform 8 balanced, constant, enduring,
resolute 9 diuturnal, perduring, permanent,
steadfast, unvarying 10 perdurable,
unchanging, unshakable

stack 4 bank, cock, heap, hill, load, mass,
pile 5 drift, mound 7 pyramid

stadium 4 bowl 5 arena 6 garden 8 coliseum 9 gymnasium

staff 3 rod 4 club, prop, rung, wand
6 cudgel 7 support *bishop's:* 7 crosier,
crozier *medical:* 8 caduceus

stage 4 give, open, play, rung, show, step
5 grade, level, mount, notch, phase, put on
6 degree, period 7 execute, perform, present, produce *direction:* 4 exit 5 enter
6 exeunt *scenery:* 8 backdrop *show:*
4 play 5 drama, revue 7 musical 9 burlesque 10 vaudeville *signal:* 3 cue *whisper:* 5 aside

stage set 5 scene 7 scenery, setting
11 mise-en-scène

stagger 4 halt, reel, sway 5 amaze, floor,
lurch, shift, stump, swing, waver, weave,
wheel 6 boggle, careen, dither, falter, puzzle, teeter, topple, totter, wobble 7 astound,
nonplus, perplex, shatter, stumble, whiffle
8 astonish, bowl over, hesitate, paralyze,
titubate 9 devastate, dumbfound, knock
over, overpower, overwhelm, vacillate

stagnant 5 stale 6 static 8 immobile,
unmoving 10 motionless, stationary

stagnate 6 stifle 7 trammel 8 stultify, vegetate

staid 4 cool, smug 5 grave, sober 6 formal, sedate, solemn, somber, stuffy 7 earnest, serious, starchy, weighty 8 composed, decorous, priggish

stain 3 dye, tar 4 blot, blur, daub, flaw,
onus, slur, smut, soil, spot 5 brand, color,
crock, odium, smear, sully, taint, tinge
6 bedaub, blotch, debase, defect, defile,
embrue, imbrue, smirch, smudge, smutch,
stigma 7 besmear, blemish, corrupt,
debauch, deprave, pervert, pigment, tarnish
8 besmirch, black eye, colorant, discolor,
dyestuff, tincture *combining form:*
5 macul 6 maculi, maculo

staircase *handrail:* 8 banister *outdoor:*
6 perron *post:* 5 newel 8 baluster

stake 3 bet, lay, pot, set 4 ante, back,
game, play 5 claim, put on, share, wager
6 gamble 7 finance 8 bankroll, interest
10 capitalize

stale 4 rank 5 dusty, fetid, fusty, moldy,
musty, tired, trite 6 cliché, smelly 7 clichéd,
noisome, reeking, stenchy 8 shopworn,
timeworn 9 hackneyed 10 malodorous
11 commonplace, stereotyped

stalemate 3 tie 4 draw 7 dogfall 8 deadlock, standoff

stalk 4 hunt, prey 5 chase, drive, march,
sling, track 6 ambush, follow, pursue,
stride, walk up 8 flush out *flower:* 8 peduncle *leaf:* 7 petiole *short:* 5 stipe

stall 4 halt 5 booth, brake, check, kiosk,
stand 6 arrest, put off 7 hold off 11 compartment

stalwart 4 bold 5 brave, husky, stout,
tough 6 brawny, sinewy, strong, sturdy
7 valiant 8 athletic, fearless, intrepid, muscular, unafraid, valorous 9 dauntless, tenacious, undaunted 10 courageous

stamen *combining form:* 4 andr 5 andro
9 stemonous *part:* 6 anther 8 filament

stamina 9 endurance, tolerance 10 toleration

stammer 6 gibber, jabber 7 sputter, stutter 8 hesitate, splutter

stamp 3 ilk, lot 4 cast, etch, kind, mint,
mold, seal, sort, type 5 clomp, clump,
drive, grave, infix, pound, print, tromp
6 hammer, incuse, stripe 7 impress,

imprint, sticker, trample 8 hallmark, inscribe
9 character 10 impression

stampede 4 bolt, dash, rout, rush, tear
5 chase, fling, shoot 6 charge 8 pell-mell

stamps 7 postage

stance 4 pose 5 color 7 posture 8 attitude, carriage, position, positure

stanch 4 stem, stop

stanchion 4 prop 5 brace 7 support

stand 4 bear, take 5 abide, booth, brook,
kiosk, treat 6 endure, suffer 7 stomach,
swallow 8 attitude, position, tolerate
artist's: 5 easel *having three legs:* 6 tripod, trivet *ornamental:* 7 étagère *stiffly:*
7 bristle

standard 3 law, par 4 flag, jack, mean,
norm, rule 5 axiom, color, gauge, ideal,
model 6 assize, banner, belief, ensign,
median, mirror, pennon 7 average, example, measure, pattern, pennant 8 bannerol,
ensample, exemplar, paradigm, streamer
9 archetype, banderole, beau ideal, benchmark, criterion, principle, yardstick
10 touchstone 11 fundamental

stand-in 3 sub 6 second 9 alternate,
assistant, surrogate 10 substitute 11 locum
tenens, pinch hitter, replacement, succedaneum

standing 4 rank, term 5 place 6 cachet,
status 7 dignity, footing, station, stature
8 capacity, position, prestige 9 character,
situation 11 consequence

standoff see **stalemate**

standoffish 5 aloof 7 distant 8 eremitic,
reserved, solitary 9 reclusive, withdrawn
10 antisocial, insociable, unsociable
12 misanthropic

stand out 3 jut 4 bulk, loom, poke, pout
5 bulge, pouch 6 beetle 7 project 8 overhang, protrude

standpatter 4 tory 7 diehard 8 old liner,
rightist 11 bitter-ender, right-winger
12 conservative

standpoint 4 side 5 angle, slant 7 outlook 9 direction

standstill 4 halt, stop 5 check, pause
6 arrest 8 deadlock 9 cessation

Stanford site 8 Palo Alto

Stanley Kowalski's wife 6 Stella

Stanley's car 7 steamer

Stan's pal 5 Ollie

stanza 7 strophe *combining form:* 5 stich
of eight lines: 6 octave 8 octonary *of four
lines:* 6 ballad 8 quatrain *of six lines:*
6 sestet, sextet 7 sextain *of three lines:*
6 tercet 7 triplet 8 tristich *Persian:* 8 rubaiyat

star 4 main, nova 5 actor, chief, major,
novae (plural) 6 étoile 7 actress, capital
8 asterisk, dominant 9 principal 10 preeminent 11 outstanding, predominant *bright:*

4 Vega 5 Deneb, Rigel, Spica 6 Altair, Pollux, Sirius 7 Antares, Canopus, Capella,
Procyon 8 Arcturus 9 Aldebaran, Archer-
nar, Fomalhaut 10 Beta Crucis, Betelgeuse
11 Alpha Crucis 12 Beta Centauri
13 Alpha Centauri *combining form:* 4 astr
5 aster, astro 6 astero, sidero *five-pointed:*
8 pentacle *giant:* 10 Betelgeuse *six-
pointed:* 8 hexagram *suffix:* 2 id

starch 2 go 3 pep 4 bang, push, snap
5 drive, getup, punch, vigor 6 amylum
7 stiffen 8 vitality *combining form:* 4 amyl
5 amylo

star-crossed 6 doomed 7 hapless,
unhappy, unlucky 8 ill-fated, luckless, untoward 10 ill-starred 11 unfortunate 12 misfortunate

Stardust composer 10 Carmichael
(Hoagy)

stare 3 eye 4 bore, gape, gawk, gaze,
look, ogle, peer 5 gloat 6 goggle 7 fisheye
10 rubberneck

stark 3 raw 4 bare, firm, nude, pure
5 bleak, clear, empty, naked, quite, rigid,
sheer, stout, utter 6 barren, robust, strict,
unclad, vacant, wholly 8 absolute, complete, desolate, stripped 9 au naturel, out-
and-out 10 absolutely

starry 6 astral 7 stellar 8 sidereal 9 stellular

Star-Spangled Banner writer 3 Key
(Francis Scott)

start 4 bolt, dawn, draw, edge, jump, leap,
odds, open 5 alpha, arise, begin, bound,
bulge, crank, enter, found, intro, onset,
quail, set up, wince 6 blanch, blench,
bounce, create, embark, flinch, get off,
launch, outset, recoil, setout, shrink, spring,
take up, tee off 7 actuate, dawning, genesis, infancy, kickoff, opening, pioneer, proceed, squinch, trigger, vantage 8 activate,
commence, drawback, embark on, handicap, initiate, organize 9 advantage, allowance, beginning, establish, institute,
originate 10 inaugurate 12 commencement

startle 3 awe 4 bolt, jolt, jump 5 alarm,
scare, shock, spook 8 affright, astonish,
frighten, surprise

starved 6 hungry 8 famished, ravenous,
underfed

stash 4 bury, hide 5 cache, hoard, plant
7 conceal, secrete 8 ensconce, squirrel

stasis 5 poise 7 balance 9 equipoise
11 equilibrium

state 3 air, put, say 4 aver, mode, rank,
tell, vent 5 opine, place, utter 6 affirm,
assert, cachet, define, recite, relate, report
7 declare, deliver, dignity, enounce, explain,
expound, express, footing, narrate, posture,
recount 8 attitude, bring out, capacity,
describe, position, prestige, set forth, stand-

ing **9** character, condition, elucidate, enunciate, interpret, situation, ventilate **11** body politic *subdivison:* **6** county *suffix:* **2** cy, th **3** ate, dom, ery, ion, ism, ity **4** ance, ancy, ence, ency, hood, ment, ness, oses (plural), osis, ship **5** ation **7** isation, ization

state *easternmost:* **5** Maine *largest:* **6** Alaska *smallest:* **11** Rhode Island *southernmost:* **6** Hawaii

State abbreviation *Alabama:* **2** AL **3** Ala. *Alaska:* **2** AK **4** Alas. *Arizona:* **2** AZ **4** Ariz. *Arkansas:* **2** AR **3** Ark. *California:* **2** CA **3** Cal. **5** Calif. *Colorado:* **2** CO **3** Col. **4** Colo *Connecticut:* **2** CT **4** Conn. *Delaware:* **2** DE **3** Del. *Florida:* **2** FL **3** Fla. *Georgia:* **2** GA *Hawaii:* **2** Hi *Idaho:* **2** ID **3** Ida. *Illinois:* **2** IL **3** Ill. *Indiana:* **2** IN **3** Ind. *Iowa:* **2** IA, Io. *Kansas:* **2** KS **3** Kan., Kas. **4** Kans. *Kentucky:* **2** KY **3** Ken. *Louisiana:* **2** LA *Maine:* **2** ME *Maryland:* **2** MD *Massachusetts:* **2** MA **4** Mass. *Michigan:* **2** MI **4** Mich. *Minnesota:* **2** MN **4** Minn. *Mississippi:* **2** MS **4** Miss. *Missouri:* **2** MO *Montana:* **2** MT **4** Mont. *Nebraska:* **2** NE **3** Neb. **4** Nebr. *Nevada:* **2** NV **3** Nev. *New Hampshire:* **2** NH *New Jersey:* **2** NJ *New Mexico:* **2** NM **4** N. Mex. *New York:* **2** NY *North Carolina:* **2** NC **4** N. Car. *North Dakota:* **2** ND **4** N. Dak. *Ohio:* **2** OH *Oklahoma:* **2** OK **4** Okla. *Oregon:* **2** OR **3** Ore. **4** Oreg. *Pennsylvania:* **2** PA **4** Penn. **5** Penna. *Rhode Island:* **2** RI *South Carolina:* **2** SC **4** S. Car. *South Dakota:* **2** SD **4** S. Dak. *Tennessee:* **2** TN **4** Tenn. *Texas:* **2** TX **3** Tex. *Utah:* **2** UT *Vermont:* **2** VT **4** Verm. *Virginia:* **2** VA **4** Virg. *Washington:* **2** WA **4** Wash. *West Virginia:* **2** WV **3** W. Va. *Wisconsin:* **2** WI **3** Wis. **4** Wisc. *Wyoming:* **2** WY **3** Wyo.

stately **5** grand, noble, preux, regal, royal **6** august, formal, kingly, lordly, solemn **7** courtly, gallant **8** gracious, imperial, imposing, magnific, majestic, princely **9** dignified, grandiose **10** ceremonial **11** ceremonious, magnificent

statement **3** tab **4** bill, vent, word **5** score, voice **6** dictum **7** account, invoice, recital **9** narrative, reckoning, testimony, utterance **10** deposition, expression **11** description **12** vocalization **13** verbalization *introductory:* **7** preface **8** foreword, prologue

stateroom **5** cabin

statesman **10** politician *American:* **3** Hay (John Milton) **4** Clay (Henry), Hull (Cordell), Otis (James), Root (Elihu) **5** Henry (Patrick), Lodge (Henry Cabot), Vance (Cyrus) **6** Bunche (Ralph), Bunker (Ellsworth), Dulles (John Foster), Kennan (George F.), Morris (Gouverneur), Sumner (Charles) **7** Acheson (Dean), Hancock (John), Kellogg (Frank B.), Lansing (Robert), Sherman (John, Roger), Stimson (Henry L.), Webster (Daniel) **8** Franklin (Benjamin), Hamilton (Alexander), Harriman (Averell), Pinckney (Charles, Thomas), Randolph (Edmund Jennings, John, Payton), Rutledge (John), Stevenson (Adlai), Trumbull (Jonathan, Joseph) **9** Kissinger (Henry) **10** Stettinius (Edward Reilly) *Australian:* **9** Wentworth (William Charles) *Austrian:* **6** Renner (Karl) **7** Kaunitz (Wenzel von) **8** Dollfuss (Engelbert) **10** Metternich (Klemens von) **13** Schwarzenberg (Felix zu) *Canadian:* **4** King (William Lyon Mackenzie) **7** Laurier (Wilfrid) **8** Thompson (John Sparrow) **9** Macdonald (John Alexander, John Sandfield), Mackenzie (Alexander, William Lyon) *Chinese:* **3** Yen (Hsishan) **4** Kung (Hsiang-hsi), Wang (Anshih, Chingwei), Yuan (Shih-kai) **9** Sun Yat-Sen *Dutch:* **6** de Witt (Johan de) **7** Grotius (Hugo), Stikker (Dirk) *East German:* **8** Ulbricht (Walter) *English:* **3** Fox (Charles, Henry) **4** Eden (Anthony, George, William), More (Thomas), Peel (Arthur, Robert, William), Pitt (William), Vane (Henry) **5** Cecil (Robert, William), North (Francis, Frederick, Roger) **6** Morley (John), Sidney (Algernon, Henry, Philip, Robert), Temple (Henry, William), Wolsey (Thomas) **7** Halifax (Earl of), Reading (Marquis of), Russell (John, William), Stanley (Edward George, Edward Henry), Stewart (Robert), Warwick (Earl of) **8** Cromwell (Oliver, Thomas), Disraeli (Benjamin), Robinson (George Frederick Samuel), Villiers (George) **9** Cavendish (Spencer, William), Churchill (Randolph, Winston), Gladstone (William), Salisbury (Earl, Marquis of), Strafford (Earl of), Wellesley (Arthur, Richard Colley) **10** Palmerston (Lord), Rockingham (Marquis of), Sunderland (Earl of), Walsingham (Francis), Wellington (Duke of) **11** Chamberlain (Austen, Joseph, Neville), Shaftesbury (Earl of) **12** Chesterfield (Earl of) *Finnish:* **9** Stahlberg (Kaarlo Juho) *French:* **5** Sully (Duc de) **6** Guizot (Francois-Pierre-Guillaume), Thiers (Louis-Adolphe), Turgot (Anne-Robert-Jacques) **7** Herriot (Edouard), Mazarin (Jules), Schuman (Robert), Viviani (Rene) **8** Hanotaux (Gabriel) **9** Lafayette (Marquis de), Millerand (Alexandre), Richelieu (Duc de) **10** Clemenceau (Georges) **11** Tocqueville (Alexis de) *German:* **5** Wirth (Joseph) **10** Stresemann (Gustav) *German-Danish:* **9** Struensee (Johann Friedrich) *Greek:* **6** Zaimis (Alexandros) **8** Pericles **9** Aristides **11** Cleisthenes, Demosthenes **12** Themistocles *Israeli:* **5** Begin (Menachem), Dayan (Moshe) *Italian:* 6 Cavour (Conte di), Crispi (Francesco) 7 Orlando (Vittorio Emanuele) 11 Machiavelli (Niccolo) *Japanese:* 5 genro, Kanoe 6 Kanoye *Norwegian:* 6 Nansen (Fridtjof) *Polish:* 7 Zaleski (August) 9 Pilsudski (Jozef) 10 Paderewski (Ignacy) *Prussian:* 5 Stein (Karl) *Roman:* 4 Cato (Marcus Porcius) 6 Cicero (Marcus Tullius), Pompey, Seneca (Lucius Annaeus) 7 Agrippa (Marcus Vipsanius) 8 Gracchus (Gaius, Tiberius), Maecenas (Gaius) 9 Symmachus (Quintus Aurelius) *Russian:* 5 Witte (Sergey) 7 Molotov (Vyacheslav) 8 Potemkin (Grigory) 9 Vyshinsky (Andrey) *Scottish:* 4 Knox (John) *South American:* 9 San Martin (Jose de) *Swiss:* 4 Ador (Gustave) 5 Welti (Emil)

static 5 fixed, inert, rigid, stuck 6 stable, steady, sticky 7 stabile, stalled, stopped 8 constant, immobile, inactive, stagnant, unmoving 9 immovable 10 unchanging 13 unfluctuating

station 3 set 4 post, rank, site, spot 5 depot, locus, place, point, state, where 6 assign 7 appoint, footing 8 capacity, standing 9 character

stationary 5 fixed 6 static 8 immobile, stagnant, unmoving 9 immovable 10 motionless, stock-still

statue *base:* 6 plinth 8 pedestal *gigantic:* 8 Colossus *Greek:* 5 atlas 7 telamon 8 caryatid *religious:* 5 Pietà *small:* 8 figurine

statuesque 4 tall, trim 7 shapely 10 well-turned 11 clean-limbed

stature see status

status 4 rank 5 merit, place, worth 6 cachet, rating, renown 7 caliber, dignity, footing, posture, quality 8 capacity, eminence, position, prestige, standing 9 character, condition, situation 10 prominence 11 consequence, distinction

statute 3 act, law 4 rule 5 canon, edict 6 assize, decree 7 precept 8 decretum 9 enactment, ordinance 10 regulation

staunch 4 fast, firm, sure, true 5 liege, loyal 6 ardent, secure, stable, strong 8 constant, faithful, resolute 9 allegiant, steadfast

stave off 4 ward 5 avert, block, deter, parry, rebut, repel 6 rebuff 7 forfend, obviate, prevent, repulse, rule out, ward off 8 preclude 9 forestall

stay 3 lag 4 base, bide, halt, live, prop, rest, stop, wait 5 abide, brace, check, dally, defer, delay, dwell, found, remit, shore, tarry, visit 6 arrest, bottom, column, ground, linger, loiter, put off, remain, shelve 7 adjourn, sojourn, support, suspend 8 buttress, hold over, intermit, postpone, pro-

rogue, stop over 9 establish, interrupt, predicate 10 dillydally, hang around 11 stick around

steadfast 4 firm, sure, true 5 fixed, liege, loyal, rigid 6 ardent 7 abiding, adamant, patient, staunch 8 constant, enduring, faithful, immobile, immotile, immotive, obdurate, resolute, stubborn 9 allegiant, immovable, unbending, unmovable 10 inexorable, inflexible, relentless, unwavering, unyielding 11 irremovable, unfaltering, unflinching, unqualified 12 never-failing, single-minded, wholehearted 13 unquestioning

steady 3 set 4 beau, even, fast, sure 5 fixed, flame, liege, lover, loyal, poise 6 ardent, stable, static 7 abiding, ballast, beloved, certain, durable, equable, stabile, staunch, uniform 8 constant, enduring, faithful, ladylove, reliable, resolute, truelove, unshaken 9 allegiant, boyfriend, inamorata, inamorato, stabilify, stabilize, unvarying 10 changeless, girl friend, sweetheart, unchanging, unswerving, unwavering 11 unfaltering 12 unchangeable, unflickering, wholehearted 13 unfluctuating

steak 4 club, cube 5 chuck, flank, round, T-bone 6 rib eye 7 sirloin 9 Delmonico, hamburger, Salisbury 10 tenderloin 11 porterhouse 13 chateaubriand

steal 3 cop, nab, nim, nip, rob 4 glom, grab, hook, kite, lift, loot, lurk, slip, take 5 annex, creep, filch, glide, grasp, heist, mooch, mouse, pinch, poach, prowl, rifle, seize, shirk, sidle, skulk, slide, slink, sneak, swipe, theft 6 burgle, collar, fleece, hijack, pilfer, pocket, rustle, smouch, snatch, snitch, thieve, tiptoe 7 bargain, gumshoe, larceny, pillage, plunder, purloin 8 shanghai, shoplift, thievery, thieving 9 pussyfoot 10 burglarize 11 appropriate *a vehicle:* 6 hijack 8 highjack

stealing 7 larceny *combining form:* 5 klept 6 klepto

stealthy 3 sly 4 wily 5 catty, quiet, sneak 6 covert, crafty, feline, secret, shifty, silent, slinky, sneaky 7 catlike, cunning, furtive, sub-rosa 8 hush-hush, skulking, slinking, sneaking 9 noiseless 10 pantherine, pantherish, undercover 11 clandestine 12 hugger-mugger 13 surreptitious

steam 5 force, might, power, sinew 6 energy, muscle 7 potency 8 strength 9 puissance *combining form:* 5 atmid 6 atmido

steam bath 5 sauna

steamboat structure 5 texas

steamer 4 boat, clam, ship

steam organ 8 calliope

steamship abbreviation 2 SS

steed 5 horse 7 charger

steel 4 gird 5 brace, cheer, nerve, rally, ready 6 buck up 7 animate, chirk up, fortify, hearten, prepare 8 embolden, inspirit 9 encourage, enhearten, reinforce 10 strengthen

steep 3 sop 4 high, soak 5 dizzy, imbue, lofty, sheer 6 abrupt, drench, infuse 7 arduous, extreme, suffuse 8 elevated, saturate 9 excessive 10 exorbitant, immoderate, impregnate, inordinate 11 precipitate, precipitous

steeple 5 spire 6 flèche

steer 3 see, tip 4 lead, show 5 guide, pilot, point, route 6 direct, escort, tip-off 7 channel, conduct 8 shepherd *a racing rowboat:* 3 cox 8 coxswain *a ship:* 4 conn, helm, luff 7 boxhaul

stein 3 cup, mug 5 stoup 6 goblet, seidel 7 tankard

Steinbeck novel 10 Cannery Row, East of Eden 12 Of Mice and Men, Tortilla Flat 13 Grapes of Wrath

Steinway product 5 piano

stellar 4 main 5 chief, major 6 astral, starry 7 capital, shining 8 dominant, gleaming, luminous, lustrous, sidereal, starlike 9 principal 10 preeminent 11 outstanding, predominant

stem 4 flow, head, rise, stop 5 arise, check, issue 6 arrest, spring, stanch 7 control, emanate, proceed 8 peduncle 9 originate 10 derive from *covering:* 5 ocrea *plant:* 4 halm 5 haulm *suffix:* 3 ome *underground:* 5 tuber 7 rhizoma, rhizome

stench 4 funk, reek 5 smell, stink

stenchful see smelly

stentorian 4 loud 5 rough 7 blaring, orotund, roaring 8 gravelly, piercing 9 clamorous 10 loud-voiced, vociferous 11 fullmouthed, loudmouthed 12 earsplitting 13 clarion-voiced

step 3 act 4 hoof, move, pace, rung, walk 5 dance, grade, notch, spoor, stage, stair, track, tract, tread, troop 6 action, degree, prance 7 measure, traipse 8 ambulate 9 footprint, procedure 10 proceeding *dance:* 3 pas *one of a series:* 6 gradin 7 gradine

step-by-step 7 gradual 9 piecemeal

stepmotherly 8 novercal

steppe 5 plain *Kazakhstan:* 6 Kirgiz 10 Betpak-Dala

Steppenwolf author 5 Hesse (Hermann)

stereotypical 4 hack 5 stale, trite 6 cliché, common 7 clichéd 8 bathetic, shopworn, timeworn 9 hackneyed 11 commonplace

sterile 3 dry 4 arid, bare, dead, flat 5 stale, vapid 6 barren, effete, fallow, jejune 7 insipid, worn-out 8 desolate, impo-

tent, infecund 9 fruitless, infertile 10 uncreative, unfruitful, uninspired, unoriginal, unprolific 12 unproductive

sterilize 3 fix 4 geld, spay 5 alter, unsex 6 change, neuter 8 caponize, castrate, mutilate, sanitate, sanitize 10 emasculate, poulardize

sterilized 7 aseptic

sterling 4 pure, true 5 noble 6 worthy 9 estimable, honorable

stern 4 grim 5 sober, stony 6 flinty, severe, strict 7 ascetic, austere 9 mortified 10 astringent, implacable, inexorable, inflexible 11 unrelenting

sternward 3 aft

Sterope *father:* 5 Atlas *mother:* 7 Pleione *sisters:* 8 Pleiades

Stevenson novel 9 Kidnapped

stew 4 boil, brew, cark, flap, fret, fume, fuss, hash, olio, olla, slum, snit 5 civet, daube, salmi, sweat, tizzy, worry 6 burgoo, dither, jumble, lather, medley, paella, pother, ragout, salmis, scouse, seethe, simmer, swivet, tumult 7 goulash, mélange, parboil, puchero, turmoil 8 mishmash, mulligan, pot-au-feu 9 agitation, Brunswick, cassoulet, commotion, confusion, pasticcio, potpourri 10 capilotade, hodgepodge, hotchpotch, miscellany, turbulence 11 olla podrida, ratatouille, slumgullion 13 bouillabaisse

steward 6 manage 7 manager

Stheno see Gorgon

stick 3 bar, dig, fix, gag, get, jib, lay, nod, put, ram, rod, run, set, shy 4 balk, beat, clip, glue, milk, pole, rook, sink, skin, slab, soak, stab 5 affix, baton, bleed, blind, cling, decoy, demur, drive, ingot, mulct, paste, place, shill, strip, stump, sweat 6 adhere, attach, billet, boggle, capper, cement, cleave, cohere, fasten, fleece, plunge, settle, strain, thrust 7 buffalo, nonplus, scruple, stumble 9 establish, shillaber 10 overcharge *combining form:* 5 rhabd 6 rhabdo

stick around 4 bide, stay, wait 5 abide, tarry 6 linger, remain

sticker 4 seal 5 stamp

stick-in-the-mud 4 fogy 6 fogram, fossil, square 8 mossback 10 fuddy-duddy

stick out 3 jut 4 bear, poke, pout, push, take 5 abide, brook, bulge, pouch, stand 6 beetle, endure, strike 7 project, protend, stomach, support 8 overhang, protrude, tolerate 9 outthrust 10 outstretch

stick up 3 rob 4 loot 5 rifle 7 plunder, ransack, relieve 9 knock over

sticky 4 hard 5 gluey, gooey, gummy, heavy, humid, muggy, mushy, rough, soggy, tacky 6 cloggy, knotty, resiny, rugged, slushy, stodgy, sultry, viscid 7 maudlin, mawkish, operose, viscous 8 adhesive, bathetic, resinous, romantic 9 difficult, laborious, strenuous 10 formidable 11 sentimental, tear-jerking

stiff 3 dry, set 4 arid, body, dull, hard, lush, mort, skin 5 drunk, miser, nabal, rigid, stark, steep, stock, tense, undue 6 boozer, corpse, mulish, wooden 7 buckram, cadaver, carcass, extreme, guzzler, muddled, niggard, scrooge, stilted, studied, swiller 8 drunkard, hardened, tightwad, towering 9 cardboard, disguised, excessive, impliable, inebriate, inelastic, obstinate, petrified, pixilated, resistant, skinflint, unbending 10 boozehound, bullheaded, cheapskate, exorbitant, hardheaded, immoderate, inebriated, inflexible, inordinate, mechanical, self-willed, unflexible, unyielding 11 extravagant, immalleable, incompliant, intoxicated, intractable 12 closed-minded, pertinacious

stiffen 6 harden, tauten 7 bolster, buckram, support, thicken 8 rigidify, solidify 9 constrict, formalize, stabilize 10 immobilize

stifle 4 mute 5 burke, choke 6 dampen, deaden, hush up, muffle 7 smother, trammel 8 stagnate, stultify, suppress 9 suffocate 10 asphyxiate

stigma 4 blot, blur, onus, slur, spot 5 brand, odium, shame, stain, taint 6 smudge, smutch 8 black eye, disgrace, dishonor, tainting 11 bar sinister 12 besmirchment

stigmatize 7 censure 8 denounce, identify 9 designate

still 3 too, yet 4 also, balm, calm, even, hush, lull, more 5 allay, along, quiet, shush, whist 6 as well, becalm, hushed, placid, serene, settle, shut up, silent, though, withal 7 besides, compose, deathly, halcyon, howbeit, however, hushful, silence 8 after all, choke off, likewise, moreover, peaceful, quietude, stagnant, tranquil 9 deathlike, noiseless, quietness, soundless 10 motionless, untroubled 11 furthermore, nonetheless, tranquilize, unperturbed 12 additionally, nevertheless

stilt 4 bird, pole 8 longlegs

stilted 4 prim 6 formal, la-di-da, too-too, wooden 7 aureate, buckram, flowery, genteel 8 affected, decorous, sonorous 9 bombastic, cardboard 10 euphuistic

stilt-like bird 6 avocet

stimulant 4 goad, spur 7 caffein, impetus, impulse 8 caffeine, catalyst, excitant 9 incentive 10 incitation, incitement, motivation

stimulate 4 move, whet 5 pique, rouse, set up 6 arouse, excite, vivify 7 commove, enliven, innerve, inspire, provoke, quicken 8 activate, dynamize, energize, motivate, spirit up, vitalize 9 galvanize, innervate 10 exhilarate

stimulus 4 goad, push, spur 5 boost, cause 6 motive, urging 7 impetus, impulse, piquing 8 catalyst, stressor 9 incentive 10 excitement, incitation, incitement, inducement, invitation, motivation, propellant 11 instigation, provocation, provocative 13 encouragement

sting 4 bite, burn 5 smart

stinging 8 aculeate

stingy 4 mean 5 close, scant, tight 6 frugal, narrow, scrimy 7 chinchy, costive, miserly, niggard, save-all, scrimpy, sparing, thrifty 8 pinching, ungiving 9 niggardly, penny-wise, penurious 10 economical, hardfisted, hardhanded, ironfisted, pinchpenny, ungenerous 11 closefisted, tightfisted 12 cheeseparing, parsimonious 13 narrowhearted, penny-pinching

stink 4 funk, reek 5 smell 6 stench 7 malodor 8 malaroma

stinker 3 cur, dog 4 scum, snot 5 skunk, snake

stinking see smelly

stinky see smelly

stint 2 go 3 job 4 bout, duty, task, time, tour, turn 5 chare, chore, cramp, pinch, scant, screw, share, shift, short, skimp, spare, spell, trick 6 amount, devoir, scrape, scrimp, skinch 8 quantity 9 allotment, stricture 10 assignment, limitation 11 restriction

stipend 3 fee, pay 4 hire, wage 5 award 6 salary 7 payment 9 emolument 13 consideration

stipple 3 dot 5 speck 6 pepper, streak 7 freckle, speckle 8 sprinkle 9 bespeckle

stipulate 5 state 6 detail 7 provide, specify 9 designate 13 particularize

stipulation 5 limit, terms 7 proviso, strings 9 provision

stir 3 ado, can, din, jug, mix, pen, set 4 abet, boil, fuss, jail, keep, moil, move, rout, wake, whet 5 awake, churn, drive, impel, raise, rally, rouse, roust, set on, waken, whirl 6 arouse, awaken, bubble, bustle, excite, flurry, foment, furore, hubbub, incite, kindle, motion, pother, seethe, simmer, tumult, whip up 7 actuate, agitate, ferment, inspire, provoke, quicken 8 activate, energize, movement, vitalize 9 agitation, challenge, commotion, galvanize, instigate, stimulate 11 disturbance, pandemonium

stirrup 6 stapes

stithy 5 anvil

stock 4 clan, folk, fund, have, hope, keep, race 5 carry, faith, hoard, house, tribe, trust 6 family, supply 7 backlog, furnish, kindred, lineage, nest egg, reserve 8 estimate, judgment, reliance 9 appraisal, inventory, reservoir 10 assessment, confidence, dependence, estimation, evaluation

stockade 3 can, jug 4 coop, jail 6 cooler, lockup, prison 8 hoosegow 9 calaboose, guardroom

stock exchange 6 bourse

stockings 4 hose 7 hosiery

stockpile 4 bank, heap, hill, hive, mass 5 amass, drift, hoard, lay up, mound, stack, store, uplay 6 garner, roll up 7 backlog, nest egg, pyramid, reserve, store up 8 cumulate, mountain 9 inventory, reservoir 10 accumulate

stocky 3 fat 5 bunty, cobby, dumpy, lumpy, plump, pudgy, short, squab, squat, thick 6 chuffy, chumpy, chunky, low-set, squdgy, stubby, stuggy, stumpy 7 lumpish 8 heavyset, thickset 9 corpulent 11 thickbodied

stodge 4 cloy, fill, flut, jade, pall, plod, sate, slog, slop, toil 5 gorge 6 trudge 7 filling, satiate, surfeit 8 footslog, plunther

stodgy 4 blah, dull 5 dowdy, dumpy, gluey, gooey, gummy, heavy, tacky 6 boring, claggy, clarty, cloggy, dreary, frumpy, sticky 7 humdrum, weighty 8 banausic, frumpish, outmoded, pedantic, plodding 9 hidebound, out-of-date, ponderous, unstylish 10 monotonous, pedestrian, unexciting

stoic 3 dry 5 aloof 7 patient, Spartan 8 detached, resigned 9 apathetic, impassive 10 phlegmatic 11 indifferent, indomitable, unconcerned

stoicism 4 grit, guts, sand 5 pluck 6 apathy 8 backbone 9 fortitude, stolidity 11 impassivity 13 insensibility *founder:* 4 Zeno

stoke 4 feed, poke, stir, tend 6 supply

Stoker, Bram *novel:* 7 Dracula

stolid 3 dry 4 dull, dumb, slow 5 blunt, dense, inert 6 bovine, obtuse, supine 7 passive 8 inactive, rocklike 9 apathetic, impassive 10 phlegmatic

stomach 3 gut 4 bear, craw, take 5 abide, belly, brook, stand, taste, tummy 6 digest, endure, paunch, venter 7 abdomen, swallow 8 appetite, tolerate 9 appetence *combining form:* 5 gastr 6 gaster, gastro, ventri, ventro 7 gastero, gastria *enzyme:* 6 pepsin, rennin *muscle:* 7 pylorus *ruminant:* 5 rumen 6 omasum 8 abomasum 9 reticulum *Scottish:* 4 kyte

stomachache 5 colic, gripe 6 misery 8 distress 12 collywobbles

stomp 5 tramp 7 trample

stone 3 gem 4 buhr, rock 5 lapis, logan, stane 6 pebble, testis 7 boulder, lapides (plural), surface 8 calculus *base:* 6 plinth *block of:* 8 monolith *chip:* 5 spall 6 gallet

combining form: 4 lite, lith, lyte *cosmic:* 6 meteor 9 chondrite, meteorite *for grinding grains:* 6 metate *fruit:* 5 drupe *memorial:* 7 obelisk *monument:* 8 megalith *of a fruit:* 3 pit 6 pyrene *precious:* 6 ligure

_____ **Stone** 7 Blarney, Rosetta

stonecrop 5 sedum

stoned 4 high 5 boozy, doped, drunk 6 canned, lushed, zonked 7 drugged, muddled 8 hopped-up, turned on, wiped out 9 disguised, pixilated, plastered, spaced-out 10 inebriated, tripped out 11 intoxicated

stonelike 7 lithoid

Stooge 3 Moe (Howard) 5 Curly (Howard), Larry (Fine)

stool pigeon 3 rat 4 fink, nark, pimp, sing 5 peach 6 canary, inform, snitch, squeak, squeal 7 tipster

stoop 3 dip 4 duck, sink, thaw 5 deign, favor, kneel, porch, relax 6 accord, crouch, oblige, unbend 7 concede, descend, portico 10 condescend 11 accommodate

stop 3 bar, can, dam, end, see 4 balk, call, clog, fill, halt, plug, quit, stay, stem, wall 5 block, brake, cease, check, choke, close, stall, tarry 6 arrest, cut off, desist, draw up, ending, haul up, hinder, kibosh, lay off, pull up, stanch 7 barrier, break up, bring up, closing, congest, disrupt, occlude, prevent, shut off, sojourn, suspend, turn off 8 blockade, knock off, leave off, obstruct, surcease 9 barricade, cessation, interrupt, roadblock, terminate 10 conclusion, desistance, standstill 11 discontinue, refrain from, termination *blood:* 6 stanch *up:* 4 cork, plug 7 occlude 8 obturate

stopgap 5 shift 6 refuge, resort 8 recourse, resource 9 expedient, makeshift 10 expediency, substitute 11 provisional

stopover 5 visit 7 sojourn 9 tarriance *for troops:* 5 étape

stoppage 6 strike *combining form:* 5 stasi 6 stases (plural), stasia, stasis *work:* 6 hartal, strike

stopper 4 clog, fill, plug 5 block, choke, close 7 congest, occlude 8 obstruct

store 3 bin 4 fund, hive, pack, shop, tank 5 amass, cache, depot, hoard, lay up, stash 6 bestow, bought, garner, market, outlet, roll up, shoppe, supply 7 arsenal, backlog, deposit, nest egg, reserve 8 cumulate, emporium, magazine, mothball, showroom, squirrel 9 inventory, reservoir, stockpile, warehouse 10 accumulate, depository, repository *candle:* 9 chandlery *in a silo:* 6 ensile 8 ensilage *shoe:* 7 bootery

storehouse 5 depot 7 arsenal, granary 8 magazine 10 depository, repository

storekeeper 8 merchant

storeroom 6 larder, pantry 7 buttery

storm 4 hail, to-do 5 beset, buran, burst, salvo 6 assail, attack, bustle, clamor, easter, fall on, hassle, hubbub, pother, strike, volley 7 aggress, assault, barrage, clatter, ruction, typhoon 8 drumfire, fall upon 9 broadside, cannonade, commotion, fusillade 10 hurly-burly 11 bombardment

storm trooper 10 brownshirt

stormy 4 foul, wild 5 dirty, dusty, murky, rough 6 raging 7 furious, howling, roaring 8 blustery 9 turbulent 10 blustering, riproaring 11 tempestuous, threatening

story 3 fib, lie 4 tale, yarn 5 conte, fable 6 canard, legend, report 7 account, falsity, fiction, märchen, untruth, version 8 allegory, anecdote, folktale 9 chronicle, fairy tale, falsehood, narration, narrative 11 description, fabrication 13 prevarication *involved:* 8 megillah *moral:* 7 parable *short:* 5 conte 8 anecdote

storyteller 4 liar 6 fibber 8 fabulist 9 raconteur

stoup 4 font 5 basin 6 flagon 7 tankard

stout 3 ale, fat 4 bold, brew, hard 5 brave, heavy, obese, tough 6 fleshy, heroic, portly, strong, sturdy 7 porcine, valiant, weighty 8 fearless, intrepid, resolute, stalwart, valorous 9 corpulent, steadfast, tenacious 10 courageous, invincible, overweight 11 indomitable, thick-bodied

Stout detective 5 Wolfe (Nero)

stouthearted 4 bold 5 brave 7 doughty, valiant 8 fearless, intrepid, unafraid 9 dauntless, undaunted 10 courageous

stove 4 kiln 5 range 8 potbelly

stow 4 pack 6 steeve 9 warehouse

stower 9 stevedore

Stowe work 4 Dred

strabismus 6 squint

straddle 6 ramble, sprawl, stride 8 bestride, scramble, sprangle 11 spreadeagle

straggle 4 roam, rove 5 drift, range, stray 6 ramble, wander 7 maunder, meander

straight 4 fair, good, neat, pure 5 plain, right 6 at once, direct, honest, linear, square 7 unmixed 8 directly, first off, orthodox 9 forthwith, instanter, right away, undiluted 10 aboveboard, button-down, forthright, unmodified 11 immediately 12 concentrated, conventional, plain dealing 13 unadulterated, undeviatingly, uninterrupted *combining form:* 4 orth, rect 5 ortho, recti

straightaway 3 now 6 at once 8 directly, first off 9 forthwith, instanter 11 immediately

straightedge 5 razor

straighten 4 true 5 align 6 unbend, uncurl *up:* 4 tidy

straightforward 5 frank 6 candid, direct, honest 7 precise 8 clearcut 9 outspoken 11 undeviating

strain 3 air, irk, lay, tax, try, tug 4 hint, mind, moil, mood, ooze, pull, seep, toil, tone, tune, vein, work 5 drive, labor, shade, sweat, tinge, touch, trace 6 harass, melody, streak, stress, strive, warble 7 descant, measure, melisma, soupçon, tension, trouble 8 diapason, distress, pressure, transude 9 suspicion 10 suggestion

strait 4 bind, pass 5 pinch 6 crisis 7 squeeze 8 exigency, hardship, juncture 9 crossroad, emergency 10 difficulty, perplexity 11 contingency *Adriatic Sea-Ionian Sea:* 7 Otranto *Africa-Madagascar:* 10 Mozambique *Alaska:* 3 Icy *Alaska-Russia:* 6 Bering *Albania-Greece:* 5 Corfu *Asia-Europe:* 11 Dardanelles *Atlantic-Baffin Island:* 5 Davis *Atlantic-Gulf of Mexico:* 7 Florida *Atlantic-Mediterranean:* 9 Gibraltar *Atlantic-Nantucket Sound:* 8 Muskeget *Atlantic-North Sea:* 7 English *Atlantic-Pacific:* 5 Drake 8 Magellan *Atlantic-Saint Lawrence:* 5 Cabot *Baffin Island-Quebec:* 6 Hudson *Bering Sea-Sea of Okhotsk:* 5 Kuril 6 Kurile *Bismarck Sea-Solomon Sea:* 6 Vitiaz *Canada:* 3 Rae 5 Dease *East China Sea:* 5 Korea 8 Tsushima *East China-South China:* 6 Taiwan 7 Formosa *England-France:* 5 Dover *Flores Sea-Indian Ocean:* 4 Sape *Flores Sea-Savu Sea:* 4 Alor *Indian Ocean-Java Sea:* 5 Sunda *India-Sri Lanka:* 4 Palk *Indonesia:* 4 Alas, Alor, Bali 5 Tioro 6 Lombok 7 Dampier, Makasar 8 Makassar, Surabaja *Inner Hebrides:* 5 Tiree *Iran-Oman:* 6 Hormuz *Italy:* 7 Messina *Japan:* 4 Yura 5 Bungo, Kitan 7 Hayasui *Japan-Sakhalin Island:* 4 Sōya *Lake Huron:* 10 Mississagi *Lake Huron-Lake Michigan:* 8 Mackinac *Malay Archipelago:* 5 Wetar *Malaysia-Singapore:* 6 Johore *Malay-Sumatra:* 7 Malacca *New Jersey-Staten Island:* 7 van Kull *New South Wales-Tasmania:* 4 Bass *New Zealand:* 4 Cook *Northwest Territories:* 6 Barrow 8 Franklin, Victoria 13 Prince of Wales *Nova Scotia:* 5 Canso *Pacific-San Francisco Bay:* 10 Golden Gate *Pacific-South China Sea:* 5 Luzon *Philippines:* 5 Bohol, Tanon 6 Iloilo 7 Basilan *Russia:* 4 Kara *Suvu Sea-Timor Sea:* 4 Roti *Sea of Azov-Black Sea:* 5 Kerch 7 Enikale *Sea of Japan:* 5 Tatar *Solomon Islands:* 12 Bougainville *South China Sea:* 7 Mindoro 9 Singapore *Turkey:* 8 Bosporus 9 Karadeniz *Vancouver-Washington:* 10 Juan de Fuca *Wales:* 5 Menai *Washington Sound:* 4 Haro

straitlaced 4 prig, prim 6 narrow, prissy, strict, stuffy 7 genteel, prudish 8 priggish, rigorous 9 hidebound, Victorian 10 intolerant 11 puritanical 12 narrow-minded

strand 4 bank 5 beach, coast, shore, wreck 6 pile up 8 cast away 9 shipwreck

strange 3 new, odd 5 alien, crazy, fishy, funny, kinky, kooky, nutty, outré, queer, weird 6 exotic, far-out, freaky, quaint 7 amazing, bizarre, curious, erratic, oddball, offbeat, uncanny, uncouth, unknown, unusual 8 aberrant, abnormal, atypical, peculiar, romantic, singular, wondrous 9 eccentric, fantastic, grotesque, marvelous, wonderful 10 astounding, miraculous, mysterious, off-the-wall, outlandish, stupendous, surprising, unfamiliar 11 astonishing, exceptional, spectacular 12 unaccustomed 13 idiosyncratic *combining form:* 3 xen 4 xeno

Strange Interlude author 6 O'Neill (Eugene)

stranger 4 unco 5 alien 7 inconnu, visitor 8 outcomer, outsider, wanderer 9 auslander, foreigner, immigrant, transient

strangle 5 burke, choke, shush 6 garote, muffle, quelch 7 garotte, garrote 8 suppress, throttle

strapping 6 robust

stratagem 4 play, plot, ploy, ruse, wile 5 feint, trick 6 device, gambit 8 artifice, intrigue, maneuver 10 conspiracy 11 machination

strategy 4 plan 6 design, scheme 7 project 8 game plan 9 blueprint

stratum 3 bed 5 layer

Strauss *opera:* 6 Salome 7 Elektra 13 Rosenkavalier *tone poem:* 7 Don Juan 10 Don Quixote

straw 3 sow 5 blond 6 flaxen, golden, thatch *braided:* 6 sennit *bundle:* 0 windling *Japanese:* 4 toyo *mat:* 6 tatami *plaited:* 7 leghorn

strawberry nettle 6 urtica

stray 3 err, gad 4 roam, rove 5 range 6 depart, errant, ramble, random, wander 7 deviate, devious, digress, diverge, erratic, excurse, meander, runaway, traipse 8 divagate, sporadic 9 gallivant, wandering

streak 4 hint, spot, vein 5 fleck, shade, tinge, touch, trace 6 dapple, marble, mottle, strain, strake, stripe 7 striate 8 tincture 9 suspicion, variegate 10 intimation, suggestion *of color:* 5 vitta

streaked 8 brindled, grizzled

stream 3 run 4 burn, flow, flux, gill, gush, pour, race, roll, rush, tide 5 bourn, brook, creek, drift, flood, spate, surge 6 bourne, branch, rindle, runlet, runnel, sluice 7 current, rivulet 8 affluent *combining form:* 5 fluvi 6 fluvio *rapid:* 7 torrent *small:* 4 sike, syke *verbal:* 10 blue streak

streamer 4 flag, jack 5 color 6 banner, ensign, pennon 7 pendant, pennant 8 banderol, bannerol, standard

streamline 8 simplify

street 3 way 4 drag, path, road 5 drive, track 6 artery, avenue, ruelle 7 highway, roadway 9 boulevard 12 thoroughfare *border:* 7 curbing *material:* 6 cobble 7 asphalt 11 cobblestone *narrow:* 4 wynd *show:* 5 raree

streetcar 4 tram 7 trolley

Streetcar Named Desire, A *author:* 8 Williams (Tennessee) *character:* 6 Stella 7 Blanche, Stanley

Street Scene author 4 Rice (Elmer)

strength 5 brawn, force, might, power, sense, sinew 6 burden, energy, muscle 7 potency, purport 8 firmness, security 9 soundness, stability, substance, toughness 10 stableness, steadiness, sturdiness

strengthen 4 beef, gird 5 brace, ready, sinew, steel 6 anneal, tone up 7 animate, chirk up, ensteel, fortify, hearten, prepare, support, toughen 8 embolden, energize, fortress, inspirit 9 encourage, enhearten, reinforce, undergird 10 invigorate

strenuous 4 hard, mean 5 lusty, tough, vital 6 uphill, wicked 7 dynamic, operose, toilful 8 toilsome, vigorous 9 difficult, effortful, energetic, Herculean, laborious

Strephon 8 shepherd *beloved:* 5 Chloe 6 Urania

stress 3 irk, try 4 pain 5 pinch 6 accent, burden, harass, import, play up, strain, weight 7 feature, tension, trouble 8 emphasis, pressure 9 emphasize, italicize, underline 10 importance, underscore 12 accentuation *in poetry:* 5 ictus

stretch 3 run 4 area, draw, time 5 fudge, range, reach, scope, space, spell, sweep, tract, while 6 extend, extent, length, limber, region, spread, supple, whippy 7 breadth, compass, draw out, elastic, expanse, magnify, prolong, purview, spin out, springy, tighten 8 distance, elongate, flexible, lengthen, protract 9 amplitude, dimension, embellish, embroider, expansion, overstate, resilient 10 exaggerate *on a frame:* 6 tenter *out:* 3 lie 4 rest 6 repose, sprawl

stretchable 7 elastic, tensile 8 tensible

stretched 4 taut

stretcher 5 dooly 6 dhooly, gurney, leader, litter 7 tall fly 8 tall tale

strew 3 sow 4 dust 5 cover 6 pepper, spread 7 diffuse, disject, radiate, scatter 8 disperse, sprinkle 9 broadcast, circulate, dissipate, propagate 10 distribute 11 disseminate

strict 4 dour, grim, just, true 5 harsh, right, rigid, tough 8 exacting, faithful, rigorous 9 draconian, unsparing, veracious, veridical 10 forbidding, hard-boiled, ironhanded, oppressive 11 undistorted 12 unpermissive

stricture 4 slam, slur 5 cramp, stint 7 obloquy 9 aspersion 10 limitation, reflection 11 restriction 12 ball and chain 13 animadversion

stride 5 march, sling, stalk 8 straddle

strident 4 loud 5 harsh 6 hoarse 7 blatant, dinsome, grating, jarring, rasping, raucous, squawky 9 clamorous 10 boisterous, stentorian, stertorous, vociferant, vociferous 11 loudmouthed 12 obstreperous

strife 4 fray 5 brawl, broil, fight 6 affray, combat, fracas 7 contest, discord, dispute, dissent, quarrel, rivalry, warfare, wrangle 8 argument, conflict, disunity, squabble, tug-of-war, variance 9 disaccord, emulation 10 contention, difference, dissension, dissidence 11 altercation, competition, controversy

strike 3 hit, pop, rap 4 bang, bash, beat, dash, deal, ding, give, kick, knap, mace, poke, rack, slam, slap, slog, slug, sock, swat, whap, whop 5 beset, carry, clout, crash, flick, knack, knock, occur, punch, smack, smite, storm, swipe, thump, whack 6 affect, assail, attack, cudgel, fall on, fillip, hammer, harrow, pummel, thrash 7 afflict, aggress, assault, deliver, impress, inflict, inspire, percuss, torment, torture 8 fall upon 9 detection, discovery, influence

striking 5 showy, vivid 6 cogent, marked, signal 7 salient, telling 8 forceful, powerful 9 arresting, arrestive, prominent 10 compelling, noticeable, remarkable 11 conspicuous, outstanding

Strindberg play 6 Easter 8 Comrades 9 Miss Julie, The Father 10 Master Olaf 12 Dance of Death, Gustavus Vasa, The Creditors

string 3 row 4 file, line, rank, tier 5 chain, order, queue, shift, train 6 refuge, resort, sequel, series 7 echelon, stopgap 8 recourse, resource, sequence 9 expedient, makeshift 10 substitute, succession *up:* 4 hang 5 noose, scrag 6 gibbet

string along 3 toy 4 fool 5 dally, flirt 6 coquet, lead on, trifle, wanton

stringent see **strict**

stringy 4 ropy, wiry 6 sinewy 7 fibrous 8 muscular

strip 3 bar, rod 4 band, bare, doff, flay, husk, peel, sack, skin, slab 5 ingot, scale, stick, waste 6 billet, denude, devest, divest, expose, fillet, flitch, ravage, ribbon 7 bandeau, banding, deprive, disrobe, pillage, take off, uncover, undress 8 bankrupt, denudate, desolate, spoliate, unclothe

9 depredate, desecrate, devastate, dismantle 11 decorticate, excorticate *leather:* 5 thong *of wood:* 4 lath, slat *skin:* 6 flench, flense

stripe 3 ilk 4 band, flog, hide, kind, lash, sort, type, whip 5 breed, order, whale 6 fillet, kidney, lather, ribbon, strake, streak, striate, thrash 7 bandeau, banding, feather, scourge, species, variety 10 flagellate

stripling 3 boy, lad

stripper 6 peeler, teaser 9 ecdysiast

stripteaser see **stripper**

strive 3 try, tug, vie 4 cope, moil, seek, toil, work 5 assay, essay, labor, offer 6 resist, strain 7 attempt, travail 8 endeavor, struggle 9 undertake

stroke 3 hit, pet 4 hone, whet 6 caress, soothe 8 apoplexy 9 heartbeat

stroll 4 mope, muck, turn, walk 5 amble, drift, mosey, paseo 6 bummel, linger, ramble 7 saunter

stroller 4 pram 5 tramp 6 go-cart 7 vagrant

strong 4 fast, firm, hard, rich, sure 5 hardy, large, lusty, stout, tough 6 ardent, brawny, heroic, mighty, potent, robust, rugged, secure, sinewy, stable, sturdy, wieldy 7 durable, staunch, unmixed 8 enduring, forceful, muscular, powerful, stalwart, straight, vigorous 9 strapping, tenacious, undiluted 10 able-bodied, full-bodied, spirituous 12 concentrated

strong-arm 5 bully 6 bounce, hector 7 dragoon 8 bludgeon, browbeat, bulldoze, bullyrag 9 terrorize 10 intimidate

strongbox 6 coffer

stronghold 4 fort 7 citadel, redoubt 8 fastness, fortress

strong point 5 forte

strong suit 5 forte 6 medium, métier, oyster 8 eminency

strontium *symbol:* 2 Sr

strophe 6 stanza

structure 4 form, pile 5 build, frame 6 fabric, format, makeup, system 7 anatomy, complex, edifice, network 8 building, erection, skeleton 9 framework 10 morphology 11 arrangement, composition 12 construction *combining form:* 5 morph 6 morpho

struggle 3 try, vie 4 agon 5 assay, essay, offer, trial 6 hassle, strive, tussle 7 attempt, compete, grapple, scuffle 8 endeavor, flounder, striving 9 undertake 11 undertaking

strumpet 4 jade, slut 5 hussy, tramp, trull, wench 6 harlot, wanton 7 jezebel, trollop 8 slattern

strut 6 flaunt, parade, prance, sashay 7 flounce, peacock, swagger

stub 4 snag 5 fence, guard 6 strike 9 pulverize

stubborn 5 balky, rigid, stunt 6 dogged, mulish, ornery, wilful 7 adamant, bullish, wayward, willful 8 obdurate 9 obstinate, pigheaded, steadfast, unbending 10 bullheaded, headstrong, inexorable, inflexible, rebellious, refractory, relentless, unyielding 11 intractable 12 cantankerous, contumacious, single-minded

stubby 5 dumpy, puggy, squat 6 chumpy, chunky, squdgy, stocky, stuggy, stumpy 7 puggish 8 heavyset 11 thick-bodied

stuck-up 4 vain 8 conceity 9 conceited 12 narcissistic, vainglorious

stud 3 dot 4 male, nail, post, spot 5 cleat 6 button, pillar, pimple 7 speckle, upright 8 sprinkle

student 5 pupil 6 premed 7 protégé *college:* 13 undergraduate *combining form:* 3 log 5 logue *female:* 4 coed *first-year:* 8 freshman *fourth-year:* 6 senior *French:* 5 élève 8 étudiant *military:* 5 cadet *Muslim:* 5 softa *naval officer:* 5 middy 10 midshipman *of a guru:* 5 chela *placement:* 8 tracking *second-year:* 9 sophomore *third-year:* 6 junior *wandering:* 7 goliard

studio 4 shop 7 atelier, bottega 8 workroom, workshop

Studs Lonigan creator 7 Farrell (James T.)

study 3 con, den, vet 4 heed, mind, muse, view 5 learn, weigh 6 debate, lesson, musing, ponder, survey, trance 7 analyze, canvass, check up, examine, inspect, reverie 8 consider, exercise, memorize, think out, weighing 9 attention, check over, pondering, think over 10 excogitate, meditation, rumination, scrutinize 11 abstraction, application, contemplate 12 deliberation 13 concentration, consideration, contemplation *combining form:* 5 sophy *group:* 7 seminar *hard:* 4 cram *suffix:* 3 ics

stuff 3 jam, ram 4 cram, pith, soul, tamp 5 being, crowd, gorge 6 entity, marrow, matter, object, things 7 essence, jam-pack 8 material, overcram, overfill 9 substance 10 individual, virtuality 12 essentiality, quintessence

stuffed shirt 4 prig, smug 5 Blimp, prude 7 diehard 10 fuddy-duddy 12 Colonel Blimp

stuffing 3 gut, tar 6 tripes 7 innards, insides, inwards, pudding, viscera 8 dressing, entrails 9 internals

stuffy 4 dull, prim 5 close, fuggy, heavy, humid, stivy, thick, wiggy 6 narrow, prissy, proper, shut-up, stodgy, sultry 7 airless, bloated, genteel, humdrum, pompous, prudish 8 arrogant, priggish, stagnant, stifling 9 hidebound, illiberal, important, Victorian 10 breathless, oppressive, pontifical, tight-laced 11 magisterial, puritanical, strait-laced, suffocating 12 narrow-minded 13 self-important

stultify 4 dull 5 check 6 deaden, impair, stifle, weaken 7 inhibit, nullify, repress, smother, trammel 8 enfeeble, restrain, stagnate, suppress 9 suffocate 10 constipate, discourage, invalidate

stumble 3 err, sin 4 slip, trip 5 demur, error 6 falter 7 blunder, scruple, stagger, stammer 8 hesitate

stump 3 get 4 beat, dare, defi, defy 5 barge, stick 6 cartel, lumber 7 buffalo, galumph, nonplus 8 defiance 9 challenge

stun 4 daze 5 amaze 6 bedaze, bemuse, benumb, dazzle 7 astound, nonplus, petrify, stupefy 8 bewilder, knock out, paralyze 11 flabbergast

stunt 4 curb, feat 5 check, dwarf, runty, trick 6 impair, runted 7 runtish, scrunty 8 hold back, suppress

stupefy 4 daze, dull, faze 5 addle, blunt 6 bedaze, bemuse, benumb, rattle 7 nonplus, petrify 8 hebetate, paralyze

stupendous 7 amazing, massive 8 cracking, towering, wondrous 9 fantastic, marvelous, monstrous, wonderful 10 astounding, miraculous, monumental, prodigious, staggering 11 astonishing, spectacular

stupid 4 dull, dumb, slow 5 brute, crass, dense, dopey, dummy, dunce, heavy, idiot, moron, silly, thick 6 dummel, goosey, oafish, simple, torpid 7 asinine, brutish, doltish, dullard, fatuous, foolish, idiotic, lumpish, pinhead 8 backward, blockish, comatose, dullhead, dumbbell, dummkopf, duncical, ignorant, retarded, sluggish 9 blear-eyed, fatheaded, half-assed, ignoramus, imbecilic, lethargic, lumbering, pinheaded, simpleton 10 beefheaded, beef-witted, half-witted, numskulled, slow-witted, slumberous 11 blockheaded, thickheaded, thick-witted 12 beetleheaded, hammerheaded, hebetudinous 13 chuckleheaded

stupor 4 coma 5 sleep 6 torpor 7 languor, slumber 8 dullness, hebetude, lethargy, narcosis 9 lassitude, torpidity 10 anesthesia 13 insensibility *combining form:* 4 narc 5 narco

sturdy 5 sound, stout, tough 6 strong 7 healthy 8 stalwart 9 tenacious 11 substantial

sturgeon 6 beluga *roe:* 6 caviar 7 caviare

Sturm und Drang 6 unrest 7 ailment, ferment, turmoil 8 disquiet 10 inquietude 11 disquietude, restiveness 12 restlessness

St. Vitus' ___ 5 dance

sty 3 den, pen 4 dump, sink 5 Sodom
6 pigpen 7 cesspit, piggery 8 cesspool

stygian 7 avernal, hellish 8 infernal, plutonic 9 cimmerian, plutonian 11 pandemoniac

style 3 fad, way 4 chic, mode, rage, tone, vein 5 craze, decor, thing, vogue 6 manner 7 fashion, wording 9 designate 10 dernier cri 11 appellation, appellative *hair:* 4 coif 8 coiffure *suffix:* 5 esque

stylish 2 in 3 mod, new 4 chic, posh, tony, trig 5 doggy, natty, nifty, ritzy, sassy, sharp, showy, sleek, slick, smart, swank, swell 6 chichi, classy, dapper, dressy, modern, modish, new-day, rakish, snappy, snazzy, spiffy, tonish, trendy, with-it 7 à la mode, dashing, doggish, swagger 8 spiffing, up-to-date 9 exclusive 10 newfangled 11 fashionable, modernistic, pretentious 12 new-fashioned, ostentatious

Stymphalides' slayer 8 Heracles, Hercules

styx 5 nymph, river 7 hateful *father:* 7 Oceanus *ferryman:* 6 Charon *location:* 5 Hades *mother:* 6 Tethys

Suah's father 6 Zophah

suave 5 bland, slick 6 genial, polite, smooth, urbane 7 affable, cordial, courtly, fulsome, politic, refined, tactful, worldly 8 cultured, gracious, polished, sociable, unctuous, well-bred 9 courteous, distingué 10 cultivated, diplomatic, soft-spoken 12 ingratiating 13 sophisticated

sub 5 under 6 fill-in 7 stand-in 9 alternate, dependent, secondary 10 collateral 11 locum tenens, pinch hitter, replacement

subaltern 8 inferior 9 secondary, underling

subdue 5 crush, quash, quell 6 defeat, master, quench, reduce 7 conquer, put down, squelch 8 bear down, beat down, suppress, vanquish 9 overpower, subjugate

subdued 4 soft, tame 5 quiet, sober 6 low-key, mellow 7 neutral, serious 8 low-keyed, softened, tasteful, tempered 9 moderated, toned down 10 controlled, restrained, submissive 11 inobtrusive, unobtrusive

subjacent 3 low 5 lower, under 6 lesser, nether 8 inferior

subject 3 apt 4 core, head, meat, open, text 5 motif, point, prone, theme, topic, under 6 expose, liable, likely, matter, motive 7 citizen, exposed, lay open, problem, servile, slavish, uncover 8 argument, material, notional, question 9 dependent, leitmotif, leitmotiv, obnoxious, secondary, sensitive, substance, tributary 10 collateral 11 subordinate, subservient, susceptible

subjective 6 biased 10 prejudiced

subjugate see **subdue**

sublime 4 holy 5 erect, exalt, grand, honor, ideal, lofty, noble, proud 6 august, divine, sacred, superb 7 dignify, ennoble, exalted, glorify, magnify, stately 8 elevated, glorious, gorgeous, majestic, splendid 9 spiritual 10 aggrandize 11 distinguish, magnificent, resplendent, splendorous 12 transcendent 13 splendiferous

submarine *detector:* 5 sonar

submerge 3 dip 4 duck, dunk, sink, soak 5 douse, drown, flood, souse, swamp, whelm 6 deluge, drench, engulf, go down 7 founder, go under, immerse 8 inundate, overflow, saturate

submerse see **submerge**

submissive 4 tame 6 menial 7 obeying, servile, slavish, subdued, unerect 8 resigned, uxorious, yielding 9 complying 10 bowing down 11 acquiescent, conformable, subservient, unresistant, unresisting 12 nonresistant, nonresisting

submit 3 bow 4 cave, fall 5 bring, defer, offer, refer, yield 6 go down, hand in, send in, tender 7 deliver, go under, knuckle, present, proffer, provide, succumb, suggest 8 theorize 9 surrender 10 capitulate 11 buckle under 12 knuckle under

subordinate 5 minor, scrub, under 7 adjunct, subject 8 adjuvant, inferior, parergal 9 accessory, auxiliary, dependent, satellite, secondary, subaltern, tributary, underling 10 collateral, subsidiary

suborn 6 incite, induce 9 instigate

sub rosa 8 covertly, in camera, secretly 9 by stealth, furtively, privately 10 stealthily 12 hugger-mugger 13 clandestinely

subscribe 3 ink, yes 4 sign 5 agree, favor 6 accede, adhere, assent 7 approve, consent, endorse 8 sanction 9 acquiesce, autograph, signature 10 contribute

subsequent 4 next 5 after, later 6 serial 7 ensuing 9 following, posterior, resultant, resulting, succedent 10 sequential, succeeding, successive 11 consecutive *prefix:* 4 post

subservient 4 mean 6 abject, menial 7 fawning, ignoble, servile, slavish 8 adjuvant, cowering, cringing, obeisant, resigned 9 accessory, ancillary, auxiliary, compliant, truckling 10 collateral, obsequious, submissive 11 acquiescent

subside 3 ebb 4 fall, lull, wane 5 abate, let up 7 die away, die down, ease off, slacken 8 moderate

subsidiary 5 minor 6 back-up 8 adjuvant 9 accessory, ancillary, tributary 10 collateral

subsidize 4 back, fund, help 5 endow 7 finance, promote

subsidy 4 gift 5 grant 6 reward 10 subvention 13 appropriation
subsist 2 be 4 live, move 7 breathe
subsistence 4 keep, salt 5 bread 6 living
7 alimony, support 10 sustenance
11 maintenance 12 alimentation
substance 3 nub 4 body, bulk, core, crux,
gist, mass, meat, pith, soul 5 being, drift,
focus, heart, point, sense, short, stuff,
tenor, thing, worth 6 amount, bottom, burden, center, corpus, entity, import, kernel,
marrow, matter, nubbin, object, riches, staple, thrust, upshot, wealth 7 essence, fortune, meaning, nucleus, purport 8 additive,
material, property, strength, sum total
9 resources 10 individual, virtuality
12 essentiality, quintessence *combining
form:* 3 hyl 4 hylo 5 phane, state *transparent:* 6 hyalin 7 hyaline
substantial 3 big 4 easy, snug, well
5 gross, solid 6 strong 7 weighty, well-off
8 material, physical, sensible, tangible, well-
to-do 9 corporeal, important, momentous,
objective, well-fixed 10 meaningful, phenomenal, prosperous, well-heeled 11 comfortable, significant 12 considerable
substantiate 3 try 4 test 5 prove
6 embody, verify 7 bear out, confirm, justify
8 manifest, validate 9 incarnate, objectify,
personify, personize 11 corroborate, demonstrate, exteriorize, externalize, materialize, personalize 12 authenticate
substantive 4 firm, noun, real 5 solid
8 definite 9 essential
substitute 4 mock, sham, swap
5 dummy, false, locum, other, proxy, trade
6 back-up, change, deputy, double, ersatz,
fill-in, refuge, resort, second, switch
7 another, replace, reserve, standby, stand-
in, stopgap 8 exchange, recourse,
resource, spurious, supplant 9 alternate,
expedient, imitation, makeshift, simulated,
surrogate 10 additional, artificial, expediency, suppletory, understudy 11 alternative, locum tenens, pinch hitter, replacement, succedaneum *combining form:*
5 pseud 6 pseudo *suffix:* 4 ette
substratum 4 base, core, meat, root, seat
5 basis, stuff 6 bottom, ground 7 bedrock,
footing 10 foundation, groundwork
12 underpinning
substructure 4 base, seat 5 basis 6 bottom 10 foundation, groundwork
subsume 4 have 6 embody, take in
7 contain, embrace, include, involve
9 encompass 10 comprehend
subterfuge 5 cheat, fraud 6 dupery 7 chicane 8 trickery 9 chicanery, deception
10 dishonesty 11 highbinding 13 double-
dealing

subterranean 4 cave 6 cavern, grotto
9 underfoot 10 underearth 11 underground
subtile 4 rare, thin 7 elusive, tenuous
8 rarefied
subtle 3 sly 4 deep, fine, foxy, nice, wily
6 artful, astute, crafty 7 cunning, logical,
refined 8 analytic, delicate, finespun, guileful, hairline, skillful 9 dexterous, insidious
10 analytical
subtract 4 take 6 deduct 7 take off, take
out 8 discount, draw back, knock off, take
away
subtraction 6 rebate 8 discount 9 abatement *word:* 7 minuend 9 remainder
suburbs 7 fringes 8 environs, outskirt,
purlieus
subversion 8 sabotage, wreckage, wrecking 10 destroying 11 demolishing, destruction, undermining
subvert 4 ruin 5 upset, wreck 6 debase
7 corrupt, deprave, destroy 8 demolish,
overturn, sabotage 9 overthrow, undermine
subway *British:* 4 tube 11 underground
French: 5 métro
succeed 2 go 4 boom 5 click, ensue,
score 6 arrive, follow, go over, pan out,
thrive, win out 7 catch on, come off, make
out, prevail, prosper, triumph 8 flourish,
get ahead, prove out 9 supervene
10 accomplish
success 3 hit 7 arrival, killing, triumph,
victory 10 attainment, prosperity
11 achievement
successful 5 smash 7 notable 8 smashing, thriving 10 noteworthy, prosperous
11 flourishing
succession 3 row 5 chain, cycle, order,
round, suite, train 6 course, sequel, series,
string 8 sequence 11 consecution
succinct 4 curt 5 blunt, brief, short, terse
7 brusque, concise, laconic, summary
11 compendiary, compendious 12 breviloquent
succor 3 aid 4 hand, help, lift 6 assist,
relief 7 comfort, secours, support 8 ministry 10 assistance, sustenance 11 maintenance, nourishment 12 ministration
succubus 5 demon, devil, fiend, Satan
9 archfiend
succulent 5 juicy, sappy
succumb 3 bow, die 4 cave, drop, fall,
pass, wilt 5 defer, yield 6 cash in, cave in,
demise, depart, expire, go down, peg out,
perish, resign, submit 7 decease, give out,
go under, knuckle 8 collapse, pass away
9 break down, surrender 10 capitulate
11 buckle under 12 knuckle under
such 4 akin, like, said, that 5 alike 7 similar 8 parallel 9 aforesaid, analogous
10 comparable, equivalent 13 corresponding

suck 3 lap, sip 4 draw 5 nurse 6 absorb, imbibe, inhale

sucker 3 gyp, sap 4 beat, bilk, dupe, fool, gull, mark 5 cheat, chump, cozen, leech 6 diddle, pigeon, sponge 7 defraud, fall guy, saphead, sponger 8 barnacle, hanger-on, parasite 9 schlemiel 10 freeloader

suckle 5 nurse 7 nourish 10 breast-feed

Sudan *capital:* 8 Khartoum *monetary unit:* 5 pound

sudden 4 fast 5 fleet, hasty, rapid, swift 6 abrupt 7 hurried, rushing 8 headlong 9 forthwith, impetuous, quickened 11 precipitant, precipitate, precipitous, subitaneous

suds 4 beer, foam, soap 5 froth, spume 6 lather

sue 3 woo 5 court, spark 6 appeal 7 address, implead 8 litigate, make up to, petition

suer 8 litigant

suet 3 fat 6 tallow *combining form:* 5 steat 6 steato

Suez Canal *builder:* 9 de Lesseps (Ferdinand-Marie) *city:* 8 Ismailia, Port Said

suffer 3 bow, let, see 4 bear, have, know, lump, take 5 abide, admit, allow, brook, leave, stand, yield 6 accept, endure, permit, submit 7 agonize, anguish, receive, stomach, sustain, swallow, undergo 8 tolerate 9 acquiesce 10 experience 11 countenance

sufferance 5 leave 6 permit 7 consent 8 sanction 10 permission 13 authorization

sufferer 6 victim *combining form:* 4 path

suffering 5 agony, dolor 6 misery 7 passion 8 distress 9 adversity 10 misfortune *combining form:* 5 pathy 6 pathic

suffice 2 do 5 serve 6 enough

sufficient 3 due 5 ample 6 common, decent, enough, plenty 8 adequacy, adequate, all right, pleasing 9 agreeable, competent, plenteous, plentiful, tolerable 10 acceptable, competence 11 comfortable 12 commensurate, satisfactory 13 commensurable, proportionate, unexceptional *poetic:* 4 enow

suffix *adjective:* 2 al, an, ar, er, ic, ly 3 ant, ary, ean, ent, ese, est, eth, fic, ful, ial, ian, ile, ine, ish, ist, oid, ory, ose, ous 4 able, eous, ible, ical, ious, less 5 ative, istic, oidal, ulent 6 escent, itious 7 istical *noun:* 2 ad, al, cy, ee, er, et, il, on, or, th, ty 3 ade, ana, ant, ard, ata, ate, dom, een, eer, ery, ese, ice, ics, ier, ile, ine, ing, ion, ism, ist, ite, ity, ium, ive, ode, oma, ome, one, ote, sis 4 ance, ancy, ence, ency, esis, ette, etum, iana, itis, ling, ment, ness, osis, ship, ster, trix, tron 5 arian, arium, aster, ation, iasis, ician, onium, orium, tress

7 escence, isation, ization *verb:* 2 ed, en, fy, le 3 ate, ify, ing, ise, ize 4 lyse, lyze

suffocate 5 burke, choke, stive 6 stifle 7 quackle, smother 8 strangle 10 asphyxiate

suffrage 4 vote 5 voice 6 ballot 9 franchise

suffragist 4 Catt (Carrie Chapman), Howe (Julia), Paul (Alice) 5 Stone (Lucy) 7 Anthony (Susan B.), Stanton (Elizabeth Cady) 8 Woodhull (Victoria Claflin) 9 Pankhurst (Emmeline)

suffuse 5 imbue, steep 6 invest, leaven 7 ingrain 9 inoculate, interject, interpose, introduce

sugar 6 aldose, fucose, xylose 7 glucose, lactose, maltose, mannose, pentose, sorbose, sucrose, sweeten 8 fructose, furanose, levulose 10 saccharose *combining form:* 3 lyx 4 gluc, glyc, lyxo, sucr, thre 5 gluco, glyco, sucro, threo 7 sacchar 8 sacchari, saccharo *from palm sap:* 7 jaggery *Mexican:* 7 panocha, panoche *source:* 4 beet, cane, corn 5 maple *suffix:* 3 ose 5 ulose

sugarcane refuse 7 bagasse

sugarcoat 5 candy, honey, white 6 veneer, whiten 7 sweeten, varnish 8 palliate 9 extenuate, gloss over, gloze over, whitewash 10 blanch over, edulcorate

suggest 3 put 4 hint, pose 5 imply, point 6 prefer, submit 7 connote, propose 8 indicate, intimate, propound, theorize 9 adumbrate, insinuate

suggestion 3 cue 4 clue, hint, vein, wind 5 shade, smack, tinge, trace 6 advice, strain 7 inkling, proffer 8 allusion, innuendo, overtone, proposal, reminder, telltale 9 suspicion, undertone

suggestive 4 blue, racy, sexy 5 broad, salty, shady, spicy 6 erotic, purple, risqué, wicked 8 off-color 9 evocative

suicidal pilot 8 kamikaze

suicide 8 felo-de-se, hara-kiri 10 self-murder 13 self-slaughter *Japanese:* 7 seppuku

suit 2 do, go 3 fit 4 case, jibe, plea 5 adapt, agree, befit, cause, check, serve, tally 6 accord, action, adjust, appeal, asking, become, go with, orison, please, prayer, square, tailor 7 conform, enhance, flatter, lawsuit, request, satisfy, suffice 8 check out, entreaty, petition, quadrate 9 agree with, reconcile 10 go together, requesting, soliciting, tailor-make 11 accommodate, application, imploration, imprecation 12 solicitation, supplication 13 harmonize with *type:* 4 zoot 6 monkey, vested 9 paternity 10 pin-striped 11 class action

suitable 3 apt, due, fit 4 good, just, meet, nice 5 happy, right 6 proper, seemly, useful 7 condign, fitting, merited 8 deserved, eligible, rightful 9 requisite 10 convenient, felicitous 11 appropriate

suitcase 3 bag 4 grip 6 valise

suite 3 lot, row, set 4 body, flat, sort 5 array, batch, chain, group, rooms, train 6 clutch, parcel, rental, sequel, series, string 7 battery, lodging, retinue 8 chambers, sequence, tenement 9 apartment, entourage, following

suitor 4 beau 5 asker, lover, spark, swain, wooer 7 gallant, sparker 8 cavalier, paramour 9 boyfriend 10 petitioner

sulfur 9 brimstone *combining form:* 3 thi 4 thio

sulk 4 mope, pout 5 brood, frown, gloom, grump, scowl 6 glower

sulky 4 cart, dour, glum 5 huffy, moody, surly, testy 6 cranky, gloomy, morose, touchy 7 crabbed 9 irritable, querulous, saturnine 12 cantankerous

sullen 4 dour, glum, mean, sour, ugly 5 black, cross, moody, pouty, surly 6 crabby, gloomy, grumpy, morose 7 crabbed, cynical, fretful, hostile, mumpish, peevish, pouting 8 frowning, lowering, petulant, scowling 9 glowering, saturnine, tenebrose, tenebrous 10 ill-humored, malevolent, sourpussed, tenebrific 11 pessimistic

Sullivan's partner 7 Gilbert (William Schwenck)

sully 3 tar 4 soil 5 shame, smear, stain, taint 6 defile 7 besmear, pollute, tarnish 8 besmirch, discolor, disgrace

Sultan of Swat 8 Babe Ruth

sultry 3 hot 5 close, humid, livid, lurid, mucky, muggy, soggy, stivy 6 baking, redhot, sticky, stuffy, torrid 7 airless, burning, tabloid 8 broiling, sizzling, smothery, stifling 9 scorching 10 breathless, sweltering 11 sensational

sum 3 add, all, tot 4 bulk, mass, tote 5 gross, total, whole 6 amount, digest, entity, figure, resumé, system 7 epitome 8 condense, entirety, integral, nutshell, totality, totalize 9 aggregate, epitomize, integrate, inventory, synopsize *small:* 7 peanuts 8 pittance

Sumatra *country:* 9 Indonesia *highest peak:* 8 Kerintji *largest city:* 5 Medan *shrew:* 4 tana

Sumerian *city:* 2 Ur 4 Umma *dragon:* 3 Kur *god:* 2 An 3 Abu, Kur, Utu 4 Enki 5 Enlil, Lahar, Nanna, Nintu 6 Dumuzi, Nergal, Ninazu 7 Enkimdu *goddess:* 2 Ki 6 Ningal, Ninlil

summarize 5 brief, recap 6 digest, resumé 8 condense, nutshell 9 epitomize,

inventory, synopsize 10 retrograde 12 recapitulate

summary 4 curt 5 brief, short, terse 6 aperçu, précis, resumé 7 compact, compend, concise, epitome, laconic, outline, roundup, rundown 8 drumhead, overview, scenario, succinct, synopses (plural), synopsis 9 compacted, inventory 11 compendiary, compendious 12 breviloquent

summerhouse 6 alcove, gazebo, pagoda 9 belvedere

summery 7 estival 8 aestival

summit 3 top 4 acme, apex, peak, roof 5 crest, crown 6 apogee, climax, vertex, zenith 8 capsheaf, capstone, meridian, pinnacle 9 fastigium 11 culmination *combining form:* 3 ace, acr, akr 4 acro, akro, apic 5 apici, apico

summon 3 bid 4 beck, call, cite 5 order 6 beckon, call in, enjoin, muster 7 command, conjure, convene, convoke, subpena 8 assemble, subpoena

sump 3 bog, fen 4 mire, quag 5 marsh, swamp 6 morass, slough 8 quagmire 9 swampland

sumptuous 4 lush, rich 5 grand, plush 6 Capuan, deluxe, lavish, superb 7 opulent 8 gorgeous, imposing, luscious, palatial, splendid 9 grandiose, luxuriant, luxurious 10 impressive 11 resplendent 12 aweinspiring

sun 3 orb, Sol 4 bask, star 7 daystar, phoebus 8 daylight, insolate, luminary, radiance 9 radiation 13 celestial body *combining form:* 4 heli 5 helio *disk:* 4 Aten *god:* 2 Ra 3 Lug, Sol, Tem, Utu 4 Amen, Atmu, Atum, Inti, Lleu, Llew, Lugh, Utug 5 Horus, Sunna, Surya 6 Apollo, Babbar, Helios, Marduk 7 Khepera, Ninurta, Phoebus, Shamash 8 Hyperion, Merodach

Sun Also Rises, The *author:* 9 Hemingway (Ernest) *character:* 6 Ashley (Brett), Barnes (Jake)

sunder 3 cut, rip 4 rend, rive 5 break, carve, sever, slice, split 6 cleave, divide 7 break up, disjoin, disrupt, dissect, divorce 8 disjoint, dissever, disunite, separate 11 dichotomize

sundew 7 drosera

sundial part 6 gnomon

sundries 7 notions 8 oddments 9 etceteras 11 odds and ends

sundry 4 many, some 6 divers, legion 7 diverse, several, various 8 manifold, numerous, populous 9 different 10 voluminous 12 multifarious, multitudinal 13 miscellaneous, multitudinous

sunfish 4 opah 8 bluegill

Sunflower State 6 Kansas

sun-god see at sun

Sun King 8 Louis XIV
sunny 4 fair, fine, warm 5 clear, happy 6 blithe, bright, cheery, chirpy, golden 7 clarion 8 cheerful, chirrupy, pleasant, rainless 9 brilliant, cloudless, lightsome, unclouded 10 undarkened
sunrise 4 dawn, morn 5 light 6 aurora 7 dawning, morning 8 cockcrow, daybreak, daylight *goddess:* 3 Eos 6 Aurora
sun-room 8 solarium
sunset 3 eve 4 dusk 7 evening 8 twilight
Sunset State 6 Oregon
Sunshine State 7 Florida 11 South Dakota
sunspot portion 5 umbra 8 penumbra
sunup see **sunrise**
sup 3 eat 4 dine 5 drink, quaff 6 imbibe 7 swallow 8 mouthful
superannuate 6 retire 7 outdate, outmode 8 obsolete 9 antiquate, obsolesce 10 pension off
superb 4 best, fine, rich 5 grand, lofty, noble, prime, proud, super 7 elegant, exalted, optimal, optimum, opulent, rousing, stately, sublime, supreme 8 crashing, elevated, glorious, gorgeous, imposing, majestic, slambang, splendid, standout 9 excellent, marvelous, wonderful 11 magnificent, outstanding, resplendent, sensational, splendorous, superlative 13 splendiferous
supercilious 5 proud 6 lordly, sniffy, snifty, snippy, snuffy 7 haughty 8 arrogant, cavalier, insolent, sneering, sniffish, snobbish, superior 10 disdainful 11 overbearing 13 high-and-mighty
superficial 5 hasty, shoal 6 casual, slight 7 cursory, general, shallow, sketchy, surface 8 skin-deep, smattery 9 depthless 10 uncritical
superfluity 5 frill, luxus 6 excess, luxury 7 amenity, surfeit, surplus, teeming 8 overflow, overkill, overmuch, overplus, plethora, swarming 10 surplusage 11 overflowing, prodigality 12 extravagance 13 overabundance
superfluous 4 over 5 extra, spare 6 de trop, excess 7 surplus, unasked, useless 8 needless, unneeded, unwanted 9 excessive, redundant 10 gratuitous 11 dispensable, uncalled-for, unnecessary 12 nonessential
superhuman 6 divine 7 demigod, uncanny 8 numinous 9 unearthly, unnatural 10 miraculous 13 extraordinary, preternatural
superintend 4 boss 5 guide 6 direct, manage, survey 7 control, oversee 8 chaperon, overlook 10 administer 11 quarterback
superintendence 4 care 6 charge 7 conduct, running 8 handling 9 authority, direction, oversight 10 management, presidence
superior 4 fine, head, lord, over, rare 5 above, dandy, elder, lofty, major, prime, proud, upper 6 better, choice, dainty, famous, higher, select, senior 7 capital, elegant, greater, haughty, premium, primary, unusual 8 arrogant, brass hat, cavalier, delicate, dominant, five-star, higher-up, insolent, numinous 9 excellent, exquisite, firstrate, marvelous, overlying, recherché, unearthly 10 disdainful, first-class, miraculous, noteworthy, preeminant, preferable, remarkable, suprahuman 11 exceptional, first-string, heavyweight, overbearing, predominant 13 high-and-mighty, preternatural
superiority 6 better 7 victory 8 whip hand 9 advantage, dominance, seniority, supremacy, upper hand 10 ascendancy
superjacent 4 over 6 higher 7 greater 9 overlying
superlative 4 best 8 finished, peerless, standout 10 consummate 11 magnificent, outstanding 12 accomplished
superlative degree *suffix:* 3 est
Superman 9 Clark Kent *cartoonist:* 7 Shuster (Joe) *girl friend:* 8 Lois Lane
supernatural 5 magic 6 divine 7 uncanny, unusual 8 heavenly, numinous 9 celestial, spiritual, unearthly 10 miraculous, paranormal, phenomenal 12 metaphysical 13 extraordinary
supernatural being 3 elf, god 5 angel, deity, demon, fairy, gnome, nymph, troll 6 seraph, spirit 7 banshee, goddess 10 leprechaun *Muslim:* 4 jinn *Persian:* 4 peri
supernumerary 5 extra, spare 6 de trop, excess 7 surplus
supersede 7 replace, succeed 8 displace, outplace, set aside, supplant
supervene 5 ensue 6 follow 7 succeed
supervise 3 run 4 boss 5 guide, steer 6 direct, govern, manage, survey 7 conduct, control, monitor, oversee, proctor, referee 8 chaperon, overlook 10 administer 11 quarterback
supervision 4 care 6 charge 7 conduct, running 8 handling 9 oversight 10 intendance, management
supervisor 7 foreman
supine 5 inert, prone, slack 6 abject 7 passive 8 inactive, indolent 11 indifferent
supper club 4 café 6 nitery 7 cabaret, hot spot 8 nightery 9 night spot
supplant 4 oust 5 eject, expel, usurp 6 bounce, cut out 7 cast out, replace 8 crowd out, displace, force out, outplace 9 overthrow, supersede
supple 4 wiry 5 agile, lithe, withy 6 limber, nimble, pliant, whippy 7 ductile, elastic, lis-

some, plastic, pliable, springy, stretch, willowy 8 flexible, graceful, moldable, stretchy 9 adaptable, lithesome, malleable, resilient

supplement 3 add, eke 5 rider 6 append 7 adjunct, codicil 8 addendum, addition, appendix 9 accessory 10 complement

suppliant 5 asker 6 beggar, prayer, suitor 9 solicitor 10 petitioner

supplicant see **suppliant**

supplicate 3 beg, sue 4 pray 5 crave, plead 6 appeal, invoke 7 beseech, entreat, implore, solicit 8 petition 9 importune

supplication 4 plea, suit 6 appeal, orison, prayer 8 entreaty, petition 11 application, imploration, imprecation

supplies 8 matériel 9 materials

supply 3 fit, man 4 feed, find, fund, give, hand, help 5 cache, equip, hoard, stock, store 6 outfit, purvey, succor 7 deliver, fulfill, furnish, provide, reserve, surplus 8 dispense, hand over, transfer, turn over 9 inventory, provision, reservoir, stockpile 12 accumulation

support 3 aid 4 back, base, bear, hand, help, keep, lift, prop, root, side, stay, take 5 abide, adopt, boost, brace, bread, brook, carry, favor, shore, strut, truss 6 anchor, assist, bear up, behalf, buoy up, column, crutch, defend, endure, girder, living, pillar, relief, second, succor, suffer, upbear, uphold, verify 7 alimony, applaud, approve, backing, bolster, bracing, comfort, confirm, embrace, endorse, espouse, footing, fortify, fulcrum, nourish, nurture, pull for, secours, shore up, stiffen, sustain, toehold 8 advocate, backstop, buttress, champion, foothold, mainstay, maintain, sanction, side with, underpin 9 encourage, reinforce, underprop 10 assistance, foundation, livelihood, provide for, strengthen, sustenance 11 corroborate, maintenance, subsistence, underpinner 12 alimentation, sustentation, underpinning *of a bridge:* 8 abutment

supporter 4 ally 6 cohort, patron 7 booster, sectary 8 adherent, advocate, champion, disciple, exponent, follower, henchman, partisan, sectator 9 expounder, proponent, satellite *combining form:* 4 crat 5 ocrat *suffix:* 3 ite

suppose 4 deem, take 5 allow, guess, infer, judge, opine, think 6 assume, expect, gather, reckon, repute, theory 7 believe, imagine, perhaps, presume, pretend, surmise, suspect 8 conclude, consider 10 conjecture, understand 11 speculation

supposition 5 posit 6 theory, thesis 7 premise, surmise 9 apriorism, postulate 10 assumption, conjecture, estimation, hypothesis 11 postulation, presumption, speculation

supposititious 6 unreal 7 dubious, fictive, reputed 8 doubtful, fanciful, illusory, putative, spurious 9 fantastic, fictional, imaginary, pretended, simulated 10 chimerical, fictitious, fraudulent 11 conjectural 12 hypothetical, questionable

suppress 4 cool, curb, hide, kill, rein, stop 5 burke, check, choke, crush, drown, dwarf, quash, quell, shush, spike, stunt 6 arrest, censor, cut off, hush up, muffle, quench, retard, squash, stifle, subdue 7 abolish, collect, compose, conceal, control, destroy, prevent, put down, silence, smother, squelch, swallow 8 prohibit, restrain, slap down, strangle, withhold 9 overpower, overthrow 10 annihilate, extinguish

suppurate 6 fester

supra 5 above

supremacy 4 sway 5 power 7 control, mastery 8 dominion 9 ascendant, authority, dominance, masterdom 10 ascendancy, domination, mastership, prepotence, prepotency 11 preeminence, sovereignty, superiority 12 predominance, principality 13 preponderance, preponderancy, transcendence

supreme 4 last 5 alone, chief, final 6 master, superb, utmost 7 highest, maximum, perfect 8 absolute, crowning, foremost, peerless, towering, ultimate 9 excellent, marvelous, paramount, sovereign, unequaled, unmatched, unrivaled 10 preeminent, surpassing 11 unequalable, unmatchable, unsurpassed 12 incomparable, transcendent, unparalleled 13 unsurpassable

Supreme Being 3 God 5 Allah 7 creator, Jehovah 11 the Almighty

surcease 3 end 4 halt, quit, rest, stop 6 desist 7 refrain, suspend 8 give over, knock off, leave off, postpone 9 cessation 11 discontinue

sure 3 set 4 fast, firm, safe 5 cocky, fixed 6 indeed, secure, stable, steady, strong 7 abiding, certain, staunch 8 absolute, arrogant, cocksure, definite, enduring, inerrant, positive, reliable, surefire, unerring, unshaken 9 confident, convinced, inerrable, steadfast 10 convincing, dependable, infallible, undeniable, unshakable, unwavering 11 indubitable, trustworthy, unequivocal, unfaltering, unqualified 12 indisputable, never-failing, wholehearted 13 incontestable, uncontestable, unquestioning

sure thing 6 shoo-in, winner 9 certainty

surety 4 bail, bond 5 angel 6 backer, patron, pledge 7 sponsor 8 backer-up, guaranty, security, warranty 9 certainty, certitude, guarantee, guarantor 10 confidence, conviction

surface 3 top 4 face, pave, rise, skin
5 cover, facet 6 come up, facing, finish, patina, veneer 7 outside 8 covering, exterior
11 superficial

surfeit 4 cloy, fill, glut, jade, pall, sate
5 gorge, stall 6 excess, stodge 7 replete,
satiate, satisfy, surplus 8 overfill, overflow,
overkill, overmuch, overplus, plethora
10 surplusage 11 overindulge, superfluity
13 overabundance

surge 4 flow, gush, pour, rise, roll, rush,
wave 5 swell 6 billow, sluice, stream
7 upswell

surgeon 8 sawbones *American:* 4 Mayo
(Charles, William), Reed (Walter) 6 Thorek
(Max) 7 Cushing (Harvey), DeBakey
(Michael) 8 McDowell (Ephraim) *British:*
6 Hunter (John) *English:* 5 Paget (James)
6 Lister (Joseph) *French:* 4 Paré (Ambroise) 5 Broca (Paul) *heart:* 7 Barnard
(Christiaan) *South African:* 7 Barnard
(Christiaan) *Swiss:* 6 Kocher (Emil Theodor) *type:* 4 oral 5 brain, heart 7 plastic
8 thoracic

surgery 9 operation *instrument:* 5 clamp,
curet, lance, probe 6 gorget, lancet, splint,
stylet, trocar 7 forceps, scalpel

surgical removal 8 ablation *combining
form:* 6 ectomy

surly 4 dour, glum, rude, ugly 5 cross,
gruff, sulky 6 crusty, grumpy, morose, sullen 7 bearish, boorish, crabbed, haughty,
waspish 8 churlish, snappish 9 fractious,
irritable, saturnine 10 ungracious 11 ill-
mannered 12 discourteous

surmise see **suppose**

surmount 3 cap, top 4 best, down, leap,
lick, over 5 clear, crest, crown, excel,
outdo, throw, vault 6 better, finish, hurdle,
master, outtop 7 conquer, surpass 8 outstrip, outtower, overcome, overleap
9 negotiate, terminate, transcend

surpass 3 cap, cob, top 4 beat, best,
pass, rank 5 excel, outdo, outgo, trump
6 better, exceed, outrun, outvie 7 eclipse,
outpace, outrank, outstep 8 distance, outclass, outmatch, outpoint, outrange, outri-
val, outshine, outstrip, outweigh, overstep
9 transcend 10 outperform, overshadow
11 outdistance

surplice 5 cotta, ephod 8 vestment

surplus 5 extra, spare 6 de trop, excess
7 overage, reserve, surfeit 8 overflow, overkill, overmuch, plethora 9 overstock,
remainder 10 oversupply 11 superfluent,
superfluity, superfluous 13 overabundance,
supernumerary

surprise 4 faze, grab, stun 5 amaze,
catch, floor, grasp, seize 6 ambush, dismay, lay for, rattle, waylay, wonder
7 astound, capture, nonplus, stagger, star-

tle, stupefy 8 astonish, bewilder, bowl over,
confound, dry-gulch, overcome 9 amazement, bushwhack, discomfit, dumbfound,
overpower 10 disconcert 11 flabbergast
12 astonishment

surrender 4 cede, fall 5 leave, waive,
yield 6 commit, give in, give up, go down,
resign, submit 7 abandon, concede, consign, go under, succumb 8 dedition, hand
over, yielding 9 relenting 10 capitulate,
relinquish, submission, succumbing
11 appeasement 12 capitulation *sign:*
9 white flag

surreptitious see **stealthy**

surrogate 3 sub 6 deputy, fill-in, refuge,
resort 7 stand-in, stopgap 8 recourse,
resource 9 alternate, expedient, makeshift
10 expediency, substitute 11 alternative,
locum tenens, pinch hitter, replacement,
succedaneum

surround 3 hem, rim 4 edge, gird, loop,
ring 5 beset, bound, limit, round, skirt,
verge 6 begird, border, circle, engulf,
fringe, girdle, margin 7 compass, confine,
embosom, enclave, enclose, envelop, environ, outline 8 encircle 9 encompass 10 circumvent 12 circumscribe

surrounding 5 about 12 circumjacent
prefix: 4 peri 6 circum

surroundings 6 medium, milieu 7 ambient, climate 8 ambience 10 atmosphere
11 environment, mise-en-scène

surveillance 3 eye, tab 4 tout 5 vigil,
watch 7 lookout 8 eagle eye, scrutiny,
stakeout 9 vigilance

survey 3 con, vet 4 boss, rate, scan, view
5 assay, audit, set at, study, value
6 aperçu, assess, digest, précis, review,
search, sketch 7 canvass, check up, examine, inspect, oversee, pandect, preview, sylloge, valuate 8 analysis, appraise, chaperon, estimate, evaluate, overlook, scrutiny,
syllabus 9 check over, supervise 10 compendium, inspection, scrutinize 11 examination, quarterback, superintend 13 perlustration

survive 4 last 6 endure, revive 7 carry on,
outlast, outlive, outwear, persist, recover,
ride out 8 continue, live down 11 come
through, pull through

Surya 6 sun-god *son:* 4 Manu, Yama
5 Karna 6 Asvins 7 Sugriva *temple site:*
7 Konarak

susceptible 4 easy, open 5 naive, prone
6 liable 7 exposed, sensile, subject 8 disposed, gullible, inclined, sensible, sentient
9 obnoxious, receptive, sensitive 10 fleeceable, responsive, vulnerable 11 impressible, predisposed 12 nonresistant

Susi's son 5 Gaddi

suspect 4 open 5 doubt, guess, shaky, think 6 assume, expect, gather, unsure 7 believe, dubious, imagine, suppose, unclear 8 conceive, distrust, doubtful, misdoubt, mistrust 9 doubtable, uncertain 10 disbelieve, understand 11 problematic

suspend 3 bar 4 bate, hang, stay, stop 5 debar, defer, delay, hover, sling 6 dangle, depend, except, hold up, put off, shelve 7 adjourn, exclude, hold off, rule out 8 count out, intermit, postpone, prorogue 9 eliminate 11 discontinue

suspended 7 hanging, pendant, pensile 8 dangling, swinging 9 pendulant, pendulous

suspenders 6 braces 8 galluses

suspense 5 worry 6 unease 7 anxiety, concern, mystery 11 uncertainty 12 apprehension

suspension 4 stop 5 delay 7 latency 8 abeyance, abeyancy, doldrums, dormancy, stoppage 9 remission 10 moratorium, quiescence, quiescency 11 cold storage, withholding 12 intermission, interruption

suspicion 4 cast, hint 5 doubt, shade, smell, tinge, touch, trace, whiff 6 wonder 7 concern, dubiety 8 distrust, mistrust 9 dubiosity, misgiving 10 foreboding, intimation, skepticism, suggestion 11 incertitude, uncertainty, uncertitude

suspicious 4 wary 5 chary, leery, queer, shaky 6 unsure 7 careful, dubious, jealous, suspect 8 cautious, doubtful, watchful 9 doubtable, skeptical, uncertain 10 borderline 11 distrustful, mistrustful, problematic, unbelieving 12 questionable

suspire 4 sigh

sustain 4 bear, feed, prop, save 5 abide, brace, brook, carry, stand 6 bear up, buoy up, endure, foster, hold up, keep up, succor, suffer, upbear, uphold 7 bolster, confirm, nourish, nurture, prolong, receive, shore up, stomach, support, undergo 8 buttress, continue, preserve, tolerate 9 underprop, withstand 10 experience, strengthen

sustenance 3 pap 4 food, keep, meat, salt 5 bread 6 living, viands 7 aliment, alimony, pabulum, support 9 nutriment 10 livelihood 11 maintenance, nourishment, subsistence 12 alimentation

susurration 6 mumble, murmur, mutter, rustle 7 whisper 9 undertone

suture 4 line, seam 6 stitch

swab 3 mop 5 clean

swaddle 4 roll, wrap 5 drape 6 enwrap, swathe, wrap up 7 bandage, envelop 8 enswathe

swag 3 yaw 4 flag, loot, tilt, wilt 5 booty, droop, lurch, money, pitch, prize, spoil 6 boodle, seesaw, tilter 7 plunder 10 plunderage

swagger 4 brag, cock, lord 5 boast, strut, swank, swash, swell 7 bluster, peacock 8 flourish 11 pontificate, swashbuckle

swain 4 beau 5 lover, spark, wooer 6 suitor 7 admirer, sparker 9 boyfriend

swallow 3 sip 4 bear, bolt, down, gulp, take 5 abide, brook, drink, quaff, stand 6 absorb, accept, digest, endure, imbibe, ingest 7 believe, consume, stomach 8 bear with, tolerate 11 ingurgitate

swamp 3 bog, fen 4 mire, moss, muck, quag 5 drown, flood, glade, marsh, whelm 6 deluge, engulf, morass, muskeg, slough 7 baygall, bottoms 8 inundate, overcome, overflow, quagmire, submerge 9 marshland, overwhelm *Everglades:* 10 Big Cypress *Georgia:* 10 Okefenokee *North Carolina-Virginia:* 6 Dismal 11 Great Dismal

Swamp Fox 6 Marion (Francis)

swan *female:* 3 pen *male:* 3 cob 4 cobb *young:* 6 cygnet

Swanhild *father:* 6 Sigurd *mother:* 6 Gudrun

swank 4 cock, lord, tony, trig 5 sharp, showy, swell, swish 6 chichi, classy, lively, snappy, tonish, trendy, with-it 7 peacock, splashy, stylish, swagger 8 peacocky 10 flamboyant, peacockish 11 pontificate, pretentious 12 orchidaceous, ostentatious

swap 5 trade, truck 6 barter, change, switch 7 bargain, traffic 8 exchange 10 substitute

swarm 4 flow, host, teem 5 crawl, crowd, flock, group, horde 6 abound, throng 7 overrun 9 multitude, pullulate 10 congregate

swarthy 4 dark 5 dusky 8 bistered 11 black-a-vised, dark-skinned

swash 3 lap 4 dash, slop 5 douse, plash, slosh 6 bubble, burble, gurgle, splash, splosh 7 bluster, spatter, splurge, spurtle, swagger 8 splatter

swat 3 bat, box, hit, rap 4 belt, blow, cuff, lick, slog, slug, sock 5 clout, knock, smack, smash, smite, swipe, whack 6 buffet, strike, wallop 7 clobber

swathe see swaddle

sway 3 get 4 bend, bias, move, rock, rule 5 carry, lurch, might, power, range, reach, reign, scope, sweep, swing, touch, waver, weave 6 affect, careen, direct, govern, manage, spread, strike, totter, waddle, wobble 7 command, dispose, expanse, impress, incline, inspire, mastery, stagger, stretch, strings 8 overrule 9 amplitude, authority, dominance, influence, oscillate, pendulate, vacillate 10 domination, predispose 11 fluctuation 12 jurisdiction

swear 3 vow 4 bind, cuss, damn, oath, rail, rant 5 abuse, curse 6 adjure, affirm, assert, attest, bedamn, depone, depose, pledge, plight, revile, vilify 7 declare, promise, testify 8 covenant, cussword, execrate 9 blaspheme, expletive, imprecate 10 asseverate, vituperate

swearword 4 cuss, oath 5 curse 9 expletive, obscenity 10 scurrility

sweat 4 emit, fume, milk, moil, ooze, rook, seep, snit, stew, toil, weep, work 5 bleed, exude, grind, labor, mulct, stick, tizzy 6 fleece, strain, swivet 7 excrete, slavery, travail 8 bullwork, drudgery, perspire, transude 10 donkeywork *combining form:* 4 hidr 5 hidro

sweater 8 cardigan, pullover, slipover

sweat out 2 go 4 bear, lump, take, wait 5 abide, brook, stand 6 endure 7 stomach 8 tolerate

sweaty 3 wet 6 clammy, sticky 7 labored 8 perspiry 10 perspiring

Sweden *capital:* 9 Stockholm *monetary unit:* 5 krona

Swedish Nightingale 4 Lind (Jenny)

sweep 3 fly 4 flit, sail, wing 5 ambit, broom, clean, clear, drive, fleet, orbit, range, reach, scope, surge 6 extent, radius 7 compass, purview 9 extension

sweeping 6 all-out 7 blanket, general, overall 8 whole-hog 9 all-around, extensive, inclusive, out-and-out, wholesale 12 all-embracing 13 comprehensive, thoroughgoing

sweepings 4 dust, junk 5 trash, waste 6 debris, litter, refuse 7 garbage, rubbish

sweet 5 candy, honey, spicy 6 aromal, dulcet, lovely, savory, sugary, syrupy 7 angelic, dessert, melodic, odorous, perfumy, scented, winning, winsome 8 aromatic, engaging, euphonic, fragrant, heavenly, loveling, luscious, perfumed, pleasant, pleasing, redolent 9 agreeable, ambrosial, beautiful, delicious 10 delectable, delightful *combining form:* 4 glyc 5 glyco

Sweet ____, song 7 Adeline

sweeten 5 candy, honey, sugar 6 pacify, refine, soften, solace 7 appease, assuage, lighten, mollify, placate, relieve 9 sugarcoat, sugar over 10 conciliate, propitiate

sweet potato 3 yam

sweet-talk 3 con 4 coax 6 banter, cajole 7 blarney, wheedle 8 blandish, soft-soap

swell 4 cock, grow, keen, lord, neat, pout, puff 5 bloat, bulge, dandy, nifty, pouch, super, surge, swank 6 billow, blow up, dilate, expand, groovy, tumefy 7 amplify, augment, balloon, distend, inflate, peacock, swagger, upsurge 8 increase, overblow, terrific 9 marvelous, wonderful *British:* 3 nob 4 toff

swelled head 5 pride 6 egoism 7 conceit, egotism 9 arrogance, vainglory 10 narcissism 11 amour propre 13 conceitedness

swelling 3 sty 4 bubo, gall, node 5 edema, tumid, tumor 6 bunion, growth 7 aureate, flowery, gibbous 8 tubercle 9 bombastic, carbuncle, chilblain, tumescent 10 euphuistic, rhetorical 12 inflammation, magniloquent 13 grandiloquent

sweltering 3 hot 5 fiery 6 baking, sultry, torrid 7 burning 8 broiling, sizzling 9 scorching

swerve 3 dip, err 4 skew, slue, turn, veer 5 sheer, shift, stray, waver 6 depart, totter, wander 7 deflect, deviate, digress, diverge 8 train off

swift 4 fast 5 fleet, hasty, quick, rapid, ready 6 prompt, raking, snappy, speedy, sudden 7 flat-out, fleetly, quickly, rapidly 8 full tilt, headlong, promptly, speedily 9 breakneck 10 harefooted

____ Swift 3 Tom 8 Jonathan *character:* 8 Gulliver

swiftness 4 gait, pace 5 haste, hurry, speed 6 hustle, rustle 8 celerity, dispatch, rapidity, velocity 9 quickness, rapidness 10 expedition, speediness

swig 4 drag, pull 5 booze, draft, drink, swill 6 guzzle, imbibe, tipple 7 swizzle

swill 4 slop, swig, tope 5 booze, draft, drink, offal, rinse, slops, trash, waste 6 debris, guzzle, refuse, spilth, tank up, tipple 7 consume, garbage, hogwash, put away, put down, rubbish, swizzle 9 polish off

swim 4 reel, spin, turn 5 float, swoon, whirl 9 dizziness

swimmer 7 natator

swimming stroke 5 crawl 7 dolphin, trudgen 9 butterfly, dogpaddle

swindle 3 con, gyp 4 beat, bilk, dupe, fake, hoax, rook, scam, sell, sham, skin 5 bunco, cheat, cozen, fraud, phony, rogue 6 chouse, diddle, humbug 7 defraud 8 flimflam 9 imposture, victimize

swine see hog

swing 3 ply, wag 4 beat, hang, rock, roll, sway, turn, veer, wave, whip 5 avert, flail, knack, lurch, meter, pivot, rhyme, sheer, trick, weave, wheel, whirl, wield 6 careen, divert, handle, jiggle, rhythm, rotate, stroke, switch, waggle, wiggle, wigwag, wobble 7 cadence, cadency, deflect, measure, revolve, stagger, vibrate 8 brandish, dispense, maneuver, undulate 9 fluctuate, oscillate, pendulate 10 manipulate

swinish 5 brute, feral, gross 6 animal, brutal, coarse, ferine, greedy 7 beastly, bestial, boarish, brutish, porcine, sensual

swipe 3 cop, hit, nab, rap 4 blow, conk, hook, lick, lift, swat, wipe 5 draft, heist, knock, pinch, steal 6 pilfer, snatch, snitch, strike

swirl 4 eddy, purl, roil 5 curve, gurge, twist, whirl, whorl 6 swoosh, vortex 9 whirlpool 11 convolution

swish 2 in 4 buzz, fizz, flog, hiss, tony, whiz 5 smart, swank, whisk 6 classy, fizzle, sizzle, tonish, trendy, wheeze, whoosh, with-it 7 stylish 8 sibilate 9 exclusive

Swiss Family Robinson author 4 Wyss (Johann David)

switch 3 rod, wag 4 beat, flog, lash, swap, wand, wave, whip 5 shift, shunt, trade, whisk 6 change, strike, waggle, woggle 7 scourge 8 exchange 9 sidetrack 10 substitute

Switzerland *capital:* 4 Bern *largest city:* 6 Zurich *monetary unit:* 5 franc

swivel 4 turn 5 swing

swivet see **snit**

swizzle see **swig**

swollen 5 bulgy, tumid 6 turgid 7 aureate, bulbous, bulging, flowery, pompous 8 enlarged, inflated, varicose 9 bombastic, distended, tumescent 10 euphuistic, rhetorical 12 magniloquent 13 grandiloquent *combining form:* 4 phys 5 physo

swoon 4 coma, daze, fade 5 drown, faint 6 torpor 7 die away, pass out, rapture, syncope 8 black out

swoosh 4 eddy, gush, purl 5 gurge, swirl, whirl, whorl

sword 4 épée, foil, kris, pata 5 estoc, saber 6 barong, bilboa, creese, rapier, toledo 7 cutlass 8 claymore, falchion, scimitar, yataghan

sword of ___ 8 Damocles

sword-shaped 6 ensate 8 ensiform

sworn 6 avowed 7 devoted, settled 8 affirmed 9 confirmed, hard-shell 10 deep-rooted, deep-seated, entrenched, inveterate

sybarite 7 epicure 8 hedonist 10 voluptuary

sybaritic 6 carnal 7 sensual 8 sensuous 9 epicurean, luxurious 10 apolaustic, hedonistic, voluptuous 13 self-indulgent

sycophancy 7 calumny, scandal, slander 8 toadying 10 backbiting, defamation, detraction 12 backstabbing, belittlement, depreciation 13 disparagement

sycophant 5 toady 6 flunky, lackey, minion, stooge, yes-man 7 defamer, fawning 8 bootlick, cowering, cringing, groveler, lickspit, parasite, toadying, toadyish 9 easy rider, flatterer, groveling, kowtowing, parasitic, slanderer 10 bootlicker, self-seeker 11 bootlicking, lickspittle 13 apple-polisher

sycophantic 7 fawning, servile, slavish 8 cowering, cringing, toadying, toadyish 9 groveling, kowtowing, parasitic, truckling 10 defamatory, obsequious, slanderous 11 bootlicking

Sycorax's son 7 Caliban

syllable 3 bit, jot 4 atom, iota, whit 5 crumb, ounce, shred 7 modicum 8 particle *deletion:* 7 apocope *last:* 6 ultima *lengthening of:* 7 ectasis *next to last:* 6 penult *shortening:* 7 elision, systole *stressed:* 5 arsis

syllabus 6 aperçu, digest, précis, sketch, survey 7 epitome, outline, pandect, summary 8 abstract, headnote, synopsis 10 compendium

sylvan 5 bosky, woody 6 rustic, wooded *deity:* 3 Pan 4 Faun 5 dryad, satyr 6 Faunus 7 Silenus 8 Arethusa, Silvanus, Sylvanus

symbol 4 logo, mark, note, sign, type 5 badge, motif, stamp, token 6 design, device, emblem, figure, mascot 7 pattern 9 attribute, character 10 indication *chemical:* see individual element *Egyptian:* 4 ankh *musical:* 4 clef, flat, hold, note, rest, turn 5 presa, shake, sharp, trill 7 fermata, mordent, natural 8 arpeggio 9 crescendo 10 diminuendo 11 decrescendo

symbolic 10 emblematic 11 allegorical

symbolist poet 7 Rimbaud (Arthur) 8 Mallarmé (Stéphane), Verlaine (Paul)

symbolize 6 embody, mirror, typify 7 express, signify 9 body forth, epitomize, exemplify, personify, represent 10 illustrate 11 emblematize

symmetrical 5 equal 7 regular 8 balanced 12 commensurate, proportional 13 commensurable

symmetry 5 order 7 balance, harmony 8 equality, evenness 9 agreement, congruity 10 conformity, proportion, regularity 11 arrangement

sympathetic 4 kind, warm 6 benign, humane, kindly, tender 8 amenable, favoring, friendly 9 agreeable, approving, benignant, congenial, congruous, consonant, favorable, receptive 10 compatible, consistent, responsive 11 kindhearted, softhearted, warmhearted 12 appreciating, well-disposed 13 compassionate, comprehending, understanding

sympathize 4 ache, pity 7 condole, feel for 10 appreciate, comprehend, understand 11 commiserate 13 compassionate

sympathy 3 rue 4 pity, ruth 5 heart 6 accord, warmth 7 empathy, harmony 8 affinity, kindness 9 agreement 10 benignancy, benignness, compassion, condolence, kindliness, tenderness 11 sensitivity 13 commiseration

symphonic 7 chiming, musical 8 blending, harmonic 9 consonant 10 harmonious
symphony 4 band 7 concord, harmony 9 orchestra 10 consonance 11 concert band 12 philharmonic
symptom 4 mark, note, sign 5 index, token 7 indicia 8 evidence 10 indication 11 significant
symptoms 8 syndrome
synagogue 8 assembly, building 9 community 12 congregation
synchronize 5 agree 6 concur 8 coincide
synchronous 6 coeval 8 existing 10 coetaneous, coexistent, coexisting, concurrent 11 concomitant 12 contemporary, simultaneous
syncope 4 coma 5 faint, swoon 8 blackout
syndicate 4 pool 5 chain, group, trust, union 6 cartel 7 combine 11 association, partnership 12 conglomerate, organization
syndrome 3 ill 6 malady 7 ailment, disease 8 disorder, sickness 9 affection, complaint, condition, infirmity 11 concurrence
synergic 8 coacting, coactive, conjoint
synod 4 body 7 council, meeting 8 assembly 10 convention, judicatory 11 convocation
synopsis 5 brief 7 epitome, summary 8 abstract, boildown, breviary, breviate 10 abridgment, conspectus 12 condensation

synopsize 3 sum 5 sum up 6 digest 7 summate 8 condense, nutshell 9 epitomize, inventory, summarize
synthesis 5 blend, union 11 combination 13 incorporation
synthesize 5 blend, unify 7 combine 9 harmonize, integrate
synthetic 7 man-made 10 artificial, fabricated
Syria *capital:* 8 Damascus *monetary unit:* 5 pound
Syrinx 5 nymph 7 panpipe *pursuer:* 3 Pan
syrup 4 corn 5 maple 7 sorghum 8 molasses *almond-flavored:* 6 orgeat
syrupy 5 gooey, moist, mushy, sappy, sobby, sweet 6 drippy, dulcet, slushy, sticky 7 maudlin 11 sentimental
system 3 sum, way 4 code, mode, plan, wise 5 modus, order, setup, whole 6 entity, manner, method, scheme 7 complex, fashion, network, pattern, process, regimen 9 technique 10 regularity 11 arrangement, disposition, orderliness
systematic 7 logical, ordered, orderly, regular 8 arranged, methodic 9 organized 10 analytical, methodical 12 businesslike
systematize 5 array, order 6 adjust, codify 7 arrange, catalog, dispose, marshal 8 classify, organize, regiment 9 methodize
system of weights 4 troy 11 avoirdupois

T

tab 3 eye, tag 4 bill, cost, rate 5 check, price, score, watch 6 charge, tariff 7 account, invoice 8 eagle eye, price tag, scrutiny 9 reckoning, statement 12 surveillance

tabard 4 cape, coat 5 tunic 7 pendant

tabby 3 cat 6 feline, gossip 7 rumorer 8 gossiper, quidnunc, telltale 9 carrytale 10 newsmonger, talebearer 12 gossipmonger 13 scandalmonger

tabellion 6 scribe

tabernacle 6 church, temple 10 house of God 13 house of prayer

tabes 7 atrophy, wasting

Tabitha's Greek name 6 Dorcas

table 4 fare, list 5 bench, board, chart, stand 6 buffet, record, teapoy, upland 7 counter, plateau 8 mahogany 9 sideboard *ornament:* 7 epergne 11 centerpiece *spread:* 4 oleo 6 butter *wheeled:* 4 cart *writing:* 4 desk 9 secretary 10 escritoire

table d' ___ 4 hôte

table game see at game

tableland 4 mesa 6 upland 7 plateau *Alabama-West Virginia:* 10 Cumberland *Arizona:* 5 Kanab 6 Kaibob *England:* 8 Dartmoor *India:* 5 Malwa; (see also plateau)

tablet 3 bar, pad 4 cake, disk, pill, slab 5 panel, slate 6 troche 7 lozenge *combining form:* 4 plac 5 pinac, pinak, placo 6 pinaco *ornamental:* 9 cartouche *stone:* 5 stela, stele *writing:* 3 pad 7 fanfold 8 triptych

Table Talk author 6 Selden (John)

table talk expert 13 deipnosophist

tableware 4 cups 5 bowls, forks 6 dishes, knives, plates, silver, spoons 7 glasses, saucers

tabloid 5 livid, lurid, short 9 newspaper 11 sensational

taboo 3 ban 4 don't 6 enjoin, forbid, outlaw 7 inhibit 8 prohibit, sanction 9 interdict, restraint 10 inhibition, limitation, regulation 11 forbiddance, prohibition, reservation, restriction 12 interdiction, proscription

tabor 4 drum

taboret 5 stand, stool 7 cabinet

Tabrimmon *father:* 6 Hezion *son:* 8 Benhadad

tabula ___ 4 rasa

tabulation 5 chart, tally

tache 5 clasp 6 buckle

tacit 6 silent, unsaid 7 assumed, implied 8 hinted at, implicit, inferred, unspoken, unvoiced 9 alluded to, intimated, suggested, unuttered 10 undeclared, understood 11 unexpressed 12 inarticulate

taciturn 5 close 6 silent 7 laconic 8 reserved, reticent, wordless 10 silentious 11 close-lipped, tight-lipped 12 closemouthed

Tacitus work 7 Annales 8 Germania 9 Historiae

tack 3 pin, yaw 4 bend, brad, link, nail, turn 5 shift 6 double, swerve, zigzag 7 tangent 9 deviation 10 alteration, deflection, digression

tackle 3 rig 4 gear 5 throw 6 attack, burton, outfit, take on 7 lineman, rigging 8 matériel, set about 9 apparatus, equipment, machinery, undertake 10 footballer, plunge into 11 clothesline, habiliments 13 accouterments, paraphernalia

tacky 5 cheap, crude, dingy, dowdy, faded, gaudy, messy, seedy 6 blowsy, frowsy, frumpy, shabby, sloppy, sticky, stodgy, tagrag, untidy 7 run-down, unkempt 8 frumpish, outmoded, slovenly 9 incorrect, inelegant, out-of-date, tasteless, unstylish 10 broken-down, down-at-heel, threadbare, unbecoming, unsuitable 11 dilapidated

tact 5 poise, skill 6 acumen 7 finesse, suavity 8 civility, courtesy, deftness, urbanity 9 diplomacy, gallantry 10 adroitness, perception, politeness, smoothness 11 delicatesse, savoir faire, sensitivity

tactful 4 deft 5 suave 6 adroit, urbane 7 politic, skilled 8 delicate, discreet, polished, skillful 9 sensitive 10 diplomatic, perceptive

tactical 4 wise 7 politic, prudent 8 delicate 9 advisable, expedient 10 diplomatic, short-range

tactics 4 plan 6 method, system 9 maneuvers

tactile 8 palpable, tangible 9 touchable

taction 5 touch 7 contact 9 palpation

tad 3 bit, boy, lad, son 5 child 6 laddie 9 shaveling, stripling

tadpole 8 polliwog, pollywog

taffy 5 candy 8 flattery

tag 3 dog, end 4 flap, game, tail 5 bedog, label, trail 6 cliché, follow, shadow, ticket, truism 7 bromide 8 banality, prosaism 9 platitude 10 prosaicism, shibboleth

tagrag 5 dingy, faded, seedy, tacky 6 shabby 7 run-down 10 bedraggled, down-at-heel, threadbare 11 dilapidated

Tahan's father 7 Ephraim

Tahash's father 5 Nahor

Tahath's father 5 Bered 7 Eleadah

Tahiti *capital:* 7 Papeete *painter:* 7 Gauguin (Paul)

tail 3 dog, end, eye, tag 4 butt, rear 5 bedog, cauda, hound, trail 6 follow, pursue, shadow 7 hind end, rear end 8 backside, buttocks 9 posterior *relating to:* 6 caudal *short:* 4 scut

tailed 7 caudate

tailless 7 acaudal, anurous 8 ecaudate

tailor 3 fit, sew 4 suit 5 adapt, alter, style 6 adjust, sartor, square 7 conform, shape up 8 clothier, dovetail, quadrate, seamster 9 reconcile 11 accommodate *Hindu:* 5 darzi 6 durzee

taint 3 hue, rot, tar 4 blur, foul, harm, hurt, smut, soil, turn 5 brand, cloud, color, decay, dirty, smear, spoil, stain, sully 6 befoul, damage, defile, molder, smudge, smutch 7 besmear, blacken, crumble, pollute, putrefy, tarnish 8 besmirch, discolor 9 break down, decompose, discredit 10 stigmatize 11 contaminate

taipan 5 snake 8 merchant

Taiwan 7 Formosa *capital:* 6 Taipei

taj 3 cap

Taj Mahal 9 mausoleum *builder:* 9 Shah Jahan *site:* 4 Agra

take 3 bag, buy, cut, eat, get, gyp, nab, use, win 4 bear, beat, bilk, cull, down, draw, grab, grip, haul, pick 5 abide, admit, annex, brook, catch, charm, cheat, clasp, cozen, grasp, seize, share, stand, think, treat 6 accept, allure, assume, choose, clutch, collar, deduct, devour, endure, follow, gather, income, ingest, obtain, opt for, prefer, secure, select, snatch, strike, suffer 7 attract, believe, call for, capture, consume, defraud, enchant, grapple, imagine, receive, require, stomach, suppose, swallow 8 arrogate, contract, deal with, discount, flimflam, knock off, proceeds, purchase, receipts, subtract, tolerate 9 apprehend, captivate, fascinate, partake of, single out, substract 10 commandeer, comprehend, confiscate, sicken with, understand 11 appropriate 12 come down with *account of:* 6 notice *advantage of:* 5 abuse 7 exploit *after:* 6 follow 8 resemble *apart:* 7 analyze, dissect 9 dismantle

care: 6 beware *care of:* 3 fix 4 tend 5 nurse 6 attend *exception:* 6 object *five:* 4 rest *from:* 7 deprive, detract 8 subtract *it easy:* 5 relax *on the:* 7 corrupt *part:* 4 join 5 share 11 participate *place:* 5 occur 6 happen *the cake:* 3 win *to:* 4 like *to task:* 5 scold 7 reprove *turns:* 9 alternate *unawares:* 8 surprise

take away 5 decry, wrest 6 deduct, remove 7 deprive, detract 8 belittle, derogate, diminish, discount, draw back, knock off, minimize, subtract, withdraw, write off 9 disparage, substract 10 depreciate 11 detract from

take back 5 unsay 6 abjure, recall, recant, return 7 replace, restore, retract 8 forswear, palinode, withdraw 9 repossess, restitute

take down 5 lower 6 reduce, tackle 8 dismount 9 dismantle, dismember 11 disassemble

take in 3 see 4 fool, have 5 admit, bluff, catch, grasp, trick 6 absorb, accept, betray, delude, embody, follow, illude 7 beguile, compass, contain, deceive, embrace, include, involve, receive, subsume 8 flimflam 9 apprehend, encompass, four-flush 10 assimilate, comprehend, understand 11 double cross

take off 2 go 3 ape 4 doff, down, exit, head, kill, kite, mock, quit, slay 5 douse, leave, mimic, scram 6 begone, decamp, deduct, depart, finish, get out, lay low, parody, remove, set out 7 destroy, get away, imitate, pull out, put away, skiddoo, vamoose 8 clear out, discount, dispatch, draw back, hightail, light out, subtract, withdraw 9 burlesque, skedaddle, strike out, substract

takeoff 4 jato, rato 6 launch, parody, send-up 7 lift-off 8 blast-off, travesty 9 burlesque 10 caricature *area:* 3 pad 6 runway

take on 3 add, don 4 face, hire, meet, pull 5 adopt, annex 6 append, assume, employ, engage, strike 7 embrace, espouse, subjoin 9 encounter

take out 4 date, vent 5 loose 6 deduct, remove 7 release, unleash 8 discount, draw back, knock off, subtract, withdraw 9 clear away, eliminate, substract

take over 5 seize, spell, usurp 7 relieve

take up 3 use 4 lift, open, rear 5 adopt, begin, enter, hoist, raise, renew, set to, start 6 assume, resume, tackle, uphold, uplift, uprear 7 elevate, embrace, espouse, kick off, restart, upraise 8 commence, continue, initiate 10 recommence

talc 4 mica 6 powder 7 agalite 8 steatite 9 soapstone

tale 3 fib, lie, sum 4 myth, saga, tote, yarn 5 fable, story, total, whole 6 canard, legend

7 calumny, falsity, fiction, scandal, slander, untruth **8** anecdote, entirety, sum total, totality, untruism **9** aggregate, falsehood, narration, narrative **10** backbiting, defamation, detraction **12** backstabbing, belittlement, depreciation **13** disparagement, prevarication *epic:* **4** saga *woeful:* **8** jeremiad

talebearer **4** fink **5** tabby **6** canary, gossip, snitch **7** rumorer, tattler, tipster **8** gossiper, informer, quidnunc, squealer **10** newsmonger **11** rumormonger, stool pigeon **13** scandalmonger

talent **4** bent, gift, nose **5** craft, flair, forte, money, skill **6** genius **7** aptness, faculty **9** endowment, expertise

Tale of Two Cities, A *author:* **7** Dickens (Charles) *character:* **6** Carton (Sidney), Darnay (Charles) **7** Defarge, Manette (Alexander), Manette (Lucie)

Tales of a Traveller author **6** Irving (Washington)

Tales of a Wayside Inn author **10** Longfellow (Henry Wadsworth)

Tales of Hoffman composer **9** Offenbach (Jacques)

talipot **4** palm

talisman **4** juju, luck, zemi **5** charm, saffi **6** amulet, fetish, mascot, saphie **7** periapt **10** phylactery

Talisman, The *author:* **5** Scott (Walter)

talk **3** gab, rap, yak **4** blab, buzz, chat, chin, sing, yarn **5** on-dit, prate, rumor, run on, speak, utter, voice **6** babble, dialog, gabble, gossip, parley, patter, powwow, report, speech, squeal, tattle **7** address, chatter, declaim, gabfest, hearsay, lecture, prattle **8** causerie, colloque, colloquy, converse, dialogue, harangue, perorate, vocalize **9** discourse, grapevine, hold forth, speechify, utterance, verbalize **10** allocution, discussion **11** scuttlebutt **12** conversation, deliberation **13** confabulation, verbalization *about:* **7** discuss *back:* **4** sass *combining form:* **3** log **4** logy **5** logia, logue *foolish:* **4** bunk **6** babble **7** chatter, palaver *indistinctly:* **6** mumble, mutter *over:* **7** discuss *slowly:* **5** drawl *small:* **8** chitchat *wildly:* **4** rant, rave

talkative **4** glib **5** gabby, vocal **6** chatty, fluent, mouthy **7** gossipy, voluble **9** garrulous **10** babblative, loquacious **11** loose-lipped **12** loose-tongued, multiloquent **13** multiloquious

tall **4** high **5** lanky, lofty, rangy **8** towering **11** skyscraping **12** altitudinous

tallow **3** fat **4** suet **6** grease *combining form:* **4** sebi, sebo **5** stear, steat **6** stearo, steato

tally **4** jibe **5** agree, count, fit in, match, score **6** accord, number, square **7** balance, catalog, conform, itemize **8** numerate

9 catalogue, enumerate, harmonize, inventory **10** correspond

Talmai *daughter:* **6** Maacah *father:* **4** Anak *grandson:* **7** Absalom

talon **4** claw

talus **5** ankle, scree, slope

tam **3** cap

Tamar *brother:* **7** Absalom *father:* **5** David **7** Absalom *father-in-law:* **5** Judah *half brother:* **5** Amnon *husband:* **2** Er *seducer:* **5** Amnon *son:* **5** Perez, Zerah

tamarisk **4** atle **5** athel, atlee

tambour **3** cup **4** bell, drum, wall **7** drummer

tambourine **4** dove, drum **7** timbrel

Tamburlaine the Great author **7** Marlowe (Christopher)

tame **4** meek, mild **6** docile, gentle, master, pliant **7** pliable, subdued, trained **8** amenable, biddable, broken in, domestic, obedient **9** tractable **10** submissive **11** domesticate, domesticize, domiciliate, housebroken **12** domesticated

Taming of the Shrew, The *character:* **6** Bianca **8** Baptista **9** Katharina, Potruchio

Tammany boss **5** Tweed (William)

Tammuz' lover **6** Ishtar

tam-o'-shanter **3** cap

tamp **3** jam, mat, ram **4** cram, pack **5** pound, stuff

tampion **4** plug

tan **3** sun, taw **4** beat, ecru, flog, whip **5** beige, brown, toast **6** bronze, darken, thrash

tanager **4** bird, yeni

Tancred, Tancredi *beloved:* **8** Clorinda *father:* **3** Odo *mother:* **4** Emma *victim:* **8** Clorinda

tandem **4** pair **8** carriage

tang **3** nip **4** bite, odor, zest **5** aroma, sapor, savor, smack, taste **6** flavor, relish **8** piquancy, pungency, sapidity **9** spiciness

tangible **7** tactile **8** embodied, material, palpable, physical, sensible **9** corporeal, touchable **10** detectable, observable, phenomenal **11** appreciable, discernible, perceptible, substantial

tangle **3** mat, web **4** knot, maze, mesh, muck, trap **5** benet, catch, mix up, ravel, skein, snare, snarl **6** entrap, foul up, jungle, morass, muddle **7** catch up, embroil, ensnare, ensnarl, involve, mizmaze, perplex **9** implicate, labyrinth **10** complicate

Tanglewood Tales author **9** Hawthorne (Nathaniel)

tango **5** dance

tank **3** vat **5** basin **7** cistern, pachuca, vehicle **8** aquarium **9** container, reservoir *American:* **7** Sherman *German:* **6** panzer *part:* **6** turret

tankard 3 mug 5 stoup 6 flagon 9 black-jack

tanker 4 ship 5 oiler

Tannhäuser composer 6 Wagner (Richard)

tantalize 4 bait, gnaw 5 annoy, harry, taunt, tease, worry 6 harass, pester, plague 7 bedevil, hagride, torment 9 beleaguer, frustrate

Tantalus *daughter:* 5 Niobe *father:* 4 Zeus *son:* 6 Pelops

tantamount 4 same 5 alike, equal 8 selfsame 9 duplicate, identical 10 equivalent

tantara 5 blare 7 fanfare

tantivy 4 rush 6 gallop 8 headlong

tantrum 3 fit

Tanzania *capital:* 11 Dar es Salaam *monetary unit:* 8 shilling

Taoism founder 6 Lao Tzu

tap 3 bar, bob, hit, pub, rap 4 cock, draw, name, pump, tunk 5 draft, drain, knock, nudge, thump, valve 6 faucet, finger, siphon, spigot, strike 7 appoint, barroom, draw off, hydrant, petcock 8 nominate, stopcock 9 designate

tape 4 band, belt, bind 5 strip 6 fillet, record, ribbon 7 bandage, measure *kind:* 5 inkle 6 ferret 7 masking 8 adhesive 9 measuring *machine:* 8 recorder

taper 4 wick 5 abate, close, spire 6 lessen, reduce 7 dwindle 8 decrease, diminish 9 drain away

tapering 5 conic, spiry 6 terete 7 conical, pointed 8 fusiform, subulate 9 acuminate

tapestry 5 arras, kilim 6 dossal 7 curtain, Gobelin, hanging *pattern:* 7 cartoon *tool:* 6 broché

tapeworm 6 taenia 8 parasite *body:* 8 strobila *combining form:* 4 taen 5 taeni 6 taenio *head:* 6 scolex

Taphath's father 7 Solomon

tapioca 7 cassava, pudding

Tappuah's father 6 Hebron

taproom 3 bar, pub 6 saloon, tavern

tapster 6 barman 7 barmaid 9 barkeeper, bartender 10 mixologist

tar 4 jack, pave, salt, soil 5 pitch, smear, stain, sully, taint 6 defile, sailor, seaman 7 asphalt, besmear, mariner 8 besmirch 9 sailorman

taradiddle 3 fib, lie 5 story 6 canard 7 falsity 9 falsehood 13 prevarication

tarantella 5 dance

tarantula 6 spider

Taras Bulba author 5 Gogol (Nikolay)

tarboosh 3 fez, hat

tardy 3 lax 4 late, slow 7 belated, delayed, laggard, overdue 8 detained, dilatory 10 behindhand, delinquent, unpunctual

tare 4 seed 5 vetch 6 weight

target 3 aim 4 butt, goal, mark 6 object, victim 9 objective, quaesitum 11 sitting duck *center:* 8 bull's-eye *shooter's:* 10 clay pigeon

Tar Heel State 13 North Carolina

tariff 3 tab, tax 4 cost, duty, levy, rate 5 price 6 charge, impost 8 price tag 10 assessment

Tarkington, Booth *character:* 6 Penrod

tarn 4 lake, pool

tarnish 3 dim, mar, tar 4 dull, fade, foul, harm, hurt, pale, soil 5 dirty, grime, muddy, smear, spoil, sully, taint 6 besoil, damage, impair, injure, smirch, smudge, smutch 7 begrime, besmear, blemish 8 besmirch, discolor

taro 4 dalo, eddo, gabe, gabi 5 aroid, tania 6 yautia 7 dasheen, malanga *product:* 3 poi

tarpaulin 4 jack, salt 5 cover 6 sailor, seaman 7 mariner 9 sailorman

tarpon 4 fish 5 oxeye

tarry 3 lag 4 bide, drag, poke, stay, wait 5 abide, dally, delay, trail, visit 6 linger, loiter, put off, remain 8 stop over 11 stick around 13 procrastinate

Tarshish's father 6 Bilhan

tarsus 5 ankle

tart 3 dry, pie 4 acid, sour 5 acerb, sharp 6 pastry 7 acerbic, acetose, piquant, pungent 9 acidulous

Tartar 6 Mongol 7 Turkish 8 Mongolic 9 Mongolian

Tartuffe author 7 Molière

Tarzan *creator:* 9 Burroughs (Edgar Rice) *mate:* 4 Jane

task 3 job 4 duty, lade, load, toil, work 5 chare, chore, labor, stint, weigh 6 burden, charge, devoir, errand, lumber, saddle, weight 7 mission, project 8 encumber 10 assignment 11 undertaking

Tasmanian 4 wolf 5 devil *pine:* 4 Huon

Tasmania's capital 6 Hobart

tassel 4 tuft 5 adorn 6 fringe 7 pendant 8 ornament

Tasso *patron:* 4 Este (Alfonso II d') *work:* 6 Aminta 7 Rinaldo 18 Jerusalem Delivered

taste 3 eat, sip, try 4 dash, feel, hint, tang, zest 5 grace, gusto, heart, sapor, savor, smack, tinge, touch, whiff 6 degust, flavor, liking, palate, polish, relish, trifle 7 finesse, stomach 8 appetite, elegance, fondness, sapidity, soft spot, tincture, weakness 9 appetence 10 experience, partiality, refinement, sprinkling 11 inclination *combining form:* 6 geusia *kind:* 4 salt, sour 5 sweet 6 bitter *lacking:* (see **tasteless**) *organ:* 3 bud

tasteless 4 dull, flat, wild 5 bland, vapid 6 vulgar 7 insipid 8 barbaric, unsavory

9 barbarian, barbarous, graceless, inelegant, savorless, unrefined **10** flavorless, outlandish, unflavored, unpolished **11** ill-flavored, unpalatable **12** unappetizing **13** uninteresting

tasty 5 sapid **6** savory, toothy **9** palatable, relishing, toothsome **10** appetizing, flavorsome

Tate 7 Gallery

tatou 9 armadillo

tatter 3 rag, rip **4** tear **5** shred

tattered 5 dingy, seedy, tacky **6** frayed, ragged, shabby, tagrag **7** run-down, shreddy **8** frazzled **10** bedraggled, broken-down, threadbare **11** dilapidated

tattle 4 blab, buzz, talk **5** rumor **6** gossip, report **7** hearsay **9** grapevine **11** scuttlebutt

tattler see talebearer

tattletale see talebearer

tatty 4 base, mean, poor **5** cheap **6** common, paltry, shoddy, sleazy, trashy **8** rubbishy

taunt 4 gibe, lout, mock, razz, twit **5** scout, tease **6** deride **7** provoke **8** reproach, ridicule

taurine 6 bovine

Taurus 4 bull *star:* **9** Aldebaran

taut 5 close, tense, tight

tautology 8 pleonasm, verbiage **9** verbality **10** periphrase, redundancy, roundabout **11** periphrasis **13** circumambages

tavern 3 bar, inn, pub **5** hotel, lodge **6** bistro, hostel, saloon **7** auberge, barroom, hospice, taproom **8** alehouse, drinkery, hostelry **9** roadhouse **11** caravansary, public house **12** watering hole

taverner 8 boniface, publican **9** barkeeper, innholder, innkeeper, saloonist **12** saloonkeeper

taw 5 stake **6** marble

tawdry 4 loud **5** gaudy **6** brazen, flashy, garish, tinsel **7** blatant, chintzy, glaring **12** meretricious

tawny 3 tan **4** dark **5** brown **6** tanned *combining form:* **5** fusco, pyrrh, pyrro **6** pyrrho

tax 4 duty, lade, levy, load, onus, scot, toll **5** abuse, tithe **6** assess, burden, cumber, impost, saddle, strain, tariff, weight **7** tollage, tribute **8** encumber **10** assessment, deadweight *agency:* **3** IRS *feudal:* **7** scutage, tallage *kind:* **4** geld **5** sales, tithe **6** excise, income **7** chevage, prisage **8** property **9** surcharge *on salt:* **7** gabelle *rate:* **10** assessment

taxi 3 cab, car **4** hack

taxing 5 tough **6** trying **7** exigent, onerous, weighty **8** exacting, grievous **9** demanding **10** burdensome, oppressive

Taygeta *father:* 5 Atlas *mother:* **7** Pleione *sisters:* **8** Pleiades

tazza 3 cup **4** vase

Tchaikovsky, Peter *ballet:* 8 Swan Lake **10** Nutcracker *opera:* **12** Eugene Onegin **13** Queen of Spades

tea 5 drink, party **6** repast **8** beverage **9** marijuana, reception *black:* **5** bohea, oopak, pekoe **8** souchong *cake:* **6** cookie *genus:* **4** Thea *ingredient:* **8** caffeine *kind:* **4** herb, Java **5** Assam, black, bohea, green, hyson, ledum, pekoe **6** Ceylon, congou, oolong **7** cambric **8** souchong **9** sassafras *of India:* **10** Darjeeling

teach 5 coach, train, tutor **6** impart, school **7** educate, instill **8** instruct **9** enlighten, inculcate **12** indoctrinate

teacher 4 guru, prof **5** coach, guide, tutor **6** docent, master, mentor, pedant **7** edifier, maestro, trainer **8** educator, magister **9** pedagogue, preceptor, professor **10** instructor **12** schoolmaster *Hindu:* **5** swami *Jewish:* **5** rabbi **7** rabboni *Muslim:* **3** pir **5** mulla **6** mollah, mullah *organization:* **3** NEA *religious:* **8** mystagog **9** catechist

Tea for Two composer 7 Youmans (Vincent)

team 4 club, crew, gang, join, pair, side, yoke **5** group, squad, wagon **8** carriage *baseball:* **4** nine *basketball:* **4** five **7** quintet *football:* **6** eleven *kind:* **2** JV **6** jayvee **7** varsity *supporter:* **3** fan

tear 3 cut, rip, run **4** bolt, dash, gash, lash, race, rend, rift, rive, rush, slit **5** chase, fling, sever, shoot, shred, slash, speed, split **6** career, charge, cleave, course, incise, sunder, tatter **8** lacerate

tear away 6 avulse

tear down 4 raze, ruin, slur **5** smear, wrack, wreck **6** defame, malign **7** asperse, destroy, shatter, slander **8** demolish, destruct **9** denigrate **10** annihilate, calumniate, scandalize

tearful 3 sad **5** weepy **6** crying **7** bawling, sobbing, weeping **8** mourning **9** lamenting, sniveling **10** blubbering, lachrymose

tear-jerking 5 mushy **6** slushy, sticky **7** maudlin, mawkish **8** bathetic, romantic **11** sentimental

teary see tearful

teary-eyed 5 blear

tease 3 kid, rip **4** gnaw, josh, twit **5** annoy, chaff, harry, taunt, worry **6** harass, pester, plague **7** bedevil **8** ridicule **9** beleaguer

teaser *television:* 5 promo

Tebah *father:* 5 Nahor *mother:* **6** Reumah

teched 4 daft **5** batty, crazy **6** crazed, insane **7** cracked, lunatic **8** demented, deranged **9** bedlamite

technicality 6 detail 8 loophole

technique 3 way 4 mode, wise 5 modus 6 manner, method, system 7 fashion *combining form:* 4 urgy

tectonic 10 structural

ted 5 strew 6 spread 7 scatter

tedious 3 dry 4 arid, dull 5 dusty 6 boring, tiring 7 insipid, irksome 8 boresome, bromidic, drudging, weariful 9 dryasdust, wearisome 13 uninteresting

tedium 4 yawn 5 ennui 7 boredom 8 doldrums, dullness, monotony

teem 4 flow 5 crawl, swarm 6 abound 9 pullulate

teeming 4 lush, rife 5 alive 6 aswarm 7 replete 8 swarming, thronged 9 abounding 11 overflowing

teen 5 youth 8 juvenile 9 youngster 10 adolescent

tee off 4 open 5 begin, drive, enter, start 6 take up 8 commence, initiate

teeter 5 lurch 6 falter, seesaw, topple, totter, wobble 7 stagger, stumble

teeth *false:* 8 dentures *grinding:* 7 bruxism *having:* 7 dentate *problem:* 5 decay 6 caries 8 overbite *relating to:* 6 dental; (see also **tooth**)

teg 3 doe 4 deer 5 sheep

tegua 8 moccasin

teju 6 lizard

telamon 5 atlas *counterpart:* 8 caryatid

Telamon *brother:* 6 Peleus *father:* 6 Aeacus *half-brother:* 6 Phocus *son:* 4 Ajax 6 Teucer

Telegonus *father:* 7 Ulysses 8 Odysseus *mother:* 5 Circe

telegraph 4 wire 5 cable 6 signal *code:* 5 Morse

Telemachus *father:* 7 Ulysses 8 Odysseus *mother:* 8 Penelope

telephone 4 buzz, call, dial, ring 5 phone 6 ring up *inventor:* 4 Bell (Alexander Graham)

Telephus *father:* 8 Heracles, Hercules *mother:* 4 Auge

telescope 5 glass 8 compress, condense, spyglass

television 2 TV 4 tube 5 video 8 boob tube *antenna:* 10 rabbit ears *award:* 4 Emmy *British:* 5 telly *children's:* 6 kidvid *frequency:* 3 UHF, VHF *interference:* 4 snow *network:* 3 ABC, BBC, CBS, Fox, NBC, NET, PBS *pioneer:* 5 Baird (John Logie) 8 Zworykin (Vladimir) *program:* 4 news, show 5 rerun 6 series, sitcom 7 western 8 game show, talk show 9 broadcast, docudrama, soap opera 11 infomercial 12 infotainment *tube:* 4 kine 9 kinescope

tell 3 bid, say 4 clew, clue, post, tale, warn 5 mouth, order, spill, state, tally, utter 6 advise, betray, charge, direct, enjoin, fill in, inform, notify, number, relate, reveal, wise up 7 blab out, command, declare, divulge, narrate 8 bring out, disclose, discover, give away, instruct, numerate

teller 5 clerk 7 cashier, counter 8 informer, narrator

telling 5 solid, sound, valid 6 cogent 10 convincing, satisfying 12 satisfactory

tell off 3 jaw 4 rail 5 scold 6 berate, revile 7 bawl out, chew out, upbraid 8 call down 10 tongue-lash, vituperate

tell on 6 snitch, tattle

telltale 3 cue 4 clue, hint, wind 5 clack, tabby 6 gossip, notion 7 inkling 8 gossiper, quidnunc 9 carrytale 10 indication, intimation, newsmonger, suggestion, talebearer 12 gossipmonger 13 scandalmonger

tellurian 6 earthy 7 earthly, mundane, terrene, worldly 9 sublunary 11 terrestrial, uncelestial

tellurium *symbol:* 2 Te

Tema's father 7 Ishmael

temblor 5 quake, shake, shock 6 quaker, tremor 10 earthquake

temerarious 4 rash 6 daring 8 heedless, reckless 9 audacious, daredevil, foolhardy, imprudent, venturous 10 incautious 11 adventurous, injudicious, venturesome 13 adventuresome

temerity 4 gall 5 nerve 6 daring 8 audacity, rashness 9 assurance, brashness, hardihood, hardiness 11 impetuosity 12 heedlessness, impertinence, recklessness 13 foolhardiness

temper 4 curb, mind, mood, tone, vein 5 humor 6 dilute, makeup, season, soften, spirit, strain, timbre 7 passion 8 moderate, modulate, restrain, tone down 10 complexion 11 personality 13 individualism, individuality

temperament 4 mood 5 humor 6 makeup, nature 9 character 10 complexion 11 disposition, personality

temperamental 5 moody 6 fickle 8 ticklish, unstable, variable, volatile 9 humorsome, mercurial, uncertain 10 capricious, changeable, inconstant

temperance 7 control, measure 8 sobriety 9 austerity 10 abstinence, continence, moderation 11 refrainment, self-control 12 moderateness *advocate of:* 6 Nation (Carry) 7 Willard (Frances)

temperate 4 calm, even 5 sober 6 modest, steady 8 discreet, moderate 9 abstinent, continent, regulated, unextreme 10 abstemious, controlled, reasonable, restrained 11 abstentious, unexcessive 12 conservative 13 unimpassioned temperature 4 heat 5 fever 6 warmth 9 intensity

tempest 4 gale, rage, wind 5 storm 6 tumult, uproar 9 commotion, hurricane

Tempest, The *character:* 5 Ariel 7 Caliban, Miranda 8 Prospero 9 Ferdinand

tempestuous 4 wild 5 rough 6 raging, stormy 7 furious, violent 8 blustery 9 turbulent, unbridled 10 blustering, tumultuous

temple 4 fane 6 church 10 house of God, tabernacle 13 house of prayer *ancient:* 4 naos 5 speos 8 pantheon *Aztec:* 6 teopan 8 teocalli *Buddhist:* 2 ta 3 taa, wat *Eastern:* 6 pagoda *Greek:* 6 hieron 9 Parthenon *sanctuary:* 5 cella 6 adytum 10 penetralia

tempo 4 pace, rate, time 5 speed 6 rhythm *fast:* 6 presto 7 allegro *moderate:* 7 andante *slow:* 5 grave, lento 6 adagio

temporal 3 lay 6 earthy 7 mundane, profane, secular, sensual, worldly 8 banausic, unsacred 13 materialistic

temporary 6 acting, pro tem, supply 7 interim 9 ad interim, transient 10 pro tempore

tempt 3 woo 4 bait, lure, risk, vamp 5 decoy, train 6 allure, entice, entrap, invite, lead on, seduce 7 solicit 8 inveigle 9 tantalize

temptation 4 bait, lure, trap 5 decoy, snare 6 come-on 10 allurement, enticement, seducement 12 inveiglement

temptress 4 vamp 5 siren 7 Delilah, Lorelei 10 seductress 11 femme fatale

ten *cents:* 4 dime *combining form:* 3 dec, dek 4 deca, deka 5 decem *dollars:* 7 sawbuck *mills:* 4 cent *thousand:* 6 myriad *years:* 6 decade

tenacious 3 set 4 fast, firm, true 5 fixed, stout, tight, tough 6 dogged, secure, strong, sturdy, viscid 7 viscose, viscous 8 stalwart, stubborn 9 obstinate, steadfast 10 bulldogged, persisting 11 bulldoggish, persevering 12 pertinacious

tenacity 8 firmness 10 resolution 11 persistence

tenant 6 holder, lessee, occupy, people, renter 7 boarder, dweller, inhabit 8 occupant, populate 9 collibert *feudal:* 4 leud 6 bordar, vassal 7 socager, sokeman *Indian:* 7 chakdar *Irish:* 7 cottier

tenantable 7 livable 9 habitable, lodgeable 10 occupiable 11 inhabitable

Ten Commandments 9 Decalogue

tend 4 care, lean, look, mind, till, work 5 dress, labor, nurse, serve, watch 7 care for, conduce, incline, redound 8 minister 10 contribute

tendency 3 run 4 bent, bias 5 drift, tenor, trend 7 current, leaning 8 penchant

9 inclining 10 proclivity, propensity 11 disposition, inclination 12 predilection *combining form:* 5 phily 6 philia *suffix:* 4 itis

tendentious 6 biased 7 colored, partial 8 one-sided, partisan 10 prejudiced

tender 4 fond, give, mild, pose, soft, sore, warm 5 offer 6 extend, gentle, humane, loving, submit 7 hold out, lenient, present, proffer, propose 8 yielding 9 forgiving 10 benevolent, charitable, responsive 11 considerate, kindhearted, softhearted, sympathetic, warmhearted 12 affectionate 13 commiserative, compassionate

tenderfoot 4 colt, tyro 6 novice, rookie 8 beginner, freshman, neophyte, newcomer 9 novitiate 10 apprentice

Tender is the Night author 10 Fitzgerald (F. Scott)

tendon 4 band, cord 5 sinew

tendril 4 curl 6 cirrus 7 ringlet

tenebrific 5 black, bleak 6 dismal, dreary, gloomy, somber 8 funereal 10 oppressive 11 dispiriting 13 disheartening

tenebrous 3 dim 4 dark, dusk 5 dusky, murky, vague 6 gloomy 7 obscure, unclear 9 ambiguous, equivocal, lightless, sibylline, uncertain 10 caliginous, unexplicit 13 unilluminated

tenement 4 flat 5 rooms, suite 6 rental 7 lodging 8 building 9 apartment

tenet 3 ism 5 canon, dogma 8 doctrine

tenfold 6 denary

Tennessee *capital:* 9 Nashville *college, university:* 5 Bryan 10 Vanderbilt *largest city:* 7 Memphis *nickname:* 14 Volunteer State *state flower:* 4 iris

tennis *award:* 8 Davis Cup *item:* 3 net 4 ball 6 racket 7 racquet *kind:* 5 table 7 doubles, singles 8 platform *score:* 4 love 5 deuce *serve:* 3 ace *shoe:* 7 sneaker *stroke:* 3 cut, lob 4 chop, drop 5 serve, slice 6 volley 8 backhand, forehand *term:* 3 let, set 5 court, fault 7 service 9 advantage, backcourt

tennis champ 4 Ashe (Arthur), Borg (Bjorn), Cash (Pat), Graf (Steffi), King (Billie Jean), Noah (Yannick), Wade (Virginia) 5 Budge (Don), Chang (Michael), Court (Margaret Smith), Evert (Chris), Gomez (Andres), Laver (Rod), Lendl (Ivan), Perry (Fred), Seles (Monica), Stich (Michael), Vilas (Guillermo), Wills (Helen) 6 Agassi (André), Austin (Tracy), Becker (Boris), Edberg (Stephan), Fraser (Neale), Gibson (Althea), Kramer (Jack), Muster (Thomas), Pierce (Mary), Stolle (Fred), Tilden (Bill) 7 Connors (Jimmy), Courier (Jim), Emerson (Roy), Lacoste (Rene), McEnroe (John), Nastase (Ilie), Sampras (Pete) 8 Bruguera (Sergi), Connolly (Maureen), Gonzalez (Pancho), Martinez (Conchita), Newcombe

(John), Rosewall (Ken), Sabatini (Gabriela), Wilander (Mats) **10** Mandlikova (Hana) **11** Navratilova (Martina) **14** Sanchez Vicario (Arantxa)

Tennyson poem **4** Maud **7** Ulysses **8** Tiresias **10** Enoch Arden, In Memoriam **12** Locksley Hall

tenor **3** run **4** body, mood, tone **5** drift, voice **6** singer **7** current, meaning, purport **8** tendency **9** substance *American:* **5** Lanza (Mario) **6** Hadley (Jerry), Peerce (Jan), Tucker (Richard) **8** Melchior (Lauritz) **9** McCormack (John), McCracken (James) *Canadian:* **7** Vickers (Jon) *Czech:* **6** Slezak (Leo) *German:* **10** Wunderlich (Fritz) *Italian:* **5** Gigli (Beniamino) **6** Caruso (Enrico) **7** Corelli (Franco) **8** Bergonzi (Carlo) **9** del Monaco (Mario), di Stefano (Giuseppe), Pavarotti (Luciano) *Spanish:* **7** Domingo (Placido) **8** Carreras (Jose) *Swedish:* **5** Gedda (Nicolai) **8** Björling (Jussi) **9** Bjoerling (Jussi)

tenpins **7** bowling

tense **4** edgy, taut **5** nervy, tight **6** uneasy **7** anxious, jittery, restive, uptight **8** strained *grammatical:* **4** past **6** future **7** perfect, present **8** preterit **9** preterite **10** pluperfect **11** progressive

tension **6** nerves, strain, stress, unease **7** anxiety **8** pressure, tautness **9** agitation **10** discomfort, uneasiness **11** nervousness, uptightness

tent **4** camp **5** bivvy, cover, lodge **6** canopy, encamp, laager, maroon **7** bivouac, shelter *Eskimo:* **5** tupik *kind:* **3** pup **4** bell, pawl, yort **5** Baker, tepee **6** teepee, wigwam **7** kibitka, marquee, wickiup **8** pavilion; umbrella *maker:* **4** Omar *material:* **6** canvas *part:* **3** fly, guy, peg **4** pole

tentacle **3** arm **6** feeler

tentative **4** test **5** trial **6** wobbly **7** halting **8** hesitant **9** faltering, makeshift, provisory, uncertain **10** irresolute **11** conditional, provisional, vacillating, vacillatory **12** provisionary

tenth **5** tithe *combining form:* **4** deci

tenuous **4** rare, slim, thin, weak **5** reedy **6** feeble, flimsy, slight, stalky, subtle, twiggy **7** slender, squinny, subtile **8** ethereal, rarefied **9** attenuate **10** attenuated **11** implausible **13** insubstantial, unsubstantial

tenure **4** grip, hold, term **5** clamp, clasp, grasp, gripe **6** clench, clinch, clutch, estate **7** grapple *feudal:* **7** burgage

tepid **4** mild, warm **7** warmish **8** lukewarm, milk-warm **9** temperate **11** halfhearted, indifferent

tequila source **6** mescal

Terah's son **5** Abram, Haran, Nahor **7** Abraham

teras **7** monster

terbium *symbol:* **2** Tb

Terentia's husband **6** Cicero

Tereus *son:* **4** Itys *wife:* **6** Procne

tergiversate **3** rat **4** turn **5** dodge, evade, hedge **6** defect, desert, weasel **7** shuffle **8** renounce, sidestep **9** pussyfoot, repudiate **10** apostatize, equivocate

term **3** dub **4** call, name, span, time, word **5** bound, hitch, spell **6** detail, period, tenure **7** article, baptize, stretch **8** christen, duration **9** designate **10** denominate, limitation, particular

termagant **5** harpy, rowdy, scold, shrew, vixen **6** amazon, ogress, unruly, virago **7** raucous **8** fishwife **5** rowdy **9** turbulent, Xanthippe **10** boisterous, disorderly, rowdydowdy, tumultuous **11** rumbustious

terminable **6** finite **7** endable, limited **9** limitable

terminal **3** end, lag **4** last **5** depot, final **6** latest, latter **7** closing, station **8** eventual, hindmost, ultimate **10** concluding *negative:* **7** cathode *positive:* **5** anode

terminate **2** ax **3** end **4** drop, fire, halt, quit, rise, sack, stop **5** close, leave **6** bounce, finish, recess, resign, wind up, wrap up **7** abolish, adjourn, boot out, cashier, dismiss, kick out **8** complete, conclude, dissolve, prorogue, ultimate **9** determine, discharge, prorogate **10** extinguish **11** discontinue

terminology **4** cant **6** jargon **7** lexicon, palaver **8** language **10** dictionary, vocabulary

termite **3** ant

tern **4** trio **5** scray **8** schooner *genus:* **6** Sterna

ternary **6** triple **9** threefold

terpsichore see **Muse**

terrace **4** bank, dais, deck, roof, step **5** bench, porch **7** balcony, portico **8** platform

terra-cotta **4** clay **7** pottery

terra firma **4** dirt, land, soil **5** earth **6** ground **7** dry land

terrain **4** turf, walk **5** field **6** domain, sphere **7** demesne **8** dominion, province **9** bailiwick, champaign, territory **10** topography

terrapin **6** turtle

terrestrial **6** earthy **7** earthly, mundane, profane, prosaic, secular, terrene, worldly **8** telluric **9** earthlike, sublunary, tellurian **10** earthbound

terrible **3** bad **4** grim, hard **5** awful, heavy, tough **6** fierce, grisly, horrid, severe **7** arduous, fearful, furious, ghastly, hideous, intense, macabre, vicious, violent **8** dreadful, gruesome, horrible, horrific, shocking, toilsome, vehement **9** appalling, desperate, difficult, exquisite, frightful, laborious, strenuous **10** formidable, horrifying *combining form:* **3** din **4** dein, dino **5** deino

terrier **3** dog *kind:* **3** fox **4** blue, bull, Skye **5** cairn, Irish, Welsh **6** Boston **8** Airedale, Lakeland **9** Yorkshire

terrific **5** super, swell **6** superb **7** fearful **8** dreadful, glorious, horrible, horrific, shocking **9** appalling, frightful, marvelous, upsetting, wonderful **10** formidable **11** magnificent, sensational, terrorizing

terrify **3** awe **4** stun **5** alarm, scare **7** startle **8** affright, frighten **9** terrorize

terrifying **4** grim **6** grisly, horrid **7** ghastly, hideous, macabre **8** gruesome, horrible, terrible **10** horrifying

territory **4** area, belt, land, turf, walk, zone **5** field, tract **6** domain, region, sphere **7** demesne, terrain **8** dominion, province **9** bailiwick, champaign

terror **4** fear **5** alarm, dread, panic **6** dismay, fright, horror **9** trepidity **11** fearfulness, trepidation **13** consternation

terrorist **4** thug **6** bomber **7** Jacobin **8** alarmist

terrorize **3** cow **5** alarm, bully, scare **6** fright, hector **7** dragoon **8** affright, bludgeon, browbeat, bulldoze, bullyrag, frighten **9** strong-arm **10** intimidate

terry **4** loop **6** fabric **8** toweling

terse **4** curt, taut **5** brief, crisp, pithy, short **7** compact, concise, laconic, summary **8** succinct **11** compendiary, compendious **12** breviloquent

tertiary **5** third

tessera **3** die **4** tile **6** tablet, ticket

test **3** try **4** exam, quiz **5** assay, check, essay, final, prove, trial, try on **6** sample, trying, try out, verify **7** confirm, examine, mid-term, proving **8** sounding, trial run **10** experiment **11** demonstrate, examination **12** experimental

testa **4** coat **5** shell **8** episperm **10** integument

testament **4** will **5** proof **7** witness **8** evidence **9** scripture, testimony **11** attestation, testimonial **12** confirmation

tester **5** frame **6** canopy, prover **7** assayer

testifier **7** witness **8** deponent **9** proselyte

testify **5** argue, swear **6** attest, depone, depose **7** bespeak, betoken, point to, witness **8** announce, indicate

testimonial **5** proof, salvo, token **6** salute **7** tribute, witness **8** evidence, memorial, monument **9** character, reference, testament **10** indication **11** attestation, credentials **12** appreciation, confirmation

testimony **5** proof **7** witness **8** evidence **10** indication **11** affirmation, attestation **12** confirmation **13** documentation

testy **5** cross, ratty **6** cranky, tetchy, touchy **7** grouchy **8** choleric **9** irascible, irritable, temperish **10** ill-humored **12** cantankerous **13** quick-tempered

tetanus **7** lockjaw, trismus

tetchy see testy

tête-à-tête **4** chat, coze, talk **7** vis-à-vis **8** causerie **10** discussion **12** conversation

tether **3** tie **4** bind, rope **5** cable, chain, scope **6** fasten

Tethys *daughters:* **9** Oceanides *father:* **6** Uranus *husband:* **7** Oceanus *mother:* **2** Ge **4** Gaea **5** Terra

tetrad **4** four **7** quartet, quatuor **8** foursome **9** quartetto **10** quaternion

Teucer *father:* **7** Telamon **9** Scamander *stepbrother:* **4** Ajax

Teutonic **6** German **8** Germanic *language:* **5** Dutch **6** Danish, German, Gothic **7** English, Flemish, Frisian, Swedish **9** Afrikaans, Norwegian

Texas *capital:* **6** Austin *college, university:* **3** SMU **4** Rice **5** Lamar, Wiley **6** Baylor *largest city:* **7** Houston *nickname:* **13** Lone Star State *state flower:* **10** bluebonnet

text **4** head **5** motif, point, theme, topic **6** matter, motive **7** subject **8** argument **13** subject matter

textbook **6** manual, primer

textile **6** fabric *dealer:* **6** mercer *machine:* **8** calender *shop:* **7** mercery *treat:* **9** mercerize

texture **3** web **5** being, fiber **6** fabric, nature **7** essence

Thackeray novel **9** Pendennis **10** Vanity Fair **11** Henry Esmond

Thailand **4** Siam *capital:* **7** Bangkok *language:* **3** Lao *monetary unit:* **4** baht **5** tical *temple:* **3** wat

Thaïs **7** hetaera **9** courtesan *author:* **6** France (Anatole) *composer:* **8** Massenet (Jules)

thalassic **6** marine **7** oceanic **8** maritime

Thalia see Graces; Muse

thallium *symbol:* **2** Tl

Thanatopsis author **6** Bryant (William Cullen)

Thanatos **5** death *brother:* **6** Hypnos *mother:* **3** Nyx

thankful **7** obliged **8** grateful **12** appreciative

thanks **2** ta **5** grace **8** blessing **9** gratitude **11** benediction **12** appreciation, thanksgiving

Thanksgiving **5** feast **7** holiday *first celebrant:* **6** Indian **7** Pilgrim *food:* **6** turkey

thatch **4** roof **5** cover

that is **2** i.e. *Latin:* **5** id est

Thaumas *daughter:* **4** Iris **5** Aello, Harpy **7** Celaeno, Ocypete *daughters:* **7** Harpies *father:* **6** Pontus *mother:* **2** Ge **4** Gaea *wife:* **7** Electra

thaumaturgic 5 magic 6 magian, mystic, witchy 7 magical 8 wizardly 9 sorcerous 11 necromantic

thaumaturgy 5 magic 7 sorcery 8 witchery, wizardry 9 conjuring 10 necromancy, witchcraft 11 bewitchment, enchantment, incantation

thaw 3 run 4 flux, fuse, melt 7 liquefy 8 dissolve, liquesce 10 deliquesce

the 7 article *French:* 2 la, le 3 les *German:* 3 das, der, die *Italian:* 2 il, la *Spanish:* 2 el, la 3 las, los

Thea *daughter:* 6 Selene *father:* 6 Uranus *husband:* 8 Hyperion *mother:* 2 Ge 4 Gaea

theater 4 hall 5 drama, house, odeum, stage 6 boards 9 playhouse 10 footlights *award:* 4 Tony *entrance:* 5 foyer, lobby *Greek:* 5 odeum *movie:* 6 cinema *outdoor:* 7 drive-in *part:* 3 box, pit 4 loge 5 skene, stage, wings 7 balcony, parodos, parquet 10 proscenium

theatrical 5 stagy 6 staged 8 affected, dramatic, mannered, thespian 10 artificial, histrionic 11 dramaturgic, exaggerated 12 melodramatic *agent:* 6 Morris (William) *device:* 4 prop *group:* 6 troupe

Theban Eagle 6 Pindar

Thebes *founder:* 6 Cadmus *king:* 5 Laius 7 Oedipus *queen:* 7 Jocasta

theft 4 lift 5 pinch, steal 6 piracy 7 larceny, robbery, robbing, swiping 8 burglary, filching, stealage, stealing, thievery, thieving 9 pilferage, pilfering 10 purloining *combining form:* 5 klept 6 klepto

The Golden 3 Ass 4 Bowl 5 Bough 6 Fleece, Legend

theme 4 head, text 5 essay, motif, paper, point, topic 6 matter, motive, thesis 7 article, subject 8 argument 11 composition 13 subject matter

Themis *father:* 6 Uranus *goddess of:* 3 law 7 justice *husband:* 4 Zeus 7 Jupiter *mother:* 2 Ge 4 Gaea

then 2 so 4 also, anon, ergo, thus, when 5 again, hence 7 besides, further 9 therefore, thereupon 10 in addition 11 accordingly 12 additionally, consequently

thence 4 away 7 thereof 9 therefrom

theologian *American:* 7 Edwards (Jonathan), Niebuhr (Reinhold), Tillich (Paul), Walther (Carl) *Dutch:* 6 Jansen (Cornelis) *English:* 4 Bede (Venerable) 5 Pusey (Edward), Watts (Isaac) 6 Alcuin, Wesley (John) 7 Langton (Stephen) 8 Pelagius, Wycliffe (John) *French:* 6 Calvin (John) 7 William (of Auvergne, of Auxerre) 8 Sabatier (Auguste) *German:* 6 Rahner (Karl) 7 Eckhart (Meister) 9 Niemoller (Martin) 14 Albertus Magnus *Greek:*

9 Zygomalas (Theodore) *Italian:* 7 Aquinas (Thomas), Socinus (Fausto, Laelius) *Scottish:* 10 Duns Scotus (John) *Spanish:* 6 Suarez (Francisco) 7 Vitoria (Francisco de) 8 Servetus (Michael) *Swedish:* 9 Soderblom (Nathan) *Swiss:* 5 Barth (Karl), Vinet (Alexandre-Rodolphe)

Theologica 5 Summa

theological *school:* 8 seminary *virtue:* 4 hope 5 faith 7 charity

theorbo 4 lute 8 archlute

theorem 3 law 4 rule 5 axiom 9 principle 10 principium 11 fundamental

theoretical 5 ideal 8 abstract, academic, notional, unproved 11 conjectural, speculative 12 hypothetical, transcendent 13 problematical, suppositional

theorize 6 submit 7 suggest 9 postulate

theory 7 perhaps, premise, suppose, surmise 8 supposal 10 conjecture, hypothesis 11 speculation, supposition *astronomical:* 7 big bang *combining form:* 4 logy 5 logia, ology *suffix:* 3 ism

therapy 9 treatment *combining form:* 5 pathy 6 pathic

therefore 2 so 4 ergo, then, thus 5 hence 11 accordingly 12 consequently

therefrom 6 thence

thereupon 4 then 6 at once

therm 7 calorie

thermal 3 hot 4 warm *unit:* 3 Btu 6 degree 7 calorie

thermometer 9 indicator *kind:* 7 Celsius, Reaumur 10 centigrade, Fahrenheit

Thersander's father 9 Polynices

Thersites' slayer 8 Achilles

The Saint 12 Simon Templar

the same 4 idem 5 ditto 8 likewise 9 identical

thesaurus 7 lexicon 10 dictionary *editor:* 5 Roget (Peter Mark)

Theseus *father:* 6 Aegeus *mother:* 6 Aethra *slayer:* 9 Lycomedes *son:* 10 Hippolytus *victim:* 6 Sciron 8 Minotaur 10 Procrustes *wife:* 7 Phaedra

thesis 5 essay, point, posit 6 belief, memoir 7 premise 8 tractate, treatise 9 apriorism, discourse, monograph, postulate 10 contention, exposition, monography 11 postulation, proposition, supposition 12 disquisition, dissertation

thespian 4 mime 5 actor, mimic 6 mummer, player 7 trouper 8 dramatic, theatral, theatric 9 performer, playactor 10 histrionic, theatrical 11 dramaturgic 12 impersonator

Thespis' forte 5 drama 7 tragedy

Thessalian hero 5 Jason 8 Achilles

_____ the Terrible 4 Ivan

"The Thinker" sculptor 5 Rodin (Auguste)

Thetis 6 Nereid *father:* 6 Nereus *husband:* 6 Peleus *mother:* 5 Doris *son:* 8 Achilles

theurgist 8 magician

thew 4 beef 5 brawn, might, power, sinew 6 muscle 8 strength

thick 3 fat 4 dull, dumb, wide 5 broad, bulky, burly, close, dense, dumpy, husky, obese, squat 6 chummy, chunky, flimsy, obtuse, stocky, stupid 7 compact, crammed, crowded, doltish, massive, viscous 8 blockish, duncical, familiar, heavyset, intimate 10 numskulled *combining form:* 4 dasy, hadr 5 hadro, pachy

thicket 4 bosk, bush, wood 5 clump, copse, grove 6 bosket, tangle 7 boscage, coppice, spinney 9 brushwood, chaparral *Scottish:* 4 rone

thickness 5 layer 7 density 9 callosity

thief 3 dip, nip 4 prig 5 ganef 6 bandit, lifter, looter, nimmer, pirate, robber 7 booster, burglar, filcher, stealer 8 hijacker, larcener, pilferer 9 larcenist, purloiner 10 cat burglar, pickpocket, shoplifter 12 housebreaker

thieve 3 nip 4 hook, lift 5 filch, pinch, steal, swipe 6 pilfer, snitch 7 purloin

thievery see theft

thievish 9 larcenous

thigh 3 ham 5 flank 6 gammon *bone:* 5 femur *combining form:* 3 mer 4 mero 5 cruro, merus 6 femoro *relating to:* 6 crural

thimble 3 cup 5 cover

thin 3 cut 4 fine, high, lank, lean, puny, rare, slim, weak 5 acute, gaunt, lanky, reedy, sharp, spare, wispy 6 argute, dilute, flimsy, meager, piping, rarefy, shrill, skinny, slight, sparse, stalky, treble, twiggy, watery, weaken 7 scrawny, slender, squinny, subtile, tenuous 8 piercing, rarefied, rawboned, skeletal, twiglike, wiredraw 9 attenuate, extenuate 10 attenuated 11 implausible, watered-down 12 unconvincing 13 unsubstantial *combining form:* 4 lept 5 lepto

thing 2 go 3 act, cry, fad 4 deed, item, mode, rage 5 being, craze, doing, event, mania, point, stuff, style, vogue 6 action, affair, detail, entity, fetish, furore, matter, object 7 article, concern, element, episode, fashion 8 business, existent, fixation, incident, material, occasion 9 existence, happening, obsession, substance 10 dernier cri, individual, occurrence, phenomenon *additional:* 5 bonus *in law:* 3 res *insignificant:* 6 trifle *rare:* 4 oner *single:* 4 unit *suffix:* 2 ia (plural) 3 ant, ory 4 oria (plural)

5 orium *to do:* 3 job 5 chore *unusual:* 5 freak 6 oddity *worthless:* 4 junk 5 waste

thingamajig 5 gizmo 6 dingus, doodad, gadget, jigger 7 dofunny 9 doohickey 10 thingumbob

things 4 duds, togs 5 dress, goods, stuff, traps 6 attire, tricks 7 apparel, clothes, effects, plunder, raiment 8 chattels, clothing, movables 10 attirement, belongings, habiliment, possession *for sale:* 11 merchandise

think 4 deem, feel, mull, muse 5 brood, fancy, guess, opine, study, weigh 6 assume, expect, gather, ideate, ponder, reason 7 believe, imagine, perpend, presume, realize, reflect, suppose, surmise, suspect 8 cogitate, conceive, consider, envisage, envision, logicize, meditate, ruminate 9 cerebrate, speculate, visualize 10 conjecture, deliberate, excogitate, logicalize 11 contemplate, rationalize *out:* 4 plan *piece:* 7 article

third 8 tertiary *combining form:* 4 trit 5 trito *power:* 4 cube

third degree 5 grill 8 grilling 13 interrogation

third estate 5 plebs 6 people, plebes 8 populace 9 commonage, commoners, plebeians 10 commonalty 11 rank and file

Third Man, The *author:* 6 Greene (Graham)

thirst 3 yen 4 ache, itch, long, lust, pine 5 crave, yearn 6 hanker, hunger

thirsty 3 dry 4 agog, arid, avid, keen, sere 5 eager 6 ardent 7 anxious, athirst, bonedry, parched 8 appetent, droughty 9 impatient, unwatered, waterless 12 moistureless

this and that 8 oddments, sundries 9 etceteras 11 odds and ends

Thisbe's lover 7 Pyramus

This Side of Paradise author 10 Fitzgerald (F. Scott)

thistle 4 weed 7 caltrop *Russian:* 10 tumbleweed

thistlebird 9 goldfinch

thither 3 yon 5 there 6 yonder

thole 3 peg, pin

____ Thomas, Welsh author 5 Dylan

Thomas à ____ 6 Becket, Kempis

Thomas' Greek name 7 Didymus

Thomas opera 6 Mignon

Thompson 5 Sadie 7 Dorothy, Francis, J. Walter 8 Benjamin

thong 4 lace, lash, rein 5 romal, strap, strip 7 amentum, babiche, latchet 8 whiplash

Thor 5 Donar *father:* 4 Odin *god of:* 7 thunder *hammer:* 8 Mjollnir *mother:* 5 Jordh, Jorth

thorax 5 chest

Thoreau, Henry David *friend:* 7 Emerson (Ralph Waldo) *work:* 6 Walden

thorium *symbol:* 2 Th

thorn 5 briar, brier, spine 7 acantha, spinule 9 annoyance 10 irritation *combining form:* 4 spin 5 spini, spino 6 acanth 7 acantho, spinoso 8 acanthus

thorny 5 sharp, spiny 6 tricky 7 prickly, spinate 9 difficult, vexatious 10 nettlesome 11 troublesome

thorough 4 full 6 minute 8 complete, detailed, itemized, whole-hog 9 clocklike 10 blow-by-blow, exhaustive

thoroughbred 5 horse 8 pedigree, purebred 9 pedigreed, pureblood 11 full-blooded

thoroughfare 3 way 4 drag, path, road 5 track 6 artery, avenue, street 7 highway 9 boulevard

thoroughgoing 4 rank 5 gross, utter 8 absolute, complete, outright, whole-hog 9 out-and-out 10 consummate, exhaustive 11 straight-out, unmitigated

though 3 yet 5 still, while 6 albeit 7 however, whereas 8 after all 11 nonetheless 12 nevertheless

thought 4 idea, mind 5 image 6 musing, notion 7 concept, opinion 9 brainwork, pondering 10 cogitation, conception, meditation, reflection, rumination 11 cerebration, speculation 12 deliberation, intellection 13 contemplation *combining form:* 3 log 4 logo

thoughtful 6 polite 7 careful, gallant, heedful, logical, mindful, pensive, serious 8 gracious, rational, studious, thinking 9 attentive, courteous, pondering, regardful 10 cogitative, meditative, reflecting, reflective, ruminative, solicitous 11 considerate 12 intellectual 13 contemplative

thoughtless 4 rash, rude 5 brash, hasty 6 madcap 7 selfish 8 careless, feckless, heedless, impolite, reckless, uncaring 9 hotheaded, unheeding, unrecking 10 ill-advised, incautious, mad-brained, ungracious, unthinking 11 inadvertent 12 discourteous, irreflective, unreflective 13 inconsiderate

thousand *combining form:* 4 kilo *dollars:* 5 grand *years:* 10 millennium

thousandth 10 millesimal *combining form:* 5 milli

thrall 4 yoke 7 bondage, helotry, peonage, serfdom, slavery 9 servitude, villenage 11 enslavement

thrash 4 beat, drub, flog, hide, lash, lick, maul, pelt, whip 5 paste, pound, smear, whale 6 batter, buffet, larrup, pummel, stripe, wallop 7 belabor, scourge, shellac 8 lambaste 10 flagellate

thrash out 4 moot 5 argue 6 debate 7 agitate, canvass, discept, discuss, dispute 10 kick around, toss around

thread 4 line, vein, yard 5 fiber, reeve, weave 6 strand, stream, string 8 filament *ball of:* 4 clew, clue *combining form:* 3 mit, nem 4 fili, mito, nema, neme, nemo 5 nemat 6 nemata (plural), nemato *dental:* 5 floss *holder:* 6 bobbin *kind:* 4 silk, yarn 5 floss, lisle, watap 6 cotton, lingel 8 surgical *loose:* 8 raveling 9 ravelling *surgical:* 5 seton 6 catgut, suture

threadbare 4 hack, worn 5 dingy, faded, seedy, stale, tacky, tired, trite 6 cliché, frayed, ragged, shabby, tagrag 7 clichéd, run-down, worn-out 8 bathetic, shopworn, tattered, timeworn, well-worn 10 down-at-heel 11 commonplace, dilapidated

threadlike 6 filose

threads 8 clothing

threat 6 duress, menace 7 warning

threaten 3 cow 4 warn 5 augur 6 menace 7 caution, portend, presage 8 browbeat, bulldoze, forebode, forewarn 10 intimidate

three 4 trey 5 crowd *combining form:* 3 ter, tri *group of:* (see **threesome**)

threefold 5 trine 6 thrice, triple

Three Musketeers 5 Athos 6 Aramis 7 Porthos *author:* 5 Dumas (Alexandre)

Threepenny Opera, The *author:* 6 Brecht (Bertolt) *music:* 5 Weill (Kurt)

threescore 5 sixty

Three Sisters, The 4 Olga 5 Irina, Masha *author:* 7 Chekhov (Anton)

Three Soldiers author 9 Dos Passos (John)

threesome 4 trio 5 triad, trine 6 triple, triune, troika 7 trinity 11 triumvirate

three-wheeler 8 tricycle

threnody 5 dirge, elegy

thresh 4 beat, flog, whip 5 flail 6 strike

threshold 3 eve 4 edge, gate 5 brink, limen, point, verge

thrice 9 threefold *a day:* 3 t.i.d. 8 ter in die

thrift 7 economy 8 prudence 9 frugality, husbandry 11 economizing

thriftiness see **thrift**

thrifty 5 canny, chary 6 frugal, robust, saving 7 booming, roaring, sparing 8 thriving 9 provident, stewardly 10 conserving, economical, preserving, prospering, prosperous, unwasteful 11 flourishing

thrill 4 bang, boot, kick, send 6 excite, wallop 7 enthuse 9 electrify, galvanize 10 excitement 11 titillation

thriller 6 gothic 7 chiller, mystery, shocker 9 dime novel 13 penny dreadful

thrive 2 go 4 boom, grow 5 score 6 arrive
7 develop, make out, prosper, succeed
8 flourish

throat 3 maw 4 gula, tube 6 groove, gullet
7 channel, weasand, weazand *combining
form:* 3 der 4 dero 6 bronch 7 broncho
inflammation: 5 croup 6 angina, quinsy
10 laryngitis *relating to:* 8 guttural *upper:*
4 gula *warmer:* 5 scarf

throb 4 ache, beat 5 pulse 7 pulsate
9 palpitate

throe 3 fit 4 ache, pain, pang 5 spell
6 access, attack, stitch, twinge 7 seizure
10 convulsion

thrombus 4 clot

throne 4 apse, seat 5 chair, gaddi, power
8 cathedra 11 sovereignty

throng 4 host, pack, push 5 bunch, crowd,
crush, drove, flock, group, horde, press
6 squash 9 multitude

throttle 5 choke 7 garrote 8 strangle
11 accelerator

through 2 by 3 per, via 4 done, over,
past, with 5 about, due to, ended, round
6 around, direct 7 by way of, done for,
owing to 8 by dint of, complete, finished,
straight, washed-up 9 because of, by
means of, completed, concluded 10 by virtue of, terminated, throughout 13 uninterrupted *prefix:* 2 di 3 dia, per

throughout 3 mid 4 amid, over 5 about,
midst, round 6 around, during 7 all over,
overall 10 everyplace, everywhere, far and
near, far and wide, high and low *combining form:* 3 hol 4 holo

Through the Looking Glass *author:*
7 Carroll (Lewis) *character:* 5 Alice

throw 3 peg, put 4 cast, fire, hurl, toss
5 fling, heave, pitch, sling 6 launch, propel,
unseat 7 buck off, project, unhorse *in the
towel:* 4 quit 6 give up

throw away 4 blow, cast, junk, shed
5 scrap, waste 6 reject, slough 7 cashier,
consume, discard, fritter 8 jettison, squander

throw back 6 reject, revert 7 regress
10 retrogress

throwback 7 atavism 9 reversion

throw down 4 fell 5 level 6 lay low
8 bowl over 9 knock over, overthrow, prostrate *the gauntlet:* 4 defy 9 challenge

throw off 3 rid 4 emit, lose, shed, slip,
vent 5 addle, eject, expel, issue, mix up,
shake 6 ball up 7 confuse, fluster, give out,
release 8 befuddle, bewilder, distract,
unburden *the track:* 6 derail 7 confuse,
mislead

throw out 4 cast, junk, shed 5 addle,
chuck, eject, evict, mix up, scrap 6 ball up,
reject, slough 7 cashier, confuse, discard,

dismiss, extrude, fluster 8 befuddle, bewilder, distract, jettison

throw up 4 barf 5 heave, vomit
7 upchuck 8 disgorge 10 jerry-build

thrush 4 bird 5 robin, veery 8 bluebird
European: 5 mavis, ousel, ouzel 6 mistle
9 blackbird, mistletoe 11 nightingale

thrust 3 dig, jab, ram, run 4 core, gist,
meat, pith, push, sink, stab 5 drive, sense,
short, shove, stick 6 burden, plunge, propel, upshot 7 intrude, purport, riposte
9 substance

thug 3 mug 4 goon, hood, punk 5 bully,
rough, rowdy, tough, yahoo 6 gunman,
mucker 7 hoodlum, mobster, ruffian
8 gangster, hooligan, plug-ugly 9 cutthroat,
roughneck, strong arm 10 hatchet man

thulium *symbol:* 2 Tm

thumb 5 digit, hitch 6 pollex 8 pollices
(plural) 9 hitchhike

thumb through 4 scan 6 browse 7 dip
into, run over 8 glance at 10 glance over

thunder 4 bang, roar 6 rumble 8 rumbling
11 fulmination *combining form:* 5 bront
6 bronto, ceraun 7 cerauno, kerauno

thunderbolt 9 lightning

thunderclap see thunder

thunder lizard 10 brontosaur

thunderstruck 5 agape 6 aghast
7 shocked, stunned 8 dismayed 9 stag-
gered 10 bewildered, confounded
11 dumbfounded, overwhelmed

Thurber character 11 Walter Mitty

thurify 5 cense

thus 2 so 3 sic 4 ergo, then 5 hence
9 therefore, thereupon, thus and so
11 accordingly 12 consequently *French:*
5 ainsi

Thus Spoke Zarathustra *author:*
9 Nietzsche (Friedrich)

thwack 3 bop 4 biff, blow, sock, whop
5 crack, pound, smack, whack

thwart 4 balk, beat, bilk, curb, dash, foil,
ruin 6 arrest, baffle, scotch, stymie 8 traverse 9 checkmate, crosswise, frustrate
10 circumvent, disappoint, transverse
11 transversal

Thyestes *brother:* 6 Atreus *daughter:*
7 Pelopia *father:* 6 Pelops *mother:* 10 Hippodamia *son:* 9 Aegisthus

Tiamat *husband:* 4 Apsu *slayer:* 6 Marduk

tiara 5 crown 6 diadem 9 headdress

Tibetan *animal:* 3 yak 5 manul *coin:*
5 tanga *gazelle:* 3 goa *monk:* 4 lama *people:* 6 Bhotia, Sherpa

Tibet's capital 5 Lhasa

tibia 8 shinbone

Tibni's father 6 Ginath

tic 5 spasm 6 twitch 9 twitching

tick 6 credit, insect 8 arachnid, parasite 11 bloodsucker *combining form:* 4 acar 5 acari, acaro

ticker 4 bomb 5 clock, heart, watch

ticket 3 key, tag 4 vote 5 label, slate 6 ballot 8 passport, password 10 open sesame 12 carte d'entrée *seller:* 7 cashier, scalper

tickle 4 stir 5 amuse, tease, touch 6 arouse, excite, please, tingle 7 delight, gratify, provoke 9 stimulate, titillate

ticklish 5 risky, rocky 6 fickle, touchy, tricky 8 delicate, unstable, variable, volatile 9 mercurial, sensitive, uncertain 10 capricious, changeable, inconstant, precarious

tick off 3 irk 4 list 5 chide 6 monish, rebuke 7 reprove 8 admonish, call down, numerate, reproach 9 enumerate, reprimand

tidal flood 4 bore 5 eagre

tidbit 5 goody, treat 6 dainty, morsel 8 delicacy, kickshaw 11 bonne bouche

tide 4 flow, flux, rush 5 drift, flood, spate, surge 6 stream 7 current, holiday *lowest:* 4 neap *type:* 3 ebb, low 4 high, neap 5 flood 6 spring

tidings 4 news, word 6 advice 7 message 9 speerings 11 information 12 intelligence

tidy 4 neat, snug, trig, trim 7 chipper, orderly 9 shipshape 11 uncluttered, well-groomed 12 spick-and-span

tie 3 rod, wed 4 band, bind, bond, cord, draw, gird, join, knot, lash, link, mate, moor, rope, yoke 5 ascot, cinch, equal, jabot, leash, marry, match, nexus 6 attach, cravat, fasten, fetter, hamper, hobble, secure, splice 7 connect, dogfall, shackle, trammel, truss up 8 deadlock, fastener, ligament, ligature, standoff, vinculum 9 entrammel, fastening, stalemate 10 attachment, four-in-hand

tier 3 row 4 file, line, rank 5 class, grade, group, queue, story 6 league, string 7 echelon 8 category, grouping

tiff 3 row 4 spat 5 run-in, scrap 6 bicker 7 brabble, dispute, fall out, quarrel, rhubarb, wrangle 8 squabble 9 bickering, caterwaul 10 falling-out 11 altercation

tiffany 5 gauze 11 cheesecloth

tiger 3 cat 6 feline 9 carnivore *young:* 3 cub

tight 3 set 4 fast, firm, hard, snug, taut, trim 5 cheap, close, dense, drunk, fixed, tense, thick 6 firmly, secure, stingy 7 compact, crowded, drunken, fixedly, miserly, solidly 9 niggardly, penurious, tenacious 10 contracted, inebriated 11 closefisted, constricted, intoxicated, steadfastly 12 cheeseparing, parsimonious 13 penny-pinching

tightfisted see stingy

tight-lipped 5 close 6 silent 8 reserved, reticent, taciturn 12 closemouthed, close-tongued

tightwad 4 skin 5 miser, nabal, stiff 7 niggard, scrooge 9 skinflint 10 cheapskate 11 cheeseparer

Tikvah's son 7 Shallum 8 Jahaziah

tile 3 hat 5 brick, guard, plate, slate 6 domino, tegula 7 abacula, tessera *roofing:* 7 pantile

till 2 to 3 sow 4 plow, tend, turn, up to, work 5 until 6 before, harrow 7 prior to 9 cultivate 11 in advance of

tillable 6 arable 10 cultivable 12 cultivatable

tillage 4 farm, land 5 crops 11 cultivation

tiller 4 helm 6 farmer, rudder 7 steerer

Tilon's father 6 Shimon

tilt 3 tip, yaw 4 cant, cock, heel, lean, list, swag 5 grade, lurch, pitch, slant, slope 6 seesaw 7 incline, leaning, recline 8 gradient 11 inclination

timbal 4 drum 10 kettledrum

timber 3 log 4 balk, beam, tree, wood 5 board, joist, plank, trees, weald, woods 6 forest, girder, lumber, rafter 8 woodland *decay:* 4 dote, doze *joint:* 4 coak *mine:* 5 stull *Philippine:* 5 lauan *ship's:* 3 rib 4 bibb, keel, mast, skeg 7 stemson 8 sternson *supporting:* 4 stud 6 purlin, putlog, rafter 8 puncheon *uncut:* 8 stumpage *wolf:* 4 lobo

timbre 4 mood, tone 6 spirit, temper

timbrel 4 drum 10 tambourine

time 2 go 3 age, bit, day, era 4 book, bout, date, hour, pace, plan, shot, show, span, term, tour, turn 5 break, clock, epoch, set up, shift, space, spell, stint, tempo, trick, while 6 chance, look-in, moment, period, season, squeak 7 instant, opening, program, stretch 8 duration, occasion, schedule 11 opportunity *ahead of:* 5 early *combining form:* 5 chron, semic 6 chrono 8 chronous *gone by:* 4 past 9 yesterday *long:* 3 age, eon, era 4 aeon *of day:* 4 dawn, dusk, noon 5 night 6 sunset 7 evening, morning, sunrise 8 daybreak, twilight 9 afternoon *olden:* 4 yore 10 yesteryear *period:* 3 age, day, eon, era 4 aeon, hour, week, year 5 epoch, month 6 decade, minute, moment, second 7 century, instant 9 fortnight 10 millennium *present:* 3 now *relating to:* 8 temporal *short:* 5 jiffy 6 moment, second 7 instant *suffix:* 2 ad *to come:* 6 future 8 tomorrow *waste:* 4 loaf 5 dally 6 loiter

time and again 3 oft 5 often 8 ofttimes 10 frequently, oftentimes, repeatedly 11 over and over

timeless 7 ageless, endless, eternal 8 dateless, unending 9 ceaseless, continual, perpetual, unceasing 10 intemporal 11 everlasting, unremitting 12 interminable

timely 3 fit 4 meet, soon 5 early 6 likely, prompt, proper 7 betimes, fitting, timeous 8 punctual, suitable 9 favorable, opportune, promising, well-timed 10 auspicious, propitious, prosperous, seasonable, seasonably 11 appropriate

Time Machine, The *author:* 5 Wells (Herbert George)

Time magazine founder 4 Luce (Henry Robinson) 6 Hadden (Briton)

Time of Your Life, The *author:* 7 Saroyan (William)

timepiece 5 clock, watch 7 horloge, sundial 8 horologe 9 clepsydra 11 chronograph, chronometer, chronoscope

timetable 4 card, plan, sked 6 agenda, docket 7 program 8 calendar, schedule

timeworn 3 old 4 aged, hack 5 hoary, stale, trite 6 age-old 8 Noachian 9 hackneyed, venerable 12 antediluvian

time zone, U.S. 7 central, eastern, Pacific 8 mountain

timid 3 coy, shy 4 mild, wary 5 chary, mousy, pavid 6 afraid, demure, gentle, modest, yellow 7 bashful, chicken, fearful, halting, nervous, panicky, rabbity 9 diffident, faltering, milk-toast, mouselike, shrinking, tentative, unassured, uncertain 10 irresolute 11 unassertive, vacillating, vacillatory 12 apprehensive, fainthearted

Timna *brother:* 5 Lotan *father:* 4 Seir *son:* 6 Amalek

Timon's servant 7 Flavius

timorous 5 timid 7 fearful 8 quailing, undaring 9 quivering, recoiling, shivering, shrinking, trembling 10 shuddering

Timothy's associate 4 Paul

tin 3 box, can 5 metal 7 element, stannum 9 container *combining form:* 5 stann 6 stanni, stanno *mining region:* 8 stannary *relating to:* 7 stannic 8 stannous *sheet:* 6 latten *symbol:* 2 Sn

tincture 3 dye 4 cast, hint, tint 5 color, shade, stain, tinge, touch, trace 6 streak 8 colorant, dyestuff 10 complexion, intimation, suggestion

tinder 4 punk 8 kindling

tine 5 point, prong, spike 6 branch

tinge 3 dye, hue 4 cast, hint, tint, tone 5 color, shade, tinct, touch, trace 6 strain 8 tincture 10 complexion, intimation, sprinkling, suggestion

tinker 3 fix 4 mend, mess 6 doodle, fiddle, mender, potter, puddle, putter, repair 9 repairman 10 mess around

tinkle 3 gab, gas, jaw, yak 4 chat, ting 5 chink, clack, clink, plink 6 babble, jangle, jingle, rattle, tingle 7 chatter, prattle

tinny 4 thin 5 cheap, harsh 8 metallic

Tin Pan Alley acronym 5 ASCAP

tinsel 4 loud 5 gaudy 6 brazen, flashy, garish, tawdry 7 blatant, chintzy, glaring 8 ornament 9 clinquant 12 meretricious

tint 3 dye, hue 4 cast, tone, wash 5 color, shade, tinge, touch 7 touch up 8 tincture 10 coloration, complexion 12 pigmentation

tiny 3 wee 5 bitsy, dwarf, minim, pygmy, small, teeny, weeny 6 midget, minute, peewee, pocket, teensy, teenty, weensy 7 minikin 8 dwarfish, pint-size 9 itsy-bitsy, itty-bitty, miniature, minuscule 10 diminutive, minuscular, pocket-size, teeny-weeny 11 liliputian, microscopic 12 teensy-weensy 13 infinitesimal

tip 3 cap, cue, top 4 apex, cant, clue, cusp, heel, hint, lean, list, peak, perk, tilt 5 point, slant, slope, steer, upset 6 advice, topple 7 cumshaw, incline, largess, overset, pointer, recline 8 forecast, gratuity, overturn, turn over 9 baksheesh, knock over, lagniappe, overthrow, pourboire 10 perquisite, prediction 11 information *combining form:* 3 acr, akr 4 acro, akro, apic 5 apici, apico

tip-off 4 hint 5 point, steer 7 pointer, warning 8 giveaway, jump ball 10 indication

Tippecanoe and ___ too 5 Tyler

tippet 4 band, barb, cape 5 scarf

tipple 3 bib, sip 4 grog, soak, swig 5 booze, drink, swill 6 guzzle, imbibe, liquor, spirit, tank up 7 swizzle 8 liquor up 9 aqua vitae, firewater

tippler 3 sot 4 lush, soak 5 drunk, toper 6 bibber, boozer 7 tosspot 8 drunkard 9 inebriate

tipstaff 7 bailiff

tipster 4 fink, nark 6 canary, snitch 7 tattler 8 betrayer, informer, squealer 10 talebearer 11 stool pigeon

tipsy 5 drunk, tight 7 drunken 8 unsteady 10 inebriated 11 intoxicated

tiptoe 5 creep, steal 7 gumshoe 9 pussyfoot

tirade 4 rant 5 abuse 6 screed 7 censure 8 berating, diatribe, harangue, jeremiad 9 invective, philippic 10 revilement 11 rodomontade 12 condemnation, denunciation, vituperation 13 tongue-lashing

tire 3 sap 4 bore, hoop, jade, pall, poop, wear 5 drain, ennui, weary, wheel 6 tucker, weaken 7 exhaust, fatigue, wear out 8 enervate, enfeeble, wear down 10 debilitate *airless:* 4 flat 7 blowout *kind:* 4 bias, snow 6 radial 7 retread 9 whitewall

tiredness 7 fatigue 8 collapse 9 lassitude, weariness 10 exhaustion 11 prostration

tireless 4 busy 6 active 8 untiring 9 weariless 10 unflagging, unwearying

11 unwearable 12 enthusiastic 13 indefatigable, inexhaustible

Tiresias 4 seer 10 soothsayer

tiresome 4 dull, hard 6 boring, jading, tiring 7 irksome, onerous, tedious 8 boresome, drudging 9 difficult, wearisome 10 burdensome, oppressive

Tirhanah *father:* 5 Caleb *mother:* 6 Maacah *uncle:* 9 Jerahmeel

Tirlac of tennis 3 Ion

tiring see tiresome

Tirol, Tyrol *capital:* 9 Innsbruck *country:* 7 Austria *mountains:* 4 Alps

Tirzah's father 10 Zelophehad

Tisiphone see Erinyes

tissue 3 web 4 mesh 5 fiber, gauze, paper 6 fabric *anatomical:* 4 tela 5 fiber 6 diploe 8 ganglion 10 epithelium *combining form:* 4 hist 5 histi, histo, hypho 6 histio *connective:* 6 stroma, tendon 9 cartilage *kind:* 3 fat 5 nerve 6 muscle 7 nervous 8 muscular 10 connective, epithelial *layer:* 6 dermis 7 stratum *plant:* 4 bast, wood 5 xylem 6 phloem

Titan *father:* 6 Uranus *female:* 4 Rhea 6 Tethys, Themis *male:* 6 Cronus 7 Iapetus, Oceanus *mother:* 2 Ge 4 Gaea

Titan, The *author:* 7 Dreiser (Theodore)

Titania's husband 6 Oberon

titanic 4 huge 5 great 6 mighty 8 colossal, enormous, gigantic 9 cyclopean, Herculean, monstrous 10 gargantuan, tremendous

titanium *symbol:* 2 Ti

tithe 3 tax 5 tenth

Tithonus *beloved by:* 3 Eos *father:* 8 Laomedon

Titian painting 5 Danaë 8 Ecce Homo 10 Holy Family 12 Rape of Europa 13 Maltese Knight, Medea and Venus, Venus and Cupid 14 Worship of Venus

title 3 dub, due 4 call, deed, dibs, name, term 5 claim, merit, nomen 7 baptize, caption, heading 8 christen, cognomen, pretense 9 designate 10 denominate, pretension 11 appellation, appellative, designation 12 championship, compellation, denomination *Dutch:* 7 mynheer *ecclesiastic:* 8 reverend *feminine:* 2 Ms. 3 Mrs. 4 dame, lady, ma'am, miss 5 madam 6 milady, missus 8 mistress *French:* 6 madame 8 monsieur 12 mademoiselle *German:* 4 Frau, Herr 8 Fraulein *holder:* 5 noble 8 champion *Indian:* 3 sri 4 raja, shri 5 sahib 7 bahadur *Islamic:* 6 sayyid 9 ayatollah *Italian:* 5 donna 6 signor 7 signora 9 signorina *monk's:* 3 fra 7 brother *of nobility:* 3 sir 4 Duke, Earl, King, Lord, sire 5 Baron, Count, Queen 6 Prince 7 Baronet, Marquis

8 Archduke, Princess, Viscount *Oriental:* 4 khan *Persian:* 5 mirza

titmouse 4 bird 6 tomtit, verdin 7 bushtit 9 chickadee

Tito 4 Broz (Josip)

titter 5 laugh, tehee 6 giggle, guffaw, heehaw 7 chortle, chuckle, snicker

tittle 3 bit, jot 4 atom, iota, mite 5 minim, speck 6 smitch 7 smidgen 8 particle

titular 6 formal 7 nominal 8 so-called

Tityus *father:* 4 Zeus *slayer:* 6 Apollo

Tiu see Tyr

tizzy 4 fume, snit, stew 5 sweat 6 dither, swivet

T-man 5 agent 8 revenuer

TNT 8 dynamite 9 explosive

to 2 at 3 ere, for 4 ante, till 5 until 6 before, toward, up till 7 against, ahead of, prior to 8 opposite, touching 9 preceding 11 in advance of *be sure:* 6 indeed 9 certainly *prefix:* 2 ac, ad; af, ag, al, ap, as, at *Scottish:* 3 tae *wit:* 3 viz 6 namely 8 scilicet

toad 4 agua, hyla, scum 6 anuran, peeper 7 crapaud, stinker 8 lickspit, truckler 9 amphibian, sycophant 10 batrachian, bootlicker, footlicker 11 lickspittle *combining form:* 7 batrach 8 batracho 9 batrachus *genus:* 4 Bufo

toady 4 fawn 5 cower, kotow 6 cringe, flunky, grovel, kowtow 7 honey up, truckle 8 bootlick, lickspit, truckler 9 brownnose, sycophant 10 bootlicker, footlicker 11 apple-polish, lickspittle

To Althea from ___ 6 Prison *author:* 8 Lovelace (Richard)

toast 5 bread, brown, drink, skoal 6 cheers, pledge, prosit, salute 7 wassail *Jewish:* 7 lehayim 8 lechayim *kind:* 5 melba 6 French 8 zwieback

toastmaster 2 MC 5 emcee

To a Waterfowl author 6 Bryant (William Cullen)

tobacco 4 leaf, weed *cask:* 8 hogshead *chewing:* 4 chaw, quid *Cuban:* 4 capa *ingredient:* 3 tar 8 nicotine *juice:* 6 ambeer *kind:* 4 shag 5 bogie, snuff 6 bright, burley 7 caporal, perique, Turkish 9 broadleaf, mundungus *pipe:* 4 heel 6 dottle *rolled:* 5 cigar *Turkish:* 7 latakia

Tobacco Road author 8 Caldwell (Erskine)

to be *Latin:* 4 esse

Tobias *father:* 5 Tobit *son:* 8 Hyrcanus

toboggan 4 sled 7 coaster

toby 3 cup, mug 5 cigar

tocsin 3 SOS 4 sign 5 alarm, alert 6 alarum, signal

today 3 now 7 present 8 nowadays 9 presently

toddle 4 walk 6 stroll 7 saunter

toddy 3 sap 5 drink

to-do 4 coil, fuss 5 whirl 6 clamor, furore, hassle, hubbub, hurrah, pother, ruckus, rumpus, shindy, tumult, uproar 7 turmoil 9 commotion 10 hurly-burly

toe 3 tip 5 digit, touch *big:* 6 hallux *combining form:* 6 dactyl, digiti 7 dactylo, dactyly 8 dactylia 9 dactylism, dactylous *little:* 7 minimus

toehold 7 footing

toffee 5 candy

toga 4 gown, rope, wrap 5 tunic

together 6 at once, joined, united 7 jointly 8 mutually 10 conjointly 11 concertedly 12 coincidently, collectively, concurrently *prefix:* 2 co 3 col, com, con, cor, sym, syn

togetherness 5 union 7 cahoots 8 alliance, cohesion 10 connection, solidarity 11 affiliation, association, combination, conjunction, partnership

Togo *capital:* 4 Lome *monetary unit:* 5 franc

tog out 5 fix up, slick, spiff 6 doll up 7 dress up, gussy up 8 spruce up 9 smarten up

togs 4 duds 5 dress 6 attire, things 7 apparel, clothes, raiment 8 clothing 10 attirement, habiliment

To Have and to Hold author 8 Johnston (Mary)

To His Coy Mistress author 7 Marvell (Andrew)

toil 3 net, tug 4 grub, plod, slog, slop, work 5 drive, grind, labor, slave, sweat 6 drudge, stodge, strain, strive, trudge 7 travail 8 bullwork, drudgery, footslog, plunther, slogging

toiler 4 peon 5 slave 6 drudge, slavey 9 dray horse, workhorse 11 galley slave

toilet 4 head, john 5 dress, privy 6 johnny 7 latrine 8 bathroom, lavatory 11 convenience, water closet *British:* 3 loo

toilsome 4 hard 6 uphill 7 arduous, labored, operose 9 difficult, effortful, laborious, strenuous

Toi's son 5 Joram 7 Hadoram, Jehoram

Tokay 4 wine

token 4 mark, pawn, sign 5 index, relic 6 pledge, trophy 7 earnest, gesture, indicia, memento, minimal, symptom, warrant 8 evidence, keepsake, memorial, reminder, security, souvenir 9 indicator 10 expression, indication 11 remembrance 12 remembrancer

Tokyo *formerly:* 3 Edo *island:* 6 Honshu

Tola's father 4 Puah 8 Issachar

tolerable 2 OK 4 fair 6 common, decent 7 livable 8 adequate, all right, bearable 9 endurable 10 acceptable, sufferable, sufficient 11 presentable, respectable, supportable, sustainable 12 satisfactory

tolerably 4 so-so 6 enough, fairly, pretty, rather 8 passably 9 averagely 10 moderately

tolerance 7 stamina 8 clemency, lenience, leniency, patience 9 endurance 10 indulgence, resistance, steadiness, sufferance 11 forbearance 13 steadfastness

tolerant 4 easy 5 broad 7 clement, lenient, liberal 9 condoning, forgiving, indulgent 10 charitable, forbearing, open-minded, permissive 11 broad-minded, progressive, sympathetic 13 understanding

tolerate 4 bear, take 5 abide, allow, brook, stand 6 accept, endure, permit, suffer 7 condone, stomach, swallow 8 bear with, tough out 11 countenance

Tolkien creature 3 Ent 6 Hobbit

toll 3 tax 4 bait, bell, bong, cost, lure, peal, ring 5 chime, decoy, knell, price, tempt 6 allure, charge, entice, entrap, lead on, seduce 7 expense, lockage 8 inveigle

tollbooth 11 customhouse

Tolstoy novel 11 War and Peace 12 Anna Karenina

tomato 5 fruit 9 love apple

tomb 4 bury 5 grave, inter, plant 6 burial, inhume 7 lay away, put away 8 mausolea (plural) 9 mausoleum, sepulcher, sepulture 11 ensepulcher *ancient Egyptian:* 7 mastaba 8 mastabah *circular:* 6 tholoi (plural), tholos *empty:* 8 cenotaph

tomboy 6 gamine, hoyden

Tom Brown's School Days *author:* 6 Hughes (Thomas)

tombstone 6 ledger 8 memorial, monument 11 grave marker *inscription:* 3 RIP 8 hic jacet

tome 4 book 6 volume

tomfool 3 ass 4 fool, jerk 5 crazy, idiot, loony, ninny, silly 6 absurd, donkey, insane 7 foolish, jackass 8 imbecile 9 fantastic 10 nincompoop 11 harebrained 12 preposterous

tomfoolery 4 dido, lark 5 antic, caper, prank, shine, trick 6 frolic 7 hogwash, rubbish, twaddle 8 claptrap, malarkey, nonsense 9 poppycock 10 balderdash, shenanigan 11 monkeyshine 12 blatherskite

Tom Jones author 8 Fielding (Henry)

tommyrot 4 bash, bull, crap 5 bilge, hooey, trash 7 hogwash, rubbish 8 nonsense

Tom o'Bedlam 3 nut 4 loon 5 loony 6 dement, madman, maniac 7 lunatic, madling 9 bedlamite, non compos

tomorrow 6 future, mañana

Tom Sawyer *author:* 5 Twain (Mark) *character:* 5 Becky 8 Huck Finn, Injun Joe 9 Aunt Polly 10 Muff Potter

Tom Thumb 4 runt 5 dwarf, midge,

pygmy 6 midget, peewee 7 manikin 10 homunculus 11 lilliputian

ton 3 fad 4 chic, rage 5 craze, style, vogue 6 furore 7 fashion

tone 3 hue 4 cast, mode, mood, tint, vein 5 color, humor, pitch, shade, style, tinge 6 accent, manner, spirit, strain, temper, timbre 7 fashion 10 inflection *combining form:* 4 phon 5 phono

toned down 4 mute, soft 5 sober 6 lowkey, mellow 7 subdued 8 low-keyed, softened

tongue 4 lick 6 glossa, lingua, speech 7 dialect 8 language 10 vernacular *click of:* 3 tch *combining form:* 4 glot 5 gloss, lingu 6 glossa, glosso, lingua, lingui, linguo 7 glossia

tongue-lash 3 wig 4 lash, rail 5 scold 6 berate 7 bawl out, chew out, tell off, upbraid

tonguelike part 7 languet

tonic 5 sharp 7 bracing 8 renewing, roborant 9 animating 10 astringent, quickening, refreshing, vitalizing 11 restorative, stimulating, stimulative 12 exhilarating, exhilarative, invigorating 13 strengthening *extract:* 4 cola 9 berberine

tonsorialist 6 barber

tony 2 in 4 chic 5 swank, swish 6 modish 7 a la mode, stylish 9 exclusive 11 fashionable

too 4 also, ever, more, over, very 5 along 6 as well, highly, overly, unduly, withal 7 awfully, besides, greatly, notably 8 likewise, moreover, overfull, overmuch 9 extremely, immensely 10 remarkably, strikingly 11 exceedingly, excessively, furthermore 12 additionally, exorbitantly, immoderately, inordinately, unmeasurably 13 exceptionally

tool 3 awl, zax 4 pawn 5 drive 6 puppet, rimmer, stooge 7 cat's-paw, hayfork, machine, rounder, utensil 8 picklock 9 implement, mechanism 10 instrument *axlike:* 3 adz *barrel making:* 5 croze 6 crozer *boring:* 5 auger, drill *carving:* 6 veiner *cleaving:* 4 froe *cobbler's:* 3 awl *cutting:* 2 ax 3 adz, axe, saw 4 adze 5 knife 6 shears 8 billhook *digging:* 4 pick 7 mattock *engraving:* 5 burin 7 scauper *farm:* 6 seeder *filing:* 4 rasp 7 riffler *garden:* 3 hoe 4 rake 5 spade 6 trowel, weeder *grasping:* 6 pincer 7 tweezer 8 tweezers *mining:* 6 trepan *prehistoric:* 5 flint 6 eolith *pruning:* 6 shears 8 secateur *rubbing:* 9 burnisher *scooping:* 6 router *toothed:* 3 saw 7 rippler *woodworking:* 3 saw 5 bevel, plane 6 chisel, hammer

toot 3 bat, jag 4 bust, tear 5 binge, drunk, sound, spree 6 bender 7 blowoff, carouse

tooth 5 molar 7 incisor 8 bicuspid, premolar *combining form:* 4 dent, odon, odus 5 denti, dento, odont 6 odonta, odonto, odonty 7 dentate, odontes, odontia *cuspid:* 6 canine 8 dogtooth, eyetooth *cutting:* 10 carnassial *decay:* 6 caries *doctor:* 7 dentist *pointed:* 4 fang 6 canine, cuspid *small:* 8 denticle *surface:* 5 mensa

toothless 8 edentate

toothsome 5 sapid, tasty 6 savory 8 pleasant, pleasing, tasteful 9 agreeable, delicious, palatable, relishing 10 appetizing, attractive 11 good-tasting

top 3 cap, tip 4 acme, apex, beat, best, clip, crop, cusp, dock, face, fine, head, peak, pick, roof 5 cream, crest, crown, elite, excel, outdo, point, pride, prime, prize 6 apical, better, choice, climax, exceed, height, summit, utmost, vertex 7 capital, highest, maximal, maximum, outside, pollard, surface, surpass 8 five-star, loftiest, outshine, outstrip, pinnacle, superior, surmount 9 excellent, fastigium, first-rate, transcend, uppermost 10 first-class 11 culmination, first-string *combining form:* 3 acr, akr 4 acro, akro

tope 3 nip 4 soak 5 booze, drink, shark 6 guzzle, imbibe, tank up, tipple 7 swizzle 8 liquor up

toper 3 sot 4 lush, soak 5 drunk 6 bibber, boozer 7 tippler, tosspot 8 drunkard 9 inebriate

Tophet 4 hell 5 hades, Sheol 6 blazes 7 Gehenna, inferno 9 barathrum, perdition 10 underworld 11 Pandemonium

topic 4 head, text 5 issue, motif, point, theme 6 matter, motive 7 subject 8 argument 11 proposition 13 subject matter

top-notch 4 fine 5 prime 7 capital 8 fivestar, superior 9 excellent, first-rate 10 firstclass 11 first-string

top off 3 cap 5 crown 6 climax 8 round off 9 culminate, finish off

topography 7 terrain

topple 4 drop, fall 5 lurch, pitch, slump, upset 6 falter, go down, plunge, teeter, totter, tumble, wobble 7 overset, stagger, stumble, tip over, unhorse 8 keel over, overturn, turn over 9 knock over, overthrow

topsy-turvy 8 cockeyed, inverted, unhinged 10 disjointed, disordered, downside-up, upside-down 11 disarranged

toque 3 cap, hat

tor 4 hill, peak 5 mound 8 pinnacle

torch 7 firebug 8 arsonist, flambeau 10 incendiary

toreador 6 torero 7 matador 11 bullfighter

torment 3 try 4 bait, hurt, pain, rack 5 smite, wring 6 harass, harrow, heckle, molest, plague 7 afflict, agonize, crucify, torture, trouble **8** distress **9** persecute **10** excruciate

torn 4 rent **7** mangled **9** lacerated

tornado 7 cyclone, twister **9** whirlwind

toro 4 bull

torpedo 3 gun **4** mine **6** gunman, hit man **8** assassin **9** cutthroat, explosive **10** gunslinger, hatchet man, projectile, triggerman

torpid 5 dopey **8** comatose, sluggish **9** lethargic **10** slumberous **12** hebetudinous

torpor 4 coma **5** sleep **6** stupor **7** languor **8** dullness, hebetude, lethargy **9** lassitude, passivity, stolidity **10** stagnation **12** listlessness

torque 5 chain, twist **6** collar

torrent 5 flood, spate **6** deluge **7** niagara **8** cataract, flooding, overflow **9** cataclysm **10** inundation, outpouring

torrid 3 hot **5** fiery **6** ardent, fervid, heated, red-hot, sultry **7** blazing, burning, flaming **8** broiling, scalding, sizzling, white-hot **9** scorching **10** hot-blooded, passionate, sweltering **11** impassioned

tort 3 sin **4** evil **5** crime, wrong **8** iniquity **9** diablerie **10** wrongdoing

tortilla 4 cake, taco

Tortilla Flat author 9 Steinbeck (John)

tortoise 6 turtle **8** terrapin **9** chelonian *freshwater:* **4** emyd *shell:* **8** carapace

tortuous 5 snaky **7** sinuous, winding **8** flexuous, involute, involved **9** meandrous **10** convoluted, meandering, serpentine **11** anfractuous, vermiculate

torture 3 try **4** hurt, maim, rack, warp **5** smite, wring **6** deform, harrow, mangle **7** afflict, agonize, contort, crucify, distort, oppress, torment **8** misshape, mutilate **10** excruciate

tory 5 right **7** diehard, fogyish, old-line **8** loyalist, old liner, orthodox, rightist, standpat **11** bitter-ender, reactionary, right-winger, standpatter **12** conservative

Tosca *character:* **5** Mario **7** Scarpia *composer:* **7** Puccini (Giacomo)

___ **Toscanini 6** Arturo

tosh 5 bilge, hooey **6** bunkum **7** eyewash **8** malarkey, nonsense, pishposh

toss 4 cast, fire, flip, hurl, rock, roll **5** bandy, drink, fling, heave, pitch, quaff, sling, throw **6** imbibe, launch, seesaw, squirm, writhe **7** agonize

tosspot see **tippler**

tot 3 add, nip, sum **4** cast, dram, drop, foot, jolt, shot, slug **5** child, snort, total **6** figure **7** snifter, summate, toddler

totable 8 portable

total 3 add, all, sum **4** body, bulk, cast, come, foot, full, tale **5** add up, equal, gross, run to, smash, sum to, utter, whole, wreck,

yield **6** all-out, amount, budget, entire, figure, number **7** crack up, destroy, full-out, overall, perfect, plenary, quantum, run into, stack up, sum into, summate **8** absolute, complete, comprise, demolish, entirety, outright, positive, quantity, result in **9** aggregate, consist of, full-blown, full-scale, inclusive, out-and-out, unlimited **10** consummate, unreserved **11** unmitigated **13** comprehensive, thoroughgoing *combining form:* **3** hol **4** holo

totalitarian 6 all-out **7** full-out **8** absolute **9** full-blown, full-scale, unlimited **11** dictatorial **13** authoritarian

totality 3 all, sum **4** tale **5** gross, whole **6** entity, system **7** allness, oneness **8** entirety, integral **9** aggregate, integrate, wholeness **10** entireness **12** completeness

totalize 3 add, sum, tot **6** figure **7** summate

tote 3 add, lug **4** bear, buck, cart, haul, pack **5** carry, ferry **6** convey, figure **7** summate **9** transport

totem 4 clan, pole **6** emblem *pole:* **3** xat

To the Lighthouse author 5 Woolf (Virginia)

totter 4 reel **5** lurch, wheel **6** falter, topple, wobble **7** stagger, stammer **8** titubate

touch 3 dab, pat, paw, rub **4** abut, dash, feel, hand, hint, join, line, meet, move, palm, stir, sway **5** brush, carry, graze, march, probe, shade, smack, thumb, tinge, verge **6** adjoin, affect, amount, arouse, border, butt on, caress, excite, finger, fondle, handle, streak, strike, stroke **7** contact, feeling, impress, inspire, palpate, quicken, taction, toy with, verge on **9** influence, palpation, stimulate, tactility *combining form:* **6** thigmo

touchable 7 tactile **8** palpable, tangible

touch down 4 land **5** light, perch, roost **6** alight, settle **9** six points

touching 2 to **4** as to, in re **5** about, anent, as for **6** moving, tender **7** against, apropos, meeting, piteous, pitiful, tangent **8** abutting, adjacent, pitiable, poignant, stirring **9** adjoining, affecting, as regards, bordering, impinging **10** approximal, as respects, concerning, contiguous, impressive, juxtaposed, responsive **11** overlapping, sympathetic, tear-jerking **12** conterminous **13** compassionate

touchstone 4 test **5** check, gauge, proof, scale, trial **7** measure **8** standard **9** barometer, benchmark, criterion, yardstick **13** demonstration

touch up 4 do up **5** fix up **6** polish **7** brush up, improve, perfect

touchy 5 cross, dicey, miffy, ratty, risky, testy **6** cranky, tetchy, tricky, unsafe **7** harmful **8** choleric, delicate, ticklish, volatile **9** hazardous, irascible, sensitive, temperish **10** precarious **11** thin-skinned **13** oversensitive, quick-tempered, temperamental, unpredictable

tough 3 bad, fit, mug **4** goon, hard, hood, punk, taut, thug **5** bully, fixed, hardy, harsh, lusty, rigid, rough, rowdy, stiff, stout, teuch, teugh, yahoo **6** accept, anneal, flinty, ghetto, mucker, mulish, narrow, robust, rugged, severe, strict, strong, sturdy, taxing, trying, unsafe, uphill, viscid **7** arduous, drastic, exigent, healthy, hoodlum, labored, onerous, ruffian, steeled, toilful, viscose, viscous, weighty **8** bullyboy, exacting, grievous, hardcase, hardened, hard-line, hooligan, obdurate, plug-ugly, rigorous, seasoned, stalwart, stubborn, toilsome, vigorous **9** arbitrary, confirmed, dangerous, demanding, difficult, effortful, hard-shell, immutable, inner city, laborious, obstinate, pigheaded, resistant, roughneck, strenuous, tenacious **10** bullheaded, burdensome, disorderly, hard-bitten, hard-boiled, hardfisted, hardhanded, hardheaded, headstrong, inflexible, oppressive, refractory, self-willed, unyielding **11** conditioned, intractable, procrustean, unalterable, unbreakable **12** pertinacious, withstanding

toughen 6 anneal, harden, season **7** develop **9** acclimate, climatize **10** strengthen **11** acclimatize

toughie 4 punk **5** heavy, rough, rowdy, yahoo **6** mucker **7** ruffian **8** bullyboy **9** roughneck

toupee 3 wig **6** peruke, wiglet **7** periwig, wiggery

tour 4 bout, time, trip, turn **5** round, shift, spell, stint, trick **6** travel, troupe **7** circuit **9** round trip **10** roundabout

tour de force 4 deed, feat **7** classic, exploit **10** magnum opus, masterwork **11** achievement, chef d'oeuvre, masterpiece

tour guide 8 cicerone

tourist 7 tripper, visitor **8** traveler **9** sightseer, traveller **10** day-tripper, rubberneck **12** excursionist

tournament 4 tilt **5** joust **7** tourney

tousle 4 mess, muss **6** rumple **8** dishevel, disorder

tout 4 laud, plug **5** vigil, watch **6** herald, praise **7** acclaim, lookout, promote, trumpet **8** ballyhoo, proclaim **9** publicize, vigilance

tow 3 lug, tug **4** drag, draw, haul, pull

toward 6 contra, facing **7** against, apropos, benefic, helpful, vis-à-vis **8** favoring, fronting **9** favorable, regarding **10** beneficial, propitious *prefix:* **2** ac, ad, af, ag, al, ap, as, at, il, im, in, ir **4** pros *suffix:* **2** ad

towel word 3 his **4** hers

tower 5 spire **7** overtop **8** dominate, look down, overlook *Babylonian:* **8** ziggurat *on a mosque:* **7** minaret *small:* **6** turret

towering 4 airy, high, tall **5** dizzy, lofty, undue **6** aerial **7** extreme, massive, soaring, spiring, supreme **8** ultimate **10** exorbitant, immoderate, inordinate, monumental, preeminent, prodigious, stupendous, surpassing, tremendous **11** extravagant, skyscraping **12** altitudinous, overpowering, overwhelming, transcendent

towhee 5 finch

to wit 3 viz **6** namely **8** scilicet **9** videlicetis

town 4 burg **6** podunk **7** borough, village *medieval:* **5** bourg

town and ___ 4 gown **7** country

townsman 3 cit **6** townee **7** burgher, citizen, oppidan

town square *Italian:* **6** piazza

toxic 6 poison **8** mephitic, venomous, virulent **9** poisonous

toxin 5 venin, venom **6** poison

toy 3 pet **4** fool, play **5** curio, dally, flirt, sport, tease **6** bauble, caress, coquet, cosset, cuddle, dandle, frolic, gewgaw, lead on, popgun, trifle, wanton **7** bibelot, disport, dreidel, novelty, trinket, whatnot **8** gimcrack, pinwheel **9** plaything **10** fiddle with, knickknack **11** string along

trace 4 hint, mark **5** relic, shade, smell, tinge, track, trail, tread, whiff **6** nuance, shadow, strain, streak **7** memento, soupçon, vestige **9** suspicion **10** intimation

trachea 8 windpipe

track 3 dog, way **4** drag, find, mark, path, road, sign, step, tail, walk **5** chase, cover, print, spoor, trace, trail, tread **6** artery, avenue, follow, pursue, shadow, street, travel **7** footway, highway, imprint, monitor, pathway, vestige **8** footpath, footstep, hunt down, pass over, smell out, traverse **9** footprint *combining form:* **4** ichn **5** ichno

track-and-field event 4 dash, race **7** shot put **8** footrace, high jump, long jump **9** broad jump, decathlon, pole vault, relay race **10** heptathlon, pentathlon, triple jump **11** discus throw **12** steeplechase

tract 3 lot **4** area, belt, plat, plot, zone **6** parcel, region **7** portion, terrain **9** territory

tractable 6 docile, pliant **7** pliable, subdued **8** amenable, biddable, flexible, obedient **10** manageable

tractate 6 memoir, thesis **8** treatise **9** discourse, monograph **10** monography **12** disquisition, dissertation

tractor *maker:* **5** Deere (John)

trade 3 art **4** deal, sell, swap, work **5** craft, truck **6** barter, change, custom, market, métier, peddle, switch **7** bargain, calling, pursuit, traffic **8** business, commerce,

exchange, industry, merchant, vocation
9 patronage 10 employment, handicraft,
occupation, profession, substitute 11 merchandise *illicit:* 11 black market *suffix:*
3 ery

trademark 4 logo 5 brand 8 logotype
trade route 7 sea-lane
tradition 4 lore, myth 6 custom, legacy,
legend, mythos 8 folklore, heritage
9 mythology 10 convention
traditional 3 old 4 oral 5 fixed, usual
6 common, spoken, verbal 7 popular
8 habitual, orthodox 9 ancestral, customary, unwritten 10 immemorial 11 established, word-of-mouth 12 acknowledged,
conventional, tralatitious
traditionalist 6 purist 9 precisian 12 precisionist
traditionalistic 4 tory 5 right 7 die-hard,
fogyish, old-line 8 orthodox 11 reactionary
12 conservative
traduce 5 libel 6 betray, defame, malign,
vilify 7 asperse, slander, violate 8 disgrace
9 denigrate 10 calumniate, scandalize
Trafalgar commander 6 Nelson (Horatio)
traffic 4 push, swap 5 fence, trade, truck
6 barter, custom, deal in, travel 7 bargain,
bootleg 8 business, commerce, dealings,
exchange, industry 9 communion, patronage 11 black market, intercourse
trafficker 6 dealer, trader
tragedy 3 lot 4 blow, woes 5 curse, shock
6 mishap 8 calamity, disaster 9 adversity,
cataclysm, mischance 10 misfortune
11 catastrophe, contretemps 12 misadventure
trail 3 dog, lag, tag 4 drag, flag, halt, path,
plod, poke, tail 5 bedog, chase, chivy,
dally, delay, tarry, trace, track 6 dawdle,
falter, follow, linger, loiter, pursue, shadow,
trudge 7 draggle, footway, gumshoe, pathway, traipse 8 footpath, footwalk 10 bridle
path *emigrant:* 6 Oregon *Florida:* 7 Tamiami *Georgia-Maine:* 11 Appalachian
Indian: 5 Great
trailer truck 4 semi
train 3 aim, lay, row, run 4 bait, cast, head,
line, lure, tier, toll, turn 5 chain, coach,
decoy, level, order, point, scale, shape,
suite, teach, tempt 6 allure, course, direct,
entice, harden, lead on, school, season,
seduce, sequel, series, thread, zero in
7 develop, educate, incline, retinue 8 accustom, instruct, inveigle, sequence 9 cultivate, entourage, following, gradation, habituate 10 discipline, succession
11 alternation, consecution, progression
training 7 tuition 8 teaching, tutelage
9 education, schooling 11 instruction
horses: 6 manege

train off 3 dip 4 skew, slue, veer 5 sheer
6 swerve
traipse 3 gad 4 dowd, drab, drag, hoof,
pace, roam, rove, slut, step, walk 5 dowdy,
drift, mooch, range, trail, tread, troop 6 foot
it, ramble, wander 7 draggle, meander
8 ambulate, slattern 9 gallivant 11 draggletail
trait 4 mark 5 point, savor 6 virtue 7 feature, quality 8 property 9 affection, attribute, birthmark, character 11 denominator
traitor 5 Judas 6 Arnold 8 betrayer, quisling, renegade, renegado, traditor, turncoat
traitorous 5 false 6 untrue 7 unloyal
8 apostate, disloyal, mutinous, recreant, renegade 9 alienated, estranged, faithless,
seditious 10 perfidious, rebellious, unfaithful 11 disaffected, treacherous, unpatriotic
traject 4 pipe 5 carry 6 convey, funnel,
siphon 7 channel, conduct 8 transmit
tram 3 car 7 trolley 9 streetcar
trammel 3 tie 4 bind, clog, curb 5 leash,
limit 6 enmesh, fetter, hamper, hobble,
hog-tie, stifle 7 confine, enchain, ensnarl,
manacle, shackle 8 entangle, handcuff,
stagnate, stultify 9 embrangle, entrammel
12 circumscribe
tramontane 7 foreign 10 outlandish
11 transalpine
tramp 3 vag 4 hike, hobo, jade, plod, thud,
walk 5 march, stamp, stomp 6 ramble,
stodge, stroll, trudge 7 drifter, floater, saunter, traipse, vagrant 8 derelict, footslog,
vagabond 9 walkabout 10 street arab
trample 5 pound, stamp, stomp, tromp
7 tread on 8 override
trance 4 muse 5 study 6 ravish 7 reverie
8 enravish, hypnosis 9 enrapture, transport
10 brown study
tranquil 4 calm, easy 5 quiet, still 6 irenic,
placid, poised, serene, stable, steady
7 pacific, restful 8 composed, peaceful
9 collected, easygoing 13 self-possessed
tranquilize 4 balm, calm, hush, lull
5 quiet, still 6 becalm, sedate, settle,
soothe, subdue 7 compose
tranquilizer 6 downer, opiate 8 diazepam, pacifier, sedative 10 depressant
transaction 4 bond, pact 7 bargain, compact, dealing 8 contract, covenant 9 agreement 10 convention
transcend 3 top 4 beat, best 5 excel,
outdo 6 better, exceed 7 surpass 8 outshine, outstrip
transcendent 5 ideal 7 perfect, supreme
8 abstract, towering 10 consummate, preeminent, surpassing 11 theoretical, unequalable, unmatchable 12 hypothetical,
incomparable 13 unsurpassable
Transcendentalist 7 Emerson (Ralph
Waldo), Thoreau (Henry David)

transcribe 4 copy 5 write 6 record
9 translate 13 transliterate
transfer 4 cede, deed, feed, find, give,
hand, move, ship 5 alien, carry, shift
6 assign, change, convey, remise, remove,
supply 7 convert, deliver, devolve, disturb,
provide 8 alienate, dispense, hand over,
make over, relocate, sign over, turn over
9 carry over, dislocate 10 abalienate
transfix 4 spit 5 lance, spear, spike
6 impale, skewer, skiver
transform 5 alter 6 change, mutate
7 commute, convert 8 denature 12 metamorphize, metamorphose
transformation 5 shift 10 alteration,
changeover, conversion
transfuse 6 charge 7 pervade 8 permeate, saturate 9 penetrate, percolate
10 impregnate 11 impenetrate
transgress 3 sin 5 break 6 breach,
offend 7 infract, violate 8 infringe, overstep, trespass 10 contravene
transient 7 passing 8 fleeting, flitting, fugitive, temporal, unstable, volatile 9 ephemeral, fugacious, momentary, temporary
10 evanescent, short-lived, transitory
11 impermanent 12 momentaneous
13 insubstantial
transit 5 shift 6 travel 7 passage 8 carriage, carrying 9 transport 10 alteration,
conveyance 12 transporting
transition 5 shift 6 change, growth 7 passage 8 progress 9 evolution 10 alteration,
conversion 11 development 13 metamorphosis *musical:* 5 segue
transitory see **transient**
translate 3 put 4 turn 6 change, render,
reword 7 commute, convert, restate
8 rephrase 9 interpret 10 paraphrase
12 metamorphose
translation 7 version 9 rendering
10 paraphrase 11 restatement
translucent 5 clear, lucid 6 limpid 7 crystal, obvious 8 apparent, clear-cut, luminous, pellucid 9 unblurred 10 see-through
combining form: 4 hyal 5 hyalo
transmarine 7 oversea 8 overseas
transmission 7 gearbox *combining
form:* 8 phoreses (plural), phoresis
transmit 4 pipe, send, ship 5 break, carry,
radio, route 6 convey, funnel, hand on,
impart, pass on, siphon 7 address, channel, conduct, consign, forward, instill, traject
8 bequeath, dispatch, hand down
transmogrify see **transform**
transmute see **transform**
transoceanic message 9 cablegram
transparent 5 clear, filmy, gauzy, lucid,
plain, sheer 6 flimsy, limpid, lucent 7 crystal, tiffany 8 clear-cut, gossamer, luminous,

pellucid 9 tralucent, unblurred 10 diaphanous, seethrough, translucid 11 crystalline,
translucent *combining form:* 4 hyal
5 hyalo 7 diaphan 8 diaphano
transpire 3 hap, out 4 leak 5 occur
6 befall, betide, chance, happen 7 develop
transport 3 lug, wow 4 bear, buck, move,
oust, pack, send, slay, tote 5 ardor, carry,
exile, expel, ferry, truck 6 banish, convey,
deport, excite, fervor, heaven, ravish, stir
up, thrill, trance, uplift 7 agitate, cast out,
delight, ecstasy, elevate, expulse, inflame,
passion, provoke, quicken, rapture, transit,
vehicle 8 carriage, carrying, displace, enravish, entrance, relegate, rhapsody 9 carry
away, enrapture, happiness, stimulate
10 conveyance, enthusiasm, imparadise
transportation 6 moving 7 hauling, transit, vehicle 8 carriage, carrying 10 conveyance
transpose 4 turn 6 change, invert, render,
revert 7 commute, convert, inverse,
reverse 12 metamorphose
transubstantiate see **transform**
transude 4 ooze, seep, weep 5 bleed,
sweat 6 strain
Transvaal *capital:* 8 Pretoria *natives:*
7 Bushmen 10 Hottentots *resource:*
4 gold
transversal 4 bent 6 thwart 8 crossing
9 crosswise 12 intersecting
transverse 5 cross 6 across, thwart
7 crossed, oblique 8 crossing, diagonal
9 crosswise
trap 3 net 4 bait, lure, plot, ploy, ruse,
snag, tree, wile 5 benet, catch, decoy,
feint, snare 6 ambush, come-on, gambit,
tangle 7 catch up, ensnare 8 artifice, bird-
lime, entangle, intrigue, maneuver
9 ambuscade, stratagem 10 allurement,
conspiracy, enticement, seducement,
temptation 11 machination 12 inveiglement
an animal: 8 deadfall
trappings 4 gear 5 dress 10 decoration
13 embellishment
Trappist 4 monk *writer:* 6 Merton
(Thomas)
trash 3 mob, rot 4 bosh, crap, junk, plod,
scum, slog, slop, toil 5 bilge, dregs, hokum,
offal, waste, wreck 6 bunkum, debris, kelter, litter, masses, rabble, refuse, shlock,
stodge, trudge 7 garbage, rubbish
8 canaille, claptrap, doggerel, dustheap,
footslog, leavings, malarkey, nonsense,
plunther, riffraff, unwashed 9 sweepings,
vandalize 11 proletariat
trash can 7 dustbin
trashy 4 base, mean, poor 5 cheap, tatty
6 common, cruddy, paltry, shoddy, sleazy
8 rubbishy 9 third-rate

trauma 4 blow 5 shock, upset 6 stress 8 collapse 11 disturbance

travail 4 moil, task, toil, work 5 grind, labor, pains 6 drudge 7 slavery 8 bullwork, drudgery, plugging, struggle 10 birth pangs, childbirth 11 parturition 12 childbearing, contractions

travel 2 go 3 hie 4 fare, pass, roam, tour, trek, wend 5 cover, cross, jaunt, track 6 move on, push on, repair, voyage 7 explore, journey, passage, proceed, process, traffic, transit 8 pass over

travelable 8 passable 9 navigable 10 negotiable

traveling library 10 bookmobile

traverse 3 bar, rub 4 buck, deny, duel, snag, walk 5 cover, cross, fight, repel 6 combat, hamper, hurdle, impugn, negate, oppose, patrol, resist, thwart, travel 7 contest, dispute, gainsay 8 crossing, negative, obstacle, pass over 9 crosswise, disaffirm, withstand 10 contradict, contravene, crisscross, impediment 11 obstruction, perambulate

travesty 3 ape 4 mock, sham 5 farce, mimic 6 parody 7 imitate, mimicry, mockery, take off 8 ridicule 9 burlesque 10 caricature, distortion 12 exaggeration *satanic:* 9 Black Mass

Traviata, La *character:* 7 Alfredo, Germont 8 Violetta *composer:* 5 Verdi (Giuseppe)

trawl 3 net 4 fish 5 troll 7 setline

tray 6 salver, server 7 platter 8 teaboard *revolving:* 9 lazy Susan

treacherous 5 false, hairy, Punic, risky 6 chancy, tricky, untrue, wicked 7 unloyal, unsound 8 disloyal, perilous, recreant, ticklish 9 betraying, dangerous, deceptive, faithless, hazardous, unhealthy 10 jeopardous, misleading, perfidious, precarious, traitorous, unfaithful 12 falsehearted

treachery 7 perfidy, sellout, treason 9 falseness 10 disloyalty, infidelity 11 double cross 13 double dealing, faithlessness

treacle 5 syrup 6 remedy 8 molasses

tread 4 hoof, pace, step, walk 5 dance, march, stamp, stomp, trace, track, tramp, tromp, troop 6 foot it, hoof it, prance, stride 7 traipse, trample 8 ambulate

treadle 5 lever, pedal

treadmill 3 rut 4 pace, rote 5 grind 6 groove 7 routine

treason 6 deceit 7 perfidy 8 betrayal, sedition 9 duplicity, treachery 10 disloyalty, misprision 13 deceitfulness, faithlessness, seditiousness

treasure 4 find, plum, save 5 catch, guard, pearl, prize, trove, value 6 esteem, revere 7 apprize, cherish, idolize, worship

8 conserve, preserve, venerate 9 reverence 10 appreciate

Treasure Island *author:* 9 Stevenson (Robert Louis) *narrator:* 10 Jim Hawkins

treasurer 6 bursar, purser 11 chamberlain

Treasure State 7 Montana

treasure trove 4 find, mine 7 bonanza 8 eldorado, Golconda, gold mine

treasury 4 mine 5 chest 6 coffer, museum 7 bonanza, gallery 8 archives, eldorado, Golconda, gold mine, war chest 9 exchequer 10 depositary, depository, repository, storehouse *state:* 4 fisc

treat 3 use 5 goody, nurse, serve 6 advise, confab, confer, dainty, doctor, do with, handle, huddle, manage, morsel, parley, physic, powwow, regard, tidbit, titbit 7 care for, consult 8 collogue, deal with, delicacy, kickshaw, medicate, medicine 10 minister to 11 bonne bouche, confabulate *animals:* 3 vet *leather:* 3 tan, taw 6 shammy, shamoy 7 chamois, tanning

treatise 4 book 6 memoir, thesis 7 writing 8 argument, tractate 9 discourse, monograph 10 discussion, exposition, monography 12 disquisition, dissertation *combining form:* 3 log 4 logy 5 logia, logue *suffix:* 3 ics

treatment 4 care 7 therapy *combining form:* 6 praxes (plural), praxis

treaty 4 pact 6 accord 7 charter, compact, concord 8 contract, covenant 9 agreement, concordat 10 convention

treble 4 high, thin 5 acute, sharp 6 argute, piping, shrill 8 piercing

tree *African:* 4 akee, cola, shea 5 limba, sassy 6 baobab 7 avodire, bubinga 8 sasswood 9 berberine *Asian:* 4 dhak, upas 6 banyan, kamala *Australian:* 7 blue gum 8 lacewood, quandong 9 casuarina *branch:* 5 bough *Brazilian:* 3 apa, ule 7 arariba, seringa, wallaba *Chinese:* 4 tung 5 yulan 6 gingko, ginkgo, litchi 7 kumquat *citrus:* 4 lime 5 lemon 6 orange 8 bergamot 10 calamondin *combining form:* 3 dry 4 dryo 5 dendr 6 dendra (plural), dendro 7 dendron *coniferous:* 3 fir, yew 4 pine 5 alder, cedar, larch 6 spruce 7 cypress, hemlock, juniper, redwood, sequoia *dwarf:* 8 arbuscle 10 chinquapin *East Indian:* 4 neem, poon, teak, toon 6 banyan, deodar, durian, durion 7 amboina, amboyna, cajaput, cajeput, cajuput, champac, champak, deodara 11 chaulmoogra *elm:* 4 wych *Ethiopian:* 5 cusso, kusso 6 kousso *Eurasian:* 5 abele, rowan 6 medlar *European:* 5 osier 8 bourtree, caprifig *European oak:* 7 murmast *evergreen:* 3 fir, yew 4 atle, pine, titi 5 athel, bunya, carob, cedar, piñon, taxus, thuja, thuya 6 arbute, cullay, dahoon, jarrah, loquat, mallee, pinyon, sapota 7 arbutus, camphor, conifer, inkwood, juniper, lentisk, madrona, madrone, madrono, peebeen, quillai, redwood, sequoia 8 eucalypt, loblolly, longleaf, tamarisk 9 balsam fir 12 balm of Gilead *evergreen oak:* 6 encina *fig:* 5 pipal 6 peepul *flowering:* 5 sumac 6 acacia, sumach 7 dogwood 8 sourwood *hardwood:* 3 oak 5 beech, birch, ebony, maple 6 cherry, copalm, cornel, walnut 7 bilsted, hickory, shittah 8 chestnut, mahogany 9 primavera *Japanese:* 4 kaki 7 zelkova *linden:* 8 basswood *mulberry:* 8 sycamine *North African:* 5 babul 7 babool *nut-bearing:* 4 cola, kola 5 hazel, pecan, piñon 6 almond, cashew 7 buckeye, filbert, hickory 9 pistachio *oak:* 5 roble 8 bluejack *oil-yielding:* 3 ebo 4 eboe, tung 7 cajaput, cajeput, cajuput *ornamental:* 3 box 5 holly 6 gingko, ginkgo, mimosa, myrtle, redbud 8 laburnum, magnolia 9 poinciana 12 rhododendron *palm:* 4 coco, nipa 5 ratan 6 cohune, gomuti, grugru, pinang, raffia, raphia, rattan 7 babassu, coquito, talipot 8 carnauba, ladypalm *Peruvian:* 8 cinchona *Philippine:* 4 dita, pili 6 bataan, molave 7 tindalo 10 calamondin *resinous:* 10 candlewood *rubber:* 3 ule *shade:* 3 elm, oak 5 maple 6 linden 8 sycamore 10 chinaberry *softwood:* 5 alamo 6 tupelo 8 black gum, corkwood; (see also **coniferous**) *South American:* 3 apa 4 ombu 7 wallaba 8 oiticica 9 Brazil nut *swamp:* 11 bald cypress *tropical:* 4 akee, ohia, sago, teak 5 areca, assai, balsa, cacao, ceiba, genip, lehua, mahoe, mamey, mamie 6 acajou, balata, baobab, bustic, citrus, degame, degami, fustic, kabiki, mammee, mammey, padauk, padouk, santol, souari 7 arnotto, bebeeri, genipap, logwood, majagua, mameyes, palmyra, quassia, soursop 8 allspice, barbasco, cocobola, cocobolo, jelutong, mahogany, mangrove, milkwood, palmetto, porkwood, rosewood, simaruba, soapbark, sweetsop, tamarind 9 candlenut, cherimoya, jacaranda 10 breadfruit, manchineel 11 candleberry, coconut palm *trunk:* 4 bole *willow:* 5 osier, sauch, saugh 6 poplar *young:* 7 sapling

tree frog *genus:* 4 Hyla
trefoil 4 leaf 6 clover *part:* 3 arc
trek 4 trip 7 journey, travels 10 expedition
trellis 6 screen 7 lattice
tremble 3 jar 5 quake, shake 6 dither, quaver, quiver, shiver, tremor 7 shudder, twitter, vibrate *Scottish:* 4 dirl
tremblor see temblor
tremendous 4 huge, vast 5 awful 6 mighty, mortal 7 fearful, immense, mas-

sive, titanic 8 colossal, cracking, dreadful, enormous, gigantic, horrible, shocking, terrible, terrific, towering 9 appalling, fantastic, frightful, monstrous 10 formidable, monumental, prodigious, stupendous

tremolo 7 vibrato
tremor 3 jar 5 quake, shake, shock 6 dither, quaver, quiver, shiver 7 shudder, temblor, tremble, twitter, vibrate 8 tremblor 10 earthquake *muscular:* 8 dystaxia *Scottish:* 6 dindle
tremulous 5 aspen, quaky, shaky 6 aguish, aquake, ashake 7 aquiver, ashiver, quaking, quivery, shaking, shivery 9 quivering, shivering, trembling, tremorous, tremulant, vibrating 11 palpitating
trench 4 sink 5 ditch, drain, drill, fosse, gully, verge 6 border, furrow, trough 8 approach *Caribbean:* 6 Cayman *combining form:* 5 bothr 6 bothro
trenchant 5 acrid, crisp, salty 6 biting 7 caustic, cutting, ingoing, mordant, probing, satiric 8 clear-cut, incisive, piercing, sardonic, scathing 9 sarcastic 10 mordacious, razor-sharp 11 penetrating
trencher 4 tray 7 platter
trend 3 fad, run 4 flow, mode, rage, wind 5 craze, drift, style, swing, tenor, vogue 6 furore 7 current, fashion 8 movement, tendency 9 direction 10 dernier cri
trendy 2 in 3 hep, hip 4 tony 5 faddy 6 modish, tonish, with-it 7 a la mode, faddish, stylish 11 fashionable, ultramodern
Trent's Last Case author 7 Bentley (Edmund Clerihew)
trepidation 4 fear 5 alarm, dread, panic 6 dismay, fright, horror, terror 13 consternation
trepidity 4 fear 5 alarm, dread, panic 6 dismay, fright, horror, terror 13 consternation
trespass 3 err, sin 5 lapse, poach 6 breach, invade, offend 7 intrude 8 encroach, entrench, infringe, invasion 9 interlope, intrusion, obtrusion, violation 10 infraction, transgress 11 intermeddle 12 encroachment, infringement 13 contravention, transgression
tress 4 curl, hair, lock 5 braid, plait
trestle 4 buck 5 horse 7 sawbuck 8 sawhorse 9 workhorse
tret 9 allowance
triad 4 trio 5 trine 6 triple, triune, troika 7 trinity 9 threesome 11 triumvirate
trial 3 try, woe 4 care, test 5 agony, cross, essay, grief, rigor, worry 6 hassle, misery, ordeal, sorrow 7 anguish, attempt, calvary, trouble 8 crucible, distress, endeavor, hardship, striving, struggle 9 adversity, suffering 10 affliction, difficulty, experiment, heart-

break, misfortune, visitation 11 tribulation
12 experimental

trial balloon 6 feeler

trial run 4 test 10 experiment

triangle type 5 right 6 obtuse 7 scalene
9 isosceles 11 equilateral

triangular 6 cuneal 7 cuneate, hastate
combining form: 6 trigon 7 trigono

tribal unit 7 phratry

tribe 4 clan, folk, race 5 house, stock
6 family 7 kindred, lineage *combining
form:* 4 phyl 5 phylo

tribulation 5 cross, trial 6 ordeal 7 calvary 8 crucible, wronging 10 affliction,
oppression, visitation 11 persecution

tribunal 3 bar 5 court 8 lawcourt

tributary 3 sub 5 minor, under 7 subject
8 influent 9 dependent, satellite, secondary
10 collateral 11 subordinate

tribute 5 salvo 6 eulogy 8 citation, encomium 9 panegyric 10 salutation 11 recognition, testimonial 12 appreciation *feudal:*
6 heriot

trice 4 wink 5 shake 6 moment, second
7 instant 9 twinkling 11 split second

trick 3 jig 4 bout, dupe, feat, fool, gull,
hang, hoax, lark, play, ploy, ruse, sham,
tour, turn, wile 5 antic, blind, bluff, caper,
craft, cully, curve, dodge, feint, fraud,
knack, prank, shaky, shift, slick, spell, stall,
stint, stunt 6 chouse, device, didoes, frolic,
gambit, outwit, praxis, scheme, shines,
touchy 7 boutade, chicane, dodgery, finagle, gimmick, sleight 8 artifice, escapade,
flimflam, hoodwink, maneuver, outtrump,
skin game, unstable 9 bamboozle, deception, defective, diversion, stratagem, victimize 10 expediency, red herring, shenanigan, tomfoolery, unreliable 11 contrivance,
hornswoggle, monkeyshine 12 undependable 13 practical joke, untrustworthy *Scottish:* 6 shavie

trickery 5 cheat, fraud 7 chicane, knavery
8 hokypoky 9 chicanery, deception, fourberie 10 hanky-panky 11 double-cross,
highbinding 13 double-dealing, sharp practice

trickle 4 drib, drip, drop, weep 5 trill 7 distill, dribble

trickster 5 cheat 6 con man 7 cheater,
diddler, grifter, sharper 8 conjurer, magician, swindler 9 defrauder 11 flimflammer,
illusionist 12 double-dealer

tricksy 5 rough, tight 6 trying 7 arduous
8 prankish

tricky 3 sly 4 foxy, wily 5 rocky 6 artful,
astute, crafty, quirky, shifty, touchy 7 cunning 8 delicate, delusive, delusory, gim-
micky, guileful, ticklish, unstable 9 deceitful, deceptive, difficult, dishonest, insidious,

sensitive 10 misleading, precarious
12 undependable

trident 5 spear 7 scepter

tried 6 proved, secure, tested, trusty
7 staunch 8 approved, faithful, reliable
9 certified, steadfast 10 dependable
11 trustworthy

tried and true 6 secure, trusty 8 reliable
10 dependable 11 trustworthy

trifle 3 toy 4 fico, fool, mash, muck, play
5 curio, dally, flirt, use up, waste 6 bauble,
burn up, coquet, fiddle, fidget, gewgaw,
lead on, misuse, mucker, wanton 7 bibelot,
consume, fribble, fritter, novelty, trinket,
twiddle, whatnot 8 fool away, gimcrack,
kickshaw, play with, squander 9 dissipate,
objet d'art, philander, throw away 10 frivol
away, knickknack, mess around, potter
away 11 prodigalize, string along

trifolium 6 clover 8 shamrock

trig 4 chic, neat, prim, snug, tidy, trim
5 sharp, smart, swank 6 classy, modish,
snappy 7 chipper, dashing, orderly, stylish
9 shipshape 11 fashionable, spic-and-span,
uncluttered, well-groomed 12 spic-and-
span

triggerman 3 gun 5 bravo 6 gunman, hit
man 7 torpedo 8 assassin 9 cutthroat
10 gunslinger, hatchet man

trigonometric function see at function

trill 4 drib, drip, drop, weep 5 shake 7 distill, dribble, trickle

trillion *combining form:* 4 tera, treg
5 trega

trillionth *combining form:* 4 pico

trim 3 cut, fit 4 beat, clip, crop, deck, drub,
lick, neat, pare, snug, tidy, trig, whip
5 adorn, order, prank, prune, shape, shave,
shear, skive 6 barber, bedeck, dapper, fettle, kilter, repair, ricrac, spruce, sprucy,
thrash 7 chipper, dress up, fitness, garnish,
orderly, shapely, shellac 8 beautify, clean-
cut, decorate, lambaste, manicure, ornament, rickrack, shapeful 9 condition, embellish, shipshape 10 statuesque, well-turned
11 clean-limbed, spic-and-span, stream-
lined, uncluttered, well-groomed 12 spick-
and-span *a tree:* 5 prune 7 pollard

trine see triad

Trinidad and Tobago *capital:* 11 Port
of Spain *monetary unit:* 6 dollar

trinity see triad

trinket 5 curio 6 bauble, gewgaw, tinsel,
trifle 7 bibelot, novelty, whatnot 8 frippery,
gimcrack, kickshaw, nicknack 9 plaything
10 knickknack

trinkets 10 bijouterie

trio *of goddesses:* 5 Fates 6 Furies,
Graces; (see also **triad**)

trip 3 hop, run 4 bull, lope, skip, slip, tour, trek 5 boner, error, fluff, lapse 6 bungle, spring 7 blooper, blunder, journey, mistake, skitter, stumble, travels 10 expedition

tripes 4 guts 7 innards, insides, inwards, viscera 8 entrails, stuffing 9 internals

triple 4 trio 5 triad, trine 6 treble, triune, troika 7 trinity 9 threesome 11 triumvirate

Triple Crown winner *1919:* 9 Sir Barton *1930:* 10 Gallant Fox *1935:* 5 Omaha *1937:* 10 War Admiral *1941:* 9 Whirlaway *1943:* 10 Count Fleet *1946:* 7 Assault *1948:* 8 Citation *1973:* 11 Secretariat *1977:* 11 Seattle Slew *1978:* 8 Affirmed

tripped out 4 high 5 doped 6 stoned, zonked 7 drugged 8 hopped-up, turned on, wiped out 9 spaced-out

Triptolemus *father:* 6 Celeus *gift to man:* 5 grain *mother:* 9 Metaneira

Tristan, Tristam *beloved:* 6 Iseult, Isolde

triste 3 sad 7 joyless 8 mournful 9 saddening 10 depressing, melancholy 11 melancholic

Tristram Shandy author 6 Sterne (Laurence)

trite 3 set 4 dull, flat, hack 5 banal, chain, corny, musty, stale, stock, tired, vapid 6 cliché, common, jejune, old hat, used-up 7 clichéd, drained, prosaic, worn-out 8 bathetic, bromidic, mildewed, ordinary, shopworn, timeworn, well-worn 9 hackneyed 10 threadbare 11 commonplace, stereotyped 13 platitudinous, stereotypical

triton 3 eft 4 newt 10 salamander

Triton 6 merman *attribute:* 5 conch *father:* 7 Neptune 8 Poseidon *mother:* 10 Amphitrite

triturate 4 bray, buck 5 crush, grind 6 powder 9 comminute, pulverize

triumph 3 joy, win 4 beat, best, gain 5 exult, glory 6 master 7 conquer, delight, prevail, prosper, succeed, victory 8 conquest, jubilate, overcome, reveling, surmount 9 exultance, festivity, jubilance 10 ascendancy, exultation, jubilation 11 surmounting, vanquishing 12 vanquishment

triumphal see **triumphant**

triumphant 8 exultant, exulting, jubilant 9 rejoicing

triumvirate see **triad**

Triumvirate, First *member:* 6 Caesar (Julius), Pompey (the Great) 7 Crassus (Marcus Licinius)

Triumvirate, Second *member:* 6 Antony (Marc) 7 Lepidus (Marcus Aemilius) 8 Octavius (Gaius)

triune see **triad**

trivet 4 rack 5 stand 6 tripod

trivia 8 minutiae 9 small beer 11 small change 13 small potatoes

trivial 4 puny 5 light, minor, petty 6 casual, little, measly, paltry, slight 7 shallow 8 captious, picayune, trifling 9 fribbling, frivolous, small-beer 10 negligible, picayunish, shoestring 11 Mickey Mouse, superficial, unimportant 13 insignificant

troche 6 tablet 7 lozenge 8 pastille

troglodyte 7 caveman 11 cave dweller

troika 8 carriage; (see also **triad**)

Troilus *beloved:* 8 Cressida *father:* 5 Priam *mother:* 6 Hecuba *slayer:* 8 Achilles

Troilus and ____ 8 Cressida, Criseyde

Trojan *horse builder:* 5 Epeus *king:* 5 Priam *priest:* 7 Laocoon *soothsayer:* 7 Helenus 9 Cassandra *warrior:* 5 Paris 6 Aeneas, Agenor, Hector 9 Euphorbus

Trojan Horse builder 5 Epeus 6 Epeius

troll 4 fish, lure, roll, sing 5 angle, dwarf, giant

trolley 3 car 4 cart, tram 8 carriage 9 streetcar

Trollope, Anthony *novel:* 11 Ayala's Angel, Phineas Finn 12 Phineas Redux 13 The Claverings

trombone 4 wind 5 brass 7 sackbut

tromp 4 beat, drub, hike, pelt, slog 5 pound, stamp, stomp, tramp 6 batter, buffet, pummel, thrash, trudge 7 belabor, trample 8 lambaste

troop 4 army, band, hoof, host, pace, step, walk 5 corps, tread 6 foot it, forces, legion, outfit 7 company, traipse 8 ambulate, assembly, military, soldiers 9 gathering, multitude 10 collection, combatants, servicemen 11 armed forces

trope 5 irony 6 simile 8 metaphor, metonymy 10 synecdoche

Trophonius *brother:* 8 Agamedes *temple site:* 6 Delphi

trophy 5 relic, token 7 memento 8 keepsake, memorial, reminder, souvenir 11 remembrance 12 remembrancer

tropical 3 hot 4 warm 6 jungly, sultry, torrid 10 equatorial

tropical cyclone see **typhoon**

tropical storm see **typhoon**

Tropic of Cancer author 6 Miller (Henry)

Tros' son 4 Ilus 8 Ganymede

trot 3 jog 4 crib, gait, lope, pony 11 translation

troth 8 espousal 10 engagement

trot out 4 show 5 flash 6 expose, flaunt, parade 7 display, disport, exhibit, show off 8 brandish

Trotsky, Leon *associate:* 5 Lenin (Vladimir)

troubadour 4 bard, poet 6 rhymer 8 jongleur, minstrel, musician 9 balladist, rhymester

trouble 3 ado, ail, irk, try, vex 4 care, cark, fret, fuss, pain 5 annoy, Dutch, harry, haunt, pains, rowel, trial, upset, while, worry 6 bother, bustle, effort, flurry, harass, kiaugh, pester, plague, pother, put out, strain, stress 7 afflict, agitate, disturb, intrude, perturb, torment 8 disquiet, distress, exertion, hardship, hot water, impose on, irritate, mischief, put about, vexation 9 disoblige, incommode 10 difficulty, discommode, discompose, disconcert, impose upon 11 bedevilment, elbow grease, predicament 13 inconvenience

troublemaker 6 heller 7 hellion, inciter 8 agitator, inflamer 10 instigator

troublesome 4 mean, ugly 5 pesky 6 vexing, wicked 7 painful 8 alarming, annoying 9 upsetting, vexatious 10 bothersome, disturbing 11 disquieting

troublous 4 mean, ugly 5 pesky 6 stormy, wicked 9 turbulent, vexatious

trough 3 hod 4 bowl, tank 5 basin, drain 6 manger, vessel 7 channel 9 container *combining form:* 5 bothr 6 bothro

trounce 4 beat, drub, rout, trim, whip 5 whomp 6 thrash, wallop 7 clobber, shellac 9 overwhelm

troupe 4 band 5 corps, party 6 outfit 7 company

trouper 4 mime 5 actor, mimic 6 mummer, player 7 artiste 8 thespian 9 performer, playactor 11 entertainer 12 impersonator

trousers 5 pants 6 slacks 8 britches *tartan:* 5 trews

trout *kind:* 3 sea 4 char, lake 5 brook, brown, river 7 rainbow 8 speckled 9 steelhead

Trovatore, Il *character:* 7 Azucena, Leonora, Manrico 11 Count di Luna *composer:* 5 Verdi (Giuseppe)

trove 5 hoard 9 amassment, colluvies 10 collection, cumulation 11 aggregation 12 accumulation 13 agglomeration

Troy 5 Ilium *epic of:* 5 Iliad *excavator:* 10 Schliemann (Heinrich) *founder:* 4 Ilus *modern site:* 9 Hissarlik; (see also Trojan)

truant 4 idle 7 shirker 8 shirking 13 irresponsible

truce 4 lull 5 letup, pause, peace 6 accord 7 respite 9 armistice, cease-fire

truck 3 van 4 swap 5 lorry, trade 6 barter, handle, peddle, retail 7 bargain, traffic 8 commerce, dealings, exchange *military:* 6 camion

truckers' communicators 3 CBs

truckle 3 tag 4 fawn, tail 5 cower, toady, trail 6 cringe, follow, grovel, kowtow 7 honey up, succumb 8 bootlick 11 applepolish

truckler 4 toad 5 toady 7 spaniel 8 lickspit 9 sycophant, toadeater 10 bootlicker, footlicker 11 lickspittle

truculent 4 fell, grim 5 cruel, harsh, rough, sharp 6 cowing, fierce, savage, severe 7 abusive, inhuman, scrappy, warlike, wolfish 8 bullying, inhumane, militant, scathing, scurrile 9 barbarous, bellicose, combative, ferocious, invective, trenchant, vitriolic 10 pugnacious, scurrilous, terrifying, vituperous 11 belligerent, browbeating, contentious, frightening, opprobrious, quarrelsome, terrorizing 12 contumelious, gladiatorial, intimidating, vituperative, vituperatory

trudge 4 plod, slog, slop, toil, trek 6 stodge 8 footslog, plunther

true 4 just, real, very 5 liege, loyal, right, sooth, valid 6 actual, ardent, honest, kosher, strict, trusty 7 factual, genuine, precise, staunch, unfaked, upright 8 accurate, bona fide, constant, faithful, resolute, rightful, unfabled 9 allegiant, authentic, honorable, steadfast, trustable, undoubted, unfeigned, veracious, veridical, veritable 10 creditable, dependable, legitimate, sureenough, undeniable 11 appropriate, indubitable, trustworthy, undesigning, undistorted 12 indisputable, undissembled 13 authoritative *combining form:* 2 eu 4 orth 5 ortho

true-blue 5 loyal 8 faithful 10 unswerving

truism 4 rule 5 axiom, gnome, maxim, moral 6 cliché, dictum, gospel, verity 7 brocard, bromide 8 aphorism, apothegm, veracity 9 platitude 10 shibboleth 11 commonplace

Truk Island 3 Tol 4 Moen, Udot, Uman 5 Fefan 6 Dublon

truly 3 yea 4 even, very, well 6 easily, indeed, really, surely, verily 7 de facto 8 actually 9 genuinely, veritably 10 absolutely, positively 11 confidently, doubtlessly, undoubtedly

Truman, Harry S *birthplace:* 5 Lamar (Missouri) *predecessor:* 3 FDR *successor:* 3 DDE

trump 3 cap, top 4 beat, best, pass, ruff 5 excel, outdo 6 better 7 manille, surpass 8 clincher, outstrip, spadille

trumpery 4 base, mean, poor 5 bilge, cheap, hokum 6 bunkum, bushwa, cheesy, common, paltry, shoddy, trashy 7 twaddle 8 claptrap, flimflam, malarkey, nonsense, rubbishy 10 double-talk

trumpet 4 horn, tout 6 herald 8 ballyhoo *call:* 6 sennet *ram's horn:* 6 shofar

trumpeter 4 Hirt (Al) 5 André (Maurice), Baker (Chet), Davis (Miles), James (Harry)

6 Alpert (Herb), Voisin (Roger) 7 Schwarz (Gerard) 8 Eldridge (Roy) 9 Armstrong (Louis), Gillespie (Dizzy) 10 McPartland (Jimmy)

truncate 3 lop, top 4 crop 5 shear 6 cut off 7 abridge, pollard 10 abbreviate

truncheon 3 bat 4 club, mace 5 billy 6 cudgel 8 bludgeon 9 billy club 10 knobkerrie, nightstick

trundle 3 bed, tub 4 bowl, cart, haul, push, roll 5 churn, wheel 6 lumber

trunk 3 box 4 body, case, stem 5 chest, torso 7 channel, circuit, luggage *elephant:* 9 proboscis *tree:* 4 bole

truss 3 tie 4 bind, pack 5 brace 7 support 9 supporter 10 strengthen

trust 4 care, hope, pool, rely, ward 5 chain, faith, group, lot on, stock 6 assume, bank on, belief, cartel, charge, commit, credit, rely on 7 build on, combine, confide, consign, count on, custody, keeping, presume 8 bank upon, credence, depend on, reckon on, reliance, rely upon, sureness 9 assurance, certainty, certitude, syndicate 10 confidence, conviction, dependence, depend upon 11 calculate on, safekeeping 12 conglomerate, guardianship, positiveness *Scottish:* 6 lippen

trustworthy 4 true 5 exact, tried, valid 6 honest, secure 7 upright 8 accurate, credible, faithful, reliable 9 authentic, realistic, veracious 10 convincing, dependable, scrupulous 12 tried and true 13 authoritative

trusty 4 firm 5 sound, tried 6 secure, stable 7 convict, turnkey 8 credible, faithful, reliable 9 authentic 10 convincing, dependable 11 predictable, responsible 12 tried and true

truth 5 axiom, maxim, sooth 6 candor, gospel, verity 7 lowdown, reality, veritas 8 veracity 9 precision, rightness 11 genuineness 12 authenticity, veridicality 13 veraciousness, veritableness *goddess:* 4 Maat *serum:* 11 scopolamine

truthful 4 real 5 frank 6 candid, honest 7 factual, sincere, veridic 8 accurate 9 realistic, veracious, veridical

truthfulness 5 truth 6 verity 8 veracity 12 veridicality 13 veraciousness

try 2 go 3 aim, irk, pop, vex 4 pain, rack, seek, shot, slap, stab, test 5 annoy, assay, check, crack, essay, exert, fling, offer, prove, trial, whack, whirl, wring 6 aspire, bother, harass, harrow, hassle, martyr, strain, stress, strive 7 afflict, agonize, attempt, crucify, test out, torment, torture, trouble 8 distress, endeavor, striving, struggle 9 undertake 10 excruciate, experiment

trying 5 rough, tight, tough 6 sticky, taxing, tricky, vexing 7 arduous, exigent, irk-

some, onerous, tricksy, weighty 8 annoying, exacting 9 demanding, strenuous 10 bothersome, burdensome, irritating, oppressive 11 troublesome

try out 8 audition

tryst 4 date 7 meeting 10 engagement, rendezvous 11 appointment, assignation

tsetse fly 8 glossina

tsunami 9 tidal wave

"____ tu"(aria) 3 Eri

tub 3 vat 4 bath, wash 5 keeve 6 shower 8 dumpling 10 butterball

tuba 7 helicon

Tubalcain *father:* 6 Lamech *mother:* 6 Zillah

Tubal's father 7 Japheth

tubby 5 plump, podgy, pudgy 6 chubby, plumpy, rotund 8 plumpish, roly-poly 10 roundabout

tube 2 TV 4 duct, hose, pipe 5 buret, pipet 6 siphon, subway, tunnel, vessel 7 burette, conduit, cuvette, pipette, syringe 8 pipe-line *anatomical:* 3 vas 4 duct, vasa (plural) 7 salpinx 9 salpinges (plural) *combining form:* 5 solen 6 siphon, soleno, syring 7 siphoni, siphono, syringo

tuber 4 bulb, corm, stem 6 potato 7 rhizome

tuberculosis 2 TB 8 phthisis 11 consumption, white plague

tuck 2 go 3 pep 4 birr, chow, eats, feed, food, grub, meat 5 bread, moxie, scoff, vigor 6 energy, viands 7 potency 9 hardihood, provender

tucker 4 poop, wilt 5 gruel 7 exhaust, frazzle, tire out, wear out 8 knock out 9 prostrate

tuft 5 clump, mound 7 cluster *combining form:* 4 loph 5 lophi, lopho 6 lophio *of feathers:* 7 panache *of hair:* 4 tate *ornamental:* 6 pompon *vascular:* 6 glomus

tufted 8 floccose

tug 3 lug, tow, war 4 drag, draw, haul, moil, pull, toil, work 5 drive, fight, labor 6 battle, oppugn, strain, strive 7 contend

tug-of-war 6 strife 7 contest, rivalry, warfare 8 conflict, striving 9 emulation 11 competition

tuition 8 teaching, training, tutelage 9 education, schooling 11 instruction

tumble 3 dip, hit 4 bump, down, drop, fall, fell, hash, hear, luck, mash, meet, skid, trip 5 floor, learn, level, light, mix up, pitch, snafu, upset 6 chance, foul up, go down, happen, jumble, litter, mess up, muddle, muss up, plunge, topple 7 catch on, clutter, confuse, descend, disturb, find out, flatten, overset, plummet, rummage, shuffle, snarl up, unearth, unhorse 8 bowl down, bowl over, come down, disarray, discover, disorder, keel over, mishmash, nose-dive, over-

turn, scramble, unsettle 9 ascertain, bring down, determine, knock down, knock over, overthrow 10 disarrange, discompose
tumbledown 7 rickety 10 ramshackle
tumbler 5 glass 11 cartwheeler
tumbrel 4 cart 5 wagon 7 vehicle 8 dumpcart
tumescent 6 turgid 7 aureate, bloated, bulging, flowery, swollen 8 dropsied, inflated, swelling 9 bombastic, dropsical, flatulent, overblown 10 euphuistic, rhetorical 12 magniloquent 13 grandiloquent
tumid see **tumescent**
tummy 3 gut 5 belly 6 paunch, venter 7 abdomen, stomach
tumor 3 wen 4 cyst 5 myoma 6 emerod, glioma, lipoma, myxoma 7 desmoid, emeroid, myeloma, neuroma, osteoma, sarcoma 8 blastoma, hepatoma, lymphoma, neoplasm, teratoma 9 carcinoma *benign:* 7 fibroid, fibroma *combining form:* 3 oma 4 cele, myom, onco 5 myomo, omato (plural), oncho 6 gangli 7 ganglio *hard:* 8 scirrhus *soft:* 5 gumma
tumult 3 din 4 flap, stew, to-do 5 babel, noise, whirl 6 clamor, dither, hassle, hubbub, jangle, lather, outcry, pother, racket, uproar, upturn 7 ferment, turmoil 8 disorder, paroxysm, seething, upheaval 9 agitation, commotion, confusion, maelstrom 10 convulsion, hullabaloo, hurly burly, turbulence 11 disturbance, pandemonium 12 unsettlement
tumultuous 5 rowdy 6 unruly 7 raucous 8 rowdyish 9 termagant, turbulent 10 boisterous, disorderly, rowdydowdy 11 rumbustious
tumulus 4 hill 5 mound 6 barrow 7 hillock
tun 3 keg, vat 4 butt, cask, pipe 6 barrel 8 hogshead
tuna 6 bonito 7 bluefin 8 albacore, dogtooth, skipjack 9 yellowfin
tune 3 air, fix, lay 4 dial, sing, sync 5 carol, chant, chime, order, range, synch 6 accord, adjust, chorus, extent, matter, melody, strain, warble 7 concert, concord, conform, descant, harmony, measure, melisma, melodia 8 diapason, regulate, vicinity, vocalize 9 agreement, harmonize, integrate, magnitude, reconcile 10 consonance, coordinate, proportion 11 accommodate, composition, concordance 12 neighborhood, reconciliate
tuneful 5 sweet, tuned 6 dulcet 7 lyrical, melodic, musical, songful 8 euphonic 9 melodious 10 euphonious 11 mellisonant
tungsten 7 wolfram
tunic 5 gipon, jupon 6 caftan, kaftan, kirtle *Greek:* 6 chiton
tunicate 4 salp 5 salpa 6 salpid 8 ascidian, doliolid 9 sea squirt

Tunisia *monetary unit:* 5 dinar *ruins:* 8 Carthage
tunnel 4 tube 6 burrow 7 conduit 8 crawlway *Alps:* 7 Simplon *France:* 4 Rove *Hudson river:* 7 Holland, Lincoln *Nevada:* 5 Sutro *railroad:* 6 Hoosac 7 Cascade
tunny 4 tuna 7 bluefin
Turandot *character:* 3 Liu 5 Calaf *composer:* 7 Puccini (Giacomo) *suitor:* 5 Calaf
turban 6 pugree 7 pugaree, puggree 8 bandanna, puggaree 9 headdress
turbid 4 dark 5 dense, mucky, muddy, murky, riley, roily, smoky, thick 6 cloudy, opaque 7 clouded, obscure
turbulence 3 din 4 flap, stew 5 babel, fight 6 dither, fracas, lather, pother, tumult, uproar 7 turmoil 9 agitation, commotion, confusion 10 unruliness 11 pandemonium
turbulent 4 fast, wild 5 roily, rough, rowdy 6 raging, stormy, unruly 7 boiling, furious, howling, moiling, raucous, riotous, roaring, ruffled 8 agitated, blustery, brawling, mutinous, rowdyish, stormful, swirling 9 clamorous, convulsed, stirred up, termagant 10 blustering, boisterous, disorderly, riproaring, roisterous, roughhouse, rowdydowdy, tumultuous 11 rumbustious, tempestuous, uninhibited 12 rambunctious 13 tempest-tossed
turf 3 sod 4 area 5 divot, track 6 region, sphere, swarth 7 terrain 9 racetrack, territory
turgid see **tumescent**
turkey *disease:* 9 blackhead *female:* 3 hen *head growth:* 5 snood 7 dewbill *male:* 3 tom 7 gobbler *throat pouch:* 6 wattle *young:* 5 poult
Turkey *capital:* 6 Ankara *largest city:* 8 Istanbul *monetary unit:* 4 lira 5 pound
turkey buzzard 4 aura
Turkey in the ____ 5 Straw
Turkish *empire:* 7 Ottoman *governor:* 4 vali *inn:* 6 imaret *music:* 9 janissary *palace:* 5 serai *province:* 7 vilayet *soldier:* 5 nizam 8 janizary 9 janissary *sultan:* 5 Ahmed, Selim 7 Bajazet, Bayezid, Ilderim *sword:* 8 yataghan *title:* 3 aga, bey 4 agha 5 pasha 6 vizier
turmeric 4 herb 5 spice 8 curcumin 9 bloodroot
turmoil 4 flap, moil, riot, stew, to-do 5 whirl 6 clamor, dither, hassle, hubbub, lather, pother, strife, tumult, unease, unrest, uproar 7 anxiety, ferment, garboil 8 disorder, disquiet, distress, upheaval 9 agitation, commotion, confusion 10 disruption, hurly burly, inquietude, turbulence, uneasiness 11 anxiousness, disquietude, jitteriness, nervousness, restiveness 12 restlessness 13 Sturm und Drang

turn 3 aim, yaw, zag, zig 4 bend, bias, bout, cast, eddy, grow, gyre, plow, reel, roll, sour, spin, swim, tack, tour, vary, veer, whip, wind 5 alter, angle, avert, curve, orbit, pivot, point, refer, round, sheer, shunt, spell, stint, swing, swirl, train, twirl, twist, upset, weave, whirl 6 become, change, circle, defect, desert, detour, direct, divert, gyrate, hang on, invert, modify, mutate, obvert, plow up, render, repair, resort, revert, rotate, sicken, sprain, switch, swivel, wrench, zero in, zigzag 7 circuit, convert, deflect, derange, deviate, digress, diverge, flexure, hinge on, inverse, passade, reflect, reverse, revolve 8 disorder, flection, gyration, mutation, renounce, reversal, rotation, unsettle 9 about-face, deviation, oscillate, pirouette, rechannel, refashion, repudiate, reversion, sidetrack, translate, transpose, variation, volte-face 10 alteration, apostatize, change into, circumduct, deflection, double back, revolution, right-about, tergiverse, transplace 11 changeabout, reversement 12 modification, tergiversate *combining form:* 4 trop 5 trope, tropy 6 tropic 7 trophic, tropism, tropous *to stone:* 8 lapidify

turnabout 3 rat 6 coward 7 quitter, reverse 8 apostate, defector, recreant, renegade, reversal, runagate 9 about-face, reversion, volte-face 10 backslider, right-about 11 changeabout, reversement 13 tergiversator

turn aside or away 4 skew, veer, ward 5 avert, shunt 6 divert 7 deflect, shuttle

turn back 5 react, recur, repel 6 return, revert 10 recrudesce

turncoat 3 rat, spy 7 quisler, traitor 8 apostate, betrayer, defector, deserter, quisling, recreant, renegade, runagate 9 straggler, turnabout 13 tergiversator

turn down 4 veto 5 spurn 6 refuse, reject 7 decline, dismiss 9 reprobate, repudiate 10 disapprove

turned on 4 high 5 doped 6 stoned, zonked 7 drugged 8 hopped-up 9 spaced-out 10 tripped out

turn in 3 bed 5 rat on 6 betray, retire 7 deliver, produce 8 hand over, inform on

turning point 4 crux 5 pivot 6 climax, crisis 8 landmark

turnip 5 swede 8 rutabaga *Scottish:* 4 neep

turnip-shaped 8 napiform

turn left 3 haw

Turn of the Screw, The *author:* 5 James (Henry) *character:* 5 Flora, Miles 10 Peter Quint *composer:* 7 Britten (Benjamin)

turn over 4 feed, find, give, hand, muse, plow, roll 5 break, upset 6 assign, commit, give up, plow up, ponder, supply, topple 7 commend, confide, consign, deliver, entrust, furnish, overset, provide, revolve 8 delegate, meditate, ruminate, transfer 9 overthrow 10 deliberate, relinquish

turnpike 4 road 7 highway, tollway 8 toll road

turn right 3 gee

turn up 3 get 4 come, espy, find, show, spot 5 catch, get in, hit on, pop in, reach 6 appear, arrive, descry, detect, louden, roll in, show up 7 hit upon, uncover, unearth 8 meet with 9 encounter, track down 11 materialize

Turnus *beloved:* 7 Lavinia *slayer:* 6 Aeneas

turpentine 7 galipot, solvent, thinner *ingredient:* 6 pinene *tree:* 4 pine 9 terebinth

turret 5 tower 8 bartizan

turtle 8 terrapin, tortoise 9 chelonian *edible part:* 7 calipee 8 calipash *sea:* 6 ridley 8 hawkbill *shell:* 8 carapace *shell part:* 8 plastron

Tuscany *city:* 4 Pisa 8 Florence *river:* 4 Arno *tower:* 4 Pisa *wine:* 7 chianti

tusk 4 fang 5 ivory, tooth

tussle 4 spar 5 scrap 6 hassle 7 grapple, scuffle, wrestle 8 skirmish

tutelage see tuition

tutor 5 coach, teach 6 docent, mentor 7 teacher 9 pedagogue 10 instructor

Tut's tomb discoverer 6 Carter (Howard)

TV see television

twaddle 3 jaw, yak 4 bosh, chat 5 clack, drool, prate, run on 6 babble, dither, drivel, gabble, hot air 7 blabber, blather, chatter, prattle 8 claptrap, malarkey, nonsense, tommyrot, wish-wash 9 poppycock 10 balderdash

Twain biographer 5 Paine (Albert)

tweak 3 jog 4 jerk, pull 5 pinch 6 snatch, twitch

Twelfth Night character 5 Maria, Viola 6 Olivia 8 Malvolio 9 Sebastian, Toby Belch

twelve *combining form:* 5 dodec 6 dodeca

twenty *combining form:* 4 icos 5 icosa, icosi

twerp 4 brat, fool, jerk 5 sprat 6 squirt 7 upstart

twibil 2 ax 3 axe 8 battle-ax 9 battle-axe

twice 3 bis 7 twofold *combining form:* 2 di 3 bis *prefix:* 2 bi 3 dis

twice a day 3 b.i.d. 8 bis in die

twice a year 8 biannual

Twice-Told Tales author 9 Hawthorne (Nathaniel)

twig 5 shoot, sprig 6 branch *bundle of:* 5 fagot 6 faggot

twiggy 4 slim, thin 5 reedy 6 slight, stalky 7 slender, squinny, tenuous 9 attenuate

twilight 3 end, eve 4 dusk 5 gloom 6 sunset 8 gloaming, glooming, owl light 9 attenuate, nightfall

Twilight of the Gods 8 Ragnarok

twill 5 cloth, serge, weave 6 fabric 9 gabardine 11 herringbone

twin 4 dual, like, mate 5 match 6 bifold, binary, double, fellow, paired 7 matched, similar, twofold 8 matching 9 companion, duplicate, identical 10 coordinate, reciprocal *combining form:* 5 didym 6 didymo

Twin Cities 6 St. Paul 11 Minneapolis

twine 4 coil, curl, wind 5 twist 6 enmesh, spiral, tangle 7 entwine, wreathe 8 entangle 9 corkscrew 10 interweave

twinge 4 ache, pain, pang 5 throe 6 stitch

twinkle 3 bat 4 wink 5 blink, flash, gleam, glint, light, shake, shine, trice 6 minute, moment, second 7 flicker, glimmer, glisten, glitter, instant, light up, nictate, shimmer, sparkle 9 coruscate, nictitate, twinkling 10 illuminate 11 coruscation, scintillate, split second 13 scintillation

twin stars 6 Castor, Pollux

twirl 4 gyre, spin 5 whirl 6 gyrate 9 pirouette, whirligig

twist 3 wry 4 coil, curl, kink, slub, turn, warp, wind, wisp 5 belie, color, gnarl, pivot, quirk, thraw, twine, wring 6 garble, intort, spiral, sprain, squirm, torque, widdle, wrench, writhe 7 contort, distort, entwine, falsify, intwine, pervert, wreathe, wriggle 8 miscolor, misstate, squiggle 9 corkscrew 12 misrepresent *combining form:* 4 spir 5 spiri, spiro

twisted 3 wry 4 awry 5 askew 6 knurly, thrawn, warped 7 tortile

twister 7 cyclone, tornado 9 whirlwind

twit 4 jive, josh, lout, mock, quiz, razz 5 blame, chide, rally, scout, taunt, tease 6 deride 7 censure, reprove 8 reproach, ridicule 9 reprehend

twitch 3 lug, nip, tic 4 jerk, snap, yank 5 grasp, lurch, pinch, pluck, tweak 6 clutch, snatch 9 vellicate

twitter 3 gab, jaw 4 chat, chip, peep 5 cheep, chirp, quake, run on, shake, tweet 6 babble, cackle, dither, quaver, quiver, rattle, shiver, tremor 7 chatter, chipper, chirrup, chitter, prattle, shudder, tremble, tweedle

twittery 5 jumpy, nervy 6 goosey, spooky 7 fidgety, jittery, nervous 9 flustered 10 high-strung

two 3 duo 4 duet, pair 5 twain 6 couple *combining form:* 2 dy 3 bis, duo, dyo *divide into:* 4 fork 6 bisect 9 bifurcate *prefix:* 2 bi 3 twi

twofold 4 dual, twin 5 binal, duple 6 binary, double, duplex, dyadic, paired 9 dualistic *combining form:* 2 di 4 dipl 5 diphy, diplo 6 diphyo

Two Gentlemen of Verona *character:* 5 Julia 6 Silvia, Thurio 7 Proteus 9 Valentine

two-horned 10 bicornuate

twosome 3 duo 4 dyad, pair 5 brace 6 couple 7 doublet

two-time 5 bluff 6 delude, humbug, illude, juggle, take in 7 beguile, deceive, mislead 11 double-cross

two-wheeler 4 bike 5 cycle 7 bicycle, scooter 10 velocipede

two-winged 9 dipterous

Two Years Before the Mast *author* 4 Dana (Richard Henry)

Tybalt *cousin:* 6 Juliet *family:* 7 Capulet *slayer:* 5 Romeo *victim:* 8 Mercutio

Tyche *goddess of:* 7 fortune

tycoon 4 czar, king 5 baron, mogul, nabob 6 prince 7 magnate

tyke 3 dog 5 child, hound 6 canine 7 mongrel

tympanum 7 eardrum 9 middle ear

Tyndareus *kingdom:* 6 Sparta *wife:* 4 Leda

type 3 cut, ilk, lot, way 4 cast, form, kind, mold, sort 5 breed, class, genre, order, print, serif, stamp 6 kidney, nature, stripe 7 feather, species, variety 8 category 9 character 10 persuasion 11 description *bar:* 4 slug *combining form:* 5 morph 6 morpho *jumbled:* 2 pi 3 pie *measure:* 2 em, en 4 pica 5 point *set:* 7 compose *setter:* 10 compositor *size:* 4 pica 5 agate, pearl *stroke:* 5 serif *style:* 5 roman 6 Gothic, italic 7 Fraktur 8 boldface, sanserif 9 lightface, sans serif *tray:* 6 galley

Typee *author:* 8 Melville (Herman) *character:* 4 Toby

typewriter *part:* 3 key 6 platen, spacer *type size:* 4 pica 5 elite

Typhon 3 Set 7 monster 8 Typhoeus *offspring:* 6 Sphinx 7 Chimera 8 Cerberus, Chimaera *wife:* 7 Echidna

typhoon 9 hurricane 13 tropical storm

typical 5 ideal, model, usual 6 common, normal, old hat 7 classic, general, natural, regular 9 exemplary, prevalent 11 commonplace

typical of *suffix:* 2 ic, ly 3 ish, ist 4 ical 5 istic 7 istical

typify 6 embody, mirror 9 body forth, epitomize, exemplify, personify, represent, symbolize 10 illustrate 11 emblematize

typo 5 error 8 misprint
typographer 7 printer 10 compositor
Tyr 3 Tiu *brother:* 4 Thor *father:* 4 Odin
  god of: 3 war *mother:* 5 Jordh, Jorth
tyrannical 5 harsh 6 brutal 8 absolute,
  despotic 9 arbitrary, autarchic, roughshod
  10 autocratic, monocratic, oppressive
tyrannize 5 crush 7 dictate, oppress,
  shackle, trample 8 dominate, domineer,
  overlord 9 despotize, terrorize
tyrannous 6 lordly 8 absolute, despotic
  9 arbitrary, autarchic, fascistic 10 autocratic, monocratic 12 totalitarian

tyranny 7 fascism 8 totality 9 autocracy,
  despotism, terrorism 10 absolutism, domination, oppression 12 dictatorship
tyrant 4 duce 6 despot 8 autocrat, dictator
  9 oppressor, strong man 12 totalitarian
Tyrian ___ 6 purple
tyro 4 colt 6 novice, rookie 7 amateur,
  dabbler 8 beginner, freshman, neophyte,
  newcomer 9 novitiate, smatterer
  10 apprentice, dilettante, tenderfoot, uninitiate 11 abecedarian
Tyrol see Tirol
Tzar see czar

U

übermensch 7 overman 8 superman
ubiquitous 7 allover 9 universal
  10 everywhere 11 omnipresent
Uel's father 4 Bani
Uganda *capital:* 7 Kampala *monetary
  unit:* 8 shilling
ugly 3 bad, low 4 base, dour, fell, foul,
  glum, mean, ugly, vile 5 awful, cross,
  grave, major, pesky, plain, sulky, surly,
  toady 6 cranky, gloomy, homely, morose,
  sordid, sullen, wicked 7 bizarre, crabbed,
  hideous, ignoble, low-down, serious, servile, vicious 8 grievous, gruesome,
  uncomely, unlovely, wretched 9 dangerous,
  grotesque, repelling, repugnant, repulsive,
  saturnine, troublous, unsightly, vexatious
  10 despicable, ill-favored, ill-looking, unin-
  viting, unpleasing 11 ill-tempered, threatening, troublesome, unbeautiful 12 unattractive
Ugly Duckling author 8 Andersen
  (Hans Christian)
ugni blanc 4 wine 9 Trebbiano
ukase 5 edict, order 6 decree, ruling
  7 command 9 directive 12 proclamation
Ukraine *capital:* 4 Kiev *folk dance:*
  5 gopak *soldier:* 7 cossack
Ulalume author 3 Poe (Edgar Allan)
Ulam's father 5 Eshek
ulcer 4 sore *kind:* 6 peptic 8 duodenal
  mouth: 10 canker sore
uliginous 3 wet 4 damp, oozy 5 moist,
  muddy 6 swampy
ulna 5 cubit 7 cubitus, forearm
Ulrica 5 sibyl, sybil, witch

Ulster hero 4 Emer, Medb 5 Cu Roi,
  Etain, Noisi 6 Ailill, Fergus 7 Cathbad, Con-
  aire, Da Derga, Deirdre 8 MacDatho
  9 Conchobar, Cuchullin, Finnabair
  10 Cuchulainn
ulterior 4 dark 5 later, privy 6 buried,
  covert, future, hidden, latent 7 cryptic, further, guarded, obscure, remoter, thither
  8 obscured, shrouded 9 ambiguous, concealed, enigmatic, equivocal 10 subsequent, succeeding 11 undisclosed
ultimate 3 end, lag 4 dire, last 5 basic,
  close, final, grand, lofty 6 finish, latest, latter, utmost, wind up, wrap up 7 closing,
  epitome, exalted, extreme, maximum, sublime, supreme 8 absolute, complete, conclude, earliest, empyreal, empyrean, eventual, farthest, hindmost, last word, original,
  terminal, towering 9 determine, elemental,
  terminate 10 apotheosis, concluding, consummate, preeminent, surpassing 11 categorical, fundamental, unequalable, unmatchable 12 incomparable, quintessence,
  transcendent 13 unsurpassable
ultimatum 5 order 6 demand, threat
ultra 5 kinky, outré, rabid 6 beyond, far-out
  7 extreme, fanatic, forward, radical
  9 excessive, extremist, fanatical 10 outlandish 11 extravagant
ultraconservative 4 tory 5 blimp, white
  7 Bourbon, diehard 8 royalist 9 right-wing
  11 reactionary, reactionist 13 reactionarist
ultraist 5 rabid 7 extreme, fanatic, radical
  9 extremist
ultramarine 7 new blue, oversea 8 over-

seas **10** French blue **11** lapis lazuli, trans-marine

ululate 3 bay **4** hoot, howl, wail, yelp **5** quest **6** bewail, lament **7** screech

Ulysses *author:* **5** Joyce (James) *character:* **5** Bloom, Molly **6** Boylan **7** Dedalus (Stephen); (see also **Odysseus**)

umber 5 brown, shade **6** darken, shadow **8** grayling **9** hammerkop

umbilicus 4 core **5** heart, hilum, navel *combining form:* **6** omphal **7** omphalo

umbra 4 fish **5** ghost, shade **6** shadow **7** eidolon, phantom **8** darkness, phantasm, revenant **10** apparition

umbrage 3 ire **4** fury, huff, miff, rage **5** anger, doubt, pique, shade, trace, umbra, wrath **6** enrage, irking, madden, offend, screen, shadow **7** dudgeon, foliage, incense, leafage, offense, pretext, steam up, verdure **8** nettling, vexation **9** annoyance, infuriate, provoking, semblance, suspicion **10** irritation, resentment **11** displeasure **12** exasperation

umbrageous 5 shady **6** shaded, shadow **7** shadowy **8** shadowed **9** resentful **11** belligerent

umbrella 5 guard, shade **6** brolly, pileus, screen **7** parasol, shelter **10** protection **11** bumbershoot *large:* **4** gamp

umbrous 5 shady **6** shaded, shadow **7** shadowy **8** shadowed

umph see **oomph**

umpire 5 judge **7** adjudge, arbiter, referee **9** arbitrate **10** adjudicate, arbitrator *call:* **3** out **4** balk, ball, safe **6** strike

unabashed 6 arrant, brassy, brazen **7** blatant **8** impudent, overbold **9** barefaced, shameless **10** unblushing **11** brazenfaced

unabbreviated see **unabridged**

unable 8 helpless, impotent **9** incapable **11** incompetent, inefficient, unqualified **13** incapacitated

unabridged 5 uncut, whole **6** entire, intact **8** complete, undocked **11** uncondensed, whole-length **13** unabbreviated

unacceptable 4 poor **7** boorish **8** below par, unwanted **9** unwelcome **10** ill-favored, unpleasing, unsuitable **11** undesirable **12** inadmissible **13** below standard, exceptionable, objectionable

unaccompanied 4 bare, sole **5** alone, apart **6** single **7** isolate, removed **8** detached, isolated

unaccomplished 7 jackleg **8** dabbling, ungifted **9** unskilled **10** amateurish, dilettante, incomplete, unfinished **12** dilettantish, dilettantist

unaccountable 6 arcane, mystic **7** strange **8** numinous **9** mysterial, unguessed **10** cabalistic, mysterious,

unknowable **11** inscrutable **12** impenetrable, inexplicable, unfathomable **13** inexplainable, irresponsible, unexplainable

unaccustomed 3 new **6** unused **7** strange **8** uncommon **10** unfamiliar

unacquainted 7 strange, unaware, unusual **8** ignorant **9** oblivious, unknowing, unwitting **10** unfamiliar, uninformed **11** incognizant **12** inconversant, uninstructed **13** inexperienced

unacquired 6 inborn, innate, native **7** connate, natural **9** inherited **10** congenital, connatural, indigenous

unadorned 3 dry **4** bald, bare **5** naked, plain, stark **6** rustic, simple **7** austere **11** undecorated, unelaborate, ungarnished **12** unbeautified, unornamented **13** unembellished, unembroidered, unpretentious

unadulterated 4 neat, pure **5** plain, sheer **6** honest, simple **7** genuine, perfect, sincere, unmixed **8** absolute, straight **9** unalloyed, undiluted **11** unmitigated, unqualified

unadvisable see **inadvisable**

unaffable 7 aseptic **8** retiring **9** shrinking, withdrawn **10** restrained **11** unexpansive

unaffected 4 easy, real **5** naive, plain **6** rustic, simple **7** artless, natural, sincere **9** ingenuous, unstudied, untouched, untutored **10** unschooled **12** unartificial, uninfluenced

unafraid 4 bold, cool, sure **5** brave **7** assured, defiant, valiant **8** composed, fearless, intrepid, valorous **9** audacious, confident, dauntless, undaunted **10** courageous **13** imperturbable

unaimed 6 random **7** aimless **9** desultory, haphazard, hit-or-miss, unplanned **10** designless **11** purposeless **12** unconsidered

unalike 7 distant, diverse, unequal, various **9** different, disparate, divergent, unsimilar **10** dissimilar

unalloyed 4 deep, pure **5** sheer, solid **6** simple, virgin **7** genuine, perfect, unmixed **8** absolute **9** undiluted **11** unmitigated, unqualified **13** unadulterated

unalluring 5 plain **6** homely **8** uncomely, unpretty **10** unhandsome **11** unbeauteous, unbeautiful **12** unattractive

unalterable see **inalterable**

unambiguous 5 clear, lucid, plain **6** patent **7** crystal, evident, express, obvious **8** apparent, clean-cut, clear-cut, definite, distinct, explicit, luminous, manifest, palpable, pellucid, specific **9** unblurred **10** definitive **11** categorical, translucent, transparent **12** transpicuous

unanimated 4 cold, dead, dull, flat **5** vapid **6** asleep **7** insipid

unanimous 5 solid 6 agreed, united 8 agreeing, univocal 10 concordant, concurrent, harmonious 11 consentient 13 consentaneous

unanimously 5 as one

unappeasable 4 grim 6 mortal 8 ruthless 9 insatiate, merciless, unsatiate 10 implacable, insatiable, ironfisted, quenchless, relentless, unyielding 11 unflinching, unrelenting 12 unquenchable 13 unsatisfiable

unappetizing 4 flat 7 insipid 8 unsavory 9 savorless, tasteless 10 flavorless 11 distasteful, ill-flavored, unpalatable 12 unattractive 13 uninteresting

unappreciative 9 thankless 10 ungrateful, unthankful

unapproachable 5 aloof 6 offish 7 distant, stately 8 reserved 9 unbending, withdrawn 10 insociable, unsociable 11 standoffish, ungetatable, unreachable 12 inaccessible, unattainable

unarm see **disarm**

unarmed 4 bare 5 inerm 8 unbarbed 11 defenseless *combining form:* 5 anopl 6 anoplo

unartful 5 naive 6 simple 7 artless, natural 9 ingenuous, unstudied 10 unaffected, unschooled 12 unartificial

unarticulate see **inarticulate**

unasked 5 unbid 6 wanton 8 arrogant, impudent, unbidden, unsought, unwanted 9 uninvited, unwelcome, voluntary 10 gratuitous 11 overbearing, spontaneous, uncalled-for, unrequested 12 presumptuous, supererogant, unacceptable

unassailable 5 stout, tough 6 secure, strong, sturdy 8 stalwart 9 tenacious 10 invincible, unbeatable 11 impregnable, indomitable 12 inexpugnable, invulnerable, undefeatable 13 inconquerable, unconquerable

unassertive 3 shy 4 meek 5 timid 6 modest 7 bashful, rabbity 8 backward, retiring 9 diffident, unassured 12 self-effacing

unassuming 3 shy 4 meek 5 lowly 6 humble, modest, simple 7 natural 8 retiring

unassured 3 shy 5 timid 6 modest, unsafe, unsure 7 bashful, rabbity 8 backward, insecure, retiring 9 diffident 10 unreliable 11 unassertive, unconfident 12 self-effacing, undependable 13 untrustworthy

unattached 4 free 5 loose 6 single 9 unmarried

unattractive 4 rude, ugly 5 plain 6 homely 8 frumpish, uncomely, unpretty 9 unlikable 10 unalluring, ungracious, unhandsome, unlikeable 11 unbeauteous, unbeautiful

unauthentic 7 bastard 8 spurious 9 ungenuine 10 apocryphal

unavailing 4 vain 6 futile 7 useless 8 abortive, bootless, gainless 9 fruitless 11 ineffective, ineffectual 12 unproductive

unavoidable 7 certain 9 necessary 10 ineludible, inevasible, inevitable, returnless, unevadable 11 ineluctable, inescapable, unescapable

unavoidably 8 perforce 10 helplessly, inevitably, willy-nilly 11 inescapably, whether or no

unaware 5 aback, short 6 sudden 7 unready 8 ignorant, suddenly 9 oblivious, unknowing, unwitting 10 unfamiliar, uninformed, unprepared 11 incognizant 12 inconversant, unacquainted, unexpectedly, uninstructed

unawares 5 aback, short 8 suddenly 12 unexpectedly

unbalance 5 craze 6 frenzy, lunacy, madden 7 derange, madness, unhinge 8 distract, insanity 10 aberration, alienation, insaneness 11 derangement, distraction, instability, psychopathy

unbalanced 3 mad 4 daft 5 batty, wacky 6 crazed, insane, uneven 7 unequal, unsound 8 demented, deranged, lopsided 9 irregular 10 asymmetric 13 unsymmetrical

unbeautiful 4 ugly 5 plain 6 homely 7 hideous 8 uncomely, unpretty 9 unsightly 10 ill-favored, ill-looking, unalluring, unhandsome 12 unattractive

unbecoming 4 rude 5 inapt, inept, rough, undue 6 clumsy, gauche, indign, unmeet 7 awkward, beneath, ungodly 8 improper, indecent, uncomely, unseemly, untimely, untoward, unworthy 9 incorrect, inelegant, maladroit 10 indecorous, indelicate, malapropos, malodorous, undecorous, unsuitable 11 disgraceful, unbefitting 12 unattractive, unseasonable 13 inappropriate

unbefitting see **unbecoming**

unbelievable 4 thin, weak 5 thick 6 flimsy 8 fabulous 9 fantastic 10 improbable, incredible 11 implausible, incogitable, unthinkable 12 insupposable, unconvincing, unimaginable 13 inconceivable, unsubstantial

unbeliever 5 pagan 6 giaour 7 atheist, doubter, heretic, infidel, scoffer, skeptic, zetetic 8 agnostic 10 headshaker, Pyrrhonian, Pyrrhonist 11 free-thinker

unbelieving 6 show-me 8 aporetic, doubting 9 quizzical, skeptical 11 distrusting, incredulous, questioning 12 disbelieving

unbending 5 aloof, rigid, stern, stiff 6 offish 7 distant 8 obdurate, reserved, resolute 9 impliable, inelastic, withdrawn 10 brassbound, inexorable, inflexible, insociable, relentless, unflexible, unsociable, unswayable, unyielding 11 immalleable, incompliant, standoffish 12 single-minded

unbiased 4 fair, just 5 aloof, equal 8 detached, tolerant 9 equitable, impartial, objective, uncolored 12 uninterested, unprejudiced 13 dispassionate

unbidden 7 unasked 8 unsought 9 uninvited 11 unrequested

unbind 4 free, undo 5 loose, unfix, untie 6 detach, loosen, ungird 7 absolve, deliver, manumit, release, unchain, unloose 8 dissolve, liberate, unfasten, unloosen, unswathe 9 discharge, disengage, unshackle 10 emancipate

unblamable 4 good, pure 8 innocent, virtuous 9 exemplary, guiltless, righteous 10 inculpable

unblemished 4 pure 5 clean, sound, whole 6 chaste, decent, intact, modest, unhurt 7 perfect 8 flawless, spotless, unmarred 9 stainless, undamaged, undefiled, uninjured, unsullied 10 immaculate, unimpaired

unblock 3 ope 4 open, undo 6 unshut, unstop 7 unclose

unblunted 4 keen 5 honed, sharp 7 whetted 10 razor-sharp

unblurred 5 clear, lucid 7 crystal 8 clearcut, luminous, pellucid 11 translucent, transparent, unambiguous 12 transpicuous

unbolt 4 open 5 unbar, unpin 6 loosen, unlock 8 unfasten

unbosom 4 open, tell 6 betray, reveal, unveil 7 divulge, unclose, uncover 8 disclose, discover 9 uncurtain

unbound 4 free 5 loose 10 unconfined, unfastened

unbounded 4 huge, open 7 endless 8 infinite 9 boundless, limitless, unchecked, unlimited 10 indefinite, unmeasured 11 measureless 12 immeasurable, uncontrolled, unrestrained

unbridled 4 free 5 loose 7 violent 9 dissolute, unchecked 10 licentious, ungoverned 11 uninhibited 12 uncontrolled, unrestrained

unbroken 3 one 5 solid, sound, whole 6 entire, intact, single, unhurt 7 perfect, untamed 8 straight, unmarred, unplowed 9 continual, undamaged, undivided, uninjured, unsubdued 10 continuous, unimpaired 13 uninterrupted

unburden 3 rid 4 ease, lose 5 clear, empty 6 unload 7 relieve 8 shake off, throw off 9 discharge 11 disencumber

uncalled-for 4 rude 5 silly 6 absurd, wanton 7 foolish, incivil, unasked, uncivil 8 baseless, impolite, needless, unneeded 9 intrusive, officious, unfounded, unneedful

10 bottomless, gratuitous, groundless, ungracious, ungrounded, unrequired 11 disgracious, ill-mannered, impertinent, inessential, unessential, unnecessary, unwarranted 12 discourteous, preposterous, supererogant 13 disrespectful

uncanny 4 eery 5 eerie, scary, weird 6 creepy, spooky 7 ghostly, strange 9 unearthly, unnatural 10 mysterious, superhuman 11 supernormal, supranormal 12 supernatural 13 superordinary

uncared-for 7 run-down 8 untended 9 neglected

uncareful 4 wild 8 feckless, reckless 10 incautious 13 irresponsible

uncaring 8 feckless, heedless 9 oblivious, unheeding, unrecking 10 unthinking 11 inadvertent, thoughtless 12 irreflective, unreflective

unceasing 7 endless, eternal 8 constant, unending 9 ceaseless, continual, incessant, perpetual 10 continuous 11 everlasting, unremitting 12 interminable 13 uninterrupted

unceremonious 4 curt 5 bluff, blunt, sharp, short 6 abrupt 8 familiar, informal 9 irregular 10 ungracious, unofficial 11 thoughtless 13 inconsiderate

uncertain 4 asea, dark, hazy, iffy, moot, open 5 fluky, vague 6 chancy, fickle, fitful, queasy, shifty, unsure, wobbly 7 dubious, erratic, halting, mutable, obscure, protean, suspect, unclear 8 aleatory, arguable, doubtful, flickery, hesitant, insecure, mootable, slippery, ticklish, unstable, unsteady, variable, volatile 9 ambiguous, debatable, equivocal, faltering, fluctuant, mercurial, sibylline, tenebrous, tentative, undecided, unsettled, whimsical 10 borderline, capricious, changeable, disputable, inconstant, indecisive, indefinite, irresolute, lubricious, precarious, unexplicit 11 problematic, vacillating, vacillatory 12 incalculable, questionable, undependable, unexpectable, wigglewaggle 13 indeterminate, problematical, temperamental, unforeseeable, unpredictable, untrustworthy

uncertainty 5 doubt, maybe, query, worry 6 bother, gamble, wonder 7 anxiety, concern, dubiety, reserve, trouble 8 disfaith, disquiet, distress, distrust, mistrust, suspense 9 agitation, dubiosity, dubitancy, suspicion 10 hesitation, skepticism, uneasiness 12 doubtfulness, perturbation

unchain 4 free 5 loose 6 loosen, unbind 7 manumit, release 8 liberate 9 discharge, unshackle 10 emancipate

unchangeable 4 fast 5 fixed 7 eternal 8 constant 9 immovable, immutable, unmovable 10 inflexible, invariable 11 inalterable, unalterable 12 unmodifiable

unchanging 4 even, same 6 stable, static, steady 7 equable, eternal, forever, settled, stabile, uniform 8 constant 9 immutable, steadfast, unfailing, unvarying 10 consistent, invariable, stationary 13 unfluctuating

unchaste 4 easy, fast, lewd 5 bawdy, dirty, light, loose 6 coarse, impure, wanton 7 haggard, immoral, obscene, scarlet, unclean 9 uncleanly

unchecked 4 free 5 loose 7 rampant 9 unbounded, unbridled 11 uninhibited

uncivil 4 rude, wild 5 crass, crude, rough 6 brutal, coarse, crusty, Gothic, rugged, savage 7 Hunnish, ill-bred, incivil 8 barbaric, clownish, impolite 9 barbarian, barbarous 10 indecorous, ungracious, unsuitable 11 disgracious, ill-mannered, impertinent, uncivilized, uncourteous 12 discourteous, uncultivated 13 disrespectful

uncivilized 4 rude, wild 6 brutal, Gothic, Hunnic, rugged, savage, unholy, wicked 7 boorish, Hunnish, ill-bred, loutish, low-bred, ungodly 8 barbaric, churlish, cloddish 9 barbarian, barbarous, unrefined 10 outrageous, uncultured, unmannerly, unpolished 12 uncultivated 13 unenlightened

unclad see **unclothed**

uncle *Dutch:* 3 oom *Scottish:* 3 eme *Spanish:* 3 tio

unclean 4 foul, tref, vile 5 black, dirty, nasty, soily 6 common, filthy, grubby, impure 7 defiled, immoral, obscene, squalid 8 polluted, profaned, unchaste 10 desecrated 11 unwholesome

unclear 3 dim 4 hazy, open 6 bleary, blurry, opaque, unsure 7 dubious, obscure, shadowy, suspect 8 doubtful, nebulose, nebulous 9 ambiguous, equivocal, tenebrous, uncertain, undefined, unsettled 10 ill-defined, indistinct, unexplicit 11 problematic

Uncle Remus creator 6 Harris (Joel Chandler)

Uncle Tom's Cabin *author:* 5 Stowe (Harriet Beecher) *character:* 5 Eliza, Topsy 6 Legree (Simon) 9 Little Eva

Uncle Vanya author 7 Chekhov (Anton)

uncloak 6 debunk, expose, show up, unmask 7 undress 8 discover, unshroud

unclothe 5 strip 6 denude, devest, divest, expose, reveal, unveil 7 display, disrobe, uncloak, uncover, undress 8 disclose 10 dishabillé

unclothed 3 raw 4 nude 5 naked 6 unclad 8 buff-bare, stripped 9 au naturel, undressed 10 stark-naked

unclouded 4 fair, fine, open 5 clear, sunny 7 clarion 8 pleasant, rainless, sunshiny 10 undarkened

uncluttered 4 neat, snug, tidy, trig, trim 7 chipper, orderly 9 shipshape 11 spic-and-span, well-groomed 12 spick-and-span

uncolored 4 fair, just 5 equal 8 unbiased 9 equitable, impartial, objective 12 unprejudiced 13 dispassionate

uncombed 5 messy 6 sloppy, unneat, untidy 7 unkempt 8 ill-kempt, slipshod, slovenly 10 disheveled 12 unfastidious

uncombine 4 free, part 5 loose, sever 6 divide, sunder 7 disjoin 8 disjoint, dissever, disunite, separate 11 dichotomize

uncomely 4 ugly 5 inapt, inept, plain, undue 6 homely 7 hideous 8 improper, indecent, unpretty, untimely 9 unsightly 10 ill-favored, ill-looking, malapropos, unalluring, unbecoming, unhandsome, unsuitable 11 unbeauteous, unbeautiful, unbefitting 12 unattractive 13 inappropriate

uncomfortable 4 sick 5 harsh 6 queasy, uneasy 7 prickly 8 easeless, scratchy 11 distressing 13 disconcerting

uncommon 3 few, odd 4 rare 5 novel 6 choice, scarce, seldom, unique 7 special, strange, unusual 8 esoteric, especial, singular, sporadic, unwonted 10 infrequent, occasional, remarkable, unfrequent, unordinary 11 exceptional, unthinkable 12 unaccustomed, unimaginable 13 extraordinary

uncommunicative 4 dumb 5 aloof, close 6 offish, silent 7 distant, private 8 reserved, reticent, taciturn 9 unbending, withdrawn 10 insociable, unsociable 11 close-lipped, standoffish, tight-lipped 12 closemouthed, close-tongued, tight-mouthed

uncompassionate 5 stony 7 callous 8 obdurate 9 heartless, unfeeling 10 hard-boiled 11 coldhearted, hardhearted, unemotional 12 stony-hearted 13 unsympathetic

uncompliant 5 rigid 8 obdurate 9 untending 10 brassbound, inexorable, inflexible, unswayable, unyielding 12 single-minded

uncomplicated 5 basic, plain 6 honest, simple 10 elementary

uncomplimentary 9 slighting 10 derogatory, detracting, pejorative 11 disparaging, dyslogistic 12 depreciative, depreciatory

uncomprehensible see **incomprehensible**

uncompromising 4 firm 5 rigid, stern, tough 6 strict 7 extreme 8 hard-line, obdurate 9 unbending 10 brassbound, determined, inexorable, inflexible, relentless, unyielding 11 uncompliant 12 intransigent, single-minded

unconcealed 4 bare, open 5 frank, overt, plain 6 candid 8 apparent 11 openhearted, undisguised, unvarnished 12 undissembled 13 undissembling

unconcern 4 cool 6 apathy 8 coolness, lethargy 9 disregard, lassitude 11 disinterest, insouciance, nonchalance 12 heedlessness, indifference, listlessness 13 unmindfulness

unconcerned 4 cool 5 aloof 6 casual, remote 8 composed, detached 9 apathetic, collected, incurious, lethargic, uncurious, unmindful, withdrawn 10 nonchalant 11 indifferent 12 uninterested 13 disinterested

unconditional 4 free 5 frank, utter 6 simple 8 absolute, explicit, termless 10 unreserved

unconfined 3 lax 4 free 5 loose 9 boundless, limitless, unlimited 12 unrestrained

uncongenial 8 aversive, kindless 9 repellent, repugnant, unlikable 10 discordant, unpleasing 11 displeasing, inconsonant 12 antipathetic, inharmonious, unattractive, unharmonious 13 unsympathetic

unconnected 5 gappy 7 muddled 8 detached, inchoate, rambling, separate 10 disjointed, disordered, incoherent, incohesive 11 unorganized 12 uncontinuous 13 discontinuous

unconquerable 6 secure 9 resistant 10 impassable, invincible, unbeatable 11 impregnable, indomitable, insuperable 12 inexpugnable, invulnerable, unassailable, undefeatable

unconscionable 5 undue 6 unholy, wicked 7 extreme, ungodly 8 towering 9 barbarous, excessive 10 exorbitant, immoderate, inordinate, outrageous 11 extravagant, unchristian, uncivilized, unwarranted 12 unmeasurable, unprincipled, unreasonable, unscrupulous 13 unjustifiable, unwarrantable

unconscious 3 out 4 cold 5 brute 6 asleep, blotto, torpid 7 out cold, stunned, unaware 8 comatose, ignorant, mindless 10 insensible

unconsciousness 4 coma 5 faint 6 torpor, trance

unconsidered 4 puny, rash 5 brash, hasty, petty, small 6 paltry, random 7 aimless, trivial 8 picayune, reckless, trifling 9 desultory, haphazard, hit-or-miss, hotheaded, unadvised, unplanned 10 designless, ill-advised, incautious, objectless 11 promiscuous, thoughtless 12 inconsequent

unconsolable see inconsolable

unconstrained 4 easy, free 6 casual, dégagé, simple 7 natural, relaxed, unfussy 8 familiar, informal, outgoing 9 easygoing,

expansive 10 unreserved 11 low-pressure 13 demonstrative

unconstraint 4 ease 7 abandon, freedom, naiveté 10 simplicity 11 naturalness, spontaneity 13 impulsiveness, ingenuousness

uncontrollable 4 wild 6 unruly 8 indocile 9 fractious 11 indomitable, intractable 12 recalcitrant, unmanageable 13 insuppressive, irrepressible, uncontainable, undisciplined

uncontrolled 4 free, wild 5 loose 9 irregular, unbounded, unmanaged 10 hysterical, licentious, ungoverned 11 unregulated 12 unrestrained

unconventional 3 odd 5 loose, outré, queer 6 casual 7 devious, offbeat, strange, unusual 8 Bohemian, informal 10 unorthodox 13 unceremonious

unconversant 3 raw 5 green, young 6 callow 7 untried 8 unversed 9 unfleshed 10 unseasoned 11 unpracticed 13 inexperienced

unconvincing 4 thin, weak 5 fishy, thick 6 flimsy 10 improbable, incredible 11 implausible 12 unbelievable 13 inconceivable, unsubstantial

uncooked 3 raw

uncork 6 unplug 7 release

uncorrectable 8 cureless, hopeless 9 incurable, insanable, uncurable 10 impossible 11 immedicable, irreparable 12 irremediable 13 unrecoverable

uncorrupted 4 pure 5 naive 6 virgin 8 innocent, pristine 9 unspoiled

uncouple 3 cut 5 loose, unfix 6 detach 8 abstract, unfasten 9 disengage 10 disconnect, dissociate 12 disassociate

uncourteous 4 rude 7 uncivil 8 impolite 10 ungracious 11 disgracious, ill-mannered, impertinent, uncalled-for 13 disrespectful

uncouth 3 odd, raw 4 lorn, rude 5 crass, crude, gross, queer, rough, rummy 6 coarse, quaint, vulgar 7 awkward, bizarre, boorish, curious, erratic, ill-bred, loutish, oddball, strange, uncivil 8 backwood, derelict, deserted, desolate, forsaken, impolite, solitary, ungainly 9 abandoned, eccentric, inelegant, unrefined 10 uncultured, unpolished 11 disgracious, ill-mannered, impertinent, uncalled-for 12 discourteous, uncultivated 13 disrespectful *person:* 3 oaf 4 boor, lout 5 yokel 6 bumkin, rustic 7 bumpkin

uncover 4 bare, open, tell 5 strip 6 betray, denude, detect, divest, expose, remove, reveal, unmask, unveil 7 display, divulge, lay open, subject, unbosom, unclose, undrape, unearth 8 disclose, unclothe 9 uncurtain

uncovered 4 bare, open 5 naked
6 peeled 7 denuded, exposed 8 stripped,
unmasked

uncritical 6 casual 7 cursory, inexact, offhand, shallow, sketchy 8 careless, slipshod
9 depthless, imprecise 10 inaccurate
11 perfunctory, superficial

uncrown 6 depose, unmake 8 dethrone,
discrown, displace 9 disthrone 11 disenthrone

unction 3 oil 4 balm 5 cream, salve
6 cerate, chrism 7 suavity 8 ointment

unctuous 3 fat 4 oily 5 fatty, slick, soapy,
suave 6 greasy, smarmy 7 fulsome
10 oleaginous

uncultivated 3 raw 4 arid, rude, wild
5 crass, crude, feral, gross, rough
6 coarse, desert, fallow, Gothic, incult,
native, savage, sloven 7 deserty, Hunnish,
natural, uncivil 8 agrarian, agrestal, barbaric 9 barbarian, barbarous, inelegant
11 uncivilized

uncultured 3 raw 4 rude 5 crass, crude,
gross, rough 6 coarse, incult, vulgar 7 artless, boorish, ill-bred, loutish, lowbred,
uncouth 8 churlish, cloddish 9 unrefined
10 unpolished 11 clodhopping, uncivilized

uncurbed 9 audacious 10 ungoverned,
unhampered 11 uninhibited, untrammeled
12 uncontrolled, unrestrained

uncustomary 4 rare 6 unique 7 unusual
8 singular, uncommon, unwonted 10 unordinary 11 exceptional, unthinkable
13 extraordinary

uncut 5 whole 6 entire 8 complete,
undocked 10 full-length, unabridged
11 uncondensed, whole-length 13 unabbreviated

undamaged 5 sound, whole 6 intact,
unhurt 8 flawless, unbroken, unmarred
9 uninjured 10 unimpaired 11 unblemished

undaring 5 timid 8 timorous

undarkened 4 fair, fine 5 clear, sunny
7 clarion 8 pleasant, rainless, sunshiny
9 cloudless, unclouded

undaunted 4 bold 5 brave 7 Spartan, valiant 8 fearless, intrepid, valorous 9 audacious, confident 10 courageous 11 uncon-
quered

undeceive 5 purge 8 disabuse, undelude
11 disillusion

undecided 4 moot, open 6 unsure
7 dubious, pendent, pending, unclear
8 doubtful, wavering 9 equivocal, uncertain,
unsettled 10 borderline, indecisive
12 undetermined

undecipherable 9 illegible 10 unreadable

undecisive see **indecisive**

undeclared 5 tacit 6 secret, unsaid
7 implied 8 implicit, inferred, unspoken,
wordless 9 unuttered 10 understood
11 unexpressed

undecorated 5 plain 6 homely, simple
9 unadorned 11 inelaborate, ungarnished
12 unbeautified, unornamented 13 unembellished, unembroidered

undefiled 4 pure 5 clean 6 chaste,
decent, intact, modest, virgin 8 innocent,
spotless, virtuous 9 stainless, unsullied
10 immaculate 11 unblemished

undefined 3 dim 5 faint, vague 6 bleary
7 obscure, shadowy, unclear 10 indistinct
12 undetermined

undemonstrated 7 untried 8 unproved,
untested 11 unpracticed

undemonstrative 3 icy 4 calm, cold,
cool 5 aloof, chill 6 frigid 7 aseptic, distant,
glacial, laconic 8 reserved, retiring 9 shrinking, unaffable, withdrawn 10 restrained,
unsociable 11 emotionless, indifferent,
standoffish, unemotional, unexpansive
12 uninterested

undeniable 4 real, true 6 actual 7 certain
8 positive, unfabled 9 veridical 10 inarguable 11 indubitable, unequivocal 12 indisputable, undisputable 13 incontestable,
uncontestable

undependable 5 trick 6 casual, tricky,
unsafe, unsure 7 dubious, erratic
8 untrusty 9 trustless, unassured 10 fly-by-
night, unreliable 12 questionable 13 irresponsible, untrustworthy

under 3 low, sub 5 below, lower, neath
6 lesser, nether 7 beneath, subject 8 inferior 9 dependent, secondary, subjacent,
tributary 10 collateral, underneath 11 subordinate *prefix:* 3 hyp, sub 4 hypo

underage 4 lack 7 deficit, failure 8 shortage 10 deficiency, inadequacy, scantiness
11 defalcation 13 insufficience, insufficiency

undercarriage 5 frame 6 struts 8 supports 9 framework 11 landing gear

undercover 6 covert, secret 7 furtive, sub
rosa 8 hush-hush 11 clandestine 12 hugger-mugger 13 hole-and-corner, surreptitious, under-the-table *person:* 3 spy
4 mole 5 agent, spook 9 detective
10 counterspy 12 counteragent

undercroft 5 crypt, vault 7 chamber
8 catacomb

underdeveloped 7 dwarfed, stunted
8 backward 10 behindhand 13 unprogressive

underdog 4 prey 5 loser 6 victim 8 casualty 9 dark horse

underdone 4 rare

underestimate 8 disprize, minimize
9 underrate 10 undervalue

undergarment 3 bra 4 slip 5 teddy
6 bodice, briefs, cilise, corset, girdle, shorts,

skivvy, undies 7 chemise, dessous, drawers, panties, step-ins 8 flimsies, knickers, lingerie, pretties, skivvies 9 brassiere, petticoat, underwear 10 foundation

undergo 3 bow, see 4 bear, have, know, pass 5 abide, carry, defer, serve, yield 6 endure, submit, suffer 7 sustain 8 tolerate 10 experience

undergoer *suffix:* 2 ee

undergraduate 4 coed 6 junior, senior 7 student 8 freshman 9 sophomore

underground 5 train 6 hidden, secret, subway 7 beneath, illegal, off-beat 8 hypogeal, hypogean 9 underfoot 10 undercover, underearth 11 disapproved 12 subterranean 13 surreptitious 14 counterculture

underhand 3 sly 4 mean, wily 5 shady 6 crafty, secret, shifty, sneaky, tricky, unfair 7 crooked, cunning, devious, furtive, hangdog, oblique, stealth 8 guileful, indirect, sinister, sneaking 9 deceitful, dishonest, insidious 10 circuitous, fraudulent 11 duplicitous

underhanded 3 sly 4 mean 5 shady 6 secret, shifty, sneaky, unfair 7 devious 8 guileful, indirect, sneaking, unfairly 9 deceitful 10 circuitous, fraudulent 11 clandestine, duplicitous, shorthanded, undermanned 12 understaffed

underived 5 prime 7 primary 8 original 9 primitive

underlease 6 sublet 8 sublease, underlet

underlet 6 sublet 8 sublease 10 underlease

underlie 4 bear 7 subtend, support

underline 4 mark 6 legend, play up, stress 7 caption, feature 9 emphasize, italicize 10 underscore

underling 5 scrub 6 menial, minion 8 inferior 9 secondary, subaltern 11 subordinate 12 poor relation

underlying 5 basal, basic, vital 6 bottom, covert 7 crucial, needful, obscure, primary, radical 8 cardinal, critical, implicit 9 elemental, essential, necessary, primitive 10 elementary, substratal 11 fundamental 12 foundational 13 indispensable

Under Milk Wood author 6 Thomas (Dylan)

undermine 3 sap 4 cave, foil, ruin 5 blunt, drain, erode, wreck 6 impair, thwart, weaken 7 cripple, disable, founder, subvert, unbrace 8 enfeeble, sabotage, supplant 9 attenuate, frustrate 10 debilitate, demoralize 12 unstrengthen

undermost 6 bottom, lowest 9 lowermost 10 bottommost, nethermost, rock-bottom

underneath 4 sole 5 below 6 bottom, secret 9 underside 10 undercover

12 undersurface 13 surreptitious *prefix:* 5 intra

underpin 4 base, prop, root, seat, stay 5 brace, shore 7 justify, support 8 buttress, maintain 12 substantiate

underpinning 4 base, prop, root, seat, stay 5 basis, brace, shore 6 column, ground 7 bedrock, footing, seating, support 8 buttress 10 foundation, groundwork, substratum 12 substruction, substructure 13 underpropping

underpowered 4 slow, weak 6 anemic 8 sluggish

underprivileged 4 poor 5 needy 7 hapless, unlucky 8 deprived, ill-fated 9 depressed 10 ill-starred 11 handicapped, unfortunate 12 impoverished 13 disadvantaged

underprize 5 decry, lower 7 devalue 9 devaluate, write down 10 depreciate, devalorize, undervalue

underprop 4 stay 5 brace, shore 6 buoy up, uphold 7 bolster, support, sustain 8 buttress

underpropping 4 prop, stay 5 brace, shore 6 column 7 support 8 buttress

underrate 5 decry, lower 7 devalue 8 discount, mark down, write off 9 devaluate, write down 10 depreciate, devalorize, undervalue 13 underestimate

underscore 6 play up, stress 7 feature 9 emphasize, italicize, underline

undersexed 4 cold 6 frigid 9 inhibited 11 passionless 12 unresponsive

underside 4 sole 6 bottom 10 underneath 12 undersurface *combining form:* 6 infero

undersized 4 puny 5 dwarf, runty, scrub, small 6 little 7 scrubby, stunted

understand 3 con, dig, get, ken, see 4 have, know, sabe, take, twig 5 catch, fancy, grasp, guess, infer, savvy, seize, sense, think 6 accept, assume, deduce, expect, fathom, figure, follow, gather, reason, take in 7 believe, cognize, discern, imagine, presume, realize, suppose, surmise, suspect 8 conceive, conclude, consider, perceive 9 apprehend, interpret, penetrate 10 appreciate, comprehend, conjecture

understandable 3 lay 5 clear, lucid, plain 6 simple 7 popular 8 clear-cut, exoteric, knowable, luminous 9 graspable, unblurred 10 fathomable 11 unambiguous 12 intelligible 13 apprehensible

understanding 3 ken, wit 4 deal, idea 5 grasp, sense 6 accord, humane, import, kindly, notion, reason, treaty 7 compact, concept, empathy, entente, insight, knowing, meaning, message, purport 8 attitude, contract, daylight, judgment, sympathy

9 agreement, awareness, diagnosis, intellect, intuition, knowledge, tolerance
10 acceptance, intendment 11 acceptation, discernment, intelligent, penetration, sympathetic 12 apprehension, intelligence, significance, significancy 13 comprehension, signification

understatement 7 litotes

understood 5 clear, lucid, tacit 6 unsaid 7 implied 8 implicit, inferred, unspoken, wordless 9 unuttered 10 undeclared 11 unexpressed

understudy 6 double 7 stand-in 10 substitute 11 replacement

undertake 2 do, go 3 try 4 dare, pass, seek 5 assay, begin, essay, offer, start 6 accept, assume, engage, incept, pledge, strive, take on, take up 7 attempt, certify, emprise, execute, perform, promise, warrant 8 commence, contract, covenant, endeavor, struggle

undertaker 8 embalmer 9 mortician 12 entrepreneur

undertaking 3 job, try 4 task 5 essay, trial 6 cautio, charge, effort, hassle, scheme, voyage 7 attempt, calling, emprise, emprize, project, venture 8 covenant, endeavor, striving, struggle 9 adventure 10 enterprise 11 proposition

under-the-table 6 covert, secret 7 furtive, sub-rosa 8 stealthy 10 undercover 11 clandestine 13 surreptitious

undertone 4 hint 5 aside, rumor 6 mumble, murmur, mutter 7 inkling, subtone, whisper 8 overtone 10 suggestion 11 association, connotation, implication, susurration

undertow 4 eddy 6 vortex 7 current, riptide, sea puss 8 seapoose, sea purse

undervalue see underrate

underwater 9 submarine 10 subaquatic, subaqueous *breathing apparatus:* 5 scuba *captain:* 4 Nemo *chamber:* 7 caisson *device:* 8 paravane *missile:* 7 torpedo *sound detector:* 5 sonar

underwear see undergarment

underwood 5 frith 7 boscage, coppice 10 underbrush 11 undergrowth

underworld 4 hell 5 abyss, hades, Orcus, Sheol 6 Erebus, Tophet 7 Gehenna, inferno, xibalba 8 gangland 9 barathrum 11 netherworld, Pandemonium *boatman:* 6 Charon *deity:* 3 Dis 4 Bran 5 Pluto 6 Osiris 8 Dispater *goddess:* 6 Hecate 10 Persephone *organization:* 5 Mafia *relating to:* 8 chthonic *watchdog:* 8 Cerberus

underwrite 4 back, sign 6 assure, insure, pay for 7 endorse, finance, sponsor, support 9 subscribe

undesigning 4 real, true 6 honest, simple 7 artless, genuine, sincere 9 unfeigned 10 heart-whole 12 undissembled

undesirable 8 unwanted 9 unwelcome 10 ill-favored 12 inadmissible, unacceptable 13 exceptionable, objectionable

undesired 8 unsought, unwanted, unwished 9 unwelcome 10 quenchless

undestroyable see indestructible

undetermined 3 dim 5 faint, unset, vague 6 bleary 7 dubious, obscure, pendent, pending, shadowy, unclear 8 aoristic, doubtful 9 equivocal, undecided, undefined, unsettled 10 ill-defined, indistinct

undeveloped 5 crude 6 latent 7 archaic 8 backward, immature, juvenile 9 primitive, unevolved 10 behindhand, persistent 13 unprogressive

undiluted 4 mere, neat, pure 5 plain, sheer 6 simple 7 perfect, unmixed 8 absolute, straight 9 unalloyed 11 unmitigated, unqualified 13 unadulterated

undiplomatic 5 brash 8 tactless 9 impolitic, maladroit, unpolitic, untactful

undisciplined 4 wild 6 unruly, wanton 8 untoward 9 fractious, untrained 11 intractable 12 recalcitrant, ungovernable, unmanageable

undisclosed 6 hidden, sealed, secret 8 ulterior 12 confidential

undisguised 4 bald, open 5 frank, overt, plain 6 candid 9 barefaced 11 openhearted, unconcealed, unvarnished 12 undissembled 13 undissembling

undissembled 4 open, real, true 5 frank, plain 6 candid, honest 7 genuine, sincere 9 unfeigned 10 heart-whole 11 openhearted, unconcealed, undesigning, undisguised, unvarnished

undistinguished 5 gross 6 common 8 mediocre, noteless 9 unnotable 12 unnoteworthy

undistorted 4 just, true 5 clear, right 6 strict 8 faithful 9 veracious, veridical

undivided 3 one 5 fixed, total, whole 6 entire, intact 8 complete, unbroken 10 continuous, unswerving 12 concentrated, undistracted

undo 3 ope 4 have, open, raze, ruin 5 abate, annul, loose, quash, unfix, untie, wrack, wreck 6 defeat, diddle, negate, outfox, outwit, seduce, unbind, unmake, unshut, unsnap, unstop 7 abolish, debauch, destroy, nullify, unblock, unbuild, unclose, unframe, unloose, unravel, vitiate 8 abrogate, decimate, demolish, outreach, outslick, outsmart, unfasten, unloosen 9 disengage, outjockey, overreach 10 annihilate, invalidate, outgeneral 11 outmaneuver

undoing 4 bane, ruin 8 downfall 9 destroyer, overthrow, ruination 11 destruction

undoubtedly 4 well 5 truly 6 easily, indeed, really, surely 7 frankly 11 doubtlessly, indubitably

undoubtful 6 secure 7 assured 8 sanguine 9 confident 11 self-assured 13 self-confident

undress see **unclothe**

undressed 3 raw 4 nude, rude 5 crude, naked, rough 6 unclad, unhewn 8 buffbare, stripped, unformed, unworked 9 au naturel, roughhewn, unclothed 10 starknaked, unfinished, unpolished 11 unfashioned

undue 5 dizzy, inapt, inept, unapt 7 extreme 8 ill-timed, improper, towering, untimely 9 excessive, unfitting 10 exorbitant, immoderate, inordinate, unsuitable 11 extravagant, unwarranted 12 unreasonable, unseasonable 13 inappropriate, unjustifiable, unwarrantable

undulant fever 11 brucellosis

undulate 4 roll, swag, sway, wave 5 snake, swing 6 ripple 7 slidder, slither 9 fluctuate

unduly 3 too 4 ever, over 6 overly 8 overfull, overmuch 9 extremely, immensely 11 excessively 12 inordinately

undutiful 7 impious

undying 7 ageless, endless, eternal 8 immortal, unending 9 continual, deathless, unceasing 10 continuing, persistent 12 imperishable, interminable, unquenchable

uneager 3 shy 5 loath 6 afraid, averse 8 backward, hesitant 9 reluctant, unwilling 10 indisposed 11 disinclined

unearth 3 dig, see 4 hear, show 5 delve, learn 6 exhume, expose, reveal, tumble 7 catch on, exhibit, find out, uncover 8 disclose, discover 9 ascertain, determine

unearthly 4 eery 5 balmy, crazy, eerie, loony, silly, wacky, weird 6 absurd, insane, spooky 7 awesome, foolish, uncanny, ungodly 8 numinous, superior, terrific 9 appalling, fantastic 10 miraculous, mysterious, outlandish, superhuman, suprahuman 12 preposterous, supermundane, supernatural, supranatural 13 preternatural

unease 4 care 5 worry 6 unrest 7 anxiety, concern, tension, trouble 8 disquiet 9 abashment, confusion 10 discomfort, discontent, solicitude 11 concernment, displeasure, disquietude, uptightness 12 apprehension, discomfiture, discomposure 13 disconcertion, embarrassment

uneasiness see **unease**

uneasy 4 edgy 5 nervy, shaky, tense 6 unsure 7 anxious, awkward, careful, fidgety, restive, suspect, unquiet, uptight, worried 8 agitated, doubtful, restless 9 ambiguous, concerned, difficult, disturbed, doubtable, perturbed, uncertain, unrestful, unsettled 10 borderline, disquieted, precarious, solicitous, unpeaceful, untranquil 13 uncomfortable

uneducated 4 rude 6 simple 8 ignorant, untaught 9 benighted, untutored 10 illiterate, unlettered, unschooled 11 emptyheaded, know-nothing 12 uninstructed

unembellished 3 dry 5 plain 6 simple 7 austere, prosaic 9 unadorned 11 undecorated, unelaborate, ungarnished 12 unbeautified, unornamented 13 unembroidered, unpretentious

unembroidered see **unembellished**

unemotional 3 dry, icy 4 cold, cool 5 chill, stoic, stony 6 frigid 7 callous, glacial, stoical 8 obdurate 9 heartless, impassive, unfeeling 10 hard-boiled, phlegmatic 11 coldhearted, hardhearted, indifferent 12 stonyhearted 13 dispassionate, unsympathetic

unemployed 4 free, idle 5 fired 6 otiose, unused 7 jobless, laid off 8 inactive, workless 9 unengaged 10 unoccupied

unending 7 eternal, undying 8 constant, immortal, timeless 9 ceaseless, continual, perpetual 10 continuous 11 amaranthine, everlasting, unremitting 12 interminable 13 uninterrupted

unenlightened 7 heathen 8 backward, ignorant 9 benighted 13 unprogressive

unenthusiastic 4 cold, cool 8 lukewarm 9 apathetic, unexcited 10 spiritless 11 perfunctory 12 uninterested

unequal 5 impar 6 uneven, unfair, unjust, unlike 7 distant, diverse, unalike, various 8 inferior, lopsided, variable 9 different, disparate, divergent, irregular, unsimilar 10 asymmetric, dissimilar, off-balance 11 fluctuating 12 overbalanced 13 unsymmetrical *combining form:* 4 anis 5 aniso

unequalable 7 supreme 8 towering, ultimate 10 preeminent, surpassing 11 unmatchable 12 incomparable, transcendent 13 unsurpassable

unequaled 4 only 5 alone 6 unique 7 supreme 8 nonesuch, peerless 9 matchless, unmatched, unrivaled 10 surpassing 11 unparagoned 12 unparalleled 13 unprecedented

unequipped 5 unfit 8 unfitted 9 incapable 10 ineligible, unprepared 11 incompetent, unqualified 12 disqualified

unequivocal 5 clear, plain 6 direct, patent 7 certain, decided, evident, obvious 8 apparent, definite, distinct, explicit, manifest, palpable, positive 10 undeniable 11 categorical, indubitable 12 indisputable, undisputable 13 incontestable, uncontestable

unerasable see inerasable

unerring 4 dead, sure, true 5 exact 7 certain, correct, precise 8 accurate, reliable 9 unfailing 10 dependable, infallible 11 trustworthy

unescapable see inevitable

unessential 8 needless, unneeded 9 extrinsic, unneedful 10 unrequired 11 dispensable, uncalled-for, unimportant, unnecessary 13 insubstantial

unethical 5 venal, wrong 6 amoral 7 corrupt, immoral 9 mercenary 10 praetorian 12 unprincipled, unscrupulous

unevadable see inevitable

uneven 3 odd 4 wavy 5 bumpy, erose, harsh, jaggy, rough 6 craggy, jagged, patchy, rugged, spotty, unfair, unjust, unlike 7 scraggy, streaky, unequal, unlevel, varying 8 asperous, lopsided, scabrous, scraggly, scratchy, unsmooth 9 anomalous, differing, disparate, irregular 10 asymmetric, discrepant, ill-matched, off-balance, unbalanced 11 fluctuating 12 inconsistent, overbalanced 13 unsymmetrical

unevenness 4 bump, wave 7 anomaly 8 asperity, imparity 9 disparity, roughness 10 inequality 12 irregularity 13 disproportion

uneventful 6 common 7 prosaic 8 ordinary 11 commonplace 12 unnoteworthy 13 unexceptional

unexampled 4 lone, only, sole, solo 5 alone 6 unique 8 singular, solitary 12 unrepeatable

unexceptional 5 usual 6 common, decent 7 prosaic, regular 8 adequate, all right, ordinary 9 tolerable 10 acceptable, sufficient, uneventful 11 commonplace 12 satisfactory, unnoteworthy 13 unimpeachable

unexcited 4 calm 5 level, stoic 7 stoical 8 tranquil

unexciting 4 dead, dull, tame 6 boring 7 prosaic 13 uninteresting

unexpectedly 5 aback, short 6 sudden 7 unaware 8 abruptly, suddenly, unawares 10 unawaredly 12 accidentally

unexpended 6 saving 7 reserve, surplus 8 left over 9 remaining

unexperienced see inexperienced

unexpired 5 alive, valid 8 left over 9 operative, remaining

unexplicit 4 hazy 5 vague 7 obscure, unclear 8 nebulous, nubilous 9 ambiguous, equivocal, tenebrous, uncertain 10 indistinct

unexpressed 5 tacit 6 silent, unsaid 7 implied 8 implicit, inferred, unspoken,

wordless 9 unuttered, voiceless 10 undeclared, understood

unfadable 4 fast 7 sunfast 9 colorfast

unfaded 5 fresh 6 bright

unfailing 4 same, sure 6 deadly 7 certain 8 constant, reliable, surefire, unerring 9 unvarying 10 consistent, infallible, invariable, unchanging, unflagging 13 inexhaustible

unfair 4 foul, hard 5 wrong 6 biased, shabby, uneven, unjust 7 devious, unequal 8 wrongful 9 dishonest, inequable, unethical 11 inequitable, underhanded, unequitable, unrighteous 12 dishonorable

unfairness 5 wrong 8 inequity 9 injustice 10 unjustness

unfaithful 5 false 6 untrue 7 infidel, traitor, unloyal 8 disloyal, recreant, turncoat 9 faithless 10 adulterous, inaccurate, perfidious, traitorous 11 treacherous 13 untrustworthy

unfaltering 4 firm, sure, true 5 brave 6 steady 7 abiding 8 enduring, unerring 9 steadfast 11 unqualified 12 never-failing, wholehearted 13 unquestioning

unfamiliar 3 new 6 exotic 7 curious, foreign, strange, unaware, unknown 8 ignorant, peculiar 9 oblivious, unknowing, unwitting 10 remarkable, uninformed 11 incognizant 12 inconversant, unaccustomed, unacquainted, uninstructed

unfamiliarity 9 ignorance, innocence, inscience, nescience 11 unawareness 13 unknowingness

unfashionable 5 dated, passé 6 démodé 8 outmoded 9 out-of-date

unfasten 4 free, open, undo 5 loose, unbar, unfix, unpin, untie 6 detach, loosen, unbind, unlace, unlock, unsnap 7 unhitch, unloose 8 unanchor, unloosen, untether 9 disengage

unfathomable 7 abysmal 8 profound 9 plumbless, soundless 10 bottomless, fathomless, mysterious, unknowable 11 inscrutable, ungraspable 12 impenetrable, incognizable

unfavorable 3 bad, ill 4 evil, foul, poor 6 averse, unfair, unkind 7 adverse, awkward, froward, hostile, unhappy 8 backward, contrary, inimical, negative, sinister, unkindly 11 detrimental *prefix:* 3 dys

unfavorably 4 awry 5 amiss, badly, wrong 6 afield, astray

unfearful 4 bold 5 brave 7 valiant 8 fearless, intrepid, valorous 9 audacious, dauntless, undaunted 10 courageous

unfeasible 10 impossible, infeasible, unworkable 11 impractical 12 irrealizable, unattainable, unrealizable 13 impracticable

unfeeling 4 cold, dead, dull, hard, numb 5 crass, cruel, harsh, stern, stony, surly, tough 6 asleep, brutal, leaden, marble, numbed, severe, stolid, unkind 7 callous 8 benumbed, churlish, deadened, exacting, hardened, obdurate, pitiless, ruthless 9 apathetic, bloodless, crotchety, heartless, inanimate, indurated, insensate, merciless, senseless, unamiable, uncordial 10 hardboiled, insensible, insentient 11 coldblooded, coldhearted, hardhearted, insensitive, ironhearted, unemotional 12 anesthetized, cantankerous, curmudgeonly, roughhearted, stonyhearted 13 marblehearted, unsusceptible, unsympathetic

unfeigned 4 open, real, true 6 hearty, honest 7 genuine, natural, sincere 9 heartfelt 11 undesigning 12 undissembled, wholehearted

unfertile see **infertile**

unfinished 3 raw 4 rude 5 crude, rough 6 unhewn 7 jackleg, sketchy 8 dabbling, unformed, ungifted, unworked 9 imperfect, roughhewn, undressed, unskilled 10 amateurish, dilettante, incomplete, unpolished 11 unfashioned 12 dilettantish, dilettantist

Unfinished Symphony composer 8 Schubert (Franz)

unfit 3 bad 4 sick 5 inapt, inept, wrong 6 faulty, unmeet 7 awkward, unhandy 8 bungling, disabled, improper, inexpert, unsuited 9 ill-suited, incapable, maladroit 10 blundering, discordant, ill-adapted, ineligible, unbecoming, unequipped, unskillful, unsuitable 11 handicapped, heavyhanded, incompetent, incongruous, inefficient, maladjusted, uncongenial, unqualified 12 disqualified, incompatible, infelicitous, inharmonious, unproficient 13 inappropriate, incapacitated *Jewish law:* 4 tref 6 trefah 7 terefah

unfitting 5 inapt, inept, unapt 8 improper, unseemly 10 malapropos, unbecoming, unsuitable 13 inappropriate

unfix 4 undo 5 loose 6 detach, loosen, unbind 7 unloose 8 abstract, dissolve, uncouple, unfasten, unloosen, unsettle 9 disengage 10 disconnect, dissociate 12 disassociate

unflagging 6 steady 8 constant, tireless, untiring 9 weariless 10 unwearying 11 unweariable 13 indefatigable, inexhaustible

unflappable 4 cool, easy 7 relaxed 8 composed 9 collected, unruffled 10 nonchalant 13 imperturbable

unflawed 7 perfect 8 absolute, flawless 9 feckless 10 impeccable 11 note-perfect 12 indefectible

unfledged 5 green, young 6 callow, infant, unripe 8 immature, juvenile, youthful 11 undeveloped, unfeathered

unflexible see **inflexible**

unflinching 4 firm, grim 5 level 6 mortal 7 staunch 8 resolute, ruthless 9 merciless, steadfast 10 implacable, ironfisted, relentless, unwavering, unyielding 11 unrelenting 12 unappeasable

unfluctuating 4 even 6 stable, steady 7 equable, stabile, uniform 8 constant 9 unvarying 10 unchanging

unfold 4 open, show 5 break, burst, solve 6 deploy, evince, evolve, expand, expose, extend, fan out, flower, reveal, spread, unfurl, unroll, untuck, unwrap 7 blossom, clear up, develop, display, divulge, dope out, exhibit, explain, release, resolve, unravel 8 decipher, disclose, dissolve, evidence, manifest, unriddle 9 elaborate, explicate, figure out, outspread, puzzle out 10 outstretch 11 demonstrate

unforbearing 9 impatient 10 intolerant 11 unindulgent

unforced 4 easy 7 natural, willful, willing, witting 9 voluntary 10 deliberate 11 intentional 12 unprescribed

unforeseen 6 sudden 10 accidental, unexpected

unforgivable 9 untenable 10 inexpiable 11 inexcusable 12 indefensible, unpardonable 13 unjustifiable

unformed 4 rude 5 crude, rough 6 callow, unhewn 8 formless, inchoate, unshaped, unworked 9 amorphous, roughhewn, shapeless, uncreated, undressed 10 unfinished, unpolished 11 undeveloped, unfashioned

unfortunate 3 bad, ill, sad 4 dire, poor 5 inept 6 woeful, wretch 7 awkward, hapless, malefic, unhappy, unlucky 8 grievous, ill-fated, luckless, untoward, wretched 9 graceless, ill-chosen, miserable 10 afflictive, calamitous, deplorable, ill-starred, lamentable 11 distressing, regrettable, starcrossed 12 inauspicious, infelicitous, misfortunate, unsuccessful 13 heartbreaking

unfounded 4 idle, vain 8 baseless 9 deceptive, dishonest 10 bottomless, chimerical, gratuitous, groundless, mendacious, misleading, ungrounded, untruthful 11 uncalled-for, unwarranted

unfrequented 5 empty 6 lonely 8 isolated, solitary

unfriendly 3 ill 4 cold, cool, foul 5 chill 6 bitter, chilly, fierce, frosty, remote 7 hostile 8 inimical, unsocial 10 inimicable

unfruitful 6 barren, effete, wasted 7 sterile, useless 8 impotent, infecund 9 infertile 12 unproductive, unprofitable

unfurl 4 open 6 spread, unfold, unroll, unwind 7 develop

unfurnished 4 bare 6 vacant

unfussy 6 casual, common, dégagé 7 relaxed 8 informal 9 easygoing 10 unreserved 11 low-pressure 13 unconstrained

ungainly 5 gawky, lanky, splay 6 clumsy 7 awkward, boorish, lumpish, uncouth 8 clownish, lubberly, unlicked, unwieldy 9 lumbering, maladroit 10 blundering 11 elephantine, splathering

ungarnished 3 dry 5 plain 6 modest, simple 9 unadorned 11 inelaborate, unelaborate 12 unornamented 13 unembellished, unembroidered

ungenerous 4 mean, puny 5 close, harsh, nasty, petty, small, tight 6 paltry, peanut, shabby, stingy 7 miserly 8 grudging, picayune, trifling, ungiving 9 niggardly, penurious 12 inconsequent, parsimonious 13 pennypinching

ungenuine 7 bastard 8 spurious 10 apocryphal 11 unauthentic

ungiving 4 mean 5 close, tight 6 stingy 7 miserly, save-all 9 niggardly, penurious 11 tightfisted 12 parsimonious

ungodly see unholy

ungovernable 4 wild 6 unruly 7 froward 8 untoward 9 fractious, unbridled 10 disorderly, headstrong, rebellious 11 intractable 12 recalcitrant, unmanageable 13 irrepressible, undisciplined

ungoverned 8 uncurbed 9 audacious 10 unhampered 11 uninhibited, untrammeled 12 unrestrained

ungraceful 5 lanky 6 clumsy 7 angular, awkward, halting 8 untoward 9 inelegant

ungracious 4 hard, rude 5 gruff, sharp, short 7 uncivil 8 churlish, impolite, snappish 9 offensive 10 unmannerly, unpleasant 11 disgracious, ill-mannered, impertinent, thoughtless, uncalled-for, uncourteous 12 discourteous, unattractive 13 disrespectful, inconsiderate, unceremonious

ungraded 3 raw 5 crude 6 impure, native 8 unsorted 9 run-of-mine, unrefined

ungraspable 10 unknowable 12 impenetrable, incognizable, unfathomable

ungrateful 4 foul 6 unkind 7 hideous 8 horrible 9 loathsome, offensive, repellent, repugnant, repulsive, revolting, thankless 10 disgusting, unthankful 13 unappreciated

ungratified 9 uncontent 10 discontent, malcontent 11 disgruntled, uncontented, unsatisfied 12 discontented, dissatisfied, malcontented

ungrounded 8 baseless 9 unfounded 10 bottomless, gratuitous, groundless, uninformed 11 uncalled-for, unwarranted 12 uninstructed

unguarded 6 unwary 7 unalert 8 careless 9 imprudent 10 incautious, unvigilant, unwatchful 11 defenseless, thoughtless, unprotected

unguent 4 balm 5 cream, salve 6 cerate, ceroma, chrism 7 unction 8 ointment 9 lubricant

ungulate 3 hog, pig 4 deer 5 horse, tapir 6 hoofed 8 amblypod, elephant 10 rhinoceros

unhallowed 6 impure, unholy 7 demonic, impious, profane, satanic, ungodly 8 demoniac, demonian, devilish, diabolic, fiendish 10 desecrated, irreverent, serpentine 11 diabolonian 13 irreverential

unhampered 4 free 5 loose 6 direct 8 uncurbed 9 audacious, expedited 10 ungoverned 11 expeditious, uninhibited, untrammeled 12 unrestrained

unhandsome 4 mean, rude 5 plain 6 homely 7 ill-bred, uncivil 8 impolite, uncomely, unpretty 10 unalluring, unbecoming, ungracious 11 disgracious, ill-mannered, impertinent, unbeauteous, unbeautiful 12 discourteous, unattractive 13 disrespectful

unhandy 5 inapt, inept, unapt 6 clumsy, gauche, wooden 7 awkward, halting, inadept, unhappy 8 bumbling, cumbrous, inexpert, unfacile, unwieldy 9 ham-handed, maladroit, ponderous 10 cumbersome, unskillful 11 undexterous 12 inconvenient, unproficient

unhappiness 3 woe 5 blues, dolor, dumps, gloom, grief, worry 6 misery, mishap, sorrow, unrest 7 dismals, ill-luck, sadness 9 dejection 10 depression, melancholy 12 mournfulness, wretchedness

unhappy 3 bad, sad 4 evil, sour 5 black, bleak, inept, sorry 6 clumsy, dismal, dreary, gauche, gloomy, rotten, wooden 7 awkward, halting, joyless, unhandy, unlucky 8 bumbling, chiselly, dejected, illfated, luckless, mournful, saddened, untoward, wretched 9 cheerless, graceless, illchosen, maladroit, woebegone 10 depressant, ill-starred, melancholy, oppressive, unpleasant 11 dispiriting, displeasing, heavyhanded, melancholic, starcrossed, unfortunate 12 disagreeable, heavyhearted, inauspicious, infelicitous, misfortunate

unharmed 4 safe 6 unhurt 9 unscathed 10 scatheless

unharness 6 disarm, divest, ungear 7 outspan, unhitch, unhorse, unstrap 8 untackle

unhealthiness 7 disease, illness, malaise 8 debility, disorder, sickness 9 infirmity 10 affliction, feebleness, infirmness, sickliness 11 decrepitude 12 diseasedness 13 indisposition

unhealthy 3 bad, ill 4 sick 5 hairy, risky 6 chancy, infirm, putrid, queasy, rotten, sickly, unhale, wicked 7 corrupt, noisome, noxious, unsound, vicious 8 depraved, diseased, perilous, perverse 9 dangerous, hazardous, nefarious 10 degenerate, flagitious, insalutary, jeopardous, unsalutary, villainous 11 treacherous, unwholesome 12 insalubrious

unheard-of 3 new 7 obscure, strange, unfamed, unknown, unnoted 8 nameless 10 unrenowned 12 uncelebrated 13 extraordinary, unprecedented

unheeding 4 deaf 8 careless, feckless, heedless, ignoring, uncaring 9 unrecking 10 unnoticing, unthinking, unwatchful 11 inadvertent, inattentive, inobservant, insensitive, thoughtless, unobservant, unobserving 12 disregarding, irreflective, unperceiving, unreflective

unhesitating 4 free 5 ready 8 haltless 9 immediate 10 forthright 12 wholehearted

unhinge 4 turn 5 craze, upset 6 bother, flurry, frenzy, madden, sicken, untune 7 agitate, derange, disturb, fluster, perturb 8 disorder, disquiet, distract, unsettle 9 unbalance 10 discompose

unholy 5 amiss, rough 6 guilty, impure, sinful, wicked 7 corrupt, impious, profane, raucous, ungodly 8 blamable, blameful, culpable, dreadful, fiendish, god-awful, improper, indecent, shocking, unseemly, untoward 9 atheistic, atrocious, barbarous, frightful, malicious, unearthly 10 censurable, indecorous, indelicate, irreverent, malodorous, outrageous, scandalous, unbecoming, undecorous, unhallowed 11 blameworthy, unbelieving, unchristian, uncivilized 13 demeritorious, irreverential, reprehensible

unhorse 5 pitch, throw 6 topple, tumble, unseat 7 buck off, overset 8 dislodge, dismount, overturn, unsaddle 9 overthrow

unhurried 4 easy, slow 7 laggard, unhasty 8 dilatory 9 leisurely 10 deliberate

unhurt 4 safe 5 sound, whole 6 entire, intact 7 perfect 8 unbroken, unharmed, unmarred 9 undamaged, uninjured 10 unimpaired

unicity 7 oneness 8 uniquity 10 singleness, uniqueness

unicorn *antelope:* 5 takin *Chinese:* 5 kilin, kylin 6 chi-lin *fish:* 7 narwhal

unidealistic 4 hard 5 sober 9 practical, pragmatic, realistic 10 hard-boiled, hardheaded 11 down-to-earth, unfantastic 12 matter-of-fact

unification 5 union 6 hookup, merger 7 joining, linkage, melding, merging 8 alliance, coupling, mergence 9 coalition 10 connection 11 affiliation, coadunation, combination 12 interlocking 13 consolidation

uniform 4 akin, even, like, suit 5 alike, blues, dress, equal, khaki, level 6 agnate, livery, outfit, stable, steady, whites 7 equable, ordered, orderly, regular, similar, stabile 8 constant, parallel 9 analogous, consonant, unvarying 10 comparable, compatible, consistent, invariable, monotonous, unchanging 11 homogeneous 13 corresponding, unfluctuating *combining form:* 2 is 3 iso

uniformity 7 oneness 8 equality, evenness, monotony, sameness

uniformly 6 always, evenly, flatly, smooth 8 smoothly

unify 3 tie 4 bind 5 blend, merge, order, unite 6 cement 7 arrange, compact 8 coalesce, organize 9 harmonize, integrate 10 articulate, centralize, symphonize, synthesize 11 concatenate, concentrate, consolidate, orchestrate, systematize

unilluminated 3 dim 4 dark, dusk 5 dusky, murky 6 gloomy 7 obscure 9 lightless, tenebrous 10 caliginous

unimaginable 4 rare 6 unique 7 unusual 8 singular, uncommon, unwonted 10 incredible, unknowable, unordinary 11 exceptional, incogitable, unthinkable 12 insupposable, unbelievable 13 extraordinary, inconceivable

unimaginative 4 dull 7 limited, literal, prosaic 10 pedestrian

unimpaired 4 free 5 fresh, sound, whole 6 entire, intact, unhurt 7 perfect 8 unbroken, unmarred 9 undamaged, uninjured

unimpassioned 4 calm, cold 5 sober, stoic 6 placid, steady, stolid 8 moderate, tranquil 9 impassive, temperate 10 impersonal, phlegmatic 11 cold-blooded, emotionless 12 matter-of-fact

unimpeachable 6 common, decent 8 adequate, all right 9 blameless, faultless, tolerable 10 acceptable, sufficient 12 satisfactory 13 unexceptional

unimportant 5 light, minor, petty, small 6 casual, little, paltry 7 trivial 9 small-beer 10 negligible, shoestring 13 insignificant

unindifferent 6 biased 7 colored, partial 8 one-sided, partisan 9 jaundiced, unneutral 10 prejudiced 11 tendentious 12 prepossessed

uninformed 7 unaware 8 ignorant 9 oblivious, unknowing, unwitting 10 unfamiliar 11 incognizant 12 inconversant, unacquainted, uninstructed

uninhabited 4 wild 5 empty 6 desert, vacant 8 deserted, desolate

uninhibited 3 lax 4 free, open 5 loose 8 uncurbed 9 audacious 10 boisterous,

ungoverned, unhampered **11** untrammeled
12 unrestrained

uninitiate 4 tyro **7** amateur, dabbler
9 smatterer **10** dilettante **11** abecedarian

uninjured 5 sound, whole **6** entire, intact,
unhurt **7** perfect **8** unbroken, unmarred
9 undamaged **10** unimpaired

uninspired 4 dull **6** stodgy **7** sterile
9 ponderous **10** uncreative, unoriginal
11 elephantine, heavy-footed, heavy-
handed, noncreative, uninventive **13** un-
originative

uninstructed 4 rude **7** unaware **8** ignorant, untaught **9** benighted, oblivious,
unknowing, untutored, unwitting **10** illiterate, uneducated, unfamiliar, uninformed,
unlettered **11** empty-headed, incognizant,
know-nothing **12** inconversant, unacquainted

unintelligent 4 dumb **5** brute **6** obtuse,
simple, stupid, unwise **7** asinine, fatuous,
foolish, vacuous, witless **8** ignorant, mindless **9** brainless, insensate, senseless
10 irrational, weak-headed, weak-minded

unintended see unintentional

unintentional 6 chance, random **9** cause-
less, haphazard, undevised, unplanned,
unthought, unwitting **10** accidental, undesigned, unexpected, unforeseen, unpurposed, unthinking **11** inadvertent, purposeless, unlooked-for **13** unanticipated

uninterested 5 aloof **6** casual, remote
8 detached **9** incurious, uncurious, withdrawn **11** indifferent, unconcerned

uninteresting 3 dry **4** arid, drab, dull, flat
5 dusty, stale **6** boring, jejune, prolix, stupid
7 humdrum, insipid, tedious **8** bromidic,
tiresome, weariful **9** colorless, dryasdust,
wearisome **10** unexciting

uninterrupted 6 direct **7** endless, eternal, through **8** constant, straight, unending
9 ceaseless, continual, incessant, perpetual, unceasing **10** continuous **11** everlasting, unremitting **12** interminable

uninvited 7 unasked **8** unbidden,
unsought **11** unrequested

union 4 bloc, club, seam **5** alloy, group,
guild, hansa, hanse, joint, order **6** enosis,
fusion, league, merger **7** amalgam, joining,
melding, merging, society **8** alliance, congress, coupling, junction, juncture, marriage, mergence, sodality, together
9 anschluss, coalition **10** connection, federation, fellowship **11** association, brotherhood, coadunation, coalescence, combination, confederacy, unification
13 confederation, consolidation *combining
form:* **3** zyg **4** gamy, zygo **6** gamous
labor: **3** AFL, CIO, UAW **5** ILGWU *of two
gametes:* **7** zygoses (plural), zygosis

**Union Of Soviet Socialist Repub-
lics** see U.S.S.R.

unique 3 odd, one **4** lone, only, rare, sole,
solo **5** alone, queer **6** single **7** special,
strange, unusual **8** peculiar, peerless, separate, singular, solitary, uncommon,
unwonted **9** matchless, unequaled,
unmatched, unrivaled **10** particular, unexampled, unordinary **11** exceptional, unparagoned **12** unparalleled, unrepeatable
13 extraordinary

uniqueness 4 mark, note **6** import,
moment, oddity **7** oneness, unicity
10 notability, quaintness, singleness
11 curiousness, peculiarity, singularity,
strangeness, unusualness **12** memorability,
significance

____-Unis **5** Etats

unit 3 one **4** item **5** digit, group, monad,
whole **6** entity **7** element, measure **10** individual *administrative:* **6** agency, bureau
8 district *boy scout:* **5** troop *educational:*
6 course *military:* (see at military) *of acceleration:* **3** gal *of action:* **7** episode *of
advertising space:* **4** line **6** column **7** mil-
line *of a fire department:* **9** battalion *of an
element:* **4** atom **8** molecule *of angular
measure:* **6** radian **7** centrad *of area:*
4 acre **6** morgen **7** hectare *of astronomical distance:* **6** parsec **9** light-year *of
brightness:* **5** stilb **7** lambert *of capacity:*
2 cc, ml **4** gill, peck, pint **5** liter, litre,
minim, ounce, quart **6** bushel, firkin, gallon
8 fluidram *of computer information:* **3** bit
of conductance: **3** mho **7** siemens *of distance:* **4** mile **5** meter **7** furlong *of electricity:* **3** amp **4** volt, watt **6** ampere
7 coulomb *of electromotive force:* **4** volt
of energy: **3** erg **5** joule **7** quantum
8 watt-hour *of explosive force:* **7** megaton
of fineness: **5** carat, karat *of fluidity:*
3 rhe *of force:* **4** dyne **6** newton
7 poundal *of frequency:* **5** hertz **7** fresnel
of grain: **5** sheaf **6** thrave *of heat:* **3** BTU
5 therm **7** calorie *of illumination:* **3** lux
4 phot *of inductance:* **5** gauss, henry *of
length:* **3** mil **4** foot, inch, yard **5** fermi,
meter **6** micron *of loudness:* **4** phon, sone
7 decibel *of lumber:* **9** board foot *of magnetic flux:* **5** weber **7** maxwell *of magnetic induction:* **5** tesla *of magnetic
intensity:* **5** gamma **7** oersted *of magne-
tomotive force:* **7** gilbert *of pressure:*
3 bar **4** torr **5** barye **10** atmosphere *of
radiation:* **3** rad **8** roentgen *of radioactiv-
ity:* **5** curie *of resistance:* **3** ohm *of solar
radiation:* **7** langley *of sound absorption:*
5 sabin *of speech:* **4** word **6** toneme
7 phoneme **8** morpheme, syllable *of speed:*
3 CPS, MPH, RPM **4** knot *of temperature:*
6 degree, kelvin *of time:* **3** day **4** beat,

bell, hour, week 5 month 6 minute, season, second 8 svedberg *of viscosity:* 5 poise *of weight:* 3 ton 4 dram, gram, tael 5 carat, grain, ounce, pound, stein, tonne 6 drachm, kantar 7 gigaton, kiloton, millier, quintal, scruple *ancient Roman:* 5 libra *Asian:* 5 Picul, tical 6 cattie, miskal *British:* 3 tod *Chinese:* 5 liang *Hebrew:* 5 gerah *Indian:* 3 ser 4 tola *Muslim:* 4 rotl *Russian:* 4 pood *Turkish:* 3 oka, oke *of work:* 3 erg 5 ergon, joule *social:* 4 clan 5 tribe 6 family 7 chapter

unite 3 add, mix, sew, tie, wed 4 ally, band, bind, bond, fuse, join, knit, link, weld 5 blend, graft, marry, merge, unify 6 adhere, adjoin, attach, cement, concur, couple, gather, league, mingle, relate, solder, splice 7 combine, conjoin, connect 8 assemble, coadjute, coalesce, compound, copulate, federate 9 affiliate, aggregate, associate, commingle, cooperate 10 amalgamate, federalize 11 concentrate, confederate, incorporate 12 conglutinate

United Arab Emirates 5 Ajman, Dubai 7 Sharjah 8 Abu Dhabi, Fujairah

United Kingdom *capital:* 6 London *monetary unit:* 5 pound *part:* 5 Wales 7 England 8 Scotland

United Nations *secretary-general:* 3 Lie (Trygve) 5 Thant (U) 8 Waldheim (Kurt) 12 Boutros-Ghali (Boutros), Hammarskjold (Dag) 14 Perez de Cuellar (Javier)

unities, dramatic 4 time 5 place 6 action

unity 5 union 7 concord, harmony, oneness, rapport 8 identity, sodality, soleness, uniquity 9 agreement, communion, congruity 10 singleness, solidarity, uniformity, uniqueness 11 conformance, conjunction, singularity 12 selfsameness, singularness 13 individuality

universal 3 all 5 broad, total, whole 6 common, cosmic, entire, global 7 allover, general, generic 8 catholic, ecumenic, sweeping 9 extensive, planetary, unlimited, worldwide 10 ecumenical, ubiquitous 11 omnipresent 12 all-embracing, all-inclusive, all-pervading, cosmopolitan *combining form:* 3 omn 4 omni

universe 3 all 5 world 6 cosmos, nature, system 8 creation, megacosm 9 macrocosm 10 macrocosmos *combining form:* 4 cosm 5 cosmo

unjust 4 hard 5 cruel, wrong 6 unfair, wicked 7 unequal 8 improper, wrongful 9 dishonest, inequable 10 iniquitous 11 inequitable, unequitable, unrighteous

unjustifiable 5 undue 7 invalid 9 untenable 10 inexpiable 11 inexcusable, unwarranted

unkempt 5 messy 6 frowsy, frowzy, shaggy, sloppy, unneat, untidy 7 ruffled, tousled 8 draggled, ill-kempt, scraggly, slipshod, slovenly, strubbly, uncombed 10 disarrayed, disheveled 12 unfastidious

unkind 3 bad, ill 4 mean, vile 5 cruel, harsh, rough, stern 6 severe 8 ungenial 9 inclement 10 ungenerous, ungracious 11 unfavorable

unknit 4 undo 5 ravel, relax, untie 7 unravel

unknowable 6 arcane, mystic 8 mystical, numinous 9 enigmatic, mysterial, unguessed 10 cabalistic, mysterious 11 inscrutable, ungraspable 12 impenetrable, incognizable, unexaminable, unfathomable, unimaginable 13 inconceivable

unknowing 7 unaware 8 ignorant 9 oblivious, unwitting 10 unfamiliar, uninformed 11 incognizant 12 inconversant, unacquainted, uninstructed

unknown 6 nobody, secret 7 obscure, strange, unfamed, unnoted 8 nameless 9 anonymous, incognito, unheard-of 10 unfamiliar, unrenowned 12 uncelebrated *Scottish:* 6 unkent

unlawful 7 bootleg, illegal, illicit, lawless 8 criminal, improper, wrongful 9 irregular, nefarious 10 contraband, flagitious, iniquitous 11 black-market, intolerable 12 illegitimate 13 exceptionable, objectionable

unlearned 7 natural 8 ignorant, untaught 9 inerudite, unbookish, untutored 10 illiterate, uneducated, unstudious 11 instinctive, unscholarly

unleash 4 free, vent 5 loose 7 release

unless 3 but 4 save 6 except, saving 7 without 9 excepting

unlettered see **uneducated**

unlike 7 distant, diverse, unequal, various 9 different, disparate, divergent, unsimilar 10 dissimilar

unlikely 5 unfit 7 dubious 8 doubtful 10 improbable, unsuitable 11 unpromising 12 questionable, unattractive

unlikeness 8 alterity, contrast 9 otherness 10 difference, divergence, divergency 11 discrepancy, distinction 12 disagreement, dissemblance 13 dissimilarity, dissimilitude, inconsistence

unlimited 4 vast 5 total 6 all-out 7 endless, full-out 8 infinite 9 boundless, full-blown, full-scale, unbounded, undefined, universal 10 indefinite, unconfined, unmeasured 11 measureless, untrammeled 12 immeasurable, totalitarian, unrestricted 13 indeterminate

unload 4 drop, dump, land 5 empty, unbox 6 debark, remove, unlade, unpack, unship, unstow 7 deliver, lighten, off-load, relieve, uncrate 8 jettison 9 disburden, dis-

charge, disembark, liquidate, stevedore
11 disencumber

unloose, unloosen 4 undo 5 unfix
6 unbind 7 unrivet 8 unfasten 9 disengage

unloyal see **disloyal**

unlucky 3 bad, ill 4 dire 7 baleful, baneful, direful, doomful, fateful, hapless, ominous, unhappy 8 ill-fated, tragical, untoward 9 ill-boding, ill-omened
10 calamitous, disastrous, ill-starred
11 apocalyptic, cataclysmic, star-crossed,
unfortunate 12 catastrophic, misfortunate

unman 4 undo 5 abase, crush, drain, unfit
7 degrade, deplete, exhaust, unnerve
8 castrate, enervate, paralyze, unstring
9 prostrate 10 disqualify, emasculate,
impoverish

unmanageable 4 wild 6 unruly 7 restive
8 indocile 9 fractious 10 disorderly
11 indomitable, intractable 12 recalcitrant,
ungovernable 13 undisciplined

unmanly 5 sissy 6 coward, craven, prissy
7 chicken, epicene, gutless 8 childish, cowardly, poltroon 9 pansified, sissified, spunkless 10 effeminate 11 lily-livered 12 Miss-
Nancyish, poor-spirited 13 pusillanimous

unmannered 4 open, rude 5 frank, plain
6 candid 7 boorish, ill-bred, uncivil 8 impolite, man-to-man 10 ungracious, unmannerly 11 disgracious, openhearted, undisguised, unvarnished 12 discourteous,
undissembled 13 disrespectful

unmarred 5 sound, whole 6 entire, intact,
unhurt 7 perfect 8 pristine, unbroken

unmarried 4 lone, sole 5 unwed 6 single
10 spouseless

unmask 6 debunk, expose, reveal, show
up, unveil 7 uncloak, undress 8 disclose,
discover, unshroud

unmatchable 7 supreme 8 towering, ultimate 10 preeminent, surpassing 11 unequalable 12 incomparable, transcendent
13 unsurpassable

unmatched 3 odd 4 only 5 alone
6 unique 8 peerless, unpaired 9 matchless, unequaled, unrivaled 11 unparagoned
12 unparalleled

unmerciful 5 cruel 8 pitiless, ruthless
9 merciless, unpitying 10 relentless

unmethodical 7 cursory, erratic 9 desultory

unmindful 7 unaware 8 careless, heedless 9 forgetful, negligent, oblivious, unwitting 10 neglectful 11 inattentive

unmistakable 4 flat, open 5 clear, frank,
plain 6 patent 7 evident, express 8 apparent, distinct, manifest, palpable, univocal

unmitigated 4 mere, pure, rank 5 gross,
sheer, utter 6 arrant, damned, simple
7 perfect, unmixed 8 absolute, clearcut,
complete, outright 9 out-and-out, unalloyed,

undiluted 10 unmodified 11 straight-out,
unqualified 13 thoroughgoing, unadulterated

unmixed 4 deep, mere, neat, pure 5 plain,
sheer, utter 6 simple 7 perfect, sincere
8 absolute, straight 9 unalloyed, undiluted
11 unmitigated, unqualified 13 unadulterated

unmodern 3 old 5 dated, passé
7 antique, archaic, old-time, vintage 9 out-
of-date 10 antiquated, oldfangled 12 old-
fashioned

unmodifiable 5 fixed 8 constant, straight
9 immovable, immutable, unmovable
10 inflexible, invariable 11 inalterable, unalterable 12 unchangeable

unmovable see **immovable**

unmoved 4 calm, cool, firm 5 stony
6 serene 7 adamant 8 obdurate, stubborn,
unshaken 9 apathetic, impassive

unmoving 5 inert 6 static 8 immobile,
stagnant 10 stationary

unnamed 8 nameless 9 anonymous
10 innominate 12 undesignated

unnatural 6 off-key 7 deviant, uncanny
8 abnormal 9 anomalous, divergent, irregular, unregular 10 superhuman 11 supernormal, supranormal 13 superordinary

unneat 5 messy 6 sloppy, untidy
7 unkempt 8 careless, ill-kempt, slipshod,
slovenly, uncombed 12 unfastidious

unnecessary 6 excess, lavish 7 profuse,
surplus 8 needless, prodigal 9 redundant
10 gratuitous, unrequired 11 inessential,
superfluous, uncalled-for, unessential

unneeded see **unnecessary**

unnerve 3 sap 5 unman, upset 6 weaken
7 agitate, perturb 8 bewilder, castrate, confound, distract, enervate, enfeeble, unstring
9 undermine 10 emasculate

unneutral 6 biased, warped 7 colored,
partial 8 one-sided, partisan 9 jaundiced
10 prejudiced 11 tendentious 12 prepossessed

unnoted 7 obscure, unfamed, unknown
8 nameless 9 unheard-of 10 unobserved,
unremarked, unrenowned 12 uncelebrated,
unconsidered

unobservant 9 unheeding 10 unnoticing,
unwatchful 11 inattentive 12 unperceiving

unobserving see **unobservant**

unobstructed 4 open 5 clear 8 unclosed

unobtrusive 5 quiet, tasty 7 subdued
8 tasteful 10 restrained

unoccupied 4 free, idle 5 empty
10 unemployed

unofficial 8 informal 9 irregular 13 unceremonious

unorganized 7 muddled 8 inchoate
10 disjointed, disordered, incoherent, inco-

hesive 11 unconnected 12 disconnected, uncontinuous 13 discontinuous

unoriginal 3 dry 4 arid, dull 5 staid 6 barren, stodgy, stuffy 7 prosaic, sterile, unfired 10 uncreative, uninspired 11 noncreative, uninventive

unornamented 3 dry 5 plain 6 simple 9 unadorned 11 inelaborate, unelaborate, ungarnished 12 unbeautified 13 unembellished, unembroidered

unorthodox 9 dissident, heretical, sectarian 10 schismatic 13 nonconformist

unorthodoxy 6 heresy, schism 7 dissent 9 disbelief 10 dissidence 13 nonconformism, nonconformity

unpaid 3 due 5 owing 6 mature 7 overdue, payable 8 freewill, wageless 9 unsettled, voluntary, volunteer 10 gratuitous 11 outstanding 13 uncompensated, unrecompensed, unremunerated

unpalatable 4 flat, thin, weak 5 washy 6 bitter, watery 7 galling, insipid, painful 8 grievous, nauseous, unsavory 9 loathsome, savorless, sickening, tasteless 10 afflictive, flavorless 11 distasteful, ill-flavored 12 unappetizing

unparalleled 5 alone 6 unique 8 peerless 9 matchless, unequaled, unmatched, unrivaled

unperceiving see unobservant

unpermissive 5 rigid 6 strict 8 rigorist, rigorous 9 draconian, stringent 10 ironhanded

unphysical 8 bodiless 9 asomatous 10 discarnate, immaterial, unembodied 11 disembodied, incorporeal, nonmaterial

unpierceable 10 impervious 11 impregnable 12 impenetrable

unpitying 9 merciless 10 unmerciful

unplanned 6 random 7 aimless, unaimed 9 desultory, haphazard, hit-or-miss, undevised, unthought 10 designless, undesigned, unintended, unpurposed 11 inadvertent, purposeless 12 unconsidered 13 unintentional

unpleasant 3 bad 4 sour 5 seamy 6 rotten 7 unhappy 11 displeasing, distasteful 12 disagreeable *combining form:* 3 cac 4 caco

unpliable 6 mulish 8 perverse, stubborn 9 obstinate, pigheaded 10 bullheaded, headstrong, self-willed 12 pertinacious

unplug 3 ope 4 open 6 uncork 7 unblock 10 disconnect

unpolished 4 rude 5 crude, rough 6 unhewn 7 boorish, ill-bred, incivil, loutish, lowbred, uncivil 8 churlish, cloddish, impolite, unformed, unworked 9 roughhewn, undressed, unrefined 10 uncultured, unfinished, ungracious 11 clodhopping, disgra-

cious, ill-mannered, uncivilized, unfashioned 12 discourteous 13 disrespectful

unpracticed 3 raw 5 fresh, green 6 callow 7 untried 8 untested, unversed 13 inexperienced

unpredictable 4 iffy 6 chancy 7 erratic 9 fluctuant, uncertain, whimsical 10 capricious

unprejudiced 4 fair, just 5 equal 8 unbiased 9 equitable, impartial, objective, uncolored 13 dispassionate

unpressed 7 wrinkly

unpretentious 5 plain 6 modest, simple 10 unaffected 11 inelaborate, unelaborate, ungarnished 12 unbeautified 13 unembellished

unpretty 5 plain 6 homely 8 uncomely 10 unalluring, unhandsome 11 unbeauteous, unbeautiful 12 unattractive

unprincipled 5 venal 7 corrupt, crooked 9 abandoned, dishonest, dissolute, mercenary, reprobate, unethical 10 licentious, praetorian, profligate 12 unscrupulous

unproductive 4 vain 6 barren, futile 7 useless 8 impotent, infecund 9 fruitless, infertile, unbearing, unfertile 10 unavailing 11 ineffectual, unavailable 12 hardscrabble

unprofitable 4 idle, vain 7 useless

unprogressive 8 backward, ignorant 9 benighted 10 behindhand 11 undeveloped 13 unenlightened

unpropitious 4 dire 7 adverse, baleful, baneful, counter, fateful, ominous, unlucky 9 ill-boding, ill-omened 11 threatening 12 antagonistic

unprosperous 3 low 4 poor 5 broke, needy 8 indigent 9 destitute, penurious 11 fortuneless, impecunious 12 impoverished

unprotected 6 unsafe 8 helpless, insecure 9 unguarded 10 undefended, unshielded 11 defenseless, unsheltered

unproved 7 untried 8 untested

unpunctual 4 late 5 lated, tardy 7 belated, overdue 10 behindhand

unqualified 4 firm, pure, rank, sure 5 clear, gross, sheer, unfit, utter 6 entire, simple, steady 7 abiding, blasted, blessed, express, perfect, unmixed 8 absolute, complete, enduring, explicit, infernal, unfitted 9 incapable, out-and-out, steadfast, unalloyed, undiluted, unlimited, unskilled 10 confounded, ineligible, unequipped, unreserved, unsuitable 11 incompetent, unfaltering, unmitigated 12 never-failing, wholehearted 13 unadulterated, unconditional

unquenchable 9 insatiate, unsatiate 10 insatiable

unquestionable 4 flat, real, true, very 7 certain, genuine 8 bona fide, positive 9 authentic, downright, undoubted, up-and-down 10 sure-enough 11 established, well-founded 12 wellgrounded

unquestioning 4 firm, sure 5 fixed 6 steady 7 abiding 8 enduring, unshaken 9 steadfast 10 unshakable 12 never-failing

unravel 5 break, solve 6 unfold, unknit 7 dope out, resolve, unsnarl 8 decipher, dissolve, unriddle, untangle 9 extricate, figure out, puzzle out 11 disentangle

unreadable 9 illegible

unreal 7 fictive 8 chimeric, fanciful, illusory 9 fantastic, fictional, imaginary 10 chimerical, fictitious 12 supposititious *combining form:* 5 pseud 6 pseudo

unrealistic 8 fanciful 10 ivory-tower 11 impractical, unpractical 12 ivory-towered 13 ivory-towerish

unreasonable 3 mad 5 loose, undue 7 invalid 8 improper, overmuch, unlawful, wrongful 9 arbitrary, excessive, illogical, sophistic 10 fallacious, immoderate, inordinate, irrational, peremptory, reasonless, unrightful 11 incongruous, nonrational, unwarranted

unreasoned 3 mad 7 invalid 9 illogical, sophistic 10 fallacious, irrational, reasonless 11 nonrational

unrecompensed 6 unpaid 13 uncompensated

unrefined 3 raw 4 rude 5 crass, crude, gross, rough 6 coarse, impure, native, vulgar 7 boorish, ill-bred, loutish, lowbred, natural, uncouth 8 churlish, cloddish, ungraded, unsorted 9 inelegant, roughcast, roughhewn, run-of-mine, undressed 10 uncultured, unpolished 11 clodhopping, uncivilized, unprocessed

unreflective 8 careless, feckless, heedless, uncaring 9 unheeding 10 unthinking 11 inadvertent, thoughtless

unrehearsed 7 offhand 9 extempore, impromptu, unstudied 10 improvised 11 extemporary

unrelated 8 discrete, separate 9 disjoined

unrelenting 4 grim 6 mortal 8 ruthless 9 merciless 10 implacable, ironfisted, unyielding 11 unflinching 12 unappeasable

unreliable 5 false, slick 6 fickle, shifty, tricky, unsafe, unsure, untrue 7 dubious, inexact 8 slippery, untrusty 9 faithless, trustless, unassured 10 fly-by-night, inaccurate, inconstant, perfidious, unfaithful 11 vacillating 12 falsehearted 13 untrustworthy

unreligious 7 godless

unremarkable 5 plain, usual 7 routine 8 everyday, ordinary, workaday 9 plain Jane, quotidian

unremitting 7 endless 8 constant, unending 9 ceaseless, continual, perpetual,

unceasing 12 interminable 13 uninterrupted

unremorseful 7 unsorry 10 impenitent, regretless, uncontrite

unremunerated 6 unpaid

unrenowned 7 obscure, unfamed, unknown, unnoted 8 nameless 9 unheard-of 12 uncelebrated

unrepentant 7 unsorry 10 impenitent, regretless, uncontrite 11 remorseless

unrepresentative 7 deviant 8 aberrant, abnormal, atypical 9 anomalous, untypical 11 heteroclite

unrequested 7 unasked 8 unbidden, unsought 9 uninvited

unrequired 8 needless, unneeded 9 omissible, unneedful 11 dispensable, inessential, uncalled-for, unessential, unnecessary 12 nonessential

unreserved 4 open 5 frank, plain 6 breezy, candid, casual, dégagé 7 relaxed, unfussy 8 informal, outgoing, outright 9 easygoing, expansive 11 low-pressure, openhearted, unconcealed, undisguised, unvarnished 12 undissembled 13 demonstrative, unconstrained

unresolved 8 hesitant, wavering 9 faltering, uncertain 10 hesitating, indecisive, irresolute, undecisive 11 vacillating 12 shilly-shally

unrespectable 5 shady 6 shabby, shoddy 8 shameful 10 inglorious 11 disgraceful, ignominious

unresponsive 4 cold 6 frigid 9 inhibited 10 insentient, undersexed 11 insensitive, passionless 13 insusceptible, unimpressible, unsusceptible

unresponsiveness 6 apathy, phlegm 8 stoicism 9 stolidity 11 impassivity 13 insensibility

unrest 5 chaos 6 tumult 7 ailment, anarchy, ferment, turmoil, unquiet 8 disorder, disquiet, upheaval 9 agitation, commotion, confusion 10 convulsion, inquietude, turbulence 11 disquietude, restiveness 13 Sturm und Drang

unrestrained 4 free, open 5 bluff, blunt, frank, loose 6 candid 7 brusque, rampant 8 outgoing, reinless, uncurbed 9 audacious, excessive, expansive 10 forthright, immoderate, inordinate, ungoverned, unhampered, untempered 11 intemperate, plainspoken, uninhibited, untrammeled 13 demonstrative, overindulgent

unrestraint 4 ease 7 abandon 11 naturalness, spontaneity 13 impulsiveness

unrestricted 4 free, open 6 public 10 accessible

unrighteous 6 unfair, unjust 9 inequable 11 inequitable, unequitable

unripe 5 green, young 6 callow, infant 8 immature, juvenile, youthful 9 unfledged

unrivaled 4 only 5 alone 6 unique 8 peerless 9 matchless, unmatched 11 unparagoned 12 unparalleled

unrobe see unclothe

unroll 6 extend, uncoil, unfurl, unwind 7 open out

unromantic 4 cool, hard 5 sober 9 practical, pragmatic, realistic 10 hard-boiled, hardheaded 11 down-to-earth 12 matter-of-fact 13 unsentimental

unruffled 4 calm, cool 6 serene 8 composed, tranquil 9 collected 10 nonchalant 11 unflappable 13 imperturbable

unruly 4 hard, wild 5 rowdy, tough 7 froward, naughty, raffish, raucous, wayward 8 contrary, indocile, perverse, rowdyish, untoward 9 fractious, obstinate, ruffianly, termagant, turbulent 10 boisterous, disorderly, rampageous, rebellious, rowdydowdy, tumultuous 11 disobedient, indomitable, intractable, rumbustious 12 contumacious, incorrigible, obstreperous, rambunctious, recalcitrant, ungovernable, unmanageable 13 insubordinate, undisciplined

unsacred 3 lay 7 profane, secular 8 temporal

unsafe 5 risky, shaky 6 chancy 7 erratic, tottery, unsound 8 insecure, perilous, unstable 9 dangerous, hazardous, unassured, uncertain 10 jeopardous, unreliable 12 undependable 13 untrustworthy

unsaid 5 tacit 7 implied 8 implicit, inferred, nonvocal, unspoken, wordless 9 unuttered 10 undeclared, understood 11 unexpressed

unsalutary 7 noisome, noxious 9 unhealthy 11 unhealthful, unwholesome 12 insalubrious

unsatisfactory 3 bad, bum 4 poor, punk 5 amiss, wrong 6 rotten

unsatisfiable 9 insatiate 10 quenchless

unsavory 4 flat 7 insipid 9 tasteless 10 flavorless 11 distasteful, ill-flavored, unpalatable 12 unappetizing

unsay 6 abjure, recall, recant 7 retract 8 forswear, palinode, take back, withdraw

unscathed 4 safe 8 unharmed

unscented 8 odorless

unschooled 5 naive 6 simple 7 artless, natural 8 ignorant, untaught 9 benighted, ingenuous, unstudied, untutored 10 illiterate, unaffected, uneducated, unlettered 11 emptyheaded, know-nothing 12 unartificial, uninstructed

unscramble 5 untie 7 untwine 8 untangle 9 extricate 10 disembroil, disentwine, unentangle 11 disencumber, disentangle 12 disembarrass

unscrupulous 5 shady, venal 6 crafty 7 corrupt, crooked 8 improper, scheming, sinister, unseemly, wrongful 9 deceitful, dishonest, mercenary, underhand, unethical 10 praetorian 12 questionable, unprincipled

unseasonable 5 inapt, inept, unapt, undue 8 ill-timed, improper, mistimed, untimely 10 malapropos, unbecoming 11 inopportune, unfortunate 12 inauspicious, inconvenient, infelicitous 13 inappropriate

unseasoned 3 raw 5 fresh, green, young 6 callow 7 untried 8 unversed 9 unfleshed 11 unpracticed 13 inexperienced

unseat 5 pitch, throw 6 depose, remove 7 buck off, unhorse 8 dethrone

unseemliness 9 indecorum 10 inelegance 11 impropriety

unseemly 5 crude, inapt, inept, rough, rowdy, unapt 6 coarse 7 raffish, ungodly 8 ill-timed, improper, indecent, untoward 9 inelegant, ruffianly, unrefined 10 indecorous, indelicate, malapropos, malodorous, unbecoming, undecorous, unsuitable 11 unbefitting 13 inappropriate

unseen 9 invisible

unsentimental see unromantic

unserviceable 7 useless 11 impractical 12 univ ersal 13 nonfunctional

unsettle 4 turn 5 upset 6 bother, flurry, jumble, sicken 7 agitate, derange, disturb, fluster, perturb, rummage, trouble, unhinge 8 disarray, disorder, disquiet 9 incommode 10 disarrange, discommode, discompose 11 disorganize

unsettled 3 due 4 back, open 5 fluid 6 mature, mobile, queasy, remote, uneasy, unpaid 7 clouded, dubious, mutable, overdue, payable, pendent, pending, protean, unclear, unquiet 8 doubtful, frontier, restless, unstable, unsteady, variable, weathery 9 changeful, dubitable, uncertain, undecided, unrestful 10 changeable, indecisive, unpeaceful, untranquil 11 outstanding, problematic 12 undetermined

unsex 3 fix 4 geld 5 alter 6 change, neuter 8 castrate, mutilate 9 sterilize 11 desexualize

unshackle 4 free 5 loose 6 loosen, unbind 7 manumit, release, unchain 8 liberate 9 discharge 10 emancipate

unshakable 4 firm, sure 5 fixed 6 steady 7 abiding 9 steadfast 10 unwavering 11 unfaltering 12 never-failing 13 unquestioning

unshaped 8 formless, inchoate, unformed 9 amorphous

unshared 4 sole 6 single 9 exclusive

unship 6 unlade, unload, unstow 7 offload 9 disburden, discharge

unshod 8 barefoot, shoeless 10 unsandaled

unshroud 6 debunk, expose, show up, unmask 7 uncloak, undress 8 discover

unshut 3 ope 4 open, undo 6 unstop 7 unblock, unclose

unsightly 4 drab, dull, ugly 7 hideous 8 uncomely 9 ill-shaped, unshapely 10 ill-favored, ill-looking, lackluster, unesthetic 11 unbeautiful

unsimilar 6 unlike 7 distant, diverse, unalike, unequal, various 9 different, disparate, divergent

unskilled 5 green, inept 7 amateur, jackleg 10 amateurish 12 dilettantish, dilettantist 13 unworkmanlike

unskillful 5 inapt, inept, unapt 6 clumsy, gauche 7 awkward, inadept, unhandy, unready 8 inexpert, unexpert, unfacile, unfitted 9 butcherly, incapable 11 incompetent, inefficient, undexterous, unqualified 12 unproficient 13 unworkmanlike

unsleeping 5 alert 7 wakeful 8 open-eyed, vigilant, watchful 9 wide-awake

unsmooth 5 harsh, rough 6 craggy, jagged, ruffly, rugged, uneven 7 scraggy, unlevel 8 asperous, scabrous

unsnarl see untangle

unsociable 3 shy 4 cool 5 aloof, timid 6 offish, remote, shut-in 7 distant, prickly 8 brooding, reserved, solitary, standoff 9 diffident, exclusive, secretive, sensitive, unbending, withdrawn 11 indifferent, standoffish 12 inaccessible

unsoiled 5 clean 7 cleanly 8 spotless 9 taintless, unsullied 10 immaculate

unsophisticated 5 crude, green, naive 6 callow, simple 7 artless, genuine, natural, uncouth 9 ingenuous, untutored, unworldly 10 unaffected, unschooled 12 unartificial

unsorted 3 raw 5 crude, mixed 6 impure, motley, native, varied 8 ungraded 9 unrefined 11 promiscuous 12 multifarious 13 heterogeneous, miscellaneous

unsought 7 unasked 8 unbidden, unwanted, unwished 9 undesired, uninvited, unwelcome 11 unrequested

unsound 3 mad 4 daft, weak 5 batty, false, frail, hairy, risky, wrong 6 chancy, crazed, faulty, flawed, flimsy, infirm, insane, untrue, weakly, wicked 7 cracked, damaged, fragile, lunatic 8 decrepit, demented, deranged, perilous, specious 9 dangerous, erroneous, hazardous, imperfect, incorrect, unhealthy 10 inaccurate, jeopardous, unbalanced 11 treacherous 13 insubstantial, unsubstantial *mentally:* 6 insane

unsparing 4 free 6 severe 7 liberal 8 generous, handsome 9 bounteous, bountiful 10 freehanded, munificent, open-handed

unspeakable 6 odious 7 hateful 9 atrocious, loathsome, obnoxious, offensive, repellent, repugnant, repulsive, revolting 10 disgusting, outrageous 11 distasteful 13 inexpressible, unexpressible

unspoiled 6 intact, virgin 8 pristine, untapped, virginal 9 undefiled, untouched

unspoken 4 mute 5 tacit 6 hinted, silent, unsaid 7 implied 8 implicit, inferred, unstated, unvoiced, wordless 9 intimated, suggested, unuttered 10 undeclared, understood 11 unexpressed

unstable 4 weak 5 fluid, rocky, shaky 6 dickey, fickle, mobile, moving, shifty, tricky, unsure, wobbly 7 buoyant, dubious, elastic, protean, suspect 8 doubtful, freakish, insecure, rootless, slippery, ticklish, volatile, wavering, weathery 9 ambiguous, changeful, fluctuant, mercurial, resilient, uncertain, unsettled 10 borderline, capricious, inconstant, lubricious, precarious 11 vacillating 12 effervescent 13 temperamental

unsteady 5 fluid, rocky, tippy 6 jiggly, mobile, moving, shifty, wobbly 7 movable, mutable, protean, rickety, tottery 8 slippery, staggery, tittuppy, variable, weathery 9 changeful, uncertain, unsettled 10 changeable, inconstant *British:* 5 wonky

unsteel 5 unarm 6 disarm 7 win over

unstop 3 ope 4 open, undo 6 uncork, unplug, unshut 7 unblock, unclose

unstow 6 unlade, unload, unship 7 offload 9 disburden, discharge

unstrengthen 3 sap 5 blunt 6 weaken 7 cripple, disable, unbrace 8 enfeeble 9 attenuate, undermine 10 debilitate

unstudied 5 naive 6 simple 7 artless, natural, offhand 8 unversed 9 extempore, impromptu, ingenuous, unlearned, untutored 10 improvised, unaffected, unschooled 11 extemporary, spontaneous, unrehearsed 12 unartificial

unstylish 5 dowdy, tacky 6 démodé, frumpy, stodgy 8 frumpish, outmoded 9 out-of-date

unsubstantial 4 thin, weak 5 frail, shaky 6 feeble, flimsy, infirm, weakly 7 fragile, tenuous, unsound 8 bodiless, decrepit, insecure 9 spiritual 10 immaterial, improbable, incredible, unembodied, unphysical 11 implausible, incorporeal, nonmaterial, nonphysical 12 metaphysical, unbelievable, unconvincing, undependable 13 inconceivable

unsuccess 4 bomb, flop 6 defeat 7 failure, reverse, setback

unsuitable 5 inapt, inept, undue, unfit 6 unmeet 7 unhappy 8 ill-timed, improper, unfitted, untimely 9 ill-suited 10 ill-adapted, unbecoming 11 unbefitting 13 inappropriate

unsuited 5 inapt, unfit 6 unmeet 8 unfitted 10 ill-adapted, inadequate 12 inadmissible, unacceptable 13 disappointing, inappropriate, objectionable

unsullied 4 pure 5 clean 6 chaste, decent, modest 7 cleanly 8 spotless, unsoiled 9 stainless, taintless, undefiled 10 immaculate 11 unblemished

unsure 4 open, weak 5 shaky 6 dickey, wobbly 7 dubious, unclear 8 doubtful, insecure, rootless, unstable, untrusty, wavering 9 fluctuant, trustless, unassured, uncertain, undecided 10 borderline, indecisive, suspicious, unreliable 11 problematic, unconfident, vacillating 12 questionable, undependable 13 untrustworthy

unsurpassable 7 supreme 8 towering, ultimate 10 preeminent 12 transcendent

unsusceptible 9 impassive 10 insentient 11 insensitive 12 unresponsive

unsuspecting 6 unwary 9 credulous

unsuspicious see **unsuspecting**

unswayable 5 rigid 8 obdurate 10 inflexible, relentless, unyielding 11 uncompliant 12 single-minded

unswerving see **unfaltering**

unsymmetrical 6 uneven 7 unequal 8 lopsided 9 irregular 10 off-balance 12 overbalanced

unsympathetic 4 cold, cool 6 frigid 7 callous 8 aversive, kindless, lukewarm, obdurate, ungenial 9 heartless, repellent, repugnant, unfeeling, unlikable 10 dislikable, hard-boiled, unpleasant, unpleasing 11 coldhearted, displeasing, halfhearted, hardhearted, indifferent, uncongenial, unemotional 12 stonyhearted 13 disinterested

untactful 5 brash 9 impolitic, maladroit, unpolitic 12 undiplomatic

untamed 4 wild 5 feral 9 unsubdued

untangle 7 unsnarl, untwine, untwist 9 discumber, extricate 10 disembroil, disentwine, unscramble 11 disencumber 12 disembarrass

untapped 6 virgin 8 virginal 9 unspoiled, untouched

untaught 8 ignorant 9 benighted, untutored 10 illiterate, uneducated, unlettered, unschooled 11 empty-headed, know-nothing 12 uninstructed

untempered 9 excessive 10 immoderate, inordinate 12 unrestrained 13 overindulgent

untended 7 run-down 9 neglected 10 uncared-for

Unter den ____ 6 Linden

untested 7 untried 8 unproved 11 unpracticed

unthankful 9 thankless 10 ungrateful

unthinkable 4 rare 6 unique 7 unusual 8 singular, uncommon, unwonted 10 incredible, unordinary 11 exceptional 13 extraordinary

unthinking 8 careless, feckless, heedless, uncaring 9 unheeding 11 inadvertent, thoughtless 12 irreflective, unreflective

unthorough 5 messy 6 botchy, sloppy, untidy 8 careless, slapdash, slipshod, slovenly

unthought 9 undevised, unplanned 10 undesigned, unintended, unpurposed 11 inadvertent 13 unintentional

unthrift 5 waste 6 lavish, waster 7 spender, wastrel 8 prodigal, squander 9 overdoing 10 high roller, lavishness, profligate, squanderer 11 improvident, prodigality, scattergood 12 extravagance, extravagancy, wastefulness

unthrifty 6 lavish 8 prodigal, wasteful 10 thriftless 11 extravagant, improvident

untidy 5 messy 6 botchy, sloppy, unneat 7 unkempt 8 careless, ill-kempt, slapdash, slipshod, slovenly, uncombed 10 disheveled, unthorough 12 unfastidious

untie 6 loosen, unknot, unlace, unlash 8 unstring 9 extricate 10 disembroil, disentwine, unentangle, unscramble 11 disencumber, disentangle 12 disembarrass

untighten 3 lax 4 ease 5 loose, relax, slack 6 loosen 7 ease off, slacken

until 2 to 4 till, up to 5 since 6 before 7 prior to 11 in advance of

untimely 4 soon 5 early, inapt, unapt, undue 8 ill-timed, improper, mistimed, oversoon, previous 9 overearly, premature 10 malapropos, unsuitable 11 ill-seasoned, inopportune 12 intempestive, unseasonable 13 inappropriate

untiring 8 tireless 9 weariless 10 unflagging, unwearying 11 unweariable 13 indefatigable, inexhaustible

untold 4 huge, vast 6 mighty 7 immense, mammoth, titanic 8 enormous, gigantic 9 countless, monstrous, uncounted, unrelated 10 innumerous, numberless, prodigious, unnumbered 11 innumerable, uncountable 12 unnumberable

untouchable 5 leper 6 pariah 7 Ishmael, outcast 8 castaway, déclassé, derelict, outcaste, outsider 10 Ishmaelite 11 offscouring

untouched 4 pure 5 sound, whole 6 entire, intact, virgin 7 perfect 8 flawless, pristine, unmarred, untapped, virginal 9 undamaged, unspoiled 11 unblemished

untoward 4 wild 5 rough 6 unruly 7 hapless, ungodly, unhappy, unlucky 8 ill-fated, improper, indecent, indocile, luckless, unseemly **9** fractious **10** ill-starred, indecorous, indelicate, unbecoming, undecorous **11** intractable, star-crossed, unfortunate **12** misfortunate, recalcitrant, ungovernable, unmanageable **13** undisciplined

untrained see **unskilled**

untrammeled **8** uncurbed **9** audacious **10** ungoverned, unhampered **11** uninhibited **12** unrestrained

untried **3** raw **5** fresh, green **6** callow, unripe **8** immature, unproved, untested, unversed **9** half-baked **10** unseasoned **11** unpracticed **12** unconversant **13** inexperienced

untroubled **4** calm **5** quiet, still **6** hushed, placid, stilly **7** halcyon

untroublesome **4** easy **5** light, royal **6** facile, simple, smooth **10** effortless

untrue **5** false, wrong **7** inexact, unloyal, unsound **8** disloyal, forsworn, perjured, recreant, specious **9** erroneous, faithless, imprecise, incorrect, unprecise **10** inaccurate, perfidious, traitorous, unfaithful **11** treacherous *combining form:* **5** pseud **6** pseudo

untruism **3** fib, lie **4** tale **5** story **6** canard **7** bouncer **9** falsehood **13** prevarication

untrustworthy **6** unsafe, unsure **7** dubious **9** unassured **10** fly-by-night, unreliable **12** questionable, undependable

untruth **3** fib, lie **4** tale **5** error, story **6** canard **7** fallacy, falsity **9** falsehood, falseness **13** erroneousness, prevarication

untruthful **5** false, lying, wrong **6** shifty **7** knavish, roguish **8** delusive, delusory, unhonest **9** deceitful, deceptive, dishonest, incorrect **10** inaccurate, mendacious, misleading

untruthfulness **7** fibbery **9** falsehood, mendacity **10** unveracity

untune **5** upset **6** bother, flurry **7** agitate, disturb, fluster, perturb, unhinge **8** disquiet **10** discompose

untutored see **unschooled**

untwine see **untangle**

untwist see **untangle**

untypical see **unusual**

unusable **7** useless **11** impractical **12** unfunctional **13** nonfunctional

unused **4** idle **6** vacant

unusual **3** odd **4** rare **6** freaky, quaint, unique **7** bizarre, curious, deviant, oddball, strange **8** aberrant, abnormal, freakish, peculiar, singular, uncommon, unwonted **9** anomalous, eccentric, untypical **10** outlandish, unordinary **11** exceptional, unthinkable **12** unimaginable **13** extraordinary *combining form:* **4** anom **5** anomo

unusually **5** extra **6** rarely **8** uncommon **9** extremely **10** uncommonly

unutterable **5** awful **7** awesome **8** wondrous **9** marvelous, wonderful **10** incredible, prodigious **13** inexpressible, unexpressible

unuttered see **unspoken**

unvaried **5** alike **7** uniform **10** monotonous

unvarnished see **undisguised**

unvarying see **unchanging**

unveil see **uncover**

unversed **3** raw **5** fresh, green **6** callow **7** untried **9** unfleshed **10** unseasoned **11** unpracticed **12** unconversant **13** inexperienced

unvigilant **6** unwary **7** unalert **9** unguarded **10** incautious, unwatchful

unvital **5** petty **6** paltry, peanut **7** trivial **8** piddling, trifling **12** inconsequent

unvoiced see **unspoken**

unwanted see **unwelcome**

unwarranted **5** undue **8** baseless **9** unfounded **10** bottomless, gratuitous, groundless, ungrounded **11** uncalled-for **12** unreasonable **13** unjustifiable

unwary **4** rash **5** brash, hasty **7** unalert **8** reckless **9** credulous, hotheaded, unadvised, unguarded **10** ill-advised, incautious, unvigilant **11** thoughtless **12** unsuspecting, unsuspicious **13** inconsiderate

unwashed **3** low, mob **4** base, mean, scum **5** dregs, lowly, trash **6** humble, masses, rabble **7** ignoble, lowborn **8** baseborn, canaille, plebeian, riffraff **10** unennobled **11** proletariat

unwasteful **5** canny, chary **6** frugal, saving **7** sparing, thrifty **9** provident, stewardly **10** economical

unwatchful **7** unalert **9** unguarded, unheeding **10** incautious, unnoticing, unvigilant **11** inattentive, inobservant, unobservant, unobserving **12** unperceiving

unwatered **3** dry **4** arid, sere **7** bone-dry, thirsty **8** droughty **9** waterless **12** moistureless

unwavering see **unfaltering**

unwearying **6** steady **8** constant, tireless, untiring **9** unceasing, weariless **10** unflagging **12** interminable **13** indefatigable, inexhaustible

unwed see **unmarried**

unwelcome **7** unasked **8** unsought, unwanted, unwished **9** obnoxious, repellent, undesired **10** ill-favored, unpleasant, unpleasing **11** distasteful, undesirable **12** inadmissible, unacceptable **13** exceptionable, objectionable

unwell **3** ill, low **4** mean, sick **5** frail, rocky, shaky **6** ailing, feeble, infirm, offish, poorly, queasy, sickly, weakly, wobbly **7** underly **8** off-color, qualmish **9** squeamish **10** indisposed

unwholesome 4 foul 6 sickly 7 baneful, harmful, hideous, hurtful, noxious, obscene 8 horrible 9 injurious, offensive, repellent, repulsive, unhealthy 10 disgusting, insalutary, pernicious, unsalutary 11 deleterious, detrimental, unhealthful 12 insalubrious

unwieldy 5 bulky, heavy 6 clumsy 7 awkward, massive, onerous, unhandy 8 cumbrous 9 lumbering, ponderous 10 burdensome, cumbersome 11 encumbering 12 inconvenient, unmanageable

unwilling 4 loth 5 loath 6 afraid, averse 7 uneager 8 backward, hesitant 9 reluctant 10 indisposed 11 disinclined

unwind 5 relax, unlax 6 unbend, unreel, unroll 7 ease off 8 loosen up

unwise 5 inane, inept, naive 7 fatuous, foolish, unsound, witless 8 childish, immature 9 ill-judged, impolitic, imprudent, misguided, senseless 10 ill-advised, indiscreet 11 impractical, injudicious, thoughtless, undesirable, unfortunate 13 inappropriate, unintelligent

unwished see unwelcome

unwishful 4 loth 5 loath 6 afraid, averse 7 uneager 8 backward, hesitant 9 reluctant 10 indisposed 11 disinclined

unwitting 7 unaware 8 ignorant 9 forgetful, oblivious, unknowing, unmindful 10 unfamiliar, uninformed 11 incognizant 12 inconversant, unacquainted, uninstructed

unwitty 5 silly 6 simple 7 asinine, fatuous, foolish, witless 8 mindless 9 brainless 10 weak-headed, weak-minded

unwonted 4 rare 6 unique 7 unusual 8 singular, uncommon 10 unordinary 11 exceptional, unthinkable 12 unimaginable 13 extraordinary

unworkable 7 useless 10 impossible, infeasible, unfeasible 11 impractical 12 unfunctional 13 nonfunctional

unworked 4 rude 5 crude, rough 6 unhewn 8 unformed 9 roughhewn, undressed 10 unfinished, unpolished 11 unfashioned

unworkmanlike 5 inept 8 inexpert, unexpert 9 incapable, unskilled 10 unskillful 11 incompetent, inefficient

unworldly 5 naive 6 astral, dreamy, simple 7 artless, natural 9 daydreamy, ingenuous, unstudied, untutored, visionary 10 unaffected, unschooled 11 daydreaming 12 unartificial

unworthy 6 drossy, no-good 7 inutile, nothing 9 no-account, valueless, worthless

unwrap see uncover

unwrinkled 6 smooth

unwritten 4 oral 6 spoken, verbal 11 traditional, word-of-mouth

unwrought see unworked

unyielding 4 firm, grim, hard 5 fixed, rigid, stern, stiff, tough 6 mortal, mulish 8 hardcore, hard-line, obdurate, ruthless, stubborn 9 impliable, inelastic, merciless, obstinate, pigheaded 10 bullheaded, headstrong, implacable, inexorable, inflexible, ironfisted, refractory, relentless, self-willed, unflexible, unswayable 11 immalleable, incompliant, intractable, uncompliant, unflinching, unrelenting 12 pertinacious, single-minded, unappeasable

unyoke 5 untie 6 unbind, unlink 7 disjoin, outspan, unhitch

up 4 hike, jump, lift, rise, soar 5 arise, boost, mount, raise 6 ascend, aspire, au fait, red-hot, uprear, versed 7 abreast, versant 8 familiar, increase, informed 9 au courant 10 acquainted, conversant, down-to-date 12 contemporary *prefix:* 2 an 3 ana, sur

up-and-coming 4 keen 5 alert, eager, ready 7 go-ahead 9 gumptious 12 enterprising

upbear 4 prop 5 brace, carry 7 bolster, shore up, support, sustain 8 buttress

upbeat 4 fond 8 sanguine 10 optimistic 12 Pollyannaish

upbraid 4 lash, rate 5 scold 6 berate, revile 7 bawl out, chew out 8 bless out 10 tongue-lash, vituperate

upchuck 4 barf, spew 5 vomit 6 spit up 7 bring up, throw up 8 disgorge

upcoming 7 nearing 8 foreseen 11 approaching, prospective

up-country 4 bush 6 sticks 8 backland, backwash, frontier 9 backwater, backwoods, boondocks 10 hinterland

update 5 renew 7 refresh, restore 8 renovate 9 modernize, refurbish 10 rejuvenate

Updike novel 10 Rabbit, Run, The Centaur, Bech is Back 11 Rabbit Redux 12 Rabbit at Rest, Rabbit is Rich

upend 4 beat, drub, lick, trim, whip 6 wallop 7 clobber, shellac, trounce 9 overwhelm

upgrade 3 wax 4 hike, rise 5 boost 6 prefer 7 advance, elevate, promote 8 increase 12 breakthrough

upgrowth 8 progress 9 evolution, flowering, unfolding 10 evolvement 11 development, progression

upheaval 6 change, clamor, outcry, tumult, upturn 7 ferment, heaving 8 churning, disaster, stirring 9 cataclysm, commotion 10 alteration, convulsion 11 catastrophe

uphill 4 hard 6 rugged 7 arduous, labored, operose 8 toilsome 9 difficult, effortful, laborious, strenuous

uphold 3 aid 4 back, help, lift, prop, rear 5 brace, carry, hoist, raise 6 assist, bear up, buoy up, defend, pick up, take up, upbear, uplift, uprear **7** bolster, elevate, justify, shore up, support, sustain, upraise **8** advocate, backstop, buttress, champion, maintain, side with **9** underprop, vindicate

upland 5 table **7** plateau

uplift 4 rear **5** edify, hoist, raise **6** illume, pick up, take up, uphold, uprear **7** elevate, improve, upraise **8** illumine **9** enlighten, irradiate **10** illuminate

upon 4 atop *prefix:* **2** ep **3** eph, epi

upper class 5 elite **6** flower, gentry **7** quality, society, who's who **9** blue blood, gentility **11** aristocracy

upper crust see **upper class**

upper hand 6 better **7** victory **9** advantage **11** superiority

uppermost 3 top **6** apical **7** highest **8** loftiest

uppity 5 brash **7** forward, pushful, pushing **9** presuming **11** overweening **12** presumptuous **13** self-asserting, self-assertive

upraise 4 lift, rear **5** cheer, hoist **6** buck up, pick up, solace, take up, uphold, uplift, uprear **7** comfort, console, elevate

uprear 4 lift, rise, soar **5** arise, build, erect, exalt, hoist, honor, mount, put up, raise **6** ascend, aspire, pick up, take up, uphold, uplift **7** dignify, elevate, ennoble, glorify, magnify, sublime, upraise **9** construct **10** aggrandize **11** distinguish

upright 4 fair, good, just, pure, true **5** erect, moral, noble **6** arrect, honest, raised **8** ethical, stand-up **8** elevated, virtuous **9** blameless, equitable, exemplary, honorable, impartial, righteous **10** high-minded, principled, scrupulous, straight-up, upstanding **13** conscientious *combining form:* **4** orth **5** ortho

uprightness 6 virtue **7** honesty, probity **8** morality, nobility **9** integrity, rectitude **12** reputability

uprising 6 revolt **9** rebellion **10** revolution **12** insurrection

uproar 3 din **4** coil, to-do **5** babel, brawl, broil, chaos, furor, melee, whirl **6** clamor, fracas, furore, hassle, hubbub, jangle, pother, racket, ruckus, rumpus, shindy, tumult **7** shindig, turmoil **8** brouhaha, disorder, foofaraw **9** commotion, confusion **10** hullabaloo, hurly-burly, tintamarre, turbulence **11** pandemonium

uproarious 5 noisy **7** rackety **8** clattery, noiseful, sonorous **10** clangorous

uproot 4 grub, move **5** abate, shift **6** uptear **7** abolish, blot out, destroy, replace, subvert, wipe out **8** demolish, displace, overturn, supplant, uncreate **9** eradicate, extirpate, overthrow, supersede **10** annihilate, transplant **11** exterminate

upset 3 ail **4** bend, cark, turn **5** curve, lay up, mix up, unman, worry **6** bother, flurry, invert, jumble, muddle, sicken, suffer, topple, tumble **7** afflict, agitate, derange, disturb, fluster, invalid, perturb, reverse, rummage, tip over, trouble, unhinge, unnerve **8** bewilder, confound, disarray, disorder, disquiet, distract, distress, overturn, turn over, unsettle **9** indispose, knock over, overthrow **10** debilitate, disarrange, discompose **12** incapacitate

upshot 4 core, gist, meat, pith **5** event, issue, sense, short **6** burden, climax, effect, ending, finish, result, sequel, thrust **7** outcome, purport **9** aftermath, substance **10** completion, conclusion **11** aftereffect, consequence, culmination, eventuality, termination

upside-down 5 snafu **7** chaotic, haywire, jumbled, mixed-up **8** confused, fouled-up, inverted, reversed **10** downside-up, topsy-turvy **13** helter-skelter

upspring 4 flow, head, rise **5** arise, get up, issue **6** uprise **7** emanate, proceed, stand up **9** originate **10** derive from

upstanding see **upright**

upstart 3 cad **4** boor, lout, slob **5** comer, rowdy **6** mucker **7** bounder, parvenu **8** outsider, roturier **9** arriviste, roughneck, vulgarian **11** guttersnipe **12** nouveau riche **13** social climber

upsurge 3 wax **4** rise **5** build, mount **6** expand **7** augment, enlarge **8** heighten, increase, multiply

uptight 4 edgy **5** nervy, tense **6** uneasy **7** restive

uptightness 6 unease **7** tension

up till 2 to **5** until **6** before **7** prior to **11** in advance of

up to 4 till **5** until **6** before **11** in advance of

up-to-date 6 modern, modish, red-hot, timely **7** abreast, a la mode, dashing, fitting, stylish **8** advanced, suitable **9** au courant, expedient, opportune **10** convenient **12** contemporary

Urania see **Muse**

Uranus *mother, wife:* **2** Ge **4** Gaea *offspring:* **6** Titans **8** Cyclopes *overthrower, son:* **6** Cronus

urban 4 city, town **5** civic **6** public **7** burghal, oppidan, popular, village **9** inner city, municipal **12** metropolitan

urbane 5 bland, civil, suave **6** poised, smooth **7** affable, genteel, refined **8** balanced, cultured, gracious, obliging, polished, well-bred **9** civilized, courteous, distingué **10** cultivated **12** cosmopolitan, metropolitan

urbanize 6 citify

urchin 3 imp 4 brat 5 child, gamin, scamp, whelp 7 dickens, mudlark 8 bratling 10 ragamuffin, street arab 11 guttersnipe, hobbledehoy *combining form:* 6 echino

Urdur, Urth see Norn

urge 3 egg, sic 4 coax, goad, itch, lust, prod, push, rush, sick, spur 5 drive, egg on, hurry, impel, press, prick, set on, shove, tar on, tarre 6 cajole, compel, desire, exhort, hustle, incite, motive, needle, prompt, propel, spring 7 craving, impulse, passion, provoke, solicit, wheedle 8 appetite, blandish, pressure 9 constrain, encourage, incentive 10 appetition 12 high-pressure

urgency 8 entreaty, exigence, instancy, pressure 10 insistence 11 importunity

urgent 6 crying 7 burning, clamant, driving, instant 8 pressing 9 clamorous, demanding, impelling, insistent 10 imperative 11 importunate

Uriah, Urijah *father:* 8 Shemaiah *slayer:* 9 Jehoiakim *son:* 8 Meremoth *wife:* 9 Bathsheba

Uriel 9 archangel *father:* 6 Kohath *grandson:* 6 Abijah

Uris, Leon *novel:* 5 QBVII 6 Exodus, The Haj, Trinity 9 Battle Cry 13 The Angry Hills

Uri's son 5 Geber 7 Bezalel

urn 4 vase 7 samovar *Greek:* 7 amphora

Ursa Major 9 Great Bear

Ursa Minor 10 Little Bear *star:* 7 Polaris

Ur's son 7 Eliphal

Uruguay *capital:* 10 Montevideo *monetary unit:* 4 peso

usable 4 open 9 operative 10 accessible, functional

usage 3 way 4 form, lead, wont 5 habit, trick 6 choice, custom, manner, praxis 7 guiding, process 8 ceremony, guidance, habitude, practice 9 formality, procedure 10 convenance, convention, preference, proceeding *combining form:* 4 nomo

use 3 ply, run, way 4 duty, goal, mark, need, play, take, talk, wont, work 5 apply, avail, habit, inure, serve, speak, treat, trick, value, wield, worth 6 bestow, custom, demand, employ, govern, handle, manage, manner, object, parley, praxis, profit, target 7 account, benefit, control, exploit, fitness, operate, purpose, service, utility, utilize 8 accustom, ceremony, deal with, efficacy, exercise, exertion, function, habitude, impose on, occasion, practice, regulate 9 advantage, appliance, formality, habituate, objective, operation, relevance 10 converse in, employment, exercising, impose

upon, manipulate 11 application, familiarize 12 adaptability, availability 13 applicability

used 8 shopworn 10 secondhand

used up 5 all in, spent 6 bleary, effete 7 drained, far-gone, worn-out 8 depleted 9 exhausted, washed-out

useful 3 fit 4 good, meet 5 brave, handy, utile 6 proper, toward 7 benefic, helpful 8 favoring, suitable 9 favorable, practical 10 beneficial, convenient, functional, propitious 11 appropriate, practicable, serviceable 12 advantageous

usefulness 7 account, service, utility 9 advantage, relevance 13 applicability

useless 4 vain 6 futile 7 fustian, inutile 8 abortive, unusable 10 unavailing, unpurposed, unworkable 11 impractical, ineffective, ineffectual, unavailable 12 unfunctional, unproductive 13 impracticable, nonfunctional, unserviceable

user 6 addict 7 pothead 8 utilizer *suffix:* 4 ster

use up 3 eat 4 draw 5 drain, spend 6 devour, expend, finish 7 consume, deplete, exhaust 8 bankrupt, draw down 10 impoverish, run through

usher 4 lead 7 precede, preface 9 introduce

usher in 5 set up 6 launch 8 initiate 9 institute, introduce, originate 10 inaugurate

U.S.S.R, former *capital:* 6 Moscow *leader:* 5 Beria (Lavrenty), Lenin (Vladimir) 6 Stalin (Joseph) 7 Gromyko (Andrey), Kosygin (Aleksey), Molotov (Vyacheslav) 8 Andropov (Yury), Brezhnev (Leonid), Bukharin (Nikolay), Podgorny (Nikolay), Zinovyev (Grigory) 9 Chernenko (Konstantin), Gorbachev (Mikhail) 10 Khrushchev (Nikita) *monetary unit:* 5 ruble *republic:* 5 Tajik, Uzbek 6 Kazakh, Kirgiz, Latvia, Russia 7 Armenia, Estonia, Georgia, Tadzhik, Turkmen, Ukraine 8 Moldavia 9 Kirgiziya, Lithuania 10 Azerbaijan, Belorussia, Kazakhstan, Tajikistan, Uzbekistan 12 Turkmenistan

usual 4 rife 5 plain, typic 6 common, normal, wonted 7 chronic, current, general, natural, regular, routine, typical 8 accepted, everyday, familiar, ordinary, workaday 9 customary, plain Jane, prevalent, quotidian 10 accustomed, prevailing 11 commonplace 12 unremarkable

usually 7 as a rule 8 commonly, wontedly 9 sometimes 10 by ordinary, frequently, now and then, ordinarily 11 customarily, now and again 12 consistently, once and again

usurer 7 Shylock 9 loan shark

usurp 6 assume, cutout 7 preempt

8 accroach, arrogate, displace, supplant **10** commandeer **11** appropriate

Utah *capital:* **12** Salt Lake City *college, university:* **10** Weber State **12** Brigham Young *neighbor:* **5** Idaho **6** Nevada **7** Arizona, Wyoming **8** Colorado *nickname:* **11** Mormon State **12** Beehive State *state flower:* **8** sego lily

utensil 4 fork, tool **5** knife, spoon **8** coquille, teaspoon **9** implement **10** instrument *cooking:* (see at **kitchen**)

uterus 4 womb

Uther Pendragon *son:* **6** Arthur *wife:* **6** Ygerne **7** Igraine

utile 5 handy **6** useful **9** practical **10** functional **11** practicable, serviceable

utilitarian 4 hard **7** practic **9** practical, pragmatic, realistic **10** unromantic **11** down-to-earth, pragmatical **12** matter-of-fact, unidealistic *philosopher:* **4** Mill (John Stuart) **7** Bentham (Jeremy)

utility 3 use **7** account, fitness, service **9** advantage, relevance **10** usefulness

utilize 3 use **5** apply **6** bestow, employ, handle **7** advance, exploit, forward, further, promote **8** exercise

utmost 3 top **7** extreme, maximal, maximum, outside **8** damndest, darndest, farthest, furthest, remotest **9** damnedest, darnedest

utopia 4 Zion **6** heaven **7** arcadia **8** paradise **9** Cockaigne, dreamland, fairyland, Shangri-la **10** dreamworld, lubberland, never-never, wonderland **12** promised land

Utopia author 4 More (Thomas)

utopian 5 ideal, lofty **6** edenic **7** dreamer **8** abstract, arcadian, idealist **9** ambitious, grandiose, ideologue, visionary **10** idealistic, impossible, millennial, unfeasible **11** pretentious **12** otherworldly **13** castle-builder, impracticable

Uttar Pradesh *capital:* **7** Lucknow *country:* **5** India

utter 3 say **4** blue, dang, darn, durn, pure, rank, talk, tell **5** black, blank, gross, sheer, speak, stark, state, total, voice **6** arrant, blamed, dashed, deuced **7** blasted, blessed, chime in, declare, deliver, doggone, flat-out, goldarn, perfect, regular **8** absolute, all-fired, blighted, blinding, bring out, complete, crashing, infernal, outright, positive, throw-out, vocalize **9** dad-blamed, dad-burned, downright, out-and-out, verbalize **10** blithering, confounded, consummate, dad-blasted, double-dyed **11** come out with, straight-out, unmitigated, unqualified **13** blankety-blank, thoroughgoing

utterance 4 talk, vent, word **5** parol, voice **6** speech **8** speaking, vocalism **9** discourse, statement **10** expression **12** articulation, vocalization **13** verbalization

utterly 3 all **4** just, well **5** à fond, fully, plumb, quite **6** in toto, purely, wholly **7** exactly, totally **8** all in all, entirely **9** perfectly **10** altogether, completely, thoroughly

uttermost 7 extreme **8** farthest, furthest, remotest

Utu 6 sun-god *father:* **5** Nanna *mother:* **6** Ningal

Uzai's son 5 Palal

Uzal's father 6 Joktan

Uzbek capital 8 Tashkent

Uzzah *father:* **6** Shimei **8** Abinadab *son:* **6** Shimea

Uzzi *father:* **4** Bani **5** Bukki **6** Michri *son:* **4** Elah **8** Zerahiah

Uzziah *father:* **5** Harim, Shaul **7** Amaziah *son:* **6** Jotham **8** Jonathan

Uzziel *brother:* **5** Amram, Izhar *father:* **6** Kohath **8** Harhaiah, Jeduthun *grandfather:* **4** Levi *son:* **6** Sithri **7** Mishael **8** Elzaphan **9** Elizaphan

V

vacancy 4 void 6 vacuum 7 vacuity 8 voidness 9 blankness, emptiness 11 vacuousness 12 desertedness

vacant 4 bare, idle, void 5 blank, clear, empty, inane, stark, unlet 6 unused 7 deadpan, untaken, vacuous, witless 8 unfilled 10 tenantless, unoccupied 11 emptyheaded, thoughtless 12 inexpressive, unexpressive

vacate 4 quit, void 5 annul, clear, empty, leave, quash 6 give up, repeal, revoke 7 abandon, rescind, retract, reverse 8 abrogate, dissolve, part from, part with 9 discharge 10 relinquish

vacation 4 rest, trip 5 break, leave 6 recess 7 holiday, respite, time off 8 furlough 12 intermission *resort:* 3 spa

vacationer 7 tourist, tripper

vaccination 4 shot 7 booster 9 injection 11 inoculation

vaccine 4 shot 5 serum *Inventor:* 6 Jenner (Edward)

vacillate 3 wag 4 halt, swag, sway 5 dally, waver 6 dawdle, dither, falter, seesaw, teeter, waggle, wigwag, wobble 7 stagger, swither, whiffle 8 hesitate 9 alternate 12 fiddle-faddle, shilly-shally, teeter-totter, wiggle-waggle

vacillating 4 weak 5 shaky, timid 6 dickey, fickle, unsure, wobbly 7 erratic, halting, unfixed 8 dallying, dawdling, doubtful, doubting, hesitant, insecure, rootless, shifting, stalling, unstable, unsteady, volatile, wavering 9 demurring, eccentric, faltering, fluctuant, mercurial, pendulous, tentative, uncertain, unsettled, weak-kneed, whiffling 10 changeable, hesitating, inconstant, indecisive, irresolute, undecisive, unresolved 11 fluctuating, oscillating 12 double-minded, shilly-shally, wigglewaggle 13 dillydallying

vacillation 5 doubt 8 dallying, demurral, stalling, to-and-fro, wavering 9 hesitancy 10 hesitation, indecision 12 irresolution, shilly-shally 13 dillydallying

vacuity 4 hole, nada, void 6 cavity, hollow 7 inanity, nullity, vacancy 8 bareness, dullness, nihility, voidness 9 blankness, bleakness, emptiness, inaneness, stupidity 10 barrenness, hollowness 11 nothingness,

vacuousness 12 desolateness, nonexistence

vacuous 4 bare, dull, void 5 blank, clear, empty, inane, silly, stark 6 stupid, vacant 7 foolish, shallow 11 empty-headed, superficial

vacuousness 7 vacancy, vacuity 8 voidness 9 blankness, emptiness

vacuum 4 void 5 space 9 emptiness

vacuum tube 5 diode 6 triode 7 pentode, tetrode *casing:* 4 bulb *suffix:* 4 tron

vade mecum 5 guide 6 manual 8 Baedeker, handbook 9 guidebook 10 compendium 11 enchiridion

vadimonium 4 bond 6 pledge 8 contract, security

____ **Vadis** 3 Quo

vagabond 3 bum 4 hobo, roam, rove 5 drift, gypsy, piker, range, rogue, rover, stiff, stray, tramp 6 beggar, boomer, canter, picaro, ramble, roamer, roving, wander 7 drifter, floater, gangrel, meander, migrant, nomadic, swagger, swagman, traipse, tramper, vagrant 8 bohemian, clochard, derelict, picaroon, roadster, runabout, runagate, straggle, traveler, wanderer 9 itinerant, itinerate, straggler, transient, wandering, wayfaring 10 street arab 11 perambulant, peripatetic, Weary Willie 13 parambulatory

vagarious 5 kinky 7 erratic 8 freakish, whimsied 9 arbitrary, whimsical 10 capricious 12 unreasonable

vagary 3 bee 4 kink, whim 5 dream, fancy, freak, humor, quirk 6 megrim 7 boutade, caprice, conceit, fantasy 8 crotchet, day-dream

vagrancy 6 roving 7 hoboism, roaming 8 nomadism, rambling 9 itineracy, wandering 10 itinerancy

vagrant see **vagabond**

vague 3 dim 4 hazy 5 blear, faint, foggy, misty, muddy, mushy 6 bleary, blurry, cloudy, dreamy, opaque, vapory 7 bleared, obscure, shadowy, unclear, unplain 8 nebulous, vaporous 9 ambiguous, dreamlike, equivocal, tenebrous, uncertain 10 illdefined, indefinite, indistinct, unexplicit 12 undetermined 13 indeterminate, unsubstantial

vain 4 idle, puny, void 5 empty, pensy, petty, proud 6 futile, hollow, otiose, paltry 7 foppish, haughty, stuck-up, trivial, useless 8 abortive, arrogant, boastful, bootless, conceity, dandyish, delusive, delusory, egoistic, nugatory, trifling 9 conceited, fruitless, valueless, worthless 10 egocentric, misleading, profitless, unavailing 11 coxcombical, ineffective, ineffectual, unavailable 12 narcissistic, self-exalting, unproductive, unprofitable, vainglorious 13 inefficacious, self-conceited, self-important, swollen-headed

vainglorious 7 stuck-up 8 boastful, bragging, conceity, insolent, vaunting 9 conceited 10 disdainful 12 narcissistic, supercilious 13 self-conceited

vainglory 5 pride 6 egoism 7 bombast, conceit, egotism 8 parading 9 arrogance, flaunting, self-glory, self-pride 10 exhibition 11 haughtiness, self-opinion 12 boastfulness

vainness see vanity

valance 5 drape 7 curtain, drapery

vale 4 dale, glen 5 combe 6 valley 8 farewell

valediction 7 good-bye 8 farewell

valedictory 7 good-bye, parting 8 farewell 9 departing

valentine 4 card 7 beloved 10 sweetheart

Valentine *beloved:* 6 Silvia *sister:* 8 Margaret *slayer:* 5 Faust *twin brother:* 5 Orson *wife:* 9 Clerimond

valet 3 man 4 goad 7 servant 10 manservant

Vali *father:* 4 Odin *guardian of:* 7 justice *mother:* 4 Rind 5 Rindr *victim:* 5 Hoder

valiance see valor

valiant see valorous

valid 4 just, true 5 legal, licit, solid, sound 6 cogent, lawful, potent, strong 7 telling 8 attested, decisive, verified 9 confirmed, effective, effectual 10 acceptable, conclusive, convincing, definitive, determined, persuasive, satisfying 11 established 12 corroborated, demonstrated, satisfactory 13 determinative, substantiated

validate 5 prove 6 ratify, verify 7 approve, bear out, confirm, endorse, justify, probate 8 legalize, sanction 11 corroborate, rubberstamp 12 authenticate, substantiate

validity 5 force, point, punch 7 cogency, gravity, potency 8 efficacy 9 soundness 13 effectiveness

validness see validity

valise 3 bag 4 grip 7 luggage 8 gripsack, suitcase

Valjean's pursuer 6 Javert

Valkyrie 6 maiden 8 Brynhild

valley 4 dale, dell, glen, vale 5 basin, combe, gorge, gully, swale 6 canyon, din-

gle, hollow, ravine, rincon 10 depression *Africa-Asia:* 4 Rift 9 Great Rift *Alps:* 11 Grindelwald *ancient Greece:* 5 Nemea *arid:* 6 bolson *California:* 4 Napa 5 Death, Squaw 8 Imperial, Yosemite 11 San Fernando *Dead Sea area:* 6 Arabah *Dominican Republic:* 5 Cibao *Egypt:* 6 Kharga *England:* 5 Doone *Germany:* 4 Ruhr *Greece:* 5 Tembi, Tempe *India:* 4 Kulu *Ireland:* 5 Avoca, Ovoca *Israel:* 4 Elah *Lebanon:* 4 Bika *moon:* 5 rille *New York:* 6 Sleepy 12 Sleepy Hollow *Pennsylvania:* 7 Nittany *Scotland:* 7 Glen Roy *steep:* 6 ravine *Switzerland:* 5 Hasli *Virginia:* 10 Shenandoah *volcanic:* 5 atrio *Washington:* 11 Grand Coulee

vallum 4 wall 7 rampart

Valmiki's epic 8 Ramayana

valor 4 guts, sand 6 mettle, spirit 7 bravery, courage, heroism, prowess 8 backbone, tenacity, valiance, valiancy 9 fortitude, gallantry 10 resolution

valorous 4 bold 5 brave 7 doughty, valiant 8 fearless, intrepid 9 audacious, dauntless, undaunted 10 courageous

valuable 4 dear 6 costly, prized, worthy 7 admired 8 esteemed, precious, property 9 expensive, priceless, respected, treasured 11 appreciated

valuate 4 rate 5 assay, set at 6 assess, survey 8 appraise, estimate

valuation 4 cost 5 price, worth 6 charge, rating 7 account, opinion 8 estimate, judgment 9 appraisal 10 assessment, estimation 12 appraisement

value 4 cost, rate 5 assay, gauge, merit, price, prize, set at, worth 6 assess, charge, esteem, figure, reckon, revere, survey, virtue 7 account, apprize, caliber, care for, cherish, compute, expense, quality, stature 8 appraise, estimate, treasure, venerate 9 appraisal, reverence 10 appreciate, assessment *Scottish:* 4 feck

valueless 6 draffy, drossy, no-good 7 inutile, nothing 8 unworthy 9 worthless

valve 3 tap 4 cock, gate 6 faucet, poppet, spigot 7 hydrant, petcock, shutoff 8 stopcock *cardiac:* 6 mitral 8 bicuspid

vamoose 3 git 4 kite, scat 5 scram 6 begone, decamp, get out 7 skiddoo, take off 8 clear out, hightail 9 skedaddle

vamp 3 fix 4 do up, mend 5 fix up, flirt, frame, patch, siren 6 cook up, devise, invent, make up, repair 7 brush up, charmer, concoct, dream up, enticer, furbish, hatch up, rebuild, touch up 8 contrive, coquette, overhaul 9 formulate, inveigler, refurbish, temptress 10 gold digger, seductress 11 enchantress, femme fatale, recondition, reconstruct

vampire 3 bat 7 Dracula 9 Nosferatu 11 bloodsucker

van 3 car 4 head, lead 5 truck, wagon 6 leader 7 vehicle

vandal 4 lout 6 looter, ruiner 7 defacer, hoodlum, ravager, ruffian, spoiler, wrecker 8 hooligan, pillager, ruinator 9 despoiler, destroyer, plunderer, spoliator 10 devastator, iconoclast

vandalize 3 mar 5 trash, wreck 6 deface, rip off, tear up 7 destroy

Vandal king 8 Genseric

Vandyke 5 beard

vane 3 arm 9 indicator 11 weathercock

vanguard 9 forefront

Vaniah's father 4 Bani

vanilla 7 extract

vanish 3 die 4 fade, melt 5 clear 8 dissolve, evanesce, melt away 9 disappear, evaporate 13 dematerialize

vanity 6 egoism 7 conceit 8 self-love 9 vainglory

Vanity Fair author 9 Thackeray (William Makepeace)

vanquish 4 beat 5 crush 6 defeat, humble, reduce, subdue 7 conquer, subvert, trample 8 bear down, beat down, overturn, surmount 9 overpower, subjugate

vanquisher 5 champ 6 master, victor, winner 7 subduer 8 champion, defeater 9 conqueror 10 subjugator

vanquishment 4 rout 6 defeat 7 beating, debacle, licking, mastery, subdual 8 drubbing 9 overthrow, trouncing 10 defeasance 11 shellacking, subjugation

vantage 4 draw, edge, odds 5 bulge, start 8 deadwood, handicap 9 allowance, head start

vapid 4 dull, flat, weak 5 inane 6 jejune 7 insipid, sapless 9 driveling, innocuous, milk-toast, tasteless 10 flavorless, namby-pamby, wishy-washy 13 unimaginative, uninteresting

vapor 3 fog, gas 4 haze, mist, smog 5 brume, cloud, smoke, steam 6 breath, nimbus *combining form:* 3 atm 4 atmo, mano 5 atmid 6 atmido 7 pneumat 8 pneumato *condensed:* 3 dew *frozen:* 4 rime 5 frost *noxious:* 6 miasma

vaporize 4 boil 9 evaporate

vaporous 4 airy, hazy 5 foggy, gassy, misty, mushy, vague, wispy 6 aerial, cloudy, unreal 7 gaseous 8 ethereal, illusory 13 unsubstantial

vaquero 6 cowboy 8 herdsman

varia 10 miscellany

variable 5 fluid 6 fickle, fitful, mobile, shifty 7 mutable, protean, unequal 8 slippery, ticklish, unstable, unsteady, volatile, weathery 9 changeful, irregular, mercurial, spasmodic, uncertain, unequable, unset-

tled, ununiform 10 capricious, changeable, inconstant 13 temperamental

variance 6 change, strife 7 discord, dissent 8 conflict, disunity, division, severing 9 deviation, disaccord, sundering, variation 10 contention, difference, dissension, dissidence, separation 11 fluctuation

variation 4 turn 5 shift 6 change 8 mutation, variance 9 disparity 10 alteration, deflection, difference, divergence 11 discrepancy 12 modification 13 dissimilarity

varicolored see **variegated**

varicose 7 cirsoid, dilated, swollen

varied 5 mixed 6 motley 8 assorted, chowchow 11 promiscuous 12 conglomerate, multifarious 13 heterogeneous, miscellaneous

variegated 4 pied 5 pinto 6 calico, motley, mottle 7 checked, dappled, flecked, freaked, marbled, mottled, piebald, spotted 8 discolor, skewbald, speckled, stippled, streaked 9 checkered, multihued, spattered 10 multicolor, parti-color, polychrome, versicolor 11 varicolored 12 multicolored, particolored, versicolored 13 polychromatic

variety 3 ilk 4 kind, rank, sort, type 5 grade 6 medley, nature, stripe 7 species 8 multeity 9 character, diversity, variation 10 assortment, miscellany 11 description, diverseness, variousness 12 multiformity, multiplicity 13 heterogeneity

various 4 many, some 6 divers, legion, sundry, unlike, varied 7 certain, distant, diverse, several, unalike, unequal, variant, varying 8 assorted, changing, discrete, distinct, numerous, peculiar, populous, separate 9 different, disparate, divergent, unsimilar 10 dissimilar, individual, omnigenous, voluminous 11 distinctive 12 multifarious, multitudinal 13 heterogeneous, miscellaneous, multitudinous

varlet 5 knave 6 rascal 9 scoundrel

varmint 6 animal, rascal 7 critter

varnish 4 coat 5 glaze, japan, white 6 veneer, whiten 7 shellac 8 palliate 9 extenuate, gloss over, gloze over, sugarcoat, whitewash 10 blanch over *component:* 5 resin

vary 3 run 4 part, turn 5 alter, range 6 change, depart, differ, divide, extend, modify, mutate 7 deviate, digress, discord, dissent, diverge, qualify 8 disagree, modulate, separate 9 disaccord, refashion

vase 3 jar, urn 4 ewer 6 crater, krater, vessel 7 amphora, potiche 8 boughpot

Vashni's father 6 Samuel

Vashti's husband 6 Xerxes 9 Ahasuerus

vassal 4 esne, leud, serf 5 helot, liege, slave 6 tenant, varlet 7 bondman, feodary, homager, peasant, servant, subject 8 liege-

man 9 dependent, underling 11 beneficiary, subordinate *high-ranking:* 7 vavasor
8 vavasour *office:* 5 feoff

vast 3 big 4 huge, wide 5 ample, broad,
giant, large 6 cosmic 7 immense, titanic
8 colossal, enormous, far-flung, gigantic,
spacious, whopping 9 capacious, expansive 10 monumental, tremendous, widespread 12 astronomical

vastness 8 enormity, hugeness 9 immensity, magnitude 12 enormousness

vat 3 tub, tun 4 back, beck, cask, kier, tank
5 keeve, kieve 6 barrel, vessel 7 cistern
8 cauldron *cheese:* 7 chessel

vatic 6 mantic 7 fatidic 8 Delphian, oracular 9 prophetic, sibylline 11 apocalyptic,
prophetical

Vatican *chapel:* 7 Sistine *church:*
11 Saint Peter's *ruler:* 4 Pope *site:*
4 Rome

vaticinal see vatic

vaticinate 4 call 5 augur 7 portend, predict, presage 8 forecast, foretell, prophesy
9 adumbrate 13 prognosticate

vaudeville 4 song 5 revue 7 variety
9 burlesque 13 entertainment

vaudevillian 5 actor, comic 6 dancer,
singer 7 acrobat 9 performer 11 entertainer

vault 3 hop, lop, pit 4 arch, cave, dome,
jump, leap, over, rise, room, soar, tomb
5 bound, clear, crypt, mount 6 ascend,
bounce, cavern, cellar, hurdle, spring,
upleap 7 saltate 8 catacomb, overjump,
overleap, surmount, upspring 9 negotiate
10 undercroft

vaulting 7 emulous 8 aspiring 9 ambitious 12 enthusiastic 13 opportunistic

vaunt 4 blow, brag, crow, puff 5 boast,
mouth, prate 6 expose, flaunt, parade
7 display, exhibit, show off 8 brandish
9 gasconade 11 rodomontade

Ve *brother:* 4 Odin, Vili *victim:* 4 Ymir

veal 4 calf *cutlet:* 9 schnitzel *roasted:*
10 fricandeau *shank:* 8 osso buco

vector 7 carrier

Vedic *god:* 4 Agni, Soma, Vayu, Yama
5 Aditi, Bhaga, Dyaus, Indra, Mitra, Rudra
6 Aditya, Varuna 7 Savitar *goddess:*
4 Usas 5 Ushas *hymn:* 6 mantra *language:* 8 Sanskrit *treatise:* 9 Upanishad
writing: 7 Samhita

veer 3 dip, yaw 4 skew, slue, turn, whip
5 avert, pivot, sheer, shift, twist, wheel,
whirl 6 depart, divert, swerve 7 bear off,
deflect, deviate, digress, diverge 8 angle
off, train off 9 volte-face

vega 5 plain 6 meadow

vegetable 3 pea, soy, yam 4 bean, beet,
corn, kale, leek, okra, soya, taro, wort

5 chive, cress, green, onion, plant 6 carrot,
celery, cowpea, endive, garlic, lentil, peanut, pepper, potato, radish, sorrel, squash,
tomato, turnip 7 cabbage, chayote, dullard,
lettuce, mustard, parsley, parsnip, pumpkin,
rhubarb, salsify, shallot, soybean, spinach
8 broccoli, collards, cucumber, eggplant,
kohlrabi, lima bean, rutabaga, scallion
9 artichoke, asparagus, muskmelon
10 watermelon 11 cauliflower, horseradish,
sweet potato *dish:* 5 salad *mold:* 5 humus
oyster: 7 salsify *pear:* 7 chayote *seller:*
6 grocer 7 grocery 12 costermonger
sponge: 5 luffa *spread:* 4 oleo 9 margarine

vegetarian 9 herbivore

vegetate 4 idle, laze 8 languish, stagnate
9 hibernate

vegetation 5 flora 6 growth, plants 7 verdure 8 greenery *floating:* 4 sudd 8 pleus-
ton

vehement 3 hot 4 wild 5 rabid 6 ardent,
fervid, fierce, hearty, heated, lively, potent
7 fervent, frantic, furious, intense, vicious,
violent, zealous 8 emphatic, forceful, powerful, terrible 9 delirious, desperate, energetic, exquisite, perfervid 10 passionate,
pronounced 11 impassioned 12 concentrated

vehicle 3 bus, car, van 4 auto, tool
5 agent, buggy, means, organ, sedan,
wagon 6 agency, medium, vector 7 carrier,
channel 8 ministry 9 implement, transport
10 automobile, conveyance, instrument
baby's: 4 pram 8 carriage, stroller *child's:*
4 bike 5 trike 7 bicycle, scooter 8 tricycle
combining form: 6 mobile *farm:* 4 wain
7 tractor *horse-drawn:* 4 cart, dray
5 buggy, lorry, sulky, wagon 6 hansom,
landau 8 carriage *military:* 4 jeep, tank
one-wheeled: 8 unicycle *passenger:*
3 bus, cab, car 4 auto, taxi 7 ricksha *public:* 3 bus 4 tram 5 train 6 subway
7 omnibus, trolley *Roman:* 7 chariot *winter:*
4 sled 6 sleigh 8 snowplow

veil 4 hide, mask, wrap 5 cloak, color,
cover, front, guise 6 enfold, enwrap,
facade, invest, mantle, screen, shroud
7 blanket, conceal, cover up, curtain,
enclose, envelop, secrete 8 calyptra, coloring, disguise, enshroud 10 camouflage,
false front, overspread, spread over *Muslim:* 7 yashmak *netting:* 6 maline
7 malines

vein 3 way 4 hint, line, lode, mind, mode,
mood, seam, tone, tube, vena 5 humor,
shade, style, tenor, tinge, touch, trace 6 fettle, manner, nature, spirit, strain, streak,
temper, vessel 7 channel, fashion 8 tincture 9 character, suspicion 10 complexion,

suggestion **11** disposition, temperament *combining form:* **3** ven **4** veni, veno **5** phleb **6** phlebo *deposit:* **3** ore *fluid:* **5** blood *leaf:* **3** rib *leg:* **7** saphena *neck:* **7** jugular *small:* **6** venule *varicose:* **5** varix

velar 7 palatal

veldt 5 plain **6** meadow **9** grassland

velitation 5 brush, run-in, set-to **8** skirmish **9** encounter

velleity 4 mind, will, wish **5** fancy **6** liking **8** pleasure, volition **11** inclination

vellicate 3 jig, lug, nip **4** jerk, snap, yank **5** lurch, pinch **6** fidget, jiggle, twitch

velocipede 4 bike **5** cycle **7** bicycle **10** two-wheeler

velocity 3 bat **4** gait, pace **5** haste, hurry, speed **7** headway, impetus **8** celerity, dispatch, momentum, rapidity **9** quickness, rapidness, swiftness **10** expedition

velum 4 veil **8** membrane

velvet 5 cloth **6** fabric, profit **8** winnings *on:* **4** rich, safe **7** wealthy

velvety 4 soft **5** plush, silky, sleek, slick **6** glossy, plushy, satiny, silken, smooth **7** cottony **10** velutinous

venal 4 hack, paid **6** sordid **7** buyable, corrupt, crooked, ignoble, vicious **8** bribable, hireling, infamous **9** mercenary, nefarious, unethical **10** flagitious, iniquitous, praetorian **11** corruptible, purchasable **12** unprincipled, unscrupulous

vend 4 give, hawk, sell, toot **5** sound **6** blazon, market, monger, peddle **7** declare, publish **8** announce, huckster, proclaim **9** advertise, broadcast **10** promulgate

vendee 5 buyer **6** emptor **9** purchaser

vendetta 4 feud **9** blood feud

vendible 7 salable **8** sellable **10** marketable

vendibles 5 goods, wares **11** commodities, merchandise

vendor 6 duffer, hawker, seller **7** higgler, packman, peddler, roadman **8** huckster, merchant, outcrier, salesman **9** cheap-jack, cheap-john

vendue 4 sale **7** auction

veneer 4 face, mask, show, veil **5** cover, front, gloss, white **6** facade, whiten **7** coating, varnish **8** disguise, palliate **9** extenuate, gloss over, gloze over, sugarcoat, whitewash **10** blanch over, false front

venerable 3 old **4** aged **5** hoary **6** age-old, sacred **7** ancient, antique, elderly, honored, revered, stately **8** imposing, Noachian, reverend, timeworn **9** admirable, dignified, estimable, honorable **10** reverenced, worshipful **11** patriarchal, reverential **12** antediluvian

venerate 5 adore, honor **6** revere **7** idolize, worship **9** reverence

veneration 3 awe **5** dulia, honor **6** esteem, homage **7** respect, worship **9** reverence

venery 4 game **5** chase **7** hunting

venesection 10 phlebotomy **12** bloodletting

Venetian *boat:* **7** gondola *boatman:* **9** gondolier *canal:* **3** rii (plural), rio *ruler:* **4** doge *street:* **5** canal

Venezuela *capital:* **7** Caracas *monetary unit:* **7** bolivar

Venezuelan *herdsman:* **7** llanero *liberator:* **7** Bolívar (Simón) *people:* **5** Carib **6** Timote

venge 7 redress **9** vindicate

vengeance 6 return **7** revenge **8** avenging, reprisal, requital, revanche **9** repayment **10** avengement **11** counterblow, retaliation, retribution

vengeful 7 hostile **8** inimical, wreakful **9** rancorous **10** vindictive **12** antagonistic

venial 5 minor **7** trivial **8** harmless, trifling **9** allowable, excusable, tolerable **10** forgivable, pardonable, remittable **13** insignificant

Venice of the East 7 Bangkok

Venice of the North 9 Stockholm

Veni, Creator ___ 8 Spiritus

venireman 5 juror

venison 4 deer

veni, vidi, ___ 4 vici

venom 4 bane **5** virus **6** poison, rancor **7** ill will, vitriol **9** contagion, malignity, virulence

venomous 5 toxic **6** deadly, malign, poison **7** baleful, malefic **8** mephitic, toxicant, viperish, viperous, virulent **9** malignant, poisonous, viperlike **10** maleficent, malevolent

vent 3 air, put **4** emit, give, hole, slit, slot **5** issue, loose, state, utter, voice **6** assert, outlet **7** cast out, declare, exhaust, express, give off, give out, opening, orifice, release, unleash **8** aperture, throw off **9** discharge, statement, take out on, utterance **10** expression **12** articulation, vocalization **13** verbalization

venter 3 gut **5** belly **6** paunch **7** abdomen, stomach

ventilate 3 air, put **4** give, moot **5** state **6** broach, debate, go into, take up, talk of **7** bring up, discuss, express, publish **8** rap about, talk over **9** advertise, broadcast, introduce, thresh out **10** deliberate

ventral area 7 abdomen *combining form:* **5** gastr **6** gaster, gastri, gastro **7** gastero

ventricle 7 chamber *combining form:* **4** cele, coel **5** coele

ventriloquist *companion:* **5** dummy *famous:* **6** Bergen (Edgar)

venture 3 bet, try 4 dare, defy, face, feat, gest, risk 5 beard, brave, crack, fling, front, peril, stake, wager 6 banter, chance, expose, gamble, hazard 7 attempt, emprise, exploit, imperil, jeopard, lay open, operate, outdare, outface, play for 8 endanger, jeopardy 9 adventure, challenge, speculate 10 enterprise, jeopardize 11 speculation, undertaking

venturesome 4 bold, rash 5 brave, stout 6 daring, sturdy 8 overbold, reckless, stalwart 9 audacious, daredevil, foolhardy 11 adventurous, temerarious

venturous see venturesome

venue 4 side, site 5 place 6 ground, locale

Venus 6 planet, Vesper 8 Hesperus; (see also **Aphrodite**)

Venus de ___ 4 Milo

___ vera 4 aloe

veracious 4 just, true 5 right, valid 6 direct, strict 8 accurate, faithful, truthful 9 veridical 11 true-tongued, undeceitful, undeceptive, undistorted, unvarnished 12 truth-telling 13 truth-speaking

veracity 4 fact 5 truth 6 gospel, truism, verity 7 honesty 8 accuracy 9 actuality, exactness, frankness 11 correctness, factualness 12 truthfulness, veridicality

veranda 5 lanai, porch 6 piazza 7 balcony, gallery, portico

verb *auxiliary:* 2 am, be, do, is 3 are, can, did, had, has, may, was 4 have, must, were, will 5 could, might, shall, would 6 should *form:* 6 active, gerund 7 passive 10 infinitive, participle *kind:* 10 transitive 12 intransitive *linking:* 6 copula *mood:* 8 optative 10 imperative, indicative 11 subjunctive *suffix:* (see at **suffix**) *tense:* 4 past 6 aorist, future 7 perfect, present 9 predicate 10 pluperfect

verbal 4 oral 6 spoken 7 literal 8 verbatim 9 unwritten 11 traditional, word-for-word, word-of-mouth

verbalism 6 phrase 7 diction, styling, wordage, wording 8 parlance, phrasing, verbiage 9 prolixity, verbosity, windiness, wordiness 10 prolixness 11 phraseology, verboseness

verbalization 4 talk 6 speech 8 speaking 9 discourse, utterance

verbalize 3 air, say 4 give, talk, vent, word 5 speak, state, utter, voice 7 express 8 vocalize 9 ventilate

verbatim 5 close, exact 6 direct, strict, verbal 7 exactly, literal, precise 8 directly, faithful 9 literally, literatim, precisely 10 accurately 11 word-for-word

verbiage 6 phrase 7 diction, wordage, wording 8 parlance, phrasing, pleonasm 9 floridity, tautology, verbalism, verbality,

verbosity 10 floridness, periphrase, redundancy, roundabout 11 periphrasis, phraseology

verbose 5 windy, wordy 6 prolix 7 diffuse, flowery 9 redundant 10 long-winded, palaverous, pleonastic 11 tautologous 12 magniloquent, periphrastic 13 grandiloquent

verboseness see verbosity

verbosity 7 bombast 8 verbiage 9 prolixity, verbalism, windiness, wordiness 10 prolixness, redundancy 11 verboseness

verboten 5 taboo 6 banned 8 outlawed 9 forbidden 10 disallowed, prohibited, unlicensed 11 disapproved 12 unauthorized, unsanctioned

verdant 3 raw 5 green 6 grassy

verdict 6 ruling 7 finding, opinion 8 decision, judgment

Verdi opera 4 Aida 6 Ernani, Oberto, Otello 7 Nabucco 8 Don Carlo, Falstaff 9 Rigoletto 10 La Traviata 11 Il Trovatore

verdure 5 green 7 foliage, leafage, umbrage 8 greenery 10 vegetation

verge 3 hem, lip, rim 4 abut, brim, edge, join, lean, line 5 bound, brink, march, point, skirt, touch 6 adjoin, border, butt on, fringe, margin, tend to, trench 7 incline, outline, selvage, touch on 8 approach, neighbor, surround 9 threshold, touch upon 10 border line, tend toward 11 butt against, communicate

Vergil *epic:* 6 Aeneid *poems:* 8 Bucolics, Georgics

veridical see veracious

verification 5 proof 12 confirmation

verify 3 try 4 test 5 prove 6 settle 7 bear out, confirm, justify 8 document, validate 9 establish 11 corroborate, demonstrate 12 authenticate, substantiate

verily 3 yea 4 even 5 truly 6 indeed

verisimility 5 color 12 plausibility

veritable 4 real, true, very 6 actual 7 factual, genuine 8 bona fide, undenied 9 authentic, undoubted, unrefuted 10 sure-enough 11 indubitable

verity 5 truth 6 gospel, truism 8 veracity 12 truthfulness, veridicality 13 veraciousness

vermeil 4 ruby

vermiform 8 wormlike

vermilion 3 red

vermin 4 lice, mice, rats 5 fleas 7 bedbugs

verminous 6 filthy 7 noxious 9 offensive

Vermont *capital:* 10 Montpelier *college, university:* 7 Norwich 10 Middlebury, St. Michael's *state bird:* 12 hermit thrush *state flower:* 9 red clover

vernacular 4 cant 5 argot, idiom, lingo, slang 6 jargon, patois, patter, speech, tongue, vulgar **7** dialect, vulgate **8** language **10** colloquial **12** mother tongue

vernacularism   8 slangism, solecism **9** barbarism, vulgarism **10** corruption **11** impropriety

vernal   6 spring **10** springlike

Verne, Jules *character:* **4** Fogg (Phileas), Nemo **12** Passepartout *submarine:* **8** Nautilus

versant   2 up **6** au fait **7** abreast **8** familiar, informed **9** au courant **10** acquainted

versatile   4 able **5** handy **6** adroit, facile, gifted, mobile **7** elastic, plastic, pliable, skilled **8** flexible, skillful, talented **9** adaptable, all-around, dexterous, many-sided **10** conversant **11** well-rounded

verse   3 lay, ode **4** epic, poem, rune, song **5** lyric, poesy, rhyme, stich **6** ballad, jingle, poetry, sonnet, stanza **11** familiarize *analysis:* **8** scansion *four-line:* **8** quatrain *six-line:* **6** sestet *three-line:* **6** tercet *two-line:* **7** couplet *writer:* **4** poet; (see also **poem**)

versed   2 up **3** old, vet **5** adept **6** au fait **7** abreast, old-time, skilled, versant, veteran **8** familiar, informed, seasoned **9** au courant, competent, practical, practiced **10** acquainted, conversant **11** experienced

verseman   4 bard, poet **6** rhymer **9** poetaster, rhymester, versifier **12** balladmonger

versicolor   see **variegated**

versifier   see **verseman**

version   4 tale **5** story **6** report **7** account, history, reading **9** chronicle, narrative, rendering, rendition, rewording **10** paraphrase **11** restatement, translation **12** condensation **13** clarification, restipulation

versus   3 con **6** contra **7** against, vis-à-vis **11** over against

vertebra   4 bone *combining form:* **7** spondyl **8** spondyli (plural), spondylo **9** spondylus *kind:* **6** dorsal, lumbar, sacral **8** cervical, thoracic

vertebrae   4 back **5** spine **6** rachis **8** backbone **12** spinal column

vertebrate   6 animal *characteristic:* **5** spine **7** cranium *kind:* **4** bird, fish, frog **5** shark **6** mammal **7** lamprey, reptile

vertex   3 cap, top **4** apex, peak, roof **5** crest, crown **6** apogee, summit, tip-top, zenith **9** fastigium

Verthandi   see **Norn**

vertical   5 erect, plumb, sheer, steep **7** upright **9** up-and-down **10** straight-up **13** perpendicular *combining form:* **4** orth **5** ortho

vertiginous   5 dizzy, giddy, light **6** rotary, swimmy **8** swimming **11** light-headed

vertigo   6 megrim **9** dizziness

verve   3 pep, vim, zip **4** brio, dash, élan, fire, life, zest, zing **5** gusto, oomph **6** bounce, esprit, spirit, spring **8** buoyancy,

vivacity **9** animation **10** elasticity, liveliness, resiliency

very   2 so **3** too **4** bare, mere, most, much, real, same, true **5** ideal, model, pesky, quite, super, truly **6** damned, highly, hugely, mighty, really **7** awfully, de facto, genuine, greatly, notably, parlous, precise, vitally **8** actually, bona fide, mightily, mortally, rattling, selfsame, snapping, spanking, terribly, whacking, whopping **9** authentic, eminently, extremely, genuinely, identical, tellingly, undoubted, veritable, veritably **10** dreadfully, insatiably, remarkably, strikingly, sure-enough, thoroughly **11** exceedingly, indubitable **12** surpassingly **13** exceptionally *French:* **4** très *German:* **4** sehr *Scottish:* **3** gey

vesicle   3 sac **4** cyst **6** cavity **7** bladder, blister

Vesper   5 Venus **8** Hesperus **11** evening star

vespers   6 prayer **7** service **8** evensong

_____ Vespucci   7 Amerigo

vessel   3 ama, can, cup, jar, pan, pot, pyx, tub, urn **4** boat, bowl, drum, ewer, pail, ship, tank, tube, vase, vein **5** canal, craft, cruse, laver **6** artery, barrel, bottle, bucket, firkin, flagon, kettle, krater, pottle, situla **7** cresset, pitcher **8** crucible **10** receptacle *combining form:* **3** vas **4** ange, angi, vasi, vaso **5** angia (plural), angio **6** angium, arteri, vascul **7** arterio, vasculo *drinking:* **3** cup, mug **4** toby **5** cylix, flask, glass, gourd, kylix, stein, stoup **6** goblet, seidel **7** tankard, tumbler *Indian:* **4** lota **5** lotah *sailing:* (see at **ship**) *Scottish:* **3** cog **6** cootie, quaich, quaigh **7** yetling

vest   4 coat **6** belong, invest, jacket, weskit **7** empower, pertain **9** appertain, authorize, waistcoat

Vesta   see **Hestia**

vestal   3 nun **4** pure **6** chaste, virgin **8** virginal

vestibule   4 hall **5** entry, foyer, lobby **6** portal **7** narthex, portico **8** anteroom, entryway **11** antechamber **12** entrance hall

vestige   3 rag, tag **4** path, step **5** relic, scrap, spoor, trace, track, tract, trail **6** shadow **7** memento, remains, remnant **8** footstep **9** footprint, remainder

vestment   3 alb **4** cope, garb, gown, pall, robe **5** amice, cotta, dress, fanon, orale, stole, tunic **6** rochet, sakkos **7** cassock, garment, maniple, pallium, tunicle **8** chasuble, cincture, dalmatic, parament, surplice **9** phelonion *ancient Hebrew:* **5** ephod

vestry   4 room **6** closet **8** sacristy

vesture   5 cover **6** clothe **7** apparel, costume, envelop, garment **8** clothing

Vesuvius   7 volcano

vetch   4 tare *bitter:* **3** ers **5** ervil

veteran 4 wise 6 expert, master, versed 7 old hand, old-time, skilled, worldly 8 old-timer, seasoned 9 longtimer, practical, practiced 10 past master 11 experienced 13 sophisticated

veto 3 nix 4 deny, kill 6 defeat, forbid, refuse, reject 7 decline 8 disallow, negative, prohibit 9 blackball, non-placet

vex 3 bug, ire, irk 4 chaw, fret, gall 5 anger, annoy, chafe, tease 6 abrade, bother, plague 7 provoke, torment 8 exercise 9 embarrass, infuriate

vexation 6 irking 9 annoyance, bothering, provoking 10 harassment, irritation 11 aggravation, bedevilment, provocation

vexatious 4 mean, ugly 5 pesky 6 wicked 9 troublous 11 troublesome

via 2 by 3 per 4 over, road, with 5 along 7 by way of, passage, through 8 by dint of 9 by means of 10 by virtue of

viable 6 doable 8 feasible, possible, workable 11 practicable

viaduct 6 bridge

vial 5 ampul, flask, glass, phial 6 ampule, beaker, bottle, vessel 7 ampoule 8 test tube

viands 4 eats, fare, feed, food, grub 7 edibles, nurture 8 victuals 9 provender 10 provisions 11 comestibles

viator 8 traveler, wayfarer

vibrant 5 alive, round, vital 6 rotund 7 orotund, ringing 8 plangent, resonant, sonorant, sonorous 9 consonant 10 resounding

vibrate 3 jar 4 rock 5 quake, shake, trill, twang 6 shiver, tremor 7 shudder, tremble

vibration 4 vibe 5 quake, shake, trill 6 quaver, quiver, tremor 7 flutter, shaking 8 fremitus 9 trembling 11 oscillation *Scottish:* 6 dindle

vicar 6 priest 8 minister 9 clergyman

Vicar of Wakefield *author:* 9 Goldsmith (Oliver) *character:* 8 Primrose

vice 3 ill, sin 4 evil, flaw 5 fault, wrong 6 defect, foible 7 blemish, failing, frailty 9 depravity, indecency 10 corruption, debasement, debauchery, immorality, perversion, unchastity, wickedness 11 shortcoming

vice-president 4 veep 9 executive *American:* 4 Burr (Aaron), Bush (George), Ford (Gerald), Gore (Albert), King (William) 5 Adams (John), Agnew (Spiro), Dawes (Charles), Gerry (Elbridge), Nixon (Richard Milhous), Tyler (John) 6 Arthur (Chester), Colfax (Schuyler), Curtis (Charles), Dallas (George), Garner (John Nance), Hamlin (Hannibal), Hobart (Garret), Morton (Levi), Quayle (Dan), Truman (Harry), Wilson (Woodrow) 7 Barkley (Alben), Calhoun (John Caldwell), Clinton (George), Johnson (Andrew, Lyndon Baines, Richard Mentor),

Mondale (Walter), Sherman (James Schoolcraft), Wallace (Henry), Wheeler (William) 8 Coolidge (Calvin), Fillmore (Millard), Humphrey (Hubert Horatio), Marshall (Thomas), Tompkins (Daniel), Van Buren (Martin) 9 Fairbanks (Charles), Hendricks (Thomas), Jefferson (Thomas), Roosevelt (Theodore), Stevenson (Adlai) 11 Rockefeller (Nelson) 12 Breckinridge (John)

viceroy 5 nabob, ruler 6 exarch, satrap 7 khedive 8 governor 9 butterfly

vice versa 10 contrawise, conversely 12 contrariwise

vicinage 4 area 8 district, locality, vicinity 12 neighborhood

vicinity 4 area 5 range 6 extent, matter, region 8 district, locality, nearness, vicinage 9 magnitude, proximity 12 neighborhood

vicious 4 evil, mean, wild 5 feral, wrong 6 fierce, malign, putrid, rotten, savage, sinful, wicked 7 brutish, corrupt, furious, hateful, immoral, intense, violent 8 depraved, infamous, perverse, spiteful, terrible, vehement 9 desperate, malicious, malignant, miscreant, nefarious, rancorous, reprobate 10 degenerate, despiteful, flagitious, iniquitous, malevolent, villainous 12 blood-thirsty

vicissitude 5 rigor, trial 6 change 7 novelty, variety 8 asperity, hardness, hardship, mutation, reversal 9 adversity, diversity, mischance 10 affliction, difficulty, innovation, misfortune 11 permutation, progression, tribulation, ups and downs

victim 4 butt, dupe, fool, gull, mark, prey 5 chump 6 pigeon, quarry, sucker 7 fall guy, gudgeon 8 casualty, offering, underdog 9 bottom dog, sacrifice

victimize 4 dupe, fool, gull, hoax 5 trick 6 pigeon 8 flimflam, hoodwink, immolate 9 bamboozle, sacrifice 11 hornswoggle

victor 3 top 5 champ, first 6 master, winner 7 subduer 8 champion, defeater 9 conquerer 10 subjugator, vanquisher

Victoria, Queen *family:* 7 Hanover *father:* 6 Edward *husband:* 6 Albert *son:* 6 Edward

Victorian 4 prig, prim 6 prissy, stuffy 10 old-maidish, tight-laced 11 puritanical, straitlaced 12 old-fashioned

victory 3 win 6 better 7 command, control, mastery, success, triumph 8 conquest, dominion, walkaway, walkover, whip hand 9 advantage, supremacy, upper hand 11 subjugation, superiority *costly:* 7 Pyrrhic *easy:* 8 cakewalk, walkaway *monument:* 4 arch 13 Arc de Triomphe *reward:* 6 spoils *sign:* 3 vee *symbol:* 4 flag 6 laurel, wreath

Victory author 6 Conrad (Joseph)

victuals 4 chow, eats, feed, food, grub 6 viands 7 edibles 9 provender 10 provisions 11 comestibles

___ Vidal 4 Gore

videlicet 3 viz 5 to wit 6 namely 8 scilicet

vie 3 pit 5 match, rival 6 oppose, outvie 7 compete, contend, contest, counter, play off 9 challenge

Viennese *city hall:* 7 Rathaus *family:* 8 Hapsburg *palace:* 7 Hofburg *park:* 6 Prater

Vientiane's land 4 Laos

Vietnam *capital:* 5 Hanoi *monetary unit:* 4 dong

Vietnamese New Year 3 Tet

view 3 aim, con, eye, see, vet 4 deem, espy, goal, look, mark, mind, plan, scan 5 audit, scene, sight, study, vista 6 behold, belief, descry, design, look at, notice, notion, object, regard, review, survey 7 canvass, check up, discern, examine, feeling, inspect, observe, opinion, outlook, picture, scenery 8 analysis, consider, gaze upon, look upon, panorama, perceive, prospect, scrutiny 9 check over, objective, sentiment 10 conviction, inspection, persuasion, scrutinize 11 contemplate, distinguish, examination, perlustrate 13 perlustration

viewable 6 ocular, visual 7 seeable, visible

viewer 7 watcher, witness 8 beholder, bysitter, looker-on, observer, onlooker 9 bystander, spectator 10 eyewitness

viewing instrument 5 glass, scope 7 glasses 9 telescope 10 binoculars, microscope *combining form:* 5 scope

viewpoint 3 eye 4 side 5 angle, slant, stand 7 outlook, posture 8 attitude, position 9 direction 10 estimation, standpoint 11 perspective

vigil 4 tout 5 watch 7 lookout 12 surveillance, watch and ward

vigilance see **vigil**

vigilant 4 agog, avid, keen 5 acute, alert, awake, aware, eager, sharp 7 anxious, wakeful 8 open-eyed, watchful 9 attentive, sharp-eyed, wide-awake 10 unsleeping

vignette 5 scene 6 sketch 7 picture 8 ornament

vigor 3 pep, vim, zip 4 bang, beef, birr, dash, fire, push, snap, tuck, zing 5 drive, force, getup, might, moxie, oomph, power, punch, steam 6 bounce, energy, muscle, spirit, starch 7 ability, potency 8 dynamism, strength, virility, vitality 9 hardihood, lustiness, manliness, puissance, soundness 10 capability, enterprise, get-up-and-go 11 healthiness

vigorous 5 brisk, hardy, husky, lusty, proud, stout, tough, vital 6 hearty, lively, potent, robust, sinewy, strong, sturdy 7 dashing, driving, dynamic, healthy, zealous 8 athletic, bouncing, muscular, powerful, slashing, spirited 9 energetic, exuberant, masterful, strenuous 10 mettlesome, red-blooded, survigrous 11 hard-driving, hard-hitting 13 rough-and-ready

Viking see **Norse**

vile 3 low 4 base, evil, foul, mean, ugly 5 gross, nasty 6 coarse, horrid, sordid, vulgar 7 debased, ignoble, low-down, noisome, obscene, servile, squalid 8 depraved, wretched 9 abhorrent, corrupted, debauched, loathsome, offensive, perverted, repugnant, repulsive, revolting 10 despicable, disgusting 12 contemptible

Vili *brother:* 2 Ve 4 Odin *victim:* 4 Ymir

vilify 5 abuse, libel 6 assail, attack, berate, defame, malign, misuse 7 asperse, outrage, slander, traduce 8 denounce, mistreat, tear down 9 denigrate 10 calumniate, villainize

villa 5 manor 6 castle, estate 7 chateau, mansion

village 4 burg, town 5 bourg, thorp 6 hamlet 7 townlet *African:* 4 dorp, stad 5 kraal *Indian:* 6 bustee, pueblo *Japanese:* 4 mura *Jewish:* 6 shtetl *Malay:* 7 campong, kampong *Russian:* 3 mir

Village Blacksmith author 10 Longfellow (Henry Wadsworth)

villain 4 heel 5 devil, heavy, knave, rogue, scamp 6 meanie, rascal, sinner 7 lowlife 8 criminal, evildoer, mischief, offender, roperipe, scalawag 9 miscreant, reprobate, scoundrel, skeezicks 10 blackguard, malefactor 11 rapscallion *classic:* 4 Iago

villainous 6 putrid, rotten 7 corrupt, debased, heinous, vicious 8 contrary, infamous, perverse 9 abandoned, atrocious, dissolute, miscreant, nefarious, offensive, perverted 10 degenerate, detestable, flagitious, outrageous, profligate 13 objectionable

villainy 5 crime 9 depravity

villein 7 peasant 8 villager

villenage 4 yoke 6 thrall 7 bondage, helotry, peonage, serfdom, slavery 9 servitude, thralldom 11 enslavement

vim 4 brio, dash, élan, kick, life, push, zing 5 oomph, verve 6 esprit, pepper, spirit 9 animation

vinaigrette 3 box 4 cart 5 sauce, wagon 6 bottle

vinculum 3 tie 4 bond, knot, link, yoke 5 nexus 8 ligament, ligature

vindicable 6 venial 7 tenable 9 excusable 10 condonable, defensible 11 inoffensive, justifiable, warrantable

vindicate 4 free 5 argue, claim, clear, guard, prove, venge 6 acquit, assert,

avenge, defend, refute, second, shield,
uphold **7** absolve, bear out, confute, contend, justify, protect, redress, revenge, support, warrant **8** advocate, disprove, maintain, plead for **9** exculpate, exonerate **10** disculpate **11** rationalize

vindictive 5 nasty **6** malign **8** punitive, spiteful, vengeful, wreakful **9** malicious, malignant, merciless **10** implacable, relentless, revengeful **11** unrelenting

vine 3 hop, ivy, pea **4** gogo, soma **5** betel, buaze, guaco, kudzu, liana, liane, luffa, maile **6** cowage, cowpea, loofah, maypop **7** chayote, climber, copihue, creeper, cupseed **8** catbrier, clematis **10** chile-bells **11** bittersweet *combining form:* **4** viti *East Indian:* **6** pikake

vinegar 3 vim **6** acetum **8** sourness *combining form:* **4** acet **5** aceto *relating to:* **6** acetic *steep in:* **6** pickle

vinegarish 4 sour **5** waspy **6** bitter, cranky, ornery **7** bearish, waspish **8** cankered **9** crotchety, irascible **12** cantankerous, cross-grained

Vinegar Joe 8 Stilwell (Joseph)

vinegary 4 sour **6** acetic **7** acetose, acetous

vineyard 7 grapery *French:* **3** cru

Vinland discoverer 8 Ericsson, Eriksson (Leif)

vintage 3 old **4** crop, wine **5** dated, passé **6** démodé **7** antique, archaic, classic, harvest **8** outdated, outmoded **9** classical **10** antiquated **12** old-fashioned

Viola *brother:* **9** Sebastian *husband:* **6** Orsino

Viola da ___ 5 gamba

violate 3 err, sin **4** rape **5** break, force, spoil **6** breach, defile, offend, ravish **7** infract, outrage **8** deflower, infringe, overpass, trespass **9** deflorate, disregard, trample on **10** contravene, transgress **11** trample upon

violation 5 break, crime, wrong **6** breach **7** offense **8** defacing, trespass **9** blasphemy, sacrilege **10** defacement, illegality, infraction **11** desecration, misdemeanor, profanation **12** encroachment, infringement **13** contravention, transgression

violence 4 fury, riot **5** clash, force **6** attack, duress, frenzy, tumult, uproar **7** assault, rampage **8** coercion, foul play, savagery, struggle **9** onslaught **10** compulsion, constraint

violent 5 acute, harsh, rough **6** fierce, mighty, potent, strong **7** cutting, extreme, furious, intense, vicious **8** forceful, forcible, piercing, powerful, terrible, vehement **9** desperate, exquisite, splitting **10** immoderate, inordinate **11** destructive **12** concentrated

violently 4 hard **5** madly **6** wildly **8** fiercely, stormily **9** furiously, ruinously **10** frenziedly **11** combatively, frantically, turbulently **12** tumultuously **13** destructively

violet 5 mauve **6** flower, purple

violin 6 fiddle **10** instrument *kind:* **4** bass **5** Amati, cello, Strad **7** quinton **10** double bass, Guarnerius, Stradivari **12** Stradivarius *part:* **3** bow, nut, peg, rib **4** neck **5** belly **6** bridge, corner, pegbox, saddle, scroll, string **8** chin rest, purfling **11** fingerboard *precursor:* **5** gigue, rabab, rebec **6** vielle

violinist *American:* **5** Elman (Mischa), Fodor (Eugene), Rabin (Michael), Ricci (Ruggiero), Stern (Isaac) **6** Midori, Powell (Maud), Rosand (Aaron) **7** Heifetz (Jascha), Menuhin (Yehudi), Szigeti (Joseph) **8** Kreisler (Fritz), Milstein (Nathan), Spalding (Albert), Zukofsky (Paul) **9** Zimbalist (Efrem) *Belgian:* **5** Ysaye (Eugene-Auguste) **8** Grumiaux (Arthur) *Canadian:* **6** Staryk (Steven) *Chinese:* **4** Chen (Chong) *Czech:* **3** Suk (Josef) *French:* **12** Francescatti (Zino) *German:* **6** Mutter (Anne-Sophie) **9** Hindemith (Paul) *Hungarian:* **6** Tatrai (Vilmos) **7** Joachim (Joseph) *Israeli:* **7** Perlman (Itzhak) **8** Zukerman (Pinchas) *Italian:* **6** Viotti (Giovanne Battista) **7** Corelli (Arcangelo), Vivaldi (Antonio) **8** Paganini (Niccolo) **9** Geminiani (Francesco) *Romanian:* **6** Enescu (George) *Russian:* **8** Oistrakh (David), Spivakov (Vladimir)

violin maker 4 Salo (Gasparo da) **5** Amati (Andrea, Antonio, Girolamo, Nicolo) **7** Maggini (Giovanni) **8** Guarneri (Andrea, Giuseppe, Pietro) **10** Stradivari (Antonio, Francesco, Omobono)

VIP 4 lion **6** biggie, bigwig, fat cat, leader **7** big shot, notable, someone **8** big wheel, luminary, somebody **9** big cheese

viper 3 asp **5** adder, snake **10** bushmaster, copperhead, fer-de-lance **11** rattlesnake

virago 5 harpy, scold, shrew, vixen **6** amazon, ogress **8** fishwife **9** termagant, Xanthippe

Virgil see Vergil

virgin 3 new **4** pure **5** fresh, unwed **6** intact, maiden, single, vestal **8** celibate, innocent, primeval, pristine, unmarred, untapped **9** abstinent, unmarried, unspoiled, unsullied, untouched **10** spouseless **12** undeflowered *combining form:* **7** parthen **8** partheno

virginal 4 pure **6** intact, maiden **8** untapped **9** unspoiled, untouched **12** undeflowered

Virgin Goddess 5 Diana **7** Artemis

Virginia *capital:* 8 Richmond *college, institute, university:* 7 Hampton 8 Richmond 11 Old Dominion 13 Randolph Macon 14 William and Mary *nickname:* 11 Old Dominion *state bird:* 8 cardinal
Virginian, The *author:* 6 Wister (Owen) *character:* 7 Trampas
Virginia willow 4 itea
Virgin Islands of the U.S. 6 St. John 7 St. Croix 8 St. Thomas
virginity 6 purity 8 chastity 10 chasteness, maidenhead, maidenhood
Virgin Queen 10 Elizabeth I
Virgo star 5 Spica
viridity 5 youth 9 freshness, greenness, innocence
virile 4 male 5 manly 6 manful, potent, robust 7 driving, manlike, mannish 8 decisive, forceful 9 energetic, masculine
virose 5 fetid 6 poison 9 poisonous
virtual 5 basic 8 implicit 9 essential, practical 11 fundamental 12 constructive
virtuality 4 pith, soul 5 stuff 6 bottom, marrow 7 essence 9 substance 12 essentiality, quintessence
virtually 6 almost, nearly 7 morally 8 actually 9 basically, in essence 10 absolutely 11 essentially, practically 13 fundamentally
virtue 4 dint, mark 5 arête, merit, piety, trait, value, vigor, worth 7 caliber, feature, potency, probity, quality, stature 8 efficacy, goodness, morality, property 9 affection, attribute, character, puissance, rectitude, rightness 10 excellence, excellency, perfection 11 uprightness 13 effectiveness, effectualness, righteousness *cardinal:* 4 hope 5 faith 7 charity, justice 8 prudence 9 fortitude 10 temperance
virtuosic 4 ripe 6 expert 8 finished 9 masterful, perfected 10 consummate 12 accomplished
virtuoso 4 whiz 6 artist, expert, master, musico, wizard 7 artiste, dabster 8 musician 9 authority 10 past master 12 professional
virtuous 4 good, pure 5 moral, noble 6 worthy 7 ethical, sinless 8 innocent, spotless 9 blameless, effective, effectual, efficient, exemplary, faultless, guiltless, righteous, unsullied, untainted 10 inculpable, moralistic, principled, unblamable 11 efficacious, right-minded, untarnished
virulent 5 sharp, toxic 6 biting, bitter, malign, poison 7 cutting, hateful, hostile 8 mephitic, scathing, spiteful, stabbing, toxicant, venomous 9 malignant, poisonous, rancorous, vitriolic 10 unfriendly 12 antagonistic
virus 4 bane, germ 5 venom 6 poison 9 contagion, infection
vis 5 force, might, power

visage 3 mug 4 cast, face, look, phiz 6 kisser 8 features 10 expression 11 countenance
vis-à-vis 6 contra, facing, toward, versus 7 against 8 fronting, opposite 9 tête-à-tête 10 coordinate 11 counterpart, over against
viscera 4 guts 7 innards, insides, inwards 8 entrails, stuffing 9 internals *combining form:* 9 splanchno
visceral 3 gut 5 inner 8 interior, internal, intimate 9 intuitive 11 instinctive, instinctual
viscid see **viscous**
viscount 4 peer 7 sheriff 8 nobleman
viscous 4 ropy, sizy 5 gummy, slimy, stiff, thick, tough 6 sticky 9 glutinous, semifluid, tenacious
vise 4 grip, tool 5 clamp
Vishnu 4 Hare, Hari *avatar:* 4 Rama 5 Kurma 6 Buddha, Matsya, Vamena, Varaha 7 Krishna 9 Narasinha *consort:* 3 Sri 4 Shri 7 Lakshmi *home:* 4 Meru
visible 4 seen 6 ocular, visual 7 seeable 8 apparent, viewable
Visigoth *conquest:* 4 Rome *king:* 6 Alaric
vision 3 eye 4 muse 5 dream, fancy, image, sight, think 6 beauty, oracle, seeing 7 fantasy, feature, imagine, realize 8 conceive, daydream, envisage, eyesight, phantasm, phantasy, presence, prophecy 9 nightmare, visualize 10 apocalypse, apparition, phenomenon, revelation *combining form:* 4 opsy, opto 5 opsia, opsis 6 optico *deceptive:* 6 mirage *defect:* (see at **eye**) *in bright light:* 8 photopia *in dim light:* 8 scotopia *relating to:* 5 optic 6 visual 7 optical *without:* 5 blind
visionary 5 ideal, lofty, noble 6 astral, dreamy, musing 7 dreamer, exalted, radical, utopian 8 idealist 9 ambitious, daydreamy, grandiose, ideologue, unworldly 10 abstracted, idealistic 11 daydreaming, impractical, pretentious 12 otherworldly 13 castle-builder, introspective
visionless 4 dark 5 blind 7 eyeless 9 sightless 10 stone-blind
Vision of Sir Launfal, The *author* 6 Lowell (James Russell)
visit 3 gam, see 4 call, chat, chin, pain, stay, talk, yarn 5 pop in, run in, tarry, wreak, wreck 6 avenge, bother, come by, drop by, drop in, impose, look in, look up, punish, reside, step in, stop by, stop in 7 afflict, force on, inflict, sojourn, trouble 8 colloque, come over, converse, frequent, stopover 9 force upon, tarriance *often:* 8 frequent
visitation 4 call 5 cross, trial 6 ordeal 7 calvary 8 calamity, crucible, disaster

9 mischance 10 affliction 11 catastrophe, tribulation

visitor 5 guest 6 caller 7 company, invitee

vison 4 mink

visor 4 bill, mask, peak 6 domino, vizard 8 eyeshade 9 doughface, false face

vista 4 view 5 range, scape, scene, scope, sight 6 survey 7 lookout, outlook 8 panorama, prospect 11 perspective

visual 5 optic 6 ocular 7 optical, seeable, visible 8 viewable, visional 11 discernible, perceivable, perceptible

visualize 3 see 4 view 5 fancy, image, think 6 call up, divine 7 feature, foresee, imagine, picture, preknow, previse, realize 8 conceive, envisage, envision, forefeel, foreknow 9 apprehend, conjure up, objectify, prevision 10 anticipate

vital 5 alive, lusty 6 living, needed, zoetic 7 animate, dynamic, needful 8 animated, cardinal, integral, required, vigorous 9 breathing, energetic, essential, requisite, strenuous 10 red-blooded 11 fundamental 12 constitutive, prerequisite 13 indispensable

vital force 4 soul 5 anima 6 animus, pneuma, psyche, spirit 9 élan vital

vitality see **vigor**

vitalize 5 liven, pep up 6 actify, excite, vivify 7 animate, enliven, provoke, quicken 8 activate, activize, dynamize, energize 9 galvanize, stimulate 10 invigorate, strengthen

vitally 4 very 6 hugely 7 notably, parlous 9 extremely 10 remarkably, strikingly 11 exceedingly 12 surpassingly 13 exceptionally

vitals see **viscera**

vitamin 6 biotin, niacin 7 choline, folacin 8 carotene, inositol, thiamine 9 cobalamin, folic acid, pyridoxal 10 calciferol, pyridoxine, riboflavin, tocopherol 12 ascorbic acid, bioflavonoid, meso-inositol

Vito Nuova, La *author:* 5 Dante

vitellus 4 yolk

vitiate 3 mar 4 harm, hurt, soil, undo 5 abate, annul, quash, spoil, sully, taint 6 damage, debase, defile, impair, injure, negate 7 abolish, blemish, corrupt, debased, debauch, deprave, nullify, pervert, tarnish 8 abrogate, depraved 9 brutalize, corrupted, debauched, perverted, prejudice 10 annihilate, bastardize, bestialize, demoralize, invalidate

vitreous 6 glassy

vitriol 7 sulfate 9 virulence

vitriolic 6 bitter 7 hostile 8 virulent 9 rancorous 12 antagonistic

vituperate 4 lash, rail, rate 5 abuse, curse, scold 6 bark at, berate, malign, revile, yell at 7 asperse, bawl out, chew out, condemn, growl at, upbraid 8 lambaste 10 tongue-lash

vituperation 5 abuse, blame 7 censure, obloquy 8 scolding 9 contumely, invective 10 revilement, scurrility 12 billingsgate 13 tongue-lashing

vituperative 6 severe 7 abusive, railing 8 critical, scolding, scurrile 9 invective, truculent 10 censorious, scurrilous 11 opprobrious 12 contumelious

vivacious 3 gay 4 cant, keen 5 alert, brash, canty, zesty 6 breezy, lively 7 animate, playful, vibrant 8 animated, spirited, sportive 9 ebullient, exuberant, sprightly 10 frolicsome 12 effervescent, high-spirited

vivacity see **verve**

Vivaldi, Antonio *epithet:* 12 il prete rosso, the red priest

____ **vivant** 3 bon

vivarium 3 zoo

vivid 3 gay 4 keen, rich 5 acute, alive, brave, sharp 6 bright, colory, lively, living 7 graphic, intense 8 animated, colorful, dramatic, eloquent, spirited, vigorous 9 pictorial 10 expressive, meaningful, theatrical 11 dramaturgic, picturesque 12 photographic

vivify 5 liven, renew 6 excite, revive 7 animate, enliven, quicken, refresh, restore 9 galvanize

vixen 3 fox, nag 5 harpy, scold, shrew 6 amazon, ogress, virago 8 fishwife 9 termagant, Xanthippe

viz 5 to wit 6 namely 8 scilicet 9 videlicet

vizard 4 mask 5 visor 6 domino 9 doughface, false face

vocabulary 4 cant 5 words 6 jargon 7 lexicon, palaver 8 language 9 wordhoard, word-stock 10 dictionary 11 phraseology, terminology

vocal 4 oral 6 fluent, sonant, spoken, voiced 7 uttered, voicing 8 eloquent 9 expressed, intonated, outspoken 10 articulate, expressing, expressive, free-spoken

vocalic 5 vowel 6 vowely 9 vowellike

vocalist 6 singer 8 songster 9 performer 11 entertainer

vocalization 5 mouth, voice 6 speech 7 diction, voicing 8 mouthing, sounding, speaking, uttering 9 utterance 11 enunciation 12 articulation 13 verbalization

vocalize 4 sing, talk, tune 5 chant, speak, utter, voice 6 convey, impart, let out 7 express 9 enunciate, pronounce, verbalize 11 communicate

vocal organ 6 larynx *bird:* 6 syrinx

vocation 3 art, job 4 work 5 craft, trade 6 métier 7 calling, mission 8 lifework 10 handicraft, occupation, profession

vocative 4 case 6 fluent 7 voluble 9 garrulous

vociferate 3 cry 4 call, yell 5 hallo, hollo, shout 6 holler

vociferous 4 loud 5 noisy 6 shrill 7 blatant, dinsome 8 strident 9 clamorous 10 boisterous, multivocal 11 distracting, loudmouthed, openmouthed 12 obstreperous

vogue 3 cry, fad 4 chic, mode, rage 5 craze, style, trend 6 bon ton, furore 7 fashion 10 dernier cri 11 stylishness

voice 3 put, say 4 talk, tell, vent 5 say-so, sound, speak, utter 6 phrase, speech 7 present, recount 8 vocalize 9 enunciate, formulate, pronounce, statement, utterance, verbalize 10 articulate, expression *combining form:* 4 phon 5 phone, phono, phony 6 phonia *female:* 4 alto 5 mezzo 7 soprano 9 contralto *high:* 5 tenor 7 soprano 8 falsetto *in grammar:* 6 active 7 passive *Latin:* 3 vox *male:* 4 bass 5 tenor 8 baritone *quality:* 5 pitch 6 timbre *quiet:* 7 whisper *relating to:* 5 vocal 8 phonetic *without:* 4 dumb, mute

voice box 6 larynx

voiced 4 oral 5 vocal 6 sonant, spoken 10 articulate

voiceless 3 mum 4 dumb, mute 6 silent 10 speechless 12 inarticulate, unarticulate

void 3 bad, gap 4 bare, emit, flow, hole, null, pour 5 abyss, annul, clear, drain, eject, empty, quash, scant, short 6 bereft, cavity, devoid, hollow, remove, vacant, vacate, vacuum 7 denuded, deplete, give off, invalid, negated, vacuity, vacuous 8 abrogate, deprived, dissolve, evacuate, innocent, throw out 9 destitute, discharge, eliminate 10 disembogue

voiture 3 car 8 carriage

volage 5 dizzy, giddy 7 flighty 9 frivolous 10 bird-witted 11 empty-headed, harebrained 13 rattlebrained

volant 4 spry, yare 5 agile, brisk, catty, zippy 6 active, lively, nimble 9 sprightly

volary 6 aviary 8 birdcage

volatile 4 airy, edgy 6 bouncy, fickle, lively 7 buoyant, elastic, flighty, protean 8 agitable, fleeting, flippant, fugitive, skittery, skittish, ticklish, unstable, variable 9 alarmable, ephemeral, excitable, expansive, explosive, frivolous, fugacious, mercurial, momentary, resilient, startlish, transient 10 capricious, changeable, evanescent, inconstant, lubricious, short-lived, transitory 11 impermanent, light-minded 12 effervescent 13 temperamental

volatility 6 levity 9 animation, flippancy, frivolity, lightness 11 flightiness, inconstancy, instability, variability 13 changeability, mercurialness, sprightliness

volcanic *crater:* 4 maar *explosion:* 8 eruption *glass:* 8 obsidian *matter:* 3 ash 4 lava, tufa, tuff 5 magma, trass 6 scoria *mound:* 4 cone 7 hornito *passage:* 6 throat 7 conduit *vent:* 8 fumarole 9 solfatara

volcano 8 mountain *Alaska:* 11 Mount Katmai *Andes:* 5 Omate 12 Huaina Putina *Antarctica:* 11 Mount Erebus *Azores:* 4 Alto *California:* 10 Lassen Peak *Canaries:* 5 Teide 8 Tenerife *Colombia:* 5 Huila, Pasto 6 Purace 7 Galeras *Costa Rica:* 4 Poás 5 Barba, Irazú *Ecuador:* 8 Cotopaxi *extinct:* 5 Iriga 8 Mauna Kea 9 Mount Popa 10 Mount Kenya *Guatemala:* 4 Agua 5 Fuego 7 Atitlán *Hawaii:* 8 Mauna Loa *Honshu:* 4 Nasu 5 Asama, Azuma 6 Bandai 8 Nasudake 9 Asamayama *Iceland:* 5 Askja, Hekla *Indonesia:* 7 Tambora 9 Gunung Awu 10 Peak of Bali 11 Gunung Agung *island:* 8 Krakatau, Krakatoa *Italy:* 8 Vesuvius 9 Stromboli *Japan:* 3 Aso 5 Unzen 6 Asosan *Java:* 4 Gede 5 Bromo, Gedeh, Kelud, Salak *Madeira:* 5 Ruivo *Martinique:* 10 Mount Pelee *Mexico:* 6 Colima 7 Orizaba 9 Paricutin 12 Popocatepetl *New Zealand:* 7 Ruapehu 9 Ngauruhoe *Philippines:* 4 Taal 10 Mount Mayon 13 Mount Pinatubo *Saint Vincent:* 9 Soufrière *Sicily:* 4 Etna 5 Aetna *Solomons:* 5 Balbi *South America:* 5 Lanín, Maipo *Sumatra:* 5 Dempo *Washington:* 16 Mount Saint Helens

____ **volente** 3 Deo

volition 4 will 6 choice, desire, option 8 election 9 selection 10 preference

volley 4 hail, shot 5 burst, round, salvo, storm 6 shower 7 barrage 8 drumfire

volplane 5 glide

Volpone 3 fox *author:* 6 Jonson (Ben) *servant:* 5 Mosca

Volsung *grandson:* 6 Sigurd 9 Siegfried *great-grandfather:* 4 Odin *son:* 7 Sigmund

Voltaire *drama:* 5 Zaïre 6 Alzire, Brutus, Mèrope, Oedipe 7 Mahomet 8 Tancrède *novel:* 5 Zadig 7 Candide *real name:* 6 Arouet (François Marie)

volte-face 4 turn, veer, whip 5 avert, pivot, sheer, wheel, whirl 6 divert 7 deflect, reverse 8 reversal 9 about-face, face about, reversion, turnabout 10 right-about 11 changeabout, reversement

voluble 4 glib 6 fickle, fluent 8 vocative 9 talkative 13 silver-tongued

volume 4 body, book, bulk, mass, size, tome 6 amount, object 7 content 8 capacity, loudness, quantity

voluminous 4 full, many 6 legion, sundry 7 several, various 8 numerous 12 multifarious, multitudinal 13 multitudinous

Volumnia's son 10 Coriolanus

Völund 5 smith 7 Wayland *brother:* 4 Egil 5 Egill

voluntary 4 free 5 opted 6 chosen 7 elected, willful, willing, witting 8 elective, optional, unforced 10 autonomous, deliberate, volitional 11 independent, intentional 12 unprescribed

volunteer 5 offer 6 enlist *hospital:* 12 candy striper

Volunteer State 9 Tennessee

voluptuous 4 lush 6 wanton 7 sensual 8 luscious, sensuous 9 abandoned, dissolute, epicurean, excessive, indulgent, luxurious 10 dissipated 12 sensualistic

volute 6 scroll, spiral

volution 5 twist, whorl

vomit 3 gag 4 barf, spew 5 eject, expel, retch 6 spit up 7 bring up, throw up, upchuck 8 disgorge 11 regurgitate

vomiting 6 emesis

Von Flotow opera 6 Martha

Vonnegut, Kurt *work:* 10 Cat's Cradle 11 Player Piano 16 The Sirens of Titan 18 Slaughterhouse Five 20 Breakfast of Champions 22 Happy Birthday Wanda June

Von Stroheim film 5 Greed 10 Queen Kelly 12 Foolish Wives 13 Blind Husbands, Grand Illusion, The Merry Widow 15 Sunset Boulevard

voodoo 3 hex 4 jinx, mage 5 charm, magus, obeah, spell, witch 6 whammy, wizard 7 bewitch, enchant, warlock 8 conjurer, magician, sorcerer 9 enchanter, ensorcell 10 Indian sign 11 necromancer

voodooist 4 mage 5 magus 6 wizard 7 charmer, warlock 8 conjurer, magician, sorcerer 9 enchanter 11 necromancer

Vophsi's son 5 Nahbi

voracious 4 avid 6 greedy, hungry, sating 7 gorging 8 covetous, edacious, grasping, ravening, ravenous 9 devouring, rapacious, satiating 10 gluttonous, insatiable, surfeiting 11 acquisitive

vorago 5 abyss, chasm

vortex 4 eddy, gyre 5 spout, whirl 6 spiral 9 maelstrom, whirlpool

votary 3 fan 4 buff 5 freak, hound, lover 6 addict, zealot 7 admirer, amateur, devotee, fancier, habitué 8 disciple 10 aficionado

vote 4 poll 5 elect 6 ballot, choice, choose, decide, ratify, ticket 7 opinion 8 election, suffrage 9 franchise *affirmative:* 3 aye, nod, yea, yes 6 placet *kind:* 5 proxy, straw, voice 6 secret 7 write-in 10 plebi-

scite, referendum *negative:* 2 no 3 nay *right to:* 8 suffrage 9 franchise

voter 7 chooser, elector *kind:* 8 absentee

vouch 5 prove 6 assure, attest, uphold, verify 7 certify, confirm, support, witness 9 guarantee 11 corroborate 12 substantiate

voucher 4 chit 5 proof 7 receipt 9 affidavit 10 credential 11 certificate

vouchsafe 4 give 5 award, deign, favor, grant, stoop 6 accord, oblige 7 concede 10 condescend 11 accommodate

vow 4 oath, swan 5 swear 6 assert, pledge, plight, prayer 7 declare, promise 8 covenant

vowel 5 vocal 6 letter *kind:* 4 long 5 glide, schwa, short 9 diphthong *omission:* 7 aphesis 11 contraction *variation:* 6 ablaut, umlaut

vowely 5 vocal 7 vocalic

voyage 4 tour, trip 6 cruise, travel 7 journey 9 excursion 10 expedition, pilgrimage

voyeur 6 peeper 10 peeping Tom

Vronski's lover 12 Anna Karenina

Vulcan see **Hephaestus**

vulgar 3 low, raw 4 base, rude, vile, wild 5 crass, crude, dirty, gross, nasty, rough 6 coarse, public, ribald, smutty, spoken 7 general, obscene, popular, profane, uncouth 8 barbaric, barnyard, improper, indecent, unseemly 9 barbarian, barbarous, graceless, idiomatic, incorrect, inelegant, loathsome, offensive, repulsive, revolting, tasteless, unrefined 10 colloquial, indecorous, indelicate, outlandish, ungraceful, unpolished, vernacular 12 scatological

vulgarism 8 slangism, solecism 9 barbarism 10 corruption 11 impropriety 13 vernacularism, vernacularity

vulgate 6 patois 10 colloquial, vernacular

Vulgate translator 6 Jerome

vulnerability 8 exposure, openness, weakness 9 liability 11 vincibility

vulnerable 4 open, weak 6 liable 7 exposed

vulnerary 6 curing 7 healing 8 curative, remedial, sanative, sanatory 9 remedying, wholesome 11 restorative

vulpine 3 sly 4 foxy, wily 6 artful, astute, crafty, tricky 7 cunning 8 guileful 9 insidious

vulture 4 hook, lift 5 filch, pinch, steal, swipe 6 condor, snitch 7 buzzard 8 aasvogel 11 lammergeier *food:* 7 carrion

vulturine 9 predative, predatory, rapacious, raptorial 10 predacious 11 predatorial

W

wacky 3 mad 4 nuts 5 crazy, loony, silly
6 absurd, crazed, insane 7 cracked, foolish, lunatic 8 demented, deranged 11 harebrained 12 preposterous

wad 3 gob, pot 4 bomb, clod, hunk, lump,
mint, pile 5 chunk, clump, hunch 6 boodle,
bundle, nugget, packet 7 fortune

waddy 3 peg 4 club 5 stick 6 cowboy
7 rustler

wade 4 ford, plod *into:* 6 attack

wadi 3 bed 4 wash 5 gully 6 ravine

wafer 4 cake, disk 7 cracker

waft 4 gust, puff, wave 5 drift, float, whiff

wag 3 wit 4 beat, card, lash, wave, zany
5 clown, comic, cutup, droll, joker, shake
6 jester, kidder, madcap, switch, twitch,
waggle, wiggle, wigwag, woggle 7 farceur,
show-off 8 comedian, funnyman, humorist,
jokester, quipster 9 oscillate, prankster
11 wisecracker

wage 3 fee, pay 4 hire, take 6 income,
return, reward, salary 7 stipend 8 earnings,
receipts 9 emolument 10 recompense
12 compensation, remuneration

wager 3 bet, lay, pot, set 4 ante, game,
play, risk 5 put on, stake 6 chance, gamble, hazard, impone 7 venture 9 adventure

waggery 3 gag 4 jape, jest, joke, quip
5 crack 7 devilry, roguery 8 deviltry, drollery, mischief 9 devilment, wisecrack, witticism 10 impishness 11 roguishness, waggishness 12 sportiveness

waggish 4 arch, pert 5 antic, comic, droll,
funny, saucy, witty 6 impish, jocose 7 comical, jocular, playful, puckish, roguish
8 humorous, prankish, sportive 9 facetious,
laughable, ludicrous 10 frolicsome 11 mischievous

waggle 4 beat, lash, sway, wave 6 switch,
waddle, wobble

Wagner, Richard *birthplace:* 7 Leipzig
deathplace: 6 Venice *father-in-law:*
5 Liszt (Franz) *heroine:* 5 Senta *opera:*
6 Rienzi 8 Parsifal 9 Lohengrin, Siegfried
10 Die Walküre, Tannhäuser 12 Das
Rheingold *recurring theme:* 9 leitmotif,
leitmotiv *wife:* 5 Minna 6 Cosima

wagon 3 car, van 4 cart, dray, wain 5 gilly
6 telega 7 fourgon, vehicle

wah 5 panda

wahoo 4 fish 5 shrub 8 basswood, mackerel 11 burning bush

waif 5 stray 7 vagrant 8 wanderer
9 foundling

wail 3 bay, cry, sob 4 bawl, blub, fuss,
howl, keen, kick, weep, yowl 5 quest,
whine 6 boohoo, murmur, repine, squall
7 blubber, ululate 8 complain

wailful 6 rueful, woeful 7 doleful 8 dolesome, mournful 9 plaintive, sorrowful
10 lamentable, lugubrious, melancholy

wain 5 wagon

waistband 4 belt, sash 6 girdle 8 ceinture, cincture

waistcoat 4 vest 6 jerkin

wait 4 bide, stay 5 abide, nurse, serve,
tarry 6 expect, linger, mother, remain
7 care for, foresee 10 anticipate, minister to
11 stick around

waiter 6 garçon 7 servant 9 attendant

Waiting for ____ 5 Godot, Lefty

waive 4 cede, stay 5 allow, defer, delay,
grant, leave, yield 6 give up, hold up, put
off, resign, shelve 7 abandon, concede,
hold off, suspend 8 hand over, hold over,
postpone 9 surrender 10 relinquish

wake 4 stir, whet 5 arise, get up, rally,
renew, rouse 6 arouse, bestir, kindle
7 freshen, roll out 9 challenge *mower's:*
5 swath

wakeful 5 alert 8 restless, vigilant, watchful 9 sleepless

waken see wake

Walden author 7 Thoreau (Henry David)

wale 3 rib 4 weal, welt 5 ridge, wheal,
whelk

Wales 5 Cymru *capital:* 7 Cardiff *language:* 6 Cymric *Latin name:* 7 Cambria
patron saint: 5 David

walk 3 leg, run 4 foot, hike, hoof, pace,
plod, race, reel, slog, step, turn 5 amble,
field, march, mince, strut, stump, tramp,
tread, troop 6 airing, domain, foot it, lumber, parade, ramble, sashay, sphere, stride,
stroll, strunt, toddle, trudge 7 alameda,
demesne, saunter, stretch, terrain, traipse
8 ambulate, dominion, province, traverse
9 bailiwick, champaign, promenade, territory 11 base on balls, perambulate
12 deambulation

walkaway 4 romp, rout
walking shorts 8 Bermudas
walking stick 4 cane 5 staff 6 kebbie
8 ashplant
walk out 5 leave 6 strike
walkway 4 path 7 catwalk 9 promenade
ancient Greek: 4 stoa
wall 3 bar, hem 4 cage, coop, stop
5 block, fence, hedge 6 corral, immure
7 barrier, close in, enclose, envelop 8 blockade 9 barricade, roadblock *hanging:* 8 tapestry *painting:* 5 mural *protective:* 7 parapet *top of:* 6 coping
wallaba tree 3 apa
wallaby 8 kangaroo
wallet 8 billfold 10 pocketbook *items:*
5 bills
wallop 3 bat, bop, jar 4 bang, bash, beat,
belt, blow, boot, bump, drub, jolt, kick, lick,
pelt, slam, slug, trim, whip, whop 5 baste,
blast, clash, crash, paste, pound, shock,
smack, smash 6 buffet, impact, pummel,
thrash, thrill, thwack 7 belabor, shellac,
trounce 8 lambaste 9 collision 10 percussion
walloping 4 huge 5 giant 7 immense,
mammoth, monster 8 colossal, enormous,
gigantic 10 gargantuan, prodigious
wallow 4 bask, roll 5 enjoy, lurch, revel
6 welter 7 blunder, indulge, rollick, stumble
8 flounder 9 delight in, luxuriate
____ **Walpole, writer** 6 Horace
walrus 6 mammal *relative:* 4 seal *tooth:*
4 tusk
____ **Walton, writer** 5 Izaak
waltz 3 zip 6 breeze
Waltz King 7 Strauss (Johann)
Wampanoag chief 9 Massasoit, Metacomet 10 King Philip
wampum 5 beads, money, sewan
6 shells
wan 4 ashy, pale, weak, worn 5 ashen,
livid, waxen 6 anemic, doughy, pallid,
sickly 7 haggard 8 blanched, bleached,
boneless, impotent 9 bloodless, colorless,
forceless, spineless, washed-out 10 cadaverous, emasculate 11 ineffective, ineffectual, slack-spined 12 invertebrate
wand 3 rod 4 pole, tube 5 baton, staff
combining form: 5 rhabd 6 rhabdo
wander 3 bat, bum, err, gad 4 roam, roll,
rove 5 amble, drift, gypsy, mooch, range,
stray, tramp 6 depart, gander, ramble, stroll
7 deviate, digress, diverge, excurse, maunder, meander, saunter, traipse 8 divagate,
straggle, vagabond 9 gallivant
wanderer 5 nomad, rover 6 errant,
roamer 7 drifter, pilgrim, rambler, tzigane,
vagrant 9 meanderer 12 rolling stone

wane 3 ebb 4 fail, fall 5 abate, let up
6 relent, shrink, weaken 7 decline, die
away, die down, dwindle, ease off, slacken,
subside 8 moderate 9 fall short, waste
away
wangle 7 finagle 8 engineer, maneuver,
outflank 9 machinate, overreach 10 outgeneral 11 outmaneuver
want 4 lack, must, need, wish 5 covet,
crave, ought 6 dearth, defect, demand,
desire, penury, should 7 absence, default,
poverty, require 8 exigency, poorness
9 indigence, necessity, neediness, privation
10 desiderate, inadequacy, meagerness,
scantiness, skimpiness 11 destitution,
requirement 12 exiguousness 13 insufficiency
wanting 3 shy 4 away, gone, sans
5 minus, scant, short 6 absent, scanty,
scarce 7 failing, lacking, missing, omitted,
without 9 defective, deficient 10 inadequate, incomplete, uncomplete 12 insufficient, unsufficient
wanton 3 lax, toy 4 doxy, easy, fast, fool,
jade, slut 5 cruel, dally, flirt, hussy, light,
loose, slack, tramp, trull, wench 6 coquet,
harlot, lead on, trifle 7 baggage, cyprian,
jezebel, trollop, unasked, wayward, whorish
8 contrary, perverse, slattern, spiteful,
strumpet, unchaste 9 malicious 10 gratuitous, malevolent, prostitute 11 string
along, uncalled-for 12 supererogant
wapiti 3 elk 4 deer, stag
war 3 tug 4 feud 5 fight 6 battle, combat,
oppugn, strife 7 contend, crusade 8 struggle *German:* 5 krieg 10 blitzkrieg *god:*
3 Tyr 4 Ares, Mars, Odin 5 Wodan, Woden
goddess: 4 Enyo 5 Anath 6 Inanna, Ishtar 7 Bellona *Latin:* 6 bellum *Muslim:*
5 jehad, jihad *relating to:* 7 martial
War and Peace *author:* 7 Tolstoy (Leo)
composer: 9 Prokofiev (Sergey)
warble 3 air, lay 4 sing, tune 6 melody,
strain 7 descant, measure, melisma, melodia 8 diapason
warbler 7 kinglet 8 songster 9 blackpoll
11 gnatcatcher *European:* 10 chiffchaff
war club 3 bat 4 mace 5 baton 6 cudgel
8 bludgeon 9 truncheon 10 knobkerrie
war cry 5 motto 6 slogan *Greek:* 5 alala
ward 4 balk, care, fend, foil, halt, stay, turn
5 aegis, armor, avert, block, check, deter,
guard, parry, rebut, repel, trust, watch
6 divert, picket, rebuff, sentry, shield, stymie, thwart 7 custody, defense, deflect,
fend off, forfend, hold off, keeping, keep off,
lookout, obviate, prevent, repulse, rule out
8 armament, preclude, security, sentinel,
stave off, watchman 9 forestall, frustrate,

interrupt, safeguard 10 protection 11 safekeeping 12 guardianship

warden 6 custos, jailer, keeper, ranger
8 cerberus, claviger, guardian, watchdog
9 custodian

wardrobe 4 room 5 trunk 6 closet
7 armoire 12 clothespress

ware 4 shun 5 avoid, awake, aware, cloth,
goods 7 fabrics, knowing, pottery 8 sensible 9 cognizant, conscious

warehouse 4 pack, stow 5 étape, guard,
store 6 bestow 7 protect, shelter, storage
8 entrepôt 11 accommodate *oriental:*
6 godown

wares 4 line 5 goods 9 vendibles 11 commodities, merchandise

warfare 6 strife 7 contest, rivalry 8 conflict, striving 9 emulation 11 competition
combining form: 5 machy

warhorse 7 charger, courser

warlike 7 hawkish, martial, warring 8 battling, fighting, militant, military, ructious
9 bellicose, combative, truculent 10 contending, pugnacious 11 belligerent, contentious, quarrelsome 12 gladiatorial

warlock 4 mage 5 magus 6 wizard
7 charmer 8 conjurer, magician, sorcerer
9 enchanter, voodooist 11 necromancer

warm 4 heat 5 tepid 6 ardent 7 affable,
cordial, fervent, sincere, zealous 8 gracious
9 heartfelt 10 passionate, responsive
11 kindhearted, softhearted, sympathetic
12 enthusiastic, wholehearted 13 compassionate *air:* 7 thermal

warmed-over 5 stale, tired, trite 6 old hat
7 clichéd 8 shopworn, timeworn, well-worn
9 hackneyed, twice-told

warmhearted 4 kind, warm 6 benign,
kindly, tender 8 outgoing 9 benignant
10 responsive 11 sympathetic 13 compassionate

warn 3 bid, tip 4 clew, clue, post, tell
5 alert, guide, order 6 advise, beacon,
charge, direct, enjoin, fill in, inform, monish,
notify, wise up 7 apprise, caution, command, counsel 8 acquaint, instruct

warning 3 tip 4 hint 6 advice, caveat
7 caution, counsel, sematic 8 guidance,
monition, monitory 10 admonition, admonitory, cautionary, cautioning, monitorial, suggestion 11 admonishing, commonition
legal: 6 caveat

War of the Worlds author 5 Wells
(Herbert George)

warp 4 bend, kink, wind 5 color, twist,
wrest 6 debase, deform, garble, wrench
7 confuse, contort, corrupt, debauch,
deprave, distort, pervert, torture, vitiate
8 miscolor, misshape 9 brutalize 10 bastardize, bestialize, demoralize 12 misrepresent

warrant 4 back, pawn, word 5 argue,
basis, claim, state, token 6 affirm, assert,
assure, defend, ensure, insure, pledge,
secure 7 call for, certify, contend, earnest,
justify, require, sponsor 8 guaranty, maintain, mittimus, security 9 assurance, guarantee, stipulate, vindicate 10 foundation

warranty 4 bail, bond 6 surety 8 guaranty, security 9 guarantee

warrior 2 GI 4 hero, swad 7 fighter, soldier 9 man-at-arms 10 serviceman
11 fighting man *female:* 6 Amazon *Japanese:* 7 samurai

Warsaw *castle:* 5 Zamek *river:* 7 Vistula

warship see **ship,** *military*

wart 6 lesion 7 verruca

wary 4 safe 5 canny, chary, leery 6 frugal,
saving, scotch 7 careful, guarded, sceptic,
skeptic, sparing, thrifty 8 cautious, discreet,
doubting, gingerly, vigilant, watchful 9 provident, stewardly 10 suspicious, unwasteful
11 calculating, circumspect, considerate,
distrustful

wash 3 lap, lip, tub 4 lave, ride, suds
5 bathe, clean, drift, float, slosh, swash
6 bubble, burble, gurgle, shower, sluice
7 launder, shampoo

washed-out 5 all in, spent 6 bleary,
effete, used up 7 drained, far-gone, worn-
out 8 depleted 9 exhausted

washed-up 4 done 7 done for, through
8 finished

washing 4 bath 6 lavage 8 ablution *ceremonial:* 6 lavabo

Washington *capital:* 7 Olympia *largest
city:* 7 Seattle *nickname:* 12 Chinook
State 14 Evergreen State *state bird:*
9 goldfinch *state flower:* 12 rhododendron

Washington, D.C. designer 7 L'Enfant
(Pierre-Charles)

Washington's home 11 Mount Vernon

Washington Square author 5 James
(Henry)

wash out 4 cast, fail, flop, junk, shed
5 elute, scrap 6 reject, slough 7 cashier,
discard, flummox 8 jettison 9 throw away

wasp 6 hornet, vespid

waspish 5 huffy, sharp 6 cranky, ornery
7 bearish, crabbed, fretful, peevish, pettish
8 cankered, contrary, perverse, petulant,
snappish, spiteful 9 crotchety, fractious,
impatient, irritable, malicious, querulous
10 vinegarish 12 cantankerous, cross-
grained

waspy see **waspish**

wassail 3 bat 4 bust, hell, riot, soak, tear
5 binge, revel, spree 6 bender, frolic, ran-
tan 7 carouse, revelry, roister, whoopee,

whoopla, whoop-up 8 carousal 9 high jinks, revelment 10 skylarking

waste 4 blow, fail, junk, sack, wane, wild 5 offal, trash 6 barren, debris, desert, devour, drivel, kelter, litter, ravage, refuse, sewage, shrink, trifle, weaken 7 badland, consume, despoil, dwindle, fritter, garbage, pillage, rubbish, sullage 8 cast away, desolate, emaciate, fool away, misspend, riot away, spoilage, spoliate, squander, unthrift, wild land, wildness 9 depredate, desecrate, devastate, dissipate, fall short, overdoing, sweepings, throw away 10 frivol away, lavishness, muddle away, potter away, trifle away, wilderness 11 blunder away, dribble away, prodigality, prodigalize 12 extravagance, extravagancy *allowance:* 4 tret *from a mine:* 7 mullock *maker:* 5 haste *time:* 5 dally 6 dawdle, footle, piddle

waste away 4 fail, wane 5 dwine 7 atrophy, decline

wasted 4 worn 5 gaunt 6 meager 7 wizened 8 skeletal, withered 9 emaciated, shriveled 10 cadaverous

wasteful 6 lavish 8 prodigal 10 thriftless 11 extravagant, improvident

wastefulness 8 squander, unthrift 9 overdoing 10 lavishness 11 prodigality 12 extravagance, extravagancy

wasteland 4 wild 6 barren, desert 8 wildness 10 wilderness

Waste Land author 5 Eliot (Thomas Stearns)

waster 5 idler 6 loafer, no-good 7 lounger, rounder, spender, wastrel 8 prodigal, unthrift 9 fritterer 10 dissipater, high roller, ne'er-do-well, profligate, scapegrace, squanderer 11 scattergood, spendthrift

wastrel 3 rip 4 rake, roué 5 idler, knave, rogue, scamp 6 lecher, loafer, no-good, rascal 7 lounger, rounder, spender 8 prodigal, scalawag, unthrift 9 fritterer, libertine, scoundrel 10 blackguard, black sheep, dissipater, high roller, ne'er-do-well, profligate, scapegrace, squanderer 11 rapscallion, scattergood, spendthrift

watch 3 eye, see, spy, tab 4 look, mind, scan, tend, tout, ward 5 guard, vigil 6 attend, follow, picket, sentry 7 care for, examine, eyeball, inspect, lookout, monitor, surveil 8 eagle eye, scrutiny, sentinel, watchman 9 timepiece, vigilance 10 scrutinize 11 chronograph, chronometer 12 surveillance *chain:* 3 fob *maker:* 10 horologist

watchdog 6 custos, keeper, warden 8 cerberus, claviger, guardian 9 custodian

watcher 6 viewer 7 guarder, lookout, witness 8 beholder, by-sitter, guardian, looker-on, observer, onlooker 9 bystander,

spectator 10 eyewitness *combining form:* 6 scopus

watchfire 6 beacon

watchful 4 wary 5 alert, chary, quick, ready 6 prompt 7 wakeful 8 cautious, open-eyed, vigilant 9 wide-awake 10 unsleeping 11 circumspect *Scottish:* 5 tenty 6 tentie

watchman 4 ward 5 guard 6 picket, sentry 7 lookout 8 sentinel

watch out 4 mind 6 beware 7 look out

watchtower 7 lookout 10 lighthouse

watchword 6 slogan 10 shibboleth 11 catchphrase, countersign

water 5 fluid 6 dilute, liquid 7 moisten 8 irrigate, moisture, snowmelt *body:* 3 bay, sea 4 gulf, lake, pool 5 ocean 6 lagoon, strait 9 reservoir *combining form:* 4 aqua, aqui, aquo, hydr 5 hydat, hydro 6 hydato, limnia (plural) 7 limnion *French:* 3 eau *goddess:* 4 Nina 7 Anahita, Anaitis *Latin:* 4 aqua *Spanish:* 4 agua

water buffalo 4 arna 7 carabao *female:* 5 arnee

water clock 9 clepsydra

water closet 2 WC 4 head, john 5 privy 6 johnny, toilet 7 latrine 8 lavatory 11 convenience *British:* 3 loo

watercourse 4 duct 5 canal 6 course 7 channel, conduit 8 aqueduct, headrace, tailrace

water cow 7 manatee

water eagle 6 osprey

watered-down 4 thin, weak 5 washy 6 dilute, watery 7 diluted 8 waterish

water elephant 12 hippopotamus

waterfall 4 eddy 5 chute, falls, sault, shoot, spout, surge 6 rapids, riffle, vortex 7 cascade 8 cataract 9 whirlpool *California:* 8 Yosemite *Canada:* 5 Grand *Canada-U.S.:* 7 Niagara *former Nile:* 5 Ripon *Kentucky:* 5 Great 10 Cumberland *Niagara:* 8 American, Canadian 9 Horseshoe *Oregon:* 9 Multnomah *Snake river:* 4 Twin 8 Shoshone *Washington:* 10 Snoqualmie *world's highest:* 5 Angel *Yellowstone:* 5 Tower *Zambezi:* 8 Victoria

waterfinder 6 dowser

water hole *desert:* 5 oasis

water horse 6 kelpie 11 hippocampus

watering hole 3 bar, pub 4 café 5 haunt, oasis 6 lounge, nitery, resort, saloon, tavern 7 barroom, cabaret, hangout, hot spot, purlieu 8 drinkery, nightery 9 nightclub, nightspot 10 rendezvous, supper club 11 discotheque

water jar 4 ewer, lota, olla 5 banga, lotah 6 hydria, kalpis

waterless 3 dry 4 arid, sere 7 bone-dry, thirsty 8 droughty 9 unwatered 12 mois-

tureless *combining form:* 6 anhydr
7 anhydro

waterlog 3 sap 4 soak 5 souse, steep
6 drench, sodden 7 insteep 8 saturate

water nymph 4 lily 5 naiad 6 Nereid
7 Oceanid 9 dragonfly *female:* 5 nixie

water oscillation 6 seiche

water pipe 5 hooka 6 hookah 8 narghile,
nargileh

water plant 7 aquatic 10 hydrophyte

water rat 4 vole 6 rodent 7 muskrat

water spirit 6 undine

waterspout 6 funnel 10 cloudburst

water sprite see **water nymph**

water tank 7 cistern

waterwheel 5 noria 6 sakieh

watery 4 pale, thin, weak 5 banal, bland,
vapid, washy 6 anemic, dilute, jejune, pallid, sluicy 7 diluted, insipid, sapless 9 bloodless 10 namby-pamby, wishy-washy

wattle 3 rod 4 pole 10 interweave

wattle and ___ 4 daub

wave 3 wag 4 beat, flap, lash 6 marcel,
ripple, switch, waggle, woggle 7 flutter, rip-
plet 8 brandish, undulate *combining form:*
3 cym, kym 4 cymo, kymo *large:* 7 tsunami

waver 4 halt, trim 5 hedge, shift 6 dither,
falter, palter, seesaw, teeter 7 flicker, stagger, whiffle 8 hesitate 9 vacillate 12 shilly-
shally, wiggle-waggle

wavering 4 weak 5 shaky 6 dickey,
unsure, wobbly 7 halting 8 insecure, rootless, to-and-fro, unstable 9 faltering, fluctuant, hesitancy, vacillant, whiffling 10 hesitating, hesitation, indecision 11 vacillating,
vacillation, vacillatory 12 irresolution, shilly-
shally, wiggle-waggle

Waverly author 5 Scott (Walter)

wavy pattern 5 moiré

wax 3 get, run 4 come, grow, hike, rise,
turn 5 boost, build, lipid, mount 6 become,
expand 7 augment, enlarge, upgrade,
upsurge 8 heighten, increase, multiply, paraffin, simonize *combining form:* 3 cer
4 cero

waxen 3 wan 4 ashy, pale 5 ashen, livid
6 doughy, pallid 8 blanched 9 colorless

waxlike 9 ceraceous

way 3 ilk 4 adit, door, kind, lane, mode,
path, road, sort, type, wise, wont 5 alley,
breed, class, entry, habit, modus, order,
route, style, track, trick, usage 6 access,
artery, avenue, course, custom, entrée,
manner, method, praxis, street, system
7 fashion, ingress, species, variety 8 distance, entrance, habitude, practice 9 admission, boulevard, technique 10 admittance,
consuetude 12 thoroughfare *combining
form:* 3 ode

wayfaring 6 roving 7 nomadic, vagrant
8 vagabond 9 itinerant, itinerate, wandering
11 perambulant, peripatetic 13 perambulatory

waylay 6 ambush 8 surprise

Way of All Flesh author 6 Butler
(Samuel)

Way of the World author 8 Congreve
(William)

way or sea ___ 5 farer

wayward 5 balky 6 fickle, ornery
7 erratic, froward, restive 8 contrary, freakish, perverse, unstable, variable, whimsied
9 arbitrary, vagarious, whimsical 10 capricious, inconstant 11 wrongheaded
12 cross-grained

we *French:* 4 nous *German:* 3 wir *Italian:*
3 noi *Spanish:* 8 nosotros

weak 3 wan 4 puny, thin 5 faint, frail,
shaky, washy 6 dickey, dilute, feeble,
flimsy, infirm, sickly, unsure, watery, wobbly
7 diluted, fragile, rickety, sapless, spindly,
unsound 8 boneless, decrepit, impotent,
insecure, rootless, thewless, unstable,
wavering 9 enfeebled, fluctuant, forceless,
powerless, spineless, uncertain 10 emasculate, improbable, impuissant, inadequate,
incredible, irresolute, unreliable 11 debilitated, implausible, ineffective, ineffectual,
slack-spined, vacillating, watered-down
12 invertebrate, unbelievable, unconvincing,
undependable 13 insubstantial, unsubstantial *combining form:* 4 lept 5 lepto
6 asthen 7 astheno

weaken 3 cut, sap 4 fade, fail, flag, thin,
wane 5 blunt, unman 6 damage, dilute,
impair, infirm, injure, lessen, reduce, shrink,
soften 7 cripple, decline, disable, dwindle,
unbrace, unnerve 8 enervate, enfeeble, languish, minimize, paralyze 9 attenuate, fall
short, undermine, waste away 10 debilitate,
emasculate 11 deteriorate 12 incapacitate,
unstrengthen

weak-kneed 5 timid 6 wobbly 8 wavering
9 faltering, uncertain, whiffling 10 irresolute
11 vacillating 12 double-minded, wiggle-
waggle

weakling 3 sop 4 baby, butt, drip, mark
5 sissy 6 misfit, sucker 7 doormat, milksop, sad sack 8 mama's boy, pushover
9 jellyfish 10 mother's boy, namby-pamby,
pantywaist, sissy-pants 11 Milquetoast,
mollycoddle 12 invertebrate 13 sissy-
britches

weakness 5 taste 6 foible, liking 7 frailty
8 adynamia, appetite, fondness, soft spot
12 Achilles' heel

weal 4 wale, welt 5 ridge, wheal, whelk
6 stripe 7 welfare 9 well-being

weald 5 woods 6 forest, timber 8 woodland 10 timberland

wealth 4 mean, pelf 5 goods, worth 6 assets, estate, mammon, riches 7 capital, fortune 8 golconda, holdings, nabobism, opulence, property 9 resources, substance 11 possessions *combining form:* 4 plut 5 pluto

Wealth of Nations author 5 Smith (Adam)

wealthy 4 rich 7 moneyed, opulent 8 affluent

wean 5 alien, spean 8 alienate, disunify, disunite, estrange 9 disaffect

weapon 3 gun 4 bola, bolo, club, dart, dirk, épée, foil, mace, nuke, pike 5 arrow, knife, lance, rifle, saber, sabre, sling, spear, sword 6 dagger, magnum, musket, pistol, poleax, rapier 7 bazooka, carbine, firearm, halberd, halbert, javelin, machete, missile, poleaxe, shotgun, trident 8 battle-ax, catapult, crossbow, petronel, revolver, spontoon, tomahawk 9 battle-axe, blackjack, boomerang, derringer 11 blunderbuss 13 brass knuckles

weapons 7 arsenal

wear 3 rub 4 fray, gall, jade, tire 5 chafe, drain, erode, graze, grind, weary 6 abrade, ruffle, tatter 7 corrode, fatigue, frazzle

wear away 3 eat 4 bite, gnaw 5 erode, scour 6 abrade 7 corrode

wear down 4 jade, tire 5 drain, weary 6 weaken 7 exhaust, fatigue

weariness 5 ennui 7 fatigue 9 lassitude, tiredness 10 exhaustion

wearisome see **tiresome**

wear out 3 fag 4 poop 6 tucker 7 exhaust, frazzle, outtire 8 knock out, overstay, overtoil 9 prostrate

weary 4 bore, jade, pall, sick, tire, worn 5 drain, fed up, jaded, tired 6 tucker, weaken 7 fatigue 8 enfeeble, fatigued, footsore, footworn, overtire, overwork, wear down, worn down 9 disgusted 10 debilitate

weasand 6 gullet, throat 8 windpipe

weasel 5 dodge, evade, hedge, slink, sneak, stoat 6 ermine, ferret 7 shuffle, sneaker 8 sidestep, sneaksby 9 pussyfoot 10 equivocate, tergiverse 12 tergiversate *Scottish:* 8 whittret

weather 5 clime 7 climate *combining form:* 6 meteor 7 meteoro

weathercock 4 vane

weave 4 reed, spin, sway 5 braid, lurch, swing, twill 6 careen, damask, pleach, raddle, tissue, wattle, wobble 7 stagger, texture

weaverbird 4 taha 6 whidah, whydah 8 avadavat

Weaver of Raveloe 6 Marner (Silas)

weaver's reed 4 slay, sley

web 3 net 4 knot, maze, mesh 5 fiber, skein, snare, snarl, toils 6 cobweb, fabric, jungle, meshes, morass, tangle 7 ensnare, mizmaze, network, texture 8 entangle 9 labyrinth 10 enmeshment, entrapment 11 embroilment, ensnarement, involvement 12 entanglement *combining form:* 5 hypho *of a feather:* 5 vexil 8 vexillum

Weber opera 6 Oberon 9 Euryanthe 13 Der Freischütz

___ Webster 4 Noah 6 Daniel

wed 3 tie 4 join, link, mate, yoke 5 catch, marry, unite 6 marrow, relate, splice 7 combine, conjoin, connect, espouse 9 associate

wedded 7 marital, married, nuptial, spousal 8 conjugal, hymeneal 9 connubial 11 matrimonial

wedding 6 bridal 7 spousal 8 espousal, marriage, nuptials

wedding anniversary *fifteenth:* 7 crystal *fifth:* 6 wooden *fiftieth:* 6 golden *first:* 5 paper *seventy-fifth:* 7 diamond *tenth:* 3 tin *twentieth:* 5 china *twenty-fifth:* 6 silver

wedge-shaped 7 cuneate, sphenic

wedlock 8 marriage 9 matrimony 11 conjugality 12 connubiality

wee 4 tiny 5 teeny 6 minute, teensy, weensy 7 teentsy 9 miniature 10 diminutive, teeny-weeny 11 lilliputian 12 teensy-weensy

weed 4 dock, tare 5 chess 6 darnel, dodder, lupine, nettle, sorrel, teasel 7 burdock, burseed, hemlock, mullein, solanum, thistle, tobacco 8 amaranth, charlock, gromwell, purslane, toadflax 9 cocklebur, dandelion, glasswort, goldenrod, horsetail, knotgrass, marijuana, poison ivy, poison oak, stickseed 10 cinquefoil *European:* 6 spurry 7 spurrey 8 pingrass *killer:* 8 paraquat 9 herbicide *Western:* 4 loco

week 8 hebdomad *two weeks:* 9 fortnight

weep 3 cry, sob 4 blub, drib, drip, drop, moan, ooze, seep, wail 5 bleed, exude, greet, sweat, trill 6 bemoan, bewail, boohoo, grieve, lament, strain 7 blubber, deplore, distill, dribble, trickle 8 transude

weepy 5 teary 7 maudlin, tearful 10 lachrymose

weevil 4 boll 7 billbug 8 curculio *tropical:* 7 zyzzyva

weft 3 web 4 pick, woof, yarn 6 fabric, thread

weigh 3 tax 4 lade, load, mind, rate, tare 5 count, study 6 burden, charge, cumber, lumber, ponder, saddle, weight 7 balance, perpend 8 appraise, consider, encumber, evaluate, militate, think out 9 think over 10 excogitate 11 contemplate

weigh down 5 press 6 sadden 7 depress, oppress

weight 3 tax 4 duty, lade, load, onus, pith, task 6 burden, charge, credit, cumber, debase, import, lumber, moment, saddle 7 potency 8 efficacy, encumber, prestige 9 authority, influence, magnitude, millstone 10 adulterate, importance 11 consequence 12 forcefulness, forcibleness, powerfulness, significance *allowance:* 4 tare, tret 7 scalage *apothecary:* 4 dram 5 grain, pound 7 scruple *Asian:* 6 cattle *combining form:* 3 bar 4 baro *gem:* 5 carat *measure of:* 3 ton 4 dram, gram 5 grain, ounce, pound 7 long ton, scruple 8 kilogram, short ton 9 metric ton *system:* 3 net 4 troy 6 metric 10 apothecary 11 avoirdupois

weightiness 4 pith 6 import, moment, weight 9 magnitude 10 importance 11 consequence 12 significance

weight lift 5 press 6 snatch 12 clean and jerk

weighty 3 big, fat 5 grave, gross, heavy, hefty, obese, sober, staid, stout, tough 6 fleshy, portly, sedate, severe, solemn, somber, taxing 7 earnest, exigent, massive, onerous, porcine, serious 8 cumbrous, exacting, grievous, material 9 corpulent, demanding, important, momentous, ponderous 10 burdensome, cumbersome, meaningful, no-nonsense, oppressive, overweight, sobersided 11 significant, substantial 12 considerable 13 consequential

weir 3 dam 9 fishgarth

weird 3 lot, odd 4 cast, doom, eery, fate 5 awful, eerie, moira, queer 6 creepy, kismet, spooky 7 bizarre, curious, destiny, eldrich, fearful, oddball, portion, strange, uncanny, uncouth 8 dreadful, eldritch, forecast, haunting, horrific, peculiar, prophecy, singular, supernal 9 eccentric, prevision, prognosis, unearthly, unnatural 10 mysterious, outlandish, prediction 11 foretelling, inscrutable 12 awe-inspiring, circumstance, supernatural 13 preternatural

welcome 4 hail 5 greet 6 genial 7 cordial 8 pleasant, pleasing 9 agreeable, congenial, favorable 10 contenting, gratifying, satisfying 11 pleasurable, pleasureful, sympathetic

weld 5 unite 6 solder 11 consolidate

welfare 4 good 7 benefit, fortune, success 8 interest 9 advantage, happiness, well-being 10 prosperity

welkin 3 sky 7 heavens 9 firmament

well 3 far, fit 4 easy, hale, sane 5 amply, clear, fitly, fully, happy, lucky, quite, right, sound, truly 6 aright, freely, indeed, justly, kindly, likely, nicely, origin, rather, really, source, wholly 7 happily, healthy, lightly, perhaps, readily, rightly, roundly, utterly 8 decently, entirely, facilely, fountain, possibly, probably, properly, smoothly, some-

what, suitably 9 correctly, favorably, fittingly, fortunate, inception, perfectly, tolerably, wholesome 10 acceptably, adequately, altogether, becomingly, completely, decorously, generously, pleasantly, prosperous, provenance, swimmingly, thoroughly 11 approvingly, befittingly, comfortable, doubtlessly, fortunately, provenience, substantial 12 considerably, effortlessly, fountainhead, prosperously, providential, satisfyingly, successfully 13 appropriately, significantly *combining form:* 2 eu

well-being 4 ease, good 7 benefit, welfare 8 euphoria, interest, thriving 9 abundance, advantage 10 easy street, prosperity

well-bred 6 urbane 7 genteel, refined 8 cultured, polished 9 distingué 10 cultivated

well-built 5 hunky, solid

well-developed 5 curvy 7 rounded 9 curvesome, Junoesque 10 curvaceous 11 curvilinear

well-disposed 8 friendly 9 receptive 11 sympathetic

Welles movie 7 Macbeth, Othello 8 The Trial 11 Citizen Kane, The Third Man, Touch of Evil 16 Chimes at Midnight

well-favored 4 fair 6 comely, lovely, pretty 8 handsome 9 beauteous, beautiful 10 attractive 11 good-looking

well-fixed see well-to-do

well-founded 4 good, just 5 meaty, pithy, sound, valid 6 cogent 7 telling 8 rational, reasoned 9 justified 10 reasonable 11 fundamental, substantial

well-groomed 4 neat, snug, tidy, trig, trim 5 doggy, natty, sassy 6 dapper, spiffy, spruce, sprucy 7 chipper, doggish, orderly 8 sparkish 9 shipshape 11 spic-and-span, uncluttered 12 spick-and-span

wellhead see wellspring

well-heeled see well-to-do

Wellington *horse:* 10 Copenhagen *victory:* 7 Vitoria 8 Talavera, Waterloo 9 Salamanca

well-known 5 noted 6 famous 7 leading, popular 9 important, notorious, prominent 11 conspicuous, outstanding

well-liked 7 favored, popular 8 favorite 9 preferred

well-mannered 5 civil 6 polite 7 genteel 9 courteous

well-nigh 4 most, much, nigh 5 about 6 all but, almost, nearly 8 as good as, as much as 11 essentially, practically

well-off see well-to-do

well-paying 7 gainful 9 lucrative 10 profitable, worthwhile 11 moneymaking 12 advantageous, remunerative

well-proportioned see well-turned

wellspring 4 root 6 origin, source 8 fountain 9 inception 10 provenance 11 provenience 12 fountainhead

well-thought-of 7 reputed 9 estimable, reputable 10 creditable 11 respectable

well-timed 7 timeous 9 favorable, opportune 10 auspicious, propitious, prosperous, seasonable

well-to-do 4 easy, rich 7 wealthy 8 affluent 10 prosperous 11 comfortable, substantial

well-turned 4 trim 7 shapely 8 shapeful 10 statuesque 11 clean-limbed

well-worn 5 stale, tired, trite 9 hackneyed 10 threadbare 11 commonplace, stereotyped

welsh 6 cry off, renege, resile 7 back off, back out 8 back down 9 backpedal, backwater 10 declare off 11 crawfish out

Welsh see Cymric

welt 4 wale, weal 5 ridge, wheal, whelk

welter 4 bask, roll, wilt 5 dry up, mummy, revel, wizen 6 wallow, wither 7 indulge, mummify, rollick, shrivel 9 luxuriate

_____ Welty, writer 6 Eudora

wen 4 cyst 6 growth 11 excrescence

wench 3 gal 4 girl, jade, lass, maid, miss 5 hussy, missy, tramp, trull 6 damsel, lassie, maiden, wanton 7 jezebel, servant, trollop 8 slattern, strumpet

wend 2 go 3 hie 4 fare, pass 6 push on, repair, travel 7 journey, proceed

werewolf 11 lycanthrope

Werther's beloved 5 Lotte

Wesleyan 9 Methodist

West 8 Occident

West African _baboon:_ 5 drill 8 mandrill _city:_ 5 Accra, Dakar, Lagos _country:_ 4 Togo 5 Benin, Gabon, Ghana 6 Gambia, Guinea 7 Liberia, Nigeria, Senegal 8 Cameroon 10 Ivory Coast 11 Sierra Leone _fetish:_ 4 juju _native:_ 3 Ibo 5 Hausa 7 Ashanti

western 5 oater 9 shoot-em-up 10 horse opera

Western novelist 4 Grey (Zane) 5 Short (Luke) 6 Judson (Edward Zane Carroll), L'Amour (Louis), Wister (Owen) 7 Guthrie (Alfred Bertram) 8 McMurtry (Larry)

Western organization 3 OAS 4 NATO

Western Samoa _capital:_ 4 Apia _monetary unit:_ 4 tala

West Indies _boat:_ 7 drogher _country:_ 4 Cuba 5 Haiti 7 Grenada, Jamaica 8 Dominica 10 Saint Lucia 13 Bahama Islands _language:_ 6 Creole, French 7 English, Spanish

West Point _father of:_ 6 Thayer (Sylvanus) _freshman:_ 5 plebe _student:_ 5 cadet

West Side Story _composer:_ 9 Bernstein (Leonard) _heroine:_ 5 Maria _lyricist:_ 8 Sondheim (Stephen)

West Virginia _capital:_ 10 Charleston _nickname:_ 13 Mountain State _state bird:_ 8 cardinal _state flower:_ 12 rhododendron

west wind see at wind

wet 3 dew, sop 4 damp, dank, lave, soak, wash 5 bedew, douse, drown, drunk, madid, moist, rainy, rinse, soggy, soppy, souse, water 6 dampen, deluge, drench, drippy, soaked, sodden, soused, sweaty, vapory 7 moisten, slopped, soaking, sopping 8 drenched, dripping, humidify, irrigate, saturate 9 saturated 10 inebriated 11 intoxicated _combining form:_ 4 hygr 5 hygro

wet blanket 7 killjoy 10 spoilsport

wether 4 goat 5 sheep

wetland 3 bog, fen 5 marsh, swamp

whack 2 go 3 bat, hit, pop, try 4 bash, blow, ding, shot, slap, slog, sock, stab, whop 5 catch, crack, fling, smack, smash, whirl 6 strike, thwack, wallop 7 stagger

whale 4 flog, hide, lash, whip 5 giant 6 stripe, thrash 7 mammoth, monster, scourge 8 behemoth 9 leviathan 10 flagellate _arctic:_ 7 bowhead _combining form:_ 3 cet 4 ceto _group:_ 3 pod _killer:_ 4 orca _kind:_ 3 sei 4 blue 5 right, sperm 6 baleen, beluga, killer 7 narwhal, rorqual 8 cachalot _tale:_ 8 Moby Dick _toothed:_ 9 blackfish _young:_ 4 calf

whalebone 6 baleen

wham 4 bang, boom, clap, slam 5 blast, burst, crack, crash, smash

whammy 3 hex 4 jinx 6 hoodoo, voodoo 10 Indian sign

wharf 4 dock, pier, quay, slip 5 berth, jetty, levee

Wharton novel 10 Ethan Frome 12 House of Mirth 13 The Buccaneers 16 Age of Innocence

whatnot 5 curio 6 bauble, gewgaw, trifle 7 bibelot, novelty, trinket 8 gimcrack 9 objet d'art 10 knickknack

wheal 4 wale, welt 5 whelk 6 strake, streak, stripe

wheat 5 durum, emmer, spelt, trigo 6 speltz 7 einkorn _beard:_ 3 awn _beat:_ 6 thresh _chaff:_ 4 bran _crushed:_ 6 bulgur _disease:_ 4 rust, smut

wheedle 3 con 4 coax 6 cajole 7 blarney 8 blandish, soft-soap 9 sweet-talk

wheel 4 auto, gyre, loop, reel, tire, tool, turn, veer, whip 5 avert, cycle, dolly, drive, motor, pilot, pivot, round, sheer, whirl 6 circle, divert, league, totter 7 circuit, deflect, stagger 8 gyration, rotation, titubate 9 volte-face 10 charioteer, conference, rev-

olution 11 association, circulation *combining form:* 5 troch 6 trocho *part:* 3 hub,
rim 5 spoke *rim:* 5 felly 6 felloe *spoke:*
6 radius *toothed:* 3 cog 4 gear
wheel-like 8 rotiform
wheelman 6 driver 7 cyclist 8 helmsman
wheel-shaped 5 round 7 trochal 8 circular
wheeze 4 buzz, fizz, hiss, lark 5 antic,
caper, prank, swish, trick 6 didoes, fizzle,
frolic, shines, sizzle, whoosh 7 whisper
8 sibilate 10 shenanigan 11 monkeyshine
whelk 4 wale, weal, welt 5 wheal
whelm 5 drown, flood, swamp 6 deluge,
engulf 8 inundate, overcome, overflow,
submerge 9 knock over, overpower, overwhelm, prostrate
whelp 3 boy, cub, pup 4 girl 5 child,
puppy
when 4 anon 5 again, while 6 albeit, much
as, though 7 howbeit, whereas 8 although
where 4 site, spot 5 locus, place, point
7 station, whither 8 location, position 9 situation
whereas 2 as 3 for, now 4 when 5 since,
while 6 albeit, much as, seeing, though
7 because, howbeit 8 although, as long as
10 inasmuch as 11 considering
wherefore 3 why 5 proof 6 ground, reason, whyfor 8 argument
wherewithal 5 means, money
9 resources
wherry 4 boat 5 barge 7 rowboat
whet 4 edge, hone, stir, wake 5 rally,
rouse, waken 6 arouse, awaken, bestir, kindle 7 sharpen, zakuska 9 antipasto, appetizer, challenge 11 hors d'oeuvre
whiff 4 dash, hint 5 shade, smack, tinge,
trace 6 breath, trifle 7 soupçon 8 tincture
whiffet 4 zero 5 zilch 6 cipher, nobody
7 nothing, nullity 8 whipster 9 nonentity
whiffle 4 halt 5 waver 6 dither, falter
7 stagger 8 hesitate 9 vacillate 12 shilly-
shally, wiggle-waggle
while 2 as 3 bit 4 pass, time, when
5 fleet, pains, space, spell, spend 6 albeit,
effort, moment, much as, though 7 beguile,
howbeit, instant, stretch, trouble, whereas
8 although, exertion, occasion
whim 3 bee 4 idea 5 dream, fancy, freak,
humor 6 megrim, vagary, vision 7 boutade,
caprice, conceit, fantasy, thought
8 crotchet 11 disposition, inclination
whimper 3 cry 4 mewl, pule 5 whine
whimsical 4 iffy 6 chancy 7 erratic, wayward 8 freakish, whimsied 9 arbitrary, fluctuant, uncertain, vagarious 10 capricious
12 incalculable 13 unpredictable
whimsy 4 idea 5 dream, fancy, freak,
humor 6 megrim, vagary, vision 7 boutade,

caprice, conceit, fantasy, thought
8 crotchet 9 capriccio 11 disposition, inclination
whine 4 fuss, kick, pule, wail 6 murmur,
repine, snivel, yammer 7 whimper 8 complain
whinny 5 neigh 6 nicker 7 whicker
whiny 5 raspy, waspy 6 snappy, twitty
7 peevish, raspish, waspish 8 snappish
9 irritable, querulous
whip 3 set 4 abet, beat, cane, drub, dust,
flog, hide, lash, lick, rout, trim, turn, veer
5 avert, blast, curry, mop up, pivot, quirt,
raise, set on, sheer, upend, whale, wheel,
whirl, whisk, whomp 6 cudgel, defeat,
divert, foment, incite, lather, stir up, stripe,
subdue, switch, thrash, wallop 7 curbash,
deflect, kurbash, overrun, provoke, rawhide,
scourge, shellac, trounce 8 bludgeon, cour-
bash, kourbash, lambaste, overcome, vanquish 9 bastinado, instigate, overwhelm
10 flagellate 13 cat-o'-nine-tails *braided:*
10 blacksnake *combining form:* 6 mastig,
mastix 7 mastigo *riding:* 4 crop
whippersnapper see whiffet
whipping boy 4 goat 5 patsy 7 fall guy
9 scapegoat
whippy 6 supple 7 elastic, springy, stretch
8 flexible, stretchy 9 resilient
whir 3 fly 4 buzz 5 chirr 6 chirre
7 revolve, vibrate
whirl 2 go 3 ado, pop, try 4 eddy, flit, fuss,
gyre, moil, reel, shot, slap, spin, stab, stir,
swim, turn, veer, whip, whiz 5 avert, crack,
fleet, fling, gurge, hurry, pivot, round, sheer,
speed, stave, storm, twirl, whack, wheel,
whish, whisk 6 barrel, bullet, bustle, divert,
flurry, furore, gyrate, hassle, hubbub,
pother, swoosh, vortex 7 circuit, clatter,
deflect, ruction, stagger, whoopla 8 gyration, rotation, rowdydow 9 commotion,
maelstrom, pirouette 10 hurly-burly, revolution 11 circulation
whirligig 4 gyre, spin 6 bootle, gyrate
8 carousel 9 carrousel, pirouette 12 merry-
go-round
whirlpool 3 ado 4 eddy, fuss, purl, stir
5 gurge, whorl 6 bustle, flurry, furore,
pother, swoosh, vortex 8 vortices (plural)
9 maelstrom, whirlwind *combining form:*
4 dino
whirlwind 2 oe 3 ado 4 fuss, stir 6 bustle, flurry, furore, pother, whirly 7 tornado
9 dust devil, hurricane, rainspout, sand
spout 10 sand column, waterspout
whish 3 fly 4 buzz, fizz, flit, hiss, whiz
5 fleet, hurry, speed, stave, whirl 6 bullet,
fizzle, sizzle, wheeze 7 whisper 8 sibilate
whisk 3 fly, zip 4 beat, flit, whip, whiz
5 hurry, speed 6 barrel, bullet

whisker 3 ace 4 hair 11 hairbreadth

whiskered 5 hairy 6 fleecy, pilose, woolly 7 barbate, bearded, hirsute, pileous

whiskers 5 beard 6 beaver

whiskey 3 rye 5 hooch, usque 6 hootch, Scotch 7 bourbon 8 usquabae, usquebae *with beer chaser:* 11 boilermaker

whisper 4 buzz, dash, fizz, hint, hiss, whiz 5 rumor, shade, swish, tinge, touch, trace, whiff 6 breath, fizzle, mumble, murmur, mutter, rustle, sizzle, wheeze, whoosh 7 breathe, confide 8 sibilate 9 suspicion, undertone 11 susurration

whist 4 game, hush 5 quiet, still 6 silent, stilly 7 hushful 9 noiseless, soundless *card hand:* 10 Yarborough

whistle 4 pipe 5 flute 6 signal

whit 3 bit, jot 4 atom, damn, hoot, iota 5 shred, whoop 7 modicum 8 particle

white 5 hoary, milky 6 albino, benign, blanch, bleach, blench, bright, dexter 7 decolor 8 palliate 9 canescent, extenuate, favorable, fortunate, gloss over, gloze over, sugarcoat 10 auspicious, blanch over, decolorize, propitious *combining form:* 3 alb 4 albo, cali, calo, leuc, leuk 5 callo, leuco, leuko *egg's:* 5 glair 6 glaire 7 albumen

white cliffs of ___ 5 Dover

White Fang author 6 London (Jack)

White House *designer:* 5 Hoban (James) *first occupant:* 5 Adams (Abigail, John)

white lightning 7 bootleg 9 moonshine 10 bathtub gin 11 mountain dew

whiten 3 dim 4 dull, fade, pale 5 frost 6 blanch, bleach, blench, silver, veneer 7 decolor, grizzle, lighten, varnish 8 etiolate, palliate 9 extenuate, gloss over, gloze over, sugarcoat 10 blanch over, decolorize

white plague 2 TB 8 phthisis 11 consumption 12 tuberculosis

whitewash 6 veneer 7 varnish 8 palliate 9 extenuate, gloss over, gloze over, sugarcoat 10 blanch over

whither 5 where 7 whereto 9 whereunto 11 whereabouts

whiting 4 fish, hake

Whitsunday 9 Pentecost

Whittier poem 7 Ichabod, Laus Deo 9 Snow-Bound 10 Maud Muller 11 Barefoot Boy 14 Telling the Bees 16 Barbara Frietchie

whittle 3 cut 4 pare 5 carve, shape

whiz 3 fly, zip 4 buzz, fizz, flit, hiss, zoom 5 adept, hurry, speed, swish, whirl, whish, whisk 6 bullet, expert, fizzle, master, sizzle, wheeze, whoosh, wizard 7 whisper 8 sibilate, virtuoso 10 past master 12 professional

whole 3 all, fit, sum 4 full, hale, sane 5 fixed, gross, right, sound, total 6 choate, entire, entity, intact, system, unhurt, unrent 7 gestalt, perfect, plenary 8 complete, entirety, flawless, integral, outright, sum total, totality, unbroken, unmarred 9 aggregate, exclusive, integrate, undamaged, undivided, uninjured, untouched 10 unimpaired, unswerving 11 unblemished 12 concentrated, undistracted *combining form:* 3 hol, pan 4 holo, pano, toti 7 integri

wholehearted 4 sure 6 ardent, hearty, steady 7 abiding, earnest, fervent, genuine, serious, sincere 8 bona fide, enduring 9 authentic, heartfelt, steadfast, unfeigned 10 passionate, unwavering 11 impassioned, unfaltering, unqualified 13 unquestioning

whole-hog 8 complete, thorough 9 fulldress 10 exhaustive 13 thoroughgoing

wholeness 5 vigor 6 health 7 allness, oneness 8 entirety, haleness, totality 9 integrity, soundness 10 entireness, heartiness, perfection, robustness 11 healthiness 12 completeness

whole note 9 semibreve

whole number 5 digit 6 cipher, figure 7 chiffer, integer, numeral

wholesome 3 fit 4 good, hale, safe, sane, well 5 right, sound 6 curing 7 healing, healthy 8 curative, hygienic, remedial, salutary, sanative, sanatory 9 healthful, remedying, vulnerary 10 salubrious, well-liking 11 restorative

wholly 3 all 4 just, well 5 fully, quite 6 in toto, purely 7 exactly, roundly, totally, utterly 8 all in all, entirely 9 perfectly 10 altogether, completely, thoroughly *combining form:* 4 toti

whomp 4 beat, drub, whip 5 smear 6 thrash, wallop 7 shellac, trounce 8 lambaste

whoopee 3 fun 5 revel 6 gaiety 7 jollity, revelry, wassail 8 reveling 9 festivity, high jinks, merriment, revelment 10 skylarking 11 merrymaking

whoopla 4 to-do 5 revel, whirl 6 clamor, hassle, pother, tumult, uproar 7 revelry, turmoil, wassail 9 commotion, high jinks, revelment 10 hurly-burly, skylarking

whop 3 bat, bop 4 bash, beat, biff, blow, drub, sock 5 baste, pound, smack, whack 6 batter, buffet, hammer, pummel, thwack, wallop 7 belabor 8 lambaste

whopping 4 huge, much, very 6 damned, highly, hugely, mighty 7 awfully, immense 8 colossal, enormous, gigantic 10 gargantuan, prodigious 11 exceedingly

whorl 4 eddy, purl 5 gurge, swirl 6 swoosh 9 whirlpool *combining form:* 7 spondyl 8 spondylo

why 5 proof 6 enigma, ground, puzzle, reason, riddle 7 mystery 8 argument 9 conundrum, wherefore 10 puzzlement 13 Chinese puzzle, mystification

wicked 3 bad 4 blue, evil, mean, racy, ugly 5 antic, broad, hairy, pesky, risky, salty, shady, spicy, wrong 6 adroit, au fait, chancy, clever, cursed, impish, malign, pranky, purple, risqué, sinful, unholy 7 hateful, heinous, immoral, larkish, playful, roguish, ungodly, unsound, vicious 8 fiendish, off-color, perilous, prankful, prankish, spiteful 9 barbarous, dangerous, hazardous, malicious, malignant, rancorous, reprobate, troublous, unhealthy, vexatious 10 despiteful, iniquitous, jeopardous, malevolent, outrageous, suggestive 11 mischievous, treacherous, troublesome, unchristian, uncivilized

wickedness 3 sin 4 debt, evil, vice 5 wrong 9 depravity 10 corruption, immorality

wicker 3 rod 4 twig 5 osier, withe

wicket 4 arch, door, gate, hoop 6 window

wickiup 3 hut 5 lodge, tepee 7 shelter

wide 5 ample, broad, roomy 6 scopic, sweepy 7 liberal, radical 8 advanced, extended, scopious, spacious, tolerant 9 capacious, expansive, extensive 10 commodious 11 broad-minded, progressive *combining form:* 4 eury, lati

widen 4 ream 6 dilate 7 broaden 9 breadthen

wideness 5 scope 7 breadth 8 fullness 9 amplitude

widespread 4 rife 6 ruling 7 current, popular, rampant, regnant 9 prevalent 10 prevailing

widget 5 gizmo 6 gadget, jigger 7 gimmick

width 5 ambit, orbit, range, scope 6 circle, length, radius 7 breadth, compass 8 panorama 9 extension

wield 3 ply 5 exert, swing, throw 6 handle, put out 7 conduct, control 8 dispense, exercise, maneuver 10 manipulate *the gavel:* 7 preside

wieldy 6 mighty, strong 8 powerful

wiener 3 dog 5 frank 6 hot dog 11 frankfurter, wienerwurst

wife 3 Mrs. 4 mate 5 bride 6 matron, missis, missus, spouse 7 consort, dowager 8 helpmate, helpmeet 9 other half *Latin:* 4 uxor *of a rajah:* 4 rani 5 ranee

wifely 7 uxorial

wig 3 jaw, rap 4 rail, rate 5 scold 6 berate, peruke, rebuke, revile, toupee 7 bawl out, chiding, reproof, upbraid 8 reproach 9 reprimand 10 admonition, tongue-lash 12 admonishment

wiggle 4 worm 6 squirm, writhe 8 squiggle *Scottish:* 5 hotch

wight 5 being, human 6 mortal, person 8 creature 9 personage 10 human being, individual

wigwam 3 hut 5 lodge, tepee

wild 3 mad 4 fast 5 crazy, dirty, feral, rabid, rough, waste 6 barren, brutal, desert, ferine, Gothic, raging, rakish, savage, stormy, unruly, vulgar 7 badland, frantic, furious, Hunnish, natural, raffish, uncivil, untamed, vicious 8 agrarian, agrestal, barbaric, blustery, carefree, feckless, frenetic, frenzied, rakehell, reckless, stormful, untoward 9 barbarian, barbarous, delirious, fantastic, fractious, graceless, tasteless, turbulent, uncareful, unsubdued, wasteland 10 blustering, corybantic, incautious, outlandish, wilderness 11 extravagant, intractable, tempestuous, uncivilized 12 devil-may-care, preposterous, recalcitrant, uncultivated, ungovernable, unmanageable 13 irresponsible, undisciplined *combining form:* 5 agrio

wild ass 5 kiang 6 onager

Wild Duck author 5 Ibsen (Henrik)

wildebeest 3 gnu

wilderness 5 waste 6 barren, desert 7 badland 9 backlands, wasteland 10 hinterland 11 backcountry

Wilder play 7 Our Town 13 The Matchmaker 17 The Skin of Our Teeth

wild-eyed 6 raving 7 radical 9 visionary

wild ox 4 anoa

wile 4 draw, ploy, ruse 5 charm, feint, guile, trick 6 allure, deceit, device, gambit 7 attract, beguile, bewitch, chicane, cunning, enchant, gimmick 8 artifice, maneuver, trickery 9 captivate, chicanery, fascinate, magnetize, stratagem 13 dissimulation

wiliness 3 art 5 craft 7 cunning, slyness 8 artifice, foxiness 9 cageyness, canniness 10 artfulness, craftiness

will 4 like, mind, wish 5 elect, fancy, leave 6 choose, devise, legate, liking, please 8 bequeath, pleasure, velleity, volition 9 testament 10 discipline 11 inclination, self-command, self-control, self-mastery 13 determination, self-restraint *addition:* 7 codicil *maker:* 8 testator 9 testatrix *without:* 9 intestate

willful 6 dogged, mulish, unruly 7 decided 8 factious, perverse, resolved, stubborn, unforced 9 obstinate, pigheaded, purposive, voluntary 10 deliberate, determined, headstrong 11 intentional, intractable, stiffnecked, wrongheaded 12 contumacious, pertinacious, unprescribed

Williams play 10 Camino Real 13 The Rose Tattoo 16 Cat on a Hot Tin Roof,

Sweet Bird of Youth **17** The Glass Menagerie **18** Suddenly Last Summer

William Tell composer 7 Rossini
(Gioacchino)

willies 5 jumps **6** creeps, dither, shakes
7 jitters, shivers **9** whim-whams **13** heebie-
jeebies

willing 3 apt **4** fair, game, open **5** prone,
ready **6** minded, prompt **7** forward, witting
8 disposed, inclined, unforced **9** agreeable,
compliant, favorable, voluntary **10** deliberate **11** intentional, predisposed **12** unprescribed

willow 5 osier, salix **6** sallow *flower cluster:* **6** catkin *kind:* **5** crack, pussy, white
6 basket **7** weeping

willowy 4 tall **5** lithe **6** pliant **7** slender
8 graceful

wilt 3 sag **4** drop, flag, swag **5** droop, dry
up, mummy, wizen **6** cave in, peg out, welter, wither **7** give out, mummify, shrivel,
succumb **8** collapse **9** break down

wily 3 sly **4** deep, foxy **6** artful, astute,
clever, crafty, shrewd, tricky **7** cunning,
knowing **8** guileful **9** insidious, sagacious

wimble 4 bore **5** auger, brace, scoop
6 gimlet

Wimbledon's game 6 tennis

wimple 4 veil, wrap **6** ripple *wearer:*
3 nun

win 3 get **4** beat, earn, gain, have, make,
take **5** annex, reach, score, yield **6** attain,
defeat, obtain, pick up, rack up, secure
7 achieve, acquire, bring in, chalk up, conquer, procure, produce, realize, triumph, victory **8** conquest, drag down, draw down,
overcome **9** knock down **10** accomplish
over: **6** disarm, induce **8** convince, persuade, talk into **9** prevail on

wince 5 cower, quail, start **6** blanch,
blench, cringe, flinch, recoil, shrink
7 squinch

wind 3 fan, nil **4** bend, blow, clue, coil,
curl, gale, gird, gust, hint, reel, warp, wrap
5 curve, spool, twine, twist, weave
6 breath, breeze, circle, deform, enlace, girdle, naught, notion, nought, ruffle, spiral,
winnow, zephyr **7** contort, distort, enclose,
entwine, envelop, inkling, meander, monsoon, nothing, torture, wreathe **8** easterly,
encircle, misshape, surround, westerly
9 corkscrew **10** indication, intimation, suggestion *California:* **8** Santa Ana *cold:*
4 bise, bora **6** sansar, sarsar **7** mistral,
pampero, wulliwa **8** williwaw, willywaw
combining form: **4** anem **5** anemo, venti,
vento *east:* **5** Eurus *gentle:* **6** breeze,
zephyr **7** cat's-paw *hot:* **6** ghibli, samiel,
shamal, simoom, solano **7** sirocco *instrument:* **3** sax **4** horn, oboe, tuba, vane
5 flute **7** bassoon, trumpet **8** trombone

10 anemometer **11** weather vane *into:*
8 aweather *measure of speed:* **4** knot
Mediterranean: **7** etesian **8** levanter *north:*
6 Boreas *scale:* **8** Beaufort *south:*
5 Notus **6** Auster *southwest:* **8** libeccio
stormy: **4** gale **7** cyclone, tornado, twister
9 hurricane **11** northeaster *warm:* **4** föhn
5 foehn **7** chinook *west:* **6** zephyr
8 Favonius, Zephyrus

winding 5 snaky **6** spiral **7** bending, coil-
ing, crooked, curving, devious, sinuous
8 flexuous, indirect, tortuous, twisting
9 meandrous **10** circuitous, convoluted,
meandering, roundabout, serpentine
11 anfractuous

windmill *fighter:* **9** Don Quixote *sail:*
3 awe

window 3 bay, eye **4** pane **5** oriel **6** dormer **7** fenster, lucarne, luthern, opening
8 aperture, casement, jalousie *cover:*
5 blind **7** curtain, shutter *French:* **7** fenêtre
over a door: **7** transom **8** fanlight *part:*
4 came, pane, sash, sill **5** frame *projecting:* **3** bay **5** oriel *relating to:* **9** fenestral
roof's: **6** dormer **8** skylight *Scottish:*
7 winnock *ship's:* **4** port **8** porthole *ticket:*
7 guichet

windpipe 6 throat **7** trachea *combining
form:* **6** bronch, trache **7** bronchi, broncho,
tracheo **8** bronchio

windrow 4 bank, heap, hill, mass, pile
5 drift, mound, stack **6** furrow **7** pyramid
8 mountain

wind up 3 end **4** halt **5** close **6** finish, settle, wrap up **7** clean up **8** complete, conclude **9** determine, terminate

windup 3 end **5** close **6** ending, finale, finish **10** conclusion

windy 4 airy **5** blowy, brisk, fresh, gusty,
tumid, wordy **6** breezy, drafty, prolix, turgid
7 diffuse, verbose **8** blustery, dropsied,
inflated **9** dropsical, flatulent, overblown,
redundant **10** palaverous

wine 4 vino **5** drink, juice **8** beverage *aro-
matized:* **8** vermouth **9** hippocras, Quin-
quina *beverage:* **5** clary, mulse, negus,
punch **6** bishop **8** sangaree **9** hippocras
bottle: **6** fiasco, magnum **8** decanter, jeroboam, rehoboam **9** balthazar **10** methuselah, salmanazar **14** nebuchadnezzar *cabi-
net:* **8** cellaret *cask:* **3** tun, vat **4** butt, pipe
8 puncheon *cellar:* **6** bodega *combining
form:* **2** en **3** eno, oen **4** oeno *discoverer:*
4 Noah *disorder:* **5** casse *distillate:*
6 brandy, cognac *dry:* **3** sec **4** brut *film:*
8 beeswing *flavor:* **4** mull *fortified:* **4** port
6 Malaga, sherry **7** Madeira, marsala *fragrance:* **4** nose **7** bouquet *golden:* **4** Bual
7 Amoroso, Madeira, Moscato, Oloroso,
Sercial **8** Bucellas, Moscatel, muscatel
lover: **9** oenophile **11** oenophilist *maker:*

7 vintner **8** vigneron **13** viticulturist *merchant:* **7** vintner *pitcher:* **4** olpe **5** olpae (plural) **8** oenochoe *red:* **4** port, tent **5** Gamay, Macon, Marco, Medoc, Rioja **6** Aleyor, Barolo, Beaune, claret, Shiraz, Volnay **7** Almissa, Barbera, Chianti, Falerno, Inferno, Margaux **8** Aleatico, Alicante, Ambonnay, Bordeaux, Burgundy, cabernet, Gragnano, Julienas, Nebbiolo, Sassella **9** Adlesberg, Hermitage, Lambrusco, Pinot Noir, St. Emilion, zinfandel **10** Barbaresco, Beaujolais, Roussillon, Sangiovese, Valtellina, Verdicchio **11** Affenthaler, Mavrodaphne, Petite Sirah **12** Valpolicella *relating to:* **5** vinic **6** vinous *residue:* **4** marc *rice:* **4** sake *richness:* **4** body *sediment:* **4** lees **5** dregs *shop:* **6** bistro, bodega *sparkling:* **4** sekt **8** cold duck, mousseux, sparkler, Spumante **9** champagne, Lambrusco *specialist:* **9** enologist **10** oenologist *spiced:* **9** hippocras *steward:* **9** sommelier *study of:* **7** enology **8** oenology *sweet:* **4** Bual, port, tent **5** Almus, Tokay **6** Albana, canary, d'Yquem, Malaga, muscat **7** Almissa, bastard, Catawba, Madeira, malmsey, marsala, Moscato, Oloroso, Orvieto, Vouvray **8** Aleatico, Alicante, Malvasia, Moscatel, muscadel, muscatel, sauterne **9** Sauternes **11** Mavrodaphne, scuppernong *sweeten:* **4** mull *unfermented:* **4** must *vessel:* **3** ama **5** amula **7** chalice *white:* **4** hock, sock **5** Almus, Rhine, Soave **6** Alella, Barsac, Gentil, Graves, Saumur, Valmur **7** Banyuls, Catawba, Chablis, Chacoli, Conthey, Dezaley, Falerno, Moselle, Orvieto, Vouvray **8** Aiglerie, Amarante, Bordeaux, Frascati, Riesling, Semillon, Sylvaner, Traminer, Vaudesir, vermouth **9** champagne, Hermitage, Meursault, Neuchatel, Sansevero, Teneriffe, Zeltinger **10** chardonnay, Hochheimer, Montrachet **11** Chenin Blanc, Niersteiner, Rudesheimer, scuppernong **12** Gelsenhelmer **13** liebfraumilch **14** sauvignon blanc *year:* **7** vintage

wing **3** ala, arm, ell, fly **4** flit, limb, sail **5** annex, block, bulge, fleet, pinna, sweep **9** expansion, extension **10** projection, protrusion **12** prolongation, protuberance *combining form:* **3** ali **4** pter **5** ptera, ptero **6** pterus, pteryg **7** pterous, pterygo *relating to:* **4** alar **5** alary **6** pteric

winged **5** alate **7** pennate *deity:* **4** Amor, Eros, Nike **5** Cupid **6** Hermes **7** Mercury *horse:* **7** Pegasus *monster:* **5** harpy

wingless **7** apteral **8** apterous

winglike **4** alar **7** aliform *part:* **3** ala **4** alae (plural)

wink **3** bat **5** blink, shake, trice **6** minute, moment, second **7** instant, nictate, twinkle **9** nictitate, twinkling **11** split second

winner **6** victor **8** champion **9** conqueror

Winnie-the-Pooh *author:* **5** Milne (Alan Alexander) *character:* **3** Roo **5** Kanga **6** Piglet, Tigger

winning **5** sweet **6** dulcet, profit **8** conquest, engaging

winnow **3** fan **4** blow, comb, sift, sort, wind **6** delete, remove, ruffle **8** separate

winsome **5** sweet **6** dulcet **7** lovable, winning **8** adorable, cheerful, engaging, lovesome

winter **6** season *French:* **5** hiver *Spanish:* **8** invierno

Winter's Tale character **7** Camillo, Leontes, Perdita **8** Florizel, Hermione **9** Polixenes

wintry **3** icy **4** cold **5** hoary, snowy **6** frigid, hiemal, stormy **8** hibernal, storming

wipe **3** mop **4** x out **5** abate, annul, erase, towel **6** cancel, delete, efface **7** abolish, blot out, expunge **8** black out, decimate, massacre **9** eradicate, extirpate, slaughter **10** annihilate, extinguish, obliterate **11** exterminate

wire **3** rod **4** cord, line **5** cable **6** thread **7** message **8** telegram **9** telegraph *measure:* **3** mil **5** gauge

wireless **5** radio

wiry **4** lean, ropy **6** sinewy **7** fibrous, stringy **8** muscular

Wisconsin *capital:* **7** Madison *college, university:* **5** Ripon **9** Marquette *largest city:* **9** Milwaukee *nickname:* **11** Badger State *state bird:* **5** robin *state flower:* **6** violet

wisdom **4** lore **5** sense **7** insight, science **8** gumption, judgment, sagacity, sageness, saneness, sapience **9** good sense, knowledge **10** horse sense, shrewdness **11** common sense, information **12** perspicacity **13** judiciousness, sagaciousness *combining form:* **5** sophy

wise **3** hep, hip, way **4** bold, clew, clue, flip, keen, mode, pert, post, sage, sane, tell, warn, wily **5** acute, alert, aware, brash, cagey, canny, cocky, fresh, lippy, modus, nervy, quick, sassy, saucy, sharp, slick, smart **6** advise, artful, astute, bright, cheeky, crafty, fill in, inform, manner, method, notify, shrewd, smooth, sophic, system, tricky **7** apprise, cunning, fashion, forward, gnostic, knowing, politic, prudent, sapient **8** acquaint, arrogant, discreet, flippant, impudent, insolent, sensible, slippery, tactical **9** advisable, bold-faced, expedient, insighted, intuitive, judgmatic, judicious, provident, sagacious **10** cogitative, discerning, insightful, perceptive, procacious, reflective, thoughtful **11** foresighted, impertinent, intelligent, quick-witted, sharp-witted, smart-alecky **12** nimble-witted **13** contemplative,

knowledgeable, perspicacious *old man:*
6 Nestor *person:* 4 sage 6 savant
7 scholar

wiseacre see **wise guy**

wisecrack 3 gag 4 jape, jest, joke, quip
5 sally 7 waggery 9 witticism

wise guy 6 smarty 9 know-it-all 10 smart
aleck 11 smarty-pants

Wise Men see **Magi**

wish 4 hope, like, long, want, will 5 covet,
crave, elect, fancy, foist, yearn 6 desire,
expect, impose, please 7 longing 10 desiderate

wishbone 7 furcula 8 furculum

wishful 5 eager 7 longing 8 desirous

wishy-washy 4 weak 5 banal, bland,
vapid 6 jejune, watery 7 insipid, languid,
sapless 8 listless, waterish 9 enervated,
savorless 10 flavorless, namby-pamby,
pantywaist, spiritless 13 characterless

wisp 5 strip 6 streak 7 handful 8 fragment

wispy 5 frail 8 nebulous

wisteria 4 fuji, vine

Wister novel 12 The Virginian

wistful 3 sad 7 pensive 10 meditative,
melancholy

wit 3 ESP, wag 4 head, mind 5 brain,
comic, droll, grasp, humor, joker, sense
6 acumen, brains, esprit, jester, reason, sanity, satire, senses, wisdom 7 balance,
insight, punster, sensing 8 astuicity, comedian, funnyman, humorist, jokester, keenness, lucidity, prudence, quipster, repartee,
sagacity, sageness, saneness, sapience,
wordplay 9 alertness, awareness, mentality, smartness, soundness 10 astuteness,
brainpower, brilliance, cleverness, divination, gray matter, perception, shrewdness
11 discernment, penetration, percipience,
rationality 12 apprehension, clairvoyance,
intelligence, perspicacity 13 comprehension, sagaciousness, understanding

witch 3 hag, hex 4 drab, trot 5 biddy,
bruja, charm, crone, lamia, spell 6 beldam,
voodoo 7 enchant 8 magician, sorcerer
9 ensorcell, sorceress 11 enchantress *companion:* 3 cat *group:* 5 coven *male:* 6 wizard 7 warlock *meeting:* 6 sabbat *Scottish:*
6 cummer *town:* 5 Endor *vehicle:*
5 broom

witchcraft 5 charm, magic 6 allure,
appeal, voodoo 7 glamour, hexerei, sorcery
8 charisma, witchery, wizardry 9 conjuring,
magnetism 10 black magic, necromancy
11 enchantment, fascination, incantation,
thaumaturgy

witch hazel 8 hornbeam 11 tobacco-
wood, winterbloom *lotion:* 9 hamamelin

witchy 5 magic 6 magian, mystic 7 magi-

cal 8 wizardly 9 sorcerous 11 necromantic
12 thaumaturgic

with 2 by, on 3 for, per, pro, via 4 over,
upon 5 about 7 by way of, through 8 by
dint of 9 by means of, in favor of 10 by virtue of *French:* 4 avec *German:* 3 mit *Italian:* 3 con *Latin:* 3 cum *prefix:* 2 co
3 col, com, con, cor, sym, syn

withal 3 too, yea, yet 4 also, more 5 still
6 as well, though 7 besides, howbeit, however 8 after all, moreover 9 per contra
11 furthermore, nonetheless 12 additionally, nevertheless

withdraw 2 go 4 exit, quit, 5 leave, quail,
unsay 6 abjure, depart, get off, recall,
recant, recede, recoil, remove, retire,
secede, shrink 7 get away, retract, retreat,
take off, take out 8 fall back, forswear, give
back, palinode, run along, take away, take
back

withdrawal 4 exit 6 egress, exodus
7 exiting, pullout, retreat 8 offgoing
9 departure, egression 10 setting-out *from
reality:* 6 autism

withdrawn 4 cool 5 aloof 6 casual, offish,
remote 7 aseptic, distant 8 detached,
reserved, retiring, solitary 9 incurious,
shrinking, unaffable, uncurious
10 restrained, unsociable 11 indifferent,
standoffish, unconcerned, unexpansive
12 uninterested *from reality:* 8 autistic

wither 3 age, dry 4 wane, wilt 5 dry up,
mummy, wizen 6 shrink, welter 7 decline,
mummify, shrivel

withered 4 sere 8 shrunken

withhold 3 bit 4 curb, deny, keep 5 check
6 bridle, detain, refuse, retain 7 abstain,
forbear, inhibit, keep out, refrain, reserve
8 disallow, keep back, restrain 9 constrain

within 4 into 5 among 6 inside 7 indoors,
inwards 8 interior *combining form:* 3 end,
ent 4 endo, ento *prefix:* 2 il, im, in, ir
5 infra, inter, intra, intro

with-it 2 in 4 tony 5 swank, swish 6 modish, tonish, trendy 7 à la mode, stylish
11 fashionable

without 4 open, past, sans 5 after, minus
6 beyond 7 lacking, open air, outside, wanting 8 awanting, outdoors 10 out-of-doors
combining form: 4 lipo *Latin:* 4 sine *suffix:* 4 less

with respect to 2 re 4 as to 5 as for
7 apropos 8 touching 9 as regards, regarding 10 concerning

withstand 4 bear, buck, duel 5 abide,
fight, repel 6 combat, endure, oppose,
resist, suffer 7 contest, dispute 8 tolerate,
traverse

withy 4 twig 5 osier 6 branch, willow

witless 4 daft 5 crazy, silly 6 crazed, insane, simple, stupid 7 asinine, cracked, unwitty 8 demented, deranged, mindless 9 bedlamite, brainless, nitwitted, senseless 10 reasonless, weak-headed, weak-minded

witlessness 5 folly 7 inanity 8 insanity 9 absurdity, craziness, dottiness, silliness 11 foolishness 13 senselessness

witness 3 see 4 view 5 argue, proof, vouch 6 attest, viewer 7 bespeak, betoken, certify, testify, watcher 8 announce, beholder, by-sitter, evidence, indicate, looker-on, observer, onlooker 9 bystander, spectator, testament, testimony 11 attestation, testimonial 12 confirmation

witticism 3 gag, mot, pun 4 jape, jest, joke, quip 5 crack 6 bon mot 7 waggery 8 drollery 9 wisecrack

wittiness 5 humor 6 comedy 8 drollery 9 drollness, funniness

witting 4 ware 5 alive, awake, aware 7 knowing, willful, willing 8 sensible, sentient, unforced 9 cognizant, conscious, voluntary 10 deliberate 11 intentional

witty 5 funny 6 clever, jocose 7 amusing, jocular, probing, risible 8 humorous, piercing 9 diverting, facetious, sparkling 10 ridiculous 11 penetrating 12 entertaining 13 scintillating

witty saying 3 mot 4 quip 7 epigram 8 facetiae (plural)

wiz 6 artist, expert, master 8 virtuoso 9 authority 10 past master

wizard 4 mage, sage, whiz 5 magus 6 artist, expert, master 7 warlock 8 conjurer, magician, sorcerer, virtuoso 9 archimage, authority, enchanter 10 past master, proficient 11 necromancer

wizardly 5 magic 6 magian, mystic, witchy 7 magical 9 sorcerous 11 necromantic 12 thaumaturgic

Wizard of Menlo Park 6 Edison (Thomas Alva)

Wizard of Oz *author:* 4 Baum (Lyman Frank) *character:* 7 Dorothy 9 Scarecrow 10 Tin Woodman 12 Cowardly Lion *dog:* 4 Toto

wizardry 5 magic 7 sorcery 8 witchery 9 conjuring, magicking 10 necromancy, witchcraft 11 bewitchment, enchantment, incantation

wizen 3 dry 4 wilt 5 dry up, mummy 6 welter, wither 7 mummify, shrivel

wobble 4 sway 5 lurch, quake, shake, swing, waver, weave 6 careen, dither, falter, quaver, quiver, shimmy, shiver, teeter, topple, totter 7 shudder, stagger, stumble

wobbly 4 weak 5 shaky 6 dickey, unsure 7 halting, rackety, rickety, shaking 8 hesitant, insecure, rachitic, rootless, unstable,

unsteady, wavering 9 faltering, fluctuant, tentative, uncertain 10 irresolute, rattletrap 11 vacillating, vacillatory 12 wiggle-waggle

Wodehouse character 6 Jeeves, Psmith 7 Wooster 8 Mulliner

Woden see Odin

woe 3 rue 4 care 5 grief 6 misery, regret, sorrow 7 anguish, sadness, trouble 9 bemoaning, bewailing, deploring, heartache 10 affliction, heartbreak 11 lamentation, unhappiness 12 wretchedness

woebegone 3 low 4 blue, down, worn 5 black, bleak 6 dismal, dreary, gloomy, shabby 8 dejected, downcast, funereal 9 depressed 10 depressing, dispirited, lugubrious, melancholy, oppressive, tenebrific 11 crestfallen, dilapidated, dispiriting, downhearted 12 disconsolate

woeful 3 sad 4 dire 5 grave, wrung 6 dismal, dolent, paltry, racked, rueful 7 crushed 8 dejected, dolesome, dolorous, downcast, grievous, harrowed, mournful, overcome, stricken, tortured, wretched 9 afflicted, depressed, heartsick, miserable, plaintive, sorrowful 10 afflictive, calamitous, deplorable, dispirited, lamentable, lugubrious, melancholy 11 distressing, downhearted, low-spirited, regrettable, unfortunate 12 disconsolate, inconsolable 13 heartbreaking, unprecedented

wold 5 plain

wolf 4 bolt, cram, grub, gulp, lobo, roué, slop 6 canine, chaser, coyote, englut, gobble, guzzle, lecher, masher 7 amorist, Don Juan, rounder 8 Casanova, lothario, womanize 9 ladies' man, libertine, philander, womanizer 10 fool around, lady-killer, mess around, play around, profligate 11 ingurgitate, philanderer *combining form:* 3 lyc 4 lyco *genus:* 5 Canis *group:* 4 pack *young:* 5 whelp

wolfish 4 fell, grim 5 cruel 6 fierce, lupine, savage 7 inhuman 8 inhumane 9 barbarous, ferocious, truculent

wolverine 8 carcajou *European:* 7 glutton *genus:* 4 Gulo

Wolverine State 8 Michigan

woman 4 dame, lady 5 madam 6 female, matron 8 mistress *attractive:* 4 peri 5 belle 6 beauty, eyeful, looker 7 stunner 8 knockout *Australian:* 4 bint *combining form:* 3 gyn 4 gyne, gyno, gyny 5 gynec, gyneo 6 gynaec, gynaeo, gyneo, gynous 7 gynaeco *courageous:* 7 heroine *dignified:* 6 matron 7 dowager 10 grande dame *dowdy:* 5 frump *Dutch:* 4 vrow 5 vrouw *English:* 6 milady *first, biblical:* 3 Eve *first, mythological:* 7 Pandora *French:* 5 femme *German:* 4 frau 8 fräulein *Hawaiian:* 6 wahine *Indian:* 5 squaw

intellectual: 12 bluestocking *Italian:*
5 donna 7 signora *lewd:* 5 hussy 6 harlot,
wanton 7 trollop *little:* 3 Mrs. 4 wife *old:*
3 hag 4 dame 5 crone 6 beldam, carlin,
gammer, granny *pregnant:* 7 gravida
resembling: 8 gynecoid *royal:* 5 queen
8 princess *sailor:* 4 Wave *scheming:*
7 jezebel *servant:* 4 maid *slovenly:*
8 slattern *soldier:* 3 Wac *Spanish:* 4 doña
6 senora *strong:* 6 amazon, virago *unmarried:* 4 miss 6 maiden 8 spinster *young:*
4 girl, lass 6 lassie, maiden

womanize 4 wolf 9 philander 10 fool
around, mess around, play around

womanizer 4 wolf 6 chaser, masher
7 Don Juan 8 Casanova 9 ladies' man, philander 10 lady-killer 11 philanderer

womb 6 uterus *combining form:* 4 metr,
uter 5 metra, metro, utero 6 hyster, metria
(plural) 7 hystero, metrium

wombat 9 marsupial

women *hatred of:* 8 misogyny *organization of:* 3 DAR, NOW 7 sorosis 8 sorority

Women in Love author 8 Lawrence
(David Herbert)

wonder 3 awe 5 amaze, doubt 6 marvel
7 concern, dubiety, miracle, portent, prodigy, stunner 8 mistrust 9 amazement, dubiosity, marveling, sensation, suspicion
10 admiration, phenomenon, skepticism
11 incertitude, uncertainty, uncertitude
12 astonishment, bewilderment

wonderful 5 great, super, swell 6 divine,
groovy, peachy 7 amazing, strange 8 glorious, terrific, wondrous 9 marvelous
10 astounding, miraculous, staggering, stupendous, surprising 11 astonishing, sensational

wondrous 7 amazing, strange 9 marvelous, wonderful 10 astounding, miraculous,
stupendous, surprising 11 astonishing,
spectacular

wont 3 apt, use, way 5 habit, inure, trick,
usage 6 custom, manner 8 accustom, habitude, practice 9 habituate 10 consuetude
11 familiarize

wonted 5 usual 7 chronic, routine
8 accepted, habitual 9 customary
10 accustomed

woo 3 sue 5 court, spark 6 pursue
7 address 8 make up to 10 sweetheart

wood 5 weald 6 forest, lumber, timber
10 timberland *combining form:* 3 hyl, xyl
4 hylo, lign, xylo 5 ligni, ligno, xylon, xylum
decayed: 4 punk *eater:* 7 termite *for burning:* 5 fagot 6 tinder 8 kindling *golf:*
5 spoon 6 driver 7 brassie *hard:* 3 elm,
eng, oak 4 ebon, poon, rata, teak 5 beech,
birch, ebony, maple 6 cherry, walnut
8 chestnut, mahogany, sycamore *imperfection:* 4 knot 5 gnarl *kind:* 5 xylem

6 phloem *light:* 5 balsa *made of:* 5 treen
pattern in: 5 grain 6 figure *product:* 3 tar
5 paper 10 turpentine *soft:* 4 pine

wood alcohol 6 methyl 8 methanol

woodchuck 6 marmot 9 groundhog

wood coal 7 lignite

wooded 5 bosky 6 sylvan 8 sylvatic

wooden 4 dull 5 inept, stiff, treen
6 clumsy, gauche 7 buckram, halting,
stilted, unhandy 8 bumbling 9 cardboard,
ham-handed, maladroit 11 heavy-handed,
muscle-bound

woodland 5 weald, woods 6 forest,
timber

wood nymph 5 dryad

woodpecker 7 flicker, piculet, wryneck
9 sapsucker *genus:* 5 Picus *kind:*
5 downy, green, hairy 8 imperial, pileated
9 redheaded 11 ivory-billed *relating to:*
6 picine 8 piciform

woodsman 6 logger, ranger 7 bushman
8 forester 11 bushwhacker

wood sorrel 3 oca 6 oxalis 7 begonia
8 shamrock

woodsy 6 rustic, sylvan

woodwind 4 oboe 5 flute 7 bassoon
8 clarinet 9 saxophone 10 instrument

woodworker 9 carpenter 12 cabinetmaker

woody 6 xyloid 8 ligneous
(see also **wooded**)

Woody Allen film 5 Alice, Zelig
7 Bananas, Sleeper 9 Annie Hall, Interiors,
Manhattan, Radio Days, September
12 Love and Death 16 Husbands and
Wives

wooer 4 beau 5 spark, swain 6 suitor
7 sparker

woof 4 weft, yarn 5 weave 6 fabric, thread
7 texture

wool 3 fur 4 coat, hair 6 fleece *coarse:*
3 abb *combining form:* 3 lan 4 erio, lani,
lano *cut:* 5 shear *fabric:* 4 felt 5 baize,
crepe, serge, tweed 6 covert, kersey,
mohair, poplin, shoddy, velour 7 duvetyn,
flannel, worsted 8 cashmere, chenille
9 gabardine 10 broadcloth *fat:* 7 lanolin
kind: 4 hogg 6 angora, hogget, virgin *low-
quality:* 5 mungo 6 shoddy *matted:*
7 daglock, taglock *musk-ox:* 6 qiviut *process:* 7 carding 8 skirting *source:* 4 goat,
lamb 5 camel, llama, sheep

woolly 5 hairy 6 fleecy, lanate, lanose,
pilose 7 hirsute, lanated, pileous 9 whiskered

woozy 4 sick, weak 5 dizzy 6 blurry
8 nauseous

word 3 cry, put, say, vow 4 buzz, news,
oath, talk, tell, term 5 order, rumor, state
6 advice, behest, charge, convey, gossip,
pledge, plight, report, rumble, saying 7 bid-

ding, command, dictate, express, hearsay, mandate, message, promise, tidings, vocable, warrant **8** locution **9** assurance, directive, formulate, guarantee, speerings, statement, utterance **10** commitment, expression, injunction **11** countersign, declaration, information, scuttlebutt **12** announcement, intelligence **13** communication, pronouncement *combining form:* **3** log **4** logo, onym **7** onomato *connective:* **11** conjunction *group:* **6** clause, phrase **8** sentence *misused:* **8** malaprop **11** malapropism *naming:* **4** noun *new:* **7** coinage **9** neologism *of action:* **4** verb *of honor:* **4** oath **7** promise *origin:* **9** etymology *part:* **8** syllable *root:* **6** etymon *scrambled:* **7** anagram *shortened:* **11** contraction **12** abbreviation *square:* **10** palindrome *with opposite meaning:* **7** antonym *with same meaning:* **7** synonym *with same pronunciation:* **7** homonym **9** homophone *with same spelling:* **7** homonym **9** homograph

wordbook 7 lexicon **8** libretto **9** thesaurus **10** dictionary

word for word 8 verbatim

wordiness 8 verbiage **9** prolixity, verbalism, verbosity, windiness **10** prolixness **11** verboseness

word-of-mouth 4 oral **6** spoken, verbal **9** unwritten

wordy 4 glib **5** tumid, windy **6** prolix, turgid **7** diffuse, verbose, voluble **8** inflated **9** bombastic, flatulent, garrulous, redundant, talkative **10** long-winded, loquacious, palaverous, rhetorical

work 2 go **3** act, fix, job, run, tug, use **4** duty, line, moil, opus, take, tend, till, toil **5** chore, craft, dress, drive, grind, labor, react, solve, sweat, trade **6** behave, drudge, effort, handle, métier, racket, strain, strive **7** calling, operate, perform, pursuit, resolve, slavery, travail, trouble **8** bullwork, business, drudgery, exertion, function, plugging, slogging, striving, vocation **9** cultivate **10** employment, handicraft, occupation, profession *combining form:* **3** erg **4** ergo *together:* **9** cooperate **11** collaborate *unit:* **3** erg **5** joule

workaday 4 dull **5** lowly, plain, usual **7** mundane, prosaic, routine **8** everyday, ordinary **9** quotidian **11** commonplace

worker 4 doer, hand **6** toiler, wallah **7** artisan, laborer **8** employee, mechanic, operator **9** craftsman, operative **10** roustabout *combining form:* **5** ergat **6** ergato *fellow:* **7** comrade, partner **9** colleague *group:* **4** crew, gang **5** shift, staff, union *hard:* **5** slave **6** beaver, drudge *itinerant:* **6** boomer **7** migrant *slow:* **7** plodder *unskilled:* **4** peon **7** jackleg, laborer

working 4 busy, live **5** alive **6** active **7** dynamic, engaged, running **8** employed, occupied **9** operative **11** functioning *not:* **5** kaput **6** broken

workless 4 idle **7** jobless **10** unemployed

workman see worker

work out 3 fix **5** solve, train **7** resolve **8** exercise

workout 8 exercise, practice

work over 4 redo **6** beat up, redraw, rehash, revamp, revise, rework **7** redraft, restyle, rewrite **9** manhandle

workroom 3 lab **4** shop **6** studio **7** atelier **10** laboratory

works 4 mill **5** plant **7** factory

Works and Days author 6 Hesiod

world 5 earth, globe **6** cosmos, kosmos, nature, planet **8** creation, megacosm, universe **9** macrocosm **11** macrocosmos *combining form:* **4** cosm **5** cosmo

worldly 5 blasé **6** earthy **7** earthly, knowing, mundane, sensual, terrene **8** banausic, mondaine, telluric, temporal **9** sublunary, tellurian **11** terrestrial **12** disenchanted, sophisticate **13** disillusioned, materialistic, sophisticated

World War I *battle:* **5** Marne, Somme, Ypres **6** Verdun **7** Jutland, Lemberg **10** Tannenberg *battle line:* **9** Siegfried *hero:* **4** York (Alvin) **8** Pershing (John J.) **12** Rickenbacker (Eddie) *treaty:* **10** Versailles

World War II *admiral:* **6** Halsey (William "Bull"), Nimitz (Chester) *alliance:* **4** Axis **6** Allies *battle:* **5** Anzio, Bulge **6** Bataan, Midway, Tarawa, Warsaw **7** Iwo Jima, Okinawa **8** Normandy **10** Stalingrad *general:* **6** Patton (George), Rommel (Erwin) **7** Bradley (Omar) **10** Eisenhower (Dwight David), Montgomery (Bernard) *hero:* **6** Murphy (Audie) *journalist:* **4** Pyle (Ernie) *vehicle:* **4** jeep *weapon:* **5** A-bomb **6** rocket

worldwide 6 cosmic, global **8** catholic **9** planetary, universal **10** ecumenical **12** cosmopolitan *combining form:* **5** globo

worm 3 eel, loa, lug **4** grub, nema **5** borer, fluke, leech **6** edge in, maggot, mucker, nogood, squirm, wiggle, work in, wretch, writhe **7** carbora, distome, lowlife, serpent, triclad, wriggle **8** helminth, nematode, squiggle **9** insinuate, planarium, trematode **10** infiltrate *combining form:* **5** nemat, vermi **6** nemato, scolec, scolex **7** scoleco **8** helminth **9** helmintho *marine:* **3** lug **4** naid **6** nereis, palolo **7** annelid, tubifex **11** chaetognath *parasitic:* **5** fluke, leech **7** ascarid, ascaris, cestode, filaria **8** strongyle, trichina *relating to:* **7** vermian *resembling:* **11** helminthoid

worm-eaten 6 pitted 7 decayed, worn-out 10 antiquated

worn 5 drawn, erose, jaded, tired, weary 6 eroded 7 haggard, pinched, wearied 8 careworn, fatigued

worn-out 4 sere 5 all in, spent, stale, tired, trite 6 bleary, effete, used up 7 cli-chéd, drained, far-gone 8 depleted 9 exhausted, hackneyed, washed out 10 threadbare 11 stereotyped

worried 8 distrait, harassed, troubled 9 tormented 10 distracted, distraught, distressed

worry 3 ail, dun, nag, tew, try, vex 4 care, cark, fret, fuss, gnaw, stew, test 5 annoy, beset, harry, tease, trial, upset 6 bother, harass, needle, pester, plague, pother, unease 7 afflict, anguish, anxiety, bedevil, disturb, hagride, oppress, torment, torture, trouble 8 aggrieve, distress 9 beleaguer, tantalize 10 solicitude, uneasiness 11 concernment, disquietude *without:* 8 carefree

worrywart 7 fusspot 9 Cassandra, pessimist 11 crepehanger

worse 4 less 6 poorer 8 inferior

worsen 3 rot 4 sink 6 debase 7 decline, degrade, descend 10 degenerate, retro-grade 11 deteriorate

worship 4 love 5 adore 6 dote on, revere 7 idolize, lionize, liturgy 8 dote upon, idola-try, venerate 9 adoration, affection, rever-ence 10 veneration 11 idolization *combining form:* 5 latry *object of:* 3 god 4 icon, idol *place of:* 5 altar 6 church, mosque, shrine, temple 9 cathedral, synagogue

worshiper 6 votary 7 devotee 8 disciple *combining form:* 5 later

worst 4 beat, best, down 5 least, outdo 6 defeat, lowest

worsted 4 yarn 5 serge 6 fabric, poplin 9 gabardine

wort 4 herb 5 plant

worth 4 mark, note 5 merit, price, value 6 moment, riches, wealth 7 account, cali-ber, fortune, quality, stature 8 property 9 resources, substance, valuation

worthless 4 mean 5 junky, sorry 6 draffy, drossy, no-good, trashy 7 fustian, inutile, nothing, useless 8 feckless, unworthy 9 cheapjack, incapable, valueless 11 incompetent, meaningless, purposeless, unqualified 12 contemptible

worthwhile 4 good 6 paying 7 gainful 9 lucrative 10 profitable, well-paying 11 moneymaking 12 advantageous, remu-nerative

worthy 4 good 5 noble 6 divine 8 laud-able, pleasing, precious, sterling 9 admira-ble, deserving, desirable, estimable, honora-ble, meritable, praisable, priceless

10 invaluable, satisfying 11 commendable, meritorious

Wotan see Odin

Wouk *novel* 13 The Winds of War 14 The Caine Mutiny

wound 3 cut 4 blow, harm, hurt 6 dam-age, injure, injury, lesion, trauma 8 lacerate 10 laceration *combining form:* 7 traumat 8 traumato *discharge:* 3 pus *sign:* 4 scab, scar 5 blood 7 blister

wow 3 hit 4 bang 5 smash 7 success 9 succès fou 10 bell ringer 11 exclamation

Wozzeck composer 4 Berg (Alban)

wrack 4 kelp, raze, ruin, undo 5 wreck 6 unmake 7 destroy, seaweed, unbuild, unframe 8 decimate, demolish

wraith 5 ghost, shade, spook 6 shadow, spirit 7 phantom, specter 8 phantasm 10 apparition

wrangle 3 row 4 spat, tiff 5 argue, fight, scrap 6 argufy, bicker, fracas, hassle 7 brabble, dispute, fall out, quarrel, quibble 8 squabble 9 bickering, caterwaul 11 alter-cation

wrangler 6 cowboy 9 disputant

wrap 4 foil, mask, roll, veil 5 cloak, drape, paper, shawl 6 enfold, invest, muffle, shroud, swathe 7 blanket, enclose, envelop, muffler, swaddle 8 bundle up, enshroud, enswathe, wax paper 10 camou-flage

wrapped up 4 deep, rapt 6 intent 7 engaged 8 absorbed, immersed 9 engrossed 11 preoccupied

wrapper 4 gown 5 cover, shawl 6 jacket

wrap up see wind up

wrath 3 ire 4 fury, rage 5 anger 8 acer-bity, acrimony, asperity 10 resentment 11 indignation

wrathful 3 mad 4 waxy 5 angry, irate, wroth 6 heated, ireful, wrothy

wreak 5 exact, visit, wreck 6 impose 7 force on, inflict 9 force upon

wreath 3 lei 4 bays 5 crown, torse 6 ana-dem, laurel 7 chaplet, coronal, coronet, garland

wreathe 4 coil, curl, wind 5 twine, twist 6 spiral 7 contort, entwine 9 corkscrew

wreck 3 dog 4 do in, heap, hulk, raze, ruin, undo 5 beach, crash, crate, smash, total, visit, wrack, wreak 6 damage, impose, jalopy, junker, pileup, ravage, strand, unmake 7 clunker, crack-up, deba-cle, despoil, destroy, disable, force on, inflict, plunder, smashup, subvert, unbuild, unframe 8 bankrupt, cast away, collapse, decimate, demolish, sabotage 9 break-down, force upon, undermine, vandalize

wreckage 6 jetsam 7 flotsam 8 sabotage 9 driftwood 10 subversion 11 undermining

wrench 3 wry 4 pull, tool, turn, warp 5 exact, force, gouge, pinch, screw, twist, wrest, wring 6 coerce, compel, extort, garble, sprain 7 distort, pervert, squeeze 9 constrain, shake down 12 misrepresent *kind:* 6 monkey 7 ratchet

wrest 3 wry 4 warp 5 exact, gouge, pinch, screw, twist, wring 6 extort, garble, wrench 7 confuse, distort, extract, pervert, squeeze 9 shake down 12 misrepresent

wrestle 4 moil, toil 5 essay, exert, fight, labor 6 strain, strive, tussle 7 contend, grapple, scuffle, stretch, travail 8 endeavor, struggle

wrestling *hold:* 4 lock 6 nelson 8 headlock, scissors *kind:* 4 sumo *term:* 3 pin 4 fall 5 throw 8 takedown

wretch 3 cur, dog 4 scum, snot, toad, worm 5 devil, knave, rogue, skunk, snake 6 mucker, no-good, rascal, rotter 7 caitiff, lowlife, stinker, villain 8 scalawag, stinkard, wormling 9 scoundrel, stinkaroo 10 blackguard, ne'er-do-well 11 rapscallion

wretched 3 low 4 base, mean, vile 6 abject, dismal, dolent, paltry, rueful, scurvy, sordid, woeful 7 doleful, forlorn, ignoble, piteous, pitiful, ruthful, servile 8 dolorous, hopeless, pitiable 9 afflicted, miserable, sorrowful 10 despairing, despicable, despondent, melancholy

wretchedness 3 woe 6 misery 11 unhappiness

wriggle 4 worm 6 squirm, writhe 8 squiggle

wring 3 wry 4 rack 5 exact, gouge, pinch, screw, wrest 6 extort, harrow, martyr, wrench 7 afflict, agonize, torment, torture 10 excruciate *the neck:* 5 scrag

wringing-wet 5 soppy 6 soaked, sodden, soused 7 soaking, sopping 8 drenched, dripping 9 saturated

wrinkle 4 fold, line, ruck, ruga, seam 5 crimp, plica, ridge, rivel, screw 6 crease, furrow, method, rimple, ruck up, rumple 7 crimple, crinkle, crumple, novelty, scrunch, shrivel 9 crow's foot 10 innovation 11 corrugation

wrinkled 5 lined 6 rugate, rugose, rugous, rumply 8 rugulose

wrist 5 joint 6 carpus *bone:* 6 carpal, hamate, lunate 8 capitate, pisiform 9 navicular 10 triangular 11 multangular *combining form:* 4 carp 5 carpo

writ 5 breve, brief, order, tales 6 capias, elegit, venire 7 mandate, precipe, summons, warrant 8 document, mandamus, mittimus, praecipe, replevin, subpoena 10 certiorari, distringas, injunction 12 habeas corpus

write 3 ink, jot, pen 4 draw, note, sign 5 chalk, draft 6 author, indite, pencil, scrawl, scribe 7 compose, dot down, engross, scratch 8 inscribe, scribble 10 correspond

write down 4 note 6 record

write off 5 decry, lower 6 cancel 7 devalue, downcry, run down 8 belittle, derogate, discount, mark down, minimize 9 devaluate, disparage, downgrade, underrate 10 depreciate, undervalue 11 detract from

writer 4 poet 6 penman, scribe 7 penster 8 composer, novelist *bad:* 4 hack *combining form:* 7 grapher; (see also **author**)

writhe 4 bend, curl, toss, worm 5 twist 6 squirm, wiggle 7 agonize, contort, distort, wriggle 8 squiggle

writing 4 book, hand 5 essay, paper, print, prose, words 6 letter, script 7 epistle 8 document, longhand 9 allograph, signature 10 literature, manuscript, penmanship 11 calligraphy, composition, inscription, publication *character:* 6 letter 9 cuneiform 10 hieroglyph *combining form:* 4 gram 6 grapho, graphy 7 graphia *for the blind:* 7 braille *instrument:* 3 pen 5 chalk, quill 6 pencil, stylus *kind:* 5 prose, verse 6 poetry *sacred:* 5 Bible, Koran 6 Talmud, Tantra 9 scripture *secret:* 4 code *surface:* 5 board, paper, slate 6 scroll 9 parchment

wrong 3 bad, ill, off, sin 4 awry, debt, evil, harm, hurt, poor, tort 5 abuse, amiss, badly, crime, false, inapt, unfit 6 afield, astray, injure, injury, offend, rotten, sinful, untrue, wicked 7 immoral, oppress, outrage, vicious 8 aggrieve, ill-treat, improper, inequity, iniquity, maltreat, mistaken, mistreat 9 diablerie, erroneous, grievance, incorrect, injustice, misguided, persecute, reprobate, unfitting 10 inaccurate, iniquitous, unfairness, unjustness, unsuitable, wickedness 11 unfavorably 12 infelicitous 13 inappropriate *prefix:* 3 mis

wrongdoer 5 felon 6 sinner 8 criminal, offender 9 miscreant 10 malefactor

wrongdoing 3 sin 4 evil, tort 5 crime 7 misdeed, offense 8 iniquity 9 diablerie, violation 10 misconduct 11 malefaction, misbehavior

wrongful 7 illegal, illicit, lawless 8 criminal, unlawful 12 illegitimate

wrongheaded 5 balky 6 mulish, ornery 7 froward, restive, wayward 8 contrary, perverse, stubborn 9 obstinate 10 self-willed 11 stiff-necked 12 cross-grained, pertinacious

wrought 4 made 6 formed, shaped, worked 7 created 8 finished, hammered 9 fashioned, processed 10 ornamented 12 manufactured *up:* 7 excited, stirred

wry 4 bent 5 twist, wrest, wring 6 ironic, wrench 7 cynical, twisted 8 sardonic
wryneck 10 woodpecker
Wuthering Heights *author:* 6 Brontë (Emily) *character:* 7 Hindley 9 Catherine 10 Heathcliff

Wycliffite 7 Lollard
Wyoming *capital:* 8 Cheyenne *city:* 6 Casper 7 Laramie *nickname:* 13 Equality State *state bird:* 10 meadowlark

x 3 chi, ten 4 kiss, mark 5 annul, cross, erase, error, times, wrong 6 cancel, delete, efface 7 blot out, expunge, mistake, wipe out 8 abscissa, black out 9 signature 10 obliterate
Xanadu *country:* 5 China *river:* 4 Alph
xanthic 6 yellow 9 yellowish
Xanthippe 3 nag 5 harpy, scold, shrew, vixen 6 nagger, ogress, virago 8 fishwife 9 termagant *husband:* 8 Socrates
xanthous 6 yellow
xebec 4 boat, ship 6 vessel 10 pirate ship
xenium 4 gift 7 present
xenon *symbol:* 2 Xe
Xenophon work 8 Anabasis 9 Cyropedia, Hellenica
Xeres 4 wine 5 Jerez 6 sherry

xerophyte 6 cactus
xerosis 7 dryness
Xerxes *defeat:* 7 Salamis *father:* 6 Darius *kingdom:* 6 Persia *mother:* 6 Atossa *wife:* 6 Esther
Xmas 4 Noel, yule 8 Nativity, yuletide 9 Christmas
X ray *discoverer:* 8 Roentgen (Wilhelm) *science:* 9 radiology 13 roentgenology
xurel 4 scad 6 saurel
xyloid 5 woody 8 ligneous
xylophone 5 saron, vibes 7 gambang, gamelan, marimba 8 gamelang, gigelira, sticcado 10 vibraphone
xystus 4 stoa, walk 5 porch 7 portico, terrace

Y

yacht 4 boat, race, sail, ship 5 craft
6 cruise, sonder 8 keelboat

yahoo 4 lout, punk 5 brute, clown, rough,
rowdy, tough 6 mucker, savage 7 bumpkin, ruffian, toughie 8 bullyboy 9 roughneck

Yahweh 3 God 6 Jahvah 7 Jehovah

yak 2 ox 3 gab, jaw 4 blab, chat 5 clack,
laugh, prate 6 babble, gabble, jabber, sar-
lak, sarlyk, yammer 7 blabber, buffalo, chatter, palaver, prattle

yakety-yak 3 gab, jaw 4 blab, chat
5 clack, prate 6 babble, gabble, jabber
7 blabber, chatter, palaver, prattle

Yale 3 Eli 4 lock 10 university

Yalta participant 6 Stalin (Joseph)
9 Churchill (Winston), Roosevelt (Franklin
Delano)

yam 3 ube, ubi 5 tugui 6 igname, potato
7 boniata 11 sweet potato

yammer 3 cry, gab, jaw, yak 4 chat, crab,
fuss, yaup, yawp, yell 5 bleat, clack, gripe,
whine, yearn 6 babble, clamor, gabble,
squawk 7 chatter, grumble, prattle 8 complain 9 bellyache, yakety-yak

yank 3 lug, tug 4 grab, jerk, pull, snap, tear
5 hoick, lurch 6 clutch, evulse, snatch,
twitch 7 extract 9 vellicate

yap 4 bark, hick, jake, yelp 5 clown, mouth,
scold 6 bowwow, rustic 7 bumpkin, chatter,
hayseed 9 hillbilly 10 clodhopper, provincial 12 backwoodsman

yard 4 lawn, quad, spar 5 court, garth,
patio, stick 9 curtilage, enclosure 10 play-
ground, quadrangle *enclosed:* 5 garth,
patio *five and one-half:* 3 rod *part of:*
4 foot, nail *shelter:* 6 gazebo *sixteenth of:*
4 nail *two hundred and twenty:* 7 furlong

yardstick 5 gauge 7 measure 8 standard
9 benchmark, criterion 10 touchstone

yare 4 spry 5 agile, brisk, catty, ready
6 active, brisky, lively, nimble, volant
9 sprightly

yarn 3 rap 4 chat, chin, garn, tale, talk
5 fiber, floss, grain, prose, story, visit 6 caddis, cotton, crewel, strand, thread 7 caddice, genappe, schappe 8 anecdote, causerie, colloque, converse 9 narration,
narrative *ball of:* 4 clew, clue *coll:* 5 skein
6 skeane *cotton:* 10 candlewick *for fas-*
tening a sail: 6 roband, robbin *woolen:*
6 crewel, worset 7 worsted 8 shetland

yate 8 eucalypt

yaw 4 bend, gape, swag, tack, tilt, turn,
veer, yawn 5 lurch, pitch, shift 6 double,
seesaw, swerve, tilter 7 deviate 9 deviation
10 deflection

yawn 4 gape 5 ennui 6 tedium 7 boredom
8 doldrums

yawning 5 agape, bored 6 gaping
7 chasmal 8 oscitant 9 cavernous

yawp 3 bay, caw, cry 4 bawl, crab, fuss,
gape 5 bleat, gripe 6 squall, squark,
squawk, yammer 8 complain

yaws 4 pian 9 frambesia

yea 2 ay, OK 3 aye, nay, too, yes, yet
4 also, even, more, okay 5 along, truly
6 agreed, assent, as well, indeed, really, verily 7 besides 8 all right, likewise, moreover,
positive 11 affirmative 12 additionally

yeanling 3 kid 4 lamb 7 newborn

year *academic:* 7 session *combining*
form: 6 ennial *division:* 5 month 6 season 9 trimester *kind:* 4 leap 5 lunar, solar
6 fiscal 8 calendar, sidereal, tropical
12 astronomical *Latin:* 5 annus *Scottish:*
7 towmond, towmont

yearbook 5 annal 6 annual 7 almanac,
annuary

yearling 4 colt

Yearling *author:* 8 Rawlings (Marjorie
Kinnan) *character:* 4 Jody

yearly 6 annual 8 annually

yearn 3 yen 4 ache, burn, long, lust, pant,
pine, sigh, wish 5 covet, crave, dream
6 desire, grieve, hanker, hunger, thirst,
yammer

yearning 4 wish 5 eager 6 desire, hanker
7 craving, wistful 8 homesick, lovesick

years *eight:* 9 octennial *five:* 7 lustrum
12 quinquennial, quinquennium *four:*
11 quadrennial, quadrennium *one hundred:*
7 century 9 centenary 10 centennial *one*
thousand: 10 millennium *ten:* 6 decade
9 decennary, decennial, decennium, decennium *three:* 9 triennial, triennium

yeast 3 bee 4 barm, foam, suds 5 froth,
spume 6 lather, leaven 7 ferment

yeasty 5 dizzy, giddy, light 6 frothy

7 flighty **8** restless **9** exuberant, fribbling, frivolous **11** light-headed

Yeats *beloved:* **9** Maud Gonne *birthplace:* **6** Dublin *play:* **7** Deirdre **9** Purgatory **12** The Herne's Egg *poem:* **9** Byzantium **11** Lapis Lazuli

yegg **5** thief **6** robber **7** burglar **8** criminal **11** safecracker

yell **3** cry, yip **4** call, howl, roar, wail, weep, yowl **5** cheer, hallo, hollo, shout, whoop **6** bellow, bemoan, bewail, clamor, holler, lament, outcry, scream, shriek, squall, squeal, yammer **7** deplore, roaring **10** vociferate

yellow **4** mean **5** amber, blake, favel, lemon, ochre **6** coward, craven, flavid, flaxen, golden, sallow **7** gutless, mustard, saffron, unmanly, xanthic **8** cowardly, xanthous **9** jaundiced, spunkless **11** lily-livered **12** dishonorable **13** pusillanimous *brownish:* **3** dun **5** aloma, amber, straw **6** manila *combining form:* **4** flav **5** chrys, flavo, luteo, xanth **6** chryso, xantho *dye:* **5** morin **6** orlean **7** annatto **9** morindone *grayish:* **4** ecru *greenish:* **5** olive **6** acacia **10** chartreuse

yellowbelly **3** rat **4** funk **6** coward, craven, funker **7** chicken, dastard, quitter **8** poltroon

yellow dog **3** cad, cur **6** rotter **7** bounder

yellowhammer **5** ammer, finch, skite **6** gladdy **7** bunting, flicker, yeldrin **8** yoldring

yellowish brown **4** gold **7** mustard **9** butternut **12** butterscotch

Yellowstone attraction **4** bear **6** geyser **11** Old Faithful

yelp **3** cry, yap, yip **4** bark **5** boast, shout **6** outcry, squeal **8** complain

Yemen *capital:* **4** San'a *monetary unit:* **4** rial **5** dinar, riyal

yen **4** ache, long, lust, pine, sigh, urge **5** crave, yearn **6** desire, hanker, hunger, thirst **7** craving, longing

yeoman **5** churl, clerk **6** farmer **7** freeman **8** retainer **9** assistant, attendant, beefeater, landowner **10** freeholder **11** subordinate

yeomanly **5** brave, loyal **6** sturdy **8** faithful **9** laborious **11** hardworking

yes **2** OK **3** aye, yea, yeh, yep, yup **4** okay, yeah **5** agree **6** accede, agreed, assent, gladly **7** consent, exactly **8** all right **9** acquiesce, assuredly, certainly, precisely, subscribe, willingly **11** affirmation, affirmative, undoubtedly *French:* **3** oui *German:* **2** ja *Italian:* **2** si *Russian:* **2** da *Spanish:* **2** si

yes-man **5** dummy, toady **6** minion, stooge **7** spaniel **8** bootlick, groveler, truckler **9** sycophant **10** bootlicker

yesterday **4** past, yore **8** foretime *French:* **4** hier

yesteryear **4** past, yore **8** foretime

yet **3** but, too **4** also, even, more, only, save **5** along, so far, still **6** as well, except, though, withal **7** besides, earlier, finally, further, howbeit, however, someday, thus far **8** after all, hitherto, likewise, moreover, sometime, somewhen **10** eventually, ultimately **11** furthermore, nonetheless, still and all **12** additionally, nevertheless

Yevtushenko poem **7** Babi Yar

Ygerne see **Igraine**

yield **3** bow, net, pay **4** bear, bend, cave, cede, cess, crop, emit, fail, fold, give, obey, quit, vent **5** admit, agree, allow, award, break, bring, defer, eject, grant, leave, offer, repay, waive **6** accede, accord, afford, bounty, buckle, comply, fold up, give up, impart, output, profit, relent, render, resign, return, reward, soften, submit, supply, tender **7** abandon, bring in, concede, consent, crumple, deliver, furnish, harvest, hold out, indulge, knuckle, outturn, produce, product, proffer, provide, revenue, succumb, truckle, turnout **8** collapse, hand over **9** acquiesce, discharge, surrender **10** capitulate, production, recompense, relinquish **11** buckle under **12** knuckle under

yielding **4** meek, soft, waxy **5** mushy, pappy, pulpy **6** feeble, flabby, limber, pliant, quaggy, spongy, supple **7** bearing, flaccid, flexile, passive, squashy, squishy, squushy **8** flexible, resigned, squelchy **9** tractable **10** manageable, submissive **11** acquiescent, unresistant, unresisting **12** nonresistant, nonresisting *combining form:* **6** ferous

yin and ___ **4** yang

yip **4** howl, yell, yelp, yowl **6** scream, squeal

yoga *posture:* **5** asana

yoke **3** tie, wed **4** bail, bond, join, knot, link, pair, span, team **5** bangy, hitch, marry, nexus, unite **6** banghy, couple, inspan, tackle **7** bondage, combine, conjoin, connect, harness, helotry, oppress, peonage, serfage, serfdom, slavery **8** ligament, ligature, vinculum **9** associate, conjugate, servility, servitude, thralldom **10** oppression **11** enslavement *combining form:* **3** zyg **4** zygo *part:* **5** oxbow

yokel **3** oaf **4** boor, clod, hick, jake, rube **6** rustic **7** bucolic, bumpkin, hayseed **8** Abderite **9** chawbacon, hillbilly **10** clodhopper **12** backwoodsman

yolk **6** center, yellow **7** essence *combining form:* **6** lecith, vitell **7** lecitho, vitello *egg:* **8** vitellus

yon see **yonder**

yonder 5 there 7 farther, further, thither

yore 4 past 8 foretime 10 yesteryear

you 2 ye 3 one 4 thee, thou *French:* 2 te, tu 4 vous *German:* 2 du 3 sie

young 3 fry, new, raw 4 baby, rude, tyro, weak 5 brood, fresh, green 6 callow, infant, junior, litter, unripe 7 untried 8 childish, immature, juvenile, unformed, unversed, youthful 9 unfledged, unfleshed 10 unfinished, unseasoned 11 unpracticed 13 inexperienced *animal:* 3 cub, fry, pup 4 calf, colt, fawn, foal, joey, lamb 5 puppy *bird:* 5 chick *hare:* 7 leveret *sheep, goat:* 6 yeelin 8 yeanling

younger 6 junior

youngling see youngster

Young Lions author 4 Shaw (Irwin)

youngster 3 boy, cub, kid, lad, tad, tot 4 girl, lass, tike 5 chick, child 6 moppet, shaver, urchin 8 juvenile *suffix:* 4 ling

youth 5 prime 6 spring 7 puberty 8 juvenile, teenager 9 fledgling, stripling 10 adolescent, callowness, immaturity, juvenility, pubescence, springtide, springtime 11 adolescence 12 inexperience *ancient Greek:* 7 ephebos, ephebus *goddess of:* 4 Hebe *mythological:* 6 Adonis, Apollo, Icarus 8 Ganymede *time of:* 9 salad days; (see also **youngster**)

youthful 5 fresh, green, young 6 boyish, callow, infant, junior, maiden, unripe, virgin 7 puerile 8 immature, juvenile, virginal 9 beardless, unfledged

yowl 3 cry, yip 4 bawl, howl, wail, yell, yelp 6 scream, squall, squeal

yucca 5 palma 9 bear grass

Yugoslavia *capital:* 8 Belgrade *monetary unit:* 5 dinar *president:* 4 Broz (Josip), Tito (Marshal) *former republic:* 7 Croatia 8 Slovenia 9 Macedonia 17 Bosnia-Herzegovina *republic:* 6 Kosovo, Serbia 9 Vojvodina 10 Montenegro

Yukon *capital:* 10 Whitehorse *region:* 8 Klondike *town:* 6 Dawson

yule 4 Noel, Xmas 8 Nativity, yuletide 9 Christmas 13 Christmastide

Z

Zabbai *father:* 5 Bebai *son:* 6 Baruch

Zabud's father 6 Nathan

Zaccur *father:* 4 Imri 5 Asaph 7 Jaaziah 9 Mattaniah *son:* 5 Hanan

Zacharias *father:* 9 Barachias *son:* 4 John 6 Joseph *wife:* 9 Elisabeth

Zadoke *daughter:* 7 Jerusha *father:* 5 Baana, Immer 6 Ahitub 8 Meraioth *grandson:* 6 Jotham *son:* 7 Ahimaaz, Shallum

Zaire *capital:* 8 Kinshasa *former name:* 5 Congo 12 Belgian Congo

zakuska 4 whet 9 antipasto, appetizer 11 hors d'oeuvre

Zalmunna's slayer 6 Gideon

Zambia *capital:* 6 Lusaka *monetary unit:* 6 kwacha

zampogna 7 bagpipe, panpipe

zany 3 wag 4 card, fool 5 ament, clown, comic, crazy, cutup, dotty, idiot, joker, moron, nutty 6 cretin 7 buffoon, farceur, half-wit, pranker 8 clowning, clownish, comedian, funnyman, humorist, imbecile, jokester 9 harlequin, prankster, simpleton, trickster

Zauberflöte composer 6 Mozart (Wolfgang Amadeus)

zeal 4 fire, zest 5 ardor, gusto 6 desire, energy, fervor, hurrah, spirit 7 avidity, passion, urgency 8 devotion, keenness 9 calenture, eagerness, intensity, readiness, sincerity, vehemence 10 enthusiasm, fanaticism, fierceness 11 earnestness, seriousness

zealot 3 bug, nut 5 bigot, fiend, freak 6 maniac, votary 7 devotee, fanatic, sectary 8 adherent, disciple, follower, partisan 10 enthusiast

zealous 4 avid, keen, warm 5 afire, eager, fired, nutty, rabid 6 ardent, fervid, gung ho, hearty 7 devoted, earnest, fanatic, fervent 8 frenetic, obsessed, wild-eyed 9 dedicated, possessed 12 enthusiastic

Zebadiah *father:* 6 Asahel 7 Jeroham 11 Meshelemiah *uncle:* 4 Joab

Zebah's slayer 6 Gideon

Zebedee *son:* 4 John 5 James *wife:* 6 Salome

zebra 4 duaw *extinct:* 6 quagga *resembling:* 7 zebrine, zebroid

Zebulun *brother:* 4 Levi 5 Judah 6 Simeon *father:* 5 Jacob *mother:* 4 Leah *son:* 4 Elon 5 Sered 7 Jahleel

zecchino 6 sequin

Zechariah *daughter:* 3 Abi 6 Abijah *father:* 4 Elam, Iddo 5 Bebai, Hosah 7 Isshiah 8 Jehoiada, Jeroboam, Jonathan 9 Berechiah 11 Jeberechiah, Jehoshaphat, Meshelemiah *grandson:* 8 Hezekiah *slayer:* 7 Jehoram, Shallum *son:* 4 Iddo 8 Jahaziel

Zedekiah *brother:* 8 Jehoahaz *father:* 6 Josiah 8 Hananiah, Jeconiah, Maaseiah 9 Chenaanah *mother:* 7 Hamutal

Zeeb's slayer 6 Gideon

zenana 5 harem, harim 8 seraglio

zenith 4 acme, apex, peak 6 apogee, climax, height, summit, vertex 8 capstone, meridian, pinnacle 11 culmination *opposite:* 5 nadir

Zenobia *husband:* 9 Odenathus *kingdom:* 7 Palmyra

Zeno follower 5 stoic

Zephaniah *father:* 8 Maaseiah *son:* 6 Josiah

Zephi, Zepho *father:* 7 Eliphaz *grandfather:* 4 Esau

Zephon's father 3 Gad

Zephyrus 4 wind 6 breeze 8 west wind *father:* 6 Aeolus 8 Astraeus *mother:* 3 Eos 6 Aurora *wife:* 4 Iris

zeppelin 5 blimp 7 airship 9 dirigible

Zerah *brother:* 5 Perez *father:* 5 Judah, Reuel 6 Simeon *grandfather:* 4 Esau *mother:* 5 Tamar

Zerbino *beloved:* 8 Isabella *friend:* 7 Orlando *sister:* 7 Ginevra *slayer:* 11 Mandricardo

Zeresh's husband 5 Haman

zero 2 oh 3 aim, lay, nil, nul 4 cast, head, nowt, null, turn, void 5 aught, blank, empty, level, ought, point, train, zilch 6 cipher, direct, naught, nobody, nought 7 address, nothing, nullity, scratch, whiffet 8 goose egg, whipster 9 nonentity

Zeruah *husband:* 5 Nebat *son:* 8 Jeroboam

Zerubbabel *daughter:* 9 Shelomith *father:* 7 Pedaiah *grandfather:* 10 Jehoiachin *son:* 4 Ohel

Zeruiah *brother:* 5 David *sister:* 7 Abigail *son:* 4 Joab 6 Asahel 7 Abishai

zest 4 edge, élan, tang, zeal 5 ardor, gusto, heart, taste 6 fervor, flavor, palate, relish 7 delight, ecstasy, elation, passion 8 piquancy, pleasure 9 eagerness, enjoyment 10 enthusiasm 11 delectation 12 satisfaction

zesty 4 racy 5 spicy 6 breezy, hearty, snappy 7 peppery, piquant, pungent 8 poignant

Zetes *brother:* 6 Calais *father:* 6 Boreas *mother:* 8 Orithyia *slayer:* 8 Heracles, Hercules

zetetic 6 seeker 7 doubter, skeptic 10 headshaker, pyrrhonian, pyrrhonist, unbeliever

Zethus *brother:* 7 Amphion *father:* 4 Zeus 7 Jupiter *mother:* 7 Antiope

Zeus 7 Jupiter *brother:* 5 Hades 8 Poseidon *daughter:* 3 Ate 4 Hebe, Kore 5 Helen, Irene 6 Athena 7 Artemis, Astraea 9 Aphrodite 10 Persephone, Proserpina 12 Clytemnestra *father:* 6 Cronus *lover:* 2 Io 4 Leda, Leto, Maia 5 Danae, Dione, Metis 6 Aegina, Europa, Latona, Semele, Themis 7 Alcmene, Antiope, Demeter 8 Callisto, Eurynome *messenger:* 4 Iris *mother:* 4 Rhea *nurse:* 8 Cynosura *oracle:* 6 Dodona *shield:* 5 aegis *sister:* 4 Hera, Juno 6 Hestia *son:* 4 Ares 5 Arcas, Argus, Minos 6 Aeacus, Apollo, Hermes, Zethus 7 Amphion, Perseus 8 Dionysus, Heracles, Hercules, Sarpedon, Tantalus *tree:* 3 oak *wife:* 4 Hera, Juno 5 Metis 6 Themis

Zibiah *husband:* 7 Ahaziah *son:* 7 Jehoash

Zichri *father:* 5 Asaph 6 Shimei 7 Jeroham, Shashak *son:* 4 Joel 7 Amasiah, Eliezer 10 Elishaphat *victim:* 8 Maaseiah

zigzag 4 tack, turn 5 angle, crank, weave 7 chevron 8 flexuose, flexuous

zilch 4 zero 5 aught, ought 6 cipher, naught, nobody, nought 7 nothing, nullity, whiffet 8 goose egg, whipster 9 nonentity

Zillah *husband:* 6 Lamech *son:* 9 Tubal-cain

Zilpah's son 3 Gad 5 Asher

zimarra 5 cloak 7 cassock, soutane

Zimbabwe *capital:* 6 Harare *former name:* 8 Rhodesia

Zimran *father:* 7 Abraham *mother:* 7 Keturah

Zimri *father:* 5 Zerah *grandfather:* 5 Judah *victim:* 4 Elah

zinc *impure oxide:* 5 tutty *ingot:* 7 spelter *ore:* 6 blende 10 sphalerite *symbol:* 2 Zn

zing 3 pep, vim, zip 4 brio, dash, élan, life, snap 5 ardor, force, oomph, verve, vigor 6 energy, esprit, spirit 9 animation, eagerness 10 enthusiasm

zingel 5 perch

Zion 5 bliss 6 canaan, heaven, Israel, utopia 7 arcadia, elysium, nirvana 8 empyrean, paradise 9 cockaigne, fairyland, Shangri-la 10 Civitas Dei, wonderland 12 New Jerusalem, promised land 13 Abraham's bosom

Zionist *American:* 5 Szold (Henrietta) *English:* 8 Zangwill (Israel) *German:*

6 Nordau (Max Simon) *Hungarian:* 5 Herzl (Theodor) *Israeli:* 5 Buber (Martin) 8 Weizmann (Chaim)

zip 3 fly, pep, vim 4 dash, rush, snap, whiz, zing 5 force, hurry, speed, waltz, whisk 6 breeze, bustle, energy, hasten, hustle

zipper 8 fastener

Zipporah *father:* 5 Reuel 6 Jethro *husband:* 5 Moses *son:* 7 Eliezer, Gershom

Zippor's son 5 Balak

zippy 4 keen, spry, yare 5 agile, alert, brisk, catty, ready 6 active, brisky, lively, nimble, snappy 7 dynamic, intense 8 forceful 9 sprightly

zircon 6 jargon 7 jargoon *variety:* 7 jacinth 8 hyacinth, starlite

zirconium *symbol:* 2 Zr

zither *Chinese:* 3 kin *Japanese:* 4 koto

Ziza *father:* 8 Rehoboam *mother:* 6 Maacah

zodiac sign 3 Leo (the Lion) 5 Aries (the Ram), Libra (the Balance), Virgo (the Virgin) 6 Cancer (the Crab), Gemini (the Twins), Pisces (the Fishes), Taurus (the Bull) 7 Scorpio (the Scorpion) 8 Aquarius (the Water Bearer) 9 Capricorn (the Goat) 11 Sagittarius (the Archer)

zoetic 5 alive, vital 6 living 7 animate 8 animated

Zohar *father:* 6 Simeon *son:* 6 Ephron

Zoheth's father 4 Ishi

Zoilus 5 momus 6 carper, critic 7 caviler, knocker 9 aristarch, belittler 10 criticizer 11 faultfinder, smellfungus

Zola, Emile *work:* 4 Nana 6 Verité

7 J'accuse 8 Germinal 9 La Débâcle 10 L'Assommoir 13 Thérèse Raquin

zombie 5 drink, snake 6 python 8 cocktail

zone 4 area, band, belt 5 tract 6 region, sector 7 section, segment 9 territory *ecological:* 7 ecotone

zonked 4 high 5 doped, drunk, tight 6 stoned 7 drugged, drunken 8 hopped-up, turned on 9 spaced-out 10 inebriated, tripped out 11 intoxicated

zoologist *American:* 5 Clark (Eugenie), Hyatt (Alpheus) 6 Carson (Rachel), Fossey (Dian), Kinsey (Alfred), Osborn (Henry Fairfield), Yerkes (Robert) 7 Ditmars (Raymond), Merriam (Clinton) *British:* 6 Darwin (Charles), Huxley (Julian, Thomas) 7 Goodall (Jane), Medawar (Peter) 9 Lankester (Edwin) *Dutch:* 10 Swammerdam (Jan) *French:* 6 Cuvier (Georges) *German:* 7 Haeckel (Ernst), Spemann (Hans) *Norwegian:* 6 Nansen (Fridtjof) *South African:* 5 Broom (Robert) *Swedish:* 8 Linnaeus (Carolus)

zoophyte 5 coral 6 sponge 7 hydroid 8 bryozoan 9 gorgonian 10 sea anemone 12 invertebrate

Zoroastrian *demon:* 4 deva *god:* 10 Ahura Mazda *sacred writings:* 6 Avesta

zucchetto 7 calotte 8 skullcap

Zur *brother:* 4 Kish *daughter:* 5 Cozbi *father:* 5 Jeiel

Zuriel's father 7 Abihail

zweiback 5 bread, toast 7 biscuit

zygomatic bone 5 malar 9 cheekbone

zygote 6 oocyst 7 oosperm